P9-ANZ-399

PRESENTED

Mary Lukes

TO

I bought this book from Mark, who got it from MSOE student.

BY

ON

Nov 20, 1998

THE NIV QUIET TIME BIBLE

NEW INTERNATIONAL VERSION

A LIFEGUIDE®
BIBLE

InterVarsity Press
Downers Grove, Illinois

InterVarsity Press® is the book-publishing division of InterVarsity Christian Fellowship®, a student movement active on cam at hundreds of universities, colleges and schools of nursing in the United States of America, and a member movement of the International Fwship of Evangelical Students. For information about local and regional activities, write Public Relations Dept., InterVarsity Christian owship, 6400 Schroeder Rd., P.O. Box 7895, Madison, WI 53707-7895.

Cover photograph: J. C. Leacock
ISBN 0-8308-2104-X (cloth)
ISBN 0-8308-2105-8 (paper)
ISBN 0-8308-2106-6 (leather)
Printed in the United States of America ♾

Library of Congress Cataloging-in-Publication Data

18 17 16 15 14 13 12 11 10 9 8 7 6 5 4 3 2 1
11 10 09 08 07 06 05 04 03 02 01 00 99 98 97 96

CONTENTS

THE NIV QUIET TIME BIBLE
STAFF & CONTRIBUTORS

GENERAL EDITOR
Cindy Bunch

EDITORIAL ADVISORS
Ken DeRuiter, James Hoover, Nancy Iglesias, Andrew T. Le Peau and Don Stephenson

DESIGNER
Kathy Lay Burrows

WORD PROCESSING
Gloria Duncan-Bevilacqua

PROOFREADING
Michele Pelton-Fall, Al Hsu and Rebecca Cooper

PRODUCTION
Nancy Fox, Don Frye and Marjorie Sire

QUIET TIME WRITERS
Genesis: Charles and Anne Hummel
Exodus: James Reapsome
Leviticus: Dale and Sandy Larsen, Carolyn Nystrom and Ruth Goring
Numbers: Rob Suggs and Gladys Hunt
Deuteronomy: Stephen Eyre
Joshua: Donald Baker
Judges: Donald Baker
Ruth: Gladys Hunt
1 Samuel: Jack Kuhatschek, Pete Scazzero, Hazel Offner and Gladys Hunt
2 Samuel: Jack Kuhatschek, Brian Wallace, Cindy Bunch and Scott Hotaling
1 Kings: Carolyn Nystrom, Pete Scazzero, Cindy Bunch and Phyllis J. Le Peau
2 Kings: Carolyn Nystrom, Andrea and Howard Louthan, Gladys Hunt and Phyllis J. Le Peau
1 Chronicles: Dale and Sandy Larsen and Jack Kuhatschek
2 Chronicles: Dale and Sandy Larsen, Carolyn Nystrom, Cindy Bunch and Scott Hotaling
Ezra: Tom Parker
Nehemiah: Don Fields
Esther: Patty Pell
Job: Paul Stevens
Psalms: Cindy Bunch, Isaac Canales, Stephen Eyre, Phyllis J. Le Peau, Jack Kuhatschek, Mary Fisher, Linda Gehrs, Dietrich Gruen, Dan Harrison, David Healey, Carolyn Nystrom, Hazel Offner, Eugene Peterson, Dale and Juanita Ryan, Bill Syrios and Brian Wallace
Proverbs: William Mouser
Ecclesiastes: Bill and Teresa Syrios
Song of Songs: Cindy Bunch
Isaiah: Howard Peskett
Jeremiah: Stephen Eyre, Dale and Sandy Larsen
Lamentations: Lin Johnson
Ezekiel: Paul Stevens
Daniel: Douglas Connelly
Hosea: Tom Parker
Joel: Doug and Doris Haugen
Amos: Doug and Doris Haugen
Obadiah: Dale and Sandy Larsen
Jonah: Doug and Doris Haugen
Micah: Tom Parker
Nahum: Rob Suggs
Habakkuk: Bob and Carolyn Hunter, Carolyn Nystrom
Zephaniah: Lin Johnson
Haggai: Lin Johnson
Zechariah: Jack Kuhatschek
Malachi: Carolyn Nystrom
Matthew: Stephen and Jacalyn Eyre
Mark: James Hoover
Luke: Ada Lum
John: Douglas Connelly
Acts: Phyllis J. Le Peau
Romans: Jack Kuhatschek
1 Corinthians: Paul Stevens and Dan Williams
2 Corinthians: Paul Stevens
Galatians: Jack Kuhatschek
Ephesians: Andrew T. and Phyllis J. Le Peau
Philippians: Donald Baker
Colossians: Martha Reapsome
1 & 2 Thessalonians: Donald Baker
1 & 2 Timothy: Pete Sommer
Titus: Pete Sommer
Philemon: Martha Reapsome
Hebrews: James Reapsome
James: Andrew T. and Phyllis J. Le Peau
1 & 2 Peter: Carolyn Nystrom
1, 2, 3 John: Ron Blankley
Jude: Carolyn Nystrom
Revelation: Paul Stevens and Scott Hotaling

ABBREVIATIONS

Books of the Bible

Genesis	Ge	Isaiah	Is	Romans	Ro
Exodus	Ex	Jeremiah	Jer	1 Corinthians	1Co
Leviticus	Lev	Lamentations	La	2 Corinthians	2Co
Numbers	Nu	Ezekiel	Eze	Galatians	Gal
Deuteronomy	Dt	Daniel	Da	Ephesians	Eph
Joshua	Jos	Hosea	Hos	Philippians	Php
Judges	Jdg	Joel	Joel	Colossians	Col
Ruth	Ru	Amos	Am	1 Thessalonians	1Th
1 Samuel	1Sa	Obadiah	Ob	2 Thessalonians	2Th
2 Samuel	2Sa	Jonah	Jnh	1 Timothy	1Ti
1 Kings	1Ki	Micah	Mic	2 Timothy	2Ti
2 Kings	2Ki	Nahum	Na	Titus	Tit
1 Chronicles	1Ch	Habakkuk	Hab	Philemon	Phm
2 Chronicles	2Ch	Zephaniah	Zep	Hebrews	Heb
Ezra	Ezr	Haggai	Hag	James	Jas
Nehemiah	Ne	Zechariah	Zec	1 Peter	1Pe
Esther	Est	Malachi	Mal	2 Peter	2Pe
Job	Job	Matthew	Mt	1 John	1Jn
Psalms	Ps	Mark	Mk	2 John	2Jn
Proverbs	Pr	Luke	Lk	3 John	3Jn
Ecclesiastes	Ecc	John	Jn	Jude	Jude
Song of Songs	SS	Acts	Ac	Revelation	Rev

TOPICAL BIBLE READINGS

Here are some quiet times you can turn to when you are looking for some answers to questions you are facing, encouragement from God through the difficult times or when you want to rejoice and praise God for the good things in your life. More topics are listed in the index on pages 1597-1601.

Angels Around Us
Psalm 91
Hebrews 1
Revelation 8—9

Assurance of Salvation
Psalms 25, 73
Luke 13:22—14:35
2 Corinthians 1:1-11

Battling Temptation
2 Samuel 11
Daniel 3
Mark 1:1-15
John 18:1-27

Comfort from God
Psalms 19, 86, 145
John 14
1 Peter 5

Decision-Making
Psalm 119:1-24
1 Corinthians 3
Revelation 14—15

Experiencing Burnout
1 Kings 19:1-18
Mark 6:6-56

Expressing Anger
Job 9—10
Psalms 4; 18:1-24; 94; 109
Jonah 4
Nahum 1
Mark 11:1-25

Facing Pressure
Daniel 1
Psalm 31
Mark 2:18—3:35
Galatians 6:11-18
Revelation 2

Feeling Lonely
Psalms 3, 22
Luke 6:12-49
John 12
2 Timothy 1

Finding Joy in God
Psalms 66, 126
Romans 5
Philippians 3:1-21

Grieving
Psalm 102
2 Corinthians 6:14—7:16

Handling Guilt
Leviticus 16
Psalm 130
1 Timothy 1

Loving Others
1 John 4:1-12
2 John 1-13

The Power of God
Nahum 3
Acts 9:32—10:48

Repentance
Psalm 32
Luke 3:1-20

Sources of Hope
Genesis 45:16—47:31
Psalms 33, 42—43, 146
Isaiah 11—12; 49; 65:17—66:24
Luke 1
Romans 4
1 Peter 1:1-12
Revelation 1:1-8

Spiritual Battles
Joshua 5:13—6:27
Psalm 110
John 7:1-52
Ephesians 6:10-24
1 John 5:1-12
Revelation 12, 13

Suffering
Job 20—21
Psalm 6
Lamentations 3, 4—5
John 18:28—19:16
Acts 8
2 Corinthians 12
Philippians 1:12-30
Hebrews 4:14—5:10
1 Peter 3:8-22; 4

Thanking God
Psalms 47, 50, 65
Philippians 4:10-23
Colossians 1:1-14

Times of Waiting
Psalms 27, 40, 44
Mark 13:1-37
Hebrews 9

BIBLE READING PLAN

The plan outlined below offers some variety in reading between Old and New Testament and types of literature with some effort to follow a historical sequence of events. Following it will help you better understand the whole of Scripture. Check off the boxes as you go to keep track of your reading. You can also use this plan and follow a different order; just look for the italic book titles and check off each passage. The quiet times cover all of the New Testament and selected passages from every Old Testament book. Bold type indicates that there is a quiet time with the passage. Every verse is represented in a readable unit, whether or not there is a quiet time. If you complete one quiet time each day, you will cover all of the quiet times in two years.

John
☐ **Jn 1**
☐ **Jn 2**
☐ **Jn 3**
☐ **Jn 4**
☐ **Jn 5**
☐ **Jn 6**
☐ **Jn 7:1-52**
☐ **Jn 7:53—8:11**
☐ **Jn 8:12-59**
☐ **Jn 9**
☐ **Jn 10**
☐ **Jn 11**
☐ **Jn 12**
☐ **Jn 13:1-17**
☐ **Jn 13:18-38**
☐ **Jn 14**
☐ **Jn 15:1-17**
☐ **Jn 15:18—16:4**
☐ **Jn 16:5-33**
☐ **Jn 17:1-26**
☐ **Jn 18:1-27**
☐ **Jn 18:28—19:16**
☐ **Jn 19:17-42**
☐ **Jn 20**
☐ **Jn 21**

Genesis
☐ **Ge 1:1—2:3**
☐ **Ge 2:4-25**
☐ **Ge 3**
☐ **Ge 4—5**
☐ **Ge 6—7**
☐ **Ge 8:1—9:17**
☐ **Ge 9:18—11:32**
☐ **Ge 12—13**
☐ **Ge 14—15**
☐ **Ge 16—17**
☐ **Ge 18—19**
☐ **Ge 20—21**
☐ **Ge 22—23**
☐ **Ge 24:1—25:11**
☐ **Ge 25:12—27:40**
☐ **Ge 27:41—30:24**
☐ **Ge 30:25—31:55**
☐ **Ge 32—33**
☐ **Ge 34—36**
☐ **Ge 37—38**
☐ **Ge 39—40**
☐ **Ge 41—42**
☐ **Ge 43:1—45:15**
☐ **Ge 45:16—47:31**
☐ **Ge 48—49**
☐ **Ge 50**

Psalms 1—13
☐ **Ps 1**
☐ **Ps 2**
☐ **Ps 3**
☐ **Ps 4**
☐ **Ps 5**
☐ **Ps 6**
☐ Ps 7
☐ **Ps 8**
☐ Ps 9
☐ **Ps 10**
☐ Ps 11—12
☐ **Ps 13**

1 Thessalonians
☐ **1Th 1**
☐ **1Th 2:1-16**
☐ **1Th 2:17—3:13**
☐ **1Th 4:1-12**
☐ **1Th 4:13—5:11**
☐ **1Th 5:12-28**

2 Thessalonians
☐ **2Th 1**
☐ **2Th 2**
☐ **2Th 3**

Exodus
☐ **Ex 1**
☐ **Ex 2**
☐ **Ex 3—4**
☐ **Ex 5:1—7:7**
☐ **Ex 7:8—10:29**
☐ **Ex 11:1—12:28**
☐ **Ex 12:29—13:16**
☐ **Ex 13:17—14:31**
☐ **Ex 15:1-21**
☐ **Ex 15:22—17:16**
☐ **Ex 18**
☐ **Ex 19**
☐ **Ex 20:1-21**
☐ **Ex 20:22—23:19**
☐ **Ex 23:20—24:18**
☐ **Ex 25—27**
☐ **Ex 28:1—29:37**
☐ **Ex 29:38—31:18**
☐ **Ex 32**
☐ **Ex 33**
☐ **Ex 34**
☐ **Ex 35—36**
☐ **Ex 37:1—39:31**
☐ **Ex 39:32—40:38**

Ecclesiastes
☐ **Ecc 1:1-11**
☐ **Ecc 1:12—2:16**
☐ **Ecc 2:17-26**
☐ **Ecc 3:1—4:3**
☐ **Ecc 4:4—5:7**
☐ **Ecc 5:8—6:12**
☐ **Ecc 7:1—8:1**
☐ **Ecc 8:2-17**
☐ **Ecc 9:1-12**
☐ **Ecc 9:13—10:20**
☐ **Ecc 11:1—12:8**
☐ **Ecc 12:9-14**

Song of Songs
☐ **SS 1—2**
☐ **SS 3**
☐ **SS 4**
☐ **SS 5—6**
☐ **SS 7—8**

Luke
☐ **Lk 1**
☐ **Lk 2**
☐ **Lk 3:1-20**
☐ **Lk 3:21—4:13**
☐ **Lk 4:14—5:16**
☐ **Lk 5:17—6:11**
☐ **Lk 6:12-49**
☐ **Lk 7**
☐ **Lk 8:1-21**
☐ **Lk 8:22-56**
☐ **Lk 9:1-50**
☐ **Lk 9:51—10:24**
☐ **Lk 10:25—11:13**
☐ **Lk 11:14—12:12**
☐ **Lk 12:13—13:21**
☐ **Lk 13:22—14:35**
☐ **Lk 15**
☐ **Lk 16**
☐ **Lk 17:1—18:14**
☐ **Lk 18:15—19:10**
☐ **Lk 19:11-48**
☐ **Lk 20:1—21:4**
☐ **Lk 21:5-38**
☐ **Lk 22:1-46**
☐ **Lk 22:47—23:56**
☐ **Lk 24**

Leviticus
☐ **Lev 1**
☐ Lev 2—4
☐ Lev 5—7
☐ **Lev 8**
☐ Lev 9
☐ **Lev 10**
☐ Lev 11—12
☐ Lev 13
☐ Lev 14—15
☐ **Lev 16**
☐ Lev 17—18
☐ **Lev 19**
☐ Lev 20—22
☐ **Lev 23**
☐ Lev 24
☐ **Lev 25**
☐ **Lev 26**
☐ Lev 27

Acts
☐ **Ac 1**
☐ **Ac 2**
☐ **Ac 3**
☐ **Ac 4:1-31**
☐ **Ac 4:32—5:16**
☐ **Ac 5:17—6:7**
☐ **Ac 6:8—7:60**
☐ **Ac 8**
☐ **Ac 9:1-31**
☐ **Ac 9:32—10:48**
☐ **Ac 11**
☐ **Ac 12**
☐ **Ac 13—14**
☐ **Ac 15**
☐ **Ac 16**
☐ **Ac 17**
☐ **Ac 18**
☐ **Ac 19:1—20:12**
☐ **Ac 20:13-38**
☐ **Ac 21:1—22:21**
☐ **Ac 22:22—23:35**
☐ **Ac 24:1—25:12**
☐ **Ac 25:13—26:32**
☐ **Ac 27—28**

Psalms 14—29
☐ Ps 14
☐ **Ps 15**
☐ **Ps 16**
☐ Ps 17
☐ **Ps 18:1-24**
☐ **Ps 18:25-50**
☐ **Ps 19**
☐ Ps 20—21
☐ **Ps 22**
☐ **Ps 23**
☐ **Ps 24**
☐ **Ps 25**
☐ Ps 26
☐ **Ps 27**
☐ Ps 28
☐ **Ps 29**

Jonah

- ☐ **Jnh 1**
- ☐ **Jnh 2**
- ☐ **Jnh 3**
- ☐ **Jnh 4**

Galatians

- ☐ **Gal 1:1-10**
- ☐ **Gal 1:11—2:10**
- ☐ **Gal 2:11-21**
- ☐ **Gal 3:1-14**
- ☐ **Gal 3:15-29**
- ☐ **Gal 4:1-20**
- ☐ **Gal 4:21—5:1**
- ☐ **Gal 5:2-15**
- ☐ **Gal 5:16-26**
- ☐ **Gal 6:1-10**
- ☐ **Gal 6:11-18**

Isaiah

- ☐ **Isa 1**
- ☐ **Isa 2**
- ☐ Isa 3—4
- ☐ **Isa 5**
- ☐ **Isa 6**
- ☐ **Isa 7**
- ☐ Isa 8:1-10
- ☐ **Isa 8:11—9:7**
- ☐ Isa 9:8—10:34
- ☐ **Isa 11—12**
- ☐ Isa 13—14
- ☐ Isa 15—16
- ☐ Isa 17—18
- ☐ Isa 19—20
- ☐ Isa 21—22
- ☐ Isa 23
- ☐ **Isa 24**
- ☐ **Isa 25**
- ☐ Isa 26—27
- ☐ Isa 28—29
- ☐ **Isa 30:1-18**
- ☐ Isa 30:19—32:20
- ☐ Isa 33—35
- ☐ **Isa 36—37**
- ☐ **Isa 38—39**
- ☐ **Isa 40**
- ☐ Isa 41
- ☐ **Isa 42**
- ☐ **Isa 43:1—44:5**
- ☐ Isa 44:6-28
- ☐ **Isa 45**
- ☐ Isa 46—48
- ☐ **Isa 49**
- ☐ Isa 50:1—52:12
- ☐ **Isa 52:13—53:12**
- ☐ **Isa 54—55**
- ☐ Isa 56—57
- ☐ **Isa 58**
- ☐ Isa 59—60
- ☐ **Isa 61**
- ☐ **Isa 62**
- ☐ Isa 63:1-6
- ☐ **Isa 63:7—64:12**
- ☐ Isa 65:1-16
- ☐ **Isa 65:17—66:24**

Matthew

- ☐ **Mt 1—2**
- ☐ **Mt 3**
- ☐ **Mt 4**
- ☐ **Mt 5:1—6:18**
- ☐ **Mt 6:19—7:29**
- ☐ **Mt 8:1—9:34**
- ☐ **Mt 9:35—11:30**
- ☐ **Mt 12**
- ☐ **Mt 13**
- ☐ **Mt 14**
- ☐ **Mt 15:1—16:20**
- ☐ **Mt 16:21—17:27**
- ☐ **Mt 18**
- ☐ **Mt 19—20**
- ☐ **Mt 21:1-27**
- ☐ **Mt 21:28—22:46**
- ☐ **Mt 23**
- ☐ **Mt 24**
- ☐ **Mt 25**
- ☐ **Mt 26**
- ☐ **Mt 27**
- ☐ **Mt 28**

Psalms 30—41

- ☐ **Ps 30**
- ☐ **Ps 31**
- ☐ **Ps 32**
- ☐ **Ps 33**
- ☐ **Ps 34**
- ☐ **Ps 35**
- ☐ **Ps 36**
- ☐ **Ps 37:1-17**
- ☐ **Ps 37:18-40**
- ☐ **Ps 38**
- ☐ **Ps 39**
- ☐ **Ps 40**
- ☐ Ps 41

Romans

- ☐ **Rm 1:1-17**
- ☐ **Rm 1:18-32**
- ☐ **Rm 2**
- ☐ **Rm 3:1-20**
- ☐ **Rm 3:21-31**
- ☐ **Rm 4**
- ☐ **Rm 5**
- ☐ **Rm 6:1—7:6**
- ☐ **Rm 7:7-25**
- ☐ **Rm 8:1-17**
- ☐ **Rm 8:18-39**
- ☐ **Rm 9:1-29**
- ☐ **Rm 9:30—10:21**
- ☐ **Rm 11**
- ☐ **Rm 12**
- ☐ **Rm 13**
- ☐ **Rm 14**
- ☐ **Rm 15:1-13**
- ☐ **Rm 15:14—16:27**

Numbers

- ☐ **Nu 1**
- ☐ Nu 2—3
- ☐ Nu 4—6
- ☐ Nu 7
- ☐ Nu 8
- ☐ **Nu 9**
- ☐ Nu 10
- ☐ **Nu 11**
- ☐ **Nu 12**
- ☐ **Nu 13:1—14:12**
- ☐ Nu 14:13—15:41
- ☐ Nu 16
- ☐ **Nu 17**
- ☐ Nu 18—19
- ☐ **Nu 20:1-13**
- ☐ Nu 20:14-29
- ☐ **Nu 21:1-9**
- ☐ Nu 21:10—22:41
- ☐ Nu 23—25
- ☐ Nu 26:1—27:11
- ☐ **Nu 27:12-23**
- ☐ Nu 28—29
- ☐ Nu 30—31
- ☐ **Nu 32**
- ☐ Nu 33—34
- ☐ Nu 35—36

Amos

- ☐ **Am 1—2**
- ☐ **Am 3**
- ☐ **Am 4**
- ☐ **Am 5—6**
- ☐ **Am 7—8**
- ☐ **Am 9**

Hosea

- ☐ **Hos 1:1—2:1**
- ☐ **Hos 2:2—3:5**
- ☐ **Hos 4**
- ☐ **Hos 5:1—6:11**
- ☐ **Hos 6:11—8:14**
- ☐ **Hos 9—10**
- ☐ **Hos 11:1-11**
- ☐ **Hos 11:12—13:16**
- ☐ **Hos 14**

1 Corinthians

- ☐ **1 Co 1**
- ☐ **1 Co 2**
- ☐ **1 Co 3**
- ☐ **1 Co 4**
- ☐ **1 Co 5—6**
- ☐ **1 Co 7**
- ☐ **1 Co 8—9**
- ☐ **1 Co 10:1—11:1**
- ☐ **1 Co 11:2-34**
- ☐ **1 Co 12**
- ☐ **1 Co 13**
- ☐ **1 Co 14**
- ☐ **1 Co 15—16**

Deuteronomy

- ☐ Dt 1
- ☐ Dt 2:1—3:20
- ☐ **Dt 3:21-29**
- ☐ **Dt 4:1-14**
- ☐ **Dt 4:15-40**
- ☐ Dt 4:41-49
- ☐ **Dt 5**
- ☐ **Dt 6**
- ☐ **Dt 7**
- ☐ **Dt 8**
- ☐ Dt 9—10
- ☐ Dt 11
- ☐ **Dt 12:1-14**
- ☐ Dt 12:15—13:18
- ☐ Dt 14
- ☐ **Dt 15:1-11**
- ☐ Dt 15:12—16:20
- ☐ Dt 16:21—18:22
- ☐ Dt 19—20
- ☐ Dt 21:1—23:14
- ☐ **Dt 23:15-25**
- ☐ Dt 24—25
- ☐ Dt 26—27
- ☐ Dt 28
- ☐ Dt 29
- ☐ **Dt 30**
- ☐ **Dt 31:1-13**
- ☐ Dt 31:14—34:12

2 Corinthians

- ☐ **2 Co 1:1-11**
- ☐ **2 Co 1:12—2:11**
- ☐ **2 Co 2:12—3:6**
- ☐ **2 Co 3:7-18**
- ☐ **2 Co 4:1—5:10**
- ☐ **2 Co 5:11—6:13**
- ☐ **2 Co 6:14—7:16**
- ☐ **2 Co 8:1—9:15**
- ☐ **2 Co 10**
- ☐ **2 Co 11**
- ☐ **2 Co 12**
- ☐ **2 Co 13**

Psalms 42—61

- ☐ **Ps 42—43**
- ☐ **Ps 44**
- ☐ **Ps 45**
- ☐ **Ps 46**
- ☐ **Ps 47**
- ☐ Ps 48—49
- ☐ **Ps 50**
- ☐ **Ps 51**
- ☐ Ps 52—54
- ☐ **Ps 55**
- ☐ Ps 56
- ☐ **Ps 57**
- ☐ Ps 58—59
- ☐ Ps 60—61

Micah

- ☐ Mic 1
- ☐ **Mic 2**
- ☐ **Mic 3**
- ☐ **Mic 4**
- ☐ **Mic 5**
- ☐ **Mic 6**
- ☐ **Mic 7**

Joshua

- ☐ **Jos 1**
- ☐ **Jos 2**
- ☐ **Jos 3:1—5:12**
- ☐ **Jos 5:13—6:27**
- ☐ **Jos 7—8**
- ☐ **Jos 9**
- ☐ **Jos 10—12**
- ☐ Jos 13
- ☐ **Jos 14—18**
- ☐ Jos 19
- ☐ **Jos 20—21**
- ☐ **Jos 22**
- ☐ **Jos 23**
- ☐ **Jos 24**

1 Timothy

- ☐ **1Ti 1**
- ☐ **1Ti 2**
- ☐ **1Ti 3**
- ☐ **1Ti 4**
- ☐ **1Ti 5:1—6:2**
- ☐ **1Ti 6:3-20**

Joel

- ☐ **Joel 1**
- ☐ **Joel 2:1-27**
- ☐ **Joel 2:28—3:21**

2 Timothy

- ☐ **2Ti 1**
- ☐ **2Ti 2**
- ☐ **2Ti 3**
- ☐ **2Ti 4**

Obadiah

- ☐ **Ob 1-21**

Titus

- ☐ **Tit 1—3**

Judges

- ☐ Jdg 1:1—2:5

- ☐ **Jdg 2:6-23**
- ☐ Jdg 3:1-11
- ☐ **Jdg 3:12-31**
- ☐ **Jdg 4**
- ☐ Jdg 5
- ☐ **Jdg 6:1-32**
- ☐ **Jdg 6:33—7:25**
- ☐ Jdg 8
- ☐ **Jdg 9**
- ☐ Jdg 10
- ☐ **Jdg 11—12**
- ☐ **Jdg 13**
- ☐ **Jdg 14—15**
- ☐ **Jdg 16**
- ☐ **Jdg 17—18**
- ☐ Jdg 19—20
- ☐ **Jdg 21**

Ruth

- ☐ **Ru 1—2**
- ☐ **Ru 3—4**

1 Samuel

- ☐ **1Sa 1:1—2:11**
- ☐ 1Sa 2:12-36
- ☐ **1Sa 3**
- ☐ 1Sa 4—5
- ☐ 1Sa 6—7
- ☐ **1Sa 8**
- ☐ **1Sa 9:1—10:8**
- ☐ 1Sa 10:9—12:25
- ☐ 1Sa 13—14
- ☐ **1Sa 15**
- ☐ **1Sa 16**
- ☐ **1Sa 17**
- ☐ **1Sa 18**
- ☐ 1Sa 19
- ☐ **1Sa 20**
- ☐ 1Sa 21—23
- ☐ **1Sa 24**
- ☐ **1Sa 25**
- ☐ **1Sa 26**
- ☐ 1Sa 27—29
- ☐ **1Sa 30**
- ☐ 1Sa 31

Ephesians

- ☐ **Eph 1:1-14**
- ☐ **Eph 1:15-23**
- ☐ **Eph 2:1-10**
- ☐ **Eph 2:11-22**
- ☐ **Eph 3**
- ☐ **Eph 4:1-16**
- ☐ **Eph 4:17-32**
- ☐ **Eph 5:1-20**
- ☐ **Eph 5:21-33**
- ☐ **Eph 6:1-9**
- ☐ **Eph 6:10-24**

2 Samuel

- ☐ 2Sa 1—2
- ☐ 2Sa 3—5
- ☐ **2Sa 6**
- ☐ **2Sa 7**
- ☐ 2Sa 8
- ☐ **2Sa 9**
- ☐ 2Sa 10
- ☐ **2Sa 11**
- ☐ **2Sa 12**
- ☐ **2Sa 13**
- ☐ 2Sa 14
- ☐ **2Sa 15**
- ☐ 2Sa 16:1—18:18
- ☐ **2Sa 18:19—19:10**
- ☐ 2Sa 19:11—20:26
- ☐ 2Sa 21—22
- ☐ 2Sa 23—24

Psalms 62—84

- ☐ **Ps 62**
- ☐ **Ps 63**
- ☐ Ps 64
- ☐ **Ps 65**
- ☐ **Ps 66**
- ☐ **Ps 67**
- ☐ Ps 68
- ☐ Ps 69—70
- ☐ Ps 71
- ☐ Ps 72
- ☐ **Ps 73**
- ☐ Ps 74
- ☐ Ps 75—76
- ☐ **Ps 77**
- ☐ Ps 78
- ☐ Ps 79
- ☐ Ps 80—81
- ☐ Ps 82—83
- ☐ **Ps 84**

1 Kings

- ☐ 1Ki 1
- ☐ 1Ki 2
- ☐ **1Ki 3**
- ☐ 1Ki 4
- ☐ 1Ki 5—6
- ☐ 1Ki 7
- ☐ 1Ki 8
- ☐ 1Ki 9—10
- ☐ **1Ki 11**
- ☐ **1Ki 12**
- ☐ 1Ki 13—14
- ☐ 1Ki 15—16
- ☐ **1Ki 17**
- ☐ **1Ki 18**
- ☐ **1Ki 19:1-18**
- ☐ 1Ki 19:19—20:43
- ☐ **1Ki 21**
- ☐ **1Ki 22:1-40**
- ☐ 1Ki 22:41-53

2 Kings

- ☐ 2Ki 1
- ☐ **2Ki 2**
- ☐ 2Ki 3:1—4:7
- ☐ **2Ki 4:8-37**
- ☐ 2Ki 4:38-44
- ☐ **2Ki 5**
- ☐ 2Ki 6:1-23
- ☐ **2Ki 6:24—7:20**
- ☐ 2Ki 8
- ☐ **2Ki 9—10**
- ☐ 2Ki 11—12
- ☐ **2Ki 13**
- ☐ 2Ki 14—15
- ☐ **2Ki 16**
- ☐ **2Ki 17**
- ☐ 2Ki 18:1-16
- ☐ **2Ki 18:17-37**
- ☐ **2Ki 19**
- ☐ **2Ki 20:1—21:18**
- ☐ 2Ki 21:19-26
- ☐ **2Ki 22:1—23:35**
- ☐ **2Ki 23:36—25:30**

Philippians

- ☐ **Php 1:1-11**
- ☐ **Php 1:12-30**
- ☐ **Php 2:1-18**
- ☐ **Php 2:19-30**
- ☐ **Php 3**
- ☐ **Php 4:1-9**
- ☐ **Php 4:10-23**

1 Chronicles

- ☐ 1Ch 1—4
- ☐ 1Ch 5—6
- ☐ 1Ch 7—8
- ☐ 1Ch 9—10
- ☐ **1Ch 11**
- ☐ 1Ch 12—14
- ☐ **1Ch 15:1—16:6**
- ☐ 1Ch 16:7-43
- ☐ **1Ch 17**
- ☐ 1Ch 18
- ☐ **1Ch 19**
- ☐ 1Ch 20
- ☐ **1Ch 21:1—22:1**
- ☐ 1Ch 22:2—23:32
- ☐ 1Ch 24—27
- ☐ **1Ch 28**
- ☐ **1Ch 29**

2 Chronicles

- ☐ **2Ch 1**
- ☐ 2Ch 2—3
- ☐ 2Ch 4—5
- ☐ **2Ch 6—7**
- ☐ 2Ch 8—9
- ☐ 2Ch 10—11
- ☐ 2Ch 12—13
- ☐ **2Ch 14—15**
- ☐ 2Ch 16—17
- ☐ **2Ch 18:1—19:3**
- ☐ 2Ch 19:4-11
- ☐ **2Ch 20:1-30**
- ☐ 2Ch 20:31—22:12
- ☐ **2Ch 23—24**
- ☐ 2Ch 25—26
- ☐ 2Ch 27—28
- ☐ 2Ch 29
- ☐ 2Ch 30—31
- ☐ 2Ch 32—33
- ☐ **2Ch 34**
- ☐ 2Ch 35—36

Colossians

- ☐ **Col 1:1-14**
- ☐ **Col 1:15-23**
- ☐ **Col 1:24—2:5**
- ☐ **Col 2:6-23**
- ☐ **Col 3:1-11**
- ☐ **Col 3:12-17**
- ☐ **Col 3:18—4:1**
- ☐ **Col 4:2-18**

Philemon

- ☐ **Phm 1-25**

Esther

- ☐ **Est 1**
- ☐ **Est 2**
- ☐ **Est 3**
- ☐ **Est 4**
- ☐ **Est 5**
- ☐ **Est 6**
- ☐ **Est 7**
- ☐ **Est 8**
- ☐ **Est 9—10**

Ezra

- ☐ **Ezr 1—2**
- ☐ **Ezr 3**
- ☐ **Ezr 4**
- ☐ **Ezr 5—6**
- ☐ **Ezr 7**
- ☐ **Ezr 8**
- ☐ **Ezr 9**
- ☐ **Ezr 10**

1 Peter

- ☐ **1Pe 1:1-12**
- ☐ **1Pe 1:13-25**
- ☐ **1Pe 2:1-12**
- ☐ **1Pe 2:13—3:7**
- ☐ **1Pe 3:8-22**
- ☐ **1Pe 4**
- ☐ **1Pe 5**

Nehemiah

- ☐ **Ne 1**
- ☐ **Ne 2**
- ☐ **Ne 3**
- ☐ **Ne 4**
- ☐ **Ne 5**
- ☐ **Ne 6**
- ☐ **Ne 7**
- ☐ **Ne 8**
- ☐ **Ne 9**
- ☐ **Ne 10**
- ☐ **Ne 11**
- ☐ **Ne 12**
- ☐ **Ne 13**

2 Peter

- ☐ **2Pe 1:1-11**
- ☐ **2Pe 1:12-21**
- ☐ **2Pe 2**
- ☐ **2Pe 3**

Jude

- ☐ **Jude 1-25**

Psalms 85—106

- ☐ Ps 85
- ☐ **Ps 86**
- ☐ Ps 87
- ☐ **Ps 88**
- ☐ Ps 89
- ☐ **Ps 90**
- ☐ **Ps 91**
- ☐ Ps 92—93
- ☐ **Ps 94**
- ☐ **Ps 95**
- ☐ **Ps 96**
- ☐ Ps 97—98
- ☐ **Ps 99**
- ☐ **Ps 100**
- ☐ Ps 101
- ☐ **Ps 102**
- ☐ **Ps 103**
- ☐ **Ps 104**
- ☐ Ps 105
- ☐ Ps 106

Job

- ☐ **Job 1:1—2:10**
- ☐ **Job 2:11—4:17**
- ☐ Job 4:18—5:27
- ☐ **Job 6**
- ☐ Job 7—8
- ☐ **Job 9—10**
- ☐ Job 11—12
- ☐ **Job 13—14**
- ☐ Job 15
- ☐ **Job 16—17**
- ☐ Job 18—19
- ☐ **Job 20—21**
- ☐ Job 22
- ☐ **Job 23**
- ☐ Job 24—26

- ☐ Job 27—28
- ☐ Job 29—31
- ☐ Job 32—33
- ☐ Job 34
- ☐ **Job 35**
- ☐ Job 36—37
- ☐ **Job 38**
- ☐ Job 39
- ☐ **Job 40**
- ☐ Job 41
- ☐ **Job 42**

James

- ☐ **Jas 1:1-18**
- ☐ **Jas 1:19-27**
- ☐ **Jas 2:1-13**
- ☐ **Jas 2:14-26**
- ☐ **Jas 3:1-12**
- ☐ **Jas 3:13—4:10**
- ☐ **Jas 4:11-17**
- ☐ **Jas 5:1-11**
- ☐ **Jas 5:12-20**

Proverbs

- ☐ Pr 1
- ☐ Pr 2—3
- ☐ Pr 4—5
- ☐ **Pr 6:1-19**
- ☐ Pr 6:20-35
- ☐ **Pr 7**
- ☐ Pr 8
- ☐ **Pr 9**
- ☐ **Pr 10**
- ☐ Pr 11—12
- ☐ **Pr 13—14**
- ☐ **Pr 15—16**
- ☐ **Pr 17—18**
- ☐ **Pr 19**
- ☐ Pr 20
- ☐ **Pr 21**
- ☐ Pr 22:1—24:22
- ☐ **Pr 24:23-34**
- ☐ Pr 25—26
- ☐ **Pr 27**
- ☐ Pr 28—29
- ☐ **Pr 30**
- ☐ Pr 31

Zephaniah

- ☐ **Zep 1**
- ☐ **Zep 2**
- ☐ **Zep 3**

Nahum

- ☐ **Na 1**
- ☐ **Na 2**
- ☐ **Na 3**

Ezekiel

- ☐ **Eze 1**
- ☐ **Eze 2:1—3:15**
- ☐ Eze 3:16-27
- ☐ **Eze 4—5**
- ☐ **Eze 6—7**
- ☐ **Eze 8**
- ☐ Eze 9—10
- ☐ **Eze 11**
- ☐ Eze 12—13
- ☐ Eze 14—15
- ☐ **Eze 16**
- ☐ Eze 17
- ☐ **Eze 18**
- ☐ Eze 19—20
- ☐ Eze 21—22
- ☐ Eze 23:1—24:14
- ☐ **Eze 24:15-27**
- ☐ Eze 25—26
- ☐ **Eze 27—28**
- ☐ Eze 29—30
- ☐ Eze 31—32
- ☐ **Eze 33**
- ☐ **Eze 34**
- ☐ Eze 35—36
- ☐ **Eze 37**
- ☐ Eze 38—39
- ☐ **Eze 40—41**
- ☐ Eze 42
- ☐ **Eze 43:1-12**
- ☐ Eze 43:13—44:31
- ☐ Eze 45—46
- ☐ **Eze 47:1-12**
- ☐ Eze 47:13—48:35

1 John

- ☐ **1Jn 1**
- ☐ **1Jn 2:1-11**
- ☐ **1Jn 2:12-17**
- ☐ **1Jn 2:18-27**
- ☐ **1Jn 2:28—3:10**
- ☐ **1Jn 3:11-24**
- ☐ **1Jn 4:1-12**
- ☐ **1Jn 4:13-21**
- ☐ **1Jn 5:1-12**
- ☐ **1Jn 5:13-21**

Habakkuk

- ☐ **Hab 1:1—2:1**
- ☐ **Hab 2:2-20**
- ☐ **Hab 3**

2 John

- ☐ **2Jn 1-13**

3 John

- ☐ **3Jn 1-14**

Jeremiah

- ☐ **Jer 1**
- ☐ Jer 2:1—3:5
- ☐ **Jer 3:6—4:4**
- ☐ Jer 4:5-31
- ☐ **Jer 5**
- ☐ Jer 6
- ☐ **Jer 7:1-20**
- ☐ Jer 7:21—8:22
- ☐ Jer 9
- ☐ **Jer 10:1-16**
- ☐ Jer 10:17—11:23
- ☐ **Jer 12**
- ☐ **Jer 13**
- ☐ Jer 14—15
- ☐ Jer 16:1—17:4
- ☐ **Jer 17:5-18**
- ☐ Jer 17:19-27
- ☐ **Jer 18:1-17**
- ☐ Jer 18:18—19:15
- ☐ Jer 20—21
- ☐ **Jer 22**
- ☐ **Jer 23**
- ☐ **Jer 24**
- ☐ Jer 25:1-14
- ☐ **Jer 25:15-38**
- ☐ Jer 26
- ☐ **Jer 27**
- ☐ **Jer 28**
- ☐ **Jer 29:1-23**
- ☐ Jer 29:24—30:24
- ☐ **Jer 31**
- ☐ **Jer 32:1-25**
- ☐ Jer 32:26-44
- ☐ **Jer 33**
- ☐ Jer 34—35
- ☐ **Jer 36**
- ☐ Jer 37
- ☐ **Jer 38**
- ☐ Jer 39—40
- ☐ Jer 41—43
- ☐ **Jer 44**
- ☐ Jer 45—47
- ☐ Jer 48—49
- ☐ **Jer 50:1-20**
- ☐ Jer 50:21—51:64
- ☐ **Jer 52**

Psalms 107—129

- ☐ **Ps 107**
- ☐ Ps 108
- ☐ **Ps 109**
- ☐ **Ps 110**
- ☐ Ps 111—114
- ☐ **Ps 115**
- ☐ **Ps 116**
- ☐ Ps 117
- ☐ **Ps 118**
- ☐ **Ps 119:1-24**
- ☐ **Ps 119:25-40**
- ☐ Ps 119:41—120:7
- ☐ **Ps 121**
- ☐ **Ps 122**
- ☐ Ps 123—125
- ☐ **Ps 126**
- ☐ **Ps 127**
- ☐ Ps 128—129

Lamentations

- ☐ **La 1—2**
- ☐ **La 3**
- ☐ **La 4—5**

Haggai

- ☐ **Hag 1—2**

Mark

- ☐ **Mk 1:1-15**
- ☐ **Mk 1:16-39**
- ☐ **Mk 1:40—2:17**
- ☐ **Mk 2:18—3:35**
- ☐ **Mk 4:1-34**
- ☐ **Mk 4:35—6:6**
- ☐ **Mk 6:6-56**
- ☐ **Mk 7**
- ☐ **Mk 8:1—9:1**
- ☐ **Mk 9:2-32**
- ☐ **Mk 9:33-50**
- ☐ **Mk 10:1-31**
- ☐ **Mk 10:32-52**
- ☐ **Mk 11:1-25**
- ☐ **Mk 11:27—12:27**
- ☐ **Mk 12:28-44**
- ☐ **Mk 13**
- ☐ **Mk 14:1-42**
- ☐ **Mk 14:43-72**
- ☐ **Mk 15:1—16:8**

Zechariah

- ☐ **Zec 1**
- ☐ **Zec 2—3**
- ☐ **Zec 4—5**
- ☐ **Zec 6**
- ☐ **Zec 7**
- ☐ **Zec 8**
- ☐ **Zec 9—10**
- ☐ **Zec 11**
- ☐ **Zec 12—13**
- ☐ **Zec 14**

Daniel

- ☐ **Da 1**
- ☐ **Da 2:1-30**
- ☐ **Da 2:31-49**
- ☐ **Da 3**
- ☐ **Da 4**
- ☐ **Da 5**
- ☐ **Da 6**
- ☐ **Da 7**
- ☐ **Da 8**
- ☐ **Da 9**
- ☐ **Da 10:1—11:35**
- ☐ **Da 11:36—12:13**

Malachi

- ☐ **Mal 1:1—2:16**
- ☐ **Mal 2:17—3:18**
- ☐ **Mal 4**

Hebrews

- ☐ **Heb 1**
- ☐ **Heb 2**
- ☐ **Heb 3**
- ☐ **Heb 4:1-13**
- ☐ **Heb 4:14—5:10**
- ☐ **Heb 5:11—6:20**
- ☐ **Heb 7**
- ☐ **Heb 8**
- ☐ **Heb 9**
- ☐ **Heb 10**
- ☐ **Heb 11**
- ☐ **Heb 12**
- ☐ **Heb 13**

Psalms 130—150

- ☐ **Ps 130**
- ☐ Ps 131—132
- ☐ **Ps 133**
- ☐ Ps 134—135
- ☐ Ps 136
- ☐ **Ps 137**
- ☐ Ps 138
- ☐ **Ps 139**
- ☐ Ps 140—141
- ☐ **Ps 142**
- ☐ **Ps 143**
- ☐ Ps 144
- ☐ **Ps 145**
- ☐ **Ps 146**
- ☐ Ps 147
- ☐ **Ps 148**
- ☐ Ps 149
- ☐ **Ps 150**

Revelation

- ☐ **Rev 1:1-8**
- ☐ **Rev 1:9-20**
- ☐ **Rev 2**
- ☐ **Rev 3**
- ☐ **Rev 4—5**
- ☐ **Rev 6**
- ☐ **Rev 7**
- ☐ **Rev 8—9**
- ☐ **Rev 10—11**
- ☐ **Rev 12**
- ☐ **Rev 13**
- ☐ **Rev 14—15**
- ☐ **Rev 16**
- ☐ **Rev 17—18**
- ☐ **Rev 19**
- ☐ **Rev 20**
- ☐ **Rev 21—22**

Getting the Most Out of *The NIV Quiet Time Bible*

Cindy Bunch & Andrew T. Le Peau

Quiet time can seem like an impossible dream to many of us. We face so many demands—work, family, friends, maintaining a home, schoolwork, church obligations each day—that we have little time left for peaceful reflection. Yet this can be one of the most renewing and vitalizing experiences of our Christian lives.

Whether you call it quiet time, devotions, or Bible study and prayer, what we are talking about is a portion of your day that is set aside to be in solitude. It is a time to connect with God and to hear what he has to say to you, to study Scripture, to apply the Word to your life, to offer praise and worship to God, and to pray. This may also be a time when you record what you are learning in a spiritual journal.

God is calling us to be with him. We cannot neglect this honor.

Why a Quiet Time Bible?

The NIV Quiet Time Bible puts us in direct touch with God's Word. It leads us to discover what the Bible says rather than simply telling us what it says. In the same way, this Bible does not tell you how to apply the Word to your life; rather it guides us with God's help to apply the Scripture ourselves. It uncovers the questions we have, the issues we face and the challenges that lie ahead. In this way, God's Word becomes as current as this morning's breakfast conversations.

How does *The NIV Quiet Time Bible* accomplish all this? Not by giving you study notes, extensive background notes or cross-references. Instead, it helps you discover for yourself the meaning of Scripture by asking thought-provoking questions. This question format is known as *inductive Bible study*.

We tend to remember very little of what others tell us. But we remember a large percentage of what we discover ourselves. As it has been said, "Tell me, and I will forget. Show me, and I may remember. Involve me, and I will understand." This is why inductive study works so well. Even if other sources of spiritual nourishment are hard to find, if we learn how to feed ourselves from the Word of God, we will never go hungry.

The quiet times in this Bible are personal. The questions expose us to the promises, assurances, exhortations and challenges of God's Word. They are designed to allow the Scriptures to renew our minds so that we can be transformed by the Spirit of God. Our goal as Christians is not just to know *about* God, but to actually know him as one person knows another. He is our Friend, our Father, our Comforter, our Helper, our Guide and our Lord. Knowing him in this way, talking with him in this way calls for responses of joy, of worship, of repentance and sorrow, of hope and expectation. Loving God more. That's what this Bible is all about.

How to Use *The NIV Quiet Time Bible*

Because you will be making discoveries about yourself and about God, you may want to keep a special notebook to record what you are learning each day. You may want to note commitments that you make and keep a list of prayer concerns so that you can look back and discover how God has been working in your life.

At the beginning of each book of the Bible you will find a brief introduction which provides important information on who wrote the book, who it was written to and why it was written. The outline in each introduction provides an overview of all the quiet times in each book (but excludes text not covered in the quiet times). It will also include historical background and maps or charts in some cases. All of this is important to understanding each book.

Each quiet time has several components:

Warming Up to God. Sometimes a question that draws you into the theme for the day, sometimes a topic to reflect on or pray about, this portion is designed to help you prepare your heart and mind for what you will be learning from Scripture.

Daily Scripture Reading. Read and reread the assigned Bible passage to familiarize yourself with what the author is saying. When you begin a new section you may want to read the entire book along with the introduction to that book. This will give you a helpful overview of its contents. It might be good to have a Bible dictionary handy. You could use it to look up any unfamiliar words, names or places.

Discovering the Word. The studies ask three different kinds of questions. *Observation* questions help us to understand the content of the passage by asking about the basic facts: who, what, when, where and how. *Interpretation* questions delve into the meaning of the passage. *Application* questions help us discover its implications for growing in Christ. These three keys unlock the treasures of the biblical writings and help us live them out.

Applying the Word. This is your opportunity to make the study personal. How has God's Word spoken to you? What actions do you need to take as a result of what you have learned?

Responding in Prayer. The suggestion here is to help you begin to seek God's wisdom in the area you've studied. You will also want to pray about your daily concerns, for family and friends, and about national and world events.

The introductory articles that follow will help you to better understand each of the parts of the study and show you how to get the most out of them. If you've never had a quiet time before, you'll discover the reason to have one in John White's article. Steve Eyre offers help on how to approach the discipline of quiet time, while Jack Kuhatschek and James Nyquist help with how Bible study works. Finally, Bill Hybels overviews the components of prayer and journaling.

The studies are designed to take fifteen or twenty minutes. You'll want to set aside additional time for prayer. Feel free to work at your own pace. Sometimes you may want to spend two days on one quiet time; other times you might want to do two in one day (one psalm and one New Testament study, for example). There are a total of 730 quiet times, which will allow you to read the Bible in two years. However, this schedule should not be something you feel bound to. Go at your own pace and as the Spirit leads you. Not all of the psalms are covered in the quiet times, but you may want to read them all as you go along.

A plan is provided at the front of the Bible interspersing the Old and New Testament books. You can follow that or can move around according to your needs and interests and keep track of what you have covered. Another option would be to read the New Testament and the Psalms in one year and the Old Testament in a second year. The topical index offers help in areas of personal need. It's a place to turn when you feel sad or lonely or are in need of forgiveness. Each quiet time is indexed at the end of the Bible so that you can locate particular topics. Generally, you'll find that you gain the best grasp of each Bible book if you work through the book from beginning to end, rather than skipping around.

If you are in a Bible study group, you may be interested in knowing that our LifeGuide® Bible Study Series includes companion guides on each New Testament book and many Old Testament books. You may want to double up on your learning by using those guides, which provide studies forty-five to sixty minutes long and include leader's notes, in a group context.

It is our hope that these quiet times will be an encouragement and a source of growth for your life with Christ. May the Holy Spirit be with you as you meet God each day.

Why Have a Quiet Time?

John White

Quiet times work. Prayer and Bible study change us—and the people around us. Our values alter once we start meeting regularly with God. Some things that once seemed important shrivel, while others swell in significance.

We see people differently. We pity people we once feared, and pray for people who once enraged us.

We will, to be sure, approach problems differently, feel different about our work, our studies, our job, our future. Our goals will have changed so that life slowly takes on new meaning. The changes are understandable since we are influenced by our Creator God who we spend time with daily.

But do I recommend that we have a daily quiet time solely for these reasons? As a matter of fact, no. There's much more to be gained.

To commune with God is to touch both infinity and eternity. We have opened a window to both a beyondness and an immediacy which time and space are powerless to provide and which we can experience in no other way. The most widely read person has only rubbed shoulders with a few obscurity-bound professors or dipped into a selection of "the world's great books"—a contradictory jumble of finite perspectives. Yet we are invited to private tutorials with the fountain of ultimate wisdom.

We are invited to collaborate in the creation of destiny, not to be a mere spectator but a coauthor. God does not want to determine all things in splendid solitude by the word of his power. He wants the painting of the future to be a family project in which we all play a part under his benign direction. Earth's policymakers are but actors in a drama written in heaven, and we are offered a pen to do some of the writing. Can we imagine anything better?

For Love's Sake

Yet not even for any of these reasons but for love's sake would I urge us to meet God daily!

As the deer pants for streams of water,
so my soul pants for you, O God.
My soul thirsts for God, for the living God.
When can I go and meet with God?
(Ps 42:1-2)

Our quest must be that of a suitor too blinded by beauty to descend to calculating self-interest, too intoxicated with love to care about the cost or the consequences of his suit.

It must be the love of Mary, sitting at Jesus' feet, enchanted by his words and grace, but deaf and blind to the frustration of her resentful sister (Lk 10:38-42). An enchantment of that sort will not be broken, nor its pleasures denied. It is time we forgot about our spiritual performance and our spiritual needs and gave ourselves up to passion.

"Beautiful!" you sigh. "I wish I felt that way. But I don't love God like that. So what can I do? How can I love when my heart is cold, when all I experience is the nagging guilt of knowing my love is a sorry thing not worth offering?"

But wait. A moment ago when you read the words of the psalmist, wasn't there a faint stirring of envy in you, an echo of the longing the psalmist expressed? If there was—and it matters not how feeble or faint—then your love is not absent but suppressed. It lies dormant beneath the weight of unbelief and discouragement.

Our love for God lies within many of us like a coiled spring, inactive but straining for release. It is a potential volcano, a dangerous thing that we fear to set free lest we shall have to cope with raging fire. Unless we take the risk of loving, we will only be half alive. But we should not be afraid of the longing within; it is more than matched by the greater longing of a God who planted it there.

Come, then, for love's sake. Come boldly defying fears. Enter into a love-pact to meet Christ daily. Come trembling to confess inadequacies. He is gentle and will understand. He will not force us or hurry the pace beyond what we are able to tolerate.

Come to his footstool. Come trusting. And come for love of him.

How to Have a Quiet Time

Stephen D. Eyre

One of the questions I frequently ask in counseling and discipling is "How is your quiet time?" If the person is having one, usually there is a slight pause and then the answer "I am having it regularly." Or, "I have been studying the Scriptures diligently."

Both responses are good, but not what I am after. I want to know more than just frequency or diligence in Scripture. What I want to know is, What is happening in your personal encounter with God?

Only as I get a glimpse of what's happening in the heart in touch with God can I give helpful spiritual guidance. Is there a sense of worship, or a sense of deadness? Perhaps so many concerns come to mind that we can't focus on the Scriptures. Or our prayer may be jumbled and distracted. All these things mean something, indicating both our needs and what God may be doing in our hearts.

I also want to know what is happening in a quiet time because I have found that it is possible to be blind to the presence of God and not even know it. When this happens, quiet times become merely an empty formality. Scripture becomes a book of principles to be applied. Prayer is a shopping list of things God is supposed to do. Difficulties in life are problems God is supposed to solve.

When we are blind to God, what God is doing in us in the midst of difficulties is overlooked. That God might want us to listen rather than do all the talking in prayer never occurs to us. And that God might want to meet us in Scripture is lost in our search for principles.

The Presence of God

The Lord's presence is the birthright of every believer and the heart of every quiet time. Before Jesus was born he was named *Immanuel*—God with us. During his discipling of the apostles, Jesus promised them, and us, that he would not leave us as orphans but make his home with us (Jn 14:15-21). His last words in the Gospel of Matthew were his promise to be with us to the end of the age (Mt 28:20).

This is more than an abstract promise or an intellectual idea. Nor is it an exotic mystical experience. It is merely a matter of relationship. God intends for us to know that he is with us. Meeting with God is very similar to being with a friend when you know each other well. There is a sense of connection that is much deeper than what we say to each other or the things we do together.

Sometimes you can know the presence of the Lord as a warm, quiet affection that wells up as you sit quietly before him. At other times the sense of his presence may come as a deep sense of heaviness and grief over your sinfulness. Or perhaps you know the Lord is with you as you read the Scriptures—a sense of inner nourishment as you read about God's work in the lives of people in the Old and New Testaments.

God's presence gives strength for living. And, we should note, the presence of God with us is not merely for our benefit. Others too will sense a depth about our lives that stirs spiritual hunger within them.

Using Your Emotions

All relationships involve our emotions, and our relationship with God is no different. Just as ignoring our emotions will leave us feeling separate and distant from people, the same will be true of our relationship with God if we ignore its emotional dimension.

So if we are to grow in spiritual perception, then we need to understand that emotions play an important role. With my emotions I sense God's affection for me, embrace his Word and react to his commands.

I realize that to bring in emotions is to invite controversy. Talking about emotions among Christians can be, well, emotional. Some pride themselves on their emotional restraint. Others take pride in their ability to display emotion. For those who value emotional restraint, let me say that, while I am suggesting that we must open ourselves up to emotion, I am not necessarily advocating outward displays of emotion. For those who have found great benefit in the feeling side of faith, you should keep in mind that emotions are natural responses that vary from time to time and should not be forced or manipulated.

Both in Scripture and in history we see godly people whose emotions were central in their encounters with God. David, as many psalms testify, experienced tremendous heights and great depths. Elijah, Jeremiah, Jonah and Habakkuk, to mention a few, had their times of ups and lots of downs.

Our emotions are more than mere reactions. They mean something. The writer of Psalm 42 begins, "As the deer pants for streams of water, so my soul pants for you, O God." He continues, "Why are you downcast, O my soul? Why so disturbed within me?" (vv. 5, 11). Today we would just consider ourselves depressed. The psalmist, in contrast, knew that his soul was "downcast" for a reason; he was thirsty for a fresh encounter with God.

This is not to say that strong emotions are a guarantee that God's Spirit is at work. Satan can duplicate almost anything. The way to discern true spiritual affection is in our love for God. Are we growing in appreciation of God's might, majesty and beauty? And when we are emotionally down, are we pitying ourselves or are we reaching out to seek God's consolation?

Once we are open to our emotions before the Lord, fresh springs of spiritual life can open up. And there is no better place to embrace our emotions than in our quiet times.

Quiet Time Phases

Because knowing God is a dynamic personal relationship, just like any other relationship, it tends to shift and vary with time and circumstances. If we are unaware of this dynamic, we may expect the same thing to happen each time we sit down to enjoy time with God. But the reality is that our quiet times are full of variety. Sometimes they are rich and sweet, other times dry and boring. Sometimes they require great determination, and other times they seem fresh and spontaneous. Sometimes we may go for long periods in which we do not consistently have quiet times, while at other times we are easily able to maintain the discipline of meeting God regularly.

We should not feel guilty about these ebbs and flows. If we think of quiet times as merely something we do, a method to be followed, then this variety will bother us. But if we know that our quiet times are always changing because our relationship with God is always growing and developing, then we can view these changes in our quiet times with deeper spiritual insight.

Personality and Spiritual Disciplines

Our temperaments have a great deal to do with our spiritual disciplines. I have observed that people who are methodical and detail oriented—accountants and engineers, for example—may have a hard time getting beyond staying in a routine, focusing on rigorously doing one's spiritual duty. On the other hand, those who tend to be spontaneous—say, artists, musicians and designers—may struggle to maintain a routine, but meet God on a more intimate level.

I am of the spontaneous temperament. I don't like to settle into one way of doing things for very long. I have a natural inclination to avoid set daily quiet times. I deal with this tendency in two ways. Sometimes I find it necessary to be very determined on a daily basis. At other times, I make it a goal to have four or five quiet times during the week and feel good about it if I have three or four.

Whatever our quiet time experience, there is no place for self-condemnation or pride. When we do well, it is surely a gift of God's grace to us. When we do poorly, being either irregular or legalistic, we shouldn't be surprised. God isn't. I don't condemn myself when I miss the mark. I am grateful for what times I have. I know the Lord is glad to be with me, and I determine to do better next time.

Each person has to move through the spiritual journey in his or her own way. Wherever we are in our spiritual lives, we should keep in mind that our goal in having a quiet time is to live with a heart-sense of devotion in the presence of God.

Inexpressible Joy

Quiet times are so much more than a duty. A quiet time is a divine encounter. God is with us. The purpose of a quiet time is to meet with him. If we are not listening for him, if we are not looking for him, we may miss the meeting.

On the other hand, if we are looking and listening through carefully developed spiritual disciplines, we will, in the words of Peter, be "filled with an inexpressible and glorious joy" (1Pe 1:8).

The Lord is present in his world, and all creation declares his glory. In our work, our family, our recreation, whatever we do, we can be filled with a sense of his presence.

However, unless we practice the discipline of a quiet time, we will be apt to miss his glory that swirls and sings around us. A fruitful quiet time will allow us to be before him in such a way that we sense his presence in everything we do.

How to Study the Bible

James F. Nyquist & Jack Kuhatschek

Sherlock Holmes was known for his brilliant powers of observation. One day a stranger came into Holmes's study. The detective looked over the gentleman carefully and then remarked to Watson: "Beyond the obvious facts that he has at some time done manual labour, that he takes snuff, that he is a Freemason, that he has been in China, and that he has done considerable amount of writing lately, I can deduce nothing else."[1]

Watson was so astounded by his abilities that he commented: "I could not help laughing at the ease with which he explained his process of deduction. 'When I hear you give your reasons,' I remarked, 'the thing always appears to me to be so ridiculously simple that I could easily do it myself, though at each successive instance of your reasoning I am baffled, until you explain your process. And yet I believe that my eyes are as good as yours.'

" 'Quite so,' he answered . . . throwing himself down into an armchair. 'You see, but you do not observe.' "[2]

Step One: Observation

The first step in personal Bible study is to make several *observations* about the passage or book you are studying. Like a good detective, we must train our eyes to see the obvious and the not so obvious. We can learn to do this by bombarding the book or passage with questions. Rudyard Kipling once wrote:

> I have six faithful serving men
> Who taught me all I know,
> Their names are *What* and *Where* and *When*
> And *How* and *Why* and *Who*.

Who—Who is the author of the book? To whom is he writing? Who are the major and minor characters?

Where—Where do the events occur? Are there any references to towns, cities, provinces? If you are reading a letter, where do the recipients live?

When—Are there any references to the time, day, month or year, or to when events took place in relation to other events?

What—What actions or events are taking place? What words or ideas are repeated or are central to the passage? What is the mood (joyous, somber)?

Why—Does the passage offer any reasons, explanations, statements of purpose?

How—How is the passage written? Is it a letter, speech, poem, parable? Does the author use any figures of speech (similes, metaphors)? How is it organized (around ideas, people, geography)?

The observation questions in the quiet times (which often begin with one of these six words) help us probe a book or passage and uncover many important facts. *Writing down* our observations in a notebook helps us make sure we are observing clearly and allows us to refer to these facts later in our study.

The importance of careful observation cannot be

overstressed since your observations will form the basis for your interpretations. In one of his most baffling cases, Sherlock Holmes commented to Watson: "I had . . . come to an entirely erroneous conclusion, which shows, my dear Watson, how dangerous it always is to reason from insufficient data."[3]

Sometimes observation may seem simplistic and dull. But it is extremely important. As Holmes suggests, faulty or inadequate data could lead us to wrong conclusions about what the passage means, which is the next step in the process.

Step Two: Interpretation

When we interpret we seek to understand those facts discovered through careful observation.

Were there any words you didn't understand? Define them.

Did the author use figurative language? This needs to be unraveled.

Were major ideas presented? Try to grasp their meaning and significance.

Did you encounter any difficulties? Seek to resolve them.

Meaning, significance, explanation—these are the goals of the interpreter. How do you reach these goals? And once you have reached them, how do you know you are not mistaken?

For example, have you ever been discussing a passage of Scripture with someone when suddenly he or she says, "That's just *your* interpretation," as if to say, "You have your interpretation and I have mine, and mine is just as good as yours!"

The person is half right. People often disagree on how the Bible should be interpreted. But just because there are many different interpretations of a passage doesn't mean they are all *good* interpretations. A good interpretation must pass one crucial test—it must conform to the *author's* intended meaning. You may have a seemingly wonderful interpretation of Scripture, but if it is different from what the author intended, it is incorrect.

How then can we discover the author's meaning? By following five steps:

1. Discover the historical context of the book. The events described in the Bible took place thousands of years ago. Therefore, we often lack important information regarding the background or context in which these events took place. For example, almost every New Testament letter was written to address a particular problem or set of problems: the Galatians were seeking to be justified by law; the Corinthians wanted answers to questions about marriage, spiritual gifts, meat offered to idols and so on; Timothy needed to know how to restore order to a church.

Sometimes the background or context of a psalm, prophetic book or New Testament letter can be found within the book or passage itself. For example, in 1 John we read, "I am writing these things to you about those who are trying to lead you astray" (1Jn 2:26). The introductions to each book in *The NIV Quiet Time Bible* also give you much of the basic information you'll need. If you want more, you can always consult a good reference work like the *New Bible Dictionary*.

2. Identify the type of literature you are studying. The biblical authors communicated in a variety of ways—through stories, letters, poems, proverbs, parables and symbols. The *way* they say things adds richness and beauty to *what* they say.

The literature of the Bible has been classified into various types. These include discourse (for example, the New Testament letters), prose narrative (the style used in the Gospels re-creating scenes and events from biblical history), poetry (the Psalms), proverbs (wise sayings such as those in the book of Proverbs), parables (Jesus used parables to explain a spiritual truth by means of a story or analogy), prophetic literature (for example, Isaiah) and apocalyptic literature (Revelation, which makes heavy use of symbolism, fits here).

3. Get an overview of the book. In Bible study it is helpful to get an overview of the book you are studying. And you may want to do this before starting on the quiet times in any given book. The parts of the book only take on their true significance in light of the whole. But remember that the way a book is put together will be closely related to its literary type. An epistle such as Romans is organized around ideas. Historical narratives are put together in a variety of ways. Genesis (after chapter 11) is organized around people: Abraham, Isaac, Jacob and Joseph. The Gospel of John focuses primarily on several "signs" which Jesus did. Psalm 119 is structured around the letters of the Hebrew alphabet!

Begin by reading quickly through the book. As you read, try to discover its overall theme. Next, look for major sections or divisions within the book. Look for connections or relationships between the sections, subsections and paragraphs. Look also for contracts, for cause and effect, for movement from general to specific and so on. Continually ask yourself how these paragraphs, subsections and sections contribute to the overall theme of the book.

4. Study the book passage by passage. Once you have an overview of the structure and contents of a book, begin studying it passage by passage, which are already clearly divided for you in this Bible. Many of the questions you will find in the quiet times will help you identify the main *subject* of the passage, what the author is *saying* about it, the *context* of the passage you are studying and its *atmosphere* or *mood.*

5. Compare your interpretation with a good commentary. Once you feel you have understood the main subject of the passage and what the author is saying about it, compare your interpretation with that of a good commentary, such as the *New Bible Commentary,* which can give you additional insights that you might have missed. It can also serve as a corrective if you have misunderstood something the author has said. But do your best to understand the passage on your own before consulting a commentary.

Step Three: Application

To properly apply the Scriptures, we must remember the nature of Scripture. We mentioned earlier that almost every book of the Bible was written to address specific problems, needs and questions of the people living *at that time.*

We face many of these same problems and questions today. It is still possible to take a fellow believer to court, and we still have questions about marriage. In fact there are hundreds of ways in which our problems and needs correspond to those faced by the people in the Bible. This is natural since we share a common humanity.

This leads us to the first principle of application:

> Rule #1: *Whenever our situation corresponds to that faced by the original readers, God's Word to us is exactly the same as it was to them.*

But there are also situations from their day which do not have an exact counterpart today. This, too, is to be expected because of the differences between modern and biblical culture. In such cases we should follow the second principle of application:

> Rule #2: *Whenever our situation does not correspond to that faced by the original readers, we should look for the* principle *underlying God's Word to them. We can then apply that principle to comparable situations today.*

For example, what was the principle underlying Paul's words about food sacrificed to idols? He was concerned that the Corinthians not do anything that would lead someone with a weak conscience to sin: "Therefore, if what I eat causes my brother to fall into sin, I will never eat meat again, so that I will not cause him to fall" (1Co 8:13). This principle might be applicable to many situations today, such as whether a Christian should drink alcoholic beverages around someone who is a former alcoholic—or drink at all.

Once we understand these principles of application, we can think of unlimited ways in which God's Word applies today.

Practice Makes Perfect (Well, Almost)

Learning to study the Bible is like learning any other skill—the more you do it, the easier it becomes. One of the side benefits of using *The NIV Quiet Time Bible* regularly is that you will be trained to better observe, interpret and apply Scripture. At first, it may seem mechanical, like learning how to type. And remember, you are not alone in Bible study. The Holy Spirit did not write Scripture in order to confuse us. He will help you to understand and apply the Bible as you pray, study diligently and make use of many of the study aids available today. Bon appetit!

---

[1]*The Illustrated Sherlock Holmes Treasury* (New York: Avenel Books, 1976), p. 17.

[2]Ibid., p. 2 (emphasis added).

[3]Ibid., p. 112.

Prayer and Journaling

Bill Hybels

According to a well-known business axiom, "if you want to know something, ask an expert." If you want to learn about sailboat racing, ask Dennis Connor. If you want to know about broadcast journalism, ask Diane Sawyer. If you want to find out how to turn around a large corporation, ask Lee Iacocca.

It makes sense, then, if you want to learn how to pray, to ask the number-one expert—Jesus Christ himself. Jesus' disciples recognized his expertise. Once they stumbled upon him while he was praying privately (see Lk 11:1). They were so moved by his earnestness and intensity that when he finally got up from his knees, one of them timidly asked, "Would you teach us to pray?" They knew that in comparison to their Master, they were mere neophytes—first-graders in the school of prayer.

Jesus did not object to their question. Instead, he took the opportunity to teach them how to pray. This is what he said:

> When you pray, do not be like the hypocrites, for they love to pray standing in the synagogues and on the street corners to be seen by men. . . . When you pray, go into your room, close the door and pray to your Father, who is unseen. Then your Father, who sees what is done in secret, will reward you. And when you pray, do not keep on babbling like pagans, for they think they will be heard because of their many words. Do not be like them, for your Father knows what you need before you ask him.
>
> This, then, is how you should pray:
>
> "Our Father in heaven, hallowed be your name, your kingdom come, your will be done on earth as it is in heaven. Give us today our daily bread. Forgive us our debts, as we also have forgiven our debtors. And lead us not into temptation, but deliver us from the evil one." (Mt 6:5-13)

No other passage in Scripture tells so straightforwardly how to pray, and the advice Jesus offered his disciples two thousand years ago applies to all of us today: (1) pray secretly, (2) pray sincerely and (3) pray specifically.

Getting Away from Distractions

Some people pray in public places, at social gatherings and at mealtimes, just so they can be seen and heard and assumed to be religious. But prayer, Jesus says, is not a spectator sport. It is not something we are to engage in to give off signals of spirituality. Forget that idea, says Jesus. When you pray, go into your room and shut the door. Find a closet, an empty office, the workshop out in the garage, some secret place away from people and alone with God. That's where you can pray most effectively.

Why the emphasis on privacy? Why shut the door? First, there is an obvious, practical reason. A private place ensures a minimum of distractions, and most people find distractions deadly when it comes to making connection with God. Almost any kind of noise—voices, music, a ringing phone, kids, dogs, birds—can cause me to lose my concentration during a time of prayer. Even a ticking clock can catch me up in its rhythm until I'm tapping my foot and singing a country song to its beat. Jesus knows how our minds are put together, and he counsels, "Don't bother fighting distractions, because you'll lose. Avoid them. Find a quiet place where you can pray without interruption."

The practical reasons for privacy are important, but I think there is also a more subtle wisdom in Jesus' advice to pray in a secret place. Once you identify such a place and begin to use it regularly, a kind of aura surrounds it. Your prayer room becomes to you what the garden of Gethsemane became to Jesus—a holy place, the place where God meets with you.

I created such a prayer room near the credenza in a corner of my former office. In my prayer place I put an open Bible, a sign that says "God is able," a crown of thorns to remind me of the suffering

Savior and a shepherd's staff that I often hold up while making requests.

That office corner became a holy place for me. I arrived there around six o'clock in the morning when no one was around and the phone was unlikely to ring, and there I communed with the Lord. I poured out my heart to him, worshiped him, prayed for members of my congregation and received remarkable answers to my prayer.

My office has recently been relocated, and I now have a new prayer corner. But I miss the old one—not because there is anything holy about the corner itself, but because of what happened there. Every morning for several years I met with the Lord, and he met faithfully with me. Thinking of that corner is like thinking of home.

If you want to learn how to pray, find yourself a quiet place, free of distractions. It doesn't have to be a chapel. It can be the utility room, the kitchen pantry, the barn, your office or the front seat of your pickup truck, as long as the surroundings are familiar and quiet.

Meaning What We Say

Not only did Jesus tell his disciples to pray secretly; he also told them to pray sincerely. "Do not keep on babbling," he said. Be careful of clichés. Don't fall into the habit of using meaningless repetition.

How easy it is to use sanctified jargon while praying! Certain phrases sound so appropriate, so spiritual, so pious, that many believers learn to string them together and call that prayer. They may not even think of the implications of what they are saying.

For example, I sometimes hear a mature believer say very earnestly, "Dear Lord, please be with me as I go on this new job interview," or "Please be with me as I go on this trip." When you first hear it, this request sounds holy. Unfortunately, it doesn't make sense. I'm often tempted to ask the one doing the praying, "Why do you ask God to do what he is already doing?" We don't need to ask God to be with us if we are members of his family. Instead, we need to pray that we will be *aware* of his presence, that we will be confident because of it. Asking God to be with us when he is already there is one kind of "babbling."

Another kind of meaningless repetition is often heard at the dinner table. A believer sits down to a meal that is a nutritional nightmare. The grease is bubbling, the salt is glistening, the sugared drink stands ready to slosh the stuff down. "Dear Lord," the person prays, "bless this food to our bodies, and grant us strength and nourishment from it so that we may do your will." God's will might be for the believer to say, "Amen," push back from the table and give the meal to the dog—except that dogs matter to God too!

The apostle Paul tells us God's will in 1 Corinthians 6:20: "Honor God with your body." That means putting the right things into your body. Don't ask God to bless junk food and miraculously transform it so that it has nutritional value. Doing that is acting like the fifth-grader who, after taking the geography test, prayed, "Dear God, please make Detroit the capital of Michigan." That's not how God works.

Praying Specifically

God-honoring prayers are not simply shopping lists. They are more than cries for help, strength, mercy and miracles. Authentic prayer should include worship: "Our Father in heaven, hallowed be your name" (Mt 6:9). It should include submission: "Your will be done on earth as it is in heaven" (v. 10). Requests are certainly appropriate: "Give us today our daily bread" (v. 11); as are confessions: "Forgive us our debts, as we also have forgiven our debtors" (v. 12).

The Lord's Prayer is an excellent model, but it was never intended to be a magical incantation to get God's attention. Jesus didn't give this prayer as a paragraph to be recited; in fact, he had just warned against using repetitious phrases. Instead, he gave it as a pattern to suggest the variety of elements that should be included when we pray.

Putting Prayers on Paper

A good way to learn to pray specifically is to write out your prayers and then read them to God. Many people find they are better able to concentrate if they put pen to paper and arrange their assorted thoughts into an organized format. I've been doing this for several years, and I find that it helps me in several ways. It forces me to be specific; broad generalities don't look good on paper. It keeps my mind from wandering. And it helps me see when

God answers prayers.

At the end of each month, I read over my prayer journal and see where God has done miraculous things. Whenever my faith feels weak, I turn to my journal and see evidence that God is answering my prayers. If I can list a number of answers to specific prayers in January, I feel better prepared to trust God in February.

I write out my prayers every day; I have not been able to grow in my prayer life any other way. Experiment and see what works best for you. Try writing out your prayers once a week at first. If you find it helpful, do it more often. If it cramps your style and makes you uncomfortable, find another way that is more effective for you. But however you do it, pray Jesus' way: make your prayers private, sincere and specific.

Remember that God's prevailing power is released through prayer. He is interested in you and your needs. He is able to meet any need, and he has invited you to pray. His Son, Jesus, the expert on prayer, has given instructions so that you know just how to pray.

Here's an assignment to get your prayer routine started. Take a sheet of paper and draw three horizontal lines across it, dividing it into four sections. Label the sections A, C, T and S.

In the first section, write a paragraph of adoration. List God's characteristics that especially move you today. In the second, write a paragraph of confession. Specifically identify the sins that are on your conscience. (You can burn this paper when you're done with it!) In the third, list God's blessings for which you are thankful. And in the fourth, make your requests, whatever they may be.

Do this again tomorrow, and the next day. Experiment with the ACTS routine. Adapt the categories to fit your situation, but be sure to include each category each time you pray. Experience the blessings of balance.

And see what God does in your life.

PREFACE

The New International Version of the Holy Bible is a completely new translation made by over a hundred scholars working directly from the best available Greek texts. It had its beginning in 1965 when, after several years of exploratory study by committees from the Christian Reformed Church and the National Association of Evangelicals, a group of scholars met at Palos Heights, Illinois, and concurred in the need for a new translation of the Bible in contemporary English. This group, though not made up of official church representatives, was transdenominational. Its conclusion was endorsed by a large number of leaders from many denominations who met in Chicago in 1966.

Responsibility for the new version was delegated by the Palos Heights group to a self-governing body of fifteen, the Committee on Bible Translation, composed for the most part of biblical scholars from colleges, universities and seminaries. In 1967 the New York Bible Society (now the International Bible Society) generously undertook the financial sponsorship of the project—a sponsorship that made it possible to enlist the help of many distinguished scholars. The fact that participants from the United States, Great Britain, Canada, Australia and New Zealand worked together gave the project its international scope. That they were from many denominations—including Anglican, Assemblies of God, Baptist, Brethren, Christian Reformed, Church of Christ, Evangelical Free, Lutheran, Mennonite, Methodist, Nazarene, Presbyterian, Wesleyan and other churches helped to safeguard the translation from sectarian bias.

How it was made helps to give the New International Version its distinctiveness. The translation of each book was assigned to a team of scholars. Next, one of the Intermediate Editorial Committees revised the initial translation, with constant reference to the Hebrew, Aramaic or Greek. Their work then went to one of the General Editorial Committees, which checked it in detail and made another thorough revision. This revision in turn was carefully reviewed by the Committee on Bible Translation, which made further changes and then released the final version for publication. In this way the entire Bible underwent three revisions, during each of which the translation was examined for its faithfulness to the original languages and for its English style.

All this involved many thousands of hours of research and discussion regarding the meaning of the texts and the precise way of putting them into English. It may well be that no other translation has been made by a more thorough process of review and revision from committee to committee than this one.

From the beginning of the project, the Committee on Bible Translation held to certain goals for the New International Version: that it would be an accurate translation and one that would have clarity and literary quality and so prove suitable for public and private reading, teaching, preaching, memorizing and liturgical use. The Committee also sought to preserve some measure of continuity with the long tradition of translating the Scriptures into English.

In working toward these goals, the translators were united in their commitment to the authority and infallibility of the Bible as God's Word in written form. They believe that it contains the divine answer to the deepest needs of humanity, that it sheds unique light on our path in a dark world, and that it sets forth the way to our eternal well-being.

The first concern of the translators has been the accuracy of the translation and its fidelity to the thought of the biblical writers. They have striven for more than a word-for-word translation. Because thought patterns and syntax differ from language to language, faithful communication of the meaning of the writers of the Bible demands frequent modifications in sentence structure and constant regard for the contextual meanings of words.

The Committee on Bible Translation submitted the developing version to a number of stylistic consultants. Samples of the translation were tested for clarity and ease of reading by various kinds of people—young and old, highly educated and less well educated, ministers and laymen. Concern for clear and natural English motivated the translators and consultants. In view of the international use of English, the translators sought to avoid obvious Americanisms on the one hand and obvious Anglicisms on the other. A British edition reflects the comparatively few differences of significant idiom and of spelling.

As for the traditional pronouns "thou," "thee" and "thine" in reference to the Deity, the translators judged that to use these archaisms (along with the old verb forms such as "doest," "wouldest" and "hadst") would violate accuracy in translation. Greek does not use special pronouns for the persons of the Godhead. A present-day translation is not enhanced by forms that in the time of the King James Version were used in everyday speech, whether referring to God or man.

The Greek text used in translating the New Testament was an eclectic one. No other piece of ancient literature has such an abundance of manuscript witnesses as does the New Testament. Where existing manuscripts differ, the translators made their choice of readings according to accepted principles of New Testament textual criticism. Footnotes call attention to places where there was uncertainty about what the original text was. The best current printed texts of the Greek New Testament were used.

There is a sense in which the work of translation is never wholly finished. This applies to all great literature and uniquely so to the Bible. In 1973 the New Testament in the New International Version was published. Since then, suggestions for corrections and revisions have been received from various sources. The Committee on Bible Translation carefully considered the suggestions and adopted a number of them. These were incorporated in the first printing of the entire Bible in 1978. Additional revisions were made by the Committee on Bible Translation in 1983 and appear in printings after that date.

As in other ancient documents, the precise meaning of the biblical texts is sometimes uncertian. This is more often the case with the Hebrew and Aramaic texts than with the Greek text. Although archaeological and linguistic discoveries in this century aid in understanding difficult passages, some uncertainties remain. The more significant of these have been called to the reader's attention in the footnotes.

In regard to the divine name *YHWH,* commonly referred to as the *Tetragrammaton,* the translators adopted the device used in most English versions of rendering that name as "LORD" in capital letters to distinguish it from *Adonai,* another Hebrew word rendered "Lord," for which small letters are used. Wherever the two names stand together in the Old Testament as a compound name of God, they are rendered "Sovereign LORD."

Because for most readers today the phrases "the LORD of hosts" and "God of hosts" have little meaning, this version renders them "the LORD Almighty" and "God Almighty." These renderings convey the sense of the Hebrew, namely, "he who is sovereign over all the 'hosts' (powers) in heaven and on earth, especially over the 'hosts' (armies) of Israel." For readers unacquainted with Hebrew this does not make clear the distinction between *Sabaoth* ("hosts" or "Almighty") and *Shaddai* (which can also be translated "Almighty"), but the latter occurs infrequently and is always footnoted. When *Adonai* and *YHWH Sabaoth* occur together, they are rendered "the Lord, the LORD Almighty."

As for other proper nouns, the familiar spellings of the King James Version are generally retained. Names traditionally spelled with "ch," except where it is final, are usually spelled in this translation with "k" or "c," since the biblical languages do not have the sound that "ch" frequently indicates in English—for example, in *chant.* For well-known names such as Zechariah, however, the traditional spelling has been retained. Variation in the spelling of names in the original languages has usually not been indicated. Where a person or place has two or more different names in the Hebrew, Aramaic or Greek texts, the more familiar one has generally been used, with footnotes where needed.

To achieve clarity the translators sometimes supplied words not in the original texts but required by the context. If there was uncertainty about such material, it is enclosed in brackets. Also for the sake of clarity or style, nouns, including some proper nouns, are sometimes substituted for pronouns, and vice versa. As an aid to the reader, italicized sectional headings are inserted in most of the books. They are not to be regarded as part of the NIV text, are not for oral reading, and are not intended to dictate the interpretation of the sections they head.

The footnotes in this version are of several kinds, most of which need no explanation. Those giving alternative translations begin with "Or" and generally introduce the alternative with the last word preceding it in the text, except when it is a single-word alternative; in poetry quoted in a footnote a slant mark indicates a line division. Footnotes introduced by "Or" do not have uniform significance. In some cases two possible translations were considered to have about equal validity. In other cases, though the translators were convinced that the translation in the text was correct, they judged that another interpretation was possible and of sufficient importance to be represented in a footnote.

In the New Testament, footnotes that refer to uncertainty regarding the original text are introduced by "Some manuscripts" or similar expressions. In the Old Testament, evidence for the reading chosen is given first and evidence for the alternative is added after a semicolon (for example: Septuagint; Hebrew *father*). In such notes the term "Hebrew" refers to the Masoretic Text.

It should be noted that minerals, flora and fauna, architectural details, articles of clothing and jewelry, musical instruments and other articles cannot always be identified with precision. Also measures of capacity in the biblical period are particularly uncertain.

Like all translations of the Bible, made as they are by imperfect man, this one undoubtedly falls short of its goals. Yet we are grateful to God for the extent to which he has enabled us to realize these goals and for the strength he has given us and our colleagues to complete our task. We offer this version of the Bible to him in whose name and for whose glory it has been made. We pray that it will lead many into a better understanding of the Holy Scriptures and a fuller knowledge of Jesus Christ the incarnate Word, of whom the Scriptures so faithfully testify.

The Committee on Bible Translation

June 1978
(Revised August 1983)

Names of the translators and editors
may be secured
from the International Bible Society,
translation sponsors of the
New International Version,
P.O. Box 62970,
Colorado Springs, Colorado
80962-2970 U.S.A.

TABLE OF WEIGHTS AND MEASURES

Biblical Unit		*Approximate American Equivalent*	*Approximate Metric Equivalent*
		WEIGHTS	
talent	*(60 minas)*	75 pounds	34 kilograms
mina	*(50 shekels)*	1¼ pounds	0.6 kilogram
shekel	*(2 bekas)*	⅗ ounce	11.5 grams
pim	*(⅔ shekel)*	⅓ ounce	7.6 grams
beka	*(10 gerahs)*	⅕ ounce	5.5 grams
gerah		1/50 ounce	0.6 gram
		LENGTH	
cubit		18 inches	0.5 meter
span		9 inches	23 centimeters
handbreadth		3 inches	8 centimeters
		CAPACITY	
		Dry Measure	
cor [homer]	*(10 ephahs)*	6 bushels	220 liters
lethek	*(5 ephahs)*	3 bushels	110 liters
ephah	*(10 omers)*	⅗ bushel	22 liters
seah	*(⅓ ephah)*	7 quarts	7.3 liters
omer	*(1/10 ephah)*	2 quarts	2 liters
cab	*(1/18 ephah)*	1 quart	1 liter
		Liquid Measure	
bath	*(1 ephah)*	6 gallons	22 liters
hin	*(⅙ bath)*	4 quarts	4 liters
log	*(1/72 bath)*	⅓ quart	0.3 liter

The figures of the table are calculated on the basis of a shekel equaling 11.5 grams, a cubit equaling 18 inches and an ephah equaling 22 liters. The quart referred to is either a dry quart (slightly larger than a liter) or a liquid quart (slightly smaller than a liter), whichever is applicable. The ton referred to in the footnotes is the American ton of 2,000 pounds.

This table is based on the best available information, but it is not intended to be mathematically precise; like the measurement equivalents in the footnotes, it merely gives approximate amounts and distances. Weights and measures differed somewhat at various times and places in the ancient world. There is uncertainty particularly about the ephah and the bath; further discoveries may give more light on these units of capacity.

THE
OLD TESTAMENT

Genesis

We all look back and wonder about beginnings. Children are fascinated with stories of their birth and babyhood. Families trace their genealogies. Nations produce histories of their origin. The pressures of the present and hopes for the future take on new meaning when we know more about how it all began.

Genesis is a book of beginnings: the origin of the universe, birth of the human race and founding of the Hebrew nation. Yet this book is more than a record of origins. It provides the foundation for many of the great themes so prominent throughout the Old and New Testaments. Here we learn about God, humanity and nature in their mutual relationships. The Creator and Controller of the universe reveals himself as the Lord and Judge of history, which has both a purpose and a goal. Concepts of covenant and grace, election and redemption permeate God's saving activity to overcome the consequences of evil and sin. These great doctrines of creation, sin and salvation trace their beginnings to this remarkable book.

It should not surprise us that Genesis, more than any other part of the Bible, has been the scene of historical, literary, theological and scientific battles. Some of these issues have made their way out of church and seminary into our schools and courts. Since much discussion of these controversial questions is based on misinformation and secondhand opinion, we should find out for ourselves what the text says and, equally important, what it does *not* say. The purpose of these quiet times is to help you discover the meaning of Genesis for those who first heard its message and then for us today. You may be surprised to find how clear Genesis is when we let the author have his say and refrain from importing questions he never intended to answer.

Historical Context

Genesis is the first of five books called the Pentateuch. The New Testament attributes these writings to Moses. During the last century many critics have questioned the Mosaic authorship of the Pentateuch. Liberal scholarship attributes these writings to unknown authors or redactors long after Moses, probably late in the monarchy. Nevertheless, a strong case can be made for the traditional view that Moses wrote most of the Pentateuch, even though he may have used existing sources for Genesis and some of the material may have been edited after his death. At any rate, we will assume that the message of Genesis was given to Israel during their years in the wilderness, around 1250 B.C. Therefore, we need to know something of Israel's cultural and religious situation in order to understand what the author intends to teach.

For about four hundred years the Hebrews had languished in Egypt, far from the land promised to Abraham. Those centuries took a spiritual as well as a physical toll. The Hebrews had no Scriptures, only some oral patriarchal traditions. Except for a few midwives who remained faithful, the people had supplanted the fear of the Lord with cultic worship of the gods of other nations. Even after they were miraculously delivered from slavery and led toward Canaan, the people apparently had little knowledge of the God of their forefather Abraham.

When the Hebrews arrived at Mount Sinai, their worldview and lifestyle differed little from that of neighboring nations. Their culture was essentially pagan. Now God was calling them to keep his covenant, to become "a kingdom of priests and a holy nation" (Ex 19:6). Although the people assented enthusiastically, their yes was just the beginning of a long, painful process by which God would create a new culture to fulfill their vocation.

Moses faced a formidable task. The people needed a radically different theology to know God and his purpose in history, a new religious institution to guide their worship, another lifestyle for moral and ethical living, and a new cosmology to reorient their attitudes toward the natural world. These five books of Moses were designed to make the Hebrews a people of God through a new, divinely instituted culture. For this reason the Pentateuch provides strong antipagan teaching to help God's people make a clean break with the past and learn to look at all of life from his point of view.

The Role of Genesis

This first book opens with an account of the beginning of the universe that lays the foundation for Israel's new cosmology. The narrative strikes hard not only at the nature gods worshiped by Israel's pagan neighbors but also at an array of false philosophies which have led large sections of the human race astray in every century.

The creation of the world culminates in God's forming a man and woman. But they soon rebel against their Creator and plunge humanity into sin, with devastating consequences. From then on Genesis recounts the drama of God's mighty acts of judgment and mercy as his redemptive purpose unfolds.

Throughout these narratives a central and organizing motif is the "call of God." His creative word initially calls the whole creation into being. God then calls into existence a covenant community to be his special people. Genesis and the whole Old Testament look forward to his new creation and covenant in Jesus Christ, into whose fellowship we also are called.

Outline

Part 1: Creation and Primeval History

Part 2: The Emergence of Israel

Part 3: Migration to Egypt

1 / *Genesis 1:1—2:3*
Our Place in the World

HAVE YOU EVER been involved in a discussion about creation? Do you wonder why this first chapter of Genesis generates so much controversy and what it is really meant to teach? This study will help you understand the author's purpose in writing and what his message taught Israel about their God, his creation and their special place in the natural world. It will also help you to consider how this account is relevant today. Remember that Genesis 1, like other books in the Bible, describes natural events in popular and nontechnical language. It reports them as they appear to the average person without explaining exactly *how* they took place. The emphasis is on the *who* and *why*, the Creator and his purposes in creation.

Warming Up to God Isn't it amazing? The Creator of the universe is also the God who wants to be with you today. Sit quietly and let him come to you now.

Read Genesis 1:1—2:3.

1 In the beginning God created the heavens
and the earth. 2Now the earth was[a]
formless and empty, darkness was over
the surface of the deep, and the Spirit of God
was hovering over the waters.

3And God said, "Let there be light," and there
was light. 4God saw that the light was good,
and he separated the light from the darkness.
5God called the light "day," and the darkness
he called "night." And there was evening, and
there was morning—the first day.
6And God said, "Let there be an expanse be-
tween the waters to separate water from wa-
ter." 7So God made the expanse and sepa-
rated the water under the expanse from the
water above it. And it was so. 8God called the
expanse "sky." And there was evening, and
there was morning—the second day.
9And God said, "Let the water under the sky be
gathered to one place, and let dry ground ap-
pear." And it was so. 10God called the dry
ground "land," and the gathered waters he
called "seas." And God saw that it was good.
11Then God said, "Let the land produce
vegetation: seed-bearing plants and trees on
the land that bear fruit with seed in it, ac-
cording to their various kinds." And it was
so. 12The land produced vegetation: plants
bearing seed according to their kinds and
trees bearing fruit with seed in it according to
their kinds. And God saw that it was good.
13And there was evening, and there was
morning—the third day.
14And God said, "Let there be lights in the ex-
panse of the sky to separate the day from the
night, and let them serve as signs to mark
seasons and days and years, 15and let them be
lights in the expanse of the sky to give light
on the earth." And it was so. 16God made two
great lights—the greater light to govern the
day and the lesser light to govern the night.
He also made the stars. 17God set them in the
expanse of the sky to give light on the earth,
18to govern the day and the night, and to sep-
arate light from darkness. And God saw that
it was good. 19And there was evening, and
there was morning—the fourth day.
20And God said, "Let the water teem with living
creatures, and let birds fly above the earth
across the expanse of the sky." 21So God cre-
ated the great creatures of the sea and every
living and moving thing with which the water
teems, according to their kinds, and every
winged bird according to its kind. And God
saw that it was good. 22God blessed them and
said, "Be fruitful and increase in number and
fill the water in the seas, and let the birds
increase on the earth." 23And there was eve-
ning, and there was morning—the fifth day.
24And God said, "Let the land produce living
creatures according to their kinds: livestock,
creatures that move along the ground, and
wild animals, each according to its kind."
And it was so. 25God made the wild animals
according to their kinds, the livestock ac-
cording to their kinds, and all the creatures
that move along the ground according to
their kinds. And God saw that it was good.
26Then God said, "Let us make man in our

[a]2 Or possibly *became*

image, in our likeness, and let them rule over
the fish of the sea and the birds of the air,
over the livestock, over all the earth,[b] and
over all the creatures that move along the
ground."

27 So God created man in his own image,
in the image of God he created him;
male and female he created them.

28 God blessed them and said to them, "Be
fruitful and increase in number; fill the earth
and subdue it. Rule over the fish of the sea
and the birds of the air and over every living
creature that moves on the ground."
29 Then God said, "I give you every seed-
bearing plant on the face of the whole earth
and every tree that has fruit with seed in it.
They will be yours for food. 30 And to all the
beasts of the earth and all the birds of the
air and all the creatures that move on the
ground—everything that has the breath of
life in it—I give every green plant for food."
And it was so.
31 God saw all that he had made, and it was
very good. And there was evening, and there
was morning—the sixth day.

2 Thus the heavens and the earth were
completed in all their vast array.
2 By the seventh day God had finished the
work he had been doing; so on the seventh
day he rested[c] from all his work. 3 And God
blessed the seventh day and made it holy, be-
cause on it he rested from all the work of
creating that he had done.

[b]26 Hebrew; Syriac *all the wild animals* [c]2 Or *ceased*; also in verse 3

Discovering the Word 1. In what ways do God's creative commands during the first three days add form to the formless earth (1:3–13)? 2. How do God's commands during the next three days add fullness to the empty earth (1:14–25)? 3. In what ways do you think God views his creation as being good (1:4, 10, 12, 18, 21, 25)? 4. In what ways are man and woman unique among God's creation (1:26–27)? 5. What special commands and provisions does God give to the man and woman in his creation (1:28–31)? 6. According to 1:26, the man and woman are made in the image and likeness of God. What similarities are there between God's own work in creation and the commands and responsibilities he gives to the man and woman?

Applying the Word 1. The creation account reveals that God brings order, beauty and harmony out of an originally chaotic situation. In what areas do you need to trust God to produce these qualities in your life? 2. As you look around at God's creation, how does it give you a greater appreciation for the Creator?

Responding in Prayer Thank God for the magnificence of his creation and for allowing you to play such an important role in it.

2 / *Genesis 2:4–25*
Life as God Intended It

For of all sad words of tongue or pen,
The saddest are these: "It might have been!"

THESE WORDS TAKE on special significance when we consider life as God originally intended it. Genesis 2 still provides the basis for understanding who we were meant to be in relation to God, nature and each other. This narrative is different from the first in both content and style. It quickly moves from the world at large to the narrow stage of "a garden in the east." The literary style also changes significantly with its more colorful and detailed descriptions. Yet it continues to be history, rather than parable or myth, as it supplements the brief account of the creation of man and woman in 1:26–30.

Warming Up to God Close your eyes and think of a lush tropical forest, gloriously scented and teeming with life. Drink in the beautiful world God made for his people. Allow thanksgiving to well up inside until you are a bubbling spring of praise for God.

Read Genesis 2:4–25.

4This is the account of the heavens and the earth when they were created.

When the LORD God made the earth and the heavens— 5and no shrub of the field had yet appeared on the earth[d] and no plant of the field had yet sprung up, for the LORD God had not sent rain on the earth[d] and there was no man to work the ground, 6but streams[e] came up from the earth and watered the whole surface of the ground— 7the LORD God formed the man[f] from the dust of the ground and breathed into his nostrils the breath of life, and the man became a living being.

8Now the LORD God had planted a garden in the east, in Eden; and there he put the man he had formed. 9And the LORD God made all kinds of trees grow out of the ground—trees that were pleasing to the eye and good for food. In the middle of the garden were the tree of life and the tree of the knowledge of good and evil.

10A river watering the garden flowed from Eden; from there it was separated into four headwaters. 11The name of the first is the Pishon; it winds through the entire land of Havilah, where there is gold. 12(The gold of that land is good; aromatic resin[g] and onyx are also there.) 13The name of the second river is the Gihon; it winds through the entire land of Cush.[h] 14The name of the third river is the Tigris; it runs along the east side of Asshur. And the fourth river is the Euphrates.

15The LORD God took the man and put him in the Garden of Eden to work it and take care of it. 16And the LORD God commanded the man, "You are free to eat from any tree in the garden; 17but you must not eat from the tree of the knowledge of good and evil, for when you eat of it you will surely die."

18The LORD God said, "It is not good for the man to be alone. I will make a helper suitable for him."

19Now the LORD God had formed out of the ground all the beasts of the field and all the birds of the air. He brought them to the man to see what he would name them; and whatever the man called each living creature, that was its name. 20So the man gave names to all the livestock, the birds of the air and all the beasts of the field.

But for Adam[i] no suitable helper was found. 21So the LORD God caused the man to fall into a deep sleep; and while he was sleeping, he took one of the man's ribs[j] and closed up the place with flesh. 22Then the LORD God made a woman from the rib[k] he had taken out of the man, and he brought her to the man.

23The man said,

"This is now bone of my bones
  and flesh of my flesh;
she shall be called 'woman,[l]'
  for she was taken out of man."

24For this reason a man will leave his father and mother and be united to his wife, and they will become one flesh.

25The man and his wife were both naked, and they felt no shame.

[d]5 Or *land*; also in verse 6 [e]6 Or *mist* [f]7 The Hebrew for *man (adam)* sounds like and may be related to the Hebrew for *ground (adamah)*; it is also the name *Adam* (see Gen. 2:20). [g]12 Or *good; pearls* [h]13 Possibly southeast Mesopotamia [i]20 Or *the man* [j]21 Or *took part of the man's side* [k]22 Or *part* [l]23 The Hebrew for *woman* sounds like the Hebrew for *man.*

Discovering the Word 1. The author describes the creation of man in verse 7. In what ways is his creation unique? 2. What are we told about the garden God has prepared for Adam (vv. 8–14)? 3. What responsibility, freedom and limitation does God give to the man (vv. 15–17)? 4. How does Adam's name for his new partner reflect his appreciation of her (v. 23)? 5. Explain in your own words what verse 24 teaches about marriage.

Applying the Word 1. Note the social dimension of being created in the image of God (v. 18). What implications does this have for your relationships with other people? 2. How has this passage helped you understand who you were created to be in relation to God, nature and other people?

Responding in Prayer Thank your heavenly Father for making you in his image and likeness.

3 / *Genesis 3*
How Can We Deal with Temptation?

IF GOD IS good and powerful, why does he allow so much evil and pain? Although the Bible doesn't answer this question directly, it shows how sin and its consequences entered the world. The last chapter left Adam and Eve in Eden at peace with God, themselves and the natural world over which they had been given stewardship. They had the freedom to fulfill this responsibility and eat any fruit in the garden, with one exception. The tree of the knowledge of good and evil would be the test of their obedience to the Creator. In this study we see how they met this test and what lessons we can learn from their experience.

Warming Up to God Remember that no sin is any different or worse than the first sin in the Garden of Eden. Tell Jesus about your sin—and let him forgive you.

Read Genesis 3.

3 Now the serpent was more crafty than any of the wild animals the LORD God had made. He said to the woman, "Did God really say, 'You must not eat from any tree in the garden'?"

2The woman said to the serpent, "We may eat fruit from the trees in the garden, 3but God did say, 'You must not eat fruit from the tree that is in the middle of the garden, and you must not touch it, or you will die.' "

4"You will not surely die," the serpent said to the woman. 5"For God knows that when you eat of it your eyes will be opened, and you will be like God, knowing good and evil."

6When the woman saw that the fruit of the tree was good for food and pleasing to the eye, and also desirable for gaining wisdom, she took some and ate it. She also gave some to her husband, who was with her, and he ate it. 7Then the eyes of both of them were opened, and they realized they were naked; so they sewed fig leaves together and made coverings for themselves.

8Then the man and his wife heard the sound of the LORD God as he was walking in the garden in the cool of the day, and they hid from the LORD God among the trees of the garden. 9But the LORD God called to the man, "Where are you?"

10He answered, "I heard you in the garden, and I was afraid because I was naked; so I hid."

11And he said, "Who told you that you were naked? Have you eaten from the tree that I commanded you not to eat from?"

12The man said, "The woman you put here with me—she gave me some fruit from the tree, and I ate it."

13Then the LORD God said to the woman, "What is this you have done?"

The woman said, "The serpent deceived me, and I ate."

14So the LORD God said to the serpent, "Because you have done this,

"Cursed are you above all the livestock
and all the wild animals!
You will crawl on your belly
and you will eat dust
all the days of your life.
15And I will put enmity
between you and the woman,
and between your offspring[m] and hers;
he will crush[n] your head,
and you will strike his heel."

16To the woman he said,

"I will greatly increase your pains in childbearing;
with pain you will give birth to children.
Your desire will be for your husband,
and he will rule over you."

17To Adam he said, "Because you listened to your wife and ate from the tree about which I commanded you, 'You must not eat of it,'

"Cursed is the ground because of you;
through painful toil you will eat of it
all the days of your life.
18It will produce thorns and thistles for you,
and you will eat the plants of the field.
19By the sweat of your brow
you will eat your food
until you return to the ground,

[m]15 *Or seed* [n]15 *Or strike*

since from it you were taken;
for dust you are
and to dust you will return."

20Adam[o] named his wife Eve,[p] because she
would become the mother of all the living.
21The LORD God made garments of skin for
Adam and his wife and clothed them. 22And the
LORD God said, "The man has now become like
one of us, knowing good and evil. He must not be
allowed to reach out his hand and take also from
the tree of life and eat, and live forever." 23So the
LORD God banished him from the Garden of Eden
to work the ground from which he had been
taken. 24After he drove the man out, he placed on
the east side[q] of the Garden of Eden cherubim
and a flaming sword flashing back and forth to
guard the way to the tree of life.

[o]20 Or *The man* [p]20 *Eve* probably means *living.* [q]24 Or *placed in front*

Discovering the Word 1. How does Eve's answer misrepresent God's command (vv. 2–3)? 2. The serpent now becomes more direct (vv. 4–5). What statements does he make about the purpose and results of the command? 3. How have the serpent's words distorted Eve's thinking (v. 6)? 4. How did Adam and Eve's sin immediately affect their attitude toward themselves, each other and God (vv. 7–13)? 5. What judgments does the Lord God pronounce on the serpent (vv. 14–15), the woman (v. 16) and the man (vv. 17–19)? (Describe them in your own words.) 6. What actions does God finally take to end this era in Eden (vv. 21–24)?

Applying the Word 1. Adam and Eve made several mistakes: they listened to a creature instead of the Creator, followed their own impressions against his instructions, doubted God's concern for their best interests and made self-fulfillment their goal. In what situations have any of these led you to disobey a command of God? 2. What one lesson have you learned from this study that can help you recognize and resist a temptation you are facing?

Responding in Prayer Romans 5:12 and 15 tell us that in the same way that sin entered the world through one person, it is redeemed by one man, our Lord Jesus Christ. Thank him for his love that erased our first sin in the garden and gave his wonderful grace.

4 / *Genesis 4—5*
Consequences of Sin

A LUTHERAN BISHOP in East Germany who suffered persecution first by the Nazis and then the Communists declared: "When God is not God, man is not man!" He had seen how the rejection of divine authority inevitably led to inhuman actions. In the previous chapter Adam and Eve's disobedience to God fractured their relationship with him. Now we see sin spreading to family relationships as hateful attitudes lead to violent actions.

Warming Up to God Jesus your Savior wants to care for you today. Hide under his shadow and tell him your concerns. He is listening and offers you peace.

Read Genesis 4—5.

4 Adam[r] lay with his wife Eve, and she
became pregnant and gave birth to
Cain.[s] She said, "With the help of the
LORD I have brought forth[t] a man." 2Later she
gave birth to his brother Abel.
Now Abel kept flocks, and Cain worked the
soil. 3In the course of time Cain brought some of
the fruits of the soil as an offering to the LORD.
4But Abel brought fat portions from some of the
firstborn of his flock. The LORD looked with favor
on Abel and his offering, 5but on Cain and his
offering he did not look with favor. So Cain was
very angry, and his face was downcast.
6Then the LORD said to Cain, "Why are you
angry? Why is your face downcast? 7If you do
what is right, will you not be accepted? But if you

[r]1 Or *The man* [s]1 *Cain* sounds like the Hebrew for *brought forth* or *acquired.* [t]1 Or *have acquired*

do not do what is right, sin is crouching at your
door; it desires to have you, but you must mas-
ter it."

8Now Cain said to his brother Abel, "Let's go
out to the field."[u] And while they were in the
field, Cain attacked his brother Abel and killed
him.

9Then the LORD said to Cain, "Where is your
brother Abel?"

"I don't know," he replied. "Am I my brother's
keeper?"

10The LORD said, "What have you done? Listen!
Your brother's blood cries out to me from the
ground. 11Now you are under a curse and driven
from the ground, which opened its mouth to re-
ceive your brother's blood from your hand.
12When you work the ground, it will no longer
yield its crops for you. You will be a restless wan-
derer on the earth."

13Cain said to the LORD, "My punishment is
more than I can bear. 14Today you are driving me
from the land, and I will be hidden from your
presence; I will be a restless wanderer on the
earth, and whoever finds me will kill me."

15But the LORD said to him, "Not so[v]; if anyone
kills Cain, he will suffer vengeance seven times
over." Then the LORD put a mark on Cain so that
no one who found him would kill him. 16So Cain
went out from the LORD's presence and lived in
the land of Nod,[w] east of Eden.

17Cain lay with his wife, and she became preg-
nant and gave birth to Enoch. Cain was then
building a city, and he named it after his son
Enoch. 18To Enoch was born Irad, and Irad was
the father of Mehujael, and Mehujael was the fa-
ther of Methushael, and Methushael was the fa-
ther of Lamech.

19Lamech married two women, one named
Adah and the other Zillah. 20Adah gave birth to
Jabal; he was the father of those who live in tents
and raise livestock. 21His brother's name was Ju-
bal; he was the father of all who play the harp and
flute. 22Zillah also had a son, Tubal-Cain, who
forged all kinds of tools out of[x] bronze and iron.
Tubal-Cain's sister was Naamah.

23Lamech said to his wives,

"Adah and Zillah, listen to me;
  wives of Lamech, hear my words.
I have killed[y] a man for wounding me,
  a young man for injuring me.
24If Cain is avenged seven times,
  then Lamech seventy-seven times."

25Adam lay with his wife again, and she gave
birth to a son and named him Seth,[z] saying,
"God has granted me another child in place of
Abel, since Cain killed him." 26Seth also had a
son, and he named him Enosh.

At that time men began to call on[a] the name
of the LORD.

5 This is the written account of Adam's
line.

When God created man, he made him in
the likeness of God. 2He created them male and
female and blessed them. And when they were
created, he called them "man.[b]"

3When Adam had lived 130 years, he had a son
in his own likeness, in his own image; and he
named him Seth. 4After Seth was born, Adam
lived 800 years and had other sons and daughters.
5Altogether, Adam lived 930 years, and then he
died.

6When Seth had lived 105 years, he became the
father[c] of Enosh. 7And after he became the fa-
ther of Enosh, Seth lived 807 years and had other
sons and daughters. 8Altogether, Seth lived 912
years, and then he died.

9When Enosh had lived 90 years, he became
the father of Kenan. 10And after he became the
father of Kenan, Enosh lived 815 years and had
other sons and daughters. 11Altogether, Enosh
lived 905 years, and then he died.

12When Kenan had lived 70 years, he became
the father of Mahalalel. 13And after he became the
father of Mahalalel, Kenan lived 840 years and
had other sons and daughters. 14Altogether, Ke-
nan lived 910 years, and then he died.

15When Mahalalel had lived 65 years, he be-
came the father of Jared. 16And after he became
the father of Jared, Mahalalel lived 830 years and
had other sons and daughters. 17Altogether, Ma-
halalel lived 895 years, and then he died.

18When Jared had lived 162 years, he became
the father of Enoch. 19And after he became the
father of Enoch, Jared lived 800 years and had
other sons and daughters. 20Altogether, Jared
lived 962 years, and then he died.

21When Enoch had lived 65 years, he became

[u]8 Samaritan Pentateuch, Septuagint, Vulgate and Syriac; Masoretic Text does not have *"Let's go out to the field."* [v]*15* Septuagint, Vulgate and Syriac; Hebrew *Very well* [w]*16 Nod* means *wandering* (see verses 12 and 14). [x]22 Or *who instructed all who work in* [y]23 Or *I will kill* [z]25 *Seth* probably means *granted.* [a]26 Or *to proclaim* [b]2 Hebrew *adam* [c]6 *Father* may mean *ancestor*; also in verses 7-26.

the father of Methuselah. 22And after he became
the father of Methuselah, Enoch walked with God
300 years and had other sons and daughters. 23Al-
together, Enoch lived 365 years. 24Enoch walked
with God; then he was no more, because God
took him away.

25When Methuselah had lived 187 years, he be-
came the father of Lamech. 26And after he became
the father of Lamech, Methuselah lived 782 years
and had other sons and daughters. 27Altogether,
Methuselah lived 969 years, and then he died.

28When Lamech had lived 182 years, he had a
son. 29He named him Noah[d] and said, "He will
comfort us in the labor and painful toil of our
hands caused by the ground the LORD has cursed."
30After Noah was born, Lamech lived 595 years
and had other sons and daughters. 31Altogether,
Lamech lived 777 years, and then he died.

32After Noah was 500 years old, he became the
father of Shem, Ham and Japheth.

[d]29 *Noah* sounds like the Hebrew for *comfort*.

Discovering the Word 1. Why do you think the Lord looked with favor on Abel and his offering but not on Cain and his offering (vv. 3–7)? 2. How does 4:7 illustrate the nature of sin and our response to it? 3. The Lord confronts Adam, Eve and Cain with their sin by using a question (3:11, 13; 4:9–10). What might be some of the reasons for this approach? 4. In what way is Cain's punishment (4:10–16) a logical consequence of his sin? 5. How do Lamech's attitude and action expressed in his taunting song go beyond that of Cain's (4:23–24)?

Applying the Word 1. The lifestyle of Cain's family is a picture of humanity—technical progress matched by moral decline. How do you see this trend reflected in our own civilization? 2. How have you experienced God's judgment as a logical result of a wrong action? 3. How has this chapter helped you to understand the nature and consequences of sin?

Responding in Prayer Ask God to heal relationships in your life damaged by the effects of the Fall.

---

5 / *Genesis 6—7*
How Should We Live?

DOES IT REALLY make much difference how we live? Good so often goes unrewarded while evil persists without punishment. No wonder that we find life so perplexing. Even though these chapters don't answer all our questions, they show that eventually God's justice becomes evident in human affairs. The last chapter recorded how sin became more flagrant in Cain's family. Now the author describes the spread of this moral cancer throughout the human race. He contrasts two radically different ways of living and their results.

Warming Up to God Today is a day full of sin and struggle—and it is a day made and consecrated by the Lord. Tell him about the events of your day and let anxiety slip away.

Read Genesis 6—7.

---

6 When men began to increase in number
on the earth and daughters were born to
them, 2the sons of God saw that the
daughters of men were beautiful, and they mar-
ried any of them they chose. 3Then the LORD said,
"My Spirit will not contend with[e] man forever,
for he is mortal[f]; his days will be a hundred and
twenty years."

4The Nephilim were on the earth in those
days—and also afterward—when the sons of God
went to the daughters of men and had children by
them. They were the heroes of old, men of re-
nown.

5The LORD saw how great man's wickedness on
the earth had become, and that every inclination
of the thoughts of his heart was only evil all the
time. 6The LORD was grieved that he had made

[e]3 Or *My spirit will not remain in* [f]3 Or *corrupt*

man on the earth, and his heart was filled with pain. 7So the LORD said, "I will wipe mankind, whom I have created, from the face of the earth—men and animals, and creatures that move along the ground, and birds of the air—for I am grieved that I have made them." 8But Noah found favor in the eyes of the LORD.

9This is the account of Noah.

Noah was a righteous man, blameless among the people of his time, and he walked with God. 10Noah had three sons: Shem, Ham and Japheth.

11Now the earth was corrupt in God's sight and was full of violence. 12God saw how corrupt the earth had become, for all the people on earth had corrupted their ways. 13So God said to Noah, "I am going to put an end to all people, for the earth is filled with violence because of them. I am surely going to destroy both them and the earth. 14So make yourself an ark of cypress[g] wood; make rooms in it and coat it with pitch inside and out. 15This is how you are to build it: The ark is to be 450 feet long, 75 feet wide and 45 feet high.[h] 16Make a roof for it and finish[i] the ark to within 18 inches[j] of the top. Put a door in the side of the ark and make lower, middle and upper decks. 17I am going to bring floodwaters on the earth to destroy all life under the heavens, every creature that has the breath of life in it. Everything on earth will perish. 18But I will establish my covenant with you, and you will enter the ark—you and your sons and your wife and your sons' wives with you. 19You are to bring into the ark two of all living creatures, male and female, to keep them alive with you. 20Two of every kind of bird, of every kind of animal and of every kind of creature that moves along the ground will come to you to be kept alive. 21You are to take every kind of food that is to be eaten and store it away as food for you and for them."

22Noah did everything just as God commanded him.

7 The LORD then said to Noah, "Go into the ark, you and your whole family, because I have found you righteous in this generation. 2Take with you seven[k] of every kind of clean animal, a male and its mate, and two of every kind of unclean animal, a male and its mate, 3and also seven of every kind of bird, male and female, to keep their various kinds alive throughout the earth. 4Seven days from now I will send rain on the earth for forty days and forty nights, and I will wipe from the face of the earth every living creature I have made."

5And Noah did all that the LORD commanded him.

6Noah was six hundred years old when the floodwaters came on the earth. 7And Noah and his sons and his wife and his sons' wives entered the ark to escape the waters of the flood. 8Pairs of clean and unclean animals, of birds and of all creatures that move along the ground, 9male and female, came to Noah and entered the ark, as God had commanded Noah. 10And after the seven days the floodwaters came on the earth.

11In the six hundredth year of Noah's life, on the seventeenth day of the second month—on that day all the springs of the great deep burst forth, and the floodgates of the heavens were opened. 12And rain fell on the earth forty days and forty nights.

13On that very day Noah and his sons, Shem, Ham and Japheth, together with his wife and the wives of his three sons, entered the ark. 14They had with them every wild animal according to its kind, all livestock according to their kinds, every creature that moves along the ground according to its kind and every bird according to its kind, everything with wings. 15Pairs of all creatures that have the breath of life in them came to Noah and entered the ark. 16The animals going in were male and female of every living thing, as God had commanded Noah. Then the LORD shut him in.

17For forty days the flood kept coming on the earth, and as the waters increased they lifted the ark high above the earth. 18The waters rose and increased greatly on the earth, and the ark floated on the surface of the water. 19They rose greatly on the earth, and all the high mountains under the entire heavens were covered. 20The waters rose and covered the mountains to a depth of more than twenty feet.[l,m] 21Every living thing that moved on the earth perished—birds, livestock, wild animals, all the creatures that swarm over the earth, and all mankind. 22Everything on dry land that had the breath of life in its nostrils died. 23Every living thing on the face of the earth was wiped out; men and animals and the creatures that move along the ground and the birds of the

g14 The meaning of the Hebrew for this word is uncertain.
h15 Hebrew *300 cubits long, 50 cubits wide and 30 cubits high* (about 140 meters long, 23 meters wide and 13.5 meters high)
i16 Or *Make an opening for light by finishing*
j16 Hebrew *a cubit* (about 0.5 meter)
k2 Or *seven pairs*; also in verse 3
l20 Hebrew *fifteen cubits* (about 6.9 meters)
m20 Or *rose more than twenty feet, and the mountains were covered*

air were wiped from the earth. Only Noah was
left, and those with him in the ark.
24The waters flooded the earth for a hundred
and fifty days.

Discovering the Word 1. When the Lord looks at the human condition in the time of Noah, what does he see (6:5–13)? 2. How has God's attitude toward creation changed since the beginning (1:31; 6:6–7, 11–13, 17)? 3. How is Noah different from his contemporaries (6:9; 7:1)? 4. What provisions does God make for Noah and for the various living creatures to preserve life after the flood (7:14–22)? 5. What details are given about the flood and its results (7:17–24)?

Applying the Word 1. In what situations have you felt embarrassed because of your obedience to God? 2. What do chapters 6 and 7 reveal about the severity and grace of God? 3. The New Testament compares the severe judgment in the days of Noah with the judgment that will be poured out at the return of Christ. How can you urge those around you to seek refuge in Christ?

Responding in Prayer Think of someone you want to come to salvation. Pray to God and ask him to "flood" that person with love and forgiveness.

6 / *Genesis 8:1—9:17*
God's Promises

HOW DO YOU feel when you see the long-awaited fulfillment of one of God's promises? Perhaps your response is similar to that of Noah and his family. In the previous study we saw them safe within the ark as the deluge destroyed all life on earth and eventually covered the mountains. Now we see how God fulfills his promises to them and how Noah's response can be an example to us today.

Warming Up to God As you come to Jesus today, let the truth of his love that was poured out for you sink into your soul. Reflect quietly for a few moments on the beauty of his love.

Read Genesis 8:1—9:17.

8 But God remembered Noah and all the
wild animals and the livestock that were
with him in the ark, and he sent a wind
over the earth, and the waters receded. 2Now the
springs of the deep and the floodgates of the
heavens had been closed, and the rain had
stopped falling from the sky. 3The water receded
steadily from the earth. At the end of the hundred
and fifty days the water had gone down, 4and on
the seventeenth day of the seventh month the ark
came to rest on the mountains of Ararat. 5The
waters continued to recede until the tenth month,
and on the first day of the tenth month the tops
of the mountains became visible.
6After forty days Noah opened the window he
had made in the ark 7and sent out a raven, and it
kept flying back and forth until the water had
dried up from the earth. 8Then he sent out a dove
to see if the water had receded from the surface of
the ground. 9But the dove could find no place to
set its feet because there was water over all the
surface of the earth; so it returned to Noah in the
ark. He reached out his hand and took the dove
and brought it back to himself in the ark. 10He
waited seven more days and again sent out the
dove from the ark. 11When the dove returned to
him in the evening, there in its beak was a freshly
plucked olive leaf! Then Noah knew that the wa-
ter had receded from the earth. 12He waited seven
more days and sent the dove out again, but this
time it did not return to him.
13By the first day of the first month of Noah's
six hundred and first year, the water had dried up
from the earth. Noah then removed the covering
from the ark and saw that the surface of the
ground was dry. 14By the twenty-seventh day of
the second month the earth was completely dry.
15Then God said to Noah, 16"Come out of the
ark, you and your wife and your sons and their
wives. 17Bring out every kind of living creature

that is with you—the birds, the animals, and all the creatures that move along the ground—so they can multiply on the earth and be fruitful and increase in number upon it."

18 So Noah came out, together with his sons and his wife and his sons' wives. 19 All the animals and all the creatures that move along the ground and all the birds—everything that moves on the earth—came out of the ark, one kind after another.

20 Then Noah built an altar to the LORD and, taking some of all the clean animals and clean birds, he sacrificed burnt offerings on it. 21 The LORD smelled the pleasing aroma and said in his heart: "Never again will I curse the ground because of man, even though[n] every inclination of his heart is evil from childhood. And never again will I destroy all living creatures, as I have done.

22 "As long as the earth endures,
 seedtime and harvest,
 cold and heat,
 summer and winter,
 day and night
 will never cease."

9 Then God blessed Noah and his sons, saying to them, "Be fruitful and increase in number and fill the earth. 2 The fear and dread of you will fall upon all the beasts of the earth and all the birds of the air, upon every creature that moves along the ground, and upon all the fish of the sea; they are given into your hands. 3 Everything that lives and moves will be food for you. Just as I gave you the green plants, I now give you everything.

4 "But you must not eat meat that has its lifeblood still in it. 5 And for your lifeblood I will surely demand an accounting. I will demand an accounting from every animal. And from each man, too, I will demand an accounting for the life of his fellow man.

6 "Whoever sheds the blood of man,
 by man shall his blood be shed;
for in the image of God
 has God made man.

7 As for you, be fruitful and increase in number; multiply on the earth and increase upon it."

8 Then God said to Noah and to his sons with him: 9 "I now establish my covenant with you and with your descendants after you 10 and with every living creature that was with you—the birds, the livestock and all the wild animals, all those that came out of the ark with you—every living creature on earth. 11 I establish my covenant with you: Never again will all life be cut off by the waters of a flood; never again will there be a flood to destroy the earth."

12 And God said, "This is the sign of the covenant I am making between me and you and every living creature with you, a covenant for all generations to come: 13 I have set my rainbow in the clouds, and it will be the sign of the covenant between me and the earth. 14 Whenever I bring clouds over the earth and the rainbow appears in the clouds, 15 I will remember my covenant between me and you and all living creatures of every kind. Never again will the waters become a flood to destroy all life. 16 Whenever the rainbow appears in the clouds, I will see it and remember the everlasting covenant between God and all living creatures of every kind on the earth."

17 So God said to Noah, "This is the sign of the covenant I have established between me and all life on the earth."

[n]21 Or *man, for*

Discovering the Word 1. What do we learn about God's concern for the passengers of the ark and his activity to end the flood (8:1-5)? 2. What initiative does Noah take during this period (8:6-12)? 3. Noah's first action after emptying the ark is to offer a sacrifice to God (8:20). What does this reveal about his priorities amid the pressure of urgent tasks calling for immediate attention? 4. What commission does God now give Noah and his family (9:1-7)? 5. In 9:17 God makes a covenant as unconditional as it is undeserved. What do we learn about the extent and purpose of this first covenant?

Applying the Word 1. How has God's grace been evident throughout this passage? 2. How has his grace been evident in your life lately? 3. What aspect of Noah's example—his obedience, faith, courage, endurance—is most meaningful to you in a situation you are facing?

Responding in Prayer Spend time in prayer, thanking God for his grace to you, who deserve his judgment.

7 / *Genesis 9:18—11:32*
Family Problems

A RECURRING PROBLEM in every generation is self-centered disrespect for authority, both human and divine. This attitude continued after the flood in Noah's own family, then on a larger scale in society. In the previous study we saw that Noah's new commission was similar to the one given to Adam. Now we see how sin again spreads from father to son to succeeding generations in both the private and public realms as self-indulgence generates waves of evil in ever-widening circles.

Warming Up to God Does the evil in this world sometimes weigh heavily on you? Tell Jesus your frustrations and let him renew your hope in his sovereignty.

Read Genesis 9:18—11:32.

18The sons of Noah who came out of the ark
were Shem, Ham and Japheth. (Ham was the fa-
ther of Canaan.) 19These were the three sons of
Noah, and from them came the people who were
scattered over the earth.

20Noah, a man of the soil, proceeded[o] to plant
a vineyard. 21When he drank some of its wine, he
became drunk and lay uncovered inside his tent.
22Ham, the father of Canaan, saw his father's na-
kedness and told his two brothers outside. 23But
Shem and Japheth took a garment and laid it
across their shoulders; then they walked in back-
ward and covered their father's nakedness. Their
faces were turned the other way so that they
would not see their father's nakedness.

24When Noah awoke from his wine and found
out what his youngest son had done to him, 25he
said,

"Cursed be Canaan!
The lowest of slaves
will he be to his brothers."

26He also said,

"Blessed be the LORD, the God of Shem!
May Canaan be the slave of Shem.[p]
27May God extend the territory of Japheth[q];
may Japheth live in the tents of Shem,
and may Canaan be his[r] slave."

28After the flood Noah lived 350 years.
29Altogether, Noah lived 950 years, and then he
died.

10 This is the account of Shem, Ham
and Japheth, Noah's sons, who
themselves had sons after the flood.
2The sons[s] of Japheth:
Gomer, Magog, Madai, Javan, Tubal, Me-
shech and Tiras.
3The sons of Gomer:
Ashkenaz, Riphath and Togarmah.
4The sons of Javan:
Elishah, Tarshish, the Kittim and the
Rodanim.[t] 5(From these the maritime
peoples spread out into their territories
by their clans within their nations, each
with its own language.)
6The sons of Ham:
Cush, Mizraim,[u] Put and Canaan.
7The sons of Cush:
Seba, Havilah, Sabtah, Raamah and Sab-
teca.
The sons of Raamah:
Sheba and Dedan.

8Cush was the father[v] of Nimrod, who grew
to be a mighty warrior on the earth. 9He was a
mighty hunter before the LORD; that is why it is
said, "Like Nimrod, a mighty hunter before the
LORD." 10The first centers of his kingdom were
Babylon, Erech, Akkad and Calneh, in[w] Shinar.[x]
11From that land he went to Assyria, where he
built Nineveh, Rehoboth Ir,[y] Calah 12and Resen,
which is between Nineveh and Calah; that is the
great city.

13Mizraim was the father of
the Ludites, Anamites, Lehabites, Naph-
tuhites, 14Pathrusites, Casluhites (from

[o]20 Or *soil, was the first* [p]26 Or *be his slave* [q]27 *Japheth* sounds like the Hebrew for *extend.* [r]27 Or *their* [s]2 *Sons* may mean *descendants* or *successors* or *nations*; also in verses 3, 4, 6, 7, 20-23, 29 and 31. [t]4 Some manuscripts of the Masoretic Text and Samaritan Pentateuch (see also Septuagint and 1 Chron. 1:7); most manuscripts of the Masoretic Text *Dodanim* [u]6 That is, Egypt; also in verse 13 [v]8 *Father* may mean *ancestor* or *predecessor* or *founder*; also in verses 13, 15, 24 and 26.

whom the Philistines came) and Caphto-
rites.
15Canaan was the father of
Sidon his firstborn,[z] and of the Hittites,
16Jebusites, Amorites, Girgashites, 17Hi-
vites, Arkites, Sinites, 18Arvadites, Zema-
rites and Hamathites.

Later the Canaanite clans scattered 19and the
borders of Canaan reached from Sidon toward
Gerar as far as Gaza, and then toward Sodom,
Gomorrah, Admah and Zeboiim, as far as Lasha.
20These are the sons of Ham by their clans and
languages, in their territories and nations.

21Sons were also born to Shem, whose older
brother was[a] Japheth; Shem was the ancestor of
all the sons of Eber.

22The sons of Shem:
Elam, Asshur, Arphaxad, Lud and Aram.
23The sons of Aram:
Uz, Hul, Gether and Meshech.[b]
24Arphaxad was the father of[c] Shelah,
and Shelah the father of Eber.
25Two sons were born to Eber:
One was named Peleg,[d] because in his
time the earth was divided; his brother
was named Joktan.
26Joktan was the father of
Almodad, Sheleph, Hazarmaveth, Jerah,
27Hadoram, Uzal, Diklah, 28Obal, Abim-
ael, Sheba, 29Ophir, Havilah and Jobab.
All these were sons of Joktan.

30The region where they lived stretched from Me-
sha toward Sephar, in the eastern hill country.
31These are the sons of Shem by their clans and
languages, in their territories and nations.

32These are the clans of Noah's sons, according
to their lines of descent, within their nations.
From these the nations spread out over the earth
after the flood.

11

Now the whole world had one lan-
guage and a common speech. 2As
men moved eastward,[e] they found
a plain in Shinar[x] and settled there.
3They said to each other, "Come, let's make
bricks and bake them thoroughly." They used
brick instead of stone, and tar for mortar. 4Then
they said, "Come, let us build ourselves a city,
with a tower that reaches to the heavens, so that
we may make a name for ourselves and not be
scattered over the face of the whole earth."
5But the LORD came down to see the city and
the tower that the men were building. 6The LORD
said, "If as one people speaking the same lan-
guage they have begun to do this, then nothing
they plan to do will be impossible for them.
7Come, let us go down and confuse their lan-
guage so they will not understand each other."
8So the LORD scattered them from there over all
the earth, and they stopped building the city.
9That is why it was called Babel[f]—because there
the LORD confused the language of the whole
world. From there the LORD scattered them over
the face of the whole earth.

10This is the account of Shem.

Two years after the flood, when Shem was 100
years old, he became the father[g] of Arphaxad.
11And after he became the father of Arphaxad,
Shem lived 500 years and had other sons and
daughters.
12When Arphaxad had lived 35 years, he be-
came the father of Shelah. 13And after he became
the father of Shelah, Arphaxad lived 403 years
and had other sons and daughters.[h]
14When Shelah had lived 30 years, he became
the father of Eber. 15And after he became the fa-
ther of Eber, Shelah lived 403 years and had other
sons and daughters.
16When Eber had lived 34 years, he became the
father of Peleg. 17And after he became the father
of Peleg, Eber lived 430 years and had other sons
and daughters.
18When Peleg had lived 30 years, he became
the father of Reu. 19And after he became the fa-
ther of Reu, Peleg lived 209 years and had other
sons and daughters.
20When Reu had lived 32 years, he became the
father of Serug. 21And after he became the father
of Serug, Reu lived 207 years and had other sons
and daughters.

[w] 10 Or *Erech and Akkad—all of them in* [x] 10,2 That is, Babylonia [y] 11 Or *Nineveh with its city squares* [z] 15 Or *of the Sidonians, the foremost* [a] 21 Or *Shem, the older brother of* [b] 23 See Septuagint and 1 Chron. 1:17; Hebrew *Mash* [c] 24 Hebrew; Septuagint *father of Cainan, and Cainan was the father of* [d] 25 *Peleg* means *division.* [e] 2 Or *from the east*; or *in the east* [f] 9 That is, Babylon; *Babel* sounds like the Hebrew for *confused.* [g] 10 *Father* may mean *ancestor*; also in verses 11-25. [h] 12,13 Hebrew; Septuagint (see also Luke 3:35, 36 and note at Gen. 10:24) *35 years, he became the father of Cainan. 13And after he became the father of Cainan, Arphaxad lived 430 years and had other sons and daughters, and then he died. When Cainan had lived 130 years, he became the father of Shelah. And after he became the father of Shelah, Cainan lived 330 years and had other sons and daughters*

22When Serug had lived 30 years, he became
the father of Nahor. 23And after he became the
father of Nahor, Serug lived 200 years and had
other sons and daughters.
24When Nahor had lived 29 years, he became
the father of Terah. 25And after he became the
father of Terah, Nahor lived 119 years and had
other sons and daughters.
26After Terah had lived 70 years, he became the
father of Abram, Nahor and Haran.

27This is the account of Terah.

Terah became the father of Abram, Nahor and
Haran. And Haran became the father of Lot.
28While his father Terah was still alive, Haran
died in Ur of the Chaldeans, in the land of
his birth. 29Abram and Nahor both married.
The name of Abram's wife was Sarai, and the
name of Nahor's wife was Milcah; she was the
daughter of Haran, the father of both Milcah
and Iscah. 30Now Sarai was barren; she had no
children.
31Terah took his son Abram, his grandson
Lot son of Haran, and his daughter-in-law Sarai,
the wife of his son Abram, and together they
set out from Ur of the Chaldeans to go to Canaan. But when they came to Haran, they settled
there.
32Terah lived 205 years, and he died in
Haran.

Discovering the Word 1. Describe what happens in the brief story of Noah and his three sons (9:20–23). 2. What curse does Noah pronounce on Canaan (Ham's son) and his descendants (9:24–27)? 3. What interesting facts does chapter 10 reveal about the spread of humanity after the flood? (Note especially 10:5, 8–15, 25.) 4. What action do the people of Babel take, and what is their motive (11:1–9)? 5. It is amusing that the Lord must come down (11:5) to see this tower that will reach to the heavens. What is his reaction (11:5–9)? 6. Genesis 11:10–32 traces the line from Shem to Abram. Why do you think the author is beginning to shift from all the families of the earth to one family?

Applying the Word 1. In what specific ways do families today suffer from a disrespect for parents and animosity among the children? 2. How have you recently hurt someone through failure to communicate, and what steps toward healing can you take?

Responding in Prayer Ask the Father to show you one specific way you can be a minister of the gospel of Christ to your family or community.

8/ *Genesis 12—13*
Following God into the Unknown

SUPPOSE GOD CALLED you to leave all that is familiar—your home, family, friends—and follow him into another part of the country or world with a radically different lifestyle. How would you feel as you said goodby and moved out into the unknown? In this study we see how Abram responds to such a call and how his faith matures.

Warming Up to God Free your hands of books or pencils and fold them across your lap. Close your eyes and think of the characteristics of God. Let God draw near to you in these quiet moments.

Read Genesis 12—13.

12 The LORD had said to Abram,
"Leave your country, your people
and your father's household and go
to the land I will show you.

2"I will make you into a great nation
and I will bless you;
I will make your name great,
and you will be a blessing.

3I will bless those who bless you,
and whoever curses you I will curse;
and all peoples on earth
will be blessed through you."

4So Abram left, as the LORD had told him; and
Lot went with him. Abram was seventy-five years
old when he set out from Haran. 5He took his
wife Sarai, his nephew Lot, all the possessions
they had accumulated and the people they had
acquired in Haran, and they set out for the land of
Canaan, and they arrived there.
6Abram traveled through the land as far as the
site of the great tree of Moreh at Shechem. At that
time the Canaanites were in the land. 7The LORD
appeared to Abram and said, "To your offspring[i]
I will give this land." So he built an altar there to
the LORD, who had appeared to him.
8From there he went on toward the hills east of
Bethel and pitched his tent, with Bethel on the
west and Ai on the east. There he built an altar to
the LORD and called on the name of the LORD.
9Then Abram set out and continued toward the
Negev.
10Now there was a famine in the land, and
Abram went down to Egypt to live there for a
while because the famine was severe. 11As he was
about to enter Egypt, he said to his wife Sarai, "I
know what a beautiful woman you are. 12When
the Egyptians see you, they will say, 'This is his
wife.' Then they will kill me but will let you live.
13Say you are my sister, so that I will be treated
well for your sake and my life will be spared be-
cause of you."
14When Abram came to Egypt, the Egyptians
saw that she was a very beautiful woman. 15And
when Pharaoh's officials saw her, they praised her
to Pharaoh, and she was taken into his palace.
16He treated Abram well for her sake, and Abram
acquired sheep and cattle, male and female
donkeys, menservants and maidservants, and
camels.
17But the LORD inflicted serious diseases on
Pharaoh and his household because of Abram's
wife Sarai. 18So Pharaoh summoned Abram.
"What have you done to me?" he said. "Why
didn't you tell me she was your wife? 19Why did
you say, 'She is my sister,' so that I took her to be
my wife? Now then, here is your wife. Take her
and go!" 20Then Pharaoh gave orders about
Abram to his men, and they sent him on his way,
with his wife and everything he had.

13

So Abram went up from Egypt to
the Negev, with his wife and every-
thing he had, and Lot went with
him. 2Abram had become very wealthy in live-
stock and in silver and gold.
3From the Negev he went from place to place
until he came to Bethel, to the place between
Bethel and Ai where his tent had been earlier 4and
where he had first built an altar. There Abram
called on the name of the LORD.
5Now Lot, who was moving about with Abram,
also had flocks and herds and tents. 6But the land
could not support them while they stayed to-
gether, for their possessions were so great that
they were not able to stay together. 7And quarrel-
ing arose between Abram's herdsmen and the
herdsmen of Lot. The Canaanites and Perizzites
were also living in the land at that time.
8So Abram said to Lot, "Let's not have any
quarreling between you and me, or between your
herdsmen and mine, for we are brothers. 9Is not
the whole land before you? Let's part company. If
you go to the left, I'll go to the right; if you go to
the right, I'll go to the left."
10Lot looked up and saw that the whole plain of
the Jordan was well watered, like the garden of
the LORD, like the land of Egypt, toward Zoar.
(This was before the LORD destroyed Sodom and
Gomorrah.) 11So Lot chose for himself the whole
plain of the Jordan and set out toward the east.
The two men parted company: 12Abram lived in
the land of Canaan, while Lot lived among the
cities of the plain and pitched his tents near
Sodom. 13Now the men of Sodom were wicked
and were sinning greatly against the LORD.
14The LORD said to Abram after Lot had parted
from him, "Lift up your eyes from where you are
and look north and south, east and west. 15All the
land that you see I will give to you and your
offspring[j] forever. 16I will make your offspring
like the dust of the earth, so that if anyone could
count the dust, then your offspring could
be counted. 17Go, walk through the length
and breadth of the land, for I am giving it to
you."
18So Abram moved his tents and went to live
near the great trees of Mamre at Hebron, where
he built an altar to the LORD.

i7 Or *seed* j15 Or *seed*; also in verse 16

Discovering the Word 1. What command and promise does the Lord give to Abram (12:1–3)? 2. What additional promise and encouragement does God give to Abram as he arrives in Canaan (12:6–9)? 3. How does Abram's scheming about himself and Sarai evidence a lack of faith (12:10–16)? 4. Describe the problem which arises between Abram and Lot (13:1–7). 5. Abram, as the older man, has the right to choose the best land. How does his action here demonstrate a greater confidence in God's promise to take care of him (13:8–13)? 6. What renewed and expanded promises does the Lord give to Abram (13:14–17)?

Applying the Word 1. Describe a time when you took matters into your own hands instead of trusting in God's faithfulness. 2. How can Abram's experiences in chapters 12 and 13 encourage you to entrust your needs more fully to God?

Responding in Prayer Thank God for his faithfulness in keeping promises—and ask him to increase your faith while you wait to see your requests come to fruition.

9 / *Genesis 14—15*
Tests of Faith

IF YOU WANT your faith to increase, don't be surprised or disheartened over difficulties which demand faith. The muscles of faith grow strong through training and testing that is sometimes painful. Abram continues to learn this lesson after parting from his nephew Lot. In this study we see Abram's trials and the resources God provides to help him meet the challenge and persevere.

Warming Up to God What do you think really makes your faith grow? Write down any specific events in your life that God has used to increase your faith.

Read Genesis 14—15.

14 At this time Amraphel king of Shinar,[k] Arioch king of Ellasar, Kedorlaomer king of Elam and Tidal king of Goiim [2]went to war against Bera king of Sodom, Birsha king of Gomorrah, Shinab king of Admah, Shemeber king of Zeboiim, and the king of Bela (that is, Zoar). [3]All these latter kings joined forces in the Valley of Siddim (the Salt Sea[l]). [4]For twelve years they had been subject to Kedorlaomer, but in the thirteenth year they rebelled.

[5]In the fourteenth year, Kedorlaomer and the kings allied with him went out and defeated the Rephaites in Ashteroth Karnaim, the Zuzites in Ham, the Emites in Shaveh Kiriathaim [6]and the Horites in the hill country of Seir, as far as El Paran near the desert. [7]Then they turned back and went to En Mishpat (that is, Kadesh), and they conquered the whole territory of the Amalekites, as well as the Amorites who were living in Hazazon Tamar.

[8]Then the king of Sodom, the king of Gomorrah, the king of Admah, the king of Zeboiim and the king of Bela (that is, Zoar) marched out and drew up their battle lines in the Valley of Siddim [9]against Kedorlaomer king of Elam, Tidal king of Goiim, Amraphel king of Shinar and Arioch king of Ellasar—four kings against five. [10]Now the Valley of Siddim was full of tar pits, and when the kings of Sodom and Gomorrah fled, some of the men fell into them and the rest fled to the hills. [11]The four kings seized all the goods of Sodom and Gomorrah and all their food; then they went away. [12]They also carried off Abram's nephew Lot and his possessions, since he was living in Sodom.

[13]One who had escaped came and reported this to Abram the Hebrew. Now Abram was living near the great trees of Mamre the Amorite, a brother[m] of Eshcol and Aner, all of whom were allied with Abram. [14]When Abram heard that his relative had been taken captive, he called out the 318 trained men born in his household and went in pursuit as far as Dan. [15]During the night

[k]1 That is, Babylonia; also in verse 9 [l]3 That is, the Dead Sea
[m]13 Or *a relative*; or *an ally*

Abram divided his men to attack them and he routed them, pursuing them as far as Hobah, north of Damascus. [16]He recovered all the goods and brought back his relative Lot and his possessions, together with the women and the other people.

[17]After Abram returned from defeating Kedorlaomer and the kings allied with him, the king of Sodom came out to meet him in the Valley of Shaveh (that is, the King's Valley).

[18]Then Melchizedek king of Salem[n] brought out bread and wine. He was priest of God Most High, [19]and he blessed Abram, saying,

"Blessed be Abram by God Most High,
Creator[o] of heaven and earth.
[20]And blessed be[p] God Most High,
who delivered your enemies into your hand."

Then Abram gave him a tenth of everything.

[21]The king of Sodom said to Abram, "Give me the people and keep the goods for yourself."

[22]But Abram said to the king of Sodom, "I have raised my hand to the LORD, God Most High, Creator of heaven and earth, and have taken an oath [23]that I will accept nothing belonging to you, not even a thread or the thong of a sandal, so that you will never be able to say, 'I made Abram rich.' [24]I will accept nothing but what my men have eaten and the share that belongs to the men who went with me—to Aner, Eshcol and Mamre. Let them have their share."

15

After this, the word of the LORD came to Abram in a vision:

"Do not be afraid, Abram.
I am your shield,[q]
your very great reward.[r]"

[2]But Abram said, "O Sovereign LORD, what can you give me since I remain childless and the one who will inherit[s] my estate is Eliezer of Damascus?" [3]And Abram said, "You have given me no children; so a servant in my household will be my heir."

[4]Then the word of the LORD came to him: "This man will not be your heir, but a son coming from your own body will be your heir." [5]He took him outside and said, "Look up at the heavens and count the stars—if indeed you can count them." Then he said to him, "So shall your offspring be."

[6]Abram believed the LORD, and he credited it to him as righteousness.

[7]He also said to him, "I am the LORD, who brought you out of Ur of the Chaldeans to give you this land to take possession of it."

[8]But Abram said, "O Sovereign LORD, how can I know that I will gain possession of it?"

[9]So the LORD said to him, "Bring me a heifer, a goat and a ram, each three years old, along with a dove and a young pigeon."

[10]Abram brought all these to him, cut them in two and arranged the halves opposite each other; the birds, however, he did not cut in half. [11]Then birds of prey came down on the carcasses, but Abram drove them away.

[12]As the sun was setting, Abram fell into a deep sleep, and a thick and dreadful darkness came over him. [13]Then the LORD said to him, "Know for certain that your descendants will be strangers in a country not their own, and they will be enslaved and mistreated four hundred years. [14]But I will punish the nation they serve as slaves, and afterward they will come out with great possessions. [15]You, however, will go to your fathers in peace and be buried at a good old age. [16]In the fourth generation your descendants will come back here, for the sin of the Amorites has not yet reached its full measure."

[17]When the sun had set and darkness had fallen, a smoking firepot with a blazing torch appeared and passed between the pieces. [18]On that day the LORD made a covenant with Abram and said, "To your descendants I give this land, from the river[t] of Egypt to the great river, the Euphrates— [19]the land of the Kenites, Kenizzites, Kadmonites, [20]Hittites, Perizzites, Rephaites, [21]Amorites, Canaanites, Girgashites and Jebusites."

[n]18 That is, Jerusalem [o]19 Or *Possessor;* also in verse 22 [p]20 Or *And praise be to* [q]1 Or *sovereign* [r]1 Or *shield; / your reward will be very great* [s]2 The meaning of the Hebrew for this phrase is uncertain. [t]18 Or *Wadi*

Discovering the Word 1. What political and military situation is described in 14:1-4, and how is it similar to today? 2. Since Abram lived in tents away from the cities, his people were not involved in this military campaign. When he learns of Lot's capture, what strategy does Abram devise (14:13-16)? 3. Who is Melchizedek, and what does he do (14:18-20)? 4. What is Abram's main problem in chapter 15, and how does he propose to solve it (15:2-3)? 5. How would God's message to Abram at this point renew his confidence (15:1, 4, 5)?

6. Genesis 15:6 is the first time we read that Abram *believes* the Lord. Explain in your own words what it means that his faith is credited to him as righteousness.

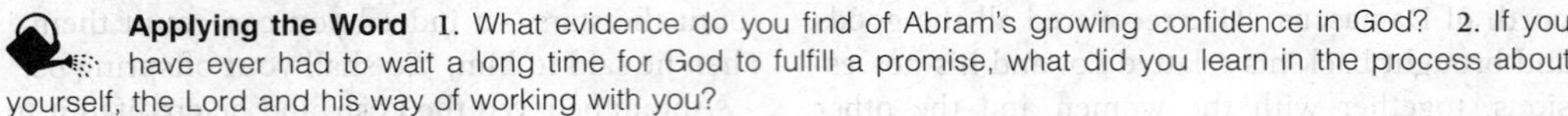

Applying the Word 1. What evidence do you find of Abram's growing confidence in God? 2. If you have ever had to wait a long time for God to fulfill a promise, what did you learn in the process about yourself, the Lord and his way of working with you?

Responding in Prayer Thank Jesus for his death, which enables our belief to be credited as righteousness in God's eyes.

10 / *Genesis 16—17*
When Faith Falters

DO YOU EVER get tired of waiting for God to act? Do you sometimes wonder whether your faith is simply foolishness? At such times it is tempting to become an activist. "If *God* won't help me, I'll do it *myself!*" As this passage opens, we find that Sarai and Abram are frustrated by the passing of years without a son. Taking matters into their own hands, they devise their own strategy for "fulfilling" God's promise.

Warming Up to God You are like a jar of clay filled with the Spirit of Christ. Pour out to him your weariness, sin or discouragement and let him pour into you his cool water of grace and peace.

Read Genesis 16—17.

16 Now Sarai, Abram's wife, had borne
him no children. But she had an
Egyptian maidservant named Ha-
gar; 2so she said to Abram, "The Lord has kept me
from having children. Go, sleep with my maidser-
vant; perhaps I can build a family through her."
Abram agreed to what Sarai said. 3So after
Abram had been living in Canaan ten years, Sarai
his wife took her Egyptian maidservant Hagar and
gave her to her husband to be his wife. 4He slept
with Hagar, and she conceived.
When she knew she was pregnant, she began to
despise her mistress. 5Then Sarai said to Abram,
"You are responsible for the wrong I am suffering.
I put my servant in your arms, and now that she
knows she is pregnant, she despises me. May the
Lord judge between you and me."
6"Your servant is in your hands," Abram said.
"Do with her whatever you think best." Then Sa-
rai mistreated Hagar; so she fled from her.
7The angel of the Lord found Hagar near a
spring in the desert; it was the spring that is be-
side the road to Shur. 8And he said, "Hagar, ser-
vant of Sarai, where have you come from, and
where are you going?"
"I'm running away from my mistress Sarai," she
answered.
9Then the angel of the Lord told her, "Go back
to your mistress and submit to her." 10The angel
added, "I will so increase your descendants that
they will be too numerous to count."
11The angel of the Lord also said to her:

"You are now with child
and you will have a son.
You shall name him Ishmael,[u]
for the Lord has heard of your misery.
12He will be a wild donkey of a man;
his hand will be against everyone
and everyone's hand against him,
and he will live in hostility
toward[v] all his brothers."

13She gave this name to the Lord who spoke to
her: "You are the God who sees me," for she said,
"I have now seen[w] the One who sees me." 14That
is why the well was called Beer Lahai Roi[x]; it is
still there, between Kadesh and Bered.
15So Hagar bore Abram a son, and Abram gave
the name Ishmael to the son she had borne.
16Abram was eighty-six years old when Hagar
bore him Ishmael.

[u]11 *Ishmael means God hears.* [v]12 *Or live to the east / of* [w]13 *Or seen the back of* [x]14 *Beer Lahai Roi means well of the Living One who sees me.*

17 When Abram was ninety-nine years old, the LORD appeared to him and said, "I am God Almighty[y]; walk before me and be blameless. 2I will confirm my covenant between me and you and will greatly increase your numbers."

3Abram fell facedown, and God said to him, 4"As for me, this is my covenant with you: You will be the father of many nations. 5No longer will you be called Abram[z]; your name will be Abraham,[a] for I have made you a father of many nations. 6I will make you very fruitful; I will make nations of you, and kings will come from you. 7I will establish my covenant as an everlasting covenant between me and you and your descendants after you for the generations to come, to be your God and the God of your descendants after you. 8The whole land of Canaan, where you are now an alien, I will give as an everlasting possession to you and your descendants after you; and I will be their God."

9Then God said to Abraham, "As for you, you must keep my covenant, you and your descendants after you for the generations to come. 10This is my covenant with you and your descendants after you, the covenant you are to keep: Every male among you shall be circumcised. 11You are to undergo circumcision, and it will be the sign of the covenant between me and you. 12For the generations to come every male among you who is eight days old must be circumcised, including those born in your household or bought with money from a foreigner—those who are not your offspring. 13Whether born in your household or bought with your money, they must be circumcised. My covenant in your flesh is to be an everlasting covenant. 14Any uncircumcised male, who has not been circumcised in the flesh, will be cut off from his people; he has broken my covenant."

15God also said to Abraham, "As for Sarai your wife, you are no longer to call her Sarai; her name will be Sarah. 16I will bless her and will surely give you a son by her. I will bless her so that she will be the mother of nations; kings of peoples will come from her."

17Abraham fell facedown; he laughed and said to himself, "Will a son be born to a man a hundred years old? Will Sarah bear a child at the age of ninety?" 18And Abraham said to God, "If only Ishmael might live under your blessing!"

19Then God said, "Yes, but your wife Sarah will bear you a son, and you will call him Isaac.[b] I will establish my covenant with him as an everlasting covenant for his descendants after him. 20And as for Ishmael, I have heard you: I will surely bless him; I will make him fruitful and will greatly increase his numbers. He will be the father of twelve rulers, and I will make him into a great nation. 21But my covenant I will establish with Isaac, whom Sarah will bear to you by this time next year." 22When he had finished speaking with Abraham, God went up from him.

23On that very day Abraham took his son Ishmael and all those born in his household or bought with his money, every male in his household, and circumcised them, as God told him. 24Abraham was ninety-nine years old when he was circumcised, 25and his son Ishmael was thirteen; 26Abraham and his son Ishmael were both circumcised on that same day. 27And every male in Abraham's household, including those born in his household or bought from a foreigner, was circumcised with him.

[y]1 Hebrew *El-Shaddai* [z]5 *Abram* means *exalted father.* [a]5 *Abraham* means *father of many.* [b]19 *Isaac* means *he laughs.*

Discovering the Word 1. Sarai and Abram's action seems strange to us, but it was an acceptable custom in ancient Near Eastern culture. Yet how might their action indicate a lack of faith? 2. Hagar flees to the wilderness of Shur on the northeast frontier of Egypt, her native land. What promises and encouragement does the angel give to her (16:7–12)? 3. What does Hagar learn about the Lord through this traumatic experience (16:13–14)? 4. In 17:1–8 "God Almighty" appears to Abram and, ironically, changes his name from *Abram* ("exalted father") to *Abraham* ("father of many"). What covenant promises does the Lord reiterate in these verses? 5. In 17:18 Abraham expressed his concern about Ishmael. How does God respond to Abraham's request (17:19–22)? 6. How did Abraham fulfill his responsibility in the covenant (17:23–27)?

Applying the Word 1. How can impatience with God's timetable and way of working lead us to unbelief and even disobedience? 2. Have you ever gone through a difficult time in which you gained new insight into God's concern for you? Explain.

Responding in Prayer Ask God to teach you to be obedient in the face of ambiguous or difficult circumstances.

11 / *Genesis 18—19*
God's Judgment on Society

CONTEMPORARY CHRISTIANITY HAS been described as "privately engaging but socially irrelevant." Many of us concern ourselves only with family and church to the neglect of the broader arenas of work and community—the economic, social and political fabric of our society. So far we have seen Abraham wrapped up in his personal and family concerns. But in this passage he broadens his perspective. He becomes involved in the problems of a neighboring city whose lifestyle is the antithesis of everything he stands for. Abraham's reaction to the news of impending judgment can instruct us today concerning responsible Christian action in our own society.

Warming Up to God What problems do you see in your community that weigh on your heart and mind?

Read Genesis 18—19.

18 The LORD appeared to Abraham near the great trees of Mamre while he was sitting at the entrance to his tent in the heat of the day. 2Abraham looked up and saw three men standing nearby. When he saw them, he hurried from the entrance of his tent to meet them and bowed low to the ground.

3He said, "If I have found favor in your eyes, my lord,[c] do not pass your servant by. 4Let a little water be brought, and then you may all wash your feet and rest under this tree. 5Let me get you something to eat, so you can be refreshed and then go on your way—now that you have come to your servant."

"Very well," they answered, "do as you say."

6So Abraham hurried into the tent to Sarah. "Quick," he said, "get three seahs[d] of fine flour and knead it and bake some bread."

7Then he ran to the herd and selected a choice, tender calf and gave it to a servant, who hurried to prepare it. 8He then brought some curds and milk and the calf that had been prepared, and set these before them. While they ate, he stood near them under a tree.

9"Where is your wife Sarah?" they asked him.

"There, in the tent," he said.

10Then the LORD[e] said, "I will surely return to you about this time next year, and Sarah your wife will have a son."

Now Sarah was listening at the entrance to the tent, which was behind him. 11Abraham and Sarah were already old and well advanced in years, and Sarah was past the age of childbearing. 12So Sarah laughed to herself as she thought, "After I am worn out and my master[f] is old, will I now have this pleasure?"

13Then the LORD said to Abraham, "Why did Sarah laugh and say, 'Will I really have a child, now that I am old?' 14Is anything too hard for the LORD? I will return to you at the appointed time next year and Sarah will have a son."

15Sarah was afraid, so she lied and said, "I did not laugh."

But he said, "Yes, you did laugh."

16When the men got up to leave, they looked down toward Sodom, and Abraham walked along with them to see them on their way. 17Then the LORD said, "Shall I hide from Abraham what I am about to do? 18Abraham will surely become a great and powerful nation, and all nations on earth will be blessed through him. 19For I have chosen him, so that he will direct his children and his household after him to keep the way of the LORD by doing what is right and just, so that the LORD will bring about for Abraham what he has promised him."

20Then the LORD said, "The outcry against Sodom and Gomorrah is so great and their sin so grievous 21that I will go down and see if what they have done is as bad as the outcry that has reached me. If not, I will know."

22The men turned away and went toward Sodom, but Abraham remained standing before the LORD.[g] 23Then Abraham approached him and said: "Will you sweep away the righteous with the wicked? 24What if there are fifty righteous people

[c]3 Or *O Lord* [d]6 That is, probably about 20 quarts (about 22 liters) [e]10 Hebrew *Then he* [f]12 Or *husband* [g]22 Masoretic Text; an ancient Hebrew scribal tradition *but the LORD remained standing before Abraham*

in the city? Will you really sweep it away and not spare[h] the place for the sake of the fifty righteous people in it? 25Far be it from you to do such a thing—to kill the righteous with the wicked, treating the righteous and the wicked alike. Far be it from you! Will not the Judge[i] of all the earth do right?"

26The LORD said, "If I find fifty righteous people in the city of Sodom, I will spare the whole place for their sake."

27Then Abraham spoke up again: "Now that I have been so bold as to speak to the Lord, though I am nothing but dust and ashes, 28what if the number of the righteous is five less than fifty? Will you destroy the whole city because of five people?"

"If I find forty-five there," he said, "I will not destroy it."

29Once again he spoke to him, "What if only forty are found there?"

He said, "For the sake of forty, I will not do it."

30Then he said, "May the Lord not be angry, but let me speak. What if only thirty can be found there?"

He answered, "I will not do it if I find thirty there."

31Abraham said, "Now that I have been so bold as to speak to the Lord, what if only twenty can be found there?"

He said, "For the sake of twenty, I will not destroy it."

32Then he said, "May the Lord not be angry, but let me speak just once more. What if only ten can be found there?"

He answered, "For the sake of ten, I will not destroy it."

33When the LORD had finished speaking with Abraham, he left, and Abraham returned home.

19

The two angels arrived at Sodom in the evening, and Lot was sitting in the gateway of the city. When he saw them, he got up to meet them and bowed down with his face to the ground. 2"My lords," he said, "please turn aside to your servant's house. You can wash your feet and spend the night and then go on your way early in the morning."

"No," they answered, "we will spend the night in the square."

3But he insisted so strongly that they did go with him and entered his house. He prepared a meal for them, baking bread without yeast, and they ate. 4Before they had gone to bed, all the men from every part of the city of Sodom—both young and old—surrounded the house. 5They called to Lot, "Where are the men who came to you tonight? Bring them out to us so that we can have sex with them."

6Lot went outside to meet them and shut the door behind him 7and said, "No, my friends. Don't do this wicked thing. 8Look, I have two daughters who have never slept with a man. Let me bring them out to you, and you can do what you like with them. But don't do anything to these men, for they have come under the protection of my roof."

9"Get out of our way," they replied. And they said, "This fellow came here as an alien, and now he wants to play the judge! We'll treat you worse than them." They kept bringing pressure on Lot and moved forward to break down the door.

10But the men inside reached out and pulled Lot back into the house and shut the door. 11Then they struck the men who were at the door of the house, young and old, with blindness so that they could not find the door.

12The two men said to Lot, "Do you have anyone else here—sons-in-law, sons or daughters, or anyone else in the city who belongs to you? Get them out of here, 13because we are going to destroy this place. The outcry to the LORD against its people is so great that he has sent us to destroy it."

14So Lot went out and spoke to his sons-in-law, who were pledged to marry[j] his daughters. He said, "Hurry and get out of this place, because the LORD is about to destroy the city!" But his sons-in-law thought he was joking.

15With the coming of dawn, the angels urged Lot, saying, "Hurry! Take your wife and your two daughters who are here, or you will be swept away when the city is punished."

16When he hesitated, the men grasped his hand and the hands of his wife and of his two daughters and led them safely out of the city, for the LORD was merciful to them. 17As soon as they had brought them out, one of them said, "Flee for

[h]24 Or *forgive*; also in verse 26 [i]25 Or *Ruler* [j]14 Or *were married to*

your lives! Don't look back, and don't stop any-
where in the plain! Flee to the mountains or you
will be swept away!"
[18]But Lot said to them, "No, my lords,[k] please!
[19]Your[l] servant has found favor in your[l]
eyes, and you[l] have shown great kindness
to me in sparing my life. But I can't flee to the
mountains; this disaster will overtake me, and
I'll die. [20]Look, here is a town near enough
to run to, and it is small. Let me flee to it—
it is very small, isn't it? Then my life will be
spared."
[21]He said to him, "Very well, I will grant this
request too; I will not overthrow the town you
speak of. [22]But flee there quickly, because I can-
not do anything until you reach it." (That is why
the town was called Zoar.[m])
[23]By the time Lot reached Zoar, the sun
had risen over the land. [24]Then the LORD rained
down burning sulfur on Sodom and Gomor-
rah—from the LORD out of the heavens. [25]Thus
he overthrew those cities and the entire
plain, including all those living in the cities—
and also the vegetation in the land. [26]But Lot's
wife looked back, and she became a pillar of
salt.
[27]Early the next morning Abraham got up and
returned to the place where he had stood before
the LORD. [28]He looked down toward Sodom and
Gomorrah, toward all the land of the plain, and
he saw dense smoke rising from the land, like
smoke from a furnace.
[29]So when God destroyed the cities of the
plain, he remembered Abraham, and he brought
Lot out of the catastrophe that overthrew the cit-
ies where Lot had lived.
[30]Lot and his two daughters left Zoar and set-
tled in the mountains, for he was afraid to stay in
Zoar. He and his two daughters lived in a cave.
[31]One day the older daughter said to the younger,
"Our father is old, and there is no man around
here to lie with us, as is the custom all over the
earth. [32]Let's get our father to drink wine and
then lie with him and preserve our family line
through our father."
[33]That night they got their father to drink wine,
and the older daughter went in and lay with him.
He was not aware of it when she lay down or
when she got up.
[34]The next day the older daughter said to the
younger, "Last night I lay with my father. Let's get
him to drink wine again tonight, and you go in
and lie with him so we can preserve our family
line through our father." [35]So they got their father
to drink wine that night also, and the younger
daughter went and lay with him. Again he was
not aware of it when she lay down or when she
got up.
[36]So both of Lot's daughters became pregnant
by their father. [37]The older daughter had a son,
and she named him Moab[n]; he is the father of
the Moabites of today. [38]The younger daugh-
ter also had a son, and she named him Ben-
Ammi[o]; he is the father of the Ammonites of
today.

[k]18 Or *No, Lord*; or *No, my lord* [l]19 The Hebrew is singular.
[m]22 *Zoar* means *small*. [n]37 *Moab* sounds like the Hebrew for *from father*. [o]38 *Ben-Ammi* means *son of my people*.

Discovering the Word 1. In 18:1-8 what elements of hospitality does Abraham show even to visiting strangers? 2. Why does the Lord decide to tell Abraham about his decision to destroy Sodom and Gomorrah (18:16-19)? 3. In the long conversation that follows (18:20-33), what do you learn about Abraham's attitude toward the wicked cities and toward the Lord? 4. In chapter 19 we get a close look at the people in Sodom. How do their actions help us understand why they were under God's judgment? 5. How is the Lord's mercy evident in his treatment of Lot and his family (19:10-22)? 6. Describe how God's judgment works out in Sodom and in Lot's family (19:23-28).

Applying the Word 1. In what areas could we intercede with God for our city, state or country because of its sins? 2. What can we do to avert the judgment of God on ourselves and those around us?

Responding in Prayer Pray for the city or town you live in, that you might be spared God's judgment.

12 / *Genesis 20—21*
The Consequences of Unbelief

HAVE YOU EVER gotten into trouble because you didn't trust God to take care of you? Did you take matters into your own hands and in the process cut some moral or ethical corners? If so, you have company. Even Abraham gave in to his fears and failed to tell the truth in a potentially dangerous situation. The Bible has no plaster saints. It doesn't cover over the sins of its heroes. So we can learn from their *failures* as well as their successes. In the previous study we saw Abraham at his best as he showed concern for a sinful city. In this study we find him near his worst as he pursues a course of action with potentially disastrous consequences for everyone concerned.

Warming Up to God What have you struggled with recently? Tell Christ about it and let him take it from you as you come near to him in Scripture.

Read Genesis 20—21.

20 Now Abraham moved on from
there into the region of the Negev
and lived between Kadesh and
Shur. For a while he stayed in Gerar, 2and there
Abraham said of his wife Sarah, "She is my sis-
ter." Then Abimelech king of Gerar sent for Sarah
and took her.

3But God came to Abimelech in a dream one
night and said to him, "You are as good as dead
because of the woman you have taken; she is a
married woman."

4Now Abimelech had not gone near her, so he
said, "Lord, will you destroy an innocent nation?
5Did he not say to me, 'She is my sister,' and
didn't she also say, 'He is my brother'? I have
done this with a clear conscience and clean
hands."

6Then God said to him in the dream, "Yes, I
know you did this with a clear conscience, and so
I have kept you from sinning against me. That is
why I did not let you touch her. 7Now return the
man's wife, for he is a prophet, and he will pray
for you and you will live. But if you do not return
her, you may be sure that you and all yours will
die."

8Early the next morning Abimelech summoned
all his officials, and when he told them all that
had happened, they were very much afraid. 9Then
Abimelech called Abraham in and said, "What
have you done to us? How have I wronged you
that you have brought such great guilt upon me
and my kingdom? You have done things to me
that should not be done." 10And Abimelech asked
Abraham, "What was your reason for doing this?"

11Abraham replied, "I said to myself, 'There is
surely no fear of God in this place, and they will
kill me because of my wife.' 12Besides, she really
is my sister, the daughter of my father though not
of my mother; and she became my wife. 13And
when God had me wander from my father's
household, I said to her, 'This is how you can
show your love to me: Everywhere we go, say of
me, "He is my brother." ' "

14Then Abimelech brought sheep and cattle
and male and female slaves and gave them to
Abraham, and he returned Sarah his wife to him.
15And Abimelech said, "My land is before you;
live wherever you like."

16To Sarah he said, "I am giving your brother a
thousand shekels[p] of silver. This is to cover the
offense against you before all who are with you;
you are completely vindicated."

17Then Abraham prayed to God, and God
healed Abimelech, his wife and his slave girls so
they could have children again, 18for the LORD had
closed up every womb in Abimelech's household
because of Abraham's wife Sarah.

21 Now the LORD was gracious to
Sarah as he had said, and the LORD
did for Sarah what he had prom-
ised. 2Sarah became pregnant and bore a son to
Abraham in his old age, at the very time God had
promised him. 3Abraham gave the name Isaac[q]
to the son Sarah bore him. 4When his son Isaac
was eight days old, Abraham circumcised him, as
God commanded him. 5Abraham was a hundred
years old when his son Isaac was born to him.

6Sarah said, "God has brought me laughter, and
everyone who hears about this will laugh with
me." 7And she added, "Who would have said to

p16 That is, about 25 pounds (about 11.5 kilograms) q3 *Isaac* means *he laughs*.

Abraham that Sarah would nurse children? Yet I
have borne him a son in his old age."
8The child grew and was weaned, and on the
day Isaac was weaned Abraham held a great feast.
9But Sarah saw that the son whom Hagar the
Egyptian had borne to Abraham was mocking,
10and she said to Abraham, "Get rid of that slave
woman and her son, for that slave woman's son
will never share in the inheritance with my son
Isaac."
11The matter distressed Abraham greatly be-
cause it concerned his son. 12But God said to him,
"Do not be so distressed about the boy and your
maidservant. Listen to whatever Sarah tells you,
because it is through Isaac that your offspring[r]
will be reckoned. 13I will make the son of the
maidservant into a nation also, because he is your
offspring."
14Early the next morning Abraham took some
food and a skin of water and gave them to Hagar.
He set them on her shoulders and then sent her
off with the boy. She went on her way and wan-
dered in the desert of Beersheba.
15When the water in the skin was gone, she put
the boy under one of the bushes. 16Then she went
off and sat down nearby, about a bowshot away,
for she thought, "I cannot watch the boy die."
And as she sat there nearby, she[s] began to sob.
17God heard the boy crying, and the angel of
God called to Hagar from heaven and said to her,
"What is the matter, Hagar? Do not be afraid;
God has heard the boy crying as he lies there.
18Lift the boy up and take him by the hand, for I
will make him into a great nation."
19Then God opened her eyes and she saw a well
of water. So she went and filled the skin with
water and gave the boy a drink.
20God was with the boy as he grew up. He lived
in the desert and became an archer. 21While he
was living in the Desert of Paran, his mother got
a wife for him from Egypt.
22At that time Abimelech and Phicol the com-
mander of his forces said to Abraham, "God is
with you in everything you do. 23Now swear to
me here before God that you will not deal falsely
with me or my children or my descendants. Show
to me and the country where you are living as an
alien the same kindness I have shown to you."
24Abraham said, "I swear it."
25Then Abraham complained to Abimelech
about a well of water that Abimelech's servants
had seized. 26But Abimelech said, "I don't know
who has done this. You did not tell me, and I
heard about it only today."
27So Abraham brought sheep and cattle and
gave them to Abimelech, and the two men made
a treaty. 28Abraham set apart seven ewe lambs
from the flock, 29and Abimelech asked Abraham,
"What is the meaning of these seven ewe lambs
you have set apart by themselves?"
30He replied, "Accept these seven lambs from
my hand as a witness that I dug this well."
31So that place was called Beersheba,[t] because
the two men swore an oath there.
32After the treaty had been made at Beersheba,
Abimelech and Phicol the commander of his
forces returned to the land of the Philistines.
33Abraham planted a tamarisk tree in Beersheba,
and there he called upon the name of the LORD,
the Eternal God. 34And Abraham stayed in the
land of the Philistines for a long time.

[r]12 Or *seed* [s]16 Hebrew; Septuagint *the child* [t]31 *Beersheba* can mean *well of seven* or *well of the oath.*

Discovering the Word 1. Describe Abraham's situation and how God deals with it (20:1-7). 2. What do the questions Abimelech asks the next day reveal about his attitude toward Abraham (20:8-10)? 3. How does the patriarch try to explain his way out of this difficulty (20:11-13)? 4. The name *Isaac* means "he laughs." Describe Sarah's reaction and how she feels after waiting so long for this joyful event (21:1-7). 5. What problem does Abraham face in 21:8-14, and how is it resolved? 6. How does God help and encourage Hagar in her hour of crisis (21:15-21)?

Applying the Word 1. Think of a difficult situation in which fear or unbelief led you to a course of action that didn't honor God. What were the consequences and lessons you learned? 2. How can Sarah and Abraham's experience encourage us to be more patient and faithful in waiting for unanswered prayer?

Responding in Prayer Thank your Father for the laughter he's brought into your heart.

13 / *Genesis 22—23*
Ultimate Faith

SUPPOSE GOD ASKED you to give up someone or something at the very center of your life—a loved one, your home, profession or plans for the future. How would you respond? In this study we walk with Abraham through such a valley of testing. He comes to the climax of his career as he faces a soul-shattering event. Abraham's experience can teach us how God provides for those who honor him with such faith and obedience.

Warming Up to God Tell God about any pain you are suffering right now. Remember that James says trials develop perseverance. Ask God to purify your character while you endure.

Read Genesis 22—23.

22 Some time later God tested Abra-
ham. He said to him, "Abraham!"
"Here I am," he replied.
2Then God said, "Take your son, your only
son, Isaac, whom you love, and go to the region
of Moriah. Sacrifice him there as a burnt offer-
ing on one of the mountains I will tell you
about."
3Early the next morning Abraham got up and
saddled his donkey. He took with him two of his
servants and his son Isaac. When he had cut
enough wood for the burnt offering, he set out for
the place God had told him about. 4On the third
day Abraham looked up and saw the place in the
distance. 5He said to his servants, "Stay here with
the donkey while I and the boy go over there.
We will worship and then we will come back to
you."
6Abraham took the wood for the burnt offering
and placed it on his son Isaac, and he himself
carried the fire and the knife. As the two of them
went on together, 7Isaac spoke up and said to his
father Abraham, "Father?"
"Yes, my son?" Abraham replied.
"The fire and wood are here," Isaac said, "but
where is the lamb for the burnt offering?"
8Abraham answered, "God himself will provide
the lamb for the burnt offering, my son." And the
two of them went on together.
9When they reached the place God had told
him about, Abraham built an altar there and ar-
ranged the wood on it. He bound his son Isaac
and laid him on the altar, on top of the wood.
10Then he reached out his hand and took the
knife to slay his son. 11But the angel of the LORD
called out to him from heaven, "Abraham! Abra-
ham!"
"Here I am," he replied.
12"Do not lay a hand on the boy," he said. "Do
not do anything to him. Now I know that you fear
God, because you have not withheld from me
your son, your only son."
13Abraham looked up and there in a thicket he
saw a ram[u] caught by its horns. He went over
and took the ram and sacrificed it as a burnt of-
fering instead of his son. 14So Abraham called that
place The LORD Will Provide. And to this day it is
said, "On the mountain of the LORD it will be pro-
vided."
15The angel of the LORD called to Abraham from
heaven a second time 16and said, "I swear by my-
self, declares the LORD, that because you have
done this and have not withheld your son, your
only son, 17I will surely bless you and make your
descendants as numerous as the stars in the sky
and as the sand on the seashore. Your descen-
dants will take possession of the cities of their
enemies, 18and through your offspring[v] all na-
tions on earth will be blessed, because you have
obeyed me."
19Then Abraham returned to his servants, and
they set off together for Beersheba. And Abraham
stayed in Beersheba.
20Some time later Abraham was told, "Milcah is
also a mother; she has borne sons to your brother
Nahor: 21Uz the firstborn, Buz his brother, Kem-
uel (the father of Aram), 22Kesed, Hazo, Pildash,
Jidlaph and Bethuel." 23Bethuel became the father
of Rebekah. Milcah bore these eight sons to Abra-
ham's brother Nahor. 24His concubine, whose
name was Reumah, also had sons: Tebah, Gaham,
Tahash and Maacah.

[u] *13* Many manuscripts of the Masoretic Text, Samaritan Pentateuch, Septuagint and Syriac; most manuscripts of the Masoretic Text *a ram behind ⌊him⌋* [v] *18* Or *seed*

23 Sarah lived to be a hundred and twenty-seven years old. 2She died at Kiriath Arba (that is, Hebron) in the land of Canaan, and Abraham went to mourn for Sarah and to weep over her.

3Then Abraham rose from beside his dead wife and spoke to the Hittites.[w] He said, 4"I am an alien and a stranger among you. Sell me some property for a burial site here so I can bury my dead."

5The Hittites replied to Abraham, 6"Sir, listen to us. You are a mighty prince among us. Bury your dead in the choicest of our tombs. None of us will refuse you his tomb for burying your dead."

7Then Abraham rose and bowed down before the people of the land, the Hittites. 8He said to them, "If you are willing to let me bury my dead, then listen to me and intercede with Ephron son of Zohar on my behalf 9so he will sell me the cave of Machpelah, which belongs to him and is at the end of his field. Ask him to sell it to me for the full price as a burial site among you."

10Ephron the Hittite was sitting among his people and he replied to Abraham in the hearing of all the Hittites who had come to the gate of his city. 11"No, my lord," he said. "Listen to me; I give[x] you the field, and I give[x] you the cave that is in it. I give[x] it to you in the presence of my people. Bury your dead."

12Again Abraham bowed down before the people of the land 13and he said to Ephron in their hearing, "Listen to me, if you will. I will pay the price of the field. Accept it from me so I can bury my dead there."

14Ephron answered Abraham, 15"Listen to me, my lord; the land is worth four hundred shekels[y] of silver, but what is that between me and you? Bury your dead."

16Abraham agreed to Ephron's terms and weighed out for him the price he had named in the hearing of the Hittites: four hundred shekels of silver, according to the weight current among the merchants.

17So Ephron's field in Machpelah near Mamre—both the field and the cave in it, and all the trees within the borders of the field—was deeded 18to Abraham as his property in the presence of all the Hittites who had come to the gate of the city. 19Afterward Abraham buried his wife Sarah in the cave in the field of Machpelah near Mamre (which is at Hebron) in the land of Canaan. 20So the field and the cave in it were deeded to Abraham by the Hittites as a burial site.

w3 Or *the sons of Heth*; also in verses 5, 7, 10, 16, 18 and 20
x11 Or *sell* y15 That is, about 10 pounds (about 4.5 kilograms)

Discovering the Word 1. In God's command to Abraham what phrases emphasize the magnitude and painfulness of this sacrifice (22:1–2)? 2. What do the details of the narrative reveal about Abraham's response to this incredibly difficult situation (22:3–10)? 3. How does God's provision for Abraham in 22:13–14 fulfill the confidence he expressed earlier (22:5, 8)? 4. When Abraham decides to bury Sarah among the Hittites, how do they react to his first request (23:1–6)? 5. What steps does Abraham go through to observe the laws of the land (23:7–16)? 6. At the time of Sarah's death, she and Abraham had not seen the fulfillment of most of God's promises. How was her burial a silent testimony to their future fulfillment (23:17–19)?

Applying the Word 1. In 22:12 the Lord says, "Now I know that you fear God, because you have not withheld from me your son, your only son." Based on Abraham's example, what do you think it means to fear God? 2. Have you ever faced a situation in which obedience to God required you to give up someone or something you loved? Explain.

Responding in Prayer Praise God for this foreshadowing of his ultimate act of sacrifice—the willful surrender of his Son's life to give us forgiveness and salvation.

14/ *Genesis 24:1—25:11*
God's Guidance and Care

HOW DO YOU go about discovering God's will in a specific situation? When you think you understand his will, do you simply wait for it or do you work toward its fulfillment? Although the Bible gives no formulas or blueprints, it does illustrate certain principles we can apply. In this study Abraham continues to wind up his affairs by arranging for the sure succession of his line. Here we have the fascinating story of the way he went about securing the right wife for his son Isaac.

Warming Up to God God wants to give you the desires of your heart. What are you yearning for today?

Read Genesis 24:1—25:11.

24 Abraham was now old and well ad-
vanced in years, and the LORD had
blessed him in every way. 2He said
to the chief[z] servant in his household, the one in
charge of all that he had, "Put your hand under
my thigh. 3I want you to swear by the LORD, the
God of heaven and the God of earth, that you will
not get a wife for my son from the daughters of
the Canaanites, among whom I am living, 4but
will go to my country and my own relatives and
get a wife for my son Isaac."
5The servant asked him, "What if the woman is
unwilling to come back with me to this land?
Shall I then take your son back to the country you
came from?"
6"Make sure that you do not take my son back
there," Abraham said. 7"The LORD, the God of
heaven, who brought me out of my father's
household and my native land and who spoke to
me and promised me on oath, saying, 'To your
offspring[a] I will give this land'—he will send his
angel before you so that you can get a wife for my
son from there. 8If the woman is unwilling to
come back with you, then you will be released
from this oath of mine. Only do not take my son
back there." 9So the servant put his hand under
the thigh of his master Abraham and swore an
oath to him concerning this matter.
10Then the servant took ten of his master's
camels and left, taking with him all kinds of good
things from his master. He set out for Aram Na-
haraim[b] and made his way to the town of Nahor.
11He had the camels kneel down near the well
outside the town; it was toward evening, the time
the women go out to draw water.
12Then he prayed, "O LORD, God of my master
Abraham, give me success today, and show kind-
ness to my master Abraham. 13See, I am standing
beside this spring, and the daughters of the
townspeople are coming out to draw water. 14May
it be that when I say to a girl, 'Please let down
your jar that I may have a drink,' and she says,
'Drink, and I'll water your camels too'—let her be
the one you have chosen for your servant Isaac.
By this I will know that you have shown kindness
to my master."
15Before he had finished praying, Rebekah
came out with her jar on her shoulder. She was
the daughter of Bethuel son of Milcah, who was
the wife of Abraham's brother Nahor. 16The girl
was very beautiful, a virgin; no man had ever lain
with her. She went down to the spring, filled her
jar and came up again.
17The servant hurried to meet her and said,
"Please give me a little water from your jar."
18"Drink, my lord," she said, and quickly low-
ered the jar to her hands and gave him a drink.
19After she had given him a drink, she said, "I'll
draw water for your camels too, until they have
finished drinking." 20So she quickly emptied her
jar into the trough, ran back to the well to draw
more water, and drew enough for all his camels.
21Without saying a word, the man watched her
closely to learn whether or not the LORD had made
his journey successful.
22When the camels had finished drinking, the
man took out a gold nose ring weighing a beka[c]
and two gold bracelets weighing ten shekels.[d]
23Then he asked, "Whose daughter are you?
Please tell me, is there room in your father's
house for us to spend the night?"
24She answered him, "I am the daughter of Be-

[z]2 Or *oldest* [a]7 Or *seed* [b]10 That is, Northwest Mesopotamia
[c]22 That is, about 1/5 ounce (about 5.5 grams) [d]22 That is, about 4 ounces (about 110 grams)

thuel, the son that Milcah bore to Nahor." 25And she added, "We have plenty of straw and fodder, as well as room for you to spend the night."

26Then the man bowed down and worshiped the LORD, 27saying, "Praise be to the LORD, the God of my master Abraham, who has not abandoned his kindness and faithfulness to my master. As for me, the LORD has led me on the journey to the house of my master's relatives."

28The girl ran and told her mother's household about these things. 29Now Rebekah had a brother named Laban, and he hurried out to the man at the spring. 30As soon as he had seen the nose ring, and the bracelets on his sister's arms, and had heard Rebekah tell what the man said to her, he went out to the man and found him standing by the camels near the spring. 31"Come, you who are blessed by the LORD," he said. "Why are you standing out here? I have prepared the house and a place for the camels."

32So the man went to the house, and the camels were unloaded. Straw and fodder were brought for the camels, and water for him and his men to wash their feet. 33Then food was set before him, but he said, "I will not eat until I have told you what I have to say."

"Then tell us," ⌊Laban⌋ said.

34So he said, "I am Abraham's servant. 35The LORD has blessed my master abundantly, and he has become wealthy. He has given him sheep and cattle, silver and gold, menservants and maidservants, and camels and donkeys. 36My master's wife Sarah has borne him a son in her[e] old age, and he has given him everything he owns. 37And my master made me swear an oath, and said, 'You must not get a wife for my son from the daughters of the Canaanites, in whose land I live, 38but go to my father's family and to my own clan, and get a wife for my son.'

39"Then I asked my master, 'What if the woman will not come back with me?'

40"He replied, 'The LORD, before whom I have walked, will send his angel with you and make your journey a success, so that you can get a wife for my son from my own clan and from my father's family. 41Then, when you go to my clan, you will be released from my oath even if they refuse to give her to you—you will be released from my oath.'

42"When I came to the spring today, I said, 'O LORD, God of my master Abraham, if you will, please grant success to the journey on which I have come. 43See, I am standing beside this spring; if a maiden comes out to draw water and I say to her, "Please let me drink a little water from your jar," 44and if she says to me, "Drink, and I'll draw water for your camels too," let her be the one the LORD has chosen for my master's son.'

45"Before I finished praying in my heart, Rebekah came out, with her jar on her shoulder. She went down to the spring and drew water, and I said to her, 'Please give me a drink.'

46"She quickly lowered her jar from her shoulder and said, 'Drink, and I'll water your camels too.' So I drank, and she watered the camels also.

47"I asked her, 'Whose daughter are you?'

"She said, 'The daughter of Bethuel son of Nahor, whom Milcah bore to him.'

"Then I put the ring in her nose and the bracelets on her arms, 48and I bowed down and worshiped the LORD. I praised the LORD, the God of my master Abraham, who had led me on the right road to get the granddaughter of my master's brother for his son. 49Now if you will show kindness and faithfulness to my master, tell me; and if not, tell me, so I may know which way to turn."

50Laban and Bethuel answered, "This is from the LORD; we can say nothing to you one way or the other. 51Here is Rebekah; take her and go, and let her become the wife of your master's son, as the LORD has directed."

52When Abraham's servant heard what they said, he bowed down to the ground before the LORD. 53Then the servant brought out gold and silver jewelry and articles of clothing and gave them to Rebekah; he also gave costly gifts to her brother and to her mother. 54Then he and the men who were with him ate and drank and spent the night there.

When they got up the next morning, he said, "Send me on my way to my master."

55But her brother and her mother replied, "Let the girl remain with us ten days or so; then you[f] may go."

56But he said to them, "Do not detain me, now that the LORD has granted success to my journey. Send me on my way so I may go to my master."

57Then they said, "Let's call the girl and ask her about it." 58So they called Rebekah and asked her, "Will you go with this man?"

"I will go," she said.

[e]36 Or *his* [f]55 Or *she*

59So they sent their sister Rebekah on her way,
along with her nurse and Abraham's servant and
his men. 60And they blessed Rebekah and said to
her,

"Our sister, may you increase
to thousands upon thousands;
may your offspring possess
the gates of their enemies."

61Then Rebekah and her maids got ready and
mounted their camels and went back with the
man. So the servant took Rebekah and left.
62Now Isaac had come from Beer Lahai Roi, for
he was living in the Negev. 63He went out to the
field one evening to meditate,[g] and as he looked
up, he saw camels approaching. 64Rebekah also
looked up and saw Isaac. She got down from her
camel 65and asked the servant, "Who is that man
in the field coming to meet us?"

"He is my master," the servant answered. So
she took her veil and covered herself.
66Then the servant told Isaac all he had done.
67Isaac brought her into the tent of his mother
Sarah, and he married Rebekah. So she became
his wife, and he loved her; and Isaac was comforted
after his mother's death.

25 Abraham took[h] another wife,
whose name was Keturah. 2She
bore him Zimran, Jokshan, Medan,
Midian, Ishbak and Shuah. 3Jokshan was the father
of Sheba and Dedan; the descendants of Dedan
were the Asshurites, the Letushites and the
Leummites. 4The sons of Midian were Ephah,
Epher, Hanoch, Abida and Eldaah. All these were
descendants of Keturah.
5Abraham left everything he owned to Isaac.
6But while he was still living, he gave gifts to the
sons of his concubines and sent them away from
his son Isaac to the land of the east.
7Altogether, Abraham lived a hundred and seventy-five
years. 8Then Abraham breathed his last
and died at a good old age, an old man and full of
years; and he was gathered to his people. 9His
sons Isaac and Ishmael buried him in the cave of
Machpelah near Mamre, in the field of Ephron
son of Zohar the Hittite, 10the field Abraham had
bought from the Hittites.[i] There Abraham was
buried with his wife Sarah. 11After Abraham's
death, God blessed his son Isaac, who then lived
near Beer Lahai Roi.

[g]63 The meaning of the Hebrew for this word is uncertain. [h]1 Or *had taken* [i]10 Or *the sons of Heth*

Discovering the Word 1. What main concerns are evident in Abraham's commands to his servant (24:1–9)? 2. As the servant arrives at Nahor he offers the first prayer for personal guidance recorded in the Bible. What does he specifically ask of God (24:12–14)? 3. How does the servant's account in 24:33–49 reveal his excitement and awe at the Lord's guidance? 4. How does Rebekah's family react to these sudden, unexpected events (24:50–53)? 5. In what way is Rebekah involved in the decision to go with the servant (24:54–60)? 6. What do we learn about Abraham's final years (25:1–11)?

Applying the Word 1. The servant had not asked for a vision or miraculous event but for guidance through clear signs in natural circumstances. When has God guided you in this way? 2. What is the most important lesson you have learned from studying the life of Abraham?

Responding in Prayer Thank the Lord for giving you the model of the not-so-perfect, but God-directed, life of Abraham.

15 / *Genesis 25:12—27:40*
A Family Feud

CONTROVERSY AND QUARRELING among brothers, euphemistically called sibling rivalry, is prevalent in most families and is a part of growing up. It can be contained, however, if it is dealt with consistently and fairly. But when the parents show partiality and take sides, this struggle often becomes malignant and fatal to family unity. This study opens with the joy of long-awaited birth. After twenty years, Isaac and Rebekah have not just one son but twins. As the boys grow up, parental partiality develops with tragic consequences for family relationships. Yet throughout these events God works out his sovereign purpose and remains merciful to this family in spite of their failures. Not only can we profit from their mistakes, but we can also be encouraged by God's love for us even when we fail.

Warming Up to God What one new event or piece of news can you share with Jesus today? Tell him a story and ask him to teach you as you continue reading the stories of Abraham, Isaac and now Jacob.

Read Genesis 25:12—27:40.

12This is the account of Abraham's son Ishmael, whom Sarah's maidservant, Hagar the Egyptian, bore to Abraham.

13These are the names of the sons of Ishmael, listed in the order of their birth: Nebaioth the firstborn of Ishmael, Kedar, Adbeel, Mibsam,
14Mishma, Dumah, Massa, 15Hadad, Tema, Jetur,
Naphish and Kedemah. 16These were the sons of Ishmael, and these are the names of the twelve tribal rulers according to their settlements and
camps. 17Altogether, Ishmael lived a hundred and thirty-seven years. He breathed his last and died, and he was gathered to his people. 18His descendants settled in the area from Havilah to Shur, near the border of Egypt, as you go toward Asshur. And they lived in hostility toward[j] all their brothers.

19This is the account of Abraham's son Isaac.

Abraham became the father of Isaac, 20and
Isaac was forty years old when he married Rebekah daughter of Bethuel the Aramean from Paddan Aram[k] and sister of Laban the Aramean.
21Isaac prayed to the LORD on behalf of his wife, because she was barren. The LORD answered his prayer, and his wife Rebekah became pregnant.
22The babies jostled each other within her, and she said, "Why is this happening to me?" So she went to inquire of the LORD.
23The LORD said to her,

"Two nations are in your womb,
and two peoples from within you will be separated;
one people will be stronger than the other,
and the older will serve the younger."

24When the time came for her to give birth, there were twin boys in her womb. 25The first to come out was red, and his whole body was like a hairy garment; so they named him Esau.[l] 26After
this, his brother came out, with his hand grasping Esau's heel; so he was named Jacob.[m] Isaac was sixty years old when Rebekah gave birth to them.
27The boys grew up, and Esau became a skillful hunter, a man of the open country, while Jacob was a quiet man, staying among the tents. 28Isaac,
who had a taste for wild game, loved Esau, but Rebekah loved Jacob.

29Once when Jacob was cooking some stew, Esau came in from the open country, famished.
30He said to Jacob, "Quick, let me have some of that red stew! I'm famished!" (That is why he was also called Edom.[n])
31Jacob replied, "First sell me your birthright."
32"Look, I am about to die," Esau said. "What good is the birthright to me?"
33But Jacob said, "Swear to me first." So he swore an oath to him, selling his birthright to Jacob.
34Then Jacob gave Esau some bread and some lentil stew. He ate and drank, and then got up and left.

So Esau despised his birthright.

26 Now there was a famine in the land—besides the earlier famine of Abraham's time—and Isaac went to Abimelech king of the Philistines in Gerar. 2The
LORD appeared to Isaac and said, "Do not go down to Egypt; live in the land where I tell you to live.
3Stay in this land for a while, and I will be with you and will bless you. For to you and your descendants I will give all these lands and will confirm the oath I swore to your father Abraham.
4I will make your descendants as numerous as the stars in the sky and will give them all these lands, and through your offspring[o] all nations on earth will be blessed, 5because Abraham obeyed me and kept my requirements, my commands, my decrees and my laws." 6So Isaac stayed in Gerar.
7When the men of that place asked him about his wife, he said, "She is my sister," because he was afraid to say, "She is my wife." He thought, "The men of this place might kill me on account of Rebekah, because she is beautiful."
8When Isaac had been there a long time, Abim-

[j]18 Or *lived to the east of* [k]20 That is, Northwest Mesopotamia
[l]25 *Esau* may mean *hairy*; he was also called Edom, which means *red*.
[m]26 *Jacob* means *he grasps the heel* (figuratively, *he deceives*).
[n]30 *Edom* means *red*. [o]4 Or *seed*

elech king of the Philistines looked down from a window and saw Isaac caressing his wife Rebekah. 9So Abimelech summoned Isaac and said, "She is really your wife! Why did you say, 'She is my sister'?"

Isaac answered him, "Because I thought I might lose my life on account of her."

10Then Abimelech said, "What is this you have done to us? One of the men might well have slept with your wife, and you would have brought guilt upon us."

11So Abimelech gave orders to all the people: "Anyone who molests this man or his wife shall surely be put to death."

12Isaac planted crops in that land and the same year reaped a hundredfold, because the LORD blessed him. 13The man became rich, and his wealth continued to grow until he became very wealthy. 14He had so many flocks and herds and servants that the Philistines envied him. 15So all the wells that his father's servants had dug in the time of his father Abraham, the Philistines stopped up, filling them with earth.

16Then Abimelech said to Isaac, "Move away from us; you have become too powerful for us."

17So Isaac moved away from there and encamped in the Valley of Gerar and settled there. 18Isaac reopened the wells that had been dug in the time of his father Abraham, which the Philistines had stopped up after Abraham died, and he gave them the same names his father had given them.

19Isaac's servants dug in the valley and discovered a well of fresh water there. 20But the herdsmen of Gerar quarreled with Isaac's herdsmen and said, "The water is ours!" So he named the well Esek,[p] because they disputed with him. 21Then they dug another well, but they quarreled over that one also; so he named it Sitnah.[q] 22He moved on from there and dug another well, and no one quarreled over it. He named it Rehoboth,[r] saying, "Now the LORD has given us room and we will flourish in the land."

23From there he went up to Beersheba. 24That night the LORD appeared to him and said, "I am the God of your father Abraham. Do not be afraid, for I am with you; I will bless you and will increase the number of your descendants for the sake of my servant Abraham."

25Isaac built an altar there and called on the name of the LORD. There he pitched his tent, and there his servants dug a well.

26Meanwhile, Abimelech had come to him from Gerar, with Ahuzzath his personal adviser and Phicol the commander of his forces. 27Isaac asked them, "Why have you come to me, since you were hostile to me and sent me away?"

28They answered, "We saw clearly that the LORD was with you; so we said, 'There ought to be a sworn agreement between us'—between us and you. Let us make a treaty with you 29that you will do us no harm, just as we did not molest you but always treated you well and sent you away in peace. And now you are blessed by the LORD."

30Isaac then made a feast for them, and they ate and drank. 31Early the next morning the men swore an oath to each other. Then Isaac sent them on their way, and they left him in peace.

32That day Isaac's servants came and told him about the well they had dug. They said, "We've found water!" 33He called it Shibah,[s] and to this day the name of the town has been Beersheba.[t]

34When Esau was forty years old, he married Judith daughter of Beeri the Hittite, and also Basemath daughter of Elon the Hittite. 35They were a source of grief to Isaac and Rebekah.

27 When Isaac was old and his eyes were so weak that he could no longer see, he called for Esau his older son and said to him, "My son."

"Here I am," he answered.

2Isaac said, "I am now an old man and don't know the day of my death. 3Now then, get your weapons—your quiver and bow—and go out to the open country to hunt some wild game for me. 4Prepare me the kind of tasty food I like and bring it to me to eat, so that I may give you my blessing before I die."

5Now Rebekah was listening as Isaac spoke to his son Esau. When Esau left for the open country to hunt game and bring it back, 6Rebekah said to her son Jacob, "Look, I overheard your father say to your brother Esau, 7'Bring me some game and prepare me some tasty food to eat, so that I may give you my blessing in the presence of the LORD before I die.' 8Now, my son, listen carefully and do what I tell you: 9Go out to the flock and bring me two choice young goats, so I can prepare some tasty food for your father, just the way he likes it. 10Then take it to your father to eat, so that he may give you his blessing before he dies."

[p]20 *Esek* means *dispute.* [q]21 *Sitnah* means *opposition.* [r]22 *Rehoboth* means *room.* [s]33 *Shibah* can mean *oath* or *seven.* [t]33 *Beersheba* can mean *well of the oath* or *well of seven.*

11Jacob said to Rebekah his mother, "But my
brother Esau is a hairy man, and I'm a man with
smooth skin. 12What if my father touches me? I
would appear to be tricking him and would bring
down a curse on myself rather than a blessing."
13His mother said to him, "My son, let the
curse fall on me. Just do what I say; go and get
them for me."
14So he went and got them and brought them
to his mother, and she prepared some tasty food,
just the way his father liked it. 15Then Rebekah
took the best clothes of Esau her older son, which
she had in the house, and put them on her youn-
ger son Jacob. 16She also covered his hands and
the smooth part of his neck with the goatskins.
17Then she handed to her son Jacob the tasty food
and the bread she had made.
18He went to his father and said, "My father."
"Yes, my son," he answered. "Who is it?"
19Jacob said to his father, "I am Esau your first-
born. I have done as you told me. Please sit up
and eat some of my game so that you may give me
your blessing."
20Isaac asked his son, "How did you find it so
quickly, my son?"
"The LORD your God gave me success," he re-
plied.
21Then Isaac said to Jacob, "Come near so I can
touch you, my son, to know whether you really
are my son Esau or not."
22Jacob went close to his father Isaac, who
touched him and said, "The voice is the voice of
Jacob, but the hands are the hands of Esau." 23He
did not recognize him, for his hands were hairy
like those of his brother Esau; so he blessed him.
24"Are you really my son Esau?" he asked.
"I am," he replied.
25Then he said, "My son, bring me some of
your game to eat, so that I may give you my bless-
ing."
Jacob brought it to him and he ate; and he
brought some wine and he drank. 26Then his fa-
ther Isaac said to him, "Come here, my son, and
kiss me."
27So he went to him and kissed him. When
Isaac caught the smell of his clothes, he blessed
him and said,

"Ah, the smell of my son
  is like the smell of a field
  that the LORD has blessed.
28May God give you of heaven's dew
  and of earth's richness—
  an abundance of grain and new wine.
29May nations serve you
  and peoples bow down to you.
Be lord over your brothers,
  and may the sons of your mother bow
    down to you.
May those who curse you be cursed
  and those who bless you be blessed."

30After Isaac finished blessing him and Jacob
had scarcely left his father's presence, his brother
Esau came in from hunting. 31He too prepared
some tasty food and brought it to his father. Then
he said to him, "My father, sit up and eat some of
my game, so that you may give me your blessing."
32His father Isaac asked him, "Who are you?"
"I am your son," he answered, "your firstborn,
Esau."
33Isaac trembled violently and said, "Who was
it, then, that hunted game and brought it to me?
I ate it just before you came and I blessed him—
and indeed he will be blessed!"
34When Esau heard his father's words, he burst
out with a loud and bitter cry and said to his
father, "Bless me—me too, my father!"
35But he said, "Your brother came deceitfully
and took your blessing."
36Esau said, "Isn't he rightly named Jacob[u]?
He has deceived me these two times: He took
my birthright, and now he's taken my blessing!"
Then he asked, "Haven't you reserved any bless-
ing for me?"
37Isaac answered Esau, "I have made him lord
over you and have made all his relatives his ser-
vants, and I have sustained him with grain and
new wine. So what can I possibly do for you, my
son?"
38Esau said to his father, "Do you have only
one blessing, my father? Bless me too, my father!"
Then Esau wept aloud.
39His father Isaac answered him,

"Your dwelling will be
  away from the earth's richness,
  away from the dew of heaven above.
40You will live by the sword
  and you will serve your brother.
But when you grow restless,
  you will throw his yoke
  from off your neck."

[u]36 *Jacob* means *he grasps the heel* (figuratively, *he deceives*).

Discovering the Word 1. What difficulties and tests of faith do Isaac and Rebekah encounter in connection with the birth of their sons (25:19–22)? 2. What does the incident in 25:29–34 reveal about the character of the two brothers? 3. What specific promises does the Lord make to Isaac in reaffirming his covenant with Abraham (26:2–6, 23–25)? 4. In 25:28 we learned that "Isaac, who had a taste for wild game, loved Esau, but Rebekah loved Jacob." How does this parental favoritism work itself out in the struggle recounted in 27:1–17? 5. How does Jacob succeed in deceiving his father (27:18–29)?

Applying the Word 1. Verse 34 states that Esau despised his birthright (his double portion of the inheritance and future role as head of the family). In what areas are you tempted to give up something spiritually valuable for the sake of something of little or no value? 2. In what ways have you experienced the strength of your parents or been influenced by their weaknesses? 3. How can you show equal love and care to family members with radically different personalities?

Responding in Prayer Ask God to show you how to encourage better relationships in your own family or living situation.

16 / *Genesis 27:41—30:24*

God's Mercy and Justice

HOW DO YOU cope with the consequences of sin in your life? What effect does your disobedience to God have on his purposes for you? Jacob's experience can provide helpful answers to these questions. In the last study we saw how parental partiality increased the natural rivalry between Esau and Jacob. As Isaac and Rebekah took sides to work against each other, the family relationships became strained. In this study we see how they finally fractured, with unforeseen consequences.

Warming Up to God What words would you use to describe the mercy of God? Thank him for each way he has shown mercy to you.

Read Genesis 27:41—30:24.

41Esau held a grudge against Jacob because of
the blessing his father had given him. He said to
himself, "The days of mourning for my father are
near; then I will kill my brother Jacob."
42When Rebekah was told what her older son
Esau had said, she sent for her younger son Jacob
and said to him, "Your brother Esau is consoling
himself with the thought of killing you. 43Now
then, my son, do what I say: Flee at once to my
brother Laban in Haran. 44Stay with him for a
while until your brother's fury subsides. 45When
your brother is no longer angry with you and
forgets what you did to him, I'll send word for
you to come back from there. Why should I lose
both of you in one day?"
46Then Rebekah said to Isaac, "I'm disgusted
with living because of these Hittite women. If Jacob takes a wife from among the women of this
land, from Hittite women like these, my life will
not be worth living."

28 So Isaac called for Jacob and
blessed[v] him and commanded
him: "Do not marry a Canaanite
woman. 2Go at once to Paddan Aram,[w] to the
house of your mother's father Bethuel. Take a
wife for yourself there, from among the daughters
of Laban, your mother's brother. 3May God Almighty[x] bless you and make you fruitful and increase your numbers until you become a community of peoples. 4May he give you and your
descendants the blessing given to Abraham, so
that you may take possession of the land where
you now live as an alien, the land God gave to
Abraham." 5Then Isaac sent Jacob on his way,
and he went to Paddan Aram, to Laban son of
Bethuel the Aramean, the brother of Rebekah,
who was the mother of Jacob and Esau.
6Now Esau learned that Isaac had blessed Jacob
and had sent him to Paddan Aram to take a wife

[v] *1* Or *greeted* [w] *2* That is, Northwest Mesopotamia; also in verses 5, 6 and 7 [x] *3* Hebrew *El-Shaddai*

from there, and that when he blessed him he commanded him, "Do not marry a Canaanite woman," 7and that Jacob had obeyed his father and mother and had gone to Paddan Aram. 8Esau then realized how displeasing the Canaanite women were to his father Isaac; 9so he went to Ishmael and married Mahalath, the sister of Nebaioth and daughter of Ishmael son of Abraham, in addition to the wives he already had.

10Jacob left Beersheba and set out for Haran. 11When he reached a certain place, he stopped for the night because the sun had set. Taking one of the stones there, he put it under his head and lay down to sleep. 12He had a dream in which he saw a stairway[y] resting on the earth, with its top reaching to heaven, and the angels of God were ascending and descending on it. 13There above it[z] stood the LORD, and he said: "I am the LORD, the God of your father Abraham and the God of Isaac. I will give you and your descendants the land on which you are lying. 14Your descendants will be like the dust of the earth, and you will spread out to the west and to the east, to the north and to the south. All peoples on earth will be blessed through you and your offspring. 15I am with you and will watch over you wherever you go, and I will bring you back to this land. I will not leave you until I have done what I have promised you."

16When Jacob awoke from his sleep, he thought, "Surely the LORD is in this place, and I was not aware of it." 17He was afraid and said, "How awesome is this place! This is none other than the house of God; this is the gate of heaven."

18Early the next morning Jacob took the stone he had placed under his head and set it up as a pillar and poured oil on top of it. 19He called that place Bethel,[a] though the city used to be called Luz.

20Then Jacob made a vow, saying, "If God will be with me and will watch over me on this journey I am taking and will give me food to eat and clothes to wear 21so that I return safely to my father's house, then the LORD[b] will be my God 22and[c] this stone that I have set up as a pillar will be God's house, and of all that you give me I will give you a tenth."

29 Then Jacob continued on his journey and came to the land of the eastern peoples. 2There he saw a well in the field, with three flocks of sheep lying near it because the flocks were watered from that well. The stone over the mouth of the well was large. 3When all the flocks were gathered there, the shepherds would roll the stone away from the well's mouth and water the sheep. Then they would return the stone to its place over the mouth of the well.

4Jacob asked the shepherds, "My brothers, where are you from?"

"We're from Haran," they replied.

5He said to them, "Do you know Laban, Nahor's grandson?"

"Yes, we know him," they answered.

6Then Jacob asked them, "Is he well?"

"Yes, he is," they said, "and here comes his daughter Rachel with the sheep."

7"Look," he said, "the sun is still high; it is not time for the flocks to be gathered. Water the sheep and take them back to pasture."

8"We can't," they replied, "until all the flocks are gathered and the stone has been rolled away from the mouth of the well. Then we will water the sheep."

9While he was still talking with them, Rachel came with her father's sheep, for she was a shepherdess. 10When Jacob saw Rachel daughter of Laban, his mother's brother, and Laban's sheep, he went over and rolled the stone away from the mouth of the well and watered his uncle's sheep. 11Then Jacob kissed Rachel and began to weep aloud. 12He had told Rachel that he was a relative of her father and a son of Rebekah. So she ran and told her father.

13As soon as Laban heard the news about Jacob, his sister's son, he hurried to meet him. He embraced him and kissed him and brought him to his home, and there Jacob told him all these things. 14Then Laban said to him, "You are my own flesh and blood."

After Jacob had stayed with him for a whole month, 15Laban said to him, "Just because you are a relative of mine, should you work for me for nothing? Tell me what your wages should be."

16Now Laban had two daughters; the name of the older was Leah, and the name of the younger was Rachel. 17Leah had weak[d] eyes, but Rachel was lovely in form, and beautiful. 18Jacob was in love with Rachel and said, "I'll work for you seven years in return for your younger daughter Rachel."

[y]12 Or *ladder* [z]13 Or *There beside him* [a]19 *Bethel* means *house of God.* [b]20,21 Or *Since God . . . father's house, the LORD* [c]21,22 Or *house, and the LORD will be my God, 22then* [d]17 Or *delicate*

19Laban said, "It's better that I give her to you than to some other man. Stay here with me." 20So Jacob served seven years to get Rachel, but they seemed like only a few days to him because of his love for her.

21Then Jacob said to Laban, "Give me my wife. My time is completed, and I want to lie with her."

22So Laban brought together all the people of the place and gave a feast. 23But when evening came, he took his daughter Leah and gave her to Jacob, and Jacob lay with her. 24And Laban gave his servant girl Zilpah to his daughter as her maidservant.

25When morning came, there was Leah! So Jacob said to Laban, "What is this you have done to me? I served you for Rachel, didn't I? Why have you deceived me?"

26Laban replied, "It is not our custom here to give the younger daughter in marriage before the older one. 27Finish this daughter's bridal week; then we will give you the younger one also, in return for another seven years of work."

28And Jacob did so. He finished the week with Leah, and then Laban gave him his daughter Rachel to be his wife. 29Laban gave his servant girl Bilhah to his daughter Rachel as her maidservant. 30Jacob lay with Rachel also, and he loved Rachel more than Leah. And he worked for Laban another seven years.

31When the LORD saw that Leah was not loved, he opened her womb, but Rachel was barren. 32Leah became pregnant and gave birth to a son. She named him Reuben,[e] for she said, "It is because the LORD has seen my misery. Surely my husband will love me now."

33She conceived again, and when she gave birth to a son she said, "Because the LORD heard that I am not loved, he gave me this one too." So she named him Simeon.[f]

34Again she conceived, and when she gave birth to a son she said, "Now at last my husband will become attached to me, because I have borne him three sons." So he was named Levi.[g]

35She conceived again, and when she gave birth to a son she said, "This time I will praise the LORD." So she named him Judah.[h] Then she stopped having children.

30 When Rachel saw that she was not bearing Jacob any children, she became jealous of her sister. So she said to Jacob, "Give me children, or I'll die!"

2Jacob became angry with her and said, "Am I in the place of God, who has kept you from having children?"

3Then she said, "Here is Bilhah, my maidservant. Sleep with her so that she can bear children for me and that through her I too can build a family."

4So she gave him her servant Bilhah as a wife. Jacob slept with her, 5and she became pregnant and bore him a son. 6Then Rachel said, "God has vindicated me; he has listened to my plea and given me a son." Because of this she named him Dan.[i]

7Rachel's servant Bilhah conceived again and bore Jacob a second son. 8Then Rachel said, "I have had a great struggle with my sister, and I have won." So she named him Naphtali.[j]

9When Leah saw that she had stopped having children, she took her maidservant Zilpah and gave her to Jacob as a wife. 10Leah's servant Zilpah bore Jacob a son. 11Then Leah said, "What good fortune!"[k] So she named him Gad.[l]

12Leah's servant Zilpah bore Jacob a second son. 13Then Leah said, "How happy I am! The women will call me happy." So she named him Asher.[m]

14During wheat harvest, Reuben went out into the fields and found some mandrake plants, which he brought to his mother Leah. Rachel said to Leah, "Please give me some of your son's mandrakes."

15But she said to her, "Wasn't it enough that you took away my husband? Will you take my son's mandrakes too?"

"Very well," Rachel said, "he can sleep with you tonight in return for your son's mandrakes."

16So when Jacob came in from the fields that evening, Leah went out to meet him. "You must sleep with me," she said. "I have hired you with my son's mandrakes." So he slept with her that night.

17God listened to Leah, and she became pregnant and bore Jacob a fifth son. 18Then Leah said, "God has rewarded me for giving my maidservant to my husband." So she named him Issachar.[n]

19Leah conceived again and bore Jacob a sixth son. 20Then Leah said, "God has presented me

[e]32 *Reuben* sounds like the Hebrew for *he has seen my misery*; the name means *see, a son.* [f]33 *Simeon* probably means *one who hears.* [g]34 *Levi* sounds like and may be derived from the Hebrew for *attached.* [h]35 *Judah* sounds like and may be derived from the Hebrew for *praise.* [i]6 *Dan* here means *he has vindicated.* [j]8 *Naphtali* means *my struggle.* [k]11 Or *"A troop is coming!"* [l]11 *Gad* can mean *good fortune* or *a troop.* [m]13 *Asher* means *happy.* [n]18 *Issachar* sounds like the Hebrew for *reward.*

with a precious gift. This time my husband will
treat me with honor, because I have borne him
six sons." So she named him Zebulun.[o]
21Some time later she gave birth to a daughter
and named her Dinah.
22Then God remembered Rachel; he listened to
her and opened her womb. 23She became preg-
nant and gave birth to a son and said, "God has
taken away my disgrace." 24She named him Jo-
seph,[p] and said, "May the LORD add to me an-
other son."

[o]20 *Zebulun* probably means *honor*. [p]24 *Joseph* means *may he add*.

Discovering the Word 1. When Rebekah hears of Esau's plan to kill Jacob, what strategy does she devise, and how does she persuade her son and husband to carry it out (27:41-46)? 2. Describe what happens to Jacob on his first night away from home (28:10-15). 3. From Jacob's response to the dream, what clue can we get about his relationship to God at this point (28:16-22)? 4. In what ways is Jacob's initial experience in Haran similar to and different from that of Abraham's chief servant many years earlier (29:1-18; see also 24:10-28)? 5. Jacob meets his match and means of discipline in Laban. In what way does the latter's trickery repay Jacob for the exploitation of his father's blindness (29:19-24), and how is this situation resolved (29:25-30)? 6. What impresses you about the relationships between Rachel and Leah (30:1-24)?

Applying the Word 1. A past sin or disobedience to God can leave us with a burden of guilt or failure. How can Jacob's experience renew our confidence in God's grace? 2. Spiritual maturity often comes through suffering. In what difficult situation do you now believe God is working to strengthen your faith and character?

Responding in Prayer Spend time thanking God for his care and discipline in your life.

17 / *Genesis 30:25—31:55*
Rivalry and Its Results

DO YOU CURRENTLY have a strained or fractured relationship with a family member, friend or colleague at work? Has the cancer of resentment or anger been eating away at you? In this passage we find Jacob and Laban in just such a situation. In the previous chapter, after marrying both Leah and Rachel, Jacob was obligated to serve their father for another seven years. Now he wants to return to his homeland with his family. But Laban persuades Jacob to stay on with a new contract. We will see how the rivalry between these two men escalates to the point of open conflict.

Warming Up to God Why are you coming to be with the Lord today? Tell him with honesty and frankness your thoughts and feelings. Extend them as gifts of obedience, and he will accept them as a fragrant offering.

Read Genesis 30:25—31:55.

25After Rachel gave birth to Joseph, Jacob said
to Laban, "Send me on my way so I can go back
to my own homeland. 26Give me my wives and
children, for whom I have served you, and I will
be on my way. You know how much work I've
done for you."
27But Laban said to him, "If I have found favor
in your eyes, please stay. I have learned by divina-
tion that[q] the LORD has blessed me because of
you." 28He added, "Name your wages, and I will
pay them."
29Jacob said to him, "You know how I have
worked for you and how your livestock has fared
under my care. 30The little you had before I came
has increased greatly, and the LORD has blessed
you wherever I have been. But now, when may I
do something for my own household?"

[q]27 Or possibly *have become rich and*

31“What shall I give you?” he asked.

“Don’t give me anything,” Jacob replied. “But if you will do this one thing for me, I will go on tending your flocks and watching over them: 32Let me go through all your flocks today and remove from them every speckled or spotted sheep, every dark-colored lamb and every spotted or speckled goat. They will be my wages. 33And my honesty will testify for me in the future, whenever you check on the wages you have paid me. Any goat in my possession that is not speckled or spotted, or any lamb that is not dark-colored, will be considered stolen.”

34“Agreed,” said Laban. “Let it be as you have said.” 35That same day he removed all the male goats that were streaked or spotted, and all the speckled or spotted female goats (all that had white on them) and all the dark-colored lambs, and he placed them in the care of his sons. 36Then he put a three-day journey between himself and Jacob, while Jacob continued to tend the rest of Laban’s flocks.

37Jacob, however, took fresh-cut branches from poplar, almond and plane trees and made white stripes on them by peeling the bark and exposing the white inner wood of the branches. 38Then he placed the peeled branches in all the watering troughs, so that they would be directly in front of the flocks when they came to drink. When the flocks were in heat and came to drink, 39they mated in front of the branches. And they bore young that were streaked or speckled or spotted. 40Jacob set apart the young of the flock by themselves, but made the rest face the streaked and dark-colored animals that belonged to Laban. Thus he made separate flocks for himself and did not put them with Laban’s animals. 41Whenever the stronger females were in heat, Jacob would place the branches in the troughs in front of the animals so they would mate near the branches, 42but if the animals were weak, he would not place them there. So the weak animals went to Laban and the strong ones to Jacob. 43In this way the man grew exceedingly prosperous and came to own large flocks, and maidservants and menservants, and camels and donkeys.

31 Jacob heard that Laban’s sons were saying, “Jacob has taken everything our father owned and has gained all this wealth from what belonged to our father.” 2And Jacob noticed that Laban’s attitude toward him was not what it had been.

3Then the LORD said to Jacob, “Go back to the land of your fathers and to your relatives, and I will be with you.”

4So Jacob sent word to Rachel and Leah to come out to the fields where his flocks were. 5He said to them, “I see that your father’s attitude toward me is not what it was before, but the God of my father has been with me. 6You know that I’ve worked for your father with all my strength, 7yet your father has cheated me by changing my wages ten times. However, God has not allowed him to harm me. 8If he said, ‘The speckled ones will be your wages,’ then all the flocks gave birth to speckled young; and if he said, ‘The streaked ones will be your wages,’ then all the flocks bore streaked young. 9So God has taken away your father’s livestock and has given them to me.

10“In breeding season I once had a dream in which I looked up and saw that the male goats mating with the flock were streaked, speckled or spotted. 11The angel of God said to me in the dream, ‘Jacob.’ I answered, ‘Here I am.’ 12And he said, ‘Look up and see that all the male goats mating with the flock are streaked, speckled or spotted, for I have seen all that Laban has been doing to you. 13I am the God of Bethel, where you anointed a pillar and where you made a vow to me. Now leave this land at once and go back to your native land.’ ”

14Then Rachel and Leah replied, “Do we still have any share in the inheritance of our father’s estate? 15Does he not regard us as foreigners? Not only has he sold us, but he has used up what was paid for us. 16Surely all the wealth that God took away from our father belongs to us and our children. So do whatever God has told you.”

17Then Jacob put his children and his wives on camels, 18and he drove all his livestock ahead of him, along with all the goods he had accumulated in Paddan Aram,[r] to go to his father Isaac in the land of Canaan.

19When Laban had gone to shear his sheep, Rachel stole her father’s household gods. 20Moreover, Jacob deceived Laban the Aramean by not telling him he was running away. 21So he fled with all he had, and crossing the River,[s] he headed for the hill country of Gilead.

22On the third day Laban was told that Jacob had fled. 23Taking his relatives with him, he pursued Jacob for seven days and caught up with him

[r] *18* That is, Northwest Mesopotamia [s] *21* That is, the Euphrates

in the hill country of Gilead. 24Then God came to Laban the Aramean in a dream at night and said to him, "Be careful not to say anything to Jacob, either good or bad."

25Jacob had pitched his tent in the hill country of Gilead when Laban overtook him, and Laban and his relatives camped there too. 26Then Laban said to Jacob, "What have you done? You've deceived me, and you've carried off my daughters like captives in war. 27Why did you run off secretly and deceive me? Why didn't you tell me, so I could send you away with joy and singing to the music of tambourines and harps? 28You didn't even let me kiss my grandchildren and my daughters good-by. You have done a foolish thing. 29I have the power to harm you; but last night the God of your father said to me, 'Be careful not to say anything to Jacob, either good or bad.' 30Now you have gone off because you longed to return to your father's house. But why did you steal my gods?"

31Jacob answered Laban, "I was afraid, because I thought you would take your daughters away from me by force. 32But if you find anyone who has your gods, he shall not live. In the presence of our relatives, see for yourself whether there is anything of yours here with me; and if so, take it." Now Jacob did not know that Rachel had stolen the gods.

33So Laban went into Jacob's tent and into Leah's tent and into the tent of the two maidservants, but he found nothing. After he came out of Leah's tent, he entered Rachel's tent. 34Now Rachel had taken the household gods and put them inside her camel's saddle and was sitting on them. Laban searched through everything in the tent but found nothing.

35Rachel said to her father, "Don't be angry, my lord, that I cannot stand up in your presence; I'm having my period." So he searched but could not find the household gods.

36Jacob was angry and took Laban to task. "What is my crime?" he asked Laban. "What sin have I committed that you hunt me down? 37Now that you have searched through all my goods, what have you found that belongs to your household? Put it here in front of your relatives and mine, and let them judge between the two of us.

38"I have been with you for twenty years now. Your sheep and goats have not miscarried, nor have I eaten rams from your flocks. 39I did not bring you animals torn by wild beasts; I bore the loss myself. And you demanded payment from me for whatever was stolen by day or night. 40This was my situation: The heat consumed me in the daytime and the cold at night, and sleep fled from my eyes. 41It was like this for the twenty years I was in your household. I worked for you fourteen years for your two daughters and six years for your flocks, and you changed my wages ten times. 42If the God of my father, the God of Abraham and the Fear of Isaac, had not been with me, you would surely have sent me away empty-handed. But God has seen my hardship and the toil of my hands, and last night he rebuked you."

43Laban answered Jacob, "The women are my daughters, the children are my children, and the flocks are my flocks. All you see is mine. Yet what can I do today about these daughters of mine, or about the children they have borne? 44Come now, let's make a covenant, you and I, and let it serve as a witness between us."

45So Jacob took a stone and set it up as a pillar. 46He said to his relatives, "Gather some stones." So they took stones and piled them in a heap, and they ate there by the heap. 47Laban called it Jegar Sahadutha,[t] and Jacob called it Galeed.[u]

48Laban said, "This heap is a witness between you and me today." That is why it was called Galeed. 49It was also called Mizpah,[v] because he said, "May the LORD keep watch between you and me when we are away from each other. 50If you mistreat my daughters or if you take any wives besides my daughters, even though no one is with us, remember that God is a witness between you and me."

51Laban also said to Jacob, "Here is this heap, and here is this pillar I have set up between you and me. 52This heap is a witness, and this pillar is a witness, that I will not go past this heap to your side to harm you and that you will not go past this heap and pillar to my side to harm me. 53May the God of Abraham and the God of Nahor, the God of their father, judge between us."

So Jacob took an oath in the name of the Fear of his father Isaac. 54He offered a sacrifice there in the hill country and invited his relatives to a meal. After they had eaten, they spent the night there.

55Early the next morning Laban kissed his grandchildren and his daughters and blessed them. Then he left and returned home.

[t]47 The Aramaic *Jegar Sahadutha* means *witness heap.* [u]47 The Hebrew *Galeed* means *witness heap.* [v]49 *Mizpah* means *watchtower.*

Discovering the Word 1. Why does Jacob want to leave, and why does Laban want him to stay (30:25–30)? 2. Describe Jacob's way of getting back at Laban to increase the strength of his own flocks (30:37–43). 3. What new factors in Jacob's situation now prompt his decision to leave Laban's employ and return home (31:1–13)? 4. How has God protected and provided for Jacob in the midst of his unjust treatment by Laban (31:1–21)? 5. How do Laban and Jacob reconcile their differences (31:43–55)?

Applying the Word 1. Why is it often so difficult for us to see the other person's point of view in a controversy? 2. What have we learned in this passage that can help us in dealing with a strained or fractured relationship?

Responding in Prayer Decide now what steps you can take in a personal conflict you face, and pray for courage to follow through.

18 / *Genesis 32—33*
Planning and Praying

THE CHRISTIAN LIFE is a mysterious mixture of God's work and ours, his gracious provision and our effort. Sometimes we are perplexed over who should make the next move. We see this pattern in the life of Jacob, whose planning and praying, laboring and believing are prominent in this narrative. The previous study ended with reconciliation and peaceful departure. Now Jacob resolutely heads toward another confrontation with his adversary of twenty years earlier—his brother Esau, whom he cheated. Jacob combines planning and prayer as he obeys God's command to return to his country and relatives. His struggle can teach us how to redress past wrongs and effect reconciliation with someone we have injured.

Warming Up to God As you sit before your Father, remember that he has also come to be with you. Rest with him and enjoy his presence while he teaches you about himself.

Read Genesis 32—33.

32 Jacob also went on his way, and the
angels of God met him. 2When Ja-
cob saw them, he said, "This is the
camp of God!" So he named that place Maha-
naim.[w]
3Jacob sent messengers ahead of him to his
brother Esau in the land of Seir, the country of
Edom. 4He instructed them: "This is what you are
to say to my master Esau: 'Your servant Jacob
says, I have been staying with Laban and have
remained there till now. 5I have cattle and don-
keys, sheep and goats, menservants and maidser-
vants. Now I am sending this message to my lord,
that I may find favor in your eyes.' "
6When the messengers returned to Jacob, they
said, "We went to your brother Esau, and now he
is coming to meet you, and four hundred men are
with him."
7In great fear and distress Jacob divided the
people who were with him into two groups,[x]
and the flocks and herds and camels as well. 8He
thought, "If Esau comes and attacks one group,[y]
the group[y] that is left may escape."
9Then Jacob prayed, "O God of my father Abra-
ham, God of my father Isaac, O LORD, who said to
me, 'Go back to your country and your relatives,
and I will make you prosper,' 10I am unworthy of
all the kindness and faithfulness you have shown
your servant. I had only my staff when I crossed
this Jordan, but now I have become two groups.
11Save me, I pray, from the hand of my brother
Esau, for I am afraid he will come and attack me,
and also the mothers with their children. 12But
you have said, 'I will surely make you prosper and
will make your descendants like the sand of the
sea, which cannot be counted.' "
13He spent the night there, and from what he
had with him he selected a gift for his brother
Esau: 14two hundred female goats and twenty
male goats, two hundred ewes and twenty rams,
15thirty female camels with their young, forty

[w]2 *Mahanaim* means *two camps.* [x]7 Or *camps;* also in verse 10
[y]8 Or *camp*

cows and ten bulls, and twenty female donkeys and ten male donkeys. 16He put them in the care of his servants, each herd by itself, and said to his servants, "Go ahead of me, and keep some space between the herds."

17He instructed the one in the lead: "When my brother Esau meets you and asks, 'To whom do you belong, and where are you going, and who owns all these animals in front of you?' 18then you are to say, 'They belong to your servant Jacob. They are a gift sent to my lord Esau, and he is coming behind us.' "

19He also instructed the second, the third and all the others who followed the herds: "You are to say the same thing to Esau when you meet him. 20And be sure to say, 'Your servant Jacob is coming behind us.' " For he thought, "I will pacify him with these gifts I am sending on ahead; later, when I see him, perhaps he will receive me." 21So Jacob's gifts went on ahead of him, but he himself spent the night in the camp.

22That night Jacob got up and took his two wives, his two maidservants and his eleven sons and crossed the ford of the Jabbok. 23After he had sent them across the stream, he sent over all his possessions. 24So Jacob was left alone, and a man wrestled with him till daybreak. 25When the man saw that he could not overpower him, he touched the socket of Jacob's hip so that his hip was wrenched as he wrestled with the man. 26Then the man said, "Let me go, for it is daybreak."

But Jacob replied, "I will not let you go unless you bless me."

27The man asked him, "What is your name?"

"Jacob," he answered.

28Then the man said, "Your name will no longer be Jacob, but Israel,[z] because you have struggled with God and with men and have overcome."

29Jacob said, "Please tell me your name."

But he replied, "Why do you ask my name?" Then he blessed him there.

30So Jacob called the place Peniel,[a] saying, "It is because I saw God face to face, and yet my life was spared."

31The sun rose above him as he passed Peniel,[b] and he was limping because of his hip. 32Therefore to this day the Israelites do not eat the tendon attached to the socket of the hip, because the socket of Jacob's hip was touched near the tendon.

33

Jacob looked up and there was Esau, coming with his four hundred men; so he divided the children among Leah, Rachel and the two maidservants. 2He put the maidservants and their children in front, Leah and her children next, and Rachel and Joseph in the rear. 3He himself went on ahead and bowed down to the ground seven times as he approached his brother.

4But Esau ran to meet Jacob and embraced him; he threw his arms around his neck and kissed him. And they wept. 5Then Esau looked up and saw the women and children. "Who are these with you?" he asked.

Jacob answered, "They are the children God has graciously given your servant."

6Then the maidservants and their children approached and bowed down. 7Next, Leah and her children came and bowed down. Last of all came Joseph and Rachel, and they too bowed down.

8Esau asked, "What do you mean by all these droves I met?"

"To find favor in your eyes, my lord," he said.

9But Esau said, "I already have plenty, my brother. Keep what you have for yourself."

10"No, please!" said Jacob. "If I have found favor in your eyes, accept this gift from me. For to see your face is like seeing the face of God, now that you have received me favorably. 11Please accept the present that was brought to you, for God has been gracious to me and I have all I need." And because Jacob insisted, Esau accepted it.

12Then Esau said, "Let us be on our way; I'll accompany you."

13But Jacob said to him, "My lord knows that the children are tender and that I must care for the ewes and cows that are nursing their young. If they are driven hard just one day, all the animals will die. 14So let my lord go on ahead of his servant, while I move along slowly at the pace of the droves before me and that of the children, until I come to my lord in Seir."

15Esau said, "Then let me leave some of my men with you."

"But why do that?" Jacob asked. "Just let me find favor in the eyes of my lord."

16So that day Esau started on his way back to Seir. 17Jacob, however, went to Succoth, where he built a place for himself and made shelters for his

[z]28 *Israel* means *he struggles with God.* [a]30 *Peniel* means *face of God.* [b]31 Hebrew *Penuel,* a variant of *Peniel*

livestock. That is why the place is called Suc-
coth.[c]
[18]After Jacob came from Paddan Aram,[d] he ar-
rived safely at the[e] city of Shechem in Canaan
and camped within sight of the city. [19]For a hun-
dred pieces of silver,[f] he bought from the sons
of Hamor, the father of Shechem, the plot of
ground where he pitched his tent. [20]There he set
up an altar and called it El Elohe Israel.[g]

[c]17 *Succoth* means *shelters*. [d]18 That is, Northwest Mesopotamia [e]18 Or *arrived at Shalem, a* [f]19 Hebrew *hundred kesitahs*; a kesitah was a unit of money of unknown weight and value. [g]20 *El Elohe Israel* can mean *God, the God of Israel* or *mighty is the God of Israel.*

Discovering the Word 1. After Jacob receives the ominous report brought back by the servants (32:6), he alternately plans and prays. How does his prayer in 32:9–12 reflect his relationship with God at this point? 2. To what extent do you think Jacob's plans are consistent or inconsistent with his prayer (32:13–21)? 3. How does the struggle with the unknown man give insight into Jacob's personality (32:22–32)? 4. How does the change of Jacob's name from *he deceives* to *he struggles with God* indicate the development of his character? 5. In what ways does this meeting between Jacob and Esau (chapter 33) contrast with the last time they saw each other (chapter 27)?

Applying the Word 1. In what ways can Jacob's prayer be a model for our own praying? 2. In what areas do you struggle to trust and obey the Lord? 3. In what areas can Jacob's actions toward Esau be a model for us of repentance and reconciliation?

Responding in Prayer Praise the God of the world, your Father, for being a God who changes names. Ask him to "rename" you as one in the image of his Son.

19/ *Genesis 34—36*
The Cost of Discipleship

IN OUR CHRISTIAN life both compromise and commitment are costly. When we falter and compromise, the consequences take their toll on us personally and often on our family and friends. Nevertheless, God graciously calls us to repentance and renewed commitment. In the last chapter Jacob bought a plot of land in Shechem among the Canaanites instead of going on to Bethel as God commanded. Now his compromise with a pagan community results in a multiple tragedy. We see how God again rescues his servant from a dangerous situation and reaffirms his covenant promise.

Warming Up to God What expectations do you place on this time with the Lord? (Do you feel pressure to "accomplish" something?) Allow yourself to just *be* with Jesus today.

Read Genesis 34—36.

34 Now Dinah, the daughter Leah had
borne to Jacob, went out to visit the
women of the land. [2]When She-
chem son of Hamor the Hivite, the ruler of that
area, saw her, he took her and violated her. [3]His
heart was drawn to Dinah daughter of Jacob, and
he loved the girl and spoke tenderly to her. [4]And
Shechem said to his father Hamor, "Get me this
girl as my wife."
[5]When Jacob heard that his daughter Dinah
had been defiled, his sons were in the fields with
his livestock; so he kept quiet about it until they
came home.
[6]Then Shechem's father Hamor went out to talk
with Jacob. [7]Now Jacob's sons had come in from
the fields as soon as they heard what had hap-
pened. They were filled with grief and fury, be-
cause Shechem had done a disgraceful thing in[h]
Israel by lying with Jacob's daughter—a thing
that should not be done.
[8]But Hamor said to them, "My son Shechem
has his heart set on your daughter. Please give her

[h]7 Or *against*

to him as his wife. 9Intermarry with us; give us your daughters and take our daughters for yourselves. 10You can settle among us; the land is open to you. Live in it, trade[i] in it, and acquire property in it."

11Then Shechem said to Dinah's father and brothers, "Let me find favor in your eyes, and I will give you whatever you ask. 12Make the price for the bride and the gift I am to bring as great as you like, and I'll pay whatever you ask me. Only give me the girl as my wife."

13Because their sister Dinah had been defiled, Jacob's sons replied deceitfully as they spoke to Shechem and his father Hamor. 14They said to them, "We can't do such a thing; we can't give our sister to a man who is not circumcised. That would be a disgrace to us. 15We will give our consent to you on one condition only: that you become like us by circumcising all your males. 16Then we will give you our daughters and take your daughters for ourselves. We'll settle among you and become one people with you. 17But if you will not agree to be circumcised, we'll take our sister[j] and go."

18Their proposal seemed good to Hamor and his son Shechem. 19The young man, who was the most honored of all his father's household, lost no time in doing what they said, because he was delighted with Jacob's daughter. 20So Hamor and his son Shechem went to the gate of their city to speak to their fellow townsmen. 21"These men are friendly toward us," they said. "Let them live in our land and trade in it; the land has plenty of room for them. We can marry their daughters and they can marry ours. 22But the men will consent to live with us as one people only on the condition that our males be circumcised, as they themselves are. 23Won't their livestock, their property and all their other animals become ours? So let us give our consent to them, and they will settle among us."

24All the men who went out of the city gate agreed with Hamor and his son Shechem, and every male in the city was circumcised.

25Three days later, while all of them were still in pain, two of Jacob's sons, Simeon and Levi, Dinah's brothers, took their swords and attacked the unsuspecting city, killing every male. 26They put Hamor and his son Shechem to the sword and took Dinah from Shechem's house and left. 27The sons of Jacob came upon the dead bodies and looted the city where[k] their sister had been defiled. 28They seized their flocks and herds and donkeys and everything else of theirs in the city and out in the fields. 29They carried off all their wealth and all their women and children, taking as plunder everything in the houses.

30Then Jacob said to Simeon and Levi, "You have brought trouble on me by making me a stench to the Canaanites and Perizzites, the people living in this land. We are few in number, and if they join forces against me and attack me, I and my household will be destroyed."

31But they replied, "Should he have treated our sister like a prostitute?"

35

Then God said to Jacob, "Go up to Bethel and settle there, and build an altar there to God, who appeared to you when you were fleeing from your brother Esau."

2So Jacob said to his household and to all who were with him, "Get rid of the foreign gods you have with you, and purify yourselves and change your clothes. 3Then come, let us go up to Bethel, where I will build an altar to God, who answered me in the day of my distress and who has been with me wherever I have gone." 4So they gave Jacob all the foreign gods they had and the rings in their ears, and Jacob buried them under the oak at Shechem. 5Then they set out, and the terror of God fell upon the towns all around them so that no one pursued them.

6Jacob and all the people with him came to Luz (that is, Bethel) in the land of Canaan. 7There he built an altar, and he called the place El Bethel,[l] because it was there that God revealed himself to him when he was fleeing from his brother.

8Now Deborah, Rebekah's nurse, died and was buried under the oak below Bethel. So it was named Allon Bacuth.[m]

9After Jacob returned from Paddan Aram,[n] God appeared to him again and blessed him. 10God said to him, "Your name is Jacob,[o] but you will no longer be called Jacob; your name will be Israel.[p]" So he named him Israel.

11And God said to him, "I am God Almighty[q]; be fruitful and increase in number. A nation and a community of nations will come from you, and kings will come from your body. 12The land I

[i] 10 Or *move about freely*; also in verse 21 [j] 17 Hebrew *daughter* [k] 27 Or *because* [l] 7 *El Bethel* means *God of Bethel.* [m] 8 *Allon Bacuth* means *oak of weeping.* [n] 9 That is, Northwest Mesopotamia; also in verse 26 [o] 10 *Jacob* means *he grasps the heel* (figuratively, *he deceives*). [p] 10 *Israel* means *he struggles with God.* [q] 11 Hebrew *El-Shaddai*

gave to Abraham and Isaac I also give to you, and I will give this land to your descendants after you." [13]Then God went up from him at the place where he had talked with him.

[14]Jacob set up a stone pillar at the place where God had talked with him, and he poured out a drink offering on it; he also poured oil on it. [15]Jacob called the place where God had talked with him Bethel.[r]

[16]Then they moved on from Bethel. While they were still some distance from Ephrath, Rachel began to give birth and had great difficulty. [17]And as she was having great difficulty in childbirth, the midwife said to her, "Don't be afraid, for you have another son." [18]As she breathed her last—for she was dying—she named her son Ben-Oni.[s] But his father named him Benjamin.[t]

[19]So Rachel died and was buried on the way to Ephrath (that is, Bethlehem). [20]Over her tomb Jacob set up a pillar, and to this day that pillar marks Rachel's tomb.

[21]Israel moved on again and pitched his tent beyond Migdal Eder. [22]While Israel was living in that region, Reuben went in and slept with his father's concubine Bilhah, and Israel heard of it.

Jacob had twelve sons:

[23]The sons of Leah:
Reuben the firstborn of Jacob,
Simeon, Levi, Judah, Issachar and Zebulun.

[24]The sons of Rachel:
Joseph and Benjamin.

[25]The sons of Rachel's maidservant Bilhah:
Dan and Naphtali.

[26]The sons of Leah's maidservant Zilpah:
Gad and Asher.

These were the sons of Jacob, who were born to him in Paddan Aram.

[27]Jacob came home to his father Isaac in Mamre, near Kiriath Arba (that is, Hebron), where Abraham and Isaac had stayed. [28]Isaac lived a hundred and eighty years. [29]Then he breathed his last and died and was gathered to his people, old and full of years. And his sons Esau and Jacob buried him.

36

This is the account of Esau (that is, Edom).

[2]Esau took his wives from the women of Canaan: Adah daughter of Elon the Hittite, and Oholibamah daughter of Anah and granddaughter of Zibeon the Hivite— [3]also Basemath daughter of Ishmael and sister of Nebaioth.

[4]Adah bore Eliphaz to Esau, Basemath bore Reuel, [5]and Oholibamah bore Jeush, Jalam and Korah. These were the sons of Esau, who were born to him in Canaan.

[6]Esau took his wives and sons and daughters and all the members of his household, as well as his livestock and all his other animals and all the goods he had acquired in Canaan, and moved to a land some distance from his brother Jacob. [7]Their possessions were too great for them to remain together; the land where they were staying could not support them both because of their livestock. [8]So Esau (that is, Edom) settled in the hill country of Seir.

[9]This is the account of Esau the father of the Edomites in the hill country of Seir.

[10]These are the names of Esau's sons:
Eliphaz, the son of Esau's wife Adah, and Reuel, the son of Esau's wife Basemath.

[11]The sons of Eliphaz:
Teman, Omar, Zepho, Gatam and Kenaz.
[12]Esau's son Eliphaz also had a concubine named Timna, who bore him Amalek. These were grandsons of Esau's wife Adah.

[13]The sons of Reuel:
Nahath, Zerah, Shammah and Mizzah. These were grandsons of Esau's wife Basemath.

[14]The sons of Esau's wife Oholibamah daughter of Anah and granddaughter of Zibeon, whom she bore to Esau:
Jeush, Jalam and Korah.

[15]These were the chiefs among Esau's descendants:

The sons of Eliphaz the firstborn of Esau:
Chiefs Teman, Omar, Zepho, Kenaz, [16]Korah,[u] Gatam and Amalek. These were the chiefs descended from Eliphaz in Edom; they were grandsons of Adah.

[17]The sons of Esau's son Reuel:
Chiefs Nahath, Zerah, Shammah and Mizzah. These were the chiefs descended

[r]15 *Bethel* means *house of God.* [s]18 *Ben-Oni* means *son of my trouble.* [t]18 *Benjamin* means *son of my right hand.*
[u]16 Masoretic Text; Samaritan Pentateuch (see also Gen. 36:11 and 1 Chron. 1:36) does not have *Korah.*

from Reuel in Edom; they were grand-
sons of Esau's wife Basemath.
18The sons of Esau's wife Oholibamah:
Chiefs Jeush, Jalam and Korah. These
were the chiefs descended from Esau's
wife Oholibamah daughter of Anah.
19These were the sons of Esau (that is, Edom),
and these were their chiefs.

20These were the sons of Seir the Horite, who
were living in the region:
Lotan, Shobal, Zibeon, Anah, 21Dishon,
Ezer and Dishan. These sons of Seir in
Edom were Horite chiefs.
22The sons of Lotan:
Hori and Homam.[v] Timna was Lotan's
sister.
23The sons of Shobal:
Alvan, Manahath, Ebal, Shepho and
Onam.
24The sons of Zibeon:
Aiah and Anah. This is the Anah who dis-
covered the hot springs[w] in the desert
while he was grazing the donkeys of his
father Zibeon.
25The children of Anah:
Dishon and Oholibamah daughter of
Anah.
26The sons of Dishon[x]:
Hemdan, Eshban, Ithran and Keran.
27The sons of Ezer:
Bilhan, Zaavan and Akan.
28The sons of Dishan:
Uz and Aran.
29These were the Horite chiefs:
Lotan, Shobal, Zibeon, Anah, 30Dishon,
Ezer and Dishan. These were the Horite
chiefs, according to their divisions, in the
land of Seir.

31These were the kings who reigned in Edom
before any Israelite king reigned[y]:
32Bela son of Beor became king of Edom.
His city was named Dinhabah.
33When Bela died, Jobab son of Zerah from
Bozrah succeeded him as king.
34When Jobab died, Husham from the land of
the Temanites succeeded him as king.
35When Husham died, Hadad son of Bedad,
who defeated Midian in the country of
Moab, succeeded him as king. His city
was named Avith.
36When Hadad died, Samlah from Masrekah
succeeded him as king.
37When Samlah died, Shaul from Rehoboth
on the river[z] succeeded him as king.
38When Shaul died, Baal-Hanan son of Acbor
succeeded him as king.
39When Baal-Hanan son of Acbor died, Ha-
dad[a] succeeded him as king. His city
was named Pau, and his wife's name was
Mehetabel daughter of Matred, the
daughter of Me-Zahab.

40These were the chiefs descended from Esau,
by name, according to their clans and regions:
Timna, Alvah, Jetheth, 41Oholibamah,
Elah, Pinon, 42Kenaz, Teman, Mibzar,
43Magdiel and Iram. These were the
chiefs of Edom, according to their settle-
ments in the land they occupied.

This was Esau the father of the Edomites.

[v] 22 Hebrew *Hemam,* a variant of *Homam* (see 1 Chron. 1:39) [w] 24 Vulgate; Syriac *discovered water;* the meaning of the Hebrew for this word is uncertain. [x] 26 Hebrew *Dishan,* a variant of *Dishon* [y] 31 Or *before an Israelite king reigned over them* [z] 37 Possibly the Euphrates [a] 39 Many manuscripts of the Masoretic Text, Samaritan Pentateuch and Syriac (see also 1 Chron. 1:50); most manuscripts of the Masoretic Text *Hadar*

Discovering the Word 1. What is Shechem's attitude toward Dinah (34:1–4)? 2. In Genesis 35:1 God renews his call for Jacob to settle in Bethel. What is the cost of this commitment for Jacob and the members of his household (35:2–7)? 3. What specific promises does God reaffirm to Jacob and to his descendants (35:9–13)? 4. What new griefs come into Jacob's life (35:16–29)? 5. What do the comments in 35:29 and 36:6–8 show about the relationship between Jacob and Esau?

Applying the Word 1. In what way does this tragedy illustrate the dangers of spiritual compromise or disobedience? 2. Have you become aware of any "foreign god" in your life, something which is taking the place of God? Explain. 3. How can we, like Jacob, transform the pain of losing someone we love into confidence and courage for the future?

Responding in Prayer Praise God for the remarkable example of his faithfulness to his chosen children through the life of Jacob.

20/ *Genesis 37—38*
Pride and Prejudice

WE OFTEN SEE how children tend to duplicate the weaknesses as well as the strengths of their parents. This is evident in many families of the Old Testament. Jacob suffered from parental favoritism as a boy. Now we see how he perpetuates this practice in his relationship with Joseph—with disastrous results.

Warming Up to God How have you seen the harmful effects of "playing favorites" in your family?

Read Genesis 37—38.

37 Jacob lived in the land where his father had stayed, the land of Canaan.

2This is the account of Jacob.

Joseph, a young man of seventeen, was tending the flocks with his brothers, the sons of Bilhah and the sons of Zilpah, his father's wives, and he brought their father a bad report about them.

3Now Israel loved Joseph more than any of his other sons, because he had been born to him in his old age; and he made a richly ornamented[b] robe for him. 4When his brothers saw that their father loved him more than any of them, they hated him and could not speak a kind word to him.

5Joseph had a dream, and when he told it to his brothers, they hated him all the more. 6He said to them, "Listen to this dream I had: 7We were binding sheaves of grain out in the field when suddenly my sheaf rose and stood upright, while your sheaves gathered around mine and bowed down to it."

8His brothers said to him, "Do you intend to reign over us? Will you actually rule us?" And they hated him all the more because of his dream and what he had said.

9Then he had another dream, and he told it to his brothers. "Listen," he said, "I had another dream, and this time the sun and moon and eleven stars were bowing down to me."

10When he told his father as well as his brothers, his father rebuked him and said, "What is this dream you had? Will your mother and I and your brothers actually come and bow down to the ground before you?" 11His brothers were jealous of him, but his father kept the matter in mind.

12Now his brothers had gone to graze their father's flocks near Shechem, 13and Israel said to Joseph, "As you know, your brothers are grazing the flocks near Shechem. Come, I am going to send you to them."

"Very well," he replied.

14So he said to him, "Go and see if all is well with your brothers and with the flocks, and bring word back to me." Then he sent him off from the Valley of Hebron.

When Joseph arrived at Shechem, 15a man found him wandering around in the fields and asked him, "What are you looking for?"

16He replied, "I'm looking for my brothers. Can you tell me where they are grazing their flocks?"

17"They have moved on from here," the man answered. "I heard them say, 'Let's go to Dothan.'"

So Joseph went after his brothers and found them near Dothan. 18But they saw him in the distance, and before he reached them, they plotted to kill him.

19"Here comes that dreamer!" they said to each other. 20"Come now, let's kill him and throw him into one of these cisterns and say that a ferocious animal devoured him. Then we'll see what comes of his dreams."

21When Reuben heard this, he tried to rescue him from their hands. "Let's not take his life," he said. 22"Don't shed any blood. Throw him into this cistern here in the desert, but don't lay a hand on him." Reuben said this to rescue him from them and take him back to his father.

23So when Joseph came to his brothers, they stripped him of his robe—the richly ornamented robe he was wearing— 24and they took him and threw him into the cistern. Now the cistern was empty; there was no water in it.

25As they sat down to eat their meal, they

b3 The meaning of the Hebrew for *richly ornamented* is uncertain; also in verses 23 and 32.

looked up and saw a caravan of Ishmaelites coming from Gilead. Their camels were loaded with spices, balm and myrrh, and they were on their way to take them down to Egypt.

[26]Judah said to his brothers, "What will we gain if we kill our brother and cover up his blood? [27]Come, let's sell him to the Ishmaelites and not lay our hands on him; after all, he is our brother, our own flesh and blood." His brothers agreed.

[28]So when the Midianite merchants came by, his brothers pulled Joseph up out of the cistern and sold him for twenty shekels[c] of silver to the Ishmaelites, who took him to Egypt.

[29]When Reuben returned to the cistern and saw that Joseph was not there, he tore his clothes. [30]He went back to his brothers and said, "The boy isn't there! Where can I turn now?"

[31]Then they got Joseph's robe, slaughtered a goat and dipped the robe in the blood. [32]They took the ornamented robe back to their father and said, "We found this. Examine it to see whether it is your son's robe."

[33]He recognized it and said, "It is my son's robe! Some ferocious animal has devoured him. Joseph has surely been torn to pieces."

[34]Then Jacob tore his clothes, put on sackcloth and mourned for his son many days. [35]All his sons and daughters came to comfort him, but he refused to be comforted. "No," he said, "in mourning will I go down to the grave[d] to my son." So his father wept for him.

[36]Meanwhile, the Midianites[e] sold Joseph in Egypt to Potiphar, one of Pharaoh's officials, the captain of the guard.

38

At that time, Judah left his brothers and went down to stay with a man of Adullam named Hirah. [2]There Judah met the daughter of a Canaanite man named Shua. He married her and lay with her; [3]she became pregnant and gave birth to a son, who was named Er. [4]She conceived again and gave birth to a son and named him Onan. [5]She gave birth to still another son and named him Shelah. It was at Kezib that she gave birth to him.

[6]Judah got a wife for Er, his firstborn, and her name was Tamar. [7]But Er, Judah's firstborn, was wicked in the LORD's sight; so the LORD put him to death.

[8]Then Judah said to Onan, "Lie with your brother's wife and fulfill your duty to her as a brother-in-law to produce offspring for your brother." [9]But Onan knew that the offspring would not be his; so whenever he lay with his brother's wife, he spilled his semen on the ground to keep from producing offspring for his brother. [10]What he did was wicked in the LORD's sight; so he put him to death also.

[11]Judah then said to his daughter-in-law Tamar, "Live as a widow in your father's house until my son Shelah grows up." For he thought, "He may die too, just like his brothers." So Tamar went to live in her father's house.

[12]After a long time Judah's wife, the daughter of Shua, died. When Judah had recovered from his grief, he went up to Timnah, to the men who were shearing his sheep, and his friend Hirah the Adullamite went with him.

[13]When Tamar was told, "Your father-in-law is on his way to Timnah to shear his sheep," [14]she took off her widow's clothes, covered herself with a veil to disguise herself, and then sat down at the entrance to Enaim, which is on the road to Timnah. For she saw that, though Shelah had now grown up, she had not been given to him as his wife.

[15]When Judah saw her, he thought she was a prostitute, for she had covered her face. [16]Not realizing that she was his daughter-in-law, he went over to her by the roadside and said, "Come now, let me sleep with you."

"And what will you give me to sleep with you?" she asked.

[17]"I'll send you a young goat from my flock," he said.

"Will you give me something as a pledge until you send it?" she asked.

[18]He said, "What pledge should I give you?"

"Your seal and its cord, and the staff in your hand," she answered. So he gave them to her and slept with her, and she became pregnant by him. [19]After she left, she took off her veil and put on her widow's clothes again.

[20]Meanwhile Judah sent the young goat by his friend the Adullamite in order to get his pledge back from the woman, but he did not find her. [21]He asked the men who lived there, "Where is the shrine prostitute who was beside the road at Enaim?"

"There hasn't been any shrine prostitute here," they said.

[c]28 That is, about 8 ounces (about 0.2 kilogram) [d]35 Hebrew *Sheol*
[e]36 Samaritan Pentateuch, Septuagint, Vulgate and Syriac (see also verse 28); Masoretic Text *Medanites*

[22]So he went back to Judah and said, "I didn't find her. Besides, the men who lived there said, 'There hasn't been any shrine prostitute here.' "

[23]Then Judah said, "Let her keep what she has, or we will become a laughingstock. After all, I did send her this young goat, but you didn't find her."

[24]About three months later Judah was told, "Your daughter-in-law Tamar is guilty of prostitution, and as a result she is now pregnant."

Judah said, "Bring her out and have her burned to death!"

[25]As she was being brought out, she sent a message to her father-in-law. "I am pregnant by the man who owns these," she said. And she added, "See if you recognize whose seal and cord and staff these are."

[26]Judah recognized them and said, "She is more righteous than I, since I wouldn't give her to my son Shelah." And he did not sleep with her again.

[27]When the time came for her to give birth, there were twin boys in her womb. [28]As she was giving birth, one of them put out his hand; so the midwife took a scarlet thread and tied it on his wrist and said, "This one came out first." [29]But when he drew back his hand, his brother came out, and she said, "So this is how you have broken out!" And he was named Perez.[f] [30]Then his brother, who had the scarlet thread on his wrist, came out and he was given the name Zerah.[g]

[f]29 Perez means *breaking out.* [g]30 Zerah can mean *scarlet* or *brightness.*

Discovering the Word 1. Describe the family relationships at the outset of the story (37:1–4). 2. We have already seen in the examples of Abimelech, Jacob and Laban that dreams are a medium through which God reveals his will. This time, however, the communication is not through words. How are the symbols in Joseph's two dreams interpreted by his family (37:5–11)? 3. What are the varied reactions of Joseph's brothers when they see him approaching (37:12–22)? 4. What motive do you see in the way the brothers report to their father the news of Joseph's disappearance (37:29–35)? 5. In spite of having three sons, how does Judah find his lineage to be in jeopardy (38:1–11)? 6. What strategy does Tamar work out to establish her status as matriarch of Judah's line (38:12–30)?

Applying the Word 1. Jacob's favoritism, Joseph's arrogance and the brothers' envy contribute to this tragedy of rivalry and hatred. To what extent are you involved in a family situation, either your own or that of a friend, with some of these elements? 2. Perez (38:29) is listed in the genealogies of David (Ru 4:18–22) and Joseph, the husband of Mary (Mt 1:3). How can this fact help us to appreciate God's grace?

Responding in Prayer Ask God to give you endurance when painful circumstances make his will seem unsure.

21 / *Genesis 39—40*
Performance Under Pressure

HOW DO YOU react when you are treated unjustly? How do you feel when you do everything you can to serve God well, only to have the bottom drop out of your life? Joseph faced these difficulties after he became a slave in Egypt. His example of perseverance under pressure and the way he coped with a shattering reversal can be instructive to us in similar situations.

Warming Up to God Like Joseph, we sometimes face hardships we don't understand. Tell God about your worries, and ask him to remind you of his faithfulness to you, his child.

Read Genesis 39—40.

39 Now Joseph had been taken down
to Egypt. Potiphar, an Egyptian
who was one of Pharaoh's officials,
the captain of the guard, bought him from the
Ishmaelites who had taken him there.
2The LORD was with Joseph and he prospered,
and he lived in the house of his Egyptian master.
3When his master saw that the LORD was with him
and that the LORD gave him success in everything
he did, 4Joseph found favor in his eyes and be-
came his attendant. Potiphar put him in charge of
his household, and he entrusted to his care every-
thing he owned. 5From the time he put him in
charge of his household and of all that he owned,
the LORD blessed the household of the Egyptian
because of Joseph. The blessing of the LORD was
on everything Potiphar had, both in the house
and in the field. 6So he left in Joseph's care every-
thing he had; with Joseph in charge, he did not
concern himself with anything except the food he
ate.
Now Joseph was well-built and handsome,
7and after a while his master's wife took notice of
Joseph and said, "Come to bed with me!"
8But he refused. "With me in charge," he told
her, "my master does not concern himself with
anything in the house; everything he owns he has
entrusted to my care. 9No one is greater in this
house than I am. My master has withheld nothing
from me except you, because you are his wife.
How then could I do such a wicked thing and sin
against God?" 10And though she spoke to Joseph
day after day, he refused to go to bed with her or
even be with her.
11One day he went into the house to attend to
his duties, and none of the household servants
was inside. 12She caught him by his cloak and
said, "Come to bed with me!" But he left his cloak
in her hand and ran out of the house.
13When she saw that he had left his cloak in
her hand and had run out of the house, 14she
called her household servants. "Look," she said to
them, "this Hebrew has been brought to us to
make sport of us! He came in here to sleep with
me, but I screamed. 15When he heard me scream
for help, he left his cloak beside me and ran out
of the house."
16She kept his cloak beside her until his master
came home. 17Then she told him this story: "That
Hebrew slave you brought us came to me to make
sport of me. 18But as soon as I screamed for help,
he left his cloak beside me and ran out of the
house."
19When his master heard the story his wife told
him, saying, "This is how your slave treated me,"
he burned with anger. 20Joseph's master took him
and put him in prison, the place where the king's
prisoners were confined.
But while Joseph was there in the prison, 21the
LORD was with him; he showed him kindness and
granted him favor in the eyes of the prison war-
den. 22So the warden put Joseph in charge of all
those held in the prison, and he was made re-
sponsible for all that was done there. 23The war-
den paid no attention to anything under Joseph's
care, because the LORD was with Joseph and gave
him success in whatever he did.

40 Some time later, the cupbearer and
the baker of the king of Egypt of-
fended their master, the king of
Egypt. 2Pharaoh was angry with his two officials,
the chief cupbearer and the chief baker, 3and put
them in custody in the house of the captain of the
guard, in the same prison where Joseph was con-
fined. 4The captain of the guard assigned them to
Joseph, and he attended them.
After they had been in custody for some time,
5each of the two men—the cupbearer and the
baker of the king of Egypt, who were being held
in prison—had a dream the same night, and each
dream had a meaning of its own.
6When Joseph came to them the next morning,
he saw that they were dejected. 7So he asked
Pharaoh's officials who were in custody with him
in his master's house, "Why are your faces so sad
today?"
8"We both had dreams," they answered, "but
there is no one to interpret them."
Then Joseph said to them, "Do not interpreta-
tions belong to God? Tell me your dreams."
9So the chief cupbearer told Joseph his dream.
He said to him, "In my dream I saw a vine in front
of me, 10and on the vine were three branches. As
soon as it budded, it blossomed, and its clusters
ripened into grapes. 11Pharaoh's cup was in my
hand, and I took the grapes, squeezed them into
Pharaoh's cup and put the cup in his hand."
12"This is what it means," Joseph said to him.
"The three branches are three days. 13Within
three days Pharaoh will lift up your head and
restore you to your position, and you will put
Pharaoh's cup in his hand, just as you used to do
when you were his cupbearer. 14But when all goes

well with you, remember me and show me kindness; mention me to Pharaoh and get me out of this prison. 15For I was forcibly carried off from the land of the Hebrews, and even here I have done nothing to deserve being put in a dungeon."

16When the chief baker saw that Joseph had given a favorable interpretation, he said to Joseph, "I too had a dream: On my head were three baskets of bread.[h] 17In the top basket were all kinds of baked goods for Pharaoh, but the birds were eating them out of the basket on my head."

18"This is what it means," Joseph said. "The three baskets are three days. 19Within three days Pharaoh will lift off your head and hang you on a tree.[i] And the birds will eat away your flesh."

20Now the third day was Pharaoh's birthday, and he gave a feast for all his officials. He lifted up the heads of the chief cupbearer and the chief baker in the presence of his officials: 21He restored the chief cupbearer to his position, so that he once again put the cup into Pharaoh's hand, 22but he hanged[j] the chief baker, just as Joseph had said to them in his interpretation.

23The chief cupbearer, however, did not remember Joseph; he forgot him.

[h]16 Or *three wicker baskets* [i]19 Or *and impale you on a pole* [j]22 Or *impaled*

Discovering the Word 1. Trace the development of Joseph's ability and responsibility from the time he enters Potiphar's house (39:1-6). 2. Describe the temptation and increasing pressure Joseph now experiences (39:6-12). 3. Notice the symmetry between verses 1-6 and 20-23 in chapter 39. From the latter description of Joseph's activities, what can we surmise about his attitude toward his new, more humiliating situation? 4. Describe the new situation in which Joseph finds himself (40:1-8). 5. In 40:9-19 what similarities and differences do you find in the cupbearer's and baker's dreams and Joseph's interpretations? 6. What are the consequences for the three men (40:20-23)?

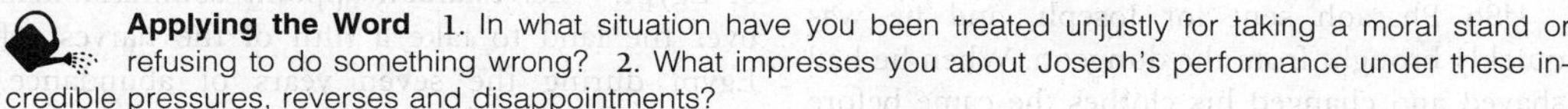

Applying the Word 1. In what situation have you been treated unjustly for taking a moral stand or refusing to do something wrong? 2. What impresses you about Joseph's performance under these incredible pressures, reverses and disappointments?

Responding in Prayer Ask your heavenly Father, your shield and protector, to give you moral courage and stamina during these difficult days.

22 / *Genesis 41—42*
Faithful Service Rewarded

WE OFTEN TAKE a short-term view of the Christian life that concentrates on what God does *for* us *now*. Yet God has longer-range purposes that focus on what he wants to accomplish *in* us for the *future*. This principle has been at work in Joseph's life. Through adversity and disappointment God developed his character and gave him invaluable training. Now a sudden crisis and opportunity reveal what kind of person he has become—an example that can encourage us in our life and service for God.

Warming Up to God What are some tangible ways that God has blessed you recently? Thank him for each gift. Rejoice that every day is full of his blessings.

Read Genesis 41—42.

41 When two full years had passed, Pharaoh had a dream: He was standing by the Nile, 2when out of the river there came up seven cows, sleek and fat, and they grazed among the reeds. 3After them, seven other cows, ugly and gaunt, came up out of the Nile and stood beside those on the riverbank. 4And the cows that were ugly and gaunt ate up the seven sleek, fat cows. Then Pharaoh woke up.

5He fell asleep again and had a second dream: Seven heads of grain, healthy and good, were growing on a single stalk. 6After them, seven other heads of grain sprouted—thin and scorched by the east wind. 7The thin heads of grain swallowed up the seven healthy, full heads. Then Pharaoh woke up; it had been a dream.

8In the morning his mind was troubled, so he sent for all the magicians and wise men of Egypt. Pharaoh told them his dreams, but no one could interpret them for him.

9Then the chief cupbearer said to Pharaoh, "Today I am reminded of my shortcomings. 10Pharaoh was once angry with his servants, and he imprisoned me and the chief baker in the house of the captain of the guard. 11Each of us had a dream the same night, and each dream had a meaning of its own. 12Now a young Hebrew was there with us, a servant of the captain of the guard. We told him our dreams, and he interpreted them for us, giving each man the interpretation of his dream. 13And things turned out exactly as he interpreted them to us: I was restored to my position, and the other man was hanged.[k]"

14So Pharaoh sent for Joseph, and he was quickly brought from the dungeon. When he had shaved and changed his clothes, he came before Pharaoh.

15Pharaoh said to Joseph, "I had a dream, and no one can interpret it. But I have heard it said of you that when you hear a dream you can interpret it."

16"I cannot do it," Joseph replied to Pharaoh, "but God will give Pharaoh the answer he desires."

17Then Pharaoh said to Joseph, "In my dream I was standing on the bank of the Nile, 18when out of the river there came up seven cows, fat and sleek, and they grazed among the reeds. 19After them, seven other cows came up—scrawny and very ugly and lean. I had never seen such ugly cows in all the land of Egypt. 20The lean, ugly cows ate up the seven fat cows that came up first. 21But even after they ate them, no one could tell that they had done so; they looked just as ugly as before. Then I woke up.

22"In my dreams I also saw seven heads of grain, full and good, growing on a single stalk. 23After them, seven other heads sprouted—withered and thin and scorched by the east wind. 24The thin heads of grain swallowed up the seven good heads. I told this to the magicians, but none could explain it to me."

25Then Joseph said to Pharaoh, "The dreams of Pharaoh are one and the same. God has revealed to Pharaoh what he is about to do. 26The seven good cows are seven years, and the seven good heads of grain are seven years; it is one and the same dream. 27The seven lean, ugly cows that came up afterward are seven years, and so are the seven worthless heads of grain scorched by the east wind: They are seven years of famine.

28"It is just as I said to Pharaoh: God has shown Pharaoh what he is about to do. 29Seven years of great abundance are coming throughout the land of Egypt, 30but seven years of famine will follow them. Then all the abundance in Egypt will be forgotten, and the famine will ravage the land. 31The abundance in the land will not be remembered, because the famine that follows it will be so severe. 32The reason the dream was given to Pharaoh in two forms is that the matter has been firmly decided by God, and God will do it soon.

33"And now let Pharaoh look for a discerning and wise man and put him in charge of the land of Egypt. 34Let Pharaoh appoint commissioners over the land to take a fifth of the harvest of Egypt during the seven years of abundance. 35They should collect all the food of these good years that are coming and store up the grain under the authority of Pharaoh, to be kept in the cities for food. 36This food should be held in reserve for the country, to be used during the seven years of famine that will come upon Egypt, so that the country may not be ruined by the famine."

37The plan seemed good to Pharaoh and to all his officials. 38So Pharaoh asked them, "Can we find anyone like this man, one in whom is the spirit of God[l]?"

39Then Pharaoh said to Joseph, "Since God has made all this known to you, there is no one so discerning and wise as you. 40You shall be in charge of my palace, and all my people are to submit to your orders. Only with respect to the throne will I be greater than you."

41So Pharaoh said to Joseph, "I hereby put you in charge of the whole land of Egypt." 42Then Pharaoh took his signet ring from his finger and put it on Joseph's finger. He dressed him in robes of fine linen and put a gold chain around his neck. 43He had him ride in a chariot as his second-in-command,[m] and men shouted before

[k]13 Or *impaled* [l]38 Or *of the gods* [m]43 Or *in the chariot of his second-in-command*; or *in his second chariot*

him, "Make way[n]!" Thus he put him in charge of the whole land of Egypt.

44Then Pharaoh said to Joseph, "I am Pharaoh, but without your word no one will lift hand or foot in all Egypt." 45Pharaoh gave Joseph the name Zaphenath-Paneah and gave him Asenath daughter of Potiphera, priest of On,[o] to be his wife. And Joseph went throughout the land of Egypt.

46Joseph was thirty years old when he entered the service of Pharaoh king of Egypt. And Joseph went out from Pharaoh's presence and traveled throughout Egypt. 47During the seven years of abundance the land produced plentifully. 48Joseph collected all the food produced in those seven years of abundance in Egypt and stored it in the cities. In each city he put the food grown in the fields surrounding it. 49Joseph stored up huge quantities of grain, like the sand of the sea; it was so much that he stopped keeping records because it was beyond measure.

50Before the years of famine came, two sons were born to Joseph by Asenath daughter of Potiphera, priest of On. 51Joseph named his firstborn Manasseh[p] and said, "It is because God has made me forget all my trouble and all my father's household." 52The second son he named Ephraim[q] and said, "It is because God has made me fruitful in the land of my suffering."

53The seven years of abundance in Egypt came to an end, 54and the seven years of famine began, just as Joseph had said. There was famine in all the other lands, but in the whole land of Egypt there was food. 55When all Egypt began to feel the famine, the people cried to Pharaoh for food. Then Pharaoh told all the Egyptians, "Go to Joseph and do what he tells you."

56When the famine had spread over the whole country, Joseph opened the storehouses and sold grain to the Egyptians, for the famine was severe throughout Egypt. 57And all the countries came to Egypt to buy grain from Joseph, because the famine was severe in all the world.

42

When Jacob learned that there was grain in Egypt, he said to his sons, "Why do you just keep looking at each other?" 2He continued, "I have heard that there is grain in Egypt. Go down there and buy some for us, so that we may live and not die."

3Then ten of Joseph's brothers went down to buy grain from Egypt. 4But Jacob did not send Benjamin, Joseph's brother, with the others, because he was afraid that harm might come to him. 5So Israel's sons were among those who went to buy grain, for the famine was in the land of Canaan also.

6Now Joseph was the governor of the land, the one who sold grain to all its people. So when Joseph's brothers arrived, they bowed down to him with their faces to the ground. 7As soon as Joseph saw his brothers, he recognized them, but he pretended to be a stranger and spoke harshly to them. "Where do you come from?" he asked.

"From the land of Canaan," they replied, "to buy food."

8Although Joseph recognized his brothers, they did not recognize him. 9Then he remembered his dreams about them and said to them, "You are spies! You have come to see where our land is unprotected."

10"No, my lord," they answered. "Your servants have come to buy food. 11We are all the sons of one man. Your servants are honest men, not spies."

12"No!" he said to them. "You have come to see where our land is unprotected."

13But they replied, "Your servants were twelve brothers, the sons of one man, who lives in the land of Canaan. The youngest is now with our father, and one is no more."

14Joseph said to them, "It is just as I told you: You are spies! 15And this is how you will be tested: As surely as Pharaoh lives, you will not leave this place unless your youngest brother comes here. 16Send one of your number to get your brother; the rest of you will be kept in prison, so that your words may be tested to see if you are telling the truth. If you are not, then as surely as Pharaoh lives, you are spies!" 17And he put them all in custody for three days.

18On the third day, Joseph said to them, "Do this and you will live, for I fear God: 19If you are honest men, let one of your brothers stay here in prison, while the rest of you go and take grain back for your starving households. 20But you must bring your youngest brother to me, so that your words may be verified and that you may not die." This they proceeded to do.

21They said to one another, "Surely we are being punished because of our brother. We saw how distressed he was when he pleaded with us

[n]43 Or *Bow down* [o]45 That is, Heliopolis; also in verse 50
[p]51 *Manasseh* sounds like and may be derived from the Hebrew for *forget.* [q]52 *Ephraim* sounds like the Hebrew for *twice fruitful.*

for his life, but we would not listen; that's why this distress has come upon us."

22 Reuben replied, "Didn't I tell you not to sin against the boy? But you wouldn't listen! Now we must give an accounting for his blood." 23 They did not realize that Joseph could understand them, since he was using an interpreter.

24 He turned away from them and began to weep, but then turned back and spoke to them again. He had Simeon taken from them and bound before their eyes.

25 Joseph gave orders to fill their bags with grain, to put each man's silver back in his sack, and to give them provisions for their journey. After this was done for them, 26 they loaded their grain on their donkeys and left.

27 At the place where they stopped for the night one of them opened his sack to get feed for his donkey, and he saw his silver in the mouth of his sack. 28 "My silver has been returned," he said to his brothers. "Here it is in my sack."

Their hearts sank and they turned to each other trembling and said, "What is this that God has done to us?"

29 When they came to their father Jacob in the land of Canaan, they told him all that had happened to them. They said, 30 "The man who is lord over the land spoke harshly to us and treated us as though we were spying on the land. 31 But we said to him, 'We are honest men; we are not spies. 32 We were twelve brothers, sons of one father. One is no more, and the youngest is now with our father in Canaan.'

33 "Then the man who is lord over the land said to us, 'This is how I will know whether you are honest men: Leave one of your brothers here with me, and take food for your starving households and go. 34 But bring your youngest brother to me so I will know that you are not spies but honest men. Then I will give your brother back to you, and you can trade[r] in the land.' "

35 As they were emptying their sacks, there in each man's sack was his pouch of silver! When they and their father saw the money pouches, they were frightened. 36 Their father Jacob said to them, "You have deprived me of my children. Joseph is no more and Simeon is no more, and now you want to take Benjamin. Everything is against me!"

37 Then Reuben said to his father, "You may put both of my sons to death if I do not bring him back to you. Entrust him to my care, and I will bring him back."

38 But Jacob said, "My son will not go down there with you; his brother is dead and he is the only one left. If harm comes to him on the journey you are taking, you will bring my gray head down to the grave[s] in sorrow."

[r] 34 Or *move about freely* [s] 38 Hebrew *Sheol*

Discovering the Word 1. How does Joseph's sudden opportunity come about (41:8–14)? 2. How do Joseph's interpretation and proposal demonstrate discernment and wisdom (41:15–36)? 3. Describe Joseph's new position and the responsibilities Pharaoh gives him (41:37–49). 4. Joseph's brothers sold him into slavery twenty years before this event. He is now about thirty-seven (see 37:2; 41:46). Trace the events which lead Joseph's brothers into his presence and fulfill his earlier dreams (42:1–9). 5. Do you think the brothers are genuinely repentant at this point (42:21–22)? Explain. 6. How does Reuben's response to his father's despair show his willingness to shoulder family responsibility (42:35–37)?

Applying the Word 1. How have you seen God use a difficult assignment to prepare you for a later responsibility? 2. How has adversity or pressure helped you become more mature in your responsibility for others?

Responding in Prayer Ask God to help you strive for excellence in all that you do to the glory of his name (1Co 10:31).

23 / *Genesis 43:1—45:15*
Family Reconciliation

WHAT MAKES RECONCILIATION possible? What elements are necessary on each side of a hurt or wrong to heal a damaged relationship? This study provides answers to these crucial questions. Joseph's brothers have now returned home from Egypt with a report of their traumatic experience. As the grain purchased on the first visit to Egypt runs out, Jacob and his sons face increasingly difficult decisions. Although our experience may be less traumatic, we can learn principles of reconciliation from this complex family situation.

Warming Up to God Why does it seem so hard to freely accept God's forgiveness? Today, let yourself rest with confidence in the truth that God's forgiveness covers over every one of your sins. Jesus forgives you now.

Read Genesis 43:1—45:15.

---

43 Now the famine was still severe in
the land. 2So when they had eaten
all the grain they had brought from
Egypt, their father said to them, "Go back and
buy us a little more food."

3But Judah said to him, "The man warned us
solemnly, 'You will not see my face again unless
your brother is with you.' 4If you will send our
brother along with us, we will go down and buy
food for you. 5But if you will not send him, we
will not go down, because the man said to us,
'You will not see my face again unless your
brother is with you.' "

6Israel asked, "Why did you bring this trouble
on me by telling the man you had another
brother?"

7They replied, "The man questioned us closely
about ourselves and our family. 'Is your father
still living?' he asked us. 'Do you have another
brother?' We simply answered his questions. How
were we to know he would say, 'Bring your
brother down here'?"

8Then Judah said to Israel his father, "Send the
boy along with me and we will go at once, so that
we and you and our children may live and not
die. 9I myself will guarantee his safety; you can
hold me personally responsible for him. If I do
not bring him back to you and set him here be-
fore you, I will bear the blame before you all my
life. 10As it is, if we had not delayed, we could
have gone and returned twice."

11Then their father Israel said to them, "If it
must be, then do this: Put some of the best prod-
ucts of the land in your bags and take them down
to the man as a gift—a little balm and a little
honey, some spices and myrrh, some pistachio
nuts and almonds. 12Take double the amount of
silver with you, for you must return the silver
that was put back into the mouths of your sacks.
Perhaps it was a mistake. 13Take your brother
also and go back to the man at once. 14And may
God Almighty[t] grant you mercy before the man
so that he will let your other brother and Benja-
min come back with you. As for me, if I am be-
reaved, I am bereaved."

15So the men took the gifts and double the
amount of silver, and Benjamin also. They hur-
ried down to Egypt and presented themselves to
Joseph. 16When Joseph saw Benjamin with them,
he said to the steward of his house, "Take these
men to my house, slaughter an animal and pre-
pare dinner; they are to eat with me at noon."

17The man did as Joseph told him and took
the men to Joseph's house. 18Now the men were
frightened when they were taken to his house.
They thought, "We were brought here because of
the silver that was put back into our sacks the
first time. He wants to attack us and overpower
us and seize us as slaves and take our donkeys."

19So they went up to Joseph's steward and
spoke to him at the entrance to the house.
20"Please, sir," they said, "we came down here the
first time to buy food. 21But at the place where we
stopped for the night we opened our sacks and
each of us found his silver—the exact weight—in
the mouth of his sack. So we have brought it back
with us. 22We have also brought additional silver
with us to buy food. We don't know who put our
silver in our sacks."

23"It's all right," he said. "Don't be afraid. Your
God, the God of your father, has given you trea-

[t]14 Hebrew *El-Shaddai*

sure in your sacks; I received your silver." Then he brought Simeon out to them.

24The steward took the men into Joseph's house, gave them water to wash their feet and provided fodder for their donkeys. 25They prepared their gifts for Joseph's arrival at noon, because they had heard that they were to eat there.

26When Joseph came home, they presented to him the gifts they had brought into the house, and they bowed down before him to the ground. 27He asked them how they were, and then he said, "How is your aged father you told me about? Is he still living?"

28They replied, "Your servant our father is still alive and well." And they bowed low to pay him honor.

29As he looked about and saw his brother Benjamin, his own mother's son, he asked, "Is this your youngest brother, the one you told me about?" And he said, "God be gracious to you, my son." 30Deeply moved at the sight of his brother, Joseph hurried out and looked for a place to weep. He went into his private room and wept there.

31After he had washed his face, he came out and, controlling himself, said, "Serve the food."

32They served him by himself, the brothers by themselves, and the Egyptians who ate with him by themselves, because Egyptians could not eat with Hebrews, for that is detestable to Egyptians. 33The men had been seated before him in the order of their ages, from the firstborn to the youngest; and they looked at each other in astonishment. 34When portions were served to them from Joseph's table, Benjamin's portion was five times as much as anyone else's. So they feasted and drank freely with him.

44

Now Joseph gave these instructions to the steward of his house: "Fill the men's sacks with as much food as they can carry, and put each man's silver in the mouth of his sack. 2Then put my cup, the silver one, in the mouth of the youngest one's sack, along with the silver for his grain." And he did as Joseph said.

3As morning dawned, the men were sent on their way with their donkeys. 4They had not gone far from the city when Joseph said to his steward, "Go after those men at once, and when you catch up with them, say to them, 'Why have you repaid good with evil? 5Isn't this the cup my master drinks from and also uses for divination? This is a wicked thing you have done.' "

6When he caught up with them, he repeated these words to them. 7But they said to him, "Why does my lord say such things? Far be it from your servants to do anything like that! 8We even brought back to you from the land of Canaan the silver we found inside the mouths of our sacks. So why would we steal silver or gold from your master's house? 9If any of your servants is found to have it, he will die; and the rest of us will become my lord's slaves."

10"Very well, then," he said, "let it be as you say. Whoever is found to have it will become my slave; the rest of you will be free from blame."

11Each of them quickly lowered his sack to the ground and opened it. 12Then the steward proceeded to search, beginning with the oldest and ending with the youngest. And the cup was found in Benjamin's sack. 13At this, they tore their clothes. Then they all loaded their donkeys and returned to the city.

14Joseph was still in the house when Judah and his brothers came in, and they threw themselves to the ground before him. 15Joseph said to them, "What is this you have done? Don't you know that a man like me can find things out by divination?"

16"What can we say to my lord?" Judah replied. "What can we say? How can we prove our innocence? God has uncovered your servants' guilt. We are now my lord's slaves—we ourselves and the one who was found to have the cup."

17But Joseph said, "Far be it from me to do such a thing! Only the man who was found to have the cup will become my slave. The rest of you, go back to your father in peace."

18Then Judah went up to him and said: "Please, my lord, let your servant speak a word to my lord. Do not be angry with your servant, though you are equal to Pharaoh himself. 19My lord asked his servants, 'Do you have a father or a brother?' 20And we answered, 'We have an aged father, and there is a young son born to him in his old age. His brother is dead, and he is the only one of his mother's sons left, and his father loves him.'

21"Then you said to your servants, 'Bring him down to me so I can see him for myself.' 22And we said to my lord, 'The boy cannot leave his father; if he leaves him, his father will die.' 23But you told your servants, 'Unless your youngest brother comes down with you, you will not see my face again.' 24When we went back to your servant my father, we told him what my lord had said.

25"Then our father said, 'Go back and buy a little more food.' 26But we said, 'We cannot go down. Only if our youngest brother is with us will we go. We cannot see the man's face unless our youngest brother is with us.'

27"Your servant my father said to us, 'You know that my wife bore me two sons. 28One of them went away from me, and I said, "He has surely been torn to pieces." And I have not seen him since. 29If you take this one from me too and harm comes to him, you will bring my gray head down to the grave[u] in misery.'

30"So now, if the boy is not with us when I go back to your servant my father and if my father, whose life is closely bound up with the boy's life, 31sees that the boy isn't there, he will die. Your servants will bring the gray head of our father down to the grave in sorrow. 32Your servant guaranteed the boy's safety to my father. I said, 'If I do not bring him back to you, I will bear the blame before you, my father, all my life!'

33"Now then, please let your servant remain here as my lord's slave in place of the boy, and let the boy return with his brothers. 34How can I go back to my father if the boy is not with me? No! Do not let me see the misery that would come upon my father."

45 Then Joseph could no longer control himself before all his attendants, and he cried out, "Have everyone leave my presence!" So there was no one with Joseph when he made himself known to his brothers. 2And he wept so loudly that the Egyptians heard him, and Pharaoh's household heard about it.

3Joseph said to his brothers, "I am Joseph! Is my father still living?" But his brothers were not able to answer him, because they were terrified at his presence.

4Then Joseph said to his brothers, "Come close to me." When they had done so, he said, "I am your brother Joseph, the one you sold into Egypt! 5And now, do not be distressed and do not be angry with yourselves for selling me here, because it was to save lives that God sent me ahead of you. 6For two years now there has been famine in the land, and for the next five years there will not be plowing and reaping. 7But God sent me ahead of you to preserve for you a remnant on earth and to save your lives by a great deliverance.[v]

8"So then, it was not you who sent me here, but God. He made me father to Pharaoh, lord of his entire household and ruler of all Egypt. 9Now hurry back to my father and say to him, 'This is what your son Joseph says: God has made me lord of all Egypt. Come down to me; don't delay. 10You shall live in the region of Goshen and be near me—you, your children and grandchildren, your flocks and herds, and all you have. 11I will provide for you there, because five years of famine are still to come. Otherwise you and your household and all who belong to you will become destitute.'

12"You can see for yourselves, and so can my brother Benjamin, that it is really I who am speaking to you. 13Tell my father about all the honor accorded me in Egypt and about everything you have seen. And bring my father down here quickly."

14Then he threw his arms around his brother Benjamin and wept, and Benjamin embraced him, weeping. 15And he kissed all his brothers and wept over them. Afterward his brothers talked with him.

[u]29 Hebrew *Sheol*; also in verse 31 [v]7 Or *save you as a great band of survivors*

Discovering the Word 1. As Jacob instructs his sons and takes the risk of losing Benjamin, where does his confidence lie (43:11–14)? 2. What insights do verses 26–34 of chapter 43 give us into Joseph's character? 3. The stage is now set for the climax of this drama (chapter 44). What final strategy does Joseph devise in verses 1–17? 4. Judah's appeal is one of the great intercessions in the Bible. How does his attitude differ from that shown by him and his brothers twenty-three years earlier (44:18–34)? 5. How does Joseph explain to his brothers the reason for his being sold into Egypt and the purpose of his sufferings (45:1–11)?

Applying the Word 1. Think of a difficult situation you are currently facing. How can you entrust it to God Almighty, the one for whom nothing is impossible? 2. Restoring a relationship fractured by injustice and injury requires repentance, confession and acceptance of responsibility for the consequences. In what way have you, like Joseph's brothers, been involved in such a process? 3. How can this perspective toward your own suffering make it possible for you to forgive someone who has grievously wronged or hurt you?

 **Responding in Prayer** Think of one step you need to take to encourage reconciliation with someone you know. Ask God to give you the love, patience and courage to follow through.

24 / *Genesis 45:16—47:31*
God Preserves His People

DO YOU EVER wonder how the bits and pieces of your life fit together? This study shows how the seemingly unrelated and perplexing events of the preceding chapters now serve God's purpose to preserve Jacob's family during the coming famine. This account can strengthen our faith and hope as we work through difficult situations we cannot understand.

 **Warming Up to God** After years of separation and trials, Jacob and Joseph are reunited. What relationships or areas of your life seem untouchable by God's grace? Pray for God to renew your hope—and to answer your "hopeless" requests.

 **Read Genesis 45:16—47:31.**

16When the news reached Pharaoh's palace that
Joseph's brothers had come, Pharaoh and all his
officials were pleased. 17Pharaoh said to Joseph,
"Tell your brothers, 'Do this: Load your animals
and return to the land of Canaan, 18and bring
your father and your families back to me. I will
give you the best of the land of Egypt and you can
enjoy the fat of the land.'

19"You are also directed to tell them, 'Do this:
Take some carts from Egypt for your children and
your wives, and get your father and come.
20Never mind about your belongings, because the
best of all Egypt will be yours.' "

21So the sons of Israel did this. Joseph gave
them carts, as Pharaoh had commanded, and he
also gave them provisions for their journey. 22To
each of them he gave new clothing, but to Benja-
min he gave three hundred shekels[w] of silver and
five sets of clothes. 23And this is what he sent
to his father: ten donkeys loaded with the best
things of Egypt, and ten female donkeys loaded
with grain and bread and other provisions for his
journey. 24Then he sent his brothers away, and as
they were leaving he said to them, "Don't quarrel
on the way!"

25So they went up out of Egypt and came to
their father Jacob in the land of Canaan. 26They
told him, "Joseph is still alive! In fact, he is ruler
of all Egypt." Jacob was stunned; he did not be-
lieve them. 27But when they told him everything
Joseph had said to them, and when he saw the
carts Joseph had sent to carry him back, the spirit
of their father Jacob revived. 28And Israel said,
"I'm convinced! My son Joseph is still alive. I will
go and see him before I die."

46 So Israel set out with all that was
his, and when he reached Beer-
sheba, he offered sacrifices to the
God of his father Isaac.

2And God spoke to Israel in a vision at night
and said, "Jacob! Jacob!"

"Here I am," he replied.

3"I am God, the God of your father," he said.
"Do not be afraid to go down to Egypt, for I will
make you into a great nation there. 4I will go
down to Egypt with you, and I will surely bring
you back again. And Joseph's own hand will close
your eyes."

5Then Jacob left Beersheba, and Israel's sons
took their father Jacob and their children and
their wives in the carts that Pharaoh had sent to
transport him. 6They also took with them their
livestock and the possessions they had acquired
in Canaan, and Jacob and all his offspring went to
Egypt. 7He took with him to Egypt his sons and
grandsons and his daughters and granddaugh-
ters—all his offspring.

8These are the names of the sons of Israel (Ja-
cob and his descendants) who went to Egypt:

Reuben the firstborn of Jacob.
9The sons of Reuben:

w22 That is, about 7 1/2 pounds (about 3.5 kilograms)

Hanoch, Pallu, Hezron and Carmi.
[10]The sons of Simeon:
Jemuel, Jamin, Ohad, Jakin, Zohar and Shaul the son of a Canaanite woman.
[11]The sons of Levi:
Gershon, Kohath and Merari.
[12]The sons of Judah:
Er, Onan, Shelah, Perez and Zerah (but Er and Onan had died in the land of Canaan).
The sons of Perez:
Hezron and Hamul.
[13]The sons of Issachar:
Tola, Puah,[x] Jashub[y] and Shimron.
[14]The sons of Zebulun:
Sered, Elon and Jahleel.
[15]These were the sons Leah bore to Jacob in Paddan Aram,[z] besides his daughter Dinah. These sons and daughters of his were thirty-three in all.

[16]The sons of Gad:
Zephon,[a] Haggi, Shuni, Ezbon, Eri, Arodi and Areli.
[17]The sons of Asher:
Imnah, Ishvah, Ishvi and Beriah.
Their sister was Serah.
The sons of Beriah:
Heber and Malkiel.
[18]These were the children born to Jacob by Zilpah, whom Laban had given to his daughter Leah—sixteen in all.

[19]The sons of Jacob's wife Rachel:
Joseph and Benjamin. [20]In Egypt, Manasseh and Ephraim were born to Joseph by Asenath daughter of Potiphera, priest of On.[b]
[21]The sons of Benjamin:
Bela, Beker, Ashbel, Gera, Naaman, Ehi, Rosh, Muppim, Huppim and Ard.
[22]These were the sons of Rachel who were born to Jacob—fourteen in all.

[23]The son of Dan:
Hushim.
[24]The sons of Naphtali:
Jahziel, Guni, Jezer and Shillem.
[25]These were the sons born to Jacob by Bilhah, whom Laban had given to his daughter Rachel—seven in all.

[26]All those who went to Egypt with Jacob—those who were his direct descendants, not counting his sons' wives—numbered sixty-six persons. [27]With the two sons[c] who had been born to Joseph in Egypt, the members of Jacob's family, which went to Egypt, were seventy[d] in all.

[28]Now Jacob sent Judah ahead of him to Joseph to get directions to Goshen. When they arrived in the region of Goshen, [29]Joseph had his chariot made ready and went to Goshen to meet his father Israel. As soon as Joseph appeared before him, he threw his arms around his father[e] and wept for a long time.

[30]Israel said to Joseph, "Now I am ready to die, since I have seen for myself that you are still alive."

[31]Then Joseph said to his brothers and to his father's household, "I will go up and speak to Pharaoh and will say to him, 'My brothers and my father's household, who were living in the land of Canaan, have come to me. [32]The men are shepherds; they tend livestock, and they have brought along their flocks and herds and everything they own.' [33]When Pharaoh calls you in and asks, 'What is your occupation?' [34]you should answer, 'Your servants have tended livestock from our boyhood on, just as our fathers did.' Then you will be allowed to settle in the region of Goshen, for all shepherds are detestable to the Egyptians."

47

Joseph went and told Pharaoh, "My father and brothers, with their flocks and herds and everything they own, have come from the land of Canaan and are now in Goshen." [2]He chose five of his brothers and presented them before Pharaoh.

[3]Pharaoh asked the brothers, "What is your occupation?"

"Your servants are shepherds," they replied to Pharaoh, "just as our fathers were." [4]They also said to him, "We have come to live here awhile, because the famine is severe in Canaan and your servants' flocks have no pasture. So now, please let your servants settle in Goshen."

[5]Pharaoh said to Joseph, "Your father and your brothers have come to you, [6]and the land of Egypt is before you; settle your father and your brothers in the best part of the land. Let them live

[x]13 Samaritan Pentateuch and Syriac (see also 1 Chron. 7:1); Masoretic Text *Puvah* [y]13 Samaritan Pentateuch and some Septuagint manuscripts (see also Num. 26:24 and 1 Chron. 7:1); Masoretic Text *Iob* [z]15 That is, Northwest Mesopotamia [a]16 Samaritan Pentateuch and Septuagint (see also Num. 26:15); Masoretic Text *Ziphion* [b]20 That is, Heliopolis [c]27 Hebrew; Septuagint *the nine children* [d]27 Hebrew (see also Exodus 1:5 and footnote); Septuagint (see also Acts 7:14) *seventy-five* [e]29 Hebrew *around him*

in Goshen. And if you know of any among them with special ability, put them in charge of my own livestock."

[7]Then Joseph brought his father Jacob in and presented him before Pharaoh. After Jacob blessed[f] Pharaoh, [8]Pharaoh asked him, "How old are you?"

[9]And Jacob said to Pharaoh, "The years of my pilgrimage are a hundred and thirty. My years have been few and difficult, and they do not equal the years of the pilgrimage of my fathers." [10]Then Jacob blessed[g] Pharaoh and went out from his presence.

[11]So Joseph settled his father and his brothers in Egypt and gave them property in the best part of the land, the district of Rameses, as Pharaoh directed. [12]Joseph also provided his father and his brothers and all his father's household with food, according to the number of their children.

[13]There was no food, however, in the whole region because the famine was severe; both Egypt and Canaan wasted away because of the famine. [14]Joseph collected all the money that was to be found in Egypt and Canaan in payment for the grain they were buying, and he brought it to Pharaoh's palace. [15]When the money of the people of Egypt and Canaan was gone, all Egypt came to Joseph and said, "Give us food. Why should we die before your eyes? Our money is used up."

[16]"Then bring your livestock," said Joseph. "I will sell you food in exchange for your livestock, since your money is gone." [17]So they brought their livestock to Joseph, and he gave them food in exchange for their horses, their sheep and goats, their cattle and donkeys. And he brought them through that year with food in exchange for all their livestock.

[18]When that year was over, they came to him the following year and said, "We cannot hide from our lord the fact that since our money is gone and our livestock belongs to you, there is nothing left for our lord except our bodies and our land. [19]Why should we perish before your eyes—we and our land as well? Buy us and our land in exchange for food, and we with our land will be in bondage to Pharaoh. Give us seed so that we may live and not die, and that the land may not become desolate."

[20]So Joseph bought all the land in Egypt for Pharaoh. The Egyptians, one and all, sold their fields, because the famine was too severe for them. The land became Pharaoh's, [21]and Joseph reduced the people to servitude,[h] from one end of Egypt to the other. [22]However, he did not buy the land of the priests, because they received a regular allotment from Pharaoh and had food enough from the allotment Pharaoh gave them. That is why they did not sell their land.

[23]Joseph said to the people, "Now that I have bought you and your land today for Pharaoh, here is seed for you so you can plant the ground. [24]But when the crop comes in, give a fifth of it to Pharaoh. The other four-fifths you may keep as seed for the fields and as food for yourselves and your households and your children."

[25]"You have saved our lives," they said. "May we find favor in the eyes of our lord; we will be in bondage to Pharaoh."

[26]So Joseph established it as a law concerning land in Egypt—still in force today—that a fifth of the produce belongs to Pharaoh. It was only the land of the priests that did not become Pharaoh's.

[27]Now the Israelites settled in Egypt in the region of Goshen. They acquired property there and were fruitful and increased greatly in number.

[28]Jacob lived in Egypt seventeen years, and the years of his life were a hundred and forty-seven. [29]When the time drew near for Israel to die, he called for his son Joseph and said to him, "If I have found favor in your eyes, put your hand under my thigh and promise that you will show me kindness and faithfulness. Do not bury me in Egypt, [30]but when I rest with my fathers, carry me out of Egypt and bury me where they are buried."

"I will do as you say," he said.

[31]"Swear to me," he said. Then Joseph swore to him, and Israel worshiped as he leaned on the top of his staff.[i]

[f]7 Or *greeted* [g]10 Or *said farewell to* [h]21 Samaritan Pentateuch and Septuagint (see also Vulgate); Masoretic Text *and he moved the people into the cities* [i]31 Or *Israel bowed down at the head of his bed*

Discovering the Word 1. What is Pharaoh's reaction to the news that Joseph's brothers have arrived (45:16–24)? 2. Beersheba had been Isaac's center of worship. As God confirms this move to Egypt, what encouragement does he give Jacob for both the immediate and distant future (46:1–4)? 3. How do verses 5–27 of chapter 46 underscore God's faithfulness to the promises he made to Abraham, Isaac and Jacob? 4. How does Joseph's skill as a planner and administrator continue to show itself as he arranges for his father's family to settle in Goshen (46:28–34)? 5. What does 47:13–27 reveal about God's purpose in bringing Joseph to Egypt? 6. How does Jacob's last request of Joseph show his faith in God's promise regarding his descendants and their own land (47:28–30)?

Applying the Word 1. Has God ever allowed you to see how seemingly unrelated events fit into the tapestry of his will? Explain. 2. What important promise or prayer request are you patiently waiting for God to fulfill?

Responding in Prayer Thank God for his loving control over the lives of Abraham, Isaac and Jacob. Praise him for ordering your steps according to his benevolent will.

25 / *Genesis 48—49*
The Life of Faith

OUR SELF-CENTERED TECHNOLOGICAL society seeks instant gratification and immediate results. The good life emblazoned on television is measured by what we have and use now. The elderly are usually considered obsolete rather than examples of how to live fully for the long run. But for those with eyes to see, Jacob can teach us valuable lessons about the satisfaction of persevering in the life of faith. This study views his final days as he evaluates the past and peers into the future.

Warming Up to God Paint a picture of God in your mind. What is he like? Write down what you see. Let God come to you now and broaden your perspective.

Read Genesis 48—49.

48 Some time later Joseph was told, "Your father is ill." So he took his two sons Manasseh and Ephraim along with him. 2When Jacob was told, "Your son Joseph has come to you," Israel rallied his strength and sat up on the bed.

3Jacob said to Joseph, "God Almighty[j] appeared to me at Luz in the land of Canaan, and there he blessed me 4and said to me, 'I am going to make you fruitful and will increase your numbers. I will make you a community of peoples, and I will give this land as an everlasting possession to your descendants after you.'

5"Now then, your two sons born to you in Egypt before I came to you here will be reckoned as mine; Ephraim and Manasseh will be mine, just as Reuben and Simeon are mine. 6Any children born to you after them will be yours; in the territory they inherit they will be reckoned under the names of their brothers. 7As I was returning from Paddan,[k] to my sorrow Rachel died in the land of Canaan while we were still on the way, a little distance from Ephrath. So I buried her there beside the road to Ephrath" (that is, Bethlehem).

8When Israel saw the sons of Joseph, he asked, "Who are these?"

9"They are the sons God has given me here," Joseph said to his father.

Then Israel said, "Bring them to me so I may bless them."

10Now Israel's eyes were failing because of old age, and he could hardly see. So Joseph brought his sons close to him, and his father kissed them and embraced them.

11Israel said to Joseph, "I never expected to see your face again, and now God has allowed me to see your children too."

12Then Joseph removed them from Israel's knees and bowed down with his face to the ground. 13And Joseph took both of them, Ephraim on his right toward Israel's left hand and Manasseh on his left toward Israel's right hand, and brought them close to him. 14But Israel reached out his right hand and put it on Ephraim's head, though he was the younger, and crossing his arms, he put his left hand on Manas-

j3 Hebrew *El-Shaddai* k7 That is, Northwest Mesopotamia

seh's head, even though Manasseh was the first-
born.
15Then he blessed Joseph and said,

"May the God before whom my fathers
Abraham and Isaac walked,
the God who has been my shepherd
all my life to this day,
16the Angel who has delivered me from all
harm
—may he bless these boys.
May they be called by my name
and the names of my fathers Abraham and
Isaac,
and may they increase greatly
upon the earth."

17When Joseph saw his father placing his right
hand on Ephraim's head he was displeased; so he
took hold of his father's hand to move it from
Ephraim's head to Manasseh's head. 18Joseph said
to him, "No, my father, this one is the firstborn;
put your right hand on his head."
19But his father refused and said, "I know, my
son, I know. He too will become a people, and he
too will become great. Nevertheless, his younger
brother will be greater than he, and his descen-
dants will become a group of nations." 20He
blessed them that day and said,

"In your[l] name will Israel pronounce this
blessing:
'May God make you like Ephraim and
Manasseh.' "

So he put Ephraim ahead of Manasseh.
21Then Israel said to Joseph, "I am about to die,
but God will be with you[m] and take you[m] back
to the land of your[m] fathers. 22And to you, as one
who is over your brothers, I give the ridge of
land[n] I took from the Amorites with my sword
and my bow."

49 Then Jacob called for his sons and
said: "Gather around so I can tell
you what will happen to you in
days to come.

2"Assemble and listen, sons of Jacob;
listen to your father Israel.

3"Reuben, you are my firstborn,
my might, the first sign of my strength,
excelling in honor, excelling in power.
4Turbulent as the waters, you will no longer
excel,
for you went up onto your father's bed,
onto my couch and defiled it.

5"Simeon and Levi are brothers—
their swords[o] are weapons of violence.
6Let me not enter their council,
let me not join their assembly,
for they have killed men in their anger
and hamstrung oxen as they pleased.
7Cursed be their anger, so fierce,
and their fury, so cruel!
I will scatter them in Jacob
and disperse them in Israel.

8"Judah,[p] your brothers will praise you;
your hand will be on the neck of your
enemies;
your father's sons will bow down to you.
9You are a lion's cub, O Judah;
you return from the prey, my son.
Like a lion he crouches and lies down,
like a lioness—who dares to rouse him?
10The scepter will not depart from Judah,
nor the ruler's staff from between his feet,
until he comes to whom it belongs[q]
and the obedience of the nations is his.
11He will tether his donkey to a vine,
his colt to the choicest branch;
he will wash his garments in wine,
his robes in the blood of grapes.
12His eyes will be darker than wine,
his teeth whiter than milk.[r]

13"Zebulun will live by the seashore
and become a haven for ships;
his border will extend toward Sidon.

14"Issachar is a rawboned[s] donkey
lying down between two saddlebags.[t]
15When he sees how good is his resting place
and how pleasant is his land,
he will bend his shoulder to the burden
and submit to forced labor.

16"Dan[u] will provide justice for his people
as one of the tribes of Israel.
17Dan will be a serpent by the roadside,
a viper along the path,
that bites the horse's heels
so that its rider tumbles backward.

[l]20 The Hebrew is singular. [m]21 The Hebrew is plural. [n]22 Or *And to you I give one portion more than to your brothers—the portion*
[o]5 The meaning of the Hebrew for this word is uncertain. [p]8 *Judah* sounds like and may be derived from the Hebrew for *praise.*
[q]10 Or *until Shiloh comes;* or *until he comes to whom tribute belongs*
[r]12 Or *will be dull from wine, / his teeth white from milk* [s]14 Or *strong* [t]14 Or *campfires* [u]16 *Dan* here means *he provides justice.*

18 "I look for your deliverance, O LORD.

19 "Gad[v] will be attacked by a band of raiders,
but he will attack them at their heels.

20 "Asher's food will be rich;
he will provide delicacies fit for a king.

21 "Naphtali is a doe set free
that bears beautiful fawns.[w]

22 "Joseph is a fruitful vine,
a fruitful vine near a spring,
whose branches climb over a wall.[x]
23 With bitterness archers attacked him;
they shot at him with hostility.
24 But his bow remained steady,
his strong arms stayed[y] limber,
because of the hand of the Mighty One of Jacob,
because of the Shepherd, the Rock of Israel,
25 because of your father's God, who helps you,
because of the Almighty,[z] who blesses you
with blessings of the heavens above,
blessings of the deep that lies below,
blessings of the breast and womb.
26 Your father's blessings are greater
than the blessings of the ancient mountains,
than[a] the bounty of the age-old hills.
Let all these rest on the head of Joseph,
on the brow of the prince among[b] his brothers.

27 "Benjamin is a ravenous wolf;
in the morning he devours the prey,
in the evening he divides the plunder."

28 All these are the twelve tribes of Israel, and this is what their father said to them when he blessed them, giving each the blessing appropriate to him.

29 Then he gave them these instructions: "I am about to be gathered to my people. Bury me with my fathers in the cave in the field of Ephron the Hittite, 30 the cave in the field of Machpelah, near Mamre in Canaan, which Abraham bought as a burial place from Ephron the Hittite, along with the field. 31 There Abraham and his wife Sarah were buried, there Isaac and his wife Rebekah were buried, and there I buried Leah. 32 The field and the cave in it were bought from the Hittites.[c]"

33 When Jacob had finished giving instructions to his sons, he drew his feet up into the bed, breathed his last and was gathered to his people.

[v] 19 *Gad* can mean *attack* and *band of raiders.* [w] 21 Or *free; / he utters beautiful words* [x] 22 Or *Joseph is a wild colt, / a wild colt near a spring, / a wild donkey on a terraced hill* [y] 23,24 Or *archers will attack . . . will shoot . . . will remain . . . will stay* [z] 25 Hebrew *Shaddai* [a] 26 Or *of my progenitors, / as great as* [b] 26 Or *the one separated from* [c] 32 Or *the sons of Heth*

Discovering the Word 1. In what ways is Jacob's faith evident as he blesses Ephraim and Manasseh (48:8–20)? 2. In 49:3–7 how are the blessings given to Reuben, Simeon and Levi related to their past actions (see Ge 34; 35:22)? 3. What future does Jacob see for Judah (49:8–12)? 4. After blessing six of his other sons (49:13–21), Jacob gives a rich and lengthy blessing to Joseph. How is Joseph's blessing related to his past actions (49:22–26)? 5. Recall events in Joseph's life which illustrate the names given to God in 49:24–25. 6. How do Jacob's last words demonstrate the faith and hope with which he finished the course of his life (48:21–22; 49:29–32)?

Applying the Word 1. Although our past failures and sins affect our future, how can God's forgiveness and grace help us triumph over these consequences? 2. In what specific areas are you having to trust God for the future?

Responding in Prayer Ask God to help you remember that his plans are much greater than our own. Praise him for the miracles he's shown you in the life of Jacob.

Exodus

When we're young we can hardly wait to get our independence. Responsibility rarely crosses our minds. Our parents, on the other hand, think about responsibility a great deal. They cautiously increase our independence bit by bit, anxiously waiting for signs of growing maturity. But that's just the beginning. For the rest of our lives we walk the tightrope between independence and responsibility.

Long ago this issue was dramatized for us in ancient Israel's struggle to gain its independence and to show responsible obedience to God. Moses was "the anxious parent" deputized by God to lead the nation to independence and to teach them responsible freedom.

The book of Exodus tells it all. Written by Moses himself, Exodus is the story of abject slavery and glorious liberation. God patiently teaches what human responsibility means, both in worship and in our relationships with others.

Just like children struggling through adolescence to responsible adulthood, Israel had its good and bad days. Their exodus to freedom did not give them the right to do as they pleased. They had to learn loyalty and obedience to God as a consequence of his giving them their independence. For them, learning to trust and obey God was rooted in God's gracious deliverance from bondage.

In effect, God owned them because he had redeemed them from bondage. The story of Israel's exodus thus becomes a prototype of every Christian's exodus from the enslaving power of sin. Jesus Christ the redeemer becomes Lord of those who would acknowledge his saving love and power.

All this and more is bound up in the book of Exodus. Serious students will find a gold mine of insight and practical values that relate to living today. This is history with a punch. Allow yourself the benefit of careful reflection. Take time to cross 3,500 years and think about both victories and defeats among God's people. Thrill to Moses' encounters with Pharaoh, with his own rebellious people and with God at Mount Sinai. Grasp the significance of the Ten Commandments and the worship of the true and living God. Meditate on new ideas about the meaning of worship, music, and the consecration of one's possessions and talents to the glory of God.

Exodus begins with Moses' account of cruel bondage in Egypt, moves through the bitter struggle with Pharaoh for deliverance, continues on to Mount Sinai and the giving of the Ten

Commandments, and climaxes with the building of a place of worship and the establishment of a priesthood. It covers a period of close to one hundred years.

Major themes include the name and glory of God, the covenants (agreements) between God and Israel, the Law and the tabernacle. The institution of the Passover points to salvation through the death of Christ. The tabernacle and the priesthood speak of the God-given principles of how we worship God and the privileges we have to praise and glorify him.

Because there is much historical data to be covered, some of it is not included in the questions. The quiet times are organized around the major events in the story, their significance for Israel and what we can learn from them about Christian living. You will need to develop the skill of scanning blocks of text, looking for highlights. Pertinent New Testament doctrines and applications for Christian living are also considered.

The questions are designed to help you discover the facts and reflect on their significance for your life. The apostle Paul wrote that these ancient accounts were given to teach and warn us (1Co 10:11). May God help you to grasp life-changing truth as you grow in your ability to trust and obey him. •

Outline

1 / *Exodus 1*
Evil Plans, Courageous Resistance

OPPRESSION IS A nasty word, but it grabs the headlines because it's the reason for much conflict today. Scenes out of this chapter fit totalitarian societies. Only the methods of oppression change. God's people were not spared in 1700 B.C., and they are not always spared now. But in this study you will find a bright spot of courageous resistance.

Warming Up to God Today you begin the account of the nation of Israel, the descendants of the promises made to Abraham, Isaac and Jacob. How are you seeing God's promises fulfilled in your life?

Read Exodus 1.

1 These are the names of the sons of Israel who went to Egypt with Jacob, each with his family: 2Reuben, Simeon, Levi and Judah; 3Issachar, Zebulun and Benjamin; 4Dan and Naphtali; Gad and Asher. 5The descendants of Jacob numbered seventy[a] in all; Joseph was already in Egypt.

6Now Joseph and all his brothers and all that generation died, 7but the Israelites were fruitful and multiplied greatly and became exceedingly numerous, so that the land was filled with them.

8Then a new king, who did not know about Joseph, came to power in Egypt. 9"Look," he said to his people, "the Israelites have become much too numerous for us. 10Come, we must deal shrewdly with them or they will become even more numerous and, if war breaks out, will join our enemies, fight against us and leave the country."

11So they put slave masters over them to oppress them with forced labor, and they built Pithom and Rameses as store cities for Pharaoh. 12But the more they were oppressed, the more they multiplied and spread; so the Egyptians came to dread the Israelites 13and worked them ruthlessly. 14They made their lives bitter with hard labor in brick and mortar and with all kinds of work in the fields; in all their hard labor the Egyptians used them ruthlessly.

15The king of Egypt said to the Hebrew midwives, whose names were Shiphrah and Puah, 16"When you help the Hebrew women in childbirth and observe them on the delivery stool, if it is a boy, kill him; but if it is a girl, let her live." 17The midwives, however, feared God and did not do what the king of Egypt had told them to do; they let the boys live. 18Then the king of Egypt summoned the midwives and asked them, "Why have you done this? Why have you let the boys live?"

19The midwives answered Pharaoh, "Hebrew women are not like Egyptian women; they are vigorous and give birth before the midwives arrive."

20So God was kind to the midwives and the people increased and became even more numerous. 21And because the midwives feared God, he gave them families of their own.

22Then Pharaoh gave this order to all his people: "Every boy that is born[b] you must throw into the Nile, but let every girl live."

[a]5 Masoretic Text (see also Gen. 46:27); Dead Sea Scrolls and Septuagint (see also Acts 7:14 and note at Gen. 46:27) *seventy-five*
[b]22 Masoretic Text; Samaritan Pentateuch, Septuagint and Targums *born to the Hebrews*

Discovering the Word 1. How did "the sons of Israel" (Jacob's descendants) fare in Egypt (vv. 1–7)? 2. What was their situation under a king who had forgotten Joseph's role (Ge 41) in saving the country (vv. 8–14)? 3. Why did Pharaoh's strategy backfire (v. 12)? 4. What new population control plans did Pharaoh devise (vv. 15–22)? 5. Imagine the emotions of the king and the midwives when he summoned them (v. 18). What was the secret of the women's self-control and wisdom (vv. 17, 21)?

Applying the Word 1. How does your fear of God motivate right moral conduct and give you the courage to withstand the temptation to do evil? 2. In what circumstances have you felt oppressed by unreasonable demands? 3. How did you find God's help?

Responding in Prayer Thank God for your personal freedom and ask him to give you endurance when you are faced with oppression.

2 / *Exodus 2*
A Mother's Faith, a Son's Brashness

WORKING DOWNTOWN ON an engineering maintenance project, the man knew that his friend's wife lay dying in a hospital only four blocks away. But he didn't go to see the woman. Lack of appropriate dress demolished his courage to do something bold in Christ's name. Few of us can brag about how bravely we have responded in crisis. Faith, for us, is a comfortable intellectual exercise, not something that demands bold action. That definition becomes even more attractive when we're not sure how to distinguish between faith and foolishness. This study contrasts a privileged kid's brashness with a woman's courageous faith in action.

Warming Up to God What has been the most costly thing you have had to do for God?

Read Exodus 2.

2 Now a man of the house of Levi married a Levite woman, 2and she became pregnant and gave birth to a son. When she saw that he was a fine child, she hid him for three months. 3But when she could hide him no longer, she got a papyrus basket for him and coated it with tar and pitch. Then she placed the child in it and put it among the reeds along the bank of the Nile. 4His sister stood at a distance to see what would happen to him.

5Then Pharaoh's daughter went down to the Nile to bathe, and her attendants were walking along the river bank. She saw the basket among the reeds and sent her slave girl to get it. 6She opened it and saw the baby. He was crying, and she felt sorry for him. "This is one of the Hebrew babies," she said.

7Then his sister asked Pharaoh's daughter, "Shall I go and get one of the Hebrew women to nurse the baby for you?"

8"Yes, go," she answered. And the girl went and got the baby's mother. 9Pharaoh's daughter said to her, "Take this baby and nurse him for me, and I will pay you." So the woman took the baby and nursed him. 10When the child grew older, she took him to Pharaoh's daughter and he became her son. She named him Moses,[c] saying, "I drew him out of the water."

11One day, after Moses had grown up, he went out to where his own people were and watched them at their hard labor. He saw an Egyptian beating a Hebrew, one of his own people. 12Glancing this way and that and seeing no one, he killed the Egyptian and hid him in the sand. 13The next day he went out and saw two Hebrews fighting. He asked the one in the wrong, "Why are you hitting your fellow Hebrew?"

14The man said, "Who made you ruler and judge over us? Are you thinking of killing me as you killed the Egyptian?" Then Moses was afraid and thought, "What I did must have become known."

15When Pharaoh heard of this, he tried to kill Moses, but Moses fled from Pharaoh and went to live in Midian, where he sat down by a well. 16Now a priest of Midian had seven daughters, and they came to draw water and fill the troughs to water their father's flock. 17Some shepherds came along and drove them away, but Moses got up and came to their rescue and watered their flock.

18When the girls returned to Reuel their father, he asked them, "Why have you returned so early today?"

19They answered, "An Egyptian rescued us from the shepherds. He even drew water for us and watered the flock."

20"And where is he?" he asked his daughters. "Why did you leave him? Invite him to have something to eat."

21Moses agreed to stay with the man, who gave his daughter Zipporah to Moses in marriage. 22Zipporah gave birth to a son, and Moses named him Gershom,[d] saying, "I have become an alien in a foreign land."

23During that long period, the king of Egypt died. The Israelites groaned in their slavery and

[c]10 *Moses* sounds like the Hebrew for *draw out.* [d]22 *Gershom* sounds like the Hebrew for *an alien there.*

cried out, and their cry for help because of their
slavery went up to God. 24God heard their groan-
ing and he remembered his covenant with Abra-
ham, with Isaac and with Jacob. 25So God looked
on the Israelites and was concerned about
them.

Discovering the Word 1. How did God plan for the infant Moses to survive Pharaoh's murderous edict (vv. 1–10)? 2. What did Moses' survival cost his mother? 3. Why did Moses flee to Midian (vv. 11–15)? (He was 40 years old at the time.) 4. Meanwhile, what was happening to the Israelites in Egypt (v. 23)? 5. How did their condition affect God and why (vv. 24–25)?

Applying the Word 1. How has God confronted you recently with a demand for courageous faith? 2. God hears the cries of his people today. What difference does that make when you are confronted by circumstances you are powerless to change?

Responding in Prayer Ask God to use you in his plans to creatively address the difficult situations in your life.

3 / *Exodus 3—4*
Stubborn Reluctance Overcome

THE MILESTONES OF history are marked by people who have met impossible demands. Battlefield monuments utter mute testimony to these events. Modern Turkey owes its existence to Kemal Ataturk, who rallied his troops with the impossible demand that they drive back the enemy from Gallipoli. Your most impossible demand may seem small in comparison—but not at the time the challenge presented itself. Perhaps it was writing an academic paper without adequate time or expertise. Or maybe it was the time when your church group decided to talk to people on the beach about Jesus Christ. This study shows how God put an impossible demand on Moses and propelled him into national leadership.

Warming Up to God Remember today that God has chosen you to do great works through him. Ask God to give you courage and to teach you from the example of Moses.

Read Exodus 3—4.

3 Now Moses was tending the flock of
Jethro his father-in-law, the priest of Mid-
ian, and he led the flock to the far side of
the desert and came to Horeb, the mountain of
God. 2There the angel of the Lord appeared to
him in flames of fire from within a bush. Moses
saw that though the bush was on fire it did not
burn up. 3So Moses thought, "I will go over and
see this strange sight—why the bush does not
burn up."
4When the Lord saw that he had gone over to
look, God called to him from within the bush,
"Moses! Moses!"
And Moses said, "Here I am."
5"Do not come any closer," God said. "Take off
your sandals, for the place where you are stand-
ing is holy ground." 6Then he said, "I am the God
of your father, the God of Abraham, the God of
Isaac and the God of Jacob." At this, Moses hid
his face, because he was afraid to look at God.
7The Lord said, "I have indeed seen the misery
of my people in Egypt. I have heard them crying
out because of their slave drivers, and I am con-
cerned about their suffering. 8So I have come
down to rescue them from the hand of the Egyp-
tians and to bring them up out of that land into a
good and spacious land, a land flowing with milk
and honey—the home of the Canaanites, Hittites,

Amorites, Perizzites, Hivites and Jebusites. 9And now the cry of the Israelites has reached me, and I have seen the way the Egyptians are oppressing them. 10So now, go. I am sending you to Pharaoh to bring my people the Israelites out of Egypt."

11But Moses said to God, "Who am I, that I should go to Pharaoh and bring the Israelites out of Egypt?"

12And God said, "I will be with you. And this will be the sign to you that it is I who have sent you: When you have brought the people out of Egypt, you[e] will worship God on this mountain."

13Moses said to God, "Suppose I go to the Israelites and say to them, 'The God of your fathers has sent me to you,' and they ask me, 'What is his name?' Then what shall I tell them?"

14God said to Moses, "I AM WHO I AM.[f] This is what you are to say to the Israelites: 'I AM has sent me to you.' "

15God also said to Moses, "Say to the Israelites, 'The LORD,[g] the God of your fathers—the God of Abraham, the God of Isaac and the God of Jacob—has sent me to you.' This is my name forever, the name by which I am to be remembered from generation to generation.

16"Go, assemble the elders of Israel and say to them, 'The LORD, the God of your fathers—the God of Abraham, Isaac and Jacob—appeared to me and said: I have watched over you and have seen what has been done to you in Egypt. 17And I have promised to bring you up out of your misery in Egypt into the land of the Canaanites, Hittites, Amorites, Perizzites, Hivites and Jebusites—a land flowing with milk and honey.'

18"The elders of Israel will listen to you. Then you and the elders are to go to the king of Egypt and say to him, 'The LORD, the God of the Hebrews, has met with us. Let us take a three-day journey into the desert to offer sacrifices to the LORD our God.' 19But I know that the king of Egypt will not let you go unless a mighty hand compels him. 20So I will stretch out my hand and strike the Egyptians with all the wonders that I will perform among them. After that, he will let you go.

21"And I will make the Egyptians favorably disposed toward this people, so that when you leave you will not go empty-handed. 22Every woman is to ask her neighbor and any woman living in her house for articles of silver and gold and for clothing, which you will put on your sons and daughters. And so you will plunder the Egyptians."

4 Moses answered, "What if they do not believe me or listen to me and say, 'The LORD did not appear to you'?"

2Then the LORD said to him, "What is that in your hand?"

"A staff," he replied.

3The LORD said, "Throw it on the ground."

Moses threw it on the ground and it became a snake, and he ran from it. 4Then the LORD said to him, "Reach out your hand and take it by the tail." So Moses reached out and took hold of the snake and it turned back into a staff in his hand. 5"This," said the LORD, "is so that they may believe that the LORD, the God of their fathers—the God of Abraham, the God of Isaac and the God of Jacob—has appeared to you."

6Then the LORD said, "Put your hand inside your cloak." So Moses put his hand into his cloak, and when he took it out, it was leprous,[h] like snow.

7"Now put it back into your cloak," he said. So Moses put his hand back into his cloak, and when he took it out, it was restored, like the rest of his flesh.

8Then the LORD said, "If they do not believe you or pay attention to the first miraculous sign, they may believe the second. 9But if they do not believe these two signs or listen to you, take some water from the Nile and pour it on the dry ground. The water you take from the river will become blood on the ground."

10Moses said to the LORD, "O Lord, I have never been eloquent, neither in the past nor since you have spoken to your servant. I am slow of speech and tongue."

11The LORD said to him, "Who gave man his mouth? Who makes him deaf or mute? Who gives him sight or makes him blind? Is it not I, the LORD? 12Now go; I will help you speak and will teach you what to say."

13But Moses said, "O Lord, please send someone else to do it."

14Then the LORD's anger burned against Moses and he said, "What about your brother, Aaron the Levite? I know he can speak well. He is already on his way to meet you, and his heart will be glad when he sees you. 15You shall speak to him and

[e] 12 The Hebrew is plural. [f] 14 Or I WILL BE WHAT I WILL BE
[g] 15 The Hebrew for LORD sounds like and may be derived from the Hebrew for I AM in verse 14. [h] 6 The Hebrew word was used for various diseases affecting the skin—not necessarily leprosy.

put words in his mouth; I will help both of you speak and will teach you what to do. 16He will speak to the people for you, and it will be as if he were your mouth and as if you were God to him. 17But take this staff in your hand so you can perform miraculous signs with it."

18Then Moses went back to Jethro his father-in-law and said to him, "Let me go back to my own people in Egypt to see if any of them are still alive."

Jethro said, "Go, and I wish you well."

19Now the LORD had said to Moses in Midian, "Go back to Egypt, for all the men who wanted to kill you are dead." 20So Moses took his wife and sons, put them on a donkey and started back to Egypt. And he took the staff of God in his hand.

21The LORD said to Moses, "When you return to Egypt, see that you perform before Pharaoh all the wonders I have given you the power to do. But I will harden his heart so that he will not let the people go. 22Then say to Pharaoh, 'This is what the LORD says: Israel is my firstborn son, 23and I told you, "Let my son go, so he may worship me." But you refused to let him go; so I will kill your firstborn son.' "

24At a lodging place on the way, the LORD met ⌞Moses⌟[i] and was about to kill him. 25But Zipporah took a flint knife, cut off her son's foreskin and touched ⌞Moses'⌟ feet with it.[j] "Surely you are a bridegroom of blood to me," she said. 26So the LORD let him alone. (At that time she said "bridegroom of blood," referring to circumcision.)

27The LORD said to Aaron, "Go into the desert to meet Moses." So he met Moses at the mountain of God and kissed him. 28Then Moses told Aaron everything the LORD had sent him to say, and also about all the miraculous signs he had commanded him to perform.

29Moses and Aaron brought together all the elders of the Israelites, 30and Aaron told them everything the LORD had said to Moses. He also performed the signs before the people, 31and they believed. And when they heard that the LORD was concerned about them and had seen their misery, they bowed down and worshiped.

[i]24 Or *⌞Moses' son⌟*; Hebrew *him* [j]25 Or *and drew near ⌞Moses'⌟ feet*

Discovering the Word 1. What motivates God to act on behalf of his people (3:7–10)? 2. How does Moses respond to God's assignment and why (3:11–13)? 3. What reassurance does God give Moses (3:12–22)? 4. What other doubts and fears does Moses have (4:1, 10)? 5. How does God deal with these inadequacies (4:2–9, 11–12)? 6. How do the events in 4:27–31 confirm the Lord's promises to Moses?

Applying the Word 1. When have you felt inadequate to do something God wanted you to do? 2. When you are sure God is speaking to you, and a specific "Yes, Lord" is expected of you, what things influence your answer?

Responding in Prayer Confess your fears and feelings of inadequacy to the Lord, and boldly ask him to call you to participate in his plans.

4 / *Exodus 5:1—7:7*
Rebuff and Resolution

THE CHRISTIAN STUDENT group discovered a sure-fire winner for its outreach meeting. Here was a famous businessman who was sure to attract a crowd. Confidently, the Christians plugged away at inviting their friends, and their work was rewarded with a packed room. An hour or so later they fled the room in defeat. They had tried to obey God, but their venture failed. In a word, their hero speaker bombed. Discouragement enveloped the group like a dense fog. No doubt Moses felt the same way, except the stakes were higher. In this study, he and Aaron are soundly rebuffed, though they doggedly pursue God's will with obedient courage.

Warming Up to God What struggles have you faced today? Tell God about them, and let him show you through Scripture how he deals with evil.

 **Read Exodus 5:1—7:7.**

5 Afterward Moses and Aaron went to Pharaoh and said, "This is what the LORD, the God of Israel, says: 'Let my people go, so that they may hold a festival to me in the desert.' "

2Pharaoh said, "Who is the LORD, that I should obey him and let Israel go? I do not know the LORD and I will not let Israel go."

3Then they said, "The God of the Hebrews has met with us. Now let us take a three-day journey into the desert to offer sacrifices to the LORD our God, or he may strike us with plagues or with the sword."

4But the king of Egypt said, "Moses and Aaron, why are you taking the people away from their labor? Get back to your work!" 5Then Pharaoh said, "Look, the people of the land are now numerous, and you are stopping them from working."

6That same day Pharaoh gave this order to the slave drivers and foremen in charge of the people: 7"You are no longer to supply the people with straw for making bricks; let them go and gather their own straw. 8But require them to make the same number of bricks as before; don't reduce the quota. They are lazy; that is why they are crying out, 'Let us go and sacrifice to our God.' 9Make the work harder for the men so that they keep working and pay no attention to lies."

10Then the slave drivers and the foremen went out and said to the people, "This is what Pharaoh says: 'I will not give you any more straw. 11Go and get your own straw wherever you can find it, but your work will not be reduced at all.' " 12So the people scattered all over Egypt to gather stubble to use for straw. 13The slave drivers kept pressing them, saying, "Complete the work required of you for each day, just as when you had straw." 14The Israelite foremen appointed by Pharaoh's slave drivers were beaten and were asked, "Why didn't you meet your quota of bricks yesterday or today, as before?"

15Then the Israelite foremen went and appealed to Pharaoh: "Why have you treated your servants this way? 16Your servants are given no straw, yet we are told, 'Make bricks!' Your servants are being beaten, but the fault is with your own people."

17Pharaoh said, "Lazy, that's what you are—lazy! That is why you keep saying, 'Let us go and sacrifice to the LORD.' 18Now get to work. You will not be given any straw, yet you must produce your full quota of bricks."

19The Israelite foremen realized they were in trouble when they were told, "You are not to reduce the number of bricks required of you for each day." 20When they left Pharaoh, they found Moses and Aaron waiting to meet them, 21and they said, "May the LORD look upon you and judge you! You have made us a stench to Pharaoh and his officials and have put a sword in their hand to kill us."

22Moses returned to the LORD and said, "O Lord, why have you brought trouble upon this people? Is this why you sent me? 23Ever since I went to Pharaoh to speak in your name, he has brought trouble upon this people, and you have not rescued your people at all."

6 Then the LORD said to Moses, "Now you will see what I will do to Pharaoh: Because of my mighty hand he will let them go; because of my mighty hand he will drive them out of his country."

2God also said to Moses, "I am the LORD. 3I appeared to Abraham, to Isaac and to Jacob as God Almighty,[k] but by my name the LORD[l] I did not make myself known to them.[m] 4I also established my covenant with them to give them the land of Canaan, where they lived as aliens. 5Moreover, I have heard the groaning of the Israelites, whom the Egyptians are enslaving, and I have remembered my covenant.

6"Therefore, say to the Israelites: 'I am the LORD, and I will bring you out from under the yoke of the Egyptians. I will free you from being slaves to them, and I will redeem you with an outstretched arm and with mighty acts of judgment. 7I will take you as my own people, and I will be your God. Then you will know that I am the LORD your God, who brought you out from under the yoke of the Egyptians. 8And I will bring you to the land I swore with uplifted hand to give to Abraham, to Isaac and to Jacob. I will give it to you as a possession. I am the LORD.' "

9Moses reported this to the Israelites, but they

k3 Hebrew *El-Shaddai* l3 See note at Exodus 3:15. m3 Or *Almighty, and by my name the LORD did I not let myself be known to them?*

did not listen to him because of their discouragement and cruel bondage.

10 Then the LORD said to Moses, 11 "Go, tell Pharaoh king of Egypt to let the Israelites go out of his country."

12 But Moses said to the LORD, "If the Israelites will not listen to me, why would Pharaoh listen to me, since I speak with faltering lips[n]?"

13 Now the LORD spoke to Moses and Aaron about the Israelites and Pharaoh king of Egypt, and he commanded them to bring the Israelites out of Egypt.

14 These were the heads of their families[o]:

The sons of Reuben the firstborn son of Israel were Hanoch and Pallu, Hezron and Carmi. These were the clans of Reuben.

15 The sons of Simeon were Jemuel, Jamin, Ohad, Jakin, Zohar and Shaul the son of a Canaanite woman. These were the clans of Simeon.

16 These were the names of the sons of Levi according to their records: Gershon, Kohath and Merari. Levi lived 137 years.

17 The sons of Gershon, by clans, were Libni and Shimei.

18 The sons of Kohath were Amram, Izhar, Hebron and Uzziel. Kohath lived 133 years.

19 The sons of Merari were Mahli and Mushi.

These were the clans of Levi according to their records.

20 Amram married his father's sister Jochebed, who bore him Aaron and Moses. Amram lived 137 years.

21 The sons of Izhar were Korah, Nepheg and Zicri.

22 The sons of Uzziel were Mishael, Elzaphan and Sithri.

23 Aaron married Elisheba, daughter of Amminadab and sister of Nahshon, and she bore him Nadab and Abihu, Eleazar and Ithamar.

24 The sons of Korah were Assir, Elkanah and Abiasaph. These were the Korahite clans.

25 Eleazar son of Aaron married one of the daughters of Putiel, and she bore him Phinehas.

These were the heads of the Levite families, clan by clan.

26 It was this same Aaron and Moses to whom the LORD said, "Bring the Israelites out of Egypt by their divisions." 27 They were the ones who spoke to Pharaoh king of Egypt about bringing the Israelites out of Egypt. It was the same Moses and Aaron.

28 Now when the LORD spoke to Moses in Egypt, 29 he said to him, "I am the LORD. Tell Pharaoh king of Egypt everything I tell you."

30 But Moses said to the LORD, "Since I speak with faltering lips, why would Pharaoh listen to me?"

7 Then the LORD said to Moses, "See, I have made you like God to Pharaoh, and your brother Aaron will be your prophet. 2 You are to say everything I command you, and your brother Aaron is to tell Pharaoh to let the Israelites go out of his country. 3 But I will harden Pharaoh's heart, and though I multiply my miraculous signs and wonders in Egypt, 4 he will not listen to you. Then I will lay my hand on Egypt and with mighty acts of judgment I will bring out my divisions, my people the Israelites. 5 And the Egyptians will know that I am the LORD when I stretch out my hand against Egypt and bring the Israelites out of it."

6 Moses and Aaron did just as the LORD commanded them. 7 Moses was eighty years old and Aaron eighty-three when they spoke to Pharaoh.

[n] 12 Hebrew *I am uncircumcised of lips*; also in verse 30 [o] 14 The Hebrew for *families* here and in verse 25 refers to units larger than clans.

Discovering the Word 1. What were the major outcomes of the first encounter between Moses and Aaron and Pharaoh (Ex 5)? 2. Describe Moses' feelings and the logic of his cry to God (5:22–23). 3. The statement "I am the LORD" is repeated four times in 6:1–8. What does God emphasize about himself in response to Moses' complaint (6:1–5)? 4. What does the Lord's message to Israel emphasize about his plans for them (6:6–8)? 5. Moses is concerned that Pharaoh won't listen to him (6:30). Yet how will Pharaoh's stubbornness help to fulfill God's plans for Egypt (7:3–5)? 6. In spite of defeat and discouragement (5:2; 6:9, 12, 30), Moses "did just as the LORD commanded" (7:6). What do you think brought him to this decisive obedience?

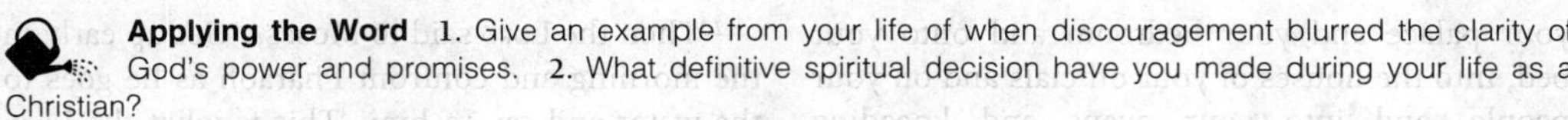

Applying the Word 1. Give an example from your life of when discouragement blurred the clarity of God's power and promises. 2. What definitive spiritual decision have you made during your life as a Christian?

Responding in Prayer Thank God for the people and circumstances he used to influence your walk with Christ.

5 / *Exodus 7:8—10:29*

God's Power on the Line

GOD'S AUTHORITY IS on the line any time a world leader like Pharaoh decides to take charge. It's also on the line when his children decide to play the game their own way. We have the benefit of looking at a historical book like Exodus to tell us the futility of resisting God. But somehow we find ourselves engaged in a recurring battle in our lives, not too dissimilar to Pharaoh's. Pharaoh opposed God, with devastating consequences. God will also challenge your right to do as you please. This lesson shows that it's futile to resist.

Warming Up to God When do you feel that the world is spinning out of control? What do you need from God in those times?

Read Exodus 7:8—10:29.

8The LORD said to Moses and Aaron, 9"When Pharaoh says to you, 'Perform a miracle,' then say to Aaron, 'Take your staff and throw it down before Pharaoh,' and it will become a snake."

10So Moses and Aaron went to Pharaoh and did just as the LORD commanded. Aaron threw his staff down in front of Pharaoh and his officials, and it became a snake. 11Pharaoh then summoned wise men and sorcerers, and the Egyptian magicians also did the same things by their secret arts: 12Each one threw down his staff and it became a snake. But Aaron's staff swallowed up their staffs. 13Yet Pharaoh's heart became hard and he would not listen to them, just as the LORD had said.

14Then the LORD said to Moses, "Pharaoh's heart is unyielding; he refuses to let the people go. 15Go to Pharaoh in the morning as he goes out to the water. Wait on the bank of the Nile to meet him, and take in your hand the staff that was changed into a snake. 16Then say to him, 'The LORD, the God of the Hebrews, has sent me to say to you: Let my people go, so that they may worship me in the desert. But until now you have not listened. 17This is what the LORD says: By this you will know that I am the LORD: With the staff that is in my hand I will strike the water of the Nile, and it will be changed into blood. 18The fish in the Nile will die, and the river will stink; the Egyptians will not be able to drink its water.' "

19The LORD said to Moses, "Tell Aaron, 'Take your staff and stretch out your hand over the waters of Egypt—over the streams and canals, over the ponds and all the reservoirs'—and they will turn to blood. Blood will be everywhere in Egypt, even in the wooden buckets and stone jars."

20Moses and Aaron did just as the LORD had commanded. He raised his staff in the presence of Pharaoh and his officials and struck the water of the Nile, and all the water was changed into blood. 21The fish in the Nile died, and the river smelled so bad that the Egyptians could not drink its water. Blood was everywhere in Egypt.

22But the Egyptian magicians did the same things by their secret arts, and Pharaoh's heart became hard; he would not listen to Moses and Aaron, just as the LORD had said. 23Instead, he turned and went into his palace, and did not take even this to heart. 24And all the Egyptians dug along the Nile to get drinking water, because they could not drink the water of the river.

25Seven days passed after the LORD struck the Nile.

8 1Then the LORD said to Moses, "Go to Pharaoh and say to him, 'This is what the LORD says: Let my people go, so that they may worship me. 2If you refuse to let them go, I will plague your whole country with frogs. 3The Nile will teem with frogs. They will come up into

your palace and your bedroom and onto your bed, into the houses of your officials and on your people, and into your ovens and kneading troughs. 4The frogs will go up on you and your people and all your officials.' "

5Then the LORD said to Moses, "Tell Aaron, 'Stretch out your hand with your staff over the streams and canals and ponds, and make frogs come up on the land of Egypt.' "

6So Aaron stretched out his hand over the waters of Egypt, and the frogs came up and covered the land. 7But the magicians did the same things by their secret arts; they also made frogs come up on the land of Egypt.

8Pharaoh summoned Moses and Aaron and said, "Pray to the LORD to take the frogs away from me and my people, and I will let your people go to offer sacrifices to the LORD."

9Moses said to Pharaoh, "I leave to you the honor of setting the time for me to pray for you and your officials and your people that you and your houses may be rid of the frogs, except for those that remain in the Nile."

10"Tomorrow," Pharaoh said.

Moses replied, "It will be as you say, so that you may know there is no one like the LORD our God. 11The frogs will leave you and your houses, your officials and your people; they will remain only in the Nile."

12After Moses and Aaron left Pharaoh, Moses cried out to the LORD about the frogs he had brought on Pharaoh. 13And the LORD did what Moses asked. The frogs died in the houses, in the courtyards and in the fields. 14They were piled into heaps, and the land reeked of them. 15But when Pharaoh saw that there was relief, he hardened his heart and would not listen to Moses and Aaron, just as the LORD had said.

16Then the LORD said to Moses, "Tell Aaron, 'Stretch out your staff and strike the dust of the ground,' and throughout the land of Egypt the dust will become gnats." 17They did this, and when Aaron stretched out his hand with the staff and struck the dust of the ground, gnats came upon men and animals. All the dust throughout the land of Egypt became gnats. 18But when the magicians tried to produce gnats by their secret arts, they could not. And the gnats were on men and animals.

19The magicians said to Pharaoh, "This is the finger of God." But Pharaoh's heart was hard and he would not listen, just as the LORD had said.

20Then the LORD said to Moses, "Get up early in the morning and confront Pharaoh as he goes to the water and say to him, 'This is what the LORD says: Let my people go, so that they may worship me. 21If you do not let my people go, I will send swarms of flies on you and your officials, on your people and into your houses. The houses of the Egyptians will be full of flies, and even the ground where they are.

22" 'But on that day I will deal differently with the land of Goshen, where my people live; no swarms of flies will be there, so that you will know that I, the LORD, am in this land. 23I will make a distinction[p] between my people and your people. This miraculous sign will occur tomorrow.' "

24And the LORD did this. Dense swarms of flies poured into Pharaoh's palace and into the houses of his officials, and throughout Egypt the land was ruined by the flies.

25Then Pharaoh summoned Moses and Aaron and said, "Go, sacrifice to your God here in the land."

26But Moses said, "That would not be right. The sacrifices we offer the LORD our God would be detestable to the Egyptians. And if we offer sacrifices that are detestable in their eyes, will they not stone us? 27We must take a three-day journey into the desert to offer sacrifices to the LORD our God, as he commands us."

28Pharaoh said, "I will let you go to offer sacrifices to the LORD your God in the desert, but you must not go very far. Now pray for me."

29Moses answered, "As soon as I leave you, I will pray to the LORD, and tomorrow the flies will leave Pharaoh and his officials and his people. Only be sure that Pharaoh does not act deceitfully again by not letting the people go to offer sacrifices to the LORD."

30Then Moses left Pharaoh and prayed to the LORD, 31and the LORD did what Moses asked: The flies left Pharaoh and his officials and his people; not a fly remained. 32But this time also Pharaoh hardened his heart and would not let the people go.

9 Then the LORD said to Moses, "Go to Pharaoh and say to him, 'This is what the LORD, the God of the Hebrews, says: "Let my people go, so that they may worship me." 2If you refuse to let them go and continue to hold

p23 Septuagint and Vulgate; Hebrew *will put a deliverance*

them back, 3the hand of the LORD will bring a terrible plague on your livestock in the field—on your horses and donkeys and camels and on your cattle and sheep and goats. 4But the LORD will make a distinction between the livestock of Israel and that of Egypt, so that no animal belonging to the Israelites will die.' "

5The LORD set a time and said, "Tomorrow the LORD will do this in the land." 6And the next day the LORD did it: All the livestock of the Egyptians died, but not one animal belonging to the Israelites died. 7Pharaoh sent men to investigate and found that not even one of the animals of the Israelites had died. Yet his heart was unyielding and he would not let the people go.

8Then the LORD said to Moses and Aaron, "Take handfuls of soot from a furnace and have Moses toss it into the air in the presence of Pharaoh. 9It will become fine dust over the whole land of Egypt, and festering boils will break out on men and animals throughout the land."

10So they took soot from a furnace and stood before Pharaoh. Moses tossed it into the air, and festering boils broke out on men and animals. 11The magicians could not stand before Moses because of the boils that were on them and on all the Egyptians. 12But the LORD hardened Pharaoh's heart and he would not listen to Moses and Aaron, just as the LORD had said to Moses.

13Then the LORD said to Moses, "Get up early in the morning, confront Pharaoh and say to him, 'This is what the LORD, the God of the Hebrews, says: Let my people go, so that they may worship me, 14or this time I will send the full force of my plagues against you and against your officials and your people, so you may know that there is no one like me in all the earth. 15For by now I could have stretched out my hand and struck you and your people with a plague that would have wiped you off the earth. 16But I have raised you up[q] for this very purpose, that I might show you my power and that my name might be proclaimed in all the earth. 17You still set yourself against my people and will not let them go. 18Therefore, at this time tomorrow I will send the worst hailstorm that has ever fallen on Egypt, from the day it was founded till now. 19Give an order now to bring your livestock and everything you have in the field to a place of shelter, because the hail will fall on every man and animal that has not been brought in and is still out in the field, and they will die.' "

20Those officials of Pharaoh who feared the word of the LORD hurried to bring their slaves and their livestock inside. 21But those who ignored the word of the LORD left their slaves and livestock in the field.

22Then the LORD said to Moses, "Stretch out your hand toward the sky so that hail will fall all over Egypt—on men and animals and on everything growing in the fields of Egypt." 23When Moses stretched out his staff toward the sky, the LORD sent thunder and hail, and lightning flashed down to the ground. So the LORD rained hail on the land of Egypt; 24hail fell and lightning flashed back and forth. It was the worst storm in all the land of Egypt since it had become a nation. 25Throughout Egypt hail struck everything in the fields—both men and animals; it beat down everything growing in the fields and stripped every tree. 26The only place it did not hail was the land of Goshen, where the Israelites were.

27Then Pharaoh summoned Moses and Aaron. "This time I have sinned," he said to them. "The LORD is in the right, and I and my people are in the wrong. 28Pray to the LORD, for we have had enough thunder and hail. I will let you go; you don't have to stay any longer."

29Moses replied, "When I have gone out of the city, I will spread out my hands in prayer to the LORD. The thunder will stop and there will be no more hail, so you may know that the earth is the LORD's. 30But I know that you and your officials still do not fear the LORD God."

31(The flax and barley were destroyed, since the barley had headed and the flax was in bloom. 32The wheat and spelt, however, were not destroyed, because they ripen later.)

33Then Moses left Pharaoh and went out of the city. He spread out his hands toward the LORD; the thunder and hail stopped, and the rain no longer poured down on the land. 34When Pharaoh saw that the rain and hail and thunder had stopped, he sinned again: He and his officials hardened their hearts. 35So Pharaoh's heart was hard and he would not let the Israelites go, just as the LORD had said through Moses.

10 Then the LORD said to Moses, "Go to Pharaoh, for I have hardened his heart and the hearts of his officials so that I may perform these miraculous signs of mine among them 2that you may tell your chil-

q16 Or *have spared you*

dren and grandchildren how I dealt harshly with the Egyptians and how I performed my signs among them, and that you may know that I am the LORD."

[3]So Moses and Aaron went to Pharaoh and said to him, "This is what the LORD, the God of the Hebrews, says: 'How long will you refuse to humble yourself before me? Let my people go, so that they may worship me. [4]If you refuse to let them go, I will bring locusts into your country tomorrow. [5]They will cover the face of the ground so that it cannot be seen. They will devour what little you have left after the hail, including every tree that is growing in your fields. [6]They will fill your houses and those of all your officials and all the Egyptians—something neither your fathers nor your forefathers have ever seen from the day they settled in this land till now.'" Then Moses turned and left Pharaoh.

[7]Pharaoh's officials said to him, "How long will this man be a snare to us? Let the people go, so that they may worship the LORD their God. Do you not yet realize that Egypt is ruined?"

[8]Then Moses and Aaron were brought back to Pharaoh. "Go, worship the LORD your God," he said. "But just who will be going?"

[9]Moses answered, "We will go with our young and old, with our sons and daughters, and with our flocks and herds, because we are to celebrate a festival to the LORD."

[10]Pharaoh said, "The LORD be with you—if I let you go, along with your women and children! Clearly you are bent on evil.[r] [11]No! Have only the men go; and worship the LORD, since that's what you have been asking for." Then Moses and Aaron were driven out of Pharaoh's presence.

[12]And the LORD said to Moses, "Stretch out your hand over Egypt so that locusts will swarm over the land and devour everything growing in the fields, everything left by the hail."

[13]So Moses stretched out his staff over Egypt, and the LORD made an east wind blow across the land all that day and all that night. By morning the wind had brought the locusts; [14]they invaded all Egypt and settled down in every area of the country in great numbers. Never before had there been such a plague of locusts, nor will there ever be again. [15]They covered all the ground until it was black. They devoured all that was left after the hail—everything growing in the fields and the fruit on the trees. Nothing green remained on tree or plant in all the land of Egypt.

[16]Pharaoh quickly summoned Moses and Aaron and said, "I have sinned against the LORD your God and against you. [17]Now forgive my sin once more and pray to the LORD your God to take this deadly plague away from me."

[18]Moses then left Pharaoh and prayed to the LORD. [19]And the LORD changed the wind to a very strong west wind, which caught up the locusts and carried them into the Red Sea.[s] Not a locust was left anywhere in Egypt. [20]But the LORD hardened Pharaoh's heart, and he would not let the Israelites go.

[21]Then the LORD said to Moses, "Stretch out your hand toward the sky so that darkness will spread over Egypt—darkness that can be felt." [22]So Moses stretched out his hand toward the sky, and total darkness covered all Egypt for three days. [23]No one could see anyone else or leave his place for three days. Yet all the Israelites had light in the places where they lived.

[24]Then Pharaoh summoned Moses and said, "Go, worship the LORD. Even your women and children may go with you; only leave your flocks and herds behind."

[25]But Moses said, "You must allow us to have sacrifices and burnt offerings to present to the LORD our God. [26]Our livestock too must go with us; not a hoof is to be left behind. We have to use some of them in worshiping the LORD our God, and until we get there we will not know what we are to use to worship the LORD."

[27]But the LORD hardened Pharaoh's heart, and he was not willing to let them go. [28]Pharaoh said to Moses, "Get out of my sight! Make sure you do not appear before me again! The day you see my face you will die."

[29]"Just as you say," Moses replied, "I will never appear before you again."

[r]10 Or *Be careful, trouble is in store for you!* [s]19 Hebrew *Yam Suph*; that is, Sea of Reeds

Discovering the Word 1. What was the sign of God's supremacy (7:8–13)? 2. How did Pharaoh react to these "mighty acts of judgment," as God called them (7:4; 8:8, 25–32)? 3. What was the basic issue between God and Pharaoh (7:5, 17; 8:10, 22)? 4. What new disclosure does God make to Pharaoh about his power (8:22–23)? 5. Some of the Egyptians responded positively to this outbreak of judgments (9:20). How do people interpret natural disasters today? **6.** What pattern of behavior has by this time become well established in Pharaoh (8:15, 30–32; 9:34–35)?

Applying the Word 1. In what matters is God in conflict with earthly powers today? 2. When you are humbled by God, how can you regain your self-confidence and your trust in God?

Responding in Prayer Give thanks to your loving, gracious Father, who "has raised you up for this very purpose"—to demonstrate his power and proclaim his name in all the earth.

6 / *Exodus 11:1—12:28*

Night of Death and Deliverance

DEATH IS A powerful, painful lesson. It gets our attention as nothing else does. It's also unavoidable. It was God's final recourse in showing both his supremacy to Pharaoh and his power to liberate his people. When Pharaoh refused God's ultimatum, thousands perished; when Israel heeded his way of deliverance, thousands lived. The final act of judgment is thus a stark portrayal of how every person's fate hinges on either believing or disbelieving the one true and living God in heaven.

Warming Up to God Sit quietly for a few moments and recall the events of your salvation. Thank the Lord for the way he "drew you out of Egypt."

Read Exodus 11:1—12:28.

11 Now the LORD had said to Moses, "I will bring one more plague on Pharaoh and on Egypt. After that, he will let you go from here, and when he does, he will drive you out completely. 2Tell the people that men and women alike are to ask their neighbors for articles of silver and gold." 3(The LORD made the Egyptians favorably disposed toward the people, and Moses himself was highly regarded in Egypt by Pharaoh's officials and by the people.)

4So Moses said, "This is what the LORD says: 'About midnight I will go throughout Egypt. 5Every firstborn son in Egypt will die, from the firstborn son of Pharaoh, who sits on the throne, to the firstborn son of the slave girl, who is at her hand mill, and all the firstborn of the cattle as well. 6There will be loud wailing throughout Egypt—worse than there has ever been or ever will be again. 7But among the Israelites not a dog will bark at any man or animal.' Then you will know that the LORD makes a distinction between Egypt and Israel. 8All these officials of yours will come to me, bowing down before me and saying, 'Go, you and all the people who follow you!' After that I will leave." Then Moses, hot with anger, left Pharaoh.

9The LORD had said to Moses, "Pharaoh will refuse to listen to you—so that my wonders may be multiplied in Egypt." 10Moses and Aaron performed all these wonders before Pharaoh, but the LORD hardened Pharaoh's heart, and he would not let the Israelites go out of his country.

12 The LORD said to Moses and Aaron in Egypt, 2"This month is to be for you the first month, the first month of your year. 3Tell the whole community of Israel that on the tenth day of this month each man is to take a lamb[t] for his family, one for each household. 4If any household is too small for a whole lamb, they must share one with their nearest neighbor, having taken into account the number of people there are. You are to determine the amount of lamb needed in accordance with what each person will eat. 5The animals you choose must be year-old males without defect, and you may take them from the sheep or the goats. 6Take care of them until the fourteenth day of the month, when all the people of the community of Israel must slaughter them at twilight. 7Then they are to take some of the blood and put it on the sides and tops of the doorframes of the houses where they eat the lambs. 8That same night they

t3 The Hebrew word can mean *lamb* or *kid*; also in verse 4.

are to eat the meat roasted over the fire, along
with bitter herbs, and bread made without yeast.
9Do not eat the meat raw or cooked in water, but
roast it over the fire—head, legs and inner parts.
10Do not leave any of it till morning; if some is
left till morning, you must burn it. 11This is how
you are to eat it: with your cloak tucked into your
belt, your sandals on your feet and your staff in
your hand. Eat it in haste; it is the LORD's Pass-
over.

12"On that same night I will pass through
Egypt and strike down every firstborn—both
men and animals—and I will bring judgment on
all the gods of Egypt. I am the LORD. 13The blood
will be a sign for you on the houses where you
are; and when I see the blood, I will pass over
you. No destructive plague will touch you when I
strike Egypt.

14"This is a day you are to commemorate; for
the generations to come you shall celebrate it as a
festival to the LORD—a lasting ordinance. 15For
seven days you are to eat bread made without
yeast. On the first day remove the yeast from your
houses, for whoever eats anything with yeast in it
from the first day through the seventh must be
cut off from Israel. 16On the first day hold a sa-
cred assembly, and another one on the seventh
day. Do no work at all on these days, except to
prepare food for everyone to eat—that is all you
may do.

17"Celebrate the Feast of Unleavened Bread, be-
cause it was on this very day that I brought your
divisions out of Egypt. Celebrate this day as a
lasting ordinance for the generations to come.
18In the first month you are to eat bread made
without yeast, from the evening of the fourteenth
day until the evening of the twenty-first day.
19For seven days no yeast is to be found in your
houses. And whoever eats anything with yeast in
it must be cut off from the community of Israel,
whether he is an alien or native-born. 20Eat noth-
ing made with yeast. Wherever you live, you
must eat unleavened bread."

21Then Moses summoned all the elders of Israel
and said to them, "Go at once and select the ani-
mals for your families and slaughter the Passover
lamb. 22Take a bunch of hyssop, dip it into the
blood in the basin and put some of the blood on
the top and on both sides of the doorframe. Not
one of you shall go out the door of his house until
morning. 23When the LORD goes through the land
to strike down the Egyptians, he will see the
blood on the top and sides of the doorframe and
will pass over that doorway, and he will not per-
mit the destroyer to enter your houses and strike
you down.

24"Obey these instructions as a lasting ordi-
nance for you and your descendants. 25When you
enter the land that the LORD will give you as he
promised, observe this ceremony. 26And when
your children ask you, 'What does this ceremony
mean to you?' 27then tell them, 'It is the Passover
sacrifice to the LORD, who passed over the houses
of the Israelites in Egypt and spared our homes
when he struck down the Egyptians.'" Then the
people bowed down and worshiped. 28The Israel-
ites did just what the LORD commanded Moses
and Aaron.

Discovering the Word 1. What is God's promise and instruction to Moses (11:1–2)? 2. How do you account for the Egyptians' change in attitude toward God's people and Moses (11:3)? 3. What is to be the nature, scope and result of God's final judgment on Egypt (11:4–7)? 4. What steps are the Israelites to take to be spared (12:1–13)? 5. Why were they to eat the meal "in haste" (12:11)? 6. Describe the memorial Feast of Unleavened Bread (12:14–20).

Applying the Word 1. Like Moses, how can we continue to trust God in the face of seemingly irresistible unbelief among friends, family or relatives? 2. The shield against the "destroyer" (12:23) in Egypt was the blood of a perfect lamb. Christ's blood secures the Christian's deliverance from eternal death (Jn 1:29; Heb 9:14; Rev 5:13). As you reflect on the powerful imagery of the Lord's Passover, and also on Christ's sacrifice, what response and deeds would be appropriate?

Responding in Prayer Thank Jesus for being your Passover lamb and for the remarkable foreshadowing of his coming to earth in the Israelites' exodus from Egypt.

7 / Exodus 12:29—13:16
Freedom and Its Cost

FREEDOM HAS A high price. For some political refugees today it means a perilous sea journey along the coast of Southeast Asia. For others, a dangerous trek over Central American mountains. In Europe it often costs job and even family. In this study we find what Israel's freedom cost—for both the losers and the winners. God secured the liberation of his people, but this in turn cost them the rights to their most precious possessions.

Warming Up to God What does it mean to be "free in Christ"?

Read Exodus 12:29—13:16.

29At midnight the LORD struck down all the
firstborn in Egypt, from the firstborn of Pharaoh,
who sat on the throne, to the firstborn of the
prisoner, who was in the dungeon, and the first-
born of all the livestock as well. 30Pharaoh and all
his officials and all the Egyptians got up during
the night, and there was loud wailing in Egypt,
for there was not a house without someone dead.
31During the night Pharaoh summoned Moses
and Aaron and said, "Up! Leave my people, you
and the Israelites! Go, worship the LORD as you
have requested. 32Take your flocks and herds, as
you have said, and go. And also bless me."
33The Egyptians urged the people to hurry and
leave the country. "For otherwise," they said, "we
will all die!" 34So the people took their dough
before the yeast was added, and carried it on their
shoulders in kneading troughs wrapped in cloth-
ing. 35The Israelites did as Moses instructed and
asked the Egyptians for articles of silver and gold
and for clothing. 36The LORD had made the Egyp-
tians favorably disposed toward the people, and
they gave them what they asked for; so they plun-
dered the Egyptians.
37The Israelites journeyed from Rameses to
Succoth. There were about six hundred thousand
men on foot, besides women and children.
38Many other people went up with them, as well
as large droves of livestock, both flocks and
herds. 39With the dough they had brought from
Egypt, they baked cakes of unleavened bread. The
dough was without yeast because they had been
driven out of Egypt and did not have time to
prepare food for themselves.
40Now the length of time the Israelite people
lived in Egypt[u] was 430 years. 41At the end of the
430 years, to the very day, all the LORD's divisions
left Egypt. 42Because the LORD kept vigil that night
to bring them out of Egypt, on this night all the
Israelites are to keep vigil to honor the LORD for
the generations to come.
43The LORD said to Moses and Aaron, "These
are the regulations for the Passover:
"No foreigner is to eat of it. 44Any slave you
have bought may eat of it after you have circum-
cised him, 45but a temporary resident and a hired
worker may not eat of it.
46"It must be eaten inside one house; take none
of the meat outside the house. Do not break any
of the bones. 47The whole community of Israel
must celebrate it.
48"An alien living among you who wants to cel-
ebrate the LORD's Passover must have all the males
in his household circumcised; then he may take
part like one born in the land. No uncircumcised
male may eat of it. 49The same law applies to the
native-born and to the alien living among you."
50All the Israelites did just what the LORD had
commanded Moses and Aaron. 51And on that very
day the LORD brought the Israelites out of Egypt
by their divisions.

13 The LORD said to Moses, 2"Conse-
crate to me every firstborn male.
The first offspring of every womb
among the Israelites belongs to me, whether man
or animal."
3Then Moses said to the people, "Commemo-
rate this day, the day you came out of Egypt, out
of the land of slavery, because the LORD brought
you out of it with a mighty hand. Eat nothing
containing yeast. 4Today, in the month of Abib,
you are leaving. 5When the LORD brings you into
the land of the Canaanites, Hittites, Amorites, Hi-
vites and Jebusites—the land he swore to your

u40 Masoretic Text; Samaritan Pentateuch and Septuagint *Egypt and Canaan*

forefathers to give you, a land flowing with milk and honey—you are to observe this ceremony in this month: 6For seven days eat bread made without yeast and on the seventh day hold a festival to the LORD. 7Eat unleavened bread during those seven days; nothing with yeast in it is to be seen among you, nor shall any yeast be seen anywhere within your borders. 8On that day tell your son, 'I do this because of what the LORD did for me when I came out of Egypt.' 9This observance will be for you like a sign on your hand and a reminder on your forehead that the law of the LORD is to be on your lips. For the LORD brought you out of Egypt with his mighty hand. 10You must keep this ordinance at the appointed time year after year.

11"After the LORD brings you into the land of the Canaanites and gives it to you, as he promised on oath to you and your forefathers, 12you are to give over to the LORD the first offspring of every womb. All the firstborn males of your livestock belong to the LORD. 13Redeem with a lamb every firstborn donkey, but if you do not redeem it, break its neck. Redeem every firstborn among your sons.

14"In days to come, when your son asks you, 'What does this mean?' say to him, 'With a mighty hand the LORD brought us out of Egypt, out of the land of slavery. 15When Pharaoh stubbornly refused to let us go, the LORD killed every firstborn in Egypt, both man and animal. This is why I sacrifice to the LORD the first male offspring of every womb and redeem each of my firstborn sons.' 16And it will be like a sign on your hand and a symbol on your forehead that the LORD brought us out of Egypt with his mighty hand."

Discovering the Word 1. What contrasts do you observe between Pharaoh's attitude and behavior now and his earlier encounters with Moses and Aaron (12:29–32)? 2. God fulfilled his warnings and promises (see 3:20–22; 4:23). What significance would this have for Israel's understanding of God's nature and character? 3. How would the Passover restrictions (12:43–49) encourage foreigners and others to worship God and, at the same time, preserve Israel from religious compromise and contamination? 4. God calls Israel to dedicate to him that which he has just delivered—the whole nation, not just the firstborn of man and beast. What plan does God have for perpetuating this ordinance (13:8–10, 14–15)? 5. What was the basis of God's authority to claim the firstborn as his own?

Applying the Word 1. How can we guard the essential elements of our faith in Jesus Christ and, at the same time, extend his offer of salvation to all people? 2. How do you maintain fresh impressions of your own deliverance from the guilt and enslavement of sin?

Responding in Prayer Ask the Lord to show you how to balance freedom in him with the responsibilities of service.

8 / *Exodus 13:17—14:31*

From Crisis to Triumph

IMPOSSIBLE JAMS CONVERGE on us at the most unlikely moments. One minute we're cruising down the freeway at 60 mph, and the next instant we slam on the brakes. For the next two hours we're stuck. Wouldn't it be wonderful if we could wave a magic wand and unclog the whole mess? Life is like that. God leads us in and out of jams to test our mettle. In this study, Israel's moment of glorious freedom was shattered by an advancing army. Seemingly, disaster loomed. But God had some things to prove to Egypt, Israel and Moses. Painful lessons indeed.

Warming Up to God Think of a miracle you've experienced. Respond from your heart to the God who loves to surprise you with his tremendous power and creativity.

Read Exodus 13:17—14:31.

17When Pharaoh let the people go, God did not lead them on the road through the Philistine country, though that was shorter. For God said, "If they face war, they might change their minds and return to Egypt." 18So God led the people around by the desert road toward the Red Sea.[v] The Israelites went up out of Egypt armed for battle.

19Moses took the bones of Joseph with him because Joseph had made the sons of Israel swear an oath. He had said, "God will surely come to your aid, and then you must carry my bones up with you from this place."[w]

20After leaving Succoth they camped at Etham on the edge of the desert. 21By day the LORD went ahead of them in a pillar of cloud to guide them on their way and by night in a pillar of fire to give them light, so that they could travel by day or night. 22Neither the pillar of cloud by day nor the pillar of fire by night left its place in front of the people.

14 Then the LORD said to Moses, 2"Tell the Israelites to turn back and encamp near Pi Hahiroth, between Migdol and the sea. They are to encamp by the sea, directly opposite Baal Zephon. 3Pharaoh will think, 'The Israelites are wandering around the land in confusion, hemmed in by the desert.' 4And I will harden Pharaoh's heart, and he will pursue them. But I will gain glory for myself through Pharaoh and all his army, and the Egyptians will know that I am the LORD." So the Israelites did this.

5When the king of Egypt was told that the people had fled, Pharaoh and his officials changed their minds about them and said, "What have we done? We have let the Israelites go and have lost their services!" 6So he had his chariot made ready and took his army with him. 7He took six hundred of the best chariots, along with all the other chariots of Egypt, with officers over all of them. 8The LORD hardened the heart of Pharaoh king of Egypt, so that he pursued the Israelites, who were marching out boldly. 9The Egyptians—all Pharaoh's horses and chariots, horsemen[x] and troops—pursued the Israelites and overtook them as they camped by the sea near Pi Hahiroth, opposite Baal Zephon.

10As Pharaoh approached, the Israelites looked up, and there were the Egyptians, marching after them. They were terrified and cried out to the LORD. 11They said to Moses, "Was it because there were no graves in Egypt that you brought us to the desert to die? What have you done to us by bringing us out of Egypt? 12Didn't we say to you in Egypt, 'Leave us alone; let us serve the Egyptians'? It would have been better for us to serve the Egyptians than to die in the desert!"

13Moses answered the people, "Do not be afraid. Stand firm and you will see the deliverance the LORD will bring you today. The Egyptians you see today you will never see again. 14The LORD will fight for you; you need only to be still."

15Then the LORD said to Moses, "Why are you crying out to me? Tell the Israelites to move on. 16Raise your staff and stretch out your hand over the sea to divide the water so that the Israelites can go through the sea on dry ground. 17I will harden the hearts of the Egyptians so that they will go in after them. And I will gain glory through Pharaoh and all his army, through his chariots and his horsemen. 18The Egyptians will know that I am the LORD when I gain glory through Pharaoh, his chariots and his horsemen."

19Then the angel of God, who had been traveling in front of Israel's army, withdrew and went behind them. The pillar of cloud also moved from in front and stood behind them, 20coming between the armies of Egypt and Israel. Throughout the night the cloud brought darkness to the one side and light to the other side; so neither went near the other all night long.

21Then Moses stretched out his hand over the sea, and all that night the LORD drove the sea back with a strong east wind and turned it into dry land. The waters were divided, 22and the Israelites went through the sea on dry ground, with a wall of water on their right and on their left.

23The Egyptians pursued them, and all Pharaoh's horses and chariots and horsemen followed them into the sea. 24During the last watch of the night the LORD looked down from the pillar of fire and cloud at the Egyptian army and threw it into confusion. 25He made the wheels of their chariots come off[y] so that they had difficulty driving. And the Egyptians said, "Let's get away from the Israelites! The LORD is fighting for them against Egypt."

26Then the LORD said to Moses, "Stretch out your hand over the sea so that the waters may flow back over the Egyptians and their chariots

[v] *18* Hebrew *Yam Suph*; that is, Sea of Reeds [w] *19* See Gen. 50:25.
[x] *9* Or *charioteers*; also in verses 17, 18, 23, 26 and 28 [y] *25* Or *He jammed the wheels of their chariots* (see Samaritan Pentateuch, Septuagint and Syriac)

and horsemen." 27Moses stretched out his hand
over the sea, and at daybreak the sea went back to
its place. The Egyptians were fleeing toward[z] it,
and the LORD swept them into the sea. 28The water
flowed back and covered the chariots and horse-
men—the entire army of Pharaoh that had fol-
lowed the Israelites into the sea. Not one of them
survived.

29But the Israelites went through the sea on dry
ground, with a wall of water on their right and on
their left. 30That day the LORD saved Israel from
the hands of the Egyptians, and Israel saw the
Egyptians lying dead on the shore. 31And when
the Israelites saw the great power the LORD dis-
played against the Egyptians, the people feared
the LORD and put their trust in him and in Moses
his servant.

[z]27 Or *from*

Discovering the Word 1. Why did God not take Israel the shortest route to Palestine? 2. What plan does God reveal to Moses (14:1–4)? 3. How did the Israelites react to the onslaught of the Egyptians and why (14:10–12)? 4. Compare each part of Moses' commands (14:13–14) with the Israelites' conditions and attitudes (14:10–12). 5. What did God's plan for escape require of Moses and the people (14:15–18)? 6. What was the outcome of this hair-raising experience for the Egyptians, Moses and Israel (14:17–18, 30–31)?

Applying the Word 1. Faith operates both long-range (Joseph) and short-range (following the cloud pillar). What areas of your life require long-range or short-range trust in God? 2. Think about times when you have felt like Israel, trapped between the Egyptians and the Red Sea. What did you do and why?

Responding in Prayer Thank the Lord for the ways he has miraculously delivered you—either physically or spiritually—from "the Egyptians" in your life.

9 / *Exodus 15:1–21*
Praise for the Past and Hope for the Future

MUSIC PLAYS A vital role in Christian worship. Sometimes, however, music causes contention: the old favorites versus the new gospel tunes; organs versus guitars. Overlooked is the fact that God gave us music and singing to praise and glorify his name. Nowhere is this seen more clearly than in the thrilling song service that broke out on the eastern shore of the Red Sea. Moses the statesman, Moses the voice of God became Israel's song leader. Praise and honor to God marked the final triumph over Egypt. How much more do Christians need to sing to God for his victory in Christ.

Warming Up to God For what do you have reason to praise the Father? List the many ways God has blessed you.

Read Exodus 15:1–21.

15 Then Moses and the Israelites sang
this song to the LORD:
"I will sing to the LORD,
for he is highly exalted.
The horse and its rider
he has hurled into the sea.
2The LORD is my strength and my song;
he has become my salvation.
He is my God, and I will praise him,
my father's God, and I will exalt him.
3The LORD is a warrior;
the LORD is his name.
4Pharaoh's chariots and his army
he has hurled into the sea.
The best of Pharaoh's officers
are drowned in the Red Sea.[a]
5The deep waters have covered them;
they sank to the depths like a stone.
6"Your right hand, O LORD,

[a]4 Hebrew *Yam Suph*; that is, Sea of Reeds; also in verse 22

was majestic in power.
Your right hand, O LORD,
shattered the enemy.
7In the greatness of your majesty
you threw down those who opposed you.
You unleashed your burning anger;
it consumed them like stubble.
8By the blast of your nostrils
the waters piled up.
The surging waters stood firm like a wall;
the deep waters congealed in the heart of
the sea.

9"The enemy boasted,
'I will pursue, I will overtake them.
I will divide the spoils;
I will gorge myself on them.
I will draw my sword
and my hand will destroy them.'
10But you blew with your breath,
and the sea covered them.
They sank like lead
in the mighty waters.
11"Who among the gods is like you, O LORD?
Who is like you—
majestic in holiness,
awesome in glory,
working wonders?
12You stretched out your right hand
and the earth swallowed them.
13"In your unfailing love you will lead
the people you have redeemed.
In your strength you will guide them
to your holy dwelling.
14The nations will hear and tremble;
anguish will grip the people of Philistia.
15The chiefs of Edom will be terrified,
the leaders of Moab will be seized with
trembling,
the people[b] of Canaan will melt away;
16 terror and dread will fall upon them.
By the power of your arm
they will be as still as a stone—
until your people pass by, O LORD,
until the people you bought[c] pass by.
17You will bring them in and plant them
on the mountain of your inheritance—
the place, O LORD, you made for your
dwelling,
the sanctuary, O Lord, your hands
established.
18The LORD will reign
for ever and ever."

19When Pharaoh's horses, chariots and horse-
men[d] went into the sea, the LORD brought the
waters of the sea back over them, but the Israel-
ites walked through the sea on dry ground.
20Then Miriam the prophetess, Aaron's sister,
took a tambourine in her hand, and all the
women followed her, with tambourines and danc-
ing. 21Miriam sang to them:

"Sing to the LORD,
for he is highly exalted.
The horse and its rider
he has hurled into the sea."

[b]15 Or *rulers* [c]16 Or *created* [d]19 Or *charioteers*

Discovering the Word 1. What inspired this song of victory (v. 1)? 2. What conclusions about God do the people draw from the Red Sea victory (vv. 3–11)? 3. After rehearsing the past, the people look to the future. What enemies lie ahead (vv. 14–15)? 4. What will be the effect of the exodus on these nations (vv. 14–16)? 5. On what basis do the people exude confidence for their future (vv. 13–18)? 6. What role did Miriam and the other women play in the victory celebration and why (vv. 20–21)?

Applying the Word 1. Against what adversaries do you need to see a demonstration of God's power, majesty and holiness? 2. How does the knowledge of God's character and past faithfulness encourage you in anticipation of the future?

Responding in Prayer Pray aloud and tell God his characteristics and qualities.

10 / *Exodus 15:22—17:16*
Adversities of the Desert

ONE OF THE premier sports events in America is the Super Bowl, a football game played each January for the championship of the National Football League. Contending teams get two weeks to prepare. Players and coaches get the best of everything in order to win. Suppose the teams ran out of water and food. Suppose the players mutinied. If that happened, suppose you were the coach. Could you possibly concentrate on your game plans? Of course not. But that's what confronted Moses as he led team Israel. This study chronicles not only defection in the ranks but also attack from outside. Not a pretty picture, really, until we see how God intervened.

Warming Up to God What needs or longings do you have? Present them to God—and let his peace dwell in your heart and the knowledge that God promises to meet your needs.

Read Exodus 15:22—17:16.

22Then Moses led Israel from the Red Sea and
they went into the Desert of Shur. For three days
they traveled in the desert without finding water.
23When they came to Marah, they could not drink
its water because it was bitter. (That is why the
place is called Marah.[e]) 24So the people grum-
bled against Moses, saying, "What are we to
drink?"
25Then Moses cried out to the LORD, and the
LORD showed him a piece of wood. He threw it
into the water, and the water became sweet.

There the LORD made a decree and a law for
them, and there he tested them. 26He said, "If you
listen carefully to the voice of the LORD your God
and do what is right in his eyes, if you pay atten-
tion to his commands and keep all his decrees,
I will not bring on you any of the diseases I
brought on the Egyptians, for I am the LORD, who
heals you."
27Then they came to Elim, where there were
twelve springs and seventy palm trees, and they
camped there near the water.

16 The whole Israelite community set out from Elim and came to the Desert of Sin, which is between Elim and Sinai, on the fifteenth day of the second
month after they had come out of Egypt. 2In the
desert the whole community grumbled against
Moses and Aaron. 3The Israelites said to them, "If
only we had died by the LORD's hand in Egypt!
There we sat around pots of meat and ate all the
food we wanted, but you have brought us out
into this desert to starve this entire assembly to
death."
4Then the LORD said to Moses, "I will rain down
bread from heaven for you. The people are to go
out each day and gather enough for that day. In
this way I will test them and see whether they will
follow my instructions. 5On the sixth day they are
to prepare what they bring in, and that is to be
twice as much as they gather on the other days."
6So Moses and Aaron said to all the Israelites,
"In the evening you will know that it was the
LORD who brought you out of Egypt, 7and in the
morning you will see the glory of the LORD, be-
cause he has heard your grumbling against him.
Who are we, that you should grumble against
us?" 8Moses also said, "You will know that it was
the LORD when he gives you meat to eat in the
evening and all the bread you want in the morn-
ing, because he has heard your grumbling against
him. Who are we? You are not grumbling against
us, but against the LORD."
9Then Moses told Aaron, "Say to the entire Is-
raelite community, 'Come before the LORD, for he
has heard your grumbling.' "
10While Aaron was speaking to the whole Isra-
elite community, they looked toward the desert,
and there was the glory of the LORD appearing in
the cloud.
11The LORD said to Moses, 12"I have heard the
grumbling of the Israelites. Tell them, 'At twilight
you will eat meat, and in the morning you will be
filled with bread. Then you will know that I am
the LORD your God.' "
13That evening quail came and covered the
camp, and in the morning there was a layer of
dew around the camp. 14When the dew was gone,
thin flakes like frost on the ground appeared on
the desert floor. 15When the Israelites saw it, they

[e]23 *Marah* means *bitter.*

said to each other, "What is it?" For they did not know what it was.

Moses said to them, "It is the bread the LORD has given you to eat. 16This is what the LORD has commanded: 'Each one is to gather as much as he needs. Take an omer[f] for each person you have in your tent.' "

17The Israelites did as they were told; some gathered much, some little. 18And when they measured it by the omer, he who gathered much did not have too much, and he who gathered little did not have too little. Each one gathered as much as he needed.

19Then Moses said to them, "No one is to keep any of it until morning."

20However, some of them paid no attention to Moses; they kept part of it until morning, but it was full of maggots and began to smell. So Moses was angry with them.

21Each morning everyone gathered as much as he needed, and when the sun grew hot, it melted away. 22On the sixth day, they gathered twice as much—two omers[g] for each person—and the leaders of the community came and reported this to Moses. 23He said to them, "This is what the LORD commanded: 'Tomorrow is to be a day of rest, a holy Sabbath to the LORD. So bake what you want to bake and boil what you want to boil. Save whatever is left and keep it until morning.' "

24So they saved it until morning, as Moses commanded, and it did not stink or get maggots in it. 25"Eat it today," Moses said, "because today is a Sabbath to the LORD. You will not find any of it on the ground today. 26Six days you are to gather it, but on the seventh day, the Sabbath, there will not be any."

27Nevertheless, some of the people went out on the seventh day to gather it, but they found none. 28Then the LORD said to Moses, "How long will you[h] refuse to keep my commands and my instructions? 29Bear in mind that the LORD has given you the Sabbath; that is why on the sixth day he gives you bread for two days. Everyone is to stay where he is on the seventh day; no one is to go out." 30So the people rested on the seventh day.

31The people of Israel called the bread manna.[i] It was white like coriander seed and tasted like wafers made with honey. 32Moses said, "This is what the LORD has commanded: 'Take an omer of manna and keep it for the generations to come, so they can see the bread I gave you to eat in the desert when I brought you out of Egypt.' "

33So Moses said to Aaron, "Take a jar and put an omer of manna in it. Then place it before the LORD to be kept for the generations to come."

34As the LORD commanded Moses, Aaron put the manna in front of the Testimony, that it might be kept. 35The Israelites ate manna forty years, until they came to a land that was settled; they ate manna until they reached the border of Canaan.

36(An omer is one tenth of an ephah.)

17 The whole Israelite community set out from the Desert of Sin, traveling from place to place as the LORD commanded. They camped at Rephidim, but there was no water for the people to drink. 2So they quarreled with Moses and said, "Give us water to drink."

Moses replied, "Why do you quarrel with me? Why do you put the LORD to the test?"

3But the people were thirsty for water there, and they grumbled against Moses. They said, "Why did you bring us up out of Egypt to make us and our children and livestock die of thirst?"

4Then Moses cried out to the LORD, "What am I to do with these people? They are almost ready to stone me."

5The LORD answered Moses, "Walk on ahead of the people. Take with you some of the elders of Israel and take in your hand the staff with which you struck the Nile, and go. 6I will stand there before you by the rock at Horeb. Strike the rock, and water will come out of it for the people to drink." So Moses did this in the sight of the elders of Israel. 7And he called the place Massah[j] and Meribah[k] because the Israelites quarreled and because they tested the LORD saying, "Is the LORD among us or not?"

8The Amalekites came and attacked the Israelites at Rephidim. 9Moses said to Joshua, "Choose some of our men and go out to fight the Amalekites. Tomorrow I will stand on top of the hill with the staff of God in my hands."

10So Joshua fought the Amalekites as Moses had ordered, and Moses, Aaron and Hur went to the top of the hill. 11As long as Moses held up his hands, the Israelites were winning, but whenever he lowered his hands, the Amalekites were winning. 12When Moses' hands grew tired, they took a stone and put it under him and he sat on it. Aaron and Hur held his hands up—one on one

[f]16 That is, probably about 2 quarts (about 2 liters); also in verses 18, 32, 33 and 36 [g]22 That is, probably about 4 quarts (about 4.5 liters) [h]28 The Hebrew is plural. [i]31 *Manna* means *What is it?* (see verse 15). [j]7 *Massah* means *testing.* [k]7 *Meribah* means *quarreling.*

side, one on the other—so that his hands remained steady till sunset. 13So Joshua overcame the Amalekite army with the sword.

14Then the LORD said to Moses, "Write this on a scroll as something to be remembered and make sure that Joshua hears it, because I will completely blot out the memory of Amalek from under heaven."

15Moses built an altar and called it The LORD is my Banner. 16He said, "For hands were lifted up to the throne of the LORD. The[l] LORD will be at war against the Amalekites from generation to generation."

[l]16 Or *"Because a hand was against the throne of the* LORD, *the*

Discovering the Word 1. Put yourself in the shoes of an Israelite three days into the desert with no water. How would you feel? 2. Faced with starvation, the Israelites attacked Moses and Aaron (16:1–3). In what sense were they groaning against God (16:7–8)? 3. Why and how did God respond to Israel's complaints (16:9–15)? 4. In what ways did Israel violate God's commands and why (16:16–30)? 5. Israel's next hurdle is an enemy attack (17:8–16). What was God's plan for victory over the Amalekites? 6. Reflect on how Moses summarized the day. What did he do, what did he emphasize, and why (17:15–16)?

Applying the Word 1. When you have reached the end of the rope, what do you say to God and to those whom you think are to blame? Why? 2. Reflect on God's meeting your needs in emergencies. How might you be able to keep such events as a testimony to future generations?

Responding in Prayer What happens after the miracle? Ask God to help you be obedient even after he "parts the Red Sea."

11 / *Exodus 18*
Wise Counsel

IN-LAWS ARE THE favorite butt of jokes. Rarely are they portrayed in a positive light. But God places us in extended families to give us added wisdom and to shave off our rough edges. Jethro, Moses' father-in-law, brought Moses' wife and sons back to him. He also brought praise and worship to God. But he didn't stop there. This study shows how he made Moses face up to a weak link in his command. Jethro could be accused of meddling, but he was God's deliverer for Moses and Israel, just as much as Joshua and his soldiers were (17:8–16). Jethro forces us to examine our motives in doing Christian service.

Warming Up to God What burdens have you felt today as a result of your responsibilities? Tell God about them and let your anxiety slip away.

Read Exodus 18.

18 Now Jethro, the priest of Midian and father-in-law of Moses, heard of everything God had done for Moses and for his people Israel, and how the LORD had brought Israel out of Egypt.

2After Moses had sent away his wife Zipporah, his father-in-law Jethro received her 3and her two sons. One son was named Gershom,[m] for Moses said, "I have become an alien in a foreign land"; 4and the other was named Eliezer,[n] for he said, "My father's God was my helper; he saved me from the sword of Pharaoh."

5Jethro, Moses' father-in-law, together with Moses' sons and wife, came to him in the desert,

[m]3 *Gershom* sounds like the Hebrew for *an alien there.* [n]4 *Eliezer* means *my God is helper.*

where he was camped near the mountain of God. [6]Jethro had sent word to him, "I, your father-in-law Jethro, am coming to you with your wife and her two sons."

[7]So Moses went out to meet his father-in-law and bowed down and kissed him. They greeted each other and then went into the tent. [8]Moses told his father-in-law about everything the LORD had done to Pharaoh and the Egyptians for Israel's sake and about all the hardships they had met along the way and how the LORD had saved them.

[9]Jethro was delighted to hear about all the good things the LORD had done for Israel in rescuing them from the hand of the Egyptians. [10]He said, "Praise be to the LORD, who rescued you from the hand of the Egyptians and of Pharaoh, and who rescued the people from the hand of the Egyptians. [11]Now I know that the LORD is greater than all other gods, for he did this to those who had treated Israel arrogantly." [12]Then Jethro, Moses' father-in-law, brought a burnt offering and other sacrifices to God, and Aaron came with all the elders of Israel to eat bread with Moses' father-in-law in the presence of God.

[13]The next day Moses took his seat to serve as judge for the people, and they stood around him from morning till evening. [14]When his father-in-law saw all that Moses was doing for the people, he said, "What is this you are doing for the people? Why do you alone sit as judge, while all these people stand around you from morning till evening?"

[15]Moses answered him, "Because the people come to me to seek God's will. [16]Whenever they have a dispute, it is brought to me, and I decide between the parties and inform them of God's decrees and laws."

[17]Moses' father-in-law replied, "What you are doing is not good. [18]You and these people who come to you will only wear yourselves out. The work is too heavy for you; you cannot handle it alone. [19]Listen now to me and I will give you some advice, and may God be with you. You must be the people's representative before God and bring their disputes to him. [20]Teach them the decrees and laws, and show them the way to live and the duties they are to perform. [21]But select capable men from all the people—men who fear God, trustworthy men who hate dishonest gain—and appoint them as officials over thousands, hundreds, fifties and tens. [22]Have them serve as judges for the people at all times, but have them bring every difficult case to you; the simple cases they can decide themselves. That will make your load lighter, because they will share it with you. [23]If you do this and God so commands, you will be able to stand the strain, and all these people will go home satisfied."

[24]Moses listened to his father-in-law and did everything he said. [25]He chose capable men from all Israel and made them leaders of the people, officials over thousands, hundreds, fifties and tens. [26]They served as judges for the people at all times. The difficult cases they brought to Moses, but the simple ones they decided themselves.

[27]Then Moses sent his father-in-law on his way, and Jethro returned to his own country.

Discovering the Word 1. What facts do we learn about Jethro and Moses' family (vv. 1–4)? 2. What do the names of Moses' sons recall for him and his family (vv. 3–4)? 3. Why was worship the appropriate response to Moses' report (vv. 9–12)? 4. What did Jethro observe about Moses' daily routine and the toll this was taking on Moses and the people (vv. 13–18)? 5. How did Moses respond to Jethro's counsel (vv. 19–26)?

Applying the Word 1. What impressions do you have of Moses' ego at this time in his life? 2. Why could it have been easy to overlook God's hand at work in this family reunion, compared to his provision of water, food and victories over the Egyptians and the Amalekites? 3. If you are in a leadership position, think about planning to share the load. What will this do for you, for others and especially for younger leaders coming along?

Responding in Prayer Thank God for the people in your life who have given you wise counsel.

12 / *Exodus 19*
Preparing for God

DO YOU TUNE in or tune out when the pastor stands to read the Scripture? You've heard it before? Probably. How then can Christians who have heard the Bible so often recapture the expectancy of hearing it for the first time? A very practical problem indeed. When God spoke to his people the first time, a thunderstorm erupted. We can't expect that every Sunday, so perhaps we have to look within. How eager are we to hear God speak? To listen and obey? In this study we find not only thunder and lightning but a prepared, excited—even fearful—people. The New Testament reminds us that God is still a consuming fire.

Warming Up to God Spend some time quietly meditating on the nature of God. Prepare your heart to be met by the Lord today.

Read Exodus 19.

19 In the third month after the Israelites left Egypt—on the very day—they came to the Desert of Sinai. 2After they set out from Rephidim, they entered the Desert of Sinai, and Israel camped there in the desert in front of the mountain.

3Then Moses went up to God, and the LORD called to him from the mountain and said, "This is what you are to say to the house of Jacob and what you are to tell the people of Israel: 4'You yourselves have seen what I did to Egypt, and how I carried you on eagles' wings and brought you to myself. 5Now if you obey me fully and keep my covenant, then out of all nations you will be my treasured possession. Although the whole earth is mine, 6you[o] will be for me a kingdom of priests and a holy nation.' These are the words you are to speak to the Israelites."

7So Moses went back and summoned the elders of the people and set before them all the words the LORD had commanded him to speak. 8The people all responded together, "We will do everything the LORD has said." So Moses brought their answer back to the LORD.

9The LORD said to Moses, "I am going to come to you in a dense cloud, so that the people will hear me speaking with you and will always put their trust in you." Then Moses told the LORD what the people had said.

10And the LORD said to Moses, "Go to the people and consecrate them today and tomorrow. Have them wash their clothes 11and be ready by the third day, because on that day the LORD will come down on Mount Sinai in the sight of all the people. 12Put limits for the people around the mountain and tell them, 'Be careful that you do not go up the mountain or touch the foot of it. Whoever touches the mountain shall surely be put to death. 13He shall surely be stoned or shot with arrows; not a hand is to be laid on him. Whether man or animal, he shall not be permitted to live.' Only when the ram's horn sounds a long blast may they go up to the mountain."

14After Moses had gone down the mountain to the people, he consecrated them, and they washed their clothes. 15Then he said to the people, "Prepare yourselves for the third day. Abstain from sexual relations."

16On the morning of the third day there was thunder and lightning, with a thick cloud over the mountain, and a very loud trumpet blast. Everyone in the camp trembled. 17Then Moses led the people out of the camp to meet with God, and they stood at the foot of the mountain. 18Mount Sinai was covered with smoke, because the LORD descended on it in fire. The smoke billowed up from it like smoke from a furnace, the whole mountain[p] trembled violently, 19and the sound of the trumpet grew louder and louder. Then Moses spoke and the voice of God answered him.[q]

20The LORD descended to the top of Mount Sinai and called Moses to the top of the mountain. So Moses went up 21and the LORD said to him, "Go down and warn the people so they do not force their way through to see the LORD and many of them perish. 22Even the priests, who approach the LORD, must consecrate themselves, or the LORD will break out against them."

23Moses said to the LORD, "The people cannot come up Mount Sinai, because you yourself

[o]5,6 Or *possession, for the whole earth is mine.* 6*You* [p]18 Most Hebrew manuscripts; a few Hebrew manuscripts and Septuagint *all the people* [q]19 Or *and God answered him with thunder*

warned us, 'Put limits around the mountain and
set it apart as holy.' "
[24]The Lord replied, "Go down and bring Aaron
up with you. But the priests and the people must
not force their way through to come up to the
Lord, or he will break out against them."
[25]So Moses went down to the people and told
them.

Discovering the Word 1. What prospect did God hold out for his people after three months on the road (vv. 1–6)? 2. What preparations did the people have to make for God's appearance and why (vv. 10–15)? 3. What message was God conveying about himself and about his words (vv. 6, 23)? 4. How and why did the people react to the signs of God's presence on the mountain (vv. 16–19)? 5. Why would the Israelites be tempted to "force their way through to see the Lord" (v. 21)?

Applying the Word 1. Moses "consecrated" the people so they could meet God (v. 14). What is required of you to meet him? Why? 2. Moses acts as mediator between God and his people. In what sense is Jesus our mediator now (1Ti 2:5–6)? 3. The events of these days cause the people to hear and obey. How can we hold God's Word in holy awe?

Responding in Prayer Ask the Lord to help you prepare your heart for worship before you come to church.

13 / *Exodus 20:1–21*

Ten Keys to God's Character

THE MOST CONVINCING orders are those issued in simple words: Stop! Go! No misunderstanding them. In military training, soldiers learn split-second obedience to concise commands. Their survival depends on it! In Exodus 20, God speaks ten words—the most majestic moral commands ever spoken, the clearest rules for humanity's welfare. They are the foundation of personal and national life. They also reveal God's character. In this passage Israel learns that God is much more than the God of food, water, military victories and natural calamities.

Warming Up to God What part, if any, have the Ten Commandments had in forming your faith?

Read Exodus 20:1–21.

20 And God spoke all these words:
[2]"I am the Lord your God, who
brought you out of Egypt, out of
the land of slavery.
[3]"You shall have no other gods before[r]
me.
[4]"You shall not make for yourself an idol in
the form of anything in heaven above
or on the earth beneath or in the waters
below. [5]You shall not bow down to
them or worship them; for I, the Lord
your God, am a jealous God, punishing
the children for the sin of the fathers
to the third and fourth generation of
those who hate me, [6]but showing love
to a thousand ⌞generations⌟ of those
who love me and keep my command-
ments.
[7]"You shall not misuse the name of the Lord
your God, for the Lord will not hold
anyone guiltless who misuses his
name.
[8]"Remember the Sabbath day by keeping it
holy. [9]Six days you shall labor and do
all your work, [10]but the seventh day is
a Sabbath to the Lord your God. On it
you shall not do any work, neither you,
nor your son or daughter, nor your
manservant or maidservant, nor your
animals, nor the alien within your
gates. [11]For in six days the Lord made
the heavens and the earth, the sea, and

[r]3 Or *besides*

all that is in them, but he rested on
the seventh day. Therefore the LORD
blessed the Sabbath day and made it
holy.
12"Honor your father and your mother, so
that you may live long in the land the
LORD your God is giving you.
13"You shall not murder.
14"You shall not commit adultery.
15"You shall not steal.
16"You shall not give false testimony against
your neighbor.
17"You shall not covet your neighbor's house.
You shall not covet your neighbor's
wife, or his manservant or maidservant, his ox or donkey, or anything
that belongs to your neighbor."

18When the people saw the thunder and lightning and heard the trumpet and saw the mountain in smoke, they trembled with fear. They
stayed at a distance 19and said to Moses, "Speak
to us yourself and we will listen. But do not have
God speak to us or we will die."
20Moses said to the people, "Do not be afraid.
God has come to test you, so that the fear of God
will be with you to keep you from sinning."
21The people remained at a distance, while Moses approached the thick darkness where God
was.

Discovering the Word 1. What right did God have to issue these commands (v. 2)? 2. What reasons does God give for prohibiting idolatry (v. 4)? 3. How would you interpret the promise given to those who honor their parents (v. 12)? 4. Murder and adultery (vv. 13–14) are not just external acts; they are matters of the heart (see Mt 5:21–30). What, then, does it mean to obey these commands? 5. In what way is coveting (v. 17) a wrong not only against our neighbor but against God?

Applying the Word 1. What "other gods" or idols compete for your allegiance? 2. In today's world, how can we observe God's sabbath principle (vv. 8–11)?

Responding in Prayer Reflect on all the commands and, as needed, follow the promise of 1 John 1:9, asking God to purify your heart and life anew.

14 / *Exodus 20:22—23:19*
A Well-Ordered Society

"DO NOT COOK a young goat in its mother's milk." That law seems to have about as much relevance as the 55 mph speed limit. But long before Congress got into the act, God gave laws to his nation that addressed serious social ills that still plague us today. Not goat's-milk stew or speed limits—but what about murder, robbery and rape? What about justice and bribery? Who cares for the helpless? In this study Moses conveys God's plan for a newly born nation, whose fundamental credo was "You are to be my holy people" (22:31). Holiness is never outdated.

Warming Up to God What is the purpose for rules in society? Think of ways God's law has protected you, and thank God for instituting it.

Read Exodus 20:22—23:19.

22Then the LORD said to Moses, "Tell the Israelites this: 'You have seen for yourselves that I have
spoken to you from heaven: 23Do not make any
gods to be alongside me; do not make for yourselves gods of silver or gods of gold.
24" 'Make an altar of earth for me and sacrifice
on it your burnt offerings and fellowship offerings,[s] your sheep and goats and your cattle.
Wherever I cause my name to be honored, I will
come to you and bless you. 25If you make an altar
of stones for me, do not build it with dressed
stones, for you will defile it if you use a tool on it.
26And do not go up to my altar on steps, lest your
nakedness be exposed on it.'

[s]24 Traditionally *peace offerings*

21

“These are the laws you are to set before them:

2“If you buy a Hebrew servant, he is to serve you for six years. But in the seventh year, he shall go free, without paying anything. 3If he comes alone, he is to go free alone; but if he has a wife when he comes, she is to go with him. 4If his master gives him a wife and she bears him sons or daughters, the woman and her children shall belong to her master, and only the man shall go free.

5“But if the servant declares, ‘I love my master and my wife and children and do not want to go free,’ 6then his master must take him before the judges.[t] He shall take him to the door or the doorpost and pierce his ear with an awl. Then he will be his servant for life.

7“If a man sells his daughter as a servant, she is not to go free as menservants do. 8If she does not please the master who has selected her for himself,[u] he must let her be redeemed. He has no right to sell her to foreigners, because he has broken faith with her. 9If he selects her for his son, he must grant her the rights of a daughter. 10If he marries another woman, he must not deprive the first one of her food, clothing and marital rights. 11If he does not provide her with these three things, she is to go free, without any payment of money.

12“Anyone who strikes a man and kills him shall surely be put to death. 13However, if he does not do it intentionally, but God lets it happen, he is to flee to a place I will designate. 14But if a man schemes and kills another man deliberately, take him away from my altar and put him to death.

15“Anyone who attacks[v] his father or his mother must be put to death.

16“Anyone who kidnaps another and either sells him or still has him when he is caught must be put to death.

17“Anyone who curses his father or mother must be put to death.

18“If men quarrel and one hits the other with a stone or with his fist[w] and he does not die but is confined to bed, 19the one who struck the blow will not be held responsible if the other gets up and walks around outside with his staff; however, he must pay the injured man for the loss of his time and see that he is completely healed.

20“If a man beats his male or female slave with a rod and the slave dies as a direct result, he must be punished, 21but he is not to be punished if the slave gets up after a day or two, since the slave is his property.

22“If men who are fighting hit a pregnant woman and she gives birth prematurely[x] but there is no serious injury, the offender must be fined whatever the woman’s husband demands and the court allows. 23But if there is serious injury, you are to take life for life, 24eye for eye, tooth for tooth, hand for hand, foot for foot, 25burn for burn, wound for wound, bruise for bruise.

26“If a man hits a manservant or maidservant in the eye and destroys it, he must let the servant go free to compensate for the eye. 27And if he knocks out the tooth of a manservant or maidservant, he must let the servant go free to compensate for the tooth.

28“If a bull gores a man or a woman to death, the bull must be stoned to death, and its meat must not be eaten. But the owner of the bull will not be held responsible. 29If, however, the bull has had the habit of goring and the owner has been warned but has not kept it penned up and it kills a man or woman, the bull must be stoned and the owner also must be put to death. 30However, if payment is demanded of him, he may redeem his life by paying whatever is demanded. 31This law also applies if the bull gores a son or daughter. 32If the bull gores a male or female slave, the owner must pay thirty shekels[y] of silver to the master of the slave, and the bull must be stoned.

33“If a man uncovers a pit or digs one and fails to cover it and an ox or a donkey falls into it, 34the owner of the pit must pay for the loss; he must pay its owner, and the dead animal will be his.

35“If a man’s bull injures the bull of another and it dies, they are to sell the live one and divide both the money and the dead animal equally. 36However, if it was known that the bull had the habit of goring, yet the owner did not keep it penned up, the owner must pay, animal for animal, and the dead animal will be his.

22

“If a man steals an ox or a sheep and slaughters it or sells it, he must pay back five head of cattle for the ox and four sheep for the sheep.

[t]6 Or *before God* [u]8 Or *master so that he does not choose her* [v]15 Or *kills* [w]18 Or *with a tool* [x]22 Or *she has a miscarriage* [y]32 That is, about 12 ounces (about 0.3 kilogram)

2"If a thief is caught breaking in and is struck so that he dies, the defender is not guilty of bloodshed; 3but if it happens[z] after sunrise, he is guilty of bloodshed.

"A thief must certainly make restitution, but if he has nothing, he must be sold to pay for his theft.

4"If the stolen animal is found alive in his possession—whether ox or donkey or sheep—he must pay back double.

5"If a man grazes his livestock in a field or vineyard and lets them stray and they graze in another man's field, he must make restitution from the best of his own field or vineyard.

6"If a fire breaks out and spreads into thornbushes so that it burns shocks of grain or standing grain or the whole field, the one who started the fire must make restitution.

7"If a man gives his neighbor silver or goods for safekeeping and they are stolen from the neighbor's house, the thief, if he is caught, must pay back double. 8But if the thief is not found, the owner of the house must appear before the judges[a] to determine whether he has laid his hands on the other man's property. 9In all cases of illegal possession of an ox, a donkey, a sheep, a garment, or any other lost property about which somebody says, 'This is mine,' both parties are to bring their cases before the judges. The one whom the judges declare[b] guilty must pay back double to his neighbor.

10"If a man gives a donkey, an ox, a sheep or any other animal to his neighbor for safekeeping and it dies or is injured or is taken away while no one is looking, 11the issue between them will be settled by the taking of an oath before the LORD that the neighbor did not lay hands on the other person's property. The owner is to accept this, and no restitution is required. 12But if the animal was stolen from the neighbor, he must make restitution to the owner. 13If it was torn to pieces by a wild animal, he shall bring in the remains as evidence and he will not be required to pay for the torn animal.

14"If a man borrows an animal from his neighbor and it is injured or dies while the owner is not present, he must make restitution. 15But if the owner is with the animal, the borrower will not have to pay. If the animal was hired, the money paid for the hire covers the loss.

16"If a man seduces a virgin who is not pledged to be married and sleeps with her, he must pay the bride-price, and she shall be his wife. 17If her father absolutely refuses to give her to him, he must still pay the bride-price for virgins.

18"Do not allow a sorceress to live.

19"Anyone who has sexual relations with an animal must be put to death.

20"Whoever sacrifices to any god other than the LORD must be destroyed.[c]

21"Do not mistreat an alien or oppress him, for you were aliens in Egypt.

22"Do not take advantage of a widow or an orphan. 23If you do and they cry out to me, I will certainly hear their cry. 24My anger will be aroused, and I will kill you with the sword; your wives will become widows and your children fatherless.

25"If you lend money to one of my people among you who is needy, do not be like a moneylender; charge him no interest.[d] 26If you take your neighbor's cloak as a pledge, return it to him by sunset, 27because his cloak is the only covering he has for his body. What else will he sleep in? When he cries out to me, I will hear, for I am compassionate.

28"Do not blaspheme God[e] or curse the ruler of your people.

29"Do not hold back offerings from your granaries or your vats.[f]

"You must give me the firstborn of your sons. 30Do the same with your cattle and your sheep. Let them stay with their mothers for seven days, but give them to me on the eighth day.

31"You are to be my holy people. So do not eat the meat of an animal torn by wild beasts; throw it to the dogs.

23

"Do not spread false reports. Do not help a wicked man by being a malicious witness.

2"Do not follow the crowd in doing wrong. When you give testimony in a lawsuit, do not pervert justice by siding with the crowd, 3and do not show favoritism to a poor man in his lawsuit.

4"If you come across your enemy's ox or donkey wandering off, be sure to take it back to him. 5If you see the donkey of someone who hates you fallen down under its load, do not leave it there; be sure you help him with it.

6"Do not deny justice to your poor people in

z3 Or *if he strikes him* a8 Or *before God*; also in verse 9 b9 Or *whom God declares* c20 The Hebrew term refers to the irrevocable giving over of things or persons to the LORD, often by totally destroying them. d25 Or *excessive interest* e28 Or *Do not revile the judges* f29 The meaning of the Hebrew for this phrase is uncertain.

their lawsuits. 7Have nothing to do with a false charge and do not put an innocent or honest person to death, for I will not acquit the guilty.

8"Do not accept a bribe, for a bribe blinds those who see and twists the words of the righteous.

9"Do not oppress an alien; you yourselves know how it feels to be aliens, because you were aliens in Egypt.

10"For six years you are to sow your fields and harvest the crops, 11but during the seventh year let the land lie unplowed and unused. Then the poor among your people may get food from it, and the wild animals may eat what they leave. Do the same with your vineyard and your olive grove.

12"Six days do your work, but on the seventh day do not work, so that your ox and your donkey may rest and the slave born in your household, and the alien as well, may be refreshed.

13"Be careful to do everything I have said to you. Do not invoke the names of other gods; do not let them be heard on your lips.

14"Three times a year you are to celebrate a festival to me.

15"Celebrate the Feast of Unleavened Bread; for seven days eat bread made without yeast, as I commanded you. Do this at the appointed time in the month of Abib, for in that month you came out of Egypt.

"No one is to appear before me empty-handed.

16"Celebrate the Feast of Harvest with the firstfruits of the crops you sow in your field.

"Celebrate the Feast of Ingathering at the end of the year, when you gather in your crops from the field.

17"Three times a year all the men are to appear before the Sovereign LORD.

18"Do not offer the blood of a sacrifice to me along with anything containing yeast.

"The fat of my festival offerings must not be kept until morning.

19"Bring the best of the firstfruits of your soil to the house of the LORD your God.

"Do not cook a young goat in its mother's milk.

Discovering the Word 1. These laws were intended to improve the conditions of slaves. Why do you think slavery of any kind was permitted (21:1-11)? 2. What crimes are subject to capital punishment and why (21:12-17)? 3. What legal principle underlies punishment of those guilty of causing personal injuries (21:23-25)? 4. Restitution had to be made in certain cases. How does being liable for restitution contribute to the protection of property (22:1-15)? 5. In these miscellaneous laws, what do you sense is God's prime concern (22:16-31)? Why? 6. How does God's concern for justice and mercy stand out here (23:1-9)?

Applying the Word 1. How would you explain your social responsibilities based on the principles here? 2. Compared to what Israel's religious festivals might cost the average Israelite (23:10-19), what does your worship of God cost you?

Responding in Prayer Ask the Lord to give you a proper perspective of the law in your life.

15 / *Exodus 23:20—24:18*
Ratifying the Covenant

PEACE TREATIES AND home mortgages are ratified by signatures of the parties involved. Marriages are ratified by vows spoken before witnesses. The point is the same: promises are made and solemnly sealed. God called forth such an agreement at the birth of Israel. A written document was agreed to. Public vows were made. The blood of sacrificial animals sealed the covenant—a landmark in Israel's history. A marriage, as it were, was begun between God and his people. As this study reveals, our commitments to God carry awesome responsibilities.

Warming Up to God List three promises in Scripture given to you by the Father. Let these promises encourage your heart and give you peace as you seek the face of God today.

Read Exodus 23:20—24:18.

20"See, I am sending an angel ahead of you to guard you along the way and to bring you to the place I have prepared. 21Pay attention to him and listen to what he says. Do not rebel against him; he will not forgive your rebellion, since my Name is in him. 22If you listen carefully to what he says and do all that I say, I will be an enemy to your enemies and will oppose those who oppose you. 23My angel will go ahead of you and bring you into the land of the Amorites, Hittites, Perizzites, Canaanites, Hivites and Jebusites, and I will wipe them out. 24Do not bow down before their gods or worship them or follow their practices. You must demolish them and break their sacred stones to pieces. 25Worship the LORD your God, and his blessing will be on your food and water. I will take away sickness from among you, 26and none will miscarry or be barren in your land. I will give you a full life span.

27"I will send my terror ahead of you and throw into confusion every nation you encounter. I will make all your enemies turn their backs and run. 28I will send the hornet ahead of you to drive the Hivites, Canaanites and Hittites out of your way. 29But I will not drive them out in a single year, because the land would become desolate and the wild animals too numerous for you. 30Little by little I will drive them out before you, until you have increased enough to take possession of the land.

31"I will establish your borders from the Red Sea[g] to the Sea of the Philistines,[h] and from the desert to the River.[i] I will hand over to you the people who live in the land and you will drive them out before you. 32Do not make a covenant with them or with their gods. 33Do not let them live in your land, or they will cause you to sin against me, because the worship of their gods will certainly be a snare to you."

24

Then he said to Moses, "Come up to the LORD, you and Aaron, Nadab and Abihu, and seventy of the elders of Israel. You are to worship at a distance, 2but Moses alone is to approach the LORD; the others must not come near. And the people may not come up with him."

3When Moses went and told the people all the LORD's words and laws, they responded with one voice, "Everything the LORD has said we will do." 4Moses then wrote down everything the LORD had said.

He got up early the next morning and built an altar at the foot of the mountain and set up twelve stone pillars representing the twelve tribes of Israel. 5Then he sent young Israelite men, and they offered burnt offerings and sacrificed young bulls as fellowship offerings[j] to the LORD. 6Moses took half of the blood and put it in bowls, and the other half he sprinkled on the altar. 7Then he took the Book of the Covenant and read it to the people. They responded, "We will do everything the LORD has said; we will obey."

8Moses then took the blood, sprinkled it on the people and said, "This is the blood of the covenant that the LORD has made with you in accordance with all these words."

9Moses and Aaron, Nadab and Abihu, and the seventy elders of Israel went up 10and saw the God of Israel. Under his feet was something like a pavement made of sapphire,[k] clear as the sky itself. 11But God did not raise his hand against these leaders of the Israelites; they saw God, and they ate and drank.

12The LORD said to Moses, "Come up to me on the mountain and stay here, and I will give you the tablets of stone, with the law and commands I have written for their instruction."

13Then Moses set out with Joshua his aide, and Moses went up on the mountain of God. 14He said to the elders, "Wait here for us until we come back to you. Aaron and Hur are with you, and anyone involved in a dispute can go to them."

15When Moses went up on the mountain, the cloud covered it, 16and the glory of the LORD settled on Mount Sinai. For six days the cloud covered the mountain, and on the seventh day the LORD called to Moses from within the cloud. 17To the Israelites the glory of the LORD looked like a consuming fire on top of the mountain. 18Then Moses entered the cloud as he went on up the mountain. And he stayed on the mountain forty days and forty nights.

g31 Hebrew *Yam Suph*; that is, Sea of Reeds h31 That is, the Mediterranean i31 That is, the Euphrates j5 Traditionally *peace offerings* k10 Or *lapis lazuli*

Discovering the Word 1. What perils and temptations lie ahead for the Israelites? 2. In light of these, what commands and promises does God give? 3. After Israel's response (24:3) and Moses' steps to ensure that a public record of the laws would be kept (24:4), why was sacrifice appropriate (24:5)? 4. How would you summarize the basic points of this agreement (covenant) between God and his people? 5. What is the purpose of this mountaintop meeting with God (24:9–18)?

Applying the Word 1. What perils or temptations are you facing? 2. How does God help you to meet them? 3. God showed his glory to Israel (24:15–18). In what ways have you seen God display his glory in your life?

Responding in Prayer Praise God for his incredible covenant—the solid assurance that God will always be with his children and you, his child.

16 / *Exodus 25—27*
God's Blueprint for Worship

CHURCH BUILDINGS TODAY appear to be designed primarily for functional purposes. We don't build Gothic cathedrals anymore. We struggle to find God's presence in our sanctuaries. For some, architecture is unimportant. For others, it's a prime source of inspiration. Moses and the Israelites didn't have to debate the matter. God gave them his plan for their sanctuary. Beyond the plans, however, were important spiritual lessons. Fortunately for us, the New Testament gives us the fulfillment of these plans in Christ and his church.

Warming Up to God Where in your life do you need God's guidance? Reflect on this question and ask God to show you the correct path.

Read Exodus 25—27.

25 The LORD said to Moses, 2“Tell the Israelites to bring me an offering. You are to receive the offering for me from each man whose heart prompts him to give. 3These are the offerings you are to receive from them: gold, silver and bronze; 4blue, purple and scarlet yarn and fine linen; goat hair; 5ram skins dyed red and hides of sea cows[l]; acacia wood; 6olive oil for the light; spices for the anointing oil and for the fragrant incense; 7and onyx stones and other gems to be mounted on the ephod and breastpiece.

8“Then have them make a sanctuary for me, and I will dwell among them. 9Make this tabernacle and all its furnishings exactly like the pattern I will show you.

10“Have them make a chest of acacia wood—two and a half cubits long, a cubit and a half wide, and a cubit and a half high.[m] 11Overlay it with pure gold, both inside and out, and make a gold molding around it. 12Cast four gold rings for it and fasten them to its four feet, with two rings on one side and two rings on the other. 13Then make poles of acacia wood and overlay them with gold. 14Insert the poles into the rings on the sides of the chest to carry it. 15The poles are to remain in the rings of this ark; they are not to be removed. 16Then put in the ark the Testimony, which I will give you.

17“Make an atonement cover[n] of pure gold—two and a half cubits long and a cubit and a half wide.[o] 18And make two cherubim out of hammered gold at the ends of the cover. 19Make one cherub on one end and the second cherub on the other; make the cherubim of one piece with the cover, at the two ends. 20The cherubim are to have their wings spread upward, overshadowing the cover with them. The cherubim are to face each other, looking toward the cover. 21Place the cover on top of the ark and put in the ark the Testimony, which I will give you. 22There, above the cover between the two cherubim that are over the ark of the Testimony, I will meet with you

[l]5 That is, dugongs [m]10 That is, about 3 3/4 feet (about 1.1 meters) long and 2 1/4 feet (about 0.7 meter) wide and high
[n]17 Traditionally *a mercy seat* [o]17 That is, about 3 3/4 feet (about 1.1 meters) long and 2 1/4 feet (about 0.7 meter) wide

and give you all my commands for the Israelites.
23“Make a table of acacia wood—two cubits
long, a cubit wide and a cubit and a half high.[p]
24Overlay it with pure gold and make a gold
molding around it. 25Also make around it a rim a
handbreadth[q] wide and put a gold molding on
the rim. 26Make four gold rings for the table and
fasten them to the four corners, where the four
legs are. 27The rings are to be close to the rim to
hold the poles used in carrying the table. 28Make
the poles of acacia wood, overlay them with gold
and carry the table with them. 29And make its
plates and dishes of pure gold, as well as its pitch-
ers and bowls for the pouring out of offerings.
30Put the bread of the Presence on this table to be
before me at all times.

31“Make a lampstand of pure gold and hammer
it out, base and shaft; its flowerlike cups, buds
and blossoms shall be of one piece with it. 32Six
branches are to extend from the sides of the
lampstand—three on one side and three on the
other. 33Three cups shaped like almond flowers
with buds and blossoms are to be on one branch,
three on the next branch, and the same for all six
branches extending from the lampstand. 34And
on the lampstand there are to be four cups shaped
like almond flowers with buds and blossoms.
35One bud shall be under the first pair of
branches extending from the lampstand, a second
bud under the second pair, and a third bud under
the third pair—six branches in all. 36The buds
and branches shall all be of one piece with the
lampstand, hammered out of pure gold.

37“Then make its seven lamps and set them up
on it so that they light the space in front of it.
38Its wick trimmers and trays are to be of pure
gold. 39A talent[r] of pure gold is to be used for
the lampstand and all these accessories. 40See that
you make them according to the pattern shown
you on the mountain.

26 “Make the tabernacle with ten cur-
tains of finely twisted linen and
blue, purple and scarlet yarn, with
cherubim worked into them by a skilled crafts-
man. 2All the curtains are to be the same size—
twenty-eight cubits long and four cubits wide.[s]
3Join five of the curtains together, and do the
same with the other five. 4Make loops of blue
material along the edge of the end curtain in one
set, and do the same with the end curtain in the
other set. 5Make fifty loops on one curtain and
fifty loops on the end curtain of the other set,
with the loops opposite each other. 6Then make
fifty gold clasps and use them to fasten the cur-
tains together so that the tabernacle is a unit.

7“Make curtains of goat hair for the tent over
the tabernacle—eleven altogether. 8All eleven
curtains are to be the same size—thirty cubits
long and four cubits wide.[t] 9Join five of the cur-
tains together into one set and the other six into
another set. Fold the sixth curtain double at the
front of the tent. 10Make fifty loops along the edge
of the end curtain in one set and also along the
edge of the end curtain in the other set. 11Then
make fifty bronze clasps and put them in the
loops to fasten the tent together as a unit. 12As for
the additional length of the tent curtains, the half
curtain that is left over is to hang down at the rear
of the tabernacle. 13The tent curtains will be a
cubit[u] longer on both sides; what is left will
hang over the sides of the tabernacle so as to
cover it. 14Make for the tent a covering of ram
skins dyed red, and over that a covering of hides
of sea cows.[v]

15“Make upright frames of acacia wood for the
tabernacle. 16Each frame is to be ten cubits long
and a cubit and a half wide,[w] 17with two projec-
tions set parallel to each other. Make all the
frames of the tabernacle in this way. 18Make
twenty frames for the south side of the tabernacle
19and make forty silver bases to go under them—
two bases for each frame, one under each projec-
tion. 20For the other side, the north side of the
tabernacle, make twenty frames 21and forty silver
bases—two under each frame. 22Make six frames
for the far end, that is, the west end of the taber-
nacle, 23and make two frames for the corners at
the far end. 24At these two corners they must be
double from the bottom all the way to the top,
and fitted into a single ring; both shall be like
that. 25So there will be eight frames and sixteen
silver bases—two under each frame.

26“Also make crossbars of acacia wood: five for
the frames on one side of the tabernacle, 27five for
those on the other side, and five for the frames on
the west, at the far end of the tabernacle. 28The
center crossbar is to extend from end to end at
the middle of the frames. 29Overlay the frames

[p] *23* That is, about 3 feet (about 0.9 meter) long and 1 1/2 feet (about 0.5 meter) wide and 2 1/4 feet (about 0.7 meter) high [q] *25* That is, about 3 inches (about 8 centimeters) [r] *39* That is, about 75 pounds (about 34 kilograms) [s] *2* That is, about 42 feet (about 12.5 meters) long and 6 feet (about 1.8 meters) wide [t] *8* That is, about 45 feet (about 13.5 meters) long and 6 feet (about 1.8 meters) wide [u] *13* That is, about 1 1/2 feet (about 0.5 meter) [v] *14* That is, dugongs [w] *16* That is, about 15 feet (about 4.5 meters) long and 2 1/4 feet (about 0.7 meter) wide

with gold and make gold rings to hold the crossbars. Also overlay the crossbars with gold.

[30]"Set up the tabernacle according to the plan shown you on the mountain.

[31]"Make a curtain of blue, purple and scarlet yarn and finely twisted linen, with cherubim worked into it by a skilled craftsman. [32]Hang it with gold hooks on four posts of acacia wood overlaid with gold and standing on four silver bases. [33]Hang the curtain from the clasps and place the ark of the Testimony behind the curtain. The curtain will separate the Holy Place from the Most Holy Place. [34]Put the atonement cover on the ark of the Testimony in the Most Holy Place. [35]Place the table outside the curtain on the north side of the tabernacle and put the lampstand opposite it on the south side.

[36]"For the entrance to the tent make a curtain of blue, purple and scarlet yarn and finely twisted linen—the work of an embroiderer. [37]Make gold hooks for this curtain and five posts of acacia wood overlaid with gold. And cast five bronze bases for them.

27

"Build an altar of acacia wood, three cubits[x] high; it is to be square, five cubits long and five cubits wide.[y] [2]Make a horn at each of the four corners, so that the horns and the altar are of one piece, and overlay the altar with bronze. [3]Make all its utensils of bronze—its pots to remove the ashes, and its shovels, sprinkling bowls, meat forks and firepans. [4]Make a grating for it, a bronze network, and make a bronze ring at each of the four corners of the network. [5]Put it under the ledge of the altar so that it is halfway up the altar. [6]Make poles of acacia wood for the altar and overlay them with bronze. [7]The poles are to be inserted into the rings so they will be on two sides of the altar when it is carried. [8]Make the altar hollow, out of boards. It is to be made just as you were shown on the mountain.

[9]"Make a courtyard for the tabernacle. The south side shall be a hundred cubits[z] long and is to have curtains of finely twisted linen, [10]with twenty posts and twenty bronze bases and with silver hooks and bands on the posts. [11]The north side shall also be a hundred cubits long and is to have curtains, with twenty posts and twenty bronze bases and with silver hooks and bands on the posts.

[12]"The west end of the courtyard shall be fifty cubits[a] wide and have curtains, with ten posts and ten bases. [13]On the east end, toward the sunrise, the courtyard shall also be fifty cubits wide. [14]Curtains fifteen cubits[b] long are to be on one side of the entrance, with three posts and three bases, [15]and curtains fifteen cubits long are to be on the other side, with three posts and three bases.

[16]"For the entrance to the courtyard, provide a curtain twenty cubits[c] long, of blue, purple and scarlet yarn and finely twisted linen—the work of an embroiderer—with four posts and four bases. [17]All the posts around the courtyard are to have silver bands and hooks, and bronze bases. [18]The courtyard shall be a hundred cubits long and fifty cubits wide,[d] with curtains of finely twisted linen five cubits[e] high, and with bronze bases. [19]All the other articles used in the service of the tabernacle, whatever their function, including all the tent pegs for it and those for the courtyard, are to be of bronze.

[20]"Command the Israelites to bring you clear oil of pressed olives for the light so that the lamps may be kept burning. [21]In the Tent of Meeting, outside the curtain that is in front of the Testimony, Aaron and his sons are to keep the lamps burning before the LORD from evening till morning. This is to be a lasting ordinance among the Israelites for the generations to come.

[x]*1* That is, about 4 1/2 feet (about 1.3 meters) [y]*1* That is, about 7 1/2 feet (about 2.3 meters) long and wide [z]*9* That is, about 150 feet (about 46 meters); also in verse 11 [a]*12* That is, about 75 feet (about 23 meters); also in verse 13 [b]*14* That is, about 22 1/2 feet (about 6.9 meters); also in verse 15 [c]*16* That is, about 30 feet (about 9 meters) [d]*18* That is, about 150 feet (about 46 meters) long and 75 feet (about 23 meters) wide [e]*18* That is, about 7 1/2 feet (about 2.3 meters)

Discovering the Word 1. Why would an Israelite feel prompted to give building materials for the tabernacle (25:2)? 2. What was the purpose of the sanctuary (25:8)? 3. Since God does not dwell in a building now (Eph 2:19–22), why should we have church sanctuaries? 4. The wooden chest called the ark held God's Law ("the Testimony"). God promised to meet his people there and teach them his commands (25:16, 22). As Christians, how is our access to God and his commands superior to what is described here? 5. The bread of the Presence (25:30) symbolized that the fruit of our labors comes from and belongs to God. Why would Israel need this daily reminder? 6. What does the value of the materials that went into the tabernacle suggest about the message God was trying to convey to his people (Ex 26)?

Applying the Word 1. Israel's tabernacle "was only a copy of the true one . . . heaven itself" (Heb 9:24). How does this fact enhance your appreciation of what Jesus has done and is doing for you (Heb 9:1-5, 23-28)? 2. How can we carry on the tradition of the bread of the Presence, reminding ourselves that all we have comes from God?

Responding in Prayer Ask God to fill his tabernacle, your heart, with his glory and mercy.

17 / *Exodus 28:1—29:37*
God's Holiness

DEPENDING ON YOUR religious background, you might venerate, despise or just tolerate priests. Regardless of our church affiliation and the various names we give our leaders, we recognize their role in corporate worship. Too often we see the man or woman in leadership and fail to focus on God himself. The focal point of worship is, after all, God, and not the priest or pastor. God's plan for Israel's priesthood pointed to his own holiness and to human sin. Priests and worshipers alike needed atonement for their sins. This study will help you examine your own motives in worship.

Warming Up to God What do you need to tell God before you read his Word? Confess today's sin or today's frustrations—and let God listen to you as your loving Father.

Read Exodus 28:1—29:37.

28 "Have Aaron your brother brought
to you from among the Israelites,
along with his sons Nadab and
Abihu, Eleazar and Ithamar, so they may serve
me as priests. 2Make sacred garments for your
brother Aaron, to give him dignity and honor.
3Tell all the skilled men to whom I have given
wisdom in such matters that they are to make
garments for Aaron, for his consecration, so he
may serve me as priest. 4These are the garments
they are to make: a breastpiece, an ephod, a robe,
a woven tunic, a turban and a sash. They are to
make these sacred garments for your brother
Aaron and his sons, so they may serve me as
priests. 5Have them use gold, and blue, purple
and scarlet yarn, and fine linen.

6"Make the ephod of gold, and of blue, purple
and scarlet yarn, and of finely twisted linen—the
work of a skilled craftsman. 7It is to have two
shoulder pieces attached to two of its corners, so
it can be fastened. 8Its skillfully woven waistband
is to be like it—of one piece with the ephod and
made with gold, and with blue, purple and scarlet
yarn, and with finely twisted linen.

9"Take two onyx stones and engrave on them
the names of the sons of Israel 10in the order of
their birth—six names on one stone and the remaining six on the other. 11Engrave the names of
the sons of Israel on the two stones the way a gem
cutter engraves a seal. Then mount the stones in
gold filigree settings 12and fasten them on the
shoulder pieces of the ephod as memorial stones
for the sons of Israel. Aaron is to bear the names
on his shoulders as a memorial before the LORD.
13Make gold filigree settings 14and two braided
chains of pure gold, like a rope, and attach the
chains to the settings.

15"Fashion a breastpiece for making decisions—the work of a skilled craftsman. Make it
like the ephod: of gold, and of blue, purple and
scarlet yarn, and of finely twisted linen. 16It is to
be square—a span[f] long and a span wide—and
folded double. 17Then mount four rows of precious stones on it. In the first row there shall be
a ruby, a topaz and a beryl; 18in the second row a
turquoise, a sapphire[g] and an emerald; 19in the
third row a jacinth, an agate and an amethyst; 20in
the fourth row a chrysolite, an onyx and a jasper.[h] Mount them in gold filigree settings.
21There are to be twelve stones, one for each of
the names of the sons of Israel, each engraved like

f16 That is, about 9 inches (about 22 centimeters) g18 Or *lapis lazuli* h20 The precise identification of some of these precious stones is uncertain.

a seal with the name of one of the twelve tribes.

22"For the breastpiece make braided chains of pure gold, like a rope. 23Make two gold rings for it and fasten them to two corners of the breastpiece. 24Fasten the two gold chains to the rings at the corners of the breastpiece, 25and the other ends of the chains to the two settings, attaching them to the shoulder pieces of the ephod at the front. 26Make two gold rings and attach them to the other two corners of the breastpiece on the inside edge next to the ephod. 27Make two more gold rings and attach them to the bottom of the shoulder pieces on the front of the ephod, close to the seam just above the waistband of the ephod. 28The rings of the breastpiece are to be tied to the rings of the ephod with blue cord, connecting it to the waistband, so that the breastpiece will not swing out from the ephod.

29"Whenever Aaron enters the Holy Place, he will bear the names of the sons of Israel over his heart on the breastpiece of decision as a continuing memorial before the LORD. 30Also put the Urim and the Thummim in the breastpiece, so they may be over Aaron's heart whenever he enters the presence of the LORD. Thus Aaron will always bear the means of making decisions for the Israelites over his heart before the LORD.

31"Make the robe of the ephod entirely of blue cloth, 32with an opening for the head in its center. There shall be a woven edge like a collar[i] around this opening, so that it will not tear. 33Make pomegranates of blue, purple and scarlet yarn around the hem of the robe, with gold bells between them. 34The gold bells and the pomegranates are to alternate around the hem of the robe. 35Aaron must wear it when he ministers. The sound of the bells will be heard when he enters the Holy Place before the LORD and when he comes out, so that he will not die.

36"Make a plate of pure gold and engrave on it as on a seal: HOLY TO THE LORD. 37Fasten a blue cord to it to attach it to the turban; it is to be on the front of the turban. 38It will be on Aaron's forehead, and he will bear the guilt involved in the sacred gifts the Israelites consecrate, whatever their gifts may be. It will be on Aaron's forehead continually so that they will be acceptable to the LORD.

39"Weave the tunic of fine linen and make the turban of fine linen. The sash is to be the work of an embroiderer. 40Make tunics, sashes and headbands for Aaron's sons, to give them dignity and honor. 41After you put these clothes on your brother Aaron and his sons, anoint and ordain them. Consecrate them so they may serve me as priests.

42"Make linen undergarments as a covering for the body, reaching from the waist to the thigh. 43Aaron and his sons must wear them whenever they enter the Tent of Meeting or approach the altar to minister in the Holy Place, so that they will not incur guilt and die.

"This is to be a lasting ordinance for Aaron and his descendants.

29 "This is what you are to do to consecrate them, so they may serve me as priests: Take a young bull and two rams without defect. 2And from fine wheat flour, without yeast, make bread, and cakes mixed with oil, and wafers spread with oil. 3Put them in a basket and present them in it—along with the bull and the two rams. 4Then bring Aaron and his sons to the entrance to the Tent of Meeting and wash them with water. 5Take the garments and dress Aaron with the tunic, the robe of the ephod, the ephod itself and the breastpiece. Fasten the ephod on him by its skillfully woven waistband. 6Put the turban on his head and attach the sacred diadem to the turban. 7Take the anointing oil and anoint him by pouring it on his head. 8Bring his sons and dress them in tunics 9and put headbands on them. Then tie sashes on Aaron and his sons.[j] The priesthood is theirs by a lasting ordinance. In this way you shall ordain Aaron and his sons.

10"Bring the bull to the front of the Tent of Meeting, and Aaron and his sons shall lay their hands on its head. 11Slaughter it in the LORD's presence at the entrance to the Tent of Meeting. 12Take some of the bull's blood and put it on the horns of the altar with your finger, and pour out the rest of it at the base of the altar. 13Then take all the fat around the inner parts, the covering of the liver, and both kidneys with the fat on them, and burn them on the altar. 14But burn the bull's flesh and its hide and its offal outside the camp. It is a sin offering.

15"Take one of the rams, and Aaron and his sons shall lay their hands on its head. 16Slaughter it and take the blood and sprinkle it against the altar on all sides. 17Cut the ram into pieces and wash the inner parts and the legs, putting them

[i]32 The meaning of the Hebrew for this word is uncertain.
[j]9 Hebrew; Septuagint *on them*

with the head and the other pieces. 18Then burn
the entire ram on the altar. It is a burnt offering
to the LORD, a pleasing aroma, an offering made to
the LORD by fire.

19"Take the other ram, and Aaron and his sons
shall lay their hands on its head. 20Slaughter it,
take some of its blood and put it on the lobes
of the right ears of Aaron and his sons, on the
thumbs of their right hands, and on the big toes
of their right feet. Then sprinkle blood against the
altar on all sides. 21And take some of the blood on
the altar and some of the anointing oil and sprin-
kle it on Aaron and his garments and on his sons
and their garments. Then he and his sons and
their garments will be consecrated.

22"Take from this ram the fat, the fat tail, the
fat around the inner parts, the covering of the
liver, both kidneys with the fat on them, and the
right thigh. (This is the ram for the ordination.)
23From the basket of bread made without yeast,
which is before the LORD, take a loaf, and a cake
made with oil, and a wafer. 24Put all these in the
hands of Aaron and his sons and wave them be-
fore the LORD as a wave offering. 25Then take them
from their hands and burn them on the altar
along with the burnt offering for a pleasing aroma
to the LORD, an offering made to the LORD by fire.
26After you take the breast of the ram for Aaron's
ordination, wave it before the LORD as a wave of-
fering, and it will be your share.

27"Consecrate those parts of the ordination ram
that belong to Aaron and his sons: the breast that
was waved and the thigh that was presented.
28This is always to be the regular share from the
Israelites for Aaron and his sons. It is the contri-
bution the Israelites are to make to the LORD from
their fellowship offerings.[k]

29"Aaron's sacred garments will belong to his
descendants so that they can be anointed and or-
dained in them. 30The son who succeeds him as
priest and comes to the Tent of Meeting to minis-
ter in the Holy Place is to wear them seven days.

31"Take the ram for the ordination and cook
the meat in a sacred place. 32At the entrance to
the Tent of Meeting, Aaron and his sons are to eat
the meat of the ram and the bread that is in the
basket. 33They are to eat these offerings by which
atonement was made for their ordination and
consecration. But no one else may eat them, be-
cause they are sacred. 34And if any of the meat of
the ordination ram or any bread is left over till
morning, burn it up. It must not be eaten, be-
cause it is sacred.

35"Do for Aaron and his sons everything I have
commanded you, taking seven days to ordain
them. 36Sacrifice a bull each day as a sin offering
to make atonement. Purify the altar by making
atonement for it, and anoint it to consecrate it.
37For seven days make atonement for the altar
and consecrate it. Then the altar will be most
holy, and whatever touches it will be holy.

[k]28 Traditionally *peace offerings*

Discovering the Word 1. How and why did God give special status to the sons of Aaron? 2. What would the precious stones mean to the Israelites in their relationship with God (28:9–12, 21, 29)? 3. What facts about God's nature are emphasized by these garments (28:35–36, 38, 43)? 4. What do they teach about our spiritual condition and its consequences? 5. What offerings were made for the priests (29:1–3)? 6. Why do you think God went to such elaborate measures for his priests' garments and for their ordination?

Applying the Word 1. How can we develop an appreciation of our own sin and God's holiness in our worship? 2. If you had been one of Aaron's sons, what would have been your major feelings and impressions about God and about your ministry? 3. Jesus is our great high priest. What benefits do we receive from him (Heb 2:14–18; 5:1–3, 7–10; 9:11–15; 10:19–25)?

Responding in Prayer Pour out your requests to God, knowing that Jesus, your High Priest, will plead to the Father on your behalf.

18 / *Exodus 29:38—31:18*
God's Revelation in People and Things

"BACK TO THE drawing board" is often said after a failed experiment or project. Sometimes Christians behave as though the worship of God is a do-it-yourself project. Some lack a sense of responding to God himself. Church leaders experiment and fiddle with changes in the order of worship. But God is a God of economy and order. No wasted, botched plans or experiments with him. Moses and the Israelites received a specific plan, precise in every detail and dimension. Each part of the plan said something about God. Careful study of the plan pays off in new insights about God and about worship.

Warming Up to God As you sit before the Bible allow yourself to sit spiritually before the Lord. Rest silently for a few minutes and allow yourself to become relaxed and focused before you begin your study.

Read Exodus 29:38—31:18.

38"This is what you are to offer on the altar
regularly each day: two lambs a year old. 39Offer
one in the morning and the other at twilight.
40With the first lamb offer a tenth of an ephah[l]
of fine flour mixed with a quarter of a hin[m] of oil
from pressed olives, and a quarter of a hin of wine
as a drink offering. 41Sacrifice the other lamb at
twilight with the same grain offering and its drink offering as in the morning—a pleasing aroma, an offering made to the LORD by fire.

42"For the generations to come this burnt offering is to be made regularly at the entrance to the Tent of Meeting before the LORD. There I will
meet you and speak to you; 43there also I will
meet with the Israelites, and the place will be consecrated by my glory.

44"So I will consecrate the Tent of Meeting and the altar and will consecrate Aaron and his sons
to serve me as priests. 45Then I will dwell among
the Israelites and be their God. 46They will know
that I am the LORD their God, who brought them out of Egypt so that I might dwell among them. I am the LORD their God.

30 "Make an altar of acacia wood for burning incense. 2It is to be square,
a cubit long and a cubit wide, and two cubits high[n]—its horns of one piece with it.
3Overlay the top and all the sides and the horns with pure gold, and make a gold molding around
it. 4Make two gold rings for the altar below the molding—two on opposite sides—to hold the
poles used to carry it. 5Make the poles of acacia
wood and overlay them with gold. 6Put the altar
in front of the curtain that is before the ark of the Testimony—before the atonement cover that is over the Testimony—where I will meet with you.
7"Aaron must burn fragrant incense on the altar every morning when he tends the lamps. 8He
must burn incense again when he lights the lamps at twilight so incense will burn regularly before
the LORD for the generations to come. 9Do not
offer on this altar any other incense or any burnt offering or grain offering, and do not pour a drink
offering on it. 10Once a year Aaron shall make
atonement on its horns. This annual atonement must be made with the blood of the atoning sin offering for the generations to come. It is most holy to the LORD."

11Then the LORD said to Moses, 12"When you
take a census of the Israelites to count them, each one must pay the LORD a ransom for his life at the time he is counted. Then no plague will come on
them when you number them. 13Each one who
crosses over to those already counted is to give a half shekel,[o] according to the sanctuary shekel, which weighs twenty gerahs. This half shekel is
an offering to the LORD. 14All who cross over,
those twenty years old or more, are to give an
offering to the LORD. 15The rich are not to give
more than a half shekel and the poor are not to give less when you make the offering to the LORD
to atone for your lives. 16Receive the atonement
money from the Israelites and use it for the service of the Tent of Meeting. It will be a memorial for the Israelites before the LORD, making atonement for your lives."

17Then the LORD said to Moses, 18"Make a

[l]40 That is, probably about 2 quarts (about 2 liters) [m]40 That is, probably about 1 quart (about 1 liter) [n]2 That is, about 1 1/2 feet (about 0.5 meter) long and wide and about 3 feet (about 0.9 meter) high [o]13 That is, about 1/5 ounce (about 6 grams); also in verse 15

bronze basin, with its bronze stand, for washing. Place it between the Tent of Meeting and the altar, and put water in it. 19Aaron and his sons are to wash their hands and feet with water from it. 20Whenever they enter the Tent of Meeting, they shall wash with water so that they will not die. Also, when they approach the altar to minister by presenting an offering made to the LORD by fire, 21they shall wash their hands and feet so that they will not die. This is to be a lasting ordinance for Aaron and his descendants for the generations to come."

22Then the LORD said to Moses, 23"Take the following fine spices: 500 shekels[p] of liquid myrrh, half as much (that is, 250 shekels) of fragrant cinnamon, 250 shekels of fragrant cane, 24500 shekels of cassia—all according to the sanctuary shekel—and a hin[q] of olive oil. 25Make these into a sacred anointing oil, a fragrant blend, the work of a perfumer. It will be the sacred anointing oil. 26Then use it to anoint the Tent of Meeting, the ark of the Testimony, 27the table and all its articles, the lampstand and its accessories, the altar of incense, 28the altar of burnt offering and all its utensils, and the basin with its stand. 29You shall consecrate them so they will be most holy, and whatever touches them will be holy.

30"Anoint Aaron and his sons and consecrate them so they may serve me as priests. 31Say to the Israelites, 'This is to be my sacred anointing oil for the generations to come. 32Do not pour it on men's bodies and do not make any oil with the same formula. It is sacred, and you are to consider it sacred. 33Whoever makes perfume like it and whoever puts it on anyone other than a priest must be cut off from his people.' "

34Then the LORD said to Moses, "Take fragrant spices—gum resin, onycha and galbanum—and pure frankincense, all in equal amounts, 35and make a fragrant blend of incense, the work of a perfumer. It is to be salted and pure and sacred. 36Grind some of it to powder and place it in front of the Testimony in the Tent of Meeting, where I will meet with you. It shall be most holy to you. 37Do not make any incense with this formula for yourselves; consider it holy to the LORD. 38Whoever makes any like it to enjoy its fragrance must be cut off from his people."

31

Then the LORD said to Moses, 2"See, I have chosen Bezalel son of Uri, the son of Hur, of the tribe of Judah, 3and I have filled him with the Spirit of God, with skill, ability and knowledge in all kinds of crafts— 4to make artistic designs for work in gold, silver and bronze, 5to cut and set stones, to work in wood, and to engage in all kinds of craftsmanship. 6Moreover, I have appointed Oholiab son of Ahisamach, of the tribe of Dan, to help him. Also I have given skill to all the craftsmen to make everything I have commanded you: 7the Tent of Meeting, the ark of the Testimony with the atonement cover on it, and all the other furnishings of the tent— 8the table and its articles, the pure gold lampstand and all its accessories, the altar of incense, 9the altar of burnt offering and all its utensils, the basin with its stand— 10and also the woven garments, both the sacred garments for Aaron the priest and the garments for his sons when they serve as priests, 11and the anointing oil and fragrant incense for the Holy Place. They are to make them just as I commanded you."

12Then the LORD said to Moses, 13"Say to the Israelites, 'You must observe my Sabbaths. This will be a sign between me and you for the generations to come, so you may know that I am the LORD, who makes you holy.[r]

14" 'Observe the Sabbath, because it is holy to you. Anyone who desecrates it must be put to death; whoever does any work on that day must be cut off from his people. 15For six days, work is to be done, but the seventh day is a Sabbath of rest, holy to the LORD. Whoever does any work on the Sabbath day must be put to death. 16The Israelites are to observe the Sabbath, celebrating it for the generations to come as a lasting covenant. 17It will be a sign between me and the Israelites forever, for in six days the LORD made the heavens and the earth, and on the seventh day he abstained from work and rested.' "

18When the LORD finished speaking to Moses on Mount Sinai, he gave him the two tablets of the Testimony, the tablets of stone inscribed by the finger of God.

p23 That is, about 12 1/2 pounds (about 6 kilograms) q24 That is, probably about 4 quarts (about 4 liters) r13 Or *who sanctifies you;* or *who sets you apart as holy*

Discovering the Word 1. How does God summarize the purposes of worship (29:42-46)? 2. Incense speaks of the prayers of God's people (Rev 5:8). Why would Israel need such a reminder (30:1-10)? 3. What aspect of worship would be inspired by paying atonement money (30:11-16)? 4. Why do you think it was important that rich and poor gave the same small amount (30:15)? 5. The shepherds of Israel had neither artistic skills nor craftsmanship. What does God's plan to remedy this reveal about his concern for beauty (31:1-11)? 6. Exodus 31:12-18 is the third instruction and warning regarding the Sabbath (see 20:8-11; 23:10-13). What new emphasis is added here regarding the purpose of the Sabbath and the punishment of those who disregard it?

Applying the Word 1. The Bible speaks of the cleansing effect of Scripture (Ps 119:9; Jn 15:3). Why is it important to be washed daily by God's Word? 2. From these forty days' instructions (Ex 25—31) from God, what major impressions do you receive about him and about worshiping him?

Responding in Prayer Spend time worshiping the Lord. Choose your own way to express yourself and ascribe worth to God.

19 / *Exodus 32*
Idolatry's Fearful Toll

PROBABLY NOTHING SHOCKS us as much as defection. Selling out to the enemy is hard to understand. Loyalty rightly stands near the top of qualities we admire. When traitors are exposed, we smugly assume that we would never do such a thing. But who knows where we are the most vulnerable? On the heels of glorious triumph Israel plunged into idolatry with the flimsiest of excuses. God's nation flunked the loyalty test, with disastrous consequences.

Warming Up to God Sit quietly as you recall recent events in your life. Confess your sins to Jesus and acknowledge that every one of them is forgiven and blotted from the memory of the Father.

Read Exodus 32.

32 When the people saw that Moses was so long in coming down from the mountain, they gathered around Aaron and said, "Come, make us gods[s] who will go before us. As for this fellow Moses who brought us up out of Egypt, we don't know what has happened to him."

2Aaron answered them, "Take off the gold earrings that your wives, your sons and your daughters are wearing, and bring them to me." 3So all the people took off their earrings and brought them to Aaron. 4He took what they handed him and made it into an idol cast in the shape of a calf, fashioning it with a tool. Then they said, "These are your gods,[t] O Israel, who brought you up out of Egypt."

5When Aaron saw this, he built an altar in front of the calf and announced, "Tomorrow there will be a festival to the LORD." 6So the next day the people rose early and sacrificed burnt offerings and presented fellowship offerings.[u] Afterward they sat down to eat and drink and got up to indulge in revelry.

7Then the LORD said to Moses, "Go down, because your people, whom you brought up out of Egypt, have become corrupt. 8They have been quick to turn away from what I commanded them and have made themselves an idol cast in the shape of a calf. They have bowed down to it and sacrificed to it and have said, 'These are your gods, O Israel, who brought you up out of Egypt.'

9"I have seen these people," the LORD said to Moses, "and they are a stiff-necked people. 10Now leave me alone so that my anger may burn against them and that I may destroy them. Then I will make you into a great nation."

11But Moses sought the favor of the LORD his God. "O LORD," he said, "why should your anger burn against your people, whom you brought out of Egypt with great power and a mighty hand? 12Why should the Egyptians say, 'It was with evil

[s] 1 Or *a god*; also in verses 23 and 31 [t] 4 Or *This is your god*; also in verse 8 [u] 6 Traditionally *peace offerings*

intent that he brought them out, to kill them in the mountains and to wipe them off the face of the earth'? Turn from your fierce anger; relent and do not bring disaster on your people. 13Remember your servants Abraham, Isaac and Israel, to whom you swore by your own self: 'I will make your descendants as numerous as the stars in the sky and I will give your descendants all this land I promised them, and it will be their inheritance forever.' " 14Then the LORD relented and did not bring on his people the disaster he had threatened.

15Moses turned and went down the mountain with the two tablets of the Testimony in his hands. They were inscribed on both sides, front and back. 16The tablets were the work of God; the writing was the writing of God, engraved on the tablets.

17When Joshua heard the noise of the people shouting, he said to Moses, "There is the sound of war in the camp."

18Moses replied:

"It is not the sound of victory,
  it is not the sound of defeat;
  it is the sound of singing that I hear."

19When Moses approached the camp and saw the calf and the dancing, his anger burned and he threw the tablets out of his hands, breaking them to pieces at the foot of the mountain. 20And he took the calf they had made and burned it in the fire; then he ground it to powder, scattered it on the water and made the Israelites drink it.

21He said to Aaron, "What did these people do to you, that you led them into such great sin?"

22"Do not be angry, my lord," Aaron answered. "You know how prone these people are to evil. 23They said to me, 'Make us gods who will go before us. As for this fellow Moses who brought us up out of Egypt, we don't know what has happened to him.' 24So I told them, 'Whoever has any gold jewelry, take it off.' Then they gave me the gold, and I threw it into the fire, and out came this calf!"

25Moses saw that the people were running wild and that Aaron had let them get out of control and so become a laughingstock to their enemies. 26So he stood at the entrance to the camp and said, "Whoever is for the LORD, come to me." And all the Levites rallied to him.

27Then he said to them, "This is what the LORD, the God of Israel, says: 'Each man strap a sword to his side. Go back and forth through the camp from one end to the other, each killing his brother and friend and neighbor.' " 28The Levites did as Moses commanded, and that day about three thousand of the people died. 29Then Moses said, "You have been set apart to the LORD today, for you were against your own sons and brothers, and he has blessed you this day."

30The next day Moses said to the people, "You have committed a great sin. But now I will go up to the LORD; perhaps I can make atonement for your sin."

31So Moses went back to the LORD and said, "Oh, what a great sin these people have committed! They have made themselves gods of gold. 32But now, please forgive their sin—but if not, then blot me out of the book you have written."

33The LORD replied to Moses, "Whoever has sinned against me I will blot out of my book. 34Now go, lead the people to the place I spoke of, and my angel will go before you. However, when the time comes for me to punish, I will punish them for their sin."

35And the LORD struck the people with a plague because of what they did with the calf Aaron had made.

Discovering the Word 1. Who instigated the idolatry and why (v. 1)? 2. What impresses you about the dialogue between God and Moses (vv. 9–14)? 3. How did Moses react when he saw the Israelites' idolatrous worship (vv. 19–24)? 4. How was God's judgment against idolatry carried out (vv. 27–28, 35)? 5. What did it cost the Levites to take a public stand for God? 6. Moses offered his life to atone for Israel's sin (vv. 30–32). What did God promise instead (vv. 33–34)?

Applying the Word 1. In what ways can we emulate Moses in our relation to God and in our care for sinning people? 2. What spiritual disciplines could help you maintain faithfulness to God?

Responding in Prayer Praise God for this example of grace—even in Exodus, long before Christ ever came to earth.

20/ *Exodus 33*
God's Presence and Glory

I REMEMBER TAKING my son to school the first time. I dragged him all the way. My presence was not enough to enable him to face this terrible prospect. The command to go was clear, but that wasn't enough for him. In the same way God commanded Israel to go to the good land he had promised to give them. God's leader asked for God's presence before he would move out. In this study we see more of God's loving patience with Moses and Israel and how this speaks to our own basic spiritual goals.

Warming Up to God Sit quietly and imagine you are a glass of water, full of words, thoughts, ideas and sins that distract. Pour yourself out in front of the Lord and let the Spirit refill you with his good, refreshing water.

Read Exodus 33.

33 Then the LORD said to Moses,
"Leave this place, you and the peo-
ple you brought up out of Egypt,
and go up to the land I promised on oath to Abra-
ham, Isaac and Jacob, saying, 'I will give it to your
descendants.' 2I will send an angel before you and
drive out the Canaanites, Amorites, Hittites, Per-
izzites, Hivites and Jebusites. 3Go up to the land
flowing with milk and honey. But I will not go
with you, because you are a stiff-necked people
and I might destroy you on the way."

4When the people heard these distressing
words, they began to mourn and no one put on
any ornaments. 5For the LORD had said to Moses,
"Tell the Israelites, 'You are a stiff-necked people.
If I were to go with you even for a moment, I
might destroy you. Now take off your ornaments
and I will decide what to do with you.' " 6So the
Israelites stripped off their ornaments at Mount
Horeb.

7Now Moses used to take a tent and pitch it
outside the camp some distance away, calling it
the "tent of meeting." Anyone inquiring of the
LORD would go to the tent of meeting outside the
camp. 8And whenever Moses went out to the tent,
all the people rose and stood at the entrances to
their tents, watching Moses until he entered the
tent. 9As Moses went into the tent, the pillar of
cloud would come down and stay at the entrance,
while the LORD spoke with Moses. 10Whenever the
people saw the pillar of cloud standing at the en-
trance to the tent, they all stood and worshiped,
each at the entrance to his tent. 11The LORD would
speak to Moses face to face, as a man speaks with
his friend. Then Moses would return to the camp,
but his young aide Joshua son of Nun did not
leave the tent.

12Moses said to the LORD, "You have been tell-
ing me, 'Lead these people,' but you have not let
me know whom you will send with me. You have
said, 'I know you by name and you have found
favor with me.' 13If you are pleased with me,
teach me your ways so I may know you and con-
tinue to find favor with you. Remember that this
nation is your people."

14The LORD replied, "My Presence will go with
you, and I will give you rest."

15Then Moses said to him, "If your Presence
does not go with us, do not send us up from here.
16How will anyone know that you are pleased
with me and with your people unless you go with
us? What else will distinguish me and your peo-
ple from all the other people on the face of the
earth?"

17And the LORD said to Moses, "I will do the
very thing you have asked, because I am pleased
with you and I know you by name."

18Then Moses said, "Now show me your glory."

19And the LORD said, "I will cause all my good-
ness to pass in front of you, and I will proclaim
my name, the LORD, in your presence. I will have
mercy on whom I will have mercy, and I will have
compassion on whom I will have compassion.
20But," he said, "you cannot see my face, for no
one may see me and live."

21Then the LORD said, "There is a place near me
where you may stand on a rock. 22When my glory
passes by, I will put you in a cleft in the rock and
cover you with my hand until I have passed by.
23Then I will remove my hand and you will see
my back; but my face must not be seen."

Discovering the Word 1. What commands, promises and warnings did God give Israel? 2. What occurred at the tent of meeting and why? 3. What do these verses reveal about Moses' relationship with God and the effect it had on others? 4. Look at the development of Moses' requests (vv. 13, 15, 18). How do they increase in spiritual wisdom and depth and reveal Moses' deepest desire? 5. In God's answer to Moses (vv. 19–23), what do you learn about his nature and character?

Applying the Word 1. Moses could not see God's face. What is our privilege and responsibility in light of John 14:8–14 and Hebrews 1:1–4? 2. In what ways do you demonstrate a desire to know God and to see his glory?

Responding in Prayer Thank the Father for showing you his glory incarnate in his son, Jesus Christ.

21 / *Exodus 34*
Renewing the Covenant

THE CYNICAL STATEMENT of some historians is that treaties are made to be broken. Sadly, that's often been the case. Humanity's record of keeping treaties is abysmal, but nations keep on making treaties, hoping for a more secure future. Israel fell into idolatry and soon broke faith with God (Ex 19:8; 24:3). Likewise, we can recall solemn vows and promises shattered by expediency, fear and unfaithfulness. But God doesn't quit on us. That's not his nature. In this study, he calls Moses to the mountain a second time and reaffirms principles of holy living.

Warming Up to God Think of an experience in which you were given a second chance. How did it make you feel? Why?

Read Exodus 34.

34 The LORD said to Moses, "Chisel out
two stone tablets like the first ones,
and I will write on them the words
that were on the first tablets, which you broke.
2Be ready in the morning, and then come up on
Mount Sinai. Present yourself to me there on top
of the mountain. 3No one is to come with you or
be seen anywhere on the mountain; not even the
flocks and herds may graze in front of the mountain."
4So Moses chiseled out two stone tablets like
the first ones and went up Mount Sinai early in
the morning, as the LORD had commanded him;
and he carried the two stone tablets in his hands.
5Then the LORD came down in the cloud and
stood there with him and proclaimed his name,
the LORD. 6And he passed in front of Moses, proclaiming, "The LORD, the LORD, the compassionate
and gracious God, slow to anger, abounding in
love and faithfulness, 7maintaining love to thousands, and forgiving wickedness, rebellion and
sin. Yet he does not leave the guilty unpunished;
he punishes the children and their children for
the sin of the fathers to the third and fourth generation."
8Moses bowed to the ground at once and worshiped. 9"O Lord, if I have found favor in your
eyes," he said, "then let the Lord go with us. Although this is a stiff-necked people, forgive our
wickedness and our sin, and take us as your inheritance."
10Then the LORD said: "I am making a covenant
with you. Before all your people I will do wonders
never before done in any nation in all the world.
The people you live among will see how awesome
is the work that I, the LORD, will do for you.
11Obey what I command you today. I will drive
out before you the Amorites, Canaanites, Hittites,
Perizzites, Hivites and Jebusites. 12Be careful not
to make a treaty with those who live in the land
where you are going, or they will be a snare
among you. 13Break down their altars, smash
their sacred stones and cut down their Asherah
poles.[v] 14Do not worship any other god, for the
LORD, whose name is Jealous, is a jealous God.

v13 That is, symbols of the goddess Asherah

15“Be careful not to make a treaty with those
who live in the land; for when they prostitute
themselves to their gods and sacrifice to them,
they will invite you and you will eat their sacri-
fices. 16And when you choose some of their
daughters as wives for your sons and those
daughters prostitute themselves to their gods,
they will lead your sons to do the same.

17“Do not make cast idols.

18“Celebrate the Feast of Unleavened Bread.
For seven days eat bread made without yeast, as I
commanded you. Do this at the appointed time in
the month of Abib, for in that month you came
out of Egypt.

19“The first offspring of every womb belongs to
me, including all the firstborn males of your live-
stock, whether from herd or flock. 20Redeem the
firstborn donkey with a lamb, but if you do not
redeem it, break its neck. Redeem all your first-
born sons.

“No one is to appear before me empty-handed.

21“Six days you shall labor, but on the seventh
day you shall rest; even during the plowing sea-
son and harvest you must rest.

22“Celebrate the Feast of Weeks with the first-
fruits of the wheat harvest, and the Feast of In-
gathering at the turn of the year.[w] 23Three times
a year all your men are to appear before the Sov-
ereign LORD, the God of Israel. 24I will drive out
nations before you and enlarge your territory, and
no one will covet your land when you go up three
times each year to appear before the LORD your
God.

25“Do not offer the blood of a sacrifice to me
along with anything containing yeast, and do not
let any of the sacrifice from the Passover Feast
remain until morning.

26“Bring the best of the firstfruits of your soil to
the house of the LORD your God.

“Do not cook a young goat in its mother’s
milk.”

27Then the LORD said to Moses, “Write down
these words, for in accordance with these words I
have made a covenant with you and with Israel.”
28Moses was there with the LORD forty days and
forty nights without eating bread or drinking wa-
ter. And he wrote on the tablets the words of the
covenant—the Ten Commandments.

29When Moses came down from Mount Sinai
with the two tablets of the Testimony in his
hands, he was not aware that his face was radiant
because he had spoken with the LORD. 30When
Aaron and all the Israelites saw Moses, his face
was radiant, and they were afraid to come near
him. 31But Moses called to them; so Aaron and all
the leaders of the community came back to him,
and he spoke to them. 32Afterward all the Israel-
ites came near him, and he gave them all the com-
mands the LORD had given him on Mount Sinai.

33When Moses finished speaking to them, he
put a veil over his face. 34But whenever he en-
tered the LORD’s presence to speak with him, he
removed the veil until he came out. And when he
came out and told the Israelites what he had been
commanded, 35they saw that his face was radiant.
Then Moses would put the veil back over his face
until he went in to speak with the LORD.

w22 That is, in the fall

Discovering the Word 1. In order to meet God, what was required of Moses (vv. 1–3)? 2. How would you describe God, based on what he proclaimed to Moses (vv. 6–7)? 3. What request did Moses make and why (vv. 8–9)? 4. How would you summarize the covenant God made with Israel? 5. What effect did this meeting with God have on Moses, the leaders and the people (vv. 29–32)? 6. What practice was then established and why (vv. 33–35)?

Applying the Word 1. God calls us to live among those who do not honor his name. In what ways can they be a “snare” for us (v. 12)? 2. What principles of godly living in the New Testament would correspond to God’s concern for Israel here (Gal 5:16–26; Eph 4:20–32)?

Responding in Prayer Praise God for being a God of second chances.

22 / *Exodus 35—36*
Building the Tabernacle

HARDLY A DAY passes that we aren't asked to contribute to some worthy cause or implored to work on a needed project. The avalanche of appeals dulls our senses and makes it hard to sort out priorities. It's tempting to do nothing. In this study, God launches a tabernacle building project. He asks for money (donated goods) and services (labor). Israel was called a "stiff-necked people"—not the best prospects for a building fund drive—but their response to God is surprising.

Warming Up to God Spend a few minutes telling God about the events of your day—your joys and worries. Lay them at his feet and leave them behind as you look into the Word.

Read Exodus 35—36.

35 Moses assembled the whole Israelite community and said to them, "These are the things the LORD has commanded you to do: [2]For six days, work is to be done, but the seventh day shall be your holy day, a Sabbath of rest to the LORD. Whoever does any work on it must be put to death. [3]Do not light a fire in any of your dwellings on the Sabbath day."

[4]Moses said to the whole Israelite community, "This is what the LORD has commanded: [5]From what you have, take an offering for the LORD. Everyone who is willing is to bring to the LORD an offering of gold, silver and bronze; [6]blue, purple and scarlet yarn and fine linen; goat hair; [7]ram skins dyed red and hides of sea cows[x]; acacia wood; [8]olive oil for the light; spices for the anointing oil and for the fragrant incense; [9]and onyx stones and other gems to be mounted on the ephod and breastpiece.

[10]"All who are skilled among you are to come and make everything the LORD has commanded: [11]the tabernacle with its tent and its covering, clasps, frames, crossbars, posts and bases; [12]the ark with its poles and the atonement cover and the curtain that shields it; [13]the table with its poles and all its articles and the bread of the Presence; [14]the lampstand that is for light with its accessories, lamps and oil for the light; [15]the altar of incense with its poles, the anointing oil and the fragrant incense; the curtain for the doorway at the entrance to the tabernacle; [16]the altar of burnt offering with its bronze grating, its poles and all its utensils; the bronze basin with its stand; [17]the curtains of the courtyard with its posts and bases, and the curtain for the entrance to the courtyard; [18]the tent pegs for the tabernacle and for the courtyard, and their ropes; [19]the woven garments worn for ministering in the sanctuary—both the sacred garments for Aaron the priest and the garments for his sons when they serve as priests."

[20]Then the whole Israelite community withdrew from Moses' presence, [21]and everyone who was willing and whose heart moved him came and brought an offering to the LORD for the work on the Tent of Meeting, for all its service, and for the sacred garments. [22]All who were willing, men and women alike, came and brought gold jewelry of all kinds: brooches, earrings, rings and ornaments. They all presented their gold as a wave offering to the LORD. [23]Everyone who had blue, purple or scarlet yarn or fine linen, or goat hair, ram skins dyed red or hides of sea cows brought them. [24]Those presenting an offering of silver or bronze brought it as an offering to the LORD, and everyone who had acacia wood for any part of the work brought it. [25]Every skilled woman spun with her hands and brought what she had spun—blue, purple or scarlet yarn or fine linen. [26]And all the women who were willing and had the skill spun the goat hair. [27]The leaders brought onyx stones and other gems to be mounted on the ephod and breastpiece. [28]They also brought spices and olive oil for the light and for the anointing oil and for the fragrant incense. [29]All the Israelite men and women who were willing brought to the LORD freewill offerings for all the work the LORD through Moses had commanded them to do.

[30]Then Moses said to the Israelites, "See, the LORD has chosen Bezalel son of Uri, the son of Hur, of the tribe of Judah, [31]and he has filled him with the Spirit of God, with skill, ability and

[x]7 That is, dugongs; also in verse 23

knowledge in all kinds of crafts— [32]to make artistic designs for work in gold, silver and bronze, [33]to cut and set stones, to work in wood and to engage in all kinds of artistic craftsmanship. [34]And he has given both him and Oholiab son of Ahisamach, of the tribe of Dan, the ability to teach others. [35]He has filled them with skill to do all kinds of work as craftsmen, designers, embroiderers in blue, purple and scarlet yarn and fine linen, and weavers—all of them master craftsmen and designers.

36

[1]So Bezalel, Oholiab and every skilled person to whom the LORD has given skill and ability to know how to carry out all the work of constructing the sanctuary are to do the work just as the Lord has commanded."

[2]Then Moses summoned Bezalel and Oholiab and every skilled person to whom the LORD had given ability and who was willing to come and do the work. [3]They received from Moses all the offerings the Israelites had brought to carry out the work of constructing the sanctuary. And the people continued to bring freewill offerings morning after morning. [4]So all the skilled craftsmen who were doing all the work on the sanctuary left their work [5]and said to Moses, "The people are bringing more than enough for doing the work the LORD commanded to be done."

[6]Then Moses gave an order and they sent this word throughout the camp: "No man or woman is to make anything else as an offering for the sanctuary." And so the people were restrained from bringing more, [7]because what they already had was more than enough to do all the work.

[8]All the skilled men among the workmen made the tabernacle with ten curtains of finely twisted linen and blue, purple and scarlet yarn, with cherubim worked into them by a skilled craftsman. [9]All the curtains were the same size—twenty-eight cubits long and four cubits wide.[y] [10]They joined five of the curtains together and did the same with the other five. [11]Then they made loops of blue material along the edge of the end curtain in one set, and the same was done with the end curtain in the other set. [12]They also made fifty loops on one curtain and fifty loops on the end curtain of the other set, with the loops opposite each other. [13]Then they made fifty gold clasps and used them to fasten the two sets of curtains together so that the tabernacle was a unit.

[14]They made curtains of goat hair for the tent over the tabernacle—eleven altogether. [15]All eleven curtains were the same size—thirty cubits long and four cubits wide.[z] [16]They joined five of the curtains into one set and the other six into another set. [17]Then they made fifty loops along the edge of the end curtain in one set and also along the edge of the end curtain in the other set. [18]They made fifty bronze clasps to fasten the tent together as a unit. [19]Then they made for the tent a covering of ram skins dyed red, and over that a covering of hides of sea cows.[a]

[20]They made upright frames of acacia wood for the tabernacle. [21]Each frame was ten cubits long and a cubit and a half wide,[b] [22]with two projections set parallel to each other. They made all the frames of the tabernacle in this way. [23]They made twenty frames for the south side of the tabernacle [24]and made forty silver bases to go under them—two bases for each frame, one under each projection. [25]For the other side, the north side of the tabernacle, they made twenty frames [26]and forty silver bases—two under each frame. [27]They made six frames for the far end, that is, the west end of the tabernacle, [28]and two frames were made for the corners of the tabernacle at the far end. [29]At these two corners the frames were double from the bottom all the way to the top and fitted into a single ring; both were made alike. [30]So there were eight frames and sixteen silver bases—two under each frame.

[31]They also made crossbars of acacia wood: five for the frames on one side of the tabernacle, [32]five for those on the other side, and five for the frames on the west, at the far end of the tabernacle. [33]They made the center crossbar so that it extended from end to end at the middle of the frames. [34]They overlaid the frames with gold and made gold rings to hold the crossbars. They also overlaid the crossbars with gold.

[35]They made the curtain of blue, purple and scarlet yarn and finely twisted linen, with cherubim worked into it by a skilled craftsman. [36]They made four posts of acacia wood for it and overlaid them with gold. They made gold hooks for them and cast their four silver bases. [37]For the entrance to the tent they made a curtain of blue, purple and scarlet yarn and finely twisted linen—the

[y] *9* That is, about 42 feet (about 12.5 meters) long and 6 feet (about 1.8 meters) wide [z] *15* That is, about 45 feet (about 13.5 meters) long and 6 feet (about 1.8 meters) wide [a] *19* That is, dugongs [b] *21* That is, about 15 feet (about 4.5 meters) long and 2 1/4 feet (about 0.7 meter) wide

work of an embroiderer; 38and they made five
posts with hooks for them. They overlaid the tops
of the posts and their bands with gold and made
their five bases of bronze.

Discovering the Word 1. What was God's plan for the provision of materials (vv. 4–9)? 2. Of what value and importance would it be for the Israelites to give their own possessions and to build the tabernacle themselves (35:10)? 3. The Israelites responded to God's call for an offering (35:20–29). How do you account for this outpouring of goods and materials (see 36:3–7)? 4. In God's plan, how was it possible for everyone to give something (see 3:21–22; 12:35–36)? 5. How did the nomadic Israelites—shepherds in Egypt for more than four centuries—suddenly develop skills in design, building and craftsmanship (35:30–35)? 6. Who came to do the work (36:1–2)?

Applying the Word 1. What possessions and abilities do you have for God to use? 2. What keeps God's people today from giving willingly, sacrificially and generously?

Responding in Prayer Ask the Lord to teach you how to give graciously.

23 / *Exodus 37:1—39:31*

God Speaks Powerfully in Wood, Gold, Silver, Linen and Wool

HOW IMPORTANT IS the furniture in your church? What about the clothes people wear? What do they say to you and others? In God's plan for Israel's worship, he spoke powerfully through furniture and clothing. God has also given us spiritual dress—both inner qualities and outward deeds—to help people know and understand him. He also speaks to us in the beauty of the sanctuary. This study looks at outward things, so look for their hidden meaning and significance. The medium is the message in this case.

Warming Up to God Confess the ways you've forgotten your Savior today. Let his forgiveness fall on you like gentle rain—and regain your strength to press on.

Read Exodus 37:1—39:31.

37 Bezalel made the ark of acacia
wood—two and a half cubits long,
a cubit and a half wide, and a cubit
and a half high.[c] 2He overlaid it with pure gold,
both inside and out, and made a gold molding
around it. 3He cast four gold rings for it and fas-
tened them to its four feet, with two rings on one
side and two rings on the other. 4Then he made
poles of acacia wood and overlaid them with gold.
5And he inserted the poles into the rings on the
sides of the ark to carry it.

6He made the atonement cover of pure gold—
two and a half cubits long and a cubit and a half
wide.[d] 7Then he made two cherubim out of ham-
mered gold at the ends of the cover. 8He made
one cherub on one end and the second cherub on
the other; at the two ends he made them of one
piece with the cover. 9The cherubim had their
wings spread upward, overshadowing the cover
with them. The cherubim faced each other, look-
ing toward the cover.

10They[e] made the table of acacia wood—two
cubits long, a cubit wide, and a cubit and a half
high.[f] 11Then they overlaid it with pure gold and
made a gold molding around it. 12They also made
around it a rim a handbreadth[g] wide and put a
gold molding on the rim. 13They cast four gold
rings for the table and fastened them to the four
corners, where the four legs were. 14The rings
were put close to the rim to hold the poles used

[c] 1 That is, about 3 3/4 feet (about 1.1 meters) long and 2 1/4 feet (about 0.7 meter) wide and high [d] 6 That is, about 3 3/4 feet (about 1.1 meters) long and 2 1/4 feet (about 0.7 meter) wide [e] 10 Or He; also in verses 11-29 [f] 10 That is, about 3 feet (about 0.9 meter) long, 1 1/2 feet (about 0.5 meter) wide, and 2 1/4 feet (about 0.7 meter) high [g] 12 That is, about 3 inches (about 8 centimeters)

in carrying the table. 15The poles for carrying the table were made of acacia wood and were overlaid with gold. 16And they made from pure gold the articles for the table—its plates and dishes and bowls and its pitchers for the pouring out of drink offerings.

17They made the lampstand of pure gold and hammered it out, base and shaft; its flowerlike cups, buds and blossoms were of one piece with it. 18Six branches extended from the sides of the lampstand—three on one side and three on the other. 19Three cups shaped like almond flowers with buds and blossoms were on one branch, three on the next branch and the same for all six branches extending from the lampstand. 20And on the lampstand were four cups shaped like almond flowers with buds and blossoms. 21One bud was under the first pair of branches extending from the lampstand, a second bud under the second pair, and a third bud under the third pair—six branches in all. 22The buds and the branches were all of one piece with the lampstand, hammered out of pure gold.

23They made its seven lamps, as well as its wick trimmers and trays, of pure gold. 24They made the lampstand and all its accessories from one talent[h] of pure gold.

25They made the altar of incense out of acacia wood. It was square, a cubit long and a cubit wide, and two cubits high[i]—its horns of one piece with it. 26They overlaid the top and all the sides and the horns with pure gold, and made a gold molding around it. 27They made two gold rings below the molding—two on opposite sides—to hold the poles used to carry it. 28They made the poles of acacia wood and overlaid them with gold.

29They also made the sacred anointing oil and the pure, fragrant incense—the work of a perfumer.

38 They[j] built the altar of burnt offering of acacia wood, three cubits[k] high; it was square, five cubits long and five cubits wide.[l] 2They made a horn at each of the four corners, so that the horns and the altar were of one piece, and they overlaid the altar with bronze. 3They made all its utensils of bronze—its pots, shovels, sprinkling bowls, meat forks and firepans. 4They made a grating for the altar, a bronze network, to be under its ledge, halfway up the altar. 5They cast bronze rings to hold the poles for the four corners of the bronze grating. 6They made the poles of acacia wood and overlaid them with bronze. 7They inserted the poles into the rings so they would be on the sides of the altar for carrying it. They made it hollow, out of boards.

8They made the bronze basin and its bronze stand from the mirrors of the women who served at the entrance to the Tent of Meeting.

9Next they made the courtyard. The south side was a hundred cubits[m] long and had curtains of finely twisted linen, 10with twenty posts and twenty bronze bases, and with silver hooks and bands on the posts. 11The north side was also a hundred cubits long and had twenty posts and twenty bronze bases, with silver hooks and bands on the posts.

12The west end was fifty cubits[n] wide and had curtains, with ten posts and ten bases, with silver hooks and bands on the posts. 13The east end, toward the sunrise, was also fifty cubits wide. 14Curtains fifteen cubits[o] long were on one side of the entrance, with three posts and three bases, 15and curtains fifteen cubits long were on the other side of the entrance to the courtyard, with three posts and three bases. 16All the curtains around the courtyard were of finely twisted linen. 17The bases for the posts were bronze. The hooks and bands on the posts were silver, and their tops were overlaid with silver; so all the posts of the courtyard had silver bands.

18The curtain for the entrance to the courtyard was of blue, purple and scarlet yarn and finely twisted linen—the work of an embroiderer. It was twenty cubits[p] long and, like the curtains of the courtyard, five cubits[q] high, 19with four posts and four bronze bases. Their hooks and bands were silver, and their tops were overlaid with silver. 20All the tent pegs of the tabernacle and of the surrounding courtyard were bronze.

21These are the amounts of the materials used for the tabernacle, the tabernacle of the Testimony, which were recorded at Moses' command by the Levites under the direction of Ithamar son of Aaron, the priest. 22(Bezalel son of Uri, the son of Hur, of the tribe of Judah, made everything the LORD commanded Moses; 23with him was Oholiab

[h] *24* That is, about 75 pounds (about 34 kilograms) [i] *25* That is, about 1 1/2 feet (about 0.5 meter) long and wide, and about 3 feet (about 0.9 meter) high [j] *1* Or *He*; also in verses 2-9 [k] *1* That is, about 4 1/2 feet (about 1.3 meters) [l] *1* That is, about 7 1/2 feet (about 2.3 meters) long and wide [m] *9* That is, about 150 feet (about 46 meters) [n] *12* That is, about 75 feet (about 23 meters) [o] *14* That is, about 22 1/2 feet (about 6.9 meters) [p] *18* That is, about 30 feet (about 9 meters) [q] *18* That is, about 7 1/2 feet (about 2.3 meters)

son of Ahisamach, of the tribe of Dan—a craftsman and designer, and an embroiderer in blue, purple and scarlet yarn and fine linen.) 24The total amount of the gold from the wave offering used for all the work on the sanctuary was 29 talents and 730 shekels,[r] according to the sanctuary shekel.

25The silver obtained from those of the community who were counted in the census was 100 talents and 1,775 shekels,[s] according to the sanctuary shekel— 26one beka per person, that is, half a shekel,[t] according to the sanctuary shekel, from everyone who had crossed over to those counted, twenty years old or more, a total of 603,550 men. 27The 100 talents[u] of silver were used to cast the bases for the sanctuary and for the curtain—100 bases from the 100 talents, one talent for each base. 28They used the 1,775 shekels[v] to make the hooks for the posts, to overlay the tops of the posts, and to make their bands.

29The bronze from the wave offering was 70 talents and 2,400 shekels.[w] 30They used it to make the bases for the entrance to the Tent of Meeting, the bronze altar with its bronze grating and all its utensils, 31the bases for the surrounding courtyard and those for its entrance and all the tent pegs for the tabernacle and those for the surrounding courtyard.

39

From the blue, purple and scarlet yarn they made woven garments for ministering in the sanctuary. They also made sacred garments for Aaron, as the LORD commanded Moses.

2They[x] made the ephod of gold, and of blue, purple and scarlet yarn, and of finely twisted linen. 3They hammered out thin sheets of gold and cut strands to be worked into the blue, purple and scarlet yarn and fine linen—the work of a skilled craftsman. 4They made shoulder pieces for the ephod, which were attached to two of its corners, so it could be fastened. 5Its skillfully woven waistband was like it—of one piece with the ephod and made with gold, and with blue, purple and scarlet yarn, and with finely twisted linen, as the LORD commanded Moses.

6They mounted the onyx stones in gold filigree settings and engraved them like a seal with the names of the sons of Israel. 7Then they fastened them on the shoulder pieces of the ephod as memorial stones for the sons of Israel, as the LORD commanded Moses.

8They fashioned the breastpiece—the work of a skilled craftsman. They made it like the ephod: of gold, and of blue, purple and scarlet yarn, and of finely twisted linen. 9It was square—a span[y] long and a span wide—and folded double. 10Then they mounted four rows of precious stones on it. In the first row there was a ruby, a topaz and a beryl; 11in the second row a turquoise, a sapphire[z] and an emerald; 12in the third row a jacinth, an agate and an amethyst; 13in the fourth row a chrysolite, an onyx and a jasper.[a] They were mounted in gold filigree settings. 14There were twelve stones, one for each of the names of the sons of Israel, each engraved like a seal with the name of one of the twelve tribes.

15For the breastpiece they made braided chains of pure gold, like a rope. 16They made two gold filigree settings and two gold rings, and fastened the rings to two of the corners of the breastpiece. 17They fastened the two gold chains to the rings at the corners of the breastpiece, 18and the other ends of the chains to the two settings, attaching them to the shoulder pieces of the ephod at the front. 19They made two gold rings and attached them to the other two corners of the breastpiece on the inside edge next to the ephod. 20Then they made two more gold rings and attached them to the bottom of the shoulder pieces on the front of the ephod, close to the seam just above the waistband of the ephod. 21They tied the rings of the breastpiece to the rings of the ephod with blue cord, connecting it to the waistband so that the breastpiece would not swing out from the ephod—as the LORD commanded Moses.

22They made the robe of the ephod entirely of blue cloth—the work of a weaver— 23with an opening in the center of the robe like the opening of a collar,[b] and a band around this opening, so that it would not tear. 24They made pomegranates of blue, purple and scarlet yarn and finely twisted linen around the hem of the robe. 25And they made bells of pure gold and attached them around the hem between the pomegranates. 26The bells and pomegranates alternated around the

r24 The weight of the gold was a little over one ton (about 1 metric ton). s25 The weight of the silver was a little over 3 3/4 tons (about 3.4 metric tons). t26 That is, about 1/5 ounce (about 5.5 grams) u27 That is, about 3 3/4 tons (about 3.4 metric tons) v28 That is, about 45 pounds (about 20 kilograms) w29 The weight of the bronze was about 2 1/2 tons (about 2.4 metric tons). x2 Or *He*; also in verses 7, 8 and 22 y9 That is, about 9 inches (about 22 centimeters) z11 Or *lapis lazuli* a13 The precise identification of some of these precious stones is uncertain. b23 The meaning of the Hebrew for this word is uncertain.

hem of the robe to be worn for ministering, as the LORD commanded Moses.

27For Aaron and his sons, they made tunics of fine linen—the work of a weaver— 28and the turban of fine linen, the linen headbands and the undergarments of finely twisted linen. 29The sash was of finely twisted linen and blue, purple and scarlet yarn—the work of an embroiderer—as the LORD commanded Moses.

30They made the plate, the sacred diadem, out of pure gold and engraved on it, like an inscription on a seal: HOLY TO THE LORD. 31Then they fastened a blue cord to it to attach it to the turban, as the LORD commanded Moses.

Discovering the Word 1. How would the ark, table, lampstand, altar of incense and altar of burnt offering assist the Israelites in their worship of God? 2. What aspect of God's nature and character does each article depict? 3. How does each article illustrate some aspect of our own relation to God? 4. What message was God trying to convey about himself and worship through the priests' ephod, breastpiece, robe and tunic (Ex 39)?

Applying the Word 1. What advantages do we have in knowing and worshiping God that the Israelites did not have (Heb 9:1–15)? 2. The New Testament refers to Christians as priests (1Pe 2:5, 9). What is our function as priests? 3. What priestly garments are we called to wear (Col 3:12–14)?

Responding in Prayer Praise God for revealing himself to us. Pray that he will use you in his service.

24 / *Exodus 39:32—40:38*
Time for Praise and Reflection

DEDICATIONS OF NEW churches are special. Such services evoke pride and appreciation. But with every privilege and blessing from God comes new responsibilities. Our church buildings, in a sense, call us to faithful worship, witness and obedience to God's will. Although God's glory may not be visible, it is present in our hearts. Join with Moses and the Israelites in this study and celebrate God's goodness to them and to us.

Warming Up to God What have you learned about God through these quiet times in Exodus? Reflect on the ways you've grown and thank God for molding you in the image of his Son.

Read Exodus 39:32—40:38.

32So all the work on the tabernacle, the Tent of Meeting, was completed. The Israelites did everything just as the LORD commanded Moses. 33Then they brought the tabernacle to Moses: the tent and all its furnishings, its clasps, frames, crossbars, posts and bases; 34the covering of ram skins dyed red, the covering of hides of sea cows[c] and the shielding curtain; 35the ark of the Testimony with its poles and the atonement cover; 36the table with all its articles and the bread of the Presence; 37the pure gold lampstand with its row of lamps and all its accessories, and the oil for the light; 38the gold altar, the anointing oil, the fragrant incense, and the curtain for the entrance to the tent; 39the bronze altar with its bronze grating, its poles and all its utensils; the basin with its stand; 40the curtains of the courtyard with its posts and bases, and the curtain for the entrance to the courtyard; the ropes and tent pegs for the courtyard; all the furnishings for the tabernacle, the Tent of Meeting; 41and the woven garments worn for ministering in the sanctuary, both the sacred garments for Aaron the priest and the garments for his sons when serving as priests.

42The Israelites had done all the work just as the LORD had commanded Moses. 43Moses inspected the work and saw that they had done it just as the LORD had commanded. So Moses blessed them.

40 Then the LORD said to Moses: 2"Set up the tabernacle, the Tent of Meeting, on the first day of the first month. 3Place the ark of the Testimony in it and shield the ark with the curtain. 4Bring in the table

c34 That is, dugongs

and set out what belongs on it. Then bring in the lampstand and set up its lamps. 5Place the gold altar of incense in front of the ark of the Testimony and put the curtain at the entrance to the tabernacle.

6"Place the altar of burnt offering in front of the entrance to the tabernacle, the Tent of Meeting; 7place the basin between the Tent of Meeting and the altar and put water in it. 8Set up the courtyard around it and put the curtain at the entrance to the courtyard.

9"Take the anointing oil and anoint the tabernacle and everything in it; consecrate it and all its furnishings, and it will be holy. 10Then anoint the altar of burnt offering and all its utensils; consecrate the altar, and it will be most holy. 11Anoint the basin and its stand and consecrate them.

12"Bring Aaron and his sons to the entrance to the Tent of Meeting and wash them with water. 13Then dress Aaron in the sacred garments, anoint him and consecrate him so he may serve me as priest. 14Bring his sons and dress them in tunics. 15Anoint them just as you anointed their father, so they may serve me as priests. Their anointing will be to a priesthood that will continue for all generations to come." 16Moses did everything just as the LORD commanded him.

17So the tabernacle was set up on the first day of the first month in the second year. 18When Moses set up the tabernacle, he put the bases in place, erected the frames, inserted the crossbars and set up the posts. 19Then he spread the tent over the tabernacle and put the covering over the tent, as the LORD commanded him.

20He took the Testimony and placed it in the ark, attached the poles to the ark and put the atonement cover over it. 21Then he brought the ark into the tabernacle and hung the shielding curtain and shielded the ark of the Testimony, as the LORD commanded him.

22Moses placed the table in the Tent of Meeting on the north side of the tabernacle outside the curtain 23and set out the bread on it before the LORD, as the LORD commanded him.

24He placed the lampstand in the Tent of Meeting opposite the table on the south side of the tabernacle 25and set up the lamps before the LORD, as the LORD commanded him.

26Moses placed the gold altar in the Tent of Meeting in front of the curtain 27and burned fragrant incense on it, as the LORD commanded him. 28Then he put up the curtain at the entrance to the tabernacle.

29He set the altar of burnt offering near the entrance to the tabernacle, the Tent of Meeting, and offered on it burnt offerings and grain offerings, as the LORD commanded him.

30He placed the basin between the Tent of Meeting and the altar and put water in it for washing, 31and Moses and Aaron and his sons used it to wash their hands and feet. 32They washed whenever they entered the Tent of Meeting or approached the altar, as the LORD commanded Moses.

33Then Moses set up the courtyard around the tabernacle and altar and put up the curtain at the entrance to the courtyard. And so Moses finished the work.

34Then the cloud covered the Tent of Meeting, and the glory of the LORD filled the tabernacle. 35Moses could not enter the Tent of Meeting because the cloud had settled upon it, and the glory of the LORD filled the tabernacle.

36In all the travels of the Israelites, whenever the cloud lifted from above the tabernacle, they would set out; 37but if the cloud did not lift, they did not set out—until the day it lifted. 38So the cloud of the LORD was over the tabernacle by day, and fire was in the cloud by night, in the sight of all the house of Israel during all their travels.

Discovering the Word 1. What feelings do you think the Israelites had in working "just as the Lord had commanded" and in showing their work to Moses? 2. Why was it necessary to anoint everything, burn incense and make offerings (40:9–10, 26–29)? 3. Buildings and furnishings today are not holy, as the tabernacle and its furnishings were. What are the components of God's dwelling place today (Eph 2:19–22)? 4. How did God reveal his presence (40:34–38)?

Applying the Word 1. As you invest your life for God, what satisfaction have you gained from following his plan? 2. In what circumstances have you especially felt God's presence? 3. How does God reveal his glory and presence in our midst today?

Responding in Prayer Thank God for the ways he has used the stories of Exodus to strengthen you and draw you closer to himself.

Leviticus

"You're spending your quiet time reading *Leviticus?* Isn't it just a list of laws? And hasn't that all been replaced by grace?"

Those are some of the astonished responses you're likely to get when you tell people you're reading this book of the Bible. It's true, Leviticus has never made popular devotional reading. But for those who dare to venture into it daily, it brings us face to face with realities about God, the world and ourselves.

The book is concerned with living out the sacred trust of holiness. *Leviticus* means "pertaining to the Levites." To the descendants of Levi, Jacob's son, God gave special responsibilities for worship (Nu 1:47–53; 3:5–13). The Lord set them apart as his priests who were to make sure that the tabernacle—and the people—remained holy.

The first seven chapters are instructions for various offerings. Chapters 8—10 relate the ordination of Aaron and his sons as priests. Chapters 11—15 are about cleansing. In chapter 16 the all-important Day of Atonement (Yom Kippur) is instituted. The last eleven chapters deal with moral laws for everyday living, priestly behavior, festivals and the results to be expected from obeying or disobeying God.

Except for brief narrative portions, the book presents itself as spoken by God to Moses. No proof is offered. It simply says, "The Lord said to Moses," or sometimes, "The Lord said to Moses and Aaron." The time is shortly after the Israelites' exodus from Egypt, an event long dated c. 1220 B.C., though recent discoveries indicate it may have been earlier, c. 1440 B.C.

This is all historically interesting and deserves study—but is it appropriate for a Christian's quiet time? Why concern ourselves with Old Testament sacrifices and purification when Christ has fulfilled all the law? What do we gain today from a devotional reading of Leviticus?

First of all, Leviticus shows us God. It says that God is holy, a truth that made the prophet Isaiah cry out, "Woe is me!" Yet this holy God talks to Moses, a man sometimes of timidity and temper, and, through Moses, he talks to ordinary people, explaining how to live and how to know him.

Leviticus also shows us ourselves. It tells us we can know God. It says that we are not holy unless God makes us so. It portrays people trying to get around God's laws—something we all still try in various ways. And it promises that a broken relationship with God can be restored through his mercy.

Finally, Leviticus shows us the world, mostly indirectly, by telling us how God's people are different from the world. Some differences are external, but they are primarily internal because God has already made us different from the rest of humanity. Leviticus tells us that as we live in this world we are bound to be distinctive simply because we belong to God.

God commands his people: "Be holy, because I am holy" (Lev 11:44). He also assures us: "I am the LORD, who makes you holy" (Lev 20:8). May you grow in holiness as you meditate on this book of holiness.

Outline

1 / *Leviticus 1*
A Holy Sacrifice

DROPPING A FEW coins in the Salvation Army kettle at Christmas or giving used items to Goodwill Industries has become routine for most of us. But what if you were asked to contribute your best suit or your best set of china? God asked the Israelites to give their best as a sacrifice to him. No doubt some did it with secret grumblings, while others did it with joy.

Warming Up to God Reflect on a time when you made some difficult sacrifices and the Lord made the cost worth it. Allow your words of praise and gratitude to well up in response.

Read Leviticus 1.

1 The Lord called to Moses and spoke to
him from the Tent of Meeting. He said,
2“Speak to the Israelites and say to them:
‘When any of you brings an offering to the Lord,
bring as your offering an animal from either the
herd or the flock.
3“ ‘If the offering is a burnt offering from the
herd, he is to offer a male without defect. He must
present it at the entrance to the Tent of Meeting
so that it[a] will be acceptable to the Lord. 4He is
to lay his hand on the head of the burnt offering,
and it will be accepted on his behalf to make
atonement for him. 5He is to slaughter the young
bull before the Lord, and then Aaron’s sons the
priests shall bring the blood and sprinkle it
against the altar on all sides at the entrance to the
Tent of Meeting. 6He is to skin the burnt offering
and cut it into pieces. 7The sons of Aaron the
priest are to put fire on the altar and arrange
wood on the fire. 8Then Aaron’s sons the priests
shall arrange the pieces, including the head
and the fat, on the burning wood that is on
the altar. 9He is to wash the inner parts and the
legs with water, and the priest is to burn all
of it on the altar. It is a burnt offering, an
offering made by fire, an aroma pleasing to the
Lord.
10“ ‘If the offering is a burnt offering from
the flock, from either the sheep or the goats,
he is to offer a male without defect. 11He is to
slaughter it at the north side of the altar before
the Lord, and Aaron’s sons the priests shall
sprinkle its blood against the altar on all sides.
12He is to cut it into pieces, and the priest shall
arrange them, including the head and the fat,
on the burning wood that is on the altar. 13He
is to wash the inner parts and the legs with water,
and the priest is to bring all of it and burn
it on the altar. It is a burnt offering, an offer-
ing made by fire, an aroma pleasing to the
Lord.
14“ ‘If the offering to the Lord is a burnt offering
of birds, he is to offer a dove or a young pigeon.
15The priest shall bring it to the altar, wring off
the head and burn it on the altar; its blood shall
be drained out on the side of the altar. 16He is to
remove the crop with its contents[b] and throw it
to the east side of the altar, where the ashes are.
17He shall tear it open by the wings, not severing
it completely, and then the priest shall burn it on
the wood that is on the fire on the altar. It is a
burnt offering, an offering made by fire, an aroma
pleasing to the Lord.

[a]3 Or *he* [b]16 Or *crop and the feathers*; the meaning of the Hebrew for this word is uncertain.

Discovering the Word 1. When the Israelites brought offerings from their herds or flocks, what requirements did they need to meet (vv. 3–10)? 2. How were the givers to identify themselves with the offering (v. 4)? 3. What was the purpose of the offering (v. 4)? 4. What part did the priests play in the offering (vv. 5–17)? 5. How was an offering of birds different from one from the herd or flock (vv. 14–17)?

Applying the Word 1. In Romans 12:1 Paul urges us: “Offer your bodies as living sacrifices, holy and pleasing to God—this is your spiritual act of worship.” How is this sacrifice different from the burnt offerings of Leviticus 1? How is it the same? 2. Verses 9, 13 and 17 describe how the offering creates “an aroma pleasing to the Lord.” How is your life pleasing to God?

Responding in Prayer Give thanks for Christ's sacrifice and the salvation it has made available to you. Pray for guidance in how you can offer your body as a living sacrifice today.

Leviticus 2—7

2 " 'When someone brings a grain offering to the LORD, his offering is to be of fine flour. He is to pour oil on it, put incense on it 2and take it to Aaron's sons the priests. The priest shall take a handful of the fine flour and oil, together with all the incense, and burn this as a memorial portion on the altar, an offering made by fire, an aroma pleasing to the LORD. 3The rest of the grain offering belongs to Aaron and his sons; it is a most holy part of the offerings made to the LORD by fire.

4" 'If you bring a grain offering baked in an oven, it is to consist of fine flour: cakes made without yeast and mixed with oil, or[c] wafers made without yeast and spread with oil. 5If your grain offering is prepared on a griddle, it is to be made of fine flour mixed with oil, and without yeast. 6Crumble it and pour oil on it; it is a grain offering. 7If your grain offering is cooked in a pan, it is to be made of fine flour and oil. 8Bring the grain offering made of these things to the LORD; present it to the priest, who shall take it to the altar. 9He shall take out the memorial portion from the grain offering and burn it on the altar as an offering made by fire, an aroma pleasing to the LORD. 10The rest of the grain offering belongs to Aaron and his sons; it is a most holy part of the offerings made to the LORD by fire.

11" 'Every grain offering you bring to the LORD must be made without yeast, for you are not to burn any yeast or honey in an offering made to the LORD by fire. 12You may bring them to the LORD as an offering of the firstfruits, but they are not to be offered on the altar as a pleasing aroma. 13Season all your grain offerings with salt. Do not leave the salt of the covenant of your God out of your grain offerings; add salt to all your offerings.

14" 'If you bring a grain offering of firstfruits to the LORD, offer crushed heads of new grain roasted in the fire. 15Put oil and incense on it; it is a grain offering. 16The priest shall burn the memorial portion of the crushed grain and the oil, together with all the incense, as an offering made to the LORD by fire.

3 " 'If someone's offering is a fellowship offering,[d] and he offers an animal from the herd, whether male or female, he is to present before the LORD an animal without defect. 2He is to lay his hand on the head of his offering and slaughter it at the entrance to the Tent of Meeting. Then Aaron's sons the priests shall sprinkle the blood against the altar on all sides. 3From the fellowship offering he is to bring a sacrifice made to the LORD by fire: all the fat that covers the inner parts or is connected to them, 4both kidneys with the fat on them near the loins, and the covering of the liver, which he will remove with the kidneys. 5Then Aaron's sons are to burn it on the altar on top of the burnt offering that is on the burning wood, as an offering made by fire, an aroma pleasing to the LORD.

6" 'If he offers an animal from the flock as a fellowship offering to the LORD, he is to offer a male or female without defect. 7If he offers a lamb, he is to present it before the LORD. 8He is to lay his hand on the head of his offering and slaughter it in front of the Tent of Meeting. Then Aaron's sons shall sprinkle its blood against the altar on all sides. 9From the fellowship offering he is to bring a sacrifice made to the LORD by fire: its fat, the entire fat tail cut off close to the backbone, all the fat that covers the inner parts or is connected to them, 10both kidneys with the fat on them near the loins, and the covering of the liver, which he will remove with the kidneys. 11The priest shall burn them on the altar as food, an offering made to the LORD by fire.

12" 'If his offering is a goat, he is to present it before the LORD. 13He is to lay his hand on its head and slaughter it in front of the Tent of Meeting. Then Aaron's sons shall sprinkle its blood against the altar on all sides. 14From what he offers he is to make this offering to the LORD by fire: all the fat that covers the inner parts or is connected to them, 15both kidneys with the fat on them near the loins, and the covering of the liver, which he will remove with the kidneys. 16The

[c]4 Or *and* [d]1 Traditionally *peace offering*; also in verses 3, 6 and 9

priest shall burn them on the altar as food, an offering made by fire, a pleasing aroma. All the fat is the LORD's.

17" 'This is a lasting ordinance for the generations to come, wherever you live: You must not eat any fat or any blood.' "

4 The LORD said to Moses, 2"Say to the Israelites: 'When anyone sins unintentionally and does what is forbidden in any of the LORD's commands—

3" 'If the anointed priest sins, bringing guilt on the people, he must bring to the LORD a young bull without defect as a sin offering for the sin he has committed. 4He is to present the bull at the entrance to the Tent of Meeting before the LORD. He is to lay his hand on its head and slaughter it before the LORD. 5Then the anointed priest shall take some of the bull's blood and carry it into the Tent of Meeting. 6He is to dip his finger into the blood and sprinkle some of it seven times before the LORD, in front of the curtain of the sanctuary. 7The priest shall then put some of the blood on the horns of the altar of fragrant incense that is before the LORD in the Tent of Meeting. The rest of the bull's blood he shall pour out at the base of the altar of burnt offering at the entrance to the Tent of Meeting. 8He shall remove all the fat from the bull of the sin offering—the fat that covers the inner parts or is connected to them, 9both kidneys with the fat on them near the loins, and the covering of the liver, which he will remove with the kidneys— 10just as the fat is removed from the ox[e] sacrificed as a fellowship offering.[f] Then the priest shall burn them on the altar of burnt offering. 11But the hide of the bull and all its flesh, as well as the head and legs, the inner parts and offal— 12that is, all the rest of the bull—he must take outside the camp to a place ceremonially clean, where the ashes are thrown, and burn it in a wood fire on the ash heap.

13" 'If the whole Israelite community sins unintentionally and does what is forbidden in any of the LORD's commands, even though the community is unaware of the matter, they are guilty. 14When they become aware of the sin they committed, the assembly must bring a young bull as a sin offering and present it before the Tent of Meeting. 15The elders of the community are to lay their hands on the bull's head before the LORD, and the bull shall be slaughtered before the LORD. 16Then the anointed priest is to take some of the bull's blood into the Tent of Meeting. 17He shall dip his finger into the blood and sprinkle it before the LORD seven times in front of the curtain. 18He is to put some of the blood on the horns of the altar that is before the LORD in the Tent of Meeting. The rest of the blood he shall pour out at the base of the altar of burnt offering at the entrance to the Tent of Meeting. 19He shall remove all the fat from it and burn it on the altar, 20and do with this bull just as he did with the bull for the sin offering. In this way the priest will make atonement for them, and they will be forgiven. 21Then he shall take the bull outside the camp and burn it as he burned the first bull. This is the sin offering for the community.

22" 'When a leader sins unintentionally and does what is forbidden in any of the commands of the LORD his God, he is guilty. 23When he is made aware of the sin he committed, he must bring as his offering a male goat without defect. 24He is to lay his hand on the goat's head and slaughter it at the place where the burnt offering is slaughtered before the LORD. It is a sin offering. 25Then the priest shall take some of the blood of the sin offering with his finger and put it on the horns of the altar of burnt offering and pour out the rest of the blood at the base of the altar. 26He shall burn all the fat on the altar as he burned the fat of the fellowship offering. In this way the priest will make atonement for the man's sin, and he will be forgiven.

27" 'If a member of the community sins unintentionally and does what is forbidden in any of the LORD's commands, he is guilty. 28When he is made aware of the sin he committed, he must bring as his offering for the sin he committed a female goat without defect. 29He is to lay his hand on the head of the sin offering and slaughter it at the place of the burnt offering. 30Then the priest is to take some of the blood with his finger and put it on the horns of the altar of burnt offering and pour out the rest of the blood at the base of the altar. 31He shall remove all the fat, just as the fat is removed from the fellowship offering, and the priest shall burn it on the altar as an aroma pleasing to the LORD. In this way the priest will make atonement for him, and he will be forgiven.

32" 'If he brings a lamb as his sin offering, he is to bring a female without defect. 33He is to lay his

e10 The Hebrew word can include both male and female.
f10 Traditionally *peace offering*; also in verses 26, 31 and 35

hand on its head and slaughter it for a sin offering
at the place where the burnt offering is slaugh-
tered. 34Then the priest shall take some of the
blood of the sin offering with his finger and put it
on the horns of the altar of burnt offering and
pour out the rest of the blood at the base of the
altar. 35He shall remove all the fat, just as the fat
is removed from the lamb of the fellowship offer-
ing, and the priest shall burn it on the altar on top
of the offerings made to the LORD by fire. In this
way the priest will make atonement for him for
the sin he has committed, and he will be forgiven.

5 " 'If a person sins because he does not
speak up when he hears a public charge
to testify regarding something he has seen
or learned about, he will be held responsible.
2" 'Or if a person touches anything ceremoni-
ally unclean—whether the carcasses of unclean
wild animals or of unclean livestock or of unclean
creatures that move along the ground—even
though he is unaware of it, he has become un-
clean and is guilty.
3" 'Or if he touches human uncleanness—any-
thing that would make him unclean—even
though he is unaware of it, when he learns of it he
will be guilty.
4" 'Or if a person thoughtlessly takes an oath to
do anything, whether good or evil—in any matter
one might carelessly swear about—even though
he is unaware of it, in any case when he learns of
it he will be guilty.
5" 'When anyone is guilty in any of these ways,
he must confess in what way he has sinned 6and,
as a penalty for the sin he has committed, he must
bring to the LORD a female lamb or goat from the
flock as a sin offering; and the priest shall make
atonement for him for his sin.
7" 'If he cannot afford a lamb, he is to bring two
doves or two young pigeons to the LORD as a pen-
alty for his sin—one for a sin offering and the
other for a burnt offering. 8He is to bring them to
the priest, who shall first offer the one for the sin
offering. He is to wring its head from its neck, not
severing it completely, 9and is to sprinkle some of
the blood of the sin offering against the side of
the altar; the rest of the blood must be drained
out at the base of the altar. It is a sin offering.
10The priest shall then offer the other as a burnt
offering in the prescribed way and make atone-
ment for him for the sin he has committed, and
he will be forgiven.
11" 'If, however, he cannot afford two doves or
two young pigeons, he is to bring as an offering
for his sin a tenth of an ephah[g] of fine flour for
a sin offering. He must not put oil or incense on
it, because it is a sin offering. 12He is to bring it to
the priest, who shall take a handful of it as a
memorial portion and burn it on the altar on top
of the offerings made to the LORD by fire. It is a sin
offering. 13In this way the priest will make atone-
ment for him for any of these sins he has commit-
ted, and he will be forgiven. The rest of the offer-
ing will belong to the priest, as in the case of the
grain offering.' "
14The LORD said to Moses: 15"When a person
commits a violation and sins unintentionally in
regard to any of the LORD's holy things, he is to
bring to the LORD as a penalty a ram from the
flock, one without defect and of the proper value
in silver, according to the sanctuary shekel.[h] It is
a guilt offering. 16He must make restitution for
what he has failed to do in regard to the holy
things, add a fifth of the value to that and give it
all to the priest, who will make atonement for
him with the ram as a guilt offering, and he will
be forgiven.
17"If a person sins and does what is forbidden
in any of the LORD's commands, even though he
does not know it, he is guilty and will be held
responsible. 18He is to bring to the priest as a guilt
offering a ram from the flock, one without defect
and of the proper value. In this way the priest will
make atonement for him for the wrong he has
committed unintentionally, and he will be for-
given. 19It is a guilt offering; he has been guilty
of[i] wrongdoing against the LORD."

6 The LORD said to Moses: 2"If anyone sins
and is unfaithful to the LORD by deceiving
his neighbor about something entrusted
to him or left in his care or stolen, or if he cheats
him, 3or if he finds lost property and lies about it,
or if he swears falsely, or if he commits any such
sin that people may do— 4when he thus sins and
becomes guilty, he must return what he has sto-
len or taken by extortion, or what was entrusted
to him, or the lost property he found, 5or what-
ever it was he swore falsely about. He must make
restitution in full, add a fifth of the value to it and
give it all to the owner on the day he presents his
guilt offering. 6And as a penalty he must bring to

[g] *11* That is, probably about 2 quarts (about 2 liters) [h] *15* That is, about 2/5 ounce (about 11.5 grams) [i] *19* Or *has made full expiation for his*

the priest, that is, to the LORD, his guilt offering, a ram from the flock, one without defect and of the proper value. [7]In this way the priest will make atonement for him before the LORD, and he will be forgiven for any of these things he did that made him guilty."

[8]The LORD said to Moses: [9]"Give Aaron and his sons this command: 'These are the regulations for the burnt offering: The burnt offering is to remain on the altar hearth throughout the night, till morning, and the fire must be kept burning on the altar. [10]The priest shall then put on his linen clothes, with linen undergarments next to his body, and shall remove the ashes of the burnt offering that the fire has consumed on the altar and place them beside the altar. [11]Then he is to take off these clothes and put on others, and carry the ashes outside the camp to a place that is ceremonially clean. [12]The fire on the altar must be kept burning; it must not go out. Every morning the priest is to add firewood and arrange the burnt offering on the fire and burn the fat of the fellowship offerings[j] on it. [13]The fire must be kept burning on the altar continuously; it must not go out.

[14]" 'These are the regulations for the grain offering: Aaron's sons are to bring it before the LORD, in front of the altar. [15]The priest is to take a handful of fine flour and oil, together with all the incense on the grain offering, and burn the memorial portion on the altar as an aroma pleasing to the LORD. [16]Aaron and his sons shall eat the rest of it, but it is to be eaten without yeast in a holy place; they are to eat it in the courtyard of the Tent of Meeting. [17]It must not be baked with yeast; I have given it as their share of the offerings made to me by fire. Like the sin offering and the guilt offering, it is most holy. [18]Any male descendant of Aaron may eat it. It is his regular share of the offerings made to the LORD by fire for the generations to come. Whatever touches them will become holy.[k]' "

[19]The LORD also said to Moses, [20]"This is the offering Aaron and his sons are to bring to the LORD on the day he[l] is anointed: a tenth of an ephah[m] of fine flour as a regular grain offering, half of it in the morning and half in the evening. [21]Prepare it with oil on a griddle; bring it well-mixed and present the grain offering broken[n] in pieces as an aroma pleasing to the LORD. [22]The son who is to succeed him as anointed priest shall prepare it. It is the LORD's regular share and is to be burned completely. [23]Every grain offering of a priest shall be burned completely; it must not be eaten."

[24]The LORD said to Moses, [25]"Say to Aaron and his sons: 'These are the regulations for the sin offering: The sin offering is to be slaughtered before the LORD in the place the burnt offering is slaughtered; it is most holy. [26]The priest who offers it shall eat it; it is to be eaten in a holy place, in the courtyard of the Tent of Meeting. [27]Whatever touches any of the flesh will become holy, and if any of the blood is spattered on a garment, you must wash it in a holy place. [28]The clay pot the meat is cooked in must be broken; but if it is cooked in a bronze pot, the pot is to be scoured and rinsed with water. [29]Any male in a priest's family may eat it; it is most holy. [30]But any sin offering whose blood is brought into the Tent of Meeting to make atonement in the Holy Place must not be eaten; it must be burned.

7 " 'These are the regulations for the guilt offering, which is most holy: [2]The guilt offering is to be slaughtered in the place where the burnt offering is slaughtered, and its blood is to be sprinkled against the altar on all sides. [3]All its fat shall be offered: the fat tail and the fat that covers the inner parts, [4]both kidneys with the fat on them near the loins, and the covering of the liver, which is to be removed with the kidneys. [5]The priest shall burn them on the altar as an offering made to the LORD by fire. It is a guilt offering. [6]Any male in a priest's family may eat it, but it must be eaten in a holy place; it is most holy.

[7]" 'The same law applies to both the sin offering and the guilt offering: They belong to the priest who makes atonement with them. [8]The priest who offers a burnt offering for anyone may keep its hide for himself. [9]Every grain offering baked in an oven or cooked in a pan or on a griddle belongs to the priest who offers it, [10]and every grain offering, whether mixed with oil or dry, belongs equally to all the sons of Aaron.

[11]" 'These are the regulations for the fellowship offering[o] a person may present to the LORD:

[12]" 'If he offers it as an expression of thankfulness, then along with this thank offering he is to offer cakes of bread made without yeast and

[j]12 Traditionally *peace offerings* [k]18 Or *Whoever touches them must be holy*; similarly in verse 27 [l]20 Or *each* [m]20 That is, probably about 2 quarts (about 2 liters) [n]21 The meaning of the Hebrew for this word is uncertain. [o]11 Traditionally *peace offering*; also in verses 13-37

mixed with oil, wafers made without yeast and
spread with oil, and cakes of fine flour well-
kneaded and mixed with oil. [13]Along with his fel-
lowship offering of thanksgiving he is to present
an offering with cakes of bread made with yeast.
[14]He is to bring one of each kind as an offering, a
contribution to the LORD; it belongs to the priest
who sprinkles the blood of the fellowship offer-
ings. [15]The meat of his fellowship offering of
thanksgiving must be eaten on the day it is of-
fered; he must leave none of it till morning.

[16]" 'If, however, his offering is the result of a
vow or is a freewill offering, the sacrifice shall be
eaten on the day he offers it, but anything left
over may be eaten on the next day. [17]Any meat of
the sacrifice left over till the third day must be
burned up. [18]If any meat of the fellowship offer-
ing is eaten on the third day, it will not be ac-
cepted. It will not be credited to the one who
offered it, for it is impure; the person who eats
any of it will be held responsible.

[19]" 'Meat that touches anything ceremonially
unclean must not be eaten; it must be burned up.
As for other meat, anyone ceremonially clean may
eat it. [20]But if anyone who is unclean eats any
meat of the fellowship offering belonging to the
LORD, that person must be cut off from his people.
[21]If anyone touches something unclean—whether
human uncleanness or an unclean animal or any
unclean, detestable thing—and then eats any of
the meat of the fellowship offering belonging to
the LORD, that person must be cut off from his
people.' "

[22]The LORD said to Moses, [23]"Say to the Israel-
ites: 'Do not eat any of the fat of cattle, sheep or
goats. [24]The fat of an animal found dead or torn
by wild animals may be used for any other pur-
pose, but you must not eat it. [25]Anyone who eats
the fat of an animal from which an offering by fire
may be[p] made to the LORD must be cut off from
his people. [26]And wherever you live, you must
not eat the blood of any bird or animal. [27]If any-
one eats blood, that person must be cut off from
his people.' "

[28]The LORD said to Moses, [29]"Say to the Israel-
ites: 'Anyone who brings a fellowship offering to
the LORD is to bring part of it as his sacrifice to the
LORD. [30]With his own hands he is to bring the
offering made to the LORD by fire; he is to bring
the fat, together with the breast, and wave the
breast before the LORD as a wave offering. [31]The
priest shall burn the fat on the altar, but the
breast belongs to Aaron and his sons. [32]You are to
give the right thigh of your fellowship offerings to
the priest as a contribution. [33]The son of Aaron
who offers the blood and the fat of the fellowship
offering shall have the right thigh as his share.
[34]From the fellowship offerings of the Israelites, I
have taken the breast that is waved and the thigh
that is presented and have given them to Aaron
the priest and his sons as their regular share from
the Israelites.' "

[35]This is the portion of the offerings made to
the LORD by fire that were allotted to Aaron and
his sons on the day they were presented to serve
the LORD as priests. [36]On the day they were
anointed, the LORD commanded that the Israelites
give this to them as their regular share for the
generations to come.

[37]These, then, are the regulations for the burnt
offering, the grain offering, the sin offering, the
guilt offering, the ordination offering and the fel-
lowship offering, [38]which the LORD gave Moses on
Mount Sinai on the day he commanded the Israel-
ites to bring their offerings to the LORD, in the
Desert of Sinai.

p25 Or *fire is*

2 / *Leviticus 8*
A Chosen Priesthood

"YOU HAVE BEEN selected for this once-in-a-lifetime opportunity to own a piece of Paradise!" Maybe we'd feel more specially chosen if the sales letter weren't a computer-generated form letter. We would like to be singled out personally for a gift or an honor. The Lord is building all believers into a "holy priesthood" (1Pe 2:5). Our priesthood is foreshadowed in the original ordination ceremony of the priests of the Lord.

Warming Up to God Recall a time you felt called by the Lord for a particular task or role. Thank him for how he helped you fulfill it and for what the experience showed you about yourself and about God.

Read Leviticus 8.

8

The LORD said to Moses, 2“Bring Aaron and his sons, their garments, the anointing oil, the bull for the sin offering, the two rams and the basket containing bread made without yeast, 3and gather the entire assembly at the entrance to the Tent of Meeting.” 4Moses did as the LORD commanded him, and the assembly gathered at the entrance to the Tent of Meeting.

5Moses said to the assembly, “This is what the LORD has commanded to be done.” 6Then Moses brought Aaron and his sons forward and washed them with water. 7He put the tunic on Aaron, tied the sash around him, clothed him with the robe and put the ephod on him. He also tied the ephod to him by its skillfully woven waistband; so it was fastened on him. 8He placed the breastpiece on him and put the Urim and Thummim in the breastpiece. 9Then he placed the turban on Aaron's head and set the gold plate, the sacred diadem, on the front of it, as the LORD commanded Moses.

10Then Moses took the anointing oil and anointed the tabernacle and everything in it, and so consecrated them. 11He sprinkled some of the oil on the altar seven times, anointing the altar and all its utensils and the basin with its stand, to consecrate them. 12He poured some of the anointing oil on Aaron's head and anointed him to consecrate him. 13Then he brought Aaron's sons forward, put tunics on them, tied sashes around them and put headbands on them, as the LORD commanded Moses.

14He then presented the bull for the sin offering, and Aaron and his sons laid their hands on its head. 15Moses slaughtered the bull and took some of the blood, and with his finger he put it on all the horns of the altar to purify the altar. He poured out the rest of the blood at the base of the altar. So he consecrated it to make atonement for it. 16Moses also took all the fat around the inner parts, the covering of the liver, and both kidneys and their fat, and burned it on the altar. 17But the bull with its hide and its flesh and its offal he burned up outside the camp, as the LORD commanded Moses.

18He then presented the ram for the burnt offering, and Aaron and his sons laid their hands on its head. 19Then Moses slaughtered the ram and sprinkled the blood against the altar on all sides. 20He cut the ram into pieces and burned the head, the pieces and the fat. 21He washed the inner parts and the legs with water and burned the whole ram on the altar as a burnt offering, a pleasing aroma, an offering made to the LORD by fire, as the LORD commanded Moses.

22He then presented the other ram, the ram for the ordination, and Aaron and his sons laid their hands on its head. 23Moses slaughtered the ram and took some of its blood and put it on the lobe of Aaron's right ear, on the thumb of his right hand and on the big toe of his right foot. 24Moses also brought Aaron's sons forward and put some of the blood on the lobes of their right ears, on the thumbs of their right hands and on the big toes of their right feet. Then he sprinkled blood against the altar on all sides. 25He took the fat, the fat tail, all the fat around the inner parts, the covering of the liver, both kidneys and their fat and the right thigh. 26Then from the basket of bread made without yeast, which was before the LORD, he took a cake of bread, and one made with oil, and a wafer; he put these on the fat portions and on the right thigh. 27He put all these in the hands of Aaron and his sons and waved them before the LORD as a wave offering. 28Then Moses took them from their hands and burned them on the altar on top of the burnt offering as an ordination offering, a pleasing aroma, an offering made to the LORD by fire. 29He also took the breast—Moses' share of the ordination ram—and waved it before the LORD as a wave offering, as the LORD commanded Moses.

30Then Moses took some of the anointing oil and some of the blood from the altar and sprinkled them on Aaron and his garments and on his sons and their garments. So he consecrated Aaron and his garments and his sons and their garments.

31Moses then said to Aaron and his sons, “Cook the meat at the entrance to the Tent of Meeting and eat it there with the bread from the basket of ordination offerings, as I commanded,

saying,[q] 'Aaron and his sons are to eat it.' 32 Then
burn up the rest of the meat and the bread. 33 Do
not leave the entrance to the Tent of Meeting for
seven days, until the days of your ordination are
completed, for your ordination will last seven
days. 34 What has been done today was com-
manded by the LORD to make atonement for you.
35 You must stay at the entrance to the Tent of
Meeting day and night for seven days and do
what the LORD requires, so you will not die; for
that is what I have been commanded." 36 So Aaron
and his sons did everything the LORD commanded
through Moses.

[q]31 Or *I was commanded:*

Discovering the Word 1. How were Aaron and his sons singled out in front of the assembly of all the Israelites (vv. 1–13)? 2. Recalling the atonement sacrifice (Lev 1:4), what is the significance of Aaron and his sons' laying their hands on the heads of the offerings (vv. 14, 18, 22)? 3. How was the blood of the ordination lamb used to anoint Aaron and his sons (vv. 23–24)? 4. What message would this ceremony carry to the watching Israelites? 5. How would Aaron and his sons feel honored by this ceremony of ordination as God's priests? 6. How might they feel inadequate for the job?

Applying the Word 1. How do you feel honored for the role in which God has placed you? 2. In what ways do you feel inadequate?

Responding in Prayer Thank the Lord for the privileges and responsibilities of your priesthood. Bring your sins, fears and inadequacies to him for his cleansing and renewing.

Leviticus 9

9 On the eighth day Moses summoned
Aaron and his sons and the elders of Is-
rael. 2 He said to Aaron, "Take a bull calf
for your sin offering and a ram for your burnt
offering, both without defect, and present them
before the LORD. 3 Then say to the Israelites: 'Take
a male goat for a sin offering, a calf and a lamb—
both a year old and without defect—for a burnt
offering, 4 and an ox[r] and a ram for a fellowship
offering[s] to sacrifice before the LORD, together
with a grain offering mixed with oil. For today
the LORD will appear to you.'"

5 They took the things Moses commanded to
the front of the Tent of Meeting, and the entire
assembly came near and stood before the LORD.
6 Then Moses said, "This is what the LORD has
commanded you to do, so that the glory of the
LORD may appear to you."

7 Moses said to Aaron, "Come to the altar and
sacrifice your sin offering and your burnt offering
and make atonement for yourself and the people;
sacrifice the offering that is for the people and
make atonement for them, as the LORD has com-
manded."

8 So Aaron came to the altar and slaughtered
the calf as a sin offering for himself. 9 His sons
brought the blood to him, and he dipped his fin-
ger into the blood and put it on the horns of the
altar; the rest of the blood he poured out at the
base of the altar. 10 On the altar he burned the fat,
the kidneys and the covering of the liver from the
sin offering, as the LORD commanded Moses; 11 the
flesh and the hide he burned up outside the
camp.

12 Then he slaughtered the burnt offering. His
sons handed him the blood, and he sprinkled it
against the altar on all sides. 13 They handed him
the burnt offering piece by piece, including the
head, and he burned them on the altar. 14 He
washed the inner parts and the legs and burned
them on top of the burnt offering on the altar.

15 Aaron then brought the offering that was for
the people. He took the goat for the people's sin
offering and slaughtered it and offered it for a sin
offering as he did with the first one.

16 He brought the burnt offering and offered it
in the prescribed way. 17 He also brought the grain
offering, took a handful of it and burned it on the
altar in addition to the morning's burnt offering.

18 He slaughtered the ox and the ram as the
fellowship offering for the people. His sons

[r]4 The Hebrew word can include both male and female; also in verses 18 and 19. [s]4 Traditionally *peace offering;* also in verses 18 and 22

handed him the blood, and he sprinkled it against the altar on all sides. 19But the fat portions of the ox and the ram—the fat tail, the layer of fat, the kidneys and the covering of the liver— 20these they laid on the breasts, and then Aaron burned the fat on the altar. 21Aaron waved the breasts and the right thigh before the LORD as a wave offering, as Moses commanded.

22Then Aaron lifted his hands toward the people and blessed them. And having sacrificed the sin offering, the burnt offering and the fellowship offering, he stepped down.

23Moses and Aaron then went into the Tent of Meeting. When they came out, they blessed the people; and the glory of the LORD appeared to all the people. 24Fire came out from the presence of the LORD and consumed the burnt offering and the fat portions on the altar. And when all the people saw it, they shouted for joy and fell facedown.

3/ *Leviticus 10*
Where Flippancy Doesn't Fit

"THE PRESIDENT IS on the phone!" "It's the Queen calling—she wants to talk to you!" Most of us would gulp and take the phone with a shaking hand. We're far less nervous about approaching the Lord. Certainly we do have confident access to God through Christ. Still it's all too easy to forget that God is holy and only through his mercy can we approach at all.

Warming Up to God Think about your focus when you enter a worship service. Are you preoccupied with responsibilities and other plans, or are you aware of the wonder of worshiping a holy God?

Read Leviticus 10.

10 Aaron's sons Nadab and Abihu took their censers, put fire in them and added incense; and they offered unauthorized fire before the LORD, contrary to his command. 2So fire came out from the presence of the LORD and consumed them, and they died before the LORD. 3Moses then said to Aaron, "This is what the LORD spoke of when he said:

" 'Among those who approach me
I will show myself holy;
in the sight of all the people
I will be honored.' "

Aaron remained silent.

4Moses summoned Mishael and Elzaphan, sons of Aaron's uncle Uzziel, and said to them, "Come here; carry your cousins outside the camp, away from the front of the sanctuary." 5So they came and carried them, still in their tunics, outside the camp, as Moses ordered.

6Then Moses said to Aaron and his sons Eleazar and Ithamar, "Do not let your hair become unkempt,[t] and do not tear your clothes, or you will die and the LORD will be angry with the whole community. But your relatives, all the house of Israel, may mourn for those the LORD has destroyed by fire. 7Do not leave the entrance to the Tent of Meeting or you will die, because the LORD's anointing oil is on you." So they did as Moses said.

8Then the LORD said to Aaron, 9"You and your sons are not to drink wine or other fermented drink whenever you go into the Tent of Meeting, or you will die. This is a lasting ordinance for the generations to come. 10You must distinguish between the holy and the common, between the unclean and the clean, 11and you must teach the Israelites all the decrees the LORD has given them through Moses."

12Moses said to Aaron and his remaining sons, Eleazar and Ithamar, "Take the grain offering left over from the offerings made to the LORD by fire and eat it prepared without yeast beside the altar, for it is most holy. 13Eat it in a holy place, because it is your share and your sons' share of the offerings made to the LORD by fire; for so I have been commanded. 14But you and your sons and your

[t]6 Or *Do not uncover your heads*

daughters may eat the breast that was waved and
the thigh that was presented. Eat them in a cere-
monially clean place; they have been given to you
and your children as your share of the Israelites'
fellowship offerings.[u] 15The thigh that was pre-
sented and the breast that was waved must be
brought with the fat portions of the offerings
made by fire, to be waved before the LORD as a
wave offering. This will be the regular share for
you and your children, as the LORD has com-
manded."

16When Moses inquired about the goat of the
sin offering and found that it had been burned
up, he was angry with Eleazar and Ithamar,
Aaron's remaining sons, and asked, 17"Why didn't
you eat the sin offering in the sanctuary area? It is
most holy; it was given to you to take away the
guilt of the community by making atonement for
them before the LORD. 18Since its blood was not
taken into the Holy Place, you should have eaten
the goat in the sanctuary area, as I commanded."

19Aaron replied to Moses, "Today they sacri-
ficed their sin offering and their burnt offering
before the LORD, but such things as this have hap-
pened to me. Would the LORD have been pleased
if I had eaten the sin offering today?" 20When
Moses heard this, he was satisfied.

[u]14 Traditionally *peace offerings*

Discovering the Word 1. What led to Nadab and Abihu's tragedy (vv. 1–2)? 2. What reason did Moses offer for God's extreme reaction (vv. 2–3)? 3. How were Aaron and his two surviving sons to mourn differently from the rest of the people (vv. 6–7)? 4. How else was God's holiness to be esteemed by the priests (vv. 8–11)? 5. Notice the detailed instructions Moses gives regarding the remains of offerings (vv. 12–20). How do his admonitions reflect his concern for the holiness of God?

Applying the Word 1. During worship, what typically distracts you from the sense of God's holy presence? 2. In what ways have you approached God with presumption?

Responding in Prayer We don't have to attend a worship service to approach the Lord. Acknowledge God's holy presence with you now, and worship him in your heart.

Leviticus 11—15

11 The LORD said to Moses and Aaron,
2"Say to the Israelites: 'Of all the
animals that live on land, these are
the ones you may eat: 3You may eat any animal
that has a split hoof completely divided and that
chews the cud.

4" 'There are some that only chew the cud or
only have a split hoof, but you must not eat them.
The camel, though it chews the cud, does not
have a split hoof; it is ceremonially unclean for
you. 5The coney,[v] though it chews the cud, does
not have a split hoof; it is unclean for you. 6The
rabbit, though it chews the cud, does not have a
split hoof; it is unclean for you. 7And the pig,
though it has a split hoof completely divided,
does not chew the cud; it is unclean for you. 8You
must not eat their meat or touch their carcasses;
they are unclean for you.

9" 'Of all the creatures living in the water of the
seas and the streams, you may eat any that have
fins and scales. 10But all creatures in the seas or
streams that do not have fins and scales—
whether among all the swarming things or among
all the other living creatures in the water—you
are to detest. 11And since you are to detest them,
you must not eat their meat and you must detest
their carcasses. 12Anything living in the water
that does not have fins and scales is to be detest-
able to you.

13" 'These are the birds you are to detest and
not eat because they are detestable: the eagle, the
vulture, the black vulture, 14the red kite, any kind
of black kite, 15any kind of raven, 16the horned
owl, the screech owl, the gull, any kind of hawk,
17the little owl, the cormorant, the great owl,
18the white owl, the desert owl, the osprey, 19the
stork, any kind of heron, the hoopoe and the
bat.[w]

20" 'All flying insects that walk on all fours are
to be detestable to you. 21There are, however,

[v]5 That is, the hyrax or rock badger [w]19 The precise identification of some of the birds, insects and animals in this chapter is uncertain.

some winged creatures that walk on all fours that you may eat: those that have jointed legs for hopping on the ground. 22Of these you may eat any kind of locust, katydid, cricket or grasshopper. 23But all other winged creatures that have four legs you are to detest.

24" 'You will make yourselves unclean by these; whoever touches their carcasses will be unclean till evening. 25Whoever picks up one of their carcasses must wash his clothes, and he will be unclean till evening.

26" 'Every animal that has a split hoof not completely divided or that does not chew the cud is unclean for you; whoever touches ⌞the carcass of⌟ any of them will be unclean. 27Of all the animals that walk on all fours, those that walk on their paws are unclean for you; whoever touches their carcasses will be unclean till evening. 28Anyone who picks up their carcasses must wash his clothes, and he will be unclean till evening. They are unclean for you.

29" 'Of the animals that move about on the ground, these are unclean for you: the weasel, the rat, any kind of great lizard, 30the gecko, the monitor lizard, the wall lizard, the skink and the chameleon. 31Of all those that move along the ground, these are unclean for you. Whoever touches them when they are dead will be unclean till evening. 32When one of them dies and falls on something, that article, whatever its use, will be unclean, whether it is made of wood, cloth, hide or sackcloth. Put it in water; it will be unclean till evening, and then it will be clean. 33If one of them falls into a clay pot, everything in it will be unclean, and you must break the pot. 34Any food that could be eaten but has water on it from such a pot is unclean, and any liquid that could be drunk from it is unclean. 35Anything that one of their carcasses falls on becomes unclean; an oven or cooking pot must be broken up. They are unclean, and you are to regard them as unclean. 36A spring, however, or a cistern for collecting water remains clean, but anyone who touches one of these carcasses is unclean. 37If a carcass falls on any seeds that are to be planted, they remain clean. 38But if water has been put on the seed and a carcass falls on it, it is unclean for you.

39" 'If an animal that you are allowed to eat dies, anyone who touches the carcass will be unclean till evening. 40Anyone who eats some of the carcass must wash his clothes, and he will be unclean till evening. Anyone who picks up the carcass must wash his clothes, and he will be unclean till evening.

41" 'Every creature that moves about on the ground is detestable; it is not to be eaten. 42You are not to eat any creature that moves about on the ground, whether it moves on its belly or walks on all fours or on many feet; it is detestable. 43Do not defile yourselves by any of these creatures. Do not make yourselves unclean by means of them or be made unclean by them. 44I am the LORD your God; consecrate yourselves and be holy, because I am holy. Do not make yourselves unclean by any creature that moves about on the ground. 45I am the LORD who brought you up out of Egypt to be your God; therefore be holy, because I am holy.

46" 'These are the regulations concerning animals, birds, every living thing that moves in the water and every creature that moves about on the ground. 47You must distinguish between the unclean and the clean, between living creatures that may be eaten and those that may not be eaten.' "

12 The LORD said to Moses, 2"Say to the Israelites: 'A woman who becomes pregnant and gives birth to a son will be ceremonially unclean for seven days, just as she is unclean during her monthly period. 3On the eighth day the boy is to be circumcised. 4Then the woman must wait thirty-three days to be purified from her bleeding. She must not touch anything sacred or go to the sanctuary until the days of her purification are over. 5If she gives birth to a daughter, for two weeks the woman will be unclean, as during her period. Then she must wait sixty-six days to be purified from her bleeding.

6" 'When the days of her purification for a son or daughter are over, she is to bring to the priest at the entrance to the Tent of Meeting a year-old lamb for a burnt offering and a young pigeon or a dove for a sin offering. 7He shall offer them before the LORD to make atonement for her, and then she will be ceremonially clean from her flow of blood.

" 'These are the regulations for the woman who gives birth to a boy or a girl. 8If she cannot afford a lamb, she is to bring two doves or two young pigeons, one for a burnt offering and the other for a sin offering. In this way the priest will make atonement for her, and she will be clean.' "

13 The LORD said to Moses and Aaron,
2"When anyone has a swelling or a
rash or a bright spot on his skin
that may become an infectious skin disease,[x] he
must be brought to Aaron the priest or to one of
his sons[y] who is a priest. 3The priest is to exam-
ine the sore on his skin, and if the hair in the sore
has turned white and the sore appears to be more
than skin deep,[z] it is an infectious skin disease.
When the priest examines him, he shall pro-
nounce him ceremonially unclean. 4If the spot on
his skin is white but does not appear to be more
than skin deep and the hair in it has not turned
white, the priest is to put the infected person in
isolation for seven days. 5On the seventh day the
priest is to examine him, and if he sees that the
sore is unchanged and has not spread in the skin,
he is to keep him in isolation another seven days.
6On the seventh day the priest is to examine him
again, and if the sore has faded and has not
spread in the skin, the priest shall pronounce him
clean; it is only a rash. The man must wash his
clothes, and he will be clean. 7But if the rash does
spread in his skin after he has shown himself to
the priest to be pronounced clean, he must ap-
pear before the priest again. 8The priest is to ex-
amine him, and if the rash has spread in the skin,
he shall pronounce him unclean; it is an infec-
tious disease.

9"When anyone has an infectious skin disease,
he must be brought to the priest. 10The priest is to
examine him, and if there is a white swelling in
the skin that has turned the hair white and if
there is raw flesh in the swelling, 11it is a chronic
skin disease and the priest shall pronounce him
unclean. He is not to put him in isolation, be-
cause he is already unclean.

12"If the disease breaks out all over his skin
and, so far as the priest can see, it covers all the
skin of the infected person from head to foot,
13the priest is to examine him, and if the disease
has covered his whole body, he shall pronounce
that person clean. Since it has all turned white, he
is clean. 14But whenever raw flesh appears on
him, he will be unclean. 15When the priest sees
the raw flesh, he shall pronounce him unclean.
The raw flesh is unclean; he has an infectious
disease. 16Should the raw flesh change and turn
white, he must go to the priest. 17The priest is to
examine him, and if the sores have turned white,
the priest shall pronounce the infected person
clean; then he will be clean.

18"When someone has a boil on his skin and it
heals, 19and in the place where the boil was, a
white swelling or reddish-white spot appears, he
must present himself to the priest. 20The priest is
to examine it, and if it appears to be more than
skin deep and the hair in it has turned white, the
priest shall pronounce him unclean. It is an infec-
tious skin disease that has broken out where the
boil was. 21But if, when the priest examines it,
there is no white hair in it and it is not more than
skin deep and has faded, then the priest is to put
him in isolation for seven days. 22If it is spreading
in the skin, the priest shall pronounce him un-
clean; it is infectious. 23But if the spot is un-
changed and has not spread, it is only a scar from
the boil, and the priest shall pronounce him
clean.

24"When someone has a burn on his skin and a
reddish-white or white spot appears in the raw
flesh of the burn, 25the priest is to examine the
spot, and if the hair in it has turned white, and it
appears to be more than skin deep, it is an infec-
tious disease that has broken out in the burn. The
priest shall pronounce him unclean; it is an infec-
tious skin disease. 26But if the priest examines it
and there is no white hair in the spot and if it is
not more than skin deep and has faded, then the
priest is to put him in isolation for seven days.
27On the seventh day the priest is to examine
him, and if it is spreading in the skin, the priest
shall pronounce him unclean; it is an infectious
skin disease. 28If, however, the spot is unchanged
and has not spread in the skin but has faded, it is
a swelling from the burn, and the priest shall pro-
nounce him clean; it is only a scar from the burn.

29"If a man or woman has a sore on the head or
on the chin, 30the priest is to examine the sore,
and if it appears to be more than skin deep and
the hair in it is yellow and thin, the priest shall
pronounce that person unclean; it is an itch, an
infectious disease of the head or chin. 31But if,
when the priest examines this kind of sore, it
does not seem to be more than skin deep and
there is no black hair in it, then the priest is to
put the infected person in isolation for seven
days. 32On the seventh day the priest is to exam-
ine the sore, and if the itch has not spread and
there is no yellow hair in it and it does not appear
to be more than skin deep, 33he must be shaved

x2 Traditionally *leprosy*; the Hebrew word was used for various diseases affecting the skin—not necessarily leprosy; also elsewhere in this chapter. y2 Or *descendants* z3 Or *be lower than the rest of the skin*; also elsewhere in this chapter

except for the diseased area, and the priest is to keep him in isolation another seven days. 34On the seventh day the priest is to examine the itch, and if it has not spread in the skin and appears to be no more than skin deep, the priest shall pronounce him clean. He must wash his clothes, and he will be clean. 35But if the itch does spread in the skin after he is pronounced clean, 36the priest is to examine him, and if the itch has spread in the skin, the priest does not need to look for yellow hair; the person is unclean. 37If, however, in his judgment it is unchanged and black hair has grown in it, the itch is healed. He is clean, and the priest shall pronounce him clean.

38"When a man or woman has white spots on the skin, 39the priest is to examine them, and if the spots are dull white, it is a harmless rash that has broken out on the skin; that person is clean.

40"When a man has lost his hair and is bald, he is clean. 41If he has lost his hair from the front of his scalp and has a bald forehead, he is clean. 42But if he has a reddish-white sore on his bald head or forehead, it is an infectious disease breaking out on his head or forehead. 43The priest is to examine him, and if the swollen sore on his head or forehead is reddish-white like an infectious skin disease, 44the man is diseased and is unclean. The priest shall pronounce him unclean because of the sore on his head.

45"The person with such an infectious disease must wear torn clothes, let his hair be unkempt,[a] cover the lower part of his face and cry out, 'Unclean! Unclean!' 46As long as he has the infection he remains unclean. He must live alone; he must live outside the camp.

47"If any clothing is contaminated with mildew—any woolen or linen clothing, 48any woven or knitted material of linen or wool, any leather or anything made of leather— 49and if the contamination in the clothing, or leather, or woven or knitted material, or any leather article, is greenish or reddish, it is a spreading mildew and must be shown to the priest. 50The priest is to examine the mildew and isolate the affected article for seven days. 51On the seventh day he is to examine it, and if the mildew has spread in the clothing, or the woven or knitted material, or the leather, whatever its use, it is a destructive mildew; the article is unclean. 52He must burn up the clothing, or the woven or knitted material of wool or linen, or any leather article that has the contamination in it, because the mildew is destructive; the article must be burned up.

53"But if, when the priest examines it, the mildew has not spread in the clothing, or the woven or knitted material, or the leather article, 54he shall order that the contaminated article be washed. Then he is to isolate it for another seven days. 55After the affected article has been washed, the priest is to examine it, and if the mildew has not changed its appearance, even though it has not spread, it is unclean. Burn it with fire, whether the mildew has affected one side or the other. 56If, when the priest examines it, the mildew has faded after the article has been washed, he is to tear the contaminated part out of the clothing, or the leather, or the woven or knitted material. 57But if it reappears in the clothing, or in the woven or knitted material, or in the leather article, it is spreading, and whatever has the mildew must be burned with fire. 58The clothing, or the woven or knitted material, or any leather article that has been washed and is rid of the mildew, must be washed again, and it will be clean."

59These are the regulations concerning contamination by mildew in woolen or linen clothing, woven or knitted material, or any leather article, for pronouncing them clean or unclean.

14

The LORD said to Moses, 2"These are the regulations for the diseased person at the time of his ceremonial cleansing, when he is brought to the priest: 3The priest is to go outside the camp and examine him. If the person has been healed of his infectious skin disease,[b] 4the priest shall order that two live clean birds and some cedar wood, scarlet yarn and hyssop be brought for the one to be cleansed. 5Then the priest shall order that one of the birds be killed over fresh water in a clay pot. 6He is then to take the live bird and dip it, together with the cedar wood, the scarlet yarn and the hyssop, into the blood of the bird that was killed over the fresh water. 7Seven times he shall sprinkle the one to be cleansed of the infectious disease and pronounce him clean. Then he is to release the live bird in the open fields.

8"The person to be cleansed must wash his clothes, shave off all his hair and bathe with water; then he will be ceremonially clean. After this he may come into the camp, but he must stay

[a]45 Or *clothes, uncover his head* [b]3 Traditionally *leprosy*; the Hebrew word was used for various diseases affecting the skin—not necessarily leprosy; also elsewhere in this chapter.

outside his tent for seven days. 9On the seventh day he must shave off all his hair; he must shave his head, his beard, his eyebrows and the rest of his hair. He must wash his clothes and bathe himself with water, and he will be clean.

10"On the eighth day he must bring two male lambs and one ewe lamb a year old, each without defect, along with three-tenths of an ephah[c] of fine flour mixed with oil for a grain offering, and one log[d] of oil. 11The priest who pronounces him clean shall present both the one to be cleansed and his offerings before the LORD at the entrance to the Tent of Meeting.

12"Then the priest is to take one of the male lambs and offer it as a guilt offering, along with the log of oil; he shall wave them before the LORD as a wave offering. 13He is to slaughter the lamb in the holy place where the sin offering and the burnt offering are slaughtered. Like the sin offering, the guilt offering belongs to the priest; it is most holy. 14The priest is to take some of the blood of the guilt offering and put it on the lobe of the right ear of the one to be cleansed, on the thumb of his right hand and on the big toe of his right foot. 15The priest shall then take some of the log of oil, pour it in the palm of his own left hand, 16dip his right forefinger into the oil in his palm, and with his finger sprinkle some of it before the LORD seven times. 17The priest is to put some of the oil remaining in his palm on the lobe of the right ear of the one to be cleansed, on the thumb of his right hand and on the big toe of his right foot, on top of the blood of the guilt offering. 18The rest of the oil in his palm the priest shall put on the head of the one to be cleansed and make atonement for him before the LORD.

19"Then the priest is to sacrifice the sin offering and make atonement for the one to be cleansed from his uncleanness. After that, the priest shall slaughter the burnt offering 20and offer it on the altar, together with the grain offering, and make atonement for him, and he will be clean.

21"If, however, he is poor and cannot afford these, he must take one male lamb as a guilt offering to be waved to make atonement for him, together with a tenth of an ephah[e] of fine flour mixed with oil for a grain offering, a log of oil, 22and two doves or two young pigeons, which he can afford, one for a sin offering and the other for a burnt offering.

23"On the eighth day he must bring them for his cleansing to the priest at the entrance to the Tent of Meeting, before the LORD. 24The priest is to take the lamb for the guilt offering, together with the log of oil, and wave them before the LORD as a wave offering. 25He shall slaughter the lamb for the guilt offering and take some of its blood and put it on the lobe of the right ear of the one to be cleansed, on the thumb of his right hand and on the big toe of his right foot. 26The priest is to pour some of the oil into the palm of his own left hand, 27and with his right forefinger sprinkle some of the oil from his palm seven times before the LORD. 28Some of the oil in his palm he is to put on the same places he put the blood of the guilt offering—on the lobe of the right ear of the one to be cleansed, on the thumb of his right hand and on the big toe of his right foot. 29The rest of the oil in his palm the priest shall put on the head of the one to be cleansed, to make atonement for him before the LORD. 30Then he shall sacrifice the doves or the young pigeons, which the person can afford, 31one[f] as a sin offering and the other as a burnt offering, together with the grain offering. In this way the priest will make atonement before the LORD on behalf of the one to be cleansed."

32These are the regulations for anyone who has an infectious skin disease and who cannot afford the regular offerings for his cleansing.

33The LORD said to Moses and Aaron, 34"When you enter the land of Canaan, which I am giving you as your possession, and I put a spreading mildew in a house in that land, 35the owner of the house must go and tell the priest, 'I have seen something that looks like mildew in my house.' 36The priest is to order the house to be emptied before he goes in to examine the mildew, so that nothing in the house will be pronounced unclean. After this the priest is to go in and inspect the house. 37He is to examine the mildew on the walls, and if it has greenish or reddish depressions that appear to be deeper than the surface of the wall, 38the priest shall go out the doorway of the house and close it up for seven days. 39On the seventh day the priest shall return to inspect the house. If the mildew has spread on the walls, 40he is to order that the contaminated stones be torn out and thrown into an unclean place outside the town. 41He must have all the inside walls of the house scraped and the material that is scraped off

[c] *10* That is, probably about 6 quarts (about 6.5 liters) [d] *10* That is, probably about 2/3 pint (about 0.3 liter); also in verses 12, 15, 21 and 24 [e] *21* That is, probably about 2 quarts (about 2 liters)
[f] *31* Septuagint and Syriac; Hebrew 31*such as the person can afford, one*

dumped into an unclean place outside the town. 42 Then they are to take other stones to replace these and take new clay and plaster the house.

43 "If the mildew reappears in the house after the stones have been torn out and the house scraped and plastered, 44 the priest is to go and examine it and, if the mildew has spread in the house, it is a destructive mildew; the house is unclean. 45 It must be torn down—its stones, timbers and all the plaster—and taken out of the town to an unclean place.

46 "Anyone who goes into the house while it is closed up will be unclean till evening. 47 Anyone who sleeps or eats in the house must wash his clothes.

48 "But if the priest comes to examine it and the mildew has not spread after the house has been plastered, he shall pronounce the house clean, because the mildew is gone. 49 To purify the house he is to take two birds and some cedar wood, scarlet yarn and hyssop. 50 He shall kill one of the birds over fresh water in a clay pot. 51 Then he is to take the cedar wood, the hyssop, the scarlet yarn and the live bird, dip them into the blood of the dead bird and the fresh water, and sprinkle the house seven times. 52 He shall purify the house with the bird's blood, the fresh water, the live bird, the cedar wood, the hyssop and the scarlet yarn. 53 Then he is to release the live bird in the open fields outside the town. In this way he will make atonement for the house, and it will be clean."

54 These are the regulations for any infectious skin disease, for an itch, 55 for mildew in clothing or in a house, 56 and for a swelling, a rash or a bright spot, 57 to determine when something is clean or unclean.

These are the regulations for infectious skin diseases and mildew.

15 The LORD said to Moses and Aaron, 2 "Speak to the Israelites and say to them: 'When any man has a bodily discharge, the discharge is unclean. 3 Whether it continues flowing from his body or is blocked, it will make him unclean. This is how his discharge will bring about uncleanness:

4 " 'Any bed the man with a discharge lies on will be unclean, and anything he sits on will be unclean. 5 Anyone who touches his bed must wash his clothes and bathe with water, and he will be unclean till evening. 6 Whoever sits on anything that the man with a discharge sat on must wash his clothes and bathe with water, and he will be unclean till evening.

7 " 'Whoever touches the man who has a discharge must wash his clothes and bathe with water, and he will be unclean till evening.

8 " 'If the man with the discharge spits on someone who is clean, that person must wash his clothes and bathe with water, and he will be unclean till evening.

9 " 'Everything the man sits on when riding will be unclean, 10 and whoever touches any of the things that were under him will be unclean till evening; whoever picks up those things must wash his clothes and bathe with water, and he will be unclean till evening.

11 " 'Anyone the man with a discharge touches without rinsing his hands with water must wash his clothes and bathe with water, and he will be unclean till evening.

12 " 'A clay pot that the man touches must be broken, and any wooden article is to be rinsed with water.

13 " 'When a man is cleansed from his discharge, he is to count off seven days for his ceremonial cleansing; he must wash his clothes and bathe himself with fresh water, and he will be clean. 14 On the eighth day he must take two doves or two young pigeons and come before the LORD to the entrance to the Tent of Meeting and give them to the priest. 15 The priest is to sacrifice them, the one for a sin offering and the other for a burnt offering. In this way he will make atonement before the LORD for the man because of his discharge.

16 " 'When a man has an emission of semen, he must bathe his whole body with water, and he will be unclean till evening. 17 Any clothing or leather that has semen on it must be washed with water, and it will be unclean till evening. 18 When a man lies with a woman and there is an emission of semen, both must bathe with water, and they will be unclean till evening.

19 " 'When a woman has her regular flow of blood, the impurity of her monthly period will last seven days, and anyone who touches her will be unclean till evening.

20 " 'Anything she lies on during her period will be unclean, and anything she sits on will be unclean. 21 Whoever touches her bed must wash his clothes and bathe with water, and he will be unclean till evening. 22 Whoever touches anything she sits on must wash his clothes and bathe with

water, and he will be unclean till evening.
23Whether it is the bed or anything she was sit-
ting on, when anyone touches it, he will be un-
clean till evening.
24" 'If a man lies with her and her monthly flow
touches him, he will be unclean for seven days;
any bed he lies on will be unclean.
25" 'When a woman has a discharge of blood for
many days at a time other than her monthly pe-
riod or has a discharge that continues beyond her
period, she will be unclean as long as she has the
discharge, just as in the days of her period. 26Any
bed she lies on while her discharge continues will
be unclean, as is her bed during her monthly pe-
riod, and anything she sits on will be unclean, as
during her period. 27Whoever touches them will
be unclean; he must wash his clothes and bathe
with water, and he will be unclean till evening.
28" 'When she is cleansed from her discharge,
she must count off seven days, and after that she
will be ceremonially clean. 29On the eighth day
she must take two doves or two young pigeons
and bring them to the priest at the entrance to the
Tent of Meeting. 30The priest is to sacrifice one
for a sin offering and the other for a burnt offer-
ing. In this way he will make atonement for her
before the LORD for the uncleanness of her dis-
charge.
31" 'You must keep the Israelites separate from
things that make them unclean, so they will not
die in their uncleanness for defiling my dwelling
place,[g] which is among them.' "
32These are the regulations for a man with a
discharge, for anyone made unclean by an emis-
sion of semen, 33for a woman in her monthly pe-
riod, for a man or a woman with a discharge, and
for a man who lies with a woman who is cere-
monially unclean.

g31 Or *my tabernacle*

4 / *Leviticus 16*
Facing Temptation

"I HAVEN'T SINNED for seventeen years," says one fervent Christian.

"I sin every day," says another, equally fervent.

These two Christians may define *sin* differently, but each knows the insistent battle of temptation. One knows the constant guardedness it takes to resist a small lie, a cutting remark, an inclination to laziness. The other knows the equally constant wash of God's grace as confession assures forgiveness and a continued walk with Christ. But no matter how we view sin, temptation is a battle for us all. And guilt often results from our battles with sin.

Warming Up to God Sit quietly before God. What have you felt guilty about recently? Talk to God about it.

Read Leviticus 16.

16 The LORD spoke to Moses after the
death of the two sons of Aaron who
died when they approached the
LORD. 2The LORD said to Moses: "Tell your brother
Aaron not to come whenever he chooses into the
Most Holy Place behind the curtain in front of the
atonement cover on the ark, or else he will die,
because I appear in the cloud over the atonement
cover.
3"This is how Aaron is to enter the sanctuary
area: with a young bull for a sin offering and a
ram for a burnt offering. 4He is to put on the
sacred linen tunic, with linen undergarments
next to his body; he is to tie the linen sash around
him and put on the linen turban. These are sacred
garments; so he must bathe himself with water
before he puts them on. 5From the Israelite com-
munity he is to take two male goats for a sin
offering and a ram for a burnt offering.
6"Aaron is to offer the bull for his own sin of-
fering to make atonement for himself and his
household. 7Then he is to take the two goats and
present them before the LORD at the entrance to
the Tent of Meeting. 8He is to cast lots for the two

goats—one lot for the LORD and the other for the scapegoat.[h] 9Aaron shall bring the goat whose lot falls to the LORD and sacrifice it for a sin offering. 10But the goat chosen by lot as the scapegoat shall be presented alive before the LORD to be used for making atonement by sending it into the desert as a scapegoat.

11"Aaron shall bring the bull for his own sin offering to make atonement for himself and his household, and he is to slaughter the bull for his own sin offering. 12He is to take a censer full of burning coals from the altar before the LORD and two handfuls of finely ground fragrant incense and take them behind the curtain. 13He is to put the incense on the fire before the LORD, and the smoke of the incense will conceal the atonement cover above the Testimony, so that he will not die. 14He is to take some of the bull's blood and with his finger sprinkle it on the front of the atonement cover; then he shall sprinkle some of it with his finger seven times before the atonement cover.

15"He shall then slaughter the goat for the sin offering for the people and take its blood behind the curtain and do with it as he did with the bull's blood: He shall sprinkle it on the atonement cover and in front of it. 16In this way he will make atonement for the Most Holy Place because of the uncleanness and rebellion of the Israelites, whatever their sins have been. He is to do the same for the Tent of Meeting, which is among them in the midst of their uncleanness. 17No one is to be in the Tent of Meeting from the time Aaron goes in to make atonement in the Most Holy Place until he comes out, having made atonement for himself, his household and the whole community of Israel.

18"Then he shall come out to the altar that is before the LORD and make atonement for it. He shall take some of the bull's blood and some of the goat's blood and put it on all the horns of the altar. 19He shall sprinkle some of the blood on it with his finger seven times to cleanse it and to consecrate it from the uncleanness of the Israelites.

20"When Aaron has finished making atonement for the Most Holy Place, the Tent of Meeting and the altar, he shall bring forward the live goat. 21He is to lay both hands on the head of the live goat and confess over it all the wickedness and rebellion of the Israelites—all their sins—and put them on the goat's head. He shall send the goat away into the desert in the care of a man appointed for the task. 22The goat will carry on itself all their sins to a solitary place; and the man shall release it in the desert.

23"Then Aaron is to go into the Tent of Meeting and take off the linen garments he put on before he entered the Most Holy Place, and he is to leave them there. 24He shall bathe himself with water in a holy place and put on his regular garments. Then he shall come out and sacrifice the burnt offering for himself and the burnt offering for the people, to make atonement for himself and for the people. 25He shall also burn the fat of the sin offering on the altar.

26"The man who releases the goat as a scapegoat must wash his clothes and bathe himself with water; afterward he may come into the camp. 27The bull and the goat for the sin offerings, whose blood was brought into the Most Holy Place to make atonement, must be taken outside the camp; their hides, flesh and offal are to be burned up. 28The man who burns them must wash his clothes and bathe himself with water; afterward he may come into the camp.

29"This is to be a lasting ordinance for you: On the tenth day of the seventh month you must deny yourselves[i] and not do any work—whether native-born or an alien living among you— 30because on this day atonement will be made for you, to cleanse you. Then, before the LORD, you will be clean from all your sins. 31It is a sabbath of rest, and you must deny yourselves; it is a lasting ordinance. 32The priest who is anointed and ordained to succeed his father as high priest is to make atonement. He is to put on the sacred linen garments 33and make atonement for the Most Holy Place, for the Tent of Meeting and the altar, and for the priests and all the people of the community.

34"This is to be a lasting ordinance for you: Atonement is to be made once a year for all the sins of the Israelites."

And it was done, as the LORD commanded Moses.

[h]8 That is, the goat of removal; Hebrew *azazel*; also in verses 10 and 26 [i]29 Or *must fast*; also in verse 31

Discovering the Word 1. As you visualize all that was to happen on the Day of Atonement, what pictures remind you that God is holy and that he expects holiness from his people? 2. What personal preparation was Aaron to make for his work of atonement (vv. 1–14)? 3. What did this preparation symbolize about Aaron and his role before God and the people? 4. How is each sacrificial goat a visual symbol of sin (vv. 7–10, 15–19, 20–24)? 5. What practical good could come from this method of atoning for sin?

Applying the Word 1. Imagine yourself as a Hebrew of this era. How do you think you would feel on the days just before and just after the Day of Atonement? 2. What do you do when you feel guilty about something?

Responding in Prayer If this study points to sin that needs to be confessed, do so now. If you have already done this, ask God to help you experience his forgiveness.

Leviticus 17—18

17 The LORD said to Moses, 2“Speak to
Aaron and his sons and to all the
Israelites and say to them: ‘This is
what the LORD has commanded: 3Any Israelite
who sacrifices an ox,[j] a lamb or a goat in the
camp or outside of it 4instead of bringing it to the
entrance to the Tent of Meeting to present it as an
offering to the LORD in front of the tabernacle of
the LORD—that man shall be considered guilty of
bloodshed; he has shed blood and must be cut off
from his people. 5This is so the Israelites will
bring to the LORD the sacrifices they are now mak-
ing in the open fields. They must bring them to
the priest, that is, to the LORD, at the entrance to
the Tent of Meeting and sacrifice them as fellow-
ship offerings.[k] 6The priest is to sprinkle the
blood against the altar of the LORD at the entrance
to the Tent of Meeting and burn the fat as an
aroma pleasing to the LORD. 7They must no longer
offer any of their sacrifices to the goat idols[l] to
whom they prostitute themselves. This is to be a
lasting ordinance for them and for the genera-
tions to come.’

8“Say to them: ‘Any Israelite or any alien living
among them who offers a burnt offering or sacri-
fice 9and does not bring it to the entrance to the
Tent of Meeting to sacrifice it to the LORD—that
man must be cut off from his people.

10“ ‘Any Israelite or any alien living among
them who eats any blood—I will set my face
against that person who eats blood and will cut
him off from his people. 11For the life of a crea-
ture is in the blood, and I have given it to you to
make atonement for yourselves on the altar; it is
the blood that makes atonement for one’s life.
12Therefore I say to the Israelites, “None of you
may eat blood, nor may an alien living among you
eat blood.”

13“ ‘Any Israelite or any alien living among you
who hunts any animal or bird that may be eaten
must drain out the blood and cover it with earth,
14because the life of every creature is its blood.
That is why I have said to the Israelites, “You
must not eat the blood of any creature, because
the life of every creature is its blood; anyone who
eats it must be cut off.”

15“ ‘Anyone, whether native-born or alien, who
eats anything found dead or torn by wild animals
must wash his clothes and bathe with water, and
he will be ceremonially unclean till evening; then
he will be clean. 16But if he does not wash his
clothes and bathe himself, he will be held respon-
sible.’ ”

18 The LORD said to Moses, 2“Speak to
the Israelites and say to them: ‘I am
the LORD your God. 3You must not
do as they do in Egypt, where you used to live,
and you must not do as they do in the land of
Canaan, where I am bringing you. Do not follow
their practices. 4You must obey my laws and be
careful to follow my decrees. I am the LORD your
God. 5Keep my decrees and laws, for the man
who obeys them will live by them. I am the LORD.

6“ ‘No one is to approach any close relative to
have sexual relations. I am the LORD.

7“ ‘Do not dishonor your father by having sex-
ual relations with your mother. She is your
mother; do not have relations with her.

8“ ‘Do not have sexual relations with your fa-
ther’s wife; that would dishonor your father.

j3 The Hebrew word can include both male and female.
k5 Traditionally *peace offerings*
l7 Or *demons*

9“ ‘Do not have sexual relations with your sister, either your father’s daughter or your mother’s daughter, whether she was born in the same home or elsewhere.

10“ ‘Do not have sexual relations with your son’s daughter or your daughter’s daughter; that would dishonor you.

11“ ‘Do not have sexual relations with the daughter of your father’s wife, born to your father; she is your sister.

12“ ‘Do not have sexual relations with your father’s sister; she is your father’s close relative.

13“ ‘Do not have sexual relations with your mother’s sister, because she is your mother’s close relative.

14“ ‘Do not dishonor your father’s brother by approaching his wife to have sexual relations; she is your aunt.

15“ ‘Do not have sexual relations with your daughter-in-law. She is your son’s wife; do not have relations with her.

16“ ‘Do not have sexual relations with your brother’s wife; that would dishonor your brother.

17“ ‘Do not have sexual relations with both a woman and her daughter. Do not have sexual relations with either her son’s daughter or her daughter’s daughter; they are her close relatives. That is wickedness.

18“ ‘Do not take your wife’s sister as a rival wife and have sexual relations with her while your wife is living.

19“ ‘Do not approach a woman to have sexual relations during the uncleanness of her monthly period.

20“ ‘Do not have sexual relations with your neighbor’s wife and defile yourself with her.

21“ ‘Do not give any of your children to be sacrificed[m] to Molech, for you must not profane the name of your God. I am the LORD.

22“ ‘Do not lie with a man as one lies with a woman; that is detestable.

23“ ‘Do not have sexual relations with an animal and defile yourself with it. A woman must not present herself to an animal to have sexual relations with it; that is a perversion.

24“ ‘Do not defile yourselves in any of these ways, because this is how the nations that I am going to drive out before you became defiled.
25Even the land was defiled; so I punished it for its sin, and the land vomited out its inhabitants.
26But you must keep my decrees and my laws. The native-born and the aliens living among you must not do any of these detestable things, 27for all these things were done by the people who lived in the land before you, and the land became defiled. 28And if you defile the land, it will vomit you out as it vomited out the nations that were before you.

29“ ‘Everyone who does any of these detestable things—such persons must be cut off from their people. 30Keep my requirements and do not follow any of the detestable customs that were practiced before you came and do not defile yourselves with them. I am the LORD your God.’ ”

[m]21 *Or to be passed through ⌊the fire⌋*

5 / *Leviticus 19*
Laws with a Purpose

“A POLICY? WHAT do we need a policy for?” That’s how a group of junior highers reacted when we announced a policy for an upcoming overnight trip. They knew “policy” was a fancy name for “rules.” But when it came to curbing the behavior of certain obnoxious group members, they saw a need for rules. Good rules have a purpose beyond rule-keeping. God’s rules, faithfully followed, will yield a better life for people.

Warming Up to God Think about the rules you’ve had to follow in life. When have you found following rules difficult? Some rules are better than others. Compare your experiences with unreasonable rules to what it’s like to follow God’s laws. Allow this to be a source of praise to God for caring enough to give us his good laws.

Read Leviticus 19.

19 The LORD said to Moses, 2“Speak to the entire assembly of Israel and say to them: ‘Be holy because I, the LORD your God, am holy.

3“ ‘Each of you must respect his mother and father, and you must observe my Sabbaths. I am the LORD your God.

4“ ‘Do not turn to idols or make gods of cast metal for yourselves. I am the LORD your God.

5“ ‘When you sacrifice a fellowship offering[n] to the LORD, sacrifice it in such a way that it will be accepted on your behalf. 6It shall be eaten on the day you sacrifice it or on the next day; anything left over until the third day must be burned up. 7If any of it is eaten on the third day, it is impure and will not be accepted. 8Whoever eats it will be held responsible because he has desecrated what is holy to the LORD; that person must be cut off from his people.

9“ ‘When you reap the harvest of your land, do not reap to the very edges of your field or gather the gleanings of your harvest. 10Do not go over your vineyard a second time or pick up the grapes that have fallen. Leave them for the poor and the alien. I am the LORD your God.

11“ ‘Do not steal.

“ ‘Do not lie.

“ ‘Do not deceive one another.

12“ ‘Do not swear falsely by my name and so profane the name of your God. I am the LORD.

13“ ‘Do not defraud your neighbor or rob him.

“ ‘Do not hold back the wages of a hired man overnight.

14“ ‘Do not curse the deaf or put a stumbling block in front of the blind, but fear your God. I am the LORD.

15“ ‘Do not pervert justice; do not show partiality to the poor or favoritism to the great, but judge your neighbor fairly.

16“ ‘Do not go about spreading slander among your people.

“ ‘Do not do anything that endangers your neighbor’s life. I am the LORD.

17“ ‘Do not hate your brother in your heart. Rebuke your neighbor frankly so you will not share in his guilt.

18“ ‘Do not seek revenge or bear a grudge against one of your people, but love your neighbor as yourself. I am the LORD.

19“ ‘Keep my decrees.

“ ‘Do not mate different kinds of animals.

“ ‘Do not plant your field with two kinds of seed.

“ ‘Do not wear clothing woven of two kinds of material.

20“ ‘If a man sleeps with a woman who is a slave girl promised to another man but who has not been ransomed or given her freedom, there must be due punishment. Yet they are not to be put to death, because she had not been freed. 21The man, however, must bring a ram to the entrance to the Tent of Meeting for a guilt offering to the LORD. 22With the ram of the guilt offering the priest is to make atonement for him before the LORD for the sin he has committed, and his sin will be forgiven.

23“ ‘When you enter the land and plant any kind of fruit tree, regard its fruit as forbidden.[o] For three years you are to consider it forbidden[o]; it must not be eaten. 24In the fourth year all its fruit will be holy, an offering of praise to the LORD. 25But in the fifth year you may eat its fruit. In this way your harvest will be increased. I am the LORD your God.

26“ ‘Do not eat any meat with the blood still in it.

“ ‘Do not practice divination or sorcery.

27“ ‘Do not cut the hair at the sides of your head or clip off the edges of your beard.

28“ ‘Do not cut your bodies for the dead or put tattoo marks on yourselves. I am the LORD.

29“ ‘Do not degrade your daughter by making her a prostitute, or the land will turn to prostitution and be filled with wickedness.

30“ ‘Observe my Sabbaths and have reverence for my sanctuary. I am the LORD.

31“ ‘Do not turn to mediums or seek out spiritists, for you will be defiled by them. I am the LORD your God.

32“ ‘Rise in the presence of the aged, show respect for the elderly and revere your God. I am the LORD.

33“ ‘When an alien lives with you in your land, do not mistreat him. 34The alien living with you must be treated as one of your native-born. Love him as yourself, for you were aliens in Egypt. I am the LORD your God.

35“ ‘Do not use dishonest standards when mea-

[n]5 Traditionally *peace offering* [o]23 Hebrew *uncircumcised*

suring length, weight or quantity. [36]Use honest
scales and honest weights, an honest ephah[p] and
an honest hin.[q] I am the LORD your God, who
brought you out of Egypt.

[37]" 'Keep all my decrees and all my laws and
follow them. I am the LORD.' "

[p]36 An ephah was a dry measure. [q]36 A hin was a liquid measure.

Discovering the Word 1. God said, "Be holy because I, the LORD your God, am holy" (v. 2). What do the various laws that follow reveal about the holiness of God? 2. Consider the laws in verses 3, 11, 16–17, 32 and 35–36. How would obedience to these laws create better relationships between people? 3. Consider the laws in verses 9–10, 14 and 33–34, and imagine a society observing these laws. How would life be better for disadvantaged people? 4. Jesus quoted "love your neighbor as yourself" (v. 18) as one of the two greatest commandments, second only to loving God. Why is it a good summary of all the laws in this chapter (as well as all God's other laws)? 5. What do these laws reveal about God's concern for his people?

Applying the Word 1. Which of the laws in this chapter particularly stir your heart with their "rightness" (that is, you're glad to find them in the Bible)? 2. Which of the laws would you find hardest to obey?

Responding in Prayer Praise God for showing you his character through his principles. Ask for his continuing help in living as he wants.

Leviticus 20—22

20 The LORD said to Moses, [2]"Say to
the Israelites: 'Any Israelite or any
alien living in Israel who gives[r]
any of his children to Molech must be put to
death. The people of the community are to stone
him. [3]I will set my face against that man and I will
cut him off from his people; for by giving his
children to Molech, he has defiled my sanctuary
and profaned my holy name. [4]If the people of the
community close their eyes when that man gives
one of his children to Molech and they fail to put
him to death, [5]I will set my face against that man
and his family and will cut off from their people
both him and all who follow him in prostituting
themselves to Molech.
[6]" 'I will set my face against the person who
turns to mediums and spiritists to prostitute him-
self by following them, and I will cut him off from
his people.
[7]" 'Consecrate yourselves and be holy, because
I am the LORD your God. [8]Keep my decrees and
follow them. I am the LORD, who makes you holy.[s]
[9]" 'If anyone curses his father or mother, he
must be put to death. He has cursed his father or
his mother, and his blood will be on his own
head.
[10]" 'If a man commits adultery with another
man's wife—with the wife of his neighbor—both
the adulterer and the adulteress must be put to
death.
[11]" 'If a man sleeps with his father's wife, he has
dishonored his father. Both the man and the
woman must be put to death; their blood will be
on their own heads.
[12]" 'If a man sleeps with his daughter-in-law,
both of them must be put to death. What they
have done is a perversion; their blood will be on
their own heads.
[13]" 'If a man lies with a man as one lies with a
woman, both of them have done what is detest-
able. They must be put to death; their blood will
be on their own heads.
[14]" 'If a man marries both a woman and her
mother, it is wicked. Both he and they must be
burned in the fire, so that no wickedness will be
among you.
[15]" 'If a man has sexual relations with an ani-
mal, he must be put to death, and you must kill
the animal.
[16]" 'If a woman approaches an animal to have
sexual relations with it, kill both the woman and
the animal. They must be put to death; their
blood will be on their own heads.
[17]" 'If a man marries his sister, the daughter of
either his father or his mother, and they have
sexual relations, it is a disgrace. They must be cut
off before the eyes of their people. He has dishon-
ored his sister and will be held responsible.

[r]2 Or *sacrifices*; also in verses 3 and 4 [s]8 Or *who sanctifies you*; or *who sets you apart as holy*

18“ ‘If a man lies with a woman during her monthly period and has sexual relations with her, he has exposed the source of her flow, and she has also uncovered it. Both of them must be cut off from their people.

19“ ‘Do not have sexual relations with the sister of either your mother or your father, for that would dishonor a close relative; both of you would be held responsible.

20“ ‘If a man sleeps with his aunt, he has dishonored his uncle. They will be held responsible; they will die childless.

21“ ‘If a man marries his brother’s wife, it is an act of impurity; he has dishonored his brother. They will be childless.

22“ ‘Keep all my decrees and laws and follow them, so that the land where I am bringing you to live may not vomit you out. 23You must not live according to the customs of the nations I am going to drive out before you. Because they did all these things, I abhorred them. 24But I said to you, “You will possess their land; I will give it to you as an inheritance, a land flowing with milk and honey.” I am the LORD your God, who has set you apart from the nations.

25“ ‘You must therefore make a distinction between clean and unclean animals and between unclean and clean birds. Do not defile yourselves by any animal or bird or anything that moves along the ground—those which I have set apart as unclean for you. 26You are to be holy to me[t] because I, the LORD, am holy, and I have set you apart from the nations to be my own.

27“ ‘A man or woman who is a medium or spiritist among you must be put to death. You are to stone them; their blood will be on their own heads.’ ”

21

The LORD said to Moses, “Speak to the priests, the sons of Aaron, and say to them: ‘A priest must not make himself ceremonially unclean for any of his people who die, 2except for a close relative, such as his mother or father, his son or daughter, his brother, 3or an unmarried sister who is dependent on him since she has no husband—for her he may make himself unclean. 4He must not make himself unclean for people related to him by marriage,[u] and so defile himself.

5“ ‘Priests must not shave their heads or shave off the edges of their beards or cut their bodies. 6They must be holy to their God and must not profane the name of their God. Because they present the offerings made to the LORD by fire, the food of their God, they are to be holy.

7“ ‘They must not marry women defiled by prostitution or divorced from their husbands, because priests are holy to their God. 8Regard them as holy, because they offer up the food of your God. Consider them holy, because I the LORD am holy—I who make you holy.[v]

9“ ‘If a priest’s daughter defiles herself by becoming a prostitute, she disgraces her father; she must be burned in the fire.

10“ ‘The high priest, the one among his brothers who has had the anointing oil poured on his head and who has been ordained to wear the priestly garments, must not let his hair become unkempt[w] or tear his clothes. 11He must not enter a place where there is a dead body. He must not make himself unclean, even for his father or mother, 12nor leave the sanctuary of his God or desecrate it, because he has been dedicated by the anointing oil of his God. I am the LORD.

13“ ‘The woman he marries must be a virgin. 14He must not marry a widow, a divorced woman, or a woman defiled by prostitution, but only a virgin from his own people, 15so he will not defile his offspring among his people. I am the LORD, who makes him holy.[x]’ ”

16The LORD said to Moses, 17“Say to Aaron: ‘For the generations to come none of your descendants who has a defect may come near to offer the food of his God. 18No man who has any defect may come near: no man who is blind or lame, disfigured or deformed; 19no man with a crippled foot or hand, 20or who is hunchbacked or dwarfed, or who has any eye defect, or who has festering or running sores or damaged testicles. 21No descendant of Aaron the priest who has any defect is to come near to present the offerings made to the LORD by fire. He has a defect; he must not come near to offer the food of his God. 22He may eat the most holy food of his God, as well as the holy food; 23yet because of his defect, he must not go near the curtain or approach the altar, and so desecrate my sanctuary. I am the LORD, who makes them holy.[y]’ ”

24So Moses told this to Aaron and his sons and to all the Israelites.

[t]26 Or *be my holy ones* [u]4 Or *unclean as a leader among his people* [v]8 Or *who sanctify you; or who set you apart as holy* [w]10 Or *not uncover his head* [x]15 Or *who sanctifies him; or who sets him apart as holy* [y]23 Or *who sanctifies them; or who sets them apart as holy*

22

The LORD said to Moses, 2“Tell Aaron and his sons to treat with respect the sacred offerings the Israelites consecrate to me, so they will not profane my holy name. I am the LORD.

3“Say to them: ‘For the generations to come, if any of your descendants is ceremonially unclean and yet comes near the sacred offerings that the Israelites consecrate to the LORD, that person must be cut off from my presence. I am the LORD.

4“ ‘If a descendant of Aaron has an infectious skin disease[z] or a bodily discharge, he may not eat the sacred offerings until he is cleansed. He will also be unclean if he touches something defiled by a corpse or by anyone who has an emission of semen, 5or if he touches any crawling thing that makes him unclean, or any person who makes him unclean, whatever the uncleanness may be. 6The one who touches any such thing will be unclean till evening. He must not eat any of the sacred offerings unless he has bathed himself with water. 7When the sun goes down, he will be clean, and after that he may eat the sacred offerings, for they are his food. 8He must not eat anything found dead or torn by wild animals, and so become unclean through it. I am the LORD.

9“ ‘The priests are to keep my requirements so that they do not become guilty and die for treating them with contempt. I am the LORD, who makes them holy.[a]

10“ ‘No one outside a priest’s family may eat the sacred offering, nor may the guest of a priest or his hired worker eat it. 11But if a priest buys a slave with money, or if a slave is born in his household, that slave may eat his food. 12If a priest’s daughter marries anyone other than a priest, she may not eat any of the sacred contributions. 13But if a priest’s daughter becomes a widow or is divorced, yet has no children, and she returns to live in her father’s house as in her youth, she may eat of her father’s food. No unauthorized person, however, may eat any of it.

14“ ‘If anyone eats a sacred offering by mistake, he must make restitution to the priest for the offering and add a fifth of the value to it. 15The priests must not desecrate the sacred offerings the Israelites present to the LORD 16by allowing them to eat the sacred offerings and so bring upon them guilt requiring payment. I am the LORD, who makes them holy.’ ”

17The LORD said to Moses, 18“Speak to Aaron and his sons and to all the Israelites and say to them: ‘If any of you—either an Israelite or an alien living in Israel—presents a gift for a burnt offering to the LORD, either to fulfill a vow or as a freewill offering, 19you must present a male without defect from the cattle, sheep or goats in order that it may be accepted on your behalf. 20Do not bring anything with a defect, because it will not be accepted on your behalf. 21When anyone brings from the herd or flock a fellowship offering[b] to the LORD to fulfill a special vow or as a freewill offering, it must be without defect or blemish to be acceptable. 22Do not offer to the LORD the blind, the injured or the maimed, or anything with warts or festering or running sores. Do not place any of these on the altar as an offering made to the LORD by fire. 23You may, however, present as a freewill offering an ox[c] or a sheep that is deformed or stunted, but it will not be accepted in fulfillment of a vow. 24You must not offer to the LORD an animal whose testicles are bruised, crushed, torn or cut. You must not do this in your own land, 25and you must not accept such animals from the hand of a foreigner and offer them as the food of your God. They will not be accepted on your behalf, because they are deformed and have defects.’ ”

26The LORD said to Moses, 27“When a calf, a lamb or a goat is born, it is to remain with its mother for seven days. From the eighth day on, it will be acceptable as an offering made to the LORD by fire. 28Do not slaughter a cow or a sheep and its young on the same day.

29“When you sacrifice a thank offering to the LORD, sacrifice it in such a way that it will be accepted on your behalf. 30It must be eaten that same day; leave none of it till morning. I am the LORD.

31“Keep my commands and follow them. I am the LORD. 32Do not profane my holy name. I must be acknowledged as holy by the Israelites. I am the LORD, who makes[d] you holy[e] 33and who brought you out of Egypt to be your God. I am the LORD.”

[z]4 Traditionally *leprosy*; the Hebrew word was used for various diseases affecting the skin—not necessarily leprosy. [a]9 Or *who sanctifies them*; or *who sets them apart as holy*; also in verse 16
[b]21 Traditionally *peace offering* [c]23 The Hebrew word can include both male and female. [d]32 Or *made* [e]32 Or *who sanctifies you*; or *who sets you apart as holy*

6 / *Leviticus 23*
Feasts of Remembrance

"I CAN'T COME to class tomorrow," Tanya told me. "It's my mother's birthday, and we're going to lay flowers on her grave." A birthday is not a time we normally think of visiting a grave, and we certainly wouldn't miss an entire day of school to do it. Tanya, however, was one of my students in the Ukraine, where both birthdays and visits to graves are momentous occasions—times of remembrance. From the flow of the Israelites' year God carved out regular celebrations of remembrance so they would never forget who they were and where they came from.

Warming Up to God What observances help you most to celebrate your history with the Lord? (They may be ones common to all Christians, such as Christmas and Easter, or your own private remembrances, such as the date of your salvation or baptism.)

Read Leviticus 23.

23 The LORD said to Moses, 2"Speak to
the Israelites and say to them:
'These are my appointed feasts, the
appointed feasts of the LORD, which you are to
proclaim as sacred assemblies.
3" 'There are six days when you may work, but
the seventh day is a Sabbath of rest, a day of sa-
cred assembly. You are not to do any work; wher-
ever you live, it is a Sabbath to the LORD.
4" 'These are the LORD's appointed feasts, the
sacred assemblies you are to proclaim at their ap-
pointed times: 5The LORD's Passover begins at twi-
light on the fourteenth day of the first month.
6On the fifteenth day of that month the LORD's
Feast of Unleavened Bread begins; for seven days
you must eat bread made without yeast. 7On the
first day hold a sacred assembly and do no regular
work. 8For seven days present an offering made
to the LORD by fire. And on the seventh day hold
a sacred assembly and do no regular work.' "
9The LORD said to Moses, 10"Speak to the Israel-
ites and say to them: 'When you enter the land I
am going to give you and you reap its harvest,
bring to the priest a sheaf of the first grain you
harvest. 11He is to wave the sheaf before the LORD
so it will be accepted on your behalf; the priest is
to wave it on the day after the Sabbath. 12On the
day you wave the sheaf, you must sacrifice as a
burnt offering to the LORD a lamb a year old with-
out defect, 13together with its grain offering of
two-tenths of an ephah[f] of fine flour mixed with
oil—an offering made to the LORD by fire, a pleas-
ing aroma—and its drink offering of a quarter of
a hin[g] of wine. 14You must not eat any bread, or
roasted or new grain, until the very day you bring
this offering to your God. This is to be a lasting
ordinance for the generations to come, wherever
you live.
15" 'From the day after the Sabbath, the day you
brought the sheaf of the wave offering, count off
seven full weeks. 16Count off fifty days up to the
day after the seventh Sabbath, and then present
an offering of new grain to the LORD. 17From
wherever you live, bring two loaves made of two-
tenths of an ephah of fine flour, baked with yeast,
as a wave offering of firstfruits to the LORD.
18Present with this bread seven male lambs, each
a year old and without defect, one young bull and
two rams. They will be a burnt offering to the
LORD, together with their grain offerings and
drink offerings—an offering made by fire, an
aroma pleasing to the LORD. 19Then sacrifice one
male goat for a sin offering and two lambs, each
a year old, for a fellowship offering.[h] 20The priest
is to wave the two lambs before the LORD as a
wave offering, together with the bread of the first-
fruits. They are a sacred offering to the LORD for
the priest. 21On that same day you are to proclaim
a sacred assembly and do no regular work. This is
to be a lasting ordinance for the generations to
come, wherever you live.
22" 'When you reap the harvest of your land, do
not reap to the very edges of your field or gather
the gleanings of your harvest. Leave them for the
poor and the alien. I am the LORD your God.' "
23The LORD said to Moses, 24"Say to the Israel-
ites: 'On the first day of the seventh month you
are to have a day of rest, a sacred assembly com-
memorated with trumpet blasts. 25Do no regular

[f]13 That is, probably about 4 quarts (about 4.5 liters); also in verse 17
[g]13 That is, probably about 1 quart (about 1 liter) [h]19 Traditionally *peace offering*

work, but present an offering made to the LORD by fire.' "

26The LORD said to Moses, 27"The tenth day of this seventh month is the Day of Atonement. Hold a sacred assembly and deny yourselves,[i] and present an offering made to the LORD by fire. 28Do no work on that day, because it is the Day of Atonement, when atonement is made for you before the LORD your God. 29Anyone who does not deny himself on that day must be cut off from his people. 30I will destroy from among his people anyone who does any work on that day. 31You shall do no work at all. This is to be a lasting ordinance for the generations to come, wherever you live. 32It is a sabbath of rest for you, and you must deny yourselves. From the evening of the ninth day of the month until the following evening you are to observe your sabbath."

33The LORD said to Moses, 34"Say to the Israelites: 'On the fifteenth day of the seventh month the LORD's Feast of Tabernacles begins, and it lasts for seven days. 35The first day is a sacred assembly; do no regular work. 36For seven days present offerings made to the LORD by fire, and on the eighth day hold a sacred assembly and present an offering made to the LORD by fire. It is the closing assembly; do no regular work.

37(" 'These are the LORD's appointed feasts, which you are to proclaim as sacred assemblies for bringing offerings made to the LORD by fire—the burnt offerings and grain offerings, sacrifices and drink offerings required for each day. 38These offerings are in addition to those for the LORD's Sabbaths and[j] in addition to your gifts and whatever you have vowed and all the freewill offerings you give to the LORD.)

39" 'So beginning with the fifteenth day of the seventh month, after you have gathered the crops of the land, celebrate the festival to the LORD for seven days; the first day is a day of rest, and the eighth day also is a day of rest. 40On the first day you are to take choice fruit from the trees, and palm fronds, leafy branches and poplars, and rejoice before the LORD your God for seven days. 41Celebrate this as a festival to the LORD for seven days each year. This is to be a lasting ordinance for the generations to come; celebrate it in the seventh month. 42Live in booths for seven days: All native-born Israelites are to live in booths 43so your descendants will know that I had the Israelites live in booths when I brought them out of Egypt. I am the LORD your God.' "

44So Moses announced to the Israelites the appointed feasts of the LORD.

[i]27 Or *and fast*; also in verses 29 and 32 [j]38 Or *These feasts are in addition to the LORD's Sabbaths, and these offerings are*

Discovering the Word 1. What are the various feasts ordained by God? 2. There are variations in the feasts, but what features do they have in common? 3. Notice the place offerings have in the feasts (vv. 8, 12–13, 16–19, 27, 36–37). Why do you think they included offerings? 4. What value would the feasts have in the yearly cycle of life for Israel? 5. How would giving common dates of remembrance to all Israel help ensure their observance?

Applying the Word 1. What do we gain from regular—even enforced—remembrance of our past? 2. What is the value of celebrating what God has done "by the calendar" and not just whenever we feel like it? 3. How can you commemorate some particular act of God on your behalf? (Remember these feasts were joyful parties!)

Responding in Prayer Thank the Lord for his faithfulness to you and to all his people. Ask him to bring to your mind some of his acts for you that you have forgotten.

Leviticus 24

24 The LORD said to Moses, 2"Command the Israelites to bring you clear oil of pressed olives for the light so that the lamps may be kept burning continually. 3Outside the curtain of the Testimony in the Tent of Meeting, Aaron is to tend the lamps before the LORD from evening till morning, continually. This is to be a lasting ordinance for the generations to come. 4The lamps on the pure gold lampstand before the LORD must be tended continually.

5"Take fine flour and bake twelve loaves of

Wont the stoners be put to death then also for stoning someone else to death?

bread, using two-tenths of an ephah[k] for each loaf. 6Set them in two rows, six in each row, on the table of pure gold before the LORD. 7Along each row put some pure incense as a memorial portion to represent the bread and to be an offering made to the LORD by fire. 8This bread is to be set out before the LORD regularly, Sabbath after Sabbath, on behalf of the Israelites, as a lasting covenant. 9It belongs to Aaron and his sons, who are to eat it in a holy place, because it is a most holy part of their regular share of the offerings made to the LORD by fire."

10Now the son of an Israelite mother and an Egyptian father went out among the Israelites, and a fight broke out in the camp between him and an Israelite. 11The son of the Israelite woman blasphemed the Name with a curse; so they brought him to Moses. (His mother's name was Shelomith, the daughter of Dibri the Danite.) 12They put him in custody until the will of the LORD should be made clear to them.

13Then the LORD said to Moses: 14"Take the blasphemer outside the camp. All those who heard him are to lay their hands on his head, and the entire assembly is to stone him. 15Say to the Israelites: 'If anyone curses his God, he will be held responsible; 16anyone who blasphemes the name of the LORD must be put to death. The entire assembly must stone him. Whether an alien or native-born, when he blasphemes the Name, he must be put to death.

17" 'If anyone takes the life of a human being, he must be put to death. 18Anyone who takes the life of someone's animal must make restitution—life for life. 19If anyone injures his neighbor, whatever he has done must be done to him: 20fracture for fracture, eye for eye, tooth for tooth. As he has injured the other, so he is to be injured. 21Whoever kills an animal must make restitution, but whoever kills a man must be put to death. 22You are to have the same law for the alien and the native-born. I am the LORD your God.' "

23Then Moses spoke to the Israelites, and they took the blasphemer outside the camp and stoned him. The Israelites did as the LORD commanded Moses.

k5 That is, probably about 4 quarts (about 4.5 liters)

7 / *Leviticus 25*
A Garden to Tend

FOR MANY OF us, farming—even gardening—is an alien occupation practiced by loners who wear flannel shirts and overalls and are separated from neighbors by many miles. Most of us live severed from the earth, unaware of our profound daily dependence on its bounty. God gave Israel, an agricultural society, guidelines for establishing just practices. Even those of us who are urban need to understand the link between environmental stewardship and justice.

Warming Up to God Today's quiet time deals with how we are to care for God's creation. Recall a place in nature that has touched you. As you bring that place to mind, praise God for how he created it.

Read Leviticus 25.

25 The LORD said to Moses on Mount Sinai, 2"Speak to the Israelites and say to them: 'When you enter the land I am going to give you, the land itself must observe a sabbath to the LORD. 3For six years sow your fields, and for six years prune your vineyards and gather their crops. 4But in the seventh year the land is to have a sabbath of rest, a sabbath to the LORD. Do not sow your fields or prune your vineyards. 5Do not reap what grows of itself or harvest the grapes of your untended vines. The land is to have a year of rest. 6Whatever the land yields during the sabbath year will be food for you—for yourself, your manservant and maidservant, and the hired worker and temporary resident who live among you, 7as well as for your livestock and the wild animals in your land. Whatever the land produces may be eaten.

8“ ‘Count off seven sabbaths of years—seven
times seven years—so that the seven sabbaths of
years amount to a period of forty-nine years.
9Then have the trumpet sounded everywhere on
the tenth day of the seventh month; on the Day of
Atonement sound the trumpet throughout your
land. 10Consecrate the fiftieth year and proclaim
liberty throughout the land to all its inhabitants.
It shall be a jubilee for you; each one of you is to
return to his family property and each to his own
clan. 11The fiftieth year shall be a jubilee for you;
do not sow and do not reap what grows of itself
or harvest the untended vines. 12For it is a jubilee
and is to be holy for you; eat only what is taken
directly from the fields.

13“ ‘In this Year of Jubilee everyone is to return
to his own property.

14“ ‘If you sell land to one of your countrymen
or buy any from him, do not take advantage of
each other. 15You are to buy from your country-
man on the basis of the number of years since the
Jubilee. And he is to sell to you on the basis of the
number of years left for harvesting crops. 16When
the years are many, you are to increase the price,
and when the years are few, you are to decrease
the price, because what he is really selling you is
the number of crops. 17Do not take advantage of
each other, but fear your God. I am the LORD your
God.

18“ ‘Follow my decrees and be careful to obey
my laws, and you will live safely in the land.
19Then the land will yield its fruit, and you will
eat your fill and live there in safety. 20You may
ask, “What will we eat in the seventh year if we
do not plant or harvest our crops?” 21I will send
you such a blessing in the sixth year that the land
will yield enough for three years. 22While you
plant during the eighth year, you will eat from the
old crop and will continue to eat from it until the
harvest of the ninth year comes in.

23“ ‘The land must not be sold permanently, be-
cause the land is mine and you are but aliens and
my tenants. 24Throughout the country that you
hold as a possession, you must provide for the
redemption of the land.

25“ ‘If one of your countrymen becomes poor
and sells some of his property, his nearest relative
is to come and redeem what his countryman has
sold. 26If, however, a man has no one to redeem
it for him but he himself prospers and acquires
sufficient means to redeem it, 27he is to determine
the value for the years since he sold it and refund
the balance to the man to whom he sold it; he can
then go back to his own property. 28But if he does
not acquire the means to repay him, what he sold
will remain in the possession of the buyer until
the Year of Jubilee. It will be returned in the Jubi-
lee, and he can then go back to his property.

29“ ‘If a man sells a house in a walled city, he
retains the right of redemption a full year after its
sale. During that time he may redeem it. 30If it is
not redeemed before a full year has passed, the
house in the walled city shall belong permanently
to the buyer and his descendants. It is not to be
returned in the Jubilee. 31But houses in villages
without walls around them are to be considered
as open country. They can be redeemed, and they
are to be returned in the Jubilee.

32“ ‘The Levites always have the right to redeem
their houses in the Levitical towns, which they
possess. 33So the property of the Levites is re-
deemable—that is, a house sold in any town they
hold—and is to be returned in the Jubilee, be-
cause the houses in the towns of the Levites are
their property among the Israelites. 34But the pas-
tureland belonging to their towns must not be
sold; it is their permanent possession.

35“ ‘If one of your countrymen becomes poor
and is unable to support himself among you, help
him as you would an alien or a temporary resi-
dent, so he can continue to live among you. 36Do
not take interest of any kind[l] from him, but fear
your God, so that your countryman may continue
to live among you. 37You must not lend him
money at interest or sell him food at a profit. 38I
am the LORD your God, who brought you out of
Egypt to give you the land of Canaan and to be
your God.

39“ ‘If one of your countrymen becomes poor
among you and sells himself to you, do not make
him work as a slave. 40He is to be treated as a
hired worker or a temporary resident among you;
he is to work for you until the Year of Jubilee.
41Then he and his children are to be released, and
he will go back to his own clan and to the prop-
erty of his forefathers. 42Because the Israelites are
my servants, whom I brought out of Egypt, they
must not be sold as slaves. 43Do not rule over
them ruthlessly, but fear your God.

44“ ‘Your male and female slaves are to come
from the nations around you; from them you may

[l]36 Or *take excessive interest*; similarly in verse 37

buy slaves. 45You may also buy some of the tem-
porary residents living among you and members
of their clans born in your country, and they will
become your property. 46You can will them to
your children as inherited property and can make
them slaves for life, but you must not rule over
your fellow Israelites ruthlessly.

47" 'If an alien or a temporary resident among
you becomes rich and one of your countrymen
becomes poor and sells himself to the alien living
among you or to a member of the alien's clan,
48he retains the right of redemption after he has
sold himself. One of his relatives may redeem
him: 49An uncle or a cousin or any blood relative
in his clan may redeem him. Or if he prospers, he
may redeem himself. 50He and his buyer are to
count the time from the year he sold himself up
to the Year of Jubilee. The price for his release is
to be based on the rate paid to a hired man for
that number of years. 51If many years remain, he
must pay for his redemption a larger share of the
price paid for him. 52If only a few years remain
until the Year of Jubilee, he is to compute that
and pay for his redemption accordingly. 53He is to
be treated as a man hired from year to year; you
must see to it that his owner does not rule over
him ruthlessly.

54" 'Even if he is not redeemed in any of these
ways, he and his children are to be released in the
Year of Jubilee, 55for the Israelites belong to me as
servants. They are my servants, whom I brought
out of Egypt. I am the LORD your God.

Discovering the Word 1. What is the primary way the Israelites are to care for their land (vv. 3–5, 11)? 2. What would a sabbath year for the land be like for the people of Israel (vv. 4–7)? 3. What are the key provisions of the Year of Jubilee (vv. 13–22)? 4. How do the guidelines for observing the Year of Jubilee show the link that exists between care of the land and justice for people? 5. What images does the phrase "redemption of the land" bring to mind (v. 24)? 6. Verses 25–55 contain principles for living on the land with others. What do these principles tell you about God's desires for the land and the people?

Applying the Word 1. In what ways is taking good care of the land linked to justice for people in today's world? 2. How is the misuse of land related to the oppression of people?

Responding in Prayer Pray for those who suffer because we do not properly care for God's creation.

8 / *Leviticus 26*
Reaping Results

"SHE HAD IT coming." "I should have known." "It was his own fault." "Well, what did they expect?" In these and a hundred other ways we affirm that people reap what they sow. While that is often said negatively, it can be positive too: "It really paid off." "That's your reward." "You earned it!" Before Israel entered the Promised Land, the Lord told them what they could expect from both obedience and disobedience.

Warming Up to God In what ways has God rewarded your faith and obedience to him?

Read Leviticus 26.

26 " 'Do not make idols or set up an
image or a sacred stone for your-
selves, and do not place a carved
stone in your land to bow down before it. I am
the LORD your God.

2" 'Observe my Sabbaths and have reverence for
my sanctuary. I am the LORD.

3" 'If you follow my decrees and are careful to
obey my commands, 4I will send you rain in its
season, and the ground will yield its crops and

the trees of the field their fruit. 5Your threshing
will continue until grape harvest and the grape
harvest will continue until planting, and you will
eat all the food you want and live in safety in your
land.
6" 'I will grant peace in the land, and you will
lie down and no one will make you afraid. I will
remove savage beasts from the land, and the
sword will not pass through your country. 7You
will pursue your enemies, and they will fall by the
sword before you. 8Five of you will chase a hun-
dred, and a hundred of you will chase ten thou-
sand, and your enemies will fall by the sword
before you.
9" 'I will look on you with favor and make you
fruitful and increase your numbers, and I will
keep my covenant with you. 10You will still be
eating last year's harvest when you will have to
move it out to make room for the new. 11I will
put my dwelling place[m] among you, and I will
not abhor you. 12I will walk among you and be
your God, and you will be my people. 13I am the
LORD your God, who brought you out of Egypt so
that you would no longer be slaves to the Egyp-
tians; I broke the bars of your yoke and enabled
you to walk with heads held high.
14" 'But if you will not listen to me and carry
out all these commands, 15and if you reject my
decrees and abhor my laws and fail to carry out
all my commands and so violate my covenant,
16then I will do this to you: I will bring upon you
sudden terror, wasting diseases and fever that will
destroy your sight and drain away your life. You
will plant seed in vain, because your enemies will
eat it. 17I will set my face against you so that you
will be defeated by your enemies; those who hate
you will rule over you, and you will flee even
when no one is pursuing you.
18" 'If after all this you will not listen to me, I
will punish you for your sins seven times over. 19I
will break down your stubborn pride and make
the sky above you like iron and the ground be-
neath you like bronze. 20Your strength will be
spent in vain, because your soil will not yield its
crops, nor will the trees of the land yield their
fruit.
21" 'If you remain hostile toward me and refuse
to listen to me, I will multiply your afflictions
seven times over, as your sins deserve. 22I will
send wild animals against you, and they will rob
you of your children, destroy your cattle and
make you so few in number that your roads will
be deserted.
23" 'If in spite of these things you do not accept
my correction but continue to be hostile toward
me, 24I myself will be hostile toward you and will
afflict you for your sins seven times over. 25And
I will bring the sword upon you to avenge the
breaking of the covenant. When you withdraw
into your cities, I will send a plague among you,
and you will be given into enemy hands. 26When
I cut off your supply of bread, ten women will be
able to bake your bread in one oven, and they will
dole out the bread by weight. You will eat, but
you will not be satisfied.
27" 'If in spite of this you still do not listen to
me but continue to be hostile toward me, 28then
in my anger I will be hostile toward you, and I
myself will punish you for your sins seven times
over. 29You will eat the flesh of your sons and the
flesh of your daughters. 30I will destroy your high
places, cut down your incense altars and pile your
dead bodies on the lifeless forms of your idols,
and I will abhor you. 31I will turn your cities into
ruins and lay waste your sanctuaries, and I will
take no delight in the pleasing aroma of your of-
ferings. 32I will lay waste the land, so that your
enemies who live there will be appalled. 33I will
scatter you among the nations and will draw out
my sword and pursue you. Your land will be laid
waste, and your cities will lie in ruins. 34Then the
land will enjoy its sabbath years all the time that
it lies desolate and you are in the country of your
enemies; then the land will rest and enjoy its sab-
baths. 35All the time that it lies desolate, the land
will have the rest it did not have during the sab-
baths you lived in it.
36" 'As for those of you who are left, I will make
their hearts so fearful in the lands of their ene-
mies that the sound of a windblown leaf will put
them to flight. They will run as though fleeing
from the sword, and they will fall, even though
no one is pursuing them. 37They will stumble
over one another as though fleeing from the
sword, even though no one is pursuing them. So
you will not be able to stand before your enemies.
38You will perish among the nations; the land of
your enemies will devour you. 39Those of you
who are left will waste away in the lands of
their enemies because of their sins; also be-

m 11 *Or my tabernacle*

cause of their fathers' sins they will waste away.

40" 'But if they will confess their sins and the sins of their fathers—their treachery against me and their hostility toward me, 41which made me hostile toward them so that I sent them into the land of their enemies—then when their uncircumcised hearts are humbled and they pay for their sin, 42I will remember my covenant with Jacob and my covenant with Isaac and my covenant with Abraham, and I will remember the land. 43For the land will be deserted by them and will enjoy its sabbaths while it lies desolate without them. They will pay for their sins because they rejected my laws and abhorred my decrees. 44Yet in spite of this, when they are in the land of their enemies, I will not reject them or abhor them so as to destroy them completely, breaking my covenant with them. I am the LORD their God. 45But for their sake I will remember the covenant with their ancestors whom I brought out of Egypt in the sight of the nations to be their God. I am the LORD.' "

46These are the decrees, the laws and the regulations that the LORD established on Mount Sinai between himself and the Israelites through Moses.

Discovering the Word 1. How would the Lord bless Israel for obeying him (vv. 3–13)? 2. How would he chastise them for disobeying (vv. 14–39)? 3. How do verses 18, 21, 23 and 27 show that God would keep giving Israel another chance to obey? 4. Even after the extreme chastisement of being banished from their land, what did God promise if they repented (vv. 40–45)? 5. How do the punishments, as well as the rewards, demonstrate God's generous grace?

Applying the Word 1. This Scripture should not lead us to interpret *every* event as God's reward or punishment. Nevertheless, we can all think of events through which God spoke to us about our behavior. How has the Lord affirmed or reprimanded you through something that happened? 2. When remarkable events occur, how open are you to what the Lord might be saying to you through them?

Responding in Prayer Thank the Lord for communicating to you through happenings in your life. Renew your commitment to follow him in obedience.

Leviticus 27

27 The LORD said to Moses, 2"Speak to the Israelites and say to them: 'If anyone makes a special vow to dedicate persons to the LORD by giving equivalent values, 3set the value of a male between the ages of twenty and sixty at fifty shekels[n] of silver, according to the sanctuary shekel[o]; 4and if it is a female, set her value at thirty shekels.[p] 5If it is a person between the ages of five and twenty, set the value of a male at twenty shekels[q] and of a female at ten shekels.[r] 6If it is a person between one month and five years, set the value of a male at five shekels[s] of silver and that of a female at three shekels[t] of silver. 7If it is a person sixty years old or more, set the value of a male at fifteen shekels[u] and of a female at ten shekels. 8If anyone making the vow is too poor to pay the specified amount, he is to present the person to the priest, who will set the value for him according to what the man making the vow can afford.

9" 'If what he vowed is an animal that is acceptable as an offering to the LORD, such an animal given to the LORD becomes holy. 10He must not exchange it or substitute a good one for a bad one, or a bad one for a good one; if he should substitute one animal for another, both it and the substitute become holy. 11If what he vowed is a ceremonially unclean animal—one that is not acceptable as an offering to the LORD—the animal must be presented to the priest, 12who will judge its quality as good or bad. Whatever value the priest then sets, that is what it will be. 13If the owner wishes to redeem the animal, he must add a fifth to its value.

14" 'If a man dedicates his house as something holy to the LORD, the priest will judge its quality as good or bad. Whatever value the priest then

[n]3 That is, about 1 1/4 pounds (about 0.6 kilogram); also in verse 16 [o]3 That is, about 2/5 ounce (about 11.5 grams); also in verse 25 [p]4 That is, about 12 ounces (about 0.3 kilogram) [q]5 That is, about 8 ounces (about 0.2 kilogram) [r]5 That is, about 4 ounces (about 110 grams); also in verse 7 [s]6 That is, about 2 ounces (about 55 grams) [t]6 That is, about 1 1/4 ounces (about 35 grams) [u]7 That is, about 6 ounces (about 170 grams)

sets, so it will remain. 15If the man who dedicates his house redeems it, he must add a fifth to its value, and the house will again become his.

16" 'If a man dedicates to the LORD part of his family land, its value is to be set according to the amount of seed required for it—fifty shekels of silver to a homer[v] of barley seed. 17If he dedicates his field during the Year of Jubilee, the value that has been set remains. 18But if he dedicates his field after the Jubilee, the priest will determine the value according to the number of years that remain until the next Year of Jubilee, and its set value will be reduced. 19If the man who dedicates the field wishes to redeem it, he must add a fifth to its value, and the field will again become his. 20If, however, he does not redeem the field, or if he has sold it to someone else, it can never be redeemed. 21When the field is released in the Jubilee, it will become holy, like a field devoted to the LORD; it will become the property of the priests.[w]

22" 'If a man dedicates to the LORD a field he has bought, which is not part of his family land, 23the priest will determine its value up to the Year of Jubilee, and the man must pay its value on that day as something holy to the LORD. 24In the Year of Jubilee the field will revert to the person from whom he bought it, the one whose land it was. 25Every value is to be set according to the sanctuary shekel, twenty gerahs to the shekel.

26" 'No one, however, may dedicate the firstborn of an animal, since the firstborn already belongs to the LORD; whether an ox[x] or a sheep, it is the LORD's. 27If it is one of the unclean animals, he may buy it back at its set value, adding a fifth of the value to it. If he does not redeem it, it is to be sold at its set value.

28" 'But nothing that a man owns and devotes[y] to the LORD—whether man or animal or family land—may be sold or redeemed; everything so devoted is most holy to the LORD.

29" 'No person devoted to destruction[z] may be ransomed; he must be put to death.

30" 'A tithe of everything from the land, whether grain from the soil or fruit from the trees, belongs to the LORD; it is holy to the LORD. 31If a man redeems any of his tithe, he must add a fifth of the value to it. 32The entire tithe of the herd and flock—every tenth animal that passes under the shepherd's rod—will be holy to the LORD. 33He must not pick out the good from the bad or make any substitution. If he does make a substitution, both the animal and its substitute become holy and cannot be redeemed.' "

34These are the commands the LORD gave Moses on Mount Sinai for the Israelites.

[v] *16* That is, probably about 6 bushels (about 220 liters) [w] *21* Or *priest* [x] *26* The Hebrew word can include both male and female. [y] *28* The Hebrew term refers to the irrevocable giving over of things or persons to the LORD. [z] *29* The Hebrew term refers to the irrevocable giving over of things or persons to the LORD, often by totally destroying them.

Numbers

One month after the close of the book of Exodus, Moses commands a census of all the Jews. He finds that an Israelite army would number 603,550 fighting men. A generation later (Nu 26) he will commission a new count. These human inventories —the numbering of God's people—provide the title of the Pentateuch's fourth book.

But the ancients had another name for this account: they called it "In the Wilderness." That title is a fitting one for the story of a wandering people caught in transition between slavery and freedom. Having fled Pharaoh's tyranny in Egypt, God's people seek the permanent homeland of their dreams. But reality interferes with their dreams; they face the crises and trials of nomadic life.

Along with its colorful and gripping narrative, Numbers offers a metaphor for the wilderness experience every human must encounter. We experience life as a pilgrimage like that of Moses and his people, with past struggles behind us and dreams yet to fulfill. Along the way, there is heartbreak and disappointment. But the voice of God is consistent, calling on us to face every challenge with steadfast obedience. Like the Israelites, we discover that the hardest times produce the strongest lessons, and that at the other end of the wilderness journey we find ourselves wiser and more capable. To obey God is to move forward in life with direction and purpose.

But disobedience has consequences. When God's people rebel against his command to enter Canaan, the results are painful and far-reaching. We learn that our own failures have implications for generations yet unborn. There is nowhere in the Bible a more graphic picture of the social consequences of sin.

Numbers begins with the exodus generation. It ends thirty-nine years later with the story of their children fighting to solidify their place in Canaan. It begins shortly after the Israelites receive the Law from Mount Sinai. It ends as they struggle to live by that Law in a world of hostile neighbors. It begins with a leader, Moses, at the peak of his power. It ends as Moses, forbidden from entering the Promised Land, gives way to a new leader. These are thirty-nine pivotal years in the spiritual history of a nation.

As you study Numbers, watch for these themes: obedience, purity, leadership, guidance, discouragement, deliverance. What can you learn and apply from the lessons of Moses' people? As those themes play out in the book of Numbers, so will they be repeated in the wilderness experiences of our own lives.

Outline

1/ Numbers 1 ——— *People Count!*

2/ Numbers 9 ——— *Looking Back; Looking Ahead*

3/ Numbers 11 ——— *No Thanks*

4/ Numbers 12 ——— *A Critical Spirit*

5/ Numbers 13:1—14:12 ——— *Taking Risks*

6/ Numbers 17 ——— *Budding Leadership*

7/ Numbers 20:1–13 ——— *God's Work; God's Way*

8/ Numbers 21:1–9 ——— *The Serpent That Saved*

9/ Numbers 27:12–23 ——— *Passing the Torch*

10/ Numbers 32 ——— *United We Stand*

1 / *Numbers 1*
People Count!

WE LIVE IN the age of the survey. Demographic studies measure every possible facet of modern life. We seem to have an obsession with categorizing people. In Numbers categories play an important part—two censuses are recorded. The Israelites have secured their freedom from Egyptian slavery, and Moses calls for a count of the twelve tribes.

Warming Up to God What groups do you feel particularly a part of and identify with?

Read Numbers 1.

---

1 The LORD spoke to Moses in the Tent of
Meeting in the Desert of Sinai on the first
day of the second month of the second
year after the Israelites came out of Egypt. He
said: 2“Take a census of the whole Israelite com-
munity by their clans and families, listing every
man by name, one by one. 3You and Aaron are to
number by their divisions all the men in Israel
twenty years old or more who are able to serve in
the army. 4One man from each tribe, each the
head of his family, is to help you. 5These are the
names of the men who are to assist you:

from Reuben, Elizur son of Shedeur;
6from Simeon, Shelumiel son of Zurishaddai;
7from Judah, Nahshon son of Amminadab;
8from Issachar, Nethanel son of Zuar;
9from Zebulun, Eliab son of Helon;
10from the sons of Joseph:
from Ephraim, Elishama son of Ammihud;
from Manasseh, Gamaliel son of Pedahzur;
11from Benjamin, Abidan son of Gideoni;
12from Dan, Ahiezer son of Ammishaddai;
13from Asher, Pagiel son of Ocran;
14from Gad, Eliasaph son of Deuel;
15from Naphtali, Ahira son of Enan.”

16These were the men appointed from the com-
munity, the leaders of their ancestral tribes. They
were the heads of the clans of Israel.
17Moses and Aaron took these men whose
names had been given, 18and they called the
whole community together on the first day of the
second month. The people indicated their ances-
try by their clans and families, and the men
twenty years old or more were listed by name,
one by one, 19as the LORD commanded Moses.
And so he counted them in the Desert of Sinai:

20From the descendants of Reuben the firstborn son of Israel:
All the men twenty years old or more
who were able to serve in the army were
listed by name, one by one, according to
the records of their clans and families.
21The number from the tribe of Reuben
was 46,500.

22From the descendants of Simeon:
All the men twenty years old or more
who were able to serve in the army were
counted and listed by name, one by one,
according to the records of their clans
and families. 23The number from the tribe
of Simeon was 59,300.

24From the descendants of Gad:
All the men twenty years old or more
who were able to serve in the army were
listed by name, according to the records
of their clans and families. 25The number
from the tribe of Gad was 45,650.

26From the descendants of Judah:
All the men twenty years old or more
who were able to serve in the army were
listed by name, according to the records
of their clans and families. 27The number
from the tribe of Judah was 74,600.

28From the descendants of Issachar:
All the men twenty years old or more
who were able to serve in the army were
listed by name, according to the records
of their clans and families. 29The number
from the tribe of Issachar was 54,400.

30 From the descendants of Zebulun:

All the men twenty years old or more who were able to serve in the army were listed by name, according to the records of their clans and families. 31 The number from the tribe of Zebulun was 57,400.

32 From the sons of Joseph:
From the descendants of Ephraim:

All the men twenty years old or more who were able to serve in the army were listed by name, according to the records of their clans and families. 33 The number from the tribe of Ephraim was 40,500.

34 From the descendants of Manasseh:

All the men twenty years old or more who were able to serve in the army were listed by name, according to the records of their clans and families. 35 The number from the tribe of Manasseh was 32,200.

36 From the descendants of Benjamin:

All the men twenty years old or more who were able to serve in the army were listed by name, according to the records of their clans and families. 37 The number from the tribe of Benjamin was 35,400.

38 From the descendants of Dan:

All the men twenty years old or more who were able to serve in the army were listed by name, according to the records of their clans and families. 39 The number from the tribe of Dan was 62,700.

40 From the descendants of Asher:

All the men twenty years old or more who were able to serve in the army were listed by name, according to the records of their clans and families. 41 The number from the tribe of Asher was 41,500.

42 From the descendants of Naphtali:

All the men twenty years old or more who were able to serve in the army were listed by name, according to the records of their clans and families. 43 The number from the tribe of Naphtali was 53,400.

44 These were the men counted by Moses and Aaron and the twelve leaders of Israel, each one representing his family. 45 All the Israelites twenty years old or more who were able to serve in Israel's army were counted according to their families. 46 The total number was 603,550.

47 The families of the tribe of Levi, however, were not counted along with the others. 48 The LORD had said to Moses: 49 "You must not count the tribe of Levi or include them in the census of the other Israelites. 50 Instead, appoint the Levites to be in charge of the tabernacle of the Testimony—over all its furnishings and everything belonging to it. They are to carry the tabernacle and all its furnishings; they are to take care of it and encamp around it. 51 Whenever the tabernacle is to move, the Levites are to take it down, and whenever the tabernacle is to be set up, the Levites shall do it. Anyone else who goes near it shall be put to death. 52 The Israelites are to set up their tents by divisions, each man in his own camp under his own standard. 53 The Levites, however, are to set up their tents around the tabernacle of the Testimony so that wrath will not fall on the Israelite community. The Levites are to be responsible for the care of the tabernacle of the Testimony."

54 The Israelites did all this just as the LORD commanded Moses.

Discovering the Word 1. For what reasons does God ask Moses to take a census of all the people (vv. 2–3)? 2. Why do you think it was important for the Israelites to maintain their tribal identities? 3. God sets apart the Levites to take care of the tabernacle (vv. 47–53). Why is it important for those with spiritual responsibilities to be singled out? 4. What special challenges might there have been for nomadic people maintaining the tabernacle and God's laws?

Applying the Word 1. What personal characteristics about you might God count as most important? 2. How can you specifically build up your "tribe" (this could mean family, church or group) as a unit mobilized to serve God?

Responding in Prayer In God's eyes people count. Praise him for caring about the details of our lives. Ask him to help you today to make your "tribe" a stronger one.

Numbers 2—8

2 The LORD said to Moses and Aaron: [2]"The Israelites are to camp around the Tent of Meeting some distance from it, each man under his standard with the banners of his family."

[3]On the east, toward the sunrise, the divisions of the camp of Judah are to encamp under their standard. The leader of the people of Judah is Nahshon son of Amminadab. [4]His division numbers 74,600.

[5]The tribe of Issachar will camp next to them. The leader of the people of Issachar is Nethanel son of Zuar. [6]His division numbers 54,400.

[7]The tribe of Zebulun will be next. The leader of the people of Zebulun is Eliab son of Helon. [8]His division numbers 57,400.

[9]All the men assigned to the camp of Judah, according to their divisions, number 186,400. They will set out first.

[10]On the south will be the divisions of the camp of Reuben under their standard. The leader of the people of Reuben is Elizur son of Shedeur. [11]His division numbers 46,500.

[12]The tribe of Simeon will camp next to them. The leader of the people of Simeon is Shelumiel son of Zurishaddai. [13]His division numbers 59,300.

[14]The tribe of Gad will be next. The leader of the people of Gad is Eliasaph son of Deuel.[a] [15]His division numbers 45,650.

[16]All the men assigned to the camp of Reuben, according to their divisions, number 151,450. They will set out second.

[17]Then the Tent of Meeting and the camp of the Levites will set out in the middle of the camps. They will set out in the same order as they encamp, each in his own place under his standard.

[18]On the west will be the divisions of the camp of Ephraim under their standard. The leader of the people of Ephraim is Elishama son of Ammihud. [19]His division numbers 40,500.

[20]The tribe of Manasseh will be next to them. The leader of the people of Manasseh is Gamaliel son of Pedahzur. [21]His division numbers 32,200.

[22]The tribe of Benjamin will be next. The leader of the people of Benjamin is Abidan son of Gideoni. [23]His division numbers 35,400.

[24]All the men assigned to the camp of Ephraim, according to their divisions, number 108,100. They will set out third.

[25]On the north will be the divisions of the camp of Dan, under their standard. The leader of the people of Dan is Ahiezer son of Ammishaddai. [26]His division numbers 62,700.

[27]The tribe of Asher will camp next to them. The leader of the people of Asher is Pagiel son of Ocran. [28]His division numbers 41,500.

[29]The tribe of Naphtali will be next. The leader of the people of Naphtali is Ahira son of Enan. [30]His division numbers 53,400.

[31]All the men assigned to the camp of Dan number 157,600. They will set out last, under their standards.

[32]These are the Israelites, counted according to their families. All those in the camps, by their divisions, number 603,550. [33]The Levites, however, were not counted along with the other Israelites, as the LORD commanded Moses.

[34]So the Israelites did everything the LORD commanded Moses; that is the way they encamped under their standards, and that is the way they set out, each with his clan and family.

3 This is the account of the family of Aaron and Moses at the time the LORD talked with Moses on Mount Sinai.

[2]The names of the sons of Aaron were Nadab the firstborn and Abihu, Eleazar and Ithamar. [3]Those were the names of Aaron's sons, the anointed priests, who were ordained to serve as priests. [4]Nadab and Abihu, however, fell dead before the LORD when they made an offering with unauthorized fire before him in the Desert of Sinai. They had no sons; so only Eleazar and Itha-

[a]14 Many manuscripts of the Masoretic Text, Samaritan Pentateuch and Vulgate (see also Num. 1:14); most manuscripts of the Masoretic Text *Reuel*

mar served as priests during the lifetime of their father Aaron.

5The LORD said to Moses, 6"Bring the tribe of Levi and present them to Aaron the priest to assist him. 7They are to perform duties for him and for the whole community at the Tent of Meeting by doing the work of the tabernacle. 8They are to take care of all the furnishings of the Tent of Meeting, fulfilling the obligations of the Israelites by doing the work of the tabernacle. 9Give the Levites to Aaron and his sons; they are the Israelites who are to be given wholly to him.[b] 10Appoint Aaron and his sons to serve as priests; anyone else who approaches the sanctuary must be put to death."

11The LORD also said to Moses, 12"I have taken the Levites from among the Israelites in place of the first male offspring of every Israelite woman. The Levites are mine, 13for all the firstborn are mine. When I struck down all the firstborn in Egypt, I set apart for myself every firstborn in Israel, whether man or animal. They are to be mine. I am the LORD."

14The LORD said to Moses in the Desert of Sinai, 15"Count the Levites by their families and clans. Count every male a month old or more." 16So Moses counted them, as he was commanded by the word of the LORD.

17These were the names of the sons of Levi:

Gershon, Kohath and Merari.

18These were the names of the Gershonite clans:

Libni and Shimei.

19The Kohathite clans:

Amram, Izhar, Hebron and Uzziel.

20The Merarite clans:

Mahli and Mushi.

These were the Levite clans, according to their families.

21To Gershon belonged the clans of the Libnites and Shimeites; these were the Gershonite clans. 22The number of all the males a month old or more who were counted was 7,500. 23The Gershonite clans were to camp on the west, behind the tabernacle. 24The leader of the families of the Gershonites was Eliasaph son of Lael. 25At the Tent of Meeting the Gershonites were responsible for the care of the tabernacle and tent, its coverings, the curtain at the entrance to the Tent of Meeting, 26the curtains of the courtyard, the curtain at the entrance to the courtyard surrounding the tabernacle and altar, and the ropes—and everything related to their use.

27To Kohath belonged the clans of the Amramites, Izharites, Hebronites and Uzzielites; these were the Kohathite clans. 28The number of all the males a month old or more was 8,600.[c] The Kohathites were responsible for the care of the sanctuary. 29The Kohathite clans were to camp on the south side of the tabernacle. 30The leader of the families of the Kohathite clans was Elizaphan son of Uzziel. 31They were responsible for the care of the ark, the table, the lampstand, the altars, the articles of the sanctuary used in ministering, the curtain, and everything related to their use. 32The chief leader of the Levites was Eleazar son of Aaron, the priest. He was appointed over those who were responsible for the care of the sanctuary.

33To Merari belonged the clans of the Mahlites and the Mushites; these were the Merarite clans. 34The number of all the males a month old or more who were counted was 6,200. 35The leader of the families of the Merarite clans was Zuriel son of Abihail; they were to camp on the north side of the tabernacle. 36The Merarites were appointed to take care of the frames of the tabernacle, its crossbars, posts, bases, all its equipment, and everything related to their use, 37as well as the posts of the surrounding courtyard with their bases, tent pegs and ropes.

38Moses and Aaron and his sons were to camp to the east of the tabernacle, toward the sunrise, in front of the Tent of Meeting. They were responsible for the care of the sanctuary on behalf of the Israelites. Anyone else who approached the sanctuary was to be put to death.

39The total number of Levites counted at the LORD's command by Moses and Aaron according to their clans, including every male a month old or more, was 22,000.

40The LORD said to Moses, "Count all the firstborn Israelite males who are a month old or more and make a list of their names. 41Take the Levites for me in place of all the firstborn of the Israelites, and the livestock of the Levites in place of all the firstborn of the livestock of the Israelites. I am the LORD."

[b]9 Most manuscripts of the Masoretic Text; some manuscripts of the Masoretic Text, Samaritan Pentateuch and Septuagint (see also Num. 8:16) *to me* [c]28 Hebrew; some Septuagint manuscripts *8,300*

42So Moses counted all the firstborn of the Israelites, as the LORD commanded him. 43The total number of firstborn males a month old or more, listed by name, was 22,273.

44The LORD also said to Moses, 45"Take the Levites in place of all the firstborn of Israel, and the livestock of the Levites in place of their livestock. The Levites are to be mine. I am the LORD. 46To redeem the 273 firstborn Israelites who exceed the number of the Levites, 47collect five shekels[d] for each one, according to the sanctuary shekel, which weighs twenty gerahs. 48Give the money for the redemption of the additional Israelites to Aaron and his sons."

49So Moses collected the redemption money from those who exceeded the number redeemed by the Levites. 50From the firstborn of the Israelites he collected silver weighing 1,365 shekels,[e] according to the sanctuary shekel. 51Moses gave the redemption money to Aaron and his sons, as he was commanded by the word of the LORD.

4 The LORD said to Moses and Aaron: 2"Take a census of the Kohathite branch of the Levites by their clans and families. 3Count all the men from thirty to fifty years of age who come to serve in the work in the Tent of Meeting.

4"This is the work of the Kohathites in the Tent of Meeting: the care of the most holy things. 5When the camp is to move, Aaron and his sons are to go in and take down the shielding curtain and cover the ark of the Testimony with it. 6Then they are to cover this with hides of sea cows,[f] spread a cloth of solid blue over that and put the poles in place.

7"Over the table of the Presence they are to spread a blue cloth and put on it the plates, dishes and bowls, and the jars for drink offerings; the bread that is continually there is to remain on it. 8Over these they are to spread a scarlet cloth, cover that with hides of sea cows and put its poles in place.

9"They are to take a blue cloth and cover the lampstand that is for light, together with its lamps, its wick trimmers and trays, and all its jars for the oil used to supply it. 10Then they are to wrap it and all its accessories in a covering of hides of sea cows and put it on a carrying frame.

11"Over the gold altar they are to spread a blue cloth and cover that with hides of sea cows and put its poles in place.

12"They are to take all the articles used for ministering in the sanctuary, wrap them in a blue cloth, cover that with hides of sea cows and put them on a carrying frame.

13"They are to remove the ashes from the bronze altar and spread a purple cloth over it. 14Then they are to place on it all the utensils used for ministering at the altar, including the firepans, meat forks, shovels and sprinkling bowls. Over it they are to spread a covering of hides of sea cows and put its poles in place.

15"After Aaron and his sons have finished covering the holy furnishings and all the holy articles, and when the camp is ready to move, the Kohathites are to come to do the carrying. But they must not touch the holy things or they will die. The Kohathites are to carry those things that are in the Tent of Meeting.

16"Eleazar son of Aaron, the priest, is to have charge of the oil for the light, the fragrant incense, the regular grain offering and the anointing oil. He is to be in charge of the entire tabernacle and everything in it, including its holy furnishings and articles."

17The LORD said to Moses and Aaron, 18"See that the Kohathite tribal clans are not cut off from the Levites. 19So that they may live and not die when they come near the most holy things, do this for them: Aaron and his sons are to go into the sanctuary and assign to each man his work and what he is to carry. 20But the Kohathites must not go in to look at the holy things, even for a moment, or they will die."

21The LORD said to Moses, 22"Take a census also of the Gershonites by their families and clans. 23Count all the men from thirty to fifty years of age who come to serve in the work at the Tent of Meeting.

24"This is the service of the Gershonite clans as they work and carry burdens: 25They are to carry the curtains of the tabernacle, the Tent of Meeting, its covering and the outer covering of hides of sea cows, the curtains for the entrance to the Tent of Meeting, 26the curtains of the courtyard surrounding the tabernacle and altar, the curtain for the entrance, the ropes and all the equipment used in its service. The Gershonites are to do all that needs to be done with these things. 27All their service, whether carrying or doing other work, is to be done under the direction of Aaron

[d]47 That is, about 2 ounces (about 55 grams) [e]50 That is, about 35 pounds (about 15.5 kilograms) [f]6 That is, dugongs; also in verses 8, 10, 11, 12, 14 and 25

and his sons. You shall assign to them as their responsibility all they are to carry. [28]This is the service of the Gershonite clans at the Tent of Meeting. Their duties are to be under the direction of Ithamar son of Aaron, the priest.

[29]"Count the Merarites by their clans and families. [30]Count all the men from thirty to fifty years of age who come to serve in the work at the Tent of Meeting. [31]This is their duty as they perform service at the Tent of Meeting: to carry the frames of the tabernacle, its crossbars, posts and bases, [32]as well as the posts of the surrounding courtyard with their bases, tent pegs, ropes, all their equipment and everything related to their use. Assign to each man the specific things he is to carry. [33]This is the service of the Merarite clans as they work at the Tent of Meeting under the direction of Ithamar son of Aaron, the priest."

[34]Moses, Aaron and the leaders of the community counted the Kohathites by their clans and families. [35]All the men from thirty to fifty years of age who came to serve in the work in the Tent of Meeting, [36]counted by clans, were 2,750. [37]This was the total of all those in the Kohathite clans who served in the Tent of Meeting. Moses and Aaron counted them according to the LORD's command through Moses.

[38]The Gershonites were counted by their clans and families. [39]All the men from thirty to fifty years of age who came to serve in the work at the Tent of Meeting, [40]counted by their clans and families, were 2,630. [41]This was the total of those in the Gershonite clans who served at the Tent of Meeting. Moses and Aaron counted them according to the LORD's command.

[42]The Merarites were counted by their clans and families. [43]All the men from thirty to fifty years of age who came to serve in the work at the Tent of Meeting, [44]counted by their clans, were 3,200. [45]This was the total of those in the Merarite clans. Moses and Aaron counted them according to the LORD's command through Moses.

[46]So Moses, Aaron and the leaders of Israel counted all the Levites by their clans and families. [47]All the men from thirty to fifty years of age who came to do the work of serving and carrying the Tent of Meeting [48]numbered 8,580. [49]At the LORD's command through Moses, each was assigned his work and told what to carry.

Thus they were counted, as the LORD commanded Moses.

5

The LORD said to Moses, [2]"Command the Israelites to send away from the camp anyone who has an infectious skin disease[g] or a discharge of any kind, or who is ceremonially unclean because of a dead body. [3]Send away male and female alike; send them outside the camp so they will not defile their camp, where I dwell among them." [4]The Israelites did this; they sent them outside the camp. They did just as the LORD had instructed Moses.

[5]The LORD said to Moses, [6]"Say to the Israelites: 'When a man or woman wrongs another in any way[h] and so is unfaithful to the LORD, that person is guilty [7]and must confess the sin he has committed. He must make full restitution for his wrong, add one fifth to it and give it all to the person he has wronged. [8]But if that person has no close relative to whom restitution can be made for the wrong, the restitution belongs to the LORD and must be given to the priest, along with the ram with which atonement is made for him. [9]All the sacred contributions the Israelites bring to a priest will belong to him. [10]Each man's sacred gifts are his own, but what he gives to the priest will belong to the priest.' "

[11]Then the LORD said to Moses, [12]"Speak to the Israelites and say to them: 'If a man's wife goes astray and is unfaithful to him [13]by sleeping with another man, and this is hidden from her husband and her impurity is undetected (since there is no witness against her and she has not been caught in the act), [14]and if feelings of jealousy come over her husband and he suspects his wife and she is impure—or if he is jealous and suspects her even though she is not impure— [15]then he is to take his wife to the priest. He must also take an offering of a tenth of an ephah[i] of barley flour on her behalf. He must not pour oil on it or put incense on it, because it is a grain offering for jealousy, a reminder offering to draw attention to guilt.

[16]" 'The priest shall bring her and have her stand before the LORD. [17]Then he shall take some holy water in a clay jar and put some dust from the tabernacle floor into the water. [18]After the priest has had the woman stand before the LORD, he shall loosen her hair and place in her hands the reminder offering, the grain offering for jealousy, while he himself holds the bitter water that

[g]2 Traditionally *leprosy*; the Hebrew word was used for various diseases affecting the skin—not necessarily leprosy. [h]6 Or *woman commits any wrong common to mankind* [i]15 That is, probably about 2 quarts (about 2 liters)

brings a curse. 19Then the priest shall put the woman under oath and say to her, "If no other man has slept with you and you have not gone astray and become impure while married to your husband, may this bitter water that brings a curse not harm you. 20But if you have gone astray while married to your husband and you have defiled yourself by sleeping with a man other than your husband"— 21here the priest is to put the woman under this curse of the oath—"may the LORD cause your people to curse and denounce you when he causes your thigh to waste away and your abdomen to swell.[j] 22May this water that brings a curse enter your body so that your abdomen swells and your thigh wastes away.[k]"

" 'Then the woman is to say, "Amen. So be it."

23" 'The priest is to write these curses on a scroll and then wash them off into the bitter water. 24He shall have the woman drink the bitter water that brings a curse, and this water will enter her and cause bitter suffering. 25The priest is to take from her hands the grain offering for jealousy, wave it before the LORD and bring it to the altar. 26The priest is then to take a handful of the grain offering as a memorial offering and burn it on the altar; after that, he is to have the woman drink the water. 27If she has defiled herself and been unfaithful to her husband, then when she is made to drink the water that brings a curse, it will go into her and cause bitter suffering; her abdomen will swell and her thigh waste away,[l] and she will become accursed among her people. 28If, however, the woman has not defiled herself and is free from impurity, she will be cleared of guilt and will be able to have children.

29" 'This, then, is the law of jealousy when a woman goes astray and defiles herself while married to her husband, 30or when feelings of jealousy come over a man because he suspects his wife. The priest is to have her stand before the LORD and is to apply this entire law to her. 31The husband will be innocent of any wrongdoing, but the woman will bear the consequences of her sin.' "

6 The LORD said to Moses, 2"Speak to the Israelites and say to them: 'If a man or woman wants to make a special vow, a vow of separation to the LORD as a Nazirite, 3he must abstain from wine and other fermented drink and must not drink vinegar made from wine or from other fermented drink. He must not drink grape juice or eat grapes or raisins. 4As long as he is a Nazirite, he must not eat anything that comes from the grapevine, not even the seeds or skins.

5" 'During the entire period of his vow of separation no razor may be used on his head. He must be holy until the period of his separation to the LORD is over; he must let the hair of his head grow long. 6Throughout the period of his separation to the LORD he must not go near a dead body. 7Even if his own father or mother or brother or sister dies, he must not make himself ceremonially unclean on account of them, because the symbol of his separation to God is on his head. 8Throughout the period of his separation he is consecrated to the LORD.

9" 'If someone dies suddenly in his presence, thus defiling the hair he has dedicated, he must shave his head on the day of his cleansing—the seventh day. 10Then on the eighth day he must bring two doves or two young pigeons to the priest at the entrance to the Tent of Meeting. 11The priest is to offer one as a sin offering and the other as a burnt offering to make atonement for him because he sinned by being in the presence of the dead body. That same day he is to consecrate his head. 12He must dedicate himself to the LORD for the period of his separation and must bring a year-old male lamb as a guilt offering. The previous days do not count, because he became defiled during his separation.

13" 'Now this is the law for the Nazirite when the period of his separation is over. He is to be brought to the entrance to the Tent of Meeting. 14There he is to present his offerings to the LORD: a year-old male lamb without defect for a burnt offering, a year-old ewe lamb without defect for a sin offering, a ram without defect for a fellowship offering,[m] 15together with their grain offerings and drink offerings, and a basket of bread made without yeast—cakes made of fine flour mixed with oil, and wafers spread with oil.

16" 'The priest is to present them before the LORD and make the sin offering and the burnt offering. 17He is to present the basket of unleavened bread and is to sacrifice the ram as a fellowship offering to the LORD, together with its grain offering and drink offering.

18" 'Then at the entrance to the Tent of Meeting, the Nazirite must shave off the hair that he

[j] 21 Or *causes you to have a miscarrying womb and barrenness*
[k] 22 Or *body and cause you to be barren and have a miscarrying womb*
[l] 27 Or *suffering; she will have barrenness and a miscarrying womb*
[m] 14 Traditionally *peace offering*; also in verses 17 and 18

dedicated. He is to take the hair and put it in the
fire that is under the sacrifice of the fellowship
offering.
19" 'After the Nazirite has shaved off the hair of
his dedication, the priest is to place in his hands
a boiled shoulder of the ram, and a cake and a
wafer from the basket, both made without yeast.
20The priest shall then wave them before the LORD
as a wave offering; they are holy and belong to the
priest, together with the breast that was waved
and the thigh that was presented. After that, the
Nazirite may drink wine.
21" 'This is the law of the Nazirite who vows his
offering to the LORD in accordance with his sepa-
ration, in addition to whatever else he can afford.
He must fulfill the vow he has made, according to
the law of the Nazirite.' "
22The LORD said to Moses, 23"Tell Aaron and his
sons, 'This is how you are to bless the Israelites.
Say to them:

24" ' "The LORD bless you
and keep you;
25the LORD make his face shine upon you
and be gracious to you;
26the LORD turn his face toward you
and give you peace." '

27"So they will put my name on the Israelites,
and I will bless them."

7 When Moses finished setting up the tab-
ernacle, he anointed it and consecrated it
and all its furnishings. He also anointed
and consecrated the altar and all its utensils.
2Then the leaders of Israel, the heads of families
who were the tribal leaders in charge of those
who were counted, made offerings. 3They
brought as their gifts before the LORD six covered
carts and twelve oxen—an ox from each leader
and a cart from every two. These they presented
before the tabernacle.
4The LORD said to Moses, 5"Accept these from
them, that they may be used in the work at the
Tent of Meeting. Give them to the Levites as each
man's work requires."
6So Moses took the carts and oxen and gave
them to the Levites. 7He gave two carts and four
oxen to the Gershonites, as their work required,
8and he gave four carts and eight oxen to the
Merarites, as their work required. They were all
under the direction of Ithamar son of Aaron, the
priest. 9But Moses did not give any to the Kohath-
ites, because they were to carry on their shoulders
the holy things, for which they were responsible.
10When the altar was anointed, the leaders
brought their offerings for its dedication and pre-
sented them before the altar. 11For the LORD had
said to Moses, "Each day one leader is to bring his
offering for the dedication of the altar."

12The one who brought his offering on the first
day was Nahshon son of Amminadab of the tribe
of Judah.
13His offering was one silver plate weighing a
hundred and thirty shekels,[n] and one silver
sprinkling bowl weighing seventy shekels,[o]
both according to the sanctuary shekel, each
filled with fine flour mixed with oil as a
grain offering; 14one gold dish weighing ten
shekels,[p] filled with incense; 15one young
bull, one ram and one male lamb a year old,
for a burnt offering; 16one male goat for a sin
offering; 17and two oxen, five rams, five male
goats and five male lambs a year old, to be
sacrificed as a fellowship offering.[q] This
was the offering of Nahshon son of Ammina-
dab.

18On the second day Nethanel son of Zuar, the
leader of Issachar, brought his offering.
19The offering he brought was one silver
plate weighing a hundred and thirty shekels,
and one silver sprinkling bowl weighing sev-
enty shekels, both according to the sanctuary
shekel, each filled with fine flour mixed with
oil as a grain offering; 20one gold dish weigh-
ing ten shekels, filled with incense; 21one
young bull, one ram and one male lamb a
year old, for a burnt offering; 22one male
goat for a sin offering; 23and two oxen, five
rams, five male goats and five male lambs a
year old, to be sacrificed as a fellowship of-
fering. This was the offering of Nethanel son
of Zuar.

24On the third day, Eliab son of Helon, the leader
of the people of Zebulun, brought his offering.
25His offering was one silver plate weighing a
hundred and thirty shekels, and one silver
sprinkling bowl weighing seventy shekels,
both according to the sanctuary shekel, each
filled with fine flour mixed with oil as a
grain offering; 26one gold dish weighing ten

[n] 13 That is, about 3 1/4 pounds (about 1.5 kilograms); also elsewhere in this chapter [o] 13 That is, about 1 3/4 pounds (about 0.8 kilogram); also elsewhere in this chapter [p] 14 That is, about 4 ounces (about 110 grams); also elsewhere in this chapter [q] 17 Traditionally *peace offering*; also elsewhere in this chapter

shekels, filled with incense; 27one young bull, one ram and one male lamb a year old, for a burnt offering; 28one male goat for a sin offering; 29and two oxen, five rams, five male goats and five male lambs a year old, to be sacrificed as a fellowship offering. This was the offering of Eliab son of Helon.

30On the fourth day Elizur son of Shedeur, the leader of the people of Reuben, brought his offering.

31His offering was one silver plate weighing a hundred and thirty shekels, and one silver sprinkling bowl weighing seventy shekels, both according to the sanctuary shekel, each filled with fine flour mixed with oil as a grain offering; 32one gold dish weighing ten shekels, filled with incense; 33one young bull, one ram and one male lamb a year old, for a burnt offering; 34one male goat for a sin offering; 35and two oxen, five rams, five male goats and five male lambs a year old, to be sacrificed as a fellowship offering. This was the offering of Elizur son of Shedeur.

36On the fifth day Shelumiel son of Zurishaddai, the leader of the people of Simeon, brought his offering.

37His offering was one silver plate weighing a hundred and thirty shekels, and one silver sprinkling bowl weighing seventy shekels, both according to the sanctuary shekel, each filled with fine flour mixed with oil as a grain offering; 38one gold dish weighing ten shekels, filled with incense; 39one young bull, one ram and one male lamb a year old, for a burnt offering; 40one male goat for a sin offering; 41and two oxen, five rams, five male goats and five male lambs a year old, to be sacrificed as a fellowship offering. This was the offering of Shelumiel son of Zurishaddai.

42On the sixth day Eliasaph son of Deuel, the leader of the people of Gad, brought his offering.

43His offering was one silver plate weighing a hundred and thirty shekels, and one silver sprinkling bowl weighing seventy shekels, both according to the sanctuary shekel, each filled with fine flour mixed with oil as a grain offering; 44one gold dish weighing ten shekels, filled with incense; 45one young bull, one ram and one male lamb a year old, for a burnt offering; 46one male goat for a sin offering; 47and two oxen, five rams, five male goats and five male lambs a year old, to be sacrificed as a fellowship offering. This was the offering of Eliasaph son of Deuel.

48On the seventh day Elishama son of Ammihud, the leader of the people of Ephraim, brought his offering.

49His offering was one silver plate weighing a hundred and thirty shekels, and one silver sprinkling bowl weighing seventy shekels, both according to the sanctuary shekel, each filled with fine flour mixed with oil as a grain offering; 50one gold dish weighing ten shekels, filled with incense; 51one young bull, one ram and one male lamb a year old, for a burnt offering; 52one male goat for a sin offering; 53and two oxen, five rams, five male goats and five male lambs a year old, to be sacrificed as a fellowship offering. This was the offering of Elishama son of Ammihud.

54On the eighth day Gamaliel son of Pedahzur, the leader of the people of Manasseh, brought his offering.

55His offering was one silver plate weighing a hundred and thirty shekels, and one silver sprinkling bowl weighing seventy shekels, both according to the sanctuary shekel, each filled with fine flour mixed with oil as a grain offering; 56one gold dish weighing ten shekels, filled with incense; 57one young bull, one ram and one male lamb a year old, for a burnt offering; 58one male goat for a sin offering; 59and two oxen, five rams, five male goats and five male lambs a year old, to be sacrificed as a fellowship offering. This was the offering of Gamaliel son of Pedahzur.

60On the ninth day Abidan son of Gideoni, the leader of the people of Benjamin, brought his offering.

61His offering was one silver plate weighing a hundred and thirty shekels, and one silver sprinkling bowl weighing seventy shekels, both according to the sanctuary shekel, each filled with fine flour mixed with oil as a grain offering; 62one gold dish weighing ten shekels, filled with incense; 63one young bull, one ram and one male lamb a year old, for a burnt offering; 64one male goat for a sin offering; 65and two oxen, five rams, five male goats and five male lambs a year old, to be sacrificed as a fellowship offering. This was the offering of Abidan son of Gideoni.

66On the tenth day Ahiezer son of Ammishaddai, the leader of the people of Dan, brought his offering.

67His offering was one silver plate weighing a hundred and thirty shekels, and one silver sprinkling bowl weighing seventy shekels, both according to the sanctuary shekel, each filled with fine flour mixed with oil as a grain offering; 68one gold dish weighing ten shekels, filled with incense; 69one young bull, one ram and one male lamb a year old, for a burnt offering; 70one male goat for a sin offering; 71and two oxen, five rams, five male goats and five male lambs a year old, to be sacrificed as a fellowship offering. This was the offering of Ahiezer son of Ammishaddai.

72On the eleventh day Pagiel son of Ocran, the leader of the people of Asher, brought his offering.

73His offering was one silver plate weighing a hundred and thirty shekels, and one silver sprinkling bowl weighing seventy shekels, both according to the sanctuary shekel, each filled with fine flour mixed with oil as a grain offering; 74one gold dish weighing ten shekels, filled with incense; 75one young bull, one ram and one male lamb a year old, for a burnt offering; 76one male goat for a sin offering; 77and two oxen, five rams, five male goats and five male lambs a year old, to be sacrificed as a fellowship offering. This was the offering of Pagiel son of Ocran.

78On the twelfth day Ahira son of Enan, the leader of the people of Naphtali, brought his offering.

79His offering was one silver plate weighing a hundred and thirty shekels, and one silver sprinkling bowl weighing seventy shekels, both according to the sanctuary shekel, each filled with fine flour mixed with oil as a grain offering; 80one gold dish weighing ten shekels, filled with incense; 81one young bull, one ram and one male lamb a year old, for a burnt offering; 82one male goat for a sin offering; 83and two oxen, five rams, five male goats and five male lambs a year old, to be sacrificed as a fellowship offering. This was the offering of Ahira son of Enan.

84These were the offerings of the Israelite leaders for the dedication of the altar when it was anointed: twelve silver plates, twelve silver sprinkling bowls and twelve gold dishes. 85Each silver plate weighed a hundred and thirty shekels, and each sprinkling bowl seventy shekels. Altogether, the silver dishes weighed two thousand four hundred shekels,[r] according to the sanctuary shekel. 86The twelve gold dishes filled with incense weighed ten shekels each, according to the sanctuary shekel. Altogether, the gold dishes weighed a hundred and twenty shekels.[s] 87The total number of animals for the burnt offering came to twelve young bulls, twelve rams and twelve male lambs a year old, together with their grain offering. Twelve male goats were used for the sin offering. 88The total number of animals for the sacrifice of the fellowship offering came to twenty-four oxen, sixty rams, sixty male goats and sixty male lambs a year old. These were the offerings for the dedication of the altar after it was anointed.

89When Moses entered the Tent of Meeting to speak with the LORD, he heard the voice speaking to him from between the two cherubim above the atonement cover on the ark of the Testimony. And he spoke with him.

8 The LORD said to Moses, 2"Speak to Aaron and say to him, 'When you set up the seven lamps, they are to light the area in front of the lampstand.' "

3Aaron did so; he set up the lamps so that they faced forward on the lampstand, just as the LORD commanded Moses. 4This is how the lampstand was made: It was made of hammered gold—from its base to its blossoms. The lampstand was made exactly like the pattern the LORD had shown Moses.

5The LORD said to Moses: 6"Take the Levites from among the other Israelites and make them ceremonially clean. 7To purify them, do this: Sprinkle the water of cleansing on them; then have them shave their whole bodies and wash their clothes, and so purify themselves. 8Have them take a young bull with its grain offering of fine flour mixed with oil; then you are to take a second young bull for a sin offering. 9Bring the Levites to the front of the Tent of Meeting and assemble the whole Israelite community. 10You are to bring the Levites before the LORD, and the

[r]85 That is, about 60 pounds (about 28 kilograms) [s]86 That is, about 3 pounds (about 1.4 kilograms)

Israelites are to lay their hands on them. 11Aaron
is to present the Levites before the LORD as a wave
offering from the Israelites, so that they may be
ready to do the work of the LORD.

12"After the Levites lay their hands on the
heads of the bulls, use the one for a sin offering to
the LORD and the other for a burnt offering, to
make atonement for the Levites. 13Have the Le-
vites stand in front of Aaron and his sons and
then present them as a wave offering to the LORD.
14In this way you are to set the Levites apart
from the other Israelites, and the Levites will be
mine.

15"After you have purified the Levites and pre-
sented them as a wave offering, they are to come
to do their work at the Tent of Meeting. 16They
are the Israelites who are to be given wholly to
me. I have taken them as my own in place of the
firstborn, the first male offspring from every Isra-
elite woman. 17Every firstborn male in Israel,
whether man or animal, is mine. When I struck
down all the firstborn in Egypt, I set them apart
for myself. 18And I have taken the Levites in place
of all the firstborn sons in Israel. 19Of all the Isra-
elites, I have given the Levites as gifts to Aaron
and his sons to do the work at the Tent of Meet-
ing on behalf of the Israelites and to make atone-
ment for them so that no plague will strike the
Israelites when they go near the sanctuary."

20Moses, Aaron and the whole Israelite com-
munity did with the Levites just as the LORD com-
manded Moses. 21The Levites purified themselves
and washed their clothes. Then Aaron presented
them as a wave offering before the LORD and made
atonement for them to purify them. 22After that,
the Levites came to do their work at the Tent of
Meeting under the supervision of Aaron and his
sons. They did with the Levites just as the LORD
commanded Moses.

23The LORD said to Moses, 24"This applies to the
Levites: Men twenty-five years old or more shall
come to take part in the work at the Tent of Meet-
ing, 25but at the age of fifty, they must retire from
their regular service and work no longer. 26They
may assist their brothers in performing their du-
ties at the Tent of Meeting, but they themselves
must not do the work. This, then, is how you are
to assign the responsibilities of the Levites."

2 / *Numbers 9*

Looking Back; Looking Ahead

WHAT TRADITIONS DO you look forward to each year? Caroling at Christmas? Decorating Easter eggs? A family cookout in July? The Bible deals frequently with the importance of tradition and commemoration of important events. In Numbers 9 we learn the power of remembering the past as we face the future.

Warming Up to God Think of a tradition that is meaningful for you. How does it nurture you? Thank God for the joy you gain through traditions.

Read Numbers 9.

9 The LORD spoke to Moses in the Desert of
Sinai in the first month of the second year
after they came out of Egypt. He said,
2"Have the Israelites celebrate the Passover at the
appointed time. 3Celebrate it at the appointed
time, at twilight on the fourteenth day of this
month, in accordance with all its rules and regu-
lations."

4So Moses told the Israelites to celebrate the
Passover, 5and they did so in the Desert of Sinai at
twilight on the fourteenth day of the first month.
The Israelites did everything just as the LORD
commanded Moses.

6But some of them could not celebrate the
Passover on that day because they were cere-
monially unclean on account of a dead body. So
they came to Moses and Aaron that same day
7and said to Moses, "We have become unclean
because of a dead body, but why should we
be kept from presenting the LORD's offering
with the other Israelites at the appointed
time?"

8Moses answered them, "Wait until I find out what the LORD commands concerning you."

9Then the LORD said to Moses, 10"Tell the Israelites: 'When any of you or your descendants are unclean because of a dead body or are away on a journey, they may still celebrate the LORD's Passover. 11They are to celebrate it on the fourteenth day of the second month at twilight. They are to eat the lamb, together with unleavened bread and bitter herbs. 12They must not leave any of it till morning or break any of its bones. When they celebrate the Passover, they must follow all the regulations. 13But if a man who is ceremonially clean and not on a journey fails to celebrate the Passover, that person must be cut off from his people because he did not present the LORD's offering at the appointed time. That man will bear the consequences of his sin.

14" 'An alien living among you who wants to celebrate the LORD's Passover must do so in accordance with its rules and regulations. You must have the same regulations for the alien and the native-born.' "

15On the day the tabernacle, the Tent of the Testimony, was set up, the cloud covered it. From evening till morning the cloud above the tabernacle looked like fire. 16That is how it continued to be; the cloud covered it, and at night it looked like fire. 17Whenever the cloud lifted from above the Tent, the Israelites set out; wherever the cloud settled, the Israelites encamped. 18At the LORD's command the Israelites set out, and at his command they encamped. As long as the cloud stayed over the tabernacle, they remained in camp. 19When the cloud remained over the tabernacle a long time, the Israelites obeyed the LORD's order and did not set out. 20Sometimes the cloud was over the tabernacle only a few days; at the LORD's command they would encamp, and then at his command they would set out. 21Sometimes the cloud stayed only from evening till morning, and when it lifted in the morning, they set out. Whether by day or by night, whenever the cloud lifted, they set out. 22Whether the cloud stayed over the tabernacle for two days or a month or a year, the Israelites would remain in camp and not set out; but when it lifted, they would set out. 23At the LORD's command they encamped, and at the LORD's command they set out. They obeyed the LORD's order, in accordance with his command through Moses.

Discovering the Word 1. God establishes celebration of the Passover at the beginning of chapter 9 (Exodus 12 provides the background). Why might he want the Israelites to commemorate this recent spiritual event? 2. Verses 6–13 involve purity during the Passover celebration. What is the relationship between purity and worship? 3. Soon after, God begins to lead the Israelites using a cloud (vv. 15–23). How will it help the Israelites to keep a sense of the past as they move into the future? 4. What do the "cloud patterns" (that is, the cloud's day-to-day status) reveal about the process of following God's guidance?

Applying the Word 1. How can you commemorate the important events in your personal spiritual pilgrimage? 2. In what direction is God leading you in current life decisions?

Responding in Prayer Praise God for the strength he gives us through memories, and ask him to help you be patient in the guidance he provides from day to day.

Numbers 10

10 The LORD said to Moses: 2"Make two trumpets of hammered silver, and use them for calling the community together and for having the camps set out. 3When both are sounded, the whole community is to assemble before you at the entrance to the Tent of Meeting. 4If only one is sounded, the leaders—the heads of the clans of Israel—are to assemble before you. 5When a trumpet blast is sounded, the tribes camping on the east are to set out. 6At the sounding of a second blast, the camps on the south are to set out. The blast will be the signal for setting out. 7To gather the assembly, blow the trumpets, but not with the same signal.

8"The sons of Aaron, the priests, are to blow the trumpets. This is to be a lasting ordinance for you and the generations to come. 9When you go into battle in your own land against an enemy who is oppressing you, sound a blast on the trumpets. Then you will be remembered by the LORD your God and rescued from your enemies. 10Also at your times of rejoicing—your appointed feasts and New Moon festivals—you are to sound the trumpets over your burnt offerings and fellowship offerings,[t] and they will be a memorial for you before your God. I am the LORD your God."

11On the twentieth day of the second month of the second year, the cloud lifted from above the tabernacle of the Testimony. 12Then the Israelites set out from the Desert of Sinai and traveled from place to place until the cloud came to rest in the Desert of Paran. 13They set out, this first time, at the LORD's command through Moses.

14The divisions of the camp of Judah went first, under their standard. Nahshon son of Amminadab was in command. 15Nethanel son of Zuar was over the division of the tribe of Issachar, 16and Eliab son of Helon was over the division of the tribe of Zebulun. 17Then the tabernacle was taken down, and the Gershonites and Merarites, who carried it, set out.

18The divisions of the camp of Reuben went next, under their standard. Elizur son of Shedeur was in command. 19Shelumiel son of Zurishaddai was over the division of the tribe of Simeon, 20and Eliasaph son of Deuel was over the division of the tribe of Gad. 21Then the Kohathites set out, carrying the holy things. The tabernacle was to be set up before they arrived.

22The divisions of the camp of Ephraim went next, under their standard. Elishama son of Ammihud was in command. 23Gamaliel son of Pedahzur was over the division of the tribe of Manasseh, 24and Abidan son of Gideoni was over the division of the tribe of Benjamin.

25Finally, as the rear guard for all the units, the divisions of the camp of Dan set out, under their standard. Ahiezer son of Ammishaddai was in command. 26Pagiel son of Ocran was over the division of the tribe of Asher, 27and Ahira son of Enan was over the division of the tribe of Naphtali. 28This was the order of march for the Israelite divisions as they set out.

29Now Moses said to Hobab son of Reuel the Midianite, Moses' father-in-law, "We are setting out for the place about which the LORD said, 'I will give it to you.' Come with us and we will treat you well, for the LORD has promised good things to Israel."

30He answered, "No, I will not go; I am going back to my own land and my own people."

31But Moses said, "Please do not leave us. You know where we should camp in the desert, and you can be our eyes. 32If you come with us, we will share with you whatever good things the LORD gives us."

33So they set out from the mountain of the LORD and traveled for three days. The ark of the covenant of the LORD went before them during those three days to find them a place to rest. 34The cloud of the LORD was over them by day when they set out from the camp.

35Whenever the ark set out, Moses said,

"Rise up, O LORD!
May your enemies be scattered;
may your foes flee before you."

36Whenever it came to rest, he said,

"Return, O LORD,
to the countless thousands of Israel."

[t]10 Traditionally *peace offerings*

3 / *Numbers 11*
No Thanks

"WHAT HAVE YOU done for me lately?" It's just human nature. We quickly take for granted what we have, and wish we had more. In this chapter, God's people begin to grumble, forgetting the many blessings and miracles they've experienced on the journey.

Warming Up to God Some things we take completely for granted; it takes losing them to fully appreciate them. When have you had this experience? Thank God for three good things in your life you would normally ignore.

 **Read Numbers 11.**

11 Now the people complained about
their hardships in the hearing of
the LORD, and when he heard them
his anger was aroused. Then fire from the LORD
burned among them and consumed some of the
outskirts of the camp. 2When the people cried out
to Moses, he prayed to the LORD and the fire died
down. 3So that place was called Taberah,[u] be-
cause fire from the LORD had burned among them.
4The rabble with them began to crave other
food, and again the Israelites started wailing and
said, "If only we had meat to eat! 5We remember
the fish we ate in Egypt at no cost—also the cu-
cumbers, melons, leeks, onions and garlic. 6But
now we have lost our appetite; we never see any-
thing but this manna!"
7The manna was like coriander seed and
looked like resin. 8The people went around gath-
ering it, and then ground it in a handmill or
crushed it in a mortar. They cooked it in a pot or
made it into cakes. And it tasted like something
made with olive oil. 9When the dew settled on the
camp at night, the manna also came down.
10Moses heard the people of every family wail-
ing, each at the entrance to his tent. The LORD
became exceedingly angry, and Moses was trou-
bled. 11He asked the LORD, "Why have you
brought this trouble on your servant? What have
I done to displease you that you put the burden of
all these people on me? 12Did I conceive all these
people? Did I give them birth? Why do you tell
me to carry them in my arms, as a nurse carries
an infant, to the land you promised on oath to
their forefathers? 13Where can I get meat for all
these people? They keep wailing to me, 'Give us
meat to eat!' 14I cannot carry all these people by
myself; the burden is too heavy for me. 15If this is
how you are going to treat me, put me to death
right now—if I have found favor in your eyes—
and do not let me face my own ruin."
16The LORD said to Moses: "Bring me seventy of
Israel's elders who are known to you as leaders
and officials among the people. Have them come
to the Tent of Meeting, that they may stand there
with you. 17I will come down and speak with you
there, and I will take of the Spirit that is on you
and put the Spirit on them. They will help you
carry the burden of the people so that you will
not have to carry it alone.
18"Tell the people: 'Consecrate yourselves in
preparation for tomorrow, when you will eat
meat. The LORD heard you when you wailed, "If
only we had meat to eat! We were better off in
Egypt!" Now the LORD will give you meat, and
you will eat it. 19You will not eat it for just one
day, or two days, or five, ten or twenty days, 20but
for a whole month—until it comes out of your
nostrils and you loathe it—because you have re-
jected the LORD, who is among you, and have
wailed before him, saying, "Why did we ever
leave Egypt?"'"
21But Moses said, "Here I am among six hun-
dred thousand men on foot, and you say, 'I will
give them meat to eat for a whole month!'
22Would they have enough if flocks and herds
were slaughtered for them? Would they have
enough if all the fish in the sea were caught for
them?"
23The LORD answered Moses, "Is the LORD's arm
too short? You will now see whether or not what
I say will come true for you."
24So Moses went out and told the people what
the LORD had said. He brought together seventy of
their elders and had them stand around the Tent.
25Then the LORD came down in the cloud and
spoke with him, and he took of the Spirit that was
on him and put the Spirit on the seventy elders.
When the Spirit rested on them, they prophesied,
but they did not do so again.[v]
26However, two men, whose names were Eldad
and Medad, had remained in the camp. They
were listed among the elders, but did not go out
to the Tent. Yet the Spirit also rested on them,
and they prophesied in the camp. 27A young man
ran and told Moses, "Eldad and Medad are proph-
esying in the camp."
28Joshua son of Nun, who had been Moses' aide
since youth, spoke up and said, "Moses, my lord,
stop them!"
29But Moses replied, "Are you jealous for my
sake? I wish that all the LORD's people were
prophets and that the LORD would put his Spirit
on them!" 30Then Moses and the elders of Israel
returned to the camp.
31Now a wind went out from the LORD and
drove quail in from the sea. It brought them[w]

[u]3 *Taberah* means *burning*. [v]25 Or *prophesied and continued to do so* [w]31 Or *They flew*

down all around the camp to about three feet[x] above the ground, as far as a day's walk in any direction. 32All that day and night and all the next day the people went out and gathered quail. No one gathered less than ten homers.[y] Then they spread them out all around the camp. 33But while the meat was still between their teeth and before it could be consumed, the anger of the LORD burned against the people, and he struck them with a severe plague. 34Therefore the place was named Kibroth Hattaavah,[z] because there they buried the people who had craved other food.

35From Kibroth Hattaavah the people traveled to Hazeroth and stayed there.

[x]31 Hebrew *two cubits* (about 1 meter) [y]32 That is, probably about 60 bushels (about 2.2 kiloliters) [z]34 *Kibroth Hattaavah* means *graves of craving.*

Discovering the Word 1. What do you learn about the Israelites from these verses? 2. Considering God's method for feeding the people, why do you think he is particularly angered by their response (vv. 4–10)? 3. Moses himself complains to God (vv. 11–15). Why do you think God takes his complaint seriously? 4. If Moses were a discontented person, how might he have reacted differently to the events in verses 24–28? 5. What lesson does God teach the people through granting their request (vv. 18–20, 31–35)?

Applying the Word 1. How should God's statement in verse 23 influence your tendency to complain? 2. With what area of your life do you most often feel dissatisfaction? 3. What can you do to keep God's blessings before you in such a way that you will be more grateful?

Responding in Prayer Spend time in prayer exclusively thanking God for all he has provided—even those things that are hard to appreciate. Then, follow Moses' example in presenting your frustrations honestly as you seek his guidance.

4 / *Numbers 12*
A Critical Spirit

WHO HASN'T BEEN critical of someone else and said, either aloud or inwardly, "Who does he think he is?" Often we don't understand the details of someone's actions or have all the facts. Our anxiety comes out of our mouths, and we not only hurt ourselves but sometimes damage the loyalty and well-being of others. This passage warns us about the dangers of criticism. When the children of Israel left Egypt, they had little sense of national identity and were not used to following a leader. Imagine what could have happened to Moses' confidence and to the people when the members of Moses' own family began to criticize his leadership.

Warming Up to God What have you been thinking critical thoughts about lately?

Read Numbers 12.

12 Miriam and Aaron began to talk against Moses because of his Cushite wife, for he had married a Cushite. 2"Has the LORD spoken only through Moses?" they asked. "Hasn't he also spoken through us?" And the LORD heard this.

3(Now Moses was a very humble man, more humble than anyone else on the face of the earth.)

4At once the LORD said to Moses, Aaron and Miriam, "Come out to the Tent of Meeting, all three of you." So the three of them came out. 5Then the LORD came down in a pillar of cloud; he stood at the entrance to the Tent and summoned Aaron and Miriam. When both of them stepped forward, 6he said, "Listen to my words:

"When a prophet of the LORD is among you,
I reveal myself to him in visions,
I speak to him in dreams.
7But this is not true of my servant Moses;
he is faithful in all my house.
8With him I speak face to face,

clearly and not in riddles;
he sees the form of the LORD.
Why then were you not afraid
to speak against my servant Moses?"

9The anger of the LORD burned against them,
and he left them.

10When the cloud lifted from above the Tent,
there stood Miriam—leprous,[a] like snow. Aaron
turned toward her and saw that she had leprosy;
11and he said to Moses, "Please, my lord, do not
hold against us the sin we have so foolishly com-
mitted. 12Do not let her be like a stillborn infant
coming from its mother's womb with its flesh half
eaten away."

13So Moses cried out to the LORD, "O God,
please heal her!"

14The LORD replied to Moses, "If her father had
spit in her face, would she not have been in dis-
grace for seven days? Confine her outside the
camp for seven days; after that she can be brought
back." 15So Miriam was confined outside the
camp for seven days, and the people did not move
on till she was brought back.

16After that, the people left Hazeroth and en-
camped in the Desert of Paran.

[a] *10* The Hebrew word was used for various diseases affecting the skin—not necessarily leprosy.

Discovering the Word 1. Of what two things are Miriam and Aaron critical? 2. How does their view differ from God's evaluation of Moses? 3. Miriam and Aaron's attack on their brother may have been provoked by his appointing seventy elders over Israel (11:16–17). How might the appointment of elders affect Miriam's status and feelings? 4. How does the Lord respond to the criticisms of Miriam and Aaron (vv. 4–10)? 5. What do we learn about Aaron and Moses from their response to this traumatic event (vv. 10–13)? 6. Why do you think God carried out a seven-day punishment for Miriam (vv. 14–15)? Why didn't he punish Aaron in the same way?

Applying the Word 1. How do you react when you feel your status or position is threatened? 2. Why is the criticism of spiritual leaders especially dangerous?

Responding in Prayer Sometimes God does give us important insights into situations. Pray that God will give you the knowledge to use this insight with a godly spirit, not a critical spirit.

5 / *Numbers 13:1—14:12*
Taking Risks

THOSE WHO CHALLENGE society's standards risk disapproval or even ostracism. We are constantly warned about the folly of taking risks. From life insurance to safe long-term investments, we are encouraged to save and conserve our resources. While this might be prudent financial advice, it can have a dangerous effect in the lives of Christians. We tend to adapt all too easily to a safe and comfortable lifestyle. In our walk with Christ we often follow the path of least resistance, avoiding challenges which intimidate us. Today's passage reminds us that an essential element of faithfulness to Christ is the willingness to risk. On the threshold of the Promised Land the children of Israel are faced with a critical choice. They can opt for the path of least resistance or dare to trust their God.

Warming Up to God What aspect of following Christ frightens or challenges you the most? God knows your fears and wants to comfort you.

Read Numbers 13:1—14:12.

13 The LORD said to Moses, 2"Send
some men to explore the land of
Canaan, which I am giving to the
Israelites. From each ancestral tribe send one of
its leaders."

3So at the LORD's command Moses sent them
out from the Desert of Paran. All of them were
leaders of the Israelites. 4These are their names:

from the tribe of Reuben, Shammua son of
Zaccur;
5from the tribe of Simeon, Shaphat son of
Hori;
6from the tribe of Judah, Caleb son of Je-
phunneh;
7from the tribe of Issachar, Igal son of Jo-
seph;
8from the tribe of Ephraim, Hoshea son of
Nun;
9from the tribe of Benjamin, Palti son of Ra-
phu;
10from the tribe of Zebulun, Gaddiel son of
Sodi;
11from the tribe of Manasseh (a tribe of Jo-
seph), Gaddi son of Susi;
12from the tribe of Dan, Ammiel son of Ge-
malli;
13from the tribe of Asher, Sethur son of Mi-
chael;
14from the tribe of Naphtali, Nahbi son of
Vophsi;
15from the tribe of Gad, Geuel son of Maki.

16These are the names of the men Moses sent to
explore the land. (Moses gave Hoshea son of Nun
the name Joshua.)

17When Moses sent them to explore Canaan,
he said, "Go up through the Negev and on into
the hill country. 18See what the land is like and
whether the people who live there are strong or
weak, few or many. 19What kind of land do they
live in? Is it good or bad? What kind of towns
do they live in? Are they unwalled or fortified?
20How is the soil? Is it fertile or poor? Are there
trees on it or not? Do your best to bring back
some of the fruit of the land." (It was the season
for the first ripe grapes.)

21So they went up and explored the land from
the Desert of Zin as far as Rehob, toward Lebo[b]
Hamath. 22They went up through the Negev and
came to Hebron, where Ahiman, Sheshai and Tal-
mai, the descendants of Anak, lived. (Hebron had
been built seven years before Zoan in Egypt.)
23When they reached the Valley of Eshcol,[c] they
cut off a branch bearing a single cluster of grapes.
Two of them carried it on a pole between them,
along with some pomegranates and figs. 24That
place was called the Valley of Eshcol because of
the cluster of grapes the Israelites cut off there.
25At the end of forty days they returned from ex-
ploring the land.

26They came back to Moses and Aaron and the
whole Israelite community at Kadesh in the
Desert of Paran. There they reported to them and
to the whole assembly and showed them the fruit
of the land. 27They gave Moses this account: "We
went into the land to which you sent us, and it
does flow with milk and honey! Here is its fruit.
28But the people who live there are powerful, and
the cities are fortified and very large. We even
saw descendants of Anak there. 29The Amalekites
live in the Negev; the Hittites, Jebusites and Amo-
rites live in the hill country; and the Canaanites
live near the sea and along the Jordan."

30Then Caleb silenced the people before Moses
and said, "We should go up and take possession
of the land, for we can certainly do it."

31But the men who had gone up with him said,
"We can't attack those people; they are stronger
than we are." 32And they spread among the Israel-
ites a bad report about the land they had ex-
plored. They said, "The land we explored devours
those living in it. All the people we saw there are
of great size. 33We saw the Nephilim there (the
descendants of Anak come from the Nephilim).
We seemed like grasshoppers in our own eyes,
and we looked the same to them."

14

That night all the people of the
community raised their voices and
wept aloud. 2All the Israelites
grumbled against Moses and Aaron, and the
whole assembly said to them, "If only we had
died in Egypt! Or in this desert! 3Why is the LORD
bringing us to this land only to let us fall by the
sword? Our wives and children will be taken as
plunder. Wouldn't it be better for us to go back to
Egypt?" 4And they said to each other, "We should
choose a leader and go back to Egypt."

5Then Moses and Aaron fell facedown in front
of the whole Israelite assembly gathered there.
6Joshua son of Nun and Caleb son of Jephunneh,
who were among those who had explored the
land, tore their clothes 7and said to the entire
Israelite assembly, "The land we passed through
and explored is exceedingly good. 8If the LORD is
pleased with us, he will lead us into that land, a
land flowing with milk and honey, and will give it
to us. 9Only do not rebel against the LORD. And do
not be afraid of the people of the land, because we
will swallow them up. Their protection is gone,
but the LORD is with us. Do not be afraid of them."

[b]21 *Or toward the entrance to* verse 24.
[c]23 *Eshcol* means *cluster*; also in

[10]But the whole assembly talked about stoning
them. Then the glory of the LORD appeared at the
Tent of Meeting to all the Israelites. [11]The LORD
said to Moses, "How long will these people treat
me with contempt? How long will they refuse to
believe in me, in spite of all the miraculous signs
I have performed among them? [12]I will strike
them down with a plague and destroy them, but
I will make you into a nation greater and stronger
than they."

Discovering the Word 1. What kind of information does Moses ask the Israelite leaders to gather (13:18–20)? 2. What negative and positive aspects of the land do the spies describe in their report to the Israelite community (13:27–29)? 3. How does Caleb's perception of the situation (13:30) contrast with that of the other spies (13:31–33)? 4. How do the Israelites respond to the conflicting assessments of the land the spies have explored (14:1–4)? 5. What do Caleb and Joshua remind the people about their identity (14:8–9)?

Applying the Word 1. In your Christian experience, have you ever reached a point when you wanted to "go back to Egypt"? Explain. 2. In verse 10 the people respond to Moses, Aaron, Joshua and Caleb by talking about stoning them. Clearly, their stance for God had put them in physical danger. What type of risks might Christians in your situation face by trusting God despite the opposition of a majority? 3. Where might God be calling you to step out in faith in a risky situation?

Responding in Prayer Ask God to make you a person who is ready to take risks for his sake.

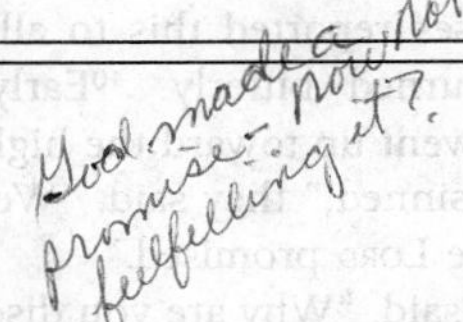

Numbers 14:13—16:50

[13]Moses said to the LORD, "Then the Egyptians
will hear about it! By your power you brought
these people up from among them. [14]And they
will tell the inhabitants of this land about it. They
have already heard that you, O LORD, are with
these people and that you, O LORD, have been
seen face to face, that your cloud stays over them,
and that you go before them in a pillar of cloud
by day and a pillar of fire by night. [15]If you put
these people to death all at one time, the nations
who have heard this report about you will say,
[16]'The LORD was not able to bring these people
into the land he promised them on oath; so he
slaughtered them in the desert.'
[17]"Now may the Lord's strength be displayed,
just as you have declared: [18]'The LORD is slow to
anger, abounding in love and forgiving sin and
rebellion. Yet he does not leave the guilty unpun-
ished; he punishes the children for the sin of the
fathers to the third and fourth generation.' [19]In
accordance with your great love, forgive the sin of
these people, just as you have pardoned them
from the time they left Egypt until now."
[20]The LORD replied, "I have forgiven them, as
you asked. [21]Nevertheless, as surely as I live and
as surely as the glory of the LORD fills the whole
earth, [22]not one of the men who saw my glory
and the miraculous signs I performed in Egypt
and in the desert but who disobeyed me and
tested me ten times— [23]not one of them will ever
see the land I promised on oath to their forefa-
thers. No one who has treated me with contempt
will ever see it. [24]But because my servant Caleb
has a different spirit and follows me wholeheart-
edly, I will bring him into the land he went to,
and his descendants will inherit it. [25]Since the
Amalekites and Canaanites are living in the val-
leys, turn back tomorrow and set out toward the
desert along the route to the Red Sea.[d]"
[26]The LORD said to Moses and Aaron: [27]"How
long will this wicked community grumble against
me? I have heard the complaints of these grum-
bling Israelites. [28]So tell them, 'As surely as I live,
declares the LORD, I will do to you the very things
I heard you say: [29]In this desert your bodies will
fall—every one of you twenty years old or more
who was counted in the census and who has
grumbled against me. [30]Not one of you will enter
the land I swore with uplifted hand to make your
home, except Caleb son of Jephunneh and Joshua
son of Nun. [31]As for your children that you said
would be taken as plunder, I will bring them in to
enjoy the land you have rejected. [32]But you—
your bodies will fall in this desert. [33]Your chil-
dren will be shepherds here for forty years, suffer-

[d]25 Hebrew *Yam Suph;* that is, Sea of Reeds

ing for your unfaithfulness, until the last of your bodies lies in the desert. 34For forty years—one year for each of the forty days you explored the land—you will suffer for your sins and know what it is like to have me against you.' 35I, the LORD, have spoken, and I will surely do these things to this whole wicked community, which has banded together against me. They will meet their end in this desert; here they will die."

36So the men Moses had sent to explore the land, who returned and made the whole community grumble against him by spreading a bad report about it— 37these men responsible for spreading the bad report about the land were struck down and died of a plague before the LORD. 38Of the men who went to explore the land, only Joshua son of Nun and Caleb son of Jephunneh survived.

39When Moses reported this to all the Israelites, they mourned bitterly. 40Early the next morning they went up toward the high hill country. "We have sinned," they said. "We will go up to the place the LORD promised."

41But Moses said, "Why are you disobeying the LORD's command? This will not succeed! 42Do not go up, because the LORD is not with you. You will be defeated by your enemies, 43for the Amalekites and Canaanites will face you there. Because you have turned away from the LORD, he will not be with you and you will fall by the sword."

44Nevertheless, in their presumption they went up toward the high hill country, though neither Moses nor the ark of the LORD's covenant moved from the camp. 45Then the Amalekites and Canaanites who lived in that hill country came down and attacked them and beat them down all the way to Hormah.

15 The LORD said to Moses, 2"Speak to the Israelites and say to them: 'After you enter the land I am giving you as a home 3and you present to the LORD offerings made by fire, from the herd or the flock, as an aroma pleasing to the LORD—whether burnt offerings or sacrifices, for special vows or freewill offerings or festival offerings— 4then the one who brings his offering shall present to the LORD a grain offering of a tenth of an ephah[e] of fine flour mixed with a quarter of a hin[f] of oil. 5With each lamb for the burnt offering or the sacrifice, prepare a quarter of a hin of wine as a drink offering.

6" 'With a ram prepare a grain offering of two-tenths of an ephah[g] of fine flour mixed with a third of a hin[h] of oil, 7and a third of a hin of wine as a drink offering. Offer it as an aroma pleasing to the LORD.

8" 'When you prepare a young bull as a burnt offering or sacrifice, for a special vow or a fellowship offering[i] to the LORD, 9bring with the bull a grain offering of three-tenths of an ephah[j] of fine flour mixed with half a hin[k] of oil. 10Also bring half a hin of wine as a drink offering. It will be an offering made by fire, an aroma pleasing to the LORD. 11Each bull or ram, each lamb or young goat, is to be prepared in this manner. 12Do this for each one, for as many as you prepare.

13" 'Everyone who is native-born must do these things in this way when he brings an offering made by fire as an aroma pleasing to the LORD. 14For the generations to come, whenever an alien or anyone else living among you presents an offering made by fire as an aroma pleasing to the LORD, he must do exactly as you do. 15The community is to have the same rules for you and for the alien living among you; this is a lasting ordinance for the generations to come. You and the alien shall be the same before the LORD: 16The same laws and regulations will apply both to you and to the alien living among you.' "

17The LORD said to Moses, 18"Speak to the Israelites and say to them: 'When you enter the land to which I am taking you 19and you eat the food of the land, present a portion as an offering to the LORD. 20Present a cake from the first of your ground meal and present it as an offering from the threshing floor. 21Throughout the generations to come you are to give this offering to the LORD from the first of your ground meal.

22" 'Now if you unintentionally fail to keep any of these commands the LORD gave Moses— 23any of the LORD's commands to you through him, from the day the LORD gave them and continuing through the generations to come— 24and if this is done unintentionally without the community being aware of it, then the whole community is to offer a young bull for a burnt offering as an aroma pleasing to the LORD, along with its prescribed grain offering and drink offering, and a male goat for a sin offering. 25The priest is to make atone-

[e]4 That is, probably about 2 quarts (about 2 liters) [f]4 That is, probably about 1 quart (about 1 liter); also in verse 5 [g]6 That is, probably about 4 quarts (about 4.5 liters) [h]6 That is, probably about 1 1/4 quarts (about 1.2 liters); also in verse 7 [i]8 Traditionally *peace offering* [j]9 That is, probably about 6 quarts (about 6.5 liters) [k]9 That is, probably about 2 quarts (about 2 liters); also in verse 10

ment for the whole Israelite community, and they
will be forgiven, for it was not intentional and
they have brought to the LORD for their wrong an
offering made by fire and a sin offering. 26The
whole Israelite community and the aliens living
among them will be forgiven, because all the peo-
ple were involved in the unintentional wrong.
27" 'But if just one person sins unintentionally,
he must bring a year-old female goat for a sin
offering. 28The priest is to make atonement before
the LORD for the one who erred by sinning unin-
tentionally, and when atonement has been made
for him, he will be forgiven. 29One and the same
law applies to everyone who sins unintentionally,
whether he is a native-born Israelite or an alien.
30" 'But anyone who sins defiantly, whether na-
tive-born or alien, blasphemes the LORD, and that
person must be cut off from his people. 31Because
he has despised the LORD's word and broken his
commands, that person must surely be cut off; his
guilt remains on him.' "
32While the Israelites were in the desert, a man
was found gathering wood on the Sabbath day.
33Those who found him gathering wood brought
him to Moses and Aaron and the whole assembly,
34and they kept him in custody, because it was
not clear what should be done to him. 35Then the
LORD said to Moses, "The man must die. The
whole assembly must stone him outside the
camp." 36So the assembly took him outside the
camp and stoned him to death, as the LORD com-
manded Moses.
37The LORD said to Moses, 38"Speak to the Isra-
elites and say to them: 'Throughout the genera-
tions to come you are to make tassels on the cor-
ners of your garments, with a blue cord on each
tassel. 39You will have these tassels to look at and
so you will remember all the commands of the
LORD, that you may obey them and not prostitute
yourselves by going after the lusts of your own
hearts and eyes. 40Then you will remember to
obey all my commands and will be consecrated
to your God. 41I am the LORD your God, who
brought you out of Egypt to be your God. I am
the LORD your God.' "

16 Korah son of Izhar, the son of Ko-
hath, the son of Levi, and certain
Reubenites—Dathan and Abiram,
sons of Eliab, and On son of Peleth—became in-
solent[l] 2and rose up against Moses. With them
were 250 Israelite men, well-known community
leaders who had been appointed members of the
council. 3They came as a group to oppose Moses
and Aaron and said to them, "You have gone too
far! The whole community is holy, every one of
them, and the LORD is with them. Why then do
you set yourselves above the LORD's assembly?"
4When Moses heard this, he fell facedown.
5Then he said to Korah and all his followers: "In
the morning the LORD will show who belongs to
him and who is holy, and he will have that person
come near him. The man he chooses he will cause
to come near him. 6You, Korah, and all your fol-
lowers are to do this: Take censers 7and tomor-
row put fire and incense in them before the LORD.
The man the LORD chooses will be the one who is
holy. You Levites have gone too far!"
8Moses also said to Korah, "Now listen, you
Levites! 9Isn't it enough for you that the God of
Israel has separated you from the rest of the Isra-
elite community and brought you near himself to
do the work at the LORD's tabernacle and to stand
before the community and minister to them? 10He
has brought you and all your fellow Levites near
himself, but now you are trying to get the priest-
hood too. 11It is against the LORD that you and
all your followers have banded together. Who is
Aaron that you should grumble against him?"
12Then Moses summoned Dathan and Abiram,
the sons of Eliab. But they said, "We will not
come! 13Isn't it enough that you have brought us
up out of a land flowing with milk and honey to
kill us in the desert? And now you also want to
lord it over us? 14Moreover, you haven't brought
us into a land flowing with milk and honey or
given us an inheritance of fields and vineyards.
Will you gouge out the eyes of[m] these men? No,
we will not come!"
15Then Moses became very angry and said to
the LORD, "Do not accept their offering. I have not
taken so much as a donkey from them, nor have
I wronged any of them."
16Moses said to Korah, "You and all your fol-
lowers are to appear before the LORD tomorrow—
you and they and Aaron. 17Each man is to take his
censer and put incense in it—250 censers in all—
and present it before the LORD. You and Aaron are
to present your censers also." 18So each man took
his censer, put fire and incense in it, and stood
with Moses and Aaron at the entrance to the Tent
of Meeting. 19When Korah had gathered all his
followers in opposition to them at the entrance to

[l] 1 Or *Peleth—took ⌞men⌟* [m] 14 Or *you make slaves of*; or *you deceive*

the Tent of Meeting, the glory of the LORD appeared to the entire assembly. 20The LORD said to Moses and Aaron, 21"Separate yourselves from this assembly so I can put an end to them at once."

22But Moses and Aaron fell facedown and cried out, "O God, God of the spirits of all mankind, will you be angry with the entire assembly when only one man sins?"

23Then the LORD said to Moses, 24"Say to the assembly, 'Move away from the tents of Korah, Dathan and Abiram.' "

25Moses got up and went to Dathan and Abiram, and the elders of Israel followed him. 26He warned the assembly, "Move back from the tents of these wicked men! Do not touch anything belonging to them, or you will be swept away because of all their sins." 27So they moved away from the tents of Korah, Dathan and Abiram. Dathan and Abiram had come out and were standing with their wives, children and little ones at the entrances to their tents.

28Then Moses said, "This is how you will know that the LORD has sent me to do all these things and that it was not my idea: 29If these men die a natural death and experience only what usually happens to men, then the LORD has not sent me. 30But if the LORD brings about something totally new, and the earth opens its mouth and swallows them, with everything that belongs to them, and they go down alive into the grave,[n] then you will know that these men have treated the LORD with contempt."

31As soon as he finished saying all this, the ground under them split apart 32and the earth opened its mouth and swallowed them, with their households and all Korah's men and all their possessions. 33They went down alive into the grave, with everything they owned; the earth closed over them, and they perished and were gone from the community. 34At their cries, all the Israelites around them fled, shouting, "The earth is going to swallow us too!"

35And fire came out from the LORD and consumed the 250 men who were offering the incense.

36The LORD said to Moses, 37"Tell Eleazar son of Aaron, the priest, to take the censers out of the smoldering remains and scatter the coals some distance away, for the censers are holy— 38the censers of the men who sinned at the cost of their lives. Hammer the censers into sheets to overlay the altar, for they were presented before the LORD and have become holy. Let them be a sign to the Israelites."

39So Eleazar the priest collected the bronze censers brought by those who had been burned up, and he had them hammered out to overlay the altar, 40as the LORD directed him through Moses. This was to remind the Israelites that no one except a descendant of Aaron should come to burn incense before the LORD, or he would become like Korah and his followers.

41The next day the whole Israelite community grumbled against Moses and Aaron. "You have killed the LORD's people," they said.

42But when the assembly gathered in opposition to Moses and Aaron and turned toward the Tent of Meeting, suddenly the cloud covered it and the glory of the LORD appeared. 43Then Moses and Aaron went to the front of the Tent of Meeting, 44and the LORD said to Moses, 45"Get away from this assembly so I can put an end to them at once." And they fell facedown.

46Then Moses said to Aaron, "Take your censer and put incense in it, along with fire from the altar, and hurry to the assembly to make atonement for them. Wrath has come out from the LORD; the plague has started." 47So Aaron did as Moses said, and ran into the midst of the assembly. The plague had already started among the people, but Aaron offered the incense and made atonement for them. 48He stood between the living and the dead, and the plague stopped. 49But 14,700 people died from the plague, in addition to those who had died because of Korah. 50Then Aaron returned to Moses at the entrance to the Tent of Meeting, for the plague had stopped.

[n]30 Hebrew *Sheol*; also in verse 33

6 / *Numbers 17*
Budding Leadership

WANTED: STRONG LEADERS. No matter what group or organization is being discussed, that statement applies. Good leaders are hard to find, hard to train, and hard to keep. In Numbers 17 God affirms the leaders set before Israel in a time of crisis.

Warming Up to God Think of the leaders who have made a difference in your life. They might be from church, family or school. Reflect on the leadership gifts that most impressed and influenced you, and thank God for bringing them into your life.

Read Numbers 17.

17 The LORD said to Moses, 2“Speak to
the Israelites and get twelve staffs
from them, one from the leader of
each of their ancestral tribes. Write the name of
each man on his staff. 3On the staff of Levi write
Aaron's name, for there must be one staff for the
head of each ancestral tribe. 4Place them in the
Tent of Meeting in front of the Testimony, where
I meet with you. 5The staff belonging to the man
I choose will sprout, and I will rid myself of this
constant grumbling against you by the Israelites.”
6So Moses spoke to the Israelites, and their
leaders gave him twelve staffs, one for the leader
of each of their ancestral tribes, and Aaron's staff
was among them. 7Moses placed the staffs before
the LORD in the Tent of the Testimony.
8The next day Moses entered the Tent of the
Testimony and saw that Aaron's staff, which rep-
resented the house of Levi, had not only sprouted
but had budded, blossomed and produced al-
monds. 9Then Moses brought out all the staffs
from the LORD's presence to all the Israelites. They
looked at them, and each man took his own
staff.
10The LORD said to Moses, “Put back Aaron's
staff in front of the Testimony, to be kept as a
sign to the rebellious. This will put an end to
their grumbling against me, so that they will not
die.” 11Moses did just as the LORD commanded
him.
12The Israelites said to Moses, “We will die!
We are lost, we are all lost! 13Anyone who even
comes near the tabernacle of the LORD will die.
Are we all going to die?”

Discovering the Word 1. Why does God set up this test (v. 5)? 2. Why do you think he uses this test instead of simply punishing the troublemakers? 3. How does the staff make an appropriate object for God's lesson (see, for example, Ps 23:4)? 4. Why do you think the staffs are placed in front of the ark and Ten Commandments? 5. How would the display of the staffs serve as a good deterrent to grumbling (v. 10)?

Applying the Word 1. How can you provide stronger support to those in leadership in your church or fellowship? 2. How can you seek confirmation of God's approval for your own service?

Responding in Prayer Ask God to make you aware of the place of leadership in daily life. Pray for the wisdom to be a stronger supporter and a wiser leader.

Numbers 18—19

18 The LORD said to Aaron, “You, your
sons and your father's family are to
bear the responsibility for offenses
against the sanctuary, and you and your sons
alone are to bear the responsibility for offenses
against the priesthood. 2Bring your fellow Levites
from your ancestral tribe to join you and assist
you when you and your sons minister before the
Tent of the Testimony. 3They are to be responsi-
ble to you and are to perform all the duties of the
Tent, but they must not go near the furnishings of
the sanctuary or the altar, or both they and you

will die. 4They are to join you and be responsible for the care of the Tent of Meeting—all the work at the Tent—and no one else may come near where you are.

5"You are to be responsible for the care of the sanctuary and the altar, so that wrath will not fall on the Israelites again. 6I myself have selected your fellow Levites from among the Israelites as a gift to you, dedicated to the LORD to do the work at the Tent of Meeting. 7But only you and your sons may serve as priests in connection with everything at the altar and inside the curtain. I am giving you the service of the priesthood as a gift. Anyone else who comes near the sanctuary must be put to death."

8Then the LORD said to Aaron, "I myself have put you in charge of the offerings presented to me; all the holy offerings the Israelites give me I give to you and your sons as your portion and regular share. 9You are to have the part of the most holy offerings that is kept from the fire. From all the gifts they bring me as most holy offerings, whether grain or sin or guilt offerings, that part belongs to you and your sons. 10Eat it as something most holy; every male shall eat it. You must regard it as holy.

11"This also is yours: whatever is set aside from the gifts of all the wave offerings of the Israelites. I give this to you and your sons and daughters as your regular share. Everyone in your household who is ceremonially clean may eat it.

12"I give you all the finest olive oil and all the finest new wine and grain they give the LORD as the firstfruits of their harvest. 13All the land's firstfruits that they bring to the LORD will be yours. Everyone in your household who is ceremonially clean may eat it.

14"Everything in Israel that is devoted[o] to the LORD is yours. 15The first offspring of every womb, both man and animal, that is offered to the LORD is yours. But you must redeem every firstborn son and every firstborn male of unclean animals. 16When they are a month old, you must redeem them at the redemption price set at five shekels[p] of silver, according to the sanctuary shekel, which weighs twenty gerahs.

17"But you must not redeem the firstborn of an ox, a sheep or a goat; they are holy. Sprinkle their blood on the altar and burn their fat as an offering made by fire, an aroma pleasing to the LORD. 18Their meat is to be yours, just as the breast of the wave offering and the right thigh are yours. 19Whatever is set aside from the holy offerings the Israelites present to the LORD I give to you and your sons and daughters as your regular share. It is an everlasting covenant of salt before the LORD for both you and your offspring."

20The LORD said to Aaron, "You will have no inheritance in their land, nor will you have any share among them; I am your share and your inheritance among the Israelites.

21"I give to the Levites all the tithes in Israel as their inheritance in return for the work they do while serving at the Tent of Meeting. 22From now on the Israelites must not go near the Tent of Meeting, or they will bear the consequences of their sin and will die. 23It is the Levites who are to do the work at the Tent of Meeting and bear the responsibility for offenses against it. This is a lasting ordinance for the generations to come. They will receive no inheritance among the Israelites. 24Instead, I give to the Levites as their inheritance the tithes that the Israelites present as an offering to the LORD. That is why I said concerning them: 'They will have no inheritance among the Israelites.' "

25The LORD said to Moses, 26"Speak to the Levites and say to them: 'When you receive from the Israelites the tithe I give you as your inheritance, you must present a tenth of that tithe as the LORD's offering. 27Your offering will be reckoned to you as grain from the threshing floor or juice from the winepress. 28In this way you also will present an offering to the LORD from all the tithes you receive from the Israelites. From these tithes you must give the LORD's portion to Aaron the priest. 29You must present as the LORD's portion the best and holiest part of everything given to you.'

30"Say to the Levites: 'When you present the best part, it will be reckoned to you as the product of the threshing floor or the winepress. 31You and your households may eat the rest of it anywhere, for it is your wages for your work at the Tent of Meeting. 32By presenting the best part of it you will not be guilty in this matter; then you will not defile the holy offerings of the Israelites, and you will not die.' "

19

The LORD said to Moses and Aaron: 2"This is a requirement of the law that the LORD has commanded: Tell the Israelites to bring you a red heifer without

o14 The Hebrew term refers to the irrevocable giving over of things or persons to the LORD. *p16* That is, about 2 ounces (about 55 grams)

defect or blemish and that has never been under
a yoke. 3Give it to Eleazar the priest; it is to be
taken outside the camp and slaughtered in his
presence. 4Then Eleazar the priest is to take some
of its blood on his finger and sprinkle it seven
times toward the front of the Tent of Meeting.
5While he watches, the heifer is to be burned—its
hide, flesh, blood and offal. 6The priest is to take
some cedar wood, hyssop and scarlet wool and
throw them onto the burning heifer. 7After that,
the priest must wash his clothes and bathe him-
self with water. He may then come into the camp,
but he will be ceremonially unclean till evening.
8The man who burns it must also wash his
clothes and bathe with water, and he too will be
unclean till evening.

9"A man who is clean shall gather up the ashes
of the heifer and put them in a ceremonially clean
place outside the camp. They shall be kept by
the Israelite community for use in the water of
cleansing; it is for purification from sin. 10The
man who gathers up the ashes of the heifer must
also wash his clothes, and he too will be unclean
till evening. This will be a lasting ordinance both
for the Israelites and for the aliens living among
them.

11"Whoever touches the dead body of anyone
will be unclean for seven days. 12He must purify
himself with the water on the third day and on
the seventh day; then he will be clean. But if he
does not purify himself on the third and seventh
days, he will not be clean. 13Whoever touches the
dead body of anyone and fails to purify himself
defiles the LORD's tabernacle. That person must be
cut off from Israel. Because the water of cleansing
has not been sprinkled on him, he is unclean; his
uncleanness remains on him.

14"This is the law that applies when a person
dies in a tent: Anyone who enters the tent and
anyone who is in it will be unclean for seven
days, 15and every open container without a lid
fastened on it will be unclean.

16"Anyone out in the open who touches some-
one who has been killed with a sword or someone
who has died a natural death, or anyone who
touches a human bone or a grave, will be unclean
for seven days.

17"For the unclean person, put some ashes
from the burned purification offering into a jar
and pour fresh water over them. 18Then a man
who is ceremonially clean is to take some hyssop,
dip it in the water and sprinkle the tent and all
the furnishings and the people who were there.
He must also sprinkle anyone who has touched a
human bone or a grave or someone who has been
killed or someone who has died a natural death.
19The man who is clean is to sprinkle the unclean
person on the third and seventh days, and on the
seventh day he is to purify him. The person being
cleansed must wash his clothes and bathe with
water, and that evening he will be clean. 20But if
a person who is unclean does not purify himself,
he must be cut off from the community, because
he has defiled the sanctuary of the LORD. The wa-
ter of cleansing has not been sprinkled on him,
and he is unclean. 21This is a lasting ordinance for
them.

"The man who sprinkles the water of cleansing
must also wash his clothes, and anyone who
touches the water of cleansing will be unclean
till evening. 22Anything that an unclean person
touches becomes unclean, and anyone who
touches it becomes unclean till evening."

7 / *Numbers 20:1–13*
God's Work; God's Way

THERE'S NO JOY in being left out—especially when you feel you've earned something. Imagine how Moses must have felt. For nearly forty years he had led the Israelites through the wilderness, often serving as the only influence for godly obedience. But in Numbers 20, the leader discovers he will never realize his goal. What sin could be great enough to bear such a price? This chapter reveals the answer.

Warming Up to God What is your greatest personal dream? What would happen if you were told today you would never attain it? Could you still trust God?

Read Numbers 20:1–13.

20 In the first month the whole Israel-
ite community arrived at the Desert
of Zin, and they stayed at Kadesh.
There Miriam died and was buried.
2Now there was no water for the community,
and the people gathered in opposition to Moses
and Aaron. 3They quarreled with Moses and said,
"If only we had died when our brothers fell dead
before the LORD! 4Why did you bring the LORD's
community into this desert, that we and our live-
stock should die here? 5Why did you bring us up
out of Egypt to this terrible place? It has no grain
or figs, grapevines or pomegranates. And there is
no water to drink!"
6Moses and Aaron went from the assembly to
the entrance to the Tent of Meeting and fell face-
down, and the glory of the LORD appeared to
them. 7The LORD said to Moses, 8"Take the staff,
and you and your brother Aaron gather the as-
sembly together. Speak to that rock before their
eyes and it will pour out its water. You will bring
water out of the rock for the community so they
and their livestock can drink."
9So Moses took the staff from the LORD's pres-
ence, just as he commanded him. 10He and Aaron
gathered the assembly together in front of the
rock and Moses said to them, "Listen, you rebels,
must we bring you water out of this rock?"
11Then Moses raised his arm and struck the rock
twice with his staff. Water gushed out, and the
community and their livestock drank.
12But the LORD said to Moses and Aaron, "Be-
cause you did not trust in me enough to honor
me as holy in the sight of the Israelites, you will
not bring this community into the land I give
them."
13These were the waters of Meribah,[q] where
the Israelites quarreled with the LORD and where
he showed himself holy among them.

q13 *Meribah* means *quarreling.*

Discovering the Word 1. This story is set at the very place a similar rebellion had happened twenty years earlier (see Ex 17:1–7). How would this fact affect the thinking of Moses and of the people? 2. How do Moses' actions compare with or differ from those in Exodus 17? 3. What is it about Moses' actions that so angers God? 4. What effect do you think this lesson had on the observers?

Applying the Word 1. What external pressures are likely to influence the way in which you carry out God's commands? 2. What good things might you currently be doing in ways and with attitudes other than God's? List a few.

Responding in Prayer Take some time to reflect on the current pressures and conflicts in your life. Acknowledge God as sovereign over them. Thank him for giving you wisdom to handle these, and ask him to especially guard your spirit in today's events.

Numbers 20:14–29

14Moses sent messengers from Kadesh to the
king of Edom, saying:

"This is what your brother Israel says: You know about all the hardships that have come upon us. 15Our forefathers went down into Egypt, and we lived there many years. The Egyptians mistreated us and our fathers, 16but when we cried out to the LORD, he heard our cry and sent an angel and brought us out of Egypt.

"Now we are here at Kadesh, a town on the edge of your territory. 17Please let us pass through your country. We will not go through any field or vineyard, or drink water from any well. We will travel along the king's highway and not turn to the right or to the left until we have passed through your territory."

18But Edom answered:

"You may not pass through here; if you

try, we will march out and attack you with the sword."

[19]The Israelites replied:

"We will go along the main road, and if we or our livestock drink any of your water, we will pay for it. We only want to pass through on foot—nothing else."

[20]Again they answered:

"You may not pass through."

Then Edom came out against them with a large and powerful army. [21]Since Edom refused to let them go through their territory, Israel turned away from them.

[22]The whole Israelite community set out from Kadesh and came to Mount Hor. [23]At Mount Hor, near the border of Edom, the LORD said to Moses and Aaron, [24]"Aaron will be gathered to his people. He will not enter the land I give the Israelites, because both of you rebelled against my command at the waters of Meribah. [25]Get Aaron and his son Eleazar and take them up Mount Hor. [26]Remove Aaron's garments and put them on his son Eleazar, for Aaron will be gathered to his people; he will die there."

[27]Moses did as the LORD commanded: They went up Mount Hor in the sight of the whole community. [28]Moses removed Aaron's garments and put them on his son Eleazar. And Aaron died there on top of the mountain. Then Moses and Eleazar came down from the mountain, [29]and when the whole community learned that Aaron had died, the entire house of Israel mourned for him thirty days.

8 / *Numbers 21:1–9*
The Serpent That Saved

CRISIS STRIKES. WE feel surrounded by uncontrollable forces and a hopeless situation. At times like this the weakest fall into sin; the strongest lift their eyes to God and find new power. In this remarkable story, we learn of God's provision in the wilderness for those who believe. And we see in the incident the foreshadowing of God's provision through Christ, more than a thousand years later.

Warming Up to God What is the most difficult crisis you've faced over the past couple of years? How did you seek God in that situation?

Read Numbers 21:1–9.

21 When the Canaanite king of Arad, who lived in the Negev, heard that Israel was coming along the road to Atharim, he attacked the Israelites and captured some of them. [2]Then Israel made this vow to the LORD: "If you will deliver these people into our hands, we will totally destroy[r] their cities." [3]The LORD listened to Israel's plea and gave the Canaanites over to them. They completely destroyed them and their towns; so the place was named Hormah.[s]

[4]They traveled from Mount Hor along the route to the Red Sea,[t] to go around Edom. But the people grew impatient on the way; [5]they spoke against God and against Moses, and said, "Why have you brought us up out of Egypt to die in the desert? There is no bread! There is no water! And we detest this miserable food!"

[6]Then the LORD sent venomous snakes among them; they bit the people and many Israelites died. [7]The people came to Moses and said, "We sinned when we spoke against the LORD and against you. Pray that the LORD will take the snakes away from us." So Moses prayed for the people.

[8]The LORD said to Moses, "Make a snake and put it up on a pole; anyone who is bitten can look

[r]2 The Hebrew term refers to the irrevocable giving over of things or persons to the LORD, often by totally destroying them; also in verse 3.
[s]3 *Hormah* means *destruction.*
[t]4 Hebrew *Yam Suph*; that is, Sea of Reeds

at it and live." 9So Moses made a bronze snake and put it up on a pole. Then when anyone was bitten by a snake and looked at the bronze snake, he lived.

Discovering the Word 1. In the previous chapter, Aaron and Miriam have died; Moses has been punished. How would the state of mind of the Israelites contribute to this crisis? 2. How do the Israelites' complaints in verses 4–5 contrast with the events of verses 1–3? 3. Why do you think God chooses a snake as the central symbol of his salvation, considering how snakes have just been used (vv. 6–9)? 4. John 3:14–15 compares Jesus to the bronze snake. What similarities can you find?

Applying the Word 1. Crisis events seem to separate the strong from the weak. If an unforeseen catastrophe happened today, how would you look to God for strength? 2. How can you help others to seek God in trying times?

Responding in Prayer Praise God the deliverer as you seek him in prayer today. Review the times he has been there to provide comfort and deliverance. Particularly give thanks that he has lifted up his Son, like the snake, so that we can keep our vision focused.

Numbers 21:10—27:11

10The Israelites moved on and camped at Oboth. 11Then they set out from Oboth and camped in Iye Abarim, in the desert that faces Moab toward the sunrise. 12From there they moved on and camped in the Zered Valley. 13They set out from there and camped alongside the Arnon, which is in the desert extending into Amorite territory. The Arnon is the border of Moab, between Moab and the Amorites. 14That is why the Book of the Wars of the LORD says:

"... Waheb in Suphah[u] and the ravines,
the Arnon 15and[v] the slopes of the ravines
that lead to the site of Ar
and lie along the border of Moab."

16From there they continued on to Beer, the well where the LORD said to Moses, "Gather the people together and I will give them water."

17Then Israel sang this song:

"Spring up, O well!
Sing about it,
18about the well that the princes dug,
that the nobles of the people sank—
the nobles with scepters and staffs."

Then they went from the desert to Mattanah, 19from Mattanah to Nahaliel, from Nahaliel to Bamoth, 20and from Bamoth to the valley in Moab where the top of Pisgah overlooks the wasteland.

21Israel sent messengers to say to Sihon king of the Amorites:

22"Let us pass through your country. We will not turn aside into any field or vineyard, or drink water from any well. We will travel along the king's highway until we have passed through your territory."

23But Sihon would not let Israel pass through his territory. He mustered his entire army and marched out into the desert against Israel. When he reached Jahaz, he fought with Israel. 24Israel, however, put him to the sword and took over his land from the Arnon to the Jabbok, but only as far as the Ammonites, because their border was fortified. 25Israel captured all the cities of the Amorites and occupied them, including Heshbon and all its surrounding settlements. 26Heshbon was the city of Sihon king of the Amorites, who had fought against the former king of Moab and had taken from him all his land as far as the Arnon.

27That is why the poets say:

"Come to Heshbon and let it be rebuilt;
let Sihon's city be restored.

28"Fire went out from Heshbon,
a blaze from the city of Sihon.
It consumed Ar of Moab,
the citizens of Arnon's heights.
29Woe to you, O Moab!
You are destroyed, O people of Chemosh!
He has given up his sons as fugitives

[u]14 The meaning of the Hebrew for this phrase is uncertain.
[v]14,15 Or *"I have been given from Suphah and the ravines / of the Arnon 15to*

and his daughters as captives
to Sihon king of the Amorites.

30“But we have overthrown them;
Heshbon is destroyed all the way to Dibon.
We have demolished them as far as Nophah,
which extends to Medeba.”

31So Israel settled in the land of the Amorites.

32After Moses had sent spies to Jazer, the Israelites captured its surrounding settlements and drove out the Amorites who were there. 33Then they turned and went up along the road toward Bashan, and Og king of Bashan and his whole army marched out to meet them in battle at Edrei.

34The LORD said to Moses, “Do not be afraid of him, for I have handed him over to you, with his whole army and his land. Do to him what you did to Sihon king of the Amorites, who reigned in Heshbon.”

35So they struck him down, together with his sons and his whole army, leaving them no survivors. And they took possession of his land.

22

Then the Israelites traveled to the plains of Moab and camped along the Jordan across from Jericho.[w]

2Now Balak son of Zippor saw all that Israel had done to the Amorites, 3and Moab was terrified because there were so many people. Indeed, Moab was filled with dread because of the Israelites.

4The Moabites said to the elders of Midian, “This horde is going to lick up everything around us, as an ox licks up the grass of the field.”

So Balak son of Zippor, who was king of Moab at that time, 5sent messengers to summon Balaam son of Beor, who was at Pethor, near the River,[x] in his native land. Balak said:

“A people has come out of Egypt; they cover the face of the land and have settled next to me. 6Now come and put a curse on these people, because they are too powerful for me. Perhaps then I will be able to defeat them and drive them out of the country. For I know that those you bless are blessed, and those you curse are cursed.”

7The elders of Moab and Midian left, taking with them the fee for divination. When they came to Balaam, they told him what Balak had said.

8“Spend the night here,” Balaam said to them, “and I will bring you back the answer the LORD gives me.” So the Moabite princes stayed with him.

9God came to Balaam and asked, “Who are these men with you?”

10Balaam said to God, “Balak son of Zippor, king of Moab, sent me this message: 11‘A people that has come out of Egypt covers the face of the land. Now come and put a curse on them for me. Perhaps then I will be able to fight them and drive them away.’ ”

12But God said to Balaam, “Do not go with them. You must not put a curse on those people, because they are blessed.”

13The next morning Balaam got up and said to Balak’s princes, “Go back to your own country, for the LORD has refused to let me go with you.” 14So the Moabite princes returned to Balak and said, “Balaam refused to come with us.”

15Then Balak sent other princes, more numerous and more distinguished than the first. 16They came to Balaam and said:

“This is what Balak son of Zippor says: Do not let anything keep you from coming to me, 17because I will reward you handsomely and do whatever you say. Come and put a curse on these people for me.”

18But Balaam answered them, “Even if Balak gave me his palace filled with silver and gold, I could not do anything great or small to go beyond the command of the LORD my God. 19Now stay here tonight as the others did, and I will find out what else the LORD will tell me.”

20That night God came to Balaam and said, “Since these men have come to summon you, go with them, but do only what I tell you.”

21Balaam got up in the morning, saddled his donkey and went with the princes of Moab. 22But God was very angry when he went, and the angel of the LORD stood in the road to oppose him. Balaam was riding on his donkey, and his two servants were with him. 23When the donkey saw the angel of the LORD standing in the road with a drawn sword in his hand, she turned off the road into a field. Balaam beat her to get her back on the road.

24Then the angel of the LORD stood in a narrow path between two vineyards, with walls on both sides. 25When the donkey saw the angel of the

[w] 1 Hebrew *Jordan of Jericho*; possibly an ancient name for the Jordan River [x] 5 That is, the Euphrates

Lord, she pressed close to the wall, crushing Ba-
laam's foot against it. So he beat her again.
26Then the angel of the Lord moved on ahead
and stood in a narrow place where there was no
room to turn, either to the right or to the left.
27When the donkey saw the angel of the Lord, she
lay down under Balaam, and he was angry and
beat her with his staff. 28Then the Lord opened
the donkey's mouth, and she said to Balaam,
"What have I done to you to make you beat me
these three times?"
29Balaam answered the donkey, "You have
made a fool of me! If I had a sword in my hand,
I would kill you right now."
30The donkey said to Balaam, "Am I not your
own donkey, which you have always ridden, to
this day? Have I been in the habit of doing this to
you?"

"No," he said.

31Then the Lord opened Balaam's eyes, and he
saw the angel of the Lord standing in the road
with his sword drawn. So he bowed low and fell
facedown.
32The angel of the Lord asked him, "Why have
you beaten your donkey these three times? I have
come here to oppose you because your path is a
reckless one before me.[y] 33The donkey saw me
and turned away from me these three times. If she
had not turned away, I would certainly have
killed you by now, but I would have spared her."
34Balaam said to the angel of the Lord, "I have
sinned. I did not realize you were standing in the
road to oppose me. Now if you are displeased, I
will go back."
35The angel of the Lord said to Balaam, "Go
with the men, but speak only what I tell you." So
Balaam went with the princes of Balak.
36When Balak heard that Balaam was coming,
he went out to meet him at the Moabite town on
the Arnon border, at the edge of his territory.
37Balak said to Balaam, "Did I not send you an
urgent summons? Why didn't you come to me?
Am I really not able to reward you?"
38"Well, I have come to you now," Balaam re-
plied. "But can I say just anything? I must speak
only what God puts in my mouth."
39Then Balaam went with Balak to Kiriath Hu-
zoth. 40Balak sacrificed cattle and sheep, and gave
some to Balaam and the princes who were with
him. 41The next morning Balak took Balaam up to
Bamoth Baal, and from there he saw part of the
people.

23

Balaam said, "Build me seven altars
here, and prepare seven bulls and
seven rams for me." 2Balak did as
Balaam said, and the two of them offered a bull
and a ram on each altar.
3Then Balaam said to Balak, "Stay here beside
your offering while I go aside. Perhaps the Lord
will come to meet with me. Whatever he reveals
to me I will tell you." Then he went off to a bar-
ren height.
4God met with him, and Balaam said, "I have
prepared seven altars, and on each altar I have
offered a bull and a ram."
5The Lord put a message in Balaam's mouth
and said, "Go back to Balak and give him this
message."
6So he went back to him and found him stand-
ing beside his offering, with all the princes of
Moab. 7Then Balaam uttered his oracle:

"Balak brought me from Aram,
the king of Moab from the eastern
mountains.
'Come,' he said, 'curse Jacob for me;
come, denounce Israel.'
8How can I curse
those whom God has not cursed?
How can I denounce
those whom the Lord has not denounced?
9From the rocky peaks I see them,
from the heights I view them.
I see a people who live apart
and do not consider themselves one of the
nations.
10Who can count the dust of Jacob
or number the fourth part of Israel?
Let me die the death of the righteous,
and may my end be like theirs!"

11Balak said to Balaam, "What have you done
to me? I brought you to curse my enemies, but
you have done nothing but bless them!"
12He answered, "Must I not speak what the
Lord puts in my mouth?"
13Then Balak said to him, "Come with me to
another place where you can see them; you will
see only a part but not all of them. And from
there, curse them for me." 14So he took him to the
field of Zophim on the top of Pisgah, and there he
built seven altars and offered a bull and a ram on
each altar.

y32 The meaning of the Hebrew for this clause is uncertain.

15Balaam said to Balak, "Stay here beside your
offering while I meet with him over there."
16The LORD met with Balaam and put a message
in his mouth and said, "Go back to Balak and give
him this message."
17So he went to him and found him standing
beside his offering, with the princes of Moab. Ba-
lak asked him, "What did the LORD say?"
18Then he uttered his oracle:

"Arise, Balak, and listen;
hear me, son of Zippor.
19God is not a man, that he should lie,
nor a son of man, that he should change
his mind.
Does he speak and then not act?
Does he promise and not fulfill?
20I have received a command to bless;
he has blessed, and I cannot change it.

21"No misfortune is seen in Jacob,
no misery observed in Israel.[z]
The LORD their God is with them;
the shout of the King is among them.
22God brought them out of Egypt;
they have the strength of a wild ox.
23There is no sorcery against Jacob,
no divination against Israel.
It will now be said of Jacob
and of Israel, 'See what God has done!'
24The people rise like a lioness;
they rouse themselves like a lion
that does not rest till he devours his prey
and drinks the blood of his victims."

25Then Balak said to Balaam, "Neither curse
them at all nor bless them at all!"
26Balaam answered, "Did I not tell you I must
do whatever the LORD says?"
27Then Balak said to Balaam, "Come, let me
take you to another place. Perhaps it will please
God to let you curse them for me from there."
28And Balak took Balaam to the top of Peor, over-
looking the wasteland.
29Balaam said, "Build me seven altars here, and
prepare seven bulls and seven rams for me." 30Ba-
lak did as Balaam had said, and offered a bull and
a ram on each altar.

24 Now when Balaam saw that it
pleased the LORD to bless Israel, he
did not resort to sorcery as at other
times, but turned his face toward the desert.
2When Balaam looked out and saw Israel en-
camped tribe by tribe, the Spirit of God came
upon him 3and he uttered his oracle:

"The oracle of Balaam son of Beor,
the oracle of one whose eye sees clearly,
4the oracle of one who hears the words of
God,
who sees a vision from the Almighty,[a]
who falls prostrate, and whose eyes are
opened:

5"How beautiful are your tents, O Jacob,
your dwelling places, O Israel!

6"Like valleys they spread out,
like gardens beside a river,
like aloes planted by the LORD,
like cedars beside the waters.
7Water will flow from their buckets;
their seed will have abundant water.

"Their king will be greater than Agag;
their kingdom will be exalted.

8"God brought them out of Egypt;
they have the strength of a wild ox.
They devour hostile nations
and break their bones in pieces;
with their arrows they pierce them.
9Like a lion they crouch and lie down,
like a lioness—who dares to rouse them?

"May those who bless you be blessed
and those who curse you be cursed!"

10Then Balak's anger burned against Balaam.
He struck his hands together and said to him, "I
summoned you to curse my enemies, but you
have blessed them these three times. 11Now leave
at once and go home! I said I would reward you
handsomely, but the LORD has kept you from be-
ing rewarded."
12Balaam answered Balak, "Did I not tell the
messengers you sent me, 13'Even if Balak gave me
his palace filled with silver and gold, I could not
do anything of my own accord, good or bad, to go
beyond the command of the LORD—and I must
say only what the LORD says'? 14Now I am going
back to my people, but come, let me warn you of
what this people will do to your people in days to
come."
15Then he uttered his oracle:

"The oracle of Balaam son of Beor,

[z]21 Or *He has not looked on Jacob's offenses / or on the wrongs found in Israel.* [a]4 Hebrew *Shaddai*; also in verse 16

the oracle of one whose eye sees clearly,
16 the oracle of one who hears the words of
God,
who has knowledge from the Most High,
who sees a vision from the Almighty,
who falls prostrate, and whose eyes are
opened:

17 "I see him, but not now;
I behold him, but not near.
A star will come out of Jacob;
a scepter will rise out of Israel.
He will crush the foreheads of Moab,
the skulls[b] of[c] all the sons of Sheth.[d]
18 Edom will be conquered;
Seir, his enemy, will be conquered,
but Israel will grow strong.
19 A ruler will come out of Jacob
and destroy the survivors of the city."

20 Then Balaam saw Amalek and uttered his ora-
cle:

"Amalek was first among the nations,
but he will come to ruin at last."

21 Then he saw the Kenites and uttered his ora-
cle:

"Your dwelling place is secure,
your nest is set in a rock;
22 yet you Kenites will be destroyed
when Asshur takes you captive."

23 Then he uttered his oracle:

"Ah, who can live when God does this?[e]
24 Ships will come from the shores of Kittim;
they will subdue Asshur and Eber,
but they too will come to ruin."

25 Then Balaam got up and returned home and
Balak went his own way.

25

While Israel was staying in Shittim,
the men began to indulge in sexual
immorality with Moabite women,
2 who invited them to the sacrifices to their gods.
The people ate and bowed down before these
gods. 3 So Israel joined in worshiping the Baal of
Peor. And the LORD's anger burned against them.
4 The LORD said to Moses, "Take all the leaders
of these people, kill them and expose them in
broad daylight before the LORD, so that the LORD's
fierce anger may turn away from Israel."
5 So Moses said to Israel's judges, "Each of you
must put to death those of your men who have
joined in worshiping the Baal of Peor."
6 Then an Israelite man brought to his family a
Midianite woman right before the eyes of Moses
and the whole assembly of Israel while they were
weeping at the entrance to the Tent of Meeting.
7 When Phinehas son of Eleazar, the son of Aaron,
the priest, saw this, he left the assembly, took a
spear in his hand 8 and followed the Israelite into
the tent. He drove the spear through both of
them—through the Israelite and into the
woman's body. Then the plague against the Israel-
ites was stopped; 9 but those who died in the
plague numbered 24,000.
10 The LORD said to Moses, 11 "Phinehas son of
Eleazar, the son of Aaron, the priest, has turned
my anger away from the Israelites; for he was as
zealous as I am for my honor among them, so that
in my zeal I did not put an end to them. 12 There-
fore tell him I am making my covenant of peace
with him. 13 He and his descendants will have a
covenant of a lasting priesthood, because he was
zealous for the honor of his God and made atone-
ment for the Israelites."
14 The name of the Israelite who was killed with
the Midianite woman was Zimri son of Salu, the
leader of a Simeonite family. 15 And the name of
the Midianite woman who was put to death was
Cozbi daughter of Zur, a tribal chief of a Midian-
ite family.
16 The LORD said to Moses, 17 "Treat the Midian-
ites as enemies and kill them, 18 because they
treated you as enemies when they deceived you
in the affair of Peor and their sister Cozbi, the
daughter of a Midianite leader, the woman who
was killed when the plague came as a result of
Peor."

26

After the plague the LORD said to
Moses and Eleazar son of Aaron,
the priest, 2 "Take a census of the
whole Israelite community by families—all those
twenty years old or more who are able to serve in
the army of Israel." 3 So on the plains of Moab by
the Jordan across from Jericho,[f] Moses and Elea-
zar the priest spoke with them and said, 4 "Take a
census of the men twenty years old or more, as
the LORD commanded Moses."

[b] 17 Samaritan Pentateuch (see also Jer. 48:45); the meaning of the word in the Masoretic Text is uncertain. [c] 17 Or possibly *Moab, / batter* [d] 17 Or *all the noisy boasters* [e] 23 Masoretic Text; with a different word division of the Hebrew *A people will gather from the north.* [f] 3 Hebrew *Jordan of Jericho*; possibly an ancient name for the Jordan River; also in verse 63

These were the Israelites who came out of Egypt:

[5]The descendants of Reuben, the firstborn son of Israel, were:

through Hanoch, the Hanochite clan;
through Pallu, the Palluite clan;
[6]through Hezron, the Hezronite clan;
through Carmi, the Carmite clan.

[7]These were the clans of Reuben; those numbered were 43,730.

[8]The son of Pallu was Eliab, [9]and the sons of
Eliab were Nemuel, Dathan and Abiram. The
same Dathan and Abiram were the community
officials who rebelled against Moses and Aaron
and were among Korah's followers when they re-
belled against the LORD. [10]The earth opened its
mouth and swallowed them along with Korah,
whose followers died when the fire devoured the
250 men. And they served as a warning sign.
[11]The line of Korah, however, did not die out.

[12]The descendants of Simeon by their clans were:

through Nemuel, the Nemuelite clan;
through Jamin, the Jaminite clan;
through Jakin, the Jakinite clan;
[13]through Zerah, the Zerahite clan;
through Shaul, the Shaulite clan.

[14]These were the clans of Simeon; there were 22,200 men.

[15]The descendants of Gad by their clans were:

through Zephon, the Zephonite clan;
through Haggi, the Haggite clan;
through Shuni, the Shunite clan;
[16]through Ozni, the Oznite clan;
through Eri, the Erite clan;
[17]through Arodi,[g] the Arodite clan;
through Areli, the Arelite clan.

[18]These were the clans of Gad; those numbered were 40,500.

[19]Er and Onan were sons of Judah, but they died in Canaan.

[20]The descendants of Judah by their clans were:

through Shelah, the Shelanite clan;
through Perez, the Perezite clan;
through Zerah, the Zerahite clan.

[21]The descendants of Perez were:

through Hezron, the Hezronite clan;
through Hamul, the Hamulite clan.

[22]These were the clans of Judah; those numbered were 76,500.

[23]The descendants of Issachar by their clans were:

through Tola, the Tolaite clan;
through Puah, the Puite[h] clan;
[24]through Jashub, the Jashubite clan;
through Shimron, the Shimronite clan.

[25]These were the clans of Issachar; those numbered were 64,300.

[26]The descendants of Zebulun by their clans were:

through Sered, the Seredite clan;
through Elon, the Elonite clan;
through Jahleel, the Jahleelite clan.

[27]These were the clans of Zebulun; those numbered were 60,500.

[28]The descendants of Joseph by their clans through Manasseh and Ephraim were:

[29]The descendants of Manasseh:

through Makir, the Makirite clan (Makir was the father of Gilead);
through Gilead, the Gileadite clan.

[30]These were the descendants of Gilead:

through Iezer, the Iezerite clan;
through Helek, the Helekite clan;
[31]through Asriel, the Asrielite clan;
through Shechem, the Shechemite clan;
[32]through Shemida, the Shemidaite clan;
through Hepher, the Hepherite clan.
[33](Zelophehad son of Hepher had no sons; he had only daughters, whose names were Mahlah, Noah, Hoglah, Milcah and Tirzah.)

[34]These were the clans of Manasseh; those numbered were 52,700.

[35]These were the descendants of Ephraim by their clans:

through Shuthelah, the Shuthelahite clan;
through Beker, the Bekerite clan;
through Tahan, the Tahanite clan.

[36]These were the descendants of Shuthelah:

through Eran, the Eranite clan.

[37]These were the clans of Ephraim; those numbered were 32,500.

These were the descendants of Joseph by their clans.

[38]The descendants of Benjamin by their clans were:

[g]17 Samaritan Pentateuch and Syriac (see also Gen. 46:16); Masoretic Text *Arod* [h]23 Samaritan Pentateuch, Septuagint, Vulgate and Syriac (see also 1 Chron. 7:1); Masoretic Text *through Puvah, the Punite*

through Bela, the Belaite clan;
through Ashbel, the Ashbelite clan;
through Ahiram, the Ahiramite clan;
39through Shupham,[i] the Shuphamite clan;
through Hupham, the Huphamite clan.
40The descendants of Bela through Ard and Naaman were:
through Ard,[j] the Ardite clan;
through Naaman, the Naamite clan.
41These were the clans of Benjamin; those numbered were 45,600.

42These were the descendants of Dan by their clans:
through Shuham, the Shuhamite clan.
These were the clans of Dan: 43All of them were
Shuhamite clans; and those numbered were 64,400.

44The descendants of Asher by their clans were:
through Imnah, the Imnite clan;
through Ishvi, the Ishvite clan;
through Beriah, the Beriite clan;
45and through the descendants of Beriah:
through Heber, the Heberite clan;
through Malkiel, the Malkielite clan.
46(Asher had a daughter named Serah.)
47These were the clans of Asher; those numbered were 53,400.

48The descendants of Naphtali by their clans were:
through Jahzeel, the Jahzeelite clan;
through Guni, the Gunite clan;
49through Jezer, the Jezerite clan;
through Shillem, the Shillemite clan.
50These were the clans of Naphtali; those numbered were 45,400.

51The total number of the men of Israel was 601,730.

52The LORD said to Moses, 53"The land is to be
allotted to them as an inheritance based on the
number of names. 54To a larger group give a
larger inheritance, and to a smaller group a
smaller one; each is to receive its inheritance according to the number of those listed. 55Be sure
that the land is distributed by lot. What each
group inherits will be according to the names for
its ancestral tribe. 56Each inheritance is to be distributed by lot among the larger and smaller
groups."

57These were the Levites who were counted by their clans:
through Gershon, the Gershonite clan;
through Kohath, the Kohathite clan;
through Merari, the Merarite clan.
58These also were Levite clans:
the Libnite clan,
the Hebronite clan,
the Mahlite clan,
the Mushite clan,
the Korahite clan.
(Kohath was the forefather of Amram; 59the
name of Amram's wife was Jochebed, a
descendant of Levi, who was born to the Levites[k] in Egypt. To Amram she bore Aaron,
Moses and their sister Miriam. 60Aaron was
the father of Nadab and Abihu, Eleazar and
Ithamar. 61But Nadab and Abihu died when
they made an offering before the LORD with unauthorized fire.)

62All the male Levites a month old or more numbered 23,000. They were not counted along with the other Israelites because they received no inheritance among them.

63These are the ones counted by Moses and Eleazar the priest when they counted the Israelites
on the plains of Moab by the Jordan across from
Jericho. 64Not one of them was among those
counted by Moses and Aaron the priest when
they counted the Israelites in the Desert of Sinai.
65For the LORD had told those Israelites they
would surely die in the desert, and not one of
them was left except Caleb son of Jephunneh and Joshua son of Nun.

27 The daughters of Zelophehad son of Hepher, the son of Gilead, the son of Makir, the son of Manasseh,
belonged to the clans of Manasseh son of Joseph.
The names of the daughters were Mahlah, Noah,
Hoglah, Milcah and Tirzah. They approached 2the
entrance to the Tent of Meeting and stood before
Moses, Eleazar the priest, the leaders and the
whole assembly, and said, 3"Our father died in
the desert. He was not among Korah's followers,
who banded together against the LORD, but he
died for his own sin and left no sons. 4Why

[i] 39 A few manuscripts of the Masoretic Text, Samaritan Pentateuch, Vulgate and Syriac (see also Septuagint); most manuscripts of the Masoretic Text *Shephupham* [j] 40 Samaritan Pentateuch and Vulgate (see also Septuagint); Masoretic Text does not have *through Ard.*
[k] 59 Or *Jochebed, a daughter of Levi, who was born to Levi*

should our father's name disappear from his clan
because he had no son? Give us property among
our father's relatives."

[5]So Moses brought their case before the LORD
[6]and the LORD said to him, [7]"What Zelophehad's
daughters are saying is right. You must certainly
give them property as an inheritance among their
father's relatives and turn their father's inheri-
tance over to them.

[8]"Say to the Israelites, 'If a man dies and leaves
no son, turn his inheritance over to his daughter.
[9]If he has no daughter, give his inheritance to his
brothers. [10]If he has no brothers, give his inheri-
tance to his father's brothers. [11]If his father had
no brothers, give his inheritance to the nearest
relative in his clan, that he may possess it. This is
to be a legal requirement for the Israelites, as the
LORD commanded Moses.' "

9 / *Numbers 27:12–23*
Passing the Torch

WHO CARRIES ON for the great leaders? The best of them become living legends and seem irreplaceable. Moses led the Israelites for forty years. A generation had grown up who had known no other leader. But the time came, even for Moses, to pass the torch. Numbers 27:12–23 details how God's people can make such a transition.

Warming Up to God Think of a time you have lost a beloved pastor, Sunday-school teacher or important spiritual influence. How did you accept the new leader?

Read Numbers 27:12–23.

[12]Then the LORD said to Moses, "Go up this
mountain in the Abarim range and see the land I
have given the Israelites. [13]After you have seen it,
you too will be gathered to your people, as your
brother Aaron was, [14]for when the community
rebelled at the waters in the Desert of Zin, both of
you disobeyed my command to honor me as holy
before their eyes." (These were the waters of Mer-
ibah Kadesh, in the Desert of Zin.)

[15]Moses said to the LORD, [16]"May the LORD, the
God of the spirits of all mankind, appoint a man
over this community [17]to go out and come in be-
fore them, one who will lead them out and bring
them in, so the LORD's people will not be like
sheep without a shepherd."

[18]So the LORD said to Moses, "Take Joshua son
of Nun, a man in whom is the spirit,[l] and lay
your hand on him. [19]Have him stand before Elea-
zar the priest and the entire assembly and com-
mission him in their presence. [20]Give him some
of your authority so the whole Israelite commu-
nity will obey him. [21]He is to stand before Eleazar
the priest, who will obtain decisions for him by
inquiring of the Urim before the LORD. At his
command he and the entire community of the
Israelites will go out, and at his command they
will come in."

[22]Moses did as the LORD commanded him. He
took Joshua and had him stand before Eleazar the
priest and the whole assembly. [23]Then he laid his
hands on him and commissioned him, as the LORD
instructed through Moses.

[l]18 Or *Spirit*

Discovering the Word 1. Moses has been forbidden from entering the Promised Land. How do you account for God's command for Moses to look at the land from the mountains (vv. 12–14)? 2. What does Moses' statement (vv. 15–17) reveal about his state of mind? 3. From this passage (v. 18) and Numbers 14 (vv. 6–9, 30, 36–38) what do you know about Joshua's credentials for leadership? 4. What formalities are commanded for the installation of Joshua (vv. 19–21)? 5. Why is it important for Joshua to be commissioned in this way?

Applying the Word 1. What credentials should you seek in a spiritual leader? 2. How can you build and affirm trust in your church's or Christian group's leaders?

Responding in Prayer Thank God for the wise leaders he has provided in the past, as well as the ones he has placed before you now. Affirm to him that you will respect and support those leaders.

Numbers 28—31

28 The LORD said to Moses, 2“Give this command to the Israelites and say to them: ‘See that you present to me at the appointed time the food for my offerings made by fire, as an aroma pleasing to me.’ 3Say to them: ‘This is the offering made by fire that you are to present to the LORD: two lambs a year old without defect, as a regular burnt offering each day. 4Prepare one lamb in the morning and the other at twilight, 5together with a grain offering of a tenth of an ephah[m] of fine flour mixed with a quarter of a hin[n] of oil from pressed olives. 6This is the regular burnt offering instituted at Mount Sinai as a pleasing aroma, an offering made to the LORD by fire. 7The accompanying drink offering is to be a quarter of a hin of fermented drink with each lamb. Pour out the drink offering to the LORD at the sanctuary. 8Prepare the second lamb at twilight, along with the same kind of grain offering and drink offering that you prepare in the morning. This is an offering made by fire, an aroma pleasing to the LORD.

9“ ‘On the Sabbath day, make an offering of two lambs a year old without defect, together with its drink offering and a grain offering of two-tenths of an ephah[o] of fine flour mixed with oil. 10This is the burnt offering for every Sabbath, in addition to the regular burnt offering and its drink offering.

11“ ‘On the first of every month, present to the LORD a burnt offering of two young bulls, one ram and seven male lambs a year old, all without defect. 12With each bull there is to be a grain offering of three-tenths of an ephah[p] of fine flour mixed with oil; with the ram, a grain offering of two-tenths of an ephah of fine flour mixed with oil; 13and with each lamb, a grain offering of a tenth of an ephah of fine flour mixed with oil. This is for a burnt offering, a pleasing aroma, an offering made to the LORD by fire. 14With each bull there is to be a drink offering of half a hin[q] of wine; with the ram, a third of a hin[r]; and with each lamb, a quarter of a hin. This is the monthly burnt offering to be made at each new moon during the year. 15Besides the regular burnt offering with its drink offering, one male goat is to be presented to the LORD as a sin offering.

16“ ‘On the fourteenth day of the first month the LORD’s Passover is to be held. 17On the fifteenth day of this month there is to be a festival; for seven days eat bread made without yeast. 18On the first day hold a sacred assembly and do no regular work. 19Present to the LORD an offering made by fire, a burnt offering of two young bulls, one ram and seven male lambs a year old, all without defect. 20With each bull prepare a grain offering of three-tenths of an ephah of fine flour mixed with oil; with the ram, two-tenths; 21and with each of the seven lambs, one-tenth. 22Include one male goat as a sin offering to make atonement for you. 23Prepare these in addition to the regular morning burnt offering. 24In this way prepare the food for the offering made by fire every day for seven days as an aroma pleasing to the LORD; it is to be prepared in addition to the regular burnt offering and its drink offering. 25On the seventh day hold a sacred assembly and do no regular work.

26“ ‘On the day of firstfruits, when you present to the LORD an offering of new grain during the Feast of Weeks, hold a sacred assembly and do no regular work. 27Present a burnt offering of two young bulls, one ram and seven male lambs a year old as an aroma pleasing to the LORD. 28With each bull there is to be a grain offering of three-tenths of an ephah of fine flour mixed with oil; with the ram, two-tenths; 29and with each of the seven lambs, one-tenth. 30Include one male goat to make atonement for you. 31Prepare these together with their drink offerings, in addition to the regular burnt offering and its grain offering. Be sure the animals are without defect.

29 “ ‘On the first day of the seventh month hold a sacred assembly and do no regular work. It is a day for

[m]5 That is, probably about 2 quarts (about 2 liters); also in verses 13, 21 and 29 [n]5 That is, probably about 1 quart (about 1 liter); also in verses 7 and 14 [o]9 That is, probably about 4 quarts (about 4.5 liters); also in verses 12, 20 and 28 [p]12 That is, probably about 6 quarts (about 6.5 liters); also in verses 20 and 28 [q]14 That is, probably about 2 quarts (about 2 liters) [r]14 That is, probably about 1 1/4 quarts (about 1.2 liters)

you to sound the trumpets. 2As an aroma pleasing to the LORD, prepare a burnt offering of one young bull, one ram and seven male lambs a year old, all without defect. 3With the bull prepare a grain offering of three-tenths of an ephah[s] of fine flour mixed with oil; with the ram, two-tenths[t]; 4and with each of the seven lambs, one-tenth.[u] 5Include one male goat as a sin offering to make atonement for you. 6These are in addition to the monthly and daily burnt offerings with their grain offerings and drink offerings as specified. They are offerings made to the LORD by fire—a pleasing aroma.

7" 'On the tenth day of this seventh month hold a sacred assembly. You must deny yourselves[v] and do no work. 8Present as an aroma pleasing to the LORD a burnt offering of one young bull, one ram and seven male lambs a year old, all without defect. 9With the bull prepare a grain offering of three-tenths of an ephah of fine flour mixed with oil; with the ram, two-tenths; 10and with each of the seven lambs, one-tenth. 11Include one male goat as a sin offering, in addition to the sin offering for atonement and the regular burnt offering with its grain offering, and their drink offerings.

12" 'On the fifteenth day of the seventh month, hold a sacred assembly and do no regular work. Celebrate a festival to the LORD for seven days. 13Present an offering made by fire as an aroma pleasing to the LORD, a burnt offering of thirteen young bulls, two rams and fourteen male lambs a year old, all without defect. 14With each of the thirteen bulls prepare a grain offering of three-tenths of an ephah of fine flour mixed with oil; with each of the two rams, two-tenths; 15and with each of the fourteen lambs, one-tenth. 16Include one male goat as a sin offering, in addition to the regular burnt offering with its grain offering and drink offering.

17" 'On the second day prepare twelve young bulls, two rams and fourteen male lambs a year old, all without defect. 18With the bulls, rams and lambs, prepare their grain offerings and drink offerings according to the number specified. 19Include one male goat as a sin offering, in addition to the regular burnt offering with its grain offering, and their drink offerings.

20" 'On the third day prepare eleven bulls, two rams and fourteen male lambs a year old, all without defect. 21With the bulls, rams and lambs, prepare their grain offerings and drink offerings according to the number specified. 22Include one male goat as a sin offering, in addition to the regular burnt offering with its grain offering and drink offering.

23" 'On the fourth day prepare ten bulls, two rams and fourteen male lambs a year old, all without defect. 24With the bulls, rams and lambs, prepare their grain offerings and drink offerings according to the number specified. 25Include one male goat as a sin offering, in addition to the regular burnt offering with its grain offering and drink offering.

26" 'On the fifth day prepare nine bulls, two rams and fourteen male lambs a year old, all without defect. 27With the bulls, rams and lambs, prepare their grain offerings and drink offerings according to the number specified. 28Include one male goat as a sin offering, in addition to the regular burnt offering with its grain offering and drink offering.

29" 'On the sixth day prepare eight bulls, two rams and fourteen male lambs a year old, all without defect. 30With the bulls, rams and lambs, prepare their grain offerings and drink offerings according to the number specified. 31Include one male goat as a sin offering, in addition to the regular burnt offering with its grain offering and drink offering.

32" 'On the seventh day prepare seven bulls, two rams and fourteen male lambs a year old, all without defect. 33With the bulls, rams and lambs, prepare their grain offerings and drink offerings according to the number specified. 34Include one male goat as a sin offering, in addition to the regular burnt offering with its grain offering and drink offering.

35" 'On the eighth day hold an assembly and do no regular work. 36Present an offering made by fire as an aroma pleasing to the LORD, a burnt offering of one bull, one ram and seven male lambs a year old, all without defect. 37With the bull, the ram and the lambs, prepare their grain offerings and drink offerings according to the number specified. 38Include one male goat as a sin offering, in addition to the regular burnt offering with its grain offering and drink offering.

39" 'In addition to what you vow and your freewill offerings, prepare these for the LORD at your appointed feasts: your burnt offerings, grain offerings, drink offerings and fellowship offerings.[w]' "

[s]3 That is, probably about 6 quarts (about 6.5 liters); also in verses 9 and 14 [t]3 That is, probably about 4 quarts (about 4.5 liters); also in verses 9 and 14 [u]4 That is, probably about 2 quarts (about 2 liters); also in verses 10 and 15 [v]7 Or *must fast* [w]39 Traditionally *peace offerings*

[40]Moses told the Israelites all that the LORD commanded him.

30 Moses said to the heads of the tribes of Israel: "This is what the LORD commands: [2]When a man makes a vow to the LORD or takes an oath to obligate himself by a pledge, he must not break his word but must do everything he said.

[3]"When a young woman still living in her father's house makes a vow to the LORD or obligates herself by a pledge [4]and her father hears about her vow or pledge but says nothing to her, then all her vows and every pledge by which she obligated herself will stand. [5]But if her father forbids her when he hears about it, none of her vows or the pledges by which she obligated herself will stand; the LORD will release her because her father has forbidden her.

[6]"If she marries after she makes a vow or after her lips utter a rash promise by which she obligates herself [7]and her husband hears about it but says nothing to her, then her vows or the pledges by which she obligated herself will stand. [8]But if her husband forbids her when he hears about it, he nullifies the vow that obligates her or the rash promise by which she obligates herself, and the LORD will release her.

[9]"Any vow or obligation taken by a widow or divorced woman will be binding on her.

[10]"If a woman living with her husband makes a vow or obligates herself by a pledge under oath [11]and her husband hears about it but says nothing to her and does not forbid her, then all her vows or the pledges by which she obligated herself will stand. [12]But if her husband nullifies them when he hears about them, then none of the vows or pledges that came from her lips will stand. Her husband has nullified them, and the LORD will release her. [13]Her husband may confirm or nullify any vow she makes or any sworn pledge to deny herself. [14]But if her husband says nothing to her about it from day to day, then he confirms all her vows or the pledges binding on her. He confirms them by saying nothing to her when he hears about them. [15]If, however, he nullifies them some time after he hears about them, then he is responsible for her guilt."

[16]These are the regulations the LORD gave Moses concerning relationships between a man and his wife, and between a father and his young daughter still living in his house.

31 The LORD said to Moses, [2]"Take vengeance on the Midianites for the Israelites. After that, you will be gathered to your people."

[3]So Moses said to the people, "Arm some of your men to go to war against the Midianites and to carry out the LORD's vengeance on them. [4]Send into battle a thousand men from each of the tribes of Israel." [5]So twelve thousand men armed for battle, a thousand from each tribe, were supplied from the clans of Israel. [6]Moses sent them into battle, a thousand from each tribe, along with Phinehas son of Eleazar, the priest, who took with him articles from the sanctuary and the trumpets for signaling.

[7]They fought against Midian, as the LORD commanded Moses, and killed every man. [8]Among their victims were Evi, Rekem, Zur, Hur and Reba—the five kings of Midian. They also killed Balaam son of Beor with the sword. [9]The Israelites captured the Midianite women and children and took all the Midianite herds, flocks and goods as plunder. [10]They burned all the towns where the Midianites had settled, as well as all their camps. [11]They took all the plunder and spoils, including the people and animals, [12]and brought the captives, spoils and plunder to Moses and Eleazar the priest and the Israelite assembly at their camp on the plains of Moab, by the Jordan across from Jericho.[x]

[13]Moses, Eleazar the priest and all the leaders of the community went to meet them outside the camp. [14]Moses was angry with the officers of the army—the commanders of thousands and commanders of hundreds—who returned from the battle.

[15]"Have you allowed all the women to live?" he asked them. [16]"They were the ones who followed Balaam's advice and were the means of turning the Israelites away from the LORD in what happened at Peor, so that a plague struck the LORD's people. [17]Now kill all the boys. And kill every woman who has slept with a man, [18]but save for yourselves every girl who has never slept with a man.

[19]"All of you who have killed anyone or touched anyone who was killed must stay outside the camp seven days. On the third and seventh days you must purify yourselves and your cap-

[x]12 Hebrew *Jordan of Jericho*; possibly an ancient name for the Jordan River

tives. 20Purify every garment as well as everything made of leather, goat hair or wood."

21Then Eleazar the priest said to the soldiers who had gone into battle, "This is the requirement of the law that the LORD gave Moses: 22Gold, silver, bronze, iron, tin, lead 23and anything else that can withstand fire must be put through the fire, and then it will be clean. But it must also be purified with the water of cleansing. And whatever cannot withstand fire must be put through that water. 24On the seventh day wash your clothes and you will be clean. Then you may come into the camp."

25The LORD said to Moses, 26"You and Eleazar the priest and the family heads of the community are to count all the people and animals that were captured. 27Divide the spoils between the soldiers who took part in the battle and the rest of the community. 28From the soldiers who fought in the battle, set apart as tribute for the LORD one out of every five hundred, whether persons, cattle, donkeys, sheep or goats. 29Take this tribute from their half share and give it to Eleazar the priest as the LORD's part. 30From the Israelites' half, select one out of every fifty, whether persons, cattle, donkeys, sheep, goats or other animals. Give them to the Levites, who are responsible for the care of the LORD's tabernacle." 31So Moses and Eleazar the priest did as the LORD commanded Moses.

32The plunder remaining from the spoils that the soldiers took was 675,000 sheep, 3372,000 cattle, 3461,000 donkeys 35and 32,000 women who had never slept with a man.

36The half share of those who fought in the battle was:

> 337,500 sheep, 37of which the tribute for the LORD was 675;
>
> 3836,000 cattle, of which the tribute for the LORD was 72;
>
> 3930,500 donkeys, of which the tribute for the LORD was 61;
>
> 4016,000 people, of which the tribute for the LORD was 32.

41Moses gave the tribute to Eleazar the priest as the LORD's part, as the LORD commanded Moses.

42The half belonging to the Israelites, which Moses set apart from that of the fighting men— 43the community's half—was 337,500 sheep, 4436,000 cattle, 4530,500 donkeys 46and 16,000 people. 47From the Israelites' half, Moses selected one out of every fifty persons and animals, as the LORD commanded him, and gave them to the Levites, who were responsible for the care of the LORD's tabernacle.

48Then the officers who were over the units of the army—the commanders of thousands and commanders of hundreds—went to Moses 49and said to him, "Your servants have counted the soldiers under our command, and not one is missing. 50So we have brought as an offering to the LORD the gold articles each of us acquired—armlets, bracelets, signet rings, earrings and necklaces—to make atonement for ourselves before the LORD."

51Moses and Eleazar the priest accepted from them the gold—all the crafted articles. 52All the gold from the commanders of thousands and commanders of hundreds that Moses and Eleazar presented as a gift to the LORD weighed 16,750 shekels.[y] 53Each soldier had taken plunder for himself. 54Moses and Eleazar the priest accepted the gold from the commanders of thousands and commanders of hundreds and brought it into the Tent of Meeting as a memorial for the Israelites before the LORD.

[y] 52 That is, about 420 pounds (about 190 kilograms)

10 / *Numbers 32*
United We Stand

NEARLY FORTY YEARS together in the wilderness—and now the great moment has arrived. It's time for the Israelites to cross the Jordan, face the opposition, and claim their land. But two tribes announce their intention not to make the trip. Are they exercising their prerogative? Or are the destinies of the twelve tribes intertwined? To what extent must we consider the effect on others when making a decision?

Warming Up to God Finish this sentence: Others depend on me for . . . What would happen if you were to abandon a large responsibility at home, work or school? Who would suffer? Ask God to make you aware of your important leadership roles.

Read Numbers 32.

32 The Reubenites and Gadites, who had very large herds and flocks, saw that the lands of Jazer and Gilead were suitable for livestock. [2]So they came to Moses and Eleazar the priest and to the leaders of the community, and said, [3]"Ataroth, Dibon, Jazer, Nimrah, Heshbon, Elealeh, Sebam, Nebo and Beon— [4]the land the LORD subdued before the people of Israel—are suitable for livestock, and your servants have livestock. [5]If we have found favor in your eyes," they said, "let this land be given to your servants as our possession. Do not make us cross the Jordan."

[6]Moses said to the Gadites and Reubenites, "Shall your countrymen go to war while you sit here? [7]Why do you discourage the Israelites from going over into the land the LORD has given them? [8]This is what your fathers did when I sent them from Kadesh Barnea to look over the land. [9]After they went up to the Valley of Eshcol and viewed the land, they discouraged the Israelites from entering the land the LORD had given them. [10]The LORD's anger was aroused that day and he swore this oath: [11]'Because they have not followed me wholeheartedly, not one of the men twenty years old or more who came up out of Egypt will see the land I promised on oath to Abraham, Isaac and Jacob— [12]not one except Caleb son of Jephunneh the Kenizzite and Joshua son of Nun, for they followed the LORD wholeheartedly.' [13]The LORD's anger burned against Israel and he made them wander in the desert forty years, until the whole generation of those who had done evil in his sight was gone.

[14]"And here you are, a brood of sinners, standing in the place of your fathers and making the LORD even more angry with Israel. [15]If you turn away from following him, he will again leave all this people in the desert, and you will be the cause of their destruction."

[16]Then they came up to him and said, "We would like to build pens here for our livestock and cities for our women and children. [17]But we are ready to arm ourselves and go ahead of the Israelites until we have brought them to their place. Meanwhile our women and children will live in fortified cities, for protection from the inhabitants of the land. [18]We will not return to our homes until every Israelite has received his inheritance. [19]We will not receive any inheritance with them on the other side of the Jordan, because our inheritance has come to us on the east side of the Jordan."

[20]Then Moses said to them, "If you will do this—if you will arm yourselves before the LORD for battle, [21]and if all of you will go armed over the Jordan before the LORD until he has driven his enemies out before him— [22]then when the land is subdued before the LORD, you may return and be free from your obligation to the LORD and to Israel. And this land will be your possession before the LORD.

[23]"But if you fail to do this, you will be sinning against the LORD; and you may be sure that your sin will find you out. [24]Build cities for your women and children, and pens for your flocks, but do what you have promised."

[25]The Gadites and Reubenites said to Moses, "We your servants will do as our lord commands. [26]Our children and wives, our flocks and herds will remain here in the cities of Gilead. [27]But your servants, every man armed for battle, will cross over to fight before the LORD, just as our lord says."

[28]Then Moses gave orders about them to Eleazar the priest and Joshua son of Nun and to the family heads of the Israelite tribes. [29]He said to them, "If the Gadites and Reubenites, every man armed for battle, cross over the Jordan with you before the LORD, then when the land is subdued before you, give them the land of Gilead as their possession. [30]But if they do not cross over with you armed, they must accept their possession with you in Canaan."

[31]The Gadites and Reubenites answered, "Your servants will do what the LORD has said. [32]We will cross over before the LORD into Canaan armed, but the property we inherit will be on this side of the Jordan."

[33]Then Moses gave to the Gadites, the Reubenites and the half-tribe of Manasseh son of Joseph the kingdom of Sihon king of the Amorites and

the kingdom of Og king of Bashan—the whole
land with its cities and the territory around them.
34The Gadites built up Dibon, Ataroth, Aroer,
35Atroth Shophan, Jazer, Jogbehah, 36Beth Nim-
rah and Beth Haran as fortified cities, and built
pens for their flocks. 37And the Reubenites rebuilt
Heshbon, Elealeh and Kiriathaim, 38as well as
Nebo and Baal Meon (these names were changed)
and Sibmah. They gave names to the cities they
rebuilt.
39The descendants of Makir son of Manasseh
went to Gilead, captured it and drove out the Am-
orites who were there. 40So Moses gave Gilead to
the Makirites, the descendants of Manasseh, and
they settled there. 41Jair, a descendant of Manas-
seh, captured their settlements and called them
Havvoth Jair.[z] 42And Nobah captured Kenath
and its surrounding settlements and called it No-
bah after himself.

[z]41 Or *them the settlements of Jair*

Discovering the Word 1. How would you evaluate the two tribes' justification for not crossing the river into Canaan (vv. 1–5)? 2. What important principles does Moses remind them of (vv. 6–15)? 3. What practical considerations might have concerned Moses about the division in destinations? 4. How would you evaluate the compromise offered by the two tribes (vv. 16–19)? 5. Why was this arrangement satisfactory to Moses (vv. 20–24)?

Applying the Word 1. What real or potential divisions can you detect in your church or Christian group? 2. Like Moses, how can you guard unity among believers?

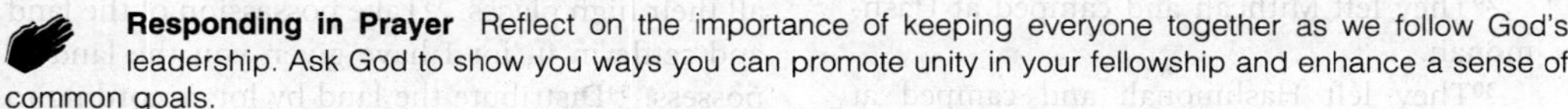

Responding in Prayer Reflect on the importance of keeping everyone together as we follow God's leadership. Ask God to show you ways you can promote unity in your fellowship and enhance a sense of common goals.

Numbers 33—36

33 Here are the stages in the journey
of the Israelites when they came
out of Egypt by divisions under the
leadership of Moses and Aaron. 2At the LORD's
command Moses recorded the stages in their
journey. This is their journey by stages:

3The Israelites set out from Rameses on
the fifteenth day of the first month, the day
after the Passover. They marched out boldly
in full view of all the Egyptians, 4who were
burying all their firstborn, whom the LORD
had struck down among them; for the LORD
had brought judgment on their gods.
5The Israelites left Rameses and camped at
Succoth.
6They left Succoth and camped at Etham,
on the edge of the desert.
7They left Etham, turned back to Pi Hahi-
roth, to the east of Baal Zephon, and camped
near Migdol.
8They left Pi Hahiroth[a] and passed
through the sea into the desert, and when
they had traveled for three days in the Desert
of Etham, they camped at Marah.
9They left Marah and went to Elim, where
there were twelve springs and seventy palm
trees, and they camped there.
10They left Elim and camped by the Red
Sea.[b]
11They left the Red Sea and camped in the
Desert of Sin.
12They left the Desert of Sin and camped
at Dophkah.
13They left Dophkah and camped at Alush.
14They left Alush and camped at Rephi-
dim, where there was no water for the people
to drink.
15They left Rephidim and camped in the
Desert of Sinai.
16They left the Desert of Sinai and camped
at Kibroth Hattaavah.
17They left Kibroth Hattaavah and camped
at Hazeroth.

[a]8 Many manuscripts of the Masoretic Text, Samaritan Pentateuch and Vulgate; most manuscripts of the Masoretic Text *left from before Hahiroth*
[b]10 Hebrew *Yam Suph*; that is, Sea of Reeds; also in verse 11

18 They left Hazeroth and camped at Rithmah.

19 They left Rithmah and camped at Rimmon Perez.

20 They left Rimmon Perez and camped at Libnah.

21 They left Libnah and camped at Rissah.

22 They left Rissah and camped at Kehelathah.

23 They left Kehelathah and camped at Mount Shepher.

24 They left Mount Shepher and camped at Haradah.

25 They left Haradah and camped at Makheloth.

26 They left Makheloth and camped at Tahath.

27 They left Tahath and camped at Terah.

28 They left Terah and camped at Mithcah.

29 They left Mithcah and camped at Hashmonah.

30 They left Hashmonah and camped at Moseroth.

31 They left Moseroth and camped at Bene Jaakan.

32 They left Bene Jaakan and camped at Hor Haggidgad.

33 They left Hor Haggidgad and camped at Jotbathah.

34 They left Jotbathah and camped at Abronah.

35 They left Abronah and camped at Ezion Geber.

36 They left Ezion Geber and camped at Kadesh, in the Desert of Zin.

37 They left Kadesh and camped at Mount Hor, on the border of Edom. 38 At the LORD's command Aaron the priest went up Mount Hor, where he died on the first day of the fifth month of the fortieth year after the Israelites came out of Egypt. 39 Aaron was a hundred and twenty-three years old when he died on Mount Hor.

40 The Canaanite king of Arad, who lived in the Negev of Canaan, heard that the Israelites were coming.

41 They left Mount Hor and camped at Zalmonah.

42 They left Zalmonah and camped at Punon.

43 They left Punon and camped at Oboth.

44 They left Oboth and camped at Iye Abarim, on the border of Moab.

45 They left Iyim[c] and camped at Dibon Gad.

46 They left Dibon Gad and camped at Almon Diblathaim.

47 They left Almon Diblathaim and camped in the mountains of Abarim, near Nebo.

48 They left the mountains of Abarim and camped on the plains of Moab by the Jordan across from Jericho.[d] 49 There on the plains of Moab they camped along the Jordan from Beth Jeshimoth to Abel Shittim.

50 On the plains of Moab by the Jordan across from Jericho the LORD said to Moses, 51 "Speak to the Israelites and say to them: 'When you cross the Jordan into Canaan, 52 drive out all the inhabitants of the land before you. Destroy all their carved images and their cast idols, and demolish all their high places. 53 Take possession of the land and settle in it, for I have given you the land to possess. 54 Distribute the land by lot, according to your clans. To a larger group give a larger inheritance, and to a smaller group a smaller one. Whatever falls to them by lot will be theirs. Distribute it according to your ancestral tribes.

55 " 'But if you do not drive out the inhabitants of the land, those you allow to remain will become barbs in your eyes and thorns in your sides. They will give you trouble in the land where you will live. 56 And then I will do to you what I plan to do to them.' "

34 The LORD said to Moses, 2 "Command the Israelites and say to them: 'When you enter Canaan, the land that will be allotted to you as an inheritance will have these boundaries:

3 " 'Your southern side will include some of the Desert of Zin along the border of Edom. On the east, your southern boundary will start from the end of the Salt Sea,[e] 4 cross south of Scorpion[f] Pass, continue on to Zin and go south of Kadesh Barnea. Then it will go to Hazar Addar and over to Azmon, 5 where it will turn, join the Wadi of Egypt and end at the Sea.[g]

6 " 'Your western boundary will be the coast of the Great Sea. This will be your boundary on the west.

[c]45 That is, Iye Abarim [d]48 Hebrew *Jordan of Jericho*; possibly an ancient name for the Jordan River; also in verse 50 [e]3 That is, the Dead Sea; also in verse 12 [f]4 Hebrew *Akrabbim* [g]5 That is, the Mediterranean; also in verses 6 and 7

7" 'For your northern boundary, run a line from the Great Sea to Mount Hor 8and from Mount Hor to Lebo[h] Hamath. Then the boundary will go to Zedad, 9continue to Ziphron and end at Hazar Enan. This will be your boundary on the north.

10" 'For your eastern boundary, run a line from Hazar Enan to Shepham. 11The boundary will go down from Shepham to Riblah on the east side of Ain and continue along the slopes east of the Sea of Kinnereth.[i] 12Then the boundary will go down along the Jordan and end at the Salt Sea.

" 'This will be your land, with its boundaries on every side.' "

13Moses commanded the Israelites: "Assign this land by lot as an inheritance. The LORD has ordered that it be given to the nine and a half tribes, 14because the families of the tribe of Reuben, the tribe of Gad and the half-tribe of Manasseh have received their inheritance. 15These two and a half tribes have received their inheritance on the east side of the Jordan of Jericho,[j] toward the sunrise."

16The LORD said to Moses, 17"These are the names of the men who are to assign the land for you as an inheritance: Eleazar the priest and Joshua son of Nun. 18And appoint one leader from each tribe to help assign the land. 19These are their names:

Caleb son of Jephunneh,
  from the tribe of Judah;
20Shemuel son of Ammihud,
  from the tribe of Simeon;
21Elidad son of Kislon,
  from the tribe of Benjamin;
22Bukki son of Jogli,
  the leader from the tribe of Dan;
23Hanniel son of Ephod,
  the leader from the tribe of Manasseh son of Joseph;
24Kemuel son of Shiphtan,
  the leader from the tribe of Ephraim son of Joseph;
25Elizaphan son of Parnach,
  the leader from the tribe of Zebulun;
26Paltiel son of Azzan,
  the leader from the tribe of Issachar;
27Ahihud son of Shelomi,
  the leader from the tribe of Asher;
28Pedahel son of Ammihud,
  the leader from the tribe of Naphtali."

29These are the men the LORD commanded to assign the inheritance to the Israelites in the land of Canaan.

35

On the plains of Moab by the Jordan across from Jericho,[k] the LORD said to Moses, 2"Command the Israelites to give the Levites towns to live in from the inheritance the Israelites will possess. And give them pasturelands around the towns. 3Then they will have towns to live in and pasturelands for their cattle, flocks and all their other livestock.

4"The pasturelands around the towns that you give the Levites will extend out fifteen hundred feet[l] from the town wall. 5Outside the town, measure three thousand feet[m] on the east side, three thousand on the south side, three thousand on the west and three thousand on the north, with the town in the center. They will have this area as pastureland for the towns.

6"Six of the towns you give the Levites will be cities of refuge, to which a person who has killed someone may flee. In addition, give them forty-two other towns. 7In all you must give the Levites forty-eight towns, together with their pasturelands. 8The towns you give the Levites from the land the Israelites possess are to be given in proportion to the inheritance of each tribe: Take many towns from a tribe that has many, but few from one that has few."

9Then the LORD said to Moses: 10"Speak to the Israelites and say to them: 'When you cross the Jordan into Canaan, 11select some towns to be your cities of refuge, to which a person who has killed someone accidentally may flee. 12They will be places of refuge from the avenger, so that a person accused of murder may not die before he stands trial before the assembly. 13These six towns you give will be your cities of refuge. 14Give three on this side of the Jordan and three in Canaan as cities of refuge. 15These six towns will be a place of refuge for Israelites, aliens and any other people living among them, so that anyone who has killed another accidentally can flee there.

16" 'If a man strikes someone with an iron object so that he dies, he is a murderer; the murderer shall be put to death. 17Or if anyone has a

[h]8 Or *to the entrance to* [i]11 That is, Galilee [j]15 *Jordan of Jericho* was possibly an ancient name for the Jordan River.
[k]1 Hebrew *Jordan of Jericho*; possibly an ancient name for the Jordan River [l]4 Hebrew *a thousand cubits* (about 450 meters)
[m]5 Hebrew *two thousand cubits* (about 900 meters)

stone in his hand that could kill, and he strikes someone so that he dies, he is a murderer; the murderer shall be put to death. 18Or if anyone has a wooden object in his hand that could kill, and he hits someone so that he dies, he is a murderer; the murderer shall be put to death. 19The avenger of blood shall put the murderer to death; when he meets him, he shall put him to death. 20If anyone with malice aforethought shoves another or throws something at him intentionally so that he dies 21or if in hostility he hits him with his fist so that he dies, that person shall be put to death; he is a murderer. The avenger of blood shall put the murderer to death when he meets him.

22" 'But if without hostility someone suddenly shoves another or throws something at him unintentionally 23or, without seeing him, drops a stone on him that could kill him, and he dies, then since he was not his enemy and he did not intend to harm him, 24the assembly must judge between him and the avenger of blood according to these regulations. 25The assembly must protect the one accused of murder from the avenger of blood and send him back to the city of refuge to which he fled. He must stay there until the death of the high priest, who was anointed with the holy oil.

26" 'But if the accused ever goes outside the limits of the city of refuge to which he has fled 27and the avenger of blood finds him outside the city, the avenger of blood may kill the accused without being guilty of murder. 28The accused must stay in his city of refuge until the death of the high priest; only after the death of the high priest may he return to his own property.

29" 'These are to be legal requirements for you throughout the generations to come, wherever you live.

30" 'Anyone who kills a person is to be put to death as a murderer only on the testimony of witnesses. But no one is to be put to death on the testimony of only one witness.

31" 'Do not accept a ransom for the life of a murderer, who deserves to die. He must surely be put to death.

32" 'Do not accept a ransom for anyone who has fled to a city of refuge and so allow him to go back and live on his own land before the death of the high priest.

33" 'Do not pollute the land where you are. Bloodshed pollutes the land, and atonement cannot be made for the land on which blood has been shed, except by the blood of the one who shed it. 34Do not defile the land where you live and where I dwell, for I, the LORD, dwell among the Israelites.' "

36

The family heads of the clan of Gilead son of Makir, the son of Manasseh, who were from the clans of the descendants of Joseph, came and spoke before Moses and the leaders, the heads of the Israelite families. 2They said, "When the LORD commanded my lord to give the land as an inheritance to the Israelites by lot, he ordered you to give the inheritance of our brother Zelophehad to his daughters. 3Now suppose they marry men from other Israelite tribes; then their inheritance will be taken from our ancestral inheritance and added to that of the tribe they marry into. And so part of the inheritance allotted to us will be taken away. 4When the Year of Jubilee for the Israelites comes, their inheritance will be added to that of the tribe into which they marry, and their property will be taken from the tribal inheritance of our forefathers."

5Then at the LORD's command Moses gave this order to the Israelites: "What the tribe of the descendants of Joseph is saying is right. 6This is what the LORD commands for Zelophehad's daughters: They may marry anyone they please as long as they marry within the tribal clan of their father. 7No inheritance in Israel is to pass from tribe to tribe, for every Israelite shall keep the tribal land inherited from his forefathers. 8Every daughter who inherits land in any Israelite tribe must marry someone in her father's tribal clan, so that every Israelite will possess the inheritance of his fathers. 9No inheritance may pass from tribe to tribe, for each Israelite tribe is to keep the land it inherits."

10So Zelophehad's daughters did as the LORD commanded Moses. 11Zelophehad's daughters—Mahlah, Tirzah, Hoglah, Milcah and Noah—married their cousins on their father's side. 12They married within the clans of the descendants of Manasseh son of Joseph, and their inheritance remained in their father's clan and tribe.

13These are the commands and regulations the LORD gave through Moses to the Israelites on the plains of Moab by the Jordan across from Jericho.[n]

[n] 13 Hebrew *Jordan of Jericho*; possibly an ancient name for the Jordan River

Deuteronomy

Deuteronomy offers great riches of wisdom to strengthen and sustain our faith. It is striking that all three of Jesus' quotes from Scripture as he resisted the temptations of Satan came from Deuteronomy (Lk 4:4, 8, 12). A book so significant in the life of our Lord must have much to say to us as well.

The word *Deuteronomy* means "the second giving of the law." It's an appropriate title, because that is what the book of Deuteronomy is. The Ten Commandments were given at Mount Sinai forty years earlier. Now, in Deuteronomy Moses repeats the Ten Commandments, reminding the nation of Israel about the circumstances under which they were given and explaining again what they mean.

The difference between the first and second giving of the law is striking. The first time Israel had just been delivered from slavery in Egypt. They hardly knew God at all, and Moses was their new leader. Now they have had forty years of experience following God under Moses' direction. The first time the law was given, they were merely a collection of slaves who had just fled from Pharaoh. They were terrified of the people whose land they were about to invade. Now they are a unified nation experienced in combat.

The book of Deuteronomy is divided into four sections. In the first three sections Moses reminds the nation of what they need to know before they march into the land. In 1:1—4:44 Moses rehearses their history. The second section, 4:44—28:68, contains the Ten Commandments and the covenant commitments that God and Israel have made to each other. In the third section Moses address the consequences of unfaithfulness to the law and issues a call to determined and heartfelt commitment to God. The final section, 29—34, records Moses' goodbys and his death.

Moses was laying down his burden of leadership and turning it over to Joshua. For forty years he had lead the nation. How hard it must have been for him to let go! With great care and passion Moses speaks from his heart. You can feel his aching desire to make sure that he had done everything possible to get his people ready for the blessings and challenges of life in the Promised Land.

As we read the words of Moses in Deuteronomy, there is much we can learn about being the people of God today. Throughout the book, Moses issues a call that rings down through the centuries, through the Old Testament to the New: "Love the LORD your God with all your heart and with all your soul and with all your strength" (6:5). That is something we need to hear again and again and again.

Outline

Deuteronomy 1:1—3:20

1 These are the words Moses spoke to all Israel in the desert east of the Jordan—that is, in the Arabah—opposite Suph, between Paran and Tophel, Laban, Hazeroth and Dizahab. 2(It takes eleven days to go from Horeb to Kadesh Barnea by the Mount Seir road.)

3In the fortieth year, on the first day of the eleventh month, Moses proclaimed to the Israelites all that the LORD had commanded him concerning them. 4This was after he had defeated Sihon king of the Amorites, who reigned in Heshbon, and at Edrei had defeated Og king of Bashan, who reigned in Ashtaroth.

5East of the Jordan in the territory of Moab, Moses began to expound this law, saying:

6The LORD our God said to us at Horeb, "You have stayed long enough at this mountain. 7Break camp and advance into the hill country of the Amorites; go to all the neighboring peoples in the Arabah, in the mountains, in the western foothills, in the Negev and along the coast, to the land of the Canaanites and to Lebanon, as far as the great river, the Euphrates. 8See, I have given you this land. Go in and take possession of the land that the LORD swore he would give to your fathers—to Abraham, Isaac and Jacob—and to their descendants after them."

9At that time I said to you, "You are too heavy a burden for me to carry alone. 10The LORD your God has increased your numbers so that today you are as many as the stars in the sky. 11May the LORD, the God of your fathers, increase you a thousand times and bless you as he has promised! 12But how can I bear your problems and your burdens and your disputes all by myself? 13Choose some wise, understanding and respected men from each of your tribes, and I will set them over you."

14You answered me, "What you propose to do is good."

15So I took the leading men of your tribes, wise and respected men, and appointed them to have authority over you—as commanders of thousands, of hundreds, of fifties and of tens and as tribal officials. 16And I charged your judges at that time: Hear the disputes between your brothers and judge fairly, whether the case is between brother Israelites or between one of them and an alien. 17Do not show partiality in judging; hear both small and great alike. Do not be afraid of any man, for judgment belongs to God. Bring me any case too hard for you, and I will hear it. 18And at that time I told you everything you were to do.

19Then, as the LORD our God commanded us, we set out from Horeb and went toward the hill country of the Amorites through all that vast and dreadful desert that you have seen, and so we reached Kadesh Barnea. 20Then I said to you, "You have reached the hill country of the Amorites, which the LORD our God is giving us. 21See, the LORD your God has given you the land. Go up and take possession of it as the LORD, the God of your fathers, told you. Do not be afraid; do not be discouraged."

22Then all of you came to me and said, "Let us send men ahead to spy out the land for us and bring back a report about the route we are to take and the towns we will come to."

23The idea seemed good to me; so I selected twelve of you, one man from each tribe. 24They left and went up into the hill country, and came to the Valley of Eshcol and explored it. 25Taking with them some of the fruit of the land, they brought it down to us and reported, "It is a good land that the LORD our God is giving us."

26But you were unwilling to go up; you rebelled against the command of the LORD your God. 27You grumbled in your tents and said, "The LORD hates us; so he brought us out of Egypt to deliver us into the hands of the Amorites to destroy us. 28Where can we go? Our brothers have made us lose heart. They say, 'The people are stronger and taller than we are; the cities are large, with walls up to the sky. We even saw the Anakites there.' "

29Then I said to you, "Do not be terrified; do not be afraid of them. 30The LORD your God, who is going before you, will fight for you, as he did for you in Egypt, before your very eyes, 31and in the desert. There you saw how the LORD your God carried you, as a father carries his son, all the way you went until you reached this place."

32In spite of this, you did not trust in the LORD your God, 33who went ahead of you on your journey, in fire by night and in a cloud by day, to search out places for you to camp and to show you the way you should go.

34When the LORD heard what you said, he was

angry and solemnly swore: 35“Not a man of this evil generation shall see the good land I swore to give your forefathers, 36except Caleb son of Jephunneh. He will see it, and I will give him and his descendants the land he set his feet on, because he followed the LORD wholeheartedly.”

37Because of you the LORD became angry with me also and said, “You shall not enter it, either. 38But your assistant, Joshua son of Nun, will enter it. Encourage him, because he will lead Israel to inherit it. 39And the little ones that you said would be taken captive, your children who do not yet know good from bad—they will enter the land. I will give it to them and they will take possession of it. 40But as for you, turn around and set out toward the desert along the route to the Red Sea.[a]”

41Then you replied, “We have sinned against the LORD. We will go up and fight, as the LORD our God commanded us.” So every one of you put on his weapons, thinking it easy to go up into the hill country.

42But the LORD said to me, “Tell them, ‘Do not go up and fight, because I will not be with you. You will be defeated by your enemies.’ ”

43So I told you, but you would not listen. You rebelled against the LORD’s command and in your arrogance you marched up into the hill country. 44The Amorites who lived in those hills came out against you; they chased you like a swarm of bees and beat you down from Seir all the way to Hormah. 45You came back and wept before the LORD, but he paid no attention to your weeping and turned a deaf ear to you. 46And so you stayed in Kadesh many days—all the time you spent there.

2

Then we turned back and set out toward the desert along the route to the Red Sea,[a] as the LORD had directed me. For a long time we made our way around the hill country of Seir.

2Then the LORD said to me, 3“You have made your way around this hill country long enough; now turn north. 4Give the people these orders: ‘You are about to pass through the territory of your brothers the descendants of Esau, who live in Seir. They will be afraid of you, but be very careful. 5Do not provoke them to war, for I will not give you any of their land, not even enough to put your foot on. I have given Esau the hill country of Seir as his own. 6You are to pay them in silver for the food you eat and the water you drink.’ ”

7The LORD your God has blessed you in all the work of your hands. He has watched over your journey through this vast desert. These forty years the LORD your God has been with you, and you have not lacked anything.

8So we went on past our brothers the descendants of Esau, who live in Seir. We turned from the Arabah road, which comes up from Elath and Ezion Geber, and traveled along the desert road of Moab.

9Then the LORD said to me, “Do not harass the Moabites or provoke them to war, for I will not give you any part of their land. I have given Ar to the descendants of Lot as a possession.”

10(The Emites used to live there—a people strong and numerous, and as tall as the Anakites. 11Like the Anakites, they too were considered Rephaites, but the Moabites called them Emites. 12Horites used to live in Seir, but the descendants of Esau drove them out. They destroyed the Horites from before them and settled in their place, just as Israel did in the land the LORD gave them as their possession.)

13And the LORD said, “Now get up and cross the Zered Valley.” So we crossed the valley.

14Thirty-eight years passed from the time we left Kadesh Barnea until we crossed the Zered Valley. By then, that entire generation of fighting men had perished from the camp, as the LORD had sworn to them. 15The LORD’s hand was against them until he had completely eliminated them from the camp.

16Now when the last of these fighting men among the people had died, 17the LORD said to me, 18“Today you are to pass by the region of Moab at Ar. 19When you come to the Ammonites, do not harass them or provoke them to war, for I will not give you possession of any land belonging to the Ammonites. I have given it as a possession to the descendants of Lot.”

20(That too was considered a land of the Rephaites, who used to live there; but the Ammonites called them Zamzummites. 21They were a people strong and numerous, and as tall as the Anakites. The LORD destroyed them from before the Ammonites, who drove them out and settled in their place. 22The LORD had done the same for the descendants of Esau, who lived in Seir, when he destroyed the Horites from before them. They drove them out and have lived in their place to

[a]40,1 Hebrew *Yam Suph*; that is, Sea of Reeds

this day. 23And as for the Avvites who lived in
villages as far as Gaza, the Caphtorites coming
out from Caphtor[b] destroyed them and settled in
their place.)

24"Set out now and cross the Arnon Gorge. See,
I have given into your hand Sihon the Amorite,
king of Heshbon, and his country. Begin to take
possession of it and engage him in battle. 25This
very day I will begin to put the terror and fear of
you on all the nations under heaven. They will
hear reports of you and will tremble and be in
anguish because of you."

26From the desert of Kedemoth I sent messen-
gers to Sihon king of Heshbon offering peace and
saying, 27"Let us pass through your country. We
will stay on the main road; we will not turn aside
to the right or to the left. 28Sell us food to eat and
water to drink for their price in silver. Only let us
pass through on foot— 29as the descendants of
Esau, who live in Seir, and the Moabites, who live
in Ar, did for us—until we cross the Jordan into
the land the LORD our God is giving us." 30But
Sihon king of Heshbon refused to let us pass
through. For the LORD your God had made his
spirit stubborn and his heart obstinate in order to
give him into your hands, as he has now done.

31The LORD said to me, "See, I have begun to
deliver Sihon and his country over to you. Now
begin to conquer and possess his land."

32When Sihon and all his army came out to
meet us in battle at Jahaz, 33the LORD our God
delivered him over to us and we struck him
down, together with his sons and his whole army.
34At that time we took all his towns and com-
pletely destroyed[c] them—men, women and chil-
dren. We left no survivors. 35But the livestock and
the plunder from the towns we had captured we
carried off for ourselves. 36From Aroer on the rim
of the Arnon Gorge, and from the town in the
gorge, even as far as Gilead, not one town was too
strong for us. The LORD our God gave us all of
them. 37But in accordance with the command of
the LORD our God, you did not encroach on any of
the land of the Ammonites, neither the land along
the course of the Jabbok nor that around the
towns in the hills.

3 Next we turned and went up along the
road toward Bashan, and Og king of Ba-
shan with his whole army marched out to
meet us in battle at Edrei. 2The LORD said to me,
"Do not be afraid of him, for I have handed him
over to you with his whole army and his land. Do
to him what you did to Sihon king of the Amo-
rites, who reigned in Heshbon."

3So the LORD our God also gave into our hands
Og king of Bashan and all his army. We struck
them down, leaving no survivors. 4At that time
we took all his cities. There was not one of the
sixty cities that we did not take from them—the
whole region of Argob, Og's kingdom in Bashan.
5All these cities were fortified with high walls and
with gates and bars, and there were also a great
many unwalled villages. 6We completely de-
stroyed[c] them, as we had done with Sihon king
of Heshbon, destroying[c] every city—men,
women and children. 7But all the livestock and
the plunder from their cities we carried off for
ourselves.

8So at that time we took from these two kings
of the Amorites the territory east of the Jordan,
from the Arnon Gorge as far as Mount Hermon.
9(Hermon is called Sirion by the Sidonians; the
Amorites call it Senir.) 10We took all the towns on
the plateau, and all Gilead, and all Bashan as far
as Salecah and Edrei, towns of Og's kingdom in
Bashan. 11(Only Og king of Bashan was left of the
remnant of the Rephaites. His bed[d] was made of
iron and was more than thirteen feet long and six
feet wide.[e] It is still in Rabbah of the Ammon-
ites.)

12Of the land that we took over at that time, I
gave the Reubenites and the Gadites the territory
north of Aroer by the Arnon Gorge, including
half the hill country of Gilead, together with its
towns. 13The rest of Gilead and also all of Bashan,
the kingdom of Og, I gave to the half tribe of
Manasseh. (The whole region of Argob in Bashan
used to be known as a land of the Rephaites.
14Jair, a descendant of Manasseh, took the whole
region of Argob as far as the border of the Geshu-
rites and the Maacathites; it was named after him,
so that to this day Bashan is called Havvoth
Jair.[f]) 15And I gave Gilead to Makir. 16But to the
Reubenites and the Gadites I gave the territory
extending from Gilead down to the Arnon Gorge
(the middle of the gorge being the border) and
out to the Jabbok River, which is the border of
the Ammonites. 17Its western border was the Jor-
dan in the Arabah, from Kinnereth to the Sea of

[b]23 That is, Crete [c]34,6 The Hebrew term refers to the irrevocable giving over of things or persons to the LORD, often by totally destroying them. [d]11 Or *sarcophagus* [e]11 Hebrew *nine cubits long and four cubits wide* (about 4 meters long and 1.8 meters wide) [f]14 Or *called the settlements of Jair*

the Arabah (the Salt Sea[g]), below the slopes of
Pisgah.
18I commanded you at that time: "The LORD
your God has given you this land to take posses-
sion of it. But all your able-bodied men, armed
for battle, must cross over ahead of your brother
Israelites. 19However, your wives, your children
and your livestock (I know you have much live-
stock) may stay in the towns I have given you,
20until the LORD gives rest to your brothers as he
has to you, and they too have taken over the land
that the LORD your God is giving them, across the
Jordan. After that, each of you may go back to the
possession I have given you."

g17 That is, the Dead Sea

1 / *Deuteronomy 3:21–29*

Passing the Baton

I KNEW THAT a new training position would be necessary in the next couple of years for our ministry, and I wanted to be the one who got it. However, it went to someone else. I was angry with those in authority who passed me over; I was angry with my friends who didn't support me; I was angry at God who had the power to make things come out differently. I had to work through the grief and pain back to the point of trusting that God knew what he was doing. And I had to come to terms with the fact that I cannot always have things my way. Moses also had to face a bitter disappointment. He didn't get to take the people of Israel into the Promised Land. That job, one that he had been waiting for all his life, was to go to Joshua. Moses was disappointed with God and angry at others.

Warming Up to God This is a time of transition for Moses and the Israelites, moving from the wilderness to the Promised Land and changing from one leader to another. What major transitions in your personal, professional or spiritual life have you faced, and how did they affect you?

Read Deuteronomy 3:21–29.

21At that time I commanded Joshua: "You have
seen with your own eyes all that the LORD your
God has done to these two kings. The LORD will
do the same to all the kingdoms over there where
you are going. 22Do not be afraid of them; the
LORD your God himself will fight for you."
23At that time I pleaded with the LORD: 24"O
Sovereign LORD, you have begun to show to your
servant your greatness and your strong hand. For
what god is there in heaven or on earth who can
do the deeds and mighty works you do? 25Let
me go over and see the good land beyond the
Jordan—that fine hill country and Lebanon."
26But because of you the LORD was angry with
me and would not listen to me. "That is enough,"
the LORD said. "Do not speak to me anymore
about this matter. 27Go up to the top of Pisgah
and look west and north and south and east. Look
at the land with your own eyes, since you are not
going to cross this Jordan. 28But commission
Joshua, and encourage and strengthen him, for he
will lead this people across and will cause them to
inherit the land that you will see." 29So we stayed
in the valley near Beth Peor.

Discovering the Word 1. What issues is Moses facing as he comes to the end of his life and ministry? 2. As Moses recounts his "forced retirement," how would you describe his interaction with God? 3. What is Moses doing to see that things carry on when he is gone (vv. 21–22, 28)? 4. What might Moses have felt as he stood on the top of Pisgah and looked over at the Promised Land (v. 27)?

Applying the Word 1. Moses had to turn over the leadership of Israel. Recall tasks that you have had to turn over to someone else. What was difficult about doing this? 2. Moses encouraged Joshua to take up leadership responsibilities for Israel. What responsibilities do you have, and how do you feel a need for encouragement? 3. Moses bolstered Joshua's confidence by reminding him of battles that had been won through the help of God. As you reflect on your life, what "battles" has God helped you to win?

Responding in Prayer Pray that the leaders in your church will have the wisdom to know when to take charge and when to step back. Ask God to give you a sense of his empowering presence as you face the responsibilities he has called you to.

2 / *Deuteronomy 4:1–14*
Remembering When and Why

WEDDINGS ARE life-changing events for everyone from the bride and groom to their parents and their friends. That may be one of the reasons that so much planning goes into a wedding and the service is so elaborate. The bride in her white dress accompanied by her attendants, the groom and groomsmen in their tuxedos, the walk down the aisle. These rituals show outwardly that this is a turning point in life. In the years to come the wedding service will become a fond memory to be shared with children and mused on in passing moments between husband and wife.

The giving of the Ten Commandments was just such a life-changing event. Not just for two people, but for a couple of million people. In fact, in many ways it was like a marriage ceremony. Israel was making a commitment to God and God was making a commitment to Israel. And so God made sure that there was an elaborate display of his glory. God wanted to create an event that would be recalled with reverence and awe by generations to come.

Warming Up to God Recall a time when God seemed very close and caring. What impressed you about him, and what difference did it make in your life? How can recalling that previous experience be a help and encouragement to you right now?

Read Deuteronomy 4:1–14.

4 Hear now, O Israel, the decrees and laws
I am about to teach you. Follow them so
that you may live and may go in and take
possession of the land that the LORD, the God of
your fathers, is giving you. 2Do not add to what I
command you and do not subtract from it, but
keep the commands of the LORD your God that I
give you.
3You saw with your own eyes what the LORD
did at Baal Peor. The LORD your God destroyed
from among you everyone who followed the Baal
of Peor, 4but all of you who held fast to the LORD
your God are still alive today.
5See, I have taught you decrees and laws as the
LORD my God commanded me, so that you may
follow them in the land you are entering to take
possession of it. 6Observe them carefully, for this
will show your wisdom and understanding to the
nations, who will hear about all these decrees and
say, "Surely this great nation is a wise and under-
standing people." 7What other nation is so great
as to have their gods near them the way the LORD
our God is near us whenever we pray to him?
8And what other nation is so great as to have such
righteous decrees and laws as this body of laws I
am setting before you today?
9Only be careful, and watch yourselves closely
so that you do not forget the things your eyes
have seen or let them slip from your heart as long
as you live. Teach them to your children and to
their children after them. 10Remember the day
you stood before the LORD your God at Horeb,
when he said to me, "Assemble the people before
me to hear my words so that they may learn to
revere me as long as they live in the land and may
teach them to their children." 11You came near
and stood at the foot of the mountain while it
blazed with fire to the very heavens, with black
clouds and deep darkness. 12Then the LORD spoke
to you out of the fire. You heard the sound of
words but saw no form; there was only a voice.
13He declared to you his covenant, the Ten Com-
mandments, which he commanded you to fol-
low and then wrote them on two stone tablets.
14And the LORD directed me at that time to teach
you the decrees and laws you are to follow in
the land that you are crossing the Jordan to
possess.

Discovering the Word 1. What responsibilities do the Israelites have regarding the law (look throughout the passage)? 2. What benefits were to come to Israel through the Ten Commandments? 3. How was the law to make Israel an international witness (vv. 6–8)? 4. If you were standing at the mountain when the law was given, according to verses 11–13, what would you have seen and heard? 5. How would it have affected your attitude toward the law?

Applying the Word 1. In what ways might we add to or subtract from God's law (v. 2)? 2. What benefits have come to you through God's laws? 3. Moses warns Israel to be careful so they won't forget or let God's Word "slip" from their hearts. Note several things you can do to keep God's laws fresh in your heart and mind.

Responding in Prayer Ask God to give you an appreciation for his law. Pray that your faithful obedience to his law will make you a witness to others who don't yet know the privilege and freedom of obedience to him.

3/ *Deuteronomy 4:15–40*
Only God Can Save

SOMETIMES I FORGET what Christianity is all about. In the midst of Bible studies, worship services, committee meetings and service projects I end up just going through the motions. Somehow the Christian faith collapses into a set of obligations that I am required to fulfill and a set of activities that I am supposed to be doing. And then, as sunlight coming through the clouds, the central truth breaks through. I am reminded that God is a saving God, a liberating God, a God who wants freedom for his people. The passage that you are about to read is one you need to fix in your mind and read from time to time. It summarizes the central message of the Bible. God took his people from slavery in Egypt to freedom. There is no one like him. When that shift takes place in my mind, the pressure of obligation changes to gratitude and heartfelt service.

Warming Up to God List your obligations regarding church, work and family. As you do, commit them to the Lord's keeping. Sit in quiet for a few moments and practice gratitude for the freedom that he brings to you.

Read Deuteronomy 4:15–40.

15 You saw no form of any kind the day the LORD
spoke to you at Horeb out of the fire. Therefore
watch yourselves very carefully, 16 so that you do
not become corrupt and make for yourselves an
idol, an image of any shape, whether formed like
a man or a woman, 17 or like any animal on earth
or any bird that flies in the air, 18 or like any crea-
ture that moves along the ground or any fish in
the waters below. 19 And when you look up to the
sky and see the sun, the moon and the stars—all
the heavenly array—do not be enticed into bow-
ing down to them and worshiping things the LORD
your God has apportioned to all the nations un-
der heaven. 20 But as for you, the LORD took you
and brought you out of the iron-smelting furnace,
out of Egypt, to be the people of his inheritance,
as you now are.
21 The LORD was angry with me because of you,
and he solemnly swore that I would not cross the
Jordan and enter the good land the LORD your
God is giving you as your inheritance. 22 I will die
in this land; I will not cross the Jordan; but you
are about to cross over and take possession of that
good land. 23 Be careful not to forget the covenant
of the LORD your God that he made with you; do
not make for yourselves an idol in the form of
anything the LORD your God has forbidden. 24 For
the LORD your God is a consuming fire, a jealous
God.
25 After you have had children and grandchil-
dren and have lived in the land a long time—if
you then become corrupt and make any kind of
idol, doing evil in the eyes of the LORD your God
and provoking him to anger, 26 I call heaven and
earth as witnesses against you this day that you
will quickly perish from the land that you are
crossing the Jordan to possess. You will not live
there long but will certainly be destroyed. 27 The

LORD will scatter you among the peoples, and only
a few of you will survive among the nations to
which the LORD will drive you. [28]There you will
worship man-made gods of wood and stone,
which cannot see or hear or eat or smell. [29]But if
from there you seek the LORD your God, you will
find him if you look for him with all your heart
and with all your soul. [30]When you are in distress
and all these things have happened to you, then
in later days you will return to the LORD your God
and obey him. [31]For the LORD your God is a mer-
ciful God; he will not abandon or destroy you or
forget the covenant with your forefathers, which
he confirmed to them by oath.

[32]Ask now about the former days, long before
your time, from the day God created man on the
earth; ask from one end of the heavens to the
other. Has anything so great as this ever hap-
pened, or has anything like it ever been heard of?
[33]Has any other people heard the voice of God[h]
speaking out of fire, as you have, and lived? [34]Has
any god ever tried to take for himself one nation
out of another nation, by testings, by miraculous
signs and wonders, by war, by a mighty hand and
an outstretched arm, or by great and awesome
deeds, like all the things the LORD your God did
for you in Egypt before your very eyes?

[35]You were shown these things so that you
might know that the LORD is God; besides him
there is no other. [36]From heaven he made you
hear his voice to discipline you. On earth he
showed you his great fire, and you heard his
words from out of the fire. [37]Because he loved
your forefathers and chose their descendants after
them, he brought you out of Egypt by his Pres-
ence and his great strength, [38]to drive out before
you nations greater and stronger than you and to
bring you into their land to give it to you for your
inheritance, as it is today.

[39]Acknowledge and take to heart this day that
the LORD is God in heaven above and on the earth
below. There is no other. [40]Keep his decrees and
commands, which I am giving you today, so that
it may go well with you and your children after
you and that you may live long in the land the
LORD your God gives you for all time.

[h]33 Or *of a god*

Discovering the Word 1. What different types of idolatry are the people warned against (vv. 15–31)? 2. What are the results of idolatry (vv. 21–31)? 3. Look at verses 32–38. What had God done to achieve Israel's salvation? 4. What response should Israel have to God's saving work (vv. 35, 39–40)? 5. What benefits will come to the people if they take this admonition to heart (vv. 37–40)?

Applying the Word 1. Israel's salvation was deliverance from slavery. A Christian's salvation is deliverance from sin. How is God's power at work in both? 2. For Israel, one of the gifts coming with their salvation was the Promised Land. What are some of the benefits that come to Christians through Christ's achievement of salvation on the cross? 3. What can you do to keep from taking your salvation for granted as Israel was in danger of doing?

Responding in Prayer Ask God to give you a heart of gratitude for his saving work in Jesus Christ. Pray that you would grow in your exclusive commitment to him and responsiveness to his leading and law.

Deuteronomy 4:41–49

[41]Then Moses set aside three cities east of the
Jordan, [42]to which anyone who had killed a per-
son could flee if he had unintentionally killed his
neighbor without malice aforethought. He could
flee into one of these cities and save his life. [43]The
cities were these: Bezer in the desert plateau, for
the Reubenites; Ramoth in Gilead, for the Gad-
ites; and Golan in Bashan, for the Manassites.

[44]This is the law Moses set before the Israelites.
[45]These are the stipulations, decrees and laws
Moses gave them when they came out of Egypt
[46]and were in the valley near Beth Peor east of the
Jordan, in the land of Sihon king of the Amorites,
who reigned in Heshbon and was defeated by Mo-
ses and the Israelites as they came out of Egypt.
[47]They took possession of his land and the land of

Og king of Bashan, the two Amorite kings east of
the Jordan. 48This land extended from Aroer on
the rim of the Arnon Gorge to Mount Siyon[i]
(that is, Hermon), 49and included all the Arabah
east of the Jordan, as far as the Sea of the Arabah,[j] below the slopes of Pisgah.

[i] 48 Hebrew; Syriac (see also Deut. 3:9) *Sirion* [j] 49 That is, the Dead Sea

4 / *Deuteronomy 5*
Keeping God at a Distance

ONE OF THE most memorable passages for me in C. S. Lewis's Chronicles of Narnia comes in the first book, *The Lion, the Witch and the Wardrobe.* When Peter, Susan and Lucy first hear about Aslan, the lion Lord of Narnia, they experience a thrill of fear. One of the children asks if Aslan's "safe." The answer is "No, he's not safe, but he's good."

With those words Lewis captures the heart of the passage you are about to read. As God reveals his glory at Mount Sinai, his voice thunders the Ten Commandments, and the top of the mountain is ablaze with fire. The response of the people, appropriately, is fear. But God is interested in creating a special kind of fear, a fear that is afraid of evil and disobedience and is respectfully desirous of doing good. The writer of Proverbs summarizes it this way, "The fear of the LORD is the beginning of knowledge" (1:7).

Warming Up to God Approaching God creates a variety of heart responses. Often we experience a sense of gratitude. And, frequently, we should have a sense of awe and respect. Pause now to consider the expanse of the galaxies and the brutality of Christ's cross. Write down any responses you have.

Read Deuteronomy 5.

5 Moses summoned all Israel and said:
Hear, O Israel, the decrees and laws I declare in your hearing today. Learn them
and be sure to follow them. 2The LORD our God
made a covenant with us at Horeb. 3It was not
with our fathers that the LORD made this covenant, but with us, with all of us who are alive
here today. 4The LORD spoke to you face to face
out of the fire on the mountain. 5(At that time I
stood between the LORD and you to declare to you
the word of the LORD, because you were afraid of
the fire and did not go up the mountain.) And he
said:

6"I am the LORD your God, who brought you out of Egypt, out of the land of slavery.
7"You shall have no other gods before[k] me.
8"You shall not make for yourself an idol in the form of anything in heaven above or on the earth beneath or in the waters
below. 9You shall not bow down to them or worship them; for I, the LORD your God, am a jealous God, punishing the children for the sin of the fathers to the third and fourth generation of those who hate me, 10but showing love to a thousand ⌊generations⌋ of those who love me and keep my commandments.
11"You shall not misuse the name of the LORD your God, for the LORD will not hold anyone guiltless who misuses his name.
12"Observe the Sabbath day by keeping it holy, as the LORD your God has commanded you. 13Six days you shall labor
and do all your work, 14but the seventh day is a Sabbath to the LORD your God. On it you shall not do any work, neither you, nor your son or daughter, nor your manservant or maidservant, nor your ox, your donkey or any of your animals, nor the alien within your gates, so that your manservant and maidservant may rest, as you do. 15Re-
member that you were slaves in Egypt and that the LORD your God brought you out of there with a mighty hand and an outstretched arm. Therefore the

[k] 7 Or *besides*

LORD your God has commanded you to
observe the Sabbath day.
16“Honor your father and your mother, as the
LORD your God has commanded you, so
that you may live long and that it may
go well with you in the land the LORD
your God is giving you.
17“You shall not murder.
18“You shall not commit adultery.
19“You shall not steal.
20“You shall not give false testimony against
your neighbor.
21“You shall not covet your neighbor’s wife.
You shall not set your desire on your
neighbor’s house or land, his manser-
vant or maidservant, his ox or donkey,
or anything that belongs to your neigh-
bor.”

22These are the commandments the LORD pro-
claimed in a loud voice to your whole assembly
there on the mountain from out of the fire, the
cloud and the deep darkness; and he added noth-
ing more. Then he wrote them on two stone tab-
lets and gave them to me.
23When you heard the voice out of the dark-
ness, while the mountain was ablaze with fire, all
the leading men of your tribes and your elders
came to me. 24And you said, “The LORD our God
has shown us his glory and his majesty, and we
have heard his voice from the fire. Today we have
seen that a man can live even if God speaks with
him. 25But now, why should we die? This great
fire will consume us, and we will die if we hear
the voice of the LORD our God any longer. 26For
what mortal man has ever heard the voice of the
living God speaking out of fire, as we have, and
survived? 27Go near and listen to all that the LORD
our God says. Then tell us whatever the LORD our
God tells you. We will listen and obey.”
28The LORD heard you when you spoke to me
and the LORD said to me, “I have heard what this
people said to you. Everything they said was
good. 29Oh, that their hearts would be inclined to
fear me and keep all my commands always, so
that it might go well with them and their children
forever!
30“Go, tell them to return to their tents. 31But
you stay here with me so that I may give you all
the commands, decrees and laws you are to teach
them to follow in the land I am giving them to
possess.”
32So be careful to do what the LORD your God
has commanded you; do not turn aside to the
right or to the left. 33Walk in all the way that the
LORD your God has commanded you, so that you
may live and prosper and prolong your days in
the land that you will possess.

Discovering the Word 1. What positive and negative aspects of fear run through these verses? 2. Note the response of the people in verses 23–27. Why do you think the experience of receiving the law produced such fear? 3. In response to the law, what role is Moses given by the people (vv. 24–27)? 4. According to verses 28–29, how does God feel about the suggestion of the Israelite leaders regarding Moses’ role? 5. What benefits are to come to the nation from living by the law?

Applying the Word 1. How can the fear of the Lord be a positive influence in your life and conduct? 2. In what way may the fear of the Lord be a problem for you that keeps you from spending time with him? 3. In Jesus Christ we no longer come to God through a mediator. How does this encourage a more personal relationship with him than the people had in the Old Testament?

Responding in Prayer Ask God to give you the courage to seek his presence, and then spend some time in quiet worship. Pray that the fear of the Lord would be a helpful presence in guiding your heartfelt obedience.

5/ *Deuteronomy 6*
Loving and Fearing the Law Giver

WHILE KNOWLEDGE BEGINS with the fear of the Lord (Pr 1:7), it is not the end. Fearing God goes hand-in-hand with heartfelt love. Yet this fact often slips from our minds and hearts. What we need to fix in our minds as firmly as we can is that God loves us, and he wants us to love him. The Scriptures are the tool that he has given us to keep our hearts alive. They are to be logs on the hearth of hearts feeding the flame of devotion. As we read the record of his loving acts as recorded in Scripture, we are to be reminded that he is the God who saves us from our chains and provides abundantly for our needs.

Warming Up to God God deserves our love. From the cross of Jesus Christ to the food that you have eaten today, make a record of things to be grateful for. Offer your praise to the Lord from that list. Ask him to breathe life into the embers of your heart. Sit with him and cultivate a quiet that is filled with heartfelt affection.

Read Deuteronomy 6.

6 These are the commands, decrees and laws the LORD your God directed me to teach you to observe in the land that you are crossing the Jordan to possess, [2]so that you, your children and their children after them may fear the LORD your God as long as you live by keeping all his decrees and commands that I give you, and so that you may enjoy long life. [3]Hear, O Israel, and be careful to obey so that it may go well with you and that you may increase greatly in a land flowing with milk and honey, just as the LORD, the God of your fathers, promised you.

[4]Hear, O Israel: The LORD our God, the LORD is one.[1] [5]Love the LORD your God with all your heart and with all your soul and with all your strength. [6]These commandments that I give you today are to be upon your hearts. [7]Impress them on your children. Talk about them when you sit at home and when you walk along the road, when you lie down and when you get up. [8]Tie them as symbols on your hands and bind them on your foreheads. [9]Write them on the doorframes of your houses and on your gates.

[10]When the LORD your God brings you into the land he swore to your fathers, to Abraham, Isaac and Jacob, to give you—a land with large, flourishing cities you did not build, [11]houses filled with all kinds of good things you did not provide, wells you did not dig, and vineyards and olive groves you did not plant—then when you eat and are satisfied, [12]be careful that you do not forget the LORD, who brought you out of Egypt, out of the land of slavery.

[13]Fear the LORD your God, serve him only and take your oaths in his name. [14]Do not follow other gods, the gods of the peoples around you; [15]for the LORD your God, who is among you, is a jealous God and his anger will burn against you, and he will destroy you from the face of the land. [16]Do not test the LORD your God as you did at Massah. [17]Be sure to keep the commands of the LORD your God and the stipulations and decrees he has given you. [18]Do what is right and good in the LORD's sight, so that it may go well with you and you may go in and take over the good land that the LORD promised on oath to your forefathers, [19]thrusting out all your enemies before you, as the LORD said.

[20]In the future, when your son asks you, "What is the meaning of the stipulations, decrees and laws the LORD our God has commanded you?" [21]tell him: "We were slaves of Pharaoh in Egypt, but the LORD brought us out of Egypt with a mighty hand. [22]Before our eyes the LORD sent miraculous signs and wonders—great and terrible—upon Egypt and Pharaoh and his whole household. [23]But he brought us out from there to bring us in and give us the land that he promised on oath to our forefathers. [24]The LORD commanded us to obey all these decrees and to fear the LORD our God, so that we might always prosper and be kept alive, as is the case today. [25]And if we are careful to obey all this law before the LORD our God, as he has commanded us, that will be our righteousness."

[1]4 Or *The LORD our God is one LORD*; or *The LORD is our God, the LORD is one*; or *The LORD is our God, the LORD alone*

Discovering the Word 1. How are both fear and love important motivations in these verses? 2. How is love of the Lord to affect the way children are to be raised in the new land (vv. 4–9)? 3. What is the difference between passing the law on out of obligation and passing it on out of love? 4. What dangers will the Israelites face, and how will the fear of the Lord be helpful (vv. 10–19)? 5. How will the law be an aid in keeping the memory of God's salvation fresh (vv. 20–25)?

Applying the Word 1. Love for God was to be passed on from generation to generation. What attitudes have you picked up toward God from your parents? (If you are a parent, consider as well what attitudes toward God you are passing on to your children.) 2. Consider your own motivations. In what areas do you live by God's law out of obligation and in what ways do you follow God's law because of your affection for him? 3. The Israelites were to be careful not to take God's gift of the new land for granted. What do you tend to take for granted about God's saving work in your life?

Responding in Prayer Ask God to help you grow in a love-filled faith. Pray that the members of your church would pass on a love for God from adults to children.

6 / *Deuteronomy 7*
Being a Holy People

STEPPING ACROSS THE border from the U.S. to Mexico or getting off a plane at Heathrow airport in London, you know that you are in a different country. Expressed in the difference in clothes and architecture are attitudes, values and beliefs which make each country unique. And behind all the differences is the way God or a god is worshiped. In the midst of the cultural and racial mix of the Middle East God wanted to make his people distinct. God set up firm limits as if to say to his children, "We don't do that in our family." In their customs, relationships, government and religion they were to be a distinct people of freedom, salvation and liberation for all the world to see.

Warming Up to God How do your experiences of worship, both on Sunday morning at church and on your own, affect the way you live?

Read Deuteronomy 7.

7 When the LORD your God brings you into
the land you are entering to possess and
drives out before you many nations—the
Hittites, Girgashites, Amorites, Canaanites, Periz-
zites, Hivites and Jebusites, seven nations larger
and stronger than you— 2and when the LORD
your God has delivered them over to you and you
have defeated them, then you must destroy them
totally.[m] Make no treaty with them, and show
them no mercy. 3Do not intermarry with them.
Do not give your daughters to their sons or take
their daughters for your sons, 4for they will turn
your sons away from following me to serve other
gods, and the LORD's anger will burn against you
and will quickly destroy you. 5This is what you
are to do to them: Break down their altars, smash
their sacred stones, cut down their Asherah
poles[n] and burn their idols in the fire. 6For you
are a people holy to the LORD your God. The LORD
your God has chosen you out of all the peoples
on the face of the earth to be his people, his trea-
sured possession.
7The LORD did not set his affection on you and
choose you because you were more numerous
than other peoples, for you were the fewest of all
peoples. 8But it was because the LORD loved you
and kept the oath he swore to your forefathers
that he brought you out with a mighty hand and
redeemed you from the land of slavery, from the
power of Pharaoh king of Egypt. 9Know therefore
that the LORD your God is God; he is the faithful
God, keeping his covenant of love to a thousand
generations of those who love him and keep his
commands. 10But

those who hate him he will repay to their face
by destruction;

m2 The Hebrew term refers to the irrevocable giving over of things or persons to the LORD, often by totally destroying them; also in verse 26.
n5 That is, symbols of the goddess Asherah; here and elsewhere in Deuteronomy

he will not be slow to repay to their face
those who hate him.

11Therefore, take care to follow the commands, decrees and laws I give you today.

12If you pay attention to these laws and are careful to follow them, then the LORD your God will keep his covenant of love with you, as he swore to your forefathers. 13He will love you and bless you and increase your numbers. He will bless the fruit of your womb, the crops of your land—your grain, new wine and oil—the calves of your herds and the lambs of your flocks in the land that he swore to your forefathers to give you. 14You will be blessed more than any other people; none of your men or women will be childless, nor any of your livestock without young. 15The LORD will keep you free from every disease. He will not inflict on you the horrible diseases you knew in Egypt, but he will inflict them on all who hate you. 16You must destroy all the peoples the LORD your God gives over to you. Do not look on them with pity and do not serve their gods, for that will be a snare to you.

17You may say to yourselves, "These nations are stronger than we are. How can we drive them out?" 18But do not be afraid of them; remember well what the LORD your God did to Pharaoh and to all Egypt. 19You saw with your own eyes the great trials, the miraculous signs and wonders, the mighty hand and outstretched arm, with which the LORD your God brought you out. The LORD your God will do the same to all the peoples you now fear. 20Moreover, the LORD your God will send the hornet among them until even the survivors who hide from you have perished. 21Do not be terrified by them, for the LORD your God, who is among you, is a great and awesome God. 22The LORD your God will drive out those nations before you, little by little. You will not be allowed to eliminate them all at once, or the wild animals will multiply around you. 23But the LORD your God will deliver them over to you, throwing them into great confusion until they are destroyed. 24He will give their kings into your hand, and you will wipe out their names from under heaven. No one will be able to stand up against you; you will destroy them. 25The images of their gods you are to burn in the fire. Do not covet the silver and gold on them, and do not take it for yourselves, or you will be ensnared by it, for it is detestable to the LORD your God. 26Do not bring a detestable thing into your house or you, like it, will be set apart for destruction. Utterly abhor and detest it, for it is set apart for destruction.

Discovering the Word 1. What obligations come to Israel in its special relationship with God? 2. From these verses, how would you define the word *holy*? 3. Intermarriage was forbidden and destruction of foreign altars was required (vv. 1-7). Why would you think these instructions are so harsh and uncompromising? 4. Israel is told that they have a special relationship with God (v. 6). How does Moses seek to deal with the potential danger of national arrogance (vv. 7-11)? 5. What blessings come with keeping these laws (vv. 12-26)?

Applying the Word 1. How do you seek to be separate from ungodly forms of worship and behavior? 2. What are some sources of temptation that cause you to turn from the Lord? 3. As Christians, we are also God's chosen people. How is this a cause for both gratitude and humility?

Responding in Prayer Ask the Lord to teach you what it means to be *in* but not *of* the world. Ask God to make your church a place where people feel special and important in Christ.

7 / *Deuteronomy 8*
Remembering to Be Grateful

I HAVE A houseful of stuff now, but I can remember when I could put everything I owned in the trunk and back seat of my car. I had some good times in those student days, but I am having some good times now too. I suppose the real difference is that I've got more to be thankful for. I wonder if the depth of my gratitude has kept pace with the increase in God's blessings? I don't think so. Gratitude is a skill that requires disciplined cultivation throughout our lives. After all, God continues to give and give. Shouldn't we continue to say we appreciate it?

Warming Up to God Considering your current state of spiritual gratitude in comparison to the blessings you have been given, how would you rate yourself? After you have done that, make a list of as many things as you can to thank God for.

Read Deuteronomy 8.

8 Be careful to follow every command I am
giving you today, so that you may live
and increase and may enter and possess
the land that the LORD promised on oath to your
forefathers. 2Remember how the LORD your God
led you all the way in the desert these forty years,
to humble you and to test you in order to know
what was in your heart, whether or not you
would keep his commands. 3He humbled you,
causing you to hunger and then feeding you with
manna, which neither you nor your fathers had
known, to teach you that man does not live on
bread alone but on every word that comes from
the mouth of the LORD. 4Your clothes did not wear
out and your feet did not swell during these forty
years. 5Know then in your heart that as a man
disciplines his son, so the LORD your God disci-
plines you.
6Observe the commands of the LORD your God,
walking in his ways and revering him. 7For the
LORD your God is bringing you into a good land—
a land with streams and pools of water, with
springs flowing in the valleys and hills; 8a land
with wheat and barley, vines and fig trees, pome-
granates, olive oil and honey; 9a land where bread
will not be scarce and you will lack nothing; a
land where the rocks are iron and you can dig
copper out of the hills.
10When you have eaten and are satisfied, praise
the LORD your God for the good land he has given
you. 11Be careful that you do not forget the LORD
your God, failing to observe his commands, his
laws and his decrees that I am giving you this day.
12Otherwise, when you eat and are satisfied, when
you build fine houses and settle down, 13and
when your herds and flocks grow large and your
silver and gold increase and all you have is multi-
plied, 14then your heart will become proud and
you will forget the LORD your God, who brought
you out of Egypt, out of the land of slavery. 15He
led you through the vast and dreadful desert, that
thirsty and waterless land, with its venomous
snakes and scorpions. He brought you water out
of hard rock. 16He gave you manna to eat in the
desert, something your fathers had never known,
to humble and to test you so that in the end it
might go well with you. 17You may say to your-
self, "My power and the strength of my hands
have produced this wealth for me." 18But remem-
ber the LORD your God, for it is he who gives you
the ability to produce wealth, and so confirms his
covenant, which he swore to your forefathers, as
it is today.
19If you ever forget the LORD your God and fol-
low other gods and worship and bow down to
them, I testify against you today that you will
surely be destroyed. 20Like the nations the LORD
destroyed before you, so you will be destroyed for
not obeying the LORD your God.

Discovering the Word 1. Summarize what Israel needs to know to continually enjoy the fruits of the Promised Land. 2. Describe the character of God's discipline (vv. 1–5). 3. How might the discipline of God have prepared Israel for living in the Promised Land? 4. Why was the testing and waiting in the wilderness worth the wait (vv. 6–9)? 5. What were the dangers to be faced in the Promised Land (vv. 10–18)? 6. Describe the relationship between forgetfulness and disobedience (vv. 19–20).

Applying the Word 1. While God disciplined and tested Israel, he also provided for "daily bread" during their time of testing. How has God provided for you during times of testing? 2. After God's time of testing, he brought Israel into the blessing of the Promised Land. What parallels can you draw to your own experience of God's leading in your life?

Responding in Prayer Ask God to give you a grateful heart that trusts and obeys in the times of blessing and testing.

Deuteronomy 9—11

9 Hear, O Israel. You are now about to cross the Jordan to go in and dispossess nations greater and stronger than you, with large cities that have walls up to the sky. 2The people are strong and tall—Anakites! You know about them and have heard it said: "Who can stand up against the Anakites?" 3But be assured today that the LORD your God is the one who goes across ahead of you like a devouring fire. He will destroy them; he will subdue them before you. And you will drive them out and annihilate them quickly, as the LORD has promised you.

4After the LORD your God has driven them out before you, do not say to yourself, "The LORD has brought me here to take possession of this land because of my righteousness." No, it is on account of the wickedness of these nations that the LORD is going to drive them out before you. 5It is not because of your righteousness or your integrity that you are going in to take possession of their land; but on account of the wickedness of these nations, the LORD your God will drive them out before you, to accomplish what he swore to your fathers, to Abraham, Isaac and Jacob. 6Understand, then, that it is not because of your righteousness that the LORD your God is giving you this good land to possess, for you are a stiff-necked people.

7Remember this and never forget how you provoked the LORD your God to anger in the desert. From the day you left Egypt until you arrived here, you have been rebellious against the LORD. 8At Horeb you aroused the LORD's wrath so that he was angry enough to destroy you. 9When I went up on the mountain to receive the tablets of stone, the tablets of the covenant that the LORD had made with you, I stayed on the mountain forty days and forty nights; I ate no bread and drank no water. 10The LORD gave me two stone tablets inscribed by the finger of God. On them were all the commandments the LORD proclaimed to you on the mountain out of the fire, on the day of the assembly.

11At the end of the forty days and forty nights, the LORD gave me the two stone tablets, the tablets of the covenant. 12Then the LORD told me, "Go down from here at once, because your people whom you brought out of Egypt have become corrupt. They have turned away quickly from what I commanded them and have made a cast idol for themselves."

13And the LORD said to me, "I have seen this people, and they are a stiff-necked people indeed! 14Let me alone, so that I may destroy them and blot out their name from under heaven. And I will make you into a nation stronger and more numerous than they."

15So I turned and went down from the mountain while it was ablaze with fire. And the two tablets of the covenant were in my hands.[o] 16When I looked, I saw that you had sinned against the LORD your God; you had made for yourselves an idol cast in the shape of a calf. You had turned aside quickly from the way that the LORD had commanded you. 17So I took the two tablets and threw them out of my hands, breaking them to pieces before your eyes.

18Then once again I fell prostrate before the LORD for forty days and forty nights; I ate no bread and drank no water, because of all the sin you had committed, doing what was evil in the LORD's sight and so provoking him to anger. 19I feared the anger and wrath of the LORD, for he was angry enough with you to destroy you. But again the LORD listened to me. 20And the LORD was angry enough with Aaron to destroy him, but at that time I prayed for Aaron too. 21Also I took that sinful thing of yours, the calf you had made, and burned it in the fire. Then I crushed it and ground it to powder as fine as dust and threw the dust into a stream that flowed down the mountain.

22You also made the LORD angry at Taberah, at Massah and at Kibroth Hattaavah.

23And when the LORD sent you out from Kadesh Barnea, he said, "Go up and take possession of the land I have given you." But you rebelled against the command of the LORD your God. You did not trust him or obey him. 24You have been rebellious against the LORD ever since I have known you.

25I lay prostrate before the LORD those forty days and forty nights because the LORD had said he would destroy you. 26I prayed to the LORD and said, "O Sovereign LORD, do not destroy your peo-

[o]15 Or *And I had the two tablets of the covenant with me, one in each hand*

ple, your own inheritance that you redeemed by your great power and brought out of Egypt with a mighty hand. 27 Remember your servants Abraham, Isaac and Jacob. Overlook the stubbornness of this people, their wickedness and their sin. 28 Otherwise, the country from which you brought us will say, 'Because the LORD was not able to take them into the land he had promised them, and because he hated them, he brought them out to put them to death in the desert.' 29 But they are your people, your inheritance that you brought out by your great power and your outstretched arm."

10 At that time the LORD said to me, "Chisel out two stone tablets like the first ones and come up to me on the mountain. Also make a wooden chest.[p] 2 I will write on the tablets the words that were on the first tablets, which you broke. Then you are to put them in the chest."

3 So I made the ark out of acacia wood and chiseled out two stone tablets like the first ones, and I went up on the mountain with the two tablets in my hands. 4 The LORD wrote on these tablets what he had written before, the Ten Commandments he had proclaimed to you on the mountain, out of the fire, on the day of the assembly. And the LORD gave them to me. 5 Then I came back down the mountain and put the tablets in the ark I had made, as the LORD commanded me, and they are there now.

6 (The Israelites traveled from the wells of the Jaakanites to Moserah. There Aaron died and was buried, and Eleazar his son succeeded him as priest. 7 From there they traveled to Gudgodah and on to Jotbathah, a land with streams of water. 8 At that time the LORD set apart the tribe of Levi to carry the ark of the covenant of the LORD, to stand before the LORD to minister and to pronounce blessings in his name, as they still do today. 9 That is why the Levites have no share or inheritance among their brothers; the LORD is their inheritance, as the LORD your God told them.)

10 Now I had stayed on the mountain forty days and nights, as I did the first time, and the LORD listened to me at this time also. It was not his will to destroy you. 11 "Go," the LORD said to me, "and lead the people on their way, so that they may enter and possess the land that I swore to their fathers to give them."

12 And now, O Israel, what does the LORD your God ask of you but to fear the LORD your God, to walk in all his ways, to love him, to serve the LORD your God with all your heart and with all your soul, 13 and to observe the LORD's commands and decrees that I am giving you today for your own good?

14 To the LORD your God belong the heavens, even the highest heavens, the earth and everything in it. 15 Yet the LORD set his affection on your forefathers and loved them, and he chose you, their descendants, above all the nations, as it is today. 16 Circumcise your hearts, therefore, and do not be stiff-necked any longer. 17 For the LORD your God is God of gods and Lord of lords, the great God, mighty and awesome, who shows no partiality and accepts no bribes. 18 He defends the cause of the fatherless and the widow, and loves the alien, giving him food and clothing. 19 And you are to love those who are aliens, for you yourselves were aliens in Egypt. 20 Fear the LORD your God and serve him. Hold fast to him and take your oaths in his name. 21 He is your praise; he is your God, who performed for you those great and awesome wonders you saw with your own eyes. 22 Your forefathers who went down into Egypt were seventy in all, and now the LORD your God has made you as numerous as the stars in the sky.

11 Love the LORD your God and keep his requirements, his decrees, his laws and his commands always. 2 Remember today that your children were not the ones who saw and experienced the discipline of the LORD your God: his majesty, his mighty hand, his outstretched arm; 3 the signs he performed and the things he did in the heart of Egypt, both to Pharaoh king of Egypt and to his whole country; 4 what he did to the Egyptian army, to its horses and chariots, how he overwhelmed them with the waters of the Red Sea[q] as they were pursuing you, and how the LORD brought lasting ruin on them. 5 It was not your children who saw what he did for you in the desert until you arrived at this place, 6 and what he did to Dathan and Abiram, sons of Eliab the Reubenite, when the earth opened its mouth right in the middle of all Israel and swallowed them up with their households, their tents and every living thing that belonged to them. 7 But it was your own eyes that saw all these great things the LORD has done.

8 Observe therefore all the commands I am giv-

p1 That is, an ark q4 Hebrew *Yam Suph*; that is, Sea of Reeds

ing you today, so that you may have the strength to go in and take over the land that you are crossing the Jordan to possess, 9and so that you may live long in the land that the LORD swore to your forefathers to give to them and their descendants, a land flowing with milk and honey. 10The land you are entering to take over is not like the land of Egypt, from which you have come, where you planted your seed and irrigated it by foot as in a vegetable garden. 11But the land you are crossing the Jordan to take possession of is a land of mountains and valleys that drinks rain from heaven. 12It is a land the LORD your God cares for; the eyes of the LORD your God are continually on it from the beginning of the year to its end.

13So if you faithfully obey the commands I am giving you today—to love the LORD your God and to serve him with all your heart and with all your soul— 14then I will send rain on your land in its season, both autumn and spring rains, so that you may gather in your grain, new wine and oil. 15I will provide grass in the fields for your cattle, and you will eat and be satisfied.

16Be careful, or you will be enticed to turn away and worship other gods and bow down to them. 17Then the LORD's anger will burn against you, and he will shut the heavens so that it will not rain and the ground will yield no produce, and you will soon perish from the good land the LORD is giving you. 18Fix these words of mine in your hearts and minds; tie them as symbols on your hands and bind them on your foreheads. 19Teach them to your children, talking about them when you sit at home and when you walk along the road, when you lie down and when you get up. 20Write them on the doorframes of your houses and on your gates, 21so that your days and the days of your children may be many in the land that the LORD swore to give your forefathers, as many as the days that the heavens are above the earth.

22If you carefully observe all these commands I am giving you to follow—to love the LORD your God, to walk in all his ways and to hold fast to him— 23then the LORD will drive out all these nations before you, and you will dispossess nations larger and stronger than you. 24Every place where you set your foot will be yours: Your territory will extend from the desert to Lebanon, and from the Euphrates River to the western sea.[r] 25No man will be able to stand against you. The LORD your God, as he promised you, will put the terror and fear of you on the whole land, wherever you go.

26See, I am setting before you today a blessing and a curse— 27the blessing if you obey the commands of the LORD your God that I am giving you today; 28the curse if you disobey the commands of the LORD your God and turn from the way that I command you today by following other gods, which you have not known. 29When the LORD your God has brought you into the land you are entering to possess, you are to proclaim on Mount Gerizim the blessings, and on Mount Ebal the curses. 30As you know, these mountains are across the Jordan, west of the road,[s] toward the setting sun, near the great trees of Moreh, in the territory of those Canaanites living in the Arabah in the vicinity of Gilgal. 31You are about to cross the Jordan to enter and take possession of the land the LORD your God is giving you. When you have taken it over and are living there, 32be sure that you obey all the decrees and laws I am setting before you today.

[r]24 That is, the Mediterranean [s]30 Or *Jordan, westward*

8 / *Deuteronomy 12:1-14*
One Place of Worship

VISIT LONDON AND two of the "must sees" are Westminster Abbey and St. Paul's Cathedral. In Paris Notre Dame will be on your sightseeing list. And a cathedral will be on your tour of many other major cities in Europe. Wandering through these huge buildings with their myriad statues, soaring arches and rainbow-colored windows, you may pause to consider what motivated such massive efforts of religious construction. Why is it that some continue to serve living communities of faith and others are only museums? A place of worship embodies the values, beliefs and practices that unify a people and contributes to their formation as a community.

Warming Up to God How does your church building contribute to (or hinder) your experience of worship?

Read Deuteronomy 12:1–14.

12 These are the decrees and laws you
must be careful to follow in the
land that the LORD, the God of your
fathers, has given you to possess—as long as you
live in the land. [2]Destroy completely all the places
on the high mountains and on the hills and under
every spreading tree where the nations you are
dispossessing worship their gods. [3]Break down
their altars, smash their sacred stones and burn
their Asherah poles in the fire; cut down the idols
of their gods and wipe out their names from those
places.
[4]You must not worship the LORD your God in
their way. [5]But you are to seek the place the LORD
your God will choose from among all your tribes
to put his Name there for his dwelling. To that
place you must go; [6]there bring your burnt offer-
ings and sacrifices, your tithes and special gifts,
what you have vowed to give and your free-
will offerings, and the firstborn of your herds
and flocks. [7]There, in the presence of the LORD
your God, you and your families shall eat and
shall rejoice in everything you have put your
hand to, because the LORD your God has blessed
you.
[8]You are not to do as we do here today, every-
one as he sees fit, [9]since you have not yet reached
the resting place and the inheritance the LORD
your God is giving you. [10]But you will cross the
Jordan and settle in the land the LORD your God is
giving you as an inheritance, and he will give you
rest from all your enemies around you so that you
will live in safety. [11]Then to the place the LORD
your God will choose as a dwelling for his
Name—there you are to bring everything I com-
mand you: your burnt offerings and sacrifices,
your tithes and special gifts, and all the choice
possessions you have vowed to the LORD. [12]And
there rejoice before the LORD your God, you, your
sons and daughters, your menservants and maid-
servants, and the Levites from your towns, who
have no allotment or inheritance of their own.
[13]Be careful not to sacrifice your burnt offerings
anywhere you please. [14]Offer them only at the
place the LORD will choose in one of your tribes,
and there observe everything I command you.

Discovering the Word 1. How will the worship of God change after Israel enters the land? 2. What verbs are used in verses 2–3 to describe how Israel is to treat the worship centers of the Canaanite gods? What's the point? 3. From verses 7 and 12 describe the tone of a typical worship experience in the land. 4. How would the plan for worship described here be superior to the current practices—"everyone as he sees fit" (v. 8)? 5. What limitations would having a national worship center place on the frequency and style of the worship in Israel? 6. What benefits and protection might a central place of worship provide for Israel as they enter the land?

Applying the Word 1. Although a central place of worship was abolished with the coming of Christ, Christians still gather at church—the place which has become our worship center. What benefits do you get out of your church's worship? 2. Israel's worship was to be characterized by rejoicing in the presence of the Lord for his blessings of prosperity. How would you describe your church's worship? 3. Israel needed a centralized place of worship to counter the influence of Canaanite idolatry. What worship guidelines might you need to counter the patterns of ungodliness of our present time?

Responding in Prayer Ask God to make worship a time of gratitude and celebration in your life, and praise him for the places where Jesus Christ is worshiped that are scattered all around the world.

Deuteronomy 12:15—14:29

15Nevertheless, you may slaughter your animals in any of your towns and eat as much of the meat as you want, as if it were gazelle or deer, according to the blessing the LORD your God gives you. Both the ceremonially unclean and the clean may eat it. 16But you must not eat the blood; pour it out on the ground like water. 17You must not eat in your own towns the tithe of your grain and new wine and oil, or the firstborn of your herds and flocks, or whatever you have vowed to give, or your freewill offerings or special gifts. 18Instead, you are to eat them in the presence of the LORD your God at the place the LORD your God will choose—you, your sons and daughters, your menservants and maidservants, and the Levites from your towns—and you are to rejoice before the LORD your God in everything you put your hand to. 19Be careful not to neglect the Levites as long as you live in your land.

20When the LORD your God has enlarged your territory as he promised you, and you crave meat and say, "I would like some meat," then you may eat as much of it as you want. 21If the place where the LORD your God chooses to put his Name is too far away from you, you may slaughter animals from the herds and flocks the LORD has given you, as I have commanded you, and in your own towns you may eat as much of them as you want. 22Eat them as you would gazelle or deer. Both the ceremonially unclean and the clean may eat. 23But be sure you do not eat the blood, because the blood is the life, and you must not eat the life with the meat. 24You must not eat the blood; pour it out on the ground like water. 25Do not eat it, so that it may go well with you and your children after you, because you will be doing what is right in the eyes of the LORD.

26But take your consecrated things and whatever you have vowed to give, and go to the place the LORD will choose. 27Present your burnt offerings on the altar of the LORD your God, both the meat and the blood. The blood of your sacrifices must be poured beside the altar of the LORD your God, but you may eat the meat. 28Be careful to obey all these regulations I am giving you, so that it may always go well with you and your children after you, because you will be doing what is good and right in the eyes of the LORD your God.

29The LORD your God will cut off before you the nations you are about to invade and dispossess. But when you have driven them out and settled in their land, 30and after they have been destroyed before you, be careful not to be ensnared by inquiring about their gods, saying, "How do these nations serve their gods? We will do the same." 31You must not worship the LORD your God in their way, because in worshiping their gods, they do all kinds of detestable things the LORD hates. They even burn their sons and daughters in the fire as sacrifices to their gods.

32See that you do all I command you; do not add to it or take away from it.

13 If a prophet, or one who foretells by dreams, appears among you and announces to you a miraculous sign or wonder, 2and if the sign or wonder of which he has spoken takes place, and he says, "Let us follow other gods" (gods you have not known) "and let us worship them," 3you must not listen to the words of that prophet or dreamer. The LORD your God is testing you to find out whether you love him with all your heart and with all your soul. 4It is the LORD your God you must follow, and him you must revere. Keep his commands and obey him; serve him and hold fast to him. 5That prophet or dreamer must be put to death, because he preached rebellion against the LORD your God, who brought you out of Egypt and redeemed you from the land of slavery; he has tried to turn you from the way the LORD your God commanded you to follow. You must purge the evil from among you.

6If your very own brother, or your son or daughter, or the wife you love, or your closest friend secretly entices you, saying, "Let us go and worship other gods" (gods that neither you nor your fathers have known, 7gods of the peoples around you, whether near or far, from one end of the land to the other), 8do not yield to him or listen to him. Show him no pity. Do not spare him or shield him. 9You must certainly put him to death. Your hand must be the first in putting him to death, and then the hands of all the people. 10Stone him to death, because he tried to turn you away from the LORD your God, who brought you out of Egypt, out of the land of slavery. 11Then all Israel will hear and be afraid, and no one among you will do such an evil thing again.

12If you hear it said about one of the towns the
LORD your God is giving you to live in 13that
wicked men have arisen among you and have led
the people of their town astray, saying, "Let us
go and worship other gods" (gods you have not
known), 14then you must inquire, probe and in-
vestigate it thoroughly. And if it is true and it has
been proved that this detestable thing has been
done among you, 15you must certainly put to the
sword all who live in that town. Destroy it com-
pletely,[t] both its people and its livestock.
16Gather all the plunder of the town into the mid-
dle of the public square and completely burn the
town and all its plunder as a whole burnt offering
to the LORD your God. It is to remain a ruin for-
ever, never to be rebuilt. 17None of those con-
demned things[t] shall be found in your hands, so
that the LORD will turn from his fierce anger; he
will show you mercy, have compassion on you,
and increase your numbers, as he promised on
oath to your forefathers, 18because you obey the
LORD your God, keeping all his commands that I
am giving you today and doing what is right in
his eyes.

14 You are the children of the LORD
your God. Do not cut yourselves or
shave the front of your heads for
the dead, 2for you are a people holy to the LORD
your God. Out of all the peoples on the face of the
earth, the LORD has chosen you to be his treasured
possession.

3Do not eat any detestable thing. 4These are the
animals you may eat: the ox, the sheep, the goat,
5the deer, the gazelle, the roe deer, the wild goat,
the ibex, the antelope and the mountain sheep.[u]
6You may eat any animal that has a split hoof
divided in two and that chews the cud. 7However,
of those that chew the cud or that have a split
hoof completely divided you may not eat the
camel, the rabbit or the coney.[v] Although they
chew the cud, they do not have a split hoof; they
are ceremonially unclean for you. 8The pig is also
unclean; although it has a split hoof, it does not
chew the cud. You are not to eat their meat or
touch their carcasses.

9Of all the creatures living in the water, you
may eat any that has fins and scales. 10But any-
thing that does not have fins and scales you may
not eat; for you it is unclean.

11You may eat any clean bird. 12But these you
may not eat: the eagle, the vulture, the black vul-
ture, 13the red kite, the black kite, any kind of
falcon, 14any kind of raven, 15the horned owl, the
screech owl, the gull, any kind of hawk, 16the
little owl, the great owl, the white owl, 17the
desert owl, the osprey, the cormorant, 18the stork,
any kind of heron, the hoopoe and the bat.

19All flying insects that swarm are unclean to
you; do not eat them. 20But any winged creature
that is clean you may eat.

21Do not eat anything you find already dead.
You may give it to an alien living in any of your
towns, and he may eat it, or you may sell it to a
foreigner. But you are a people holy to the LORD
your God.

Do not cook a young goat in its mother's milk.

22Be sure to set aside a tenth of all that your
fields produce each year. 23Eat the tithe of your
grain, new wine and oil, and the firstborn of
your herds and flocks in the presence of the LORD
your God at the place he will choose as a dwell-
ing for his Name, so that you may learn to revere
the LORD your God always. 24But if that place is
too distant and you have been blessed by the LORD
your God and cannot carry your tithe (because
the place where the LORD will choose to put his
Name is so far away), 25then exchange your tithe
for silver, and take the silver with you and go to
the place the LORD your God will choose. 26Use
the silver to buy whatever you like: cattle, sheep,
wine or other fermented drink, or anything you
wish. Then you and your household shall eat
there in the presence of the LORD your God and
rejoice. 27And do not neglect the Levites living in
your towns, for they have no allotment or inheri-
tance of their own.

28At the end of every three years, bring all the
tithes of that year's produce and store it in your
towns, 29so that the Levites (who have no allot-
ment or inheritance of their own) and the aliens,
the fatherless and the widows who live in your
towns may come and eat and be satisfied, and so
that the LORD your God may bless you in all the
work of your hands.

[t] *15,17* The Hebrew term refers to the irrevocable giving over of things or persons to the LORD, often by totally destroying them. [u] *5* The precise identification of some of the birds and animals in this chapter is uncertain. [v] *7* That is, the hyrax or rock badger

9 / *Deuteronomy 15:1–11*
The Year of Freedom

IT SEEMS LIKE every couple of nights I get a phone call from some credit card company. They offer me the opportunity to go further into debt through the use of their card at some great interest rate. My response is "No, thanks. I'm deep enough in debt as it is." No one has ever called up and offered to take the load of my debt and cancel it, no interest, no charge. It's inconceivable. Yet in ancient Israel something equivalent to that happened every seven years. Why? God's salvation is an offer of freedom—not just religious freedom, not just political freedom, but economic freedom as well.

Warming Up to God Jesus teaches us to pray, "Give us this day our daily bread." What difference would it make in your attitude toward your work today if you didn't feel that earning your living was totally up to you?

Read Deuteronomy 15:1–11.

---

15 At the end of every seven years you must cancel debts. [2]This is how it is to be done: Every creditor shall cancel the loan he has made to his fellow Israelite. He shall not require payment from his fellow Israelite or brother, because the LORD's time for canceling debts has been proclaimed. [3]You may require payment from a foreigner, but you must cancel any debt your brother owes you. [4]However, there should be no poor among you, for in the land the LORD your God is giving you to possess as your inheritance, he will richly bless you, [5]if only you fully obey the LORD your God and are careful to follow all these commands I am giving you today. [6]For the LORD your God will bless you as he has promised, and you will lend to many nations but will borrow from none. You will rule over many nations but none will rule over you.

[7]If there is a poor man among your brothers in any of the towns of the land that the LORD your God is giving you, do not be hardhearted or tightfisted toward your poor brother. [8]Rather be openhanded and freely lend him whatever he needs. [9]Be careful not to harbor this wicked thought: "The seventh year, the year for canceling debts, is near," so that you do not show ill will toward your needy brother and give him nothing. He may then appeal to the LORD against you, and you will be found guilty of sin. [10]Give generously to him and do so without a grudging heart; then because of this the LORD your God will bless you in all your work and in everything you put your hand to. [11]There will always be poor people in the land. Therefore I command you to be openhanded toward your brothers and toward the poor and needy in your land.

Discovering the Word 1. What provisions are being made for the poor after they enter the land? 2. Note the colorful words in verses 7–10 which describe those who refuse to follow this law. What attitude does Moses want to see among the citizens of the land? 3. What provision is made for those who would seek to avoid the spirit of this law (vv. 8–9)? 4. Moses sets high standards, yet he is also realistic. How would you explain the apparent conflict between verses 4 and 11?

Applying the Word 1. What is there about the intent of this law that could be applied in your country? 2. What is there about the intent of this law that could be applied in the church? 3. How will the spirit of these economic principles make a difference in the way that you use your money?

Responding in Prayer Pray for those who have financial needs in your church. Ask God to touch the hearts of members of your church to be a help to them. Pray for those who have adequate financial resources, that they would be willing to be an aid and resource for those in need.

Deuteronomy 15:12—23:14

12If a fellow Hebrew, a man or a woman, sells himself to you and serves you six years, in the seventh year you must let him go free. 13And when you release him, do not send him away empty-handed. 14Supply him liberally from your flock, your threshing floor and your winepress. Give to him as the LORD your God has blessed you. 15Remember that you were slaves in Egypt and the LORD your God redeemed you. That is why I give you this command today.

16But if your servant says to you, "I do not want to leave you," because he loves you and your family and is well off with you, 17then take an awl and push it through his ear lobe into the door, and he will become your servant for life. Do the same for your maidservant.

18Do not consider it a hardship to set your servant free, because his service to you these six years has been worth twice as much as that of a hired hand. And the LORD your God will bless you in everything you do.

19Set apart for the LORD your God every firstborn male of your herds and flocks. Do not put the firstborn of your oxen to work, and do not shear the firstborn of your sheep. 20Each year you and your family are to eat them in the presence of the LORD your God at the place he will choose. 21If an animal has a defect, is lame or blind, or has any serious flaw, you must not sacrifice it to the LORD your God. 22You are to eat it in your own towns. Both the ceremonially unclean and the clean may eat it, as if it were gazelle or deer. 23But you must not eat the blood; pour it out on the ground like water.

16 Observe the month of Abib and celebrate the Passover of the LORD your God, because in the month of Abib he brought you out of Egypt by night. 2Sacrifice as the Passover to the LORD your God an animal from your flock or herd at the place the LORD will choose as a dwelling for his Name. 3Do not eat it with bread made with yeast, but for seven days eat unleavened bread, the bread of affliction, because you left Egypt in haste—so that all the days of your life you may remember the time of your departure from Egypt. 4Let no yeast be found in your possession in all your land for seven days. Do not let any of the meat you sacrifice on the evening of the first day remain until morning.

5You must not sacrifice the Passover in any town the LORD your God gives you 6except in the place he will choose as a dwelling for his Name. There you must sacrifice the Passover in the evening, when the sun goes down, on the anniversary[w] of your departure from Egypt. 7Roast it and eat it at the place the LORD your God will choose. Then in the morning return to your tents. 8For six days eat unleavened bread and on the seventh day hold an assembly to the LORD your God and do no work.

9Count off seven weeks from the time you begin to put the sickle to the standing grain. 10Then celebrate the Feast of Weeks to the LORD your God by giving a freewill offering in proportion to the blessings the LORD your God has given you. 11And rejoice before the LORD your God at the place he will choose as a dwelling for his Name—you, your sons and daughters, your menservants and maidservants, the Levites in your towns, and the aliens, the fatherless and the widows living among you. 12Remember that you were slaves in Egypt, and follow carefully these decrees.

13Celebrate the Feast of Tabernacles for seven days after you have gathered the produce of your threshing floor and your winepress. 14Be joyful at your Feast—you, your sons and daughters, your menservants and maidservants, and the Levites, the aliens, the fatherless and the widows who live in your towns. 15For seven days celebrate the Feast to the LORD your God at the place the LORD will choose. For the LORD your God will bless you in all your harvest and in all the work of your hands, and your joy will be complete.

16Three times a year all your men must appear before the LORD your God at the place he will choose: at the Feast of Unleavened Bread, the Feast of Weeks and the Feast of Tabernacles. No man should appear before the LORD empty-handed: 17Each of you must bring a gift in proportion to the way the LORD your God has blessed you.

18Appoint judges and officials for each of your tribes in every town the LORD your God is giving you, and they shall judge the people fairly. 19Do not pervert justice or show partiality. Do not ac-

w6 *Or down, at the time of day*

cept a bribe, for a bribe blinds the eyes of the wise and twists the words of the righteous. 20Follow justice and justice alone, so that you may live and possess the land the LORD your God is giving you.

21Do not set up any wooden Asherah pole[x] beside the altar you build to the LORD your God, 22and do not erect a sacred stone, for these the LORD your God hates.

17 Do not sacrifice to the LORD your God an ox or a sheep that has any defect or flaw in it, for that would be detestable to him.

2If a man or woman living among you in one of the towns the LORD gives you is found doing evil in the eyes of the LORD your God in violation of his covenant, 3and contrary to my command has worshiped other gods, bowing down to them or to the sun or the moon or the stars of the sky, 4and this has been brought to your attention, then you must investigate it thoroughly. If it is true and it has been proved that this detestable thing has been done in Israel, 5take the man or woman who has done this evil deed to your city gate and stone that person to death. 6On the testimony of two or three witnesses a man shall be put to death, but no one shall be put to death on the testimony of only one witness. 7The hands of the witnesses must be the first in putting him to death, and then the hands of all the people. You must purge the evil from among you.

8If cases come before your courts that are too difficult for you to judge—whether bloodshed, lawsuits or assaults—take them to the place the LORD your God will choose. 9Go to the priests, who are Levites, and to the judge who is in office at that time. Inquire of them and they will give you the verdict. 10You must act according to the decisions they give you at the place the LORD will choose. Be careful to do everything they direct you to do. 11Act according to the law they teach you and the decisions they give you. Do not turn aside from what they tell you, to the right or to the left. 12The man who shows contempt for the judge or for the priest who stands ministering there to the LORD your God must be put to death. You must purge the evil from Israel. 13All the people will hear and be afraid, and will not be contemptuous again.

14When you enter the land the LORD your God is giving you and have taken possession of it and settled in it, and you say, "Let us set a king over us like all the nations around us," 15be sure to appoint over you the king the LORD your God chooses. He must be from among your own brothers. Do not place a foreigner over you, one who is not a brother Israelite. 16The king, moreover, must not acquire great numbers of horses for himself or make the people return to Egypt to get more of them, for the LORD has told you, "You are not to go back that way again." 17He must not take many wives, or his heart will be led astray. He must not accumulate large amounts of silver and gold.

18When he takes the throne of his kingdom, he is to write for himself on a scroll a copy of this law, taken from that of the priests, who are Levites. 19It is to be with him, and he is to read it all the days of his life so that he may learn to revere the LORD his God and follow carefully all the words of this law and these decrees 20and not consider himself better than his brothers and turn from the law to the right or to the left. Then he and his descendants will reign a long time over his kingdom in Israel.

18 The priests, who are Levites—indeed the whole tribe of Levi—are to have no allotment or inheritance with Israel. They shall live on the offerings made to the LORD by fire, for that is their inheritance. 2They shall have no inheritance among their brothers; the LORD is their inheritance, as he promised them.

3This is the share due the priests from the people who sacrifice a bull or a sheep: the shoulder, the jowls and the inner parts. 4You are to give them the firstfruits of your grain, new wine and oil, and the first wool from the shearing of your sheep, 5for the LORD your God has chosen them and their descendants out of all your tribes to stand and minister in the LORD's name always.

6If a Levite moves from one of your towns anywhere in Israel where he is living, and comes in all earnestness to the place the LORD will choose, 7he may minister in the name of the LORD his God like all his fellow Levites who serve there in the presence of the LORD. 8He is to share equally in their benefits, even though he has received money from the sale of family possessions.

9When you enter the land the LORD your God is giving you, do not learn to imitate the detestable ways of the nations there. 10Let no one be found among you who sacrifices his son or daughter

[x]21 Or *Do not plant any tree dedicated to Asherah*

in[y] the fire, who practices divination or sorcery, interprets omens, engages in witchcraft, 11or casts spells, or who is a medium or spiritist or who consults the dead. 12Anyone who does these things is detestable to the LORD, and because of these detestable practices the LORD your God will drive out those nations before you. 13You must be blameless before the LORD your God.

14The nations you will dispossess listen to those who practice sorcery or divination. But as for you, the LORD your God has not permitted you to do so. 15The LORD your God will raise up for you a prophet like me from among your own brothers. You must listen to him. 16For this is what you asked of the LORD your God at Horeb on the day of the assembly when you said, "Let us not hear the voice of the LORD our God nor see this great fire anymore, or we will die."

17The LORD said to me: "What they say is good. 18I will raise up for them a prophet like you from among their brothers; I will put my words in his mouth, and he will tell them everything I command him. 19If anyone does not listen to my words that the prophet speaks in my name, I myself will call him to account. 20But a prophet who presumes to speak in my name anything I have not commanded him to say, or a prophet who speaks in the name of other gods, must be put to death."

21You may say to yourselves, "How can we know when a message has not been spoken by the LORD?" 22If what a prophet proclaims in the name of the LORD does not take place or come true, that is a message the LORD has not spoken. That prophet has spoken presumptuously. Do not be afraid of him.

19 When the LORD your God has destroyed the nations whose land he is giving you, and when you have driven them out and settled in their towns and houses, 2then set aside for yourselves three cities centrally located in the land the LORD your God is giving you to possess. 3Build roads to them and divide into three parts the land the LORD your God is giving you as an inheritance, so that anyone who kills a man may flee there.

4This is the rule concerning the man who kills another and flees there to save his life—one who kills his neighbor unintentionally, without malice aforethought. 5For instance, a man may go into the forest with his neighbor to cut wood, and as he swings his ax to fell a tree, the head may fly off and hit his neighbor and kill him. That man may flee to one of these cities and save his life. 6Otherwise, the avenger of blood might pursue him in a rage, overtake him if the distance is too great, and kill him even though he is not deserving of death, since he did it to his neighbor without malice aforethought. 7This is why I command you to set aside for yourselves three cities.

8If the LORD your God enlarges your territory, as he promised on oath to your forefathers, and gives you the whole land he promised them, 9because you carefully follow all these laws I command you today—to love the LORD your God and to walk always in his ways—then you are to set aside three more cities. 10Do this so that innocent blood will not be shed in your land, which the LORD your God is giving you as your inheritance, and so that you will not be guilty of bloodshed.

11But if a man hates his neighbor and lies in wait for him, assaults him, and then flees to one of these cities, 12the elders of his town shall send for him, bring him back from the city, and hand him over to the avenger of blood to die. 13Show him no pity. You must purge from Israel the guilt of shedding innocent blood, so that it may go well with you.

14Do not move your neighbor's boundary stone set up by your predecessors in the inheritance you receive in the land the LORD your God is giving you to possess.

15One witness is not enough to convict a man accused of any crime or offense he may have committed. A matter must be established by the testimony of two or three witnesses.

16If a malicious witness takes the stand to accuse a man of a crime, 17the two men involved in the dispute must stand in the presence of the LORD before the priests and the judges who are in office at the time. 18The judges must make a thorough investigation, and if the witness proves to be a liar, giving false testimony against his brother, 19then do to him as he intended to do to his brother. You must purge the evil from among you. 20The rest of the people will hear of this and be afraid, and never again will such an evil thing be done among you. 21Show no pity: life for life, eye for eye, tooth for tooth, hand for hand, foot for foot.

y10 Or who makes his son or daughter pass through

20

When you go to war against your enemies and see horses and chariots and an army greater than yours, do not be afraid of them, because the LORD your God, who brought you up out of Egypt, will be with you. 2When you are about to go into battle, the priest shall come forward and address the army. 3He shall say: "Hear, O Israel, today you are going into battle against your enemies. Do not be fainthearted or afraid; do not be terrified or give way to panic before them. 4For the LORD your God is the one who goes with you to fight for you against your enemies to give you victory."

5The officers shall say to the army: "Has anyone built a new house and not dedicated it? Let him go home, or he may die in battle and someone else may dedicate it. 6Has anyone planted a vineyard and not begun to enjoy it? Let him go home, or he may die in battle and someone else enjoy it. 7Has anyone become pledged to a woman and not married her? Let him go home, or he may die in battle and someone else marry her." 8Then the officers shall add, "Is any man afraid or fainthearted? Let him go home so that his brothers will not become disheartened too." 9When the officers have finished speaking to the army, they shall appoint commanders over it.

10When you march up to attack a city, make its people an offer of peace. 11If they accept and open their gates, all the people in it shall be subject to forced labor and shall work for you. 12If they refuse to make peace and they engage you in battle, lay siege to that city. 13When the LORD your God delivers it into your hand, put to the sword all the men in it. 14As for the women, the children, the livestock and everything else in the city, you may take these as plunder for yourselves. And you may use the plunder the LORD your God gives you from your enemies. 15This is how you are to treat all the cities that are at a distance from you and do not belong to the nations nearby.

16However, in the cities of the nations the LORD your God is giving you as an inheritance, do not leave alive anything that breathes. 17Completely destroy[z] them—the Hittites, Amorites, Canaanites, Perizzites, Hivites and Jebusites—as the LORD your God has commanded you. 18Otherwise, they will teach you to follow all the detestable things they do in worshiping their gods, and you will sin against the LORD your God.

19When you lay siege to a city for a long time, fighting against it to capture it, do not destroy its trees by putting an ax to them, because you can eat their fruit. Do not cut them down. Are the trees of the field people, that you should besiege them?[a] 20However, you may cut down trees that you know are not fruit trees and use them to build siege works until the city at war with you falls.

21

If a man is found slain, lying in a field in the land the LORD your God is giving you to possess, and it is not known who killed him, 2your elders and judges shall go out and measure the distance from the body to the neighboring towns. 3Then the elders of the town nearest the body shall take a heifer that has never been worked and has never worn a yoke 4and lead her down to a valley that has not been plowed or planted and where there is a flowing stream. There in the valley they are to break the heifer's neck. 5The priests, the sons of Levi, shall step forward, for the LORD your God has chosen them to minister and to pronounce blessings in the name of the LORD and to decide all cases of dispute and assault. 6Then all the elders of the town nearest the body shall wash their hands over the heifer whose neck was broken in the valley, 7and they shall declare: "Our hands did not shed this blood, nor did our eyes see it done. 8Accept this atonement for your people Israel, whom you have redeemed, O LORD, and do not hold your people guilty of the blood of an innocent man." And the bloodshed will be atoned for. 9So you will purge from yourselves the guilt of shedding innocent blood, since you have done what is right in the eyes of the LORD.

10When you go to war against your enemies and the LORD your God delivers them into your hands and you take captives, 11if you notice among the captives a beautiful woman and are attracted to her, you may take her as your wife. 12Bring her into your home and have her shave her head, trim her nails 13and put aside the clothes she was wearing when captured. After she has lived in your house and mourned her father and mother for a full month, then you may go to her and be her husband and she shall be your wife. 14If you are not pleased with her, let her go wherever she wishes. You must not sell her or treat her as a slave, since you have dishonored her.

[z] 17 The Hebrew term refers to the irrevocable giving over of things or persons to the LORD, often by totally destroying them. [a] 19 Or *down to use in the siege, for the fruit trees are for the benefit of man.*

15If a man has two wives, and he loves one but not the other, and both bear him sons but the firstborn is the son of the wife he does not love, 16when he wills his property to his sons, he must not give the rights of the firstborn to the son of the wife he loves in preference to his actual firstborn, the son of the wife he does not love. 17He must acknowledge the son of his unloved wife as the firstborn by giving him a double share of all he has. That son is the first sign of his father's strength. The right of the firstborn belongs to him.

18If a man has a stubborn and rebellious son who does not obey his father and mother and will not listen to them when they discipline him, 19his father and mother shall take hold of him and bring him to the elders at the gate of his town. 20They shall say to the elders, "This son of ours is stubborn and rebellious. He will not obey us. He is a profligate and a drunkard." 21Then all the men of his town shall stone him to death. You must purge the evil from among you. All Israel will hear of it and be afraid.

22If a man guilty of a capital offense is put to death and his body is hung on a tree, 23you must not leave his body on the tree overnight. Be sure to bury him that same day, because anyone who is hung on a tree is under God's curse. You must not desecrate the land the LORD your God is giving you as an inheritance.

22

If you see your brother's ox or sheep straying, do not ignore it but be sure to take it back to him. 2If the brother does not live near you or if you do not know who he is, take it home with you and keep it until he comes looking for it. Then give it back to him. 3Do the same if you find your brother's donkey or his cloak or anything he loses. Do not ignore it.

4If you see your brother's donkey or his ox fallen on the road, do not ignore it. Help him get it to its feet.

5A woman must not wear men's clothing, nor a man wear women's clothing, for the LORD your God detests anyone who does this.

6If you come across a bird's nest beside the road, either in a tree or on the ground, and the mother is sitting on the young or on the eggs, do not take the mother with the young. 7You may take the young, but be sure to let the mother go, so that it may go well with you and you may have a long life.

8When you build a new house, make a parapet around your roof so that you may not bring the guilt of bloodshed on your house if someone falls from the roof.

9Do not plant two kinds of seed in your vineyard; if you do, not only the crops you plant but also the fruit of the vineyard will be defiled.[b]

10Do not plow with an ox and a donkey yoked together.

11Do not wear clothes of wool and linen woven together.

12Make tassels on the four corners of the cloak you wear.

13If a man takes a wife and, after lying with her, dislikes her 14and slanders her and gives her a bad name, saying, "I married this woman, but when I approached her, I did not find proof of her virginity," 15then the girl's father and mother shall bring proof that she was a virgin to the town elders at the gate. 16The girl's father will say to the elders, "I gave my daughter in marriage to this man, but he dislikes her. 17Now he has slandered her and said, 'I did not find your daughter to be a virgin.' But here is the proof of my daughter's virginity." Then her parents shall display the cloth before the elders of the town, 18and the elders shall take the man and punish him. 19They shall fine him a hundred shekels of silver[c] and give them to the girl's father, because this man has given an Israelite virgin a bad name. She shall continue to be his wife; he must not divorce her as long as he lives.

20If, however, the charge is true and no proof of the girl's virginity can be found, 21she shall be brought to the door of her father's house and there the men of her town shall stone her to death. She has done a disgraceful thing in Israel by being promiscuous while still in her father's house. You must purge the evil from among you.

22If a man is found sleeping with another man's wife, both the man who slept with her and the woman must die. You must purge the evil from Israel.

23If a man happens to meet in a town a virgin pledged to be married and he sleeps with her, 24you shall take both of them to the gate of that town and stone them to death—the girl because she was in a town and did not scream for help, and the man because he violated another man's wife. You must purge the evil from among you.

[b] *9* Or *be forfeited to the sanctuary*
[c] *19* That is, about 2 1/2 pounds (about 1 kilogram)

25But if out in the country a man happens to meet a girl pledged to be married and rapes her, only the man who has done this shall die. 26Do nothing to the girl; she has committed no sin deserving death. This case is like that of someone who attacks and murders his neighbor, 27for the man found the girl out in the country, and though the betrothed girl screamed, there was no one to rescue her.

28If a man happens to meet a virgin who is not pledged to be married and rapes her and they are discovered, 29he shall pay the girl's father fifty shekels of silver.[d] He must marry the girl, for he has violated her. He can never divorce her as long as he lives.

30A man is not to marry his father's wife; he must not dishonor his father's bed.

23 No one who has been emasculated by crushing or cutting may enter the assembly of the LORD.

2No one born of a forbidden marriage[e] nor any of his descendants may enter the assembly of the LORD, even down to the tenth generation.

3No Ammonite or Moabite or any of his descendants may enter the assembly of the LORD, even down to the tenth generation. 4For they did not come to meet you with bread and water on your way when you came out of Egypt, and they hired Balaam son of Beor from Pethor in Aram Naharaim[f] to pronounce a curse on you. 5However, the LORD your God would not listen to Balaam but turned the curse into a blessing for you, because the LORD your God loves you. 6Do not seek a treaty of friendship with them as long as you live.

7Do not abhor an Edomite, for he is your brother. Do not abhor an Egyptian, because you lived as an alien in his country. 8The third generation of children born to them may enter the assembly of the LORD.

9When you are encamped against your enemies, keep away from everything impure. 10If one of your men is unclean because of a nocturnal emission, he is to go outside the camp and stay there. 11But as evening approaches he is to wash himself, and at sunset he may return to the camp.

12Designate a place outside the camp where you can go to relieve yourself. 13As part of your equipment have something to dig with, and when you relieve yourself, dig a hole and cover up your excrement. 14For the LORD your God moves about in your camp to protect you and to deliver your enemies to you. Your camp must be holy, so that he will not see among you anything indecent and turn away from you.

[d]29 That is, about 1 1/4 pounds (about 0.6 kilogram) [e]2 Or *one of illegitimate birth* [f]4 That is, Northwest Mesopotamia

10 / *Deuteronomy 23:15-25*
The Laws of Freedom

ONE CHARACTERISTIC OF a good insurance policy is the details. Every contingency is covered—no possibilities are left open. The verses you read in this section of Scripture fit into the category of the insurance policy. They are a collection of miscellaneous laws that don't appear to be intrinsically related to each other, but they are worth considering, as are other difficult passages. What you will discover is that God's wise care for the freedom of his people extends to the smallest details of personal conduct and community concerns.

Warming Up to God God reveals himself to us in the details of our daily experiences. Think back over your activities for the past several days. Consider how God might have been caring, guiding and instructing you through all that you've experienced.

Read Deuteronomy 23:15-25.

15If a slave has taken refuge with you, do not hand him over to his master. 16Let him live among you wherever he likes and in whatever town he chooses. Do not oppress him.

17No Israelite man or woman is to become a shrine prostitute. 18You must not bring the earn-

ings of a female prostitute or of a male prosti-
tute[g] into the house of the LORD your God to pay
any vow, because the LORD your God detests them
both.
19Do not charge your brother interest, whether
on money or food or anything else that may earn
interest. 20You may charge a foreigner interest,
but not a brother Israelite, so that the LORD
your God may bless you in everything you
put your hand to in the land you are entering to
possess.
21If you make a vow to the LORD your God, do
not be slow to pay it, for the LORD your God will
certainly demand it of you and you will be guilty
of sin. 22But if you refrain from making a vow,
you will not be guilty. 23Whatever your lips utter
you must be sure to do, because you made your
vow freely to the LORD your God with your own
mouth.
24If you enter your neighbor's vineyard, you
may eat all the grapes you want, but do not put
any in your basket. 25If you enter your neighbor's
grainfield, you may pick kernels with your hands,
but you must not put a sickle to his standing
grain.

[g]18 Hebrew *of a dog*

Discovering the Word 1. What different community problems are addressed in these verses? 2. In what different ways do these laws protect the Israelites and encourage them to live as a community of freed people? 3. What abuses of worship are addressed in verses 17–18 and 21–23? 4. What do these provisions tell you about how worship is to be approached? 5. What potential problems in a farming community do verses 24–25 address?

Applying the Word 1. God's law is meant to maintain the freedom he gave Israel when he rescued them from slavery in Egypt. How can this insight affect the way you read both the Old and New Testament? 2. The law about shrine prostitution addresses the issue of acceptable offerings. What do you think God expects from you when you make a pledge or an offering at your church? 3. Look at verses 19–20. The laws in Deuteronomy were given for an agricultural society. What principles regarding the use of money might we draw from these verses for a capitalist society that is built on the principle of lending and interest?

Responding in Prayer Thank God for the freedom his law brings. Pray that God will make you wise and honest in the use of the financial resources he has given to you.

Deuteronomy 24—29

24 If a man marries a woman who be-
comes displeasing to him because
he finds something indecent about
her, and he writes her a certificate of divorce,
gives it to her and sends her from his house, 2and
if after she leaves his house she becomes the wife
of another man, 3and her second husband dislikes
her and writes her a certificate of divorce, gives it
to her and sends her from his house, or if he dies,
4then her first husband, who divorced her, is not
allowed to marry her again after she has been
defiled. That would be detestable in the eyes of
the LORD. Do not bring sin upon the land the LORD
your God is giving you as an inheritance.
5If a man has recently married, he must not be
sent to war or have any other duty laid on him.
For one year he is to be free to stay at home and
bring happiness to the wife he has married.
6Do not take a pair of millstones—not even the
upper one—as security for a debt, because that
would be taking a man's livelihood as security.
7If a man is caught kidnapping one of his
brother Israelites and treats him as a slave or sells
him, the kidnapper must die. You must purge the
evil from among you.
8In cases of leprous[h] diseases be very careful
to do exactly as the priests, who are Levites, in-
struct you. You must follow carefully what I have
commanded them. 9Remember what the LORD
your God did to Miriam along the way after you
came out of Egypt.
10When you make a loan of any kind to your
neighbor, do not go into his house to get what he
is offering as a pledge. 11Stay outside and let the

[h]8 The Hebrew word was used for various diseases affecting the skin—not necessarily leprosy.

man to whom you are making the loan bring the pledge out to you. 12If the man is poor, do not go to sleep with his pledge in your possession. 13Return his cloak to him by sunset so that he may sleep in it. Then he will thank you, and it will be regarded as a righteous act in the sight of the LORD your God.

14Do not take advantage of a hired man who is poor and needy, whether he is a brother Israelite or an alien living in one of your towns. 15Pay him his wages each day before sunset, because he is poor and is counting on it. Otherwise he may cry to the LORD against you, and you will be guilty of sin.

16Fathers shall not be put to death for their children, nor children put to death for their fathers; each is to die for his own sin.

17Do not deprive the alien or the fatherless of justice, or take the cloak of the widow as a pledge. 18Remember that you were slaves in Egypt and the LORD your God redeemed you from there. That is why I command you to do this.

19When you are harvesting in your field and you overlook a sheaf, do not go back to get it. Leave it for the alien, the fatherless and the widow, so that the LORD your God may bless you in all the work of your hands. 20When you beat the olives from your trees, do not go over the branches a second time. Leave what remains for the alien, the fatherless and the widow. 21When you harvest the grapes in your vineyard, do not go over the vines again. Leave what remains for the alien, the fatherless and the widow. 22Remember that you were slaves in Egypt. That is why I command you to do this.

25 When men have a dispute, they are to take it to court and the judges will decide the case, acquitting the innocent and condemning the guilty. 2If the guilty man deserves to be beaten, the judge shall make him lie down and have him flogged in his presence with the number of lashes his crime deserves, 3but he must not give him more than forty lashes. If he is flogged more than that, your brother will be degraded in your eyes.

4Do not muzzle an ox while it is treading out the grain.

5If brothers are living together and one of them dies without a son, his widow must not marry outside the family. Her husband's brother shall take her and marry her and fulfill the duty of a brother-in-law to her. 6The first son she bears shall carry on the name of the dead brother so that his name will not be blotted out from Israel.

7However, if a man does not want to marry his brother's wife, she shall go to the elders at the town gate and say, "My husband's brother refuses to carry on his brother's name in Israel. He will not fulfill the duty of a brother-in-law to me." 8Then the elders of his town shall summon him and talk to him. If he persists in saying, "I do not want to marry her," 9his brother's widow shall go up to him in the presence of the elders, take off one of his sandals, spit in his face and say, "This is what is done to the man who will not build up his brother's family line." 10That man's line shall be known in Israel as The Family of the Unsandaled.

11If two men are fighting and the wife of one of them comes to rescue her husband from his assailant, and she reaches out and seizes him by his private parts, 12you shall cut off her hand. Show her no pity.

13Do not have two differing weights in your bag—one heavy, one light. 14Do not have two differing measures in your house—one large, one small. 15You must have accurate and honest weights and measures, so that you may live long in the land the LORD your God is giving you. 16For the LORD your God detests anyone who does these things, anyone who deals dishonestly.

17Remember what the Amalekites did to you along the way when you came out of Egypt. 18When you were weary and worn out, they met you on your journey and cut off all who were lagging behind; they had no fear of God. 19When the LORD your God gives you rest from all the enemies around you in the land he is giving you to possess as an inheritance, you shall blot out the memory of Amalek from under heaven. Do not forget!

26 When you have entered the land the LORD your God is giving you as an inheritance and have taken possession of it and settled in it, 2take some of the firstfruits of all that you produce from the soil of the land the LORD your God is giving you and put them in a basket. Then go to the place the LORD your God will choose as a dwelling for his Name 3and say to the priest in office at the time, "I declare today to the LORD your God that I have come to the land the LORD swore to our forefathers to give us." 4The priest shall take the basket from your hands and set it down in front of the

altar of the LORD your God. 5 Then you shall de-
clare before the LORD your God: "My father was
a wandering Aramean, and he went down into
Egypt with a few people and lived there and be-
came a great nation, powerful and numerous.
6 But the Egyptians mistreated us and made us
suffer, putting us to hard labor. 7 Then we cried
out to the LORD, the God of our fathers, and the
LORD heard our voice and saw our misery, toil and
oppression. 8 So the LORD brought us out of Egypt
with a mighty hand and an outstretched arm,
with great terror and with miraculous signs and
wonders. 9 He brought us to this place and gave us
this land, a land flowing with milk and honey;
10 and now I bring the firstfruits of the soil that
you, O LORD, have given me." Place the basket
before the LORD your God and bow down before
him. 11 And you and the Levites and the aliens
among you shall rejoice in all the good things the
LORD your God has given to you and your house-
hold.

12 When you have finished setting aside a tenth
of all your produce in the third year, the year of
the tithe, you shall give it to the Levite, the alien,
the fatherless and the widow, so that they may eat
in your towns and be satisfied. 13 Then say to the
LORD your God: "I have removed from my house
the sacred portion and have given it to the Levite,
the alien, the fatherless and the widow, according
to all you commanded. I have not turned aside
from your commands nor have I forgotten any of
them. 14 I have not eaten any of the sacred portion
while I was in mourning, nor have I removed any
of it while I was unclean, nor have I offered any
of it to the dead. I have obeyed the LORD my God;
I have done everything you commanded me.
15 Look down from heaven, your holy dwelling
place, and bless your people Israel and the land
you have given us as you promised on oath to our
forefathers, a land flowing with milk and honey."

16 The LORD your God commands you this day
to follow these decrees and laws; carefully ob-
serve them with all your heart and with all your
soul. 17 You have declared this day that the LORD is
your God and that you will walk in his ways, that
you will keep his decrees, commands and laws,
and that you will obey him. 18 And the LORD has
declared this day that you are his people, his trea-
sured possession as he promised, and that you are
to keep all his commands. 19 He has declared that
he will set you in praise, fame and honor high
above all the nations he has made and that you
will be a people holy to the LORD your God, as he
promised.

27 Moses and the elders of Israel com-
manded the people: "Keep all these
commands that I give you today.
2 When you have crossed the Jordan into the land
the LORD your God is giving you, set up some
large stones and coat them with plaster. 3 Write on
them all the words of this law when you have
crossed over to enter the land the LORD your God
is giving you, a land flowing with milk and
honey, just as the LORD, the God of your fathers,
promised you. 4 And when you have crossed the
Jordan, set up these stones on Mount Ebal, as I
command you today, and coat them with plaster.
5 Build there an altar to the LORD your God, an
altar of stones. Do not use any iron tool upon
them. 6 Build the altar of the LORD your God with
fieldstones and offer burnt offerings on it to the
LORD your God. 7 Sacrifice fellowship offerings[i]
there, eating them and rejoicing in the presence
of the LORD your God. 8 And you shall write very
clearly all the words of this law on these stones
you have set up."

9 Then Moses and the priests, who are Levites,
said to all Israel, "Be silent, O Israel, and listen!
You have now become the people of the LORD
your God. 10 Obey the LORD your God and follow
his commands and decrees that I give you today."

11 On the same day Moses commanded the peo-
ple:

12 When you have crossed the Jordan, these
tribes shall stand on Mount Gerizim to bless the
people: Simeon, Levi, Judah, Issachar, Joseph and
Benjamin. 13 And these tribes shall stand on
Mount Ebal to pronounce curses: Reuben, Gad,
Asher, Zebulun, Dan and Naphtali.

14 The Levites shall recite to all the people of
Israel in a loud voice:

15 "Cursed is the man who carves an image
or casts an idol—a thing detestable to the
LORD, the work of the craftsman's hands—
and sets it up in secret."

Then all the people shall say, "Amen!"

16 "Cursed is the man who dishonors his
father or his mother."

Then all the people shall say, "Amen!"

17 "Cursed is the man who moves his
neighbor's boundary stone."

Then all the people shall say, "Amen!"

i7 Traditionally *peace offerings*

[18]"Cursed is the man who leads the blind astray on the road."

Then all the people shall say, "Amen!"

[19]"Cursed is the man who withholds justice from the alien, the fatherless or the widow."

Then all the people shall say, "Amen!"

[20]"Cursed is the man who sleeps with his father's wife, for he dishonors his father's bed."

Then all the people shall say, "Amen!"

[21]"Cursed is the man who has sexual relations with any animal."

Then all the people shall say, "Amen!"

[22]"Cursed is the man who sleeps with his sister, the daughter of his father or the daughter of his mother."

Then all the people shall say, "Amen!"

[23]"Cursed is the man who sleeps with his mother-in-law."

Then all the people shall say, "Amen!"

[24]"Cursed is the man who kills his neighbor secretly."

Then all the people shall say, "Amen!"

[25]"Cursed is the man who accepts a bribe to kill an innocent person."

Then all the people shall say, "Amen!"

[26]"Cursed is the man who does not uphold the words of this law by carrying them out."

Then all the people shall say, "Amen!"

28

If you fully obey the LORD your God and carefully follow all his commands I give you today, the LORD your God will set you high above all the nations on earth. [2]All these blessings will come upon you and accompany you if you obey the LORD your God:

[3]You will be blessed in the city and blessed
in the country.

[4]The fruit of your womb will be blessed,
and the crops of your land and the young of your livestock—the calves of your herds and the lambs of your flocks.

[5]Your basket and your kneading trough
will be blessed.

[6]You will be blessed when you come in
and blessed when you go out.

[7]The LORD will grant that the enemies who rise up against you will be defeated before you. They will come at you from one direction but flee from you in seven.

[8]The LORD will send a blessing on your barns and on everything you put your hand to. The LORD your God will bless you in the land he is giving you.

[9]The LORD will establish you as his holy people, as he promised you on oath, if you keep the commands of the LORD your God and walk in his ways. [10]Then all the peoples on earth will see that you are called by the name of the LORD, and they will fear you. [11]The LORD will grant you abundant prosperity—in the fruit of your womb, the young of your livestock and the crops of your ground—in the land he swore to your forefathers to give you.

[12]The LORD will open the heavens, the storehouse of his bounty, to send rain on your land in season and to bless all the work of your hands. You will lend to many nations but will borrow from none. [13]The LORD will make you the head, not the tail. If you pay attention to the commands of the LORD your God that I give you this day and carefully follow them, you will always be at the top, never at the bottom. [14]Do not turn aside from any of the commands I give you today, to the right or to the left, following other gods and serving them.

[15]However, if you do not obey the LORD your God and do not carefully follow all his commands and decrees I am giving you today, all these curses will come upon you and overtake you:

[16]You will be cursed in the city and cursed
in the country.

[17]Your basket and your kneading trough
will be cursed.

[18]The fruit of your womb will be cursed,
and the crops of your land, and the calves of your herds and the lambs of your flocks.

[19]You will be cursed when you come in
and cursed when you go out.

[20]The LORD will send on you curses, confusion and rebuke in everything you put your hand to, until you are destroyed and come to sudden ruin because of the evil you have done in forsaking him.[j] [21]The LORD will plague you with diseases until he has destroyed you from the land you are entering to possess. [22]The LORD will strike you with wasting disease, with fever and inflamma-

[j]20 Hebrew *me*

tion, with scorching heat and drought, with blight and mildew, which will plague you until you perish. 23The sky over your head will be bronze, the ground beneath you iron. 24The LORD will turn the rain of your country into dust and powder; it will come down from the skies until you are destroyed.

25The LORD will cause you to be defeated before your enemies. You will come at them from one direction but flee from them in seven, and you will become a thing of horror to all the kingdoms on earth. 26Your carcasses will be food for all the birds of the air and the beasts of the earth, and there will be no one to frighten them away. 27The LORD will afflict you with the boils of Egypt and with tumors, festering sores and the itch, from which you cannot be cured. 28The LORD will afflict you with madness, blindness and confusion of mind. 29At midday you will grope about like a blind man in the dark. You will be unsuccessful in everything you do; day after day you will be oppressed and robbed, with no one to rescue you.

30You will be pledged to be married to a woman, but another will take her and ravish her. You will build a house, but you will not live in it. You will plant a vineyard, but you will not even begin to enjoy its fruit. 31Your ox will be slaughtered before your eyes, but you will eat none of it. Your donkey will be forcibly taken from you and will not be returned. Your sheep will be given to your enemies, and no one will rescue them. 32Your sons and daughters will be given to another nation, and you will wear out your eyes watching for them day after day, powerless to lift a hand. 33A people that you do not know will eat what your land and labor produce, and you will have nothing but cruel oppression all your days. 34The sights you see will drive you mad. 35The LORD will afflict your knees and legs with painful boils that cannot be cured, spreading from the soles of your feet to the top of your head.

36The LORD will drive you and the king you set over you to a nation unknown to you or your fathers. There you will worship other gods, gods of wood and stone. 37You will become a thing of horror and an object of scorn and ridicule to all the nations where the LORD will drive you.

38You will sow much seed in the field but you will harvest little, because locusts will devour it. 39You will plant vineyards and cultivate them but you will not drink the wine or gather the grapes, because worms will eat them. 40You will have olive trees throughout your country but you will not use the oil, because the olives will drop off. 41You will have sons and daughters but you will not keep them, because they will go into captivity. 42Swarms of locusts will take over all your trees and the crops of your land.

43The alien who lives among you will rise above you higher and higher, but you will sink lower and lower. 44He will lend to you, but you will not lend to him. He will be the head, but you will be the tail.

45All these curses will come upon you. They will pursue you and overtake you until you are destroyed, because you did not obey the LORD your God and observe the commands and decrees he gave you. 46They will be a sign and a wonder to you and your descendants forever. 47Because you did not serve the LORD your God joyfully and gladly in the time of prosperity, 48therefore in hunger and thirst, in nakedness and dire poverty, you will serve the enemies the LORD sends against you. He will put an iron yoke on your neck until he has destroyed you.

49The LORD will bring a nation against you from far away, from the ends of the earth, like an eagle swooping down, a nation whose language you will not understand, 50a fierce-looking nation without respect for the old or pity for the young. 51They will devour the young of your livestock and the crops of your land until you are destroyed. They will leave you no grain, new wine or oil, nor any calves of your herds or lambs of your flocks until you are ruined. 52They will lay siege to all the cities throughout your land until the high fortified walls in which you trust fall down. They will besiege all the cities throughout the land the LORD your God is giving you.

53Because of the suffering that your enemy will inflict on you during the siege, you will eat the fruit of the womb, the flesh of the sons and daughters the LORD your God has given you. 54Even the most gentle and sensitive man among you will have no compassion on his own brother or the wife he loves or his surviving children, 55and he will not give to one of them any of the flesh of his children that he is eating. It will be all he has left because of the suffering your enemy will inflict on you during the siege of all your cities. 56The most gentle and sensitive woman among you—so sensitive and gentle that she would not venture to touch the ground with the sole of her foot—will begrudge the husband she

loves and her own son or daughter 57the after-
birth from her womb and the children she bears.
For she intends to eat them secretly during the
siege and in the distress that your enemy will
inflict on you in your cities.

58If you do not carefully follow all the words of
this law, which are written in this book, and do
not revere this glorious and awesome name—the
LORD your God— 59the LORD will send fearful
plagues on you and your descendants, harsh and
prolonged disasters, and severe and lingering ill-
nesses. 60He will bring upon you all the diseases
of Egypt that you dreaded, and they will cling to
you. 61The LORD will also bring on you every kind
of sickness and disaster not recorded in this Book
of the Law, until you are destroyed. 62You who
were as numerous as the stars in the sky will be
left but few in number, because you did not obey
the LORD your God. 63Just as it pleased the LORD to
make you prosper and increase in number, so it
will please him to ruin and destroy you. You will
be uprooted from the land you are entering to
possess.

64Then the LORD will scatter you among all na-
tions, from one end of the earth to the other.
There you will worship other gods—gods of
wood and stone, which neither you nor your fa-
thers have known. 65Among those nations you
will find no repose, no resting place for the sole of
your foot. There the LORD will give you an anx-
ious mind, eyes weary with longing, and a de-
spairing heart. 66You will live in constant sus-
pense, filled with dread both night and day, never
sure of your life. 67In the morning you will say,
"If only it were evening!" and in the evening, "If
only it were morning!"—because of the terror
that will fill your hearts and the sights that your
eyes will see. 68The LORD will send you back in
ships to Egypt on a journey I said you should
never make again. There you will offer yourselves
for sale to your enemies as male and female
slaves, but no one will buy you.

29

These are the terms of the covenant
the LORD commanded Moses to
make with the Israelites in Moab,
in addition to the covenant he had made with
them at Horeb.

2Moses summoned all the Israelites and said to
them:

Your eyes have seen all that the LORD did in
Egypt to Pharaoh, to all his officials and to all his
land. 3With your own eyes you saw those great
trials, those miraculous signs and great wonders.
4But to this day the LORD has not given you a
mind that understands or eyes that see or ears
that hear. 5During the forty years that I led you
through the desert, your clothes did not wear out,
nor did the sandals on your feet. 6You ate no
bread and drank no wine or other fermented
drink. I did this so that you might know that I am
the LORD your God.

7When you reached this place, Sihon king of
Heshbon and Og king of Bashan came out to fight
against us, but we defeated them. 8We took their
land and gave it as an inheritance to the Reuben-
ites, the Gadites and the half-tribe of Manasseh.

9Carefully follow the terms of this covenant, so
that you may prosper in everything you do. 10All
of you are standing today in the presence of the
LORD your God—your leaders and chief men,
your elders and officials, and all the other men of
Israel, 11together with your children and your
wives, and the aliens living in your camps who
chop your wood and carry your water. 12You are
standing here in order to enter into a covenant
with the LORD your God, a covenant the LORD is
making with you this day and sealing with an
oath, 13to confirm you this day as his people, that
he may be your God as he promised you and as
he swore to your fathers, Abraham, Isaac and Ja-
cob. 14I am making this covenant, with its oath,
not only with you 15who are standing here with
us today in the presence of the LORD our God but
also with those who are not here today.

16You yourselves know how we lived in Egypt
and how we passed through the countries on the
way here. 17You saw among them their detestable
images and idols of wood and stone, of silver and
gold. 18Make sure there is no man or woman, clan
or tribe among you today whose heart turns away
from the LORD our God to go and worship the
gods of those nations; make sure there is no root
among you that produces such bitter poison.

19When such a person hears the words of this
oath, he invokes a blessing on himself and there-
fore thinks, "I will be safe, even though I persist
in going my own way." This will bring disaster on
the watered land as well as the dry.[k] 20The LORD
will never be willing to forgive him; his wrath and
zeal will burn against that man. All the curses
written in this book will fall upon him, and the

[k]19 *Or way, in order to add drunkenness to thirst."*

LORD will blot out his name from under heaven. 21The LORD will single him out from all the tribes of Israel for disaster, according to all the curses of the covenant written in this Book of the Law.

22Your children who follow you in later generations and foreigners who come from distant lands will see the calamities that have fallen on the land and the diseases with which the LORD has afflicted it. 23The whole land will be a burning waste of salt and sulfur—nothing planted, nothing sprouting, no vegetation growing on it. It will be like the destruction of Sodom and Gomorrah, Admah and Zeboiim, which the LORD overthrew in fierce anger. 24All the nations will ask: "Why has the LORD done this to this land? Why this fierce, burning anger?"

25And the answer will be: "It is because this people abandoned the covenant of the LORD, the God of their fathers, the covenant he made with them when he brought them out of Egypt. 26They went off and worshiped other gods and bowed down to them, gods they did not know, gods he had not given them. 27Therefore the LORD's anger burned against this land, so that he brought on it all the curses written in this book. 28In furious anger and in great wrath the LORD uprooted them from their land and thrust them into another land, as it is now."

29The secret things belong to the LORD our God, but the things revealed belong to us and to our children forever, that we may follow all the words of this law.

11 / *Deuteronomy 30*
A Scattered Future

THE HISTORY OF Israel for the past three thousand years has been a turbulent one. They have experienced numerous invasions and massive deportation and persecution. I find it amazing that they were able to maintain their sense of national identity for nearly two thousand years without sovereign control of their homeland. The hand of God has been at work. Moses foretold the dispersion even before they set foot in the land. As he is giving his final words, he tells the people that they will not stay faithful to the covenant. And he wants Israel to know in no uncertain terms that they will be severely disciplined for future unfaithfulness. However, threat of judgment is not the last word. As Moses looks into the future, he gives Israel hope on the other side of judgment.

Warming Up to God In the Ten Commandments God describes himself as a jealous God. What are some of the painful and positive consequences of worshiping a God who cares whether you love him or ignore him?

Read Deuteronomy 30.

30 When all these blessings and curses I have set before you come upon you and you take them to heart wherever the LORD your God disperses you among the nations, 2and when you and your children return to the LORD your God and obey him with all your heart and with all your soul according to everything I command you today, 3then the LORD your God will restore your fortunes[1] and have compassion on you and gather you again from all the nations where he scattered you. 4Even if you have been banished to the most distant land under the heavens, from there the LORD your God will gather you and bring you back. 5He will bring you to the land that belonged to your fathers, and you will take possession of it. He will make you more prosperous and numerous than your fathers. 6The LORD your God will circumcise your hearts and the hearts of your descendants, so that you may love him with all your heart and with all your soul, and live. 7The LORD your God will put all these curses on your enemies who hate and persecute you. 8You will again obey the LORD and follow all his commands I am giving you today. 9Then the LORD your God will make you most prosperous in all the work of your hands and in the fruit of your womb, the young of your livestock and the crops of your land. The LORD will

[1]3 Or *will bring you back from captivity*

again delight in you and make you prosperous,
just as he delighted in your fathers, [10]if you obey
the LORD your God and keep his commands and
decrees that are written in this Book of the Law
and turn to the LORD your God with all your heart
and with all your soul.
[11]Now what I am commanding you today is not
too difficult for you or beyond your reach. [12]It is
not up in heaven, so that you have to ask, "Who
will ascend into heaven to get it and proclaim it
to us so we may obey it?" [13]Nor is it beyond the
sea, so that you have to ask, "Who will cross the
sea to get it and proclaim it to us so we may obey
it?" [14]No, the word is very near you; it is in
your mouth and in your heart so you may obey
it.
[15]See, I set before you today life and prosperity,
death and destruction. [16]For I command you to-
day to love the LORD your God, to walk in his
ways, and to keep his commands, decrees and
laws; then you will live and increase, and the LORD
your God will bless you in the land you are enter-
ing to possess.
[17]But if your heart turns away and you are not
obedient, and if you are drawn away to bow down
to other gods and worship them, [18]I declare to
you this day that you will certainly be destroyed.
You will not live long in the land you are crossing
the Jordan to enter and possess.
[19]This day I call heaven and earth as witnesses
against you that I have set before you life and
death, blessings and curses. Now choose life, so
that you and your children may live [20]and that
you may love the LORD your God, listen to his
voice, and hold fast to him. For the LORD is your
life, and he will give you many years in the land
he swore to give to your fathers, Abraham, Isaac
and Jacob.

Discovering the Word 1. What is going to happen to Israel in the future? 2. How is the Lord's justice and mercy embodied in these verses? 3. How might an Israelite who had yet to enter the land respond to the warnings here? 4. Compare and contrast the choice between life and death (vv. 11–20). What is involved in each? 5. Read the passage again. What issues of the heart are woven throughout? 6. How are these verses a summary of the entire book?

Applying the Word 1. The curses and the blessings for obedience were aimed at cultivating a community of people with spiritually responsive hearts. How would you characterize the spiritual responsiveness of your own heart? 2. In what area of your life do you need the reassurance of verses 11–14, that you are able to follow God's commands?

Responding in Prayer Thank God for his love that won't let you live in disobedience. Pray that God will give you a heart that is open to learning from his loving discipline.

12 / *Deuteronomy 31:1–13*
Saying Goodby

"DO YOU HAVE your notebook? How about your lunch? What about your coat? Don't forget the permission slip I signed for you last night." These are the questions a parent asks as a child leaves for school. So it is with Moses as he prepares Israel for their entrance into the Promised Land without him. How hard it must have been to turn over the reins of leadership and step out of the way! And how must the people have felt? Moses was the only leader they had ever known. He knew God, he knew the law, and he always seemed to know what to do. No doubt about it, the parting, for all, was difficult. However, both Moses and the nation needed to understand that the nation had made a covenant with God, not with Moses. They needed to grasp that God was their Savior, not Moses. If Moses had continued, it wouldn't have been good for the nation, nor would it have been good for Moses himself.

Warming Up to God We must look beyond our spiritual leaders to the God they serve. Think of someone who has been a spiritual influence in your life. Consider how they have been a means of pointing to the presence and character of God. Thank God for that person and for his grace in working through him or her.

Read Deuteronomy 31:1–13.

31 Then Moses went out and spoke these words to all Israel: 2"I am now a hundred and twenty years old and I am no longer able to lead you. The LORD has said to me, 'You shall not cross the Jordan.' 3The LORD your God himself will cross over ahead of you. He will destroy these nations before you, and you will take possession of their land. Joshua also will cross over ahead of you, as the LORD said. 4And the LORD will do to them what he did to Sihon and Og, the kings of the Amorites, whom he destroyed along with their land. 5The LORD will deliver them to you, and you must do to them all that I have commanded you. 6Be strong and courageous. Do not be afraid or terrified because of them, for the LORD your God goes with you; he will never leave you nor forsake you."

7Then Moses summoned Joshua and said to him in the presence of all Israel, "Be strong and courageous, for you must go with this people into the land that the LORD swore to their forefathers to give them, and you must divide it among them as their inheritance. 8The LORD himself goes before you and will be with you; he will never leave you nor forsake you. Do not be afraid; do not be discouraged."

9So Moses wrote down this law and gave it to the priests, the sons of Levi, who carried the ark of the covenant of the LORD, and to all the elders of Israel. 10Then Moses commanded them: "At the end of every seven years, in the year for canceling debts, during the Feast of Tabernacles, 11when all Israel comes to appear before the LORD your God at the place he will choose, you shall read this law before them in their hearing. 12Assemble the people—men, women and children, and the aliens living in your towns—so they can listen and learn to fear the LORD your God and follow carefully all the words of this law. 13Their children, who do not know this law, must hear it and learn to fear the LORD your God as long as you live in the land you are crossing the Jordan to possess."

Discovering the Word 1. How would you characterize the tone of these goodby words from Moses? 2. What is the Lord's part and what is Israel's part in taking the land (vv. 3–6)? 3. How would you describe Joshua's commission from Moses (vv. 7–8)? 4. What provision is made for keeping the law a central part of the nation's life (vv. 9–13)? 5. Look through the whole chapter again. In what specific ways does Moses assure the people that the presence of God will be a help to them?

Applying the Word 1. Moses reminds the people of what God has done as they prepare to enter the land. How does the knowledge of what God did for Israel help you to trust him for the challenges you face? 2. The presence of God was to provide a sense of confidence and courage in the time of leadership transition. How can the presence of God provide confidence and courage as you face your tasks and transitions? 3. The presence of God does not take away the need to "be strong and courageous." In what areas do you need to exercise strength and courage?

Responding in Prayer Pray that the leaders of your church would find their strength and courage in the presence of God. Ask that God would give you a love for his law that will keep you stable and faithful throughout the duration of your Christian pilgrimage.

Deuteronomy 31:14—34:12

14The LORD said to Moses, "Now the day of your death is near. Call Joshua and present yourselves at the Tent of Meeting, where I will commission him." So Moses and Joshua came and presented themselves at the Tent of Meeting.

15Then the LORD appeared at the Tent in a pillar of cloud, and the cloud stood over the entrance to the Tent. 16And the LORD said to Moses: "You are going to rest with your fathers, and these people will soon prostitute themselves to the foreign gods of the land they are entering. They will forsake me and break the covenant I made with them. 17On that day I will become angry with them and forsake them; I will hide my face from them, and they will be destroyed. Many disasters and difficulties will come upon them, and on that day they will ask, 'Have not these disasters come upon us because our God is not with us?' 18And

I will certainly hide my face on that day because
of all their wickedness in turning to other gods.
19“Now write down for yourselves this song
and teach it to the Israelites and have them sing
it, so that it may be a witness for me against them.
20When I have brought them into the land flow-
ing with milk and honey, the land I promised on
oath to their forefathers, and when they eat their
fill and thrive, they will turn to other gods and
worship them, rejecting me and breaking my cov-
enant. 21And when many disasters and difficulties
come upon them, this song will testify against
them, because it will not be forgotten by their
descendants. I know what they are disposed to
do, even before I bring them into the land I prom-
ised them on oath.” 22So Moses wrote down this
song that day and taught it to the Israelites.
23The LORD gave this command to Joshua son
of Nun: “Be strong and courageous, for you will
bring the Israelites into the land I promised them
on oath, and I myself will be with you.”
24After Moses finished writing in a book the
words of this law from beginning to end, 25he
gave this command to the Levites who carried the
ark of the covenant of the LORD: 26“Take this Book
of the Law and place it beside the ark of the cov-
enant of the LORD your God. There it will remain
as a witness against you. 27For I know how rebel-
lious and stiff-necked you are. If you have been
rebellious against the LORD while I am still alive
and with you, how much more will you rebel
after I die! 28Assemble before me all the elders of
your tribes and all your officials, so that I can
speak these words in their hearing and call
heaven and earth to testify against them. 29For I
know that after my death you are sure to become
utterly corrupt and to turn from the way I have
commanded you. In days to come, disaster will
fall upon you because you will do evil in the sight
of the LORD and provoke him to anger by what
your hands have made.”
30And Moses recited the words of this song
from beginning to end in the hearing of the whole
assembly of Israel:

32 Listen, O heavens, and I will speak;
hear, O earth, the words of my mouth.
2Let my teaching fall like rain
and my words descend like dew,
like showers on new grass,
like abundant rain on tender plants.
3I will proclaim the name of the LORD.
Oh, praise the greatness of our God!
4He is the Rock, his works are perfect,
and all his ways are just.
A faithful God who does no wrong,
upright and just is he.

5They have acted corruptly toward him;
to their shame they are no longer his children,
but a warped and crooked generation.[m]
6Is this the way you repay the LORD,
O foolish and unwise people?
Is he not your Father, your Creator,[n]
who made you and formed you?

7Remember the days of old;
consider the generations long past.
Ask your father and he will tell you,
your elders, and they will explain to you.
8When the Most High gave the nations their inheritance,
when he divided all mankind,
he set up boundaries for the peoples
according to the number of the sons of Israel.[o]
9For the LORD's portion is his people,
Jacob his allotted inheritance.

10In a desert land he found him,
in a barren and howling waste.
He shielded him and cared for him;
he guarded him as the apple of his eye,
11like an eagle that stirs up its nest
and hovers over its young,
that spreads its wings to catch them
and carries them on its pinions.
12The LORD alone led him;
no foreign god was with him.

13He made him ride on the heights of the land
and fed him with the fruit of the fields.
He nourished him with honey from the rock,
and with oil from the flinty crag,
14with curds and milk from herd and flock
and with fattened lambs and goats,
with choice rams of Bashan
and the finest kernels of wheat.
You drank the foaming blood of the grape.

[m]5 Or *Corrupt are they and not his children, / a generation warped and twisted to their shame* [n]6 Or *Father, who bought you*
[o]8 Masoretic Text; Dead Sea Scrolls (see also Septuagint) *sons of God*

15Jeshurun[p] grew fat and kicked;
filled with food, he became heavy and sleek.
He abandoned the God who made him
and rejected the Rock his Savior.
16They made him jealous with their foreign gods
and angered him with their detestable idols.
17They sacrificed to demons, which are not God—
gods they had not known,
gods that recently appeared,
gods your fathers did not fear.
18You deserted the Rock, who fathered you;
you forgot the God who gave you birth.

19The LORD saw this and rejected them
because he was angered by his sons and daughters.
20"I will hide my face from them," he said,
"and see what their end will be;
for they are a perverse generation,
children who are unfaithful.
21They made me jealous by what is no god
and angered me with their worthless idols.
I will make them envious by those who are not a people;
I will make them angry by a nation that has no understanding.
22For a fire has been kindled by my wrath,
one that burns to the realm of death[q] below.
It will devour the earth and its harvests
and set afire the foundations of the mountains.

23"I will heap calamities upon them
and spend my arrows against them.
24I will send wasting famine against them,
consuming pestilence and deadly plague;
I will send against them the fangs of wild beasts,
the venom of vipers that glide in the dust.
25In the street the sword will make them childless;
in their homes terror will reign.
Young men and young women will perish,
infants and gray-haired men.
26I said I would scatter them
and blot out their memory from mankind,
27but I dreaded the taunt of the enemy,
lest the adversary misunderstand
and say, 'Our hand has triumphed;
the LORD has not done all this.'"
28They are a nation without sense,
there is no discernment in them.
29If only they were wise and would understand this
and discern what their end will be!
30How could one man chase a thousand,
or two put ten thousand to flight,
unless their Rock had sold them,
unless the LORD had given them up?
31For their rock is not like our Rock,
as even our enemies concede.
32Their vine comes from the vine of Sodom
and from the fields of Gomorrah.
Their grapes are filled with poison,
and their clusters with bitterness.
33Their wine is the venom of serpents,
the deadly poison of cobras.

34"Have I not kept this in reserve
and sealed it in my vaults?
35It is mine to avenge; I will repay.
In due time their foot will slip;
their day of disaster is near
and their doom rushes upon them."

36The LORD will judge his people
and have compassion on his servants
when he sees their strength is gone
and no one is left, slave or free.
37He will say: "Now where are their gods,
the rock they took refuge in,
38the gods who ate the fat of their sacrifices
and drank the wine of their drink offerings?
Let them rise up to help you!
Let them give you shelter!

39"See now that I myself am He!
There is no god besides me.
I put to death and I bring to life,
I have wounded and I will heal,
and no one can deliver out of my hand.
40I lift my hand to heaven and declare:
As surely as I live forever,
41when I sharpen my flashing sword
and my hand grasps it in judgment,
I will take vengeance on my adversaries
and repay those who hate me.
42I will make my arrows drunk with blood,
while my sword devours flesh:
the blood of the slain and the captives,

p15 *Jeshurun* means *the upright one,* that is, Israel. q22 Hebrew *to Sheol*

the heads of the enemy leaders."

43 Rejoice, O nations, with his people,[r,s]
for he will avenge the blood of his servants;
he will take vengeance on his enemies
and make atonement for his land and
people.

44 Moses came with Joshua[t] son of Nun and
spoke all the words of this song in the hearing of
the people. 45 When Moses finished reciting all
these words to all Israel, 46 he said to them, "Take
to heart all the words I have solemnly declared to
you this day, so that you may command your
children to obey carefully all the words of this
law. 47 They are not just idle words for you—they
are your life. By them you will live long in the
land you are crossing the Jordan to possess."
48 On that same day the LORD told Moses, 49 "Go
up into the Abarim Range to Mount Nebo in
Moab, across from Jericho, and view Canaan, the
land I am giving the Israelites as their own pos-
session. 50 There on the mountain that you have
climbed you will die and be gathered to your peo-
ple, just as your brother Aaron died on Mount
Hor and was gathered to his people. 51 This is be-
cause both of you broke faith with me in the pres-
ence of the Israelites at the waters of Meribah
Kadesh in the Desert of Zin and because you did
not uphold my holiness among the Israelites.
52 Therefore, you will see the land only from a
distance; you will not enter the land I am giving
to the people of Israel."

33

This is the blessing that Moses the
man of God pronounced on the Is-
raelites before his death. 2 He said:

"The LORD came from Sinai
and dawned over them from Seir;
he shone forth from Mount Paran.
He came with[u] myriads of holy ones
from the south, from his mountain
slopes.[v]
3 Surely it is you who love the people;
all the holy ones are in your hand.
At your feet they all bow down,
and from you receive instruction,
4 the law that Moses gave us,
the possession of the assembly of Jacob.
5 He was king over Jeshurun[w]
when the leaders of the people assembled,
along with the tribes of Israel.

6 "Let Reuben live and not die,
nor[x] his men be few."

7 And this he said about Judah:

"Hear, O LORD, the cry of Judah;
bring him to his people.
With his own hands he defends his cause.
Oh, be his help against his foes!"

8 About Levi he said:

"Your Thummim and Urim belong
to the man you favored.
You tested him at Massah;
you contended with him at the waters of
Meribah.
9 He said of his father and mother,
'I have no regard for them.'
He did not recognize his brothers
or acknowledge his own children,
but he watched over your word
and guarded your covenant.
10 He teaches your precepts to Jacob
and your law to Israel.
He offers incense before you
and whole burnt offerings on your altar.
11 Bless all his skills, O LORD,
and be pleased with the work of his hands.
Smite the loins of those who rise up against
him;
strike his foes till they rise no more."

12 About Benjamin he said:

"Let the beloved of the LORD rest secure in
him,
for he shields him all day long,
and the one the LORD loves rests between
his shoulders."

13 About Joseph he said:

"May the LORD bless his land
with the precious dew from heaven above
and with the deep waters that lie below;
14 with the best the sun brings forth
and the finest the moon can yield;
15 with the choicest gifts of the ancient
mountains
and the fruitfulness of the everlasting hills;
16 with the best gifts of the earth and its fullness

[r] 43 Or *Make his people rejoice, O nations* [s] 43 Masoretic Text; Dead Sea Scrolls (see also Septuagint) *people, / and let all the angels worship him /* [t] 44 Hebrew *Hoshea,* a variant of *Joshua* [u] 2 Or *from*
[v] 2 The meaning of the Hebrew for this phrase is uncertain.
[w] 5 *Jeshurun* means *the upright one,* that is, Israel; also in verse 26.
[x] 6 Or *but let*

and the favor of him who dwelt in the
burning bush.
Let all these rest on the head of Joseph,
on the brow of the prince among[y] his
brothers.
17In majesty he is like a firstborn bull;
his horns are the horns of a wild ox.
With them he will gore the nations,
even those at the ends of the earth.
Such are the ten thousands of Ephraim;
such are the thousands of Manasseh."

18About Zebulun he said:

"Rejoice, Zebulun, in your going out,
and you, Issachar, in your tents.
19They will summon peoples to the mountain
and there offer sacrifices of righteousness;
they will feast on the abundance of the seas,
on the treasures hidden in the sand."

20About Gad he said:

"Blessed is he who enlarges Gad's domain!
Gad lives there like a lion,
tearing at arm or head.
21He chose the best land for himself;
the leader's portion was kept for him.
When the heads of the people assembled,
he carried out the LORD's righteous will,
and his judgments concerning Israel."

22About Dan he said:

"Dan is a lion's cub,
springing out of Bashan."

23About Naphtali he said:

"Naphtali is abounding with the favor of the
LORD
and is full of his blessing;
he will inherit southward to the lake."

24About Asher he said:

"Most blessed of sons is Asher;
let him be favored by his brothers,
and let him bathe his feet in oil.
25The bolts of your gates will be iron and
bronze,
and your strength will equal your days.

26"There is no one like the God of Jeshurun,
who rides on the heavens to help you
and on the clouds in his majesty.
27The eternal God is your refuge,
and underneath are the everlasting arms.
He will drive out your enemy before you,
saying, 'Destroy him!'
28So Israel will live in safety alone;
Jacob's spring is secure
in a land of grain and new wine,
where the heavens drop dew.
29Blessed are you, O Israel!
Who is like you,
a people saved by the LORD?
He is your shield and helper
and your glorious sword.
Your enemies will cower before you,
and you will trample down their high
places.[z]"

34

Then Moses climbed Mount Nebo
from the plains of Moab to the top
of Pisgah, across from Jericho.
There the LORD showed him the whole land—
from Gilead to Dan, 2all of Naphtali, the territory
of Ephraim and Manasseh, all the land of Judah
as far as the western sea,[a] 3the Negev and the
whole region from the Valley of Jericho, the City
of Palms, as far as Zoar. 4Then the LORD said to
him, "This is the land I promised on oath to Abra-
ham, Isaac and Jacob when I said, 'I will give it to
your descendants.' I have let you see it with your
eyes, but you will not cross over into it."
5And Moses the servant of the LORD died there
in Moab, as the LORD had said. 6He buried him[b]
in Moab, in the valley opposite Beth Peor, but to
this day no one knows where his grave is. 7Moses
was a hundred and twenty years old when he
died, yet his eyes were not weak nor his strength
gone. 8The Israelites grieved for Moses in the
plains of Moab thirty days, until the time of weep-
ing and mourning was over.
9Now Joshua son of Nun was filled with the
spirit[c] of wisdom because Moses had laid his
hands on him. So the Israelites listened to him
and did what the LORD had commanded Moses.
10Since then, no prophet has risen in Israel like
Moses, whom the LORD knew face to face, 11who
did all those miraculous signs and wonders the
LORD sent him to do in Egypt—to Pharaoh and to
all his officials and to his whole land. 12For no
one has ever shown the mighty power or per-
formed the awesome deeds that Moses did in the
sight of all Israel.

[y]16 Or *of the one separated from* [z]29 Or *will tread upon their bodies*
[a]2 That is, the Mediterranean [b]6 Or *He was buried* [c]9 Or *Spirit*

Joshua

Can we count on God to keep his promises?

Thousands of years ago God promised Abraham, "I will make you into a great nation" (Ge 12:2). "To your descendants I give this land, from the river of Egypt to the great river, the Euphrates" (Ge 15:18). These same promises were renewed with each generation of Abraham's descendants, but hundreds of years passed and his children still had no land to call their own. Even worse, they lived as slaves for four hundred years and wandered in the desert forty years after that. They hardly qualified as a great nation!

The book of Joshua is the story of God's making good on his promises. It tells how Israel entered and conquered the land God had promised them. In fact, God's faithfulness is so complete that at the end of the book we hear this proclamation: "You know with all your heart and soul that not one of all the good promises the LORD your God gave you has failed. Every promise has been fulfilled; not one has failed" (Jos 23:14).

Can we count on God to keep his promises? The answer from Joshua is a resounding yes! God is utterly dependable, and we can trust him completely. Joshua is a book for those whose prayers seem to go unanswered, for those who wonder if God is really alive and active, and for those who desire fresh assurance of God's dependability.

Joshua is also a fast-paced book. In it we share the excitement of the Israelites, who through God's power saw a river dry up and a city wall tumble. We watch them face overwhelming odds and emerge victorious.

The book of Joshua picks up the story of Israel's history after the death of Moses and carries it through the entry, conquest and division of the Promised Land. The events recorded began around 1406 B.C. and ended about twenty-four years later.

Although the author of the book is not identified, the traditional view is that it was written by Joshua himself, with a few additions made by Eleazar or Phinehas (for example, the reference to Joshua's death in 24:29–30). However, some scholars believe that the book may have been written by a younger contemporary of Joshua, and still others think it was not written until the beginning of the monarchy by someone who had access to various records of the actual events.

Outline

1 / *Joshua 1*
Get Ready to Go

GOD SOMETIMES ASKS us to do things that seem far beyond our abilities. He might ask us to assume a position of leadership, or take on a demanding project, or begin a Bible study with our non-Christian friends. At such times it is easy to feel underqualified and overwhelmed. Imagine trying to fill the shoes of someone as legendary as Moses! This was the task Joshua faced. You will notice that the name Moses pops up many times in the book of Joshua. At times Joshua must have felt that the memory of Moses hung over him like a dark cloud. Now that it was his turn to lead, Joshua needed to know if the people would follow him as they had Moses. More importantly, he needed to know if God intended to help him as he had Moses.

Warming Up to God God has a unique task for you. It is possible that he is calling you to do some work for him even now. Ask God to make you open to doing his will.

Read Joshua 1.

---

1 After the death of Moses the servant of the LORD, the LORD said to Joshua son of Nun, Moses' aide: 2"Moses my servant is dead. Now then, you and all these people, get ready to cross the Jordan River into the land I am about to give to them—to the Israelites. 3I will give you every place where you set your foot, as I promised Moses. 4Your territory will extend from the desert to Lebanon, and from the great river, the Euphrates—all the Hittite country—to the Great Sea[a] on the west. 5No one will be able to stand up against you all the days of your life. As I was with Moses, so I will be with you; I will never leave you nor forsake you.

6"Be strong and courageous, because you will lead these people to inherit the land I swore to their forefathers to give them. 7Be strong and very courageous. Be careful to obey all the law my servant Moses gave you; do not turn from it to the right or to the left, that you may be successful wherever you go. 8Do not let this Book of the Law depart from your mouth; meditate on it day and night, so that you may be careful to do everything written in it. Then you will be prosperous and successful. 9Have I not commanded you? Be strong and courageous. Do not be terrified; do not be discouraged, for the LORD your God will be with you wherever you go."

10So Joshua ordered the officers of the people: 11"Go through the camp and tell the people, 'Get your supplies ready. Three days from now you will cross the Jordan here to go in and take possession of the land the LORD your God is giving you for your own.' "

12But to the Reubenites, the Gadites and the half-tribe of Manasseh, Joshua said, 13"Remember the command that Moses the servant of the LORD gave you: 'The LORD your God is giving you rest and has granted you this land.' 14Your wives, your children and your livestock may stay in the land that Moses gave you east of the Jordan, but all your fighting men, fully armed, must cross over ahead of your brothers. You are to help your brothers 15until the LORD gives them rest, as he has done for you, and until they too have taken possession of the land that the LORD your God is giving them. After that, you may go back and occupy your own land, which Moses the servant of the LORD gave you east of the Jordan toward the sunrise."

16Then they answered Joshua, "Whatever you have commanded us we will do, and wherever you send us we will go. 17Just as we fully obeyed Moses, so we will obey you. Only may the LORD your God be with you as he was with Moses. 18Whoever rebels against your word and does not obey your words, whatever you may command them, will be put to death. Only be strong and courageous!"

[a]4 That is, the Mediterranean

Discovering the Word 1. What promises does the Lord make to Joshua (vv. 1–9)? 2. How would these promises strengthen and encourage Joshua? 3. What commands does the Lord give to Joshua (vv. 6–9)? 4. What is the relationship between God's promises and his commands? 5. How is God's presence made evident in the response he receives from the tribes (vv. 16–18)?

Applying the Word 1. How do you react when faced with something you feel totally unqualified to do? 2. What challenging task do you face in the near future?

Responding in Prayer Thank God for his presence and strength as you seek to obey him in the challenges you face.

2 / *Joshua 2*
Rahab's Life-Changing Faith

HOW CAN WE recognize genuine faith? What does it look like? How does it act? In this study we meet a woman of faith, a member of the only family in Jericho God allowed Israel to spare. Because of Rahab's faith, not only was her life spared but God extended to her the promises he had made to Israel. She became an ancestor of both King David and Jesus. She is mentioned in James as an example of saving faith. She is also honored in Hebrews 11, "The Faith Hall of Fame." Not bad for someone known throughout history as "Rahab the prostitute"!

Warming Up to God Reflect on the past week. How has your faith made a difference in your life? Praise God for his care for you.

Read Joshua 2.

2 Then Joshua son of Nun secretly sent two
spies from Shittim. "Go, look over the
land," he said, "especially Jericho." So
they went and entered the house of a prostitute[b]
named Rahab and stayed there.
2The king of Jericho was told, "Look! Some of
the Israelites have come here tonight to spy out
the land." 3So the king of Jericho sent this message to Rahab: "Bring out the men who came to
you and entered your house, because they have
come to spy out the whole land."
4But the woman had taken the two men and
hidden them. She said, "Yes, the men came to me,
but I did not know where they had come from.
5At dusk, when it was time to close the city gate,
the men left. I don't know which way they went.
Go after them quickly. You may catch up with
them." 6(But she had taken them up to the roof
and hidden them under the stalks of flax she had
laid out on the roof.) 7So the men set out in pursuit of the spies on the road that leads to the fords
of the Jordan, and as soon as the pursuers had
gone out, the gate was shut.
8Before the spies lay down for the night, she
went up on the roof 9and said to them, "I know
that the LORD has given this land to you and that
a great fear of you has fallen on us, so that all who
live in this country are melting in fear because of
you. 10We have heard how the LORD dried up the
water of the Red Sea[c] for you when you came
out of Egypt, and what you did to Sihon and Og,
the two kings of the Amorites east of the Jordan,
whom you completely destroyed.[d] 11When we
heard of it, our hearts melted and everyone's
courage failed because of you, for the LORD your
God is God in heaven above and on the earth
below. 12Now then, please swear to me by the
LORD that you will show kindness to my family,
because I have shown kindness to you. Give me a
sure sign 13that you will spare the lives of my
father and mother, my brothers and sisters, and
all who belong to them, and that you will save us
from death."
14"Our lives for your lives!" the men assured
her. "If you don't tell what we are doing, we will
treat you kindly and faithfully when the LORD
gives us the land."
15So she let them down by a rope through the

[b]1 Or possibly *an innkeeper* [c]10 Hebrew *Yam Suph*; that is, Sea of Reeds [d]10 The Hebrew term refers to the irrevocable giving over of things or persons to the LORD, often by totally destroying them.

window, for the house she lived in was part of the
city wall. 16Now she had said to them, "Go to the
hills so the pursuers will not find you. Hide your-
selves there three days until they return, and then
go on your way."
17The men said to her, "This oath you made us
swear will not be binding on us 18unless, when
we enter the land, you have tied this scarlet cord
in the window through which you let us down,
and unless you have brought your father and
mother, your brothers and all your family into
your house. 19If anyone goes outside your house
into the street, his blood will be on his own head;
we will not be responsible. As for anyone who is
in the house with you, his blood will be on our
head if a hand is laid on him. 20But if you tell
what we are doing, we will be released from the
oath you made us swear."
21"Agreed," she replied. "Let it be as you say."
So she sent them away and they departed. And
she tied the scarlet cord in the window.
22When they left, they went into the hills and
stayed there three days, until the pursuers had
searched all along the road and returned with-
out finding them. 23Then the two men started
back. They went down out of the hills, forded
the river and came to Joshua son of Nun
and told him everything that had happened to
them. 24They said to Joshua, "The LORD has
surely given the whole land into our hands;
all the people are melting in fear because
of us."

Discovering the Word 1. What risks does Rahab take in protecting the spies (vv. 1–7)? 2. What does Rahab know and believe about the God of Israel (vv. 8–11)? 3. What deal does Rahab make in exchange for helping the spies (vv. 12–16)? 4. What conditions must she and her family fulfill in order to be saved (vv. 17–21)? 5. A missionary named Jim Elliot once made the statement "He is no fool who gives what he cannot keep to gain what he cannot lose." How might this statement apply to Rahab? 6. Why must a genuine faith express itself in actions?

Applying the Word 1. What actions have you taken recently as a direct result of your faith in Christ? 2. How can our faith have a positive effect on both Christians and non-Christians?

Responding in Prayer Ask God to make you ready to take the risks your faith requires.

3 / *Joshua 3:1—5:12*
Crossing the Jordan

GOD'S BLESSINGS ARE given for a purpose. He wants us to grow in our love for him as we experience kindness upon kindness. These chapters contain several reminders of all God did in leading Israel from Egypt to the Promised Land. They teach us the importance of remembering and celebrating what God has done for us.

Warming Up to God How have God's blessings recently encouraged growth in your life?

Read Joshua 3:1—5:12.

3 Early in the morning Joshua and all the
Israelites set out from Shittim and went to
the Jordan, where they camped before
crossing over. 2After three days the officers went
throughout the camp, 3giving orders to the peo-
ple: "When you see the ark of the covenant of the
LORD your God, and the priests, who are Levites,
carrying it, you are to move out from your posi-
tions and follow it. 4Then you will know which
way to go, since you have never been this way
before. But keep a distance of about a thousand
yards[e] between you and the ark; do not go
near it."

e4 Hebrew *about two thousand cubits* (about 900 meters)

5Joshua told the people, "Consecrate yourselves, for tomorrow the LORD will do amazing things among you."

6Joshua said to the priests, "Take up the ark of the covenant and pass on ahead of the people." So they took it up and went ahead of them.

7And the LORD said to Joshua, "Today I will begin to exalt you in the eyes of all Israel, so they may know that I am with you as I was with Moses. 8Tell the priests who carry the ark of the covenant: 'When you reach the edge of the Jordan's waters, go and stand in the river.' "

9Joshua said to the Israelites, "Come here and listen to the words of the LORD your God. 10This is how you will know that the living God is among you and that he will certainly drive out before you the Canaanites, Hittites, Hivites, Perizzites, Girgashites, Amorites and Jebusites. 11See, the ark of the covenant of the Lord of all the earth will go into the Jordan ahead of you. 12Now then, choose twelve men from the tribes of Israel, one from each tribe. 13And as soon as the priests who carry the ark of the LORD—the Lord of all the earth—set foot in the Jordan, its waters flowing downstream will be cut off and stand up in a heap."

14So when the people broke camp to cross the Jordan, the priests carrying the ark of the covenant went ahead of them. 15Now the Jordan is at flood stage all during harvest. Yet as soon as the priests who carried the ark reached the Jordan and their feet touched the water's edge, 16the water from upstream stopped flowing. It piled up in a heap a great distance away, at a town called Adam in the vicinity of Zarethan, while the water flowing down to the Sea of the Arabah (the Salt Sea[f]) was completely cut off. So the people crossed over opposite Jericho. 17The priests who carried the ark of the covenant of the LORD stood firm on dry ground in the middle of the Jordan, while all Israel passed by until the whole nation had completed the crossing on dry ground.

4 When the whole nation had finished crossing the Jordan, the LORD said to Joshua, 2"Choose twelve men from among the people, one from each tribe, 3and tell them to take up twelve stones from the middle of the Jordan from right where the priests stood and to carry them over with you and put them down at the place where you stay tonight."

4So Joshua called together the twelve men he had appointed from the Israelites, one from each tribe, 5and said to them, "Go over before the ark of the LORD your God into the middle of the Jordan. Each of you is to take up a stone on his shoulder, according to the number of the tribes of the Israelites, 6to serve as a sign among you. In the future, when your children ask you, 'What do these stones mean?' 7tell them that the flow of the Jordan was cut off before the ark of the covenant of the LORD. When it crossed the Jordan, the waters of the Jordan were cut off. These stones are to be a memorial to the people of Israel forever."

8So the Israelites did as Joshua commanded them. They took twelve stones from the middle of the Jordan, according to the number of the tribes of the Israelites, as the LORD had told Joshua; and they carried them over with them to their camp, where they put them down. 9Joshua set up the twelve stones that had been[g] in the middle of the Jordan at the spot where the priests who carried the ark of the covenant had stood. And they are there to this day.

10Now the priests who carried the ark remained standing in the middle of the Jordan until everything the LORD had commanded Joshua was done by the people, just as Moses had directed Joshua. The people hurried over, 11and as soon as all of them had crossed, the ark of the LORD and the priests came to the other side while the people watched. 12The men of Reuben, Gad and the half-tribe of Manasseh crossed over, armed, in front of the Israelites, as Moses had directed them. 13About forty thousand armed for battle crossed over before the LORD to the plains of Jericho for war.

14That day the LORD exalted Joshua in the sight of all Israel; and they revered him all the days of his life, just as they had revered Moses.

15Then the LORD said to Joshua, 16"Command the priests carrying the ark of the Testimony to come up out of the Jordan."

17So Joshua commanded the priests, "Come up out of the Jordan."

18And the priests came up out of the river carrying the ark of the covenant of the LORD. No sooner had they set their feet on the dry ground than the waters of the Jordan returned to their place and ran at flood stage as before.

19On the tenth day of the first month the people went up from the Jordan and camped at Gilgal on the eastern border of Jericho. 20And Joshua set

f16 That is, the Dead Sea   g9 Or *Joshua also set up twelve stones*

up at Gilgal the twelve stones they had taken out
of the Jordan. 21He said to the Israelites, "In the
future when your descendants ask their fathers,
'What do these stones mean?' 22tell them, 'Israel
crossed the Jordan on dry ground.' 23For the LORD
your God dried up the Jordan before you until
you had crossed over. The LORD your God did to
the Jordan just what he had done to the Red Sea[h]
when he dried it up before us until we had
crossed over. 24He did this so that all the peoples
of the earth might know that the hand of the LORD
is powerful and so that you might always fear the
LORD your God."

5 Now when all the Amorite kings west of
the Jordan and all the Canaanite kings
along the coast heard how the LORD had
dried up the Jordan before the Israelites until we
had crossed over, their hearts melted and they no
longer had the courage to face the Israelites.

2At that time the LORD said to Joshua, "Make
flint knives and circumcise the Israelites again."
3So Joshua made flint knives and circumcised the
Israelites at Gibeath Haaraloth.[i]

4Now this is why he did so: All those who came
out of Egypt—all the men of military age—died
in the desert on the way after leaving Egypt. 5All
the people that came out had been circumcised,
but all the people born in the desert during the
journey from Egypt had not. 6The Israelites had
moved about in the desert forty years until all the
men who were of military age when they left
Egypt had died, since they had not obeyed the
LORD. For the LORD had sworn to them that they
would not see the land that he had solemnly
promised their fathers to give us, a land flowing
with milk and honey. 7So he raised up their sons
in their place, and these were the ones Joshua
circumcised. They were still uncircumcised be-
cause they had not been circumcised on the way.
8And after the whole nation had been circum-
cised, they remained where they were in camp
until they were healed.

9Then the LORD said to Joshua, "Today I have
rolled away the reproach of Egypt from you." So
the place has been called Gilgal[j] to this day.

10On the evening of the fourteenth day of the
month, while camped at Gilgal on the plains of
Jericho, the Israelites celebrated the Passover.
11The day after the Passover, that very day, they
ate some of the produce of the land: unleavened
bread and roasted grain. 12The manna stopped
the day after[k] they ate this food from the land;
there was no longer any manna for the Israelites,
but that year they ate of the produce of Canaan.

[h]23 Hebrew *Yam Suph*; that is, Sea of Reeds [i]3 *Gibeath Haaraloth* means *hill of foreskins.* [j]9 *Gilgal* sounds like the Hebrew for *roll.* [k]12 Or *the day*

Discovering the Word 1. Picture life with the Israelites during their three days of encampment along the Jordan. What thoughts and conversations do you imagine they had? 2. Describe the sequence of events the Israelites would have seen as they crossed the Jordan (3:3–4, 8–17). 3. Why was this miraculous crossing especially important for Joshua's leadership (3:7 and 4:14)? 4. What other goals did this miracle accomplish (3:10; 4:24; see 5:1)? 5. How would the twelve stones from the Jordan River serve as a memorial for future generations (4:1–7, 19–24)? 6. Circumcision was the sign of the covenant between God and Israel. Why was it important for the Israelites to be circumcised at this time?

Applying the Word 1. What memorials do you have to remind yourself and future generations of what God has done? 2. What have these chapters taught you about remembering and celebrating the things God has done?

Responding in Prayer Praise God for the things you have seen him do—in your life and your church.

4 / *Joshua 5:13—6:27*
Jericho Falls

WE FIGHT MANY battles in life—financial, physical, emotional and spiritual. How can we be victorious in these struggles, especially when the odds against us seem overwhelming?

Conquering the Promised Land was an enormous task. Forty years earlier the Israelites had lamented, "The land we explored devours those living in it. All the people we saw there are of great size. . . . We seemed like grasshoppers in our own eyes, and we looked the same to them" (Nu 13:32-33). Yet in spite of these obstacles, Joshua and the people of Israel now set out to conquer the first Canaanite stronghold—Jericho. As they do so, the Lord teaches them and us how to be victorious.

Warming Up to God When have you felt that God was fighting your battles for you? How did you feel?

Read Joshua 5:13—6:27.

13Now when Joshua was near Jericho, he looked up and saw a man standing in front of him with a drawn sword in his hand. Joshua went up to him and asked, "Are you for us or for our enemies?"

14"Neither," he replied, "but as commander of the army of the LORD I have now come." Then Joshua fell facedown to the ground in reverence, and asked him, "What message does my Lord[l] have for his servant?"

15The commander of the LORD's army replied, "Take off your sandals, for the place where you are standing is holy." And Joshua did so.

6 Now Jericho was tightly shut up because of the Israelites. No one went out and no one came in.

2Then the LORD said to Joshua, "See, I have delivered Jericho into your hands, along with its king and its fighting men. 3March around the city once with all the armed men. Do this for six days. 4Have seven priests carry trumpets of rams' horns in front of the ark. On the seventh day, march around the city seven times, with the priests blowing the trumpets. 5When you hear them sound a long blast on the trumpets, have all the people give a loud shout; then the wall of the city will collapse and the people will go up, every man straight in."

6So Joshua son of Nun called the priests and said to them, "Take up the ark of the covenant of the LORD and have seven priests carry trumpets in front of it." 7And he ordered the people, "Advance! March around the city, with the armed guard going ahead of the ark of the LORD."

8When Joshua had spoken to the people, the seven priests carrying the seven trumpets before the LORD went forward, blowing their trumpets, and the ark of the LORD's covenant followed them. 9The armed guard marched ahead of the priests who blew the trumpets, and the rear guard followed the ark. All this time the trumpets were sounding. 10But Joshua had commanded the people, "Do not give a war cry, do not raise your voices, do not say a word until the day I tell you to shout. Then shout!" 11So he had the ark of the LORD carried around the city, circling it once. Then the people returned to camp and spent the night there.

12Joshua got up early the next morning and the priests took up the ark of the LORD. 13The seven priests carrying the seven trumpets went forward, marching before the ark of the LORD and blowing the trumpets. The armed men went ahead of them and the rear guard followed the ark of the LORD, while the trumpets kept sounding. 14So on the second day they marched around the city once and returned to the camp. They did this for six days.

15On the seventh day, they got up at daybreak and marched around the city seven times in the same manner, except that on that day they circled the city seven times. 16The seventh time around, when the priests sounded the trumpet blast, Joshua commanded the people, "Shout! For the LORD has given you the city! 17The city and all that is in it are to be devoted[m] to the LORD. Only Rahab the prostitute[n] and all who are with her in

[l]14 Or *lord* [m]17 The Hebrew term refers to the irrevocable giving over of things or persons to the LORD, often by totally destroying them; also in verses 18 and 21. [n]17 Or possibly *innkeeper*; also in verses 22 and 25

her house shall be spared, because she hid the
spies we sent. [18]But keep away from the devoted
things, so that you will not bring about your own
destruction by taking any of them. Otherwise you
will make the camp of Israel liable to destruction
and bring trouble on it. [19]All the silver and gold
and the articles of bronze and iron are sacred to
the LORD and must go into his treasury."

[20]When the trumpets sounded, the people
shouted, and at the sound of the trumpet, when
the people gave a loud shout, the wall collapsed;
so every man charged straight in, and they took
the city. [21]They devoted the city to the LORD and
destroyed with the sword every living thing in
it—men and women, young and old, cattle, sheep
and donkeys.

[22]Joshua said to the two men who had spied
out the land, "Go into the prostitute's house and
bring her out and all who belong to her, in accordance
with your oath to her." [23]So the young men
who had done the spying went in and brought
out Rahab, her father and mother and brothers
and all who belonged to her. They brought out
her entire family and put them in a place outside
the camp of Israel.

[24]Then they burned the whole city and everything
in it, but they put the silver and gold and
the articles of bronze and iron into the treasury of
the LORD's house. [25]But Joshua spared Rahab the
prostitute, with her family and all who belonged
to her, because she hid the men Joshua had sent
as spies to Jericho—and she lives among the Israelites
to this day.

[26]At that time Joshua pronounced this solemn
oath: "Cursed before the LORD is the man who
undertakes to rebuild this city, Jericho:

"At the cost of his firstborn son
 will he lay its foundations;
at the cost of his youngest
 will he set up its gates."

[27]So the LORD was with Joshua, and his fame
spread throughout the land.

Discovering the Word 1. How do you think the visit by the commander of the army of the Lord affected Joshua (5:13–15)? 2. In what ways do the Lord's instructions for the conquest of Jericho seem strange (6:1–5)? 3. How do you think the Israelites felt during this seven-day spectacle (6:6–16)? 4. What lessons was God teaching the Israelites during their seven days of marching? 5. What did it mean for this city and its contents to be devoted to the Lord (6:17–25)? 6. Why didn't God allow the Israelites to keep any of the spoils of war (6:19, 24)?

Applying the Word 1. How is our spiritual warfare today similar to and different from Israel's conquest of Jericho (see 2Co 10:3–5)? 2. What spiritual battles are you currently fighting?

Responding in Prayer Pray for victory for yourself and others you know who are fighting spiritual battles.

5 / *Joshua 7—8*
Defeat, Confession and Victory

SUCCESS CAN LEAD to complacency. We feel confident, in control, optimistic—then suddenly the bottom drops out of our lives. Israel had tasted success. They had entered the Promised Land, they had won an important battle, and God was obviously with them. Conquering the city of Ai would be a piece of cake! But their confidence collapsed when they attacked the city and were routed. What had gone wrong? Had God failed them? Why hadn't God kept his promise?

Warming Up to God Think of a time when you failed at something. How did you feel, and why?

Read Joshua 7—8.

7 But the Israelites acted unfaithfully in regard to the devoted things[o]; Achan son of Carmi, the son of Zimri,[p] the son of Zerah, of the tribe of Judah, took some of them. So the LORD's anger burned against Israel.

2Now Joshua sent men from Jericho to Ai, which is near Beth Aven to the east of Bethel, and told them, "Go up and spy out the region." So the men went up and spied out Ai.

3When they returned to Joshua, they said, "Not all the people will have to go up against Ai. Send two or three thousand men to take it and do not weary all the people, for only a few men are there." 4So about three thousand men went up; but they were routed by the men of Ai, 5who killed about thirty-six of them. They chased the Israelites from the city gate as far as the stone quarries[q] and struck them down on the slopes. At this the hearts of the people melted and became like water.

6Then Joshua tore his clothes and fell facedown to the ground before the ark of the LORD, remaining there till evening. The elders of Israel did the same, and sprinkled dust on their heads. 7And Joshua said, "Ah, Sovereign LORD, why did you ever bring this people across the Jordan to deliver us into the hands of the Amorites to destroy us? If only we had been content to stay on the other side of the Jordan! 8O Lord, what can I say, now that Israel has been routed by its enemies? 9The Canaanites and the other people of the country will hear about this and they will surround us and wipe out our name from the earth. What then will you do for your own great name?"

10The LORD said to Joshua, "Stand up! What are you doing down on your face? 11Israel has sinned; they have violated my covenant, which I commanded them to keep. They have taken some of the devoted things; they have stolen, they have lied, they have put them with their own possessions. 12That is why the Israelites cannot stand against their enemies; they turn their backs and run because they have been made liable to destruction. I will not be with you anymore unless you destroy whatever among you is devoted to destruction.

13"Go, consecrate the people. Tell them, 'Consecrate yourselves in preparation for tomorrow; for this is what the LORD, the God of Israel, says: That which is devoted is among you, O Israel. You cannot stand against your enemies until you remove it.

14" 'In the morning, present yourselves tribe by tribe. The tribe that the LORD takes shall come forward clan by clan; the clan that the LORD takes shall come forward family by family; and the family that the LORD takes shall come forward man by man. 15He who is caught with the devoted things shall be destroyed by fire, along with all that belongs to him. He has violated the covenant of the LORD and has done a disgraceful thing in Israel!' "

16Early the next morning Joshua had Israel come forward by tribes, and Judah was taken. 17The clans of Judah came forward, and he took the Zerahites. He had the clan of the Zerahites come forward by families, and Zimri was taken. 18Joshua had his family come forward man by man, and Achan son of Carmi, the son of Zimri, the son of Zerah, of the tribe of Judah, was taken.

19Then Joshua said to Achan, "My son, give glory to the LORD,[r] the God of Israel, and give him the praise.[s] Tell me what you have done; do not hide it from me."

20Achan replied, "It is true! I have sinned against the LORD, the God of Israel. This is what I have done: 21When I saw in the plunder a beautiful robe from Babylonia,[t] two hundred shekels[u] of silver and a wedge of gold weighing fifty shekels,[v] I coveted them and took them. They are hidden in the ground inside my tent, with the silver underneath."

22So Joshua sent messengers, and they ran to the tent, and there it was, hidden in his tent, with the silver underneath. 23They took the things from the tent, brought them to Joshua and all the Israelites and spread them out before the LORD.

24Then Joshua, together with all Israel, took Achan son of Zerah, the silver, the robe, the gold wedge, his sons and daughters, his cattle, donkeys and sheep, his tent and all that he had, to the Valley of Achor. 25Joshua said, "Why have you brought this trouble on us? The LORD will bring trouble on you today."

Then all Israel stoned him, and after they had stoned the rest, they burned them. 26Over Achan they heaped up a large pile of rocks, which remains to this day. Then the LORD turned from his

[o]*1* The Hebrew term refers to the irrevocable giving over of things or persons to the LORD, often by totally destroying them; also in verses 11, 12, 13 and 15. [p]*1* See Septuagint and 1 Chron. 2:6; Hebrew *Zabdi*; also in verses 17 and 18. [q]*5* Or *as far as Shebarim* [r]*19* A solemn charge to tell the truth [s]*19* Or *and confess to him* [t]*21* Hebrew *Shinar* [u]*21* That is, about 5 pounds (about 2.3 kilograms) [v]*21* That is, about 1 1/4 pounds (about 0.6 kilogram)

fierce anger. Therefore that place has been called the Valley of Achor[w] ever since.

8 Then the LORD said to Joshua, "Do not be afraid; do not be discouraged. Take the whole army with you, and go up and attack Ai. For I have delivered into your hands the king of Ai, his people, his city and his land. 2You shall do to Ai and its king as you did to Jericho and its king, except that you may carry off their plunder and livestock for yourselves. Set an ambush behind the city."

3So Joshua and the whole army moved out to attack Ai. He chose thirty thousand of his best fighting men and sent them out at night 4with these orders: "Listen carefully. You are to set an ambush behind the city. Don't go very far from it. All of you be on the alert. 5I and all those with me will advance on the city, and when the men come out against us, as they did before, we will flee from them. 6They will pursue us until we have lured them away from the city, for they will say, 'They are running away from us as they did before.' So when we flee from them, 7you are to rise up from ambush and take the city. The LORD your God will give it into your hand. 8When you have taken the city, set it on fire. Do what the LORD has commanded. See to it; you have my orders."

9Then Joshua sent them off, and they went to the place of ambush and lay in wait between Bethel and Ai, to the west of Ai—but Joshua spent that night with the people.

10Early the next morning Joshua mustered his men, and he and the leaders of Israel marched before them to Ai. 11The entire force that was with him marched up and approached the city and arrived in front of it. They set up camp north of Ai, with the valley between them and the city. 12Joshua had taken about five thousand men and set them in ambush between Bethel and Ai, to the west of the city. 13They had the soldiers take up their positions—all those in the camp to the north of the city and the ambush to the west of it. That night Joshua went into the valley.

14When the king of Ai saw this, he and all the men of the city hurried out early in the morning to meet Israel in battle at a certain place overlooking the Arabah. But he did not know that an ambush had been set against him behind the city. 15Joshua and all Israel let themselves be driven back before them, and they fled toward the desert. 16All the men of Ai were called to pursue them, and they pursued Joshua and were lured away from the city. 17Not a man remained in Ai or Bethel who did not go after Israel. They left the city open and went in pursuit of Israel.

18Then the LORD said to Joshua, "Hold out toward Ai the javelin that is in your hand, for into your hand I will deliver the city." So Joshua held out his javelin toward Ai. 19As soon as he did this, the men in the ambush rose quickly from their position and rushed forward. They entered the city and captured it and quickly set it on fire.

20The men of Ai looked back and saw the smoke of the city rising against the sky, but they had no chance to escape in any direction, for the Israelites who had been fleeing toward the desert had turned back against their pursuers. 21For when Joshua and all Israel saw that the ambush had taken the city and that smoke was going up from the city, they turned around and attacked the men of Ai. 22The men of the ambush also came out of the city against them, so that they were caught in the middle, with Israelites on both sides. Israel cut them down, leaving them neither survivors nor fugitives. 23But they took the king of Ai alive and brought him to Joshua.

24When Israel had finished killing all the men of Ai in the fields and in the desert where they had chased them, and when every one of them had been put to the sword, all the Israelites returned to Ai and killed those who were in it. 25Twelve thousand men and women fell that day—all the people of Ai. 26For Joshua did not draw back the hand that held out his javelin until he had destroyed[x] all who lived in Ai. 27But Israel did carry off for themselves the livestock and plunder of this city, as the LORD had instructed Joshua.

28So Joshua burned Ai and made it a permanent heap of ruins, a desolate place to this day. 29He hung the king of Ai on a tree and left him there until evening. At sunset, Joshua ordered them to take his body from the tree and throw it down at the entrance of the city gate. And they raised a large pile of rocks over it, which remains to this day.

30Then Joshua built on Mount Ebal an altar to the LORD, the God of Israel, 31as Moses the servant of the LORD had commanded the Israelites. He built it according to what is written in the Book of the Law of Moses—an altar of uncut stones, on

[w]26 *Achor* means *trouble*. [x]26 The Hebrew term refers to the irrevocable giving over of things or persons to the LORD, often by totally destroying them.

which no iron tool had been used. On it they
offered to the LORD burnt offerings and sacrificed
fellowship offerings.[y] 32There, in the presence of
the Israelites, Joshua copied on stones the law of
Moses, which he had written. 33All Israel, aliens
and citizens alike, with their elders, officials and
judges, were standing on both sides of the ark of
the covenant of the LORD, facing those who car-
ried it—the priests, who were Levites. Half of the
people stood in front of Mount Gerizim and half
of them in front of Mount Ebal, as Moses the
servant of the LORD had formerly commanded
when he gave instructions to bless the people of
Israel.

34Afterward, Joshua read all the words of the
law—the blessings and the curses—just as it is
written in the Book of the Law. 35There was not
a word of all that Moses had commanded that
Joshua did not read to the whole assembly of Is-
rael, including the women and children, and the
aliens who lived among them.

[y]31 Traditionally *peace offerings*

Discovering the Word 1. What are Joshua's concerns after this defeat (7:6–9)? 2. How do God's concerns differ from Joshua's (7:10–15)? 3. Joshua urged Achan to "give glory to the LORD" by admitting his crime (7:19). How does confession glorify God? 4. How did the second attack on Ai differ from the first (8:1–29)? 5. If you had been an Israelite, what thoughts would have come to mind each time you saw the rock piles mentioned in 7:26 and 8:29? 6. What impact would the reading of the law have had on the Israelites (8:32–35)?

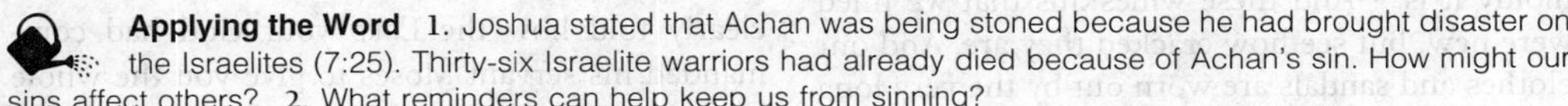

Applying the Word 1. Joshua stated that Achan was being stoned because he had brought disaster on the Israelites (7:25). Thirty-six Israelite warriors had already died because of Achan's sin. How might our sins affect others? 2. What reminders can help keep us from sinning?

Responding in Prayer Bring any sin in your life before God. Confess it to him with a penitent heart.

6 / *Joshua 9*
Deceived

SATAN'S PRIMARY STRATEGY is deceit. He seduces us into believing that a lie is truth, that evil is good and that a "suicidal plunge is really a leap into life" (Derek Kidner, *Genesis* [Downers Grove, Ill.: InterVarsity Press, 1967], p. 68).

Warming Up to God How do you decide whether to make a decision on your own or to pray about it first?

Read Joshua 9.

9 Now when all the kings west of the Jor-
dan heard about these things—those in
the hill country, in the western foothills,
and along the entire coast of the Great Sea[z] as far
as Lebanon (the kings of the Hittites, Amorites,
Canaanites, Perizzites, Hivites and Jebusites)—
2they came together to make war against Joshua
and Israel.

3However, when the people of Gibeon heard
what Joshua had done to Jericho and Ai, 4they
resorted to a ruse: They went as a delegation
whose donkeys were loaded[a] with worn-out
sacks and old wineskins, cracked and mended.
5The men put worn and patched sandals on their
feet and wore old clothes. All the bread of their
food supply was dry and moldy. 6Then they went
to Joshua in the camp at Gilgal and said to him
and the men of Israel, "We have come from a
distant country; make a treaty with us."

[z]1 That is, the Mediterranean [a]4 Most Hebrew manuscripts; some Hebrew manuscripts, Vulgate and Syriac (see also Septuagint) *They prepared provisions and loaded their donkeys*

7The men of Israel said to the Hivites, "But perhaps you live near us. How then can we make a treaty with you?"

8"We are your servants," they said to Joshua.

But Joshua asked, "Who are you and where do you come from?"

9They answered: "Your servants have come from a very distant country because of the fame of the LORD your God. For we have heard reports of him: all that he did in Egypt, 10and all that he did to the two kings of the Amorites east of the Jordan—Sihon king of Heshbon, and Og king of Bashan, who reigned in Ashtaroth. 11And our elders and all those living in our country said to us, 'Take provisions for your journey; go and meet them and say to them, "We are your servants; make a treaty with us." ' 12This bread of ours was warm when we packed it at home on the day we left to come to you. But now see how dry and moldy it is. 13And these wineskins that we filled were new, but see how cracked they are. And our clothes and sandals are worn out by the very long journey."

14The men of Israel sampled their provisions but did not inquire of the LORD. 15Then Joshua made a treaty of peace with them to let them live, and the leaders of the assembly ratified it by oath.

16Three days after they made the treaty with the Gibeonites, the Israelites heard that they were neighbors, living near them. 17So the Israelites set out and on the third day came to their cities: Gibeon, Kephirah, Beeroth and Kiriath Jearim. 18But the Israelites did not attack them, because the leaders of the assembly had sworn an oath to them by the LORD, the God of Israel.

The whole assembly grumbled against the leaders, 19but all the leaders answered, "We have given them our oath by the LORD, the God of Israel, and we cannot touch them now. 20This is what we will do to them: We will let them live, so that wrath will not fall on us for breaking the oath we swore to them." 21They continued, "Let them live, but let them be woodcutters and water carriers for the entire community." So the leaders' promise to them was kept.

22Then Joshua summoned the Gibeonites and said, "Why did you deceive us by saying, 'We live a long way from you,' while actually you live near us? 23You are now under a curse: You will never cease to serve as woodcutters and water carriers for the house of my God."

24They answered Joshua, "Your servants were clearly told how the LORD your God had commanded his servant Moses to give you the whole land and to wipe out all its inhabitants from before you. So we feared for our lives because of you, and that is why we did this. 25We are now in your hands. Do to us whatever seems good and right to you."

26So Joshua saved them from the Israelites, and they did not kill them. 27That day he made the Gibeonites woodcutters and water carriers for the community and for the altar of the LORD at the place the LORD would choose. And that is what they are to this day.

Discovering the Word 1. When they hear about Israel's victories, how does the Gibeonites' reaction differ from that of the kings west of the Jordan (vv. 1–6)? 2. What made the Gibeonites' deception so convincing to the Israelites (vv. 7–13)? 3. The Israelites were fooled because they "did not inquire of the LORD" (v. 14). Why should they have known that this was not a decision to be made on their own? 4. Why did the Israelites take their oath so seriously, even though it was based on a lie (vv. 16–19)? 5. The Gibeonites are similar to Rahab in that, for both, their faith led them to lie (vv. 22–27). Why aren't the Gibeonites commended for their faith as Rahab was?

Applying the Word 1. What tricks does Satan use to keep us from seeking God's guidance? 2. In what areas are we tempted to make peace with a sinful world?

Responding in Prayer Pray for those who are even now under Satan's deceitful influence.

7 / Joshua 10—12
The Lord Fights for Israel

GOD DEMONSTRATES HIS faithfulness to every Christian. He strengthens us when we are weak, comforts us when we are suffering, heals us when we are sick. He provides for all of our physical, emotional and spiritual needs. After all this, why do we often find it difficult to trust him? Joshua and Israel had miraculously crossed the Jordan and conquered the cities of Jericho and Ai. Yet in spite of these victories, they still needed to be reassured that God was with them.

Warming Up to God Why is it often hard to trust God for the future even though he has been faithful in the past?

Read Joshua 10—12.

---

10 Now Adoni-Zedek king of Jerusalem heard that Joshua had taken Ai and totally destroyed[b] it, doing to Ai and its king as he had done to Jericho and its king, and that the people of Gibeon had made a treaty of peace with Israel and were living near them. 2He and his people were very much alarmed at this, because Gibeon was an important city, like one of the royal cities; it was larger than Ai, and all its men were good fighters. 3So Adoni-Zedek king of Jerusalem appealed to Hoham king of Hebron, Piram king of Jarmuth, Japhia king of Lachish and Debir king of Eglon. 4"Come up and help me attack Gibeon," he said, "because it has made peace with Joshua and the Israelites."

5Then the five kings of the Amorites—the kings of Jerusalem, Hebron, Jarmuth, Lachish and Eglon—joined forces. They moved up with all their troops and took up positions against Gibeon and attacked it.

6The Gibeonites then sent word to Joshua in the camp at Gilgal: "Do not abandon your servants. Come up to us quickly and save us! Help us, because all the Amorite kings from the hill country have joined forces against us."

7So Joshua marched up from Gilgal with his entire army, including all the best fighting men. 8The LORD said to Joshua, "Do not be afraid of them; I have given them into your hand. Not one of them will be able to withstand you."

9After an all-night march from Gilgal, Joshua took them by surprise. 10The LORD threw them into confusion before Israel, who defeated them in a great victory at Gibeon. Israel pursued them along the road going up to Beth Horon and cut them down all the way to Azekah and Makkedah. 11As they fled before Israel on the road down from Beth Horon to Azekah, the LORD hurled large hailstones down on them from the sky, and more of them died from the hailstones than were killed by the swords of the Israelites.

12On the day the LORD gave the Amorites over to Israel, Joshua said to the LORD in the presence of Israel:

"O sun, stand still over Gibeon,
O moon, over the Valley of Aijalon."
13So the sun stood still,
and the moon stopped,
till the nation avenged itself on[c] its
enemies,

as it is written in the Book of Jashar.

The sun stopped in the middle of the sky and delayed going down about a full day. 14There has never been a day like it before or since, a day when the LORD listened to a man. Surely the LORD was fighting for Israel!

15Then Joshua returned with all Israel to the camp at Gilgal.

16Now the five kings had fled and hidden in the cave at Makkedah. 17When Joshua was told that the five kings had been found hiding in the cave at Makkedah, 18he said, "Roll large rocks up to the mouth of the cave, and post some men there to guard it. 19But don't stop! Pursue your enemies, attack them from the rear and don't let them reach their cities, for the LORD your God has given them into your hand."

20So Joshua and the Israelites destroyed them completely—almost to a man—but the few who were left reached their fortified cities. 21The whole army then returned safely to Joshua in the

b1 The Hebrew term refers to the irrevocable giving over of things or persons to the LORD, often by totally destroying them; also in verses 28, 35, 37, 39 and 40. c13 Or *nation triumphed over*

camp at Makkedah, and no one uttered a word against the Israelites.

22Joshua said, "Open the mouth of the cave and bring those five kings out to me." 23So they brought the five kings out of the cave—the kings of Jerusalem, Hebron, Jarmuth, Lachish and Eglon. 24When they had brought these kings to Joshua, he summoned all the men of Israel and said to the army commanders who had come with him, "Come here and put your feet on the necks of these kings." So they came forward and placed their feet on their necks.

25Joshua said to them, "Do not be afraid; do not be discouraged. Be strong and courageous. This is what the LORD will do to all the enemies you are going to fight." 26Then Joshua struck and killed the kings and hung them on five trees, and they were left hanging on the trees until evening.

27At sunset Joshua gave the order and they took them down from the trees and threw them into the cave where they had been hiding. At the mouth of the cave they placed large rocks, which are there to this day.

28That day Joshua took Makkedah. He put the city and its king to the sword and totally destroyed everyone in it. He left no survivors. And he did to the king of Makkedah as he had done to the king of Jericho.

29Then Joshua and all Israel with him moved on from Makkedah to Libnah and attacked it. 30The LORD also gave that city and its king into Israel's hand. The city and everyone in it Joshua put to the sword. He left no survivors there. And he did to its king as he had done to the king of Jericho.

31Then Joshua and all Israel with him moved on from Libnah to Lachish; he took up positions against it and attacked it. 32The LORD handed Lachish over to Israel, and Joshua took it on the second day. The city and everyone in it he put to the sword, just as he had done to Libnah. 33Meanwhile, Horam king of Gezer had come up to help Lachish, but Joshua defeated him and his army—until no survivors were left.

34Then Joshua and all Israel with him moved on from Lachish to Eglon; they took up positions against it and attacked it. 35They captured it that same day and put it to the sword and totally destroyed everyone in it, just as they had done to Lachish.

36Then Joshua and all Israel with him went up from Eglon to Hebron and attacked it. 37They took the city and put it to the sword, together with its king, its villages and everyone in it. They left no survivors. Just as at Eglon, they totally destroyed it and everyone in it.

38Then Joshua and all Israel with him turned around and attacked Debir. 39They took the city, its king and its villages, and put them to the sword. Everyone in it they totally destroyed. They left no survivors. They did to Debir and its king as they had done to Libnah and its king and to Hebron.

40So Joshua subdued the whole region, including the hill country, the Negev, the western foothills and the mountain slopes, together with all their kings. He left no survivors. He totally destroyed all who breathed, just as the LORD, the God of Israel, had commanded. 41Joshua subdued them from Kadesh Barnea to Gaza and from the whole region of Goshen to Gibeon. 42All these kings and their lands Joshua conquered in one campaign, because the LORD, the God of Israel, fought for Israel.

43Then Joshua returned with all Israel to the camp at Gilgal.

11 When Jabin king of Hazor heard of this, he sent word to Jobab king of Madon, to the kings of Shimron and Acshaph, 2and to the northern kings who were in the mountains, in the Arabah south of Kinnereth, in the western foothills and in Naphoth Dor[d] on the west; 3to the Canaanites in the east and west; to the Amorites, Hittites, Perizzites and Jebusites in the hill country; and to the Hivites below Hermon in the region of Mizpah. 4They came out with all their troops and a large number of horses and chariots—a huge army, as numerous as the sand on the seashore. 5All these kings joined forces and made camp together at the Waters of Merom, to fight against Israel.

6The LORD said to Joshua, "Do not be afraid of them, because by this time tomorrow I will hand all of them over to Israel, slain. You are to hamstring their horses and burn their chariots."

7So Joshua and his whole army came against them suddenly at the Waters of Merom and attacked them, 8and the LORD gave them into the

[d]2 *Or in the heights of Dor*

hand of Israel. They defeated them and pursued them all the way to Greater Sidon, to Misrephoth Maim, and to the Valley of Mizpah on the east, until no survivors were left. 9Joshua did to them as the LORD had directed: He hamstrung their horses and burned their chariots.

10At that time Joshua turned back and captured Hazor and put its king to the sword. (Hazor had been the head of all these kingdoms.) 11Everyone in it they put to the sword. They totally destroyed[e] them, not sparing anything that breathed, and he burned up Hazor itself.

12Joshua took all these royal cities and their kings and put them to the sword. He totally destroyed them, as Moses the servant of the LORD had commanded. 13Yet Israel did not burn any of the cities built on their mounds—except Hazor, which Joshua burned. 14The Israelites carried off for themselves all the plunder and livestock of these cities, but all the people they put to the sword until they completely destroyed them, not sparing anyone that breathed. 15As the LORD commanded his servant Moses, so Moses commanded Joshua, and Joshua did it; he left nothing undone of all that the LORD commanded Moses.

16So Joshua took this entire land: the hill country, all the Negev, the whole region of Goshen, the western foothills, the Arabah and the mountains of Israel with their foothills, 17from Mount Halak, which rises toward Seir, to Baal Gad in the Valley of Lebanon below Mount Hermon. He captured all their kings and struck them down, putting them to death. 18Joshua waged war against all these kings for a long time. 19Except for the Hivites living in Gibeon, not one city made a treaty of peace with the Israelites, who took them all in battle. 20For it was the LORD himself who hardened their hearts to wage war against Israel, so that he might destroy them totally, exterminating them without mercy, as the LORD had commanded Moses.

21At that time Joshua went and destroyed the Anakites from the hill country: from Hebron, Debir and Anab, from all the hill country of Judah, and from all the hill country of Israel. Joshua totally destroyed them and their towns. 22No Anakites were left in Israelite territory; only in Gaza, Gath and Ashdod did any survive. 23So Joshua took the entire land, just as the LORD had directed Moses, and he gave it as an inheritance to Israel according to their tribal divisions.

Then the land had rest from war.

12

These are the kings of the land whom the Israelites had defeated and whose territory they took over east of the Jordan, from the Arnon Gorge to Mount Hermon, including all the eastern side of the Arabah:

2Sihon king of the Amorites,
who reigned in Heshbon. He ruled from Aroer on the rim of the Arnon Gorge—from the middle of the gorge—to the Jabbok River, which is the border of the Ammonites. This included half of Gilead. 3He also ruled over the eastern Arabah from the Sea of Kinnereth[f] to the Sea of the Arabah (the Salt Sea[g]), to Beth Jeshimoth, and then southward below the slopes of Pisgah.

4And the territory of Og king of Bashan,
one of the last of the Rephaites, who reigned in Ashtaroth and Edrei. 5He ruled over Mount Hermon, Salecah, all of Bashan to the border of the people of Geshur and Maacah, and half of Gilead to the border of Sihon king of Heshbon.

6Moses, the servant of the LORD, and the Israelites conquered them. And Moses the servant of the LORD gave their land to the Reubenites, the Gadites and the half-tribe of Manasseh to be their possession.

7These are the kings of the land that Joshua and the Israelites conquered on the west side of the Jordan, from Baal Gad in the Valley of Lebanon to Mount Halak, which rises toward Seir (their lands Joshua gave as an inheritance to the tribes of Israel according to their tribal divisions— 8the hill country, the western foothills, the Arabah, the mountain slopes, the desert and the Negev—the lands of the Hittites, Amorites, Canaanites, Perizzites, Hivites and Jebusites):

9the king of Jericho one
the king of Ai (near Bethel) one
10the king of Jerusalem one
the king of Hebron one
11the king of Jarmuth one
the king of Lachish one
12the king of Eglon one
the king of Gezer one
13the king of Debir one

[e]11 The Hebrew term refers to the irrevocable giving over of things or persons to the LORD, often by totally destroying them; also in verses 12, 20 and 21. [f]3 That is, Galilee [g]3 That is, the Dead Sea

the king of Geder one
14 the king of Hormah one
the king of Arad one
15 the king of Libnah one
the king of Adullam one
16 the king of Makkedah one
the king of Bethel one
17 the king of Tappuah one
the king of Hepher one
18 the king of Aphek one
the king of Lasharon one
19 the king of Madon one
the king of Hazor one
20 the king of Shimron Meron one
the king of Acshaph one
21 the king of Taanach one
the king of Megiddo one
22 the king of Kedesh one
the king of Jokneam in Carmel one
23 the king of Dor (in Naphoth Dor[h]) one
the king of Goyim in Gilgal one
24 the king of Tirzah one
thirty-one kings in all.

[h]23 Or *in the heights of Dor*

Discovering the Word 1. The Lord tells Joshua, "Do not be afraid of them; I have given them into your hand" (10:8). After miraculously crossing the Jordan and conquering Jericho and Ai, why would Joshua need this reassurance? 2. Verse 14 concludes, "Surely the LORD was fighting for Israel!" How is this obvious from 10:9–15? 3. After the Lord reassures him, how does Joshua reassure his army about future battles (10:16–27)? 4. How does the Lord demonstrate his faithfulness to Israel during the southern campaign (10:29–43)? 5. During the northern campaign, how does Joshua demonstrate his obedience to the Lord (11:6–23)? 6. In chapters 11—12 we do not read of any miraculous intervention by God as we did in previous chapters. How did the Israelites know that God was still the one giving them the victory?

Applying the Word 1. In spite of past victories, in what areas do you need to be reassured of God's presence and power? Explain. 2. What can we do to encourage others about God's faithfulness? 3. Why is our obedience an important factor if we wish to see God's power?

Responding in Prayer Pray that God would make his presence real to you.

Joshua 13

13 When Joshua was old and well ad-
vanced in years, the LORD said to
him, "You are very old, and there
are still very large areas of land to be taken over.
2 "This is the land that remains: all the re-
gions of the Philistines and Geshurites:
3 from the Shihor River on the east of Egypt
to the territory of Ekron on the north, all of
it counted as Canaanite (the territory of the
five Philistine rulers in Gaza, Ashdod, Ash-
kelon, Gath and Ekron—that of the Av-
vites); 4 from the south, all the land of the
Canaanites, from Arah of the Sidonians as far
as Aphek, the region of the Amorites, 5 the
area of the Gebalites[i]; and all Lebanon to
the east, from Baal Gad below Mount Her-
mon to Lebo[j] Hamath.
6 "As for all the inhabitants of the mountain re-
gions from Lebanon to Misrephoth Maim, that is,
all the Sidonians, I myself will drive them out
before the Israelites. Be sure to allocate this land
to Israel for an inheritance, as I have instructed
you, 7 and divide it as an inheritance among the
nine tribes and half of the tribe of Manasseh."
8 The other half of Manasseh,[k] the Reubenites
and the Gadites had received the inheritance that
Moses had given them east of the Jordan, as he,
the servant of the LORD, had assigned it to them.
9 It extended from Aroer on the rim of the
Arnon Gorge, and from the town in the mid-
dle of the gorge, and included the whole pla-
teau of Medeba as far as Dibon, 10 and all the
towns of Sihon king of the Amorites, who
ruled in Heshbon, out to the border of the

[i]5 That is, the area of Byblos [j]5 Or *to the entrance to*
[k]8 Hebrew *With it* (that is, with the other half of Manasseh)

Ammonites. [11]It also included Gilead, the territory of the people of Geshur and Maacah, all of Mount Hermon and all Bashan as far as Salecah— [12]that is, the whole kingdom of Og in Bashan, who had reigned in Ashtaroth and Edrei and had survived as one of the last of the Rephaites. Moses had defeated them and taken over their land. [13]But the Israelites did not drive out the people of Geshur and Maacah, so they continue to live among the Israelites to this day.

[14]But to the tribe of Levi he gave no inheritance, since the offerings made by fire to the LORD, the God of Israel, are their inheritance, as he promised them.

[15]This is what Moses had given to the tribe of Reuben, clan by clan:

[16]The territory from Aroer on the rim of the Arnon Gorge, and from the town in the middle of the gorge, and the whole plateau past Medeba [17]to Heshbon and all its towns on the plateau, including Dibon, Bamoth Baal, Beth Baal Meon, [18]Jahaz, Kedemoth, Mephaath, [19]Kiriathaim, Sibmah, Zereth Shahar on the hill in the valley, [20]Beth Peor, the slopes of Pisgah, and Beth Jeshimoth [21]—all the towns on the plateau and the entire realm of Sihon king of the Amorites, who ruled at Heshbon. Moses had defeated him and the Midianite chiefs, Evi, Rekem, Zur, Hur and Reba—princes allied with Sihon—who lived in that country. [22]In addition to those slain in battle, the Israelites had put to the sword Balaam son of Beor, who practiced divination. [23]The boundary of the Reubenites was the bank of the Jordan. These towns and their villages were the inheritance of the Reubenites, clan by clan.

[24]This is what Moses had given to the tribe of Gad, clan by clan:

[25]The territory of Jazer, all the towns of Gilead and half the Ammonite country as far as Aroer, near Rabbah; [26]and from Heshbon to Ramath Mizpah and Betonim, and from Mahanaim to the territory of Debir; [27]and in the valley, Beth Haram, Beth Nimrah, Succoth and Zaphon with the rest of the realm of Sihon king of Heshbon (the east side of the Jordan, the territory up to the end of the Sea of Kinnereth[l]). [28]These towns and their villages were the inheritance of the Gadites, clan by clan.

[29]This is what Moses had given to the half-tribe of Manasseh, that is, to half the family of the descendants of Manasseh, clan by clan:

[30]The territory extending from Mahanaim and including all of Bashan, the entire realm of Og king of Bashan—all the settlements of Jair in Bashan, sixty towns, [31]half of Gilead, and Ashtaroth and Edrei (the royal cities of Og in Bashan). This was for the descendants of Makir son of Manasseh—for half of the sons of Makir, clan by clan.

[32]This is the inheritance Moses had given when he was in the plains of Moab across the Jordan east of Jericho. [33]But to the tribe of Levi, Moses had given no inheritance; the LORD, the God of Israel, is their inheritance, as he promised them.

[l]27 That is, Galilee

8 / *Joshua 14—18*
Joshua Divides the Land

CHRISTIANS OFTEN FEEL more like captives than conquerors. What hinders our spiritual progress? Why do we sometimes experience so little when we are promised so much? God had proven himself to Israel throughout their many battles. He had promised to be with them in the conquest of Canaan and had kept his promise. Yet in spite of many victories, much of the land remained to be conquered. These chapters look at why Israel had failed to possess all that God had promised.

Warming Up to God In what one area of your life would you most like to see spiritual progress?

Read Joshua 14—18.

14 Now these are the areas the Israelites received as an inheritance in the land of Canaan, which Eleazar the priest, Joshua son of Nun and the heads of the tribal clans of Israel allotted to them. 2Their inheritances were assigned by lot to the nine-and-a-half tribes, as the LORD had commanded through Moses. 3Moses had granted the two-and-a-half tribes their inheritance east of the Jordan but had not granted the Levites an inheritance among the rest, 4for the sons of Joseph had become two tribes—Manasseh and Ephraim. The Levites received no share of the land but only towns to live in, with pasturelands for their flocks and herds. 5So the Israelites divided the land, just as the LORD had commanded Moses.

6Now the men of Judah approached Joshua at Gilgal, and Caleb son of Jephunneh the Kenizzite said to him, "You know what the LORD said to Moses the man of God at Kadesh Barnea about you and me. 7I was forty years old when Moses the servant of the LORD sent me from Kadesh Barnea to explore the land. And I brought him back a report according to my convictions, 8but my brothers who went up with me made the hearts of the people melt with fear. I, however, followed the LORD my God wholeheartedly. 9So on that day Moses swore to me, 'The land on which your feet have walked will be your inheritance and that of your children forever, because you have followed the LORD my God wholeheartedly.'[m]

10"Now then, just as the LORD promised, he has kept me alive for forty-five years since the time he said this to Moses, while Israel moved about in the desert. So here I am today, eighty-five years old! 11I am still as strong today as the day Moses sent me out; I'm just as vigorous to go out to battle now as I was then. 12Now give me this hill country that the LORD promised me that day. You yourself heard then that the Anakites were there and their cities were large and fortified, but, the LORD helping me, I will drive them out just as he said."

13Then Joshua blessed Caleb son of Jephunneh and gave him Hebron as his inheritance. 14So Hebron has belonged to Caleb son of Jephunneh the Kenizzite ever since, because he followed the LORD, the God of Israel, wholeheartedly. 15(Hebron used to be called Kiriath Arba after Arba, who was the greatest man among the Anakites.)

Then the land had rest from war.

15 The allotment for the tribe of Judah, clan by clan, extended down to the territory of Edom, to the Desert of Zin in the extreme south.

2Their southern boundary started from the bay at the southern end of the Salt Sea,[n] 3crossed south of Scorpion[o] Pass, continued on to Zin and went over to the south of Kadesh Barnea. Then it ran past Hezron up to Addar and curved around to Karka. 4It then passed along to Azmon and joined the Wadi of Egypt, ending at the sea. This is their[p] southern boundary.

5The eastern boundary is the Salt Sea as far as the mouth of the Jordan.

The northern boundary started from the bay of the sea at the mouth of the Jordan, 6went up to Beth Hoglah and continued north of Beth Arabah to the Stone of Bohan son of Reuben. 7The boundary then went up to Debir from the Valley of Achor and turned north to Gilgal, which faces the Pass of Adummim south of the gorge. It continued along to the waters of En Shemesh and came out at En Rogel. 8Then it ran up the Valley of Ben Hinnom along the southern slope of the Jebusite city (that is, Jerusalem). From there it climbed to the top of the hill west of the Hinnom Valley at the northern end of the Valley of Rephaim. 9From the hilltop the boundary headed toward the spring of the waters of Nephtoah, came out at the towns of Mount Ephron and went down toward Baalah (that is, Kiriath Jearim). 10Then it curved westward from Baalah to Mount Seir, ran along the northern slope of Mount Jearim (that is, Kesalon), continued down to Beth Shemesh and crossed to Timnah. 11It went to the northern slope of Ekron, turned toward Shikkeron, passed along to Mount

m9 Deut. 1:36 n2 That is, the Dead Sea; also in verse 5
o3 Hebrew *Akrabbim* p4 Hebrew *your*

Baalah and reached Jabneel. The boundary
ended at the sea.

12The western boundary is the coastline of
the Great Sea.[q]

These are the boundaries around the people of
Judah by their clans.

13In accordance with the LORD's command to
him, Joshua gave to Caleb son of Jephunneh a
portion in Judah—Kiriath Arba, that is, Hebron.
(Arba was the forefather of Anak.) 14From He-
bron Caleb drove out the three Anakites—She-
shai, Ahiman and Talmai—descendants of Anak.
15From there he marched against the people liv-
ing in Debir (formerly called Kiriath Sepher).
16And Caleb said, "I will give my daughter Acsah
in marriage to the man who attacks and captures
Kiriath Sepher." 17Othniel son of Kenaz, Caleb's
brother, took it; so Caleb gave his daughter Acsah
to him in marriage.

18One day when she came to Othniel, she
urged him[r] to ask her father for a field. When
she got off her donkey, Caleb asked her, "What
can I do for you?"

19She replied, "Do me a special favor. Since you
have given me land in the Negev, give me also
springs of water." So Caleb gave her the upper
and lower springs.

20This is the inheritance of the tribe of Judah,
clan by clan:

21The southernmost towns of the tribe of Judah in
the Negev toward the boundary of Edom were:

Kabzeel, Eder, Jagur, 22Kinah, Dimonah,
Adadah, 23Kedesh, Hazor, Ithnan, 24Ziph,
Telem, Bealoth, 25Hazor Hadattah, Kerioth
Hezron (that is, Hazor), 26Amam, Shema,
Moladah, 27Hazar Gaddah, Heshmon, Beth
Pelet, 28Hazar Shual, Beersheba, Biziothiah,
29Baalah, Iim, Ezem, 30Eltolad, Kesil, Hor-
mah, 31Ziklag, Madmannah, Sansannah,
32Lebaoth, Shilhim, Ain and Rimmon—a to-
tal of twenty-nine towns and their villages.

33In the western foothills:

Eshtaol, Zorah, Ashnah, 34Zanoah, En
Gannim, Tappuah, Enam, 35Jarmuth, Adul-
lam, Socoh, Azekah, 36Shaaraim, Adithaim
and Gederah (or Gederothaim)[s]—fourteen
towns and their villages.

37Zenan, Hadashah, Migdal Gad, 38Dilean,
Mizpah, Joktheel, 39Lachish, Bozkath, Eglon,
40Cabbon, Lahmas, Kitlish, 41Gederoth, Beth
Dagon, Naamah and Makkedah—sixteen
towns and their villages.

42Libnah, Ether, Ashan, 43Iphtah, Ashnah,
Nezib, 44Keilah, Aczib and Mareshah—nine
towns and their villages.

45Ekron, with its surrounding settlements
and villages; 46west of Ekron, all that were in
the vicinity of Ashdod, together with their
villages; 47Ashdod, its surrounding settle-
ments and villages; and Gaza, its settlements
and villages, as far as the Wadi of Egypt and
the coastline of the Great Sea.

48In the hill country:

Shamir, Jattir, Socoh, 49Dannah, Kiriath
Sannah (that is, Debir), 50Anab, Eshtemoh,
Anim, 51Goshen, Holon and Giloh—eleven
towns and their villages.

52Arab, Dumah, Eshan, 53Janim, Beth Tap-
puah, Aphekah, 54Humtah, Kiriath Arba
(that is, Hebron) and Zior—nine towns and
their villages.

55Maon, Carmel, Ziph, Juttah, 56Jezreel,
Jokdeam, Zanoah, 57Kain, Gibeah and Tim-
nah—ten towns and their villages.

58Halhul, Beth Zur, Gedor, 59Maarath,
Beth Anoth and Eltekon—six towns and
their villages.

60Kiriath Baal (that is, Kiriath Jearim) and
Rabbah—two towns and their villages.

61In the desert:

Beth Arabah, Middin, Secacah, 62Nibshan,
the City of Salt and En Gedi—six towns and
their villages.

63Judah could not dislodge the Jebusites, who
were living in Jerusalem; to this day the Jebusites
live there with the people of Judah.

16 The allotment for Joseph be-
gan at the Jordan of Jericho,[t]
east of the waters of Jericho,
and went up from there through the desert
into the hill country of Bethel. 2It went on
from Bethel (that is, Luz),[u] crossed over to
the territory of the Arkites in Ataroth, 3de-
scended westward to the territory of the
Japhletites as far as the region of Lower Beth
Horon and on to Gezer, ending at the sea.

[q]12 That is, the Mediterranean; also in verse 47 [r]18 Hebrew and some Septuagint manuscripts; other Septuagint manuscripts (see also note at Judges 1:14) *Othniel, he urged her* [s]36 Or *Gederah and Gederothaim* [t]1 *Jordan of Jericho* was possibly an ancient name for the Jordan River. [u]2 Septuagint; Hebrew *Bethel to Luz*

4So Manasseh and Ephraim, the descendants of
Joseph, received their inheritance.

5This was the territory of Ephraim, clan by clan:

The boundary of their inheritance went
from Ataroth Addar in the east to Upper Beth
Horon 6and continued to the sea. From Mic-
methath on the north it curved eastward to
Taanath Shiloh, passing by it to Janoah on
the east. 7Then it went down from Janoah to
Ataroth and Naarah, touched Jericho and
came out at the Jordan. 8From Tappuah the
border went west to the Kanah Ravine and
ended at the sea. This was the inheritance of
the tribe of the Ephraimites, clan by clan. 9It
also included all the towns and their villages
that were set aside for the Ephraimites
within the inheritance of the Manassites.

10They did not dislodge the Canaanites living in
Gezer; to this day the Canaanites live among the
people of Ephraim but are required to do forced
labor.

17 This was the allotment for the tribe
of Manasseh as Joseph's firstborn,
that is, for Makir, Manasseh's first-
born. Makir was the ancestor of the Gileadites,
who had received Gilead and Bashan because the
Makirites were great soldiers. 2So this allotment
was for the rest of the people of Manasseh—the
clans of Abiezer, Helek, Asriel, Shechem, Hepher
and Shemida. These are the other male descen-
dants of Manasseh son of Joseph by their clans.

3Now Zelophehad son of Hepher, the son of
Gilead, the son of Makir, the son of Manasseh,
had no sons but only daughters, whose names
were Mahlah, Noah, Hoglah, Milcah and Tirzah.
4They went to Eleazar the priest, Joshua son of
Nun, and the leaders and said, "The LORD com-
manded Moses to give us an inheritance among
our brothers." So Joshua gave them an inheri-
tance along with the brothers of their father, ac-
cording to the LORD's command. 5Manasseh's
share consisted of ten tracts of land besides Gil-
ead and Bashan east of the Jordan, 6because the
daughters of the tribe of Manasseh received an
inheritance among the sons. The land of Gilead
belonged to the rest of the descendants of Manas-
seh.

7The territory of Manasseh extended from
Asher to Micmethath east of Shechem. The
boundary ran southward from there to in-
clude the people living at En Tappuah. 8(Ma-
nasseh had the land of Tappuah, but Tap-
puah itself, on the boundary of Manasseh,
belonged to the Ephraimites.) 9Then the
boundary continued south to the Kanah Ra-
vine. There were towns belonging to
Ephraim lying among the towns of Manas-
seh, but the boundary of Manasseh was the
northern side of the ravine and ended at the
sea. 10On the south the land belonged to
Ephraim, on the north to Manasseh. The ter-
ritory of Manasseh reached the sea and bor-
dered Asher on the north and Issachar on the
east.

11Within Issachar and Asher, Manasseh
also had Beth Shan, Ibleam and the people of
Dor, Endor, Taanach and Megiddo, together
with their surrounding settlements (the third
in the list is Naphoth[v]).

12Yet the Manassites were not able to occupy
these towns, for the Canaanites were determined
to live in that region. 13However, when the Israel-
ites grew stronger, they subjected the Canaanites
to forced labor but did not drive them out com-
pletely.

14The people of Joseph said to Joshua, "Why
have you given us only one allotment and one
portion for an inheritance? We are a numerous
people and the LORD has blessed us abundantly."

15"If you are so numerous," Joshua answered,
"and if the hill country of Ephraim is too small
for you, go up into the forest and clear land for
yourselves there in the land of the Perizzites and
Rephaites."

16The people of Joseph replied, "The hill coun-
try is not enough for us, and all the Canaanites
who live in the plain have iron chariots, both
those in Beth Shan and its settlements and those
in the Valley of Jezreel."

17But Joshua said to the house of Joseph—to
Ephraim and Manasseh—"You are numerous and
very powerful. You will have not only one allot-
ment 18but the forested hill country as well. Clear
it, and its farthest limits will be yours; though the
Canaanites have iron chariots and though they
are strong, you can drive them out."

18 The whole assembly of the Israel-
ites gathered at Shiloh and set up
the Tent of Meeting there. The
country was brought under their control, 2but

v11 That is, Naphoth Dor

there were still seven Israelite tribes who had not
yet received their inheritance.
3So Joshua said to the Israelites: "How long will
you wait before you begin to take possession of
the land that the LORD, the God of your fathers,
has given you? 4Appoint three men from each
tribe. I will send them out to make a survey of the
land and to write a description of it, according to
the inheritance of each. Then they will return to
me. 5You are to divide the land into seven parts.
Judah is to remain in its territory on the south
and the house of Joseph in its territory on the
north. 6After you have written descriptions of the
seven parts of the land, bring them here to me
and I will cast lots for you in the presence of the
LORD our God. 7The Levites, however, do not get
a portion among you, because the priestly service
of the LORD is their inheritance. And Gad, Reuben
and the half-tribe of Manasseh have already re-
ceived their inheritance on the east side of the
Jordan. Moses the servant of the LORD gave it to
them."

8As the men started on their way to map out
the land, Joshua instructed them, "Go and make
a survey of the land and write a description of it.
Then return to me, and I will cast lots for you
here at Shiloh in the presence of the LORD." 9So
the men left and went through the land. They
wrote its description on a scroll, town by town, in
seven parts, and returned to Joshua in the camp
at Shiloh. 10Joshua then cast lots for them in Shi-
loh in the presence of the LORD, and there he dis-
tributed the land to the Israelites according to
their tribal divisions.

11The lot came up for the tribe of Benjamin, clan
by clan. Their allotted territory lay between the
tribes of Judah and Joseph:

12On the north side their boundary began
at the Jordan, passed the northern slope of
Jericho and headed west into the hill coun-
try, coming out at the desert of Beth Aven.
13From there it crossed to the south slope of
Luz (that is, Bethel) and went down to Ata-
roth Addar on the hill south of Lower Beth
Horon.

14From the hill facing Beth Horon on the
south the boundary turned south along the
western side and came out at Kiriath Baal
(that is, Kiriath Jearim), a town of the people
of Judah. This was the western side.

15The southern side began at the outskirts
of Kiriath Jearim on the west, and the
boundary came out at the spring of the wa-
ters of Nephtoah. 16The boundary went
down to the foot of the hill facing the Valley
of Ben Hinnom, north of the Valley of Reph-
aim. It continued down the Hinnom Valley
along the southern slope of the Jebusite city
and so to En Rogel. 17It then curved north,
went to En Shemesh, continued to Geliloth,
which faces the Pass of Adummim, and ran
down to the Stone of Bohan son of Reuben.
18It continued to the northern slope of Beth
Arabah[w] and on down into the Arabah. 19It
then went to the northern slope of Beth Hog-
lah and came out at the northern bay of the
Salt Sea,[x] at the mouth of the Jordan in the
south. This was the southern boundary.

20The Jordan formed the boundary on the
eastern side.

These were the boundaries that marked out the
inheritance of the clans of Benjamin on all sides.

21The tribe of Benjamin, clan by clan, had the
following cities:

Jericho, Beth Hoglah, Emek Keziz, 22Beth
Arabah, Zemaraim, Bethel, 23Avvim, Parah,
Ophrah, 24Kephar Ammoni, Ophni and
Geba—twelve towns and their villages.

25Gibeon, Ramah, Beeroth, 26Mizpah, Ke-
phirah, Mozah, 27Rekem, Irpeel, Taralah,
28Zelah, Haeleph, the Jebusite city (that is,
Jerusalem), Gibeah and Kiriath—fourteen
towns and their villages.

This was the inheritance of Benjamin for its clans.

w18 Septuagint; Hebrew *slope facing the Arabah* x19 That is, the Dead Sea

Discovering the Word 1. How is Caleb's faith just as strong at eighty-five as it had been at forty? 2. Note 15:63, 16:10 and 17:12–13. God had promised to drive these Canaanites out of the land. Why then do you think Israel had difficulty dislodging them (see also Ex 23:29–30 and Dt 7:22–24)? 3. How does the attitude of the people of Joseph contrast with that of Caleb? 4. How does Joshua deal with their complaint (17:17–18)? 5. Seven tribes had not yet received their inheritance. What was their problem (18:1–10)? 6. As you look back over these chapters, what reasons can you give for why Israel had difficulty taking full possession of the land?

Applying the Word 1. Which reasons help to explain why God's promises to us are sometimes only partially fulfilled? (For example, his promise to purify our lives of sin.) Explain. 2. We sometimes act like the people of Joseph, complaining about how little God has given us when we have not fully used what we have. How do you think Joshua would respond to our complaints and excuses?

Responding in Prayer Ask God to mold your faith to be like Caleb's.

Joshua 19

19 The second lot came out for the tribe of Simeon, clan by clan. Their inheritance lay within the territory of Judah. 2It included:

Beersheba (or Sheba),[y] Moladah, 3Hazar Shual, Balah, Ezem, 4Eltolad, Bethul, Hormah, 5Ziklag, Beth Marcaboth, Hazar Susah, 6Beth Lebaoth and Sharuhen—thirteen towns and their villages;

7Ain, Rimmon, Ether and Ashan—four towns and their villages— 8and all the villages around these towns as far as Baalath Beer (Ramah in the Negev).

This was the inheritance of the tribe of the Simeonites, clan by clan. 9The inheritance of the Simeonites was taken from the share of Judah, because Judah's portion was more than they needed. So the Simeonites received their inheritance within the territory of Judah.

10The third lot came up for Zebulun, clan by clan:

The boundary of their inheritance went as far as Sarid. 11Going west it ran to Maralah, touched Dabbesheth, and extended to the ravine near Jokneam. 12It turned east from Sarid toward the sunrise to the territory of Kisloth Tabor and went on to Daberath and up to Japhia. 13Then it continued eastward to Gath Hepher and Eth Kazin; it came out at Rimmon and turned toward Neah. 14There the boundary went around on the north to Hannathon and ended at the Valley of Iphtah El. 15Included were Kattath, Nahalal, Shimron, Idalah and Bethlehem. There were twelve towns and their villages.

16These towns and their villages were the inheritance of Zebulun, clan by clan.

17The fourth lot came out for Issachar, clan by clan. 18Their territory included:

Jezreel, Kesulloth, Shunem, 19Hapharaim, Shion, Anaharath, 20Rabbith, Kishion, Ebez, 21Remeth, En Gannim, En Haddah and Beth Pazzez. 22The boundary touched Tabor, Shahazumah and Beth Shemesh, and ended at the Jordan. There were sixteen towns and their villages.

23These towns and their villages were the inheritance of the tribe of Issachar, clan by clan.

24The fifth lot came out for the tribe of Asher, clan by clan. 25Their territory included:

Helkath, Hali, Beten, Acshaph, 26Allammelech, Amad and Mishal. On the west the boundary touched Carmel and Shihor Libnath. 27It then turned east toward Beth Dagon, touched Zebulun and the Valley of Iphtah El, and went north to Beth Emek and Neiel, passing Cabul on the left. 28It went to Abdon,[z] Rehob, Hammon and Kanah, as far as Greater Sidon. 29The boundary then turned back toward Ramah and went to the fortified city of Tyre, turned toward Hosah and came out at the sea in the region of Aczib, 30Ummah, Aphek and Rehob. There were twenty-two towns and their villages.

31These towns and their villages were the inheritance of the tribe of Asher, clan by clan.

32The sixth lot came out for Naphtali, clan by clan:

33Their boundary went from Heleph and the large tree in Zaanannim, passing Adami Nekeb and Jabneel to Lakkum and ending at the Jordan. 34The boundary ran west through Aznoth Tabor and came out at Hukkok. It touched Zebulun on the south, Asher on the west and the Jordan[a] on the east. 35The fortified cities were Ziddim, Zer, Hammath, Rakkath, Kinnereth, 36Adamah, Ramah, Hazor, 37Kedesh, Edrei, En Hazor,

[y]2 Or *Beersheba, Sheba;* 1 Chron. 4:28 does not have *Sheba.* [z]28 Some Hebrew manuscripts (see also Joshua 21:30); most Hebrew manuscripts *Ebron* [a]34 Septuagint; Hebrew *west, and Judah, the Jordan,*

[38]Iron, Migdal El, Horem, Beth Anath and Beth Shemesh. There were nineteen towns and their villages.

[39]These towns and their villages were the inheritance of the tribe of Naphtali, clan by clan.

[40]The seventh lot came out for the tribe of Dan, clan by clan. [41]The territory of their inheritance included:

Zorah, Eshtaol, Ir Shemesh, [42]Shaalabbin, Aijalon, Ithlah, [43]Elon, Timnah, Ekron, [44]Eltekeh, Gibbethon, Baalath, [45]Jehud, Bene Berak, Gath Rimmon, [46]Me Jarkon and Rakkon, with the area facing Joppa.

[47](But the Danites had difficulty taking possession of their territory, so they went up and attacked Leshem, took it, put it to the sword and occupied it. They settled in Leshem and named it Dan after their forefather.)

[48]These towns and their villages were the inheritance of the tribe of Dan, clan by clan.

[49]When they had finished dividing the land into its allotted portions, the Israelites gave Joshua son of Nun an inheritance among them, [50]as the LORD had commanded. They gave him the town he asked for—Timnath Serah[b] in the hill country of Ephraim. And he built up the town and settled there.

[51]These are the territories that Eleazar the priest, Joshua son of Nun and the heads of the tribal clans of Israel assigned by lot at Shiloh in the presence of the LORD at the entrance to the Tent of Meeting. And so they finished dividing the land.

[b]*50* Also known as *Timnath Heres* (see Judges 2:9)

9 / *Joshua 20—21*
The Lord Fulfills His Promises

HOW DOES FAITH differ from wishful thinking? Why should we expect God to answer our prayers, to provide us with food and clothing, or to be involved in jobs or family? How do we know our faith isn't simply foolishness? Scripture tells us that true faith must be grounded in God's promises. If God has promised to do something, then we can trust him wholeheartedly. If he has not promised to do something, then all the faith in the world won't make it happen. In Joshua 20—21 we see the final outcome of God's promises to Israel.

Warming Up to God Think of a time recently when you trusted God for something. Which of his promises applied to that situation?

Read Joshua 20—21.

20 Then the LORD said to Joshua: [2]"Tell the Israelites to designate the cities of refuge, as I instructed you through Moses, [3]so that anyone who kills a person accidentally and unintentionally may flee there and find protection from the avenger of blood.

[4]"When he flees to one of these cities, he is to stand in the entrance of the city gate and state his case before the elders of that city. Then they are to admit him into their city and give him a place to live with them. [5]If the avenger of blood pursues him, they must not surrender the one accused, because he killed his neighbor unintentionally and without malice aforethought. [6]He is to stay in that city until he has stood trial before the assembly and until the death of the high priest who is serving at that time. Then he may go back to his own home in the town from which he fled."

[7]So they set apart Kedesh in Galilee in the hill country of Naphtali, Shechem in the hill country of Ephraim, and Kiriath Arba (that is, Hebron) in the hill country of Judah. [8]On the east side of the Jordan of Jericho[c] they designated Bezer in the desert on the plateau in the tribe of Reuben, Ramoth in Gilead in the tribe of Gad, and Golan in Bashan in the tribe of Manasseh. [9]Any of the Israelites or any alien living among them who killed

[c]*8* *Jordan of Jericho* was possibly an ancient name for the Jordan River.

someone accidentally could flee to these designated cities and not be killed by the avenger of blood prior to standing trial before the assembly.

21 Now the family heads of the Levites approached Eleazar the priest, Joshua son of Nun, and the heads of the other tribal families of Israel 2at Shiloh in Canaan and said to them, "The LORD commanded through Moses that you give us towns to live in, with pasturelands for our livestock." 3So, as the LORD had commanded, the Israelites gave the Levites the following towns and pasturelands out of their own inheritance:

4The first lot came out for the Kohathites, clan by clan. The Levites who were descendants of Aaron the priest were allotted thirteen towns from the tribes of Judah, Simeon and Benjamin. 5The rest of Kohath's descendants were allotted ten towns from the clans of the tribes of Ephraim, Dan and half of Manasseh.

6The descendants of Gershon were allotted thirteen towns from the clans of the tribes of Issachar, Asher, Naphtali and the half-tribe of Manasseh in Bashan.

7The descendants of Merari, clan by clan, received twelve towns from the tribes of Reuben, Gad and Zebulun.

8So the Israelites allotted to the Levites these towns and their pasturelands, as the LORD had commanded through Moses.

9From the tribes of Judah and Simeon they allotted the following towns by name 10(these towns were assigned to the descendants of Aaron who were from the Kohathite clans of the Levites, because the first lot fell to them):

11They gave them Kiriath Arba (that is, Hebron), with its surrounding pastureland, in the hill country of Judah. (Arba was the forefather of Anak.) 12But the fields and villages around the city they had given to Caleb son of Jephunneh as his possession.

13So to the descendants of Aaron the priest they gave Hebron (a city of refuge for one accused of murder), Libnah, 14Jattir, Eshtemoa, 15Holon, Debir, 16Ain, Juttah and Beth Shemesh, together with their pasturelands—nine towns from these two tribes.

17And from the tribe of Benjamin they gave them Gibeon, Geba, 18Anathoth and Almon, together with their pasturelands—four towns.

19All the towns for the priests, the descendants of Aaron, were thirteen, together with their pasturelands.

20The rest of the Kohathite clans of the Levites were allotted towns from the tribe of Ephraim:

21In the hill country of Ephraim they were given Shechem (a city of refuge for one accused of murder) and Gezer, 22Kibzaim and Beth Horon, together with their pasturelands—four towns.

23Also from the tribe of Dan they received Eltekeh, Gibbethon, 24Aijalon and Gath Rimmon, together with their pasturelands—four towns.

25From half the tribe of Manasseh they received Taanach and Gath Rimmon, together with their pasturelands—two towns.

26All these ten towns and their pasturelands were given to the rest of the Kohathite clans.

27The Levite clans of the Gershonites were given:
from the half-tribe of Manasseh,
Golan in Bashan (a city of refuge for one accused of murder) and Be Eshtarah, together with their pasturelands—two towns;
28from the tribe of Issachar,
Kishion, Daberath, 29Jarmuth and En Gannim, together with their pasturelands—four towns;
30from the tribe of Asher,
Mishal, Abdon, 31Helkath and Rehob, together with their pasturelands—four towns;
32from the tribe of Naphtali,
Kedesh in Galilee (a city of refuge for one accused of murder), Hammoth Dor and Kartan, together with their pasturelands—three towns.

33All the towns of the Gershonite clans were thirteen, together with their pasturelands.

34The Merarite clans (the rest of the Levites) were given:
from the tribe of Zebulun,
Jokneam, Kartah, 35Dimnah and Nahalal, together with their pasturelands—four towns;
36from the tribe of Reuben,
Bezer, Jahaz, 37Kedemoth and Mephaath, together with their pasturelands—four towns;
38from the tribe of Gad,
Ramoth in Gilead (a city of refuge for one accused of murder), Mahanaim, 39Heshbon

and Jazer, together with their pasturelands—four towns in all.
40All the towns allotted to the Merarite clans, who were the rest of the Levites, were twelve.

41The towns of the Levites in the territory held by the Israelites were forty-eight in all, together with their pasturelands. 42Each of these towns had pasturelands surrounding it; this was true for all these towns.

43So the LORD gave Israel all the land he had sworn to give their forefathers, and they took possession of it and settled there. 44The LORD gave them rest on every side, just as he had sworn to their forefathers. Not one of their enemies withstood them; the LORD handed all their enemies over to them. 45Not one of all the LORD's good promises to the house of Israel failed; every one was fulfilled.

Discovering the Word 1. What was the purpose of the cities of refuge (20:1–6)? 2. What does the command to establish these cities teach us about the Lord? 3. How did the Levites differ from the other tribes (see 13:14, 33; 14:3–4; 18:7)? 4. What do you think God's purpose was in scattering the Levites throughout the land? 5. How does 21:43–45 provide the climax to the book of Joshua?

Applying the Word 1. What are some of the promises God has made to us as Christians? 2. In what ways have you seen God fulfill these promises in your life?

Responding in Prayer Praise God for his faithfulness in keeping his promises to us.

10/ *Joshua 22*
Will the Nation Survive?

THE TRIBES WHICH had been given land on the east side of the Jordan had fulfilled their commitment to the rest of Israel. They had entered the Promised Land with the others and had helped them to fight. Now it was time for them to return to their own homes. But since the Israelites would be living on both sides of the river, the Jordan Rift Valley became a natural barrier which hindered the unity of the twelve tribes. Could Israel still remain unified? Their response to a national crisis illustrates principles for maintaining Christian unity.

Warming Up to God God is glorified by your praise and worship. Spend some time offering your thanks for who he is.

Read Joshua 22.

22 Then Joshua summoned the Reubenites, the Gadites and the half-tribe of Manasseh 2and said to them, "You have done all that Moses the servant of the LORD commanded, and you have obeyed me in everything I commanded. 3For a long time now—to this very day—you have not deserted your brothers but have carried out the mission the LORD your God gave you. 4Now that the LORD your God has given your brothers rest as he promised, return to your homes in the land that Moses the servant of the LORD gave you on the other side of the Jordan. 5But be very careful to keep the commandment and the law that Moses the servant of the LORD gave you: to love the LORD your God, to walk in all his ways, to obey his commands, to hold fast to him and to serve him with all your heart and all your soul."

6Then Joshua blessed them and sent them away, and they went to their homes. 7(To the half-tribe of Manasseh Moses had given land in Bashan, and to the other half of the tribe Joshua gave land on the west side of the Jordan with their brothers.) When Joshua sent them home, he blessed them, 8saying, "Return to your homes with your great wealth—with large herds of livestock, with silver, gold, bronze and iron, and a great quantity of clothing—and divide with your brothers the plunder from your enemies."

9So the Reubenites, the Gadites and the half-tribe of Manasseh left the Israelites at Shiloh in Canaan to return to Gilead, their own land, which they had acquired in accordance with the command of the LORD through Moses.

10When they came to Geliloth near the Jordan in the land of Canaan, the Reubenites, the Gadites and the half-tribe of Manasseh built an imposing altar there by the Jordan. 11And when the Israelites heard that they had built the altar on the border of Canaan at Geliloth near the Jordan on the Israelite side, 12the whole assembly of Israel gathered at Shiloh to go to war against them.

13So the Israelites sent Phinehas son of Eleazar, the priest, to the land of Gilead—to Reuben, Gad and the half-tribe of Manasseh. 14With him they sent ten of the chief men, one for each of the tribes of Israel, each the head of a family division among the Israelite clans.

15When they went to Gilead—to Reuben, Gad and the half-tribe of Manasseh—they said to them: 16"The whole assembly of the LORD says: 'How could you break faith with the God of Israel like this? How could you turn away from the LORD and build yourselves an altar in rebellion against him now? 17Was not the sin of Peor enough for us? Up to this very day we have not cleansed ourselves from that sin, even though a plague fell on the community of the LORD! 18And are you now turning away from the LORD?

" 'If you rebel against the LORD today, tomorrow he will be angry with the whole community of Israel. 19If the land you possess is defiled, come over to the LORD's land, where the LORD's tabernacle stands, and share the land with us. But do not rebel against the LORD or against us by building an altar for yourselves, other than the altar of the LORD our God. 20When Achan son of Zerah acted unfaithfully regarding the devoted things,[d] did not wrath come upon the whole community of Israel? He was not the only one who died for his sin.' "

21Then Reuben, Gad and the half-tribe of Manasseh replied to the heads of the clans of Israel: 22"The Mighty One, God, the LORD! The Mighty One, God, the LORD! He knows! And let Israel know! If this has been in rebellion or disobedience to the LORD, do not spare us this day. 23If we have built our own altar to turn away from the LORD and to offer burnt offerings and grain offerings, or to sacrifice fellowship offerings[e] on it, may the LORD himself call us to account.

24"No! We did it for fear that some day your descendants might say to ours, 'What do you have to do with the LORD, the God of Israel? 25The LORD has made the Jordan a boundary between us and you—you Reubenites and Gadites! You have no share in the LORD.' So your descendants might cause ours to stop fearing the LORD.

26"That is why we said, 'Let us get ready and build an altar—but not for burnt offerings or sacrifices.' 27On the contrary, it is to be a witness between us and you and the generations that follow, that we will worship the LORD at his sanctuary with our burnt offerings, sacrifices and fellowship offerings. Then in the future your descendants will not be able to say to ours, 'You have no share in the LORD.'

28"And we said, 'If they ever say this to us, or to our descendants, we will answer: Look at the replica of the LORD's altar, which our fathers built, not for burnt offerings and sacrifices, but as a witness between us and you.'

29"Far be it from us to rebel against the LORD and turn away from him today by building an altar for burnt offerings, grain offerings and sacrifices, other than the altar of the LORD our God that stands before his tabernacle."

30When Phinehas the priest and the leaders of the community—the heads of the clans of the Israelites—heard what Reuben, Gad and Manasseh had to say, they were pleased. 31And Phinehas son of Eleazar, the priest, said to Reuben, Gad and Manasseh, "Today we know that the LORD is with us, because you have not acted unfaithfully toward the LORD in this matter. Now you have rescued the Israelites from the LORD's hand."

32Then Phinehas son of Eleazar, the priest, and the leaders returned to Canaan from their meeting with the Reubenites and Gadites in Gilead and reported to the Israelites. 33They were glad to hear the report and praised God. And they talked no more about going to war against them to devastate the country where the Reubenites and the Gadites lived.

34And the Reubenites and the Gadites gave the altar this name: A Witness Between Us that the LORD is God.

[d]20 The Hebrew term refers to the irrevocable giving over of things or persons to the LORD, often by totally destroying them.
[e]23 Traditionally *peace offerings*; also in verse 27

Discovering the Word 1. Why does Joshua commend the tribes of Reuben, Gad and Manasseh (vv. 1–4)? 2. What blessings had these tribes received from God because of their faithful service (vv. 6–9)? 3. Why were the western tribes prepared to do battle over the issue of the altar (vv. 10–20; see also Deut 12:1–14)? 4. What reasons did the eastern tribes have for building the altar (vv. 21–29)? 5. How did both sides in this dispute show that they were honoring God (vv. 30–34)?

Applying the Word 1. What can we learn from this story about confronting those whose actions seem offensive? 2. What should our attitude be toward those who have misunderstood our actions? 3. What principles do you find in this chapter for restoring and maintaining unity in your church or fellowship group?

Responding in Prayer Pray that God would bring unity to his church around the world.

11 / *Joshua* 23
Joshua's Farewell

GREAT LEADERS INSPIRE us to obey God. We depend on their encouragement and their example. But what happens when such leaders are no longer around? About twenty years elapsed between the end of the war and Joshua's death. During that time, Joshua's influence kept Israel loyal to God. Now Joshua knows that he is about to die, and he is concerned that Israel's loyalty to God might not continue in his absence. Therefore, he calls the Israelites together to hear a farewell message of challenge and warning.

Warming Up to God If you were giving a farewell address, what words of thanks would you offer to God?

Read Joshua 23.

23 After a long time had passed and
the LORD had given Israel rest from
all their enemies around them,
Joshua, by then old and well advanced in years,
2summoned all Israel—their elders, leaders,
judges and officials—and said to them: "I am old
and well advanced in years. 3You yourselves have
seen everything the LORD your God has done to all
these nations for your sake; it was the LORD your
God who fought for you. 4Remember how I have
allotted as an inheritance for your tribes all the
land of the nations that remain—the nations I
conquered—between the Jordan and the Great
Sea[f] in the west. 5The LORD your God himself
will drive them out of your way. He will push
them out before you, and you will take possession
of their land, as the LORD your God promised you.
6"Be very strong; be careful to obey all that is
written in the Book of the Law of Moses, without
turning aside to the right or to the left. 7Do not
associate with these nations that remain among
you; do not invoke the names of their gods or
swear by them. You must not serve them or bow
down to them. 8But you are to hold fast to the
LORD your God, as you have until now.
9"The LORD has driven out before you great and
powerful nations; to this day no one has been able
to withstand you. 10One of you routs a thousand,
because the LORD your God fights for you, just as
he promised. 11So be very careful to love the LORD
your God.
12"But if you turn away and ally yourselves
with the survivors of these nations that remain
among you and if you intermarry with them and
associate with them, 13then you may be sure that
the LORD your God will no longer drive out these
nations before you. Instead, they will become
snares and traps for you, whips on your backs
and thorns in your eyes, until you perish from
this good land, which the LORD your God has
given you.
14"Now I am about to go the way of all the
earth. You know with all your heart and soul that
not one of all the good promises the LORD your
God gave you has failed. Every promise has been
fulfilled; not one has failed. 15But just as every
good promise of the LORD your God has come
true, so the LORD will bring on you all the evil he
has threatened, until he has destroyed you from

f4 That is, the Mediterranean

this good land he has given you. [16]If you violate
the covenant of the LORD your God, which he
commanded you, and go and serve other gods
and bow down to them, the LORD's anger will
burn against you, and you will quickly perish
from the good land he has given you."

Discovering the Word 1. How does Joshua exalt God in his farewell address? 2. What promises and commands does Joshua give to Israel (vv. 5–11)? 3. What does it mean for us to "hold fast to the LORD" and "to love the LORD" (vv. 8, 11)? 4. Why weren't the Israelites allowed to associate with the nations around them (vv. 7–8, 12–13)? 5. Joshua warns that the Lord is faithful not only to his promises but also to his threats (vv. 14–16). What threats had the Lord made to Israel (vv. 15–16)?

Applying the Word 1. Today, what aspects of non-Christian culture can become snares, traps, whips on our backs and thorns in our eyes? 2. We obviously cannot and should not avoid non-Christians today. How then can we resist the temptation to live like them? 3. How does Joshua's farewell address motivate you to be faithful to the Lord?

Responding in Prayer Ask God to make you faithful. Pray that your pastor and the leaders of your church would be faithful as well.

12 / *Joshua 24*
Who Will Serve the Lord?

THROUGHOUT THE BOOK of Joshua the Lord has demonstrated his faithfulness and his power. Every promise he made was fulfilled; every battle he fought was won. Now at the conclusion of the book he asks Israel and us to reaffirm the most important decision of our lives: "Choose for yourselves this day whom you will serve" (v. 15).

Warming Up to God God has given us the ability to make choices. What are some of the inherent benefits and dangers of this freedom for you?

Read Joshua 24.

24 Then Joshua assembled all the
tribes of Israel at Shechem. He
summoned the elders, leaders,
judges and officials of Israel, and they presented
themselves before God.
[2]Joshua said to all the people, "This is what the
LORD, the God of Israel, says: 'Long ago your fore-
fathers, including Terah the father of Abraham
and Nahor, lived beyond the River[g] and wor-
shiped other gods. [3]But I took your father Abra-
ham from the land beyond the River and led him
throughout Canaan and gave him many descen-
dants. I gave him Isaac, [4]and to Isaac I gave Jacob
and Esau. I assigned the hill country of Seir to
Esau, but Jacob and his sons went down to Egypt.
[5]" 'Then I sent Moses and Aaron, and I afflicted
the Egyptians by what I did there, and I brought
you out. [6]When I brought your fathers out of
Egypt, you came to the sea, and the Egyptians
pursued them with chariots and horsemen[h] as
far as the Red Sea.[i] [7]But they cried to the LORD
for help, and he put darkness between you and
the Egyptians; he brought the sea over them and
covered them. You saw with your own eyes what
I did to the Egyptians. Then you lived in the
desert for a long time.
[8]" 'I brought you to the land of the Amorites
who lived east of the Jordan. They fought against
you, but I gave them into your hands. I destroyed
them from before you, and you took possession of
their land. [9]When Balak son of Zippor, the king
of Moab, prepared to fight against Israel, he sent
for Balaam son of Beor to put a curse on you.
[10]But I would not listen to Balaam, so he blessed
you again and again, and I delivered you out of
his hand.
[11]" 'Then you crossed the Jordan and came to
Jericho. The citizens of Jericho fought against
you, as did also the Amorites, Perizzites, Canaan-
ites, Hittites, Girgashites, Hivites and Jebusites,

[g]2 That is, the Euphrates; also in verses 3, 14 and 15 [h]6 Or *charioteers* [i]6 Hebrew *Yam Suph*; that is, Sea of Reeds

but I gave them into your hands. 12I sent the hornet ahead of you, which drove them out before you—also the two Amorite kings. You did not do it with your own sword and bow. 13So I gave you a land on which you did not toil and cities you did not build; and you live in them and eat from vineyards and olive groves that you did not plant.'

14"Now fear the LORD and serve him with all faithfulness. Throw away the gods your forefathers worshiped beyond the River and in Egypt, and serve the LORD. 15But if serving the LORD seems undesirable to you, then choose for yourselves this day whom you will serve, whether the gods your forefathers served beyond the River, or the gods of the Amorites, in whose land you are living. But as for me and my household, we will serve the LORD."

16Then the people answered, "Far be it from us to forsake the LORD to serve other gods! 17It was the LORD our God himself who brought us and our fathers up out of Egypt, from that land of slavery, and performed those great signs before our eyes. He protected us on our entire journey and among all the nations through which we traveled. 18And the LORD drove out before us all the nations, including the Amorites, who lived in the land. We too will serve the LORD, because he is our God."

19Joshua said to the people, "You are not able to serve the LORD. He is a holy God; he is a jealous God. He will not forgive your rebellion and your sins. 20If you forsake the LORD and serve foreign gods, he will turn and bring disaster on you and make an end of you, after he has been good to you."

21But the people said to Joshua, "No! We will serve the LORD."

22Then Joshua said, "You are witnesses against yourselves that you have chosen to serve the LORD."

"Yes, we are witnesses," they replied.

23"Now then," said Joshua, "throw away the foreign gods that are among you and yield your hearts to the LORD, the God of Israel."

24And the people said to Joshua, "We will serve the LORD our God and obey him."

25On that day Joshua made a covenant for the people, and there at Shechem he drew up for them decrees and laws. 26And Joshua recorded these things in the Book of the Law of God. Then he took a large stone and set it up there under the oak near the holy place of the LORD.

27"See!" he said to all the people. "This stone will be a witness against us. It has heard all the words the LORD has said to us. It will be a witness against you if you are untrue to your God."

28Then Joshua sent the people away, each to his own inheritance.

29After these things, Joshua son of Nun, the servant of the LORD, died at the age of a hundred and ten. 30And they buried him in the land of his inheritance, at Timnath Serah[j] in the hill country of Ephraim, north of Mount Gaash.

31Israel served the LORD throughout the lifetime of Joshua and of the elders who outlived him and who had experienced everything the LORD had done for Israel.

32And Joseph's bones, which the Israelites had brought up from Egypt, were buried at Shechem in the tract of land that Jacob bought for a hundred pieces of silver[k] from the sons of Hamor, the father of Shechem. This became the inheritance of Joseph's descendants.

33And Eleazar son of Aaron died and was buried at Gibeah, which had been allotted to his son Phinehas in the hill country of Ephraim.

j30 Also known as *Timnath Heres* (see Judges 2:9) k32 Hebrew *hundred kesitahs*; a kesitah was a unit of money of unknown weight and value.

Discovering the Word 1. Why do you think the Lord recounts Israel's history from beginning to end (vv. 1–13)? 2. Joshua and the Israelites repeat the word *serve* thirteen times in verses 14–27. Why is this a good word to describe our duty to God? 3. Why might serving the Lord seem undesirable to the Israelites (v. 15)? 4. Why doesn't Joshua accept the Israelites' first pledge to serve the Lord (v. 19)? 5. What is the purpose of the witnesses mentioned in verses 22 and 27?

Applying the Word 1. Israel must choose whom they will serve (v. 15). What choices to you have about whom to serve? 2. In what ways is serving the Lord difficult for you? 3. What makes serving him worthwhile?

Responding in Prayer Pray that God will give you courage to rise to the challenge of Joshua—to obey God more fully.

Judges

Despicable people doing deplorable things. That pretty much sums up the book of Judges. Why would the Bible even contain such trashy tales about dysfunctional characters? As I read the book, I find it difficult to find any sympathy for those—even the heroes—involved in these violent and abusive accounts.

Who can love people who maltreat others? Who would care about people who complicate and sabotage their own lives and then refuse the hope that is offered? Who would have patience with people who refuse to learn from their mistakes but instead pass them on as a legacy to the next generation? The answer is that only God could care about creatures such as these. So the book of Judges is not really about the judges who held court in Israel. It is about the God of mercy and patience who loves even the most dysfunctional and resistant among us.

The book of Judges covers the history of Israel between the death of Joshua and the appearance of Samuel (approximately 1220–1050 B.C.). For Israel this was a time without a formal government. The people were supposed to look to God for leadership, but when they failed to do so, they were doomed to a continuing cycle of disobedience, suffering, cries for help and deliverance.

How can you benefit from the book of Judges? You will learn of the great depth of God's love and mercy as you see it continually offered to people who do not deserve or appreciate it. You will be able to learn from the mistakes of others. Perhaps you will be able to break cycles of dysfunction which persist in your own life or home. Most of all, the study of Judges should help you to hand the throne of your life over to God, the true king. The writer of the book of Judges often uses the phrase "in those days Israel had no king." Without God reigning in our hearts, our lives are destined to become as disastrous as the characters of this book.

To gain these benefits, it is important to study the book of Judges correctly. If you look to the characters of these stories as role models, you will be sorely disappointed. Even the judges whom God uses to save Israel are depraved and fallen creatures. The point of these stories is not the character qualities of the judges, but the fact that God works through people such as these. The only true hero of this book is God.

It is also important that you refrain from becoming smug about your own enlightenment. As you read Judges, you will encounter characters who treat women as possessions and who settle problems with angry outbursts of violence (and these are supposedly the good guys!). These are stories of people in a much more primitive time who were struggling to understand God, themselves and forgiveness. Although they acted out in a much more dramatic and childish way, their passions and their rebellion against God were the same as yours and mine. So as you read, look for the sins you have in common with the characters and ask yourself what would happen if you were to give full reign to every passion.

In your quiet times, may you come to understand the condition of humankind and the mercy of God with new clarity and depth.

Outline

Judges 1:1—2:5

1 After the death of Joshua, the Israelites asked the LORD, "Who will be the first to go up and fight for us against the Canaanites?"

2The LORD answered, "Judah is to go; I have given the land into their hands."

3Then the men of Judah said to the Simeonites their brothers, "Come up with us into the territory allotted to us, to fight against the Canaanites. We in turn will go with you into yours." So the Simeonites went with them.

4When Judah attacked, the LORD gave the Canaanites and Perizzites into their hands and they struck down ten thousand men at Bezek. 5It was there that they found Adoni-Bezek and fought against him, putting to rout the Canaanites and Perizzites. 6Adoni-Bezek fled, but they chased him and caught him, and cut off his thumbs and big toes.

7Then Adoni-Bezek said, "Seventy kings with their thumbs and big toes cut off have picked up scraps under my table. Now God has paid me back for what I did to them." They brought him to Jerusalem, and he died there.

8The men of Judah attacked Jerusalem also and took it. They put the city to the sword and set it on fire.

9After that, the men of Judah went down to fight against the Canaanites living in the hill country, the Negev and the western foothills. 10They advanced against the Canaanites living in Hebron (formerly called Kiriath Arba) and defeated Sheshai, Ahiman and Talmai.

11From there they advanced against the people living in Debir (formerly called Kiriath Sepher). 12And Caleb said, "I will give my daughter Acsah in marriage to the man who attacks and captures Kiriath Sepher." 13Othniel son of Kenaz, Caleb's younger brother, took it; so Caleb gave his daughter Acsah to him in marriage.

14One day when she came to Othniel, she urged him[a] to ask her father for a field. When she got off her donkey, Caleb asked her, "What can I do for you?"

15She replied, "Do me a special favor. Since you have given me land in the Negev, give me also springs of water." Then Caleb gave her the upper and lower springs.

16The descendants of Moses' father-in-law, the Kenite, went up from the City of Palms[b] with the men of Judah to live among the people of the Desert of Judah in the Negev near Arad.

17Then the men of Judah went with the Simeonites their brothers and attacked the Canaanites living in Zephath, and they totally destroyed[c] the city. Therefore it was called Hormah.[d] 18The men of Judah also took[e] Gaza, Ashkelon and Ekron—each city with its territory.

19The LORD was with the men of Judah. They took possession of the hill country, but they were unable to drive the people from the plains, because they had iron chariots. 20As Moses had promised, Hebron was given to Caleb, who drove from it the three sons of Anak. 21The Benjamites, however, failed to dislodge the Jebusites, who were living in Jerusalem; to this day the Jebusites live there with the Benjamites.

22Now the house of Joseph attacked Bethel, and the LORD was with them. 23When they sent men to spy out Bethel (formerly called Luz), 24the spies saw a man coming out of the city and they said to him, "Show us how to get into the city and we will see that you are treated well." 25So he showed them, and they put the city to the sword but spared the man and his whole family. 26He then went to the land of the Hittites, where he built a city and called it Luz, which is its name to this day.

27But Manasseh did not drive out the people of Beth Shan or Taanach or Dor or Ibleam or Megiddo and their surrounding settlements, for the Canaanites were determined to live in that land. 28When Israel became strong, they pressed the Canaanites into forced labor but never drove them out completely. 29Nor did Ephraim drive out the Canaanites living in Gezer, but the Canaanites continued to live there among them. 30Neither did Zebulun drive out the Canaanites living in Kitron or Nahalol, who remained among them; but they did subject them to forced labor. 31Nor did Asher drive out those living in Acco or

[a]14 Hebrew; Septuagint and Vulgate *Othniel, he urged her* [b]16 That is, Jericho [c]17 The Hebrew term refers to the irrevocable giving over of things or persons to the LORD, often by totally destroying them. [d]17 *Hormah* means *destruction.* [e]18 Hebrew; Septuagint *Judah did not take*

Sidon or Ahlab or Aczib or Helbah or Aphek or
Rehob, 32and because of this the people of Asher
lived among the Canaanite inhabitants of the
land. 33Neither did Naphtali drive out those living
in Beth Shemesh or Beth Anath; but the Naphtalites too lived among the Canaanite inhabitants of
the land, and those living in Beth Shemesh and
Beth Anath became forced laborers for them.
34The Amorites confined the Danites to the hill
country, not allowing them to come down into
the plain. 35And the Amorites were determined
also to hold out in Mount Heres, Aijalon and Shaalbim, but when the power of the house of Joseph
increased, they too were pressed into forced labor. 36The boundary of the Amorites was from
Scorpion[f] Pass to Sela and beyond.

2 The angel of the LORD went up from Gilgal to Bokim and said, "I brought you up out of Egypt and led you into the land that I swore to give to your forefathers. I said, 'I will never break my covenant with you, 2and you shall
not make a covenant with the people of this land,
but you shall break down their altars.' Yet you
have disobeyed me. Why have you done this?
3Now therefore I tell you that I will not drive
them out before you; they will be ⌞thorns⌟ in your
sides and their gods will be a snare to you."

4When the angel of the LORD had spoken these
things to all the Israelites, the people wept aloud,
5and they called that place Bokim.[g] There they
offered sacrifices to the LORD.

f36 Hebrew *Akrabbim* g5 *Bokim* means *weepers.*

1 / *Judges 2:6–23*
The Cycle of Misery

UNDER THE INSPIRED leadership of Joshua, the Israelite people marched into the land which God had promised to give them. Through many brilliant military campaigns, the pagan populace was destroyed and the Israelites were left clearly in charge. Joshua had been able to retire with pride, leaving a bright and promising future for the young nation. However, it wasn't long before the golden future turned to hopeless despair. The people had foolishly destroyed the gift they had been given and now they needed to be rescued. It was the first round of a cycle that was to be repeated again and again.

Warming Up to God It is said that "no one touches a hot stove twice." What "hot stoves" have plagued your life?

Read Judges 2:6–23.

6After Joshua had dismissed the Israelites, they
went to take possession of the land, each to his
own inheritance. 7The people served the LORD
throughout the lifetime of Joshua and of the elders who outlived him and who had seen all the
great things the LORD had done for Israel.

8Joshua son of Nun, the servant of the LORD,
died at the age of a hundred and ten. 9And they
buried him in the land of his inheritance, at Timnath Heres[h] in the hill country of Ephraim,
north of Mount Gaash.

10After that whole generation had been gathered to their fathers, another generation grew up,
who knew neither the LORD nor what he had done
for Israel. 11Then the Israelites did evil in the eyes
of the LORD and served the Baals. 12They forsook
the LORD, the God of their fathers, who had
brought them out of Egypt. They followed and
worshiped various gods of the peoples around
them. They provoked the LORD to anger 13because
they forsook him and served Baal and the Ashtoreths. 14In his anger against Israel the LORD
handed them over to raiders who plundered
them. He sold them to their enemies all around,
whom they were no longer able to resist. 15Whenever Israel went out to fight, the hand of the LORD
was against them to defeat them, just as he had
sworn to them. They were in great distress.

16Then the LORD raised up judges,[i] who saved
them out of the hands of these raiders. 17Yet they

h9 Also known as *Timnath Serah* (see Joshua 19:50 and 24:30)
i16 Or *leaders*; similarly in verses 17-19

would not listen to their judges but prostituted
themselves to other gods and worshiped them.
Unlike their fathers, they quickly turned from the
way in which their fathers had walked, the way of
obedience to the LORD's commands. [18]Whenever
the LORD raised up a judge for them, he was with
the judge and saved them out of the hands of
their enemies as long as the judge lived; for the
LORD had compassion on them as they groaned
under those who oppressed and afflicted them.
[19]But when the judge died, the people returned to
ways even more corrupt than those of their fa-
thers, following other gods and serving and wor-
shiping them. They refused to give up their evil
practices and stubborn ways.
[20]Therefore the LORD was very angry with Israel
and said, "Because this nation has violated the
covenant that I laid down for their forefathers and
has not listened to me, [21]I will no longer drive out
before them any of the nations Joshua left when
he died. [22]I will use them to test Israel and see
whether they will keep the way of the LORD and
walk in it as their forefathers did." [23]The LORD had
allowed those nations to remain; he did not drive
them out at once by giving them into the hands of
Joshua.

Discovering the Word 1. What cycle of behavior do these verses describe? 2. How did the second generation differ from the first (vv. 10–15)? 3. What does God's work through the judges reveal about his character (vv. 16–19)? 4. Why do you think the Israelites refused to listen to the judges? 5. In what ways did God use and control the enemies of Israel (vv. 20–23)?

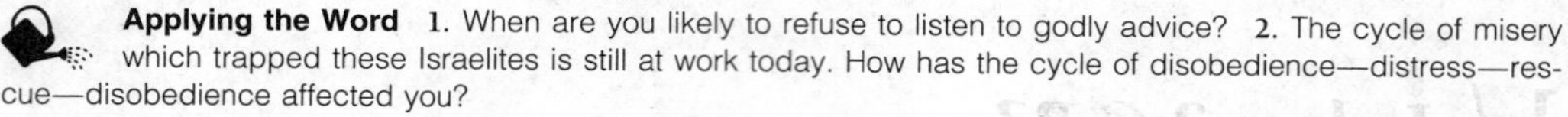

Applying the Word 1. When are you likely to refuse to listen to godly advice? 2. The cycle of misery which trapped these Israelites is still at work today. How has the cycle of disobedience—distress—rescue—disobedience affected you?

Responding in Prayer Consider how you might be currently disobeying God. Let your memories of his past faithfulness to you call you back to obedience.

Judges 3:1–11

3 These are the nations the LORD left to test
all those Israelites who had not experi-
enced any of the wars in Canaan [2](he did
this only to teach warfare to the descendants of
the Israelites who had not had previous battle ex-
perience): [3]the five rulers of the Philistines, all
the Canaanites, the Sidonians, and the Hivites liv-
ing in the Lebanon mountains from Mount Baal
Hermon to Lebo[j] Hamath. [4]They were left to
test the Israelites to see whether they would obey
the LORD's commands, which he had given their
forefathers through Moses.
[5]The Israelites lived among the Canaanites,
Hittites, Amorites, Perizzites, Hivites and Jebu-
sites. [6]They took their daughters in marriage and
gave their own daughters to their sons, and
served their gods.
[7]The Israelites did evil in the eyes of the LORD;
they forgot the LORD their God and served the
Baals and the Asherahs. [8]The anger of the LORD
burned against Israel so that he sold them into
the hands of Cushan-Rishathaim king of Aram
Naharaim,[k] to whom the Israelites were subject
for eight years. [9]But when they cried out to the
LORD, he raised up for them a deliverer, Othniel
son of Kenaz, Caleb's younger brother, who saved
them. [10]The Spirit of the LORD came upon him, so
that he became Israel's judge[l] and went to war.
The LORD gave Cushan-Rishathaim king of Aram
into the hands of Othniel, who overpowered him.
[11]So the land had peace for forty years, until Oth-
niel son of Kenaz died.

[j]3 Or *to the entrance to*
[k]8 That is, Northwest Mesopotamia
[l]10 Or *leader*

2 / *Judges 3:12-31*
A Left-Handed Leader

IN ONE OF those cheaply produced local television commercials, a large, smirking man smoking a huge cigar is identified as the greedy landlord. He is grabbing money from a line of discouraged-looking tenants and stuffing it into his already full pockets. But when the announcer shows how you can buy a new home and make payments lower than rent, the tenants triumphantly toss Mr. Landlord into his swimming pool. Like those discouraged tenants, the Israelites found themselves paying tribute to a greedy king. Their unwise choices to ignore God had caused the loss of their independence, so they were desperate for someone like the television announcer who would help them throw the greedy king off their back.

Warming Up to God What would happen in your life if you gradually stopped worshiping God? Ask God to use this passage to strengthen your character through your worship.

Read Judges 3:12-31.

12Once again the Israelites did evil in the eyes of the LORD, and because they did this evil the LORD gave Eglon king of Moab power over Israel. 13Getting the Ammonites and Amalekites to join him, Eglon came and attacked Israel, and they took possession of the City of Palms.[m] 14The Israelites were subject to Eglon king of Moab for eighteen years.

15Again the Israelites cried out to the LORD, and he gave them a deliverer—Ehud, a left-handed man, the son of Gera the Benjamite. The Israelites sent him with tribute to Eglon king of Moab. 16Now Ehud had made a double-edged sword about a foot and a half[n] long, which he strapped to his right thigh under his clothing. 17He presented the tribute to Eglon king of Moab, who was a very fat man. 18After Ehud had presented the tribute, he sent on their way the men who had carried it. 19At the idols[o] near Gilgal he himself turned back and said, "I have a secret message for you, O king."

The king said, "Quiet!" And all his attendants left him.

20Ehud then approached him while he was sitting alone in the upper room of his summer palace[p] and said, "I have a message from God for you." As the king rose from his seat, 21Ehud reached with his left hand, drew the sword from his right thigh and plunged it into the king's belly. 22Even the handle sank in after the blade, which came out his back. Ehud did not pull the sword out, and the fat closed in over it. 23Then Ehud went out to the porch[q]; he shut the doors of the upper room behind him and locked them.

24After he had gone, the servants came and found the doors of the upper room locked. They said, "He must be relieving himself in the inner room of the house." 25They waited to the point of embarrassment, but when he did not open the doors of the room, they took a key and unlocked them. There they saw their lord fallen to the floor, dead.

26While they waited, Ehud got away. He passed by the idols and escaped to Seirah. 27When he arrived there, he blew a trumpet in the hill country of Ephraim, and the Israelites went down with him from the hills, with him leading them.

28"Follow me," he ordered, "for the LORD has given Moab, your enemy, into your hands." So they followed him down and, taking possession of the fords of the Jordan that led to Moab, they allowed no one to cross over. 29At that time they struck down about ten thousand Moabites, all vigorous and strong; not a man escaped. 30That day Moab was made subject to Israel, and the land had peace for eighty years.

31After Ehud came Shamgar son of Anath, who struck down six hundred Philistines with an oxgoad. He too saved Israel.

[m]13 That is, Jericho [n]16 Hebrew *a cubit* (about 0.5 meter) [o]19 Or *the stone quarries*; also in verse 26 [p]20 The meaning of the Hebrew for this phrase is uncertain. [q]23 The meaning of the Hebrew for this word is uncertain.

Discovering the Word 1. How do the attitudes and emotions of the Israelite people change in this story (vv. 12–15, 27–30)? 2. The conquering Moabites attempted to keep Israel weak by forcing them to pay a heavy tax called *tribute.* In verses 15–19 Ehud delivers the tribute to King Eglon. How does this picture highlight the painful consequences of poor choices? 3. Why do you think the Bible gives such a gory description of how Israel was saved? 4. Which of Ehud's qualities did God use in fulfilling his plan? 5. Ehud's left-handedness was considered to be a handicap. What does this tell you about God's surprises?

Applying the Word 1. The Israelites paid a high price for ignoring God. What has been the price of your bad choices? 2. Which of your weaknesses would you be surprised to find God developing into assets? 3. What has this story taught you about the way back to God?

Responding in Prayer What bad choices have you recently made? Make confession a part of your prayer as you ask God to build your character.

3 / *Judges 4*
Trust and Betrayal

"ET TU, BRUTE?" These words from the Shakespearean play *Julius Caesar* sum up the shock and pain of betrayal. The dagger twisted in the back by a trusted friend is a double agony. But it isn't only our friends who betray us. After a recent earthquake, Californians talked about their fears that they couldn't trust the ground to remain firm. A friend who lost hours of computer input during a power failure said he felt betrayed by technology. If friends, nature, knowledge and things all have the potential to turn against us, then where can we turn in a time of crisis?

Warming Up to God What people and things have you assumed would be there to rescue you if you needed them?

Read Judges 4.

4 After Ehud died, the Israelites once again
did evil in the eyes of the LORD. 2So the
LORD sold them into the hands of Jabin, a
king of Canaan, who reigned in Hazor. The com-
mander of his army was Sisera, who lived in Ha-
rosheth Haggoyim. 3Because he had nine hundred
iron chariots and had cruelly oppressed the Isra-
elites for twenty years, they cried to the LORD for
help.
4Deborah, a prophetess, the wife of Lappidoth,
was leading[r] Israel at that time. 5She held court
under the Palm of Deborah between Ramah and
Bethel in the hill country of Ephraim, and the
Israelites came to her to have their disputes de-
cided. 6She sent for Barak son of Abinoam from
Kedesh in Naphtali and said to him, "The LORD,
the God of Israel, commands you: 'Go, take with
you ten thousand men of Naphtali and Zebulun
and lead the way to Mount Tabor. 7I will lure
Sisera, the commander of Jabin's army, with his
chariots and his troops to the Kishon River and
give him into your hands.' "
8Barak said to her, "If you go with me, I will go;
but if you don't go with me, I won't go."
9"Very well," Deborah said, "I will go with you.
But because of the way you are going about
this,[s] the honor will not be yours, for the LORD
will hand Sisera over to a woman." So Deborah
went with Barak to Kedesh, 10where he sum-
moned Zebulun and Naphtali. Ten thousand men
followed him, and Deborah also went with him.
11Now Heber the Kenite had left the other Ke-
nites, the descendants of Hobab, Moses' brother-
in-law,[t] and pitched his tent by the great tree in
Zaanannim near Kedesh.
12When they told Sisera that Barak son of Abin-
oam had gone up to Mount Tabor, 13Sisera gath-
ered together his nine hundred iron chariots and
all the men with him, from Harosheth Haggoyim
to the Kishon River.
14Then Deborah said to Barak, "Go! This is the
day the LORD has given Sisera into your hands.
Has not the LORD gone ahead of you?" So Barak

[r]4 Traditionally *judging* [s]9 Or *But on the expedition you are undertaking* [t]11 Or *father-in-law*

went down Mount Tabor, followed by ten thou-
sand men. 15At Barak's advance, the LORD routed
Sisera and all his chariots and army by the sword,
and Sisera abandoned his chariot and fled on foot.
16But Barak pursued the chariots and army as far
as Harosheth Haggoyim. All the troops of Sisera
fell by the sword; not a man was left.

17Sisera, however, fled on foot to the tent of
Jael, the wife of Heber the Kenite, because there
were friendly relations between Jabin king of Ha-
zor and the clan of Heber the Kenite.

18Jael went out to meet Sisera and said to him,
"Come, my lord, come right in. Don't be afraid."
So he entered her tent, and she put a covering
over him.

19"I'm thirsty," he said. "Please give me some
water." She opened a skin of milk, gave him a
drink, and covered him up.

20"Stand in the doorway of the tent," he told
her. "If someone comes by and asks you, 'Is any-
one here?' say 'No.' "

21But Jael, Heber's wife, picked up a tent peg
and a hammer and went quietly to him while he
lay fast asleep, exhausted. She drove the peg
through his temple into the ground, and he
died.

22Barak came by in pursuit of Sisera, and Jael
went out to meet him. "Come," she said, "I will
show you the man you're looking for." So he went
in with her, and there lay Sisera with the tent peg
through his temple—dead.

23On that day God subdued Jabin, the Canaan-
ite king, before the Israelites. 24And the hand of
the Israelites grew stronger and stronger against
Jabin, the Canaanite king, until they destroyed
him.

Discovering the Word 1. What gifts and skills did Deborah possess (vv. 4–14)? 2. What difference did Deborah's presence make during a godless period of Israel's history? 3. Why was it wrong for Barak to ask Deborah to go with him (v. 8)? 4. What assumptions did Sisera make regarding his safety (vv. 15–21)? 5. How did each of the things Sisera trusted to protect him fail?

Applying the Word 1. Consider where each of the leading characters of this story—Deborah, Barak, Jael and Sisera—put his or her trust. Which of them are you most like? Why? 2. What has this study helped you to discover about your trust in God?

Responding in Prayer Ask God to show you where your trust is. Ask him to be the stable foundation of your trust.

Judges 5

5 On that day Deborah and Barak son of
Abinoam sang this song:

2"When the princes in Israel take the
lead,
when the people willingly offer
themselves—
praise the LORD!

3"Hear this, you kings! Listen, you rulers!
I will sing to[u] the LORD, I will sing;
I will make music to[v] the LORD, the God of
Israel.

4"O LORD, when you went out from Seir,
when you marched from the land of Edom,
the earth shook, the heavens poured,
the clouds poured down water.
5The mountains quaked before the LORD, the
One of Sinai,
before the LORD, the God of Israel.

6"In the days of Shamgar son of Anath,
in the days of Jael, the roads were
abandoned;
travelers took to winding paths.
7Village life[w] in Israel ceased,
ceased until I,[x] Deborah, arose,
arose a mother in Israel.
8When they chose new gods,

[u]3 Or *of* [v]3 Or / *with song I will praise* [w]7 Or *Warriors*
[x]7 Or *you*

war came to the city gates,
and not a shield or spear was seen
among forty thousand in Israel.
9My heart is with Israel's princes,
with the willing volunteers among the people.
Praise the LORD!

10"You who ride on white donkeys,
sitting on your saddle blankets,
and you who walk along the road,
consider 11the voice of the singers[y] at the watering places.
They recite the righteous acts of the LORD,
the righteous acts of his warriors[z] in Israel.

"Then the people of the LORD
went down to the city gates.
12'Wake up, wake up, Deborah!
Wake up, wake up, break out in song!
Arise, O Barak!
Take captive your captives, O son of Abinoam.'

13"Then the men who were left
came down to the nobles;
the people of the LORD
came to me with the mighty.
14Some came from Ephraim, whose roots were in Amalek;
Benjamin was with the people who followed you.
From Makir captains came down,
from Zebulun those who bear a commander's staff.
15The princes of Issachar were with Deborah;
yes, Issachar was with Barak,
rushing after him into the valley.
In the districts of Reuben
there was much searching of heart.
16Why did you stay among the campfires[a]
to hear the whistling for the flocks?
In the districts of Reuben
there was much searching of heart.
17Gilead stayed beyond the Jordan.
And Dan, why did he linger by the ships?
Asher remained on the coast
and stayed in his coves.
18The people of Zebulun risked their very lives;
so did Naphtali on the heights of the field.

19"Kings came, they fought;
the kings of Canaan fought
at Taanach by the waters of Megiddo,
but they carried off no silver, no plunder.
20From the heavens the stars fought,
from their courses they fought against Sisera.
21The river Kishon swept them away,
the age-old river, the river Kishon.
March on, my soul; be strong!
22Then thundered the horses' hoofs—
galloping, galloping go his mighty steeds.
23'Curse Meroz,' said the angel of the LORD.
'Curse its people bitterly,
because they did not come to help the LORD,
to help the LORD against the mighty.'

24"Most blessed of women be Jael,
the wife of Heber the Kenite,
most blessed of tent-dwelling women.
25He asked for water, and she gave him milk;
in a bowl fit for nobles she brought him curdled milk.
26Her hand reached for the tent peg,
her right hand for the workman's hammer.
She struck Sisera, she crushed his head,
she shattered and pierced his temple.
27At her feet he sank,
he fell; there he lay.
At her feet he sank, he fell;
where he sank, there he fell—dead.

28"Through the window peered Sisera's mother;
behind the lattice she cried out,
'Why is his chariot so long in coming?
Why is the clatter of his chariots delayed?'
29The wisest of her ladies answer her;
indeed, she keeps saying to herself,
30'Are they not finding and dividing the spoils:
a girl or two for each man,
colorful garments as plunder for Sisera,
colorful garments embroidered,
highly embroidered garments for my neck—
all this as plunder?'

31"So may all your enemies perish, O LORD!
But may they who love you be like the sun
when it rises in its strength."
Then the land had peace forty years.

y11 Or *archers*; the meaning of the Hebrew for this word is uncertain.
z11 Or *villagers* a16 Or *saddlebags*

4 / *Judges 6:1–32*
Real Repentance

OH, NO! GOD'S people are at it again. By this time in your study, you are probably getting used to the disappointing litany "Again the Israelites did evil in the eyes of the LORD." You know what's coming: punishment, repentance and rescue. But what happens when the people become so hard-hearted that even punishment fails to cause them to see the error of their ways? What happens when their cry to God carries only regret and no repentance? In Judges 6 you will see God take the initiative to win his people back to himself.

Warming Up to God In what ways was God at work in your life even before you met him?

Read Judges 6:1–32.

6 Again the Israelites did evil in the eyes
of the LORD, and for seven years he gave
them into the hands of the Midianites.
2 Because the power of Midian was so oppressive,
the Israelites prepared shelters for themselves in
mountain clefts, caves and strongholds. 3 When-
ever the Israelites planted their crops, the Midian-
ites, Amalekites and other eastern peoples in-
vaded the country. 4 They camped on the land and
ruined the crops all the way to Gaza and did not
spare a living thing for Israel, neither sheep nor
cattle nor donkeys. 5 They came up with their live-
stock and their tents like swarms of locusts. It
was impossible to count the men and their cam-
els; they invaded the land to ravage it. 6 Midian so
impoverished the Israelites that they cried out to
the LORD for help.
7 When the Israelites cried to the LORD because
of Midian, 8 he sent them a prophet, who said,
"This is what the LORD, the God of Israel, says: I
brought you up out of Egypt, out of the land of
slavery. 9 I snatched you from the power of Egypt
and from the hand of all your oppressors. I drove
them from before you and gave you their land. 10 I
said to you, 'I am the LORD your God; do not
worship the gods of the Amorites, in whose land
you live.' But you have not listened to me."
11 The angel of the LORD came and sat down
under the oak in Ophrah that belonged to Joash
the Abiezrite, where his son Gideon was thresh-
ing wheat in a winepress to keep it from the Midi-
anites. 12 When the angel of the LORD appeared to
Gideon, he said, "The LORD is with you, mighty
warrior."
13 "But sir," Gideon replied, "if the LORD is with
us, why has all this happened to us? Where are all
his wonders that our fathers told us about when
they said, 'Did not the LORD bring us up out of
Egypt?' But now the LORD has abandoned us and
put us into the hand of Midian."
14 The LORD turned to him and said, "Go in the
strength you have and save Israel out of Midian's
hand. Am I not sending you?"
15 "But Lord,[b]" Gideon asked, "how can I save
Israel? My clan is the weakest in Manasseh, and I
am the least in my family."
16 The LORD answered, "I will be with you, and
you will strike down all the Midianites together."
17 Gideon replied, "If now I have found favor in
your eyes, give me a sign that it is really you
talking to me. 18 Please do not go away until I
come back and bring my offering and set it before
you."
And the LORD said, "I will wait until you re-
turn."
19 Gideon went in, prepared a young goat, and
from an ephah[c] of flour he made bread without
yeast. Putting the meat in a basket and its broth
in a pot, he brought them out and offered them to
him under the oak.
20 The angel of God said to him, "Take the meat
and the unleavened bread, place them on this
rock, and pour out the broth." And Gideon did
so. 21 With the tip of the staff that was in his hand,
the angel of the LORD touched the meat and the
unleavened bread. Fire flared from the rock, con-
suming the meat and the bread. And the angel of
the LORD disappeared. 22 When Gideon realized
that it was the angel of the LORD, he exclaimed,
"Ah, Sovereign LORD! I have seen the angel of the
LORD face to face!"
23 But the LORD said to him, "Peace! Do not be
afraid. You are not going to die."

[b] *15* Or *sir* [c] *19* That is, probably about 3/5 bushel (about 22 liters)

24So Gideon built an altar to the LORD there and
called it The LORD is Peace. To this day it stands
in Ophrah of the Abiezrites.
25That same night the LORD said to him, "Take
the second bull from your father's herd, the one
seven years old.[d] Tear down your father's altar to
Baal and cut down the Asherah pole[e] beside it.
26Then build a proper kind of[f] altar to the LORD
your God on the top of this height. Using the
wood of the Asherah pole that you cut down,
offer the second[g] bull as a burnt offering."
27So Gideon took ten of his servants and did as
the LORD told him. But because he was afraid of
his family and the men of the town, he did it at
night rather than in the daytime.
28In the morning when the men of the town got
up, there was Baal's altar, demolished, with the
Asherah pole beside it cut down and the second
bull sacrificed on the newly built altar!
29They asked each other, "Who did this?"
When they carefully investigated, they were
told, "Gideon son of Joash did it."
30The men of the town demanded of Joash,
"Bring out your son. He must die, because he has
broken down Baal's altar and cut down the Ashe-
rah pole beside it."
31But Joash replied to the hostile crowd around
him, "Are you going to plead Baal's cause? Are
you trying to save him? Whoever fights for him
shall be put to death by morning! If Baal really
is a god, he can defend himself when someone
breaks down his altar." 32So that day they called
Gideon "Jerub-Baal,[h]" saying, "Let Baal contend
with him," because he broke down Baal's altar.

[d]25 Or *Take a full-grown, mature bull from your father's herd* [e]25 That is, a symbol of the goddess Asherah; here and elsewhere in Judges [f]26 Or *build with layers of stone an* [g]26 Or *full-grown*; also in verse 28 [h]32 *Jerub-Baal* means *let Baal contend.*

Discovering the Word 1. Imagine life during the years of Midianite occupation (vv. 1–6). What about this situation would have been most distressing to you? 2. When the Israelites finally cried out to God, he first sent a prophet (vv. 7–10). What evidence is there that the Israelites' repentance was not real? 3. Compare the words of God to the words of Gideon in verses 7–15. How did Gideon's view of the problem and its solution differ from God's? 4. How did the miracle of verse 21 change Gideon? 5. God's first command to Gideon was to tear down his father's altar to Baal (vv. 25–27). How did Gideon's obedience differ from God's intention? 6. How could true obedience have made an even greater impact on Gideon's family and community (vv. 28–30)?

Applying the Word 1. When has your repentance and obedience been less than complete? 2. What have been the results of false repentance in your life?

Responding in Prayer Take some time to thank God for his initiative in your life. Ask him to guide you to true repentance.

5 / *Judges 6:33—7:25*
Building Faith

"FAITH IS [OUR] response to God's initiative," says John White in *The Fight* (Downers Grove, Ill.: InterVarsity Press, 1976, p. 97). Given this definition, faith is shown not in how devotedly we believe, but in how powerfully we take action. It can be illustrated by Gideon, who entered public life as a timid and uncertain man, constantly second-guessing himself. Yet Gideon took action when God asked him to do so. Our passage for this study chronicles the metamorphosis of Gideon from reluctant leader to confident man of faith.

Warming Up to God How has John White's definition of faith been true in your life?

Read Judges 6:33—7:25.

33Now all the Midianites, Amalekites and other eastern peoples joined forces and crossed over the Jordan and camped in the Valley of Jezreel. 34Then the Spirit of the LORD came upon Gideon, and he blew a trumpet, summoning the Abiezrites to follow him. 35He sent messengers throughout Manasseh, calling them to arms, and also into Asher, Zebulun and Naphtali, so that they too went up to meet them.

36Gideon said to God, "If you will save Israel by my hand as you have promised— 37look, I will place a wool fleece on the threshing floor. If there is dew only on the fleece and all the ground is dry, then I will know that you will save Israel by my hand, as you said." 38And that is what happened. Gideon rose early the next day; he squeezed the fleece and wrung out the dew—a bowlful of water.

39Then Gideon said to God, "Do not be angry with me. Let me make just one more request. Allow me one more test with the fleece. This time make the fleece dry and the ground covered with dew." 40That night God did so. Only the fleece was dry; all the ground was covered with dew.

7 Early in the morning, Jerub-Baal (that is, Gideon) and all his men camped at the spring of Harod. The camp of Midian was north of them in the valley near the hill of Moreh. 2The LORD said to Gideon, "You have too many men for me to deliver Midian into their hands. In order that Israel may not boast against me that her own strength has saved her, 3announce now to the people, 'Anyone who trembles with fear may turn back and leave Mount Gilead.' " So twenty-two thousand men left, while ten thousand remained.

4But the LORD said to Gideon, "There are still too many men. Take them down to the water, and I will sift them for you there. If I say, 'This one shall go with you,' he shall go; but if I say, 'This one shall not go with you,' he shall not go."

5So Gideon took the men down to the water. There the LORD told him, "Separate those who lap the water with their tongues like a dog from those who kneel down to drink." 6Three hundred men lapped with their hands to their mouths. All the rest got down on their knees to drink.

7The LORD said to Gideon, "With the three hundred men that lapped I will save you and give the Midianites into your hands. Let all the other men go, each to his own place." 8So Gideon sent the rest of the Israelites to their tents but kept the three hundred, who took over the provisions and trumpets of the others.

Now the camp of Midian lay below him in the valley. 9During that night the LORD said to Gideon, "Get up, go down against the camp, because I am going to give it into your hands. 10If you are afraid to attack, go down to the camp with your servant Purah 11and listen to what they are saying. Afterward, you will be encouraged to attack the camp." So he and Purah his servant went down to the outposts of the camp. 12The Midianites, the Amalekites and all the other eastern peoples had settled in the valley, thick as locusts. Their camels could no more be counted than the sand on the seashore.

13Gideon arrived just as a man was telling a friend his dream. "I had a dream," he was saying. "A round loaf of barley bread came tumbling into the Midianite camp. It struck the tent with such force that the tent overturned and collapsed."

14His friend responded, "This can be nothing other than the sword of Gideon son of Joash, the Israelite. God has given the Midianites and the whole camp into his hands."

15When Gideon heard the dream and its interpretation, he worshiped God. He returned to the camp of Israel and called out, "Get up! The LORD has given the Midianite camp into your hands." 16Dividing the three hundred men into three companies, he placed trumpets and empty jars in the hands of all of them, with torches inside.

17"Watch me," he told them. "Follow my lead. When I get to the edge of the camp, do exactly as I do. 18When I and all who are with me blow our trumpets, then from all around the camp blow yours and shout, 'For the LORD and for Gideon.' "

19Gideon and the hundred men with him reached the edge of the camp at the beginning of the middle watch, just after they had changed the guard. They blew their trumpets and broke the jars that were in their hands. 20The three companies blew the trumpets and smashed the jars. Grasping the torches in their left hands and holding in their right hands the trumpets they were to blow, they shouted, "A sword for the LORD and for Gideon!" 21While each man held his position around the camp, all the Midianites ran, crying out as they fled.

22When the three hundred trumpets sounded, the LORD caused the men throughout the camp to turn on each other with their swords. The army fled to Beth Shittah toward Zererah as far as the border of Abel Meholah near Tabbath. 23Israelites from Naphtali, Asher and all Manasseh were called out, and they pursued the Midianites. 24Gideon sent messengers throughout the hill country of Ephraim, saying, "Come down against the Midianites and seize the waters of the Jordan ahead of them as far as Beth Barah."

So all the men of Ephraim were called out and they took the waters of the Jordan as far as Beth Barah. 25They also captured two of the Midianite leaders, Oreb and Zeeb. They killed Oreb at the rock of Oreb, and Zeeb at the winepress of Zeeb. They pursued the Midianites and brought the heads of Oreb and Zeeb to Gideon, who was by the Jordan.

Discovering the Word 1. Gideon called the people to battle (6:34–35) before he laid out the fleece (6:36–40). What do you think would have happened if he had asked for the proof first? 2. Many people have sought spiritual guidance by asking for a specific sign. Because they base this on what Gideon did, this practice is sometimes referred to as "fleecing." What does Gideon's experience teach you about this practice? 3. How would Gideon have felt when over two-thirds of his men went home (7:3)? 4. How were Gideon and the Israelite army like a barley loaf (7:13–15)? 5. How was Gideon changed by these events (7:15–25)?

Applying the Word 1. How do you seek God's guidance? 2. How has God given you encouragement when you wavered in your faith?

Responding in Prayer Pray that God will give you faith to carry out the tasks that he has for you.

Judges 8

8 Now the Ephraimites asked Gideon, "Why have you treated us like this? Why didn't you call us when you went to fight Midian?" And they criticized him sharply.

2But he answered them, "What have I accomplished compared to you? Aren't the gleanings of Ephraim's grapes better than the full grape harvest of Abiezer? 3God gave Oreb and Zeeb, the Midianite leaders, into your hands. What was I able to do compared to you?" At this, their resentment against him subsided.

4Gideon and his three hundred men, exhausted yet keeping up the pursuit, came to the Jordan and crossed it. 5He said to the men of Succoth, "Give my troops some bread; they are worn out, and I am still pursuing Zebah and Zalmunna, the kings of Midian."

6But the officials of Succoth said, "Do you already have the hands of Zebah and Zalmunna in your possession? Why should we give bread to your troops?"

7Then Gideon replied, "Just for that, when the LORD has given Zebah and Zalmunna into my hand, I will tear your flesh with desert thorns and briers."

8From there he went up to Peniel[i] and made the same request of them, but they answered as the men of Succoth had. 9So he said to the men of Peniel, "When I return in triumph, I will tear down this tower."

10Now Zebah and Zalmunna were in Karkor with a force of about fifteen thousand men, all that were left of the armies of the eastern peoples; a hundred and twenty thousand swordsmen had fallen. 11Gideon went up by the route of the nomads east of Nobah and Jogbehah and fell upon the unsuspecting army. 12Zebah and Zalmunna, the two kings of Midian, fled, but he pursued them and captured them, routing their entire army.

13Gideon son of Joash then returned from the battle by the Pass of Heres. 14He caught a young man of Succoth and questioned him, and the young man wrote down for him the names of the seventy-seven officials of Succoth, the elders of the town. 15Then Gideon came and said to the men of Succoth, "Here are Zebah and Zalmunna, about whom you taunted me by saying, 'Do you already have the hands of Zebah and Zalmunna in your possession? Why should we give bread to your exhausted men?' " 16He took the elders of the town and taught the men of Succoth a lesson by punishing them with desert thorns and briers.

[i]8 Hebrew *Penuel*, a variant of *Peniel*; also in verses 9 and 17

[17]He also pulled down the tower of Peniel and killed the men of the town.

[18]Then he asked Zebah and Zalmunna, "What kind of men did you kill at Tabor?"

"Men like you," they answered, "each one with the bearing of a prince."

[19]Gideon replied, "Those were my brothers, the sons of my own mother. As surely as the LORD lives, if you had spared their lives, I would not kill you." [20]Turning to Jether, his oldest son, he said, "Kill them!" But Jether did not draw his sword, because he was only a boy and was afraid.

[21]Zebah and Zalmunna said, "Come, do it yourself. 'As is the man, so is his strength.' " So Gideon stepped forward and killed them, and took the ornaments off their camels' necks.

[22]The Israelites said to Gideon, "Rule over us—you, your son and your grandson—because you have saved us out of the hand of Midian."

[23]But Gideon told them, "I will not rule over you, nor will my son rule over you. The LORD will rule over you." [24]And he said, "I do have one request, that each of you give me an earring from your share of the plunder." (It was the custom of the Ishmaelites to wear gold earrings.)

[25]They answered, "We'll be glad to give them." So they spread out a garment, and each man threw a ring from his plunder onto it. [26]The weight of the gold rings he asked for came to seventeen hundred shekels,[j] not counting the ornaments, the pendants and the purple garments worn by the kings of Midian or the chains that were on their camels' necks. [27]Gideon made the gold into an ephod, which he placed in Ophrah, his town. All Israel prostituted themselves by worshiping it there, and it became a snare to Gideon and his family.

[28]Thus Midian was subdued before the Israelites and did not raise its head again. During Gideon's lifetime, the land enjoyed peace forty years.

[29]Jerub-Baal son of Joash went back home to live. [30]He had seventy sons of his own, for he had many wives. [31]His concubine, who lived in Shechem, also bore him a son, whom he named Abimelech. [32]Gideon son of Joash died at a good old age and was buried in the tomb of his father Joash in Ophrah of the Abiezrites.

[33]No sooner had Gideon died than the Israelites again prostituted themselves to the Baals. They set up Baal-Berith as their god and [34]did not remember the LORD their God, who had rescued them from the hands of all their enemies on every side. [35]They also failed to show kindness to the family of Jerub-Baal (that is, Gideon) for all the good things he had done for them.

[j]26 That is, about 43 pounds (about 19.5 kilograms)

6 / *Judges 9*
Integrity Lost

A MOTTO ON the wall of a German school read:

When wealth is lost, nothing is lost;
When health is lost, something is lost;
When character is lost, all is lost!

The people of Shechem serve as an illustration of this motto. By failing to stand up for what was right, they soon found their lives ruled by evil. Once character was gone, they lost freedom. All of the choices presented to them were merely different paths through a vile maze which led inexorably to a final death trap.

Warming Up to God When have you felt pressured to make a decision you were uncomfortable with?

Read Judges 9.

9 Abimelech son of Jerub-Baal went to his mother's brothers in Shechem and said to them and to all his mother's clan, 2"Ask all the citizens of Shechem, 'Which is better for you: to have all seventy of Jerub-Baal's sons rule over you, or just one man?' Remember, I am your flesh and blood."

3When the brothers repeated all this to the citizens of Shechem, they were inclined to follow Abimelech, for they said, "He is our brother." 4They gave him seventy shekels[k] of silver from the temple of Baal-Berith, and Abimelech used it to hire reckless adventurers, who became his followers. 5He went to his father's home in Ophrah and on one stone murdered his seventy brothers, the sons of Jerub-Baal. But Jotham, the youngest son of Jerub-Baal, escaped by hiding. 6Then all the citizens of Shechem and Beth Millo gathered beside the great tree at the pillar in Shechem to crown Abimelech king.

7When Jotham was told about this, he climbed up on the top of Mount Gerizim and shouted to them, "Listen to me, citizens of Shechem, so that God may listen to you. 8One day the trees went out to anoint a king for themselves. They said to the olive tree, 'Be our king.'

9"But the olive tree answered, 'Should I give up my oil, by which both gods and men are honored, to hold sway over the trees?'

10"Next, the trees said to the fig tree, 'Come and be our king.'

11"But the fig tree replied, 'Should I give up my fruit, so good and sweet, to hold sway over the trees?'

12"Then the trees said to the vine, 'Come and be our king.'

13"But the vine answered, 'Should I give up my wine, which cheers both gods and men, to hold sway over the trees?'

14"Finally all the trees said to the thornbush, 'Come and be our king.'

15"The thornbush said to the trees, 'If you really want to anoint me king over you, come and take refuge in my shade; but if not, then let fire come out of the thornbush and consume the cedars of Lebanon!'

16"Now if you have acted honorably and in good faith when you made Abimelech king, and if you have been fair to Jerub-Baal and his family, and if you have treated him as he deserves—17and to think that my father fought for you, risked his life to rescue you from the hand of Midian 18(but today you have revolted against my father's family, murdered his seventy sons on a single stone, and made Abimelech, the son of his slave girl, king over the citizens of Shechem because he is your brother)— 19if then you have acted honorably and in good faith toward Jerub-Baal and his family today, may Abimelech be your joy, and may you be his, too! 20But if you have not, let fire come out from Abimelech and consume you, citizens of Shechem and Beth Millo, and let fire come out from you, citizens of Shechem and Beth Millo, and consume Abimelech!"

21Then Jotham fled, escaping to Beer, and he lived there because he was afraid of his brother Abimelech.

22After Abimelech had governed Israel three years, 23God sent an evil spirit between Abimelech and the citizens of Shechem, who acted treacherously against Abimelech. 24God did this in order that the crime against Jerub-Baal's seventy sons, the shedding of their blood, might be avenged on their brother Abimelech and on the citizens of Shechem, who had helped him murder his brothers. 25In opposition to him these citizens of Shechem set men on the hilltops to ambush and rob everyone who passed by, and this was reported to Abimelech.

26Now Gaal son of Ebed moved with his brothers into Shechem, and its citizens put their confidence in him. 27After they had gone out into the fields and gathered the grapes and trodden them, they held a festival in the temple of their god. While they were eating and drinking, they cursed Abimelech. 28Then Gaal son of Ebed said, "Who is Abimelech, and who is Shechem, that we should be subject to him? Isn't he Jerub-Baal's son, and isn't Zebul his deputy? Serve the men of Hamor, Shechem's father! Why should we serve Abimelech? 29If only this people were under my command! Then I would get rid of him. I would say to Abimelech, 'Call out your whole army!' "[l]

30When Zebul the governor of the city heard what Gaal son of Ebed said, he was very angry. 31Under cover he sent messengers to Abimelech, saying, "Gaal son of Ebed and his brothers have come to Shechem and are stirring up the city against you. 32Now then, during the night you and your men should come and lie in wait in the fields. 33In the morning at sunrise, advance against the city. When Gaal and his men come

[k]4 That is, about 1 3/4 pounds (about 0.8 kilogram) [l]29 Septuagint; Hebrew *him." Then he said to Abimelech, "Call out your whole army!"*

out against you, do whatever your hand finds to do."

34So Abimelech and all his troops set out by night and took up concealed positions near Shechem in four companies. 35Now Gaal son of Ebed had gone out and was standing at the entrance to the city gate just as Abimelech and his soldiers came out from their hiding place.

36When Gaal saw them, he said to Zebul, "Look, people are coming down from the tops of the mountains!"

Zebul replied, "You mistake the shadows of the mountains for men."

37But Gaal spoke up again: "Look, people are coming down from the center of the land, and a company is coming from the direction of the soothsayers' tree."

38Then Zebul said to him, "Where is your big talk now, you who said, 'Who is Abimelech that we should be subject to him?' Aren't these the men you ridiculed? Go out and fight them!"

39So Gaal led out[m] the citizens of Shechem and fought Abimelech. 40Abimelech chased him, and many fell wounded in the flight—all the way to the entrance to the gate. 41Abimelech stayed in Arumah, and Zebul drove Gaal and his brothers out of Shechem.

42The next day the people of Shechem went out to the fields, and this was reported to Abimelech. 43So he took his men, divided them into three companies and set an ambush in the fields. When he saw the people coming out of the city, he rose to attack them. 44Abimelech and the companies with him rushed forward to a position at the entrance to the city gate. Then two companies rushed upon those in the fields and struck them down. 45All that day Abimelech pressed his attack against the city until he had captured it and killed its people. Then he destroyed the city and scattered salt over it.

46On hearing this, the citizens in the tower of Shechem went into the stronghold of the temple of El-Berith. 47When Abimelech heard that they had assembled there, 48he and all his men went up Mount Zalmon. He took an ax and cut off some branches, which he lifted to his shoulders. He ordered the men with him, "Quick! Do what you have seen me do!" 49So all the men cut branches and followed Abimelech. They piled them against the stronghold and set it on fire over the people inside. So all the people in the tower of Shechem, about a thousand men and women, also died.

50Next Abimelech went to Thebez and besieged it and captured it. 51Inside the city, however, was a strong tower, to which all the men and women—all the people of the city—fled. They locked themselves in and climbed up on the tower roof. 52Abimelech went to the tower and stormed it. But as he approached the entrance to the tower to set it on fire, 53a woman dropped an upper millstone on his head and cracked his skull.

54Hurriedly he called to his armor-bearer, "Draw your sword and kill me, so that they can't say, 'A woman killed him.' " So his servant ran him through, and he died. 55When the Israelites saw that Abimelech was dead, they went home.

56Thus God repaid the wickedness that Abimelech had done to his father by murdering his seventy brothers. 57God also made the men of Shechem pay for all their wickedness. The curse of Jotham son of Jerub-Baal came on them.

[m]39 Or *Gaal went out in the sight of*

Discovering the Word 1. If you were assigned the task of writing an obituary for Abimelech, what would you say about him? 2. When the people offered to make Gideon their king, he turned them down (8:22–23). His children apparently didn't feel the same way. What dilemmas did this present for the people of Shechem (vv. 1–6)? 3. What truths was Jotham attempting to illustrate by his fable (vv. 7–15)? 4. Jotham had shouted, "If then you have acted honorably and in good faith toward Jerub-Baal and his family today, may Abimelech be your joy, and may you be his, too!" (v. 19). What prevented this blessing of joy from occurring? 5. How was Jotham's prophecy in verse 20 fulfilled?

Applying the Word 1. The story ends by stating, "Thus God repaid the wickedness" (v. 56). What does this passage teach you about God's justice and integrity? 2. What do you as a citizen learn from this passage about the importance of choosing leaders who have integrity?

Responding in Prayer Pray that your spiritual leaders and elected officials would be people of character and integrity.

Judges 10

10 After the time of Abimelech a man
of Issachar, Tola son of Puah, the
son of Dodo, rose to save Israel. He
lived in Shamir, in the hill country of Ephraim.
2He led[n] Israel twenty-three years; then he died,
and was buried in Shamir.

3He was followed by Jair of Gilead, who led
Israel twenty-two years. 4He had thirty sons, who
rode thirty donkeys. They controlled thirty towns
in Gilead, which to this day are called Havvoth
Jair.[o] 5When Jair died, he was buried in
Kamon.

6Again the Israelites did evil in the eyes of the
LORD. They served the Baals and the Ashtoreths,
and the gods of Aram, the gods of Sidon, the gods
of Moab, the gods of the Ammonites and the gods
of the Philistines. And because the Israelites for-
sook the LORD and no longer served him, 7he be-
came angry with them. He sold them into the
hands of the Philistines and the Ammonites, 8who
that year shattered and crushed them. For eigh-
teen years they oppressed all the Israelites on the
east side of the Jordan in Gilead, the land of the
Amorites. 9The Ammonites also crossed the Jor-
dan to fight against Judah, Benjamin and the
house of Ephraim; and Israel was in great distress.
10Then the Israelites cried out to the LORD, "We
have sinned against you, forsaking our God and
serving the Baals."

11The LORD replied, "When the Egyptians, the
Amorites, the Ammonites, the Philistines, 12the
Sidonians, the Amalekites and the Maonites[p] op-
pressed you and you cried to me for help, did I
not save you from their hands? 13But you have
forsaken me and served other gods, so I will no
longer save you. 14Go and cry out to the gods you
have chosen. Let them save you when you are in
trouble!"

15But the Israelites said to the LORD, "We have
sinned. Do with us whatever you think best,
but please rescue us now." 16Then they got rid
of the foreign gods among them and served
the LORD. And he could bear Israel's misery no
longer.

17When the Ammonites were called to arms
and camped in Gilead, the Israelites assembled
and camped at Mizpah. 18The leaders of the peo-
ple of Gilead said to each other, "Whoever will
launch the attack against the Ammonites will be
the head of all those living in Gilead."

n2 Traditionally *judged*; also in verse 3 o4 Or *called the settlements of Jair* p12 Hebrew; some Septuagint manuscripts *Midianites*

7 / *Judges 11—12*

God's Dysfunctional Family

IF OUR FAMILIES were perfect, none of us would ever feel worthless or unloved, our relationships with each other would bring joy and satisfaction, and we would experience intimacy with God. Unfortunately, we are all products of a fallen world. Pains from our past continue to bring a destructive element into our present relationships. The intimacy and acceptance we crave slip away from us. Does God love us even when our own dysfunctions cause us to run from him? In the story of Jephthah, God uses this man with a broken and hurting past to illustrate what he will do to heal a broken, pain-driven world.

Warming Up to God What effect do past pains have on your current relationships? Prepare your heart for God's healing through the story in this passage.

Read Judges 11—12.

11

Jephthah the Gileadite was a
mighty warrior. His father was Gil-
ead; his mother was a prostitute.
2Gilead's wife also bore him sons, and when they
were grown up, they drove Jephthah away. "You
are not going to get any inheritance in our fam-
ily," they said, "because you are the son of an-
other woman." 3So Jephthah fled from his broth-
ers and settled in the land of Tob, where a group
of adventurers gathered around him and followed
him.

4Some time later, when the Ammonites made
war on Israel, 5the elders of Gilead went to get
Jephthah from the land of Tob. 6"Come," they
said, "be our commander, so we can fight the
Ammonites."

7Jephthah said to them, "Didn't you hate me
and drive me from my father's house? Why do
you come to me now, when you're in trouble?"

8The elders of Gilead said to him, "Neverthe-
less, we are turning to you now; come with us to
fight the Ammonites, and you will be our head
over all who live in Gilead."

9Jephthah answered, "Suppose you take me
back to fight the Ammonites and the LORD gives
them to me—will I really be your head?"

10The elders of Gilead replied, "The LORD is our
witness; we will certainly do as you say." 11So
Jephthah went with the elders of Gilead, and the
people made him head and commander over
them. And he repeated all his words before the
LORD in Mizpah.

12Then Jephthah sent messengers to the Am-
monite king with the question: "What do you
have against us that you have attacked our coun-
try?"

13The king of the Ammonites answered Jeph-
thah's messengers, "When Israel came up out of
Egypt, they took away my land from the Arnon to
the Jabbok, all the way to the Jordan. Now give it
back peaceably."

14Jephthah sent back messengers to the Am-
monite king, 15saying:

"This is what Jephthah says: Israel did not
take the land of Moab or the land of the
Ammonites. 16But when they came up out of
Egypt, Israel went through the desert to the
Red Sea[q] and on to Kadesh. 17Then Israel
sent messengers to the king of Edom, saying,
'Give us permission to go through your
country,' but the king of Edom would not
listen. They sent also to the king of Moab,
and he refused. So Israel stayed at Kadesh.

18"Next they traveled through the desert,
skirted the lands of Edom and Moab, passed
along the eastern side of the country of
Moab, and camped on the other side of the
Arnon. They did not enter the territory of
Moab, for the Arnon was its border.

19"Then Israel sent messengers to Sihon
king of the Amorites, who ruled in Heshbon,
and said to him, 'Let us pass through your
country to our own place.' 20Sihon, however,
did not trust Israel[r] to pass through his ter-
ritory. He mustered all his men and en-
camped at Jahaz and fought with Israel.

21"Then the LORD, the God of Israel, gave
Sihon and all his men into Israel's hands, and
they defeated them. Israel took over all the
land of the Amorites who lived in that coun-
try, 22capturing all of it from the Arnon to
the Jabbok and from the desert to the Jordan.

23"Now since the LORD, the God of Israel,
has driven the Amorites out before his peo-
ple Israel, what right have you to take it
over? 24Will you not take what your god
Chemosh gives you? Likewise, whatever the
LORD our God has given us, we will possess.
25Are you better than Balak son of Zippor,
king of Moab? Did he ever quarrel with Is-
rael or fight with them? 26For three hundred
years Israel occupied Heshbon, Aroer, the
surrounding settlements and all the towns
along the Arnon. Why didn't you retake
them during that time? 27I have not wronged
you, but you are doing me wrong by waging
war against me. Let the LORD, the Judge,[s]
decide the dispute this day between the Isra-
elites and the Ammonites."

28The king of Ammon, however, paid no atten-
tion to the message Jephthah sent him.

29Then the Spirit of the LORD came upon Jeph-
thah. He crossed Gilead and Manasseh, passed
through Mizpah of Gilead, and from there he ad-
vanced against the Ammonites. 30And Jephthah
made a vow to the LORD: "If you give the Ammon-
ites into my hands, 31whatever comes out of the
door of my house to meet me when I return in
triumph from the Ammonites will be the LORD's,
and I will sacrifice it as a burnt offering."

q16 Hebrew *Yam Suph;* that is, Sea of Reeds r20 Or *however, would not make an agreement for Israel* s27 Or *Ruler*

32 Then Jephthah went over to fight the Ammonites, and the LORD gave them into his hands. 33 He devastated twenty towns from Aroer to the vicinity of Minnith, as far as Abel Keramim. Thus Israel subdued Ammon.

34 When Jephthah returned to his home in Mizpah, who should come out to meet him but his daughter, dancing to the sound of tambourines! She was an only child. Except for her he had neither son nor daughter. 35 When he saw her, he tore his clothes and cried, "Oh! My daughter! You have made me miserable and wretched, because I have made a vow to the LORD that I cannot break."

36 "My father," she replied, "you have given your word to the LORD. Do to me just as you promised, now that the LORD has avenged you of your enemies, the Ammonites. 37 But grant me this one request," she said. "Give me two months to roam the hills and weep with my friends, because I will never marry."

38 "You may go," he said. And he let her go for two months. She and the girls went into the hills and wept because she would never marry. 39 After the two months, she returned to her father and he did to her as he had vowed. And she was a virgin.

From this comes the Israelite custom 40 that each year the young women of Israel go out for four days to commemorate the daughter of Jephthah the Gileadite.

12

The men of Ephraim called out their forces, crossed over to Zaphon and said to Jephthah, "Why did you go to fight the Ammonites without calling us to go with you? We're going to burn down your house over your head."

2 Jephthah answered, "I and my people were engaged in a great struggle with the Ammonites, and although I called, you didn't save me out of their hands. 3 When I saw that you wouldn't help, I took my life in my hands and crossed over to fight the Ammonites, and the LORD gave me the victory over them. Now why have you come up today to fight me?"

4 Jephthah then called together the men of Gilead and fought against Ephraim. The Gileadites struck them down because the Ephraimites had said, "You Gileadites are renegades from Ephraim and Manasseh." 5 The Gileadites captured the fords of the Jordan leading to Ephraim, and whenever a survivor of Ephraim said, "Let me cross over," the men of Gilead asked him, "Are you an Ephraimite?" If he replied, "No," 6 they said, "All right, say 'Shibboleth.' " If he said, "Sibboleth," because he could not pronounce the word correctly, they seized him and killed him at the fords of the Jordan. Forty-two thousand Ephraimites were killed at that time.

7 Jephthah led[t] Israel six years. Then Jephthah the Gileadite died, and was buried in a town in Gilead.

8 After him, Ibzan of Bethlehem led Israel. 9 He had thirty sons and thirty daughters. He gave his daughters away in marriage to those outside his clan, and for his sons he brought in thirty young women as wives from outside his clan. Ibzan led Israel seven years. 10 Then Ibzan died, and was buried in Bethlehem.

11 After him, Elon the Zebulunite led Israel ten years. 12 Then Elon died, and was buried in Aijalon in the land of Zebulun.

13 After him, Abdon son of Hillel, from Pirathon, led Israel. 14 He had forty sons and thirty grandsons, who rode on seventy donkeys. He led Israel eight years. 15 Then Abdon son of Hillel died, and was buried at Pirathon in Ephraim, in the hill country of the Amalekites.

[t]7 Traditionally *judged*; also in verses 8-14

Discovering the Word 1. Imagine that you are a psychologist and that Jephthah and the people of Israel have come to your office for family counseling. What problems do you see in this family? 2. What expectations did Jephthah and the people of Gilead bring to their reconciliation (11:4–11)? 3. Why did Jephthah make and keep his tragic vow to God (11:30–35)? 4. After winning a great victory and sacrificing a beloved daughter, Jephthah still did not find the approval he craved (12:1). How does Jephthah deal with this latest rejection? 5. Even though God provided a great victory, the characters in this story were unable to celebrate or appreciate it. How did their dysfunctions prevent them from celebrating God's mighty act?

Applying the Word 1. How have you dealt with rejection in your life? 2. When have your own relational dysfunctions caused you to miss celebrating a gift from God? 3. How could changes in the way you relate to other people make a positive difference in the way you relate to God?

Responding in Prayer Pray that God will build you into a person of gentleness and discernment so that you can show acceptance to others.

8 / *Judges 13*
God Forges a New Tool

FINDING A GOOD pair of scissors in my house can often be difficult. One day in frustration, I bought a new pair, put them in my private drawer and forbid the rest of the family to touch them. Since that day, I (almost always) have been able to locate scissors when I need them. God's sending of Samson was similar to my purchase of scissors. Samson was to be set apart for God's use alone. When it was time to once again save the Israelites, God's implement of salvation would be readily at hand.

Warming Up to God Imagine yourself as God's tool. How would you describe yourself? For example, would you say that you are in the toolbox waiting to be used? misplaced and can't be found? in God's hands? Or being used for someone else's project?

Read Judges 13.

13 Again the Israelites did evil in the
eyes of the LORD, so the LORD deliv-
ered them into the hands of the
Philistines for forty years.
[2]A certain man of Zorah, named Manoah, from
the clan of the Danites, had a wife who was sterile
and remained childless. [3]The angel of the LORD
appeared to her and said, "You are sterile and
childless, but you are going to conceive and have
a son. [4]Now see to it that you drink no wine or
other fermented drink and that you do not eat
anything unclean, [5]because you will conceive
and give birth to a son. No razor may be used
on his head, because the boy is to be a Nazirite,
set apart to God from birth, and he will begin
the deliverance of Israel from the hands of the
Philistines."
[6]Then the woman went to her husband and
told him, "A man of God came to me. He looked
like an angel of God, very awesome. I didn't ask
him where he came from, and he didn't tell me
his name. [7]But he said to me, 'You will conceive
and give birth to a son. Now then, drink no wine
or other fermented drink and do not eat anything
unclean, because the boy will be a Nazirite of God
from birth until the day of his death.' "
[8]Then Manoah prayed to the LORD: "O Lord, I
beg you, let the man of God you sent to us come
again to teach us how to bring up the boy who is
to be born."
[9]God heard Manoah, and the angel of God
came again to the woman while she was out in
the field; but her husband Manoah was not with
her. [10]The woman hurried to tell her husband,
"He's here! The man who appeared to me the
other day!"
[11]Manoah got up and followed his wife. When
he came to the man, he said, "Are you the one
who talked to my wife?"
"I am," he said.
[12]So Manoah asked him, "When your words
are fulfilled, what is to be the rule for the boy's
life and work?"
[13]The angel of the LORD answered, "Your wife
must do all that I have told her. [14]She must not
eat anything that comes from the grapevine, nor
drink any wine or other fermented drink nor eat
anything unclean. She must do everything I have
commanded her."
[15]Manoah said to the angel of the LORD, "We
would like you to stay until we prepare a young
goat for you."
[16]The angel of the LORD replied, "Even though
you detain me, I will not eat any of your food. But
if you prepare a burnt offering, offer it to the
LORD." (Manoah did not realize that it was the
angel of the LORD.)
[17]Then Manoah inquired of the angel of the
LORD, "What is your name, so that we may honor
you when your word comes true?"
[18]He replied, "Why do you ask my name? It is
beyond understanding.[u]" [19]Then Manoah took a

[u]18 *Or is wonderful*

young goat, together with the grain offering, and sacrificed it on a rock to the LORD. And the LORD did an amazing thing while Manoah and his wife watched: [20]As the flame blazed up from the altar toward heaven, the angel of the LORD ascended in the flame. Seeing this, Manoah and his wife fell with their faces to the ground. [21]When the angel of the LORD did not show himself again to Manoah and his wife, Manoah realized that it was the angel of the LORD.

[22]"We are doomed to die!" he said to his wife. "We have seen God!"

[23]But his wife answered, "If the LORD had meant to kill us, he would not have accepted a burnt offering and grain offering from our hands, nor shown us all these things or now told us this."

[24]The woman gave birth to a boy and named him Samson. He grew and the LORD blessed him, [25]and the Spirit of the LORD began to stir him while he was in Mahaneh Dan, between Zorah and Eshtaol.

Discovering the Word 1. What did God require of Manoah, his wife and Samson (vv. 4–5)? 2. How would keeping the Nazirite vow have prepared Samson for God's service? 3. What does God's second visit to Samson's parents add to the first (vv. 9–21)? 4. What does God reveal about himself to Samson's parents, and what does he hold back (vv. 16–21)? 5. Why were Samson's parents afraid when they realized they had seen God (vv. 22–23)?

Applying the Word 1. What does this passage teach you about how God prepares us for service? 2. How has God prepared you for his service?

Responding in Prayer Ask God to make you a useful tool in his service.

9 / *Judges 14—15*
The Need for Conflict

"THERE IS IN truth no such thing as harmonious co-existence between church and world, for where there is no conflict it is because the world has taken over," writes Michael Wilcock (*The Message of Judges* [Downers Grove, Ill.: InterVarsity Press, 1992], p. 142). In each of the previous occupations described in Judges, there is conflict. We are at least told that the people cry out to God for deliverance. Not so with the Philistine conquest. The people have lived under the Philistines' thumb for forty years without complaining. In surprising ways God uses Samson to create conflict where none existed. The message to today's church is clear—conflict is a necessary part of our message.

Warming Up to God What conflict do you see between the church and the world today? In what ways do you feel caught up in that conflict?

Read Judges 14—15.

14 Samson went down to Timnah and saw there a young Philistine woman. [2]When he returned, he said to his father and mother, "I have seen a Philistine woman in Timnah; now get her for me as my wife."

[3]His father and mother replied, "Isn't there an acceptable woman among your relatives or among all our people? Must you go to the uncircumcised Philistines to get a wife?"

But Samson said to his father, "Get her for me. She's the right one for me." [4](His parents did not know that this was from the LORD, who was seeking an occasion to confront the Philistines; for at that time they were ruling over Israel.) [5]Samson went down to Timnah together with his father and mother. As they approached the vineyards of Timnah, suddenly a young lion came roaring toward him. 6The Spirit of the LORD came upon him in power so that he tore the lion apart with his bare hands as he might have torn a young goat. But he told neither his father nor his mother what he had done. 7Then he went down and talked with the woman, and he liked her.

8Some time later, when he went back to marry her, he turned aside to look at the lion's carcass. In it was a swarm of bees and some honey, 9which he scooped out with his hands and ate as he went along. When he rejoined his parents, he gave them some, and they too ate it. But he did not tell them that he had taken the honey from the lion's carcass.

10Now his father went down to see the woman. And Samson made a feast there, as was customary for bridegrooms. 11When he appeared, he was given thirty companions.

12"Let me tell you a riddle," Samson said to them. "If you can give me the answer within the seven days of the feast, I will give you thirty linen garments and thirty sets of clothes. 13If you can't tell me the answer, you must give me thirty linen garments and thirty sets of clothes."

"Tell us your riddle," they said. "Let's hear it."

14He replied,

"Out of the eater, something to eat;
out of the strong, something sweet."

For three days they could not give the answer.

15On the fourth[v] day, they said to Samson's wife, "Coax your husband into explaining the riddle for us, or we will burn you and your father's household to death. Did you invite us here to rob us?"

16Then Samson's wife threw herself on him, sobbing, "You hate me! You don't really love me. You've given my people a riddle, but you haven't told me the answer."

"I haven't even explained it to my father or mother," he replied, "so why should I explain it to you?" 17She cried the whole seven days of the feast. So on the seventh day he finally told her, because she continued to press him. She in turn explained the riddle to her people.

18Before sunset on the seventh day the men of the town said to him,

"What is sweeter than honey?
What is stronger than a lion?"

Samson said to them,

"If you had not plowed with my heifer,
you would not have solved my riddle."

19Then the Spirit of the LORD came upon him in power. He went down to Ashkelon, struck down thirty of their men, stripped them of their belongings and gave their clothes to those who had explained the riddle. Burning with anger, he went up to his father's house. 20And Samson's wife was given to the friend who had attended him at his wedding.

15 Later on, at the time of wheat harvest, Samson took a young goat and went to visit his wife. He said, "I'm going to my wife's room." But her father would not let him go in.

2"I was so sure you thoroughly hated her," he said, "that I gave her to your friend. Isn't her younger sister more attractive? Take her instead."

3Samson said to them, "This time I have a right to get even with the Philistines; I will really harm them." 4So he went out and caught three hundred foxes and tied them tail to tail in pairs. He then fastened a torch to every pair of tails, 5lit the torches and let the foxes loose in the standing grain of the Philistines. He burned up the shocks and standing grain, together with the vineyards and olive groves.

6When the Philistines asked, "Who did this?" they were told, "Samson, the Timnite's son-in-law, because his wife was given to his friend."

So the Philistines went up and burned her and her father to death. 7Samson said to them, "Since you've acted like this, I won't stop until I get my revenge on you." 8He attacked them viciously and slaughtered many of them. Then he went down and stayed in a cave in the rock of Etam.

9The Philistines went up and camped in Judah, spreading out near Lehi. 10The men of Judah asked, "Why have you come to fight us?"

"We have come to take Samson prisoner," they answered, "to do to him as he did to us."

11Then three thousand men from Judah went down to the cave in the rock of Etam and said to Samson, "Don't you realize that the Philistines are rulers over us? What have you done to us?"

He answered, "I merely did to them what they did to me."

12They said to him, "We've come to tie you up and hand you over to the Philistines."

v15 Some Septuagint manuscripts and Syriac; Hebrew *seventh*

Samson said, “Swear to me that you won’t kill me yourselves.”

13“Agreed,” they answered. “We will only tie you up and hand you over to them. We will not kill you.” So they bound him with two new ropes and led him up from the rock. 14As he approached Lehi, the Philistines came toward him shouting. The Spirit of the LORD came upon him in power. The ropes on his arms became like charred flax, and the bindings dropped from his hands. 15Finding a fresh jawbone of a donkey, he grabbed it and struck down a thousand men.

16Then Samson said,

“With a donkey’s jawbone
  I have made donkeys of them.[w]
With a donkey’s jawbone
  I have killed a thousand men.”

17When he finished speaking, he threw away the jawbone; and the place was called Ramath Lehi.[x]

18Because he was very thirsty, he cried out to the LORD, “You have given your servant this great victory. Must I now die of thirst and fall into the hands of the uncircumcised?” 19Then God opened up the hollow place in Lehi, and water came out of it. When Samson drank, his strength returned and he revived. So the spring was called En Hakkore,[y] and it is still there in Lehi.

20Samson led[z] Israel for twenty years in the days of the Philistines.

[w]16 Or *made a heap or two*; the Hebrew for *donkey* sounds like the Hebrew for *heap.* [x]17 *Ramath Lehi* means *jawbone hill.* [y]19 *En Hakkore* means *caller’s spring.* [z]20 Traditionally *judged*

Discovering the Word 1. What did Samson’s parents seem to expect their son would be like (14:1–4)? 2. What did Samson’s marriage and subsequent acts of vengeance accomplish (14:19—15:8)? 3. What do Samson’s actions reveal about his character? 4. What attitude did the men of Judah have toward the Philistines (15:9–13)? 5. Samson was the only judge without an army. All of his exploits were performed single-handedly. What does this tell you about the moral and spiritual condition of Israel?

Applying the Word 1. What similarities do you see between Israel’s situation and the moral and spiritual conditions of today? 2. What action might God be calling you to take that would be in conflict with the ways of the world?

Responding in Prayer Pray that the Christian church will be united in facing conflict with a world that rejects God.

10 / *Judges 16*
Victorious Defeat

IMAGINE A PASSION play starring a notorious sinner in the role of Jesus. Instead of traveling the countryside preaching and healing, this hero visits brothels and brawls in bar fights. You would probably walk out of such a sacrilegious production, yet this is what God presents to us in the story of Samson. Samson represents both the best and the worst in each of us; called by the grace of God, bound to him by promise, repeatedly empowered, greatly gifted, yet faithless, self-indulgent, and only too ready to fraternize with the enemy.

Warming Up to God When has a “sinner” surprised you by demonstrating God’s grace?

Read Judges 16.

16 One day Samson went to Gaza, where he saw a prostitute. He went in to spend the night with her. 2The people of Gaza were told, “Samson is here!” So they surrounded the place and lay in wait for him all night at the city gate. They made no move during the night, saying, “At dawn we’ll kill him.”

3But Samson lay there only until the middle of the night. Then he got up and took hold of the doors of the city gate, together with the two posts, and tore them loose, bar and all. He lifted them to his shoulders and carried them to the top of the hill that faces Hebron.

4Some time later, he fell in love with a woman in the Valley of Sorek whose name was Delilah. 5The rulers of the Philistines went to her and said, "See if you can lure him into showing you the secret of his great strength and how we can overpower him so we may tie him up and subdue him. Each one of us will give you eleven hundred shekels[a] of silver."

6So Delilah said to Samson, "Tell me the secret of your great strength and how you can be tied up and subdued."

7Samson answered her, "If anyone ties me with seven fresh thongs[b] that have not been dried, I'll become as weak as any other man."

8Then the rulers of the Philistines brought her seven fresh thongs that had not been dried, and she tied him with them. 9With men hidden in the room, she called to him, "Samson, the Philistines are upon you!" But he snapped the thongs as easily as a piece of string snaps when it comes close to a flame. So the secret of his strength was not discovered.

10Then Delilah said to Samson, "You have made a fool of me; you lied to me. Come now, tell me how you can be tied."

11He said, "If anyone ties me securely with new ropes that have never been used, I'll become as weak as any other man."

12So Delilah took new ropes and tied him with them. Then, with men hidden in the room, she called to him, "Samson, the Philistines are upon you!" But he snapped the ropes off his arms as if they were threads.

13Delilah then said to Samson, "Until now, you have been making a fool of me and lying to me. Tell me how you can be tied."

He replied, "If you weave the seven braids of my head into the fabric ⌊on the loom⌋ and tighten it with the pin, I'll become as weak as any other man." So while he was sleeping, Delilah took the seven braids of his head, wove them into the fabric 14and[c] tightened it with the pin.

Again she called to him, "Samson, the Philistines are upon you!" He awoke from his sleep and pulled up the pin and the loom, with the fabric.

15Then she said to him, "How can you say, 'I love you,' when you won't confide in me? This is the third time you have made a fool of me and haven't told me the secret of your great strength." 16With such nagging she prodded him day after day until he was tired to death.

17So he told her everything. "No razor has ever been used on my head," he said, "because I have been a Nazirite set apart to God since birth. If my head were shaved, my strength would leave me, and I would become as weak as any other man."

18When Delilah saw that he had told her everything, she sent word to the rulers of the Philistines, "Come back once more; he has told me everything." So the rulers of the Philistines returned with the silver in their hands. 19Having put him to sleep on her lap, she called a man to shave off the seven braids of his hair, and so began to subdue him.[d] And his strength left him.

20Then she called, "Samson, the Philistines are upon you!"

He awoke from his sleep and thought, "I'll go out as before and shake myself free." But he did not know that the LORD had left him.

21Then the Philistines seized him, gouged out his eyes and took him down to Gaza. Binding him with bronze shackles, they set him to grinding in the prison. 22But the hair on his head began to grow again after it had been shaved.

23Now the rulers of the Philistines assembled to offer a great sacrifice to Dagon their god and to celebrate, saying, "Our god has delivered Samson, our enemy, into our hands."

24When the people saw him, they praised their god, saying,

"Our god has delivered our enemy
 into our hands,
the one who laid waste our land
 and multiplied our slain."

25While they were in high spirits, they shouted, "Bring out Samson to entertain us." So they called Samson out of the prison, and he performed for them.

When they stood him among the pillars, 26Samson said to the servant who held his hand, "Put me where I can feel the pillars that support the temple, so that I may lean against them." 27Now the temple was crowded with men and women; all the rulers of the Philistines were there, and on the roof were about three thousand men and women watching Samson perform.

[a]5 That is, about 28 pounds (about 13 kilograms) [b]7 Or *bowstrings*; also in verses 8 and 9 [c]13,14 Some Septuagint manuscripts; Hebrew *"⌊I can⌋ if you weave the seven braids of my head into the fabric ⌊on the loom⌋." 14So she* [d]19 Hebrew; some Septuagint manuscripts *and he began to weaken*

28Then Samson prayed to the LORD, "O Sovereign
LORD, remember me. O God, please strengthen
me just once more, and let me with one blow
get revenge on the Philistines for my two eyes."
29Then Samson reached toward the two central
pillars on which the temple stood. Bracing him-
self against them, his right hand on the one and
his left hand on the other, 30Samson said, "Let me
die with the Philistines!" Then he pushed with all
his might, and down came the temple on the rul-
ers and all the people in it. Thus he killed many
more when he died than while he lived.
31Then his brothers and his father's whole fam-
ily went down to get him. They brought him back
and buried him between Zorah and Eshtaol in the
tomb of Manoah his father. He had led[e] Israel
twenty years.

[e]31 Traditionally *judged*

Discovering the Word 1. What clues suggest Samson's spiritual condition at the beginning of this chapter (vv. 1–4)? 2. Why do you think Samson revealed the secret of his strength to Delilah (vv. 15–17)? 3. Imagine the scene in verse 20 when Samson discovers that the Lord has left him. What thoughts, emotions and regrets would have gone through his mind? 4. How did Samson change after his capture (vv. 25–30)? 5. What has Samson taught you?

Applying the Word 1. In what ways do you, like Samson, take God's gifts for granted? 2. How would your life be different if the Lord suddenly "left" you?

Responding in Prayer In his arrest and death Samson can remind us of Jesus' great gift to us. Tell Jesus how grateful you are for his sacrifice.

11/ *Judges 17—18*
A Moral Collapse

IN HIS JANUARY 27, 1838, address before the Young Men's Lyceum, Springfield, Illinois, Abraham Lincoln said:

> At what point shall we expect the approach of danger? By what means shall we fortify against it? Shall we expect some trans-Atlantic military giant, to step the ocean, and crush us at a blow?
>
> Never!
>
> At what point then is the approach of danger to be expected?
>
> I answer, if it ever reaches us, it must spring up amongst us. It cannot come from abroad. If destruction be our lot, we ourselves must be its author and finisher. As a nation of free men, we must live through all times, or die by suicide.

The last five chapters of Judges show us a picture of a society destroying itself by a moral and spiritual collapse.

Warming Up to God What dangers are your nation, church and family facing? God grieves when we turn from him. Take some time to reflect on how God must feel as he looks on the world he created.

Read Judges 17—18.

17 Now a man named Micah from the
hill country of Ephraim 2said to his
mother, "The eleven hundred shek-
els[f] of silver that were taken from you and about
which I heard you utter a curse—I have that sil-
ver with me; I took it."
Then his mother said, "The LORD bless you, my
son!"
3When he returned the eleven hundred shekels
of silver to his mother, she said, "I solemnly con-
secrate my silver to the LORD for my son to make
a carved image and a cast idol. I will give it back
to you."
4So he returned the silver to his mother, and
she took two hundred shekels[g] of silver and gave
them to a silversmith, who made them into the

[f]2 That is, about 28 pounds (about 13 kilograms) [g]4 That is, about 5 pounds (about 2.3 kilograms)

image and the idol. And they were put in Micah's
house.
[5]Now this man Micah had a shrine, and he
made an ephod and some idols and installed one
of his sons as his priest. [6]In those days Israel had
no king; everyone did as he saw fit.
[7]A young Levite from Bethlehem in Judah, who
had been living within the clan of Judah, [8]left that
town in search of some other place to stay. On his
way[h] he came to Micah's house in the hill coun-
try of Ephraim.
[9]Micah asked him, "Where are you from?"
"I'm a Levite from Bethlehem in Judah," he
said, "and I'm looking for a place to stay."
[10]Then Micah said to him, "Live with me and
be my father and priest, and I'll give you ten shek-
els[i] of silver a year, your clothes and your food."
[11]So the Levite agreed to live with him, and the
young man was to him like one of his sons.
[12]Then Micah installed the Levite, and the young
man became his priest and lived in his house.
[13]And Micah said, "Now I know that the LORD will
be good to me, since this Levite has become my
priest."

18 In those days Israel had no king.
And in those days the tribe of the
Danites was seeking a place of their
own where they might settle, because they had
not yet come into an inheritance among the tribes
of Israel. [2]So the Danites sent five warriors from
Zorah and Eshtaol to spy out the land and ex-
plore it. These men represented all their clans.
They told them, "Go, explore the land."
The men entered the hill country of Ephraim
and came to the house of Micah, where they
spent the night. [3]When they were near Micah's
house, they recognized the voice of the young
Levite; so they turned in there and asked him,
"Who brought you here? What are you doing in
this place? Why are you here?"
[4]He told them what Micah had done for him,
and said, "He has hired me and I am his priest."
[5]Then they said to him, "Please inquire of God
to learn whether our journey will be successful."
[6]The priest answered them, "Go in peace. Your
journey has the LORD's approval."
[7]So the five men left and came to Laish, where
they saw that the people were living in safety, like
the Sidonians, unsuspecting and secure. And
since their land lacked nothing, they were pros-
perous.[j] Also, they lived a long way from the
Sidonians and had no relationship with anyone
else.[k]
[8]When they returned to Zorah and Eshtaol,
their brothers asked them, "How did you find
things?"
[9]They answered, "Come on, let's attack them!
We have seen that the land is very good. Aren't
you going to do something? Don't hesitate to go
there and take it over. [10]When you get there, you
will find an unsuspecting people and a spacious
land that God has put into your hands, a land that
lacks nothing whatever."
[11]Then six hundred men from the clan of the
Danites, armed for battle, set out from Zorah and
Eshtaol. [12]On their way they set up camp near
Kiriath Jearim in Judah. This is why the place
west of Kiriath Jearim is called Mahaneh Dan[l] to
this day. [13]From there they went on to the hill
country of Ephraim and came to Micah's house.
[14]Then the five men who had spied out the
land of Laish said to their brothers, "Do you
know that one of these houses has an ephod,
other household gods, a carved image and a cast
idol? Now you know what to do." [15]So they
turned in there and went to the house of the
young Levite at Micah's place and greeted him.
[16]The six hundred Danites, armed for battle,
stood at the entrance to the gate. [17]The five men
who had spied out the land went inside and took
the carved image, the ephod, the other household
gods and the cast idol while the priest and the six
hundred armed men stood at the entrance to the
gate.
[18]When these men went into Micah's house
and took the carved image, the ephod, the other
household gods and the cast idol, the priest said
to them, "What are you doing?"
[19]They answered him, "Be quiet! Don't say a
word. Come with us, and be our father and priest.
Isn't it better that you serve a tribe and clan in
Israel as priest rather than just one man's house-
hold?" [20]Then the priest was glad. He took the
ephod, the other household gods and the carved
image and went along with the people. [21]Putting
their little children, their livestock and their pos-
sessions in front of them, they turned away and
left.
[22]When they had gone some distance from Mi-
cah's house, the men who lived near Micah were

[h]8 Or *To carry on his profession* [i]10 That is, about 4 ounces (about 110 grams) [j]7 The meaning of the Hebrew for this clause is uncertain. [k]7 Hebrew; some Septuagint manuscripts *with the Arameans* [l]12 *Mahaneh Dan* means *Dan's camp.*

called together and overtook the Danites. 23As they shouted after them, the Danites turned and said to Micah, "What's the matter with you that you called out your men to fight?"

24He replied, "You took the gods I made, and my priest, and went away. What else do I have? How can you ask, 'What's the matter with you?' "

25The Danites answered, "Don't argue with us, or some hot-tempered men will attack you, and you and your family will lose your lives." 26So the Danites went their way, and Micah, seeing that they were too strong for him, turned around and went back home.

27Then they took what Micah had made, and his priest, and went on to Laish, against a peaceful and unsuspecting people. They attacked them with the sword and burned down their city. 28There was no one to rescue them because they lived a long way from Sidon and had no relationship with anyone else. The city was in a valley near Beth Rehob.

The Danites rebuilt the city and settled there. 29They named it Dan after their forefather Dan, who was born to Israel—though the city used to be called Laish. 30There the Danites set up for themselves the idols, and Jonathan son of Gershom, the son of Moses,[m] and his sons were priests for the tribe of Dan until the time of the captivity of the land. 31They continued to use the idols Micah had made, all the time the house of God was in Shiloh.

[m]*30* An ancient Hebrew scribal tradition, some Septuagint manuscripts and Vulgate; Masoretic Text *Manasseh*

Discovering the Word 1. What happens to the stolen silver throughout this tale? 2. Describe Micah's mother (17:1-4). What was her relationship to God and to her son? 3. What actions does Micah take in this narrative (17:1-3, 10-13; 18:22-26)? 4. How did the Levite pervert religion (17:10-13; 18:4-6, 18-20)? 5. What do you learn about the tribe of Dan?

Applying the Word 1. What individuals or groups in your community most resemble Micah's mother, Micah, the Levite and the Danites? 2. By which of their sins are you most tempted? 3. What role could you have in calling people back to God?

Responding in Prayer Pray for the people in your city or town and for yourself.

Judges 19—20

19

In those days Israel had no king.

Now a Levite who lived in a remote area in the hill country of Ephraim took a concubine from Bethlehem in Judah. 2But she was unfaithful to him. She left him and went back to her father's house in Bethlehem, Judah. After she had been there four months, 3her husband went to her to persuade her to return. He had with him his servant and two donkeys. She took him into her father's house, and when her father saw him, he gladly welcomed him. 4His father-in-law, the girl's father, prevailed upon him to stay; so he remained with him three days, eating and drinking, and sleeping there.

5On the fourth day they got up early and he prepared to leave, but the girl's father said to his son-in-law, "Refresh yourself with something to eat; then you can go." 6So the two of them sat down to eat and drink together. Afterward the girl's father said, "Please stay tonight and enjoy yourself." 7And when the man got up to go, his father-in-law persuaded him, so he stayed there that night. 8On the morning of the fifth day, when he rose to go, the girl's father said, "Refresh yourself. Wait till afternoon!" So the two of them ate together.

9Then when the man, with his concubine and his servant, got up to leave, his father-in-law, the girl's father, said, "Now look, it's almost evening. Spend the night here; the day is nearly over. Stay and enjoy yourself. Early tomorrow morning you can get up and be on your way home." 10But, unwilling to stay another night, the man left and went toward Jebus (that is, Jerusalem), with his two saddled donkeys and his concubine.

11When they were near Jebus and the day was almost gone, the servant said to his master,

"Come, let's stop at this city of the Jebusites and spend the night."

[12]His master replied, "No. We won't go into an alien city, whose people are not Israelites. We will go on to Gibeah." [13]He added, "Come, let's try to reach Gibeah or Ramah and spend the night in one of those places." [14]So they went on, and the sun set as they neared Gibeah in Benjamin. [15]There they stopped to spend the night. They went and sat in the city square, but no one took them into his home for the night.

[16]That evening an old man from the hill country of Ephraim, who was living in Gibeah (the men of the place were Benjamites), came in from his work in the fields. [17]When he looked and saw the traveler in the city square, the old man asked, "Where are you going? Where did you come from?"

[18]He answered, "We are on our way from Bethlehem in Judah to a remote area in the hill country of Ephraim where I live. I have been to Bethlehem in Judah and now I am going to the house of the LORD. No one has taken me into his house. [19]We have both straw and fodder for our donkeys and bread and wine for ourselves your servants—me, your maidservant, and the young man with us. We don't need anything."

[20]"You are welcome at my house," the old man said. "Let me supply whatever you need. Only don't spend the night in the square." [21]So he took him into his house and fed his donkeys. After they had washed their feet, they had something to eat and drink.

[22]While they were enjoying themselves, some of the wicked men of the city surrounded the house. Pounding on the door, they shouted to the old man who owned the house, "Bring out the man who came to your house so we can have sex with him."

[23]The owner of the house went outside and said to them, "No, my friends, don't be so vile. Since this man is my guest, don't do this disgraceful thing. [24]Look, here is my virgin daughter, and his concubine. I will bring them out to you now, and you can use them and do to them whatever you wish. But to this man, don't do such a disgraceful thing."

[25]But the men would not listen to him. So the man took his concubine and sent her outside to them, and they raped her and abused her throughout the night, and at dawn they let her go. [26]At daybreak the woman went back to the house where her master was staying, fell down at the door and lay there until daylight.

[27]When her master got up in the morning and opened the door of the house and stepped out to continue on his way, there lay his concubine, fallen in the doorway of the house, with her hands on the threshold. [28]He said to her, "Get up; let's go." But there was no answer. Then the man put her on his donkey and set out for home.

[29]When he reached home, he took a knife and cut up his concubine, limb by limb, into twelve parts and sent them into all the areas of Israel. [30]Everyone who saw it said, "Such a thing has never been seen or done, not since the day the Israelites came up out of Egypt. Think about it! Consider it! Tell us what to do!"

20 Then all the Israelites from Dan to Beersheba and from the land of Gilead came out as one man and assembled before the LORD in Mizpah. [2]The leaders of all the people of the tribes of Israel took their places in the assembly of the people of God, four hundred thousand soldiers armed with swords. [3](The Benjamites heard that the Israelites had gone up to Mizpah.) Then the Israelites said, "Tell us how this awful thing happened."

[4]So the Levite, the husband of the murdered woman, said, "I and my concubine came to Gibeah in Benjamin to spend the night. [5]During the night the men of Gibeah came after me and surrounded the house, intending to kill me. They raped my concubine, and she died. [6]I took my concubine, cut her into pieces and sent one piece to each region of Israel's inheritance, because they committed this lewd and disgraceful act in Israel. [7]Now, all you Israelites, speak up and give your verdict."

[8]All the people rose as one man, saying, "None of us will go home. No, not one of us will return to his house. [9]But now this is what we'll do to Gibeah: We'll go up against it as the lot directs. [10]We'll take ten men out of every hundred from all the tribes of Israel, and a hundred from a thousand, and a thousand from ten thousand, to get provisions for the army. Then, when the army arrives at Gibeah[n] in Benjamin, it can give them what they deserve for all this vileness done in Israel." [11]So all the men of Israel got together and united as one man against the city.

[12]The tribes of Israel sent men throughout the

[n] 10 One Hebrew manuscript; most Hebrew manuscripts *Geba,* a variant of *Gibeah*

tribe of Benjamin, saying, “What about this awful crime that was committed among you? 13Now surrender those wicked men of Gibeah so that we may put them to death and purge the evil from Israel.”

But the Benjamites would not listen to their fellow Israelites. 14From their towns they came together at Gibeah to fight against the Israelites. 15At once the Benjamites mobilized twenty-six thousand swordsmen from their towns, in addition to seven hundred chosen men from those living in Gibeah. 16Among all these soldiers there were seven hundred chosen men who were left-handed, each of whom could sling a stone at a hair and not miss.

17Israel, apart from Benjamin, mustered four hundred thousand swordsmen, all of them fighting men.

18The Israelites went up to Bethel[o] and inquired of God. They said, “Who of us shall go first to fight against the Benjamites?”

The LORD replied, “Judah shall go first.”

19The next morning the Israelites got up and pitched camp near Gibeah. 20The men of Israel went out to fight the Benjamites and took up battle positions against them at Gibeah. 21The Benjamites came out of Gibeah and cut down twenty-two thousand Israelites on the battlefield that day. 22But the men of Israel encouraged one another and again took up their positions where they had stationed themselves the first day. 23The Israelites went up and wept before the LORD until evening, and they inquired of the LORD. They said, “Shall we go up again to battle against the Benjamites, our brothers?”

The LORD answered, “Go up against them.”

24Then the Israelites drew near to Benjamin the second day. 25This time, when the Benjamites came out from Gibeah to oppose them, they cut down another eighteen thousand Israelites, all of them armed with swords.

26Then the Israelites, all the people, went up to Bethel, and there they sat weeping before the LORD. They fasted that day until evening and presented burnt offerings and fellowship offerings[p] to the LORD. 27And the Israelites inquired of the LORD. (In those days the ark of the covenant of God was there, 28with Phinehas son of Eleazar, the son of Aaron, ministering before it.) They asked, “Shall we go up again to battle with Benjamin our brother, or not?”

The LORD responded, “Go, for tomorrow I will give them into your hands.”

29Then Israel set an ambush around Gibeah. 30They went up against the Benjamites on the third day and took up positions against Gibeah as they had done before. 31The Benjamites came out to meet them and were drawn away from the city. They began to inflict casualties on the Israelites as before, so that about thirty men fell in the open field and on the roads—the one leading to Bethel and the other to Gibeah.

32While the Benjamites were saying, “We are defeating them as before,” the Israelites were saying, “Let’s retreat and draw them away from the city to the roads.”

33All the men of Israel moved from their places and took up positions at Baal Tamar, and the Israelite ambush charged out of its place on the west[q] of Gibeah.[r] 34Then ten thousand of Israel’s finest men made a frontal attack on Gibeah. The fighting was so heavy that the Benjamites did not realize how near disaster was. 35The LORD defeated Benjamin before Israel, and on that day the Israelites struck down 25,100 Benjamites, all armed with swords. 36Then the Benjamites saw that they were beaten.

Now the men of Israel had given way before Benjamin, because they relied on the ambush they had set near Gibeah. 37The men who had been in ambush made a sudden dash into Gibeah, spread out and put the whole city to the sword. 38The men of Israel had arranged with the ambush that they should send up a great cloud of smoke from the city, 39and then the men of Israel would turn in the battle.

The Benjamites had begun to inflict casualties on the men of Israel (about thirty), and they said, “We are defeating them as in the first battle.” 40But when the column of smoke began to rise from the city, the Benjamites turned and saw the smoke of the whole city going up into the sky. 41Then the men of Israel turned on them, and the men of Benjamin were terrified, because they realized that disaster had come upon them. 42So they fled before the Israelites in the direction of the desert, but they could not escape the battle. And the men of Israel who came out of the towns cut them down there. 43They surrounded the

[o]18 Or *to the house of God*; also in verse 26 [p]26 Traditionally *peace offerings* [q]33 Some Septuagint manuscripts and Vulgate; the meaning of the Hebrew for this word is uncertain. [r]33 Hebrew *Geba,* a variant of *Gibeah*

Benjamites, chased them and easily[s] overran them in the vicinity of Gibeah on the east. 44Eighteen thousand Benjamites fell, all of them valiant fighters. 45As they turned and fled toward the desert to the rock of Rimmon, the Israelites cut down five thousand men along the roads. They kept pressing after the Benjamites as far as Gidom and struck down two thousand more.

46On that day twenty-five thousand Benjamite swordsmen fell, all of them valiant fighters. 47But six hundred men turned and fled into the desert to the rock of Rimmon, where they stayed four months. 48The men of Israel went back to Benjamin and put all the towns to the sword, including the animals and everything else they found. All the towns they came across they set on fire.

[s]43 The meaning of the Hebrew for this word is uncertain.

12 / *Judges 21*
The Aftermath of Moral Decay

THE MORAL DECAY of Israel continued to grow worse. In Judges 19 we are told the story of a man and his concubine who, while traveling, had stopped for the night in the town of Gibeah. Instead of offering hospitality, the residents of Gibeah tried to rape the man. To save himself, he gave the townsfolk his concubine instead. The poor woman was gang-raped and left dead on the doorstep. In an attempt to gain sympathy and to justify himself, the enraged lover cut the body of his concubine into twelve pieces and sent one to each tribe of Israel with a message demanding that justice be done. This incident resulted in a bloody and devastating civil war against not only the town of Gibeah but also the entire tribe of Benjamin (Jdg 20). In the aftermath of the civil war, the Israelites began to regret what they had done. All of the women from the tribe of Benjamin had been killed and only six hundred men remained alive.

Warming Up to God When have you made a promise foolishly? What should be done about foolish promises?

Read Judges 21.

21 The men of Israel had taken an oath at Mizpah: "Not one of us will give his daughter in marriage to a Benjamite."

2The people went to Bethel,[t] where they sat before God until evening, raising their voices and weeping bitterly. 3"O LORD, the God of Israel," they cried, "why has this happened to Israel? Why should one tribe be missing from Israel today?"

4Early the next day the people built an altar and presented burnt offerings and fellowship offerings.[u]

5Then the Israelites asked, "Who from all the tribes of Israel has failed to assemble before the LORD?" For they had taken a solemn oath that anyone who failed to assemble before the LORD at Mizpah should certainly be put to death.

6Now the Israelites grieved for their brothers, the Benjamites. "Today one tribe is cut off from Israel," they said. 7"How can we provide wives for those who are left, since we have taken an oath by the LORD not to give them any of our daughters in marriage?" 8Then they asked, "Which one of the tribes of Israel failed to assemble before the LORD at Mizpah?" They discovered that no one from Jabesh Gilead had come to the camp for the assembly. 9For when they counted the people, they found that none of the people of Jabesh Gilead were there.

10So the assembly sent twelve thousand fighting men with instructions to go to Jabesh Gilead and put to the sword those living there, including the women and children. 11"This is what you are to do," they said. "Kill every male and every woman who is not a virgin." 12They found among the people living in Jabesh Gilead four hundred young women who had never slept with a man, and they took them to the camp at Shiloh in Canaan.

13Then the whole assembly sent an offer of

[t]2 Or *to the house of God* [u]4 Traditionally *peace offerings*

peace to the Benjamites at the rock of Rimmon.
[14]So the Benjamites returned at that time and
were given the women of Jabesh Gilead who had
been spared. But there were not enough for all of
them.
[15]The people grieved for Benjamin, because the
LORD had made a gap in the tribes of Israel. [16]And
the elders of the assembly said, "With the women
of Benjamin destroyed, how shall we provide
wives for the men who are left? [17]The Benjamite
survivors must have heirs," they said, "so that a
tribe of Israel will not be wiped out. [18]We can't
give them our daughters as wives, since we Israel-
ites have taken this oath: 'Cursed be anyone who
gives a wife to a Benjamite.' [19]But look, there is
the annual festival of the LORD in Shiloh, to the
north of Bethel, and east of the road that goes
from Bethel to Shechem, and to the south of Le-
bonah."
[20]So they instructed the Benjamites, saying,
"Go and hide in the vineyards [21]and watch. When
the girls of Shiloh come out to join in the danc-
ing, then rush from the vineyards and each of you
seize a wife from the girls of Shiloh and go to the
land of Benjamin. [22]When their fathers or broth-
ers complain to us, we will say to them, 'Do us a
kindness by helping them, because we did not get
wives for them during the war, and you are inno-
cent, since you did not give your daughters to
them.' "
[23]So that is what the Benjamites did. While the
girls were dancing, each man caught one and car-
ried her off to be his wife. Then they returned to
their inheritance and rebuilt the towns and set-
tled in them.
[24]At that time the Israelites left that place and
went home to their tribes and clans, each to his
own inheritance.
[25]In those days Israel had no king; everyone
did as he saw fit.

Discovering the Word 1. The Israelites ask God, "Why has this happened to Israel? Why should one tribe be missing from Israel today?" (v. 3). How would you answer their question? 2. What is right and what is wrong about the Israelites' actions in this chapter? 3. What do you learn from this story about the importance of and the process for reconciliation? 4. What did the Israelites understand about the making and keeping of vows, and where had they gone wrong in their vow making (vv. 7, 12-23)? 5. The book of Judges ends with a phrase that is repeated often, especially in the last five chapters: "In those days Israel had no king; everyone did as he saw fit." Why is the author so concerned that we know this?

Applying the Word 1. With whom might God be calling you to reconcile? 2. How can you do this? 3. What foolish promise do you need to reconsider today?

Responding in Prayer Ask God to give you wisdom in your relationships as you reconcile brokenness and make and keep promises.

Ruth

Loyalty is a rare virtue. "I'll go with you unless someone better comes along" is a popular way to act with friends and sometimes even spouses. Who are the friends who have stuck by you during the hard times? Hopefully, a few people come to mind. These are most likely people of unusual character and courage.

Ruth was written during the period of the judges (c. 1380–1050 B.C.), which were dark and turbulent days for Israel. It provides a glimpse into the lives of ordinary people who show a care and loyalty for each other that reflect God's character.

Ruth was a Moabite. Her people descended from Lot's oldest daughter, who, though rescued from the destruction of Sodom and Gomorrah, chose to live apart from God's people (Ge 19:37). Ruth's choices are in sharp contrast to this.

After Ruth marries into an Israelite family, she becomes very devoted to them, especially to her mother-in-law, Naomi. Because Ruth chooses to identify with the people of God, she is given a place in the genealogy of Jesus Christ (Mt 1:1, 5) as the great-grandmother of David. From Ruth we learn that simple obedience, faith and loyalty can have far-reaching results.

Outline

1 / *Ruth 1—2*
The Cost of Loyalty

A UNIVERSITY STUDENT wrote to J. R. R. Tolkien after reading *Lord of the Rings,* "You have made loyalty and courage more meaningful to me." Loyalty doesn't get much "press" today. It's present in the lives of many, but isn't heralded like it used to be when people signed their letters "Your loyal friend." In Ruth we find a model of loyalty that would bring much to our friendships today.

Warming Up to God What makes it hard to be loyal to another person?

Read Ruth 1—2.

1 In the days when the judges ruled,[a] there was a famine in the land, and a man from Bethlehem in Judah, together with his wife and two sons, went to live for a while in the country of Moab. 2The man's name was Elimelech, his wife's name Naomi, and the names of his two sons were Mahlon and Kilion. They were Ephrathites from Bethlehem, Judah. And they went to Moab and lived there.

3Now Elimelech, Naomi's husband, died, and she was left with her two sons. 4They married Moabite women, one named Orpah and the other Ruth. After they had lived there about ten years, 5both Mahlon and Kilion also died, and Naomi was left without her two sons and her husband.

6When she heard in Moab that the LORD had come to the aid of his people by providing food for them, Naomi and her daughters-in-law prepared to return home from there. 7With her two daughters-in-law she left the place where she had been living and set out on the road that would take them back to the land of Judah.

8Then Naomi said to her two daughters-in-law, "Go back, each of you, to your mother's home. May the LORD show kindness to you, as you have shown to your dead and to me. 9May the LORD grant that each of you will find rest in the home of another husband."

Then she kissed them and they wept aloud 10and said to her, "We will go back with you to your people."

11But Naomi said, "Return home, my daughters. Why would you come with me? Am I going to have any more sons, who could become your husbands? 12Return home, my daughters; I am too old to have another husband. Even if I thought there was still hope for me—even if I had a husband tonight and then gave birth to sons—13would you wait until they grew up? Would you remain unmarried for them? No, my daughters. It is more bitter for me than for you, because the LORD's hand has gone out against me!"

14At this they wept again. Then Orpah kissed her mother-in-law good-by, but Ruth clung to her.

15"Look," said Naomi, "your sister-in-law is going back to her people and her gods. Go back with her."

16But Ruth replied, "Don't urge me to leave you or to turn back from you. Where you go I will go, and where you stay I will stay. Your people will be my people and your God my God. 17Where you die I will die, and there I will be buried. May the LORD deal with me, be it ever so severely, if anything but death separates you and me." 18When Naomi realized that Ruth was determined to go with her, she stopped urging her.

19So the two women went on until they came to Bethlehem. When they arrived in Bethlehem, the whole town was stirred because of them, and the women exclaimed, "Can this be Naomi?"

20"Don't call me Naomi,[b]" she told them. "Call me Mara,[c] because the Almighty[d] has made my life very bitter. 21I went away full, but the LORD has brought me back empty. Why call me Naomi? The LORD has afflicted[e] me; the Almighty has brought misfortune upon me."

22So Naomi returned from Moab accompanied by Ruth the Moabitess, her daughter-in-law, arriving in Bethlehem as the barley harvest was beginning.

[a] 1 Traditionally *judged*
[b] 20 *Naomi* means *pleasant*; also in verse 21.
[c] 20 *Mara* means *bitter.*
[d] 20 Hebrew *Shaddai*; also in verse 21
[e] 21 Or *has testified against*

2 Now Naomi had a relative on her hus-
band's side, from the clan of Elimelech, a
man of standing, whose name was Boaz.
2And Ruth the Moabitess said to Naomi, "Let
me go to the fields and pick up the leftover grain
behind anyone in whose eyes I find favor."
Naomi said to her, "Go ahead, my daughter."
3So she went out and began to glean in the fields
behind the harvesters. As it turned out, she found
herself working in a field belonging to Boaz, who
was from the clan of Elimelech.
4Just then Boaz arrived from Bethlehem and
greeted the harvesters, "The LORD be with you!"
"The LORD bless you!" they called back.
5Boaz asked the foreman of his harvesters,
"Whose young woman is that?"
6The foreman replied, "She is the Moabitess
who came back from Moab with Naomi. 7She
said, 'Please let me glean and gather among the
sheaves behind the harvesters.' She went into the
field and has worked steadily from morning till
now, except for a short rest in the shelter."
8So Boaz said to Ruth, "My daughter, listen to
me. Don't go and glean in another field and don't
go away from here. Stay here with my servant
girls. 9Watch the field where the men are harvest-
ing, and follow along after the girls. I have told
the men not to touch you. And whenever you are
thirsty, go and get a drink from the water jars the
men have filled."
10At this, she bowed down with her face to the
ground. She exclaimed, "Why have I found such
favor in your eyes that you notice me—a for-
eigner?"
11Boaz replied, "I've been told all about what
you have done for your mother-in-law since the
death of your husband—how you left your father
and mother and your homeland and came to live
with a people you did not know before. 12May the
LORD repay you for what you have done. May you
be richly rewarded by the LORD, the God of Israel,
under whose wings you have come to take ref-
uge."
13"May I continue to find favor in your eyes,
my lord," she said. "You have given me comfort
and have spoken kindly to your servant—though
I do not have the standing of one of your servant
girls."
14At mealtime Boaz said to her, "Come over
here. Have some bread and dip it in the wine
vinegar."
When she sat down with the harvesters, he of-
fered her some roasted grain. She ate all she
wanted and had some left over. 15As she got up to
glean, Boaz gave orders to his men, "Even if she
gathers among the sheaves, don't embarrass her.
16Rather, pull out some stalks for her from the
bundles and leave them for her to pick up, and
don't rebuke her."
17So Ruth gleaned in the field until evening.
Then she threshed the barley she had gathered,
and it amounted to about an ephah.[f] 18She car-
ried it back to town, and her mother-in-law saw
how much she had gathered. Ruth also brought
out and gave her what she had left over after she
had eaten enough.
19Her mother-in-law asked her, "Where did
you glean today? Where did you work? Blessed
be the man who took notice of you!"
Then Ruth told her mother-in-law about the
one at whose place she had been working. "The
name of the man I worked with today is Boaz,"
she said.
20"The LORD bless him!" Naomi said to her
daughter-in-law. "He has not stopped showing
his kindness to the living and the dead." She
added, "That man is our close relative; he is one
of our kinsman-redeemers."
21Then Ruth the Moabitess said, "He even said
to me, 'Stay with my workers until they finish
harvesting all my grain.' "
22Naomi said to Ruth her daughter-in-law, "It
will be good for you, my daughter, to go with his
girls, because in someone else's field you might be
harmed."
23So Ruth stayed close to the servant girls of
Boaz to glean until the barley and wheat harvests
were finished. And she lived with her mother-in-
law.

f17 That is, probably about 3/5 bushel (about 22 liters)

Discovering the Word 1. How does Ruth's relationship with Naomi differ from Orpah's (1:10, 14, 16–18)? 2. What are the practical implications of the choice Ruth makes in contrast to the choice Orpah makes? 3. Naomi and Ruth arrive in Bethlehem at the time of the barley harvest (1:22). What does Ruth's willingness to be a gleaner tell us about her (2:2)? 4. How does the regard that Boaz has for Ruth and her position in Israel (2:11–12) differ from Ruth's concept of herself (2:10, 13)? 5. Put yourself in Ruth's place. How would it feel to be a foreigner, needing to work hard to support your mother-in-law?

Applying the Word 1. What motivates your own loyalty? 2. What loyalties are important to you as a Christian, regardless of cost?

Responding in Prayer Ask God to build you into a person of loyalty.

2 / *Ruth 3—4*
Sadness Swallowed Up by Joy

LIFE IS LIKE a grindstone, someone once said, and whether it grinds you down or polishes you depends on the stuff you are made of. It also depends on your view of God. Some people seem to get more hard knocks in life than others, and if you say, "That's not fair," you are probably right. Life isn't always fair. But the question is, even in the hardest circumstances is God in control? If he is, that means he can change the bitterness of our hard experiences.

Warming Up to God Naomi is a case study in hardship. Despite Naomi's trials, Ruth's insistence on returning with her is strong indication of God's care. Gradually it dawns on Naomi that God has provided for her and Ruth in ways she had never expected. In these two chapters we see Naomi's bitterness turned to joy.

Read Ruth 3—4.

3 One day Naomi her mother-in-law said to her, "My daughter, should I not try to find a home[g] for you, where you will be well provided for? [2]Is not Boaz, with whose servant girls you have been, a kinsman of ours? Tonight he will be winnowing barley on the threshing floor. [3]Wash and perfume yourself, and put on your best clothes. Then go down to the threshing floor, but don't let him know you are there until he has finished eating and drinking. [4]When he lies down, note the place where he is lying. Then go and uncover his feet and lie down. He will tell you what to do."

[5]"I will do whatever you say," Ruth answered. [6]So she went down to the threshing floor and did everything her mother-in-law told her to do.

[7]When Boaz had finished eating and drinking and was in good spirits, he went over to lie down at the far end of the grain pile. Ruth approached quietly, uncovered his feet and lay down. [8]In the middle of the night something startled the man, and he turned and discovered a woman lying at his feet.

[9]"Who are you?" he asked.

"I am your servant Ruth," she said. "Spread the corner of your garment over me, since you are a kinsman-redeemer."

[10]"The LORD bless you, my daughter," he replied. "This kindness is greater than that which you showed earlier: You have not run after the younger men, whether rich or poor. [11]And now, my daughter, don't be afraid. I will do for you all you ask. All my fellow townsmen know that you are a woman of noble character. [12]Although it is true that I am near of kin, there is a kinsman-redeemer nearer than I. [13]Stay here for the night, and in the morning if he wants to redeem, good; let him redeem. But if he is not willing, as surely as the LORD lives I will do it. Lie here until morning."

[14]So she lay at his feet until morning, but got up before anyone could be recognized; and he said, "Don't let it be known that a woman came to the threshing floor."

[15]He also said, "Bring me the shawl you are wearing and hold it out." When she did so, he poured into it six measures of barley and put it on her. Then he[h] went back to town.

[16]When Ruth came to her mother-in-law, Naomi asked, "How did it go, my daughter?"

Then she told her everything Boaz had done for her [17]and added, "He gave me these six measures of barley, saying, 'Don't go back to your mother-in-law empty-handed.' "

[18]Then Naomi said, "Wait, my daughter, until you find out what happens. For the man will not rest until the matter is settled today."

g1 Hebrew *find rest* (see Ruth 1:9) h15 Most Hebrew manuscripts; many Hebrew manuscripts, Vulgate and Syriac *she*

4 Meanwhile Boaz went up to the town gate
and sat there. When the kinsman-re-
deemer he had mentioned came along,
Boaz said, “Come over here, my friend, and sit
down.” So he went over and sat down.
2Boaz took ten of the elders of the town and
said, “Sit here,” and they did so. 3Then he said to
the kinsman-redeemer, “Naomi, who has come
back from Moab, is selling the piece of land that
belonged to our brother Elimelech. 4I thought I
should bring the matter to your attention and
suggest that you buy it in the presence of these
seated here and in the presence of the elders of
my people. If you will redeem it, do so. But if
you[i] will not, tell me, so I will know. For no one
has the right to do it except you, and I am next in
line.”
“I will redeem it,” he said.
5Then Boaz said, “On the day you buy the land
from Naomi and from Ruth the Moabitess, you
acquire[j] the dead man’s widow, in order to
maintain the name of the dead with his property.”
6At this, the kinsman-redeemer said, “Then I
cannot redeem it because I might endanger my
own estate. You redeem it yourself. I cannot
do it.”
7(Now in earlier times in Israel, for the re-
demption and transfer of property to become fi-
nal, one party took off his sandal and gave it to
the other. This was the method of legalizing
transactions in Israel.)
8So the kinsman-redeemer said to Boaz, “Buy it
yourself.” And he removed his sandal.
9Then Boaz announced to the elders and all the
people, “Today you are witnesses that I have
bought from Naomi all the property of Elimelech,
Kilion and Mahlon. 10I have also acquired Ruth
the Moabitess, Mahlon’s widow, as my wife, in
order to maintain the name of the dead with his
property, so that his name will not disappear
from among his family or from the town records.
Today you are witnesses!”
11Then the elders and all those at the gate said,
“We are witnesses. May the LORD make the
woman who is coming into your home like Ra-
chel and Leah, who together built up the house of
Israel. May you have standing in Ephrathah and
be famous in Bethlehem. 12Through the offspring
the LORD gives you by this young woman, may
your family be like that of Perez, whom Tamar
bore to Judah.”
13So Boaz took Ruth and she became his wife.
Then he went to her, and the LORD enabled her
to conceive, and she gave birth to a son. 14The
women said to Naomi: “Praise be to the LORD,
who this day has not left you without a kinsman-
redeemer. May he become famous throughout Is-
rael! 15He will renew your life and sustain you
in your old age. For your daughter-in-law, who
loves you and who is better to you than seven
sons, has given him birth.”
16Then Naomi took the child, laid him in her
lap and cared for him. 17The women living there
said, “Naomi has a son.” And they named him
Obed. He was the father of Jesse, the father of
David.
18This, then, is the family line of Perez:

Perez was the father of Hezron,
19Hezron the father of Ram,
Ram the father of Amminadab,
20Amminadab the father of Nahshon,
Nahshon the father of Salmon,[k]
21Salmon the father of Boaz,
Boaz the father of Obed,
22Obed the father of Jesse,
and Jesse the father of David.

[i]4 Many Hebrew manuscripts, Septuagint, Vulgate and Syriac; most Hebrew manuscripts *he* [j]5 Hebrew; Vulgate and Syriac *Naomi, you acquire Ruth the Moabitess,* [k]20 A few Hebrew manuscripts, some Septuagint manuscripts and Vulgate (see also verse 21 and Septuagint of 1 Chron. 2:11); most Hebrew manuscripts *Salma*

Discovering the Word 1. How does Naomi plan for Ruth’s future (3:1–4)? 2. “To spread the corners of your garment over me” (3:9) was a request for marriage. Why might this be a risky plan? 3. How would you evaluate Boaz’s character from his actions in these two chapters? 4. What does the birth of Obed mean to Naomi (4:13–17)? 5. What is the turning point in Naomi’s life from the bitterness she expressed as she returned to Bethlehem (1:20) to the joy she feels at the end of the story (4:16)?

Applying the Word 1. Naomi’s grandson becomes an ancestor of King David and is mentioned in the genealogy of Jesus in Matthew 1:5. What do you learn about God from the amazing ways in which he blesses Naomi after all her tragedies? 2. In what ways has God shown his faithfulness to you and changed your sorrow to joy?

Responding in Prayer Praise God for the Redeemer he has given us in Jesus Christ. Thank him for the joy that he brings into your life.

1 Samuel

When I was a child, my hero was Superman. Like him, I wanted to be faster than a speeding bullet, able to leap tall buildings in a single bound and bend steel in my bare hands. Using a bath towel for my cape, I flew around the house, performing imaginary feats of strength and courage.

As I grew up, however, I discovered that Superman was not the best kind of hero. I found it impossible to be like him, no matter how hard I tried. Bullets simply wouldn't bounce off me and neither would harsh words, fears, disappointments, illnesses or a hundred other weaknesses that are common to frail, fallen humanity.

Bullets didn't bounce off David either. As I read about his life, I am astonished at how open and vulnerable he was. He records his weaknesses and struggles for all the world to read: "I am worn out from groaning; all night long I flood my bed with weeping and drench my couch with tears. My eyes grow weak with sorrow; they fail because of all my foes." "I know my transgressions, and my sin is always before me. Against you, you only, have I sinned and done what is evil in your sight" (Ps 6:6–7; 51:3–4).

Yet in spite of all his weaknesses, fears, doubts and sins, David was also a man of faith. His life illustrates a tenacious trust in God and an intense desire to know him: "The LORD is my light and my salvation—whom shall I fear? The LORD is the stronghold of my life—of whom shall I be afraid?" "One thing I ask of the LORD, this is what I seek: that I may dwell in the house of the LORD . . . and to seek him in his temple" (Ps 27:1, 4). Because of these qualities, God was able to use David mightily, molding and shaping him into a man after his own heart.

I believe we need this kind of three-dimensional role model today—someone who allows us to be fully human, yet who inspires us to look beyond our weaknesses and frailties to the Living God. You will meet David in these quiet times in 1 Samuel.

David's life extended from around 1040 to 970 B.C. Second Samuel 5 records that "David was thirty years old when he became king, and he reigned forty years. In Hebron he reigned over Judah seven years and six months, and in Jerusalem he reigned over all Israel and Judah thirty-three years" (vv. 4–5). The biblical writers view David as the greatest of Israel's kings and the one through whom the ultimate king, the Messiah, eventually came (see Mt 1:1; Lk 3:31).

It is my prayer that as you study 1 Samuel, you too will develop a passionate heart for God.

Outline

1 / *1 Samuel 1:1—2:11*
From Misery to Praise

WAITING IS ONE of the hardest things we do. So much of life involves waiting, and in an age of instant products, waiting irritates us. But waiting is hardest when we see the clock running on, the years going by and still our hopes and dreams are unfulfilled. Hannah knew about waiting. In a society that measured a woman's worth by her children, Hannah was barren. Year after year she waited in misery for the answer to her prayers. She had two choices: to be bitter or to continue seeking God's help. This quiet time looks at Hannah's journey from misery to praise.

Warming Up to God What cherished hope do you increasingly fear may never be realized in your life? Talk openly with God about your physical, emotional and spiritual response to this experience of waiting.

Read 1 Samuel 1:1—2:11.

---

1 There was a certain man from Ramathaim, a Zuphite[a] from the hill country of Ephraim, whose name was Elkanah son of Jeroham, the son of Elihu, the son of Tohu, the son of Zuph, an Ephraimite. [2]He had two wives; one was called Hannah and the other Peninnah. Peninnah had children, but Hannah had none.

[3]Year after year this man went up from his town to worship and sacrifice to the LORD Almighty at Shiloh, where Hophni and Phinehas, the two sons of Eli, were priests of the LORD. [4]Whenever the day came for Elkanah to sacrifice, he would give portions of the meat to his wife Peninnah and to all her sons and daughters. [5]But to Hannah he gave a double portion because he loved her, and the LORD had closed her womb. [6]And because the LORD had closed her womb, her rival kept provoking her in order to irritate her. [7]This went on year after year. Whenever Hannah went up to the house of the LORD, her rival provoked her till she wept and would not eat. [8]Elkanah her husband would say to her, "Hannah, why are you weeping? Why don't you eat? Why are you downhearted? Don't I mean more to you than ten sons?"

[9]Once when they had finished eating and drinking in Shiloh, Hannah stood up. Now Eli the priest was sitting on a chair by the doorpost of the LORD's temple.[b] [10]In bitterness of soul Hannah wept much and prayed to the LORD. [11]And she made a vow, saying, "O LORD Almighty, if you will only look upon your servant's misery and remember me, and not forget your servant but give her a son, then I will give him to the LORD for all the days of his life, and no razor will ever be used on his head."

[12]As she kept on praying to the LORD, Eli observed her mouth. [13]Hannah was praying in her heart, and her lips were moving but her voice was not heard. Eli thought she was drunk [14]and said to her, "How long will you keep on getting drunk? Get rid of your wine."

[15]"Not so, my lord," Hannah replied, "I am a woman who is deeply troubled. I have not been drinking wine or beer; I was pouring out my soul to the LORD. [16]Do not take your servant for a wicked woman; I have been praying here out of my great anguish and grief."

[17]Eli answered, "Go in peace, and may the God of Israel grant you what you have asked of him."

[18]She said, "May your servant find favor in your eyes." Then she went her way and ate something, and her face was no longer downcast.

[19]Early the next morning they arose and worshiped before the LORD and then went back to their home at Ramah. Elkanah lay with Hannah his wife, and the LORD remembered her. [20]So in the course of time Hannah conceived and gave birth to a son. She named him Samuel,[c] saying, "Because I asked the LORD for him."

[21]When the man Elkanah went up with all his family to offer the annual sacrifice to the LORD and to fulfill his vow, [22]Hannah did not go. She said to her husband, "After the boy is weaned, I will take him and present him before the LORD, and he will live there always."

[23]"Do what seems best to you," Elkanah her husband told her. "Stay here until you have

[a]1 Or *from Ramathaim Zuphim* [b]9 That is, tabernacle
[c]20 *Samuel* sounds like the Hebrew for *heard of God.*

weaned him; only may the LORD make good his[d]
word." So the woman stayed at home and nursed
her son until she had weaned him.
24After he was weaned, she took the boy with
her, young as he was, along with a three-year-old
bull,[e] an ephah[f] of flour and a skin of wine,
and brought him to the house of the LORD at Shi-
loh. 25When they had slaughtered the bull, they
brought the boy to Eli, 26and she said to him, "As
surely as you live, my lord, I am the woman who
stood here beside you praying to the LORD. 27I
prayed for this child, and the LORD has granted me
what I asked of him. 28So now I give him to the
LORD. For his whole life he will be given over to
the LORD." And he worshiped the LORD there.

2

Then Hannah prayed and said:

"My heart rejoices in the LORD;
in the LORD my horn[g] is lifted high.
My mouth boasts over my enemies,
for I delight in your deliverance.

2"There is no one holy[h] like the LORD;
there is no one besides you;
there is no Rock like our God.

3"Do not keep talking so proudly
or let your mouth speak such arrogance,
for the LORD is a God who knows,
and by him deeds are weighed.

4"The bows of the warriors are broken,
but those who stumbled are armed with strength.
5Those who were full hire themselves out for food,
but those who were hungry hunger no more.
She who was barren has borne seven children,
but she who has had many sons pines away.

6"The LORD brings death and makes alive;
he brings down to the grave[i] and raises up.
7The LORD sends poverty and wealth;
he humbles and he exalts.
8He raises the poor from the dust
and lifts the needy from the ash heap;
he seats them with princes
and has them inherit a throne of honor.

"For the foundations of the earth are the LORD's;
upon them he has set the world.
9He will guard the feet of his saints,
but the wicked will be silenced in darkness.

"It is not by strength that one prevails;
10 those who oppose the LORD will be shattered.
He will thunder against them from heaven;
the LORD will judge the ends of the earth.

"He will give strength to his king
and exalt the horn of his anointed."

11Then Elkanah went home to Ramah, but the
boy ministered before the LORD under Eli the
priest.

[d]23 Masoretic Text; Dead Sea Scrolls, Septuagint and Syriac *your*
[e]24 Dead Sea Scrolls, Septuagint and Syriac; Masoretic Text *with three bulls*
[f]24 That is, probably about 3/5 bushel (about 22 liters)
[g]1 *Horn* here symbolizes strength; also in verse 10.
[h]2 Or *no Holy One*
[i]6 Hebrew *Sheol*

Discovering the Word 1. Why is Hannah's pain so intense (1:2-7)? 2. Hannah turns to God in desperation. What does her prayer reveal about her (1:9-11)? 3. Look at chapter 2. What shift do you see in Hannah's focus between chapters 1 and 2? 4. What does Hannah believe about God? (Find several strong beliefs.) 5. If you were describing Hannah to a friend, what would you say about her? about her gifts? about her spiritual life?

Applying the Word 1. When you are bitter about your disappointments, to whom (or what) do you turn? 2. What specific things can you learn from Hannah about the solution to the pain of unfulfilled hopes?

Responding in Prayer Try speaking or writing out your own song of praise, telling God what you believe about him.

1 Samuel 2:12–36

12Eli's sons were wicked men; they had no regard for the LORD. 13Now it was the practice of the priests with the people that whenever anyone offered a sacrifice and while the meat was being boiled, the servant of the priest would come with a three-pronged fork in his hand. 14He would plunge it into the pan or kettle or caldron or pot, and the priest would take for himself whatever the fork brought up. This is how they treated all the Israelites who came to Shiloh. 15But even before the fat was burned, the servant of the priest would come and say to the man who was sacrificing, "Give the priest some meat to roast; he won't accept boiled meat from you, but only raw."

16If the man said to him, "Let the fat be burned up first, and then take whatever you want," the servant would then answer, "No, hand it over now; if you don't, I'll take it by force."

17This sin of the young men was very great in the LORD's sight, for they[j] were treating the LORD's offering with contempt.

18But Samuel was ministering before the LORD—a boy wearing a linen ephod. 19Each year his mother made him a little robe and took it to him when she went up with her husband to offer the annual sacrifice. 20Eli would bless Elkanah and his wife, saying, "May the LORD give you children by this woman to take the place of the one she prayed for and gave to the LORD." Then they would go home. 21And the LORD was gracious to Hannah; she conceived and gave birth to three sons and two daughters. Meanwhile, the boy Samuel grew up in the presence of the LORD.

22Now Eli, who was very old, heard about everything his sons were doing to all Israel and how they slept with the women who served at the entrance to the Tent of Meeting. 23So he said to them, "Why do you do such things? I hear from all the people about these wicked deeds of yours. 24No, my sons; it is not a good report that I hear spreading among the LORD's people. 25If a man sins against another man, God[k] may mediate for him; but if a man sins against the LORD, who will intercede for him?" His sons, however, did not listen to their father's rebuke, for it was the LORD's will to put them to death.

26And the boy Samuel continued to grow in stature and in favor with the LORD and with men.

27Now a man of God came to Eli and said to him, "This is what the LORD says: 'Did I not clearly reveal myself to your father's house when they were in Egypt under Pharaoh? 28I chose your father out of all the tribes of Israel to be my priest, to go up to my altar, to burn incense, and to wear an ephod in my presence. I also gave your father's house all the offerings made with fire by the Israelites. 29Why do you[l] scorn my sacrifice and offering that I prescribed for my dwelling? Why do you honor your sons more than me by fattening yourselves on the choice parts of every offering made by my people Israel?'

30"Therefore the LORD, the God of Israel, declares: 'I promised that your house and your father's house would minister before me forever.' But now the LORD declares: 'Far be it from me! Those who honor me I will honor, but those who despise me will be disdained. 31The time is coming when I will cut short your strength and the strength of your father's house, so that there will not be an old man in your family line 32and you will see distress in my dwelling. Although good will be done to Israel, in your family line there will never be an old man. 33Every one of you that I do not cut off from my altar will be spared only to blind your eyes with tears and to grieve your heart, and all your descendants will die in the prime of life.

34" 'And what happens to your two sons, Hophni and Phinehas, will be a sign to you—they will both die on the same day. 35I will raise up for myself a faithful priest, who will do according to what is in my heart and mind. I will firmly establish his house, and he will minister before my anointed one always. 36Then everyone left in your family line will come and bow down before him for a piece of silver and a crust of bread and plead, "Appoint me to some priestly office so I can have food to eat." ' "

[j]17 Or *men* [k]25 Or *the judges* [l]29 The Hebrew is plural.

2 / *1 Samuel 3*
Hearing God's Voice

AMID THE HUSTLE and bustle of daily life, we often find it hard to hear God's voice. Many "voices" shout for our attention—deadlines to meet, bills to pay, meetings to attend, phone calls to make, children to care for. We try to read our Bible but struggle to be still and receive a word from God.

In the days of Samuel few people were listening to God's voice. Politically and spiritually Israel was in terrible shape as they "had no king" and "everyone did as he saw fit" (Jdg 21:25). In this study we observe Samuel as a young man, hearing the word of the Lord for the first time and beginning his prophetic ministry.

Warming Up to God How have you heard God speak to you?

Read 1 Samuel 3.

3 The boy Samuel ministered before the LORD under Eli. In those days the word of the LORD was rare; there were not many visions.

2One night Eli, whose eyes were becoming so weak that he could barely see, was lying down in his usual place. 3The lamp of God had not yet gone out, and Samuel was lying down in the temple[m] of the LORD, where the ark of God was. 4Then the LORD called Samuel.

Samuel answered, "Here I am." 5And he ran to Eli and said, "Here I am; you called me."

But Eli said, "I did not call; go back and lie down." So he went and lay down.

6Again the LORD called, "Samuel!" And Samuel got up and went to Eli and said, "Here I am; you called me."

"My son," Eli said, "I did not call; go back and lie down."

7Now Samuel did not yet know the LORD: The word of the LORD had not yet been revealed to him.

8The LORD called Samuel a third time, and Samuel got up and went to Eli and said, "Here I am; you called me."

Then Eli realized that the LORD was calling the boy. 9So Eli told Samuel, "Go and lie down, and if he calls you, say, 'Speak, LORD, for your servant is listening.'" So Samuel went and lay down in his place.

10The LORD came and stood there, calling as at the other times, "Samuel! Samuel!"

Then Samuel said, "Speak, for your servant is listening."

11And the LORD said to Samuel: "See, I am about to do something in Israel that will make the ears of everyone who hears of it tingle. 12At that time I will carry out against Eli everything I spoke against his family—from beginning to end. 13For I told him that I would judge his family forever because of the sin he knew about; his sons made themselves contemptible,[n] and he failed to restrain them. 14Therefore, I swore to the house of Eli, 'The guilt of Eli's house will never be atoned for by sacrifice or offering.'"

15Samuel lay down until morning and then opened the doors of the house of the LORD. He was afraid to tell Eli the vision, 16but Eli called him and said, "Samuel, my son."

Samuel answered, "Here I am."

17"What was it he said to you?" Eli asked. "Do not hide it from me. May God deal with you, be it ever so severely, if you hide from me anything he told you." 18So Samuel told him everything, hiding nothing from him. Then Eli said, "He is the LORD; let him do what is good in his eyes."

19The LORD was with Samuel as he grew up, and he let none of his words fall to the ground. 20And all Israel from Dan to Beersheba recognized that Samuel was attested as a prophet of the LORD. 21The LORD continued to appear at Shiloh, and there he revealed himself to Samuel through his word.

[m]3 That is, tabernacle [n]13 Masoretic Text; an ancient Hebrew scribal tradition and Septuagint *sons blasphemed God*

Discovering the Word 1. Why do you think Samuel has difficulty discerning God's voice from Eli's (vv. 4–8)? 2. What do you think Samuel thought and felt as he listened to Eli and then returned to his bed (vv. 9–10)? 3. Why is the attitude "Speak, for your servant is listening" (v. 10) so important in order to hear from God? 4. Why would God's message in verses 11–14 have been particularly hard for Samuel to hear? 5. How does Samuel's obedience affect his relationship to God and his future ministry (vv. 19–21)?

Applying the Word 1. How does Samuel's openness to hear from God compare with yours? 2. When are you most tempted to hide God's word from others? Explain. 3. What is the greatest obstacle that prevents you from hearing God's voice?

Responding in Prayer Ask God to make you more open and attentive to his voice.

1 Samuel 4—7

4 And Samuel's word came to all Israel.
Now the Israelites went out to fight
against the Philistines. The Israelites
camped at Ebenezer, and the Philistines at Aphek.
2The Philistines deployed their forces to meet Is-
rael, and as the battle spread, Israel was defeated
by the Philistines, who killed about four thou-
sand of them on the battlefield. 3When the sol-
diers returned to camp, the elders of Israel asked,
"Why did the LORD bring defeat upon us today
before the Philistines? Let us bring the ark of the
LORD's covenant from Shiloh, so that it[o] may go
with us and save us from the hand of our ene-
mies."
4So the people sent men to Shiloh, and they
brought back the ark of the covenant of the LORD
Almighty, who is enthroned between the cheru-
bim. And Eli's two sons, Hophni and Phinehas,
were there with the ark of the covenant of God.
5When the ark of the LORD's covenant came
into the camp, all Israel raised such a great shout
that the ground shook. 6Hearing the uproar, the
Philistines asked, "What's all this shouting in the
Hebrew camp?"
When they learned that the ark of the LORD had
come into the camp, 7the Philistines were afraid.
"A god has come into the camp," they said.
"We're in trouble! Nothing like this has happened
before. 8Woe to us! Who will deliver us from the
hand of these mighty gods? They are the gods
who struck the Egyptians with all kinds of
plagues in the desert. 9Be strong, Philistines! Be
men, or you will be subject to the Hebrews, as
they have been to you. Be men, and fight!"
10So the Philistines fought, and the Israelites
were defeated and every man fled to his tent. The
slaughter was very great; Israel lost thirty thou-
sand foot soldiers. 11The ark of God was cap-
tured, and Eli's two sons, Hophni and Phinehas,
died.
12That same day a Benjamite ran from the bat-
tle line and went to Shiloh, his clothes torn and
dust on his head. 13When he arrived, there was
Eli sitting on his chair by the side of the road,
watching, because his heart feared for the ark of
God. When the man entered the town and told
what had happened, the whole town sent up a
cry.
14Eli heard the outcry and asked, "What is the
meaning of this uproar?"
The man hurried over to Eli, 15who was ninety-
eight years old and whose eyes were set so that he
could not see. 16He told Eli, "I have just come
from the battle line; I fled from it this very day."
Eli asked, "What happened, my son?"
17The man who brought the news replied, "Is-
rael fled before the Philistines, and the army has
suffered heavy losses. Also your two sons,
Hophni and Phinehas, are dead, and the ark of
God has been captured."
18When he mentioned the ark of God, Eli fell
backward off his chair by the side of the gate. His
neck was broken and he died, for he was an old
man and heavy. He had led[p] Israel forty years.
19His daughter-in-law, the wife of Phinehas,
was pregnant and near the time of delivery. When
she heard the news that the ark of God had been
captured and that her father-in-law and her hus-
band were dead, she went into labor and gave
birth, but was overcome by her labor pains. 20As
she was dying, the women attending her said,

[o]3 Or *he* [p]18 Traditionally *judged*

"Don't despair; you have given birth to a son."
But she did not respond or pay any attention.
21She named the boy Ichabod,[q] saying, "The
glory has departed from Israel"—because of the
capture of the ark of God and the deaths of her
father-in-law and her husband. 22She said, "The
glory has departed from Israel, for the ark of God
has been captured."

5 After the Philistines had captured the ark
of God, they took it from Ebenezer to
Ashdod. 2Then they carried the ark into
Dagon's temple and set it beside Dagon. 3When
the people of Ashdod rose early the next day,
there was Dagon, fallen on his face on the ground
before the ark of the LORD! They took Dagon and
put him back in his place. 4But the following
morning when they rose, there was Dagon, fallen
on his face on the ground before the ark of the
LORD! His head and hands had been broken off
and were lying on the threshold; only his body
remained. 5That is why to this day neither the
priests of Dagon nor any others who enter Da-
gon's temple at Ashdod step on the threshold.
6The LORD's hand was heavy upon the people of
Ashdod and its vicinity; he brought devastation
upon them and afflicted them with tumors.[r]
7When the men of Ashdod saw what was happen-
ing, they said, "The ark of the god of Israel must
not stay here with us, because his hand is heavy
upon us and upon Dagon our god." 8So they
called together all the rulers of the Philistines and
asked them, "What shall we do with the ark of
the god of Israel?"

They answered, "Have the ark of the god of
Israel moved to Gath." So they moved the ark of
the God of Israel.
9But after they had moved it, the LORD's hand
was against that city, throwing it into a great
panic. He afflicted the people of the city, both
young and old, with an outbreak of tumors.[s]
10So they sent the ark of God to Ekron.

As the ark of God was entering Ekron, the peo-
ple of Ekron cried out, "They have brought the
ark of the god of Israel around to us to kill us and
our people." 11So they called together all the rul-
ers of the Philistines and said, "Send the ark of
the god of Israel away; let it go back to its own
place, or it[t] will kill us and our people." For
death had filled the city with panic; God's hand
was very heavy upon it. 12Those who did not die
were afflicted with tumors, and the outcry of the
city went up to heaven.

6 When the ark of the LORD had been in
Philistine territory seven months, 2the
Philistines called for the priests and the
diviners and said, "What shall we do with the ark
of the LORD? Tell us how we should send it back
to its place."
3They answered, "If you return the ark of the
god of Israel, do not send it away empty, but by
all means send a guilt offering to him. Then you
will be healed, and you will know why his hand
has not been lifted from you."
4The Philistines asked, "What guilt offering
should we send to him?"

They replied, "Five gold tumors and five gold
rats, according to the number of the Philistine
rulers, because the same plague has struck both
you and your rulers. 5Make models of the tumors
and of the rats that are destroying the country,
and pay honor to Israel's god. Perhaps he will lift
his hand from you and your gods and your land.
6Why do you harden your hearts as the Egyptians
and Pharaoh did? When he[u] treated them
harshly, did they not send the Israelites out so
they could go on their way?
7"Now then, get a new cart ready, with two
cows that have calved and have never been
yoked. Hitch the cows to the cart, but take their
calves away and pen them up. 8Take the ark of
the LORD and put it on the cart, and in a chest
beside it put the gold objects you are sending
back to him as a guilt offering. Send it on its way,
9but keep watching it. If it goes up to its own
territory, toward Beth Shemesh, then the LORD has
brought this great disaster on us. But if it does
not, then we will know that it was not his hand
that struck us and that it happened to us by
chance."
10So they did this. They took two such cows
and hitched them to the cart and penned up their
calves. 11They placed the ark of the LORD on the
cart and along with it the chest containing the
gold rats and the models of the tumors. 12Then
the cows went straight up toward Beth Shemesh,
keeping on the road and lowing all the way; they
did not turn to the right or to the left. The rulers
of the Philistines followed them as far as the bor-
der of Beth Shemesh.
13Now the people of Beth Shemesh were har-
vesting their wheat in the valley, and when they

[q]21 *Ichabod* means *no glory.* [r]6 Hebrew; Septuagint and Vulgate *tumors. And rats appeared in their land, and death and destruction were throughout the city* [s]9 Or *with tumors in the groin* (see Septuagint) [t]11 Or *he* [u]6 That is, God

looked up and saw the ark, they rejoiced at the sight. 14 The cart came to the field of Joshua of Beth Shemesh, and there it stopped beside a large rock. The people chopped up the wood of the cart and sacrificed the cows as a burnt offering to the LORD. 15 The Levites took down the ark of the LORD, together with the chest containing the gold objects, and placed them on the large rock. On that day the people of Beth Shemesh offered burnt offerings and made sacrifices to the LORD. 16 The five rulers of the Philistines saw all this and then returned that same day to Ekron.

17 These are the gold tumors the Philistines sent as a guilt offering to the LORD—one each for Ashdod, Gaza, Ashkelon, Gath and Ekron. 18 And the number of the gold rats was according to the number of Philistine towns belonging to the five rulers—the fortified towns with their country villages. The large rock, on which[v] they set the ark of the LORD, is a witness to this day in the field of Joshua of Beth Shemesh.

19 But God struck down some of the men of Beth Shemesh, putting seventy[w] of them to death because they had looked into the ark of the LORD. The people mourned because of the heavy blow the LORD had dealt them, 20 and the men of Beth Shemesh asked, "Who can stand in the presence of the LORD, this holy God? To whom will the ark go up from here?"

21 Then they sent messengers to the people of Kiriath Jearim, saying, "The Philistines have returned the ark of the LORD. Come down and take

7 it up to your place." 1 So the men of Kiriath Jearim came and took up the ark of the LORD. They took it to Abinadab's house on the hill and consecrated Eleazar his son to guard the ark of the LORD.

2 It was a long time, twenty years in all, that the ark remained at Kiriath Jearim, and all the people of Israel mourned and sought after the LORD. 3 And Samuel said to the whole house of Israel, "If you are returning to the LORD with all your hearts, then rid yourselves of the foreign gods and the Ashtoreths and commit yourselves to the LORD and serve him only, and he will deliver you out of the hand of the Philistines." 4 So the Israelites put away their Baals and Ashtoreths, and served the LORD only.

5 Then Samuel said, "Assemble all Israel at Mizpah and I will intercede with the LORD for you." 6 When they had assembled at Mizpah, they drew water and poured it out before the LORD. On that day they fasted and there they confessed, "We have sinned against the LORD." And Samuel was leader[x] of Israel at Mizpah.

7 When the Philistines heard that Israel had assembled at Mizpah, the rulers of the Philistines came up to attack them. And when the Israelites heard of it, they were afraid because of the Philistines. 8 They said to Samuel, "Do not stop crying out to the LORD our God for us, that he may rescue us from the hand of the Philistines." 9 Then Samuel took a suckling lamb and offered it up as a whole burnt offering to the LORD. He cried out to the LORD on Israel's behalf, and the LORD answered him.

10 While Samuel was sacrificing the burnt offering, the Philistines drew near to engage Israel in battle. But that day the LORD thundered with loud thunder against the Philistines and threw them into such a panic that they were routed before the Israelites. 11 The men of Israel rushed out of Mizpah and pursued the Philistines, slaughtering them along the way to a point below Beth Car.

12 Then Samuel took a stone and set it up between Mizpah and Shen. He named it Ebenezer,[y] saying, "Thus far has the LORD helped us." 13 So the Philistines were subdued and did not invade Israelite territory again.

Throughout Samuel's lifetime, the hand of the LORD was against the Philistines. 14 The towns from Ekron to Gath that the Philistines had captured from Israel were restored to her, and Israel delivered the neighboring territory from the power of the Philistines. And there was peace between Israel and the Amorites.

15 Samuel continued as judge over Israel all the days of his life. 16 From year to year he went on a circuit from Bethel to Gilgal to Mizpah, judging Israel in all those places. 17 But he always went back to Ramah, where his home was, and there he also judged Israel. And he built an altar there to the LORD.

[v] 18 A few Hebrew manuscripts (see also Septuagint); most Hebrew manuscripts *villages as far as Greater Abel, where* [w] 19 A few Hebrew manuscripts; most Hebrew manuscripts and Septuagint *50,070* [x] 6 Traditionally *judge* [y] 12 *Ebenezer* means *stone of help.*

3 / *1 Samuel 8*
Status Symbols

DO YOU REMEMBER the alligators? For a while the Izod symbol was the trendiest inch-long animal to have positioned on the left side of your knit shirt. In rebellion I wore a shirt with a small frog on it. Trends come and go, but they inevitably carry us along. In this passage the Israelites decide that a king would be a great status symbol so they could be like the countries around them.

Warming Up to God Reflect on your own patterns of living—home, clothing, car, possessions, even your yard. In what ways has your imagination been captured by current trends?

Read 1 Samuel 8.

8 When Samuel grew old, he appointed his
sons as judges for Israel. 2The name of his
firstborn was Joel and the name of his
second was Abijah, and they served at Beersheba.
3But his sons did not walk in his ways. They
turned aside after dishonest gain and accepted
bribes and perverted justice.
4So all the elders of Israel gathered together
and came to Samuel at Ramah. 5They said to him,
"You are old, and your sons do not walk in your
ways; now appoint a king to lead[z] us, such as all
the other nations have."
6But when they said, "Give us a king to lead
us," this displeased Samuel; so he prayed to the
LORD. 7And the LORD told him: "Listen to all that
the people are saying to you; it is not you they
have rejected, but they have rejected me as their
king. 8As they have done from the day I brought
them up out of Egypt until this day, forsaking me
and serving other gods, so they are doing to you.
9Now listen to them; but warn them solemnly and
let them know what the king who will reign over
them will do."
10Samuel told all the words of the LORD to the
people who were asking him for a king. 11He said,
"This is what the king who will reign over you
will do: He will take your sons and make them
serve with his chariots and horses, and they will
run in front of his chariots. 12Some he will assign
to be commanders of thousands and commanders
of fifties, and others to plow his ground and reap
his harvest, and still others to make weapons of
war and equipment for his chariots. 13He will take
your daughters to be perfumers and cooks and
bakers. 14He will take the best of your fields and
vineyards and olive groves and give them to his
attendants. 15He will take a tenth of your grain
and of your vintage and give it to his officials and
attendants. 16Your menservants and maidservants
and the best of your cattle[a] and donkeys he will
take for his own use. 17He will take a tenth of
your flocks, and you yourselves will become his
slaves. 18When that day comes, you will cry out
for relief from the king you have chosen, and the
LORD will not answer you in that day."
19But the people refused to listen to Samuel.
"No!" they said. "We want a king over us. 20Then
we will be like all the other nations, with a king
to lead us and to go out before us and fight our
battles."
21When Samuel heard all that the people said,
he repeated it before the LORD. 22The LORD an-
swered, "Listen to them and give them a king."
Then Samuel said to the men of Israel, "Every-
one go back to his town."

[z]5 Traditionally *judge*; also in verses 6 and 20 [a]16 Septuagint; Hebrew *young men*

Discovering the Word 1. What do we learn about Samuel's sons in verses 1–3? 2. What reasons do the elders give for wanting a king (vv. 4–5)? 3. It seems that the elders have good reasons for being dissatisfied with Samuel's sons, but what other motivations are behind their request (vv. 7–8, 19–20)? 4. Notice all the terrible results that will come from having a king (vv. 11–18). Why do you think the people continue asking despite these warnings? 5. Why do you think the Lord repeatedly tells Samuel to "listen to the people" (vv. 7, 9, 22)?

Applying the Word 1. When are you most likely to be influenced by trends? 2. What trends are you following despite the warnings you may have had?

 **Responding in Prayer** Tell the Lord how you have replaced him as king (v. 7) with status symbols. Ask him to help you reform your ways.

4 / *1 Samuel 9:1—10:8*
Citizenship

LEIF SERVES ON his local public school board. The board must make a decision about a public health clinic located in the high school. The health clinic provides immunizations and physical examinations, and gives emergency care for injuries. It provides counsel to students with drug and alcohol problems. It supplies nutrition advice for pregnant women, birth control information, adoption agency referrals and phone numbers for abortion clinics. Recently the board has received a rash of complaints about the health clinic. One side says that the public school ought to be in the business of education, not providing fancy health services. The other complaints are from those who want birth control and abortion information ceased. And they want the clinic closed if that's what it takes.

Leif believes that abortion is wrong. And he believes that sex outside of marriage is wrong. He also knows that a certain percentage of these high-school students will have problem pregnancies—whether or not the clinic is open. And without the clinic, many kids at that high school will get no medical care at all. What position should Leif take on the upcoming school board decision?

 **Warming Up to God** In what area of your life do you see potential conflict between civil policy and moral principle?

 **Read 1 Samuel 9:1—10:8.**

9 There was a Benjamite, a man of standing,
whose name was Kish son of Abiel, the
son of Zeror, the son of Becorath, the son
of Aphiah of Benjamin. 2He had a son named
Saul, an impressive young man without equal
among the Israelites—a head taller than any of
the others.
3Now the donkeys belonging to Saul's father
Kish were lost, and Kish said to his son Saul,
"Take one of the servants with you and go and
look for the donkeys." 4So he passed through the
hill country of Ephraim and through the area
around Shalisha, but they did not find them. They
went on into the district of Shaalim, but the donkeys were not there. Then he passed through the
territory of Benjamin, but they did not find them.
5When they reached the district of Zuph, Saul
said to the servant who was with him, "Come,
let's go back, or my father will stop thinking
about the donkeys and start worrying about us."
6But the servant replied, "Look, in this town
there is a man of God; he is highly respected, and
everything he says comes true. Let's go there now.
Perhaps he will tell us what way to take."
7Saul said to his servant, "If we go, what can we
give the man? The food in our sacks is gone. We
have no gift to take to the man of God. What do
we have?"
8The servant answered him again. "Look," he
said, "I have a quarter of a shekel[b] of silver. I will
give it to the man of God so that he will tell us
what way to take." 9(Formerly in Israel, if a man
went to inquire of God, he would say, "Come, let
us go to the seer," because the prophet of today
used to be called a seer.)
10"Good," Saul said to his servant. "Come, let's
go." So they set out for the town where the man
of God was.
11As they were going up the hill to the town,
they met some girls coming out to draw water,
and they asked them, "Is the seer here?"
12"He is," they answered. "He's ahead of you.
Hurry now; he has just come to our town today,
for the people have a sacrifice at the high place.
13As soon as you enter the town, you will find
him before he goes up to the high place to eat.
The people will not begin eating until he comes,
because he must bless the sacrifice; afterward,
those who are invited will eat. Go up now; you
should find him about this time."
14They went up to the town, and as they were

[b]8 That is, about 1/10 ounce (about 3 grams)

entering it, there was Samuel, coming toward them on his way up to the high place.

15Now the day before Saul came, the LORD had revealed this to Samuel: 16"About this time tomorrow I will send you a man from the land of Benjamin. Anoint him leader over my people Israel; he will deliver my people from the hand of the Philistines. I have looked upon my people, for their cry has reached me."

17When Samuel caught sight of Saul, the LORD said to him, "This is the man I spoke to you about; he will govern my people."

18Saul approached Samuel in the gateway and asked, "Would you please tell me where the seer's house is?"

19"I am the seer," Samuel replied. "Go up ahead of me to the high place, for today you are to eat with me, and in the morning I will let you go and will tell you all that is in your heart. 20As for the donkeys you lost three days ago, do not worry about them; they have been found. And to whom is all the desire of Israel turned, if not to you and all your father's family?"

21Saul answered, "But am I not a Benjamite, from the smallest tribe of Israel, and is not my clan the least of all the clans of the tribe of Benjamin? Why do you say such a thing to me?"

22Then Samuel brought Saul and his servant into the hall and seated them at the head of those who were invited—about thirty in number. 23Samuel said to the cook, "Bring the piece of meat I gave you, the one I told you to lay aside."

24So the cook took up the leg with what was on it and set it in front of Saul. Samuel said, "Here is what has been kept for you. Eat, because it was set aside for you for this occasion, from the time I said, 'I have invited guests.'" And Saul dined with Samuel that day.

25After they came down from the high place to the town, Samuel talked with Saul on the roof of his house. 26They rose about daybreak and Samuel called to Saul on the roof, "Get ready, and I will send you on your way." When Saul got ready, he and Samuel went outside together. 27As they were going down to the edge of the town, Samuel said to Saul, "Tell the servant to go on ahead of us"—and the servant did so—"but you stay here awhile, so that I may give you a message from God."

10 Then Samuel took a flask of oil and poured it on Saul's head and kissed him, saying, "Has not the LORD anointed you leader over his inheritance?[c] 2When you leave me today, you will meet two men near Rachel's tomb, at Zelzah on the border of Benjamin. They will say to you, 'The donkeys you set out to look for have been found. And now your father has stopped thinking about them and is worried about you. He is asking, "What shall I do about my son?"'

3"Then you will go on from there until you reach the great tree of Tabor. Three men going up to God at Bethel will meet you there. One will be carrying three young goats, another three loaves of bread, and another a skin of wine. 4They will greet you and offer you two loaves of bread, which you will accept from them.

5"After that you will go to Gibeah of God, where there is a Philistine outpost. As you approach the town, you will meet a procession of prophets coming down from the high place with lyres, tambourines, flutes and harps being played before them, and they will be prophesying. 6The Spirit of the LORD will come upon you in power, and you will prophesy with them; and you will be changed into a different person. 7Once these signs are fulfilled, do whatever your hand finds to do, for God is with you.

8"Go down ahead of me to Gilgal. I will surely come down to you to sacrifice burnt offerings and fellowship offerings,[d] but you must wait seven days until I come to you and tell you what you are to do."

c1 Hebrew; Septuagint and Vulgate *over his people Israel? You will reign over the LORD's people and save them from the power of their enemies round about. And this will be a sign to you that the LORD has anointed you leader over his inheritance:* d8 Traditionally *peace offerings*

Discovering the Word 1. What events lead to a meeting between Saul and Samuel? 2. What reasons did Saul have to trust Samuel? 3. Given the information here, what do you see as Samuel's civil responsibilities? 4. What do you see as Samuel's spiritual responsibilities? 5. What do you think would be hard about Samuel's dual position?

Applying the Word 1. Review the dilemma Leif faced with his school board. If you were Leif, what decision would you urge on your fellow board members? 2. How would the recommendation you have chosen meet your responsibilities to all of the people in your school district? 3. How would it meet your responsibilities as a heavenly citizen?

Responding in Prayer Take time now to pray for one of your own civil leaders.

1 Samuel 10:9—14:52

9As Saul turned to leave Samuel, God changed
Saul's heart, and all these signs were fulfilled that
day. 10When they arrived at Gibeah, a procession
of prophets met him; the Spirit of God came upon
him in power, and he joined in their prophesying.
11When all those who had formerly known him
saw him prophesying with the prophets, they
asked each other, "What is this that has happened
to the son of Kish? Is Saul also among the proph-
ets?"

12A man who lived there answered, "And who
is their father?" So it became a saying: "Is Saul
also among the prophets?" 13After Saul stopped
prophesying, he went to the high place.

14Now Saul's uncle asked him and his servant,
"Where have you been?"

"Looking for the donkeys," he said. "But when we saw they were not to be found, we went to Samuel."

15Saul's uncle said, "Tell me what Samuel said
to you."

16Saul replied, "He assured us that the donkeys
had been found." But he did not tell his uncle
what Samuel had said about the kingship.

17Samuel summoned the people of Israel to the
LORD at Mizpah 18and said to them, "This is what
the LORD, the God of Israel, says: 'I brought Israel
up out of Egypt, and I delivered you from the
power of Egypt and all the kingdoms that op-
pressed you.' 19But you have now rejected your
God, who saves you out of all your calamities and
distresses. And you have said, 'No, set a king over
us.' So now present yourselves before the LORD by
your tribes and clans."

20When Samuel brought all the tribes of Israel
near, the tribe of Benjamin was chosen. 21Then he
brought forward the tribe of Benjamin, clan by
clan, and Matri's clan was chosen. Finally Saul
son of Kish was chosen. But when they looked for
him, he was not to be found. 22So they inquired
further of the LORD, "Has the man come here yet?"

And the LORD said, "Yes, he has hidden himself among the baggage."

23They ran and brought him out, and as he
stood among the people he was a head taller than
any of the others. 24Samuel said to all the people,
"Do you see the man the LORD has chosen? There
is no one like him among all the people."

Then the people shouted, "Long live the king!"

25Samuel explained to the people the regula-
tions of the kingship. He wrote them down on a
scroll and deposited it before the LORD. Then Sam-
uel dismissed the people, each to his own home.
26Saul also went to his home in Gibeah, accom-
panied by valiant men whose hearts God had
touched. 27But some troublemakers said, "How
can this fellow save us?" They despised him and
brought him no gifts. But Saul kept silent.

11 Nahash the Ammonite went up and
besieged Jabesh Gilead. And all the
men of Jabesh said to him, "Make a
treaty with us, and we will be subject to you."
2But Nahash the Ammonite replied, "I will
make a treaty with you only on the condition that
I gouge out the right eye of every one of you and
so bring disgrace on all Israel."

3The elders of Jabesh said to him, "Give us
seven days so we can send messengers through-
out Israel; if no one comes to rescue us, we will
surrender to you."

4When the messengers came to Gibeah of Saul
and reported these terms to the people, they all
wept aloud. 5Just then Saul was returning from
the fields, behind his oxen, and he asked, "What
is wrong with the people? Why are they weep-
ing?" Then they repeated to him what the men of
Jabesh had said.

6When Saul heard their words, the Spirit of
God came upon him in power, and he burned
with anger. 7He took a pair of oxen, cut them
into pieces, and sent the pieces by messengers
throughout Israel, proclaiming, "This is what will

be done to the oxen of anyone who does not follow Saul and Samuel." Then the terror of the LORD fell on the people, and they turned out as one man. 8When Saul mustered them at Bezek, the men of Israel numbered three hundred thousand and the men of Judah thirty thousand.

9They told the messengers who had come, "Say to the men of Jabesh Gilead, 'By the time the sun is hot tomorrow, you will be delivered.' " When the messengers went and reported this to the men of Jabesh, they were elated. 10They said to the Ammonites, "Tomorrow we will surrender to you, and you can do to us whatever seems good to you."

11The next day Saul separated his men into three divisions; during the last watch of the night they broke into the camp of the Ammonites and slaughtered them until the heat of the day. Those who survived were scattered, so that no two of them were left together.

12The people then said to Samuel, "Who was it that asked, 'Shall Saul reign over us?' Bring these men to us and we will put them to death."

13But Saul said, "No one shall be put to death today, for this day the LORD has rescued Israel."

14Then Samuel said to the people, "Come, let us go to Gilgal and there reaffirm the kingship." 15So all the people went to Gilgal and confirmed Saul as king in the presence of the LORD. There they sacrificed fellowship offerings[e] before the LORD, and Saul and all the Israelites held a great celebration.

12 Samuel said to all Israel, "I have listened to everything you said to me and have set a king over you. 2Now you have a king as your leader. As for me, I am old and gray, and my sons are here with you. I have been your leader from my youth until this day. 3Here I stand. Testify against me in the presence of the LORD and his anointed. Whose ox have I taken? Whose donkey have I taken? Whom have I cheated? Whom have I oppressed? From whose hand have I accepted a bribe to make me shut my eyes? If I have done any of these, I will make it right."

4"You have not cheated or oppressed us," they replied. "You have not taken anything from anyone's hand."

5Samuel said to them, "The LORD is witness against you, and also his anointed is witness this day, that you have not found anything in my hand."

"He is witness," they said.

6Then Samuel said to the people, "It is the LORD who appointed Moses and Aaron and brought your forefathers up out of Egypt. 7Now then, stand here, because I am going to confront you with evidence before the LORD as to all the righteous acts performed by the LORD for you and your fathers.

8"After Jacob entered Egypt, they cried to the LORD for help, and the LORD sent Moses and Aaron, who brought your forefathers out of Egypt and settled them in this place.

9"But they forgot the LORD their God; so he sold them into the hand of Sisera, the commander of the army of Hazor, and into the hands of the Philistines and the king of Moab, who fought against them. 10They cried out to the LORD and said, 'We have sinned; we have forsaken the LORD and served the Baals and the Ashtoreths. But now deliver us from the hands of our enemies, and we will serve you.' 11Then the LORD sent Jerub-Baal,[f] Barak,[g] Jephthah and Samuel,[h] and he delivered you from the hands of your enemies on every side, so that you lived securely.

12"But when you saw that Nahash king of the Ammonites was moving against you, you said to me, 'No, we want a king to rule over us'—even though the LORD your God was your king. 13Now here is the king you have chosen, the one you asked for; see, the LORD has set a king over you. 14If you fear the LORD and serve and obey him and do not rebel against his commands, and if both you and the king who reigns over you follow the LORD your God—good! 15But if you do not obey the LORD, and if you rebel against his commands, his hand will be against you, as it was against your fathers.

16"Now then, stand still and see this great thing the LORD is about to do before your eyes! 17Is it not wheat harvest now? I will call upon the LORD to send thunder and rain. And you will realize what an evil thing you did in the eyes of the LORD when you asked for a king."

18Then Samuel called upon the LORD, and that same day the LORD sent thunder and rain. So all the people stood in awe of the LORD and of Samuel.

19The people all said to Samuel, "Pray to the LORD your God for your servants so that we will

[e]15 Traditionally *peace offerings* [f]11 Also called *Gideon*
[g]11 Some Septuagint manuscripts and Syriac; Hebrew *Bedan*
[h]11 Hebrew; some Septuagint manuscripts and Syriac *Samson*

not die, for we have added to all our other sins the evil of asking for a king."

20"Do not be afraid," Samuel replied. "You have done all this evil; yet do not turn away from the LORD, but serve the LORD with all your heart. 21Do not turn away after useless idols. They can do you no good, nor can they rescue you, because they are useless. 22For the sake of his great name the LORD will not reject his people, because the LORD was pleased to make you his own. 23As for me, far be it from me that I should sin against the LORD by failing to pray for you. And I will teach you the way that is good and right. 24But be sure to fear the LORD and serve him faithfully with all your heart; consider what great things he has done for you. 25Yet if you persist in doing evil, both you and your king will be swept away."

13

Saul was ⌞thirty⌟[i] years old when he became king, and he reigned over Israel ⌞forty-⌟[j] two years.

2Saul[k] chose three thousand men from Israel; two thousand were with him at Micmash and in the hill country of Bethel, and a thousand were with Jonathan at Gibeah in Benjamin. The rest of the men he sent back to their homes.

3Jonathan attacked the Philistine outpost at Geba, and the Philistines heard about it. Then Saul had the trumpet blown throughout the land and said, "Let the Hebrews hear!" 4So all Israel heard the news: "Saul has attacked the Philistine outpost, and now Israel has become a stench to the Philistines." And the people were summoned to join Saul at Gilgal.

5The Philistines assembled to fight Israel, with three thousand[l] chariots, six thousand charioteers, and soldiers as numerous as the sand on the seashore. They went up and camped at Micmash, east of Beth Aven. 6When the men of Israel saw that their situation was critical and that their army was hard pressed, they hid in caves and thickets, among the rocks, and in pits and cisterns. 7Some Hebrews even crossed the Jordan to the land of Gad and Gilead.

Saul remained at Gilgal, and all the troops with him were quaking with fear. 8He waited seven days, the time set by Samuel; but Samuel did not come to Gilgal, and Saul's men began to scatter. 9So he said, "Bring me the burnt offering and the fellowship offerings.[m]" And Saul offered up the burnt offering. 10Just as he finished making the offering, Samuel arrived, and Saul went out to greet him.

11"What have you done?" asked Samuel.

Saul replied, "When I saw that the men were scattering, and that you did not come at the set time, and that the Philistines were assembling at Micmash, 12I thought, 'Now the Philistines will come down against me at Gilgal, and I have not sought the LORD's favor.' So I felt compelled to offer the burnt offering."

13"You acted foolishly," Samuel said. "You have not kept the command the LORD your God gave you; if you had, he would have established your kingdom over Israel for all time. 14But now your kingdom will not endure; the LORD has sought out a man after his own heart and appointed him leader of his people, because you have not kept the LORD's command."

15Then Samuel left Gilgal[n] and went up to Gibeah in Benjamin, and Saul counted the men who were with him. They numbered about six hundred.

16Saul and his son Jonathan and the men with them were staying in Gibeah[o] in Benjamin, while the Philistines camped at Micmash. 17Raiding parties went out from the Philistine camp in three detachments. One turned toward Ophrah in the vicinity of Shual, 18another toward Beth Horon, and the third toward the borderland overlooking the Valley of Zeboim facing the desert.

19Not a blacksmith could be found in the whole land of Israel, because the Philistines had said, "Otherwise the Hebrews will make swords or spears!" 20So all Israel went down to the Philistines to have their plowshares, mattocks, axes and sickles[p] sharpened. 21The price was two thirds of a shekel[q] for sharpening plowshares and mattocks, and a third of a shekel[r] for sharpening forks and axes and for repointing goads.

22So on the day of the battle not a soldier with Saul and Jonathan had a sword or spear in his hand; only Saul and his son Jonathan had them.

23Now a detachment of Philistines had gone

[i] *1* A few late manuscripts of the Septuagint; Hebrew does not have *thirty.* [j] *1* See the round number in Acts 13:21; Hebrew does not have *forty-.* [k] *1,2* Or *and when he had reigned over Israel two years, 2he* [l] *5* Some Septuagint manuscripts and Syriac; Hebrew *thirty thousand* [m] *9* Traditionally *peace offerings* [n] *15* Hebrew; Septuagint *Gilgal and went his way; the rest of the people went after Saul to meet the army, and they went out of Gilgal* [o] *16* Two Hebrew manuscripts; most Hebrew manuscripts *Geba,* a variant of *Gibeah* [p] *20* Septuagint; Hebrew *plowshares* [q] *21* Hebrew *pim*; that is, about 1/4 ounce (about 8 grams) [r] *21* That is, about 1/8 ounce (about 4 grams)

14 out to the pass at Micmash. 1One day Jonathan son of Saul said to the young man bearing his armor, "Come, let's go over to the Philistine outpost on the other side." But he did not tell his father.

2Saul was staying on the outskirts of Gibeah under a pomegranate tree in Migron. With him were about six hundred men, 3among whom was Ahijah, who was wearing an ephod. He was a son of Ichabod's brother Ahitub son of Phinehas, the son of Eli, the LORD's priest in Shiloh. No one was aware that Jonathan had left.

4On each side of the pass that Jonathan intended to cross to reach the Philistine outpost was a cliff; one was called Bozez, and the other Seneh. 5One cliff stood to the north toward Micmash, the other to the south toward Geba.

6Jonathan said to his young armor-bearer, "Come, let's go over to the outpost of those uncircumcised fellows. Perhaps the LORD will act in our behalf. Nothing can hinder the LORD from saving, whether by many or by few."

7"Do all that you have in mind," his armor-bearer said. "Go ahead; I am with you heart and soul."

8Jonathan said, "Come, then; we will cross over toward the men and let them see us. 9If they say to us, 'Wait there until we come to you,' we will stay where we are and not go up to them. 10But if they say, 'Come up to us,' we will climb up, because that will be our sign that the LORD has given them into our hands."

11So both of them showed themselves to the Philistine outpost. "Look!" said the Philistines. "The Hebrews are crawling out of the holes they were hiding in." 12The men of the outpost shouted to Jonathan and his armor-bearer, "Come up to us and we'll teach you a lesson."

So Jonathan said to his armor-bearer, "Climb up after me; the LORD has given them into the hand of Israel."

13Jonathan climbed up, using his hands and feet, with his armor-bearer right behind him. The Philistines fell before Jonathan, and his armor-bearer followed and killed behind him. 14In that first attack Jonathan and his armor-bearer killed some twenty men in an area of about half an acre.[s]

15Then panic struck the whole army—those in the camp and field, and those in the outposts and raiding parties—and the ground shook. It was a panic sent by God.[t]

16Saul's lookouts at Gibeah in Benjamin saw the army melting away in all directions. 17Then Saul said to the men who were with him, "Muster the forces and see who has left us." When they did, it was Jonathan and his armor-bearer who were not there.

18Saul said to Ahijah, "Bring the ark of God." (At that time it was with the Israelites.)[u] 19While Saul was talking to the priest, the tumult in the Philistine camp increased more and more. So Saul said to the priest, "Withdraw your hand."

20Then Saul and all his men assembled and went to the battle. They found the Philistines in total confusion, striking each other with their swords. 21Those Hebrews who had previously been with the Philistines and had gone up with them to their camp went over to the Israelites who were with Saul and Jonathan. 22When all the Israelites who had hidden in the hill country of Ephraim heard that the Philistines were on the run, they joined the battle in hot pursuit. 23So the LORD rescued Israel that day, and the battle moved on beyond Beth Aven.

24Now the men of Israel were in distress that day, because Saul had bound the people under an oath, saying, "Cursed be any man who eats food before evening comes, before I have avenged myself on my enemies!" So none of the troops tasted food.

25The entire army[v] entered the woods, and there was honey on the ground. 26When they went into the woods, they saw the honey oozing out, yet no one put his hand to his mouth, because they feared the oath. 27But Jonathan had not heard that his father had bound the people with the oath, so he reached out the end of the staff that was in his hand and dipped it into the honeycomb. He raised his hand to his mouth, and his eyes brightened.[w] 28Then one of the soldiers told him, "Your father bound the army under a strict oath, saying, 'Cursed be any man who eats food today!' That is why the men are faint."

29Jonathan said, "My father has made trouble for the country. See how my eyes brightened[x] when I tasted a little of this honey. 30How much better it would have been if the men had eaten today some of the plunder they took from their

[s]14 Hebrew *half a yoke*; a "yoke" was the land plowed by a yoke of oxen in one day. [t]15 Or *a terrible panic* [u]18 Hebrew; Septuagint *"Bring the ephod." (At that time he wore the ephod before the Israelites.)* [v]25 Or *Now all the people of the land* [w]27 Or *his strength was renewed* [x]29 Or *my strength was renewed*

enemies. Would not the slaughter of the Philistines have been even greater?"

31That day, after the Israelites had struck down the Philistines from Micmash to Aijalon, they were exhausted. 32They pounced on the plunder and, taking sheep, cattle and calves, they butchered them on the ground and ate them, together with the blood. 33Then someone said to Saul, "Look, the men are sinning against the LORD by eating meat that has blood in it."

"You have broken faith," he said. "Roll a large stone over here at once." 34Then he said, "Go out among the men and tell them, 'Each of you bring me your cattle and sheep, and slaughter them here and eat them. Do not sin against the LORD by eating meat with blood still in it.' "

So everyone brought his ox that night and slaughtered it there. 35Then Saul built an altar to the LORD; it was the first time he had done this.

36Saul said, "Let us go down after the Philistines by night and plunder them till dawn, and let us not leave one of them alive."

"Do whatever seems best to you," they replied.

But the priest said, "Let us inquire of God here."

37So Saul asked God, "Shall I go down after the Philistines? Will you give them into Israel's hand?" But God did not answer him that day.

38Saul therefore said, "Come here, all you who are leaders of the army, and let us find out what sin has been committed today. 39As surely as the LORD who rescues Israel lives, even if it lies with my son Jonathan, he must die." But not one of the men said a word.

40Saul then said to all the Israelites, "You stand over there; I and Jonathan my son will stand over here."

"Do what seems best to you," the men replied.

41Then Saul prayed to the LORD, the God of Israel, "Give me the right answer."[y] And Jonathan and Saul were taken by lot, and the men were cleared. 42Saul said, "Cast the lot between me and Jonathan my son." And Jonathan was taken.

43Then Saul said to Jonathan, "Tell me what you have done."

So Jonathan told him, "I merely tasted a little honey with the end of my staff. And now must I die?"

44Saul said, "May God deal with me, be it ever so severely, if you do not die, Jonathan."

45But the men said to Saul, "Should Jonathan die—he who has brought about this great deliverance in Israel? Never! As surely as the LORD lives, not a hair of his head will fall to the ground, for he did this today with God's help." So the men rescued Jonathan, and he was not put to death.

46Then Saul stopped pursuing the Philistines, and they withdrew to their own land.

47After Saul had assumed rule over Israel, he fought against their enemies on every side: Moab, the Ammonites, Edom, the kings[z] of Zobah, and the Philistines. Wherever he turned, he inflicted punishment on them.[a] 48He fought valiantly and defeated the Amalekites, delivering Israel from the hands of those who had plundered them.

49Saul's sons were Jonathan, Ishvi and Malki-Shua. The name of his older daughter was Merab, and that of the younger was Michal. 50His wife's name was Ahinoam daughter of Ahimaaz. The name of the commander of Saul's army was Abner son of Ner, and Ner was Saul's uncle. 51Saul's father Kish and Abner's father Ner were sons of Abiel.

52All the days of Saul there was bitter war with the Philistines, and whenever Saul saw a mighty or brave man, he took him into his service.

[y] 41 Hebrew; Septuagint *"Why have you not answered your servant today? If the fault is in me or my son Jonathan, respond with Urim, but if the men of Israel are at fault, respond with Thummim."*
[z] 47 Masoretic Text; Dead Sea Scrolls and Septuagint *king*
[a] 47 Hebrew; Septuagint *he was victorious*

5/ 1 Samuel 15
Doing Almost All of God's Will

PERHAPS ONE OF the cleverest schemes of the Enemy is to convince us that doing most of God's will is enough, and that by doing it we will receive God's blessings. King Saul fell into such a temptation. Instructed by God to fight and to destroy the Amalekites, he succumbed to the wishes of his fighting men and did only part of God's command.

Warming Up to God When does pressure from the people around you have a greater influence on your life than God does?

Read 1 Samuel 15.

15 Samuel said to Saul, "I am the one the LORD sent to anoint you king over his people Israel; so listen now to the message from the LORD. 2This is what the LORD Almighty says: 'I will punish the Amalekites for what they did to Israel when they waylaid them as they came up from Egypt. 3Now go, attack the Amalekites and totally destroy[b] everything that belongs to them. Do not spare them; put to death men and women, children and infants, cattle and sheep, camels and donkeys.' "

4So Saul summoned the men and mustered them at Telaim—two hundred thousand foot soldiers and ten thousand men from Judah. 5Saul went to the city of Amalek and set an ambush in the ravine. 6Then he said to the Kenites, "Go away, leave the Amalekites so that I do not destroy you along with them; for you showed kindness to all the Israelites when they came up out of Egypt." So the Kenites moved away from the Amalekites.

7Then Saul attacked the Amalekites all the way from Havilah to Shur, to the east of Egypt. 8He took Agag king of the Amalekites alive, and all his people he totally destroyed with the sword. 9But Saul and the army spared Agag and the best of the sheep and cattle, the fat calves[c] and lambs—everything that was good. These they were unwilling to destroy completely, but everything that was despised and weak they totally destroyed.

10Then the word of the LORD came to Samuel: 11"I am grieved that I have made Saul king, because he has turned away from me and has not carried out my instructions." Samuel was troubled, and he cried out to the LORD all that night.

12Early in the morning Samuel got up and went to meet Saul, but he was told, "Saul has gone to Carmel. There he has set up a monument in his own honor and has turned and gone on down to Gilgal."

13When Samuel reached him, Saul said, "The LORD bless you! I have carried out the LORD's instructions."

14But Samuel said, "What then is this bleating of sheep in my ears? What is this lowing of cattle that I hear?"

15Saul answered, "The soldiers brought them from the Amalekites; they spared the best of the sheep and cattle to sacrifice to the LORD your God, but we totally destroyed the rest."

16"Stop!" Samuel said to Saul. "Let me tell you what the LORD said to me last night."

"Tell me," Saul replied.

17Samuel said, "Although you were once small in your own eyes, did you not become the head of the tribes of Israel? The LORD anointed you king over Israel. 18And he sent you on a mission, saying, 'Go and completely destroy those wicked people, the Amalekites; make war on them until you have wiped them out.' 19Why did you not obey the LORD? Why did you pounce on the plunder and do evil in the eyes of the LORD?"

20"But I did obey the LORD," Saul said. "I went on the mission the LORD assigned me. I completely destroyed the Amalekites and brought back Agag their king. 21The soldiers took sheep and cattle from the plunder, the best of what was devoted to God, in order to sacrifice them to the LORD your God at Gilgal."

22But Samuel replied:

"Does the LORD delight in burnt offerings and
sacrifices

[b]3 The Hebrew term refers to the irrevocable giving over of things or persons to the LORD, often by totally destroying them; also in verses 8, 9, 15, 18, 20 and 21. [c]9 Or *the grown bulls*; the meaning of the Hebrew for this phrase is uncertain.

as much as in obeying the voice of the
LORD?
To obey is better than sacrifice,
and to heed is better than the fat of rams.
23For rebellion is like the sin of divination,
and arrogance like the evil of idolatry.
Because you have rejected the word of the
LORD,
he has rejected you as king."

24Then Saul said to Samuel, "I have sinned. I
violated the LORD's command and your instruc-
tions. I was afraid of the people and so I gave in
to them. 25Now I beg you, forgive my sin and
come back with me, so that I may worship the
LORD."

26But Samuel said to him, "I will not go back
with you. You have rejected the word of the LORD,
and the LORD has rejected you as king over Is-
rael!"

27As Samuel turned to leave, Saul caught hold
of the hem of his robe, and it tore. 28Samuel said
to him, "The LORD has torn the kingdom of Israel
from you today and has given it to one of your
neighbors—to one better than you. 29He who is
the Glory of Israel does not lie or change his
mind; for he is not a man, that he should change
his mind."

30Saul replied, "I have sinned. But please honor
me before the elders of my people and before Is-
rael; come back with me, so that I may worship
the LORD your God." 31So Samuel went back with
Saul, and Saul worshiped the LORD.

32Then Samuel said, "Bring me Agag king of
the Amalekites."

Agag came to him confidently,[d] thinking,
"Surely the bitterness of death is past."

33But Samuel said,

"As your sword has made women childless,
so will your mother be childless among
women."

And Samuel put Agag to death before the LORD at
Gilgal.

34Then Samuel left for Ramah, but Saul went
up to his home in Gibeah of Saul. 35Until the day
Samuel died, he did not go to see Saul again,
though Samuel mourned for him. And the LORD
was grieved that he had made Saul king over Is-
rael.

[d]32 *Or him trembling, yet*

Discovering the Word 1. What message from the Lord does Samuel deliver to Saul, and why (vv. 1–3)? 2. How does Saul begin to obey God but later change his mind (vv. 4–9)? 3. What factors probably contributed to Saul's unwillingness to carry out God's explicit command (vv. 12, 24, 30)? 4. Why do you think God equates disobedience with idolatry (vv. 22–23)? 5. Although Saul finally confesses his sin in verse 24, what do his actions suggest about the sincerity of his repentance (vv. 24–30)?

Applying the Word 1. How does the description of Saul's disobedience (vv. 22–23) differ from the way we view our sin when we do not do all of God's will? 2. What "burnt offerings" and "sacrifices" do we sometimes offer to compensate for our lack of obedience? 3. Think of one area where you have been content to do almost all of God's will. What steps should you take to complete your obedience to God?

Responding in Prayer Ask God for courage to give him your obedience.

6 / *1 Samuel 16*
The Lord Looks at the Heart

IN THE BOOK *Selling of the President,* author Joe McGinniss emphasized that in politics, image is everything. A candidate must exude confidence, charm and good looks. Never mind the real issues of the campaign. A broad smile, a warm handshake and the ability to look good on camera are much more important for selling the political product to the ultimate consumer—the registered voter. Israel's first king, Saul, was this sort of candidate—tall, handsome and impressive. Unfortunately, he was also foolish and disobedient. As Israel's second king is chosen, the Lord rejects worldly standards of leadership and selects David, a man after his own heart.

Warming Up to God How does a person's appearance affect your initial opinion of him or her?

Read 1 Samuel 16.

16

The LORD said to Samuel, "How long will you mourn for Saul, since I have rejected him as king over Israel? Fill your horn with oil and be on your way; I am sending you to Jesse of Bethlehem. I have chosen one of his sons to be king."

2But Samuel said, "How can I go? Saul will hear about it and kill me."

The LORD said, "Take a heifer with you and say, 'I have come to sacrifice to the LORD.' 3Invite Jesse to the sacrifice, and I will show you what to do. You are to anoint for me the one I indicate."

4Samuel did what the LORD said. When he arrived at Bethlehem, the elders of the town trembled when they met him. They asked, "Do you come in peace?"

5Samuel replied, "Yes, in peace; I have come to sacrifice to the LORD. Consecrate yourselves and come to the sacrifice with me." Then he consecrated Jesse and his sons and invited them to the sacrifice.

6When they arrived, Samuel saw Eliab and thought, "Surely the LORD's anointed stands here before the LORD."

7But the LORD said to Samuel, "Do not consider his appearance or his height, for I have rejected him. The LORD does not look at the things man looks at. Man looks at the outward appearance, but the LORD looks at the heart."

8Then Jesse called Abinadab and had him pass in front of Samuel. But Samuel said, "The LORD has not chosen this one either." 9Jesse then had Shammah pass by, but Samuel said, "Nor has the LORD chosen this one." 10Jesse had seven of his sons pass before Samuel, but Samuel said to him, "The LORD has not chosen these." 11So he asked Jesse, "Are these all the sons you have?"

"There is still the youngest," Jesse answered, "but he is tending the sheep."

Samuel said, "Send for him; we will not sit down[e] until he arrives."

12So he sent and had him brought in. He was ruddy, with a fine appearance and handsome features.

Then the LORD said, "Rise and anoint him; he is the one."

13So Samuel took the horn of oil and anointed him in the presence of his brothers, and from that day on the Spirit of the LORD came upon David in power. Samuel then went to Ramah.

14Now the Spirit of the LORD had departed from Saul, and an evil[f] spirit from the LORD tormented him.

15Saul's attendants said to him, "See, an evil spirit from God is tormenting you. 16Let our lord command his servants here to search for someone who can play the harp. He will play when the evil spirit from God comes upon you, and you will feel better."

17So Saul said to his attendants, "Find someone who plays well and bring him to me."

18One of the servants answered, "I have seen a son of Jesse of Bethlehem who knows how to play the harp. He is a brave man and a warrior. He speaks well and is a fine-looking man. And the LORD is with him."

19Then Saul sent messengers to Jesse and said, "Send me your son David, who is with the sheep." 20So Jesse took a donkey loaded with bread, a skin of wine and a young goat and sent them with his son David to Saul.

21David came to Saul and entered his service. Saul liked him very much, and David became one of his armor-bearers. 22Then Saul sent word to Jesse, saying, "Allow David to remain in my service, for I am pleased with him."

23Whenever the spirit from God came upon Saul, David would take his harp and play. Then relief would come to Saul; he would feel better, and the evil spirit would leave him.

[e] *11* Some Septuagint manuscripts; Hebrew *not gather around* [f] *14* Or *injurious;* also in verses 15, 16 and 23

Discovering the Word 1. What specific instructions does the Lord give Samuel for anointing a new king (vv. 1–3)? 2. Why did Samuel suppose that Eliab was the Lord's anointed (vv. 6–7; see 17:13)? 3. Why are outward qualities an unreliable way to judge a person (v. 7)? 4. If you had been given the job of finding the next king of Israel, why would David have been an unlikely choice? 5. In what sense was he also a good choice (vv. 14–23)?

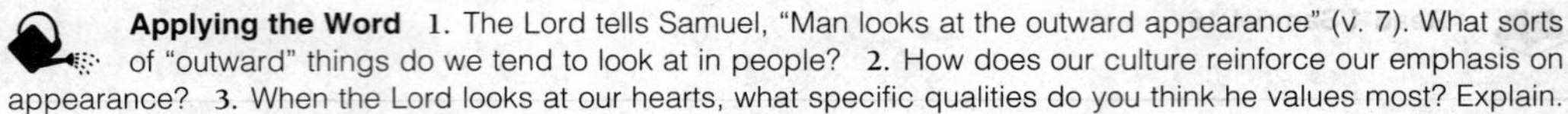

Applying the Word 1. The Lord tells Samuel, "Man looks at the outward appearance" (v. 7). What sorts of "outward" things do we tend to look at in people? 2. How does our culture reinforce our emphasis on appearance? 3. When the Lord looks at our hearts, what specific qualities do you think he values most? Explain.

Responding in Prayer Take time to pray, asking the Lord to develop these qualities within you.

7 / 1 Samuel 17
The Battle Is the Lord's

ONE OF THE myths of our culture is "If you set your mind to it, you can do anything." The heroes of that myth are self-made men and women, those who climb from obscurity to fame through sheer willpower and determination. The message is clear: victory goes to the strong, and the spoils of victory to those who are powerful. The Bible presents a very different message: " 'Not by might nor by power, but by my Spirit,' says the LORD Almighty" (Zec 4:6). In this chapter David confronts not only Goliath but also our myths of human adequacy.

Warming Up to God When you are faced with a challenge that seems beyond your abilities, how do you tend to respond?

Read 1 Samuel 17.

17 Now the Philistines gathered their
forces for war and assembled at So-
coh in Judah. They pitched camp at
at Ephes Dammim, between Socoh and Azekah.
2Saul and the Israelites assembled and camped in
the Valley of Elah and drew up their battle line to
meet the Philistines. 3The Philistines occupied
one hill and the Israelites another, with the valley
between them.

4A champion named Goliath, who was from
Gath, came out of the Philistine camp. He was
over nine feet[g] tall. 5He had a bronze helmet on
his head and wore a coat of scale armor of bronze
weighing five thousand shekels[h]; 6on his legs he
wore bronze greaves, and a bronze javelin was
slung on his back. 7His spear shaft was like a
weaver's rod, and its iron point weighed six hun-
dred shekels.[i] His shield bearer went ahead of
him.

8Goliath stood and shouted to the ranks of Is-
rael, "Why do you come out and line up for bat-
tle? Am I not a Philistine, and are you not the
servants of Saul? Choose a man and have him
come down to me. 9If he is able to fight and kill
me, we will become your subjects; but if I over-
come him and kill him, you will become our sub-
jects and serve us." 10Then the Philistine said,
"This day I defy the ranks of Israel! Give me a
man and let us fight each other." 11On hearing the
Philistine's words, Saul and all the Israelites were
dismayed and terrified.

12Now David was the son of an Ephrathite
named Jesse, who was from Bethlehem in Judah.
Jesse had eight sons, and in Saul's time he was old
and well advanced in years. 13Jesse's three oldest
sons had followed Saul to the war: The firstborn
was Eliab; the second, Abinadab; and the third,
Shammah. 14David was the youngest. The three
oldest followed Saul, 15but David went back and
forth from Saul to tend his father's sheep at Beth-
lehem.

16For forty days the Philistine came forward ev-
ery morning and evening and took his stand.

17Now Jesse said to his son David, "Take this
ephah[j] of roasted grain and these ten loaves of
bread for your brothers and hurry to their camp.
18Take along these ten cheeses to the commander
of their unit.[k] See how your brothers are and
bring back some assurance[l] from them. 19They

g4 Hebrew *was six cubits and a span* (about 3 meters) h5 That is, about 125 pounds (about 57 kilograms) i7 That is, about 15 pounds (about 7 kilograms) j17 That is, probably about 3/5 bushel (about 22 liters) k18 Hebrew *thousand* l18 Or *some token*; or *some pledge of spoils*

are with Saul and all the men of Israel in the Valley of Elah, fighting against the Philistines."

20Early in the morning David left the flock with a shepherd, loaded up and set out, as Jesse had directed. He reached the camp as the army was going out to its battle positions, shouting the war cry. 21Israel and the Philistines were drawing up their lines facing each other. 22David left his things with the keeper of supplies, ran to the battle lines and greeted his brothers. 23As he was talking with them, Goliath, the Philistine champion from Gath, stepped out from his lines and shouted his usual defiance, and David heard it. 24When the Israelites saw the man, they all ran from him in great fear.

25Now the Israelites had been saying, "Do you see how this man keeps coming out? He comes out to defy Israel. The king will give great wealth to the man who kills him. He will also give him his daughter in marriage and will exempt his father's family from taxes in Israel."

26David asked the men standing near him, "What will be done for the man who kills this Philistine and removes this disgrace from Israel? Who is this uncircumcised Philistine that he should defy the armies of the living God?"

27They repeated to him what they had been saying and told him, "This is what will be done for the man who kills him."

28When Eliab, David's oldest brother, heard him speaking with the men, he burned with anger at him and asked, "Why have you come down here? And with whom did you leave those few sheep in the desert? I know how conceited you are and how wicked your heart is; you came down only to watch the battle."

29"Now what have I done?" said David. "Can't I even speak?" 30He then turned away to someone else and brought up the same matter, and the men answered him as before. 31What David said was overheard and reported to Saul, and Saul sent for him.

32David said to Saul, "Let no one lose heart on account of this Philistine; your servant will go and fight him."

33Saul replied, "You are not able to go out against this Philistine and fight him; you are only a boy, and he has been a fighting man from his youth."

34But David said to Saul, "Your servant has been keeping his father's sheep. When a lion or a bear came and carried off a sheep from the flock, 35I went after it, struck it and rescued the sheep from its mouth. When it turned on me, I seized it by its hair, struck it and killed it. 36Your servant has killed both the lion and the bear; this uncircumcised Philistine will be like one of them, because he has defied the armies of the living God. 37The Lord who delivered me from the paw of the lion and the paw of the bear will deliver me from the hand of this Philistine."

Saul said to David, "Go, and the Lord be with you."

38Then Saul dressed David in his own tunic. He put a coat of armor on him and a bronze helmet on his head. 39David fastened on his sword over the tunic and tried walking around, because he was not used to them.

"I cannot go in these," he said to Saul, "because I am not used to them." So he took them off. 40Then he took his staff in his hand, chose five smooth stones from the stream, put them in the pouch of his shepherd's bag and, with his sling in his hand, approached the Philistine.

41Meanwhile, the Philistine, with his shield bearer in front of him, kept coming closer to David. 42He looked David over and saw that he was only a boy, ruddy and handsome, and he despised him. 43He said to David, "Am I a dog, that you come at me with sticks?" And the Philistine cursed David by his gods. 44"Come here," he said, "and I'll give your flesh to the birds of the air and the beasts of the field!"

45David said to the Philistine, "You come against me with sword and spear and javelin, but I come against you in the name of the Lord Almighty, the God of the armies of Israel, whom you have defied. 46This day the Lord will hand you over to me, and I'll strike you down and cut off your head. Today I will give the carcasses of the Philistine army to the birds of the air and the beasts of the earth, and the whole world will know that there is a God in Israel. 47All those gathered here will know that it is not by sword or spear that the Lord saves; for the battle is the Lord's, and he will give all of you into our hands."

48As the Philistine moved closer to attack him, David ran quickly toward the battle line to meet him. 49Reaching into his bag and taking out a stone, he slung it and struck the Philistine on the forehead. The stone sank into his forehead, and he fell facedown on the ground.

50So David triumphed over the Philistine with a

sling and a stone; without a sword in his hand he
struck down the Philistine and killed him.
51David ran and stood over him. He took hold
of the Philistine's sword and drew it from the
scabbard. After he killed him, he cut off his head
with the sword.
When the Philistines saw that their hero was
dead, they turned and ran. 52Then the men of
Israel and Judah surged forward with a shout and
pursued the Philistines to the entrance of Gath[m]
and to the gates of Ekron. Their dead were strewn
along the Shaaraim road to Gath and Ekron.
53When the Israelites returned from chasing the
Philistines, they plundered their camp. 54David
took the Philistine's head and brought it to Jeru-
salem, and he put the Philistine's weapons in his
own tent.
55As Saul watched David going out to meet the
Philistine, he said to Abner, commander of the
army, "Abner, whose son is that young man?"
Abner replied, "As surely as you live, O king, I
don't know."
56The king said, "Find out whose son this
young man is."
57As soon as David returned from killing the
Philistine, Abner took him and brought him be-
fore Saul, with David still holding the Philistine's
head.
58"Whose son are you, young man?" Saul asked
him.
David said, "I am the son of your servant Jesse
of Bethlehem."

m52 Some Septuagint manuscripts; Hebrew *a valley*

Discovering the Word 1. Humanly speaking, why were the Israelites justly terrified of Goliath (vv. 1–11)? 2. As David reaches the army camp, what does he learn about their situation (vv. 12–27)? 3. Why do you think David's brother is so harsh with him (vv. 28–30)? 4. From a human standpoint, why was David an unlikely choice as the champion of Israel (vv. 15, 33, 38–40)? 5. What impresses you about the conversation and battle between David and Goliath (vv. 41–49)?

Applying the Word 1. Normally, we select people who are humanly qualified to do a job. Likewise, we normally take on responsibilities for which we feel qualified. Does faith remove the need for human qualifications? Why or why not? 2. When is it proper to trust God to overcome our deficiencies? 3. What "Goliaths" are you currently facing—either at work or home or in your personal life?

Responding in Prayer Praise God for the past spiritual victories he's given you. Let those victories be a source of encouragement.

8 / *1 Samuel 18*

Bitterness

ONE OF THE darkest times in my life was when I allowed bitterness to root and grow in my heart. I was hurt. I refused to forgive or to risk being hurt again. My whole person was becoming engulfed by this monstrous plant that was growing inside of me. Others were defiled by it. If I had continued to disobey God in this way, I would have been destroyed.

Saul, ancient Israel's first king, knew those feelings. They were directed toward David, a young man from the hill country. David had changed the course of a forty-day stand-off with the Philistine army by singlehandedly killing their giant leader. Suddenly, all the people were praising this boy from the sheep pastures. Rumor had it that David would someday be king.

Warming Up to God How do you usually respond when you are afraid that someone or something important to you will be taken away?

Read 1 Samuel 18.

18

After David had finished talking with Saul, Jonathan became one in spirit with David, and he loved him as himself. 2From that day Saul kept David with him and did not let him return to his father's house. 3And Jonathan made a covenant with David because he loved him as himself. 4Jonathan took off the robe he was wearing and gave it to David, along with his tunic, and even his sword, his bow and his belt.

5Whatever Saul sent him to do, David did it so successfully[n] that Saul gave him a high rank in the army. This pleased all the people, and Saul's officers as well.

6When the men were returning home after David had killed the Philistine, the women came out from all the towns of Israel to meet King Saul with singing and dancing, with joyful songs and with tambourines and lutes. 7As they danced, they sang:

"Saul has slain his thousands,
  and David his tens of thousands."

8Saul was very angry; this refrain galled him. "They have credited David with tens of thousands," he thought, "but me with only thousands. What more can he get but the kingdom?" 9And from that time on Saul kept a jealous eye on David.

10The next day an evil[o] spirit from God came forcefully upon Saul. He was prophesying in his house, while David was playing the harp, as he usually did. Saul had a spear in his hand 11and he hurled it, saying to himself, "I'll pin David to the wall." But David eluded him twice.

12Saul was afraid of David, because the LORD was with David but had left Saul. 13So he sent David away from him and gave him command over a thousand men, and David led the troops in their campaigns. 14In everything he did he had great success,[p] because the LORD was with him. 15When Saul saw how successful[q] he was, he was afraid of him. 16But all Israel and Judah loved David, because he led them in their campaigns.

17Saul said to David, "Here is my older daughter Merab. I will give her to you in marriage; only serve me bravely and fight the battles of the LORD." For Saul said to himself, "I will not raise a hand against him. Let the Philistines do that!"

18But David said to Saul, "Who am I, and what is my family or my father's clan in Israel, that I should become the king's son-in-law?" 19So[r] when the time came for Merab, Saul's daughter, to be given to David, she was given in marriage to Adriel of Meholah.

20Now Saul's daughter Michal was in love with David, and when they told Saul about it, he was pleased. 21"I will give her to him," he thought, "so that she may be a snare to him and so that the hand of the Philistines may be against him." So Saul said to David, "Now you have a second opportunity to become my son-in-law."

22Then Saul ordered his attendants: "Speak to David privately and say, 'Look, the king is pleased with you, and his attendants all like you; now become his son-in-law.' "

23They repeated these words to David. But David said, "Do you think it is a small matter to become the king's son-in-law? I'm only a poor man and little known."

24When Saul's servants told him what David had said, 25Saul replied, "Say to David, 'The king wants no other price for the bride than a hundred Philistine foreskins, to take revenge on his enemies.' " Saul's plan was to have David fall by the hands of the Philistines.

26When the attendants told David these things, he was pleased to become the king's son-in-law. So before the allotted time elapsed, 27David and his men went out and killed two hundred Philistines. He brought their foreskins and presented the full number to the king so that he might become the king's son-in-law. Then Saul gave him his daughter Michal in marriage.

28When Saul realized that the LORD was with David and that his daughter Michal loved David, 29Saul became still more afraid of him, and he remained his enemy the rest of his days.

30The Philistine commanders continued to go out to battle, and as often as they did, David met with more success[s] than the rest of Saul's officers, and his name became well known.

[n]5 Or *wisely* [o]10 Or *injurious* [p]14 Or *he was very wise*
[q]15 Or *wise* [r]19 Or *However,* [s]30 Or *David acted more wisely*

Discovering the Word 1. What causes can you find for Saul's hostile feelings? 2. Often, if not always, fear is behind anger. What specifically was Saul afraid of (vv. 8, 12, 15, 28)? 3. How was Saul affected by the bitterness that he allowed to grow within himself? 4. What do you think is the difference between anger and bitterness? 5. What evidence is there that the problem became not only an emotional battle but a spiritual battle (vv. 10, 12, 28)? 6. What warnings do we get from this passage about the destructive nature of bitterness?

Applying the Word 1. Think about a time when you were bitter. What were you afraid of? 2. How was your relationship with others affected? 3. How was your relationship with God affected?

Responding in Prayer Ask God to help you recognize the fears and/or anger in you that could lead to bitterness. Ask him to make you sensitive to those fears in others.

1 Samuel 19

19 Saul told his son Jonathan and all the attendants to kill David. But Jonathan was very fond of David 2and warned him, "My father Saul is looking for a chance to kill you. Be on your guard tomorrow morning; go into hiding and stay there. 3I will go out and stand with my father in the field where you are. I'll speak to him about you and will tell you what I find out."

4Jonathan spoke well of David to Saul his father and said to him, "Let not the king do wrong to his servant David; he has not wronged you, and what he has done has benefited you greatly. 5He took his life in his hands when he killed the Philistine. The LORD won a great victory for all Israel, and you saw it and were glad. Why then would you do wrong to an innocent man like David by killing him for no reason?"

6Saul listened to Jonathan and took this oath: "As surely as the LORD lives, David will not be put to death."

7So Jonathan called David and told him the whole conversation. He brought him to Saul, and David was with Saul as before.

8Once more war broke out, and David went out and fought the Philistines. He struck them with such force that they fled before him.

9But an evil[t] spirit from the LORD came upon Saul as he was sitting in his house with his spear in his hand. While David was playing the harp, 10Saul tried to pin him to the wall with his spear, but David eluded him as Saul drove the spear into the wall. That night David made good his escape.

11Saul sent men to David's house to watch it and to kill him in the morning. But Michal, David's wife, warned him, "If you don't run for your life tonight, tomorrow you'll be killed." 12So Michal let David down through a window, and he fled and escaped. 13Then Michal took an idol[u] and laid it on the bed, covering it with a garment and putting some goats' hair at the head.

14When Saul sent the men to capture David, Michal said, "He is ill."

15Then Saul sent the men back to see David and told them, "Bring him up to me in his bed so that I may kill him." 16But when the men entered, there was the idol in the bed, and at the head was some goats' hair.

17Saul said to Michal, "Why did you deceive me like this and send my enemy away so that he escaped?"

Michal told him, "He said to me, 'Let me get away. Why should I kill you?' "

18When David had fled and made his escape, he went to Samuel at Ramah and told him all that Saul had done to him. Then he and Samuel went to Naioth and stayed there. 19Word came to Saul: "David is in Naioth at Ramah"; 20so he sent men to capture him. But when they saw a group of prophets prophesying, with Samuel standing there as their leader, the Spirit of God came upon Saul's men and they also prophesied. 21Saul was told about it, and he sent more men, and they prophesied too. Saul sent men a third time, and they also prophesied. 22Finally, he himself left for Ramah and went to the great cistern at Secu. And he asked, "Where are Samuel and David?"

"Over in Naioth at Ramah," they said.

23So Saul went to Naioth at Ramah. But the Spirit of God came even upon him, and he walked along prophesying until he came to Naioth. 24He stripped off his robes and also prophesied in Samuel's presence. He lay that way all that day and night. This is why people say, "Is Saul also among the prophets?"

t9 Or *injurious* u13 Hebrew *teraphim*; also in verse 16

9 / *1 Samuel 20*
True Friendship

WHEN I WAS growing up, I had a friend named David Miller. David and I met in grammar school. In the third grade we were in Cub Scouts together. In the fourth grade we both had the same girlfriend. In sixth and seventh grade we went to camp together. Our relationship continued through high school, then we lost touch with each other, and later I moved to another city.

After many years, I went home for a visit and decided to stop by and see David. He was living in the same house—now with his wife and children. After the initial shock and joy at seeing each other, he invited me in. As I stepped inside, I felt as though I was stepping back in time. All the childhood memories associated with his house flooded back into my mind. What good friends we'd been!

In this study we will explore the strong relationship between David and Jonathan. It helps us see and appreciate the qualities of true friendship.

Warming Up to God What qualities do you appreciate most in a friend, and why?

Read 1 Samuel 20.

20 Then David fled from Naioth at Ramah and went to Jonathan and asked, "What have I done? What is my crime? How have I wronged your father, that he is trying to take my life?"

2"Never!" Jonathan replied. "You are not going to die! Look, my father doesn't do anything, great or small, without confiding in me. Why would he hide this from me? It's not so!"

3But David took an oath and said, "Your father knows very well that I have found favor in your eyes, and he has said to himself, 'Jonathan must not know this or he will be grieved.' Yet as surely as the LORD lives and as you live, there is only a step between me and death."

4Jonathan said to David, "Whatever you want me to do, I'll do for you."

5So David said, "Look, tomorrow is the New Moon festival, and I am supposed to dine with the king; but let me go and hide in the field until the evening of the day after tomorrow. 6If your father misses me at all, tell him, 'David earnestly asked my permission to hurry to Bethlehem, his hometown, because an annual sacrifice is being made there for his whole clan.' 7If he says, 'Very well,' then your servant is safe. But if he loses his temper, you can be sure that he is determined to harm me. 8As for you, show kindness to your servant, for you have brought him into a covenant with you before the LORD. If I am guilty, then kill me yourself! Why hand me over to your father?"

9"Never!" Jonathan said. "If I had the least inkling that my father was determined to harm you, wouldn't I tell you?"

10David asked, "Who will tell me if your father answers you harshly?"

11"Come," Jonathan said, "let's go out into the field." So they went there together.

12Then Jonathan said to David: "By the LORD, the God of Israel, I will surely sound out my father by this time the day after tomorrow! If he is favorably disposed toward you, will I not send you word and let you know? 13But if my father is inclined to harm you, may the LORD deal with me, be it ever so severely, if I do not let you know and send you away safely. May the LORD be with you as he has been with my father. 14But show me unfailing kindness like that of the LORD as long as I live, so that I may not be killed, 15and do not ever cut off your kindness from my family—not even when the LORD has cut off every one of David's enemies from the face of the earth."

16So Jonathan made a covenant with the house of David, saying, "May the LORD call David's enemies to account." 17And Jonathan had David reaffirm his oath out of love for him, because he loved him as he loved himself.

18Then Jonathan said to David: "Tomorrow is the New Moon festival. You will be missed, because your seat will be empty. 19The day after tomorrow, toward evening, go to the place where you hid when this trouble began, and wait by the stone Ezel. 20I will shoot three arrows to the side of it, as though I were shooting at a target. 21Then I will send a boy and say, 'Go, find the arrows.' If

I say to him, 'Look, the arrows are on this side of you; bring them here,' then come, because, as surely as the LORD lives, you are safe; there is no danger. [22]But if I say to the boy, 'Look, the arrows are beyond you,' then you must go, because the LORD has sent you away. [23]And about the matter you and I discussed—remember, the LORD is witness between you and me forever."

[24]So David hid in the field, and when the New Moon festival came, the king sat down to eat. [25]He sat in his customary place by the wall, opposite Jonathan,[v] and Abner sat next to Saul, but David's place was empty. [26]Saul said nothing that day, for he thought, "Something must have happened to David to make him ceremonially unclean—surely he is unclean." [27]But the next day, the second day of the month, David's place was empty again. Then Saul said to his son Jonathan, "Why hasn't the son of Jesse come to the meal, either yesterday or today?"

[28]Jonathan answered, "David earnestly asked me for permission to go to Bethlehem. [29]He said, 'Let me go, because our family is observing a sacrifice in the town and my brother has ordered me to be there. If I have found favor in your eyes, let me get away to see my brothers.' That is why he has not come to the king's table."

[30]Saul's anger flared up at Jonathan and he said to him, "You son of a perverse and rebellious woman! Don't I know that you have sided with the son of Jesse to your own shame and to the shame of the mother who bore you? [31]As long as the son of Jesse lives on this earth, neither you nor your kingdom will be established. Now send and bring him to me, for he must die!"

[32]"Why should he be put to death? What has he done?" Jonathan asked his father. [33]But Saul hurled his spear at him to kill him. Then Jonathan knew that his father intended to kill David.

[34]Jonathan got up from the table in fierce anger; on that second day of the month he did not eat, because he was grieved at his father's shameful treatment of David.

[35]In the morning Jonathan went out to the field for his meeting with David. He had a small boy with him, [36]and he said to the boy, "Run and find the arrows I shoot." As the boy ran, he shot an arrow beyond him. [37]When the boy came to the place where Jonathan's arrow had fallen, Jonathan called out after him, "Isn't the arrow beyond you?" [38]Then he shouted, "Hurry! Go quickly! Don't stop!" The boy picked up the arrow and returned to his master. [39](The boy knew nothing of all this; only Jonathan and David knew.) [40]Then Jonathan gave his weapons to the boy and said, "Go, carry them back to town."

[41]After the boy had gone, David got up from the south side ⌞of the stone⌟ and bowed down before Jonathan three times, with his face to the ground. Then they kissed each other and wept together—but David wept the most.

[42]Jonathan said to David, "Go in peace, for we have sworn friendship with each other in the name of the LORD, saying, 'The LORD is witness between you and me, and between your descendants and my descendants forever.'" Then David left, and Jonathan went back to the town.

[v]25 Septuagint; Hebrew *wall. Jonathan arose*

Discovering the Word 1. In 1 Samuel 18:1–4 David and Jonathan make a covenant with one another. This is put to the test when Saul tries to kill David (chapter 19). What impresses you about Jonathan's and David's love for each other? 2. How does their love express itself in their commitment to each other? 3. How does Jonathan's experience with Saul demonstrate some of the cost of friendship (vv. 30–42)? 4. What do we learn about the level of intimacy between Jonathan and David (vv. 41–42)?

Applying the Word 1. What factors enhance or inhibit intimacy in a relationship? 2. Think of your closest friend. If you could pick one area in which you'd like your friendship to be more like Jonathan's and David's, what would it be? 3. What specific steps can you take to achieve that goal?

Responding in Prayer Praise God for the friends he has given you. Ask him to help you show his love to them.

1 Samuel 21—23

21 David went to Nob, to Ahimelech the priest. Ahimelech trembled when he met him, and asked, "Why are you alone? Why is no one with you?"

2 David answered Ahimelech the priest, "The king charged me with a certain matter and said to me, 'No one is to know anything about your mission and your instructions.' As for my men, I have told them to meet me at a certain place. 3 Now then, what do you have on hand? Give me five loaves of bread, or whatever you can find."

4 But the priest answered David, "I don't have any ordinary bread on hand; however, there is some consecrated bread here—provided the men have kept themselves from women."

5 David replied, "Indeed women have been kept from us, as usual whenever[w] I set out. The men's things[x] are holy even on missions that are not holy. How much more so today!" 6 So the priest gave him the consecrated bread, since there was no bread there except the bread of the Presence that had been removed from before the LORD and replaced by hot bread on the day it was taken away.

7 Now one of Saul's servants was there that day, detained before the LORD; he was Doeg the Edomite, Saul's head shepherd.

8 David asked Ahimelech, "Don't you have a spear or a sword here? I haven't brought my sword or any other weapon, because the king's business was urgent."

9 The priest replied, "The sword of Goliath the Philistine, whom you killed in the Valley of Elah, is here; it is wrapped in a cloth behind the ephod. If you want it, take it; there is no sword here but that one."

David said, "There is none like it; give it to me."

10 That day David fled from Saul and went to Achish king of Gath. 11 But the servants of Achish said to him, "Isn't this David, the king of the land? Isn't he the one they sing about in their dances:

" 'Saul has slain his thousands,
and David his tens of thousands'?"

12 David took these words to heart and was very much afraid of Achish king of Gath. 13 So he pretended to be insane in their presence; and while he was in their hands he acted like a madman, making marks on the doors of the gate and letting saliva run down his beard.

14 Achish said to his servants, "Look at the man! He is insane! Why bring him to me? 15 Am I so short of madmen that you have to bring this fellow here to carry on like this in front of me? Must this man come into my house?"

22 David left Gath and escaped to the cave of Adullam. When his brothers and his father's household heard about it, they went down to him there. 2 All those who were in distress or in debt or discontented gathered around him, and he became their leader. About four hundred men were with him.

3 From there David went to Mizpah in Moab and said to the king of Moab, "Would you let my father and mother come and stay with you until I learn what God will do for me?" 4 So he left them with the king of Moab, and they stayed with him as long as David was in the stronghold.

5 But the prophet Gad said to David, "Do not stay in the stronghold. Go into the land of Judah." So David left and went to the forest of Hereth.

6 Now Saul heard that David and his men had been discovered. And Saul, spear in hand, was seated under the tamarisk tree on the hill at Gibeah, with all his officials standing around him. 7 Saul said to them, "Listen, men of Benjamin! Will the son of Jesse give all of you fields and vineyards? Will he make all of you commanders of thousands and commanders of hundreds? 8 Is that why you have all conspired against me? No one tells me when my son makes a covenant with the son of Jesse. None of you is concerned about me or tells me that my son has incited my servant to lie in wait for me, as he does today."

9 But Doeg the Edomite, who was standing with Saul's officials, said, "I saw the son of Jesse come to Ahimelech son of Ahitub at Nob. 10 Ahimelech inquired of the LORD for him; he also gave him provisions and the sword of Goliath the Philistine."

11 Then the king sent for the priest Ahimelech son of Ahitub and his father's whole family, who were the priests at Nob, and they all came to the king. 12 Saul said, "Listen now, son of Ahitub."

[w]5 Or *from us in the past few days since* [x]5 Or *bodies*

"Yes, my lord," he answered.

[13]Saul said to him, "Why have you conspired against me, you and the son of Jesse, giving him bread and a sword and inquiring of God for him, so that he has rebelled against me and lies in wait for me, as he does today?"

[14]Ahimelech answered the king, "Who of all your servants is as loyal as David, the king's son-in-law, captain of your bodyguard and highly respected in your household? [15]Was that day the first time I inquired of God for him? Of course not! Let not the king accuse your servant or any of his father's family, for your servant knows nothing at all about this whole affair."

[16]But the king said, "You will surely die, Ahimelech, you and your father's whole family."

[17]Then the king ordered the guards at his side: "Turn and kill the priests of the LORD, because they too have sided with David. They knew he was fleeing, yet they did not tell me."

But the king's officials were not willing to raise a hand to strike the priests of the LORD.

[18]The king then ordered Doeg, "You turn and strike down the priests." So Doeg the Edomite turned and struck them down. That day he killed eighty-five men who wore the linen ephod. [19]He also put to the sword Nob, the town of the priests, with its men and women, its children and infants, and its cattle, donkeys and sheep.

[20]But Abiathar, a son of Ahimelech son of Ahitub, escaped and fled to join David. [21]He told David that Saul had killed the priests of the LORD. [22]Then David said to Abiathar: "That day, when Doeg the Edomite was there, I knew he would be sure to tell Saul. I am responsible for the death of your father's whole family. [23]Stay with me; don't be afraid; the man who is seeking your life is seeking mine also. You will be safe with me."

23 When David was told, "Look, the Philistines are fighting against Keilah and are looting the threshing floors," [2]he inquired of the LORD, saying, "Shall I go and attack these Philistines?"

The LORD answered him, "Go, attack the Philistines and save Keilah."

[3]But David's men said to him, "Here in Judah we are afraid. How much more, then, if we go to Keilah against the Philistine forces!"

[4]Once again David inquired of the LORD, and the LORD answered him, "Go down to Keilah, for I am going to give the Philistines into your hand." [5]So David and his men went to Keilah, fought the Philistines and carried off their livestock. He inflicted heavy losses on the Philistines and saved the people of Keilah. [6](Now Abiathar son of Ahimelech had brought the ephod down with him when he fled to David at Keilah.)

[7]Saul was told that David had gone to Keilah, and he said, "God has handed him over to me, for David has imprisoned himself by entering a town with gates and bars." [8]And Saul called up all his forces for battle, to go down to Keilah to besiege David and his men.

[9]When David learned that Saul was plotting against him, he said to Abiathar the priest, "Bring the ephod." [10]David said, "O LORD, God of Israel, your servant has heard definitely that Saul plans to come to Keilah and destroy the town on account of me. [11]Will the citizens of Keilah surrender me to him? Will Saul come down, as your servant has heard? O LORD, God of Israel, tell your servant."

And the LORD said, "He will."

[12]Again David asked, "Will the citizens of Keilah surrender me and my men to Saul?"

And the LORD said, "They will."

[13]So David and his men, about six hundred in number, left Keilah and kept moving from place to place. When Saul was told that David had escaped from Keilah, he did not go there.

[14]David stayed in the desert strongholds and in the hills of the Desert of Ziph. Day after day Saul searched for him, but God did not give David into his hands.

[15]While David was at Horesh in the Desert of Ziph, he learned that Saul had come out to take his life. [16]And Saul's son Jonathan went to David at Horesh and helped him find strength in God. [17]"Don't be afraid," he said. "My father Saul will not lay a hand on you. You will be king over Israel, and I will be second to you. Even my father Saul knows this." [18]The two of them made a covenant before the LORD. Then Jonathan went home, but David remained at Horesh.

[19]The Ziphites went up to Saul at Gibeah and said, "Is not David hiding among us in the strongholds at Horesh, on the hill of Hakilah, south of Jeshimon? [20]Now, O king, come down whenever it pleases you to do so, and we will be responsible for handing him over to the king."

[21]Saul replied, "The LORD bless you for your concern for me. [22]Go and make further preparation. Find out where David usually goes and who has seen him there. They tell me he is very crafty.

23Find out about all the hiding places he uses and
come back to me with definite information.[y]
Then I will go with you; if he is in the area, I will
track him down among all the clans of Judah."
24So they set out and went to Ziph ahead of
Saul. Now David and his men were in the Desert
of Maon, in the Arabah south of Jeshimon. 25Saul
and his men began the search, and when David
was told about it, he went down to the rock and
stayed in the Desert of Maon. When Saul heard
this, he went into the Desert of Maon in pursuit
of David.
26Saul was going along one side of the moun-
tain, and David and his men were on the other
side, hurrying to get away from Saul. As Saul and
his forces were closing in on David and his men
to capture them, 27a messenger came to Saul, say-
ing, "Come quickly! The Philistines are raiding
the land." 28Then Saul broke off his pursuit of
David and went to meet the Philistines. That is
why they call this place Sela Hammahlekoth.[z]
29And David went up from there and lived in the
strongholds of En Gedi.

[y]23 Or *me at Nacon* [z]28 *Sela Hammahlekoth* means *rock of parting.*

10 / *1 Samuel 24*
A Matter of Conscience

HOW DO WE determine God's will? Do we look to circumstances? the counsel of friends? the words of Scripture? In 1 Samuel 24 everything seems to indicate that David should kill Saul and take his place on the throne of Israel. Yet David rejects conventional wisdom and uses a different method for deciding what is right. His attitude should cause us to reexamine our own notions about guidance.

Warming Up to God As you begin this quiet time, consider in what area of your life you need God's guidance. Ask God to use this study to direct you.

Read 1 Samuel 24.

24 After Saul returned from pursuing
the Philistines, he was told, "David
is in the Desert of En Gedi." 2So
Saul took three thousand chosen men from all
Israel and set out to look for David and his men
near the Crags of the Wild Goats.
3He came to the sheep pens along the way; a
cave was there, and Saul went in to relieve him-
self. David and his men were far back in the cave.
4The men said, "This is the day the LORD spoke of
when he said[a] to you, 'I will give your enemy
into your hands for you to deal with as you
wish.' " Then David crept up unnoticed and cut
off a corner of Saul's robe.
5Afterward, David was conscience-stricken
for having cut off a corner of his robe. 6He
said to his men, "The LORD forbid that I should
do such a thing to my master, the LORD's anoint-
ed, or lift my hand against him; for he is the
anointed of the LORD." 7With these words David
rebuked his men and did not allow them to
attack Saul. And Saul left the cave and went his
way.
8Then David went out of the cave and called
out to Saul, "My lord the king!" When Saul
looked behind him, David bowed down and pros-
trated himself with his face to the ground. 9He
said to Saul, "Why do you listen when men say,
'David is bent on harming you'? 10This day you
have seen with your own eyes how the LORD deliv-
ered you into my hands in the cave. Some urged
me to kill you, but I spared you; I said, 'I will not
lift my hand against my master, because he is the
LORD's anointed.' 11See, my father, look at this
piece of your robe in my hand! I cut off the cor-
ner of your robe but did not kill you. Now under-
stand and recognize that I am not guilty of
wrongdoing or rebellion. I have not wronged you,
but you are hunting me down to take my life.
12May the LORD judge between you and me. And

[a]4 Or *"Today the LORD is saying*

may the LORD avenge the wrongs you have done to me, but my hand will not touch you. 13As the old saying goes, 'From evildoers come evil deeds,' so my hand will not touch you.

14"Against whom has the king of Israel come out? Whom are you pursuing? A dead dog? A flea? 15May the LORD be our judge and decide between us. May he consider my cause and uphold it; may he vindicate me by delivering me from your hand."

16When David finished saying this, Saul asked, "Is that your voice, David my son?" And he wept aloud. 17"You are more righteous than I," he said. "You have treated me well, but I have treated you badly. 18You have just now told me of the good you did to me; the LORD delivered me into your hands, but you did not kill me. 19When a man finds his enemy, does he let him get away unharmed? May the LORD reward you well for the way you treated me today. 20I know that you will surely be king and that the kingdom of Israel will be established in your hands. 21Now swear to me by the LORD that you will not cut off my descendants or wipe out my name from my father's family."

22So David gave his oath to Saul. Then Saul returned home, but David and his men went up to the stronghold.

Discovering the Word 1. What factors might have convinced David that it was God's will for him to kill Saul (vv. 1–7)? 2. Why do you think David places such importance on respecting the Lord's anointed (vv. 6, 10)? 3. What arguments does David use to convince Saul of his innocence (vv. 8–15)? 4. How does Saul respond to David's words (vv. 16–22)? 5. What do David's actions force Saul to conclude about David?

Applying the Word 1. We often rely on circumstances and the counsel of friends when making important decisions. To what extent are these reliable guides? 2. Is it ever right to go against conscience in a small area for the sake of a supposedly greater good? Explain. 3. How can we know when to take matters into our own hands and when to leave them in God's hands?

Responding in Prayer Ask God to give you wisdom in the area you are struggling with. Ask him to show you how to take action—or wait on him.

11 / *1 Samuel 25*
Secure in the Lord

IN THE TV series *The Honeymooners* Ralph Cramden used to threaten to knock his wife clear to the moon. "One of these days, Alice, *bang . . . zoom!*" We all give similar threats at one time or another: "I'll get you for this!" "You'll be sorry you ever treated me like that!" "You'll wish you had never been born!" When people mistreat us, we instinctively want revenge. We want to get even, to show them how it feels. In 1 Samuel 25 David is insulted by a man named Nabal. David's response gives us both a positive and negative example of how we should respond to those who mistreat us.

Warming Up to God How have you felt mistreated by others this week?

Read 1 Samuel 25.

25 Now Samuel died, and all Israel assembled and mourned for him; and they buried him at his home in Ramah.

Then David moved down into the Desert of Maon.[b] 2A certain man in Maon, who had property there at Carmel, was very wealthy. He had a thousand goats and three thousand sheep, which he was shearing in Carmel. 3His name was Nabal and his wife's name was Abigail. She was an intelligent and beautiful woman, but her husband, a Calebite, was surly and mean in his dealings.

4While David was in the desert, he heard that

[b]1 Some Septuagint manuscripts; Hebrew *Paran*

Nabal was shearing sheep. 5So he sent ten young men and said to them, "Go up to Nabal at Carmel and greet him in my name. 6Say to him: 'Long life to you! Good health to you and your household! And good health to all that is yours!

7" 'Now I hear that it is sheep-shearing time. When your shepherds were with us, we did not mistreat them, and the whole time they were at Carmel nothing of theirs was missing. 8Ask your own servants and they will tell you. Therefore be favorable toward my young men, since we come at a festive time. Please give your servants and your son David whatever you can find for them.' "

9When David's men arrived, they gave Nabal this message in David's name. Then they waited.

10Nabal answered David's servants, "Who is this David? Who is this son of Jesse? Many servants are breaking away from their masters these days. 11Why should I take my bread and water, and the meat I have slaughtered for my shearers, and give it to men coming from who knows where?"

12David's men turned around and went back. When they arrived, they reported every word. 13David said to his men, "Put on your swords!" So they put on their swords, and David put on his. About four hundred men went up with David, while two hundred stayed with the supplies.

14One of the servants told Nabal's wife Abigail: "David sent messengers from the desert to give our master his greetings, but he hurled insults at them. 15Yet these men were very good to us. They did not mistreat us, and the whole time we were out in the fields near them nothing was missing. 16Night and day they were a wall around us all the time we were herding our sheep near them. 17Now think it over and see what you can do, because disaster is hanging over our master and his whole household. He is such a wicked man that no one can talk to him."

18Abigail lost no time. She took two hundred loaves of bread, two skins of wine, five dressed sheep, five seahs[c] of roasted grain, a hundred cakes of raisins and two hundred cakes of pressed figs, and loaded them on donkeys. 19Then she told her servants, "Go on ahead; I'll follow you." But she did not tell her husband Nabal.

20As she came riding her donkey into a mountain ravine, there were David and his men descending toward her, and she met them. 21David had just said, "It's been useless—all my watching over this fellow's property in the desert so that nothing of his was missing. He has paid me back evil for good. 22May God deal with David,[d] be it ever so severely, if by morning I leave alive one male of all who belong to him!"

23When Abigail saw David, she quickly got off her donkey and bowed down before David with her face to the ground. 24She fell at his feet and said: "My lord, let the blame be on me alone. Please let your servant speak to you; hear what your servant has to say. 25May my lord pay no attention to that wicked man Nabal. He is just like his name—his name is Fool, and folly goes with him. But as for me, your servant, I did not see the men my master sent.

26"Now since the LORD has kept you, my master, from bloodshed and from avenging yourself with your own hands, as surely as the LORD lives and as you live, may your enemies and all who intend to harm my master be like Nabal. 27And let this gift, which your servant has brought to my master, be given to the men who follow you. 28Please forgive your servant's offense, for the LORD will certainly make a lasting dynasty for my master, because he fights the LORD's battles. Let no wrongdoing be found in you as long as you live. 29Even though someone is pursuing you to take your life, the life of my master will be bound securely in the bundle of the living by the LORD your God. But the lives of your enemies he will hurl away as from the pocket of a sling. 30When the LORD has done for my master every good thing he promised concerning him and has appointed him leader over Israel, 31my master will not have on his conscience the staggering burden of needless bloodshed or of having avenged himself. And when the LORD has brought my master success, remember your servant."

32David said to Abigail, "Praise be to the LORD, the God of Israel, who has sent you today to meet me. 33May you be blessed for your good judgment and for keeping me from bloodshed this day and from avenging myself with my own hands. 34Otherwise, as surely as the LORD, the God of Israel, lives, who has kept me from harming you, if you had not come quickly to meet me, not one male belonging to Nabal would have been left alive by daybreak."

35Then David accepted from her hand what she had brought him and said, "Go home in peace.

[c] *18* That is, probably about a bushel (about 37 liters) [d] *22* Some Septuagint manuscripts; Hebrew *with David's enemies*

I have heard your words and granted your re-
quest."
36When Abigail went to Nabal, he was in the
house holding a banquet like that of a king. He
was in high spirits and very drunk. So she told
him nothing until daybreak. 37Then in the morn-
ing, when Nabal was sober, his wife told him all
these things, and his heart failed him and he be-
came like a stone. 38About ten days later, the LORD
struck Nabal and he died.
39When David heard that Nabal was dead, he
said, "Praise be to the LORD, who has upheld my
cause against Nabal for treating me with con-
tempt. He has kept his servant from doing wrong
and has brought Nabal's wrongdoing down on his
own head."
Then David sent word to Abigail, asking her to
become his wife. 40His servants went to Carmel
and said to Abigail, "David has sent us to you to
take you to become his wife."
41She bowed down with her face to the ground
and said, "Here is your maidservant, ready to
serve you and wash the feet of my master's ser-
vants." 42Abigail quickly got on a donkey and,
attended by her five maids, went with David's
messengers and became his wife. 43David had also
married Ahinoam of Jezreel, and they both were
his wives. 44But Saul had given his daughter Mi-
chal, David's wife, to Paltiel[e] son of Laish, who
was from Gallim.

[e]44 Hebrew *Palti*, a variant of *Paltiel*

Discovering the Word 1. What does the author tell us about the two new characters in this drama (vv. 2–3)? 2. Why is David so offended by Nabal's response to his request (vv. 4–13, 21–22)? 3. Even if David's offense is justified, how would you evaluate his plan to get even with Nabal (vv. 13, 34)? 4. What impresses you about Abigail's response when she finds out what has happened (vv. 14–32)? 5. The events in this chapter are deliberately sandwiched between two accounts of David sparing Saul's life. How is David's relationship with Nabal similar to his relationship with Saul?

Applying the Word 1. What methods do we sometimes use to "get even" with those who mistreat us? 2. Think of someone who has recently mistreated you. How can this study affect your attitude and actions toward that person?

Responding in Prayer Pray for your enemies.

12 / *1 Samuel 26*
Self-Control

YOU'RE ON A diet. As you pick up a magazine, you turn innocently to the food section. "After all," you say to yourself, "pictures aren't fattening." As you pore over every page, each dessert looks better than the last one. You decide to read in the kitchen because "the light is better." After a few minutes, you begin thinking about the ice cream in the freezer. A model of restraint, you decide to get only one spoonful—well, two at the most. Pretty soon you've eaten the whole quart! Sound familiar? We all struggle with self-control. And temptations often blind our better judgment. In 1 Samuel 26 David faces the powerful temptation of choosing between self-gratification and self-control. His response can encourage us in our struggles.

Warming Up to God In what area of your life would you like to have greater self-control?

Read 1 Samuel 26.

26

The Ziphites went to Saul at Gibeah and said, "Is not David hiding on the hill of Hakilah, which faces Jeshimon?"

2So Saul went down to the Desert of Ziph, with his three thousand chosen men of Israel, to search there for David. 3Saul made his camp beside the road on the hill of Hakilah facing Jeshimon, but David stayed in the desert. When he saw that Saul had followed him there, 4he sent out scouts and learned that Saul had definitely arrived.[f]

5Then David set out and went to the place where Saul had camped. He saw where Saul and Abner son of Ner, the commander of the army, had lain down. Saul was lying inside the camp, with the army encamped around him.

6David then asked Ahimelech the Hittite and Abishai son of Zeruiah, Joab's brother, "Who will go down into the camp with me to Saul?"

"I'll go with you," said Abishai.

7So David and Abishai went to the army by night, and there was Saul, lying asleep inside the camp with his spear stuck in the ground near his head. Abner and the soldiers were lying around him.

8Abishai said to David, "Today God has delivered your enemy into your hands. Now let me pin him to the ground with one thrust of my spear; I won't strike him twice."

9But David said to Abishai, "Don't destroy him! Who can lay a hand on the LORD's anointed and be guiltless? 10As surely as the LORD lives," he said, "the LORD himself will strike him; either his time will come and he will die, or he will go into battle and perish. 11But the LORD forbid that I should lay a hand on the LORD's anointed. Now get the spear and water jug that are near his head, and let's go."

12So David took the spear and water jug near Saul's head, and they left. No one saw or knew about it, nor did anyone wake up. They were all sleeping, because the LORD had put them into a deep sleep.

13Then David crossed over to the other side and stood on top of the hill some distance away; there was a wide space between them. 14He called out to the army and to Abner son of Ner, "Aren't you going to answer me, Abner?"

Abner replied, "Who are you who calls to the king?"

15David said, "You're a man, aren't you? And who is like you in Israel? Why didn't you guard your lord the king? Someone came to destroy your lord the king. 16What you have done is not good. As surely as the LORD lives, you and your men deserve to die, because you did not guard your master, the LORD's anointed. Look around you. Where are the king's spear and water jug that were near his head?"

17Saul recognized David's voice and said, "Is that your voice, David my son?"

David replied, "Yes it is, my lord the king." 18And he added, "Why is my lord pursuing his servant? What have I done, and what wrong am I guilty of? 19Now let my lord the king listen to his servant's words. If the LORD has incited you against me, then may he accept an offering. If, however, men have done it, may they be cursed before the LORD! They have now driven me from my share in the LORD's inheritance and have said, 'Go, serve other gods.' 20Now do not let my blood fall to the ground far from the presence of the LORD. The king of Israel has come out to look for a flea—as one hunts a partridge in the mountains."

21Then Saul said, "I have sinned. Come back, David my son. Because you considered my life precious today, I will not try to harm you again. Surely I have acted like a fool and have erred greatly."

22"Here is the king's spear," David answered. "Let one of your young men come over and get it. 23The LORD rewards every man for his righteousness and faithfulness. The LORD delivered you into my hands today, but I would not lay a hand on the LORD's anointed. 24As surely as I valued your life today, so may the LORD value my life and deliver me from all trouble."

25Then Saul said to David, "May you be blessed, my son David; you will do great things and surely triumph."

So David went on his way, and Saul returned home.

f4 Or *had come to Nacon*

Discovering the Word 1. Describe the tension and dangers involved in David's plan (vv. 5–7). 2. Abishai tells David to seize this golden opportunity to kill Saul (v. 8). Why would this be a tempting suggestion? 3. Why does David resist the temptation to take matters into his own hands (vv. 9–11)? 4. From a safe distance David calls out to Abner (vv. 13–16). How would his words to Abner make Saul more receptive to him? 5. What does the passage teach about how God regards human life (vv. 21–24)?

Applying the Word 1. When we are tempted to sin, how can our attitude toward God's will affect the outcome? 2. If we know God is present to help us in our struggle, how can it be easier to exercise self-control? 3. In what ways can our commitment to doing God's will affect Christians and non-Christians as they observe us?

Responding in Prayer Think again about that area where you desire greater self-control. Ask God's Spirit to cultivate this fruit within you.

1 Samuel 27—29

27 But David thought to himself, "One
of these days I will be destroyed by
the hand of Saul. The best thing I
can do is to escape to the land of the Philistines.
Then Saul will give up searching for me anywhere
in Israel, and I will slip out of his hand."
2So David and the six hundred men with him
left and went over to Achish son of Maoch king of
Gath. 3David and his men settled in Gath with
Achish. Each man had his family with him, and
David had his two wives: Ahinoam of Jezreel and
Abigail of Carmel, the widow of Nabal. 4When
Saul was told that David had fled to Gath, he no
longer searched for him.
5Then David said to Achish, "If I have found
favor in your eyes, let a place be assigned to me in
one of the country towns, that I may live there.
Why should your servant live in the royal city
with you?"
6So on that day Achish gave him Ziklag, and it
has belonged to the kings of Judah ever since.
7David lived in Philistine territory a year and four
months.
8Now David and his men went up and raided
the Geshurites, the Girzites and the Amalekites.
(From ancient times these peoples had lived in
the land extending to Shur and Egypt.) 9When-
ever David attacked an area, he did not leave a
man or woman alive, but took sheep and cattle,
donkeys and camels, and clothes. Then he re-
turned to Achish.
10When Achish asked, "Where did you go raid-
ing today?" David would say, "Against the Negev
of Judah" or "Against the Negev of Jerahmeel" or
"Against the Negev of the Kenites." 11He did not
leave a man or woman alive to be brought to
Gath, for he thought, "They might inform on us
and say, 'This is what David did.' " And such was
his practice as long as he lived in Philistine terri-
tory. 12Achish trusted David and said to himself,
"He has become so odious to his people, the Isra-
elites, that he will be my servant forever."

28 In those days the Philistines gath-
ered their forces to fight against Is-
rael. Achish said to David, "You
must understand that you and your men will ac-
company me in the army."
2David said, "Then you will see for yourself
what your servant can do."
Achish replied, "Very well, I will make you my
bodyguard for life."
3Now Samuel was dead, and all Israel had
mourned for him and buried him in his own town
of Ramah. Saul had expelled the mediums and
spiritists from the land.
4The Philistines assembled and came and set
up camp at Shunem, while Saul gathered all the
Israelites and set up camp at Gilboa. 5When Saul
saw the Philistine army, he was afraid; terror
filled his heart. 6He inquired of the LORD, but the
LORD did not answer him by dreams or Urim or
prophets. 7Saul then said to his attendants, "Find
me a woman who is a medium, so I may go and
inquire of her."
"There is one in Endor," they said.
8So Saul disguised himself, putting on other
clothes, and at night he and two men went to the
woman. "Consult a spirit for me," he said, "and
bring up for me the one I name."
9But the woman said to him, "Surely you know
what Saul has done. He has cut off the mediums

and spiritists from the land. Why have you set a trap for my life to bring about my death?"

10Saul swore to her by the LORD, "As surely as the LORD lives, you will not be punished for this."

11Then the woman asked, "Whom shall I bring up for you?"

"Bring up Samuel," he said.

12When the woman saw Samuel, she cried out at the top of her voice and said to Saul, "Why have you deceived me? You are Saul!"

13The king said to her, "Don't be afraid. What do you see?"

The woman said, "I see a spirit[g] coming up out of the ground."

14"What does he look like?" he asked.

"An old man wearing a robe is coming up," she said.

Then Saul knew it was Samuel, and he bowed down and prostrated himself with his face to the ground.

15Samuel said to Saul, "Why have you disturbed me by bringing me up?"

"I am in great distress," Saul said. "The Philistines are fighting against me, and God has turned away from me. He no longer answers me, either by prophets or by dreams. So I have called on you to tell me what to do."

16Samuel said, "Why do you consult me, now that the LORD has turned away from you and become your enemy? 17The LORD has done what he predicted through me. The LORD has torn the kingdom out of your hands and given it to one of your neighbors—to David. 18Because you did not obey the LORD or carry out his fierce wrath against the Amalekites, the LORD has done this to you today. 19The LORD will hand over both Israel and you to the Philistines, and tomorrow you and your sons will be with me. The LORD will also hand over the army of Israel to the Philistines."

20Immediately Saul fell full length on the ground, filled with fear because of Samuel's words. His strength was gone, for he had eaten nothing all that day and night.

21When the woman came to Saul and saw that he was greatly shaken, she said, "Look, your maidservant has obeyed you. I took my life in my hands and did what you told me to do. 22Now please listen to your servant and let me give you some food so you may eat and have the strength to go on your way."

23He refused and said, "I will not eat."

But his men joined the woman in urging him, and he listened to them. He got up from the ground and sat on the couch.

24The woman had a fattened calf at the house, which she butchered at once. She took some flour, kneaded it and baked bread without yeast. 25Then she set it before Saul and his men, and they ate. That same night they got up and left.

29 The Philistines gathered all their forces at Aphek, and Israel camped by the spring in Jezreel. 2As the Philistine rulers marched with their units of hundreds and thousands, David and his men were marching at the rear with Achish. 3The commanders of the Philistines asked, "What about these Hebrews?"

Achish replied, "Is this not David, who was an officer of Saul king of Israel? He has already been with me for over a year, and from the day he left Saul until now, I have found no fault in him."

4But the Philistine commanders were angry with him and said, "Send the man back, that he may return to the place you assigned him. He must not go with us into battle, or he will turn against us during the fighting. How better could he regain his master's favor than by taking the heads of our own men? 5Isn't this the David they sang about in their dances:

"'Saul has slain his thousands,
and David his tens of thousands'?"

6So Achish called David and said to him, "As surely as the LORD lives, you have been reliable, and I would be pleased to have you serve with me in the army. From the day you came to me until now, I have found no fault in you, but the rulers don't approve of you. 7Turn back and go in peace; do nothing to displease the Philistine rulers."

8"But what have I done?" asked David. "What have you found against your servant from the day I came to you until now? Why can't I go and fight against the enemies of my lord the king?"

9Achish answered, "I know that you have been as pleasing in my eyes as an angel of God; nevertheless, the Philistine commanders have said, 'He must not go up with us into battle.' 10Now get up

[g]13 Or *see spirits*; or *see gods*

early, along with your master's servants who have come with you, and leave in the morning as soon as it is light."

[11]So David and his men got up early in the morning to go back to the land of the Philistines, and the Philistines went up to Jezreel.

13 / *1 Samuel 30*
Finding Strength in the Lord

IN A CHAPTER entitled "The False Hope of Modern Christianity," Larry Crabb writes, "Modern Christianity, in dramatic reversal of its biblical form, promises to relieve the pain of living in a fallen world. The message, whether it's from fundamentalists requiring us to live by a favored set of rules or from charismatics urging a deeper surrender of the Spirit's power, is too often the same: The promise of bliss is for NOW! Complete satisfaction can be ours this side of Heaven" (*Inside Out* [Colorado Springs: NavPress, 1988], p. 15). The life of David exposes the inadequacy of that view. In this chapter David and his men experience a devastating crisis. Yet in the midst of the crisis, they also find strength and help in the Lord.

Warming Up to God The Christian life is often portrayed as a before-and-after story, with everything "after" being sweetness and light. How do you respond to that kind of portrayal?

Read 1 Samuel 30.

30 David and his men reached Ziklag
on the third day. Now the Amalek-
ites had raided the Negev and Zik-
lag. They had attacked Ziklag and burned it, [2]and
had taken captive the women and all who were in
it, both young and old. They killed none of them,
but carried them off as they went on their way.
[3]When David and his men came to Ziklag, they
found it destroyed by fire and their wives and
sons and daughters taken captive. [4]So David and
his men wept aloud until they had no strength
left to weep. [5]David's two wives had been cap-
tured—Ahinoam of Jezreel and Abigail, the
widow of Nabal of Carmel. [6]David was greatly
distressed because the men were talking of ston-
ing him; each one was bitter in spirit because of
his sons and daughters. But David found strength
in the LORD his God.
[7]Then David said to Abiathar the priest, the son
of Ahimelech, "Bring me the ephod." Abiathar
brought it to him, [8]and David inquired of the
LORD, "Shall I pursue this raiding party? Will I
overtake them?"
"Pursue them," he answered. "You will cer-
tainly overtake them and succeed in the rescue."
[9]David and the six hundred men with him
came to the Besor Ravine, where some stayed be-
hind, [10]for two hundred men were too exhausted
to cross the ravine. But David and four hundred
men continued the pursuit.
[11]They found an Egyptian in a field and
brought him to David. They gave him water to
drink and food to eat— [12]part of a cake of pressed
figs and two cakes of raisins. He ate and was re-
vived, for he had not eaten any food or drunk any
water for three days and three nights.
[13]David asked him, "To whom do you belong,
and where do you come from?"
He said, "I am an Egyptian, the slave of an
Amalekite. My master abandoned me when I be-
came ill three days ago. [14]We raided the Negev of
the Kerethites and the territory belonging to Ju-
dah and the Negev of Caleb. And we burned Zik-
lag."
[15]David asked him, "Can you lead me down to
this raiding party?"
He answered, "Swear to me before God that
you will not kill me or hand me over to my mas-
ter, and I will take you down to them."
[16]He led David down, and there they were,
scattered over the countryside, eating, drinking
and reveling because of the great amount of plun-
der they had taken from the land of the Philis-
tines and from Judah. [17]David fought them from
dusk until the evening of the next day, and none
of them got away, except four hundred young

men who rode off on camels and fled. 18David
recovered everything the Amalekites had taken,
including his two wives. 19Nothing was missing:
young or old, boy or girl, plunder or anything
else they had taken. David brought everything
back. 20He took all the flocks and herds, and his
men drove them ahead of the other livestock, say-
ing, "This is David's plunder."

21Then David came to the two hundred men
who had been too exhausted to follow him and
who were left behind at the Besor Ravine. They
came out to meet David and the people with him.
As David and his men approached, he greeted
them. 22But all the evil men and troublemakers
among David's followers said, "Because they did
not go out with us, we will not share with them
the plunder we recovered. However, each man
may take his wife and children and go."

23David replied, "No, my brothers, you must
not do that with what the LORD has given us. He
has protected us and handed over to us the forces
that came against us. 24Who will listen to what
you say? The share of the man who stayed with
the supplies is to be the same as that of him who
went down to the battle. All will share alike."
25David made this a statute and ordinance for Is-
rael from that day to this.

26When David arrived in Ziklag, he sent some
of the plunder to the elders of Judah, who were
his friends, saying, "Here is a present for you
from the plunder of the LORD's enemies."

27He sent it to those who were in Bethel, Ra-
moth Negev and Jattir; 28to those in Aroer, Siph-
moth, Eshtemoa 29and Racal; to those in the
towns of the Jerahmeelites and the Kenites; 30to
those in Hormah, Bor Ashan, Athach 31and He-
bron; and to those in all the other places where
David and his men had roamed.

Discovering the Word 1. When David and his men return to their home in Ziklag, what do they find (vv. 1–3)? 2. What are we told about the depths of their distress (vv. 4–6)? 3. After David has found strength in the Lord, how does he also find help from the Lord (vv. 7–20)? 4. What was wrong with the logic of those who said, "Because they did not go out with us, we will not share with them the plunder we recovered" (v. 22)? 5. David declares that the Lord "has protected us and handed over to us the forces that came against us" (v. 23). If the Lord was able to do all that, why do you think he allowed the problem to arise in the first place?

Applying the Word 1. How can David's experience help us to have a realistic view of the difficulties we might face as Christians? 2. Reflect on a difficulty or distress you are currently facing. How can David's experience give you hope?

Responding in Prayer Ask God to sustain you with hope through your crisis.

1 Samuel 31

31 Now the Philistines fought against
Israel; the Israelites fled before
them, and many fell slain on Mount
Gilboa. 2The Philistines pressed hard after Saul
and his sons, and they killed his sons Jonathan,
Abinadab and Malki-Shua. 3The fighting grew
fierce around Saul, and when the archers over-
took him, they wounded him critically.

4Saul said to his armor-bearer, "Draw your
sword and run me through, or these uncircum-
cised fellows will come and run me through and
abuse me."

But his armor-bearer was terrified and would
not do it; so Saul took his own sword and fell on
it. 5When the armor-bearer saw that Saul was
dead, he too fell on his sword and died with him.
6So Saul and his three sons and his armor-bearer
and all his men died together that same day.

7When the Israelites along the valley and those
across the Jordan saw that the Israelite army had
fled and that Saul and his sons had died, they
abandoned their towns and fled. And the Philis-
tines came and occupied them.

8The next day, when the Philistines came to
strip the dead, they found Saul and his three sons
fallen on Mount Gilboa. 9They cut off his head
and stripped off his armor, and they sent messen-
gers throughout the land of the Philistines to pro-
claim the news in the temple of their idols and
among their people. 10They put his armor in the

temple of the Ashtoreths and fastened his body to
the wall of Beth Shan.
[11]When the people of Jabesh Gilead heard of
what the Philistines had done to Saul, [12]all their
valiant men journeyed through the night to Beth
Shan. They took down the bodies of Saul and his
sons from the wall of Beth Shan and went to Jabesh,
where they burned them. [13]Then they took
their bones and buried them under a tamarisk
tree at Jabesh, and they fasted seven days.

2 Samuel

Highs and lows. David's life, like our lives, was full of extremes. For David, however, God played a part through it all.

Second Samuel highlights some of David's high moments, winning battles and bringing prosperity to Israel. Chapter 7 contains God's promise that his dynasty would live forever.

In chapters 10—20 we move to the darker moments of David's life as we see him succumb to temptation and murder. The results of his sin follow him through life and are seen in the lives of his children.

At the end of the book we discover that David has not lost his hope in the Lord. Chapters 22 and 23 record his songs of praise to God. May you, like David, find that the Lord is your rock, your fortress and your deliverer (22:2) through the ups and downs of life.

Outline

2 Samuel 1—5

1 After the death of Saul, David returned from defeating the Amalekites and stayed in Ziklag two days. 2On the third day a man arrived from Saul's camp, with his clothes torn and with dust on his head. When he came to David, he fell to the ground to pay him honor.

3"Where have you come from?" David asked him.

He answered, "I have escaped from the Israelite camp."

4"What happened?" David asked. "Tell me."

He said, "The men fled from the battle. Many of them fell and died. And Saul and his son Jonathan are dead."

5Then David said to the young man who brought him the report, "How do you know that Saul and his son Jonathan are dead?"

6"I happened to be on Mount Gilboa," the young man said, "and there was Saul, leaning on his spear, with the chariots and riders almost upon him. 7When he turned around and saw me, he called out to me, and I said, 'What can I do?'

8"He asked me, 'Who are you?'

" 'An Amalekite,' I answered.

9"Then he said to me, 'Stand over me and kill me! I am in the throes of death, but I'm still alive.'

10"So I stood over him and killed him, because I knew that after he had fallen he could not survive. And I took the crown that was on his head and the band on his arm and have brought them here to my lord."

11Then David and all the men with him took hold of their clothes and tore them. 12They mourned and wept and fasted till evening for Saul and his son Jonathan, and for the army of the LORD and the house of Israel, because they had fallen by the sword.

13David said to the young man who brought him the report, "Where are you from?"

"I am the son of an alien, an Amalekite," he answered.

14David asked him, "Why were you not afraid to lift your hand to destroy the LORD's anointed?"

15Then David called one of his men and said, "Go, strike him down!" So he struck him down, and he died. 16For David had said to him, "Your blood be on your own head. Your own mouth testified against you when you said, 'I killed the LORD's anointed.' "

17David took up this lament concerning Saul and his son Jonathan, 18and ordered that the men of Judah be taught this lament of the bow (it is written in the Book of Jashar):

19"Your glory, O Israel, lies slain on your heights.
How the mighty have fallen!

20"Tell it not in Gath,
proclaim it not in the streets of Ashkelon,
lest the daughters of the Philistines be glad,
lest the daughters of the uncircumcised rejoice.

21"O mountains of Gilboa,
may you have neither dew nor rain,
nor fields that yield offerings ⌞of grain⌟.
For there the shield of the mighty was defiled,
the shield of Saul—no longer rubbed with oil.
22From the blood of the slain,
from the flesh of the mighty,
the bow of Jonathan did not turn back,
the sword of Saul did not return unsatisfied.

23"Saul and Jonathan—
in life they were loved and gracious,
and in death they were not parted.
They were swifter than eagles,
they were stronger than lions.

24"O daughters of Israel,
weep for Saul,
who clothed you in scarlet and finery,
who adorned your garments with ornaments of gold.

25"How the mighty have fallen in battle!
Jonathan lies slain on your heights.
26I grieve for you, Jonathan my brother;
you were very dear to me.
Your love for me was wonderful,
more wonderful than that of women.

27"How the mighty have fallen!
The weapons of war have perished!"

2 In the course of time, David inquired of the LORD. "Shall I go up to one of the towns of Judah?" he asked.

The LORD said, "Go up."

David asked, "Where shall I go?"

"To Hebron," the LORD answered.

2So David went up there with his two wives, Ahinoam of Jezreel and Abigail, the widow of Nabal of Carmel. 3David also took the men who were with him, each with his family, and they settled in Hebron and its towns. 4Then the men of Judah came to Hebron and there they anointed David king over the house of Judah.

When David was told that it was the men of Jabesh Gilead who had buried Saul, 5he sent messengers to the men of Jabesh Gilead to say to them, "The LORD bless you for showing this kindness to Saul your master by burying him. 6May the LORD now show you kindness and faithfulness, and I too will show you the same favor because you have done this. 7Now then, be strong and brave, for Saul your master is dead, and the house of Judah has anointed me king over them."

8Meanwhile, Abner son of Ner, the commander of Saul's army, had taken Ish-Bosheth son of Saul and brought him over to Mahanaim. 9He made him king over Gilead, Ashuri[a] and Jezreel, and also over Ephraim, Benjamin and all Israel.

10Ish-Bosheth son of Saul was forty years old when he became king over Israel, and he reigned two years. The house of Judah, however, followed David. 11The length of time David was king in Hebron over the house of Judah was seven years and six months.

12Abner son of Ner, together with the men of Ish-Bosheth son of Saul, left Mahanaim and went to Gibeon. 13Joab son of Zeruiah and David's men went out and met them at the pool of Gibeon. One group sat down on one side of the pool and one group on the other side.

14Then Abner said to Joab, "Let's have some of the young men get up and fight hand to hand in front of us."

"All right, let them do it," Joab said.

15So they stood up and were counted off—twelve men for Benjamin and Ish-Bosheth son of Saul, and twelve for David. 16Then each man grabbed his opponent by the head and thrust his dagger into his opponent's side, and they fell down together. So that place in Gibeon was called Helkath Hazzurim.[b]

17The battle that day was very fierce, and Abner and the men of Israel were defeated by David's men.

18The three sons of Zeruiah were there: Joab, Abishai and Asahel. Now Asahel was as fleet-footed as a wild gazelle. 19He chased Abner, turning neither to the right nor to the left as he pursued him. 20Abner looked behind him and asked, "Is that you, Asahel?"

"It is," he answered.

21Then Abner said to him, "Turn aside to the right or to the left; take on one of the young men and strip him of his weapons." But Asahel would not stop chasing him.

22Again Abner warned Asahel, "Stop chasing me! Why should I strike you down? How could I look your brother Joab in the face?"

23But Asahel refused to give up the pursuit; so Abner thrust the butt of his spear into Asahel's stomach, and the spear came out through his back. He fell there and died on the spot. And every man stopped when he came to the place where Asahel had fallen and died.

24But Joab and Abishai pursued Abner, and as the sun was setting, they came to the hill of Ammah, near Giah on the way to the wasteland of Gibeon. 25Then the men of Benjamin rallied behind Abner. They formed themselves into a group and took their stand on top of a hill.

26Abner called out to Joab, "Must the sword devour forever? Don't you realize that this will end in bitterness? How long before you order your men to stop pursuing their brothers?"

27Joab answered, "As surely as God lives, if you had not spoken, the men would have continued the pursuit of their brothers until morning.[c]"

28So Joab blew the trumpet, and all the men came to a halt; they no longer pursued Israel, nor did they fight anymore.

29All that night Abner and his men marched through the Arabah. They crossed the Jordan, continued through the whole Bithron[d] and came to Mahanaim.

30Then Joab returned from pursuing Abner and assembled all his men. Besides Asahel, nineteen of David's men were found missing. 31But David's men had killed three hundred and sixty Benjamites who were with Abner. 32They took Asahel and buried him in his father's tomb at Bethlehem. Then Joab and his men marched all night and arrived at Hebron by daybreak.

[a]9 Or *Asher* [b]16 *Helkath Hazzurim* means *field of daggers* or *field of hostilities.* [c]27 Or *spoken this morning, the men would not have taken up the pursuit of their brothers*; or *spoken, the men would have given up the pursuit of their brothers by morning* [d]29 Or *morning*; or *ravine*; the meaning of the Hebrew for this word is uncertain.

3 The war between the house of Saul and
the house of David lasted a long time. Da-
vid grew stronger and stronger, while the
house of Saul grew weaker and weaker.
2Sons were born to David in Hebron:
His firstborn was Amnon the son of Ahin-
oam of Jezreel;
3his second, Kileab the son of Abigail the
widow of Nabal of Carmel;
the third, Absalom the son of Maacah
daughter of Talmai king of Geshur;
4the fourth, Adonijah the son of Haggith;
the fifth, Shephatiah the son of Abital;
5and the sixth, Ithream the son of David's
wife Eglah.
These were born to David in Hebron.
6During the war between the house of Saul and
the house of David, Abner had been strengthen-
ing his own position in the house of Saul. 7Now
Saul had had a concubine named Rizpah daughter
of Aiah. And Ish-Bosheth said to Abner, "Why
did you sleep with my father's concubine?"
8Abner was very angry because of what Ish-Bo-
sheth said and he answered, "Am I a dog's
head—on Judah's side? This very day I am loyal
to the house of your father Saul and to his family
and friends. I haven't handed you over to David.
Yet now you accuse me of an offense involving
this woman! 9May God deal with Abner, be it
ever so severely, if I do not do for David what the
LORD promised him on oath 10and transfer the
kingdom from the house of Saul and establish
David's throne over Israel and Judah from Dan to
Beersheba." 11Ish-Bosheth did not dare to say an-
other word to Abner, because he was afraid of
him.
12Then Abner sent messengers on his behalf to
say to David, "Whose land is it? Make an agree-
ment with me, and I will help you bring all Israel
over to you."
13"Good," said David. "I will make an agree-
ment with you. But I demand one thing of you:
Do not come into my presence unless you bring
Michal daughter of Saul when you come to see
me." 14Then David sent messengers to Ish-Bo-
sheth son of Saul, demanding, "Give me my wife
Michal, whom I betrothed to myself for the price
of a hundred Philistine foreskins."
15So Ish-Bosheth gave orders and had her taken
away from her husband Paltiel son of Laish. 16Her
husband, however, went with her, weeping be-
hind her all the way to Bahurim. Then Abner said
to him, "Go back home!" So he went back.
17Abner conferred with the elders of Israel and
said, "For some time you have wanted to make
David your king. 18Now do it! For the LORD prom-
ised David, 'By my servant David I will rescue my
people Israel from the hand of the Philistines and
from the hand of all their enemies.' "
19Abner also spoke to the Benjamites in person.
Then he went to Hebron to tell David everything
that Israel and the whole house of Benjamin
wanted to do. 20When Abner, who had twenty
men with him, came to David at Hebron, David
prepared a feast for him and his men. 21Then Ab-
ner said to David, "Let me go at once and assem-
ble all Israel for my lord the king, so that they
may make a compact with you, and that you may
rule over all that your heart desires." So David
sent Abner away, and he went in peace.
22Just then David's men and Joab returned from
a raid and brought with them a great deal of plun-
der. But Abner was no longer with David in He-
bron, because David had sent him away, and he
had gone in peace. 23When Joab and all the sol-
diers with him arrived, he was told that Abner
son of Ner had come to the king and that the king
had sent him away and that he had gone in peace.
24So Joab went to the king and said, "What
have you done? Look, Abner came to you. Why
did you let him go? Now he is gone! 25You know
Abner son of Ner; he came to deceive you and
observe your movements and find out everything
you are doing."
26Joab then left David and sent messengers af-
ter Abner, and they brought him back from the
well of Sirah. But David did not know it. 27Now
when Abner returned to Hebron, Joab took him
aside into the gateway, as though to speak with
him privately. And there, to avenge the blood of
his brother Asahel, Joab stabbed him in the stom-
ach, and he died.
28Later, when David heard about this, he said,
"I and my kingdom are forever innocent before
the LORD concerning the blood of Abner son of
Ner. 29May his blood fall upon the head of Joab
and upon all his father's house! May Joab's house
never be without someone who has a running
sore or leprosy[e] or who leans on a crutch or who
falls by the sword or who lacks food."
30(Joab and his brother Abishai murdered Ab-

[e]29 The Hebrew word was used for various diseases affecting the skin—not necessarily leprosy.

ner because he had killed their brother Asahel in
the battle at Gibeon.)
31Then David said to Joab and all the people
with him, "Tear your clothes and put on sack-
cloth and walk in mourning in front of Abner."
King David himself walked behind the bier.
32They buried Abner in Hebron, and the king
wept aloud at Abner's tomb. All the people wept
also.
33The king sang this lament for Abner:

"Should Abner have died as the lawless die?
34 Your hands were not bound,
your feet were not fettered.
You fell as one falls before wicked men."

And all the people wept over him again.
35Then they all came and urged David to eat
something while it was still day; but David took
an oath, saying, "May God deal with me, be it
ever so severely, if I taste bread or anything else
before the sun sets!"
36All the people took note and were pleased;
indeed, everything the king did pleased them.
37So on that day all the people and all Israel knew
that the king had no part in the murder of Abner
son of Ner.
38Then the king said to his men, "Do you not
realize that a prince and a great man has fallen
in Israel this day? 39And today, though I am the
anointed king, I am weak, and these sons of Zeru-
iah are too strong for me. May the LORD repay the
evildoer according to his evil deeds!"

4 When Ish-Bosheth son of Saul heard that
Abner had died in Hebron, he lost cour-
age, and all Israel became alarmed. 2Now
Saul's son had two men who were leaders of raid-
ing bands. One was named Baanah and the other
Recab; they were sons of Rimmon the Beerothite
from the tribe of Benjamin—Beeroth is consid-
ered part of Benjamin, 3because the people of Bee-
roth fled to Gittaim and have lived there as aliens
to this day.
4(Jonathan son of Saul had a son who was lame
in both feet. He was five years old when the news
about Saul and Jonathan came from Jezreel. His
nurse picked him up and fled, but as she hurried
to leave, he fell and became crippled. His name
was Mephibosheth.)
5Now Recab and Baanah, the sons of Rimmon
the Beerothite, set out for the house of Ish-Bo-
sheth, and they arrived there in the heat of the
day while he was taking his noonday rest. 6They
went into the inner part of the house as if to get
some wheat, and they stabbed him in the stom-
ach. Then Recab and his brother Baanah slipped
away.
7They had gone into the house while he was
lying on the bed in his bedroom. After they
stabbed and killed him, they cut off his head.
Taking it with them, they traveled all night by
way of the Arabah. 8They brought the head of
Ish-Bosheth to David at Hebron and said to the
king, "Here is the head of Ish-Bosheth son of
Saul, your enemy, who tried to take your life.
This day the LORD has avenged my lord the king
against Saul and his offspring."
9David answered Recab and his brother Baa-
nah, the sons of Rimmon the Beerothite, "As
surely as the LORD lives, who has delivered me out
of all trouble, 10when a man told me, 'Saul is
dead,' and thought he was bringing good news, I
seized him and put him to death in Ziklag. That
was the reward I gave him for his news! 11How
much more—when wicked men have killed an
innocent man in his own house and on his own
bed—should I not now demand his blood from
your hand and rid the earth of you!"
12So David gave an order to his men, and they
killed them. They cut off their hands and feet and
hung the bodies by the pool in Hebron. But they
took the head of Ish-Bosheth and buried it in Ab-
ner's tomb at Hebron.

5 All the tribes of Israel came to David at
Hebron and said, "We are your own flesh
and blood. 2In the past, while Saul was
king over us, you were the one who led Israel on
their military campaigns. And the LORD said to
you, 'You will shepherd my people Israel, and you
will become their ruler.' "
3When all the elders of Israel had come to King
David at Hebron, the king made a compact with
them at Hebron before the LORD, and they
anointed David king over Israel.
4David was thirty years old when he became
king, and he reigned forty years. 5In Hebron he
reigned over Judah seven years and six months,
and in Jerusalem he reigned over all Israel and
Judah thirty-three years.
6The king and his men marched to Jerusalem
to attack the Jebusites, who lived there. The Jebu-
sites said to David, "You will not get in here; even
the blind and the lame can ward you off." They
thought, "David cannot get in here." 7Neverthe-

less, David captured the fortress of Zion, the City of David.

[8]On that day, David said, "Anyone who conquers the Jebusites will have to use the water shaft[f] to reach those 'lame and blind' who are David's enemies.[g]" That is why they say, "The 'blind and lame' will not enter the palace."

[9]David then took up residence in the fortress and called it the City of David. He built up the area around it, from the supporting terraces[h] inward. [10]And he became more and more powerful, because the LORD God Almighty was with him.

[11]Now Hiram king of Tyre sent messengers to David, along with cedar logs and carpenters and stonemasons, and they built a palace for David. [12]And David knew that the LORD had established him as king over Israel and had exalted his kingdom for the sake of his people Israel.

[13]After he left Hebron, David took more concubines and wives in Jerusalem, and more sons and daughters were born to him. [14]These are the names of the children born to him there: Shammua, Shobab, Nathan, Solomon, [15]Ibhar, Elishua, Nepheg, Japhia, [16]Elishama, Eliada and Eliphelet.

[17]When the Philistines heard that David had been anointed king over Israel, they went up in full force to search for him, but David heard about it and went down to the stronghold. [18]Now the Philistines had come and spread out in the Valley of Rephaim; [19]so David inquired of the LORD, "Shall I go and attack the Philistines? Will you hand them over to me?"

The LORD answered him, "Go, for I will surely hand the Philistines over to you."

[20]So David went to Baal Perazim, and there he defeated them. He said, "As waters break out, the LORD has broken out against my enemies before me." So that place was called Baal Perazim.[i] [21]The Philistines abandoned their idols there, and David and his men carried them off.

[22]Once more the Philistines came up and spread out in the Valley of Rephaim; [23]so David inquired of the LORD, and he answered, "Do not go straight up, but circle around behind them and attack them in front of the balsam trees. [24]As soon as you hear the sound of marching in the tops of the balsam trees, move quickly, because that will mean the LORD has gone out in front of you to strike the Philistine army." [25]So David did as the LORD commanded him, and he struck down the Philistines all the way from Gibeon[j] to Gezer.

[f]8 *Or use scaling hooks* [g]8 *Or are hated by David* [h]9 *Or the Millo* [i]20 *Baal Perazim means the lord who breaks out.*
[j]25 Septuagint (see also 1 Chron. 14:16); Hebrew *Geba*

1 / 2 *Samuel 6*
God's Wrath & Blessing

IN THE CHRONICLES of Narnia we are introduced to Aslan, the son of the great Emperor-Beyond-the-Sea, in this way:

"Don't you know who is the King of Beasts? Aslan is a lion—*the* Lion, the great Lion."

"Ooh!" said Susan, "I'd thought he was a man. Is he—quite safe? I shall feel rather nervous about meeting a lion."

"That you will, dearie, and no mistake," said Mrs. Beaver. "If there's anyone who can appear before Aslan without their knees knocking, they're either braver than most or else just silly."

"Then he isn't safe?" said Lucy.

"Safe!" said Mr. Beaver. "Don't you hear what Mrs. Beaver tells you? Who said anything about safe? 'Course he isn't safe. But he's good."

In this chapter David learns in a terrible way that the Lord, the God of Israel, isn't safe. But he also gains a greater appreciation of God's goodness.

Warming Up to God When you think of God's holiness, what ideas or images come to mind?

Read 2 Samuel 6.

6

David again brought together out of Israel chosen men, thirty thousand in all. 2He and all his men set out from Baalah of Judah[k] to bring up from there the ark of God, which is called by the Name,[l] the name of the LORD Almighty, who is enthroned between the cherubim that are on the ark. 3They set the ark of God on a new cart and brought it from the house of Abinadab, which was on the hill. Uzzah and Ahio, sons of Abinadab, were guiding the new cart 4with the ark of God on it,[m] and Ahio was walking in front of it. 5David and the whole house of Israel were celebrating with all their might before the LORD, with songs[n] and with harps, lyres, tambourines, sistrums and cymbals.

6When they came to the threshing floor of Nacon, Uzzah reached out and took hold of the ark of God, because the oxen stumbled. 7The LORD's anger burned against Uzzah because of his irreverent act; therefore God struck him down and he died there beside the ark of God.

8Then David was angry because the LORD's wrath had broken out against Uzzah, and to this day that place is called Perez Uzzah.[o]

9David was afraid of the LORD that day and said, "How can the ark of the LORD ever come to me?" 10He was not willing to take the ark of the LORD to be with him in the City of David. Instead, he took it aside to the house of Obed-Edom the Gittite. 11The ark of the LORD remained in the house of Obed-Edom the Gittite for three months, and the LORD blessed him and his entire household.

12Now King David was told, "The LORD has blessed the household of Obed-Edom and everything he has, because of the ark of God." So David went down and brought up the ark of God from the house of Obed-Edom to the City of David with rejoicing. 13When those who were carrying the ark of the LORD had taken six steps, he sacrificed a bull and a fattened calf. 14David, wearing a linen ephod, danced before the LORD with all his might, 15while he and the entire house of Israel brought up the ark of the LORD with shouts and the sound of trumpets.

16As the ark of the LORD was entering the City of David, Michal daughter of Saul watched from a window. And when she saw King David leaping and dancing before the LORD, she despised him in her heart.

17They brought the ark of the LORD and set it in its place inside the tent that David had pitched for it, and David sacrificed burnt offerings and fellowship offerings[p] before the LORD. 18After he had finished sacrificing the burnt offerings and fellowship offerings, he blessed the people in the name of the LORD Almighty. 19Then he gave a loaf of bread, a cake of dates and a cake of raisins to each person in the whole crowd of Israelites, both men and women. And all the people went to their homes.

20When David returned home to bless his household, Michal daughter of Saul came out to meet him and said, "How the king of Israel has distinguished himself today, disrobing in the sight of the slave girls of his servants as any vulgar fellow would!"

21David said to Michal, "It was before the LORD, who chose me rather than your father or anyone from his house when he appointed me ruler over the LORD's people Israel—I will celebrate before the LORD. 22I will become even more undignified than this, and I will be humiliated in my own eyes. But by these slave girls you spoke of, I will be held in honor."

23And Michal daughter of Saul had no children to the day of her death.

[k]2 That is, Kiriath Jearim; Hebrew *Baale Judah,* a variant of *Baalah of Judah* [l]2 Hebrew; Septuagint and Vulgate do not have *the Name.* [m]3,4 Dead Sea Scrolls and some Septuagint manuscripts; Masoretic Text *cart* 4*and they brought it with the ark of God from the house of Abinadab, which was on the hill* [n]5 See Dead Sea Scrolls, Septuagint and 1 Chronicles 13:8; Masoretic Text *celebrating before the LORD with all kinds of instruments made of pine.* [o]8 *Perez Uzzah* means *outbreak against Uzzah.* [p]17 Traditionally *peace offerings;* also in verse 18

Discovering the Word 1. What words would you use to describe the mood of those bringing the ark to Jerusalem (vv. 1–5)? 2. Uzzah's act of taking hold of the ark seems well intentioned (v. 6). Why then did the Lord's anger burn against him (v. 17; see also 1Ch 15:11–15)? 3. After Uzzah died, David become both angry and afraid of the Lord (vv. 8–9). How would you evaluate his emotional response? 4. Although the Lord had struck down Uzzah, he blessed the house of Obed-Edom (vv. 10–11). What was the Lord saying about himself through these events? 5. What new precautions does David take as he moves the ark to Jerusalem (vv. 12–15)? 6. In what other ways was this event marked by celebration?

Applying the Word 1. Do your times of worship tend to be somber or joyous? Explain. 2. In what ways might we make our times of worship more of a joyous celebration? 3. How does this chapter help you to understand God's holiness?

Responding in Prayer Ask God to teach you about his holiness, that you might respond in reverence to the one who is good—but not safe.

2 / 2 *Samuel 7*
God's Promise to David

AT SOME POINT in our lives, most of us want to do great things for God. We may imagine ourselves as world-famous evangelists, proclaiming the good news to thousands. Or we may aspire to be great Bible expositors, holding people spellbound with our oratory. Or perhaps we will be the next Mother Teresa, bringing care to the sick and needy. David wanted to build a magnificent temple for the Lord. However, in this passage he is surprised to discover that God's plans for David are far greater than David's plans for God.

Warming Up to God Have you ever wanted to do great things for God? Explain.

Read 2 Samuel 7.

7 After the king was settled in his palace
and the LORD had given him rest from all
his enemies around him, 2he said to Na-
than the prophet, "Here I am, living in a palace of
cedar, while the ark of God remains in a tent."
3Nathan replied to the king, "Whatever you
have in mind, go ahead and do it, for the LORD is
with you."
4That night the word of the LORD came to Na-
than, saying:
5"Go and tell my servant David, 'This is
what the LORD says: Are you the one to build
me a house to dwell in? 6I have not dwelt in
a house from the day I brought the Israelites
up out of Egypt to this day. I have been mov-
ing from place to place with a tent as my
dwelling. 7Wherever I have moved with all
the Israelites, did I ever say to any of their
rulers whom I commanded to shepherd my
people Israel, "Why have you not built me a
house of cedar?" '
8"Now then, tell my servant David, 'This
is what the LORD Almighty says: I took you
from the pasture and from following the
flock to be ruler over my people Israel. 9I
have been with you wherever you have gone,
and I have cut off all your enemies from be-
fore you. Now I will make your name great,
like the names of the greatest men of the
earth. 10And I will provide a place for my
people Israel and will plant them so that they
can have a home of their own and no longer
be disturbed. Wicked people will not op-
press them anymore, as they did at the be-
ginning 11and have done ever since the time
I appointed leaders[q] over my people Israel.
I will also give you rest from all your ene-
mies.
" 'The LORD declares to you that the LORD
himself will establish a house for you:
12When your days are over and you rest with
your fathers, I will raise up your offspring to
succeed you, who will come from your own
body, and I will establish his kingdom. 13He
is the one who will build a house for my
Name, and I will establish the throne of his
kingdom forever. 14I will be his father, and
he will be my son. When he does wrong, I
will punish him with the rod of men, with
floggings inflicted by men. 15But my love will
never be taken away from him, as I took it
away from Saul, whom I removed from be-
fore you. 16Your house and your kingdom
will endure forever before me[r]; your throne
will be established forever.' "
17Nathan reported to David all the words of
this entire revelation.
18Then King David went in and sat before the
LORD, and he said:

q11 Traditionally *judges* r16 Some Hebrew manuscripts and Septuagint; most Hebrew manuscripts *you*

"Who am I, O Sovereign LORD, and what is
my family, that you have brought me this
far? 19And as if this were not enough in your
sight, O Sovereign LORD, you have also spo-
ken about the future of the house of your
servant. Is this your usual way of dealing
with man, O Sovereign LORD?
20"What more can David say to you? For
you know your servant, O Sovereign LORD.
21For the sake of your word and according to
your will, you have done this great thing and
made it known to your servant.
22"How great you are, O Sovereign LORD!
There is no one like you, and there is no God
but you, as we have heard with our own ears.
23And who is like your people Israel—the
one nation on earth that God went out to
redeem as a people for himself, and to make
a name for himself, and to perform great and
awesome wonders by driving out nations
and their gods from before your people,
whom you redeemed from Egypt?[s] 24You
have established your people Israel as your
very own forever, and you, O LORD, have be-
come their God.
25"And now, LORD God, keep forever the
promise you have made concerning your ser-
vant and his house. Do as you promised, 26so
that your name will be great forever. Then
men will say, 'The LORD Almighty is God
over Israel!' And the house of your servant
David will be established before you.
27"O LORD Almighty, God of Israel, you
have revealed this to your servant, saying, 'I
will build a house for you.' So your servant
has found courage to offer you this prayer.
28O Sovereign LORD, you are God! Your
words are trustworthy, and you have prom-
ised these good things to your servant.
29Now be pleased to bless the house of your
servant, that it may continue forever in your
sight; for you, O Sovereign LORD, have spo-
ken, and with your blessing the house of
your servant will be blessed forever."

[s]23 See Septuagint and 1 Chron. 17:21; Hebrew *wonders for your land and before your people, whom you redeemed from Egypt, from the nations and their gods.*

Discovering the Word 1. What prompts David to want to build a house for the Lord (vv. 1-3)? 2. Throughout history, sincere people have built monuments for the Lord that he never asked for (vv. 4-7). How can we avoid involvement in these misguided projects? 3. Verses 8-16 have been called the Davidic covenant. What specific promises does God make to David? 4. How do the promises in verses 8-16 find their ultimate fulfillment in Jesus Christ (see, for example, Lk 1:30-33)? 5. After hearing God's promises to him, David prays (v. 18). Why is he astonished not only with the promises but with God himself (vv. 18-24)? 6. After praising God for his greatness, what requests does David make (vv. 25-29)?

Applying the Word 1. What insights does this passage give us into the relationship between God's sovereignty and our responsibility? 2. When have you been astonished to discover that both God and his plans are far greater than you imagined? 3. In what ways has the Lord demonstrated his greatness or goodness to you recently?

Responding in Prayer Take time to thank him for all that he has done for you.

2 Samuel 8

8 In the course of time, David defeated the
Philistines and subdued them, and he
took Metheg Ammah from the control of
the Philistines.
2David also defeated the Moabites. He
made them lie down on the ground and mea-
sured them off with a length of cord. Every
two lengths of them were put to death, and
the third length was allowed to live. So the
Moabites became subject to David and brought
tribute.
3Moreover, David fought Hadadezer son of Re-
hob, king of Zobah, when he went to restore his
control along the Euphrates River. 4David cap-
tured a thousand of his chariots, seven thousand
charioteers[t] and twenty thousand foot soldiers.

[t]4 Septuagint (see also Dead Sea Scrolls and 1 Chron. 18:4); Masoretic Text *captured seventeen hundred of his charioteers*

He hamstrung all but a hundred of the chariot horses.

5When the Arameans of Damascus came to help Hadadezer king of Zobah, David struck down twenty-two thousand of them. 6He put garrisons in the Aramean kingdom of Damascus, and the Arameans became subject to him and brought tribute. The LORD gave David victory wherever he went.

7David took the gold shields that belonged to the officers of Hadadezer and brought them to Jerusalem. 8From Tebah[u] and Berothai, towns that belonged to Hadadezer, King David took a great quantity of bronze.

9When Tou[v] king of Hamath heard that David had defeated the entire army of Hadadezer, 10he sent his son Joram[w] to King David to greet him and congratulate him on his victory in battle over Hadadezer, who had been at war with Tou. Joram brought with him articles of silver and gold and bronze.

11King David dedicated these articles to the LORD, as he had done with the silver and gold from all the nations he had subdued: 12Edom[x] and Moab, the Ammonites and the Philistines, and Amalek. He also dedicated the plunder taken from Hadadezer son of Rehob, king of Zobah.

13And David became famous after he returned from striking down eighteen thousand Edomites[y] in the Valley of Salt.

14He put garrisons throughout Edom, and all the Edomites became subject to David. The LORD gave David victory wherever he went.

15David reigned over all Israel, doing what was just and right for all his people. 16Joab son of Zeruiah was over the army; Jehoshaphat son of Ahilud was recorder; 17Zadok son of Ahitub and Ahimelech son of Abiathar were priests; Seraiah was secretary; 18Benaiah son of Jehoiada was over the Kerethites and Pelethites; and David's sons were royal advisers.[z]

u8 See some Septuagint manuscripts (see also 1 Chron. 18:8); Hebrew *Betah.* v9 Hebrew *Toi,* a variant of *Tou;* also in verse 10 w10 A variant of *Hadoram* x12 Some Hebrew manuscripts, Septuagint and Syriac (see also 1 Chron. 18:11); most Hebrew manuscripts *Aram* y13 A few Hebrew manuscripts, Septuagint and Syriac (see also 1 Chron. 18:12); most Hebrew manuscripts *Aram* (that is, Arameans) z18 Or *were priests*

3 / 2 *Samuel 9*
Integrity

I WAS IN a minor accident not long ago. It caused so little damage that the owner of the other car suggested we settle privately, without the help of our insurance companies and the police. This was an attractive offer, since the accident was my fault and I'd probably get a ticket. But I wanted to do the right thing . . . and besides, someone had already called the police. That week I felt good about having done the right thing. However, the next week when I paid my ticket and my insurance premium went up, I felt frustrated. I caught myself wishing I had taken the man's suggestion. I learned through this incident that, though I value being a man of integrity, I'm not so wild about the costs that sometimes go along with it.

Warming Up to God What is real integrity? Give an example of someone who has demonstrated strong integrity.

Read 2 Samuel 9.

9 David asked, "Is there anyone still left of the house of Saul to whom I can show kindness for Jonathan's sake?"

2Now there was a servant of Saul's household named Ziba. They called him to appear before David, and the king said to him, "Are you Ziba?"

"Your servant," he replied.

3The king asked, "Is there no one still left of the house of Saul to whom I can show God's kindness?"

Ziba answered the king, "There is still a son of Jonathan; he is crippled in both feet."

4"Where is he?" the king asked.

Ziba answered, "He is at the house of Makir son of Ammiel in Lo Debar."

5So King David had him brought from Lo Debar, from the house of Makir son of Ammiel.

6When Mephibosheth son of Jonathan, the son
of Saul, came to David, he bowed down to pay
him honor.
David said, "Mephibosheth!"
"Your servant," he replied.
7"Don't be afraid," David said to him, "for I will
surely show you kindness for the sake of your
father Jonathan. I will restore to you all the land
that belonged to your grandfather Saul, and you
will always eat at my table."
8Mephibosheth bowed down and said, "What is
your servant, that you should notice a dead dog
like me?"
9Then the king summoned Ziba, Saul's servant,
and said to him, "I have given your master's
grandson everything that belonged to Saul and
his family. 10You and your sons and your servants
are to farm the land for him and bring in the
crops, so that your master's grandson may be provided for. And Mephibosheth, grandson of your
master, will always eat at my table." (Now Ziba
had fifteen sons and twenty servants.)
11Then Ziba said to the king, "Your servant will
do whatever my lord the king commands his servant to do." So Mephibosheth ate at David's[a] table like one of the king's sons.
12Mephibosheth had a young son named Mica,
and all the members of Ziba's household were
servants of Mephibosheth. 13And Mephibosheth
lived in Jerusalem, because he always ate at the
king's table, and he was crippled in both feet.

[a] *11* Septuagint; Hebrew *my*

Discovering the Word 1. What is Mephibosheth's relationship to Jonathan and to Saul? 2. In 1 Samuel 20:12–17 David made a covenant with Jonathan. In what way is David's care for Mephibosheth a fulfillment of his promise to Jonathan? 3. What kindness does David show Mephibosheth, and what does it cost him (vv. 7–15)? 4. What does this tell us about David's character? 5. What does this say about David's attitude toward his promises?

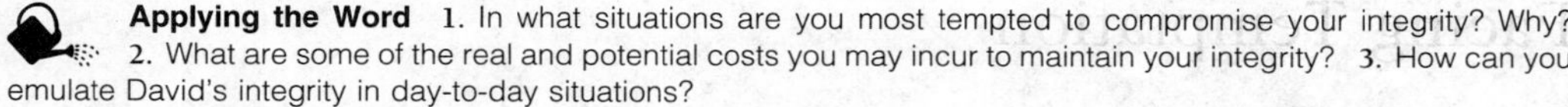

Applying the Word 1. In what situations are you most tempted to compromise your integrity? Why? 2. What are some of the real and potential costs you may incur to maintain your integrity? 3. How can you emulate David's integrity in day-to-day situations?

Responding in Prayer Pray for God's strength as you work toward being a person of integrity.

2 Samuel 10

10 In the course of time, the king of
the Ammonites died, and his son
Hanun succeeded him as king. 2David thought, "I will show kindness to Hanun son
of Nahash, just as his father showed kindness to
me." So David sent a delegation to express his
sympathy to Hanun concerning his father.
When David's men came to the land of the Ammonites, 3the Ammonite nobles said to Hanun
their lord, "Do you think David is honoring your
father by sending men to you to express sympathy? Hasn't David sent them to you to explore the
city and spy it out and overthrow it?" 4So Hanun
seized David's men, shaved off half of each man's
beard, cut off their garments in the middle at the
buttocks, and sent them away.
5When David was told about this, he sent messengers to meet the men, for they were greatly
humiliated. The king said, "Stay at Jericho till
your beards have grown, and then come back."
6When the Ammonites realized that they had
become a stench in David's nostrils, they hired
twenty thousand Aramean foot soldiers from Beth
Rehob and Zobah, as well as the king of Maacah
with a thousand men, and also twelve thousand
men from Tob.
7On hearing this, David sent Joab out with
the entire army of fighting men. 8The Ammonites came out and drew up in battle formation
at the entrance to their city gate, while the Arameans of Zobah and Rehob and the men of Tob
and Maacah were by themselves in the open
country.
9Joab saw that there were battle lines in front of
him and behind him; so he selected some of the
best troops in Israel and deployed them against

the Arameans. 10He put the rest of the men under
the command of Abishai his brother and de-
ployed them against the Ammonites. 11Joab said,
"If the Arameans are too strong for me, then you
are to come to my rescue; but if the Ammonites
are too strong for you, then I will come to rescue
you. 12Be strong and let us fight bravely for our
people and the cities of our God. The LORD will do
what is good in his sight."
13Then Joab and the troops with him advanced
to fight the Arameans, and they fled before him.
14When the Ammonites saw that the Arameans
were fleeing, they fled before Abishai and went
inside the city. So Joab returned from fighting the
Ammonites and came to Jerusalem.
15After the Arameans saw that they had been
routed by Israel, they regrouped. 16Hadadezer had
Arameans brought from beyond the River[b]; they
went to Helam, with Shobach the commander of
Hadadezer's army leading them.
17When David was told of this, he gathered all
Israel, crossed the Jordan and went to Helam. The
Arameans formed their battle lines to meet David
and fought against him. 18But they fled before Is-
rael, and David killed seven hundred of their
charioteers and forty thousand of their foot sol-
diers.[c] He also struck down Shobach the com-
mander of their army, and he died there. 19When
all the kings who were vassals of Hadadezer saw
that they had been defeated by Israel, they made
peace with the Israelites and became subject to
them.

So the Arameans were afraid to help the Ammonites anymore.

[b] 16 That is, the Euphrates [c] 18 Some Septuagint manuscripts (see also 1 Chron. 19:18); Hebrew *horsemen*

4 / *2 Samuel 11*
Facing Temptation

IN *LAKE WOBEGON Days* Garrison Keillor describes a priest named Father Emil, who presides over Our Lady of Perpetual Responsibility Catholic Church. Every year Father Emil faithfully delivers a sermon on the evils of birth control. He entitles it "If You Didn't Want to Go to Minneapolis, Why Did You Get on the Train?" His point, of course, is that if we want to avoid certain consequences, we must avoid certain actions. The story of David and Bathsheba reveals how a series of smaller sins can build to tragic and devastating results. We also discover what forces can lead "a man after God's own heart" to commit adultery and murder.

Warming Up to God When have you failed to be honest with God about sin in your life? If you have not yet done so, confess that sin to God.

Read 2 Samuel 11.

11 In the spring, at the time when
kings go off to war, David sent Joab
out with the king's men and the
whole Israelite army. They destroyed the Am-
monites and besieged Rabbah. But David re-
mained in Jerusalem.
2One evening David got up from his bed and
walked around on the roof of the palace. From
the roof he saw a woman bathing. The woman
was very beautiful, 3and David sent someone to
find out about her. The man said, "Isn't this Bath-
sheba, the daughter of Eliam and the wife of
Uriah the Hittite?" 4Then David sent messengers
to get her. She came to him, and he slept with
her. (She had purified herself from her unclean-
ness.) Then[d] she went back home. 5The woman
conceived and sent word to David, saying, "I am
pregnant."
6So David sent this word to Joab: "Send me
Uriah the Hittite." And Joab sent him to David.
7When Uriah came to him, David asked him how
Joab was, how the soldiers were and how the war
was going. 8Then David said to Uriah, "Go down
to your house and wash your feet." So Uriah left
the palace, and a gift from the king was sent after
him. 9But Uriah slept at the entrance to the palace
with all his master's servants and did not go down
to his house.

[d] 4 Or *with her. When she purified herself from her uncleanness,*

[10]When David was told, "Uriah did not go home," he asked him, "Haven't you just come from a distance? Why didn't you go home?"

[11]Uriah said to David, "The ark and Israel and Judah are staying in tents, and my master Joab and my lord's men are camped in the open fields. How could I go to my house to eat and drink and lie with my wife? As surely as you live, I will not do such a thing!"

[12]Then David said to him, "Stay here one more day, and tomorrow I will send you back." So Uriah remained in Jerusalem that day and the next. [13]At David's invitation, he ate and drank with him, and David made him drunk. But in the evening Uriah went out to sleep on his mat among his master's servants; he did not go home.

[14]In the morning David wrote a letter to Joab and sent it with Uriah. [15]In it he wrote, "Put Uriah in the front line where the fighting is fiercest. Then withdraw from him so he will be struck down and die."

[16]So while Joab had the city under siege, he put Uriah at a place where he knew the strongest defenders were. [17]When the men of the city came out and fought against Joab, some of the men in David's army fell; moreover, Uriah the Hittite died.

[18]Joab sent David a full account of the battle. [19]He instructed the messenger: "When you have finished giving the king this account of the battle, [20]the king's anger may flare up, and he may ask you, 'Why did you get so close to the city to fight? Didn't you know they would shoot arrows from the wall? [21]Who killed Abimelech son of Jerub-Besheth[e]? Didn't a woman throw an upper millstone on him from the wall, so that he died in Thebez? Why did you get so close to the wall?' If he asks you this, then say to him, 'Also, your servant Uriah the Hittite is dead.' "

[22]The messenger set out, and when he arrived he told David everything Joab had sent him to say. [23]The messenger said to David, "The men overpowered us and came out against us in the open, but we drove them back to the entrance to the city gate. [24]Then the archers shot arrows at your servants from the wall, and some of the king's men died. Moreover, your servant Uriah the Hittite is dead."

[25]David told the messenger, "Say this to Joab: 'Don't let this upset you; the sword devours one as well as another. Press the attack against the city and destroy it.' Say this to encourage Joab."

[26]When Uriah's wife heard that her husband was dead, she mourned for him. [27]After the time of mourning was over, David had her brought to his house, and she became his wife and bore him a son. But the thing David had done displeased the LORD.

[e]21 Also known as *Jerub-Baal* (that is, Gideon)

Discovering the Word 1. Sin often begins with a series of temptations, each one leading to the next. What steps led to David's sin with Bathsheba (vv. 1–5)? 2. At each stage of his temptation, what might David have done to keep from taking the next step? (Be specific.) 3. What plan does David devise to cover up his sin (vv. 6–13)? How does Uriah thwart David's plan—at least initially? 4. When deceit fails to work, how does David's plan become vicious (vv. 14–15)? 5. What other people does David draw into the wake of his sin? 6. From this chapter, how would you explain what led "a man after God's own heart" to commit adultery and murder?

Applying the Word 1. At what point does a temptation become sin? 2. Why are we tempted to cover up our sins rather than confess them? 3. In what specific ways is David's experience a warning to you?

Responding in Prayer Pray that you would be faithful in the "little things" so that you would not be led into temptation.

5 / *2 Samuel 12*
God's Severe Mercy

IT OFTEN SEEMS easier to cover up our sin than to confess it and accept the consequences. In the previous chapter, David sought desperately to hide what he had done. After his plan was frustrated again and again, he cold-bloodedly killed the one who threatened to expose his sin. The chapter concluded with the ominous words "But the thing David had done displeased the LORD." Then, when David assumes his "problem" is safely behind him, Nathan appears with a message from God. This chapter gives us a powerful example of God's severe mercy.

Warming Up to God How do you tend to respond when someone confronts you about something you know you've done wrong?

Read 2 Samuel 12.

12 The LORD sent Nathan to David.
When he came to him, he said,
"There were two men in a certain
town, one rich and the other poor. 2The rich man
had a very large number of sheep and cattle, 3but
the poor man had nothing except one little ewe
lamb he had bought. He raised it, and it grew up
with him and his children. It shared his food,
drank from his cup and even slept in his arms. It
was like a daughter to him.
4"Now a traveler came to the rich man, but the
rich man refrained from taking one of his own
sheep or cattle to prepare a meal for the traveler
who had come to him. Instead, he took the ewe
lamb that belonged to the poor man and prepared
it for the one who had come to him."
5David burned with anger against the man and
said to Nathan, "As surely as the LORD lives, the
man who did this deserves to die! 6He must pay
for that lamb four times over, because he did such
a thing and had no pity."
7Then Nathan said to David, "You are the man!
This is what the LORD, the God of Israel, says: 'I
anointed you king over Israel, and I delivered you
from the hand of Saul. 8I gave your master's
house to you, and your master's wives into your
arms. I gave you the house of Israel and Judah.
And if all this had been too little, I would have
given you even more. 9Why did you despise the
word of the LORD by doing what is evil in his eyes?
You struck down Uriah the Hittite with the sword
and took his wife to be your own. You killed him
with the sword of the Ammonites. 10Now, there-
fore, the sword will never depart from your
house, because you despised me and took the
wife of Uriah the Hittite to be your own.'
11"This is what the LORD says: 'Out of your own
household I am going to bring calamity upon
you. Before your very eyes I will take your wives
and give them to one who is close to you, and he
will lie with your wives in broad daylight. 12You
did it in secret, but I will do this thing in broad
daylight before all Israel.' "
13Then David said to Nathan, "I have sinned
against the LORD."
Nathan replied, "The LORD has taken away your
sin. You are not going to die. 14But because by
doing this you have made the enemies of the LORD
show utter contempt,[f] the son born to you will
die."
15After Nathan had gone home, the LORD struck
the child that Uriah's wife had borne to David,
and he became ill. 16David pleaded with God for
the child. He fasted and went into his house and
spent the nights lying on the ground. 17The elders
of his household stood beside him to get him up
from the ground, but he refused, and he would
not eat any food with them.
18On the seventh day the child died. David's
servants were afraid to tell him that the child was
dead, for they thought, "While the child was still
living, we spoke to David but he would not listen
to us. How can we tell him the child is dead? He
may do something desperate."
19David noticed that his servants were whisper-
ing among themselves and he realized the child
was dead. "Is the child dead?" he asked.
"Yes," they replied, "he is dead."
20Then David got up from the ground. After
he had washed, put on lotions and changed his
clothes, he went into the house of the LORD and

[f]14 Masoretic Text; an ancient Hebrew scribal tradition *this you have shown utter contempt for the LORD*

worshiped. Then he went to his own house, and
at his request they served him food, and he ate.
[21]His servants asked him, "Why are you acting
this way? While the child was alive, you fasted
and wept, but now that the child is dead, you get
up and eat!"
[22]He answered, "While the child was still alive,
I fasted and wept. I thought, 'Who knows? The
LORD may be gracious to me and let the child live.'
[23]But now that he is dead, why should I fast? Can
I bring him back again? I will go to him, but he
will not return to me."
[24]Then David comforted his wife Bathsheba,
and he went to her and lay with her. She gave
birth to a son, and they named him Solomon. The
LORD loved him; [25]and because the LORD loved
him, he sent word through Nathan the prophet to
name him Jedidiah.[g]
[26]Meanwhile Joab fought against Rabbah of the
Ammonites and captured the royal citadel. [27]Joab
then sent messengers to David, saying, "I have
fought against Rabbah and taken its water supply.
[28]Now muster the rest of the troops and besiege
the city and capture it. Otherwise I will take the
city, and it will be named after me."
[29]So David mustered the entire army and went
to Rabbah, and attacked and captured it. [30]He
took the crown from the head of their king[h]—its
weight was a talent[i] of gold, and it was set with
precious stones—and it was placed on David's
head. He took a great quantity of plunder from
the city [31]and brought out the people who were
there, consigning them to labor with saws and
with iron picks and axes, and he made them work
at brickmaking.[j] He did this to all the Ammonite
towns. Then David and his entire army returned
to Jerusalem.

g25 *Jedidiah* means *loved by the LORD.* h30 Or *of Milcom* (that is, Molech) i30 That is, about 75 pounds (about 34 kilograms) j31 The meaning of the Hebrew for this clause is uncertain.

Discovering the Word 1. Why do you think Nathan tells David a story rather than confronting him directly about his sin (vv. 1-6)? 2. Why is the Lord amazed that David despised both him and his word (vv. 7-10)? 3. How is God's justice and mercy revealed in his decision about David's sin (vv. 10-14)? 4. We normally assume that God disciplines us for our benefit (see Heb 12:5-13). Is God's treatment of David an example of beneficial discipline, or is God merely demanding a penalty for David's sin? Explain. 5. How does David respond to the news that his child is ill (vv. 15-17)? 6. After the child dies, how is God's grace again evident in David's life (vv. 23-25)?

Applying the Word 1. Why is it so difficult for us to be objective about our own sin? 2. The author of Hebrews writes: "No discipline seems pleasant at the time, but painful. Later on, however, it produces a harvest of righteousness and peace for those who have been trained by it" (12:11). In what ways has God's painful discipline had that effect in your life?

Responding in Prayer What is God trying to teach you at this point in your life? Ask him to make you open to his voice.

6 / *2 Samuel 13*
Sexual Violence

IN PREPARATION FOR writing *Stolen Childhood,* Alice Huskey did a survey of female students at a Christian college. Nineteen percent of the students reported sexual abuse before the age of eighteen. Five percent reported incest. Of those abused, eighty-nine percent knew the abuser. Less than half of the victims had told another person. Often those who did tell were ignored or even punished ([Downers Grove, Ill.: InterVarsity Press, 1989], p. 35). As these statistics show, sexual violence, among both Christians and non-Christians, is all too common. In this study we will see some of the far-reaching implications of this tragic fact.

Warming Up to God How has sexual violence affected you or someone you know? Ask God to prepare you to study this difficult topic.

Read 2 Samuel 13.

13 In the course of time, Amnon son of David fell in love with Tamar, the beautiful sister of Absalom son of David.

2Amnon became frustrated to the point of illness on account of his sister Tamar, for she was a virgin, and it seemed impossible for him to do anything to her.

3Now Amnon had a friend named Jonadab son of Shimeah, David's brother. Jonadab was a very shrewd man. 4He asked Amnon, "Why do you, the king's son, look so haggard morning after morning? Won't you tell me?"

Amnon said to him, "I'm in love with Tamar, my brother Absalom's sister."

5"Go to bed and pretend to be ill," Jonadab said. "When your father comes to see you, say to him, 'I would like my sister Tamar to come and give me something to eat. Let her prepare the food in my sight so I may watch her and then eat it from her hand.' "

6So Amnon lay down and pretended to be ill. When the king came to see him, Amnon said to him, "I would like my sister Tamar to come and make some special bread in my sight, so I may eat from her hand."

7David sent word to Tamar at the palace: "Go to the house of your brother Amnon and prepare some food for him." 8So Tamar went to the house of her brother Amnon, who was lying down. She took some dough, kneaded it, made the bread in his sight and baked it. 9Then she took the pan and served him the bread, but he refused to eat.

"Send everyone out of here," Amnon said. So everyone left him. 10Then Amnon said to Tamar, "Bring the food here into my bedroom so I may eat from your hand." And Tamar took the bread she had prepared and brought it to her brother Amnon in his bedroom. 11But when she took it to him to eat, he grabbed her and said, "Come to bed with me, my sister."

12"Don't, my brother!" she said to him. "Don't force me. Such a thing should not be done in Israel! Don't do this wicked thing. 13What about me? Where could I get rid of my disgrace? And what about you? You would be like one of the wicked fools in Israel. Please speak to the king; he will not keep me from being married to you." 14But he refused to listen to her, and since he was stronger than she, he raped her.

15Then Amnon hated her with intense hatred. In fact, he hated her more than he had loved her. Amnon said to her, "Get up and get out!"

16"No!" she said to him. "Sending me away would be a greater wrong than what you have already done to me."

But he refused to listen to her. 17He called his personal servant and said, "Get this woman out of here and bolt the door after her." 18So his servant put her out and bolted the door after her. She was wearing a richly ornamented[k] robe, for this was the kind of garment the virgin daughters of the king wore. 19Tamar put ashes on her head and tore the ornamented[l] robe she was wearing. She put her hand on her head and went away, weeping aloud as she went.

20Her brother Absalom said to her, "Has that Amnon, your brother, been with you? Be quiet now, my sister; he is your brother. Don't take this thing to heart." And Tamar lived in her brother Absalom's house, a desolate woman.

21When King David heard all this, he was furious. 22Absalom never said a word to Amnon, either good or bad; he hated Amnon because he had disgraced his sister Tamar.

23Two years later, when Absalom's sheepshearers were at Baal Hazor near the border of Ephraim, he invited all the king's sons to come there. 24Absalom went to the king and said, "Your servant has had shearers come. Will the king and his officials please join me?"

25"No, my son," the king replied. "All of us should not go; we would only be a burden to you." Although Absalom urged him, he still refused to go, but gave him his blessing.

26Then Absalom said, "If not, please let my brother Amnon come with us."

The king asked him, "Why should he go with you?" 27But Absalom urged him, so he sent with him Amnon and the rest of the king's sons.

28Absalom ordered his men, "Listen! When Amnon is in high spirits from drinking wine and I say to you, 'Strike Amnon down,' then kill him. Don't be afraid. Have not I given you this order? Be strong and brave." 29So Absalom's men did to

[k] *18* The meaning of the Hebrew for this phrase is uncertain. [l] *19* The meaning of the Hebrew for this word is uncertain.

Amnon what Absalom had ordered. Then all the king's sons got up, mounted their mules and fled.

30While they were on their way, the report came to David: "Absalom has struck down all the king's sons; not one of them is left." 31The king stood up, tore his clothes and lay down on the ground; and all his servants stood by with their clothes torn.

32But Jonadab son of Shimeah, David's brother, said, "My lord should not think that they killed all the princes; only Amnon is dead. This has been Absalom's expressed intention ever since the day Amnon raped his sister Tamar. 33My lord the king should not be concerned about the report that all the king's sons are dead. Only Amnon is dead."

34Meanwhile, Absalom had fled.

Now the man standing watch looked up and saw many people on the road west of him, coming down the side of the hill. The watchman went and told the king, "I see men in the direction of Horonaim, on the side of the hill."[m]

35Jonadab said to the king, "See, the king's sons are here; it has happened just as your servant said."

36As he finished speaking, the king's sons came in, wailing loudly. The king, too, and all his servants wept very bitterly.

37Absalom fled and went to Talmai son of Ammihud, the king of Geshur. But King David mourned for his son every day.

38After Absalom fled and went to Geshur, he stayed there three years. 39And the spirit of the king[n] longed to go to Absalom, for he was consoled concerning Amnon's death.

[m] 34 Septuagint; Hebrew does not have this sentence. [n] 39 Dead Sea Scrolls and some Septuagint manuscripts; Masoretic Text *But* ⌞*the spirit of*⌟ *David the king*

Discovering the Word 1. Summarize Amnon's situation as it is described in verses 1–2. 2. Why do you think Amnon chooses to confide in Jonadab (vv. 3–4)? 3. How does Tamar respond to Amnon's advances (vv. 11–13)? 4. Why do you think Amnon's reaction after the encounter was hatred (vv. 15–17)? 5. What is the effect of Amnon's actions on family relations (vv. 21–22, 32)?

Applying the Word 1. What are some of the effects of sexual violence on our culture? 2. What can we do with our friends or in our churches to address the issue of sexual violence? Consider both victims and perpetrators.

Responding in Prayer Absalom tells Tamar not to take it to heart, yet she is described as a "desolate woman." Pray for those who have felt the pain of sexual violence. What results of sexual violence have you seen in victims in our culture (yourself, someone you know, someone you've heard or read about)?

2 Samuel 14

14 Joab son of Zeruiah knew that the king's heart longed for Absalom. 2So Joab sent someone to Tekoa and had a wise woman brought from there. He said to her, "Pretend you are in mourning. Dress in mourning clothes, and don't use any cosmetic lotions. Act like a woman who has spent many days grieving for the dead. 3Then go to the king and speak these words to him." And Joab put the words in her mouth.

4When the woman from Tekoa went[o] to the king, she fell with her face to the ground to pay him honor, and she said, "Help me, O king!"

5The king asked her, "What is troubling you?"

She said, "I am indeed a widow; my husband is dead. 6I your servant had two sons. They got into a fight with each other in the field, and no one was there to separate them. One struck the other and killed him. 7Now the whole clan has risen up against your servant; they say, 'Hand over the one who struck his brother down, so that we may put him to death for the life of his brother whom he killed; then we will get rid of the heir as well.' They would put out the only burning coal I have left, leaving my husband neither name nor descendant on the face of the earth."

8The king said to the woman, "Go home, and I will issue an order in your behalf."

9But the woman from Tekoa said to him, "My lord the king, let the blame rest on me and on my

[o] 4 Many Hebrew manuscripts, Septuagint, Vulgate and Syriac; most Hebrew manuscripts *spoke*

father's family, and let the king and his throne be without guilt."

10The king replied, "If anyone says anything to you, bring him to me, and he will not bother you again."

11She said, "Then let the king invoke the LORD his God to prevent the avenger of blood from adding to the destruction, so that my son will not be destroyed."

"As surely as the LORD lives," he said, "not one hair of your son's head will fall to the ground."

12Then the woman said, "Let your servant speak a word to my lord the king."

"Speak," he replied.

13The woman said, "Why then have you devised a thing like this against the people of God? When the king says this, does he not convict himself, for the king has not brought back his banished son? 14Like water spilled on the ground, which cannot be recovered, so we must die. But God does not take away life; instead, he devises ways so that a banished person may not remain estranged from him.

15"And now I have come to say this to my lord the king because the people have made me afraid. Your servant thought, 'I will speak to the king; perhaps he will do what his servant asks. 16Perhaps the king will agree to deliver his servant from the hand of the man who is trying to cut off both me and my son from the inheritance God gave us.'

17"And now your servant says, 'May the word of my lord the king bring me rest, for my lord the king is like an angel of God in discerning good and evil. May the LORD your God be with you.' "

18Then the king said to the woman, "Do not keep from me the answer to what I am going to ask you."

"Let my lord the king speak," the woman said.

19The king asked, "Isn't the hand of Joab with you in all this?"

The woman answered, "As surely as you live, my lord the king, no one can turn to the right or to the left from anything my lord the king says. Yes, it was your servant Joab who instructed me to do this and who put all these words into the mouth of your servant. 20Your servant Joab did this to change the present situation. My lord has wisdom like that of an angel of God—he knows everything that happens in the land."

21The king said to Joab, "Very well, I will do it. Go, bring back the young man Absalom."

22Joab fell with his face to the ground to pay him honor, and he blessed the king. Joab said, "Today your servant knows that he has found favor in your eyes, my lord the king, because the king has granted his servant's request."

23Then Joab went to Geshur and brought Absalom back to Jerusalem. 24But the king said, "He must go to his own house; he must not see my face." So Absalom went to his own house and did not see the face of the king.

25In all Israel there was not a man so highly praised for his handsome appearance as Absalom. From the top of his head to the sole of his foot there was no blemish in him. 26Whenever he cut the hair of his head—he used to cut his hair from time to time when it became too heavy for him—he would weigh it, and its weight was two hundred shekels[p] by the royal standard.

27Three sons and a daughter were born to Absalom. The daughter's name was Tamar, and she became a beautiful woman.

28Absalom lived two years in Jerusalem without seeing the king's face. 29Then Absalom sent for Joab in order to send him to the king, but Joab refused to come to him. So he sent a second time, but he refused to come. 30Then he said to his servants, "Look, Joab's field is next to mine, and he has barley there. Go and set it on fire." So Absalom's servants set the field on fire.

31Then Joab did go to Absalom's house and he said to him, "Why have your servants set my field on fire?"

32Absalom said to Joab, "Look, I sent word to you and said, 'Come here so I can send you to the king to ask, "Why have I come from Geshur? It would be better for me if I were still there!" ' Now then, I want to see the king's face, and if I am guilty of anything, let him put me to death."

33So Joab went to the king and told him this. Then the king summoned Absalom, and he came in and bowed down with his face to the ground before the king. And the king kissed Absalom.

p26 That is, about 5 pounds (about 2.3 kilograms)

7 / 2 Samuel 15
Difficult Days

STRESS HAS BECOME a part of our Western culture. We are all familiar with it, and it affects us all in our own way. Some can't eat, some get grumpy, some sleep. Me, well, I stay awake at night. My mind and heart cannot stop thinking about the issue at hand. My body is zonked, but my head keeps going a mile a minute.

One night a few years ago, while wrestling with a sudden case of insomnia brought on by balancing the family checkbook, I was struck by how void my worry was of thoughts of God. I had considered every option a thousand times in my head, but I hadn't prayed. I had not stopped to consider God's character or the promises of his Word. That night I learned that my lack of sleep is directly linked to my lack of faith. I still occasionally find myself unable to sleep, but I now have an option that brings my heart rest. I remember God, and I give it to him.

 **Warming Up to God** What are you feeling worried about right now? How has God been part of your process of working through your stress?

 **Read 2 Samuel 15.**

15 In the course of time, Absalom provided himself with a chariot and horses and with fifty men to run ahead of him. 2He would get up early and stand by the side of the road leading to the city gate. Whenever anyone came with a complaint to be placed before the king for a decision, Absalom would call out to him, "What town are you from?" He would answer, "Your servant is from one of the tribes of Israel." 3Then Absalom would say to him, "Look, your claims are valid and proper, but there is no representative of the king to hear you." 4And Absalom would add, "If only I were appointed judge in the land! Then everyone who has a complaint or case could come to me and I would see that he gets justice."

5Also, whenever anyone approached him to bow down before him, Absalom would reach out his hand, take hold of him and kiss him. 6Absalom behaved in this way toward all the Israelites who came to the king asking for justice, and so he stole the hearts of the men of Israel.

7At the end of four[q] years, Absalom said to the king, "Let me go to Hebron and fulfill a vow I made to the LORD. 8While your servant was living at Geshur in Aram, I made this vow: 'If the LORD takes me back to Jerusalem, I will worship the LORD in Hebron.[r]' "

9The king said to him, "Go in peace." So he went to Hebron.

10Then Absalom sent secret messengers throughout the tribes of Israel to say, "As soon as you hear the sound of the trumpets, then say, 'Absalom is king in Hebron.' " 11Two hundred men from Jerusalem had accompanied Absalom. They had been invited as guests and went quite innocently, knowing nothing about the matter. 12While Absalom was offering sacrifices, he also sent for Ahithophel the Gilonite, David's counselor, to come from Giloh, his hometown. And so the conspiracy gained strength, and Absalom's following kept on increasing.

13A messenger came and told David, "The hearts of the men of Israel are with Absalom."

14Then David said to all his officials who were with him in Jerusalem, "Come! We must flee, or none of us will escape from Absalom. We must leave immediately, or he will move quickly to overtake us and bring ruin upon us and put the city to the sword."

15The king's officials answered him, "Your servants are ready to do whatever our lord the king chooses."

16The king set out, with his entire household following him; but he left ten concubines to take care of the palace. 17So the king set out, with all the people following him, and they halted at a place some distance away. 18All his men marched past him, along with all the Kerethites and Pelethites; and all the six hundred Gittites who had accompanied him from Gath marched before the king.

19The king said to Ittai the Gittite, "Why should you come along with us? Go back and stay with King Absalom. You are a foreigner, an exile from your homeland. 20You came only yesterday. And today shall I make you wander about with us, when I do not know where I am going? Go

q7 Some Septuagint manuscripts, Syriac and Josephus; Hebrew *forty*
r8 Some Septuagint manuscripts; Hebrew does not have *in Hebron.*

back, and take your countrymen. May kindness and faithfulness be with you."

21But Ittai replied to the king, "As surely as the LORD lives, and as my lord the king lives, wherever my lord the king may be, whether it means life or death, there will your servant be."

22David said to Ittai, "Go ahead, march on." So Ittai the Gittite marched on with all his men and the families that were with him.

23The whole countryside wept aloud as all the people passed by. The king also crossed the Kidron Valley, and all the people moved on toward the desert.

24Zadok was there, too, and all the Levites who were with him were carrying the ark of the covenant of God. They set down the ark of God, and Abiathar offered sacrifices[s] until all the people had finished leaving the city.

25Then the king said to Zadok, "Take the ark of God back into the city. If I find favor in the LORD's eyes, he will bring me back and let me see it and his dwelling place again. 26But if he says, 'I am not pleased with you,' then I am ready; let him do to me whatever seems good to him."

27The king also said to Zadok the priest, "Aren't you a seer? Go back to the city in peace, with your son Ahimaaz and Jonathan son of Abiathar. You and Abiathar take your two sons with you. 28I will wait at the fords in the desert until word comes from you to inform me." 29So Zadok and Abiathar took the ark of God back to Jerusalem and stayed there.

30But David continued up the Mount of Olives, weeping as he went; his head was covered and he was barefoot. All the people with him covered their heads too and were weeping as they went up. 31Now David had been told, "Ahithophel is among the conspirators with Absalom." So David prayed, "O LORD, turn Ahithophel's counsel into foolishness."

32When David arrived at the summit, where people used to worship God, Hushai the Arkite was there to meet him, his robe torn and dust on his head. 33David said to him, "If you go with me, you will be a burden to me. 34But if you return to the city and say to Absalom, 'I will be your servant, O king; I was your father's servant in the past, but now I will be your servant,' then you can help me by frustrating Ahithophel's advice. 35Won't the priests Zadok and Abiathar be there with you? Tell them anything you hear in the king's palace. 36Their two sons, Ahimaaz son of Zadok and Jonathan son of Abiathar, are there with them. Send them to me with anything you hear."

37So David's friend Hushai arrived at Jerusalem as Absalom was entering the city.

[s]24 Or *Abiathar went up*

Discovering the Word 1. What is Absalom's strategy against David (vv. 1–12)? 2. Identify Absalom's unethical behavior. What does it tell us about him? 3. What does David do in defense against Absalom's attack? 4. Why does David tell Ittai to go back at first (vv. 19–20)? 5. What does the devotion of the people tell you about David (vv. 16, 21, 23, 30)? 6. In what ways does David demonstrate and act on his faith and trust in God?

Applying the Word 1. In 2 Samuel we learn that David took some steps in his own defense; yet he also looked to God for a sign of favor. 2. What truth or truths about God might help you respond to stressful situations with rest and peace?

Responding in Prayer Spend some time praying through the issues that are troubling you.

2 Samuel 16:1—18:18

16 When David had gone a short distance beyond the summit, there was Ziba, the steward of Mephibosheth, waiting to meet him. He had a string of donkeys saddled and loaded with two hundred loaves of bread, a hundred cakes of raisins, a hundred cakes of figs and a skin of wine.

2The king asked Ziba, "Why have you brought these?"

Ziba answered, "The donkeys are for the king's household to ride on, the bread and fruit are for the men to eat, and the wine is to refresh those who become exhausted in the desert."

3The king then asked, "Where is your master's grandson?"

Ziba said to him, "He is staying in Jerusalem, because he thinks, 'Today the house of Israel will give me back my grandfather's kingdom.' "

4Then the king said to Ziba, "All that belonged to Mephibosheth is now yours."

"I humbly bow," Ziba said. "May I find favor in your eyes, my lord the king."

5As King David approached Bahurim, a man from the same clan as Saul's family came out from there. His name was Shimei son of Gera, and he cursed as he came out. 6He pelted David and all the king's officials with stones, though all the troops and the special guard were on David's right and left. 7As he cursed, Shimei said, "Get out, get out, you man of blood, you scoundrel! 8The LORD has repaid you for all the blood you shed in the household of Saul, in whose place you have reigned. The LORD has handed the kingdom over to your son Absalom. You have come to ruin because you are a man of blood!"

9Then Abishai son of Zeruiah said to the king, "Why should this dead dog curse my lord the king? Let me go over and cut off his head."

10But the king said, "What do you and I have in common, you sons of Zeruiah? If he is cursing because the LORD said to him, 'Curse David,' who can ask, 'Why do you do this?' "

11David then said to Abishai and all his officials, "My son, who is of my own flesh, is trying to take my life. How much more, then, this Benjamite! Leave him alone; let him curse, for the LORD has told him to. 12It may be that the LORD will see my distress and repay me with good for the cursing I am receiving today."

13So David and his men continued along the road while Shimei was going along the hillside opposite him, cursing as he went and throwing stones at him and showering him with dirt. 14The king and all the people with him arrived at their destination exhausted. And there he refreshed himself.

15Meanwhile, Absalom and all the men of Israel came to Jerusalem, and Ahithophel was with him. 16Then Hushai the Arkite, David's friend, went to Absalom and said to him, "Long live the king! Long live the king!"

17Absalom asked Hushai, "Is this the love you show your friend? Why didn't you go with your friend?"

18Hushai said to Absalom, "No, the one chosen by the LORD, by these people, and by all the men of Israel—his I will be, and I will remain with him. 19Furthermore, whom should I serve? Should I not serve the son? Just as I served your father, so I will serve you."

20Absalom said to Ahithophel, "Give us your advice. What should we do?"

21Ahithophel answered, "Lie with your father's concubines whom he left to take care of the palace. Then all Israel will hear that you have made yourself a stench in your father's nostrils, and the hands of everyone with you will be strengthened." 22So they pitched a tent for Absalom on the roof, and he lay with his father's concubines in the sight of all Israel.

23Now in those days the advice Ahithophel gave was like that of one who inquires of God. That was how both David and Absalom regarded all of Ahithophel's advice.

17 Ahithophel said to Absalom, "I would[t] choose twelve thousand men and set out tonight in pursuit of David. 2I would[u] attack him while he is weary and weak. I would[u] strike him with terror, and then all the people with him will flee. I would[u] strike down only the king 3and bring all the people back to you. The death of the man you seek will mean the return of all; all the people will be unharmed." 4This plan seemed good to Absalom and to all the elders of Israel.

5But Absalom said, "Summon also Hushai the Arkite, so we can hear what he has to say."

[t]1 Or *Let me* [u]2 Or *will*

6When Hushai came to him, Absalom said,
"Ahithophel has given this advice. Should we do
what he says? If not, give us your opinion."
7Hushai replied to Absalom, "The advice
Ahithophel has given is not good this time. 8You
know your father and his men; they are fighters,
and as fierce as a wild bear robbed of her cubs.
Besides, your father is an experienced fighter; he
will not spend the night with the troops. 9Even
now, he is hidden in a cave or some other place.
If he should attack your troops first,[v] whoever
hears about it will say, 'There has been a slaugh-
ter among the troops who follow Absalom.'
10Then even the bravest soldier, whose heart is
like the heart of a lion, will melt with fear, for all
Israel knows that your father is a fighter and that
those with him are brave.
11"So I advise you: Let all Israel, from Dan to
Beersheba—as numerous as the sand on the sea-
shore—be gathered to you, with you yourself
leading them into battle. 12Then we will attack
him wherever he may be found, and we will fall
on him as dew settles on the ground. Neither he
nor any of his men will be left alive. 13If he with-
draws into a city, then all Israel will bring ropes
to that city, and we will drag it down to the valley
until not even a piece of it can be found."
14Absalom and all the men of Israel said, "The
advice of Hushai the Arkite is better than that
of Ahithophel." For the LORD had determined to
frustrate the good advice of Ahithophel in order
to bring disaster on Absalom.
15Hushai told Zadok and Abiathar, the priests,
"Ahithophel has advised Absalom and the elders
of Israel to do such and such, but I have advised
them to do so and so. 16Now send a message im-
mediately and tell David, 'Do not spend the night
at the fords in the desert; cross over without fail,
or the king and all the people with him will be
swallowed up.'"
17Jonathan and Ahimaaz were staying at En Ro-
gel. A servant girl was to go and inform them, and
they were to go and tell King David, for they
could not risk being seen entering the city. 18But
a young man saw them and told Absalom. So the
two of them left quickly and went to the house of
a man in Bahurim. He had a well in his courtyard,
and they climbed down into it. 19His wife took a
covering and spread it out over the opening of the
well and scattered grain over it. No one knew
anything about it.
20When Absalom's men came to the woman at
the house, they asked, "Where are Ahimaaz and
Jonathan?"
The woman answered them, "They crossed
over the brook."[w] The men searched but found
no one, so they returned to Jerusalem.
21After the men had gone, the two climbed out
of the well and went to inform King David. They
said to him, "Set out and cross the river at once;
Ahithophel has advised such and such against
you." 22So David and all the people with him set
out and crossed the Jordan. By daybreak, no one
was left who had not crossed the Jordan.
23When Ahithophel saw that his advice had not
been followed, he saddled his donkey and set out
for his house in his hometown. He put his house
in order and then hanged himself. So he died and
was buried in his father's tomb.
24David went to Mahanaim, and Absalom
crossed the Jordan with all the men of Israel.
25Absalom had appointed Amasa over the army in
place of Joab. Amasa was the son of a man named
Jether,[x] an Israelite[y] who had married Abi-
gail,[z] the daughter of Nahash and sister of Zeru-
iah the mother of Joab. 26The Israelites and Absa-
lom camped in the land of Gilead.
27When David came to Mahanaim, Shobi son of
Nahash from Rabbah of the Ammonites, and Ma-
kir son of Ammiel from Lo Debar, and Barzillai
the Gileadite from Rogelim 28brought bedding
and bowls and articles of pottery. They also
brought wheat and barley, flour and roasted
grain, beans and lentils,[a] 29honey and curds,
sheep, and cheese from cows' milk for David and
his people to eat. For they said, "The people have
become hungry and tired and thirsty in the
desert."

18 David mustered the men who were
with him and appointed over them
commanders of thousands and
commanders of hundreds. 2David sent the troops
out—a third under the command of Joab, a third
under Joab's brother Abishai son of Zeruiah, and
a third under Ittai the Gittite. The king told the
troops, "I myself will surely march out with you."
3But the men said, "You must not go out; if we
are forced to flee, they won't care about us. Even
if half of us die, they won't care; but you are

[v]9 Or *When some of the men fall at the first attack* [w]20 Or *"They passed by the sheep pen toward the water."* [x]25 Hebrew *Ithra*, a variant of *Jether* [y]25 Hebrew and some Septuagint manuscripts; other Septuagint manuscripts (see also 1 Chron. 2:17) *Ishmaelite* or *Jezreelite* [z]25 Hebrew *Abigal*, a variant of *Abigail* [a]28 Most Septuagint manuscripts and Syriac; Hebrew *lentils, and roasted grain*

worth ten thousand of us.[b] It would be better now for you to give us support from the city."

4The king answered, "I will do whatever seems best to you."

So the king stood beside the gate while all the men marched out in units of hundreds and of thousands. 5The king commanded Joab, Abishai and Ittai, "Be gentle with the young man Absalom for my sake." And all the troops heard the king giving orders concerning Absalom to each of the commanders.

6The army marched into the field to fight Israel, and the battle took place in the forest of Ephraim. 7There the army of Israel was defeated by David's men, and the casualties that day were great—twenty thousand men. 8The battle spread out over the whole countryside, and the forest claimed more lives that day than the sword.

9Now Absalom happened to meet David's men. He was riding his mule, and as the mule went under the thick branches of a large oak, Absalom's head got caught in the tree. He was left hanging in midair, while the mule he was riding kept on going.

10When one of the men saw this, he told Joab, "I just saw Absalom hanging in an oak tree."

11Joab said to the man who had told him this, "What! You saw him? Why didn't you strike him to the ground right there? Then I would have had to give you ten shekels[c] of silver and a warrior's belt."

12But the man replied, "Even if a thousand shekels[d] were weighed out into my hands, I would not lift my hand against the king's son. In our hearing the king commanded you and Abishai and Ittai, 'Protect the young man Absalom for my sake.[e]' 13And if I had put my life in jeopardy[f]—and nothing is hidden from the king—you would have kept your distance from me."

14Joab said, "I'm not going to wait like this for you." So he took three javelins in his hand and plunged them into Absalom's heart while Absalom was still alive in the oak tree. 15And ten of Joab's armor-bearers surrounded Absalom, struck him and killed him.

16Then Joab sounded the trumpet, and the troops stopped pursuing Israel, for Joab halted them. 17They took Absalom, threw him into a big pit in the forest and piled up a large heap of rocks over him. Meanwhile, all the Israelites fled to their homes.

18During his lifetime Absalom had taken a pillar and erected it in the King's Valley as a monument to himself, for he thought, "I have no son to carry on the memory of my name." He named the pillar after himself, and it is called Absalom's Monument to this day.

[b]3 Two Hebrew manuscripts, some Septuagint manuscripts and Vulgate; most Hebrew manuscripts *care; for now there are ten thousand like us* [c]11 That is, about 4 ounces (about 115 grams) [d]12 That is, about 25 pounds (about 11 kilograms) [e]12 A few Hebrew manuscripts, Septuagint, Vulgate and Syriac; most Hebrew manuscripts may be translated *Absalom, whoever you may be.* [f]13 Or *Otherwise, if I had acted treacherously toward him*

8 / 2 *Samuel 18:19—19:10*
Receiving Counsel

I HATE LOOKING silly—looking as if I don't know what I am doing. Sometimes this fear keeps me from the simplest of tasks (asking directions, for instance). This aversion was so strong in my youth that it kept me from trying the things I enjoy so much today, like basketball and golf. I was so paralyzed by fear that I even refused instruction.

Maturity and a growing security in God's love for me have freed me from so many fears—but some still linger. Like I said, I'm occasionally stereotypically male in my reluctance to ask for directions. But experience has taught me that I'll be much better off if I seek other people's advice. I may not always look like the competent man I think people expect me to be, but I'm learning, growing and becoming more like God in humility.

Warming Up to God When has asking for advice or instruction been of significant benefit to you?

Read 2 Samuel 18:19—19:10.

19 Now Ahimaaz son of Zadok said, "Let me run and take the news to the king that the LORD has delivered him from the hand of his enemies."

20 "You are not the one to take the news today," Joab told him. "You may take the news another time, but you must not do so today, because the king's son is dead."

21 Then Joab said to a Cushite, "Go, tell the king what you have seen." The Cushite bowed down before Joab and ran off.

22 Ahimaaz son of Zadok again said to Joab, "Come what may, please let me run behind the Cushite."

But Joab replied, "My son, why do you want to go? You don't have any news that will bring you a reward."

23 He said, "Come what may, I want to run."

So Joab said, "Run!" Then Ahimaaz ran by way of the plain[g] and outran the Cushite.

24 While David was sitting between the inner and outer gates, the watchman went up to the roof of the gateway by the wall. As he looked out, he saw a man running alone. 25 The watchman called out to the king and reported it.

The king said, "If he is alone, he must have good news." And the man came closer and closer.

26 Then the watchman saw another man running, and he called down to the gatekeeper, "Look, another man running alone!"

The king said, "He must be bringing good news, too."

27 The watchman said, "It seems to me that the first one runs like Ahimaaz son of Zadok."

"He's a good man," the king said. "He comes with good news."

28 Then Ahimaaz called out to the king, "All is well!" He bowed down before the king with his face to the ground and said, "Praise be to the LORD your God! He has delivered up the men who lifted their hands against my lord the king."

29 The king asked, "Is the young man Absalom safe?"

Ahimaaz answered, "I saw great confusion just as Joab was about to send the king's servant and me, your servant, but I don't know what it was."

30 The king said, "Stand aside and wait here." So he stepped aside and stood there.

31 Then the Cushite arrived and said, "My lord the king, hear the good news! The LORD has delivered you today from all who rose up against you."

32 The king asked the Cushite, "Is the young man Absalom safe?"

The Cushite replied, "May the enemies of my lord the king and all who rise up to harm you be like that young man."

33 The king was shaken. He went up to the room over the gateway and wept. As he went, he said: "O my son Absalom! My son, my son Absalom! If only I had died instead of you—O Absalom, my son, my son!"

19

Joab was told, "The king is weeping and mourning for Absalom." 2 And for the whole army the victory that day was turned into mourning, because on that day the troops heard it said, "The king is grieving for his son." 3 The men stole into the city that day as men steal in who are ashamed when they flee from battle. 4 The king covered his face and cried aloud, "O my son Absalom! O Absalom, my son, my son!"

5 Then Joab went into the house to the king and said, "Today you have humiliated all your men, who have just saved your life and the lives of your sons and daughters and the lives of your wives and concubines. 6 You love those who hate you and hate those who love you. You have made it clear today that the commanders and their men mean nothing to you. I see that you would be pleased if Absalom were alive today and all of us were dead. 7 Now go out and encourage your men. I swear by the LORD that if you don't go out, not a man will be left with you by nightfall. This will be worse for you than all the calamities that have come upon you from your youth till now."

8 So the king got up and took his seat in the gateway. When the men were told, "The king is sitting in the gateway," they all came before him.

Meanwhile, the Israelites had fled to their homes. 9 Throughout the tribes of Israel, the people were all arguing with each other, saying, "The king delivered us from the hand of our enemies; he is the one who rescued us from the hand of the Philistines. But now he has fled the country because of Absalom; 10 and Absalom, whom we anointed to rule over us, has died in battle. So why do you say nothing about bringing the king back?"

g23 That is, the plain of the Jordan

Discovering the Word 1. What seems to be David's mood in 18:24–32? 2. Absalom was killed in 18:14 while trying to forcibly take the kingdom from David. Describe the extent of David's grief. 3. Why is David's mourning his son's death upsetting to his army (19:5–6)? 4. In your own words, what was Joab's advice to David (19:7)? 5. What did it cost David to follow the advice given to him (19:9–10)?

Applying the Word 1. What kind of advice are you eager to receive? Explain. 2. Are you good at hearing criticism? Why or why not? 3. From David's example, what are some principles we should apply when we try to evaluate advice given to us?

Responding in Prayer Ask God to build in you the character traits of humility and wisdom.

2 Samuel 19:11—24:25

11King David sent this message to Zadok and Abiathar, the priests: "Ask the elders of Judah, 'Why should you be the last to bring the king back to his palace, since what is being said throughout Israel has reached the king at his quarters? 12You are my brothers, my own flesh and blood. So why should you be the last to bring back the king?' 13And say to Amasa, 'Are you not my own flesh and blood? May God deal with me, be it ever so severely, if from now on you are not the commander of my army in place of Joab.' "

14He won over the hearts of all the men of Judah as though they were one man. They sent word to the king, "Return, you and all your men." 15Then the king returned and went as far as the Jordan.

Now the men of Judah had come to Gilgal to go out and meet the king and bring him across the Jordan. 16Shimei son of Gera, the Benjamite from Bahurim, hurried down with the men of Judah to meet King David. 17With him were a thousand Benjamites, along with Ziba, the steward of Saul's household, and his fifteen sons and twenty servants. They rushed to the Jordan, where the king was. 18They crossed at the ford to take the king's household over and to do whatever he wished.

When Shimei son of Gera crossed the Jordan, he fell prostrate before the king 19and said to him, "May my lord not hold me guilty. Do not remember how your servant did wrong on the day my lord the king left Jerusalem. May the king put it out of his mind. 20For I your servant know that I have sinned, but today I have come here as the first of the whole house of Joseph to come down and meet my lord the king."

21Then Abishai son of Zeruiah said, "Shouldn't Shimei be put to death for this? He cursed the LORD's anointed."

22David replied, "What do you and I have in common, you sons of Zeruiah? This day you have become my adversaries! Should anyone be put to death in Israel today? Do I not know that today I am king over Israel?" 23So the king said to Shimei, "You shall not die." And the king promised him on oath.

24Mephibosheth, Saul's grandson, also went down to meet the king. He had not taken care of his feet or trimmed his mustache or washed his clothes from the day the king left until the day he returned safely. 25When he came from Jerusalem to meet the king, the king asked him, "Why didn't you go with me, Mephibosheth?"

26He said, "My lord the king, since I your servant am lame, I said, 'I will have my donkey saddled and will ride on it, so I can go with the king.' But Ziba my servant betrayed me. 27And he has slandered your servant to my lord the king. My lord the king is like an angel of God; so do whatever pleases you. 28All my grandfather's descendants deserved nothing but death from my lord the king, but you gave your servant a place among those who eat at your table. So what right do I have to make any more appeals to the king?"

29The king said to him, "Why say more? I order you and Ziba to divide the fields."

30Mephibosheth said to the king, "Let him take everything, now that my lord the king has arrived home safely."

31Barzillai the Gileadite also came down from Rogelim to cross the Jordan with the king and to send him on his way from there. 32Now Barzillai was a very old man, eighty years of age. He had provided for the king during his stay in Mahanaim, for he was a very wealthy man. 33The king said to Barzillai, "Cross over with me and stay with me in Jerusalem, and I will provide for you."

[34]But Barzillai answered the king, "How many more years will I live, that I should go up to Jerusalem with the king? [35]I am now eighty years old. Can I tell the difference between what is good and what is not? Can your servant taste what he eats and drinks? Can I still hear the voices of men and women singers? Why should your servant be an added burden to my lord the king? [36]Your servant will cross over the Jordan with the king for a short distance, but why should the king reward me in this way? [37]Let your servant return, that I may die in my own town near the tomb of my father and mother. But here is your servant Kimham. Let him cross over with my lord the king. Do for him whatever pleases you."

[38]The king said, "Kimham shall cross over with me, and I will do for him whatever pleases you. And anything you desire from me I will do for you."

[39]So all the people crossed the Jordan, and then the king crossed over. The king kissed Barzillai and gave him his blessing, and Barzillai returned to his home.

[40]When the king crossed over to Gilgal, Kimham crossed with him. All the troops of Judah and half the troops of Israel had taken the king over.

[41]Soon all the men of Israel were coming to the king and saying to him, "Why did our brothers, the men of Judah, steal the king away and bring him and his household across the Jordan, together with all his men?"

[42]All the men of Judah answered the men of Israel, "We did this because the king is closely related to us. Why are you angry about it? Have we eaten any of the king's provisions? Have we taken anything for ourselves?"

[43]Then the men of Israel answered the men of Judah, "We have ten shares in the king; and besides, we have a greater claim on David than you have. So why do you treat us with contempt? Were we not the first to speak of bringing back our king?"

But the men of Judah responded even more harshly than the men of Israel.

20

Now a troublemaker named Sheba son of Bicri, a Benjamite, happened to be there. He sounded the trumpet and shouted,

"We have no share in David,
  no part in Jesse's son!
Every man to his tent, O Israel!"

[2]So all the men of Israel deserted David to follow Sheba son of Bicri. But the men of Judah stayed by their king all the way from the Jordan to Jerusalem.

[3]When David returned to his palace in Jerusalem, he took the ten concubines he had left to take care of the palace and put them in a house under guard. He provided for them, but did not lie with them. They were kept in confinement till the day of their death, living as widows.

[4]Then the king said to Amasa, "Summon the men of Judah to come to me within three days, and be here yourself." [5]But when Amasa went to summon Judah, he took longer than the time the king had set for him.

[6]David said to Abishai, "Now Sheba son of Bicri will do us more harm than Absalom did. Take your master's men and pursue him, or he will find fortified cities and escape from us." [7]So Joab's men and the Kerethites and Pelethites and all the mighty warriors went out under the command of Abishai. They marched out from Jerusalem to pursue Sheba son of Bicri.

[8]While they were at the great rock in Gibeon, Amasa came to meet them. Joab was wearing his military tunic, and strapped over it at his waist was a belt with a dagger in its sheath. As he stepped forward, it dropped out of its sheath.

[9]Joab said to Amasa, "How are you, my brother?" Then Joab took Amasa by the beard with his right hand to kiss him. [10]Amasa was not on his guard against the dagger in Joab's hand, and Joab plunged it into his belly, and his intestines spilled out on the ground. Without being stabbed again, Amasa died. Then Joab and his brother Abishai pursued Sheba son of Bicri.

[11]One of Joab's men stood beside Amasa and said, "Whoever favors Joab, and whoever is for David, let him follow Joab!" [12]Amasa lay wallowing in his blood in the middle of the road, and the man saw that all the troops came to a halt there. When he realized that everyone who came up to Amasa stopped, he dragged him from the road into a field and threw a garment over him. [13]After Amasa had been removed from the road, all the men went on with Joab to pursue Sheba son of Bicri.

[14]Sheba passed through all the tribes of Israel to Abel Beth Maacah[h] and through the entire region of the Berites, who gathered together and followed him. [15]All the troops with Joab came

[h]14 Or *Abel, even Beth Maacah*; also in verse 15

and besieged Sheba in Abel Beth Maacah. They built a siege ramp up to the city, and it stood against the outer fortifications. While they were battering the wall to bring it down, 16a wise woman called from the city, "Listen! Listen! Tell Joab to come here so I can speak to him." 17He went toward her, and she asked, "Are you Joab?"

"I am," he answered.

She said, "Listen to what your servant has to say."

"I'm listening," he said.

18She continued, "Long ago they used to say, 'Get your answer at Abel,' and that settled it. 19We are the peaceful and faithful in Israel. You are trying to destroy a city that is a mother in Israel. Why do you want to swallow up the LORD's inheritance?"

20"Far be it from me!" Joab replied, "Far be it from me to swallow up or destroy! 21That is not the case. A man named Sheba son of Bicri, from the hill country of Ephraim, has lifted up his hand against the king, against David. Hand over this one man, and I'll withdraw from the city."

The woman said to Joab, "His head will be thrown to you from the wall."

22Then the woman went to all the people with her wise advice, and they cut off the head of Sheba son of Bicri and threw it to Joab. So he sounded the trumpet, and his men dispersed from the city, each returning to his home. And Joab went back to the king in Jerusalem.

23Joab was over Israel's entire army; Benaiah son of Jehoiada was over the Kerethites and Pelethites; 24Adoniram[i] was in charge of forced labor; Jehoshaphat son of Ahilud was recorder; 25Sheva was secretary; Zadok and Abiathar were priests; 26and Ira the Jairite was David's priest.

21 During the reign of David, there was a famine for three successive years; so David sought the face of the LORD. The LORD said, "It is on account of Saul and his blood-stained house; it is because he put the Gibeonites to death."

2The king summoned the Gibeonites and spoke to them. (Now the Gibeonites were not a part of Israel but were survivors of the Amorites; the Israelites had sworn to ⌊spare⌋ them, but Saul in his zeal for Israel and Judah had tried to annihilate them.) 3David asked the Gibeonites, "What shall I do for you? How shall I make amends so that you will bless the LORD's inheritance?"

4The Gibeonites answered him, "We have no right to demand silver or gold from Saul or his family, nor do we have the right to put anyone in Israel to death."

"What do you want me to do for you?" David asked.

5They answered the king, "As for the man who destroyed us and plotted against us so that we have been decimated and have no place anywhere in Israel, 6let seven of his male descendants be given to us to be killed and exposed before the LORD at Gibeah of Saul—the LORD's chosen one."

So the king said, "I will give them to you."

7The king spared Mephibosheth son of Jonathan, the son of Saul, because of the oath before the LORD between David and Jonathan son of Saul. 8But the king took Armoni and Mephibosheth, the two sons of Aiah's daughter Rizpah, whom she had borne to Saul, together with the five sons of Saul's daughter Merab,[j] whom she had borne to Adriel son of Barzillai the Meholathite. 9He handed them over to the Gibeonites, who killed and exposed them on a hill before the LORD. All seven of them fell together; they were put to death during the first days of the harvest, just as the barley harvest was beginning.

10Rizpah daughter of Aiah took sackcloth and spread it out for herself on a rock. From the beginning of the harvest till the rain poured down from the heavens on the bodies, she did not let the birds of the air touch them by day or the wild animals by night. 11When David was told what Aiah's daughter Rizpah, Saul's concubine, had done, 12he went and took the bones of Saul and his son Jonathan from the citizens of Jabesh Gilead. (They had taken them secretly from the public square at Beth Shan, where the Philistines had hung them after they struck Saul down on Gilboa.) 13David brought the bones of Saul and his son Jonathan from there, and the bones of those who had been killed and exposed were gathered up.

14They buried the bones of Saul and his son Jonathan in the tomb of Saul's father Kish, at Zela in Benjamin, and did everything the king commanded. After that, God answered prayer in behalf of the land.

15Once again there was a battle between the Philistines and Israel. David went down with his men to fight against the Philistines, and he be-

i24 Some Septuagint manuscripts (see also 1 Kings 4:6 and 5:14); Hebrew *Adoram* j8 Two Hebrew manuscripts, some Septuagint manuscripts and Syriac (see also 1 Samuel 18:19); most Hebrew and Septuagint manuscripts *Michal*

came exhausted. 16And Ishbi-Benob, one of the
descendants of Rapha, whose bronze spearhead
weighed three hundred shekels[k] and who was
armed with a new ⌊sword⌋, said he would kill
David. 17But Abishai son of Zeruiah came to Da-
vid's rescue; he struck the Philistine down and
killed him. Then David's men swore to him, say-
ing, "Never again will you go out with us to bat-
tle, so that the lamp of Israel will not be extin-
guished."

18In the course of time, there was another bat-
tle with the Philistines, at Gob. At that time Sib-
becai the Hushathite killed Saph, one of the
descendants of Rapha.

19In another battle with the Philistines at Gob,
Elhanan son of Jaare-Oregim[l] the Bethlehemite
killed Goliath[m] the Gittite, who had a spear with
a shaft like a weaver's rod.

20In still another battle, which took place at
Gath, there was a huge man with six fingers on
each hand and six toes on each foot—twenty-
four in all. He also was descended from Rapha.
21When he taunted Israel, Jonathan son of Shim-
eah, David's brother, killed him.

22These four were descendants of Rapha in
Gath, and they fell at the hands of David and his
men.

22

David sang to the LORD the words of
this song when the LORD delivered
him from the hand of all his ene-
mies and from the hand of Saul. 2He said:

"The LORD is my rock, my fortress and my deliverer;
3 my God is my rock, in whom I take refuge,
my shield and the horn[n] of my salvation.
He is my stronghold, my refuge and my savior—
from violent men you save me.
4I call to the LORD, who is worthy of praise,
and I am saved from my enemies.

5"The waves of death swirled about me;
the torrents of destruction overwhelmed me.
6The cords of the grave[o] coiled around me;
the snares of death confronted me.
7In my distress I called to the LORD;
I called out to my God.
From his temple he heard my voice;
my cry came to his ears.

8"The earth trembled and quaked,
the foundations of the heavens[p] shook;
they trembled because he was angry.
9Smoke rose from his nostrils;
consuming fire came from his mouth,
burning coals blazed out of it.
10He parted the heavens and came down;
dark clouds were under his feet.
11He mounted the cherubim and flew;
he soared[q] on the wings of the wind.
12He made darkness his canopy around him—
the dark[r] rain clouds of the sky.
13Out of the brightness of his presence
bolts of lightning blazed forth.
14The LORD thundered from heaven;
the voice of the Most High resounded.
15He shot arrows and scattered ⌊the enemies⌋,
bolts of lightning and routed them.
16The valleys of the sea were exposed
and the foundations of the earth laid bare
at the rebuke of the LORD,
at the blast of breath from his nostrils.

17"He reached down from on high and took hold of me;
he drew me out of deep waters.
18He rescued me from my powerful enemy,
from my foes, who were too strong for me.
19They confronted me in the day of my disaster,
but the LORD was my support.
20He brought me out into a spacious place;
he rescued me because he delighted in me.

21"The LORD has dealt with me according to my righteousness;
according to the cleanness of my hands he has rewarded me.
22For I have kept the ways of the LORD;
I have not done evil by turning from my God.
23All his laws are before me;
I have not turned away from his decrees.
24I have been blameless before him
and have kept myself from sin.
25The LORD has rewarded me according to my righteousness,
according to my cleanness[s] in his sight.

[k]16 That is, about 7 1/2 pounds (about 3.5 kilograms) [l]19 Or *son of Jair the weaver* [m]19 Hebrew and Septuagint; 1 Chron. 20:5 *son of Jair killed Lahmi the brother of Goliath* [n]3 *Horn* here symbolizes strength. [o]6 Hebrew *Sheol* [p]8 Hebrew; Vulgate and Syriac (see also Psalm 18:7) *mountains* [q]11 Many Hebrew manuscripts (see also Psalm 18:10); most Hebrew manuscripts *appeared* [r]12 Septuagint and Vulgate (see also Psalm 18:11); Hebrew *massed* [s]25 Hebrew; Septuagint and Vulgate (see also Psalm 18:24) *to the cleanness of my hands*

26"To the faithful you show yourself faithful,
to the blameless you show yourself blameless,
27to the pure you show yourself pure,
but to the crooked you show yourself shrewd.
28You save the humble,
but your eyes are on the haughty to bring them low.
29You are my lamp, O LORD;
the LORD turns my darkness into light.
30With your help I can advance against a troop[t];
with my God I can scale a wall.

31"As for God, his way is perfect;
the word of the LORD is flawless.
He is a shield
for all who take refuge in him.
32For who is God besides the LORD?
And who is the Rock except our God?
33It is God who arms me with strength[u]
and makes my way perfect.
34He makes my feet like the feet of a deer;
he enables me to stand on the heights.
35He trains my hands for battle;
my arms can bend a bow of bronze.
36You give me your shield of victory;
you stoop down to make me great.
37You broaden the path beneath me,
so that my ankles do not turn.

38"I pursued my enemies and crushed them;
I did not turn back till they were destroyed.
39I crushed them completely, and they could not rise;
they fell beneath my feet.
40You armed me with strength for battle;
you made my adversaries bow at my feet.
41You made my enemies turn their backs in flight,
and I destroyed my foes.
42They cried for help, but there was no one to save them—
to the LORD, but he did not answer.
43I beat them as fine as the dust of the earth;
I pounded and trampled them like mud in the streets.
44"You have delivered me from the attacks of my people;
you have preserved me as the head of nations.
People I did not know are subject to me,
45 and foreigners come cringing to me;
as soon as they hear me, they obey me.
46They all lose heart;
they come trembling[v] from their strongholds.

47"The LORD lives! Praise be to my Rock!
Exalted be God, the Rock, my Savior!
48He is the God who avenges me,
who puts the nations under me,
49 who sets me free from my enemies.
You exalted me above my foes;
from violent men you rescued me.
50Therefore I will praise you, O LORD, among the nations;
I will sing praises to your name.
51He gives his king great victories;
he shows unfailing kindness to his anointed,
to David and his descendants forever."

23

These are the last words of David:
"The oracle of David son of Jesse,
the oracle of the man exalted by the Most High,
the man anointed by the God of Jacob,
Israel's singer of songs[w]:

2"The Spirit of the LORD spoke through me;
his word was on my tongue.
3The God of Israel spoke,
the Rock of Israel said to me:
'When one rules over men in righteousness,
when he rules in the fear of God,
4he is like the light of morning at sunrise
on a cloudless morning,
like the brightness after rain
that brings the grass from the earth.'

5"Is not my house right with God?
Has he not made with me an everlasting covenant,
arranged and secured in every part?
Will he not bring to fruition my salvation
and grant me my every desire?
6But evil men are all to be cast aside like thorns,
which are not gathered with the hand.
7Whoever touches thorns
uses a tool of iron or the shaft of a spear;
they are burned up where they lie."

[t]30 Or *can run through a barricade* [u]33 Dead Sea Scrolls, some Septuagint manuscripts, Vulgate and Syriac (see also Psalm 18:32); Masoretic Text *who is my strong refuge* [v]46 Some Septuagint manuscripts and Vulgate (see also Psalm 18:45); Masoretic Text *they arm themselves.* [w]1 Or *Israel's beloved singer*

8These are the names of David's mighty men:
Josheb-Basshebeth,[x] a Tahkemonite,[y] was
chief of the Three; he raised his spear against
eight hundred men, whom he killed[z] in one en-
counter.

9Next to him was Eleazar son of Dodai the
Ahohite. As one of the three mighty men, he was
with David when they taunted the Philistines
gathered ⌊at Pas Dammim⌋[a] for battle. Then the
men of Israel retreated, 10but he stood his ground
and struck down the Philistines till his hand grew
tired and froze to the sword. The LORD brought
about a great victory that day. The troops re-
turned to Eleazar, but only to strip the dead.

11Next to him was Shammah son of Agee the
Hararite. When the Philistines banded together at
a place where there was a field full of lentils, Is-
rael's troops fled from them. 12But Shammah took
his stand in the middle of the field. He defended
it and struck the Philistines down, and the LORD
brought about a great victory.

13During harvest time, three of the thirty chief
men came down to David at the cave of Adullam,
while a band of Philistines was encamped in the
Valley of Rephaim. 14At that time David was in
the stronghold, and the Philistine garrison was at
Bethlehem. 15David longed for water and said,
"Oh, that someone would get me a drink of water
from the well near the gate of Bethlehem!" 16So
the three mighty men broke through the Philis-
tine lines, drew water from the well near the gate
of Bethlehem and carried it back to David. But he
refused to drink it; instead, he poured it out be-
fore the LORD. 17"Far be it from me, O LORD, to do
this!" he said. "Is it not the blood of men who
went at the risk of their lives?" And David would
not drink it.

Such were the exploits of the three mighty
men.

18Abishai the brother of Joab son of Zeruiah
was chief of the Three.[b] He raised his spear
against three hundred men, whom he killed, and
so he became as famous as the Three. 19Was he
not held in greater honor than the Three? He be-
came their commander, even though he was not
included among them.

20Benaiah son of Jehoiada was a valiant fighter
from Kabzeel, who performed great exploits. He
struck down two of Moab's best men. He also
went down into a pit on a snowy day and killed a
lion. 21And he struck down a huge Egyptian. Al-
though the Egyptian had a spear in his hand, Be-
naiah went against him with a club. He snatched
the spear from the Egyptian's hand and killed him
with his own spear. 22Such were the exploits of
Benaiah son of Jehoiada; he too was as famous as
the three mighty men. 23He was held in greater
honor than any of the Thirty, but he was not
included among the Three. And David put him in
charge of his bodyguard.

24Among the Thirty were:
Asahel the brother of Joab,
Elhanan son of Dodo from Bethlehem,
25Shammah the Harodite,
Elika the Harodite,
26Helez the Paltite,
Ira son of Ikkesh from Tekoa,
27Abiezer from Anathoth,
Mebunnai[c] the Hushathite,
28Zalmon the Ahohite,
Maharai the Netophathite,
29Heled[d] son of Baanah the Netophathite,
Ithai son of Ribai from Gibeah in Benja-
min,
30Benaiah the Pirathonite,
Hiddai[e] from the ravines of Gaash,
31Abi-Albon the Arbathite,
Azmaveth the Barhumite,
32Eliahba the Shaalbonite,
the sons of Jashen,
Jonathan 33son of[f] Shammah the Hara-
rite,
Ahiam son of Sharar[g] the Hararite,
34Eliphelet son of Ahasbai the Maacathite,
Eliam son of Ahithophel the Gilonite,
35Hezro the Carmelite,
Paarai the Arbite,
36Igal son of Nathan from Zobah,
the son of Hagri,[h]
37Zelek the Ammonite,
Naharai the Beerothite, the armor-bearer
of Joab son of Zeruiah,
38Ira the Ithrite,
Gareb the Ithrite

[x]8 Hebrew; some Septuagint manuscripts suggest *Ish-Bosheth,* that is, *Esh-Baal* (see also 1 Chron. 11:11 *Jashobeam*). [y]8 Probably a variant of *Hacmonite* (see 1 Chron. 11:11) [z]8 Some Septuagint manuscripts (see also 1 Chron. 11:11); Hebrew and other Septuagint manuscripts *Three; it was Adino the Eznite who killed eight hundred men* [a]9 See 1 Chron. 11:13; Hebrew *gathered there.* [b]18 Most Hebrew manuscripts (see also 1 Chron. 11:20); two Hebrew manuscripts and Syriac *Thirty* [c]27 Hebrew; some Septuagint manuscripts (see also 1 Chron. 11:29) *Sibbecai* [d]29 Some Hebrew manuscripts and Vulgate (see also 1 Chron. 11:30); most Hebrew manuscripts *Heleb* [e]30 Hebrew; some Septuagint manuscripts (see also 1 Chron. 11:32) *Hurai* [f]33 Some Septuagint manuscripts (see also 1 Chron. 11:34); Hebrew does not have *son of.* [g]33 Hebrew; some Septuagint manuscripts (see also 1 Chron. 11:35) *Sacar* [h]36 Some Septuagint manuscripts (see also 1 Chron. 11:38); Hebrew *Haggadi*

39and Uriah the Hittite.

There were thirty-seven in all.

24

Again the anger of the LORD burned against Israel, and he incited David against them, saying, "Go and take a census of Israel and Judah."

2So the king said to Joab and the army commanders[i] with him, "Go throughout the tribes of Israel from Dan to Beersheba and enroll the fighting men, so that I may know how many there are."

3But Joab replied to the king, "May the LORD your God multiply the troops a hundred times over, and may the eyes of my lord the king see it. But why does my lord the king want to do such a thing?"

4The king's word, however, overruled Joab and the army commanders; so they left the presence of the king to enroll the fighting men of Israel.

5After crossing the Jordan, they camped near Aroer, south of the town in the gorge, and then went through Gad and on to Jazer. 6They went to Gilead and the region of Tahtim Hodshi, and on to Dan Jaan and around toward Sidon. 7Then they went toward the fortress of Tyre and all the towns of the Hivites and Canaanites. Finally, they went on to Beersheba in the Negev of Judah.

8After they had gone through the entire land, they came back to Jerusalem at the end of nine months and twenty days.

9Joab reported the number of the fighting men to the king: In Israel there were eight hundred thousand able-bodied men who could handle a sword, and in Judah five hundred thousand.

10David was conscience-stricken after he had counted the fighting men, and he said to the LORD, "I have sinned greatly in what I have done. Now, O LORD, I beg you, take away the guilt of your servant. I have done a very foolish thing."

11Before David got up the next morning, the word of the LORD had come to Gad the prophet, David's seer: 12"Go and tell David, 'This is what the LORD says: I am giving you three options. Choose one of them for me to carry out against you.' "

13So Gad went to David and said to him, "Shall there come upon you three[j] years of famine in your land? Or three months of fleeing from your enemies while they pursue you? Or three days of plague in your land? Now then, think it over and decide how I should answer the one who sent me."

14David said to Gad, "I am in deep distress. Let us fall into the hands of the LORD, for his mercy is great; but do not let me fall into the hands of men."

15So the LORD sent a plague on Israel from that morning until the end of the time designated, and seventy thousand of the people from Dan to Beersheba died. 16When the angel stretched out his hand to destroy Jerusalem, the LORD was grieved because of the calamity and said to the angel who was afflicting the people, "Enough! Withdraw your hand." The angel of the LORD was then at the threshing floor of Araunah the Jebusite.

17When David saw the angel who was striking down the people, he said to the LORD, "I am the one who has sinned and done wrong. These are but sheep. What have they done? Let your hand fall upon me and my family."

18On that day Gad went to David and said to him, "Go up and build an altar to the LORD on the threshing floor of Araunah the Jebusite." 19So David went up, as the LORD had commanded through Gad. 20When Araunah looked and saw the king and his men coming toward him, he went out and bowed down before the king with his face to the ground.

21Araunah said, "Why has my lord the king come to his servant?"

"To buy your threshing floor," David answered, "so I can build an altar to the LORD, that the plague on the people may be stopped."

22Araunah said to David, "Let my lord the king take whatever pleases him and offer it up. Here are oxen for the burnt offering, and here are threshing sledges and ox yokes for the wood. 23O king, Araunah gives all this to the king." Araunah also said to him, "May the LORD your God accept you."

24But the king replied to Araunah, "No, I insist on paying you for it. I will not sacrifice to the LORD my God burnt offerings that cost me nothing."

So David bought the threshing floor and the oxen and paid fifty shekels[k] of silver for them. 25David built an altar to the LORD there and sacrificed burnt offerings and fellowship offerings.[l] Then the LORD answered prayer in behalf of the land, and the plague on Israel was stopped.

[i]2 Septuagint (see also verse 4 and 1 Chron. 21:2); Hebrew *Joab the army commander* [j]13 Septuagint (see also 1 Chron. 21:12); Hebrew *seven* [k]24 That is, about 1 1/4 pounds (about 0.6 kilogram) [l]25 Traditionally *peace offerings*

1 Kings

What good will it do us twenty-first century Christians to study the kings who ruled a nation of Hebrews three thousand years ago? For people who get excited about battles and dates and ancient political maneuverings, the answer is obvious. All history, even Hebrew history, is great.

But what about the rest of us? God must have had some reason for designing his Holy Book so that one-third of the Old Testament recounts historical events. He wasn't just entertaining history buffs. A look at the issues surrounding these kings will give us some clues.

We see Solomon, who prayed as if he knew exactly what God desired to give, then fell into paganism under the influence of his seven hundred(!) wives. And we ask, "Do I ever place the people I love ahead of God?"

We see Jeroboam and Rehoboam, who split their nation in civil war and then split their places of worship. (Who among us has endured civil war within our church that could end in separate places of worship?)

We see Ahab, who ignored God even though prophets shouted into his spiritually deaf ears. And we look with dread upon our own potential deafness.

They ruled for four centuries, these Hebrew kings. There were forty-two of them. Some ruled only days, others for a lifetime. Some were so minor that they rate only a line of text. Others fill whole books. Some were evil; some were good. The biblical text evaluates each one at the end of his life. A reminder that we ourselves will undergo the same evaluation.

Outline

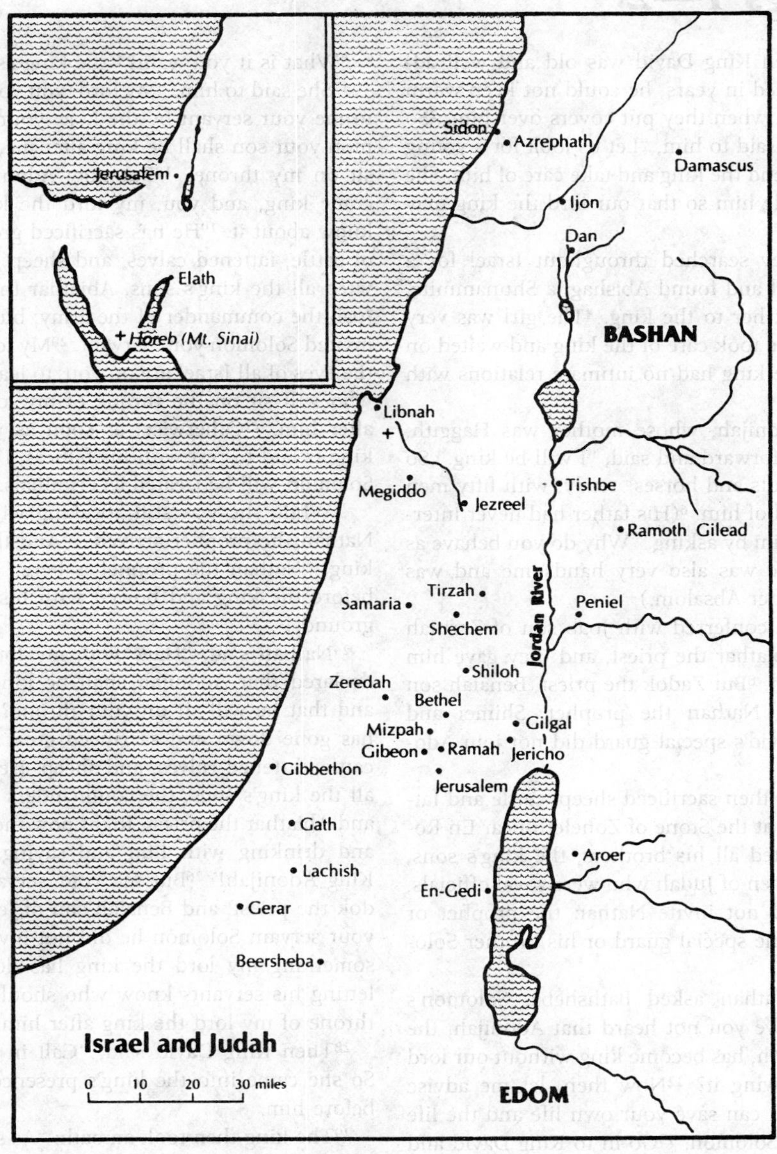
Sidon
Azrephath
Damascus
Jerusalem
Ijon
Dan
Elath
Horeb (Mt. Sinai)
BASHAN
Libnah
Megiddo
Tishbe
Jezreel
Ramoth Gilead
Tirzah
Peniel
Samaria
Shechem
Jordan River
Shiloh
Zeredah
Bethel
Gilgal
Mizpah
Gibeon
Ramah
Jericho
Jerusalem
Gibbethon
Gath
Aroer
Lachish
En-Gedi
Gerar
Beersheba
Israel and Judah
0 10 20 30 miles
EDOM

1 Kings 1—2

1 When King David was old and well advanced in years, he could not keep warm even when they put covers over him. 2So his servants said to him, "Let us look for a young virgin to attend the king and take care of him. She can lie beside him so that our lord the king may keep warm."

3Then they searched throughout Israel for a beautiful girl and found Abishag, a Shunammite, and brought her to the king. 4The girl was very beautiful; she took care of the king and waited on him, but the king had no intimate relations with her.

5Now Adonijah, whose mother was Haggith, put himself forward and said, "I will be king." So he got chariots and horses[a] ready, with fifty men to run ahead of him. 6(His father had never interfered with him by asking, "Why do you behave as you do?" He was also very handsome and was born next after Absalom.)

7Adonijah conferred with Joab son of Zeruiah and with Abiathar the priest, and they gave him their support. 8But Zadok the priest, Benaiah son of Jehoiada, Nathan the prophet, Shimei and Rei[b] and David's special guard did not join Adonijah.

9Adonijah then sacrificed sheep, cattle and fattened calves at the Stone of Zoheleth near En Rogel. He invited all his brothers, the king's sons, and all the men of Judah who were royal officials, 10but he did not invite Nathan the prophet or Benaiah or the special guard or his brother Solomon.

11Then Nathan asked Bathsheba, Solomon's mother, "Have you not heard that Adonijah, the son of Haggith, has become king without our lord David's knowing it? 12Now then, let me advise you how you can save your own life and the life of your son Solomon. 13Go in to King David and say to him, 'My lord the king, did you not swear to me your servant: "Surely Solomon your son shall be king after me, and he will sit on my throne"? Why then has Adonijah become king?' 14While you are still there talking to the king, I will come in and confirm what you have said."

15So Bathsheba went to see the aged king in his room, where Abishag the Shunammite was attending him. 16Bathsheba bowed low and knelt before the king.

"What is it you want?" the king asked.

17She said to him, "My lord, you yourself swore to me your servant by the LORD your God: 'Solomon your son shall be king after me, and he will sit on my throne.' 18But now Adonijah has become king, and you, my lord the king, do not know about it. 19He has sacrificed great numbers of cattle, fattened calves, and sheep, and has invited all the king's sons, Abiathar the priest and Joab the commander of the army, but he has not invited Solomon your servant. 20My lord the king, the eyes of all Israel are on you, to learn from you who will sit on the throne of my lord the king after him. 21Otherwise, as soon as my lord the king is laid to rest with his fathers, I and my son Solomon will be treated as criminals."

22While she was still speaking with the king, Nathan the prophet arrived. 23And they told the king, "Nathan the prophet is here." So he went before the king and bowed with his face to the ground.

24Nathan said, "Have you, my lord the king, declared that Adonijah shall be king after you, and that he will sit on your throne? 25Today he has gone down and sacrificed great numbers of cattle, fattened calves, and sheep. He has invited all the king's sons, the commanders of the army and Abiathar the priest. Right now they are eating and drinking with him and saying, 'Long live King Adonijah!' 26But me your servant, and Zadok the priest, and Benaiah son of Jehoiada, and your servant Solomon he did not invite. 27Is this something my lord the king has done without letting his servants know who should sit on the throne of my lord the king after him?"

28Then King David said, "Call in Bathsheba." So she came into the king's presence and stood before him.

29The king then took an oath: "As surely as the LORD lives, who has delivered me out of every trouble, 30I will surely carry out today what I swore to you by the LORD, the God of Israel: Solomon your son shall be king after me, and he will sit on my throne in my place."

31Then Bathsheba bowed low with her face to the ground and, kneeling before the king, said, "May my lord King David live forever!"

32King David said, "Call in Zadok the priest,

[a]5 Or *charioteers* [b]8 Or *and his friends*

Nathan the prophet and Benaiah son of Jehoiada." When they came before the king, [33]he said to them: "Take your lord's servants with you and set Solomon my son on my own mule and take him down to Gihon. [34]There have Zadok the priest and Nathan the prophet anoint him king over Israel. Blow the trumpet and shout, 'Long live King Solomon!' [35]Then you are to go up with him, and he is to come and sit on my throne and reign in my place. I have appointed him ruler over Israel and Judah."

[36]Benaiah son of Jehoiada answered the king, "Amen! May the LORD, the God of my lord the king, so declare it. [37]As the LORD was with my lord the king, so may he be with Solomon to make his throne even greater than the throne of my lord King David!"

[38]So Zadok the priest, Nathan the prophet, Benaiah son of Jehoiada, the Kerethites and the Pelethites went down and put Solomon on King David's mule and escorted him to Gihon. [39]Zadok the priest took the horn of oil from the sacred tent and anointed Solomon. Then they sounded the trumpet and all the people shouted, "Long live King Solomon!" [40]And all the people went up after him, playing flutes and rejoicing greatly, so that the ground shook with the sound.

[41]Adonijah and all the guests who were with him heard it as they were finishing their feast. On hearing the sound of the trumpet, Joab asked, "What's the meaning of all the noise in the city?"

[42]Even as he was speaking, Jonathan son of Abiathar the priest arrived. Adonijah said, "Come in. A worthy man like you must be bringing good news."

[43]"Not at all!" Jonathan answered. "Our lord King David has made Solomon king. [44]The king has sent with him Zadok the priest, Nathan the prophet, Benaiah son of Jehoiada, the Kerethites and the Pelethites, and they have put him on the king's mule, [45]and Zadok the priest and Nathan the prophet have anointed him king at Gihon. From there they have gone up cheering, and the city resounds with it. That's the noise you hear. [46]Moreover, Solomon has taken his seat on the royal throne. [47]Also, the royal officials have come to congratulate our lord King David, saying, 'May your God make Solomon's name more famous than yours and his throne greater than yours!' And the king bowed in worship on his bed [48]and said, 'Praise be to the LORD, the God of Israel, who has allowed my eyes to see a successor on my throne today.' "

[49]At this, all Adonijah's guests rose in alarm and dispersed. [50]But Adonijah, in fear of Solomon, went and took hold of the horns of the altar. [51]Then Solomon was told, "Adonijah is afraid of King Solomon and is clinging to the horns of the altar. He says, 'Let King Solomon swear to me today that he will not put his servant to death with the sword.' "

[52]Solomon replied, "If he shows himself to be a worthy man, not a hair of his head will fall to the ground; but if evil is found in him, he will die." [53]Then King Solomon sent men, and they brought him down from the altar. And Adonijah came and bowed down to King Solomon, and Solomon said, "Go to your home."

2

When the time drew near for David to die, he gave a charge to Solomon his son. [2]"I am about to go the way of all the earth," he said. "So be strong, show yourself a man, [3]and observe what the LORD your God requires: Walk in his ways, and keep his decrees and commands, his laws and requirements, as written in the Law of Moses, so that you may prosper in all you do and wherever you go, [4]and that the LORD may keep his promise to me: 'If your descendants watch how they live, and if they walk faithfully before me with all their heart and soul, you will never fail to have a man on the throne of Israel.'

[5]"Now you yourself know what Joab son of Zeruiah did to me—what he did to the two commanders of Israel's armies, Abner son of Ner and Amasa son of Jether. He killed them, shedding their blood in peacetime as if in battle, and with that blood stained the belt around his waist and the sandals on his feet. [6]Deal with him according to your wisdom, but do not let his gray head go down to the grave[c] in peace.

[7]"But show kindness to the sons of Barzillai of Gilead and let them be among those who eat at your table. They stood by me when I fled from your brother Absalom.

[8]"And remember, you have with you Shimei son of Gera, the Benjamite from Bahurim, who called down bitter curses on me the day I went to Mahanaim. When he came down to meet me at the Jordan, I swore to him by the LORD: 'I will not put you to death by the sword.' [9]But now, do not

[c]6 Hebrew *Sheol*; also in verse 9

consider him innocent. You are a man of wisdom; you will know what to do to him. Bring his gray head down to the grave in blood."

10Then David rested with his fathers and was buried in the City of David. 11He had reigned forty years over Israel—seven years in Hebron and thirty-three in Jerusalem. 12So Solomon sat on the throne of his father David, and his rule was firmly established.

13Now Adonijah, the son of Haggith, went to Bathsheba, Solomon's mother. Bathsheba asked him, "Do you come peacefully?"

He answered, "Yes, peacefully." 14Then he added, "I have something to say to you."

"You may say it," she replied.

15"As you know," he said, "the kingdom was mine. All Israel looked to me as their king. But things changed, and the kingdom has gone to my brother; for it has come to him from the LORD. 16Now I have one request to make of you. Do not refuse me."

"You may make it," she said.

17So he continued, "Please ask King Solomon—he will not refuse you—to give me Abishag the Shunammite as my wife."

18"Very well," Bathsheba replied, "I will speak to the king for you."

19When Bathsheba went to King Solomon to speak to him for Adonijah, the king stood up to meet her, bowed down to her and sat down on his throne. He had a throne brought for the king's mother, and she sat down at his right hand.

20"I have one small request to make of you," she said. "Do not refuse me."

The king replied, "Make it, my mother; I will not refuse you."

21So she said, "Let Abishag the Shunammite be given in marriage to your brother Adonijah."

22King Solomon answered his mother, "Why do you request Abishag the Shunammite for Adonijah? You might as well request the kingdom for him—after all, he is my older brother—yes, for him and for Abiathar the priest and Joab son of Zeruiah!"

23Then King Solomon swore by the LORD: "May God deal with me, be it ever so severely, if Adonijah does not pay with his life for this request! 24And now, as surely as the LORD lives—he who has established me securely on the throne of my father David and has founded a dynasty for me as he promised—Adonijah shall be put to death today!" 25So King Solomon gave orders to Benaiah son of Jehoiada, and he struck down Adonijah and he died.

26To Abiathar the priest the king said, "Go back to your fields in Anathoth. You deserve to die, but I will not put you to death now, because you carried the ark of the Sovereign LORD before my father David and shared all my father's hardships." 27So Solomon removed Abiathar from the priesthood of the LORD, fulfilling the word the LORD had spoken at Shiloh about the house of Eli.

28When the news reached Joab, who had conspired with Adonijah though not with Absalom, he fled to the tent of the LORD and took hold of the horns of the altar. 29King Solomon was told that Joab had fled to the tent of the LORD and was beside the altar. Then Solomon ordered Benaiah son of Jehoiada, "Go, strike him down!"

30So Benaiah entered the tent of the LORD and said to Joab, "The king says, 'Come out!'"

But he answered, "No, I will die here."

Benaiah reported to the king, "This is how Joab answered me."

31Then the king commanded Benaiah, "Do as he says. Strike him down and bury him, and so clear me and my father's house of the guilt of the innocent blood that Joab shed. 32The LORD will repay him for the blood he shed, because without the knowledge of my father David he attacked two men and killed them with the sword. Both of them—Abner son of Ner, commander of Israel's army, and Amasa son of Jether, commander of Judah's army—were better men and more upright than he. 33May the guilt of their blood rest on the head of Joab and his descendants forever. But on David and his descendants, his house and his throne, may there be the LORD's peace forever."

34So Benaiah son of Jehoiada went up and struck down Joab and killed him, and he was buried on his own land[d] in the desert. 35The king put Benaiah son of Jehoiada over the army in Joab's position and replaced Abiathar with Zadok the priest.

36Then the king sent for Shimei and said to him, "Build yourself a house in Jerusalem and live there, but do not go anywhere else. 37The day you leave and cross the Kidron Valley, you can be sure you will die; your blood will be on your own head."

38Shimei answered the king, "What you say is good. Your servant will do as my lord the king

d34 Or *buried in his tomb*

has said." And Shimei stayed in Jerusalem for a
long time.

39But three years later, two of Shimei's slaves
ran off to Achish son of Maacah, king of Gath,
and Shimei was told, "Your slaves are in Gath."
40At this, he saddled his donkey and went to
Achish at Gath in search of his slaves. So Shimei
went away and brought the slaves back from
Gath.

41When Solomon was told that Shimei had
gone from Jerusalem to Gath and had returned,
42the king summoned Shimei and said to him,
"Did I not make you swear by the LORD and warn
you, 'On the day you leave to go anywhere else,
you can be sure you will die'? At that time you
said to me, 'What you say is good. I will obey.'
43Why then did you not keep your oath to the
LORD and obey the command I gave you?"

44The king also said to Shimei, "You know in
your heart all the wrong you did to my father
David. Now the LORD will repay you for your
wrongdoing. 45But King Solomon will be blessed,
and David's throne will remain secure before the
LORD forever."

46Then the king gave the order to Benaiah son
of Jehoiada, and he went out and struck Shimei
down and killed him.

The kingdom was now firmly established in
Solomon's hands.

1 / *1 Kings 3*
Praying with God's Values

"HELLO, MARY? I need a listening ear. Do you have time?" Haltingly, I poured out my disappointment and sorrow about a problem that had been plaguing me for days. Mary made sympathetic noises, offered a few corrective comments and promised to pray. The situation was unchanged; yet, as the day progressed, I felt the cloud of sadness lift. I knew Mary was praying. And God, in his generosity, was granting the requests of her prayer.

Why had I chosen Mary? Because she was approachable? Partly. But more because I knew her spiritual walk. It was carefully metered by God's laws. And because she was comfortable with prayer, her prayers were specific and to the point. Like her spiritual walk, her prayers seemed closely matched to God's values.

Warming Up to God In what area of your life would you like to have someone's prayers?

Read 1 Kings 3.

3 Solomon made an alliance with Pharaoh
king of Egypt and married his daughter.
He brought her to the City of David until
he finished building his palace and the temple of
the LORD, and the wall around Jerusalem. 2The
people, however, were still sacrificing at the high
places, because a temple had not yet been built
for the Name of the LORD. 3Solomon showed his
love for the LORD by walking according to the stat-
utes of his father David, except that he offered
sacrifices and burned incense on the high places.

4The king went to Gibeon to offer sacrifices, for
that was the most important high place, and Solo-
mon offered a thousand burnt offerings on that
altar. 5At Gibeon the LORD appeared to Solomon
during the night in a dream, and God said, "Ask
for whatever you want me to give you."

6Solomon answered, "You have shown great
kindness to your servant, my father David, be-
cause he was faithful to you and righteous and
upright in heart. You have continued this great
kindness to him and have given him a son to sit
on his throne this very day.

7"Now, O LORD my God, you have made your
servant king in place of my father David. But I am
only a little child and do not know how to carry
out my duties. 8Your servant is here among the
people you have chosen, a great people, too nu-
merous to count or number. 9So give your servant
a discerning heart to govern your people and to
distinguish between right and wrong. For who is
able to govern this great people of yours?"

10The Lord was pleased that Solomon had
asked for this. 11So God said to him, "Since you

have asked for this and not for long life or wealth
for yourself, nor have asked for the death of your
enemies but for discernment in administering jus-
tice, 12I will do what you have asked. I will give
you a wise and discerning heart, so that there will
never have been anyone like you, nor will there
ever be. 13Moreover, I will give you what you
have not asked for—both riches and honor—so
that in your lifetime you will have no equal
among kings. 14And if you walk in my ways and
obey my statutes and commands as David your
father did, I will give you a long life." 15Then
Solomon awoke—and he realized it had been a
dream.

He returned to Jerusalem, stood before the ark
of the Lord's covenant and sacrificed burnt offer-
ings and fellowship offerings.[e] Then he gave a
feast for all his court.

16Now two prostitutes came to the king and
stood before him. 17One of them said, "My lord,
this woman and I live in the same house. I had a
baby while she was there with me. 18The third
day after my child was born, this woman also had
a baby. We were alone; there was no one in the
house but the two of us.

19"During the night this woman's son died be-
cause she lay on him. 20So she got up in the mid-
dle of the night and took my son from my side
while I your servant was asleep. She put him by
her breast and put her dead son by my breast.
21The next morning, I got up to nurse my son—
and he was dead! But when I looked at him
closely in the morning light, I saw that it wasn't
the son I had borne."

22The other woman said, "No! The living one is
my son; the dead one is yours."

But the first one insisted, "No! The dead one is
yours; the living one is mine." And so they argued
before the king.

23The king said, "This one says, 'My son is alive
and your son is dead,' while that one says, 'No!
Your son is dead and mine is alive.' "

24Then the king said, "Bring me a sword." So
they brought a sword for the king. 25He then gave
an order: "Cut the living child in two and give
half to one and half to the other."

26The woman whose son was alive was filled
with compassion for her son and said to the king,
"Please, my lord, give her the living baby! Don't
kill him!"

But the other said, "Neither I nor you shall
have him. Cut him in two!"

27Then the king gave his ruling: "Give the liv-
ing baby to the first woman. Do not kill him; she
is his mother."

28When all Israel heard the verdict the king had
given, they held the king in awe, because they
saw that he had wisdom from God to administer
justice.

[e]15 Traditionally *peace offerings*

Discovering the Word 1. What do Solomon's actions in the early years of his reign (vv. 1–4) say about his character? 2. Solomon answered God's question with a prayer (vv. 5–9). What does Solomon's prayer suggest about his attitude toward himself, his job and his God? 3. What did God promise Solomon (vv. 10–14)? 4. How would you describe a discerning heart? 5. In verses 16–28 we see Solomon's wisdom put to the test. Do you agree that Solomon's method of judgment was wise? Why or why not?

Applying the Word 1. Think of one of your current responsibilities that seems a bit too big for you. What would you *like* to ask of God in that area? 2. How can you begin to bring your prayers more into line with God's values?

Responding in Prayer Think of one person who particularly needs a discerning heart right now. Pray one or two sentences asking God's help for that person.

1 Kings 4—10

4 So King Solomon ruled over all Israel. [2]And these were his chief officials:

Azariah son of Zadok—the priest;
[3]Elihoreph and Ahijah, sons of Shisha—secretaries;
Jehoshaphat son of Ahilud—recorder;
[4]Benaiah son of Jehoiada—commander in chief;
Zadok and Abiathar—priests;
[5]Azariah son of Nathan—in charge of the district officers;
Zabud son of Nathan—a priest and personal adviser to the king;
[6]Ahishar—in charge of the palace;
Adoniram son of Abda—in charge of forced labor.

[7]Solomon also had twelve district governors over all Israel, who supplied provisions for the king and the royal household. Each one had to provide supplies for one month in the year. [8]These are their names:

Ben-Hur—in the hill country of Ephraim;
[9]Ben-Deker—in Makaz, Shaalbim, Beth Shemesh and Elon Bethhanan;
[10]Ben-Hesed—in Arubboth (Socoh and all the land of Hepher were his);
[11]Ben-Abinadab—in Naphoth Dor[f] (he was married to Taphath daughter of Solomon);
[12]Baana son of Ahilud—in Taanach and Megiddo, and in all of Beth Shan next to Zarethan below Jezreel, from Beth Shan to Abel Meholah across to Jokmeam;
[13]Ben-Geber—in Ramoth Gilead (the settlements of Jair son of Manasseh in Gilead were his, as well as the district of Argob in Bashan and its sixty large walled cities with bronze gate bars);
[14]Ahinadab son of Iddo—in Mahanaim;
[15]Ahimaaz—in Naphtali (he had married Basemath daughter of Solomon);
[16]Baana son of Hushai—in Asher and in Aloth;
[17]Jehoshaphat son of Paruah—in Issachar;
[18]Shimei son of Ela—in Benjamin;
[19]Geber son of Uri—in Gilead (the country of Sihon king of the Amorites and the country of Og king of Bashan). He was the only governor over the district.

[20]The people of Judah and Israel were as numerous as the sand on the seashore; they ate, they drank and they were happy. [21]And Solomon ruled over all the kingdoms from the River[g] to the land of the Philistines, as far as the border of Egypt. These countries brought tribute and were Solomon's subjects all his life.

[22]Solomon's daily provisions were thirty cors[h] of fine flour and sixty cors[i] of meal, [23]ten head of stall-fed cattle, twenty of pasture-fed cattle and a hundred sheep and goats, as well as deer, gazelles, roebucks and choice fowl. [24]For he ruled over all the kingdoms west of the River, from Tiphsah to Gaza, and had peace on all sides. [25]During Solomon's lifetime Judah and Israel, from Dan to Beersheba, lived in safety, each man under his own vine and fig tree.

[26]Solomon had four[j] thousand stalls for chariot horses, and twelve thousand horses.[k]

[27]The district officers, each in his month, supplied provisions for King Solomon and all who came to the king's table. They saw to it that nothing was lacking. [28]They also brought to the proper place their quotas of barley and straw for the chariot horses and the other horses.

[29]God gave Solomon wisdom and very great insight, and a breadth of understanding as measureless as the sand on the seashore. [30]Solomon's wisdom was greater than the wisdom of all the men of the East, and greater than all the wisdom of Egypt. [31]He was wiser than any other man, including Ethan the Ezrahite—wiser than Heman, Calcol and Darda, the sons of Mahol. And his fame spread to all the surrounding nations. [32]He spoke three thousand proverbs and his songs numbered a thousand and five. [33]He described plant life, from the cedar of Lebanon to the hyssop that grows out of walls. He also taught about animals and birds, reptiles and fish. [34]Men of all nations came to listen to Solomon's wisdom, sent by all the kings of the world, who had heard of his wisdom.

[f]11 Or *in the heights of Dor* [g]21 That is, the Euphrates; also in verse 24 [h]22 That is, probably about 185 bushels (about 6.6 kiloliters)
[i]22 That is, probably about 375 bushels (about 13.2 kiloliters)
[j]26 Some Septuagint manuscripts (see also 2 Chron. 9:25); Hebrew *forty*
[k]26 Or *charioteers*

5

When Hiram king of Tyre heard that Solomon had been anointed king to succeed his father David, he sent his envoys to Solomon, because he had always been on friendly terms with David. 2 Solomon sent back this message to Hiram:

3 "You know that because of the wars waged against my father David from all sides, he could not build a temple for the Name of the LORD his God until the LORD put his enemies under his feet. 4 But now the LORD my God has given me rest on every side, and there is no adversary or disaster. 5 I intend, therefore, to build a temple for the Name of the LORD my God, as the LORD told my father David, when he said, 'Your son whom I will put on the throne in your place will build the temple for my Name.'

6 "So give orders that cedars of Lebanon be cut for me. My men will work with yours, and I will pay you for your men whatever wages you set. You know that we have no one so skilled in felling timber as the Sidonians."

7 When Hiram heard Solomon's message, he was greatly pleased and said, "Praise be to the LORD today, for he has given David a wise son to rule over this great nation."

8 So Hiram sent word to Solomon:

"I have received the message you sent me and will do all you want in providing the cedar and pine logs. 9 My men will haul them down from Lebanon to the sea, and I will float them in rafts by sea to the place you specify. There I will separate them and you can take them away. And you are to grant my wish by providing food for my royal household."

10 In this way Hiram kept Solomon supplied with all the cedar and pine logs he wanted, 11 and Solomon gave Hiram twenty thousand cors[l] of wheat as food for his household, in addition to twenty thousand baths[m,n] of pressed olive oil. Solomon continued to do this for Hiram year after year. 12 The LORD gave Solomon wisdom, just as he had promised him. There were peaceful relations between Hiram and Solomon, and the two of them made a treaty.

13 King Solomon conscripted laborers from all Israel—thirty thousand men. 14 He sent them off to Lebanon in shifts of ten thousand a month, so that they spent one month in Lebanon and two months at home. Adoniram was in charge of the forced labor. 15 Solomon had seventy thousand carriers and eighty thousand stonecutters in the hills, 16 as well as thirty-three hundred[o] foremen who supervised the project and directed the workmen. 17 At the king's command they removed from the quarry large blocks of quality stone to provide a foundation of dressed stone for the temple. 18 The craftsmen of Solomon and Hiram and the men of Gebal[p] cut and prepared the timber and stone for the building of the temple.

6

In the four hundred and eightieth[q] year after the Israelites had come out of Egypt, in the fourth year of Solomon's reign over Israel, in the month of Ziv, the second month, he began to build the temple of the LORD.

2 The temple that King Solomon built for the LORD was sixty cubits long, twenty wide and thirty high.[r] 3 The portico at the front of the main hall of the temple extended the width of the temple, that is twenty cubits,[s] and projected ten cubits[t] from the front of the temple. 4 He made narrow clerestory windows in the temple. 5 Against the walls of the main hall and inner sanctuary he built a structure around the building, in which there were side rooms. 6 The lowest floor was five cubits[u] wide, the middle floor six cubits[v] and the third floor seven.[w] He made offset ledges around the outside of the temple so that nothing would be inserted into the temple walls.

7 In building the temple, only blocks dressed at the quarry were used, and no hammer, chisel or any other iron tool was heard at the temple site while it was being built.

8 The entrance to the lowest[x] floor was on the south side of the temple; a stairway led up to the middle level and from there to the third. 9 So he built the temple and completed it, roofing it with beams and cedar planks. 10 And he built the side rooms all along the temple. The height of each was five cubits, and they were attached to the temple by beams of cedar.

l 11 That is, probably about 125,000 bushels (about 4,400 kiloliters)
m 11 Septuagint (see also 2 Chron. 2:10); Hebrew *twenty cors*
n 11 That is, about 115,000 gallons (about 440 kiloliters)
o 16 Hebrew; some Septuagint manuscripts (see also 2 Chron. 2:2, 18) *thirty-six hundred*
p 18 That is, Byblos
q 1 Hebrew; Septuagint *four hundred and fortieth*
r 2 That is, about 90 feet (about 27 meters) long and 30 feet (about 9 meters) wide and 45 feet (about 13.5 meters) high
s 3 That is, about 30 feet (about 9 meters)
t 3 That is, about 15 feet (about 4.5 meters)
u 6 That is, about 7 1/2 feet (about 2.3 meters); also in verses 10 and 24
v 6 That is, about 9 feet (about 2.7 meters)
w 6 That is, about 10 1/2 feet (about 3.1 meters)
x 8 Septuagint; Hebrew *middle*

11The word of the LORD came to Solomon: 12"As
for this temple you are building, if you follow my
decrees, carry out my regulations and keep all my
commands and obey them, I will fulfill through
you the promise I gave to David your father.
13And I will live among the Israelites and will not
abandon my people Israel."

14So Solomon built the temple and completed
it. 15He lined its interior walls with cedar boards,
paneling them from the floor of the temple to the
ceiling, and covered the floor of the temple with
planks of pine. 16He partitioned off twenty cu-
bits[y] at the rear of the temple with cedar boards
from floor to ceiling to form within the temple an
inner sanctuary, the Most Holy Place. 17The main
hall in front of this room was forty cubits[z] long.
18The inside of the temple was cedar, carved with
gourds and open flowers. Everything was cedar;
no stone was to be seen.

19He prepared the inner sanctuary within the
temple to set the ark of the covenant of the LORD
there. 20The inner sanctuary was twenty cubits
long, twenty wide and twenty high.[a] He overlaid
the inside with pure gold, and he also overlaid the
altar of cedar. 21Solomon covered the inside of the
temple with pure gold, and he extended gold
chains across the front of the inner sanctuary,
which was overlaid with gold. 22So he overlaid
the whole interior with gold. He also overlaid
with gold the altar that belonged to the inner
sanctuary.

23In the inner sanctuary he made a pair of cher-
ubim of olive wood, each ten cubits[b] high. 24One
wing of the first cherub was five cubits long, and
the other wing five cubits—ten cubits from wing
tip to wing tip. 25The second cherub also mea-
sured ten cubits, for the two cherubim were iden-
tical in size and shape. 26The height of each
cherub was ten cubits. 27He placed the cherubim
inside the innermost room of the temple, with
their wings spread out. The wing of one cherub
touched one wall, while the wing of the other
touched the other wall, and their wings touched
each other in the middle of the room. 28He over-
laid the cherubim with gold.

29On the walls all around the temple, in both
the inner and outer rooms, he carved cherubim,
palm trees and open flowers. 30He also covered
the floors of both the inner and outer rooms of
the temple with gold.

31For the entrance of the inner sanctuary he
made doors of olive wood with five-sided jambs.
32And on the two olive wood doors he carved
cherubim, palm trees and open flowers, and over-
laid the cherubim and palm trees with beaten
gold. 33In the same way he made four-sided jambs
of olive wood for the entrance to the main hall.
34He also made two pine doors, each having two
leaves that turned in sockets. 35He carved cheru-
bim, palm trees and open flowers on them and
overlaid them with gold hammered evenly over
the carvings.

36And he built the inner courtyard of three
courses of dressed stone and one course of
trimmed cedar beams.

37The foundation of the temple of the LORD was
laid in the fourth year, in the month of Ziv. 38In
the eleventh year in the month of Bul, the eighth
month, the temple was finished in all its details
according to its specifications. He had spent
seven years building it.

7 It took Solomon thirteen years, however,
to complete the construction of his pal-
ace. 2He built the Palace of the Forest of
Lebanon a hundred cubits long, fifty wide and
thirty high,[c] with four rows of cedar columns
supporting trimmed cedar beams. 3It was roofed
with cedar above the beams that rested on the
columns—forty-five beams, fifteen to a row. 4Its
windows were placed high in sets of three, facing
each other. 5All the doorways had rectangular
frames; they were in the front part in sets of three,
facing each other.[d]

6He made a colonnade fifty cubits long and
thirty wide.[e] In front of it was a portico, and in
front of that were pillars and an overhanging roof.

7He built the throne hall, the Hall of Justice,
where he was to judge, and he covered it with
cedar from floor to ceiling.[f] 8And the palace in
which he was to live, set farther back, was similar
in design. Solomon also made a palace like this
hall for Pharaoh's daughter, whom he had mar-
ried.

9All these structures, from the outside to the
great courtyard and from foundation to eaves,
were made of blocks of high-grade stone cut to
size and trimmed with a saw on their inner and
outer faces. 10The foundations were laid with

[y]16 That is, about 30 feet (about 9 meters) [z]17 That is, about 60 feet (about 18 meters) [a]20 That is, about 30 feet (about 9 meters) long, wide and high [b]23 That is, about 15 feet (about 4.5 meters) [c]2 That is, about 150 feet (about 46 meters) long, 75 feet (about 23 meters) wide and 45 feet (about 13.5 meters) high [d]5 The meaning of the Hebrew for this verse is uncertain. [e]6 That is, about 75 feet (about 23 meters) long and 45 feet (about 13.5 meters) wide [f]7 Vulgate and Syriac; Hebrew *floor*

large stones of good quality, some measuring ten cubits[g] and some eight.[h] 11Above were high-grade stones, cut to size, and cedar beams. 12The great courtyard was surrounded by a wall of three courses of dressed stone and one course of trimmed cedar beams, as was the inner courtyard of the temple of the LORD with its portico.

13King Solomon sent to Tyre and brought Huram,[i] 14whose mother was a widow from the tribe of Naphtali and whose father was a man of Tyre and a craftsman in bronze. Huram was highly skilled and experienced in all kinds of bronze work. He came to King Solomon and did all the work assigned to him.

15He cast two bronze pillars, each eighteen cubits high and twelve cubits around,[j] by line. 16He also made two capitals of cast bronze to set on the tops of the pillars; each capital was five cubits[k] high. 17A network of interwoven chains festooned the capitals on top of the pillars, seven for each capital. 18He made pomegranates in two rows[l] encircling each network to decorate the capitals on top of the pillars.[m] He did the same for each capital. 19The capitals on top of the pillars in the portico were in the shape of lilies, four cubits[n] high. 20On the capitals of both pillars, above the bowl-shaped part next to the network, were the two hundred pomegranates in rows all around. 21He erected the pillars at the portico of the temple. The pillar to the south he named Jakin[o] and the one to the north Boaz.[p] 22The capitals on top were in the shape of lilies. And so the work on the pillars was completed.

23He made the Sea of cast metal, circular in shape, measuring ten cubits[g] from rim to rim and five cubits high. It took a line of thirty cubits[q] to measure around it. 24Below the rim, gourds encircled it—ten to a cubit. The gourds were cast in two rows in one piece with the Sea.

25The Sea stood on twelve bulls, three facing north, three facing west, three facing south and three facing east. The Sea rested on top of them, and their hindquarters were toward the center. 26It was a handbreadth[r] in thickness, and its rim was like the rim of a cup, like a lily blossom. It held two thousand baths.[s]

27He also made ten movable stands of bronze; each was four cubits long, four wide and three high.[t] 28This is how the stands were made: They had side panels attached to uprights. 29On the panels between the uprights were lions, bulls and cherubim—and on the uprights as well. Above and below the lions and bulls were wreaths of hammered work. 30Each stand had four bronze wheels with bronze axles, and each had a basin resting on four supports, cast with wreaths on each side. 31On the inside of the stand there was an opening that had a circular frame one cubit[u] deep. This opening was round, and with its basework it measured a cubit and a half.[v] Around its opening there was engraving. The panels of the stands were square, not round. 32The four wheels were under the panels, and the axles of the wheels were attached to the stand. The diameter of each wheel was a cubit and a half. 33The wheels were made like chariot wheels; the axles, rims, spokes and hubs were all of cast metal.

34Each stand had four handles, one on each corner, projecting from the stand. 35At the top of the stand there was a circular band half a cubit[w] deep. The supports and panels were attached to the top of the stand. 36He engraved cherubim, lions and palm trees on the surfaces of the supports and on the panels, in every available space, with wreaths all around. 37This is the way he made the ten stands. They were all cast in the same molds and were identical in size and shape.

38He then made ten bronze basins, each holding forty baths[x] and measuring four cubits across, one basin to go on each of the ten stands. 39He placed five of the stands on the south side of the temple and five on the north. He placed the Sea on the south side, at the southeast corner of the temple. 40He also made the basins and shovels and sprinkling bowls.

So Huram finished all the work he had undertaken for King Solomon in the temple of the LORD:

41the two pillars;
the two bowl-shaped capitals on top of the pillars;
the two sets of network decorating the two bowl-shaped capitals on top of the pillars;

[g]10,23 That is, about 15 feet (about 4.5 meters) [h]10 That is, about 12 feet (about 3.6 meters) [i]13 Hebrew *Hiram*, a variant of *Huram*; also in verses 40 and 45 [j]15 That is, about 27 feet (about 8.1 meters) high and 18 feet (about 5.4 meters) around [k]16 That is, about 7 1/2 feet (about 2.3 meters); also in verse 23 [l]18 Two Hebrew manuscripts and Septuagint; most Hebrew manuscripts *made the pillars, and there were two rows* [m]18 Many Hebrew manuscripts and Syriac; most Hebrew manuscripts *pomegranates* [n]19 That is, about 6 feet (about 1.8 meters); also in verse 38 [o]21 *Jakin* probably means *he establishes.* [p]21 *Boaz* probably means *in him is strength.* [q]23 That is, about 45 feet (about 13.5 meters) [r]26 That is, about 3 inches (about 8 centimeters) [s]26 That is, probably about 11,500 gallons (about 44 kiloliters); the Septuagint does not have this sentence. [t]27 That is, about 6 feet (about 1.8 meters) long and wide and about 4 1/2 feet (about 1.3 meters) high [u]31 That is, about 1 1/2 feet (about 0.5 meter) [v]31 That is, about 2 1/4 feet (about 0.7 meter); also in verse 32 [w]35 That is, about 3/4 foot (about 0.2 meter) [x]38 That is, about 230 gallons (about 880 liters)

42the four hundred pomegranates for the two sets of network (two rows of pomegranates for each network, decorating the bowl-shaped capitals on top of the pillars);
43the ten stands with their ten basins;
44the Sea and the twelve bulls under it;
45the pots, shovels and sprinkling bowls.

All these objects that Huram made for King Solomon for the temple of the LORD were of burnished bronze. 46The king had them cast in clay molds in the plain of the Jordan between Succoth and Zarethan. 47Solomon left all these things unweighed, because there were so many; the weight of the bronze was not determined.

48Solomon also made all the furnishings that were in the LORD's temple:

the golden altar;
the golden table on which was the bread of the Presence;
49the lampstands of pure gold (five on the right and five on the left, in front of the inner sanctuary);
the gold floral work and lamps and tongs;
50the pure gold basins, wick trimmers, sprinkling bowls, dishes and censers;
and the gold sockets for the doors of the innermost room, the Most Holy Place, and also for the doors of the main hall of the temple.

51When all the work King Solomon had done for the temple of the LORD was finished, he brought in the things his father David had dedicated—the silver and gold and the furnishings—and he placed them in the treasuries of the LORD's temple.

8 Then King Solomon summoned into his presence at Jerusalem the elders of Israel, all the heads of the tribes and the chiefs of the Israelite families, to bring up the ark of the LORD's covenant from Zion, the City of David. 2All the men of Israel came together to King Solomon at the time of the festival in the month of Ethanim, the seventh month.

3When all the elders of Israel had arrived, the priests took up the ark, 4and they brought up the ark of the LORD and the Tent of Meeting and all the sacred furnishings in it. The priests and Levites carried them up, 5and King Solomon and the entire assembly of Israel that had gathered about him were before the ark, sacrificing so many sheep and cattle that they could not be recorded or counted.

6The priests then brought the ark of the LORD's covenant to its place in the inner sanctuary of the temple, the Most Holy Place, and put it beneath the wings of the cherubim. 7The cherubim spread their wings over the place of the ark and overshadowed the ark and its carrying poles. 8These poles were so long that their ends could be seen from the Holy Place in front of the inner sanctuary, but not from outside the Holy Place; and they are still there today. 9There was nothing in the ark except the two stone tablets that Moses had placed in it at Horeb, where the LORD made a covenant with the Israelites after they came out of Egypt.

10When the priests withdrew from the Holy Place, the cloud filled the temple of the LORD. 11And the priests could not perform their service because of the cloud, for the glory of the LORD filled his temple.

12Then Solomon said, "The LORD has said that he would dwell in a dark cloud; 13I have indeed built a magnificent temple for you, a place for you to dwell forever."

14While the whole assembly of Israel was standing there, the king turned around and blessed them. 15Then he said:

"Praise be to the LORD, the God of Israel, who with his own hand has fulfilled what he promised with his own mouth to my father David. For he said, 16'Since the day I brought my people Israel out of Egypt, I have not chosen a city in any tribe of Israel to have a temple built for my Name to be there, but I have chosen David to rule my people Israel.'

17"My father David had it in his heart to build a temple for the Name of the LORD, the God of Israel. 18But the LORD said to my father David, 'Because it was in your heart to build a temple for my Name, you did well to have this in your heart. 19Nevertheless, you are not the one to build the temple, but your son, who is your own flesh and blood—he is the one who will build the temple for my Name.'

20"The LORD has kept the promise he made: I have succeeded David my father and now I sit on the throne of Israel, just as the LORD promised, and I have built the temple

for the Name of the LORD, the God of Israel.
21I have provided a place there for the ark, in
which is the covenant of the LORD that he
made with our fathers when he brought
them out of Egypt."

22Then Solomon stood before the altar of the
LORD in front of the whole assembly of Israel,
spread out his hands toward heaven 23and said:

"O LORD, God of Israel, there is no God
like you in heaven above or on earth be-
low—you who keep your covenant of love
with your servants who continue whole-
heartedly in your way. 24You have kept your
promise to your servant David my father;
with your mouth you have promised and
with your hand you have fulfilled it—as it is
today.

25"Now LORD, God of Israel, keep for your
servant David my father the promises you
made to him when you said, 'You shall never
fail to have a man to sit before me on the
throne of Israel, if only your sons are careful
in all they do to walk before me as you have
done.' 26And now, O God of Israel, let your
word that you promised your servant David
my father come true.

27"But will God really dwell on earth? The
heavens, even the highest heaven, cannot
contain you. How much less this temple I
have built! 28Yet give attention to your ser-
vant's prayer and his plea for mercy, O LORD
my God. Hear the cry and the prayer that
your servant is praying in your presence this
day. 29May your eyes be open toward this
temple night and day, this place of which
you said, 'My Name shall be there,' so that
you will hear the prayer your servant prays
toward this place. 30Hear the supplication of
your servant and of your people Israel when
they pray toward this place. Hear from
heaven, your dwelling place, and when you
hear, forgive.

31"When a man wrongs his neighbor and
is required to take an oath and he comes and
swears the oath before your altar in this tem-
ple, 32then hear from heaven and act. Judge
between your servants, condemning the
guilty and bringing down on his own head
what he has done. Declare the innocent not
guilty, and so establish his innocence.

33"When your people Israel have been de-
feated by an enemy because they have sinned
against you, and when they turn back to you
and confess your name, praying and making
supplication to you in this temple, 34then
hear from heaven and forgive the sin of your
people Israel and bring them back to the
land you gave to their fathers.

35"When the heavens are shut up and
there is no rain because your people have
sinned against you, and when they pray to-
ward this place and confess your name and
turn from their sin because you have af-
flicted them, 36then hear from heaven and
forgive the sin of your servants, your people
Israel. Teach them the right way to live, and
send rain on the land you gave your people
for an inheritance.

37"When famine or plague comes to the
land, or blight or mildew, locusts or grass-
hoppers, or when an enemy besieges them in
any of their cities, whatever disaster or dis-
ease may come, 38and when a prayer or plea
is made by any of your people Israel—each
one aware of the afflictions of his own heart,
and spreading out his hands toward this
temple— 39then hear from heaven, your
dwelling place. Forgive and act; deal with
each man according to all he does, since you
know his heart (for you alone know the
hearts of all men), 40so that they will fear
you all the time they live in the land you
gave our fathers.

41"As for the foreigner who does not be-
long to your people Israel but has come from
a distant land because of your name— 42for
men will hear of your great name and your
mighty hand and your outstretched arm—
when he comes and prays toward this tem-
ple, 43then hear from heaven, your dwelling
place, and do whatever the foreigner asks of
you, so that all the peoples of the earth may
know your name and fear you, as do your
own people Israel, and may know that this
house I have built bears your Name.

44"When your people go to war against
their enemies, wherever you send them, and
when they pray to the LORD toward the city
you have chosen and the temple I have built
for your Name, 45then hear from heaven
their prayer and their plea, and uphold their
cause.

46"When they sin against you—for there is

no one who does not sin—and you become
angry with them and give them over to the
enemy, who takes them captive to his own
land, far away or near; 47and if they have a
change of heart in the land where they are
held captive, and repent and plead with you
in the land of their conquerors and say, 'We
have sinned, we have done wrong, we have
acted wickedly'; 48and if they turn back to
you with all their heart and soul in the land
of their enemies who took them captive, and
pray to you toward the land you gave their
fathers, toward the city you have chosen and
the temple I have built for your Name;
49then from heaven, your dwelling place,
hear their prayer and their plea, and uphold
their cause. 50And forgive your people, who
have sinned against you; forgive all the of-
fenses they have committed against you, and
cause their conquerors to show them mercy;
51for they are your people and your inheri-
tance, whom you brought out of Egypt, out
of that iron-smelting furnace.

52"May your eyes be open to your servant's
plea and to the plea of your people Israel,
and may you listen to them whenever they
cry out to you. 53For you singled them out
from all the nations of the world to be your
own inheritance, just as you declared
through your servant Moses when you,
O Sovereign LORD, brought our fathers out of
Egypt."

54When Solomon had finished all these prayers
and supplications to the LORD, he rose from before
the altar of the LORD, where he had been kneeling
with his hands spread out toward heaven. 55He
stood and blessed the whole assembly of Israel in
a loud voice, saying:

56"Praise be to the LORD, who has given
rest to his people Israel just as he promised.
Not one word has failed of all the good
promises he gave through his servant Moses.
57May the LORD our God be with us as he was
with our fathers; may he never leave us nor
forsake us. 58May he turn our hearts to him,
to walk in all his ways and to keep the com-
mands, decrees and regulations he gave our
fathers. 59And may these words of mine,
which I have prayed before the LORD, be near
to the LORD our God day and night, that he
may uphold the cause of his servant and the
cause of his people Israel according to each
day's need, 60so that all the peoples of the
earth may know that the LORD is God and
that there is no other. 61But your hearts must
be fully committed to the LORD our God, to
live by his decrees and obey his commands,
as at this time."

62Then the king and all Israel with him offered
sacrifices before the LORD. 63Solomon offered a
sacrifice of fellowship offerings[y] to the LORD:
twenty-two thousand cattle and a hundred and
twenty thousand sheep and goats. So the king and
all the Israelites dedicated the temple of the LORD.

64On that same day the king consecrated the
middle part of the courtyard in front of the tem-
ple of the LORD, and there he offered burnt offer-
ings, grain offerings and the fat of the fellowship
offerings, because the bronze altar before the LORD
was too small to hold the burnt offerings, the
grain offerings and the fat of the fellowship offer-
ings.

65So Solomon observed the festival at that time,
and all Israel with him—a vast assembly, people
from Lebo[z] Hamath to the Wadi of Egypt. They
celebrated it before the LORD our God for seven
days and seven days more, fourteen days in all.
66On the following day he sent the people away.
They blessed the king and then went home, joyful
and glad in heart for all the good things the LORD
had done for his servant David and his people
Israel.

9 When Solomon had finished building the
temple of the LORD and the royal palace,
and had achieved all he had desired to do,
2the LORD appeared to him a second time, as he
had appeared to him at Gibeon. 3The LORD said to
him:

"I have heard the prayer and plea you have
made before me; I have consecrated this tem-
ple, which you have built, by putting my
Name there forever. My eyes and my heart
will always be there.

4"As for you, if you walk before me in in-
tegrity of heart and uprightness, as David
your father did, and do all I command and
observe my decrees and laws, 5I will estab-
lish your royal throne over Israel forever, as
I promised David your father when I said,

[y] 63 Traditionally *peace offerings*; also in verse 64 [z] 65 Or *from the entrance to*

'You shall never fail to have a man on the throne of Israel.'

6"But if you[a] or your sons turn away from me and do not observe the commands and decrees I have given you[a] and go off to serve other gods and worship them, 7then I will cut off Israel from the land I have given them and will reject this temple I have consecrated for my Name. Israel will then become a byword and an object of ridicule among all peoples. 8And though this temple is now imposing, all who pass by will be appalled and will scoff and say, 'Why has the LORD done such a thing to this land and to this temple?' 9People will answer, 'Because they have forsaken the LORD their God, who brought their fathers out of Egypt, and have embraced other gods, worshiping and serving them—that is why the LORD brought all this disaster on them.' "

10At the end of twenty years, during which Solomon built these two buildings—the temple of the LORD and the royal palace— 11King Solomon gave twenty towns in Galilee to Hiram king of Tyre, because Hiram had supplied him with all the cedar and pine and gold he wanted. 12But when Hiram went from Tyre to see the towns that Solomon had given him, he was not pleased with them. 13"What kind of towns are these you have given me, my brother?" he asked. And he called them the Land of Cabul,[b] a name they have to this day. 14Now Hiram had sent to the king 120 talents[c] of gold.

15Here is the account of the forced labor King Solomon conscripted to build the LORD's temple, his own palace, the supporting terraces,[d] the wall of Jerusalem, and Hazor, Megiddo and Gezer. 16(Pharaoh king of Egypt had attacked and captured Gezer. He had set it on fire. He killed its Canaanite inhabitants and then gave it as a wedding gift to his daughter, Solomon's wife. 17And Solomon rebuilt Gezer.) He built up Lower Beth Horon, 18Baalath, and Tadmor[e] in the desert, within his land, 19as well as all his store cities and the towns for his chariots and for his horses[f]—whatever he desired to build in Jerusalem, in Lebanon and throughout all the territory he ruled.

20All the people left from the Amorites, Hittites, Perizzites, Hivites and Jebusites (these peoples were not Israelites), 21that is, their descendants remaining in the land, whom the Israelites could not exterminate[g]—these Solomon conscripted for his slave labor force, as it is to this day. 22But Solomon did not make slaves of any of the Israelites; they were his fighting men, his government officials, his officers, his captains, and the commanders of his chariots and charioteers. 23They were also the chief officials in charge of Solomon's projects—550 officials supervising the men who did the work.

24After Pharaoh's daughter had come up from the City of David to the palace Solomon had built for her, he constructed the supporting terraces.

25Three times a year Solomon sacrificed burnt offerings and fellowship offerings[h] on the altar he had built for the LORD, burning incense before the LORD along with them, and so fulfilled the temple obligations.

26King Solomon also built ships at Ezion Geber, which is near Elath in Edom, on the shore of the Red Sea.[i] 27And Hiram sent his men—sailors who knew the sea—to serve in the fleet with Solomon's men. 28They sailed to Ophir and brought back 420 talents[j] of gold, which they delivered to King Solomon.

10 When the queen of Sheba heard about the fame of Solomon and his relation to the name of the LORD, she came to test him with hard questions. 2Arriving at Jerusalem with a very great caravan—with camels carrying spices, large quantities of gold, and precious stones—she came to Solomon and talked with him about all that she had on her mind. 3Solomon answered all her questions; nothing was too hard for the king to explain to her. 4When the queen of Sheba saw all the wisdom of Solomon and the palace he had built, 5the food on his table, the seating of his officials, the attending servants in their robes, his cupbearers, and the burnt offerings he made at[k] the temple of the LORD, she was overwhelmed.

6She said to the king, "The report I heard in my own country about your achievements and your wisdom is true. 7But I did not believe these things until I came and saw with my own eyes. Indeed, not even half was told me; in wisdom and wealth you have far exceeded the report I heard. 8How

[a]6 The Hebrew is plural. [b]13 *Cabul* sounds like the Hebrew for *good-for-nothing.* [c]14 That is, about 4 1/2 tons (about 4 metric tons) [d]15 Or *the Millo*; also in verse 24 [e]18 The Hebrew may also be read *Tamar.* [f]19 Or *charioteers* [g]21 The Hebrew term refers to the irrevocable giving over of things or persons to the LORD, often by totally destroying them. [h]25 Traditionally *peace offerings* [i]26 Hebrew *Yam Suph*; that is, Sea of Reeds [j]28 That is, about 16 tons (about 14.5 metric tons) [k]5 Or *the ascent by which he went up to*

happy your men must be! How happy your officials, who continually stand before you and hear your wisdom! 9Praise be to the LORD your God, who has delighted in you and placed you on the throne of Israel. Because of the LORD's eternal love for Israel, he has made you king, to maintain justice and righteousness."

10And she gave the king 120 talents[l] of gold, large quantities of spices, and precious stones. Never again were so many spices brought in as those the queen of Sheba gave to King Solomon.

11(Hiram's ships brought gold from Ophir; and from there they brought great cargoes of almugwood[m] and precious stones. 12The king used the almugwood to make supports for the temple of the LORD and for the royal palace, and to make harps and lyres for the musicians. So much almugwood has never been imported or seen since that day.)

13King Solomon gave the queen of Sheba all she desired and asked for, besides what he had given her out of his royal bounty. Then she left and returned with her retinue to her own country.

14The weight of the gold that Solomon received yearly was 666 talents,[n] 15not including the revenues from merchants and traders and from all the Arabian kings and the governors of the land.

16King Solomon made two hundred large shields of hammered gold; six hundred bekas[o] of gold went into each shield. 17He also made three hundred small shields of hammered gold, with three minas[p] of gold in each shield. The king put them in the Palace of the Forest of Lebanon.

18Then the king made a great throne inlaid with ivory and overlaid with fine gold. 19The throne had six steps, and its back had a rounded top. On both sides of the seat were armrests, with a lion standing beside each of them. 20Twelve lions stood on the six steps, one at either end of each step. Nothing like it had ever been made for any other kingdom. 21All King Solomon's goblets were gold, and all the household articles in the Palace of the Forest of Lebanon were pure gold. Nothing was made of silver, because silver was considered of little value in Solomon's days. 22The king had a fleet of trading ships[q] at sea along with the ships of Hiram. Once every three years it returned, carrying gold, silver and ivory, and apes and baboons.

23King Solomon was greater in riches and wisdom than all the other kings of the earth. 24The whole world sought audience with Solomon to hear the wisdom God had put in his heart. 25Year after year, everyone who came brought a gift—articles of silver and gold, robes, weapons and spices, and horses and mules.

26Solomon accumulated chariots and horses; he had fourteen hundred chariots and twelve thousand horses,[r] which he kept in the chariot cities and also with him in Jerusalem. 27The king made silver as common in Jerusalem as stones, and cedar as plentiful as sycamore-fig trees in the foothills. 28Solomon's horses were imported from Egypt[s] and from Kue[t]—the royal merchants purchased them from Kue. 29They imported a chariot from Egypt for six hundred shekels[u] of silver, and a horse for a hundred and fifty.[p] They also exported them to all the kings of the Hittites and of the Arameans.

[l]10 That is, about 4 1/2 tons (about 4 metric tons) [m]11 Probably a variant of *algumwood*; also in verse 12 [n]14 That is, about 25 tons (about 23 metric tons) [o]16 That is, about 7 1/2 pounds (about 3.5 kilograms) [p]17,29 That is, about 3 3/4 pounds (about 1.7 kilograms) [q]22 Hebrew *of ships of Tarshish* [r]26 Or *charioteers* [s]28 Or possibly *Muzur*, a region in Cilicia; also in verse 29 [t]28 Probably *Cilicia* [u]29 That is, about 15 pounds (about 7 kilograms)

2 / *1 Kings 11*
Faithless in Love

"I WANT TO do God's will—if only I knew what it was," the young woman said to her pastor. "God has brought Bill and me together, and he has created a great love between us. Bill wants to marry me, but I'm not sure."

"But has Bill given himself to Jesus Christ?" her pastor probed.

"No, not yet," she hesitated. "But I think he will—perhaps after we're married . . ." Her voice trailed off under her pastor's firm gaze.

"God has already shown you his will, I think," her pastor replied. "You know Paul's writings to the Christians at Corinth: 'Do not be yoked together with unbelievers.' "

God's laws may seem harsh, but they are less harsh than the results of living by our own guidelines. God seems to know what works. Solomon had occasion to discover this truth.

Warming Up to God What effect does it have on you when spiritual values are kept separate from your everyday life?

Read 1 Kings 11.

11 King Solomon, however, loved many foreign women besides Pharaoh's daughter—Moabites, Ammonites, Edomites, Sidonians and Hittites. 2They were from nations about which the LORD had told the Israelites, "You must not intermarry with them, because they will surely turn your hearts after their gods." Nevertheless, Solomon held fast to them in love. 3He had seven hundred wives of royal birth and three hundred concubines, and his wives led him astray. 4As Solomon grew old, his wives turned his heart after other gods, and his heart was not fully devoted to the LORD his God, as the heart of David his father had been. 5He followed Ashtoreth the goddess of the Sidonians, and Molech[v] the detestable god of the Ammonites. 6So Solomon did evil in the eyes of the LORD; he did not follow the LORD completely, as David his father had done.

7On a hill east of Jerusalem, Solomon built a high place for Chemosh the detestable god of Moab, and for Molech the detestable god of the Ammonites. 8He did the same for all his foreign wives, who burned incense and offered sacrifices to their gods.

9The LORD became angry with Solomon because his heart had turned away from the LORD, the God of Israel, who had appeared to him twice. 10Although he had forbidden Solomon to follow other gods, Solomon did not keep the LORD's command. 11So the LORD said to Solomon, "Since this is your attitude and you have not kept my covenant and my decrees, which I commanded you, I will most certainly tear the kingdom away from you and give it to one of your subordinates. 12Nevertheless, for the sake of David your father, I will not do it during your lifetime. I will tear it out of the hand of your son. 13Yet I will not tear the whole kingdom from him, but will give him one tribe for the sake of David my servant and for the sake of Jerusalem, which I have chosen."

14Then the LORD raised up against Solomon an adversary, Hadad the Edomite, from the royal line of Edom. 15Earlier when David was fighting with Edom, Joab the commander of the army, who had gone up to bury the dead, had struck down all the men in Edom. 16Joab and all the Israelites stayed there for six months, until they had destroyed all the men in Edom. 17But Hadad, still only a boy, fled to Egypt with some Edomite officials who had served his father. 18They set out from Midian and went to Paran. Then taking men from Paran with them, they went to Egypt, to Pharaoh king of Egypt, who gave Hadad a house and land and provided him with food.

19Pharaoh was so pleased with Hadad that he gave him a sister of his own wife, Queen Tahpenes, in marriage. 20The sister of Tahpenes bore him a son named Genubath, whom Tahpenes brought up in the royal palace. There Genubath lived with Pharaoh's own children.

21While he was in Egypt, Hadad heard that David rested with his fathers and that Joab the commander of the army was also dead. Then Hadad said to Pharaoh, "Let me go, that I may return to my own country."

22"What have you lacked here that you want to go back to your own country?" Pharaoh asked.

"Nothing," Hadad replied, "but do let me go!"

23And God raised up against Solomon another adversary, Rezon son of Eliada, who had fled from his master, Hadadezer king of Zobah. 24He gathered men around him and became the leader of a band of rebels when David destroyed the forces[w] ⌊of Zobah⌋; the rebels went to Damascus, where they settled and took control. 25Rezon was Israel's adversary as long as Solomon lived, adding to the trouble caused by Hadad. So Rezon ruled in Aram and was hostile toward Israel.

26Also, Jeroboam son of Nebat rebelled against the king. He was one of Solomon's officials, an Ephraimite from Zeredah, and his mother was a widow named Zeruah.

27Here is the account of how he rebelled against the king: Solomon had built the supporting terraces[x] and had filled in the gap in the wall of the city of David his father. 28Now Jeroboam

v5 Hebrew *Milcom*; also in verse 33
w24 Hebrew *destroyed them*
x27 Or *the Millo*

was a man of standing, and when Solomon saw
how well the young man did his work, he put
him in charge of the whole labor force of the
house of Joseph.

29About that time Jeroboam was going out of
Jerusalem, and Ahijah the prophet of Shiloh met
him on the way, wearing a new cloak. The two of
them were alone out in the country, 30and Ahijah
took hold of the new cloak he was wearing and
tore it into twelve pieces. 31Then he said to Jero-
boam, "Take ten pieces for yourself, for this is
what the LORD, the God of Israel, says: 'See, I am
going to tear the kingdom out of Solomon's hand
and give you ten tribes. 32But for the sake of my
servant David and the city of Jerusalem, which I
have chosen out of all the tribes of Israel, he will
have one tribe. 33I will do this because they
have[y] forsaken me and worshiped Ashtoreth the
goddess of the Sidonians, Chemosh the god of the
Moabites, and Molech the god of the Ammonites,
and have not walked in my ways, nor done what
is right in my eyes, nor kept my statutes and laws
as David, Solomon's father, did.

34" 'But I will not take the whole kingdom out
of Solomon's hand; I have made him ruler all the
days of his life for the sake of David my servant,
whom I chose and who observed my commands
and statutes. 35I will take the kingdom from his
son's hands and give you ten tribes. 36I will give
one tribe to his son so that David my servant may
always have a lamp before me in Jerusalem, the
city where I chose to put my Name. 37However, as
for you, I will take you, and you will rule over all
that your heart desires; you will be king over Is-
rael. 38If you do whatever I command you and
walk in my ways and do what is right in my eyes
by keeping my statutes and commands, as David
my servant did, I will be with you. I will build
you a dynasty as enduring as the one I built for
David and will give Israel to you. 39I will humble
David's descendants because of this, but not for-
ever.' "

40Solomon tried to kill Jeroboam, but Jeroboam
fled to Egypt, to Shishak the king, and stayed
there until Solomon's death.

41As for the other events of Solomon's reign—
all he did and the wisdom he displayed—are they
not written in the book of the annals of Solomon?
42Solomon reigned in Jerusalem over all Israel
forty years. 43Then he rested with his fathers and
was buried in the city of David his father. And
Rehoboam his son succeeded him as king.

y33 Hebrew; Septuagint, Vulgate and Syriac *because he has*

Discovering the Word 1. In what ways did Solomon break the first commandment, "You shall have no other gods before me" (vv. 1–13)? 2. In verse 13 God says that the consequence of Solomon's sin will be that his kingdom will be taken away. What mercy does God promise? Why? 3. What indications do you see that Hadad had the potential to become a serious threat to Solomon (vv. 14–22)? 4. What about Rezon (vv. 23–25)? 5. If Jeroboam chose to benefit from the experience of Israel's previous two kings (David and Solomon), how would it affect his reign?

Applying the Word 1. Solomon allowed his acquisition of wives to ease out his faith in God. When has your own love for a person created tensions with your faith? 2. How can we balance our love for the important people in our lives with our love for God? 3. Solomon's marriages to pagans testified to his lack of wholehearted commitment to God. In what area of your life do you struggle to keep your actions in line with your beliefs?

Responding in Prayer Verse 6 characterizes Solomon's life: "So Solomon did evil in the eyes of the LORD." Pray that your life will be characterized by faithfulness.

3 / 1 Kings 12
Internal Conflict

CIVIL WAR. AMERICAN minds turn to Yankee blue battling Confederate gray; brothers, cousins and neighbors pitted against each other; a wantonly destructive march to the sea, forever an embarrassment to both sides; a president on his knees, in tears. Three thousand years ago, Israel, too, suffered civil war with many of the same griefs. As in the U.S. Civil War, family members had to decide which side they were on. Geography wasn't always the most important factor, for this war was not only a war of politics. It was also, at least at the outset, a war of faith.

Warming Up to God How do you respond to conflict within your church or fellowship group? How does that kind of conflict affect your faith?

Read 1 Kings 12.

12 Rehoboam went to Shechem, for all the Israelites had gone there to make him king. [2]When Jeroboam son of Nebat heard this (he was still in Egypt, where he had fled from King Solomon), he returned from[z] Egypt. [3]So they sent for Jeroboam, and he and the whole assembly of Israel went to Rehoboam and said to him: [4]"Your father put a heavy yoke on us, but now lighten the harsh labor and the heavy yoke he put on us, and we will serve you."

[5]Rehoboam answered, "Go away for three days and then come back to me." So the people went away.

[6]Then King Rehoboam consulted the elders who had served his father Solomon during his lifetime. "How would you advise me to answer these people?" he asked.

[7]They replied, "If today you will be a servant to these people and serve them and give them a favorable answer, they will always be your servants."

[8]But Rehoboam rejected the advice the elders gave him and consulted the young men who had grown up with him and were serving him. [9]He asked them, "What is your advice? How should we answer these people who say to me, 'Lighten the yoke your father put on us'?"

[10]The young men who had grown up with him replied, "Tell these people who have said to you, 'Your father put a heavy yoke on us, but make our yoke lighter'—tell them, 'My little finger is thicker than my father's waist. [11]My father laid on you a heavy yoke; I will make it even heavier. My father scourged you with whips; I will scourge you with scorpions.' "

[12]Three days later Jeroboam and all the people returned to Rehoboam, as the king had said, "Come back to me in three days." [13]The king answered the people harshly. Rejecting the advice given him by the elders, [14]he followed the advice of the young men and said, "My father made your yoke heavy; I will make it even heavier. My father scourged you with whips; I will scourge you with scorpions." [15]So the king did not listen to the people, for this turn of events was from the LORD, to fulfill the word the LORD had spoken to Jeroboam son of Nebat through Ahijah the Shilonite.

[16]When all Israel saw that the king refused to listen to them, they answered the king:

"What share do we have in David,
what part in Jesse's son?
To your tents, O Israel!
Look after your own house, O David!"

So the Israelites went home. [17]But as for the Israelites who were living in the towns of Judah, Rehoboam still ruled over them.

[18]King Rehoboam sent out Adoniram,[a] who was in charge of forced labor, but all Israel stoned him to death. King Rehoboam, however, managed to get into his chariot and escape to Jerusalem. [19]So Israel has been in rebellion against the house of David to this day.

[20]When all the Israelites heard that Jeroboam had returned, they sent and called him to the assembly and made him king over all Israel. Only the tribe of Judah remained loyal to the house of David.

[21]When Rehoboam arrived in Jerusalem, he mustered the whole house of Judah and the tribe of Benjamin—a hundred and eighty thousand

[z]2 Or *he remained in* [a]18 Some Septuagint manuscripts and Syriac (see also 1 Kings 4:6 and 5:14); Hebrew *Adoram*

fighting men—to make war against the house of
Israel and to regain the kingdom for Rehoboam
son of Solomon.
22But this word of God came to Shemaiah the
man of God: 23"Say to Rehoboam son of Solomon
king of Judah, to the whole house of Judah and
Benjamin, and to the rest of the people, 24'This is
what the LORD says: Do not go up to fight against
your brothers, the Israelites. Go home, every one
of you, for this is my doing.' " So they obeyed the
word of the LORD and went home again, as the
LORD had ordered.
25Then Jeroboam fortified Shechem in the hill
country of Ephraim and lived there. From there
he went out and built up Peniel.[b]
26Jeroboam thought to himself, "The kingdom
will now likely revert to the house of David. 27If
these people go up to offer sacrifices at the temple
of the LORD in Jerusalem, they will again give their
allegiance to their lord, Rehoboam king of Judah.
They will kill me and return to King Rehoboam."
28After seeking advice, the king made two
golden calves. He said to the people, "It is too
much for you to go up to Jerusalem. Here are
your gods, O Israel, who brought you up out of
Egypt." 29One he set up in Bethel, and the other
in Dan. 30And this thing became a sin; the people
went even as far as Dan to worship the one there.
31Jeroboam built shrines on high places and ap-
pointed priests from all sorts of people, even
though they were not Levites. 32He instituted a
festival on the fifteenth day of the eighth month,
like the festival held in Judah, and offered sacri-
fices on the altar. This he did in Bethel, sacrificing
to the calves he had made. And at Bethel he also
installed priests at the high places he had made.
33On the fifteenth day of the eighth month, a
month of his own choosing, he offered sacrifices
on the altar he had built at Bethel. So he insti-
tuted the festival for the Israelites and went up to
the altar to make offerings.

[b]25 Hebrew *Penuel,* a variant of *Peniel*

Discovering the Word 1. What steps in verses 1–19 led to the division recorded in verse 20? 2. At what points did reconciliation seem possible? 3. What indications do you find that God had not abandoned his people during this time of conflict? 4. What spiritual results for the people of Israel would you expect to grow out of Jeroboam's new places of worship (vv. 26–30)? 5. What did Jeroboam do that was contrary to God's law (vv. 31–33)?

Applying the Word 1. If you were a godly person living under Jeroboam's rule, what choices would you have to make? 2. In what ways do your actions show a take-it-for-granted attitude toward your current opportunities to worship? 3. What conflict are you currently facing, and how do you need God's help to resolve it?

Responding in Prayer Praise God for the freedom you have to worship. Pray for those who don't have religious freedom.

---

1 Kings 13—16

13 By the word of the LORD a man of
God came from Judah to Bethel, as
Jeroboam was standing by the altar
to make an offering. 2He cried out against the
altar by the word of the LORD: "O altar, altar! This
is what the LORD says: 'A son named Josiah will be
born to the house of David. On you he will sacri-
fice the priests of the high places who now make
offerings here, and human bones will be burned
on you.' " 3That same day the man of God gave a
sign: "This is the sign the LORD has declared: The
altar will be split apart and the ashes on it will be
poured out."
4When King Jeroboam heard what the man of
God cried out against the altar at Bethel, he
stretched out his hand from the altar and said,
"Seize him!" But the hand he stretched out to-
ward the man shriveled up, so that he could not
pull it back. 5Also, the altar was split apart and its
ashes poured out according to the sign given by
the man of God by the word of the LORD.
6Then the king said to the man of God, "Inter-
cede with the LORD your God and pray for me that
my hand may be restored." So the man of God
interceded with the LORD, and the king's hand was
restored and became as it was before.

7The king said to the man of God, "Come home with me and have something to eat, and I will give you a gift."

8But the man of God answered the king, "Even if you were to give me half your possessions, I would not go with you, nor would I eat bread or drink water here. 9For I was commanded by the word of the LORD: 'You must not eat bread or drink water or return by the way you came.' " 10So he took another road and did not return by the way he had come to Bethel.

11Now there was a certain old prophet living in Bethel, whose sons came and told him all that the man of God had done there that day. They also told their father what he had said to the king. 12Their father asked them, "Which way did he go?" And his sons showed him which road the man of God from Judah had taken. 13So he said to his sons, "Saddle the donkey for me." And when they had saddled the donkey for him, he mounted it 14and rode after the man of God. He found him sitting under an oak tree and asked, "Are you the man of God who came from Judah?"

"I am," he replied.

15So the prophet said to him, "Come home with me and eat."

16The man of God said, "I cannot turn back and go with you, nor can I eat bread or drink water with you in this place. 17I have been told by the word of the LORD: 'You must not eat bread or drink water there or return by the way you came.' "

18The old prophet answered, "I too am a prophet, as you are. And an angel said to me by the word of the LORD: 'Bring him back with you to your house so that he may eat bread and drink water.' " (But he was lying to him.) 19So the man of God returned with him and ate and drank in his house.

20While they were sitting at the table, the word of the LORD came to the old prophet who had brought him back. 21He cried out to the man of God who had come from Judah, "This is what the LORD says: 'You have defied the word of the LORD and have not kept the command the LORD your God gave you. 22You came back and ate bread and drank water in the place where he told you not to eat or drink. Therefore your body will not be buried in the tomb of your fathers.' "

23When the man of God had finished eating and drinking, the prophet who had brought him back saddled his donkey for him. 24As he went on his way, a lion met him on the road and killed him, and his body was thrown down on the road, with both the donkey and the lion standing beside it. 25Some people who passed by saw the body thrown down there, with the lion standing beside the body, and they went and reported it in the city where the old prophet lived.

26When the prophet who had brought him back from his journey heard of it, he said, "It is the man of God who defied the word of the LORD. The LORD has given him over to the lion, which has mauled him and killed him, as the word of the LORD had warned him."

27The prophet said to his sons, "Saddle the donkey for me," and they did so. 28Then he went out and found the body thrown down on the road, with the donkey and the lion standing beside it. The lion had neither eaten the body nor mauled the donkey. 29So the prophet picked up the body of the man of God, laid it on the donkey, and brought it back to his own city to mourn for him and bury him. 30Then he laid the body in his own tomb, and they mourned over him and said, "Oh, my brother!"

31After burying him, he said to his sons, "When I die, bury me in the grave where the man of God is buried; lay my bones beside his bones. 32For the message he declared by the word of the LORD against the altar in Bethel and against all the shrines on the high places in the towns of Samaria will certainly come true."

33Even after this, Jeroboam did not change his evil ways, but once more appointed priests for the high places from all sorts of people. Anyone who wanted to become a priest he consecrated for the high places. 34This was the sin of the house of Jeroboam that led to its downfall and to its destruction from the face of the earth.

14 At that time Abijah son of Jeroboam became ill, 2and Jeroboam said to his wife, "Go, disguise yourself, so you won't be recognized as the wife of Jeroboam. Then go to Shiloh. Ahijah the prophet is there—the one who told me I would be king over this people. 3Take ten loaves of bread with you, some cakes and a jar of honey, and go to him. He will tell you what will happen to the boy." 4So Jeroboam's wife did what he said and went to Ahijah's house in Shiloh.

Now Ahijah could not see; his sight was gone because of his age. 5But the LORD had told Ahijah, "Jeroboam's wife is coming to ask you about her son, for he is ill, and you are to give her such and such an answer. When she arrives, she will pretend to be someone else."

6So when Ahijah heard the sound of her footsteps at the door, he said, "Come in, wife of Jeroboam. Why this pretense? I have been sent to you with bad news. 7Go, tell Jeroboam that this is what the LORD, the God of Israel, says: 'I raised you up from among the people and made you a leader over my people Israel. 8I tore the kingdom away from the house of David and gave it to you, but you have not been like my servant David, who kept my commands and followed me with all his heart, doing only what was right in my eyes. 9You have done more evil than all who lived before you. You have made for yourself other gods, idols made of metal; you have provoked me to anger and thrust me behind your back.

10" 'Because of this, I am going to bring disaster on the house of Jeroboam. I will cut off from Jeroboam every last male in Israel—slave or free. I will burn up the house of Jeroboam as one burns dung, until it is all gone. 11Dogs will eat those belonging to Jeroboam who die in the city, and the birds of the air will feed on those who die in the country. The LORD has spoken!'

12"As for you, go back home. When you set foot in your city, the boy will die. 13All Israel will mourn for him and bury him. He is the only one belonging to Jeroboam who will be buried, because he is the only one in the house of Jeroboam in whom the LORD, the God of Israel, has found anything good.

14"The LORD will raise up for himself a king over Israel who will cut off the family of Jeroboam. This is the day! What? Yes, even now.[c] 15And the LORD will strike Israel, so that it will be like a reed swaying in the water. He will uproot Israel from this good land that he gave to their forefathers and scatter them beyond the River,[d] because they provoked the LORD to anger by making Asherah poles.[e] 16And he will give Israel up because of the sins Jeroboam has committed and has caused Israel to commit."

17Then Jeroboam's wife got up and left and went to Tirzah. As soon as she stepped over the threshold of the house, the boy died. 18They buried him, and all Israel mourned for him, as the LORD had said through his servant the prophet Ahijah.

19The other events of Jeroboam's reign, his wars and how he ruled, are written in the book of the annals of the kings of Israel. 20He reigned for twenty-two years and then rested with his fathers. And Nadab his son succeeded him as king.

21Rehoboam son of Solomon was king in Judah. He was forty-one years old when he became king, and he reigned seventeen years in Jerusalem, the city the LORD had chosen out of all the tribes of Israel in which to put his Name. His mother's name was Naamah; she was an Ammonite.

22Judah did evil in the eyes of the LORD. By the sins they committed they stirred up his jealous anger more than their fathers had done. 23They also set up for themselves high places, sacred stones and Asherah poles on every high hill and under every spreading tree. 24There were even male shrine prostitutes in the land; the people engaged in all the detestable practices of the nations the LORD had driven out before the Israelites.

25In the fifth year of King Rehoboam, Shishak king of Egypt attacked Jerusalem. 26He carried off the treasures of the temple of the LORD and the treasures of the royal palace. He took everything, including all the gold shields Solomon had made. 27So King Rehoboam made bronze shields to replace them and assigned these to the commanders of the guard on duty at the entrance to the royal palace. 28Whenever the king went to the LORD's temple, the guards bore the shields, and afterward they returned them to the guardroom.

29As for the other events of Rehoboam's reign, and all he did, are they not written in the book of the annals of the kings of Judah? 30There was continual warfare between Rehoboam and Jeroboam. 31And Rehoboam rested with his fathers and was buried with them in the City of David. His mother's name was Naamah; she was an Ammonite. And Abijah[f] his son succeeded him as king.

15 In the eighteenth year of the reign of Jeroboam son of Nebat, Abijah[g] became king of Judah, 2and he reigned in Jerusalem three years. His mother's name was Maacah daughter of Abishalom.[h]

3He committed all the sins his father had done before him; his heart was not fully devoted to the LORD his God, as the heart of David his forefather

[c]14 The meaning of the Hebrew for this sentence is uncertain.
[d]15 That is, the Euphrates [e]15 That is, symbols of the goddess Asherah; here and elsewhere in 1 Kings [f]31 Some Hebrew manuscripts and Septuagint (see also 2 Chron. 12:16); most Hebrew manuscripts *Abijam* [g]1 Some Hebrew manuscripts and Septuagint (see also 2 Chron. 12:16); most Hebrew manuscripts *Abijam*; also in verses 7 and 8 [h]2 A variant of *Absalom*; also in verse 10

had been. 4Nevertheless, for David's sake the LORD his God gave him a lamp in Jerusalem by raising up a son to succeed him and by making Jerusalem strong. 5For David had done what was right in the eyes of the LORD and had not failed to keep any of the LORD's commands all the days of his life—except in the case of Uriah the Hittite.

6There was war between Rehoboam[i] and Jeroboam throughout ⌞Abijah's⌟ lifetime. 7As for the other events of Abijah's reign, and all he did, are they not written in the book of the annals of the kings of Judah? There was war between Abijah and Jeroboam. 8And Abijah rested with his fathers and was buried in the City of David. And Asa his son succeeded him as king.

9In the twentieth year of Jeroboam king of Israel, Asa became king of Judah, 10and he reigned in Jerusalem forty-one years. His grandmother's name was Maacah daughter of Abishalom.

11Asa did what was right in the eyes of the LORD, as his father David had done. 12He expelled the male shrine prostitutes from the land and got rid of all the idols his fathers had made. 13He even deposed his grandmother Maacah from her position as queen mother, because she had made a repulsive Asherah pole. Asa cut the pole down and burned it in the Kidron Valley. 14Although he did not remove the high places, Asa's heart was fully committed to the LORD all his life. 15He brought into the temple of the LORD the silver and gold and the articles that he and his father had dedicated.

16There was war between Asa and Baasha king of Israel throughout their reigns. 17Baasha king of Israel went up against Judah and fortified Ramah to prevent anyone from leaving or entering the territory of Asa king of Judah.

18Asa then took all the silver and gold that was left in the treasuries of the LORD's temple and of his own palace. He entrusted it to his officials and sent them to Ben-Hadad son of Tabrimmon, the son of Hezion, the king of Aram, who was ruling in Damascus. 19"Let there be a treaty between me and you," he said, "as there was between my father and your father. See, I am sending you a gift of silver and gold. Now break your treaty with Baasha king of Israel so he will withdraw from me."

20Ben-Hadad agreed with King Asa and sent the commanders of his forces against the towns of Israel. He conquered Ijon, Dan, Abel Beth Maacah and all Kinnereth in addition to Naphtali. 21When Baasha heard this, he stopped building Ramah and withdrew to Tirzah. 22Then King Asa issued an order to all Judah—no one was exempt—and they carried away from Ramah the stones and timber Baasha had been using there. With them King Asa built up Geba in Benjamin, and also Mizpah.

23As for all the other events of Asa's reign, all his achievements, all he did and the cities he built, are they not written in the book of the annals of the kings of Judah? In his old age, however, his feet became diseased. 24Then Asa rested with his fathers and was buried with them in the city of his father David. And Jehoshaphat his son succeeded him as king.

25Nadab son of Jeroboam became king of Israel in the second year of Asa king of Judah, and he reigned over Israel two years. 26He did evil in the eyes of the LORD, walking in the ways of his father and in his sin, which he had caused Israel to commit.

27Baasha son of Ahijah of the house of Issachar plotted against him, and he struck him down at Gibbethon, a Philistine town, while Nadab and all Israel were besieging it. 28Baasha killed Nadab in the third year of Asa king of Judah and succeeded him as king.

29As soon as he began to reign, he killed Jeroboam's whole family. He did not leave Jeroboam anyone that breathed, but destroyed them all, according to the word of the LORD given through his servant Ahijah the Shilonite— 30because of the sins Jeroboam had committed and had caused Israel to commit, and because he provoked the LORD, the God of Israel, to anger.

31As for the other events of Nadab's reign, and all he did, are they not written in the book of the annals of the kings of Israel? 32There was war between Asa and Baasha king of Israel throughout their reigns.

33In the third year of Asa king of Judah, Baasha son of Ahijah became king of all Israel in Tirzah, and he reigned twenty-four years. 34He did evil in the eyes of the LORD, walking in the ways of Jeroboam and in his sin, which he had caused Israel to commit.

16

Then the word of the LORD came to Jehu son of Hanani against Baasha: 2"I lifted you up from the dust and made you leader of my people Israel, but you walked in the ways of Jeroboam and caused my people Israel to sin and to provoke me to anger by

i6 Most Hebrew manuscripts; some Hebrew manuscripts and Syriac *Abijam* (that is, Abijah)

their sins. [3]So I am about to consume Baasha and his house, and I will make your house like that of Jeroboam son of Nebat. [4]Dogs will eat those belonging to Baasha who die in the city, and the birds of the air will feed on those who die in the country."

[5]As for the other events of Baasha's reign, what he did and his achievements, are they not written in the book of the annals of the kings of Israel? [6]Baasha rested with his fathers and was buried in Tirzah. And Elah his son succeeded him as king.

[7]Moreover, the word of the LORD came through the prophet Jehu son of Hanani to Baasha and his house, because of all the evil he had done in the eyes of the LORD, provoking him to anger by the things he did, and becoming like the house of Jeroboam—and also because he destroyed it.

[8]In the twenty-sixth year of Asa king of Judah, Elah son of Baasha became king of Israel, and he reigned in Tirzah two years.

[9]Zimri, one of his officials, who had command of half his chariots, plotted against him. Elah was in Tirzah at the time, getting drunk in the home of Arza, the man in charge of the palace at Tirzah. [10]Zimri came in, struck him down and killed him in the twenty-seventh year of Asa king of Judah. Then he succeeded him as king.

[11]As soon as he began to reign and was seated on the throne, he killed off Baasha's whole family. He did not spare a single male, whether relative or friend. [12]So Zimri destroyed the whole family of Baasha, in accordance with the word of the LORD spoken against Baasha through the prophet Jehu— [13]because of all the sins Baasha and his son Elah had committed and had caused Israel to commit, so that they provoked the LORD, the God of Israel, to anger by their worthless idols.

[14]As for the other events of Elah's reign, and all he did, are they not written in the book of the annals of the kings of Israel?

[15]In the twenty-seventh year of Asa king of Judah, Zimri reigned in Tirzah seven days. The army was encamped near Gibbethon, a Philistine town. [16]When the Israelites in the camp heard that Zimri had plotted against the king and murdered him, they proclaimed Omri, the commander of the army, king over Israel that very day there in the camp. [17]Then Omri and all the Israelites with him withdrew from Gibbethon and laid siege to Tirzah. [18]When Zimri saw that the city was taken, he went into the citadel of the royal palace and set the palace on fire around him. So he died, [19]because of the sins he had committed, doing evil in the eyes of the LORD and walking in the ways of Jeroboam and in the sin he had committed and had caused Israel to commit.

[20]As for the other events of Zimri's reign, and the rebellion he carried out, are they not written in the book of the annals of the kings of Israel?

[21]Then the people of Israel were split into two factions; half supported Tibni son of Ginath for king, and the other half supported Omri. [22]But Omri's followers proved stronger than those of Tibni son of Ginath. So Tibni died and Omri became king.

[23]In the thirty-first year of Asa king of Judah, Omri became king of Israel, and he reigned twelve years, six of them in Tirzah. [24]He bought the hill of Samaria from Shemer for two talents[j] of silver and built a city on the hill, calling it Samaria, after Shemer, the name of the former owner of the hill.

[25]But Omri did evil in the eyes of the LORD and sinned more than all those before him. [26]He walked in all the ways of Jeroboam son of Nebat and in his sin, which he had caused Israel to commit, so that they provoked the LORD, the God of Israel, to anger by their worthless idols.

[27]As for the other events of Omri's reign, what he did and the things he achieved, are they not written in the book of the annals of the kings of Israel? [28]Omri rested with his fathers and was buried in Samaria. And Ahab his son succeeded him as king.

[29]In the thirty-eighth year of Asa king of Judah, Ahab son of Omri became king of Israel, and he reigned in Samaria over Israel twenty-two years. [30]Ahab son of Omri did more evil in the eyes of the LORD than any of those before him. [31]He not only considered it trivial to commit the sins of Jeroboam son of Nebat, but he also married Jezebel daughter of Ethbaal king of the Sidonians, and began to serve Baal and worship him. [32]He set up an altar for Baal in the temple of Baal that he built in Samaria. [33]Ahab also made an Asherah pole and did more to provoke the LORD, the God of Israel, to anger than did all the kings of Israel before him.

[34]In Ahab's time, Hiel of Bethel rebuilt Jericho. He laid its foundations at the cost of his firstborn son Abiram, and he set up its gates at the cost of his youngest son Segub, in accordance with the word of the LORD spoken by Joshua son of Nun.

j24 That is, about 150 pounds (about 70 kilograms)

4 / *1 Kings 17*
Serving Each Other

IT SEEMED TO Elijah that he was the only person in Israel who served God. Ahab had just become the king, and he was already more evil than his father, Omri, had been. And now God was asking Elijah to give a dire prophecy about no rain in the land. All Elijah wanted to do was get away from everything and not do anything important. Most of all, he wanted someone to take care of *him* for once.

Warming Up to God When have you felt that you didn't want to be responsible for anyone else, that you just wanted to be taken care of?

Read 1 Kings 17.

17 Now Elijah the Tishbite, from
Tishbe[k] in Gilead, said to Ahab,
"As the LORD, the God of Israel,
lives, whom I serve, there will be neither dew
nor rain in the next few years except at my
word."
2Then the word of the LORD came to Elijah:
3"Leave here, turn eastward and hide in the Ke-
rith Ravine, east of the Jordan. 4You will drink
from the brook, and I have ordered the ravens to
feed you there."
5So he did what the LORD had told him.
He went to the Kerith Ravine, east of the Jordan,
and stayed there. 6The ravens brought him
bread and meat in the morning and bread and
meat in the evening, and he drank from the
brook.
7Some time later the brook dried up because
there had been no rain in the land. 8Then the
word of the LORD came to him: 9"Go at once to
Zarephath of Sidon and stay there. I have com-
manded a widow in that place to supply you with
food." 10So he went to Zarephath. When he came
to the town gate, a widow was there gather-
ing sticks. He called to her and asked, "Would
you bring me a little water in a jar so I may
have a drink?" 11As she was going to get it,
he called, "And bring me, please, a piece of
bread."
12"As surely as the LORD your God lives," she
replied, "I don't have any bread—only a handful
of flour in a jar and a little oil in a jug. I am
gathering a few sticks to take home and make a
meal for myself and my son, that we may eat it—
and die."
13Elijah said to her, "Don't be afraid. Go home
and do as you have said. But first make a small
cake of bread for me from what you have and
bring it to me, and then make something
for yourself and your son. 14For this is what the
LORD, the God of Israel, says: 'The jar of flour
will not be used up and the jug of oil will not
run dry until the day the LORD gives rain on the
land.'"
15She went away and did as Elijah had told her.
So there was food every day for Elijah and for the
woman and her family. 16For the jar of flour was
not used up and the jug of oil did not run dry, in
keeping with the word of the LORD spoken by Eli-
jah.
17Some time later the son of the woman who
owned the house became ill. He grew worse and
worse, and finally stopped breathing. 18She said
to Elijah, "What do you have against me, man of
God? Did you come to remind me of my sin and
kill my son?"
19"Give me your son," Elijah replied. He took
him from her arms, carried him to the upper
room where he was staying, and laid him on his
bed. 20Then he cried out to the LORD, "O LORD
my God, have you brought tragedy also upon
this widow I am staying with, by causing her
son to die?" 21Then he stretched himself out
on the boy three times and cried to the LORD,
"O LORD my God, let this boy's life return to
him!"
22The LORD heard Elijah's cry, and the boy's life
returned to him, and he lived. 23Elijah picked up
the child and carried him down from the room
into the house. He gave him to his mother and
said, "Look, your son is alive!"
24Then the woman said to Elijah, "Now I know
that you are a man of God and that the word of
the LORD from your mouth is the truth."

k1 Or *Tishbite, of the settlers*

Discovering the Word 1. Why does God send Elijah first into the Kerith ravine and then to the widow at Zarephath (v. 1)? 2. What service does the widow render to Elijah (vv. 7–15)? 3. What service does Elijah render to the widow (vv. 13–14, 22)? 4. How is the widow's response to her son's coming back to life (v. 24) different from her statement in verse 18? 5. What two (or more) things are accomplished by the relationship between the widow and Elijah?

Applying the Word 1. At what time in your life did you help someone in a difficult situation and find that that person had helped you also? 2. Sometimes God can't use us in the way he used the widow and Elijah in each other's lives because we aren't open to the possibility of mutual service. How do you need to change in order to be open to such a relationship?

Responding in Prayer Pray for awareness of the blessings you can give and receive through Christian service.

5 / *1 Kings 18*
Knowing God's Power

IMAGINE YOURSELF LIVING in a country where everyone is following other gods. There are no churches, no Bible studies, no fellowship, no Christian literature. As far as you know, you are the only Christian in the land. How would you respond? The prophet Elijah faced such odds. Israel had abandoned the Lord for another god, Baal. They had rejected Elijah in favor of the four hundred and fifty prophets of Baal. Yet in spite of these odds, Elijah challenged Baal and his prophets to a contest with God.

Warming Up to God How would you feel if every Christian you know abandoned the faith, and you had to stand alone in your commitment to Jesus? Consider this prayerfully and honestly before God.

Read 1 Kings 18.

18 After a long time, in the third year,
the word of the LORD came to Eli-
jah: "Go and present yourself to
Ahab, and I will send rain on the land." [2]So Elijah
went to present himself to Ahab.
Now the famine was severe in Samaria, [3]and
Ahab had summoned Obadiah, who was in
charge of his palace. (Obadiah was a devout be-
liever in the LORD. [4]While Jezebel was killing off
the LORD's prophets, Obadiah had taken a hun-
dred prophets and hidden them in two caves, fifty
in each, and had supplied them with food and
water.) [5]Ahab had said to Obadiah, "Go through
the land to all the springs and valleys. Maybe we
can find some grass to keep the horses and mules
alive so we will not have to kill any of our ani-
mals." [6]So they divided the land they were to
cover, Ahab going in one direction and Obadiah
in another.
[7]As Obadiah was walking along, Elijah met
him. Obadiah recognized him, bowed down to
the ground, and said, "Is it really you, my lord
Elijah?"
[8]"Yes," he replied. "Go tell your master, 'Elijah
is here.' "
[9]"What have I done wrong," asked Obadiah,
"that you are handing your servant over to Ahab
to be put to death? [10]As surely as the LORD your
God lives, there is not a nation or kingdom where
my master has not sent someone to look for you.
And whenever a nation or kingdom claimed you
were not there, he made them swear they could
not find you. [11]But now you tell me to go to my
master and say, 'Elijah is here.' [12]I don't know
where the Spirit of the LORD may carry you when
I leave you. If I go and tell Ahab and he doesn't
find you, he will kill me. Yet I your servant have
worshiped the LORD since my youth. [13]Haven't
you heard, my lord, what I did while Jezebel was

killing the prophets of the LORD? I hid a hundred of the LORD's prophets in two caves, fifty in each, and supplied them with food and water. 14And now you tell me to go to my master and say, 'Elijah is here.' He will kill me!"

15Elijah said, "As the LORD Almighty lives, whom I serve, I will surely present myself to Ahab today."

16So Obadiah went to meet Ahab and told him, and Ahab went to meet Elijah. 17When he saw Elijah, he said to him, "Is that you, you troubler of Israel?"

18"I have not made trouble for Israel," Elijah replied. "But you and your father's family have. You have abandoned the LORD's commands and have followed the Baals. 19Now summon the people from all over Israel to meet me on Mount Carmel. And bring the four hundred and fifty prophets of Baal and the four hundred prophets of Asherah, who eat at Jezebel's table."

20So Ahab sent word throughout all Israel and assembled the prophets on Mount Carmel. 21Elijah went before the people and said, "How long will you waver between two opinions? If the LORD is God, follow him; but if Baal is God, follow him."

But the people said nothing.

22Then Elijah said to them, "I am the only one of the LORD's prophets left, but Baal has four hundred and fifty prophets. 23Get two bulls for us. Let them choose one for themselves, and let them cut it into pieces and put it on the wood but not set fire to it. I will prepare the other bull and put it on the wood but not set fire to it. 24Then you call on the name of your god, and I will call on the name of the LORD. The god who answers by fire—he is God."

Then all the people said, "What you say is good."

25Elijah said to the prophets of Baal, "Choose one of the bulls and prepare it first, since there are so many of you. Call on the name of your god, but do not light the fire." 26So they took the bull given them and prepared it.

Then they called on the name of Baal from morning till noon. "O Baal, answer us!" they shouted. But there was no response; no one answered. And they danced around the altar they had made.

27At noon Elijah began to taunt them. "Shout louder!" he said. "Surely he is a god! Perhaps he is deep in thought, or busy, or traveling. Maybe he is sleeping and must be awakened." 28So they shouted louder and slashed themselves with swords and spears, as was their custom, until their blood flowed. 29Midday passed, and they continued their frantic prophesying until the time for the evening sacrifice. But there was no response, no one answered, no one paid attention.

30Then Elijah said to all the people, "Come here to me." They came to him, and he repaired the altar of the LORD, which was in ruins. 31Elijah took twelve stones, one for each of the tribes descended from Jacob, to whom the word of the LORD had come, saying, "Your name shall be Israel." 32With the stones he built an altar in the name of the LORD, and he dug a trench around it large enough to hold two seahs[l] of seed. 33He arranged the wood, cut the bull into pieces and laid it on the wood. Then he said to them, "Fill four large jars with water and pour it on the offering and on the wood."

34"Do it again," he said, and they did it again.

"Do it a third time," he ordered, and they did it the third time. 35The water ran down around the altar and even filled the trench.

36At the time of sacrifice, the prophet Elijah stepped forward and prayed: "O LORD, God of Abraham, Isaac and Israel, let it be known today that you are God in Israel and that I am your servant and have done all these things at your command. 37Answer me, O LORD, answer me, so these people will know that you, O LORD, are God, and that you are turning their hearts back again."

38Then the fire of the LORD fell and burned up the sacrifice, the wood, the stones and the soil, and also licked up the water in the trench.

39When all the people saw this, they fell prostrate and cried, "The LORD—he is God! The LORD—he is God!"

40Then Elijah commanded them, "Seize the prophets of Baal. Don't let anyone get away!" They seized them, and Elijah had them brought down to the Kishon Valley and slaughtered there.

41And Elijah said to Ahab, "Go, eat and drink, for there is the sound of a heavy rain." 42So Ahab went off to eat and drink, but Elijah climbed to

l32 That is, probably about 13 quarts (about 15 liters)

the top of Carmel, bent down to the ground and
put his face between his knees.
43“Go and look toward the sea,” he told his
servant. And he went up and looked.
“There is nothing there,” he said.
Seven times Elijah said, “Go back.”
44The seventh time the servant reported, “A
cloud as small as a man’s hand is rising from the
sea.”

So Elijah said, “Go and tell Ahab, ‘Hitch up
your chariot and go down before the rain stops
you.’ ”
45Meanwhile, the sky grew black with clouds,
the wind rose, a heavy rain came on and Ahab
rode off to Jezreel. 46The power of the LORD
came upon Elijah and, tucking his cloak into
his belt, he ran ahead of Ahab all the way to
Jezreel.

Discovering the Word 1. Describe the difficult position Obadiah finds himself in (vv. 9–15). 2. Why do you think Ahab agrees to Elijah’s demand for a contest? 3. Elijah challenges the people of Israel at Mount Carmel (vv. 20–21). What does their failure to answer indicate? 4. What is pathetic about the frenzied activities of Baal’s prophets and the taunts of Elijah (vv. 26–29)? 5. What do Elijah’s actions indicate about his knowledge of God’s reality and power (vv. 30–37)? 6. Summarize the dramatic outcome of the contest between Elijah and the prophets of Baal (vv. 38–40).

Applying the Word 1. In what ways are you or the people around you wavering between two gods? (For example, wavering between materialism, personal desires or ambitions and the Lord Jesus Christ.) 2. What are the “Mount Carmel” situations in which you face overwhelming odds today? (For example, at work, at school, in your family or neighborhood.) 3. How can you, like Elijah, rely on God’s power in that situation? (Take into account what your part and God’s part might be.)

Responding in Prayer Spend time in prayer, committing your situation to God’s powerful care.

6 / *1 Kings 19:1–18*
Caring for the Whole Person

ELIJAH EXPERIENCED A thrilling victory over the prophets of Baal in chapter 18. Impressed, the people worshiped the Lord. Then they helped Elijah kill all the prophets of Baal. Life was going well until suddenly Queen Jezebel stepped into Elijah’s scene.

Often we are quick to blame discontent on spiritual need. But Elijah had experienced great spiritual victory. In this passage his emotional and physical needs became evident. We are whole people—body, soul (emotions, mind and will) and spirit. And God ministered to Elijah’s whole being.

Warming Up to God Why is it sometimes difficult to hear the Lord’s voice when you are feeling especially busy and successful “doing the Lord’s work”?

Read 1 Kings 19:1–18.

19 Now Ahab told Jezebel everything
Elijah had done and how he had
killed all the prophets with the
sword. 2So Jezebel sent a messenger to Elijah to
say, “May the gods deal with me, be it ever so
severely, if by this time tomorrow I do not make
your life like that of one of them.”
3Elijah was afraid[m] and ran for his life. When
he came to Beersheba in Judah, he left his servant
there, 4while he himself went a day’s journey into
the desert. He came to a broom tree, sat down
under it and prayed that he might die. “I have had
enough, LORD,” he said. “Take my life; I am no
better than my ancestors.” 5Then he lay down
under the tree and fell asleep.

[m]3 Or *Elijah saw*

All at once an angel touched him and said, "Get up and eat." 6He looked around, and there by his head was a cake of bread baked over hot coals, and a jar of water. He ate and drank and then lay down again.

7The angel of the LORD came back a second time and touched him and said, "Get up and eat, for the journey is too much for you." 8So he got up and ate and drank. Strengthened by that food, he traveled forty days and forty nights until he reached Horeb, the mountain of God. 9There he went into a cave and spent the night.

And the word of the LORD came to him: "What are you doing here, Elijah?"

10He replied, "I have been very zealous for the LORD God Almighty. The Israelites have rejected your covenant, broken down your altars, and put your prophets to death with the sword. I am the only one left, and now they are trying to kill me too."

11The LORD said, "Go out and stand on the mountain in the presence of the LORD, for the LORD is about to pass by."

Then a great and powerful wind tore the mountains apart and shattered the rocks before the LORD, but the LORD was not in the wind. After the wind there was an earthquake, but the LORD was not in the earthquake. 12After the earthquake came a fire, but the LORD was not in the fire. And after the fire came a gentle whisper. 13When Elijah heard it, he pulled his cloak over his face and went out and stood at the mouth of the cave.

Then a voice said to him, "What are you doing here, Elijah?"

14He replied, "I have been very zealous for the LORD God Almighty. The Israelites have rejected your covenant, broken down your altars, and put your prophets to death with the sword. I am the only one left, and now they are trying to kill me too."

15The LORD said to him, "Go back the way you came, and go to the Desert of Damascus. When you get there, anoint Hazael king over Aram. 16Also, anoint Jehu son of Nimshi king over Israel, and anoint Elisha son of Shaphat from Abel Meholah to succeed you as prophet. 17Jehu will put to death any who escape the sword of Hazael, and Elisha will put to death any who escape the sword of Jehu. 18Yet I reserve seven thousand in Israel—all whose knees have not bowed down to Baal and all whose mouths have not kissed him."

Discovering the Word 1. As you look through the passage, what do you see of Elijah's emotional needs (vv. 3–4, 10, 14), physical needs (vv. 5–8) and spiritual needs (vv. 8, 10–11, 13–14)? 2. What do you think happened to the faith Elijah had so dramatically demonstrated in the previous chapters? 3. In what different ways did the angel minister to Elijah's needs (vv. 5–9)? 4. What do you think is the significance of the Lord *not* being in the wind, the earthquake or the fire—but in a gentle whisper (vv. 11–12)? 5. What emotional as well as spiritual needs of Elijah were met by his encounter with God?

Applying the Word 1. What factors in your life cause you to miss the "gentle whisper" of God? 2. What helps you to hear it?

Responding in Prayer Thank God for making you a whole person. Ask him to meet the emotional, physical and spiritual needs you have right now.

1 Kings 19:19—20:43

19So Elijah went from there and found Elisha son of Shaphat. He was plowing with twelve yoke of oxen, and he himself was driving the twelfth pair. Elijah went up to him and threw his cloak around him. 20Elisha then left his oxen and ran after Elijah. "Let me kiss my father and mother good-by," he said, "and then I will come with you."

"Go back," Elijah replied. "What have I done to you?"

21So Elisha left him and went back. He took his yoke of oxen and slaughtered them. He burned the plowing equipment to cook the meat and gave it to the people, and they ate. Then he set out to follow Elijah and became his attendant.

20 Now Ben-Hadad king of Aram mustered his entire army. Accompanied by thirty-two kings with their horses and chariots, he went up and besieged Samaria and attacked it. 2He sent messengers into the city to Ahab king of Israel, saying, "This is what Ben-Hadad says: 3'Your silver and gold are mine, and the best of your wives and children are mine.' "

4The king of Israel answered, "Just as you say, my lord the king. I and all I have are yours."

5The messengers came again and said, "This is what Ben-Hadad says: 'I sent to demand your silver and gold, your wives and your children. 6But about this time tomorrow I am going to send my officials to search your palace and the houses of your officials. They will seize everything you value and carry it away.' "

7The king of Israel summoned all the elders of the land and said to them, "See how this man is looking for trouble! When he sent for my wives and my children, my silver and my gold, I did not refuse him."

8The elders and the people all answered, "Don't listen to him or agree to his demands."

9So he replied to Ben-Hadad's messengers, "Tell my lord the king, 'Your servant will do all you demanded the first time, but this demand I cannot meet.' " They left and took the answer back to Ben-Hadad.

10Then Ben-Hadad sent another message to Ahab: "May the gods deal with me, be it ever so severely, if enough dust remains in Samaria to give each of my men a handful."

11The king of Israel answered, "Tell him: 'One who puts on his armor should not boast like one who takes it off.' "

12Ben-Hadad heard this message while he and the kings were drinking in their tents,[n] and he ordered his men: "Prepare to attack." So they prepared to attack the city.

13Meanwhile a prophet came to Ahab king of Israel and announced, "This is what the LORD says: 'Do you see this vast army? I will give it into your hand today, and then you will know that I am the LORD.' "

14"But who will do this?" asked Ahab.

The prophet replied, "This is what the LORD says: 'The young officers of the provincial commanders will do it.' "

"And who will start the battle?" he asked.

The prophet answered, "You will."

15So Ahab summoned the young officers of the provincial commanders, 232 men. Then he assembled the rest of the Israelites, 7,000 in all. 16They set out at noon while Ben-Hadad and the 32 kings allied with him were in their tents getting drunk. 17The young officers of the provincial commanders went out first.

Now Ben-Hadad had dispatched scouts, who reported, "Men are advancing from Samaria."

18He said, "If they have come out for peace, take them alive; if they have come out for war, take them alive."

19The young officers of the provincial commanders marched out of the city with the army behind them 20and each one struck down his opponent. At that, the Arameans fled, with the Israelites in pursuit. But Ben-Hadad king of Aram escaped on horseback with some of his horsemen. 21The king of Israel advanced and overpowered the horses and chariots and inflicted heavy losses on the Arameans.

22Afterward, the prophet came to the king of Israel and said, "Strengthen your position and see what must be done, because next spring the king of Aram will attack you again."

23Meanwhile, the officials of the king of Aram advised him, "Their gods are gods of the hills. That is why they were too strong for us. But if we fight them on the plains, surely we will be stronger than they. 24Do this: Remove all the kings from their commands and replace them with other officers. 25You must also raise an army like the one you lost—horse for horse and chariot for chariot—so we can fight Israel on the plains. Then surely we will be stronger than they." He agreed with them and acted accordingly.

26The next spring Ben-Hadad mustered the Arameans and went up to Aphek to fight against Israel. 27When the Israelites were also mustered and given provisions, they marched out to meet them. The Israelites camped opposite them like two small flocks of goats, while the Arameans covered the countryside.

28The man of God came up and told the king of Israel, "This is what the LORD says: 'Because the Arameans think the LORD is a god of the hills and not a god of the valleys, I will deliver this vast army into your hands, and you will know that I am the LORD.' "

29For seven days they camped opposite each

[n] 12 Or *in Succoth*; also in verse 16

other, and on the seventh day the battle was
joined. The Israelites inflicted a hundred thou-
sand casualties on the Aramean foot soldiers in
one day. 30The rest of them escaped to the city of
Aphek, where the wall collapsed on twenty-seven
thousand of them. And Ben-Hadad fled to the city
and hid in an inner room.
31His officials said to him, "Look, we have
heard that the kings of the house of Israel are
merciful. Let us go to the king of Israel with sack-
cloth around our waists and ropes around our
heads. Perhaps he will spare your life."
32Wearing sackcloth around their waists and
ropes around their heads, they went to the king of
Israel and said, "Your servant Ben-Hadad says:
'Please let me live.' "

The king answered, "Is he still alive? He is my
brother."
33The men took this as a good sign and were
quick to pick up his word. "Yes, your brother
Ben-Hadad!" they said.

"Go and get him," the king said. When Ben-
Hadad came out, Ahab had him come up into his
chariot.
34"I will return the cities my father took from
your father," Ben-Hadad offered. "You may set up
your own market areas in Damascus, as my father
did in Samaria."

⌞Ahab said,⌟ "On the basis of a treaty I will set
you free." So he made a treaty with him, and let
him go.
35By the word of the LORD one of the sons of the
prophets said to his companion, "Strike me with
your weapon," but the man refused.
36So the prophet said, "Because you have not
obeyed the LORD, as soon as you leave me a lion
will kill you." And after the man went away, a
lion found him and killed him.
37The prophet found another man and said,
"Strike me, please." So the man struck him and
wounded him. 38Then the prophet went and
stood by the road waiting for the king. He dis-
guised himself with his headband down over his
eyes. 39As the king passed by, the prophet called
out to him, "Your servant went into the thick of
the battle, and someone came to me with a cap-
tive and said, 'Guard this man. If he is missing, it
will be your life for his life, or you must pay a
talent[o] of silver.' 40While your servant was busy
here and there, the man disappeared."

"That is your sentence," the king of Israel said.
"You have pronounced it yourself."
41Then the prophet quickly removed the head-
band from his eyes, and the king of Israel recog-
nized him as one of the prophets. 42He said to the
king, "This is what the LORD says: 'You have set
free a man I had determined should die.[p] There-
fore it is your life for his life, your people for his
people.' " 43Sullen and angry, the king of Israel
went to his palace in Samaria.

[o]39 That is, about 75 pounds (about 34 kilograms) [p]42 The Hebrew term refers to the irrevocable giving over of things or persons to the LORD, often by totally destroying them.

7 / *1 Kings 21*
Manipulation

A RECENT BOOK released by a Christian publisher entitled *Not Just Any Man: A Guide to Finding Mr. Right* explains that the way to find a husband is to practice careful manipulation. For example, the author suggests that a woman should compliment men often. At the office she could say, "I really think you are the best salesman in the company." At church she might "comment on how much more perceptive he is than others or how much more he's thought through his beliefs than other men." The author concludes by saying, "Of course you should base your comparison on some supporting evidence, but don't be too literal." This kind of advice is not new. But since Old Testament days the results of manipulation have been both sin and compromise.

Warming Up to God Think of a recent time when you manipulated events to your advantage. What factors prompted you to do this? Discuss your sin openly with God.

Read 1 Kings 21.

21 Some time later there was an incident involving a vineyard belonging to Naboth the Jezreelite. The vineyard was in Jezreel, close to the palace of Ahab king of Samaria. 2Ahab said to Naboth, "Let me have your vineyard to use for a vegetable garden, since it is close to my palace. In exchange I will give you a better vineyard or, if you prefer, I will pay you whatever it is worth."

3But Naboth replied, "The LORD forbid that I should give you the inheritance of my fathers."

4So Ahab went home, sullen and angry because Naboth the Jezreelite had said, "I will not give you the inheritance of my fathers." He lay on his bed sulking and refused to eat.

5His wife Jezebel came in and asked him, "Why are you so sullen? Why won't you eat?"

6He answered her, "Because I said to Naboth the Jezreelite, 'Sell me your vineyard; or if you prefer, I will give you another vineyard in its place.' But he said, 'I will not give you my vineyard.' "

7Jezebel his wife said, "Is this how you act as king over Israel? Get up and eat! Cheer up. I'll get you the vineyard of Naboth the Jezreelite."

8So she wrote letters in Ahab's name, placed his seal on them, and sent them to the elders and nobles who lived in Naboth's city with him. 9In those letters she wrote:

> "Proclaim a day of fasting and seat Naboth in a prominent place among the people. 10But seat two scoundrels opposite him and have them testify that he has cursed both God and the king. Then take him out and stone him to death."

11So the elders and nobles who lived in Naboth's city did as Jezebel directed in the letters she had written to them. 12They proclaimed a fast and seated Naboth in a prominent place among the people. 13Then two scoundrels came and sat opposite him and brought charges against Naboth before the people, saying, "Naboth has cursed both God and the king." So they took him outside the city and stoned him to death. 14Then they sent word to Jezebel: "Naboth has been stoned and is dead."

15As soon as Jezebel heard that Naboth had been stoned to death, she said to Ahab, "Get up and take possession of the vineyard of Naboth the Jezreelite that he refused to sell you. He is no longer alive, but dead." 16When Ahab heard that Naboth was dead, he got up and went down to take possession of Naboth's vineyard.

17Then the word of the LORD came to Elijah the Tishbite: 18"Go down to meet Ahab king of Israel, who rules in Samaria. He is now in Naboth's vineyard, where he has gone to take possession of it. 19Say to him, 'This is what the LORD says: Have you not murdered a man and seized his property?' Then say to him, 'This is what the LORD says: In the place where dogs licked up Naboth's blood, dogs will lick up your blood—yes, yours!' "

20Ahab said to Elijah, "So you have found me, my enemy!"

"I have found you," he answered, "because you have sold yourself to do evil in the eyes of the LORD. 21'I am going to bring disaster on you. I will consume your descendants and cut off from Ahab every last male in Israel—slave or free. 22I will make your house like that of Jeroboam son of Nebat and that of Baasha son of Ahijah, because you have provoked me to anger and have caused Israel to sin.'

23"And also concerning Jezebel the LORD says: 'Dogs will devour Jezebel by the wall of[q] Jezreel.'

24"Dogs will eat those belonging to Ahab who die in the city, and the birds of the air will feed on those who die in the country."

25(There was never a man like Ahab, who sold himself to do evil in the eyes of the LORD, urged on by Jezebel his wife. 26He behaved in the vilest manner by going after idols, like the Amorites the LORD drove out before Israel.)

27When Ahab heard these words, he tore his clothes, put on sackcloth and fasted. He lay in sackcloth and went around meekly.

28Then the word of the LORD came to Elijah the Tishbite: 29"Have you noticed how Ahab has humbled himself before me? Because he has humbled himself, I will not bring this disaster in his day, but I will bring it on his house in the days of his son."

q23 Most Hebrew manuscripts; a few Hebrew manuscripts, Vulgate and Syriac (see also 2 Kings 9:26) *the plot of ground at*

Discovering the Word 1. Naboth refuses Ahab's request because he believes the land has been given to his family by the Lord, and he wants to keep it as his family's inheritance in the Promised Land. Describe Ahab's response from verse 4. 2. How does Jezebel react to her husband's behavior (vv. 5–7)? 3. In what ways do you think Ahab's behavior was manipulative? 4. How does Jezebel attempt to resolve the problem (vv. 8–16)? 5. After Ahab's direct approach fails, Jezebel is able to manipulate the situation to Ahab's advantage. Sometimes manipulation seems to work. However, what is the end result (vv. 17–28)?

Applying the Word 1. What kinds of actions define manipulation? 2. How does our culture encourage the use of manipulative tactics to achieve our goals and desires? 3. Think of a situation or relationship in which you are tempted to manipulate. What would be a more Christlike approach?

Responding in Prayer Recognizing the manipulative patterns in your life is a major step in overcoming them. Ask God to give you insight into the patterns in your life and courage to overcome them.

8 / *1 Kings 22:1–40*
Deaf to God

WE EACH HAVE our own methods of tuning out God. For example, singing an entire hymn without a single word registering in the mind; meticulously compiling a things-to-do list during the sermon; accidentally leaving a Bible at church and not missing it for days; feeling no compunction about a pattern of daily prayer long since abandoned and hardly remembered. There are many paths by which we can become deaf to God. Ahab's life (and death) warns us against such a route.

Warming Up to God What do you do that sometimes makes you "deaf" to God?

Read 1 Kings 22:1–40.

22 For three years there was no war
between Aram and Israel. [2]But in
the third year Jehoshaphat king of
Judah went down to see the king of Israel. [3]The
king of Israel had said to his officials, "Don't you
know that Ramoth Gilead belongs to us and yet
we are doing nothing to retake it from the king of
Aram?"
[4]So he asked Jehoshaphat, "Will you go with
me to fight against Ramoth Gilead?"
Jehoshaphat replied to the king of Israel, "I am
as you are, my people as your people, my horses
as your horses." [5]But Jehoshaphat also said to the
king of Israel, "First seek the counsel of the
LORD."
[6]So the king of Israel brought together the
prophets—about four hundred men—and asked
them, "Shall I go to war against Ramoth Gilead,
or shall I refrain?"
"Go," they answered, "for the Lord will give it
into the king's hand."
[7]But Jehoshaphat asked, "Is there not a prophet
of the LORD here whom we can inquire of?"
[8]The king of Israel answered Jehoshaphat,
"There is still one man through whom we can
inquire of the LORD, but I hate him because he
never prophesies anything good about me, but
always bad. He is Micaiah son of Imlah."
"The king should not say that," Jehoshaphat
replied.
[9]So the king of Israel called one of his officials
and said, "Bring Micaiah son of Imlah at once."
[10]Dressed in their royal robes, the king of Israel
and Jehoshaphat king of Judah were sitting on
their thrones at the threshing floor by the en-
trance of the gate of Samaria, with all the proph-
ets prophesying before them. [11]Now Zedekiah
son of Kenaanah had made iron horns and he
declared, "This is what the LORD says: 'With these
you will gore the Arameans until they are de-
stroyed.' "
[12]All the other prophets were prophesying the
same thing. "Attack Ramoth Gilead and be victo-

rious," they said, "for the LORD will give it into the
king's hand."
13The messenger who had gone to summon Mi-
caiah said to him, "Look, as one man the other
prophets are predicting success for the king. Let
your word agree with theirs, and speak favor-
ably."
14But Micaiah said, "As surely as the LORD lives,
I can tell him only what the LORD tells me."
15When he arrived, the king asked him, "Mica-
iah, shall we go to war against Ramoth Gilead, or
shall I refrain?"
"Attack and be victorious," he answered, "for
the LORD will give it into the king's hand."
16The king said to him, "How many times must
I make you swear to tell me nothing but the truth
in the name of the LORD?"
17Then Micaiah answered, "I saw all Israel scat-
tered on the hills like sheep without a shepherd,
and the LORD said, 'These people have no master.
Let each one go home in peace.' "
18The king of Israel said to Jehoshaphat,
"Didn't I tell you that he never prophesies any-
thing good about me, but only bad?"
19Micaiah continued, "Therefore hear the word
of the LORD: I saw the LORD sitting on his throne
with all the host of heaven standing around him
on his right and on his left. 20And the LORD said,
'Who will entice Ahab into attacking Ramoth Gil-
ead and going to his death there?'
"One suggested this, and another that. 21Fi-
nally, a spirit came forward, stood before the LORD
and said, 'I will entice him.'
22" 'By what means?' the LORD asked.
" 'I will go out and be a lying spirit in the
mouths of all his prophets,' he said.
" 'You will succeed in enticing him,' said the
LORD. 'Go and do it.'
23"So now the LORD has put a lying spirit in the
mouths of all these prophets of yours. The LORD
has decreed disaster for you."
24Then Zedekiah son of Kenaanah went up and
slapped Micaiah in the face. "Which way did the
spirit from[r] the LORD go when he went from me
to speak to you?" he asked.
25Micaiah replied, "You will find out on the day
you go to hide in an inner room."
26The king of Israel then ordered, "Take Mica-
iah and send him back to Amon the ruler of the
city and to Joash the king's son 27and say, 'This is
what the king says: Put this fellow in prison and
give him nothing but bread and water until I re-
turn safely.' "
28Micaiah declared, "If you ever return safely,
the LORD has not spoken through me." Then he
added, "Mark my words, all you people!"
29So the king of Israel and Jehoshaphat king of
Judah went up to Ramoth Gilead. 30The king of
Israel said to Jehoshaphat, "I will enter the battle
in disguise, but you wear your royal robes." So
the king of Israel disguised himself and went into
battle.
31Now the king of Aram had ordered his thirty-
two chariot commanders, "Do not fight with any-
one, small or great, except the king of Israel."
32When the chariot commanders saw Jehosha-
phat, they thought, "Surely this is the king of
Israel." So they turned to attack him, but when
Jehoshaphat cried out, 33the chariot commanders
saw that he was not the king of Israel and stopped
pursuing him.
34But someone drew his bow at random and hit
the king of Israel between the sections of his ar-
mor. The king told his chariot driver, "Wheel
around and get me out of the fighting. I've been
wounded." 35All day long the battle raged, and
the king was propped up in his chariot facing the
Arameans. The blood from his wound ran onto
the floor of the chariot, and that evening he died.
36As the sun was setting, a cry spread through the
army: "Every man to his town; everyone to his
land!"
37So the king died and was brought to Samaria,
and they buried him there. 38They washed the
chariot at a pool in Samaria (where the prosti-
tutes bathed),[s] and the dogs licked up his blood,
as the word of the LORD had declared.
39As for the other events of Ahab's reign, in-
cluding all he did, the palace he built and inlaid
with ivory, and the cities he fortified, are they not
written in the book of the annals of the kings of
Israel? 40Ahab rested with his fathers. And Aha-
ziah his son succeeded him as king.

[r] 24 Or *Spirit of* [s] 38 Or *Samaria and cleaned the weapons*

Discovering the Word 1. What was Ahab's proposal (vv. 1–4)? 2. How did the two kings view the project differently (vv. 4–8)? 3. What was hard about Micaiah's job (vv. 9–16)? 4. Look again at Micaiah's statements in verses 17–23. Why do you think that Ahab was easy prey for the lying prophets? 5. What did it cost Micaiah to speak God's truth? 6. During the course of his life, Ahab had many opportunities for hearing truths from God. In view of this, what do you see as the difference between hearing and receiving God's Word?

Applying the Word 1. Why do you sometimes hesitate to talk about what you know to be God's truth? 2. What precautions could you take to keep from acquiring Ahab's kind of deafness?

Responding in Prayer Ask God to give you ears to hear his truth (Mt 13:16).

1 Kings 22:41–53

[41]Jehoshaphat son of Asa became king of Judah in the fourth year of Ahab king of Israel. [42]Jehoshaphat was thirty-five years old when he became king, and he reigned in Jerusalem twenty-five years. His mother's name was Azubah daughter of Shilhi. [43]In everything he walked in the ways of his father Asa and did not stray from them; he did what was right in the eyes of the LORD. The high places, however, were not removed, and the people continued to offer sacrifices and burn incense there. [44]Jehoshaphat was also at peace with the king of Israel.

[45]As for the other events of Jehoshaphat's reign, the things he achieved and his military exploits, are they not written in the book of the annals of the kings of Judah? [46]He rid the land of the rest of the male shrine prostitutes who remained there even after the reign of his father Asa. [47]There was then no king in Edom; a deputy ruled.

[48]Now Jehoshaphat built a fleet of trading ships[t] to go to Ophir for gold, but they never set sail—they were wrecked at Ezion Geber. [49]At that time Ahaziah son of Ahab said to Jehoshaphat, "Let my men sail with your men," but Jehoshaphat refused.

[50]Then Jehoshaphat rested with his fathers and was buried with them in the city of David his father. And Jehoram his son succeeded him.

[51]Ahaziah son of Ahab became king of Israel in Samaria in the seventeenth year of Jehoshaphat king of Judah, and he reigned over Israel two years. [52]He did evil in the eyes of the LORD, because he walked in the ways of his father and mother and in the ways of Jeroboam son of Nebat, who caused Israel to sin. [53]He served and worshiped Baal and provoked the LORD, the God of Israel, to anger, just as his father had done.

[t]48 Hebrew *of ships of Tarshish*

2 Kings

The Old Testament kings faltered and failed in many ways. As we examine their lives, we can learn much about following God. We see Ahaz, who, when faced with trouble, stopped believing in God. And we wonder about our own ability to keep faith in the face of circumstantial despair.

We see Hoshea, who angered God so much by his determination to serve other gods that God destroyed his nation. And we pray for our own national leaders, and thereby for ourselves.

We see Hezekiah, who when faced with terminal illness, cried out to God. And God extended his life, which Hezekiah may have later regretted. And we wonder whether we will die with grace, or fear, or both.

We see Manasseh, the most wicked king of all. Yet God let him reign for forty-five years, the longest reign of any Hebrew king. We wonder how our faith, rattled by an afternoon of inconvenience, would endure in an era when the king killed God-worshipers every day.

We see Josiah, who became king at the age of eight, yet turned his nation to worship God. And we wonder about our influence for God on our own children—and the results of their influence on others.

We see Zedekiah, the last Hebrew king, presiding over a nation already dead. And we look for hope from a God who is not stopped by death.

When the narrative of the kings ends with the fall of Judah in 587 B.C., their names are not forgotten. In the opening pages of the New Testament, they live again. It seems that when God chose a family for his son, the infant Jesus, he chose from a line of kings. And so we read Joseph's genealogy, and we find, among all those hard-to-pronounce names, a familiar line: the kings of Israel.

Let us read from them and learn. None was perfect, and neither are we. But God was sovereign—even over the kings. And he is sovereign over us as well.

Outline

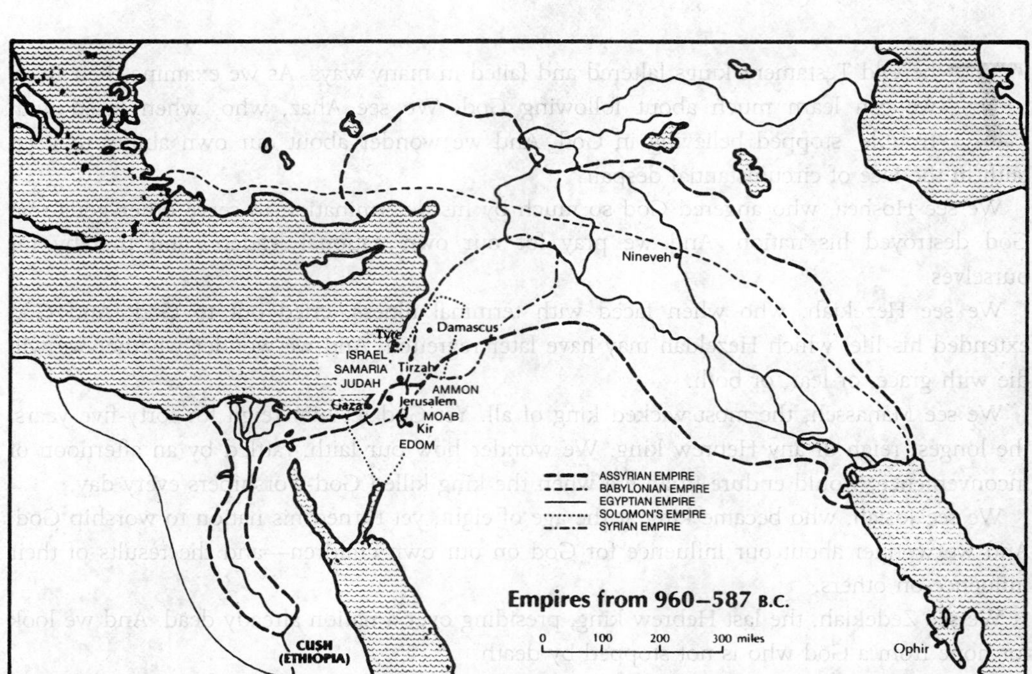

Empires from 960–587 B.C.

2 *Kings* 1

1 After Ahab's death, Moab rebelled against
Israel. 2Now Ahaziah had fallen through
the lattice of his upper room in Samaria
and injured himself. So he sent messengers, say-
ing to them, "Go and consult Baal-Zebub, the god
of Ekron, to see if I will recover from this injury."
3But the angel of the LORD said to Elijah the
Tishbite, "Go up and meet the messengers of the
king of Samaria and ask them, 'Is it because there
is no God in Israel that you are going off to con-
sult Baal-Zebub, the god of Ekron?' 4Therefore
this is what the LORD says: 'You will not leave the
bed you are lying on. You will certainly die!' " So
Elijah went.
5When the messengers returned to the king, he
asked them, "Why have you come back?"
6"A man came to meet us," they replied. "And
he said to us, 'Go back to the king who sent you
and tell him, "This is what the LORD says: Is it
because there is no God in Israel that you are
sending men to consult Baal-Zebub, the god of
Ekron? Therefore you will not leave the bed you
are lying on. You will certainly die!" ' "
7The king asked them, "What kind of man was
it who came to meet you and told you this?"
8They replied, "He was a man with a garment
of hair and with a leather belt around his waist."
The king said, "That was Elijah the Tishbite."
9Then he sent to Elijah a captain with his com-
pany of fifty men. The captain went up to Elijah,
who was sitting on the top of a hill, and said to
him, "Man of God, the king says, 'Come down!' "
10Elijah answered the captain, "If I am a man of
God, may fire come down from heaven and con-
sume you and your fifty men!" Then fire fell from
heaven and consumed the captain and his men.
11At this the king sent to Elijah another captain
with his fifty men. The captain said to him, "Man
of God, this is what the king says, 'Come down at
once!' "
12"If I am a man of God," Elijah replied, "may
fire come down from heaven and consume you
and your fifty men!" Then the fire of God fell
from heaven and consumed him and his fifty
men.
13So the king sent a third captain with his fifty
men. This third captain went up and fell on his
knees before Elijah. "Man of God," he begged,
"please have respect for my life and the lives of
these fifty men, your servants! 14See, fire has
fallen from heaven and consumed the first two
captains and all their men. But now have respect
for my life!"
15The angel of the LORD said to Elijah, "Go
down with him; do not be afraid of him." So Eli-
jah got up and went down with him to the king.
16He told the king, "This is what the LORD says:
Is it because there is no God in Israel for you to
consult that you have sent messengers to consult
Baal-Zebub, the god of Ekron? Because you have
done this, you will never leave the bed you are
lying on. You will certainly die!" 17So he died,
according to the word of the LORD that Elijah had
spoken.
Because Ahaziah had no son, Joram[a] suc-
ceeded him as king in the second year of Jehoram
son of Jehoshaphat king of Judah. 18As for all the
other events of Ahaziah's reign, and what he did,
are they not written in the book of the annals of
the kings of Israel?

[a]17 Hebrew *Jehoram*, a variant of *Joram*

1 / 2 *Kings* 2
Transition

WHEN OUR OLDEST daughter, Sheri, left for college, it was a big transition for our family. She played all four stringed instruments—and several instruments of other varieties. Her part-time job during high school was to teach younger music students. At the same time our next-oldest daughter, Lori, a cellist and a flutist, was being asked to consider picking up some of Sheri's students. It was a scary thought, walking in the footsteps of a respected older sister. Sure, Lori had studied hard and practiced a lot. But she was younger and inexperienced. The mantle was on the ground. Would she pick it up? Elisha had to make the same decision.

Warming Up to God In what area of your life are you anxious about taking on a responsibility that you think has been given to you?

Read 2 Kings 2.

2

When the Lord was about to take Elijah
up to heaven in a whirlwind, Elijah and
Elisha were on their way from Gilgal.
2Elijah said to Elisha, "Stay here; the Lord has
sent me to Bethel."

But Elisha said, "As surely as the Lord lives and
as you live, I will not leave you." So they went
down to Bethel.

3The company of the prophets at Bethel came
out to Elisha and asked, "Do you know that the
Lord is going to take your master from you to-
day?"

"Yes, I know," Elisha replied, "but do not speak
of it."

4Then Elijah said to him, "Stay here, Elisha; the
Lord has sent me to Jericho."

And he replied, "As surely as the Lord lives and
as you live, I will not leave you." So they went to
Jericho.

5The company of the prophets at Jericho went
up to Elisha and asked him, "Do you know that
the Lord is going to take your master from you
today?"

"Yes, I know," he replied, "but do not speak
of it."

6Then Elijah said to him, "Stay here; the Lord
has sent me to the Jordan."

And he replied, "As surely as the Lord lives and
as you live, I will not leave you." So the two of
them walked on.

7Fifty men of the company of the prophets
went and stood at a distance, facing the place
where Elijah and Elisha had stopped at the Jor-
dan. 8Elijah took his cloak, rolled it up and struck
the water with it. The water divided to the right
and to the left, and the two of them crossed over
on dry ground.

9When they had crossed, Elijah said to Elisha,
"Tell me, what can I do for you before I am taken
from you?"

"Let me inherit a double portion of your
spirit," Elisha replied.

10"You have asked a difficult thing," Elijah
said, "yet if you see me when I am taken from
you, it will be yours—otherwise not."

11As they were walking along and talking to-
gether, suddenly a chariot of fire and horses of
fire appeared and separated the two of them, and
Elijah went up to heaven in a whirlwind. 12Elisha
saw this and cried out, "My father! My father!
The chariots and horsemen of Israel!" And Elisha
saw him no more. Then he took hold of his own
clothes and tore them apart.

13He picked up the cloak that had fallen from
Elijah and went back and stood on the bank of
the Jordan. 14Then he took the cloak that had
fallen from him and struck the water with it.
"Where now is the Lord, the God of Elijah?" he
asked. When he struck the water, it divided to the
right and to the left, and he crossed over.

15The company of the prophets from Jericho,
who were watching, said, "The spirit of Elijah is
resting on Elisha." And they went to meet him
and bowed to the ground before him. 16"Look,"
they said, "we your servants have fifty able men.
Let them go and look for your master. Perhaps
the Spirit of the Lord has picked him up and set
him down on some mountain or in some valley."

"No," Elisha replied, "do not send them."

17But they persisted until he was too ashamed
to refuse. So he said, "Send them." And they sent
fifty men, who searched for three days but did not
find him. 18When they returned to Elisha, who
was staying in Jericho, he said to them, "Didn't I
tell you not to go?"

19The men of the city said to Elisha, "Look, our
lord, this town is well situated, as you can see,
but the water is bad and the land is unproduc-
tive."

20"Bring me a new bowl," he said, "and put salt
in it." So they brought it to him.

21Then he went out to the spring and threw the
salt into it, saying, "This is what the Lord says: 'I
have healed this water. Never again will it cause
death or make the land unproductive.' " 22And
the water has remained wholesome to this day,
according to the word Elisha had spoken.

23From there Elisha went up to Bethel. As he
was walking along the road, some youths came
out of the town and jeered at him. "Go on up, you
baldhead!" they said. "Go on up, you baldhead!"
24He turned around, looked at them and called
down a curse on them in the name of the Lord.

Then two bears came out of the woods and mauled forty-two of the youths. 25And he went on to Mount Carmel and from there returned to Samaria.

Discovering the Word 1. Why do you think Elijah kept telling Elisha to "stay here" (vv. 2, 4, 6)? 2. Why do you think Elisha insisted on following Elijah? 3. How did Elijah show that the gift Elisha requested was not within his authority to give (vv. 9–12)? 4. Three miracles occur (vv. 14, 19–22, 23–25). What effect would each have on Elisha's ministry? 5. In what ways did God provide support for Elisha in the job he had given him to do? (Use the whole chapter.)

Applying the Word 1. Think of at least one job that you are reasonably sure God has assigned to you. What help has God given you so far in doing that job? 2. What obstacles and discouragements are you likely to face in this job? 3. How might your past experiences of God's support help you through future obstacles?

Responding in Prayer Ask God to encourage you through the time of transition that you face.

2 Kings 3:1—4:7

3 Joram[b] son of Ahab became king of Israel in Samaria in the eighteenth year of Jehoshaphat king of Judah, and he reigned twelve years. 2He did evil in the eyes of the LORD, but not as his father and mother had done. He got rid of the sacred stone of Baal that his father had made. 3Nevertheless he clung to the sins of Jeroboam son of Nebat, which he had caused Israel to commit; he did not turn away from them.

4Now Mesha king of Moab raised sheep, and he had to supply the king of Israel with a hundred thousand lambs and with the wool of a hundred thousand rams. 5But after Ahab died, the king of Moab rebelled against the king of Israel. 6So at that time King Joram set out from Samaria and mobilized all Israel. 7He also sent this message to Jehoshaphat king of Judah: "The king of Moab has rebelled against me. Will you go with me to fight against Moab?"

"I will go with you," he replied. "I am as you are, my people as your people, my horses as your horses."

8"By what route shall we attack?" he asked.

"Through the Desert of Edom," he answered.

9So the king of Israel set out with the king of Judah and the king of Edom. After a roundabout march of seven days, the army had no more water for themselves or for the animals with them.

10"What!" exclaimed the king of Israel. "Has the LORD called us three kings together only to hand us over to Moab?"

11But Jehoshaphat asked, "Is there no prophet of the LORD here, that we may inquire of the LORD through him?"

An officer of the king of Israel answered, "Elisha son of Shaphat is here. He used to pour water on the hands of Elijah.[c]"

12Jehoshaphat said, "The word of the LORD is with him." So the king of Israel and Jehoshaphat and the king of Edom went down to him.

13Elisha said to the king of Israel, "What do we have to do with each other? Go to the prophets of your father and the prophets of your mother."

"No," the king of Israel answered, "because it was the LORD who called us three kings together to hand us over to Moab."

14Elisha said, "As surely as the LORD Almighty lives, whom I serve, if I did not have respect for the presence of Jehoshaphat king of Judah, I would not look at you or even notice you. 15But now bring me a harpist."

While the harpist was playing, the hand of the LORD came upon Elisha 16and he said, "This is what the LORD says: Make this valley full of ditches. 17For this is what the LORD says: You will see neither wind nor rain, yet this valley will be filled with water, and you, your cattle and your other animals will drink. 18This is an easy thing in the eyes of the LORD; he will also hand Moab over to you. 19You will overthrow every fortified city

[b]1 Hebrew *Jehoram*, a variant of *Joram*; also in verse 6 [c]11 That is, he was Elijah's personal servant.

and every major town. You will cut down every good tree, stop up all the springs, and ruin every good field with stones."

[20]The next morning, about the time for offering the sacrifice, there it was—water flowing from the direction of Edom! And the land was filled with water.

[21]Now all the Moabites had heard that the kings had come to fight against them; so every man, young and old, who could bear arms was called up and stationed on the border. [22]When they got up early in the morning, the sun was shining on the water. To the Moabites across the way, the water looked red—like blood. [23]"That's blood!" they said. "Those kings must have fought and slaughtered each other. Now to the plunder, Moab!"

[24]But when the Moabites came to the camp of Israel, the Israelites rose up and fought them until they fled. And the Israelites invaded the land and slaughtered the Moabites. [25]They destroyed the towns, and each man threw a stone on every good field until it was covered. They stopped up all the springs and cut down every good tree. Only Kir Hareseth was left with its stones in place, but men armed with slings surrounded it and attacked it as well.

[26]When the king of Moab saw that the battle had gone against him, he took with him seven hundred swordsmen to break through to the king of Edom, but they failed. [27]Then he took his firstborn son, who was to succeed him as king, and offered him as a sacrifice on the city wall. The fury against Israel was great; they withdrew and returned to their own land.

4 The wife of a man from the company of the prophets cried out to Elisha, "Your servant my husband is dead, and you know that he revered the LORD. But now his creditor is coming to take my two boys as his slaves."

[2]Elisha replied to her, "How can I help you? Tell me, what do you have in your house?"

"Your servant has nothing there at all," she said, "except a little oil."

[3]Elisha said, "Go around and ask all your neighbors for empty jars. Don't ask for just a few. [4]Then go inside and shut the door behind you and your sons. Pour oil into all the jars, and as each is filled, put it to one side."

[5]She left him and afterward shut the door behind her and her sons. They brought the jars to her and she kept pouring. [6]When all the jars were full, she said to her son, "Bring me another one."

But he replied, "There is not a jar left." Then the oil stopped flowing.

[7]She went and told the man of God, and he said, "Go, sell the oil and pay your debts. You and your sons can live on what is left."

2 / 2 *Kings 4:8–37*
Taking the Initiative

"I THOUGHT HE must be a Christian when he took me to his home for dinner and overnight," said a visiting Chinese scholar, recounting how a stranger at the airport had offered him hospitality when he was stranded. Hospitality is a trait repeatedly commended in the Bible. God is hospitable, and he wants his children to be also. In this story a woman welcomes "the man of God" into her home and is rewarded for doing so—or so it seems until the day her son dies. The initiative she shows in offering hospitality leads her to a deeper faith in expecting God to act on her behalf. Her faith and boldness, as well as her generosity, are a model for us.

Warming Up to God When is it hard for you to show hospitality?

Read 2 Kings 4:8–37.

[8]One day Elisha went to Shunem. And a well-to-do woman was there, who urged him to stay for a meal. So whenever he came by, he stopped there to eat. [9]She said to her husband, "I know that this man who often comes our way is a holy man of God. [10]Let's make a small room on the roof and put in it a bed and a table, a chair and a lamp for him. Then he can stay there whenever he comes to us."

[11]One day when Elisha came, he went up to his

room and lay down there. 12He said to his servant Gehazi, "Call the Shunammite." So he called her, and she stood before him. 13Elisha said to him, "Tell her, 'You have gone to all this trouble for us. Now what can be done for you? Can we speak on your behalf to the king or the commander of the army?' "

She replied, "I have a home among my own people."

14"What can be done for her?" Elisha asked.

Gehazi said, "Well, she has no son and her husband is old."

15Then Elisha said, "Call her." So he called her, and she stood in the doorway. 16"About this time next year," Elisha said, "you will hold a son in your arms."

"No, my lord," she objected. "Don't mislead your servant, O man of God!"

17But the woman became pregnant, and the next year about that same time she gave birth to a son, just as Elisha had told her.

18The child grew, and one day he went out to his father, who was with the reapers. 19"My head! My head!" he said to his father.

His father told a servant, "Carry him to his mother." 20After the servant had lifted him up and carried him to his mother, the boy sat on her lap until noon, and then he died. 21She went up and laid him on the bed of the man of God, then shut the door and went out.

22She called her husband and said, "Please send me one of the servants and a donkey so I can go to the man of God quickly and return."

23"Why go to him today?" he asked. "It's not the New Moon or the Sabbath."

"It's all right," she said.

24She saddled the donkey and said to her servant, "Lead on; don't slow down for me unless I tell you." 25So she set out and came to the man of God at Mount Carmel.

When he saw her in the distance, the man of God said to his servant Gehazi, "Look! There's the Shunammite! 26Run to meet her and ask her, 'Are you all right? Is your husband all right? Is your child all right?' "

"Everything is all right," she said.

27When she reached the man of God at the mountain, she took hold of his feet. Gehazi came over to push her away, but the man of God said, "Leave her alone! She is in bitter distress, but the LORD has hidden it from me and has not told me why."

28"Did I ask you for a son, my lord?" she said. "Didn't I tell you, 'Don't raise my hopes'?"

29Elisha said to Gehazi, "Tuck your cloak into your belt, take my staff in your hand and run. If you meet anyone, do not greet him, and if anyone greets you, do not answer. Lay my staff on the boy's face."

30But the child's mother said, "As surely as the LORD lives and as you live, I will not leave you." So he got up and followed her.

31Gehazi went on ahead and laid the staff on the boy's face, but there was no sound or response. So Gehazi went back to meet Elisha and told him, "The boy has not awakened."

32When Elisha reached the house, there was the boy lying dead on his couch. 33He went in, shut the door on the two of them and prayed to the LORD. 34Then he got on the bed and lay upon the boy, mouth to mouth, eyes to eyes, hands to hands. As he stretched himself out upon him, the boy's body grew warm. 35Elisha turned away and walked back and forth in the room and then got on the bed and stretched out upon him once more. The boy sneezed seven times and opened his eyes.

36Elisha summoned Gehazi and said, "Call the Shunammite." And he did. When she came, he said, "Take your son." 37She came in, fell at his feet and bowed to the ground. Then she took her son and went out.

Discovering the Word 1. What do you know about the life circumstances of the Shunammite woman from this story? 2. Why did the woman use her resources to help Elisha? 3. What do you think Elisha's concern for her needs (vv. 12–14) meant to the Shunammite woman? 4. After being given a son and raising him to boyhood, the woman now faces a terrible loss (vv. 18–20). How does she respond to the death of her son (vv. 21–30)? 5. What is the woman's strong resolve in the face of her son's death?

Applying the Word 1. Compare your own use of resources to that of the woman in this story. How can you show hospitality even with limited resources? 2. When have you spoken "accusing words" like these to God or to others? 3. Why is it important to lay a foundation of faith and trust in God before times of crisis come to us?

Responding in Prayer What wonderful works has God done on your behalf? Offer him your praise.

2 Kings 4:38–44

[38]Elisha returned to Gilgal and there was a famine in that region. While the company of the prophets was meeting with him, he said to his servant, "Put on the large pot and cook some stew for these men."

[39]One of them went out into the fields to gather herbs and found a wild vine. He gathered some of its gourds and filled the fold of his cloak. When he returned, he cut them up into the pot of stew, though no one knew what they were. [40]The stew was poured out for the men, but as they began to eat it, they cried out, "O man of God, there is death in the pot!" And they could not eat it.

[41]Elisha said, "Get some flour." He put it into the pot and said, "Serve it to the people to eat." And there was nothing harmful in the pot.

[42]A man came from Baal Shalishah, bringing the man of God twenty loaves of barley bread baked from the first ripe grain, along with some heads of new grain. "Give it to the people to eat," Elisha said.

[43]"How can I set this before a hundred men?" his servant asked.

But Elisha answered, "Give it to the people to eat. For this is what the LORD says: 'They will eat and have some left over.' " [44]Then he set it before them, and they ate and had some left over, according to the word of the LORD.

3 / 2 *Kings* 5
Physical Healing

I KNEW DIANA was growing when she was able to say, "I have come to realize that there are others all around me who are in pain. I am not the only one who is suffering. Until now I could not see the pain of others because I was so focused on mine." Often, the first step in being used by God in meeting others' needs is being able to identify those needs. Three thousand years ago, Naaman, the pagan commander of a large army, was sick. In that setting, a take-charge man learned about need—from a servant girl. And he met a God who cared.

Warming Up to God When you are in physical need, what kinds of responses or activities from people communicate to you that someone cares?

Read 2 Kings 5.

5 Now Naaman was commander of the army of the king of Aram. He was a great man in the sight of his master and highly regarded, because through him the LORD had given victory to Aram. He was a valiant soldier, but he had leprosy.[d]

[2]Now bands from Aram had gone out and had taken captive a young girl from Israel, and she served Naaman's wife. [3]She said to her mistress, "If only my master would see the prophet who is in Samaria! He would cure him of his leprosy."

[4]Naaman went to his master and told him what the girl from Israel had said. [5]"By all means, go," the king of Aram replied. "I will send a letter to the king of Israel." So Naaman left, taking with him ten talents[e] of silver, six thousand shekels[f] of gold and ten sets of clothing. [6]The letter that he took to the king of Israel read: "With this letter I am sending my servant Naaman to you so that you may cure him of his leprosy."

[7]As soon as the king of Israel read the letter, he tore his robes and said, "Am I God? Can I kill and bring back to life? Why does this fellow send someone to me to be cured of his leprosy? See how he is trying to pick a quarrel with me!"

[8]When Elisha the man of God heard that the king of Israel had torn his robes, he sent him this message: "Why have you torn your robes? Have the man come to me and he will know that there is a prophet in Israel." [9]So Naaman went with his horses and chariots and stopped at the door of

[d]1 The Hebrew word was used for various diseases affecting the skin—not necessarily leprosy; also in verses 3, 6, 7, 11 and 27.
[e]5 That is, about 750 pounds (about 340 kilograms) [f]5 That is, about 150 pounds (about 70 kilograms)

Elisha's house. 10Elisha sent a messenger to say to
him, "Go, wash yourself seven times in the Jor-
dan, and your flesh will be restored and you will
be cleansed."

11But Naaman went away angry and said, "I
thought that he would surely come out to me and
stand and call on the name of the LORD his God,
wave his hand over the spot and cure me of my
leprosy. 12Are not Abana and Pharpar, the rivers
of Damascus, better than any of the waters of Is-
rael? Couldn't I wash in them and be cleansed?"
So he turned and went off in a rage.

13Naaman's servants went to him and said, "My
father, if the prophet had told you to do some
great thing, would you not have done it? How
much more, then, when he tells you, 'Wash and
be cleansed'!" 14So he went down and dipped
himself in the Jordan seven times, as the man of
God had told him, and his flesh was restored and
became clean like that of a young boy.

15Then Naaman and all his attendants went
back to the man of God. He stood before him and
said, "Now I know that there is no God in all the
world except in Israel. Please accept now a gift
from your servant."

16The prophet answered, "As surely as the LORD
lives, whom I serve, I will not accept a thing."
And even though Naaman urged him, he refused.

17"If you will not," said Naaman, "please let
me, your servant, be given as much earth as a pair
of mules can carry, for your servant will never
again make burnt offerings and sacrifices to any
other god but the LORD. 18But may the LORD for-
give your servant for this one thing: When my
master enters the temple of Rimmon to bow
down and he is leaning on my arm and I bow
there also—when I bow down in the temple of
Rimmon, may the LORD forgive your servant for
this."

19"Go in peace," Elisha said.

After Naaman had traveled some distance,
20Gehazi, the servant of Elisha the man of God,
said to himself, "My master was too easy on Naa-
man, this Aramean, by not accepting from him
what he brought. As surely as the LORD lives, I will
run after him and get something from him."

21So Gehazi hurried after Naaman. When Naa-
man saw him running toward him, he got down
from the chariot to meet him. "Is everything all
right?" he asked.

22"Everything is all right," Gehazi answered.
"My master sent me to say, 'Two young men from
the company of the prophets have just come to
me from the hill country of Ephraim. Please give
them a talent[g] of silver and two sets of cloth-
ing.' "

23"By all means, take two talents," said Naa-
man. He urged Gehazi to accept them, and then
tied up the two talents of silver in two bags, with
two sets of clothing. He gave them to two of his
servants, and they carried them ahead of Gehazi.
24When Gehazi came to the hill, he took the
things from the servants and put them away in
the house. He sent the men away and they left.
25Then he went in and stood before his master
Elisha.

"Where have you been, Gehazi?" Elisha asked.

"Your servant didn't go anywhere," Gehazi an-
swered.

26But Elisha said to him, "Was not my spirit
with you when the man got down from his char-
iot to meet you? Is this the time to take money, or
to accept clothes, olive groves, vineyards, flocks,
herds, or menservants and maidservants? 27Naa-
man's leprosy will cling to you and to your
descendants forever." Then Gehazi went from
Elisha's presence and he was leprous, as white as
snow.

[g]22 That is, about 75 pounds (about 34 kilograms)

Discovering the Word 1. What are ways that people reached out to Naaman throughout this passage? 2. Describe Naaman and the servant girl (vv. 1–3). 3. Why was Naaman angry at Elisha (vv. 10–13)? 4. What was Naaman's response when he was cured (v. 15)? 5. Why did Gehazi follow Naaman (vv. 20–22)?

Applying the Word 1. When have you been upset because of the way God chose to work when you or someone else was in need? 2. We have considered the benefits to Naaman of the help people gave him. What benefits do you think came to those who helped? 3. What benefits do you receive from seeing others helped?

Responding in Prayer Pray that God will make you sensitive to the needs of others and will help you to gently lead them in the right steps toward healing.

2 *Kings* 6:1–23

6 The company of the prophets said to Eli-
sha, "Look, the place where we meet with
you is too small for us. 2Let us go to the
Jordan, where each of us can get a pole; and let us
build a place there for us to live."
And he said, "Go."
3Then one of them said, "Won't you please
come with your servants?"
"I will," Elisha replied. 4And he went with
them.
They went to the Jordan and began to cut down
trees. 5As one of them was cutting down a tree,
the iron axhead fell into the water. "Oh, my lord,"
he cried out, "it was borrowed!"
6The man of God asked, "Where did it fall?"
When he showed him the place, Elisha cut a stick
and threw it there, and made the iron float. 7"Lift
it out," he said. Then the man reached out his
hand and took it.
8Now the king of Aram was at war with Israel.
After conferring with his officers, he said, "I will
set up my camp in such and such a place."
9The man of God sent word to the king of Is-
rael: "Beware of passing that place, because the
Arameans are going down there." 10So the king of
Israel checked on the place indicated by the man
of God. Time and again Elisha warned the king,
so that he was on his guard in such places.
11This enraged the king of Aram. He sum-
moned his officers and demanded of them, "Will
you not tell me which of us is on the side of the
king of Israel?"
12"None of us, my lord the king," said one of
his officers, "but Elisha, the prophet who is in
Israel, tells the king of Israel the very words you
speak in your bedroom."
13"Go, find out where he is," the king ordered,
"so I can send men and capture him." The report
came back: "He is in Dothan." 14Then he sent
horses and chariots and a strong force there. They
went by night and surrounded the city.
15When the servant of the man of God got up
and went out early the next morning, an army
with horses and chariots had surrounded the city.
"Oh, my lord, what shall we do?" the servant
asked.
16"Don't be afraid," the prophet answered.
"Those who are with us are more than those who
are with them."
17And Elisha prayed, "O LORD, open his eyes so
he may see." Then the LORD opened the servant's
eyes, and he looked and saw the hills full of
horses and chariots of fire all around Elisha.
18As the enemy came down toward him, Elisha
prayed to the LORD, "Strike these people with
blindness." So he struck them with blindness, as
Elisha had asked.
19Elisha told them, "This is not the road and
this is not the city. Follow me, and I will lead you
to the man you are looking for." And he led them
to Samaria.
20After they entered the city, Elisha said, "LORD,
open the eyes of these men so they can see." Then
the LORD opened their eyes and they looked, and
there they were, inside Samaria.
21When the king of Israel saw them, he asked
Elisha, "Shall I kill them, my father? Shall I kill
them?"
22"Do not kill them," he answered. "Would you
kill men you have captured with your own sword
or bow? Set food and water before them so that
they may eat and drink and then go back to their
master." 23So he prepared a great feast for them,
and after they had finished eating and drinking,
he sent them away, and they returned to their
master. So the bands from Aram stopped raiding
Israel's territory.

4 / 2 *Kings* 6:24—7:20
Faith in Hard Times

I HAVE A friend who has been plagued by seeming disasters: One daughter joined a cult; another daughter couldn't seem to stay married—to anyone; a son died of cancer; her husband requires frequent psychiatric care.

What has she done wrong? Nothing really. She has done a better-than-average job of parenting and she possesses a more-than-normal dose of stability. Through all the trauma, she has maintained an uncomplicated trust in God. And occasionally we see a glimmer of purpose around her string of disasters. This larger view shows all of us close to her that her trust is justified.

Warming Up to God What is the biggest disaster you have had to face since you began to trust God? What did that period in your life teach you about God?

Read 2 Kings 6:24—7:20.

24Some time later, Ben-Hadad king of Aram mobilized his entire army and marched up and laid siege to Samaria. 25There was a great famine in the city; the siege lasted so long that a donkey's head sold for eighty shekels[h] of silver, and a quarter of a cab[i] of seed pods[j] for five shekels.[k]

26As the king of Israel was passing by on the wall, a woman cried to him, "Help me, my lord the king!"

27The king replied, "If the LORD does not help you, where can I get help for you? From the threshing floor? From the winepress?" 28Then he asked her, "What's the matter?"

She answered, "This woman said to me, 'Give up your son so we may eat him today, and tomorrow we'll eat my son.' 29So we cooked my son and ate him. The next day I said to her, 'Give up your son so we may eat him,' but she had hidden him."

30When the king heard the woman's words, he tore his robes. As he went along the wall, the people looked, and there, underneath, he had sackcloth on his body. 31He said, "May God deal with me, be it ever so severely, if the head of Elisha son of Shaphat remains on his shoulders today!"

32Now Elisha was sitting in his house, and the elders were sitting with him. The king sent a messenger ahead, but before he arrived, Elisha said to the elders, "Don't you see how this murderer is sending someone to cut off my head? Look, when the messenger comes, shut the door and hold it shut against him. Is not the sound of his master's footsteps behind him?"

33While he was still talking to them, the messenger came down to him. And ⌞the king⌟ said, "This disaster is from the LORD. Why should I wait for the LORD any longer?"

7 Elisha said, "Hear the word of the LORD. This is what the LORD says: About this time tomorrow, a seah[l] of flour will sell for a shekel[m] and two seahs[n] of barley for a shekel at the gate of Samaria."

2The officer on whose arm the king was leaning said to the man of God, "Look, even if the LORD should open the floodgates of the heavens, could this happen?"

"You will see it with your own eyes," answered Elisha, "but you will not eat any of it!"

3Now there were four men with leprosy[o] at the entrance of the city gate. They said to each other, "Why stay here until we die? 4If we say, 'We'll go into the city'—the famine is there, and we will die. And if we stay here, we will die. So let's go over to the camp of the Arameans and surrender. If they spare us, we live; if they kill us, then we die."

5At dusk they got up and went to the camp of the Arameans. When they reached the edge of the camp, not a man was there, 6for the Lord had caused the Arameans to hear the sound of chariots and horses and a great army, so that they said to one another, "Look, the king of Israel has hired the Hittite and Egyptian kings to attack us!" 7So they got up and fled in the dusk and abandoned their tents and their horses and donkeys. They left the camp as it was and ran for their lives.

8The men who had leprosy reached the edge of the camp and entered one of the tents. They ate and drank, and carried away silver, gold and clothes, and went off and hid them. They returned and entered another tent and took some things from it and hid them also.

9Then they said to each other, "We're not doing right. This is a day of good news and we are keeping it to ourselves. If we wait until daylight,

[h]25 That is, about 2 pounds (about 1 kilogram) [i]25 That is, probably about 1/2 pint (about 0.3 liter) [j]25 Or *of dove's dung* [k]25 That is, about 2 ounces (about 55 grams) [l]1 That is, probably about 7 quarts (about 7.3 liters); also in verses 16 and 18 [m]1 That is, about 2/5 ounce (about 11 grams); also in verses 16 and 18 [n]1 That is, probably about 13 quarts (about 15 liters); also in verses 16 and 18 [o]3 The Hebrew word is used for various diseases affecting the skin—not necessarily leprosy; also in verse 8.

punishment will overtake us. Let's go at once and
report this to the royal palace."
10So they went and called out to the city gate-
keepers and told them, "We went into the Ara-
mean camp and not a man was there—not a
sound of anyone—only tethered horses and don-
keys, and the tents left just as they were." 11The
gatekeepers shouted the news, and it was re-
ported within the palace.
12The king got up in the night and said to his
officers, "I will tell you what the Arameans have
done to us. They know we are starving; so they
have left the camp to hide in the country-
side, thinking, 'They will surely come out, and
then we will take them alive and get into the
city.'"
13One of his officers answered, "Have some
men take five of the horses that are left in the city.
Their plight will be like that of all the Israelites
left here—yes, they will only be like all these Is-
raelites who are doomed. So let us send them to
find out what happened."
14So they selected two chariots with their
horses, and the king sent them after the Aramean
army. He commanded the drivers, "Go and find
out what has happened." 15They followed them as
far as the Jordan, and they found the whole road
strewn with the clothing and equipment the Ara-
means had thrown away in their headlong flight.
So the messengers returned and reported to the
king. 16Then the people went out and plundered
the camp of the Arameans. So a seah of flour sold
for a shekel, and two seahs of barley sold for a
shekel, as the LORD had said.
17Now the king had put the officer on whose
arm he leaned in charge of the gate, and the peo-
ple trampled him in the gateway, and he died,
just as the man of God had foretold when the
king came down to his house. 18It happened as
the man of God had said to the king: "About this
time tomorrow, a seah of flour will sell for a
shekel and two seahs of barley for a shekel at the
gate of Samaria."
19The officer had said to the man of God,
"Look, even if the LORD should open the flood-
gates of the heavens, could this happen?" The
man of God had replied, "You will see it with
your own eyes, but you will not eat any of it!"
20And that is exactly what happened to him, for
the people trampled him in the gateway, and he
died.

Discovering the Word 1. What indications do you see that the situation in Samaria was desperate (6:24—7:2)? 2. Notice each reference to God in 6:24—7:2. What does each speaker seem to believe about God's relationship to the siege? 3. Why did the four lepers go to the Aramean camp (7:3–4)? 4. If you had been one of those lepers, what would you have done when you discovered the Aramean camp deserted (vv. 8–9)? 5. Why do you think the king's officer died (vv. 17–20)?

Applying the Word 1. Why is it hard to trust God during hard times? 2. What can you do during times of relative calm that would prepare you to trust God when times are hard?

Responding in Prayer Pray about the hard times you face in your life and pray for those around the world who face famine and war.

2 *Kings* 8

8 Now Elisha had said to the woman whose
son he had restored to life, "Go away with
your family and stay for a while wherever
you can, because the LORD has decreed a famine in
the land that will last seven years." 2The woman
proceeded to do as the man of God said. She and
her family went away and stayed in the land of
the Philistines seven years.
3At the end of the seven years she came back
from the land of the Philistines and went to the
king to beg for her house and land. 4The king was
talking to Gehazi, the servant of the man of God,

and had said, "Tell me about all the great things Elisha has done." 5Just as Gehazi was telling the king how Elisha had restored the dead to life, the woman whose son Elisha had brought back to life came to beg the king for her house and land.

Gehazi said, "This is the woman, my lord the king, and this is her son whom Elisha restored to life." 6The king asked the woman about it, and she told him.

Then he assigned an official to her case and said to him, "Give back everything that belonged to her, including all the income from her land from the day she left the country until now."

7Elisha went to Damascus, and Ben-Hadad king of Aram was ill. When the king was told, "The man of God has come all the way up here," 8he said to Hazael, "Take a gift with you and go to meet the man of God. Consult the LORD through him; ask him, 'Will I recover from this illness?' "

9Hazael went to meet Elisha, taking with him as a gift forty camel-loads of all the finest wares of Damascus. He went in and stood before him, and said, "Your son Ben-Hadad king of Aram has sent me to ask, 'Will I recover from this illness?' "

10Elisha answered, "Go and say to him, 'You will certainly recover'; but[p] the LORD has revealed to me that he will in fact die." 11He stared at him with a fixed gaze until Hazael felt ashamed. Then the man of God began to weep.

12"Why is my lord weeping?" asked Hazael.

"Because I know the harm you will do to the Israelites," he answered. "You will set fire to their fortified places, kill their young men with the sword, dash their little children to the ground, and rip open their pregnant women."

13Hazael said, "How could your servant, a mere dog, accomplish such a feat?"

"The LORD has shown me that you will become king of Aram," answered Elisha.

14Then Hazael left Elisha and returned to his master. When Ben-Hadad asked, "What did Elisha say to you?" Hazael replied, "He told me that you would certainly recover." 15But the next day he took a thick cloth, soaked it in water and spread it over the king's face, so that he died. Then Hazael succeeded him as king.

16In the fifth year of Joram son of Ahab king of Israel, when Jehoshaphat was king of Judah, Jehoram son of Jehoshaphat began his reign as king of Judah. 17He was thirty-two years old when he became king, and he reigned in Jerusalem eight years. 18He walked in the ways of the kings of Israel, as the house of Ahab had done, for he married a daughter of Ahab. He did evil in the eyes of the LORD. 19Nevertheless, for the sake of his servant David, the LORD was not willing to destroy Judah. He had promised to maintain a lamp for David and his descendants forever.

20In the time of Jehoram, Edom rebelled against Judah and set up its own king. 21So Jehoram[q] went to Zair with all his chariots. The Edomites surrounded him and his chariot commanders, but he rose up and broke through by night; his army, however, fled back home. 22To this day Edom has been in rebellion against Judah. Libnah revolted at the same time.

23As for the other events of Jehoram's reign, and all he did, are they not written in the book of the annals of the kings of Judah? 24Jehoram rested with his fathers and was buried with them in the City of David. And Ahaziah his son succeeded him as king.

25In the twelfth year of Joram son of Ahab king of Israel, Ahaziah son of Jehoram king of Judah began to reign. 26Ahaziah was twenty-two years old when he became king, and he reigned in Jerusalem one year. His mother's name was Athaliah, a granddaughter of Omri king of Israel. 27He walked in the ways of the house of Ahab and did evil in the eyes of the LORD, as the house of Ahab had done, for he was related by marriage to Ahab's family.

28Ahaziah went with Joram son of Ahab to war against Hazael king of Aram at Ramoth Gilead. The Arameans wounded Joram; 29so King Joram returned to Jezreel to recover from the wounds the Arameans had inflicted on him at Ramoth[r] in his battle with Hazael king of Aram.

Then Ahaziah son of Jehoram king of Judah went down to Jezreel to see Joram son of Ahab, because he had been wounded.

p10 The Hebrew may also be read *Go and say, 'You will certainly not recover,' for.* q21 Hebrew *Joram,* a variant of *Jehoram;* also in verses 23 and 24 r29 Hebrew *Ramah,* a variant of *Ramoth*

5 / 2 Kings 9—10
God's Avenger

GOD'S EXECUTIONER

Fly, killer Jehu
Riding your chariot
A madman across the plains
"He drives like Jehu?"
Swallows my messengers
And spits them out his tail

Tremble Ahab in your grave
You spilt your seed on the ground
One-hundred-fold
And Jehu rides to lick it up

 **Warming Up to God** In what way or on whom would you like to exercise vengeance?

 **Read 2 Kings 9—10.**

9 The prophet Elisha summoned a man from the company of the prophets and said to him, "Tuck your cloak into your belt, take this flask of oil with you and go to Ramoth Gilead. 2When you get there, look for Jehu son of Jehoshaphat, the son of Nimshi. Go to him, get him away from his companions and take him into an inner room. 3Then take the flask and pour the oil on his head and declare, 'This is what the LORD says: I anoint you king over Israel.' Then open the door and run; don't delay!"

4So the young man, the prophet, went to Ramoth Gilead. 5When he arrived, he found the army officers sitting together. "I have a message for you, commander," he said.

"For which of us?" asked Jehu.

"For you, commander," he replied.

6Jehu got up and went into the house. Then the prophet poured the oil on Jehu's head and declared, "This is what the LORD, the God of Israel, says: 'I anoint you king over the LORD's people Israel. 7You are to destroy the house of Ahab your master, and I will avenge the blood of my servants the prophets and the blood of all the LORD's servants shed by Jezebel. 8The whole house of Ahab will perish. I will cut off from Ahab every last male in Israel—slave or free. 9I will make the house of Ahab like the house of Jeroboam son of Nebat and like the house of Baasha son of Ahijah. 10As for Jezebel, dogs will devour her on the plot of ground at Jezreel, and no one will bury her.'" Then he opened the door and ran.

11When Jehu went out to his fellow officers, one of them asked him, "Is everything all right? Why did this madman come to you?"

"You know the man and the sort of things he says," Jehu replied.

12"That's not true!" they said. "Tell us."

Jehu said, "Here is what he told me: 'This is what the LORD says: I anoint you king over Israel.'"

13They hurried and took their cloaks and spread them under him on the bare steps. Then they blew the trumpet and shouted, "Jehu is king!"

14So Jehu son of Jehoshaphat, the son of Nimshi, conspired against Joram. (Now Joram and all Israel had been defending Ramoth Gilead against Hazael king of Aram, 15but King Joram[s] had returned to Jezreel to recover from the wounds the Arameans had inflicted on him in the battle with Hazael king of Aram.) Jehu said, "If this is the way you feel, don't let anyone slip out of the city to go and tell the news in Jezreel." 16Then he got into his chariot and rode to Jezreel, because Joram was resting there and Ahaziah king of Judah had gone down to see him.

17When the lookout standing on the tower in

s15 Hebrew *Jehoram*, a variant of *Joram*; also in verses 17 and 21-24

Jezreel saw Jehu's troops approaching, he called out, "I see some troops coming."

"Get a horseman," Joram ordered. "Send him to meet them and ask, 'Do you come in peace?' "

18The horseman rode off to meet Jehu and said, "This is what the king says: 'Do you come in peace?' "

"What do you have to do with peace?" Jehu replied. "Fall in behind me."

The lookout reported, "The messenger has reached them, but he isn't coming back."

19So the king sent out a second horseman. When he came to them he said, "This is what the king says: 'Do you come in peace?' "

Jehu replied, "What do you have to do with peace? Fall in behind me."

20The lookout reported, "He has reached them, but he isn't coming back either. The driving is like that of Jehu son of Nimshi—he drives like a madman."

21"Hitch up my chariot," Joram ordered. And when it was hitched up, Joram king of Israel and Ahaziah king of Judah rode out, each in his own chariot, to meet Jehu. They met him at the plot of ground that had belonged to Naboth the Jezreelite. 22When Joram saw Jehu he asked, "Have you come in peace, Jehu?"

"How can there be peace," Jehu replied, "as long as all the idolatry and witchcraft of your mother Jezebel abound?"

23Joram turned about and fled, calling out to Ahaziah, "Treachery, Ahaziah!"

24Then Jehu drew his bow and shot Joram between the shoulders. The arrow pierced his heart and he slumped down in his chariot. 25Jehu said to Bidkar, his chariot officer, "Pick him up and throw him on the field that belonged to Naboth the Jezreelite. Remember how you and I were riding together in chariots behind Ahab his father when the LORD made this prophecy about him: 26'Yesterday I saw the blood of Naboth and the blood of his sons, declares the LORD, and I will surely make you pay for it on this plot of ground, declares the LORD.'[t] Now then, pick him up and throw him on that plot, in accordance with the word of the LORD."

27When Ahaziah king of Judah saw what had happened, he fled up the road to Beth Haggan.[u] Jehu chased him, shouting, "Kill him too!" They wounded him in his chariot on the way up to Gur near Ibleam, but he escaped to Megiddo and died there. 28His servants took him by chariot to Jerusalem and buried him with his fathers in his tomb in the City of David. 29(In the eleventh year of Joram son of Ahab, Ahaziah had become king of Judah.)

30Then Jehu went to Jezreel. When Jezebel heard about it, she painted her eyes, arranged her hair and looked out of a window. 31As Jehu entered the gate, she asked, "Have you come in peace, Zimri, you murderer of your master?"[v]

32He looked up at the window and called out, "Who is on my side? Who?" Two or three eunuchs looked down at him. 33"Throw her down!" Jehu said. So they threw her down, and some of her blood spattered the wall and the horses as they trampled her underfoot.

34Jehu went in and ate and drank. "Take care of that cursed woman," he said, "and bury her, for she was a king's daughter." 35But when they went out to bury her, they found nothing except her skull, her feet and her hands. 36They went back and told Jehu, who said, "This is the word of the LORD that he spoke through his servant Elijah the Tishbite: On the plot of ground at Jezreel dogs will devour Jezebel's flesh.[w] 37Jezebel's body will be like refuse on the ground in the plot at Jezreel, so that no one will be able to say, 'This is Jezebel.' "

10

Now there were in Samaria seventy sons of the house of Ahab. So Jehu wrote letters and sent them to Samaria: to the officials of Jezreel,[x] to the elders and to the guardians of Ahab's children. He said, 2"As soon as this letter reaches you, since your master's sons are with you and you have chariots and horses, a fortified city and weapons, 3choose the best and most worthy of your master's sons and set him on his father's throne. Then fight for your master's house."

4But they were terrified and said, "If two kings could not resist him, how can we?"

5So the palace administrator, the city governor, the elders and the guardians sent this message to Jehu: "We are your servants and we will do anything you say. We will not appoint anyone as king; you do whatever you think best."

6Then Jehu wrote them a second letter, saying, "If you are on my side and will obey me, take the heads of your master's sons and come to me in Jezreel by this time tomorrow."

[t]26 See 1 Kings 21:19. [u]27 Or *fled by way of the garden house* [v]31 Or *"Did Zimri have peace, who murdered his master?"* [w]36 See 1 Kings 21:23. [x]1 Hebrew; some Septuagint manuscripts and Vulgate *of the city*

Now the royal princes, seventy of them, were
with the leading men of the city, who were rear-
ing them. 7When the letter arrived, these men
took the princes and slaughtered all seventy of
them. They put their heads in baskets and sent
them to Jehu in Jezreel. 8When the messenger
arrived, he told Jehu, "They have brought the
heads of the princes."

Then Jehu ordered, "Put them in two piles at
the entrance of the city gate until morning."

9The next morning Jehu went out. He stood
before all the people and said, "You are innocent.
It was I who conspired against my master and
killed him, but who killed all these? 10Know then,
that not a word the LORD has spoken against the
house of Ahab will fail. The LORD has done what
he promised through his servant Elijah." 11So
Jehu killed everyone in Jezreel who remained of
the house of Ahab, as well as all his chief men, his
close friends and his priests, leaving him no sur-
vivor.

12Jehu then set out and went toward Samaria.
At Beth Eked of the Shepherds, 13he met some
relatives of Ahaziah king of Judah and asked,
"Who are you?"

They said, "We are relatives of Ahaziah, and we
have come down to greet the families of the king
and of the queen mother."

14"Take them alive!" he ordered. So they took
them alive and slaughtered them by the well of
Beth Eked—forty-two men. He left no survivor.

15After he left there, he came upon Jehonadab
son of Recab, who was on his way to meet him.
Jehu greeted him and said, "Are you in accord
with me, as I am with you?"

"I am," Jehonadab answered.

"If so," said Jehu, "give me your hand." So he
did, and Jehu helped him up into the chariot.
16Jehu said, "Come with me and see my zeal for
the LORD." Then he had him ride along in his
chariot.

17When Jehu came to Samaria, he killed all
who were left there of Ahab's family; he destroyed
them, according to the word of the LORD spoken
to Elijah.

18Then Jehu brought all the people together
and said to them, "Ahab served Baal a little; Jehu
will serve him much. 19Now summon all the
prophets of Baal, all his ministers and all his
priests. See that no one is missing, because I am
going to hold a great sacrifice for Baal. Anyone
who fails to come will no longer live." But Jehu
was acting deceptively in order to destroy the
ministers of Baal.

20Jehu said, "Call an assembly in honor of
Baal." So they proclaimed it. 21Then he sent word
throughout Israel, and all the ministers of Baal
came; not one stayed away. They crowded into
the temple of Baal until it was full from one end
to the other. 22And Jehu said to the keeper of the
wardrobe, "Bring robes for all the ministers of
Baal." So he brought out robes for them.

23Then Jehu and Jehonadab son of Recab went
into the temple of Baal. Jehu said to the ministers
of Baal, "Look around and see that no servants of
the LORD are here with you—only ministers of
Baal." 24So they went in to make sacrifices and
burnt offerings. Now Jehu had posted eighty men
outside with this warning: "If one of you lets any
of the men I am placing in your hands escape, it
will be your life for his life."

25As soon as Jehu had finished making the
burnt offering, he ordered the guards and officers:
"Go in and kill them; let no one escape." So they
cut them down with the sword. The guards and
officers threw the bodies out and then entered the
inner shrine of the temple of Baal. 26They brought
the sacred stone out of the temple of Baal and
burned it. 27They demolished the sacred stone of
Baal and tore down the temple of Baal, and people
have used it for a latrine to this day.

28So Jehu destroyed Baal worship in Israel.
29However, he did not turn away from the sins of
Jeroboam son of Nebat, which he had caused Is-
rael to commit—the worship of the golden calves
at Bethel and Dan.

30The LORD said to Jehu, "Because you have
done well in accomplishing what is right in my
eyes and have done to the house of Ahab all I had
in mind to do, your descendants will sit on the
throne of Israel to the fourth generation." 31Yet
Jehu was not careful to keep the law of the LORD,
the God of Israel, with all his heart. He did not
turn away from the sins of Jeroboam, which he
had caused Israel to commit.

32In those days the LORD began to reduce the
size of Israel. Hazael overpowered the Israelites
throughout their territory 33east of the Jordan in
all the land of Gilead (the region of Gad, Reuben
and Manasseh), from Aroer by the Arnon Gorge
through Gilead to Bashan.

34As for the other events of Jehu's reign, all he
did, and all his achievements, are they not written
in the book of the annals of the kings of Israel?

35Jehu rested with his fathers and was buried in Samaria. And Jehoahaz his son succeeded him as king. 36The time that Jehu reigned over Israel in Samaria was twenty-eight years.

Discovering the Word 1. What disturbs you most about this account? 2. What did God tell Jehu to do (9:3–10)? 3. Note all the people Jehu killed. How was each a part of his strategy for securing his own position as king? 4. What evidence do you see that when Jehu killed the leaders of Baal-worship it was not simply because of his desire to worship the true God (10:28–31)? 5. Would you classify Jehu as a good or an evil king? Why? 6. Why do you think God allowed this slaughter by Jehu?

Applying the Word 1. If God is good and God is sovereign, how do you explain wholesale violence in our world? 2. What do you think should be the attitude of Christians toward violence?

Responding in Prayer Pray that God's justice will be exercised in the parts of the world where people suffer.

2 Kings 11—12

11 When Athaliah the mother of Ahaziah saw that her son was dead, she proceeded to destroy the whole royal family. 2But Jehosheba, the daughter of King Jehoram[y] and sister of Ahaziah, took Joash son of Ahaziah and stole him away from among the royal princes, who were about to be murdered. She put him and his nurse in a bedroom to hide him from Athaliah; so he was not killed. 3He remained hidden with his nurse at the temple of the LORD for six years while Athaliah ruled the land.

4In the seventh year Jehoiada sent for the commanders of units of a hundred, the Carites and the guards and had them brought to him at the temple of the LORD. He made a covenant with them and put them under oath at the temple of the LORD. Then he showed them the king's son. 5He commanded them, saying, "This is what you are to do: You who are in the three companies that are going on duty on the Sabbath—a third of you guarding the royal palace, 6a third at the Sur Gate, and a third at the gate behind the guard, who take turns guarding the temple— 7and you who are in the other two companies that normally go off Sabbath duty are all to guard the temple for the king. 8Station yourselves around the king, each man with his weapon in his hand. Anyone who approaches your ranks[z] must be put to death. Stay close to the king wherever he goes."

9The commanders of units of a hundred did just as Jehoiada the priest ordered. Each one took his men—those who were going on duty on the Sabbath and those who were going off duty—and came to Jehoiada the priest. 10Then he gave the commanders the spears and shields that had belonged to King David and that were in the temple of the LORD. 11The guards, each with his weapon in his hand, stationed themselves around the king—near the altar and the temple, from the south side to the north side of the temple.

12Jehoiada brought out the king's son and put the crown on him; he presented him with a copy of the covenant and proclaimed him king. They anointed him, and the people clapped their hands and shouted, "Long live the king!"

13When Athaliah heard the noise made by the guards and the people, she went to the people at the temple of the LORD. 14She looked and there was the king, standing by the pillar, as the custom was. The officers and the trumpeters were beside the king, and all the people of the land were rejoicing and blowing trumpets. Then Athaliah tore her robes and called out, "Treason! Treason!"

15Jehoiada the priest ordered the commanders of units of a hundred, who were in charge of the troops: "Bring her out between the ranks[a] and put to the sword anyone who follows her." For the priest had said, "She must not be put to death in the temple of the LORD." 16So they seized her as she reached the place where the horses enter the palace grounds, and there she was put to death.

17Jehoiada then made a covenant between the LORD and the king and people that they would be the LORD's people. He also made a covenant be-

y2 Hebrew *Joram,* a variant of *Jehoram* z8 Or *approaches the precincts* a15 Or *out from the precincts*

tween the king and the people. 18All the people of the land went to the temple of Baal and tore it down. They smashed the altars and idols to pieces and killed Mattan the priest of Baal in front of the altars.

Then Jehoiada the priest posted guards at the temple of the LORD. 19He took with him the commanders of hundreds, the Carites, the guards and all the people of the land, and together they brought the king down from the temple of the LORD and went into the palace, entering by way of the gate of the guards. The king then took his place on the royal throne, 20and all the people of the land rejoiced. And the city was quiet, because Athaliah had been slain with the sword at the palace.

21Joash[b] was seven years old when he began to reign.

12 In the seventh year of Jehu, Joash[c] became king, and he reigned in Jerusalem forty years. His mother's name was Zibiah; she was from Beersheba. 2Joash did what was right in the eyes of the LORD all the years Jehoiada the priest instructed him. 3The high places, however, were not removed; the people continued to offer sacrifices and burn incense there.

4Joash said to the priests, "Collect all the money that is brought as sacred offerings to the temple of the LORD—the money collected in the census, the money received from personal vows and the money brought voluntarily to the temple. 5Let every priest receive the money from one of the treasurers, and let it be used to repair whatever damage is found in the temple."

6But by the twenty-third year of King Joash the priests still had not repaired the temple. 7Therefore King Joash summoned Jehoiada the priest and the other priests and asked them, "Why aren't you repairing the damage done to the temple? Take no more money from your treasurers, but hand it over for repairing the temple." 8The priests agreed that they would not collect any more money from the people and that they would not repair the temple themselves.

9Jehoiada the priest took a chest and bored a hole in its lid. He placed it beside the altar, on the right side as one enters the temple of the LORD. The priests who guarded the entrance put into the chest all the money that was brought to the temple of the LORD. 10Whenever they saw that there was a large amount of money in the chest, the royal secretary and the high priest came, counted the money that had been brought into the temple of the LORD and put it into bags. 11When the amount had been determined, they gave the money to the men appointed to supervise the work on the temple. With it they paid those who worked on the temple of the LORD—the carpenters and builders, 12the masons and stonecutters. They purchased timber and dressed stone for the repair of the temple of the LORD, and met all the other expenses of restoring the temple.

13The money brought into the temple was not spent for making silver basins, wick trimmers, sprinkling bowls, trumpets or any other articles of gold or silver for the temple of the LORD; 14it was paid to the workmen, who used it to repair the temple. 15They did not require an accounting from those to whom they gave the money to pay the workers, because they acted with complete honesty. 16The money from the guilt offerings and sin offerings was not brought into the temple of the LORD; it belonged to the priests.

17About this time Hazael king of Aram went up and attacked Gath and captured it. Then he turned to attack Jerusalem. 18But Joash king of Judah took all the sacred objects dedicated by his fathers—Jehoshaphat, Jehoram and Ahaziah, the kings of Judah—and the gifts he himself had dedicated and all the gold found in the treasuries of the temple of the LORD and of the royal palace, and he sent them to Hazael king of Aram, who then withdrew from Jerusalem.

19As for the other events of the reign of Joash, and all he did, are they not written in the book of the annals of the kings of Judah? 20His officials conspired against him and assassinated him at Beth Millo, on the road down to Silla. 21The officials who murdered him were Jozabad son of Shimeath and Jehozabad son of Shomer. He died and was buried with his fathers in the City of David. And Amaziah his son succeeded him as king.

[b]21 Hebrew *Jehoash,* a variant of *Joash* [c]1 Hebrew *Jehoash,* a variant of *Joash*; also in verses 2, 4, 6, 7 and 18

6 / 2 *Kings 13*
Facing Losses

MY FRIEND JAN sat at her kitchen table and cried. Her husband had lost his job. Their living room now stood warehouse-vacant; the furniture had been repossessed. The large country home in which they lived was next in line; the bank would no longer carry the loan. And now (surprise) a new baby was on the way. Jan would also have to give up her job. Losses like these make us take a hard look at ourselves. Have we displeased God? Have we made foolish errors in planning? Or are we simply caught in the fallout of a world that is overrun by sin? Sometimes we can find no answers, but if we bring the questions to God, we will come away with something of value to sustain us through that time.

Warming Up to God How has a personal loss of your own or of a friend or relative caused you to feel abandoned by God?

Read 2 Kings 13.

13 In the twenty-third year of Joash
son of Ahaziah king of Judah, Jeho-
ahaz son of Jehu became king of
Israel in Samaria, and he reigned seventeen years.
2He did evil in the eyes of the LORD by following
the sins of Jeroboam son of Nebat, which he had
caused Israel to commit, and he did not turn
away from them. 3So the LORD's anger burned
against Israel, and for a long time he kept them
under the power of Hazael king of Aram and Ben-
Hadad his son.
4Then Jehoahaz sought the LORD's favor, and
the LORD listened to him, for he saw how severely
the king of Aram was oppressing Israel. 5The LORD
provided a deliverer for Israel, and they escaped
from the power of Aram. So the Israelites lived in
their own homes as they had before. 6But they did
not turn away from the sins of the house of Jero-
boam, which he had caused Israel to commit;
they continued in them. Also, the Asherah pole[d]
remained standing in Samaria.
7Nothing had been left of the army of Jehoahaz
except fifty horsemen, ten chariots and ten thou-
sand foot soldiers, for the king of Aram had de-
stroyed the rest and made them like the dust at
threshing time.
8As for the other events of the reign of Jehoa-
haz, all he did and his achievements, are they not
written in the book of the annals of the kings of
Israel? 9Jehoahaz rested with his fathers and was
buried in Samaria. And Jehoash[e] his son suc-
ceeded him as king.
10In the thirty-seventh year of Joash king of
Judah, Jehoash son of Jehoahaz became king of
Israel in Samaria, and he reigned sixteen years.
11He did evil in the eyes of the LORD and did not
turn away from any of the sins of Jeroboam son of
Nebat, which he had caused Israel to commit; he
continued in them.
12As for the other events of the reign of Jeho-
ash, all he did and his achievements, including
his war against Amaziah king of Judah, are they
not written in the book of the annals of the kings
of Israel? 13Jehoash rested with his fathers, and
Jeroboam succeeded him on the throne. Jehoash
was buried in Samaria with the kings of Israel.
14Now Elisha was suffering from the illness
from which he died. Jehoash king of Israel went
down to see him and wept over him. "My father!
My father!" he cried. "The chariots and horsemen
of Israel!"
15Elisha said, "Get a bow and some arrows,"
and he did so. 16"Take the bow in your hands," he
said to the king of Israel. When he had taken it,
Elisha put his hands on the king's hands.
17"Open the east window," he said, and he
opened it. "Shoot!" Elisha said, and he shot. "The
LORD's arrow of victory, the arrow of victory over
Aram!" Elisha declared. "You will completely de-
stroy the Arameans at Aphek."
18Then he said, "Take the arrows," and the
king took them. Elisha told him, "Strike the
ground." He struck it three times and stopped.
19The man of God was angry with him and said,
"You should have struck the ground five or six
times; then you would have defeated Aram and
completely destroyed it. But now you will defeat
it only three times."

[d]6 That is, a symbol of the goddess Asherah; here and elsewhere in 2 Kings [e]9 Hebrew *Joash*, a variant of *Jehoash*; also in verses 12-14 and 25

[20]Elisha died and was buried.

Now Moabite raiders used to enter the country every spring. [21]Once while some Israelites were burying a man, suddenly they saw a band of raiders; so they threw the man's body into Elisha's tomb. When the body touched Elisha's bones, the man came to life and stood up on his feet.

[22]Hazael king of Aram oppressed Israel throughout the reign of Jehoahaz. [23]But the LORD was gracious to them and had compassion and showed concern for them because of his covenant with Abraham, Isaac and Jacob. To this day he has been unwilling to destroy them or banish them from his presence.

[24]Hazael king of Aram died, and Ben-Hadad his son succeeded him as king. [25]Then Jehoash son of Jehoahaz recaptured from Ben-Hadad son of Hazael the towns he had taken in battle from his father Jehoahaz. Three times Jehoash defeated him, and so he recovered the Israelite towns.

Discovering the Word 1. Describe the conditions in Israel during the reign of Jehoahaz and Jehoash (vv. 13–10). 2. What do you think King Jehoash meant when he said to Elisha, "My father! My father! . . . The chariots and horsemen of Israel" (v. 14)? 3. Why do you think Elisha had Jehoash act out his message from God (vv. 15–19)? 4. What effect was Elisha's final miracle likely to have on the Israelites who saw it (vv. 20–21)? 5. Why did God bring relief from Hazael's attacks (vv. 22–25)?

Applying the Word 1. When have you seen evidence of God's mercy in a time of personal loss? 2. How has personal loss increased your trust in God?

Responding in Prayer Pray that God will teach you about himself through the losses you experience.

2 Kings 14—15

14 In the second year of Jehoash[f] son of Jehoahaz king of Israel, Amaziah son of Joash king of Judah began to reign. [2]He was twenty-five years old when he became king, and he reigned in Jerusalem twenty-nine years. His mother's name was Jehoaddin; she was from Jerusalem. [3]He did what was right in the eyes of the LORD, but not as his father David had done. In everything he followed the example of his father Joash. [4]The high places, however, were not removed; the people continued to offer sacrifices and burn incense there.

[5]After the kingdom was firmly in his grasp, he executed the officials who had murdered his father the king. [6]Yet he did not put the sons of the assassins to death, in accordance with what is written in the Book of the Law of Moses where the LORD commanded: "Fathers shall not be put to death for their children, nor children put to death for their fathers; each is to die for his own sins."[g]

[7]He was the one who defeated ten thousand Edomites in the Valley of Salt and captured Sela in battle, calling it Joktheel, the name it has to this day.

[8]Then Amaziah sent messengers to Jehoash son of Jehoahaz, the son of Jehu, king of Israel, with the challenge: "Come, meet me face to face."

[9]But Jehoash king of Israel replied to Amaziah king of Judah: "A thistle in Lebanon sent a message to a cedar in Lebanon, 'Give your daughter to my son in marriage.' Then a wild beast in Lebanon came along and trampled the thistle underfoot. [10]You have indeed defeated Edom and now you are arrogant. Glory in your victory, but stay at home! Why ask for trouble and cause your own downfall and that of Judah also?"

[11]Amaziah, however, would not listen, so Jehoash king of Israel attacked. He and Amaziah king of Judah faced each other at Beth Shemesh in Judah. [12]Judah was routed by Israel, and every man fled to his home. [13]Jehoash king of Israel captured Amaziah king of Judah, the son of Joash, the son of Ahaziah, at Beth Shemesh. Then Jehoash went to Jerusalem and broke down the wall of Jerusalem from the Ephraim Gate to the Corner Gate—a section about six hundred feet long.[h] [14]He took all the gold and silver and all the articles found in the temple of the LORD and in the treasuries of the

[f]1 Hebrew *Joash*, a variant of *Jehoash*; also in verses 13, 23 and 27
[g]6 Deut. 24:16
[h]13 Hebrew *four hundred cubits* (about 180 meters)

royal palace. He also took hostages and returned to Samaria.

15As for the other events of the reign of Jehoash, what he did and his achievements, including his war against Amaziah king of Judah, are they not written in the book of the annals of the kings of Israel? 16Jehoash rested with his fathers and was buried in Samaria with the kings of Israel. And Jeroboam his son succeeded him as king.

17Amaziah son of Joash king of Judah lived for fifteen years after the death of Jehoash son of Jehoahaz king of Israel. 18As for the other events of Amaziah's reign, are they not written in the book of the annals of the kings of Judah?

19They conspired against him in Jerusalem, and he fled to Lachish, but they sent men after him to Lachish and killed him there. 20He was brought back by horse and was buried in Jerusalem with his fathers, in the City of David.

21Then all the people of Judah took Azariah,[i] who was sixteen years old, and made him king in place of his father Amaziah. 22He was the one who rebuilt Elath and restored it to Judah after Amaziah rested with his fathers.

23In the fifteenth year of Amaziah son of Joash king of Judah, Jeroboam son of Jehoash king of Israel became king in Samaria, and he reigned forty-one years. 24He did evil in the eyes of the LORD and did not turn away from any of the sins of Jeroboam son of Nebat, which he had caused Israel to commit. 25He was the one who restored the boundaries of Israel from Lebo[j] Hamath to the Sea of the Arabah,[k] in accordance with the word of the LORD, the God of Israel, spoken through his servant Jonah son of Amittai, the prophet from Gath Hepher.

26The LORD had seen how bitterly everyone in Israel, whether slave or free, was suffering; there was no one to help them. 27And since the LORD had not said he would blot out the name of Israel from under heaven, he saved them by the hand of Jeroboam son of Jehoash.

28As for the other events of Jeroboam's reign, all he did, and his military achievements, including how he recovered for Israel both Damascus and Hamath, which had belonged to Yaudi,[l] are they not written in the book of the annals of the kings of Israel? 29Jeroboam rested with his fathers, the kings of Israel. And Zechariah his son succeeded him as king.

15 In the twenty-seventh year of Jeroboam king of Israel, Azariah son of Amaziah king of Judah began to reign. 2He was sixteen years old when he became king, and he reigned in Jerusalem fifty-two years. His mother's name was Jecoliah; she was from Jerusalem. 3He did what was right in the eyes of the LORD, just as his father Amaziah had done. 4The high places, however, were not removed; the people continued to offer sacrifices and burn incense there.

5The LORD afflicted the king with leprosy[m] until the day he died, and he lived in a separate house.[n] Jotham the king's son had charge of the palace and governed the people of the land.

6As for the other events of Azariah's reign, and all he did, are they not written in the book of the annals of the kings of Judah? 7Azariah rested with his fathers and was buried near them in the City of David. And Jotham his son succeeded him as king.

8In the thirty-eighth year of Azariah king of Judah, Zechariah son of Jeroboam became king of Israel in Samaria, and he reigned six months. 9He did evil in the eyes of the LORD, as his fathers had done. He did not turn away from the sins of Jeroboam son of Nebat, which he had caused Israel to commit.

10Shallum son of Jabesh conspired against Zechariah. He attacked him in front of the people,[o] assassinated him and succeeded him as king. 11The other events of Zechariah's reign are written in the book of the annals of the kings of Israel. 12So the word of the LORD spoken to Jehu was fulfilled: "Your descendants will sit on the throne of Israel to the fourth generation."[p]

13Shallum son of Jabesh became king in the thirty-ninth year of Uzziah king of Judah, and he reigned in Samaria one month. 14Then Menahem son of Gadi went from Tirzah up to Samaria. He attacked Shallum son of Jabesh in Samaria, assassinated him and succeeded him as king.

15The other events of Shallum's reign, and the conspiracy he led, are written in the book of the annals of the kings of Israel.

16At that time Menahem, starting out from Tirzah, attacked Tiphsah and everyone in the city and its vicinity, because they refused to open

[i]21 Also called *Uzziah* [j]25 Or *from the entrance to* [k]25 That is, the Dead Sea [l]28 Or *Judah* [m]5 The Hebrew word was used for various diseases affecting the skin—not necessarily leprosy. [n]5 Or *in a house where he was relieved of responsibility* [o]10 Hebrew; some Septuagint manuscripts *in Ibleam* [p]12 2 Kings 10:30

their gates. He sacked Tiphsah and ripped open all the pregnant women.

[17]In the thirty-ninth year of Azariah king of Judah, Menahem son of Gadi became king of Israel, and he reigned in Samaria ten years. [18]He did evil in the eyes of the LORD. During his entire reign he did not turn away from the sins of Jeroboam son of Nebat, which he had caused Israel to commit.

[19]Then Pul[q] king of Assyria invaded the land, and Menahem gave him a thousand talents[r] of silver to gain his support and strengthen his own hold on the kingdom. [20]Menahem exacted this money from Israel. Every wealthy man had to contribute fifty shekels[s] of silver to be given to the king of Assyria. So the king of Assyria withdrew and stayed in the land no longer.

[21]As for the other events of Menahem's reign, and all he did, are they not written in the book of the annals of the kings of Israel? [22]Menahem rested with his fathers. And Pekahiah his son succeeded him as king.

[23]In the fiftieth year of Azariah king of Judah, Pekahiah son of Menahem became king of Israel in Samaria, and he reigned two years. [24]Pekahiah did evil in the eyes of the LORD. He did not turn away from the sins of Jeroboam son of Nebat, which he had caused Israel to commit. [25]One of his chief officers, Pekah son of Remaliah, conspired against him. Taking fifty men of Gilead with him, he assassinated Pekahiah, along with Argob and Arieh, in the citadel of the royal palace at Samaria. So Pekah killed Pekahiah and succeeded him as king.

[26]The other events of Pekahiah's reign, and all he did, are written in the book of the annals of the kings of Israel.

[27]In the fifty-second year of Azariah king of Judah, Pekah son of Remaliah became king of Israel in Samaria, and he reigned twenty years. [28]He did evil in the eyes of the LORD. He did not turn away from the sins of Jeroboam son of Nebat, which he had caused Israel to commit.

[29]In the time of Pekah king of Israel, Tiglath-Pileser king of Assyria came and took Ijon, Abel Beth Maacah, Janoah, Kedesh and Hazor. He took Gilead and Galilee, including all the land of Naphtali, and deported the people to Assyria. [30]Then Hoshea son of Elah conspired against Pekah son of Remaliah. He attacked and assassinated him, and then succeeded him as king in the twentieth year of Jotham son of Uzziah.

[31]As for the other events of Pekah's reign, and all he did, are they not written in the book of the annals of the kings of Israel?

[32]In the second year of Pekah son of Remaliah king of Israel, Jotham son of Uzziah king of Judah began to reign. [33]He was twenty-five years old when he became king, and he reigned in Jerusalem sixteen years. His mother's name was Jerusha daughter of Zadok. [34]He did what was right in the eyes of the LORD, just as his father Uzziah had done. [35]The high places, however, were not removed; the people continued to offer sacrifices and burn incense there. Jotham rebuilt the Upper Gate of the temple of the LORD.

[36]As for the other events of Jotham's reign, and what he did, are they not written in the book of the annals of the kings of Judah? [37](In those days the LORD began to send Rezin king of Aram and Pekah son of Remaliah against Judah.) [38]Jotham rested with his fathers and was buried with them in the City of David, the city of his father. And Ahaz his son succeeded him as king.

q19 Also called *Tiglath-Pileser* r19 That is, about 37 tons (about 34 metric tons) s20 That is, about 1 1/4 pounds (about 0.6 kilogram)

7 / 2 *Kings 16*
Faithless in Trouble

WE HAD TWO girls, but we had planned two more children—boys, we hoped. Already, I had lost one baby in the first trimester. Pregnant again, I prayed my way through those first three months. Shortly into the second trimester I lost the baby. And I was mad! I had done all the right things. I had been especially careful about diet, medicines, activities. I had prayed constantly. But the baby had died inside me anyway. I prayed one angry prayer to God and then stopped praying altogether. For a while. But God is merciful. He gave us two boys (adopted). Later I had to ask, "Why was I so mad? Is God only God for the good times?" My response to trouble was not so different from that of King Ahaz. When the going got tough, Ahaz switched sides.

Warming Up to God Think of difficult times you have experienced, for example, a fight within your church, the death of someone you have prayed for, unemployment, family or friends going through a divorce. What are some negative ways you have responded to such situations? What are some positive ways you have responded?

Read 2 Kings 16.

16 In the seventeenth year of Pekah son of Remaliah, Ahaz son of Jotham king of Judah began to reign. 2Ahaz was twenty years old when he became king, and he reigned in Jerusalem sixteen years. Unlike David his father, he did not do what was right in the eyes of the LORD his God. 3He walked in the ways of the kings of Israel and even sacrificed his son in[t] the fire, following the detestable ways of the nations the LORD had driven out before the Israelites. 4He offered sacrifices and burned incense at the high places, on the hilltops and under every spreading tree.

5Then Rezin king of Aram and Pekah son of Remaliah king of Israel marched up to fight against Jerusalem and besieged Ahaz, but they could not overpower him. 6At that time, Rezin king of Aram recovered Elath for Aram by driving out the men of Judah. Edomites then moved into Elath and have lived there to this day.

7Ahaz sent messengers to say to Tiglath-Pileser king of Assyria, "I am your servant and vassal. Come up and save me out of the hand of the king of Aram and of the king of Israel, who are attacking me." 8And Ahaz took the silver and gold found in the temple of the LORD and in the treasuries of the royal palace and sent it as a gift to the king of Assyria. 9The king of Assyria complied by attacking Damascus and capturing it. He deported its inhabitants to Kir and put Rezin to death.

10Then King Ahaz went to Damascus to meet Tiglath-Pileser king of Assyria. He saw an altar in Damascus and sent to Uriah the priest a sketch of the altar, with detailed plans for its construction. 11So Uriah the priest built an altar in accordance with all the plans that King Ahaz had sent from Damascus and finished it before King Ahaz returned. 12When the king came back from Damascus and saw the altar, he approached it and presented offerings[u] on it. 13He offered up his burnt offering and grain offering, poured out his drink offering, and sprinkled the blood of his fellowship offerings[v] on the altar. 14The bronze altar that stood before the LORD he brought from the front of the temple—from between the new altar and the temple of the LORD—and put it on the north side of the new altar.

15King Ahaz then gave these orders to Uriah the priest: "On the large new altar, offer the morning burnt offering and the evening grain offering, the king's burnt offering and his grain offering, and the burnt offering of all the people of the land, and their grain offering and their drink offering. Sprinkle on the altar all the blood of the burnt offerings and sacrifices. But I will use the bronze altar for seeking guidance." 16And Uriah the priest did just as King Ahaz had ordered.

17King Ahaz took away the side panels and removed the basins from the movable stands. He removed the Sea from the bronze bulls that supported it and set it on a stone base. 18He took away the Sabbath canopy[w] that had been built at the temple and removed the royal entryway outside the temple of the LORD, in deference to the king of Assyria.

19As for the other events of the reign of Ahaz, and what he did, are they not written in the book of the annals of the kings of Judah? 20Ahaz rested with his fathers and was buried with them in the City of David. And Hezekiah his son succeeded him as king.

[t]3 Or *even made his son pass through* [u]12 Or *and went up* [v]13 Traditionally *peace offerings* [w]18 Or *the dais of his throne* (see Septuagint)

Discovering the Word 1. In what different ways did Ahaz express his idolatry? 2. What military crisis did Ahaz face (vv. 5–6)? (Use the map in the introduction to picture this.) 3. Why do you think Ahaz appealed to Assyria (vv. 7–9)? 4. What specific changes did Ahaz make in the temple (vv. 8, 10–18)? 5. God gave Moses specific instructions for arrangements in his tabernacle. In view of this, what was Ahaz saying by his actions in the temple?

Applying the Word 1. In what ways does your response to trouble seem to be a search for other gods and other altars? 2. To what extent does your response to trouble reflect a determined faith in God? 3. Much of our worship can become, like Ahaz's, an attempt to get what we want out of God. When this occurs, we need to ask ourselves, "Who is my god: God or me?" How can you make your worship less self-centered and more God centered?

Responding in Prayer Focus your prayers on God, reflecting on his character and good works.

8 / 2 *Kings 17*

Idolatry's Reward

WE HAD JUST bought a new house on an acre of land. I could plant fruit trees and a vegetable garden. Our children could run and yell without disturbing neighbors. All six of us could sit down at the kitchen table. Best of all, there were windows everywhere. When my brother visited, he asked matter-of-factly, "Is this house your goal in life?" He meant, "Do you plan to stay here, or are you planning to 'move up'?"

I knew what he meant, but I chose to answer what he actually asked. "No, of course not," I said stoutly. "I don't think any house could be my goal in life." I could answer with confidence because I'm just not a house person, as my grubby kitchen floor and cluttered linen closet will testify. But had Dan chosen another topic (such as work, friends, family, church), I might have had to squirm a little. Idolatry is insidious to us all.

Warming Up to God Take a private inventory of your own temptations by jotting down answers to the following questions:

I couldn't live without ______. When my mind is idle, it automatically turns to ______. If I could have anything in the world, I would choose ______. The most important thing (or person) to me is ______. I know God wants me to ______, but I can't.

Read 2 Kings 17.

17 In the twelfth year of Ahaz king of
Judah, Hoshea son of Elah became
king of Israel in Samaria, and he
reigned nine years. 2He did evil in the eyes of the
LORD, but not like the kings of Israel who pre-
ceded him.
3Shalmaneser king of Assyria came up to attack
Hoshea, who had been Shalmaneser's vassal and
had paid him tribute. 4But the king of Assyria
discovered that Hoshea was a traitor, for he had
sent envoys to So[x] king of Egypt, and he no
longer paid tribute to the king of Assyria, as he
had done year by year. Therefore Shalmaneser
seized him and put him in prison. 5The king of
Assyria invaded the entire land, marched against
Samaria and laid siege to it for three years. 6In the
ninth year of Hoshea, the king of Assyria cap-
tured Samaria and deported the Israelites to As-
syria. He settled them in Halah, in Gozan on the
Habor River and in the towns of the Medes.
7All this took place because the Israelites had
sinned against the LORD their God, who had
brought them up out of Egypt from under the
power of Pharaoh king of Egypt. They worshiped
other gods 8and followed the practices of the na-
tions the LORD had driven out before them, as well
as the practices that the kings of Israel had intro-
duced. 9The Israelites secretly did things against
the LORD their God that were not right. From
watchtower to fortified city they built themselves
high places in all their towns. 10They set up sa-
cred stones and Asherah poles on every high hill
and under every spreading tree. 11At every high
place they burned incense, as the nations whom
the LORD had driven out before them had done.

x4 Or *to Sais, to the*; *So* is possibly an abbreviation for *Osorkon.*

They did wicked things that provoked the LORD to
anger. 12They worshiped idols, though the LORD
had said, "You shall not do this."[y] 13The LORD
warned Israel and Judah through all his prophets
and seers: "Turn from your evil ways. Observe my
commands and decrees, in accordance with the
entire Law that I commanded your fathers to obey
and that I delivered to you through my servants
the prophets."

14But they would not listen and were as stiff-
necked as their fathers, who did not trust in the
LORD their God. 15They rejected his decrees and
the covenant he had made with their fathers and
the warnings he had given them. They followed
worthless idols and themselves became worthless.
They imitated the nations around them although
the LORD had ordered them, "Do not do as they
do," and they did the things the LORD had forbid-
den them to do.

16They forsook all the commands of the LORD
their God and made for themselves two idols cast
in the shape of calves, and an Asherah pole. They
bowed down to all the starry hosts, and they wor-
shiped Baal. 17They sacrificed their sons and
daughters in[z] the fire. They practiced divination
and sorcery and sold themselves to do evil in the
eyes of the LORD, provoking him to anger.

18So the LORD was very angry with Israel and
removed them from his presence. Only the tribe
of Judah was left, 19and even Judah did not keep
the commands of the LORD their God. They fol-
lowed the practices Israel had introduced.
20Therefore the LORD rejected all the people of
Israel; he afflicted them and gave them into the
hands of plunderers, until he thrust them from
his presence.

21When he tore Israel away from the house of
David, they made Jeroboam son of Nebat their
king. Jeroboam enticed Israel away from follow-
ing the LORD and caused them to commit a great
sin. 22The Israelites persisted in all the sins of
Jeroboam and did not turn away from them 23un-
til the LORD removed them from his presence, as
he had warned through all his servants the proph-
ets. So the people of Israel were taken from their
homeland into exile in Assyria, and they are still
there.

24The king of Assyria brought people from Bab-
ylon, Cuthah, Avva, Hamath and Sepharvaim and
settled them in the towns of Samaria to replace
the Israelites. They took over Samaria and lived in
its towns. 25When they first lived there, they did
not worship the LORD; so he sent lions among
them and they killed some of the people. 26It was
reported to the king of Assyria: "The people you
deported and resettled in the towns of Samaria do
not know what the god of that country requires.
He has sent lions among them, which are killing
them off, because the people do not know what
he requires."

27Then the king of Assyria gave this order:
"Have one of the priests you took captive from
Samaria go back to live there and teach the people
what the god of the land requires." 28So one of the
priests who had been exiled from Samaria came
to live in Bethel and taught them how to worship
the LORD.

29Nevertheless, each national group made its
own gods in the several towns where they settled,
and set them up in the shrines the people of Sa-
maria had made at the high places. 30The men
from Babylon made Succoth Benoth, the men
from Cuthah made Nergal, and the men from Ha-
math made Ashima; 31the Avvites made Nibhaz
and Tartak, and the Sepharvites burned their chil-
dren in the fire as sacrifices to Adrammelech and
Anammelech, the gods of Sepharvaim. 32They
worshiped the LORD, but they also appointed all
sorts of their own people to officiate for them as
priests in the shrines at the high places. 33They
worshiped the LORD, but they also served their
own gods in accordance with the customs of the
nations from which they had been brought.

34To this day they persist in their former prac-
tices. They neither worship the LORD nor adhere
to the decrees and ordinances, the laws and com-
mands that the LORD gave the descendants of Ja-
cob, whom he named Israel. 35When the LORD
made a covenant with the Israelites, he com-
manded them: "Do not worship any other gods or
bow down to them, serve them or sacrifice to
them. 36But the LORD, who brought you up out of
Egypt with mighty power and outstretched arm,
is the one you must worship. To him you shall
bow down and to him offer sacrifices. 37You must
always be careful to keep the decrees and ordi-
nances, the laws and commands he wrote for you.
Do not worship other gods. 38Do not forget the
covenant I have made with you, and do not wor-
ship other gods. 39Rather, worship the LORD your
God; it is he who will deliver you from the hand
of all your enemies."

[y] 12 Exodus 20:4, 5 [z] 17 Or *They made their sons and daughters pass through*

[40]They would not listen, however, but persisted in their former practices. [41]Even while these people were worshiping the LORD, they were serving their idols. To this day their children and grandchildren continue to do as their fathers did.

Discovering the Word 1. Notice the people and places in verses 1–6. How do these verses outline the final steps to Israel's death as a nation? 2. Review the list of sins (there are about twenty) in verses 7–22. What common characteristics do you find? 3. The writer of 2 Kings says repeatedly of Israel, "The LORD removed them from his presence." Consider the events of this chapter. What did it mean to Israel in practical terms to be removed from the presence of God (vv. 18, 20 and 23)? 4. Do you think that it is possible for people or nations today to be removed from the presence of God? Explain. 5. Why did the new Samaritans find it hard to serve one God alone (vv. 24–33)?

Applying the Word 1. Looking back to your inventory of temptations, in what areas of your life do you need to be alert to the temptation of idolatry? 2. What steps can you take to keep normal healthy interests in the world around you from turning into idolatry?

Responding in Prayer Confess your areas of weakness to the Lord. Ask him to protect you from idolatry.

2 Kings 18:1–16

18 In the third year of Hoshea son of Elah king of Israel, Hezekiah son of Ahaz king of Judah began to reign. [2]He was twenty-five years old when he became king, and he reigned in Jerusalem twenty-nine years. His mother's name was Abijah[a] daughter of Zechariah. [3]He did what was right in the eyes of the LORD, just as his father David had done. [4]He removed the high places, smashed the sacred stones and cut down the Asherah poles. He broke into pieces the bronze snake Moses had made, for up to that time the Israelites had been burning incense to it. (It was called[b] Nehushtan.[c])

[5]Hezekiah trusted in the LORD, the God of Israel. There was no one like him among all the kings of Judah, either before him or after him. [6]He held fast to the LORD and did not cease to follow him; he kept the commands the LORD had given Moses. [7]And the LORD was with him; he was successful in whatever he undertook. He rebelled against the king of Assyria and did not serve him. [8]From watchtower to fortified city, he defeated the Philistines, as far as Gaza and its territory.

[9]In King Hezekiah's fourth year, which was the seventh year of Hoshea son of Elah king of Israel, Shalmaneser king of Assyria marched against Samaria and laid siege to it. [10]At the end of three years the Assyrians took it. So Samaria was captured in Hezekiah's sixth year, which was the ninth year of Hoshea king of Israel. [11]The king of Assyria deported Israel to Assyria and settled them in Halah, in Gozan on the Habor River and in towns of the Medes. [12]This happened because they had not obeyed the LORD their God, but had violated his covenant—all that Moses the servant of the LORD commanded. They neither listened to the commands nor carried them out.

[13]In the fourteenth year of King Hezekiah's reign, Sennacherib king of Assyria attacked all the fortified cities of Judah and captured them. [14]So Hezekiah king of Judah sent this message to the king of Assyria at Lachish: "I have done wrong. Withdraw from me, and I will pay whatever you demand of me." The king of Assyria exacted from Hezekiah king of Judah three hundred talents[d] of silver and thirty talents[e] of gold. [15]So Hezekiah gave him all the silver that was found in the temple of the LORD and in the treasuries of the royal palace.

[16]At this time Hezekiah king of Judah stripped off the gold with which he had covered the doors and doorposts of the temple of the LORD, and gave it to the king of Assyria.

[a]2 Hebrew *Abi,* a variant of *Abijah* [b]4 Or *He called it*
[c]4 *Nehushtan* sounds like the Hebrew for *bronze* and *snake* and *unclean thing.* [d]14 That is, about 11 tons (about 10 metric tons)
[e]14 That is, about 1 ton (about 1 metric ton)

9 / 2 *Kings 18:17–37*
Identity

OUR SOCIETY IS locked in a longstanding identity crisis. From the troubled teen years beset with self-image problems to the midlife crisis and beyond, many of those around us do not know who they are. After the Sunday message many Christians walk out into the world only to sink back into the quagmire of their own identity crisis. We shouldn't be surprised that so many of us wrestle with this problem. God's Word makes it clear that his people live in a halfway house between heaven and hell, adherents to God's truth within a world of lies. The following passage from 2 Kings gives one such example. Besieging Jerusalem with a powerful army, the Assyrian king, Sennacherib, issues not only a threat to King Hezekiah and the kingdom of Judah but also a direct challenge to the entire identity of God's people.

Warming Up to God Every day we are challenged by our society. Sometimes our culture intimidates us and attempts to erode confidence in our identity as God's people. In what ways do you struggle with this?

Read 2 Kings 18:17–37.

[17]The king of Assyria sent his supreme commander, his chief officer and his field commander with a large army, from Lachish to King Hezekiah at Jerusalem. They came up to Jerusalem and stopped at the aqueduct of the Upper Pool, on the road to the Washerman's Field. [18]They called for the king; and Eliakim son of Hilkiah the palace administrator, Shebna the secretary, and Joah son of Asaph the recorder went out to them.

[19]The field commander said to them, "Tell Hezekiah:

"'This is what the great king, the king of Assyria, says: On what are you basing this confidence of yours? [20]You say you have strategy and military strength—but you speak only empty words. On whom are you depending, that you rebel against me? [21]Look now, you are depending on Egypt, that splintered reed of a staff, which pierces a man's hand and wounds him if he leans on it! Such is Pharaoh king of Egypt to all who depend on him. [22]And if you say to me, "We are depending on the LORD our God"—isn't he the one whose high places and altars Hezekiah removed, saying to Judah and Jerusalem, "You must worship before this altar in Jerusalem"?

[23]"'Come now, make a bargain with my master, the king of Assyria: I will give you two thousand horses—if you can put riders on them! [24]How can you repulse one officer of the least of my master's officials, even though you are depending on Egypt for chariots and horsemen[f]? [25]Furthermore, have I come to attack and destroy this place without word from the LORD? The LORD himself told me to march against this country and destroy it.'"

[26]Then Eliakim son of Hilkiah, and Shebna and Joah said to the field commander, "Please speak to your servants in Aramaic, since we understand it. Don't speak to us in Hebrew in the hearing of the people on the wall."

[27]But the commander replied, "Was it only to your master and you that my master sent me to say these things, and not to the men sitting on the wall—who, like you, will have to eat their own filth and drink their own urine?"

[28]Then the commander stood and called out in Hebrew: "Hear the word of the great king, the king of Assyria! [29]This is what the king says: Do not let Hezekiah deceive you. He cannot deliver you from my hand. [30]Do not let Hezekiah persuade you to trust in the LORD when he says, 'The LORD will surely deliver us; this city will not be given into the hand of the king of Assyria.'

[31]"Do not listen to Hezekiah. This is what the king of Assyria says: Make peace with me and come out to me. Then every one of you will eat from his own vine and fig tree and drink water from his own cistern, [32]until I come and take you to a land like your own, a land of grain and new wine, a land of bread and vineyards, a land of olive trees and honey. Choose life and not death!

"Do not listen to Hezekiah, for he is misleading you when he says, 'The LORD will deliver us.'

*f*24 *Or charioteers*

33Has the god of any nation ever delivered his
land from the hand of the king of Assyria?
34Where are the gods of Hamath and Arpad?
Where are the gods of Sepharvaim, Hena and Iv-
vah? Have they rescued Samaria from my hand?
35Who of all the gods of these countries has been
able to save his land from me? How then can the
LORD deliver Jerusalem from my hand?"

36But the people remained silent and said noth-
ing in reply, because the king had commanded,
"Do not answer him."

37Then Eliakim son of Hilkiah the palace ad-
ministrator, Shebna the secretary and Joah son of
Asaph the recorder went to Hezekiah, with their
clothes torn, and told him what the field com-
mander had said.

Discovering the Word 1. Speaking through the field commander, Sennacherib, the king of Assyria, addresses Hezekiah and his assistants. What kinds of questions does Sennacherib raise in verses 19–20? 2. How does Sennacherib try to shake Judah's confidence in verses 21–24? 3. Compare Hezekiah's exhortation (v. 30) with the offer of the king of Assyria (vv. 31–33). What are the relative benefits of these two appeals? 4. In what sense does the king of Assyria attempt to undermine their identity as God's chosen people (vv. 33–35)?

Applying the Word 1. What tactics does our culture use to cause us to question our identity as God's people? 2. In what aspect of your identity do you feel particularly vulnerable to attack? 3. What would it mean for you to "trust in the LORD" (v. 30) in responding to this threat?

Responding in Prayer Ask God to teach you what trust means for you today.

10/ *2 Kings 19*
Asking for Help

"I AM AN island." This unbiblical thought is steeped in Western culture. However, if we are to stand against the world, we must stand together. And we can start by asking God for help as Hezekiah does.

Warming Up to God How do you tend to feel and respond when your faith or confidence in God is tested?

Read 2 Kings 19.

19 When King Hezekiah heard this, he
tore his clothes and put on sack-
cloth and went into the temple of
the LORD. 2He sent Eliakim the palace administra-
tor, Shebna the secretary and the leading priests,
all wearing sackcloth, to the prophet Isaiah son of
Amoz. 3They told him, "This is what Hezekiah
says: This day is a day of distress and rebuke and
disgrace, as when children come to the point of
birth and there is no strength to deliver them. 4It
may be that the LORD your God will hear all the
words of the field commander, whom his master,
the king of Assyria, has sent to ridicule the living
God, and that he will rebuke him for the words
the LORD your God has heard. Therefore pray for
the remnant that still survives."

5When King Hezekiah's officials came to Isaiah,
6Isaiah said to them, "Tell your master, 'This is
what the LORD says: Do not be afraid of what you
have heard—those words with which the under-
lings of the king of Assyria have blasphemed me.
7Listen! I am going to put such a spirit in him
that when he hears a certain report, he will return
to his own country, and there I will have him cut
down with the sword.'"

8When the field commander heard that the
king of Assyria had left Lachish, he withdrew and
found the king fighting against Libnah.

9Now Sennacherib received a report that Tirha-
kah, the Cushite[g] king ⌞of Egypt⌟, was marching
out to fight against him. So he again sent messen-

g9 That is, from the upper Nile region

gers to Hezekiah with this word: 10“Say to Heze-
kiah king of Judah: Do not let the god you de-
pend on deceive you when he says, ‘Jerusalem
will not be handed over to the king of Assyria.’
11Surely you have heard what the kings of Assyria
have done to all the countries, destroying them
completely. And will you be delivered? 12Did the
gods of the nations that were destroyed by my
forefathers deliver them: the gods of Gozan, Ha-
ran, Rezeph and the people of Eden who were in
Tel Assar? 13Where is the king of Hamath, the
king of Arpad, the king of the city of Sepharvaim,
or of Hena or Ivvah?”

14Hezekiah received the letter from the messen-
gers and read it. Then he went up to the temple of
the LORD and spread it out before the LORD. 15And
Hezekiah prayed to the LORD: “O LORD, God of
Israel, enthroned between the cherubim, you
alone are God over all the kingdoms of the earth.
You have made heaven and earth. 16Give ear,
O LORD, and hear; open your eyes, O LORD, and
see; listen to the words Sennacherib has sent to
insult the living God.

17“It is true, O LORD, that the Assyrian kings
have laid waste these nations and their lands.
18They have thrown their gods into the fire and
destroyed them, for they were not gods but only
wood and stone, fashioned by men’s hands.
19Now, O LORD our God, deliver us from his
hand, so that all kingdoms on earth may know
that you alone, O LORD, are God.”

20Then Isaiah son of Amoz sent a message to
Hezekiah: “This is what the LORD, the God of Is-
rael, says: I have heard your prayer concerning
Sennacherib king of Assyria. 21This is the word
that the LORD has spoken against him:

“ ‘The Virgin Daughter of Zion
despises you and mocks you.
The Daughter of Jerusalem
tosses her head as you flee.
22Who is it you have insulted and blasphemed?
Against whom have you raised your voice
and lifted your eyes in pride?
Against the Holy One of Israel!
23By your messengers
you have heaped insults on the Lord.
And you have said,
“With my many chariots
I have ascended the heights of the mountains,
the utmost heights of Lebanon.
I have cut down its tallest cedars,
the choicest of its pines.
I have reached its remotest parts,
the finest of its forests.
24I have dug wells in foreign lands
and drunk the water there.
With the soles of my feet
I have dried up all the streams of Egypt.”

25“ ‘Have you not heard?
Long ago I ordained it.
In days of old I planned it;
now I have brought it to pass,
that you have turned fortified cities
into piles of stone.
26Their people, drained of power,
are dismayed and put to shame.
They are like plants in the field,
like tender green shoots,
like grass sprouting on the roof,
scorched before it grows up.

27“ ‘But I know where you stay
and when you come and go
and how you rage against me.
28Because you rage against me
and your insolence has reached my ears,
I will put my hook in your nose
and my bit in your mouth,
and I will make you return
by the way you came.’

29“This will be the sign for you, O Hezekiah:

“This year you will eat what grows by itself,
and the second year what springs from that.
But in the third year sow and reap,
plant vineyards and eat their fruit.
30Once more a remnant of the house of Judah
will take root below and bear fruit above.
31For out of Jerusalem will come a remnant,
and out of Mount Zion a band of survivors.

The zeal of the LORD Almighty will accomplish
this.

32“Therefore this is what the LORD says con-
cerning the king of Assyria:

“He will not enter this city
or shoot an arrow here.
He will not come before it with shield
or build a siege ramp against it.
33By the way that he came he will return;
he will not enter this city,
declares the LORD.

34I will defend this city and save it,
for my sake and for the sake of David my servant."

35That night the angel of the LORD went out and
put to death a hundred and eighty-five thousand
men in the Assyrian camp. When the people got
up the next morning—there were all the dead
bodies! 36So Sennacherib king of Assyria broke
camp and withdrew. He returned to Nineveh and
stayed there.
37One day, while he was worshiping in the
temple of his god Nisroch, his sons Adrammelech and Sharezer cut him down with the
sword, and they escaped to the land of Ararat.
And Esarhaddon his son succeeded him as
king.

Discovering the Word 1. Describe Hezekiah's attitude and actions in response to the ominous words of the king (vv. 1–4). 2. Compare Sennacherib's view of God and the Assyrian army (vv. 9–13) with the picture presented in Isaiah's prophecy (vv. 6–7). How do they differ? 3. Confronted with his own crisis, Hezekiah brings his dilemma before the Lord. Reread verses 3–4 and Hezekiah's prayer in verses 15–19. How has Hezekiah's perception changed? 4. Review Sennacherib's boasts in verses 10–13. How does Hezekiah now evaluate Sennacherib's claims (vv. 17–18)? 5. What assurances does Isaiah offer in his prophecy (vv. 20–34)?

Applying the Word 1. What can we learn from Hezekiah's example about confronting the lies the world feeds us? 2. How would a reaffirmation of God's character be of help when we face overt or subtle attacks on our identity as Christians?

Responding in Prayer Ask God for the help you need in the difficult situations you are facing.

---

11 / 2 *Kings 20:1—21:18*
One Giant Step Backward

MY FRIENDS BOB and Dottie and their children are missionaries to a primitive tribe of Indians in South America. After some initial awkwardness, they were well received. They donned the long white tunics of the tribal people, carried their woven handbags and wore tiny beaded necklaces. They ate native food. The Indians helped Bob and Dottie learn the language. God seemed ready to use them to help bring these people into his kingdom. Then drug traffic swept the area. Speculators bought the land or simply massacred Indians reluctant to sell. Twentieth-century viruses decimated the tribe. Only two-thirds of the Indians remained alive. And some who were left looked at my friends with hostile eyes. Can we still trust God when all the trends point counter to what we know of his purposes? One of the advantages of studying the Old Testament is seeing, in a few pages, God moving through hundreds of years of history. It may help us trust God's unseen purposes for our own small page.

Warming Up to God When in your life has it been hard to understand God's purposes?

Read 2 Kings 20:1—21:18.

---

20 In those days Hezekiah became ill
and was at the point of death. The
prophet Isaiah son of Amoz went to
him and said, "This is what the LORD says: Put
your house in order, because you are going to die;
you will not recover."
2Hezekiah turned his face to the wall and
prayed to the LORD, 3"Remember, O LORD, how I
have walked before you faithfully and with
wholehearted devotion and have done what
is good in your eyes." And Hezekiah wept
bitterly.
4Before Isaiah had left the middle court, the
word of the LORD came to him: 5"Go back and tell
Hezekiah, the leader of my people, 'This is what
the LORD, the God of your father David, says: I

have heard your prayer and seen your tears; I will
heal you. On the third day from now you will go
up to the temple of the LORD. 6I will add fifteen
years to your life. And I will deliver you and this
city from the hand of the king of Assyria. I will
defend this city for my sake and for the sake of
my servant David.' "
7Then Isaiah said, "Prepare a poultice of figs."
They did so and applied it to the boil, and he
recovered.
8Hezekiah had asked Isaiah, "What will be the
sign that the LORD will heal me and that I will go
up to the temple of the LORD on the third day
from now?"
9Isaiah answered, "This is the LORD's sign to
you that the LORD will do what he has promised:
Shall the shadow go forward ten steps, or shall it
go back ten steps?"
10"It is a simple matter for the shadow to go
forward ten steps," said Hezekiah. "Rather, have
it go back ten steps."
11Then the prophet Isaiah called upon the
LORD, and the LORD made the shadow go back the
ten steps it had gone down on the stairway of
Ahaz.
12At that time Merodach-Baladan son of Bala-
dan king of Babylon sent Hezekiah letters and a
gift, because he had heard of Hezekiah's illness.
13Hezekiah received the messengers and showed
them all that was in his storehouses—the silver,
the gold, the spices and the fine oil—his armory
and everything found among his treasures. There
was nothing in his palace or in all his kingdom
that Hezekiah did not show them.
14Then Isaiah the prophet went to King Heze-
kiah and asked, "What did those men say, and
where did they come from?"
"From a distant land," Hezekiah replied. "They
came from Babylon."
15The prophet asked, "What did they see in
your palace?"
"They saw everything in my palace," Hezekiah
said. "There is nothing among my treasures that I
did not show them."
16Then Isaiah said to Hezekiah, "Hear the word
of the LORD: 17The time will surely come when
everything in your palace, and all that your fa-
thers have stored up until this day, will be carried
off to Babylon. Nothing will be left, says the LORD.
18And some of your descendants, your own flesh
and blood, that will be born to you, will be taken
away, and they will become eunuchs in the palace
of the king of Babylon."
19"The word of the LORD you have spoken
is good," Hezekiah replied. For he thought,
"Will there not be peace and security in my
lifetime?"
20As for the other events of Hezekiah's reign, all
his achievements and how he made the pool and
the tunnel by which he brought water into the
city, are they not written in the book of the annals
of the kings of Judah? 21Hezekiah rested with his
fathers. And Manasseh his son succeeded him as
king.

21

Manasseh was twelve years old
when he became king, and he
reigned in Jerusalem fifty-five
years. His mother's name was Hephzibah. 2He did
evil in the eyes of the LORD, following the detest-
able practices of the nations the LORD had driven
out before the Israelites. 3He rebuilt the high
places his father Hezekiah had destroyed; he also
erected altars to Baal and made an Asherah pole,
as Ahab king of Israel had done. He bowed down
to all the starry hosts and worshiped them. 4He
built altars in the temple of the LORD, of which the
LORD had said, "In Jerusalem I will put my Name."
5In both courts of the temple of the LORD, he built
altars to all the starry hosts. 6He sacrificed his
own son in[h] the fire, practiced sorcery and divi-
nation, and consulted mediums and spiritists. He
did much evil in the eyes of the LORD, provoking
him to anger.
7He took the carved Asherah pole he had made
and put it in the temple, of which the LORD had
said to David and to his son Solomon, "In this
temple and in Jerusalem, which I have chosen out
of all the tribes of Israel, I will put my Name
forever. 8I will not again make the feet of
the Israelites wander from the land I gave their
forefathers, if only they will be careful to do
everything I commanded them and will keep the
whole Law that my servant Moses gave them."
9But the people did not listen. Manasseh led
them astray, so that they did more evil than
the nations the LORD had destroyed before the
Israelites.
10The LORD said through his servants the
prophets: 11"Manasseh king of Judah has commit-
ted these detestable sins. He has done more evil

[h]6 *Or He made his own son pass through*

than the Amorites who preceded him and has led
Judah into sin with his idols. 12Therefore this is
what the LORD, the God of Israel, says: I am going
to bring such disaster on Jerusalem and Judah
that the ears of everyone who hears of it will tin-
gle. 13I will stretch out over Jerusalem the mea-
suring line used against Samaria and the plumb
line used against the house of Ahab. I will wipe
out Jerusalem as one wipes a dish, wiping it and
turning it upside down. 14I will forsake the rem-
nant of my inheritance and hand them over to
their enemies. They will be looted and plundered
by all their foes, 15because they have done evil in
my eyes and have provoked me to anger from the
day their forefathers came out of Egypt until this
day."

16Moreover, Manasseh also shed so much inno-
cent blood that he filled Jerusalem from end to
end—besides the sin that he had caused Judah to
commit, so that they did evil in the eyes of the
LORD.

17As for the other events of Manasseh's reign,
and all he did, including the sin he committed,
are they not written in the book of the annals of
the kings of Judah? 18Manasseh rested with his
fathers and was buried in his palace garden, the
garden of Uzza. And Amon his son succeeded
him as king.

Discovering the Word 1. What do the details in the communication between God and Hezekiah reveal about their relationship (20:1–11)? 2. Why do you think Hezekiah treated the messengers from Babylon the way he did (20:15)? 3. What explanation can you offer for Hezekiah's response to Isaiah's prophecy (20:16–19)? 4. When you try to imagine life in Judah under Manasseh's reign, what pictures come to your mind? 5. Find as many references to the people of Judah as you can in 21:7–15. How do these help explain why Manasseh was able to make such a total reversal of his father's reforms? 6. Look back at Hezekiah's situation in 20:1–11. If Hezekiah could have known the future, including the birth of his son, do you think he would have wanted God to add fifteen years to his life? Why or why not?

Applying the Word 1. What do you know about God that helps you to stand against popular trends that go against what you know is right? 2. How can you serve God in your response to these trends?

Responding in Prayer Ask God to teach you how to trust in him even during times when the world only seems to be getting worse.

2 Kings 21:19–26

19Amon was twenty-two years old when he be-
came king, and he reigned in Jerusalem two
years. His mother's name was Meshullemeth
daughter of Haruz; she was from Jotbah. 20He did
evil in the eyes of the LORD, as his father Manasseh
had done. 21He walked in all the ways of his fa-
ther; he worshiped the idols his father had wor-
shiped, and bowed down to them. 22He forsook
the LORD, the God of his fathers, and did not walk
in the way of the LORD.

23Amon's officials conspired against him and
assassinated the king in his palace. 24Then the
people of the land killed all who had plotted
against King Amon, and they made Josiah his son
king in his place.

25As for the other events of Amon's reign, and
what he did, are they not written in the book of
the annals of the kings of Judah? 26He was buried
in his grave in the garden of Uzza. And Josiah his
son succeeded him as king.

12 / 2 *Kings 22:1—23:35*
Following God's Law

SENIORS IN HIGH school typically get a little huffy about restrictive school rules such as hall passes and washroom permits. Sometimes even teachers are not immune to similar feelings. When my daughter's music teacher, accustomed to working with diligent honors students, was confronted with the request for one more hall pass for an in-building errand, he wrote, "Sheri has my permission to be in the hall so that she can check the drug supply in her locker. Antonia is her bodyguard." (They weren't stopped.) There's something inside us that grates against laws—of any kind—unless, of course, we've had to live a long time without them. Judah had such an experience.

Warming Up to God Much of today's culture ignores God's laws. What pressures do you feel to follow the culture rather than the law of God?

Read 2 Kings 22:1—23:35.

22 Josiah was eight years old when he
became king, and he reigned in Je-
rusalem thirty-one years. His
mother's name was Jedidah daughter of Adaiah;
she was from Bozkath. 2He did what was right in
the eyes of the LORD and walked in all the ways of
his father David, not turning aside to the right or
to the left.
3In the eighteenth year of his reign, King Josiah
sent the secretary, Shaphan son of Azaliah, the
son of Meshullam, to the temple of the LORD. He
said: 4"Go up to Hilkiah the high priest and have
him get ready the money that has been brought
into the temple of the LORD, which the doorkeep-
ers have collected from the people. 5Have them
entrust it to the men appointed to supervise the
work on the temple. And have these men pay the
workers who repair the temple of the LORD— 6the
carpenters, the builders and the masons. Also
have them purchase timber and dressed stone to
repair the temple. 7But they need not account for
the money entrusted to them, because they are
acting faithfully."
8Hilkiah the high priest said to Shaphan the
secretary, "I have found the Book of the Law in
the temple of the LORD." He gave it to Shaphan,
who read it. 9Then Shaphan the secretary went to
the king and reported to him: "Your officials have
paid out the money that was in the temple of the
LORD and have entrusted it to the workers and
supervisors at the temple." 10Then Shaphan the
secretary informed the king, "Hilkiah the priest
has given me a book." And Shaphan read from it
in the presence of the king.
11When the king heard the words of the Book
of the Law, he tore his robes. 12He gave these
orders to Hilkiah the priest, Ahikam son of Sha-
phan, Acbor son of Micaiah, Shaphan the secre-
tary and Asaiah the king's attendant: 13"Go and
inquire of the LORD for me and for the people and
for all Judah about what is written in this book
that has been found. Great is the LORD's anger that
burns against us because our fathers have not
obeyed the words of this book; they have not
acted in accordance with all that is written there
concerning us."
14Hilkiah the priest, Ahikam, Acbor, Shaphan
and Asaiah went to speak to the prophetess Hul-
dah, who was the wife of Shallum son of Tikvah,
the son of Harhas, keeper of the wardrobe. She
lived in Jerusalem, in the Second District.
15She said to them, "This is what the LORD, the
God of Israel, says: Tell the man who sent you to
me, 16'This is what the LORD says: I am going to
bring disaster on this place and its people, ac-
cording to everything written in the book the
king of Judah has read. 17Because they have for-
saken me and burned incense to other gods and
provoked me to anger by all the idols their hands
have made,[i] my anger will burn against this
place and will not be quenched.' 18Tell the king of
Judah, who sent you to inquire of the LORD, 'This
is what the LORD, the God of Israel, says concern-
ing the words you heard: 19Because your heart
was responsive and you humbled yourself before
the LORD when you heard what I have spoken
against this place and its people, that they would
become accursed and laid waste, and because you
tore your robes and wept in my presence, I have
heard you, declares the LORD. 20Therefore I will
gather you to your fathers, and you will be buried

i17 Or *by everything they have done*

in peace. Your eyes will not see all the disaster I am going to bring on this place.' "

So they took her answer back to the king.

23 Then the king called together all the elders of Judah and Jerusalem. [2]He went up to the temple of the LORD with the men of Judah, the people of Jerusalem, the priests and the prophets—all the people from the least to the greatest. He read in their hearing all the words of the Book of the Covenant, which had been found in the temple of the LORD. [3]The king stood by the pillar and renewed the covenant in the presence of the LORD—to follow the LORD and keep his commands, regulations and decrees with all his heart and all his soul, thus confirming the words of the covenant written in this book. Then all the people pledged themselves to the covenant.

[4]The king ordered Hilkiah the high priest, the priests next in rank and the doorkeepers to remove from the temple of the LORD all the articles made for Baal and Asherah and all the starry hosts. He burned them outside Jerusalem in the fields of the Kidron Valley and took the ashes to Bethel. [5]He did away with the pagan priests appointed by the kings of Judah to burn incense on the high places of the towns of Judah and on those around Jerusalem—those who burned incense to Baal, to the sun and moon, to the constellations and to all the starry hosts. [6]He took the Asherah pole from the temple of the LORD to the Kidron Valley outside Jerusalem and burned it there. He ground it to powder and scattered the dust over the graves of the common people. [7]He also tore down the quarters of the male shrine prostitutes, which were in the temple of the LORD and where women did weaving for Asherah.

[8]Josiah brought all the priests from the towns of Judah and desecrated the high places, from Geba to Beersheba, where the priests had burned incense. He broke down the shrines[j] at the gates—at the entrance to the Gate of Joshua, the city governor, which is on the left of the city gate. [9]Although the priests of the high places did not serve at the altar of the LORD in Jerusalem, they ate unleavened bread with their fellow priests.

[10]He desecrated Topheth, which was in the Valley of Ben Hinnom, so no one could use it to sacrifice his son or daughter in[k] the fire to Molech. [11]He removed from the entrance to the temple of the LORD the horses that the kings of Judah had dedicated to the sun. They were in the court near the room of an official named Nathan-Melech. Josiah then burned the chariots dedicated to the sun.

[12]He pulled down the altars the kings of Judah had erected on the roof near the upper room of Ahaz, and the altars Manasseh had built in the two courts of the temple of the LORD. He removed them from there, smashed them to pieces and threw the rubble into the Kidron Valley. [13]The king also desecrated the high places that were east of Jerusalem on the south of the Hill of Corruption—the ones Solomon king of Israel had built for Ashtoreth the vile goddess of the Sidonians, for Chemosh the vile god of Moab, and for Molech[l] the detestable god of the people of Ammon. [14]Josiah smashed the sacred stones and cut down the Asherah poles and covered the sites with human bones.

[15]Even the altar at Bethel, the high place made by Jeroboam son of Nebat, who had caused Israel to sin—even that altar and high place he demolished. He burned the high place and ground it to powder, and burned the Asherah pole also. [16]Then Josiah looked around, and when he saw the tombs that were there on the hillside, he had the bones removed from them and burned on the altar to defile it, in accordance with the word of the LORD proclaimed by the man of God who foretold these things.

[17]The king asked, "What is that tombstone I see?"

The men of the city said, "It marks the tomb of the man of God who came from Judah and pronounced against the altar of Bethel the very things you have done to it."

[18]"Leave it alone," he said. "Don't let anyone disturb his bones." So they spared his bones and those of the prophet who had come from Samaria.

[19]Just as he had done at Bethel, Josiah removed and defiled all the shrines at the high places that the kings of Israel had built in the towns of Samaria that had provoked the LORD to anger. [20]Josiah slaughtered all the priests of those high places on the altars and burned human bones on them. Then he went back to Jerusalem.

[21]The king gave this order to all the people: "Celebrate the Passover to the LORD your God, as it is written in this Book of the Covenant." [22]Not since the days of the judges who led Israel, nor throughout the days of the kings of Israel and the

[j]8 Or *high places* [k]10 Or *to make his son or daughter pass through*
[l]13 Hebrew *Milcom*

kings of Judah, had any such Passover been ob-
served. [23]But in the eighteenth year of King Jo-
siah, this Passover was celebrated to the LORD in
Jerusalem.
[24]Furthermore, Josiah got rid of the mediums
and spiritists, the household gods, the idols and
all the other detestable things seen in Judah and
Jerusalem. This he did to fulfill the requirements
of the law written in the book that Hilkiah the
priest had discovered in the temple of the LORD.
[25]Neither before nor after Josiah was there a king
like him who turned to the LORD as he did—with
all his heart and with all his soul and with all his
strength, in accordance with all the Law of Moses.
[26]Nevertheless, the LORD did not turn away
from the heat of his fierce anger, which burned
against Judah because of all that Manasseh had
done to provoke him to anger. [27]So the LORD said,
"I will remove Judah also from my presence as I
removed Israel, and I will reject Jerusalem, the
city I chose, and this temple, about which I said,
'There shall my Name be.'[m]"
[28]As for the other events of Josiah's reign, and
all he did, are they not written in the book of the
annals of the kings of Judah?
[29]While Josiah was king, Pharaoh Neco king of
Egypt went up to the Euphrates River to help the
king of Assyria. King Josiah marched out to meet
him in battle, but Neco faced him and killed him
at Megiddo. [30]Josiah's servants brought his body
in a chariot from Megiddo to Jerusalem and bur-
ied him in his own tomb. And the people of the
land took Jehoahaz son of Josiah and anointed
him and made him king in place of his father.
[31]Jehoahaz was twenty-three years old when he
became king, and he reigned in Jerusalem three
months. His mother's name was Hamutal daugh-
ter of Jeremiah; she was from Libnah. [32]He did
evil in the eyes of the LORD, just as his fathers had
done. [33]Pharaoh Neco put him in chains at Riblah
in the land of Hamath[n] so that he might not
reign in Jerusalem, and he imposed on Judah a
levy of a hundred talents[o] of silver and a talent[p]
of gold. [34]Pharaoh Neco made Eliakim son of Jo-
siah king in place of his father Josiah and changed
Eliakim's name to Jehoiakim. But he took Jehoa-
haz and carried him off to Egypt, and there he
died. [35]Jehoiakim paid Pharaoh Neco the silver
and gold he demanded. In order to do so, he
taxed the land and exacted the silver and gold
from the people of the land according to their
assessments.

[m]27 1 Kings 8:29 [n]33 Hebrew; Septuagint (see also 2 Chron. 36:3) *Neco at Riblah in Hamath removed him* [o]33 That is, about 3 3/4 tons (about 3.4 metric tons) [p]33 That is, about 75 pounds (about 34 kilograms)

Discovering the Word 1. What steps led to finding the Book of the Law (22:1–8)? 2. What can you know about Huldah from verses 14–20? 3. What effect would you expect the scene in 23:1–3 to have on the people? 4. From 23:2–24 list some sixteen religious reforms that Josiah instituted. As you read through these reforms, what do you learn about the spiritual practices of the people before Josiah became king? 5. How does the description of Josiah in 23:25 contrast with the description of Jehoahaz in 23:31–34?

Applying the Word 1. What relationship do you see between our response to God's law and our concept of God? 2. Study more carefully the words in 2 Kings 23:25 describing Josiah's commitment to God and to God's law. What aspect of that description would you like to make more a part of your own commitment? 3. God's law is tied to his character. As you think of your own natural resistance to law, what steps could you take to bring your response to God's law into line with what you believe to be true of God?

Responding in Prayer Make 2 Kings 23:25 your prayer that you would turn to the Lord with all your heart, soul and strength.

13 / *2 Kings 23:36—25:30*
End of the Line

EZEKIEL 8

Dig you prophet, Dig in the wall
Probe the hole that opens to the night
Weep Ezekiel, Weep for your call

Crumble small the whitewash with your awl
Daubed by holy priests who smothered light
Dig you prophet, Dig in the wall

Dig you deeper, Dig back to the fall
Hasten shepherd, see your flock's in flight
Weep Ezekiel, Weep for your call

Hide your eyes and shrink from the small
Door that dries your bones as if you might
Not dig. You watchman, Dig in the wall

Seventy elders, sentries of God's law
Worship beasts and creatures slimed with blight
Weep Ezekiel, Weep for your call

Watch the Spirit flee among the tall
Cherubim, who bear Him out of sight
Hear the curse of God upon your wall
Weep you watchman, Weep for your call

—*Carolyn Nystrom, 1980*

Warming Up to God How do you feel when a Christian leader falls deep into sin?

Read 2 Kings 23:36—25:30.

[36]Jehoiakim was twenty-five years old when he became king, and he reigned in Jerusalem eleven years. His mother's name was Zebidah daughter of Pedaiah; she was from Rumah. [37]And he did evil in the eyes of the LORD, just as his fathers had done.

24 During Jehoiakim's reign, Nebuchadnezzar king of Babylon invaded the land, and Jehoiakim became his vassal for three years. But then he changed his mind and rebelled against Nebuchadnezzar. [2]The LORD sent Babylonian,[q] Aramean, Moabite and Ammonite raiders against him. He sent them to destroy Judah, in accordance with the word of the LORD proclaimed by his servants the prophets. [3]Surely these things happened to Judah according to the LORD's command, in order to remove them from his presence because of the sins of Manasseh and all he had done, [4]including the shedding of innocent blood. For he had filled Jerusalem with innocent blood, and the LORD was not willing to forgive.

[5]As for the other events of Jehoiakim's reign, and all he did, are they not written in the book of the annals of the kings of Judah? [6]Jehoiakim rested with his fathers. And Jehoiachin his son succeeded him as king.

[7]The king of Egypt did not march out from his own country again, because the king of Babylon had taken all his territory, from the Wadi of Egypt to the Euphrates River.

[8]Jehoiachin was eighteen years old when he became king, and he reigned in Jerusalem three months. His mother's name was Nehushta daughter of Elnathan; she was from Jerusalem. [9]He did evil in the eyes of the LORD, just as his father had done.

[10]At that time the officers of Nebuchadnezzar king of Babylon advanced on Jerusalem and laid

q2 Or *Chaldean*

siege to it, 11and Nebuchadnezzar himself came up to the city while his officers were besieging it. 12Jehoiachin king of Judah, his mother, his attendants, his nobles and his officials all surrendered to him.

In the eighth year of the reign of the king of Babylon, he took Jehoiachin prisoner. 13As the LORD had declared, Nebuchadnezzar removed all the treasures from the temple of the LORD and from the royal palace, and took away all the gold articles that Solomon king of Israel had made for the temple of the LORD. 14He carried into exile all Jerusalem: all the officers and fighting men, and all the craftsmen and artisans—a total of ten thousand. Only the poorest people of the land were left.

15Nebuchadnezzar took Jehoiachin captive to Babylon. He also took from Jerusalem to Babylon the king's mother, his wives, his officials and the leading men of the land. 16The king of Babylon also deported to Babylon the entire force of seven thousand fighting men, strong and fit for war, and a thousand craftsmen and artisans. 17He made Mattaniah, Jehoiachin's uncle, king in his place and changed his name to Zedekiah.

18Zedekiah was twenty-one years old when he became king, and he reigned in Jerusalem eleven years. His mother's name was Hamutal daughter of Jeremiah; she was from Libnah. 19He did evil in the eyes of the LORD, just as Jehoiakim had done. 20It was because of the LORD's anger that all this happened to Jerusalem and Judah, and in the end he thrust them from his presence.

Now Zedekiah rebelled against the king of Babylon.

25 So in the ninth year of Zedekiah's reign, on the tenth day of the tenth month, Nebuchadnezzar king of Babylon marched against Jerusalem with his whole army. He encamped outside the city and built siege works all around it. 2The city was kept under siege until the eleventh year of King Zedekiah. 3By the ninth day of the ⌊fourth⌋[r] month the famine in the city had become so severe that there was no food for the people to eat. 4Then the city wall was broken through, and the whole army fled at night through the gate between the two walls near the king's garden, though the Babylonians[s] were surrounding the city. They fled toward the Arabah,[t] 5but the Babylonian[u] army pursued the king and overtook him in the plains of Jericho. All his soldiers were separated from him and scattered, 6and he was captured. He was taken to the king of Babylon at Riblah, where sentence was pronounced on him. 7They killed the sons of Zedekiah before his eyes. Then they put out his eyes, bound him with bronze shackles and took him to Babylon.

8On the seventh day of the fifth month, in the nineteenth year of Nebuchadnezzar king of Babylon, Nebuzaradan commander of the imperial guard, an official of the king of Babylon, came to Jerusalem. 9He set fire to the temple of the LORD, the royal palace and all the houses of Jerusalem. Every important building he burned down. 10The whole Babylonian army, under the commander of the imperial guard, broke down the walls around Jerusalem. 11Nebuzaradan the commander of the guard carried into exile the people who remained in the city, along with the rest of the populace and those who had gone over to the king of Babylon. 12But the commander left behind some of the poorest people of the land to work the vineyards and fields.

13The Babylonians broke up the bronze pillars, the movable stands and the bronze Sea that were at the temple of the LORD and they carried the bronze to Babylon. 14They also took away the pots, shovels, wick trimmers, dishes and all the bronze articles used in the temple service. 15The commander of the imperial guard took away the censers and sprinkling bowls—all that were made of pure gold or silver.

16The bronze from the two pillars, the Sea and the movable stands, which Solomon had made for the temple of the LORD, was more than could be weighed. 17Each pillar was twenty-seven feet[v] high. The bronze capital on top of one pillar was four and a half feet[w] high and was decorated with a network and pomegranates of bronze all around. The other pillar, with its network, was similar.

18The commander of the guard took as prisoners Seraiah the chief priest, Zephaniah the priest next in rank and the three doorkeepers. 19Of those still in the city, he took the officer in charge of the fighting men and five royal advisers. He also took the secretary who was chief officer in charge of conscripting the people of the land and sixty of his men who were found in the city. 20Nebuzaradan the commander took them all and

[r]3 See Jer. 52:6. [s]4 Or *Chaldeans*; also in verses 13, 25 and 26 [t]4 Or *the Jordan Valley* [u]5 Or *Chaldean*; also in verses 10 and 24 [v]17 Hebrew *eighteen cubits* (about 8.1 meters) [w]17 Hebrew *three cubits* (about 1.3 meters)

brought them to the king of Babylon at Riblah. [21]There at Riblah, in the land of Hamath, the king had them executed.

So Judah went into captivity, away from her land.

[22]Nebuchadnezzar king of Babylon appointed Gedaliah son of Ahikam, the son of Shaphan, to be over the people he had left behind in Judah. [23]When all the army officers and their men heard that the king of Babylon had appointed Gedaliah as governor, they came to Gedaliah at Mizpah—Ishmael son of Nethaniah, Johanan son of Kareah, Seraiah son of Tanhumeth the Netophathite, Jaazaniah the son of the Maacathite, and their men. [24]Gedaliah took an oath to reassure them and their men. "Do not be afraid of the Babylonian officials," he said. "Settle down in the land and serve the king of Babylon, and it will go well with you."

[25]In the seventh month, however, Ishmael son of Nethaniah, the son of Elishama, who was of royal blood, came with ten men and assassinated Gedaliah and also the men of Judah and the Babylonians who were with him at Mizpah. [26]At this, all the people from the least to the greatest, together with the army officers, fled to Egypt for fear of the Babylonians.

[27]In the thirty-seventh year of the exile of Jehoiachin king of Judah, in the year Evil-Merodach[x] became king of Babylon, he released Jehoiachin from prison on the twenty-seventh day of the twelfth month. [28]He spoke kindly to him and gave him a seat of honor higher than those of the other kings who were with him in Babylon. [29]So Jehoiachin put aside his prison clothes and for the rest of his life ate regularly at the king's table. [30]Day by day the king gave Jehoiachin a regular allowance as long as he lived.

[x]27 Also called *Amel-Marduk*

Discovering the Word 1. Using the material you've read, trace the final steps of the nation of Judah. 2. What events in those final years make the strongest impression on your mind? Why? 3. Consider the history of Israel and Judah. What turning points do you see that led to this kind of end? 4. During the time that Zedekiah and his people were about to be deported to Babylon, the prophet Jeremiah wrote a letter to the Hebrew people already captive in Babylon. Read God's words to them in Jeremiah 29:10–14. If you had been a Hebrew captive in Babylon, what effect would these words have on the way you conducted your life during captivity?

Applying the Word 1. How might this study of Jewish history affect the way you pray for your own nation and its leaders? 2. What personal hope do the words from Jeremiah offer to you?

Responding in Prayer Take time to pray for specific national needs and leaders.

1 Chronicles

A flood devastates a community. Houses that were not swept away are filled knee-deep with mud. As the waters recede at last, the residents return and look at the damage. At first they're numb, then grief-stricken over their losses. Finally, they take courage and tackle the job of rebuilding, and soon a renewed community emerges from the wreckage.

That's the sort of situation that faced the Jews on their return to Jerusalem after their exile to Babylon. Their city and temple had been ransacked by Nebuchadnezzar in 587 B.C. (2Ki 25:8–12). After Persia took over Babylon, King Cyrus gave the Jews permission to return and rebuild. Nehemiah made an inspection tour and found massive destruction (Ne 2:11–17). It was enough to dishearten even the most loyal Jew.

Enter Ezra, the priest, traditionally considered the author of the Chronicles. (They were originally written as one book but later divided, probably because the single scroll was unwieldy for reading aloud in the synagogue.) Ezra was a man with a purpose. He made the journey back to Jerusalem to help rebuild the temple and restore the worship of God (Ezr 7:6–10). With everything in ruins, surrounded by unfriendly non-Jews who had been imported by Nebuchadnezzar, the people needed encouragement to begin—and finish—the work. They also needed admonitions to stay faithful to the Lord. The books of 1 and 2 Chronicles were apparently written to provide that encouragement and admonition.

At first glance the Chronicles don't look very encouraging! First Chronicles begins with one of those dreaded "name" lists: genealogies beginning all the way back with Adam. While it's not very interesting for us to read nine chapters of someone else's family tree, it must have been fascinating for the returning Jews to reestablish contact with their broken history.

After the genealogies, 1 Chronicles briefly sums up the life of Israel's first king, Saul, then begins a lengthy account of the life of King David. Skipping over David's sins and failures—we have to go to 2 Samuel to find those—it relates in adventure-story style the conquest of Jerusalem, triumphs of David and his warriors, the bringing of the ark of the covenant to Jerusalem, and David's dying in honor and high regard. Throughout the book the Lord's hand is seen, blessing obedience and faithfulness with success.

Our circumstances are different, but we still need encouragement to continue the work God has given us. What needs to be renewed in your life? During your quiet times in 1 Chronicles, you will discover those places where you need to seek renewal—and the courage you need to begin the process. You can praise God along with David: "In your hands are strength and power to exalt and give strength to all" (1Ch 29:12).

Outline

1 Chronicles 1—10

1 Adam, Seth, Enosh, [2]Kenan, Mahalalel, Jared, [3]Enoch, Methuselah, Lamech, Noah.

[4]The sons of Noah:[a]
Shem, Ham and Japheth.

[5]The sons[b] of Japheth:
Gomer, Magog, Madai, Javan, Tubal, Meshech and Tiras.
[6]The sons of Gomer:
Ashkenaz, Riphath[c] and Togarmah.
[7]The sons of Javan:
Elishah, Tarshish, the Kittim and the Rodanim.

[8]The sons of Ham:
Cush, Mizraim,[d] Put and Canaan.
[9]The sons of Cush:
Seba, Havilah, Sabta, Raamah and Sabteca.
The sons of Raamah:
Sheba and Dedan.
[10]Cush was the father[e] of
Nimrod, who grew to be a mighty warrior on earth.
[11]Mizraim was the father of
the Ludites, Anamites, Lehabites, Naphtuhites, [12]Pathrusites, Casluhites (from whom the Philistines came) and Caphtorites.
[13]Canaan was the father of
Sidon his firstborn,[f] and of the Hittites, [14]Jebusites, Amorites, Girgashites, [15]Hivites, Arkites, Sinites, [16]Arvadites, Zemarites and Hamathites.

[17]The sons of Shem:
Elam, Asshur, Arphaxad, Lud and Aram.
The sons of Aram[g]:
Uz, Hul, Gether and Meshech.
[18]Arphaxad was the father of Shelah,
and Shelah the father of Eber.
[19]Two sons were born to Eber:
One was named Peleg,[h] because in his time the earth was divided; his brother was named Joktan.
[20]Joktan was the father of
Almodad, Sheleph, Hazarmaveth, Jerah, [21]Hadoram, Uzal, Diklah, [22]Obal,[i] Abimael, Sheba, [23]Ophir, Havilah and Jobab. All these were sons of Joktan.

[24]Shem, Arphaxad,[j] Shelah,
[25]Eber, Peleg, Reu,
[26]Serug, Nahor, Terah
[27]and Abram (that is, Abraham).

[28]The sons of Abraham:
Isaac and Ishmael.
[29]These were their descendants:
Nebaioth the firstborn of Ishmael, Kedar, Adbeel, Mibsam, [30]Mishma, Dumah, Massa, Hadad, Tema, [31]Jetur, Naphish and Kedemah. These were the sons of Ishmael.

[32]The sons born to Keturah, Abraham's concubine:
Zimran, Jokshan, Medan, Midian, Ishbak and Shuah.
The sons of Jokshan:
Sheba and Dedan.
[33]The sons of Midian:
Ephah, Epher, Hanoch, Abida and Eldaah.
All these were descendants of Keturah.

[34]Abraham was the father of Isaac.
The sons of Isaac:
Esau and Israel.
[35]The sons of Esau:
Eliphaz, Reuel, Jeush, Jalam and Korah.
[36]The sons of Eliphaz:
Teman, Omar, Zepho,[k] Gatam and Kenaz;
by Timna: Amalek.[l]
[37]The sons of Reuel:
Nahath, Zerah, Shammah and Mizzah.

[38]The sons of Seir:

[a]4 Septuagint; Hebrew does not have *The sons of Noah:* [b]5 *Sons* may mean *descendants* or *successors* or *nations;* also in verses 6-10, 17 and 20. [c]6 Many Hebrew manuscripts and Vulgate (see also Septuagint and Gen. 10:3); most Hebrew manuscripts *Diphath* [d]8 That is, Egypt; also in verse 11 [e]10 *Father* may mean *ancestor* or *predecessor* or *founder;* also in verses 11, 13, 18 and 20. [f]13 Or *of the Sidonians, the foremost* [g]17 One Hebrew manuscript and some Septuagint manuscripts (see also Gen. 10:23); most Hebrew manuscripts do not have this line. [h]19 *Peleg* means *division.* [i]22 Some Hebrew manuscripts and Syriac (see also Gen. 10:28); most Hebrew manuscripts *Ebal* [j]24 Hebrew; some Septuagint manuscripts *Arphaxad, Cainan* (see also note at Gen. 11:10) [k]36 Many Hebrew manuscripts, some Septuagint manuscripts and Syriac (see also Gen. 36:11); most Hebrew manuscripts *Zephi* [l]36 Some Septuagint manuscripts (see also Gen. 36:12); Hebrew *Gatam, Kenaz, Timna and Amalek*

Lotan, Shobal, Zibeon, Anah, Dishon,
Ezer and Dishan.
39The sons of Lotan:
Hori and Homam. Timna was Lotan's sister.
40The sons of Shobal:
Alvan,[m] Manahath, Ebal, Shepho and Onam.
The sons of Zibeon:
Aiah and Anah.
41The son of Anah:
Dishon.
The sons of Dishon:
Hemdan,[n] Eshban, Ithran and Keran.
42The sons of Ezer:
Bilhan, Zaavan and Akan.[o]
The sons of Dishan[p]:
Uz and Aran.

43These were the kings who reigned in Edom
before any Israelite king reigned[q]:
Bela son of Beor, whose city was named Dinhabah.
44When Bela died, Jobab son of Zerah from
Bozrah succeeded him as king.
45When Jobab died, Husham from the land of
the Temanites succeeded him as king.
46When Husham died, Hadad son of Bedad,
who defeated Midian in the country of Moab, succeeded him as king. His city was named Avith.
47When Hadad died, Samlah from Masrekah
succeeded him as king.
48When Samlah died, Shaul from Rehoboth
on the river[r] succeeded him as king.
49When Shaul died, Baal-Hanan son of Acbor
succeeded him as king.
50When Baal-Hanan died, Hadad succeeded
him as king. His city was named Pau,[s] and his wife's name was Mehetabel daughter of Matred, the daughter of Me-
Zahab. 51Hadad also died.

The chiefs of Edom were:
Timna, Alvah, Jetheth, 52Oholibamah,
Elah, Pinon, 53Kenaz, Teman, Mibzar,
54Magdiel and Iram. These were the chiefs of Edom.

2

These were the sons of Israel:
Reuben, Simeon, Levi, Judah, Issachar,
Zebulun, 2Dan, Joseph, Benjamin,
Naphtali, Gad and Asher.

3The sons of Judah:
Er, Onan and Shelah. These three were born to him by a Canaanite woman, the daughter of Shua. Er, Judah's firstborn, was wicked in the LORD's sight; so the
LORD put him to death. 4Tamar, Judah's
daughter-in-law, bore him Perez and Zerah. Judah had five sons in all.

5The sons of Perez:
Hezron and Hamul.
6The sons of Zerah:
Zimri, Ethan, Heman, Calcol and Darda[t]—five in all.
7The son of Carmi:
Achar,[u] who brought trouble on Israel by violating the ban on taking devoted things.[v]
8The son of Ethan:
Azariah.
9The sons born to Hezron were:
Jerahmeel, Ram and Caleb.[w]
10Ram was the father of
Amminadab, and Amminadab the father of Nahshon, the leader of the people of
Judah. 11Nahshon was the father of Sal-
mon,[x] Salmon the father of Boaz, 12Boaz
the father of Obed and Obed the father of Jesse.
13Jesse was the father of
Eliab his firstborn; the second son was
Abinadab, the third Shimea, 14the fourth
Nethanel, the fifth Raddai, 15the sixth
Ozem and the seventh David. 16Their sisters were Zeruiah and Abigail. Zeruiah's three sons were Abishai, Joab and Asahel.
17Abigail was the mother of Amasa, whose father was Jether the Ishmaelite.

18Caleb son of Hezron had children by his wife Azubah (and by Jerioth). These were her sons: Jesher, Shobab and Ardon.
19When Azubah died, Caleb married Eph-

[m]40 Many Hebrew manuscripts and some Septuagint manuscripts (see also Gen. 36:23); most Hebrew manuscripts *Alian* [n]41 Many Hebrew manuscripts and some Septuagint manuscripts (see also Gen. 36:26); most Hebrew manuscripts *Hamran* [o]42 Many Hebrew and Septuagint manuscripts (see also Gen. 36:27); most Hebrew manuscripts *Zaavan, Jaakan* [p]42 Hebrew *Dishon*, a variant of *Dishan* [q]43 Or *before an Israelite king reigned over them* [r]48 Possibly the Euphrates [s]50 Many Hebrew manuscripts, some Septuagint manuscripts, Vulgate and Syriac (see also Gen. 36:39); most Hebrew manuscripts *Pai* [t]6 Many Hebrew manuscripts, some Septuagint manuscripts and Syriac (see also 1 Kings 4:31); most Hebrew manuscripts *Dara* [u]7 *Achar* means *trouble*; *Achar* is called *Achan* in Joshua. [v]7 The Hebrew term refers to the irrevocable giving over of things or persons to the LORD, often by totally destroying them. [w]9 Hebrew *Kelubai*, a variant of *Caleb* [x]11 Septuagint (see also Ruth 4:21); Hebrew *Salma*

rath, who bore him Hur. [20]Hur was the
father of Uri, and Uri the father of Beza-
lel.
[21]Later, Hezron lay with the daughter of Ma-
kir the father of Gilead (he had married
her when he was sixty years old), and she
bore him Segub. [22]Segub was the father of
Jair, who controlled twenty-three towns
in Gilead. [23](But Geshur and Aram cap-
tured Havvoth Jair,[y] as well as Kenath
with its surrounding settlements—sixty
towns.) All these were descendants of
Makir the father of Gilead.

[24]After Hezron died in Caleb Ephrathah, Abi-
jah the wife of Hezron bore him Ashhur
the father[z] of Tekoa.

[25]The sons of Jerahmeel the firstborn of Hez-
ron:
Ram his firstborn, Bunah, Oren, Ozem
and[a] Ahijah. [26]Jerahmeel had another
wife, whose name was Atarah; she was
the mother of Onam.
[27]The sons of Ram the firstborn of Jerahmeel:
Maaz, Jamin and Eker.
[28]The sons of Onam:
Shammai and Jada.
The sons of Shammai:
Nadab and Abishur.
[29]Abishur's wife was named Abihail, who bore
him Ahban and Molid.
[30]The sons of Nadab:
Seled and Appaim. Seled died without
children.
[31]The son of Appaim:
Ishi, who was the father of Sheshan.
Sheshan was the father of Ahlai.
[32]The sons of Jada, Shammai's brother:
Jether and Jonathan. Jether died without
children.
[33]The sons of Jonathan:
Peleth and Zaza.
These were the descendants of Jerahmeel.
[34]Sheshan had no sons—only daughters.
He had an Egyptian servant named Jarha.
[35]Sheshan gave his daughter in marriage
to his servant Jarha, and she bore him
Attai.
[36]Attai was the father of Nathan,
Nathan the father of Zabad,
[37]Zabad the father of Ephlal,
Ephlal the father of Obed,
[38]Obed the father of Jehu,
Jehu the father of Azariah,
[39]Azariah the father of Helez,
Helez the father of Eleasah,
[40]Eleasah the father of Sismai,
Sismai the father of Shallum,
[41]Shallum the father of Jekamiah,
and Jekamiah the father of Elishama.

[42]The sons of Caleb the brother of Jerahmeel:
Mesha his firstborn, who was the father
of Ziph, and his son Mareshah,[b] who
was the father of Hebron.
[43]The sons of Hebron:
Korah, Tappuah, Rekem and Shema.
[44]Shema was the father of Raham, and Ra-
ham the father of Jorkeam. Rekem was
the father of Shammai. [45]The son of
Shammai was Maon, and Maon was the
father of Beth Zur.
[46]Caleb's concubine Ephah was the mother of
Haran, Moza and Gazez. Haran was the
father of Gazez.
[47]The sons of Jahdai:
Regem, Jotham, Geshan, Pelet, Ephah
and Shaaph.
[48]Caleb's concubine Maacah was the mother
of Sheber and Tirhanah. [49]She also gave
birth to Shaaph the father of Madmannah
and to Sheva the father of Machenah and
Gibea. Caleb's daughter was Acsah.
[50]These were the descendants of Caleb.

The sons of Hur the firstborn of Ephrathah:
Shobal the father of Kiriath Jearim,
[51]Salma the father of Bethlehem, and Ha-
reph the father of Beth Gader.
[52]The descendants of Shobal the father of Kir-
iath Jearim were:
Haroeh, half the Manahathites, [53]and the
clans of Kiriath Jearim: the Ithrites, Pu-
thites, Shumathites and Mishraites. From
these descended the Zorathites and Esh-
taolites.
[54]The descendants of Salma:
Bethlehem, the Netophathites, Atroth
Beth Joab, half the Manahathites, the Zo-
rites, [55]and the clans of scribes[c] who
lived at Jabez: the Tirathites, Shimeathites
and Sucathites. These are the Kenites

[y]23 Or *captured the settlements of Jair* [z]24 *Father* may mean *civic leader* or *military leader*; also in verses 42, 45, 49-52 and possibly elsewhere. [a]25 Or *Oren and Ozem, by* [b]42 The meaning of the Hebrew for this phrase is uncertain. [c]55 Or *of the Sopherites*

who came from Hammath, the father of
the house of Recab.[d]

3 These were the sons of David born to him
in Hebron:
The firstborn was Amnon the son of
Ahinoam of Jezreel;
the second, Daniel the son of Abigail of
Carmel;
2the third, Absalom the son of Maacah
daughter of Talmai king of Geshur;
the fourth, Adonijah the son of Haggith;
3the fifth, Shephatiah the son of Abital;
and the sixth, Ithream, by his wife Eglah.
4These six were born to David in Hebron,
where he reigned seven years and six
months.
David reigned in Jerusalem thirty-three years,
5and these were the children born to him there:
Shammua,[e] Shobab, Nathan and Solo-
mon. These four were by Bathsheba[f]
daughter of Ammiel. 6There were also Ib-
har, Elishua,[g] Eliphelet, 7Nogah, Ne-
pheg, Japhia, 8Elishama, Eliada and
Eliphelet—nine in all. 9All these were the
sons of David, besides his sons by his
concubines. And Tamar was their sister.

10Solomon's son was Rehoboam,
Abijah his son,
Asa his son,
Jehoshaphat his son,
11Jehoram[h] his son,
Ahaziah his son,
Joash his son,
12Amaziah his son,
Azariah his son,
Jotham his son,
13Ahaz his son,
Hezekiah his son,
Manasseh his son,
14Amon his son,
Josiah his son.
15The sons of Josiah:
Johanan the firstborn,
Jehoiakim the second son,
Zedekiah the third,
Shallum the fourth.
16The successors of Jehoiakim:
Jehoiachin[i] his son,
and Zedekiah.
17The descendants of Jehoiachin the captive:
Shealtiel his son, 18Malkiram, Pedaiah,
Shenazzar, Jekamiah, Hoshama and Ned-
abiah.
19The sons of Pedaiah:
Zerubbabel and Shimei.
The sons of Zerubbabel:
Meshullam and Hananiah.
Shelomith was their sister.
20There were also five others:
Hashubah, Ohel, Berekiah, Hasadiah and
Jushab-Hesed.
21The descendants of Hananiah:
Pelatiah and Jeshaiah, and the sons of Re-
phaiah, of Arnan, of Obadiah and of
Shecaniah.
22The descendants of Shecaniah:
Shemaiah and his sons:
Hattush, Igal, Bariah, Neariah and Sha-
phat—six in all.
23The sons of Neariah:
Elioenai, Hizkiah and Azrikam—three in
all.
24The sons of Elioenai:
Hodaviah, Eliashib, Pelaiah, Akkub, Joha-
nan, Delaiah and Anani—seven in all.

4 The descendants of Judah:
Perez, Hezron, Carmi, Hur and Shobal.
2Reaiah son of Shobal was the father of
Jahath, and Jahath the father of Ahumai
and Lahad. These were the clans of the
Zorathites.
3These were the sons[j] of Etam:
Jezreel, Ishma and Idbash. Their sister
was named Hazzelelponi. 4Penuel was the
father of Gedor, and Ezer the father of
Hushah.
These were the descendants of Hur, the
firstborn of Ephrathah and father[k] of
Bethlehem.
5Ashhur the father of Tekoa had two wives,
Helah and Naarah.
6Naarah bore him Ahuzzam, Hepher, Tem-
eni and Haahashtari. These were the
descendants of Naarah.
7The sons of Helah:

[d]55 Or *father of Beth Recab* [e]5 Hebrew *Shimea*, a variant of *Shammua* [f]5 One Hebrew manuscript and Vulgate (see also Septuagint and 2 Samuel 11:3); most Hebrew manuscripts *Bathshua* [g]6 Two Hebrew manuscripts (see also 2 Samuel 5:15 and 1 Chron. 14:5); most Hebrew manuscripts *Elishama* [h]11 Hebrew *Joram*, a variant of *Jehoram* [i]16 Hebrew *Jeconiah*, a variant of *Jehoiachin*; also in verse 17 [j]3 Some Septuagint manuscripts (see also Vulgate); Hebrew *father* [k]4 *Father* may mean *civic leader* or *military leader*; also in verses 12, 14, 17, 18 and possibly elsewhere.

Zereth, Zohar, Ethnan, 8and Koz, who was the father of Anub and Hazzobebah and of the clans of Aharhel son of Harum.

9Jabez was more honorable than his brothers. His mother had named him Jabez,[l] saying, "I gave birth to him in pain." 10Jabez cried out to the God of Israel, "Oh, that you would bless me and enlarge my territory! Let your hand be with me, and keep me from harm so that I will be free from pain." And God granted his request.

11Kelub, Shuhah's brother, was the father of Mehir, who was the father of Eshton. 12Eshton was the father of Beth Rapha, Paseah and Tehinnah the father of Ir Nahash.[m] These were the men of Recah.

13The sons of Kenaz:
Othniel and Seraiah.
The sons of Othniel:
Hathath and Meonothai.[n] 14Meonothai was the father of Ophrah.
Seraiah was the father of Joab,
the father of Ge Harashim.[o] It was called this because its people were craftsmen.

15The sons of Caleb son of Jephunneh:
Iru, Elah and Naam.
The son of Elah:
Kenaz.

16The sons of Jehallelel:
Ziph, Ziphah, Tiria and Asarel.

17The sons of Ezrah:
Jether, Mered, Epher and Jalon. One of Mered's wives gave birth to Miriam, Shammai and Ishbah the father of Eshtemoa. 18(His Judean wife gave birth to Jered the father of Gedor, Heber the father of Soco, and Jekuthiel the father of Zanoah.) These were the children of Pharaoh's daughter Bithiah, whom Mered had married.

19The sons of Hodiah's wife, the sister of Naham:
the father of Keilah the Garmite, and Eshtemoa the Maacathite.

20The sons of Shimon:
Amnon, Rinnah, Ben-Hanan and Tilon.
The descendants of Ishi:
Zoheth and Ben-Zoheth.

21The sons of Shelah son of Judah:
Er the father of Lecah, Laadah the father of Mareshah and the clans of the linen workers at Beth Ashbea, 22Jokim, the men of Cozeba, and Joash and Saraph, who ruled in Moab and Jashubi Lehem. (These records are from ancient times.) 23They were the potters who lived at Netaim and Gederah; they stayed there and worked for the king.

24The descendants of Simeon:
Nemuel, Jamin, Jarib, Zerah and Shaul;
25Shallum was Shaul's son, Mibsam his son and Mishma his son.

26The descendants of Mishma:
Hammuel his son, Zaccur his son and Shimei his son.

27Shimei had sixteen sons and six daughters, but his brothers did not have many children; so their entire clan did not become as numerous as the people of Judah. 28They lived in Beersheba, Moladah, Hazar Shual, 29Bilhah, Ezem, Tolad, 30Bethuel, Hormah, Ziklag, 31Beth Marcaboth, Hazar Susim, Beth Biri and Shaaraim. These were their towns until the reign of David. 32Their surrounding villages were Etam, Ain, Rimmon, Token and Ashan—five towns— 33and all the villages around these towns as far as Baalath.[p] These were their settlements. And they kept a genealogical record.

34Meshobab, Jamlech, Joshah son of Amaziah, 35Joel, Jehu son of Joshibiah, the son of Seraiah, the son of Asiel, 36also Elioenai, Jaakobah, Jeshohaiah, Asaiah, Adiel, Jesimiel, Benaiah, 37and Ziza son of Shiphi, the son of Allon, the son of Jedaiah, the son of Shimri, the son of Shemaiah.

38The men listed above by name were leaders of their clans. Their families increased greatly, 39and they went to the outskirts of Gedor to the east of the valley in search of pasture for their flocks. 40They found rich, good pasture, and the land was spacious, peaceful and quiet. Some Hamites had lived there formerly.

41The men whose names were listed came in the days of Hezekiah king of Judah. They attacked the Hamites in their dwellings and also the Meunites who were there and completely destroyed[q] them, as is evident to this day. Then

[l]9 *Jabez* sounds like the Hebrew for *pain.* [m]12 Or *of the city of Nahash* [n]13 Some Septuagint manuscripts and Vulgate; Hebrew does not have *and Meonothai.* [o]14 *Ge Harashim* means *valley of craftsmen.* [p]33 Some Septuagint manuscripts (see also Joshua 19:8); Hebrew *Baal* [q]41 The Hebrew term refers to the irrevocable giving over of things or persons to the LORD, often by totally destroying them.

they settled in their place, because there was pas-
ture for their flocks. 42And five hundred of these
Simeonites, led by Pelatiah, Neariah, Rephaiah
and Uzziel, the sons of Ishi, invaded the hill
country of Seir. 43They killed the remaining Ama-
lekites who had escaped, and they have lived
there to this day.

5 The sons of Reuben the firstborn of Israel
(he was the firstborn, but when he defiled
his father's marriage bed, his rights as
firstborn were given to the sons of Joseph son of
Israel; so he could not be listed in the genealogi-
cal record in accordance with his birthright, 2and
though Judah was the strongest of his brothers
and a ruler came from him, the rights of the first-
born belonged to Joseph)— 3the sons of Reuben
the firstborn of Israel:

Hanoch, Pallu, Hezron and Carmi.

4The descendants of Joel:

Shemaiah his son, Gog his son,
Shimei his son, 5Micah his son,
Reaiah his son, Baal his son,
6and Beerah his son, whom Tiglath-Pile-
ser[r] king of Assyria took into exile. Bee-
rah was a leader of the Reubenites.

7Their relatives by clans, listed according to
their genealogical records:

Jeiel the chief, Zechariah, 8and Bela son of
Azaz, the son of Shema, the son of Joel.
They settled in the area from Aroer to
Nebo and Baal Meon. 9To the east they
occupied the land up to the edge of the
desert that extends to the Euphrates
River, because their livestock had in-
creased in Gilead.

10During Saul's reign they waged war
against the Hagrites, who were defeated at
their hands; they occupied the dwellings of
the Hagrites throughout the entire region
east of Gilead.

11The Gadites lived next to them in Bashan,
as far as Salecah:

12Joel was the chief, Shapham the second,
then Janai and Shaphat, in Bashan.

13Their relatives, by families, were:

Michael, Meshullam, Sheba, Jorai, Jacan,
Zia and Eber—seven in all.

14These were the sons of Abihail son of
Huri, the son of Jaroah, the son of Gilead,
the son of Michael, the son of Jeshishai,
the son of Jahdo, the son of Buz.

15Ahi son of Abdiel, the son of Guni, was
head of their family.

16The Gadites lived in Gilead, in Bashan and
its outlying villages, and on all the pas-
turelands of Sharon as far as they ex-
tended.

17All these were entered in the genealogical
records during the reigns of Jotham king of Judah
and Jeroboam king of Israel.

18The Reubenites, the Gadites and the half-
tribe of Manasseh had 44,760 men ready for mili-
tary service—able-bodied men who could handle
shield and sword, who could use a bow, and who
were trained for battle. 19They waged war against
the Hagrites, Jetur, Naphish and Nodab. 20They
were helped in fighting them, and God handed
the Hagrites and all their allies over to them, be-
cause they cried out to him during the battle. He
answered their prayers, because they trusted in
him. 21They seized the livestock of the Hagrites—
fifty thousand camels, two hundred fifty thou-
sand sheep and two thousand donkeys. They also
took one hundred thousand people captive, 22and
many others fell slain, because the battle was
God's. And they occupied the land until the exile.

23The people of the half-tribe of Manasseh were
numerous; they settled in the land from Bashan to
Baal Hermon, that is, to Senir (Mount Hermon).

24These were the heads of their families: Epher,
Ishi, Eliel, Azriel, Jeremiah, Hodaviah and Jah-
diel. They were brave warriors, famous men, and
heads of their families. 25But they were unfaithful
to the God of their fathers and prostituted them-
selves to the gods of the peoples of the land,
whom God had destroyed before them. 26So the
God of Israel stirred up the spirit of Pul king of
Assyria (that is, Tiglath-Pileser king of Assyria),
who took the Reubenites, the Gadites and the
half-tribe of Manasseh into exile. He took them to
Halah, Habor, Hara and the river of Gozan, where
they are to this day.

6 The sons of Levi:

Gershon, Kohath and Merari.

2The sons of Kohath:

Amram, Izhar, Hebron and Uzziel.

3The children of Amram:

Aaron, Moses and Miriam.

The sons of Aaron:

Nadab, Abihu, Eleazar and Ithamar.

r6 Hebrew *Tilgath-Pilneser,* a variant of *Tiglath-Pileser;* also in verse 26

4Eleazar was the father of Phinehas,
Phinehas the father of Abishua,
5Abishua the father of Bukki,
Bukki the father of Uzzi,
6Uzzi the father of Zerahiah,
Zerahiah the father of Meraioth,
7Meraioth the father of Amariah,
Amariah the father of Ahitub,
8Ahitub the father of Zadok,
Zadok the father of Ahimaaz,
9Ahimaaz the father of Azariah,
Azariah the father of Johanan,
10Johanan the father of Azariah (it was he
who served as priest in the temple Solo-
mon built in Jerusalem),
11Azariah the father of Amariah,
Amariah the father of Ahitub,
12Ahitub the father of Zadok,
Zadok the father of Shallum,
13Shallum the father of Hilkiah,
Hilkiah the father of Azariah,
14Azariah the father of Seraiah,
and Seraiah the father of Jehozadak.
15Jehozadak was deported when the LORD sent
Judah and Jerusalem into exile by the hand
of Nebuchadnezzar.

16The sons of Levi:
Gershon,[s] Kohath and Merari.
17These are the names of the sons of Gershon:
Libni and Shimei.
18The sons of Kohath:
Amram, Izhar, Hebron and Uzziel.
19The sons of Merari:
Mahli and Mushi.
These are the clans of the Levites listed ac-
cording to their fathers:
20Of Gershon:
Libni his son, Jehath his son,
Zimmah his son, 21Joah his son,
Iddo his son, Zerah his son
and Jeatherai his son.
22The descendants of Kohath:
Amminadab his son, Korah his son,
Assir his son, 23Elkanah his son,
Ebiasaph his son, Assir his son,
24Tahath his son, Uriel his son,
Uzziah his son and Shaul his son.
25The descendants of Elkanah:
Amasai, Ahimoth,
26Elkanah his son,[t] Zophai his son,
Nahath his son, 27Eliab his son,
Jeroham his son, Elkanah his son
and Samuel his son.[u]
28The sons of Samuel:
Joel[v] the firstborn
and Abijah the second son.
29The descendants of Merari:
Mahli, Libni his son,
Shimei his son, Uzzah his son,
30Shimea his son, Haggiah his son
and Asaiah his son.

31These are the men David put in charge of the
music in the house of the LORD after the ark came
to rest there. 32They ministered with music before
the tabernacle, the Tent of Meeting, until Solo-
mon built the temple of the LORD in Jerusalem.
They performed their duties according to the reg-
ulations laid down for them.

33Here are the men who served, together with
their sons:
From the Kohathites:
Heman, the musician,
the son of Joel, the son of Samuel,
34the son of Elkanah, the son of Jeroham,
the son of Eliel, the son of Toah,
35the son of Zuph, the son of Elkanah,
the son of Mahath, the son of Amasai,
36the son of Elkanah, the son of Joel,
the son of Azariah, the son of Zephaniah,
37the son of Tahath, the son of Assir,
the son of Ebiasaph, the son of Korah,
38the son of Izhar, the son of Kohath,
the son of Levi, the son of Israel;
39and Heman's associate Asaph, who served at
his right hand:
Asaph son of Berekiah, the son of Shimea,
40the son of Michael, the son of Baaseiah,[w]
the son of Malkijah, 41the son of Ethni,
the son of Zerah, the son of Adaiah,
42the son of Ethan, the son of Zimmah,
the son of Shimei, 43the son of Jahath,
the son of Gershon, the son of Levi;
44and from their associates, the Merarites, at
his left hand:
Ethan son of Kishi, the son of Abdi,

[s]*16* Hebrew *Gershom,* a variant of *Gershon;* also in verses 17, 20, 43, 62 and 71 [t]*26* Some Hebrew manuscripts, Septuagint and Syriac; most Hebrew manuscripts *Ahimoth 26and Elkanah. The sons of Elkanah:* [u]*27* Some Septuagint manuscripts (see also 1 Samuel 1:19,20 and 1 Chron. 6:33,34); Hebrew does not have *and Samuel his son.* [v]*28* Some Septuagint manuscripts and Syriac (see also 1 Samuel 8:2 and 1 Chron. 6:33); Hebrew does not have *Joel.* [w]*40* Most Hebrew manuscripts; some Hebrew manuscripts, one Septuagint manuscript and Syriac *Maaseiah*

the son of Malluch, [45]the son of Hasha-
biah,
the son of Amaziah, the son of Hilkiah,
[46]the son of Amzi, the son of Bani,
the son of Shemer, [47]the son of Mahli,
the son of Mushi, the son of Merari,
the son of Levi.

[48]Their fellow Levites were assigned to all the
other duties of the tabernacle, the house of God.
[49]But Aaron and his descendants were the ones
who presented offerings on the altar of burnt of-
fering and on the altar of incense in connection
with all that was done in the Most Holy Place,
making atonement for Israel, in accordance with
all that Moses the servant of God had com-
manded.

[50]These were the descendants of Aaron:
Eleazar his son, Phinehas his son,
Abishua his son, [51]Bukki his son,
Uzzi his son, Zerahiah his son,
[52]Meraioth his son, Amariah his son,
Ahitub his son, [53]Zadok his son
and Ahimaaz his son.

[54]These were the locations of their settlements
allotted as their territory (they were assigned to
the descendants of Aaron who were from the Ko-
hathite clan, because the first lot was for them):
[55]They were given Hebron in Judah with
its surrounding pasturelands. [56]But the fields
and villages around the city were given to
Caleb son of Jephunneh.
[57]So the descendants of Aaron were given
Hebron (a city of refuge), and Libnah,[x] Jat-
tir, Eshtemoa, [58]Hilen, Debir, [59]Ashan, Jut-
tah[y] and Beth Shemesh, together with their
pasturelands. [60]And from the tribe of Benja-
min they were given Gibeon,[z] Geba, Ale-
meth and Anathoth, together with their pas-
turelands.

These towns, which were distributed
among the Kohathite clans, were thirteen in
all.

[61]The rest of Kohath's descendants were allot-
ted ten towns from the clans of half the tribe of
Manasseh.

[62]The descendants of Gershon, clan by clan,
were allotted thirteen towns from the tribes of
Issachar, Asher and Naphtali, and from the part
of the tribe of Manasseh that is in Bashan.

[63]The descendants of Merari, clan by clan, were
allotted twelve towns from the tribes of Reuben,
Gad and Zebulun.

[64]So the Israelites gave the Levites these towns
and their pasturelands. [65]From the tribes of Ju-
dah, Simeon and Benjamin they allotted the pre-
viously named towns.

[66]Some of the Kohathite clans were given as
their territory towns from the tribe of Ephraim.

[67]In the hill country of Ephraim they were
given Shechem (a city of refuge), and Ge-
zer,[a] [68]Jokmeam, Beth Horon, [69]Aijalon and
Gath Rimmon, together with their pasture-
lands.

[70]And from half the tribe of Manasseh the
Israelites gave Aner and Bileam, together
with their pasturelands, to the rest of the Ko-
hathite clans.

[71]The Gershonites received the following:
From the clan of the half-tribe of Manasseh
they received Golan in Bashan and also
Ashtaroth, together with their pasture-
lands;
[72]from the tribe of Issachar
they received Kedesh, Daberath, [73]Ra-
moth and Anem, together with their pas-
turelands;
[74]from the tribe of Asher
they received Mashal, Abdon, [75]Hukok
and Rehob, together with their pasture-
lands;
[76]and from the tribe of Naphtali
they received Kedesh in Galilee, Hammon
and Kiriathaim, together with their pas-
turelands.

[77]The Merarites (the rest of the Levites) re-
ceived the following:
From the tribe of Zebulun
they received Jokneam, Kartah,[b] Rim-
mono and Tabor, together with their pas-
turelands;
[78]from the tribe of Reuben across the Jordan
east of Jericho
they received Bezer in the desert, Jahzah,
[79]Kedemoth and Mephaath, together with
their pasturelands;
[80]and from the tribe of Gad

[x]57 See Joshua 21:13; Hebrew *given the cities of refuge: Hebron, Libnah.*
[y]59 Syriac (see also Septuagint and Joshua 21:16); Hebrew does not have *Juttah.* [z]60 See Joshua 21:17; Hebrew does not have *Gibeon.*
[a]67 See Joshua 21:21; Hebrew *given the cities of refuge: Shechem, Gezer.*
[b]77 See Septuagint and Joshua 21:34; Hebrew does not have *Jokneam, Kartah.*

they received Ramoth in Gilead, Maha-
naim, 81Heshbon and Jazer, together with
their pasturelands.

7 The sons of Issachar:
Tola, Puah, Jashub and Shimron—four
in all.

2The sons of Tola:
Uzzi, Rephaiah, Jeriel, Jahmai, Ibsam and
Samuel—heads of their families. During
the reign of David, the descendants of
Tola listed as fighting men in their gene-
alogy numbered 22,600.

3The son of Uzzi:
Izrahiah.

The sons of Izrahiah:
Michael, Obadiah, Joel and Isshiah. All
five of them were chiefs. 4According to
their family genealogy, they had 36,000
men ready for battle, for they had many
wives and children.

5The relatives who were fighting men be-
longing to all the clans of Issachar, as
listed in their genealogy, were 87,000 in
all.

6Three sons of Benjamin:
Bela, Beker and Jediael.

7The sons of Bela:
Ezbon, Uzzi, Uzziel, Jerimoth and Iri,
heads of families—five in all. Their gene-
alogical record listed 22,034 fighting
men.

8The sons of Beker:
Zemirah, Joash, Eliezer, Elioenai, Omri,
Jeremoth, Abijah, Anathoth and Alemeth.
All these were the sons of Beker. 9Their
genealogical record listed the heads of
families and 20,200 fighting men.

10The son of Jediael:
Bilhan.

The sons of Bilhan:
Jeush, Benjamin, Ehud, Kenaanah, Ze-
than, Tarshish and Ahishahar. 11All these
sons of Jediael were heads of families.
There were 17,200 fighting men ready to
go out to war.

12The Shuppites and Huppites were the
descendants of Ir, and the Hushites the
descendants of Aher.

13The sons of Naphtali:
Jahziel, Guni, Jezer and Shillem[c]—the
descendants of Bilhah.

14The descendants of Manasseh:

Asriel was his descendant through his Ar-
amean concubine. She gave birth to Makir
the father of Gilead. 15Makir took a wife
from among the Huppites and Shuppites.
His sister's name was Maacah.

Another descendant was named Zelophe-
had, who had only daughters.

16Makir's wife Maacah gave birth to a son
and named him Peresh. His brother was
named Sheresh, and his sons were Ulam
and Rakem.

17The son of Ulam:
Bedan.

These were the sons of Gilead son of Makir,
the son of Manasseh. 18His sister Ham-
moleketh gave birth to Ishhod, Abiezer
and Mahlah.

19The sons of Shemida were:
Ahian, Shechem, Likhi and Aniam.

20The descendants of Ephraim:
Shuthelah, Bered his son,
Tahath his son, Eleadah his son,
Tahath his son, 21Zabad his son
and Shuthelah his son.

Ezer and Elead were killed by the native-
born men of Gath, when they went down to
seize their livestock. 22Their father Ephraim
mourned for them many days, and his rela-
tives came to comfort him. 23Then he lay
with his wife again, and she became preg-
nant and gave birth to a son. He named him
Beriah,[d] because there had been misfor-
tune in his family. 24His daughter was Shee-
rah, who built Lower and Upper Beth Ho-
ron as well as Uzzen Sheerah.

25Rephah was his son, Resheph his son,[e]
Telah his son, Tahan his son,
26Ladan his son, Ammihud his son,
Elishama his son, 27Nun his son
and Joshua his son.

28Their lands and settlements included Bethel
and its surrounding villages, Naaran to the east,
Gezer and its villages to the west, and Shechem
and its villages all the way to Ayyah and its vil-
lages. 29Along the borders of Manasseh were Beth

[c]13 Some Hebrew and Septuagint manuscripts (see also Gen. 46:24 and Num. 26:49); most Hebrew manuscripts *Shallum* [d]23 *Beriah* sounds like the Hebrew for *misfortune*. [e]25 Some Septuagint manuscripts; Hebrew does not have *his son*.

Shan, Taanach, Megiddo and Dor, together with
their villages. The descendants of Joseph son of
Israel lived in these towns.

30The sons of Asher:
Imnah, Ishvah, Ishvi and Beriah. Their
sister was Serah.
31The sons of Beriah:
Heber and Malkiel, who was the father of
Birzaith.
32Heber was the father of Japhlet, Shomer and
Hotham and of their sister Shua.
33The sons of Japhlet:
Pasach, Bimhal and Ashvath.
These were Japhlet's sons.
34The sons of Shomer:
Ahi, Rohgah,[f] Hubbah and Aram.
35The sons of his brother Helem:
Zophah, Imna, Shelesh and Amal.
36The sons of Zophah:
Suah, Harnepher, Shual, Beri, Imrah,
37Bezer, Hod, Shamma, Shilshah, Ithran[g]
and Beera.
38The sons of Jether:
Jephunneh, Pispah and Ara.
39The sons of Ulla:
Arah, Hanniel and Rizia.
40All these were descendants of Asher—heads
of families, choice men, brave warriors and out-
standing leaders. The number of men ready for
battle, as listed in their genealogy, was 26,000.

8 Benjamin was the father of Bela his first-
born,
Ashbel the second son, Aharah the
third,
2Nohah the fourth and Rapha the fifth.
3The sons of Bela were:
Addar, Gera, Abihud,[h] 4Abishua, Naa-
man, Ahoah, 5Gera, Shephuphan and Hu-
ram.
6These were the descendants of Ehud, who
were heads of families of those living in
Geba and were deported to Manahath:
7Naaman, Ahijah, and Gera, who deported
them and who was the father of Uzza and
Ahihud.
8Sons were born to Shaharaim in Moab after
he had divorced his wives Hushim and
Baara. 9By his wife Hodesh he had Jobab,
Zibia, Mesha, Malcam, 10Jeuz, Sakia and
Mirmah. These were his sons, heads of
families. 11By Hushim he had Abitub and
Elpaal.
12The sons of Elpaal:
Eber, Misham, Shemed (who built Ono
and Lod with its surrounding villages),
13and Beriah and Shema, who were heads
of families of those living in Aijalon and
who drove out the inhabitants of Gath.
14Ahio, Shashak, Jeremoth, 15Zebadiah, Arad,
Eder, 16Michael, Ishpah and Joha were
the sons of Beriah.
17Zebadiah, Meshullam, Hizki, Heber, 18Ish-
merai, Izliah and Jobab were the sons of
Elpaal.
19Jakim, Zicri, Zabdi, 20Elienai, Zillethai,
Eliel, 21Adaiah, Beraiah and Shimrath
were the sons of Shimei.
22Ishpan, Eber, Eliel, 23Abdon, Zicri, Hanan,
24Hananiah, Elam, Anthothijah, 25Iphde-
iah and Penuel were the sons of Shashak.
26Shamsherai, Shehariah, Athaliah, 27Jaare-
shiah, Elijah and Zicri were the sons of
Jeroham.
28All these were heads of families, chiefs as
listed in their genealogy, and they lived in Jerusa-
lem.

29Jeiel[i] the father[j] of Gibeon lived in Gib-
eon.
His wife's name was Maacah, 30and his
firstborn son was Abdon, followed by
Zur, Kish, Baal, Ner,[k] Nadab, 31Gedor,
Ahio, Zeker 32and Mikloth, who was the
father of Shimeah. They too lived near
their relatives in Jerusalem.
33Ner was the father of Kish, Kish the father
of Saul, and Saul the father of Jonathan,
Malki-Shua, Abinadab and Esh-Baal.[l]
34The son of Jonathan:
Merib-Baal,[m] who was the father of Mi-
cah.
35The sons of Micah:
Pithon, Melech, Tarea and Ahaz.
36Ahaz was the father of Jehoaddah, Jeho-
addah was the father of Alemeth, Azma-
veth and Zimri, and Zimri was the father
of Moza. 37Moza was the father of Binea;

[f]34 Or *of his brother Shomer: Rohgah* [g]37 Possibly a variant of *Jether* [h]3 Or *Gera the father of Ehud* [i]29 Some Septuagint manuscripts (see also 1 Chron. 9:35); Hebrew does not have *Jeiel.* [j]29 *Father* may mean *civic leader* or *military leader.* [k]30 Some Septuagint manuscripts (see also 1 Chron. 9:36); Hebrew does not have *Ner.* [l]33 Also known as *Ish-Bosheth* [m]34 Also known as *Mephibosheth*

Raphah was his son, Eleasah his son and
Azel his son.
38Azel had six sons, and these were their
names:
Azrikam, Bokeru, Ishmael, Sheariah,
Obadiah and Hanan. All these were the
sons of Azel.
39The sons of his brother Eshek:
Ulam his firstborn, Jeush the second son
and Eliphelet the third. 40The sons of
Ulam were brave warriors who could
handle the bow. They had many sons and
grandsons—150 in all.
All these were the descendants of Benjamin.

9 All Israel was listed in the genealogies re-
corded in the book of the kings of Israel.
The people of Judah were taken captive to
Babylon because of their unfaithfulness. 2Now the
first to resettle on their own property in their own
towns were some Israelites, priests, Levites and
temple servants.
3Those from Judah, from Benjamin, and from
Ephraim and Manasseh who lived in Jerusalem
were:
4Uthai son of Ammihud, the son of Omri, the
son of Imri, the son of Bani, a descendant
of Perez son of Judah.
5Of the Shilonites:
Asaiah the firstborn and his sons.
6Of the Zerahites:
Jeuel.
The people from Judah numbered 690.
7Of the Benjamites:
Sallu son of Meshullam, the son of Hoda-
viah, the son of Hassenuah;
8Ibneiah son of Jeroham; Elah son of Uzzi,
the son of Micri; and Meshullam son of
Shephatiah, the son of Reuel, the son of
Ibnijah.
9The people from Benjamin, as listed in
their genealogy, numbered 956. All these
men were heads of their families.
10Of the priests:
Jedaiah; Jehoiarib; Jakin;
11Azariah son of Hilkiah, the son of Me-
shullam, the son of Zadok, the son of Me-
raioth, the son of Ahitub, the official in
charge of the house of God;
12Adaiah son of Jeroham, the son of Pash-
hur, the son of Malkijah; and Maasai son
of Adiel, the son of Jahzerah, the son of
Meshullam, the son of Meshillemith, the
son of Immer.
13The priests, who were heads of families,
numbered 1,760. They were able men, re-
sponsible for ministering in the house of
God.
14Of the Levites:
Shemaiah son of Hasshub, the son of Az-
rikam, the son of Hashabiah, a Merarite;
15Bakbakkar, Heresh, Galal and Matta-
niah son of Mica, the son of Zicri, the son
of Asaph; 16Obadiah son of Shemaiah, the
son of Galal, the son of Jeduthun; and
Berekiah son of Asa, the son of Elkanah,
who lived in the villages of the Netopha-
thites.
17The gatekeepers:
Shallum, Akkub, Talmon, Ahiman and
their brothers, Shallum their chief 18being
stationed at the King's Gate on the east,
up to the present time. These were the
gatekeepers belonging to the camp of the
Levites. 19Shallum son of Kore, the son of
Ebiasaph, the son of Korah, and his fel-
low gatekeepers from his family (the Ko-
rahites) were responsible for guarding the
thresholds of the Tent[n] just as their fa-
thers had been responsible for guarding
the entrance to the dwelling of the LORD.
20In earlier times Phinehas son of Eleazar
was in charge of the gatekeepers, and the
LORD was with him. 21Zechariah son of
Meshelemiah was the gatekeeper at the
entrance to the Tent of Meeting.
22Altogether, those chosen to be gatekeepers at
the thresholds numbered 212. They were regis-
tered by genealogy in their villages. The gatekeep-
ers had been assigned to their positions of trust
by David and Samuel the seer. 23They and their
descendants were in charge of guarding the gates
of the house of the LORD—the house called the
Tent. 24The gatekeepers were on the four sides:
east, west, north and south. 25Their brothers in
their villages had to come from time to time and
share their duties for seven-day periods. 26But the
four principal gatekeepers, who were Levites,
were entrusted with the responsibility for the
rooms and treasuries in the house of God. 27They
would spend the night stationed around the
house of God, because they had to guard it; and

[n] 19 That is, the temple; also in verses 21 and 23

they had charge of the key for opening it each
morning.

28Some of them were in charge of the articles
used in the temple service; they counted them
when they were brought in and when they were
taken out. 29Others were assigned to take care of
the furnishings and all the other articles of the
sanctuary, as well as the flour and wine, and the
oil, incense and spices. 30But some of the priests
took care of mixing the spices. 31A Levite named
Mattithiah, the firstborn son of Shallum the Ko-
rahite, was entrusted with the responsibility for
baking the offering bread. 32Some of their Ko-
hathite brothers were in charge of preparing for
every Sabbath the bread set out on the table.

33Those who were musicians, heads of Levite
families, stayed in the rooms of the temple and
were exempt from other duties because they were
responsible for the work day and night.

34All these were heads of Levite families, chiefs
as listed in their genealogy, and they lived in Jeru-
salem.

35Jeiel the father[o] of Gibeon lived in Gibeon.
His wife's name was Maacah, 36and his
firstborn son was Abdon, followed by
Zur, Kish, Baal, Ner, Nadab, 37Gedor,
Ahio, Zechariah and Mikloth. 38Mikloth
was the father of Shimeam. They too
lived near their relatives in Jerusalem.

39Ner was the father of Kish, Kish the father
of Saul, and Saul the father of Jonathan,
Malki-Shua, Abinadab and Esh-Baal.[p]

40The son of Jonathan:
Merib-Baal,[q] who was the father of Mi-
cah.

41The sons of Micah:
Pithon, Melech, Tahrea and Ahaz.[r]

42Ahaz was the father of Jadah, Jadah[s] was
the father of Alemeth, Azmaveth and
Zimri, and Zimri was the father of Moza.
43Moza was the father of Binea; Rephaiah
was his son, Eleasah his son and Azel his
son.

44Azel had six sons, and these were their
names:
Azrikam, Bokeru, Ishmael, Sheariah,
Obadiah and Hanan. These were the sons
of Azel.

10 Now the Philistines fought against
Israel; the Israelites fled before
them, and many fell slain on Mount
Gilboa. 2The Philistines pressed hard after Saul
and his sons, and they killed his sons Jonathan,
Abinadab and Malki-Shua. 3The fighting grew
fierce around Saul, and when the archers over-
took him, they wounded him.

4Saul said to his armor-bearer, "Draw your
sword and run me through, or these uncircum-
cised fellows will come and abuse me."

But his armor-bearer was terrified and would
not do it; so Saul took his own sword and fell on
it. 5When the armor-bearer saw that Saul was
dead, he too fell on his sword and died. 6So Saul
and his three sons died, and all his house died
together.

7When all the Israelites in the valley saw that
the army had fled and that Saul and his sons had
died, they abandoned their towns and fled. And
the Philistines came and occupied them.

8The next day, when the Philistines came to
strip the dead, they found Saul and his sons fallen
on Mount Gilboa. 9They stripped him and took
his head and his armor, and sent messengers
throughout the land of the Philistines to proclaim
the news among their idols and their people.
10They put his armor in the temple of their gods
and hung up his head in the temple of Dagon.

11When all the inhabitants of Jabesh Gilead
heard of everything the Philistines had done to
Saul, 12all their valiant men went and took the
bodies of Saul and his sons and brought them to
Jabesh. Then they buried their bones under the
great tree in Jabesh, and they fasted seven days.

13Saul died because he was unfaithful to the
LORD; he did not keep the word of the LORD and
even consulted a medium for guidance, 14and did
not inquire of the LORD. So the LORD put him to
death and turned the kingdom over to David son
of Jesse.

[o]35 *Father* may mean *civic leader* or *military leader.* [p]39 Also known as *Ish-Bosheth* [q]40 Also known as *Mephibosheth*
[r]41 Vulgate and Syriac (see also Septuagint and 1 Chron. 8:35); Hebrew does not have *and Ahaz.* [s]42 Some Hebrew manuscripts and Septuagint (see also 1 Chron. 8:36); most Hebrew manuscripts *Jarah, Jarah*

1 / *1 Chronicles 11*
Famous for Bravery

"YOU MAY NOT be the best person, but you may be the only person." I pondered my friend's comment for a long time as I thought about doing something that would take nerve—nerve I didn't feel I had. I finally concluded that she meant, "Somebody else might do a better job, but nobody else is willing—except you." Sometimes that's how bravery is born. A dangerous job lies ahead of us, and we choose to go ahead and do it.

Warming Up to God When has the Lord given you courage to take a risk for him?

Read 1 Chronicles 11.

---

11 All Israel came together to David at Hebron and said, "We are your own flesh and blood. 2In the past, even while Saul was king, you were the one who led Israel on their military campaigns. And the LORD your God said to you, 'You will shepherd my people Israel, and you will become their ruler.' "

3When all the elders of Israel had come to King David at Hebron, he made a compact with them at Hebron before the LORD, and they anointed David king over Israel, as the LORD had promised through Samuel.

4David and all the Israelites marched to Jerusalem (that is, Jebus). The Jebusites who lived there 5said to David, "You will not get in here." Nevertheless, David captured the fortress of Zion, the City of David.

6David had said, "Whoever leads the attack on the Jebusites will become commander-in-chief." Joab son of Zeruiah went up first, and so he received the command.

7David then took up residence in the fortress, and so it was called the City of David. 8He built up the city around it, from the supporting terraces[t] to the surrounding wall, while Joab restored the rest of the city. 9And David became more and more powerful, because the LORD Almighty was with him.

10These were the chiefs of David's mighty men—they, together with all Israel, gave his kingship strong support to extend it over the whole land, as the LORD had promised— 11this is the list of David's mighty men:

Jashobeam,[u] a Hacmonite, was chief of the officers[v]; he raised his spear against three hundred men, whom he killed in one encounter.

12Next to him was Eleazar son of Dodai the Ahohite, one of the three mighty men. 13He was with David at Pas Dammim when the Philistines gathered there for battle. At a place where there was a field full of barley, the troops fled from the Philistines. 14But they took their stand in the middle of the field. They defended it and struck the Philistines down, and the LORD brought about a great victory.

15Three of the thirty chiefs came down to David to the rock at the cave of Adullam, while a band of Philistines was encamped in the Valley of Rephaim. 16At that time David was in the stronghold, and the Philistine garrison was at Bethlehem. 17David longed for water and said, "Oh, that someone would get me a drink of water from the well near the gate of Bethlehem!" 18So the Three broke through the Philistine lines, drew water from the well near the gate of Bethlehem and carried it back to David. But he refused to drink it; instead, he poured it out before the LORD. 19"God forbid that I should do this!" he said. "Should I drink the blood of these men who went at the risk of their lives?" Because they risked their lives to bring it back, David would not drink it.

Such were the exploits of the three mighty men.

20Abishai the brother of Joab was chief of the Three. He raised his spear against three hundred men, whom he killed, and so he became as famous as the Three. 21He was doubly honored above the Three and became their commander, even though he was not included among them.

22Benaiah son of Jehoiada was a valiant fighter from Kabzeel, who performed great exploits. He struck down two of Moab's best men. He also went down into a pit on a snowy day and killed a lion. 23And he struck down an Egyptian who was

[t]*8* Or *the Millo* [u]*11* Possibly a variant of *Jashob-Baal* [v]*11* Or *Thirty*; some Septuagint manuscripts *Three* (see also 2 Samuel 23:8)

seven and a half feet[w] tall. Although the Egyptian had a spear like a weaver's rod in his hand, Benaiah went against him with a club. He snatched the spear from the Egyptian's hand and killed him with his own spear. 24Such were the exploits of Benaiah son of Jehoiada; he too was as famous as the three mighty men. 25He was held in greater honor than any of the Thirty, but he was not included among the Three. And David put him in charge of his bodyguard.

26The mighty men were:
Asahel the brother of Joab,
Elhanan son of Dodo from Bethlehem,
27Shammoth the Harorite,
Helez the Pelonite,
28Ira son of Ikkesh from Tekoa,
Abiezer from Anathoth,
29Sibbecai the Hushathite,
Ilai the Ahohite,
30Maharai the Netophathite,
Heled son of Baanah the Netophathite,
31Ithai son of Ribai from Gibeah in Benjamin,
Benaiah the Pirathonite,
32Hurai from the ravines of Gaash,
Abiel the Arbathite,
33Azmaveth the Baharumite,
Eliahba the Shaalbonite,
34the sons of Hashem the Gizonite,
Jonathan son of Shagee the Hararite,
35Ahiam son of Sacar the Hararite,
Eliphal son of Ur,
36Hepher the Mekerathite,
Ahijah the Pelonite,
37Hezro the Carmelite,
Naarai son of Ezbai,
38Joel the brother of Nathan,
Mibhar son of Hagri,
39Zelek the Ammonite,
Naharai the Berothite, the armor-bearer of Joab son of Zeruiah,
40Ira the Ithrite,
Gareb the Ithrite,
41Uriah the Hittite,
Zabad son of Ahlai,
42Adina son of Shiza the Reubenite, who was chief of the Reubenites, and the thirty with him,
43Hanan son of Maacah,
Joshaphat the Mithnite,
44Uzzia the Ashterathite,
Shama and Jeiel the sons of Hotham the Aroerite,
45Jediael son of Shimri,
his brother Joha the Tizite,
46Eliel the Mahavite,
Jeribai and Joshaviah the sons of Elnaam,
Ithmah the Moabite,
47Eliel, Obed and Jaasiel the Mezobaite.

w23 Hebrew *five cubits* (about 2.3 meters)

Discovering the Word 1. How had David inspired others to bravery (vv. 1–2)? 2. In what ways did the capture of Zion require courageous action (vv. 4–9)? 3. How did David's "mighty men" exhibit courage (vv. 11–25)? 4. Why did David refuse the water he had longed for (vv. 17–19)? 5. How would you say this passage defines heroism?

Applying the Word 1. How do you think these "mighty men" handled their natural fears? 2. How does faith in God help us act more courageously? 3. What challenge are you now facing which requires bravery?

Responding in Prayer Bring your fears to the Lord. Trust him to be with you as you do whatever is necessary. Take the step to act in spite of your fears.

1 Chronicles 12—14

12 These were the men who came to David at Ziklag, while he was banished from the presence of Saul son of Kish (they were among the warriors who helped him in battle; 2they were armed with bows and were able to shoot arrows or to sling stones right-handed or left-handed; they were kinsmen of Saul from the tribe of Benjamin):

3Ahiezer their chief and Joash the sons of Shemaah the Gibeathite; Jeziel and Pelet the sons of Azmaveth; Beracah, Jehu the Anathothite, 4and Ishmaiah the Gibeonite, a mighty man among the Thirty, who was a leader of the Thirty; Jeremiah, Jahaziel, Johanan, Jozabad the Gederathite, 5Eluzai, Jerimoth, Bealiah, Shemariah and Shephatiah the Haruphite; 6Elkanah, Isshiah, Azarel, Joezer and Jashobeam the Korahites; 7and Joelah and Zebadiah the sons of Jeroham from Gedor.

8Some Gadites defected to David at his stronghold in the desert. They were brave warriors, ready for battle and able to handle the shield and spear. Their faces were the faces of lions, and they were as swift as gazelles in the mountains.

9Ezer was the chief,
Obadiah the second in command, Eliab the third,
10Mishmannah the fourth, Jeremiah the fifth,
11Attai the sixth, Eliel the seventh,
12Johanan the eighth, Elzabad the ninth,
13Jeremiah the tenth and Macbannai the eleventh.

14These Gadites were army commanders; the least was a match for a hundred, and the greatest for a thousand. 15It was they who crossed the Jordan in the first month when it was overflowing all its banks, and they put to flight everyone living in the valleys, to the east and to the west.

16Other Benjamites and some men from Judah also came to David in his stronghold. 17David went out to meet them and said to them, "If you have come to me in peace, to help me, I am ready to have you unite with me. But if you have come to betray me to my enemies when my hands are free from violence, may the God of our fathers see it and judge you."

18Then the Spirit came upon Amasai, chief of the Thirty, and he said:

"We are yours, O David!
We are with you, O son of Jesse!
Success, success to you,
and success to those who help you,
for your God will help you."

So David received them and made them leaders of his raiding bands.

19Some of the men of Manasseh defected to David when he went with the Philistines to fight against Saul. (He and his men did not help the Philistines because, after consultation, their rulers sent him away. They said, "It will cost us our heads if he deserts to his master Saul.") 20When David went to Ziklag, these were the men of Manasseh who defected to him: Adnah, Jozabad, Jediael, Michael, Jozabad, Elihu and Zillethai, leaders of units of a thousand in Manasseh. 21They helped David against raiding bands, for all of them were brave warriors, and they were commanders in his army. 22Day after day men came to help David, until he had a great army, like the army of God.[x]

23These are the numbers of the men armed for battle who came to David at Hebron to turn Saul's kingdom over to him, as the LORD had said:

24men of Judah, carrying shield and spear—6,800 armed for battle;
25men of Simeon, warriors ready for battle—7,100;
26men of Levi—4,600, 27including Jehoiada, leader of the family of Aaron, with 3,700 men, 28and Zadok, a brave young warrior, with 22 officers from his family;
29men of Benjamin, Saul's kinsmen—3,000, most of whom had remained loyal to Saul's house until then;
30men of Ephraim, brave warriors, famous in their own clans—20,800;
31men of half the tribe of Manasseh, designated by name to come and make David king—18,000;
32men of Issachar, who understood the times and knew what Israel should do—200

x22 *Or a great and mighty army*

chiefs, with all their relatives under their command;
33men of Zebulun, experienced soldiers prepared for battle with every type of weapon, to help David with undivided loyalty—50,000;
34men of Naphtali—1,000 officers, together with 37,000 men carrying shields and spears;
35men of Dan, ready for battle—28,600;
36men of Asher, experienced soldiers prepared for battle—40,000;
37and from east of the Jordan, men of Reuben, Gad and the half-tribe of Manasseh, armed with every type of weapon—120,000.

38All these were fighting men who volunteered to serve in the ranks. They came to Hebron fully determined to make David king over all Israel. All the rest of the Israelites were also of one mind to make David king. 39The men spent three days there with David, eating and drinking, for their families had supplied provisions for them. 40Also, their neighbors from as far away as Issachar, Zebulun and Naphtali came bringing food on donkeys, camels, mules and oxen. There were plentiful supplies of flour, fig cakes, raisin cakes, wine, oil, cattle and sheep, for there was joy in Israel.

13

David conferred with each of his officers, the commanders of thousands and commanders of hundreds. 2He then said to the whole assembly of Israel, "If it seems good to you and if it is the will of the LORD our God, let us send word far and wide to the rest of our brothers throughout the territories of Israel, and also to the priests and Levites who are with them in their towns and pasturelands, to come and join us. 3Let us bring the ark of our God back to us, for we did not inquire of[y] it[z] during the reign of Saul." 4The whole assembly agreed to do this, because it seemed right to all the people.

5So David assembled all the Israelites, from the Shihor River in Egypt to Lebo[a] Hamath, to bring the ark of God from Kiriath Jearim. 6David and all the Israelites with him went to Baalah of Judah (Kiriath Jearim) to bring up from there the ark of God the LORD, who is enthroned between the cherubim—the ark that is called by the Name.

7They moved the ark of God from Abinadab's house on a new cart, with Uzzah and Ahio guiding it. 8David and all the Israelites were celebrating with all their might before God, with songs and with harps, lyres, tambourines, cymbals and trumpets.

9When they came to the threshing floor of Kidon, Uzzah reached out his hand to steady the ark, because the oxen stumbled. 10The LORD's anger burned against Uzzah, and he struck him down because he had put his hand on the ark. So he died there before God.

11Then David was angry because the LORD's wrath had broken out against Uzzah, and to this day that place is called Perez Uzzah.[b]

12David was afraid of God that day and asked, "How can I ever bring the ark of God to me?" 13He did not take the ark to be with him in the City of David. Instead, he took it aside to the house of Obed-Edom the Gittite. 14The ark of God remained with the family of Obed-Edom in his house for three months, and the LORD blessed his household and everything he had.

14

Now Hiram king of Tyre sent messengers to David, along with cedar logs, stonemasons and carpenters to build a palace for him. 2And David knew that the LORD had established him as king over Israel and that his kingdom had been highly exalted for the sake of his people Israel.

3In Jerusalem David took more wives and became the father of more sons and daughters. 4These are the names of the children born to him there: Shammua, Shobab, Nathan, Solomon, 5Ibhar, Elishua, Elpelet, 6Nogah, Nepheg, Japhia, 7Elishama, Beeliada[c] and Eliphelet.

8When the Philistines heard that David had been anointed king over all Israel, they went up in full force to search for him, but David heard about it and went out to meet them. 9Now the Philistines had come and raided the Valley of Rephaim; 10so David inquired of God: "Shall I go and attack the Philistines? Will you hand them over to me?"

The LORD answered him, "Go, I will hand them over to you."

11So David and his men went up to Baal Perazim, and there he defeated them. He said, "As waters break out, God has broken out against my enemies by my hand." So that place was called Baal Perazim.[d] 12The Philistines had abandoned

[y]3 Or *we neglected* [z]3 Or *him* [a]5 Or *to the entrance to* [b]11 *Perez Uzzah* means *outbreak against Uzzah.* [c]7 A variant of *Eliada* [d]11 *Baal Perazim* means *the lord who breaks out.*

their gods there, and David gave orders to burn them in the fire.

13Once more the Philistines raided the valley;
14so David inquired of God again, and God answered him, "Do not go straight up, but circle around them and attack them in front of the balsam trees.
15As soon as you hear the sound of marching in the tops of the balsam trees, move out to battle, because that will mean God has gone out in front of you to strike the Philistine army."
16So David did as God commanded him, and they struck down the Philistine army, all the way from Gibeon to Gezer.

17So David's fame spread throughout every land, and the LORD made all the nations fear him.

2 / *1 Chronicles 15:1—16:6*
Joyful Celebration

THE BACKYARD WEDDING two doors away was getting noisy. It was late; everybody was singing. Fortunately, the couple seemed to have all musical friends and family, because the sound was glorious. It must have been a similar event when David and the priests and singers brought the ark of the covenant to its new place in Jerusalem in a noisy, joyful procession.

 **Warming Up to God** What makes you feel like celebrating the Lord?

 **Read 1 Chronicles 15:1—16:6.**

15 After David had constructed buildings for himself in the City of David, he prepared a place for the ark of God and pitched a tent for it.
2Then David said, "No one but the Levites may carry the ark of God, because the LORD chose them to carry the ark of the LORD and to minister before him forever."

3David assembled all Israel in Jerusalem to bring up the ark of the LORD to the place he had prepared for it.
4He called together the descendants of Aaron and the Levites:

5From the descendants of Kohath,
Uriel the leader and 120 relatives;
6from the descendants of Merari,
Asaiah the leader and 220 relatives;
7from the descendants of Gershon,[e]
Joel the leader and 130 relatives;
8from the descendants of Elizaphan,
Shemaiah the leader and 200 relatives;
9from the descendants of Hebron,
Eliel the leader and 80 relatives;
10from the descendants of Uzziel,
Amminadab the leader and 112 relatives.

11Then David summoned Zadok and Abiathar the priests, and Uriel, Asaiah, Joel, Shemaiah, Eliel and Amminadab the Levites.
12He said to them, "You are the heads of the Levitical families; you and your fellow Levites are to consecrate yourselves and bring up the ark of the LORD, the God of Israel, to the place I have prepared for it.
13It was because you, the Levites, did not bring it up the first time that the LORD our God broke out in anger against us. We did not inquire of him about how to do it in the prescribed way."
14So the priests and Levites consecrated themselves in order to bring up the ark of the LORD, the God of Israel.
15And the Levites carried the ark of God with the poles on their shoulders, as Moses had commanded in accordance with the word of the LORD.

16David told the leaders of the Levites to appoint their brothers as singers to sing joyful songs, accompanied by musical instruments: lyres, harps and cymbals.

17So the Levites appointed Heman son of Joel; from his brothers, Asaph son of Berekiah; and from their brothers the Merarites, Ethan son of Kushaiah;
18and with them their brothers next in rank: Zechariah,[f] Jaaziel, Shemiramoth, Jehiel,

[e]7 Hebrew *Gershom*, a variant of *Gershon* [f]18 Three Hebrew manuscripts and most Septuagint manuscripts (see also verse 20 and 1 Chron. 16:5); most Hebrew manuscripts *Zechariah son and* or *Zechariah, Ben and*

Unni, Eliab, Benaiah, Maaseiah, Mattithiah,
Eliphelehu, Mikneiah, Obed-Edom and Jeiel,[g]
the gatekeepers.
19 The musicians Heman, Asaph and Ethan
were to sound the bronze cymbals; 20 Zechariah,
Aziel, Shemiramoth, Jehiel, Unni, Eliab, Maaseiah
and Benaiah were to play the lyres according to
alamoth,[h] 21 and Mattithiah, Eliphelehu, Mikne-
iah, Obed-Edom, Jeiel and Azaziah were to play
the harps, directing according to *sheminith*.[h]
22 Kenaniah the head Levite was in charge of the
singing; that was his responsibility because he
was skillful at it.
23 Berekiah and Elkanah were to be doorkeepers
for the ark. 24 Shebaniah, Joshaphat, Nethanel,
Amasai, Zechariah, Benaiah and Eliezer the
priests were to blow trumpets before the ark of
God. Obed-Edom and Jehiah were also to be
doorkeepers for the ark.
25 So David and the elders of Israel and the
commanders of units of a thousand went to bring
up the ark of the covenant of the LORD from the
house of Obed-Edom, with rejoicing. 26 Because
God had helped the Levites who were carrying
the ark of the covenant of the LORD, seven bulls
and seven rams were sacrificed. 27 Now David was
clothed in a robe of fine linen, as were all the
Levites who were carrying the ark, and as were
the singers, and Kenaniah, who was in charge of
the singing of the choirs. David also wore a linen
ephod. 28 So all Israel brought up the ark of the
covenant of the LORD with shouts, with the sound-
ing of rams' horns and trumpets, and of cymbals,
and the playing of lyres and harps.
29 As the ark of the covenant of the LORD was
entering the City of David, Michal daughter of
Saul watched from a window. And when she saw
King David dancing and celebrating, she despised
him in her heart.

16 They brought the ark of God and
set it inside the tent that David had
pitched for it, and they presented
burnt offerings and fellowship offerings[i] before
God. 2 After David had finished sacrificing the
burnt offerings and fellowship offerings, he
blessed the people in the name of the LORD. 3 Then
he gave a loaf of bread, a cake of dates and a cake
of raisins to each Israelite man and woman.
4 He appointed some of the Levites to minister
before the ark of the LORD, to make petition, to
give thanks, and to praise the LORD, the God of
Israel: 5 Asaph was the chief, Zechariah second,
then Jeiel, Shemiramoth, Jehiel, Mattithiah, Eliab,
Benaiah, Obed-Edom and Jeiel. They were to play
the lyres and harps, Asaph was to sound the cym-
bals, 6 and Benaiah and Jahaziel the priests were to
blow the trumpets regularly before the ark of the
covenant of God.

[g]18 Hebrew; Septuagint (see also verse 21) *Jeiel and Azaziah*
[h]20,21 Probably a musical term [i]1 Traditionally *peace offerings*; also in verse 2

Discovering the Word 1. Before this, the ark of the covenant was in temporary lodging. It had never been in Jerusalem. How did King David make preparations for bringing it into his new capital (15:1–15)? 2. What was the importance of singing as the ark was moved (15:16–22)? 3. How did David conduct himself during the procession (15:25–29)? 4. If you had been an observer there, what would you have thought of the king? 5. Why do you think Michal, one of David's wives, reacted negatively (15:29)? 6. In what ways did they celebrate when they got the ark inside the tent (16:1–6)?

Applying the Word 1. How do you feel about unrestrained celebration by Christians in worship? 2. How open are you to worship styles different from the one you prefer? 3. What helps you to express your joy in the Lord?

Responding in Prayer Praise the Lord in some joyful way today through motion, spoken words, music, writing, artwork or whatever is natural to you.

1 Chronicles 16:7–43

[7]That day David first committed to Asaph and
his associates this psalm of thanks to the LORD:

[8]Give thanks to the LORD, call on his name;
make known among the nations what he has done.
[9]Sing to him, sing praise to him;
tell of all his wonderful acts.
[10]Glory in his holy name;
let the hearts of those who seek the LORD rejoice.
[11]Look to the LORD and his strength;
seek his face always.
[12]Remember the wonders he has done,
his miracles, and the judgments he pronounced,
[13]O descendants of Israel his servant,
O sons of Jacob, his chosen ones.

[14]He is the LORD our God;
his judgments are in all the earth.
[15]He remembers[j] his covenant forever,
the word he commanded, for a thousand generations,
[16]the covenant he made with Abraham,
the oath he swore to Isaac.
[17]He confirmed it to Jacob as a decree,
to Israel as an everlasting covenant:
[18]"To you I will give the land of Canaan
as the portion you will inherit."
[19]When they were but few in number,
few indeed, and strangers in it,
[20]they[k] wandered from nation to nation,
from one kingdom to another.
[21]He allowed no man to oppress them;
for their sake he rebuked kings:
[22]"Do not touch my anointed ones;
do my prophets no harm."

[23]Sing to the LORD, all the earth;
proclaim his salvation day after day.
[24]Declare his glory among the nations,
his marvelous deeds among all peoples.
[25]For great is the LORD and most worthy of praise;
he is to be feared above all gods.
[26]For all the gods of the nations are idols,
but the LORD made the heavens.
[27]Splendor and majesty are before him;
strength and joy in his dwelling place.
[28]Ascribe to the LORD, O families of nations,
ascribe to the LORD glory and strength,
[29] ascribe to the LORD the glory due his name.
Bring an offering and come before him;
worship the LORD in the splendor of his[l] holiness.
[30]Tremble before him, all the earth!
The world is firmly established; it cannot be moved.
[31]Let the heavens rejoice, let the earth be glad;
let them say among the nations, "The LORD reigns!"
[32]Let the sea resound, and all that is in it;
let the fields be jubilant, and everything in them!
[33]Then the trees of the forest will sing,
they will sing for joy before the LORD,
for he comes to judge the earth.

[34]Give thanks to the LORD, for he is good;
his love endures forever.
[35]Cry out, "Save us, O God our Savior;
gather us and deliver us from the nations,
that we may give thanks to your holy name,
that we may glory in your praise."
[36]Praise be to the LORD, the God of Israel,
from everlasting to everlasting.

Then all the people said "Amen" and "Praise the LORD."

[37]David left Asaph and his associates before the
ark of the covenant of the LORD to minister there
regularly, according to each day's requirements.
[38]He also left Obed-Edom and his sixty-eight as-
sociates to minister with them. Obed-Edom son
of Jeduthun, and also Hosah, were gatekeepers.
[39]David left Zadok the priest and his fellow
priests before the tabernacle of the LORD at the
high place in Gibeon [40]to present burnt offerings
to the LORD on the altar of burnt offering regu-
larly, morning and evening, in accordance with
everything written in the Law of the LORD, which
he had given Israel. [41]With them were Heman
and Jeduthun and the rest of those chosen and
designated by name to give thanks to the LORD,

[j]15 Some Septuagint manuscripts (see also Psalm 105:8); Hebrew *Remember* [k]18-20 One Hebrew manuscript, Septuagint and Vulgate (see also Psalm 105:12); most Hebrew manuscripts *inherit, / [19]though you are but few in number, / few indeed, and strangers in it." / [20]They* [l]29 Or LORD *with the splendor of*

"for his love endures forever." [42]Heman and Jeduthun were responsible for the sounding of the trumpets and cymbals and for the playing of the other instruments for sacred song. The sons of Jeduthun were stationed at the gate.

[43]Then all the people left, each for his own home, and David returned home to bless his family.

3 / *1 Chronicles 17*
Honored by God's Promises

A MAGAZINE AD campaign has for its theme "a promise." The picture always shows people who are committed to each other, and the words give lavish promises of security. I find the ads unclear, but apparently this insurance company will help the people in the ad keep their promises. Sometimes we extract promises from people against their will. In today's Scripture God gave David an unexpected promise.

Warming Up to God Think about a time the Lord kept a promise to you. How did it deepen your relationship with him?

Read 1 Chronicles 17.

17 After David was settled in his palace, he said to Nathan the prophet, "Here I am, living in a palace of cedar, while the ark of the covenant of the LORD is under a tent."

[2]Nathan replied to David, "Whatever you have in mind, do it, for God is with you."

[3]That night the word of God came to Nathan, saying:

[4]"Go and tell my servant David, 'This is what the LORD says: You are not the one to build me a house to dwell in. [5]I have not dwelt in a house from the day I brought Israel up out of Egypt to this day. I have moved from one tent site to another, from one dwelling place to another. [6]Wherever I have moved with all the Israelites, did I ever say to any of their leaders[m] whom I commanded to shepherd my people, "Why have you not built me a house of cedar?" '

[7]"Now then, tell my servant David, 'This is what the LORD Almighty says: I took you from the pasture and from following the flock, to be ruler over my people Israel. [8]I have been with you wherever you have gone, and I have cut off all your enemies from before you. Now I will make your name like the names of the greatest men of the earth. [9]And I will provide a place for my people Israel and will plant them so that they can have a home of their own and no longer be disturbed. Wicked people will not oppress them anymore, as they did at the beginning [10]and have done ever since the time I appointed leaders over my people Israel. I will also subdue all your enemies.

" 'I declare to you that the LORD will build a house for you: [11]When your days are over and you go to be with your fathers, I will raise up your offspring to succeed you, one of your own sons, and I will establish his kingdom. [12]He is the one who will build a house for me, and I will establish his throne forever. [13]I will be his father, and he will be my son. I will never take my love away from him, as I took it away from your predecessor. [14]I will set him over my house and my kingdom forever; his throne will be established forever.' "

[15]Nathan reported to David all the words of this entire revelation.

[16]Then King David went in and sat before the LORD, and he said:

"Who am I, O LORD God, and what is my family, that you have brought me this far? [17]And as if this were not enough in your

[m]6 Traditionally *judges*; also in verse 10

sight, O God, you have spoken about the fu-
ture of the house of your servant. You have
looked on me as though I were the most ex-
alted of men, O LORD God.
18“What more can David say to you for
honoring your servant? For you know your
servant, 19O LORD. For the sake of your ser-
vant and according to your will, you have
done this great thing and made known all
these great promises.
20“There is no one like you, O LORD, and
there is no God but you, as we have heard
with our own ears. 21And who is like your
people Israel—the one nation on earth
whose God went out to redeem a people for
himself, and to make a name for yourself,
and to perform great and awesome wonders
by driving out nations from before your peo-
ple, whom you redeemed from Egypt? 22You
made your people Israel your very own for-
ever, and you, O LORD, have become their
God.
23“And now, LORD, let the promise you
have made concerning your servant and his
house be established forever. Do as you
promised, 24so that it will be established and
that your name will be great forever. Then
men will say, ‘The LORD Almighty, the God
over Israel, is Israel’s God!’ And the house of
your servant David will be established before
you.
25“You, my God, have revealed to your
servant that you will build a house for him.
So your servant has found courage to pray to
you. 26O LORD, you are God! You have prom-
ised these good things to your servant.
27Now you have been pleased to bless the
house of your servant, that it may continue
forever in your sight; for you, O LORD, have
blessed it, and it will be blessed forever.”

Discovering the Word 1. The ark of the covenant had been brought to Jerusalem and set up in the tabernacle (tent). What did David plan to do next (v. 1)? 2. How did God use Nathan to intervene in David's plans (vv. 2–6)? 3. What did the Lord promise David (vv. 7–14)? 4. David could have gotten huffy about the Lord not letting *him* build a temple. Instead, how did he respond to the revelation of this unexpected promise (vv. 16–19)? 5. How did David express his confidence in God's promise (vv. 20–27)?

Applying the Word 1. How do you feel about the promises God makes to us? 2. In times of anxiety, what promises of God do you hold on to?

Responding in Prayer Thank the Lord for his promises. Think of specific ones and how they apply to you, and praise him for his faithfulness.

1 Chronicles 18

18 In the course of time, David de-
feated the Philistines and subdued
them, and he took Gath and its sur-
rounding villages from the control of the Philis-
tines.
2David also defeated the Moabites, and they be-
came subject to him and brought tribute.
3Moreover, David fought Hadadezer king of
Zobah, as far as Hamath, when he went to estab-
lish his control along the Euphrates River. 4David
captured a thousand of his chariots, seven thou-
sand charioteers and twenty thousand foot sol-
diers. He hamstrung all but a hundred of the
chariot horses.
5When the Arameans of Damascus came to
help Hadadezer king of Zobah, David struck
down twenty-two thousand of them. 6He put gar-
risons in the Aramean kingdom of Damascus, and
the Arameans became subject to him and brought
tribute. The LORD gave David victory everywhere
he went.
7David took the gold shields carried by the offi-
cers of Hadadezer and brought them to Jerusa-
lem. 8From Tebah[n] and Cun, towns that be-
longed to Hadadezer, David took a great quantity
of bronze, which Solomon used to make the
bronze Sea, the pillars and various bronze arti-
cles.
9When Tou king of Hamath heard that David
had defeated the entire army of Hadadezer king of

[n]8 Hebrew *Tibhath*, a variant of *Tebah*

Zobah, [10]he sent his son Hadoram to King David to greet him and congratulate him on his victory in battle over Hadadezer, who had been at war with Tou. Hadoram brought all kinds of articles of gold and silver and bronze.

[11]King David dedicated these articles to the LORD, as he had done with the silver and gold he had taken from all these nations: Edom and Moab, the Ammonites and the Philistines, and Amalek.

[12]Abishai son of Zeruiah struck down eighteen thousand Edomites in the Valley of Salt. [13]He put garrisons in Edom, and all the Edomites became subject to David. The LORD gave David victory everywhere he went.

[14]David reigned over all Israel, doing what was just and right for all his people. [15]Joab son of Zeruiah was over the army; Jehoshaphat son of Ahilud was recorder; [16]Zadok son of Ahitub and Ahimelech[o] son of Abiathar were priests; Shavsha was secretary; [17]Benaiah son of Jehoiada was over the Kerethites and Pelethites; and David's sons were chief officials at the king's side.

[o]16 Some Hebrew manuscripts, Vulgate and Syriac (see also 2 Samuel 8:17); most Hebrew manuscripts *Abimelech*

4 / *1 Chronicles 19*
Misunderstood Sympathy

WE KNOW ONE home where it's not safe to inquire about family members; you might mention the name of whoever's in the doghouse right now. In many families and workplaces—even churches—there's one person who keeps things stirred up with rumors. When we start guessing and second-guessing people's motives, there's no end in sight. In this case a misunderstanding inflated into war.

Warming Up to God When have your motives been misunderstood? How did God help you deal with it?

Read 1 Chronicles 19.

19 In the course of time, Nahash king of the Ammonites died, and his son succeeded him as king. [2]David thought, "I will show kindness to Hanun son of Nahash, because his father showed kindness to me." So David sent a delegation to express his sympathy to Hanun concerning his father.

When David's men came to Hanun in the land of the Ammonites to express sympathy to him, [3]the Ammonite nobles said to Hanun, "Do you think David is honoring your father by sending men to you to express sympathy? Haven't his men come to you to explore and spy out the country and overthrow it?" [4]So Hanun seized David's men, shaved them, cut off their garments in the middle at the buttocks, and sent them away.

[5]When someone came and told David about the men, he sent messengers to meet them, for they were greatly humiliated. The king said, "Stay at Jericho till your beards have grown, and then come back."

[6]When the Ammonites realized that they had become a stench in David's nostrils, Hanun and the Ammonites sent a thousand talents[p] of silver to hire chariots and charioteers from Aram Naharaim,[q] Aram Maacah and Zobah. [7]They hired thirty-two thousand chariots and charioteers, as well as the king of Maacah with his troops, who came and camped near Medeba, while the Ammonites were mustered from their towns and moved out for battle.

[8]On hearing this, David sent Joab out with the entire army of fighting men. [9]The Ammonites came out and drew up in battle formation at the entrance to their city, while the kings who had come were by themselves in the open country.

[10]Joab saw that there were battle lines in front of him and behind him; so he selected some of the best troops in Israel and deployed them against the Arameans. [11]He put the rest of the

[p]6 That is, about 37 tons (about 34 metric tons) [q]6 That is, Northwest Mesopotamia

men under the command of Abishai his brother, and they were deployed against the Ammonites. 12 Joab said, "If the Arameans are too strong for me, then you are to rescue me; but if the Ammonites are too strong for you, then I will rescue you. 13 Be strong and let us fight bravely for our people and the cities of our God. The LORD will do what is good in his sight."

14 Then Joab and the troops with him advanced to fight the Arameans, and they fled before him. 15 When the Ammonites saw that the Arameans were fleeing, they too fled before his brother Abishai and went inside the city. So Joab went back to Jerusalem.

16 After the Arameans saw that they had been routed by Israel, they sent messengers and had Arameans brought from beyond the River,[r] with Shophach the commander of Hadadezer's army leading them.

17 When David was told of this, he gathered all Israel and crossed the Jordan; he advanced against them and formed his battle lines opposite them. David formed his lines to meet the Arameans in battle, and they fought against him. 18 But they fled before Israel, and David killed seven thousand of their charioteers and forty thousand of their foot soldiers. He also killed Shophach the commander of their army.

19 When the vassals of Hadadezer saw that they had been defeated by Israel, they made peace with David and became subject to him.

So the Arameans were not willing to help the Ammonites anymore.

[r]16 That is, the Euphrates

Discovering the Word 1. What was David's intention in sending the delegation to the Ammonites (vv. 1–2)? 2. How did suspicion poison their mission (vv. 3–4)? 3. How did the Ammonites escalate their aggression against Israel (vv. 6–7)? 4. What was the outcome of the conflict (vv. 14–19)? 5. How could the conflict have been avoided?

Applying the Word 1. Why are we so prone to take offense at what might be innocent gestures? 2. When have you seen something innocent escalate into a fight? 3. What can you do to prevent such tragic misunderstandings?

Responding in Prayer Pray for patience and wisdom to avoid leaping to conclusions about other people's motives.

1 Chronicles 20

20 In the spring, at the time when kings go off to war, Joab led out the armed forces. He laid waste the land of the Ammonites and went to Rabbah and besieged it, but David remained in Jerusalem. Joab attacked Rabbah and left it in ruins. 2 David took the crown from the head of their king[s]—its weight was found to be a talent[t] of gold, and it was set with precious stones—and it was placed on David's head. He took a great quantity of plunder from the city 3 and brought out the people who were there, consigning them to labor with saws and with iron picks and axes. David did this to all the Ammonite towns. Then David and his entire army returned to Jerusalem.

4 In the course of time, war broke out with the Philistines, at Gezer. At that time Sibbecai the Hushathite killed Sippai, one of the descendants of the Rephaites, and the Philistines were subjugated.

5 In another battle with the Philistines, Elhanan son of Jair killed Lahmi the brother of Goliath the Gittite, who had a spear with a shaft like a weaver's rod.

6 In still another battle, which took place at Gath, there was a huge man with six fingers on each hand and six toes on each foot—twenty-four in all. He also was descended from Rapha. 7 When he taunted Israel, Jonathan son of Shimea, David's brother, killed him.

8 These were descendants of Rapha in Gath, and they fell at the hands of David and his men.

[s]2 Or *of Milcom,* that is, Molech [t]2 That is, about 75 pounds (about 34 kilograms)

5 / *1 Chronicles 21:1—22:1*
Misplaced Trust

WHAT MAKES YOU feel secure? Is it a steady job? a large savings account? good health? family and friends? Each of these can be a gift from the Lord and a reason for giving thanks. However, when we begin to trust in the gift rather than the Giver, we are headed for trouble. In this chapter David discovers the terrible consequences of misplaced trust.

Warming Up to God What sorts of things contribute to your feelings of security?

Read 1 Chronicles 21:1—22:1.

21 Satan rose up against Israel and in-
cited David to take a census of Is-
rael. 2So David said to Joab and the
commanders of the troops, "Go and count the
Israelites from Beersheba to Dan. Then report
back to me so that I may know how many there
are."
3But Joab replied, "May the LORD multiply his
troops a hundred times over. My lord the king,
are they not all my lord's subjects? Why does my
lord want to do this? Why should he bring guilt
on Israel?"
4The king's word, however, overruled Joab; so
Joab left and went throughout Israel and then
came back to Jerusalem. 5Joab reported the num-
ber of the fighting men to David: In all Israel
there were one million one hundred thousand
men who could handle a sword, including four
hundred and seventy thousand in Judah.
6But Joab did not include Levi and Benjamin in
the numbering, because the king's command was
repulsive to him. 7This command was also evil in
the sight of God; so he punished Israel.
8Then David said to God, "I have sinned greatly
by doing this. Now, I beg you, take away the
guilt of your servant. I have done a very foolish
thing."
9The LORD said to Gad, David's seer, 10"Go and
tell David, 'This is what the LORD says: I am giving
you three options. Choose one of them for me to
carry out against you.' "
11So Gad went to David and said to him, "This
is what the LORD says: 'Take your choice: 12three
years of famine, three months of being swept
away[u] before your enemies, with their swords
overtaking you, or three days of the sword of the
LORD—days of plague in the land, with the angel
of the LORD ravaging every part of Israel.' Now
then, decide how I should answer the one who
sent me."
13David said to Gad, "I am in deep distress. Let
me fall into the hands of the LORD, for his mercy
is very great; but do not let me fall into the hands
of men."
14So the LORD sent a plague on Israel, and sev-
enty thousand men of Israel fell dead. 15And God
sent an angel to destroy Jerusalem. But as the
angel was doing so, the LORD saw it and was
grieved because of the calamity and said to the
angel who was destroying the people, "Enough!
Withdraw your hand." The angel of the LORD was
then standing at the threshing floor of Araunah[v]
the Jebusite.
16David looked up and saw the angel of the
LORD standing between heaven and earth, with a
drawn sword in his hand extended over Jerusa-
lem. Then David and the elders, clothed in sack-
cloth, fell facedown.
17David said to God, "Was it not I who ordered
the fighting men to be counted? I am the one who
has sinned and done wrong. These are but sheep.
What have they done? O LORD my God, let your
hand fall upon me and my family, but do not let
this plague remain on your people."
18Then the angel of the LORD ordered Gad to
tell David to go up and build an altar to the LORD
on the threshing floor of Araunah the Jebusite.
19So David went up in obedience to the word that
Gad had spoken in the name of the LORD.
20While Araunah was threshing wheat, he
turned and saw the angel; his four sons who were
with him hid themselves. 21Then David ap-
proached, and when Araunah looked and saw

[u] 12 Hebrew; Septuagint and Vulgate (see also 2 Samuel 24:13) *of fleeing*
[v] 15 Hebrew *Ornan*, a variant of *Araunah*; also in verses 18-28

him, he left the threshing floor and bowed down
before David with his face to the ground.
22David said to him, "Let me have the site of
your threshing floor so I can build an altar to
the LORD, that the plague on the people may be
stopped. Sell it to me at the full price."
23Araunah said to David, "Take it! Let my lord
the king do whatever pleases him. Look, I will
give the oxen for the burnt offerings, the thresh-
ing sledges for the wood, and the wheat for the
grain offering. I will give all this."
24But King David replied to Araunah, "No, I
insist on paying the full price. I will not take for
the LORD what is yours, or sacrifice a burnt offer-
ing that costs me nothing."
25So David paid Araunah six hundred shekels[w]
of gold for the site. 26David built an altar to the
LORD there and sacrificed burnt offerings and fel-
lowship offerings.[x] He called on the LORD, and
the LORD answered him with fire from heaven on
the altar of burnt offering.
27Then the LORD spoke to the angel, and he put
his sword back into its sheath. 28At that time,
when David saw that the LORD had answered him
on the threshing floor of Araunah the Jebusite, he
offered sacrifices there. 29The tabernacle of the
LORD, which Moses had made in the desert, and
the altar of burnt offering were at that time on the
high place at Gibeon. 30But David could not go
before it to inquire of God, because he was afraid
of the sword of the angel of the LORD.
22 Then David said, "The house of the
LORD God is to be here, and also the
altar of burnt offering for Israel."

[w]25 That is, about 15 pounds (about 7 kilograms) [x]26 Traditionally *peace offerings*

Discovering the Word 1. In what ways does the author make it clear that David's action was evil (21:1, 3, 6, 8)? 2. Unfortunately, the author does not tell us *why* David's action was sinful. Why might the Lord have viewed David's action as sinful? 3. In what sense was the plague on Israel (21:14) an appropriate punishment for David's sin? 4. What contributes to the mood of fear and urgency in 21:16–27? 5. Why was this an appropriate site for building the house of the Lord (22:1)?

Applying the Word 1. Why are we often tempted to trust in human strength and resources rather than in the Lord? 2. Animal sacrifices are no longer necessary to atone for our sins (Heb 10:11–12). What then should we do when we discover we are guilty of misplaced trust?

Responding in Prayer If you are aware of any such areas of your life, take time now to confess them to the Lord. Thank him for the forgiveness and security we have in Christ.

1 Chronicles 22:2—27:34

2So David gave orders to assemble the aliens
living in Israel, and from among them he ap-
pointed stonecutters to prepare dressed stone for
building the house of God. 3He provided a large
amount of iron to make nails for the doors of the
gateways and for the fittings, and more bronze
than could be weighed. 4He also provided more
cedar logs than could be counted, for the Sidoni-
ans and Tyrians had brought large numbers of
them to David.
5David said, "My son Solomon is young and
inexperienced, and the house to be built for the
LORD should be of great magnificence and fame
and splendor in the sight of all the nations.
Therefore I will make preparations for it." So Da-
vid made extensive preparations before his death.
6Then he called for his son Solomon and
charged him to build a house for the LORD, the
God of Israel. 7David said to Solomon: "My son, I
had it in my heart to build a house for the Name
of the LORD my God. 8But this word of the LORD
came to me: 'You have shed much blood and have
fought many wars. You are not to build a house
for my Name, because you have shed much blood
on the earth in my sight. 9But you will have a son
who will be a man of peace and rest, and I will
give him rest from all his enemies on every side.
His name will be Solomon,[y] and I will grant Is-
rael peace and quiet during his reign. 10He is the
one who will build a house for my Name. He will
be my son, and I will be his father. And I will

[y]9 *Solomon* sounds like and may be derived from the Hebrew for *peace.*

establish the throne of his kingdom over Israel forever.'

11"Now, my son, the LORD be with you, and may you have success and build the house of the LORD your God, as he said you would. 12May the LORD give you discretion and understanding when he puts you in command over Israel, so that you may keep the law of the LORD your God. 13Then you will have success if you are careful to observe the decrees and laws that the LORD gave Moses for Israel. Be strong and courageous. Do not be afraid or discouraged.

14"I have taken great pains to provide for the temple of the LORD a hundred thousand talents[z] of gold, a million talents[a] of silver, quantities of bronze and iron too great to be weighed, and wood and stone. And you may add to them. 15You have many workmen: stonecutters, masons and carpenters, as well as men skilled in every kind of work 16in gold and silver, bronze and iron—craftsmen beyond number. Now begin the work, and the LORD be with you."

17Then David ordered all the leaders of Israel to help his son Solomon. 18He said to them, "Is not the LORD your God with you? And has he not granted you rest on every side? For he has handed the inhabitants of the land over to me, and the land is subject to the LORD and to his people. 19Now devote your heart and soul to seeking the LORD your God. Begin to build the sanctuary of the LORD God, so that you may bring the ark of the covenant of the LORD and the sacred articles belonging to God into the temple that will be built for the Name of the LORD."

23 When David was old and full of years, he made his son Solomon king over Israel.

2He also gathered together all the leaders of Israel, as well as the priests and Levites. 3The Levites thirty years old or more were counted, and the total number of men was thirty-eight thousand. 4David said, "Of these, twenty-four thousand are to supervise the work of the temple of the LORD and six thousand are to be officials and judges. 5Four thousand are to be gatekeepers and four thousand are to praise the LORD with the musical instruments I have provided for that purpose."

6David divided the Levites into groups corresponding to the sons of Levi: Gershon, Kohath and Merari.

7Belonging to the Gershonites:
Ladan and Shimei.

8The sons of Ladan:
Jehiel the first, Zetham and Joel—three in all.

9The sons of Shimei:
Shelomoth, Haziel and Haran—three in all.
These were the heads of the families of Ladan.

10And the sons of Shimei:
Jahath, Ziza,[b] Jeush and Beriah.
These were the sons of Shimei—four in all.
11Jahath was the first and Ziza the second, but Jeush and Beriah did not have many sons; so they were counted as one family with one assignment.

12The sons of Kohath:
Amram, Izhar, Hebron and Uzziel—four in all.

13The sons of Amram:
Aaron and Moses.
Aaron was set apart, he and his descendants forever, to consecrate the most holy things, to offer sacrifices before the LORD, to minister before him and to pronounce blessings in his name forever. 14The sons of Moses the man of God were counted as part of the tribe of Levi.

15The sons of Moses:
Gershom and Eliezer.

16The descendants of Gershom:
Shubael was the first.

17The descendants of Eliezer:
Rehabiah was the first.
Eliezer had no other sons, but the sons of Rehabiah were very numerous.

18The sons of Izhar:
Shelomith was the first.

19The sons of Hebron:
Jeriah the first, Amariah the second, Jahaziel the third and Jekameam the fourth.

20The sons of Uzziel:
Micah the first and Isshiah the second.

21The sons of Merari:
Mahli and Mushi.
The sons of Mahli:

[z] *14* That is, about 3,750 tons (about 3,450 metric tons) [a] *14* That is, about 37,500 tons (about 34,500 metric tons) [b] *10* One Hebrew manuscript, Septuagint and Vulgate (see also verse 11); most Hebrew manuscripts *Zina*

Eleazar and Kish.

22Eleazar died without having sons: he had only daughters. Their cousins, the sons of Kish, married them.

23The sons of Mushi:

Mahli, Eder and Jerimoth—three in all.

24These were the descendants of Levi by their families—the heads of families as they were registered under their names and counted individually, that is, the workers twenty years old or more who served in the temple of the LORD. 25For David had said, "Since the LORD, the God of Israel, has granted rest to his people and has come to dwell in Jerusalem forever, 26the Levites no longer need to carry the tabernacle or any of the articles used in its service." 27According to the last instructions of David, the Levites were counted from those twenty years old or more.

28The duty of the Levites was to help Aaron's descendants in the service of the temple of the LORD: to be in charge of the courtyards, the side rooms, the purification of all sacred things and the performance of other duties at the house of God. 29They were in charge of the bread set out on the table, the flour for the grain offerings, the unleavened wafers, the baking and the mixing, and all measurements of quantity and size. 30They were also to stand every morning to thank and praise the LORD. They were to do the same in the evening 31and whenever burnt offerings were presented to the LORD on Sabbaths and at New Moon festivals and at appointed feasts. They were to serve before the LORD regularly in the proper number and in the way prescribed for them.

32And so the Levites carried out their responsibilities for the Tent of Meeting, for the Holy Place and, under their brothers the descendants of Aaron, for the service of the temple of the LORD.

24

These were the divisions of the sons of Aaron:

The sons of Aaron were Nadab, Abihu, Eleazar and Ithamar. 2But Nadab and Abihu died before their father did, and they had no sons; so Eleazar and Ithamar served as the priests. 3With the help of Zadok a descendant of Eleazar and Ahimelech a descendant of Ithamar, David separated them into divisions for their appointed order of ministering. 4A larger number of leaders were found among Eleazar's descendants than among Ithamar's, and they were divided accordingly: sixteen heads of families from Eleazar's descendants and eight heads of families from Ithamar's descendants. 5They divided them impartially by drawing lots, for there were officials of the sanctuary and officials of God among the descendants of both Eleazar and Ithamar.

6The scribe Shemaiah son of Nethanel, a Levite, recorded their names in the presence of the king and of the officials: Zadok the priest, Ahimelech son of Abiathar and the heads of families of the priests and of the Levites—one family being taken from Eleazar and then one from Ithamar.

7The first lot fell to Jehoiarib,
the second to Jedaiah,
8the third to Harim,
the fourth to Seorim,
9the fifth to Malkijah,
the sixth to Mijamin,
10the seventh to Hakkoz,
the eighth to Abijah,
11the ninth to Jeshua,
the tenth to Shecaniah,
12the eleventh to Eliashib,
the twelfth to Jakim,
13the thirteenth to Huppah,
the fourteenth to Jeshebeab,
14the fifteenth to Bilgah,
the sixteenth to Immer,
15the seventeenth to Hezir,
the eighteenth to Happizzez,
16the nineteenth to Pethahiah,
the twentieth to Jehezkel,
17the twenty-first to Jakin,
the twenty-second to Gamul,
18the twenty-third to Delaiah
and the twenty-fourth to Maaziah.

19This was their appointed order of ministering when they entered the temple of the LORD, according to the regulations prescribed for them by their forefather Aaron, as the LORD, the God of Israel, had commanded him.

20As for the rest of the descendants of Levi:
from the sons of Amram: Shubael;
from the sons of Shubael: Jehdeiah.
21As for Rehabiah, from his sons:
Isshiah was the first.
22From the Izharites: Shelomoth;
from the sons of Shelomoth: Jahath.
23The sons of Hebron: Jeriah the first,[c] Ama-

[c]23 Two Hebrew manuscripts and some Septuagint manuscripts (see also 1 Chron. 23:19); most Hebrew manuscripts *The sons of Jeriah:*

were in the care of Shelomith and his relatives.

29 From the Izharites: Kenaniah and his sons were assigned duties away from the temple, as officials and judges over Israel.

30 From the Hebronites: Hashabiah and his
relatives—seventeen hundred able
men—were responsible in Israel west of
the Jordan for all the work of the LORD
and for the king's service. 31 As for the He-
bronites, Jeriah was their chief according
to the genealogical records of their fami-
lies. In the fortieth year of David's reign a
search was made in the records, and ca-
pable men among the Hebronites were
found at Jazer in Gilead. 32 Jeriah had
twenty-seven hundred relatives, who
were able men and heads of families, and
King David put them in charge of the
Reubenites, the Gadites and the half-tribe
of Manasseh for every matter pertaining
to God and for the affairs of the king.

27

This is the list of the Israelites—heads of families, commanders of thousands and commanders of hundreds, and their officers, who served the king in all that concerned the army divisions that were on duty month by month throughout the year. Each division consisted of 24,000 men.

2 In charge of the first division, for the first
month, was Jashobeam son of Zabdiel. There
were 24,000 men in his division. 3 He was a
descendant of Perez and chief of all the army
officers for the first month.

4 In charge of the division for the second month was Dodai the Ahohite; Mikloth was the leader of his division. There were 24,000 men in his division.

5 The third army commander, for the third
month, was Benaiah son of Jehoiada the
priest. He was chief and there were 24,000
men in his division. 6 This was the Benaiah
who was a mighty man among the Thirty and
was over the Thirty. His son Ammizabad was
in charge of his division.

7 The fourth, for the fourth month, was Asahel the brother of Joab; his son Zebadiah was his successor. There were 24,000 men in his division.

8 The fifth, for the fifth month, was the commander Shamhuth the Izrahite. There were 24,000 men in his division.

9 The sixth, for the sixth month, was Ira the son of Ikkesh the Tekoite. There were 24,000 men in his division.

10 The seventh, for the seventh month, was Helez the Pelonite, an Ephraimite. There were 24,000 men in his division.

11 The eighth, for the eighth month, was Sibbecai the Hushathite, a Zerahite. There were 24,000 men in his division.

12 The ninth, for the ninth month, was Abiezer the Anathothite, a Benjamite. There were 24,000 men in his division.

13 The tenth, for the tenth month, was Maharai the Netophathite, a Zerahite. There were 24,000 men in his division.

14 The eleventh, for the eleventh month, was Benaiah the Pirathonite, an Ephraimite. There were 24,000 men in his division.

15 The twelfth, for the twelfth month, was Heldai the Netophathite, from the family of Othniel. There were 24,000 men in his division.

16 The officers over the tribes of Israel:

over the Reubenites: Eliezer son of Zicri;
over the Simeonites: Shephatiah son of Maacah;
17 over Levi: Hashabiah son of Kemuel;
over Aaron: Zadok;
18 over Judah: Elihu, a brother of David;
over Issachar: Omri son of Michael;
19 over Zebulun: Ishmaiah son of Obadiah;
over Naphtali: Jerimoth son of Azriel;
20 over the Ephraimites: Hoshea son of Azaziah;
over half the tribe of Manasseh: Joel son of Pedaiah;
21 over the half-tribe of Manasseh in Gilead: Iddo son of Zechariah;
over Benjamin: Jaasiel son of Abner;
22 over Dan: Azarel son of Jeroham.

These were the officers over the tribes of Israel.

23 David did not take the number of the men
twenty years old or less, because the LORD had
promised to make Israel as numerous as the stars
in the sky. 24 Joab son of Zeruiah began to count
the men but did not finish. Wrath came on Israel
on account of this numbering, and the number

was not entered in the book[m] of the annals of King David.

25Azmaveth son of Adiel was in charge of the royal storehouses.

Jonathan son of Uzziah was in charge of the storehouses in the outlying districts, in the towns, the villages and the watchtowers.

26Ezri son of Kelub was in charge of the field workers who farmed the land.

27Shimei the Ramathite was in charge of the vineyards.

Zabdi the Shiphmite was in charge of the produce of the vineyards for the wine vats.

28Baal-Hanan the Gederite was in charge of the olive and sycamore-fig trees in the western foothills.

Joash was in charge of the supplies of olive oil.

29Shitrai the Sharonite was in charge of the herds grazing in Sharon. Shaphat son of Adlai was in charge of the herds in the valleys.

30Obil the Ishmaelite was in charge of the camels.

Jehdeiah the Meronothite was in charge of the donkeys.

31Jaziz the Hagrite was in charge of the flocks.

All these were the officials in charge of King David's property.

32Jonathan, David's uncle, was a counselor, a man of insight and a scribe. Jehiel son of Hacmoni took care of the king's sons.

33Ahithophel was the king's counselor.

Hushai the Arkite was the king's friend.

34Ahithophel was succeeded by Jehoiada son of Benaiah and by Abiathar.

Joab was the commander of the royal army.

m24 Septuagint; Hebrew *number*

6 / *1 Chronicles 28*
A Legacy of Humble Service

OUR CHURCH IS full of plaques memorializing those who gave the stained glass windows, the organ, the furnishings in the small chapel, the ceiling lights. The names go largely unnoticed, but what would the building be like without those things? People several generations back started the Sunday school, began the choir, collected the first missions offering. Today we carry on the work they started. As David passes his dreams for the temple on to Solomon—despite his disappointment at not being able to build it himself—he too leaves a legacy for those to come.

Warming Up to God How much of your work for the Lord was actually started by a previous generation? Consider the people who came before you to lay the foundation, and thank God for them.

Read 1 Chronicles 28.

28 David summoned all the officials of Israel to assemble at Jerusalem: the officers over the tribes, the commanders of the divisions in the service of the king, the commanders of thousands and commanders of hundreds, and the officials in charge of all the property and livestock belonging to the king and his sons, together with the palace officials, the mighty men and all the brave warriors.

2King David rose to his feet and said: "Listen to me, my brothers and my people. I had it in my heart to build a house as a place of rest for the ark of the covenant of the LORD, for the footstool of our God, and I made plans to build it. 3But God said to me, 'You are not to build a house for my Name, because you are a warrior and have shed blood.'

4"Yet the LORD, the God of Israel, chose me from my whole family to be king over Israel forever. He chose Judah as leader, and from the house of Judah he chose my family, and from my father's sons he was pleased to make me king over all Israel. 5Of all my sons—and the LORD has given me many—he has chosen my son Solomon to sit on the throne of the kingdom of the LORD over Israel. 6He said to me: 'Solomon your son is the one who will build my house and my courts, for I have chosen him to be my son, and I will be his father. 7I will establish his kingdom forever if he is unswerving in carrying out my commands and laws, as is being done at this time.'

8"So now I charge you in the sight of all Israel and of the assembly of the LORD, and in the hearing of our God: Be careful to follow all the commands of the LORD your God, that you may possess this good land and pass it on as an inheritance to your descendants forever.

9"And you, my son Solomon, acknowledge the God of your father, and serve him with wholehearted devotion and with a willing mind, for the LORD searches every heart and understands every motive behind the thoughts. If you seek him, he will be found by you; but if you forsake him, he will reject you forever. 10Consider now, for the LORD has chosen you to build a temple as a sanctuary. Be strong and do the work."

11Then David gave his son Solomon the plans for the portico of the temple, its buildings, its storerooms, its upper parts, its inner rooms and the place of atonement. 12He gave him the plans of all that the Spirit had put in his mind for the courts of the temple of the LORD and all the surrounding rooms, for the treasuries of the temple of God and for the treasuries for the dedicated things. 13He gave him instructions for the divisions of the priests and Levites, and for all the work of serving in the temple of the LORD, as well as for all the articles to be used in its service. 14He designated the weight of gold for all the gold articles to be used in various kinds of service, and the weight of silver for all the silver articles to be used in various kinds of service: 15the weight of gold for the gold lampstands and their lamps, with the weight for each lampstand and its lamps; and the weight of silver for each silver lampstand and its lamps, according to the use of each lampstand; 16the weight of gold for each table for consecrated bread; the weight of silver for the silver tables; 17the weight of pure gold for the forks, sprinkling bowls and pitchers; the weight of gold for each gold dish; the weight of silver for each silver dish; 18and the weight of the refined gold for the altar of incense. He also gave him the plan for the chariot, that is, the cherubim of gold that spread their wings and shelter the ark of the covenant of the LORD.

19"All this," David said, "I have in writing from the hand of the LORD upon me, and he gave me understanding in all the details of the plan."

20David also said to Solomon his son, "Be strong and courageous, and do the work. Do not be afraid or discouraged, for the LORD God, my God, is with you. He will not fail you or forsake you until all the work for the service of the temple of the LORD is finished. 21The divisions of the priests and Levites are ready for all the work on the temple of God, and every willing man skilled in any craft will help you in all the work. The officials and all the people will obey your every command."

Discovering the Word 1. David was admitting to the officials that the Lord had denied him the privilege of building the temple in favor of his son Solomon. What do his actions throughout this passage tell you about how he's handling this news? 2. How did David encourage Solomon to act (vv. 9–10)? 3. How did David provide for Solomon to carry out the building of the temple (vv. 11–19)? 4. How did David conclude his address (vv. 20–21)? 5. What do you learn about David's character from his reaction to this disappointment?

Applying the Word 1. When are you likely to pout about God's plans for you? (For example, when God gives someone else a job you'd like to have.) 2. How can your attitude be helped by getting the "long view" of God's plans in the world? 3. In what ways would you like to handle disappointment more like David does?

Responding in Prayer If you are aware of being overpossessive about some aspect of your life or ministry, confess your attitude to the Lord. Ask him to teach you humility and give you energy to serve him in the places he's called you to.

7 / 1 Chronicles 29
Generous Giving

GIVING HAS BECOME a sore spot for many Christians. Every day we are bombarded with appeals for money—from television and radio evangelists, from missionaries, from parachurch organizations, from relief agencies, and from our own churches. Sometimes we feel like shouting, "Enough is enough!" David had a very different attitude toward giving. In this chapter he illustrates what it means to give joyously and generously to the Lord.

Warming Up to God Reflect on a time when you have recently enjoyed giving something to someone else. Thank God for the joy of giving.

Read 1 Chronicles 29.

29 Then King David said to the whole
assembly: "My son Solomon, the
one whom God has chosen, is
young and inexperienced. The task is great, be-
cause this palatial structure is not for man but for
the LORD God. 2With all my resources I have pro-
vided for the temple of my God—gold for the
gold work, silver for the silver, bronze for the
bronze, iron for the iron and wood for the wood,
as well as onyx for the settings, turquoise,[n]
stones of various colors, and all kinds of fine
stone and marble—all of these in large quantities.
3Besides, in my devotion to the temple of my God
I now give my personal treasures of gold and sil-
ver for the temple of my God, over and above
everything I have provided for this holy temple:
4three thousand talents[o] of gold (gold of Ophir)
and seven thousand talents[p] of refined silver,
for the overlaying of the walls of the buildings,
5for the gold work and the silver work, and
for all the work to be done by the craftsmen.
Now, who is willing to consecrate himself today
to the LORD?"
6Then the leaders of families, the officers of the
tribes of Israel, the commanders of thousands and
commanders of hundreds, and the officials in
charge of the king's work gave willingly. 7They
gave toward the work on the temple of God five
thousand talents[q] and ten thousand darics[r] of
gold, ten thousand talents[s] of silver, eighteen
thousand talents[t] of bronze and a hundred thou-
sand talents[u] of iron. 8Any who had precious
stones gave them to the treasury of the temple of
the LORD in the custody of Jehiel the Gershonite.
9The people rejoiced at the willing response of
their leaders, for they had given freely and whole-
heartedly to the LORD. David the king also re-
joiced greatly.
10David praised the LORD in the presence of the
whole assembly, saying,

"Praise be to you, O LORD,
God of our father Israel,
from everlasting to everlasting.
11Yours, O LORD, is the greatness and the power
and the glory and the majesty and the
splendor,
for everything in heaven and earth is yours.
Yours, O LORD, is the kingdom;
you are exalted as head over all.
12Wealth and honor come from you;
you are the ruler of all things.
In your hands are strength and power
to exalt and give strength to all.
13Now, our God, we give you thanks,
and praise your glorious name.

14"But who am I, and who are my people, that
we should be able to give as generously as this?
Everything comes from you, and we have given
you only what comes from your hand. 15We are
aliens and strangers in your sight, as were all our
forefathers. Our days on earth are like a shadow,
without hope. 16O LORD our God, as for all this
abundance that we have provided for building
you a temple for your Holy Name, it comes from
your hand, and all of it belongs to you. 17I know,
my God, that you test the heart and are pleased
with integrity. All these things have I given will-
ingly and with honest intent. And now I have
seen with joy how willingly your people who are
here have given to you. 18O LORD, God of our fa-

[n]2 The meaning of the Hebrew for this word is uncertain. [o]4 That is, about 110 tons (about 100 metric tons) [p]4 That is, about 260 tons (about 240 metric tons) [q]7 That is, about 190 tons (about 170 metric tons) [r]7 That is, about 185 pounds (about 84 kilograms) [s]7 That is, about 375 tons (about 345 metric tons) [t]7 That is, about 675 tons (about 610 metric tons) [u]7 That is, about 3,750 tons (about 3,450 metric tons)

thers Abraham, Isaac and Israel, keep this desire in the hearts of your people forever, and keep their hearts loyal to you. 19And give my son Solomon the wholehearted devotion to keep your commands, requirements and decrees and to do everything to build the palatial structure for which I have provided."

20Then David said to the whole assembly, "Praise the LORD your God." So they all praised the LORD, the God of their fathers; they bowed low and fell prostrate before the LORD and the king.

21The next day they made sacrifices to the LORD and presented burnt offerings to him: a thousand bulls, a thousand rams and a thousand male lambs, together with their drink offerings, and other sacrifices in abundance for all Israel. 22They ate and drank with great joy in the presence of the LORD that day.

Then they acknowledged Solomon son of David as king a second time, anointing him before the LORD to be ruler and Zadok to be priest. 23So Solomon sat on the throne of the LORD as king in place of his father David. He prospered and all Israel obeyed him. 24All the officers and mighty men, as well as all of King David's sons, pledged their submission to King Solomon.

25The LORD highly exalted Solomon in the sight of all Israel and bestowed on him royal splendor such as no king over Israel ever had before.

26David son of Jesse was king over all Israel. 27He ruled over Israel forty years—seven in Hebron and thirty-three in Jerusalem. 28He died at a good old age, having enjoyed long life, wealth and honor. His son Solomon succeeded him as king.

29As for the events of King David's reign, from beginning to end, they are written in the records of Samuel the seer, the records of Nathan the prophet and the records of Gad the seer, 30together with the details of his reign and power, and the circumstances that surrounded him and Israel and the kingdoms of all the other lands.

Discovering the Word 1. How does David provide an excellent example of what it means to give generously to God (vv. 1–5)? 2. What effect does David's example have on the leaders of Israel and the people (vv. 6–9)? 3. What does David's prayer in verses 10–13 reveal about his view of God? 4. David might have felt boastful about his giving. What do verses 14–19 reveal about his reasons for humility? 5. David might also have felt remorse about parting with so much of his wealth. Instead, what spiritual and emotional impact did it have on him and the people (vv. 20–25)?

Applying the Word 1. How is our view of God related to our willingness or unwillingness to give generously? 2. In what ways have you been motivated to give more generously or to dedicate yourself more fully by observing the personal example of Christian leaders? 3. In what ways have you been challenged by David's example?

Responding in Prayer Ask God to show you how you should be giving of your resources (time, money, talent and so on).

2 Chronicles

What do you want out of life? Money? Prestige? Significant relationships? God told Solomon to ask for whatever he wanted. Second Chronicles begins with Solomon's answer. You may find it surprising!

Solomon was given the huge responsibility of building the temple that his father, David, had put much of his life into planning. Several chapters of lavish detail are devoted to the construction and dedication of the temple in Jerusalem. The temple continues to be prominent throughout the book.

Revolt soon splits Solomon's kingdom in two (Israel and Judah) when Jeroboam rebels against Solomon's son Rehoboam. Though the sins of ungodly kings are briefly mentioned and condemned, most of the book is devoted to spiritual reform and renewal under the Judean kings Asa, Jehoshaphat, Joash, Hezekiah and Josiah. Perhaps the most dramatic moment comes when among the debris of the unused temple, Hilkiah the priest finds the lost Torah—the law of Moses (34:14–32). The fall of Jerusalem to Nebuchadnezzar is explained as the result of sin, but the book ends positively, with Cyrus king of Persia authorizing the rebuilding of the temple.

Throughout 2 Chronicles the Lord's hand is seen blessing obedience with success. This book will be an encouragement to you as you try to stay faithful to the Lord. It was said of King Uzziah, "As long as he sought the LORD, God gave him success" (26:5).

What places in your life would you like to rebuild? In 2 Chronicles you'll find courage to begin the process and see it through to completion.

Outline

1 / *2 Chronicles 1*
Give Me Wisdom

POWERFUL TECHNOLOGICAL CONNECTIONS are bringing us almost unlimited access to information. Yet we have been unable to achieve our highest ideals of human rights and strong families. Knowledge is power, but power does not necessarily bring morality. Solomon asked for godly wisdom, the kind of knowledge that would make him a fit leader for God's people.

Warming Up to God Reflect on a time that you did not know what to do and God gave you insight and direction.

Read 2 Chronicles 1.

1 Solomon son of David established himself firmly over his kingdom, for the LORD his God was with him and made him exceedingly great.

2 Then Solomon spoke to all Israel—to the commanders of thousands and commanders of hundreds, to the judges and to all the leaders in Israel, the heads of families— 3 and Solomon and the whole assembly went to the high place at Gibeon, for God's Tent of Meeting was there, which Moses the LORD's servant had made in the desert. 4 Now David had brought up the ark of God from Kiriath Jearim to the place he had prepared for it, because he had pitched a tent for it in Jerusalem. 5 But the bronze altar that Bezalel son of Uri, the son of Hur, had made was in Gibeon in front of the tabernacle of the LORD; so Solomon and the assembly inquired of him there. 6 Solomon went up to the bronze altar before the LORD in the Tent of Meeting and offered a thousand burnt offerings on it.

7 That night God appeared to Solomon and said to him, "Ask for whatever you want me to give you."

8 Solomon answered God, "You have shown great kindness to David my father and have made me king in his place. 9 Now, LORD God, let your promise to my father David be confirmed, for you have made me king over a people who are as numerous as the dust of the earth. 10 Give me wisdom and knowledge, that I may lead this people, for who is able to govern this great people of yours?"

11 God said to Solomon, "Since this is your heart's desire and you have not asked for wealth, riches or honor, nor for the death of your enemies, and since you have not asked for a long life but for wisdom and knowledge to govern my people over whom I have made you king, 12 therefore wisdom and knowledge will be given you. And I will also give you wealth, riches and honor, such as no king who was before you ever had and none after you will have."

13 Then Solomon went to Jerusalem from the high place at Gibeon, from before the Tent of Meeting. And he reigned over Israel.

14 Solomon accumulated chariots and horses; he had fourteen hundred chariots and twelve thousand horses,[a] which he kept in the chariot cities and also with him in Jerusalem. 15 The king made silver and gold as common in Jerusalem as stones, and cedar as plentiful as sycamore-fig trees in the foothills. 16 Solomon's horses were imported from Egypt[b] and from Kue[c]—the royal merchants purchased them from Kue. 17 They imported a chariot from Egypt for six hundred shekels[d] of silver, and a horse for a hundred and fifty.[e] They also exported them to all the kings of the Hittites and of the Arameans.

[a]14 Or *charioteers* [b]16 Or possibly *Muzur,* a region in Cilicia; also in verse 17 [c]16 Probably Cilicia [d]17 That is, about 15 pounds (about 7 kilograms) [e]17 That is, about 3 3/4 pounds (about 1.7 kilograms)

Discovering the Word 1. What does verse 1 tell you about the relationship between God and Solomon? 2. What significant choices does Solomon make as he goes to worship God in verses 2–6? (Consider the people involved, the place and the symbolism of the elements he includes.) 3. What does the way in which God approaches Solomon suggest about their relationship (v. 7)? 4. What did Solomon ask of God, and why (vv. 8–10)? 5. How did God fulfill even what Solomon had not asked for (vv. 11–17)?

Applying the Word 1. In what area of your life do you need wisdom and knowledge? 2. In order to make your request of God, what must you believe about him?

Responding in Prayer Bring to the Lord all situations where you feel bewildered or stymied. Admit that you don't know what to do, and trust him for an answer.

2 Chronicles 2—5

2 Solomon gave orders to build a temple for
the Name of the LORD and a royal palace
for himself. 2He conscripted seventy
thousand men as carriers and eighty thousand as
stonecutters in the hills and thirty-six hundred as
foremen over them.

3Solomon sent this message to Hiram[f] king of
Tyre:

"Send me cedar logs as you did for my
father David when you sent him cedar to
build a palace to live in. 4Now I am about to
build a temple for the Name of the LORD my
God and to dedicate it to him for burning
fragrant incense before him, for setting out
the consecrated bread regularly, and for
making burnt offerings every morning and
evening and on Sabbaths and New Moons
and at the appointed feasts of the LORD our
God. This is a lasting ordinance for Israel.

5"The temple I am going to build will be
great, because our God is greater than all
other gods. 6But who is able to build a tem-
ple for him, since the heavens, even the
highest heavens, cannot contain him? Who
then am I to build a temple for him, except
as a place to burn sacrifices before him?

7"Send me, therefore, a man skilled to
work in gold and silver, bronze and iron, and
in purple, crimson and blue yarn, and expe-
rienced in the art of engraving, to work in
Judah and Jerusalem with my skilled crafts-
men, whom my father David provided.

8"Send me also cedar, pine and algum[g]
logs from Lebanon, for I know that your men
are skilled in cutting timber there. My men
will work with yours 9to provide me with
plenty of lumber, because the temple I build
must be large and magnificent. 10I will give
your servants, the woodsmen who cut the
timber, twenty thousand cors[h] of ground
wheat, twenty thousand cors of barley,
twenty thousand baths[i] of wine and twenty
thousand baths of olive oil."

11Hiram king of Tyre replied by letter to Solo-
mon:

"Because the LORD loves his people, he has
made you their king."

12And Hiram added:

"Praise be to the LORD, the God of Israel,
who made heaven and earth! He has given
King David a wise son, endowed with intelli-
gence and discernment, who will build a
temple for the LORD and a palace for himself.

13"I am sending you Huram-Abi, a man of
great skill, 14whose mother was from Dan
and whose father was from Tyre. He is
trained to work in gold and silver, bronze
and iron, stone and wood, and with purple
and blue and crimson yarn and fine linen. He
is experienced in all kinds of engraving and
can execute any design given to him. He will
work with your craftsmen and with those of
my lord, David your father.

15"Now let my lord send his servants the
wheat and barley and the olive oil and wine
he promised, 16and we will cut all the logs
from Lebanon that you need and will float
them in rafts by sea down to Joppa. You can
then take them up to Jerusalem."

17Solomon took a census of all the aliens who
were in Israel, after the census his father David
had taken; and they were found to be 153,600.
18He assigned 70,000 of them to be carriers and
80,000 to be stonecutters in the hills, with 3,600
foremen over them to keep the people working.

f3 Hebrew *Huram*, a variant of *Hiram*; also in verses 11 and 12
g8 Probably a variant of *almug*; possibly juniper
h10 That is, probably about 125,000 bushels (about 4,400 kiloliters)
i10 That is, probably about 115,000 gallons (about 440 kiloliters)

3 Then Solomon began to build the temple of the LORD in Jerusalem on Mount Moriah, where the LORD had appeared to his father David. It was on the threshing floor of Araunah[j] the Jebusite, the place provided by David. [2]He began building on the second day of the second month in the fourth year of his reign.

[3]The foundation Solomon laid for building the temple of God was sixty cubits long and twenty cubits wide[k] (using the cubit of the old standard). [4]The portico at the front of the temple was twenty cubits[l] long across the width of the building and twenty cubits[m] high.

He overlaid the inside with pure gold. [5]He paneled the main hall with pine and covered it with fine gold and decorated it with palm tree and chain designs. [6]He adorned the temple with precious stones. And the gold he used was gold of Parvaim. [7]He overlaid the ceiling beams, doorframes, walls and doors of the temple with gold, and he carved cherubim on the walls.

[8]He built the Most Holy Place, its length corresponding to the width of the temple—twenty cubits long and twenty cubits wide. He overlaid the inside with six hundred talents[n] of fine gold. [9]The gold nails weighed fifty shekels.[o] He also overlaid the upper parts with gold.

[10]In the Most Holy Place he made a pair of sculptured cherubim and overlaid them with gold. [11]The total wingspan of the cherubim was twenty cubits. One wing of the first cherub was five cubits[p] long and touched the temple wall, while its other wing, also five cubits long, touched the wing of the other cherub. [12]Similarly one wing of the second cherub was five cubits long and touched the other temple wall, and its other wing, also five cubits long, touched the wing of the first cherub. [13]The wings of these cherubim extended twenty cubits. They stood on their feet, facing the main hall.[q]

[14]He made the curtain of blue, purple and crimson yarn and fine linen, with cherubim worked into it.

[15]In the front of the temple he made two pillars, which ⌞together⌟ were thirty-five cubits[r] long, each with a capital on top measuring five cubits. [16]He made interwoven chains[s] and put them on top of the pillars. He also made a hundred pomegranates and attached them to the chains. [17]He erected the pillars in the front of the temple, one to the south and one to the north. The one to the south he named Jakin[t] and the one to the north Boaz.[u]

4 He made a bronze altar twenty cubits long, twenty cubits wide and ten cubits high.[v] [2]He made the Sea of cast metal, circular in shape, measuring ten cubits from rim to rim and five cubits[w] high. It took a line of thirty cubits[x] to measure around it. [3]Below the rim, figures of bulls encircled it—ten to a cubit.[y] The bulls were cast in two rows in one piece with the Sea.

[4]The Sea stood on twelve bulls, three facing north, three facing west, three facing south and three facing east. The Sea rested on top of them, and their hindquarters were toward the center. [5]It was a handbreadth[z] in thickness, and its rim was like the rim of a cup, like a lily blossom. It held three thousand baths.[a]

[6]He then made ten basins for washing and placed five on the south side and five on the north. In them the things to be used for the burnt offerings were rinsed, but the Sea was to be used by the priests for washing.

[7]He made ten gold lampstands according to the specifications for them and placed them in the temple, five on the south side and five on the north.

[8]He made ten tables and placed them in the temple, five on the south side and five on the north. He also made a hundred gold sprinkling bowls.

[9]He made the courtyard of the priests, and the large court and the doors for the court, and overlaid the doors with bronze. [10]He placed the Sea on the south side, at the southeast corner.

[11]He also made the pots and shovels and sprinkling bowls.

So Huram finished the work he had undertaken for King Solomon in the temple of God:

[12]the two pillars;

[j]1 Hebrew *Ornan*, a variant of *Araunah* [k]3 That is, about 90 feet (about 27 meters) long and 30 feet (about 9 meters) wide [l]4 That is, about 30 feet (about 9 meters); also in verses 8, 11 and 13 [m]4 Some Septuagint and Syriac manuscripts; Hebrew *and a hundred and twenty* [n]8 That is, about 23 tons (about 21 metric tons) [o]9 That is, about 1 1/4 pounds (about 0.6 kilogram) [p]11 That is, about 7 1/2 feet (about 2.3 meters); also in verse 15 [q]13 Or *facing inward* [r]15 That is, about 52 feet (about 16 meters) [s]16 Or possibly *made chains in the inner sanctuary*; the meaning of the Hebrew for this phrase is uncertain. [t]17 *Jakin* probably means *he establishes.* [u]17 *Boaz* probably means *in him is strength.* [v]1 That is, about 30 feet (about 9 meters) long and wide, and about 15 feet (about 4.5 meters) high [w]2 That is, about 7 1/2 feet (about 2.3 meters) [x]2 That is, about 45 feet (about 13.5 meters) [y]3 That is, about 1 1/2 feet (about 0.5 meter) [z]5 That is, about 3 inches (about 8 centimeters) [a]5 That is, about 17,500 gallons (about 66 kiloliters)

the two bowl-shaped capitals on top of the
pillars;
the two sets of network decorating the two
bowl-shaped capitals on top of the pillars;
13the four hundred pomegranates for the two
sets of network (two rows of pomegranates
for each network, decorating the
bowl-shaped capitals on top of the pillars);
14the stands with their basins;
15the Sea and the twelve bulls under it;
16the pots, shovels, meat forks and all related
articles.

All the objects that Huram-Abi made for King
Solomon for the temple of the LORD were of polished
bronze. 17The king had them cast in clay
molds in the plain of the Jordan between Succoth
and Zarethan.[b] 18All these things that Solomon
made amounted to so much that the weight of the
bronze was not determined.

19Solomon also made all the furnishings that
were in God's temple:

the golden altar;
the tables on which was the bread of the
Presence;
20the lampstands of pure gold with their
lamps, to burn in front of the inner sanctuary
as prescribed;
21the gold floral work and lamps and tongs
(they were solid gold);
22the pure gold wick trimmers, sprinkling
bowls, dishes and censers; and the gold
doors of the temple: the inner doors to
the Most Holy Place and the doors of the
main hall.

5 When all the work Solomon had done for
the temple of the LORD was finished, he
brought in the things his father David had
dedicated—the silver and gold and all the furnishings—and
he placed them in the treasuries of
God's temple.

2Then Solomon summoned to Jerusalem the elders
of Israel, all the heads of the tribes and the
chiefs of the Israelite families, to bring up the ark
of the LORD's covenant from Zion, the City of David.
3And all the men of Israel came together to
the king at the time of the festival in the seventh
month.

4When all the elders of Israel had arrived, the
Levites took up the ark, 5and they brought up the
ark and the Tent of Meeting and all the sacred
furnishings in it. The priests, who were Levites,
carried them up; 6and King Solomon and the entire
assembly of Israel that had gathered about
him were before the ark, sacrificing so many
sheep and cattle that they could not be recorded
or counted.

7The priests then brought the ark of the LORD's
covenant to its place in the inner sanctuary of the
temple, the Most Holy Place, and put it beneath
the wings of the cherubim. 8The cherubim spread
their wings over the place of the ark and covered
the ark and its carrying poles. 9These poles were
so long that their ends, extending from the ark,
could be seen from in front of the inner sanctuary,
but not from outside the Holy Place; and they
are still there today. 10There was nothing in the
ark except the two tablets that Moses had placed
in it at Horeb, where the LORD made a covenant
with the Israelites after they came out of Egypt.

11The priests then withdrew from the Holy
Place. All the priests who were there had consecrated
themselves, regardless of their divisions.
12All the Levites who were musicians—Asaph,
Heman, Jeduthun and their sons and relatives—stood
on the east side of the altar, dressed in fine
linen and playing cymbals, harps and lyres. They
were accompanied by 120 priests sounding trumpets.
13The trumpeters and singers joined in unison,
as with one voice, to give praise and thanks
to the LORD. Accompanied by trumpets, cymbals
and other instruments, they raised their voices in
praise to the LORD and sang:

"He is good;
his love endures forever."

Then the temple of the LORD was filled with a
cloud, 14and the priests could not perform their
service because of the cloud, for the glory of the
LORD filled the temple of God.

[b]17 Hebrew *Zeredatha*, a variant of *Zarethan*

2 / 2 Chronicles 6—7
Bearing God's Name

"I NOW PRONOUNCE you husband and wife. What God has joined, let no man put asunder." With these traditional words, a wedding ends. Two people who entered the church separately leave united. They even carry the same last name. And after that point anything that one or the other does will reflect on that name. Reasonable or not, the reputation of each person will rise and fall with the partner's behavior. It's enough to give a newly engaged couple some very solemn thoughts. But God himself takes the same risk—and not with just one person, but with a whole group. God calls them "my people, who are called by my Name" (7:14). What a great privilege to be linked to the name of God. And what a heavy responsibility.

Warming Up to God In what ways have you been a bearer of God's name this week?

Read 2 Chronicles 6—7.

6 Then Solomon said, "The LORD has said
that he would dwell in a dark cloud; 2I
have built a magnificent temple for you, a
place for you to dwell forever."
3While the whole assembly of Israel was standing there, the king turned around and blessed them. 4Then he said:

"Praise be to the LORD, the God of Israel, who with his hands has fulfilled what he promised with his mouth to my father David. For he said, 5'Since the day I brought my people out of Egypt, I have not chosen a city in any tribe of Israel to have a temple built for my Name to be there, nor have I chosen anyone to be the leader over my people Israel. 6But now I have chosen Jerusalem for my Name to be there, and I have chosen David to rule my people Israel.'

7"My father David had it in his heart to build a temple for the Name of the LORD, the God of Israel. 8But the LORD said to my father David, 'Because it was in your heart to build a temple for my Name, you did well to have this in your heart. 9Nevertheless, you are not the one to build the temple, but your son, who is your own flesh and blood—he is the one who will build the temple for my Name.'

10"The LORD has kept the promise he made. I have succeeded David my father and now I sit on the throne of Israel, just as the LORD promised, and I have built the temple for the Name of the LORD, the God of Israel. 11There I have placed the ark, in which is the covenant of the LORD that he made with the people of Israel."

12Then Solomon stood before the altar of the LORD in front of the whole assembly of Israel and spread out his hands. 13Now he had made a bronze platform, five cubits[c] long, five cubits wide and three cubits[d] high, and had placed it in the center of the outer court. He stood on the platform and then knelt down before the whole assembly of Israel and spread out his hands toward heaven. 14He said:

"O LORD, God of Israel, there is no God like you in heaven or on earth—you who keep your covenant of love with your servants who continue wholeheartedly in your way. 15You have kept your promise to your servant David my father; with your mouth you have promised and with your hand you have fulfilled it—as it is today.

16"Now LORD, God of Israel, keep for your servant David my father the promises you made to him when you said, 'You shall never fail to have a man to sit before me on the throne of Israel, if only your sons are careful in all they do to walk before me according to my law, as you have done.' 17And now, O LORD, God of Israel, let your word that you promised your servant David come true.

18"But will God really dwell on earth with men? The heavens, even the highest heavens, cannot contain you. How much less this temple I have built! 19Yet give attention to your servant's prayer and his plea for mercy, O LORD my God. Hear the cry and the prayer that your servant is praying in your pres-

c13 That is, about 7 1/2 feet (about 2.3 meters) d13 That is, about 4 1/2 feet (about 1.3 meters) ence. [20]May your eyes be open toward this temple day and night, this place of which you said you would put your Name there. May you hear the prayer your servant prays toward this place. [21]Hear the supplications of your servant and of your people Israel when they pray toward this place. Hear from heaven, your dwelling place; and when you hear, forgive.

[22]"When a man wrongs his neighbor and is required to take an oath and he comes and swears the oath before your altar in this temple, [23]then hear from heaven and act. Judge between your servants, repaying the guilty by bringing down on his own head what he has done. Declare the innocent not guilty and so establish his innocence.

[24]"When your people Israel have been defeated by an enemy because they have sinned against you and when they turn back and confess your name, praying and making supplication before you in this temple, [25]then hear from heaven and forgive the sin of your people Israel and bring them back to the land you gave to them and their fathers.

[26]"When the heavens are shut up and there is no rain because your people have sinned against you, and when they pray toward this place and confess your name and turn from their sin because you have afflicted them, [27]then hear from heaven and forgive the sin of your servants, your people Israel. Teach them the right way to live, and send rain on the land you gave your people for an inheritance.

[28]"When famine or plague comes to the land, or blight or mildew, locusts or grasshoppers, or when enemies besiege them in any of their cities, whatever disaster or disease may come, [29]and when a prayer or plea is made by any of your people Israel—each one aware of his afflictions and pains, and spreading out his hands toward this temple— [30]then hear from heaven, your dwelling place. Forgive, and deal with each man according to all he does, since you know his heart (for you alone know the hearts of men), [31]so that they will fear you and walk in your ways all the time they live in the land you gave our fathers.

[32]"As for the foreigner who does not belong to your people Israel but has come from a distant land because of your great name and your mighty hand and your outstretched arm—when he comes and prays toward this temple, [33]then hear from heaven, your dwelling place, and do whatever the foreigner asks of you, so that all the peoples of the earth may know your name and fear you, as do your own people Israel, and may know that this house I have built bears your Name.

[34]"When your people go to war against their enemies, wherever you send them, and when they pray to you toward this city you have chosen and the temple I have built for your Name, [35]then hear from heaven their prayer and their plea, and uphold their cause.

[36]"When they sin against you—for there is no one who does not sin—and you become angry with them and give them over to the enemy, who takes them captive to a land far away or near; [37]and if they have a change of heart in the land where they are held captive, and repent and plead with you in the land of their captivity and say, 'We have sinned, we have done wrong and acted wickedly'; [38]and if they turn back to you with all their heart and soul in the land of their captivity where they were taken, and pray toward the land you gave their fathers, toward the city you have chosen and toward the temple I have built for your Name; [39]then from heaven, your dwelling place, hear their prayer and their pleas, and uphold their cause. And forgive your people, who have sinned against you.

[40]"Now, my God, may your eyes be open and your ears attentive to the prayers offered in this place.

[41]"Now arise, O Lord God, and come to
 your resting place,
 you and the ark of your might.
May your priests, O Lord God, be
 clothed with salvation,
 may your saints rejoice in your
 goodness.
[42]O Lord God, do not reject your anointed
 one.
 Remember the great love promised to
 David your servant."

7 When Solomon finished praying, fire came down from heaven and consumed the burnt offering and the sacrifices, and the glory of the LORD filled the temple. 2The priests could not enter the temple of the LORD because the glory of the LORD filled it. 3When all the Israelites saw the fire coming down and the glory of the LORD above the temple, they knelt on the pavement with their faces to the ground, and they worshiped and gave thanks to the LORD, saying,

"He is good;
 his love endures forever."

4Then the king and all the people offered sacrifices before the LORD. 5And King Solomon offered a sacrifice of twenty-two thousand head of cattle and a hundred and twenty thousand sheep and goats. So the king and all the people dedicated the temple of God. 6The priests took their positions, as did the Levites with the LORD's musical instruments, which King David had made for praising the LORD and which were used when he gave thanks, saying, "His love endures forever." Opposite the Levites, the priests blew their trumpets, and all the Israelites were standing.

7Solomon consecrated the middle part of the courtyard in front of the temple of the LORD, and there he offered burnt offerings and the fat of the fellowship offerings,[e] because the bronze altar he had made could not hold the burnt offerings, the grain offerings and the fat portions.

8So Solomon observed the festival at that time for seven days, and all Israel with him—a vast assembly, people from Lebo[f] Hamath to the Wadi of Egypt. 9On the eighth day they held an assembly, for they had celebrated the dedication of the altar for seven days and the festival for seven days more. 10On the twenty-third day of the seventh month he sent the people to their homes, joyful and glad in heart for the good things the LORD had done for David and Solomon and for his people Israel.

11When Solomon had finished the temple of the LORD and the royal palace, and had succeeded in carrying out all he had in mind to do in the temple of the LORD and in his own palace, 12the LORD appeared to him at night and said:

"I have heard your prayer and have chosen this place for myself as a temple for sacrifices.

13"When I shut up the heavens so that there is no rain, or command locusts to devour the land or send a plague among my people, 14if my people, who are called by my name, will humble themselves and pray and seek my face and turn from their wicked ways, then will I hear from heaven and will forgive their sin and will heal their land. 15Now my eyes will be open and my ears attentive to the prayers offered in this place. 16I have chosen and consecrated this temple so that my Name may be there forever. My eyes and my heart will always be there.

17"As for you, if you walk before me as David your father did, and do all I command, and observe my decrees and laws, 18I will establish your royal throne, as I covenanted with David your father when I said, 'You shall never fail to have a man to rule over Israel.'

19"But if you[g] turn away and forsake the decrees and commands I have given you[g] and go off to serve other gods and worship them, 20then I will uproot Israel from my land, which I have given them, and will reject this temple I have consecrated for my Name. I will make it a byword and an object of ridicule among all peoples. 21And though this temple is now so imposing, all who pass by will be appalled and say, 'Why has the LORD done such a thing to this land and to this temple?' 22People will answer, 'Because they have forsaken the LORD, the God of their fathers, who brought them out of Egypt, and have embraced other gods, worshiping and serving them—that is why he brought all this disaster on them.' "

[e]7 Traditionally *peace offerings* [f]8 Or *from the entrance to*
[g]19 The Hebrew is plural.

Discovering the Word 1. What qualities of God are revealed in Solomon's account of Jewish history (6:1–11)? 2. What did Solomon express by the position of his body during his prayer (6:13)? 3. How does Solomon answer his own question in 6:18: "But will God really dwell on earth with men?" What does he not expect (6:19–21)? 4. In 6:22–42 what all is Solomon asking God to do? 5. In what ways did the people express their worship of God (7:1–10)? 6. What steps could the people take to restore their relationship with God (7:12–22)?

Applying the Word 1. If chapter 6 accurately describes God's nature, why might you need and want his forgiveness? 2. Prayerfully read again 7:14. Think of a group of people whose relationship with God needs restoring (your family, your church, your community, your nation). How could you, as a part of that group, begin to contribute to a restored relationship with God?

Responding in Prayer Pray for the group you thought of above and for your role in the restoration process.

2 Chronicles 8—13

8 At the end of twenty years, during which
Solomon built the temple of the LORD and
his own palace, 2Solomon rebuilt the vil-
lages that Hiram[h] had given him, and settled Is-
raelites in them. 3Solomon then went to Hamath
Zobah and captured it. 4He also built up Tadmor
in the desert and all the store cities he had built
in Hamath. 5He rebuilt Upper Beth Horon and
Lower Beth Horon as fortified cities, with walls
and with gates and bars, 6as well as Baalath and
all his store cities, and all the cities for his chari-
ots and for his horses[i]—whatever he desired to
build in Jerusalem, in Lebanon and throughout
all the territory he ruled.
7All the people left from the Hittites, Amorites,
Perizzites, Hivites and Jebusites (these peoples
were not Israelites), 8that is, their descendants re-
maining in the land, whom the Israelites had not
destroyed—these Solomon conscripted for his
slave labor force, as it is to this day. 9But Solomon
did not make slaves of the Israelites for his work;
they were his fighting men, commanders of his
captains, and commanders of his chariots and
charioteers. 10They were also King Solomon's
chief officials—two hundred and fifty officials su-
pervising the men.
11Solomon brought Pharaoh's daughter up
from the City of David to the palace he had built
for her, for he said, "My wife must not live in the
palace of David king of Israel, because the places
the ark of the LORD has entered are holy."
12On the altar of the LORD that he had built in
front of the portico, Solomon sacrificed burnt of-
ferings to the LORD, 13according to the daily re-
quirement for offerings commanded by Moses for
Sabbaths, New Moons and the three annual
feasts—the Feast of Unleavened Bread, the Feast
of Weeks and the Feast of Tabernacles. 14In keep-
ing with the ordinance of his father David, he
appointed the divisions of the priests for their
duties, and the Levites to lead the praise and to
assist the priests according to each day's require-
ment. He also appointed the gatekeepers by divi-
sions for the various gates, because this was what
David the man of God had ordered. 15They did
not deviate from the king's commands to the
priests or to the Levites in any matter, including
that of the treasuries.
16All Solomon's work was carried out, from the
day the foundation of the temple of the LORD was
laid until its completion. So the temple of the
LORD was finished.
17Then Solomon went to Ezion Geber and
Elath on the coast of Edom. 18And Hiram sent
him ships commanded by his own officers, men
who knew the sea. These, with Solomon's men,
sailed to Ophir and brought back four hundred
and fifty talents[j] of gold, which they delivered to
King Solomon.

9 When the queen of Sheba heard of Solo-
mon's fame, she came to Jerusalem to test
him with hard questions. Arriving with a
very great caravan—with camels carrying spices,
large quantities of gold, and precious stones—she
came to Solomon and talked with him about all
she had on her mind. 2Solomon answered all her
questions; nothing was too hard for him to ex-
plain to her. 3When the queen of Sheba saw the
wisdom of Solomon, as well as the palace he had
built, 4the food on his table, the seating of his
officials, the attending servants in their robes, the
cupbearers in their robes and the burnt offerings
he made at[k] the temple of the LORD, she was
overwhelmed.
5She said to the king, "The report I heard in my

[h]2 Hebrew *Huram,* a variant of *Hiram;* also in verse 18 [i]6 Or *charioteers* [j]18 That is, about 17 tons (about 16 metric tons)
[k]4 Or *the ascent by which he went up to*

own country about your achievements and your wisdom is true. 6But I did not believe what they said until I came and saw with my own eyes. Indeed, not even half the greatness of your wisdom was told me; you have far exceeded the report I heard. 7How happy your men must be! How happy your officials, who continually stand before you and hear your wisdom! 8Praise be to the LORD your God, who has delighted in you and placed you on his throne as king to rule for the LORD your God. Because of the love of your God for Israel and his desire to uphold them forever, he has made you king over them, to maintain justice and righteousness."

9Then she gave the king 120 talents[l] of gold, large quantities of spices, and precious stones. There had never been such spices as those the queen of Sheba gave to King Solomon.

10(The men of Hiram and the men of Solomon brought gold from Ophir; they also brought algumwood[m] and precious stones. 11The king used the algumwood to make steps for the temple of the LORD and for the royal palace, and to make harps and lyres for the musicians. Nothing like them had ever been seen in Judah.)

12King Solomon gave the queen of Sheba all she desired and asked for; he gave her more than she had brought to him. Then she left and returned with her retinue to her own country.

13The weight of the gold that Solomon received yearly was 666 talents,[n] 14not including the revenues brought in by merchants and traders. Also all the kings of Arabia and the governors of the land brought gold and silver to Solomon.

15King Solomon made two hundred large shields of hammered gold; six hundred bekas[o] of hammered gold went into each shield. 16He also made three hundred small shields of hammered gold, with three hundred bekas[p] of gold in each shield. The king put them in the Palace of the Forest of Lebanon.

17Then the king made a great throne inlaid with ivory and overlaid with pure gold. 18The throne had six steps, and a footstool of gold was attached to it. On both sides of the seat were armrests, with a lion standing beside each of them. 19Twelve lions stood on the six steps, one at either end of each step. Nothing like it had ever been made for any other kingdom. 20All King Solomon's goblets were gold, and all the household articles in the Palace of the Forest of Lebanon were pure gold. Nothing was made of silver, because silver was considered of little value in Solomon's day. 21The king had a fleet of trading ships[q] manned by Hiram's[r] men. Once every three years it returned, carrying gold, silver and ivory, and apes and baboons.

22King Solomon was greater in riches and wisdom than all the other kings of the earth. 23All the kings of the earth sought audience with Solomon to hear the wisdom God had put in his heart. 24Year after year, everyone who came brought a gift—articles of silver and gold, and robes, weapons and spices, and horses and mules.

25Solomon had four thousand stalls for horses and chariots, and twelve thousand horses,[s] which he kept in the chariot cities and also with him in Jerusalem. 26He ruled over all the kings from the River[t] to the land of the Philistines, as far as the border of Egypt. 27The king made silver as common in Jerusalem as stones, and cedar as plentiful as sycamore-fig trees in the foothills. 28Solomon's horses were imported from Egypt[u] and from all other countries.

29As for the other events of Solomon's reign, from beginning to end, are they not written in the records of Nathan the prophet, in the prophecy of Ahijah the Shilonite and in the visions of Iddo the seer concerning Jeroboam son of Nebat? 30Solomon reigned in Jerusalem over all Israel forty years. 31Then he rested with his fathers and was buried in the city of David his father. And Rehoboam his son succeeded him as king.

10 Rehoboam went to Shechem, for all the Israelites had gone there to make him king. 2When Jeroboam son of Nebat heard this (he was in Egypt, where he had fled from King Solomon), he returned from Egypt. 3So they sent for Jeroboam, and he and all Israel went to Rehoboam and said to him: 4"Your father put a heavy yoke on us, but now lighten the harsh labor and the heavy yoke he put on us, and we will serve you."

5Rehoboam answered, "Come back to me in three days." So the people went away.

6Then King Rehoboam consulted the elders who had served his father Solomon during his lifetime. "How would you advise me to answer these people?" he asked.

[l]9 That is, about 4 1/2 tons (about 4 metric tons) [m]10 Probably a variant of *almugwood* [n]13 That is, about 25 tons (about 23 metric tons) [o]15 That is, about 7 1/2 pounds (about 3.5 kilograms) [p]16 That is, about 3 3/4 pounds (about 1.7 kilograms) [q]21 Hebrew *of ships that could go to Tarshish* [r]21 Hebrew *Huram,* a variant of *Hiram* [s]25 Or *charioteers* [t]26 That is, the Euphrates [u]28 Or possibly *Muzur,* a region in Cilicia

[7]They replied, "If you will be kind to these peo-
ple and please them and give them a favorable
answer, they will always be your servants."
[8]But Rehoboam rejected the advice the elders
gave him and consulted the young men who had
grown up with him and were serving him. [9]He
asked them, "What is your advice? How should
we answer these people who say to me, 'Lighten
the yoke your father put on us'?"
[10]The young men who had grown up with him
replied, "Tell the people who have said to you,
'Your father put a heavy yoke on us, but make
our yoke lighter'—tell them, 'My little finger is
thicker than my father's waist. [11]My father laid on
you a heavy yoke; I will make it even heavier. My
father scourged you with whips; I will scourge
you with scorpions.' "
[12]Three days later Jeroboam and all the people
returned to Rehoboam, as the king had said,
"Come back to me in three days." [13]The king an-
swered them harshly. Rejecting the advice of the
elders, [14]he followed the advice of the young men
and said, "My father made your yoke heavy; I will
make it even heavier. My father scourged you
with whips; I will scourge you with scorpions."
[15]So the king did not listen to the people, for this
turn of events was from God, to fulfill the word
the LORD had spoken to Jeroboam son of Nebat
through Ahijah the Shilonite.
[16]When all Israel saw that the king refused to
listen to them, they answered the king:

"What share do we have in David,
what part in Jesse's son?
To your tents, O Israel!
Look after your own house, O David!"

So all the Israelites went home. [17]But as for the
Israelites who were living in the towns of Judah,
Rehoboam still ruled over them.
[18]King Rehoboam sent out Adoniram,[v] who
was in charge of forced labor, but the Israelites
stoned him to death. King Rehoboam, however,
managed to get into his chariot and escape to
Jerusalem. [19]So Israel has been in rebellion
against the house of David to this day.

11 When Rehoboam arrived in Jerusa-
lem, he mustered the house of Ju-
dah and Benjamin—a hundred and
eighty thousand fighting men—to make war
against Israel and to regain the kingdom for Re-
hoboam.
[2]But this word of the LORD came to Shemaiah
the man of God: [3]"Say to Rehoboam son of Solo-
mon king of Judah and to all the Israelites in
Judah and Benjamin, [4]'This is what the LORD says:
Do not go up to fight against your brothers. Go
home, every one of you, for this is my doing.' " So
they obeyed the words of the LORD and turned
back from marching against Jeroboam.
[5]Rehoboam lived in Jerusalem and built up
towns for defense in Judah: [6]Bethlehem, Etam,
Tekoa, [7]Beth Zur, Soco, Adullam, [8]Gath, Mare-
shah, Ziph, [9]Adoraim, Lachish, Azekah, [10]Zorah,
Aijalon and Hebron. These were fortified cities in
Judah and Benjamin. [11]He strengthened their de-
fenses and put commanders in them, with sup-
plies of food, olive oil and wine. [12]He put shields
and spears in all the cities, and made them very
strong. So Judah and Benjamin were his.
[13]The priests and Levites from all their districts
throughout Israel sided with him. [14]The Levites
even abandoned their pasturelands and property,
and came to Judah and Jerusalem because Jero-
boam and his sons had rejected them as priests of
the LORD. [15]And he appointed his own priests for
the high places and for the goat and calf idols he
had made. [16]Those from every tribe of Israel who
set their hearts on seeking the LORD, the God of
Israel, followed the Levites to Jerusalem to offer
sacrifices to the LORD, the God of their fathers.
[17]They strengthened the kingdom of Judah and
supported Rehoboam son of Solomon three years,
walking in the ways of David and Solomon during
this time.
[18]Rehoboam married Mahalath, who was the
daughter of David's son Jerimoth and of Abihail,
the daughter of Jesse's son Eliab. [19]She bore him
sons: Jeush, Shemariah and Zaham. [20]Then he
married Maacah daughter of Absalom, who bore
him Abijah, Attai, Ziza and Shelomith. [21]Reho-
boam loved Maacah daughter of Absalom more
than any of his other wives and concubines. In
all, he had eighteen wives and sixty concubines,
twenty-eight sons and sixty daughters.
[22]Rehoboam appointed Abijah son of Maacah
to be the chief prince among his brothers, in or-
der to make him king. [23]He acted wisely, dispers-
ing some of his sons throughout the districts of
Judah and Benjamin, and to all the fortified cities.
He gave them abundant provisions and took
many wives for them.

[v] 18 Hebrew *Hadoram*, a variant of *Adoniram*

12

After Rehoboam's position as king was established and he had become strong, he and all Israel[w] with him abandoned the law of the LORD. 2Because they had been unfaithful to the LORD, Shishak king of Egypt attacked Jerusalem in the fifth year of King Rehoboam. 3With twelve hundred chariots and sixty thousand horsemen and the innumerable troops of Libyans, Sukkites and Cushites[x] that came with him from Egypt, 4he captured the fortified cities of Judah and came as far as Jerusalem.

5Then the prophet Shemaiah came to Rehoboam and to the leaders of Judah who had assembled in Jerusalem for fear of Shishak, and he said to them, "This is what the LORD says, 'You have abandoned me; therefore, I now abandon you to Shishak.' "

6The leaders of Israel and the king humbled themselves and said, "The LORD is just."

7When the LORD saw that they humbled themselves, this word of the LORD came to Shemaiah: "Since they have humbled themselves, I will not destroy them but will soon give them deliverance. My wrath will not be poured out on Jerusalem through Shishak. 8They will, however, become subject to him, so that they may learn the difference between serving me and serving the kings of other lands."

9When Shishak king of Egypt attacked Jerusalem, he carried off the treasures of the temple of the LORD and the treasures of the royal palace. He took everything, including the gold shields Solomon had made. 10So King Rehoboam made bronze shields to replace them and assigned these to the commanders of the guard on duty at the entrance to the royal palace. 11Whenever the king went to the LORD's temple, the guards went with him, bearing the shields, and afterward they returned them to the guardroom.

12Because Rehoboam humbled himself, the LORD's anger turned from him, and he was not totally destroyed. Indeed, there was some good in Judah.

13King Rehoboam established himself firmly in Jerusalem and continued as king. He was forty-one years old when he became king, and he reigned seventeen years in Jerusalem, the city the LORD had chosen out of all the tribes of Israel in which to put his Name. His mother's name was Naamah; she was an Ammonite. 14He did evil because he had not set his heart on seeking the LORD.

15As for the events of Rehoboam's reign, from beginning to end, are they not written in the records of Shemaiah the prophet and of Iddo the seer that deal with genealogies? There was continual warfare between Rehoboam and Jeroboam. 16Rehoboam rested with his fathers and was buried in the City of David. And Abijah his son succeeded him as king.

13

In the eighteenth year of the reign of Jeroboam, Abijah became king of Judah, 2and he reigned in Jerusalem three years. His mother's name was Maacah,[y] a daughter[z] of Uriel of Gibeah.

There was war between Abijah and Jeroboam. 3Abijah went into battle with a force of four hundred thousand able fighting men, and Jeroboam drew up a battle line against him with eight hundred thousand able troops.

4Abijah stood on Mount Zemaraim, in the hill country of Ephraim, and said, "Jeroboam and all Israel, listen to me! 5Don't you know that the LORD, the God of Israel, has given the kingship of Israel to David and his descendants forever by a covenant of salt? 6Yet Jeroboam son of Nebat, an official of Solomon son of David, rebelled against his master. 7Some worthless scoundrels gathered around him and opposed Rehoboam son of Solomon when he was young and indecisive and not strong enough to resist them.

8"And now you plan to resist the kingdom of the LORD, which is in the hands of David's descendants. You are indeed a vast army and have with you the golden calves that Jeroboam made to be your gods. 9But didn't you drive out the priests of the LORD, the sons of Aaron, and the Levites, and make priests of your own as the peoples of other lands do? Whoever comes to consecrate himself with a young bull and seven rams may become a priest of what are not gods.

10"As for us, the LORD is our God, and we have not forsaken him. The priests who serve the LORD are sons of Aaron, and the Levites assist them. 11Every morning and evening they present burnt offerings and fragrant incense to the LORD. They set out the bread on the ceremonially clean table and light the lamps on the gold lampstand every evening. We are observing the requirements of the LORD our God. But you have forsaken him. 12God is with us; he is our leader. His priests with

[w] *1* That is, Judah, as frequently in 2 Chronicles [x] *3* That is, people from the upper Nile region [y] *2* Most Septuagint manuscripts and Syriac (see also 2 Chron. 11:20 and 1 Kings 15:2); Hebrew *Micaiah* [z] *2* Or *granddaughter*

their trumpets will sound the battle cry against
you. Men of Israel, do not fight against the LORD,
the God of your fathers, for you will not suc-
ceed."
13Now Jeroboam had sent troops around to the
rear, so that while he was in front of Judah the
ambush was behind them. 14Judah turned and
saw that they were being attacked at both front
and rear. Then they cried out to the LORD. The
priests blew their trumpets 15and the men of Ju-
dah raised the battle cry. At the sound of their
battle cry, God routed Jeroboam and all Israel
before Abijah and Judah. 16The Israelites fled
before Judah, and God delivered them into
their hands. 17Abijah and his men inflicted heavy
losses on them, so that there were five hun-
dred thousand casualties among Israel's able men.
18The men of Israel were subdued on that oc-
casion, and the men of Judah were victorious be-
cause they relied on the LORD, the God of their
fathers.
19Abijah pursued Jeroboam and took from him
the towns of Bethel, Jeshanah and Ephron, with
their surrounding villages. 20Jeroboam did not re-
gain power during the time of Abijah. And the
LORD struck him down and he died.
21But Abijah grew in strength. He married four-
teen wives and had twenty-two sons and sixteen
daughters.
22The other events of Abijah's reign, what he
did and what he said, are written in the annota-
tions of the prophet Iddo.

3 / *2 Chronicles 14—15*
Seeking God

MY FRIEND SUSAN, emotionally raw from a recent divorce, attended a Fourth of July picnic with some friends, only to discover that the one thing more lonely than being alone is being alone in a crowd. She came home feeling not only husbandless, but also that her life was without God. For twenty years she had willed God out of existence. Now, more alone than ever, she stretched out on her empty bed and spoke the hesitant beginnings of prayer: "God, if you are there . . ." So began a torturous journey toward faith—a seeking after God. And God heard her prayer; bit by bit, God Almighty revealed himself to Susan.

 **Warming Up to God** How does God draw you to himself?

 **Read 2 Chronicles 14—15.**

14 And Abijah rested with his fathers
and was buried in the City of Da-
vid. Asa his son succeeded him as
king, and in his days the country was at peace for
ten years.
2Asa did what was good and right in the eyes
of the LORD his God. 3He removed the foreign
altars and the high places, smashed the sacred
stones and cut down the Asherah poles.[a]
4He commanded Judah to seek the LORD, the
God of their fathers, and to obey his laws and
commands. 5He removed the high places and
incense altars in every town in Judah, and the
kingdom was at peace under him. 6He built
up the fortified cities of Judah, since the land
was at peace. No one was at war with him dur-
ing those years, for the LORD gave him rest.
7"Let us build up these towns," he said to Ju-
dah, "and put walls around them, with towers,
gates and bars. The land is still ours, because we
have sought the LORD our God; we sought him
and he has given us rest on every side." So they
built and prospered.
8Asa had an army of three hundred thousand
men from Judah, equipped with large shields and
with spears, and two hundred and eighty thou-
sand from Benjamin, armed with small shields
and with bows. All these were brave fighting men.
9Zerah the Cushite marched out against them
with a vast army[b] and three hundred chariots,

[a]3 That is, symbols of the goddess Asherah; here and elsewhere in 2 Chronicles [b]9 Hebrew *with an army of a thousand thousands* or *with an army of thousands upon thousands*

and came as far as Mareshah. 10Asa went out to
meet him, and they took up battle positions in the
Valley of Zephathah near Mareshah.
11Then Asa called to the LORD his God and said,
"LORD, there is no one like you to help the power-
less against the mighty. Help us, O LORD our God,
for we rely on you, and in your name we have
come against this vast army. O LORD, you are our
God; do not let man prevail against you."
12The LORD struck down the Cushites before
Asa and Judah. The Cushites fled, 13and Asa and
his army pursued them as far as Gerar. Such a
great number of Cushites fell that they could not
recover; they were crushed before the LORD and
his forces. The men of Judah carried off a large
amount of plunder. 14They destroyed all the vil-
lages around Gerar, for the terror of the LORD had
fallen upon them. They plundered all these vil-
lages, since there was much booty there. 15They
also attacked the camps of the herdsmen and car-
ried off droves of sheep and goats and camels.
Then they returned to Jerusalem.

15 The Spirit of God came upon Aza-
riah son of Oded. 2He went out to
meet Asa and said to him, "Listen
to me, Asa and all Judah and Benjamin. The LORD
is with you when you are with him. If you seek
him, he will be found by you, but if you forsake
him, he will forsake you. 3For a long time Israel
was without the true God, without a priest to
teach and without the law. 4But in their distress
they turned to the LORD, the God of Israel, and
sought him, and he was found by them. 5In those
days it was not safe to travel about, for all the
inhabitants of the lands were in great turmoil.
6One nation was being crushed by another and
one city by another, because God was troubling
them with every kind of distress. 7But as for you,
be strong and do not give up, for your work will
be rewarded."
8When Asa heard these words and the proph-
ecy of Azariah son of[c] Oded the prophet, he took
courage. He removed the detestable idols from
the whole land of Judah and Benjamin and from
the towns he had captured in the hills of
Ephraim. He repaired the altar of the LORD that
was in front of the portico of the LORD's temple.
9Then he assembled all Judah and Benjamin
and the people from Ephraim, Manasseh and Sim-
eon who had settled among them, for large num-
bers had come over to him from Israel when they
saw that the LORD his God was with him.
10They assembled at Jerusalem in the third
month of the fifteenth year of Asa's reign. 11At
that time they sacrificed to the LORD seven hun-
dred head of cattle and seven thousand sheep and
goats from the plunder they had brought back.
12They entered into a covenant to seek the LORD,
the God of their fathers, with all their heart and
soul. 13All who would not seek the LORD, the God
of Israel, were to be put to death, whether small
or great, man or woman. 14They took an oath to
the LORD with loud acclamation, with shouting
and with trumpets and horns. 15All Judah re-
joiced about the oath because they had sworn it
wholeheartedly. They sought God eagerly, and he
was found by them. So the LORD gave them rest on
every side.
16King Asa also deposed his grandmother Maa-
cah from her position as queen mother, because
she had made a repulsive Asherah pole. Asa cut
the pole down, broke it up and burned it in the
Kidron Valley. 17Although he did not remove the
high places from Israel, Asa's heart was fully com-
mitted ⌞to the LORD⌟ all his life. 18He brought into
the temple of God the silver and gold and the
articles that he and his father had dedicated.
19There was no more war until the thirty-fifth
year of Asa's reign.

c8 Vulgate and Syriac (see also Septuagint and verse 1); Hebrew does not have *Azariah son of.*

Discovering the Word 1. List the action words in 14:1–7. 2. What do these words tell you about Asa? 3. What does Asa's prayer (14:11) reveal about his relationship with God? 4. Looking at 15:1–7, what past conditions in Israel might cause Asa to listen carefully to God's message? 5. What information can you gather from this prophecy about what God expects from his followers? 6. What words and phrases in 15:8–19 show the wholeheartedness with which Asa and his people turned to God?

Applying the Word 1. These chapters show that if you seek the Lord, you will find him. What does this suggest about the nature of spiritual development?

Responding in Prayer Ask God to reveal himself to you and increase your faith so that you can believe more strongly in him.

2 Chronicles 16—17

16 In the thirty-sixth year of Asa's reign Baasha king of Israel went up against Judah and fortified Ramah to prevent anyone from leaving or entering the territory of Asa king of Judah.

2Asa then took the silver and gold out of the treasuries of the LORD's temple and of his own palace and sent it to Ben-Hadad king of Aram, who was ruling in Damascus. 3"Let there be a treaty between me and you," he said, "as there was between my father and your father. See, I am sending you silver and gold. Now break your treaty with Baasha king of Israel so he will withdraw from me."

4Ben-Hadad agreed with King Asa and sent the commanders of his forces against the towns of Israel. They conquered Ijon, Dan, Abel Maim[d] and all the store cities of Naphtali. 5When Baasha heard this, he stopped building Ramah and abandoned his work. 6Then King Asa brought all the men of Judah, and they carried away from Ramah the stones and timber Baasha had been using. With them he built up Geba and Mizpah.

7At that time Hanani the seer came to Asa king of Judah and said to him: "Because you relied on the king of Aram and not on the LORD your God, the army of the king of Aram has escaped from your hand. 8Were not the Cushites[e] and Libyans a mighty army with great numbers of chariots and horsemen[f]? Yet when you relied on the LORD, he delivered them into your hand. 9For the eyes of the LORD range throughout the earth to strengthen those whose hearts are fully committed to him. You have done a foolish thing, and from now on you will be at war."

10Asa was angry with the seer because of this; he was so enraged that he put him in prison. At the same time Asa brutally oppressed some of the people.

11The events of Asa's reign, from beginning to end, are written in the book of the kings of Judah and Israel. 12In the thirty-ninth year of his reign Asa was afflicted with a disease in his feet. Though his disease was severe, even in his illness he did not seek help from the LORD, but only from the physicians. 13Then in the forty-first year of his reign Asa died and rested with his fathers. 14They buried him in the tomb that he had cut out for himself in the City of David. They laid him on a bier covered with spices and various blended perfumes, and they made a huge fire in his honor.

17 Jehoshaphat his son succeeded him as king and strengthened himself against Israel. 2He stationed troops in all the fortified cities of Judah and put garrisons in Judah and in the towns of Ephraim that his father Asa had captured.

3The LORD was with Jehoshaphat because in his early years he walked in the ways his father David had followed. He did not consult the Baals 4but sought the God of his father and followed his commands rather than the practices of Israel. 5The LORD established the kingdom under his control; and all Judah brought gifts to Jehoshaphat, so that he had great wealth and honor. 6His heart was devoted to the ways of the LORD; furthermore, he removed the high places and the Asherah poles from Judah.

7In the third year of his reign he sent his officials Ben-Hail, Obadiah, Zechariah, Nethanel and Micaiah to teach in the towns of Judah. 8With them were certain Levites—Shemaiah, Nethaniah, Zebadiah, Asahel, Shemiramoth, Jehonathan, Adonijah, Tobijah and Tob-Adonijah—and the priests Elishama and Jehoram. 9They taught throughout Judah, taking with them the Book of the Law of the LORD; they went around to all the towns of Judah and taught the people.

10The fear of the LORD fell on all the kingdoms of the lands surrounding Judah, so that they did not make war with Jehoshaphat. 11Some Philistines brought Jehoshaphat gifts and silver as tribute, and the Arabs brought him flocks: seven thousand seven hundred rams and seven thousand seven hundred goats.

12Jehoshaphat became more and more powerful; he built forts and store cities in Judah 13and had large supplies in the towns of Judah. He also kept experienced fighting men in Jerusalem. 14Their enrollment by families was as follows:

From Judah, commanders of units of 1,000:
Adnah the commander, with 300,000 fighting men;

[d]4 Also known as *Abel Beth Maacah* [e]8 That is, people from the upper Nile region [f]8 Or *charioteers*

[15]next, Jehohanan the commander, with 280,000;
[16]next, Amasiah son of Zicri, who volunteered himself for the service of the LORD, with 200,000.
[17]From Benjamin:
Eliada, a valiant soldier, with 200,000 men armed with bows and shields;
[18]next, Jehozabad, with 180,000 men armed for battle.

[19]These were the men who served the king, besides those he stationed in the fortified cities throughout Judah.

4 / *2 Chronicles 18:1—19:3*
Unpopular Prophecy

"THAT WILL NEVER work." "Give up." "It's no use trying." Some people specialize in telling other people why their plans are hopeless. While nobody likes a wet blanket, there are times when God looks at our plans and says, "Don't do it." At those times we have to be open to change.

Warming Up to God How have you seen God at work in shaping your plans?

Read 2 Chronicles 18:1—19:3.

18 Now Jehoshaphat had great wealth
and honor, and he allied himself
with Ahab by marriage. [2]Some
years later he went down to visit Ahab in Samaria. Ahab slaughtered many sheep and cattle for him and the people with him and urged him to attack Ramoth Gilead. [3]Ahab king of Israel asked Jehoshaphat king of Judah, "Will you go with me against Ramoth Gilead?"

Jehoshaphat replied, "I am as you are, and my people as your people; we will join you in the war." [4]But Jehoshaphat also said to the king of Israel, "First seek the counsel of the LORD."

[5]So the king of Israel brought together the prophets—four hundred men—and asked them, "Shall we go to war against Ramoth Gilead, or shall I refrain?"

"Go," they answered, "for God will give it into the king's hand."

[6]But Jehoshaphat asked, "Is there not a prophet of the LORD here whom we can inquire of?"

[7]The king of Israel answered Jehoshaphat, "There is still one man through whom we can inquire of the LORD, but I hate him because he never prophesies anything good about me, but always bad. He is Micaiah son of Imlah."

"The king should not say that," Jehoshaphat replied.

[8]So the king of Israel called one of his officials and said, "Bring Micaiah son of Imlah at once."

[9]Dressed in their royal robes, the king of Israel and Jehoshaphat king of Judah were sitting on their thrones at the threshing floor by the entrance to the gate of Samaria, with all the prophets prophesying before them. [10]Now Zedekiah son of Kenaanah had made iron horns, and he declared, "This is what the LORD says: 'With these you will gore the Arameans until they are destroyed.'"

[11]All the other prophets were prophesying the same thing. "Attack Ramoth Gilead and be victorious," they said, "for the LORD will give it into the king's hand."

[12]The messenger who had gone to summon Micaiah said to him, "Look, as one man the other prophets are predicting success for the king. Let your word agree with theirs, and speak favorably."

13But Micaiah said, "As surely as the LORD lives,
I can tell him only what my God says."
14When he arrived, the king asked him, "Mica-
iah, shall we go to war against Ramoth Gilead, or
shall I refrain?"
"Attack and be victorious," he answered, "for
they will be given into your hand."
15The king said to him, "How many times must
I make you swear to tell me nothing but the truth
in the name of the LORD?"
16Then Micaiah answered, "I saw all Israel scat-
tered on the hills like sheep without a shepherd,
and the LORD said, 'These people have no master.
Let each one go home in peace.' "
17The king of Israel said to Jehoshaphat,
"Didn't I tell you that he never prophesies any-
thing good about me, but only bad?"
18Micaiah continued, "Therefore hear the word
of the LORD: I saw the LORD sitting on his throne
with all the host of heaven standing on his right
and on his left. 19And the LORD said, 'Who will
entice Ahab king of Israel into attacking Ramoth
Gilead and going to his death there?'
"One suggested this, and another that. 20Fi-
nally, a spirit came forward, stood before the LORD
and said, 'I will entice him.'
" 'By what means?' the LORD asked.
21" 'I will go and be a lying spirit in the mouths
of all his prophets,' he said.
" 'You will succeed in enticing him,' said the
LORD. 'Go and do it.'
22"So now the LORD has put a lying spirit in the
mouths of these prophets of yours. The LORD has
decreed disaster for you."
23Then Zedekiah son of Kenaanah went up and
slapped Micaiah in the face. "Which way did the
spirit from[g] the LORD go when he went from me
to speak to you?" he asked.
24Micaiah replied, "You will find out on the day
you go to hide in an inner room."
25The king of Israel then ordered, "Take Mica-
iah and send him back to Amon the ruler of the
city and to Joash the king's son, 26and say, 'This is
what the king says: Put this fellow in prison and
give him nothing but bread and water until I re-
turn safely.' "
27Micaiah declared, "If you ever return safely,
the LORD has not spoken through me." Then he
added, "Mark my words, all you people!"
28So the king of Israel and Jehoshaphat king of
Judah went up to Ramoth Gilead. 29The king of
Israel said to Jehoshaphat, "I will enter the battle
in disguise, but you wear your royal robes." So
the king of Israel disguised himself and went into
battle.
30Now the king of Aram had ordered his char-
iot commanders, "Do not fight with anyone,
small or great, except the king of Israel." 31When
the chariot commanders saw Jehoshaphat, they
thought, "This is the king of Israel." So they
turned to attack him, but Jehoshaphat cried out,
and the LORD helped him. God drew them away
from him, 32for when the chariot commanders
saw that he was not the king of Israel, they
stopped pursuing him.
33But someone drew his bow at random and hit
the king of Israel between the sections of his ar-
mor. The king told the chariot driver, "Wheel
around and get me out of the fighting. I've been
wounded." 34All day long the battle raged, and
the king of Israel propped himself up in his char-
iot facing the Arameans until evening. Then at
sunset he died.

19 When Jehoshaphat king of Judah
returned safely to his palace in Je-
rusalem, 2Jehu the seer, the son of
Hanani, went out to meet him and said to the
king, "Should you help the wicked and love[h]
those who hate the LORD? Because of this, the
wrath of the LORD is upon you. 3There is, how-
ever, some good in you, for you have rid the land
of the Asherah poles and have set your heart on
seeking God."

[g]23 Or *Spirit of* [h]2 Or *and make alliances with*

Discovering the Word 1. Ahab asked Jehoshaphat to join him in battle against Ramoth Gilead. How was God's will revealed concerning this plan? 2. Why was Ahab reluctant to inquire of Micaiah (18:7)? 3. It appears that Micaiah was speaking ironically in 18:14 or testing the king in some way. How does Micaiah's prophecy about the result of the battle change when the king insists Micaiah speak in the Lord's name (18:16–19)? 4. How did Ahab try to protect himself (18:28–29)? 5. How was Micaiah's prophecy fulfilled (18:33–34)?

Applying the Word 1. When do you resist hearing any discouraging words about your plans? 2. What set plans do you have that need to be opened up for God's examination?

Responding in Prayer Put your favorite plans and goals before the Lord. Ask him to sort out your motives and even change your plans if it's his will.

2 Chronicles 19:4–11

[4]Jehoshaphat lived in Jerusalem, and he went out again among the people from Beersheba to the hill country of Ephraim and turned them back to the LORD, the God of their fathers. [5]He appointed judges in the land, in each of the fortified cities of Judah. [6]He told them, "Consider carefully what you do, because you are not judging for man but for the LORD, who is with you whenever you give a verdict. [7]Now let the fear of the LORD be upon you. Judge carefully, for with the LORD our God there is no injustice or partiality or bribery."

[8]In Jerusalem also, Jehoshaphat appointed some of the Levites, priests and heads of Israelite families to administer the law of the LORD and to settle disputes. And they lived in Jerusalem. [9]He gave them these orders: "You must serve faithfully and wholeheartedly in the fear of the LORD. [10]In every case that comes before you from your fellow countrymen who live in the cities—whether bloodshed or other concerns of the law, commands, decrees or ordinances—you are to warn them not to sin against the LORD; otherwise his wrath will come on you and your brothers. Do this, and you will not sin.

[11]"Amariah the chief priest will be over you in any matter concerning the LORD, and Zebadiah son of Ishmael, the leader of the tribe of Judah, will be over you in any matter concerning the king, and the Levites will serve as officials before you. Act with courage, and may the LORD be with those who do well."

5 / 2 *Chronicles 20:1–30*
Battle Weary

BATTLES IN JEHOSHAPHAT'S life took the form of armies marching across the Palestinian wilderness, bloody conflicts in the valleys, hunting and hiding in the mountains. My battles are of a different kind. They are often battles of time: four children, countless ensemble rehearsals for the girls, sports practices for the boys, two weekly Bible studies, a prayer group, a seventy-family Sunday school to superintend, a weepy neighbor to console, music practice to oversee ("No, a dotted half gets three beats"), homework to enforce, a neglected manuscript scattered over the dining-room table. I am battle weary.

I once experienced God's momentary deliverance from this battle. It took the form of a Midwestern snowstorm. Each jingle of the phone announced a cancellation. Our family had a day to lounge around a popping fire with the chords of Handel's *Messiah* in the background. I did not have to fight the battle that day.

Warming Up to God What weariness do you bring to God today?

Read 2 Chronicles 20:1–30.

20 After this, the Moabites and Ammonites with some of the Meunites[i] came to make war on Jehoshaphat.

[2]Some men came and told Jehoshaphat, "A vast army is coming against you from Edom,[j] from the other side of the Sea.[k] It is already in Hazazon Tamar" (that is, En Gedi). [3]Alarmed, Jehoshaphat resolved to inquire of the LORD, and he proclaimed a fast for all Judah. [4]The people of Judah came together to seek help from the LORD; indeed,

[i]1 Some Septuagint manuscripts; Hebrew *Ammonites* [j]2 One Hebrew manuscript; most Hebrew manuscripts, Septuagint and Vulgate *Aram*
[k]2 That is, the Dead Sea

they came from every town in Judah to seek him.
5Then Jehoshaphat stood up in the assembly of
Judah and Jerusalem at the temple of the LORD in
the front of the new courtyard 6and said:

"O LORD, God of our fathers, are you not
the God who is in heaven? You rule over
all the kingdoms of the nations. Power and
might are in your hand, and no one can
withstand you. 7O our God, did you not
drive out the inhabitants of this land before
your people Israel and give it forever to the
descendants of Abraham your friend? 8They
have lived in it and have built in it a sanctu-
ary for your Name, saying, 9'If calamity
comes upon us, whether the sword of judg-
ment, or plague or famine, we will stand in
your presence before this temple that bears
your Name and will cry out to you in our
distress, and you will hear us and save us.'
10"But now here are men from Ammon,
Moab and Mount Seir, whose territory you
would not allow Israel to invade when they
came from Egypt; so they turned away from
them and did not destroy them. 11See how
they are repaying us by coming to drive us
out of the possession you gave us as an in-
heritance. 12O our God, will you not judge
them? For we have no power to face this vast
army that is attacking us. We do not know
what to do, but our eyes are upon you."

13All the men of Judah, with their wives and
children and little ones, stood there before the
LORD.
14Then the Spirit of the LORD came upon Jaha-
ziel son of Zechariah, the son of Benaiah, the son
of Jeiel, the son of Mattaniah, a Levite and
descendant of Asaph, as he stood in the assembly.
15He said: "Listen, King Jehoshaphat and all
who live in Judah and Jerusalem! This is what the
LORD says to you: 'Do not be afraid or discouraged
because of this vast army. For the battle is not
yours, but God's. 16Tomorrow march down
against them. They will be climbing up by the
Pass of Ziz, and you will find them at the end of
the gorge in the Desert of Jeruel. 17You will not
have to fight this battle. Take up your positions;
stand firm and see the deliverance the LORD will
give you, O Judah and Jerusalem. Do not be
afraid; do not be discouraged. Go out to face
them tomorrow, and the LORD will be with
you.' "
18Jehoshaphat bowed with his face to the
ground, and all the people of Judah and Jerusalem
fell down in worship before the LORD. 19Then
some Levites from the Kohathites and Korahites
stood up and praised the LORD, the God of Israel,
with very loud voice.
20Early in the morning they left for the Desert
of Tekoa. As they set out, Jehoshaphat stood and
said, "Listen to me, Judah and people of Jerusa-
lem! Have faith in the LORD your God and you
will be upheld; have faith in his prophets and you
will be successful." 21After consulting the people,
Jehoshaphat appointed men to sing to the LORD
and to praise him for the splendor of his[l] holi-
ness as they went out at the head of the army,
saying:

"Give thanks to the LORD,
for his love endures forever."

22As they began to sing and praise, the LORD set
ambushes against the men of Ammon and Moab
and Mount Seir who were invading Judah, and
they were defeated. 23The men of Ammon and
Moab rose up against the men from Mount Seir to
destroy and annihilate them. After they finished
slaughtering the men from Seir, they helped to
destroy one another.
24When the men of Judah came to the place
that overlooks the desert and looked toward the
vast army, they saw only dead bodies lying on the
ground; no one had escaped. 25So Jehoshaphat
and his men went to carry off their plunder, and
they found among them a great amount of equip-
ment and clothing[m] and also articles of value—
more than they could take away. There was so
much plunder that it took three days to collect it.
26On the fourth day they assembled in the Valley
of Beracah, where they praised the LORD. This is
why it is called the Valley of Beracah[n] to this
day.
27Then, led by Jehoshaphat, all the men of Ju-
dah and Jerusalem returned joyfully to Jerusalem,
for the LORD had given them cause to rejoice over
their enemies. 28They entered Jerusalem and went
to the temple of the LORD with harps and lutes and
trumpets.
29The fear of God came upon all the kingdoms

[l]21 Or *him with the splendor of* [m]25 Some Hebrew manuscripts and Vulgate; most Hebrew manuscripts *corpses* [n]26 *Beracah* means *praise.*

of the countries when they heard how the LORD had fought against the enemies of Israel. 30And the kingdom of Jehoshaphat was at peace, for his God had given him rest on every side.

Discovering the Word 1. How did Jehoshaphat and his people respond to the news of the army's approach (vv. 1–4)? 2. What elements of praise do you find in Jehoshaphat's prayer (vv. 6–12)? 3. Imagine yourself standing in the crowd of people described in verse 13. How would you have felt about Jahaziel's words in verses 15–17? Why? 4. What methods did God use to fulfill his prophecy of the previous day (vv. 22–24)? 5. In what different ways did the people of Judah worship God (vv. 18–30)?

Applying the Word 1. Look again at the words in 2 Chronicles 20:15–17: "For the battle is not yours. . . . You will not have to fight this battle." When do you most need to hear this kind of message from God? 2. What can you learn from Jehoshaphat about the way to pray during such situations? 3. God will not fight all of our battles for us. (He didn't fight all of Jehoshaphat's. Besides, we might even be in the wrong battle!) But what can you learn from Jehoshaphat's walk with God that will help you cope when you feel battle weary?

Responding in Prayer Pray for a spirit of peace and contentment even in what worries you most just now.

2 Chronicles 20:31—22:12

31So Jehoshaphat reigned over Judah. He was thirty-five years old when he became king of Judah, and he reigned in Jerusalem twenty-five years. His mother's name was Azubah daughter of Shilhi. 32He walked in the ways of his father Asa and did not stray from them; he did what was right in the eyes of the LORD. 33The high places, however, were not removed, and the people still had not set their hearts on the God of their fathers.

34The other events of Jehoshaphat's reign, from beginning to end, are written in the annals of Jehu son of Hanani, which are recorded in the book of the kings of Israel.

35Later, Jehoshaphat king of Judah made an alliance with Ahaziah king of Israel, who was guilty of wickedness. 36He agreed with him to construct a fleet of trading ships.[o] After these were built at Ezion Geber, 37Eliezer son of Dodavahu of Mareshah prophesied against Jehoshaphat, saying, "Because you have made an alliance with Ahaziah, the LORD will destroy what you have made." The ships were wrecked and were not able to set sail to trade.[p]

21 Then Jehoshaphat rested with his fathers and was buried with them in the City of David. And Jehoram his son succeeded him as king. 2Jehoram's brothers, the sons of Jehoshaphat, were Azariah, Jehiel, Zechariah, Azariahu, Michael and Shephatiah. All these were sons of Jehoshaphat king of Israel.[q] 3Their father had given them many gifts of silver and gold and articles of value, as well as fortified cities in Judah, but he had given the kingdom to Jehoram because he was his firstborn son.

4When Jehoram established himself firmly over his father's kingdom, he put all his brothers to the sword along with some of the princes of Israel. 5Jehoram was thirty-two years old when he became king, and he reigned in Jerusalem eight years. 6He walked in the ways of the kings of Israel, as the house of Ahab had done, for he married a daughter of Ahab. He did evil in the eyes of the LORD. 7Nevertheless, because of the covenant the LORD had made with David, the LORD was not willing to destroy the house of David. He had promised to maintain a lamp for him and his descendants forever.

8In the time of Jehoram, Edom rebelled against Judah and set up its own king. 9So Jehoram went there with his officers and all his chariots. The Edomites surrounded him and his chariot commanders, but he rose up and broke through by night. 10To this day Edom has been in rebellion against Judah.

Libnah revolted at the same time, because Jehoram had forsaken the LORD, the God of his fathers. 11He had also built high places on the hills of Judah and had caused the people of Jerusalem to prostitute themselves and had led Judah astray.

[o]36 Hebrew *of ships that could go to Tarshish* [p]37 Hebrew *sail for Tarshish* [q]2 That is, Judah, as frequently in 2 Chronicles

12Jehoram received a letter from Elijah the prophet, which said:

"This is what the LORD, the God of your father David, says: 'You have not walked in the ways of your father Jehoshaphat or of Asa king of Judah. 13But you have walked in the ways of the kings of Israel, and you have led Judah and the people of Jerusalem to prostitute themselves, just as the house of Ahab did. You have also murdered your own brothers, members of your father's house, men who were better than you. 14So now the LORD is about to strike your people, your sons, your wives and everything that is yours, with a heavy blow. 15You yourself will be very ill with a lingering disease of the bowels, until the disease causes your bowels to come out.' "

16The LORD aroused against Jehoram the hostility of the Philistines and of the Arabs who lived near the Cushites. 17They attacked Judah, invaded it and carried off all the goods found in the king's palace, together with his sons and wives. Not a son was left to him except Ahaziah,[r] the youngest.

18After all this, the LORD afflicted Jehoram with an incurable disease of the bowels. 19In the course of time, at the end of the second year, his bowels came out because of the disease, and he died in great pain. His people made no fire in his honor, as they had for his fathers.

20Jehoram was thirty-two years old when he became king, and he reigned in Jerusalem eight years. He passed away, to no one's regret, and was buried in the City of David, but not in the tombs of the kings.

22 The people of Jerusalem made Ahaziah, Jehoram's youngest son, king in his place, since the raiders, who came with the Arabs into the camp, had killed all the older sons. So Ahaziah son of Jehoram king of Judah began to reign.

2Ahaziah was twenty-two[s] years old when he became king, and he reigned in Jerusalem one year. His mother's name was Athaliah, a granddaughter of Omri.

3He too walked in the ways of the house of Ahab, for his mother encouraged him in doing wrong. 4He did evil in the eyes of the LORD, as the house of Ahab had done, for after his father's death they became his advisers, to his undoing. 5He also followed their counsel when he went with Joram[t] son of Ahab king of Israel to war against Hazael king of Aram at Ramoth Gilead. The Arameans wounded Joram; 6so he returned to Jezreel to recover from the wounds they had inflicted on him at Ramoth[u] in his battle with Hazael king of Aram.

Then Ahaziah[v] son of Jehoram king of Judah went down to Jezreel to see Joram son of Ahab because he had been wounded.

7Through Ahaziah's visit to Joram, God brought about Ahaziah's downfall. When Ahaziah arrived, he went out with Joram to meet Jehu son of Nimshi, whom the LORD had anointed to destroy the house of Ahab. 8While Jehu was executing judgment on the house of Ahab, he found the princes of Judah and the sons of Ahaziah's relatives, who had been attending Ahaziah, and he killed them. 9He then went in search of Ahaziah, and his men captured him while he was hiding in Samaria. He was brought to Jehu and put to death. They buried him, for they said, "He was a son of Jehoshaphat, who sought the LORD with all his heart." So there was no one in the house of Ahaziah powerful enough to retain the kingdom.

10When Athaliah the mother of Ahaziah saw that her son was dead, she proceeded to destroy the whole royal family of the house of Judah. 11But Jehosheba,[w] the daughter of King Jehoram, took Joash son of Ahaziah and stole him away from among the royal princes who were about to be murdered and put him and his nurse in a bedroom. Because Jehosheba,[w] the daughter of King Jehoram and wife of the priest Jehoiada, was Ahaziah's sister, she hid the child from Athaliah so she could not kill him. 12He remained hidden with them at the temple of God for six years while Athaliah ruled the land.

[r] *17* Hebrew *Jehoahaz,* a variant of *Ahaziah*
[s] 2 Some Septuagint manuscripts and Syriac (see also 2 Kings 8:26); Hebrew *forty-two*
[t] 5 Hebrew *Jehoram,* a variant of *Joram;* also in verses 6 and 7
[u] 6 Hebrew *Ramah,* a variant of *Ramoth*
[v] 6 Some Hebrew manuscripts, Septuagint, Vulgate and Syriac (see also 2 Kings 8:29); most Hebrew manuscripts *Azariah*
[w] *11* Hebrew *Jehoshabeath,* a variant of *Jehosheba*

6 / 2 Chronicles 23—24
Protégé to a Priest

A CAR LOADED with household goods stands waiting in the driveway. I hug my spiritual mentor, my best friend, goodby. I close the car door behind her and watch her drive away while a gnawing emptiness digs at my gut. My mind goes back over our intense times of searching the Scriptures together, comfortable walks in the woods, shouting rides on a snow sled, tearful problem solving, brief honest prayers for one another. And I know I can never relive those times. They are gone, with her, to the West Coast.

It hasn't happened—yet. But the scene has crossed my mind often enough for me to ask myself some hard questions: Where is my faith anchored? In her or in God? If she goes, where will I turn for spiritual nurture? Am I a grown woman, able to find constructive ways to meet my own needs? Or am I still wandering, umbilical cord in hand, looking for a place to plug it in?

Warming Up to God What person is most responsible for your own spiritual development? How has that person nurtured you?

Read 2 Chronicles 23—24.

23 In the seventh year Jehoiada
showed his strength. He made a
covenant with the commanders of
units of a hundred: Azariah son of Jeroham, Ish-
mael son of Jehohanan, Azariah son of Obed, Ma-
aseiah son of Adaiah, and Elishaphat son of Zicri.
2They went throughout Judah and gathered the
Levites and the heads of Israelite families from all
the towns. When they came to Jerusalem, 3the
whole assembly made a covenant with the king at
the temple of God.

Jehoiada said to them, "The king's son shall
reign, as the LORD promised concerning the
descendants of David. 4Now this is what you are
to do: A third of you priests and Levites who are
going on duty on the Sabbath are to keep watch at
the doors, 5a third of you at the royal palace and
a third at the Foundation Gate, and all the other
men are to be in the courtyards of the temple of
the LORD. 6No one is to enter the temple of the
LORD except the priests and Levites on duty; they
may enter because they are consecrated, but all
the other men are to guard what the LORD has
assigned to them.[x] 7The Levites are to station
themselves around the king, each man with his
weapons in his hand. Anyone who enters the
temple must be put to death. Stay close to the
king wherever he goes."

8The Levites and all the men of Judah did just
as Jehoiada the priest ordered. Each one took his
men—those who were going on duty on the Sab-
bath and those who were going off duty—for Je-
hoiada the priest had not released any of the divi-
sions. 9Then he gave the commanders of units
of a hundred the spears and the large and small
shields that had belonged to King David and that
were in the temple of God. 10He stationed all the
men, each with his weapon in his hand, around
the king—near the altar and the temple, from the
south side to the north side of the temple.

11Jehoiada and his sons brought out the king's
son and put the crown on him; they presented
him with a copy of the covenant and proclaimed
him king. They anointed him and shouted, "Long
live the king!"

12When Athaliah heard the noise of the people
running and cheering the king, she went to them
at the temple of the LORD. 13She looked, and there
was the king, standing by his pillar at the en-
trance. The officers and the trumpeters were be-
side the king, and all the people of the land were
rejoicing and blowing trumpets, and singers with
musical instruments were leading the praises.
Then Athaliah tore her robes and shouted, "Trea-
son! Treason!"

14Jehoiada the priest sent out the commanders
of units of a hundred, who were in charge of the
troops, and said to them: "Bring her out between
the ranks[y] and put to the sword anyone who
follows her." For the priest had said, "Do not put
her to death at the temple of the LORD." 15So they
seized her as she reached the entrance of the
Horse Gate on the palace grounds, and there they
put her to death.

16Jehoiada then made a covenant that he and

x6 *Or to observe the LORD's command ⌞not to enter⌟* y14 *Or out from the precincts*

the people and the king[z] would be the LORD's
people. 17All the people went to the temple of
Baal and tore it down. They smashed the altars
and idols and killed Mattan the priest of Baal in
front of the altars.
18Then Jehoiada placed the oversight of the
temple of the LORD in the hands of the priests,
who were Levites, to whom David had made as-
signments in the temple, to present the burnt of-
ferings of the LORD as written in the Law of Moses,
with rejoicing and singing, as David had ordered.
19He also stationed doorkeepers at the gates of the
LORD's temple so that no one who was in any way
unclean might enter.
20He took with him the commanders of hun-
dreds, the nobles, the rulers of the people and all
the people of the land and brought the king down
from the temple of the LORD. They went into the
palace through the Upper Gate and seated the
king on the royal throne, 21and all the people of
the land rejoiced. And the city was quiet, because
Athaliah had been slain with the sword.

24

Joash was seven years old when he
became king, and he reigned in Je-
rusalem forty years. His mother's
name was Zibiah; she was from Beersheba. 2Joash
did what was right in the eyes of the LORD all the
years of Jehoiada the priest. 3Jehoiada chose two
wives for him, and he had sons and daughters.
4Some time later Joash decided to restore the
temple of the LORD. 5He called together the priests
and Levites and said to them, "Go to the towns of
Judah and collect the money due annually from
all Israel, to repair the temple of your God. Do it
now." But the Levites did not act at once.
6Therefore the king summoned Jehoiada the
chief priest and said to him, "Why haven't you
required the Levites to bring in from Judah and
Jerusalem the tax imposed by Moses the servant
of the LORD and by the assembly of Israel for the
Tent of the Testimony?"
7Now the sons of that wicked woman Athaliah
had broken into the temple of God and had used
even its sacred objects for the Baals.
8At the king's command, a chest was made and
placed outside, at the gate of the temple of the
LORD. 9A proclamation was then issued in Judah
and Jerusalem that they should bring to the LORD
the tax that Moses the servant of God had re-
quired of Israel in the desert. 10All the officials
and all the people brought their contributions
gladly, dropping them into the chest until it was
full. 11Whenever the chest was brought in by the
Levites to the king's officials and they saw that
there was a large amount of money, the royal sec-
retary and the officer of the chief priest would
come and empty the chest and carry it back to
its place. They did this regularly and collected a
great amount of money. 12The king and Jehoiada
gave it to the men who carried out the work re-
quired for the temple of the LORD. They hired ma-
sons and carpenters to restore the LORD's temple,
and also workers in iron and bronze to repair the
temple.
13The men in charge of the work were diligent,
and the repairs progressed under them. They re-
built the temple of God according to its original
design and reinforced it. 14When they had fin-
ished, they brought the rest of the money to the
king and Jehoiada, and with it were made articles
for the LORD's temple: articles for the service and
for the burnt offerings, and also dishes and other
objects of gold and silver. As long as Jehoiada
lived, burnt offerings were presented continually
in the temple of the LORD.
15Now Jehoiada was old and full of years, and
he died at the age of a hundred and thirty. 16He
was buried with the kings in the City of David,
because of the good he had done in Israel for God
and his temple.
17After the death of Jehoiada, the officials of
Judah came and paid homage to the king, and he
listened to them. 18They abandoned the temple of
the LORD, the God of their fathers, and worshiped
Asherah poles and idols. Because of their guilt,
God's anger came upon Judah and Jerusalem.
19Although the LORD sent prophets to the people
to bring them back to him, and though they testi-
fied against them, they would not listen.
20Then the Spirit of God came upon Zechariah
son of Jehoiada the priest. He stood before the
people and said, "This is what God says: 'Why do
you disobey the LORD's commands? You will not
prosper. Because you have forsaken the LORD, he
has forsaken you.' "
21But they plotted against him, and by order of
the king they stoned him to death in the court-
yard of the LORD's temple. 22King Joash did not
remember the kindness Zechariah's father Jehoi-
ada had shown him but killed his son, who said
as he lay dying, "May the LORD see this and call
you to account."

z16 Or *covenant between* ⌞*the* LORD⌟ *and the people and the king that they* (see 2 Kings 11:17)

23At the turn of the year,[a] the army of Aram marched against Joash; it invaded Judah and Jerusalem and killed all the leaders of the people. They sent all the plunder to their king in Damascus. 24Although the Aramean army had come with only a few men, the LORD delivered into their hands a much larger army. Because Judah had forsaken the LORD, the God of their fathers, judgment was executed on Joash. 25When the Arameans withdrew, they left Joash severely wounded. His officials conspired against him for murdering the son of Jehoiada the priest, and they killed him in his bed. So he died and was buried in the City of David, but not in the tombs of the kings.

26Those who conspired against him were Zabad,[b] son of Shimeath an Ammonite woman, and Jehozabad, son of Shimrith[c] a Moabite woman. 27The account of his sons, the many prophecies about him, and the record of the restoration of the temple of God are written in the annotations on the book of the kings. And Amaziah his son succeeded him as king.

[a]23 Probably in the spring [b]26 A variant of *Jozabad* [c]26 A variant of *Shomer*

Discovering the Word 1. What groundwork did Jehoiada lay to ensure that the child Joash would safely become king (23:3–7)? 2. What steps did Jehoiada take to establish spiritual change in Judah (23:12—24:3)? 3. How would you describe the relationship between Jehoiada and Joash? 4. What indications do you see that Joash tried to make restoring the temple an honest process (24:4–14)? 5. What changes came to Judah after Jehoiada's death (24:17–27)? 6. Why would you not expect Joash to take this kind of turn?

Applying the Word 1. What could you be doing that would help you to continue to mature spiritually if your spiritual leader were removed from your life? 2. Think of one person for whom you are a spiritual guardian. How could you help that person continue growing spiritually even if you were no longer available to help?

Responding in Prayer Thank God for both those who have gone before you to lead the way of faith and those who follow after who you are privileged to lead.

2 Chronicles 25—33

25 Amaziah was twenty-five years old when he became king, and he reigned in Jerusalem twenty-nine years. His mother's name was Jehoaddin[d]; she was from Jerusalem. 2He did what was right in the eyes of the LORD, but not wholeheartedly. 3After the kingdom was firmly in his control, he executed the officials who had murdered his father the king. 4Yet he did not put their sons to death, but acted in accordance with what is written in the Law, in the Book of Moses, where the LORD commanded: "Fathers shall not be put to death for their children, nor children put to death for their fathers; each is to die for his own sins."[e]

5Amaziah called the people of Judah together and assigned them according to their families to commanders of thousands and commanders of hundreds for all Judah and Benjamin. He then mustered those twenty years old or more and found that there were three hundred thousand men ready for military service, able to handle the spear and shield. 6He also hired a hundred thousand fighting men from Israel for a hundred talents[f] of silver.

7But a man of God came to him and said, "O king, these troops from Israel must not march with you, for the LORD is not with Israel—not with any of the people of Ephraim. 8Even if you go and fight courageously in battle, God will overthrow you before the enemy, for God has the power to help or to overthrow."

9Amaziah asked the man of God, "But what about the hundred talents I paid for these Israelite troops?"

The man of God replied, "The LORD can give you much more than that."

10So Amaziah dismissed the troops who had come to him from Ephraim and sent them home. They were furious with Judah and left for home in a great rage.

11Amaziah then marshaled his strength and led his army to the Valley of Salt, where he killed ten thousand men of Seir. 12The army of Judah also

[d]1 Hebrew *Jehoaddan*, a variant of *Jehoaddin* [e]4 Deut. 24:16
[f]6 That is, about 3 3/4 tons (about 3.4 metric tons); also in verse 9

captured ten thousand men alive, took them to the top of a cliff and threw them down so that all were dashed to pieces.

[13]Meanwhile the troops that Amaziah had sent back and had not allowed to take part in the war raided Judean towns from Samaria to Beth Horon. They killed three thousand people and carried off great quantities of plunder.

[14]When Amaziah returned from slaughtering the Edomites, he brought back the gods of the people of Seir. He set them up as his own gods, bowed down to them and burned sacrifices to them. [15]The anger of the LORD burned against Amaziah, and he sent a prophet to him, who said, "Why do you consult this people's gods, which could not save their own people from your hand?"

[16]While he was still speaking, the king said to him, "Have we appointed you an adviser to the king? Stop! Why be struck down?"

So the prophet stopped but said, "I know that God has determined to destroy you, because you have done this and have not listened to my counsel."

[17]After Amaziah king of Judah consulted his advisers, he sent this challenge to Jehoash[g] son of Jehoahaz, the son of Jehu, king of Israel: "Come, meet me face to face."

[18]But Jehoash king of Israel replied to Amaziah king of Judah: "A thistle in Lebanon sent a message to a cedar in Lebanon, 'Give your daughter to my son in marriage.' Then a wild beast in Lebanon came along and trampled the thistle underfoot. [19]You say to yourself that you have defeated Edom, and now you are arrogant and proud. But stay at home! Why ask for trouble and cause your own downfall and that of Judah also?"

[20]Amaziah, however, would not listen, for God so worked that he might hand them over to ⌞Jehoash⌟, because they sought the gods of Edom. [21]So Jehoash king of Israel attacked. He and Amaziah king of Judah faced each other at Beth Shemesh in Judah. [22]Judah was routed by Israel, and every man fled to his home. [23]Jehoash king of Israel captured Amaziah king of Judah, the son of Joash, the son of Ahaziah,[h] at Beth Shemesh. Then Jehoash brought him to Jerusalem and broke down the wall of Jerusalem from the Ephraim Gate to the Corner Gate—a section about six hundred feet[i] long. [24]He took all the gold and silver and all the articles found in the temple of God that had been in the care of Obed-Edom, together with the palace treasures and the hostages, and returned to Samaria.

[25]Amaziah son of Joash king of Judah lived for fifteen years after the death of Jehoash son of Jehoahaz king of Israel. [26]As for the other events of Amaziah's reign, from beginning to end, are they not written in the book of the kings of Judah and Israel? [27]From the time that Amaziah turned away from following the LORD, they conspired against him in Jerusalem and he fled to Lachish, but they sent men after him to Lachish and killed him there. [28]He was brought back by horse and was buried with his fathers in the City of Judah.

26 Then all the people of Judah took Uzziah,[j] who was sixteen years old, and made him king in place of his father Amaziah. [2]He was the one who rebuilt Elath and restored it to Judah after Amaziah rested with his fathers.

[3]Uzziah was sixteen years old when he became king, and he reigned in Jerusalem fifty-two years. His mother's name was Jecoliah; she was from Jerusalem. [4]He did what was right in the eyes of the LORD, just as his father Amaziah had done. [5]He sought God during the days of Zechariah, who instructed him in the fear[k] of God. As long as he sought the LORD, God gave him success.

[6]He went to war against the Philistines and broke down the walls of Gath, Jabneh and Ashdod. He then rebuilt towns near Ashdod and elsewhere among the Philistines. [7]God helped him against the Philistines and against the Arabs who lived in Gur Baal and against the Meunites. [8]The Ammonites brought tribute to Uzziah, and his fame spread as far as the border of Egypt, because he had become very powerful.

[9]Uzziah built towers in Jerusalem at the Corner Gate, at the Valley Gate and at the angle of the wall, and he fortified them. [10]He also built towers in the desert and dug many cisterns, because he had much livestock in the foothills and in the plain. He had people working his fields and vineyards in the hills and in the fertile lands, for he loved the soil.

[11]Uzziah had a well-trained army, ready to go out by divisions according to their numbers as mustered by Jeiel the secretary and Maaseiah the officer under the direction of Hananiah, one of

[g]17 Hebrew *Joash*, a variant of *Jehoash*; also in verses 18, 21, 23 and 25 [h]23 Hebrew *Jehoahaz*, a variant of *Ahaziah* [i]23 Hebrew *four hundred cubits* (about 180 meters) [j]1 Also called *Azariah*
[k]5 Many Hebrew manuscripts, Septuagint and Syriac; other Hebrew manuscripts *vision*

the royal officials. 12The total number of family
leaders over the fighting men was 2,600. 13Under
their command was an army of 307,500 men
trained for war, a powerful force to support the
king against his enemies. 14Uzziah provided
shields, spears, helmets, coats of armor, bows and
slingstones for the entire army. 15In Jerusalem he
made machines designed by skillful men for use
on the towers and on the corner defenses to shoot
arrows and hurl large stones. His fame spread far
and wide, for he was greatly helped until he be-
came powerful.

16But after Uzziah became powerful, his pride
led to his downfall. He was unfaithful to the LORD
his God, and entered the temple of the LORD to
burn incense on the altar of incense. 17Azariah
the priest with eighty other courageous priests of
the LORD followed him in. 18They confronted him
and said, "It is not right for you, Uzziah, to burn
incense to the LORD. That is for the priests, the
descendants of Aaron, who have been conse-
crated to burn incense. Leave the sanctuary, for
you have been unfaithful; and you will not be
honored by the LORD God."

19Uzziah, who had a censer in his hand ready
to burn incense, became angry. While he was rag-
ing at the priests in their presence before the in-
cense altar in the LORD's temple, leprosy[l] broke
out on his forehead. 20When Azariah the chief
priest and all the other priests looked at him, they
saw that he had leprosy on his forehead, so they
hurried him out. Indeed, he himself was eager to
leave, because the LORD had afflicted him.

21King Uzziah had leprosy until the day he
died. He lived in a separate house[m]—leprous,
and excluded from the temple of the LORD. Jotham
his son had charge of the palace and governed the
people of the land.

22The other events of Uzziah's reign, from be-
ginning to end, are recorded by the prophet Isa-
iah son of Amoz. 23Uzziah rested with his fathers
and was buried near them in a field for burial that
belonged to the kings, for people said, "He had
leprosy." And Jotham his son succeeded him as
king.

27 Jotham was twenty-five years old
when he became king, and he
reigned in Jerusalem sixteen years.
His mother's name was Jerusha daughter of Za-
dok. 2He did what was right in the eyes of the
LORD, just as his father Uzziah had done, but un-
like him he did not enter the temple of the LORD.
The people, however, continued their corrupt
practices. 3Jotham rebuilt the Upper Gate of the
temple of the LORD and did extensive work on the
wall at the hill of Ophel. 4He built towns in the
Judean hills and forts and towers in the wooded
areas.

5Jotham made war on the king of the Ammon-
ites and conquered them. That year the Ammon-
ites paid him a hundred talents[n] of silver, ten
thousand cors[o] of wheat and ten thousand cors
of barley. The Ammonites brought him the same
amount also in the second and third years.

6Jotham grew powerful because he walked
steadfastly before the LORD his God.

7The other events in Jotham's reign, including
all his wars and the other things he did, are writ-
ten in the book of the kings of Israel and Judah.
8He was twenty-five years old when he became
king, and he reigned in Jerusalem sixteen years.
9Jotham rested with his fathers and was buried in
the City of David. And Ahaz his son succeeded
him as king.

28 Ahaz was twenty years old when he
became king, and he reigned in Je-
rusalem sixteen years. Unlike Da-
vid his father, he did not do what was right in the
eyes of the LORD. 2He walked in the ways of the
kings of Israel and also made cast idols for wor-
shiping the Baals. 3He burned sacrifices in the
Valley of Ben Hinnom and sacrificed his sons in
the fire, following the detestable ways of the na-
tions the LORD had driven out before the Israelites.
4He offered sacrifices and burned incense at the
high places, on the hilltops and under every
spreading tree.

5Therefore the LORD his God handed him over
to the king of Aram. The Arameans defeated him
and took many of his people as prisoners and
brought them to Damascus.

He was also given into the hands of the king of
Israel, who inflicted heavy casualties on him. 6In
one day Pekah son of Remaliah killed a hundred
and twenty thousand soldiers in Judah—because
Judah had forsaken the LORD, the God of their
fathers. 7Zicri, an Ephraimite warrior, killed Maa-
seiah the king's son, Azrikam the officer in charge
of the palace, and Elkanah, second to the king.
8The Israelites took captive from their kinsmen

[l]19 The Hebrew word was used for various diseases affecting the skin—not necessarily leprosy; also in verses 20, 21 and 23. [m]21 Or *in a house where he was relieved of responsibilities* [n]5 That is, about 3 3/4 tons (about 3.4 metric tons) [o]5 That is, probably about 62,000 bushels (about 2,200 kiloliters)

two hundred thousand wives, sons and daugh-
ters. They also took a great deal of plunder, which
they carried back to Samaria.
9But a prophet of the LORD named Oded was
there, and he went out to meet the army when it
returned to Samaria. He said to them, "Because
the LORD, the God of your fathers, was angry with
Judah, he gave them into your hand. But you
have slaughtered them in a rage that reaches to
heaven. 10And now you intend to make the men
and women of Judah and Jerusalem your slaves.
But aren't you also guilty of sins against the LORD
your God? 11Now listen to me! Send back your
fellow countrymen you have taken as prisoners,
for the LORD's fierce anger rests on you."
12Then some of the leaders in Ephraim—Aza-
riah son of Jehohanan, Berekiah son of Meshille-
moth, Jehizkiah son of Shallum, and Amasa son
of Hadlai—confronted those who were arriving
from the war. 13"You must not bring those pris-
oners here," they said, "or we will be guilty before
the LORD. Do you intend to add to our sin and
guilt? For our guilt is already great, and his fierce
anger rests on Israel."
14So the soldiers gave up the prisoners and
plunder in the presence of the officials and all the
assembly. 15The men designated by name took
the prisoners, and from the plunder they clothed
all who were naked. They provided them with
clothes and sandals, food and drink, and healing
balm. All those who were weak they put on don-
keys. So they took them back to their fellow
countrymen at Jericho, the City of Palms, and
returned to Samaria.
16At that time King Ahaz sent to the king[p] of
Assyria for help. 17The Edomites had again come
and attacked Judah and carried away prisoners,
18while the Philistines had raided towns in the
foothills and in the Negev of Judah. They cap-
tured and occupied Beth Shemesh, Aijalon and
Gederoth, as well as Soco, Timnah and Gimzo,
with their surrounding villages. 19The LORD had
humbled Judah because of Ahaz king of Israel,[q]
for he had promoted wickedness in Judah and
had been most unfaithful to the LORD. 20Tiglath-
Pileser[r] king of Assyria came to him, but he gave
him trouble instead of help. 21Ahaz took some of
the things from the temple of the LORD and from
the royal palace and from the princes and pre-
sented them to the king of Assyria, but that did
not help him.
22In his time of trouble King Ahaz became even
more unfaithful to the LORD. 23He offered sacri-
fices to the gods of Damascus, who had defeated
him; for he thought, "Since the gods of the kings
of Aram have helped them, I will sacrifice to them
so they will help me." But they were his downfall
and the downfall of all Israel.
24Ahaz gathered together the furnishings from
the temple of God and took them away.[s] He shut
the doors of the LORD's temple and set up altars at
every street corner in Jerusalem. 25In every town
in Judah he built high places to burn sacrifices to
other gods and provoked the LORD, the God of his
fathers, to anger.
26The other events of his reign and all his ways,
from beginning to end, are written in the book of
the kings of Judah and Israel. 27Ahaz rested with
his fathers and was buried in the city of Jerusa-
lem, but he was not placed in the tombs of the
kings of Israel. And Hezekiah his son succeeded
him as king.

29 Hezekiah was twenty-five years old
when he became king, and he
reigned in Jerusalem twenty-nine
years. His mother's name was Abijah daughter of
Zechariah. 2He did what was right in the eyes of
the LORD, just as his father David had done.
3In the first month of the first year of his reign,
he opened the doors of the temple of the LORD and
repaired them. 4He brought in the priests and the
Levites, assembled them in the square on the east
side 5and said: "Listen to me, Levites! Consecrate
yourselves now and consecrate the temple of the
LORD, the God of your fathers. Remove all defile-
ment from the sanctuary. 6Our fathers were un-
faithful; they did evil in the eyes of the LORD our
God and forsook him. They turned their faces
away from the LORD's dwelling place and turned
their backs on him. 7They also shut the doors of
the portico and put out the lamps. They did not
burn incense or present any burnt offerings at the
sanctuary to the God of Israel. 8Therefore, the
anger of the LORD has fallen on Judah and Jerusa-
lem; he has made them an object of dread and
horror and scorn, as you can see with your own
eyes. 9This is why our fathers have fallen by the
sword and why our sons and daughters and our
wives are in captivity. 10Now I intend to make a
covenant with the LORD, the God of Israel, so that
his fierce anger will turn away from us. 11My

[p]16 One Hebrew manuscript, Septuagint and Vulgate (see also 2 Kings 16:7); most Hebrew manuscripts *kings* [q]19 That is, Judah, as frequently in 2 Chronicles [r]20 Hebrew *Tilgath-Pilneser*, a variant of *Tiglath-Pileser* [s]24 Or *and cut them up*

sons, do not be negligent now, for the LORD has chosen you to stand before him and serve him, to minister before him and to burn incense."

12Then these Levites set to work:

from the Kohathites,
 Mahath son of Amasai and Joel son of Azariah;
from the Merarites,
 Kish son of Abdi and Azariah son of Jehallelel;
from the Gershonites,
 Joah son of Zimmah and Eden son of Joah;
13from the descendants of Elizaphan,
 Shimri and Jeiel;
from the descendants of Asaph,
 Zechariah and Mattaniah;
14from the descendants of Heman,
 Jehiel and Shimei;
from the descendants of Jeduthun,
 Shemaiah and Uzziel.

15When they had assembled their brothers and consecrated themselves, they went in to purify the temple of the LORD, as the king had ordered, following the word of the LORD. 16The priests went into the sanctuary of the LORD to purify it. They brought out to the courtyard of the LORD's temple everything unclean that they found in the temple of the LORD. The Levites took it and carried it out to the Kidron Valley. 17They began the consecration on the first day of the first month, and by the eighth day of the month they reached the portico of the LORD. For eight more days they consecrated the temple of the LORD itself, finishing on the sixteenth day of the first month.

18Then they went in to King Hezekiah and reported: "We have purified the entire temple of the LORD, the altar of burnt offering with all its utensils, and the table for setting out the consecrated bread, with all its articles. 19We have prepared and consecrated all the articles that King Ahaz removed in his unfaithfulness while he was king. They are now in front of the LORD's altar."

20Early the next morning King Hezekiah gathered the city officials together and went up to the temple of the LORD. 21They brought seven bulls, seven rams, seven male lambs and seven male goats as a sin offering for the kingdom, for the sanctuary and for Judah. The king commanded the priests, the descendants of Aaron, to offer these on the altar of the LORD. 22So they slaughtered the bulls, and the priests took the blood and sprinkled it on the altar; next they slaughtered the rams and sprinkled their blood on the altar; then they slaughtered the lambs and sprinkled their blood on the altar. 23The goats for the sin offering were brought before the king and the assembly, and they laid their hands on them. 24The priests then slaughtered the goats and presented their blood on the altar for a sin offering to atone for all Israel, because the king had ordered the burnt offering and the sin offering for all Israel.

25He stationed the Levites in the temple of the LORD with cymbals, harps and lyres in the way prescribed by David and Gad the king's seer and Nathan the prophet; this was commanded by the LORD through his prophets. 26So the Levites stood ready with David's instruments, and the priests with their trumpets.

27Hezekiah gave the order to sacrifice the burnt offering on the altar. As the offering began, singing to the LORD began also, accompanied by trumpets and the instruments of David king of Israel. 28The whole assembly bowed in worship, while the singers sang and the trumpeters played. All this continued until the sacrifice of the burnt offering was completed.

29When the offerings were finished, the king and everyone present with him knelt down and worshiped. 30King Hezekiah and his officials ordered the Levites to praise the LORD with the words of David and of Asaph the seer. So they sang praises with gladness and bowed their heads and worshiped.

31Then Hezekiah said, "You have now dedicated yourselves to the LORD. Come and bring sacrifices and thank offerings to the temple of the LORD." So the assembly brought sacrifices and thank offerings, and all whose hearts were willing brought burnt offerings.

32The number of burnt offerings the assembly brought was seventy bulls, a hundred rams and two hundred male lambs—all of them for burnt offerings to the LORD. 33The animals consecrated as sacrifices amounted to six hundred bulls and three thousand sheep and goats. 34The priests, however, were too few to skin all the burnt offerings; so their kinsmen the Levites helped them until the task was finished and until other priests had been consecrated, for the Levites had been more conscientious in consecrating themselves than the priests had been. 35There were burnt offerings in abundance, together with the fat of the

fellowship offerings[t] and the drink offerings that
accompanied the burnt offerings.

So the service of the temple of the LORD was
reestablished. 36Hezekiah and all the people re-
joiced at what God had brought about for his
people, because it was done so quickly.

30 Hezekiah sent word to all Israel and
Judah and also wrote letters to
Ephraim and Manasseh, inviting
them to come to the temple of the LORD in Jerusa-
lem and celebrate the Passover to the LORD, the
God of Israel. 2The king and his officials and the
whole assembly in Jerusalem decided to celebrate
the Passover in the second month. 3They had not
been able to celebrate it at the regular time be-
cause not enough priests had consecrated them-
selves and the people had not assembled in Jeru-
salem. 4The plan seemed right both to the king
and to the whole assembly. 5They decided to send
a proclamation throughout Israel, from Beersheba
to Dan, calling the people to come to Jerusalem
and celebrate the Passover to the LORD, the God of
Israel. It had not been celebrated in large num-
bers according to what was written.

6At the king's command, couriers went
throughout Israel and Judah with letters from the
king and from his officials, which read:

"People of Israel, return to the LORD, the
God of Abraham, Isaac and Israel, that he
may return to you who are left, who have
escaped from the hand of the kings of As-
syria. 7Do not be like your fathers and broth-
ers, who were unfaithful to the LORD, the
God of their fathers, so that he made them
an object of horror, as you see. 8Do not be
stiff-necked, as your fathers were; submit to
the LORD. Come to the sanctuary, which he
has consecrated forever. Serve the LORD your
God, so that his fierce anger will turn away
from you. 9If you return to the LORD, then
your brothers and your children will be
shown compassion by their captors and will
come back to this land, for the LORD your
God is gracious and compassionate. He will
not turn his face from you if you return to
him."

10The couriers went from town to town in
Ephraim and Manasseh, as far as Zebulun, but the
people scorned and ridiculed them. 11Neverthe-
less, some men of Asher, Manasseh and Zebulun
humbled themselves and went to Jerusalem.
12Also in Judah the hand of God was on the peo-
ple to give them unity of mind to carry out what
the king and his officials had ordered, following
the word of the LORD.

13A very large crowd of people assembled in
Jerusalem to celebrate the Feast of Unleavened
Bread in the second month. 14They removed the
altars in Jerusalem and cleared away the incense
altars and threw them into the Kidron Valley.

15They slaughtered the Passover lamb on the
fourteenth day of the second month. The priests
and the Levites were ashamed and consecrated
themselves and brought burnt offerings to the
temple of the LORD. 16Then they took up their
regular positions as prescribed in the Law of Mo-
ses the man of God. The priests sprinkled the
blood handed to them by the Levites. 17Since
many in the crowd had not consecrated them-
selves, the Levites had to kill the Passover lambs
for all those who were not ceremonially clean and
could not consecrate ⌞their lambs⌟ to the LORD.
18Although most of the many people who came
from Ephraim, Manasseh, Issachar and Zebulun
had not purified themselves, yet they ate the Pass-
over, contrary to what was written. But Hezekiah
prayed for them, saying, "May the LORD, who is
good, pardon everyone 19who sets his heart on
seeking God—the LORD, the God of his fathers—
even if he is not clean according to the rules of
the sanctuary." 20And the LORD heard Hezekiah
and healed the people.

21The Israelites who were present in Jerusalem
celebrated the Feast of Unleavened Bread for
seven days with great rejoicing, while the Levites
and priests sang to the LORD every day, accompa-
nied by the LORD's instruments of praise.[u]

22Hezekiah spoke encouragingly to all the Le-
vites, who showed good understanding of the ser-
vice of the LORD. For the seven days they ate their
assigned portion and offered fellowship offer-
ings[t] and praised the LORD, the God of their fa-
thers.

23The whole assembly then agreed to celebrate
the festival seven more days; so for another seven
days they celebrated joyfully. 24Hezekiah king of
Judah provided a thousand bulls and seven thou-
sand sheep and goats for the assembly, and the
officials provided them with a thousand bulls and
ten thousand sheep and goats. A great number of
priests consecrated themselves. 25The entire as-

t35,22 Traditionally *peace offerings* u21 Or *priests praised the LORD every day with resounding instruments belonging to the LORD*

sembly of Judah rejoiced, along with the priests
and Levites and all who had assembled from Is-
rael, including the aliens who had come from Is-
rael and those who lived in Judah. 26There was
great joy in Jerusalem, for since the days of Solo-
mon son of David king of Israel there had been
nothing like this in Jerusalem. 27The priests and
the Levites stood to bless the people, and God
heard them, for their prayer reached heaven, his
holy dwelling place.

31 When all this had ended, the Israel-
ites who were there went out to the
towns of Judah, smashed the sacred
stones and cut down the Asherah poles. They de-
stroyed the high places and the altars throughout
Judah and Benjamin and in Ephraim and Manas-
seh. After they had destroyed all of them, the Isra-
elites returned to their own towns and to their
own property.

2Hezekiah assigned the priests and Levites to
divisions—each of them according to their duties
as priests or Levites—to offer burnt offerings and
fellowship offerings,[v] to minister, to give thanks
and to sing praises at the gates of the Lord's
dwelling. 3The king contributed from his own
possessions for the morning and evening burnt
offerings and for the burnt offerings on the Sab-
baths, New Moons and appointed feasts as writ-
ten in the Law of the Lord. 4He ordered the peo-
ple living in Jerusalem to give the portion due the
priests and Levites so they could devote them-
selves to the Law of the Lord. 5As soon as the
order went out, the Israelites generously gave the
firstfruits of their grain, new wine, oil and honey
and all that the fields produced. They brought a
great amount, a tithe of everything. 6The men of
Israel and Judah who lived in the towns of Judah
also brought a tithe of their herds and flocks and
a tithe of the holy things dedicated to the Lord
their God, and they piled them in heaps. 7They
began doing this in the third month and finished
in the seventh month. 8When Hezekiah and his
officials came and saw the heaps, they praised the
Lord and blessed his people Israel.

9Hezekiah asked the priests and Levites about
the heaps; 10and Azariah the chief priest, from the
family of Zadok, answered, "Since the people be-
gan to bring their contributions to the temple of
the Lord, we have had enough to eat and plenty to
spare, because the Lord has blessed his people,
and this great amount is left over."

11Hezekiah gave orders to prepare storerooms
in the temple of the Lord, and this was done.
12Then they faithfully brought in the contribu-
tions, tithes and dedicated gifts. Conaniah, a Le-
vite, was in charge of these things, and his
brother Shimei was next in rank. 13Jehiel, Aza-
ziah, Nahath, Asahel, Jerimoth, Jozabad, Eliel, Is-
makiah, Mahath and Benaiah were supervisors
under Conaniah and Shimei his brother, by ap-
pointment of King Hezekiah and Azariah the offi-
cial in charge of the temple of God.

14Kore son of Imnah the Levite, keeper of the
East Gate, was in charge of the freewill offerings
given to God, distributing the contributions made
to the Lord and also the consecrated gifts. 15Eden,
Miniamin, Jeshua, Shemaiah, Amariah and Sheca-
niah assisted him faithfully in the towns of the
priests, distributing to their fellow priests accord-
ing to their divisions, old and young alike.

16In addition, they distributed to the males
three years old or more whose names were in the
genealogical records—all who would enter the
temple of the Lord to perform the daily duties of
their various tasks, according to their responsibil-
ities and their divisions. 17And they distributed to
the priests enrolled by their families in the gene-
alogical records and likewise to the Levites
twenty years old or more, according to their re-
sponsibilities and their divisions. 18They included
all the little ones, the wives, and the sons and
daughters of the whole community listed in these
genealogical records. For they were faithful in
consecrating themselves.

19As for the priests, the descendants of Aaron,
who lived on the farm lands around their towns
or in any other towns, men were designated by
name to distribute portions to every male among
them and to all who were recorded in the geneal-
ogies of the Levites.

20This is what Hezekiah did throughout Judah,
doing what was good and right and faithful before
the Lord his God. 21In everything that he under-
took in the service of God's temple and in obedi-
ence to the law and the commands, he sought his
God and worked wholeheartedly. And so he pros-
pered.

32 After all that Hezekiah had so faith-
fully done, Sennacherib king of As-
syria came and invaded Judah. He
laid siege to the fortified cities, thinking to con-

v2 Traditionally *peace offerings*

quer them for himself. 2When Hezekiah saw that Sennacherib had come and that he intended to make war on Jerusalem, 3he consulted with his officials and military staff about blocking off the water from the springs outside the city, and they helped him. 4A large force of men assembled, and they blocked all the springs and the stream that flowed through the land. "Why should the kings[w] of Assyria come and find plenty of water?" they said. 5Then he worked hard repairing all the broken sections of the wall and building towers on it. He built another wall outside that one and reinforced the supporting terraces[x] of the City of David. He also made large numbers of weapons and shields.

6He appointed military officers over the people and assembled them before him in the square at the city gate and encouraged them with these words: 7"Be strong and courageous. Do not be afraid or discouraged because of the king of Assyria and the vast army with him, for there is a greater power with us than with him. 8With him is only the arm of flesh, but with us is the LORD our God to help us and to fight our battles." And the people gained confidence from what Hezekiah the king of Judah said.

9Later, when Sennacherib king of Assyria and all his forces were laying siege to Lachish, he sent his officers to Jerusalem with this message for Hezekiah king of Judah and for all the people of Judah who were there:

10"This is what Sennacherib king of Assyria says: On what are you basing your confidence, that you remain in Jerusalem under siege? 11When Hezekiah says, 'The LORD our God will save us from the hand of the king of Assyria,' he is misleading you, to let you die of hunger and thirst. 12Did not Hezekiah himself remove this god's high places and altars, saying to Judah and Jerusalem, 'You must worship before one altar and burn sacrifices on it'?

13"Do you not know what I and my fathers have done to all the peoples of the other lands? Were the gods of those nations ever able to deliver their land from my hand? 14Who of all the gods of these nations that my fathers destroyed has been able to save his people from me? How then can your god deliver you from my hand? 15Now do not let Hezekiah deceive you and mislead you like this. Do not believe him, for no god of any nation or kingdom has been able to deliver his people from my hand or the hand of my fathers. How much less will your god deliver you from my hand!"

16Sennacherib's officers spoke further against the LORD God and against his servant Hezekiah. 17The king also wrote letters insulting the LORD, the God of Israel, and saying this against him: "Just as the gods of the peoples of the other lands did not rescue their people from my hand, so the god of Hezekiah will not rescue his people from my hand." 18Then they called out in Hebrew to the people of Jerusalem who were on the wall, to terrify them and make them afraid in order to capture the city. 19They spoke about the God of Jerusalem as they did about the gods of the other peoples of the world—the work of men's hands.

20King Hezekiah and the prophet Isaiah son of Amoz cried out in prayer to heaven about this. 21And the LORD sent an angel, who annihilated all the fighting men and the leaders and officers in the camp of the Assyrian king. So he withdrew to his own land in disgrace. And when he went into the temple of his god, some of his sons cut him down with the sword.

22So the LORD saved Hezekiah and the people of Jerusalem from the hand of Sennacherib king of Assyria and from the hand of all others. He took care of them[y] on every side. 23Many brought offerings to Jerusalem for the LORD and valuable gifts for Hezekiah king of Judah. From then on he was highly regarded by all the nations.

24In those days Hezekiah became ill and was at the point of death. He prayed to the LORD, who answered him and gave him a miraculous sign. 25But Hezekiah's heart was proud and he did not respond to the kindness shown him; therefore the LORD's wrath was on him and on Judah and Jerusalem. 26Then Hezekiah repented of the pride of his heart, as did the people of Jerusalem; therefore the LORD's wrath did not come upon them during the days of Hezekiah.

27Hezekiah had very great riches and honor, and he made treasures for his silver and gold and for his precious stones, spices, shields and all kinds of valuables. 28He also made buildings to

[w]4 Hebrew; Septuagint and Syriac *king* [x]5 Or *the Millo*
[y]22 Hebrew; Septuagint and Vulgate *He gave them rest*

store the harvest of grain, new wine and oil; and
he made stalls for various kinds of cattle, and
pens for the flocks. 29He built villages and ac-
quired great numbers of flocks and herds, for God
had given him very great riches.

30It was Hezekiah who blocked the upper out-
let of the Gihon spring and channeled the water
down to the west side of the City of David. He
succeeded in everything he undertook. 31But
when envoys were sent by the rulers of Bab-
ylon to ask him about the miraculous sign that
had occurred in the land, God left him to test
him and to know everything that was in his
heart.

32The other events of Hezekiah's reign and his
acts of devotion are written in the vision of the
prophet Isaiah son of Amoz in the book of the
kings of Judah and Israel. 33Hezekiah rested with
his fathers and was buried on the hill where the
tombs of David's descendants are. All Judah and
the people of Jerusalem honored him when he
died. And Manasseh his son succeeded him as
king.

33 Manasseh was twelve years old
when he became king, and he
reigned in Jerusalem fifty-five
years. 2He did evil in the eyes of the LORD, follow-
ing the detestable practices of the nations the
LORD had driven out before the Israelites. 3He re-
built the high places his father Hezekiah had de-
molished; he also erected altars to the Baals and
made Asherah poles. He bowed down to all the
starry hosts and worshiped them. 4He built altars
in the temple of the LORD, of which the LORD had
said, "My Name will remain in Jerusalem for-
ever." 5In both courts of the temple of the LORD,
he built altars to all the starry hosts. 6He sacri-
ficed his sons in[z] the fire in the Valley of Ben
Hinnom, practiced sorcery, divination and witch-
craft, and consulted mediums and spiritists. He
did much evil in the eyes of the LORD, provoking
him to anger.

7He took the carved image he had made and
put it in God's temple, of which God had said to
David and to his son Solomon, "In this temple
and in Jerusalem, which I have chosen out of all
the tribes of Israel, I will put my Name forever.
8I will not again make the feet of the Israelites
leave the land I assigned to your forefathers,
if only they will be careful to do everything
I commanded them concerning all the laws,
decrees and ordinances given through Moses."
9But Manasseh led Judah and the people of
Jerusalem astray, so that they did more evil than
the nations the LORD had destroyed before the
Israelites.

10The LORD spoke to Manasseh and his people,
but they paid no attention. 11So the LORD brought
against them the army commanders of the king of
Assyria, who took Manasseh prisoner, put a hook
in his nose, bound him with bronze shackles and
took him to Babylon. 12In his distress he sought
the favor of the LORD his God and humbled him-
self greatly before the God of his fathers. 13And
when he prayed to him, the LORD was moved
by his entreaty and listened to his plea; so
he brought him back to Jerusalem and to his
kingdom. Then Manasseh knew that the LORD
is God.

14Afterward he rebuilt the outer wall of the
City of David, west of the Gihon spring in the
valley, as far as the entrance of the Fish Gate and
encircling the hill of Ophel; he also made it much
higher. He stationed military commanders in all
the fortified cities in Judah.

15He got rid of the foreign gods and removed
the image from the temple of the LORD, as well as
all the altars he had built on the temple hill and
in Jerusalem; and he threw them out of the city.
16Then he restored the altar of the LORD and sacri-
ficed fellowship offerings[a] and thank offerings
on it, and told Judah to serve the LORD, the God of
Israel. 17The people, however, continued to sacri-
fice at the high places, but only to the LORD their
God.

18The other events of Manasseh's reign, includ-
ing his prayer to his God and the words the seers
spoke to him in the name of the LORD, the God of
Israel, are written in the annals of the kings of
Israel.[b] 19His prayer and how God was moved by
his entreaty, as well as all his sins and unfaithful-
ness, and the sites where he built high places and
set up Asherah poles and idols before he humbled
himself—all are written in the records of the
seers.[c] 20Manasseh rested with his fathers and
was buried in his palace. And Amon his son suc-
ceeded him as king.

21Amon was twenty-two years old when he be-
came king, and he reigned in Jerusalem two
years. 22He did evil in the eyes of the LORD, as his

[z]6 Or *He made his sons pass through* [a]16 Traditionally *peace offerings* [b]18 That is, Judah, as frequently in 2 Chronicles
[c]19 One Hebrew manuscript and Septuagint; most Hebrew manuscripts *of Hozai*

father Manasseh had done. Amon worshiped and
offered sacrifices to all the idols Manasseh had
made. 23But unlike his father Manasseh, he did
not humble himself before the LORD; Amon in-
creased his guilt.

24Amon's officials conspired against him and
assassinated him in his palace. 25Then the people
of the land killed all who had plotted against King
Amon, and they made Josiah his son king in his
place.

7 / 2 Chronicles 34
Loving God

ONE OF THE most frustrating aspects of being a Christian is our need for "proof" that God cares about our daily lives. Often, when we are left to ourselves, we have real doubts that God even notices our efforts to do what is right. King Josiah found himself in this situation when his servants found the book of the Law and read it to him.

Warming Up to God Think about a time when you really wanted to know that God cared about what you were doing. How did God communicate his love for you?

Read 2 Chronicles 34.

34 Josiah was eight years old when he
became king, and he reigned in Je-
rusalem thirty-one years. 2He did
what was right in the eyes of the LORD and walked
in the ways of his father David, not turning aside
to the right or to the left.
3In the eighth year of his reign, while he was
still young, he began to seek the God of his father
David. In his twelfth year he began to purge Ju-
dah and Jerusalem of high places, Asherah poles,
carved idols and cast images. 4Under his direction
the altars of the Baals were torn down; he cut to
pieces the incense altars that were above them,
and smashed the Asherah poles, the idols and the
images. These he broke to pieces and scattered
over the graves of those who had sacrificed to
them. 5He burned the bones of the priests on
their altars, and so he purged Judah and Je-
rusalem. 6In the towns of Manasseh, Ephraim
and Simeon, as far as Naphtali, and in the
ruins around them, 7he tore down the altars
and the Asherah poles and crushed the idols
to powder and cut to pieces all the incense altars
throughout Israel. Then he went back to Jeru-
salem.
8In the eighteenth year of Josiah's reign, to pu-
rify the land and the temple, he sent Shaphan son
of Azaliah and Maaseiah the ruler of the city, with
Joah son of Joahaz, the recorder, to repair the
temple of the LORD his God.
9They went to Hilkiah the high priest and gave
him the money that had been brought into the
temple of God, which the Levites who were the
doorkeepers had collected from the people of Ma-
nasseh, Ephraim and the entire remnant of Israel
and from all the people of Judah and Benjamin
and the inhabitants of Jerusalem. 10Then they en-
trusted it to the men appointed to supervise the
work on the LORD's temple. These men paid
the workers who repaired and restored the tem-
ple. 11They also gave money to the carpenters
and builders to purchase dressed stone, and
timber for joists and beams for the buildings
that the kings of Judah had allowed to fall into
ruin.
12The men did the work faithfully. Over them
to direct them were Jahath and Obadiah, Levites
descended from Merari, and Zechariah and Me-
shullam, descended from Kohath. The Levites—
all who were skilled in playing musical instru-
ments— 13had charge of the laborers and
supervised all the workers from job to job. Some
of the Levites were secretaries, scribes and door-
keepers.
14While they were bringing out the money that
had been taken into the temple of the LORD, Hil-

kiah the priest found the Book of the Law of the LORD that had been given through Moses. 15Hilkiah said to Shaphan the secretary, "I have found the Book of the Law in the temple of the LORD." He gave it to Shaphan.

16Then Shaphan took the book to the king and reported to him: "Your officials are doing everything that has been committed to them. 17They have paid out the money that was in the temple of the LORD and have entrusted it to the supervisors and workers." 18Then Shaphan the secretary informed the king, "Hilkiah the priest has given me a book." And Shaphan read from it in the presence of the king.

19When the king heard the words of the Law, he tore his robes. 20He gave these orders to Hilkiah, Ahikam son of Shaphan, Abdon son of Micah,[d] Shaphan the secretary and Asaiah the king's attendant: 21"Go and inquire of the LORD for me and for the remnant in Israel and Judah about what is written in this book that has been found. Great is the LORD's anger that is poured out on us because our fathers have not kept the word of the LORD; they have not acted in accordance with all that is written in this book."

22Hilkiah and those the king had sent with him[e] went to speak to the prophetess Huldah, who was the wife of Shallum son of Tokhath,[f] the son of Hasrah,[g] keeper of the wardrobe. She lived in Jerusalem, in the Second District.

23She said to them, "This is what the LORD, the God of Israel, says: Tell the man who sent you to me, 24'This is what the LORD says: I am going to bring disaster on this place and its people—all the curses written in the book that has been read in the presence of the king of Judah. 25Because they have forsaken me and burned incense to other gods and provoked me to anger by all that their hands have made,[h] my anger will be poured out on this place and will not be quenched.' 26Tell the king of Judah, who sent you to inquire of the LORD, 'This is what the LORD, the God of Israel, says concerning the words you heard: 27Because your heart was responsive and you humbled yourself before God when you heard what he spoke against this place and its people, and because you humbled yourself before me and tore your robes and wept in my presence, I have heard you, declares the LORD. 28Now I will gather you to your fathers, and you will be buried in peace. Your eyes will not see all the disaster I am going to bring on this place and on those who live here.' "

So they took her answer back to the king.

29Then the king called together all the elders of Judah and Jerusalem. 30He went up to the temple of the LORD with the men of Judah, the people of Jerusalem, the priests and the Levites—all the people from the least to the greatest. He read in their hearing all the words of the Book of the Covenant, which had been found in the temple of the LORD. 31The king stood by his pillar and renewed the covenant in the presence of the LORD—to follow the LORD and keep his commands, regulations and decrees with all his heart and all his soul, and to obey the words of the covenant written in this book.

32Then he had everyone in Jerusalem and Benjamin pledge themselves to it; the people of Jerusalem did this in accordance with the covenant of God, the God of their fathers.

33Josiah removed all the detestable idols from all the territory belonging to the Israelites, and he had all who were present in Israel serve the LORD their God. As long as he lived, they did not fail to follow the LORD, the God of their fathers.

[d] 20 Also called *Acbor son of Micaiah* [e] 22 One Hebrew manuscript, Vulgate and Syriac; most Hebrew manuscripts do not have *had sent with him.* [f] 22 Also called *Tikvah* [g] 22 Also called *Harhas* [h] 25 Or *by everything they have done*

Discovering the Word 1. What do verses 1-7 reveal about Josiah's relationship with God? 2. Describe the nature of the work in verses 8-13. 3. The book of the Law that was read to Josiah was most likely Deuteronomy 12—26 and 28. The guidelines for worship in this passage are specifically what Josiah's predecessors disobeyed. What image of God do you think Josiah had? (Note his reaction in verse 19.) 4. Why did Josiah send messengers for Huldah (vv. 20-21)? 5. What feelings do you think Josiah had in response to Huldah's message (vv. 23-28)? 6. What image of God did Huldah communicate to Josiah?

Applying the Word 1. Think of someone who has helped you to see God more clearly. How has this person affected you? 2. How has this experience helped you to obey God?

Responding in Prayer Thank God for the different people in your daily life whom God uses to communicate his love to you.

2 Chronicles 35—36

35 Josiah celebrated the Passover to the LORD in Jerusalem, and the Passover lamb was slaughtered on the fourteenth day of the first month. [2]He appointed the priests to their duties and encouraged them in the service of the LORD's temple. [3]He said to the Levites, who instructed all Israel and who had been consecrated to the LORD: "Put the sacred ark in the temple that Solomon son of David king of Israel built. It is not to be carried about on your shoulders. Now serve the LORD your God and his people Israel. [4]Prepare yourselves by families in your divisions, according to the directions written by David king of Israel and by his son Solomon.

[5]"Stand in the holy place with a group of Levites for each subdivision of the families of your fellow countrymen, the lay people. [6]Slaughter the Passover lambs, consecrate yourselves and prepare ⌞the lambs⌟ for your fellow countrymen, doing what the LORD commanded through Moses."

[7]Josiah provided for all the lay people who were there a total of thirty thousand sheep and goats for the Passover offerings, and also three thousand cattle—all from the king's own possessions.

[8]His officials also contributed voluntarily to the people and the priests and Levites. Hilkiah, Zechariah and Jehiel, the administrators of God's temple, gave the priests twenty-six hundred Passover offerings and three hundred cattle. [9]Also Conaniah along with Shemaiah and Nethanel, his brothers, and Hashabiah, Jeiel and Jozabad, the leaders of the Levites, provided five thousand Passover offerings and five hundred head of cattle for the Levites.

[10]The service was arranged and the priests stood in their places with the Levites in their divisions as the king had ordered. [11]The Passover lambs were slaughtered, and the priests sprinkled the blood handed to them, while the Levites skinned the animals. [12]They set aside the burnt offerings to give them to the subdivisions of the families of the people to offer to the LORD, as is written in the Book of Moses. They did the same with the cattle. [13]They roasted the Passover animals over the fire as prescribed, and boiled the holy offerings in pots, caldrons and pans and served them quickly to all the people. [14]After this, they made preparations for themselves and for the priests, because the priests, the descendants of Aaron, were sacrificing the burnt offerings and the fat portions until nightfall. So the Levites made preparations for themselves and for the Aaronic priests.

[15]The musicians, the descendants of Asaph, were in the places prescribed by David, Asaph, Heman and Jeduthun the king's seer. The gatekeepers at each gate did not need to leave their posts, because their fellow Levites made the preparations for them.

[16]So at that time the entire service of the LORD was carried out for the celebration of the Passover and the offering of burnt offerings on the altar of the LORD, as King Josiah had ordered. [17]The Israelites who were present celebrated the Passover at that time and observed the Feast of Unleavened Bread for seven days. [18]The Passover had not been observed like this in Israel since the days of the prophet Samuel; and none of the kings of Israel had ever celebrated such a Passover as did Josiah, with the priests, the Levites and all Judah and Israel who were there with the people of Jerusalem. [19]This Passover was celebrated in the eighteenth year of Josiah's reign.

[20]After all this, when Josiah had set the temple in order, Neco king of Egypt went up to fight at Carchemish on the Euphrates, and Josiah marched out to meet him in battle. [21]But Neco sent messengers to him, saying, "What quarrel is there between you and me, O king of Judah? It is not you I am attacking at this time, but the house with which I am at war. God has told me to hurry; so stop opposing God, who is with me, or he will destroy you."

[22]Josiah, however, would not turn away from him, but disguised himself to engage him in battle. He would not listen to what Neco had said at God's command but went to fight him on the plain of Megiddo.

[23]Archers shot King Josiah, and he told his officers, "Take me away; I am badly wounded." [24]So they took him out of his chariot, put him in the other chariot he had and brought him to Jerusalem, where he died. He was buried in the tombs of his fathers, and all Judah and Jerusalem mourned for him.

[25]Jeremiah composed laments for Josiah, and to

this day all the men and women singers com-
memorate Josiah in the laments. These became
a tradition in Israel and are written in the La-
ments.
26The other events of Josiah's reign and his acts
of devotion, according to what is written in the
Law of the LORD— 27all the events, from begin-
ning to end, are written in the book of the kings

36

of Israel and Judah. 1And the peo-
ple of the land took Jehoahaz son of
Josiah and made him king in Jeru-
salem in place of his father.
2Jehoahaz[i] was twenty-three years old when
he became king, and he reigned in Jerusalem
three months. 3The king of Egypt dethroned him
in Jerusalem and imposed on Judah a levy of a
hundred talents[j] of silver and a talent[k] of gold.
4The king of Egypt made Eliakim, a brother of
Jehoahaz, king over Judah and Jerusalem and
changed Eliakim's name to Jehoiakim. But Neco
took Eliakim's brother Jehoahaz and carried him
off to Egypt.
5Jehoiakim was twenty-five years old when he
became king, and he reigned in Jerusalem eleven
years. He did evil in the eyes of the LORD his God.
6Nebuchadnezzar king of Babylon attacked him
and bound him with bronze shackles to take him
to Babylon. 7Nebuchadnezzar also took to Bab-
ylon articles from the temple of the LORD and put
them in his temple[l] there.
8The other events of Jehoiakim's reign, the de-
testable things he did and all that was found
against him, are written in the book of the kings
of Israel and Judah. And Jehoiachin his son suc-
ceeded him as king.
9Jehoiachin was eighteen[m] years old when he
became king, and he reigned in Jerusalem three
months and ten days. He did evil in the eyes of
the LORD. 10In the spring, King Nebuchadnezzar
sent for him and brought him to Babylon, to-
gether with articles of value from the temple of
the LORD, and he made Jehoiachin's uncle,[n] Zed-
ekiah, king over Judah and Jerusalem.
11Zedekiah was twenty-one years old when he
became king, and he reigned in Jerusalem eleven
years. 12He did evil in the eyes of the LORD his
God and did not humble himself before Jeremiah
the prophet, who spoke the word of the LORD.
13He also rebelled against King Nebuchadnezzar,
who had made him take an oath in God's name.
He became stiff-necked and hardened his heart
and would not turn to the LORD, the God of Israel.
14Furthermore, all the leaders of the priests and
the people became more and more unfaithful, fol-
lowing all the detestable practices of the nations
and defiling the temple of the LORD, which he had
consecrated in Jerusalem.
15The LORD, the God of their fathers, sent word
to them through his messengers again and again,
because he had pity on his people and on his
dwelling place. 16But they mocked God's messen-
gers, despised his words and scoffed at his proph-
ets until the wrath of the LORD was aroused
against his people and there was no remedy. 17He
brought up against them the king of the Babyloni-
ans,[o] who killed their young men with the sword
in the sanctuary, and spared neither young man
nor young woman, old man or aged. God handed
all of them over to Nebuchadnezzar. 18He carried
to Babylon all the articles from the temple of God,
both large and small, and the treasures of the
LORD's temple and the treasures of the king and
his officials. 19They set fire to God's temple and
broke down the wall of Jerusalem; they burned all
the palaces and destroyed everything of value
there.
20He carried into exile to Babylon the remnant,
who escaped from the sword, and they became
servants to him and his sons until the kingdom of
Persia came to power. 21The land enjoyed its sab-
bath rests; all the time of its desolation it rested,
until the seventy years were completed in fulfill-
ment of the word of the LORD spoken by Jeremiah.
22In the first year of Cyrus king of Persia, in
order to fulfill the word of the LORD spoken by
Jeremiah, the LORD moved the heart of Cyrus king
of Persia to make a proclamation throughout his
realm and to put it in writing:

23"This is what Cyrus king of Persia says:
" 'The LORD, the God of heaven, has given
me all the kingdoms of the earth and he has
appointed me to build a temple for him at
Jerusalem in Judah. Anyone of his people
among you—may the LORD his God be with
him, and let him go up.' "

[i]2 Hebrew *Joahaz*, a variant of *Jehoahaz*; also in verse 4 [j]3 That is, about 3 3/4 tons (about 3.4 metric tons) [k]3 That is, about 75 pounds (about 34 kilograms) [l]7 Or *palace* [m]9 One Hebrew manuscript, some Septuagint manuscripts and Syriac (see also 2 Kings 24:8); most Hebrew manuscripts *eight* [n]10 Hebrew *brother*, that is, relative (see 2 Kings 24:17) [o]17 Or *Chaldeans*

Ezra

If you were in prison, what words would you like most to hear from your captors? Would they be "You can go home now"? King Cyrus of Persia said this to the Israelites when he freed them from captivity. And he also sent them back to their homeland with all of the treasures of the former temple of Jerusalem and with money and supplies to build a new altar and temple.

This would have been momentous to the people of Israel. More than two hundred years before (722 B.C.) the Assyrians destroyed the northern kingdom, Israel. In 587 B.C. the Babylonians conquered what remained of the southern kingdom, Judah. They destroyed the temple and took the leaders of the people into exile. Psalm 137:4 gives us a glimpse into the crisis that this was for the people of Israel: "How can we sing the songs of the LORD while in a foreign land?" The sense of loss and grief was profound.

Then came Cyrus the Persian in 538 B.C., who conquered Babylon and set in motion policies of religious tolerance and encouragement that would largely characterize the attitude of the Persian kings to follow, Darius and Artaxerxes. This policy enabled and encouraged the people of Israel to return to their homeland. No doubt it was advantageous for the kings to have a loyal buffer between them and the other major superpower of the day, Egypt, but whatever the motives of the Persian kings, the author makes it clear that God is the one who controls history.

Ezra is the first part of a divided book. Nehemiah is the second half. The Hebrew Bible treated the two books as one. They became separated due to Christian influence. If you read the two books together, the story will make better sense. There are three different return trips that take place (Ezr 1—6, 7—10; Ne 1—7), and the book concludes by a gathering of the congregation of Israel for repentance and rejoicing.

The book of Ezra focuses on several themes: the continuity of the leaders before and after the exile, the place of the community in bringing about God's work, the rebuilding of the altar and the temple, and the importance of holiness within the community. It is clear from this book that the freedom that the Israelites have received is from God. We can take encouragement for our lives from this picture of a God who is faithful to his promises.

Outline

1/ Ezra 1—2 ——— *Return from Exile*

2/ Ezra 3 ——— *The Priorities of God's People*

3/ Ezra 4 ——— *Words That Hurt*

4/ Ezra 5—6 ——— *God's Surprises*

5/ Ezra 7 ——— *Powerful Friends*

6/ Ezra 8 ——— *Practical Spirituality*

7/ Ezra 9 ——— *Turning Away from God*

8/ Ezra 10 ——— *Compromise*

1 / *Ezra 1—2*
Return from Exile

EXILE. THEIR HOMELAND was destroyed. They were forcibly removed to a strange land. There they were foreigners, losers, third-class inhabitants. Feelings ran deep—anger, shame, alienation and isolation. What hope could possibly exist in people who had not seen their homeland for over fifty years? This is where the book of Ezra starts.

Warming Up to God Have you ever had an experience of being physically or emotionally far from home? How would you describe that experience of exile?

Read Ezra 1—2.

1 In the first year of Cyrus king of Persia, in order to fulfill the word of the LORD spoken by Jeremiah, the LORD moved the heart of Cyrus king of Persia to make a proclamation throughout his realm and to put it in writing:

2"This is what Cyrus king of Persia says:

" 'The LORD, the God of heaven, has given me all the kingdoms of the earth and he has appointed me to build a temple for him at
Jerusalem in Judah. 3Anyone of his people among you—may his God be with him, and let him go up to Jerusalem in Judah and build the temple of the LORD, the God of Israel, the God who is in Jerusalem.
4And the people of any place where survivors may now be living are to provide him with silver and gold, with goods and livestock, and with freewill offerings for the temple of God in Jerusalem.' "

5Then the family heads of Judah and Benjamin, and the priests and Levites—everyone whose heart God had moved—prepared to go up and build the house of the LORD in Jerusalem.
6All their neighbors assisted them with articles of silver and gold, with goods and livestock, and with valuable gifts, in addition to all the freewill offerings.
7Moreover, King Cyrus brought out the articles belonging to the temple of the LORD, which Nebuchadnezzar had carried away from Jerusalem and had placed in the temple of his god.[a]
8Cyrus king of Persia had them brought by Mithredath the treasurer, who counted them out to Sheshbazzar the prince of Judah.
9This was the inventory:

gold dishes	30
silver dishes	1,000
silver pans[b]	29
10gold bowls	30
matching silver bowls	410
other articles	1,000

11In all, there were 5,400 articles of gold and of silver. Sheshbazzar brought all these along when the exiles came up from Babylon to Jerusalem.

2 Now these are the people of the province who came up from the captivity of the exiles, whom Nebuchadnezzar king of Babylon had taken captive to Babylon (they returned to Jerusalem and Judah, each to his own town,
2in company with Zerubbabel, Jeshua, Nehemiah, Seraiah, Reelaiah, Mordecai, Bilshan, Mispar, Bigvai, Rehum and Baanah):

The list of the men of the people of Israel:

3the descendants of Parosh	2,172
4of Shephatiah	372
5of Arah	775
6of Pahath-Moab (through the line of Jeshua and Joab)	2,812
7of Elam	1,254
8of Zattu	945
9of Zaccai	760
10of Bani	642
11of Bebai	623
12of Azgad	1,222
13of Adonikam	666
14of Bigvai	2,056
15of Adin	454
16of Ater (through Hezekiah)	98
17of Bezai	323
18of Jorah	112
19of Hashum	223
20of Gibbar	95
21the men of Bethlehem	123
22of Netophah	56

[a]7 Or *gods* [b]9 The meaning of the Hebrew for this word is uncertain.

[23]of Anathoth	128
[24]of Azmaveth	42
[25]of Kiriath Jearim,[c] Kephirah and Beeroth	743
[26]of Ramah and Geba	621
[27]of Micmash	122
[28]of Bethel and Ai	223
[29]of Nebo	52
[30]of Magbish	156
[31]of the other Elam	1,254
[32]of Harim	320
[33]of Lod, Hadid and Ono	725
[34]of Jericho	345
[35]of Senaah	3,630

[36]The priests:

the descendants of Jedaiah (through the family of Jeshua)	973
[37]of Immer	1,052
[38]of Pashhur	1,247
[39]of Harim	1,017

[40]The Levites:

the descendants of Jeshua and Kadmiel (through the line of Hodaviah)	74

[41]The singers:

the descendants of Asaph	128

[42]The gatekeepers of the temple:

the descendants of Shallum, Ater, Talmon, Akkub, Hatita and Shobai	139

[43]The temple servants:

the descendants of
Ziha, Hasupha, Tabbaoth,
[44]Keros, Siaha, Padon,
[45]Lebanah, Hagabah, Akkub,
[46]Hagab, Shalmai, Hanan,
[47]Giddel, Gahar, Reaiah,
[48]Rezin, Nekoda, Gazzam,
[49]Uzza, Paseah, Besai,
[50]Asnah, Meunim, Nephussim,
[51]Bakbuk, Hakupha, Harhur,
[52]Bazluth, Mehida, Harsha,
[53]Barkos, Sisera, Temah,
[54]Neziah and Hatipha

[55]The descendants of the servants of Solomon:

the descendants of
Sotai, Hassophereth, Peruda,
[56]Jaala, Darkon, Giddel,
[57]Shephatiah, Hattil,
Pokereth-Hazzebaim and Ami

[58]The temple servants and the descendants of the servants of Solomon	392

[59]The following came up from the towns of Tel Melah, Tel Harsha, Kerub, Addon and Immer, but they could not show that their families were descended from Israel:

[60]The descendants of Delaiah, Tobiah and Nekoda	652

[61]And from among the priests:

The descendants of
Hobaiah, Hakkoz and Barzillai (a man who had married a daughter of Barzillai the Gileadite and was called by that name).

[62]These searched for their family records, but they could not find them and so were excluded from the priesthood as unclean. [63]The governor ordered them not to eat any of the most sacred food until there was a priest ministering with the Urim and Thummim.

[64]The whole company numbered 42,360, [65]besides their 7,337 menservants and maidservants; and they also had 200 men and women singers. [66]They had 736 horses, 245 mules, [67]435 camels and 6,720 donkeys.

[68]When they arrived at the house of the Lord in Jerusalem, some of the heads of the families gave freewill offerings toward the rebuilding of the house of God on its site. [69]According to their ability they gave to the treasury for this work 61,000 drachmas[d] of gold, 5,000 minas[e] of silver and 100 priestly garments.

[70]The priests, the Levites, the singers, the gatekeepers and the temple servants settled in their own towns, along with some of the other people, and the rest of the Israelites settled in their towns.

[c]25 See Septuagint (see also Neh. 7:29); Hebrew *Kiriath Arim.*
[d]69 That is, about 1,100 pounds (about 500 kilograms) [e]69 That is, about 3 tons (about 2.9 metric tons)

Discovering the Word 1. What would it have been like to have heard the proclamation of King Cyrus (1:1-4)? 2. What were the Israelites provided with beyond their freedom (1:3-11)? 3. What might have been the thoughts and feelings of those who were chosen to return to Israel (2:1-66)? 4. Why were the returnees so generous in the offering (2:68-69) to rebuild the temple? 5. How would the prophecy of Jeremiah (2Ch 36:21) affect them as they resettled Israel (2:70)?

Applying the Word 1. How might God be calling you to return to a place or a group? 2. How can the profound gratitude of the Israelites in 2:68-69 impact your response to God?

Responding in Prayer Offer the Lord your thanks for bringing you back from the exile of sin.

2 / *Ezra 3*
The Priorities of God's People

IF YOU HAD to move away from your country next month, what would be on your "To Do" list? Cleaning and packing, of course. But who would you want to spend time with? People from work, the neighborhood or social clubs? You might find that it's the people you worship with each Sunday who are most important. Once you arrive in the new place, what would be your highest priorities? In this chapter we learn a lot about the Israelites' priorities.

Warming Up to God List your priorities as you think about establishing yourself in a new place. What stands out to you in the goals you would set for yourself?

Read Ezra 3.

3 When the seventh month came and the Israelites had settled in their towns, the people assembled as one man in Jerusalem.
2Then Jeshua son of Jozadak and his fellow priests and Zerubbabel son of Shealtiel and his associates began to build the altar of the God of Israel to sacrifice burnt offerings on it, in accordance with what is written in the Law of Moses the man of God.
3Despite their fear of the peoples around them, they built the altar on its foundation and sacrificed burnt offerings on it to the LORD, both the morning and evening sacrifices.
4Then in accordance with what is written, they celebrated the Feast of Tabernacles with the required number of burnt offerings prescribed for each day.
5After that, they presented the regular burnt offerings, the New Moon sacrifices and the sacrifices for all the appointed sacred feasts of the LORD, as well as those brought as freewill offerings to the LORD.
6On the first day of the seventh month they began to offer burnt offerings to the LORD, though the foundation of the LORD's temple had not yet been laid.

7Then they gave money to the masons and carpenters, and gave food and drink and oil to the people of Sidon and Tyre, so that they would bring cedar logs by sea from Lebanon to Joppa, as authorized by Cyrus king of Persia.

8In the second month of the second year after their arrival at the house of God in Jerusalem, Zerubbabel son of Shealtiel, Jeshua son of Jozadak and the rest of their brothers (the priests and the Levites and all who had returned from the captivity to Jerusalem) began the work, appointing Levites twenty years of age and older to supervise the building of the house of the LORD.
9Jeshua and his sons and brothers and Kadmiel and his sons (descendants of Hodaviah[f]) and the sons of Henadad and their sons and brothers—all Levites—joined together in supervising those working on the house of God.

10When the builders laid the foundation of the temple of the LORD, the priests in their vestments and with trumpets, and the Levites (the sons of Asaph) with cymbals, took their places to praise the LORD, as prescribed by David king of Israel.
11With praise and thanksgiving they sang to the LORD:

f9 Hebrew *Yehudah,* probably a variant of *Hodaviah*

"He is good;
his love to Israel endures forever."

And all the people gave a great shout of praise to
the LORD, because the foundation of the house of
the LORD was laid. 12But many of the older priests
and Levites and family heads, who had seen the
former temple, wept aloud when they saw the
foundation of this temple being laid, while many
others shouted for joy. 13No one could distin-
guish the sound of the shouts of joy from the
sound of weeping, because the people made
so much noise. And the sound was heard far
away.

Discovering the Word 1. Besides the obvious task of settling back in their homeland, what was the first priority for the returned exiles (vv. 1–2)? 2. How did the Israelites deal with their reasonable and real fears (v. 3)? 3. The seventh month was one of the most sacred and worshipful, yet the entire temple lay demolished. How did they "make do" (v. 6)? 4. What does the next project the Israelites turn their attention to tell you about their priorities (vv. 7–9)? 5. In what various ways did the people express themselves in worship (vv. 10–13)?

Applying the Word 1. How can the God-given priority of worshiping with God's people (Heb 10:25) grow in your life? 2. How could you follow the example of the Israelites in facing your fears?

Responding in Prayer Ask God to help you make your worship of him first and foremost in your life.

3 / *Ezra 4*
Words That Hurt

HAS SOMEONE EVER written or said something about you that was designed to hurt you? How much of it was true? false? To show the continued opposition Israel faced, the author jumps ahead in time to tell of a time when their neighbors wrote to the king in order to damage Israel.

Warming Up to God Talk to God about how the words of others have hurt you.

Read Ezra 4.

4 When the enemies of Judah and Benjamin
heard that the exiles were building a tem-
ple for the LORD, the God of Israel, 2they
came to Zerubbabel and to the heads of the fami-
lies and said, "Let us help you build because, like
you, we seek your God and have been sacrificing
to him since the time of Esarhaddon king of As-
syria, who brought us here."

3But Zerubbabel, Jeshua and the rest of the
heads of the families of Israel answered, "You
have no part with us in building a temple to our
God. We alone will build it for the LORD, the God
of Israel, as King Cyrus, the king of Persia, com-
manded us."

4Then the peoples around them set out to dis-
courage the people of Judah and make them
afraid to go on building.[g] 5They hired coun-
selors to work against them and frustrate their
plans during the entire reign of Cyrus king of
Persia and down to the reign of Darius king of
Persia.

6At the beginning of the reign of Xerxes,[h] they
lodged an accusation against the people of Judah
and Jerusalem.

7And in the days of Artaxerxes king of Persia,
Bishlam, Mithredath, Tabeel and the rest of his
associates wrote a letter to Artaxerxes. The letter
was written in Aramaic script and in the Aramaic
language.[i,j]

[g]4 Or *and troubled them as they built* [h]6 Hebrew *Ahasuerus*, a variant of Xerxes' Persian name [i]7 Or *written in Aramaic and translated* [j]7 The text of Ezra 4:8—6:18 is in Aramaic.

8Rehum the commanding officer and Shimshai
the secretary wrote a letter against Jerusalem to
Artaxerxes the king as follows:

9Rehum the commanding officer and Shim-
shai the secretary, together with the rest of
their associates—the judges and officials
over the men from Tripolis, Persia,[k] Erech
and Babylon, the Elamites of Susa, 10and the
other people whom the great and honorable
Ashurbanipal[l] deported and settled in the
city of Samaria and elsewhere in Trans-Eu-
phrates.

11(This is a copy of the letter they sent him.)

To King Artaxerxes,

From your servants, the men of Trans-Euphrates:

12The king should know that the Jews who
came up to us from you have gone to Jerusa-
lem and are rebuilding that rebellious and
wicked city. They are restoring the walls and
repairing the foundations.
13Furthermore, the king should know that
if this city is built and its walls are restored,
no more taxes, tribute or duty will be paid,
and the royal revenues will suffer. 14Now
since we are under obligation to the palace
and it is not proper for us to see the king
dishonored, we are sending this message to
inform the king, 15so that a search may be
made in the archives of your predecessors. In
these records you will find that this city is
a rebellious city, troublesome to kings and
provinces, a place of rebellion from ancient
times. That is why this city was destroyed.
16We inform the king that if this city is built
and its walls are restored, you will be left
with nothing in Trans-Euphrates.

17The king sent this reply:

To Rehum the commanding officer, Shimshai the secretary and the rest of their associates living in Samaria and elsewhere in Trans-Euphrates:

Greetings.

18The letter you sent us has been read and
translated in my presence. 19I issued an or-
der and a search was made, and it was found
that this city has a long history of revolt
against kings and has been a place of rebel-
lion and sedition. 20Jerusalem has had
powerful kings ruling over the whole of
Trans-Euphrates, and taxes, tribute and
duty were paid to them. 21Now issue an or-
der to these men to stop work, so that this
city will not be rebuilt until I so order. 22Be
careful not to neglect this matter. Why let
this threat grow, to the detriment of the
royal interests?

23As soon as the copy of the letter of King Ar-
taxerxes was read to Rehum and Shimshai the
secretary and their associates, they went immedi-
ately to the Jews in Jerusalem and compelled
them by force to stop.

24Thus the work on the house of God in Jerusa-
lem came to a standstill until the second year of
the reign of Darius king of Persia.

[k]9 Or *officials, magistrates and governors over the men from*
[l]10 Aramaic *Osnappar,* a variant of *Ashurbanipal*

Discovering the Word 1. If you could use one word to sum up the events in this passage, what word would it be? 2. Describe the response of the "neighbors" (vv. 1–5). 3. What reasons are given to King Artaxerxes to persuade him to stop the building in Jerusalem (vv. 12–16)? 4. Which of these reasons are true and which are not? 5. What reasons does King Artaxerxes give for having the work stopped (vv. 17–22)? 6. What do you think it was like for the Israelites to stop this long-awaited work for a year (v. 24)?

Applying the Word 1. What is it like for someone to tell the truth about you in order to hurt you? 2. How does it feel if someone lies about you? 3. What would be a godly response?

Responding in Prayer Praise God for the fact that his work continues even when it looks to us like it has been stopped dead by slander and other sins. Pray for those you know who have been hurt by lies.

4 / *Ezra 5—6*
God's Surprises

WHO WOULD YOU say is the most powerful person on earth today? Imagine you receive a letter from that person stating that they wanted to help your Christian community fulfill its mission and that all they wanted from you was a list of your needs so that they could be sure that they sent enough supplies and money. This was the joyful experience of the Israelites.

Warming Up to God Reflect on how powerful God is. What signs of his power have you recently witnessed?

Read Ezra 5—6.

5 Now Haggai the prophet and Zechariah
the prophet, a descendant of Iddo, proph-
esied to the Jews in Judah and Jerusalem
in the name of the God of Israel, who was over
them. 2Then Zerubbabel son of Shealtiel and
Jeshua son of Jozadak set to work to rebuild the
house of God in Jerusalem. And the prophets of
God were with them, helping them.
3At that time Tattenai, governor of Trans-Eu-
phrates, and Shethar-Bozenai and their associates
went to them and asked, "Who authorized you to
rebuild this temple and restore this structure?"
4They also asked, "What are the names of the
men constructing this building?"[m] 5But the eye
of their God was watching over the elders of the
Jews, and they were not stopped until a report
could go to Darius and his written reply be re-
ceived.
6This is a copy of the letter that Tattenai, gover-
nor of Trans-Euphrates, and Shethar-Bozenai and
their associates, the officials of Trans-Euphrates,
sent to King Darius. 7The report they sent him
read as follows:

To King Darius:

Cordial greetings.

8The king should know that we went to
the district of Judah, to the temple of the
great God. The people are building it with
large stones and placing the timbers in the
walls. The work is being carried on with dili-
gence and is making rapid progress under
their direction.
9We questioned the elders and asked
them, "Who authorized you to rebuild this
temple and restore this structure?" 10We also
asked them their names, so that we could
write down the names of their leaders for
your information.
11This is the answer they gave us:

"We are the servants of the God of heaven
and earth, and we are rebuilding the temple
that was built many years ago, one that a
great king of Israel built and finished. 12But
because our fathers angered the God of
heaven, he handed them over to Nebuchad-
nezzar the Chaldean, king of Babylon, who
destroyed this temple and deported the peo-
ple to Babylon.
13"However, in the first year of Cyrus king
of Babylon, King Cyrus issued a decree to
rebuild this house of God. 14He even re-
moved from the temple[n] of Babylon the
gold and silver articles of the house of God,
which Nebuchadnezzar had taken from the
temple in Jerusalem and brought to the tem-
ple[n] in Babylon.
"Then King Cyrus gave them to a man
named Sheshbazzar, whom he had appointed
governor, 15and he told him, 'Take these arti-
cles and go and deposit them in the temple
in Jerusalem. And rebuild the house of God
on its site.' 16So this Sheshbazzar came and
laid the foundations of the house of God in
Jerusalem. From that day to the present it
has been under construction but is not yet
finished."

17Now if it pleases the king, let a search be
made in the royal archives of Babylon to see
if King Cyrus did in fact issue a decree to
rebuild this house of God in Jerusalem. Then

m4 See Septuagint; Aramaic 4*We told them the names of the men constructing this building.* n14 Or *palace*

let the king send us his decision in this matter.

6 King Darius then issued an order, and they searched in the archives stored in the treasury at Babylon. 2A scroll was found in the citadel of Ecbatana in the province of Media, and this was written on it:

Memorandum:

> 3In the first year of King Cyrus, the king issued a decree concerning the temple of God in Jerusalem:
>
> Let the temple be rebuilt as a place to present sacrifices, and let its foundations be laid. It is to be ninety feet[o] high and ninety feet wide, 4with three courses of large stones and one of timbers. The costs are to be paid by the royal treasury. 5Also, the gold and silver articles of the house of God, which Nebuchadnezzar took from the temple in Jerusalem and brought to Babylon, are to be returned to their places in the temple in Jerusalem; they are to be deposited in the house of God.

6Now then, Tattenai, governor of Trans-Euphrates, and Shethar-Bozenai and you, their fellow officials of that province, stay away from there. 7Do not interfere with the work on this temple of God. Let the governor of the Jews and the Jewish elders rebuild this house of God on its site.

8Moreover, I hereby decree what you are to do for these elders of the Jews in the construction of this house of God:

The expenses of these men are to be fully paid out of the royal treasury, from the revenues of Trans-Euphrates, so that the work will not stop. 9Whatever is needed—young bulls, rams, male lambs for burnt offerings to the God of heaven, and wheat, salt, wine and oil, as requested by the priests in Jerusalem—must be given them daily without fail, 10so that they may offer sacrifices pleasing to the God of heaven and pray for the well-being of the king and his sons.

11Furthermore, I decree that if anyone changes this edict, a beam is to be pulled from his house and he is to be lifted up and impaled on it. And for this crime his house is to be made a pile of rubble. 12May God, who has caused his Name to dwell there, overthrow any king or people who lifts a hand to change this decree or to destroy this temple in Jerusalem.

I Darius have decreed it. Let it be carried out with diligence.

13Then, because of the decree King Darius had sent, Tattenai, governor of Trans-Euphrates, and Shethar-Bozenai and their associates carried it out with diligence. 14So the elders of the Jews continued to build and prosper under the preaching of Haggai the prophet and Zechariah, a descendant of Iddo. They finished building the temple according to the command of the God of Israel and the decrees of Cyrus, Darius and Artaxerxes, kings of Persia. 15The temple was completed on the third day of the month Adar, in the sixth year of the reign of King Darius.

16Then the people of Israel—the priests, the Levites and the rest of the exiles—celebrated the dedication of the house of God with joy. 17For the dedication of this house of God they offered a hundred bulls, two hundred rams, four hundred male lambs and, as a sin offering for all Israel, twelve male goats, one for each of the tribes of Israel. 18And they installed the priests in their divisions and the Levites in their groups for the service of God at Jerusalem, according to what is written in the Book of Moses.

19On the fourteenth day of the first month, the exiles celebrated the Passover. 20The priests and Levites had purified themselves and were all ceremonially clean. The Levites slaughtered the Passover lamb for all the exiles, for their brothers the priests and for themselves. 21So the Israelites who had returned from the exile ate it, together with all who had separated themselves from the unclean practices of their Gentile neighbors in order to seek the LORD, the God of Israel. 22For seven days they celebrated with joy the Feast of Unleavened Bread, because the LORD had filled them with joy by changing the attitude of the king of Assyria, so that he assisted them in the work on the house of God, the God of Israel.

[o]3 Aramaic *sixty cubits* (about 27 meters)

Discovering the Word 1. How do these chapters compare and contrast with chapter 4? 2. How would you feel after an encounter like the one in 5:3–4? 3. What good news did the Israelites hear in the letter of King Cyrus (6:1–12)? 4. How do you suppose the people of Israel felt when the temple was finally complete (6:13–15)? 5. What did they do when the temple was completed (6:16–22)?

Applying the Word 1. How can chapter 5 help you to press on in doing God's work in the face of opposition? 2. What does it mean to you that God is able to use the most powerful people on earth (like Cyrus) to further his purpose? 3. How can worship be a stronger part of your response to God's faithfulness?

Responding in Prayer Praise the God who holds the hearts and minds of the most powerful rulers in his hands.

5 / *Ezra 7*
Powerful Friends

LIFE IN A FOREIGN country can be difficult. There are new foods, unexpected customs, new ways of speaking or even a new language, different ways of dressing and much more. Something that helps a great deal in such a situation is a friend from the new culture who can help you make the adjustment and introduce you around. In this chapter Ezra finds a friend—and a benefactor—in the king. As a result, many good things come to his people as well.

Warming Up to God What connections, friends, privileges or abilities do you have which you can use to benefit the church?

Read Ezra 7.

7 After these things, during the reign of Ar-
taxerxes king of Persia, Ezra son of Sera-
iah, the son of Azariah, the son of Hil-
kiah, 2the son of Shallum, the son of Zadok, the
son of Ahitub, 3the son of Amariah, the son of
Azariah, the son of Meraioth, 4the son of Zera-
hiah, the son of Uzzi, the son of Bukki, 5the son
of Abishua, the son of Phinehas, the son of Elea-
zar, the son of Aaron the chief priest— 6this Ezra
came up from Babylon. He was a teacher well
versed in the Law of Moses, which the LORD, the
God of Israel, had given. The king had granted
him everything he asked, for the hand of the LORD
his God was on him. 7Some of the Israelites, in-
cluding priests, Levites, singers, gatekeepers and
temple servants, also came up to Jerusalem in the
seventh year of King Artaxerxes.

8Ezra arrived in Jerusalem in the fifth month of
the seventh year of the king. 9He had begun his
journey from Babylon on the first day of the first
month, and he arrived in Jerusalem on the first
day of the fifth month, for the gracious hand of
his God was on him. 10For Ezra had devoted him-
self to the study and observance of the Law of the
LORD, and to teaching its decrees and laws in Is-
rael.

11This is a copy of the letter King Artaxerxes
had given to Ezra the priest and teacher, a man
learned in matters concerning the commands and
decrees of the LORD for Israel:

12[p]Artaxerxes, king of kings,

To Ezra the priest, a teacher of the Law of the God of heaven:

Greetings.

13Now I decree that any of the Israelites in
my kingdom, including priests and Levites,
who wish to go to Jerusalem with you, may
go. 14You are sent by the king and his seven
advisers to inquire about Judah and Jerusa-
lem with regard to the Law of your God,
which is in your hand. 15Moreover, you are
to take with you the silver and gold that the
king and his advisers have freely given to the
God of Israel, whose dwelling is in Jerusa-
lem, 16together with all the silver and gold

p12 The text of Ezra 7:12-26 is in Aramaic.

you may obtain from the province of Bab-
ylon, as well as the freewill offerings of the
people and priests for the temple of their
God in Jerusalem. [17]With this money be sure
to buy bulls, rams and male lambs, together
with their grain offerings and drink offer-
ings, and sacrifice them on the altar of the
temple of your God in Jerusalem.
[18]You and your brother Jews may then do
whatever seems best with the rest of the sil-
ver and gold, in accordance with the will of
your God. [19]Deliver to the God of Jerusalem
all the articles entrusted to you for worship
in the temple of your God. [20]And anything
else needed for the temple of your God that
you may have occasion to supply, you may
provide from the royal treasury.
[21]Now I, King Artaxerxes, order all the
treasurers of Trans-Euphrates to provide
with diligence whatever Ezra the priest, a
teacher of the Law of the God of heaven,
may ask of you— [22]up to a hundred tal-
ents[q] of silver, a hundred cors[r] of wheat, a
hundred baths[s] of wine, a hundred baths[s]
of olive oil, and salt without limit. [23]What-
ever the God of heaven has prescribed, let it
be done with diligence for the temple of the
God of heaven. Why should there be wrath
against the realm of the king and of his sons?
[24]You are also to know that you have no au-
thority to impose taxes, tribute or duty on
any of the priests, Levites, singers, gatekeep-
ers, temple servants or other workers at this
house of God.
[25]And you, Ezra, in accordance with the
wisdom of your God, which you possess, ap-
point magistrates and judges to administer
justice to all the people of Trans-Euphra-
tes—all who know the laws of your God.
And you are to teach any who do not know
them. [26]Whoever does not obey the law of
your God and the law of the king must
surely be punished by death, banishment,
confiscation of property, or imprisonment.

[27]Praise be to the LORD, the God of our fathers,
who has put it into the king's heart to bring
honor to the house of the LORD in Jerusalem in
this way [28]and who has extended his good favor
to me before the king and his advisers and all the
king's powerful officials. Because the hand of the
LORD my God was on me, I took courage and
gathered leading men from Israel to go up
with me.

[q]22 That is, about 3 3/4 tons (about 3.4 metric tons) [r]22 That is, probably about 600 bushels (about 22 kiloliters) [s]22 That is, probably about 600 gallons (about 2.2 kiloliters)

Discovering the Word 1. What qualities of Ezra would have helped him to find favor in the eyes of the king (vv. 5–6, 9–10)? 2. Describe the king's generosity to Ezra and his people (vv. 13–22). 3. What commission is Ezra given by King Artaxerxes (vv. 25–26)? 4. This is most likely the same Artaxerxes who wrote the letter stopping all building in chapter 4. What does the letter suggest about why the king changed his mind about the temple (vv. 23, 27–28)? 5. Since Israel lay between the kingdom of Persia and Egypt (the other superpower of the day), it was undoubtedly useful for the king to have friendly allies as a buffer. How can God use this king with mixed motives?

Applying the Word 1. If God is able to change a king's heart as he did with Artaxerxes, how might that change your faith in God and your prayer life? 2. Ezra's lifelong preparation and faithfulness to God put him in a pivotal place to be used of God. How can you faithfully prepare yourself for such a day?

Responding in Prayer Pray for those in leadership in your country and around the world. Affirm your trust in God alone.

6 / *Ezra 8*
Practical Spirituality

IT'S DARK, AND you are in a part of town that is known to be dangerous. Unfortunately, you and those with you have to travel on foot to your destination. You naturally turn to prayer. This was the situation Ezra found himself in. And the pressure was on because he had bragged that God would protect those "who look to him." Now he had to put his life where his mouth was.

Warming Up to God We typically turn to God in crisis and forget to rely on him in daily life. In what part of your life should you particularly be looking to God for guidance? Spend some time in quiet with the Lord.

Read Ezra 8.

8 These are the family heads and those registered with them who came up with me from Babylon during the reign of King Artaxerxes:

2of the descendants of Phinehas, Gershom;
of the descendants of Ithamar, Daniel;
of the descendants of David, Hattush 3of the descendants of Shecaniah;

of the descendants of Parosh, Zechariah, and with him were registered 150 men;
4of the descendants of Pahath-Moab, Eliehoenai son of Zerahiah, and with him 200 men;
5of the descendants of Zattu,[t] Shecaniah son of Jahaziel, and with him 300 men;
6of the descendants of Adin, Ebed son of Jonathan, and with him 50 men;
7of the descendants of Elam, Jeshaiah son of Athaliah, and with him 70 men;
8of the descendants of Shephatiah, Zebadiah son of Michael, and with him 80 men;
9of the descendants of Joab, Obadiah son of Jehiel, and with him 218 men;
10of the descendants of Bani,[u] Shelomith son of Josiphiah, and with him 160 men;
11of the descendants of Bebai, Zechariah son of Bebai, and with him 28 men;
12of the descendants of Azgad, Johanan son of Hakkatan, and with him 110 men;
13of the descendants of Adonikam, the last ones, whose names were Eliphelet, Jeuel and Shemaiah, and with them 60 men;
14of the descendants of Bigvai, Uthai and Zaccur, and with them 70 men.

15I assembled them at the canal that flows toward Ahava, and we camped there three days. When I checked among the people and the priests, I found no Levites there. 16So I summoned Eliezer, Ariel, Shemaiah, Elnathan, Jarib, Elnathan, Nathan, Zechariah and Meshullam, who were leaders, and Joiarib and Elnathan, who were men of learning, 17and I sent them to Iddo, the leader in Casiphia. I told them what to say to Iddo and his kinsmen, the temple servants in Casiphia, so that they might bring attendants to us for the house of our God.
18Because the gracious hand of our God was on us, they brought us Sherebiah, a capable man, from the descendants of Mahli son of Levi, the son of Israel, and Sherebiah's sons and brothers, 18 men; 19and Hasahabiah, together with Jeshaiah from the descendants of Merari, and his brothers and nephews, 20 men. 20They also brought 220 of the temple servants— a body that David and the officials had established to assist the Levites. All were registered by name.

21There, by the Ahava Canal, I proclaimed a fast, so that we might humble ourselves before our God and ask him for a safe journey for us and our children, with all our possessions. 22I was ashamed to ask the king for soldiers and horsemen to protect us from enemies on the road, because we had told the king, "The gracious hand of our God is on everyone who looks to him, but his great anger is against all who forsake him." 23So we fasted and petitioned our God about this, and he answered our prayer.

24Then I set apart twelve of the leading priests, together with Sherebiah, Hashabiah and ten of their brothers, 25and I weighed out to them the offering of silver and gold and the articles that the king, his advisers, his officials and all Israel present there had donated for the house of our God. 26I weighed out to them 650 talents[v] of silver, silver articles weighing 100 talents,[w] 100 talents[w] of gold, 2720 bowls

t5 Some Septuagint manuscripts (also 1 Esdras 8:32); Hebrew does not have *Zattu*. u10 Some Septuagint manuscripts (also 1 Esdras 8:36); Hebrew does not have *Bani*. v26 That is, about 25 tons (about 22 metric tons) w26 That is, about 3 3/4 tons (about 3.4 metric tons)

of gold valued at 1,000 darics,[x] and two fine articles of polished bronze, as precious as gold.

28I said to them, "You as well as these articles are consecrated to the LORD. The silver and gold are a freewill offering to the LORD, the God of your fathers. 29Guard them carefully until you weigh them out in the chambers of the house of the LORD in Jerusalem before the leading priests and the Levites and the family heads of Israel." 30Then the priests and Levites received the silver and gold and sacred articles that had been weighed out to be taken to the house of our God in Jerusalem.

31On the twelfth day of the first month we set out from the Ahava Canal to go to Jerusalem. The hand of our God was on us, and he protected us from enemies and bandits along the way. 32So we arrived in Jerusalem, where we rested three days. 33On the fourth day, in the house of our God, we weighed out the silver and gold and the sacred articles into the hands of Meremoth son of Uriah, the priest. Eleazar son of Phinehas was with him, and so were the Levites Jozabad son of Jeshua and Noadiah son of Binnui. 34Everything was accounted for by number and weight, and the entire weight was recorded at that time.

35Then the exiles who had returned from captivity sacrificed burnt offerings to the God of Israel: twelve bulls for all Israel, ninety-six rams, seventy-seven male lambs and, as a sin offering, twelve male goats. All this was a burnt offering to the LORD. 36They also delivered the king's orders to the royal satraps and to the governors of Trans-Euphrates, who then gave assistance to the people and to the house of God.

x27 That is, about 19 pounds (about 8.5 kilograms)

Discovering the Word 1. Notice those mentioned in verses 1–14. What would it have been like for Ezra as the leader to gather all these people together (v. 15)? 2. Ezra sees that among those who are returning there are no Levites to assist in the day-to-day routine of the temple, so what does he do (vv. 15–20)? 3. What steps does Ezra take to prepare for the journey (vv. 21–30)? 4. What would be the benefit of weighing out (and weighing in) the articles given into his trust (vv. 24–26, 33–34)? 5. How did Ezra and the people respond to God after safely returning to Israel (vv. 35–36)? 6. Sometimes "being spiritual" is seen as better than "being practical." In what ways do you see both in Ezra?

Applying the Word 1. How can practical accountability safeguards (like weighing the gifts in vv. 24–34) protect the reputation of Christ's church and its leaders? 2. In what ways are you torn between being spiritual and being practical?

Responding in Prayer Ask God to help you see that being practical can be spiritual and that being spiritual can be practical. Pray that you will grow in both areas.

7 / *Ezra 9*
Turning Away from God

SEVEN HUNDRED WIVES! Though jokes come to mind quickly when we think of Solomon's household, the Bible does not give this fact to shock or amuse, but to warn. Besides the obvious show of pride and abuse of power, Solomon violated God's law by having foreign women among his wives. These were not foreign women who followed God like Rahab and Ruth; these were women who worshiped other gods—and led Solomon to do so as well. In today's passage Ezra receives news that his people have fallen into the same trap.

Warming Up to God How has a relationship with a non-Christian (friendship, coworker, dating, marriage) led you away from your commitment to God in some way?

Read Ezra 9.

9 After these things had been done, the
leaders came to me and said, "The people
of Israel, including the priests and the Le-
vites, have not kept themselves separate from the
neighboring peoples with their detestable prac-
tices, like those of the Canaanites, Hittites, Periz-
zites, Jebusites, Ammonites, Moabites, Egyptians
and Amorites. 2They have taken some of their
daughters as wives for themselves and their sons,
and have mingled the holy race with the peoples
around them. And the leaders and officials have
led the way in this unfaithfulness."
3When I heard this, I tore my tunic and cloak,
pulled hair from my head and beard and sat down
appalled. 4Then everyone who trembled at the
words of the God of Israel gathered around
me because of this unfaithfulness of the exiles.
And I sat there appalled until the evening sacri-
fice.
5Then, at the evening sacrifice, I rose from my
self-abasement, with my tunic and cloak torn,
and fell on my knees with my hands spread out to
the LORD my God 6and prayed:
"O my God, I am too ashamed and dis-
graced to lift up my face to you, my God,
because our sins are higher than our heads
and our guilt has reached to the heavens.
7From the days of our forefathers until now,
our guilt has been great. Because of our sins,
we and our kings and our priests have been
subjected to the sword and captivity, to pil-
lage and humiliation at the hand of foreign
kings, as it is today.
8"But now, for a brief moment, the LORD
our God has been gracious in leaving us a
remnant and giving us a firm place in his
sanctuary, and so our God gives light to our
eyes and a little relief in our bondage.
9Though we are slaves, our God has not de-
serted us in our bondage. He has shown us
kindness in the sight of the kings of Persia:
He has granted us new life to rebuild the
house of our God and repair its ruins, and he
has given us a wall of protection in Judah
and Jerusalem.
10"But now, O our God, what can we say
after this? For we have disregarded the com-
mands 11you gave through your servants the
prophets when you said: 'The land you are
entering to possess is a land polluted by the
corruption of its peoples. By their detestable
practices they have filled it with their impu-
rity from one end to the other. 12Therefore,
do not give your daughters in marriage to
their sons or take their daughters for your
sons. Do not seek a treaty of friendship with
them at any time, that you may be strong
and eat the good things of the land and leave
it to your children as an everlasting inheri-
tance.'
13"What has happened to us is a result of
our evil deeds and our great guilt, and yet,
our God, you have punished us less than our
sins have deserved and have given us a rem-
nant like this. 14Shall we again break your
commands and intermarry with the peoples
who commit such detestable practices?
Would you not be angry enough with us to
destroy us, leaving us no remnant or survi-
vor? 15O LORD, God of Israel, you are righ-
teous! We are left this day as a remnant.
Here we are before you in our guilt, though
because of it not one of us can stand in your
presence."

Discovering the Word 1. Some Jewish men were breaking their marriages to marry women who worshiped pagan gods (vv. 1–2, see also Mal 2:11–14). Describe Ezra's reaction to this news (vv. 3–5). 2. How would you outline the prayer of Ezra (vv. 6–15)? 3. What seems to be the problem with taking a foreign spouse (vv. 10–12)? 4. How would Ezra answer the question "Why hasn't God punished us yet?" (vv. 13–15)? 5. What in this passages shows that Ezra takes the holiness of God seriously?

Applying the Word 1. What compromises in the Christian community need to be mourned and confessed? 2. How can Ezra's prayer inform the way you confess your sins and the sins of your community? 3. How can you separate yourself from "detestable" practices of our culture and still reach out to those who desperately need the hope you have in Jesus?

Responding in Prayer Thank the Lord for not always treating us as we deserve to be treated. Pray that you will not take his mercy for granted, but instead take it wherever you go.

8 / *Ezra 10*
Compromise

HAVE YOU EVER compromised yourself and your beliefs? When did you realize this? The exiles who had returned a generation before Ezra had begun to merge with the neighboring cultures by marrying those who followed "detestable practices" (9:2). This lack of faithfulness broke Ezra's heart and caused him to pray the prayer found in chapter 9. When the people saw his passionate praying on their behalf, they realized their need for change.

Warming Up to God Ask God's Spirit to help you to see areas where you are giving in to your culture and compromising your faith.

Read Ezra 10.

10 While Ezra was praying and confessing, weeping and throwing himself down before the house of
God, a large crowd of Israelites—men, women
and children—gathered around him. They too
wept bitterly. 2Then Shecaniah son of Jehiel, one
of the descendants of Elam, said to Ezra, "We
have been unfaithful to our God by marrying foreign women from the peoples around us. But in
spite of this, there is still hope for Israel. 3Now let
us make a covenant before our God to send away
all these women and their children, in accordance
with the counsel of my lord and of those who fear
the commands of our God. Let it be done according to the Law. 4Rise up; this matter is in your
hands. We will support you, so take courage and
do it."

5So Ezra rose up and put the leading priests
and Levites and all Israel under oath to do what
had been suggested. And they took the oath.
6Then Ezra withdrew from before the house of
God and went to the room of Jehohanan son of
Eliashib. While he was there, he ate no food and
drank no water, because he continued to mourn
over the unfaithfulness of the exiles.

7A proclamation was then issued throughout
Judah and Jerusalem for all the exiles to assemble
in Jerusalem. 8Anyone who failed to appear
within three days would forfeit all his property, in
accordance with the decision of the officials and
elders, and would himself be expelled from the
assembly of the exiles.

9Within the three days, all the men of Judah
and Benjamin had gathered in Jerusalem. And on
the twentieth day of the ninth month, all the people were sitting in the square before the house of
God, greatly distressed by the occasion and because of the rain. 10Then Ezra the priest stood up
and said to them, "You have been unfaithful; you
have married foreign women, adding to Israel's
guilt. 11Now make confession to the LORD, the
God of your fathers, and do his will. Separate
yourselves from the peoples around you and from
your foreign wives."

12The whole assembly responded with a loud
voice: "You are right! We must do as you say.
13But there are many people here and it is the
rainy season; so we cannot stand outside. Besides,
this matter cannot be taken care of in a day or
two, because we have sinned greatly in this thing.
14Let our officials act for the whole assembly.
Then let everyone in our towns who has married
a foreign woman come at a set time, along with
the elders and judges of each town, until the
fierce anger of our God in this matter is turned
away from us." 15Only Jonathan son of Asahel
and Jahzeiah son of Tikvah, supported by Meshullam and Shabbethai the Levite, opposed
this.

16So the exiles did as was proposed. Ezra the
priest selected men who were family heads, one
from each family division, and all of them designated by name. On the first day of the tenth
month they sat down to investigate the cases,
17and by the first day of the first month they finished dealing with all the men who had married
foreign women.

18Among the descendants of the priests, the
following had married foreign women:

From the descendants of Jeshua son of Jozadak, and his brothers: Maaseiah, Eliezer,
Jarib and Gedaliah. 19(They all gave their
hands in pledge to put away their wives,

and for their guilt they each presented a ram from the flock as a guilt offering.)

20 From the descendants of Immer:
Hanani and Zebadiah.

21 From the descendants of Harim:
Maaseiah, Elijah, Shemaiah, Jehiel and Uzziah.

22 From the descendants of Pashhur:
Elioenai, Maaseiah, Ishmael, Nethanel, Jozabad and Elasah.

23 Among the Levites:

Jozabad, Shimei, Kelaiah (that is, Kelita), Pethahiah, Judah and Eliezer.

24 From the singers:
Eliashib.
From the gatekeepers:
Shallum, Telem and Uri.

25 And among the other Israelites:
From the descendants of Parosh:
Ramiah, Izziah, Malkijah, Mijamin, Eleazar, Malkijah and Benaiah.

26 From the descendants of Elam:
Mattaniah, Zechariah, Jehiel, Abdi, Jeremoth and Elijah.

27 From the descendants of Zattu:
Elioenai, Eliashib, Mattaniah, Jeremoth, Zabad and Aziza.

28 From the descendants of Bebai:
Jehohanan, Hananiah, Zabbai and Athlai.

29 From the descendants of Bani:
Meshullam, Malluch, Adaiah, Jashub, Sheal and Jeremoth.

30 From the descendants of Pahath-Moab:
Adna, Kelal, Benaiah, Maaseiah, Mattaniah, Bezalel, Binnui and Manasseh.

31 From the descendants of Harim:
Eliezer, Ishijah, Malkijah, Shemaiah, Shimeon, 32 Benjamin, Malluch and Shemariah.

33 From the descendants of Hashum:
Mattenai, Mattattah, Zabad, Eliphelet, Jeremai, Manasseh and Shimei.

34 From the descendants of Bani:
Maadai, Amram, Uel, 35 Benaiah, Bedeiah, Keluhi, 36 Vaniah, Meremoth, Eliashib, 37 Mattaniah, Mattenai and Jaasu.

38 From the descendants of Binnui:[y]
Shimei, 39 Shelemiah, Nathan, Adaiah, 40 Macnadebai, Shashai, Sharai, 41 Azarel, Shelemiah, Shemariah, 42 Shallum, Amariah and Joseph.

43 From the descendants of Nebo:
Jeiel, Mattithiah, Zabad, Zebina, Jaddai, Joel and Benaiah.

44 All these had married foreign women, and some of them had children by these wives.[z]

[y] 37,38 See Septuagint (also 1 Esdras 9:34); Hebrew *Jaasu* *38 and Bani and Binnui,* [z] 44 Or *and they sent them away with their children*

Discovering the Word 1. How does Ezra demonstrate his concerns about the decisions his people have made (vv. 1, 6)? 2. What indications are there that the repentance of the people is sincere (vv. 1–5, 7–9)? 3. How do the people respond to the call for repentance (vv. 12–15)? 4. How does Ezra empower the people of God (vv. 12–17)? 5. What do you learn about those who intermarried from the list in verses 18–44?

Applying the Word 1. How can marriage or a deep friendship strengthen one's relationship with God, and how can it weaken it? 2. Ezra is obviously not a controlling individual. He is open to suggestions and willing to delegate authority. What can you and your community learn from his style of leadership?

Responding in Prayer Thank God for the example of Ezra's passionate faith that does not consume people but attracts them to the Lord. Pray that you will grow in such faith.

Nehemiah

Nehemiah was in leadership during an extraordinary time in Israel's history. He faced opposition from all sides—both from his own people and from outside forces. A little background will help set the stage for understanding the pressures Nehemiah faced.

From antiquity, Ezra and Nehemiah have been considered almost as one book. The two books cover a period of about one hundred years. In 587 B.C. Judah was removed from the land of Israel and deported to Babylon with only a few left in the land. In 538 B.C. Cyrus sent some of the people back to rebuild the temple. Nehemiah's second return would be around 430 B.C. Zerubbabel, Ezra and Nehemiah are all wrapped up in this history. Zerubbabel built the temple, Ezra brought the law back into Israel's life and Nehemiah rebuilt the wall that made Jerusalem secure.

The amazing thing is that Israel had more autonomy and distinctiveness than at any time of their existence as a sovereign state. The Persian empire allowed the people to practice their religious convictions with seriousness, and this probably accounts for why Israel had such a pristine religious life at this time.

While Zerubbabel and Ezra worked more in the religious realm, Nehemiah was really sent to Judah to be governor of the land, and that gave him considerably more ability to make some lasting changes in the life of the people. The people needed Nehemiah's strong leadership to handle the opposition to their work.

There were three primary opposers: Sanballat, Geshem and Tobiah. Sanballat was probably governor of Samaria and was not interested in Judah's becoming an independent nation again. Geshem is thought to have been a leader of a powerful block of Arab communities. Tobiah was probably governor of Ammon and a member of an influential Jewish family.

Derek Kidner describes the importance of this period of Israel's history:

> The two centuries of the Persian empire were among the most formative periods of Jewish history. Out of the ruins of the little kingdom of Judah there had emerged the small community whose concern to be the people of God by pedigree and practice shaped it into the nation which meets us in the New Testament. Already the future prominence of the Temple and its priests of the law and its scribes, as well as the enmity between Jew and Samaritans, could be seen developing. Throughout this time the Persian regime was given a

> substantial part to play, both in sending and subsidizing the three expeditions of Zerubbabel, Ezra and Nehemiah, and in backing their authority with its own. It was not the first empire, nor the last, to be allotted some such role. (Derek Kidner, *Ezra & Nehemiah* [Downers Grove, Ill.: InterVarsity Press, 1979], p. 17.)

The Israelites living in the land were fairly passive at this point in history. They had to adapt to the culture around them because they were such a small remnant. Their intermarrying and political ties made this considerably worse.

Nehemiah's gifts in administration and perseverance enabled him to mold this people back into the "people of God" so they could obey God's commands and have a distinction from the people around them. This is where Nehemiah shines through. It was not enough to build just the wall—he had to build a people that would once again stand on their own as God led them. Putting some "backbone" back into the people was a large part of what Nehemiah had to accomplish—even if it required him to be harsh with them at times.

God has called each of us to important tasks, both as leaders and as followers. Reading Nehemiah will help us to have the courage we need to follow through even in the face of difficulty and persecution. God be with you as you study.

Outline

1 / *Nehemiah 1*
Depending on God

AT ONE TIME or another, most of us have said, "I am too busy to pray!" If the work of God or the work that we want to do for God depended on our energy and insight, then it might be true. But of course, at least theoretically, we believe that God's work can only be done through his power (Ps 127:1, "Unless the LORD builds the house, its builders labor in vain"). Yet we don't think our biggest job is to pray. If we did, it might make a big difference in what we try to accomplish for the Lord! As we go before the Lord in prayer, we gain his perspective, and we gain confidence. In this study Nehemiah models dependency on the Lord for his strength.

Warming Up to God Before you look into the Scriptures, sit quietly for a few moments and breathe deeply, allowing yourself to become relaxed and peaceful. Ask the Holy Spirit to give you discernment as you begin studying Nehemiah.

Read Nehemiah 1.

1 The words of Nehemiah son of Hacaliah:
In the month of Kislev in the twentieth
year, while I was in the citadel of Susa,
2Hanani, one of my brothers, came from Judah
with some other men, and I questioned them
about the Jewish remnant that survived the exile,
and also about Jerusalem.
3They said to me, "Those who survived the ex-
ile and are back in the province are in great trou-
ble and disgrace. The wall of Jerusalem is broken
down, and its gates have been burned with fire."
4When I heard these things, I sat down and
wept. For some days I mourned and fasted and
prayed before the God of heaven. 5Then I said:
"O LORD, God of heaven, the great and
awesome God, who keeps his covenant of
love with those who love him and obey his
commands, 6let your ear be attentive and
your eyes open to hear the prayer your ser-
vant is praying before you day and night for
your servants, the people of Israel. I confess
the sins we Israelites, including myself and
my father's house, have committed against
you. 7We have acted very wickedly toward
you. We have not obeyed the commands,
decrees and laws you gave your servant
Moses.
8"Remember the instruction you gave
your servant Moses, saying, 'If you are un-
faithful, I will scatter you among the nations,
9but if you return to me and obey my com-
mands, then even if your exiled people are at
the farthest horizon, I will gather them from
there and bring them to the place I have cho-
sen as a dwelling for my Name.'
10"They are your servants and your peo-
ple, whom you redeemed by your great
strength and your mighty hand. 11O Lord,
let your ear be attentive to the prayer of this
your servant and to the prayer of your ser-
vants who delight in revering your name.
Give your servant success today by granting
him favor in the presence of this man."

I was cupbearer to the king.

Discovering the Word 1. In verses 1–3 what event is being discussed? 2. What four things does Nehemiah do when he hears Hanani's report (v. 4)? 3. List the specific concerns that Nehemiah mentions in his prayer (vv. 5–11). 4. What evidence do you find here that Nehemiah believed God heard his prayer and would answer it? 5. What do you learn about Nehemiah's character from his reaction and his prayer?

Applying the Word 1. Nehemiah got more confident as he prayed and fasted. How does this compare with what you have experienced in prayer? 2. As you think about your ministry, are there any reports you are hearing that you need to petition God for? 3. What will you do to take a risk and become part of the answer for that prayer?

Responding in Prayer Thank the Lord for using people just like you to carry out his plans. Ask him to give you courage as you participate in his work.

2 / *Nehemiah 2*
The Planning Process

ONCE DWIGHT L. Moody was sailing on an ocean vessel and a fire broke out. One of his traveling companions said, "Don't you think we should go and pray, Brother Moody?" Moody replied, "You can go and pray, brother, but I am going to man the water buckets. There is a time to pray and a time to put the fire out!" We tend to build a dichotomy between praying and doing. Usually what trips us up in the Christian life is not finding the balance between dependency on God and action on our part. Surely both must be important in God's eyes! In this chapter Nehemiah shows evidence of careful planning on both fronts.

Warming Up to God What fears do you have that keep you from taking risks with your faith? Tell your Father about them—and let him show you how to overcome them with his strength.

Read Nehemiah 2.

2 In the month of Nisan in the twentieth year of King Artaxerxes, when wine was brought for him, I took the wine and gave it to the king. I had not been sad in his presence before; 2so the king asked me, "Why does your face look so sad when you are not ill? This can be nothing but sadness of heart."

I was very much afraid, 3but I said to the king, "May the king live forever! Why should my face not look sad when the city where my fathers are buried lies in ruins, and its gates have been destroyed by fire?"

4The king said to me, "What is it you want?"

Then I prayed to the God of heaven, 5and I answered the king, "If it pleases the king and if your servant has found favor in his sight, let him send me to the city in Judah where my fathers are buried so that I can rebuild it."

6Then the king, with the queen sitting beside him, asked me, "How long will your journey take, and when will you get back?" It pleased the king to send me; so I set a time.

7I also said to him, "If it pleases the king, may I have letters to the governors of Trans-Euphrates, so that they will provide me safe-conduct until I arrive in Judah? 8And may I have a letter to Asaph, keeper of the king's forest, so he will give me timber to make beams for the gates of the citadel by the temple and for the city wall and for the residence I will occupy?" And because the gracious hand of my God was upon me, the king granted my requests. 9So I went to the governors of Trans-Euphrates and gave them the king's letters. The king had also sent army officers and cavalry with me.

10When Sanballat the Horonite and Tobiah the Ammonite official heard about this, they were very much disturbed that someone had come to promote the welfare of the Israelites.

11I went to Jerusalem, and after staying there three days 12I set out during the night with a few men. I had not told anyone what my God had put in my heart to do for Jerusalem. There were no mounts with me except the one I was riding on.

13By night I went out through the Valley Gate toward the Jackal[a] Well and the Dung Gate, examining the walls of Jerusalem, which had been broken down, and its gates, which had been destroyed by fire. 14Then I moved on toward the Fountain Gate and the King's Pool, but there was not enough room for my mount to get through; 15so I went up the valley by night, examining the wall. Finally, I turned back and reentered through the Valley Gate. 16The officials did not know where I had gone or what I was doing, because as yet I had said nothing to the Jews or the priests or nobles or officials or any others who would be doing the work.

17Then I said to them, "You see the trouble we are in: Jerusalem lies in ruins, and its gates have been burned with fire. Come, let us rebuild the wall of Jerusalem, and we will no longer be in disgrace." 18I also told them about the gracious hand of my God upon me and what the king had said to me.

They replied, "Let us start rebuilding." So they began this good work.

19But when Sanballat the Horonite, Tobiah the Ammonite official and Geshem the Arab heard about it, they mocked and ridiculed us. "What is

[a]13 Or *Serpent* or *Fig*

this you are doing?" they asked. "Are you rebel-
ling against the king?"
20I answered them by saying, "The God of
heaven will give us success. We his servants will
start rebuilding, but as for you, you have no share
in Jerusalem or any claim or historic right to it."

Discovering the Word 1. How did Nehemiah give evidence of having a well-thought-through plan in verses 1–9? 2. What is the difference between the praying Nehemiah does in this chapter and what he did in chapter 1? 3. What evidences of thoroughness do you find in verses 11–16? 4. Why do you think Nehemiah appears so confident in verses 17–20? 5. From this chapter, what makes it reasonable for Nehemiah to be so hard-line with Sanballat, Tobiah and Geshem (vv. 18–20)?

Applying the Word 1. When you do a "great work for God," do you expect opposition? Explain. 2. Do you feel it is okay to say the "gracious hand of my God [is] upon me" (v. 18) regarding the work that you are doing? Explain why or why not.

Responding in Prayer Consider one risk or act of faith you need to take this week and ask the Lord to guide you through this test of your obedience.

3 / *Nehemiah 3*
Many Hands Make Lighter Work

A GIFTED LEADER can motivate others, but a job usually gets done because of prayer and unity among believers. This is so primarily because vision is spiritual and not material. When there is a lot of mundane work, like repairing a badly damaged wall, there must be unity for the job to be done. People need to feel they are part of the decision and the process. To miss this step of getting people "on board" dooms most projects to failure. This chapter shows how much the Israelites desired to work.

Warming Up to God Where are you today, figuratively, with the Lord? Take stock of yourself in relationship with him, confessing your sins and acknowledging his grace for you. He is listening and desires to talk with you today.

Read Nehemiah 3.

3 Eliashib the high priest and his fellow
priests went to work and rebuilt the
Sheep Gate. They dedicated it and set its
doors in place, building as far as the Tower of the
Hundred, which they dedicated, and as far as the
Tower of Hananel. 2The men of Jericho built the
adjoining section, and Zaccur son of Imri built
next to them.

3The Fish Gate was rebuilt by the sons of Has-
senaah. They laid its beams and put its doors
and bolts and bars in place. 4Meremoth son of
Uriah, the son of Hakkoz, repaired the next
section. Next to him Meshullam son of Berekiah,
the son of Meshezabel, made repairs, and next
to him Zadok son of Baana also made repairs.
5The next section was repaired by the men
of Tekoa, but their nobles would not put their
shoulders to the work under their supervisors.[b]

6The Jeshanah[c] Gate was repaired by Joiada
son of Paseah and Meshullam son of Besodeiah.
They laid its beams and put its doors and bolts
and bars in place. 7Next to them, repairs were
made by men from Gibeon and Mizpah—Mela-
tiah of Gibeon and Jadon of Meronoth—places
under the authority of the governor of Trans-Eu-
phrates. 8Uzziel son of Harhaiah, one of the gold-
smiths, repaired the next section; and Hananiah,
one of the perfume-makers, made repairs next to
that. They restored[d] Jerusalem as far as the
Broad Wall. 9Rephaiah son of Hur, ruler of a half-
district of Jerusalem, repaired the next section.
10Adjoining this, Jedaiah son of Harumaph made

[b]5 *Or their Lord or the governor* [c]6 *Or Old* [d]8 *Or They left out part of*

repairs opposite his house, and Hattush son of Hashabneiah made repairs next to him. [11]Malkijah son of Harim and Hasshub son of Pahath-Moab repaired another section and the Tower of the Ovens. [12]Shallum son of Hallohesh, ruler of a half-district of Jerusalem, repaired the next section with the help of his daughters.

[13]The Valley Gate was repaired by Hanun and the residents of Zanoah. They rebuilt it and put its doors and bolts and bars in place. They also repaired five hundred yards[e] of the wall as far as the Dung Gate.

[14]The Dung Gate was repaired by Malkijah son of Recab, ruler of the district of Beth Hakkerem. He rebuilt it and put its doors and bolts and bars in place.

[15]The Fountain Gate was repaired by Shallun son of Col-Hozeh, ruler of the district of Mizpah. He rebuilt it, roofing it over and putting its doors and bolts and bars in place. He also repaired the wall of the Pool of Siloam,[f] by the King's Garden, as far as the steps going down from the City of David. [16]Beyond him, Nehemiah son of Azbuk, ruler of a half-district of Beth Zur, made repairs up to a point opposite the tombs[g] of David, as far as the artificial pool and the House of the Heroes.

[17]Next to him, the repairs were made by the Levites under Rehum son of Bani. Beside him, Hashabiah, ruler of half the district of Keilah, carried out repairs for his district. [18]Next to him, the repairs were made by their countrymen under Binnui[h] son of Henadad, ruler of the other half-district of Keilah. [19]Next to him, Ezer son of Jeshua, ruler of Mizpah, repaired another section, from a point facing the ascent to the armory as far as the angle. [20]Next to him, Baruch son of Zabbai zealously repaired another section, from the angle to the entrance of the house of Eliashib the high priest. [21]Next to him, Meremoth son of Uriah, the son of Hakkoz, repaired another section, from the entrance of Eliashib's house to the end of it.

[22]The repairs next to him were made by the priests from the surrounding region. [23]Beyond them, Benjamin and Hasshub made repairs in front of their house; and next to them, Azariah son of Maaseiah, the son of Ananiah, made repairs beside his house. [24]Next to him, Binnui son of Henadad repaired another section, from Azariah's house to the angle and the corner, [25]and Palal son of Uzai worked opposite the angle and the tower projecting from the upper palace near the court of the guard. Next to him, Pedaiah son of Parosh [26]and the temple servants living on the hill of Ophel made repairs up to a point opposite the Water Gate toward the east and the projecting tower. [27]Next to them, the men of Tekoa repaired another section, from the great projecting tower to the wall of Ophel.

[28]Above the Horse Gate, the priests made repairs, each in front of his own house. [29]Next to them, Zadok son of Immer made repairs opposite his house. Next to him, Shemaiah son of Shecaniah, the guard at the East Gate, made repairs. [30]Next to him, Hananiah son of Shelemiah, and Hanun, the sixth son of Zalaph, repaired another section. Next to them, Meshullam son of Berekiah made repairs opposite his living quarters. [31]Next to him, Malkijah, one of the goldsmiths, made repairs as far as the house of the temple servants and the merchants, opposite the Inspection Gate, and as far as the room above the corner; [32]and between the room above the corner and the Sheep Gate the goldsmiths and merchants made repairs.

[e]13 Hebrew *a thousand cubits* (about 450 meters) [f]15 Hebrew *Shelah*, a variant of *Shiloah*, that is, Siloam [g]16 Hebrew; Septuagint, some Vulgate manuscripts and Syriac *tomb* [h]18 Two Hebrew manuscripts and Syriac (see also Septuagint and verse 24); most Hebrew manuscripts *Bavvai*

Discovering the Word 1. This chapter describes the hard work of building the wall around Jerusalem and repairing the gates. List the groups or individuals in this chapter who give themselves to the work. 2. What are some of the occupations of the repairers? 3. What was the place of women in this work (v. 12)? 4. From the chapter, what seems to be the motivation for people to work on their part of the wall? 5. Was Nehemiah privileged to have everyone committed to the work (v. 5)? Explain.

Applying the Word 1. How do you feel when facing what seems to be an impossible task—especially when there doesn't seem to be commitment from those you are working with? 2. How has cooperation played a significant part in your church or fellowship group's success in ministry? 3. Do you feel you are as motivated to work in your church or fellowship as this group of people is? Explain your response.

Responding in Prayer Ask the Lord to give you a helper or partner in your ministry—and ask him to teach you both how to work together.

4 / *Nehemiah 4*
Opposition from the Outside

"STICKS AND STONES may break my bones, but names will never hurt me!" We usually hear children say this. But when we want to oppose something because it is getting in our way, we adults have a slightly more sophisticated way of doing the same thing.

The enemies of Israel started out at the "sticks and stones" level, but they were soon into slander, intimidation and threatening with weapons. Our enemy the devil is always going to oppose the work of God. We need to expect and be able to fight opposition, if we will do God's work.

Warming Up to God How have your plans for good and faithful service to the Lord been frustrated lately? Express your feelings to the Lord and give them over to him completely, trusting he will continue to do his will on earth.

Read Nehemiah 4.

4 When Sanballat heard that we were rebuilding the wall, he became angry and was greatly incensed. He ridiculed the Jews, [2]and in the presence of his associates and the army of Samaria, he said, "What are those feeble Jews doing? Will they restore their wall? Will they offer sacrifices? Will they finish in a day? Can they bring the stones back to life from those heaps of rubble—burned as they are?"

[3]Tobiah the Ammonite, who was at his side, said, "What they are building—if even a fox climbed up on it, he would break down their wall of stones!"

[4]Hear us, O our God, for we are despised. Turn their insults back on their own heads. Give them over as plunder in a land of captivity. [5]Do not cover up their guilt or blot out their sins from your sight, for they have thrown insults in the face of[i] the builders.

[6]So we rebuilt the wall till all of it reached half its height, for the people worked with all their heart.

[7]But when Sanballat, Tobiah, the Arabs, the Ammonites and the men of Ashdod heard that the repairs to Jerusalem's walls had gone ahead and that the gaps were being closed, they were very angry. [8]They all plotted together to come and fight against Jerusalem and stir up trouble against it. [9]But we prayed to our God and posted a guard day and night to meet this threat.

[10]Meanwhile, the people in Judah said, "The strength of the laborers is giving out, and there is so much rubble that we cannot rebuild the wall."

[11]Also our enemies said, "Before they know it or see us, we will be right there among them and will kill them and put an end to the work."

[12]Then the Jews who lived near them came and told us ten times over, "Wherever you turn, they will attack us."

[13]Therefore I stationed some of the people behind the lowest points of the wall at the exposed places, posting them by families, with their swords, spears and bows. [14]After I looked things over, I stood up and said to the nobles, the officials and the rest of the people, "Don't be afraid of them. Remember the Lord, who is great and awesome, and fight for your brothers, your sons and your daughters, your wives and your homes."

[15]When our enemies heard that we were aware of their plot and that God had frustrated it, we all returned to the wall, each to his own work.

[16]From that day on, half of my men did the work, while the other half were equipped with spears, shields, bows and armor. The officers posted themselves behind all the people of Judah [17]who were building the wall. Those who carried materials did their work with one hand and held

[i]5 *Or have provoked you to anger before*

a weapon in the other, [18]and each of the builders
wore his sword at his side as he worked. But the
man who sounded the trumpet stayed with me.
[19]Then I said to the nobles, the officials and the
rest of the people, "The work is extensive and
spread out, and we are widely separated from
each other along the wall. [20]Wherever you hear
the sound of the trumpet, join us there. Our God
will fight for us!"
[21]So we continued the work with half the men
holding spears, from the first light of dawn till the
stars came out. [22]At that time I also said to the
people, "Have every man and his helper stay in-
side Jerusalem at night, so they can serve us as
guards by night and workmen by day." [23]Neither
I nor my brothers nor my men nor the guards
with me took off our clothes; each had his
weapon, even when he went for water.[j]

[j]23 The meaning of the Hebrew for this clause is uncertain.

Discovering the Word 1. Describe the progression of seriousness in how Sanballat and Tobiah threaten the Jews and the building of the wall in verses 1–3. 2. List the ways Nehemiah responds to these forms of opposition (vv. 4–6). 3. Why do you think Nehemiah is so uncharitable in his prayer in verses 4–5? 4. Note that Sanballat has inside help in his intimidation of the Jews and Nehemiah. What is it (vv. 10 and 12)? 5. In verses 13–20, how does Nehemiah handle these threats? 6. What was Nehemiah trusting in to get the work done (vv. 9, 14 and 20)?

Applying the Word 1. In what situation have you seen a creative solution keep the work moving forward? 2. Does opposition make you want to quit a job, or does it challenge you to work harder to complete it? Explain.

Responding in Prayer Pray verses 4 and 5 to the Lord, boldly asking for sinful oppression to be lifted from Christians today.

5 / *Nehemiah 5*
Opposition from Within

MOST ORGANIZATIONS AND nations fall apart because of opposition and deterioration from within rather than from without. An idea is conceived, gains adherence and grows to fruition. Then after it has served its purpose for a period of time, the work it took to get to that point is taken for granted and often personal aggrandizement corrupts the intended purpose. At the beginning there is sacrifice by the people, but someone usually figures out how to make money from the idea, and it is not long before that which helped people hurts people. That is what happens in this chapter of Nehemiah.

Warming Up to God The Lord is excited to hear from you today and wants to listen to all you have to say. Tell him about your day and your feelings for a few minutes before you begin reading the Word.

Read Nehemiah 5.

5 Now the men and their wives raised a
great outcry against their Jewish brothers.
[2]Some were saying, "We and our sons and
daughters are numerous; in order for us to eat
and stay alive, we must get grain."
[3]Others were saying, "We are mortgaging our
fields, our vineyards and our homes to get grain
during the famine."
[4]Still others were saying, "We have had to bor-
row money to pay the king's tax on our fields and
vineyards. [5]Although we are of the same flesh and
blood as our countrymen and though our sons
are as good as theirs, yet we have to subject our
sons and daughters to slavery. Some of our
daughters have already been enslaved, but we are
powerless, because our fields and our vineyards
belong to others."
[6]When I heard their outcry and these charges,
I was very angry. [7]I pondered them in my mind
and then accused the nobles and officials. I told

them, "You are exacting usury from your own
countrymen!" So I called together a large meeting
to deal with them 8and said: "As far as possible,
we have bought back our Jewish brothers who
were sold to the Gentiles. Now you are selling
your brothers, only for them to be sold back to
us!" They kept quiet, because they could find
nothing to say.
9So I continued, "What you are doing is not
right. Shouldn't you walk in the fear of our God
to avoid the reproach of our Gentile enemies? 10I
and my brothers and my men are also lending the
people money and grain. But let the exacting of
usury stop! 11Give back to them immediately
their fields, vineyards, olive groves and houses,
and also the usury you are charging them—the
hundredth part of the money, grain, new wine
and oil."
12"We will give it back," they said. "And we
will not demand anything more from them. We
will do as you say."
Then I summoned the priests and made the
nobles and officials take an oath to do what they
had promised. 13I also shook out the folds of my
robe and said, "In this way may God shake out of
his house and possessions every man who does
not keep this promise. So may such a man be
shaken out and emptied!"
At this the whole assembly said, "Amen," and
praised the LORD. And the people did as they had
promised.
14Moreover, from the twentieth year of King
Artaxerxes, when I was appointed to be their gov-
ernor in the land of Judah, until his thirty-second
year—twelve years—neither I nor my brothers
ate the food allotted to the governor. 15But the
earlier governors—those preceding me—placed a
heavy burden on the people and took forty shek-
els[k] of silver from them in addition to food and
wine. Their assistants also lorded it over the peo-
ple. But out of reverence for God I did not act like
that. 16Instead, I devoted myself to the work on
this wall. All my men were assembled there for
the work; we[l] did not acquire any land.
17Furthermore, a hundred and fifty Jews and
officials ate at my table, as well as those who
came to us from the surrounding nations. 18Each
day one ox, six choice sheep and some poultry
were prepared for me, and every ten days an
abundant supply of wine of all kinds. In spite of
all this, I never demanded the food allotted to the
governor, because the demands were heavy on
these people.
19Remember me with favor, O my God, for all
I have done for these people.

[k]*15* That is, about 1 pound (about 0.5 kilogram) [l]*16* Most Hebrew manuscripts; some Hebrew manuscripts, Septuagint, Vulgate and Syriac *I*

Discovering the Word 1. List the three forms of internal opposition in verses 1–5 that are developing against the vision of building the wall. 2. Who seem to be the people responsible for this inequity? Why do you think they would do this? 3. Make two lists. In the first cite the practices of the nobles, officials, former governors and their servants (vv. 7–12). In the second list cite the practices of Nehemiah (vv. 14–18). 4. How would you define the kind of leadership that Nehemiah exercises in dealing with this internal opposition to the wall? 5. In what ways does the chapter show Nehemiah doing all he can to not be part of this internal opposition?

Applying the Word 1. In what ways are leaders (spiritual or secular) today likely to assume privileges as these nobles and officials did? 2. How do you determine what is culturally acceptable and what God's kingdom values are? 3. What kind of internal opposition could likely come up within your church or Christian group to divert you from your real objectives?

Responding in Prayer Ask the Lord to "remember you" as you strive to serve him and carry out his will.

6 / *Nehemiah 6*
Facing Intimidation

USING POWER TO create pressure is a very effective way to get at people, especially if they are not sure of themselves or what they should be doing. However, if the objects of intimidation are quite confident in what they are doing, they may not be at all bothered by this approach.

Nehemiah had wrestled with God so thoroughly about what he was doing in building the wall that he was not sidetracked by attempts to call him away from the work. When someone reacts like Nehemiah, then the intimidator must become more and more threatening. It eventually boils down to who can intimidate the most or who is the most confident in what God's will is for the occasion. Notice in this chapter that Nehemiah doesn't give in to the intimidation.

Warming Up to God Think of a time when you had to be aggressive to fight for something you thought was right. How did you feel and act? Write down your ideas and compare them to the actions of Nehemiah.

Read Nehemiah 6.

6 When word came to Sanballat, Tobiah, Geshem the Arab and the rest of our enemies that I had rebuilt the wall and not a gap was left in it—though up to that time I had not set the doors in the gates— [2]Sanballat and Geshem sent me this message: "Come, let us meet together in one of the villages[m] on the plain of Ono."

But they were scheming to harm me; [3]so I sent messengers to them with this reply: "I am carrying on a great project and cannot go down. Why should the work stop while I leave it and go down to you?" [4]Four times they sent me the same message, and each time I gave them the same answer.

[5]Then, the fifth time, Sanballat sent his aide to me with the same message, and in his hand was an unsealed letter [6]in which was written:

"It is reported among the nations—and Geshem[n] says it is true—that you and the Jews are plotting to revolt, and therefore you are building the wall. Moreover, according to these reports you are about to become their king [7]and have even appointed prophets to make this proclamation about you in Jerusalem: 'There is a king in Judah!' Now this report will get back to the king; so come, let us confer together."

[8]I sent him this reply: "Nothing like what you are saying is happening; you are just making it up out of your head."

[9]They were all trying to frighten us, thinking, "Their hands will get too weak for the work, and it will not be completed."

⌊But I prayed,⌋ "Now strengthen my hands."

[10]One day I went to the house of Shemaiah son of Delaiah, the son of Mehetabel, who was shut in at his home. He said, "Let us meet in the house of God, inside the temple, and let us close the temple doors, because men are coming to kill you—by night they are coming to kill you."

[11]But I said, "Should a man like me run away? Or should one like me go into the temple to save his life? I will not go!" [12]I realized that God had not sent him, but that he had prophesied against me because Tobiah and Sanballat had hired him. [13]He had been hired to intimidate me so that I would commit a sin by doing this, and then they would give me a bad name to discredit me.

[14]Remember Tobiah and Sanballat, O my God, because of what they have done; remember also the prophetess Noadiah and the rest of the prophets who have been trying to intimidate me.

[15]So the wall was completed on the twenty-fifth of Elul, in fifty-two days. [16]When all our enemies heard about this, all the surrounding nations were afraid and lost their self-confidence, because they realized that this work had been done with the help of our God.

[17]Also, in those days the nobles of Judah were sending many letters to Tobiah, and replies from Tobiah kept coming to them. [18]For many in Judah were under oath to him, since he was son-in-law to Shecaniah son of Arah, and his son Jehohanan had married the daughter of Meshullam son of Berekiah. [19]Moreover, they kept reporting to me his good deeds and then telling him what I said. And Tobiah sent letters to intimidate me.

[m]2 Or *in Kephirim* [n]6 Hebrew *Gashmu,* a variant of *Geshem*

Discovering the Word 1. List all the efforts at intimidation in this chapter. 2. What kind of divided loyalties do you find in the people building the wall? 3. From this chapter, what guiding principles does Nehemiah give about how to cooperate with other religious groups? 4. How do the circumstances in verses 17–19 make it difficult for Nehemiah to keep his objectives clear?

Applying the Word 1. How is the work God has called you to do a "great work" and worthy of your full attention? 2. How could your vision be made great and clear enough so that you will not be easily sidetracked (vv. 3, 8 and 11)? 3. What do you expect by way of opposition in the job you are doing for the Lord?

Responding in Prayer Ask God to give you singlemindedness and determination as you work to proclaim his truth to those around you.

7 / *Nehemiah 7*
Family History

I REMEMBER MY grandparents talking about our family genealogy, and I thought, "How boring," so I didn't listen. Now I have 4,600 names on my computer about my genealogy, and I wish that I had listened to those conversations, because now I have lost much of the information with no way to retrieve it. I have even started recording many of the oldest relatives on tape so that I get not only the information but also their voices on tape for future generations. In this chapter of Nehemiah, we find that if people could not trace their lineage back to a preexilic Jewish relative, they were not considered bona fide descendants and could not be counted. I wonder if some of them didn't wish they had listened more to their relatives when they were talking about great-grandpa and great-grandma.

Warming Up to God Recall a fond family memory that you have from a holiday or your childhood. Thank the Lord for giving you your past as a remembrance and guide for the future.

Read Nehemiah 7.

7 After the wall had been rebuilt and I had
set the doors in place, the gatekeepers
and the singers and the Levites were ap-
pointed. 2I put in charge of Jerusalem my brother
Hanani, along with[o] Hananiah the commander
of the citadel, because he was a man of integrity
and feared God more than most men do. 3I said
to them, "The gates of Jerusalem are not to be
opened until the sun is hot. While the gatekeep-
ers are still on duty, have them shut the doors
and bar them. Also appoint residents of Jerusalem
as guards, some at their posts and some near their
own houses."
4Now the city was large and spacious, but there
were few people in it, and the houses had not yet
been rebuilt. 5So my God put it into my heart to
assemble the nobles, the officials and the com-
mon people for registration by families. I found
the genealogical record of those who had been the
first to return. This is what I found written there:
6These are the people of the province who
came up from the captivity of the exiles
whom Nebuchadnezzar king of Babylon had
taken captive (they returned to Jerusalem
and Judah, each to his own town, 7in com-
pany with Zerubbabel, Jeshua, Nehemiah,
Azariah, Raamiah, Nahamani, Mordecai, Bil-
shan, Mispereth, Bigvai, Nehum and Baa-
nah):

The list of the men of Israel:

8the descendants of Parosh	2,172
9of Shephatiah	372
10of Arah	652
11of Pahath-Moab (through the line of Jeshua and Joab)	2,818
12of Elam	1,254
13of Zattu	845
14of Zaccai	760
15of Binnui	648
16of Bebai	628

[o]2 Or *Hanani, that is,*

17 of Azgad 2,322
18 of Adonikam 667
19 of Bigvai 2,067
20 of Adin 655
21 of Ater (through Hezekiah) 98
22 of Hashum 328
23 of Bezai 324
24 of Hariph 112
25 of Gibeon 95

26 the men of Bethlehem and
Netophah 188
27 of Anathoth 128
28 of Beth Azmaveth 42
29 of Kiriath Jearim, Kephirah and
Beeroth 743
30 of Ramah and Geba 621
31 of Micmash 122
32 of Bethel and Ai 123
33 of the other Nebo 52
34 of the other Elam 1,254
35 of Harim 320
36 of Jericho 345
37 of Lod, Hadid and Ono 721
38 of Senaah 3,930

39 The priests:

the descendants of Jedaiah (through
the family of Jeshua) 973
40 of Immer 1,052
41 of Pashhur 1,247
42 of Harim 1,017

43 The Levites:

the descendants of Jeshua (through
Kadmiel through the line of
Hodaviah) 74

44 The singers:

the descendants of Asaph 148

45 The gatekeepers:

the descendants of
Shallum, Ater, Talmon, Akkub,
Hatita and Shobai 138

46 The temple servants:

the descendants of
Ziha, Hasupha, Tabbaoth,
47 Keros, Sia, Padon,
48 Lebana, Hagaba, Shalmai,
49 Hanan, Giddel, Gahar,
50 Reaiah, Rezin, Nekoda,
51 Gazzam, Uzza, Paseah,
52 Besai, Meunim, Nephussim,
53 Bakbuk, Hakupha, Harhur,
54 Bazluth, Mehida, Harsha,
55 Barkos, Sisera, Temah,
56 Neziah and Hatipha

57 The descendants of the servants of Solomon:

the descendants of
Sotai, Sophereth, Perida,
58 Jaala, Darkon, Giddel,
59 Shephatiah, Hattil,
Pokereth-Hazzebaim and Amon

60 The temple servants and the descendants
of the servants of Solomon 392

61 The following came up from the towns
of Tel Melah, Tel Harsha, Kerub, Addon and
Immer, but they could not show that their
families were descended from Israel:

62 the descendants of
Delaiah, Tobiah and Nekoda 642

63 And from among the priests:

the descendants of
Hobaiah, Hakkoz and Barzillai (a man
who had married a daughter of
Barzillai the Gileadite and was called
by that name).

64 These searched for their family records,
but they could not find them and so were
excluded from the priesthood as unclean.
65 The governor, therefore, ordered them not
to eat any of the most sacred food until there
should be a priest ministering with the Urim
and Thummim.

66 The whole company numbered 42,360,
67 besides their 7,337 menservants and maid-
servants; and they also had 245 men and
women singers. 68 There were 736 horses,
245 mules,[p] 69 435 camels and 6,720 don-
keys.

70 Some of the heads of the families con-
tributed to the work. The governor gave to
the treasury 1,000 drachmas[q] of gold, 50
bowls and 530 garments for priests. 71 Some
of the heads of the families gave to the trea-

p68 Some Hebrew manuscripts (see also Ezra 2:66); most Hebrew manuscripts do not have this verse. q70 That is, about 19 pounds (about 8.5 kilograms)

sury for the work 20,000 drachmas[r] of gold
and 2,200 minas[s] of silver. 72The total given
by the rest of the people was 20,000 drach-
mas of gold, 2,000 minas[t] of silver and 67
garments for priests.
73The priests, the Levites, the gatekeepers,
the singers and the temple servants, along
with certain of the people and the rest of the
Israelites, settled in their own towns.

[r]71 That is, about 375 pounds (about 170 kilograms); also in verse 72 [s]71 That is, about 1 1/3 tons (about 1.2 metric tons) [t]72 That is, about 1 1/4 tons (about 1.1 metric tons)

Discovering the Word 1. In verses 1–3, who is to guard the city, and what do you learn about where they are assigned to guard? 2. We previously met Hanani in 1:2. From the qualifications given in verse 2, why could Nehemiah trust him? 3. Nehemiah decides that the families who have returned should be registered. How would the registration deal with Israel's sin of mixing themselves with the people of the nations around Jerusalem (vv. 64–65)? 4. Look more closely at these lists. Why are there so many priests and so few Levites? 5. Why couldn't some of the people make connections with relatives? 6. What is significant about Nehemiah giving the priests 530 garments and the rest of the people only giving 67 garments?

Applying the Word 1. In what ways are you concerned about your family history and protecting it? 2. How does the thought that you will be in someone's Christian family tree affect you?

Responding in Prayer Think of one person you would like to invite into the family of God and ask the Lord to assist you as you witness to this person.

8 / *Nehemiah 8*
Celebration and Revival

A LOOK AT church history seems to indicate that mature Christians have a pretty wide variety of religious emotions. That is, they know how to laugh, and they know how to weep. Sometimes we avoid crying and laughing because it implies that we are not stable. When we deny the variety of religious emotions that we find in the Bible, we are robbing ourselves. In this chapter of Nehemiah we see real repentance, contrition and weeping as well as great celebration and joy in doing what God wants. Without the exhilaration of celebration our tears of repentance would lead us into morbid introspection—something that would do us no good, because only God can handle our sins and shortcomings. But without true repentance and contrition we really do not find joy of the kind this chapter demonstrates.

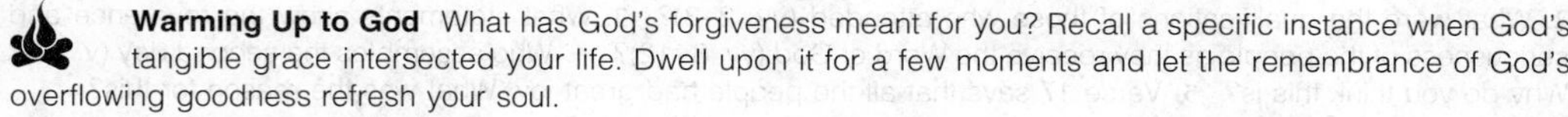

Warming Up to God What has God's forgiveness meant for you? Recall a specific instance when God's tangible grace intersected your life. Dwell upon it for a few moments and let the remembrance of God's overflowing goodness refresh your soul.

Read Nehemiah 8.

8 When the seventh month came and the Israel-
ites had settled in their towns, 1all the
people assembled as one man in the
square before the Water Gate. They told
Ezra the scribe to bring out the Book of the Law
of Moses, which the LORD had commanded
for Israel.
2So on the first day of the seventh month Ezra
the priest brought the Law before the assembly,
which was made up of men and women and all
who were able to understand. 3He read it aloud
from daybreak till noon as he faced the square
before the Water Gate in the presence of the men,
women and others who could understand. And
all the people listened attentively to the Book of
the Law.
4Ezra the scribe stood on a high wooden plat-
form built for the occasion. Beside him on his
right stood Mattithiah, Shema, Anaiah, Uriah,
Hilkiah and Maaseiah; and on his left were Peda-
iah, Mishael, Malkijah, Hashum, Hashbaddanah,
Zechariah and Meshullam.

5 Ezra opened the book. All the people could
see him because he was standing above them;
and as he opened it, the people all stood up.
6 Ezra praised the LORD, the great God; and all
the people lifted their hands and responded,
"Amen! Amen!" Then they bowed down and
worshiped the LORD with their faces to the
ground.

7 The Levites—Jeshua, Bani, Sherebiah, Jamin,
Akkub, Shabbethai, Hodiah, Maaseiah, Kelita, Az-
ariah, Jozabad, Hanan and Pelaiah—instructed
the people in the Law while the people were
standing there. 8 They read from the Book of the
Law of God, making it clear[u] and giving the
meaning so that the people could understand
what was being read.

9 Then Nehemiah the governor, Ezra the priest
and scribe, and the Levites who were instructing
the people said to them all, "This day is sacred to
the LORD your God. Do not mourn or weep." For
all the people had been weeping as they listened
to the words of the Law.

10 Nehemiah said, "Go and enjoy choice food
and sweet drinks, and send some to those who
have nothing prepared. This day is sacred to our
Lord. Do not grieve, for the joy of the LORD is
your strength."

11 The Levites calmed all the people, saying, "Be
still, for this is a sacred day. Do not grieve."

12 Then all the people went away to eat and
drink, to send portions of food and to celebrate
with great joy, because they now understood the
words that had been made known to them.

13 On the second day of the month, the heads of
all the families, along with the priests and the
Levites, gathered around Ezra the scribe to give
attention to the words of the Law. 14 They found
written in the Law, which the LORD had com-
manded through Moses, that the Israelites were
to live in booths during the feast of the seventh
month 15 and that they should proclaim this word
and spread it throughout their towns and in Jeru-
salem: "Go out into the hill country and bring
back branches from olive and wild olive trees,
and from myrtles, palms and shade trees, to make
booths"—as it is written.[v]

16 So the people went out and brought back
branches and built themselves booths on their
own roofs, in their courtyards, in the courts of the
house of God and in the square by the Water Gate
and the one by the Gate of Ephraim. 17 The whole
company that had returned from exile built
booths and lived in them. From the days of
Joshua son of Nun until that day, the Israelites
had not celebrated it like this. And their joy was
very great.

18 Day after day, from the first day to the last,
Ezra read from the Book of the Law of God. They
celebrated the feast for seven days, and on the
eighth day, in accordance with the regulation,
there was an assembly.

[u]8 *Or God, translating it* [v]15 See Lev. 23:37-40.

Discovering the Word 1. The seventh month was one of great importance to the Jews. It was to include several feasts as well as the great Day of Atonement. What prompted the people to meet together? 2. What were the qualifications of those who attended (vv. 2–3)? 3. What statements show the reverence and seriousness of the people as they receive the Word of God (vv. 3–12)? 4. Who assembles the second day (v. 13)? Why do you think this is? 5. Verse 17 says that all the people had great joy. What was the reason for this?

Applying the Word 1. How much is celebration a part of your regular Christian life? 2. How do Christians you know show the great joy they have from obeying God's Word? 3. Many Christians do not have much joy because they don't take obedience to God's Word seriously or make it a priority in their lives. How will you guard against that in your life?

Responding in Prayer Spend some time in prayer and celebrate all the many ways the Lord has provided for you and forgiven your sins.

9 / *Nehemiah 9*
Getting Back to Your Roots

FOR MANY OF us it is difficult to think about corporately confessing our sins in the sight and hearing of many people. Yet revival and renewal are always preceded by contrition and remorse for our sins. Israel is at the end of itself, and the Lord is the only one who can deliver them, so they are returning to him. We too must be humbled, broken and serious to be recipients of God's renewal.

Warming Up to God How do we get beyond the sin that keeps us from true fellowship with Christ and find true healing? Ask God to show you as you read Nehemiah 9.

Read Nehemiah 9.

9 On the twenty-fourth day of the same month, the Israelites gathered together, fasting and wearing sackcloth and having dust on their heads. 2Those of Israelite descent had separated themselves from all foreigners. They stood in their places and confessed their sins and the wickedness of their fathers. 3They stood where they were and read from the Book of the Law of the LORD their God for a quarter of the day, and spent another quarter in confession and in worshiping the LORD their God. 4Standing on the stairs were the Levites—Jeshua, Bani, Kadmiel, Shebaniah, Bunni, Sherebiah, Bani and Kenani—who called with loud voices to the LORD their God. 5And the Levites—Jeshua, Kadmiel, Bani, Hashabneiah, Sherebiah, Hodiah, Shebaniah and Pethahiah—said: "Stand up and praise the LORD your God, who is from everlasting to everlasting.[w]"

"Blessed be your glorious name, and may it be exalted above all blessing and praise. 6You alone are the LORD. You made the heavens, even the highest heavens, and all their starry host, the earth and all that is on it, the seas and all that is in them. You give life to everything, and the multitudes of heaven worship you.

7"You are the LORD God, who chose Abram and brought him out of Ur of the Chaldeans and named him Abraham. 8You found his heart faithful to you, and you made a covenant with him to give to his descendants the land of the Canaanites, Hittites, Amorites, Perizzites, Jebusites and Girgashites. You have kept your promise because you are righteous.

9"You saw the suffering of our forefathers in Egypt; you heard their cry at the Red Sea.[x] 10You sent miraculous signs and wonders against Pharaoh, against all his officials and all the people of his land, for you knew how arrogantly the Egyptians treated them. You made a name for yourself, which remains to this day. 11You divided the sea before them, so that they passed through it on dry ground, but you hurled their pursuers into the depths, like a stone into mighty waters. 12By day you led them with a pillar of cloud, and by night with a pillar of fire to give them light on the way they were to take.

13"You came down on Mount Sinai; you spoke to them from heaven. You gave them regulations and laws that are just and right, and decrees and commands that are good. 14You made known to them your holy Sabbath and gave them commands, decrees and laws through your servant Moses. 15In their hunger you gave them bread from heaven and in their thirst you brought them water from the rock; you told them to go in and take possession of the land you had sworn with uplifted hand to give them.

16"But they, our forefathers, became arrogant and stiff-necked, and did not obey your commands. 17They refused to listen and failed to remember the miracles you performed among them. They became stiff-necked and in their rebellion appointed a leader in order to return to their slavery. But you are a forgiving God, gracious and compassionate, slow to anger and abounding in love. Therefore you did not desert them, 18even when they cast for themselves an image of a calf and said, 'This is your god, who

w5 Or *God for ever and ever* x9 Hebrew *Yam Suph*; that is, Sea of Reeds brought you up out of Egypt,' or when they committed awful blasphemies.

[19]"Because of your great compassion you did not abandon them in the desert. By day the pillar of cloud did not cease to guide them on their path, nor the pillar of fire by night to shine on the way they were to take.
[20]You gave your good Spirit to instruct them. You did not withhold your manna from their mouths, and you gave them water for their thirst.
[21]For forty years you sustained them in the desert; they lacked nothing, their clothes did not wear out nor did their feet become swollen.

[22]"You gave them kingdoms and nations, allotting to them even the remotest frontiers. They took over the country of Sihon[y] king of Heshbon and the country of Og king of Bashan.
[23]You made their sons as numerous as the stars in the sky, and you brought them into the land that you told their fathers to enter and possess.
[24]Their sons went in and took possession of the land. You subdued before them the Canaanites, who lived in the land; you handed the Canaanites over to them, along with their kings and the peoples of the land, to deal with them as they pleased.
[25]They captured fortified cities and fertile land; they took possession of houses filled with all kinds of good things, wells already dug, vineyards, olive groves and fruit trees in abundance. They ate to the full and were well-nourished; they reveled in your great goodness.

[26]"But they were disobedient and rebelled against you; they put your law behind their backs. They killed your prophets, who had admonished them in order to turn them back to you; they committed awful blasphemies.
[27]So you handed them over to their enemies, who oppressed them. But when they were oppressed they cried out to you. From heaven you heard them, and in your great compassion you gave them deliverers, who rescued them from the hand of their enemies.

[28]"But as soon as they were at rest, they again did what was evil in your sight. Then you abandoned them to the hand of their enemies so that they ruled over them. And when they cried out to you again, you heard from heaven, and in your compassion you delivered them time after time.

[29]"You warned them to return to your law, but they became arrogant and disobeyed your commands. They sinned against your ordinances, by which a man will live if he obeys them. Stubbornly they turned their backs on you, became stiff-necked and refused to listen.
[30]For many years you were patient with them. By your Spirit you admonished them through your prophets. Yet they paid no attention, so you handed them over to the neighboring peoples.
[31]But in your great mercy you did not put an end to them or abandon them, for you are a gracious and merciful God.

[32]"Now therefore, O our God, the great, mighty and awesome God, who keeps his covenant of love, do not let all this hardship seem trifling in your eyes—the hardship that has come upon us, upon our kings and leaders, upon our priests and prophets, upon our fathers and all your people, from the days of the kings of Assyria until today.
[33]In all that has happened to us, you have been just; you have acted faithfully, while we did wrong.
[34]Our kings, our leaders, our priests and our fathers did not follow your law; they did not pay attention to your commands or the warnings you gave them.
[35]Even while they were in their kingdom, enjoying your great goodness to them in the spacious and fertile land you gave them, they did not serve you or turn from their evil ways.

[36]"But see, we are slaves today, slaves in the land you gave our forefathers so they could eat its fruit and the other good things it produces.
[37]Because of our sins, its abundant harvest goes to the kings you have placed over us. They rule over our bodies and our cattle as they please. We are in great distress.

[38]"In view of all this, we are making a binding agreement, putting it in writing, and our leaders, our Levites and our priests are affixing their seals to it."

[y]22 One Hebrew manuscript and Septuagint; most Hebrew manuscripts *Sihon, that is, the country of the*

Discovering the Word 1. Note that the time frame is about three weeks after the first reading of the Law. Why do you think they were wearing sackcloth and putting dust on their heads? 2. A quarter of a day is probably two to three hours. Does it seem feasible to you that they could confess sins for that long? Explain. 3. Why do you think they spent so much time confessing the sins of their ancestors? 4. What are the evidences from this passage that Ezra did not lose hope, even though the sins of Israel were many?

Applying the Word 1. How freely in your Christian life can you move between repentance for your sins and experiencing the celebration of God's forgiveness? 2. It may be surprising that the Israelites could go back so far and remember so many sins. Do you have any sense of history regarding your family sins or shortcomings? Explain your answer. 3. Now picture a time of corporate confession for your church or fellowship group. What kinds of sins should you be repenting of as a group?

Responding in Prayer Think of one act of reconciliation you need to make with members of your family, friends and the Lord himself. Pray and ask for forgiveness and commit to following through on your commitment this week.

10 / *Nehemiah 10*
A Covenant with God

MUCH OF THE world thinks that Christianity is a rip-off. Because Christians see God as the Creator and therefore the owner of everything there is, we give a tithe, and even more, to the Lord as an appropriate response. Part of the confusion is that the non-Christian sees the church or Christian leaders as getting that money. While serious Christians see all they have as belonging to God, non-Christians basically see all they have as a result of their hard work! Christians must be very honest and responsible with the money they control. Otherwise they open the body of Christ to ridicule and suspicion by the non-Christian world. There is no way the body of Christ can function well unless all God's people support those who have forgone a secular job to do the full-time work of the Lord and the body. This chapter of Nehemiah is about making such a covenant of support.

Warming Up to God What promises have you made or do you need to make with the Lord? Discuss them with him and ask for renewed energy for renewed faithfulness.

Read Nehemiah 10.

10 Those who sealed it were:

Nehemiah the governor, the son of Hacaliah.

Zedekiah, [2]Seraiah, Azariah, Jeremiah,
[3]Pashhur, Amariah, Malkijah,
[4]Hattush, Shebaniah, Malluch,
[5]Harim, Meremoth, Obadiah,
[6]Daniel, Ginnethon, Baruch,
[7]Meshullam, Abijah, Mijamin,
[8]Maaziah, Bilgai and Shemaiah.
These were the priests.

[9]The Levites:

Jeshua son of Azaniah, Binnui of the sons of Henadad, Kadmiel,
[10]and their associates: Shebaniah,
Hodiah, Kelita, Pelaiah, Hanan,
[11]Mica, Rehob, Hashabiah,
[12]Zaccur, Sherebiah, Shebaniah,
[13]Hodiah, Bani and Beninu.

[14]The leaders of the people:

Parosh, Pahath-Moab, Elam, Zattu, Bani,
[15]Bunni, Azgad, Bebai,
[16]Adonijah, Bigvai, Adin,
[17]Ater, Hezekiah, Azzur,
[18]Hodiah, Hashum, Bezai,
[19]Hariph, Anathoth, Nebai,
[20]Magpiash, Meshullam, Hezir,
[21]Meshezabel, Zadok, Jaddua,
[22]Pelatiah, Hanan, Anaiah,
[23]Hoshea, Hananiah, Hasshub,
[24]Hallohesh, Pilha, Shobek,
[25]Rehum, Hashabnah, Maaseiah,
[26]Ahiah, Hanan, Anan,

27 Malluch, Harim and Baanah.
28 "The rest of the people—priests, Levites,
gatekeepers, singers, temple servants and all
who separated themselves from the neigh-
boring peoples for the sake of the Law of
God, together with their wives and all their
sons and daughters who are able to under-
stand— 29 all these now join their brothers
the nobles, and bind themselves with a curse
and an oath to follow the Law of God given
through Moses the servant of God and to
obey carefully all the commands, regulations
and decrees of the LORD our Lord.
30 "We promise not to give our daughters
in marriage to the peoples around us or take
their daughters for our sons.
31 "When the neighboring peoples bring
merchandise or grain to sell on the Sabbath,
we will not buy from them on the Sabbath or
on any holy day. Every seventh year we will
forgo working the land and will cancel all
debts.
32 "We assume the responsibility for carry-
ing out the commands to give a third of a
shekel[z] each year for the service of the
house of our God: 33 for the bread set out on
the table; for the regular grain offerings and
burnt offerings; for the offerings on the Sab-
baths, New Moon festivals and appointed
feasts; for the holy offerings; for sin offerings
to make atonement for Israel; and for all the
duties of the house of our God.
34 "We—the priests, the Levites and the
people—have cast lots to determine when
each of our families is to bring to the house
of our God at set times each year a contribu-
tion of wood to burn on the altar of the LORD
our God, as it is written in the Law.
35 "We also assume responsibility for
bringing to the house of the LORD each year
the firstfruits of our crops and of every fruit
tree.
36 "As it is also written in the Law, we will
bring the firstborn of our sons and of our
cattle, of our herds and of our flocks to the
house of our God, to the priests ministering
there.
37 "Moreover, we will bring to the store-
rooms of the house of our God, to the
priests, the first of our ground meal, of our
⌞grain⌟ offerings, of the fruit of all our trees
and of our new wine and oil. And we will
bring a tithe of our crops to the Levites, for
it is the Levites who collect the tithes in all
the towns where we work. 38 A priest de-
scended from Aaron is to accompany the Le-
vites when they receive the tithes, and the
Levites are to bring a tenth of the tithes up to
the house of our God, to the storerooms of
the treasury. 39 The people of Israel, includ-
ing the Levites, are to bring their contribu-
tions of grain, new wine and oil to the store-
rooms where the articles for the sanctuary
are kept and where the ministering priests,
the gatekeepers and the singers stay.
"We will not neglect the house of our
God."

z32 That is, about 1/8 ounce (about 4 grams)

Discovering the Word 1. The result of hearing the Law read (chapter 8) and the result of obeying the Law (chapter 9) now produce a written agreement in chapter 10 to obey God and his commandments. Who were the groups of people mentioned in this chapter? 2. What evidence is there that everyone was included in the covenant agreement (vv. 28–29)? 3. Make a list of the things that the people covenant to do before the Lord (vv. 30–39). 4. Why would it be very important in their situation not to intermarry? 5. Do you think verse 29 is still binding on us today as it was on the people in Nehemiah's day? Explain why you give the answer that you do. 6. Who collected the tithe, and to whom did these people tithe?

Applying the Word 1. What effect would the actions the people commit to have on their life and worship? 2. Do you feel you take material things and the tithing of them as seriously as they did in this passage? Why or why not?

Responding in Prayer Reflect upon your commitments to the Lord with family, at work or school, or in your times of fellowship with him alone. Rededicate yourself in specific ways to these commitments—and promise the Lord to have renewed effort and obedience.

11 / *Nehemiah 11*
Choosing Where to Live and Work

WHEN MY FRIEND Ken is deciding where to live and work, he bases the decision on where he feels God wants him to develop a ministry and be of help in the building up of the body of Christ. Certainly people with the world's values do not choose a place to live and work on that basis. But as a Christian, the more I think about it, the more it makes sense. Not just my money belongs to the Lord, but my profession and my gifts belong to him so they can be used in the body of Christ. God would surely know better than I where I should live and work so that I would fit his plans for the building of his kingdom! Only God can balance all the variables in a way that works best for his purposes.

Warming Up to God What rests heavy on your heart today? Draw near to Jesus, who is waiting to put his arms around you as you tell him of your concerns. Let him listen to all your anxieties and allow them to become his worries for you.

Read Nehemiah 11.

11 Now the leaders of the people set-
tled in Jerusalem, and the rest of
the people cast lots to bring one out
of every ten to live in Jerusalem, the holy city,
while the remaining nine were to stay in their
own towns. 2The people commended all the men
who volunteered to live in Jerusalem.
3These are the provincial leaders who settled in
Jerusalem (now some Israelites, priests, Levites,
temple servants and descendants of Solomon's
servants lived in the towns of Judah, each on his
own property in the various towns, 4while other
people from both Judah and Benjamin lived in
Jerusalem):

From the descendants of Judah:

Athaiah son of Uzziah, the son of Zechariah,
the son of Amariah, the son of Shephatiah,
the son of Mahalalel, a descendant of Perez;
5and Maaseiah son of Baruch, the son of Col-
Hozeh, the son of Hazaiah, the son of Ada-
iah, the son of Joiarib, the son of Zechariah,
a descendant of Shelah. 6The descendants of
Perez who lived in Jerusalem totaled 468
able men.

7From the descendants of Benjamin:

Sallu son of Meshullam, the son of Joed, the
son of Pedaiah, the son of Kolaiah, the son of
Maaseiah, the son of Ithiel, the son of Jesha-
iah, 8and his followers, Gabbai and Sallai—
928 men. 9Joel son of Zicri was their chief
officer, and Judah son of Hassenuah was
over the Second District of the city.

10From the priests:

Jedaiah; the son of Joiarib; Jakin; 11Seraiah
son of Hilkiah, the son of Meshullam, the
son of Zadok, the son of Meraioth, the son
of Ahitub, supervisor in the house of God,
12and their associates, who carried on work
for the temple—822 men; Adaiah son of Je-
roham, the son of Pelaliah, the son of Amzi,
the son of Zechariah, the son of Pashhur, the
son of Malkijah, 13and his associates, who
were heads of families—242 men; Amashsai
son of Azarel, the son of Ahzai, the son of
Meshillemoth, the son of Immer, 14and his[a]
associates, who were able men—128. Their
chief officer was Zabdiel son of Haggedolim.

15From the Levites:

Shemaiah son of Hasshub, the son of Azri-
kam, the son of Hashabiah, the son of Bunni;
16Shabbethai and Jozabad, two of the heads
of the Levites, who had charge of the outside
work of the house of God; 17Mattaniah son
of Mica, the son of Zabdi, the son of Asaph,
the director who led in thanksgiving and
prayer; Bakbukiah, second among his associ-
ates; and Abda son of Shammua, the son of
Galal, the son of Jeduthun. 18The Levites in
the holy city totaled 284.

19The gatekeepers:

Akkub, Talmon and their associates, who
kept watch at the gates—172 men.

20The rest of the Israelites, with the priests and
Levites, were in all the towns of Judah, each on
his ancestral property.

[a]14 Most Septuagint manuscripts; Hebrew *their*

21The temple servants lived on the hill of
Ophel, and Ziha and Gishpa were in charge of
them.
22The chief officer of the Levites in Jerusalem
was Uzzi son of Bani, the son of Hashabiah, the
son of Mattaniah, the son of Mica. Uzzi was one
of Asaph's descendants, who were the singers re-
sponsible for the service of the house of God.
23The singers were under the king's orders, which
regulated their daily activity.
24Pethahiah son of Meshezabel, one of the
descendants of Zerah son of Judah, was the king's
agent in all affairs relating to the people.
25As for the villages with their fields, some of
the people of Judah lived in Kiriath Arba and its
surrounding settlements, in Dibon and its settle-
ments, in Jekabzeel and its villages, 26in Jeshua, in
Moladah, in Beth Pelet, 27in Hazar Shual, in Beer-
sheba and its settlements, 28in Ziklag, in Meconah
and its settlements, 29in En Rimmon, in Zorah, in
Jarmuth, 30Zanoah, Adullam and their villages, in
Lachish and its fields, and in Azekah and its set-
tlements. So they were living all the way from
Beersheba to the Valley of Hinnom.
31The descendants of the Benjamites from Geba
lived in Micmash, Aija, Bethel and its settlements,
32in Anathoth, Nob and Ananiah, 33in Hazor, Ra-
mah and Gittaim, 34in Hadid, Zeboim and Nebal-
lat, 35in Lod and Ono, and in the Valley of the
Craftsmen.
36Some of the divisions of the Levites of Judah
settled in Benjamin.

Discovering the Word 1. How did the Jews in chapter 11 decide who would live in Jerusalem? 2. Why do you think the people did not want to live in Jerusalem (v. 2)? 3. What reasons can you think of for these five groups of people to live in Jerusalem (v. 3)? 4. How (from chapter 10) would all of these people be taken care of materially? 5. How was Nehemiah making the city ready for the people?

Applying the Word 1. What factors do you consider in determining where you should live? (Consider occupation, salary, school, church, ministry, family and so on.) 2. Since our barter system is money, in what ways does our lifestyle free us up to be more involved in kingdom building? 3. As you read this passage, what personal decisions (past or future) about where you live and how that impacts your service to God come to mind?

Responding in Prayer Ask the Lord to help you live in obedience—your hardest daily decision no matter where God leads you.

12 / *Nehemiah 12*
Important Work

"IF A JOB is worth doing, it is worth doing well!" I would like to have a dollar for every time I heard that growing up. I don't think that I understood the saying nearly as well as I do after years of working on it. Integrity and respect come to those who do a good job. We recognize excellence when we see it, and we are offended by a job half-done. We would be of much better use to God, others and ourselves if we didn't volunteer for everything that came along, but rather did a better job on the things we can realistically complete. If I do my part faithfully, God will do the rest in building his kingdom.

Warming Up to God How is your kingdom workload? Are you feeling overwhelmed by commitments to your church or fellowship? Or are you ready for a new challenge? Reflect on your commitments of service to God before you begin.

Read Nehemiah 12.

12 These were the priests and Levites
who returned with Zerubbabel son
of Shealtiel and with Jeshua:
Seraiah, Jeremiah, Ezra,
2Amariah, Malluch, Hattush,
3Shecaniah, Rehum, Meremoth,
4Iddo, Ginnethon,[b] Abijah,
5Mijamin,[c] Moadiah, Bilgah,
6Shemaiah, Joiarib, Jedaiah,
7Sallu, Amok, Hilkiah and Jedaiah.
These were the leaders of the priests and their
associates in the days of Jeshua.
8The Levites were Jeshua, Binnui, Kadmiel,
Sherebiah, Judah, and also Mattaniah, who, to-
gether with his associates, was in charge of the
songs of thanksgiving. 9Bakbukiah and Unni,
their associates, stood opposite them in the ser-
vices.
10Jeshua was the father of Joiakim, Joiakim the
father of Eliashib, Eliashib the father of Joiada,
11Joiada the father of Jonathan, and Jonathan the
father of Jaddua.
12In the days of Joiakim, these were the heads
of the priestly families:
of Seraiah's family, Meraiah;
of Jeremiah's, Hananiah;
13of Ezra's, Meshullam;
of Amariah's, Jehohanan;
14of Malluch's, Jonathan;
of Shecaniah's,[d] Joseph;
15of Harim's, Adna;
of Meremoth's,[e] Helkai;
16of Iddo's, Zechariah;
of Ginnethon's, Meshullam;
17of Abijah's, Zicri;
of Miniamin's and of Moadiah's, Piltai;
18of Bilgah's, Shammua;
of Shemaiah's, Jehonathan;
19of Joiarib's, Mattenai;
of Jedaiah's, Uzzi;
20of Sallu's, Kallai;
of Amok's, Eber;
21of Hilkiah's, Hashabiah;
of Jedaiah's, Nethanel.
22The family heads of the Levites in the days of
Eliashib, Joiada, Johanan and Jaddua, as well as
those of the priests, were recorded in the reign of
Darius the Persian. 23The family heads among the
descendants of Levi up to the time of Johanan son
of Eliashib were recorded in the book of the an-
nals. 24And the leaders of the Levites were Hasha-
biah, Sherebiah, Jeshua son of Kadmiel, and their
associates, who stood opposite them to give
praise and thanksgiving, one section responding
to the other, as prescribed by David the man of
God.
25Mattaniah, Bakbukiah, Obadiah, Meshullam,
Talmon and Akkub were gatekeepers who
guarded the storerooms at the gates. 26They
served in the days of Joiakim son of Jeshua, the
son of Jozadak, and in the days of Nehemiah the
governor and of Ezra the priest and scribe.
27At the dedication of the wall of Jerusalem, the
Levites were sought out from where they lived
and were brought to Jerusalem to celebrate joy-
fully the dedication with songs of thanksgiving
and with the music of cymbals, harps and lyres.
28The singers also were brought together from the
region around Jerusalem—from the villages of
the Netophathites, 29from Beth Gilgal, and from
the area of Geba and Azmaveth, for the singers
had built villages for themselves around Jerusa-
lem. 30When the priests and Levites had purified
themselves ceremonially, they purified the peo-
ple, the gates and the wall.
31I had the leaders of Judah go up on top[f] of
the wall. I also assigned two large choirs to give
thanks. One was to proceed on top[g] of the wall
to the right, toward the Dung Gate. 32Hoshaiah
and half the leaders of Judah followed them,
33along with Azariah, Ezra, Meshullam, 34Judah,
Benjamin, Shemaiah, Jeremiah, 35as well as some
priests with trumpets, and also Zechariah son of
Jonathan, the son of Shemaiah, the son of Matta-
niah, the son of Micaiah, the son of Zaccur, the
son of Asaph, 36and his associates—Shemaiah,
Azarel, Milalai, Gilalai, Maai, Nethanel, Judah
and Hanani—with musical instruments ⌊pre-
scribed by⌋ David the man of God. Ezra the scribe
led the procession. 37At the Fountain Gate they
continued directly up the steps of the City of Da-
vid on the ascent to the wall and passed above the
house of David to the Water Gate on the east.
38The second choir proceeded in the opposite
direction. I followed them on top[h] of the wall,
together with half the people—past the Tower of
the Ovens to the Broad Wall, 39over the Gate of
Ephraim, the Jeshanah[i] Gate, the Fish Gate, the
Tower of Hananel and the Tower of the Hundred,

[b]4 Many Hebrew manuscripts and Vulgate (see also Neh. 12:16); most Hebrew manuscripts *Ginnethoi* [c]5 A variant of *Miniamin*
[d]14 Very many Hebrew manuscripts, some Septuagint manuscripts and Syriac (see also Neh. 12:3); most Hebrew manuscripts *Shebaniah's*
[e]15 Some Septuagint manuscripts (see also Neh. 12:3); Hebrew *Meraioth's* [f]31 Or *go alongside* [g]31 Or *proceed alongside*
[h]38 Or *them alongside* [i]39 Or *Old*

as far as the Sheep Gate. At the Gate of the Guard
they stopped.
40The two choirs that gave thanks then took
their places in the house of God; so did I, together
with half the officials, 41as well as the priests—
Eliakim, Maaseiah, Miniamin, Micaiah, Elioenai,
Zechariah and Hananiah with their trumpets—
42and also Maaseiah, Shemaiah, Eleazar, Uzzi, Je-
hohanan, Malkijah, Elam and Ezer. The choirs
sang under the direction of Jezrahiah. 43And on
that day they offered great sacrifices, rejoicing
because God had given them great joy. The
women and children also rejoiced. The sound
of rejoicing in Jerusalem could be heard far
away.
44At that time men were appointed to be in
charge of the storerooms for the contributions,
firstfruits and tithes. From the fields around the
towns they were to bring into the storerooms the
portions required by the Law for the priests and
the Levites, for Judah was pleased with the minis-
tering priests and Levites. 45They performed the
service of their God and the service of purifica-
tion, as did also the singers and gatekeepers, ac-
cording to the commands of David and his son
Solomon. 46For long ago, in the days of David and
Asaph, there had been directors for the singers
and for the songs of praise and thanksgiving to
God. 47So in the days of Zerubbabel and of Nehe-
miah, all Israel contributed the daily portions for
the singers and gatekeepers. They also set aside
the portion for the other Levites, and the Levites
set aside the portion for the descendants of
Aaron.

Discovering the Word 1. Why do you think the author mentions so many people in this chapter? 2. How would you feel if you were Meshullam in verse 25 and were recognized for guarding the storerooms? 3. Consider verses 8 and 24. Do you think most people would have wanted these jobs? Why or why not? 4. From the book of Nehemiah so far, what is the reason for their great rejoicing (v. 43)? 5. How important do you think the collection of these goods was to the effective running of Jerusalem and providing the worship and celebration that Jerusalem represented (vv. 44–47)?

Applying the Word 1. Since in our culture we see the up-front gifts as more significant than the supporting or helping gifts, would you see being in the choir as an important ministry? Why or why not? 2. What are some of the supporting roles you think of in the church? 3. How could you give (financially and with your encouragement) to sustain the supporting people (that is, pastors, missionaries, youth workers, denominational headquarters) in your church or fellowship?

Responding in Prayer Thank the Lord for giving you a job in his kingdom, and recommit yourself to be faithful in your tasks.

13 / *Nehemiah 13*
Spiritual Decay

"I KNOW THEY are sinning against the Lord, but I love them too much to reprimand them." Sometimes we emphasize loving people and not endangering our relationships with them over challenging them to get right with the Lord. When we think like this, we have accepted the world's values and not kingdom values! If relationship with God is the most important thing in the world, then to help people get back into right relationship with God is the best thing we can do for them. When we don't do this, what we are really saying is that we are more concerned about what that person thinks than what God thinks. We must be freed from this kind of bondage, or we are not of much use to God, others or ourselves. When we are biblically directed, we will be respected and others will hear God's Word through us.

Warming Up to God Do you need forgiveness from the Lord today? Stop now and tell him about your pride or selfishness today—and let the solid truth of 1 John 1:9 that you are forgiven and cleansed cause you to rejoice and be refreshed.

Read Nehemiah 13.

13 On that day the Book of Moses was read aloud in the hearing of the people and there it was found written that no Ammonite or Moabite should ever be admitted into the assembly of God, 2because they had not met the Israelites with food and water but had hired Balaam to call a curse down on them. (Our God, however, turned the curse into a blessing.) 3When the people heard this law, they excluded from Israel all who were of foreign descent.

4Before this, Eliashib the priest had been put in charge of the storerooms of the house of our God. He was closely associated with Tobiah, 5and he had provided him with a large room formerly used to store the grain offerings and incense and temple articles, and also the tithes of grain, new wine and oil prescribed for the Levites, singers and gatekeepers, as well as the contributions for the priests.

6But while all this was going on, I was not in Jerusalem, for in the thirty-second year of Artaxerxes king of Babylon I had returned to the king. Some time later I asked his permission 7and came back to Jerusalem. Here I learned about the evil thing Eliashib had done in providing Tobiah a room in the courts of the house of God. 8I was greatly displeased and threw all Tobiah's household goods out of the room. 9I gave orders to purify the rooms, and then I put back into them the equipment of the house of God, with the grain offerings and the incense.

10I also learned that the portions assigned to the Levites had not been given to them, and that all the Levites and singers responsible for the service had gone back to their own fields. 11So I rebuked the officials and asked them, "Why is the house of God neglected?" Then I called them together and stationed them at their posts.

12All Judah brought the tithes of grain, new wine and oil into the storerooms. 13I put Shelemiah the priest, Zadok the scribe, and a Levite named Pedaiah in charge of the storerooms and made Hanan son of Zaccur, the son of Mattaniah, their assistant, because these men were considered trustworthy. They were made responsible for distributing the supplies to their brothers.

14Remember me for this, O my God, and do not blot out what I have so faithfully done for the house of my God and its services.

15In those days I saw men in Judah treading winepresses on the Sabbath and bringing in grain and loading it on donkeys, together with wine, grapes, figs and all other kinds of loads. And they were bringing all this into Jerusalem on the Sabbath. Therefore I warned them against selling food on that day. 16Men from Tyre who lived in Jerusalem were bringing in fish and all kinds of merchandise and selling them in Jerusalem on the Sabbath to the people of Judah. 17I rebuked the nobles of Judah and said to them, "What is this wicked thing you are doing—desecrating the Sabbath day? 18Didn't your forefathers do the same things, so that our God brought all this calamity upon us and upon this city? Now you are stirring up more wrath against Israel by desecrating the Sabbath."

19When evening shadows fell on the gates of Jerusalem before the Sabbath, I ordered the doors to be shut and not opened until the Sabbath was over. I stationed some of my own men at the gates so that no load could be brought in on the Sabbath day. 20Once or twice the merchants and sellers of all kinds of goods spent the night outside Jerusalem. 21But I warned them and said, "Why do you spend the night by the wall? If you do this again, I will lay hands on you." From that time on they no longer came on the Sabbath. 22Then I commanded the Levites to purify themselves and go and guard the gates in order to keep the Sabbath day holy.

Remember me for this also, O my God, and show mercy to me according to your great love.

23Moreover, in those days I saw men of Judah who had married women from Ashdod, Ammon and Moab. 24Half of their children spoke the language of Ashdod or the language of one of the other peoples, and did not know how to speak the language of Judah. 25I rebuked them and called curses down on them. I beat some of the men and pulled out their hair. I made them take an oath in God's name and said: "You are not to give your daughters in marriage to their sons, nor are you to take their daughters in marriage for your sons or for yourselves. 26Was it not because of marriages like these that Solomon king of Israel sinned? Among the many nations there was no king like him. He was loved by his

God, and God made him king over all Israel, but even he was led into sin by foreign women. [27]Must we hear now that you too are doing all this terrible wickedness and are being unfaithful to our God by marrying foreign women?"

[28]One of the sons of Joiada son of Eliashib the high priest was son-in-law to Sanballat the Horonite. And I drove him away from me.

[29]Remember them, O my God, because they defiled the priestly office and the covenant of the priesthood and of the Levites.

[30]So I purified the priests and the Levites of everything foreign, and assigned them duties, each to his own task. [31]I also made provision for contributions of wood at designated times, and for the firstfruits.

Remember me with favor, O my God.

Discovering the Word 1. Note from 2:1 and 13:6 that Nehemiah spent twelve years in Jerusalem before going back to Artaxerxes. We don't know how long it was before Nehemiah came back to Jerusalem to check up on things, but it was probably several years. List the things in this chapter that indicate the Israelites have backslidden before the Lord. 2. Considering the people made such a strong covenant in chapter 10, how do you think they could have gone this far astray in chapter 13? 3. What does the passage reveal about how Nehemiah felt when he came back and saw how bad things were spiritually? 4. Compare 10:30 with 13:23–28. Do you see anything in the text that shows you why Israel has backslidden? 5. Nehemiah's response in verse 25 is very dramatic and physical. What principles does this suggest to you for how we should deal with sin today?

Applying the Word 1. Why is it so much harder to confront leaders who are sinning, as in this chapter? 2. In what ways do you need to be more direct with others about their sin? 3. How would you like others to help you in dealing with your own sin?

Responding in Prayer Ask the Lord to make you more like Nehemiah, who pursued righteousness and called others to holy living. Pray as he did: "Remember me with favor, O my God."

Esther

"Just Do It" has been a successful and popular slogan the past few years for the athletic company Nike. It refers to getting in shape and participating in athletics no matter what the physical or mental strain. But the slogan brings something else to my mind after spending time in the book of Esther: it reminds me to *just do it*—just do the right thing no matter what the consequences.

In the book of Esther we see the lives of several characters played out. There are those people who are selfish and prideful, seeking only personal recognition, and there are those who risk everything for others and choose integrity in the face of great opposition. Esther is a book about developing godly character. In the midst of a culture which emphasizes doing what is right, this book speaks to us in profound ways.

As we read through the events of Esther, we are given a description of what godly character is and what it is not. But there is another very strong theme that weaves in and around the theme of character. It is the idea that God is working in the circumstances and events of people's lives to bring about his plans. God is the director, the conductor, the weaver. As God works in our lives, we must choose what is right so that we can be a part of God's plan.

The events of this powerful book take place in Persia during the reign of King Xerxes from 486 to 465 B.C. It has been over one hundred years since the beginning of the exile, and some Jews have returned to Jerusalem. The story is set in the city of Susa, which is where the king has his winter palace. It involves the whole of the Jewish people, but revolves around the lives of King Xerxes; Esther; her cousin, Mordecai; and Haman, the king's highest noble.

Esther's story presents the last major threat to the Jewish people in the Old Testament period. The threat and the Jews' deliverance is recorded in this book. The Jewish festival of Purim, which is still celebrated today, is established in Esther, which accounts for the book's great popularity among the Jewish people. It is a wonderful story of God's providence and the character of his people told with humor, irony, repetition and contrast.

Esther will stir us to examine our character, the deep aspects of our hearts. It will encourage us in taking a stand for what is right and give us courage that God is still in control. It is a book that we need to study so that we can glorify God with our whole beings and begin to be witnesses in our world because of our integrity. If we allow the themes of Esther to penetrate our lives, we will begin to stop and question our actions and thoughts and align them with God's desire.

May your study in Esther produce in you a longing for consistent godly character.

Outline

1/ Esther 1 ———— *A Little Respect*

2/ Esther 2 ———— *Trusting God's Work*

3/ Esther 3 ———— *Evaluating Advice*

4/ Esther 4 ———— *Doing the Right Thing*

5/ Esther 5 ———— *The Heart of the Matter*

6/ Esther 6 ———— *Recognizing Unrighteousness*

7/ Esther 7 ———— *Character No Matter What*

8/ Esther 8 ———— *Praising God's Faithfulness*

9/ Esther 9—10 ———— *Remembering and Celebrating*

1 / *Esther 1*
A Little Respect

ONE OF MY favorite and most influential teachers was a high-school English teacher. His class was extremely difficult and challenging, but I loved it and worked diligently in order to do well. The reason I respected this teacher so much is that he listened to me and valued me. We would all like to be respected by others, and so we try many ways of gaining that respect. Some try to gain it through controlling others or by demanding it. However, one of the ways respect is gained is by appreciating others and showing them respect.

Warming Up to God Think of one person whom you respect. What are some characteristics of this person? How did he or she gain your respect?

Read Esther 1.

1 This is what happened during the time of Xerxes,[a] the Xerxes who ruled over 127 provinces stretching from India to Cush[b]: 2At that time King Xerxes reigned from his royal throne in the citadel of Susa, 3and in the third year of his reign he gave a banquet for all his nobles and officials. The military leaders of Persia and Media, the princes, and the nobles of the provinces were present.

4For a full 180 days he displayed the vast wealth of his kingdom and the splendor and glory of his majesty. 5When these days were over, the king gave a banquet, lasting seven days, in the enclosed garden of the king's palace, for all the people from the least to the greatest, who were in the citadel of Susa. 6The garden had hangings of white and blue linen, fastened with cords of white linen and purple material to silver rings on marble pillars. There were couches of gold and silver on a mosaic pavement of porphyry, marble, mother-of-pearl and other costly stones. 7Wine was served in goblets of gold, each one different from the other, and the royal wine was abundant, in keeping with the king's liberality. 8By the king's command each guest was allowed to drink in his own way, for the king instructed all the wine stewards to serve each man what he wished.

9Queen Vashti also gave a banquet for the women in the royal palace of King Xerxes.

10On the seventh day, when King Xerxes was in high spirits from wine, he commanded the seven eunuchs who served him—Mehuman, Biztha, Harbona, Bigtha, Abagtha, Zethar and Carcas—11to bring before him Queen Vashti, wearing her royal crown, in order to display her beauty to the people and nobles, for she was lovely to look at. 12But when the attendants delivered the king's command, Queen Vashti refused to come. Then the king became furious and burned with anger.

13Since it was customary for the king to consult experts in matters of law and justice, he spoke with the wise men who understood the times 14and were closest to the king—Carshena, Shethar, Admatha, Tarshish, Meres, Marsena and Memucan, the seven nobles of Persia and Media who had special access to the king and were highest in the kingdom.

15"According to law, what must be done to Queen Vashti?" he asked. "She has not obeyed the command of King Xerxes that the eunuchs have taken to her."

16Then Memucan replied in the presence of the king and the nobles, "Queen Vashti has done wrong, not only against the king but also against all the nobles and the peoples of all the provinces of King Xerxes. 17For the queen's conduct will become known to all the women, and so they will despise their husbands and say, 'King Xerxes commanded Queen Vashti to be brought before him, but she would not come.' 18This very day the Persian and Median women of the nobility who have heard about the queen's conduct will respond to all the king's nobles in the same way. There will be no end of disrespect and discord.

19"Therefore, if it pleases the king, let him issue a royal decree and let it be written in the laws of Persia and Media, which cannot be repealed, that Vashti is never again to enter the presence of King Xerxes. Also let the king give her royal position to someone else who is better than she. 20Then

[a]1 Hebrew *Ahasuerus*, a variant of Xerxes' Persian name; here and throughout Esther [b]1 That is, the upper Nile region

when the king's edict is proclaimed throughout
all his vast realm, all the women will respect their
husbands, from the least to the greatest."
[21]The king and his nobles were pleased with
this advice, so the king did as Memucan pro-
posed. [22]He sent dispatches to all parts of the
kingdom, to each province in its own script and
to each people in its own language, proclaiming
in each people's tongue that every man should be
ruler over his own household.

Discovering the Word 1. Describe the celebration given by King Xerxes (vv. 2–8). 2. Why might the king have given such an extravagant party? 3. Why does King Xerxes ask Queen Vashti to come to him (vv. 10–11)? 4. Why did the wise men perceive Queen Vashti's refusal to be so dangerous to the kingdom (vv. 16–20)? 5. The wise men mention respect several times in this chapter. In their view how was respect gained and maintained?

Applying the Word 1. In what ways have you been shown appreciation and regard by those around you? 2. Describe one thing that you can do this week to show someone respect.

Responding in Prayer Ask God to teach you how to give respect and to make you a person worthy of respect.

2 / *Esther 2*
Trusting God's Work

THE MOST IMPORTANT person in a play is not on the stage. The director is the one who has instructed the cast for months before on where to stand and sit and when and how to say a line. The director is behind the scenes giving final instructions, touching up makeup and encouraging the players—orchestrating every detail.

In the book of Esther God is not mentioned, but he is the key figure in the story. He works through the circumstances to place everything in order so that his plans will be accomplished. God is the director of our lives as well. As we look back at different times in our lives, we can see his handprints all over. Our response to him is to look for his hand moving and to trust his direction.

Warming Up to God Recall a time in your past when you saw God work through circumstances in your life to bring something about. Allow your praise for God's good work to well up in response.

Read Esther 2.

2 Later when the anger of King Xerxes had
subsided, he remembered Vashti and
what she had done and what he had de-
creed about her. [2]Then the king's personal atten-
dants proposed, "Let a search be made for beauti-
ful young virgins for the king. [3]Let the king
appoint commissioners in every province of his
realm to bring all these beautiful girls into the
harem at the citadel of Susa. Let them be placed
under the care of Hegai, the king's eunuch, who
is in charge of the women; and let beauty treat-
ments be given to them. [4]Then let the girl who
pleases the king be queen instead of Vashti." This
advice appealed to the king, and he followed it.
[5]Now there was in the citadel of Susa a Jew of
the tribe of Benjamin, named Mordecai son of
Jair, the son of Shimei, the son of Kish, [6]who had
been carried into exile from Jerusalem by Nebu-
chadnezzar king of Babylon, among those taken
captive with Jehoiachin[c] king of Judah. [7]Morde-
cai had a cousin named Hadassah, whom he had
brought up because she had neither father nor
mother. This girl, who was also known as Esther,
was lovely in form and features, and Mordecai
had taken her as his own daughter when her fa-
ther and mother died.
[8]When the king's order and edict had been pro-
claimed, many girls were brought to the citadel of
Susa and put under the care of Hegai. Esther also
was taken to the king's palace and entrusted to
Hegai, who had charge of the harem. [9]The girl

[c]6 Hebrew *Jeconiah*, a variant of *Jehoiachin*

pleased him and won his favor. Immediately he provided her with her beauty treatments and special food. He assigned to her seven maids selected from the king's palace and moved her and her maids into the best place in the harem.

10Esther had not revealed her nationality and family background, because Mordecai had forbidden her to do so. 11Every day he walked back and forth near the courtyard of the harem to find out how Esther was and what was happening to her.

12Before a girl's turn came to go in to King Xerxes, she had to complete twelve months of beauty treatments prescribed for the women, six months with oil of myrrh and six with perfumes and cosmetics. 13And this is how she would go to the king: Anything she wanted was given her to take with her from the harem to the king's palace. 14In the evening she would go there and in the morning return to another part of the harem to the care of Shaashgaz, the king's eunuch who was in charge of the concubines. She would not return to the king unless he was pleased with her and summoned her by name.

15When the turn came for Esther (the girl Mordecai had adopted, the daughter of his uncle Abihail) to go to the king, she asked for nothing other than what Hegai, the king's eunuch who was in charge of the harem, suggested. And Esther won the favor of everyone who saw her. 16She was taken to King Xerxes in the royal residence in the tenth month, the month of Tebeth, in the seventh year of his reign.

17Now the king was attracted to Esther more than to any of the other women, and she won his favor and approval more than any of the other virgins. So he set a royal crown on her head and made her queen instead of Vashti. 18And the king gave a great banquet, Esther's banquet, for all his nobles and officials. He proclaimed a holiday throughout the provinces and distributed gifts with royal liberality.

19When the virgins were assembled a second time, Mordecai was sitting at the king's gate. 20But Esther had kept secret her family background and nationality just as Mordecai had told her to do, for she continued to follow Mordecai's instructions as she had done when he was bringing her up.

21During the time Mordecai was sitting at the king's gate, Bigthana[d] and Teresh, two of the king's officers who guarded the doorway, became angry and conspired to assassinate King Xerxes. 22But Mordecai found out about the plot and told Queen Esther, who in turn reported it to the king, giving credit to Mordecai. 23And when the report was investigated and found to be true, the two officials were hanged on a gallows.[e] All this was recorded in the book of the annals in the presence of the king.

d21 Hebrew *Bigthan,* a variant of *Bigthana* e23 Or *were hung* (or *impaled*) *on poles*; similarly elsewhere in Esther

Discovering the Word 1. Summarize the plan to find a new queen that King Xerxes put into action (vv. 1–4). 2. How does Esther enter the story and become the queen (vv. 5–17)? 3. It is mentioned three times that Esther won approval in someone's eyes (vv. 9, 15, 17). What does this tell us about Esther? 4. How does Mordecai enter into the plot of the story (vv. 19–23)? 5. Even though God has not been directly mentioned in the book, where do you see his hand moving in the story so far?

Applying the Word 1. Where do you see God's hand moving in circumstances in your life right now? 2. How do you think he wants you to respond?

Responding in Prayer Ask God to give you confidence in his work in your life.

3 / *Esther 3*
Evaluating Advice

NO ONE HAS "any right to counsel others who is not ready to hear and follow the counsel of the Lord." This quote from A. W. Tozer reminds me of the responsibility we have in giving advice to others. It is a serious thing to give counsel, and it is also a serious step to take the counsel of our friends. So often we can give quick advice to one another without truly understanding the situation or without pure motives. Part of godly character is knowing how to evaluate the advice we receive and in turn to offer sound and wise counsel.

Warming Up to God When in your life have you received good advice and when have you received poor advice?

Read Esther 3.

3 After these events, King Xerxes honored
Haman son of Hammedatha, the Agagite,
elevating him and giving him a seat of
honor higher than that of all the other nobles.
2All the royal officials at the king's gate knelt
down and paid honor to Haman, for the king had
commanded this concerning him. But Mordecai
would not kneel down or pay him honor.
3Then the royal officials at the king's gate asked
Mordecai, "Why do you disobey the king's com-
mand?" 4Day after day they spoke to him but he
refused to comply. Therefore they told Haman
about it to see whether Mordecai's behavior
would be tolerated, for he had told them he was
a Jew.
5When Haman saw that Mordecai would not
kneel down or pay him honor, he was enraged.
6Yet having learned who Mordecai's people were,
he scorned the idea of killing only Mordecai. In-
stead Haman looked for a way to destroy all Mor-
decai's people, the Jews, throughout the whole
kingdom of Xerxes.
7In the twelfth year of King Xerxes, in the first
month, the month of Nisan, they cast the *pur*
(that is, the lot) in the presence of Haman to
select a day and month. And the lot fell on[f] the
twelfth month, the month of Adar.
8Then Haman said to King Xerxes, "There is a
certain people dispersed and scattered among the
peoples in all the provinces of your kingdom
whose customs are different from those of all
other people and who do not obey the king's
laws; it is not in the king's best interest to tolerate
them. 9If it pleases the king, let a decree be issued
to destroy them, and I will put ten thousand tal-
ents[g] of silver into the royal treasury for the men
who carry out this business."
10So the king took his signet ring from his fin-
ger and gave it to Haman son of Hammedatha,
the Agagite, the enemy of the Jews. 11"Keep the
money," the king said to Haman, "and do with
the people as you please."
12Then on the thirteenth day of the first month
the royal secretaries were summoned. They wrote
out in the script of each province and in the lan-
guage of each people all Haman's orders to the
king's satraps, the governors of the various prov-
inces and the nobles of the various peoples. These
were written in the name of King Xerxes himself
and sealed with his own ring. 13Dispatches were
sent by couriers to all the king's provinces with
the order to destroy, kill and annihilate all the
Jews—young and old, women and little chil-
dren—on a single day, the thirteenth day of the
twelfth month, the month of Adar, and to plunder
their goods. 14A copy of the text of the edict was
to be issued as law in every province and made
known to the people of every nationality so they
would be ready for that day.
15Spurred on by the king's command, the cou-
riers went out, and the edict was issued in the
citadel of Susa. The king and Haman sat down to
drink, but the city of Susa was bewildered.

f7 Septuagint; Hebrew does not have *And the lot fell on.* g9 That is, about 375 tons (about 345 metric tons)

Discovering the Word 1. List all the words and phrases in this chapter which bring to mind tragedy or conflict. 2. What is the conflict between Haman and Mordecai which causes Haman's intense reaction to Mordecai (vv. 2–6)? 3. How does Haman persuade the king to adopt his plan to destroy the Jews (vv. 8–9)? 4. In verses 12–14 the words *each, every* and *all* are repeated frequently. What might the author have been trying to communicate in this detailed description of the edict? 5. This chapter gives us even more detail about who King Xerxes was. What do we learn about him?

Applying the Word 1. How might you guard against giving unwise advice? 2. What are some ways you can evaluate the advice you receive from others?

 **Responding in Prayer** Pray that you will be given wise counselors who will give you godly advice.

4 / *Esther 4*
Doing the Right Thing

LASZLO TOKES WAS a pastor in Timisoara, Romania, during the reign of the communist regime under Ceausescu. He had dedicated his life to bringing about revival in the church in Romania despite opposition and danger. He risked his life to preach the gospel and stand up against the communist government. Because of his courage and integrity he helped the people to win their freedom. We may never face circumstances like those of Laszlo Tokes, but doing what is right means little things: giving back extra change when a cashier makes a mistake or letting the cable company know about the free service that's been coming in. Whether the stakes are large or small, it takes the same character qualities of courage and moral strength to choose what is right.

 **Warming Up to God** Recall an instance in your life where obeying God's call meant taking a risk or facing a difficulty. How did you feel? What did you pray?

 **Read Esther 4.**

4 When Mordecai learned of all that had
been done, he tore his clothes, put on
sackcloth and ashes, and went out into
the city, wailing loudly and bitterly. 2But he went
only as far as the king's gate, because no one
clothed in sackcloth was allowed to enter it. 3In
every province to which the edict and order of the
king came, there was great mourning among the
Jews, with fasting, weeping and wailing. Many lay
in sackcloth and ashes.
4When Esther's maids and eunuchs came and
told her about Mordecai, she was in great distress.
She sent clothes for him to put on instead of his
sackcloth, but he would not accept them. 5Then
Esther summoned Hathach, one of the king's eu-
nuchs assigned to attend her, and ordered him
to find out what was troubling Mordecai and
why.
6So Hathach went out to Mordecai in the open
square of the city in front of the king's gate. 7Mor-
decai told him everything that had happened to
him, including the exact amount of money Ha-
man had promised to pay into the royal treasury
for the destruction of the Jews. 8He also gave him
a copy of the text of the edict for their annihila-
tion, which had been published in Susa, to show
to Esther and explain it to her, and he told him to
urge her to go into the king's presence to beg for
mercy and plead with him for her people.
9Hathach went back and reported to Esther
what Mordecai had said. 10Then she instructed
him to say to Mordecai, 11"All the king's officials
and the people of the royal provinces know that
for any man or woman who approaches the king
in the inner court without being summoned the
king has but one law: that he be put to death. The
only exception to this is for the king to extend the
gold scepter to him and spare his life. But thirty
days have passed since I was called to go to the
king."
12When Esther's words were reported to Mor-
decai, 13he sent back this answer: "Do not think
that because you are in the king's house you
alone of all the Jews will escape. 14For if you re-
main silent at this time, relief and deliverance for
the Jews will arise from another place, but you
and your father's family will perish. And who
knows but that you have come to royal position
for such a time as this?"
15Then Esther sent this reply to Mordecai:
16"Go, gather together all the Jews who are in
Susa, and fast for me. Do not eat or drink for
three days, night or day. I and my maids will fast
as you do. When this is done, I will go to the

king, even though it is against the law. And if I
perish, I perish."
17So Mordecai went away and carried out all of
Esther's instructions.

Discovering the Word 1. Describe the response of Mordecai and the Jews to Haman's plot (vv. 1–3). 2. Why do you think Mordecai was so confident in his plan to stop the annihilation of the Jews (vv. 6–8)? 3. What is Esther's first reaction to Mordecai's request that she go to the king (vv. 9–11)? 4. How do Mordecai's arguments in verses 12–14 persuade Esther to go to the king? 5. In this chapter how do we see God's sovereignty and people's responses working together? 6. What character qualities does Esther show in her response to Mordecai's second message?

Applying the Word 1. Think of a present context in which God has placed you to do his will. What risks do you face in doing the right thing in this context? 2. What character qualities must you exhibit in order to do the right thing?

Responding in Prayer Pray that doing the right thing will be more than a slogan for you—that it will be a way of life.

5 / *Esther 5*
The Heart of the Matter

MY SCHOOLTEACHER HUSBAND came home one day from work with an unpleasant note from a parent. The note expressed anger and concern over his performance as a teacher. In the face of a situation that could have led my husband to bitterness I watched him respond with courage, compassion and humility as he made an appointment to meet with the parent the next day. Because of his response, the misunderstanding was clarified and the relationship was reconciled.

Our character comes through especially in times where we are facing a difficult task or situations or people that anger us. Our response to these kinds of occurrences in our life tells a great deal about our character. Do we face them with courage and humility or with anger, bitterness and pride? In their contrasting responses Esther and Haman show the condition of their hearts.

Warming Up to God What example comes to mind when you think of a person acting with courage or humility?

Read Esther 5.

5 On the third day Esther put on her royal
robes and stood in the inner court of the
palace, in front of the king's hall. The
king was sitting on his royal throne in the hall,
facing the entrance. 2When he saw Queen Esther
standing in the court, he was pleased with her
and held out to her the gold scepter that was in
his hand. So Esther approached and touched the
tip of the scepter.
3Then the king asked, "What is it, Queen Es-
ther? What is your request? Even up to half the
kingdom, it will be given you."
4"If it pleases the king," replied Esther, "let the
king, together with Haman, come today to a ban-
quet I have prepared for him."
5"Bring Haman at once," the king said, "so that
we may do what Esther asks."
So the king and Haman went to the banquet
Esther had prepared. 6As they were drinking
wine, the king again asked Esther, "Now what is
your petition? It will be given you. And what is
your request? Even up to half the kingdom, it will
be granted."
7Esther replied, "My petition and my request
is this: 8If the king regards me with favor and
if it pleases the king to grant my petition and
fulfill my request, let the king and Haman
come tomorrow to the banquet I will prepare
for them. Then I will answer the king's ques-
tion."

9Haman went out that day happy and in high spirits. But when he saw Mordecai at the king's gate and observed that he neither rose nor showed fear in his presence, he was filled with rage against Mordecai. 10Nevertheless, Haman restrained himself and went home.

Calling together his friends and Zeresh, his wife, 11Haman boasted to them about his vast wealth, his many sons, and all the ways the king had honored him and how he had elevated him above the other nobles and officials. 12"And that's not all," Haman added. "I'm the only person Queen Esther invited to accompany the king to the banquet she gave. And she has invited me along with the king tomorrow. 13But all this gives me no satisfaction as long as I see that Jew Mordecai sitting at the king's gate."

14His wife Zeresh and all his friends said to him, "Have a gallows built, seventy-five feet[h] high, and ask the king in the morning to have Mordecai hanged on it. Then go with the king to the dinner and be happy." This suggestion delighted Haman, and he had the gallows built.

[h]14 Hebrew *fifty cubits* (about 23 meters)

Discovering the Word 1. What risks does Esther take in verses 1–8? 2. The second time the king asks Esther to make her request known, she answers him. What do her words reveal about her character (vv. 7–8)? 3. What characteristics do we see in Haman (vv. 9–14)? 4. Haman boasts about having everything: sons, wealth, position and recognition. Why do you think Haman is still so consumed with Mordecai? 5. How does the passage contrast Esther's character and Haman's character?

Applying the Word 1. Where in your own life do you see the qualities of Esther, and where do you see the qualities of Haman? 2. In what current situation can you try to respond with the courage and humility of Esther? 3. Esther 4:15–16 tells us how Esther was supported by the Jewish people. How could the support of other believers be helpful to you in the midst of a trial you are going through now?

Responding in Prayer Pray that God will be molding you into a person of character who responds out of humility rather than pride.

6 / *Esther 6*
Recognizing Unrighteousness

WHEN I TAKE an honest look at myself, I see many ugly spots that mar my character. One of the ugliest traits is my desire to make myself look better than others. This ungodly character trait seeps into my relationships and damages intimacy. For each of us there are things about our character which are displeasing to God; perhaps it is pride or arrogance, selfish ambition or manipulation. Because we let those things grow in our lives rather than allowing God to remove them, we experience various consequences of our unrighteousness.

Warming Up to God What is one aspect of your character you would like to be more Christlike? Take time to talk openly with God about how you want to change.

Read Esther 6.

6 That night the king could not sleep; so he ordered the book of the chronicles, the record of his reign, to be brought in and read to him. 2It was found recorded there that Mordecai had exposed Bigthana and Teresh, two of the king's officers who guarded the doorway, who had conspired to assassinate King Xerxes.

3"What honor and recognition has Mordecai received for this?" the king asked.

"Nothing has been done for him," his attendants answered.

4The king said, "Who is in the court?" Now Haman had just entered the outer court of the palace to speak to the king about hanging Mordecai on the gallows he had erected for him.

5His attendants answered, "Haman is standing
in the court."
"Bring him in," the king ordered.
6When Haman entered, the king asked him,
"What should be done for the man the king de-
lights to honor?"
Now Haman thought to himself, "Who is there
that the king would rather honor than me?" 7So
he answered the king, "For the man the king de-
lights to honor, 8have them bring a royal robe the
king has worn and a horse the king has ridden,
one with a royal crest placed on its head. 9Then
let the robe and horse be entrusted to one of the
king's most noble princes. Let them robe the man
the king delights to honor, and lead him on the
horse through the city streets, proclaiming before
him, 'This is what is done for the man the king
delights to honor!' "
10"Go at once," the king commanded Haman.
"Get the robe and the horse and do just as you
have suggested for Mordecai the Jew, who sits at
the king's gate. Do not neglect anything you have
recommended."
11So Haman got the robe and the horse. He
robed Mordecai, and led him on horseback
through the city streets, proclaiming before him,
"This is what is done for the man the king de-
lights to honor!"
12Afterward Mordecai returned to the king's
gate. But Haman rushed home, with his head
covered in grief, 13and told Zeresh his wife and
all his friends everything that had happened to
him.
His advisers and his wife Zeresh said to him,
"Since Mordecai, before whom your downfall has
started, is of Jewish origin, you cannot stand
against him—you will surely come to ruin!"
14While they were still talking with him, the
king's eunuchs arrived and hurried Haman away
to the banquet Esther had prepared.

Discovering the Word 1. How does the king respond to discovering Mordecai's role in thwarting the assassination plot (vv. 2–6)? 2. Where do you see irony in King Xerxes' and Haman's actions on this particular night (vv. 1–6 and 5:14)? 3. What else can we discern about Haman's character through his response to the king's question in verses 7–9? 4. Haman sought comfort from his wife and friends after his ride through the city with Mordecai, but he receives a very different response. How do his wife and advisors interpret the situation and react to Haman (vv. 12–14)? Why? 5. How has the ungodliness in Haman's character led to his humiliation?

Applying the Word 1. Think back to the characteristic in your life which is not always Christlike. What might be (or have been) some negative consequences of this trait? 2. What is one thing that you can do this week, with God's help, to reform your character?

Responding in Prayer Offer your praise to Jesus Christ for what you have learned about yourself through this study. Ask him for the help you need to become more like him.

7 / *Esther 7*
Character No Matter What

> This is what the wicked are like—
> always carefree, they increase in wealth.
> Surely in vain have I kept my heart pure;
> in vain have I washed my hands in innocence. (Ps 73:12-13)

THE PSALMIST IS wrestling with the fact that he does not see justice being carried out; instead, the wicked prosper and the righteous are plagued. In a similar way Esther and Mordecai have chosen to do what is right all along, yet they face destruction. Haman, who is prideful, angry and bitter, has been successful in plotting against the Jews. Finally, in chapter 7 Esther and Mordecai see justice taking place. However, in our lives we do not always see justice when we choose to do what is right. The people of God must have consistent character whether or not justice prevails in this life.

Warming Up to God When does the injustice of the world most weigh on your mind and heart?

 **Read Esther 7.**

7 So the king and Haman went to dine with
Queen Esther, 2and as they were drinking
wine on that second day, the king again
asked, "Queen Esther, what is your petition? It
will be given you. What is your request? Even up
to half the kingdom, it will be granted."
3Then Queen Esther answered, "If I have found
favor with you, O king, and if it pleases your maj-
esty, grant me my life—this is my petition. And
spare my people—this is my request. 4For I and
my people have been sold for destruction and
slaughter and annihilation. If we had merely been
sold as male and female slaves, I would have kept
quiet, because no such distress would justify dis-
turbing the king.[i]"
5King Xerxes asked Queen Esther, "Who is he?
Where is the man who has dared to do such a
thing?"
6Esther said, "The adversary and enemy is this
vile Haman."
Then Haman was terrified before the king and
queen. 7The king got up in a rage, left his wine
and went out into the palace garden. But Haman,
realizing that the king had already decided his
fate, stayed behind to beg Queen Esther for his
life.
8Just as the king returned from the palace gar-
den to the banquet hall, Haman was falling on the
couch where Esther was reclining.
The king exclaimed, "Will he even molest the
queen while she is with me in the house?"
As soon as the word left the king's mouth, they
covered Haman's face. 9Then Harbona, one of the
eunuchs attending the king, said, "A gallows sev-
enty-five feet[j] high stands by Haman's house. He
had it made for Mordecai, who spoke up to help
the king."
The king said, "Hang him on it!" 10So they
hanged Haman on the gallows he had prepared
for Mordecai. Then the king's fury subsided.

[i]4 Or *quiet, but the compensation our adversary offers cannot be compared with the loss the king would suffer* [j]9 Hebrew *fifty cubits* (about 23 meters)

Discovering the Word 1. Name all of the truths that were previously hidden but are now revealed in this chapter. 2. This chapter revolves around Queen Esther, King Xerxes and Haman. What might each of them be feeling at the beginning of the banquet? 3. What thoughts and emotions might the king and Haman have experienced when Esther presented her request (vv. 6–7)? 4. How do you see justice carried out in the lives of Esther, Mordecai and Haman?

Applying the Word 1. As Christians, when should we expect to see justice served and when should we be satisfied with doing what is right? Give examples from your experience. 2. How can you seek justice in a situation where you currently see injustice? 3. How will you respond if justice is not served?

 **Responding in Prayer** Justice begins with prayer. Ask God to show you how he would like to use you in the pursuit of justice.

8 / *Esther 8*
Praising God's Faithfulness

AS THE SUNSHINE filtered through the sanctuary windows, the pastor stood and asked for the congregation to tell how God had been faithful. One by one the people rose to their feet and spoke. There were testimonies about marriages restored, physical healings, new passion for service, children coming to Christ and spiritual growth. I listened with a joyful heart; certainly God was faithful!

The book of Esther shows that God brings justice in his time and in his way. But one thing remains certain: God is faithful. From overwhelming opposition to the smallest concern, God provides for us. In this chapter God provides not only for Esther and Mordecai, but for all of his people, and they respond with rejoicing and celebrating. Our response to God should be no different.

Warming Up to God Recall in detail a time when God has proven himself faithful to you in a difficult situation. Thank God for all the ways he helped you.

Read Esther 8.

8 That same day King Xerxes gave Queen
Esther the estate of Haman, the enemy of
the Jews. And Mordecai came into the
presence of the king, for Esther had told how he
was related to her. [2]The king took off his signet
ring, which he had reclaimed from Haman, and
presented it to Mordecai. And Esther appointed
him over Haman's estate.
[3]Esther again pleaded with the king, falling at
his feet and weeping. She begged him to put an
end to the evil plan of Haman the Agagite, which
he had devised against the Jews. [4]Then the king
extended the gold scepter to Esther and she arose
and stood before him.
[5]"If it pleases the king," she said, "and if he
regards me with favor and thinks it the right
thing to do, and if he is pleased with me, let an
order be written overruling the dispatches that
Haman son of Hammedatha, the Agagite, devised
and wrote to destroy the Jews in all the king's
provinces. [6]For how can I bear to see disaster fall
on my people? How can I bear to see the destruction of my family?"
[7]King Xerxes replied to Queen Esther and to
Mordecai the Jew, "Because Haman attacked the
Jews, I have given his estate to Esther, and they
have hanged him on the gallows. [8]Now write an-
other decree in the king's name in behalf of the
Jews as seems best to you, and seal it with the
king's signet ring—for no document written in
the king's name and sealed with his ring can be
revoked."
[9]At once the royal secretaries were summoned—on the twenty-third day of the third
month, the month of Sivan. They wrote out all
Mordecai's orders to the Jews, and to the satraps,
governors and nobles of the 127 provinces
stretching from India to Cush.[k] These orders
were written in the script of each province and
the language of each people and also to the Jews
in their own script and language. [10]Mordecai
wrote in the name of King Xerxes, sealed the dispatches with the king's signet ring, and sent them
by mounted couriers, who rode fast horses especially bred for the king.
[11]The king's edict granted the Jews in every city
the right to assemble and protect themselves; to
destroy, kill and annihilate any armed force of
any nationality or province that might attack
them and their women and children; and to plunder the property of their enemies. [12]The day ap-
pointed for the Jews to do this in all the provinces
of King Xerxes was the thirteenth day of the
twelfth month, the month of Adar. [13]A copy of
the text of the edict was to be issued as law in every province and made known to the people of every nationality so that the Jews would be ready on
that day to avenge themselves on their enemies.
[14]The couriers, riding the royal horses, raced
out, spurred on by the king's command. And the
edict was also issued in the citadel of Susa.
[15]Mordecai left the king's presence wearing
royal garments of blue and white, a large crown
of gold and a purple robe of fine linen. And the
city of Susa held a joyous celebration. [16]For the
Jews it was a time of happiness and joy, gladness
and honor. [17]In every province and in every city,
wherever the edict of the king went, there was joy
and gladness among the Jews, with feasting and
celebrating. And many people of other nationalities became Jews because fear of the Jews had
seized them.

[k]9 That is, the upper Nile region

Discovering the Word 1. List all the ways in this chapter that Esther and Mordecai are rewarded by God through the actions of the king. 2. In verses 3–6 we see a little of Esther's heart. How does she feel toward her people? 3. How does King Xerxes respond to Esther's plea (vv. 7–10)? 4. God provides for the Jews through the edict Mordecai issued in the king's name. How did the edict (vv. 11–13) provide what Esther was asking for in verses 5–6 without breaking the first edict (3:12–14)? 5. Describe the response of the Jews to God's provision and protection (vv. 15–17).

Applying the Word 1. Esther felt deep concern and compassion for her people. For what person or group of people would you like to have that same kind of concern? 2. How might you develop your compassion for them? 3. How can we be faithful when we are waiting for God to act in our lives?

Responding in Prayer Think over the past week and share how God has been faithful to you. Express to God your joy and gladness about his provision for you.

9/ *Esther 9—10*
Remembering and Celebrating

IT WAS A beautiful spring day and I was walking along a dirt road that wound through the mountains outside Bear Trap Ranch in Colorado. I was pouring out my heart to God and wrestling with where he wanted to take me in my life. As I strolled among the pine trees, God opened my eyes to the abundant life that lay before me if I would commit my future to his service. It was that moment that changed the course of my life, and I am eternally grateful to the Lord. Every time I visit Bear Trap Ranch I walk along that very road and remember that moment and God's faithfulness to me. Celebrating God's goodness helps me keep my perspective and empowers me to go on in my commitment to his service.

Warming Up to God What is something you or your family commemorated, and how was it celebrated?

Read Esther 9—10.

9 On the thirteenth day of the twelfth month, the month of Adar, the edict commanded by the king was to be carried out.
On this day the enemies of the Jews had hoped to overpower them, but now the tables were turned and the Jews got the upper hand over those who
hated them. 2The Jews assembled in their cities in all the provinces of King Xerxes to attack those seeking their destruction. No one could stand against them, because the people of all the other
nationalities were afraid of them. 3And all the nobles of the provinces, the satraps, the governors and the king's administrators helped the Jews, be-
cause fear of Mordecai had seized them. 4Morde-
cai was prominent in the palace; his reputation spread throughout the provinces, and he became more and more powerful.
5The Jews struck down all their enemies with the sword, killing and destroying them, and they did what they pleased to those who hated them.
6In the citadel of Susa, the Jews killed and destroyed five hundred men. 7They also killed Par-
shandatha, Dalphon, Aspatha, 8Poratha, Adalia,
Aridatha, 9Parmashta, Arisai, Aridai and Vaizatha,
10the ten sons of Haman son of Hammedatha, the enemy of the Jews. But they did not lay their hands on the plunder.
11The number of those slain in the citadel of Susa was reported to the king that same day.
12The king said to Queen Esther, "The Jews have killed and destroyed five hundred men and the ten sons of Haman in the citadel of Susa. What have they done in the rest of the king's provinces? Now what is your petition? It will be given you. What is your request? It will also be granted."
13"If it pleases the king," Esther answered, "give the Jews in Susa permission to carry out this day's edict tomorrow also, and let Haman's ten sons be hanged on gallows."
14So the king commanded that this be done. An edict was issued in Susa, and they hanged the ten
sons of Haman. 15The Jews in Susa came together on the fourteenth day of the month of Adar, and they put to death in Susa three hundred men, but they did not lay their hands on the plunder.
16Meanwhile, the remainder of the Jews who were in the king's provinces also assembled to protect themselves and get relief from their enemies. They killed seventy-five thousand of them
but did not lay their hands on the plunder. 17This happened on the thirteenth day of the month of Adar, and on the fourteenth they rested and made it a day of feasting and joy.
18The Jews in Susa, however, had assembled on the thirteenth and fourteenth, and then on the fifteenth they rested and made it a day of feasting and joy.
19That is why rural Jews—those living in villages—observe the fourteenth of the month of

Adar as a day of joy and feasting, a day for giving presents to each other.

[20]Mordecai recorded these events, and he sent letters to all the Jews throughout the provinces of King Xerxes, near and far, [21]to have them celebrate annually the fourteenth and fifteenth days of the month of Adar [22]as the time when the Jews got relief from their enemies, and as the month when their sorrow was turned into joy and their mourning into a day of celebration. He wrote them to observe the days as days of feasting and joy and giving presents of food to one another and gifts to the poor.

[23]So the Jews agreed to continue the celebration they had begun, doing what Mordecai had written to them. [24]For Haman son of Hammedatha, the Agagite, the enemy of all the Jews, had plotted against the Jews to destroy them and had cast the *pur* (that is, the lot) for their ruin and destruction. [25]But when the plot came to the king's attention,[l] he issued written orders that the evil scheme Haman had devised against the Jews should come back onto his own head, and that he and his sons should be hanged on the gallows. [26](Therefore these days were called Purim, from the word *pur*.) Because of everything written in this letter and because of what they had seen and what had happened to them, [27]the Jews took it upon themselves to establish the custom that they and their descendants and all who join them should without fail observe these two days every year, in the way prescribed and at the time appointed. [28]These days should be remembered and observed in every generation by every family, and in every province and in every city. And these days of Purim should never cease to be celebrated by the Jews, nor should the memory of them die out among their descendants.

[29]So Queen Esther, daughter of Abihail, along with Mordecai the Jew, wrote with full authority to confirm this second letter concerning Purim. [30]And Mordecai sent letters to all the Jews in the 127 provinces of the kingdom of Xerxes—words of goodwill and assurance— [31]to establish these days of Purim at their designated times, as Mordecai the Jew and Queen Esther had decreed for them, and as they had established for themselves and their descendants in regard to their times of fasting and lamentation. [32]Esther's decree confirmed these regulations about Purim, and it was written down in the records.

10

King Xerxes imposed tribute throughout the empire, to its distant shores. [2]And all his acts of power and might, together with a full account of the greatness of Mordecai to which the king had raised him, are they not written in the book of the annals of the kings of Media and Persia? [3]Mordecai the Jew was second in rank to King Xerxes, preeminent among the Jews, and held in high esteem by his many fellow Jews, because he worked for the good of his people and spoke up for the welfare of all the Jews.

[l]25 Or *when Esther came before the king*

Discovering the Word 1. Summarize the events of the thirteenth, fourteenth and fifteenth days of Adar. 2. Describe the people that the Jews actually destroyed on these days in the month of Adar (9:5-17). 3. The author mentions three separate times that the Jews did not lay their hands on their enemies' plunder. Why might the Jews have left the plunder despite the king's permission to take it (9:10, 15-16)? 4. Mordecai and Esther proclaimed and established the celebration of Purim as a holiday for all the Jews. What was the purpose of the celebration (9:20-27)? 5. God has saved his people and blessed Esther and Mordecai for their obedience to him. Summarize what happens to Esther and Mordecai at the end of the story (9:29—10:3).

Applying the Word 1. Throughout Scripture God instructs his people to commemorate the times when he acted to provide and save his people. Why is remembering God's acts of faithfulness important for us as Christians? 2. What is one thing that God has done for you that you would truly like to remember? 3. What are some ways you could celebrate it?

Responding in Prayer Begin your tradition of celebrating right now by offering your praise and thanksgiving to God.

Job

One thing we can count on in this life is *trouble!* Becoming a Christian, contrary to what some say, does not so much deliver us from problems as delivers us *in* them. We still get sick, lose jobs, worry about our children and struggle with loneliness. On a deeper level a personal encounter with God brings at the same time exquisite joy and a new set of questions. Sometimes, like Job, we are led through a dark valley without seeing the path out, why we are suffering, whether God has a redeeming purpose in it all and how we are to respond. Are we to just patiently take it all?

Mention the name *Job* and one immediately thinks of patience, partly because of one misunderstood New Testament reference to this Old Testament saint (Jas 5:11). Job did suffer, but not patiently. He rebelled.

Job's saintly friends tried to "explain" his problems by appealing to the logic of good orthodox theology. In the end, Job's almost irreverent appeal to God for an explanation led to his justification and approval by God. While Job's orthodox friends were rejected (Job 42:7), he persevered; that is the real point of the New Testament reference. Perhaps among other things, this surprising reversal can be explained by the fact that Job spoke *to* God about his suffering while Job's friends spoke *about* God to Job. But this is not the only mystery encompassed by this fascinating Old Testament book.

Job raises as many questions as it answers. Indeed, when God finally speaks to Job in the whirlwind (chapters 38—41), God himself asks questions! Traditionally theology has wrestled with how a good and all-powerful God could at the same time allow or even *cause* (as Job claims) suffering and evil in the world. But the usual abstract arguments, spoken smoothly by Job's three friends—Eliphaz, Bildad and Zophar—are not only rejected by God and his beloved Job, they are not even the point of the book.

This is not a book of rational, systematic theology. This is the story of one human being—one very human and very righteous being—who loses his possessions, his family and his health. But it is a story that takes place within the household of faith. And it is faith that rebels and a God who loves the rebel that is the surprise of the story.

Job—and we—have problems with innocent suffering precisely because we have faith in God, whose goodness is known in the land of the living. There is no answer either in jettisoning belief in the goodness of God or in rejecting the hope that *in this life* there should be both satisfaction and justice. In the end, *and only in the end,* Job finds peace with God through his sufferings and not in spite of them. Ultimately, Job's passion points to the death, resurrection and vindication of Jesus as God's final answer to the problem of the innocent suffering.

The gospel-bearing quality of Job is all the more remarkable because the book may be very ancient. There is no mention of temple, monarchy or prophets. We do not know who wrote the book, when or where the author lived, though there is no adequate reason to deny the unity of the book. For date, authorship and textual questions read Francis I. Anderson, *Job,* Tyndale Old Testament Commentaries (Downers Grove, Ill.: InterVarsity Press, 1976), pages 15–76.

The book contains an astonishing mixture of riddles, hymns, curses, proverbs and nature poems. The introduction (1:1—2:13) and conclusion (42:7–17) are in prose, while the speeches of Job, the three friends, the young man Elihu and God himself (3:1—42:6) are in poetry. No wonder the Jewish rabbis were unsure where to place Job in Scripture. Though they eventually chose the Writings section, this book fits just as well alongside the great exodus, David and Ruth.

Like all biblical stories, this one catches us in its plot and invites us in its mysterious and ironic way to find God not in talking *about* God, but in talking *to* him at the point of our deepest questions about the meaning of life and of God himself, not in leisure-time spirituality, but in the middle of life where it is hardest. According to the *New Bible Commentary,* "The book takes its place in the testimony of the ages that there is a blank in the human heart which Jesus alone can fill."

Outline

1/ Job 1:1—2:10 ———— *Dueling with the Devil*

2/ Job 2:11—4:17 ———— *God in the Dark*

3/ Job 6 ———— *God-Talk*

4/ Job 9—10 ———— *If God Were Only Human!*

5/ Job 13—14 ———— *The Faith That Rebels*

6/ Job 16—17 ———— *Our Heavenly Guarantor*

7/ Job 20—21 ———— *The Problem of Pain*

8/ Job 23 ———— *The Silence of God*

9/ Job 35 ———— *Songs in the Night*

10/ Job 38 ———— *God in the Storm*

11/ Job 40 ———— *The Joy of Repentance*

12/ Job 42 ———— *Is Faith Always Worthwhile?*

1 / *Job 1:1—2:10*
Dueling with the Devil

IS IT POSSIBLE to love God for God's sake, and not merely for the benefits of being faithful, even when there *are* benefits? And what if these benefits are all removed and one is left with no benefit but God alone? This is the question Satan poses to God regarding his faithful servant, Job.

Warming Up to God How would you respond to someone who charges that religion is only for those who can't make it on their own?

Read Job 1:1—2:10.

1 In the land of Uz there lived a man whose name was Job. This man was blameless and upright; he feared God and shunned evil. 2He had seven sons and three daughters, 3and he owned seven thousand sheep, three thousand camels, five hundred yoke of oxen and five hundred donkeys, and had a large number of servants. He was the greatest man among all the people of the East.

4His sons used to take turns holding feasts in their homes, and they would invite their three sisters to eat and drink with them. 5When a period of feasting had run its course, Job would send and have them purified. Early in the morning he would sacrifice a burnt offering for each of them, thinking, "Perhaps my children have sinned and cursed God in their hearts." This was Job's regular custom.

6One day the angels[a] came to present themselves before the LORD, and Satan[b] also came with them. 7The LORD said to Satan, "Where have you come from?"

Satan answered the LORD, "From roaming through the earth and going back and forth in it."

8Then the LORD said to Satan, "Have you considered my servant Job? There is no one on earth like him; he is blameless and upright, a man who fears God and shuns evil."

9"Does Job fear God for nothing?" Satan replied. 10"Have you not put a hedge around him and his household and everything he has? You have blessed the work of his hands, so that his flocks and herds are spread throughout the land. 11But stretch out your hand and strike everything he has, and he will surely curse you to your face."

12The LORD said to Satan, "Very well, then, everything he has is in your hands, but on the man himself do not lay a finger."

Then Satan went out from the presence of the LORD.

13One day when Job's sons and daughters were feasting and drinking wine at the oldest brother's house, 14a messenger came to Job and said, "The oxen were plowing and the donkeys were grazing nearby, 15and the Sabeans attacked and carried them off. They put the servants to the sword, and I am the only one who has escaped to tell you!"

16While he was still speaking, another messenger came and said, "The fire of God fell from the sky and burned up the sheep and the servants, and I am the only one who has escaped to tell you!"

17While he was still speaking, another messenger came and said, "The Chaldeans formed three raiding parties and swept down on your camels and carried them off. They put the servants to the sword, and I am the only one who has escaped to tell you!"

18While he was still speaking, yet another messenger came and said, "Your sons and daughters were feasting and drinking wine at the oldest brother's house, 19when suddenly a mighty wind swept in from the desert and struck the four corners of the house. It collapsed on them and they are dead, and I am the only one who has escaped to tell you!"

20At this, Job got up and tore his robe and shaved his head. Then he fell to the ground in worship 21and said:

"Naked I came from my mother's womb,
and naked I will depart.[c]
The LORD gave and the LORD has taken away;
may the name of the LORD be praised."

[a]6 Hebrew *the sons of God* [b]6 *Satan means accuser.* [c]21 Or *will return there*

22In all this, Job did not sin by charging God
with wrongdoing.

2 On another day the angels[d] came to
present themselves before the LORD, and
Satan also came with them to present
himself before him. 2And the LORD said to Satan,
"Where have you come from?"

Satan answered the LORD, "From roaming
through the earth and going back and forth in it."

3Then the LORD said to Satan, "Have you con-
sidered my servant Job? There is no one on earth
like him; he is blameless and upright, a man who
fears God and shuns evil. And he still maintains
his integrity, though you incited me against him
to ruin him without any reason."

4"Skin for skin!" Satan replied. "A man will
give all he has for his own life. 5But stretch out
your hand and strike his flesh and bones, and he
will surely curse you to your face."

6The LORD said to Satan, "Very well, then, he is
in your hands; but you must spare his life."

7So Satan went out from the presence of the
LORD and afflicted Job with painful sores from the
soles of his feet to the top of his head. 8Then Job
took a piece of broken pottery and scraped him-
self with it as he sat among the ashes.

9His wife said to him, "Are you still holding on
to your integrity? Curse God and die!"

10He replied, "You are talking like a foolish[e]
woman. Shall we accept good from God, and not
trouble?"

In all this, Job did not sin in what he said.

[d]1 Hebrew *the sons of God* [e]10 The Hebrew word rendered *foolish* denotes moral deficiency.

Discovering the Word 1. What indications are there that Job's righteousness was not directly related to his being blessed with material prosperity (1:1–8)? 2. In this very ancient document Satan appears as an angelic adversary with free access to God's presence, unlike the devil in the New Testament. What does Satan accuse Job of (1:9–11)? 3. For what good reasons could God agree to a contest that would affect Job and his family so painfully? 4. How does Job react to the first test (1:20–22)? 5. Why do you think God agreed to the second test (2:1–6)? 6. Why would the suggestion Job's wife made be especially dangerous to Job's faith (2:9–10)?

Applying the Word 1. Suffering is a mystery, and the opening scenes of this book deepen the mystery by showing how inadequate are our "reasons" for misfortune. What have you already learned about accepting trouble from God (2:10)? 2. What difference will this make to your own attitude toward hard times?

Responding in Prayer This passage may have raised some difficult questions and feelings for you. Talk openly with God about your response to what you have read.

2 / *Job 2:11—4:17*
God in the Dark

FOR EVERY TEN people that can withstand the temptations of adversity, only one can stand prosperity—or so it is said. It was different with our Old Testament hero. Job has handled his prosperity as a ministry, and later defends his stewardship of abundance (29:7–25; 31:24–25). But now he is plunged into excruciating loss, a living death. This new test will examine whether his belief in the goodness of God can be subverted by hopelessly negative circumstances. Job will ask the questions that we asked when life is hardest.

Warming Up to God When have you been tempted to doubt God's goodness? What questions did you ask? What thoughts, if any, did you have of God?

Read Job 2:11—4:17.

11When Job's three friends, Eliphaz the Teman-
ite, Bildad the Shuhite and Zophar the Naama-
thite, heard about all the troubles that had come
upon him, they set out from their homes and met
together by agreement to go and sympathize with
him and comfort him. 12When they saw him from

a distance, they could hardly recognize him; they
began to weep aloud, and they tore their robes
and sprinkled dust on their heads. 13Then they
sat on the ground with him for seven days and
seven nights. No one said a word to him, because
they saw how great his suffering was.

3 After this, Job opened his mouth and
cursed the day of his birth. 2He said:

3"May the day of my birth perish,
and the night it was said, 'A boy is born!'
4That day—may it turn to darkness;
may God above not care about it;
may no light shine upon it.
5May darkness and deep shadow[f] claim it
once more;
may a cloud settle over it;
may blackness overwhelm its light.
6That night—may thick darkness seize it;
may it not be included among the days of
the year
nor be entered in any of the months.
7May that night be barren;
may no shout of joy be heard in it.
8May those who curse days[g] curse that day,
those who are ready to rouse Leviathan.
9May its morning stars become dark;
may it wait for daylight in vain
and not see the first rays of dawn,
10for it did not shut the doors of the womb on
me
to hide trouble from my eyes.

11"Why did I not perish at birth,
and die as I came from the womb?
12Why were there knees to receive me
and breasts that I might be nursed?
13For now I would be lying down in peace;
I would be asleep and at rest
14with kings and counselors of the earth,
who built for themselves places now lying
in ruins,
15with rulers who had gold,
who filled their houses with silver.
16Or why was I not hidden in the ground like a
stillborn child,
like an infant who never saw the light of
day?
17There the wicked cease from turmoil,
and there the weary are at rest.
18Captives also enjoy their ease;
they no longer hear the slave driver's shout.
19The small and the great are there,
and the slave is freed from his master.

20"Why is light given to those in misery,
and life to the bitter of soul,
21to those who long for death that does not
come,
who search for it more than for hidden
treasure,
22who are filled with gladness
and rejoice when they reach the grave?
23Why is life given to a man
whose way is hidden,
whom God has hedged in?
24For sighing comes to me instead of food;
my groans pour out like water.
25What I feared has come upon me;
what I dreaded has happened to me.
26I have no peace, no quietness;
I have no rest, but only turmoil."

4 Then Eliphaz the Temanite replied:

2"If someone ventures a word with
you, will you be impatient?
But who can keep from speaking?
3Think how you have instructed many,
how you have strengthened feeble hands.
4Your words have supported those who
stumbled;
you have strengthened faltering knees.
5But now trouble comes to you, and you are
discouraged;
it strikes you, and you are dismayed.
6Should not your piety be your confidence
and your blameless ways your hope?

7"Consider now: Who, being innocent, has
ever perished?
Where were the upright ever destroyed?
8As I have observed, those who plow evil
and those who sow trouble reap it.
9At the breath of God they are destroyed;
at the blast of his anger they perish.
10The lions may roar and growl,
yet the teeth of the great lions are broken.
11The lion perishes for lack of prey,
and the cubs of the lioness are scattered.

12"A word was secretly brought to me,
my ears caught a whisper of it.
13Amid disquieting dreams in the night,
when deep sleep falls on men,

f5 *Or and the shadow of death* g8 *Or the sea*

14 fear and trembling seized me
and made all my bones shake.
15 A spirit glided past my face,
and the hair on my body stood on end.
16 It stopped,
but I could not tell what it was.
A form stood before my eyes,
and I heard a hushed voice:
17 'Can a mortal be more righteous than God?
Can a man be more pure than his Maker?

Discovering the Word 1. At this point in the story Job's three friends travel a considerable distance to console Job. What actions of the friends indicate they understood how deeply Job was suffering (2:11–13)? 2. From chapters 3 through 31 the story moves from prose to poetry as Job's three friends discuss the meaning of his adversity and where—if anywhere—God was present in the darkness. In what ways does Job's response to his suffering go beyond asking the usual why (3:1–10)? 3. What does Job think God's role is in all this (3:11, 16)? 4. What new questions does Job ask in 3:20–26? 5. Each of Job's three friends makes a speech, with Job responding—a cycle that gets repeated three times in the book. Eliphaz responds cautiously at first and then attacks. Why does Eliphaz think Job is suffering (4:7–11)?

Applying the Word 1. Eliphaz thinks he has God's word (4:12–17). Job only has dark questions. What have you learned so far about finding God in the midst of pain and loss? 2. How do you feel about living with unanswered questions?

Responding in Prayer Initially, Job's friends were good comforters (2:11–13) simply by being there. Pray for someone you know who needs comfort. Ask God to show you what you can offer that person.

Job 4:18—5:27

18 If God places no trust in his servants,
if he charges his angels with error,
19 how much more those who live in houses of clay,
whose foundations are in the dust,
who are crushed more readily than a moth!
20 Between dawn and dusk they are broken to pieces;
unnoticed, they perish forever.
21 Are not the cords of their tent pulled up,
so that they die without wisdom?'[h]

5 "Call if you will, but who will answer you?
To which of the holy ones will you turn?
2 Resentment kills a fool,
and envy slays the simple.
3 I myself have seen a fool taking root,
but suddenly his house was cursed.
4 His children are far from safety,
crushed in court without a defender.
5 The hungry consume his harvest,
taking it even from among thorns,
and the thirsty pant after his wealth.
6 For hardship does not spring from the soil,
nor does trouble sprout from the ground.
7 Yet man is born to trouble
as surely as sparks fly upward.

8 "But if it were I, I would appeal to God;
I would lay my cause before him.
9 He performs wonders that cannot be fathomed,
miracles that cannot be counted.
10 He bestows rain on the earth;
he sends water upon the countryside.
11 The lowly he sets on high,
and those who mourn are lifted to safety.
12 He thwarts the plans of the crafty,
so that their hands achieve no success.
13 He catches the wise in their craftiness,
and the schemes of the wily are swept away.
14 Darkness comes upon them in the daytime;
at noon they grope as in the night.
15 He saves the needy from the sword in their mouth;
he saves them from the clutches of the powerful.
16 So the poor have hope,
and injustice shuts its mouth.

17 "Blessed is the man whom God corrects;

h 21 Some interpreters end the quotation after verse 17.

so do not despise the discipline of the
Almighty.[i]
18For he wounds, but he also binds up;
he injures, but his hands also heal.
19From six calamities he will rescue you;
in seven no harm will befall you.
20In famine he will ransom you from death,
and in battle from the stroke of the sword.
21You will be protected from the lash of the
tongue,
and need not fear when destruction comes.
22You will laugh at destruction and famine,
and need not fear the beasts of the earth.
23For you will have a covenant with the stones
of the field,
and the wild animals will be at peace with
you.
24You will know that your tent is secure;
you will take stock of your property and
find nothing missing.
25You will know that your children will be
many,
and your descendants like the grass of the
earth.
26You will come to the grave in full vigor,
like sheaves gathered in season.
27"We have examined this, and it is true.
So hear it and apply it to yourself."

i17 Hebrew *Shaddai*; here and throughout Job

3 / *Job 6*
God-Talk

"WITH FRIENDS LIKE these, who needs enemies!" might well be Job's heart-cry, and sometimes our own. Even our worst experiences of friendship do not quench our desire for soul friends, people who will walk with us through life's hardest moments and who will point us to God without preaching at us or judging our spirituality. Most of us are lonely, as was our Old Testament hero. "Job's comforters," the cynical title given to Eliphaz, Bildad and Zophar—and later the young man Elihu—didn't help his situation.

Warming Up to God Reflect on the friend who has been most encouraging in your spiritual journey. Use single words to characterize your relationship with that person.

Read Job 6.

6 Then Job replied:

2"If only my anguish could be weighed
and all my misery be placed on the scales!
3It would surely outweigh the sand of the
seas—
no wonder my words have been impetuous.
4The arrows of the Almighty are in me,
my spirit drinks in their poison;
God's terrors are marshaled against me.
5Does a wild donkey bray when it has grass,
or an ox bellow when it has fodder?
6Is tasteless food eaten without salt,
or is there flavor in the white of an egg[j]?
7I refuse to touch it;
such food makes me ill.
8"Oh, that I might have my request,
that God would grant what I hope for,
9that God would be willing to crush me,
to let loose his hand and cut me off!
10Then I would still have this consolation—
my joy in unrelenting pain—
that I had not denied the words of the Holy
One.

11"What strength do I have, that I should still
hope?
What prospects, that I should be patient?
12Do I have the strength of stone?
Is my flesh bronze?
13Do I have any power to help myself,
now that success has been driven from me?

14"A despairing man should have the devotion
of his friends,

j6 The meaning of the Hebrew for this phrase is uncertain.

even though he forsakes the fear of the
Almighty.
15But my brothers are as undependable as
intermittent streams,
as the streams that overflow
16when darkened by thawing ice
and swollen with melting snow,
17but that cease to flow in the dry season,
and in the heat vanish from their channels.
18Caravans turn aside from their routes;
they go up into the wasteland and perish.
19The caravans of Tema look for water,
the traveling merchants of Sheba look in
hope.
20They are distressed, because they had been
confident;
they arrive there, only to be disappointed.
21Now you too have proved to be of no help;
you see something dreadful and are afraid.
22Have I ever said, 'Give something on my
behalf,
pay a ransom for me from your wealth,
23deliver me from the hand of the enemy,
ransom me from the clutches of the
ruthless'?

24"Teach me, and I will be quiet;
show me where I have been wrong.
25How painful are honest words!
But what do your arguments prove?
26Do you mean to correct what I say,
and treat the words of a despairing man as
wind?
27You would even cast lots for the fatherless
and barter away your friend.

28"But now be so kind as to look at me.
Would I lie to your face?
29Relent, do not be unjust;
reconsider, for my integrity is at stake.[k]
30Is there any wickedness on my lips?
Can my mouth not discern malice?

[k]29 Or *my righteousness still stands*

Discovering the Word 1. Instead of responding to Eliphaz's accusation that his suffering was a result of his sin or his children's sin, Job explores his problem on a deeper level. For what new reason does he want God to end it all (v. 10)? 2. What word pictures does Job use to describe his friends (vv. 15–21)? 3. What reason does Job see underlying his friends' failure to minister to him (v. 21)? 4. What does Job need from his friends in this time of suffering? 5. How could his friends have confidence in Job's integrity (v. 29) even though they have no explanation for his problem except God's discipline?

Applying the Word 1. Look at verse 14. Is it always right to maintain a friendship even if your friend "loses" faith or goes through a period of rebellion? 2. Later Job will comment, "Men at ease have contempt for misfortune" (12:5). What would enable you to be of help to others in the pit of despair even though you are doing fine yourself?

Responding in Prayer Reflect on the friends God has given you, and thank him for their gifts. Ask him to teach you to be a faithful friend.

Job 7—8

7 "Does not man have hard service on
earth?
Are not his days like those of a hired
man?
2Like a slave longing for the evening shadows,
or a hired man waiting eagerly for his
wages,
3so I have been allotted months of futility,
and nights of misery have been assigned to
me.
4When I lie down I think, 'How long before I
get up?'
The night drags on, and I toss till dawn.
5My body is clothed with worms and scabs,
my skin is broken and festering.

6"My days are swifter than a weaver's shuttle,
and they come to an end without hope.
7Remember, O God, that my life is but a
breath;

my eyes will never see happiness again.
[8]The eye that now sees me will see me no longer;
you will look for me, but I will be no more.
[9]As a cloud vanishes and is gone,
so he who goes down to the grave[l] does not return.
[10]He will never come to his house again;
his place will know him no more.

[11]"Therefore I will not keep silent;
I will speak out in the anguish of my spirit,
I will complain in the bitterness of my soul.
[12]Am I the sea, or the monster of the deep,
that you put me under guard?
[13]When I think my bed will comfort me
and my couch will ease my complaint,
[14]even then you frighten me with dreams
and terrify me with visions,
[15]so that I prefer strangling and death,
rather than this body of mine.
[16]I despise my life; I would not live forever.
Let me alone; my days have no meaning.

[17]"What is man that you make so much of him,
that you give him so much attention,
[18]that you examine him every morning
and test him every moment?
[19]Will you never look away from me,
or let me alone even for an instant?
[20]If I have sinned, what have I done to you,
O watcher of men?
Why have you made me your target?
Have I become a burden to you?[m]
[21]Why do you not pardon my offenses
and forgive my sins?
For I will soon lie down in the dust;
you will search for me, but I will be no more."

8

Then Bildad the Shuhite replied:

[2]"How long will you say such things?
Your words are a blustering wind.
[3]Does God pervert justice?
Does the Almighty pervert what is right?
[4]When your children sinned against him,
he gave them over to the penalty of their sin.
[5]But if you will look to God
and plead with the Almighty,
[6]if you are pure and upright,
even now he will rouse himself on your behalf
and restore you to your rightful place.
[7]Your beginnings will seem humble,
so prosperous will your future be.

[8]"Ask the former generations
and find out what their fathers learned,
[9]for we were born only yesterday and know nothing,
and our days on earth are but a shadow.
[10]Will they not instruct you and tell you?
Will they not bring forth words from their understanding?
[11]Can papyrus grow tall where there is no marsh?
Can reeds thrive without water?
[12]While still growing and uncut,
they wither more quickly than grass.
[13]Such is the destiny of all who forget God;
so perishes the hope of the godless.
[14]What he trusts in is fragile[n];
what he relies on is a spider's web.
[15]He leans on his web, but it gives way;
he clings to it, but it does not hold.
[16]He is like a well-watered plant in the sunshine,
spreading its shoots over the garden;
[17]it entwines its roots around a pile of rocks
and looks for a place among the stones.
[18]But when it is torn from its spot,
that place disowns it and says, 'I never saw you.'
[19]Surely its life withers away,
and[o] from the soil other plants grow.

[20]"Surely God does not reject a blameless man
or strengthen the hands of evildoers.
[21]He will yet fill your mouth with laughter
and your lips with shouts of joy.
[22]Your enemies will be clothed in shame,
and the tents of the wicked will be no more."

[l]9 Hebrew *Sheol* [m]20 A few manuscripts of the Masoretic Text, an ancient Hebrew scribal tradition and Septuagint; most manuscripts of the Masoretic Text *I have become a burden to myself.* [n]14 The meaning of the Hebrew for this word is uncertain. [o]19 Or *Surely all the joy it has / is that*

4 / *Job 9—10*
If God Were Only Human!

WHEN THE BOTTOM falls out of life, we cry, "Where is God when I am hurting? Does he really understand? Can he *do* anything? Does God dwell in heaven unmoved by our cries?" Sometimes the Bible presents the most important truths not in a frontal attack or a prophetic pronouncement, but in a pregnant hint. This passage is a case in point. It takes us one step farther to the edge of the greatest of all discoveries, the gospel itself—that God should become a human being, making himself totally accessible to his own creature.

Warming Up to God Try to remember your first pictures or impressions of God. Was God distant, close, awesomely different, totally unlike anyone human, or very similar to your earthly father or mother? Explain.

Read Job 9—10.

9 Then Job replied:

2"Indeed, I know that this is true.
But how can a mortal be righteous before God?
3Though one wished to dispute with him,
he could not answer him one time out of a thousand.
4His wisdom is profound, his power is vast.
Who has resisted him and come out unscathed?
5He moves mountains without their knowing it
and overturns them in his anger.
6He shakes the earth from its place
and makes its pillars tremble.
7He speaks to the sun and it does not shine;
he seals off the light of the stars.
8He alone stretches out the heavens
and treads on the waves of the sea.
9He is the Maker of the Bear and Orion,
the Pleiades and the constellations of the south.
10He performs wonders that cannot be fathomed,
miracles that cannot be counted.
11When he passes me, I cannot see him;
when he goes by, I cannot perceive him.
12If he snatches away, who can stop him?
Who can say to him, 'What are you doing?'
13God does not restrain his anger;
even the cohorts of Rahab cowered at his feet.

14"How then can I dispute with him?
How can I find words to argue with him?
15Though I were innocent, I could not answer him;
I could only plead with my Judge for mercy.
16Even if I summoned him and he responded,
I do not believe he would give me a hearing.
17He would crush me with a storm
and multiply my wounds for no reason.
18He would not let me regain my breath
but would overwhelm me with misery.
19If it is a matter of strength, he is mighty!
And if it is a matter of justice, who will summon him[p]?
20Even if I were innocent, my mouth would condemn me;
if I were blameless, it would pronounce me guilty.

21"Although I am blameless,
I have no concern for myself;
I despise my own life.
22It is all the same; that is why I say,
'He destroys both the blameless and the wicked.'
23When a scourge brings sudden death,
he mocks the despair of the innocent.
24When a land falls into the hands of the wicked,
he blindfolds its judges.
If it is not he, then who is it?

25"My days are swifter than a runner;
they fly away without a glimpse of joy.
26They skim past like boats of papyrus,
like eagles swooping down on their prey.
27If I say, 'I will forget my complaint,
I will change my expression, and smile,'
28I still dread all my sufferings,
for I know you will not hold me innocent.
29Since I am already found guilty,
why should I struggle in vain?

p 19 See Septuagint; Hebrew *me.*

30Even if I washed myself with soap[q]
and my hands with washing soda,
31you would plunge me into a slime pit
so that even my clothes would detest me.

32"He is not a man like me that I might answer him,
that we might confront each other in court.
33If only there were someone to arbitrate between us,
to lay his hand upon us both,
34someone to remove God's rod from me,
so that his terror would frighten me no more.
35Then I would speak up without fear of him,
but as it now stands with me, I cannot.

10

"I loathe my very life;
therefore I will give free rein to my complaint
and speak out in the bitterness of my soul.
2I will say to God: Do not condemn me,
but tell me what charges you have against me.
3Does it please you to oppress me,
to spurn the work of your hands,
while you smile on the schemes of the wicked?
4Do you have eyes of flesh?
Do you see as a mortal sees?
5Are your days like those of a mortal
or your years like those of a man,
6that you must search out my faults
and probe after my sin—
7though you know that I am not guilty
and that no one can rescue me from your hand?

8"Your hands shaped me and made me.
Will you now turn and destroy me?
9Remember that you molded me like clay.
Will you now turn me to dust again?
10Did you not pour me out like milk
and curdle me like cheese,
11clothe me with skin and flesh
and knit me together with bones and sinews?
12You gave me life and showed me kindness,
and in your providence watched over my spirit.

13"But this is what you concealed in your heart,
and I know that this was in your mind:
14If I sinned, you would be watching me
and would not let my offense go unpunished.
15If I am guilty—woe to me!
Even if I am innocent, I cannot lift my head,
for I am full of shame
and drowned in[r] my affliction.
16If I hold my head high, you stalk me like a lion
and again display your awesome power against me.
17You bring new witnesses against me
and increase your anger toward me;
your forces come against me wave upon wave.

18"Why then did you bring me out of the womb?
I wish I had died before any eye saw me.
19If only I had never come into being,
or had been carried straight from the womb to the grave!
20Are not my few days almost over?
Turn away from me so I can have a moment's joy
21before I go to the place of no return,
to the land of gloom and deep shadow,[s]
22to the land of deepest night,
of deep shadow and disorder,
where even the light is like darkness."

[q]30 Or *snow* [r]15 Or *and aware of* [s]21 Or *and the shadow of death*; also in verse 22

Discovering the Word 1. Notice that Job's friends talk *about* God, but Job talks *to* God. How does Job characterize God (9:1–13)? 2. Why does Job feel it is becoming pointless to complain to God (9:14–20)? 3. Why is it equally pointless to put on a happy face (9:27–31)? 4. What does Job feel is wrong about his God (9:32–35 and 10:1–7)? 5. In none of his petitions does Job ask for his sickness to be cured. Describe what it is he wants from God.

Applying the Word 1. In what ways has Jesus Christ made Job's deepest dream a reality? 2. When tragedy strikes what difference does it make to know that God has come in the flesh (Jn 1:14)?

Responding in Prayer Follow Job's model and talk *to* God about the concerns on your heart—even if you are concerned about God's own character.

Job 11—12

11 Then Zophar the Naamathite replied:

2"Are all these words to go unanswered?
Is this talker to be vindicated?
3Will your idle talk reduce men to silence?
Will no one rebuke you when you mock?
4You say to God, 'My beliefs are flawless
and I am pure in your sight.'
5Oh, how I wish that God would speak,
that he would open his lips against you
6and disclose to you the secrets of wisdom,
for true wisdom has two sides.
Know this: God has even forgotten some of your sin.

7"Can you fathom the mysteries of God?
Can you probe the limits of the Almighty?
8They are higher than the heavens—what can you do?
They are deeper than the depths of the grave[t]—what can you know?
9Their measure is longer than the earth
and wider than the sea.

10"If he comes along and confines you in prison
and convenes a court, who can oppose him?
11Surely he recognizes deceitful men;
and when he sees evil, does he not take note?
12But a witless man can no more become wise
than a wild donkey's colt can be born a man.[u]

13"Yet if you devote your heart to him
and stretch out your hands to him,
14if you put away the sin that is in your hand
and allow no evil to dwell in your tent,
15then you will lift up your face without shame;
you will stand firm and without fear.
16You will surely forget your trouble,
recalling it only as waters gone by.
17Life will be brighter than noonday,
and darkness will become like morning.
18You will be secure, because there is hope;
you will look about you and take your rest in safety.
19You will lie down, with no one to make you afraid,
and many will court your favor.
20But the eyes of the wicked will fail,
and escape will elude them;
their hope will become a dying gasp."

12 Then Job replied:

2"Doubtless you are the people,
and wisdom will die with you!
3But I have a mind as well as you;
I am not inferior to you.
Who does not know all these things?

4"I have become a laughingstock to my friends,
though I called upon God and he answered—
a mere laughingstock, though righteous and blameless!
5Men at ease have contempt for misfortune
as the fate of those whose feet are slipping.
6The tents of marauders are undisturbed,
and those who provoke God are secure—
those who carry their god in their hands.[v]

7"But ask the animals, and they will teach you,
or the birds of the air, and they will tell you;
8or speak to the earth, and it will teach you,
or let the fish of the sea inform you.
9Which of all these does not know
that the hand of the LORD has done this?
10In his hand is the life of every creature
and the breath of all mankind.
11Does not the ear test words
as the tongue tastes food?
12Is not wisdom found among the aged?
Does not long life bring understanding?

13"To God belong wisdom and power;
counsel and understanding are his.
14What he tears down cannot be rebuilt;
the man he imprisons cannot be released.
15If he holds back the waters, there is drought;
if he lets them loose, they devastate the land.
16To him belong strength and victory;
both deceived and deceiver are his.
17He leads counselors away stripped
and makes fools of judges.

[t]8 Hebrew *than Sheol* [u]12 *Or wild donkey can be born tame*
[v]6 *Or secure / in what God's hand brings them*

[18]He takes off the shackles put on by kings
and ties a loincloth[w] around their waist.
[19]He leads priests away stripped
and overthrows men long established.
[20]He silences the lips of trusted advisers
and takes away the discernment of elders.
[21]He pours contempt on nobles
and disarms the mighty.
[22]He reveals the deep things of darkness
and brings deep shadows into the light.
[23]He makes nations great, and destroys them;
he enlarges nations, and disperses them.
[24]He deprives the leaders of the earth of their
reason;
he sends them wandering through a
trackless waste.
[25]They grope in darkness with no light;
he makes them stagger like drunkards.

[w]18 *Or shackles of kings / and ties a belt*

5 / *Job 13—14*
The Faith That Rebels

LOSS OF WORK, loss of loved ones, loss of opportunities, excruciating disease and withering judgments from close friends—these are experiences of the faithful. But how should we respond? Simply accept them, fight them or try to ignore them? No. Those who get blessed by God are not those who ask nothing of God but those who will do almost anything to know God. The kingdom is not for the mildly interested but the desperate (Ge 32:26). Jesus said it is for the hungry, the thirsty, the poor (Mt 5:3-6) and the bold (Lk 11:8).

Job is a case in point. He experienced the loss of everything, even the comfort of his best friends. Yet he refuses to accept his friends' explanations, or to accept the absence of God as God's final answer. There is more reverence in Job's "irreverence" than in the friends' deference. This study will show us that faith sometimes requires us to rebel—in the right direction!

Warming Up to God In what life experiences have you been tempted to "lie down and take it" or give up compliantly?

Read Job 13—14.

13 "My eyes have seen all this,
my ears have heard and
understood it.
[2]What you know, I also know;
I am not inferior to you.
[3]But I desire to speak to the Almighty
and to argue my case with God.
[4]You, however, smear me with lies;
you are worthless physicians, all of you!
[5]If only you would be altogether silent!
For you, that would be wisdom.

[6]Hear now my argument;
listen to the plea of my lips.
[7]Will you speak wickedly on God's behalf?
Will you speak deceitfully for him?
[8]Will you show him partiality?
Will you argue the case for God?
[9]Would it turn out well if he examined you?
Could you deceive him as you might
deceive men?
[10]He would surely rebuke you
if you secretly showed partiality.
[11]Would not his splendor terrify you?
Would not the dread of him fall on you?
[12]Your maxims are proverbs of ashes;
your defenses are defenses of clay.

[13]"Keep silent and let me speak;
then let come to me what may.
[14]Why do I put myself in jeopardy
and take my life in my hands?
[15]Though he slay me, yet will I hope in him;
I will surely[x] defend my ways to his face.
[16]Indeed, this will turn out for my deliverance,
for no godless man would dare come before
him!
[17]Listen carefully to my words;
let your ears take in what I say.
[18]Now that I have prepared my case,

[x]15 *Or He will surely slay me; I have no hope — / yet I will*

I know I will be vindicated.
[19]Can anyone bring charges against me?
If so, I will be silent and die.

[20]"Only grant me these two things, O God,
and then I will not hide from you:
[21]Withdraw your hand far from me,
and stop frightening me with your terrors.
[22]Then summon me and I will answer,
or let me speak, and you reply.
[23]How many wrongs and sins have I committed?
Show me my offense and my sin.
[24]Why do you hide your face
and consider me your enemy?
[25]Will you torment a windblown leaf?
Will you chase after dry chaff?
[26]For you write down bitter things against me
and make me inherit the sins of my youth.
[27]You fasten my feet in shackles;
you keep close watch on all my paths
by putting marks on the soles of my feet.
[28]"So man wastes away like something rotten,
like a garment eaten by moths.

14

"Man born of woman
is of few days and full of trouble.
[2]He springs up like a flower and withers away;
like a fleeting shadow, he does not endure.
[3]Do you fix your eye on such a one?
Will you bring him[y] before you for judgment?
[4]Who can bring what is pure from the impure?
No one!
[5]Man's days are determined;
you have decreed the number of his months
and have set limits he cannot exceed.
[6]So look away from him and let him alone,
till he has put in his time like a hired man.

[7]"At least there is hope for a tree:
If it is cut down, it will sprout again,
and its new shoots will not fail.
[8]Its roots may grow old in the ground
and its stump die in the soil,
[9]yet at the scent of water it will bud
and put forth shoots like a plant.
[10]But man dies and is laid low;
he breathes his last and is no more.
[11]As water disappears from the sea
or a riverbed becomes parched and dry,
[12]so man lies down and does not rise;
till the heavens are no more, men will not awake
or be roused from their sleep.

[13]"If only you would hide me in the grave[z]
and conceal me till your anger has passed!
If only you would set me a time
and then remember me!
[14]If a man dies, will he live again?
All the days of my hard service
I will wait for my renewal[a] to come.
[15]You will call and I will answer you;
you will long for the creature your hands have made.
[16]Surely then you will count my steps
but not keep track of my sin.
[17]My offenses will be sealed up in a bag;
you will cover over my sin.

[18]"But as a mountain erodes and crumbles
and as a rock is moved from its place,
[19]as water wears away stones
and torrents wash away the soil,
so you destroy man's hope.
[20]You overpower him once for all, and he is gone;
you change his countenance and send him away.
[21]If his sons are honored, he does not know it;
if they are brought low, he does not see it.
[22]He feels but the pain of his own body
and mourns only for himself."

[y]3 Septuagint, Vulgate and Syriac; Hebrew *me* [z]13 Hebrew *Sheol*
[a]14 Or *release*

Discovering the Word 1. The third of Job's friends, Zophar, has delivered his message (chapter 11). Why are the friends worthless physicians (13:4)? 2. Job speaks directly to God in 13:20–28. What does Job request of God (13:20–22)? 3. What makes Job feel hopeless (14:7–12), even though he claims to have hope in God (13:15)? 4. In what ways did Job rebel in the right direction?

Applying the Word 1. If you could speak directly with God, what unanswered questions would you ask? 2. What unfair experiences would you want God to explain? 3. What impact has this quiet time had on your own response to the hardest experiences of life?

Responding in Prayer Ask God to give you insight into the hard times of your life that this passage may have brought to mind. Ask him to show you how he is leading you from that place into the future.

Job 15

15 Then Eliphaz the Temanite replied:

2"Would a wise man answer with empty notions
or fill his belly with the hot east wind?
3Would he argue with useless words,
with speeches that have no value?
4But you even undermine piety
and hinder devotion to God.
5Your sin prompts your mouth;
you adopt the tongue of the crafty.
6Your own mouth condemns you, not mine;
your own lips testify against you.

7"Are you the first man ever born?
Were you brought forth before the hills?
8Do you listen in on God's council?
Do you limit wisdom to yourself?
9What do you know that we do not know?
What insights do you have that we do not have?
10The gray-haired and the aged are on our side,
men even older than your father.
11Are God's consolations not enough for you,
words spoken gently to you?
12Why has your heart carried you away,
and why do your eyes flash,
13so that you vent your rage against God
and pour out such words from your mouth?

14"What is man, that he could be pure,
or one born of woman, that he could be righteous?
15If God places no trust in his holy ones,
if even the heavens are not pure in his eyes,
16how much less man, who is vile and corrupt,
who drinks up evil like water!

17"Listen to me and I will explain to you;
let me tell you what I have seen,
18what wise men have declared,
hiding nothing received from their fathers
19(to whom alone the land was given
when no alien passed among them):
20All his days the wicked man suffers torment,
the ruthless through all the years stored up for him.
21Terrifying sounds fill his ears;
when all seems well, marauders attack him.
22He despairs of escaping the darkness;
he is marked for the sword.
23He wanders about—food for vultures[b];
he knows the day of darkness is at hand.
24Distress and anguish fill him with terror;
they overwhelm him, like a king poised to attack,
25because he shakes his fist at God
and vaunts himself against the Almighty,
26defiantly charging against him
with a thick, strong shield.

27"Though his face is covered with fat
and his waist bulges with flesh,
28he will inhabit ruined towns
and houses where no one lives,
houses crumbling to rubble.
29He will no longer be rich and his wealth will not endure,
nor will his possessions spread over the land.
30He will not escape the darkness;
a flame will wither his shoots,
and the breath of God's mouth will carry him away.
31Let him not deceive himself by trusting what is worthless,
for he will get nothing in return.
32Before his time he will be paid in full,
and his branches will not flourish.
33He will be like a vine stripped of its unripe grapes,
like an olive tree shedding its blossoms.
34For the company of the godless will be barren,
and fire will consume the tents of those who love bribes.
35They conceive trouble and give birth to evil;
their womb fashions deceit."

[b]23 Or *about, looking for food*

6 / *Job 16—17*
Our Heavenly Guarantor

WE LONG TO be sure—sure that we are accepted by God, sure that our sins are *really* forgiven, not to crop up again to haunt us like a long-suppressed secret, sure that we will be with God when we die and sure that God is *for* us. Mike Mason suggests that one of our deepest questions is whether God likes us. "Of course God loves us, he loves everybody, indiscriminately, even the people he is going to send to hell. . . . The real question is not whether God loves us, but whether he approves of us, whether we are pleasing to him" (as quoted in *Job* by Francis Andersen). In the end our question—like Job's—is "Is there a Friend in the universe?"

Warming Up to God Of what do you feel most sure in your life at this point? Explain.

Read Job 16—17.

16 Then Job replied:

2"I have heard many things like these;
miserable comforters are you all!
3Will your long-winded speeches never end?
What ails you that you keep on arguing?
4I also could speak like you,
if you were in my place;
I could make fine speeches against you
and shake my head at you.
5But my mouth would encourage you;
comfort from my lips would bring you relief.

6"Yet if I speak, my pain is not relieved;
and if I refrain, it does not go away.
7Surely, O God, you have worn me out;
you have devastated my entire household.
8You have bound me—and it has become a witness;
my gauntness rises up and testifies against me.
9God assails me and tears me in his anger
and gnashes his teeth at me;
my opponent fastens on me his piercing eyes.
10Men open their mouths to jeer at me;
they strike my cheek in scorn
and unite together against me.
11God has turned me over to evil men
and thrown me into the clutches of the wicked.
12All was well with me, but he shattered me;
he seized me by the neck and crushed me.
He has made me his target;
13 his archers surround me.
Without pity, he pierces my kidneys
and spills my gall on the ground.
14Again and again he bursts upon me;
he rushes at me like a warrior.

15"I have sewed sackcloth over my skin
and buried my brow in the dust.
16My face is red with weeping,
deep shadows ring my eyes;
17yet my hands have been free of violence
and my prayer is pure.

18"O earth, do not cover my blood;
may my cry never be laid to rest!
19Even now my witness is in heaven;
my advocate is on high.
20My intercessor is my friend[c]
as my eyes pour out tears to God;
21on behalf of a man he pleads with God
as a man pleads for his friend.

22"Only a few years will pass
before I go on the journey of no return.

17 1My spirit is broken,
my days are cut short,
the grave awaits me.
2Surely mockers surround me;
my eyes must dwell on their hostility.

3"Give me, O God, the pledge you demand.
Who else will put up security for me?
4You have closed their minds to understanding;
therefore you will not let them triumph.
5If a man denounces his friends for reward,
the eyes of his children will fail.

c20 Or *My friends treat me with scorn*

6“God has made me a byword to everyone,
a man in whose face people spit.
7My eyes have grown dim with grief;
my whole frame is but a shadow.
8Upright men are appalled at this;
the innocent are aroused against the ungodly.
9Nevertheless, the righteous will hold to their ways,
and those with clean hands will grow stronger.

10“But come on, all of you, try again!
I will not find a wise man among you.
11My days have passed, my plans are shattered,
and so are the desires of my heart.
12These men turn night into day;
in the face of darkness they say, ‘Light is near.’
13If the only home I hope for is the grave,[d]
if I spread out my bed in darkness,
14if I say to corruption, ‘You are my father,’
and to the worm, ‘My mother’ or ‘My sister,’
15where then is my hope?
Who can see any hope for me?
16Will it go down to the gates of death[d]?
Will we descend together into the dust?”

[d]13,16 Hebrew *Sheol*

Discovering the Word 1. In chapter 15 Eliphaz started the second round of speeches, trying once again to cut Job down to size. What words does Job use to emphasize that not only his friends but also God has become his enemy (16:7–14)? 2. In what sense could Job say his “prayer is pure” (16:17)? 3. What certainty is impressed on Job’s soul as he prays through his tears (16:18–21)? 4. Job looks to God for a pledge of security (17:3). How is it possible that Job could appeal for help from God when it is God who is apparently attacking him? 5. Look at Job 19:23–27. Bildad has had his second turn (chapter 18) at accusing Job. In what ways does this great breakthrough answer the deepest quest of his prayers?

Applying the Word 1. While discovering hope, Job must still exercise faith. Why is it important that the guarantees of our future should still require personal faith? 2. There are several images of God’s provision in this study: witness, advocate, intercessor, guarantor, redeemer-kinsman. Which one especially gives you hope? 3. What difference will this make to the uncertainties you face?

Responding in Prayer Bring your insecurities to your heavenly Guarantor.

Job 18—19

18 Then Bildad the Shuhite replied:

2“When will you end these speeches?
Be sensible, and then we can talk.
3Why are we regarded as cattle
and considered stupid in your sight?
4You who tear yourself to pieces in your anger,
is the earth to be abandoned for your sake?
Or must the rocks be moved from their place?

5“The lamp of the wicked is snuffed out;
the flame of his fire stops burning.
6The light in his tent becomes dark;
the lamp beside him goes out.
7The vigor of his step is weakened;
his own schemes throw him down.
8His feet thrust him into a net
and he wanders into its mesh.
9A trap seizes him by the heel;
a snare holds him fast.
10A noose is hidden for him on the ground;
a trap lies in his path.
11Terrors startle him on every side
and dog his every step.
12Calamity is hungry for him;
disaster is ready for him when he falls.
13It eats away parts of his skin;
death’s firstborn devours his limbs.
14He is torn from the security of his tent
and marched off to the king of terrors.
15Fire resides[e] in his tent;

[e]15 Or *Nothing he had remains*

burning sulfur is scattered over his
dwelling.
16His roots dry up below
and his branches wither above.
17The memory of him perishes from the earth;
he has no name in the land.
18He is driven from light into darkness
and is banished from the world.
19He has no offspring or descendants among his
people,
no survivor where once he lived.
20Men of the west are appalled at his fate;
men of the east are seized with horror.
21Surely such is the dwelling of an evil man;
such is the place of one who knows not
God."

19

Then Job replied:

2"How long will you torment me
and crush me with words?
3Ten times now you have reproached me;
shamelessly you attack me.
4If it is true that I have gone astray,
my error remains my concern alone.
5If indeed you would exalt yourselves above
me
and use my humiliation against me,
6then know that God has wronged me
and drawn his net around me.

7"Though I cry, 'I've been wronged!' I get no
response;
though I call for help, there is no justice.
8He has blocked my way so I cannot pass;
he has shrouded my paths in darkness.
9He has stripped me of my honor
and removed the crown from my head.
10He tears me down on every side till I am
gone;
he uproots my hope like a tree.
11His anger burns against me;
he counts me among his enemies.
12His troops advance in force;
they build a siege ramp against me
and encamp around my tent.

13"He has alienated my brothers from me;
my acquaintances are completely estranged
from me.
14My kinsmen have gone away;
my friends have forgotten me.
15My guests and my maidservants count me a
stranger;
they look upon me as an alien.
16I summon my servant, but he does not
answer,
though I beg him with my own mouth.
17My breath is offensive to my wife;
I am loathsome to my own brothers.
18Even the little boys scorn me;
when I appear, they ridicule me.
19All my intimate friends detest me;
those I love have turned against me.
20I am nothing but skin and bones;
I have escaped with only the skin of my
teeth.[f]

21"Have pity on me, my friends, have pity,
for the hand of God has struck me.
22Why do you pursue me as God does?
Will you never get enough of my flesh?

23"Oh, that my words were recorded,
that they were written on a scroll,
24that they were inscribed with an iron tool
on[g] lead,
or engraved in rock forever!
25I know that my Redeemer[h] lives,
and that in the end he will stand upon the
earth.[i]
26And after my skin has been destroyed,
yet[j] in[k] my flesh I will see God;
27I myself will see him
with my own eyes—I, and not another.
How my heart yearns within me!

28"If you say, 'How we will hound him,
since the root of the trouble lies in him,[l]'
29you should fear the sword yourselves;
for wrath will bring punishment by the
sword,
and then you will know that there is
judgment.[m]"

[f]20 *Or only my gums* [g]24 *Or and* [h]25 *Or defender* [i]25 *Or upon my grave* [j]26 *Or And after I awake, / though this ⌞body⌟ has been destroyed, / then* [k]26 *Or / apart from* [l]28 Many Hebrew manuscripts, Septuagint and Vulgate; most Hebrew manuscripts *me* [m]29 *Or / that you may come to know the Almighty*

7 / *Job 20—21*
The Problem of Pain

WARS, DISEASE, CONGENITAL deformities, earthquakes and the seismic disturbances in our daily lives—all of these leave us with questions about the goodness of God and his active control of the world. Job himself suffered economic, familial, physical and social disaster, so much so that he despaired of life and longed for death. How could a good God cause all this (as Job firmly believed), or even allow this (as most moderns would say)? The classic way of putting the matter is this: If God is all-powerful, he is not good; if he is good, he is not all-powerful.

Job will not get his answer in these chapters. Indeed, he does not get a satisfying theological answer even in the end when God finally speaks—he will get something even better! But his dialogue with his friend Zophar will push his thinking and praying a step closer to the belief that God's love is not confined to rewards and punishments.

Warming Up to God What have you witnessed or experienced in life that has made it difficult for you to believe there is a good God running the world?

Read Job 20—21.

---

20 Then Zophar the Naamathite replied:

2"My troubled thoughts prompt me to answer
because I am greatly disturbed.
3I hear a rebuke that dishonors me,
and my understanding inspires me to reply.

4"Surely you know how it has been from of old,
ever since man[n] was placed on the earth,
5that the mirth of the wicked is brief,
the joy of the godless lasts but a moment.
6Though his pride reaches to the heavens
and his head touches the clouds,
7he will perish forever, like his own dung;
those who have seen him will say, 'Where is he?'
8Like a dream he flies away, no more to be found,
banished like a vision of the night.
9The eye that saw him will not see him again;
his place will look on him no more.
10His children must make amends to the poor;
his own hands must give back his wealth.
11The youthful vigor that fills his bones
will lie with him in the dust.

12"Though evil is sweet in his mouth
and he hides it under his tongue,
13though he cannot bear to let it go
and keeps it in his mouth,
14yet his food will turn sour in his stomach;
it will become the venom of serpents within him.
15He will spit out the riches he swallowed;
God will make his stomach vomit them up.
16He will suck the poison of serpents;
the fangs of an adder will kill him.
17He will not enjoy the streams,
the rivers flowing with honey and cream.
18What he toiled for he must give back uneaten;
he will not enjoy the profit from his trading.
19For he has oppressed the poor and left them destitute;
he has seized houses he did not build.

20"Surely he will have no respite from his craving;
he cannot save himself by his treasure.
21Nothing is left for him to devour;
his prosperity will not endure.
22In the midst of his plenty, distress will overtake him;
the full force of misery will come upon him.
23When he has filled his belly,
God will vent his burning anger against him
and rain down his blows upon him.
24Though he flees from an iron weapon,
a bronze-tipped arrow pierces him.
25He pulls it out of his back,
the gleaming point out of his liver.
Terrors will come over him;
26 total darkness lies in wait for his treasures.

n4 Or *Adam*

A fire unfanned will consume him
and devour what is left in his tent.
27The heavens will expose his guilt;
the earth will rise up against him.
28A flood will carry off his house,
rushing waters[o] on the day of God's wrath.
29Such is the fate God allots the wicked,
the heritage appointed for them by God."

21 Then Job replied:

2"Listen carefully to my words;
let this be the consolation you give me.
3Bear with me while I speak,
and after I have spoken, mock on.

4"Is my complaint directed to man?
Why should I not be impatient?
5Look at me and be astonished;
clap your hand over your mouth.
6When I think about this, I am terrified;
trembling seizes my body.
7Why do the wicked live on,
growing old and increasing in power?
8They see their children established around them,
their offspring before their eyes.
9Their homes are safe and free from fear;
the rod of God is not upon them.
10Their bulls never fail to breed;
their cows calve and do not miscarry.
11They send forth their children as a flock;
their little ones dance about.
12They sing to the music of tambourine and harp;
they make merry to the sound of the flute.
13They spend their years in prosperity
and go down to the grave[p] in peace.[q]
14Yet they say to God, 'Leave us alone!
We have no desire to know your ways.
15Who is the Almighty, that we should serve him?
What would we gain by praying to him?'
16But their prosperity is not in their own hands,
so I stand aloof from the counsel of the wicked.

17"Yet how often is the lamp of the wicked snuffed out?
How often does calamity come upon them,
the fate God allots in his anger?
18How often are they like straw before the wind,
like chaff swept away by a gale?
19⌞It is said,⌟ 'God stores up a man's punishment for his sons.'
Let him repay the man himself, so that he will know it!
20Let his own eyes see his destruction;
let him drink of the wrath of the Almighty.[r]
21For what does he care about the family he leaves behind
when his allotted months come to an end?
22"Can anyone teach knowledge to God,
since he judges even the highest?
23One man dies in full vigor,
completely secure and at ease,
24his body[s] well nourished,
his bones rich with marrow.
25Another man dies in bitterness of soul,
never having enjoyed anything good.
26Side by side they lie in the dust,
and worms cover them both.

27"I know full well what you are thinking,
the schemes by which you would wrong me.
28You say, 'Where now is the great man's house,
the tents where wicked men lived?'
29Have you never questioned those who travel?
Have you paid no regard to their accounts—
30that the evil man is spared from the day of calamity,
that he is delivered from[t] the day of wrath?
31Who denounces his conduct to his face?
Who repays him for what he has done?
32He is carried to the grave,
and watch is kept over his tomb.
33The soil in the valley is sweet to him;
all men follow after him,
and a countless throng goes[u] before him.

34"So how can you console me with your nonsense?
Nothing is left of your answers but falsehood!"

[o] 28 Or *The possessions in his house will be carried off, / washed away*
[p] 13 Hebrew *Sheol* [q] 13 Or *in an instant* [r] 17-20 Verses 17 and 18 may be taken as exclamations and 19 and 20 as declarations.
[s] 24 The meaning of the Hebrew for this word is uncertain. [t] 30 Or *man is reserved for the day of calamity, / that he is brought forth to*
[u] 33 Or */ as a countless throng went*

Discovering the Word 1. What words and phrases are used to describe the wicked in chapter 20? 2. What is Zophar's view of God's righteousness? 3. How does Job's reality check in chapter 21 contrast with Zophar's view (20:29)? 4. Job 21:14-15 expresses the spiritual question the wicked might ask: "What would we gain by praying to him?" On the basis of the discussion thus far, how do you think Zophar would answer that question? 5. How would Job reply?

Applying the Word 1. It has been said that Job and the others were trying to fit together the pieces of a puzzle without having all the pieces. How can the discoveries Job is making (consider the last study too) help you deal with the problem of pain? 2. What have you learned in this study about helping people find answers to questions about the goodness of God?

Responding in Prayer Ask God to help you grow in your understanding of who he is and how he works in the world.

Job 22

22 Then Eliphaz the Temanite replied:

2"Can a man be of benefit to God?
Can even a wise man benefit him?
3What pleasure would it give the Almighty if you were righteous?
What would he gain if your ways were blameless?

4"Is it for your piety that he rebukes you
and brings charges against you?
5Is not your wickedness great?
Are not your sins endless?
6You demanded security from your brothers for no reason;
you stripped men of their clothing, leaving them naked.
7You gave no water to the weary
and you withheld food from the hungry,
8though you were a powerful man, owning land—
an honored man, living on it.
9And you sent widows away empty-handed
and broke the strength of the fatherless.
10That is why snares are all around you,
why sudden peril terrifies you,
11why it is so dark you cannot see,
and why a flood of water covers you.

12"Is not God in the heights of heaven?
And see how lofty are the highest stars!
13Yet you say, 'What does God know?
Does he judge through such darkness?
14Thick clouds veil him, so he does not see us
as he goes about in the vaulted heavens.'
15Will you keep to the old path
that evil men have trod?
16They were carried off before their time,
their foundations washed away by a flood.
17They said to God, 'Leave us alone!
What can the Almighty do to us?'
18Yet it was he who filled their houses with good things,
so I stand aloof from the counsel of the wicked.

19"The righteous see their ruin and rejoice;
the innocent mock them, saying,
20'Surely our foes are destroyed,
and fire devours their wealth.'

21"Submit to God and be at peace with him;
in this way prosperity will come to you.
22Accept instruction from his mouth
and lay up his words in your heart.
23If you return to the Almighty, you will be restored:
If you remove wickedness far from your tent
24and assign your nuggets to the dust,
your gold of Ophir to the rocks in the ravines,
25then the Almighty will be your gold,
the choicest silver for you.
26Surely then you will find delight in the Almighty
and will lift up your face to God.
27You will pray to him, and he will hear you,
and you will fulfill your vows.

28What you decide on will be done,
and light will shine on your ways.
29When men are brought low and you say, 'Lift
them up!'
then he will save the downcast.
30He will deliver even one who is not innocent,
who will be delivered through the cleanness
of your hands."

8 / *Job 23*
The Silence of God

WE HAVE ALL experienced someone's mindless chatter or withering judgment at a moment when we needed to be deeply understood. But when we listen—really listen—we "speak" with our ears. We communicate our respect, prize the person and encourage the movement of God in someone's life. Could it be that it's the same with God? Does he communicate his love to us sometimes by listening as we pour out our hearts, rather than finishing our sentences for us and telling us how to feel, what to do, where to go? For twenty-two chapters God has not spoken directly to Job. But God has listened in silence.

Warming Up to God Recall a time when a friend or family member really listened to you. How did you feel? How did that person's listening help you?

Read Job 23.

23 Then Job replied:

2"Even today my complaint is
bitter;
his hand[v] is heavy in spite of[w] my
groaning.
3If only I knew where to find him;
if only I could go to his dwelling!
4I would state my case before him
and fill my mouth with arguments.
5I would find out what he would answer me,
and consider what he would say.
6Would he oppose me with great power?
No, he would not press charges against me.
7There an upright man could present his case
before him,
and I would be delivered forever from my
judge.

8"But if I go to the east, he is not there;
if I go to the west, I do not find him.
9When he is at work in the north, I do not see
him;
when he turns to the south, I catch no
glimpse of him.
10But he knows the way that I take;
when he has tested me, I will come forth as
gold.
11My feet have closely followed his steps;
I have kept to his way without turning
aside.
12I have not departed from the commands of
his lips;
I have treasured the words of his mouth
more than my daily bread.

13"But he stands alone, and who can oppose
him?
He does whatever he pleases.
14He carries out his decree against me,
and many such plans he still has in store.
15That is why I am terrified before him;
when I think of all this, I fear him.
16God has made my heart faint;
the Almighty has terrified me.
17Yet I am not silenced by the darkness,
by the thick darkness that covers my face.

[v]2 Septuagint and Syriac; Hebrew / *the hand on me* [w]2 Or *heavy on me in*

Discovering the Word 1. What does Job now want more than anything (see also 29:4–5)? Why? 2. Why do you think Job finds God so elusive (vv. 8–9)? 3. Job longs for an opportunity to renew friendship with God and present his case, and he is not simply waiting passively. What has he been doing (vv. 10–12)?

4. What appears to be Job's main remaining problem in establishing his righteousness with God (vv. 13–17)? 5. How does Job's experience show the difference between a God who comforts through silence and an absent god who is not really there at all?

Applying the Word 1. Why do you think people sometimes find God unresponsive when they say they are seeking him wholeheartedly? 2. The Bible suggests that the people who received mystical experiences of God (Moses, Isaiah, John, and even Job—42:5) were not seeking an overwhelming encounter with God; these experiences were given by God at God's initiative. What does Job's case teach us about waiting? 3. How does Job's attitude help you to wait for God?

Responding in Prayer After you pray about the needs in your life, listen for God's response. Allow even silence to bring you comfort as you trust in his listening ear.

Job 24—34

24 "Why does the Almighty not set
times for judgment?
Why must those who know him
look in vain for such days?
2Men move boundary stones;
they pasture flocks they have stolen.
3They drive away the orphan's donkey
and take the widow's ox in pledge.
4They thrust the needy from the path
and force all the poor of the land into hiding.
5Like wild donkeys in the desert,
the poor go about their labor of foraging food;
the wasteland provides food for their children.
6They gather fodder in the fields
and glean in the vineyards of the wicked.
7Lacking clothes, they spend the night naked;
they have nothing to cover themselves in the cold.
8They are drenched by mountain rains
and hug the rocks for lack of shelter.
9The fatherless child is snatched from the breast;
the infant of the poor is seized for a debt.
10Lacking clothes, they go about naked;
they carry the sheaves, but still go hungry.
11They crush olives among the terraces[x];
they tread the winepresses, yet suffer thirst.
12The groans of the dying rise from the city,
and the souls of the wounded cry out for help.
But God charges no one with wrongdoing.

13"There are those who rebel against the light,
who do not know its ways
or stay in its paths.
14When daylight is gone, the murderer rises up
and kills the poor and needy;
in the night he steals forth like a thief.
15The eye of the adulterer watches for dusk;
he thinks, 'No eye will see me,'
and he keeps his face concealed.
16In the dark, men break into houses,
but by day they shut themselves in;
they want nothing to do with the light.
17For all of them, deep darkness is their morning[y];
they make friends with the terrors of darkness.[z]

18"Yet they are foam on the surface of the water;
their portion of the land is cursed,
so that no one goes to the vineyards.
19As heat and drought snatch away the melted snow,
so the grave[a] snatches away those who have sinned.
20The womb forgets them,
the worm feasts on them;
evil men are no longer remembered
but are broken like a tree.
21They prey on the barren and childless woman,
and to the widow show no kindness.
22But God drags away the mighty by his power;
though they become established, they have no assurance of life.

[x]11 Or *olives between the millstones*; the meaning of the Hebrew for this word is uncertain. [y]17 Or *them, their morning is like the shadow of death* [z]17 Or *of the shadow of death* [a]19 Hebrew *Sheol*

23He may let them rest in a feeling of security,
but his eyes are on their ways.
24For a little while they are exalted, and then they are gone;
they are brought low and gathered up like all others;
they are cut off like heads of grain.

25"If this is not so, who can prove me false
and reduce my words to nothing?"

25

Then Bildad the Shuhite replied:

2"Dominion and awe belong to God;
he establishes order in the heights of heaven.
3Can his forces be numbered?
Upon whom does his light not rise?
4How then can a man be righteous before God?
How can one born of woman be pure?
5If even the moon is not bright
and the stars are not pure in his eyes,
6how much less man, who is but a maggot—
a son of man, who is only a worm!"

26

Then Job replied:

2"How you have helped the powerless!
How you have saved the arm that is feeble!
3What advice you have offered to one without wisdom!
And what great insight you have displayed!
4Who has helped you utter these words?
And whose spirit spoke from your mouth?

5"The dead are in deep anguish,
those beneath the waters and all that live in them.
6Death[a] is naked before God;
Destruction[b] lies uncovered.
7He spreads out the northern ⌊skies⌋ over empty space;
he suspends the earth over nothing.
8He wraps up the waters in his clouds,
yet the clouds do not burst under their weight.
9He covers the face of the full moon,
spreading his clouds over it.
10He marks out the horizon on the face of the waters
for a boundary between light and darkness.
11The pillars of the heavens quake,
aghast at his rebuke.
12By his power he churned up the sea;
by his wisdom he cut Rahab to pieces.
13By his breath the skies became fair;
his hand pierced the gliding serpent.
14And these are but the outer fringe of his works;
how faint the whisper we hear of him!
Who then can understand the thunder of his power?"

27

And Job continued his discourse:

2"As surely as God lives, who has denied me justice,
the Almighty, who has made me taste bitterness of soul,
3as long as I have life within me,
the breath of God in my nostrils,
4my lips will not speak wickedness,
and my tongue will utter no deceit.
5I will never admit you are in the right;
till I die, I will not deny my integrity.
6I will maintain my righteousness and never let go of it;
my conscience will not reproach me as long as I live.

7"May my enemies be like the wicked,
my adversaries like the unjust!
8For what hope has the godless when he is cut off,
when God takes away his life?
9Does God listen to his cry
when distress comes upon him?
10Will he find delight in the Almighty?
Will he call upon God at all times?

11"I will teach you about the power of God;
the ways of the Almighty I will not conceal.
12You have all seen this yourselves.
Why then this meaningless talk?

13"Here is the fate God allots to the wicked,
the heritage a ruthless man receives from the Almighty:
14However many his children, their fate is the sword;
his offspring will never have enough to eat.
15The plague will bury those who survive him,

[a]6 Hebrew *Sheol* [b]6 Hebrew *Abaddon*

and their widows will not weep for them.
16Though he heaps up silver like dust
and clothes like piles of clay,
17what he lays up the righteous will wear,
and the innocent will divide his silver.
18The house he builds is like a moth's cocoon,
like a hut made by a watchman.
19He lies down wealthy, but will do so no more;
when he opens his eyes, all is gone.
20Terrors overtake him like a flood;
a tempest snatches him away in the night.
21The east wind carries him off, and he is gone;
it sweeps him out of his place.
22It hurls itself against him without mercy
as he flees headlong from its power.
23It claps its hands in derision
and hisses him out of his place.

28

"There is a mine for silver
and a place where gold is refined.
2Iron is taken from the earth,
and copper is smelted from ore.
3Man puts an end to the darkness;
he searches the farthest recesses
for ore in the blackest darkness.
4Far from where people dwell he cuts a shaft,
in places forgotten by the foot of man;
far from men he dangles and sways.
5The earth, from which food comes,
is transformed below as by fire;
6sapphires[c] come from its rocks,
and its dust contains nuggets of gold.
7No bird of prey knows that hidden path,
no falcon's eye has seen it.
8Proud beasts do not set foot on it,
and no lion prowls there.
9Man's hand assaults the flinty rock
and lays bare the roots of the mountains.
10He tunnels through the rock;
his eyes see all its treasures.
11He searches[d] the sources of the rivers
and brings hidden things to light.

12"But where can wisdom be found?
Where does understanding dwell?
13Man does not comprehend its worth;
it cannot be found in the land of the living.
14The deep says, 'It is not in me';
the sea says, 'It is not with me.'
15It cannot be bought with the finest gold,
nor can its price be weighed in silver.
16It cannot be bought with the gold of Ophir,
with precious onyx or sapphires.
17Neither gold nor crystal can compare with it,
nor can it be had for jewels of gold.
18Coral and jasper are not worthy of mention;
the price of wisdom is beyond rubies.
19The topaz of Cush cannot compare with it;
it cannot be bought with pure gold.

20"Where then does wisdom come from?
Where does understanding dwell?
21It is hidden from the eyes of every living thing,
concealed even from the birds of the air.
22Destruction[e] and Death say,
'Only a rumor of it has reached our ears.'
23God understands the way to it
and he alone knows where it dwells,
24for he views the ends of the earth
and sees everything under the heavens.
25When he established the force of the wind
and measured out the waters,
26when he made a decree for the rain
and a path for the thunderstorm,
27then he looked at wisdom and appraised it;
he confirmed it and tested it.
28And he said to man,
'The fear of the Lord—that is wisdom,
and to shun evil is understanding.'"

29

Job continued his discourse:
2"How I long for the months gone by,
for the days when God watched over me,
3when his lamp shone upon my head
and by his light I walked through darkness!
4Oh, for the days when I was in my prime,
when God's intimate friendship blessed my house,
5when the Almighty was still with me
and my children were around me,
6when my path was drenched with cream
and the rock poured out for me streams of olive oil.

7"When I went to the gate of the city
and took my seat in the public square,
8the young men saw me and stepped aside
and the old men rose to their feet;
9the chief men refrained from speaking
and covered their mouths with their hands;

[c]6 Or *lapis lazuli*; also in verse 16 [d]11 Septuagint, Aquila and Vulgate; Hebrew *He dams up* [e]22 Hebrew *Abaddon*

for my door was always open to the
traveler—
33 if I have concealed my sin as men do,[m]
by hiding my guilt in my heart
34 because I so feared the crowd
and so dreaded the contempt of the clans
that I kept silent and would not go outside

35 ("Oh, that I had someone to hear me!
I sign now my defense—let the Almighty
answer me;
let my accuser put his indictment in
writing.
36 Surely I would wear it on my shoulder,
I would put it on like a crown.
37 I would give him an account of my every
step;
like a prince I would approach him.)—
38 "if my land cries out against me
and all its furrows are wet with tears,
39 if I have devoured its yield without payment
or broken the spirit of its tenants,
40 then let briers come up instead of wheat
and weeds instead of barley."

The words of Job are ended.

32

So these three men stopped an-
swering Job, because he was righ-
teous in his own eyes. 2 But Elihu
son of Barakel the Buzite, of the family of Ram,
became very angry with Job for justifying himself
rather than God. 3 He was also angry with the
three friends, because they had found no way to
refute Job, and yet had condemned him.[n] 4 Now
Elihu had waited before speaking to Job because
they were older than he. 5 But when he saw that
the three men had nothing more to say, his anger
was aroused.

6 So Elihu son of Barakel the Buzite said:

"I am young in years,
and you are old;
that is why I was fearful,
not daring to tell you what I know.
7 I thought, 'Age should speak;
advanced years should teach wisdom.'
8 But it is the spirit[o] in a man,
the breath of the Almighty, that gives him
understanding.
9 It is not only the old[p] who are wise,
not only the aged who understand what is
right.

10 "Therefore I say: Listen to me;
I too will tell you what I know.
11 I waited while you spoke,
I listened to your reasoning;
while you were searching for words,
12 I gave you my full attention.
But not one of you has proved Job wrong;
none of you has answered his arguments.
13 Do not say, 'We have found wisdom;
let God refute him, not man.'
14 But Job has not marshaled his words against
me,
and I will not answer him with your
arguments.

15 "They are dismayed and have no more to say;
words have failed them.
16 Must I wait, now that they are silent,
now that they stand there with no reply?
17 I too will have my say;
I too will tell what I know.
18 For I am full of words,
and the spirit within me compels me;
19 inside I am like bottled-up wine,
like new wineskins ready to burst.
20 I must speak and find relief;
I must open my lips and reply.
21 I will show partiality to no one,
nor will I flatter any man;
22 for if I were skilled in flattery,
my Maker would soon take me away.

33

"But now, Job, listen to my
words;
pay attention to everything I say.
2 I am about to open my mouth;
my words are on the tip of my tongue.
3 My words come from an upright heart;
my lips sincerely speak what I know.
4 The Spirit of God has made me;
the breath of the Almighty gives me life.
5 Answer me then, if you can;
prepare yourself and confront me.
6 I am just like you before God;
I too have been taken from clay.
7 No fear of me should alarm you,
nor should my hand be heavy upon you.

8 "But you have said in my hearing—
I heard the very words—

m33 Or *as Adam did* n3 Masoretic Text; an ancient Hebrew scribal tradition *Job, and so had condemned God* o8 Or *Spirit*; also in verse 18 p9 Or *many*; or *great*

9'I am pure and without sin;
I am clean and free from guilt.
10Yet God has found fault with me;
he considers me his enemy.
11He fastens my feet in shackles;
he keeps close watch on all my paths.'

12"But I tell you, in this you are not right,
for God is greater than man.
13Why do you complain to him
that he answers none of man's words[q]?
14For God does speak—now one way, now
another—
though man may not perceive it.
15In a dream, in a vision of the night,
when deep sleep falls on men
as they slumber in their beds,
16he may speak in their ears
and terrify them with warnings,
17to turn man from wrongdoing
and keep him from pride,
18to preserve his soul from the pit,[r]
his life from perishing by the sword.[s]
19Or a man may be chastened on a bed of pain
with constant distress in his bones,
20so that his very being finds food repulsive
and his soul loathes the choicest meal.
21His flesh wastes away to nothing,
and his bones, once hidden, now stick out.
22His soul draws near to the pit,[t]
and his life to the messengers of death.[u]

23"Yet if there is an angel on his side
as a mediator, one out of a thousand,
to tell a man what is right for him,
24to be gracious to him and say,
'Spare him from going down to the pit[v];
I have found a ransom for him'—
25then his flesh is renewed like a child's;
it is restored as in the days of his youth.
26He prays to God and finds favor with him,
he sees God's face and shouts for joy;
he is restored by God to his righteous state.
27Then he comes to men and says,
'I sinned, and perverted what was right,
but I did not get what I deserved.
28He redeemed my soul from going down to the
pit,[w]
and I will live to enjoy the light.'

29"God does all these things to a man—
twice, even three times—
30to turn back his soul from the pit,[x]
that the light of life may shine on him.

31"Pay attention, Job, and listen to me;
be silent, and I will speak.
32If you have anything to say, answer me;
speak up, for I want you to be cleared.
33But if not, then listen to me;
be silent, and I will teach you wisdom."

34

Then Elihu said:

2"Hear my words, you wise men;
listen to me, you men of learning.
3For the ear tests words
as the tongue tastes food.
4Let us discern for ourselves what is right;
let us learn together what is good.

5"Job says, 'I am innocent,
but God denies me justice.
6Although I am right,
I am considered a liar;
although I am guiltless,
his arrow inflicts an incurable wound.'
7What man is like Job,
who drinks scorn like water?
8He keeps company with evildoers;
he associates with wicked men.
9For he says, 'It profits a man nothing
when he tries to please God.'

10"So listen to me, you men of understanding.
Far be it from God to do evil,
from the Almighty to do wrong.
11He repays a man for what he has done;
he brings upon him what his conduct
deserves.
12It is unthinkable that God would do wrong,
that the Almighty would pervert justice.
13Who appointed him over the earth?
Who put him in charge of the whole
world?
14If it were his intention
and he withdrew his spirit[y] and breath,
15all mankind would perish together
and man would return to the dust.

16"If you have understanding, hear this;
listen to what I say.
17Can he who hates justice govern?
Will you condemn the just and mighty One?

[q]13 *Or that he does not answer for any of his actions* [r]18 *Or preserve him from the grave* [s]18 *Or from crossing the River* [t]22 *Or He draws near to the grave* [u]22 *Or to the dead* [v]24 *Or grave* [w]28 *Or redeemed me from going down to the grave* [x]30 *Or turn him back from the grave* [y]14 *Or Spirit*

[18]Is he not the One who says to kings, 'You are worthless,'
and to nobles, 'You are wicked,'
[19]who shows no partiality to princes
and does not favor the rich over the poor,
for they are all the work of his hands?
[20]They die in an instant, in the middle of the night;
the people are shaken and they pass away;
the mighty are removed without human hand.

[21]"His eyes are on the ways of men;
he sees their every step.
[22]There is no dark place, no deep shadow,
where evildoers can hide.
[23]God has no need to examine men further,
that they should come before him for judgment.
[24]Without inquiry he shatters the mighty
and sets up others in their place.
[25]Because he takes note of their deeds,
he overthrows them in the night and they are crushed.
[26]He punishes them for their wickedness
where everyone can see them,
[27]because they turned from following him
and had no regard for any of his ways.
[28]They caused the cry of the poor to come before him,
so that he heard the cry of the needy.
[29]But if he remains silent, who can condemn him?
If he hides his face, who can see him?
Yet he is over man and nation alike,
30 to keep a godless man from ruling,
from laying snares for the people.

[31]"Suppose a man says to God,
'I am guilty but will offend no more.
[32]Teach me what I cannot see;
if I have done wrong, I will not do so again.'
[33]Should God then reward you on your terms,
when you refuse to repent?
You must decide, not I;
so tell me what you know.

[34]"Men of understanding declare,
wise men who hear me say to me,
[35]'Job speaks without knowledge;
his words lack insight.'
[36]Oh, that Job might be tested to the utmost
for answering like a wicked man!
[37]To his sin he adds rebellion;
scornfully he claps his hands among us
and multiplies his words against God."

9 / *Job 35*
Songs in the Night

KIERKEGAARD ONCE SAID that whatever it may be that one comes to as a matter of course because of aging, it is not wisdom. So we see that Job's three friends, all senior, have tried to explain Job's suffering and to defend God. Now a young man, Elihu, comes into the picture. Elihu waited in the sidelines because, as he says, "Age should speak" (32:7). He is exasperated with Eliphaz, Bildad and Zophar because they have failed to deal adequately with Job. But he is also angry with Job "for justifying himself rather than God" (32:2). So he jumps into the discussion offering his only slightly revised version of the stock answers, with one important variation.

Warming Up to God Recall a situation in your life when someone "jumped to a conclusion." How did you feel?

Read Job 35.

35 Then Elihu said:

[2]"Do you think this is just?
You say, 'I will be cleared by God.[z]'
[3]Yet you ask him, 'What profit is it to me,[a]
and what do I gain by not sinning?'

[z]2 Or *My righteousness is more than God's* [a]3 Or *you*

4 “I would like to reply to you
and to your friends with you.
5 Look up at the heavens and see;
gaze at the clouds so high above you.
6 If you sin, how does that affect him?
If your sins are many, what does that do to him?
7 If you are righteous, what do you give to him,
or what does he receive from your hand?
8 Your wickedness affects only a man like yourself,
and your righteousness only the sons of men.

9 “Men cry out under a load of oppression;
they plead for relief from the arm of the powerful.
10 But no one says, ‘Where is God my Maker,
who gives songs in the night,
11 who teaches more to us than to[b] the beasts of the earth
and makes us wiser than[c] the birds of the air?’
12 He does not answer when men cry out
because of the arrogance of the wicked.
13 Indeed, God does not listen to their empty plea;
the Almighty pays no attention to it.
14 How much less, then, will he listen
when you say that you do not see him,
that your case is before him
and you must wait for him,
15 and further, that his anger never punishes
and he does not take the least notice of wickedness.[d]
16 So Job opens his mouth with empty talk;
without knowledge he multiplies words.”

[b] 11 Or *teaches us by* [c] 11 Or *us wise by* [d] 15 Symmachus, Theodotion and Vulgate; the meaning of the Hebrew for this word is uncertain.

Discovering the Word 1. In verse 3 Elihu claims that Job wants to know “What profit is it to me, and what do I gain by not sinning?” yet Job has never said this. Why is this question important to the discussion? 2. How does Elihu answer the question he poses (vv. 4–8)? 3. From verses 1–8 what is Elihu’s view of God? 4. In verses 9–16 Elihu deals with a second question—one that *was* asked by Job: Why doesn’t God answer prayer? What is Elihu’s answer to this question? 5. Why does Elihu’s “ministry” not offer any substantial help to Job?

Applying the Word 1. Not all of Elihu’s advice is misguided. He does propose that God, if he were sought, would give cheer and comfort in the night when things seem more hopeless than ever (35:10). When, if ever, have you received from God a “song in the night”? 2. Chapter 36 is the last passage in which Job’s friends attempt to explain his situation and comfort him. What have you learned about ministering to people in distress?

Responding in Prayer Praise God for bringing us hope even in the midst of pain.

Job 36—37

36

Elihu continued:

2 “Bear with me a little longer and I will show you
that there is more to be said in God’s behalf.
3 I get my knowledge from afar;
I will ascribe justice to my Maker.
4 Be assured that my words are not false;
one perfect in knowledge is with you.

5 “God is mighty, but does not despise men;
he is mighty, and firm in his purpose.
6 He does not keep the wicked alive
but gives the afflicted their rights.
7 He does not take his eyes off the righteous;
he enthrones them with kings
and exalts them forever.
8 But if men are bound in chains,
held fast by cords of affliction,
9 he tells them what they have done—
that they have sinned arrogantly.
10 He makes them listen to correction
and commands them to repent of their evil.

[11]If they obey and serve him,
they will spend the rest of their days in prosperity
and their years in contentment.
[12]But if they do not listen,
they will perish by the sword[e]
and die without knowledge.

[13]"The godless in heart harbor resentment;
even when he fetters them, they do not cry for help.
[14]They die in their youth,
among male prostitutes of the shrines.
[15]But those who suffer he delivers in their suffering;
he speaks to them in their affliction.

[16]"He is wooing you from the jaws of distress
to a spacious place free from restriction,
to the comfort of your table laden with choice food.
[17]But now you are laden with the judgment due the wicked;
judgment and justice have taken hold of you.
[18]Be careful that no one entices you by riches;
do not let a large bribe turn you aside.
[19]Would your wealth
or even all your mighty efforts
sustain you so you would not be in distress?
[20]Do not long for the night,
to drag people away from their homes.[f]
[21]Beware of turning to evil,
which you seem to prefer to affliction.

[22]"God is exalted in his power.
Who is a teacher like him?
[23]Who has prescribed his ways for him,
or said to him, 'You have done wrong'?
[24]Remember to extol his work,
which men have praised in song.
[25]All mankind has seen it;
men gaze on it from afar.
[26]How great is God—beyond our understanding!
The number of his years is past finding out.

[27]"He draws up the drops of water,
which distill as rain to the streams[g];
[28]the clouds pour down their moisture
and abundant showers fall on mankind.
[29]Who can understand how he spreads out the clouds,
how he thunders from his pavilion?
[30]See how he scatters his lightning about him,
bathing the depths of the sea.
[31]This is the way he governs[h] the nations
and provides food in abundance.
[32]He fills his hands with lightning
and commands it to strike its mark.
[33]His thunder announces the coming storm;
even the cattle make known its approach.[i]

37

"At this my heart pounds
and leaps from its place.
[2]Listen! Listen to the roar of his voice,
to the rumbling that comes from his mouth.
[3]He unleashes his lightning beneath the whole heaven
and sends it to the ends of the earth.
[4]After that comes the sound of his roar;
he thunders with his majestic voice.
When his voice resounds,
he holds nothing back.
[5]God's voice thunders in marvelous ways;
he does great things beyond our understanding.
[6]He says to the snow, 'Fall on the earth,'
and to the rain shower, 'Be a mighty downpour.'
[7]So that all men he has made may know his work,
he stops every man from his labor.[j]
[8]The animals take cover;
they remain in their dens.
[9]The tempest comes out from its chamber,
the cold from the driving winds.
[10]The breath of God produces ice,
and the broad waters become frozen.
[11]He loads the clouds with moisture;
he scatters his lightning through them.
[12]At his direction they swirl around
over the face of the whole earth
to do whatever he commands them.
[13]He brings the clouds to punish men,
or to water his earth[k] and show his love.

[14]"Listen to this, Job;
stop and consider God's wonders.
[15]Do you know how God controls the clouds

[e]12 Or *will cross the River* [f]20 The meaning of the Hebrew for verses 18-20 is uncertain. [g]27 Or *distill from the mist as rain* [h]31 Or *nourishes* [i]33 Or *announces his coming— / the One zealous against evil* [j]7 Or */ he fills all men with fear by his power* [k]13 Or *to favor them*

and makes his lightning flash?
16Do you know how the clouds hang poised,
those wonders of him who is perfect in knowledge?
17You who swelter in your clothes
when the land lies hushed under the south wind,
18can you join him in spreading out the skies,
hard as a mirror of cast bronze?
19"Tell us what we should say to him;
we cannot draw up our case because of our darkness.
20Should he be told that I want to speak?
Would any man ask to be swallowed up?
21Now no one can look at the sun,
bright as it is in the skies
after the wind has swept them clean.
22Out of the north he comes in golden splendor;
God comes in awesome majesty.
23The Almighty is beyond our reach and exalted in power;
in his justice and great righteousness, he does not oppress.
24Therefore, men revere him,
for does he not have regard for all the wise in heart?[l]"

[l]24 Or *for he does not have regard for any who think they are wise.*

10/ *Job 38*
God in the Storm

SURPRISE IS ONE thing you can count on when dealing with the living God. We have had thirty-seven chapters of gut-wrenching dialogue between Job and his friends, heart-rending prayers by Job to his elusive God, and life-and-death questions hurled by Job at God to make sense of the suffering of the innocent. Job, we think, deserves a comprehensive answer from the supreme Being of the universe. He gets a surprise. For four chapters God speaks in the whirlwind. This is no "still small voice" speaking. God is thundering. But what he thunders is *more questions.*

Warming Up to God What experiences of God have led you to worship?

Read Job 38.

38 Then the LORD answered Job out of the storm. He said:

2"Who is this that darkens my counsel
with words without knowledge?
3Brace yourself like a man;
I will question you,
and you shall answer me.

4"Where were you when I laid the earth's foundation?
Tell me, if you understand.
5Who marked off its dimensions? Surely you know!
Who stretched a measuring line across it?
6On what were its footings set,
or who laid its cornerstone—
7while the morning stars sang together
and all the angels[m] shouted for joy?

8"Who shut up the sea behind doors
when it burst forth from the womb,
9when I made the clouds its garment
and wrapped it in thick darkness,
10when I fixed limits for it
and set its doors and bars in place,
11when I said, 'This far you may come and no farther;
here is where your proud waves halt'?

12"Have you ever given orders to the morning,
or shown the dawn its place,
13that it might take the earth by the edges
and shake the wicked out of it?
14The earth takes shape like clay under a seal;
its features stand out like those of a garment.
15The wicked are denied their light,
and their upraised arm is broken.

[m]7 Hebrew *the sons of God*

16"Have you journeyed to the springs of the sea
or walked in the recesses of the deep?
17Have the gates of death been shown to you?
Have you seen the gates of the shadow of death[n]?
18Have you comprehended the vast expanses of the earth?
Tell me, if you know all this.

19"What is the way to the abode of light?
And where does darkness reside?
20Can you take them to their places?
Do you know the paths to their dwellings?
21Surely you know, for you were already born!
You have lived so many years!

22"Have you entered the storehouses of the snow
or seen the storehouses of the hail,
23which I reserve for times of trouble,
for days of war and battle?
24What is the way to the place where the lightning is dispersed,
or the place where the east winds are scattered over the earth?
25Who cuts a channel for the torrents of rain,
and a path for the thunderstorm,
26to water a land where no man lives,
a desert with no one in it,
27to satisfy a desolate wasteland
and make it sprout with grass?
28Does the rain have a father?
Who fathers the drops of dew?
29From whose womb comes the ice?
Who gives birth to the frost from the heavens
30when the waters become hard as stone,
when the surface of the deep is frozen?

31"Can you bind the beautiful[o] Pleiades?
Can you loose the cords of Orion?
32Can you bring forth the constellations in their seasons[p]
or lead out the Bear[q] with its cubs?
33Do you know the laws of the heavens?
Can you set up ⌊God's[r]⌋ dominion over the earth?

34"Can you raise your voice to the clouds
and cover yourself with a flood of water?
35Do you send the lightning bolts on their way?
Do they report to you, 'Here we are'?
36Who endowed the heart[s] with wisdom
or gave understanding to the mind[s]?
37Who has the wisdom to count the clouds?
Who can tip over the water jars of the heavens
38when the dust becomes hard
and the clods of earth stick together?

39"Do you hunt the prey for the lioness
and satisfy the hunger of the lions
40when they crouch in their dens
or lie in wait in a thicket?
41Who provides food for the raven
when its young cry out to God
and wander about for lack of food?

[n]17 Or *gates of deep shadows* [o]31 Or *the twinkling;* or *the chains of the* [p]32 Or *the morning star in its season* [q]32 Or *out Leo* [r]33 Or *his;* or *their* [s]36 The meaning of the Hebrew for this word is uncertain.

Discovering the Word 1. What common theme do all of God's questions have? 2. Why does God emphasize that Job was not around when he created the world (vv. 4–7)? 3. God lists more things that Job *cannot* do in verses 8–41. What kinds of things are under God's control? 4. What purpose can God have in telling Job that God does things which no human being will ever appreciate or even see? 5. What effect will all these questions have on Job's view of himself and of God?

Applying the Word 1. Do you think that in every complaint against God there is an implicit revolt against our being creatures? Explain. 2. Why do you think it is sometimes more important in our spiritual journey to get more questions than answers? 3. How have questions helped you to grow spiritually?

Responding in Prayer Thank God for allowing you to freely come to him with your questions.

Job 39

39 "Do you know when the
mountain goats give birth?
Do you watch when the doe bears
her fawn?
2Do you count the months till they bear?
Do you know the time they give birth?
3They crouch down and bring forth their young;
their labor pains are ended.
4Their young thrive and grow strong in the wilds;
they leave and do not return.

5"Who let the wild donkey go free?
Who untied his ropes?
6I gave him the wasteland as his home,
the salt flats as his habitat.
7He laughs at the commotion in the town;
he does not hear a driver's shout.
8He ranges the hills for his pasture
and searches for any green thing.

9"Will the wild ox consent to serve you?
Will he stay by your manger at night?
10Can you hold him to the furrow with a
harness?
Will he till the valleys behind you?
11Will you rely on him for his great strength?
Will you leave your heavy work to him?
12Can you trust him to bring in your grain
and gather it to your threshing floor?

13"The wings of the ostrich flap joyfully,
but they cannot compare with the pinions
and feathers of the stork.
14She lays her eggs on the ground
and lets them warm in the sand,
15unmindful that a foot may crush them,
that some wild animal may trample them.
16She treats her young harshly, as if they were
not hers;
she cares not that her labor was in vain,
17for God did not endow her with wisdom
or give her a share of good sense.
18Yet when she spreads her feathers to run,
she laughs at horse and rider.

19"Do you give the horse his strength
or clothe his neck with a flowing mane?
20Do you make him leap like a locust,
striking terror with his proud snorting?
21He paws fiercely, rejoicing in his strength,
and charges into the fray.
22He laughs at fear, afraid of nothing;
he does not shy away from the sword.
23The quiver rattles against his side,
along with the flashing spear and lance.
24In frenzied excitement he eats up the ground;
he cannot stand still when the trumpet
sounds.
25At the blast of the trumpet he snorts, 'Aha!'
He catches the scent of battle from afar,
the shout of commanders and the battle cry.

26"Does the hawk take flight by your wisdom
and spread his wings toward the south?
27Does the eagle soar at your command
and build his nest on high?
28He dwells on a cliff and stays there at night;
a rocky crag is his stronghold.
29From there he seeks out his food;
his eyes detect it from afar.
30His young ones feast on blood,
and where the slain are, there is he."

11 / *Job 40*

The Joy of Repentance

HARDLY ANYONE WOULD speak of repentance as desirable. But it is! Repentance is not joyless self-hatred but blessed God-discovery. Repentance is the experience of coming home. In this climactic chapter Job finally repents. *But of what?* That surely is one of the burning questions evoked by the book, the answer to which will provide a profound clue for our own spiritual journeys. Job is an exemplary saint (1:8) and has thus far rightly resisted caving in to his friends' insistence that he repent of a long list of moral failures. But Job is not exempt from the need to repent.

Warming Up to God How do you feel when someone tells you, "You *must* repent"?

Read Job 40.

40 The LORD said to Job:

2"Will the one who contends
with the Almighty correct him?
Let him who accuses God answer him!"

3Then Job answered the LORD:

4"I am unworthy—how can I reply to you?
I put my hand over my mouth.
5I spoke once, but I have no answer—
twice, but I will say no more."

6Then the LORD spoke to Job out of the storm:

7"Brace yourself like a man;
I will question you,
and you shall answer me.

8"Would you discredit my justice?
Would you condemn me to justify
yourself?
9Do you have an arm like God's,
and can your voice thunder like his?
10Then adorn yourself with glory and splendor,
and clothe yourself in honor and majesty.
11Unleash the fury of your wrath,
look at every proud man and bring him
low,
12look at every proud man and humble him,
crush the wicked where they stand.
13Bury them all in the dust together;
shroud their faces in the grave.
14Then I myself will admit to you
that your own right hand can save you.

15"Look at the behemoth,[t]
which I made along with you
and which feeds on grass like an ox.
16What strength he has in his loins,
what power in the muscles of his belly!
17His tail[u] sways like a cedar;
the sinews of his thighs are close-knit.
18His bones are tubes of bronze,
his limbs like rods of iron.
19He ranks first among the works of God,
yet his Maker can approach him with his
sword.
20The hills bring him their produce,
and all the wild animals play nearby.
21Under the lotus plants he lies,
hidden among the reeds in the marsh.
22The lotuses conceal him in their shadow;
the poplars by the stream surround him.
23When the river rages, he is not alarmed;
he is secure, though the Jordan should
surge against his mouth.
24Can anyone capture him by the eyes,[v]
or trap him and pierce his nose?

[t]15 Possibly the hippopotamus or the elephant [u]17 Possibly trunk
[v]24 Or *by a water hole*

Discovering the Word 1. What three words does God use to describe what Job has been doing up until now (v. 2)? 2. Describe Job's first response to God's self-revelation (vv. 3–5). 3. What indication is there in verses 6–14 that Job has not fully repented even though he is in a more subdued frame of mind? 4. How has Job discredited God in his attempt to justify himself (v. 8)? 5. Through what means does God expand Job's grasp of his personal dilemma (vv. 15–24)?

Applying the Word 1. What have you learned from this passage about true repentance? 2. In what area of your life do you need to come to full repentance?

Responding in Prayer St. Teresa said, "As I see it, we shall never succeed in knowing ourselves unless we seek to know God." Reflect on this thought as you come before God in repentance.

Job 41

41 "Can you pull in the leviathan[w]
with a fishhook
or tie down his tongue with a
rope?
2Can you put a cord through his nose
or pierce his jaw with a hook?
3Will he keep begging you for mercy?
Will he speak to you with gentle words?
4Will he make an agreement with you
for you to take him as your slave for life?
5Can you make a pet of him like a bird
or put him on a leash for your girls?
6Will traders barter for him?
Will they divide him up among the
merchants?
7Can you fill his hide with harpoons
or his head with fishing spears?
8If you lay a hand on him,
you will remember the struggle and never
do it again!
9Any hope of subduing him is false;
the mere sight of him is overpowering.
10No one is fierce enough to rouse him.
Who then is able to stand against me?
11Who has a claim against me that I must pay?
Everything under heaven belongs to me.

12"I will not fail to speak of his limbs,
his strength and his graceful form.
13Who can strip off his outer coat?
Who would approach him with a bridle?
14Who dares open the doors of his mouth,
ringed about with his fearsome teeth?
15His back has[x] rows of shields
tightly sealed together;
16each is so close to the next
that no air can pass between.
17They are joined fast to one another;
they cling together and cannot be parted.
18His snorting throws out flashes of light;
his eyes are like the rays of dawn.
19Firebrands stream from his mouth;
sparks of fire shoot out.
20Smoke pours from his nostrils
as from a boiling pot over a fire of reeds.
21His breath sets coals ablaze,
and flames dart from his mouth.
22Strength resides in his neck;
dismay goes before him.
23The folds of his flesh are tightly joined;
they are firm and immovable.
24His chest is hard as rock,
hard as a lower millstone.
25When he rises up, the mighty are terrified;
they retreat before his thrashing.
26The sword that reaches him has no effect,
nor does the spear or the dart or the
javelin.
27Iron he treats like straw
and bronze like rotten wood.
28Arrows do not make him flee;
slingstones are like chaff to him.
29A club seems to him but a piece of straw;
he laughs at the rattling of the lance.
30His undersides are jagged potsherds,
leaving a trail in the mud like a threshing
sledge.
31He makes the depths churn like a boiling
caldron
and stirs up the sea like a pot of ointment.
32Behind him he leaves a glistening wake;
one would think the deep had white hair.
33Nothing on earth is his equal—
a creature without fear.
34He looks down on all that are haughty;
he is king over all that are proud."

w1 Possibly the crocodile x15 Or *His pride is his*

12 / *Job 42*
Is Faith Always Worthwhile?

SO WHAT DO we get out of faith? Money? Power? Success? Every believer comes to these questions at some time or other. It is, after all, Satan's question in the first chapter. And so the fateful test is designed—the test to see whether Job's faith is without any ulterior motive or, as Satan believes, merely a commercial contract rather than a covenant of belonging. After Job prays for his friends, he has his fortune restored and is given a new family. The story ends with Job living happily ever after and dying "old and full of years." But was Satan right? Is unselfish faith possible? or even desirable?

Warming Up to God How do you react when you hear someone talking about the benefits of following Jesus (such as health and wealth) when you have never received some of these blessings?

Read Job 42.

42 Then Job replied to the LORD:

2"I know that you can do all things;
no plan of yours can be thwarted.
3⌞You asked,⌟ 'Who is this that obscures my counsel without knowledge?'
Surely I spoke of things I did not understand,
things too wonderful for me to know.

4⌞"You said,⌟ 'Listen now, and I will speak;
I will question you,
and you shall answer me.'
5My ears had heard of you
but now my eyes have seen you.
6Therefore I despise myself
and repent in dust and ashes."

7After the LORD had said these things to Job, he
said to Eliphaz the Temanite, "I am angry with
you and your two friends, because you have not
spoken of me what is right, as my servant Job has.
8So now take seven bulls and seven rams and go
to my servant Job and sacrifice a burnt offering
for yourselves. My servant Job will pray for you,
and I will accept his prayer and not deal with you
according to your folly. You have not spoken of
me what is right, as my servant Job has." 9So Eli-
phaz the Temanite, Bildad the Shuhite and Zo-
phar the Naamathite did what the LORD told them;
and the LORD accepted Job's prayer.
10After Job had prayed for his friends, the LORD
made him prosperous again and gave him twice
as much as he had before. 11All his brothers and
sisters and everyone who had known him before
came and ate with him in his house. They com-
forted and consoled him over all the trouble the
LORD had brought upon him, and each one gave
him a piece of silver[y] and a gold ring.
12The LORD blessed the latter part of Job's life
more than the first. He had fourteen thousand
sheep, six thousand camels, a thousand yoke of
oxen and a thousand donkeys. 13And he also had
seven sons and three daughters. 14The first
daughter he named Jemimah, the second Keziah
and the third Keren-Happuch. 15Nowhere in all
the land were there found women as beautiful as
Job's daughters, and their father granted them an
inheritance along with their brothers.
16After this, Job lived a hundred and forty
years; he saw his children and their children to
the fourth generation. 17And so he died, old and
full of years.

y11 Hebrew *him a kesitah*; a kesitah was a unit of money of unknown weight and value.

Discovering the Word 1. After God's speech in 40:15—41:34, Job is moved to full repentance. What words does Job use to describe his direct experience of God (vv. 1–6)? 2. What does Job now know about God and about himself? 3. What do verses 7–17 say about God's evaluation of each of the characters in the drama? 4. Job's friends would probably have agreed with all that God said to Job in chapters 38—41. Why is God angry with them? 5. In what sense has Job spoken of what is right about God (v. 7)? 6. How do you think Job would now answer the question "Why are you suffering?"

Applying the Word 1. In what sense may suffering Christians look forward to the blessing of God? 2. What have you learned through this study about loving God for God's sake?

Responding in Prayer Praise God for what you have learned about him and the way he works in the world through the book of Job.

Psalms

People look into mirrors to see how they look; they look into the Psalms to find out who they are. With a mirror we detect a new wrinkle here, an old wart there. We use a mirror when shaving or applying makeup to improve, if we can, the face we present to the world. With the Psalms we bring into awareness an ancient sorrow, we release a latent joy. We use the Psalms to present ourselves before God as honestly and thoroughly as we are able. A mirror shows us the shape of our nose and the curve of our chin, things we otherwise know only through the reports of others. The Psalms show us the shape of our souls and the curve of our sin, realities deep within us, hidden and obscured, for which we need focus and names.

The Psalms are poetry and the Psalms are prayer. These two features, the poetry and the prayer, need to be kept in mind always. If either is forgotten the Psalms will not only be misunderstood but misused.

Poetry is language used with intensity. It is not, as so many suppose, decorative speech. Poets tell us what our eyes, blurred with too much gawking, and our ears, dulled with too much chatter, miss around and within us. Poets use words to drag us into the depths of reality itself, not by reporting on how life is but by pushing/pulling us into the middle of it. Poetry gets at the heart of existence. Far from being cosmetic language, it is intestinal. It is root language. Poetry doesn't so much tell us something we never knew as bring into recognition what was latent or forgotten or overlooked. The Psalms are almost entirely this kind of language. Knowing this, we will not be looking primarily for ideas about God in the Psalms or for direction in moral conduct. We will expect, rather, to find exposed and sharpened what it means to be human beings before God.

Prayer is language used in relation to God. It gives utterance to what we sense or want or respond to before God. God speaks to us; our answers are our prayers. The answers are not always articulate. Silence, sighs, groaning—these also constitute responses. But God is always involved, whether in darkness or light, whether in faith or despair. This is hard to get used to. Our habit is to talk *about* God, not to him. We love discussing God. But the Psalms resist such discussions. They are provided not to teach us about God but to train us in responding to him. We don't learn the Psalms until we are praying them.

Those two features, the poetry and the prayer, account for both the excitement and the difficulty in studying the Psalms. The *poetry* requires that we deal with our actual humanity—these words dive beneath the surfaces of prose and pretense straight into the depths. We are more comfortable with prose, the laid-back language of our ordinary discourse. The *prayer* requires that we deal with God—this God who is determined on nothing less than the total renovation of our lives. We would rather have a religious bull session.

One editorial feature of the Psalms helps to keep these distinctive qualities of the Psalms before us. The Psalms are arranged into five books. At the end of Psalms 41, 72, 89, 106 and 150 formula sentences indicate a conclusion. Because of these miniconclusions the Psalms are usually printed (in English translations) as Book I (Psalms 1—41), Book II (42—72), Book III (73—89), Book IV (90—106) and Book V (107—150).

This five-book arrangement matches the five-book beginning of the Bible, deeply embedded in our minds as the five books of Moses. The five books of Moses are matched by the five books of David like two five-fingered hands clasping one another in greeting. In the five books of Moses God addresses us by his word, calling us into being and shaping our salvation. In the five books of David we personally respond to this word that addresses us. Prayer is answering speech. Every word that God speaks to us must be answered by us. God's Word has not done its complete work until it evokes an answer from us. All our answers are prayers. The Psalms train us in this answering speech, this language that responds to all God's creating and saving words targeted to our lives.

It is important to notice this well, for it shifts our interpretive stance. Our usual approach to God's Word is to ask, What is God saying to me? That is almost always the correct question when reading Scripture. But in the Psalms the question is, How do I answer the God who speaks to me? In the Psalms we do not primarily learn what God *says* to us, but how to honestly, devoutly and faithfully *answer* his words to us. In the course of acquiring language we learn how to answer our parents, our teachers, our employers and our friends, but we do not get very much practice in answering God. The Psalms train us in answering God. And so we bring a somewhat different mindset to the Psalms than we do to the rest of Scripture—we are learning to *pray,* not study, although the two activities will always be interconnected.

We know almost nothing of the circumstances in which the 150 psalms were written. David is the most named author, but most are anonymous. But that hardly matters, for the settings of the Psalms are not geographical or cultural but *interior*. Calvin called them "an anatomy of all the parts of the soul." Everything that anyone can feel or experience in relation to God is in these prayers. You will find them the best place in Scripture to explore all the parts of your life and then to say who you are and what is in you—guilt, anger, salvation, praise—to the God who loves, judges and saves you in Jesus Christ.

Outline

1/ Psalm 1 —— *Praying Our Inattention*

2/ Psalm 2 —— *Praying Our Intimidation*

3/ Psalm 3 —— *Praying Our Trouble*

4/ Psalm 4 —— *Dealing with Anger*

5/ Psalm 5 —— *Relying on God*

6/ Psalm 6 —— *Praying Our Tears*

1 / *Psalm 1*
Praying Our Inattention

PSALM 1 IS the biblical preparation for a life of prayer. Step by step it detaches us from activities and words that distract us from God so that we can be attentive before him. Most of us can't step immediately from the noisy, high-stimulus world into the quiet concentration of prayer. We need a way of transition. Psalm 1 provides a kind of entryway into the place of prayer.

Warming Up to God Do you feel a gap (or chasm!) between "real life" (work, school, family) and your prayer life? Explain. Ask God to help you begin to make prayer a part of your life.

Read Psalm 1.

BOOK I
Psalms 1–41

Psalm 1

1 Blessed is the man
who does not walk in the counsel of the wicked
or stand in the way of sinners
or sit in the seat of mockers.
2 But his delight is in the law of the LORD,
and on his law he meditates day and night.
3 He is like a tree planted by streams of water,
which yields its fruit in season
and whose leaf does not wither.
Whatever he does prospers.

4 Not so the wicked!
They are like chaff
that the wind blows away.
5 Therefore the wicked will not stand in the judgment,
nor sinners in the assembly of the righteous.

6 For the LORD watches over the way of the righteous,
but the way of the wicked will perish.

Discovering the Word 1. What contrasts do you notice in the psalm? 2. What significance do you see in the progression from *walk* to *stand* to *sit* (v. 1)? 3. "The law of the LORD" is contrasted with the words *counsel, way* and *seat.* What does this contrast bring out? 4. *Tree* is the central metaphor of the psalm (v. 3). Put your imagination to use. How are law-delighting people like trees? 5. In what ways are the wicked like chaff (vv. 4-6)?

Applying the Word 1. How do these two radically different portraits (the tree-righteous and the chaff-wicked) motivate you to delight in God's Word? 2. How does meditation—listening to God speak to us through Scripture—prepare us for prayer? 3. A *life* of prayer requires preparation, a procedure for moving from inattention to attention. The same procedure will not suit everyone. How can you develop a procedure that fits your circumstances and development?

Responding in Prayer As you turn to prayer, spend careful time in preparation.

2 / *Psalm 2*
Praying Our Intimidation

WE WAKE UP each day in a world noisy with boasting, violent with guns, arrogant with money. How can we avoid being intimidated? What use can prayer have in the face of governments and armies and millionaires? None, if God is not at work; all, if God is. God is as much at work in the public sphere as he is in the personal, and our prayers are as needful there as in our personal lives.

Warming Up to God How do you feel when you consider the needs of our world and try to pray for them? Know that God is in control. Spend time reflecting on that fact before you begin.

Read Psalm 2.

Psalm 2

1Why do the nations conspire[a]
and the peoples plot in vain?
2The kings of the earth take their stand
and the rulers gather together
against the LORD
and against his Anointed One.[b]
3"Let us break their chains," they say,
"and throw off their fetters."

4The One enthroned in heaven laughs;
the Lord scoffs at them.
5Then he rebukes them in his anger
and terrifies them in his wrath, saying,
6"I have installed my King[c]
on Zion, my holy hill."

7I will proclaim the decree of the LORD:

He said to me, "You are my Son[d];
today I have become your Father.[e]
8Ask of me,
and I will make the nations your
inheritance,
the ends of the earth your possession.
9You will rule them with an iron scepter[f];
you will dash them to pieces like pottery."

10Therefore, you kings, be wise;
be warned, you rulers of the earth.
11Serve the LORD with fear
and rejoice with trembling.
12Kiss the Son, lest he be angry
and you be destroyed in your way,
for his wrath can flare up in a moment.
Blessed are all who take refuge in him.

[a]1 Hebrew; Septuagint *rage* [b]2 Or *anointed one* [c]6 Or *king* [d]7 Or *son*; also in verse 12 [e]7 Or *have begotten you* [f]9 Or *will break them with a rod of iron*

Discovering the Word 1. Compare the opening nouns and verbs in Psalm 1:1-3 with those in Psalm 2:1-3. What differences in orientation do they suggest between these two psalms? 2. How does the Lord view the vaunted power of nations (vv. 4-6)? 3. "Anointed One" in verse 2 is a translation of the Hebrew word *Messiah*. What in this psalm reminds you of Jesus? 4. The psalm begins and ends with references to kings and rulers (vv. 2-3, 10-12). How do they relate to the King enthroned by the Lord (v. 6)?

Applying the Word 1. It is always easier to pray for personal needs than political situations. But Psalm 2 is entirely political. Therefore, as citizens of Christ's kingdom, what responsibility do we have as citizens of an earthly nation? 2. How does Christ's relationship with kings and rulers impact your prayers for the world?

Responding in Prayer Think of three rulers (presidents, kings, prime ministers or dictators). Pray for them.

---

3 / *Psalm 3*
Praying Our Trouble

PRAYER BEGINS IN a realization that we cannot help ourselves, so we must reach out to God. "Help!" is the basic prayer. We are in trouble, deep trouble. If God cannot get us out, we are lost; if God can get us out, we are saved. If we don't know that we need help, prayer will always be peripheral to our lives, a matter of mood and good manners. But the moment we know we are in trouble, prayer is a life-or-death matter.

Warming Up to God What is the worst trouble you were in this last week? Where did you go for help? Did you get help? God is your help. Talk to him about what you need today.

Read Psalm 3.

Psalm 3

A psalm of David. When he fled from his son Absalom.

1O LORD, how many are my foes!
How many rise up against me!
2Many are saying of me,
"God will not deliver him." *Selah*[g]

3But you are a shield around me, O LORD;
you bestow glory on me and lift[h] up my head.
4To the LORD I cry aloud,
and he answers me from his holy hill. *Selah*

5I lie down and sleep;
I wake again, because the LORD sustains me.
6I will not fear the tens of thousands
drawn up against me on every side.

7Arise, O LORD!
Deliver me, O my God!
Strike all my enemies on the jaw;
break the teeth of the wicked.

8From the LORD comes deliverance.
May your blessing be on your people. *Selah*

g2 A word of uncertain meaning, occurring frequently in the Psalms; possibly a musical term h3 Or *LORD, / my Glorious One, who lifts*

Discovering the Word 1. *Deliver/deliverance* is a key word in this psalm. What do we learn about the nature of deliverance through its various uses here? 2. David's prayer naturally divides into five sections: verses 1–2, 3–4, 5–6, 7 and 8. What progression do you see from each section to the next? 3. What actions is God described as taking in this psalm? 4. Are you used to thinking of God in these ways? Explain. 5. What actions is David described as taking in the psalm?

Applying the Word 1. David describes his foes in verses 1–2. Do you ever feel overwhelmed by threatening people or circumstances? Give an example. 2. What kind of trouble are you in right now? 3. What in this psalm do you think will help you to pray your trouble?

Responding in Prayer Take an image or phrase from Psalm 3 and use it to pray your trouble.

4 / *Psalm 4*
Dealing with Anger

ANGER IS AN emotion common to all people. Anger in itself is not sin. It is simply an emotion, a God-given part of life as a human being. It's a natural reaction to threats or injuries; yet anger is all too often expressed in ways that spread the harm around. The Old Testament is full of references to God's righteous anger or indignation against sin, and this emotional aspect of God's character also appears in the New Testament through Christ. How can we learn to "be angry, but sin not"?

Warming Up to God How do you generally respond when you are angry? (For example, do you talk about it or do you keep it to yourself?)

Read Psalm 4.

Psalm 4

For the director of music. With stringed instruments. A psalm of David.

1 Answer me when I call to you,
O my righteous God.
Give me relief from my distress;
be merciful to me and hear my prayer.

2 How long, O men, will you turn my glory into shame[i]?
How long will you love delusions and seek false gods[j]? *Selah*
3 Know that the LORD has set apart the godly for himself;
the LORD will hear when I call to him.

4 In your anger do not sin;
when you are on your beds,
search your hearts and be silent. *Selah*
5 Offer right sacrifices
and trust in the LORD.

6 Many are asking, "Who can show us any good?"
Let the light of your face shine upon us,
O LORD.
7 You have filled my heart with greater joy
than when their grain and new wine abound.
8 I will lie down and sleep in peace,
for you alone, O LORD,
make me dwell in safety.

i2 Or *you dishonor my Glorious One* j2 Or *seek lies*

Discovering the Word 1. What is David angry about (v. 2)? 2. How does David deal with his anger (vv. 1, 3)? 3. In verse 4 David suggests that we can be angry and not sin. How do you think that could be possible? 4. What do you think David means by the phrase "search your hearts and be silent" (v. 4)?

Applying the Word 1. How can reflecting on angry feelings be a healthy way of dealing with anger? 2. How can knowing the joy of the Lord (vv. 6–7) help you deal with anger?

Responding in Prayer Talk to God about any anger you are dealing with right now. Ask him to help you express it directly and not hold it in.

5 / *Psalm 5*
Relying on God

FEELING BETRAYED, PERSECUTED or fearful are common human experiences. Christians are not immune from such emotions. Indeed, because of the opposition of the fallen world to Christ, we will inevitably face them. How do we pray in these circumstances? Instead of allowing our fear or anger to dominate our thinking, we need to focus on God. Psalm 5 is one example of a prayer written in the face of opposition.

Warming Up to God What happens to your relationship with God (especially your prayer life) when you find yourself facing opposition or persecution?

Read Psalm 5.

Psalm 5

For the director of music. For flutes. A psalm of David.

1 Give ear to my words, O LORD,
consider my sighing.
2 Listen to my cry for help,
my King and my God,
for to you I pray.
3 In the morning, O LORD, you hear my voice;
in the morning I lay my requests before you
and wait in expectation.

4 You are not a God who takes pleasure in evil;
with you the wicked cannot dwell.

5The arrogant cannot stand in your
presence;
you hate all who do wrong.
6You destroy those who tell lies;
bloodthirsty and deceitful men
the LORD abhors.

7But I, by your great mercy,
will come into your house;
in reverence will I bow down
toward your holy temple.
8Lead me, O LORD, in your righteousness
because of my enemies—
make straight your way before me.
9Not a word from their mouth can
be trusted;
their heart is filled with destruction.
Their throat is an open grave;
with their tongue they speak deceit.
10Declare them guilty, O God!
Let their intrigues be their downfall.
Banish them for their many sins,
for they have rebelled against you.

11But let all who take refuge in you
be glad;
let them ever sing for joy.
Spread your protection over them,
that those who love your name may rejoice
in you.
12For surely, O LORD, you bless the
righteous;
you surround them with your favor as with
a shield.

Discovering the Word 1. List the characteristics of the wicked and the righteous from David's descriptions in the passage. 2. When we are opposed or persecuted by others, it is easy to want to take revenge or become aggressive toward them. What is David's strategy for dealing with opposition? 3. David appears confident of God hearing his prayer and shielding him. What grounds are there in the passage for such confidence? 4. What does the passage show us about David's relationship with God? 5. David is clearly accustomed to beginning his day with prayer (v. 3). What are the benefits of this model?

Applying the Word 1. The psalm gives us a clear picture of how God opposes the wicked and deals with them. How does this help in coping with opposition or persecution on a day-to-day basis? 2. Both Christians and non-Christians often blame God for the pain, suffering or persecution that they encounter. How does Psalm 5 help us to understand the pain, suffering and persecution from God's perspective? 3. What aspects of David's prayer in this passage are a helpful model for you?

Responding in Prayer Think of any situations that represent a threat or pressure for you. Spend some time praying about those situations, trying to focus particularly on God's power and supremacy over the situation (while being realistic about the difficulties!).

6 / *Psalm 6*
Praying Our Tears

TEARS ARE A biological gift of God. They are a physical means for expressing emotional and spiritual experience. But it is hard to know what to do with them. If we indulge our tears, we cultivate self-pity. If we suppress our tears, we lose touch with our feelings. But if we *pray* our tears, we enter into sadnesses that integrate our sorrows with our Lord's sorrows and discover both the source of and the relief from our sadness.

Warming Up to God How do you feel about crying (is it always negative, positive or mixed)?

Read Psalm 6.

Psalm 6

For the director of music. With stringed instruments. According to *sheminith*.[k] A psalm of David.

1O LORD, do not rebuke me in your anger
or discipline me in your wrath.
2Be merciful to me, LORD, for I am faint;
O LORD, heal me, for my bones are in agony.
3My soul is in anguish.
How long, O LORD, how long?

4Turn, O LORD, and deliver me;
save me because of your unfailing love.
5No one remembers you when he is dead.
Who praises you from the grave[l]?

6I am worn out from groaning;
all night long I flood my bed with weeping
and drench my couch with tears.
7My eyes grow weak with sorrow;
they fail because of all my foes.

8Away from me, all you who do evil,
for the LORD has heard my weeping.
9The LORD has heard my cry for mercy;
the LORD accepts my prayer.
10All my enemies will be ashamed and dismayed;
they will turn back in sudden disgrace.

[k]Title: Probably a musical term [l]5 Hebrew *Sheol*

Discovering the Word 1. Compare the first verse with the last. Are the tears because of the Lord or the enemies? Explain. 2. What is the cumulative effect of the three verbs *turn, deliver* and *save* in verse 4? 3. The emotional center of this prayer is verses 6–7. How many different ways is weeping expressed? 4. Why the tears? (Go through the psalm and note every possible source.) 5. In verses 8–9 there are three phrases in parallel: *weeping, cry for mercy* and *prayer*. Are these aspects of one thing or three different things? Explain.

Applying the Word 1. "How long?" (v. 3) is a frequent question in prayer. Considering the frequency with which it is uttered in Scripture, God must welcome it. What in your life, past or present, evokes this question? 2. Tears are often considered a sign that something is wrong with us—depression, unhappiness, frustration—and are therefore to be either avoided or cured. But what if they are a sign of something right with us? What rightness could they be evidence of?

Responding in Prayer Who do you know who is in grief? Pray for them now, using phrases from Psalm 6 to express their sorrow.

Psalm 7

Psalm 7

A *shiggaion*[m] of David, which he sang to the LORD concerning Cush, a Benjamite.

1O LORD my God, I take refuge in you;
save and deliver me from all who pursue me,
2or they will tear me like a lion
and rip me to pieces with no one to rescue me.

3O LORD my God, if I have done this
and there is guilt on my hands—
4if I have done evil to him who is at peace with me
or without cause have robbed my foe—
5then let my enemy pursue and overtake me;
let him trample my life to the ground
and make me sleep in the dust. *Selah*

6Arise, O LORD, in your anger;
rise up against the rage of my enemies.
Awake, my God; decree justice.
7Let the assembled peoples gather around you.
Rule over them from on high;
8 let the LORD judge the peoples.
Judge me, O LORD, according to my righteousness,
according to my integrity, O Most High.
9O righteous God,
who searches minds and hearts,
bring to an end the violence of the wicked
and make the righteous secure.

10My shield[n] is God Most High,

[m]Title: Probably a literary or musical term [n]10 Or *sovereign*

who saves the upright in heart.
11God is a righteous judge,
a God who expresses his wrath every day.
12If he does not relent,
he[o] will sharpen his sword;
he will bend and string his bow.
13He has prepared his deadly weapons;
he makes ready his flaming arrows.

14He who is pregnant with evil
and conceives trouble gives birth to
disillusionment.
15He who digs a hole and scoops it out
falls into the pit he has made.
16The trouble he causes recoils on himself;
his violence comes down on his own head.

17I will give thanks to the LORD because of his
righteousness
and will sing praise to the name of the LORD
Most High.

[o]12 Or *If a man does not repent, / God*

7/ *Psalm 8*
Praying Our Creation

DISORIENTATION IS A terrible experience. If we cannot locate our place, we are in confusion and anxiety. We are also in danger, for we are apt to act inappropriately. If we are among enemies and don't know it, we may lose our life. If we are among friends and don't know it, we may miss good relationships. If we are alongside a cliff and don't know it, we may lose our footing. In Psalm 8, we find out where we are and some important aspects of who we are.

Warming Up to God When traveling, have you ever awakened and not known where you were? The bed is unfamiliar; the room is strange; you look out the window and don't recognize anything. What does it feel like to be disoriented?

Read Psalm 8.

Psalm 8

For the director of music. According to *gittith*.[p] A psalm of David.

1O LORD, our Lord,
how majestic is your name in all the earth!

You have set your glory
above the heavens.
2From the lips of children and infants
you have ordained praise[q]
because of your enemies,
to silence the foe and the avenger.

3When I consider your heavens,
the work of your fingers,
the moon and the stars,
which you have set in place,
4what is man that you are mindful of him,
the son of man that you care for him?
5You made him a little lower than the
heavenly beings[r]
and crowned him with glory and honor.

6You made him ruler over the works of your
hands;
you put everything under his feet:
7all flocks and herds,
and the beasts of the field,
8the birds of the air,
and the fish of the sea,
all that swim the paths of the seas.

9O LORD, our Lord,
how majestic is your name in all the earth!

[p]Title: Probably a musical term [q]2 Or *strength* [r]5 Or *than God*

Applying the Word 1. Notice the author's various perspectives of God. The prayer begins with an absent God: "Where are you, God?" In the middle the author risks asking God to respond on his behalf: "Arise, Lord!" The prayer ends with praise to the God who hears and defends the oppressed. Which of these perspectives of God have you experienced? 2. When you feel helpless, how would it help you if you experienced God as acting on your behalf?

Responding in Prayer How would you like God to respond to your feelings of helplessness?

Psalms 11—12

Psalm 11

For the director of music. Of David.

[1]In the LORD I take refuge.
How then can you say to me:
"Flee like a bird to your mountain.
[2]For look, the wicked bend their bows;
they set their arrows against the strings
to shoot from the shadows
at the upright in heart.
[3]When the foundations are being destroyed,
what can the righteous do[w]?"

[4]The LORD is in his holy temple;
the LORD is on his heavenly throne.
He observes the sons of men;
his eyes examine them.
[5]The LORD examines the righteous,
but the wicked[x] and those who love violence
his soul hates.
[6]On the wicked he will rain
fiery coals and burning sulfur;
a scorching wind will be their lot.

[7]For the LORD is righteous,
he loves justice;
upright men will see his face.

Psalm 12

For the director of music. According to *sheminith.*[y] A psalm of David.

[1]Help, LORD, for the godly are no more;
the faithful have vanished from among men.
[2]Everyone lies to his neighbor;
their flattering lips speak with deception.

[3]May the LORD cut off all flattering lips
and every boastful tongue
[4]that says, "We will triumph with our tongues;
we own our lips[z]—who is our master?"

[5]"Because of the oppression of the weak
and the groaning of the needy,
I will now arise," says the LORD.
"I will protect them from those who malign them."
[6]And the words of the LORD are flawless,
like silver refined in a furnace of clay,
purified seven times.

[7]O LORD, you will keep us safe
and protect us from such people forever.
[8]The wicked freely strut about
when what is vile is honored among men.

[w]3 Or *what is the Righteous One doing* [x]5 Or *The LORD, the Righteous One, examines the wicked, /* [y]Title: Probably a musical term [z]4 Or */ our lips are our plowshares*

9/ *Psalm 13*
A Prayer of Self-Doubt

PEOPLE ASK ABOUT God: "Why did God let this happen?" "Was he unable to respond to my prayers?" "Was it my fault?" "Was my faith too weak?" These painful questions and the doubts which they represent are difficult to discuss with other people. They can also be very difficult to share with God.

Fortunately, the Bible itself gives voice to these painful questions. God is not shocked by our struggles with doubt. May knowing that God is able to respond to doubt in helpful ways give you the courage to pray when your heart is full of unanswerable questions.

Warming Up to God At what times in your life have you struggled with doubt? Talk openly with God about it; he wants to know your true feelings.

Read Psalm 13.

Psalm 13

For the director of music. A psalm of David.

[1]How long, O LORD? Will you forget me
forever?
How long will you hide your face from me?
[2]How long must I wrestle with my thoughts
and every day have sorrow in my heart?
How long will my enemy triumph over me?

[3]Look on me and answer, O LORD my God.
Give light to my eyes, or I will sleep in
death;
[4]my enemy will say, "I have overcome him,"
and my foes will rejoice when I fall.

[5]But I trust in your unfailing love;
my heart rejoices in your salvation.
[6]I will sing to the LORD,
for he has been good to me.

Discovering the Word 1. The author begins with two questions that express his doubts about God. What are his concerns? 2. In verse 2 what reasons does he give for his sorrow? 3. Why is it helpful to express our doubts to God? 4. The author not only has questions about God, he also has questions about himself. He asks, "How long must I wrestle with my thoughts and every day have sorrow in my heart?" What is it about the experience of doubt that causes people to question themselves? 5. The writer ends the prayer of doubt with a statement of trust (vv. 5–6). How is it possible to doubt and trust at the same time?

Applying the Word 1. When is it difficult for you to follow the writer's example in expressing your doubts about God? 2. How might it give you courage in your spiritual struggle to know that the Bible gives voice to doubts?

Responding in Prayer What doubts would you like to express to God?

Psalm 14

Psalm 14

For the director of music. Of David.

[1]The fool[a] says in his heart,
"There is no God."
They are corrupt, their deeds are vile;
there is no one who does good.

[2]The LORD looks down from heaven
on the sons of men
to see if there are any who understand,
any who seek God.

[a]1 The Hebrew words rendered *fool* in Psalms denote one who is morally deficient.

[3]All have turned aside,
they have together become corrupt;
there is no one who does good,
not even one.

[4]Will evildoers never learn—
those who devour my people as men eat bread
and who do not call on the LORD?
[5]There they are, overwhelmed with dread,
for God is present in the company of the righteous.
[6]You evildoers frustrate the plans of the poor,
but the LORD is their refuge.

[7]Oh, that salvation for Israel would come out of Zion!
When the LORD restores the fortunes of his people,
let Jacob rejoice and Israel be glad!

10 / *Psalm 15*
A Person of Honesty

A LIE CONTAMINATES everyone close to it. Worst of all, it rots the character of the person who tells the lie.

Warming Up to God Reflect on the past week. How have you failed to be honest? Take your failings to Christ. What does he have to say to you?

Read Psalm 15.

Psalm 15

A psalm of David.

[1]LORD, who may dwell in your sanctuary?
Who may live on your holy hill?

[2]He whose walk is blameless
and who does what is righteous,
who speaks the truth from his heart
[3] and has no slander on his tongue,
who does his neighbor no wrong
and casts no slur on his fellowman,
[4]who despises a vile man
but honors those who fear the LORD,
who keeps his oath
even when it hurts,
[5]who lends his money without usury
and does not accept a bribe against the innocent.

He who does these things
will never be shaken.

Discovering the Word 1. What must a person do to be worthy to approach the Lord ("dwell in your sanctuary") (vv. 2–5)? 2. What, according to this psalm, keeps a person from being shaken? 3. What would it be like to live "on the holy hill" of the Lord? 4. When is it hard to keep a promise (v. 4)?

Applying the Word 1. How might this psalm help you to make specific choices for honesty in your dealings with other people? 2. What forms of self-discipline would you recommend to someone who wanted to become more truthful? 3. What help in being honest do you need?

Responding in Prayer Ask God to help you to have a walk that is blameless.

11 / *Psalm 16*
Finding Balance in Life

JOE IS A Christian businessman. He has significant responsibility at work and puts in long hours. He enjoys his work and is productive. He is also active in his church, teaching Sunday school and serving as a deacon. His wife also works outside the home, so Joe often takes a turn cooking and cleaning. Additionally, he enjoys spending time with his family—playing a game of softball or going out to dinner together.

Joe is the Christian many of us strive to be. He is able to juggle many responsibilities and demands. He seems to be able to maintain a godly balance of values. But does he really exist? This study is about how we can discover God's values for our lives.

Warming Up to God In what areas of your life do you struggle for balance?

Read Psalm 16.

Psalm 16

A *miktam*[b] of David.

1Keep me safe, O God,
for in you I take refuge.

2I said to the LORD, "You are my Lord;
apart from you I have no good thing."
3As for the saints who are in the land,
they are the glorious ones in whom is all my delight.[c]
4The sorrows of those will increase
who run after other gods.
I will not pour out their libations of blood
or take up their names on my lips.

5LORD, you have assigned me my portion and my cup;
you have made my lot secure.
6The boundary lines have fallen for me in pleasant places;
surely I have a delightful inheritance.
7I will praise the LORD, who counsels me;
even at night my heart instructs me.
8I have set the LORD always before me.
Because he is at my right hand,
I will not be shaken.

9Therefore my heart is glad and my tongue rejoices;
my body also will rest secure,
10because you will not abandon me to the grave,[d]
nor will you let your Holy One[e] see decay.
11You have made[f] known to me the path of life;
you will fill me with joy in your presence,
with eternal pleasures at your right hand.

[b]Title: Probably a literary or musical term [c]3 Or *As for the pagan priests who are in the land / and the nobles in whom all delight, I said:* [d]10 Hebrew *Sheol* [e]10 Or *your faithful one* [f]11 Or *You will make*

Discovering the Word 1. According to this passage, what has the Lord done for David? 2. What body imagery does David use to describe his relationship with God (vv. 5, 7–11)? 3. Describe the spirit of David's comments about the land in verses 5–6. 4. What is the significance of the Lord's being at David's right hand (vv. 8–11)? 5. Look back through the entire passage. What is important to people who follow God? 6. How do those values contrast with worldly values?

Applying the Word 1. In what specific ways do you need to bring your values in line with God's values? 2. What would help you to do that?

Responding in Prayer Make thanking God for the "inheritance" he has given you a focus for prayer. Try to be aware of the different roles (counselor, protector, sustainer, refuge) God plays in your daily life.

Psalm 17

Psalm 17

A prayer of David.

1Hear, O LORD, my righteous plea;
listen to my cry.
Give ear to my prayer—
it does not rise from deceitful lips.
2May my vindication come from you;
may your eyes see what is right.

3Though you probe my heart and examine me at night,
though you test me, you will find nothing;
I have resolved that my mouth will not sin.
4As for the deeds of men—
by the word of your lips
I have kept myself
from the ways of the violent.
5My steps have held to your paths;
my feet have not slipped.

6I call on you, O God, for you will answer me;
give ear to me and hear my prayer.
7Show the wonder of your great love,
you who save by your right hand
those who take refuge in you from their foes.
8Keep me as the apple of your eye;
hide me in the shadow of your wings
9from the wicked who assail me,
from my mortal enemies who surround me.

10They close up their callous hearts,
and their mouths speak with arrogance.
11They have tracked me down, they now surround me,
with eyes alert, to throw me to the ground.
12They are like a lion hungry for prey,
like a great lion crouching in cover.

13Rise up, O LORD, confront them, bring them down;
rescue me from the wicked by your sword.
14O LORD, by your hand save me from such men,
from men of this world whose reward is in this life.

You still the hunger of those you cherish;
their sons have plenty,
and they store up wealth for their children.
15And I—in righteousness I will see your face;
when I awake, I will be satisfied with seeing your likeness.

12 / *Psalm 18:1–24*
A Prayer for Justice

IT MAY COME as a surprise that God is angry at those who take advantage of others. God shares our anger at injustice. In the text for this study, the author suggests that God's response to the wicked is anger so intense that the earth itself trembles.

Warming Up to God When have you felt angry at injustice toward you or toward others?

Read Psalm 18:1–24.

Psalm 18

For the director of music. Of David the servant of the LORD. He sang to the LORD the words of this song when the LORD delivered him from the hand of all his enemies and from the hand of Saul. He said:

[1]I love you, O LORD, my strength.

[2]The LORD is my rock, my fortress and my deliverer;
my God is my rock, in whom I take refuge.
He is my shield and the horn[g] of my salvation, my stronghold.
[3]I call to the LORD, who is worthy of praise,
and I am saved from my enemies.
[4]The cords of death entangled me;
the torrents of destruction overwhelmed me.
[5]The cords of the grave[h] coiled around me;
the snares of death confronted me.
[6]In my distress I called to the LORD;
I cried to my God for help.
From his temple he heard my voice;
my cry came before him, into his ears.

[7]The earth trembled and quaked,
and the foundations of the mountains shook;
they trembled because he was angry.
[8]Smoke rose from his nostrils;
consuming fire came from his mouth,
burning coals blazed out of it.
[9]He parted the heavens and came down;
dark clouds were under his feet.
[10]He mounted the cherubim and flew;
he soared on the wings of the wind.
[11]He made darkness his covering, his canopy around him—
the dark rain clouds of the sky.
[12]Out of the brightness of his presence clouds advanced,
with hailstones and bolts of lightning.
[13]The LORD thundered from heaven;
the voice of the Most High resounded.[i]
[14]He shot his arrows and scattered ⌞the enemies⌟,
great bolts of lightning and routed them.
[15]The valleys of the sea were exposed
and the foundations of the earth laid bare
at your rebuke, O LORD,
at the blast of breath from your nostrils.

[16]He reached down from on high and took hold of me;
he drew me out of deep waters.
[17]He rescued me from my powerful enemy,
from my foes, who were too strong for me.
[18]They confronted me in the day of my disaster,
but the LORD was my support.
[19]He brought me out into a spacious place;
he rescued me because he delighted in me.

[20]The LORD has dealt with me according to my righteousness;
according to the cleanness of my hands he has rewarded me.
[21]For I have kept the ways of the LORD;
I have not done evil by turning from my God.
[22]All his laws are before me;
I have not turned away from his decrees.
[23]I have been blameless before him
and have kept myself from sin.
[24]The LORD has rewarded me according to my righteousness,
according to the cleanness of my hands in his sight.

g2 *Horn* here symbolizes strength. h5 Hebrew *Sheol* i13 Some Hebrew manuscripts and Septuagint (see also 2 Samuel 22:14); most Hebrew manuscripts *resounded, / amid hailstones and bolts of lightning*

Discovering the Word 1. How does David describe the distress he has experienced (vv. 4–6)? 2. What does the text say God actually does to our enemies (vv. 7–15)? 3. What does the Lord do to help David (vv. 16–19)? 4. For what reasons does God deliver David (vv. 20–24)?

Applying the Word 1. How do the author's feelings compare with your own? 2. What thoughts and feelings do you have as you read this powerful description of God's response to a cry for help?

Responding in Prayer What would you like to say to the God who shares your anger about injustice and who delights in you?

13 / *Psalm 18:25–50*
A Prayer for Equipping

WRESTLERS, BOXERS AND fencers know that for every move there is an equal and opposite move meant to block it, counterpunch, or parry the thrust. So also God provides just the right protection and timely provision for his people. Here God enables David to alternately evade and thwart his enemies, particularly Saul, eventually overcoming and crushing them.

Warming Up to God God is our fight coach too. The Lord does not guide where he does not also provide. Think about what battles God may be leading you into and what you need to emerge victorious. Thank God that he will make every provision to help you overcome enemies and obstacles along the way.

Read Psalm 18:25–50.

25To the faithful you show yourself faithful,
to the blameless you show yourself blameless,
26to the pure you show yourself pure,
but to the crooked you show yourself shrewd.
27You save the humble
but bring low those whose eyes are haughty.
28You, O LORD, keep my lamp burning;
my God turns my darkness into light.
29With your help I can advance against a troop[j];
with my God I can scale a wall.

30As for God, his way is perfect;
the word of the LORD is flawless.
He is a shield
for all who take refuge in him.
31For who is God besides the LORD?
And who is the Rock except our God?
32It is God who arms me with strength
and makes my way perfect.
33He makes my feet like the feet of a deer;
he enables me to stand on the heights.
34He trains my hands for battle;
my arms can bend a bow of bronze.
35You give me your shield of victory,
and your right hand sustains me;
you stoop down to make me great.
36You broaden the path beneath me,
so that my ankles do not turn.

37I pursued my enemies and overtook them;
I did not turn back till they were destroyed.
38I crushed them so that they could not rise;
they fell beneath my feet.
39You armed me with strength for battle;
you made my adversaries bow at my feet.
40You made my enemies turn their backs in flight,
and I destroyed my foes.
41They cried for help, but there was no one to save them—
to the LORD, but he did not answer.
42I beat them as fine as dust borne on the wind;
I poured them out like mud in the streets.

43You have delivered me from the attacks of the people;
you have made me the head of nations;
people I did not know are subject to me.
44As soon as they hear me, they obey me;
foreigners cringe before me.
45They all lose heart;
they come trembling from their strongholds.

46The LORD lives! Praise be to my Rock!
Exalted be God my Savior!
47He is the God who avenges me,
who subdues nations under me,
48 who saves me from my enemies.
You exalted me above my foes;
from violent men you rescued me.
49Therefore I will praise you among the nations,
O LORD;
I will sing praises to your name.
50He gives his king great victories;
he shows unfailing kindness to his anointed,
to David and his descendants forever.

j29 Or *can run through a barricade*

Discovering the Word 1. Previously, the psalmist noted that the earth trembled and quaked as an expression of God's anger (v. 7). Now it's the enemies of God's people who tremble or quake in their boots (v. 45). What has God done on David's behalf to bring this about? 2. What was David's part in securing this victory in cooperation with God (vv. 25–29)? 3. In what ways did God the Warrior specifically equip or provide for the warrior David (vv. 30–36)? 4. What reversal of fortune do David and the surrounding nations experience as a result of the Lord coming to his rescue (vv. 37–45)? 5. How does the conclusion of this psalm (vv. 46–50) compare with its beginning (vv. 1–6)? 6. What does that tell you about God the warrior?

Applying the Word 1. At what points (feelings, circumstances, outcomes) can you identify with David? 2. Think about the fights God may be preparing you for. What equipping do you need? (Where can God strengthen a particular weakness of yours? What can you praise him for already?)

Responding in Prayer Trust God to fight evil and avenge any wrongs done to you. If you have experienced God's justice in the face of evil, praise him. Recount the ways he has led you and equipped you every step of the way.

14 / *Psalm 19*

Comfort from Scripture

TOM WAS FRIGHTENED before going to surgery. I shared thoughts with him from Psalm 23 about our Shepherd who gives us all we need and goes with us through dark valleys. Tom didn't have to be afraid, because Jesus was with him. He seemed to be at peace. Sharing Scripture may not always be the right thing to help someone, but often it is. Psalm 19 describes what Scripture is like and how it can offer comfort.

Warming Up to God Reflect on some of your favorite words from Scripture. You may want to turn to the passage and reread it. Drink in the comfort those familiar words bring.

Read Psalm 19.

Psalm 19

For the director of music. A psalm of David.

1The heavens declare the glory of God;
the skies proclaim the work of his hands.
2Day after day they pour forth speech;
night after night they display knowledge.
3There is no speech or language
where their voice is not heard.[k]
4Their voice[l] goes out into all the earth,
their words to the ends of the world.

In the heavens he has pitched a tent for the sun,
5 which is like a bridegroom coming forth from his pavilion,
like a champion rejoicing to run his course.
6It rises at one end of the heavens
and makes its circuit to the other;
nothing is hidden from its heat.

7The law of the LORD is perfect,
reviving the soul.
The statutes of the LORD are trustworthy,
making wise the simple.
8The precepts of the LORD are right,
giving joy to the heart.
The commands of the LORD are radiant,
giving light to the eyes.
9The fear of the LORD is pure,
enduring forever.
The ordinances of the LORD are sure
and altogether righteous.
10They are more precious than gold,
than much pure gold;
they are sweeter than honey,
than honey from the comb.
11By them is your servant warned;
in keeping them there is great reward.

12Who can discern his errors?

k3 Or *They have no speech, there are no words; / no sound is heard from them* l4 Septuagint, Jerome and Syriac; Hebrew *line*

Forgive my hidden faults.
13Keep your servant also from willful sins;
may they not rule over me.
Then will I be blameless,
innocent of great transgression.
14May the words of my mouth and the
meditation of my heart
be pleasing in your sight,
O LORD, my Rock and my Redeemer.

Discovering the Word 1. What does creation reveal about God (vv. 1–6)? 2. The terms *law, statutes, precepts, commands* and *ordinances* in this passage are synonyms for Scripture. In verses 7–11, how are the Scriptures described? 3. What do they do? 4. What is the overall effect of the psalmist's encounter with God through nature and the Scriptures (vv. 12–14)?

Applying the Word 1. From which of the effects of Scripture listed in verses 7–11 have you benefited? 2. How has this psalm been helpful to you by offering insight or comfort? 3. Sharing Scripture can be done in three ways. The first and most obvious way is sharing a passage or verse directly. The second is sharing how we have been affected or changed by Scripture. The third is simply living out the principles of Scripture. How might you appropriately and effectively share Scripture with someone in need this week?

Responding in Prayer Ask God to make Scripture alive and active in you this week. Pray that he will help you share his Word, either directly or through actions, with someone in need.

Psalms 20—21

Psalm 20

For the director of music. A psalm of David.

1May the LORD answer you when you are in
distress;
may the name of the God of Jacob protect
you.
2May he send you help from the sanctuary
and grant you support from Zion.
3May he remember all your sacrifices
and accept your burnt offerings. *Selah*
4May he give you the desire of your heart
and make all your plans succeed.
5We will shout for joy when you are victorious
and will lift up our banners in the name of
our God.
May the LORD grant all your requests.
6Now I know that the LORD saves his anointed;
he answers him from his holy heaven
with the saving power of his right hand.
7Some trust in chariots and some in horses,
but we trust in the name of the LORD our
God.
8They are brought to their knees and fall,
but we rise up and stand firm.
9O LORD, save the king!
Answer[m] us when we call!

Psalm 21

For the director of music. A psalm of David.

1O LORD, the king rejoices in your strength.
How great is his joy in the victories you
give!
2You have granted him the desire of his heart
and have not withheld the request of his
lips. *Selah*
3You welcomed him with rich blessings
and placed a crown of pure gold on his
head.
4He asked you for life, and you gave it to
him—
length of days, for ever and ever.
5Through the victories you gave, his glory is
great;
you have bestowed on him splendor and
majesty.
6Surely you have granted him eternal blessings
and made him glad with the joy of your
presence.
7For the king trusts in the LORD;
through the unfailing love of the Most High
he will not be shaken.
8Your hand will lay hold on all your enemies;

m9 *Or save! / O King, answer*

your right hand will seize your foes.
[9]At the time of your appearing
you will make them like a fiery furnace.
In his wrath the LORD will swallow them up,
and his fire will consume them.
[10]You will destroy their descendants from the earth,
their posterity from mankind.
[11]Though they plot evil against you
and devise wicked schemes, they cannot succeed;
[12]for you will make them turn their backs
when you aim at them with drawn bow.

[13]Be exalted, O LORD, in your strength;
we will sing and praise your might.

15 / *Psalm 22*
A Prayer of Anguish

THIS PRAYER OF anguish parallels the experience of our Lord, who took Psalm 22 to heart and spoke it from the cross. No other psalm is quoted as often in the New Testament. Persecuted saints and lonely Christians ever since have used this prayer to draw near to their God at times when they feel most abandoned.

Warming Up to God We jokingly refer to places we despise, or would never want to go near or visit again, as "Godforsaken." But being forsaken or abandoned by others is no laughing matter. Do you have a "Godforsaken place" in your past experience? What was that like?

Read Psalm 22.

Psalm 22

For the director of music. To ⌞the tune of⌟ "The Doe of the Morning." A psalm of David.

[1]My God, my God, why have you forsaken me?
Why are you so far from saving me,
so far from the words of my groaning?
[2]O my God, I cry out by day, but you do not answer,
by night, and am not silent.
[3]Yet you are enthroned as the Holy One;
you are the praise of Israel.[n]
[4]In you our fathers put their trust;
they trusted and you delivered them.
[5]They cried to you and were saved;
in you they trusted and were not disappointed.

[6]But I am a worm and not a man,
scorned by men and despised by the people.
[7]All who see me mock me;
they hurl insults, shaking their heads:
[8]"He trusts in the LORD;
let the LORD rescue him.
Let him deliver him,
since he delights in him."

[9]Yet you brought me out of the womb;
you made me trust in you
even at my mother's breast.
[10]From birth I was cast upon you;
from my mother's womb you have been my God.
[11]Do not be far from me,
for trouble is near
and there is no one to help.

[12]Many bulls surround me;
strong bulls of Bashan encircle me.
[13]Roaring lions tearing their prey
open their mouths wide against me.
[14]I am poured out like water,
and all my bones are out of joint.
My heart has turned to wax;
it has melted away within me.
[15]My strength is dried up like a potsherd,
and my tongue sticks to the roof of my mouth;

[n]3 Or *Yet you are holy, / enthroned on the praises of Israel*

you lay me[o] in the dust of death.
16Dogs have surrounded me;
a band of evil men has encircled me,
they have pierced[p] my hands and my feet.
17I can count all my bones;
people stare and gloat over me.
18They divide my garments among them
and cast lots for my clothing.

19But you, O LORD, be not far off;
O my Strength, come quickly to help me.
20Deliver my life from the sword,
my precious life from the power of the dogs.
21Rescue me from the mouth of the lions;
save[q] me from the horns of the wild oxen.

22I will declare your name to my brothers;
in the congregation I will praise you.
23You who fear the LORD, praise him!
All you descendants of Jacob, honor him!
Revere him, all you descendants of Israel!
24For he has not despised or disdained
the suffering of the afflicted one;
he has not hidden his face from him
but has listened to his cry for help.
25From you comes the theme of my praise in the great assembly;
before those who fear you[r] will I fulfill my vows.
26The poor will eat and be satisfied;
they who seek the LORD will praise him—
may your hearts live forever!
27All the ends of the earth
will remember and turn to the LORD,
and all the families of the nations
will bow down before him,
28for dominion belongs to the LORD
and he rules over the nations.
29All the rich of the earth will feast and worship;
all who go down to the dust will kneel before him—
those who cannot keep themselves alive.
30Posterity will serve him;
future generations will be told about the Lord.
31They will proclaim his righteousness
to a people yet unborn—
for he has done it.

[o]15 Or / *I am laid* [p]16 Some Hebrew manuscripts, Septuagint and Syriac; most Hebrew manuscripts / *like the lion,* [q]21 Or / *you have heard* [r]25 Hebrew *him*

Discovering the Word 1. David did not shrink back from asking tough "why" questions. Neither did Jesus in quoting verse 1 (Mt 27:46; Mk 15:34). What were David and Jesus experiencing at the time they prayed this prayer (vv. 1–2, 6–8)? 2. Being abandoned by friends and surrounded by enemies can feel all the more stark in contrast to one's history of being close to God and his people. What kind of relationship have this psalmist and his people enjoyed with their God (vv. 3–5, 9–10)? 3. What are his attackers like (vv. 12–18)? 4. What does he pray for (vv. 11, 19–21)? 5. In anticipation of God's sure deliverance, what does the psalmist vow (vv. 22, 25)? 6. Who joins him in this chorus of praise and why (vv. 23, 26–31)?

Applying the Word 1. This psalm conjures up images of sword fights, bull fights, dog fights and a lion's den. What scenes of violence contemporary to your experience does this psalm conjure up for you? 2. The Gospel writers applied this psalm to Jesus (see Mt 27:35, 39, 43 and 46). In what ways does Psalm 22 fit the circumstances of Jesus' crucifixion? 3. At what points can you identify with the psalmist or with Jesus?

Responding in Prayer Pour out your anguish before God, as he will listen to your cry for help. Trust God to deliver you from physical circumstances and emotional moods that cause you to feel forsaken. Remember what God has done for you in the past, and join others in praising God for what he will do in the future.

16/ *Psalm 23*
Praying Our Fear

THE WORLD IS a fearsome place. If we manage with the help of parents, teachers and friends to survive the dangers of infancy and childhood, we find ourselves launched in an adult world that is ringed with terror—accident, assault, disease, violence, conflicts. Prayer brings fear into focus and faces it. But prayer does more than bravely face fear; it affirms God's presence in it.

Warming Up to God Spend some time trying to bring your fears into focus. Know that God is with you in the midst of your fear.

Read Psalm 23.

Psalm 23

A psalm of David.

1The LORD is my shepherd, I shall not be in
want.
2 He makes me lie down in green pastures,
he leads me beside quiet waters,
3 he restores my soul.
He guides me in paths of righteousness
for his name's sake.
4Even though I walk
through the valley of the shadow of
death,[s]
I will fear no evil,
for you are with me;
your rod and your staff,
they comfort me.

5You prepare a table before me
in the presence of my enemies.
You anoint my head with oil;
my cup overflows.
6Surely goodness and love will follow me
all the days of my life,
and I will dwell in the house of the LORD
forever.

[s]4 Or *through the darkest valley*

Discovering the Word 1. There are two large metaphors in the psalm: the shepherd (vv. 1–4) and the host (vv. 5–6). Compare and contrast these two images. 2. Look carefully at the shepherd. How exactly does he care for his sheep (vv. 1–4)? 3. "I will fear no evil" (v. 4) is a bold statement. What does it mean for you to say that? 4. Look carefully at the host. How exactly does he provide for his guest (vv. 5–6)?

Applying the Word 1. Enemies are prominent in the psalm prayers and appear here. Who are your enemies? 2. What is the most comforting thing that you have experienced in the life of faith? 3. Psalm 23 is a weapon against fear. What fear in your life will you go to war against with this prayer as your cannon?

Responding in Prayer Name your fears and ask Christ the Shepherd and Christ the Host to relieve them.

17 / *Psalm 24*
A Prayer of Ascension

DAVID MAY HAVE composed this psalm on the occasion of bringing the Ark of the Covenant back to Jerusalem or in commemoration of that historic event. This prayer by worshipers ascending to Mount Zion has long been used by the church to celebrate Christ's ascension to the heavenly Jerusalem, paving the way for others to follow and stand in God's holy presence. Psalm 24 affirms that Jerusalem is the royal site for inaugurating the kingdom of God.

Warming Up to God What is the longest journey or pilgrimage you have made? What was arriving like for you?

Read Psalm 24.

Psalm 24

Of David. A psalm.

1The earth is the LORD's, and everything in it,
the world, and all who live in it;
2for he founded it upon the seas
and established it upon the waters.

3Who may ascend the hill of the LORD?
Who may stand in his holy place?
4He who has clean hands and a pure heart,
who does not lift up his soul to an idol
or swear by what is false.[t]
5He will receive blessing from the LORD
and vindication from God his Savior.
6Such is the generation of those who seek him,
who seek your face, O God of Jacob.[u]
Selah

7Lift up your heads, O you gates;
be lifted up, you ancient doors,
that the King of glory may come in.
8Who is this King of glory?
The LORD strong and mighty,
the LORD mighty in battle.
9Lift up your heads, O you gates;
lift them up, you ancient doors,
that the King of glory may come in.
10Who is he, this King of glory?
The LORD Almighty—
he is the King of glory. *Selah*

[t]4 Or *swear falsely* [u]6 Two Hebrew manuscripts and Syriac (see also Septuagint); most Hebrew manuscripts *face, Jacob*

Discovering the Word 1. Verses 1–2 echo themes from creation in reference to the founding of a city and the temple. What feelings and images does that backdrop evoke for this worshiper? 2. What kind of person may enter the Lord's sanctuary (vv. 3–6)? 3. Do these restrictions render the temple accessible to the public, only to priests, or to the one and only King? 4. Who is this "King of glory," and how is he described? 5. What glorious things has he done as Lord of creation (vv. 1–2) and God of Jacob (v. 6)?

Applying the Word 1. This psalm raises the doors of our hearts and the standards of readiness for corporate worship. What steps in preparation for worship does this psalm conjure up for you? 2. Paul quotes verse 1, which had become a Jewish blessing at mealtimes, to underscore the believer's freedom to eat meat without a troubled conscience (1Co 10:25–26). What new freedoms does knowing the sovereignty of God, affirmed in Psalm 24, give you?

Responding in Prayer As you seek God's face, prepare to meet his standards of acceptance—pure motives, integrity, trusting totally in God to vindicate you. This may prompt you to confession. Then lift up the gates and doors of your life, with thanksgiving and praise, to let more of the King into your worship.

---

18 / *Psalm 25*
Integrity in Times of Doubt

IN PHILIP YANCEY'S thoughtful book *Disappointment with God*, the writer speaks of Richard—a new and enthusiastic convert to the Christian faith. Richard studied the Bible with diligence and prayed every day. He transferred from a university to a Christian college, graduated, and went on to a Christian graduate school.

Then Richard's parents separated. Richard dropped out of school for a while to try to mend his family. He prayed constantly that God would bring his parents back together. His parents remained apart. Next Richard lost an important job. Then his fiancée jilted him. And his health began to deteriorate.

One night, Richard stayed up all night to pray. For four hours he pleaded with God to reveal himself. Nothing. Finally, Richard got up from his knees, gathered up his Bible and his theology textbooks, and went out to a backyard brick barbecue. There, in the last hours of darkness, Richard burned his books—and his faith.

Why? As Yancey said, "The theology he had learned in school and had written about in his book no longer *worked for him.*" He was disappointed with God. Is faith in God good only as long as it "works"?

Warming Up to God When you are in a difficult situation, what kind of prayer are you likely to pray to God?

Read Psalm 25.

Psalm 25[v]

Of David.

[1]To you, O LORD, I lift up my soul;
[2] in you I trust, O my God.
Do not let me be put to shame,
nor let my enemies triumph over me.
[3]No one whose hope is in you
will ever be put to shame,
but they will be put to shame
who are treacherous without excuse.

[4]Show me your ways, O LORD,
teach me your paths;
[5]guide me in your truth and teach me,
for you are God my Savior,
and my hope is in you all day long.
[6]Remember, O LORD, your great mercy and love,
for they are from of old.
[7]Remember not the sins of my youth
and my rebellious ways;
according to your love remember me,
for you are good, O LORD.

[8]Good and upright is the LORD;
therefore he instructs sinners in his ways.
[9]He guides the humble in what is right
and teaches them his way.
[10]All the ways of the LORD are loving and faithful
for those who keep the demands of his covenant.
[11]For the sake of your name, O LORD,
forgive my iniquity, though it is great.
[12]Who, then, is the man that fears the LORD?
He will instruct him in the way chosen for him.
[13]He will spend his days in prosperity,
and his descendants will inherit the land.
[14]The LORD confides in those who fear him;
he makes his covenant known to them.
[15]My eyes are ever on the LORD,
for only he will release my feet from the snare.

[16]Turn to me and be gracious to me,
for I am lonely and afflicted.
[17]The troubles of my heart have multiplied;
free me from my anguish.
[18]Look upon my affliction and my distress
and take away all my sins.
[19]See how my enemies have increased
and how fiercely they hate me!
[20]Guard my life and rescue me;
let me not be put to shame,
for I take refuge in you.
[21]May integrity and uprightness protect me,
because my hope is in you.

[22]Redeem Israel, O God,
from all their troubles!

[v]This psalm is an acrostic poem, the verses of which begin with the successive letters of the Hebrew alphabet.

Discovering the Word 1. Psalm 25 divides into four stanzas. Give a topic-title to each (vv. 1–3, 4–7, 8–15, 16–22). 2. What does it mean to "lift up" your soul to God? 3. Study stanza 2. What all does David ask God to do? 4. Study stanza 3. David began his prayer by saying that he trusted God. In what ways does stanza 3 show that God has integrity—and therefore ought to be trusted? 5. Study stanza 4. What words and phrases here help you to understand David's current situation? 6. Compare David's position, described in stanza 4, with what he hopes from God in verses 12–13. In view of the differences, what does David's prayer say about his own integrity?

Applying the Word 1. Three times David uses the term *remember.* What would you want God to remember (and not remember) about you? 2. What do you count on God to do and to be?

Responding in Prayer Before you pray, meditate on God's character as David did. Ask God to make you a person of integrity.

Psalm 26

Psalm 26

Of David.

[1]Vindicate me, O LORD,
for I have led a blameless life;
I have trusted in the LORD
without wavering.
[2]Test me, O LORD, and try me,
examine my heart and my mind;
[3]for your love is ever before me,
and I walk continually in your truth.
[4]I do not sit with deceitful men,
nor do I consort with hypocrites;
[5]I abhor the assembly of evildoers
and refuse to sit with the wicked.
[6]I wash my hands in innocence,
and go about your altar, O LORD,
[7]proclaiming aloud your praise
and telling of all your wonderful deeds.
[8]I love the house where you live, O LORD,
the place where your glory dwells.

[9]Do not take away my soul along with sinners,
my life with bloodthirsty men,
[10]in whose hands are wicked schemes,
whose right hands are full of bribes.
[11]But I lead a blameless life;
redeem me and be merciful to me.

[12]My feet stand on level ground;
in the great assembly I will praise the LORD.

19 / *Psalm 27* Waiting for the Lord

* I like this one.

ONE OF SAMUEL Beckett's most famous plays is entitled *Waiting for Godot*. Throughout the play the characters wait and wait for Godot to appear, but he never does. The play is Beckett's way of saying that hope is futile—especially hope in God.

In contrast to Beckett's despair, the Bible offers hope to the sufferer. When we feel overwhelmed and ready to give up, Psalm 27 encourages us to "wait for the Lord." When we see no possibility of relief, David assures us, "I am still confident of this: I will see the goodness of the Lord in the land of the living."

Warming Up to God In what kinds of situations do you find it hardest to wait?

Read Psalm 27.

Psalm 27

Of David.

[1]The LORD is my light and my salvation—
whom shall I fear?
The LORD is the stronghold of my life—
of whom shall I be afraid?
[2]When evil men advance against me
to devour my flesh,[w]
when my enemies and my foes attack me,
they will stumble and fall.
[3]Though an army besiege me,
my heart will not fear;
though war break out against me,
even then will I be confident.

[4]One thing I ask of the LORD,
this is what I seek:

[w]2 Or *to slander me*

that I may dwell in the house of the LORD
all the days of my life,
to gaze upon the beauty of the LORD
and to seek him in his temple.
5For in the day of trouble
he will keep me safe in his dwelling;
he will hide me in the shelter of his tabernacle
and set me high upon a rock.
6Then my head will be exalted
above the enemies who surround me;
at his tabernacle will I sacrifice with shouts of joy;
I will sing and make music to the LORD.

7Hear my voice when I call, O LORD;
be merciful to me and answer me.
8My heart says of you, "Seek his[x] face!"
Your face, LORD, I will seek.
9Do not hide your face from me,
do not turn your servant away in anger;
you have been my helper.
Do not reject me or forsake me,
O God my Savior.
10Though my father and mother forsake me,
the LORD will receive me.
11Teach me your way, O LORD;
lead me in a straight path
because of my oppressors.
12Do not turn me over to the desire of my foes,
for false witnesses rise up against me,
breathing out violence.

13I am still confident of this:
I will see the goodness of the LORD
in the land of the living.
14Wait for the LORD;
be strong and take heart
and wait for the LORD.

x8 Or *To you, O my heart, he has said, "Seek my*

Discovering the Word 1. Why is David able to be fearless in the face of evil men, armies, and even war (vv. 1–3)? 2. What images of safety does David apply to the Lord in verses 1–2 and 5–6? 3. David seeks not only the Lord's protection but also the Lord himself (v. 4). How is David's intense desire for God revealed in this psalm (vv. 4, 8, 11)? 4. David's confident statements about the Lord (vv. 1–6) lead up to his prayer in verses 7–12. What is the substance of his prayer? 5. What real dangers does he seem to be facing? 6. Why must your hope not only be confident but also patient (v. 14)?

Applying the Word 1. How does it give you hope to know that the Lord is your stronghold (or "mighty fortress") during battle and your shelter from life's storms? 2. The psalm ends as it begins—with David's confidence in the Lord's help (vv. 13–14). How can David's view of God help you to "be strong and take heart" in the midst of suffering?

Responding in Prayer Ask God to strengthen your confidence in his promises and to make you patient as you wait for his answers.

Psalm 28

Psalm 28

Of David.

1To you I call, O LORD my Rock;
do not turn a deaf ear to me.
For if you remain silent,
I will be like those who have gone down to the pit.
2Hear my cry for mercy
as I call to you for help,
as I lift up my hands
toward your Most Holy Place.
3Do not drag me away with the wicked,
with those who do evil,
who speak cordially with their neighbors
but harbor malice in their hearts.
4Repay them for their deeds
and for their evil work;
repay them for what their hands have done
and bring back upon them what they deserve.
5Since they show no regard for the works of the LORD
and what his hands have done,
he will tear them down

and never build them up again.

6Praise be to the LORD,
for he has heard my cry for mercy.
7The LORD is my strength and my shield;
my heart trusts in him, and I am helped.
My heart leaps for joy
and I will give thanks to him in song.

8The LORD is the strength of his people,
a fortress of salvation for his anointed one.
9Save your people and bless your inheritance;
be their shepherd and carry them forever.

20 / *Psalm 29*
The Voice of the Lord

WHAT ARE THE ways that God chooses to speak to us? He uses the counsel of friends or the subtlety of our own conscience, and often he uses his own Word. But sometimes he speaks so that he can be heard loud and clear, and so that no one can be mistaken about what he is saying. This passage explores the ways we hear the voice of the Lord.

Warming Up to God Recall a time in your life when you felt that God was speaking to you specifically. Thank him for coming to you, and ask him now to speak to your listening heart.

Read Psalm 29.

Psalm 29

A psalm of David.

1Ascribe to the LORD, O mighty ones,
ascribe to the LORD glory and strength.
2Ascribe to the LORD the glory due his name;
worship the LORD in the splendor of his[y]
holiness.

3The voice of the LORD is over the waters;
the God of glory thunders,
the LORD thunders over the mighty waters.
4The voice of the LORD is powerful;
the voice of the LORD is majestic.
5The voice of the LORD breaks the cedars;
the LORD breaks in pieces the cedars of
Lebanon.
6He makes Lebanon skip like a calf,
Sirion[z] like a young wild ox.
7The voice of the LORD strikes
with flashes of lightning.
8The voice of the LORD shakes the desert;
the LORD shakes the Desert of Kadesh.
9The voice of the LORD twists the oaks[a]
and strips the forests bare.
And in his temple all cry, "Glory!"

10The LORD sits[b] enthroned over the flood;
the LORD is enthroned as King forever.
11The LORD gives strength to his people;
the LORD blesses his people with peace.

y2 Or *LORD with the splendor of* z6 That is, Mount Hermon a9 Or *LORD makes the deer give birth* b10 Or *sat*

Discovering the Word 1. The psalmist addresses a specific audience in verse 1—"mighty ones." Why do you think he speaks to them? 2. David urges his audience to "ascribe to the Lord glory and strength" (v. 1). How does his psalm accomplish this? 3. What does "the voice of the Lord" do (vv. 3–9)? 4. What characteristics of God do these verses bring to mind? 5. What does verse 9 tell us about the proper response to hearing the voice of God? 6. Most of Psalm 29 describes the actions of God as a mighty and powerful rainstorm, inspiring not only awe, but even fear. However, the psalm ends (v. 11) describing the actions of God in quite a different fashion. How does this complete the picture of God that David has painted?

Applying the Word 1. How does observing the power of God in both nature and in his own actions help us understand the nature and role of worship in our lives? 2. Sometimes God uses a storm to draw our attention to him and cause us to fall before him in awe, but he also "blesses his people with peace." How can this passage help you to better understand the ways of God and his workings in your life?

Responding in Prayer Take some time to "ascribe to the Lord" some of the marvelous deeds he has done for you.

21 / *Psalm 30*
Waiting for Security

MAJOR CORPORATIONS ARE laying off large numbers in the latest rage of downsizing. Those who have gotten a pink slip do their best to cover it, but you can see the pain in their eyes.

One of our basic human needs is security. In the end, if our security, in any area, is dependent on our own resources and abilities, then we must live in constant vigilance. How much better if the Creator of the universe were in charge of protecting us! In this psalm David relates the experience of looking to God for his security. He found it both a humbling and thrilling experience.

Warming Up to God Imagine that you have turned off the radio that is blaring away inside you. Sit for a while in the quiet. You may find that there are protests inside. What are your thoughts and impressions?

Read Psalm 30.

Psalm 30

A psalm. A song. For the dedication of the temple.[c] Of David.

1 I will exalt you, O LORD,
for you lifted me out of the depths
and did not let my enemies gloat over me.
2 O LORD my God, I called to you for help
and you healed me.
3 O LORD, you brought me up from the grave[d];
you spared me from going down into the pit.

4 Sing to the LORD, you saints of his;
praise his holy name.
5 For his anger lasts only a moment,
but his favor lasts a lifetime;
weeping may remain for a night,
but rejoicing comes in the morning.

6 When I felt secure, I said,
"I will never be shaken."
7 O LORD, when you favored me,
you made my mountain[e] stand firm;
but when you hid your face,
I was dismayed.

8 To you, O LORD, I called;
to the Lord I cried for mercy:
9 "What gain is there in my destruction,[f]
in my going down into the pit?
Will the dust praise you?
Will it proclaim your faithfulness?
10 Hear, O LORD, and be merciful to me;
O LORD, be my help."

11 You turned my wailing into dancing;
you removed my sackcloth and clothed me with joy,
12 that my heart may sing to you and not be silent.
O LORD my God, I will give you thanks forever.

[c]Title: Or *palace* [d]3 Hebrew *Sheol* [e]7 Or *hill country* [f]9 Or *there if I am silenced*

Discovering the Word 1. No one knows for sure what the problem was, but from the words "depths," "healed," "enemies," "grave" and "pit" what possible dangers may David have been facing? 2. Read the whole psalm again. List the range of emotions that is described. 3. What insight into life does David gain by acknowledging that painful as well as pleasurable experiences come from God (v. 5)? 4. How do verses 6–7 describe David's sense of dependence on God? 5. What reasons does David present to God in favor of his deliverance (vv. 9–10)? 6. Look over the entire psalm. How would you describe David's relationship with God?

Applying the Word 1. Difficult circumstances can cause us to reflect on the character of God. How have the circumstances of your life affected your relationship with God? 2. David expresses some of the ups and downs of his life. Consider the last six months to year of your life and chart your ups and downs. 3. Picture the Lord with you through the ups and downs of your life. How does it help you to know God is with you?

Responding in Prayer Give thanks to God for the ways he has been a help to you in the hard places of your life.

22 / *Psalm 31*
Rescued from Idolaters

WE LIVE IN a turbulent time. While the turbulence created by clashing belief systems seems new, the clash has been going on in different forms for thousands of years. In this psalm David affirms his choice to trust in the Lord rather than the popular idols of his age. In the current culture war we need to do the same.

Warming Up to God Make a list of everything you have to do and give it over to God. If God blesses you with a sense of peace, just sit for a while and enjoy his presence before you move on to study.

Read Psalm 31.

Psalm 31

For the director of music. A psalm of David.

1In you, O LORD, I have taken refuge;
let me never be put to shame;
deliver me in your righteousness.
2Turn your ear to me,
come quickly to my rescue;
be my rock of refuge,
a strong fortress to save me.
3Since you are my rock and my fortress,
for the sake of your name lead and guide me.
4Free me from the trap that is set for me,
for you are my refuge.
5Into your hands I commit my spirit;
redeem me, O LORD, the God of truth.

6I hate those who cling to worthless idols;
I trust in the LORD.
7I will be glad and rejoice in your love,
for you saw my affliction
and knew the anguish of my soul.
8You have not handed me over to the enemy
but have set my feet in a spacious place.
9Be merciful to me, O LORD, for I am in distress;
my eyes grow weak with sorrow,
my soul and my body with grief.
10My life is consumed by anguish
and my years by groaning;
my strength fails because of my affliction,[g]
and my bones grow weak.
11Because of all my enemies,
I am the utter contempt of my neighbors;
I am a dread to my friends—
those who see me on the street flee from me.
12I am forgotten by them as though I were dead;
I have become like broken pottery.
13For I hear the slander of many;
there is terror on every side;
they conspire against me
and plot to take my life.

14But I trust in you, O LORD;
I say, "You are my God."
15My times are in your hands;
deliver me from my enemies
and from those who pursue me.

g10 Or guilt

16Let your face shine on your servant;
save me in your unfailing love.
17Let me not be put to shame, O LORD,
for I have cried out to you;
but let the wicked be put to shame
and lie silent in the grave.[h]
18Let their lying lips be silenced,
for with pride and contempt
they speak arrogantly against the
righteous.

19How great is your goodness,
which you have stored up for those who
fear you,
which you bestow in the sight of men
on those who take refuge in you.
20In the shelter of your presence you
hide them
from the intrigues of men;
in your dwelling you keep them safe
from accusing tongues.

21Praise be to the LORD,
for he showed his wonderful love
to me
when I was in a besieged city.
22In my alarm I said,
"I am cut off from your sight!"
Yet you heard my cry for mercy
when I called to you for help.

23Love the LORD, all his saints!
The LORD preserves the faithful,
but the proud he pays back in full.
24Be strong and take heart,
all you who hope in the LORD.

[h]17 Hebrew *Sheol*

Discovering the Word 1. This is a psalm of urgency. What does David want from God (vv. 1–4)? 2. David feels threatened. What words does he use in these verses to describe his plight? 3. What words and ideas in verses 9–13 convey David's sense of isolation? 4. According to verses 14–18, what are several of the things David wants from God? 5. David's response to God's help is praise. What specific things does David praise God for?

Applying the Word 1. Consider a time in your life when you felt that others (perhaps non-Christians) held you in contempt and avoided you. How did it affect you? 2. What was your relationship with God like at that time? 3. What encouragement from God do you need to continue in a harsh world?

Responding in Prayer Tell God that you trust him with the "times" of your life. Ask him to make himself known in new ways to you and your family.

23 / *Psalm 32*
Confession and Forgiveness

JUST AS CHOLESTEROL is the silent killer of the physical heart, guilt is the silent killer of our souls. Cholesterol accumulates slowly over the years, residue left by a poor diet, inadequate exercise and perhaps genetic malfunction. So it is with guilt. Little by little, with each act of envy, lust, anger, resentment or other sin, guilt accumulates around our spiritual hearts. The good news is that God won't let us succumb to guilt without many warnings. The exposure of guilt is not for the purpose of condemnation (as it is with Satan) but for cleansing our hearts and restoring the flow of his love.

Warming Up to God What is causing you to feel frustrated or envious or resentful today? Give your feelings over to God one by one.

Read Psalm 32.

Psalm 32

Of David. A *maskil.*[i]

[1]Blessed is he
whose transgressions are forgiven,
whose sins are covered.
[2]Blessed is the man
whose sin the LORD does not count against
him
and in whose spirit is no deceit.

[3]When I kept silent,
my bones wasted away
through my groaning all day long.
[4]For day and night
your hand was heavy upon me;
my strength was sapped
as in the heat of summer. *Selah*
[5]Then I acknowledged my sin to you
and did not cover up my iniquity.
I said, "I will confess
my transgressions to the LORD"—
and you forgave
the guilt of my sin. *Selah*

[6]Therefore let everyone who is godly pray to
you
while you may be found;
surely when the mighty waters rise,
they will not reach him.
[7]You are my hiding place;
you will protect me from trouble
and surround me with songs of deliverance.
Selah

[8]I will instruct you and teach you in the way
you should go;
I will counsel you and watch over you.
[9]Do not be like the horse or the mule,
which have no understanding
but must be controlled by bit and bridle
or they will not come to you.
[10]Many are the woes of the wicked,
but the LORD's unfailing love
surrounds the man who trusts in him.

[11]Rejoice in the LORD and be glad, you
righteous;
sing, all you who are upright in heart!

[i]Title: Probably a literary or musical term

Discovering the Word 1. Verses 1 and 2 begin with the word *blessed.* How would you define *blessed* from the way David uses it in these verses? 2. David had a responsive conscience. How did his unexpressed sin affect him (vv. 3–4)? 3. It feels good to be forgiven. How does David respond in verses 6–11? 4. It is interesting that David experienced a sense of protection after receiving forgiveness (v. 7). How might unconfessed sin have made him feel vulnerable and exposed? 5. In verses 8–9 David records the Lord's promise of guidance. From these verses, what is the condition of receiving God's guidance?

Applying the Word 1. Consider whether there are things in the past for which you are guilty but have never sought forgiveness. Name those things. 2. Are there things in the past for which you feel guilty but for which there was really no wrong done? Explain.

Responding in Prayer Ask God's forgiveness for what you have done wrong, and experience his grace.

24 / *Psalm 33*
Hoping in the Word

AFTER MY CONVERSION I was shocked at what happened when I picked up the Bible. I found myself enticed, confronted, spoken to and challenged. I couldn't get enough of it. Now almost thirty years later, I still can't get enough. The words that God has spoken are never outdated. In this psalm David meditates on the powerful Word of God by which he creates and sustains his world. Because of the nature of God's Word, we need to open our ears to hear as we read to understand.

Warming Up to God In order to spend time with God today—stop! Don't try to run your own life, and don't tell God what to do. Present your life to God. Ask God to bring in his order.

Read Psalm 33.

Psalm 33

1 Sing joyfully to the LORD, you righteous;
it is fitting for the upright to praise him.
2 Praise the LORD with the harp;
make music to him on the ten-stringed
lyre.
3 Sing to him a new song;
play skillfully, and shout for joy.

4 For the word of the LORD is right and true;
he is faithful in all he does.
5 The LORD loves righteousness and justice;
the earth is full of his unfailing love.

6 By the word of the LORD were the heavens
made,
their starry host by the breath of his
mouth.
7 He gathers the waters of the sea into jars[j];
he puts the deep into storehouses.
8 Let all the earth fear the LORD;
let all the people of the world revere him.
9 For he spoke, and it came to be;
he commanded, and it stood firm.
10 The LORD foils the plans of the nations;
he thwarts the purposes of the peoples.
11 But the plans of the LORD stand firm forever,
the purposes of his heart through all
generations.
12 Blessed is the nation whose God is the LORD,
the people he chose for his inheritance.
13 From heaven the LORD looks down
and sees all mankind;
14 from his dwelling place he watches
all who live on earth—
15 he who forms the hearts of all,
who considers everything they do.
16 No king is saved by the size of his army;
no warrior escapes by his great strength.
17 A horse is a vain hope for deliverance;
despite all its great strength it cannot save.
18 But the eyes of the LORD are on those who
fear him,
on those whose hope is in his unfailing
love,
19 to deliver them from death
and keep them alive in famine.

20 We wait in hope for the LORD;
he is our help and our shield.
21 In him our hearts rejoice,
for we trust in his holy name.
22 May your unfailing love rest upon us, O LORD,
even as we put our hope in you.

j7 Or *sea as into a heap*

Discovering the Word 1. What is the emotional tone of this psalm? 2. The word of the Lord is one of the themes of this psalm. What can you learn about God's word from verses 1–11? 3. This psalm gives a big picture of God. Other nations thought of their god as a national deity with a limited realm of authority. Over what things does Israel's God have power (vv. 6–11)? 4. According to verses 12–22, what is God's relationship to the world he created? 5. What is his special relationship with "those who fear him" (vv. 18–22)?

Applying the Word 1. Imagine that God watched you conduct your day from beginning to end. What would he see about your actions? 2. How do they express your priorities, values and commitments? 3. What hopes for success do you have that are misdirected? (Consider whether you are trusting in your skills, your background, your education, your intelligence, your money, your influence, your friends . . . or a thousand other things.)

Responding in Prayer After you have identified your false hopes, turn them over to God. Ask him to take them from you.

25 / *Psalm 34*
Deliverance from Trouble

DAVID WRITES THIS psalm for the spiritually immature, who need to be instructed in the ways of God. One thing David thinks we need to know is how to live in a way that brings the blessing of God. How do we face the hard times? When we hurt, we want to know: Have we done something wrong? Has God deserted us? What do we need to do to receive God's help? These are good questions. If we pay attention to David, we will get some answers.

Warming Up to God It assaults our pride to acknowledge that there are things we don't know or problems we can't overcome. But when we stop trying to do it ourselves, we are in a position to receive the help God sends. List questions that you have for God. Don't tell him what to do, just ask. Then sit quietly for a while and listen.

Read Psalm 34.

Psalm 34[k]

Of David. When he pretended to be insane before Abimelech, who drove him away, and he left.

1 I will extol the LORD at all times;
his praise will always be on my lips.
2 My soul will boast in the LORD;
let the afflicted hear and rejoice.
3 Glorify the LORD with me;
let us exalt his name together.

4 I sought the LORD, and he answered me;
he delivered me from all my fears.
5 Those who look to him are radiant;
their faces are never covered with shame.
6 This poor man called, and the LORD heard
him;
he saved him out of all his troubles.
7 The angel of the LORD encamps around those
who fear him,
and he delivers them.
8 Taste and see that the LORD is good;
blessed is the man who takes refuge in him.
9 Fear the LORD, you his saints,
for those who fear him lack nothing.
10 The lions may grow weak and hungry,
but those who seek the LORD lack no good
thing.

11 Come, my children, listen to me;
I will teach you the fear of the LORD.
12 Whoever of you loves life
and desires to see many good days,
13 keep your tongue from evil
and your lips from speaking lies.
14 Turn from evil and do good;
seek peace and pursue it.

15 The eyes of the LORD are on the righteous
and his ears are attentive to their cry;
16 the face of the LORD is against those who do
evil,
to cut off the memory of them from the
earth.

17 The righteous cry out, and the LORD hears
them;
he delivers them from all their troubles.
18 The LORD is close to the brokenhearted
and saves those who are crushed in spirit.

19 A righteous man may have many troubles,
but the LORD delivers him from them all;
20 he protects all his bones,
not one of them will be broken.

21 Evil will slay the wicked;
the foes of the righteous will be
condemned.
22 The LORD redeems his servants;
no one will be condemned who takes
refuge in him.

[k] This psalm is an acrostic poem, the verses of which begin with the successive letters of the Hebrew alphabet.

Discovering the Word 1. What words does David use in verses 1–10 to express his feelings toward God? 2. What benefits are mentioned in verses 1–10 that come to those who seek God's help? 3. What do you think David means by inviting his readers to "taste and see that the Lord is good"? 4. From verses 11–22, describe a righteous person. 5. According to what David writes, righteousness doesn't guarantee a trouble-free life. What assurances of comfort do the righteous have during times of pain?

Applying the Word 1. How can the goodness of God be a means of strength in the problems that you face? 2. *Fear of the Lord* is an Old Testament term for "respect and submission to God." We should be afraid of offending God with conscious acts of disobedience. What temptations are you facing now? 3. How can learning the fear of the Lord keep you acting and thinking righteously?

Responding in Prayer Ask God to increase your ability to "taste and see" that he is with you and that he is good.

26 / *Psalm 35*
Protection from My Enemies

YOU MIGHT BE tempted to look at this psalm as barbaric and primitive. It contains angry thoughts of revenge. When David feels hurt, the anger pours forth in an eloquent torrent. There is no sense of "I'm not supposed to feel this way." Christian maturity is not about reducing the highs and lows of emotions to a level plane, but of feeling deeply in a godly way. The issue is not how or what we feel, but what we do with our emotions. David shows the way.

Warming Up to God Those who know God hunger for him. Before you begin your study, allow a desire for God to rise within you.

Read Psalm 35.

Psalm 35

Of David.

1Contend, O LORD, with those who contend
with me;
fight against those who fight against me.
2Take up shield and buckler;
arise and come to my aid.
3Brandish spear and javelin[l]
against those who pursue me.
Say to my soul,
"I am your salvation."

4May those who seek my life
be disgraced and put to shame;
may those who plot my ruin
be turned back in dismay.
5May they be like chaff before the wind,
with the angel of the LORD driving them
away;
6may their path be dark and slippery,
with the angel of the LORD pursuing them.
7Since they hid their net for me without cause
and without cause dug a pit for me,
8may ruin overtake them by surprise—
may the net they hid entangle them,
may they fall into the pit, to their ruin.
9Then my soul will rejoice in the LORD
and delight in his salvation.
10My whole being will exclaim,
"Who is like you, O LORD?
You rescue the poor from those too strong for
them,
the poor and needy from those who rob
them."

11Ruthless witnesses come forward;
they question me on things I know nothing
about.
12They repay me evil for good
and leave my soul forlorn.
13Yet when they were ill, I put on sackcloth
and humbled myself with fasting.
When my prayers returned to me
unanswered,
14 I went about mourning
as though for my friend or brother.
I bowed my head in grief
as though weeping for my mother.
15But when I stumbled, they gathered in glee;

[l]3 Or *and block the way*

attackers gathered against me when I was
unaware.
They slandered me without ceasing.
16 Like the ungodly they maliciously mocked[m];
they gnashed their teeth at me.
17 O Lord, how long will you look on?
Rescue my life from their ravages,
my precious life from these lions.
18 I will give you thanks in the great
assembly;
among throngs of people I will
praise you.

19 Let not those gloat over me
who are my enemies without cause;
let not those who hate me without reason
maliciously wink the eye.
20 They do not speak peaceably,
but devise false accusations
against those who live quietly in
the land.
21 They gape at me and say, "Aha! Aha!
With our own eyes we have seen it."

22 O LORD, you have seen this; be not silent.
Do not be far from me, O Lord.
23 Awake, and rise to my defense!
Contend for me, my God and Lord.
24 Vindicate me in your righteousness, O LORD
my God;
do not let them gloat over me.
25 Do not let them think, "Aha, just what we
wanted!"
or say, "We have swallowed him up."

26 May all who gloat over my distress
be put to shame and confusion;
may all who exalt themselves over me
be clothed with shame and disgrace.
27 May those who delight in my vindication
shout for joy and gladness;
may they always say, "The LORD be
exalted,
who delights in the well-being of his
servant."
28 My tongue will speak of your righteousness
and of your praises all day long.

m 16 Septuagint; Hebrew may mean *ungodly circle of mockers.*

Discovering the Word 1. In your own words describe the different kinds of misfortune David would like to see inflicted on those who have hurt him (vv. 4–6, 8, 26). 2. What reasons does David give for being so hurt and angry (vv. 4, 7, 11–16, 19–21)? 3. What do verses 11–16 reveal about David's enemies? 4. What does the cry "How long will you look on?" (v. 17) imply about David's sense of God's help? 5. David continues with the description of his adversaries' behavior. What have his enemies done in verses 19–28 to hurt him?

Applying the Word 1. We may not feel gracious toward those who hurt us, but we choose to act that way, not from feelings but from obedience to Jesus Christ. Who do you feel hostility and anger toward? 2. When we come through a trying experience with a sense of victory, it is natural to think about what a good job we have done and how cleverly we have faced our problems. David, however, avoids the temptation of personal boasting and gives praise to God. How does waiting on the Lord for help keep us from taking credit that belongs to God?

Responding in Prayer Ask God to bless those who have hurt you.

27 / *Psalm 36*
The Fountain of the Lord's Love

I FIND LOVE difficult to talk about. For one thing, my need for love is embarrassing. When I acknowledge that I need love, it means that I am not complete in myself. To receive love, I must look to someone else. To make matters worse, I find that my need for love is inexhaustible. Yesterday's love is not enough for today.

Our need for love means we need people—friends, spouses, family members. However, our need for love is such that even if all those people loved us perfectly, we still wouldn't have enough love to meet our need. David celebrates the good news that God's supply of love is more than sufficient. God's love reaches to the heavens and has more substance than the biggest mountains.

Warming Up to God Consider how open you are to receiving love from God, your family, friends and fellow Christians. Ask God to soften your heart as you prepare to spend time in his Word. Give over to God any hardening factors that you can discern.

Read Psalm 36.

Psalm 36

For the director of music. Of David the servant of the LORD.

1 An oracle is within my heart
concerning the sinfulness of the wicked:[n]
There is no fear of God
before his eyes.
2 For in his own eyes he flatters himself
too much to detect or hate his sin.
3 The words of his mouth are wicked and deceitful;
he has ceased to be wise and to do good.
4 Even on his bed he plots evil;
he commits himself to a sinful course
and does not reject what is wrong.

5 Your love, O LORD, reaches to the heavens,
your faithfulness to the skies.
6 Your righteousness is like the mighty mountains,
your justice like the great deep.
O LORD, you preserve both man and beast.
7 How priceless is your unfailing love!
Both high and low among men
find[o] refuge in the shadow of your wings.
8 They feast on the abundance of your house;
you give them drink from your river of delights.
9 For with you is the fountain of life;
in your light we see light.

10 Continue your love to those who know you,
your righteousness to the upright in heart.
11 May the foot of the proud not come against me,
nor the hand of the wicked drive me away.
12 See how the evildoers lie fallen—
thrown down, not able to rise!

[n]1 *Or heart: / Sin proceeds from the wicked.* [o]7 *Or love, O God! / Men find; or love! / Both heavenly beings and men / find*

Discovering the Word 1. Describe the character of a wicked person from verses 1–4. 2. Describe the dynamics of a wicked person's relationship to God. 3. What decisions does a wicked person make that lead to a sinful life (vv. 2–4)? 4. David observes that there is no fear of the Lord before the eyes of the wicked. From verses 5–9, what is it that they are blind to? 5. Initially David seems to jump without transition from musing on the wicked to writing on the love of God. However, in verses 10–12 he ties the two themes together. What do these verses tell you about David's experiences?

Applying the Word 1. We all have sinful thoughts from time to time. The wicked, however, do not reject such thoughts. Instead they choose to entertain them and then make a commitment to act upon them. What are some thoughts you have chosen to reject recently because you knew they were wrong? 2. Consider your own ability to accept the Lord's love and his benefits. What hesitations do you have that the Lord loves you? 3. What would have to happen for you to be more open to his love?

Responding in Prayer After you have done that, give thanks to God that he has been so active in helping you choose what is right. If you find that you have let some ungodly ideas settle in your heart, reject them now and ask God to cleanse and redirect your thinking patterns.

28 / *Psalm 37:1–17*
The Peace of the Lord

COMING TO A narrow spot in the road during a Sunday afternoon ride, I got off and walked my bike. I'd gone only a short distance when a car swerved toward me. I dove for the ditch. As the car drove off, I was filled with indignation and rage. What the driver did was foolish, but I was surprised at the intensity of my fuming response. I wanted to yell and shake my fist. Something was out of place in my spirit. In my quiet time a couple of days later, I discovered a list of unresolved hurts and growing grudges. I set aside my Bible reading for the day and had a time of heart cleaning with the Lord.

David says that for us to enjoy peace in the land we have to "refrain from anger and turn from wrath." If you pay attention to what he says, then you will find a new way of coping with anger.

Warming Up to God The first step in receiving God's peace is to stop shouting so loud. (If we aren't actually shouting out loud, we are usually doing so in our hearts.) Once we stop, he can sort things out. Put down the burdens and fights you face. Give them to God and allow him to speak peace to your heart.

Read Psalm 37:1–17.

Psalm 37[p]

Of David.

1Do not fret because of evil men
or be envious of those who do wrong;
2for like the grass they will soon wither,
like green plants they will soon die away.

3Trust in the LORD and do good;
dwell in the land and enjoy safe pasture.
4Delight yourself in the LORD
and he will give you the desires of your heart.

5Commit your way to the LORD;
trust in him and he will do this:
6He will make your righteousness shine like the dawn,
the justice of your cause like the noonday sun.

7Be still before the LORD and wait patiently for him;
do not fret when men succeed in their ways,
when they carry out their wicked schemes.
8Refrain from anger and turn from wrath;
do not fret—it leads only to evil.
9For evil men will be cut off,
but those who hope in the LORD will inherit the land.

10A little while, and the wicked will be no more;
though you look for them, they will not be found.
11But the meek will inherit the land
and enjoy great peace.

12The wicked plot against the righteous
and gnash their teeth at them;
13but the Lord laughs at the wicked,
for he knows their day is coming.

14The wicked draw the sword
and bend the bow
to bring down the poor and needy,
to slay those whose ways are upright.
15But their swords will pierce their own hearts,
and their bows will be broken.

16Better the little that the righteous have
than the wealth of many wicked;
17for the power of the wicked will be broken,
but the LORD upholds the righteous.

[p] This psalm is an acrostic poem, the stanzas of which begin with the successive letters of the Hebrew alphabet.

Discovering the Word 1. David gives an unusually extensive list of exhortations to his readers in verses 1–7. List them in your own words. 2. What benefits does God give to those who live this way? 3. We are not to worry when those who are evil succeed (v. 6). Why not? 4. What are the contrasts between the righteous and the wicked in verses 8–17? 5. Against the backdrop of the wicked, how is God's promise of peace and land an encouragement?

Applying the Word 1. David encourages you to "delight yourself in the Lord." What do you find delightful about knowing God? 2. What hesitations do you have that would keep you from delighting in God?

Responding in Prayer Pray for those who are angry at you. Ask God to bless them.

29 / *Psalm 37:18–40*
Our Inheritance

AS A NEW Christian, I was sure that life would be easier than it had been. I had been in deep trouble emotionally, spiritually and academically. My salvation brought visible, revolutionary changes to all those areas. Everyone knew that *something* had happened. Now looking back several decades, the changes were real. But I'm not so quick to say that becoming a Christian makes life easier. However, it is worth it. This psalm is written from David's perspective of knowing God for over eighty years. David affirms that God keeps his promises and brings rewards to those who trust him.

Warming Up to God Consider the staggering fact that the Creator of time and eternity loves you. Write down ten things you can think of about the love of God.

Read Psalm 37:18–40.

18The days of the blameless are known to the
LORD,
and their inheritance will endure forever.
19In times of disaster they will not wither;
in days of famine they will enjoy plenty.

20But the wicked will perish:
The LORD's enemies will be like the beauty
of the fields,
they will vanish—vanish like smoke.
21The wicked borrow and do not repay,
but the righteous give generously;
22those the LORD blesses will inherit the land,
but those he curses will be cut off.

23If the LORD delights in a man's way,
he makes his steps firm;
24though he stumble, he will not fall,
for the LORD upholds him with his hand.

25I was young and now I am old,
yet I have never seen the righteous forsaken
or their children begging bread.
26They are always generous and lend freely;
their children will be blessed.

27Turn from evil and do good;
then you will dwell in the land forever.
28For the LORD loves the just
and will not forsake his faithful ones.
They will be protected forever,
but the offspring of the wicked will be cut
off;
29the righteous will inherit the land
and dwell in it forever.

30The mouth of the righteous man utters
wisdom,
and his tongue speaks what is just.
31The law of his God is in his heart;
his feet do not slip.

32The wicked lie in wait for the righteous,
seeking their very lives;
33but the LORD will not leave them in their
power
or let them be condemned when brought to
trial.

34Wait for the LORD
and keep his way.
He will exalt you to inherit the land;
when the wicked are cut off, you will see
it.

35I have seen a wicked and ruthless man
flourishing like a green tree in its native
soil,
36but he soon passed away and was no more;
though I looked for him, he could not be
found.

[37]Consider the blameless, observe the upright;
  there is a future[q] for the man of peace.
[38]But all sinners will be destroyed;
  the future[r] of the wicked will be cut off.

[39]The salvation of the righteous comes from the
    LORD;
  he is their stronghold in time of trouble.
[40]The LORD helps them and delivers them;
  he delivers them from the wicked and saves
    them,
  because they take refuge in him.

[q]37 *Or there will be posterity* [r]38 *Or posterity*

Discovering the Word 1. What are the contrasts between the blameless and the wicked in verses 18–24? 2. What can we know about the future of the wicked (vv. 20, 22, 28, 33–35)? 3. What are the benefits that come to the righteous in the end (vv. 18, 25, 28–29, 33, 37, 39–40)? 4. From verses 25–36, describe the character and actions of the righteous. 5. Describe the relationship between the wicked and the righteous in verses 32–40.

Applying the Word 1. David emphasizes the theme of inheritance in these verses. How can the anticipation of a future inheritance affect the way you live today in your relationships and the way you use your money and your possessions? 2. Let's get more specific. If you knew that all you could want would be coming to you in five years, how would it affect your actions and decisions today?

Responding in Prayer Pray for those you know who are facing hard times. Ask God to bring his comfort, protection and provision.

30 / *Psalm 38*
Rebuke and Judgment

IF I AM willing to acknowledge that God blesses me, I must be willing to acknowledge that he disciplines me as well. As the author of Hebrews writes, "the Lord disciplines those he loves." God refuses to let me go my own way. This is good news indeed! At the same time, when I talk about the blessing or the judgment of God, I must be careful. I don't understand all that the Lord does. What appears to be a blessing may not be, while what appears to be judgment may not be either. Let's see if we can gain a little light on this difficult issue from David.

Warming Up to God God is constantly rescuing us from tight spots. Some of those tight spots we are aware of; most we are not. Make a list of thank-yous to God for as many instances of his help as you can think of.

Read Psalm 38.

Psalm 38

A psalm of David. A petition.

[1]O LORD, do not rebuke me in your anger
  or discipline me in your wrath.
[2]For your arrows have pierced me,
  and your hand has come down upon me.
[3]Because of your wrath there is no health in
    my body;
  my bones have no soundness because of my
    sin.
[4]My guilt has overwhelmed me
  like a burden too heavy to bear.

[5]My wounds fester and are loathsome
  because of my sinful folly.
[6]I am bowed down and brought very low;
  all day long I go about mourning.
[7]My back is filled with searing pain;
  there is no health in my body.
[8]I am feeble and utterly crushed;
  I groan in anguish of heart.

[9]All my longings lie open before you, O Lord;
  my sighing is not hidden from you.
[10]My heart pounds, my strength fails me;
  even the light has gone from my eyes.

11 My friends and companions avoid me because
of my wounds;
my neighbors stay far away.
12 Those who seek my life set their traps,
those who would harm me talk of
my ruin;
all day long they plot deception.

13 I am like a deaf man, who cannot
hear,
like a mute, who cannot open his
mouth;
14 I have become like a man who does
not hear,
whose mouth can offer no reply.
15 I wait for you, O LORD;
you will answer, O Lord my God.
16 For I said, "Do not let them gloat
or exalt themselves over me when my foot
slips."
17 For I am about to fall,
and my pain is ever with me.
18 I confess my iniquity;
I am troubled by my sin.
19 Many are those who are my vigorous
enemies;
those who hate me without reason are
numerous.
20 Those who repay my good with evil
slander me when I pursue what is good.

21 O LORD, do not forsake me;
be not far from me, O my God.
22 Come quickly to help me,
O Lord my Savior.

Discovering the Word 1. David writes during a time of great pain. What images does he use to describe his situation (vv. 2–14)? 2. What reasons can you discover for his all-encompassing pain in these verses? 3. What physical, social and spiritual afflictions is David experiencing in these verses? 4. Describe David's attitude toward God in the midst of his afflictions. 5. What specific things does David want God to do to help him with his pain (vv. 15–16, 21–22)?

Applying the Word 1. What dangers and what benefits come from thinking of our physical, emotional and spiritual states as being the result of the discipline of God? 2. Although David is experiencing rejection and persecution, he acknowledges that he has sinned and shares in the responsibility for his affliction. When have you experienced pain that was at least partly your fault? How did you handle it? 3. What can you learn from David's example?

Responding in Prayer Pray for those whom you have offended this past year. Ask God's blessing on them.

---

31 / *Psalm 39*
Facing Life's End

JANE WALMSLEY, TELEVISION correspondent and commentator on American life, says that an essential element of the American psyche is the fervent belief and hope that somehow it is possible to elude death. That hope of eluding death flies in the face of reality. No one has. Life this side of the Fall is 100 percent fatal. There are some, and David would be among them, who would say that only those who have faced their death can really live life properly. In this psalm he asks God to help him take a long-term view of life, and as you shall read, that includes the impending prospect of death.

Warming Up to God While we can never quite get our minds around this, the good news is that an eternal God can offer eternal life. Express praise and thanksgiving to our immortal God.

Read Psalm 39.

Psalm 39

For the director of music. For Jeduthun.
A psalm of David.

1I said, "I will watch my ways
and keep my tongue from sin;
I will put a muzzle on my mouth
as long as the wicked are in my presence."
2But when I was silent and still,
not even saying anything good,
my anguish increased.
3My heart grew hot within me,
and as I meditated, the fire burned;
then I spoke with my tongue:
4"Show me, O LORD, my life's end
and the number of my days;
let me know how fleeting is my life.
5You have made my days a mere handbreadth;
the span of my years is as nothing before you.
Each man's life is but a breath. *Selah*
6Man is a mere phantom as he goes to and fro:
He bustles about, but only in vain;
he heaps up wealth, not knowing who will get it.
7"But now, Lord, what do I look for?
My hope is in you.
8Save me from all my transgressions;
do not make me the scorn of fools.
9I was silent; I would not open my mouth,
for you are the one who has done this.
10Remove your scourge from me;
I am overcome by the blow of your hand.
11You rebuke and discipline men for their sin;
you consume their wealth like a moth—
each man is but a breath. *Selah*

12"Hear my prayer, O LORD,
listen to my cry for help;
be not deaf to my weeping.
For I dwell with you as an alien,
a stranger, as all my fathers were.
13Look away from me, that I may rejoice again
before I depart and am no more."

Discovering the Word 1. Remembering that the psalms combine life experience, knowledge of God and emotions, how would you describe David's mood and situation in this psalm? 2. David chooses to be silent in the presence of some hostile people. What effect does David's silence have on him in verses 1–6? 3. When David breaks his silence, he does so by offering a prayer to face his mortality. What does David know (vv. 5–6), and what does he want to know (v. 4)? 4. This is a psalm of judgment. In your own words describe God's approach toward sin in verses 7–13. 5. What does David desire from God for himself (vv. 8, 10)? 6. How does David seem to have come to terms with his death at the end of this passage?

Applying the Word 1. How does considering your own mortality affect the way you think of the present and the future, your possessions, and your relationships? 2. How does the knowledge of eternal life through Jesus Christ affect your reflections?

Responding in Prayer Following David's example, ask God to help you see as much about your own mortality as you can handle. Sit quietly and wait for the Lord's insight. Write down what benefits you can perceive from facing your own death.

32 / *Psalm 40*
Learning to Wait on the Lord

JUDY HAD A portable phone beside her. Her son's wife was expecting, and Judy was about to become a grandmother for the first time. During the entire Bible study, Judy contributed to our discussion. However, if that phone had rung with news of her daughter-in-law's labor, Judy would have been out of there in a minute. Just as Judy was prepared to receive a call and ready to respond when it came, so we should be waiting on the Lord.

Warming Up to God Jesus calls his disciples to deny themselves, take up their cross and follow him. Commit yourself, body and soul, to him. As reservations or objections rise to the surface, ask Jesus to take them from you.

Read Psalm 40.

Psalm 40

For the director of music. Of David.
A psalm.

1 I waited patiently for the LORD;
he turned to me and heard my cry.
2 He lifted me out of the slimy pit,
out of the mud and mire;
he set my feet on a rock
and gave me a firm place to stand.
3 He put a new song in my mouth,
a hymn of praise to our God.
Many will see and fear
and put their trust in the LORD.

4 Blessed is the man
who makes the LORD his trust,
who does not look to the proud,
to those who turn aside to false gods.[s]
5 Many, O LORD my God,
are the wonders you have done.
The things you planned for us
no one can recount to you;
were I to speak and tell of them,
they would be too many to declare.

6 Sacrifice and offering you did not desire,
but my ears you have pierced[t,u];
burnt offerings and sin offerings
you did not require.
7 Then I said, "Here I am, I have come—
it is written about me in the scroll.[v]
8 I desire to do your will, O my God;
your law is within my heart."

9 I proclaim righteousness in the great
assembly;
I do not seal my lips,
as you know, O LORD.
10 I do not hide your righteousness in my heart;
I speak of your faithfulness and salvation.
I do not conceal your love and your truth
from the great assembly.

11 Do not withhold your mercy from me,
O LORD;
may your love and your truth always
protect me.
12 For troubles without number surround me;
my sins have overtaken me, and I cannot
see.
They are more than the hairs of my head,
and my heart fails within me.

13 Be pleased, O LORD, to save me;
O LORD, come quickly to help me.
14 May all who seek to take my life
be put to shame and confusion;
may all who desire my ruin
be turned back in disgrace.
15 May those who say to me, "Aha! Aha!"
be appalled at their own shame.
16 But may all who seek you
rejoice and be glad in you;
may those who love your salvation always
say,
"The LORD be exalted!"

17 Yet I am poor and needy;
may the Lord think of me.
You are my help and my deliverer;
O my God, do not delay.

[s]4 Or *to falsehood* [t]6 Hebrew; Septuagint *but a body you have prepared for me* (see also Symmachus and Theodotion) [u]6 Or *opened* [v]7 Or *come / with the scroll written for me*

Discovering the Word 1. In response to God's help, David proclaims righteousness, doesn't seal his lips, doesn't hide God's righteousness and does not conceal God's love. From your reading of verses 1–10, what is he eager to make known? 2. Compare verses 1–10 with verses 11–17. How does the psalm's tone change in the second half? 3. Considering David's attitude in these verses, put into your own words David's description of life's dilemma. 4. What effect does it have on him? 5. David begins this psalm by saying he waited patiently. He concludes by asking that God would not delay. What do the elements of patience and the need for a speedy answer contribute to your understanding of what it means to wait on God?

Applying the Word 1. Waiting in a slimy pit—what a graphic picture of needing God's help! Imagine that you are in a slimy pit from which you need deliverance. What things in your life have placed you in that pit, and what makes it "slimy"? 2. As you call out for God to deliver you, what is it like to wait on God? 3. Imagine that you knew Jesus Christ was coming back in one week. How would you spend your week waiting?

Responding in Prayer Pray for your loved ones that don't yet have a relationship with Jesus Christ. Ask the Spirit to give them hungry hearts for his love.

Psalm 41

Psalm 41

For the director of music. A psalm of David.

1Blessed is he who has regard for the weak;
the LORD delivers him in times of trouble.
2The LORD will protect him and preserve his life;
he will bless him in the land
and not surrender him to the desire of his foes.
3The LORD will sustain him on his sickbed
and restore him from his bed of illness.

4I said, "O LORD, have mercy on me;
heal me, for I have sinned against you."
5My enemies say of me in malice,
"When will he die and his name perish?"
6Whenever one comes to see me,
he speaks falsely, while his heart gathers slander;
then he goes out and spreads it abroad.

7All my enemies whisper together against me;
they imagine the worst for me, saying,
8"A vile disease has beset him;
he will never get up from the place where he lies."
9Even my close friend, whom I trusted,
he who shared my bread,
has lifted up his heel against me.

10But you, O LORD, have mercy on me;
raise me up, that I may repay them.
11I know that you are pleased with me,
for my enemy does not triumph over me.
12In my integrity you uphold me
and set me in your presence forever.

13Praise be to the LORD, the God of Israel,
from everlasting to everlasting.
Amen and Amen.

33 / *Psalms 42—43*
Hoping in the Lord

THE AUTHOR OF Psalm 42 was a musician who used to lead the procession of worshipers to the temple in Jerusalem. But now the holy temple of God lay in ruins; the fields and vineyards were burned, and this former spiritual leader sat six hundred miles away—an exile in Babylon.

The psalmist grieved over his circumstances. Like the other holy people of his era, he had linked drawing near to God with going up to God's temple. How could he worship God now? And, as his taunters reminded him, where was God anyway?

Warming Up to God When is it hard for you to worship God? Talk honestly with God about your struggles.

Read Psalms 42—43.

BOOK II

Psalms 42–72

Psalm 42[w]

For the director of music. A *maskil*[x] of the Sons of Korah.

1As the deer pants for streams of water,
so my soul pants for you, O God.
2My soul thirsts for God, for the living God.
When can I go and meet with God?
3My tears have been my food
day and night,
while men say to me all day long,
"Where is your God?"
4These things I remember
as I pour out my soul:
how I used to go with the multitude,
leading the procession to the house of God,
with shouts of joy and thanksgiving
among the festive throng.

5Why are you downcast, O my soul?
Why so disturbed within me?
Put your hope in God,
for I will yet praise him,
my Savior and 6my God.

My[y] soul is downcast within me;
therefore I will remember you
from the land of the Jordan,
the heights of Hermon—from Mount Mizar.
7Deep calls to deep
in the roar of your waterfalls;
all your waves and breakers
have swept over me.

8By day the LORD directs his love,
at night his song is with me—
a prayer to the God of my life.

9I say to God my Rock,
"Why have you forgotten me?
Why must I go about mourning,
oppressed by the enemy?"
10My bones suffer mortal agony
as my foes taunt me,
saying to me all day long,
"Where is your God?"

11Why are you downcast, O my soul?
Why so disturbed within me?
Put your hope in God,
for I will yet praise him,
my Savior and my God.

Psalm 43[w]

1Vindicate me, O God,
and plead my cause against an ungodly nation;
rescue me from deceitful and wicked men.
2You are God my stronghold.
Why have you rejected me?
Why must I go about mourning,
oppressed by the enemy?
3Send forth your light and your truth,
let them guide me;
let them bring me to your holy mountain,
to the place where you dwell.
4Then will I go to the altar of God,
to God, my joy and my delight.
I will praise you with the harp,
O God, my God.

5Why are you downcast, O my soul?
Why so disturbed within me?
Put your hope in God,
for I will yet praise him,
my Savior and my God.

[w] In many Hebrew manuscripts Psalms 42 and 43 constitute one psalm.
[x] Title: Probably a literary or musical term
[y] 5,6 A few Hebrew manuscripts, Septuagint and Syriac; most Hebrew manuscripts *praise him for his saving help. / 6O my God, my*

Discovering the Word 1. 42:5 and 11 and 43:5 form a refrain for this psalm. What do you find in this refrain that makes it important enough to repeat? 2. The psalmist speaks honestly and openly to God. What words does he use to tell how he is feeling? 3. Why might the psalmist's honest words with God about his past and his present help to strengthen his faith? 4. Not all of what the psalmist says is about himself and his past. He also focuses on God. What aspects of God's character does he acknowledge (42:5, 8–9; 43:2, 3)? 5. How might a firm belief in a God of this character bring hope—even to an ancient Hebrew in exile?

Applying the Word 1. What kinds of things are likely to throw you into depression? 2. What do you talk about with God and with others when you are depressed? 3. Based on these psalms, when depression comes, what measures can you take to begin to cope with it?

4In your majesty ride forth victoriously
in behalf of truth, humility and
righteousness;
let your right hand display awesome deeds.
5Let your sharp arrows pierce the hearts of the
king's enemies;
let the nations fall beneath your feet.
6Your throne, O God, will last for ever and
ever;
a scepter of justice will be the scepter of
your kingdom.
7You love righteousness and hate wickedness;
therefore God, your God, has set you above
your companions
by anointing you with the oil of joy.
8All your robes are fragrant with myrrh and
aloes and cassia;
from palaces adorned with ivory
the music of the strings makes you glad.
9Daughters of kings are among your honored
women;
at your right hand is the royal bride in gold
of Ophir.
10Listen, O daughter, consider and give ear:
Forget your people and your father's house.
11The king is enthralled by your beauty;
honor him, for he is your lord.
12The Daughter of Tyre will come with a gift,[c]
men of wealth will seek your favor.

13All glorious is the princess within her
chamber;
her gown is interwoven with gold.
14In embroidered garments she is led to the
king;
her virgin companions follow her
and are brought to you.
15They are led in with joy and gladness;
they enter the palace of the king.

16Your sons will take the place of your fathers;
you will make them princes throughout the
land.
17I will perpetuate your memory through all
generations;
therefore the nations will praise you for
ever and ever.

[c]12 Or *A Tyrian robe is among the gifts*

Discovering the Word 1. Psalm 45 is a wedding song celebrating the marriage of a king of David's dynasty to a foreign princess. Twice in the psalm the poet refers to himself. What does he say are his purposes for writing (vv. 1, 17)? 2. What are the characteristics of this king? 3. How could these verses (particularly 6–7) refer to more than David's reign? 4. Verses 6 and 7 are quoted in Hebrews 1 and are used to describe the reign of Jesus Christ. How could the description of the king in this passage be applied to Christ? 5. What are the characteristics of the bride, and what is the attitude surrounding her coming (vv. 10–16)?

Applying the Word 1. We are Christ's bride. What promises do you see for yourself in this passage? 2. What kind of a response does seeing the majesty of Christ cause in your own life?

Responding in Prayer Thank God that your heart has been "stirred by a noble theme"—the promises of the King coming for his bride. Praise him for his majesty and the overwhelming awe that you feel because he has chosen *you* to be his bride.

36/ *Psalm 46*
Still Point in a Turning World

MARTIN LUTHER'S FAMOUS hymn "A Mighty Fortress Is Our God" is based on Psalm 46. This psalm celebrates Jerusalem as the city of God, the sure foundation for the kingdom of God. Today we can find spiritual strength and security in this psalm, especially when everything else is so topsy-turvy.

Warming Up to God Consider the times of loss, tragedy or high anxiety when you thought your world was falling apart. How were you able to find the strength to face the dawn of another day?

 **Read Psalm 46.**

Psalm 46

For the director of music. Of the Sons of Korah. According to *alamoth*.[d] A song.

1God is our refuge and strength,
an ever-present help in trouble.
2Therefore we will not fear, though the earth give way
and the mountains fall into the heart of the sea,
3though its waters roar and foam
and the mountains quake with their surging. *Selah*
4There is a river whose streams make glad the city of God,
the holy place where the Most High dwells.
5God is within her, she will not fall;
God will help her at break of day.
6Nations are in uproar, kingdoms fall;
he lifts his voice, the earth melts.

7The LORD Almighty is with us;
the God of Jacob is our fortress. *Selah*

8Come and see the works of the LORD,
the desolations he has brought on the earth.
9He makes wars cease to the ends of the earth;
he breaks the bow and shatters the spear,
he burns the shields[e] with fire.
10"Be still, and know that I am God;
I will be exalted among the nations,
I will be exalted in the earth."

11The LORD Almighty is with us;
the God of Jacob is our fortress. *Selah*

[d]Title: Probably a musical term [e]9 Or *chariots*

Discovering the Word 1. This psalm readily falls into three stanzas (vv. 1–3, 4–6 and 8–10) plus two refrains, or chorus lines (vv. 7, 11). What themes emerge in each section? 2. What images of a world falling apart do you see in these verses? 3. What truth about God is conveyed here in contrast to the world? 4. What effect does God's triumph over the nations have on the people who draw their strength from him (vv. 8–10)? 5. Where does one find stillness and security in the midst of violent forces unleashed all around (vv. 10–11)?

Applying the Word 1. What in your life is threatening or pounding away at your sense of security in God? 2. How can you remain still (v. 10) and know God's fortresslike strength (vv. 7, 11) in the midst of a world falling apart?

Responding in Prayer As God has triumphed, and will triumph, over all that wars against the city of Jerusalem and the soul of the believer, how can you exalt him among the nations? Spend some time being still and centering on him.

37 / *Psalm 47*
Being Devoted to God

THE SIGN OF a spiritually healthy heart is gratitude and affection. You will discover that after you have spent time with God, there rises from within your heart a deep sense of gratitude. Galatians 4:6 says, "Because you are sons, God sent the Spirit of his Son into our hearts, the Spirit who calls out, '*Abba,* Father.' " We can actually sense the Spirit within us as he cries, "Abba, Father."

Warming Up to God Make a list of things you are thankful for. While you may not be able to express gratitude right now, it will come in time if you continue to walk in this inner spiritual pilgrimage. If you do feel gratitude, sit for a while in heartfelt thanks to God.

 **Read Psalm 47.**

Psalm 47

For the director of music. Of the Sons of Korah. A psalm.

1Clap your hands, all you nations;
shout to God with cries of joy.
2How awesome is the LORD Most High,
the great King over all the earth!
3He subdued nations under us,
peoples under our feet.
4He chose our inheritance for us,
the pride of Jacob, whom he loved. *Selah*

5God has ascended amid shouts of joy,
the LORD amid the sounding of trumpets.
6Sing praises to God, sing praises;
sing praises to our King, sing praises.

7For God is the King of all the earth;
sing to him a psalm[f] of praise.
8God reigns over the nations;
God is seated on his holy throne.
9The nobles of the nations assemble
as the people of the God of Abraham,
for the kings[g] of the earth belong to God;
he is greatly exalted.

f7 Or *a maskil* (probably a literary or musical term) g9 Or *shields*

Discovering the Word 1. What is the psalmist thankful for (vv. 2–4)? 2. How is God described in each verse? 3. What is revealed about God's relationship with the people? 4. What actions of joy and gratitude do you see in these verses (vv. 1, 5–7)?

Applying the Word 1. How would you feel using the same outward expressions of joy as the psalmist? 2. The psalmist sings, claps, sacrifices and invites others to share in his joy in God. What ways can you outwardly show your joy in the Lord? 3. The Holy Spirit within us is continually offering praise. If you can, allow yourself to join the Spirit in praise. Try to write a psalm to the Lord, including in it reasons you enjoy knowing God. If you haven't come to the place of heartfelt worship, don't try to generate what you don't feel. You might want to sing a song or hymn that you can sing with meaning. Or perhaps play some recorded music that reflects your mood.

Responding in Prayer Ask God to give you the courage to walk in honesty until he brings you into the place of inner praise.

Psalms 48—49

Psalm 48

A song. A psalm of the Sons of Korah.

1Great is the LORD, and most worthy of praise,
in the city of our God, his holy mountain.
2It is beautiful in its loftiness,
the joy of the whole earth.
Like the utmost heights of Zaphon[h] is Mount Zion,
the[i] city of the Great King.
3God is in her citadels;
he has shown himself to be her fortress.

4When the kings joined forces,
when they advanced together,
5they saw ⌊her⌋ and were astounded;
they fled in terror.
6Trembling seized them there,
pain like that of a woman in labor.
7You destroyed them like ships of Tarshish
shattered by an east wind.

8As we have heard,
so have we seen
in the city of the LORD Almighty,
in the city of our God:
God makes her secure forever. *Selah*

9Within your temple, O God,
we meditate on your unfailing love.
10Like your name, O God,
your praise reaches to the ends of the earth;
your right hand is filled with righteousness.
11Mount Zion rejoices,
the villages of Judah are glad
because of your judgments.

12Walk about Zion, go around her,

h2 *Zaphon* can refer to a sacred mountain or the direction north.
i2 Or *earth, / Mount Zion, on the northern side / of the*

count her towers,
13consider well her ramparts,
view her citadels,
that you may tell of them to the next
generation.
14For this God is our God for ever and ever;
he will be our guide even to the end.

Psalm 49

For the director of music. Of the Sons of Korah. A psalm.

1Hear this, all you peoples;
listen, all who live in this world,
2both low and high,
rich and poor alike:
3My mouth will speak words of wisdom;
the utterance from my heart will give
understanding.
4I will turn my ear to a proverb;
with the harp I will expound my riddle:

5Why should I fear when evil days come,
when wicked deceivers surround me—
6those who trust in their wealth
and boast of their great riches?
7No man can redeem the life of another
or give to God a ransom for him—
8the ransom for a life is costly,
no payment is ever enough—
9that he should live on forever
and not see decay.

10For all can see that wise men die;
the foolish and the senseless alike perish
and leave their wealth to others.
11Their tombs will remain their houses[j]
forever,
their dwellings for endless generations,
though they had[k] named lands after
themselves.

12But man, despite his riches, does not endure;
he is[l] like the beasts that perish.

13This is the fate of those who trust in
themselves,
and of their followers, who approve their
sayings. *Selah*
14Like sheep they are destined for the grave,[m]
and death will feed on them.
The upright will rule over them in the
morning;
their forms will decay in the grave,[m]
far from their princely mansions.
15But God will redeem my life[n] from the grave;
he will surely take me to himself. *Selah*

16Do not be overawed when a man grows rich,
when the splendor of his house increases;
17for he will take nothing with him when he
dies,
his splendor will not descend with him.
18Though while he lived he counted himself
blessed—
and men praise you when you prosper—
19he will join the generation of his fathers,
who will never see the light ⌞of life⌟.

20A man who has riches without understanding
is like the beasts that perish.

[j]11 Septuagint and Syriac; Hebrew *In their thoughts their houses will remain* [k]11 Or / *for they have* [l]12 Hebrew; Septuagint and Syriac read verse 12 the same as verse 20. [m]14 Hebrew *Sheol*; also in verse 15 [n]15 Or *soul*

38 / *Psalm 50*
Offering Thanks

"HOW ARE YOU?" we ask, and the response generally comes back, "Fine." Often we follow that with the question "Been busy?" and the answer is invariably yes. We live in a culture of busyness, and sometimes that overlaps into our Christian lives. We can become so busy working for God, doing good deeds, that we don't have time to offer him our praise and thanksgiving. This psalm helps us get our focus back to the fact that we are created to worship God.

Warming Up to God When have you gotten caught up in the things you *do* for God to the extent that you neglected worshiping him?

Read Psalm 50.

Psalm 50

A psalm of Asaph.

1The Mighty One, God, the LORD,
speaks and summons the earth
from the rising of the sun to the place
where it sets.
2From Zion, perfect in beauty,
God shines forth.
3Our God comes and will not be silent;
a fire devours before him,
and around him a tempest rages.
4He summons the heavens above,
and the earth, that he may judge his
people:
5"Gather to me my consecrated ones,
who made a covenant with me by
sacrifice."
6And the heavens proclaim his righteousness,
for God himself is judge. *Selah*

7"Hear, O my people, and I will speak,
O Israel, and I will testify against you:
I am God, your God.
8I do not rebuke you for your sacrifices
or your burnt offerings, which are ever
before me.
9I have no need of a bull from your stall
or of goats from your pens,
10for every animal of the forest is mine,
and the cattle on a thousand hills.
11I know every bird in the mountains,
and the creatures of the field are mine.
12If I were hungry I would not tell you,
for the world is mine, and all that is in it.
13Do I eat the flesh of bulls
or drink the blood of goats?
14Sacrifice thank offerings to God,
fulfill your vows to the Most High,
15and call upon me in the day of trouble;
I will deliver you, and you will honor me."

16But to the wicked, God says:

"What right have you to recite my laws
or take my covenant on your lips?
17You hate my instruction
and cast my words behind you.
18When you see a thief, you join with him;
you throw in your lot with adulterers.
19You use your mouth for evil
and harness your tongue to deceit.
20You speak continually against your brother
and slander your own mother's son.
21These things you have done and I kept silent;
you thought I was altogether[o] like you.
But I will rebuke you
and accuse you to your face.

22"Consider this, you who forget God,
or I will tear you to pieces, with none to
rescue:
23He who sacrifices thank offerings honors me,
and he prepares the way
so that I may show him[p] the salvation of
God."

[o] 21 *Or thought the 'I AM' was* [p] 23 *Or and to him who considers his way / I will show*

Discovering the Word 1. How is God described in verses 1–6? 2. God does not say that sacrifices are wrong (v. 8), but what does he want the people to understand about their offerings to him (vv. 9–15)? 3. How does the tone of verses 16–22 change? 4. What evil deeds have the wicked done (vv. 16–22)? 5. How would "thank offerings" help them to understand salvation (vv. 14–15, 23)?

Applying the Word 1. What would a "thank offering" to God look like for you? 2. God promised that we can call upon him "in the day of trouble" and he will deliver us (v. 15). In what way would you like to call upon God today?

Responding in Prayer Make your prayers an offering of praise and thanksgiving for God's work in your life.

39 / *Psalm 51*
Praying Our Sin

ALONGSIDE THE BASIC fact that God made us good (Ps 8) is the equally basic fact that we have gone wrong. We pray our sins to get to the truth about ourselves and to find out how God treats sinners. Our experience of sin does not consist in doing some bad things but in being bad. It is a fundamental condition of our existence, not a temporary lapse into error. Praying our sin isn't resolving not to sin anymore; it is discovering what God has resolved to do with us as sinners.

Warming Up to God As Christians, we know we are sinful. Why then is it so painful to be confronted with a specific sin? What sin have you been avoiding talking to God about? Take it to God and experience his forgiveness.

Read Psalm 51.

Psalm 51

For the director of music. A psalm of David. When the prophet Nathan came to him after David had committed adultery with Bathsheba.

1 Have mercy on me, O God,
according to your unfailing love;
according to your great compassion
blot out my transgressions.
2 Wash away all my iniquity
and cleanse me from my sin.

3 For I know my transgressions,
and my sin is always before me.
4 Against you, you only, have I sinned
and done what is evil in your sight,
so that you are proved right when you speak
and justified when you judge.
5 Surely I was sinful at birth,
sinful from the time my mother conceived me.
6 Surely you desire truth in the inner parts[q];
you teach[r] me wisdom in the inmost place.

7 Cleanse me with hyssop, and I will be clean;
wash me, and I will be whiter than snow.
8 Let me hear joy and gladness;
let the bones you have crushed rejoice.
9 Hide your face from my sins
and blot out all my iniquity.

10 Create in me a pure heart, O God,
and renew a steadfast spirit within me.
11 Do not cast me from your presence
or take your Holy Spirit from me.
12 Restore to me the joy of your salvation
and grant me a willing spirit, to sustain me.

13 Then I will teach transgressors your ways,
and sinners will turn back to you.
14 Save me from bloodguilt, O God,
the God who saves me,
and my tongue will sing of your righteousness.
15 O Lord, open my lips,
and my mouth will declare your praise.
16 You do not delight in sacrifice, or I would bring it;
you do not take pleasure in burnt offerings.
17 The sacrifices of God are[s] a broken spirit;
a broken and contrite heart,
O God, you will not despise.

18 In your good pleasure make Zion prosper;
build up the walls of Jerusalem.
19 Then there will be righteous sacrifices,
whole burnt offerings to delight you;
then bulls will be offered on your altar.

q6 The meaning of the Hebrew for this phrase is uncertain. r6 Or *you desired . . . ; / you taught* s17 Or *My sacrifice, O God, is*

Discovering the Word 1. List the different synonyms for sin in David's prayer. 2. What is God asked to do about sin? (Count and name the verbs.) 3. Verse 10 is the center sentence. How does it center the prayer? 4. Forgiveness is an internal action with external consequences. What are some of them (vv. 13–17)? 5. What do you understand a "broken and contrite heart" to be (v. 17)? 6. According to verses 18–19, what is the relationship between personal forgiveness and social righteousness?

Applying the Word 1. When have you had a "broken and contrite heart"? 2. Psalm 51 makes us aware of how sinful we are, and it makes us less actively sinful. How do you see it working that way in you?

Responding in Prayer Be quiet before God. In silence confess your sins to him. Accept his forgiveness and grace.

Psalms 52—54

Psalm 52

For the director of music. A *maskil*[t] of David. When Doeg the Edomite had gone to Saul and told him: "David has gone to the house of Ahimelech."

1Why do you boast of evil, you mighty man?
Why do you boast all day long,
you who are a disgrace in the eyes of God?
2Your tongue plots destruction;
it is like a sharpened razor,
you who practice deceit.
3You love evil rather than good,
falsehood rather than speaking the truth.
Selah
4You love every harmful word,
O you deceitful tongue!

5Surely God will bring you down to everlasting ruin:
He will snatch you up and tear you from your tent;
he will uproot you from the land of the living. *Selah*
6The righteous will see and fear;
they will laugh at him, saying,
7"Here now is the man
who did not make God his stronghold
but trusted in his great wealth
and grew strong by destroying others!"

8But I am like an olive tree
flourishing in the house of God;
I trust in God's unfailing love
for ever and ever.
9I will praise you forever for what you have done;
in your name I will hope, for your name is good.
I will praise you in the presence of your saints.

Psalm 53

For the director of music. According to *mahalath*.[u] A *maskil*[t] of David.

1The fool says in his heart,
"There is no God."
They are corrupt, and their ways are vile;
there is no one who does good.

2God looks down from heaven
on the sons of men
to see if there are any who understand,
any who seek God.
3Everyone has turned away,
they have together become corrupt;
there is no one who does good,
not even one.

4Will the evildoers never learn—
those who devour my people as men eat bread
and who do not call on God?
5There they were, overwhelmed with dread,
where there was nothing to dread.
God scattered the bones of those who attacked you;
you put them to shame, for God despised them.

6Oh, that salvation for Israel would come out of Zion!
When God restores the fortunes of his people,
let Jacob rejoice and Israel be glad!

[t]Title: Probably a literary or musical term [u]Title: Probably a musical term

Psalm 54

For the director of music. With stringed instruments. A *maskil*[v] of David. When the Ziphites had gone to Saul and said, "Is not David hiding among us?"

1Save me, O God, by your name;
vindicate me by your might.
2Hear my prayer, O God;
listen to the words of my mouth.

3Strangers are attacking me;
ruthless men seek my life—
men without regard for God. *Selah*

4Surely God is my help;
the Lord is the one who sustains me.

5Let evil recoil on those who slander me;
in your faithfulness destroy them.

6I will sacrifice a freewill offering to you;
I will praise your name, O LORD,
for it is good.
7For he has delivered me from all my troubles,
and my eyes have looked in triumph on my foes.

[v]Title: Probably a literary or musical term

40 / *Psalm 55*
Expressing Feelings to God

"I WISH I could talk to God about this. But I just can't. I can't get the words out. I feel so guilty because I can't trust him with the things that are most important to me."

Learning to express our feelings to God is not easy. The passionate, emotionally unrestrained prayers of the Bible may not be the kind we grew up with. We may find, in fact, that the prayers of the Bible make us anxious. We wonder how God would respond if we told him what we really felt.

Learning to express our feelings to God is a vital part of growing in intimacy with him. When we can tell him of our sorrow and anger and confusion and joy, we will experience his faithful love in new ways. In his Word we find many models of godly people who openly expressed their deepest feelings to God.

Warming Up to God When you are sad or angry and you are talking to God, how do you expect him to respond? Talk to God about your concerns and fears.

Read Psalm 55.

Psalm 55

For the director of music. With stringed instruments. A *maskil*[w] of David.

1Listen to my prayer, O God,
do not ignore my plea;
2 hear me and answer me.
My thoughts trouble me and I am distraught
3 at the voice of the enemy,
at the stares of the wicked;
for they bring down suffering upon me
and revile me in their anger.

4My heart is in anguish within me;
the terrors of death assail me.
5Fear and trembling have beset me;
horror has overwhelmed me.
6I said, "Oh, that I had the wings of a dove!
I would fly away and be at rest—
7I would flee far away
and stay in the desert; *Selah*
8I would hurry to my place of shelter,
far from the tempest and storm."

9Confuse the wicked, O Lord, confound their speech,
for I see violence and strife in the city.
10Day and night they prowl about on its walls;
malice and abuse are within it.
11Destructive forces are at work in the city;
threats and lies never leave its streets.

12If an enemy were insulting me,
I could endure it;
if a foe were raising himself against me,

[w]Title: Probably a literary or musical term

I could hide from him.
13But it is you, a man like myself,
my companion, my close friend,
14with whom I once enjoyed sweet fellowship
as we walked with the throng at the house
of God.

15Let death take my enemies by surprise;
let them go down alive to the grave,[x]
for evil finds lodging among them.

16But I call to God,
and the LORD saves me.
17Evening, morning and noon
I cry out in distress,
and he hears my voice.
18He ransoms me unharmed
from the battle waged against me,
even though many oppose me.
19God, who is enthroned forever,
will hear them and afflict them— *Selah*
men who never change their ways
and have no fear of God.

20My companion attacks his friends;
he violates his covenant.
21His speech is smooth as butter,
yet war is in his heart;
his words are more soothing than oil,
yet they are drawn swords.

22Cast your cares on the LORD
and he will sustain you;
he will never let the righteous fall.
23But you, O God, will bring down the wicked
into the pit of corruption;
bloodthirsty and deceitful men
will not live out half their days.

But as for me, I trust in you.

[x]15 Hebrew *Sheol*

Discovering the Word 1. What feelings are described in each section of Psalm 55? 2. Describe the image of God that you find in this passage. 3. What seems to be causing the psalmist to suffer (vv. 12–15, 20–21)? 4. What does the psalmist expect God to do for him (vv. 16–19, 22–23)?

Applying the Word 1. We often have a negative response to our "negative" feelings. What thoughts do you typically have in response to your feelings of anger, depression or fear? 2. How does it affect you to know that God is near to you when you are in pain?

Responding in Prayer How would you like God to help you to grow in your ability to express your feelings to him?

Psalm 56

Psalm 56

For the director of music. To ⌞the tune of⌟ "A Dove on Distant Oaks." Of David. A *miktam*.[y] When the Philistines had seized him in Gath.

1Be merciful to me, O God, for men hotly
pursue me;
all day long they press their attack.
2My slanderers pursue me all day long;
many are attacking me in their pride.

3When I am afraid,
I will trust in you.
4In God, whose word I praise,
in God I trust; I will not be afraid.
What can mortal man do to me?

5All day long they twist my words;
they are always plotting to harm me.
6They conspire, they lurk,
they watch my steps,
eager to take my life.

7On no account let them escape;
in your anger, O God, bring down the
nations.
8Record my lament;
list my tears on your scroll[z]—
are they not in your record?

9Then my enemies will turn back
when I call for help.
By this I will know that God is for me.

[y]Title: Probably a literary or musical term [z]8 Or / *put my tears in your wineskin*

10In God, whose word I praise,
in the LORD, whose word I praise—
11in God I trust; I will not be afraid.
What can man do to me?

12I am under vows to you, O God;
I will present my thank offerings to you.

13For you have delivered me[a] from death
and my feet from stumbling,
that I may walk before God
in the light of life.[b]

[a]13 Or *my soul* [b]13 Or *the land of the living*

41 / *Psalm 57*
A Prayer of Distress

OUR NEED FOR God's presence and care in our lives is a daily reality. However, when life is good we may be unaware of our need. As C. S. Lewis wrote in *A Grief Observed*, sometimes "life is so good," we may be "tempted to forget our need of him." But there are times in our lives when we are acutely aware of our need of God. In times of distress, when we are threatened with loss or harm or even with death, we remember our need for God and we turn to him with great urgency. Some people feel that they cannot bring their troubles to God. I have often heard people say, "I can't turn to God when I am in distress if I haven't been doing this all along." And I have heard other people say, "I can't bother God with this. There are many people hurting more than I am." But God invites us to turn to him when we are in distress. Repeatedly in the Scriptures God says to us, "Call on me in the day of trouble and I will answer you." This is exactly what this psalm helps us to do.

Warming Up to God What mental pictures does the word *distress* create for you?

Read Psalm 57.

Psalm 57

For the director of music. ⌞To the tune of⌟ "Do Not Destroy." Of David. A *miktam*.[c] When he had fled from Saul into the cave.

1Have mercy on me, O God, have mercy on me,
for in you my soul takes refuge.
I will take refuge in the shadow of your wings
until the disaster has passed.

2I cry out to God Most High,
to God, who fulfills ⌞his purpose⌟ for me.
3He sends from heaven and saves me,
rebuking those who hotly pursue me; *Selah*
God sends his love and his faithfulness.

4I am in the midst of lions;
I lie among ravenous beasts—
men whose teeth are spears and arrows,
whose tongues are sharp swords.

5Be exalted, O God, above the heavens;
let your glory be over all the earth.

6They spread a net for my feet—
I was bowed down in distress.
They dug a pit in my path—
but they have fallen into it themselves. *Selah*

7My heart is steadfast, O God,
my heart is steadfast;
I will sing and make music.
8Awake, my soul!
Awake, harp and lyre!
I will awaken the dawn.

9I will praise you, O Lord, among the nations;
I will sing of you among the peoples.
10For great is your love, reaching to the heavens;
your faithfulness reaches to the skies.

11Be exalted, O God, above the heavens;
let your glory be over all the earth.

[c]Title: Probably a literary or musical term

Discovering the Word 1. The title and the introduction to this psalm suggest that this psalm was written by David when he fled into a cave, hiding from King Saul, who wanted to kill him. What image does David use in verse 1 to describe his experience of God as a safe shelter? 2. What metaphors does David use in verse 4 to describe the danger he found himself in? 3. In his time of distress David cried out to God (v. 2). What does it mean to "cry out" to God? 4. How did God intervene for David in his time of distress (vv. 3, 6)? 5. David responds to God's care in verse 7 by saying that his heart is steadfast. What is the significance of this response?

Applying the Word 1. Think of a time when you were in distress. What was your experience of God like during that time? 2. How might this psalm encourage you in times of distress?

Responding in Prayer David responds to God's care with praise in verses 9–11. Offer your praises to God for his work in your life.

Psalms 58—61

Psalm 58

For the director of music. ⌊To the tune of⌋ "Do Not Destroy." Of David. A *miktam*.[d]

1 Do you rulers indeed speak justly?
Do you judge uprightly among men?
2 No, in your heart you devise injustice,
and your hands mete out violence on the earth.
3 Even from birth the wicked go astray;
from the womb they are wayward and speak lies.
4 Their venom is like the venom of a snake,
like that of a cobra that has stopped its ears,
5 that will not heed the tune of the charmer,
however skillful the enchanter may be.

6 Break the teeth in their mouths, O God;
tear out, O LORD, the fangs of the lions!
7 Let them vanish like water that flows away;
when they draw the bow, let their arrows be blunted.
8 Like a slug melting away as it moves along,
like a stillborn child, may they not see the sun.

9 Before your pots can feel ⌊the heat of⌋ the thorns—
whether they be green or dry—the wicked will be swept away.[e]
10 The righteous will be glad when they are avenged,
when they bathe their feet in the blood of the wicked.
11 Then men will say,
"Surely the righteous still are rewarded;
surely there is a God who judges the earth."

Psalm 59

For the director of music. ⌊To the tune of⌋ "Do Not Destroy." Of David. A *miktam*.[d] When Saul had sent men to watch David's house in order to kill him.

1 Deliver me from my enemies, O God;
protect me from those who rise up against me.
2 Deliver me from evildoers
and save me from bloodthirsty men.

3 See how they lie in wait for me!
Fierce men conspire against me
for no offense or sin of mine, O LORD.
4 I have done no wrong, yet they are ready to attack me.
Arise to help me; look on my plight!
5 O LORD God Almighty, the God of Israel,
rouse yourself to punish all the nations;
show no mercy to wicked traitors. *Selah*

6 They return at evening,
snarling like dogs,
and prowl about the city.
7 See what they spew from their mouths—
they spew out swords from their lips,
and they say, "Who can hear us?"
8 But you, O LORD, laugh at them;
you scoff at all those nations.

9 O my Strength, I watch for you;

[d] Title: Probably a literary or musical term [e] 9 The meaning of the Hebrew for this verse is uncertain.

you, O God, are my fortress, [10]my loving
God.

God will go before me
and will let me gloat over those who
slander me.
[11]But do not kill them, O Lord our shield,[f]
or my people will forget.
In your might make them wander about,
and bring them down.
[12]For the sins of their mouths,
for the words of their lips,
let them be caught in their pride.
For the curses and lies they utter,
[13] consume them in wrath,
consume them till they are no more.
Then it will be known to the ends of the
earth
that God rules over Jacob. *Selah*

[14]They return at evening,
snarling like dogs,
and prowl about the city.
[15]They wander about for food
and howl if not satisfied.
[16]But I will sing of your strength,
in the morning I will sing of your love;
for you are my fortress,
my refuge in times of trouble.

[17]O my Strength, I sing praise to you;
you, O God, are my fortress, my loving
God.

Psalm 60

For the director of music. To ⌞the tune of⌟ "The Lily of the Covenant." A *miktam*[g] of David. For teaching. When he fought Aram Naharaim[h] and Aram Zobah,[i] and when Joab returned and struck down twelve thousand Edomites in the Valley of Salt.

[1]You have rejected us, O God, and burst forth
upon us;
you have been angry—now restore us!
[2]You have shaken the land and torn it open;
mend its fractures, for it is quaking.
[3]You have shown your people desperate times;
you have given us wine that makes us
stagger.

[4]But for those who fear you, you have raised a
banner
to be unfurled against the bow. *Selah*
[5]Save us and help us with your right hand,
that those you love may be delivered.
[6]God has spoken from his sanctuary:
"In triumph I will parcel out Shechem
and measure off the Valley of Succoth.
[7]Gilead is mine, and Manasseh is mine;
Ephraim is my helmet,
Judah my scepter.
[8]Moab is my washbasin,
upon Edom I toss my sandal;
over Philistia I shout in triumph."

[9]Who will bring me to the fortified city?
Who will lead me to Edom?
[10]Is it not you, O God, you who have rejected
us
and no longer go out with our armies?
[11]Give us aid against the enemy,
for the help of man is worthless.
[12]With God we will gain the victory,
and he will trample down our enemies.

Psalm 61

For the director of music. With stringed instruments. Of David.

[1]Hear my cry, O God;
listen to my prayer.

[2]From the ends of the earth I call to you,
I call as my heart grows faint;
lead me to the rock that is higher than I.
[3]For you have been my refuge,
a strong tower against the foe.

[4]I long to dwell in your tent forever
and take refuge in the shelter of your
wings. *Selah*
[5]For you have heard my vows, O God;
you have given me the heritage of those
who fear your name.

[6]Increase the days of the king's life,
his years for many generations.
[7]May he be enthroned in God's presence
forever;
appoint your love and faithfulness to
protect him.

[8]Then will I ever sing praise to your name
and fulfill my vows day after day.

[f]11 Or *sovereign* [g]Title: Probably a literary or musical term
[h]Title: That is, Arameans of Northwest Mesopotamia [i]Title: That is, Arameans of central Syria

42 / *Psalm 62*
A Prayer of Trust

HUMANS COME INTO the world as vulnerable creatures, completely dependent on their parents for their survival. For people to develop a healthy capacity to trust, they need to experience an emotional attachment with a nurturing parent. If children are not greeted with nurturing, empathic responses to their physical, emotional and social needs, or if the relationship with the parent is disrupted, the attachment will be threatened and the capacity to trust will be damaged. Later in life it will be difficult for them to trust God. Trust is based on a person's character, ability and truthfulness. It is an act of committing oneself to another's good intentions and care. This psalm invites us to risk trusting. It calls us to commit ourselves to God's care.

Warming Up to God What makes a person trustworthy?

Read Psalm 62.

Psalm 62

For the director of music. For Jeduthun.
A psalm of David.

1My soul finds rest in God alone;
my salvation comes from him.
2He alone is my rock and my salvation;
he is my fortress, I will never be shaken.

3How long will you assault a man?
Would all of you throw him down—
this leaning wall, this tottering fence?
4They fully intend to topple him
from his lofty place;
they take delight in lies.
With their mouths they bless,
but in their hearts they curse. *Selah*

5Find rest, O my soul, in God alone;
my hope comes from him.
6He alone is my rock and my salvation;
he is my fortress, I will not be shaken.
7My salvation and my honor depend on God[j];
he is my mighty rock, my refuge.
8Trust in him at all times, O people;
pour out your hearts to him,
for God is our refuge. *Selah*

9Lowborn men are but a breath,
the highborn are but a lie;
if weighed on a balance, they are nothing;
together they are only a breath.
10Do not trust in extortion
or take pride in stolen goods;
though your riches increase,
do not set your heart on them.

11One thing God has spoken,
two things have I heard:
that you, O God, are strong,
12 and that you, O Lord, are loving.
Surely you will reward each person
according to what he has done.

j7 Or / *God Most High is my salvation and my honor*

Discovering the Word 1. How does the writer contrast God and humanity? 2. The psalmist talks about resting in God. What pictures come to your mind with these words? 3. In verse 8, the psalmist draws a parallel between trusting in God and pouring out one's heart to God. How are these related? 4. Verse 10 warns against trusting in material wealth. Why is this such a strong temptation? 5. The last two verses depict God as strong and as loving. What images of a strong and loving God are presented in the psalm?

Applying the Word 1. Where else might you be tempted to place your trust, other than in God? 2. How does seeing God as strong help you to trust him? 3. How does seeing God as loving help you to trust him?

Responding in Prayer Express your hesitations and your desires to trust God.

43 / *Psalm 63*
A Prayer of Longing for God

SOMETIMES WE FEEL separated from God. During these times we may feel much like small children feel when they are separated from their parents—frightened, angry. And we may experience an intense longing for our Parent to return. Many things can create this sense of separation from God. It might come as a result of a loss or crisis in our life which leaves us feeling forgotten or uncared for by God. It might come during a time of personal sin or failure when we struggle with fear that God might condemn or reject us. It might come, as it did for this psalmist, as a result of being removed from our community of faith. Whatever the reason, a sense of separation from God can generate life's deepest pain, that of an intense longing for God. This psalm helps us express our longing for God in times when we feel separated from him.

Warming Up to God Think of a time when you felt especially close to God. What was the experience like for you?

Read Psalm 63.

Psalm 63

A psalm of David. When he was in the Desert of Judah.

1 O God, you are my God,
earnestly I seek you;
my soul thirsts for you,
my body longs for you,
in a dry and weary land
where there is no water.

2 I have seen you in the sanctuary
and beheld your power and your glory.
3 Because your love is better than life,
my lips will glorify you.
4 I will praise you as long as I live,
and in your name I will lift up my hands.
5 My soul will be satisfied as with the richest of foods;
with singing lips my mouth will praise you.

6 On my bed I remember you;
I think of you through the watches of the night.
7 Because you are my help,
I sing in the shadow of your wings.
8 My soul clings to you;
your right hand upholds me.

9 They who seek my life will be destroyed;
they will go down to the depths of the earth.
10 They will be given over to the sword
and become food for jackals.

11 But the king will rejoice in God;
all who swear by God's name will praise him,
while the mouths of liars will be silenced.

Discovering the Word 1. The psalmist describes his experience of longing for God in verse 1 with the strong physical metaphor of being thirsty in a desert with no sign of water. What does this image convey? 2. In verses 2 and 3 the psalmist describes how in the past he experienced God's presence. What did he experience of God? 3. Because of his longing for connection with God, the psalmist says he will seek God, he will remember God and he will cling to God. The first action he takes is to earnestly seek God. What does it mean to seek God? 4. The second action he takes is "remembering." Where, when, what and how does the psalmist say he "remembers" God? 5. The third action he describes is "clinging." In verse 8 he describes how he clings to God and how God holds him. What is your response to the image of clinging to God?

Applying the Word 1. Verse 1 describes a soul which is thirsty, with no chance of finding water. In stark contrast, verse 5 describes a soul which is satisfied with the richest of foods. These pictures contrast the experience of being separated from God and the experience of being close to God. What words or images would you use to describe times when you have felt separated from God? 2. What words or images would you use to describe times when you felt close to God? 3. As you think about the actions of seeking, remembering and clinging to God, which of these most closely describes what would be most helpful to you at this time? Explain.

Responding in Prayer Talk to God about your longing for him and your sense of deep satisfaction and joy in his presence.

Psalm 64

Psalm 64

For the director of music. A psalm of David.

1Hear me, O God, as I voice my complaint;
protect my life from the threat of the enemy.
2Hide me from the conspiracy of the wicked,
from that noisy crowd of evildoers.
3They sharpen their tongues like swords
and aim their words like deadly arrows.
4They shoot from ambush at the innocent man;
they shoot at him suddenly, without fear.

5They encourage each other in evil plans,
they talk about hiding their snares;
they say, "Who will see them[k]?"
6They plot injustice and say,
"We have devised a perfect plan!"
Surely the mind and heart of man are cunning.

7But God will shoot them with arrows;
suddenly they will be struck down.
8He will turn their own tongues against them
and bring them to ruin;
all who see them will shake their heads in scorn.

9All mankind will fear;
they will proclaim the works of God
and ponder what he has done.
10Let the righteous rejoice in the LORD
and take refuge in him;
let all the upright in heart praise him!

[k]5 Or *us*

44 / *Psalm 65*

A Prayer of Gratitude

BECAUSE I HAVE difficulty receiving gifts or compliments from others, I have had to remind myself to look people in the eyes when they offer me a gift or a compliment and say thank you. When we are unable to receive the good things that others offer us, we cheat ourselves, and we cheat them. When we are able to say thank you for gifts given, we are able to take the gift in, enjoy it and engage in a personal, intimate way with the giver of the gift. In the same way, when we express gratitude to God, we enter into a cycle of joyful relating with him. We take in his love, feel a deeper connection with him and experience joy. This psalm invites us to express gratitude to God for his good gifts.

Warming Up to God What is it like for you to receive a gift or a compliment? What is it like for you to be on the receiving end of someone else's gratitude?

Read Psalm 65.

Psalm 65

For the director of music. A psalm of David. A song.

1Praise awaits[l] you, O God, in Zion;
to you our vows will be fulfilled.
2O you who hear prayer,
to you all men will come.
3When we were overwhelmed by sins,
you forgave[m] our transgressions.
4Blessed are those you choose
and bring near to live in your courts!
We are filled with the good things of your house,
of your holy temple.
5You answer us with awesome deeds of righteousness,
O God our Savior,
the hope of all the ends of the earth
and of the farthest seas,
6who formed the mountains by your power,
having armed yourself with strength,
7who stilled the roaring of the seas,
the roaring of their waves,
and the turmoil of the nations.
8Those living far away fear your wonders;
where morning dawns and evening fades
you call forth songs of joy.
9You care for the land and water it;
you enrich it abundantly.
The streams of God are filled with water
to provide the people with grain,
for so you have ordained it.[n]
10You drench its furrows
and level its ridges;
you soften it with showers
and bless its crops.
11You crown the year with your bounty,
and your carts overflow with abundance.
12The grasslands of the desert overflow;
the hills are clothed with gladness.
13The meadows are covered with flocks
and the valleys are mantled with grain;
they shout for joy and sing.

[l]1 Or *befits*; the meaning of the Hebrew for this word is uncertain. [m]3 Or *made atonement for* [n]9 Or *for that is how you prepare the land*

Discovering the Word 1. God's great power is acknowledged in this psalm. How is God's power a gift to us? 2. In verse 5 God is called "our Savior, the hope of all the ends of the earth and of the farthest seas." In what ways is God the hope of all the earth and seas? 3. The psalmist mentions several of God's awesome deeds in verses 6 and 7. What other awesome deeds might you add to the list? 4. Verse 8 offers a picture of the fears and joys common to all people of the earth. How do God's wonders cause us to experience fear? 5. How do God's wonders call forth songs of joy?

Applying the Word 1. Verses 9–13 describe the specific ways in which God tenderly loves and cares for the earth. What thoughts and feelings does this description evoke for you? 2. What implications does God's care for the earth have for the ways in which we treat the earth? 3. What personal value does expressing gratitude to God have for you?

Responding in Prayer What are you grateful for today? Express your thanks to God.

45 / *Psalm 66*
A Prayer of Joy

LIFE WAS NOT intended by God to be a joyless ordeal. As much as it might surprise some of us, it is actually God's desire for us to experience joy. Joy is an act of relating to God with vulnerable, unselfconscious gratitude for the good gifts he gives. Joy comes when we experience and acknowledge God's love and care for us, when we allow ourselves to express our gratitude for his love with great energy. This psalm invites us to experience joy.

Warming Up to God Think of a time when you experienced joy. What evoked this feeling in you?

Read Psalm 66.

Psalm 66

For the director of music. A song. A psalm.

[1]Shout with joy to God, all the earth!
[2] Sing the glory of his name;
make his praise glorious!
[3]Say to God, "How awesome are your deeds!
So great is your power
that your enemies cringe before you.
[4]All the earth bows down to you;
they sing praise to you,
they sing praise to your name." *Selah*

[5]Come and see what God has done,
how awesome his works in man's behalf!
[6]He turned the sea into dry land,
they passed through the waters on foot—
come, let us rejoice in him.
[7]He rules forever by his power,
his eyes watch the nations—
let not the rebellious rise up against him.
Selah

[8]Praise our God, O peoples,
let the sound of his praise be heard;
[9]he has preserved our lives
and kept our feet from slipping.
[10]For you, O God, tested us;
you refined us like silver.
[11]You brought us into prison
and laid burdens on our backs.
[12]You let men ride over our heads;
we went through fire and water,
but you brought us to a place of
abundance.

[13]I will come to your temple with burnt
offerings
and fulfill my vows to you—
[14]vows my lips promised and my mouth spoke
when I was in trouble.
[15]I will sacrifice fat animals to you
and an offering of rams;
I will offer bulls and goats. *Selah*

[16]Come and listen, all you who fear God;
let me tell you what he has done for me.
[17]I cried out to him with my mouth;
his praise was on my tongue.
[18]If I had cherished sin in my heart,
the Lord would not have listened;
[19]but God has surely listened
and heard my voice in prayer.
[20]Praise be to God,
who has not rejected my prayer
or withheld his love from me!

Discovering the Word 1. The writer calls us to action (vv. 1, 2, 3, 5, 8 and 16). What all does he call us to do? 2. How are each of these behaviors related to the experience or the expression of joy? 3. What does the section in the middle of this psalm (vv. 8–12) tell us about the cause for this particular expression of joy? 4. How might this kind of experience lead to joy? 5. Verses 16–20 are a more personal account of what the Lord has done. What does the writer say the Lord has done for him? 6. How might this kind of experience lead to joy?

Applying the Word 1. What other ways of expressing joy to God would you add to the psalmist's list? 2. Why is it important to allow ourselves to experience and express joy? 3. How might this psalm help you to experience and express joy?

Responding in Prayer What joy would you like to express to God?

46 / *Psalm 67*
God's Love for All Creatures

Jesus loves the little children—
All the children of the world.
Red, brown, yellow, black, and white—
They are precious in his sight.
Jesus loves the little children of the world.

JESUS LOVES EVERY culture he created. Its members are his little children, and he longs for them to fully experience the healing of his compassion. That's what redemption is all about. Because some of our sincere attempts to bring others into this love have been clumsy and insulting to other cultures, we are bombarded with accusations of destroying other cultures with Christianity. Some of those accusations are true and worth listening to. Yet these mistakes are not the true picture of our ministry. The gospel is good news to all societies, and God has always called and is still calling his people to bear his redemptive love to every place and people group on the earth.

Warming Up to God How have you recently seen God's power being revealed in your nation?

Read Psalm 67.

Psalm 67

For the director of music. With stringed instruments. A psalm. A song.

1May God be gracious to us and bless us
and make his face shine upon us, *Selah*
2that your ways may be known on earth,
your salvation among all nations.

3May the peoples praise you, O God;
may all the peoples praise you.

4May the nations be glad and sing for joy,
for you rule the peoples justly
and guide the nations of the earth. *Selah*
5May the peoples praise you, O God;
may all the peoples praise you.

6Then the land will yield its harvest,
and God, our God, will bless us.
7God will bless us,
and all the ends of the earth will fear him.

Discovering the Word 1. What words do you notice being repeated throughout this passage? 2. Identify the blessings the Lord wants to bring to the nations. 3. What does this reveal about how God regards the nations?

Applying the Word 1. What would these blessings look like if they came to your own culture? 2. How would these blessings affect some other nation in the world (say, Bosnia or South Africa)?

Responding in Prayer Thank God for his compassion for the nations.

Psalms 68—72

Psalm 68

For the director of music. Of David.
A psalm. A song.

1May God arise, may his enemies be scattered;
may his foes flee before him.
2As smoke is blown away by the wind,
may you blow them away;
as wax melts before the fire,
may the wicked perish before God.
3But may the righteous be glad
and rejoice before God;
may they be happy and joyful.

4Sing to God, sing praise to his name,
extol him who rides on the clouds[o]—
his name is the LORD—
and rejoice before him.
5A father to the fatherless, a defender of widows,
is God in his holy dwelling.
6God sets the lonely in families,[p]
he leads forth the prisoners with singing;
but the rebellious live in a sun-scorched land.

7When you went out before your people, O God,
when you marched through the wasteland, *Selah*
8the earth shook,
the heavens poured down rain,
before God, the One of Sinai,
before God, the God of Israel.
9You gave abundant showers, O God;
you refreshed your weary inheritance.
10Your people settled in it,
and from your bounty, O God, you provided for the poor.

11The Lord announced the word,
and great was the company of those who proclaimed it:
12"Kings and armies flee in haste;
in the camps men divide the plunder.
13Even while you sleep among the campfires,[q]
the wings of ⌊my⌋ dove are sheathed with silver,
its feathers with shining gold."
14When the Almighty[r] scattered the kings in the land,
it was like snow fallen on Zalmon.

15The mountains of Bashan are majestic mountains;
rugged are the mountains of Bashan.
16Why gaze in envy, O rugged mountains,
at the mountain where God chooses to reign,
where the LORD himself will dwell forever?
17The chariots of God are tens of thousands
and thousands of thousands;
the Lord ⌊has come⌋ from Sinai into his sanctuary.
18When you ascended on high,
you led captives in your train;
you received gifts from men,
even from[s] the rebellious—
that you,[t] O LORD God, might dwell there.

19Praise be to the Lord, to God our Savior,
who daily bears our burdens. *Selah*
20Our God is a God who saves;
from the Sovereign LORD comes escape from death.
21Surely God will crush the heads of his enemies,
the hairy crowns of those who go on in their sins.
22The Lord says, "I will bring them from Bashan;
I will bring them from the depths of the sea,
23that you may plunge your feet in the blood of your foes,
while the tongues of your dogs have their share."

24Your procession has come into view, O God,
the procession of my God and King into the sanctuary.
25In front are the singers, after them the musicians;
with them are the maidens playing tambourines.
26Praise God in the great congregation;

[o]4 Or / *prepare the way for him who rides through the deserts* [p]6 Or *the desolate in a homeland* [q]13 Or *saddlebags* [r]14 Hebrew *Shaddai* [s]18 Or *gifts for men, / even* [t]18 Or *they*

praise the LORD in the assembly of Israel.
27There is the little tribe of Benjamin, leading them,
there the great throng of Judah's princes,
and there the princes of Zebulun and of Naphtali.

28Summon your power, O God[u];
show us your strength, O God, as you have done before.
29Because of your temple at Jerusalem
kings will bring you gifts.
30Rebuke the beast among the reeds,
the herd of bulls among the calves of the nations.
Humbled, may it bring bars of silver.
Scatter the nations who delight in war.
31Envoys will come from Egypt;
Cush[v] will submit herself to God.

32Sing to God, O kingdoms of the earth,
sing praise to the Lord, *Selah*
33to him who rides the ancient skies above,
who thunders with mighty voice.
34Proclaim the power of God,
whose majesty is over Israel,
whose power is in the skies.
35You are awesome, O God, in your sanctuary;
the God of Israel gives power and strength to his people.

Praise be to God!

Psalm 69

For the director of music. To ⌊the tune of⌋ "Lilies." Of David.

1Save me, O God,
for the waters have come up to my neck.
2I sink in the miry depths,
where there is no foothold.
I have come into the deep waters;
the floods engulf me.
3I am worn out calling for help;
my throat is parched.
My eyes fail,
looking for my God.
4Those who hate me without reason
outnumber the hairs of my head;
many are my enemies without cause,
those who seek to destroy me.
I am forced to restore
what I did not steal.

5You know my folly, O God;
my guilt is not hidden from you.
6May those who hope in you
not be disgraced because of me,
O Lord, the LORD Almighty;
may those who seek you
not be put to shame because of me,
O God of Israel.
7For I endure scorn for your sake,
and shame covers my face.
8I am a stranger to my brothers,
an alien to my own mother's sons;
9for zeal for your house consumes me,
and the insults of those who insult you fall on me.
10When I weep and fast,
I must endure scorn;
11when I put on sackcloth,
people make sport of me.
12Those who sit at the gate mock me,
and I am the song of the drunkards.
13But I pray to you, O LORD,
in the time of your favor;
in your great love, O God,
answer me with your sure salvation.
14Rescue me from the mire,
do not let me sink;
deliver me from those who hate me,
from the deep waters.
15Do not let the floodwaters engulf me
or the depths swallow me up
or the pit close its mouth over me.
16Answer me, O LORD, out of the goodness of your love;
in your great mercy turn to me.
17Do not hide your face from your servant;
answer me quickly, for I am in trouble.
18Come near and rescue me;
redeem me because of my foes.
19You know how I am scorned, disgraced and shamed;
all my enemies are before you.
20Scorn has broken my heart
and has left me helpless;
I looked for sympathy, but there was none,
for comforters, but I found none.
21They put gall in my food
and gave me vinegar for my thirst.

[u] 28 Many Hebrew manuscripts, Septuagint and Syriac; most Hebrew manuscripts *Your God has summoned power for you* [v] 31 That is, the upper Nile region

[22]May the table set before them become a snare;
may it become retribution and[w] a trap.
[23]May their eyes be darkened so they cannot see,
and their backs be bent forever.
[24]Pour out your wrath on them;
let your fierce anger overtake them.
[25]May their place be deserted;
let there be no one to dwell in their tents.
[26]For they persecute those you wound
and talk about the pain of those you hurt.
[27]Charge them with crime upon crime;
do not let them share in your salvation.
[28]May they be blotted out of the book of life
and not be listed with the righteous.

[29]I am in pain and distress;
may your salvation, O God, protect me.

[30]I will praise God's name in song
and glorify him with thanksgiving.
[31]This will please the LORD more than an ox,
more than a bull with its horns and hoofs.
[32]The poor will see and be glad—
you who seek God, may your hearts live!
[33]The LORD hears the needy
and does not despise his captive people.

[34]Let heaven and earth praise him,
the seas and all that move in them,
[35]for God will save Zion
and rebuild the cities of Judah.
Then people will settle there and possess it;
[36] the children of his servants will inherit it,
and those who love his name will dwell there.

Psalm 70

For the director of music. Of David.
A petition.

[1]Hasten, O God, to save me;
O LORD, come quickly to help me.
[2]May those who seek my life
be put to shame and confusion;
may all who desire my ruin
be turned back in disgrace.
[3]May those who say to me, "Aha! Aha!"
turn back because of their shame.
[4]But may all who seek you
rejoice and be glad in you;
may those who love your salvation always say,
"Let God be exalted!"
[5]Yet I am poor and needy;
come quickly to me, O God.
You are my help and my deliverer;
O LORD, do not delay.

Psalm 71

[1]In you, O LORD, I have taken refuge;
let me never be put to shame.
[2]Rescue me and deliver me in your righteousness;
turn your ear to me and save me.
[3]Be my rock of refuge,
to which I can always go;
give the command to save me,
for you are my rock and my fortress.
[4]Deliver me, O my God, from the hand of the wicked,
from the grasp of evil and cruel men.

[5]For you have been my hope, O Sovereign LORD,
my confidence since my youth.
[6]From birth I have relied on you;
you brought me forth from my mother's womb.
I will ever praise you.
[7]I have become like a portent to many,
but you are my strong refuge.
[8]My mouth is filled with your praise,
declaring your splendor all day long.

[9]Do not cast me away when I am old;
do not forsake me when my strength is gone.
[10]For my enemies speak against me;
those who wait to kill me conspire together.
[11]They say, "God has forsaken him;
pursue him and seize him,
for no one will rescue him."
[12]Be not far from me, O God;
come quickly, O my God, to help me.
[13]May my accusers perish in shame;
may those who want to harm me
be covered with scorn and disgrace.

[14]But as for me, I will always have hope;
I will praise you more and more.
[15]My mouth will tell of your righteousness,
of your salvation all day long,

[w]22 *Or snare / and their fellowship become*

though I know not its measure.
16I will come and proclaim your mighty acts,
O Sovereign LORD;
I will proclaim your righteousness, yours alone.
17Since my youth, O God, you have taught me,
and to this day I declare your marvelous deeds.
18Even when I am old and gray,
do not forsake me, O God,
till I declare your power to the next generation,
your might to all who are to come.

19Your righteousness reaches to the skies, O God,
you who have done great things.
Who, O God, is like you?
20Though you have made me see troubles, many and bitter,
you will restore my life again;
from the depths of the earth
you will again bring me up.
21You will increase my honor
and comfort me once again.

22I will praise you with the harp
for your faithfulness, O my God;
I will sing praise to you with the lyre,
O Holy One of Israel.
23My lips will shout for joy
when I sing praise to you—
I, whom you have redeemed.
24My tongue will tell of your righteous acts
all day long,
for those who wanted to harm me
have been put to shame and confusion.

Psalm 72

Of Solomon.

1Endow the king with your justice, O God,
the royal son with your righteousness.
2He will[x] judge your people in righteousness,
your afflicted ones with justice.
3The mountains will bring prosperity to the people,
the hills the fruit of righteousness.
4He will defend the afflicted among the people
and save the children of the needy;
he will crush the oppressor.
5He will endure[y] as long as the sun,
as long as the moon, through all generations.
6He will be like rain falling on a mown field,
like showers watering the earth.
7In his days the righteous will flourish;
prosperity will abound till the moon is no more.

8He will rule from sea to sea
and from the River[z] to the ends of the earth.[a]
9The desert tribes will bow before him
and his enemies will lick the dust.
10The kings of Tarshish and of distant shores
will bring tribute to him;
the kings of Sheba and Seba
will present him gifts.
11All kings will bow down to him
and all nations will serve him.

12For he will deliver the needy who cry out,
the afflicted who have no one to help.
13He will take pity on the weak and the needy
and save the needy from death.
14He will rescue them from oppression and violence,
for precious is their blood in his sight.

15Long may he live!
May gold from Sheba be given him.
May people ever pray for him
and bless him all day long.
16Let grain abound throughout the land;
on the tops of the hills may it sway.
Let its fruit flourish like Lebanon;
let it thrive like the grass of the field.
17May his name endure forever;
may it continue as long as the sun.

All nations will be blessed through him,
and they will call him blessed.

18Praise be to the LORD God, the God of Israel,
who alone does marvelous deeds.
19Praise be to his glorious name forever;
may the whole earth be filled with his glory.
Amen and Amen.

20This concludes the prayers of David son of Jesse.

x2 Or *May he*; similarly in verses 3-11 and 17 y5 Septuagint; Hebrew *You will be feared* z8 That is, the Euphrates a8 Or *the end of the land*

47 / *Psalm 73*
Praying Our Doubt

DOUBT IS NOT a sin. It is an essential element in belief. Doubt is honesty. We see contradictions between what we believe and what we experience. What is going on here? Did God give us a bum steer? Why aren't things turning out the way we were taught to expect? No mature faith avoids or denies doubt. Doubt forces faith to bedrock.

Warming Up to God What doubts have you had or do you have about the Christian life? Express them to God without fear.

Read Psalm 73.

BOOK III
Psalms 73–89

Psalm 73

A psalm of Asaph.

1Surely God is good to Israel,
to those who are pure in heart.

2But as for me, my feet had almost slipped;
I had nearly lost my foothold.
3For I envied the arrogant
when I saw the prosperity of the wicked.

4They have no struggles;
their bodies are healthy and strong.[b]
5They are free from the burdens common to man;
they are not plagued by human ills.
6Therefore pride is their necklace;
they clothe themselves with violence.
7From their callous hearts comes iniquity[c];
the evil conceits of their minds know no limits.
8They scoff, and speak with malice;
in their arrogance they threaten oppression.
9Their mouths lay claim to heaven,
and their tongues take possession of the earth.
10Therefore their people turn to them
and drink up waters in abundance.[d]
11They say, "How can God know?
Does the Most High have knowledge?"

12This is what the wicked are like—
always carefree, they increase in wealth.

13Surely in vain have I kept my heart pure;
in vain have I washed my hands in innocence.
14All day long I have been plagued;
I have been punished every morning.

15If I had said, "I will speak thus,"
I would have betrayed your children.
16When I tried to understand all this,
it was oppressive to me
17till I entered the sanctuary of God;
then I understood their final destiny.

18Surely you place them on slippery ground;
you cast them down to ruin.
19How suddenly are they destroyed,
completely swept away by terrors!
20As a dream when one awakes,
so when you arise, O Lord,
you will despise them as fantasies.

21When my heart was grieved
and my spirit embittered,
22I was senseless and ignorant;
I was a brute beast before you.

23Yet I am always with you;
you hold me by my right hand.
24You guide me with your counsel,
and afterward you will take me into glory.
25Whom have I in heaven but you?
And earth has nothing I desire besides you.
26My flesh and my heart may fail,
but God is the strength of my heart
and my portion forever.

27Those who are far from you will perish;
you destroy all who are unfaithful to you.
28But as for me, it is good to be near God.
I have made the Sovereign LORD my refuge;
I will tell of all your deeds.

[b]4 With a different word division of the Hebrew; Masoretic Text *struggles at their death; / their bodies are healthy* [c]7 Syriac (see also Septuagint); Hebrew *Their eyes bulge with fat* [d]10 The meaning of the Hebrew for this verse is uncertain.

Discovering the Word 1. How would you paraphrase the doubt expressed in verses 2–12? 2. Who do you know who is, as they say, "getting away with murder"? 3. The key word and the pivotal center of the psalm is the word *till* in verse 17. What takes place here in the sanctuary? 4. The *yet* in verse 23 links two contrasting statements. What are they? 5. The prosperity of the wicked occupied the first part of the psalm (vv. 1–16). The presence of the Lord occupies the second (vv. 17–28). What is more vivid to you, the wicked or the Lord? Explain.

Applying the Word 1. Self-pity is like a deadly virus. How would you express, in terms of your own life, what the psalmist says in verses 13–14? 2. The appearance of the wicked whom we envy is in utter and complete contrast to their reality (vv. 18–20). How do you discern between what you *see* (and are tempted to envy) and what *is* (and so is affirmed in obedience)? 3. Worship is the pivotal act in this prayer. The Christian consensus is that it is the pivotal act every week. How can worship become a more pivotal part of your experience?

Responding in Prayer In your time of prayer spend five minutes in silence, savoring God's presence, letting him restore your perspective. Then speak your praises.

Psalms 74—76

Psalm 74

A *maskil*[e] of Asaph.

1Why have you rejected us forever, O God?
Why does your anger smolder against the sheep of your pasture?
2Remember the people you purchased of old,
the tribe of your inheritance, whom you redeemed—
Mount Zion, where you dwelt.
3Turn your steps toward these everlasting ruins,
all this destruction the enemy has brought on the sanctuary.

4Your foes roared in the place where you met with us;
they set up their standards as signs.
5They behaved like men wielding axes
to cut through a thicket of trees.
6They smashed all the carved paneling
with their axes and hatchets.
7They burned your sanctuary to the ground;
they defiled the dwelling place of your Name.
8They said in their hearts, "We will crush them completely!"
They burned every place where God was worshiped in the land.
9We are given no miraculous signs;
no prophets are left,
and none of us knows how long this will be.
10How long will the enemy mock you, O God?
Will the foe revile your name forever?
11Why do you hold back your hand, your right hand?
Take it from the folds of your garment and destroy them!
12But you, O God, are my king from of old;
you bring salvation upon the earth.
13It was you who split open the sea by your power;
you broke the heads of the monster in the waters.
14It was you who crushed the heads of Leviathan
and gave him as food to the creatures of the desert.
15It was you who opened up springs and streams;
you dried up the ever flowing rivers.
16The day is yours, and yours also the night;
you established the sun and moon.
17It was you who set all the boundaries of the earth;
you made both summer and winter.

18Remember how the enemy has mocked you, O LORD,
how foolish people have reviled your name.
19Do not hand over the life of your dove to wild beasts;
do not forget the lives of your afflicted people forever.

[e]Title: Probably a literary or musical term

[20]Have regard for your covenant,
because haunts of violence fill the dark places of the land.
[21]Do not let the oppressed retreat in disgrace;
may the poor and needy praise your name.

[22]Rise up, O God, and defend your cause;
remember how fools mock you all day long.
[23]Do not ignore the clamor of your adversaries,
the uproar of your enemies, which rises continually.

Psalm 75

For the director of music. ⌊To the tune of⌋ "Do Not Destroy." A psalm of Asaph. A song.

[1]We give thanks to you, O God,
we give thanks, for your Name is near;
men tell of your wonderful deeds.

[2]You say, "I choose the appointed time;
it is I who judge uprightly.
[3]When the earth and all its people quake,
it is I who hold its pillars firm. *Selah*
[4]To the arrogant I say, 'Boast no more,'
and to the wicked, 'Do not lift up your horns.
[5]Do not lift your horns against heaven;
do not speak with outstretched neck.' "

[6]No one from the east or the west
or from the desert can exalt a man.
[7]But it is God who judges:
He brings one down, he exalts another.
[8]In the hand of the LORD is a cup
full of foaming wine mixed with spices;
he pours it out, and all the wicked of the earth
drink it down to its very dregs.

[9]As for me, I will declare this forever;
I will sing praise to the God of Jacob.
[10]I will cut off the horns of all the wicked,
but the horns of the righteous will be lifted up.

Psalm 76

For the director of music. With stringed instruments. A psalm of Asaph. A song.

[1]In Judah God is known;
his name is great in Israel.
[2]His tent is in Salem,
his dwelling place in Zion.
[3]There he broke the flashing arrows,
the shields and the swords, the weapons of war. *Selah*

[4]You are resplendent with light,
more majestic than mountains rich with game.
[5]Valiant men lie plundered,
they sleep their last sleep;
not one of the warriors
can lift his hands.
[6]At your rebuke, O God of Jacob,
both horse and chariot lie still.
[7]You alone are to be feared.
Who can stand before you when you are angry?
[8]From heaven you pronounced judgment,
and the land feared and was quiet—
[9]when you, O God, rose up to judge,
to save all the afflicted of the land. *Selah*
[10]Surely your wrath against men brings you praise,
and the survivors of your wrath are restrained.[f]

[11]Make vows to the LORD your God and fulfill them;
let all the neighboring lands
bring gifts to the One to be feared.
[12]He breaks the spirit of rulers;
he is feared by the kings of the earth.

[f]10 Or *Surely the wrath of men brings you praise, / and with the remainder of wrath you arm yourself*

48/ *Psalm 77*
Praying Our Discontent

"THE ROOM IS too cold. Why were we seated way back in the corner? You'd think a restaurant like this would have more selection on the menu. When is our food going to get here? I don't even think this waitress deserves a tip . . ."

Perhaps you've had a meal with a person who complains like this. Some people are never satisfied with what they are given. Such people are tiring to be with. In contrast, the person who is aware of God's never-ending good gifts (and a person who seems to have comparatively less) is a joy to be around. Where do you fall on this spectrum?

Warming Up to God Name three things you're grateful for. Reflect on your response. (How long did it take you to think of things you're grateful for? Did they come to mind quickly or slowly? How conscious are you of God's good gifts?) What did you learn about yourself?

Read Psalm 77.

Psalm 77

For the director of music. For Jeduthun.
Of Asaph. A psalm.

1 I cried out to God for help;
I cried out to God to hear me.
2 When I was in distress, I sought the Lord;
at night I stretched out untiring hands
and my soul refused to be comforted.

3 I remembered you, O God, and I groaned;
I mused, and my spirit grew faint. *Selah*
4 You kept my eyes from closing;
I was too troubled to speak.
5 I thought about the former days,
the years of long ago;
6 I remembered my songs in the night.
My heart mused and my spirit inquired:

7 "Will the Lord reject forever?
Will he never show his favor again?
8 Has his unfailing love vanished forever?
Has his promise failed for all time?
9 Has God forgotten to be merciful?
Has he in anger withheld his compassion?"
Selah

10 Then I thought, "To this I will appeal:
the years of the right hand of the Most
High."
11 I will remember the deeds of the LORD;
yes, I will remember your miracles of long
ago.
12 I will meditate on all your works
and consider all your mighty deeds.

13 Your ways, O God, are holy.
What god is so great as our God?
14 You are the God who performs miracles;
you display your power among the peoples.
15 With your mighty arm you redeemed your
people,
the descendants of Jacob and Joseph. *Selah*

16 The waters saw you, O God,
the waters saw you and writhed;
the very depths were convulsed.
17 The clouds poured down water,
the skies resounded with thunder;
your arrows flashed back and forth.
18 Your thunder was heard in the whirlwind,
your lightning lit up the world;
the earth trembled and quaked.
19 Your path led through the sea,
your way through the mighty waters,
though your footprints were not seen.

20 You led your people like a flock
by the hand of Moses and Aaron.

Discovering the Word 1. What words and phrases does the psalmist use to describe his emotion? 2. Why does he "groan" at the memory of God (vv. 3–9)? 3. How does the tone of the passage change in verses 10–15? 4. What is the source of the change? 5. How do verses 16–20 emphasize God's power?

Applying the Word 1. The psalmist's discontent makes him "too troubled to speak." When have you experienced this? 2. Sometimes our culture leads us to believe that material things and achievements, such as a promotion at work, social status, the right relationship, a new car or the perfect house, will bring contentment. What false sources of contentment do you put faith in? 3. What in this passage could help you reform your thinking?

Responding in Prayer The psalmist finds his source of contentment in who God is. Make God's character—rather than your needs—a focus of prayer.

Psalms 78—83

Psalm 78

A *maskil*[g] of Asaph.

[1]O my people, hear my teaching;
listen to the words of my mouth.
[2]I will open my mouth in parables,
I will utter hidden things, things from of old—
[3]what we have heard and known,
what our fathers have told us.
[4]We will not hide them from their children;
we will tell the next generation
the praiseworthy deeds of the LORD,
his power, and the wonders he has done.
[5]He decreed statutes for Jacob
and established the law in Israel,
which he commanded our forefathers
to teach their children,
[6]so the next generation would know them,
even the children yet to be born,
and they in turn would tell their children.
[7]Then they would put their trust in God
and would not forget his deeds
but would keep his commands.
[8]They would not be like their forefathers—
a stubborn and rebellious generation,
whose hearts were not loyal to God,
whose spirits were not faithful to him.

[9]The men of Ephraim, though armed with bows,
turned back on the day of battle;
[10]they did not keep God's covenant
and refused to live by his law.
[11]They forgot what he had done,
the wonders he had shown them.
[12]He did miracles in the sight of their fathers
in the land of Egypt, in the region of Zoan.
[13]He divided the sea and led them through;
he made the water stand firm like a wall.
[14]He guided them with the cloud by day
and with light from the fire all night.
[15]He split the rocks in the desert
and gave them water as abundant as the seas;
[16]he brought streams out of a rocky crag
and made water flow down like rivers.

[17]But they continued to sin against him,
rebelling in the desert against the Most High.
[18]They willfully put God to the test
by demanding the food they craved.
[19]They spoke against God, saying,
"Can God spread a table in the desert?
[20]When he struck the rock, water gushed out,
and streams flowed abundantly.
But can he also give us food?
Can he supply meat for his people?"
[21]When the LORD heard them, he was very angry;
his fire broke out against Jacob,
and his wrath rose against Israel,
[22]for they did not believe in God
or trust in his deliverance.
[23]Yet he gave a command to the skies above
and opened the doors of the heavens;
[24]he rained down manna for the people to eat,
he gave them the grain of heaven.
[25]Men ate the bread of angels;
he sent them all the food they could eat.
[26]He let loose the east wind from the heavens
and led forth the south wind by his power.
[27]He rained meat down on them like dust,
flying birds like sand on the seashore.
[28]He made them come down inside their camp,
all around their tents.
[29]They ate till they had more than enough,
for he had given them what they craved.
[30]But before they turned from the food they craved,
even while it was still in their mouths,
[31]God's anger rose against them;
he put to death the sturdiest among them,

[g]Title: Probably a literary or musical term

cutting down the young men of Israel.

[32]In spite of all this, they kept on sinning;
in spite of his wonders, they did not believe.
[33]So he ended their days in futility
and their years in terror.
[34]Whenever God slew them, they would seek him;
they eagerly turned to him again.
[35]They remembered that God was their Rock,
that God Most High was their Redeemer.
[36]But then they would flatter him with their mouths,
lying to him with their tongues;
[37]their hearts were not loyal to him,
they were not faithful to his covenant.
[38]Yet he was merciful;
he forgave their iniquities
and did not destroy them.
Time after time he restrained his anger
and did not stir up his full wrath.
[39]He remembered that they were but flesh,
a passing breeze that does not return.

[40]How often they rebelled against him in the desert
and grieved him in the wasteland!
[41]Again and again they put God to the test;
they vexed the Holy One of Israel.
[42]They did not remember his power—
the day he redeemed them from the oppressor,
[43]the day he displayed his miraculous signs in Egypt,
his wonders in the region of Zoan.
[44]He turned their rivers to blood;
they could not drink from their streams.
[45]He sent swarms of flies that devoured them,
and frogs that devastated them.
[46]He gave their crops to the grasshopper,
their produce to the locust.
[47]He destroyed their vines with hail
and their sycamore-figs with sleet.
[48]He gave over their cattle to the hail,
their livestock to bolts of lightning.
[49]He unleashed against them his hot anger,
his wrath, indignation and hostility—
a band of destroying angels.
[50]He prepared a path for his anger;
he did not spare them from death
but gave them over to the plague.
[51]He struck down all the firstborn of Egypt,
the firstfruits of manhood in the tents of Ham.
[52]But he brought his people out like a flock;
he led them like sheep through the desert.
[53]He guided them safely, so they were unafraid;
but the sea engulfed their enemies.
[54]Thus he brought them to the border of his holy land,
to the hill country his right hand had taken.
[55]He drove out nations before them
and allotted their lands to them as an inheritance;
he settled the tribes of Israel in their homes.

[56]But they put God to the test
and rebelled against the Most High;
they did not keep his statutes.
[57]Like their fathers they were disloyal and faithless,
as unreliable as a faulty bow.
[58]They angered him with their high places;
they aroused his jealousy with their idols.
[59]When God heard them, he was very angry;
he rejected Israel completely.
[60]He abandoned the tabernacle of Shiloh,
the tent he had set up among men.
[61]He sent ⌞the ark of⌟ his might into captivity,
his splendor into the hands of the enemy.
[62]He gave his people over to the sword;
he was very angry with his inheritance.
[63]Fire consumed their young men,
and their maidens had no wedding songs;
[64]their priests were put to the sword,
and their widows could not weep.

[65]Then the Lord awoke as from sleep,
as a man wakes from the stupor of wine.
[66]He beat back his enemies;
he put them to everlasting shame.
[67]Then he rejected the tents of Joseph,
he did not choose the tribe of Ephraim;
[68]but he chose the tribe of Judah,
Mount Zion, which he loved.
[69]He built his sanctuary like the heights,
like the earth that he established forever.
[70]He chose David his servant
and took him from the sheep pens;
[71]from tending the sheep he brought him
to be the shepherd of his people Jacob,
of Israel his inheritance.

72And David shepherded them with integrity of heart;
with skillful hands he led them.

Psalm 79

A psalm of Asaph.

1O God, the nations have invaded your inheritance;
they have defiled your holy temple,
they have reduced Jerusalem to rubble.
2They have given the dead bodies of your servants
as food to the birds of the air,
the flesh of your saints to the beasts of the earth.
3They have poured out blood like water
all around Jerusalem,
and there is no one to bury the dead.
4We are objects of reproach to our neighbors,
of scorn and derision to those around us.

5How long, O LORD? Will you be angry forever?
How long will your jealousy burn like fire?
6Pour out your wrath on the nations
that do not acknowledge you,
on the kingdoms
that do not call on your name;
7for they have devoured Jacob
and destroyed his homeland.
8Do not hold against us the sins of the fathers;
may your mercy come quickly to meet us,
for we are in desperate need.

9Help us, O God our Savior,
for the glory of your name;
deliver us and forgive our sins
for your name's sake.
10Why should the nations say,
"Where is their God?"
Before our eyes, make known among the nations
that you avenge the outpoured blood of your servants.
11May the groans of the prisoners come before you;
by the strength of your arm
preserve those condemned to die.

12Pay back into the laps of our neighbors seven times
the reproach they have hurled at you, O Lord.
13Then we your people, the sheep of your pasture,
will praise you forever;
from generation to generation
we will recount your praise.

Psalm 80

For the director of music. To ⌊the tune of⌋ "The Lilies of the Covenant." Of Asaph. A psalm.

1Hear us, O Shepherd of Israel,
you who lead Joseph like a flock;
you who sit enthroned between the cherubim, shine forth
2 before Ephraim, Benjamin and Manasseh.
Awaken your might;
come and save us.

3Restore us, O God;
make your face shine upon us,
that we may be saved.

4O LORD God Almighty,
how long will your anger smolder
against the prayers of your people?
5You have fed them with the bread of tears;
you have made them drink tears by the bowlful.
6You have made us a source of contention to our neighbors,
and our enemies mock us.

7Restore us, O God Almighty;
make your face shine upon us,
that we may be saved.

8You brought a vine out of Egypt;
you drove out the nations and planted it.
9You cleared the ground for it,
and it took root and filled the land.
10The mountains were covered with its shade,
the mighty cedars with its branches.
11It sent out its boughs to the Sea,[h]
its shoots as far as the River.[i]

12Why have you broken down its walls
so that all who pass by pick its grapes?
13Boars from the forest ravage it
and the creatures of the field feed on it.
14Return to us, O God Almighty!

[h]11 Probably the Mediterranean [i]11 That is, the Euphrates

Look down from heaven and see!
Watch over this vine,
15 the root your right hand has planted,
the son[j] you have raised up for yourself.

16Your vine is cut down, it is burned with fire;
at your rebuke your people perish.
17Let your hand rest on the man at your right hand,
the son of man you have raised up for yourself.
18Then we will not turn away from you;
revive us, and we will call on your name.

19Restore us, O LORD God Almighty;
make your face shine upon us,
that we may be saved.

Psalm 81

For the director of music. According to *gittith.*[k] Of Asaph.

1Sing for joy to God our strength;
shout aloud to the God of Jacob!
2Begin the music, strike the tambourine,
play the melodious harp and lyre.

3Sound the ram's horn at the New Moon,
and when the moon is full, on the day of our Feast;
4this is a decree for Israel,
an ordinance of the God of Jacob.
5He established it as a statute for Joseph
when he went out against Egypt,
where we heard a language we did not understand.[l]

6He says, "I removed the burden from their shoulders;
their hands were set free from the basket.
7In your distress you called and I rescued you,
I answered you out of a thundercloud;
I tested you at the waters of Meribah. *Selah*

8"Hear, O my people, and I will warn you—
if you would but listen to me, O Israel!
9You shall have no foreign god among you;
you shall not bow down to an alien god.
10I am the LORD your God,
who brought you up out of Egypt.
Open wide your mouth and I will fill it.

11"But my people would not listen to me;
Israel would not submit to me.
12So I gave them over to their stubborn hearts
to follow their own devices.

13"If my people would but listen to me,
if Israel would follow my ways,
14how quickly would I subdue their enemies
and turn my hand against their foes!
15Those who hate the LORD would cringe before him,
and their punishment would last forever.
16But you would be fed with the finest of wheat;
with honey from the rock I would satisfy you."

Psalm 82

A psalm of Asaph.

1God presides in the great assembly;
he gives judgment among the "gods":

2"How long will you[m] defend the unjust
and show partiality to the wicked? *Selah*
3Defend the cause of the weak and fatherless;
maintain the rights of the poor and oppressed.
4Rescue the weak and needy;
deliver them from the hand of the wicked.

5"They know nothing, they understand nothing.
They walk about in darkness;
all the foundations of the earth are shaken.

6"I said, 'You are "gods";
you are all sons of the Most High.'
7But you will die like mere men;
you will fall like every other ruler."

8Rise up, O God, judge the earth,
for all the nations are your inheritance.

Psalm 83

A song. A psalm of Asaph.

1O God, do not keep silent;
be not quiet, O God, be not still.
2See how your enemies are astir,
how your foes rear their heads.
3With cunning they conspire against your people;

[j]15 Or *branch* [k]Title: Probably a musical term [l]5 Or / *and we heard a voice we had not known* [m]2 The Hebrew is plural.

they plot against those you cherish.
4"Come," they say, "let us destroy them as a nation,
that the name of Israel be remembered no more."
5With one mind they plot together;
they form an alliance against you—
6the tents of Edom and the Ishmaelites,
of Moab and the Hagrites,
7Gebal,[n] Ammon and Amalek,
Philistia, with the people of Tyre.
8Even Assyria has joined them
to lend strength to the descendants of Lot.
Selah

9Do to them as you did to Midian,
as you did to Sisera and Jabin at the river Kishon,
10who perished at Endor
and became like refuse on the ground.
11Make their nobles like Oreb and Zeeb,
all their princes like Zebah and Zalmunna,
12who said, "Let us take possession
of the pasturelands of God."

13Make them like tumbleweed, O my God,
like chaff before the wind.
14As fire consumes the forest
or a flame sets the mountains ablaze,
15so pursue them with your tempest
and terrify them with your storm.
16Cover their faces with shame
so that men will seek your name, O LORD.

17May they ever be ashamed and dismayed;
may they perish in disgrace.
18Let them know that you, whose name is the LORD—
that you alone are the Most High over all the earth.

[n]7 That is, Byblos

49 / *Psalm 84*
A Prayer of Yearning

CONTINUOUS ACCESS AND warm intimacy with God is sometimes difficult to maintain. Times of spiritual dryness, "busyness" and adversity may capture our attention more and rob us of regular meeting times with God. Psalm 84 reflects a time of spiritual dryness common to many believers experientially and to Israel historically. This psalmist laments his forced and prolonged separation from God (likely during the Babylonian exile), which has robbed him of the appointed duties, freedom of access and the warm intimacy he once enjoyed.

Warming Up to God Think back to where you were living when you were twelve years old. What was the center of warmth in your home then?

Read Psalm 84.

Psalm 84

For the director of music. According to *gittith.*[o] Of the Sons of Korah. A psalm.

1How lovely is your dwelling place,
O LORD Almighty!
2My soul yearns, even faints,
for the courts of the LORD;
my heart and my flesh cry out
for the living God.
3Even the sparrow has found a home,
and the swallow a nest for herself,
where she may have her young—
a place near your altar,
O LORD Almighty, my King and my God.
4Blessed are those who dwell in your house;
they are ever praising you. *Selah*

5Blessed are those whose strength is in you,
who have set their hearts on pilgrimage.
6As they pass through the Valley of Baca,
they make it a place of springs;
the autumn rains also cover it with pools.[p]

[o]Title: Probably a musical term [p]6 Or *blessings*

[7]They go from strength to strength,
till each appears before God in Zion.

[8]Hear my prayer, O LORD God Almighty;
listen to me, O God of Jacob. *Selah*
[9]Look upon our shield,[q] O God;
look with favor on your anointed one.
[10]Better is one day in your courts
than a thousand elsewhere;
I would rather be a doorkeeper in the house
of my God
than dwell in the tents of the wicked.
[11]For the LORD God is a sun and shield;
the LORD bestows favor and honor;
no good thing does he withhold
from those whose walk is blameless.

[12]O LORD Almighty,
blessed is the man who trusts in you.

[q] 9 Or *sovereign*

Discovering the Word 1. What is the psalmist yearning for (vv. 2–3, 10)? 2. What names and metaphors for God can you find in this psalm? 3. The "Valley of Baca" (v. 6) was an arid stretch of desert that brought tears of adversity to pilgrims who had to traverse it en route to Jerusalem. What does that valley symbolize—historically and spiritually? 4. What are the benefits or blessings of trusting God as this psalmist does (vv. 4–5, 11–12)?

Applying the Word 1. If you could have one wish come true regarding your Christian life, what one thing would you yearn for? 2. How do you usually address God in prayer? Why? 3. Try to visualize where and when God has been closest to you. Put yourself in that picture as a "doorkeeper." How do you feel at those intimate times?

Responding in Prayer Spend time with the Lord of the universe in prayer, fellowship and worship.

Psalm 85

Psalm 85

For the director of music. Of the Sons of Korah. A psalm.

[1]You showed favor to your land, O LORD;
you restored the fortunes of Jacob.
[2]You forgave the iniquity of your people
and covered all their sins. *Selah*
[3]You set aside all your wrath
and turned from your fierce anger.

[4]Restore us again, O God our Savior,
and put away your displeasure toward us.
[5]Will you be angry with us forever?
Will you prolong your anger through all
generations?
[6]Will you not revive us again,
that your people may rejoice in you?
[7]Show us your unfailing love, O LORD,
and grant us your salvation.

[8]I will listen to what God the LORD will say;
he promises peace to his people, his
saints—
but let them not return to folly.
[9]Surely his salvation is near those who fear
him,
that his glory may dwell in our land.

[10]Love and faithfulness meet together;
righteousness and peace kiss each other.
[11]Faithfulness springs forth from the earth,
and righteousness looks down from heaven.
[12]The LORD will indeed give what is good,
and our land will yield its harvest.
[13]Righteousness goes before him
and prepares the way for his steps.

50 / *Psalm 86* A Prayer of Dependence

OUR RELATIONSHIP WITH God is that of children to a parent, sheep to a shepherd, creators to the Creator. We are dependent on him for life, for breath, for sustenance, for help in trouble, for love, for forgiveness, for mercy. We may like to think of ourselves as independent and self-sufficient. But we are not. We need God. It is vital that we acknowledge our need for him because it is the beginning place of our relationship with him. This psalm helps us give voice to our dependence on God.

Warming Up to God Think of a time when you needed to rely on someone for emotional or physical support. What feelings did you have about depending on them for help?

Read Psalm 86.

Psalm 86

A prayer of David.

1 Hear, O LORD, and answer me,
for I am poor and needy.
2 Guard my life, for I am devoted to you.
You are my God; save your servant
who trusts in you.
3 Have mercy on me, O Lord,
for I call to you all day long.
4 Bring joy to your servant,
for to you, O Lord,
I lift up my soul.

5 You are forgiving and good, O Lord,
abounding in love to all who call
to you.
6 Hear my prayer, O LORD;
listen to my cry for mercy.
7 In the day of my trouble I will call
to you,
for you will answer me.

8 Among the gods there is none like you,
O Lord;
no deeds can compare with yours.
9 All the nations you have made
will come and worship before you, O Lord;
they will bring glory to your name.
10 For you are great and do marvelous deeds;
you alone are God.
11 Teach me your way, O LORD,
and I will walk in your truth;
give me an undivided heart,
that I may fear your name.
12 I will praise you, O Lord my God, with all
my heart;
I will glorify your name forever.
13 For great is your love toward me;
you have delivered me from the depths of
the grave.[r]

14 The arrogant are attacking me,
O God;
a band of ruthless men seeks
my life—
men without regard for you.
15 But you, O Lord, are a compassionate and
gracious God,
slow to anger, abounding in love and
faithfulness.
16 Turn to me and have mercy on me;
grant your strength to your servant
and save the son of your maidservant.[s]
17 Give me a sign of your goodness,
that my enemies may see it and be put to
shame,
for you, O LORD, have helped me and
comforted me.

[r] 13 Hebrew *Sheol* [s] 16 Or *save your faithful son*

Discovering the Word 1. What is the overall sense you get about the nature of the psalmist's relationship with God? 2. List the many requests the psalmist makes of God. 3. The psalmist sees God as loving, powerful and actively involved in caring for him. What are some of the specific statements he makes about God? 4. What impact would this view of God have on a person's ability to depend on God? 5. How does the psalmist show his dependence on God throughout this psalm?

 **Applying the Word** 1. What reactions do you have to this kind of dependency on God? 2. How might the psalmist's dependency on God encourage you to depend more fully on God? 3. In what areas of your life do you need to acknowledge your dependence on God?

Responding in Prayer Freely express your sense of need for God and your struggles to depend on him.

Psalm 87

Psalm 87

Of the Sons of Korah. A psalm. A song.

1He has set his foundation on the holy
mountain;
2 the LORD loves the gates of Zion
more than all the dwellings of Jacob.
3Glorious things are said of you,
O city of God: *Selah*
4"I will record Rahab[t] and Babylon
among those who acknowledge me—
Philistia too, and Tyre, along with
Cush[u]—
and will say, 'This[v] one was born in
Zion.' "

5Indeed, of Zion it will be said,
"This one and that one were born in her,
and the Most High himself will establish
her."
6The LORD will write in the register of the
peoples:
"This one was born in Zion." *Selah*
7As they make music they will sing,
"All my fountains are in you."

[t]4 A poetic name for Egypt [u]4 That is, the upper Nile region [v]4 Or *"O Rahab and Babylon, / Philistia, Tyre and Cush, / I will record concerning those who acknowledge me: / 'This*

51 / *Psalm 88*
A Prayer of Despair

"I GIVE UP," Nancy said as she buried her face in her hands. Nancy was not a passive person. She worked hard as a single mother to provide for her children. She had developed a good support system for herself. She was actively, compassionately engaged in life. But a series of losses had left her deeply shaken. Everything she had worked so hard for seemed to be gone. Nancy felt defeated. And without hope. Despair is giving up. Or, as the psalmist expresses it, despair is a time when "darkness" becomes our "closest friend."

 **Warming Up to God** What pictures come to mind when you think of a person who is experiencing despair?

 **Read Psalm 88.**

Psalm 88

A song. A psalm of the Sons of Korah. For the director of music. According to *mahalath leannoth.*[w] A *maskil*[x] of Heman the Ezrahite.

1O LORD, the God who saves me,
day and night I cry out before you.
2May my prayer come before you;
turn your ear to my cry.
3For my soul is full of trouble
and my life draws near the grave.[y]
4I am counted among those who go down to
the pit;
I am like a man without strength.
5I am set apart with the dead,

[w]Title: Possibly a tune, "The Suffering of Affliction" [x]Title: Probably a literary or musical term [y]3 Hebrew *Sheol*

like the slain who lie in the grave,
whom you remember no more,
who are cut off from your care.
6You have put me in the lowest pit,
in the darkest depths.
7Your wrath lies heavily upon me;
you have overwhelmed me with all your
waves. *Selah*
8You have taken from me my closest friends
and have made me repulsive to them.
I am confined and cannot escape;
9 my eyes are dim with grief.

I call to you, O LORD, every day;
I spread out my hands to you.
10Do you show your wonders to the dead?
Do those who are dead rise up and praise
you? *Selah*
11Is your love declared in the grave,
your faithfulness in Destruction[z]?
12Are your wonders known in the place of
darkness,
or your righteous deeds in the land of
oblivion?

13But I cry to you for help, O LORD;
in the morning my prayer comes before
you.
14Why, O LORD, do you reject me
and hide your face from me?

15From my youth I have been afflicted and
close to death;
I have suffered your terrors and am in
despair.
16Your wrath has swept over me;
your terrors have destroyed me.
17All day long they surround me like a flood;
they have completely engulfed me.
18You have taken my companions and loved
ones from me;
the darkness is my closest friend.

[z]11 Hebrew *Abaddon*

Discovering the Word 1. What evidence is there of despair in this psalm? 2. What emotional impact did you experience as you read this psalm? 3. Contrast the first and last verses of this psalm. Most psalms which express strong doubts end with hope or praise. This psalm ends with doubt and despair. What is it like to be left with unresolved questions? 4. The writer blames God for his desperate situation. What does he say in blaming God (vv. 6–9, 15–18)? 5. In spite of his sense that God has rejected him and hurt him, the psalmist continues to talk with God. What does this say about his relationship with God?

Applying the Word 1. What reactions do you have to the psalmist blaming God? 2. Think of a time when it was difficult for you to talk to God. What was that experience like for you?

Responding in Prayer What would you like to say to God about the areas in life that feel "dark" or hopeless to you?

Psalm 89

Psalm 89

A *maskil*[a] of Ethan the Ezrahite.

1I will sing of the LORD's great love
forever;
with my mouth I will make your
faithfulness known through all
generations.
2I will declare that your love stands firm
forever,
that you established your faithfulness in
heaven itself.
3You said, "I have made a covenant with my
chosen one,
I have sworn to David my servant,
4'I will establish your line forever
and make your throne firm through all
generations.' " *Selah*
5The heavens praise your wonders, O LORD,
your faithfulness too, in the assembly of the
holy ones.
6For who in the skies above can compare with
the LORD?

[a]Title: Probably a literary or musical term

Who is like the LORD among the heavenly
beings?
7In the council of the holy ones God is greatly
feared;
he is more awesome than all who surround
him.
8O LORD God Almighty, who is like you?
You are mighty, O LORD, and your
faithfulness surrounds you.

9You rule over the surging sea;
when its waves mount up, you still them.
10You crushed Rahab like one of the slain;
with your strong arm you scattered your
enemies.
11The heavens are yours, and yours also the
earth;
you founded the world and all that is in it.
12You created the north and the south;
Tabor and Hermon sing for joy at your
name.
13Your arm is endued with power;
your hand is strong, your right hand
exalted.

14Righteousness and justice are the foundation
of your throne;
love and faithfulness go before you.
15Blessed are those who have learned to acclaim
you,
who walk in the light of your presence,
O LORD.
16They rejoice in your name all day long;
they exult in your righteousness.
17For you are their glory and strength,
and by your favor you exalt our horn.[b]
18Indeed, our shield[c] belongs to the LORD,
our king to the Holy One of Israel.

19Once you spoke in a vision,
to your faithful people you said:
"I have bestowed strength on a warrior;
I have exalted a young man from among
the people.
20I have found David my servant;
with my sacred oil I have anointed him.
21My hand will sustain him;
surely my arm will strengthen him.
22No enemy will subject him to tribute;
no wicked man will oppress him.
23I will crush his foes before him
and strike down his adversaries.
24My faithful love will be with him,
and through my name his horn[d] will be
exalted.
25I will set his hand over the sea,
his right hand over the rivers.
26He will call out to me, 'You are my Father,
my God, the Rock my Savior.'
27I will also appoint him my firstborn,
the most exalted of the kings of the earth.
28I will maintain my love to him forever,
and my covenant with him will never fail.
29I will establish his line forever,
his throne as long as the heavens endure.

30"If his sons forsake my law
and do not follow my statutes,
31if they violate my decrees
and fail to keep my commands,
32I will punish their sin with the rod,
their iniquity with flogging;
33but I will not take my love from him,
nor will I ever betray my faithfulness.
34I will not violate my covenant
or alter what my lips have uttered.
35Once for all, I have sworn by my holiness—
and I will not lie to David—
36that his line will continue forever
and his throne endure before me like the
sun;
37it will be established forever like the moon,
the faithful witness in the sky." *Selah*

38But you have rejected, you have spurned,
you have been very angry with your
anointed one.
39You have renounced the covenant with your
servant
and have defiled his crown in the dust.
40You have broken through all his walls
and reduced his strongholds to ruins.
41All who pass by have plundered him;
he has become the scorn of his neighbors.
42You have exalted the right hand of his foes;
you have made all his enemies rejoice.
43You have turned back the edge of his sword
and have not supported him in battle.
44You have put an end to his splendor
and cast his throne to the ground.
45You have cut short the days of his youth;
you have covered him with a mantle of
shame. *Selah*

[b]17 *Horn* here symbolizes strong one. [c]18 Or *sovereign*
[d]24 *Horn* here symbolizes strength.

46How long, O LORD? Will you hide yourself
forever?
How long will your wrath burn like fire?
47Remember how fleeting is my life.
For what futility you have created all
men!
48What man can live and not see death,
or save himself from the power of the
grave[e]? *Selah*
49O Lord, where is your former great love,
which in your faithfulness you swore to
David?
50Remember, Lord, how your servant has[f]
been mocked,
how I bear in my heart the taunts of all the
nations,
51the taunts with which your enemies have
mocked, O LORD,
with which they have mocked every step of
your anointed one.

52Praise be to the LORD forever!
Amen and Amen.

[e]48 Hebrew *Sheol* [f]50 Or *your servants have*

52 / *Psalm 90*
Praying Our Death

DEATH IS NOT a popular subject. We live in a society characterized by the denial of death. This is unusual. Most people who have lived on this earth have given a great deal of attention to death. Preparing for a good death has been, in every century except our own, an accepted goal in life. Psalm 90 has been part of that preparation for millions of Christians.

Warming Up to God When you think about your own death, what do you think about? What do you feel?

Read Psalm 90.

BOOK IV
Psalms 90–106

Psalm 90

A prayer of Moses the man of God.

1Lord, you have been our dwelling place
throughout all generations.
2Before the mountains were born
or you brought forth the earth and the
world,
from everlasting to everlasting you are God.

3You turn men back to dust,
saying, "Return to dust, O sons of men."
4For a thousand years in your sight
are like a day that has just gone by,
or like a watch in the night.
5You sweep men away in the sleep of death;
they are like the new grass of the
morning—
6though in the morning it springs up new,
by evening it is dry and withered.

7We are consumed by your anger
and terrified by your indignation.
8You have set our iniquities before you,
our secret sins in the light of your
presence.
9All our days pass away under your wrath;
we finish our years with a moan.
10The length of our days is seventy years—
or eighty, if we have the strength;
yet their span[g] is but trouble and sorrow,
for they quickly pass, and we fly away.

11Who knows the power of your anger?
For your wrath is as great as the fear that is
due you.
12Teach us to number our days aright,
that we may gain a heart of wisdom.

13Relent, O LORD! How long will it be?
Have compassion on your servants.

[g]10 Or *yet the best of them*

14Satisfy us in the morning with your unfailing
love,
that we may sing for joy and be glad all
our days.
15Make us glad for as many days as you have
afflicted us,
for as many years as we have seen trouble.
16May your deeds be shown to your servants,
your splendor to their children.
17May the favor[h] of the Lord our God rest
upon us;
establish the work of our hands for us—
yes, establish the work of our hands.

[h]17 Or *beauty*

Discovering the Word 1. Read Psalm 90. Death sets a limit to our lives and stimulates reflection on the context of life, which is not death, but God. In verses 1–2 how does the psalmist set death within his view of God? 2. How does the psalmist describe God's anger and its effects on our lives (vv. 7–11)? 3. How do you integrate this view of God with John's well-known statement "God is love"? 4. Luther commented on verse 12: "Lord, teach us all to be such arithmeticians!" What does it mean to number our days aright? 5. Study the verbs in verses 14–17. What emerges as most important for you—what you do for the rest of your life or what God will do in your life? Explain.

Applying the Word 1. How long do you expect to live? 2. How do you plan to live the years left to you? 3. Plato believed that philosophy was nothing more than a study of death. In the Middle Ages pastoral care concentrated on preparing you for a good death. How does your meditation on death affect the way you live your life?

Responding in Prayer Express your awareness that you will die. In your prayers be conscious of Christ's death.

53 / *Psalm 91*
Angels Among Us

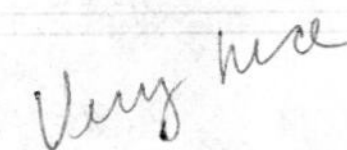

ANGEL STORIES ARE gaining wider acceptance today. People see angels taking various forms and functions—as messengers of glad tidings, spirits of people who have died, invisible guardians of our safety, angels in disguise as do-gooders or cherubs of romantic love. Many of the popular depictions of angels have nothing to do with the biblical perspective. The angels invoked in this psalm are heralds and harbingers of God's power. The psalm glows with testimony to the security of godly worshipers.

Warming Up to God In your mind's eye, what do angels look like? What do they spend their time doing?

Read Psalm 91.

Psalm 91

1He who dwells in the shelter of the Most
High
will rest in the shadow of the Almighty.[i]
2I will say[j] of the Lord, "He is my refuge and
my fortress,
my God, in whom I trust."

3Surely he will save you from the fowler's
snare
and from the deadly pestilence.
4He will cover you with his feathers,
and under his wings you will find refuge;
his faithfulness will be your shield and
rampart.
5You will not fear the terror of night,
nor the arrow that flies by day,
6nor the pestilence that stalks in the darkness,
nor the plague that destroys at midday.
7A thousand may fall at your side,
ten thousand at your right hand,

[i]1 Hebrew *Shaddai* [j]2 Or *He says*

but it will not come near you.
[8]You will only observe with your eyes
and see the punishment of the wicked.

[9]If you make the Most High your dwelling—
even the LORD, who is my refuge—
[10]then no harm will befall you,
no disaster will come near your tent.
[11]For he will command his angels concerning you
to guard you in all your ways;
[12]they will lift you up in their hands,
so that you will not strike your foot against a stone.
[13]You will tread upon the lion and the cobra;
you will trample the great lion and the serpent.

[14]"Because he loves me," says the LORD, "I will rescue him;
I will protect him, for he acknowledges my name.
[15]He will call upon me, and I will answer him;
I will be with him in trouble,
I will deliver him and honor him.
[16]With long life will I satisfy him
and show him my salvation."

Discovering the Word 1. The psalm divides into two stanzas: vv. 1–8 and vv. 9–16. What theme is common to the opening couplet of each stanza (vv. 1–2, 9–10)? 2. What threatens the security of the believer, even those who take refuge in God (vv. 3–6, 13)? 3. Is the godly believer protected *from* calamity and sorrow, or is he promised God's presence *amidst* terrible circumstances? Explain your answer from the passage. 4. What is the basis for the psalmist's assurance that he will be safe and secure (vv. 9–12, 14–15)? 5. In this psalm, what does "my [God's] salvation" (v. 16) look like?

Applying the Word 1. What are you particularly anxious about these days, for which God is waiting on you to call his name and acknowledge your need? 2. How can you make God your dwelling place, your refuge, your shield in times of trouble?

Responding in Prayer God is waiting to hear from his people who love him and acknowledge their need of him. Tell him whatever is on your mind, whatever fears you have and whatever terrible circumstances you are facing. Trust him to answer.

Psalms 92—93

Psalm 92

A psalm. A song. For the Sabbath day.

[1]It is good to praise the LORD
and make music to your name, O Most High,
[2]to proclaim your love in the morning
and your faithfulness at night,
[3]to the music of the ten-stringed lyre
and the melody of the harp.

[4]For you make me glad by your deeds, O LORD;
I sing for joy at the works of your hands.
[5]How great are your works, O LORD,
how profound your thoughts!
[6]The senseless man does not know,
fools do not understand,
[7]that though the wicked spring up like grass
and all evildoers flourish,
they will be forever destroyed.

[8]But you, O LORD, are exalted forever.

[9]For surely your enemies, O LORD,
surely your enemies will perish;
all evildoers will be scattered.
[10]You have exalted my horn[k] like that of a wild ox;
fine oils have been poured upon me.
[11]My eyes have seen the defeat of my adversaries;
my ears have heard the rout of my wicked foes.

[12]The righteous will flourish like a palm tree,
they will grow like a cedar of Lebanon;
[13]planted in the house of the LORD,
they will flourish in the courts of our God.
[14]They will still bear fruit in old age,
they will stay fresh and green,

[k]10 *Horn* here symbolizes strength.

15proclaiming, "The LORD is upright;
he is my Rock, and there is no wickedness in him."

Psalm 93

1The LORD reigns, he is robed in majesty;
the LORD is robed in majesty
and is armed with strength.
The world is firmly established;
it cannot be moved.
2Your throne was established long ago;
you are from all eternity.
3The seas have lifted up, O LORD,
the seas have lifted up their voice;
the seas have lifted up their pounding waves.
4Mightier than the thunder of the great waters,
mightier than the breakers of the sea—
the LORD on high is mighty.

5Your statutes stand firm;
holiness adorns your house
for endless days, O LORD.

54 / *Psalm 94*
A Prayer of Anger

MIKE AND JOHN had something in common—they had both been ripped off by their business partners and they were both angry. Very angry. As they shared their experiences with each other, they discovered an important difference, however. Mike was baffled by what to do with his strong feelings. His anger frightened him and did not seem very spiritual, so most of the time he kept quiet about his sense of outrage at the unfairness of it all. John, on the other hand, had grown up in a church that prayed the psalms together. Together they had spoken the words of anger and outrage to God. As a result, John was able to talk to God about his anger. He knew he had been grievously wronged and that he was deeply angry. And he knew he could take his anger to God. This psalm is one of the psalms that can help us speak freely to God about our anger.

Warming Up to God Is it difficult or relatively easy for you to tell God about your anger? Explain.

Read Psalm 94.

Psalm 94

1O LORD, the God who avenges,
O God who avenges, shine forth.
2Rise up, O Judge of the earth;
pay back to the proud what they deserve.
3How long will the wicked, O LORD,
how long will the wicked be jubilant?

4They pour out arrogant words;
all the evildoers are full of boasting.
5They crush your people, O LORD;
they oppress your inheritance.
6They slay the widow and the alien;
they murder the fatherless.
7They say, "The LORD does not see;
the God of Jacob pays no heed."

8Take heed, you senseless ones among the people;
you fools, when will you become wise?
9Does he who implanted the ear not hear?
Does he who formed the eye not see?
10Does he who disciplines nations not punish?
Does he who teaches man lack knowledge?
11The LORD knows the thoughts of man;
he knows that they are futile.

12Blessed is the man you discipline, O LORD,
the man you teach from your law;
13you grant him relief from days of trouble,
till a pit is dug for the wicked.
14For the LORD will not reject his people;
he will never forsake his inheritance.
15Judgment will again be founded on righteousness,
and all the upright in heart will follow it.
16Who will rise up for me against the wicked?

Who will take a stand for me against
evildoers?
17Unless the LORD had given me help,
I would soon have dwelt in the silence of
death.
18When I said, "My foot is slipping,"
your love, O LORD, supported me.
19When anxiety was great within me,
your consolation brought joy to my soul.

20Can a corrupt throne be allied with you—
one that brings on misery by its decrees?
21They band together against the righteous
and condemn the innocent to death.
22But the LORD has become my fortress,
and my God the rock in whom I take
refuge.
23He will repay them for their sins
and destroy them for their wickedness;
the LORD our God will destroy them.

Discovering the Word 1. The psalmist addresses God as the Judge and as the one who avenges (vv. 1–2). What is the meaning of this for the psalmist? 2. In pleading his case before God, what does the psalmist say the wicked have done (vv. 4–7)? 3. In verses 8, 9 and 10 the psalmist asks several rhetorical questions of God. What statement is he making in these questions? 4. What hope does the psalmist express in verses 12–15? 5. Verse 16 captures the question the psalmist is wrestling with. What words would you use to express this question? 6. In verses 17 through 19 the psalmist expresses himself in vulnerable terms. How does he describe the experience of danger and fear that generated his anger?

Applying the Word 1. The psalmist concludes with statements that God will take care of justice, that God will judge. Why is this important to remember when we are feeling powerless and outraged in the face of injustice? 2. This psalm models several constructive ways we can behave when we are angry. It models honesty with ourselves and with God, stating our case to God, acknowledging our vulnerability, trusting God's care and letting God take care of justice. How might this example help you in times of anger? 3. Which of these behavioral examples might be especially important for you to follow when you are angry? Explain.

Responding in Prayer Talk to God about any feelings of anger—fresh or lingering—that you have.

55 / *Psalm 95*
A Psalm of Rest

SO OFTEN GOD gives us the consequences of our choices; other times he withholds or spares us the punishment our rebellion or hardheartedness deserves. That is an act of his mercy, for which this psalmist and all believers can give thanks. This psalm acknowledges God as Lord of the earth and Shepherd King of his people. The writer reflects on times of rebellion when the Israelites put God to the test and ended up missing out on God's rest.

Warming Up to God Picture the place where you go to enjoy peace and serenity, rest from your labors, and listen to God. If you don't have a place like that, make one up. Where is that place? (Does it have mountain peaks, sandy beaches, desert calm, green pastures?)

Read Psalm 95.

Psalm 95

1Come, let us sing for joy to the LORD;
let us shout aloud to the Rock of our
salvation.
2Let us come before him with thanksgiving
and extol him with music and song.
3For the LORD is the great God,
the great King above all gods.
4In his hand are the depths of the earth,
and the mountain peaks belong to him.
5The sea is his, for he made it,
and his hands formed the dry land.

6Come, let us bow down in worship,
let us kneel before the LORD our Maker;
7for he is our God
and we are the people of his pasture,
the flock under his care.

Today, if you hear his voice,
8 do not harden your hearts as you did at
Meribah,[l]
as you did that day at Massah[m] in the
desert,
9where your fathers tested and tried me,
though they had seen what I did.
10For forty years I was angry with that
generation;
I said, "They are a people whose hearts go
astray,
and they have not known my ways."
11So I declared on oath in my anger,
"They shall never enter my rest."

[l]8 *Meribah* means *quarreling.* [m]8 *Massah* means *testing.*

Discovering the Word 1. Where does this psalmist envision God ruling as Lord and King (vv. 3–5)? 2. Meribah and Massah are places where the Israelites rebelled in the desert and tested the Lord about whether he was with them or not (vv. 8–9). What happened as a result of that testing (vv. 10–11)? 3. What is the "rest" from which the rebellious Israelites were banned with an oath of God, but which a later generation would enjoy (v. 11)? 4. Imagine life without God's promised rest. What must that have been like? 5. What warning does the psalmist derive from that experience as he contemplates "Meribah" and "Massah" recurring for the present generation of God's people?

Applying the Word 1. Imagine life for you without God's promised rest. If your life and well-being were constantly threatened with adversaries in the land where you live and work, what would you be praying for? 2. During those times in your past when your heart strayed from God's ways (v. 10), how did God bring you back to himself? 3. As you listen to God's voice "today" (v. 7), what is he saying to you?

Responding in Prayer Whatever the past or present circumstances of your relationship with him may be, this psalm invites you to come into God's presence today. Try kneeling in his presence, acknowledging him as Lord of your life, even during those times you have strayed. Soften your heart and give him the praise and thanksgiving he deserves.

56 / *Psalm 96*
Worldwide Worship

OUR GOD IS a missionary God. He wants all nations, every living thing, to bow down in worship of him. And God wants us to take that message—in word and deed, in song and praise—to the ends of the earth. The psalmist bids us to be most inclusive in our worship of the one true God.

Warming Up to God Think about the greatness of God. What hymns come to mind that prompt you with the melody, the lyrics and reasons to praise him for the great things he has done?

Read Psalm 96.

Psalm 96

1Sing to the LORD a new song;
sing to the LORD, all the earth.
2Sing to the LORD, praise his name;
proclaim his salvation day after
day.
3Declare his glory among the nations,
his marvelous deeds among all peoples.
4For great is the LORD and most worthy of
praise;
he is to be feared above all gods.
5For all the gods of the nations are idols,
but the LORD made the heavens.
6Splendor and majesty are before him;
strength and glory are in his sanctuary.

7Ascribe to the LORD, O families of nations,

ascribe to the LORD glory and strength.
8 Ascribe to the LORD the glory due his name;
bring an offering and come into his courts.
9 Worship the LORD in the splendor of his[n]
holiness;
tremble before him, all the earth.

10 Say among the nations, "The LORD reigns."
The world is firmly established, it cannot
be moved;
he will judge the peoples with equity.
11 Let the heavens rejoice, let the earth be glad;
let the sea resound, and all that is in it;
12 let the fields be jubilant, and everything in
them.
Then all the trees of the forest will sing for
joy;
13 they will sing before the LORD, for he
comes,
he comes to judge the earth.
He will judge the world in righteousness
and the peoples in his truth.

[n]9 Or *LORD with the splendor of*

Discovering the Word 1. This psalm is divided up into four parts that are identifiable by repeated words or refrains: verses 1–3, 4–6, 7–9 and 10–13. What repetition do you see in each of these sections? 2. What "marvelous deeds" (v. 3) come to mind that would prompt a believer to sing God's praises? 3. Why is the Lord "most worthy of" (entitled to) praise (vv. 4–6, 10, 13)? 4. Like an orchestra conductor that bids different sections to join in the ensemble, the psalmist bids different sections to join in the chorus of praise to God. How extensive or inclusive is this call to "ascribe glory to" (worship) God (vv. 7–13)?

Applying the Word 1. In light of this universal call to worship, think of those around you and on the other side of the globe. What does this psalmist prompt you to do about those who don't know God? 2. This psalm invites us to sing a "new song" declaring his glory to others (in witness) and ascribing glory directly to God (in worship). How would someone who is not musically inclined be creative in this kind of witness and worship? 3. Let the joy of knowing God bubble up within you and burst forth in a "new song" of worship. Be spontaneous and let this psalm be the wellspring for singing out or jotting down words of praise. (Later see if you, or someone you know, could set those words to music.)

Responding in Prayer Pray for someone who does not yet know God. Pray about inviting that person to join you in worship.

Psalms 97—98

Psalm 97

1 The LORD reigns, let the earth be glad;
let the distant shores rejoice.

2 Clouds and thick darkness surround him;
righteousness and justice are the foundation
of his throne.
3 Fire goes before him
and consumes his foes on every side.
4 His lightning lights up the world;
the earth sees and trembles.
5 The mountains melt like wax before the LORD,
before the Lord of all the earth.
6 The heavens proclaim his righteousness,
and all the peoples see his glory.

7 All who worship images are put to shame,
those who boast in idols—
worship him, all you gods!

8 Zion hears and rejoices
and the villages of Judah are glad
because of your judgments, O LORD.
9 For you, O LORD, are the Most High over all
the earth;
you are exalted far above all gods.

10 Let those who love the LORD hate evil,
for he guards the lives of his faithful ones
and delivers them from the hand of the
wicked.
11 Light is shed upon the righteous
and joy on the upright in heart.
12 Rejoice in the LORD, you who are righteous,
and praise his holy name.

Psalm 98

A psalm.

[1]Sing to the LORD a new song,
for he has done marvelous things;
his right hand and his holy arm
have worked salvation for him.
[2]The LORD has made his salvation known
and revealed his righteousness to the nations.
[3]He has remembered his love
and his faithfulness to the house of Israel;
all the ends of the earth have seen
the salvation of our God.

[4]Shout for joy to the LORD, all the earth,
burst into jubilant song with music;
[5]make music to the LORD with the harp,
with the harp and the sound of singing,
[6]with trumpets and the blast of the ram's horn—
shout for joy before the LORD, the King.

[7]Let the sea resound, and everything in it,
the world, and all who live in it.
[8]Let the rivers clap their hands,
let the mountains sing together for joy;
[9]let them sing before the LORD,
for he comes to judge the earth.
He will judge the world in righteousness
and the peoples with equity.

57 / *Psalm 99*
Hail to the King of Kings

THE ATTRIBUTES AND actions of our holy God inspire praise, awe and obedience in those who call on his name. This psalm calls to mind the special relationship that he had with Moses, Aaron and Samuel—a relationship that is representative and possible for all of God's people.

Warming Up to God Think about the holiness of God. What hymns come to mind that prompt you to praise God for his holiness, the justice and rightness of his ways? How do those hymns make you feel about approaching God?

Read Psalm 99.

Psalm 99

[1]The LORD reigns,
let the nations tremble;
he sits enthroned between the cherubim,
let the earth shake.
[2]Great is the LORD in Zion;
he is exalted over all the nations.
[3]Let them praise your great and awesome name—
he is holy.

[4]The King is mighty, he loves justice—
you have established equity;
in Jacob you have done
what is just and right.
[5]Exalt the LORD our God
and worship at his footstool;
he is holy.

[6]Moses and Aaron were among his priests,
Samuel was among those who called on his name;
they called on the LORD
and he answered them.
[7]He spoke to them from the pillar of cloud;
they kept his statutes and the decrees he gave them.

[8]O LORD our God,
you answered them;
you were to Israel[o] a forgiving God,
though you punished their misdeeds.[p]
[9]Exalt the LORD our God
and worship at his holy mountain,
for the LORD our God is holy.

[o]8 Hebrew *them* [p]8 Or / *an avenger of the wrongs done to them*

Discovering the Word 1. This psalm speaks of the Lord in different ways a total of seven times. (Seven is a symbol of completeness.) What aspects or characteristics of this complete Lord does the psalmist affirm? 2. Study the verbs. How do or should others respond in relation to the exalted Lord? 3. Consider the causes and effects, also the actions and explanations, in this psalm. Why should God's people worship this Lord (vv. 4–8)? 4. Out of reverence for God's unapproachable holiness, the people went through intermediaries to God. Priests such as Moses, Aaron and Samuel were the go-betweens (v. 6). How did God speak with them (vv. 6–8)?

Applying the Word 1. God is terribly awesome and holy, forgiving and punishing. What does that say about the casual God-is-my-buddy approach or the presumptuous God-is-my-bellhop approach we often take in worship and prayer? 2. What does God expect you to do in response to his holy character and righteous decrees? 3. This psalm invites us to tremble, praise, exalt and worship this Lord. How do you do that each day?

Responding in Prayer Let the awe of knowing this holy God sink in. Pray for a desire to be and do and love the things that characterize this holy God.

58 / *Psalm 100*

Seeing Myself as Human

"IT MAKES ME nervous when people say, 'I'm only human,'" said Bob. "I'm afraid that if I give myself excuses like that I will let myself off the hook instead of doing my best. I don't know why, but I need to keep pushing myself beyond my limits or I become terribly anxious."

We may not consciously think that we are superhuman, but we often try to act that way in order to avoid our vulnerability and our neediness. We may not consciously think we are subhuman either, but we may feel that way about ourselves when we cannot escape our finitude and dependency. To be human, for us, is to be a long list of things we would rather avoid. We do not like the vulnerability, the limits, the dependency or the needs. And so, all too often, we defend ourselves against our fears by trying to be God. But, we are not God. The more we are able to embrace this most fundamental of realities—that we are creatures and God is our Creator—the freer our lives can become. The text for this study will help us to see ourselves as belonging to God.

Warming Up to God God invites you to see yourself as a child of God. What obstacles might keep you from seeing yourself in this way?

Read Psalm 100.

Psalm 100

A psalm. For giving thanks.

1Shout for joy to the LORD, all the earth.
2 Worship the LORD with gladness;
come before him with joyful songs.
3Know that the LORD is God.
It is he who made us, and we are his[q];
we are his people, the sheep of his pasture.

4Enter his gates with thanksgiving
and his courts with praise;
give thanks to him and praise his name.
5For the LORD is good and his love endures forever;
his faithfulness continues through all generations.

[q]3 Or *and not we ourselves*

Discovering the Word 1. According to this psalm, who is God and what is he like? 2. This psalm also tells us about ourselves. According to this psalm, who are we? 3. The text instructs us to "know that LORD is God." What does it mean to "know that the LORD is God"? 4. What freedom might knowing this provide? 5. What things are we invited to do in response to God?

Applying the Word 1. In what area of your life do you need to quit trying to be superhuman? 2. How might it help you personally to "know that the LORD is God," that you are a creature, and "the sheep of his pasture"?

Responding in Prayer We are invited by this psalm to worship the Lord with gladness. Offer a brief song or poem or prayer of worship or praise to God.

Psalm 101

Psalm 101

Of David. A psalm.

1I will sing of your love and justice;
to you, O LORD, I will sing praise.
2I will be careful to lead a blameless life—
when will you come to me?

I will walk in my house
with blameless heart.
3I will set before my eyes
no vile thing.

The deeds of faithless men I hate;
they will not cling to me.
4Men of perverse heart shall be far
from me;
I will have nothing to do with evil.

5Whoever slanders his neighbor in
secret,
him will I put to silence;
whoever has haughty eyes and a proud
heart,
him will I not endure.

6My eyes will be on the faithful in the
land,
that they may dwell with me;
he whose walk is blameless
will minister to me.

7No one who practices deceit
will dwell in my house;
no one who speaks falsely
will stand in my presence.

8Every morning I will put to silence
all the wicked in the land;
I will cut off every evildoer
from the city of the LORD.

59 / *Psalm 102*
A Prayer of Grief

AND GRIEF STILL feels like fear. Perhaps, more strictly, like suspense. Or like waiting; just hanging around waiting for something to happen. It gives life a permanently provisional feeling. . . . The act of living is different all through. Her absence is like the sky, spread over everything. (C. S. Lewis, *A Grief Observed*, [New York: Bantam, 1976], pp. 39, 13)

Grief is an experience of deep sorrow over a significant loss. Whether the loss we have suffered is the loss of a loved one, a job, our health or our home, the physical, emotional and spiritual suffering is intense. This psalm speaks our anguish to God in times of grief.

Warming Up to God How would you describe the experience of grief?

Read Psalm 102.

Psalm 102

A prayer of an afflicted man. When he is faint and pours out his lament before the LORD.

[1]Hear my prayer, O LORD;
let my cry for help come to you.
[2]Do not hide your face from me
when I am in distress.
Turn your ear to me;
when I call, answer me quickly.

[3]For my days vanish like smoke;
my bones burn like glowing embers.
[4]My heart is blighted and withered like grass;
I forget to eat my food.
[5]Because of my loud groaning
I am reduced to skin and bones.
[6]I am like a desert owl,
like an owl among the ruins.
[7]I lie awake; I have become
like a bird alone on a roof.
[8]All day long my enemies taunt me;
those who rail against me use my name as a curse.
[9]For I eat ashes as my food
and mingle my drink with tears
[10]because of your great wrath,
for you have taken me up and thrown me aside.
[11]My days are like the evening shadow;
I wither away like grass.

[12]But you, O LORD, sit enthroned forever;
your renown endures through all generations.
[13]You will arise and have compassion on Zion,
for it is time to show favor to her;
the appointed time has come.
[14]For her stones are dear to your servants;
her very dust moves them to pity.
[15]The nations will fear the name of the LORD,
all the kings of the earth will revere your glory.
[16]For the LORD will rebuild Zion
and appear in his glory.
[17]He will respond to the prayer of the destitute;
he will not despise their plea.

[18]Let this be written for a future generation,
that a people not yet created may praise the LORD:
[19]"The LORD looked down from his sanctuary on high,
from heaven he viewed the earth,
[20]to hear the groans of the prisoners
and release those condemned to death."
[21]So the name of the LORD will be declared in Zion
and his praise in Jerusalem
[22]when the peoples and the kingdoms
assemble to worship the LORD.

[23]In the course of my life[r] he broke my strength;
he cut short my days.
[24]So I said:
"Do not take me away, O my God, in the midst of my days;
your years go on through all generations.
[25]In the beginning you laid the foundations of the earth,
and the heavens are the work of your hands.
[26]They will perish, but you remain;
they will all wear out like a garment.
Like clothing you will change them
and they will be discarded.
[27]But you remain the same,
and your years will never end.
[28]The children of your servants will live in your presence;
their descendants will be established before you."

[r]23 *Or By his power*

Discovering the Word 1. In verses 1–2 the psalmist pleads for God to hear him. Why is this need so urgent in times of grief and distress? 2. How does the psalmist describe his current physical and emotional state (vv. 2–11)? 3. The psalmist seems to be blaming God and pleading with God (vv. 1–2, 24) at the same time. What does he blame God for (vv. 8, 10, 23)? 4. The writer seems to have mixed feelings about God. What positive perspectives does he express about God (vv. 12–22, 25–28)? 5. Mixed feelings about God are common in times of suffering and grief. What is it about times of grief that might create these mixed feelings?

Applying the Word 1. How do the psalmist's descriptions compare with your experiences of grief? 2. What experience have you had with mixed feelings toward God in times of grief? 3. What grief are you aware of (over a loss you have suffered—recent or long past) that you need to express to God?

Responding in Prayer Express your feelings of grief to God, and pray for others you know who are grieving.

60 / *Psalm 103*
Praying Our Salvation

WHAT GOD HAS done for us far exceeds anything we have done for or against him. The summary word for this excessive, undeserved, unexpected act by God is *salvation.* Prayer explores the country of salvation, tramping the contours, smelling the flowers, touching the outcroppings. There is more to do than recognize the sheer fact of salvation and witness to it; there are unnumbered details of grace, of mercy, of blessing to be appreciated and savored. Prayer is the means by which we do this.

Warming Up to God Reflect on the meaning of your salvation. Allow praise for God to arise from your joy.

Read Psalm 103.

Psalm 103

Of David.

1Praise the LORD, O my soul;
all my inmost being, praise his holy name.
2Praise the LORD, O my soul,
and forget not all his benefits—
3who forgives all your sins
and heals all your diseases,
4who redeems your life from the pit
and crowns you with love and compassion,
5who satisfies your desires with good things
so that your youth is renewed like the eagle's.

6The LORD works righteousness
and justice for all the oppressed.

7He made known his ways to Moses,
his deeds to the people of Israel:
8The LORD is compassionate and gracious,
slow to anger, abounding in love.
9He will not always accuse,
nor will he harbor his anger forever;
10he does not treat us as our sins deserve
or repay us according to our iniquities.
11For as high as the heavens are above the earth,
so great is his love for those who fear him;
12as far as the east is from the west,
so far has he removed our transgressions from us.
13As a father has compassion on his children,
so the LORD has compassion on those who fear him;
14for he knows how we are formed,
he remembers that we are dust.
15As for man, his days are like grass,
he flourishes like a flower of the field;
16the wind blows over it and it is gone,
and its place remembers it no more.
17But from everlasting to everlasting
the LORD's love is with those who fear him,
and his righteousness with their children's children—
18with those who keep his covenant
and remember to obey his precepts.

19The LORD has established his throne in heaven,
and his kingdom rules over all.

20 Praise the LORD, you his angels,
you mighty ones who do his bidding,
who obey his word.
21 Praise the LORD, all his heavenly hosts,
you his servants who do his will.
22 Praise the LORD, all his works
everywhere in his dominion.

Praise the LORD, O my soul.

Discovering the Word 1. Note the first and last sentences. How does this bracketing affect your understanding of the psalm's contents? 2. Salvation is more richly complex than we sometimes think. What five actions of God add up to salvation (vv. 3–5)? 3. How did God make his ways known to Moses and Israel (v. 7)? 4. What astounding statements about God does the psalmist make in verses 8–14? 5. Carefully observe the contrast between us (vv. 15–16) and God (vv. 17–19). Does this make you feel better or worse about yourself? Explain.

Applying the Word 1. How have you benefited from your salvation? 2. How do verses 8–14 show you ways in which you would like to expand your thinking about God?

Responding in Prayer Add your personal praise to the praise in this psalm.

---

61 / *Psalm 104*
Protecting God's Creation

ONE NIGHT LAST summer, I stretched flat on my back in the grass of Trail Ridge Camp Sherith in central Wisconsin. "The stars are great at camp," my kids had all said. I was there to find out.

They emerged slowly at first, a few in the central heavens, but none near the still-lighted horizon. Could I count them? Almost. Then more and more came out. The first ones glared trumpetlike against the inky black, while others danced a gentle harmony. Even the horizon forgot the glow of sun and took on hundreds of thousands of lesser lights. Constellations, those artificial lines connecting stars like so many games of dot-to-dot, followed the patterns of my schoolgirl memory. A shooting star streaked across the sky, as if to connect the dots for me in some new constellation. Should I wish upon it?

I prayed instead. But what could I say to a God who had made all this and had somehow created in me the ability to enjoy it? For a long time I lay silent. Perhaps silence was the most sensible part of my prayer.

Warming Up to God When have you felt that God's creation helped you to know him?

Read Psalm 104.

Psalm 104

1 Praise the LORD, O my soul.

O LORD my God, you are very great;
you are clothed with splendor and majesty.
2 He wraps himself in light as with a garment;
he stretches out the heavens like a tent
3 and lays the beams of his upper chambers
on their waters.
He makes the clouds his chariot
and rides on the wings of the wind.
4 He makes winds his messengers,[s]
flames of fire his servants.

5 He set the earth on its foundations;
it can never be moved.
6 You covered it with the deep as with a
garment;
the waters stood above the mountains.
7 But at your rebuke the waters fled,
at the sound of your thunder they took to
flight;

[s] 4 Or *angels*

[8]they flowed over the mountains,
they went down into the valleys,
to the place you assigned for them.
[9]You set a boundary they cannot cross;
never again will they cover the earth.

[10]He makes springs pour water into the ravines;
it flows between the mountains.
[11]They give water to all the beasts of the field;
the wild donkeys quench their thirst.
[12]The birds of the air nest by the waters;
they sing among the branches.
[13]He waters the mountains from his upper
chambers;
the earth is satisfied by the fruit of his
work.
[14]He makes grass grow for the cattle,
and plants for man to cultivate—
bringing forth food from the earth:
[15]wine that gladdens the heart of man,
oil to make his face shine,
and bread that sustains his heart.
[16]The trees of the LORD are well watered,
the cedars of Lebanon that he planted.
[17]There the birds make their nests;
the stork has its home in the pine trees.
[18]The high mountains belong to the wild goats;
the crags are a refuge for the coneys.[t]

[19]The moon marks off the seasons,
and the sun knows when to go down.
[20]You bring darkness, it becomes night,
and all the beasts of the forest prowl.
[21]The lions roar for their prey
and seek their food from God.
[22]The sun rises, and they steal away;
they return and lie down in their dens.
[23]Then man goes out to his work,
to his labor until evening.

[24]How many are your works, O LORD!
In wisdom you made them all;
the earth is full of your creatures.
[25]There is the sea, vast and spacious,
teeming with creatures beyond number—
living things both large and small.
[26]There the ships go to and fro,
and the leviathan, which you formed to
frolic there.

[27]These all look to you
to give them their food at the proper time.
[28]When you give it to them,
they gather it up;
when you open your hand,
they are satisfied with good things.
[29]When you hide your face,
they are terrified;
when you take away their breath,
they die and return to the dust.
[30]When you send your Spirit,
they are created,
and you renew the face of the earth.

[31]May the glory of the LORD endure forever;
may the LORD rejoice in his works—
[32]he who looks at the earth, and it trembles,
who touches the mountains, and they
smoke.

[33]I will sing to the LORD all my life;
I will sing praise to my God as long as I
live.
[34]May my meditation be pleasing to him,
as I rejoice in the LORD.
[35]But may sinners vanish from the earth
and the wicked be no more.

Praise the LORD, O my soul.

Praise the LORD.[u]

[t]18 That is, the hyrax or rock badger [u]35 Hebrew *Hallelu Yah*; in the Septuagint this line stands at the beginning of Psalm 105.

Discovering the Word 1. Study verses 1–4. How does the sky serve God? 2. Study verses 5–9. What elements of earth's creation show God at work? 3. Study verses 10–18. What relationships does this description of God's creation reveal? 4. Study verses 19–26. How do these verses express an orderliness to what God has made? 5. Study verses 27–30. How do these verses show that God not only created but also personally takes care of what he has made? 6. Study verses 31–35. What responses to God are triggered by the psalmist's meditation on creation?

Applying the Word 1. When have you enjoyed some aspect of the natural rhythms described here? 2. As you meditate on what God has made, how would you like to respond to God?

Responding in Prayer Praise God for the glory of his creation.

Psalms 105—106

Psalm 105

1Give thanks to the LORD, call on his name;
make known among the nations what he has done.
2Sing to him, sing praise to him;
tell of all his wonderful acts.
3Glory in his holy name;
let the hearts of those who seek the LORD rejoice.
4Look to the LORD and his strength;
seek his face always.

5Remember the wonders he has done,
his miracles, and the judgments he pronounced,
6O descendants of Abraham his servant,
O sons of Jacob, his chosen ones.
7He is the LORD our God;
his judgments are in all the earth.

8He remembers his covenant forever,
the word he commanded, for a thousand generations,
9the covenant he made with Abraham,
the oath he swore to Isaac.
10He confirmed it to Jacob as a decree,
to Israel as an everlasting covenant:
11"To you I will give the land of Canaan
as the portion you will inherit."

12When they were but few in number,
few indeed, and strangers in it,
13they wandered from nation to nation,
from one kingdom to another.
14He allowed no one to oppress them;
for their sake he rebuked kings:
15"Do not touch my anointed ones;
do my prophets no harm."

16He called down famine on the land
and destroyed all their supplies of food;
17and he sent a man before them—
Joseph, sold as a slave.
18They bruised his feet with shackles,
his neck was put in irons,
19till what he foretold came to pass,
till the word of the LORD proved him true.
20The king sent and released him,
the ruler of peoples set him free.
21He made him master of his household,
ruler over all he possessed,
22to instruct his princes as he pleased
and teach his elders wisdom.

23Then Israel entered Egypt;
Jacob lived as an alien in the land of Ham.
24The LORD made his people very fruitful;
he made them too numerous for their foes,
25whose hearts he turned to hate his people,
to conspire against his servants.
26He sent Moses his servant,
and Aaron, whom he had chosen.
27They performed his miraculous signs among them,
his wonders in the land of Ham.
28He sent darkness and made the land dark—
for had they not rebelled against his words?
29He turned their waters into blood,
causing their fish to die.
30Their land teemed with frogs,
which went up into the bedrooms of their rulers.
31He spoke, and there came swarms of flies,
and gnats throughout their country.
32He turned their rain into hail,
with lightning throughout their land;
33he struck down their vines and fig trees
and shattered the trees of their country.
34He spoke, and the locusts came,
grasshoppers without number;
35they ate up every green thing in their land,
ate up the produce of their soil.
36Then he struck down all the firstborn in their land,
the firstfruits of all their manhood.

37He brought out Israel, laden with silver and gold,
and from among their tribes no one faltered.
38Egypt was glad when they left,
because dread of Israel had fallen on them.
39He spread out a cloud as a covering,
and a fire to give light at night.
40They asked, and he brought them quail
and satisfied them with the bread of heaven.
41He opened the rock, and water gushed out;
like a river it flowed in the desert.

42For he remembered his holy promise
given to his servant Abraham.
43He brought out his people with rejoicing,
his chosen ones with shouts of joy;
44he gave them the lands of the nations,
and they fell heir to what others had toiled for—
45that they might keep his precepts
and observe his laws.

Praise the LORD.[v]

Psalm 106

1Praise the LORD.[w]

Give thanks to the LORD, for he is good;
his love endures forever.
2Who can proclaim the mighty acts of the LORD
or fully declare his praise?
3Blessed are they who maintain justice,
who constantly do what is right.
4Remember me, O LORD, when you show favor to your people,
come to my aid when you save them,
5that I may enjoy the prosperity of your chosen ones,
that I may share in the joy of your nation
and join your inheritance in giving praise.

6We have sinned, even as our fathers did;
we have done wrong and acted wickedly.
7When our fathers were in Egypt,
they gave no thought to your miracles;
they did not remember your many kindnesses,
and they rebelled by the sea, the Red Sea.[x]
8Yet he saved them for his name's sake,
to make his mighty power known.
9He rebuked the Red Sea, and it dried up;
he led them through the depths as through a desert.
10He saved them from the hand of the foe;
from the hand of the enemy he redeemed them.
11The waters covered their adversaries;
not one of them survived.
12Then they believed his promises
and sang his praise.

13But they soon forgot what he had done
and did not wait for his counsel.
14In the desert they gave in to their craving;
in the wasteland they put God to the test.
15So he gave them what they asked for,
but sent a wasting disease upon them.

16In the camp they grew envious of Moses
and of Aaron, who was consecrated to the LORD.
17The earth opened up and swallowed Dathan;
it buried the company of Abiram.
18Fire blazed among their followers;
a flame consumed the wicked.

19At Horeb they made a calf
and worshiped an idol cast from metal.
20They exchanged their Glory
for an image of a bull, which eats grass.
21They forgot the God who saved them,
who had done great things in Egypt,
22miracles in the land of Ham
and awesome deeds by the Red Sea.
23So he said he would destroy them—
had not Moses, his chosen one,
stood in the breach before him
to keep his wrath from destroying them.

24Then they despised the pleasant land;
they did not believe his promise.
25They grumbled in their tents
and did not obey the LORD.
26So he swore to them with uplifted hand
that he would make them fall in the desert,
27make their descendants fall among the nations
and scatter them throughout the lands.

28They yoked themselves to the Baal of Peor
and ate sacrifices offered to lifeless gods;
29they provoked the LORD to anger by their wicked deeds,
and a plague broke out among them.
30But Phinehas stood up and intervened,
and the plague was checked.
31This was credited to him as righteousness
for endless generations to come.

32By the waters of Meribah they angered the LORD,
and trouble came to Moses because of them;
33for they rebelled against the Spirit of God,
and rash words came from Moses' lips.[y]

34They did not destroy the peoples
as the LORD had commanded them,
35but they mingled with the nations

[v] 45 Hebrew *Hallelu Yah* [w] 1 Hebrew *Hallelu Yah*; also in verse 48
[x] 7 Hebrew *Yam Suph*; that is, Sea of Reeds; also in verses 9 and 22
[y] 33 Or *against his spirit, / and rash words came from his lips*

and adopted their customs.
36They worshiped their idols,
which became a snare to them.
37They sacrificed their sons
and their daughters to demons.
38They shed innocent blood,
the blood of their sons and daughters,
whom they sacrificed to the idols of Canaan,
and the land was desecrated by their blood.
39They defiled themselves by what they did;
by their deeds they prostituted themselves.

40Therefore the LORD was angry with his people
and abhorred his inheritance.
41He handed them over to the nations,
and their foes ruled over them.
42Their enemies oppressed them
and subjected them to their power.
43Many times he delivered them,
but they were bent on rebellion
and they wasted away in their sin.

44But he took note of their distress
when he heard their cry;
45for their sake he remembered his covenant
and out of his great love he relented.
46He caused them to be pitied
by all who held them captive.

47Save us, O LORD our God,
and gather us from the nations,
that we may give thanks to your holy name
and glory in your praise.

48Praise be to the LORD, the God of Israel,
from everlasting to everlasting.
Let all the people say, "Amen!"
Praise the LORD.

62 / *Psalm 107*
The Goodness of God

PSALM 107 IS the classic exposition of God's goodness. J. I. Packer writes: "The whole psalm is a majestic panorama of the operations of divine goodness, transforming human lives" (*Knowing God* [Downers Grove, Ill.: InterVarsity Press, 1973], p. 148). God's actions reveal goodness in its highest and purest form. His goodness provides the standard for developing this fruit in our own lives.

Warming Up to God Try to imagine what it would be like if God were to withdraw all his goodness from you. How would your life be changed? Respond to God with praise for his presence with you.

Read Psalm 107.

BOOK V
Psalms 107–150

Psalm 107

1Give thanks to the LORD, for he is good;
his love endures forever.
2Let the redeemed of the LORD say this—
those he redeemed from the hand of the foe,
3those he gathered from the lands,
from east and west, from north and south.[z]

4Some wandered in desert wastelands,
finding no way to a city where they could settle.
5They were hungry and thirsty,
and their lives ebbed away.
6Then they cried out to the LORD in their trouble,
and he delivered them from their distress.
7He led them by a straight way
to a city where they could settle.
8Let them give thanks to the LORD for his unfailing love
and his wonderful deeds for men,
9for he satisfies the thirsty
and fills the hungry with good things.

10Some sat in darkness and the deepest gloom,
prisoners suffering in iron chains,

z3 Hebrew *north and the sea*

11for they had rebelled against the words of God
and despised the counsel of the Most High.
12So he subjected them to bitter labor;
they stumbled, and there was no one to help.
13Then they cried to the LORD in their trouble,
and he saved them from their distress.
14He brought them out of darkness and the deepest gloom
and broke away their chains.
15Let them give thanks to the LORD for his unfailing love
and his wonderful deeds for men,
16for he breaks down gates of bronze
and cuts through bars of iron.

17Some became fools through their rebellious ways
and suffered affliction because of their iniquities.
18They loathed all food
and drew near the gates of death.
19Then they cried to the LORD in their trouble,
and he saved them from their distress.
20He sent forth his word and healed them;
he rescued them from the grave.
21Let them give thanks to the LORD for his unfailing love
and his wonderful deeds for men.
22Let them sacrifice thank offerings
and tell of his works with songs of joy.

23Others went out on the sea in ships;
they were merchants on the mighty waters.
24They saw the works of the LORD,
his wonderful deeds in the deep.
25For he spoke and stirred up a tempest
that lifted high the waves.
26They mounted up to the heavens and went down to the depths;
in their peril their courage melted away.
27They reeled and staggered like drunken men;
they were at their wits' end.
28Then they cried out to the LORD in their trouble,
and he brought them out of their distress.
29He stilled the storm to a whisper;
the waves of the sea were hushed.
30They were glad when it grew calm,
and he guided them to their desired haven.
31Let them give thanks to the LORD for his unfailing love
and his wonderful deeds for men.
32Let them exalt him in the assembly of the people
and praise him in the council of the elders.

33He turned rivers into a desert,
flowing springs into thirsty ground,
34and fruitful land into a salt waste,
because of the wickedness of those who lived there.
35He turned the desert into pools of water
and the parched ground into flowing springs;
36there he brought the hungry to live,
and they founded a city where they could settle.
37They sowed fields and planted vineyards
that yielded a fruitful harvest;
38he blessed them, and their numbers greatly increased,
and he did not let their herds diminish.

39Then their numbers decreased, and they were humbled
by oppression, calamity and sorrow;
40he who pours contempt on nobles
made them wander in a trackless waste.
41But he lifted the needy out of their affliction
and increased their families like flocks.
42The upright see and rejoice,
but all the wicked shut their mouths.

43Whoever is wise, let him heed these things
and consider the great love of the LORD.

Discovering the Word 1. How do verses 1–3 introduce the major themes of the psalm? 2. The psalmist gives four illustrations of God's goodness in verses 4–9, 10–16, 17–22 and 23–32. What do each of these illustrations have in common? 3. What needs do the people have in each of these sections? 4. According to the psalmist, what are some ways we should give thanks to God for his goodness and love (vv. 22, 32)? 5. What do verses 33–42 reveal about the ups and downs of life?

Applying the Word 1. Are you likely to call out to God in the midst of your trouble as those in this passage did? Why or why not? 2. In what ways can we imitate the goodness of God displayed in this psalm?

Responding in Prayer Thank God for his goodness and unfailing love. Ask him to help you develop the fruit of goodness in your life.

Psalm 108

Psalm 108

A song. A psalm of David.

1My heart is steadfast, O God;
I will sing and make music with all my soul.
2Awake, harp and lyre!
I will awaken the dawn.
3I will praise you, O LORD, among the nations;
I will sing of you among the peoples.
4For great is your love, higher than the heavens;
your faithfulness reaches to the skies.
5Be exalted, O God, above the heavens,
and let your glory be over all the earth.

6Save us and help us with your right hand,
that those you love may be delivered.
7God has spoken from his sanctuary:
"In triumph I will parcel out Shechem
and measure off the Valley of Succoth.
8Gilead is mine, Manasseh is mine;
Ephraim is my helmet,
Judah my scepter.
9Moab is my washbasin,
upon Edom I toss my sandal;
over Philistia I shout in triumph."

10Who will bring me to the fortified city?
Who will lead me to Edom?
11Is it not you, O God, you who have rejected us
and no longer go out with our armies?
12Give us aid against the enemy,
for the help of man is worthless.
13With God we will gain the victory,
and he will trample down our enemies.

63 / *Psalm 109*
Feeling Anger

FOR MOST OF us, anger is not a comfortable emotion. For some of us, it is a terrifying emotion. We know the damage that anger can do. We know the pain it can cause. We fear our own capacity for evil when we are angry. We recognize our desire for revenge. We know that we have been hurt, and we know that anger feeds our longing to hurt back. However, avoiding anger will not make it go away, but can instead allow it to grow into bitterness. Feeling anger and expressing it honestly to God and to others makes it possible for us to continue growing toward forgiveness. There are, of course, both helpful and unhelpful things we can do with our anger. Denying, avoiding, minimizing and blaming others for it are just a few of the many unhelpful ways of responding to anger.

Warming Up to God What do you usually do when you are angry with someone who is important to you?

Read Psalm 109.

Psalm 109

For the director of music. Of David.
A psalm.

[1]O God, whom I praise,
do not remain silent,
[2]for wicked and deceitful men
have opened their mouths against me;
they have spoken against me with lying
tongues.
[3]With words of hatred they surround me;
they attack me without cause.
[4]In return for my friendship they accuse me,
but I am a man of prayer.
[5]They repay me evil for good,
and hatred for my friendship.
[6]Appoint[a] an evil man[b] to oppose him;
let an accuser[c] stand at his right hand.
[7]When he is tried, let him be found guilty,
and may his prayers condemn him.
[8]May his days be few;
may another take his place of leadership.
[9]May his children be fatherless
and his wife a widow.
[10]May his children be wandering beggars;
may they be driven[d] from their ruined
homes.
[11]May a creditor seize all he has;
may strangers plunder the fruits of his
labor.
[12]May no one extend kindness to him
or take pity on his fatherless children.
[13]May his descendants be cut off,
their names blotted out from the next
generation.
[14]May the iniquity of his fathers be remembered
before the LORD;
may the sin of his mother never be blotted
out.
[15]May their sins always remain before the LORD,
that he may cut off the memory of them
from the earth.

[16]For he never thought of doing a kindness,
but hounded to death the poor
and the needy and the brokenhearted.
[17]He loved to pronounce a curse—
may it[e] come on him;
he found no pleasure in blessing—
may it be[f] far from him.
[18]He wore cursing as his garment;
it entered into his body like water,
into his bones like oil.
[19]May it be like a cloak wrapped about him,
like a belt tied forever around him.
[20]May this be the LORD's payment to my
accusers,
to those who speak evil of me.

[21]But you, O Sovereign LORD,
deal well with me for your name's sake;
out of the goodness of your love, deliver
me.
[22]For I am poor and needy,
and my heart is wounded within me.
[23]I fade away like an evening shadow;
I am shaken off like a locust.
[24]My knees give way from fasting;
my body is thin and gaunt.
[25]I am an object of scorn to my accusers;
when they see me, they shake their heads.

[26]Help me, O LORD my God;
save me in accordance with your love.
[27]Let them know that it is your hand,
that you, O LORD, have done it.
[28]They may curse, but you will bless;
when they attack they will be put to shame,
but your servant will rejoice.
[29]My accusers will be clothed with disgrace
and wrapped in shame as in a cloak.

[30]With my mouth I will greatly extol the LORD;
in the great throng I will praise him.
[31]For he stands at the right hand of the needy
one,
to save his life from those who condemn
him.

[a]6 Or ⌞*They say:*⌟ "*Appoint* (with quotation marks at the end of verse 19) [b]6 Or *the Evil One* [c]6 Or *let Satan* [d]10 Septuagint; Hebrew *sought* [e]17 Or *curse, / and it has* [f]17 Or *blessing, / and it is*

Discovering the Word 1. To what painful experiences is the author reacting (vv. 2–5)? 2. The speaker is particularly outraged at the injustice of his accusers. "They repay me evil for good, and hatred for my friendship" (v. 5). How does this add to his sense of rage? 3. What does the author ask God to do to his enemies (vv. 6–20, 28–29)? 4. What does the author want God to do for him (vv. 20–26)?

Applying the Word 1. God is described in verse 31 as being on the side of the "needy" and "condemned." How could seeing God in this way be a practical help to you when you are angry? 2. How would expressing your anger to God be helpful to you? 3. How can other people be helpful to you in your struggle with anger?

Responding in Prayer What anger do you want to express to God today?

64 / *Psalm 110*
A Psalm of Submission

THINK ABOUT THE enemies you have. Bring to mind people you know who are opposed to Christianity. Picture them (and yourself) one day coming to Christ who will settle all disputes and rule with an iron hand. Psalm 110 acknowledges God as the eternal King-Priest who will, in fact, settle all disputes and judge all nations. This coronation hymn, although used for other kings of Israel, was viewed by Jews and Christians alike as clearly Messianic and forward-looking. Writers of the New Testament quote verses 1 and 4 on numerous occasions, making this psalm one of the most prophetic.

Warming Up to God Just as you picture your enemies settling accounts with God the Supreme Justice, picture yourself doing the same. That means submitting any of your own behaviors and beliefs that are not conformed or submissive to the Lord. How do you feel as you consider this scene?

Read Psalm 110.

Psalm 110

Of David. A psalm.

1The LORD says to my Lord:
"Sit at my right hand
until I make your enemies
a footstool for your feet."

2The LORD will extend your mighty scepter
from Zion;
you will rule in the midst of your enemies.
3Your troops will be willing
on your day of battle.
Arrayed in holy majesty,
from the womb of the dawn
you will receive the dew of your youth.[g]

4The LORD has sworn
and will not change his mind:
"You are a priest forever,
in the order of Melchizedek."

5The Lord is at your right hand;
he will crush kings on the day of his wrath.
6He will judge the nations, heaping up the
dead
and crushing the rulers of the whole earth.
7He will drink from a brook beside the way[h];
therefore he will lift up his head.

[g]3 Or / *your young men will come to you like the dew* [h]7 Or / *The One who grants succession will set him in authority*

Discovering the Word 1. Who is the psalmist referring to as "my Lord" (v. 1; see Mt 22:41–45)? 2. How will that Lord rule, and over whom (vv. 1–3, 5, 6)? 3. What is significant about the Lord swearing with a covenant oath (v. 4; Heb 6:16–18; 7:20–22)? 4. Melchizedek was the original king-priest of the God Most High in Jerusalem, who received a tithe from Abraham. His priesthood was a prototype of Christ's eternal priesthood (v. 4). What is significant about a priesthood for God's people that is permanent and irrevocable? 5. What is significant about this Lord sitting at the right hand of God (vv. 1, 5)?

Applying the Word 1. The troops are freewill offerings (v. 3) in the service of their Lord. What is your sacrificial offering to the Lord? 2. The Lord rules over all the powers that be, even enemies of his kingdom, with an iron hand and the undiminished vigor of youth (vv. 2–3). How is that good news to you and the battles you face?

Responding in Prayer Whatever battles you are engaged in right now, rest assured that the Lord will ultimately triumph and that the Lord's army will attack those problems with you. What battles or problem areas can you turn over to him now for his intercession and judgment?

Psalms 111—114

Psalm 111[i]

1Praise the LORD.[j]

I will extol the LORD with all my heart
in the council of the upright and in the assembly.

2Great are the works of the LORD;
they are pondered by all who delight in them.
3Glorious and majestic are his deeds,
and his righteousness endures forever.
4He has caused his wonders to be remembered;
the LORD is gracious and compassionate.
5He provides food for those who fear him;
he remembers his covenant forever.
6He has shown his people the power of his works,
giving them the lands of other nations.
7The works of his hands are faithful and just;
all his precepts are trustworthy.
8They are steadfast for ever and ever,
done in faithfulness and uprightness.
9He provided redemption for his people;
he ordained his covenant forever—
holy and awesome is his name.
10The fear of the LORD is the beginning of wisdom;
all who follow his precepts have good understanding.
To him belongs eternal praise.

Psalm 112[i]

1Praise the LORD.[j]

Blessed is the man who fears the LORD,
who finds great delight in his commands.

2His children will be mighty in the land;
the generation of the upright will be blessed.
3Wealth and riches are in his house,
and his righteousness endures forever.
4Even in darkness light dawns for the upright,
for the gracious and compassionate and righteous man.[k]
5Good will come to him who is generous and lends freely,
who conducts his affairs with justice.
6Surely he will never be shaken;
a righteous man will be remembered forever.
7He will have no fear of bad news;
his heart is steadfast, trusting in the LORD.
8His heart is secure, he will have no fear;
in the end he will look in triumph on his foes.
9He has scattered abroad his gifts to the poor,
his righteousness endures forever;
his horn[l] will be lifted high in honor.
10The wicked man will see and be vexed,
he will gnash his teeth and waste away;
the longings of the wicked will come to nothing.

Psalm 113

1Praise the LORD.[m]

Praise, O servants of the LORD,
praise the name of the LORD.
2Let the name of the LORD be praised,
both now and forevermore.
3From the rising of the sun to the place where it sets,
the name of the LORD is to be praised.

4The LORD is exalted over all the nations,
his glory above the heavens.
5Who is like the LORD our God,
the One who sits enthroned on high,
6who stoops down to look
on the heavens and the earth?

7He raises the poor from the dust
and lifts the needy from the ash heap;

[i] This psalm is an acrostic poem, the lines of which begin with the successive letters of the Hebrew alphabet. [j] 1 Hebrew *Hallelu Yah* [k] 4 Or / *for* ⌞*the LORD*⌟ *is gracious and compassionate and righteous* [l] 9 *Horn* here symbolizes dignity. [m] 1 Hebrew *Hallelu Yah*; also in verse 9

8he seats them with princes,
with the princes of their people.
9He settles the barren woman in her home
as a happy mother of children.

Praise the LORD.

Psalm 114

1When Israel came out of Egypt,
the house of Jacob from a people of foreign tongue,
2Judah became God's sanctuary,
Israel his dominion.

3The sea looked and fled,
the Jordan turned back;
4the mountains skipped like rams,
the hills like lambs.

5Why was it, O sea, that you fled,
O Jordan, that you turned back,
6you mountains, that you skipped like rams,
you hills, like lambs?

7Tremble, O earth, at the presence of the Lord,
at the presence of the God of Jacob,
8who turned the rock into a pool,
the hard rock into springs of water.

65 / *Psalm 115*
A Psalm of Praise

THIS PSALM PRAISES God as the one true Lord and ridicules the many cheap imitations and pretenders to the throne that prevail in the surrounding culture. The liturgical exchange between people and priests in this psalm makes it a very appropriate lead-in for public worship. In this liturgy, the cares and snares of the world are left behind and the people are called to trust God, who will abundantly bless them and receive the praise of his people.

Warming Up to God When has God seemed distant or unresponsive to you (in the past or present)? Open yourself up to the possibilities of God blessing you and your family afresh.

Read Psalm 115.

Psalm 115

1Not to us, O LORD, not to us
but to your name be the glory,
because of your love and faithfulness.

2Why do the nations say,
"Where is their God?"
3Our God is in heaven;
he does whatever pleases him.
4But their idols are silver and gold,
made by the hands of men.
5They have mouths, but cannot speak,
eyes, but they cannot see;
6they have ears, but cannot hear,
noses, but they cannot smell;
7they have hands, but cannot feel,
feet, but they cannot walk;
nor can they utter a sound with their throats.
8Those who make them will be like them,
and so will all who trust in them.
9O house of Israel, trust in the LORD—
he is their help and shield.
10O house of Aaron, trust in the LORD—
he is their help and shield.
11You who fear him, trust in the LORD—
he is their help and shield.

12The LORD remembers us and will bless us:
He will bless the house of Israel,
he will bless the house of Aaron,
13he will bless those who fear the LORD—
small and great alike.

14May the LORD make you increase,
both you and your children.
15May you be blessed by the LORD,
the Maker of heaven and earth.

16The highest heavens belong to the LORD,
but the earth he has given to man.
17It is not the dead who praise the LORD,

those who go down to silence;
18it is we who extol the Lord,
both now and forevermore.

Praise the Lord.[n]

[n]18 Hebrew *Hallelu Yah*

Discovering the Word 1. Note that this psalm divides into five parts: three stanzas spoken by the respondents—a taunt song (vv. 1–8), confession of trust (vv. 12–13) and the closing doxology (vv. 16–18)—interspersed with an invocation (vv. 9–11) and benediction (vv. 14–15) spoken by the priests. What does this response-and-revelation rhythm call forth from the worship participants and leaders? 2. How do the idols that others worship compare to the God that Israel worships (vv. 1–8)? 3. Why should anyone, but especially Israel, trust in the Lord (vv. 9–11)? 4. Who will the Lord bless, why and how (vv. 12–15)? 5. What is the reason for living granted to those who have survived the exile and a whole lot more (vv. 16–18)?

Applying the Word 1. The Lord is not the only person or object that people trust to get them through the day. What else do people trust in these days for their salvation or their guidance? 2. For what have you recently trusted God alone to provide? 3. How did God prove to be your help and shield?

Responding in Prayer Consider how vastly superior God is to all idols. Ask God to help you forsake the idols of your culture.

66/ *Psalm 116*
Talking to God

HONESTY IS A NECESSARY ingredient to all intimate relationships. If we are to grow in our intimacy with God, we will need to learn to be honest with him. This will require us to challenge our distorted images of God and to grow in our understanding of him. God invites us to talk to him. He has promised to pay attention. He does not require us to do any physical, mental or spiritual gymnastics to get his attention. He does not insist that we have our lives "together" before we can talk to him. We can talk to him even when we are in trouble. We will always find him interested and compassionate.

Warming Up to God Imagine yourself as one of the little children whom Jesus invited to come to him. Imagine yourself standing next to Jesus. Take a few minutes to close your eyes and experience his arm around your shoulder as you stand next to him. Tell him what you are thinking and feeling. What thoughts and feelings did you have during this meditation?

Read Psalm 116.

Psalm 116

1I love the Lord, for he heard my voice;
he heard my cry for mercy.
2Because he turned his ear to me,
I will call on him as long as I live.

3The cords of death entangled me,
the anguish of the grave[o] came upon me;
I was overcome by trouble and sorrow.
4Then I called on the name of the Lord:
"O Lord, save me!"

5The Lord is gracious and righteous;
our God is full of compassion.
6The Lord protects the simplehearted;
when I was in great need, he saved me.

7Be at rest once more, O my soul,
for the Lord has been good to you.

8For you, O Lord, have delivered my soul from
death,

[o]3 Hebrew *Sheol*

my eyes from tears,
my feet from stumbling,
9that I may walk before the LORD
in the land of the living.
10I believed; therefore[p] I said,
"I am greatly afflicted."
11And in my dismay I said,
"All men are liars."
12How can I repay the LORD
for all his goodness to me?
13I will lift up the cup of salvation
and call on the name of the LORD.
14I will fulfill my vows to the LORD
in the presence of all his people.
15Precious in the sight of the LORD
is the death of his saints.
16O LORD, truly I am your servant;
I am your servant, the son of your
maidservant[q];
you have freed me from my chains.

17I will sacrifice a thank offering to you
and call on the name of the LORD.
18I will fulfill my vows to the LORD
in the presence of all his people,
19in the courts of the house of the LORD—
in your midst, O Jerusalem.

Praise the LORD.[r]

p10 *Or believed even when* q16 *Or servant, your faithful son* r19 Hebrew Hallelu Yah

Discovering the Word 1. What images of God are presented here? 2. What did the author of the psalm experience when he called on God? 3. How does the psalmist respond to God (vv. 12–19)? 4. God invites us to talk to him about our troubles. He does not ask us to ignore them or minimize them or take care of them ourselves. How does this compare or contrast with your expectations of God?

Applying the Word 1. Think of a time when you had difficulty calling on God. What made it difficult for you? 2. Recall a time when you did call on God and he "answered you and showed you great and mighty things." What was this experience like for you?

Responding in Prayer What do you need to talk with God about today?

Psalm 117

Psalm 117

1Praise the LORD, all you nations;
extol him, all you peoples.
2For great is his love toward us,
and the faithfulness of the LORD endures
forever.

Praise the LORD.[s]

s2 Hebrew *Hallelu Yah*

67 / *Psalm 118*
Enduring Love

REMEMBER WHEN YOUR parents used to force you to write thank-you notes for the Christmas and birthday gifts you received from your out-of-town relatives? Although it may have been painful at the time, this discipline of thanksgiving helped you develop a grateful heart.

In like manner, the psalmist expresses thanks to God for delivering Israel from her many enemies. The historic occasion for Psalm 118 may have been Israel's defeat of a confederacy of nations or her deliverance from the Babylonian exile. In either event, the Israelites had much to thank God for, especially his love which endures forever. We who know the love of God in Christ have even more reason to give thanks through this psalm.

Warming Up to God Think of all the things and relationships in your life that have passed on or proven temporary. Contrast that with the most enduring love relationship you know, or with the times that come to mind when you hum that ditty "Happy Days Are Here Again." How does that relationship or those days compare with the enduring love of God?

Read Psalm 118.

Psalm 118

1Give thanks to the LORD, for he is good;
his love endures forever.

2Let Israel say:
"His love endures forever."
3Let the house of Aaron say:
"His love endures forever."
4Let those who fear the LORD say:
"His love endures forever."

5In my anguish I cried to the LORD,
and he answered by setting me free.
6The LORD is with me; I will not be afraid.
What can man do to me?
7The LORD is with me; he is my helper.
I will look in triumph on my enemies.

8It is better to take refuge in the LORD
than to trust in man.
9It is better to take refuge in the LORD
than to trust in princes.

10All the nations surrounded me,
but in the name of the LORD I cut them off.
11They surrounded me on every side,
but in the name of the LORD I cut them off.
12They swarmed around me like bees,
but they died out as quickly as burning thorns;
in the name of the LORD I cut them off.

13I was pushed back and about to fall,
but the LORD helped me.
14The LORD is my strength and my song;
he has become my salvation.

15Shouts of joy and victory
resound in the tents of the righteous:
"The LORD's right hand has done mighty things!
16 The LORD's right hand is lifted high;
the LORD's right hand has done mighty things!"

17I will not die but live,
and will proclaim what the LORD has done.
18The LORD has chastened me severely,
but he has not given me over to death.

19Open for me the gates of righteousness;
I will enter and give thanks to the LORD.
20This is the gate of the LORD
through which the righteous may enter.
21I will give you thanks, for you answered me;
you have become my salvation.

22The stone the builders rejected
has become the capstone;
23the LORD has done this,
and it is marvelous in our eyes.
24This is the day the LORD has made;
let us rejoice and be glad in it.

25O LORD, save us;
O LORD, grant us success.
26Blessed is he who comes in the name of the LORD.
From the house of the LORD we bless you.[t]
27The LORD is God,
and he has made his light shine upon us.
With boughs in hand, join in the festal procession
up[u] to the horns of the altar.

28You are my God, and I will give you thanks;
you are my God, and I will exalt you.
29Give thanks to the LORD, for he is good;
his love endures forever.

t26 The Hebrew is plural. u27 Or *Bind the festal sacrifice with ropes / and take it*

Discovering the Word 1. Note that this psalm divides into five parts: a liturgical call to praise at the beginning (vv. 1–4) and end (v. 29)—which sandwiches the leader's song of thanksgiving (vv. 5–21), the people's response (vv. 22–27) and the leader's final prompting (v. 28). What indicators do you see that suggest a change of voice or speaker in each section? 2. What is the significance of the many double and triple repetitions found throughout this psalm? 3. What has the Lord done for the king and/or representatively for the people (vv. 5–21)? 4. As an Israelite prompted to give thanks on the occasion of this psalm, what redemptive occasions in the life of your people come to mind? 5. What is the significance of the stone-turned-capstone (v. 22), which is being celebrated on this festive day (v. 23)?

Applying the Word 1. The early church applied verse 22 to Jesus. How is Jesus like this stone-turned-capstone? 2. For what events in your life are you particularly grateful to God? 3. How did God prove to be your helper, your strength or your salvation?

Responding in Prayer Praise God for the day(s) he has given you to rejoice (v. 24).

68 / *Psalm 119:1–24*
Searching for God's Wisdom

FEW SITUATIONS BRING life to a grinding halt like losing a contact lens. Have you ever seen it happen to a major-league baseball pitcher? Frustration turns to comedy as fellow players trickle out from the dugout and hunch over the mound on hands and knees. Fans get restless. Commentators start reminiscing about recent games. The TV audience goes on commercial break.

If we are going to have the vision to see life from God's perspective, we will regularly have to stop everything, hunker down and find out just what that perspective is. Like finding a contact lens, finding God's wisdom is simply worth whatever inconveniences may come in its pursuit.

Warming Up to God In what area of your life do you need God's wisdom?

Read Psalm 119:1–24.

Psalm 119[v]

א Aleph

1Blessed are they whose ways are blameless,
who walk according to the law of the LORD.
2Blessed are they who keep his statutes
and seek him with all their heart.
3They do nothing wrong;
they walk in his ways.
4You have laid down precepts
that are to be fully obeyed.
5Oh, that my ways were steadfast
in obeying your decrees!
6Then I would not be put to shame
when I consider all your commands.
7I will praise you with an upright heart
as I learn your righteous laws.
8I will obey your decrees;
do not utterly forsake me.

ב Beth

9How can a young man keep his way pure?
By living according to your word.
10I seek you with all my heart;
do not let me stray from your commands.
11I have hidden your word in my heart
that I might not sin against you.
12Praise be to you, O LORD;
teach me your decrees.
13With my lips I recount
all the laws that come from your mouth.
14I rejoice in following your statutes
as one rejoices in great riches.
15I meditate on your precepts
and consider your ways.
16I delight in your decrees;

[v]This psalm is an acrostic poem; the verses of each stanza begin with the same letter of the Hebrew alphabet.

I will not neglect your word.

ג Gimel

17Do good to your servant, and I will live;
I will obey your word.
18Open my eyes that I may see
wonderful things in your law.
19I am a stranger on earth;
do not hide your commands from me.
20My soul is consumed with longing
for your laws at all times.
21You rebuke the arrogant, who are cursed
and who stray from your commands.
22Remove from me scorn and contempt,
for I keep your statutes.
23Though rulers sit together and slander me,
your servant will meditate on your decrees.
24Your statutes are my delight;
they are my counselors.

Discovering the Word 1. What different words does the psalmist use to describe God's Word? 2. What benefits of knowing and following God's Word does the psalmist mention in verses 1–8? 3. How does God's Word help us to deal with sin (vv. 9–16)? 4. How does God's Word enlighten us about God's ways (vv. 17–24)? 5. What are the consequences of *not* knowing or following God's Word (vv. 5–6, 9–11, 21–22)?

Applying the Word 1. What is a way you have experienced frustration in studying Scripture? 2. What in the psalmist's example can bring encouragement to us to meditate on and delight in God's Word?

Responding in Prayer Ask God to guide you as you turn to his Word for wisdom.

69 / *Psalm 119:25–40*
Seeking God

PRAYER AND MEDITATION are not easy disciplines. Many of us have used prayer as a magical device for controlling God or for acquiring God's favor. Similarly, many use meditation as a magical tool for control. But there is nothing magical about the spiritual disciplines of prayer and meditation. Both are ways to focus our attention on God. We can talk (pray) openly, honestly, vulnerably to God, and we can listen (meditate) with humility. It is this dynamic of speaking/listening, prayer/meditation that makes it possible for us to increase our contact with God. We can experience loving and being loved by our Creator.

Warming Up to God What difficulties do you experience with prayer and meditation?

Read Psalm 119:25–40.

ד Daleth

25I am laid low in the dust;
preserve my life according to your word.
26I recounted my ways and you answered me;
teach me your decrees.
27Let me understand the teaching of your
precepts;
then I will meditate on your wonders.
28My soul is weary with sorrow;
strengthen me according to your word.
29Keep me from deceitful ways;
be gracious to me through your law.
30I have chosen the way of truth;
I have set my heart on your laws.
31I hold fast to your statutes, O LORD;
do not let me be put to shame.
32I run in the path of your commands,
for you have set my heart free.

ה He

33Teach me, O LORD, to follow your decrees;
then I will keep them to the end.
34Give me understanding, and I will keep your
law

and obey it with all my heart.
35Direct me in the path of your commands,
for there I find delight.
36Turn my heart toward your statutes
and not toward selfish gain.
37Turn my eyes away from worthless things;
preserve my life according to your word.[w]
38Fulfill your promise to your servant,
so that you may be feared.
39Take away the disgrace I dread,
for your laws are good.
40How I long for your precepts!
Preserve my life in your righteousness.

[w]37 Two manuscripts of the Masoretic Text and Dead Sea Scrolls; most manuscripts of the Masoretic Text *life in your way*

Discovering the Word 1. Restate in your own words the requests the psalmist makes of God. 2. What major needs and desires is the psalmist expressing in these requests? 3. How do these needs/desires compare with your own at this time? 4. How does the psalmist describe what he has done and what he desires to do in his pursuit of God? 5. What benefits does the psalmist suggest might come from prayer and meditation (vv. 32–40)?

Applying the Word 1. The psalmist describes himself as "laid low in the dust" and as "weary with sorrow." Describe a time when you experienced these feelings. 2. In your experience, how can prayer and meditation improve our contact with God?

Responding in Prayer Ask God to help you practice the disciplines of prayer and meditation.

Psalm 119:41—120:7

ו Waw

41May your unfailing love come to me, O LORD,
your salvation according to your promise;
42then I will answer the one who taunts me,
for I trust in your word.
43Do not snatch the word of truth from my mouth,
for I have put my hope in your laws.
44I will always obey your law,
for ever and ever.
45I will walk about in freedom,
for I have sought out your precepts.
46I will speak of your statutes before kings
and will not be put to shame,
47for I delight in your commands
because I love them.
48I lift up my hands to[x] your commands,
which I love,
and I meditate on your decrees.

ז Zayin

49Remember your word to your servant,
for you have given me hope.
50My comfort in my suffering is this:
Your promise preserves my life.
51The arrogant mock me without restraint,
but I do not turn from your law.
52I remember your ancient laws, O LORD,
and I find comfort in them.
53Indignation grips me because of the wicked,
who have forsaken your law.
54Your decrees are the theme of my song
wherever I lodge.
55In the night I remember your name, O LORD,
and I will keep your law.
56This has been my practice:
I obey your precepts.

ח Heth

57You are my portion, O LORD;
I have promised to obey your words.
58I have sought your face with all my heart;
be gracious to me according to your promise.
59I have considered my ways

[x]48 Or *for*

and have turned my steps to your statutes.
60I will hasten and not delay
to obey your commands.
61Though the wicked bind me with ropes,
I will not forget your law.
62At midnight I rise to give you thanks
for your righteous laws.
63I am a friend to all who fear you,
to all who follow your precepts.
64The earth is filled with your love, O LORD;
teach me your decrees.

ט Teth

65Do good to your servant
according to your word, O LORD.
66Teach me knowledge and good judgment,
for I believe in your commands.
67Before I was afflicted I went astray,
but now I obey your word.
68You are good, and what you do is good;
teach me your decrees.
69Though the arrogant have smeared me with lies,
I keep your precepts with all my heart.
70Their hearts are callous and unfeeling,
but I delight in your law.
71It was good for me to be afflicted
so that I might learn your decrees.
72The law from your mouth is more precious to me
than thousands of pieces of silver and gold.

י Yodh

73Your hands made me and formed me;
give me understanding to learn your commands.
74May those who fear you rejoice when they see me,
for I have put my hope in your word.
75I know, O LORD, that your laws are righteous,
and in faithfulness you have afflicted me.
76May your unfailing love be my comfort,
according to your promise to your servant.
77Let your compassion come to me that I may live,
for your law is my delight.
78May the arrogant be put to shame for wronging me without cause;
but I will meditate on your precepts.
79May those who fear you turn to me,
those who understand your statutes.
80May my heart be blameless toward your decrees,
that I may not be put to shame.

כ Kaph

81My soul faints with longing for your salvation,
but I have put my hope in your word.
82My eyes fail, looking for your promise;
I say, "When will you comfort me?"
83Though I am like a wineskin in the smoke,
I do not forget your decrees.
84How long must your servant wait?
When will you punish my persecutors?
85The arrogant dig pitfalls for me,
contrary to your law.
86All your commands are trustworthy;
help me, for men persecute me without cause.
87They almost wiped me from the earth,
but I have not forsaken your precepts.
88Preserve my life according to your love,
and I will obey the statutes of your mouth.

ל Lamedh

89Your word, O LORD, is eternal;
it stands firm in the heavens.
90Your faithfulness continues through all generations;
you established the earth, and it endures.
91Your laws endure to this day,
for all things serve you.
92If your law had not been my delight,
I would have perished in my affliction.
93I will never forget your precepts,
for by them you have preserved my life.
94Save me, for I am yours;
I have sought out your precepts.
95The wicked are waiting to destroy me,
but I will ponder your statutes.
96To all perfection I see a limit;
but your commands are boundless.

מ Mem

97Oh, how I love your law!
I meditate on it all day long.
98Your commands make me wiser than my enemies,
for they are ever with me.
99I have more insight than all my teachers,

for I meditate on your statutes.
100I have more understanding than the elders,
for I obey your precepts.
101I have kept my feet from every evil path
so that I might obey your word.
102I have not departed from your laws,
for you yourself have taught me.
103How sweet are your words to my taste,
sweeter than honey to my mouth!
104I gain understanding from your precepts;
therefore I hate every wrong path.

נ Nun

105Your word is a lamp to my feet
and a light for my path.
106I have taken an oath and confirmed it,
that I will follow your righteous laws.
107I have suffered much;
preserve my life, O LORD, according to your word.
108Accept, O LORD, the willing praise of my mouth,
and teach me your laws.
109Though I constantly take my life in my hands,
I will not forget your law.
110The wicked have set a snare for me,
but I have not strayed from your precepts.
111Your statutes are my heritage forever;
they are the joy of my heart.
112My heart is set on keeping your decrees
to the very end.

ס Samekh

113I hate double-minded men,
but I love your law.
114You are my refuge and my shield;
I have put my hope in your word.
115Away from me, you evildoers,
that I may keep the commands of my God!
116Sustain me according to your promise, and I will live;
do not let my hopes be dashed.
117Uphold me, and I will be delivered;
I will always have regard for your decrees.
118You reject all who stray from your decrees,
for their deceitfulness is in vain.
119All the wicked of the earth you discard like dross;
therefore I love your statutes.
120My flesh trembles in fear of you;
I stand in awe of your laws.

ע Ayin

121I have done what is righteous and just;
do not leave me to my oppressors.
122Ensure your servant's well-being;
let not the arrogant oppress me.
123My eyes fail, looking for your salvation,
looking for your righteous promise.
124Deal with your servant according to your love
and teach me your decrees.
125I am your servant; give me discernment
that I may understand your statutes.
126It is time for you to act, O LORD;
your law is being broken.
127Because I love your commands
more than gold, more than pure gold,
128and because I consider all your precepts right,
I hate every wrong path.

פ Pe

129Your statutes are wonderful;
therefore I obey them.
130The unfolding of your words gives light;
it gives understanding to the simple.
131I open my mouth and pant,
longing for your commands.
132Turn to me and have mercy on me,
as you always do to those who love your name.
133Direct my footsteps according to your word;
let no sin rule over me.
134Redeem me from the oppression of men,
that I may obey your precepts.
135Make your face shine upon your servant
and teach me your decrees.
136Streams of tears flow from my eyes,
for your law is not obeyed.

צ Tsadhe

137Righteous are you, O LORD,
and your laws are right.
138The statutes you have laid down are righteous;
they are fully trustworthy.
139My zeal wears me out,
for my enemies ignore your words.
140Your promises have been thoroughly tested,
and your servant loves them.
141Though I am lowly and despised,
I do not forget your precepts.

142Your righteousness is everlasting
and your law is true.
143Trouble and distress have come upon me,
but your commands are my delight.
144Your statutes are forever right;
give me understanding that I may live.

ק Qoph

145I call with all my heart; answer me, O LORD,
and I will obey your decrees.
146I call out to you; save me
and I will keep your statutes.
147I rise before dawn and cry for help;
I have put my hope in your word.
148My eyes stay open through the watches of the night,
that I may meditate on your promises.
149Hear my voice in accordance with your love;
preserve my life, O LORD, according to your laws.
150Those who devise wicked schemes are near,
but they are far from your law.
151Yet you are near, O LORD,
and all your commands are true.
152Long ago I learned from your statutes
that you established them to last forever.

ר Resh

153Look upon my suffering and deliver me,
for I have not forgotten your law.
154Defend my cause and redeem me;
preserve my life according to your promise.
155Salvation is far from the wicked,
for they do not seek out your decrees.
156Your compassion is great, O LORD;
preserve my life according to your laws.
157Many are the foes who persecute me,
but I have not turned from your statutes.
158I look on the faithless with loathing,
for they do not obey your word.
159See how I love your precepts;
preserve my life, O LORD, according to your love.
160All your words are true;
all your righteous laws are eternal.

ש Sin and Shin

161Rulers persecute me without cause,
but my heart trembles at your word.
162I rejoice in your promise
like one who finds great spoil.
163I hate and abhor falsehood
but I love your law.
164Seven times a day I praise you
for your righteous laws.
165Great peace have they who love your law,
and nothing can make them stumble.
166I wait for your salvation, O LORD,
and I follow your commands.
167I obey your statutes,
for I love them greatly.
168I obey your precepts and your statutes,
for all my ways are known to you.

ת Taw

169May my cry come before you, O LORD;
give me understanding according to your word.
170May my supplication come before you;
deliver me according to your promise.
171May my lips overflow with praise,
for you teach me your decrees.
172May my tongue sing of your word,
for all your commands are righteous.
173May your hand be ready to help me,
for I have chosen your precepts.
174I long for your salvation, O LORD,
and your law is my delight.
175Let me live that I may praise you,
and may your laws sustain me.
176I have strayed like a lost sheep.
Seek your servant,
for I have not forgotten your commands.

Psalm 120

A song of ascents.

1I call on the LORD in my distress,
and he answers me.
2Save me, O LORD, from lying lips
and from deceitful tongues.

3What will he do to you,
and what more besides, O deceitful tongue?
4He will punish you with a warrior's sharp arrows,
with burning coals of the broom tree.

5Woe to me that I dwell in Meshech,
that I live among the tents of Kedar!
6Too long have I lived
among those who hate peace.
7I am a man of peace;
but when I speak, they are for war.

70 / *Psalm 121*
A Prayer of Assurance

THE JEWS WERE on an uphill journey to Jerusalem and the temple at Mount Zion. This psalm is among the many "songs of ascent" sung (or inwardly affirmed) by individuals in the caravan along the way. Any pilgrim facing an uphill climb of faith, and all of us on life's pilgrimage from this earthly existence to the heavenly glory, will find assurance in repeating the confession of this psalm.

Warming Up to God Imagine a battle of faith that you may be facing. Think of all helpful resources you may have turned to, or could be turning to, for help. Then face the Lord who watched you go to and fro. How do you imagine God making a difference in that situation?

Read Psalm 121.

Psalm 121

A song of ascents.

1 I lift up my eyes to the hills—
where does my help come from?
2 My help comes from the LORD,
the Maker of heaven and earth.

3 He will not let your foot slip—
he who watches over you will not slumber;
4 indeed, he who watches over Israel
will neither slumber nor sleep.

5 The LORD watches over you—
the LORD is your shade at your right hand;
6 the sun will not harm you by day,
nor the moon by night.

7 The LORD will keep you from all harm—
he will watch over your life;
8 the LORD will watch over your coming and going
both now and forevermore.

Discovering the Word 1. Judging from the words and phrases most often repeated in this psalm, what is its major theme? 2. How does the second verse in each of the four verse pairs (vv. 2, 4, 6, 8) expand on the minitheme of the introductory line in each pair (vv. 1, 3, 5, 7)? 3. What kind of help does the Lord provide his people along the journey (in contrast to those idols who may slumber or slouch on the job)? 4. In light of the assurances offered in this psalm, how do you account for the fact that some people do slip and fall into harm's way?

Applying the Word 1. Imagine you are an Israelite making this pilgrimage to Mount Zion and dialoguing your way through this psalm of confession and assurance. What parts do you find most reassuring for yourself? 2. What parts do you find most reassuring for a fellow pilgrim who you know is struggling along the way? 3. Consider one time, day or night, when you slipped badly and fell into harm's way. How was God watching over you in that situation?

Responding in Prayer Consider using Psalm 121 as an appropriate prayer for all your comings and goings. Offer it at mealtimes, office breaks and bedtimes. Let it influence the prayers and counsel you offer family, friends and work associates, especially anyone facing an uphill battle.

---

71 / *Psalm 122*
A Prayer for Peace

PRAYER FOR THE "peace of Jerusalem" (vv. 6–9) distinguished this Zion hymn. (For other Zion songs, see Ps 46, 48, 76, 84, 126, 129, 137.) This prayer is not just for fellow worshipers, but for the policies and programs that bring "peace and prosperity" to the city. This call to pray for the decision-makers in government confers a benediction on their work, the result of which would be shalom for the "City of Peace."

Warming Up to God When you think about doing good and seeking the welfare of others, who comes to mind? Mentally open up today's newspaper along with the Bible to see the people and the needs that God cares most about in your city.

Read Psalm 122.

Psalm 122

A song of ascents. Of David.

1I rejoiced with those who said to me,
"Let us go to the house of the
LORD."
2Our feet are standing
in your gates, O Jerusalem.

3Jerusalem is built like a city
that is closely compacted together.
4That is where the tribes go up,
the tribes of the LORD,
to praise the name of the LORD
according to the statute given to
Israel.
5There the thrones for judgment stand,
the thrones of the house of David.

6Pray for the peace of Jerusalem:
"May those who love you be secure.
7May there be peace within your walls
and security within your citadels."
8For the sake of my brothers and friends,
I will say, "Peace be within you."
9For the sake of the house of the LORD our
God,
I will seek your prosperity.

Discovering the Word 1. What was it like for these worshipers to go to the house of the Lord in Jerusalem (Mount Zion)? 2. Describe the city of Jerusalem (vv. 3–5). 3. What things does the psalmist pray will be given to the city (vv. 6–9)? 4. What would this psalmist say to someone who wanted to first meet his own needs or those of his family before seeking the peace and prosperity of the city?

Applying the Word 1. Worship at Mount Zion was both a regular obligation (although a joyous event) and a bonding experience for temple-bound worshipers. What is "going to church" like for you? 2. Psalm 122 also evokes memories of how Jesus revered and wept over Jerusalem (Lk 9:51; 13:31–35; 19:41–44). By comparison, what tears have you shed over your beloved city? 3. "Peace within *your* walls" and "security within *your* citadels" (author's italics, v. 7) will also benefit believers, but the city itself is the end in view here, not believers. How do you go about working for the good of the city where you live and worship?

Responding in Prayer Scan the city news section of your newspaper for events and people that need God's "shalom" (peace and prosperity). Bring to God in prayer everyone you know in city hall and the key urban areas that need shalom.

Psalms 123—125

Psalm 123

A song of ascents.

1I lift up my eyes to you,
to you whose throne is in heaven.
2As the eyes of slaves look to the hand of their
master,
as the eyes of a maid look to the hand of
her mistress,
so our eyes look to the LORD our God,
till he shows us his mercy.

3Have mercy on us, O LORD, have mercy
on us,
for we have endured much contempt.
4We have endured much ridicule from the
proud,
much contempt from the arrogant.

Psalm 124

A song of ascents. Of David.

[1]If the LORD had not been on our side—
let Israel say—
[2]if the LORD had not been on our side
when men attacked us,
[3]when their anger flared against us,
they would have swallowed us alive;
[4]the flood would have engulfed us,
the torrent would have swept over us,
[5]the raging waters
would have swept us away.

[6]Praise be to the LORD,
who has not let us be torn by their
teeth.
[7]We have escaped like a bird
out of the fowler's snare;
the snare has been broken,
and we have escaped.
[8]Our help is in the name of the LORD,
the Maker of heaven and earth.

Psalm 125

A song of ascents.

[1]Those who trust in the LORD are like Mount
Zion,
which cannot be shaken but endures
forever.
[2]As the mountains surround Jerusalem,
so the LORD surrounds his people
both now and forevermore.

[3]The scepter of the wicked will not remain
over the land allotted to the righteous,
for then the righteous might use
their hands to do evil.

[4]Do good, O LORD, to those who are good,
to those who are upright in heart.
[5]But those who turn to crooked ways
the LORD will banish with the evildoers.

Peace be upon Israel.

72 / *Psalm 126*
A Song of Joy

ONE IMAGE OF happiness that sticks out in my mind is the suppertime dance that Snoopy does in the "Peanuts" comic strip. His head is flung back, his ears are flopping about, and his feet pound furiously. Have you ever felt like dancing for joy? In this passage the Israelites do.

Warming Up to God What do you do when you are filled with joy?

Read Psalm 126.

Psalm 126

A song of ascents.

[1]When the LORD brought back the captives to[a]
Zion,
we were like men who dreamed.[b]
[2]Our mouths were filled with laughter,
our tongues with songs of joy.
Then it was said among the nations,
"The LORD has done great things for them."
[3]The LORD has done great things for us,
and we are filled with joy.

[4]Restore our fortunes,[c] O LORD,
like streams in the Negev.
[5]Those who sow in tears
will reap with songs of joy.
[6]He who goes out weeping,
carrying seed to sow,
will return with songs of joy,
carrying sheaves with him.

[a]1 *Or* LORD *restored the fortunes of* [b]1 *Or men restored to health*
[c]4 *Or Bring back our captives*

Discovering the Word 1. This is a song of celebration by the exiles who returned to Zion. What emotions do you see expressed throughout this psalm? 2. What imagery is used in verses 1–2 to describe the joy the writers feel? 3. How do verses 4–6 reflect a balance between cause and effect? 4. How are sadness and joy intertwined (vv. 5–6)?

Applying the Word 1. The Israelites give God the credit for the "great things" that have happened. How do you do with giving God the credit? 2. When do you feel inhibited about freely expressing your joy?

Responding in Prayer What do you need to praise God for? Share your joy with him.

73 / *Psalm 127*
Worthwhile Work

WILL WE ALLOW technology and our society's definition of personhood to drive a wedge into our community? It can and does happen almost naturally—without our help.

As we respond to Jesus, there will be purpose in our lives and meaning within our relationships. It is the context of relationships with God and other persons that should give meaning to our work. Unfortunately, our culture elevates the possession of things and applauds compulsive work habits. We need to intervene where God's image in people is being destroyed by our society and structures. These passages encourage us to take the lead in bringing God's kingdom back into our relationships.

Warming Up to God What challenges to faith are you currently facing in your workplace?

Read Psalm 127.

Psalm 127

A song of ascents. Of Solomon.

1Unless the LORD builds the house,
its builders labor in vain.
Unless the LORD watches over the city,
the watchmen stand guard in vain.
2In vain you rise early
and stay up late,
toiling for food to eat—
for he grants sleep to[d] those he loves.

3Sons are a heritage from the LORD,
children a reward from him.
4Like arrows in the hands of a warrior
are sons born in one's youth.
5Blessed is the man
whose quiver is full of them.
They will not be put to shame
when they contend with their enemies in the gate.

[d]2 Or *eat— / for while they sleep he provides for*

Discovering the Word 1. What basis is offered in this passage for the worth of our work (v. 1)? 2. Why is it foolish to work long hours (v. 2)? 3. Children (v. 3) are a gift from God and are a sign of his favor on those who do worthwhile work. In what ways has God rewarded you for good work?

Applying the Word 1. How does your attitude toward work shape how you view your personal relationships? 2. In what way do you need the rest that the Lord grants "to those he loves"?

Responding in Prayer Ask God to build in you the attitude toward work that he wants you to have.

Psalms 128—129

Psalm 128

A song of ascents.

1Blessed are all who fear the LORD,
who walk in his ways.
2You will eat the fruit of your labor;
blessings and prosperity will be yours.
3Your wife will be like a fruitful vine
within your house;
your sons will be like olive shoots
around your table.
4Thus is the man blessed
who fears the LORD.

5May the LORD bless you from Zion
all the days of your life;
may you see the prosperity of Jerusalem,
6 and may you live to see your children's children.

Peace be upon Israel.

Psalm 129

A song of ascents.

1They have greatly oppressed me from my youth—
let Israel say—
2they have greatly oppressed me from my youth,
but they have not gained the victory over me.
3Plowmen have plowed my back
and made their furrows long.
4But the LORD is righteous;
he has cut me free from the cords of the wicked.
5May all who hate Zion
be turned back in shame.
6May they be like grass on the roof,
which withers before it can grow;
7with it the reaper cannot fill his hands,
nor the one who gathers fill his arms.
8May those who pass by not say,
"The blessing of the LORD be upon you;
we bless you in the name of the LORD."

74 / *Psalm 130*
A Prayer of Hope

HOPE IS NECESSARY. It gives us the strength to keep going through the tough times. It gives life joy and meaning in the good times. However, when hope has been repeatedly disappointed, it slips away. This psalm offers a picture of this struggle. The writer is without much hope. Yet he puts himself in a place of allowing for the possibility of hope. As we pray with him, we too can begin to wait with growing expectation. We too can nurture our hope.

Warming Up to God How would you describe the experience of hope? How would you describe the experience of hopelessness?

Read Psalm 130.

Psalm 130

A song of ascents.

1Out of the depths I cry to you, O LORD;
2 O Lord, hear my voice.
Let your ears be attentive
to my cry for mercy.
3If you, O LORD, kept a record of sins,
O Lord, who could stand?
4But with you there is forgiveness;
therefore you are feared.

5I wait for the LORD, my soul waits,
and in his word I put my hope.
6My soul waits for the Lord

more than watchmen wait for the morning,
more than watchmen wait for the morning.

7O Israel, put your hope in the LORD,
for with the LORD is unfailing love
and with him is full redemption.
8He himself will redeem Israel
from all their sins.

Discovering the Word 1. The psalm begins with a cry to the Lord from "out of the depths" (v. 1). What pictures come to mind as you read this phrase? 2. The psalmist's distress seems to be related to a struggle with guilt. How can guilt lead to hopelessness? 3. Verses 3 and 4 tell us that God forgives. How does the promise of forgiveness contribute to hope? 4. Verse 5 says, "I wait, . . . my soul waits." What is the relationship between waiting and hope? 5. The psalmist then uses the metaphor of watchmen (v. 6) to describe the experience of hope. What does he convey with this image? 6. What reasons does the psalmist give for hoping in the Lord (vv. 7–8)?

Applying the Word 1. What area of life is it difficult for you to be hopeful about? 2. What reasons do you have for hoping in the Lord?

Responding in Prayer Thank God for being the source of hope. Pray for courage when you face hopelessness.

Psalms 131—132

Psalm 131

A song of ascents. Of David.

1My heart is not proud, O LORD,
my eyes are not haughty;
I do not concern myself with great matters
or things too wonderful for me.
2But I have stilled and quieted my soul;
like a weaned child with its mother,
like a weaned child is my soul within me.

3O Israel, put your hope in the LORD
both now and forevermore.

Psalm 132

A song of ascents.

1O LORD, remember David
and all the hardships he endured.

2He swore an oath to the LORD
and made a vow to the Mighty One of Jacob:
3"I will not enter my house
or go to my bed—
4I will allow no sleep to my eyes,
no slumber to my eyelids,
5till I find a place for the LORD,
a dwelling for the Mighty One of Jacob."
6We heard it in Ephrathah,
we came upon it in the fields of Jaar[e]:[f]
7"Let us go to his dwelling place;
let us worship at his footstool—
8arise, O LORD, and come to your resting place,
you and the ark of your might.
9May your priests be clothed with righteousness;
may your saints sing for joy."

10For the sake of David your servant,
do not reject your anointed one.

11The LORD swore an oath to David,
a sure oath that he will not revoke:
"One of your own descendants
I will place on your throne—
12if your sons keep my covenant
and the statutes I teach them,
then their sons will sit
on your throne for ever and ever."

13For the LORD has chosen Zion,
he has desired it for his dwelling:
14"This is my resting place for ever and ever;
here I will sit enthroned, for I have desired it—
15I will bless her with abundant provisions;
her poor will I satisfy with food.
16I will clothe her priests with salvation,
and her saints will ever sing for joy.

e6 That is, Kiriath Jearim f6 Or *heard of it in Ephrathah, / we found it in the fields of Jaar.* (And no quotes around verses 7-9)

17"Here I will make a horn[g] grow for David
and set up a lamp for my anointed
one.
18I will clothe his enemies with shame,
but the crown on his head will be
resplendent."

[g]17 *Horn* here symbolizes strong one, that is, king.

75 / *Psalm 133*
Blessed Unity

THINK ABOUT THE many brother-to-brother and sister-to-sister loyalties and rivalries that are celebrated in our society—fraternities and sororities, sports teams, family corporations, class reunions, the Mafia (that is, "the Brotherhood"). In your mind's eye, or from your own experience, how do you picture those relationships? Do you envision any fraternal unity so blessed that it fairly oozes and drips with sweetness? David does. He waxes eloquent on this theme. Many contemporary songs which extol the blessedness of "mystic sweet communion" are based, in part, on this psalm.

Warming Up to God How does the "mystic sweet communion" enjoyed by God's people compare to the kinds of unity that you have witnessed or experienced firsthand with others? As you get into this brief Bible study, surround yourself with images of warm Christian fellowship.

Read Psalm 133.

Psalm 133

A song of ascents. Of David.

1How good and pleasant it is
when brothers live together in unity!
2It is like precious oil poured on the head,
running down on the beard,
running down on Aaron's beard,
down upon the collar of his robes.
3It is as if the dew of Hermon
were falling on Mount Zion.
For there the LORD bestows his blessing,
even life forevermore.

Discovering the Word 1. What is so good or pleasant or blessed about brothers living together in unity (v. 1)? 2. To what is this blessedness compared (vv. 2–3)? 3. If the oil of anointing that saturated Aaron's beard and priestly robes was so precious and sanctifying (v. 2; Ex 29:7; Lev 21:10), what does that say about harmony running its course through the fellowship of God's people? 4. Mount Hermon rises 9,000 feet at three snow-covered peaks, its many glaciers stretching across 20 miles in northern Israel, watering the Jordan River valleys and cities below. However, during the summer, its snow and glaciers produce a heavy dew that envelops Mount Hermon, leaving much of the surroundings arid. For the "dew of Hermon" to fall on Mount Zion (v. 3) would be most unusual. What does that say about the blessing of brotherly unity?

Applying the Word 1. What does this psalm say to those who know only the brotherhood and sisterhood as it is portrayed in the media (consider fraternity hazing, sports teams that brawl, family corporations divided by sibling rivalry)? 2. Where are you experiencing strong brother-to-brother or sister-to-sister bonds and blessings that sanctify and sustain God's people, as does "oil" and "dew"? 3. In what way could you experience more of the priestly "oil" and Mount Hermon's "dew"?

Responding in Prayer Think about the spiritual refreshment and moral accountability that strong fellowship provides you. Thank God for the brothers and sisters he has given you to sanctify and sustain you. Consider ways that you can live in harmony with your family of faith, and pray toward that end.

Psalms 134—136

Psalm 134

A song of ascents.

1Praise the LORD, all you servants of the LORD
who minister by night in the house of the
LORD.
2Lift up your hands in the sanctuary
and praise the LORD.

3May the LORD, the Maker of heaven and earth,
bless you from Zion.

Psalm 135

1Praise the LORD.[h]

Praise the name of the LORD;
praise him, you servants of the LORD,
2you who minister in the house of the LORD,
in the courts of the house of our God.

3Praise the LORD, for the LORD is good;
sing praise to his name, for that is pleasant.
4For the LORD has chosen Jacob to be his own,
Israel to be his treasured possession.

5I know that the LORD is great,
that our Lord is greater than all gods.
6The LORD does whatever pleases him,
in the heavens and on the earth,
in the seas and all their depths.
7He makes clouds rise from the ends of the
earth;
he sends lightning with the rain
and brings out the wind from his
storehouses.

8He struck down the firstborn of Egypt,
the firstborn of men and animals.
9He sent his signs and wonders into your
midst, O Egypt,
against Pharaoh and all his servants.
10He struck down many nations
and killed mighty kings—
11Sihon king of the Amorites,
Og king of Bashan
and all the kings of Canaan—
12and he gave their land as an inheritance,
an inheritance to his people Israel.

13Your name, O LORD, endures forever,
your renown, O LORD, through all
generations.
14For the LORD will vindicate his people
and have compassion on his servants.

15The idols of the nations are silver and gold,
made by the hands of men.
16They have mouths, but cannot speak,
eyes, but they cannot see;
17they have ears, but cannot hear,
nor is there breath in their mouths.
18Those who make them will be like them,
and so will all who trust in them.

19O house of Israel, praise the LORD;
O house of Aaron, praise the LORD;
20O house of Levi, praise the LORD;
you who fear him, praise the LORD.
21Praise be to the LORD from Zion,
to him who dwells in Jerusalem.

Praise the LORD.

Psalm 136

1Give thanks to the LORD, for he is good.
His love endures forever.
2Give thanks to the God of gods.
His love endures forever.
3Give thanks to the Lord of lords:
His love endures forever.

4to him who alone does great wonders,
His love endures forever.
5who by his understanding made the heavens,
His love endures forever.
6who spread out the earth upon the waters,
His love endures forever.
7who made the great lights—
His love endures forever.
8the sun to govern the day,
His love endures forever.
9the moon and stars to govern the night;
His love endures forever.

10to him who struck down the firstborn of
Egypt
His love endures forever.
11and brought Israel out from among them
His love endures forever.
12with a mighty hand and outstretched arm;
His love endures forever.

13to him who divided the Red Sea[i] asunder
His love endures forever.

[h] 1 Hebrew *Hallelu Yah;* also in verses 3 and 21 [i] 13 Hebrew *Yam Suph;* that is, Sea of Reeds; also in verse 15

[14]and brought Israel through the midst of it,
His love endures forever.
[15]but swept Pharaoh and his army into the Red Sea;
His love endures forever.
[16]to him who led his people through the desert,
His love endures forever.
[17]who struck down great kings,
His love endures forever.
[18]and killed mighty kings—
His love endures forever.
[19]Sihon king of the Amorites
His love endures forever.
[20]and Og king of Bashan—
His love endures forever.
[21]and gave their land as an inheritance,
His love endures forever.
[22]an inheritance to his servant Israel;
His love endures forever.

[23]to the One who remembered us in our low estate
His love endures forever.
[24]and freed us from our enemies,
His love endures forever.
[25]and who gives food to every creature.
His love endures forever.

[26]Give thanks to the God of heaven.
His love endures forever.

76 / *Psalm 137*
Praying Our Hate

WE PUT ON our "Sunday best" in our prayers. But when we pray the prayers of God's people, the Psalms, we find that will not do. We must pray who we actually are, not who we think we should be. Here is a prayer that brings out not the best but the worst in us; vile, venomous, vicious hate.

Warming Up to God Everyone has hated at one time or another. It is one of the basic human experiences. Be honest before God. Whom have you hated? Why?

Read Psalm 137.

Psalm 137

[1]By the rivers of Babylon we sat and wept
when we remembered Zion.
[2]There on the poplars
we hung our harps,
[3]for there our captors asked us for songs,
our tormentors demanded songs of joy;
they said, "Sing us one of the songs of Zion!"
[4]How can we sing the songs of the LORD
while in a foreign land?
[5]If I forget you, O Jerusalem,
may my right hand forget ⌞its skill⌟.
[6]May my tongue cling to the roof of my mouth
if I do not remember you,
if I do not consider Jerusalem
my highest joy.

[7]Remember, O LORD, what the Edomites did
on the day Jerusalem fell.
"Tear it down," they cried,
"tear it down to its foundations!"
[8]O Daughter of Babylon, doomed to destruction,
happy is he who repays you
for what you have done to us—
[9]he who seizes your infants
and dashes them against the rocks.

Discovering the Word 1. This psalm combines the loveliest lyric we can sing with the ugliest emotion we can feel. What makes verses 1–6 lovely? 2. What makes verses 7–9 ugly? 3. Homesickness is understandable. Sometimes it is evidence of loyalty. Sometimes it is simply irresponsibility. Remembering your own experiences of this, how would you evaluate verses 4–6? 4. The two dominant emotions in this prayer are self-pity

(vv. 1–6) and avenging hate (vv. 7–9), neither of them particularly commendable. Praying our sins doesn't, as such, launder them. What does it do?

Applying the Word 1. Jesus said, "Love your enemies and pray for those who persecute you" (Mt 5:44). How can we possibly love and pray for such people? 2. Most of us suppress our negative emotions (unless, neurotically, we advertise them). The way of prayer is not to cover them up so we will appear respectable, but to expose them so we can be healed. What negative emotion would you like healed?

Responding in Prayer Take any hate or dislike that you have uncovered and give it voice as you pray.

Psalm 138

Psalm 138

Of David.

[1]I will praise you, O LORD, with all my heart;
before the "gods" I will sing your praise.
[2]I will bow down toward your holy temple
and will praise your name
for your love and your faithfulness,
for you have exalted above all things
your name and your word.
[3]When I called, you answered me;
you made me bold and stouthearted.

[4]May all the kings of the earth praise you,
O LORD,
when they hear the words of your mouth.
[5]May they sing of the ways of the LORD,
for the glory of the LORD is great.

[6]Though the LORD is on high, he looks upon
the lowly,
but the proud he knows from afar.
[7]Though I walk in the midst of trouble,
you preserve my life;
you stretch out your hand against the anger
of my foes,
with your right hand you save me.
[8]The LORD will fulfill ⌞his purpose⌟ for me;
your love, O LORD, endures forever—
do not abandon the works of your hands.

77 / *Psalm 139*
Wonderfully Made

A CRAFTSMAN IN medieval times would work for months on a special piece that displayed his finest artistic skill. Finally, when the work was finished, he would present it to the craftsmen's guild in hopes of achieving the rank of master. The work was called his masterpiece. In Psalm 139 we see God the master craftsman, lovingly at work on his masterpiece. The psalm can have a profound impact on the way we view ourselves.

Warming Up to God Do you think of yourself as God's artwork, his masterpiece? Why or why not? Ask God to help you see yourself through his eyes as you begin this study.

Read Psalm 139.

Psalm 139

For the director of music. Of David.
A psalm.

[1]O LORD, you have searched me
and you know me.
[2]You know when I sit and when I rise;
you perceive my thoughts from afar.
[3]You discern my going out and my lying
down;
you are familiar with all my ways.
[4]Before a word is on my tongue
you know it completely, O LORD.

5You hem me in—behind and before;
you have laid your hand upon me.
6Such knowledge is too wonderful for me,
too lofty for me to attain.

7Where can I go from your Spirit?
Where can I flee from your presence?
8If I go up to the heavens, you are there;
if I make my bed in the depths,[j] you are there.
9If I rise on the wings of the dawn,
if I settle on the far side of the sea,
10even there your hand will guide me,
your right hand will hold me fast.
11If I say, "Surely the darkness will hide me
and the light become night around me,"
12even the darkness will not be dark to you;
the night will shine like the day,
for darkness is as light to you.

13For you created my inmost being;
you knit me together in my mother's womb.
14I praise you because I am fearfully and wonderfully made;
your works are wonderful,
I know that full well.
15My frame was not hidden from you
when I was made in the secret place.
When I was woven together in the depths of the earth,
16 your eyes saw my unformed body.
All the days ordained for me
were written in your book
before one of them came to be.
17How precious to[k] me are your thoughts, O God!
How vast is the sum of them!
18Were I to count them,
they would outnumber the grains of sand.
When I awake,
I am still with you.

19If only you would slay the wicked, O God!
Away from me, you bloodthirsty men!
20They speak of you with evil intent;
your adversaries misuse your name.
21Do I not hate those who hate you, O LORD,
and abhor those who rise up against you?
22I have nothing but hatred for them;
I count them my enemies.
23Search me, O God, and know my heart;
test me and know my anxious thoughts.
24See if there is any offensive way in me,
and lead me in the way everlasting.

[j] 8 Hebrew *Sheol* [k] 17 Or *concerning*

Discovering the Word 1. According to the psalmist, what specific things does the Lord know about us (vv. 1–6)? 2. The psalmist declares that God's knowledge of him is wonderful (v. 6). Yet why do you think he also feels an urge to flee from God's presence (vv. 7–12)? 3. What words are used to describe God's activity and artistry in making us (vv. 13–16)?

Applying the Word 1. How do you hide your true self from God? 2. When do you hide your true self from others? 3. How does this psalm help you to feel more loved and valued by God?

Responding in Prayer Take time to thank God for the fact that you are "fearfully and wonderfully made." Put verses 23–24 in your own words and express them to God in prayer.

Psalms 140—141

Psalm 140

For the director of music. A psalm of David.

1Rescue me, O LORD, from evil men;
protect me from men of violence,
2who devise evil plans in their hearts
and stir up war every day.
3They make their tongues as sharp as a serpent's;
the poison of vipers is on their lips. *Selah*

4Keep me, O LORD, from the hands of the wicked;
protect me from men of violence
who plan to trip my feet.
5Proud men have hidden a snare for me;

they have spread out the cords of their net
and have set traps for me along my path.
Selah

6O LORD, I say to you, "You are my God."
Hear, O LORD, my cry for mercy.
7O Sovereign LORD, my strong deliverer,
who shields my head in the day of battle—
8do not grant the wicked their desires, O LORD;
do not let their plans succeed,
or they will become proud. *Selah*

9Let the heads of those who surround me
be covered with the trouble their lips have caused.
10Let burning coals fall upon them;
may they be thrown into the fire,
into miry pits, never to rise.
11Let slanderers not be established in the land;
may disaster hunt down men of violence.

12I know that the LORD secures justice for the poor
and upholds the cause of the needy.
13Surely the righteous will praise your name
and the upright will live before you.

Psalm 141

A psalm of David.

1O LORD, I call to you; come quickly to me.
Hear my voice when I call to you.
2May my prayer be set before you like incense;
may the lifting up of my hands be like the evening sacrifice.

3Set a guard over my mouth, O LORD;
keep watch over the door of my lips.
4Let not my heart be drawn to what is evil,
to take part in wicked deeds
with men who are evildoers;
let me not eat of their delicacies.

5Let a righteous man[l] strike me—it is a kindness;
let him rebuke me—it is oil on my head.
My head will not refuse it.

Yet my prayer is ever against the deeds of evildoers;
6 their rulers will be thrown down from the cliffs,
and the wicked will learn that my words were well spoken.
7⌊They will say,⌋ "As one plows and breaks up the earth,
so our bones have been scattered at the mouth of the grave.[m]"

8But my eyes are fixed on you, O Sovereign LORD;
in you I take refuge—do not give me over to death.
9Keep me from the snares they have laid for me,
from the traps set by evildoers.
10Let the wicked fall into their own nets,
while I pass by in safety.

[l]5 Or *Let the Righteous One* [m]7 Hebrew *Sheol*

78 / *Psalm 142*
A Prayer of Desperation

"IT'S CANCER." THE words shattered the tension in the room. I had been waiting with my friend to find out the results of her biopsy. My friend was calm. She was probably too stunned to feel. I, however, felt desperate. I wanted to scream "No!" I felt frightened, powerless, outraged. Desperation is an experience of extreme need and helplessness. We feel desperate when life's circumstances overpower us. We feel desperate when our well-being is threatened and we feel unable to affect the outcome. This psalm gives voice to our experiences of desperation.

Warming Up to God Think of a time when you felt desperate. What phrases or images would you use to describe the situation you faced?

Read Psalm 142.

Psalm 142

A *maskil*[n] of David. When he was in the cave. A prayer.

1 I cry aloud to the LORD;
  I lift up my voice to the LORD for mercy.
2 I pour out my complaint before him;
  before him I tell my trouble.
3 When my spirit grows faint within me,
  it is you who know my way.
In the path where I walk
  men have hidden a snare for me.
4 Look to my right and see;
  no one is concerned for me.
I have no refuge;
  no one cares for my life.

5 I cry to you, O LORD;
  I say, "You are my refuge,
  my portion in the land of the living."
6 Listen to my cry,
  for I am in desperate need;
rescue me from those who pursue me,
  for they are too strong for me.
7 Set me free from my prison,
  that I may praise your name.

Then the righteous will gather about me
  because of your goodness to me.

[n] Title: Probably a literary or musical term

Discovering the Word 1. This psalm was written by David when he was in a cave, perhaps when he was hiding from Saul. How would you describe David's emotional state? 2. What phrases and images does David use to describe the situation he faces (vv. 3, 6 and 7)? 3. What contrast do you see between David's experiences with people and his experience with God? 4. How would you compare his view of his personal power with his view of God's power?

Applying the Word 1. What is the significance of the contrast between our power and God's power when we feel desperate? 2. Are you able to pray with this kind of directness and urgency in times of personal need? Why or why not?

Responding in Prayer Write a psalm of your own, allowing yourself to cry out to God on your own behalf or on behalf of someone else who faces a desperate situation.

79 / *Psalm 143*
Asking for Guidance

"THE WAY I was taught to pray," explained Sue, "was to list for God the things I wanted done. I would give God a long list of 'requests' that were really thinly disguised expectations or demands. It amazes me now, but I really felt I knew what everyone needed and that my job was to bring these needs to God's attention. I would decide what needed to be done and God would do it. Sound backwards? I think so. I was surprised to discover a humbler way to pray. I learned to say, 'show me your will today and give me the power to carry it out.' I stopped telling God what to do and started to ask for guidance and help. Now I pray with an awareness that I am talking to my Creator, who knows me better than I know me, who loves me more than I love me, and who is personally involved in my life."

Warming Up to God What fears might keep you from seeking to know and to do God's will?

Read Psalm 143.

Psalm 143

A psalm of David.

1 O LORD, hear my prayer,
 listen to my cry for mercy;
in your faithfulness and righteousness
 come to my relief.
2 Do not bring your servant into judgment,
 for no one living is righteous before you.
3 The enemy pursues me,
 he crushes me to the ground;
he makes me dwell in darkness
 like those long dead.
4 So my spirit grows faint within me;
 my heart within me is dismayed.

5 I remember the days of long ago;
 I meditate on all your works
 and consider what your hands have done.
6 I spread out my hands to you;
 my soul thirsts for you like a parched land.
Selah

7 Answer me quickly, O LORD;
 my spirit fails.
Do not hide your face from me
 or I will be like those who go down to the pit.
8 Let the morning bring me word of your unfailing love,
 for I have put my trust in you.
Show me the way I should go,
 for to you I lift up my soul.
9 Rescue me from my enemies, O LORD,
 for I hide myself in you.
10 Teach me to do your will,
 for you are my God;
may your good Spirit
 lead me on level ground.

11 For your name's sake, O LORD, preserve my life;
 in your righteousness, bring me out of trouble.
12 In your unfailing love, silence my enemies;
 destroy all my foes,
 for I am your servant.

Discovering the Word 1. What specifically does the psalmist say he longs for in this text (vv. 1, 7)? 2. What does the psalmist fear might happen (vv. 2, 7)? 3. Why does the psalmist need God's help (vv. 3–6)? 4. The psalmist asks for knowledge of God's will and the power to carry it out. What specifically does he ask for (vv. 8–12)? 5. The psalmist reminds God: "I have put my trust in you. . . . To you I lift up my soul. . . . I hide myself in you" (vv. 8–9). What do you think the psalmist is trying to communicate to God?

Applying the Word 1. In what area of life do you feel a need for knowledge of God's will? 2. What knowledge of God's will have you received, but are hesitant and needing power to carry out?

Responding in Prayer What guidance would you like to ask God for today?

Psalm 144

Psalm 144

Of David.

1 Praise be to the LORD my Rock,
 who trains my hands for war,
 my fingers for battle.
2 He is my loving God and my fortress,
 my stronghold and my deliverer,
my shield, in whom I take refuge,
 who subdues peoples[o] under me.

3 O LORD, what is man that you care for him,
 the son of man that you think of him?
4 Man is like a breath;
 his days are like a fleeting shadow.
5 Part your heavens, O LORD, and come down;
 touch the mountains, so that they smoke.
6 Send forth lightning and scatter ⌞the enemies⌟;
 shoot your arrows and rout them.
7 Reach down your hand from on high;
 deliver me and rescue me
from the mighty waters,
 from the hands of foreigners

[o] 2 Many manuscripts of the Masoretic Text, Dead Sea Scrolls, Aquila, Jerome and Syriac; most manuscripts of the Masoretic Text *subdues my people*

8whose mouths are full of lies,
whose right hands are deceitful.

9I will sing a new song to you, O God;
on the ten-stringed lyre I will make music
to you,
10to the One who gives victory to kings,
who delivers his servant David from the
deadly sword.

11Deliver me and rescue me
from the hands of foreigners
whose mouths are full of lies,
whose right hands are deceitful.

12Then our sons in their youth
will be like well-nurtured plants,
and our daughters will be like pillars
carved to adorn a palace.
13Our barns will be filled
with every kind of provision.
Our sheep will increase by thousands,
by tens of thousands in our fields;
14 our oxen will draw heavy loads.[p]
There will be no breaching of walls,
no going into captivity,
no cry of distress in our streets.

15Blessed are the people of whom this is true;
blessed are the people whose God is the
LORD.

p14 Or *our chieftains will be firmly established*

80 / *Psalm 145*
Relying on God

PEOPLE WHO HAVE experienced repeated disappointments with parents or other significant people can develop an image of an unreliable God. He is seen as a God who cannot be counted on. He makes promises he may not keep. He may be loving one day and unaccountably angry the next. People who have experienced unreliable parents may ask: "How do I know God will keep his promises? How do I know he listens to me? How do I know he will answer me or help me?" The image of an unreliable God stands in stark contrast to biblical images of God. The God of the Bible is the Faithful One, the Rock, the Fortress. He is the same yesterday, today and forever.

Warming Up to God Think of a person whom you see as reliable. Describe the person and your response to his or her reliability.

Read Psalm 145.

Psalm 145[q]

A psalm of praise. Of David.

1I will exalt you, my God the King;
I will praise your name for ever and ever.
2Every day I will praise you
and extol your name for ever and ever.

3Great is the LORD and most worthy of praise;
his greatness no one can fathom.
4One generation will commend your works to
another;
they will tell of your mighty acts.
5They will speak of the glorious splendor of
your majesty,
and I will meditate on your wonderful
works.[r]
6They will tell of the power of your awesome
works,
and I will proclaim your great deeds.
7They will celebrate your abundant goodness
and joyfully sing of your righteousness.

8The LORD is gracious and compassionate,
slow to anger and rich in love.
9The LORD is good to all;
he has compassion on all he has made.
10All you have made will praise you, O LORD;
your saints will extol you.
11They will tell of the glory of your kingdom
and speak of your might,
12so that all men may know of your mighty acts

qThis psalm is an acrostic poem, the verses of which (including verse 13b) begin with the successive letters of the Hebrew alphabet.
r5 Dead Sea Scrolls and Syriac (see also Septuagint); Masoretic Text *On the glorious splendor of your majesty / and on your wonderful works I will meditate*

and the glorious splendor of your kingdom.
[13]Your kingdom is an everlasting kingdom,
and your dominion endures through all
generations.

The LORD is faithful to all his promises
and loving toward all he has made.[s]
[14]The LORD upholds all those who fall
and lifts up all who are bowed down.
[15]The eyes of all look to you,
and you give them their food at the proper
time.
[16]You open your hand
and satisfy the desires of every living thing.

[17]The LORD is righteous in all his ways
and loving toward all he has made.
[18]The LORD is near to all who call on him,
to all who call on him in truth.
[19]He fulfills the desires of those who fear him;
he hears their cry and saves them.
[20]The LORD watches over all who love him,
but all the wicked he will destroy.

[21]My mouth will speak in praise of the LORD.
Let every creature praise his holy name
for ever and ever.

[s]*13* One manuscript of the Masoretic Text, Dead Sea Scrolls and Syriac (see also Septuagint); most manuscripts of the Masoretic Text do not have the last two lines of verse 13.

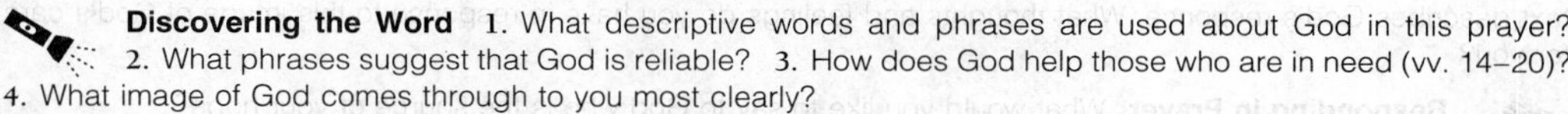

Discovering the Word 1. What descriptive words and phrases are used about God in this prayer? 2. What phrases suggest that God is reliable? 3. How does God help those who are in need (vv. 14–20)? 4. What image of God comes through to you most clearly?

Applying the Word 1. How does the picture of God here compare or contrast with your image of God's reliability? 2. Why is it important for you to know that God is reliable?

Responding in Prayer Offer God your thanks for his faithfulness.

81 / *Psalm 146*
The Source of Hope

"MY OWN MOM and Dad failed me," Linda said in her support group meeting. "Then my marriage fell apart. And then my health fell apart. Life has always been hard. I don't see why I should expect it to ever get any better. If anything, it will probably get worse. How is it possible for me to have hope?"

The Bible teaches that there is more to the story of our lives than our experiences of loss and disappointment. The planet may be fallen, but it is not forsaken by God. God is actively present in our lives, bringing gifts of life and joy into the midst of our darkness. We can dare to hope because of who God is.

Warming Up to God In what area of life is it hard for you to find hope?

Read Psalm 146.

Psalm 146

[1]Praise the LORD.[t]

Praise the LORD, O my soul.
2 I will praise the LORD all my life;
I will sing praise to my God as long as I
live.

[3]Do not put your trust in princes,
in mortal men, who cannot save.
[4]When their spirit departs, they return to the
ground;
on that very day their plans come to
nothing.

[5]Blessed is he whose help is the God of Jacob,
whose hope is in the LORD his God,
[6]the Maker of heaven and earth,

[t]*1* Hebrew *Hallelu Yah*; also in verse 10

the sea, and everything in them—
the LORD, who remains faithful forever.
7 He upholds the cause of the oppressed
and gives food to the hungry.
The LORD sets prisoners free,
8 the LORD gives sight to the blind,
the LORD lifts up those who are bowed down,
the LORD loves the righteous.
9 The LORD watches over the alien
and sustains the fatherless and the widow,
but he frustrates the ways of the wicked.

10 The LORD reigns forever,
your God, O Zion, for all generations.

Praise the LORD.

Discovering the Word 1. How does this psalm contrast the experience of hoping in God with the experience of hoping in people? 2. The psalmist mentions eight kinds of circumstances that might seem hopeless. List these situations/conditions and the reasons why they might seem hopeless. 3. Describe how God responds to people in each of these situations. 4. What do these responses from God to people in hopeless situations suggest to you about God's character?

Applying the Word 1. Which of the eight images of hopelessness do you most strongly relate to at this time? Explain. 2. Take a few minutes and allow yourself to picture God responding to you in the way this text describes God's response. What thoughts and feelings do you have in response to this image of God's care for you?

Responding in Prayer What would you like to say to God who is the source of your hope?

Psalm 147

Psalm 147

1 Praise the LORD.[u]

How good it is to sing praises to our God,
how pleasant and fitting to praise him!

2 The LORD builds up Jerusalem;
he gathers the exiles of Israel.
3 He heals the brokenhearted
and binds up their wounds.
4 He determines the number of the stars
and calls them each by name.
5 Great is our Lord and mighty in power;
his understanding has no limit.
6 The LORD sustains the humble
but casts the wicked to the ground.

7 Sing to the LORD with thanksgiving;
make music to our God on the harp.
8 He covers the sky with clouds;
he supplies the earth with rain
and makes grass grow on the hills.
9 He provides food for the cattle
and for the young ravens when they call.

10 His pleasure is not in the strength of the horse,
nor his delight in the legs of a man;
11 the LORD delights in those who fear him,
who put their hope in his unfailing love.

12 Extol the LORD, O Jerusalem;
praise your God, O Zion,
13 for he strengthens the bars of your gates
and blesses your people within you.
14 He grants peace to your borders
and satisfies you with the finest of wheat.

15 He sends his command to the earth;
his word runs swiftly.
16 He spreads the snow like wool
and scatters the frost like ashes.
17 He hurls down his hail like pebbles.
Who can withstand his icy blast?
18 He sends his word and melts them;
he stirs up his breezes, and the waters flow.

19 He has revealed his word to Jacob,
his laws and decrees to Israel.
20 He has done this for no other nation;
they do not know his laws.

Praise the LORD.

[u] 1 Hebrew *Hallelu Yah*; also in verse 20

82 / *Psalm 148*

A Symphony of Praise

THIS CALL TO praise, if heeded by all of creation, would make for quite a symphony of praise. Perhaps it would sound more like a cacophony than a symphony. Judging from the noises that all of God's creatures make individually, it boggles the mind (never mind the eardrums!) to imagine the concert called for in Psalm 148. Its location at the end of the book suggests that Psalm 148 is meant to wrap everything up on a high praise note.

Warming Up to God Think about an exciting time of corporate praise that you have been a part of. How does seeing others engaged in worship inspire your worship?

Read Psalm 148.

Psalm 148

1 Praise the LORD.[v]

Praise the LORD from the heavens,
praise him in the heights above.
2 Praise him, all his angels,
praise him, all his heavenly hosts.
3 Praise him, sun and moon,
praise him, all you shining stars.
4 Praise him, you highest heavens
and you waters above the skies.
5 Let them praise the name of the LORD,
for he commanded and they were created.
6 He set them in place for ever and ever;
he gave a decree that will never pass away.

7 Praise the LORD from the earth,
you great sea creatures and all ocean depths,
8 lightning and hail, snow and clouds,
stormy winds that do his bidding,
9 you mountains and all hills,
fruit trees and all cedars,
10 wild animals and all cattle,
small creatures and flying birds,
11 kings of the earth and all nations,
you princes and all rulers on earth,
12 young men and maidens,
old men and children.

13 Let them praise the name of the LORD,
for his name alone is exalted;
his splendor is above the earth and the heavens.
14 He has raised up for his people a horn,[w]
the praise of all his saints,
of Israel, the people close to his heart.

Praise the LORD.

[v] 1 Hebrew *Hallelu Yah*; also in verse 14 [w] 14 *Horn* here symbolizes strong one, that is, king.

Discovering the Word 1. This psalm divides into two six-verse stanzas (vv. 1–6 and 7–12), with a recap that underscores the motivation to praise (vv. 13–14). What two major chorus groups are appealed to here? 2. Within those two major choral divisions, who joins in praising God? 3. Do you see this as mere figurative (symbolic or exaggerated) language used by the psalmist to call all things in heaven and on earth, or is there some way that all the various elements actually praise God? 4. Why praise God at all (vv. 5–6, 13–14)?

Applying the Word 1. What is the closest you have come, this side of heaven, to experiencing a worldwide worship service such as this psalm announces? 2. Do you look forward to heaven when this psalm finds its fulfillment, or does praising God all day long sound boring to you? 3. How does this psalm provide a new or fresh picture of praise for you?

Responding in Prayer Imagine what it would be like to have every man, woman and child—young and old alike—participating in your church's choir. Pray (and practice) toward that end.

Psalm 149

Psalm 149

[1]Praise the LORD.[x]

Sing to the LORD a new song,
his praise in the assembly of the saints.

[2]Let Israel rejoice in their Maker;
let the people of Zion be glad in their King.
[3]Let them praise his name with dancing
and make music to him with tambourine
and harp.
[4]For the LORD takes delight in his people;
he crowns the humble with salvation.
[5]Let the saints rejoice in this honor
and sing for joy on their beds.

[6]May the praise of God be in their mouths
and a double-edged sword in their hands,
[7]to inflict vengeance on the nations
and punishment on the peoples,
[8]to bind their kings with fetters,
their nobles with shackles of iron,
[9]to carry out the sentence written against
them.
This is the glory of all his saints.

Praise the LORD.

[x]1 Hebrew *Hallelu Yah;* also in verse 9

83 / *Psalm 150*
Praying Our Praise

ALL PRAYER FINALLY, in one way or another, becomes praise. Psalm 150 is deliberately placed as the concluding prayer of the church's book of prayers. No matter how much we suffer, no matter our doubts—everything finds its way into praise, the final consummating prayer.

Warming Up to God What circumstances or feelings in the last year have, however momentarily, made a praising person out of you? Reflect on that again in joy, celebrating with Christ.

Read Psalm 150.

Psalm 150

[1]Praise the LORD.[y]

Praise God in his sanctuary;
praise him in his mighty heavens.
[2]Praise him for his acts of power;
praise him for his surpassing greatness.
[3]Praise him with the sounding of the trumpet,
praise him with the harp and lyre,
[4]praise him with tambourine and dancing,
praise him with the strings and flute,
[5]praise him with the clash of cymbals,
praise him with resounding cymbals.

[6]Let everything that has breath praise the LORD.

Praise the LORD.

[y]1 Hebrew *Hallelu Yah;* also in verse 6

Discovering the Word 1. How many times is the word *praise* used in the psalm? 2. Verse 1 tells us *where* the Lord is to be praised. What is the meaning of "in his sanctuary" and "in his mighty heavens"? 3. Verse 2 tells us *why* he is to be praised. What reasons does the psalmist give? 4. Verses 3–5 tell us *how* to praise the Lord. As you read these verses, what kind of scene do you imagine?

Applying the Word 1. Building on verse 2, what reasons can you give for praising God? 2. There are no shortcuts to praise. We can see this in many psalms that express pain. What difficult circumstances in your life have found their way into praise? 3. Augustine claimed that a "Christian should be a hallelujah from head to foot." What needs to be done to get to that point?

Responding in Prayer Gather the reflections and insights that have come from your study and turn them into a time of concluding and celebrative praise.

Proverbs

Every year thousands of books published have titles with the same first two words—*How to* . . . By reading these books you can learn how to paint like the old masters, how to get a job, how to get federal grants, a divorce, free publicity, a mortgage or even a nightclub gig. You can read about how to buy a car, a house, a small business or a personal computer. You can become a balloon artist, an astrologer, an athlete, a golfer, a fashion designer, a good dancer, a pilot, a master manipulator, a mechanic or a vampire. Experts out there will make *you* expert at petting a cat, picking lottery numbers, losing five pounds fast, building fences or bearing children.

All these books are offering us *wisdom*—skill in one area or another. Books like these proliferate because we all need wisdom to live successfully. Wisdom brings success and prosperity in our work, in dealings with family and friends, and in our relationship with God. One book of the Bible—the Proverbs of Solomon—specializes in wisdom. It gives us direction and guidance that is practical, concrete, reasonable, wholesome, understandable, shrewd and fruitful. By reading it we gain skill in *all* areas of life.

Where Did the Book of Proverbs Come From?

The book of Proverbs begins with the notice "The Proverbs of Solomon, Son of David, King of Israel." This does not mean, however, that Solomon authored every word of the book. In 1 Kings 4:32 we learn that Solomon "spoke three thousand proverbs." Undoubtedly he composed a substantial number of these proverbs himself. First Kings 4:34 mentions that kings of surrounding nations sent delegations to hear Solomon's wisdom. On the other hand, an exchange of wisdom must have developed between Solomon and those who came to learn from him.

The book of Proverbs reflects this interchange. Approximately three hundred proverbs are labeled "Proverbs of Solomon" in Proverbs 10:1—22:16. Perhaps this section formed the nucleus of the collection. Some years later, King Hezekiah's scribes added about 130 additional Solomonic proverbs, found in Proverbs 25:1—29:27. "Sayings of the Wise" appear in Proverbs 22:17—24:22, followed by "Further Sayings of the Wise" in Proverbs 24:23–34. Then come "Sayings of Agur" in Proverbs 30, "Sayings of King Lemuel" in Proverbs 31:1–9, and the acrostic poem on the virtuous wife in Proverbs 31:10–31. Clearly, the book of Proverbs as it comes to us contains a broad collection of proverbs, from a diversity of wise men and at least one woman who is identified as King Lemuel's mother.

Comparing the book of Proverbs with other ancient Near Eastern wisdom literature sheds light on how the collection arose in the first place. In order to instruct their sons, court officials in many lands would pull together the wisdom they had acquired in a lifetime of diplomatic service. From Egypt we have at least ten such collections, including *The Instruction of Ka-gem-ni* and *The Instruction of Prince Hor-dedef*, dating from the Old Kingdom (2686–2160 B.C.), and the *The Instruction of Onchsheshonqy* in the fourth or fifth century B.C. An Akkadian translation of a Sumerian original entitled *The Instructions of Shurruppak* dates from approximately 1300 B.C. Ahiquar, who served as vizier to the Assyrian kings Sennacherib and Esarhaddon in the seventh century B.C., left the *Words of Ahiquar*. The Proverbs of Solomon, Son of David, King of Israel takes its place alongside these and other collections. Prophetic authorities added Solomon's proverbs to the canon of Scripture. A manual of instruction for the king's son became available to all of God's children.

What Will Solomon's Proverbs Do for Me?

Solomon tells us the purpose of the collection in Proverbs 1:2–6:

For attaining wisdom and discipline;
  for understanding words of insight;
for acquiring a disciplined and prudent life,
  doing what is right and just and fair;
for giving prudence to the simple,
  knowledge and discretion to the young—
let the wise listen and add to their learning,
  and let the discerning get guidance—
for understanding proverbs and parables,
  the sayings and riddles of the wise.

Outline

1/ Proverbs 6:1–19 ——— *Bad Words*
2/ Proverbs 7 ——— *The Simple*
3/ Proverbs 9 ——— *Two Dinner Invitations*
4/ Proverbs 10 ——— *Good Words*
5/ Proverbs 13—14 ——— *Finding Wisdom*
6/ Proverbs 15—16 ——— *Prayer*
7/ Proverbs 17—18 ——— *Avoiding the Fool*
8/ Proverbs 19 ——— *Giving*
9/ Proverbs 21 ——— *Planning the Future*
10/ Proverbs 24:23–34 ——— *The Sluggard*
11/ Proverbs 27 ——— *Friends*
12/ Proverbs 30 ——— *Wealth & Poverty*

Proverbs 1—5

1 The proverbs of Solomon son of David, king of Israel:

[2]for attaining wisdom and discipline;
for understanding words of insight;
[3]for acquiring a disciplined and prudent life,
doing what is right and just and fair;
[4]for giving prudence to the simple,
knowledge and discretion to the young—
[5]let the wise listen and add to their learning,
and let the discerning get guidance—
[6]for understanding proverbs and parables,
the sayings and riddles of the wise.

[7]The fear of the LORD is the beginning of knowledge,
but fools[a] despise wisdom and discipline.

[8]Listen, my son, to your father's instruction
and do not forsake your mother's teaching.
[9]They will be a garland to grace your head
and a chain to adorn your neck.

[10]My son, if sinners entice you,
do not give in to them.
[11]If they say, "Come along with us;
let's lie in wait for someone's blood,
let's waylay some harmless soul;
[12]let's swallow them alive, like the grave,[b]
and whole, like those who go down to the pit;
[13]we will get all sorts of valuable things
and fill our houses with plunder;
[14]throw in your lot with us,
and we will share a common purse"—
[15]my son, do not go along with them,
do not set foot on their paths;
[16]for their feet rush into sin,
they are swift to shed blood.
[17]How useless to spread a net
in full view of all the birds!
[18]These men lie in wait for their own blood;
they waylay only themselves!
[19]Such is the end of all who go after ill-gotten gain;
it takes away the lives of those who get it.

[20]Wisdom calls aloud in the street,
she raises her voice in the public squares;
[21]at the head of the noisy streets[c] she cries out,
in the gateways of the city she makes her speech:
[22]"How long will you simple ones[d] love your simple ways?
How long will mockers delight in mockery
and fools hate knowledge?
[23]If you had responded to my rebuke,
I would have poured out my heart to you
and made my thoughts known to you.
[24]But since you rejected me when I called
and no one gave heed when I stretched out my hand,
[25]since you ignored all my advice
and would not accept my rebuke,
[26]I in turn will laugh at your disaster;
I will mock when calamity overtakes you—
[27]when calamity overtakes you like a storm,
when disaster sweeps over you like a whirlwind,
when distress and trouble overwhelm you.

[28]"Then they will call to me but I will not answer;
they will look for me but will not find me.
[29]Since they hated knowledge
and did not choose to fear the LORD,
[30]since they would not accept my advice
and spurned my rebuke,
[31]they will eat the fruit of their ways
and be filled with the fruit of their schemes.
[32]For the waywardness of the simple will kill them,
and the complacency of fools will destroy them;
[33]but whoever listens to me will live in safety
and be at ease, without fear of harm."

2 My son, if you accept my words
and store up my commands within you,
[2]turning your ear to wisdom
and applying your heart to understanding,
[3]and if you call out for insight
and cry aloud for understanding,
[4]and if you look for it as for silver
and search for it as for hidden treasure,

[a]7 The Hebrew words rendered *fool* in Proverbs, and often elsewhere in the Old Testament, denote one who is morally deficient.
[b]12 Hebrew *Sheol*
[c]21 Hebrew; Septuagint / *on the tops of the walls*
[d]22 The Hebrew word rendered *simple* in Proverbs generally denotes one without moral direction and inclined to evil.

5then you will understand the fear of the LORD
and find the knowledge of God.
6For the LORD gives wisdom,
and from his mouth come knowledge and
understanding.
7He holds victory in store for the upright,
he is a shield to those whose walk is
blameless,
8for he guards the course of the just
and protects the way of his faithful ones.

9Then you will understand what is right and
just
and fair—every good path.
10For wisdom will enter your heart,
and knowledge will be pleasant to your
soul.
11Discretion will protect you,
and understanding will guard you.

12Wisdom will save you from the ways of
wicked men,
from men whose words are perverse,
13who leave the straight paths
to walk in dark ways,
14who delight in doing wrong
and rejoice in the perverseness of evil,
15whose paths are crooked
and who are devious in their ways.

16It will save you also from the adulteress,
from the wayward wife with her seductive
words,
17who has left the partner of her youth
and ignored the covenant she made before
God.[e]
18For her house leads down to death
and her paths to the spirits of the dead.
19None who go to her return
or attain the paths of life.

20Thus you will walk in the ways of good men
and keep to the paths of the righteous.
21For the upright will live in the land,
and the blameless will remain in it;
22but the wicked will be cut off from the land,
and the unfaithful will be torn from it.

3 My son, do not forget my teaching,
but keep my commands in your heart,
2for they will prolong your life many
years
and bring you prosperity.

3Let love and faithfulness never leave you;
bind them around your neck,
write them on the tablet of your heart.
4Then you will win favor and a good name
in the sight of God and man.

5Trust in the LORD with all your heart
and lean not on your own understanding;
6in all your ways acknowledge him,
and he will make your paths straight.[f]

7Do not be wise in your own eyes;
fear the LORD and shun evil.
8This will bring health to your body
and nourishment to your bones.

9Honor the LORD with your wealth,
with the firstfruits of all your crops;
10then your barns will be filled to overflowing,
and your vats will brim over with new
wine.

11My son, do not despise the LORD's discipline
and do not resent his rebuke,
12because the LORD disciplines those he loves,
as a father[g] the son he delights in.

13Blessed is the man who finds wisdom,
the man who gains understanding,
14for she is more profitable than silver
and yields better returns than gold.
15She is more precious than rubies;
nothing you desire can compare with her.
16Long life is in her right hand;
in her left hand are riches and honor.
17Her ways are pleasant ways,
and all her paths are peace.
18She is a tree of life to those who embrace her;
those who lay hold of her will be blessed.

19By wisdom the LORD laid the earth's
foundations,
by understanding he set the heavens in
place;
20by his knowledge the deeps were divided,
and the clouds let drop the dew.

21My son, preserve sound judgment and
discernment,
do not let them out of your sight;
22they will be life for you,
an ornament to grace your neck.
23Then you will go on your way in safety,
and your foot will not stumble;

e 17 *Or covenant of her God* f 6 *Or will direct your paths*
g 12 Hebrew; Septuagint / *and he punishes*

24when you lie down, you will not be afraid;
when you lie down, your sleep will be sweet.
25Have no fear of sudden disaster
or of the ruin that overtakes the wicked,
26for the LORD will be your confidence
and will keep your foot from being snared.

27Do not withhold good from those who deserve it,
when it is in your power to act.
28Do not say to your neighbor,
"Come back later; I'll give it tomorrow"—
when you now have it with you.

29Do not plot harm against your neighbor,
who lives trustfully near you.
30Do not accuse a man for no reason—
when he has done you no harm.

31Do not envy a violent man
or choose any of his ways,
32for the LORD detests a perverse man
but takes the upright into his confidence.

33The LORD's curse is on the house of the wicked,
but he blesses the home of the righteous.
34He mocks proud mockers
but gives grace to the humble.
35The wise inherit honor,
but fools he holds up to shame.

4 Listen, my sons, to a father's instruction;
pay attention and gain understanding.
2I give you sound learning,
so do not forsake my teaching.
3When I was a boy in my father's house,
still tender, and an only child of my mother,
4he taught me and said,
"Lay hold of my words with all your heart;
keep my commands and you will live.
5Get wisdom, get understanding;
do not forget my words or swerve from them.
6Do not forsake wisdom, and she will protect you;
love her, and she will watch over you.
7Wisdom is supreme; therefore get wisdom.
Though it cost all you have,[h] get understanding.
8Esteem her, and she will exalt you;
embrace her, and she will honor you.
9She will set a garland of grace on your head
and present you with a crown of splendor."

10Listen, my son, accept what I say,
and the years of your life will be many.
11I guide you in the way of wisdom
and lead you along straight paths.
12When you walk, your steps will not be hampered;
when you run, you will not stumble.
13Hold on to instruction, do not let it go;
guard it well, for it is your life.
14Do not set foot on the path of the wicked
or walk in the way of evil men.
15Avoid it, do not travel on it;
turn from it and go on your way.
16For they cannot sleep till they do evil;
they are robbed of slumber till they make someone fall.
17They eat the bread of wickedness
and drink the wine of violence.

18The path of the righteous is like the first gleam of dawn,
shining ever brighter till the full light of day.
19But the way of the wicked is like deep darkness;
they do not know what makes them stumble.

20My son, pay attention to what I say;
listen closely to my words.
21Do not let them out of your sight,
keep them within your heart;
22for they are life to those who find them
and health to a man's whole body.
23Above all else, guard your heart,
for it is the wellspring of life.
24Put away perversity from your mouth;
keep corrupt talk far from your lips.
25Let your eyes look straight ahead,
fix your gaze directly before you.
26Make level[i] paths for your feet
and take only ways that are firm.
27Do not swerve to the right or the left;
keep your foot from evil.

[h]7 *Or Whatever else you get* [i]26 *Or Consider the*

5 My son, pay attention to my wisdom,
listen well to my words of insight,
2that you may maintain discretion
and your lips may preserve knowledge.
3For the lips of an adulteress drip honey,
and her speech is smoother than oil;
4but in the end she is bitter as gall,
sharp as a double-edged sword.
5Her feet go down to death;
her steps lead straight to the grave.[j]
6She gives no thought to the way of life;
her paths are crooked, but she knows it not.

7Now then, my sons, listen to me;
do not turn aside from what I say.
8Keep to a path far from her,
do not go near the door of her house,
9lest you give your best strength to others
and your years to one who is cruel,
10lest strangers feast on your wealth
and your toil enrich another man's house.
11At the end of your life you will groan,
when your flesh and body are spent.
12You will say, "How I hated discipline!
How my heart spurned correction!
13I would not obey my teachers
or listen to my instructors.
14I have come to the brink of utter ruin
in the midst of the whole assembly."

15Drink water from your own cistern,
running water from your own well.
16Should your springs overflow in the streets,
your streams of water in the public squares?
17Let them be yours alone,
never to be shared with strangers.
18May your fountain be blessed,
and may you rejoice in the wife of your youth.
19A loving doe, a graceful deer—
may her breasts satisfy you always,
may you ever be captivated by her love.
20Why be captivated, my son, by an adulteress?
Why embrace the bosom of another man's wife?

21For a man's ways are in full view of the LORD,
and he examines all his paths.
22The evil deeds of a wicked man ensnare him;
the cords of his sin hold him fast.
23He will die for lack of discipline,
led astray by his own great folly.

j5 Hebrew *Sheol*

1 / *Proverbs 6:1–19*
Bad Words

A CHILDHOOD TAUNT says, "Sticks and stones may break my bones, but words will never hurt me." The sentiment may be brave, but we know from painful memory that words can be exceedingly painful. Solomon's proverbs speak straightforwardly of the harm that words can work—harm when they are spoken to us, by us or about us. And for all their power to work evil, bad words can be surprisingly (and disconcertingly) pleasant to hear or to speak! The world is awash with bad words. The wise man or woman knows how to recognize them, not only so they can purge bad words from their own speech, but also to escape the menace of bad words from others.

Warming Up to God How have your words betrayed you this week—through malicious talk, gossip, sarcasm, rudeness or in other ways? Ask God to make you open to discovering how he wants you to talk.

Read Proverbs 6:1–19.

6 My son, if you have put up security for your neighbor,
if you have struck hands in pledge for another,
2if you have been trapped by what you said,
ensnared by the words of your mouth,
3then do this, my son, to free yourself,
since you have fallen into your neighbor's hands:
Go and humble yourself;

press your plea with your neighbor!
4 Allow no sleep to your eyes,
no slumber to your eyelids.
5 Free yourself, like a gazelle from the hand of the hunter,
like a bird from the snare of the fowler.

6 Go to the ant, you sluggard;
consider its ways and be wise!
7 It has no commander,
no overseer or ruler,
8 yet it stores its provisions in summer
and gathers its food at harvest.

9 How long will you lie there, you sluggard?
When will you get up from your sleep?
10 A little sleep, a little slumber,
a little folding of the hands to rest—
11 and poverty will come on you like a bandit
and scarcity like an armed man.[k]

12 A scoundrel and villain,
who goes about with a corrupt mouth,
13 who winks with his eye,
signals with his feet
and motions with his fingers,
14 who plots evil with deceit in his heart—
he always stirs up dissension.
15 Therefore disaster will overtake him in an instant;
he will suddenly be destroyed—without remedy.

16 There are six things the LORD hates,
seven that are detestable to him:
17 haughty eyes,
a lying tongue,
hands that shed innocent blood,
18 a heart that devises wicked schemes,
feet that are quick to rush into evil,
19 a false witness who pours out lies
and a man who stirs up dissension among brothers.

[k]11 *Or like a vagrant / and scarcity like a beggar*

Discovering the Word 1. What words and phrases are used to describe the effects of bad words (vv. 2, 12, 14–15, 17–19)? 2. Evil communication can occur without a word being spoken (vv. 12–14). 3. Why do you think a mischief-maker communicates in that way? 4. Why is *receiving* that kind of communication dangerous to you? 5. How are bad words a part of the seven things that are "detestable" to the Lord?

Applying the Word 1. Like smog, bad words are difficult to escape when they're "in the air." What can you do to reduce your exposure to such words in the coming weeks? 2. How can you resist adding to the pollution?

Responding in Prayer Bad words stir up dissention. Pray that your words will build unity.

Proverbs 6:20–35

20 My son, keep your father's commands
and do not forsake your mother's teaching.
21 Bind them upon your heart forever;
fasten them around your neck.
22 When you walk, they will guide you;
when you sleep, they will watch over you;
when you awake, they will speak to you.
23 For these commands are a lamp,
this teaching is a light,
and the corrections of discipline
are the way to life,
24 keeping you from the immoral woman,
from the smooth tongue of the wayward wife.
25 Do not lust in your heart after her beauty
or let her captivate you with her eyes,
26 for the prostitute reduces you to a loaf of bread,
and the adulteress preys upon your very life.
27 Can a man scoop fire into his lap
without his clothes being burned?
28 Can a man walk on hot coals
without his feet being scorched?
29 So is he who sleeps with another man's wife;
no one who touches her will go unpunished.
30 Men do not despise a thief if he steals

to satisfy his hunger when he is starving.
31Yet if he is caught, he must pay sevenfold,
though it costs him all the wealth of his house.
32But a man who commits adultery lacks judgment;
whoever does so destroys himself.
33Blows and disgrace are his lot,
and his shame will never be wiped away;
34for jealousy arouses a husband's fury,
and he will show no mercy when he takes revenge.
35He will not accept any compensation;
he will refuse the bribe, however great it is.

2 / *Proverbs 7*
The Simple

AS P. T. BARNUM was fond of saying, "A sucker is born every minute." The book of Proverbs agrees! Proverbs teaches through images and metaphors like that of the simple young man. The tale of his seduction serves as a concrete example of the way in which folly can capture a simple-minded person. From Solomon's point of view, every one of us is born "simple"—that is, gullible, credulous, naive. But while Barnum saw human gullibility as an opportunity for profit, the proverbs see the condition as a character weakness to be corrected. All around us people appeal to our gullibility in one area or another. If we're to escape with our money, health and integrity intact, we need to develop what the proverbs call *prudence.* The first practical step to wisdom is to identify the simpleton in ourselves. The proverbs in this study are a mirror which lets us see where and how we are naive. And more than that, they will set us on the road to wisdom.

Warming Up to God All of us would agree that young children are naive or simple in all areas of life. But all of us *remain* naive or simple in some areas. In what way might this be true of you?

Read Proverbs 7.

7 My son, keep my words
and store up my commands within you.
2Keep my commands and you will live;
guard my teachings as the apple of your eye.
3Bind them on your fingers;
write them on the tablet of your heart.
4Say to wisdom, "You are my sister,"
and call understanding your kinsman;
5they will keep you from the adulteress,
from the wayward wife with her seductive words.

6At the window of my house
I looked out through the lattice.
7I saw among the simple,
I noticed among the young men,
a youth who lacked judgment.
8He was going down the street near her corner,
walking along in the direction of her house
9at twilight, as the day was fading,
as the dark of night set in.

10Then out came a woman to meet him,
dressed like a prostitute and with crafty intent.
11(She is loud and defiant,
her feet never stay at home;
12now in the street, now in the squares,
at every corner she lurks.)
13She took hold of him and kissed him
and with a brazen face she said:

14"I have fellowship offerings[l] at home;
today I fulfilled my vows.
15So I came out to meet you;
I looked for you and have found you!
16I have covered my bed
with colored linens from Egypt.
17I have perfumed my bed
with myrrh, aloes and cinnamon.
18Come, let's drink deep of love till morning;
let's enjoy ourselves with love!
19My husband is not at home;
he has gone on a long journey.

[l]14 Traditionally *peace offerings*

20 He took his purse filled with money
and will not be home till full moon."
21 With persuasive words she led him astray;
she seduced him with her smooth talk.
22 All at once he followed her
like an ox going to the slaughter,
like a deer[m] stepping into a noose[n]
23 till an arrow pierces his liver,
like a bird darting into a snare,
little knowing it will cost him his life.

24 Now then, my sons, listen to me;
pay attention to what I say.
25 Do not let your heart turn to her ways
or stray into her paths.
26 Many are the victims she has brought down;
her slain are a mighty throng.
27 Her house is a highway to the grave,[o]
leading down to the chambers of death.

[m]22 Syriac (see also Septuagint); Hebrew *fool* [n]22 The meaning of the Hebrew for this line is uncertain. [o]27 Hebrew *Sheol*

Discovering the Word 1. Proverbs 7:6-23 gives us the first full-blown portrait of the simpleton. What does the seductress say that is probably true? 2. What does she say (or imply) that is actually false? 3. Men and women "without judgment" can be persuaded to do foolish things other than adultery. From your own recollections, describe a case of persuasion which follows the same pattern as Proverbs 7. 4. How are the comparisons to animals drawn in verses 22-23 appropriate? 5. Does the warning in verses 24-27 seem overly dramatic to you? Why or why not?

Applying the Word 1. All of us have spheres of living where we, like the simpleton in Proverbs 7, have little choice but to believe what we are told. What are some of these areas in your life? 2. It's one thing to know we're naive in this or that respect, and quite another to develop the character strength called *prudence*. What can you begin doing now that will make you more prudent in the future?

Responding in Prayer Jesus said, "Be as shrewd as snakes and as innocent as doves" (Mt 10:16). Pray for wisdom like that.

Proverbs 8

8 Does not wisdom call out?
Does not understanding raise her voice?
2 On the heights along the way,
where the paths meet, she takes her stand;
3 beside the gates leading into the city,
at the entrances, she cries aloud:
4 "To you, O men, I call out;
I raise my voice to all mankind.
5 You who are simple, gain prudence;
you who are foolish, gain understanding.
6 Listen, for I have worthy things to say;
I open my lips to speak what is right.
7 My mouth speaks what is true,
for my lips detest wickedness.
8 All the words of my mouth are just;
none of them is crooked or perverse.
9 To the discerning all of them are right;
they are faultless to those who have knowledge.
10 Choose my instruction instead of silver,
knowledge rather than choice gold,
11 for wisdom is more precious than rubies,
and nothing you desire can compare with her.

12 "I, wisdom, dwell together with prudence;
I possess knowledge and discretion.
13 To fear the LORD is to hate evil;
I hate pride and arrogance,
evil behavior and perverse speech.
14 Counsel and sound judgment are mine;
I have understanding and power.
15 By me kings reign
and rulers make laws that are just;
16 by me princes govern,
and all nobles who rule on earth.[p]
17 I love those who love me,
and those who seek me find me.
18 With me are riches and honor,
enduring wealth and prosperity.
19 My fruit is better than fine gold;
what I yield surpasses choice silver.
20 I walk in the way of righteousness,

[p]16 Many Hebrew manuscripts and Septuagint; most Hebrew manuscripts *and nobles—all righteous rulers*

along the paths of justice,
21bestowing wealth on those who love me
and making their treasuries full.

22"The LORD brought me forth as the first of his works,[q,r]
before his deeds of old;
23I was appointed[s] from eternity,
from the beginning, before the world began.
24When there were no oceans, I was given birth,
when there were no springs abounding with water;
25before the mountains were settled in place,
before the hills, I was given birth,
26before he made the earth or its fields
or any of the dust of the world.
27I was there when he set the heavens in place,
when he marked out the horizon on the face of the deep,
28when he established the clouds above
and fixed securely the fountains of the deep,
29when he gave the sea its boundary
so the waters would not overstep his command,
and when he marked out the foundations of the earth.
30 Then I was the craftsman at his side.
I was filled with delight day after day,
rejoicing always in his presence,
31rejoicing in his whole world
and delighting in mankind.

32"Now then, my sons, listen to me;
blessed are those who keep my ways.
33Listen to my instruction and be wise;
do not ignore it.
34Blessed is the man who listens to me,
watching daily at my doors,
waiting at my doorway.
35For whoever finds me finds life
and receives favor from the LORD.
36But whoever fails to find me harms himself;
all who hate me love death."

q22 Or *way*; or *dominion* r22 Or *The LORD possessed me at the beginning of his work*; or *The LORD brought me forth at the beginning of his work* s23 Or *fashioned*

3 / *Proverbs 9*
Two Dinner Invitations

AN INVITATION TO dinner is always welcome, until you get invitations to two *different* dinners, each held at the same time as the other. Then you have to decide which one to accept and which one to decline. Proverbs 9 presents this very dilemma—invitations to two dinners held simultaneously. How do you decide which invitation to accept? No doubt you'll make your decision based on many factors—the reputation of the host and hostess, the prospects for a good time, your own tastes in people and food. All these factors appear in the two invitations that conclude Solomon's introduction to the book of Proverbs. Other factors appear as well—such as how long you'll live and how prosperous you'll be. You see, these are no ordinary dinners, and the invitations come from no ordinary hostesses. Which one you attend will largely determine your health, your wealth and your happiness for the rest of your life.

Warming Up to God Where or how are you currently finding happiness in life?

Read Proverbs 9.

9 Wisdom has built her house;
she has hewn out its seven pillars.
2She has prepared her meat and mixed her wine;
she has also set her table.
3She has sent out her maids, and she calls
from the highest point of the city.
4"Let all who are simple come in here!"
she says to those who lack judgment.
5"Come, eat my food
and drink the wine I have mixed.
6Leave your simple ways and you will live;

walk in the way of understanding.

7"Whoever corrects a mocker invites insult;
whoever rebukes a wicked man incurs abuse.
8Do not rebuke a mocker or he will hate you;
rebuke a wise man and he will love you.
9Instruct a wise man and he will be wiser still;
teach a righteous man and he will add to his learning.

10"The fear of the LORD is the beginning of wisdom,
and knowledge of the Holy One is understanding.
11For through me your days will be many,
and years will be added to your life.
12If you are wise, your wisdom will reward you;
if you are a mocker, you alone will suffer."

13The woman Folly is loud;
she is undisciplined and without knowledge.
14She sits at the door of her house,
on a seat at the highest point of the city,
15calling out to those who pass by,
who go straight on their way.
16"Let all who are simple come in here!"
she says to those who lack judgment.
17"Stolen water is sweet;
food eaten in secret is delicious!"
18But little do they know that the dead are there,
that her guests are in the depths of the grave.[t]

[t]18 Hebrew *Sheol*

Discovering the Word 1. Do Lady Wisdom and Woman Folly invite the same people or different people to their feasts? Explain. 2. Which hostess has the greater resources to deploy in her guests' behalf? Explain. 3. What do verses 7–12 tell us about how Lady Wisdom imparts benefits to her guests? 4. After reading verse 10, do you think that knowledge and understanding must be explicitly Judeo-Christian in order to be genuine? Why or why not? 5. No matter which "invitation" you accept, your decision will result in both pleasure and pain. How do the pleasure and pain from dining at Lady Wisdom's house differ from the pleasure and pain one finds at Woman Folly's abode?

Applying the Word 1. Proverbs 9 is, of course, an extended metaphor—an allegory. Wisdom is *like* a wealthy woman inviting guests to a feast. What people do you know who embody the person of Lady Wisdom in their relationship to you? 2. In whom, or where, or in what circumstances have you encountered Woman Folly?

Responding in Prayer Pray that you would be made worthy of dinner with Lady Wisdom.

4 / *Proverbs 10*
Good Words

JESUS POWERFULLY UNDERSCORED the immense power of words to shape our destiny. Speaking of the final judgment, he said, "By your words you will be acquitted, and by your words you will be condemned" (Mt 12:37). He was reflecting a similar idea found in Proverbs 18:21: "The tongue has the power of life and death, and those who love it will eat its fruit."

Proverbs 6 displayed the awesome power for evil which words have. But they also have an awesome power for good. For all that, words are not magic; their power lies not so much in themselves as in the characters of those who speak them and those who hear them. You'll uncover some of the ways you can wisely fashion words for wholesome ends.

Warming Up to God Would you describe yourself as a person of few or many words? Explain.

Read Proverbs 10.

10 The proverbs of Solomon:
A wise son brings joy to his father,
but a foolish son grief to his mother.

2Ill-gotten treasures are of no value,
but righteousness delivers from death.

3The LORD does not let the righteous go hungry
but he thwarts the craving of the wicked.

4Lazy hands make a man poor,
but diligent hands bring wealth.

5He who gathers crops in summer is a wise son,
but he who sleeps during harvest is a disgraceful son.

6Blessings crown the head of the righteous,
but violence overwhelms the mouth of the wicked.[u]

7The memory of the righteous will be a blessing,
but the name of the wicked will rot.

8The wise in heart accept commands,
but a chattering fool comes to ruin.

9The man of integrity walks securely,
but he who takes crooked paths will be found out.

10He who winks maliciously causes grief,
and a chattering fool comes to ruin.

11The mouth of the righteous is a fountain of life,
but violence overwhelms the mouth of the wicked.

12Hatred stirs up dissension,
but love covers over all wrongs.

13Wisdom is found on the lips of the discerning,
but a rod is for the back of him who lacks judgment.

14Wise men store up knowledge,
but the mouth of a fool invites ruin.

15The wealth of the rich is their fortified city,
but poverty is the ruin of the poor.

16The wages of the righteous bring them life,
but the income of the wicked brings them punishment.

17He who heeds discipline shows the way to life,
but whoever ignores correction leads others astray.

18He who conceals his hatred has lying lips,
and whoever spreads slander is a fool.

19When words are many, sin is not absent,
but he who holds his tongue is wise.

20The tongue of the righteous is choice silver,
but the heart of the wicked is of little value.

21The lips of the righteous nourish many,
but fools die for lack of judgment.

22The blessing of the LORD brings wealth,
and he adds no trouble to it.

23A fool finds pleasure in evil conduct,
but a man of understanding delights in wisdom.

24What the wicked dreads will overtake him;
what the righteous desire will be granted.

25When the storm has swept by, the wicked are gone,
but the righteous stand firm forever.

26As vinegar to the teeth and smoke to the eyes,
so is a sluggard to those who send him.

27The fear of the LORD adds length to life,
but the years of the wicked are cut short.

28The prospect of the righteous is joy,
but the hopes of the wicked come to nothing.

29The way of the LORD is a refuge for the righteous,
but it is the ruin of those who do evil.

30The righteous will never be uprooted,
but the wicked will not remain in the land.

31The mouth of the righteous brings forth wisdom,
but a perverse tongue will be cut out.

[u]6 Or *but the mouth of the wicked conceals violence*; also in verse 11

32The lips of the righteous know what is
fitting,
but the mouth of the wicked only what is
perverse.

Discovering the Word 1. How are wise words and foolish words contrasted (vv. 8, 10, 13–14, 18–21, 31–32)? 2. The phrase "chattering fool" is used in verses 8 and 10. What images does it bring to mind? 3. Verse 19 insists that the mere quantity of words produces sin. 4. When have words been like "choice silver" (v. 20) and nourished you (v. 21)? 5. Sometimes we are able to say just the right thing in a situation. When have your lips known what was fitting (v. 32)?

Applying the Word 1. Now that you have surveyed what the proverbs say about good and bad speech, which do you think is easier—to rid yourself of unwholesome speech habits or to build wholesome speech habits? Explain. 2. What strategy might you employ to reduce or eliminate your wordiness? (Hint: don't ignore the help that a friend or spouse can provide in these settings.) 3. Who do you need to encourage with good words?

Responding in Prayer Thank God for those who have nourished you with good words. Pray that you will be like them.

Proverbs 11—12

11 The LORD abhors dishonest scales,
but accurate weights are his
delight.

2When pride comes, then comes disgrace,
but with humility comes wisdom.

3The integrity of the upright guides them,
but the unfaithful are destroyed by their
duplicity.

4Wealth is worthless in the day of wrath,
but righteousness delivers from death.

5The righteousness of the blameless makes a
straight way for them,
but the wicked are brought down by their
own wickedness.

6The righteousness of the upright delivers
them,
but the unfaithful are trapped by evil
desires.

7When a wicked man dies, his hope perishes;
all he expected from his power comes to
nothing.

8The righteous man is rescued from trouble,
and it comes on the wicked instead.

9With his mouth the godless destroys his
neighbor,
but through knowledge the righteous
escape.

10When the righteous prosper, the city rejoices;
when the wicked perish, there are shouts of
joy.

11Through the blessing of the upright a city is
exalted,
but by the mouth of the wicked it is
destroyed.

12A man who lacks judgment derides his
neighbor,
but a man of understanding holds his
tongue.

13A gossip betrays a confidence,
but a trustworthy man keeps a secret.

14For lack of guidance a nation falls,
but many advisers make victory sure.

15He who puts up security for another will
surely suffer,
but whoever refuses to strike hands in
pledge is safe.

16A kindhearted woman gains respect,
but ruthless men gain only wealth.

17A kind man benefits himself,
but a cruel man brings trouble on himself.

18The wicked man earns deceptive wages,
but he who sows righteousness reaps a sure
reward.

19The truly righteous man attains life,

but he who pursues evil goes to his death.

20The LORD detests men of perverse heart
but he delights in those whose ways are blameless.

21Be sure of this: The wicked will not go unpunished,
but those who are righteous will go free.

22Like a gold ring in a pig's snout
is a beautiful woman who shows no discretion.

23The desire of the righteous ends only in good,
but the hope of the wicked only in wrath.

24One man gives freely, yet gains even more;
another withholds unduly, but comes to poverty.

25A generous man will prosper;
he who refreshes others will himself be refreshed.

26People curse the man who hoards grain,
but blessing crowns him who is willing to sell.

27He who seeks good finds goodwill,
but evil comes to him who searches for it.

28Whoever trusts in his riches will fall,
but the righteous will thrive like a green leaf.

29He who brings trouble on his family will inherit only wind,
and the fool will be servant to the wise.

30The fruit of the righteous is a tree of life,
and he who wins souls is wise.

31If the righteous receive their due on earth,
how much more the ungodly and the sinner!

12 Whoever loves discipline loves knowledge,
but he who hates correction is stupid.

2A good man obtains favor from the LORD,
but the LORD condemns a crafty man.

3A man cannot be established through wickedness,
but the righteous cannot be uprooted.

4A wife of noble character is her husband's crown,
but a disgraceful wife is like decay in his bones.

5The plans of the righteous are just,
but the advice of the wicked is deceitful.

6The words of the wicked lie in wait for blood,
but the speech of the upright rescues them.

7Wicked men are overthrown and are no more,
but the house of the righteous stands firm.

8A man is praised according to his wisdom,
but men with warped minds are despised.

9Better to be a nobody and yet have a servant
than pretend to be somebody and have no food.

10A righteous man cares for the needs of his animal,
but the kindest acts of the wicked are cruel.

11He who works his land will have abundant food,
but he who chases fantasies lacks judgment.

12The wicked desire the plunder of evil men,
but the root of the righteous flourishes.

13An evil man is trapped by his sinful talk,
but a righteous man escapes trouble.

14From the fruit of his lips a man is filled with good things
as surely as the work of his hands rewards him.

15The way of a fool seems right to him,
but a wise man listens to advice.

16A fool shows his annoyance at once,
but a prudent man overlooks an insult.

17A truthful witness gives honest testimony,
but a false witness tells lies.

18Reckless words pierce like a sword,
but the tongue of the wise brings healing.

19Truthful lips endure forever,
but a lying tongue lasts only a moment.

20There is deceit in the hearts of those who plot evil,
but joy for those who promote peace.

21No harm befalls the righteous,

but the wicked have their fill of trouble.

22The LORD detests lying lips,
but he delights in men who are truthful.

23A prudent man keeps his knowledge to himself,
but the heart of fools blurts out folly.

24Diligent hands will rule,
but laziness ends in slave labor.

25An anxious heart weighs a man down,
but a kind word cheers him up.

26A righteous man is cautious in friendship,[v]
but the way of the wicked leads them astray.

27The lazy man does not roast[w] his game,
but the diligent man prizes his possessions.

28In the way of righteousness there is life;
along that path is immortality.

[v]26 Or *man is a guide to his neighbor* [w]27 The meaning of the Hebrew for this word is uncertain.

5 / *Proverbs 13—14*
Finding Wisdom

A FACTORY MANAGER'S assembly line was down, so he summoned a consultant to suggest remedies. After inspecting a huge piece of machinery, the consultant produced a small hammer, reached between some gears, and gave a small tap. The assembly line worked again, and the factory manager got a bill for $10,000. Aghast, the manager demanded another bill itemizing the charges. When it came, the second bill read: Tapping with hammer: $5.00/Knowing where to tap: $9,995.00.

Wisdom is "knowing where to tap." When we need some tapping done, we'll do it ourselves if we're wise enough; otherwise we'll need someone who knows where to tap. The book of Proverbs points us in both directions—by showing us "where to tap" in many areas of life, and by helping us seek out those who understand what we cannot yet perceive. The proverbs not only show us wisdom, they show us how to seek wisdom.

Warming Up to God Who do you think of when you ponder "wisdom"? Thank God for that person and what he or she has taught you as you begin.

Read Proverbs 13—14.

13 A wise son heeds his father's instruction,
but a mocker does not listen to rebuke.

2From the fruit of his lips a man enjoys good things,
but the unfaithful have a craving for violence.

3He who guards his lips guards his life,
but he who speaks rashly will come to ruin.

4The sluggard craves and gets nothing,
but the desires of the diligent are fully satisfied.

5The righteous hate what is false,
but the wicked bring shame and disgrace.

6Righteousness guards the man of integrity,
but wickedness overthrows the sinner.

7One man pretends to be rich, yet has nothing;
another pretends to be poor, yet has great wealth.

8A man's riches may ransom his life,
but a poor man hears no threat.

9The light of the righteous shines brightly,
but the lamp of the wicked is snuffed out.

10Pride only breeds quarrels,
but wisdom is found in those who take advice.

11Dishonest money dwindles away,
but he who gathers money little by little makes it grow.

[12]Hope deferred makes the heart sick,
but a longing fulfilled is a tree of life.

[13]He who scorns instruction will pay for it,
but he who respects a command is rewarded.

[14]The teaching of the wise is a fountain of life,
turning a man from the snares of death.

[15]Good understanding wins favor,
but the way of the unfaithful is hard.[x]

[16]Every prudent man acts out of knowledge,
but a fool exposes his folly.

[17]A wicked messenger falls into trouble,
but a trustworthy envoy brings healing.

[18]He who ignores discipline comes to poverty and shame,
but whoever heeds correction is honored.

[19]A longing fulfilled is sweet to the soul,
but fools detest turning from evil.

[20]He who walks with the wise grows wise,
but a companion of fools suffers harm.

[21]Misfortune pursues the sinner,
but prosperity is the reward of the righteous.

[22]A good man leaves an inheritance for his children's children,
but a sinner's wealth is stored up for the righteous.

[23]A poor man's field may produce abundant food,
but injustice sweeps it away.

[24]He who spares the rod hates his son,
but he who loves him is careful to discipline him.

[25]The righteous eat to their hearts' content,
but the stomach of the wicked goes hungry.

14 The wise woman builds her house,
but with her own hands the foolish one tears hers down.

[2]He whose walk is upright fears the LORD,
but he whose ways are devious despises him.

[3]A fool's talk brings a rod to his back,
but the lips of the wise protect them.

[4]Where there are no oxen, the manger is empty,
but from the strength of an ox comes an abundant harvest.

[5]A truthful witness does not deceive,
but a false witness pours out lies.

[6]The mocker seeks wisdom and finds none,
but knowledge comes easily to the discerning.

[7]Stay away from a foolish man,
for you will not find knowledge on his lips.

[8]The wisdom of the prudent is to give thought to their ways,
but the folly of fools is deception.

[9]Fools mock at making amends for sin,
but goodwill is found among the upright.

[10]Each heart knows its own bitterness,
and no one else can share its joy.

[11]The house of the wicked will be destroyed,
but the tent of the upright will flourish.

[12]There is a way that seems right to a man,
but in the end it leads to death.

[13]Even in laughter the heart may ache,
and joy may end in grief.

[14]The faithless will be fully repaid for their ways,
and the good man rewarded for his.

[15]A simple man believes anything,
but a prudent man gives thought to his steps.

[16]A wise man fears the LORD and shuns evil,
but a fool is hotheaded and reckless.

[17]A quick-tempered man does foolish things,
and a crafty man is hated.

[18]The simple inherit folly,
but the prudent are crowned with knowledge.

[19]Evil men will bow down in the presence of the good,
and the wicked at the gates of the righteous.

[x]15 Or *unfaithful does not endure*

20The poor are shunned even by their
neighbors,
but the rich have many friends.

21He who despises his neighbor sins,
but blessed is he who is kind to the needy.

22Do not those who plot evil go astray?
But those who plan what is good find[y]
love and faithfulness.

23All hard work brings a profit,
but mere talk leads only to poverty.

24The wealth of the wise is their crown,
but the folly of fools yields folly.

25A truthful witness saves lives,
but a false witness is deceitful.

26He who fears the LORD has a secure fortress,
and for his children it will be a refuge.

27The fear of the LORD is a fountain of life,
turning a man from the snares of death.

28A large population is a king's glory,
but without subjects a prince is ruined.

29A patient man has great understanding,
but a quick-tempered man displays folly.

30A heart at peace gives life to the body,
but envy rots the bones.

31He who oppresses the poor shows contempt
for their Maker,
but whoever is kind to the needy honors
God.

32When calamity comes, the wicked are brought
down,
but even in death the righteous have a
refuge.

33Wisdom reposes in the heart of the discerning
and even among fools she lets herself be
known.[z]

34Righteousness exalts a nation,
but sin is a disgrace to any people.

35A king delights in a wise servant,
but a shameful servant incurs his wrath.

y22 Or *show* z33 Hebrew; Septuagint and Syriac / *but in the heart of fools she is not known*

Discovering the Word 1. We often say that someone is "street smart," meaning that the person has become shrewd through enrollment in the "School of Hard Knocks." Can we get wisdom without the "hard knocks"? Defend your answer from the proverbs themselves. 2. In Solomon's day, the wisdom of Proverbs was probably taught in two places—the home and wisdom schools. Today the "wisdom school" takes many forms, from apprenticeships in trade unions to enrollment in universities. Using the proverbs above as a guide, what would you look for when trying to select such a school? 3. What do you learn from these proverbs about advice? 4. Why do you think there is often such a huge gulf between what seems right to us and what is truly wise (14:12)? 5. Wanting wisdom isn't enough. To get it we must be able to receive it. From each of the proverbs in this study, suggest a character weakness which hinders a person from becoming wise—one character weakness per proverb.

Applying the Word 1. In Proverbs to seek wisdom is to seek skill. What specific types of skill would you like to acquire in your work or in your relationships? 2. What can you do in the week ahead to begin acquiring wisdom?

Responding in Prayer Proverbs 14:33 says, "Wisdom reposes in the heart of the discerning." Pray for a discerning heart.

6 / *Proverbs 15—16*
Prayer

IF YOU SURVEYED books on prayer in a Christian bookstore, you'd find varied and often conflicting advice. Some authorities insist that successful prayer is scheduled; others favor impromptu prayer. One writer says fasting should accompany prayer, but another tells us to pray in any circumstance. Still another says that prayer is best done when alone, though someone else urges us to join with others. Some claim that prayer requires careful preparation and thought, while a conflicting authority says prayer should flow spontaneously from our hearts. Wisdom is needed as much for prayer as for any other area of human living. These proverbs furnish us wisdom for bringing our requests to God as we seek to live wisely.

Warming Up to God What has your pattern of prayer been over recent days, weeks, months, years? Where are you struggling? How are you growing? Spend some time reflecting on your prayer life.

Read Proverbs 15—16.

15 A gentle answer turns away wrath,
but a harsh word stirs up anger.

[2]The tongue of the wise
commends knowledge,
but the mouth of the fool gushes folly.

[3]The eyes of the LORD are everywhere,
keeping watch on the wicked and the good.

[4]The tongue that brings healing is a tree of life,
but a deceitful tongue crushes the spirit.

[5]A fool spurns his father's discipline,
but whoever heeds correction shows prudence.

[6]The house of the righteous contains great treasure,
but the income of the wicked brings them trouble.

[7]The lips of the wise spread knowledge;
not so the hearts of fools.

[8]The LORD detests the sacrifice of the wicked,
but the prayer of the upright pleases him.

[9]The LORD detests the way of the wicked
but he loves those who pursue righteousness.

[10]Stern discipline awaits him who leaves the path;
he who hates correction will die.

[11]Death and Destruction[a] lie open before the LORD—
how much more the hearts of men!

[12]A mocker resents correction;
he will not consult the wise.

[13]A happy heart makes the face cheerful,
but heartache crushes the spirit.

[14]The discerning heart seeks knowledge,
but the mouth of a fool feeds on folly.

[15]All the days of the oppressed are wretched,
but the cheerful heart has a continual feast.

[16]Better a little with the fear of the LORD
than great wealth with turmoil.

[17]Better a meal of vegetables where there is love
than a fattened calf with hatred.

[18]A hot-tempered man stirs up dissension,
but a patient man calms a quarrel.

[19]The way of the sluggard is blocked with thorns,
but the path of the upright is a highway.

[20]A wise son brings joy to his father,
but a foolish man despises his mother.

[21]Folly delights a man who lacks judgment,
but a man of understanding keeps a straight course.

[22]Plans fail for lack of counsel,
but with many advisers they succeed.

[23]A man finds joy in giving an apt reply—
and how good is a timely word!

[24]The path of life leads upward for the wise
to keep him from going down to the grave.[b]

[25]The LORD tears down the proud man's house
but he keeps the widow's boundaries intact.

[26]The LORD detests the thoughts of the wicked,
but those of the pure are pleasing to him.

[27]A greedy man brings trouble to his family,
but he who hates bribes will live.

[28]The heart of the righteous weighs its answers,
but the mouth of the wicked gushes evil.

[29]The LORD is far from the wicked
but he hears the prayer of the righteous.

[30]A cheerful look brings joy to the heart,
and good news gives health to the bones.

[31]He who listens to a life-giving rebuke

[a]11 Hebrew *Sheol and Abaddon* [b]24 Hebrew *Sheol*

will be at home among the wise.

32He who ignores discipline despises himself,
but whoever heeds correction gains understanding.

33The fear of the LORD teaches a man wisdom,[c]
and humility comes before honor.

16 To man belong the plans of the heart,
but from the LORD comes the reply of the tongue.

2All a man's ways seem innocent to him,
but motives are weighed by the LORD.

3Commit to the LORD whatever you do,
and your plans will succeed.

4The LORD works out everything for his own ends—
even the wicked for a day of disaster.

5The LORD detests all the proud of heart.
Be sure of this: They will not go unpunished.

6Through love and faithfulness sin is atoned for;
through the fear of the LORD a man avoids evil.

7When a man's ways are pleasing to the LORD,
he makes even his enemies live at peace with him.

8Better a little with righteousness
than much gain with injustice.

9In his heart a man plans his course,
but the LORD determines his steps.

10The lips of a king speak as an oracle,
and his mouth should not betray justice.

11Honest scales and balances are from the LORD;
all the weights in the bag are of his making.

12Kings detest wrongdoing,
for a throne is established through righteousness.

13Kings take pleasure in honest lips;
they value a man who speaks the truth.

14A king's wrath is a messenger of death,
but a wise man will appease it.

15When a king's face brightens, it means life;
his favor is like a rain cloud in spring.

16How much better to get wisdom than gold,
to choose understanding rather than silver!

17The highway of the upright avoids evil;
he who guards his way guards his life.

18Pride goes before destruction,
a haughty spirit before a fall.

19Better to be lowly in spirit and among the oppressed
than to share plunder with the proud.

20Whoever gives heed to instruction prospers,
and blessed is he who trusts in the LORD.

21The wise in heart are called discerning,
and pleasant words promote instruction.[d]

22Understanding is a fountain of life to those who have it,
but folly brings punishment to fools.

23A wise man's heart guides his mouth,
and his lips promote instruction.[e]

24Pleasant words are a honeycomb,
sweet to the soul and healing to the bones.

25There is a way that seems right to a man,
but in the end it leads to death.

26The laborer's appetite works for him;
his hunger drives him on.

27A scoundrel plots evil,
and his speech is like a scorching fire.

28A perverse man stirs up dissension,
and a gossip separates close friends.

29A violent man entices his neighbor
and leads him down a path that is not good.

30He who winks with his eye is plotting perversity;
he who purses his lips is bent on evil.

31Gray hair is a crown of splendor;
it is attained by a righteous life.

32Better a patient man than a warrior,

[c]33 Or *Wisdom teaches the fear of the LORD* [d]21 Or *words make a man persuasive* [e]23 Or *mouth / and makes his lips persuasive*

a man who controls his temper than one
who takes a city.

[33]The lot is cast into the lap,
but its every decision is from the LORD.

Discovering the Word 1. In contrast to many books on prayer, Proverbs 15:8 and 15:29 ignore the context and style of praying to focus on another factor. What is it? 2. Why is this factor sufficient by itself to account for whether God hears our prayers or not? 3. Proverbs 28:13 and other passages tell us that sin is present in everyone. How, then, can we ever be called "upright" or "righteous" in the sense of 15:8 or 15:29? 4. What does it mean to *commit* something to the Lord (16:3)? 5. What part do you think prayer plays in committing whatever you do to the Lord? 6. Proverbs 16:3 seems to promise unqualified success to those who commit their plans to the Lord. If this is not a "blank check" (and it's probably not), what is presupposed about our plans here?

Applying the Word 1. Think a moment about your own prayers. How might you begin praying more wisely? 2. In what ways does your character need to change so that your prayers will be those of the righteous?

Responding in Prayer Ask God to teach you how to pray.

7 / *Proverbs 17—18*
Avoiding the Fool

PROVERBS 27:22 MAKES one very clear point about fools—they're incorrigible: "Though you grind a fool in a mortar, grinding him like grain with a pestle, you will not remove his folly from him." But if fools can't be reformed, why do we find such an abundance of proverbs about them? The answer is simple—to help us recognize fools, their foolish behavior, and to warn us about the consequences of both. Our greatest danger from fools is meeting them unexpectedly, not recognizing them until it's too late. Recognizing and avoiding fools is our only defense from being undone by their folly. Defensive driving techniques protect us from foolish drivers. The proverbs in this study equip us for "defensive living."

Warming Up to God One of the signs of a fool we'll explore in this passage is foolish talk. What foolish talk (gossip, lies and so on) do you need to confess to God as you begin?

Read Proverbs 17—18.

17 Better a dry crust with peace and quiet
than a house full of feasting,[f] with strife.

[2]A wise servant will rule over a disgraceful son,
and will share the inheritance as one of the brothers.

[3]The crucible for silver and the furnace for gold,
but the LORD tests the heart.

[4]A wicked man listens to evil lips;
a liar pays attention to a malicious tongue.

[5]He who mocks the poor shows contempt for their Maker;
whoever gloats over disaster will not go unpunished.

[6]Children's children are a crown to the aged,
and parents are the pride of their children.

[7]Arrogant[g] lips are unsuited to a fool—
how much worse lying lips to a ruler!

[8]A bribe is a charm to the one who gives it;
wherever he turns, he succeeds.

[9]He who covers over an offense promotes love,
but whoever repeats the matter separates close friends.

[10]A rebuke impresses a man of discernment
more than a hundred lashes a fool.

f1 Hebrew *sacrifices* g7 Or *Eloquent*

11 An evil man is bent only on rebellion;
a merciless official will be sent against him.

12 Better to meet a bear robbed of her cubs
than a fool in his folly.

13 If a man pays back evil for good,
evil will never leave his house.

14 Starting a quarrel is like breaching a dam;
so drop the matter before a dispute breaks out.

15 Acquitting the guilty and condemning the innocent—
the LORD detests them both.

16 Of what use is money in the hand of a fool,
since he has no desire to get wisdom?

17 A friend loves at all times,
and a brother is born for adversity.

18 A man lacking in judgment strikes hands in pledge
and puts up security for his neighbor.

19 He who loves a quarrel loves sin;
he who builds a high gate invites destruction.

20 A man of perverse heart does not prosper;
he whose tongue is deceitful falls into trouble.

21 To have a fool for a son brings grief;
there is no joy for the father of a fool.

22 A cheerful heart is good medicine,
but a crushed spirit dries up the bones.

23 A wicked man accepts a bribe in secret
to pervert the course of justice.

24 A discerning man keeps wisdom in view,
but a fool's eyes wander to the ends of the earth.

25 A foolish son brings grief to his father
and bitterness to the one who bore him.

26 It is not good to punish an innocent man,
or to flog officials for their integrity.

27 A man of knowledge uses words with restraint,
and a man of understanding is even-tempered.

28 Even a fool is thought wise if he keeps silent,
and discerning if he holds his tongue.

18

An unfriendly man pursues selfish ends;
he defies all sound judgment.

2 A fool finds no pleasure in understanding
but delights in airing his own opinions.

3 When wickedness comes, so does contempt,
and with shame comes disgrace.

4 The words of a man's mouth are deep waters,
but the fountain of wisdom is a bubbling brook.

5 It is not good to be partial to the wicked
or to deprive the innocent of justice.

6 A fool's lips bring him strife,
and his mouth invites a beating.

7 A fool's mouth is his undoing,
and his lips are a snare to his soul.

8 The words of a gossip are like choice morsels;
they go down to a man's inmost parts.

9 One who is slack in his work
is brother to one who destroys.

10 The name of the LORD is a strong tower;
the righteous run to it and are safe.

11 The wealth of the rich is their fortified city;
they imagine it an unscalable wall.

12 Before his downfall a man's heart is proud,
but humility comes before honor.

13 He who answers before listening—
that is his folly and his shame.

14 A man's spirit sustains him in sickness,
but a crushed spirit who can bear?

15 The heart of the discerning acquires knowledge;
the ears of the wise seek it out.

16 A gift opens the way for the giver
and ushers him into the presence of the great.

17 The first to present his case seems right,
till another comes forward and questions him.

18Casting the lot settles disputes
and keeps strong opponents apart.

19An offended brother is more unyielding than
a fortified city,
and disputes are like the barred gates of a
citadel.

20From the fruit of his mouth a man's stomach
is filled;
with the harvest from his lips he is
satisfied.

21The tongue has the power of life and death,
and those who love it will eat its fruit.

22He who finds a wife finds what is good
and receives favor from the LORD.

23A poor man pleads for mercy,
but a rich man answers harshly.

24A man of many companions may come to
ruin,
but there is a friend who sticks closer than
a brother.

Discovering the Word 1. Which verses in Proverbs 17—18 speak about fools? 2. Proverbs 17:12 poses a riddle—why are you better off meeting a rampaging mother bear rather than meeting a fool in his folly? 3. Describe an episode from your experience or from the experience of someone you know which illustrates the point of Proverbs 17:12. 4. Proverbs 18:2 tells us that opinionated people are apt to be fools—they're always ready with a viewpoint and ever eager to broadcast it. How would you expect a prudent or wise person to behave differently from the fool? 5. When have you seen a fool's mouth become his or her undoing (18:17)? 6. How does 18:2 account for the truth of 18:7?

Applying the Word 1. Jesus warned, "Do not judge, or you too will be judged" (Mt 7:1). When we use the proverbs about the fool to evaluate people and conclude they are indeed foolish, do we ignore Jesus' warning? Why or why not? 2. What areas of your own character that might need work do these proverbs point to?

Responding in Prayer Who do you know that has been taken in by a fool? Pray for that person.

8 / *Proverbs 19*
Giving

WITH THE POOR come knotty questions for all who view them with compassion: How can I meet so much need from my limited resources? How do I choose whom to help and whom to pass by? How do I balance the needs of the poor with the requests for help from my children, my aged parents or my extended family? The proverbs in this study help us in two ways. First, they guide us through the moral conflicts we encounter when confronted with the material neediness of others. Second, they give an antidote to the folly which exalts acquisitiveness as a social and economic virtue. Our prosperity, it turns out, may be a result of our *giving* rather than our getting.

Warming Up to God Recall a time when you have been in need and received a gift that encouraged you. Thank God for that provision.

Read Proverbs 19.

19 Better a poor man whose walk is
blameless
than a fool whose lips are
perverse.

2It is not good to have zeal without
knowledge,
nor to be hasty and miss the way.

3A man's own folly ruins his life,
yet his heart rages against the LORD.

4Wealth brings many friends,
but a poor man's friend deserts him.

5A false witness will not go unpunished,
and he who pours out lies will not go free.

6Many curry favor with a ruler,
and everyone is the friend of a man who gives gifts.

7A poor man is shunned by all his relatives—
how much more do his friends avoid him!
Though he pursues them with pleading,
they are nowhere to be found.[h]

8He who gets wisdom loves his own soul;
he who cherishes understanding prospers.

9A false witness will not go unpunished,
and he who pours out lies will perish.

10It is not fitting for a fool to live in luxury—
how much worse for a slave to rule over princes!

11A man's wisdom gives him patience;
it is to his glory to overlook an offense.

12A king's rage is like the roar of a lion,
but his favor is like dew on the grass.

13A foolish son is his father's ruin,
and a quarrelsome wife is like a constant dripping.

14Houses and wealth are inherited from parents,
but a prudent wife is from the LORD.

15Laziness brings on deep sleep,
and the shiftless man goes hungry.

16He who obeys instructions guards his life,
but he who is contemptuous of his ways will die.

17He who is kind to the poor lends to the LORD,
and he will reward him for what he has done.

18Discipline your son, for in that there is hope;
do not be a willing party to his death.

19A hot-tempered man must pay the penalty;
if you rescue him, you will have to do it again.

20Listen to advice and accept instruction,
and in the end you will be wise.

21Many are the plans in a man's heart,
but it is the LORD's purpose that prevails.

22What a man desires is unfailing love[i];
better to be poor than a liar.

23The fear of the LORD leads to life:
Then one rests content, untouched by trouble.

24The sluggard buries his hand in the dish;
he will not even bring it back to his mouth!

25Flog a mocker, and the simple will learn prudence;
rebuke a discerning man, and he will gain knowledge.

26He who robs his father and drives out his mother
is a son who brings shame and disgrace.

27Stop listening to instruction, my son,
and you will stray from the words of knowledge.

28A corrupt witness mocks at justice,
and the mouth of the wicked gulps down evil.

29Penalties are prepared for mockers,
and beatings for the backs of fools.

[h]7 The meaning of the Hebrew for this sentence is uncertain. [i]22 Or *A man's greed is his shame*

Discovering the Word 1. When is it better to be poor (vv. 1, 22)? 2. What do you learn about the difficulties of poverty from Proverbs 19 (vv. 3, 7)? 3. What experience have you had with the problem mentioned in verse 6? 4. How can we avoid that problem? 5. Verse 17 implies a motive for giving that is almost never mentioned or, if mentioned, viewed as sub-Christian. What is it? 6. Why do you think people are uncomfortable with that kind of motive?

Applying the Word 1. When is giving to the poor difficult for you? 2. Beginning this week, how can your giving to the poor reflect the wisdom of these proverbs?

Responding in Prayer Pray for "unfailing love" (v. 22) that will allow you to give as God would want you to.

Proverbs 20

20 Wine is a mocker and beer a brawler;
whoever is led astray by them is not wise.

2A king's wrath is like the roar of a lion;
he who angers him forfeits his life.

3It is to a man's honor to avoid strife,
but every fool is quick to quarrel.

4A sluggard does not plow in season;
so at harvest time he looks but finds nothing.

5The purposes of a man's heart are deep waters,
but a man of understanding draws them out.

6Many a man claims to have unfailing love,
but a faithful man who can find?

7The righteous man leads a blameless life;
blessed are his children after him.

8When a king sits on his throne to judge,
he winnows out all evil with his eyes.

9Who can say, "I have kept my heart pure;
I am clean and without sin"?

10Differing weights and differing measures—
the LORD detests them both.

11Even a child is known by his actions,
by whether his conduct is pure and right.

12Ears that hear and eyes that see—
the LORD has made them both.

13Do not love sleep or you will grow poor;
stay awake and you will have food to spare.

14"It's no good, it's no good!" says the buyer;
then off he goes and boasts about his purchase.

15Gold there is, and rubies in abundance,
but lips that speak knowledge are a rare jewel.

16Take the garment of one who puts up security for a stranger;
hold it in pledge if he does it for a wayward woman.

17Food gained by fraud tastes sweet to a man,
but he ends up with a mouth full of gravel.

18Make plans by seeking advice;
if you wage war, obtain guidance.

19A gossip betrays a confidence;
so avoid a man who talks too much.

20If a man curses his father or mother,
his lamp will be snuffed out in pitch darkness.

21An inheritance quickly gained at the beginning
will not be blessed at the end.

22Do not say, "I'll pay you back for this wrong!"
Wait for the LORD, and he will deliver you.

23The LORD detests differing weights,
and dishonest scales do not please him.

24A man's steps are directed by the LORD.
How then can anyone understand his own way?

25It is a trap for a man to dedicate something rashly
and only later to consider his vows.

26A wise king winnows out the wicked;
he drives the threshing wheel over them.

27The lamp of the LORD searches the spirit of a man[j];
it searches out his inmost being.

28Love and faithfulness keep a king safe;
through love his throne is made secure.

29The glory of young men is their strength,
gray hair the splendor of the old.

30Blows and wounds cleanse away evil,
and beatings purge the inmost being.

j27 Or *The spirit of man is the LORD's lamp*

9 / *Proverbs 21*
Planning the Future

NO DOUBT YOU'VE glanced once or twice at an astrologer's predictions in the newspaper. Even if you felt guilty or silly for doing it, you'd hardly fault yourself for wanting every possible advantage in planning your future. Planning for the future, after all, is a major industry. Hundreds of billions of dollars ride on the forecasts of economists, investment counselors, analysts of every sort, and even astrologers! Legions of advisors will sell you opinions on what will happen in the near term and long term; whether or not you take their advice, someone else will. And that person's actions may in turn affect your prosperity, health and happiness. For all their focus on the here and now, the proverbs keep a canny eye on the future. Many proverbs, in fact, offer wisdom on how to make plans, why to make them, and what we can expect of the best plans we make. With these proverbs you'll begin training for planning your future.

Warming Up to God How often do you think about and plan for the future?

Read Proverbs 21.

21 The king's heart is in the hand of
the LORD;
he directs it like a watercourse
wherever he pleases.

2All a man's ways seem right to him,
but the LORD weighs the heart.

3To do what is right and just
is more acceptable to the LORD than
sacrifice.

4Haughty eyes and a proud heart,
the lamp of the wicked, are sin!

5The plans of the diligent lead to profit
as surely as haste leads to poverty.

6A fortune made by a lying tongue
is a fleeting vapor and a deadly snare.[k]

7The violence of the wicked will drag them
away,
for they refuse to do what is right.

8The way of the guilty is devious,
but the conduct of the innocent is upright.

9Better to live on a corner of the roof
than share a house with a quarrelsome
wife.

10The wicked man craves evil;
his neighbor gets no mercy from him.

11When a mocker is punished, the simple gain
wisdom;
when a wise man is instructed, he gets
knowledge.

12The Righteous One[l] takes note of the house
of the wicked
and brings the wicked to ruin.

13If a man shuts his ears to the cry of the poor,
he too will cry out and not be answered.

14A gift given in secret soothes anger,
and a bribe concealed in the cloak pacifies
great wrath.

15When justice is done, it brings joy to the
righteous
but terror to evildoers.

16A man who strays from the path of
understanding
comes to rest in the company of the dead.

17He who loves pleasure will become poor;
whoever loves wine and oil will never be
rich.

18The wicked become a ransom for the
righteous,
and the unfaithful for the upright.

19Better to live in a desert
than with a quarrelsome and ill-tempered
wife.

20In the house of the wise are stores of choice
food and oil,
but a foolish man devours all he has.

21He who pursues righteousness and love

k6 Some Hebrew manuscripts, Septuagint and Vulgate; most Hebrew manuscripts *vapor for those who seek death* l12 Or *The righteous man* finds life, prosperity[m] and honor.

22 A wise man attacks the city of the mighty
and pulls down the stronghold in which they trust.

23 He who guards his mouth and his tongue
keeps himself from calamity.

24 The proud and arrogant man—"Mocker" is his name;
he behaves with overweening pride.

25 The sluggard's craving will be the death of him,
because his hands refuse to work.

26 All day long he craves for more,
but the righteous give without sparing.

27 The sacrifice of the wicked is detestable—
how much more so when brought with evil intent!

28 A false witness will perish,
and whoever listens to him will be destroyed forever.[n]

29 A wicked man puts up a bold front,
but an upright man gives thought to his ways.

30 There is no wisdom, no insight, no plan
that can succeed against the LORD.

31 The horse is made ready for the day of battle,
but victory rests with the LORD.

[m] *21 Or righteousness* [n] *28 Or / but the words of an obedient man will live on*

Discovering the Word 1. The proverbs insist that character affects the success or failure of the plans a person makes. What character qualities mentioned in Proverbs 21 hinder our efforts to plan for the future (vv. 1–8, 16–17, 20–21, 23–26, 29–31)? 2. We usually evaluate a plan according to its merits, not on the basis of the character of the planner. Why does a planner's character make a difference? 3. Verse 2 points to a trap that we often fall into. Describe it. 4. Verse 5 says that a good plan by itself is not enough to yield success. Suppose you plan a picnic for a large number of people. Suppose further that you are diligent. How would your actions differ from those of a person who was not diligent? 5. Why do you think verse 21 points to just two qualities—righteousness and love—as the source of life, prosperity and honor? 6. An atheist could profitably apply much of the wisdom we've seen in these studies. Yet how do verses 30–31 also point to a divine dimension in the plans we make (and, indeed, in all wisdom)?

Applying the Word 1. When has one of your plans failed for one of the reasons mentioned in these proverbs? 2. What truths from this passage can help you with your current planning?

Responding in Prayer "Victory rests with the LORD" (v. 31). Allow that hope and promise to shape your prayers.

Proverbs 22:1—24:22

22 A good name is more desirable than great riches;
to be esteemed is better than silver or gold.

2 Rich and poor have this in common:
The LORD is the Maker of them all.

3 A prudent man sees danger and takes refuge,
but the simple keep going and suffer for it.

4 Humility and the fear of the LORD
bring wealth and honor and life.

5 In the paths of the wicked lie thorns and snares,
but he who guards his soul stays far from them.

6 Train[o] a child in the way he should go,
and when he is old he will not turn from it.

7 The rich rule over the poor,
and the borrower is servant to the lender.

8 He who sows wickedness reaps trouble,
and the rod of his fury will be destroyed.

9 A generous man will himself be blessed,
for he shares his food with the poor.

[o] *6 Or Start*

[10]Drive out the mocker, and out goes strife;
quarrels and insults are ended.

[11]He who loves a pure heart and whose speech is gracious
will have the king for his friend.

[12]The eyes of the LORD keep watch over knowledge,
but he frustrates the words of the unfaithful.

[13]The sluggard says, "There is a lion outside!"
or, "I will be murdered in the streets!"

[14]The mouth of an adulteress is a deep pit;
he who is under the LORD's wrath will fall into it.

[15]Folly is bound up in the heart of a child,
but the rod of discipline will drive it far from him.

[16]He who oppresses the poor to increase his wealth
and he who gives gifts to the rich—both come to poverty.

[17]Pay attention and listen to the sayings of the wise;
apply your heart to what I teach,
[18]for it is pleasing when you keep them in your heart
and have all of them ready on your lips.
[19]So that your trust may be in the LORD,
I teach you today, even you.
[20]Have I not written thirty[p] sayings for you,
sayings of counsel and knowledge,
[21]teaching you true and reliable words,
so that you can give sound answers
to him who sent you?

[22]Do not exploit the poor because they are poor
and do not crush the needy in court,
[23]for the LORD will take up their case
and will plunder those who plunder them.

[24]Do not make friends with a hot-tempered man,
do not associate with one easily angered,
[25]or you may learn his ways
and get yourself ensnared.

[26]Do not be a man who strikes hands in pledge
or puts up security for debts;
[27]if you lack the means to pay,
your very bed will be snatched from under you.

[28]Do not move an ancient boundary stone
set up by your forefathers.

[29]Do you see a man skilled in his work?
He will serve before kings;
he will not serve before obscure men.

23

When you sit to dine with a ruler,
note well what[q] is before you,
[2]and put a knife to your throat
if you are given to gluttony.
[3]Do not crave his delicacies,
for that food is deceptive.

[4]Do not wear yourself out to get rich;
have the wisdom to show restraint.
[5]Cast but a glance at riches, and they are gone,
for they will surely sprout wings
and fly off to the sky like an eagle.

[6]Do not eat the food of a stingy man,
do not crave his delicacies;
[7]for he is the kind of man
who is always thinking about the cost.[r]
"Eat and drink," he says to you,
but his heart is not with you.
[8]You will vomit up the little you have eaten
and will have wasted your compliments.

[9]Do not speak to a fool,
for he will scorn the wisdom of your words.

[10]Do not move an ancient boundary stone
or encroach on the fields of the fatherless,
[11]for their Defender is strong;
he will take up their case against you.

[12]Apply your heart to instruction
and your ears to words of knowledge.

[13]Do not withhold discipline from a child;
if you punish him with the rod, he will not die.
[14]Punish him with the rod
and save his soul from death.[s]

[15]My son, if your heart is wise,
then my heart will be glad;
[16]my inmost being will rejoice
when your lips speak what is right.

[p]20 *Or not formerly written; or not written excellent* [q]1 *Or who* [r]7 *Or for as he thinks within himself, / so he is; or for as he puts on a feast, / so he is* [s]14 Hebrew *Sheol*

[17]Do not let your heart envy sinners,
but always be zealous for the fear of the
LORD.
[18]There is surely a future hope for you,
and your hope will not be cut off.

[19]Listen, my son, and be wise,
and keep your heart on the right path.
[20]Do not join those who drink too much wine
or gorge themselves on meat,
[21]for drunkards and gluttons become poor,
and drowsiness clothes them in rags.

[22]Listen to your father, who gave you life,
and do not despise your mother when she
is old.
[23]Buy the truth and do not sell it;
get wisdom, discipline and understanding.
[24]The father of a righteous man has great joy;
he who has a wise son delights in him.
[25]May your father and mother be glad;
may she who gave you birth rejoice!

[26]My son, give me your heart
and let your eyes keep to my ways,
[27]for a prostitute is a deep pit
and a wayward wife is a narrow well.
[28]Like a bandit she lies in wait,
and multiplies the unfaithful among men.

[29]Who has woe? Who has sorrow?
Who has strife? Who has complaints?
Who has needless bruises? Who has
bloodshot eyes?
[30]Those who linger over wine,
who go to sample bowls of mixed wine.
[31]Do not gaze at wine when it is red,
when it sparkles in the cup,
when it goes down smoothly!
[32]In the end it bites like a snake
and poisons like a viper.
[33]Your eyes will see strange sights
and your mind imagine confusing things.
[34]You will be like one sleeping on the high
seas,
lying on top of the rigging.
[35]"They hit me," you will say, "but I'm not
hurt!
They beat me, but I don't feel it!
When will I wake up
so I can find another drink?"

24

Do not envy wicked men,
do not desire their company;
[2]for their hearts plot violence,
and their lips talk about making trouble.

[3]By wisdom a house is built,
and through understanding it is established;
[4]through knowledge its rooms are filled
with rare and beautiful treasures.

[5]A wise man has great power,
and a man of knowledge increases strength;
[6]for waging war you need guidance,
and for victory many advisers.

[7]Wisdom is too high for a fool;
in the assembly at the gate he has nothing
to say.

[8]He who plots evil
will be known as a schemer.
[9]The schemes of folly are sin,
and men detest a mocker.

[10]If you falter in times of trouble,
how small is your strength!

[11]Rescue those being led away to death;
hold back those staggering toward
slaughter.
[12]If you say, "But we knew nothing about this,"
does not he who weighs the heart perceive
it?
Does not he who guards your life know it?
Will he not repay each person according to
what he has done?

[13]Eat honey, my son, for it is good;
honey from the comb is sweet to your taste.
[14]Know also that wisdom is sweet to your soul;
if you find it, there is a future hope for
you,
and your hope will not be cut off.

[15]Do not lie in wait like an outlaw against a
righteous man's house,
do not raid his dwelling place;
[16]for though a righteous man falls seven times,
he rises again,
but the wicked are brought down by
calamity.

[17]Do not gloat when your enemy falls;
when he stumbles, do not let your heart
rejoice,
[18]or the LORD will see and disapprove

and turn his wrath away from him.

19Do not fret because of evil men
or be envious of the wicked,
20for the evil man has no future hope,
and the lamp of the wicked will be snuffed out.

21Fear the LORD and the king, my son,
and do not join with the rebellious,
22for those two will send sudden destruction upon them,
and who knows what calamities they can bring?

10 / *Proverbs 24:23-34* The Sluggard

YOU'VE FELT THE urge before; you've attended the soft voice that says: "The messy garage will still be there tomorrow; the chaotic closet won't run away. You've done enough for today. Leave that weedy flower bed till the weekend. Wait a few more days for the rest of the bills to arrive, and then you can pay them all at once! If you wash the car now, it'll rain, and then where will you be?" These seductions routinely beset a character the proverbs call *the sluggard*. We're apt to laugh in sympathy with the sluggard's feeble struggles to develop personal industry. After all, don't we know too well the sensual pleasures of a catnap? The proverbs laugh too, but it's more a snicker of scorn. The proverbs in this quiet time afford a bracing look at the sluggard.

Warming Up to God What tasks are you most tempted to put off until tomorrow?

Read Proverbs 24:23-34.

23These also are sayings of the wise:

To show partiality in judging is not good:
24Whoever says to the guilty, "You are innocent"—
peoples will curse him and nations denounce him.
25But it will go well with those who convict the guilty,
and rich blessing will come upon them.

26An honest answer
is like a kiss on the lips.

27Finish your outdoor work
and get your fields ready;
after that, build your house.

28Do not testify against your neighbor without cause,
or use your lips to deceive.
29Do not say, "I'll do to him as he has done to me;
I'll pay that man back for what he did."

30I went past the field of the sluggard,
past the vineyard of the man who lacks judgment;
31thorns had come up everywhere,
the ground was covered with weeds,
and the stone wall was in ruins.
32I applied my heart to what I observed
and learned a lesson from what I saw:
33A little sleep, a little slumber,
a little folding of the hands to rest—
34and poverty will come on you like a bandit
and scarcity like an armed man.[t]

[t]34 *Or like a vagrant / and scarcity like a beggar*

Discovering the Word 1. Although most of us are no longer farmers, how could verse 27 be good advice for us? 2. What characteristics of the sluggard do you notice (vv. 30-34)? 3. In 6:6-8 we see how the ant, in contrast, stores up provisions. How could you apply the remedy suggested by the ant to the one area of sluggardliness you mentioned previously? 4. How is the poverty that overcomes the sluggard like a bandit or an armed man (v. 34)? (What characteristics, for example, do such poverty and a bandit have in common?)

11 / *Proverbs 27*
Friends

AS E. C. McKENZIE said, "Some people make enemies instead of friends, because it is less trouble." It takes even less effort to alienate the friends we already have. On the other hand, finding and keeping a friend requires all the skill we can muster. But the reward for that effort is correspondingly great. The proverbs in this study give advice on friendship—its maintenance, how it is strengthened or weakened, and the special value of a friend. This wisdom is particularly valuable when applied to husband and wife, parent and child. But the wonder of friendship is its capacity to transcend age and gender, and to forge bonds stronger than blood.

Warming Up to God How have you recently been encouraged to spiritual growth by a friend?

Read Proverbs 27.

27 Do not boast about tomorrow,
for you do not know what a day
may bring forth.

[2]Let another praise you, and not your own mouth;
someone else, and not your own lips.

[3]Stone is heavy and sand a burden,
but provocation by a fool is heavier than both.

[4]Anger is cruel and fury overwhelming,
but who can stand before jealousy?

[5]Better is open rebuke
than hidden love.

[6]Wounds from a friend can be trusted,
but an enemy multiplies kisses.

[7]He who is full loathes honey,
but to the hungry even what is bitter tastes sweet.

[8]Like a bird that strays from its nest
is a man who strays from his home.

[9]Perfume and incense bring joy to the heart,
and the pleasantness of one's friend springs from his earnest counsel.

[10]Do not forsake your friend and the friend of your father,
and do not go to your brother's house when disaster strikes you—
better a neighbor nearby than a brother far away.

[11]Be wise, my son, and bring joy to my heart;
then I can answer anyone who treats me with contempt.

[12]The prudent see danger and take refuge,
but the simple keep going and suffer for it.

[13]Take the garment of one who puts up security for a stranger;
hold it in pledge if he does it for a wayward woman.

[14]If a man loudly blesses his neighbor early in the morning,
it will be taken as a curse.

[15]A quarrelsome wife is like
a constant dripping on a rainy day;
[16]restraining her is like restraining the wind
or grasping oil with the hand.

[17]As iron sharpens iron,
so one man sharpens another.

[18]He who tends a fig tree will eat its fruit,
and he who looks after his master will be honored.

[19]As water reflects a face,
so a man's heart reflects the man.

[20]Death and Destruction[x] are never satisfied,
and neither are the eyes of man.

[21]The crucible for silver and the furnace for gold,
but man is tested by the praise he receives.

[22]Though you grind a fool in a mortar,
grinding him like grain with a pestle,

[x]20 Hebrew *Sheol and Abaddon*

you will not remove his folly from him.

23Be sure you know the condition of your
flocks,
give careful attention to your herds;
24for riches do not endure forever,
and a crown is not secure for all
generations.
25When the hay is removed and new growth
appears
and the grass from the hills is gathered in,
26the lambs will provide you with clothing,
and the goats with the price of a field.
27You will have plenty of goats' milk
to feed you and your family
and to nourish your servant girls.

Discovering the Word 1. *Friend* in English is flexible enough in its meaning to cover everything from a casual acquaintance to an intimate soul-mate. What type of friend is being described in these verses? 2. Our enemies do not actually kiss us, any more than our friends actually wreak damage on our bodies. *Kisses* and *wounds* are figures of speech. How would you paraphrase verse 6 without using the words *kisses, wounds* or any other figurative language? 3. Describe a "kiss" you've received from an enemy and a "wound" you've received from a friend. 4. How are the kind words of friends a special pleasure (vv. 2, 17)? 5. Ancient people knew, as we do, that only a harder material effectively sharpens a softer material. What happens when two objects of the same material sharpen one another (v. 17)?

Applying the Word 1. What friendship do you currently have in which you are sharpening one another? How are you doing that? 2. How many friends (in the sense that the proverbs use the term) do you think you want? Explain.

Responding in Prayer Thank God for the friends you have who speak honestly with you—whether encouraging or rebuking—and build your relationship with Christ.

Proverbs 28—29

28 The wicked man flees though no
one pursues,
but the righteous are as bold as a
lion.

2When a country is rebellious, it has many
rulers,
but a man of understanding and knowledge
maintains order.

3A ruler[y] who oppresses the poor
is like a driving rain that leaves no crops.

4Those who forsake the law praise the wicked,
but those who keep the law resist them.

5Evil men do not understand justice,
but those who seek the LORD understand it
fully.

6Better a poor man whose walk is blameless
than a rich man whose ways are perverse.

7He who keeps the law is a discerning son,
but a companion of gluttons disgraces his
father.

8He who increases his wealth by exorbitant
interest
amasses it for another, who will be kind to
the poor.

9If anyone turns a deaf ear to the law,
even his prayers are detestable.

10He who leads the upright along an evil path
will fall into his own trap,
but the blameless will receive a good
inheritance.

11A rich man may be wise in his own eyes,
but a poor man who has discernment sees
through him.

12When the righteous triumph, there is great
elation;
but when the wicked rise to power, men go
into hiding.

13He who conceals his sins does not prosper,
but whoever confesses and renounces them
finds mercy.

y3 Or *A poor man*

[14]Blessed is the man who always fears the LORD,
but he who hardens his heart falls into trouble.

[15]Like a roaring lion or a charging bear
is a wicked man ruling over a helpless people.

[16]A tyrannical ruler lacks judgment,
but he who hates ill-gotten gain will enjoy a long life.

[17]A man tormented by the guilt of murder
will be a fugitive till death;
let no one support him.

[18]He whose walk is blameless is kept safe,
but he whose ways are perverse will suddenly fall.

[19]He who works his land will have abundant food,
but the one who chases fantasies will have his fill of poverty.

[20]A faithful man will be richly blessed,
but one eager to get rich will not go unpunished.

[21]To show partiality is not good—
yet a man will do wrong for a piece of bread.

[22]A stingy man is eager to get rich
and is unaware that poverty awaits him.

[23]He who rebukes a man will in the end gain more favor
than he who has a flattering tongue.

[24]He who robs his father or mother
and says, "It's not wrong"—
he is partner to him who destroys.

[25]A greedy man stirs up dissension,
but he who trusts in the LORD will prosper.

[26]He who trusts in himself is a fool,
but he who walks in wisdom is kept safe.

[27]He who gives to the poor will lack nothing,
but he who closes his eyes to them receives many curses.

[28]When the wicked rise to power, people go into hiding;
but when the wicked perish, the righteous thrive.

29

A man who remains stiff-necked
after many rebukes
will suddenly be destroyed—
without remedy.

[2]When the righteous thrive, the people rejoice;
when the wicked rule, the people groan.

[3]A man who loves wisdom brings joy to his father,
but a companion of prostitutes squanders his wealth.

[4]By justice a king gives a country stability,
but one who is greedy for bribes tears it down.

[5]Whoever flatters his neighbor
is spreading a net for his feet.

[6]An evil man is snared by his own sin,
but a righteous one can sing and be glad.

[7]The righteous care about justice for the poor,
but the wicked have no such concern.

[8]Mockers stir up a city,
but wise men turn away anger.

[9]If a wise man goes to court with a fool,
the fool rages and scoffs, and there is no peace.

[10]Bloodthirsty men hate a man of integrity
and seek to kill the upright.

[11]A fool gives full vent to his anger,
but a wise man keeps himself under control.

[12]If a ruler listens to lies,
all his officials become wicked.

[13]The poor man and the oppressor have this in common:
The LORD gives sight to the eyes of both.

[14]If a king judges the poor with fairness,
his throne will always be secure.

[15]The rod of correction imparts wisdom,
but a child left to himself disgraces his mother.

[16]When the wicked thrive, so does sin,
but the righteous will see their downfall.

[17]Discipline your son, and he will give you peace;
he will bring delight to your soul.

[18]Where there is no revelation, the people cast off restraint;
but blessed is he who keeps the law.
[19]A servant cannot be corrected by mere words;
though he understands, he will not respond.
[20]Do you see a man who speaks in haste?
There is more hope for a fool than for him.
[21]If a man pampers his servant from youth,
he will bring grief[z] in the end.
[22]An angry man stirs up dissension,
and a hot-tempered one commits many sins.
[23]A man's pride brings him low,
but a man of lowly spirit gains honor.
[24]The accomplice of a thief is his own enemy;
he is put under oath and dare not testify.
[25]Fear of man will prove to be a snare,
but whoever trusts in the LORD is kept safe.
[26]Many seek an audience with a ruler,
but it is from the LORD that man gets justice.
[27]The righteous detest the dishonest;
the wicked detest the upright.

[z]21 The meaning of the Hebrew for this word is uncertain.

12 / *Proverbs 30*
Wealth & Poverty

WHEN OTHERS ARE obviously rich or poor, we infer many things about their talents, education, personality, tastes and personal influence. But, from the perspective of the proverbs, wealth and poverty are poor standards to use in judging others. Furthermore, Proverbs tells us it is foolish to suppose that wealth is an unmixed blessing and that poverty is always a curse. In a world that views wealth and poverty from faulty and imperfect perspectives, we need the precise, pithy standards in the proverbs to guide our steps away from snares that lie on every side.

Warming Up to God Whether we think we're rich or poor often depends on our point of view. In what circumstances would you "feel" wealthy or poor? (Remember, we're thinking of *material* wealth and poverty.)

Read Proverbs 30.

30 The sayings of Agur son of Jakeh—
an oracle[a]:
This man declared to Ithiel,
to Ithiel and to Ucal:[b]
[2]"I am the most ignorant of men;
I do not have a man's understanding.
[3]I have not learned wisdom,
nor have I knowledge of the Holy One.
[4]Who has gone up to heaven and come down?
Who has gathered up the wind in the hollow of his hands?
Who has wrapped up the waters in his cloak?
Who has established all the ends of the earth?
What is his name, and the name of his son?
Tell me if you know!
[5]"Every word of God is flawless;
he is a shield to those who take refuge in him.
[6]Do not add to his words,
or he will rebuke you and prove you a liar.
[7]"Two things I ask of you, O LORD;
do not refuse me before I die:
[8]Keep falsehood and lies far from me;
give me neither poverty nor riches,
but give me only my daily bread.
[9]Otherwise, I may have too much and disown you
and say, 'Who is the LORD?'
Or I may become poor and steal,

[a]1 Or *Jakeh of Massa* [b]1 Masoretic Text; with a different word division of the Hebrew *declared, "I am weary, O God; / I am weary, O God, and faint.*

and so dishonor the name of my God.

[10]"Do not slander a servant to his master,
or he will curse you, and you will pay for it.

[11]"There are those who curse their fathers
and do not bless their mothers;
[12]those who are pure in their own eyes
and yet are not cleansed of their filth;
[13]those whose eyes are ever so haughty,
whose glances are so disdainful;
[14]those whose teeth are swords
and whose jaws are set with knives
to devour the poor from the earth,
the needy from among mankind.

[15]"The leech has two daughters.
'Give! Give!' they cry.

"There are three things that are never satisfied,
four that never say, 'Enough!':
[16]the grave,[c] the barren womb,
land, which is never satisfied with water,
and fire, which never says, 'Enough!'

[17]"The eye that mocks a father,
that scorns obedience to a mother,
will be pecked out by the ravens of the valley,
will be eaten by the vultures.

[18]"There are three things that are too amazing for me,
four that I do not understand:
[19]the way of an eagle in the sky,
the way of a snake on a rock,
the way of a ship on the high seas,
and the way of a man with a maiden.

[20]"This is the way of an adulteress:
She eats and wipes her mouth
and says, 'I've done nothing wrong.'

[21]"Under three things the earth trembles,
under four it cannot bear up:
[22]a servant who becomes king,
a fool who is full of food,
[23]an unloved woman who is married,
and a maidservant who displaces her mistress.

[24]"Four things on earth are small,
yet they are extremely wise:
[25]Ants are creatures of little strength,
yet they store up their food in the summer;
[26]coneys[d] are creatures of little power,
yet they make their home in the crags;
[27]locusts have no king,
yet they advance together in ranks;
[28]a lizard can be caught with the hand,
yet it is found in kings' palaces.

[29]"There are three things that are stately in their stride,
four that move with stately bearing:
[30]a lion, mighty among beasts,
who retreats before nothing;
[31]a strutting rooster, a he-goat,
and a king with his army around him.[e]

[32]"If you have played the fool and exalted yourself,
or if you have planned evil,
clap your hand over your mouth!
[33]For as churning the milk produces butter,
and as twisting the nose produces blood,
so stirring up anger produces strife."

[c]16 Hebrew *Sheol* [d]26 That is, the hyrax or rock badger [e]31 Or *king secure against revolt*

Discovering the Word 1. According to verses 8–9, what do you see to be some of the disadvantages of wealth? 2. What are the disadvantages of poverty? 3. It is simple to know if we're extravagantly rich or pitifully poor. But between these extremes the boundaries between poverty and wealth are hard to see. How does the prayer in verses 8–9 help us know when we are becoming perilously rich or poor? 4. How is extreme wealth or poverty like those things that are never satisfied (vv. 15–16)? 5. How do verses 24–28 further illustrate the need for balance in life?

Applying the Word 1. Cite an example from your experience (or the experience of someone you know about) where an increase in wealth proved *disadvantageous*. 2. Can you think of a situation where your poverty (actual or perceived) proved to be an advantage to you? Explain. 3. To what extent have you embraced the attitude "Give me only my daily bread"? Explain.

Responding in Prayer Pray for those you know who might be in danger because of having too much or not enough. Pray for yourself as well.

Proverbs 31

31 The sayings of King Lemuel—an oracle[f] his mother taught him:

2"O my son, O son of my womb,
O son of my vows,[g]
3do not spend your strength on women,
your vigor on those who ruin kings.

4"It is not for kings, O Lemuel—
not for kings to drink wine,
not for rulers to crave beer,
5lest they drink and forget what the law decrees,
and deprive all the oppressed of their rights.
6Give beer to those who are perishing,
wine to those who are in anguish;
7let them drink and forget their poverty
and remember their misery no more.

8"Speak up for those who cannot speak for themselves,
for the rights of all who are destitute.
9Speak up and judge fairly;
defend the rights of the poor and needy."

10[h]A wife of noble character who can find?
She is worth far more than rubies.
11Her husband has full confidence in her
and lacks nothing of value.
12She brings him good, not harm,
all the days of her life.
13She selects wool and flax
and works with eager hands.
14She is like the merchant ships,
bringing her food from afar.
15She gets up while it is still dark;
she provides food for her family
and portions for her servant girls.
16She considers a field and buys it;
out of her earnings she plants a vineyard.
17She sets about her work vigorously;
her arms are strong for her tasks.
18She sees that her trading is profitable,
and her lamp does not go out at night.
19In her hand she holds the distaff
and grasps the spindle with her fingers.
20She opens her arms to the poor
and extends her hands to the needy.
21When it snows, she has no fear for her household;
for all of them are clothed in scarlet.
22She makes coverings for her bed;
she is clothed in fine linen and purple.
23Her husband is respected at the city gate,
where he takes his seat among the elders of the land.
24She makes linen garments and sells them,
and supplies the merchants with sashes.
25She is clothed with strength and dignity;
she can laugh at the days to come.
26She speaks with wisdom,
and faithful instruction is on her tongue.
27She watches over the affairs of her household
and does not eat the bread of idleness.
28Her children arise and call her blessed;
her husband also, and he praises her:
29"Many women do noble things,
but you surpass them all."
30Charm is deceptive, and beauty is fleeting;
but a woman who fears the LORD is to be praised.
31Give her the reward she has earned,
and let her works bring her praise at the city gate.

f1 Or *of Lemuel king of Massa, which* g2 Or */ the answer to my prayers* h10 Verses 10-31 are an acrostic, each verse beginning with a successive letter of the Hebrew alphabet.

Ecclesiastes

Like an apple tree in the middle of an orange grove stands the book of Ecclesiastes among the other books of the Bible. At first glance, it just does not seem to fit. What place does a book which flaunts the daring assertion "Meaningless! Meaningless! Everything is meaningless" have in Scripture that intends to reveal the saving work of God?

Along with the book of Job, Ecclesiastes reminds us that God is bigger, and our life in this world more unpredictable, than we might think. The book invites us to take a realistic tour of life. The sightseeing stops will likely leave those who enjoy nice tidy answers a bit perplexed, if not downright frustrated.

Our guide for this adventure is introduced by the Hebrew title *qoheleth*. The title, which translated into Greek is *ekklēsiastēs*, comes from a Hebrew word for assembling. It suggests a type of office-bearer. Thus we have such translations as "the Preacher" (KJV, RSV, NASB), "the Speaker" (NEB), "the Philosopher" (TEV) and the one used in the NIV, "the Teacher."

The Teacher identifies himself as "son of David, king in Jerusalem" (1:1). Such an identification naturally links him with the wisest of all Israel's sages, King Solomon. Many commentators, however, believe that the Teacher was not actually Solomon but someone who wrote in the tradition and from the perspective of Solomon. (For a full discussion of Ecclesiastes' authorship, as well as other related issues, including background and date, see Michael Eaton, *Ecclesiastes*, Tyndale Old Testament Commentaries [Downers Grove, Ill.: InterVarsity Press, 1983], or Derek Kidner, *The Wisdom of Proverbs, Job and Ecclesiastes: An Introduction to Wisdom Literature* [Downers Grove, Ill.: InterVarsity Press, 1985]. Two other helpful commentaries on Ecclesiastes are Charles Swindoll, *Living on the Ragged Edge Bible Study Guide* [Fullerton, Calif.: Insight for Living, 1986], and Derek Kidner, *The Message of Ecclesiastes* [Downers Grove, Ill.: InterVarsity Press, 1976].)

The depth of insight found in the book would certainly argue for an author endowed with the kind of wisdom God granted to Solomon (see 1Ki 3:5–12). If the Teacher was not actually King Solomon, he surely qualified as a star disciple of this master sage.

As a wise man, the Teacher represented a group whose influence grew to virtual equality with Israel's prophets and priests. Israel's wise men observed the interworkings of nature and experience. From this storehouse of wisdom they made general pronouncements concerning life's most perplexing issues and counseled people who faced difficult decisions.

The three most notable works of Israel's wise men include Ecclesiastes, Job and Proverbs. Their mark on Old Testament literature may also be seen in the Song of Songs, Lamentations and a number of the psalms (such as 1, 37, 49, 73, 127, 133). This body of writing, called wisdom literature, has a strong influence on portions of the New Testament. Jesus frequently quotes proverbs and uses wise sayings. Paul often talks about the wisdom of God (see 1 Co 1:18—2:16 as an example). And the book of James provides counsel in a style similar to Old Testament wisdom literature.

The Teacher's message seems particularly aimed at the secularists—those who seek to find life's meaning outside of a practical faith in God. With despairing perception, the author explores a grim reality he calls "life under the sun"—life outside of God's control and goodness. He addresses some of life's most sensitive questions: Where can we find satisfaction? Who is really in control? What does it take to be content? How do we live wisely?

Much of the time God is left out of the discussion. But when he is introduced, everything changes. "Life under the sun" becomes "life from the hand of God." Chasing after meaning is transformed into the pursuit of God. This exploration of life's meaninglessness outside of knowing God thus becomes an invitation to know him. In its own unique way, Ecclesiastes is ultimately an introduction to the One who "came that we might have life abundantly"—Jesus Christ himself. It highlights the dilemma voiced by Peter but faced by all of us: "Lord, to whom shall we go? You have the words of eternal life" (Jn 6:68).

Understandably, then, Ecclesiastes warrants special study by anyone in a formative period of life. Colleges would do well to set up a course for their freshmen and sophomores with Ecclesiastes as required reading. They could call it "Basic Living 101."

These quiet times will help you plunge into the pessimism of Ecclesiastes in order to see the hope of a God-centered lifestyle. May the Lord use your study of Ecclesiastes as an encouragement to follow him closely in this unique and perplexing adventure we call *life*.

Outline

Part 1: Making Sense Out of Life

1/ Ecclesiastes 1:1–11 — *Is It All Meaningless?*

2/ Ecclesiastes 1:12—2:16 — *Where Can We Find Fulfillment?*

3/ Ecclesiastes 2:17–26 — *What Is the Value of Work?*

4/ Ecclesiastes 3:1—4:3 — *Who Is Really in Control?*

5/ Ecclesiastes 4:4—5:7 — *What Attitudes Should We Embrace?*

6/ Ecclesiastes 5:8—6:12 — *What Does It Take to Be Content?*

Part 2: Living Life Sensibly

7/ Ecclesiastes 7:1—8:1 — *Where Can We Find Wisdom?*

8/ Ecclesiastes 8:2–17 — *How Shall We Live Under Authority?*

9/ Ecclesiastes 9:1–12 — *What Meaning Does Death Bring to Life?*

10/ Ecclesiastes 9:13—10:20 — *How Do We Live Sensibly?*

11/ Ecclesiastes 11:1—12:8 — *How Shall We Then Live?*

12/ Ecclesiastes 12:9–14 — *What Makes Life Meaningful?*

1 / *Ecclesiastes 1:1–11*
Is It All Meaningless?

THE WATER IN the glass measures exactly at the halfway point. Now comes the classic test to determine whether you are a pessimist or an optimist: Do you consider the glass of water to be half-empty or half-full? If you answered half-empty, you will find Ecclesiastes' author, the Teacher, a fast friend. If you answered half-full, you may find it harder to relate to him. But either way, realize he is delivering pessimism with a purpose. In his introduction he answers a question before he even raises it. The question is, "Can meaning in life come outside of a God-centered universe?" The answer? Well, hang on for some of Scripture's most brutal language.

Warming Up to God Draw or imagine a line with *pure pessimist* on the left and *outrageous optimist* on the right. Where would you place yourself on the continuum? Regardless of your response, what gives you hope today?

Read Ecclesiastes 1:1–11.

1 The words of the Teacher,[a] son of David,
king in Jerusalem:

2"Meaningless! Meaningless!"
says the Teacher.
"Utterly meaningless!
Everything is meaningless."
3What does man gain from all his labor
at which he toils under the sun?
4Generations come and generations go,
but the earth remains forever.
5The sun rises and the sun sets,
and hurries back to where it rises.
6The wind blows to the south
and turns to the north;
round and round it goes,
ever returning on its course.
7All streams flow into the sea,
yet the sea is never full.
To the place the streams come from,
there they return again.
8All things are wearisome,
more than one can say.
The eye never has enough of seeing,
nor the ear its fill of hearing.
9What has been will be again,
what has been done will be done again;
there is nothing new under the sun.
10Is there anything of which one can say,
"Look! This is something new"?
It was here already, long ago;
it was here before our time.
11There is no remembrance of men of old,
and even those who are yet to come
will not be remembered
by those who follow.

[a]1 Or *leader of the assembly*; also in verses 2 and 12

Discovering the Word 1. How do you react to the theme (or thesis) of the book which the Teacher states in verses 2–3? 2. How do examples of nature support his thesis that "everything is meaningless" (vv. 5–7)? 3. From verses 9–10 describe the Teacher's view of history. 4. What might he say to a person who believes that educating people will eventually solve humanity's problems? 5. How does human mortality (vv. 4 and 11) bring the Teacher's argument to a climax?

Applying the Word 1. According to verse 8, seeking new experiences will not bring lasting satisfaction. Give a personal example to illustrate this. 2. As a Christian, on what basis would you seek to refute the Teacher's thesis? 3. What is one area in your life that has recently seemed futile or meaningless?

Responding in Prayer Reflect on ways you sense that your life lacks meaning or purpose. Ask God to help you draw on his resources to resist meaningless living and pursue his purposes.

2 / *Ecclesiastes 1:12—2:16*
Where Can We Find Fulfillment?

IMAGINE A TOTAL plunge into hedonism—following every possible avenue of self-seeking pleasure and satisfaction. Now let your imagination grow further, having the political and financial means to indulge yourself to the fullest possible extent. Imagination turns to reality in this section of Ecclesiastes—surely one of the most colorful passages in the Bible. Here is one person's attempt at something many only dream about.

Warming Up to God If by some sudden shift in perspective wordly pleasure suddenly became your overriding goal, what would you likely do? With what results? Talk to God about your deeper desires to forsake short-term self-indulgence for the long-term gain of knowing him.

Read Ecclesiastes 1:12—2:16.

[12]I, the Teacher, was king over Israel in Jerusa-
lem. [13]I devoted myself to study and to explore by
wisdom all that is done under heaven. What a
heavy burden God has laid on men! [14]I have
seen all the things that are done under the sun;
all of them are meaningless, a chasing after the
wind.

[15]What is twisted cannot be straightened;
what is lacking cannot be counted.

[16]I thought to myself, "Look, I have grown and
increased in wisdom more than anyone who has
ruled over Jerusalem before me; I have experi-
enced much of wisdom and knowledge." [17]Then I
applied myself to the understanding of wisdom,
and also of madness and folly, but I learned that
this, too, is a chasing after the wind.

[18]For with much wisdom comes much sorrow;
the more knowledge, the more grief.

2 I thought in my heart, "Come now, I will
test you with pleasure to find out what is
good." But that also proved to be mean-
ingless. [2]"Laughter," I said, "is foolish. And what
does pleasure accomplish?" [3]I tried cheering my-
self with wine, and embracing folly—my mind
still guiding me with wisdom. I wanted to see
what was worthwhile for men to do under heaven
during the few days of their lives.

[4]I undertook great projects: I built houses for
myself and planted vineyards. [5]I made gardens
and parks and planted all kinds of fruit trees in
them. [6]I made reservoirs to water groves of flour-
ishing trees. [7]I bought male and female slaves and
had other slaves who were born in my house. I
also owned more herds and flocks than anyone in
Jerusalem before me. [8]I amassed silver and gold
for myself, and the treasure of kings and prov-
inces. I acquired men and women singers, and a
harem[b] as well—the delights of the heart of
man. [9]I became greater by far than anyone in Je-
rusalem before me. In all this my wisdom stayed
with me.

[10]I denied myself nothing my eyes desired;
I refused my heart no pleasure.
My heart took delight in all my work,
and this was the reward for all my labor.
[11]Yet when I surveyed all that my hands had
done
and what I had toiled to achieve,
everything was meaningless, a chasing after
the wind;
nothing was gained under the sun.

[12]Then I turned my thoughts to consider
wisdom,
and also madness and folly.
What more can the king's successor do
than what has already been done?
[13]I saw that wisdom is better than folly,
just as light is better than darkness.
[14]The wise man has eyes in his head,
while the fool walks in the darkness;
but I came to realize
that the same fate overtakes them both.

[15]Then I thought in my heart,

"The fate of the fool will overtake me also.
What then do I gain by being wise?"

I said in my heart,
"This too is meaningless."

[b]8 The meaning of the Hebrew for this phrase is uncertain.

[16]For the wise man, like the fool, will not be
long remembered;
in days to come both will be forgotten.
Like the fool, the wise man too must die!

Discovering the Word 1. How does the Teacher describe himself and his quest? 2. Why does the author call his search for wisdom "a heavy burden" (1:13)? 3. Describe the various avenues the Teacher tested in his quest for fulfillment (2:1–16). 4. In 2:12–16 he outlines two approaches to discovering meaning in life. What are the advantages and limitations of these two approaches? 5. What prompts his change of perspective (2:14–16)? 6. In the first six chapters the Teacher repeats his thesis that "everything is meaningless" 21 times. How does he show that life is meaningless in 1:12—2:16?

Applying the Word 1. How have you been convinced of the meaninglessness of living outside of Christ's lordship? 2. What would help you turn your desire for meaning in life into a wholehearted pursuit of God?

Responding in Prayer Matthew 7:8 promises that all who seek shall find. Knock on Jesus' door right now and ask him to give you a hunger to find meaning in life through knowing him better each day.

3/ *Ecclesiastes 2:17–26*
What Is the Value of Work?

GARY HATES HIS job. The tasks are repetitive, his boss is a grouch, the other employees bicker. The job, however, pays better than anything else he could find, and his son has a medical condition that would make him uninsurable if he changes companies. Gary feels trapped. Nothing can be quite as frustrating as work. And while most of us can't fully identify with Gary, many of us can readily understand something about his predicament. In this section of Ecclesiastes, the Teacher will look back at his own life's work. If anyone had a great job, he did. Even so, he asks, "Does it really amount to anything significant?"

Warming Up to God Do you feel more like God's dutiful employee or his valued friend? Explore your perspective and tell him your heart. Remember that he is your most patient listener and he's eager to hear how you're doing.

Read Ecclesiastes 2:17–26.

[17]So I hated life, because the work that is done
under the sun was grievous to me. All of it is
meaningless, a chasing after the wind. [18]I hated
all the things I had toiled for under the sun, be-
cause I must leave them to the one who comes
after me. [19]And who knows whether he will be a
wise man or a fool? Yet he will have control over
all the work into which I have poured my effort
and skill under the sun. This too is meaningless.
[20]So my heart began to despair over all my toil-
some labor under the sun. [21]For a man may do
his work with wisdom, knowledge and skill, and
then he must leave all he owns to someone who
has not worked for it. This too is meaningless and
a great misfortune. [22]What does a man get for all
the toil and anxious striving with which he labors
under the sun? [23]All his days his work is pain and
grief; even at night his mind does not rest. This
too is meaningless.

[24]A man can do nothing better than to eat and
drink and find satisfaction in his work. This too,
I see, is from the hand of God, [25]for without him,
who can eat or find enjoyment? [26]To the man
who pleases him, God gives wisdom, knowledge
and happiness, but to the sinner he gives the task
of gathering and storing up wealth to hand it over
to the one who pleases God. This too is meaning-
less, a chasing after the wind.

Discovering the Word 1. How would you describe the Teacher's emotional state as a result of his quest for meaning so far? 2. The phrase "under the sun" appears often throughout Ecclesiastes—five times in this passage (vv. 17, 18, 19, 20, 22). Describe the "under the sun" mentality. 3. What does the Teacher say about work (vv. 21–23)? 4. What shift do you see in the way the Teacher views work (vv. 24–26)? 5. Describe the contrast between seeking pleasure (vv. 10–11) and finding enjoyment (vv. 24–26).

Applying the Word 1. When have you experienced the kind of satisfying enjoyment described here? 2. If you were to view your work as a gift from God to be enjoyed, how could that change your attitude about it?

Responding in Prayer Commit your work to the Lord and ask him to give you a heart that desires to glorify him in that context.

4 / *Ecclesiastes 3:1—4:3*
Who Is Really in Control?

"WHY DO THE innocent suffer?" is a question that has plagued the conscience of humankind. And we wonder, "Why do the unrighteous prosper?" Both of these questions can lead to despair, suggesting that life is indeed meaningless. But this famous chapter of Ecclesiastes poses a solution for life's apparent dilemma. The solution hinges on how one answers a third question—"Who is in control?" If humanity is in charge, then life is a game of chance whose rules are controlled by the most powerful among us. But if a just and loving God is in charge, then life becomes a set of ordained appointments which open the windows of eternity to us.

Warming Up to God What was a situation in which you felt as though your life was out of control? Write down a few words to describe your feelings at that time. Now speak to the Lord about them—and leave your fears and frustrations in his hands.

Read Ecclesiastes 3:1—4:3.

3 There is a time for everything,
and a season for every activity under heaven:

2 a time to be born and a time to die,
a time to plant and a time to uproot,
3 a time to kill and a time to heal,
a time to tear down and a time to build,
4 a time to weep and a time to laugh,
a time to mourn and a time to dance,
5 a time to scatter stones and a time to gather them,
a time to embrace and a time to refrain,
6 a time to search and a time to give up,
a time to keep and a time to throw away,
7 a time to tear and a time to mend,
a time to be silent and a time to speak,
8 a time to love and a time to hate,
a time for war and a time for peace.

9 What does the worker gain from his toil? 10 I
have seen the burden God has laid on men. 11 He
has made everything beautiful in its time. He has
also set eternity in the hearts of men; yet they
cannot fathom what God has done from begin-
ning to end. 12 I know that there is nothing better
for men than to be happy and do good while they
live. 13 That everyone may eat and drink, and find
satisfaction in all his toil—this is the gift of God.
14 I know that everything God does will endure
forever; nothing can be added to it and nothing
taken from it. God does it so that men will revere
him.

15 Whatever is has already been,
and what will be has been before;
and God will call the past to account.[c]

16 And I saw something else under the sun:

In the place of judgment—wickedness was there,
in the place of justice—wickedness was there.

17 I thought in my heart,

"God will bring to judgment
both the righteous and the wicked,

[c]15 Or *God calls back the past*

for there will be a time for every activity,
a time for every deed."

[18]I also thought, "As for men, God tests them
so that they may see that they are like the ani-
mals. [19]Man's fate is like that of the animals; the
same fate awaits them both: As one dies, so dies
the other. All have the same breath[d]; man has no
advantage over the animal. Everything is mean-
ingless. [20]All go to the same place; all come from
dust, and to dust all return. [21]Who knows if the
spirit of man rises upward and if the spirit of the
animal[e] goes down into the earth?"

[22]So I saw that there is nothing better for a man
than to enjoy his work, because that is his lot. For
who can bring him to see what will happen after
him?

4 Again I looked and saw all the oppression
that was taking place under the sun:

I saw the tears of the oppressed—
and they have no comforter;
power was on the side of their oppressors—
and they have no comforter.
[2]And I declared that the dead,
who had already died,
are happier than the living,
who are still alive.
[3]But better than both
is he who has not yet been,
who has not seen the evil
that is done under the sun.

[d]19 Or spirit *[e]21 Or Who knows the spirit of man, which rises upward, or the spirit of the animal, which*

Discovering the Word 1. Describe the Teacher's view of time in 3:1–8. 2. What negative and positive things does the Teacher say about time in 3:9–15? 3. What observations does the Teacher make in 3:16 and 4:1–3 about human wickedness? 4. In the future God will bring judgment (3:17). For the present, however, God brings us a test (3:18–22). What is the test and its desired results? 5. What kind of perspective results from seeing wickedness from a temporal viewpoint (4:1–3)? 6. What kind of perspective results from looking at wickedness from an eternal viewpoint (3:17)?

Applying the Word 1. How would you live your life differently if you believed God had no control? 2. How do you struggle with the tension of *knowing* God is in control and yet *seeing* wickedness in control?

Responding in Prayer Praise God for setting eternity in our hearts, and thank him for being unchangingly faithful in the midst of life in a paradoxical world.

5 / *Ecclesiastes 4:4—5:7*
What Attitudes Should We Embrace?

"THE CHURCH IS full of hypocrites!" Christians often hear this from those outside the church. We like to respond by saying, "Yes, but if you think they're bad now, you should have seen them before God got hold of them!" One way or another, when it comes to how faith should change a person's life, expectations are high. And rightly so. We become like those we live around, and if that includes the Lord, then we will see our lives begin to reflect his. In this passage the Teacher explores some everyday values and attitudes that a relationship with God should influence.

Warming Up to God Consider your usual approach to life. If you could remove one negative attitude that you struggle with, which one would it be? What difference would it make in your life if you turned this negative into a positive?

Read Ecclesiastes 4:4—5:7.

[4]And I saw that all labor and all achievement
spring from man's envy of his neighbor. This too
is meaningless, a chasing after the wind.

[5]The fool folds his hands
and ruins himself.
[6]Better one handful with tranquillity

than two handfuls with toil
and chasing after the wind.

7Again I saw something meaningless under the sun:

8There was a man all alone;
he had neither son nor brother.
There was no end to his toil,
yet his eyes were not content with his wealth.
"For whom am I toiling," he asked,
"and why am I depriving myself of enjoyment?"
This too is meaningless—
a miserable business!

9Two are better than one,
because they have a good return for their work:
10If one falls down,
his friend can help him up.
But pity the man who falls
and has no one to help him up!
11Also, if two lie down together, they will keep warm.
But how can one keep warm alone?
12Though one may be overpowered,
two can defend themselves.
A cord of three strands is not quickly broken.

13Better a poor but wise youth than an old but
foolish king who no longer knows how to take
warning. 14The youth may have come from prison
to the kingship, or he may have been born in
poverty within his kingdom. 15I saw that all who
lived and walked under the sun followed the
youth, the king's successor. 16There was no end
to all the people who were before them. But those
who came later were not pleased with the successor. This too is meaningless, a chasing after the wind.

5 Guard your steps when you go to the
house of God. Go near to listen rather
than to offer the sacrifice of fools, who do
not know that they do wrong.

2Do not be quick with your mouth,
do not be hasty in your heart
to utter anything before God.
God is in heaven
and you are on earth,
so let your words be few.
3As a dream comes when there are many cares,
so the speech of a fool when there are many words.

4When you make a vow to God, do not delay in
fulfilling it. He has no pleasure in fools; fulfill
your vow. 5It is better not to vow than to make a
vow and not fulfill it. 6Do not let your mouth lead
you into sin. And do not protest to the ⌞temple⌟
messenger, "My vow was a mistake." Why should
God be angry at what you say and destroy the
work of your hands? 7Much dreaming and many
words are meaningless. Therefore stand in awe of
God.

Discovering the Word 1. What are negative consequences of the two extreme attitudes described in 4:4–5? 2. What irony concerning the workaholic's efforts is spoken about in 4:7–8? 3. What are the benefits of partnership (4:9–12)? 4. Ecclesiastes 4:13–16 outlines a "rags to riches" story. What, however, is the ironic twist to its ending? 5. Contrast the two approaches to God described in 5:1–7.

Applying the Word 1. On a scale of 1 to 10 (1 being lazy and 10 being a workaholic), how would you rate yourself? Explain. 2. In terms of your need for other people, are you primarily a dependent or an independent person? Explain. 3. How does the Teacher's wisdom challenge you toward growth in interdependence with others?

Responding in Prayer This passage ends with the words "Therefore stand in awe of God." Pray quietly to the Lord for a few moments, allowing yourself to stand in awe of him. Humbly be silent before him who made you and is making you into his child.

6 / *Ecclesiastes 5:8—6:12*
What Does It Take to Be Content?

IF THE ADVERTISERS are right, we have a lot to feel discontent about. We don't have enough possessions, and we don't have them soon enough or up to date enough. Fulfillment is equated with wearing the right kind of clothes, driving the right kind of car, drinking the right kind of beverage. This lifestyle of discontent held similar sway for many of the Teacher's contemporaries. In this section he challenges his reader to stop seeking satisfaction from accumulating things. Instead he offers an alternative, one that leads to a lifestyle of contentment.

Warming Up to God In what areas of life do you find yourself least content? Consider Psalm 118:24: "This is the day the LORD has made; let us rejoice and be glad in it." For what do you have reason to rejoice today? Praise your God, the Lover of your soul, today before you look into his Word.

Read Ecclesiastes 5:8—6:12.

8If you see the poor oppressed in a district, and
justice and rights denied, do not be surprised at
such things; for one official is eyed by a higher
one, and over them both are others higher still.
9The increase from the land is taken by all; the
king himself profits from the fields.

10Whoever loves money never has money
enough;
whoever loves wealth is never satisfied with
his income.
This too is meaningless.

11As goods increase,
so do those who consume them.
And what benefit are they to the owner
except to feast his eyes on them?

12The sleep of a laborer is sweet,
whether he eats little or much,
but the abundance of a rich man
permits him no sleep.

13I have seen a grievous evil under the sun:

wealth hoarded to the harm of its owner,
14 or wealth lost through some misfortune,
so that when he has a son
there is nothing left for him.
15Naked a man comes from his mother's womb,
and as he comes, so he departs.
He takes nothing from his labor
that he can carry in his hand.

16This too is a grievous evil:

As a man comes, so he departs,
and what does he gain,
since he toils for the wind?
17All his days he eats in darkness,
with great frustration, affliction and anger.

18Then I realized that it is good and proper for
a man to eat and drink, and to find satisfaction in
his toilsome labor under the sun during the few
days of life God has given him—for this is his lot.
19Moreover, when God gives any man wealth and
possessions, and enables him to enjoy them, to
accept his lot and be happy in his work—this is
a gift of God. 20He seldom reflects on the days of
his life, because God keeps him occupied with
gladness of heart.

6 I have seen another evil under the sun,
and it weighs heavily on men: 2God gives
a man wealth, possessions and honor, so
that he lacks nothing his heart desires, but God
does not enable him to enjoy them, and a stranger
enjoys them instead. This is meaningless, a griev-
ous evil.
3A man may have a hundred children and live
many years; yet no matter how long he lives, if he
cannot enjoy his prosperity and does not receive
proper burial, I say that a stillborn child is better
off than he. 4It comes without meaning, it departs
in darkness, and in darkness its name is
shrouded. 5Though it never saw the sun or knew
anything, it has more rest than does that man—
6even if he lives a thousand years twice over but
fails to enjoy his prosperity. Do not all go to the
same place?

7All man's efforts are for his mouth,
yet his appetite is never satisfied.
8What advantage has a wise man
over a fool?
What does a poor man gain

by knowing how to conduct himself before
others?
[9]Better what the eye sees
than the roving of the appetite.
This too is meaningless,
a chasing after the wind.
[10]Whatever exists has already been named,
and what man is has been known;
no man can contend
with one who is stronger than he.
[11]The more the words,
the less the meaning,
and how does that profit anyone?

[12]For who knows what is good for a man in
life, during the few and meaningless days he
passes through like a shadow? Who can tell
him what will happen under the sun after he is
gone?

Discovering the Word 1. How does the Teacher describe the nature of wealth? 2. What negative effects does the desire for wealth have in public life (5:8–9) and in personal life (5:10–17)? 3. Note the contrast between 5:18–20 and 6:1–2. What role does God have in the satisfaction which wealth, possessions and honor can bring? 4. Many children and a long life were considered the greatest of blessings in the Old Testament (6:3–6). What does our society define as "the good life"? 5. In 6:7–12 the Teacher uses questions to challenge his readers. How would the questions challenge an unbeliever (see especially v. 12)?

Applying the Word 1. On a scale of 1 to 10 (1 being very little, 10 being very much), how would you rate your attachment to the things you own? 2. Give an example of how viewing possessions as a gift from God would help to change your attachment to them. 3. How could you exercise trust in God for an area in which you lack contentment?

Responding in Prayer Confess any discontent to God and ask him to help you value his goodness and sufficiency.

7/ *Ecclesiastes 7:1—8:1*
Where Can We Find Wisdom?

WHO AMONG US does not look back in regret over a past decision? Sometimes we had inadequate information to make the right judgment. But often we simply lacked the necessary wisdom to make the right choice at the right time. In this section the Teacher will address where such wisdom comes from and how we can capitalize on it for future decisions.

Warming Up to God In what way do you feel that you lack wisdom? Ask God to give you insight into his wisdom as you grow through the study of his Word.

Read Ecclesiastes 7:1—8:1.

7 A good name is better than fine
perfume,
and the day of death better than the day
of birth.
[2]It is better to go to a house of mourning
than to go to a house of feasting,
for death is the destiny of every man;
the living should take this to heart.
[3]Sorrow is better than laughter,
because a sad face is good for the heart.
[4]The heart of the wise is in the house of
mourning,
but the heart of fools is in the house of
pleasure.
[5]It is better to heed a wise man's rebuke
than to listen to the song of fools.
[6]Like the crackling of thorns under the
pot,
so is the laughter of fools.
This too is meaningless.

7Extortion turns a wise man into a fool,
and a bribe corrupts the heart.

8The end of a matter is better than its beginning,
and patience is better than pride.
9Do not be quickly provoked in your spirit,
for anger resides in the lap of fools.
10Do not say, "Why were the old days better than these?"
For it is not wise to ask such questions.

11Wisdom, like an inheritance, is a good thing
and benefits those who see the sun.
12Wisdom is a shelter
as money is a shelter,
but the advantage of knowledge is this:
that wisdom preserves the life of its possessor.

13Consider what God has done:

Who can straighten
what he has made crooked?
14When times are good, be happy;
but when times are bad, consider:
God has made the one
as well as the other.
Therefore, a man cannot discover
anything about his future.

15In this meaningless life of mine I have seen both of these:

a righteous man perishing in his righteousness,
and a wicked man living long in his wickedness.
16Do not be overrighteous,
neither be overwise—
why destroy yourself?
17Do not be overwicked,
and do not be a fool—
why die before your time?
18It is good to grasp the one
and not let go of the other.
The man who fears God will avoid all ⌞extremes⌟.[f]

19Wisdom makes one wise man more powerful
than ten rulers in a city.

20There is not a righteous man on earth
who does what is right and never sins.

21Do not pay attention to every word people say,
or you may hear your servant cursing you—
22for you know in your heart
that many times you yourself have cursed others.

23All this I tested by wisdom and I said,

"I am determined to be wise"—
but this was beyond me.
24Whatever wisdom may be,
it is far off and most profound—
who can discover it?
25So I turned my mind to understand,
to investigate and to search out wisdom
and the scheme of things
and to understand the stupidity of wickedness
and the madness of folly.

26I find more bitter than death
the woman who is a snare,
whose heart is a trap
and whose hands are chains.
The man who pleases God will escape her,
but the sinner she will ensnare.

27"Look," says the Teacher,[g] "this is what I have discovered:

"Adding one thing to another to discover the scheme of things—
28while I was still searching
but not finding—
I found one ⌞upright⌟ man among a thousand,
but not one ⌞upright⌟ woman among them all.
29This only have I found:
God made mankind upright,
but men have gone in search of many schemes."

8 Who is like the wise man?
Who knows the explanation of things?
Wisdom brightens a man's face
and changes its hard appearance.

f18 Or *will follow them both*   g27 Or *leader of the assembly*

Discovering the Word 1. What are some ways the Teacher describes wisdom? 2. Are you surprised by any of the comparisons of 7:1–6? Explain. 3. What dangers does the Teacher warn against in verses 7–10? 4. Why does he give the warning of verses 16–18 in the terms he uses? 5. Describe how fearing God puts life into perspective (v. 18). 6. What perspective does wisdom provide according to verses 19–22?

Applying the Word 1. How can suffering and sorrow offer instruction for living? 2. From this section of Ecclesiastes, Chuck Swindoll defines wisdom as "the God-given ability to see life with rare objectivity and to handle life with rare stability" (*Living on the Ragged Edge Bible Study Guide*). In what areas of your Christian life do you presently need such objectivity and stability?

Responding in Prayer Tell the Lord about one area of your life in which you need wisdom and guidance. Ask him to direct your choices and then relax in the truth that God desires to give his children good gifts.

8 / *Ecclesiastes 8:2–17*
How Shall We Live Under Authority?

DOES YOUR FOOT automatically come off the accelerator pedal when you buzz by a police car on the side of the road? Do your eyes then anxiously glance up to the rearview mirror? Sure we respect authority. But do we really appreciate how living under authority can greatly enrich our lives? In this study, the Teacher outlines some positive benefits of relating to both human and divine authority.

Warming Up to God Tell the Lord about events in your life or in world affairs that have angered you. How have you responded to that anger? Allow God to share your feelings, and remember that he too seeks an end to pain and despair.

Read Ecclesiastes 8:2–17.

2Obey the king's command, I say, because you
took an oath before God. 3Do not be in a hurry to
leave the king's presence. Do not stand up for a
bad cause, for he will do whatever he pleases.
4Since a king's word is supreme, who can say to
him, "What are you doing?"

5Whoever obeys his command will come to no
harm,
and the wise heart will know the proper
time and procedure.
6For there is a proper time and procedure for
every matter,
though a man's misery weighs heavily upon
him.
7Since no man knows the future,
who can tell him what is to come?
8No man has power over the wind to contain
it[h];
so no one has power over the day of his
death.
As no one is discharged in time of war,
so wickedness will not release those who
practice it.

9All this I saw, as I applied my mind to every-
thing done under the sun. There is a time when
a man lords it over others to his own[i] hurt.
10Then too, I saw the wicked buried—those who
used to come and go from the holy place and
receive praise[j] in the city where they did this.
This too is meaningless.

11When the sentence for a crime is not quickly
carried out, the hearts of the people are filled with
schemes to do wrong. 12Although a wicked man
commits a hundred crimes and still lives a long
time, I know that it will go better with God-fear-
ing men, who are reverent before God. 13Yet be-
cause the wicked do not fear God, it will not go
well with them, and their days will not lengthen
like a shadow.

14There is something else meaningless that oc-

[h]8 Or *over his spirit to retain it* [i]9 Or *to their* [j]10 Some Hebrew manuscripts and Septuagint (Aquila); most Hebrew manuscripts *and are forgotten*

curs on earth: righteous men who get what the
wicked deserve, and wicked men who get what
the righteous deserve. This too, I say, is meaning-
less. [15]So I commend the enjoyment of life, be-
cause nothing is better for a man under the sun
than to eat and drink and be glad. Then joy will
accompany him in his work all the days of the life
God has given him under the sun.

[16]When I applied my mind to know wisdom
and to observe man's labor on earth—his eyes not
seeing sleep day or night— [17]then I saw all that
God has done. No one can comprehend what
goes on under the sun. Despite all his efforts to
search it out, man cannot discover its meaning.
Even if a wise man claims he knows, he cannot
really comprehend it.

Discovering the Word 1. Why does the Teacher encourage obedience to authority? 2. What is significant about the fact that human authority is limited (v. 8)? 3. What unjust uses of authority are described (vv. 9–11, 14)? 4. How would you characterize the Teacher's answer to these injustices in verses 12–13? 5. How does God's authority, alluded to in verses 15–17, contrast with human limitations in verses 7–8? 6. In the face of life's injustices and uncertainties, the Teacher argues for enjoying life (v. 15). Why?

Applying the Word 1. According to verses 16–17, human wisdom is very limited. How should knowing this fact encourage you to fear and trust God? 2. What is an unsettled situation in life that you need to entrust to God?

Responding in Prayer Ask your Father to increase your faith and hope as you seek to follow him despite difficult circumstances that you do not fully understand.

9 / *Ecclesiastes 9:1–12*
What Meaning Does Death Bring to Life?

ON THE EDGE of the University of Oregon campus lies a sizable historical cemetery. For years university officials have eyed with envy this valuable slice of real estate that divides their campus. At one point some even entertained suggestions to build a superstructure of above-ground buildings over the plots! For many students the cemetery represents an unfortunate obstacle as they crisscross the campus from one class to the next. I doubt if the Teacher would share this objection. What better reminder for young people seeking to fashion lifelong values? Contemplation of death gives us the wisdom to live.

Warming Up to God When you think of your own death, what are some of your fears, anxieties—and hopes? Present these to God in prayer.

Read Ecclesiastes 9:1–12.

9 So I reflected on all this and concluded
that the righteous and the wise and what
they do are in God's hands, but no man
knows whether love or hate awaits him. [2]All
share a common destiny—the righteous and the
wicked, the good and the bad,[k] the clean and the
unclean, those who offer sacrifices and those who
do not.

As it is with the good man,
    so with the sinner;
as it is with those who take oaths,
    so with those who are afraid to take them.

[3]This is the evil in everything that happens un-
der the sun: The same destiny overtakes all. The
hearts of men, moreover, are full of evil and there
is madness in their hearts while they live, and
afterward they join the dead. [4]Anyone who is
among the living has hope[l]—even a live dog is
better off than a dead lion!

[5]For the living know that they will die,
    but the dead know nothing;
they have no further reward,

[k]2 Septuagint (Aquila), Vulgate and Syriac; Hebrew does not have *and the bad.* [l]4 Or *What then is to be chosen? With all who live, there is hope*

and even the memory of them is forgotten.
[6]Their love, their hate
and their jealousy have long since vanished;
never again will they have a part
in anything that happens under the sun.

[7]Go, eat your food with gladness, and drink
your wine with a joyful heart, for it is now that
God favors what you do. [8]Always be clothed in
white, and always anoint your head with oil. [9]En-
joy life with your wife, whom you love, all the
days of this meaningless life that God has given
you under the sun— all your meaningless days.
For this is your lot in life and in your toilsome
labor under the sun. [10]Whatever your hand finds
to do, do it with all your might, for in the grave,[m]
where you are going, there is neither working nor
planning nor knowledge nor wisdom.

[11]I have seen something else under the sun:
The race is not to the swift
or the battle to the strong,
nor does food come to the wise
or wealth to the brilliant
or favor to the learned;
but time and chance happen to them all.

[12]Moreover, no man knows when his hour will
come:

As fish are caught in a cruel net,
or birds are taken in a snare,
so men are trapped by evil times
that fall unexpectedly upon them.

[m]10 Hebrew *Sheol*

Discovering the Word 1. In what ways are the righteous and wicked described in verses 1–3? 2. What reaction might the Teacher hope to gain with his emphasis that a "common destiny" awaits all (vv. 1–3)? 3. What kind of hope does the Teacher offer in verses 4–6? 4. In what ways do verses 7–10 encourage us to enjoy life? 5. What uncertainty do the factors of time and chance bring to life (vv. 11–12)?

Applying the Word 1. What difference would it make in your life if you knew you were going to die within six months? 2. In what ways does taking death seriously help alter your values in the use of your money, time and energy? 3. How do Christ's death and resurrection give you hope in this life and in the one to come?

Responding in Prayer Reflect on the dilemna voiced by Peter but faced by all of us: "Lord, to whom shall we go? You have the words of eternal life" (Jn 6:68). Commit yourself to follow Jesus closely and thank him for the fulfillment such a life brings.

10 / *Ecclesiastes 9:13—10:20*
How Do We Live Sensibly?

COMMON SENSE. HAVE you felt that somehow you missed out on this body of wisdom that is supposedly so universal? Of course, we all lack commonsense judgment at times. But in this section, the Teacher addresses something deeper and darker, a lack of commonsense lifestyle. Such a lifestyle, called *foolishness,* results when human weakness and wickedness assert control. In this study, he will identify foolish behavior and tell us how to avoid it.

Warming Up to God When you need help making an important decision, who is your closest confidante? What qualities make that person a good listener and trusted advisor? Consider those characteristics as you read about some "contrasting" personality traits.

 **Read Ecclesiastes 9:13—10:20.**

[13]I also saw under the sun this example of wis-
dom that greatly impressed me: [14]There was once
a small city with only a few people in it. And a
powerful king came against it, surrounded it and
built huge siegeworks against it. [15]Now there
lived in that city a man poor but wise, and he

saved the city by his wisdom. But nobody remem-
bered that poor man. 16So I said, "Wisdom is bet-
ter than strength." But the poor man's wisdom is
despised, and his words are no longer heeded.

17The quiet words of the wise are more to be
heeded
than the shouts of a ruler of fools.
18Wisdom is better than weapons of war,
but one sinner destroys much good.

10 As dead flies give perfume a bad smell,
so a little folly outweighs wisdom and honor.
2The heart of the wise inclines to the right,
but the heart of the fool to the left.
3Even as he walks along the road,
the fool lacks sense
and shows everyone how stupid he is.
4If a ruler's anger rises against you,
do not leave your post;
calmness can lay great errors to rest.

5There is an evil I have seen under the sun,
the sort of error that arises from a ruler:
6Fools are put in many high positions,
while the rich occupy the low ones.
7I have seen slaves on horseback,
while princes go on foot like slaves.

8Whoever digs a pit may fall into it;
whoever breaks through a wall may be bitten by a snake.
9Whoever quarries stones may be injured by them;
whoever splits logs may be endangered by them.

10If the ax is dull
and its edge unsharpened,
more strength is needed
but skill will bring success.

11If a snake bites before it is charmed,
there is no profit for the charmer.

12Words from a wise man's mouth are gracious,
but a fool is consumed by his own lips.
13At the beginning his words are folly;
at the end they are wicked madness—
14 and the fool multiplies words.

No one knows what is coming—
who can tell him what will happen after him?

15A fool's work wearies him;
he does not know the way to town.

16Woe to you, O land whose king was a servant[n]
and whose princes feast in the morning.
17Blessed are you, O land whose king is of noble birth
and whose princes eat at a proper time—
for strength and not for drunkenness.

18If a man is lazy, the rafters sag;
if his hands are idle, the house leaks.

19A feast is made for laughter,
and wine makes life merry,
but money is the answer for everything.

20Do not revile the king even in your thoughts,
or curse the rich in your bedroom,
because a bird of the air may carry your words,
and a bird on the wing may report what you say.

[n]16 Or *king is a child*

Discovering the Word 1. Describe the ironies of wisdom and foolish behavior illustrated in 9:13–16. 2. How have you seen wisdom destroyed in the manner described in 9:18—10:1? 3. What is the significance of folly's description in 10:2–3? 4. List the common situations described in 10:8–11 that call for the exercise of good judgment. 5. What are the consequences of wise and foolish lifestyles according to 10:16–20?

Applying the Word 1. In reference to 9:17–18, do you find yourself giving more respect to those who have wisdom or to those who have status? Why? 2. What is an area of life in which you struggle to exercise good judgment? Explain. 3. James 1:5 says, "If any of you lacks wisdom, he should ask God, who gives generously." What current decision requires a wise attitude or action on your part?

Responding in Prayer Ask the Lord to teach you prayerful wisdom and to protect you from any inclination toward foolish actions. Ask for his wisdom in current decisions you must make. Ask him to nurture qualities of wisdom in your character.

11/ *Ecclesiastes 11:1—12:8*
How Shall We Then Live?

ALL WEEK I prepared myself to rappel off Inspiration II, a sheer cliff of 100 feet near Bear Trap Ranch in Colorado. Physical preparation included "learning the ropes" on smaller cliffs such as Inspiration I. Mental preparation involved watching and talking to veteran rappellers. The day that I was to go came, but I was busy with a camping trip. The next day no one was going. The day after that something else came up. From then until the end of the week I was going to make the rappelling trip . . . tomorrow. It never happened. To this day, twenty years later, I wonder: "Why didn't I go? Was I unsure of my skills, was I too timid to take up the challenge or . . . ?"

There is a risk to not taking risks. An opportunity to test our resolve or pursue a challenge may be lost forever. Failing to take spiritual risks in the life of faith has even greater consequences. In this section the Teacher will encourage us to "cast our bread upon the waters."

Warming Up to God Create a brief list of your resources, skills, funds, time, energy and possessions. Bring this list to God in a prayer of thanks. What decisions do you have about using these assets that may lead you out of your comfort zone? Meditate on God's character as it relates to these decisions.

Read Ecclesiastes 11:1—12:8.

11 Cast your bread upon the waters,
for after many days,you will find
it again.
2Give portions to seven, yes to eight,
for you do not know what disaster may
come upon the land.

3If clouds are full of water,
they pour rain upon the earth.
Whether a tree falls to the south or to the
north,
in the place where it falls, there will it lie.
4Whoever watches the wind will not plant;
whoever looks at the clouds will not reap.

5As you do not know the path of the wind,
or how the body is formed[o] in a mother's
womb,
so you cannot understand the work of God,
the Maker of all things.

6Sow your seed in the morning,
and at evening let not your hands be idle,
for you do not know which will succeed,
whether this or that,
or whether both will do equally well.

7Light is sweet,
and it pleases the eyes to see the sun.
8However many years a man may live,
let him enjoy them all.
But let him remember the days of darkness,
for they will be many.
Everything to come is meaningless.

9Be happy, young man, while you are young,
and let your heart give you joy in the days
of your youth.
Follow the ways of your heart
and whatever your eyes see,
but know that for all these things
God will bring you to judgment.
10So then, banish anxiety from your heart
and cast off the troubles of your body,
for youth and vigor are meaningless.

12 Remember your Creator
in the days of your youth,
before the days of trouble come
and the years approach when you will say,
"I find no pleasure in them"—
2before the sun and the light
and the moon and the stars grow dark,
and the clouds return after the rain;
3when the keepers of the house tremble,
and the strong men stoop,
when the grinders cease because they are few,
and those looking through the windows
grow dim;
4when the doors to the street are closed
and the sound of grinding fades;
when men rise up at the sound of birds,
but all their songs grow faint;
5when men are afraid of heights
and of dangers in the streets;
when the almond tree blossoms
and the grasshopper drags himself along

[o]5 *Or know how life (or the spirit) / enters the body being formed*

and desire no longer is stirred.
Then man goes to his eternal home
and mourners go about the streets.

6Remember him—before the silver cord is
severed,
or the golden bowl is broken;
before the pitcher is shattered at the spring,
or the wheel broken at the well,

7and the dust returns to the ground it came
from,
and the spirit returns to God who gave it.

8"Meaningless! Meaningless!" says the
Teacher.[p]
"Everything is meaningless!"

p8 Or the leader of the assembly; also in verses 9 and 10

Discovering the Word 1. What is the Teacher encouraging in 11:1–6? 2. Given what the Teacher has said in chapters 1—10, why would he encourage us to be risk-takers? 3. Describe the perspective on life found in 11:7–10. 4. What kind of relationship with God does the word *remember* imply (12:1, 6)? 5. What are the metaphors used to describe death (12:6–7)?

Applying the Word 1. What's something you've done which involved a great deal of risk? 2. How does the perspective of verses 7–10 encourage you to pursue joy? 3. Why should the eventuality of death be a strong encouragement to a risk-taking commitment to God?

Responding in Prayer Spend several minutes thanking the Lord for the life that you have found in him. Ask him to help you pursue the kind of faith-stretching life that taps into his vast resources.

12 / *Ecclesiastes 12:9–14*
What Makes Life Meaningful?

IF YOU WERE given the assignment to describe life with one word, what word would you choose? Few of us are comfortable with the Teacher's choice of *meaningless.* Consider this, however: in darkness, a few small lights will stand out clearly and become the focus of attention. These lights from Ecclesiastes—the purposes, values and priorities that should guide our lives—are now seen so much more clearly. In the final lines of the book, an observer comments on the life and writings of "the Teacher" who wrote this intriguing book. Let's take one last look at how to pursue meaning in life, Ecclesiates style.

Warming Up to God If a person who knows you well tried to summarize what you have "taught" up to this point in your life, what do you think that person would say? Remember today that it is Jesus Christ who gives you hope and a purpose for your life. Meditate on the ways he has changed your life since you met him for the first time.

Read Ecclesiastes 12:9–14.

9Not only was the Teacher wise, but also he
imparted knowledge to the people. He pondered
and searched out and set in order many proverbs.
10The Teacher searched to find just the right
words, and what he wrote was upright and
true.
11The words of the wise are like goads, their
collected sayings like firmly embedded nails—
given by one Shepherd. 12Be warned, my son, of
anything in addition to them.
Of making many books there is no end, and
much study wearies the body.

13Now all has been heard;
here is the conclusion of the matter:
Fear God and keep his commandments,
for this is the whole ⌞duty⌟ of man.
14For God will bring every deed into judgment,
including every hidden thing,
whether it is good or evil.

Discovering the Word 1. How is the Teacher's purpose described in verses 9–10? 2. Why is it significant that the Teacher's words are based on the authority of the "one Shepherd"? 3. Why do you think the commentator ends this book with the particular directives of verses 13–14? 4. Sum up the message of Ecclesiastes in a brief phrase or statement. 5. How would you characterize the Teacher's pursuit to find meaning in life? (See 1:12—6:12.)

Applying the Word 1. What does it mean for you to "fear God and keep his commandments"? 2. In light of your study of Ecclesiastes, on what basis is life meaningless to you and on what basis is it not? 3. Verse 11 says, "The words of the wise are like goads, their collected sayings like firmly embedded nails." What did you find in Ecclesiastes that goaded or irritated you toward wisdom?

Responding in Prayer Spend some time thanking the Shepherd for challenging you with the message of Ecclesiastes.

Song of Songs

"Sexuality is a gift from God." "Our bodies are beautiful and should be enjoyed." You have probably heard statements like this, but are they true—for you?

Many people, even Christians, have heard negative messages, sometimes implicit—from their parents, friends or society—which inhibit them from understanding and appreciating their own sexuality. Perhaps you have been told: "Original sin started with Adam and Eve having sex." "Women should be very modest about what they wear so they won't cause men to lust." "God made sex just so we can procreate." If so, the Song of Songs will give you a new perspective.

Interpreters of the Song of Songs have struggled with whether it is an allegory about God's love for us, or if it should be read as a love song between two people. Understanding it either way can teach us about love. However, the Song of Songs is best seen as both:

> How is one to understand the Song in terms of human and divine love? . . . The Bible suggests that these loves are united and not to be separated. . . . The union between man and woman became a primary symbol for the expression of the relationship of the Lord to His People. The covenant between God and His People is consistently portrayed as a marriage. (Roland Murphy O'Carm as quoted in Andrew Greeley, *Love Song*)

The Song of Songs is written as a play. The voice of the lover is most likely that of King Solomon, and the beloved is the feminine voice. Their friends serve as a chorus, adding dramatic effect, but perhaps also to show the importance of community relationship even in the midst of celebrating the marriage relationship. The first two chapters are the courtship between Solomon and his beloved, and chapter three describes their wedding procession. What follows is their declaration of love and their vows of commitment to the marriage.

It is our hope that these quiet times will bring you closer to God, our divine lover, and help you to understand the place of sexuality within marriage.

Outline

1/ Song of Songs 1—2 ———— *Created for Love*

2/ Song of Songs 3 ———— *Love Is Patient*

3/ Song of Songs 4 ———— *God's Good Gift*

4/ Song of Songs 5—6 ———— *Affirming One Another*

5/ Song of Songs 7—8 ———— *Love for a Lifetime*

1 / *Song of Songs 1—2*
Created for Love

DO YOU REMEMBER the first time you read the Song of Songs? Perhaps you were in junior high, flipping through your Bible during a boring sermon. You were probably surprised by the explicit language and sensual images. The Song of Songs is a celebration of married love that includes open dialogue about physical love. It's an important part of the picture of married love as God created it to be.

Warming Up to God Have you ever talked to God about how you feel about your sexual nature? Let him know of any apprehensions or positive feelings you have as you begin this book.

Read Song of Songs 1—2.

1 Solomon's Song of Songs.

[2]Let him kiss me with the kisses of his mouth—
for your love is more delightful than wine.
[3]Pleasing is the fragrance of your perfumes;
your name is like perfume poured out.
No wonder the maidens love you!
[4]Take me away with you—let us hurry!
Let the king bring me into his chambers.
We rejoice and delight in you[a];
we will praise your love more than wine.
How right they are to adore you!

[5]Dark am I, yet lovely,
O daughters of Jerusalem,
dark like the tents of Kedar,
like the tent curtains of Solomon.[b]
[6]Do not stare at me because I am dark,
because I am darkened by the sun.
My mother's sons were angry with me
and made me take care of the vineyards;
my own vineyard I have neglected.
[7]Tell me, you whom I love, where you graze your flock
and where you rest your sheep at midday.
Why should I be like a veiled woman
beside the flocks of your friends?
[8]If you do not know, most beautiful of women,
follow the tracks of the sheep
and graze your young goats
by the tents of the shepherds.
[9]I liken you, my darling, to a mare
harnessed to one of the chariots of Pharaoh.
[10]Your cheeks are beautiful with earrings,
your neck with strings of jewels.
[11]We will make you earrings of gold,
studded with silver.
[12]While the king was at his table,
my perfume spread its fragrance.
[13]My lover is to me a sachet of myrrh
resting between my breasts.
[14]My lover is to me a cluster of henna blossoms
from the vineyards of En Gedi.
[15]How beautiful you are, my darling!
Oh, how beautiful!
Your eyes are doves.
[16]How handsome you are, my lover!
Oh, how charming!
And our bed is verdant.
[17]The beams of our house are cedars;
our rafters are firs.

2 I am a rose[c] of Sharon,
a lily of the valleys.
[2]Like a lily among thorns
is my darling among the maidens.
[3]Like an apple tree among the trees of the forest
is my lover among the young men.
I delight to sit in his shade,
and his fruit is sweet to my taste.
[4]He has taken me to the banquet hall,
and his banner over me is love.
[5]Strengthen me with raisins,
refresh me with apples,
for I am faint with love.
[6]His left arm is under my head,
and his right arm embraces me.
[7]Daughters of Jerusalem, I charge you
by the gazelles and by the does of the field:
Do not arouse or awaken love
until it so desires.
[8]Listen! My lover!
Look! Here he comes,

[a]4 The Hebrew is masculine singular. [b]5 Or *Salma* [c]1 Possibly a member of the crocus family

leaping across the mountains,
bounding over the hills.
9My lover is like a gazelle or a young stag.
Look! There he stands behind our wall,
gazing through the windows,
peering through the lattice.
10My lover spoke and said to me,
"Arise, my darling,
my beautiful one, and come with me.
11See! The winter is past;
the rains are over and gone.
12Flowers appear on the earth;
the season of singing has come,
the cooing of doves
is heard in our land.
13The fig tree forms its early fruit;
the blossoming vines spread their fragrance.
Arise, come, my darling;
my beautiful one, come with me."
14My dove in the clefts of the rock,
in the hiding places on the mountainside,
show me your face,
let me hear your voice;
for your voice is sweet,
and your face is lovely.
15Catch for us the foxes,
the little foxes
that ruin the vineyards,
our vineyards that are in bloom.
16My lover is mine and I am his;
he browses among the lilies.
17Until the day breaks
and the shadows flee,
turn, my lover,
and be like a gazelle
or like a young stag
on the rugged hills.[d]

[d]17 *Or the hills of Bether*

Discovering the Word 1. What sense do you get from this passage about how the "Beloved" and the "Lover" regard one another? 2. What images do they use to describe one another (1:3, 7, 9, 10, 12–14, 15; 2:2, 3, 8–9)? 3. What do these word pictures reflect about the nature of their relationship? 4. What fears and insecurities does the beloved reveal (1:3–4, 5–7)? 5. In 1:8 how do the friends pick up on the beloved's imagery and reassure her? 6. How does the lover reassure her (1:9–11)?

Applying the Word 1. Why is it important to have supportive friends involved in a marriage relationship? 2. How does knowing that the Song of Songs is included in Scripture affect your view of married relationships?

Responding in Prayer Reflect on your own sexuality and how you respond to this picture of passionate physical love. Talk to God about how you are feeling.

2 / *Song of Songs 3*
Love Is Patient

ONE OF THE many flaws in the *Playboy* approach to sex is that it makes people into things. *Playboy* magazine and all its derivatives are nothing more than a form of idolatry. No other aspect of the person, other than his or her body, is of any interest. This is a tragic distortion of God's good creation. True love requires time—and hard work. It may even include times of searching and insecurity.

Warming Up to God Perhaps you have recently used someone you love to satisfy your desires without considering the other person. Quietly consider this before God. Confess your sin to him. Wait for his forgiveness.

Read Song of Songs 3.

3 All night long on my bed
I looked for the one my heart loves;
I looked for him but did not find him.
2I will get up now and go about the city,
through its streets and squares;
I will search for the one my heart loves.
So I looked for him but did not find him.
3The watchmen found me
as they made their rounds in the city.
"Have you seen the one my heart loves?"
4Scarcely had I passed them
when I found the one my heart loves.
I held him and would not let him go
till I had brought him to my mother's house,
to the room of the one who conceived me.
5Daughters of Jerusalem, I charge you
by the gazelles and by the does of the field:
Do not arouse or awaken love
until it so desires.

6Who is this coming up from the desert
like a column of smoke,
perfumed with myrrh and incense
made from all the spices of the merchant?
7Look! It is Solomon's carriage,
escorted by sixty warriors,
the noblest of Israel,
8all of them wearing the sword,
all experienced in battle,
each with his sword at his side,
prepared for the terrors of the night.
9King Solomon made for himself the carriage;
he made it of wood from Lebanon.
10Its posts he made of silver,
its base of gold.
Its seat was upholstered with purple,
its interior lovingly inlaid
by[e] the daughters of Jerusalem.
11Come out, you daughters of Zion,
and look at King Solomon wearing the crown,
the crown with which his mother crowned him
on the day of his wedding,
the day his heart rejoiced.

[e]10 *Or its inlaid interior a gift of love / from*

Discovering the Word 1. What shift in tone do you notice in chapter 3? 2. Verses 1–3 describe some of the insecurities that love can bring. What is it about love that can make us feel this way? 3. Describe the reunion in verse 4. 4. "Do not arouse or awaken love until it so desires" (v. 5) is repeated from 2:7. What wisdom do you see in this saying? 5. Verses 6–11 are from the perspective of the friends. How do they describe the wedding procession?

Applying the Word 1. When are you likely to feel insecure about those you love? 2. The wedding procession in this passage is a time of publicly declaring love before others. What experience in your life confirmed the love someone (that is, the romantic love of a spouse or the love of a friend or family member) has for you?

Responding in Prayer Ask God to help you better show your love to those you care about.

3 / *Song of Songs 4*
God's Good Gift

> Human passion . . . gives us a hint of God's passion for us. We are most like God's love for us when we are aroused in the presence of our beloved. And we best experience a hint of God's love for us when our beloved pursues us. (Andrew Greeley, *Love Song* [New York: Warner Books, 1989], p. 28.)

THIS EXCERPT FROM one of Andrew Greeley's novels is an appropriate description of what romantic love between a man and a woman is all about. God has given us this gift so that we can better understand what his love is like. And that is what the Song of Songs is all about.

Warming Up to God How do you feel about the quote above? Talk to God about how you experience his love.

Read Song of Songs 4.

4 How beautiful you are, my darling!
Oh, how beautiful!
Your eyes behind your veil are doves.
Your hair is like a flock of goats
descending from Mount Gilead.
2Your teeth are like a flock of sheep just
shorn,
coming up from the washing.
Each has its twin;
not one of them is alone.
3Your lips are like a scarlet ribbon;
your mouth is lovely.
Your temples behind your veil
are like the halves of a pomegranate.
4Your neck is like the tower of David,
built with elegance[f];
on it hang a thousand shields,
all of them shields of warriors.
5Your two breasts are like two fawns,
like twin fawns of a gazelle
that browse among the lilies.
6Until the day breaks
and the shadows flee,
I will go to the mountain of myrrh
and to the hill of incense.
7All beautiful you are, my darling;
there is no flaw in you.
8Come with me from Lebanon, my bride,
come with me from Lebanon.
Descend from the crest of Amana,
from the top of Senir, the summit of
Hermon,
from the lions' dens
and the mountain haunts of the
leopards.
9You have stolen my heart, my sister, my
bride;
you have stolen my heart
with one glance of your eyes,
with one jewel of your necklace.
10How delightful is your love, my sister, my
bride!
How much more pleasing is your love than
wine,
and the fragrance of your perfume than any
spice!
11Your lips drop sweetness as the honeycomb,
my bride;
milk and honey are under your tongue.
The fragrance of your garments is like that
of Lebanon.
12You are a garden locked up, my sister, my
bride;
you are a spring enclosed, a sealed
fountain.
13Your plants are an orchard of pomegranates
with choice fruits,
with henna and nard,
14 nard and saffron,
calamus and cinnamon,
with every kind of incense tree,
with myrrh and aloes
and all the finest spices.
15You are[g] a garden fountain,
a well of flowing water
streaming down from Lebanon.
16Awake, north wind,
and come, south wind!
Blow on my garden,
that its fragrance may spread abroad.
Let my lover come into his garden
and taste its choice fruits.

f4 The meaning of the Hebrew for this word is uncertain. g15 Or *I am* (spoken by the *Beloved*)

Discovering the Word 1. What kinds of emotions do you notice throughout this passage? 2. What do the lover's explicit words describing his beloved's physical beauty (vv. 1–7) reveal about their relationship? 3. What words and phrases help you understand how Solomon feels about his beloved (vv. 9–15)? 4. How does the beloved respond to the praise and adoration that is lavished upon her? 5. What does their dialogue reveal about their attitude about themselves as sexual beings?

Applying the Word 1. How does this picture compare to and contrast with the depiction of married love in current media? 2. In what ways does this passage change and/or inform your attitude toward married love?

Responding in Prayer God pursues you like the lover pursues the beloved in this passage. Praise God for his love that never lets us go.

4 / *Song of Songs 5—6*
Affirming One Another

"THAT WAS A great meal." "You look fabulous." "Thanks for remembering." We all need to be noticed and appreciated. Sometimes we forget to affirm those we are closest to—yet they are the ones who most value our opinions. In the Song of Songs we have a picture of loving, mutual affirmation.

Warming Up to God In what area of your life would you most like to be praised?

Read Song of Songs 5—6.

5 I have come into my garden, my sister,
my bride;
I have gathered my myrrh with my
spice.
I have eaten my honeycomb and my honey;
I have drunk my wine and my milk.
Eat, O friends, and drink;
drink your fill, O lovers.
2 I slept but my heart was awake.
Listen! My lover is knocking:
"Open to me, my sister, my darling,
my dove, my flawless one.
My head is drenched with dew,
my hair with the dampness of the night."
3 I have taken off my robe—
must I put it on again?
I have washed my feet—
must I soil them again?
4 My lover thrust his hand through the
latch-opening;
my heart began to pound for him.
5 I arose to open for my lover,
and my hands dripped with myrrh,
my fingers with flowing myrrh,
on the handles of the lock.
6 I opened for my lover,
but my lover had left; he was gone.
My heart sank at his departure.[h]
I looked for him but did not find him.
I called him but he did not answer.
7 The watchmen found me
as they made their rounds in the city.
They beat me, they bruised me;
they took away my cloak,
those watchmen of the walls!
8 O daughters of Jerusalem, I charge you—
if you find my lover,
what will you tell him?
Tell him I am faint with love.
9 How is your beloved better than others,
most beautiful of women?
How is your beloved better than others,
that you charge us so?
10 My lover is radiant and ruddy,
outstanding among ten thousand.
11 His head is purest gold;
his hair is wavy
and black as a raven.
12 His eyes are like doves
by the water streams,
washed in milk,
mounted like jewels.
13 His cheeks are like beds of spice
yielding perfume.
His lips are like lilies
dripping with myrrh.
14 His arms are rods of gold
set with chrysolite.
His body is like polished ivory
decorated with sapphires.[i]
15 His legs are pillars of marble
set on bases of pure gold.
His appearance is like Lebanon,
choice as its cedars.
16 His mouth is sweetness itself;

[h] 6 *Or heart had gone out to him when he spoke* [i] 14 *Or lapis lazuli*

he is altogether lovely.
This is my lover, this my friend,
O daughters of Jerusalem.

6 Where has your lover gone,
most beautiful of women?
Which way did your lover turn,
that we may look for him with you?
2 My lover has gone down to his garden,
to the beds of spices,
to browse in the gardens
and to gather lilies.
3 I am my lover's and my lover is mine;
he browses among the lilies.
4 You are beautiful, my darling, as Tirzah,
lovely as Jerusalem,
majestic as troops with banners.
5 Turn your eyes from me;
they overwhelm me.
Your hair is like a flock of goats
descending from Gilead.
6 Your teeth are like a flock of sheep
coming up from the washing.
Each has its twin,
not one of them is alone.
7 Your temples behind your veil
are like the halves of a pomegranate.
8 Sixty queens there may be,
and eighty concubines,
and virgins beyond number;
9 but my dove, my perfect one, is unique,
the only daughter of her mother,
the favorite of the one who bore her.
The maidens saw her and called her blessed;
the queens and concubines praised her.
10 Who is this that appears like the dawn,
fair as the moon, bright as the sun,
majestic as the stars in procession?
11 I went down to the grove of nut trees
to look at the new growth in the valley,
to see if the vines had budded
or the pomegranates were in bloom.
12 Before I realized it,
my desire set me among the royal chariots
of my people.[j]
13 Come back, come back, O Shulammite;
come back, come back, that we may gaze
on you!
Why would you gaze on the Shulammite
as on the dance of Mahanaim?

j12 *Or among the chariots of Amminadab; or among the chariots of the people of the prince*

Discovering the Word 1. The image of a garden runs through this passage and the whole book (5:1; 6:2–3) How is it appropriate to the picture of marital love? 2. Prompted by the friends in 5:9, the beloved describes her lover. 5:10–16 is the only place where she describes his appearance. We don't know whether he was present at that time. If he did hear her words—or if he heard about her praise—how would this have been meaningful to him? 3. Why is it important to make praise specific and concrete as in 5:10–16? 4. In 6:3 the beloved says, "I am my lover's and my lover is mine," while in 2:16 she says, "My lover is mine and I am his." What does this statement and the variation in wording tell you about the relationship?

Applying the Word 1. This is a picture of a couple who is actively adoring, courting and pursuing each other. What is the value of this in a marriage? 2. What have you seen happen when this aspect of the relationship is neglected? 3. Think of someone close to you, perhaps your spouse or a parent, that you need to affirm. How can you do this?

Responding in Prayer Ask God to make you a channel of love and affirmation to those you meet.

5 / *Song of Songs 7—8*
Love for a Lifetime

"LET'S PRETEND WE'RE married—oh, all night." This is love according to Prince. Popular songs tell us what love is. Jewelry advertisers tell us what love is. Movies show us what love is. Yet the definitions that popular culture gives us leave us empty—unfulfilled. The *NIV Student Bible* refers to the Song of Songs as "a poem about love the way it's meant to be." In this sense it shows us love as God envisions it, not as we usually see it.

Warming Up to God When are you likely to be led astray by the media's depictions of love?

Read Song of Songs 7—8.

7 How beautiful your sandaled feet,
O prince's daughter!
Your graceful legs are like jewels,
the work of a craftsman's hands.
2Your navel is a rounded goblet
that never lacks blended wine.
Your waist is a mound of wheat
encircled by lilies.
3Your breasts are like two fawns,
twins of a gazelle.
4Your neck is like an ivory tower.
Your eyes are the pools of Heshbon
by the gate of Bath Rabbim.
Your nose is like the tower of Lebanon
looking toward Damascus.
5Your head crowns you like Mount Carmel.
Your hair is like royal tapestry;
the king is held captive by its tresses.
6How beautiful you are and how pleasing,
O love, with your delights!
7Your stature is like that of the palm,
and your breasts like clusters of fruit.
8I said, "I will climb the palm tree;
I will take hold of its fruit."
May your breasts be like the clusters of the vine,
the fragrance of your breath like apples,
9 and your mouth like the best wine.
May the wine go straight to my lover,
flowing gently over lips and teeth.[k]
10I belong to my lover,
and his desire is for me.
11Come, my lover, let us go to the countryside,
let us spend the night in the villages.[l]
12Let us go early to the vineyards
to see if the vines have budded,
if their blossoms have opened,
and if the pomegranates are in bloom—
there I will give you my love.
13The mandrakes send out their fragrance,
and at our door is every delicacy,
both new and old,
that I have stored up for you, my lover.

8 If only you were to me like a brother,
who was nursed at my mother's breasts!
Then, if I found you outside,
I would kiss you,
and no one would despise me.
2I would lead you
and bring you to my mother's house—
she who has taught me.
I would give you spiced wine to drink,
the nectar of my pomegranates.
3His left arm is under my head
and his right arm embraces me.
4Daughters of Jerusalem, I charge you:
Do not arouse or awaken love
until it so desires.
5Who is this coming up from the desert
leaning on her lover?
Under the apple tree I roused you;
there your mother conceived you,
there she who was in labor gave you birth.
6Place me like a seal over your heart,
like a seal on your arm;
for love is as strong as death,
its jealousy[m] unyielding as the grave.[n]
It burns like blazing fire,
like a mighty flame.[o]
7Many waters cannot quench love;
rivers cannot wash it away.
If one were to give
all the wealth of his house for love,
it[p] would be utterly scorned.
8We have a young sister,
and her breasts are not yet grown.
What shall we do for our sister
for the day she is spoken for?
9If she is a wall,
we will build towers of silver on her.
If she is a door,
we will enclose her with panels of cedar.
10I am a wall,
and my breasts are like towers.
Thus I have become in his eyes

[k]9 Septuagint, Aquila, Vulgate and Syriac; Hebrew *lips of sleepers* [l]11 Or *henna bushes* [m]6 Or *ardor* [n]6 Hebrew *Sheol* [o]6 Or / *like the very flame of the* LORD [p]7 Or *he*

like one bringing contentment.
11Solomon had a vineyard in Baal Hamon;
he let out his vineyard to tenants.
Each was to bring for its fruit
a thousand shekels[q] of silver.
12But my own vineyard is mine to give;
the thousand shekels are for you,
O Solomon,
and two hundred[r] are for those who tend
its fruit.

13You who dwell in the gardens
with friends in attendance,
let me hear your voice!
14Come away, my lover,
and be like a gazelle
or like a young stag
on the spice-laden mountains.

[q]11 That is, about 25 pounds (about 11.5 kilograms); also in verse 12
[r]12 That is, about 5 pounds (about 2.3 kilograms)

Discovering the Word 1. The lover offers his beloved praise in exquisite detail in 7:1–9. What does this reveal about their love? 2. In 7:10 we see another variation of the refrain of 2:16 and 6:3. What truth about love and desire do you find here? 3. How does sexual love within a marriage involve discoveries "both new and old" (7:13) that a one-night stand does not? 4. The language of 8:6–7 is rich and beautiful. What qualities of love are named? 5. How are these qualities unique to the long-term commitment of marriage? 6. In what ways does marriage require a willingness to give one's self to your partner (8:12)?

Applying the Word 1. When is it difficult for you to surrender yourself to those who love you? 2. When is it difficult for you to surrender to God's love for you?

Responding in Prayer Ask God to make you responsive to his unending love for you.

Isaiah

We had planned, a pastor friend and I, a series of studies in Isaiah for his church. His enthusiasm for the studies was infectious. But when the time came, he did not attend. Why not? Some people would put it simply: "Cancer killed him." Yet from another perspective, we can say, "The Lord took him home into his presence." Thus, it was with a heart filled with sorrow and gratitude that I set off for the week in question. Filled with ideas and enthusiasm, I was convicted that "trusting God in troubled times" was the right theme for this bereaved church. I was loaded with emotion and the hope that our study times would be real encounters with God himself. And what times we had together! Times of worship, laughter and sober reflection. So it is to the memory of Eugene Kwa, to his wife, Ann Nai, and to the members of the church which he pastored that this is dedicated.

Trusting God in Troubled Times

Isaiah is a difficult and, therefore, often-neglected book. Why should we study Isaiah? First, because it is part of holy Scripture and is great literature. We should study Isaiah because it is very frequently quoted or alluded to in the New Testament. We should study these selected passages because trusting God is still essential and troubled times are our lot too.

These studies contain some fascinating passages, including (1) hard-hitting criticisms of empty religion; (2) panoramic and extraordinarily impressive views of God's coming day of judgment and the everlasting joys which follow it; (3) some of the most famous Messianic prophecies; (4) dramatic narratives of times of national crisis; (5) honest exposures of a rotten society and a heartfelt cry for revival; (6) the famous story of Isaiah's call and mysterious commission and meditations on what it means for us to be trustful, faithful servants of God; (7) robust assertions that God is the world's only Savior with worldwide purposes we are to carry out; (8) and many passages full of pastoral comfort for our "spiritual armory."

Isaiah lived through turbulent times. He was called to his work at the time when a famous Assyrian king was building his empire into the largest and cruelest that western Asia had ever seen. He saw the neighboring kingdom of Israel crack, collapse and vanish. For forty years Isaiah walked quietly in the corridors of power challenging a knock-kneed king to trust God even when he could see the campfires of the apparently invincible Assyrian army right outside his own city's locked gates and hear the threats of the general coming over the walls.

We know nothing of his wife, but Isaiah had two sons with names which were signposts to coming events. Isaiah was a social critic, remorselessly applying the yardstick of God's law to what he saw. He was a prophet—not an astrologer with cunningly ambiguous forecasts but a man who saw both the present and the future in an eternal light. He was a pastor looking with compassion on his fellow citizens and feeding them by teaching them. He was a poet, seeing events more fully, more deeply, more sharply.

It is our privilege to read his words, to be still, to observe, to receive, to meditate on what he said, and then to join in life-building, invigorating discussion in order that we too might trust God more, and thus with joy draw water from the wells of salvation.

Kosuke Koyama has pointedly contrasted Christianity as a noisy religion with the quiet religion of Buddhism. The barrage of words increases daily, amplified and multiplied by ever more sophisticated technology. We need some countermeasures. Isaiah's one hundred pages represent forty years of ministry. What then is his unusual impact? Most of the time *he lived what he talked*. By studying Isaiah, your life can also find a still center.

"This is what the Sovereign LORD, the Holy One of Israel, says: 'In repentance and rest is your salvation, in quietness and trust is your strength' " (Isa 30:15).

Outline

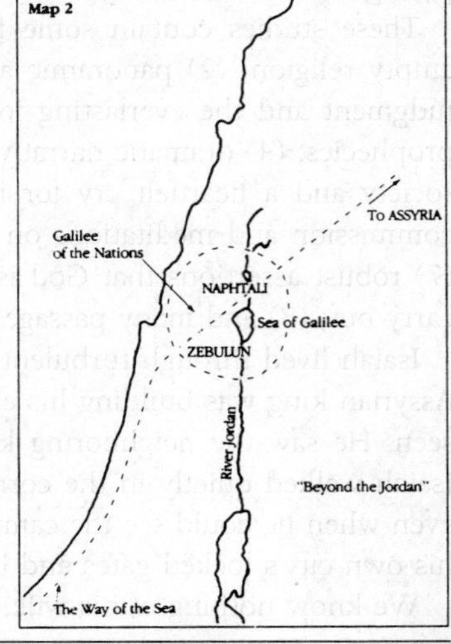

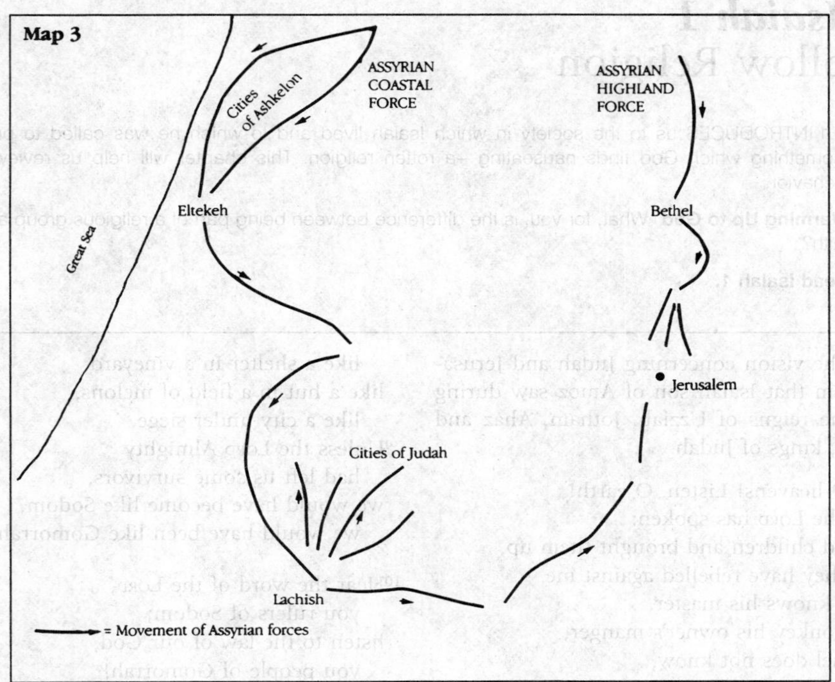

The Historical Background of Isaiah

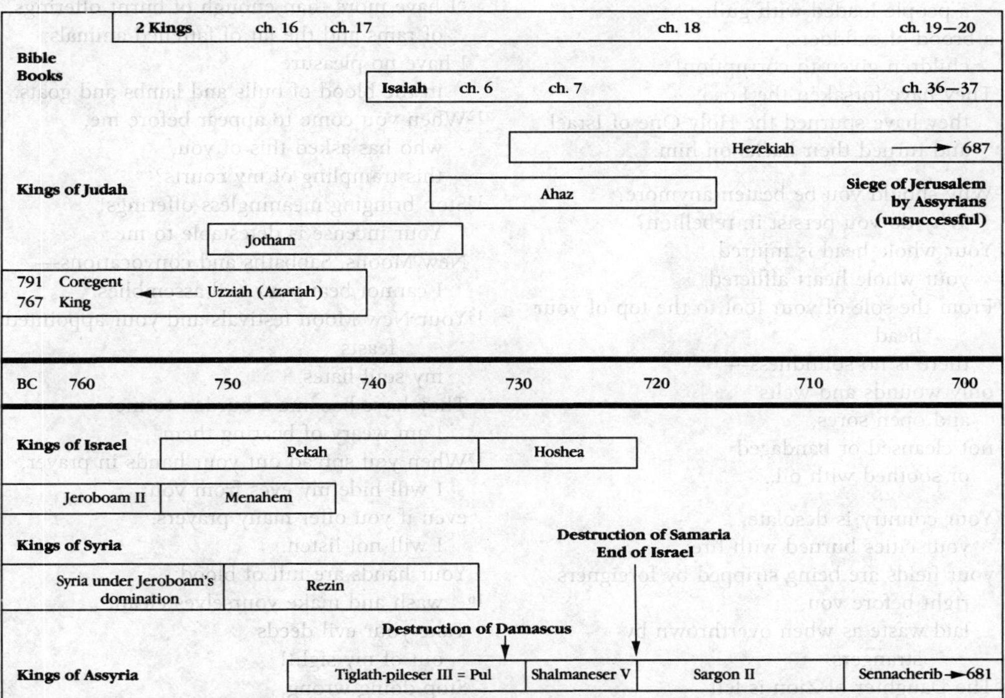

1 / *Isaiah 1*
A Hollow Religion

CHAPTER 1 INTRODUCES us to the society in which Isaiah lived and to which he was called to preach. We discover something which God finds nauseating—a rotten religion. This chapter will help us review our own religious behavior.

Warming Up to God What, for you, is the difference between being part of a religious group and having faith?

Read Isaiah 1.

1 The vision concerning Judah and Jerusalem that Isaiah son of Amoz saw during the reigns of Uzziah, Jotham, Ahaz and Hezekiah, kings of Judah.

2Hear, O heavens! Listen, O earth!
For the LORD has spoken:
"I reared children and brought them up,
but they have rebelled against me.
3The ox knows his master,
the donkey his owner's manger,
but Israel does not know,
my people do not understand."

4Ah, sinful nation,
a people loaded with guilt,
a brood of evildoers,
children given to corruption!
They have forsaken the LORD;
they have spurned the Holy One of Israel
and turned their backs on him.

5Why should you be beaten anymore?
Why do you persist in rebellion?
Your whole head is injured,
your whole heart afflicted.
6From the sole of your foot to the top of your head
there is no soundness—
only wounds and welts
and open sores,
not cleansed or bandaged
or soothed with oil.

7Your country is desolate,
your cities burned with fire;
your fields are being stripped by foreigners
right before you,
laid waste as when overthrown by strangers.
8The Daughter of Zion is left
like a shelter in a vineyard,
like a hut in a field of melons,
like a city under siege.
9Unless the LORD Almighty
had left us some survivors,
we would have become like Sodom,
we would have been like Gomorrah.

10Hear the word of the LORD,
you rulers of Sodom;
listen to the law of our God,
you people of Gomorrah!
11"The multitude of your sacrifices—
what are they to me?" says the LORD.
"I have more than enough of burnt offerings,
of rams and the fat of fattened animals;
I have no pleasure
in the blood of bulls and lambs and goats.
12When you come to appear before me,
who has asked this of you,
this trampling of my courts?
13Stop bringing meaningless offerings!
Your incense is detestable to me.
New Moons, Sabbaths and convocations—
I cannot bear your evil assemblies.
14Your New Moon festivals and your appointed feasts
my soul hates.
They have become a burden to me;
I am weary of bearing them.
15When you spread out your hands in prayer,
I will hide my eyes from you;
even if you offer many prayers,
I will not listen.
Your hands are full of blood;
16 wash and make yourselves clean.
Take your evil deeds
out of my sight!
Stop doing wrong,

17 learn to do right!
Seek justice,
encourage the oppressed.[a]
Defend the cause of the fatherless,
plead the case of the widow.

18"Come now, let us reason together,"
says the LORD.
"Though your sins are like scarlet,
they shall be as white as snow;
though they are red as crimson,
they shall be like wool.
19If you are willing and obedient,
you will eat the best from the land;
20but if you resist and rebel,
you will be devoured by the sword."
For the mouth of the LORD has spoken.

21See how the faithful city
has become a harlot!
She once was full of justice;
righteousness used to dwell in her—
but now murderers!
22Your silver has become dross,
your choice wine is diluted with water.
23Your rulers are rebels,
companions of thieves;
they all love bribes
and chase after gifts.
They do not defend the cause of the fatherless;
the widow's case does not come before them.
24Therefore the Lord, the LORD Almighty,
the Mighty One of Israel, declares:
"Ah, I will get relief from my foes
and avenge myself on my enemies.
25I will turn my hand against you;
I will thoroughly purge away your dross
and remove all your impurities.
26I will restore your judges as in days of old,
your counselors as at the beginning.
Afterward you will be called
the City of Righteousness,
the Faithful City."

27Zion will be redeemed with justice,
her penitent ones with righteousness.
28But rebels and sinners will both be broken,
and those who forsake the LORD will perish.

29"You will be ashamed because of the sacred oaks
in which you have delighted;
you will be disgraced because of the gardens
that you have chosen.
30You will be like an oak with fading leaves,
like a garden without water.
31The mighty man will become tinder
and his work a spark;
both will burn together,
with no one to quench the fire."

[a]17 Or / *rebuke the oppressor*

Discovering the Word 1. In verses 2–3 the Lord summons heaven and earth to be witnesses of his accusations against his people. What is the force of the two metaphors the Lord uses to describe his people's unreasonable and rebellious conduct? 2. Both the nation (v. 4) and the country (v. 7) are in a shocking condition. What vivid pictures of sinfulness do verses 4–9 provide? 3. These people who verses 2–9 speak of were religious! How does God react in verses 10–15 to all of their religious commotion? 4. Describe the kind of life that God is asking them to lead instead (vv. 16–17). 5. Look at verses 21–26. You will notice that these verses are framed by reference to "the faithful city" (Jerusalem or Zion). Life in the capital reflects life in the nation. What picture do these verses give of life in Jerusalem? 6. Now return to verses 18–20. Some scholars think verse 18 is cynical, but traditionally it has been understood as a gracious invitation by humanity's Judge. What does this invitation offer?

Applying the Word 1. In what ways have heaven and earth witnessed the same sinfulness and the same results in your life and your society? 2. From your own experience, explain why it is much harder to fulfill the moral requirements of verses 16–17 than just to go through the ritual activities mentioned in verses 10–15. 3. Evaluate your own religious practices in the midst of your own society with all its needs. What reorientation does your life require if your religion is not to be just a burden—to you *and* to God?

Responding in Prayer Confess your sins to God, knowing that he will make you pure.

2 / *Isaiah 2*
The Revelation of God's Glory

STANDING OUTSIDE THE Old City of Jerusalem is one of the most poignant memorials in Israel to the Six Day War of 1967. It is a futuristic sculpture made of wrecked military equipment with these words from Isaiah on it: "They will beat their swords into plowshares and their spears into pruning hooks. Nation will not take up sword against nation, nor will they train for war anymore" (Isa 2:4). These words still seem infinitely far from fulfillment. Globally, defense spending exceeds the income of the poorest half of the world's population. Yet this chapter of Isaiah tells us of a coming day of reckoning when there will be some incredible surprises. But the sorting and reassessment process begins now in people's response to God (and to Christ). Then, in that day, the process will be completed.

Warming Up to God What would you do if you knew the world would end next week?

Read Isaiah 2.

2 This is what Isaiah son of Amoz saw concerning Judah and Jerusalem:

[2]In the last days
the mountain of the LORD's temple will be established
as chief among the mountains;
it will be raised above the hills,
and all nations will stream to it.

[3]Many peoples will come and say,

"Come, let us go up to the mountain of the LORD,
to the house of the God of Jacob.
He will teach us his ways,
so that we may walk in his paths."
The law will go out from Zion,
the word of the LORD from Jerusalem.
[4]He will judge between the nations
and will settle disputes for many peoples.
They will beat their swords into plowshares
and their spears into pruning hooks.
Nation will not take up sword against nation,
nor will they train for war anymore.

[5]Come, O house of Jacob,
let us walk in the light of the LORD.

[6]You have abandoned your people,
the house of Jacob.
They are full of superstitions from the East;
they practice divination like the Philistines
and clasp hands with pagans.
[7]Their land is full of silver and gold;
there is no end to their treasures.
Their land is full of horses;
there is no end to their chariots.
[8]Their land is full of idols;
they bow down to the work of their hands,
to what their fingers have made.
[9]So man will be brought low
and mankind humbled—
do not forgive them.[b]

[10]Go into the rocks,
hide in the ground
from dread of the LORD
and the splendor of his majesty!
[11]The eyes of the arrogant man will be humbled
and the pride of men brought low;
the LORD alone will be exalted in that day.

[12]The LORD Almighty has a day in store
for all the proud and lofty,
for all that is exalted
(and they will be humbled),
[13]for all the cedars of Lebanon, tall and lofty,
and all the oaks of Bashan,
[14]for all the towering mountains
and all the high hills,
[15]for every lofty tower
and every fortified wall,
[16]for every trading ship[c]
and every stately vessel.
[17]The arrogance of man will be brought low
and the pride of men humbled;
the LORD alone will be exalted in that day,
18 and the idols will totally disappear.
[19]Men will flee to caves in the rocks
and to holes in the ground
from dread of the LORD

[b]9 Or *not raise them up* [c]16 Hebrew *every ship of Tarshish*

and the splendor of his majesty,
when he rises to shake the earth.
20In that day men will throw away
to the rodents and bats
their idols of silver and idols of gold,
which they made to worship.
21They will flee to caverns in the rocks
and to the overhanging crags
from dread of the LORD
and the splendor of his majesty,
when he rises to shake the earth.

22Stop trusting in man,
who has but a breath in his nostrils.
Of what account is he?

Discovering the Word 1. To what period or periods do the words *day* and *days* refer (vv. 2, 11–12, 17, 20)? 2. According to verses 3–4, for what purpose and in what spirit do the nations stream toward Jerusalem? 3. Verses 6–9 provide a rather sad contrast to the vision of verses 2–4. What is the land full of according to these verses? 4. Verses 10–21 mention a number of great things, some natural and some synthetic, which will be brought low in the day when the splendor of God's majesty is revealed. What things are specifically mentioned? 5. What do you think is God's purpose in this process?

Applying the Word 1. In what practical ways can you express your own commitment to global peace? 2. What incentives and encouragements do chapters 1 and 2 of Isaiah give you to trust God in troubled times?

Responding in Prayer Ask God to teach you what it means to stop trusting in humanity (v. 22) and to only rely on him.

Isaiah 3—4

3 See now, the Lord,
the LORD Almighty,
is about to take from Jerusalem and Judah
both supply and support:
all supplies of food and all supplies of water,
2 the hero and warrior,
the judge and prophet,
the soothsayer and elder,
3the captain of fifty and man of rank,
the counselor, skilled craftsman and clever enchanter.

4I will make boys their officials;
mere children will govern them.
5People will oppress each other—
man against man, neighbor against neighbor.
The young will rise up against the old,
the base against the honorable.

6A man will seize one of his brothers
at his father's home, and say,
"You have a cloak, you be our leader;
take charge of this heap of ruins!"
7But in that day he will cry out,
"I have no remedy.
I have no food or clothing in my house;
do not make me the leader of the people."

8Jerusalem staggers,
Judah is falling;
their words and deeds are against the LORD,
defying his glorious presence.
9The look on their faces testifies against them;
they parade their sin like Sodom;
they do not hide it.
Woe to them!
They have brought disaster upon themselves.

10Tell the righteous it will be well with them,
for they will enjoy the fruit of their deeds.
11Woe to the wicked! Disaster is upon them!
They will be paid back for what their hands have done.

12Youths oppress my people,
women rule over them.
O my people, your guides lead you astray;
they turn you from the path.

13The LORD takes his place in court;
he rises to judge the people.
14The LORD enters into judgment

against the elders and leaders of his people:
"It is you who have ruined my vineyard;
the plunder from the poor is in your
houses.
15What do you mean by crushing my people
and grinding the faces of the poor?"
declares the Lord, the LORD Almighty.

16The LORD says,
"The women of Zion are haughty,
walking along with outstretched necks,
flirting with their eyes,
tripping along with mincing steps,
with ornaments jingling on their ankles.
17Therefore the Lord will bring sores on the
heads of the women of Zion;
the LORD will make their scalps bald."

18In that day the Lord will snatch away their
finery: the bangles and headbands and crescent
necklaces, 19the earrings and bracelets and veils,
20the headdresses and ankle chains and sashes,
the perfume bottles and charms, 21the signet rings
and nose rings, 22the fine robes and the capes and
cloaks, the purses 23and mirrors, and the linen
garments and tiaras and shawls.

24Instead of fragrance there will be a stench;
instead of a sash, a rope;
instead of well-dressed hair, baldness;
instead of fine clothing, sackcloth;
instead of beauty, branding.
25Your men will fall by the sword,
your warriors in battle.
26The gates of Zion will lament and mourn;
destitute, she will sit on the ground.

4 In that day seven women
will take hold of one man
and say, "We will eat our own food
and provide our own clothes;
only let us be called by your name.
Take away our disgrace!"

2In that day the Branch of the LORD will be
beautiful and glorious, and the fruit of the land
will be the pride and glory of the survivors in
Israel. 3Those who are left in Zion, who remain
in Jerusalem, will be called holy, all who are re-
corded among the living in Jerusalem. 4The Lord
will wash away the filth of the women of Zion; he
will cleanse the bloodstains from Jerusalem by a
spirit[d] of judgment and a spirit[d] of fire. 5Then
the LORD will create over all of Mount Zion and
over those who assemble there a cloud of smoke
by day and a glow of flaming fire by night; over
all the glory will be a canopy. 6It will be a shelter
and shade from the heat of the day, and a refuge
and hiding place from the storm and rain.

[d]4 Or *the Spirit*

3/ *Isaiah 5*
Judah's Wild Grapes

"BE SURE YOUR sins will find you out." Do you think of this as just a quaint saying, used warningly by mothers to their children? For Isaiah this fact is a grave reality which applies to nations as well as to individuals. The setting of this chapter of Isaiah was probably during the grape harvest, a time famous for conversation and conviviality. Isaiah uses a short parable to rouse his friends' consciences, and then with mounting vehemence attacks certain sins directly.

Warming Up to God Have you ever been in a situation in which you needed to confront a friend with inconsistencies in his or her lifestyle? What happened?

Read Isaiah 5.

5 I will sing for the one I love
a song about his vineyard:
My loved one had a vineyard
on a fertile hillside.
2He dug it up and cleared it of stones
and planted it with the choicest vines.
He built a watchtower in it
and cut out a winepress as well.

Then he looked for a crop of good grapes,
but it yielded only bad fruit.

3"Now you dwellers in Jerusalem and men of Judah,
judge between me and my vineyard.
4What more could have been done for my vineyard
than I have done for it?
When I looked for good grapes,
why did it yield only bad?
5Now I will tell you
what I am going to do to my vineyard:
I will take away its hedge,
and it will be destroyed;
I will break down its wall,
and it will be trampled.
6I will make it a wasteland,
neither pruned nor cultivated,
and briers and thorns will grow there.
I will command the clouds
not to rain on it."

7The vineyard of the LORD Almighty
is the house of Israel,
and the men of Judah
are the garden of his delight.
And he looked for justice, but saw bloodshed;
for righteousness, but heard cries of distress.

8Woe to you who add house to house
and join field to field
till no space is left
and you live alone in the land.

9The LORD Almighty has declared in my hearing:

"Surely the great houses will become desolate,
the fine mansions left without occupants.
10A ten-acre[e] vineyard will produce only a bath[f] of wine,
a homer[g] of seed only an ephah[h] of grain."

11Woe to those who rise early in the morning
to run after their drinks,
who stay up late at night
till they are inflamed with wine.
12They have harps and lyres at their banquets,
tambourines and flutes and wine,
but they have no regard for the deeds of the LORD,
no respect for the work of his hands.

13Therefore my people will go into exile
for lack of understanding;
their men of rank will die of hunger
and their masses will be parched with thirst.
14Therefore the grave[i] enlarges its appetite
and opens its mouth without limit;
into it will descend their nobles and masses
with all their brawlers and revelers.
15So man will be brought low
and mankind humbled,
the eyes of the arrogant humbled.
16But the LORD Almighty will be exalted by his justice,
and the holy God will show himself holy
by his righteousness.
17Then sheep will graze as in their own pasture;
lambs will feed[j] among the ruins of the rich.

18Woe to those who draw sin along with cords of deceit,
and wickedness as with cart ropes,
19to those who say, "Let God hurry,
let him hasten his work
so we may see it.
Let it approach,
let the plan of the Holy One of Israel come,
so we may know it."

20Woe to those who call evil good
and good evil,
who put darkness for light
and light for darkness,
who put bitter for sweet
and sweet for bitter.

21Woe to those who are wise in their own eyes
and clever in their own sight.

22Woe to those who are heroes at drinking wine
and champions at mixing drinks,
23who acquit the guilty for a bribe,
but deny justice to the innocent.
24Therefore, as tongues of fire lick up straw
and as dry grass sinks down in the flames,
so their roots will decay
and their flowers blow away like dust;

[e] 10 Hebrew *ten-yoke,* that is, the land plowed by 10 yoke of oxen in one day [f] 10 That is, probably about 6 gallons (about 22 liters) [g] 10 That is, probably about 6 bushels (about 220 liters) [h] 10 That is, probably about 3/5 bushel (about 22 liters) [i] 14 Hebrew *Sheol* [j] 17 Septuagint; Hebrew / *strangers will eat*

for they have rejected the law of the LORD Almighty
and spurned the word of the Holy One of Israel.
25 Therefore the LORD's anger burns against his people;
his hand is raised and he strikes them down.
The mountains shake,
and the dead bodies are like refuse in the streets.

Yet for all this, his anger is not turned away,
his hand is still upraised.

26 He lifts up a banner for the distant nations,
he whistles for those at the ends of the earth.
Here they come,
swiftly and speedily!
27 Not one of them grows tired or stumbles,
not one slumbers or sleeps;
not a belt is loosened at the waist,
not a sandal thong is broken.
28 Their arrows are sharp,
all their bows are strung;
their horses' hoofs seem like flint,
their chariot wheels like a whirlwind.
29 Their roar is like that of the lion,
they roar like young lions;
they growl as they seize their prey
and carry it off with no one to rescue.
30 In that day they will roar over it
like the roaring of the sea.
And if one looks at the land,
he will see darkness and distress;
even the light will be darkened by the clouds.

Discovering the Word 1. Choosing carefully the occasion and form (a love song), Isaiah introduces the subject of a dear friend's vineyard. Describe the care that was lavished on the vineyard and the owner's dismay when the final product was only evil-smelling, bitter, wild grapes (vv. 1–7). 2. Dropping the disguise of the parable, Isaiah rams home the lesson to his people directly in verse 7. Contrast what God has looked for among his people with what he has found. 3. Verses 8–23 fall into six sections introduced by the word *woe.* What are the sins described in each of these sections? 4. What do these woes reveal about the society at this time? 5. What punishment does the Lord announce in verses 9–10, 13–17 and 24–25?

Applying the Word 1. Give examples of ways in which God has lavished his care upon you, only to be rewarded by a bitter harvest. 2. Consider again the image of the vineyard in verses 1–3. How is God's work in you similar to that of the vineyard owner?

Responding in Prayer God calls you to respond to him. Pray for one specific sweet fruit to grow in your life.

---

4 / *Isaiah 6*
In the Presence of God

NO ONE ALIVE today would go into a nuclear reactor without protective clothing. In a similar way, during Old Testament times merely being in the presence of God was regarded as being fatal. In this chapter Isaiah comes before the presence of God. He is so overcome by the experience that he cries out, "Woe to me!" God is gracious to Isaiah, however, and gives him a special mission. Through this famous story we will learn something about God's call to us also.

Warming Up to God When have you been confronted with the reality of God's surpassingly great holiness? How did you respond?

Read Isaiah 6.

6 In the year that King Uzziah died, I saw
the Lord seated on a throne, high and ex-
alted, and the train of his robe filled the
temple. 2Above him were seraphs, each with six
wings: With two wings they covered their faces,
with two they covered their feet, and with two
they were flying. 3And they were calling to one
another:

"Holy, holy, holy is the LORD Almighty;
 the whole earth is full of his glory."

4At the sound of their voices the doorposts and
thresholds shook and the temple was filled with
smoke.

5"Woe to me!" I cried. "I am ruined! For I am
a man of unclean lips, and I live among a people
of unclean lips, and my eyes have seen the King,
the LORD Almighty."

6Then one of the seraphs flew to me with a live
coal in his hand, which he had taken with tongs
from the altar. 7With it he touched my mouth and
said, "See, this has touched your lips; your guilt is
taken away and your sin atoned for."

8Then I heard the voice of the Lord saying,
"Whom shall I send? And who will go for us?"

And I said, "Here am I. Send me!"

9He said, "Go and tell this people:

" 'Be ever hearing, but never understanding;
 be ever seeing, but never perceiving.'
10Make the heart of this people calloused;
 make their ears dull
 and close their eyes.[k]
Otherwise they might see with their eyes,
 hear with their ears,
 understand with their hearts,
and turn and be healed."

11Then I said, "For how long, O Lord?"
And he answered:

"Until the cities lie ruined
 and without inhabitant,
until the houses are left deserted
 and the fields ruined and ravaged,
12until the LORD has sent everyone far away
 and the land is utterly forsaken.
13And though a tenth remains in the land,
 it will again be laid waste.
But as the terebinth and oak
 leave stumps when they are cut down,
 so the holy seed will be the stump in the
 land."

[k]9,10 Hebrew; Septuagint *'You will be ever hearing, but never understanding; / you will be ever seeing, but never perceiving.' / 10This people's heart has become calloused; / they hardly hear with their ears, / and they have closed their eyes*

Discovering the Word 1. Uzziah's long and prosperous reign came to an end under a cloud (see 2Ch 26:16–21). What do you think was Isaiah's purpose in verse 1 in describing God as occupying the throne? 2. Describe in your own words, as vividly as possible, what Isaiah saw (vv. 2–4). 3. What is the significance of Isaiah's cry in verse 5, especially his reference to his own and his people's lips? 4. What wonderful answer did Isaiah get to his cry of pain (vv. 6–7)? 5. In verses 8–10 Isaiah receives his call and commission. If we follow the punctuation very carefully, it appears that verse 9 is what Isaiah is to tell the people and verse 10 is God's summary of what will happen. Describe what Isaiah's ministry will be like. 6. Isaiah's surprisingly cool response to this commission is to inquire how long he should continue (v. 11). What is God's answer to this question (vv. 11–13)?

Applying the Word 1. What does this chapter tell you about what it means to be called by God and the kind of response God requires? 2. What is God calling you to?

Responding in Prayer Picture yourself in this scene in the presence of God. Respond to his holiness with worship and praise.

5 / *Isaiah 7*
Stand Firm or Lose All

IN THIS STUDY we see King Ahaz of Judah miss a crucial opportunity to trust God in troubled times. He was too frightened to trust God and too vain or proud to ask for the offered sign. Ahaz's leadership can be summarized in this way: "Faith played no part in his religion or his politics" (*The New Bible Commentary: Revised*). Isaiah's cool and calm trustfulness emerges in the most vivid contrast to Ahaz's maneuverings. Assyria was the incomparably brutal superpower of the day, threatening to engulf Syria, Israel and Judah at any time. The chill which it cast over the whole scene is comparable to modern armies like the Nazis, the Mau Mau, the Khmer Rouge and, most recently, Saddam Hussein's Republican Guard. Yet Isaiah was confident that even mighty Assyria was under his God's control.

Warming Up to God Recall a time you experienced God's grace when you were in a very tight spot or in the midst of a personal crisis. Offer your praise to God for his faithfulness.

Read Isaiah 7.

7 When Ahaz son of Jotham, the son of Uz-
ziah, was king of Judah, King Rezin of
Aram and Pekah son of Remaliah king of
Israel marched up to fight against Jerusalem, but
they could not overpower it.
2Now the house of David was told, "Aram has
allied itself with[l] Ephraim"; so the hearts of
Ahaz and his people were shaken, as the trees of
the forest are shaken by the wind.
3Then the LORD said to Isaiah, "Go out, you and
your son Shear-Jashub,[m] to meet Ahaz at the end
of the aqueduct of the Upper Pool, on the road to
the Washerman's Field. 4Say to him, 'Be careful,
keep calm and don't be afraid. Do not lose heart
because of these two smoldering stubs of fire-
wood—because of the fierce anger of Rezin and
Aram and of the son of Remaliah. 5Aram,
Ephraim and Remaliah's son have plotted your
ruin, saying, 6"Let us invade Judah; let us tear it
apart and divide it among ourselves, and make
the son of Tabeel king over it." 7Yet this is what
the Sovereign LORD says:

" 'It will not take place,
it will not happen,
8for the head of Aram is Damascus,
and the head of Damascus is only Rezin.
Within sixty-five years
Ephraim will be too shattered to be a
people.
9The head of Ephraim is Samaria,
and the head of Samaria is only Remaliah's
son.
If you do not stand firm in your faith,
you will not stand at all.' "

10Again the LORD spoke to Ahaz, 11"Ask the
LORD your God for a sign, whether in the deepest
depths or in the highest heights."
12But Ahaz said, "I will not ask; I will not put
the LORD to the test."
13Then Isaiah said, "Hear now, you house of
David! Is it not enough to try the patience of
men? Will you try the patience of my God also?
14Therefore the Lord himself will give you[n] a
sign: The virgin will be with child and will give
birth to a son, and[o] will call him Immanuel.[p]
15He will eat curds and honey when he knows
enough to reject the wrong and choose the right.
16But before the boy knows enough to reject the
wrong and choose the right, the land of the two
kings you dread will be laid waste. 17The LORD
will bring on you and on your people and on
the house of your father a time unlike any since
Ephraim broke away from Judah—he will bring
the king of Assyria."
18In that day the LORD will whistle for flies from
the distant streams of Egypt and for bees from the
land of Assyria. 19They will all come and settle in
the steep ravines and in the crevices in the rocks,
on all the thornbushes and at all the water holes.
20In that day the Lord will use a razor hired from
beyond the River[q]—the king of Assyria—to
shave your head and the hair of your legs, and to
take off your beards also. 21In that day, a man will
keep alive a young cow and two goats. 22And be-
cause of the abundance of the milk they give, he
will have curds to eat. All who remain in the land

[l]2 Or *has set up camp in* [m]3 *Shear-Jashub* means *a remnant will return.* [n]14 The Hebrew is plural. [o]14 Masoretic Text; Dead Sea Scrolls *and he* or *and they* [p]14 *Immanuel* means *God with us.* [q]20 That is, the Euphrates

will eat curds and honey. 23In that day, in every
place where there were a thousand vines worth a
thousand silver shekels,[r] there will be only bri-
ers and thorns. 24Men will go there with bow and
arrow, for the land will be covered with briers
and thorns. 25As for all the hills once cultivated
by the hoe, you will no longer go there for fear of
the briers and thorns; they will become places
where cattle are turned loose and where sheep
run.

[r]23 That is, about 25 pounds (about 11.5 kilograms)

Discovering the Word 1. Study map 1 (see introduction) to get a picture of the setting. How does God describe Ahaz's enemies in verses 3–6? 2. How does the Lord's statement "It will not happen" (vv. 7–9) challenge and encourage Ahaz to trust him? 3. Why do you think God was impatient with Ahaz (vv. 10–13)? 4. What is the significance of the sign of the virgin's child (vv. 14–17)? 5. Ahaz thought he was outwitting two small enemies by allying himself with his biggest one. What disastrous miscalculation did this involve according to verses 17 and 20? 6. Ahaz hoped to preserve his crown and kingdom, but his land would become a shambles. How do verses 18–25 expound the fateful consequences of his choice?

Applying the Word 1. When have you found verse 9—"If you do not stand firm in your faith, you will not stand at all"—to be true for you? 2. How can you better prepare to meet some real or imagined crisis by applying to yourself this very moment the exhortation that Isaiah gave to Ahaz, especially verses 4 and 9?

Responding in Prayer Pray that you will not lose heart.

Isaiah 8:1–10

8 The LORD said to me, "Take a large scroll
and write on it with an ordinary pen: Ma-
her-Shalal-Hash-Baz.[s] 2And I will call in
Uriah the priest and Zechariah son of Jeberekiah
as reliable witnesses for me."
3Then I went to the prophetess, and she con-
ceived and gave birth to a son. And the LORD said
to me, "Name him Maher-Shalal-Hash-Baz. 4Be-
fore the boy knows how to say 'My father' or 'My
mother,' the wealth of Damascus and the plunder
of Samaria will be carried off by the king of As-
syria."
5The LORD spoke to me again:

6"Because this people has rejected
the gently flowing waters of Shiloah
and rejoices over Rezin
and the son of Remaliah,
7therefore the Lord is about to bring against
them
the mighty floodwaters of the River[t]—
the king of Assyria with all his pomp.
It will overflow all its channels,
run over all its banks
8and sweep on into Judah, swirling over it,
passing through it and reaching up to the
neck.
Its outspread wings will cover the breadth of
your land,
O Immanuel[u]!"

9Raise the war cry,[v] you nations, and be
shattered!
Listen, all you distant lands.
Prepare for battle, and be shattered!
Prepare for battle, and be shattered!
10Devise your strategy, but it will be thwarted;
propose your plan, but it will not stand,
for God is with us.[w]

[s]1 *Maher-Shalal-Hash-Baz* means *quick to the plunder, swift to the spoil*; also in verse 3. [t]7 That is, the Euphrates [u]8 *Immanuel* means *God with us.* [v]9 Or *Do your worst* [w]10 Hebrew *Immanuel*

6 / *Isaiah 8:11—9:7*
To Us a Child Is Born

JUDAH HAD TURNED away from the light into the dark: to mediums and spiritists, to ghosts that gibber and squeak (8:19–20). King Ahaz has turned away from the sign God offered him, but a greater King is coming to put things right. This King is a child rather than a mighty conqueror! Yet he has shoulders adequate to the task. He shares God's character as a Wonderful Counselor. He is described as Mighty God. Paradoxically, although a son, he is described as the Everlasting Father! He is the Prince of Peace, and his kingdom shares his character. He is a descendant of David and will rule his kingdom with justice and righteousness forever. All of these characteristics distinguish his kingdom from the chronic instability of Israel and the desperate wobbling of Judah.

Warming Up to God Think of a time when you have been overwhelmed with the reality of the darkness and evil which is present in our world. How did you find comfort?

Read Isaiah 8:11—9:7.

11The LORD spoke to me with his strong hand
upon me, warning me not to follow the way of
this people. He said:

12"Do not call conspiracy
everything that these people call
conspiracy[x];
do not fear what they fear,
and do not dread it.
13The LORD Almighty is the one you are to
regard as holy,
he is the one you are to fear,
he is the one you are to dread,
14and he will be a sanctuary;
but for both houses of Israel he will be
a stone that causes men to stumble
and a rock that makes them fall.
And for the people of Jerusalem he will be
a trap and a snare.
15Many of them will stumble;
they will fall and be broken,
they will be snared and captured."

16Bind up the testimony
and seal up the law among my disciples.
17I will wait for the LORD,
who is hiding his face from the house of
Jacob.
I will put my trust in him.

18Here am I, and the children the LORD has
given me. We are signs and symbols in Israel
from the LORD Almighty, who dwells on Mount
Zion.

19When men tell you to consult mediums and
spiritists, who whisper and mutter, should not a
people inquire of their God? Why consult the
dead on behalf of the living? 20To the law and to
the testimony! If they do not speak according to
this word, they have no light of dawn. 21Dis-
tressed and hungry, they will roam through the
land; when they are famished, they will become
enraged and, looking upward, will curse their
king and their God. 22Then they will look toward
the earth and see only distress and darkness and
fearful gloom, and they will be thrust into utter
darkness.

9 Nevertheless, there will be no more
gloom for those who were in distress. In
the past he humbled the land of Zebulun
and the land of Naphtali, but in the future he will
honor Galilee of the Gentiles, by the way of the
sea, along the Jordan—

2The people walking in darkness
have seen a great light;
on those living in the land of the shadow of
death[y]
a light has dawned.
3You have enlarged the nation
and increased their joy;
they rejoice before you
as people rejoice at the harvest,
as men rejoice
when dividing the plunder.
4For as in the day of Midian's defeat,
you have shattered
the yoke that burdens them,
the bar across their shoulders,
the rod of their oppressor.
5Every warrior's boot used in battle

[x]12 Or *Do not call for a treaty / every time these people call for a treaty*
[y]2 Or *land of darkness*

and every garment rolled in blood
will be destined for burning,
will be fuel for the fire.
6For to us a child is born,
to us a son is given,
and the government will be on his
shoulders.
And he will be called
Wonderful Counselor,[z] Mighty God,
Everlasting Father, Prince of Peace.
7Of the increase of his government and peace
there will be no end.
He will reign on David's throne
and over his kingdom,
establishing and upholding it
with justice and righteousness
from that time on and forever.
The zeal of the LORD Almighty
will accomplish this.

z6 Or *Wonderful, Counselor*

Discovering the Word 1. Compare and contrast the ways of knowing God which are described in 8:11–22. 2. Where are the Israelites looking for wisdom according to 8:19–20? 3. The people are very distressed (8:21–22). Why do they curse their king and their God? 4. With the help of map 2 (in the introduction) find the regions of Zebulun, Naphtali and Galilee and the road called "the Way of the Sea." This road marked the western limits of Palestine, and the Jordan marked the eastern limits. What change from their present condition does Isaiah predict in 9:1–2? 5. The light dawns in 9:2–5. What specific changes does Isaiah predict? 6. In what ways is the coming of the kingdom of justice and righteousness mentioned in 9:7 good news for the poor, the needy and the oppressed?

Applying the Word 1. How has the Lord brought light into your dark corner of the world? 2. Which of these titles—"Wonderful Counselor, Mighty God, Everlasting Father, Prince of Peace"—particularly describes God as you have known him during a time of difficulty?

Responding in Prayer Praise God for his character and the way he has revealed himself to you.

Isaiah 9:8—10:34

8The Lord has sent a message against Jacob;
it will fall on Israel.
9All the people will know it—
Ephraim and the inhabitants of Samaria—
who say with pride
and arrogance of heart,
10"The bricks have fallen down,
but we will rebuild with dressed stone;
the fig trees have been felled,
but we will replace them with cedars."
11But the LORD has strengthened Rezin's foes
against them
and has spurred their enemies on.
12Arameans from the east and Philistines from
the west
have devoured Israel with open mouth.

Yet for all this, his anger is not turned away,
his hand is still upraised.

13But the people have not returned to him who
struck them,
nor have they sought the LORD Almighty.
14So the LORD will cut off from Israel both head
and tail,
both palm branch and reed in a single day;
15the elders and prominent men are the head,
the prophets who teach lies are the tail.
16Those who guide this people mislead them,
and those who are guided are led astray.
17Therefore the Lord will take no pleasure in
the young men,
nor will he pity the fatherless and widows,
for everyone is ungodly and wicked,
every mouth speaks vileness.

Yet for all this, his anger is not turned away,
his hand is still upraised.

18Surely wickedness burns like a fire;
it consumes briers and thorns,
it sets the forest thickets ablaze,
so that it rolls upward in a column of
smoke.

[19]By the wrath of the LORD Almighty
the land will be scorched
and the people will be fuel for the fire;
no one will spare his brother.
[20]On the right they will devour,
but still be hungry;
on the left they will eat,
but not be satisfied.
Each will feed on the flesh of his own
offspring[a]:
21 Manasseh will feed on Ephraim, and
Ephraim on Manasseh;
together they will turn against Judah.

Yet for all this, his anger is not turned away,
his hand is still upraised.

10 Woe to those who make unjust
laws,
to those who issue oppressive
decrees,
[2]to deprive the poor of their rights
and withhold justice from the oppressed of
my people,
making widows their prey
and robbing the fatherless.
[3]What will you do on the day of reckoning,
when disaster comes from afar?
To whom will you run for help?
Where will you leave your riches?
[4]Nothing will remain but to cringe among the
captives
or fall among the slain.

Yet for all this, his anger is not turned away,
his hand is still upraised.

[5]"Woe to the Assyrian, the rod of my anger,
in whose hand is the club of my wrath!
[6]I send him against a godless nation,
I dispatch him against a people who anger
me,
to seize loot and snatch plunder,
and to trample them down like mud in the
streets.
[7]But this is not what he intends,
this is not what he has in mind;
his purpose is to destroy,
to put an end to many nations.
[8]'Are not my commanders all kings?' he says.
9 'Has not Calno fared like Carchemish?
Is not Hamath like Arpad,
and Samaria like Damascus?
[10]As my hand seized the kingdoms of the idols,
kingdoms whose images excelled those of
Jerusalem and Samaria—
[11]shall I not deal with Jerusalem and her images
as I dealt with Samaria and her idols?' "

[12]When the Lord has finished all his work
against Mount Zion and Jerusalem, he will say, "I
will punish the king of Assyria for the willful
pride of his heart and the haughty look in his
eyes. [13]For he says:

" 'By the strength of my hand I have done
this,
and by my wisdom, because I have
understanding.
I removed the boundaries of nations,
I plundered their treasures;
like a mighty one I subdued[b] their kings.
[14]As one reaches into a nest,
so my hand reached for the wealth of the
nations;
as men gather abandoned eggs,
so I gathered all the countries;
not one flapped a wing,
or opened its mouth to chirp.' "

[15]Does the ax raise itself above him who swings
it,
or the saw boast against him who uses it?
As if a rod were to wield him who lifts it up,
or a club brandish him who is not wood!
[16]Therefore, the Lord, the LORD Almighty,
will send a wasting disease upon his sturdy
warriors;
under his pomp a fire will be kindled
like a blazing flame.
[17]The Light of Israel will become a fire,
their Holy One a flame;
in a single day it will burn and consume
his thorns and his briers.
[18]The splendor of his forests and fertile fields
it will completely destroy,
as when a sick man wastes away.
[19]And the remaining trees of his forests will be
so few
that a child could write them down.

[20]In that day the remnant of Israel,
the survivors of the house of Jacob,
will no longer rely on him
who struck them down

[a]20 Or *arm* [b]13 Or / *I subdued the mighty,*

but will truly rely on the LORD,
the Holy One of Israel.
21A remnant will return,[c] a remnant of Jacob
will return to the Mighty God.
22Though your people, O Israel, be like the
sand by the sea,
only a remnant will return.
Destruction has been decreed,
overwhelming and righteous.
23The Lord, the LORD Almighty, will carry out
the destruction decreed upon the whole
land.

24Therefore, this is what the Lord, the LORD Al-
mighty, says:

"O my people who live in Zion,
do not be afraid of the Assyrians,
who beat you with a rod
and lift up a club against you, as Egypt did.
25Very soon my anger against you will end
and my wrath will be directed to their
destruction."

26The LORD Almighty will lash them with a
whip,
as when he struck down Midian at the rock
of Oreb;
and he will raise his staff over the waters,
as he did in Egypt.
27In that day their burden will be lifted from
your shoulders,
their yoke from your neck;
the yoke will be broken
because you have grown so fat.[d]

28They enter Aiath;
they pass through Migron;
they store supplies at Micmash.
29They go over the pass, and say,
"We will camp overnight at Geba."
Ramah trembles;
Gibeah of Saul flees.
30Cry out, O Daughter of Gallim!
Listen, O Laishah!
Poor Anathoth!
31Madmenah is in flight;
the people of Gebim take cover.
32This day they will halt at Nob;
they will shake their fist
at the mount of the Daughter of Zion,
at the hill of Jerusalem.

33See, the Lord, the LORD Almighty,
will lop off the boughs with great power.
The lofty trees will be felled,
the tall ones will be brought low.
34He will cut down the forest thickets with an
ax;
Lebanon will fall before the Mighty One.

[c]21 Hebrew *shear-jashub*; also in verse 22 [d]27 Hebrew; Septuagint *broken / from your shoulders*

7 / *Isaiah 11—12*
The Earth Will Be Full of Knowledge

IT IS ALWAYS helpful when going through a time of trouble if you find some reason to hold on to hope for the future. In the first ten chapters of Isaiah there is a remarkable alternation of the imagery of light and darkness. In this alternation we see the true ministry of a prophet—not good news without the bad news of humanity's sinfulness; but not the bad news without the good news of God's redeeming grace. The hope expressed here is not a blind and shallow optimism. It is not a "you have never had it so good" philosophy borne along on the crest of economic prosperity. Reading the whole of Isaiah 7—12 shows how difficult and depressing the days of Ahaz were in many respects. Yet this chapter holds out in both general and specific terms a thrilling hope for the future.

Warming Up to God What does the word *hope* mean to you?

Read Isaiah 11—12.

11 A shoot will come up from the stump of Jesse;
from his roots a Branch will bear fruit.
2The Spirit of the LORD will rest on him—
the Spirit of wisdom and of understanding,
the Spirit of counsel and of power,
the Spirit of knowledge and of the fear of the LORD—
3and he will delight in the fear of the LORD.

He will not judge by what he sees with his eyes,
or decide by what he hears with his ears;
4but with righteousness he will judge the needy,
with justice he will give decisions for the poor of the earth.
He will strike the earth with the rod of his mouth;
with the breath of his lips he will slay the wicked.
5Righteousness will be his belt
and faithfulness the sash around his waist.

6The wolf will live with the lamb,
the leopard will lie down with the goat,
the calf and the lion and the yearling[e] together;
and a little child will lead them.
7The cow will feed with the bear,
their young will lie down together,
and the lion will eat straw like the ox.
8The infant will play near the hole of the cobra,
and the young child put his hand into the viper's nest.
9They will neither harm nor destroy
on all my holy mountain,
for the earth will be full of the knowledge of the LORD
as the waters cover the sea.

10In that day the Root of Jesse will stand as a
banner for the peoples; the nations will rally to
him, and his place of rest will be glorious. 11In
that day the Lord will reach out his hand a second
time to reclaim the remnant that is left of his
people from Assyria, from Lower Egypt, from Up-
per Egypt,[f] from Cush,[g] from Elam, from Bab-
ylonia,[h] from Hamath and from the islands of
the sea.

12He will raise a banner for the nations
and gather the exiles of Israel;
he will assemble the scattered people of Judah
from the four quarters of the earth.
13Ephraim's jealousy will vanish,
and Judah's enemies[i] will be cut off;
Ephraim will not be jealous of Judah,
nor Judah hostile toward Ephraim.
14They will swoop down on the slopes of Philistia to the west;
together they will plunder the people to the east.
They will lay hands on Edom and Moab,
and the Ammonites will be subject to them.
15The LORD will dry up
the gulf of the Egyptian sea;
with a scorching wind he will sweep his hand
over the Euphrates River.[j]
He will break it up into seven streams
so that men can cross over in sandals.
16There will be a highway for the remnant of his people
that is left from Assyria,
as there was for Israel
when they came up from Egypt.

12 In that day you will say:

"I will praise you, O LORD.
Although you were angry with me,
your anger has turned away
and you have comforted me.
2Surely God is my salvation;
I will trust and not be afraid.
The LORD, the LORD, is my strength and my song;
he has become my salvation."
3With joy you will draw water
from the wells of salvation.

4In that day you will say:

"Give thanks to the LORD, call on his name;
make known among the nations what he has done,
and proclaim that his name is exalted.
5Sing to the LORD, for he has done glorious things;
let this be known to all the world.
6Shout aloud and sing for joy, people of Zion,
for great is the Holy One of Israel among you."

[e]6 Hebrew; Septuagint *lion will feed* [f]11 Hebrew *from Pathros* [g]11 That is, the upper Nile region [h]11 Hebrew *Shinar* [i]13 Or *hostility* [j]15 Hebrew *the River*

Discovering the Word 1. Summarize the character of the person described as the "Branch" in 11:2-5. 2. What do verses 6-9 teach about the character of the kingdom of the One who is called the "Branch"? 3. Show how the great homecoming spoken of in 11:10-16 spells out in detail what the prophecy of 11:9 predicts. 4. How are the Branch of 11:1 and the Root of 11:10 related? 5. What are the main themes of the songs of thanksgiving in chapter 12?

Applying the Word 1. Which of the qualities of the Holy Spirit listed in 11:2 do you most want the Spirit to work in your life at this time? Why? 2. How does your church or fellowship best reflect his kingdom as it is described here? 3. In situations in your life how does trusting God mean reaffirming the truths of 12:2?

Responding in Prayer Ask the Lord to show you what it means to live in hope for the future.

Isaiah 13—23

13 An oracle concerning Babylon that Isaiah son of Amoz saw:

2Raise a banner on a bare hilltop,
shout to them;
beckon to them
to enter the gates of the nobles.
3I have commanded my holy ones;
I have summoned my warriors to carry out my wrath—
those who rejoice in my triumph.

4Listen, a noise on the mountains,
like that of a great multitude!
Listen, an uproar among the kingdoms,
like nations massing together!
The LORD Almighty is mustering
an army for war.
5They come from faraway lands,
from the ends of the heavens—
the LORD and the weapons of his wrath—
to destroy the whole country.

6Wail, for the day of the LORD is near;
it will come like destruction from the Almighty.[k]
7Because of this, all hands will go limp,
every man's heart will melt.
8Terror will seize them,
pain and anguish will grip them;
they will writhe like a woman in labor.
They will look aghast at each other,
their faces aflame.

9See, the day of the LORD is coming
—a cruel day, with wrath and fierce anger—
to make the land desolate
and destroy the sinners within it.
10The stars of heaven and their constellations
will not show their light.
The rising sun will be darkened
and the moon will not give its light.
11I will punish the world for its evil,
the wicked for their sins.
I will put an end to the arrogance of the haughty
and will humble the pride of the ruthless.
12I will make man scarcer than pure gold,
more rare than the gold of Ophir.
13Therefore I will make the heavens tremble;
and the earth will shake from its place
at the wrath of the LORD Almighty,
in the day of his burning anger.
14Like a hunted gazelle,
like sheep without a shepherd,
each will return to his own people,
each will flee to his native land.
15Whoever is captured will be thrust through;
all who are caught will fall by the sword.
16Their infants will be dashed to pieces before their eyes;
their houses will be looted and their wives ravished.

17See, I will stir up against them the Medes,
who do not care for silver
and have no delight in gold.
18Their bows will strike down the young men;
they will have no mercy on infants
nor will they look with compassion on children.
19Babylon, the jewel of kingdoms,

[k]6 Hebrew *Shaddai*

the glory of the Babylonians'[l] pride,
will be overthrown by God
like Sodom and Gomorrah.
20She will never be inhabited
or lived in through all generations;
no Arab will pitch his tent there,
no shepherd will rest his flocks there.
21But desert creatures will lie there,
jackals will fill her houses;
there the owls will dwell,
and there the wild goats will leap about.
22Hyenas will howl in her strongholds,
jackals in her luxurious palaces.
Her time is at hand,
and her days will not be prolonged.

14 The LORD will have compassion on Jacob;
once again he will choose Israel
and will settle them in their own land.
Aliens will join them
and unite with the house of Jacob.
2Nations will take them
and bring them to their own place.
And the house of Israel will possess the nations
as menservants and maidservants in the LORD's land.
They will make captives of their captors
and rule over their oppressors.

3On the day the LORD gives you relief from suf-
fering and turmoil and cruel bondage, 4you will
take up this taunt against the king of Babylon:

How the oppressor has come to an end!
How his fury[m] has ended!
5The LORD has broken the rod of the wicked,
the scepter of the rulers,
6which in anger struck down peoples
with unceasing blows,
and in fury subdued nations
with relentless aggression.
7All the lands are at rest and at peace;
they break into singing.
8Even the pine trees and the cedars of Lebanon
exult over you and say,
"Now that you have been laid low,
no woodsman comes to cut us down."

9The grave[n] below is all astir
to meet you at your coming;
it rouses the spirits of the departed to greet you—
all those who were leaders in the world;
it makes them rise from their thrones—
all those who were kings over the nations.
10They will all respond,
they will say to you,
"You also have become weak, as we are;
you have become like us."
11All your pomp has been brought down to the grave,
along with the noise of your harps;
maggots are spread out beneath you
and worms cover you.

12How you have fallen from heaven,
O morning star, son of the dawn!
You have been cast down to the earth,
you who once laid low the nations!
13You said in your heart,
"I will ascend to heaven;
I will raise my throne
above the stars of God;
I will sit enthroned on the mount of assembly,
on the utmost heights of the sacred mountain.[o]
14I will ascend above the tops of the clouds;
I will make myself like the Most High."
15But you are brought down to the grave,
to the depths of the pit.

16Those who see you stare at you,
they ponder your fate:
"Is this the man who shook the earth
and made kingdoms tremble,
17the man who made the world a desert,
who overthrew its cities
and would not let his captives go home?"

18All the kings of the nations lie in state,
each in his own tomb.
19But you are cast out of your tomb
like a rejected branch;
you are covered with the slain,
with those pierced by the sword,
those who descend to the stones of the pit.
Like a corpse trampled underfoot,
20 you will not join them in burial,
for you have destroyed your land
and killed your people.

[l] 19 Or *Chaldeans'* [m] 4 Dead Sea Scrolls, Septuagint and Syriac; the meaning of the word in the Masoretic Text is uncertain. [n] 9 Hebrew *Sheol*; also in verses 11 and 15 [o] 13 Or *the north*; Hebrew *Zaphon*

The offspring of the wicked
will never be mentioned again.
21 Prepare a place to slaughter his sons
for the sins of their forefathers;
they are not to rise to inherit the land
and cover the earth with their cities.

22 "I will rise up against them,"
declares the LORD Almighty.
"I will cut off from Babylon her name and survivors,
her offspring and descendants,"
declares the LORD.
23 "I will turn her into a place for owls
and into swampland;
I will sweep her with the broom of destruction,"
declares the LORD Almighty.

24 The LORD Almighty has sworn,

"Surely, as I have planned, so it will be,
and as I have purposed, so it will stand.
25 I will crush the Assyrian in my land;
on my mountains I will trample him down.
His yoke will be taken from my people,
and his burden removed from their shoulders."

26 This is the plan determined for the whole world;
this is the hand stretched out over all nations.
27 For the LORD Almighty has purposed, and who can thwart him?
His hand is stretched out, and who can turn it back?

28 This oracle came in the year King Ahaz died:

29 Do not rejoice, all you Philistines,
that the rod that struck you is broken;
from the root of that snake will spring up a viper,
its fruit will be a darting, venomous serpent.
30 The poorest of the poor will find pasture,
and the needy will lie down in safety.
But your root I will destroy by famine;
it will slay your survivors.

31 Wail, O gate! Howl, O city!
Melt away, all you Philistines!
A cloud of smoke comes from the north,
and there is not a straggler in its ranks.
32 What answer shall be given
to the envoys of that nation?
"The LORD has established Zion,
and in her his afflicted people will find refuge."

15

An oracle concerning Moab:

Ar in Moab is ruined,
destroyed in a night!
Kir in Moab is ruined,
destroyed in a night!
2 Dibon goes up to its temple,
to its high places to weep;
Moab wails over Nebo and Medeba.
Every head is shaved
and every beard cut off.
3 In the streets they wear sackcloth;
on the roofs and in the public squares
they all wail,
prostrate with weeping.
4 Heshbon and Elealeh cry out,
their voices are heard all the way to Jahaz.
Therefore the armed men of Moab cry out,
and their hearts are faint.

5 My heart cries out over Moab;
her fugitives flee as far as Zoar,
as far as Eglath Shelishiyah.
They go up the way to Luhith,
weeping as they go;
on the road to Horonaim
they lament their destruction.
6 The waters of Nimrim are dried up
and the grass is withered;
the vegetation is gone
and nothing green is left.
7 So the wealth they have acquired and stored up
they carry away over the Ravine of the Poplars.
8 Their outcry echoes along the border of Moab;
their wailing reaches as far as Eglaim,
their lamentation as far as Beer Elim.
9 Dimon's[p] waters are full of blood,
but I will bring still more upon Dimon[p]—
a lion upon the fugitives of Moab
and upon those who remain in the land.

p9 Masoretic Text; Dead Sea Scrolls, some Septuagint manuscripts and Vulgate *Dibon*

16 Send lambs as tribute
to the ruler of the land,
from Sela, across the desert,
to the mount of the Daughter of Zion.
2Like fluttering birds
pushed from the nest,
so are the women of Moab
at the fords of the Arnon.

3"Give us counsel,
render a decision.
Make your shadow like night—
at high noon.
Hide the fugitives,
do not betray the refugees.
4Let the Moabite fugitives stay with you;
be their shelter from the destroyer."

The oppressor will come to an end,
and destruction will cease;
the aggressor will vanish from the land.
5In love a throne will be established;
in faithfulness a man will sit on it—
one from the house[q] of David—
one who in judging seeks justice
and speeds the cause of righteousness.

6We have heard of Moab's pride—
her overweening pride and conceit,
her pride and her insolence—
but her boasts are empty.
7Therefore the Moabites wail,
they wail together for Moab.
Lament and grieve
for the men[r] of Kir Hareseth.
8The fields of Heshbon wither,
the vines of Sibmah also.
The rulers of the nations
have trampled down the choicest vines,
which once reached Jazer
and spread toward the desert.
Their shoots spread out
and went as far as the sea.
9So I weep, as Jazer weeps,
for the vines of Sibmah.
O Heshbon, O Elealeh,
I drench you with tears!
The shouts of joy over your ripened fruit
and over your harvests have been stilled.
10Joy and gladness are taken away from the
orchards;
no one sings or shouts in the vineyards;
no one treads out wine at the presses,
for I have put an end to the shouting.
11My heart laments for Moab like a harp,
my inmost being for Kir Hareseth.
12When Moab appears at her high place,
she only wears herself out;
when she goes to her shrine to pray,
it is to no avail.

13This is the word the LORD has already spoken
concerning Moab. 14But now the LORD says:
"Within three years, as a servant bound by con-
tract would count them, Moab's splendor and all
her many people will be despised, and her survi-
vors will be very few and feeble."

17 An oracle concerning Damascus:

"See, Damascus will no longer be
a city
but will become a heap of ruins.
2The cities of Aroer will be deserted
and left to flocks, which will lie down,
with no one to make them afraid.
3The fortified city will disappear from
Ephraim,
and royal power from Damascus;
the remnant of Aram will be
like the glory of the Israelites,"
declares the LORD Almighty.

4"In that day the glory of Jacob will fade;
the fat of his body will waste away.
5It will be as when a reaper gathers the
standing grain
and harvests the grain with his arm—
as when a man gleans heads of grain
in the Valley of Rephaim.
6Yet some gleanings will remain,
as when an olive tree is beaten,
leaving two or three olives on the topmost
branches,
four or five on the fruitful boughs,"
declares the LORD, the God of Israel.

7In that day men will look to their Maker
and turn their eyes to the Holy One of
Israel.
8They will not look to the altars,
the work of their hands,
and they will have no regard for the Asherah
poles[s]

q5 Hebrew *tent* r7 Or "*raisin cakes*," a wordplay s8 That is, symbols of the goddess Asherah

and the incense altars their fingers have
made.

9In that day their strong cities, which they left
because of the Israelites, will be like places aban-
doned to thickets and undergrowth. And all will
be desolation.

10You have forgotten God your Savior;
you have not remembered the Rock, your
fortress.
Therefore, though you set out the finest
plants
and plant imported vines,
11though on the day you set them out, you
make them grow,
and on the morning when you plant them,
you bring them to bud,
yet the harvest will be as nothing
in the day of disease and incurable pain.
12Oh, the raging of many nations—
they rage like the raging sea!
Oh, the uproar of the peoples—
they roar like the roaring of great waters!
13Although the peoples roar like the roar of
surging waters,
when he rebukes them they flee far away,
driven before the wind like chaff on the hills,
like tumbleweed before a gale.
14In the evening, sudden terror!
Before the morning, they are gone!
This is the portion of those who loot us,
the lot of those who plunder us.

18

Woe to the land of whirring
wings[t]
along the rivers of Cush,[u]
2which sends envoys by sea
in papyrus boats over the water.

Go, swift messengers,
to a people tall and smooth-skinned,
to a people feared far and wide,
an aggressive nation of strange speech,
whose land is divided by rivers.

3All you people of the world,
you who live on the earth,
when a banner is raised on the mountains,
you will see it,
and when a trumpet sounds,
you will hear it.
4This is what the LORD says to me:

"I will remain quiet and will look on from
my dwelling place,
like shimmering heat in the sunshine,
like a cloud of dew in the heat of harvest."
5For, before the harvest, when the blossom is
gone
and the flower becomes a ripening grape,
he will cut off the shoots with pruning
knives,
and cut down and take away the spreading
branches.
6They will all be left to the mountain birds of
prey
and to the wild animals;
the birds will feed on them all summer,
the wild animals all winter.

7At that time gifts will be brought to the LORD
Almighty

from a people tall and smooth-skinned,
from a people feared far and wide,
an aggressive nation of strange speech,
whose land is divided by rivers—

the gifts will be brought to Mount Zion, the place
of the Name of the LORD Almighty.

19

An oracle concerning Egypt:

See, the LORD rides on a swift
cloud
and is coming to Egypt.
The idols of Egypt tremble before him,
and the hearts of the Egyptians melt within
them.

2"I will stir up Egyptian against Egyptian—
brother will fight against brother,
neighbor against neighbor,
city against city,
kingdom against kingdom.
3The Egyptians will lose heart,
and I will bring their plans to nothing;
they will consult the idols and the spirits of
the dead,
the mediums and the spiritists.
4I will hand the Egyptians over
to the power of a cruel master,
and a fierce king will rule over them,"
declares the Lord, the LORD Almighty.
5The waters of the river will dry up,

t1 Or *of locusts* u1 That is, the upper Nile region

and the riverbed will be parched and dry.
6The canals will stink;
  the streams of Egypt will dwindle and dry up.
The reeds and rushes will wither,
7 also the plants along the Nile,
  at the mouth of the river.
Every sown field along the Nile
  will become parched, will blow away and be no more.
8The fishermen will groan and lament,
  all who cast hooks into the Nile;
those who throw nets on the water
  will pine away.
9Those who work with combed flax will despair,
  the weavers of fine linen will lose hope.
10The workers in cloth will be dejected,
  and all the wage earners will be sick at heart.

11The officials of Zoan are nothing but fools;
  the wise counselors of Pharaoh give senseless advice.
How can you say to Pharaoh,
  "I am one of the wise men,
  a disciple of the ancient kings"?

12Where are your wise men now?
  Let them show you and make known
what the LORD Almighty
  has planned against Egypt.
13The officials of Zoan have become fools,
  the leaders of Memphis[v] are deceived;
the cornerstones of her peoples
  have led Egypt astray.
14The LORD has poured into them
  a spirit of dizziness;
they make Egypt stagger in all that she does,
  as a drunkard staggers around in his vomit.
15There is nothing Egypt can do—
  head or tail, palm branch or reed.

16In that day the Egyptians will be like women.
They will shudder with fear at the uplifted hand
that the LORD Almighty raises against them. 17And
the land of Judah will bring terror to the Egyp-
tians; everyone to whom Judah is mentioned will
be terrified, because of what the LORD Almighty is
planning against them.
18In that day five cities in Egypt will speak the
language of Canaan and swear allegiance to the
LORD Almighty. One of them will be called the
City of Destruction.[w]
19In that day there will be an altar to the LORD
in the heart of Egypt, and a monument to the
LORD at its border. 20It will be a sign and witness
to the LORD Almighty in the land of Egypt. When
they cry out to the LORD because of their oppres-
sors, he will send them a savior and defender, and
he will rescue them. 21So the LORD will make him-
self known to the Egyptians, and in that day they
will acknowledge the LORD. They will worship
with sacrifices and grain offerings; they will make
vows to the LORD and keep them. 22The LORD
will strike Egypt with a plague; he will strike
them and heal them. They will turn to the LORD,
and he will respond to their pleas and heal
them.
23In that day there will be a highway from
Egypt to Assyria. The Assyrians will go to Egypt
and the Egyptians to Assyria. The Egyptians and
Assyrians will worship together. 24In that day Is-
rael will be the third, along with Egypt and As-
syria, a blessing on the earth. 25The LORD Al-
mighty will bless them, saying, "Blessed be Egypt
my people, Assyria my handiwork, and Israel my
inheritance."

20 In the year that the supreme com-
mander, sent by Sargon king of As-
syria, came to Ashdod and attacked
and captured it— 2at that time the LORD spoke
through Isaiah son of Amoz. He said to him,
"Take off the sackcloth from your body and the
sandals from your feet." And he did so, going
around stripped and barefoot.
3Then the LORD said, "Just as my servant Isaiah
has gone stripped and barefoot for three years, as
a sign and portent against Egypt and Cush,[x] 4so
the king of Assyria will lead away stripped and
barefoot the Egyptian captives and Cushite exiles,
young and old, with buttocks bared—to Egypt's
shame. 5Those who trusted in Cush and boasted
in Egypt will be afraid and put to shame. 6In that
day the people who live on this coast will say, 'See
what has happened to those we relied on, those
we fled to for help and deliverance from the king
of Assyria! How then can we escape?'"

[v]13 Hebrew *Noph* [w]18 Most manuscripts of the Masoretic Text; some manuscripts of the Masoretic Text, Dead Sea Scrolls and Vulgate *City of the Sun* (that is, Heliopolis) [x]3 That is, the upper Nile region; also in verse 5

21

An oracle concerning the Desert by the Sea:

Like whirlwinds sweeping through
the southland,
an invader comes from the desert,
from a land of terror.

2 A dire vision has been shown to me:
The traitor betrays, the looter takes loot.
Elam, attack! Media, lay siege!
I will bring to an end all the groaning she
caused.

3 At this my body is racked with pain,
pangs seize me, like those of a woman in
labor;
I am staggered by what I hear,
I am bewildered by what I see.
4 My heart falters,
fear makes me tremble;
the twilight I longed for
has become a horror to me.

5 They set the tables,
they spread the rugs,
they eat, they drink!
Get up, you officers,
oil the shields!

6 This is what the Lord says to me:

"Go, post a lookout
and have him report what he sees.
7 When he sees chariots
with teams of horses,
riders on donkeys
or riders on camels,
let him be alert,
fully alert."

8 And the lookout[y] shouted,

"Day after day, my lord, I stand on the
watchtower;
every night I stay at my post.
9 Look, here comes a man in a chariot
with a team of horses.
And he gives back the answer:
'Babylon has fallen, has fallen!
All the images of its gods
lie shattered on the ground!'"

10 O my people, crushed on the threshing floor,
I tell you what I have heard
from the LORD Almighty,
from the God of Israel.

11 An oracle concerning Dumah[z]:

Someone calls to me from Seir,
"Watchman, what is left of the night?
Watchman, what is left of the night?"
12 The watchman replies,
"Morning is coming, but also the night.
If you would ask, then ask;
and come back yet again."

13 An oracle concerning Arabia:

You caravans of Dedanites,
who camp in the thickets of Arabia,
14 bring water for the thirsty;
you who live in Tema,
bring food for the fugitives.
15 They flee from the sword,
from the drawn sword,
from the bent bow
and from the heat of battle.

16 This is what the Lord says to me: "Within one
year, as a servant bound by contract would count
it, all the pomp of Kedar will come to an end.
17 The survivors of the bowmen, the warriors of
Kedar, will be few." The LORD, the God of Israel,
has spoken.

22

An oracle concerning the Valley of Vision:

What troubles you now,
that you have all gone up on the roofs,
2 O town full of commotion,
O city of tumult and revelry?
Your slain were not killed by the sword,
nor did they die in battle.
3 All your leaders have fled together;
they have been captured without using the
bow.
All you who were caught were taken prisoner
together,
having fled while the enemy was still far
away.
4 Therefore I said, "Turn away from me;
let me weep bitterly.
Do not try to console me
over the destruction of my people."

5 The Lord, the LORD Almighty, has a day
of tumult and trampling and terror

[y]8 Dead Sea Scrolls and Syriac; Masoretic Text *A lion* [z]11 *Dumah* means *silence* or *stillness,* a wordplay on *Edom.*

24 See, the LORD is going to lay waste
the earth
and devastate it;
he will ruin its face
and scatter its inhabitants—
2it will be the same
for priest as for people,
for master as for servant,
for mistress as for maid,
for seller as for buyer,
for borrower as for lender,
for debtor as for creditor.
3The earth will be completely laid waste
and totally plundered.
The LORD has spoken this word.

4The earth dries up and withers,
the world languishes and withers,
the exalted of the earth languish.
5The earth is defiled by its people;
they have disobeyed the laws,
violated the statutes
and broken the everlasting covenant.
6Therefore a curse consumes the earth;
its people must bear their guilt.
Therefore earth's inhabitants are burned up,
and very few are left.
7The new wine dries up and the vine withers;
all the merrymakers groan.
8The gaiety of the tambourines is stilled,
the noise of the revelers has stopped,
the joyful harp is silent.
9No longer do they drink wine with a song;
the beer is bitter to its drinkers.
10The ruined city lies desolate;
the entrance to every house is barred.
11In the streets they cry out for wine;
all joy turns to gloom,
all gaiety is banished from the earth.
12The city is left in ruins,
its gate is battered to pieces.
13So will it be on the earth
and among the nations,
as when an olive tree is beaten,
or as when gleanings are left after the grape
harvest.

14They raise their voices, they shout for joy;
from the west they acclaim the LORD's
majesty.
15Therefore in the east give glory to the LORD;
exalt the name of the LORD, the God of
Israel,
in the islands of the sea.
16From the ends of the earth we hear singing:
"Glory to the Righteous One."

But I said, "I waste away, I waste away!
Woe to me!
The treacherous betray!
With treachery the treacherous betray!"
17Terror and pit and snare await you,
O people of the earth.
18Whoever flees at the sound of terror
will fall into a pit;
whoever climbs out of the pit
will be caught in a snare.

The floodgates of the heavens are opened,
the foundations of the earth shake.
19The earth is broken up,
the earth is split asunder,
the earth is thoroughly shaken.
20The earth reels like a drunkard,
it sways like a hut in the wind;
so heavy upon it is the guilt of its rebellion
that it falls—never to rise again.

21In that day the LORD will punish
the powers in the heavens above
and the kings on the earth below.
22They will be herded together
like prisoners bound in a dungeon;
they will be shut up in prison
and be punished[h] after many days.
23The moon will be abashed, the sun ashamed;
for the LORD Almighty will reign
on Mount Zion and in Jerusalem,
and before its elders, gloriously.

[h]22 *Or released*

Discovering the Word 1. What key words describe the Lord's devastation of the earth (vv. 1, 3–4)? 2. What is the mood of verses 4–13? 3. According to verses 4–13, why will the devastation of the earth take place? 4. How do you account for the fragment of singing which bursts out in verses 14–16, only to be abruptly silenced by Isaiah's cry of pain in the latter part of verse 16? 5. What additional aspects of God's judgment are revealed in verses 2–3?

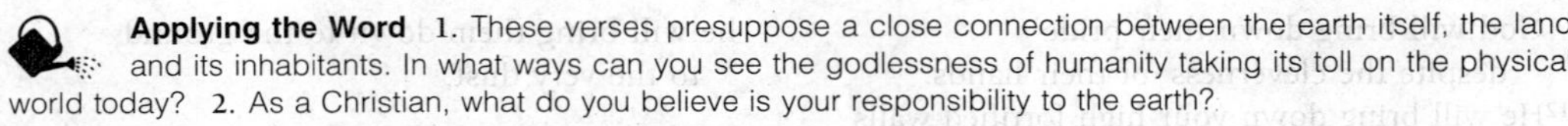

Applying the Word 1. These verses presuppose a close connection between the earth itself, the land and its inhabitants. In what ways can you see the godlessness of humanity taking its toll on the physical world today? 2. As a Christian, what do you believe is your responsibility to the earth?

Responding in Prayer Ask God to teach you about your responsibility in caring for his creation.

9 / *Isaiah 25*

Free at Last!

Free at last, free at last!
Great God Almighty,
Free at last!

THIS SONG, WITH eloquent simplicity, expresses the pervasive hope of oppressed, exploited and downtrodden people. Similarly, in this chapter a song of praise arises phoenixlike from the shattered world we saw at the end of chapter 24. Here we read of Israel's joy at the downfall of God's enemies, the end of death itself and God's final victory. Derek Kidner entitles this chapter "the great liberation," subtitling the sections: the end of tyranny (vv. 1–5), the end of darkness and death (vv. 6–8) and the end of pride (vv. 9–12). As we read of God's triumph, may it help to strengthen our faith in times of trouble.

Warming Up to God Describe an experience you have had in driving rain, a snowstorm or some other natural disaster in which you knew that God was present with you.

Read Isaiah 25.

25 O LORD, you are my God;
I will exalt you and praise your name,
for in perfect faithfulness
you have done marvelous things,
things planned long ago.
2You have made the city a heap of rubble,
the fortified town a ruin,
the foreigners' stronghold a city no more;
it will never be rebuilt.
3Therefore strong peoples will honor you;
cities of ruthless nations will revere you.
4You have been a refuge for the poor,
a refuge for the needy in his distress,
a shelter from the storm
and a shade from the heat.
For the breath of the ruthless
is like a storm driving against a wall
5 and like the heat of the desert.
You silence the uproar of foreigners;
as heat is reduced by the shadow of a cloud,
so the song of the ruthless is stilled.

6On this mountain the LORD Almighty will prepare
a feast of rich food for all peoples,
a banquet of aged wine—
the best of meats and the finest of wines.
7On this mountain he will destroy
the shroud that enfolds all peoples,
the sheet that covers all nations;
8 he will swallow up death forever.
The Sovereign LORD will wipe away the tears
from all faces;
he will remove the disgrace of his people
from all the earth.
The LORD has spoken.

9In that day they will say,

"Surely this is our God;
we trusted in him, and he saved us.
This is the LORD, we trusted in him;
let us rejoice and be glad in his salvation."

10The hand of the LORD will rest on this mountain;
but Moab will be trampled under him
as straw is trampled down in the manure.
11They will spread out their hands in it,
as a swimmer spreads out his hands to swim.

God will bring down their pride
despite the cleverness[i] of their hands.
12He will bring down your high fortified walls
and lay them low;
he will bring them down to the ground,
to the very dust.

i11 The meaning of the Hebrew for this word is uncertain.

Discovering the Word 1. How is God's character described in verse 1? 2. What repeated adjective reveals the main target of God's judgment in verses 2–5? 3. With what vivid metaphors does Isaiah describe God's relationship to the poor and needy (vv. 4–5)? 4. Look at the scene of God's banquet in verses 6–8. How does this wonderful imagery transform your understanding of death for the believer? 5. According to verses 10–12, what is the particular sin which characterized Moab (see also Isa 16:6)?

Applying the Word 1. When are you most able to identify with the delighted response of verse 9? 2. To what present trial should you make a similar response?

Responding in Prayer Pray or write your own song of praise to God for the "marvelous things" he has planned (v. 1) for your life.

Isaiah 26—29

26 In that day this song will be sung in the land of Judah:

We have a strong city;
God makes salvation
its walls and ramparts.
2Open the gates
that the righteous nation may enter,
the nation that keeps faith.
3You will keep in perfect peace
him whose mind is steadfast,
because he trusts in you.
4Trust in the LORD forever,
for the LORD, the LORD, is the Rock eternal.
5He humbles those who dwell on high,
he lays the lofty city low;
he levels it to the ground
and casts it down to the dust.
6Feet trample it down—
the feet of the oppressed,
the footsteps of the poor.
7The path of the righteous is level;
O upright One, you make the way of the righteous smooth.
8Yes, LORD, walking in the way of your laws,[j]
we wait for you;
your name and renown
are the desire of our hearts.
9My soul yearns for you in the night;
in the morning my spirit longs for you.
When your judgments come upon the earth,
the people of the world learn righteousness.
10Though grace is shown to the wicked,
they do not learn righteousness;
even in a land of uprightness they go on doing evil
and regard not the majesty of the LORD.
11O LORD, your hand is lifted high,
but they do not see it.
Let them see your zeal for your people and be put to shame;
let the fire reserved for your enemies consume them.

12LORD, you establish peace for us;
all that we have accomplished you have done for us.
13O LORD, our God, other lords besides you have ruled over us,
but your name alone do we honor.
14They are now dead, they live no more;
those departed spirits do not rise.
You punished them and brought them to ruin;
you wiped out all memory of them.
15You have enlarged the nation, O LORD;
you have enlarged the nation.
You have gained glory for yourself;
you have extended all the borders of the land.

16LORD, they came to you in their distress;
when you disciplined them,

j8 Or *judgments*

they could barely whisper a prayer.[k]
17As a woman with child and about to give
birth
writhes and cries out in her pain,
so were we in your presence, O LORD.
18We were with child, we writhed in pain,
but we gave birth to wind.
We have not brought salvation to the earth;
we have not given birth to people of the
world.

19But your dead will live;
their bodies will rise.
You who dwell in the dust,
wake up and shout for joy.
Your dew is like the dew of the morning;
the earth will give birth to her dead.
20Go, my people, enter your rooms
and shut the doors behind you;
hide yourselves for a little while
until his wrath has passed by.
21See, the LORD is coming out of his dwelling
to punish the people of the earth for their
sins.
The earth will disclose the blood shed upon
her;
she will conceal her slain no longer.

27

In that day,

the LORD will punish with his
sword,
his fierce, great and powerful sword,
Leviathan the gliding serpent,
Leviathan the coiling serpent;
he will slay the monster of the sea.

2In that day—

"Sing about a fruitful vineyard:
3 I, the LORD, watch over it;
I water it continually.
I guard it day and night
so that no one may harm it.
4 I am not angry.
If only there were briers and thorns
confronting me!
I would march against them in battle;
I would set them all on fire.
5Or else let them come to me for refuge;
let them make peace with me,
yes, let them make peace with me."

6In days to come Jacob will take root,
Israel will bud and blossom
and fill all the world with fruit.

7Has ⌞the LORD⌟ struck her
as he struck down those who struck her?
Has she been killed
as those were killed who killed her?
8By warfare[l] and exile you contend with
her—
with his fierce blast he drives her out,
as on a day the east wind blows.
9By this, then, will Jacob's guilt be atoned for,
and this will be the full fruitage of the
removal of his sin:
When he makes all the altar stones
to be like chalk stones crushed to pieces,
no Asherah poles[m] or incense altars
will be left standing.
10The fortified city stands desolate,
an abandoned settlement, forsaken like the
desert;
there the calves graze,
there they lie down;
they strip its branches bare.
11When its twigs are dry, they are broken off
and women come and make fires with
them.
For this is a people without understanding;
so their Maker has no compassion on them,
and their Creator shows them no favor.

12In that day the LORD will thresh from the
flowing Euphrates[n] to the Wadi of Egypt, and
you, O Israelites, will be gathered up one by one.
13And in that day a great trumpet will sound.
Those who were perishing in Assyria and those
who were exiled in Egypt will come and worship
the LORD on the holy mountain in Jerusalem.

28

Woe to that wreath, the pride of
Ephraim's drunkards,
to the fading flower, his glorious
beauty,
set on the head of a fertile valley—
to that city, the pride of those laid low by
wine!
2See, the Lord has one who is powerful and
strong.
Like a hailstorm and a destructive wind,
like a driving rain and a flooding downpour,
he will throw it forcefully to the ground.

[k]16 The meaning of the Hebrew for this clause is uncertain. [l]8 See Septuagint; the meaning of the Hebrew for this word is uncertain. [m]9 That is, symbols of the goddess Asherah [n]12 Hebrew *River*

[3]That wreath, the pride of Ephraim's
drunkards,
will be trampled underfoot.
[4]That fading flower, his glorious beauty,
set on the head of a fertile valley,
will be like a fig ripe before harvest—
as soon as someone sees it and takes it in
his hand,
he swallows it.

[5]In that day the LORD Almighty
will be a glorious crown,
a beautiful wreath
for the remnant of his people.
[6]He will be a spirit of justice
to him who sits in judgment,
a source of strength
to those who turn back the battle at the
gate.

[7]And these also stagger from wine
and reel from beer:
Priests and prophets stagger from beer
and are befuddled with wine;
they reel from beer,
they stagger when seeing visions,
they stumble when rendering decisions.
[8]All the tables are covered with vomit
and there is not a spot without filth.

[9]"Who is it he is trying to teach?
To whom is he explaining his message?
To children weaned from their milk,
to those just taken from the breast?
[10]For it is:
Do and do, do and do,
rule on rule, rule on rule[o];
a little here, a little there."

[11]Very well then, with foreign lips and strange
tongues
God will speak to this people,
[12]to whom he said,
"This is the resting place, let the weary
rest";
and, "This is the place of repose"—
but they would not listen.
[13]So then, the word of the LORD to them will
become:
Do and do, do and do,
rule on rule, rule on rule;
a little here, a little there—
so that they will go and fall backward,
be injured and snared and captured.

[14]Therefore hear the word of the LORD, you
scoffers
who rule this people in Jerusalem.
[15]You boast, "We have entered into a covenant
with death,
with the grave[p] we have made an
agreement.
When an overwhelming scourge sweeps by,
it cannot touch us,
for we have made a lie our refuge
and falsehood[q] our hiding place."

[16]So this is what the Sovereign LORD says:

"See, I lay a stone in Zion,
a tested stone,
a precious cornerstone for a sure foundation;
the one who trusts will never be dismayed.
[17]I will make justice the measuring line
and righteousness the plumb line;
hail will sweep away your refuge, the lie,
and water will overflow your hiding place.
[18]Your covenant with death will be annulled;
your agreement with the grave will not
stand.
When the overwhelming scourge sweeps by,
you will be beaten down by it.
[19]As often as it comes it will carry you away;
morning after morning, by day and by
night,
it will sweep through."

The understanding of this message
will bring sheer terror.
[20]The bed is too short to stretch out on,
the blanket too narrow to wrap around
you.
[21]The LORD will rise up as he did at Mount
Perazim,
he will rouse himself as in the Valley of
Gibeon—
to do his work, his strange work,
and perform his task, his alien task.
[22]Now stop your mocking,
or your chains will become heavier;
the Lord, the LORD Almighty, has told me
of the destruction decreed against the
whole land.

[23]Listen and hear my voice;
pay attention and hear what I say.

[o]*10* Hebrew / *sav lasav sav lasav / kav lakav kav lakav* (possibly meaningless sounds; perhaps a mimicking of the prophet's words); also in verse 13 [p]*15* Hebrew *Sheol*; also in verse 18 [q]*15* Or *false gods*

[24]When a farmer plows for planting, does he
plow continually?
Does he keep on breaking up and
harrowing the soil?
[25]When he has leveled the surface,
does he not sow caraway and scatter
cummin?
Does he not plant wheat in its place,[r]
barley in its plot,[r]
and spelt in its field?
[26]His God instructs him
and teaches him the right way.

[27]Caraway is not threshed with a sledge,
nor is a cartwheel rolled over cummin;
caraway is beaten out with a rod,
and cummin with a stick.
[28]Grain must be ground to make bread;
so one does not go on threshing it forever.
Though he drives the wheels of his threshing
cart over it,
his horses do not grind it.
[29]All this also comes from the LORD Almighty,
wonderful in counsel and magnificent in
wisdom.

29

Woe to you, Ariel, Ariel,
the city where David settled!
Add year to year
and let your cycle of festivals go on.
[2]Yet I will besiege Ariel;
she will mourn and lament,
she will be to me like an altar hearth.[s]
[3]I will encamp against you all around;
I will encircle you with towers
and set up my siege works against you.
[4]Brought low, you will speak from the ground;
your speech will mumble out of the dust.
Your voice will come ghostlike from the
earth;
out of the dust your speech will whisper.

[5]But your many enemies will become like fine
dust,
the ruthless hordes like blown chaff.
Suddenly, in an instant,
[6] the LORD Almighty will come
with thunder and earthquake and great noise,
with windstorm and tempest and flames of
a devouring fire.
[7]Then the hordes of all the nations that fight
against Ariel,
that attack her and her fortress and besiege
her,
will be as it is with a dream,
with a vision in the night—
[8]as when a hungry man dreams that he is
eating,
but he awakens, and his hunger remains;
as when a thirsty man dreams that he is
drinking,
but he awakens faint, with his thirst
unquenched.
So will it be with the hordes of all the nations
that fight against Mount Zion.

[9]Be stunned and amazed,
blind yourselves and be sightless;
be drunk, but not from wine,
stagger, but not from beer.
[10]The LORD has brought over you a deep sleep:
He has sealed your eyes (the prophets);
he has covered your heads (the seers).

[11]For you this whole vision is nothing but
words sealed in a scroll. And if you give the scroll
to someone who can read, and say to him, "Read
this, please," he will answer, "I can't; it is sealed."
[12]Or if you give the scroll to someone who cannot
read, and say, "Read this, please," he will answer,
"I don't know how to read."

[13]The Lord says:

"These people come near to me with their
mouth
and honor me with their lips,
but their hearts are far from me.
Their worship of me
is made up only of rules taught by men.[t]
[14]Therefore once more I will astound these
people
with wonder upon wonder;
the wisdom of the wise will perish,
the intelligence of the intelligent will
vanish."
[15]Woe to those who go to great depths
to hide their plans from the LORD,
who do their work in darkness and think,
"Who sees us? Who will know?"
[16]You turn things upside down,
as if the potter were thought to be like the
clay!

[r]25 The meaning of the Hebrew for this word is uncertain. [s]2 The Hebrew for *altar hearth* sounds like the Hebrew for *Ariel.*
[t]13 Hebrew; Septuagint *They worship me in vain; / their teachings are but rules taught by men*

Shall what is formed say to him who formed
 it,
 "He did not make me"?
Can the pot say of the potter,
 "He knows nothing"?

17In a very short time, will not Lebanon be
 turned into a fertile field
 and the fertile field seem like a forest?
18In that day the deaf will hear the words of the
 scroll,
 and out of gloom and darkness
 the eyes of the blind will see.
19Once more the humble will rejoice in the
 LORD;
 the needy will rejoice in the Holy One of
 Israel.
20The ruthless will vanish,
 the mockers will disappear,
 and all who have an eye for evil will be cut
 down—
21those who with a word make a man out to be
 guilty,
 who ensnare the defender in court
 and with false testimony deprive the
 innocent of justice.

22Therefore this is what the LORD, who re-
deemed Abraham, says to the house of Jacob:

"No longer will Jacob be ashamed;
 no longer will their faces grow pale.
23When they see among them their children,
 the work of my hands,
they will keep my name holy;
 they will acknowledge the holiness of the
 Holy One of Jacob,
 and will stand in awe of the God of Israel.
24Those who are wayward in spirit will gain
 understanding;
 those who complain will accept
 instruction."

10 / *Isaiah 30:1–18*
Who Do You Rely On?

THE TITLE OF this study is taken from Isaiah 36:4, in which Hezekiah's court officials hear the Assyrian field commander scornfully mock Jewish military capability. And indeed there were apparently many in Judah who were not at all sure that the Lord would be able to protect Jerusalem. Meanwhile, Isaiah still hammers away at the same message he has been preaching all along: "Trust in the Lord at all times." Military alliances can do little to preserve a society that is already corroded and rotten within.

Warming Up to God Describe a time when it has been difficult for you to trust in God.

Read Isaiah 30:1–18.

30 "Woe to the obstinate children,"
 declares the LORD,
 "to those who carry out plans that
 are not mine,
 forming an alliance, but not by my Spirit,
 heaping sin upon sin;
2who go down to Egypt
 without consulting me;
who look for help to Pharaoh's protection,
 to Egypt's shade for refuge.
3But Pharaoh's protection will be to your
 shame,
 Egypt's shade will bring you disgrace.
4Though they have officials in Zoan
 and their envoys have arrived in Hanes,
5everyone will be put to shame
 because of a people useless to them,
who bring neither help nor advantage,
 but only shame and disgrace."

6An oracle concerning the animals of the
Negev:

Through a land of hardship and distress,
 of lions and lionesses,
 of adders and darting snakes,

the envoys carry their riches on donkeys'
backs,
their treasures on the humps of camels,
to that unprofitable nation,
7 to Egypt, whose help is utterly useless.
Therefore I call her
Rahab the Do-Nothing.

8Go now, write it on a tablet for them,
inscribe it on a scroll,
that for the days to come
it may be an everlasting witness.
9These are rebellious people, deceitful children,
children unwilling to listen to the LORD's
instruction.
10They say to the seers,
"See no more visions!"
and to the prophets,
"Give us no more visions of what is right!
Tell us pleasant things,
prophesy illusions.
11Leave this way,
get off this path,
and stop confronting us
with the Holy One of Israel!"

12Therefore, this is what the Holy One of Israel
says:

"Because you have rejected this message,
relied on oppression
and depended on deceit,
13this sin will become for you
like a high wall, cracked and bulging,
that collapses suddenly, in an instant.
14It will break in pieces like pottery,
shattered so mercilessly
that among its pieces not a fragment will be
found
for taking coals from a hearth
or scooping water out of a cistern."

15This is what the Sovereign LORD, the Holy
One of Israel, says:

"In repentance and rest is your salvation,
in quietness and trust is your strength,
but you would have none of it.
16You said, 'No, we will flee on horses.'
Therefore you will flee!
You said, 'We will ride off on swift horses.'
Therefore your pursuers will be swift!
17A thousand will flee
at the threat of one;
at the threat of five
you will all flee away,
till you are left
like a flagstaff on a mountaintop,
like a banner on a hill."

18Yet the LORD longs to be gracious to you;
he rises to show you compassion.
For the LORD is a God of justice.
Blessed are all who wait for him!

Discovering the Word 1. Why does God object to Judah's taking shelter under the shadow of Egypt (vv. 1–5)? 2. How do verses 6–7 emphasize the utter futility of seeking Egypt's help? 3. From verses 8–11 describe the Israelites' behavior. 4. From verses 10–22 how do you think Isaiah was regarded by the people? 5. How is the metaphor Isaiah uses to depict God's judgment particularly appropriate to their sin (vv. 12–14)? 6. How do verses 16–17 depict the price of unbelief?

Applying the Word 1. What is the difference between faith and wishful thinking? 2. What sort of "Egypts" are we tempted to turn to today? 3. Consider some particular trouble you are facing at this time. What steps do you need to take in order to trust that God will be gracious to those who wait for him—as verse 18 promises?

Responding in Prayer Recall a time when you have experienced the kind of contentment verse 15 promises. Thank God for that gift, and pray that he will renew contentment in you.

Isaiah 30:19—35:10

19O people of Zion, who live in Jerusalem, you
will weep no more. How gracious he will be when
you cry for help! As soon as he hears, he will
answer you. 20Although the Lord gives you the
bread of adversity and the water of affliction, your
teachers will be hidden no more; with your own
eyes you will see them. 21Whether you turn to the
right or to the left, your ears will hear a voice
behind you, saying, "This is the way; walk in it."
22Then you will defile your idols overlaid with
silver and your images covered with gold; you
will throw them away like a menstrual cloth and
say to them, "Away with you!"

23He will also send you rain for the seed you
sow in the ground, and the food that comes from
the land will be rich and plentiful. In that day
your cattle will graze in broad meadows. 24The
oxen and donkeys that work the soil will eat fod-
der and mash, spread out with fork and shovel.
25In the day of great slaughter, when the towers
fall, streams of water will flow on every high
mountain and every lofty hill. 26The moon will
shine like the sun, and the sunlight will be seven
times brighter, like the light of seven full days,
when the LORD binds up the bruises of his people
and heals the wounds he inflicted.

27See, the Name of the LORD comes from afar,
with burning anger and dense clouds of smoke;
his lips are full of wrath,
and his tongue is a consuming fire.
28His breath is like a rushing torrent,
rising up to the neck.
He shakes the nations in the sieve of destruction;
he places in the jaws of the peoples
a bit that leads them astray.
29And you will sing
as on the night you celebrate a holy festival;
your hearts will rejoice
as when people go up with flutes
to the mountain of the LORD,
to the Rock of Israel.
30The LORD will cause men to hear his majestic voice
and will make them see his arm coming down
with raging anger and consuming fire,
with cloudburst, thunderstorm and hail.
31The voice of the LORD will shatter Assyria;
with his scepter he will strike them down.
32Every stroke the LORD lays on them
with his punishing rod
will be to the music of tambourines and harps,
as he fights them in battle with the blows of his arm.
33Topheth has long been prepared;
it has been made ready for the king.
Its fire pit has been made deep and wide,
with an abundance of fire and wood;
the breath of the LORD,
like a stream of burning sulfur,
sets it ablaze.

31 Woe to those who go down to Egypt for help,
who rely on horses,
who trust in the multitude of their chariots
and in the great strength of their horsemen,
but do not look to the Holy One of Israel,
or seek help from the LORD.
2Yet he too is wise and can bring disaster;
he does not take back his words.
He will rise up against the house of the wicked,
against those who help evildoers.
3But the Egyptians are men and not God;
their horses are flesh and not spirit.
When the LORD stretches out his hand,
he who helps will stumble,
he who is helped will fall;
both will perish together.

4This is what the LORD says to me:

"As a lion growls,
a great lion over his prey—
and though a whole band of shepherds
is called together against him,
he is not frightened by their shouts
or disturbed by their clamor—
so the LORD Almighty will come down
to do battle on Mount Zion and on its heights.
5Like birds hovering overhead,
the LORD Almighty will shield Jerusalem;

he will shield it and deliver it,
he will 'pass over' it and will rescue it."

6Return to him you have so greatly revolted
against, O Israelites. 7For in that day every one of
you will reject the idols of silver and gold your
sinful hands have made.

8"Assyria will fall by a sword that is not of man;
a sword, not of mortals, will devour them.
They will flee before the sword
and their young men will be put to forced labor.
9Their stronghold will fall because of terror;
at sight of the battle standard their commanders will panic,"
declares the LORD,
whose fire is in Zion,
whose furnace is in Jerusalem.

32

See, a king will reign in righteousness
and rulers will rule with justice.
2Each man will be like a shelter from the wind
and a refuge from the storm,
like streams of water in the desert
and the shadow of a great rock in a thirsty land.

3Then the eyes of those who see will no longer be closed,
and the ears of those who hear will listen.
4The mind of the rash will know and understand,
and the stammering tongue will be fluent and clear.
5No longer will the fool be called noble
nor the scoundrel be highly respected.
6For the fool speaks folly,
his mind is busy with evil:
He practices ungodliness
and spreads error concerning the LORD;
the hungry he leaves empty
and from the thirsty he withholds water.
7The scoundrel's methods are wicked,
he makes up evil schemes
to destroy the poor with lies,
even when the plea of the needy is just.
8But the noble man makes noble plans,
and by noble deeds he stands.

9You women who are so complacent,
rise up and listen to me;
you daughters who feel secure,
hear what I have to say!
10In little more than a year
you who feel secure will tremble;
the grape harvest will fail,
and the harvest of fruit will not come.
11Tremble, you complacent women;
shudder, you daughters who feel secure!
Strip off your clothes,
put sackcloth around your waists.
12Beat your breasts for the pleasant fields,
for the fruitful vines
13and for the land of my people,
a land overgrown with thorns and briers—
yes, mourn for all houses of merriment
and for this city of revelry.
14The fortress will be abandoned,
the noisy city deserted;
citadel and watchtower will become a wasteland forever,
the delight of donkeys, a pasture for flocks,
15till the Spirit is poured upon us from on high,
and the desert becomes a fertile field,
and the fertile field seems like a forest.
16Justice will dwell in the desert
and righteousness live in the fertile field.
17The fruit of righteousness will be peace;
the effect of righteousness will be quietness and confidence forever.
18My people will live in peaceful dwelling places,
in secure homes,
in undisturbed places of rest.
19Though hail flattens the forest
and the city is leveled completely,
20how blessed you will be,
sowing your seed by every stream,
and letting your cattle and donkeys range free.

33

Woe to you, O destroyer,
you who have not been destroyed!
Woe to you, O traitor,
you who have not been betrayed!
When you stop destroying,
you will be destroyed;
when you stop betraying,
you will be betrayed.

2O LORD, be gracious to us;
we long for you.
Be our strength every morning,
our salvation in time of distress.

[3]At the thunder of your voice, the peoples flee;
when you rise up, the nations scatter.
[4]Your plunder, O nations, is harvested as by young locusts;
like a swarm of locusts men pounce on it.

[5]The LORD is exalted, for he dwells on high;
he will fill Zion with justice and righteousness.
[6]He will be the sure foundation for your times,
a rich store of salvation and wisdom and knowledge;
the fear of the LORD is the key to this treasure.[u]

[7]Look, their brave men cry aloud in the streets;
the envoys of peace weep bitterly.
[8]The highways are deserted,
no travelers are on the roads.
The treaty is broken,
its witnesses[v] are despised,
no one is respected.
[9]The land mourns[w] and wastes away,
Lebanon is ashamed and withers;
Sharon is like the Arabah,
and Bashan and Carmel drop their leaves.

[10]"Now will I arise," says the LORD.
"Now will I be exalted;
now will I be lifted up.
[11]You conceive chaff,
you give birth to straw;
your breath is a fire that consumes you.
[12]The peoples will be burned as if to lime;
like cut thornbushes they will be set ablaze."

[13]You who are far away, hear what I have done;
you who are near, acknowledge my power!
[14]The sinners in Zion are terrified;
trembling grips the godless:
"Who of us can dwell with the consuming fire?
Who of us can dwell with everlasting burning?"
[15]He who walks righteously
and speaks what is right,
who rejects gain from extortion
and keeps his hand from accepting bribes,
who stops his ears against plots of murder
and shuts his eyes against contemplating evil—
[16]this is the man who will dwell on the heights,
whose refuge will be the mountain fortress.
His bread will be supplied,
and water will not fail him.
[17]Your eyes will see the king in his beauty
and view a land that stretches afar.
[18]In your thoughts you will ponder the former terror:
"Where is that chief officer?
Where is the one who took the revenue?
Where is the officer in charge of the towers?"
[19]You will see those arrogant people no more,
those people of an obscure speech,
with their strange, incomprehensible tongue.

[20]Look upon Zion, the city of our festivals;
your eyes will see Jerusalem,
a peaceful abode, a tent that will not be moved;
its stakes will never be pulled up,
nor any of its ropes broken.
[21]There the LORD will be our Mighty One.
It will be like a place of broad rivers and streams.
No galley with oars will ride them,
no mighty ship will sail them.
[22]For the LORD is our judge,
the LORD is our lawgiver,
the LORD is our king;
it is he who will save us.

[23]Your rigging hangs loose:
The mast is not held secure,
the sail is not spread.
Then an abundance of spoils will be divided
and even the lame will carry off plunder.
[24]No one living in Zion will say, "I am ill";
and the sins of those who dwell there will be forgiven.

34

Come near, you nations, and listen;
pay attention, you peoples!
Let the earth hear, and all that is in it,
the world, and all that comes out of it!
[2]The LORD is angry with all nations;
his wrath is upon all their armies.
He will totally destroy[x] them,
he will give them over to slaughter.

[u]6 Or *is a treasure from him* [v]8 Dead Sea Scrolls; Masoretic Text / *the cities* [w]9 Or *dries up* [x]2 The Hebrew term refers to the irrevocable giving over of things or persons to the LORD, often by totally destroying them; also in verse 5.

[3]Their slain will be thrown out,
their dead bodies will send up a stench;
the mountains will be soaked with their blood.
[4]All the stars of the heavens will be dissolved
and the sky rolled up like a scroll;
all the starry host will fall
like withered leaves from the vine,
like shriveled figs from the fig tree.

[5]My sword has drunk its fill in the heavens;
see, it descends in judgment on Edom,
the people I have totally destroyed.
[6]The sword of the LORD is bathed in blood,
it is covered with fat—
the blood of lambs and goats,
fat from the kidneys of rams.
For the LORD has a sacrifice in Bozrah
and a great slaughter in Edom.
[7]And the wild oxen will fall with them,
the bull calves and the great bulls.
Their land will be drenched with blood,
and the dust will be soaked with fat.

[8]For the LORD has a day of vengeance,
a year of retribution, to uphold Zion's cause.
[9]Edom's streams will be turned into pitch,
her dust into burning sulfur;
her land will become blazing pitch!
[10]It will not be quenched night and day;
its smoke will rise forever.
From generation to generation it will lie desolate;
no one will ever pass through it again.
[11]The desert owl[y] and screech owl[y] will possess it;
the great owl[y] and the raven will nest there.
God will stretch out over Edom
the measuring line of chaos
and the plumb line of desolation.
[12]Her nobles will have nothing there to be called a kingdom,
all her princes will vanish away.
[13]Thorns will overrun her citadels,
nettles and brambles her strongholds.
She will become a haunt for jackals,
a home for owls.
[14]Desert creatures will meet with hyenas,
and wild goats will bleat to each other;
there the night creatures will also repose
and find for themselves places of rest.
[15]The owl will nest there and lay eggs,
she will hatch them, and care for her young
under the shadow of her wings;
there also the falcons will gather,
each with its mate.

[16]Look in the scroll of the LORD and read:

None of these will be missing,
not one will lack her mate.
For it is his mouth that has given the order,
and his Spirit will gather them together.
[17]He allots their portions;
his hand distributes them by measure.
They will possess it forever
and dwell there from generation to generation.

35

The desert and the parched land
will be glad;
the wilderness will rejoice and blossom.
Like the crocus, [2]it will burst into bloom;
it will rejoice greatly and shout for joy.
The glory of Lebanon will be given to it,
the splendor of Carmel and Sharon;
they will see the glory of the LORD,
the splendor of our God.

[3]Strengthen the feeble hands,
steady the knees that give way;
[4]say to those with fearful hearts,
"Be strong, do not fear;
your God will come,
he will come with vengeance;
with divine retribution
he will come to save you."

[5]Then will the eyes of the blind be opened
and the ears of the deaf unstopped.
[6]Then will the lame leap like a deer,
and the mute tongue shout for joy.
Water will gush forth in the wilderness
and streams in the desert.
[7]The burning sand will become a pool,
the thirsty ground bubbling springs.
In the haunts where jackals once lay,
grass and reeds and papyrus will grow.

[8]And a highway will be there;
it will be called the Way of Holiness.
The unclean will not journey on it;
it will be for those who walk in that Way;

y11 The precise identification of these birds is uncertain.

wicked fools will not go about on it.[z]
9No lion will be there,
nor will any ferocious beast get up on it;
they will not be found there.
But only the redeemed will walk there,
10 and the ransomed of the LORD will return.
They will enter Zion with singing;
everlasting joy will crown their heads.
Gladness and joy will overtake them,
and sorrow and sighing will flee away.

[z]8 Or / *the simple will not stray from it*

11 / *Isaiah* 36—37
An Extraordinary Deliverance

HAVE YOU EVER been intimidated by someone's ability to present an argument? Have you ever been frustrated by someone's ability to twist your words and distort the truth? How do you respond in such situations? Isaiah and King Hezekiah were confronted with just such a situation. They remained confident in God, however, and were able to respond with force and conviction to the blasphemous words they heard.

Warming Up to God Describe a time you have heard someone distort God's words.

Read Isaiah 36—37.

36 In the fourteenth year of King Hezekiah's reign, Sennacherib king of Assyria attacked all the fortified cities of Judah and captured them. 2Then the king of Assyria sent his field commander with a large army from Lachish to King Hezekiah at Jerusalem. When the commander stopped at the aqueduct of the Upper Pool, on the road to the Washerman's Field, 3Eliakim son of Hilkiah the palace administrator, Shebna the secretary, and Joah son of Asaph the recorder went out to him.

4The field commander said to them, "Tell Hezekiah,

" 'This is what the great king, the king of Assyria, says: On what are you basing this confidence of yours? 5You say you have strategy and military strength—but you speak only empty words. On whom are you depending, that you rebel against me? 6Look now, you are depending on Egypt, that splintered reed of a staff, which pierces a man's hand and wounds him if he leans on it! Such is Pharaoh king of Egypt to all who depend on him. 7And if you say to me, "We are depending on the LORD our God"—isn't he the one whose high places and altars Hezekiah removed, saying to Judah and Jerusalem, "You must worship before this altar"?

8" 'Come now, make a bargain with my master, the king of Assyria: I will give you two thousand horses—if you can put riders on them! 9How then can you repulse one officer of the least of my master's officials, even though you are depending on Egypt for chariots and horsemen? 10Furthermore, have I come to attack and destroy this land without the LORD? The LORD himself told me to march against this country and destroy it.' "

11Then Eliakim, Shebna and Joah said to the field commander, "Please speak to your servants in Aramaic, since we understand it. Don't speak to us in Hebrew in the hearing of the people on the wall."

12But the commander replied, "Was it only to your master and you that my master sent me to say these things, and not to the men sitting on the wall—who, like you, will have to eat their own filth and drink their own urine?"

13Then the commander stood and called out in Hebrew, "Hear the words of the great king, the king of Assyria! 14This is what the king says: Do not let Hezekiah deceive you. He cannot deliver you! 15Do not let Hezekiah persuade you to trust in the LORD when he says, 'The LORD will surely deliver us; this city will not be given into the hand of the king of Assyria.'

[16]"Do not listen to Hezekiah. This is what the king of Assyria says: Make peace with me and come out to me. Then every one of you will eat from his own vine and fig tree and drink water from his own cistern, [17]until I come and take you to a land like your own—a land of grain and new wine, a land of bread and vineyards.

[18]"Do not let Hezekiah mislead you when he says, 'The LORD will deliver us.' Has the god of any nation ever delivered his land from the hand of the king of Assyria? [19]Where are the gods of Hamath and Arpad? Where are the gods of Sepharvaim? Have they rescued Samaria from my hand? [20]Who of all the gods of these countries has been able to save his land from me? How then can the LORD deliver Jerusalem from my hand?"

[21]But the people remained silent and said nothing in reply, because the king had commanded, "Do not answer him."

[22]Then Eliakim son of Hilkiah the palace administrator, Shebna the secretary, and Joah son of Asaph the recorder went to Hezekiah, with their clothes torn, and told him what the field commander had said.

37 When King Hezekiah heard this, he tore his clothes and put on sackcloth and went into the temple of the LORD. [2]He sent Eliakim the palace administrator, Shebna the secretary, and the leading priests, all wearing sackcloth, to the prophet Isaiah son of Amoz. [3]They told him, "This is what Hezekiah says: This day is a day of distress and rebuke and disgrace, as when children come to the point of birth and there is no strength to deliver them. [4]It may be that the LORD your God will hear the words of the field commander, whom his master, the king of Assyria, has sent to ridicule the living God, and that he will rebuke him for the words the LORD your God has heard. Therefore pray for the remnant that still survives."

[5]When King Hezekiah's officials came to Isaiah, [6]Isaiah said to them, "Tell your master, 'This is what the LORD says: Do not be afraid of what you have heard—those words with which the underlings of the king of Assyria have blasphemed me. [7]Listen! I am going to put a spirit in him so that when he hears a certain report, he will return to his own country, and there I will have him cut down with the sword.' "

[8]When the field commander heard that the king of Assyria had left Lachish, he withdrew and found the king fighting against Libnah.

[9]Now Sennacherib received a report that Tirhakah, the Cushite[a] king ⌞of Egypt⌟, was marching out to fight against him. When he heard it, he sent messengers to Hezekiah with this word: [10]"Say to Hezekiah king of Judah: Do not let the god you depend on deceive you when he says, 'Jerusalem will not be handed over to the king of Assyria.' [11]Surely you have heard what the kings of Assyria have done to all the countries, destroying them completely. And will you be delivered? [12]Did the gods of the nations that were destroyed by my forefathers deliver them—the gods of Gozan, Haran, Rezeph and the people of Eden who were in Tel Assar? [13]Where is the king of Hamath, the king of Arpad, the king of the city of Sepharvaim, or of Hena or Ivvah?"

[14]Hezekiah received the letter from the messengers and read it. Then he went up to the temple of the LORD and spread it out before the LORD. [15]And Hezekiah prayed to the LORD: [16]"O LORD Almighty, God of Israel, enthroned between the cherubim, you alone are God over all the kingdoms of the earth. You have made heaven and earth. [17]Give ear, O LORD, and hear; open your eyes, O LORD, and see; listen to all the words Sennacherib has sent to insult the living God.

[18]"It is true, O LORD, that the Assyrian kings have laid waste all these peoples and their lands. [19]They have thrown their gods into the fire and destroyed them, for they were not gods but only wood and stone, fashioned by human hands. [20]Now, O LORD our God, deliver us from his hand, so that all kingdoms on earth may know that you alone, O LORD, are God.[b]"

[21]Then Isaiah son of Amoz sent a message to Hezekiah: "This is what the LORD, the God of Israel, says: Because you have prayed to me concerning Sennacherib king of Assyria, [22]this is the word the LORD has spoken against him:

"The Virgin Daughter of Zion
  despises and mocks you.
The Daughter of Jerusalem
  tosses her head as you flee.
[23]Who is it you have insulted and blasphemed?
  Against whom have you raised your voice
and lifted your eyes in pride?
  Against the Holy One of Israel!
[24]By your messengers
  you have heaped insults on the Lord.

[a]9 That is, from the upper Nile region [b]20 Dead Sea Scrolls (see also 2 Kings 19:19); Masoretic Text *alone are the LORD*

And you have said,
'With my many chariots
I have ascended the heights of the mountains,
the utmost heights of Lebanon.
I have cut down its tallest cedars,
the choicest of its pines.
I have reached its remotest heights,
the finest of its forests.
25I have dug wells in foreign lands[c]
and drunk the water there.
With the soles of my feet
I have dried up all the streams of Egypt.'

26"Have you not heard?
Long ago I ordained it.
In days of old I planned it;
now I have brought it to pass,
that you have turned fortified cities
into piles of stone.
27Their people, drained of power,
are dismayed and put to shame.
They are like plants in the field,
like tender green shoots,
like grass sprouting on the roof,
scorched[d] before it grows up.

28"But I know where you stay
and when you come and go
and how you rage against me.
29Because you rage against me
and because your insolence has reached my ears,
I will put my hook in your nose
and my bit in your mouth,
and I will make you return
by the way you came.

30"This will be the sign for you, O Hezekiah:

"This year you will eat what grows by itself,
and the second year what springs from that.
But in the third year sow and reap,
plant vineyards and eat their fruit.
31Once more a remnant of the house of Judah
will take root below and bear fruit above.
32For out of Jerusalem will come a remnant,
and out of Mount Zion a band of survivors.
The zeal of the LORD Almighty
will accomplish this.

33"Therefore this is what the LORD says concerning the king of Assyria:

"He will not enter this city
or shoot an arrow here.
He will not come before it with shield
or build a siege ramp against it.
34By the way that he came he will return;
he will not enter this city,"
declares the LORD.
35"I will defend this city and save it,
for my sake and for the sake of David my servant!"

36Then the angel of the LORD went out and put
to death a hundred and eighty-five thousand men
in the Assyrian camp. When the people got up
the next morning—there were all the dead bod-
ies! 37So Sennacherib king of Assyria broke camp
and withdrew. He returned to Nineveh and stayed
there.
38One day, while he was worshiping in the
temple of his god Nisroch, his sons Adrammelech
and Sharezer cut him down with the sword, and
they escaped to the land of Ararat. And Esarhad-
don his son succeeded him as king.

[c]25 Dead Sea Scrolls (see also 2 Kings 19:24); Masoretic Text does not have *in foreign lands*. [d]27 Some manuscripts of the Masoretic Text, Dead Sea Scrolls and some Septuagint manuscripts (see also 2 Kings 19:26); most manuscripts of the Masoretic Text *roof / and terraced fields*

Discovering the Word 1. Use map 3 and the historical chart (in the introduction) to get a picture of the situation described in 36:1–3. (You may remember that the place where the Assyrian commander stood in verse 2 is the same spot where Isaiah had confronted Ahaz years earlier [see 7:3].) How do you think the Israelites and King Hezekiah were feeling at this point? 2. How does the field commander distort the truth in verse 7 and in verse 10? 3. What temptations does the king hold out in 36:16–20? 4. What attitudes are demonstrated in Hezekiah's message to Isaiah and Isaiah's reply (37:1–7)? 5. Sennacherib's response (37:9–13) is a cruder replay of the threats of his field commander in chapter 36. What is the substance of Isaiah's reply to Sennacherib's taunt? 6. Contrast the word of hope to Hezekiah (37:30–32) and the shockingly brief statement about the end of Sennacherib's campaign and the end of his life (37:36–38).

Applying the Word 1. In what respects can you see parallels between the threats of the Assyrian general and the temptations you face? 2. In what respects can you take Hezekiah's and Isaiah's responses to Sennacherib as models for your own response to intimidation?

Responding in Prayer As you face a world that is hostile toward Christianity, pray that you will be made bold in faith.

12 / *Isaiah 38—39*
Sovereign God and Forgetful King

IT WAS A miracle. Hezekiah's life was extended by fifteen years! We might expect that he would live those fifteen years in unforgettable gratitude and trustfulness, but the Bible, with its usual dogged realism, records that it was not so. In the chapter which follows we will see how Hezekiah ignored the warnings he had been given and invited a treacherous enemy into his home.

Warming Up to God Which do you believe is more dangerous to faith—adversity or prosperity? Why?

Read Isaiah 38—39.

38 In those days Hezekiah became ill
and was at the point of death. The
prophet Isaiah son of Amoz went to
him and said, "This is what the LORD says: Put
your house in order, because you are going to die;
you will not recover."
2Hezekiah turned his face to the wall and
prayed to the LORD, 3"Remember, O LORD, how I
have walked before you faithfully and with
wholehearted devotion and have done what is
good in your eyes." And Hezekiah wept bitterly.
4Then the word of the LORD came to Isaiah:
5"Go and tell Hezekiah, 'This is what the LORD,
the God of your father David, says: I have heard
your prayer and seen your tears; I will add fifteen
years to your life. 6And I will deliver you and this
city from the hand of the king of Assyria. I will
defend this city.
7" 'This is the LORD's sign to you that the LORD
will do what he has promised: 8I will make the
shadow cast by the sun go back the ten steps it
has gone down on the stairway of Ahaz.' " So the
sunlight went back the ten steps it had gone
down.

9A writing of Hezekiah king of Judah after his
illness and recovery:

10I said, "In the prime of my life
must I go through the gates of death[e]
and be robbed of the rest of my years?"
11I said, "I will not again see the LORD,
the LORD, in the land of the living;
no longer will I look on mankind,
or be with those who now dwell in this world.[f]
12Like a shepherd's tent my house
has been pulled down and taken from me.
Like a weaver I have rolled up my life,
and he has cut me off from the loom;
day and night you made an end of me.
13I waited patiently till dawn,
but like a lion he broke all my bones;
day and night you made an end of me.
14I cried like a swift or thrush,
I moaned like a mourning dove.
My eyes grew weak as I looked to the heavens.
I am troubled; O Lord, come to my aid!"
15But what can I say?
He has spoken to me, and he himself has done this.
I will walk humbly all my years
because of this anguish of my soul.
16Lord, by such things men live;
and my spirit finds life in them too.
You restored me to health
and let me live.
17Surely it was for my benefit
that I suffered such anguish.
In your love you kept me
from the pit of destruction;
you have put all my sins

[e] 10 Hebrew *Sheol* [f] 11 A few Hebrew manuscripts; most Hebrew manuscripts *in the place of cessation*

behind your back.
18For the grave[g] cannot praise you,
death cannot sing your praise;
those who go down to the pit
cannot hope for your faithfulness.
19The living, the living—they praise you,
as I am doing today;
fathers tell their children
about your faithfulness.

20The LORD will save me,
and we will sing with stringed instruments
all the days of our lives
in the temple of the LORD.

21Isaiah had said, "Prepare a poultice of figs and apply it to the boil, and he will recover."

22Hezekiah had asked, "What will be the sign that I will go up to the temple of the LORD?"

39 At that time Merodach-Baladan son of Baladan king of Babylon sent Hezekiah letters and a gift, because he had heard of his illness and recovery. 2Hezekiah received the envoys gladly and showed them what was in his storehouses—the silver, the gold, the spices, the fine oil, his entire armory and everything found among his treasures. There was nothing in his palace or in all his kingdom that Hezekiah did not show them.

3Then Isaiah the prophet went to King Hezekiah and asked, "What did those men say, and where did they come from?"

"From a distant land," Hezekiah replied. "They came to me from Babylon."

4The prophet asked, "What did they see in your palace?"

"They saw everything in my palace," Hezekiah said. "There is nothing among my treasures that I did not show them."

5Then Isaiah said to Hezekiah, "Hear the word of the LORD Almighty: 6The time will surely come when everything in your palace, and all that your fathers have stored up until this day, will be carried off to Babylon. Nothing will be left, says the LORD. 7And some of your descendants, your own flesh and blood who will be born to you, will be taken away, and they will become eunuchs in the palace of the king of Babylon."

8"The word of the LORD you have spoken is good," Hezekiah replied. For he thought, "There will be peace and security in my lifetime."

g18 Hebrew *Sheol*

Discovering the Word 1. What do you learn about prayer from the events in 38:1–8? How do you reconcile the Lord's word in verse 1 that Hezekiah would not recover and his promise in verse 5 that Hezekiah would live fifteen more years? 2. With what vivid metaphors does Hezekiah describe his deathly sickness (38:10–14)? 3. What reassurance does Hezekiah find in God's love in 38:15–20? 4. What punishment did Isaiah announce for Hezekiah's disloyalty (39:5–7)? 5. How do you interpret Hezekiah's response—his words and his thoughts (39:8)?

Applying the Word 1. What abiding truths do you find in chapter 38 to hold on to firmly in times of sickness and misfortune? 2. In what ways does this passage expand or change your understanding of who God is and how he answers our prayers?

Responding in Prayer Tell the Lord your heart's desires with confidence that he answers prayer.

13 / *Isaiah 40*
Unwearied Faith in an Unwearying God

IN ISAIAH 40 and the chapters following, the ending of the Babylonian exile is presupposed, and it is the prophet's purpose to reconstruct his people's faith and hope with prophecies of liberation from captivity and a new calling to be God's servant and a light to the nations. Through all the vicissitudes of history, God the Holy One, God the Gracious One, unwearyingly speaks to his people, revealing himself as a God of grace, an incomparably great

God, and a God who is in charge of the movements of history, even when a tyrant arises to terrify the world. The nations in terror turn to their idols. But Israel is to trust God in such world-shaking times. And so are we.

Warming Up to God What "idols" (for instance, money, power or sex) do you use as a source of comfort for your fears? Confess your sin to God and ask him to free you to hear his Word for you today.

Read Isaiah 40.

40 Comfort, comfort my people,
says your God.
2Speak tenderly to Jerusalem,
and proclaim to her
that her hard service has been completed,
that her sin has been paid for,
that she has received from the LORD's hand
double for all her sins.

3A voice of one calling:
"In the desert prepare
the way for the LORD[h];
make straight in the wilderness
a highway for our God.[i]
4Every valley shall be raised up,
every mountain and hill made low;
the rough ground shall become level,
the rugged places a plain.
5And the glory of the LORD will be revealed,
and all mankind together will see it.
For the mouth of the LORD
has spoken."

6A voice says, "Cry out."
And I said, "What shall I cry?"

"All men are like grass,
and all their glory is like the flowers of the field.
7The grass withers and the flowers fall,
because the breath of the LORD blows on them.
Surely the people are grass.
8The grass withers and the flowers fall,
but the word of our God stands forever."

9You who bring good tidings to Zion,
go up on a high mountain.
You who bring good tidings to Jerusalem,[j]
lift up your voice with a shout,
lift it up, do not be afraid;
say to the towns of Judah,
"Here is your God!"
10See, the Sovereign LORD comes with power,
and his arm rules for him.
See, his reward is with him,
and his recompense accompanies him.
11He tends his flock like a shepherd:
He gathers the lambs in his arms
and carries them close to his heart;
he gently leads those that have young.

12Who has measured the waters in the hollow of his hand,
or with the breadth of his hand marked off the heavens?
Who has held the dust of the earth in a basket,
or weighed the mountains on the scales
and the hills in a balance?
13Who has understood the mind[k] of the LORD,
or instructed him as his counselor?
14Whom did the LORD consult to enlighten him,
and who taught him the right way?
Who was it that taught him knowledge
or showed him the path of understanding?

15Surely the nations are like a drop in a bucket;
they are regarded as dust on the scales;
he weighs the islands as though they were fine dust.
16Lebanon is not sufficient for altar fires,
nor its animals enough for burnt offerings.
17Before him all the nations are as nothing;
they are regarded by him as worthless
and less than nothing.

18To whom, then, will you compare God?
What image will you compare him to?
19As for an idol, a craftsman casts it,
and a goldsmith overlays it with gold
and fashions silver chains for it.
20A man too poor to present such an offering
selects wood that will not rot.
He looks for a skilled craftsman
to set up an idol that will not topple.

21Do you not know?
Have you not heard?

[h]3 Or *A voice of one calling in the desert: / "Prepare the way for the* LORD [i]3 Hebrew; Septuagint *make straight the paths of our God* [j]9 Or *O Zion, bringer of good tidings, / go up on a high mountain. / O Jerusalem, bringer of good tidings* [k]13 Or *Spirit*; or *spirit*

Has it not been told you from the beginning?
  Have you not understood since the earth
    was founded?
22 He sits enthroned above the circle of the
    earth,
  and its people are like grasshoppers.
He stretches out the heavens like a canopy,
  and spreads them out like a tent to live in.
23 He brings princes to naught
  and reduces the rulers of this world to
    nothing.
24 No sooner are they planted,
  no sooner are they sown,
  no sooner do they take root in the ground,
than he blows on them and they wither,
  and a whirlwind sweeps them away like
    chaff.

25 "To whom will you compare me?
  Or who is my equal?" says the Holy One.
26 Lift your eyes and look to the heavens:
  Who created all these?
He who brings out the starry host one by one,
  and calls them each by name.
Because of his great power and mighty
    strength,
  not one of them is missing.

27 Why do you say, O Jacob,
  and complain, O Israel,
"My way is hidden from the LORD;
  my cause is disregarded by my God"?
28 Do you not know?
  Have you not heard?
The LORD is the everlasting God,
  the Creator of the ends of the earth.
He will not grow tired or weary,
  and his understanding no one can fathom.
29 He gives strength to the weary
  and increases the power of the weak.
30 Even youths grow tired and weary,
  and young men stumble and fall;
31 but those who hope in the LORD
  will renew their strength.
They will soar on wings like eagles;
  they will run and not grow weary,
  they will walk and not be faint.

Discovering the Word 1. A tender, wooing voice speaks to God's people in verses 1 and 2. What are the implications of the three affirmations all introduced by the word *that?* 2. A second voice is raised in verses 6–8. What vivid contrast is made in these verses? 3. The third voice, in verse 9, says, "Here is your God!" What sort of a God is he according to verses 10 and 11? 4. In what different ways is the incomparable greatness of God affirmed by the avalanche of questions and statements in verses 12–17 and 21–26? 5. How does the prophet answer Israel's complaint in verse 27?

Applying the Word 1. Deserts, valleys and mountains are hindrances to transport and communication (vv. 3–5). If all humanity is to see the glory of the Lord, these obstacles must be removed. What obstacles do you and your group or church face in both your local witness and global missions efforts? 2. How can these obstacles be removed? 3. How do these verses bring you the encouragement you need?

Responding in Prayer Make verses 28–31 your prayer to the Lord today.

Isaiah 41

41 "Be silent before me, you islands!
  Let the nations renew their
    strength!
Let them come forward and speak;
  let us meet together at the place of
    judgment.

2 "Who has stirred up one from the east,
  calling him in righteousness to his
    service[l]?
He hands nations over to him
  and subdues kings before him.
He turns them to dust with his sword,
  to windblown chaff with his bow.
3 He pursues them and moves on unscathed,
  by a path his feet have not traveled before.
4 Who has done this and carried it through,

[l]2 Or / *whom victory meets at every step*

calling forth the generations from the
beginning?
I, the LORD—with the first of them
and with the last—I am he."

5The islands have seen it and fear;
the ends of the earth tremble.
They approach and come forward;
6 each helps the other
and says to his brother, "Be strong!"
7The craftsman encourages the goldsmith,
and he who smooths with the hammer
spurs on him who strikes the anvil.
He says of the welding, "It is good."
He nails down the idol so it will not topple.
8"But you, O Israel, my servant,
Jacob, whom I have chosen,
you descendants of Abraham my friend,
9I took you from the ends of the earth,
from its farthest corners I called you.
I said, 'You are my servant';
I have chosen you and have not rejected
you.
10So do not fear, for I am with you;
do not be dismayed, for I am your God.
I will strengthen you and help you;
I will uphold you with my righteous right
hand.

11"All who rage against you
will surely be ashamed and disgraced;
those who oppose you
will be as nothing and perish.
12Though you search for your enemies,
you will not find them.
Those who wage war against you
will be as nothing at all.
13For I am the LORD, your God,
who takes hold of your right hand
and says to you, Do not fear;
I will help you.
14Do not be afraid, O worm Jacob,
O little Israel,
for I myself will help you," declares the LORD,
your Redeemer, the Holy One of Israel.
15"See, I will make you into a threshing sledge,
new and sharp, with many teeth.
You will thresh the mountains and crush
them,
and reduce the hills to chaff.
16You will winnow them, the wind will pick
them up,
and a gale will blow them away.
But you will rejoice in the LORD
and glory in the Holy One of Israel.

17"The poor and needy search for water,
but there is none;
their tongues are parched with thirst.
But I the LORD will answer them;
I, the God of Israel, will not forsake
them.
18I will make rivers flow on barren heights,
and springs within the valleys.
I will turn the desert into pools of water,
and the parched ground into springs.
19I will put in the desert
the cedar and the acacia, the myrtle and the
olive.
I will set pines in the wasteland,
the fir and the cypress together,
20so that people may see and know,
may consider and understand,
that the hand of the LORD has done this,
that the Holy One of Israel has created it.

21"Present your case," says the LORD.
"Set forth your arguments," says Jacob's
King.
22"Bring in ⌞your idols⌟ to tell us
what is going to happen.
Tell us what the former things were,
so that we may consider them
and know their final outcome.
Or declare to us the things to come,
23 tell us what the future holds,
so we may know that you are gods.
Do something, whether good or bad,
so that we will be dismayed and filled with
fear.
24But you are less than nothing
and your works are utterly worthless;
he who chooses you is detestable.

25"I have stirred up one from the north, and he
comes—
one from the rising sun who calls on my
name.
He treads on rulers as if they were mortar,
as if he were a potter treading the clay.
26Who told of this from the beginning, so we
could know,
or beforehand, so we could say, 'He was
right'?
No one told of this,

no one foretold it,
no one heard any words from you.
27I was the first to tell Zion, 'Look, here they are!'
I gave to Jerusalem a messenger of good tidings.
28I look but there is no one—
no one among them to give counsel,
no one to give answer when I ask them.
29See, they are all false!
Their deeds amount to nothing;
their images are but wind and confusion.

14 / *Isaiah 42*
God's Servant: Image and Reality

ONE OF JESUS' most memorable sayings is found in Mark 10:45: "The Son of Man did not come to be served, but to serve, and to give his life as a ransom for many." One of Jesus' most memorable actions took place in the upper room where he was having his last meal with his disciples. He washed the disciples' feet. Afterward he said, "You call me 'Teacher' and 'Lord,' and rightly so, for that is what I am. . . . I have set you an example that you should do as I have done for you" (Jn 13:13, 15). The roots of these memorable words and deeds of our Lord are in this chapter of Isaiah, in which God reveals, in gradually increasing detail, the character of the Deliverer whom he is going to provide for Israel, a mighty Deliverer who will yet be a lowly servant.

Warming Up to God How do you feel when you picture Christ as a servant?

Read Isaiah 42.

42 "Here is my servant, whom I uphold,
my chosen one in whom I delight;
I will put my Spirit on him
and he will bring justice to the nations.
2He will not shout or cry out,
or raise his voice in the streets.
3A bruised reed he will not break,
and a smoldering wick he will not snuff out.
In faithfulness he will bring forth justice;
4 he will not falter or be discouraged
till he establishes justice on earth.
In his law the islands will put their hope."

5This is what God the LORD says—
he who created the heavens and stretched them out,
who spread out the earth and all that comes out of it,
who gives breath to its people,
and life to those who walk on it:
6"I, the LORD, have called you in righteousness;
I will take hold of your hand.
I will keep you and will make you
to be a covenant for the people
and a light for the Gentiles,
7to open eyes that are blind,
to free captives from prison
and to release from the dungeon those who sit in darkness.

8"I am the LORD; that is my name!
I will not give my glory to another
or my praise to idols.
9See, the former things have taken place,
and new things I declare;
before they spring into being
I announce them to you."

10Sing to the LORD a new song,
his praise from the ends of the earth,
you who go down to the sea, and all that is in it,
you islands, and all who live in them.
11Let the desert and its towns raise their voices;
let the settlements where Kedar lives rejoice.
Let the people of Sela sing for joy;
let them shout from the mountaintops.
12Let them give glory to the LORD
and proclaim his praise in the islands.
13The LORD will march out like a mighty man,

like a warrior he will stir up his zeal;
with a shout he will raise the battle cry
and will triumph over his enemies.

14 “For a long time I have kept silent,
I have been quiet and held myself back.
But now, like a woman in childbirth,
I cry out, I gasp and pant.
15 I will lay waste the mountains and hills
and dry up all their vegetation;
I will turn rivers into islands
and dry up the pools.
16 I will lead the blind by ways they have not known,
along unfamiliar paths I will guide them;
I will turn the darkness into light before them
and make the rough places smooth.
These are the things I will do;
I will not forsake them.
17 But those who trust in idols,
who say to images, ‘You are our gods,’
will be turned back in utter shame.

18 “Hear, you deaf;
look, you blind, and see!
19 Who is blind but my servant,
and deaf like the messenger I send?
Who is blind like the one committed to me,
blind like the servant of the LORD?
20 You have seen many things, but have paid no attention;
your ears are open, but you hear nothing.”
21 It pleased the LORD
for the sake of his righteousness
to make his law great and glorious.
22 But this is a people plundered and looted,
all of them trapped in pits
or hidden away in prisons.
They have become plunder,
with no one to rescue them;
they have been made loot,
with no one to say, “Send them back.”

23 Which of you will listen to this
or pay close attention in time to come?
24 Who handed Jacob over to become loot,
and Israel to the plunderers?
Was it not the LORD,
against whom we have sinned?
For they would not follow his ways;
they did not obey his law.
25 So he poured out on them his burning anger,
the violence of war.
It enveloped them in flames, yet they did not understand;
it consumed them, but they did not take it to heart.

Discovering the Word 1. How would you summarize the servant's functions or duties according to verses 1–9? 2. What is the scope of the servant's ministry (vv. 4, 6)? 3. In what ways does the description of the servant and his ministry foreshadow our Lord's person and work? 4. What vivid metaphors do verses 10–17 use to describe the Lord at work? 5. How do verses 18–25 describe the state of the people of Israel?

Applying the Word 1. In what respect or respects does this passage challenge *you*—your character, your service? 2. Promises are needed because people are so often liars. But every word of God is a promise—what he says, he *will* do. Look in this chapter at the verbs which God is the subject of. Which one or ones can you take as a personal promise of God to you now?

Responding in Prayer Praise God for what he has done for you in Jesus Christ.

15 / *Isaiah 43:1—44:5*
Rivers in the Desert

HOW DO YOU feel when you hear the words “I love you”? We should not be ashamed to express these feelings. But many of us have never, or seldom, heard these words. And sometimes, like a radio signal cluttered with static, the true meaning of the words is distorted by their overuse in countless songs, books and movies. In this passage we will hear these words afresh so that we can be made abundantly sure of God's love for us personally.

Warming Up to God On what do you base your sense of self-worth?

Read Isaiah 43:1—44:5.

43 But now, this is what the LORD says—
he who created you, O Jacob,
he who formed you, O Israel:
"Fear not, for I have redeemed you;
I have summoned you by name; you are mine.
2 When you pass through the waters,
I will be with you;
and when you pass through the rivers,
they will not sweep over you.
When you walk through the fire,
you will not be burned;
the flames will not set you ablaze.
3 For I am the LORD, your God,
the Holy One of Israel, your Savior;
I give Egypt for your ransom,
Cush[m] and Seba in your stead.
4 Since you are precious and honored in my sight,
and because I love you,
I will give men in exchange for you,
and people in exchange for your life.
5 Do not be afraid, for I am with you;
I will bring your children from the east
and gather you from the west.
6 I will say to the north, 'Give them up!'
and to the south, 'Do not hold them back.'
Bring my sons from afar
and my daughters from the ends of the earth—
7 everyone who is called by my name,
whom I created for my glory,
whom I formed and made."

8 Lead out those who have eyes but are blind,
who have ears but are deaf.
9 All the nations gather together
and the peoples assemble.
Which of them foretold this
and proclaimed to us the former things?
Let them bring in their witnesses to prove they were right,
so that others may hear and say, "It is true."
10 "You are my witnesses," declares the LORD,
"and my servant whom I have chosen,
so that you may know and believe me
and understand that I am he.
Before me no god was formed,
nor will there be one after me.
11 I, even I, am the LORD,
and apart from me there is no savior.
12 I have revealed and saved and proclaimed—
I, and not some foreign god among you.
You are my witnesses," declares the LORD,
"that I am God.
13 Yes, and from ancient days I am he.
No one can deliver out of my hand.
When I act, who can reverse it?"

14 This is what the LORD says—
your Redeemer, the Holy One of Israel:
"For your sake I will send to Babylon
and bring down as fugitives all the Babylonians,[n]
in the ships in which they took pride.
15 I am the LORD, your Holy One,
Israel's Creator, your King."

16 This is what the LORD says—
he who made a way through the sea,
a path through the mighty waters,
17 who drew out the chariots and horses,
the army and reinforcements together,
and they lay there, never to rise again,
extinguished, snuffed out like a wick:
18 "Forget the former things;
do not dwell on the past.
19 See, I am doing a new thing!
Now it springs up; do you not perceive it?
I am making a way in the desert
and streams in the wasteland.
20 The wild animals honor me,
the jackals and the owls,
because I provide water in the desert
and streams in the wasteland,
to give drink to my people, my chosen,
21 the people I formed for myself
that they may proclaim my praise.

22 "Yet you have not called upon me, O Jacob,
you have not wearied yourselves for me, O Israel.

[m] 3 That is, the upper Nile region [n] 14 Or *Chaldeans*

23 You have not brought me sheep for burnt
offerings,
nor honored me with your sacrifices.
I have not burdened you with grain offerings
nor wearied you with demands for incense.
24 You have not bought any fragrant calamus for
me,
or lavished on me the fat of your sacrifices.
But you have burdened me with your sins
and wearied me with your offenses.

25 "I, even I, am he who blots out
your transgressions, for my own sake,
and remembers your sins no more.
26 Review the past for me,
let us argue the matter together;
state the case for your innocence.
27 Your first father sinned;
your spokesmen rebelled against me.
28 So I will disgrace the dignitaries of your
temple,
and I will consign Jacob to destruction[o]
and Israel to scorn.

44 "But now listen, O Jacob, my
servant,
Israel, whom I have chosen.
2 This is what the LORD says—
he who made you, who formed you in the
womb,
and who will help you:
Do not be afraid, O Jacob, my servant,
Jeshurun, whom I have chosen.
3 For I will pour water on the thirsty land,
and streams on the dry ground;
I will pour out my Spirit on your offspring,
and my blessing on your descendants.
4 They will spring up like grass in a meadow,
like poplar trees by flowing streams.
5 One will say, 'I belong to the LORD';
another will call himself by the name of
Jacob;
still another will write on his hand, 'The
LORD's,'
and will take the name Israel.

o28 The Hebrew term refers to the irrevocable giving over of things or persons to the LORD, often by totally destroying them.

Discovering the Word 1. Pick out the verbs in 43:1–7 of which God is the subject and God's people (Israel and her descendants) are the object. 2. Israel is called to an international assembly of idol-worshipers and their idols in 43:8–13. To what does the Lord call Israel to witness? 3. What would the significance of 43:16–17 have been for the Israelites (see Ex 14:21–22)? 4. In 43:22–24 we see Israel's slavish religiosity, which does not please God. What promise does God repeat to his people (43:25)? 5. Just as the "but now" of 43:1 shines brightly against the dark background of 42:18–25, the "but now" of 44:1 shines brightly against the dark background of 43:22–28. God's patience has not expired. What does he promise his people in 44:1–5?

Applying the Word 1. How do you feel about being the object of the loving statements in 43:1–7? 2. We read in 43:19, "See, I am doing a new thing." God is a transforming, re-creative God. He is the One who makes all things new (Rev 21:5). He is the One who brings into existence things that did not exist (Rom 4:17). What new thing do you need to look, with expectant faith, for God to do for you?

Responding in Prayer Allow the words of 43:2 to be a personal encouragement to you from the Lord as you go to him in prayer.

Isaiah 44:6–28

6 "This is what the LORD says—
Israel's King and Redeemer, the LORD
Almighty:
I am the first and I am the last;
apart from me there is no God.
7 Who then is like me? Let him proclaim it.
Let him declare and lay out before me
what has happened since I established my
ancient people,
and what is yet to come—
yes, let him foretell what will come.
8 Do not tremble, do not be afraid.
Did I not proclaim this and foretell it long
ago?
You are my witnesses. Is there any God
besides me?
No, there is no other Rock; I know not
one."

9All who make idols are nothing,
and the things they treasure are worthless.
Those who would speak up for them are blind;
they are ignorant, to their own shame.
10Who shapes a god and casts an idol,
which can profit him nothing?
11He and his kind will be put to shame;
craftsmen are nothing but men.
Let them all come together and take their stand;
they will be brought down to terror and infamy.

12The blacksmith takes a tool
and works with it in the coals;
he shapes an idol with hammers,
he forges it with the might of his arm.
He gets hungry and loses his strength;
he drinks no water and grows faint.
13The carpenter measures with a line
and makes an outline with a marker;
he roughs it out with chisels
and marks it with compasses.
He shapes it in the form of man,
of man in all his glory,
that it may dwell in a shrine.
14He cut down cedars,
or perhaps took a cypress or oak.
He let it grow among the trees of the forest,
or planted a pine, and the rain made it grow.
15It is man's fuel for burning;
some of it he takes and warms himself,
he kindles a fire and bakes bread.
But he also fashions a god and worships it;
he makes an idol and bows down to it.
16Half of the wood he burns in the fire;
over it he prepares his meal,
he roasts his meat and eats his fill.
He also warms himself and says,
"Ah! I am warm; I see the fire."
17From the rest he makes a god, his idol;
he bows down to it and worships.
He prays to it and says,
"Save me; you are my god."
18They know nothing, they understand nothing;
their eyes are plastered over so they cannot see,
and their minds closed so they cannot understand.
19No one stops to think,
no one has the knowledge or understanding to say,
"Half of it I used for fuel;
I even baked bread over its coals,
I roasted meat and I ate.
Shall I make a detestable thing from what is left?
Shall I bow down to a block of wood?"
20He feeds on ashes, a deluded heart misleads him;
he cannot save himself, or say,
"Is not this thing in my right hand a lie?"

21"Remember these things, O Jacob,
for you are my servant, O Israel.
I have made you, you are my servant;
O Israel, I will not forget you.
22I have swept away your offenses like a cloud,
your sins like the morning mist.
Return to me,
for I have redeemed you."

23Sing for joy, O heavens, for the LORD has done this;
shout aloud, O earth beneath.
Burst into song, you mountains,
you forests and all your trees,
for the LORD has redeemed Jacob,
he displays his glory in Israel.

24"This is what the LORD says—
your Redeemer, who formed you in the womb:

I am the LORD,
who has made all things,
who alone stretched out the heavens,
who spread out the earth by myself,

25who foils the signs of false prophets
and makes fools of diviners,
who overthrows the learning of the wise
and turns it into nonsense,
26who carries out the words of his servants
and fulfills the predictions of his messengers,

who says of Jerusalem, 'It shall be inhabited,'
of the towns of Judah, 'They shall be built,'
and of their ruins, 'I will restore them,'
27who says to the watery deep, 'Be dry,
and I will dry up your streams,'
28who says of Cyrus, 'He is my shepherd

and will accomplish all that I please;
he will say of Jerusalem, "Let it be rebuilt,"
and of the temple, "Let its foundations be
laid." '

16 / *Isaiah 45*
Turning to God

THERE IS A well-known story of the conversion, on January 6, 1850, of the great Baptist preacher C. H. Spurgeon. One Sunday, while he was still a teenager, he attended a service at a Primitive Methodist Chapel. Because a snowstorm had prevented the appointed preacher from arriving, one of the stewards, a shoemaker, had to teach. Having nothing much to say, he stuck to the words of his text—Isaiah 45:22: "Turn to me and be saved, all you ends of the earth; for I am God, and there is no other." Finally, recognizing Spurgeon as a stranger, he said, "Young man, you look very miserable—look to Jesus. Look. Look. Look!"

"I looked," said Spurgeon, "until I could almost have looked my eyes away; and in heaven I will look still, in joy unutterable."

Warming Up to God Spend some time looking at the Lord in worship and in awe. Focus yourself on him before you begin.

Read Isaiah 45.

45 "This is what the LORD says to his
anointed,
to Cyrus, whose right hand I take
hold of
to subdue nations before him
and to strip kings of their armor,
to open doors before him
so that gates will not be shut:
2I will go before you
and will level the mountains[p];
I will break down gates of bronze
and cut through bars of iron.
3I will give you the treasures of darkness,
riches stored in secret places,
so that you may know that I am the LORD,
the God of Israel, who summons you by
name.
4For the sake of Jacob my servant,
of Israel my chosen,
I summon you by name
and bestow on you a title of honor,
though you do not acknowledge me.
5I am the LORD, and there is no other;
apart from me there is no God.
I will strengthen you,
though you have not acknowledged me,
6so that from the rising of the sun
to the place of its setting
men may know there is none besides me.
I am the LORD, and there is no other.
7I form the light and create darkness,
I bring prosperity and create disaster;
I, the LORD, do all these things.

8"You heavens above, rain down righteousness;
let the clouds shower it down.
Let the earth open wide,
let salvation spring up,
let righteousness grow with it;
I, the LORD, have created it.
9"Woe to him who quarrels with his Maker,
to him who is but a potsherd among the
potsherds on the ground.
Does the clay say to the potter,
'What are you making?'
Does your work say,
'He has no hands'?
10Woe to him who says to his father,
'What have you begotten?'
or to his mother,
'What have you brought to birth?'

11"This is what the LORD says—
the Holy One of Israel, and its Maker:
Concerning things to come,
do you question me about my children,

p2 Dead Sea Scrolls and Septuagint; the meaning of the word in the Masoretic Text is uncertain.

or give me orders about the work of my
hands?
12It is I who made the earth
and created mankind upon it.
My own hands stretched out the heavens;
I marshaled their starry hosts.
13I will raise up Cyrus[q] in my righteousness:
I will make all his ways straight.
He will rebuild my city
and set my exiles free,
but not for a price or reward,
says the LORD Almighty."

14This is what the LORD says:
"The products of Egypt and the merchandise
of Cush,[r]
and those tall Sabeans—
they will come over to you
and will be yours;
they will trudge behind you,
coming over to you in chains.
They will bow down before you
and plead with you, saying,
'Surely God is with you, and there is no
other;
there is no other god.' "

15Truly you are a God who hides himself,
O God and Savior of Israel.
16All the makers of idols will be put to shame
and disgraced;
they will go off into disgrace together.
17But Israel will be saved by the LORD
with an everlasting salvation;
you will never be put to shame or disgraced,
to ages everlasting.

18For this is what the LORD says—
he who created the heavens,
he is God;
he who fashioned and made the earth,
he founded it;
he did not create it to be empty,
but formed it to be inhabited—
he says:
"I am the LORD,
and there is no other.
19I have not spoken in secret,
from somewhere in a land of darkness;
I have not said to Jacob's descendants,
'Seek me in vain.'
I, the LORD, speak the truth;
I declare what is right.

20"Gather together and come;
assemble, you fugitives from the nations.
Ignorant are those who carry about idols of
wood,
who pray to gods that cannot save.
21Declare what is to be, present it—
let them take counsel together.
Who foretold this long ago,
who declared it from the distant past?
Was it not I, the LORD?
And there is no God apart from me,
a righteous God and a Savior;
there is none but me.

22"Turn to me and be saved,
all you ends of the earth;
for I am God, and there is no other.
23By myself I have sworn,
my mouth has uttered in all integrity
a word that will not be revoked:
Before me every knee will bow;
by me every tongue will swear.
24They will say of me, 'In the LORD alone
are righteousness and strength.' "
All who have raged against him
will come to him and be put to shame.
25But in the LORD all the descendants of Israel
will be found righteous and will exult.

q13 Hebrew *him* r14 That is, the upper Nile region

Discovering the Word 1. In 44:28 God says of Cyrus (king of Babylon) that he is his shepherd who will cause Jerusalem and the temple to be rebuilt. What will God do for Cyrus according to 45:1–8? 2. In verses 9–13 why does Israel complain and what is God's reply? 3. What do verses 14–19 say about God's relationship with Israel? 4. In verses 20–25 the horizons widen to the "ends of the earth." What are these foreigners summoned to do? 5. What is the implication of the phrase "by myself I have sworn" in verse 23?

Applying the Word 1. What practical conclusions follow from the statements of this chapter that behind the activities of a world conqueror (v. 1), behind darkness as well as light (v. 7), behind disaster as well as prosperity (v. 7) stands the sovereign Lord God? 2. When have you complained to God? How did God reply? 3. Might it be said of you that you find righteousness and strength in the Lord (v. 24)? Why or why not?

 **Responding in Prayer** Pray for the salvation of family and friends who do not know the Lord.

Isaiah 46—48

46 Bel bows down, Nebo stoops low;
their idols are borne by beasts of burden.[s]
The images that are carried about are burdensome,
a burden for the weary.
2They stoop and bow down together;
unable to rescue the burden,
they themselves go off into captivity.
3"Listen to me, O house of Jacob,
all you who remain of the house of Israel,
you whom I have upheld since you were conceived,
and have carried since your birth.
4Even to your old age and gray hairs
I am he, I am he who will sustain you.
I have made you and I will carry you;
I will sustain you and I will rescue you.
5"To whom will you compare me or count me equal?
To whom will you liken me that we may be compared?
6Some pour out gold from their bags
and weigh out silver on the scales;
they hire a goldsmith to make it into a god,
and they bow down and worship it.
7They lift it to their shoulders and carry it;
they set it up in its place, and there it stands.
From that spot it cannot move.
Though one cries out to it, it does not answer;
it cannot save him from his troubles.

8"Remember this, fix it in mind,
take it to heart, you rebels.
9Remember the former things, those of long ago;
I am God, and there is no other;
I am God, and there is none like me.
10I make known the end from the beginning,
from ancient times, what is still to come.
I say: My purpose will stand,
and I will do all that I please.
11From the east I summon a bird of prey;
from a far-off land, a man to fulfill my purpose.
What I have said, that will I bring about;
what I have planned, that will I do.
12Listen to me, you stubborn-hearted,
you who are far from righteousness.
13I am bringing my righteousness near,
it is not far away;
and my salvation will not be delayed.
I will grant salvation to Zion,
my splendor to Israel.

47 "Go down, sit in the dust,
Virgin Daughter of Babylon;
sit on the ground without a throne,
Daughter of the Babylonians.[t]
No more will you be called
tender or delicate.
2Take millstones and grind flour;
take off your veil.
Lift up your skirts, bare your legs,
and wade through the streams.
3Your nakedness will be exposed
and your shame uncovered.
I will take vengeance;
I will spare no one."

4Our Redeemer—the LORD Almighty is his name—
is the Holy One of Israel.

5"Sit in silence, go into darkness,
Daughter of the Babylonians;
no more will you be called
queen of kingdoms.
6I was angry with my people
and desecrated my inheritance;
I gave them into your hand,
and you showed them no mercy.
Even on the aged
you laid a very heavy yoke.
7You said, 'I will continue forever—
the eternal queen!'

[s]1 Or *are but beasts and cattle* [t]1 Or *Chaldeans*; also in verse 5

But you did not consider these things
or reflect on what might happen.

8"Now then, listen, you wanton creature,
lounging in your security
and saying to yourself,
'I am, and there is none besides me.
I will never be a widow
or suffer the loss of children.'
9Both of these will overtake you
in a moment, on a single day:
loss of children and widowhood.
They will come upon you in full measure,
in spite of your many sorceries
and all your potent spells.
10You have trusted in your wickedness
and have said, 'No one sees me.'
Your wisdom and knowledge mislead you
when you say to yourself,
'I am, and there is none besides me.'
11Disaster will come upon you,
and you will not know how to conjure it away.
A calamity will fall upon you
that you cannot ward off with a ransom;
a catastrophe you cannot foresee
will suddenly come upon you.

12"Keep on, then, with your magic spells
and with your many sorceries,
which you have labored at since childhood.
Perhaps you will succeed,
perhaps you will cause terror.
13All the counsel you have received has only worn you out!
Let your astrologers come forward,
those stargazers who make predictions month by month,
let them save you from what is coming upon you.
14Surely they are like stubble;
the fire will burn them up.
They cannot even save themselves
from the power of the flame.
Here are no coals to warm anyone;
here is no fire to sit by.
15That is all they can do for you—
these you have labored with
and trafficked with since childhood.
Each of them goes on in his error;
there is not one that can save you.

48

"Listen to this, O house of Jacob,
you who are called by the name of Israel
and come from the line of Judah,
you who take oaths in the name of the LORD
and invoke the God of Israel—
but not in truth or righteousness—
2you who call yourselves citizens of the holy city
and rely on the God of Israel—
the LORD Almighty is his name:
3I foretold the former things long ago,
my mouth announced them and I made them known;
then suddenly I acted, and they came to pass.
4For I knew how stubborn you were;
the sinews of your neck were iron,
your forehead was bronze.
5Therefore I told you these things long ago;
before they happened I announced them to you
so that you could not say,
'My idols did them;
my wooden image and metal god ordained them.'
6You have heard these things; look at them all.
Will you not admit them?

"From now on I will tell you of new things,
of hidden things unknown to you.
7They are created now, and not long ago;
you have not heard of them before today.
So you cannot say,
'Yes, I knew of them.'
8You have neither heard nor understood;
from of old your ear has not been open.
Well do I know how treacherous you are;
you were called a rebel from birth.
9For my own name's sake I delay my wrath;
for the sake of my praise I hold it back from you,
so as not to cut you off.
10See, I have refined you, though not as silver;
I have tested you in the furnace of affliction.
11For my own sake, for my own sake, I do this.
How can I let myself be defamed?
I will not yield my glory to another.

12"Listen to me, O Jacob,
Israel, whom I have called:
I am he;

I am the first and I am the last.
13My own hand laid the foundations of the earth,
and my right hand spread out the heavens;
when I summon them,
they all stand up together.

14"Come together, all of you, and listen:
Which of ⌊the idols⌋ has foretold these things?
The LORD's chosen ally
will carry out his purpose against Babylon;
his arm will be against the Babylonians.[u]
15I, even I, have spoken;
yes, I have called him.
I will bring him,
and he will succeed in his mission.

16"Come near me and listen to this:

"From the first announcement I have not spoken in secret;
at the time it happens, I am there."

And now the Sovereign LORD has sent me,
with his Spirit.

17This is what the LORD says—
your Redeemer, the Holy One of Israel:
"I am the LORD your God,
who teaches you what is best for you,
who directs you in the way you should go.
18If only you had paid attention to my commands,
your peace would have been like a river,
your righteousness like the waves of the sea.
19Your descendants would have been like the sand,
your children like its numberless grains;
their name would never be cut off
nor destroyed from before me."

20Leave Babylon,
flee from the Babylonians!
Announce this with shouts of joy
and proclaim it.
Send it out to the ends of the earth;
say, "The LORD has redeemed his servant Jacob."
21They did not thirst when he led them through the deserts;
he made water flow for them from the rock;
he split the rock
and water gushed out.

22"There is no peace," says the LORD, "for the wicked."

[u]14 Or *Chaldeans*; also in verse 20

17 / *Isaiah 49*
Foundations for Service

ISAIAH 42:1–25 WAS the first passage in which the Lord began to reveal to Isaiah the character of the Mighty Deliverer he was going to send, who would yet be a lowly servant. Isaiah 49 is the second so-called servant song which reveals more about the servant and what he will be like. The words apply preeminently to our Lord, but all his servants can take them too as a pattern for their ministry.

Warming Up to God When depression, discouragement or despair comes your way, how do you deal with it?

Read Isaiah 49.

49

Listen to me, you islands;
hear this, you distant nations:
Before I was born the LORD called me;
from my birth he has made mention of my name.
2He made my mouth like a sharpened sword,
in the shadow of his hand he hid me;
he made me into a polished arrow
and concealed me in his quiver.
3He said to me, "You are my servant,
Israel, in whom I will display my splendor."

4But I said, "I have labored to no purpose;
I have spent my strength in vain and for nothing.
Yet what is due me is in the LORD's hand,
and my reward is with my God."

5And now the LORD says—
he who formed me in the womb to be his servant
to bring Jacob back to him
and gather Israel to himself,
for I am honored in the eyes of the LORD
and my God has been my strength—
6he says:
"It is too small a thing for you to be my servant
to restore the tribes of Jacob
and bring back those of Israel I have kept.
I will also make you a light for the Gentiles,
that you may bring my salvation to the ends of the earth."

7This is what the LORD says—
the Redeemer and Holy One of Israel—
to him who was despised and abhorred by the nation,
to the servant of rulers:
"Kings will see you and rise up,
princes will see and bow down,
because of the LORD, who is faithful,
the Holy One of Israel, who has chosen you."

8This is what the LORD says:

"In the time of my favor I will answer you,
and in the day of salvation I will help you;
I will keep you and will make you
to be a covenant for the people,
to restore the land
and to reassign its desolate inheritances,
9to say to the captives, 'Come out,'
and to those in darkness, 'Be free!'

"They will feed beside the roads
and find pasture on every barren hill.
10They will neither hunger nor thirst,
nor will the desert heat or the sun beat upon them.
He who has compassion on them will guide them
and lead them beside springs of water.
11I will turn all my mountains into roads,
and my highways will be raised up.
12See, they will come from afar—
some from the north, some from the west,
some from the region of Aswan.[v]"

13Shout for joy, O heavens;
rejoice, O earth;
burst into song, O mountains!
For the LORD comforts his people
and will have compassion on his afflicted ones.

14But Zion said, "The LORD has forsaken me,
the Lord has forgotten me."

15"Can a mother forget the baby at her breast
and have no compassion on the child she has borne?
Though she may forget,
I will not forget you!
16See, I have engraved you on the palms of my hands;
your walls are ever before me.
17Your sons hasten back,
and those who laid you waste depart from you.
18Lift up your eyes and look around;
all your sons gather and come to you.
As surely as I live," declares the LORD,
"you will wear them all as ornaments;
you will put them on, like a bride.

19"Though you were ruined and made desolate
and your land laid waste,
now you will be too small for your people,
and those who devoured you will be far away.
20The children born during your bereavement
will yet say in your hearing,
'This place is too small for us;
give us more space to live in.'
21Then you will say in your heart,
'Who bore me these?
I was bereaved and barren;
I was exiled and rejected.
Who brought these up?
I was left alone,
but these—where have they come from?' "

22This is what the Sovereign LORD says:

"See, I will beckon to the Gentiles,
I will lift up my banner to the peoples;
they will bring your sons in their arms

[v]12 Dead Sea Scrolls; Masoretic Text *Sinim*

and carry your daughters on their
shoulders.
23Kings will be your foster fathers,
and their queens your nursing mothers.
They will bow down before you with their
faces to the ground;
they will lick the dust at your feet.
Then you will know that I am the LORD;
those who hope in me will not be
disappointed."

24Can plunder be taken from warriors,
or captives rescued from the fierce[w]?

25But this is what the LORD says:

"Yes, captives will be taken from warriors,
and plunder retrieved from the fierce;
I will contend with those who contend with
you,
and your children I will save.
26I will make your oppressors eat their own
flesh;
they will be drunk on their own blood, as
with wine.
Then all mankind will know
that I, the LORD, am your Savior,
your Redeemer, the Mighty One of Jacob."

[w]24 Dead Sea Scrolls, Vulgate and Syriac (see also Septuagint and verse 25); Masoretic Text *righteous*

Discovering the Word 1. Review the servant's reactions in verses 1–7 to the Lord's call. How does he look to the past and to the future for his encouragement? 2. The Lord is going to save his people, and the servant is going to be the mediator of his covenant with the people. How do verses 8–12 describe different aspects of God's salvation? 3. In what ways do verses 8–12 give a foretaste of the ministry of Jesus Christ? 4. Israel (Zion) responds with a complaint—not a song—in verse 14. By what arguments does the Lord refute the complaint in verses 15–18? 5. What promises are given to the Israelites in verses 22–26?

Applying the Word 1. When have you felt disappointed or hopeless in your relationship with God? 2. Review the forces marshaled in this passage for the battle against discouragement and despair. How does this knowledge help you with the daily battles you face?

Responding in Prayer Ask God to teach you how to put your hope in him.

Isaiah 50:1—52:12

50 This is what the LORD says:

"Where is your mother's
certificate of divorce
with which I sent her away?
Or to which of my creditors
did I sell you?
Because of your sins you were sold;
because of your transgressions your mother
was sent away.
2When I came, why was there no one?
When I called, why was there no one to
answer?
Was my arm too short to ransom you?
Do I lack the strength to rescue you?
By a mere rebuke I dry up the sea,
I turn rivers into a desert;
their fish rot for lack of water
and die of thirst.
3I clothe the sky with darkness
and make sackcloth its covering."

4The Sovereign LORD has given me an
instructed tongue,
to know the word that sustains the weary.
He wakens me morning by morning,
wakens my ear to listen like one being
taught.
5The Sovereign LORD has opened my ears,
and I have not been rebellious;
I have not drawn back.
6I offered my back to those who beat me,
my cheeks to those who pulled out my
beard;
I did not hide my face
from mocking and spitting.
7Because the Sovereign LORD helps me,
I will not be disgraced.
Therefore have I set my face like flint,
and I know I will not be put to shame.

18 / *Isaiah 52:13—53:12*
The Heart of the Old Testament

THERE IS A rising note of expectancy in chapters 51—52 as the time for the Jews' release from captivity draws nearer. Isaiah 51:9–11 records a prayer for God to act and pictures the exiles coming home to Zion "crowned with never-fading gladness." Then, in 52:1 Jerusalem is told to awake and arise from the dust. Why? A runner is approaching over the mountains with good news: God is about to deliver his people. It is time to leave Babylon. In this passage we are introduced again to the servant of the Lord, whose solitary agony is the price of his people's homecoming.

Warming Up to God Think of a time when someone has suffered for you. Describe what you think the experience of suffering was like for that person.

Read Isaiah 52:13—53:12.

---

13 See, my servant will act wisely[z];
he will be raised and lifted up and highly exalted.
14 Just as there were many who were appalled at him[a]—
his appearance was so disfigured beyond that of any man
and his form marred beyond human likeness—
15 so will he sprinkle many nations,[b]
and kings will shut their mouths because of him.
For what they were not told, they will see,
and what they have not heard, they will understand.

53 Who has believed our message
and to whom has the arm of the LORD been revealed?
2 He grew up before him like a tender shoot,
and like a root out of dry ground.
He had no beauty or majesty to attract us to him,
nothing in his appearance that we should desire him.
3 He was despised and rejected by men,
a man of sorrows, and familiar with suffering.
Like one from whom men hide their faces
he was despised, and we esteemed him not.

4 Surely he took up our infirmities
and carried our sorrows,
yet we considered him stricken by God,
smitten by him, and afflicted.
5 But he was pierced for our transgressions,
he was crushed for our iniquities;
the punishment that brought us peace was upon him,
and by his wounds we are healed.
6 We all, like sheep, have gone astray,
each of us has turned to his own way;
and the LORD has laid on him
the iniquity of us all.

7 He was oppressed and afflicted,
yet he did not open his mouth;
he was led like a lamb to the slaughter,
and as a sheep before her shearers is silent,
so he did not open his mouth.
8 By oppression[c] and judgment he was taken away.
And who can speak of his descendants?
For he was cut off from the land of the living;
for the transgression of my people he was stricken.[d]
9 He was assigned a grave with the wicked,
and with the rich in his death,
though he had done no violence,
nor was any deceit in his mouth.

10 Yet it was the LORD's will to crush him and cause him to suffer,
and though the LORD makes[e] his life a guilt offering,
he will see his offspring and prolong his days,
and the will of the LORD will prosper in his hand.
11 After the suffering of his soul,

[z]13 Or *will prosper* [a]14 Hebrew *you* [b]15 Hebrew; Septuagint *so will many nations marvel at him* [c]8 Or *From arrest* [d]8 Or *away. / Yet who of his generation considered / that he was cut off from the land of the living / for the transgression of my people, / to whom the blow was due?* [e]10 Hebrew *though you make*

he will see the light ⌞of life⌟[f] and be
satisfied[g];
by his knowledge[h] my righteous servant will
justify many,
and he will bear their iniquities.
12Therefore I will give him a portion among the
great,[i]
and he will divide the spoils with the
strong,[j]
because he poured out his life unto death,
and was numbered with the transgressors.
For he bore the sin of many,
and made intercession for the transgressors.

[f]11 Dead Sea Scrolls (see also Septuagint); Masoretic Text does not have *the light ⌞of life⌟*. [g]11 Or (with Masoretic Text) [11]*He will see the result of the suffering of his soul / and be satisfied* [h]11 Or *by knowledge of him* [i]12 Or *many* [j]12 Or *numerous*

Discovering the Word 1. What reaction do many people have to the servant? Why (52:14–15)? 2. In 52:10 we are told that the Lord is going to "lay bare his holy arm"; that is, act to save his people. But when he does so, what sort of person is revealed (53:1–3)? 3. How does 53:4–6 explain the servant's sufferings? 4. How did the servant conduct himself in the midst of his suffering (53:7–9)? 5. What will be the sequel to, the result of the servant's suffering (53:10–12)? 6. Compare 1 Peter 2:21–25 to Isaiah 53. What are the parallels?

Applying the Word 1. Why do you think 53:5 is called the "burning heart" of the Old Testament and, indeed, of the whole Bible? 2. How do you respond to this graphic description of how Christ suffered for you?

Responding in Prayer Offer God your thanks and praise for Christ's suffering on your behalf.

19 / *Isaiah 54—55*
Shout for Joy

A VISITOR TO a harp shop observed that when the strings of the largest harp were plucked, all the other harps in the shop rang in unison with them. In this study the expectancy which has been heightening through previous chapters explodes into song and exhortation.

Warming Up to God Recall a time when you have been overcome with the joy of knowing God in the midst of sorrow. Allow this memory to draw you close to him in an attitude of worship.

Read Isaiah 54—55.

54 "Sing, O barren woman,
you who never bore a child;
burst into song, shout for joy,
you who were never in labor;
because more are the children of the desolate
woman
than of her who has a husband,"
says the LORD.
2"Enlarge the place of your tent,
stretch your tent curtains wide,
do not hold back;
lengthen your cords,
strengthen your stakes.
3For you will spread out to the right and to
the left;
your descendants will dispossess nations
and settle in their desolate cities.

4"Do not be afraid; you will not suffer
shame.
Do not fear disgrace; you will not be
humiliated.
You will forget the shame of your youth
and remember no more the reproach of
your widowhood.
5For your Maker is your husband—
the LORD Almighty is his name—
the Holy One of Israel is your
Redeemer;
he is called the God of all the earth.

6The LORD will call you back
as if you were a wife deserted and distressed in spirit—
a wife who married young,
only to be rejected," says your God.
7"For a brief moment I abandoned you,
but with deep compassion I will bring you back.
8In a surge of anger
I hid my face from you for a moment,
but with everlasting kindness
I will have compassion on you,"
says the LORD your Redeemer.

9"To me this is like the days of Noah,
when I swore that the waters of Noah
would never again cover the earth.
So now I have sworn not to be angry with you,
never to rebuke you again.
10Though the mountains be shaken
and the hills be removed,
yet my unfailing love for you will not be shaken
nor my covenant of peace be removed,"
says the LORD, who has compassion on you.

11"O afflicted city, lashed by storms and not comforted,
I will build you with stones of turquoise,[k]
your foundations with sapphires.[l]
12I will make your battlements of rubies,
your gates of sparkling jewels,
and all your walls of precious stones.
13All your sons will be taught by the LORD,
and great will be your children's peace.
14In righteousness you will be established:
Tyranny will be far from you;
you will have nothing to fear.
Terror will be far removed;
it will not come near you.
15If anyone does attack you, it will not be my doing;
whoever attacks you will surrender to you.

16"See, it is I who created the blacksmith
who fans the coals into flame
and forges a weapon fit for its work.
And it is I who have created the destroyer to work havoc;
17 no weapon forged against you will prevail,
and you will refute every tongue that accuses you.
This is the heritage of the servants of the LORD,
and this is their vindication from me,"
declares the LORD.

55

"Come, all you who are thirsty,
come to the waters;
and you who have no money,
come, buy and eat!
Come, buy wine and milk
without money and without cost.
2Why spend money on what is not bread,
and your labor on what does not satisfy?
Listen, listen to me, and eat what is good,
and your soul will delight in the richest of fare.
3Give ear and come to me;
hear me, that your soul may live.
I will make an everlasting covenant with you,
my faithful love promised to David.
4See, I have made him a witness to the peoples,
a leader and commander of the peoples.
5Surely you will summon nations you know not,
and nations that do not know you will hasten to you,
because of the LORD your God,
the Holy One of Israel,
for he has endowed you with splendor."

6Seek the LORD while he may be found;
call on him while he is near.
7Let the wicked forsake his way
and the evil man his thoughts.
Let him turn to the LORD, and he will have mercy on him,
and to our God, for he will freely pardon.

8"For my thoughts are not your thoughts,
neither are your ways my ways,"
declares the LORD.
9"As the heavens are higher than the earth,
so are my ways higher than your ways
and my thoughts than your thoughts.
10As the rain and the snow
come down from heaven,
and do not return to it
without watering the earth
and making it bud and flourish,

[k]11 The meaning of the Hebrew for this word is uncertain. [l]11 Or *lapis lazuli*

so that it yields seed for the sower and
bread for the eater,
11 so is my word that goes out from my mouth:
It will not return to me empty,
but will accomplish what I desire
and achieve the purpose for which I sent it.
12 You will go out in joy
and be led forth in peace;
the mountains and hills
will burst into song before you,
and all the trees of the field
will clap their hands.
13 Instead of the thornbush will grow the pine
tree,
and instead of briers the myrtle will grow.
This will be for the LORD's renown,
for an everlasting sign,
which will not be destroyed."

Discovering the Word 1. Isaiah 54:1–10 is an extended, complex metaphor applied to the relationship between Jerusalem and the Lord. What is the metaphor? 2. In Isaiah 54:11–17 the metaphor changes to that of a rebuilt city. What will characterize this city? 3. Is the fulfillment of these marvelous promises to Jerusalem in the past, present or future? 4. An amazing offer is extended in 55:1–5. Who is invited and what are they invited to? 5. A note of urgency is introduced in 55:6–7. How do these verses outline the nature of true repentance? 6. What transformations do God's thoughts and words achieve according to 55:8–13?

Applying the Word 1. God's love for you is more unshakable than the mountains (54:10, the ancient world's most immovable objects). What are the implications of this statement for your life now? 2. Here again is the place where the eternal Word of God intersects with our lives today. In what way do you need to seek the Lord (55:6) for abundant life and for free pardon?

Responding in Prayer Make your prayer a time of refreshment and praise.

Isaiah 56—57

56 This is what the LORD says:

"Maintain justice
and do what is right,
for my salvation is close at hand
and my righteousness will soon be revealed.
2 Blessed is the man who does this,
the man who holds it fast,
who keeps the Sabbath without desecrating it,
and keeps his hand from doing any evil."

3 Let no foreigner who has bound himself to
the LORD say,
"The LORD will surely exclude me from his
people."
And let not any eunuch complain,
"I am only a dry tree."

4 For this is what the LORD says:

"To the eunuchs who keep my Sabbaths,
who choose what pleases me
and hold fast to my covenant—
5 to them I will give within my temple and its
walls
a memorial and a name
better than sons and daughters;
I will give them an everlasting name
that will not be cut off.
6 And foreigners who bind themselves to the
LORD
to serve him,
to love the name of the LORD,
and to worship him,
all who keep the Sabbath without desecrating
it
and who hold fast to my covenant—
7 these I will bring to my holy mountain
and give them joy in my house of prayer.
Their burnt offerings and sacrifices
will be accepted on my altar;
for my house will be called
a house of prayer for all nations."
8 The Sovereign LORD declares—
he who gathers the exiles of Israel:
"I will gather still others to them
besides those already gathered."

9 Come, all you beasts of the field,
come and devour, all you beasts of the
forest!

10Israel's watchmen are blind,
they all lack knowledge;
they are all mute dogs,
they cannot bark;
they lie around and dream,
they love to sleep.
11They are dogs with mighty appetites;
they never have enough.
They are shepherds who lack understanding;
they all turn to their own way,
each seeks his own gain.
12"Come," each one cries, "let me get wine!
Let us drink our fill of beer!
And tomorrow will be like today,
or even far better."

57 The righteous perish,
and no one ponders it in his heart;
devout men are taken away,
and no one understands
that the righteous are taken away
to be spared from evil.
2Those who walk uprightly
enter into peace;
they find rest as they lie in death.

3"But you—come here, you sons of a sorceress,
you offspring of adulterers and prostitutes!
4Whom are you mocking?
At whom do you sneer
and stick out your tongue?
Are you not a brood of rebels,
the offspring of liars?
5You burn with lust among the oaks
and under every spreading tree;
you sacrifice your children in the ravines
and under the overhanging crags.
6⌞The idols⌟ among the smooth stones of the ravines are your portion;
they, they are your lot.
Yes, to them you have poured out drink offerings
and offered grain offerings.
In the light of these things, should I relent?
7You have made your bed on a high and lofty hill;
there you went up to offer your sacrifices.
8Behind your doors and your doorposts
you have put your pagan symbols.
Forsaking me, you uncovered your bed,
you climbed into it and opened it wide;
you made a pact with those whose beds you love,
and you looked on their nakedness.
9You went to Molech[m] with olive oil
and increased your perfumes.
You sent your ambassadors[n] far away;
you descended to the grave[o] itself!
10You were wearied by all your ways,
but you would not say, 'It is hopeless.'
You found renewal of your strength,
and so you did not faint.

11"Whom have you so dreaded and feared
that you have been false to me,
and have neither remembered me
nor pondered this in your hearts?
Is it not because I have long been silent
that you do not fear me?
12I will expose your righteousness and your works,
and they will not benefit you.
13When you cry out for help,
let your collection ⌞of idols⌟ save you!
The wind will carry all of them off,
a mere breath will blow them away.
But the man who makes me his refuge
will inherit the land
and possess my holy mountain."

14And it will be said:

"Build up, build up, prepare the road!
Remove the obstacles out of the way of my people."
15For this is what the high and lofty One says—
he who lives forever, whose name is holy:
"I live in a high and holy place,
but also with him who is contrite and lowly in spirit,
to revive the spirit of the lowly
and to revive the heart of the contrite.
16I will not accuse forever,
nor will I always be angry,
for then the spirit of man would grow faint before me—
the breath of man that I have created.
17I was enraged by his sinful greed;
I punished him, and hid my face in anger,
yet he kept on in his willful ways.

[m]9 Or *to the king* [n]9 Or *idols* [o]9 Hebrew *Sheol*

18I have seen his ways, but I will heal him;
I will guide him and restore comfort to him,
19 creating praise on the lips of the mourners in Israel.
Peace, peace, to those far and near,"
says the LORD. "And I will heal them."
20But the wicked are like the tossing sea,
which cannot rest,
whose waves cast up mire and mud.
21"There is no peace," says my God, "for the wicked."

20 / *Isaiah 58*
Unfailing Spring

HAVE YOU EVER struggled with how to balance social action and a life of worship? Have you ever felt that God wasn't recognizing the work that you were doing for him? Have you ever wondered just what God requires of you? In chapters 56—66 we return to the homeland of Israel. And we quickly see that God's people are falling far short of God's idea of true worship. These chapters reveal how true worship will strengthen us and make us like a spring that never runs dry.

Warming Up to God What frustrations do you currently have regarding the way you serve God? Make this a time of honest dialogue with the Lord.

Read Isaiah 58.

58 "Shout it aloud, do not hold back.
Raise your voice like a trumpet.
Declare to my people their rebellion
and to the house of Jacob their sins.
2For day after day they seek me out;
they seem eager to know my ways,
as if they were a nation that does what is right
and has not forsaken the commands of its God.
They ask me for just decisions
and seem eager for God to come near them.
3'Why have we fasted,' they say,
'and you have not seen it?
Why have we humbled ourselves,
and you have not noticed?'

"Yet on the day of your fasting, you do as you please
and exploit all your workers.
4Your fasting ends in quarreling and strife,
and in striking each other with wicked fists.
You cannot fast as you do today
and expect your voice to be heard on high.
5Is this the kind of fast I have chosen,
only a day for a man to humble himself?
Is it only for bowing one's head like a reed
and for lying on sackcloth and ashes?
Is that what you call a fast,
a day acceptable to the LORD?

6"Is not this the kind of fasting I have chosen:
to loose the chains of injustice
and untie the cords of the yoke,
to set the oppressed free
and break every yoke?
7Is it not to share your food with the hungry
and to provide the poor wanderer with shelter—
when you see the naked, to clothe him,
and not to turn away from your own flesh and blood?
8Then your light will break forth like the dawn,
and your healing will quickly appear;
then your righteousness[p] will go before you,
and the glory of the LORD will be your rear guard.
9Then you will call, and the LORD will answer;
you will cry for help, and he will say: Here am I.

"If you do away with the yoke of oppression,
with the pointing finger and malicious talk,

p8 *Or your righteous One*

[10]and if you spend yourselves in behalf of the hungry
and satisfy the needs of the oppressed,
then your light will rise in the darkness,
and your night will become like the noonday.
[11]The LORD will guide you always;
he will satisfy your needs in a sun-scorched land
and will strengthen your frame.
You will be like a well-watered garden,
like a spring whose waters never fail.
[12]Your people will rebuild the ancient ruins
and will raise up the age-old foundations;
you will be called Repairer of Broken Walls,
Restorer of Streets with Dwellings.

[13]"If you keep your feet from breaking the Sabbath
and from doing as you please on my holy day,
if you call the Sabbath a delight
and the LORD's holy day honorable,
and if you honor it by not going your own way
and not doing as you please or speaking idle words,
[14]then you will find your joy in the LORD,
and I will cause you to ride on the heights of the land
and to feast on the inheritance of your father Jacob."
The mouth of the LORD has spoken.

Discovering the Word 1. In verses 1–3 the people *seem* very religious (after the destruction of Jerusalem, fast days were increased). They are puzzled by God's disinterest. What evaluation do these verses give of the people's religiosity? 2. God has some counter-questions for them in verses 3–5. Why does he refuse to take note of their fasting and to hear their prayers? 3. What positive requirements are laid out in verses 6–10 as those which the Lord desires and delights in? 4. What promises of the Lord's blessings are given in verses 6–12? 5. Philanthropy is not enough. Verses 13–14 introduce the subject of the Sabbath. How is our behavior on this holy day to be characterized?

Applying the Word 1. Meditate on the metaphors of verses 10–12. Which one (or ones) describes most vividly what you would like to see in your life? 2. How is the principle of keeping the Sabbath applicable today? 3. What steps do you need to take in your religious life and in your social behavior in order that your life may be a "well-watered garden" and a "spring whose waters never fail"?

Responding in Prayer Pray that you will understand and experience true worship.

Isaiah 59—60

59 Surely the arm of the LORD is not too short to save,
nor his ear too dull to hear.
[2]But your iniquities have separated you from your God;
your sins have hidden his face from you,
so that he will not hear.
[3]For your hands are stained with blood,
your fingers with guilt.
Your lips have spoken lies,
and your tongue mutters wicked things.
[4]No one calls for justice;
no one pleads his case with integrity.
They rely on empty arguments and speak lies;
they conceive trouble and give birth to evil.
[5]They hatch the eggs of vipers
and spin a spider's web.
Whoever eats their eggs will die,
and when one is broken, an adder is hatched.
[6]Their cobwebs are useless for clothing;
they cannot cover themselves with what they make.
Their deeds are evil deeds,
and acts of violence are in their hands.
[7]Their feet rush into sin;
they are swift to shed innocent blood.
Their thoughts are evil thoughts;
ruin and destruction mark their ways.
[8]The way of peace they do not know;
there is no justice in their paths.
They have turned them into crooked roads;

no one who walks in them will know
peace.

[9]So justice is far from us,
and righteousness does not reach us.
We look for light, but all is darkness;
for brightness, but we walk in deep
shadows.
[10]Like the blind we grope along the wall,
feeling our way like men without eyes.
At midday we stumble as if it were twilight;
among the strong, we are like the dead.
[11]We all growl like bears;
we moan mournfully like doves.
We look for justice, but find none;
for deliverance, but it is far away.

[12]For our offenses are many in your sight,
and our sins testify against us.
Our offenses are ever with us,
and we acknowledge our iniquities:
[13]rebellion and treachery against the LORD,
turning our backs on our God,
fomenting oppression and revolt,
uttering lies our hearts have conceived.
[14]So justice is driven back,
and righteousness stands at a distance;
truth has stumbled in the streets,
honesty cannot enter.
[15]Truth is nowhere to be found,
and whoever shuns evil becomes a prey.

The LORD looked and was displeased
that there was no justice.
[16]He saw that there was no one,
he was appalled that there was no one to
intervene;
so his own arm worked salvation for him,
and his own righteousness sustained him.
[17]He put on righteousness as his breastplate,
and the helmet of salvation on his head;
he put on the garments of vengeance
and wrapped himself in zeal as in a cloak.
[18]According to what they have done,
so will he repay
wrath to his enemies
and retribution to his foes;
he will repay the islands their due.
[19]From the west, men will fear the name of the
LORD,
and from the rising of the sun, they will
revere his glory.
For he will come like a pent-up flood
that the breath of the LORD drives along.[q]
[20]"The Redeemer will come to Zion,
to those in Jacob who repent of their sins,"
declares the LORD.

[21]"As for me, this is my covenant with them,"
says the LORD. "My Spirit, who is on you, and my
words that I have put in your mouth will not
depart from your mouth, or from the mouths of
your children, or from the mouths of their
descendants from this time on and forever," says
the LORD.

60

"Arise, shine, for your light has
come,
and the glory of the LORD rises
upon you.
[2]See, darkness covers the earth
and thick darkness is over the peoples,
but the LORD rises upon you
and his glory appears over you.
[3]Nations will come to your light,
and kings to the brightness of your dawn.

[4]"Lift up your eyes and look about you:
All assemble and come to you;
your sons come from afar,
and your daughters are carried on the arm.
[5]Then you will look and be radiant,
your heart will throb and swell with joy;
the wealth on the seas will be brought to you,
to you the riches of the nations will come.
[6]Herds of camels will cover your land,
young camels of Midian and Ephah.
And all from Sheba will come,
bearing gold and incense
and proclaiming the praise of the LORD.
[7]All Kedar's flocks will be gathered to you,
the rams of Nebaioth will serve you;
they will be accepted as offerings on my altar,
and I will adorn my glorious temple.

[8]"Who are these that fly along like clouds,
like doves to their nests?
[9]Surely the islands look to me;
in the lead are the ships of Tarshish,[r]
bringing your sons from afar,
with their silver and gold,
to the honor of the LORD your God,
the Holy One of Israel,
for he has endowed you with splendor.

[q]19 *Or When the enemy comes in like a flood, / the Spirit of the LORD will put him to flight* [r]9 *Or the trading ships*

10"Foreigners will rebuild your walls,
and their kings will serve you.
Though in anger I struck you,
in favor I will show you compassion.
11Your gates will always stand open,
they will never be shut, day or night,
so that men may bring you the wealth of the nations—
their kings led in triumphal procession.
12For the nation or kingdom that will not serve you will perish;
it will be utterly ruined.

13"The glory of Lebanon will come to you,
the pine, the fir and the cypress together,
to adorn the place of my sanctuary;
and I will glorify the place of my feet.
14The sons of your oppressors will come bowing before you;
all who despise you will bow down at your feet
and will call you the City of the LORD,
Zion of the Holy One of Israel.

15"Although you have been forsaken and hated,
with no one traveling through,
I will make you the everlasting pride
and the joy of all generations.
16You will drink the milk of nations
and be nursed at royal breasts.
Then you will know that I, the LORD, am your Savior,
your Redeemer, the Mighty One of Jacob.
17Instead of bronze I will bring you gold,
and silver in place of iron.
Instead of wood I will bring you bronze,
and iron in place of stones.
I will make peace your governor
and righteousness your ruler.
18No longer will violence be heard in your land,
nor ruin or destruction within your borders,
but you will call your walls Salvation
and your gates Praise.
19The sun will no more be your light by day,
nor will the brightness of the moon shine on you,
for the LORD will be your everlasting light,
and your God will be your glory.
20Your sun will never set again,
and your moon will wane no more;
the LORD will be your everlasting light,
and your days of sorrow will end.
21Then will all your people be righteous
and they will possess the land forever.
They are the shoot I have planted,
the work of my hands,
for the display of my splendor.
22The least of you will become a thousand,
the smallest a mighty nation.
I am the LORD;
in its time I will do this swiftly."

21 / *Isaiah 61*
A Garment of Praise for a Spirit of Despair

WHEN JERUSALEM WAS destroyed, some people contemptuously nicknamed her "Zion for whom no one cares" (Jer 30:17). She was utterly despised and alone. But God is the only one who can delete the indelible and heal the incurable. In this chapter we see his healing and restorative work through his servant. The healing depicted here is as long as time and as wide as the created world, and we can have a part in it as well.

Warming Up to God Think of a time you felt like an outcast. Who or what brought you comfort?

Read Isaiah 61.

61

The Spirit of the Sovereign LORD is on me,
because the LORD has anointed me
to preach good news to the poor.
He has sent me to bind up the brokenhearted,
to proclaim freedom for the captives
and release from darkness for the prisoners,[s]
2to proclaim the year of the LORD's favor
and the day of vengeance of our God,
to comfort all who mourn,
3 and provide for those who grieve in Zion—
to bestow on them a crown of beauty
instead of ashes,
the oil of gladness
instead of mourning,
and a garment of praise
instead of a spirit of despair.
They will be called oaks of righteousness,
a planting of the LORD
for the display of his splendor.

4They will rebuild the ancient ruins
and restore the places long devastated;
they will renew the ruined cities
that have been devastated for generations.
5Aliens will shepherd your flocks;
foreigners will work your fields and vineyards.
6And you will be called priests of the LORD,
you will be named ministers of our God.
You will feed on the wealth of nations,
and in their riches you will boast.
7Instead of their shame
my people will receive a double portion,
and instead of disgrace
they will rejoice in their inheritance;
and so they will inherit a double portion in their land,
and everlasting joy will be theirs.

8"For I, the LORD, love justice;
I hate robbery and iniquity.
In my faithfulness I will reward them
and make an everlasting covenant with them.
9Their descendants will be known among the nations
and their offspring among the peoples.
All who see them will acknowledge
that they are a people the LORD has blessed."

10I delight greatly in the LORD;
my soul rejoices in my God.
For he has clothed me with garments of salvation
and arrayed me in a robe of righteousness,
as a bridegroom adorns his head like a priest,
and as a bride adorns herself with her jewels.
11For as the soil makes the sprout come up
and a garden causes seeds to grow,
so the Sovereign LORD will make righteousness and praise
spring up before all nations.

[s] 1 Hebrew; Septuagint *the blind*

Discovering the Word 1. Summarize the transforming ministry of the Lord's anointed servant in verses 1–3. 2. What is the significance of each metaphor in verse 3? 3. How do verses 4–9 depict Zion's transformed situation? 4. How are the two metaphors for righteousness found in the delighted outburst of song in verses 10–11 appropriate?

Applying the Word 1. How do verses 1–3 encourage you in areas of personal need? 2. There is a strong emphasis in this chapter on "righteousness" (vv. 3, 10–11) and "justice" (v. 8). How can you take a stand for justice this week for the glory of God's name?

Responding in Prayer Pray for the poor, the broken-hearted and prisoners.

22 / *Isaiah 62*
The Refugees Return

HAVE YOU EVER wondered what it is like to be a refugee? Have you ever wondered how it feels to pick up the few belongings you can carry and with a sick heart to leave your family home, your family farm, your family graves, your town, your country—perhaps never to return? But what if the chance comes to return home, for a new start under a new regime? The exultation and bridal joyousness of this chapter must be understood from the perspective of the returning refugees. The Israelites might have thought that Jerusalem had been irreversibly abandoned by the Lord—but it is not so.

Warming Up to God Picture yourself as a refugee returning home to the Lord. What do you experience?

Read Isaiah 62.

62 For Zion's sake I will not keep silent,
for Jerusalem's sake I will not remain quiet,
till her righteousness shines out like the dawn,
her salvation like a blazing torch.
2The nations will see your righteousness,
and all kings your glory;
you will be called by a new name
that the mouth of the LORD will bestow.
3You will be a crown of splendor in the LORD's hand,
a royal diadem in the hand of your God.
4No longer will they call you Deserted,
or name your land Desolate.
But you will be called Hephzibah,[t]
and your land Beulah[u];
for the LORD will take delight in you,
and your land will be married.
5As a young man marries a maiden,
so will your sons[v] marry you;
as a bridegroom rejoices over his bride,
so will your God rejoice over you.

6I have posted watchmen on your walls,
O Jerusalem;
they will never be silent day or night.
You who call on the LORD,
give yourselves no rest,
7and give him no rest till he establishes Jerusalem
and makes her the praise of the earth.

8The LORD has sworn by his right hand
and by his mighty arm:
"Never again will I give your grain
as food for your enemies,
and never again will foreigners drink the new wine
for which you have toiled;
9but those who harvest it will eat it
and praise the LORD,
and those who gather the grapes will drink it
in the courts of my sanctuary."

10Pass through, pass through the gates!
Prepare the way for the people.
Build up, build up the highway!
Remove the stones.
Raise a banner for the nations.

11The LORD has made proclamation
to the ends of the earth:
"Say to the Daughter of Zion,
'See, your Savior comes!
See, his reward is with him,
and his recompense accompanies him.' "
12They will be called the Holy People,
the Redeemed of the LORD;
and you will be called Sought After,
the City No Longer Deserted.

[t]4 *Hephzibah* means *my delight is in her.* [u]4 *Beulah* means *married.*
[v]5 Or *Builder*

Discovering the Word 1. Isaiah has not kept silent about Judah's wickedness and her judgment. What motives does verse 1 reveal about his refusal to keep silent? 2. How do verses 2–5 describe the new relationship between God and Zion? 3. What will the role of Jerusalem's watchmen be (vv. 6–7)? 4. What is promised in verses 8–9? 5. Describe the scene which verse 10 sets up.

Applying the Word 1. What role do celebratory processions and marches of witness have in the church today? 2. Pause and dwell on Zion's new names. *Hephzibah* means "my delight is in her," and *Beulah* means "married." How do you respond to these expressions of God's feelings toward you?

Responding in Prayer Respond in joyful prayer and worship to the God who calls you "Sought After, the City No Longer Deserted" (v. 12).

Isaiah 63:1–6

63 Who is this coming from Edom,
from Bozrah, with his garments
stained crimson?
Who is this, robed in splendor,
striding forward in the greatness of his
strength?

"It is I, speaking in righteousness,
mighty to save."

2Why are your garments red,
like those of one treading the winepress?

3"I have trodden the winepress alone;
from the nations no one was with me.
I trampled them in my anger
and trod them down in my wrath;
their blood spattered my garments,
and I stained all my clothing.
4For the day of vengeance was in my heart,
and the year of my redemption has come.
5I looked, but there was no one to help,
I was appalled that no one gave support;
so my own arm worked salvation for me,
and my own wrath sustained me.
6I trampled the nations in my anger;
in my wrath I made them drunk
and poured their blood on the ground."

23 / *Isaiah 63:7—64:12*
A Cry for Forgiveness and for Revival

HAVE YOU EVER been discouraged when you look at the people of God as they are today? Do you compare your church members to what they have been at various times in the past? Do you feel inadequate to the golden vision of what the church will be when Christ presents to God "a radiant church, without stain or wrinkle or any other blemish, but holy and blameless" (Eph 5:27)? It is a shattering experience for Isaiah too—to turn from the vision of radiant Zion in chapters 60—62 to Zion as she is.

Warming Up to God When have you experienced spiritual revival in your life? Allow the joy of that time to well up within you.

Read Isaiah 63:7—64:12.

7I will tell of the kindnesses of the LORD,
the deeds for which he is to be praised,
according to all the LORD has done for us—
yes, the many good things he has done
for the house of Israel,
according to his compassion and many
kindnesses.
8He said, "Surely they are my people,
sons who will not be false to me";
and so he became their Savior.

9In all their distress he too was distressed,
and the angel of his presence saved them.
In his love and mercy he redeemed them;
he lifted them up and carried them
all the days of old.
10Yet they rebelled
and grieved his Holy Spirit.
So he turned and became their enemy
and he himself fought against them.

11Then his people recalled[w] the days of old,
the days of Moses and his people—
where is he who brought them through the sea,
with the shepherd of his flock?
Where is he who set
his Holy Spirit among them,
12who sent his glorious arm of power
to be at Moses' right hand,
who divided the waters before them,
to gain for himself everlasting renown,
13who led them through the depths?
Like a horse in open country,
they did not stumble;
14like cattle that go down to the plain,
they were given rest by the Spirit of the LORD.
This is how you guided your people
to make for yourself a glorious name.

15Look down from heaven and see
from your lofty throne, holy and glorious.
Where are your zeal and your might?
Your tenderness and compassion are withheld from us.
16But you are our Father,
though Abraham does not know us
or Israel acknowledge us;
you, O LORD, are our Father,
our Redeemer from of old is your name.
17Why, O LORD, do you make us wander from your ways
and harden our hearts so we do not revere you?
Return for the sake of your servants,
the tribes that are your inheritance.
18For a little while your people possessed your holy place,
but now our enemies have trampled down your sanctuary.
19We are yours from of old;
but you have not ruled over them,
they have not been called by your name.[x]

64 Oh, that you would rend the heavens and come down,
that the mountains would tremble before you!
2As when fire sets twigs ablaze
and causes water to boil,
come down to make your name known to your enemies
and cause the nations to quake before you!
3For when you did awesome things that we did not expect,
you came down, and the mountains trembled before you.
4Since ancient times no one has heard,
no ear has perceived,
no eye has seen any God besides you,
who acts on behalf of those who wait for him.
5You come to the help of those who gladly do right,
who remember your ways.
But when we continued to sin against them,
you were angry.
How then can we be saved?
6All of us have become like one who is unclean,
and all our righteous acts are like filthy rags;
we all shrivel up like a leaf,
and like the wind our sins sweep us away.
7No one calls on your name
or strives to lay hold of you;
for you have hidden your face from us
and made us waste away because of our sins.
8Yet, O LORD, you are our Father.
We are the clay, you are the potter;
we are all the work of your hand.
9Do not be angry beyond measure, O LORD;
do not remember our sins forever.
Oh, look upon us, we pray,
for we are all your people.
10Your sacred cities have become a desert;
even Zion is a desert, Jerusalem a desolation.
11Our holy and glorious temple, where our fathers praised you,
has been burned with fire,
and all that we treasured lies in ruins.

[w]11 *Or But may he recall* [x]19 *Or We are like those you have never ruled, / like those never called by your name*

[12]After all this, O LORD, will you hold yourself
back?
Will you keep silent and punish us beyond
measure?

Discovering the Word 1. What do we learn from the way that Isaiah begins his long and passionate prayer in 63:7? 2. Isaiah 63:9 recalls how God brought his people out of slavery in Egypt. How do verses 8–9 describe the warmth of God's relationship with his people? 3. What do the chastened people remember about God's wonderful deeds (63:11–14)? 4. What striking phrase, repeated three times in 63:16—64:12, gives the prayer its special intensity (63:16; 64:8)? 5. How does Isaiah see God's hand in this sorry state of affairs, and how does Israel look to God to get them out of it (63:15, 17; 64:1, 4–5, 8)?

Applying the Word 1. God's interventions are always surprising. How do you see God's intervening in the world today through revival or in other ways? 2. How can following the model of this passage enrich and deepen your own prayer life?

Responding in Prayer Pray that God will bring revival to you and to your nation.

Isaiah 65:1–16

65 "I revealed myself to those who
did not ask for me;
I was found by those who did not
seek me.
To a nation that did not call on my name,
I said, 'Here am I, here am I.'
[2]All day long I have held out my hands
to an obstinate people,
who walk in ways not good,
pursuing their own imaginations—
[3]a people who continually provoke me
to my very face,
offering sacrifices in gardens
and burning incense on altars of brick;
[4]who sit among the graves
and spend their nights keeping secret vigil;
who eat the flesh of pigs,
and whose pots hold broth of unclean
meat;
[5]who say, 'Keep away; don't come near me,
for I am too sacred for you!'
Such people are smoke in my nostrils,
a fire that keeps burning all day.

[6]"See, it stands written before me:
I will not keep silent but will pay back in
full;
I will pay it back into their laps—
[7]both your sins and the sins of your fathers,"
says the LORD.
"Because they burned sacrifices on the
mountains
and defied me on the hills,
I will measure into their laps
the full payment for their former deeds."

[8]This is what the LORD says:

"As when juice is still found in a cluster of
grapes
and men say, 'Don't destroy it,
there is yet some good in it,'
so will I do in behalf of my servants;
I will not destroy them all.
[9]I will bring forth descendants from Jacob,
and from Judah those who will possess my
mountains;
my chosen people will inherit them,
and there will my servants live.
[10]Sharon will become a pasture for flocks,
and the Valley of Achor a resting place for
herds,
for my people who seek me.

[11]"But as for you who forsake the LORD
and forget my holy mountain,
who spread a table for Fortune
and fill bowls of mixed wine for Destiny,
[12]I will destine you for the sword,
and you will all bend down for the
slaughter;
for I called but you did not answer,
I spoke but you did not listen.
You did evil in my sight
and chose what displeases me."

[13]Therefore this is what the Sovereign LORD says:

"My servants will eat,
but you will go hungry;
my servants will drink,
but you will go thirsty;
my servants will rejoice,
but you will be put to shame.
[14]My servants will sing
out of the joy of their hearts,
but you will cry out
from anguish of heart
and wail in brokenness of spirit.
[15]You will leave your name
to my chosen ones as a curse;
the Sovereign LORD will put you to death,
but to his servants he will give another name.
[16]Whoever invokes a blessing in the land
will do so by the God of truth;
he who takes an oath in the land
will swear by the God of truth.
For the past troubles will be forgotten
and hidden from my eyes.

24 / *Isaiah 65:17—66:24* The Terror and the Glory

HOPE HAS A life-preserving character. Time and again, as prison-camp memoirs show, people who have something to live for survive, and those who lose hope die under the same conditions. All through Isaiah, the basic theme has been that God's faithful love should be the basis of his people's faithful trust. Now, as he brings his book to a climax, he describes the day when faith and hope will come to fruition. There will be a new heaven and a new earth in which love reigns. Yet this is not a fairy-tale ending. As in chapter 6, Isaiah cannot avert his eyes from the fact that some people *reject* the good news. One day their refusal will be irreversibly confirmed.

Warming Up to God What people or events have recently given you hope regarding your future?

Read Isaiah 65:17—66:24.

[17]"Behold, I will create
new heavens and a new earth.
The former things will not be remembered,
nor will they come to mind.
[18]But be glad and rejoice forever
in what I will create,
for I will create Jerusalem to be a delight
and its people a joy.
[19]I will rejoice over Jerusalem
and take delight in my people;
the sound of weeping and of crying
will be heard in it no more.

[20]"Never again will there be in it
an infant who lives but a few days,
or an old man who does not live out his years;
he who dies at a hundred
will be thought a mere youth;
he who fails to reach[y] a hundred
will be considered accursed.
[21]They will build houses and dwell in them;
they will plant vineyards and eat their fruit.
[22]No longer will they build houses and others live in them,
or plant and others eat.
For as the days of a tree,
so will be the days of my people;
my chosen ones will long enjoy
the works of their hands.
[23]They will not toil in vain
or bear children doomed to misfortune;
for they will be a people blessed by the LORD,
they and their descendants with them.
[24]Before they call I will answer;
while they are still speaking I will hear.
[25]The wolf and the lamb will feed together,
and the lion will eat straw like the ox,
but dust will be the serpent's food.

y20 Or / *the sinner who reaches*

They will neither harm nor destroy
on all my holy mountain,"
says the LORD.

66 This is what the LORD says:
"Heaven is my throne,
and the earth is my footstool.
Where is the house you will build for me?
Where will my resting place be?
2Has not my hand made all these things,
and so they came into being?"
declares the LORD.

"This is the one I esteem:
he who is humble and contrite in spirit,
and trembles at my word.
3But whoever sacrifices a bull
is like one who kills a man,
and whoever offers a lamb,
like one who breaks a dog's neck;
whoever makes a grain offering
is like one who presents pig's blood,
and whoever burns memorial incense,
like one who worships an idol.
They have chosen their own ways,
and their souls delight in their
abominations;
4so I also will choose harsh treatment for them
and will bring upon them what they dread.
For when I called, no one answered,
when I spoke, no one listened.
They did evil in my sight
and chose what displeases me."

5Hear the word of the LORD,
you who tremble at his word:
"Your brothers who hate you,
and exclude you because of my name, have
said,
'Let the LORD be glorified,
that we may see your joy!'
Yet they will be put to shame.
6Hear that uproar from the city,
hear that noise from the temple!
It is the sound of the LORD
repaying his enemies all they deserve.

7"Before she goes into labor,
she gives birth;
before the pains come upon her,
she delivers a son.
8Who has ever heard of such a thing?
Who has ever seen such things?
Can a country be born in a day
or a nation be brought forth in a moment?
Yet no sooner is Zion in labor
than she gives birth to her children.
9Do I bring to the moment of birth
and not give delivery?" says the LORD.
"Do I close up the womb
when I bring to delivery?" says your God.
10"Rejoice with Jerusalem and be glad for her,
all you who love her;
rejoice greatly with her,
all you who mourn over her.
11For you will nurse and be satisfied
at her comforting breasts;
you will drink deeply
and delight in her overflowing abundance."
12For this is what the LORD says:
"I will extend peace to her like a river,
and the wealth of nations like a flooding
stream;
you will nurse and be carried on her arm
and dandled on her knees.
13As a mother comforts her child,
so will I comfort you;
and you will be comforted over Jerusalem."

14When you see this, your heart will rejoice
and you will flourish like grass;
the hand of the LORD will be made known to
his servants,
but his fury will be shown to his foes.
15See, the LORD is coming with fire,
and his chariots are like a whirlwind;
he will bring down his anger with fury,
and his rebuke with flames of fire.
16For with fire and with his sword
the LORD will execute judgment upon all
men,
and many will be those slain by the LORD.

17"Those who consecrate and purify themselves
to go into the gardens, following the one in the
midst of[z] those who eat the flesh of pigs and rats
and other abominable things—they will meet
their end together," declares the LORD.
18"And I, because of their actions and their
imaginations, am about to come[a] and gather all
nations and tongues, and they will come and see
my glory.

[z]17 Or *gardens behind one of your temples, and* [a]18 The meaning of the Hebrew for this clause is uncertain.

19"I will set a sign among them, and I will send
some of those who survive to the nations—to
Tarshish, to the Libyans[b] and Lydians (famous
as archers), to Tubal and Greece, and to the dis-
tant islands that have not heard of my fame or
seen my glory. They will proclaim my glory
among the nations. 20And they will bring all your
brothers, from all the nations, to my holy moun-
tain in Jerusalem as an offering to the LORD—on
horses, in chariots and wagons, and on mules and
camels," says the LORD. "They will bring them,
as the Israelites bring their grain offerings, to
the temple of the LORD in ceremonially clean
vessels.
21And I will select some of them also to be priests
and Levites," says the LORD.

22"As the new heavens and the new earth that
I make will endure before me," declares the LORD,
"so will your name and descendants endure.
23From one New Moon to another and from one
Sabbath to another, all mankind will come and
bow down before me," says the LORD. 24"And they
will go out and look upon the dead bodies of
those who rebelled against me; their worm will
not die, nor will their fire be quenched, and they
will be loathsome to all mankind."

[b]19 Some Septuagint manuscripts *Put* (Libyans); Hebrew *Pul*

Discovering the Word 1. What simple joys and pleasures characterize the new heaven and new earth (65:17–19, 24)? 2. What is God's complaint in 66:1–2? 3. Which worshipers please God and which displease him (66:2–4)? 4. According to 66:7–11, the apparently barren, abandoned and childless Zion is to have children. In what ways is childbirth an appropriate metaphor here? 5. What will it be like when God finally shows his glory (66:12–24)?

Applying the Word 1. How can you best preserve the two poles of awe and intimacy that characterize true worship? 2. In what area of your life do you need to look to the Lord for hope?

Responding in Prayer Praise God for the growing trust in him that you have which enables you to have hope in a hopeless world.

Jeremiah

As a teenager, I was delighted when my pastor started a series of sermons on prophecy. I hadn't been a Christian very long, and I had the impression that the Bible was a mysterious book that spoke about the future. I suppose at that time you could say that I put the Bible, Edgar Cayce and the works of Nostradamus in the same category.

My pastor brought some cold water to my youthful fancy. I learned that the future the prophets spoke about wasn't primarily some distant utopia that had to be deciphered by hocus–pocus and hidden wisdom. Instead, the prophets of the Old Testament were only partly concerned with the future. Their primary focus was on calling God's people back to faithful obedience and worship. When the prophets spoke of the future, they did so to let Israel know that they could expect defeat at the hands of their enemies if they didn't repent.

This was not at all what I expected. As my pastor developed the series, the prophets seemed to me to be strange characters wandering around thundering the message of an angry God to people who refused to obey him. After that series, I wasn't so eager to talk about prophecy anymore. I wasn't sure I liked the prophets or their message.

Eventually I got back to the prophets in my personal study. I was convinced that if the prophets were in the Scriptures, then I needed to study them. What I discovered at that time was that, yes, many of the prophets did strange things and proclaimed lots of wrath. What was off in my understanding, however, was the impression I got of God.

The thundering message of judgment came not because God is a short-tempered despot shouting angry curses at people who break his rules, but because he is so intensely caring for those he gave himself to. In and through the message of the prophets as they proclaimed the coming judgment is a message of love. I like the way the prophet Jeremiah says it: "I have loved you with an everlasting love; I have drawn you with loving-kindness" (Jer 31:3).

In this book you will find the prophet Jeremiah behaving strangely—proclaiming wrath and impending destruction. Jeremiah lived and wrote in a dark time. For over 250 years God had been sending prophets to warn his people to change their ways. And for over 250 years the prophets were ignored, persecuted or killed. As Jeremiah began his ministry somewhere around 620 B.C., God had already sent the northern half of the kingdom into exile a hundred years previously. For the southern kingdom, Jeremiah was their last messenger, their very last chance to turn things around. God and Jeremiah knew that it wouldn't work, but they rebuked and proclaimed anyway.

Studying the ministry of the prophet Jeremiah, you will get a glimpse of what it is like to have a personal relationship with God. God called Jeremiah to a painful ministry. But with that great burden, he gave Jeremiah a great gift, the gift of himself. When you study Jeremiah you get a glimpse of what it can be like for God and a human to be together. You will see a message of love that grows from a relationship of love—a hard love, a demanding love, but love nevertheless. What you will also discover, if you pay attention, is how you can grow in your own personal relationship to God. You will be stronger and more deeply open to the love of God than you were before.

The Shape of the Study

The book of Jeremiah is challenging. It is the second longest of all the prophetic works, with 52 chapters. There are three major sections:

Jeremiah 1—20 ——————The Impending Judgment
Jeremiah 21—45 —————Living in the Midst of God's Judgment
Jeremiah 46—52 —————Oracles of International Judgment

One of the ways that Jeremiah sought to get his message across was through the use of symbols. At one time he stands at the door of the temple and uses it as a backdrop. At another time he uses a linen belt, another time a potter's house, then a clay jar, later a basket of figs and then a yoke. We will look at these symbols and the messages that accompany them.

As we ponder the symbols of Jeremiah, we will touch on the major themes of his ministry:

- ☐ The defamation of the temple and the practice of false religion
- ☐ The breaking of the covenant bond with God
- ☐ The right of God to judge Judah for their sin
- ☐ Judah's spiritual adultery with false gods
- ☐ The failure of Judah's spiritual leaders
- ☐ God's promised blessing for the captives
- ☐ God's judgment of all the nations
- ☐ Jeremiah's experience of opposition from the false prophets
- ☐ God's promise to restore people to the land after the period of judgment

Through all the symbols and themes and the proclamations of judgment there is a commitment of love. Through Jeremiah, God says:

> I will make an everlasting covenant with them: I will never stop doing good to them, and I will inspire them to fear me, so that they will never turn away from me. I will rejoice in doing them good and will assuredly plant them in this land with all my heart and soul.
>
> This is what the LORD says: As I have brought all this great calamity on this people, so I will give them all the prosperity I have promised them. (Jer 32:40–42)

When you stop to think about it, the prophets do speak of the future. God promised Israel a future on the other side of judgment and sin. It will be a time of peace, love and prosperity. A time of joy beyond which we can hardly imagine. The good news is that he invites those who have joined his people through faith in his son, Jesus Christ, to that future as well.

Outline

1 / *Jeremiah 1*
Prophet to the Nations

MAYBE IT'S BECAUSE I was in college in the sixties, but I've always wanted to do something significant with my life, to change the world. For this reason, coming into a relationship with God through Jesus Christ after my freshman year was exciting. What could be more meaningful than giving my life to God?

I've been following him for a couple of decades now. I have found it meaningful and fulfilling. But doing something significant wasn't quite what I thought it would be. Somehow I thought that making a difference would feel good and elicit loads of affirmation and appreciation from others. Well, sometimes it does and sometimes it doesn't! Jeremiah was called by God to a life of great meaning and significance. He also found lots of trouble. Why then did he do it? Read on and see.

Warming Up to God Describe a time when you were given the opportunity to do something important. How did you feel?

Read Jeremiah 1.

1 The words of Jeremiah son of Hilkiah,
one of the priests at Anathoth in the terri-
tory of Benjamin. [2]The word of the LORD
came to him in the thirteenth year of the reign of
Josiah son of Amon king of Judah, [3]and through
the reign of Jehoiakim son of Josiah king of Ju-
dah, down to the fifth month of the eleventh year
of Zedekiah son of Josiah king of Judah, when the
people of Jerusalem went into exile.

[4]The word of the LORD came to me, saying,

[5]"Before I formed you in the womb I knew[a]
you,
before you were born I set you apart;
I appointed you as a prophet to the
nations."

[6]"Ah, Sovereign LORD," I said, "I do not know
how to speak; I am only a child."
[7]But the LORD said to me, "Do not say, 'I am
only a child.' You must go to everyone I send you
to and say whatever I command you. [8]Do not be
afraid of them, for I am with you and will rescue
you," declares the LORD.
[9]Then the LORD reached out his hand and
touched my mouth and said to me, "Now, I have
put my words in your mouth. [10]See, today I ap-
point you over nations and kingdoms to uproot
and tear down, to destroy and overthrow, to build
and to plant."
[11]The word of the LORD came to me: "What do
you see, Jeremiah?"
"I see the branch of an almond tree," I replied.
[12]The LORD said to me, "You have seen cor-
rectly, for I am watching[b] to see that my word is
fulfilled."
[13]The word of the LORD came to me again:
"What do you see?"
"I see a boiling pot, tilting away from the
north," I answered.
[14]The LORD said to me, "From the north disas-
ter will be poured out on all who live in the land.
[15]I am about to summon all the peoples of the
northern kingdoms," declares the LORD.

"Their kings will come and set up their
thrones
in the entrance of the gates of Jerusalem;
they will come against all her surrounding
walls
and against all the towns of Judah.
[16]I will pronounce my judgments on my people
because of their wickedness in forsaking
me,
in burning incense to other gods
and in worshiping what their hands have
made.

[17]"Get yourself ready! Stand up and say to
them whatever I command you. Do not be terri-
fied by them, or I will terrify you before them.
[18]Today I have made you a fortified city, an iron
pillar and a bronze wall to stand against the
whole land—against the kings of Judah, its offi-
cials, its priests and the people of the land. [19]They
will fight against you but will not overcome you,
for I am with you and will rescue you," declares
the LORD.

[a]5 Or *chose* [b]12 The Hebrew for *watching* sounds like the Hebrew for *almond tree.*

Discovering the Word 1. The first three verses set the historical context. Jeremiah's ministry lasted about forty years, through one good king and then two wicked ones. From verses 1–3 alone, what do you think his ministry might have been like? 2. Describe Jeremiah's call in your own words (vv. 4–10). 3. How does the word of the Lord shape Jeremiah's identity (vv. 4–10)? 4. Jeremiah gets practice learning to see and hear God. What two pictures is he given, and how would each help the young prophet grow in his calling (vv. 11–16)? 5. Jeremiah's message will not be well received. What help does God offer him (vv. 17–19)?

Applying the Word 1. God's Word shapes the identity of all who hear it. How has it shaped you? 2. God addressed Jeremiah's fears of being too immature and inadequate. Are there ways that God has addressed your fears? 3. How might God's promise of protection and expectation of obedience be helpful for the challenges you face?

Responding in Prayer We are all called to witness of Christ's work. Pray that God will shape you into a servant who testifies of his work in you.

Jeremiah 2:1—3:5

2 The word of the LORD came to me: 2"Go
and proclaim in the hearing of Jerusalem:

" 'I remember the devotion of your youth,
how as a bride you loved me
and followed me through the desert,
through a land not sown.
3Israel was holy to the LORD,
the firstfruits of his harvest;
all who devoured her were held guilty,
and disaster overtook them,' "
declares the LORD.

4Hear the word of the LORD, O house of Jacob,
all you clans of the house of Israel.

5This is what the LORD says:

"What fault did your fathers find in me,
that they strayed so far from me?
They followed worthless idols
and became worthless themselves.
6They did not ask, 'Where is the LORD,
who brought us up out of Egypt
and led us through the barren wilderness,
through a land of deserts and rifts,
a land of drought and darkness,[c]
a land where no one travels and no one lives?'
7I brought you into a fertile land
to eat its fruit and rich produce.
But you came and defiled my land
and made my inheritance detestable.
8The priests did not ask,
'Where is the LORD?'
Those who deal with the law did not know me;
the leaders rebelled against me.
The prophets prophesied by Baal,
following worthless idols.

9"Therefore I bring charges against you again,"
declares the LORD.
"And I will bring charges against your children's children.
10Cross over to the coasts of Kittim[d] and look,
send to Kedar[e] and observe closely;
see if there has ever been anything like this:
11Has a nation ever changed its gods?
(Yet they are not gods at all.)
But my people have exchanged their[f] Glory
for worthless idols.
12Be appalled at this, O heavens,
and shudder with great horror,"
declares the LORD.
13"My people have committed two sins:
They have forsaken me,
the spring of living water,
and have dug their own cisterns,
broken cisterns that cannot hold water.
14Is Israel a servant, a slave by birth?
Why then has he become plunder?
15Lions have roared;
they have growled at him.
They have laid waste his land;
his towns are burned and deserted.
16Also, the men of Memphis[g] and Tahpanhes

[c] 6 Or *and the shadow of death* [d] 10 That is, Cyprus and western coastlands [e] 10 The home of Bedouin tribes in the Syro-Arabian desert [f] 11 Masoretic Text; an ancient Hebrew scribal tradition *my* [g] 16 Hebrew *Noph*

have shaved the crown of your head.[h]
17Have you not brought this on yourselves
by forsaking the LORD your God
when he led you in the way?
18Now why go to Egypt
to drink water from the Shihor[i]?
And why go to Assyria
to drink water from the River[j]?
19Your wickedness will punish you;
your backsliding will rebuke you.
Consider then and realize
how evil and bitter it is for you
when you forsake the LORD your God
and have no awe of me,"
declares the Lord, the LORD Almighty.

20"Long ago you broke off your yoke
and tore off your bonds;
you said, 'I will not serve you!'
Indeed, on every high hill
and under every spreading tree
you lay down as a prostitute.
21I had planted you like a choice vine
of sound and reliable stock.
How then did you turn against me
into a corrupt, wild vine?
22Although you wash yourself with soda
and use an abundance of soap,
the stain of your guilt is still before me,"
declares the Sovereign LORD.
23"How can you say, 'I am not defiled;
I have not run after the Baals'?
See how you behaved in the valley;
consider what you have done.
You are a swift she-camel
running here and there,
24a wild donkey accustomed to the desert,
sniffing the wind in her craving—
in her heat who can restrain her?
Any males that pursue her need not tire
themselves;
at mating time they will find her.
25Do not run until your feet are bare
and your throat is dry.
But you said, 'It's no use!
I love foreign gods,
and I must go after them.'

26"As a thief is disgraced when he is caught,
so the house of Israel is disgraced—
they, their kings and their officials,
their priests and their prophets.
27They say to wood, 'You are my father,'
and to stone, 'You gave me birth.'
They have turned their backs to me
and not their faces;
yet when they are in trouble, they say,
'Come and save us!'
28Where then are the gods you made for
yourselves?
Let them come if they can save you
when you are in trouble!
For you have as many gods
as you have towns, O Judah.

29"Why do you bring charges against me?
You have all rebelled against me,"
declares the LORD.
30"In vain I punished your people;
they did not respond to correction.
Your sword has devoured your prophets
like a ravening lion.

31"You of this generation, consider the word of
the LORD:

"Have I been a desert to Israel
or a land of great darkness?
Why do my people say, 'We are free to roam;
we will come to you no more'?
32Does a maiden forget her jewelry,
a bride her wedding ornaments?
Yet my people have forgotten me,
days without number.
33How skilled you are at pursuing love!
Even the worst of women can learn from
your ways.
34On your clothes men find
the lifeblood of the innocent poor,
though you did not catch them breaking in.
Yet in spite of all this
35 you say, 'I am innocent;
he is not angry with me.'
But I will pass judgment on you
because you say, 'I have not sinned.'
36Why do you go about so much,
changing your ways?
You will be disappointed by Egypt
as you were by Assyria.
37You will also leave that place
with your hands on your head,
for the LORD has rejected those you trust;
you will not be helped by them.

[h]16 Or *have cracked your skull* [i]18 That is, a branch of the Nile
[j]18 That is, the Euphrates

3 "If a man divorces his wife
and she leaves him and marries another
man,
should he return to her again?
Would not the land be completely defiled?
But you have lived as a prostitute with many
lovers—
would you now return to me?"
declares the LORD.
2"Look up to the barren heights and see.
Is there any place where you have not been
ravished?
By the roadside you sat waiting for lovers,
sat like a nomad[k] in the desert.
You have defiled the land
with your prostitution and wickedness.
3Therefore the showers have been withheld,
and no spring rains have fallen.
Yet you have the brazen look of a prostitute;
you refuse to blush with shame.
4Have you not just called to me:
'My Father, my friend from my youth,
5will you always be angry?
Will your wrath continue forever?'
This is how you talk,
but you do all the evil you can."

[k]2 *Or an Arab*

2 / *Jeremiah 3:6—4:4*
The Call to Return

"COME BACK! COME back!" Whether called out to a small child, a rebellious teenager, a wandering spouse or even a straying pet, the words ring with desperation. Spoken by God to sinful humans, the words are heartbreaking. God the Creator allows his people the freedom of wandering from him. Still, he persists in calling them back to himself.

Warming Up to God In what areas might the Lord be calling you back to a closer walk with him?

Read Jeremiah 3:6—4:4.

6During the reign of King Josiah, the LORD said
to me, "Have you seen what faithless Israel has
done? She has gone up on every high hill and
under every spreading tree and has committed
adultery there. 7I thought that after she had done
all this she would return to me but she did not,
and her unfaithful sister Judah saw it. 8I gave
faithless Israel her certificate of divorce and sent
her away because of all her adulteries. Yet I saw
that her unfaithful sister Judah had no fear; she
also went out and committed adultery. 9Because
Israel's immorality mattered so little to her, she
defiled the land and committed adultery with
stone and wood. 10In spite of all this, her unfaith-
ful sister Judah did not return to me with all her
heart, but only in pretense," declares the LORD.
11The LORD said to me, "Faithless Israel is more
righteous than unfaithful Judah. 12Go, proclaim
this message toward the north:

" 'Return, faithless Israel,' declares the LORD,
'I will frown on you no longer,
for I am merciful,' declares the LORD,
'I will not be angry forever.
13Only acknowledge your guilt—
you have rebelled against the LORD your
God,
you have scattered your favors to foreign gods
under every spreading tree,
and have not obeyed me,' "
declares the LORD.

14"Return, faithless people," declares the LORD,
"for I am your husband. I will choose you—one
from a town and two from a clan—and bring you
to Zion. 15Then I will give you shepherds after my
own heart, who will lead you with knowledge and
understanding. 16In those days, when your num-
bers have increased greatly in the land," declares
the LORD, "men will no longer say, 'The ark of the
covenant of the LORD.' It will never enter their
minds or be remembered; it will not be missed,

nor will another one be made. 17At that time they
will call Jerusalem The Throne of the LORD, and
all nations will gather in Jerusalem to honor the
name of the LORD. No longer will they follow the
stubbornness of their evil hearts. 18In those days
the house of Judah will join the house of Israel,
and together they will come from a northern land
to the land I gave your forefathers as an inheri-
tance.

19"I myself said,

" 'How gladly would I treat you like sons
and give you a desirable land,
the most beautiful inheritance of any
nation.'
I thought you would call me 'Father'
and not turn away from following me.
20But like a woman unfaithful to her husband,
so you have been unfaithful to me, O house
of Israel,"
declares the LORD.

21A cry is heard on the barren heights,
the weeping and pleading of the people of
Israel,
because they have perverted their ways
and have forgotten the LORD their God.

22"Return, faithless people;
I will cure you of backsliding."

"Yes, we will come to you,
for you are the LORD our God.
23Surely the ⌞idolatrous⌟ commotion on the hills
and mountains is a deception;
surely in the LORD our God
is the salvation of Israel.
24From our youth shameful gods have
consumed
the fruits of our fathers' labor—
their flocks and herds,
their sons and daughters.
25Let us lie down in our shame,
and let our disgrace cover us.
We have sinned against the LORD our God,
both we and our fathers;
from our youth till this day
we have not obeyed the LORD our God."

4 "If you will return, O Israel,
return to me,"
declares the LORD.
"If you put your detestable idols out of my
sight
and no longer go astray,
2and if in a truthful, just and righteous way
you swear, 'As surely as the LORD lives,'
then the nations will be blessed by him
and in him they will glory."

3This is what the LORD says to the men of Judah
and to Jerusalem:

"Break up your unplowed ground
and do not sow among thorns.
4Circumcise yourselves to the LORD,
circumcise your hearts,
you men of Judah and people of Jerusalem,
or my wrath will break out and burn like fire
because of the evil you have done—
burn with no one to quench it.

Discovering the Word 1. How had Israel been unfaithful to God (3:6–13)? 2. What does God promise if only Israel will return to him (3:14–18)? 3. What hopes did the Lord have for Israel (3:19–20)? 4. How do the people express their repentance (3:21–25)? 5. What warnings does God give Israel if they refuse to return to him (4:1–4)?

Applying the Word 1. Where have you given in to the temptation to be unfaithful to the Lord? (Think especially of "small" ways easily overlooked or excused.) 2. How do the Lord's promised blessings for repentance speak to you right now?

Responding in Prayer Confess to the Lord any wanderings and rebellion against him. Thank him for his grace which keeps calling you back.

Jeremiah 4:5–31

[5]"Announce in Judah and proclaim in
Jerusalem and say:
'Sound the trumpet throughout the land!'
Cry aloud and say:
'Gather together!
Let us flee to the fortified cities!'
[6]Raise the signal to go to Zion!
Flee for safety without delay!
For I am bringing disaster from the north,
even terrible destruction."

[7]A lion has come out of his lair;
a destroyer of nations has set out.
He has left his place
to lay waste your land.
Your towns will lie in ruins
without inhabitant.
[8]So put on sackcloth,
lament and wail,
for the fierce anger of the LORD
has not turned away from us.

[9]"In that day," declares the LORD,
"the king and the officials will lose heart,
the priests will be horrified,
and the prophets will be appalled."

[10]Then I said, "Ah, Sovereign LORD, how completely you have deceived this people and Jerusalem by saying, 'You will have peace,' when the sword is at our throats."

[11]At that time this people and Jerusalem will be
told, "A scorching wind from the barren heights
in the desert blows toward my people, but not to
winnow or cleanse; [12]a wind too strong for that
comes from me.[l] Now I pronounce my judgments against them."

[13]Look! He advances like the clouds,
his chariots come like a whirlwind,
his horses are swifter than eagles.
Woe to us! We are ruined!
[14]O Jerusalem, wash the evil from your heart
and be saved.
How long will you harbor wicked thoughts?
[15]A voice is announcing from Dan,
proclaiming disaster from the hills of
Ephraim.
[16]"Tell this to the nations,
proclaim it to Jerusalem:
'A besieging army is coming from a distant
land,
raising a war cry against the cities of Judah.
[17]They surround her like men guarding a field,
because she has rebelled against me,'"
declares the LORD.
[18]"Your own conduct and actions
have brought this upon you.
This is your punishment.
How bitter it is!
How it pierces to the heart!"

[19]Oh, my anguish, my anguish!
I writhe in pain.
Oh, the agony of my heart!
My heart pounds within me,
I cannot keep silent.
For I have heard the sound of the trumpet;
I have heard the battle cry.
[20]Disaster follows disaster;
the whole land lies in ruins.
In an instant my tents are destroyed,
my shelter in a moment.
[21]How long must I see the battle standard
and hear the sound of the trumpet?

[22]"My people are fools;
they do not know me.
They are senseless children;
they have no understanding.
They are skilled in doing evil;
they know not how to do good."

[23]I looked at the earth,
and it was formless and empty;
and at the heavens,
and their light was gone.
[24]I looked at the mountains,
and they were quaking;
all the hills were swaying.
[25]I looked, and there were no people;
every bird in the sky had flown away.
[26]I looked, and the fruitful land was a desert;
all its towns lay in ruins
before the LORD, before his fierce anger.

[27]This is what the LORD says:

"The whole land will be ruined,
though I will not destroy it completely.

[l]12 Or *comes at my command*

28Therefore the earth will mourn
and the heavens above grow dark,
because I have spoken and will not relent,
I have decided and will not turn back."

29At the sound of horsemen and archers
every town takes to flight.
Some go into the thickets;
some climb up among the rocks.
All the towns are deserted;
no one lives in them.

30What are you doing, O devastated one?
Why dress yourself in scarlet
and put on jewels of gold?
Why shade your eyes with paint?
You adorn yourself in vain.
Your lovers despise you;
they seek your life.

31I hear a cry as of a woman in labor,
a groan as of one bearing her first child—
the cry of the Daughter of Zion gasping for breath,
stretching out her hands and saying,
"Alas! I am fainting;
my life is given over to murderers."

3 / *Jeremiah 5*
Searching for Faithfulness

A NEWSPAPER AD reads "Christian carpenter. Reliable. Integrity counts." Is honesty so unusual that it merits advertisement as a unique feature of a person's work? This carpenter apparently thinks so. He is publicly committing himself to integrity and is willing to stake his work on his word. This is the sort of person God is looking for.

Warming Up to God To what extent would you say honesty characterizes your relationship with God?

Read Jeremiah 5.

5 "Go up and down the streets of Jerusalem,
look around and consider,
search through her squares.
If you can find but one person
who deals honestly and seeks the truth,
I will forgive this city.
2Although they say, 'As surely as the LORD lives,'
still they are swearing falsely."
3O LORD, do not your eyes look for truth?
You struck them, but they felt no pain;
you crushed them, but they refused correction.
They made their faces harder than stone
and refused to repent.
4I thought, "These are only the poor;
they are foolish,
for they do not know the way of the LORD,
the requirements of their God.
5So I will go to the leaders
and speak to them;
surely they know the way of the LORD,
the requirements of their God."
But with one accord they too had broken off the yoke
and torn off the bonds.
6Therefore a lion from the forest will attack them,
a wolf from the desert will ravage them,
a leopard will lie in wait near their towns
to tear to pieces any who venture out,
for their rebellion is great
and their backslidings many.

7"Why should I forgive you?
Your children have forsaken me
and sworn by gods that are not gods.
I supplied all their needs,
yet they committed adultery
and thronged to the houses of prostitutes.
8They are well-fed, lusty stallions,
each neighing for another man's wife.
9Should I not punish them for this?"
declares the LORD.

“Should I not avenge myself
on such a nation as this?

10“Go through her vineyards and ravage them,
but do not destroy them completely.
Strip off her branches,
for these people do not belong to the LORD.
11The house of Israel and the house of Judah
have been utterly unfaithful to me,”
declares the LORD.

12They have lied about the LORD;
they said, “He will do nothing!
No harm will come to us;
we will never see sword or famine.
13The prophets are but wind
and the word is not in them;
so let what they say be done to them.”

14Therefore this is what the LORD God Almighty says:

“Because the people have spoken these words,
I will make my words in your mouth a fire
and these people the wood it consumes.
15O house of Israel,” declares the LORD,
“I am bringing a distant nation against
you—
an ancient and enduring nation,
a people whose language you do not know,
whose speech you do not understand.
16Their quivers are like an open grave;
all of them are mighty warriors.
17They will devour your harvests and food,
devour your sons and daughters;
they will devour your flocks and herds,
devour your vines and fig trees.
With the sword they will destroy
the fortified cities in which you trust.

18“Yet even in those days,” declares the LORD, “I
will not destroy you completely. 19And when the
people ask, ‘Why has the LORD our God done all
this to us?’ you will tell them, ‘As you have for-
saken me and served foreign gods in your own
land, so now you will serve foreigners in a land
not your own.’

20“Announce this to the house of Jacob
and proclaim it in Judah:
21Hear this, you foolish and senseless people,
who have eyes but do not see,
who have ears but do not hear:
22Should you not fear me?” declares the LORD.
“Should you not tremble in my presence?
I made the sand a boundary for the sea,
an everlasting barrier it cannot cross.
The waves may roll, but they cannot prevail;
they may roar, but they cannot cross it.
23But these people have stubborn and rebellious
hearts;
they have turned aside and gone away.
24They do not say to themselves,
‘Let us fear the LORD our God,
who gives autumn and spring rains in season,
who assures us of the regular weeks of
harvest.’
25Your wrongdoings have kept these away;
your sins have deprived you of good.

26“Among my people are wicked men
who lie in wait like men who snare birds
and like those who set traps to catch men.
27Like cages full of birds,
their houses are full of deceit;
they have become rich and powerful
28 and have grown fat and sleek.
Their evil deeds have no limit;
they do not plead the case of the fatherless
to win it,
they do not defend the rights of the poor.
29Should I not punish them for this?”
declares the LORD.
“Should I not avenge myself
on such a nation as this?

30“A horrible and shocking thing
has happened in the land:
31The prophets prophesy lies,
the priests rule by their own authority,
and my people love it this way.
But what will you do in the end?

Discovering the Word 1. What was God searching for in the streets of Jerusalem (vv. 1–5)? 2. What did he find at different levels of society (vv. 2–5)? 3. How is mercy written into the judgments of God (vv. 6–19)? 4. How had the people lied about God and his prophets (vv. 12–13, 31)? 5. What truths about God were they ignoring or denying (vv. 21–25)?

Applying the Word 1. How will our relationship with the Lord change if we remember that he is the God of truth and hates lying? 2. In what areas can you be more honest with God, yourself and other people?

Responding in Prayer Come to the Lord in honesty about an area of life where you tend to be less than candid. Come boldly because you know God welcomes honesty and he is merciful.

Jeremiah 6

6 "Flee for safety, people of Benjamin!
Flee from Jerusalem!
Sound the trumpet in Tekoa!
Raise the signal over Beth Hakkerem!
For disaster looms out of the north,
even terrible destruction.
2I will destroy the Daughter of Zion,
so beautiful and delicate.
3Shepherds with their flocks will come against her;
they will pitch their tents around her,
each tending his own portion."

4"Prepare for battle against her!
Arise, let us attack at noon!
But, alas, the daylight is fading,
and the shadows of evening grow long.
5So arise, let us attack at night
and destroy her fortresses!"

6This is what the LORD Almighty says:

"Cut down the trees
and build siege ramps against Jerusalem.
This city must be punished;
it is filled with oppression.
7As a well pours out its water,
so she pours out her wickedness.
Violence and destruction resound in her;
her sickness and wounds are ever before me.
8Take warning, O Jerusalem,
or I will turn away from you
and make your land desolate
so no one can live in it."

9This is what the LORD Almighty says:

"Let them glean the remnant of Israel
as thoroughly as a vine;
pass your hand over the branches again,
like one gathering grapes."
10To whom can I speak and give warning?
Who will listen to me?
Their ears are closed[m]
so they cannot hear.
The word of the LORD is offensive to them;
they find no pleasure in it.
11But I am full of the wrath of the LORD,
and I cannot hold it in.

"Pour it out on the children in the street
and on the young men gathered together;
both husband and wife will be caught in it,
and the old, those weighed down with years.
12Their houses will be turned over to others,
together with their fields and their wives,
when I stretch out my hand
against those who live in the land,"
declares the LORD.
13"From the least to the greatest,
all are greedy for gain;
prophets and priests alike,
all practice deceit.
14They dress the wound of my people
as though it were not serious.
'Peace, peace,' they say,
when there is no peace.
15Are they ashamed of their loathsome conduct?
No, they have no shame at all;
they do not even know how to blush.
So they will fall among the fallen;
they will be brought down when I punish them,"
says the LORD.

16This is what the LORD says:

"Stand at the crossroads and look;
ask for the ancient paths,
ask where the good way is, and walk in it,
and you will find rest for your souls.
But you said, 'We will not walk in it.'
17I appointed watchmen over you and said,
'Listen to the sound of the trumpet!'
But you said, 'We will not listen.'
18Therefore hear, O nations;
observe, O witnesses,
what will happen to them.
19Hear, O earth:
I am bringing disaster on this people,

[m]10 Hebrew *uncircumcised*

the fruit of their schemes,
because they have not listened to my words
and have rejected my law.
20What do I care about incense from Sheba
or sweet calamus from a distant land?
Your burnt offerings are not acceptable;
your sacrifices do not please me."

21Therefore this is what the LORD says:
"I will put obstacles before this people.
Fathers and sons alike will stumble over them;
neighbors and friends will perish."

22This is what the LORD says:
"Look, an army is coming
from the land of the north;
a great nation is being stirred up
from the ends of the earth.
23They are armed with bow and spear;
they are cruel and show no mercy.
They sound like the roaring sea
as they ride on their horses;
they come like men in battle formation
to attack you, O Daughter of Zion."

24We have heard reports about them,
and our hands hang limp.
Anguish has gripped us,
pain like that of a woman in labor.
25Do not go out to the fields
or walk on the roads,
for the enemy has a sword,
and there is terror on every side.
26O my people, put on sackcloth
and roll in ashes;
mourn with bitter wailing
as for an only son,
for suddenly the destroyer
will come upon us.

27"I have made you a tester of metals
and my people the ore,
that you may observe
and test their ways.
28They are all hardened rebels,
going about to slander.
They are bronze and iron;
they all act corruptly.
29The bellows blow fiercely
to burn away the lead with fire,
but the refining goes on in vain;
the wicked are not purged out.
30They are called rejected silver,
because the LORD has rejected them."

4 / *Jeremiah 7:1–20*
Empty Religion

I AM AN ordained minster. I love the church. But there are days when I have my doubts about "organized" religion. I'm not exactly proud of the Crusades, the treatment of the Jews in the Middle Ages or the more recent fundraising scandals of the television evangelists. There are times when it seems that politics, power and social concerns are the primary moving and shaping forces of our churches. I am reminded on occasion that all that is done in the name of the Lord is not necessarily from the Lord. In front of the newly renovated temple Jeremiah called the people of Judah to examine their motives for their religious pursuits. What a shock it must have been for those who heard. Today, Jeremiah calls us to ponder: "Why do I serve God? Why am I going to church?"

Warming Up to God What would you do if someone stood at the door of your newly renovated church and told you and everyone who entered that you were hypocrites under the judgment of God?

Read Jeremiah 7:1–20.

7 This is the word that came to Jeremiah
from the LORD: 2"Stand at the gate of the
LORD's house and there proclaim this mes-
sage:

" 'Hear the word of the LORD, all you people of
Judah who come through these gates to worship
the LORD. 3This is what the LORD Almighty, the
God of Israel, says: Reform your ways and your

actions, and I will let you live in this place. 4Do
not trust in deceptive words and say, "This is the
temple of the LORD, the temple of the LORD, the
temple of the LORD!" 5If you really change your
ways and your actions and deal with each other
justly, 6if you do not oppress the alien, the father-
less or the widow and do not shed innocent blood
in this place, and if you do not follow other gods
to your own harm, 7then I will let you live in this
place, in the land I gave your forefathers for ever
and ever. 8But look, you are trusting in deceptive
words that are worthless.
9" 'Will you steal and murder, commit adultery
and perjury,[n] burn incense to Baal and follow
other gods you have not known, 10and then come
and stand before me in this house, which bears
my Name, and say, "We are safe"—safe to do all
these detestable things? 11Has this house, which
bears my Name, become a den of robbers to you?
But I have been watching! declares the LORD.
12" 'Go now to the place in Shiloh where I first
made a dwelling for my Name, and see what I did
to it because of the wickedness of my people Is-
rael. 13While you were doing all these things, de-
clares the LORD, I spoke to you again and again,
but you did not listen; I called you, but you did
not answer. 14Therefore, what I did to Shiloh I
will now do to the house that bears my Name, the
temple you trust in, the place I gave to you and
your fathers. 15I will thrust you from my pres-
ence, just as I did all your brothers, the people of
Ephraim.'
16"So do not pray for this people nor offer any
plea or petition for them; do not plead with me,
for I will not listen to you. 17Do you not see what
they are doing in the towns of Judah and in the
streets of Jerusalem? 18The children gather wood,
the fathers light the fire, and the women knead
the dough and make cakes of bread for the Queen
of Heaven. They pour out drink offerings to other
gods to provoke me to anger. 19But am I the one
they are provoking? declares the LORD. Are they
not rather harming themselves, to their own
shame?
20" 'Therefore this is what the Sovereign LORD
says: My anger and my wrath will be poured out
on this place, on man and beast, on the trees of
the field and on the fruit of the ground, and it will
burn and not be quenched.

[n]9 *Or and swear by false gods*

Discovering the Word 1. Jeremiah stands at the door of the temple and confronts those who enter. What is his message in verses 1–11? 2. In verse 4 Jeremiah repeats the phrase "The temple of the LORD" three times. What do you think he is getting at? 3. Under the reign of Josiah, Judah's last good king, the temple had been renovated and the law, which had been lost, was rediscovered. How was the law being handled by the people (vv. 4–9)? 4. How does the experience of Shiloh illustrate Jeremiah's message (vv. 12–20)? 5. God was angry with their idolatry and promised to judge it (vv. 16–20). Why do you think he was so upset with their false worship?

Applying the Word 1. In verse 11 God declares that he is watching. If God were to tell you that he was especially watching your church, what do you think he would see and say? 2. God, not the temple, should have been the object of their faith. How is it possible that the focus of our faith can drift from a person, God, to an object, like the temple? 3. What can we do to see that our own personal worship is pleasing to God?

Responding in Prayer Offer your praise to the God who is worthy of our worship.

Jeremiah 7:21—9:26

21" 'This is what the LORD Almighty, the God of
Israel, says: Go ahead, add your burnt offerings to
your other sacrifices and eat the meat yourselves!
22For when I brought your forefathers out of
Egypt and spoke to them, I did not just give them
commands about burnt offerings and sacrifices,
23but I gave them this command: Obey me, and
I will be your God and you will be my people.
Walk in all the ways I command you, that it may
go well with you. 24But they did not listen or pay
attention; instead, they followed the stubborn in-
clinations of their evil hearts. They went back-
ward and not forward. 25From the time your fore-
fathers left Egypt until now, day after day, again

and again I sent you my servants the prophets.
26 But they did not listen to me or pay attention.
They were stiff-necked and did more evil than
their forefathers.'

27 "When you tell them all this, they will not
listen to you; when you call to them, they will not
answer. 28 Therefore say to them, 'This is the na-
tion that has not obeyed the LORD its God or re-
sponded to correction. Truth has perished; it has
vanished from their lips. 29 Cut off your hair and
throw it away; take up a lament on the barren
heights, for the LORD has rejected and abandoned
this generation that is under his wrath.

30 " 'The people of Judah have done evil in my
eyes, declares the LORD. They have set up their
detestable idols in the house that bears my Name
and have defiled it. 31 They have built the high
places of Topheth in the Valley of Ben Hinnom to
burn their sons and daughters in the fire—some-
thing I did not command, nor did it enter my
mind. 32 So beware, the days are coming, declares
the LORD, when people will no longer call it To-
pheth or the Valley of Ben Hinnom, but the Val-
ley of Slaughter, for they will bury the dead in
Topheth until there is no more room. 33 Then the
carcasses of this people will become food for the
birds of the air and the beasts of the earth, and
there will be no one to frighten them away. 34 I
will bring an end to the sounds of joy and glad-
ness and to the voices of bride and bridegroom in
the towns of Judah and the streets of Jerusalem,
for the land will become desolate.

8 " 'At that time, declares the LORD, the
bones of the kings and officials of Judah,
the bones of the priests and prophets, and
the bones of the people of Jerusalem will be re-
moved from their graves. 2 They will be exposed
to the sun and the moon and all the stars of the
heavens, which they have loved and served and
which they have followed and consulted and wor-
shiped. They will not be gathered up or buried,
but will be like refuse lying on the ground.
3 Wherever I banish them, all the survivors of this
evil nation will prefer death to life, declares the
LORD Almighty.'

4 "Say to them, 'This is what the LORD says:

" 'When men fall down, do they not get up?
When a man turns away, does he not
return?
5 Why then have these people turned away?
Why does Jerusalem always turn away?
They cling to deceit;
they refuse to return.
6 I have listened attentively,
but they do not say what is right.
No one repents of his wickedness,
saying, "What have I done?"
Each pursues his own course
like a horse charging into battle.
7 Even the stork in the sky
knows her appointed seasons,
and the dove, the swift and the thrush
observe the time of their migration.
But my people do not know
the requirements of the LORD.

8 " 'How can you say, "We are wise,
for we have the law of the LORD,"
when actually the lying pen of the scribes
has handled it falsely?
9 The wise will be put to shame;
they will be dismayed and trapped.
Since they have rejected the word of the LORD,
what kind of wisdom do they have?
10 Therefore I will give their wives to other men
and their fields to new owners.
From the least to the greatest,
all are greedy for gain;
prophets and priests alike,
all practice deceit.
11 They dress the wound of my people
as though it were not serious.
"Peace, peace," they say,
when there is no peace.
12 Are they ashamed of their loathsome conduct?
No, they have no shame at all;
they do not even know how to blush.
So they will fall among the fallen;
they will be brought down when they are
punished,
says the LORD.

13 " 'I will take away their harvest,
declares the LORD.
There will be no grapes on the vine.
There will be no figs on the tree,
and their leaves will wither.
What I have given them
will be taken from them.[o]' "

14 "Why are we sitting here?
Gather together!
Let us flee to the fortified cities

[o] 13 The meaning of the Hebrew for this sentence is uncertain.

and perish there!
For the LORD our God has doomed us to perish
and given us poisoned water to drink,
because we have sinned against him.
15We hoped for peace
but no good has come,
for a time of healing
but there was only terror.
16The snorting of the enemy's horses
is heard from Dan;
at the neighing of their stallions
the whole land trembles.
They have come to devour
the land and everything in it,
the city and all who live there."

17"See, I will send venomous snakes among you,
vipers that cannot be charmed,
and they will bite you,"
declares the LORD.

18O my Comforter[p] in sorrow,
my heart is faint within me.
19Listen to the cry of my people
from a land far away:
"Is the LORD not in Zion?
Is her King no longer there?"

"Why have they provoked me to anger with their images,
with their worthless foreign idols?"

20"The harvest is past,
the summer has ended,
and we are not saved."

21Since my people are crushed, I am crushed;
I mourn, and horror grips me.
22Is there no balm in Gilead?
Is there no physician there?
Why then is there no healing
for the wound of my people?

9 1Oh, that my head were a spring of water
and my eyes a fountain of tears!
I would weep day and night
for the slain of my people.
2Oh, that I had in the desert
a lodging place for travelers,
so that I might leave my people
and go away from them;
for they are all adulterers,
a crowd of unfaithful people.

3"They make ready their tongue
like a bow, to shoot lies;
it is not by truth
that they triumph[q] in the land.
They go from one sin to another;
they do not acknowledge me,"
declares the LORD.
4"Beware of your friends;
do not trust your brothers.
For every brother is a deceiver,[r]
and every friend a slanderer.
5Friend deceives friend,
and no one speaks the truth.
They have taught their tongues to lie;
they weary themselves with sinning.
6You[s] live in the midst of deception;
in their deceit they refuse to acknowledge me,"
declares the LORD.

7Therefore this is what the LORD Almighty says:
"See, I will refine and test them,
for what else can I do
because of the sin of my people?
8Their tongue is a deadly arrow;
it speaks with deceit.
With his mouth each speaks cordially to his neighbor,
but in his heart he sets a trap for him.
9Should I not punish them for this?"
declares the LORD.
"Should I not avenge myself
on such a nation as this?"

10I will weep and wail for the mountains
and take up a lament concerning the desert pastures.
They are desolate and untraveled,
and the lowing of cattle is not heard.
The birds of the air have fled
and the animals are gone.

11"I will make Jerusalem a heap of ruins,
a haunt of jackals;
and I will lay waste the towns of Judah
so no one can live there."

12What man is wise enough to understand this?
Who has been instructed by the LORD and can

p18 The meaning of the Hebrew for this word is uncertain. q3 Or *lies; / they are not valiant for truth* r4 Or *a deceiving Jacob*
s6 That is, Jeremiah (the Hebrew is singular)

explain it? Why has the land been ruined and laid
waste like a desert that no one can cross?
13The LORD said, "It is because they have for-
saken my law, which I set before them; they have
not obeyed me or followed my law. 14Instead,
they have followed the stubbornness of their
hearts; they have followed the Baals, as their fa-
thers taught them." 15Therefore, this is what the
LORD Almighty, the God of Israel, says: "See, I will
make this people eat bitter food and drink poi-
soned water. 16I will scatter them among nations
that neither they nor their fathers have known,
and I will pursue them with the sword until I
have destroyed them."

17This is what the LORD Almighty says:

"Consider now! Call for the wailing women
to come;
send for the most skillful of them.
18Let them come quickly
and wail over us
till our eyes overflow with tears
and water streams from our eyelids.
19The sound of wailing is heard from Zion:
'How ruined we are!
How great is our shame!
We must leave our land
because our houses are in ruins.' "

20Now, O women, hear the word of the LORD;
open your ears to the words of his mouth.
Teach your daughters how to wail;
teach one another a lament.
21Death has climbed in through our windows
and has entered our fortresses;
it has cut off the children from the streets
and the young men from the public
squares.

22Say, "This is what the LORD declares:

" 'The dead bodies of men will lie
like refuse on the open field,
like cut grain behind the reaper,
with no one to gather them.' "

23This is what the LORD says:

"Let not the wise man boast of his wisdom
or the strong man boast of his strength
or the rich man boast of his riches,
24but let him who boasts boast about this:
that he understands and knows me,
that I am the LORD, who exercises kindness,
justice and righteousness on earth,
for in these I delight,"
declares the LORD.

25"The days are coming," declares the LORD,
"when I will punish all who are circumcised only
in the flesh— 26Egypt, Judah, Edom, Ammon,
Moab and all who live in the desert in distant
places.[t] For all these nations are really uncir-
cumcised, and even the whole house of Israel is
uncircumcised in heart."

[t]26 Or *desert and who clip the hair by their foreheads*

5 / *Jeremiah 10:1–16*
God or Idols?

A GARDEN CATALOG offers inflatable owls and fake falcons to scare away small birds from your fruit trees. For best effect, the catalog says, keep moving them around. Even the dumbest bird knows that a real owl or hawk doesn't sit frozen in the same spot day after day. Like those garden fakes, the idols of the nations surrounding Israel were lifeless and powerless.

Warming Up to God What has been an idol to you, and how did you come to reject it and choose the Lord?

Read Jeremiah 10:1–16.

10 Hear what the LORD says to you, O house of Israel. [2]This is what the LORD says:

“Do not learn the ways of the nations
or be terrified by signs in the sky,
though the nations are terrified by them.
[3]For the customs of the peoples are worthless;
they cut a tree out of the forest,
and a craftsman shapes it with his chisel.
[4]They adorn it with silver and gold;
they fasten it with hammer and nails
so it will not totter.
[5]Like a scarecrow in a melon patch,
their idols cannot speak;
they must be carried
because they cannot walk.
Do not fear them;
they can do no harm
nor can they do any good.”
[6]No one is like you, O LORD;
you are great,
and your name is mighty in power.
[7]Who should not revere you,
O King of the nations?
This is your due.
Among all the wise men of the nations
and in all their kingdoms,
there is no one like you.
[8]They are all senseless and foolish;
they are taught by worthless wooden idols.
[9]Hammered silver is brought from Tarshish
and gold from Uphaz.
What the craftsman and goldsmith have made
is then dressed in blue and purple—
all made by skilled workers.
[10]But the LORD is the true God;
he is the living God, the eternal King.
When he is angry, the earth trembles;
the nations cannot endure his wrath.

[11]“Tell them this: ‘These gods, who did not make the heavens and the earth, will perish from the earth and from under the heavens.’ ”[u]

[12]But God made the earth by his power;
he founded the world by his wisdom
and stretched out the heavens by his understanding.
[13]When he thunders, the waters in the heavens roar;
he makes clouds rise from the ends of the earth.
He sends lightning with the rain
and brings out the wind from his storehouses.

[14]Everyone is senseless and without knowledge;
every goldsmith is shamed by his idols.
His images are a fraud;
they have no breath in them.
[15]They are worthless, the objects of mockery;
when their judgment comes, they will perish.
[16]He who is the Portion of Jacob is not like these,
for he is the Maker of all things,
including Israel, the tribe of his inheritance—
the LORD Almighty is his name.

[u]*11* The text of this verse is in Aramaic.

Discovering the Word 1. Throughout this passage how is God contrasted with idols? 2. How do idols betray their powerlessness (v. 5)? 3. Why should people revere the Lord (vv. 6–7, 10, 12–13)? 4. What will be the fate of false gods (vv. 11, 15)? 5. How is the Lord’s power shown in his creation (vv. 12–13, 16)?

Applying the Word 1. How can the humorous images in this passage, especially verses 4–5, give you a fresh perspective on the idols that tempt you? 2. In what ways is the Lord superior to your most appealing idols?

Responding in Prayer Praise the Lord for being the only true God. Commit yourself again to worshiping him alone.

Jeremiah 10:17—11:23

17Gather up your belongings to leave the land,
you who live under siege.
18For this is what the LORD says:
"At this time I will hurl out
those who live in this land;
I will bring distress on them
so that they may be captured."

19Woe to me because of my injury!
My wound is incurable!
Yet I said to myself,
"This is my sickness, and I must endure it."
20My tent is destroyed;
all its ropes are snapped.
My sons are gone from me and are no more;
no one is left now to pitch my tent
or to set up my shelter.
21The shepherds are senseless
and do not inquire of the LORD;
so they do not prosper
and all their flock is scattered.
22Listen! The report is coming—
a great commotion from the land of the north!
It will make the towns of Judah desolate,
a haunt of jackals.

23I know, O LORD, that a man's life is not his own;
it is not for man to direct his steps.
24Correct me, LORD, but only with justice—
not in your anger,
lest you reduce me to nothing.
25Pour out your wrath on the nations
that do not acknowledge you,
on the peoples who do not call on your name.
For they have devoured Jacob;
they have devoured him completely
and destroyed his homeland.

11 This is the word that came to Jere-
miah from the LORD: 2"Listen to the
terms of this covenant and tell
them to the people of Judah and to those who live
in Jerusalem. 3Tell them that this is what the
LORD, the God of Israel, says: 'Cursed is the man
who does not obey the terms of this covenant—
4the terms I commanded your forefathers when I
brought them out of Egypt, out of the iron-smelt-
ing furnace.' I said, 'Obey me and do everything I
command you, and you will be my people, and I
will be your God. 5Then I will fulfill the oath I
swore to your forefathers, to give them a land
flowing with milk and honey'—the land you pos-
sess today."

I answered, "Amen, LORD."

6The LORD said to me, "Proclaim all these words
in the towns of Judah and in the streets of Jerusa-
lem: 'Listen to the terms of this covenant and fol-
low them. 7From the time I brought your forefa-
thers up from Egypt until today, I warned them
again and again, saying, "Obey me." 8But they did
not listen or pay attention; instead, they followed
the stubbornness of their evil hearts. So I brought
on them all the curses of the covenant I had com-
manded them to follow but that they did not
keep.' "

9Then the LORD said to me, "There is a conspir-
acy among the people of Judah and those who
live in Jerusalem. 10They have returned to the sins
of their forefathers, who refused to listen to my
words. They have followed other gods to serve
them. Both the house of Israel and the house of
Judah have broken the covenant I made with
their forefathers. 11Therefore this is what the LORD
says: 'I will bring on them a disaster they cannot
escape. Although they cry out to me, I will not
listen to them. 12The towns of Judah and the peo-
ple of Jerusalem will go and cry out to the gods to
whom they burn incense, but they will not help
them at all when disaster strikes. 13You have as
many gods as you have towns, O Judah; and the
altars you have set up to burn incense to that
shameful god Baal are as many as the streets of
Jerusalem.'

14"Do not pray for this people nor offer any
plea or petition for them, because I will not listen
when they call to me in the time of their distress.

15"What is my beloved doing in my temple
as she works out her evil schemes with many?
Can consecrated meat avert ⌞your punishment⌟?
When you engage in your wickedness,
then you rejoice.[v]"

[v]15 Or *Could consecrated meat avert your punishment? / Then you would rejoice*

16The LORD called you a thriving olive tree
with fruit beautiful in form.
But with the roar of a mighty storm
he will set it on fire,
and its branches will be broken.
17The LORD Almighty, who planted you, has de-
creed disaster for you, because the house of Israel
and the house of Judah have done evil and pro-
voked me to anger by burning incense to Baal.
18Because the LORD revealed their plot to me, I
knew it, for at that time he showed me what they
were doing. 19I had been like a gentle lamb led to
the slaughter; I did not realize that they had plot-
ted against me, saying,

"Let us destroy the tree and its fruit;
let us cut him off from the land of the
living,
that his name be remembered no
more."
20But, O LORD Almighty, you who judge
righteously
and test the heart and mind,
let me see your vengeance upon them,
for to you I have committed my cause.

21"Therefore this is what the LORD says about
the men of Anathoth who are seeking your life
and saying, 'Do not prophesy in the name of the
LORD or you will die by our hands'— 22therefore
this is what the LORD Almighty says: 'I will punish
them. Their young men will die by the sword,
their sons and daughters by famine. 23Not even a
remnant will be left to them, because I will bring
disaster on the men of Anathoth in the year of
their punishment.' "

6 / *Jeremiah 12*
An Honest Complaint

GRIPE! GRIPE! NOBODY likes a griper. One of the most surprising things about the Bible is that it faithfully records so many complaints against the Lord by his own people. God could have edited those protests out of the Scriptures, but he listened to them patiently and still lets us read them centuries later.

Warming Up to God When are you most eager to complain to God, and when are you afraid to complain?

Read Jeremiah 12.

12 You are always righteous, O LORD,
when I bring a case before you.
Yet I would speak with you about
your justice:
Why does the way of the wicked prosper?
Why do all the faithless live at ease?
2You have planted them, and they have taken
root;
they grow and bear fruit.
You are always on their lips
but far from their hearts.
3Yet you know me, O LORD;
you see me and test my thoughts about
you.
Drag them off like sheep to be butchered!
Set them apart for the day of slaughter!
4How long will the land lie parched[w]
and the grass in every field be withered?
Because those who live in it are wicked,
the animals and birds have perished.
Moreover, the people are saying,
"He will not see what happens to us."

5"If you have raced with men on foot
and they have worn you out,
how can you compete with horses?
If you stumble in safe country,[x]
how will you manage in the thickets by[y]
the Jordan?
6Your brothers, your own family—
even they have betrayed you;
they have raised a loud cry against you.
Do not trust them,

w4 Or *land mourn* x5 Or *If you put your trust in a land of safety*
y5 Or *the flooding of*

though they speak well of you.
7"I will forsake my house,
abandon my inheritance;
I will give the one I love
into the hands of her enemies.
8My inheritance has become to me
like a lion in the forest.
She roars at me;
therefore I hate her.
9Has not my inheritance become to me
like a speckled bird of prey
that other birds of prey surround and
attack?
Go and gather all the wild beasts;
bring them to devour.
10Many shepherds will ruin my vineyard
and trample down my field;
they will turn my pleasant field
into a desolate wasteland.
11It will be made a wasteland,
parched and desolate before me;
the whole land will be laid waste
because there is no one who cares.
12Over all the barren heights in the desert
destroyers will swarm,
for the sword of the LORD will devour
from one end of the land to the other;
no one will be safe.
13They will sow wheat but reap thorns;
they will wear themselves out but gain
nothing.
So bear the shame of your harvest
because of the LORD's fierce anger."

14This is what the LORD says: "As for all my
wicked neighbors who seize the inheritance I
gave my people Israel, I will uproot them from
their lands and I will uproot the house of Judah
from among them. 15But after I uproot them, I
will again have compassion and will bring each of
them back to his own inheritance and his own
country. 16And if they learn well the ways of my
people and swear by my name, saying, 'As surely
as the LORD lives'—even as they once taught my
people to swear by Baal—then they will be estab-
lished among my people. 17But if any nation does
not listen, I will completely uproot and destroy
it," declares the LORD.

Discovering the Word 1. What irked Jeremiah (vv. 1–4)? 2. How did God challenge Jeremiah (vv. 5–6)? 3. What explanation did the Lord give for letting his people be trampled on (vv. 7–13)? 4. What would be the final fate of those who devoured Israel (vv. 14–17)? 5. How would God offer mercy to Israel's enemies (vv. 15–16)?

Applying the Word 1. Think of a time you shared Jeremiah's complaint. Perhaps that time is right now. How does this passage shed light on what might be going on behind the scenes? 2. What insights has the Lord given you in response to your complaints? 3. What have you learned that can help you turn your complaints into praise?

Responding in Prayer Do not be afraid to honestly tell God how you feel about something unfair, and as you pray, stay open to what he wants to show you through unfair circumstances.

7 / *Jeremiah 13*
Spoiled Bond

FIRM COMMITMENTS ARE an important part of our lives. The bank you borrow money from wants to know your credit record and your assets to see if you can keep your commitment to repay your loan. And be careful about your business partners. Can they keep a commitment? You sign a binding contract with someone who has a history of breaking them at your peril. Think long and hard about the commitment marriage involves. Marry someone who has a series of former partners, and the chances are good that you will end up with a broken heart.

God especially doesn't like those who make commitments of convenience. He has high standards for us and for himself. When he makes a commitment, he stakes his life on it. Jesus Christ is the evidence. He expects the same sort of fidelity in return. Just as there are painful consequences when a business contract is broken or when a marriage partner cheats, so there are painful consequences when we default on our commitments to God.

Warming Up to God 1. What were the consequences of someone failing to keep their commitment to you? How did you feel?

Read Jeremiah 13.

13 This is what the LORD said to me:
"Go and buy a linen belt and put it
around your waist, but do not let it
touch water." 2So I bought a belt, as the LORD
directed, and put it around my waist.
3Then the word of the LORD came to me a sec-
ond time: 4"Take the belt you bought and are
wearing around your waist, and go now to Pe-
rath[z] and hide it there in a crevice in the rocks."
5So I went and hid it at Perath, as the LORD
told me.
6Many days later the LORD said to me, "Go now
to Perath and get the belt I told you to hide
there." 7So I went to Perath and dug up the belt
and took it from the place where I had hidden it,
but now it was ruined and completely useless.
8Then the word of the LORD came to me: 9"This
is what the LORD says: 'In the same way I will ruin
the pride of Judah and the great pride of Jerusa-
lem. 10These wicked people, who refuse to listen
to my words, who follow the stubbornness of
their hearts and go after other gods to serve and
worship them, will be like this belt—completely
useless! 11For as a belt is bound around a man's
waist, so I bound the whole house of Israel and
the whole house of Judah to me,' declares the
LORD, 'to be my people for my renown and praise
and honor. But they have not listened.'
12"Say to them: 'This is what the LORD, the God
of Israel, says: Every wineskin should be filled
with wine.' And if they say to you, 'Don't we
know that every wineskin should be filled with
wine?' 13then tell them, 'This is what the LORD
says: I am going to fill with drunkenness all who
live in this land, including the kings who sit on
David's throne, the priests, the prophets and all
those living in Jerusalem. 14I will smash them one
against the other, fathers and sons alike, declares
the LORD. I will allow no pity or mercy or compas-
sion to keep me from destroying them.' "

15Hear and pay attention,
do not be arrogant,
for the LORD has spoken.
16Give glory to the LORD your God
before he brings the darkness,
before your feet stumble
on the darkening hills.
You hope for light,
but he will turn it to thick darkness
and change it to deep gloom.
17But if you do not listen,
I will weep in secret
because of your pride;
my eyes will weep bitterly,
overflowing with tears,
because the LORD's flock will be taken captive.

18Say to the king and to the queen mother,
"Come down from your thrones,
for your glorious crowns
will fall from your heads."
19The cities in the Negev will be shut up,
and there will be no one to open them.
All Judah will be carried into exile,
carried completely away.

20Lift up your eyes and see
those who are coming from the north.
Where is the flock that was entrusted to you,
the sheep of which you boasted?
21What will you say when ⌞the LORD⌟ sets over you
those you cultivated as your special allies?
Will not pain grip you
like that of a woman in labor?
22And if you ask yourself,
"Why has this happened to me?"—
it is because of your many sins
that your skirts have been torn off
and your body mistreated.
23Can the Ethiopian[a] change his skin
or the leopard its spots?
Neither can you do good
who are accustomed to doing evil.

24"I will scatter you like chaff
driven by the desert wind.

[z]4 Or possibly *the Euphrates*; also in verses 5-7 [a]23 Hebrew *Cushite* (probably a person from the upper Nile region)

25 This is your lot,
the portion I have decreed for you,"
declares the LORD,
"because you have forgotten me
and trusted in false gods.
26 I will pull up your skirts over your face
that your shame may be seen—
27 your adulteries and lustful
neighings,
your shameless prostitution!
I have seen your detestable acts
on the hills and in the fields.
Woe to you, O Jerusalem!
How long will you be unclean?"

Discovering the Word 1. Describe the task that God gave to Jeremiah in verses 1–11. 2. What is the point of this object lesson (vv. 9–11)? 3. A linen belt was more than functional; it was an ornament of dignity and pride. How might Israel and Judah have been a source of pride to God? 4. Jeremiah's message in verses 12–17 is directed at the leaders. In what ways is pride and arrogance a problem in these verses? 5. What could be the remedy for the coming judgment (vv. 15–17, 20, 23, 25)?

Applying the Word 1. One purpose of a belt was to tie things together. What things might come apart in your life if you were no longer bound to the Lord? 2. God wants to take pride in a relationship with his people. How can this insight enrich your relationship with him? 3. How can God's Word strengthen our bonds and commitments?

Responding in Prayer Giving glory to God puts the focus back on him and puts us in our proper place. Give glory to God for yourself, your family, your work and your whole course of life.

Jeremiah 14:1—17:4

14 This is the word of the LORD to Jeremiah concerning the drought:

2 "Judah mourns,
her cities languish;
they wail for the land,
and a cry goes up from Jerusalem.
3 The nobles send their servants for water;
they go to the cisterns
but find no water.
They return with their jars unfilled;
dismayed and despairing,
they cover their heads.
4 The ground is cracked
because there is no rain in the land;
the farmers are dismayed
and cover their heads.
5 Even the doe in the field
deserts her newborn fawn
because there is no grass.
6 Wild donkeys stand on the barren heights
and pant like jackals;
their eyesight fails
for lack of pasture."
7 Although our sins testify against us,
O LORD, do something for the sake of your
name.
For our backsliding is great;
we have sinned against you.
8 O Hope of Israel,
its Savior in times of distress,
why are you like a stranger in the land,
like a traveler who stays only a night?
9 Why are you like a man taken by surprise,
like a warrior powerless to save?
You are among us, O LORD,
and we bear your name;
do not forsake us!

10 This is what the LORD says about this people:

"They greatly love to wander;
they do not restrain their feet.
So the LORD does not accept them;
he will now remember their wickedness
and punish them for their sins."

11 Then the LORD said to me, "Do not pray for
the well-being of this people. 12 Although they
fast, I will not listen to their cry; though they
offer burnt offerings and grain offerings, I will not
accept them. Instead, I will destroy them with the
sword, famine and plague."
13 But I said, "Ah, Sovereign LORD, the prophets
keep telling them, 'You will not see the sword or

suffer famine. Indeed, I will give you lasting peace
in this place.' "
14Then the LORD said to me, "The prophets are
prophesying lies in my name. I have not sent
them or appointed them or spoken to them. They
are prophesying to you false visions, divinations,
idolatries[b] and the delusions of their own minds.
15Therefore, this is what the LORD says about the
prophets who are prophesying in my name: I did
not send them, yet they are saying, 'No sword or
famine will touch this land.' Those same prophets
will perish by sword and famine. 16And the peo-
ple they are prophesying to will be thrown out
into the streets of Jerusalem because of the famine
and sword. There will be no one to bury them or
their wives, their sons or their daughters. I will
pour out on them the calamity they deserve.

17"Speak this word to them:

" 'Let my eyes overflow with tears
night and day without ceasing;
for my virgin daughter—my people—
has suffered a grievous wound,
a crushing blow.
18If I go into the country,
I see those slain by the sword;
if I go into the city,
I see the ravages of famine.
Both prophet and priest
have gone to a land they know not.' "
19Have you rejected Judah completely?
Do you despise Zion?
Why have you afflicted us
so that we cannot be healed?
We hoped for peace
but no good has come,
for a time of healing
but there is only terror.
20O LORD, we acknowledge our wickedness
and the guilt of our fathers;
we have indeed sinned against you.
21For the sake of your name do not despise us;
do not dishonor your glorious throne.
Remember your covenant with us
and do not break it.
22Do any of the worthless idols of the nations
bring rain?
Do the skies themselves send down
showers?
No, it is you, O LORD our God.
Therefore our hope is in you,
for you are the one who does all this.

15

Then the LORD said to me: "Even if
Moses and Samuel were to stand
before me, my heart would not go
out to this people. Send them away from my pres-
ence! Let them go! 2And if they ask you, 'Where
shall we go?' tell them, 'This is what the LORD
says:

" 'Those destined for death, to death;
those for the sword, to the sword;
those for starvation, to starvation;
those for captivity, to captivity.'

3"I will send four kinds of destroyers against
them," declares the LORD, "the sword to kill and
the dogs to drag away and the birds of the air and
the beasts of the earth to devour and destroy. 4I
will make them abhorrent to all the kingdoms of
the earth because of what Manasseh son of Heze-
kiah king of Judah did in Jerusalem.

5"Who will have pity on you, O Jerusalem?
Who will mourn for you?
Who will stop to ask how you are?
6You have rejected me," declares the LORD.
"You keep on backsliding.
So I will lay hands on you and destroy you;
I can no longer show compassion.
7I will winnow them with a winnowing fork
at the city gates of the land.
I will bring bereavement and destruction on
my people,
for they have not changed their ways.
8I will make their widows more numerous
than the sand of the sea.
At midday I will bring a destroyer
against the mothers of their young men;
suddenly I will bring down on them
anguish and terror.
9The mother of seven will grow faint
and breathe her last.
Her sun will set while it is still day;
she will be disgraced and humiliated.
I will put the survivors to the sword
before their enemies,"
declares the LORD.

10Alas, my mother, that you gave me birth,
a man with whom the whole land strives
and contends!
I have neither lent nor borrowed,

[b]14 *Or visions, worthless divinations*

yet everyone curses me.

11The LORD said,

"Surely I will deliver you for a good purpose;
surely I will make your enemies plead with you
in times of disaster and times of distress.

12"Can a man break iron—
iron from the north—or bronze?
13Your wealth and your treasures
I will give as plunder, without charge,
because of all your sins
throughout your country.
14I will enslave you to your enemies
in[c] a land you do not know,
for my anger will kindle a fire
that will burn against you."

15You understand, O LORD;
remember me and care for me.
Avenge me on my persecutors.
You are long-suffering—do not take me away;
think of how I suffer reproach for your sake.
16When your words came, I ate them;
they were my joy and my heart's delight,
for I bear your name,
O LORD God Almighty.
17I never sat in the company of revelers,
never made merry with them;
I sat alone because your hand was on me
and you had filled me with indignation.
18Why is my pain unending
and my wound grievous and incurable?
Will you be to me like a deceptive brook,
like a spring that fails?

19Therefore this is what the LORD says:

"If you repent, I will restore you
that you may serve me;
if you utter worthy, not worthless, words,
you will be my spokesman.
Let this people turn to you,
but you must not turn to them.
20I will make you a wall to this people,
a fortified wall of bronze;
they will fight against you
but will not overcome you,
for I am with you
to rescue and save you,"
declares the LORD.
21"I will save you from the hands of the wicked
and redeem you from the grasp of the cruel."

16 Then the word of the LORD came to
me: 2"You must not marry and have
sons or daughters in this place."
3For this is what the LORD says about the sons and
daughters born in this land and about the women
who are their mothers and the men who are their
fathers: 4"They will die of deadly diseases. They
will not be mourned or buried but will be like
refuse lying on the ground. They will perish by
sword and famine, and their dead bodies will become food for the birds of the air and the beasts
of the earth."
5For this is what the LORD says: "Do not enter a
house where there is a funeral meal; do not go to
mourn or show sympathy, because I have withdrawn my blessing, my love and my pity from
this people," declares the LORD. 6"Both high and
low will die in this land. They will not be buried
or mourned, and no one will cut himself or shave
his head for them. 7No one will offer food to comfort those who mourn for the dead—not even for
a father or a mother—nor will anyone give them
a drink to console them.
8"And do not enter a house where there is
feasting and sit down to eat and drink. 9For this
is what the LORD Almighty, the God of Israel, says:
Before your eyes and in your days I will bring an
end to the sounds of joy and gladness and to the
voices of bride and bridegroom in this place.
10"When you tell these people all this and they
ask you, 'Why has the LORD decreed such a great
disaster against us? What wrong have we done?
What sin have we committed against the LORD our
God?' 11then say to them, 'It is because your fathers forsook me,' declares the LORD, 'and followed other gods and served and worshiped
them. They forsook me and did not keep my law.
12But you have behaved more wickedly than your
fathers. See how each of you is following the
stubbornness of his evil heart instead of obeying
me. 13So I will throw you out of this land into a
land neither you nor your fathers have known,
and there you will serve other gods day and night,
for I will show you no favor.'
14"However, the days are coming," declares the
LORD, "when men will no longer say, 'As surely as
the LORD lives, who brought the Israelites up out

[c]14 Some Hebrew manuscripts, Septuagint and Syriac (see also Jer. 17:4); most Hebrew manuscripts *I will cause your enemies to bring you / into*

of Egypt,' [15]but they will say, 'As surely as the
Lord lives, who brought the Israelites up out of
the land of the north and out of all the countries
where he had banished them.' For I will restore
them to the land I gave their forefathers.

[16]"But now I will send for many fishermen,"
declares the Lord, "and they will catch them. Af-
ter that I will send for many hunters, and they
will hunt them down on every mountain and hill
and from the crevices of the rocks. [17]My eyes are
on all their ways; they are not hidden from me,
nor is their sin concealed from my eyes. [18]I will
repay them double for their wickedness and their
sin, because they have defiled my land with the
lifeless forms of their vile images and have filled
my inheritance with their detestable idols."

[19]O Lord, my strength and my fortress,
my refuge in time of distress,
to you the nations will come
from the ends of the earth and say,
"Our fathers possessed nothing but false gods,
worthless idols that did them no good.
[20]Do men make their own gods?
Yes, but they are not gods!"

[21]"Therefore I will teach them—
this time I will teach them
my power and might.
Then they will know
that my name is the Lord.

17 "Judah's sin is engraved with an
iron tool,
inscribed with a flint point,
on the tablets of their hearts
and on the horns of their altars.
[2]Even their children remember
their altars and Asherah poles[d]
beside the spreading trees
and on the high hills.
[3]My mountain in the land
and your[e] wealth and all your treasures
I will give away as plunder,
together with your high places,
because of sin throughout your country.
[4]Through your own fault you will lose
the inheritance I gave you.
I will enslave you to your enemies
in a land you do not know,
for you have kindled my anger,
and it will burn forever."

[d]2 That is, symbols of the goddess Asherah [e]2,3 Or *hills* / [3]*and the mountains of the land. / Your*

8 / *Jeremiah 17:5–18*
Blessings in Troubled Times

AFTER BEING BATTERED all day by a hot south wind, the squash vines and tomato plants in our garden drooped in the fading light. They practically cried out for water from the sprinkler. But the trees in the yard were green and flourishing, though they required far more water than the squash and tomatoes. The deep roots of the trees found a hidden source of water far below the surface where the garden plants struggled. Like those trees, people who trust in the Lord are not at the mercy of surface circumstances because we have deep roots to our eternal Source.

Warming Up to God When have you experienced God's strength in a difficult time?

Read Jeremiah 17:5–18.

[5]This is what the Lord says:

"Cursed is the one who trusts in man,
who depends on flesh for his strength
and whose heart turns away from the Lord.
[6]He will be like a bush in the wastelands;
he will not see prosperity when it comes.
He will dwell in the parched places of the
desert,
in a salt land where no one lives.
[7]"But blessed is the man who trusts in the
Lord,
whose confidence is in him.

[8]He will be like a tree planted by the water
that sends out its roots by the stream.
It does not fear when heat comes;
its leaves are always green.
It has no worries in a year of drought
and never fails to bear fruit."

[9]The heart is deceitful above all things
and beyond cure.
Who can understand it?

[10]"I the LORD search the heart
and examine the mind,
to reward a man according to his conduct,
according to what his deeds deserve."

[11]Like a partridge that hatches eggs it did not lay
is the man who gains riches by unjust means.
When his life is half gone, they will desert him,
and in the end he will prove to be a fool.

[12]A glorious throne, exalted from the beginning,
is the place of our sanctuary.
[13]O LORD, the hope of Israel,
all who forsake you will be put to shame.
Those who turn away from you will be written in the dust
because they have forsaken the LORD,
the spring of living water.

[14]Heal me, O LORD, and I will be healed;
save me and I will be saved,
for you are the one I praise.
[15]They keep saying to me,
"Where is the word of the LORD?
Let it now be fulfilled!"
[16]I have not run away from being your shepherd;
you know I have not desired the day of despair.
What passes my lips is open before you.
[17]Do not be a terror to me;
you are my refuge in the day of disaster.
[18]Let my persecutors be put to shame,
but keep me from shame;
let them be terrified,
but keep me from terror.
Bring on them the day of disaster;
destroy them with double destruction.

Discovering the Word 1. What geographical and human conditions in Jeremiah's society are described in relation to one another (vv. 5–8, 11, 15–18)? 2. Why will the person who relies on human strength be disappointed (vv. 5–6)? 3. How does God provide for the person who relies on him instead of on human strength (vv. 7–8)? 4. What is the state of the human heart before God (vv. 9–10)? 5. What did Jeremiah continue to hope for (vv. 14–18)?

Applying the Word 1. What "drought conditions" are you facing now? 2. In what ways do you find it easier to trust someone or something else besides God to see you through those circumstances? 3. How does God's promise in verses 7–8 give you confidence?

Responding in Prayer Bring the most difficult circumstances of your life to the Lord. Remembering the deceitfulness of the human heart, acknowledge any ways in which you are trusting something or someone besides God. Renew your trust in him and allow the "living water" (v. 13) to refresh you.

Jeremiah 17:19–27

[19]This is what the LORD said to me: "Go and
stand at the gate of the people, through which the
kings of Judah go in and out; stand also at all the
other gates of Jerusalem. [20]Say to them, 'Hear the
word of the LORD, O kings of Judah and all people
of Judah and everyone living in Jerusalem who
come through these gates. [21]This is what the LORD
says: Be careful not to carry a load on the Sabbath
day or bring it through the gates of Jerusalem.
[22]Do not bring a load out of your houses or do
any work on the Sabbath, but keep the Sabbath
day holy, as I commanded your forefathers. [23]Yet
they did not listen or pay attention; they were
stiff-necked and would not listen or respond to
discipline. [24]But if you are careful to obey me,
declares the LORD, and bring no load through the
gates of this city on the Sabbath, but keep the
Sabbath day holy by not doing any work on it,

[25]then kings who sit on David's throne will come through the gates of this city with their officials. They and their officials will come riding in chariots and on horses, accompanied by the men of Judah and those living in Jerusalem, and this city will be inhabited forever. [26]People will come from the towns of Judah and the villages around Jerusalem, from the territory of Benjamin and the western foothills, from the hill country and the Negev, bringing burnt offerings and sacrifices, grain offerings, incense and thank offerings to the house of the LORD. [27]But if you do not obey me to keep the Sabbath day holy by not carrying any load as you come through the gates of Jerusalem on the Sabbath day, then I will kindle an unquenchable fire in the gates of Jerusalem that will consume her fortresses.' "

9 / *Jeremiah 18:1–17*
God's Shaping Hand

ONE OF MY sons just got braces. He is not happy about it. For the next three years his mouth is going to be full of metal and rubber bands that push and pull his teeth and jaw back into shape. Three years seems like a long time, but moving flesh and bone is difficult. Braces are inconvenient and painful, but they will improve my son's mouth and health for the rest of his life.

God is interested in shaping us, not just our teeth, but our whole being. It's a big task. Shaping souls is difficult, takes time, and requires divine power and skills. Unlike gums, teeth and bone, souls don't always yield to the shaping pressures of the divine hand. If they do, it takes a lifetime of God's pressures to conform to the end goal, the image of Christ. Jeremiah didn't know about braces, nor did he know the name of Jesus Christ, but he did know that God is in the business of shaping our lives.

Warming Up to God Recall one or two major events that have been a significant shaping influence in your life. How did they affect you for good or for ill?

Read Jeremiah 18:1–17.

18 This is the word that came to Jeremiah from the LORD: [2]"Go down to the potter's house, and there I will give you my message." [3]So I went down to the potter's house, and I saw him working at the wheel. [4]But the pot he was shaping from the clay was marred in his hands; so the potter formed it into another pot, shaping it as seemed best to him.

[5]Then the word of the LORD came to me: [6]"O house of Israel, can I not do with you as this potter does?" declares the LORD. "Like clay in the hand of the potter, so are you in my hand, O house of Israel. [7]If at any time I announce that a nation or kingdom is to be uprooted, torn down and destroyed, [8]and if that nation I warned repents of its evil, then I will relent and not inflict on it the disaster I had planned. [9]And if at another time I announce that a nation or kingdom is to be built up and planted, [10]and if it does evil in my sight and does not obey me, then I will reconsider the good I had intended to do for it.

[11]"Now therefore say to the people of Judah and those living in Jerusalem, 'This is what the LORD says: Look! I am preparing a disaster for you and devising a plan against you. So turn from your evil ways, each one of you, and reform your ways and your actions.' [12]But they will reply, 'It's no use. We will continue with our own plans; each of us will follow the stubbornness of his evil heart.' "

[13]Therefore this is what the LORD says:

"Inquire among the nations:
  Who has ever heard anything like this?
A most horrible thing has been done
  by Virgin Israel.
[14]Does the snow of Lebanon
  ever vanish from its rocky slopes?
Do its cool waters from distant sources

ever cease to flow?[f]
15Yet my people have forgotten me;
they burn incense to worthless idols,
which made them stumble in their ways
and in the ancient paths.
They made them walk in bypaths
and on roads not built up.
16Their land will be laid waste,
an object of lasting scorn;
all who pass by will be appalled
and will shake their heads.
17Like a wind from the east,
I will scatter them before their enemies;
I will show them my back and not my face
in the day of their disaster."

f14 The meaning of the Hebrew for this sentence is uncertain.

Discovering the Word 1. What did Jeremiah see and hear at the potter's house (vv. 1–10)? 2. God makes it clear that his pronouncements and promises are conditional. How do you think God might respond to someone who objects that this makes him untrustworthy? 3. Jeremiah draws an analogy between human nations and clay in the potter's hand. How does the difference between humans and clay make this an analogy of hope? 4. In order to be reshaped by the potter, the clay has to be soft. How well is Judah going to do under God's hand (vv. 11–15)? 5. A primary cause of Judah's coming judgment was a determined forgetfulness (v. 15). How might forgetfulness be an expression of disobedience and unfaithfulness?

Applying the Word 1. Being reshaped by the divine potter isn't always a pleasant experience. Describe one or two times when you have been aware of God's shaping hand in your life. 2. God is the one who shapes us. What can we do to make sure that our hearts are responsive to him?

Responding in Prayer Picture yourself as clay. Ask God to make you soft and moldable. Pray that your trust in the Potter will grow stronger.

Jeremiah 18:18—21:14

18They said, "Come, let's make plans against Jeremiah; for the teaching of the law by the priest will not be lost, nor will counsel from the wise, nor the word from the prophets. So come, let's attack him with our tongues and pay no attention to anything he says."

19Listen to me, O LORD;
hear what my accusers are saying!
20Should good be repaid with evil?
Yet they have dug a pit for me.
Remember that I stood before you
and spoke in their behalf
to turn your wrath away from them.
21So give their children over to famine;
hand them over to the power of the sword.
Let their wives be made childless and widows;
let their men be put to death,
their young men slain by the sword in battle.
22Let a cry be heard from their houses
when you suddenly bring invaders against them,
for they have dug a pit to capture me
and have hidden snares for my feet.
23But you know, O LORD,
all their plots to kill me.
Do not forgive their crimes
or blot out their sins from your sight.
Let them be overthrown before you;
deal with them in the time of your anger.

19 This is what the LORD says: "Go and
buy a clay jar from a potter. Take
along some of the elders of the peo-
ple and of the priests 2and go out to the Valley of
Ben Hinnom, near the entrance of the Potsherd
Gate. There proclaim the words I tell you, 3and
say, 'Hear the word of the LORD, O kings of Judah
and people of Jerusalem. This is what the LORD
Almighty, the God of Israel, says: Listen! I am
going to bring a disaster on this place that will
make the ears of everyone who hears of it tingle.
4For they have forsaken me and made this a place
of foreign gods; they have burned sacrifices in it
to gods that neither they nor their fathers nor the
kings of Judah ever knew, and they have filled
this place with the blood of the innocent. 5They
have built the high places of Baal to burn their

sons in the fire as offerings to Baal—something I
did not command or mention, nor did it enter my
mind. 6So beware, the days are coming, declares
the LORD, when people will no longer call this
place Topheth or the Valley of Ben Hinnom, but
the Valley of Slaughter.

7" 'In this place I will ruin[g] the plans of Judah
and Jerusalem. I will make them fall by the sword
before their enemies, at the hands of those who
seek their lives, and I will give their carcasses as
food to the birds of the air and the beasts of the
earth. 8I will devastate this city and make it an
object of scorn; all who pass by will be appalled
and will scoff because of all its wounds. 9I will
make them eat the flesh of their sons and daugh-
ters, and they will eat one another's flesh during
the stress of the siege imposed on them by the
enemies who seek their lives.'

10"Then break the jar while those who go with
you are watching, 11and say to them, 'This is what
the LORD Almighty says: I will smash this nation
and this city just as this potter's jar is smashed
and cannot be repaired. They will bury the dead
in Topheth until there is no more room. 12This is
what I will do to this place and to those who live
here, declares the LORD. I will make this city like
Topheth. 13The houses in Jerusalem and those of
the kings of Judah will be defiled like this place,
Topheth—all the houses where they burned in-
cense on the roofs to all the starry hosts and
poured out drink offerings to other gods.' "

14Jeremiah then returned from Topheth, where
the LORD had sent him to prophesy, and stood in
the court of the LORD's temple and said to all the
people, 15"This is what the LORD Almighty, the
God of Israel, says: 'Listen! I am going to bring on
this city and the villages around it every disaster
I pronounced against them, because they were
stiff-necked and would not listen to my words.' "

20 When the priest Pashhur son of Im-
mer, the chief officer in the temple
of the LORD, heard Jeremiah proph-
esying these things, 2he had Jeremiah the prophet
beaten and put in the stocks at the Upper Gate of
Benjamin at the LORD's temple. 3The next day,
when Pashhur released him from the stocks, Jere-
miah said to him, "The LORD's name for you is not
Pashhur, but Magor-Missabib.[h] 4For this is what
the LORD says: 'I will make you a terror to yourself
and to all your friends; with your own eyes you
will see them fall by the sword of their enemies.
I will hand all Judah over to the king of Babylon,
who will carry them away to Babylon or put them
to the sword. 5I will hand over to their enemies all
the wealth of this city—all its products, all its
valuables and all the treasures of the kings of Ju-
dah. They will take it away as plunder and carry
it off to Babylon. 6And you, Pashhur, and all who
live in your house will go into exile to Babylon.
There you will die and be buried, you and all
your friends to whom you have prophesied lies.' "

7O LORD, you deceived[i] me, and I was
deceived[i];
you overpowered me and prevailed.
I am ridiculed all day long;
everyone mocks me.
8Whenever I speak, I cry out
proclaiming violence and destruction.
So the word of the LORD has brought me
insult and reproach all day long.
9But if I say, "I will not mention him
or speak any more in his name,"
his word is in my heart like a fire,
a fire shut up in my bones.
I am weary of holding it in;
indeed, I cannot.
10I hear many whispering,
"Terror on every side!
Report him! Let's report him!"
All my friends
are waiting for me to slip, saying,
"Perhaps he will be deceived;
then we will prevail over him
and take our revenge on him."

11But the LORD is with me like a mighty warrior;
so my persecutors will stumble and not
prevail.
They will fail and be thoroughly disgraced;
their dishonor will never be forgotten.
12O LORD Almighty, you who examine the
righteous
and probe the heart and mind,
let me see your vengeance upon them,
for to you I have committed my cause.
13Sing to the LORD!
Give praise to the LORD!
He rescues the life of the needy
from the hands of the wicked.

14Cursed be the day I was born!

g7 The Hebrew for *ruin* sounds like the Hebrew for *jar* (see verses 1 and 10). h3 *Magor-Missabib* means *terror on every side.* i7 Or *persuaded*

May the day my mother bore me not be
blessed!
[15]Cursed be the man who brought my father
the news,
who made him very glad, saying,
"A child is born to you—a son!"
[16]May that man be like the towns
the LORD overthrew without pity.
May he hear wailing in the morning,
a battle cry at noon.
[17]For he did not kill me in the womb,
with my mother as my grave,
her womb enlarged forever.
[18]Why did I ever come out of the womb
to see trouble and sorrow
and to end my days in shame?

21

The word came to Jeremiah from
the LORD when King Zedekiah sent
to him Pashhur son of Malkijah
and the priest Zephaniah son of Maaseiah. They
said: [2]"Inquire now of the LORD for us because
Nebuchadnezzar[j] king of Babylon is attacking
us. Perhaps the LORD will perform wonders for
us as in times past so that he will withdraw
from us."

[3]But Jeremiah answered them, "Tell Zedekiah,
[4]'This is what the LORD, the God of Israel, says: I
am about to turn against you the weapons of war
that are in your hands, which you are using to
fight the king of Babylon and the Babylonians[k]
who are outside the wall besieging you. And I will
gather them inside this city. [5]I myself will fight
against you with an outstretched hand and a
mighty arm in anger and fury and great wrath. [6]I
will strike down those who live in this city—both
men and animals—and they will die of a terrible
plague. [7]After that, declares the LORD, I will hand
over Zedekiah king of Judah, his officials and the
people in this city who survive the plague, sword
and famine, to Nebuchadnezzar king of Babylon
and to their enemies who seek their lives. He will
put them to the sword; he will show them no
mercy or pity or compassion.'

[8]"Furthermore, tell the people, 'This is what
the LORD says: See, I am setting before you the
way of life and the way of death. [9]Whoever stays
in this city will die by the sword, famine or
plague. But whoever goes out and surrenders to
the Babylonians who are besieging you will live;
he will escape with his life. [10]I have determined to
do this city harm and not good, declares the LORD.
It will be given into the hands of the king of
Babylon, and he will destroy it with fire.'

[11]"Moreover, say to the royal house of Judah,
'Hear the word of the LORD; [12]O house of David,
this is what the LORD says:

" 'Administer justice every morning;
rescue from the hand of his oppressor
the one who has been robbed,
or my wrath will break out and burn like fire
because of the evil you have done—
burn with no one to quench it.
[13]I am against you, ⌊Jerusalem,⌋
you who live above this valley
on the rocky plateau,
declares the LORD—
you who say, "Who can come against us?
Who can enter our refuge?"
[14]I will punish you as your deeds deserve,
declares the LORD.
I will kindle a fire in your forests
that will consume everything around you.' "

[j]2 Hebrew *Nebuchadrezzar,* of which *Nebuchadnezzar* is a variant; here and often in Jeremiah and Ezekiel [k]4 Or *Chaldeans;* also in verse 9

10 / *Jeremiah 22*
To Know the Lord

THE BOOK *ANNA and the King of Siam,* from which the musical *The King and I* was made, tells the true story of Anna Leonowens, who in 1862 became governess to the royal Siamese family. For one of her first lessons she decided to teach the children geography. The only map in the palace showed Siam at the center of the world. The Siamese king was pictured wearing a splendid crown and holding symbols of plenty and authority. Next to Siam was poor Burma, full of demons, its king without clothes or crown. It was a matter of perspective. God often sees powerful figures quite differently from the way they see themselves.

Warming Up to God How often do you say that you "know the Lord"? What does that phrase mean for you?

Read Jeremiah 22.

22 This is what the LORD says: "Go
down to the palace of the king of
Judah and proclaim this message
there: 2'Hear the word of the LORD, O king of Ju-
dah, you who sit on David's throne—you, your
officials and your people who come through these
gates. 3This is what the LORD says: Do what is just
and right. Rescue from the hand of his oppressor
the one who has been robbed. Do no wrong or
violence to the alien, the fatherless or the widow,
and do not shed innocent blood in this place.
4For if you are careful to carry out these com-
mands, then kings who sit on David's throne will
come through the gates of this palace, riding in
chariots and on horses, accompanied by their of-
ficials and their people. 5But if you do not obey
these commands, declares the LORD, I swear by
myself that this palace will become a ruin.' "
6For this is what the LORD says about the palace
of the king of Judah:

"Though you are like Gilead to me,
like the summit of Lebanon,
I will surely make you like a desert,
like towns not inhabited.
7I will send destroyers against you,
each man with his weapons,
and they will cut up your fine cedar beams
and throw them into the fire.

8"People from many nations will pass by this
city and will ask one another, 'Why has the LORD
done such a thing to this great city?' 9And the
answer will be: 'Because they have forsaken the
covenant of the LORD their God and have wor-
shiped and served other gods.' "

10Do not weep for the dead ⌞king⌟ or mourn
his loss;
rather, weep bitterly for him who is exiled,
because he will never return
nor see his native land again.

11For this is what the LORD says about Shallum[l]
son of Josiah, who succeeded his father as king
of Judah but has gone from this place: "He will
never return. 12He will die in the place where they
have led him captive; he will not see this land
again."

13"Woe to him who builds his palace by
unrighteousness,
his upper rooms by injustice,
making his countrymen work for nothing,
not paying them for their labor.
14He says, 'I will build myself a great palace
with spacious upper rooms.'
So he makes large windows in it,
panels it with cedar
and decorates it in red.

15"Does it make you a king
to have more and more cedar?
Did not your father have food and drink?
He did what was right and just,
so all went well with him.
16He defended the cause of the poor and needy,
and so all went well.
Is that not what it means to know me?"
declares the LORD.
17"But your eyes and your heart
are set only on dishonest gain,
on shedding innocent blood
and on oppression and extortion."

18Therefore this is what the LORD says about Je-
hoiakim son of Josiah king of Judah:

"They will not mourn for him:
'Alas, my brother! Alas, my sister!'
They will not mourn for him:
'Alas, my master! Alas, his splendor!'
19He will have the burial of a donkey—
dragged away and thrown
outside the gates of Jerusalem."

20"Go up to Lebanon and cry out,
let your voice be heard in Bashan,
cry out from Abarim,
for all your allies are crushed.
21I warned you when you felt secure,
but you said, 'I will not listen!'
This has been your way from your youth;
you have not obeyed me.
22The wind will drive all your shepherds away,
and your allies will go into exile.
Then you will be ashamed and disgraced

[l]11 Also called *Jehoahaz*

because of all your wickedness.
23You who live in 'Lebanon,[m]'
who are nestled in cedar buildings,
how you will groan when pangs come upon you,
pain like that of a woman in labor!

24"As surely as I live," declares the LORD, "even
if you, Jehoiachin[n] son of Jehoiakim king of Ju-
dah, were a signet ring on my right hand, I would
still pull you off. 25I will hand you over to those
who seek your life, those you fear—to Nebuchad-
nezzar king of Babylon and to the Babylonians.[o]
26I will hurl you and the mother who gave you
birth into another country, where neither of you
was born, and there you both will die. 27You will
never come back to the land you long to re-
turn to."

28Is this man Jehoiachin a despised, broken pot,
an object no one wants?
Why will he and his children be hurled out,
cast into a land they do not know?
29O land, land, land,
hear the word of the LORD!
30This is what the LORD says:
"Record this man as if childless,
a man who will not prosper in his lifetime,
for none of his offspring will prosper,
none will sit on the throne of David
or rule anymore in Judah."

[m]23 That is, the palace in Jerusalem (see 1 Kings 7:2) [n]24 Hebrew *Coniah,* a variant of *Jehoiachin;* also in verse 28 [o]25 Or *Chaldeans*

Discovering the Word 1. The kings named here were among the last to rule in Judah. What did they consider important (vv. 8–9, 14–15, 17, 20–21, 23)? 3. Verses 15–16 refer to Josiah, who led Judah into spiritual renewal a generation earlier. How is justice defined in these verses and in verse 3? 4. Why was the fate of Josaiah's son Jehoiakim to be so harsh (vv. 18–23)? 5. Why are the people told not to mourn for the king of Judah (vv. 10–12) and Jehoiakim (vv. 18–19)?

Applying the Word 1. How do you respond to the idea that doing justice is inseparable from knowing God (v. 16)? 2. How does your knowledge of God affect how fairly you treat others?

Responding in Prayer If this study reveals ways that you have been unfair or failed to stand up to injustice, confess that to the Lord. Pray for people who are being unjustly treated.

11 / *Jeremiah 23*
A Divine Coup

DURING WORLD WAR II the Japanese experimented with effective ways to run their prison camps. At one camp they removed the five percent of the prison population who had any experience in leadership or could articulate a defined set of religious beliefs and moral behavior. The results were amazing. There were less attempted escapes and more docile prisoners at that camp than at any other.

We need leaders and we need beliefs. But what happens when the leaders become corrupt or intentionally lead in an immoral way? Judah faced just such a crisis. The whole nation was headed for a cliff and the leaders weren't doing anything about it. In fact, they were leading the way to the edge. How will God respond? Jeremiah has some bad news for the leaders and some good news for the people.

Warming Up to God Recall someone who has been an influential leader in your life. What did they do, and how did it affect you?

Read Jeremiah 23.

23 "Woe to the shepherds who are de-
stroying and scattering the sheep of
my pasture!" declares the LORD.
2Therefore this is what the LORD, the God of Is-
rael, says to the shepherds who tend my people:
"Because you have scattered my flock and driven
them away and have not bestowed care on them,
I will bestow punishment on you for the evil you

have done," declares the LORD. 3"I myself will
gather the remnant of my flock out of all the
countries where I have driven them and will
bring them back to their pasture, where they will
be fruitful and increase in number. 4I will place
shepherds over them who will tend them, and
they will no longer be afraid or terrified, nor will
any be missing," declares the LORD.

5"The days are coming," declares the LORD,
"when I will raise up to David[p] a
righteous Branch,
a King who will reign wisely
and do what is just and right in the land.
6In his days Judah will be saved
and Israel will live in safety.
This is the name by which he will be called:
The LORD Our Righteousness.

7"So then, the days are coming," declares the
LORD, "when people will no longer say, 'As surely
as the LORD lives, who brought the Israelites up
out of Egypt,' 8but they will say, 'As surely as the
LORD lives, who brought the descendants of Israel
up out of the land of the north and out of all the
countries where he had banished them.' Then
they will live in their own land."

9Concerning the prophets:

My heart is broken within me;
all my bones tremble.
I am like a drunken man,
like a man overcome by wine,
because of the LORD
and his holy words.
10The land is full of adulterers;
because of the curse[q] the land lies
parched[r]
and the pastures in the desert are withered.
The ⌊prophets⌋ follow an evil course
and use their power unjustly.
11"Both prophet and priest are godless;
even in my temple I find their wickedness,"
declares the LORD.
12"Therefore their path will become slippery;
they will be banished to darkness
and there they will fall.
I will bring disaster on them
in the year they are punished,"
declares the LORD.
13"Among the prophets of Samaria
I saw this repulsive thing:
They prophesied by Baal
and led my people Israel astray.
14And among the prophets of Jerusalem
I have seen something horrible:
They commit adultery and live a lie.
They strengthen the hands of evildoers,
so that no one turns from his wickedness.
They are all like Sodom to me;
the people of Jerusalem are like Gomorrah."

15Therefore, this is what the LORD Almighty
says concerning the prophets:

"I will make them eat bitter food
and drink poisoned water,
because from the prophets of Jerusalem
ungodliness has spread throughout the
land."

16This is what the LORD Almighty says:
"Do not listen to what the prophets are
prophesying to you;
they fill you with false hopes.
They speak visions from their own minds,
not from the mouth of the LORD.
17They keep saying to those who despise me,
'The LORD says: You will have peace.'
And to all who follow the stubbornness of
their hearts
they say, 'No harm will come to you.'
18But which of them has stood in the council of
the LORD
to see or to hear his word?
Who has listened and heard his word?
19See, the storm of the LORD
will burst out in wrath,
a whirlwind swirling down
on the heads of the wicked.
20The anger of the LORD will not turn back
until he fully accomplishes
the purposes of his heart.
In days to come
you will understand it clearly.
21I did not send these prophets,
yet they have run with their message;
I did not speak to them,
yet they have prophesied.
22But if they had stood in my council,
they would have proclaimed my words to
my people

[p]5 *Or up from David's line* [q]10 *Or because of these things*
[r]10 *Or land mourns*

and would have turned them from their evil
ways
and from their evil deeds.

23"Am I only a God nearby,"
declares the LORD,
"and not a God far away?
24Can anyone hide in secret places
so that I cannot see him?"
declares the LORD.
"Do not I fill heaven and earth?"
declares the LORD.

25"I have heard what the prophets say who
prophesy lies in my name. They say, 'I had a
dream! I had a dream!' 26How long will this con-
tinue in the hearts of these lying prophets, who
prophesy the delusions of their own minds?
27They think the dreams they tell one another
will make my people forget my name, just as their
fathers forgot my name through Baal worship.
28Let the prophet who has a dream tell his dream,
but let the one who has my word speak it faith-
fully. For what has straw to do with grain?" de-
clares the LORD. 29"Is not my word like fire," de-
clares the LORD, "and like a hammer that breaks a
rock in pieces?
30"Therefore," declares the LORD, "I am against
the prophets who steal from one another words
supposedly from me. 31Yes," declares the LORD, "I
am against the prophets who wag their own
tongues and yet declare, 'The LORD declares.' 32In-
deed, I am against those who prophesy false
dreams," declares the LORD. "They tell them and
lead my people astray with their reckless lies, yet
I did not send or appoint them. They do not ben-
efit these people in the least," declares the LORD.
33"When these people, or a prophet or a priest,
ask you, 'What is the oracle[s] of the LORD?' say to
them, 'What oracle?[t] I will forsake you, declares
the LORD.' 34If a prophet or a priest or anyone else
claims, 'This is the oracle of the LORD,' I will pun-
ish that man and his household. 35This is what
each of you keeps on saying to his friend or rela-
tive: 'What is the LORD's answer?' or 'What has the
LORD spoken?' 36But you must not mention 'the
oracle of the LORD' again, because every man's
own word becomes his oracle and so you distort
the words of the living God, the LORD Almighty,
our God. 37This is what you keep saying to a
prophet: 'What is the LORD's answer to you?' or
'What has the LORD spoken?' 38Although you
claim, 'This is the oracle of the LORD,' this is what
the LORD says: You used the words, 'This is the
oracle of the LORD,' even though I told you that
you must not claim, 'This is the oracle of the
LORD.' 39Therefore, I will surely forget you and
cast you out of my presence along with the city I
gave to you and your fathers. 40I will bring upon
you everlasting disgrace—everlasting shame that
will not be forgotten."

[s]33 Or *burden* (see Septuagint and Vulgate) [t]33 Hebrew; Septuagint and Vulgate *'You are the burden.* (The Hebrew for *oracle* and *burden* is the same.)

Discovering the Word 1. How will the punishment fit the crime for Israel's leaders (vv. 1–4, 39–40)? 2. God promised a new ruler from the line of David. How will his reign be different from the current leader's (vv. 5–8)? 3. Righteousness is central to a relationship with God. Why do you think the name "The LORD Our Righteousness" (v. 6) might be significant? 4. What charges are brought against the religious leaders (vv. 9–32)? 5. What are the results of their leadership?

Applying the Word 1. If God were to bring charges against the spiritual leaders of today's church, what do think they might be? 2. What effects might such leadership be having on the life of the church and individual Christians? 3. God charges the religious leaders with failing to stand in his council (vv. 18, 22). We may not be prophets or priests, but we can learn from their example. How do you receive the counsel of the Lord?

Responding in Prayer How have you experienced the benefits of Christ as God's Shepherd King? Offer your praise to God.

12 / *Jeremiah 24*
Living with God's Judgment

AFTER THE EVENING service, a visiting preacher was invited to spend the night at the home of one of the wealthy members of the church. The host was proud of his new house and showed it off with obvious pride. He attributed his good fortune to the Lord, saying that God had blessed his business in the previous year with a fourfold increase in profits. The guest was not impressed. With a dismissive gesture he asked his host, "How do you know that your prosperity is not a trick of the devil to cause you to become proud, materialistic and greedy?"

Although the challenge of the preacher seems harsh, it's a good question. What appears to be good fortune at the present may not be so in the end. In Jeremiah's message to the exiles and those who stayed in the land after the first deportation in A.D. 596, he turns the concept of good fortune on its head and provides a different perspective.

Warming Up to God When have you changed your mind about what you initially thought was a great opportunity or positive development?

Read Jeremiah 24.

24 After Jehoiachin[u] son of Jehoiakim
king of Judah and the officials, the
craftsmen and the artisans of Judah
were carried into exile from Jerusalem to Babylon
by Nebuchadnezzar king of Babylon, the LORD
showed me two baskets of figs placed in front
of the temple of the LORD. 2One basket had very
good figs, like those that ripen early; the other
basket had very poor figs, so bad they could not
be eaten.

3Then the LORD asked me, "What do you see,
Jeremiah?"

"Figs," I answered. "The good ones are very
good, but the poor ones are so bad they cannot be
eaten."

4Then the word of the LORD came to me: 5"This
is what the LORD, the God of Israel, says: 'Like
these good figs, I regard as good the exiles from
Judah, whom I sent away from this place to the
land of the Babylonians.[v] 6My eyes will watch
over them for their good, and I will bring them
back to this land. I will build them up and not
tear them down; I will plant them and not uproot
them. 7I will give them a heart to know me, that
I am the LORD. They will be my people, and I will
be their God, for they will return to me with all
their heart.

8" 'But like the poor figs, which are so bad they
cannot be eaten,' says the LORD, 'so will I deal with
Zedekiah king of Judah, his officials and the survivors from Jerusalem, whether they remain in
this land or live in Egypt. 9I will make them abhorrent and an offense to all the kingdoms of the
earth, a reproach and a byword, an object of ridicule and cursing, wherever I banish them. 10I will
send the sword, famine and plague against them
until they are destroyed from the land I gave to
them and their fathers.' "

[u]1 Hebrew *Jeconiah,* a variant of *Jehoiachin* [v]5 Or *Chaldeans*

Discovering the Word 1. How does this vision of the figs display the continuing presence and power of God in the midst of a time of military defeat for Judah? 2. How does the vision of the figs change the way you might think about those who were taken in captivity to Babylon and those who got to stay in Jerusalem (vv. 5–10)? 4. God says that he is going to regard the exiles as "good" (v. 5). What do you think that means? 5. How might those who escaped captivity feel about themselves, the exiles and God (vv. 8–10)?

Applying the Word 1. Christians are to consider themselves blessed by God in the midst of difficult circumstances. What can we learn from the experience of the exiles that can help us experience God's blessing in difficult times? 2. What are some of the benefits that you have received from trying times?

Responding in Prayer God's ultimate act of judgment is the resurrection. Praise him for the grace offered through Christ's sacrifice.

Jeremiah 25:1–14

25 The word came to Jeremiah concerning all the people of Judah in the fourth year of Jehoiakim son of Josiah king of Judah, which was the first year of Nebuchadnezzar king of Babylon. [2]So Jeremiah the prophet said to all the people of Judah and to all those living in Jerusalem: [3]For twenty-three years—from the thirteenth year of Josiah son of Amon king of Judah until this very day—the word of the LORD has come to me and I have spoken to you again and again, but you have not listened.

[4]And though the LORD has sent all his servants the prophets to you again and again, you have not listened or paid any attention. [5]They said, "Turn now, each of you, from your evil ways and your evil practices, and you can stay in the land the LORD gave to you and your fathers for ever and ever. [6]Do not follow other gods to serve and worship them; do not provoke me to anger with what your hands have made. Then I will not harm you."

[7]"But you did not listen to me," declares the LORD, "and you have provoked me with what your hands have made, and you have brought harm to yourselves."

[8]Therefore the LORD Almighty says this: "Because you have not listened to my words, [9]I will summon all the peoples of the north and my servant Nebuchadnezzar king of Babylon," declares the LORD, "and I will bring them against this land and its inhabitants and against all the surrounding nations. I will completely destroy[w] them and make them an object of horror and scorn, and an everlasting ruin. [10]I will banish from them the sounds of joy and gladness, the voices of bride and bridegroom, the sound of millstones and the light of the lamp. [11]This whole country will become a desolate wasteland, and these nations will serve the king of Babylon seventy years.

[12]"But when the seventy years are fulfilled, I will punish the king of Babylon and his nation, the land of the Babylonians,[x] for their guilt," declares the LORD, "and will make it desolate forever. [13]I will bring upon that land all the things I have spoken against it, all that are written in this book and prophesied by Jeremiah against all the nations. [14]They themselves will be enslaved by many nations and great kings; I will repay them according to their deeds and the work of their hands."

[w]9 The Hebrew term refers to the irrevocable giving over of things or persons to the LORD, often by totally destroying them. [x]12 Or *Chaldeans*

13 / *Jeremiah 25:15–38*
International Judgment

READING ABOUT JESUS praying in the Garden of Gethsemane is painful. The night before Jesus was crucified "he fell with his face to the ground and prayed, 'My Father, if it is possible, may this cup be taken from me. Yet not as I will, but as you will'" (Mt 26:39). What was the cup Jesus was praying about? It no doubt had to do with the upcoming experience of the cross.

When we turn to this passage in Jeremiah, we can begin to get a glimpse of the pain Jesus must have felt. Jeremiah writes about the cup of God's wrath that was to be given to all the nations of the earth in order to bring judgment. The cup Jeremiah writes of was too much for the nations to drink. How then was Jesus Christ alone able to stand it? As you study this difficult passage, keep in mind the physical, spiritual and eternal issues at stake.

Warming Up to God Violence is all around us. What wars or other forms of violence are on your mind as you begin? Take time to pray about the situations that concern you.

Read Jeremiah 25:15–38.

15This is what the LORD, the God of Israel, said
to me: "Take from my hand this cup filled with
the wine of my wrath and make all the nations to
whom I send you drink it. 16When they drink
it, they will stagger and go mad because of the
sword I will send among them."

17So I took the cup from the LORD's hand and
made all the nations to whom he sent me drink it:
18Jerusalem and the towns of Judah, its kings and
officials, to make them a ruin and an object of
horror and scorn and cursing, as they are today;
19Pharaoh king of Egypt, his attendants, his offi-
cials and all his people, 20and all the foreign peo-
ple there; all the kings of Uz; all the kings of the
Philistines (those of Ashkelon, Gaza, Ekron, and
the people left at Ashdod); 21Edom, Moab and
Ammon; 22all the kings of Tyre and Sidon; the
kings of the coastlands across the sea; 23Dedan,
Tema, Buz and all who are in distant places[y];
24all the kings of Arabia and all the kings of
the foreign people who live in the desert; 25all
the kings of Zimri, Elam and Media; 26and all the
kings of the north, near and far, one after the
other—all the kingdoms on the face of the earth.
And after all of them, the king of Sheshach[z] will
drink it too.

27"Then tell them, 'This is what the LORD Al-
mighty, the God of Israel, says: Drink, get drunk
and vomit, and fall to rise no more because of the
sword I will send among you.' 28But if they refuse
to take the cup from your hand and drink, tell
them, 'This is what the LORD Almighty says: You
must drink it! 29See, I am beginning to bring di-
saster on the city that bears my Name, and will
you indeed go unpunished? You will not go un-
punished, for I am calling down a sword upon
all who live on the earth, declares the LORD Al-
mighty.'

30"Now prophesy all these words against them
and say to them:

" 'The LORD will roar from on high;
he will thunder from his holy dwelling
and roar mightily against his land.
He will shout like those who tread the grapes,
shout against all who live on the earth.
31The tumult will resound to the ends of the
earth,
for the LORD will bring charges against the
nations;
he will bring judgment on all mankind
and put the wicked to the sword,' "
declares the LORD.

32This is what the LORD Almighty says:

"Look! Disaster is spreading
from nation to nation;
a mighty storm is rising
from the ends of the earth."

33At that time those slain by the LORD will be ev-
erywhere—from one end of the earth to the
other. They will not be mourned or gathered up
or buried, but will be like refuse lying on the
ground.

34Weep and wail, you shepherds;
roll in the dust, you leaders of the flock.
For your time to be slaughtered has come;
you will fall and be shattered like fine
pottery.
35The shepherds will have nowhere to flee,
the leaders of the flock no place to escape.
36Hear the cry of the shepherds,
the wailing of the leaders of the flock,
for the LORD is destroying their pasture.
37The peaceful meadows will be laid waste
because of the fierce anger of the LORD.
38Like a lion he will leave his lair,
and their land will become desolate
because of the sword[a] of the oppressor
and because of the LORD's fierce anger.

[y]23 Or *who clip the hair by their foreheads* [z]26 *Sheshach* is a cryptogram for Babylon. [a]38 Some Hebrew manuscripts and Septuagint (see also Jer. 46:16 and 50:16); most Hebrew manuscripts *anger*

Discovering the Word 1. The central image of these verses is a cup. What does the cup stand for? 2. There is an extensive list of nations in verses 18–26. What is God's point in mentioning them one by one? 3. The nations don't have a choice about this coming war. What is the reason for God's wide-ranging judgment (vv. 27–29)? 4. Verses 30–33 emphasize the sounds of war. What will be heard, and what will the sounds mean? 5. What justification can there be for God to cause such terrible experiences? 6. Jeremiah uses the images of shepherds and a lion to describe the leaders and God. How does that help the leaders understand their situation (vv. 34–38)?

Applying the Word 1. Consider wars in the twentieth century—World War I, World War II, Vietnam, the Gulf War or others that come to mind. How do you think leaders of nations involved viewed their participation in these wars? 2. In most wars, one or even both sides claim that God is on their side. How might you respond to such a claim in light of Jeremiah's prophecy?

Responding in Prayer Pray for victims of violence and war around the world.

Jeremiah 26

26 Early in the reign of Jehoiakim son
of Josiah king of Judah, this word
came from the LORD: 2"This is what
the LORD says: Stand in the courtyard of the LORD's
house and speak to all the people of the towns of
Judah who come to worship in the house of the
LORD. Tell them everything I command you; do
not omit a word. 3Perhaps they will listen and
each will turn from his evil way. Then I will re-
lent and not bring on them the disaster I was
planning because of the evil they have done. 4Say
to them, 'This is what the LORD says: If you do not
listen to me and follow my law, which I have set
before you, 5and if you do not listen to the words
of my servants the prophets, whom I have sent to
you again and again (though you have not lis-
tened), 6then I will make this house like Shiloh
and this city an object of cursing among all the
nations of the earth.' "
7The priests, the prophets and all the people
heard Jeremiah speak these words in the house of
the LORD. 8But as soon as Jeremiah finished telling
all the people everything the LORD had com-
manded him to say, the priests, the prophets and
all the people seized him and said, "You must die!
9Why do you prophesy in the LORD's name that
this house will be like Shiloh and this city will
be desolate and deserted?" And all the people
crowded around Jeremiah in the house of the
LORD.
10When the officials of Judah heard about these
things, they went up from the royal palace to the
house of the LORD and took their places at the
entrance of the New Gate of the LORD's house.
11Then the priests and the prophets said to the
officials and all the people, "This man should be
sentenced to death because he has prophesied
against this city. You have heard it with your own
ears!"
12Then Jeremiah said to all the officials and all
the people: "The LORD sent me to prophesy
against this house and this city all the things you
have heard. 13Now reform your ways and your
actions and obey the LORD your God. Then the
LORD will relent and not bring the disaster he has
pronounced against you. 14As for me, I am in
your hands; do with me whatever you think is
good and right. 15Be assured, however, that if you
put me to death, you will bring the guilt of inno-
cent blood on yourselves and on this city and on
those who live in it, for in truth the LORD has sent
me to you to speak all these words in your hear-
ing."
16Then the officials and all the people said to
the priests and the prophets, "This man should
not be sentenced to death! He has spoken to us in
the name of the LORD our God."
17Some of the elders of the land stepped for-
ward and said to the entire assembly of people,
18"Micah of Moresheth prophesied in the days of
Hezekiah king of Judah. He told all the people of
Judah, 'This is what the LORD Almighty says:

" 'Zion will be plowed like a field,
Jerusalem will become a heap of rubble,
the temple hill a mound overgrown with
thickets.'[b]

19"Did Hezekiah king of Judah or anyone else in
Judah put him to death? Did not Hezekiah fear
the LORD and seek his favor? And did not the LORD
relent, so that he did not bring the disaster he
pronounced against them? We are about to bring
a terrible disaster on ourselves!"
20(Now Uriah son of Shemaiah from Kiriath Je-
arim was another man who prophesied in the
name of the LORD; he prophesied the same things
against this city and this land as Jeremiah did.
21When King Jehoiakim and all his officers and
officials heard his words, the king sought to put

[b]18 Micah 3:12

him to death. But Uriah heard of it and fled in
fear to Egypt. 22King Jehoiakim, however, sent
Elnathan son of Acbor to Egypt, along with some
other men. 23They brought Uriah out of Egypt
and took him to King Jehoiakim, who had him
struck down with a sword and his body thrown
into the burial place of the common people.)
24Furthermore, Ahikam son of Shaphan sup-
ported Jeremiah, and so he was not handed over
to the people to be put to death.

14 / *Jeremiah 27*
How to Prosper Anyway

HIKING ALONG A narrow ledge on a path in the Alps, a tourist slipped and fell. Just before sliding off a cliff and down into the deep ravine below, he caught hold of a tree root. About five minutes later, across the ravine, he heard a voice calling out, "Let go of the tree and swing to the left." That didn't sound like a good idea, so he continued to cling to the tree although his hands were beginning to ache and his grip was slipping. The voice called out again: "From where I am standing I can see a ledge about twenty feet below you and just off at an angle. If you drop down, you can get back to the path and walk down." The hiker had to make a decision: did he trust the voice or not? From where he hung it looked like a straight drop of hundreds of feet down to certain death. But he couldn't hang on much longer. Finally, he asked, "Is anyone else up there?"

Judah was in a difficult situation and getting strange advice from Jeremiah. Like the voice from across the ravine his message went against common sense and everything they understood about being the special people of God. Would they believe him and let go?

Warming Up to God How do you handle advice when you don't agree with it or it comes from someone you are suspicious of?

Read Jeremiah 27.

27 Early in the reign of Zedekiah[c]
son of Josiah king of Judah, this
word came to Jeremiah from the
LORD: 2This is what the LORD said to me: "Make a
yoke out of straps and crossbars and put it on
your neck. 3Then send word to the kings of
Edom, Moab, Ammon, Tyre and Sidon through
the envoys who have come to Jerusalem to Zede-
kiah king of Judah. 4Give them a message for
their masters and say, 'This is what the LORD Al-
mighty, the God of Israel, says: "Tell this to your
masters: 5With my great power and outstretched
arm I made the earth and its people and the ani-
mals that are on it, and I give it to anyone I
please. 6Now I will hand all your countries over
to my servant Nebuchadnezzar king of Babylon; I
will make even the wild animals subject to him.
7All nations will serve him and his son and his
grandson until the time for his land comes; then
many nations and great kings will subjugate him.
8" ' "If, however, any nation or kingdom will
not serve Nebuchadnezzar king of Babylon or
bow its neck under his yoke, I will punish that
nation with the sword, famine and plague, de-
clares the LORD, until I destroy it by his hand. 9So
do not listen to your prophets, your diviners,
your interpreters of dreams, your mediums or
your sorcerers who tell you, 'You will not serve
the king of Babylon.' 10They prophesy lies to you
that will only serve to remove you far from your
lands; I will banish you and you will perish. 11But
if any nation will bow its neck under the yoke of
the king of Babylon and serve him, I will let that
nation remain in its own land to till it and to live
there, declares the LORD." ' "

12I gave the same message to Zedekiah king of
Judah. I said, "Bow your neck under the yoke of
the king of Babylon; serve him and his people,
and you will live. 13Why will you and your people
die by the sword, famine and plague with which
the LORD has threatened any nation that will not
serve the king of Babylon? 14Do not listen to the
words of the prophets who say to you, 'You will
not serve the king of Babylon,' for they are proph-

c1 A few Hebrew manuscripts and Syriac (see also Jer. 27:3, 12 and 28:1); most Hebrew manuscripts *Jehoiakim* (Most Septuagint manuscripts do not have this verse.)

esying lies to you. [15]'I have not sent them,' declares the LORD. 'They are prophesying lies in my name. Therefore, I will banish you and you will perish, both you and the prophets who prophesy to you.' "

[16]Then I said to the priests and all these people, "This is what the LORD says: Do not listen to the prophets who say, 'Very soon now the articles from the LORD's house will be brought back from Babylon.' They are prophesying lies to you. [17]Do not listen to them. Serve the king of Babylon, and you will live. Why should this city become a ruin? [18]If they are prophets and have the word of the LORD, let them plead with the LORD Almighty that the furnishings remaining in the house of the LORD and in the palace of the king of Judah and in Jerusalem not be taken to Babylon. [19]For this is what the LORD Almighty says about the pillars, the Sea, the movable stands and the other furnishings that are left in this city, [20]which Nebuchadnezzar king of Babylon did not take away when he carried Jehoiachin[d] son of Jehoiakim king of Judah into exile from Jerusalem to Babylon, along with all the nobles of Judah and Jerusalem— [21]yes, this is what the LORD Almighty, the God of Israel, says about the things that are left in the house of the LORD and in the palace of the king of Judah and in Jerusalem: [22]'They will be taken to Babylon and there they will remain until the day I come for them,' declares the LORD. 'Then I will bring them back and restore them to this place.' "

[d]20 Hebrew *Jeconiah,* a variant of *Jehoiachin*

Discovering the Word 1. Jeremiah continues to function as a prophet to the nations. What is his message and who is he speaking to in verses 1–11? 2. Jeremiah also continues his use of images and object lessons. What was the purpose of giving the leaders in the Jerusalem counsel an object lesson with the yoke and a message about the coming power of Babylon? 3. How do you think the counsel of kings and envoys would have responded when Jeremiah walked in with a yoke on his neck? 4. Zedekiah received the same message as the nations. Why would this be especially upsetting and confusing to the nation who considered themselves to be God's chosen people (vv. 12–15)? 5. What challenge does Jeremiah issue to the prophets (vv. 16–18)? 6. How does God communicate that he is in charge of the whole experience of Judah's defeat (vv. 21–22)?

Applying the Word 1. When you are going through difficult times, what comfort and wisdom does the knowledge of God provide for you? 2. Jeremiah called the counsel members to risk going against common sense to receive God's deliverance. What risks has following God meant for you? 3. How can Jeremiah's courage be an example for you in the challenges you face?

Responding in Prayer Ask God to give you courage as you face difficult and challenging places in your life.

15 / *Jeremiah 28*
Destroying False Hope

HOW DO GOD'S people handle hostility? John the Baptist told his listeners they should go the second mile. Jesus told the disciples to turn the other cheek. There is a tension here. We may be inclined to think that Christians should be doormats, giving way to the forces of hostile opposition. But that is not the point. Jesus confronted the religious leaders with their hypocrisy and called for the judgment of God on them. Matthew 23 records some of his hot rhetoric. Yet, while Jesus confronted, he didn't lead a jihad, a holy war, to destroy the opposition. He trusted God to bring judgment and justice in his way and his time.

Jeremiah's ministry was full of confrontation and hostility from the opposition. In this study it becomes physical and deadly. As we watch Jeremiah, we can learn how to trust God's guidance and power in threatening situations.

Warming Up to God Recall an experience of being publicly confronted or embarrassed by someone. How did you respond?

Read Jeremiah 28.

28 In the fifth month of that same
year, the fourth year, early in the
reign of Zedekiah king of Judah,
the prophet Hananiah son of Azzur, who was
from Gibeon, said to me in the house of the LORD
in the presence of the priests and all the people:
2“This is what the LORD Almighty, the God of Is-
rael, says: ‘I will break the yoke of the king of
Babylon. 3Within two years I will bring back to
this place all the articles of the LORD’s house that
Nebuchadnezzar king of Babylon removed from
here and took to Babylon. 4I will also bring back
to this place Jehoiachin[e] son of Jehoiakim king
of Judah and all the other exiles from Judah who
went to Babylon,’ declares the LORD, ‘for I will
break the yoke of the king of Babylon.’ ”

5Then the prophet Jeremiah replied to the
prophet Hananiah before the priests and all the
people who were standing in the house of the
LORD. 6He said, “Amen! May the LORD do so! May
the LORD fulfill the words you have prophesied by
bringing the articles of the LORD’s house and all
the exiles back to this place from Babylon. 7Nev-
ertheless, listen to what I have to say in your
hearing and in the hearing of all the people:
8From early times the prophets who preceded you
and me have prophesied war, disaster and plague
against many countries and great kingdoms. 9But
the prophet who prophesies peace will be recog-
nized as one truly sent by the LORD only if his
prediction comes true.”

10Then the prophet Hananiah took the yoke off
the neck of the prophet Jeremiah and broke it,
11and he said before all the people, “This is what
the LORD says: ‘In the same way will I break the
yoke of Nebuchadnezzar king of Babylon off the
neck of all the nations within two years.’ ” At this,
the prophet Jeremiah went on his way.

12Shortly after the prophet Hananiah had bro-
ken the yoke off the neck of the prophet Jere-
miah, the word of the LORD came to Jeremiah:
13“Go and tell Hananiah, ‘This is what the LORD
says: You have broken a wooden yoke, but in its
place you will get a yoke of iron. 14This is what
the LORD Almighty, the God of Israel, says: I will
put an iron yoke on the necks of all these nations
to make them serve Nebuchadnezzar king of Bab-
ylon, and they will serve him. I will even give him
control over the wild animals.’ ”

15Then the prophet Jeremiah said to Hananiah
the prophet, “Listen, Hananiah! The LORD has not
sent you, yet you have persuaded this nation to
trust in lies. 16Therefore, this is what the LORD
says: ‘I am about to remove you from the face of
the earth. This very year you are going to die,
because you have preached rebellion against the
LORD.’ ”

17In the seventh month of that same year, Han-
aniah the prophet died.

[e] 4 Hebrew *Jeconiah*, a variant of *Jehoiachin*

Discovering the Word 1. How do you think Hananiah’s message was received by the priests and people (vv. 1–4)? 2. How would you characterize Jeremiah’s initial response to Hananiah (vv. 5–9)? 3. What test does Jeremiah give for discerning a true prophet? 4. Shortly after Hananiah broke the yoke off Jeremiah’s neck, the Lord gives Jeremiah a stern rebuttal for Hananiah (vv. 12–14). Why might he have waited for a period of time instead of speaking when Hananiah broke the yoke? 5. What do you think those who heard the encounter between Jeremiah and Hananiah might have learned?

Applying the Word 1. What insight does this incident between Jeremiah and Hananiah provide in spotting false prophets or misleading messages given by false teachers? 2. The people who hear Jeremiah and Hananiah must choose who they believe is actually speaking the word of the Lord. How can you know that the words recorded in the Bible are really words from God and not merely human words of empty hopes and dreams?

Responding in Prayer Thank God for the gifts of people and resources he has put in your life to strengthen your faith. If you have questions for God, let him know.

16 / *Jeremiah 29:1–23*
Living as Exiles

HAVING LIVED FOR several years in various countries, I admit there were times I honestly didn't want to be there. Life would have been much more familiar and comfortable in my home country where at least I understood how things were done. On those days when I really felt like a foreigner, it was good to remember that God had put me in these unfamiliar surroundings, and he would sustain me. He could transcend differences of culture and language, and he was carrying out his purposes in that place. Jeremiah needed to remind his people of these things as well.

Warming Up to God When have you felt like a foreigner? (It may have been in your own hometown.) What difference did your faith in the Lord make at those times?

Read Jeremiah 29:1–23.

29 This is the text of the letter that the
prophet Jeremiah sent from Jerusa-
lem to the surviving elders among
the exiles and to the priests, the prophets and all
the other people Nebuchadnezzar had carried
into exile from Jerusalem to Babylon. 2(This was
after King Jehoiachin[f] and the queen mother,
the court officials and the leaders of Judah and
Jerusalem, the craftsmen and the artisans had
gone into exile from Jerusalem.) 3He entrusted
the letter to Elasah son of Shaphan and to Gema-
riah son of Hilkiah, whom Zedekiah king of Ju-
dah sent to King Nebuchadnezzar in Babylon. It
said:

4This is what the LORD Almighty, the God
of Israel, says to all those I carried into exile
from Jerusalem to Babylon: 5"Build houses
and settle down; plant gardens and eat what
they produce. 6Marry and have sons and
daughters; find wives for your sons and give
your daughters in marriage, so that they too
may have sons and daughters. Increase in
number there; do not decrease. 7Also, seek
the peace and prosperity of the city to which
I have carried you into exile. Pray to the
LORD for it, because if it prospers, you too
will prosper." 8Yes, this is what the LORD Al-
mighty, the God of Israel, says: "Do not let
the prophets and diviners among you de-
ceive you. Do not listen to the dreams you
encourage them to have. 9They are prophe-
sying lies to you in my name. I have not sent
them," declares the LORD.

10This is what the LORD says: "When sev-
enty years are completed for Babylon, I will
come to you and fulfill my gracious promise
to bring you back to this place. 11For I know
the plans I have for you," declares the LORD,
"plans to prosper you and not to harm you,
plans to give you hope and a future. 12Then
you will call upon me and come and pray to
me, and I will listen to you. 13You will seek
me and find me when you seek me with all
your heart. 14I will be found by you," de-
clares the LORD, "and will bring you back
from captivity.[g] I will gather you from all
the nations and places where I have banished
you," declares the LORD, "and will bring you
back to the place from which I carried you
into exile."

15You may say, "The LORD has raised up
prophets for us in Babylon," 16but this is
what the LORD says about the king who sits
on David's throne and all the people who
remain in this city, your countrymen who
did not go with you into exile— 17yes, this is
what the LORD Almighty says: "I will send the
sword, famine and plague against them and I
will make them like poor figs that are so bad
they cannot be eaten. 18I will pursue them
with the sword, famine and plague and will
make them abhorrent to all the kingdoms of
the earth and an object of cursing and hor-
ror, of scorn and reproach, among all the
nations where I drive them. 19For they have
not listened to my words," declares the LORD,
"words that I sent to them again and again
by my servants the prophets. And you exiles
have not listened either," declares the LORD.

20Therefore, hear the word of the LORD, all

f2 Hebrew *Jeconiah*, a variant of *Jehoiachin* g14 Or *will restore your fortunes*

17 / *Jeremiah 31*
Restoration

AN ACCIDENTAL DELETE on a computer feels like a disaster. Vital material suddenly vanishes as if it never existed. Fortunately, there are usually ways to restore the lost file. Other things like broken relationships and lost opportunities are not so easy to bring back. In exile Israel must have often thought their last chance and hope were gone, but the Lord still had his purposes for them.

Warming Up to God Think of a time your closeness with the Lord was restored after something disrupted it. What brought about the restoration?

Read Jeremiah 31.

31 "At that time," declares the LORD, "I will be the God of all the clans of Israel, and they will be my people."

2This is what the LORD says:

"The people who survive the sword
will find favor in the desert;
I will come to give rest to Israel."

3The LORD appeared to us in the past,[i] saying:

"I have loved you with an everlasting love;
I have drawn you with loving-kindness.
4I will build you up again
and you will be rebuilt, O Virgin Israel.
Again you will take up your tambourines
and go out to dance with the joyful.
5Again you will plant vineyards
on the hills of Samaria;
the farmers will plant them
and enjoy their fruit.
6There will be a day when watchmen cry out
on the hills of Ephraim,
'Come, let us go up to Zion,
to the LORD our God.' "

7This is what the LORD says:

"Sing with joy for Jacob;
shout for the foremost of the nations.
Make your praises heard, and say,
'O LORD, save your people,
the remnant of Israel.'
8See, I will bring them from the land of the north
and gather them from the ends of the earth.
Among them will be the blind and the lame,
expectant mothers and women in labor;
a great throng will return.
9They will come with weeping;
they will pray as I bring them back.
I will lead them beside streams of water
on a level path where they will not stumble,
because I am Israel's father,
and Ephraim is my firstborn son.

10"Hear the word of the LORD, O nations;
proclaim it in distant coastlands:
'He who scattered Israel will gather them
and will watch over his flock like a shepherd.'
11For the LORD will ransom Jacob
and redeem them from the hand of those stronger than they.
12They will come and shout for joy on the heights of Zion;
they will rejoice in the bounty of the LORD—
the grain, the new wine and the oil,
the young of the flocks and herds.
They will be like a well-watered garden,
and they will sorrow no more.
13Then maidens will dance and be glad,
young men and old as well.
I will turn their mourning into gladness;
I will give them comfort and joy instead of sorrow.
14I will satisfy the priests with abundance,
and my people will be filled with my bounty,"
declares the LORD.

15This is what the LORD says:

"A voice is heard in Ramah,
mourning and great weeping,
Rachel weeping for her children
and refusing to be comforted,

i3 Or *LORD has appeared to us from afar*

because her children are no more."

16This is what the LORD says:

"Restrain your voice from weeping
and your eyes from tears,
for your work will be rewarded,"
declares the LORD.
"They will return from the land of the enemy.
17So there is hope for your future,"
declares the LORD.
"Your children will return to their own land.

18"I have surely heard Ephraim's moaning:
'You disciplined me like an unruly calf,
and I have been disciplined.
Restore me, and I will return,
because you are the LORD my God.
19After I strayed,
I repented;
after I came to understand,
I beat my breast.
I was ashamed and humiliated
because I bore the disgrace of my youth.'
20Is not Ephraim my dear son,
the child in whom I delight?
Though I often speak against him,
I still remember him.
Therefore my heart yearns for him;
I have great compassion for him,"
declares the LORD.

21"Set up road signs;
put up guideposts.
Take note of the highway,
the road that you take.
Return, O Virgin Israel,
return to your towns.
22How long will you wander,
O unfaithful daughter?
The LORD will create a new thing on earth—
a woman will surround[j] a man."

23This is what the LORD Almighty, the God of
Israel, says: "When I bring them back from cap-
tivity,[k] the people in the land of Judah and in its
towns will once again use these words: 'The LORD
bless you, O righteous dwelling, O sacred moun-
tain.' 24People will live together in Judah and all
its towns—farmers and those who move about
with their flocks. 25I will refresh the weary and
satisfy the faint."

26At this I awoke and looked around. My sleep
had been pleasant to me.
27"The days are coming," declares the LORD,
"when I will plant the house of Israel and the
house of Judah with the offspring of men and of
animals. 28Just as I watched over them to uproot
and tear down, and to overthrow, destroy and
bring disaster, so I will watch over them to build
and to plant," declares the LORD. 29"In those days
people will no longer say,

'The fathers have eaten sour grapes,
and the children's teeth are set on edge.'

30Instead, everyone will die for his own sin; who-
ever eats sour grapes—his own teeth will be set
on edge.

31"The time is coming," declares the LORD,
"when I will make a new covenant
with the house of Israel
and with the house of Judah.
32It will not be like the covenant
I made with their forefathers
when I took them by the hand
to lead them out of Egypt,
because they broke my covenant,
though I was a husband to[l] them,[m]"
declares the LORD.
33"This is the covenant I will make with the house of Israel
after that time," declares the LORD.
"I will put my law in their minds
and write it on their hearts.
I will be their God,
and they will be my people.
34No longer will a man teach his neighbor,
or a man his brother, saying, 'Know the LORD,'
because they will all know me,
from the least of them to the greatest,"
declares the LORD.
"For I will forgive their wickedness
and will remember their sins no more."

35This is what the LORD says,

he who appoints the sun
to shine by day,
who decrees the moon and stars
to shine by night,
who stirs up the sea

[j]22 Or *will go about* ⌞*seeking*⌟; or *will protect* [k]23 Or *I restore their fortunes* [l]32 Hebrew; Septuagint and Syriac / *and I turned away from* [m]32 Or *was their master*

so that its waves roar—
the LORD Almighty is his name:
36"Only if these decrees vanish from my
sight,"
declares the LORD,
"will the descendants of Israel ever cease
to be a nation before me."

37This is what the LORD says:

"Only if the heavens above can be measured
and the foundations of the earth below be
searched out
will I reject all the descendants of Israel
because of all they have done,"
declares the LORD.

38"The days are coming," declares the LORD,
"when this city will be rebuilt for me from the
Tower of Hananel to the Corner Gate. 39The mea-
suring line will stretch from there straight to the
hill of Gareb and then turn to Goah. 40The whole
valley where dead bodies and ashes are thrown,
and all the terraces out to the Kidron Valley on
the east as far as the corner of the Horse Gate, will
be holy to the LORD. The city will never again be
uprooted or demolished."

Discovering the Word 1. How would you sum up God's message to Jeremiah in this passage? 2. What reasons does God give for restoring Israel (vv. 3, 9, 20)? 3. How does God depict the bounty and joy which he will restore to Israel (vv. 1–2, 4–5, 12–14, 22–25, 27–28)? 4. What change of heart will Israel experience concerning their sin (vv. 9, 18–19)? 5. How will the new covenant be different from the old (vv. 31–34)? 6. How long will God's blessings last (vv. 35–37)?

Applying the Word 1. In what ways do you need to be restored by God? 2. Think of someone you know who needs restoration. It may be someone's relationship with God, a friendship, a marriage, a church fellowship. If appropriate, how can you contribute to that restoration?

Responding in Prayer Thank God for his restoring love. Pray for areas in your life where you feel broken and need his restoration. Pray for damaged relationships which need to be restored by the touch of God.

18 / *Jeremiah 32:1–25*
The Promise of Renewed Land

SOCIOLOGISTS HAVE DISCOVERED a set of behaviors which they call "deferred gratification pattern." It describes the practice of putting off a purchase or action in hope that better dividends would come in the future. Most everyone who lives by deferred gratification expects to get a good return. But what if the benefits don't come in your lifetime? In this chapter Jeremiah makes a real-estate deal that on the surface looks foolish. It is the ultimate in deferred gratification. In the transaction he demonstrates the depth of his character and the quality of his obedience to God.

Warming Up to God How do you feel when you have to put off buying something that you really want immediately?

Read Jeremiah 32:1–25.

32 This is the word that came to Jere-
miah from the LORD in the tenth
year of Zedekiah king of Judah,
which was the eighteenth year of Nebuchadnez-
zar. 2The army of the king of Babylon was then
besieging Jerusalem, and Jeremiah the prophet
was confined in the courtyard of the guard in the
royal palace of Judah.
3Now Zedekiah king of Judah had imprisoned
him there, saying, "Why do you prophesy as you
do? You say, 'This is what the LORD says: I am
about to hand this city over to the king of Bab-
ylon, and he will capture it. 4Zedekiah king of
Judah will not escape out of the hands of the
Babylonians[n] but will certainly be handed over

n4 Or *Chaldeans*; also in verses 5, 24, 25, 28, 29 and 43

to the king of Babylon, and will speak with him face to face and see him with his own eyes. 5He will take Zedekiah to Babylon, where he will remain until I deal with him, declares the LORD. If you fight against the Babylonians, you will not succeed.' "

6Jeremiah said, "The word of the LORD came to me: 7Hanamel son of Shallum your uncle is going to come to you and say, 'Buy my field at Anathoth, because as nearest relative it is your right and duty to buy it.'

8"Then, just as the LORD had said, my cousin Hanamel came to me in the courtyard of the guard and said, 'Buy my field at Anathoth in the territory of Benjamin. Since it is your right to redeem it and possess it, buy it for yourself.'

"I knew that this was the word of the LORD; 9so I bought the field at Anathoth from my cousin Hanamel and weighed out for him seventeen shekels[o] of silver. 10I signed and sealed the deed, had it witnessed, and weighed out the silver on the scales. 11I took the deed of purchase—the sealed copy containing the terms and conditions, as well as the unsealed copy— 12and I gave this deed to Baruch son of Neriah, the son of Mahseiah, in the presence of my cousin Hanamel and of the witnesses who had signed the deed and of all the Jews sitting in the courtyard of the guard.

13"In their presence I gave Baruch these instructions: 14'This is what the LORD Almighty, the God of Israel, says: Take these documents, both the sealed and unsealed copies of the deed of purchase, and put them in a clay jar so they will last a long time. 15For this is what the LORD Almighty, the God of Israel, says: Houses, fields and vineyards will again be bought in this land.'

16"After I had given the deed of purchase to Baruch son of Neriah, I prayed to the LORD:

17"Ah, Sovereign LORD, you have made the heavens and the earth by your great power and outstretched arm. Nothing is too hard for you. 18You show love to thousands but bring the punishment for the fathers' sins into the laps of their children after them. O great and powerful God, whose name is the LORD Almighty, 19great are your purposes and mighty are your deeds. Your eyes are open to all the ways of men; you reward everyone according to his conduct and as his deeds deserve. 20You performed miraculous signs and wonders in Egypt and have continued them to this day, both in Israel and among all mankind, and have gained the renown that is still yours. 21You brought your people Israel out of Egypt with signs and wonders, by a mighty hand and an outstretched arm and with great terror. 22You gave them this land you had sworn to give their forefathers, a land flowing with milk and honey. 23They came in and took possession of it, but they did not obey you or follow your law; they did not do what you commanded them to do. So you brought all this disaster upon them.

24"See how the siege ramps are built up to take the city. Because of the sword, famine and plague, the city will be handed over to the Babylonians who are attacking it. What you said has happened, as you now see. 25And though the city will be handed over to the Babylonians, you, O Sovereign LORD, say to me, 'Buy the field with silver and have the transaction witnessed.' "

o9 That is, about 7 ounces (about 200 grams)

Discovering the Word 1. Jerusalem is in a state of siege. How might Jeremiah's willingness to purchase a field have been a means of comfort to the threatened citizens? 2. Why is Jeremiah imprisoned in the courtyard, and why is Zedekiah shut up in Jerusalem? 3. Jeremiah records in detail the process of the legal transaction for the purchase of the land (vv. 9–12). What impact would this have on those who watched? 4. Why would Jeremiah make a transaction from which he would never personally benefit (vv. 14–15)? 5. After the purchase Jeremiah offered a prayer (vv. 17–25). What themes are woven throughout the prayer? 6. What further comfort and confirmation of Jeremiah does God offer in verses 38–44?

Applying the Word 1. What can we learn about Christian service and character from Jeremiah's model? 2. Jeremiah's prayer shows a familiar knowledge of God's past actions. How can this study of Jeremiah be a resource for your prayers?

Responding in Prayer Prayer is a great source of comfort in times of trouble. Talk to God about the things that are on your mind today.

Jeremiah 32:26–44

[26]Then the word of the LORD came to Jeremiah:
[27]"I am the LORD, the God of all mankind. Is anything too hard for me? [28]Therefore, this is what the LORD says: I am about to hand this city over to the Babylonians and to Nebuchadnezzar king of Babylon, who will capture it. [29]The Babylonians who are attacking this city will come in and set it on fire; they will burn it down, along with the houses where the people provoked me to anger by burning incense on the roofs to Baal and by pouring out drink offerings to other gods.

[30]"The people of Israel and Judah have done nothing but evil in my sight from their youth; indeed, the people of Israel have done nothing but provoke me with what their hands have made, declares the LORD. [31]From the day it was built until now, this city has so aroused my anger and wrath that I must remove it from my sight. [32]The people of Israel and Judah have provoked me by all the evil they have done—they, their kings and officials, their priests and prophets, the men of Judah and the people of Jerusalem. [33]They turned their backs to me and not their faces; though I taught them again and again, they would not listen or respond to discipline. [34]They set up their abominable idols in the house that bears my Name and defiled it. [35]They built high places for Baal in the Valley of Ben Hinnom to sacrifice their sons and daughters[p] to Molech, though I never commanded, nor did it enter my mind, that they should do such a detestable thing and so make Judah sin.

[36]"You are saying about this city, 'By the sword, famine and plague it will be handed over to the king of Babylon'; but this is what the LORD, the God of Israel, says: [37]I will surely gather them from all the lands where I banish them in my furious anger and great wrath; I will bring them back to this place and let them live in safety. [38]They will be my people, and I will be their God. [39]I will give them singleness of heart and action, so that they will always fear me for their own good and the good of their children after them. [40]I will make an everlasting covenant with them: I will never stop doing good to them, and I will inspire them to fear me, so that they will never turn away from me. [41]I will rejoice in doing them good and will assuredly plant them in this land with all my heart and soul.

[42]"This is what the LORD says: As I have brought all this great calamity on this people, so I will give them all the prosperity I have promised them. [43]Once more fields will be bought in this land of which you say, 'It is a desolate waste, without men or animals, for it has been handed over to the Babylonians.' [44]Fields will be bought for silver, and deeds will be signed, sealed and witnessed in the territory of Benjamin, in the villages around Jerusalem, in the towns of Judah and in the towns of the hill country, of the western foothills and of the Negev, because I will restore their fortunes,[q] declares the LORD."

p35 *Or to make their sons and daughters pass through ⌞the fire⌟*
q44 *Or will bring them back from captivity*

19 / *Jeremiah 33*
The Sure and Certain Promise

WHEN JOHN THE Baptist was in prison, he sent messengers to Jesus asking if he was the Messiah or not. The question probably came from confusion and despair. After all, hadn't John proclaimed the Coming One who would take away the sins of the world? Surely the Messiah's coming would bring freedom and fulfillment for everyone. Why was John imprisoned?

God had warned Jeremiah from the moment of his call that his ministry would be difficult. Even so, like John the Baptist, there must have been days of frustration. He was ignored, rejected, despised and imprisoned. In the midst of that darkness, God comes to Jeremiah with a candle of light. Sometimes God doesn't rescue us. Sometimes he does. Either way, he extends his love and grace.

Warming Up to God When things look dark and depressing, what do you do to gain encouragement and hope?

Read Jeremiah 33.

33 While Jeremiah was still confined
in the courtyard of the guard, the
word of the LORD came to him a sec-
ond time: [2]"This is what the LORD says, he who
made the earth, the LORD who formed it and es-
tablished it—the LORD is his name: [3]'Call to me
and I will answer you and tell you great and un-
searchable things you do not know.' [4]For this is
what the LORD, the God of Israel, says about the
houses in this city and the royal palaces of Judah
that have been torn down to be used against the
siege ramps and the sword [5]in the fight with the
Babylonians[r]: 'They will be filled with the dead
bodies of the men I will slay in my anger and
wrath. I will hide my face from this city because
of all its wickedness.
[6]" 'Nevertheless, I will bring health and healing
to it; I will heal my people and will let them enjoy
abundant peace and security. [7]I will bring Judah
and Israel back from captivity[s] and will rebuild
them as they were before. [8]I will cleanse them
from all the sin they have committed against me
and will forgive all their sins of rebellion against
me. [9]Then this city will bring me renown, joy,
praise and honor before all nations on earth that
hear of all the good things I do for it; and they
will be in awe and will tremble at the abundant
prosperity and peace I provide for it.'
[10]"This is what the LORD says: 'You say about
this place, "It is a desolate waste, without men
or animals." Yet in the towns of Judah and the
streets of Jerusalem that are deserted, inhabited
by neither men nor animals, there will be heard
once more [11]the sounds of joy and gladness, the
voices of bride and bridegroom, and the voices of
those who bring thank offerings to the house of
the LORD, saying,

"Give thanks to the LORD Almighty,
for the LORD is good;
his love endures forever."

For I will restore the fortunes of the land as they
were before,' says the LORD.

[12]"This is what the LORD Almighty says: 'In this
place, desolate and without men or animals—in
all its towns there will again be pastures for shep-
herds to rest their flocks. [13]In the towns of the
hill country, of the western foothills and of the
Negev, in the territory of Benjamin, in the villages
around Jerusalem and in the towns of Judah,
flocks will again pass under the hand of the one
who counts them,' says the LORD.
[14]" 'The days are coming,' declares the LORD,
'when I will fulfill the gracious promise I made to
the house of Israel and to the house of Judah.

[15]" 'In those days and at that time
I will make a righteous Branch sprout from
David's line;
he will do what is just and right in the
land.
[16]In those days Judah will be saved
and Jerusalem will live in safety.
This is the name by which it[t] will be called:
The LORD Our Righteousness.'

[17]For this is what the LORD says: 'David will never
fail to have a man to sit on the throne of the
house of Israel, [18]nor will the priests, who are
Levites, ever fail to have a man to stand before me
continually to offer burnt offerings, to burn grain
offerings and to present sacrifices.' "
[19]The word of the LORD came to Jeremiah:
[20]"This is what the LORD says: 'If you can break
my covenant with the day and my covenant with
the night, so that day and night no longer come at
their appointed time, [21]then my covenant with
David my servant—and my covenant with the Le-
vites who are priests ministering before me—can
be broken and David will no longer have a
descendant to reign on his throne. [22]I will make
the descendants of David my servant and the Le-
vites who minister before me as countless as the
stars of the sky and as measureless as the sand on
the seashore.' "

[r]5 *Or Chaldeans* [s]7 *Or will restore the fortunes of Judah and Israel*
[t]16 *Or he*

23The word of the LORD came to Jeremiah:
24"Have you not noticed that these people are say-
ing, 'The LORD has rejected the two kingdoms[u]
he chose'? So they despise my people and no
longer regard them as a nation. 25This is what the
LORD says: 'If I have not established my covenant
with day and night and the fixed laws of heaven
and earth, 26then I will reject the descendants of
Jacob and David my servant and will not choose
one of his sons to rule over the descendants of
Abraham, Isaac and Jacob. For I will restore their
fortunes[v] and have compassion on them.' "

[u]24 Or *families* [v]26 Or *will bring them back from captivity*

Discovering the Word 1. Jeremiah is imprisoned in Jerusalem with the Babylonian army at the gates. What does God do to offer him comfort? 2. The Hebrew meaning of the Lord's name used here is "Promise Keeper." Why do you think God repeats his name four times in verses 2–4? 3. God invites Jeremiah to call out for assurance and then immediately offers his response (vv. 4–9). In what way would God's words be comforting? 4. What is God going to do to fulfill his promises to Judah and Israel (vv. 15–18)? 5. The destruction of Israel and Judah could lead to the accusation that God was a covenant breaker. How does God answer this (vv. 20–26)?

Applying the Word 1. Have there been times in your life when you felt confined, trapped or limited? 2. How could or did the knowledge of God help? 3. How would your experience of life and your relationship with God be different if he was untrustworthy?

Responding in Prayer Offer praise to the only God worthy of your trust.

Jeremiah 34—35

34 While Nebuchadnezzar king of
Babylon and all his army and all the
kingdoms and peoples in the em-
pire he ruled were fighting against Jerusalem and
all its surrounding towns, this word came to Jere-
miah from the LORD: 2"This is what the LORD, the
God of Israel, says: Go to Zedekiah king of Judah
and tell him, 'This is what the LORD says: I am
about to hand this city over to the king of Bab-
ylon, and he will burn it down. 3You will not
escape from his grasp but will surely be captured
and handed over to him. You will see the king of
Babylon with your own eyes, and he will speak
with you face to face. And you will go to Babylon.
4" 'Yet hear the promise of the LORD,
O Zedekiah king of Judah. This is what the LORD
says concerning you: You will not die by the
sword; 5you will die peacefully. As people made a
funeral fire in honor of your fathers, the former
kings who preceded you, so they will make a fire
in your honor and lament, "Alas, O master!" I
myself make this promise, declares the LORD.' "
6Then Jeremiah the prophet told all this to Zed-
ekiah king of Judah, in Jerusalem, 7while the
army of the king of Babylon was fighting against
Jerusalem and the other cities of Judah that were
still holding out—Lachish and Azekah. These
were the only fortified cities left in Judah.
8The word came to Jeremiah from the LORD af-
ter King Zedekiah had made a covenant with all
the people in Jerusalem to proclaim freedom for
the slaves. 9Everyone was to free his Hebrew
slaves, both male and female; no one was to hold
a fellow Jew in bondage. 10So all the officials and
people who entered into this covenant agreed that
they would free their male and female slaves and
no longer hold them in bondage. They agreed,
and set them free. 11But afterward they changed
their minds and took back the slaves they had
freed and enslaved them again.
12Then the word of the LORD came to Jeremiah:
13"This is what the LORD, the God of Israel, says:
I made a covenant with your forefathers when I
brought them out of Egypt, out of the land of
slavery. I said, 14'Every seventh year each of you
must free any fellow Hebrew who has sold him-
self to you. After he has served you six years, you
must let him go free.'[w] Your fathers, however,
did not listen to me or pay attention to me. 15Re-
cently you repented and did what is right in my
sight: Each of you proclaimed freedom to his

[w]14 Deut. 15:12

countrymen. You even made a covenant before
me in the house that bears my Name. 16But now
you have turned around and profaned my name;
each of you has taken back the male and female
slaves you had set free to go where they wished.
You have forced them to become your slaves
again.

17"Therefore, this is what the LORD says: You
have not obeyed me; you have not proclaimed
freedom for your fellow countrymen. So I now
proclaim 'freedom' for you, declares the LORD—
'freedom' to fall by the sword, plague and famine.
I will make you abhorrent to all the kingdoms of
the earth. 18The men who have violated my cov-
enant and have not fulfilled the terms of the cov-
enant they made before me, I will treat like the
calf they cut in two and then walked between its
pieces. 19The leaders of Judah and Jerusalem, the
court officials, the priests and all the people of the
land who walked between the pieces of the calf,
20I will hand over to their enemies who seek their
lives. Their dead bodies will become food for the
birds of the air and the beasts of the earth.

21"I will hand Zedekiah king of Judah and his
officials over to their enemies who seek their
lives, to the army of the king of Babylon, which
has withdrawn from you. 22I am going to give the
order, declares the LORD, and I will bring them
back to this city. They will fight against it, take it
and burn it down. And I will lay waste the towns
of Judah so no one can live there."

35 This is the word that came to Jere-
miah from the LORD during the
reign of Jehoiakim son of Josiah
king of Judah: 2"Go to the Recabite family and
invite them to come to one of the side rooms of
the house of the LORD and give them wine to
drink."

3So I went to get Jaazaniah son of Jeremiah, the
son of Habazziniah, and his brothers and all his
sons—the whole family of the Recabites. 4I
brought them into the house of the LORD, into the
room of the sons of Hanan son of Igdaliah the
man of God. It was next to the room of the offi-
cials, which was over that of Maaseiah son of
Shallum the doorkeeper. 5Then I set bowls full of
wine and some cups before the men of the Recab-
ite family and said to them, "Drink some wine."

6But they replied, "We do not drink wine, be-
cause our forefather Jonadab son of Recab gave us
this command: 'Neither you nor your descen-
dants must ever drink wine. 7Also you must never
build houses, sow seed or plant vineyards; you
must never have any of these things, but must
always live in tents. Then you will live a long time
in the land where you are nomads.' 8We have
obeyed everything our forefather Jonadab son of
Recab commanded us. Neither we nor our wives
nor our sons and daughters have ever drunk wine
9or built houses to live in or had vineyards, fields
or crops. 10We have lived in tents and have fully
obeyed everything our forefather Jonadab com-
manded us. 11But when Nebuchadnezzar king of
Babylon invaded this land, we said, 'Come, we
must go to Jerusalem to escape the Babylonian[x]
and Aramean armies.' So we have remained in
Jerusalem."

12Then the word of the LORD came to Jeremiah,
saying: 13"This is what the LORD Almighty, the
God of Israel, says: Go and tell the men of Judah
and the people of Jerusalem, 'Will you not learn a
lesson and obey my words?' declares the LORD.
14'Jonadab son of Recab ordered his sons not to
drink wine and this command has been kept. To
this day they do not drink wine, because they
obey their forefather's command. But I have spo-
ken to you again and again, yet you have not
obeyed me. 15Again and again I sent all my ser-
vants the prophets to you. They said, "Each of
you must turn from your wicked ways and reform
your actions; do not follow other gods to serve
them. Then you will live in the land I have given
to you and your fathers." But you have not paid
attention or listened to me. 16The descendants of
Jonadab son of Recab have carried out the com-
mand their forefather gave them, but these people
have not obeyed me.'

17"Therefore, this is what the LORD God Al-
mighty, the God of Israel, says: 'Listen! I am go-
ing to bring on Judah and on everyone living in
Jerusalem every disaster I pronounced against
them. I spoke to them, but they did not listen; I
called to them, but they did not answer.' "

18Then Jeremiah said to the family of the Rec-
abites, "This is what the LORD Almighty, the God
of Israel, says: 'You have obeyed the command of
your forefather Jonadab and have followed all his
instructions and have done everything he or-
dered.' 19Therefore, this is what the LORD Al-
mighty, the God of Israel, says: 'Jonadab son of
Recab will never fail to have a man to serve me.' "

[x]11 Or *Chaldean*

20 / *Jeremiah 36* The Burning Scroll

A WRITER'S GREATEST fear is that the sole copy of a book manuscript will be destroyed by fire. Once burned up, those thousands of lost words can never be reconstructed. An annoyed king once tossed God's words into the flames. Still the Word of God persists and lives through any fire.

Warming Up to God Reflect on what God's Word has meant in your life. How is it precious to you?

Read Jeremiah 36.

36 In the fourth year of Jehoiakim son of Josiah king of Judah, this word came to Jeremiah from the LORD: 2"Take a scroll and write on it all the words I have spoken to you concerning Israel, Judah and all the other nations from the time I began speaking to you in the reign of Josiah till now. 3Perhaps when the people of Judah hear about every disaster I plan to inflict on them, each of them will turn from his wicked way; then I will forgive their wickedness and their sin."

4So Jeremiah called Baruch son of Neriah, and while Jeremiah dictated all the words the LORD had spoken to him, Baruch wrote them on the scroll. 5Then Jeremiah told Baruch, "I am restricted; I cannot go to the LORD's temple. 6So you go to the house of the LORD on a day of fasting and read to the people from the scroll the words of the LORD that you wrote as I dictated. Read them to all the people of Judah who come in from their towns. 7Perhaps they will bring their petition before the LORD, and each will turn from his wicked ways, for the anger and wrath pronounced against this people by the LORD are great."

8Baruch son of Neriah did everything Jeremiah the prophet told him to do; at the LORD's temple he read the words of the LORD from the scroll. 9In the ninth month of the fifth year of Jehoiakim son of Josiah king of Judah, a time of fasting before the LORD was proclaimed for all the people in Jerusalem and those who had come from the towns of Judah. 10From the room of Gemariah son of Shaphan the secretary, which was in the upper courtyard at the entrance of the New Gate of the temple, Baruch read to all the people at the LORD's temple the words of Jeremiah from the scroll.

11When Micaiah son of Gemariah, the son of Shaphan, heard all the words of the LORD from the scroll, 12he went down to the secretary's room in the royal palace, where all the officials were sitting: Elishama the secretary, Delaiah son of Shemaiah, Elnathan son of Acbor, Gemariah son of Shaphan, Zedekiah son of Hananiah, and all the other officials. 13After Micaiah told them everything he had heard Baruch read to the people from the scroll, 14all the officials sent Jehudi son of Nethaniah, the son of Shelemiah, the son of Cushi, to say to Baruch, "Bring the scroll from which you have read to the people and come." So Baruch son of Neriah went to them with the scroll in his hand. 15They said to him, "Sit down, please, and read it to us."

So Baruch read it to them. 16When they heard all these words, they looked at each other in fear and said to Baruch, "We must report all these words to the king." 17Then they asked Baruch, "Tell us, how did you come to write all this? Did Jeremiah dictate it?"

18"Yes," Baruch replied, "he dictated all these words to me, and I wrote them in ink on the scroll."

19Then the officials said to Baruch, "You and Jeremiah, go and hide. Don't let anyone know where you are."

20After they put the scroll in the room of Elishama the secretary, they went to the king in the courtyard and reported everything to him. 21The king sent Jehudi to get the scroll, and Jehudi brought it from the room of Elishama the secretary and read it to the king and all the officials standing beside him. 22It was the ninth month and the king was sitting in the winter apartment, with a fire burning in the firepot in front of him. 23Whenever Jehudi had read three or four columns of the scroll, the king cut them off with a scribe's knife and threw them into the firepot, until the entire scroll was burned in the fire. 24The king and all his attendants who heard all

these words showed no fear, nor did they tear
their clothes. 25Even though Elnathan, Delaiah
and Gemariah urged the king not to burn the
scroll, he would not listen to them. 26Instead, the
king commanded Jerahmeel, a son of the king,
Seraiah son of Azriel and Shelemiah son of Abdeel
to arrest Baruch the scribe and Jeremiah the
prophet. But the LORD had hidden them.

27After the king burned the scroll containing
the words that Baruch had written at Jeremiah's
dictation, the word of the LORD came to Jeremiah:
28"Take another scroll and write on it all the
words that were on the first scroll, which Jehoia-
kim king of Judah burned up. 29Also tell Jehoia-
kim king of Judah, 'This is what the LORD says:
You burned that scroll and said, "Why did you
write on it that the king of Babylon would cer-
tainly come and destroy this land and cut off both
men and animals from it?" 30Therefore, this is
what the LORD says about Jehoiakim king of Ju-
dah: He will have no one to sit on the throne of
David; his body will be thrown out and exposed
to the heat by day and the frost by night. 31I will
punish him and his children and his attendants
for their wickedness; I will bring on them and
those living in Jerusalem and the people of Judah
every disaster I pronounced against them, be-
cause they have not listened.' "

32So Jeremiah took another scroll and gave it to
the scribe Baruch son of Neriah, and as Jeremiah
dictated, Baruch wrote on it all the words of the
scroll that Jehoiakim king of Judah had burned in
the fire. And many similar words were added to
them.

Discovering the Word 1. What was the purpose of the scroll's being written and read (vv. 1–10)? 2. What effect did the scroll have on King Jehoiakim's officials (vv. 11–19)? 3. When the king heard the scroll read aloud, how did he react (vv. 20–26)? 4. How would you describe the king's attitude toward God's words? 5. How did God overrule the king's contempt (vv. 27–32)?

Applying the Word 1. Which of God's words do people prefer to "cut out and burn" today? 2. Jeremiah was directed to rewrite the scroll, plus more. That took courage. How can you remind people that God's Word still stands despite the contempt of some?

Responding in Prayer Praise God that his Word is eternal and can never be destroyed by unbelief or contempt. Pray that you and believers all over the world will stand up for the truth of Scripture.

Jeremiah 37

37 Zedekiah son of Josiah was made
king of Judah by Nebuchadnezzar
king of Babylon; he reigned in place
of Jehoiachin[y] son of Jehoiakim. 2Neither he nor
his attendants nor the people of the land paid
any attention to the words the LORD had spoken
through Jeremiah the prophet.

3King Zedekiah, however, sent Jehucal son of
Shelemiah with the priest Zephaniah son of Maa-
seiah to Jeremiah the prophet with this message:
"Please pray to the LORD our God for us."

4Now Jeremiah was free to come and go among
the people, for he had not yet been put in prison.
5Pharaoh's army had marched out of Egypt, and
when the Babylonians[z] who were besieging Jeru-
salem heard the report about them, they with-
drew from Jerusalem.

6Then the word of the LORD came to Jeremiah
the prophet: 7"This is what the LORD, the God of
Israel, says: Tell the king of Judah, who sent you
to inquire of me, 'Pharaoh's army, which has
marched out to support you, will go back to its
own land, to Egypt. 8Then the Babylonians will
return and attack this city; they will capture it
and burn it down.'

9"This is what the LORD says: Do not deceive
yourselves, thinking, 'The Babylonians will surely
leave us.' They will not! 10Even if you were to
defeat the entire Babylonian[a] army that is attack-
ing you and only wounded men were left in their
tents, they would come out and burn this city
down."

11After the Babylonian army had withdrawn
from Jerusalem because of Pharaoh's army, 12Jere-
miah started to leave the city to go to the territory
of Benjamin to get his share of the property

y1 Hebrew *Coniah*, a variant of *Jehoiachin* z5 Or *Chaldeans*; also in verses 8, 9, 13 and 14 a10 Or *Chaldean*; also in verse 11

among the people there. 13But when he reached
the Benjamin Gate, the captain of the guard,
whose name was Irijah son of Shelemiah, the son
of Hananiah, arrested him and said, "You are de-
serting to the Babylonians!"
14"That's not true!" Jeremiah said. "I am not
deserting to the Babylonians." But Irijah would
not listen to him; instead, he arrested Jeremiah
and brought him to the officials. 15They were an-
gry with Jeremiah and had him beaten and im-
prisoned in the house of Jonathan the secretary,
which they had made into a prison.
16Jeremiah was put into a vaulted cell in a dun-
geon, where he remained a long time. 17Then
King Zedekiah sent for him and had him brought
to the palace, where he asked him privately, "Is
there any word from the LORD?"

"Yes," Jeremiah replied, "you will be handed
over to the king of Babylon."
18Then Jeremiah said to King Zedekiah, "What
crime have I committed against you or your offi-
cials or this people, that you have put me in
prison? 19Where are your prophets who prophe-
sied to you, 'The king of Babylon will not attack
you or this land'? 20But now, my lord the king,
please listen. Let me bring my petition before
you: Do not send me back to the house of Jona-
than the secretary, or I will die there."
21King Zedekiah then gave orders for Jeremiah
to be placed in the courtyard of the guard and
given bread from the street of the bakers each
day until all the bread in the city was gone. So
Jeremiah remained in the courtyard of the
guard.

21 / *Jeremiah 38*
Sunk in the Mud

WHAT A HARD time it has been for Jeremiah! God warned him it would be difficult. Certainly it was, more than he ever imagined. In this passage we see Jeremiah thrown in the mud of a deep well and left for dead. Although he gets out of the well, he is not released from confinement and is imprisoned in Jerusalem until the very end. However, Jeremiah's ministry of faithfulness to God and God's people helped prepare the way for you and me. We can know God in ways that are deeper, richer and more powerful because Jeremiah had the courage to be faithful and the wisdom to record his words.

Warming Up to God What sort of spiritual legacy would you like to leave for your friends and family?

Read Jeremiah 38.

38 Shephatiah son of Mattan, Gedaliah
son of Pashhur, Jehucal[b] son of
Shelemiah, and Pashhur son of
Malkijah heard what Jeremiah was telling all the
people when he said, 2"This is what the LORD says:
'Whoever stays in this city will die by the sword,
famine or plague, but whoever goes over to the
Babylonians[c] will live. He will escape with his
life; he will live.' 3And this is what the LORD says:
'This city will certainly be handed over to the
army of the king of Babylon, who will cap-
ture it.' "
4Then the officials said to the king, "This man
should be put to death. He is discouraging the
soldiers who are left in this city, as well as all the
people, by the things he is saying to them. This
man is not seeking the good of these people but
their ruin."
5"He is in your hands," King Zedekiah an-
swered. "The king can do nothing to oppose
you."
6So they took Jeremiah and put him into the
cistern of Malkijah, the king's son, which was in
the courtyard of the guard. They lowered Jere-
miah by ropes into the cistern; it had no water in
it, only mud, and Jeremiah sank down into the
mud.
7But Ebed-Melech, a Cushite,[d] an official[e] in

[b]1 Hebrew *Jucal,* a variant of *Jehucal* [c]2 Or *Chaldeans;* also in verses 18, 19 and 23 [d]7 Probably from the upper Nile region [e]7 Or *a eunuch*

the royal palace, heard that they had put Jeremiah into the cistern. While the king was sitting in the Benjamin Gate, 8Ebed-Melech went out of the palace and said to him, 9"My lord the king, these men have acted wickedly in all they have done to Jeremiah the prophet. They have thrown him into a cistern, where he will starve to death when there is no longer any bread in the city."

10Then the king commanded Ebed-Melech the Cushite, "Take thirty men from here with you and lift Jeremiah the prophet out of the cistern before he dies."

11So Ebed-Melech took the men with him and went to a room under the treasury in the palace. He took some old rags and worn-out clothes from there and let them down with ropes to Jeremiah in the cistern. 12Ebed-Melech the Cushite said to Jeremiah, "Put these old rags and worn-out clothes under your arms to pad the ropes." Jeremiah did so, 13and they pulled him up with the ropes and lifted him out of the cistern. And Jeremiah remained in the courtyard of the guard.

14Then King Zedekiah sent for Jeremiah the prophet and had him brought to the third entrance to the temple of the LORD. "I am going to ask you something," the king said to Jeremiah. "Do not hide anything from me."

15Jeremiah said to Zedekiah, "If I give you an answer, will you not kill me? Even if I did give you counsel, you would not listen to me."

16But King Zedekiah swore this oath secretly to Jeremiah: "As surely as the LORD lives, who has given us breath, I will neither kill you nor hand you over to those who are seeking your life."

17Then Jeremiah said to Zedekiah, "This is what the LORD God Almighty, the God of Israel, says: 'If you surrender to the officers of the king of Babylon, your life will be spared and this city will not be burned down; you and your family will live. 18But if you will not surrender to the officers of the king of Babylon, this city will be handed over to the Babylonians and they will burn it down; you yourself will not escape from their hands.' "

19King Zedekiah said to Jeremiah, "I am afraid of the Jews who have gone over to the Babylonians, for the Babylonians may hand me over to them and they will mistreat me."

20"They will not hand you over," Jeremiah replied. "Obey the LORD by doing what I tell you. Then it will go well with you, and your life will be spared. 21But if you refuse to surrender, this is what the LORD has revealed to me: 22All the women left in the palace of the king of Judah will be brought out to the officials of the king of Babylon. Those women will say to you:

" 'They misled you and overcame you—
  those trusted friends of yours.
Your feet are sunk in the mud;
  your friends have deserted you.'

23"All your wives and children will be brought out to the Babylonians. You yourself will not escape from their hands but will be captured by the king of Babylon; and this city will[f] be burned down."

24Then Zedekiah said to Jeremiah, "Do not let anyone know about this conversation, or you may die. 25If the officials hear that I talked with you, and they come to you and say, 'Tell us what you said to the king and what the king said to you; do not hide it from us or we will kill you,' 26then tell them, 'I was pleading with the king not to send me back to Jonathan's house to die there.' "

27All the officials did come to Jeremiah and question him, and he told them everything the king had ordered him to say. So they said no more to him, for no one had heard his conversation with the king.

28And Jeremiah remained in the courtyard of the guard until the day Jerusalem was captured.

f23 Or *and you will cause this city to*

Discovering the Word 1. As Judah was besieged by Babylon, what were Jeremiah's enemies concerned about? 2. If you were in leadership and heard Jeremiah's message, what would have to happen before you would be willing to surrender to your enemies? 3. Jeremiah ends up in the well, sunk down deep into the mud. How had God prepared Jeremiah for just such a situation? 4. How did Jeremiah get out of the well (vv. 7–13)? 5. Zedekiah the king calls Jeremiah to ask for his advice (vv. 14–23). What personal and political reasons does Jeremiah give for Zedekiah to surrender? 6. How would you evaluate the success of Jeremiah's ministry?

Applying the Word 1. In what ways can Christians end up in wells today? 2. How can God help you to persevere even when you are stuck in the mud?

Responding in Prayer Ask God to mold you into his servant, someone who will leave a legacy of faith behind.

Jeremiah 39—43

39 This is how Jerusalem was taken: 1In the ninth year of Zedekiah king of Judah, in the tenth month, Nebuchadnezzar king of Babylon marched against Jerusalem with his whole army and laid siege to it. 2And on the ninth day of the fourth month of Zedekiah's eleventh year, the city wall was broken through. 3Then all the officials of the king of Babylon came and took seats in the Middle Gate: Nergal-Sharezer of Samgar, Nebo-Sarsekim[g] a chief officer, Nergal-Sharezer a high official and all the other officials of the king of Babylon. 4When Zedekiah king of Judah and all the soldiers saw them, they fled; they left the city at night by way of the king's garden, through the gate between the two walls, and headed toward the Arabah.[h]

5But the Babylonian[i] army pursued them and overtook Zedekiah in the plains of Jericho. They captured him and took him to Nebuchadnezzar king of Babylon at Riblah in the land of Hamath, where he pronounced sentence on him. 6There at Riblah the king of Babylon slaughtered the sons of Zedekiah before his eyes and also killed all the nobles of Judah. 7Then he put out Zedekiah's eyes and bound him with bronze shackles to take him to Babylon.

8The Babylonians[j] set fire to the royal palace and the houses of the people and broke down the walls of Jerusalem. 9Nebuzaradan commander of the imperial guard carried into exile to Babylon the people who remained in the city, along with those who had gone over to him, and the rest of the people. 10But Nebuzaradan the commander of the guard left behind in the land of Judah some of the poor people, who owned nothing; and at that time he gave them vineyards and fields.

11Now Nebuchadnezzar king of Babylon had given these orders about Jeremiah through Nebuzaradan commander of the imperial guard: 12"Take him and look after him; don't harm him but do for him whatever he asks." 13So Nebuzaradan the commander of the guard, Nebushazban a chief officer, Nergal-Sharezer a high official and all the other officers of the king of Babylon 14sent and had Jeremiah taken out of the courtyard of the guard. They turned him over to Gedaliah son of Ahikam, the son of Shaphan, to take him back to his home. So he remained among his own people.

15While Jeremiah had been confined in the courtyard of the guard, the word of the LORD came to him: 16"Go and tell Ebed-Melech the Cushite, 'This is what the LORD Almighty, the God of Israel, says: I am about to fulfill my words against this city through disaster, not prosperity. At that time they will be fulfilled before your eyes. 17But I will rescue you on that day, declares the LORD; you will not be handed over to those you fear. 18I will save you; you will not fall by the sword but will escape with your life, because you trust in me, declares the LORD.' "

40 The word came to Jeremiah from the LORD after Nebuzaradan commander of the imperial guard had released him at Ramah. He had found Jeremiah bound in chains among all the captives from Jerusalem and Judah who were being carried into exile to Babylon. 2When the commander of the guard found Jeremiah, he said to him, "The LORD your God decreed this disaster for this place. 3And now the LORD has brought it about; he has done just as he said he would. All this happened because you people sinned against the LORD and did not obey him. 4But today I am freeing you from the chains on your wrists. Come with me to Babylon, if you like, and I will look after you; but if you do not want to, then don't come. Look, the whole country lies before you; go wherever you please." 5However, before Jeremiah turned to go,[k] Nebuzaradan added, "Go back to Gedaliah son of Ahikam, the son of Shaphan, whom the

g3 Or *Nergal-Sharezer, Samgar-Nebo, Sarsekim* h4 Or *the Jordan Valley* i5 Or *Chaldean* j8 Or *Chaldeans* k5 Or *Jeremiah answered*

king of Babylon has appointed over the towns of Judah, and live with him among the people, or go anywhere else you please."

Then the commander gave him provisions and a present and let him go. 6So Jeremiah went to Gedaliah son of Ahikam at Mizpah and stayed with him among the people who were left behind in the land.

7When all the army officers and their men who were still in the open country heard that the king of Babylon had appointed Gedaliah son of Ahikam as governor over the land and had put him in charge of the men, women and children who were the poorest in the land and who had not been carried into exile to Babylon, 8they came to Gedaliah at Mizpah—Ishmael son of Nethaniah, Johanan and Jonathan the sons of Kareah, Seraiah son of Tanhumeth, the sons of Ephai the Netophathite, and Jaazaniah[l] the son of the Maacathite, and their men. 9Gedaliah son of Ahikam, the son of Shaphan, took an oath to reassure them and their men. "Do not be afraid to serve the Babylonians,[m]" he said. "Settle down in the land and serve the king of Babylon, and it will go well with you. 10I myself will stay at Mizpah to represent you before the Babylonians who come to us, but you are to harvest the wine, summer fruit and oil, and put them in your storage jars, and live in the towns you have taken over."

11When all the Jews in Moab, Ammon, Edom and all the other countries heard that the king of Babylon had left a remnant in Judah and had appointed Gedaliah son of Ahikam, the son of Shaphan, as governor over them, 12they all came back to the land of Judah, to Gedaliah at Mizpah, from all the countries where they had been scattered. And they harvested an abundance of wine and summer fruit.

13Johanan son of Kareah and all the army officers still in the open country came to Gedaliah at Mizpah 14and said to him, "Don't you know that Baalis king of the Ammonites has sent Ishmael son of Nethaniah to take your life?" But Gedaliah son of Ahikam did not believe them.

15Then Johanan son of Kareah said privately to Gedaliah in Mizpah, "Let me go and kill Ishmael son of Nethaniah, and no one will know it. Why should he take your life and cause all the Jews who are gathered around you to be scattered and the remnant of Judah to perish?"

16But Gedaliah son of Ahikam said to Johanan son of Kareah, "Don't do such a thing! What you are saying about Ishmael is not true."

41

In the seventh month Ishmael son of Nethaniah, the son of Elishama, who was of royal blood and had been one of the king's officers, came with ten men to Gedaliah son of Ahikam at Mizpah. While they were eating together there, 2Ishmael son of Nethaniah and the ten men who were with him got up and struck down Gedaliah son of Ahikam, the son of Shaphan, with the sword, killing the one whom the king of Babylon had appointed as governor over the land. 3Ishmael also killed all the Jews who were with Gedaliah at Mizpah, as well as the Babylonian[n] soldiers who were there.

4The day after Gedaliah's assassination, before anyone knew about it, 5eighty men who had shaved off their beards, torn their clothes and cut themselves came from Shechem, Shiloh and Samaria, bringing grain offerings and incense with them to the house of the LORD. 6Ishmael son of Nethaniah went out from Mizpah to meet them, weeping as he went. When he met them, he said, "Come to Gedaliah son of Ahikam." 7When they went into the city, Ishmael son of Nethaniah and the men who were with him slaughtered them and threw them into a cistern. 8But ten of them said to Ishmael, "Don't kill us! We have wheat and barley, oil and honey, hidden in a field." So he let them alone and did not kill them with the others. 9Now the cistern where he threw all the bodies of the men he had killed along with Gedaliah was the one King Asa had made as part of his defense against Baasha king of Israel. Ishmael son of Nethaniah filled it with the dead.

10Ishmael made captives of all the rest of the people who were in Mizpah—the king's daughters along with all the others who were left there, over whom Nebuzaradan commander of the imperial guard had appointed Gedaliah son of Ahikam. Ishmael son of Nethaniah took them captive and set out to cross over to the Ammonites.

11When Johanan son of Kareah and all the army officers who were with him heard about all the crimes Ishmael son of Nethaniah had committed, 12they took all their men and went to fight Ishmael son of Nethaniah. They caught up with him near the great pool in Gibeon. 13When all the people Ishmael had with him saw Johanan son of Kareah and the army officers who were with him,

[l]8 Hebrew *Jezaniah*, a variant of *Jaazaniah* [m]9 Or *Chaldeans*; also in verse 10 [n]3 Or *Chaldean*

they were glad. 14All the people Ishmael had taken captive at Mizpah turned and went over to Johanan son of Kareah. 15But Ishmael son of Nethaniah and eight of his men escaped from Johanan and fled to the Ammonites.

16Then Johanan son of Kareah and all the army officers who were with him led away all the survivors from Mizpah whom he had recovered from Ishmael son of Nethaniah after he had assassinated Gedaliah son of Ahikam: the soldiers, women, children and court officials he had brought from Gibeon. 17And they went on, stopping at Geruth Kimham near Bethlehem on their way to Egypt 18to escape the Babylonians.[o] They were afraid of them because Ishmael son of Nethaniah had killed Gedaliah son of Ahikam, whom the king of Babylon had appointed as governor over the land.

42 Then all the army officers, including Johanan son of Kareah and Jezaniah[p] son of Hoshaiah, and all the people from the least to the greatest approached 2Jeremiah the prophet and said to him, "Please hear our petition and pray to the LORD your God for this entire remnant. For as you now see, though we were once many, now only a few are left. 3Pray that the LORD your God will tell us where we should go and what we should do."

4"I have heard you," replied Jeremiah the prophet. "I will certainly pray to the LORD your God as you have requested; I will tell you everything the LORD says and will keep nothing back from you."

5Then they said to Jeremiah, "May the LORD be a true and faithful witness against us if we do not act in accordance with everything the LORD your God sends you to tell us. 6Whether it is favorable or unfavorable, we will obey the LORD our God, to whom we are sending you, so that it will go well with us, for we will obey the LORD our God."

7Ten days later the word of the LORD came to Jeremiah. 8So he called together Johanan son of Kareah and all the army officers who were with him and all the people from the least to the greatest. 9He said to them, "This is what the LORD, the God of Israel, to whom you sent me to present your petition, says: 10'If you stay in this land, I will build you up and not tear you down; I will plant you and not uproot you, for I am grieved over the disaster I have inflicted on you. 11Do not be afraid of the king of Babylon, whom you now fear. Do not be afraid of him, declares the LORD, for I am with you and will save you and deliver you from his hands. 12I will show you compassion so that he will have compassion on you and restore you to your land.'

13"However, if you say, 'We will not stay in this land,' and so disobey the LORD your God, 14and if you say, 'No, we will go and live in Egypt, where we will not see war or hear the trumpet or be hungry for bread,' 15then hear the word of the LORD, O remnant of Judah. This is what the LORD Almighty, the God of Israel, says: 'If you are determined to go to Egypt and you do go to settle there, 16then the sword you fear will overtake you there, and the famine you dread will follow you into Egypt, and there you will die. 17Indeed, all who are determined to go to Egypt to settle there will die by the sword, famine and plague; not one of them will survive or escape the disaster I will bring on them.' 18This is what the LORD Almighty, the God of Israel, says: 'As my anger and wrath have been poured out on those who lived in Jerusalem, so will my wrath be poured out on you when you go to Egypt. You will be an object of cursing and horror, of condemnation and reproach; you will never see this place again.'

19"O remnant of Judah, the LORD has told you, 'Do not go to Egypt.' Be sure of this: I warn you today 20that you made a fatal mistake[q] when you sent me to the LORD your God and said, 'Pray to the LORD our God for us; tell us everything he says and we will do it.' 21I have told you today, but you still have not obeyed the LORD your God in all he sent me to tell you. 22So now, be sure of this: You will die by the sword, famine and plague in the place where you want to go to settle."

43 When Jeremiah finished telling the people all the words of the LORD their God—everything the LORD had sent him to tell them— 2Azariah son of Hoshaiah and Johanan son of Kareah and all the arrogant men said to Jeremiah, "You are lying! The LORD our God has not sent you to say, 'You must not go to Egypt to settle there.' 3But Baruch son of Neriah is inciting you against us to hand us over to the Babylonians,[o] so they may kill us or carry us into exile to Babylon."

4So Johanan son of Kareah and all the army officers and all the people disobeyed the LORD's command to stay in the land of Judah. 5Instead, Johanan son of Kareah and all the army officers

o 18,3 Or *Chaldeans* p 1 Hebrew; Septuagint (see also 43:2) *Azariah*
q 20 Or *you erred in your hearts*

led away all the remnant of Judah who had come back to live in the land of Judah from all the nations where they had been scattered. 6They also led away all the men, women and children and the king's daughters whom Nebuzaradan commander of the imperial guard had left with Gedaliah son of Ahikam, the son of Shaphan, and Jeremiah the prophet and Baruch son of Neriah. 7So they entered Egypt in disobedience to the LORD and went as far as Tahpanhes.

8In Tahpanhes the word of the LORD came to Jeremiah: 9"While the Jews are watching, take some large stones with you and bury them in clay in the brick pavement at the entrance to Pharaoh's palace in Tahpanhes. 10Then say to them, 'This is what the LORD Almighty, the God of Israel, says: I will send for my servant Nebuchadnezzar king of Babylon, and I will set his throne over these stones I have buried here; he will spread his royal canopy above them. 11He will come and attack Egypt, bringing death to those destined for death, captivity to those destined for captivity, and the sword to those destined for the sword. 12He[r] will set fire to the temples of the gods of Egypt; he will burn their temples and take their gods captive. As a shepherd wraps his garment around him, so will he wrap Egypt around himself and depart from there unscathed. 13There in the temple of the sun[s] in Egypt he will demolish the sacred pillars and will burn down the temples of the gods of Egypt.' "

[r]12 Or *I* [s]13 Or *in Heliopolis*

22 / *Jeremiah 44*
Self-Destruction

THE HOUSE NEXT door to us is sinking. Not very fast, but it is definitely leaning—fortunately away from our house. It was built years ago where a ravine had been filled in. At the time the spot must have looked like a fine building site. Slowly but surely, the land has settled out from under that house.

We persist in our self-destructive habits because they offer some immediate payoff. But eventually they catch up with us when our shaky foundation starts to go.

Warming Up to God What destructive habit have you had the greatest struggle with?

Read Jeremiah 44.

44 This word came to Jeremiah concerning all the Jews living in Lower Egypt—in Migdol, Tahpanhes and Memphis[t]—and in Upper Egypt[u]: 2"This is what the LORD Almighty, the God of Israel, says: You saw the great disaster I brought on Jerusalem and on all the towns of Judah. Today they lie deserted and in ruins 3because of the evil they have done. They provoked me to anger by burning incense and by worshiping other gods that neither they nor you nor your fathers ever knew. 4Again and again I sent my servants the prophets, who said, 'Do not do this detestable thing that I hate!' 5But they did not listen or pay attention; they did not turn from their wickedness or stop burning incense to other gods. 6Therefore, my fierce anger was poured out; it raged against the towns of Judah and the streets of Jerusalem and made them the desolate ruins they are today.

7"Now this is what the LORD God Almighty, the God of Israel, says: Why bring such great disaster on yourselves by cutting off from Judah the men and women, the children and infants, and so leave yourselves without a remnant? 8Why provoke me to anger with what your hands have made, burning incense to other gods in Egypt, where you have come to live? You will destroy yourselves and make yourselves an object of cursing and reproach among all the nations on earth. 9Have you forgotten the wickedness committed by your fathers and by the kings and queens of

[t]1 Hebrew *Noph* [u]1 Hebrew *in Pathros*

Judah and the wickedness committed by you and your wives in the land of Judah and the streets of Jerusalem? [10]To this day they have not humbled themselves or shown reverence, nor have they followed my law and the decrees I set before you and your fathers.

[11]"Therefore, this is what the LORD Almighty, the God of Israel, says: I am determined to bring disaster on you and to destroy all Judah. [12]I will take away the remnant of Judah who were determined to go to Egypt to settle there. They will all perish in Egypt; they will fall by the sword or die from famine. From the least to the greatest, they will die by sword or famine. They will become an object of cursing and horror, of condemnation and reproach. [13]I will punish those who live in Egypt with the sword, famine and plague, as I punished Jerusalem. [14]None of the remnant of Judah who have gone to live in Egypt will escape or survive to return to the land of Judah, to which they long to return and live; none will return except a few fugitives."

[15]Then all the men who knew that their wives were burning incense to other gods, along with all the women who were present—a large assembly—and all the people living in Lower and Upper Egypt,[v] said to Jeremiah, [16]"We will not listen to the message you have spoken to us in the name of the LORD! [17]We will certainly do everything we said we would: We will burn incense to the Queen of Heaven and will pour out drink offerings to her just as we and our fathers, our kings and our officials did in the towns of Judah and in the streets of Jerusalem. At that time we had plenty of food and were well off and suffered no harm. [18]But ever since we stopped burning incense to the Queen of Heaven and pouring out drink offerings to her, we have had nothing and have been perishing by sword and famine."

[19]The women added, "When we burned incense to the Queen of Heaven and poured out drink offerings to her, did not our husbands know that we were making cakes like her image and pouring out drink offerings to her?"

[20]Then Jeremiah said to all the people, both men and women, who were answering him, [21]"Did not the LORD remember and think about the incense burned in the towns of Judah and the streets of Jerusalem by you and your fathers, your kings and your officials and the people of the land? [22]When the LORD could no longer endure your wicked actions and the detestable things you did, your land became an object of cursing and a desolate waste without inhabitants, as it is today. [23]Because you have burned incense and have sinned against the LORD and have not obeyed him or followed his law or his decrees or his stipulations, this disaster has come upon you, as you now see."

[24]Then Jeremiah said to all the people, including the women, "Hear the word of the LORD, all you people of Judah in Egypt. [25]This is what the LORD Almighty, the God of Israel, says: You and your wives have shown by your actions what you promised when you said, 'We will certainly carry out the vows we made to burn incense and pour out drink offerings to the Queen of Heaven.'

"Go ahead then, do what you promised! Keep your vows! [26]But hear the word of the LORD, all Jews living in Egypt: 'I swear by my great name,' says the LORD, 'that no one from Judah living anywhere in Egypt will ever again invoke my name or swear, "As surely as the Sovereign LORD lives." [27]For I am watching over them for harm, not for good; the Jews in Egypt will perish by sword and famine until they are all destroyed. [28]Those who escape the sword and return to the land of Judah from Egypt will be very few. Then the whole remnant of Judah who came to live in Egypt will know whose word will stand—mine or theirs.

[29]" 'This will be the sign to you that I will punish you in this place,' declares the LORD, 'so that you will know that my threats of harm against you will surely stand.' [30]This is what the LORD says: 'I am going to hand Pharaoh Hophra king of Egypt over to his enemies who seek his life, just as I handed Zedekiah king of Judah over to Nebuchadnezzar king of Babylon, the enemy who was seeking his life.' "

[v]15 Hebrew *in Egypt and Pathros*

Discovering the Word 1. What example is Jeremiah told to remind the exiles in Egypt about (vv. 1–6)? 2. How are they in danger of bringing destruction on themselves (vv. 7–14)? 3. What reasons do the people give for persisting in their idolatry (vv. 15–19)? 4. Through Jeremiah, how does God warn them again

(vv. 20–25)? 5. Because the Jews in Egypt failed to listen to the Lord's warning, what fate will they bring on themselves (vv. 26–30)?

Applying the Word 1. When has the Lord warned you about things in your life which harm you? 2. How might the Lord be warning you now about some self-destructive practice or attitude?

Responding in Prayer Open your life to the light of the Lord's searching. Confess any excuses you make for harmful attitudes or habits. Thank the Lord for his warnings which come because he loves you.

Jeremiah 45—49

45 This is what Jeremiah the prophet
told Baruch son of Neriah in the
fourth year of Jehoiakim son of Jo-
siah king of Judah, after Baruch had written on
a scroll the words Jeremiah was then dictating:
2"This is what the LORD, the God of Israel, says to
you, Baruch: 3You said, 'Woe to me! The LORD has
added sorrow to my pain; I am worn out with
groaning and find no rest.'"
4⌞The LORD said,⌟ "Say this to him: 'This is what
the LORD says: I will overthrow what I have built
and uproot what I have planted, throughout the
land. 5Should you then seek great things for your-
self? Seek them not. For I will bring disaster on
all people, declares the LORD, but wherever you go
I will let you escape with your life.'"

46 This is the word of the LORD that came to Jeremiah the prophet concerning the nations:

2Concerning Egypt:

This is the message against the army of Pharaoh Neco king of Egypt, which was defeated at Carchemish on the Euphrates River by Nebuchadnezzar king of Babylon in the fourth year of Jehoiakim son of Josiah king of Judah:

3"Prepare your shields, both large and small,
and march out for battle!
4Harness the horses,
mount the steeds!
Take your positions
with helmets on!
Polish your spears,
put on your armor!
5What do I see?
They are terrified,
they are retreating,
their warriors are defeated.
They flee in haste
without looking back,
and there is terror on every side,"
declares the LORD.
6"The swift cannot flee
nor the strong escape.
In the north by the River Euphrates
they stumble and fall.

7"Who is this that rises like the Nile,
like rivers of surging waters?
8Egypt rises like the Nile,
like rivers of surging waters.
She says, 'I will rise and cover the earth;
I will destroy cities and their people.'
9Charge, O horses!
Drive furiously, O charioteers!
March on, O warriors—
men of Cush[w] and Put who carry shields,
men of Lydia who draw the bow.
10But that day belongs to the Lord, the LORD Almighty—
a day of vengeance, for vengeance on his foes.
The sword will devour till it is satisfied,
till it has quenched its thirst with blood.
For the Lord, the LORD Almighty, will offer sacrifice
in the land of the north by the River Euphrates.

11"Go up to Gilead and get balm,
O Virgin Daughter of Egypt.
But you multiply remedies in vain;
there is no healing for you.
12The nations will hear of your shame;
your cries will fill the earth.
One warrior will stumble over another;
both will fall down together."

13This is the message the LORD spoke to Jere-

[w]9 That is, the upper Nile region

miah the prophet about the coming of Nebuchad-
nezzar king of Babylon to attack Egypt:

14"Announce this in Egypt, and proclaim it in
Migdol;
proclaim it also in Memphis[x] and
Tahpanhes:
'Take your positions and get ready,
for the sword devours those around you.'
15Why will your warriors be laid low?
They cannot stand, for the LORD will push
them down.
16They will stumble repeatedly;
they will fall over each other.
They will say, 'Get up, let us go back
to our own people and our native lands,
away from the sword of the oppressor.'
17There they will exclaim,
'Pharaoh king of Egypt is only a loud noise;
he has missed his opportunity.'

18"As surely as I live," declares the King,
whose name is the LORD Almighty,
"one will come who is like Tabor among the
mountains,
like Carmel by the sea.
19Pack your belongings for exile,
you who live in Egypt,
for Memphis will be laid waste
and lie in ruins without inhabitant.
20"Egypt is a beautiful heifer,
but a gadfly is coming
against her from the north.
21The mercenaries in her ranks
are like fattened calves.
They too will turn and flee together,
they will not stand their ground,
for the day of disaster is coming upon them,
the time for them to be punished.
22Egypt will hiss like a fleeing serpent
as the enemy advances in force;
they will come against her with axes,
like men who cut down trees.
23They will chop down her forest,"
declares the LORD,
"dense though it be.
They are more numerous than locusts,
they cannot be counted.
24The Daughter of Egypt will be put to shame,
handed over to the people of the north."

25The LORD Almighty, the God of Israel, says: "I
am about to bring punishment on Amon god of
Thebes,[y] on Pharaoh, on Egypt and her gods and
her kings, and on those who rely on Pharaoh. 26I
will hand them over to those who seek their lives,
to Nebuchadnezzar king of Babylon and his offi-
cers. Later, however, Egypt will be inhabited as in
times past," declares the LORD.

27"Do not fear, O Jacob my servant;
do not be dismayed, O Israel.
I will surely save you out of a distant place,
your descendants from the land of their
exile.
Jacob will again have peace and security,
and no one will make him afraid.
28Do not fear, O Jacob my servant,
for I am with you," declares the LORD.
"Though I completely destroy all the nations
among which I scatter you,
I will not completely destroy you.
I will discipline you but only with justice;
I will not let you go entirely unpunished."

47

This is the word of the LORD that
came to Jeremiah the prophet con-
cerning the Philistines before Phar-
aoh attacked Gaza:

2This is what the LORD says:

"See how the waters are rising in the north;
they will become an overflowing torrent.
They will overflow the land and everything in
it,
the towns and those who live in them.
The people will cry out;
all who dwell in the land will wail
3at the sound of the hoofs of galloping steeds,
at the noise of enemy chariots
and the rumble of their wheels.
Fathers will not turn to help their children;
their hands will hang limp.
4For the day has come
to destroy all the Philistines
and to cut off all survivors
who could help Tyre and Sidon.
The LORD is about to destroy the Philistines,
the remnant from the coasts of Caphtor.[z]
5Gaza will shave her head in mourning;
Ashkelon will be silenced.
O remnant on the plain,
how long will you cut yourselves?

[x]14 Hebrew *Noph*; also in verse 19 [y]25 Hebrew *No* [z]4 That is, Crete

6" 'Ah, sword of the LORD,' ⌞you cry,⌟
'how long till you rest?
Return to your scabbard;
cease and be still.'
7But how can it rest
when the LORD has commanded it,
when he has ordered it
to attack Ashkelon and the coast?"

48

Concerning Moab:

This is what the LORD Almighty, the God of Israel, says:

"Woe to Nebo, for it will be ruined.
Kiriathaim will be disgraced and captured;
the stronghold[a] will be disgraced and shattered.
2Moab will be praised no more;
in Heshbon[b] men will plot her downfall:
'Come, let us put an end to that nation.'
You too, O Madmen,[c] will be silenced;
the sword will pursue you.
3Listen to the cries from Horonaim,
cries of great havoc and destruction.
4Moab will be broken;
her little ones will cry out.[d]
5They go up the way to Luhith,
weeping bitterly as they go;
on the road down to Horonaim
anguished cries over the destruction are heard.
6Flee! Run for your lives;
become like a bush[e] in the desert.
7Since you trust in your deeds and riches,
you too will be taken captive,
and Chemosh will go into exile,
together with his priests and officials.
8The destroyer will come against every town,
and not a town will escape.
The valley will be ruined
and the plateau destroyed,
because the LORD has spoken.
9Put salt on Moab,
for she will be laid waste[f];
her towns will become desolate,
with no one to live in them.

10"A curse on him who is lax in doing the LORD's work!
A curse on him who keeps his sword from bloodshed!

11"Moab has been at rest from youth,
like wine left on its dregs,
not poured from one jar to another—
she has not gone into exile.
So she tastes as she did,
and her aroma is unchanged.
12But days are coming,"
declares the LORD,
"when I will send men who pour from jars,
and they will pour her out;
they will empty her jars
and smash her jugs.
13Then Moab will be ashamed of Chemosh,
as the house of Israel was ashamed
when they trusted in Bethel.

14"How can you say, 'We are warriors,
men valiant in battle'?
15Moab will be destroyed and her towns invaded;
her finest young men will go down in the slaughter,"
declares the King, whose name is the LORD Almighty.
16"The fall of Moab is at hand;
her calamity will come quickly.
17Mourn for her, all who live around her,
all who know her fame;
say, 'How broken is the mighty scepter,
how broken the glorious staff!'

18"Come down from your glory
and sit on the parched ground,
O inhabitants of the Daughter of Dibon,
for he who destroys Moab
will come up against you
and ruin your fortified cities.
19Stand by the road and watch,
you who live in Aroer.
Ask the man fleeing and the woman escaping,
ask them, 'What has happened?'
20Moab is disgraced, for she is shattered.
Wail and cry out!
Announce by the Arnon
that Moab is destroyed.
21Judgment has come to the plateau—
to Holon, Jahzah and Mephaath,
22 to Dibon, Nebo and Beth Diblathaim,
23 to Kiriathaim, Beth Gamul and Beth Meon,
24 to Kerioth and Bozrah—

[a]1 Or / *Misgab* [b]2 The Hebrew for *Heshbon* sounds like the Hebrew for *plot.* [c]2 The name of the Moabite town Madmen sounds like the Hebrew for *be silenced.* [d]4 Hebrew; Septuagint / *proclaim it to Zoar* [e]6 Or *like Aroer* [f]9 Or *Give wings to Moab, / for she will fly away*

to all the towns of Moab, far and near.
25Moab's horn[g] is cut off;
her arm is broken,"
declares the LORD.

26"Make her drunk,
for she has defied the LORD.
Let Moab wallow in her vomit;
let her be an object of ridicule.
27Was not Israel the object of your ridicule?
Was she caught among thieves,
that you shake your head in scorn
whenever you speak of her?
28Abandon your towns and dwell among the rocks,
you who live in Moab.
Be like a dove that makes its nest
at the mouth of a cave.

29"We have heard of Moab's pride—
her overweening pride and conceit,
her pride and arrogance
and the haughtiness of her heart.
30I know her insolence but it is futile,"
declares the LORD,
"and her boasts accomplish nothing.
31Therefore I wail over Moab,
for all Moab I cry out,
I moan for the men of Kir Hareseth.
32I weep for you, as Jazer weeps,
O vines of Sibmah.
Your branches spread as far as the sea;
they reached as far as the sea of Jazer.
The destroyer has fallen
on your ripened fruit and grapes.
33Joy and gladness are gone
from the orchards and fields of Moab.
I have stopped the flow of wine from the presses;
no one treads them with shouts of joy.
Although there are shouts,
they are not shouts of joy.

34"The sound of their cry rises
from Heshbon to Elealeh and Jahaz,
from Zoar as far as Horonaim and Eglath Shelishiyah,
for even the waters of Nimrim are dried up.
35In Moab I will put an end
to those who make offerings on the high places
and burn incense to their gods,"
declares the LORD.

36"So my heart laments for Moab like a flute;
it laments like a flute for the men of Kir Hareseth.
The wealth they acquired is gone.
37Every head is shaved
and every beard cut off;
every hand is slashed
and every waist is covered with sackcloth.
38On all the roofs in Moab
and in the public squares
there is nothing but mourning,
for I have broken Moab
like a jar that no one wants,"
declares the LORD.
39"How shattered she is! How they wail!
How Moab turns her back in shame!
Moab has become an object of ridicule,
an object of horror to all those around her."

40This is what the LORD says:

"Look! An eagle is swooping down,
spreading its wings over Moab.
41Kerioth[h] will be captured
and the strongholds taken.
In that day the hearts of Moab's warriors
will be like the heart of a woman in labor.
42Moab will be destroyed as a nation
because she defied the LORD.
43Terror and pit and snare await you,
O people of Moab,"
declares the LORD.
44"Whoever flees from the terror
will fall into a pit,
whoever climbs out of the pit
will be caught in a snare;
for I will bring upon Moab
the year of her punishment,"
declares the LORD.

45"In the shadow of Heshbon
the fugitives stand helpless,
for a fire has gone out from Heshbon,
a blaze from the midst of Sihon;
it burns the foreheads of Moab,
the skulls of the noisy boasters.
46Woe to you, O Moab!
The people of Chemosh are destroyed;
your sons are taken into exile
and your daughters into captivity.

g25 *Horn* here symbolizes strength. h41 Or *The cities*

47"Yet I will restore the fortunes of Moab
in days to come,"
declares the LORD.

Here ends the judgment on Moab.

49

Concerning the Ammonites:

This is what the LORD says:

"Has Israel no sons?
Has she no heirs?
Why then has Molech[i] taken possession of Gad?
Why do his people live in its towns?
2But the days are coming,"
declares the LORD,
"when I will sound the battle cry
against Rabbah of the Ammonites;
it will become a mound of ruins,
and its surrounding villages will be set on fire.
Then Israel will drive out
those who drove her out,"
says the LORD.
3"Wail, O Heshbon, for Ai is destroyed!
Cry out, O inhabitants of Rabbah!
Put on sackcloth and mourn;
rush here and there inside the walls,
for Molech will go into exile,
together with his priests and officials.
4Why do you boast of your valleys,
boast of your valleys so fruitful?
O unfaithful daughter,
you trust in your riches and say,
'Who will attack me?'
5I will bring terror on you
from all those around you,"
declares the Lord, the LORD Almighty.
"Every one of you will be driven away,
and no one will gather the fugitives.

6"Yet afterward, I will restore the fortunes of the Ammonites,"
declares the LORD.

7Concerning Edom:

This is what the LORD Almighty says:

"Is there no longer wisdom in Teman?
Has counsel perished from the prudent?
Has their wisdom decayed?
8Turn and flee, hide in deep caves,
you who live in Dedan,
for I will bring disaster on Esau
at the time I punish him.
9If grape pickers came to you,
would they not leave a few grapes?
If thieves came during the night,
would they not steal only as much as they wanted?
10But I will strip Esau bare;
I will uncover his hiding places,
so that he cannot conceal himself.
His children, relatives and neighbors will perish,
and he will be no more.
11Leave your orphans; I will protect their lives.
Your widows too can trust in me."

12This is what the LORD says: "If those who do
not deserve to drink the cup must drink it, why
should you go unpunished? You will not go un-
punished, but must drink it. 13I swear by myself,"
declares the LORD, "that Bozrah will become a ruin
and an object of horror, of reproach and of curs-
ing; and all its towns will be in ruins forever."

14I have heard a message from the LORD:
An envoy was sent to the nations to say,
"Assemble yourselves to attack it!
Rise up for battle!"

15"Now I will make you small among the nations,
despised among men.
16The terror you inspire
and the pride of your heart have deceived you,
you who live in the clefts of the rocks,
who occupy the heights of the hill.
Though you build your nest as high as the eagle's,
from there I will bring you down,"
declares the LORD.
17"Edom will become an object of horror;
all who pass by will be appalled and will scoff
because of all its wounds.
18As Sodom and Gomorrah were overthrown,
along with their neighboring towns,"
says the LORD,
"so no one will live there;
no man will dwell in it.

19"Like a lion coming up from Jordan's thickets

[i] 1 Or *their king*; Hebrew *malcam*; also in verse 3

to a rich pastureland,
I will chase Edom from its land in an instant.
Who is the chosen one I will appoint for this?
Who is like me and who can challenge me?
And what shepherd can stand against me?"
20 Therefore, hear what the LORD has planned against Edom,
what he has purposed against those who live in Teman:
The young of the flock will be dragged away;
he will completely destroy their pasture because of them.
21 At the sound of their fall the earth will tremble;
their cry will resound to the Red Sea.[j]
22 Look! An eagle will soar and swoop down,
spreading its wings over Bozrah.
In that day the hearts of Edom's warriors
will be like the heart of a woman in labor.

23 Concerning Damascus:

"Hamath and Arpad are dismayed,
for they have heard bad news.
They are disheartened,
troubled like[k] the restless sea.
24 Damascus has become feeble,
she has turned to flee
and panic has gripped her;
anguish and pain have seized her,
pain like that of a woman in labor.
25 Why has the city of renown not been abandoned,
the town in which I delight?
26 Surely, her young men will fall in the streets;
all her soldiers will be silenced in that day,"
declares the LORD Almighty.
27 "I will set fire to the walls of Damascus;
it will consume the fortresses of Ben-Hadad."

28 Concerning Kedar and the kingdoms of Hazor, which Nebuchadnezzar king of Babylon attacked:

This is what the LORD says:

"Arise, and attack Kedar
and destroy the people of the East.
29 Their tents and their flocks will be taken;
their shelters will be carried off
with all their goods and camels.
Men will shout to them,
'Terror on every side!'
30 "Flee quickly away!
Stay in deep caves, you who live in Hazor,"
declares the LORD.
"Nebuchadnezzar king of Babylon has plotted against you;
he has devised a plan against you.

31 "Arise and attack a nation at ease,
which lives in confidence,"
declares the LORD,
"a nation that has neither gates nor bars;
its people live alone.
32 Their camels will become plunder,
and their large herds will be booty.
I will scatter to the winds those who are in distant places[l]
and will bring disaster on them from every side,"
declares the LORD.
33 "Hazor will become a haunt of jackals,
a desolate place forever.
No one will live there;
no man will dwell in it."

34 This is the word of the LORD that came to
Jeremiah the prophet concerning Elam, early in
the reign of Zedekiah king of Judah:

35 This is what the LORD Almighty says:

"See, I will break the bow of Elam,
the mainstay of their might.
36 I will bring against Elam the four winds
from the four quarters of the heavens;
I will scatter them to the four winds,
and there will not be a nation
where Elam's exiles do not go.
37 I will shatter Elam before their foes,
before those who seek their lives;
I will bring disaster upon them,
even my fierce anger,"
declares the LORD.
"I will pursue them with the sword
until I have made an end of them.
38 I will set my throne in Elam
and destroy her king and officials,"
declares the LORD.

39 "Yet I will restore the fortunes of Elam
in days to come,"
declares the LORD.

[j] 21 Hebrew *Yam Suph*; that is, Sea of Reeds
[k] 23 Hebrew *on* or *by*
[l] 32 Or *who clip the hair by their foreheads*

23 / *Jeremiah 50:1–20*
Babylon Shouldn't Gloat

"IT WAS BAD enough that I fell down flat on the ice," said our friend who was just learning to ice skate, "but then this little kid skated around me in a circle and asked, 'Are you all right?' " At humiliating times like those, we need somebody to take our side and literally pick us up. When we've fallen on our faces and it feels like evil is gloating over good, God yearns jealously for us and does not forget us.

Warming Up to God Recall a time you felt defeated. How did the Lord show you he still cared?

Read Jeremiah 50:1–20.

50 This is the word the LORD spoke through Jeremiah the prophet concerning Babylon and the land of the Babylonians[m]:

2"Announce and proclaim among the nations,
lift up a banner and proclaim it;
keep nothing back, but say,
'Babylon will be captured;
Bel will be put to shame,
Marduk filled with terror.
Her images will be put to shame
and her idols filled with terror.'
3A nation from the north will attack her
and lay waste her land.
No one will live in it;
both men and animals will flee away.

4"In those days, at that time,"
declares the LORD,
"the people of Israel and the people of Judah together
will go in tears to seek the LORD their God.
5They will ask the way to Zion
and turn their faces toward it.
They will come and bind themselves to the LORD
in an everlasting covenant
that will not be forgotten.

6"My people have been lost sheep;
their shepherds have led them astray
and caused them to roam on the mountains.
They wandered over mountain and hill
and forgot their own resting place.
7Whoever found them devoured them;
their enemies said, 'We are not guilty,
for they sinned against the LORD, their true pasture,
the LORD, the hope of their fathers.'

8"Flee out of Babylon;
leave the land of the Babylonians,
and be like the goats that lead the flock.
9For I will stir up and bring against Babylon
an alliance of great nations from the land of the north.
They will take up their positions against her,
and from the north she will be captured.
Their arrows will be like skilled warriors
who do not return empty-handed.
10So Babylonia[n] will be plundered;
all who plunder her will have their fill,"
declares the LORD.

11"Because you rejoice and are glad,
you who pillage my inheritance,
because you frolic like a heifer threshing grain
and neigh like stallions,
12your mother will be greatly ashamed;
she who gave you birth will be disgraced.
She will be the least of the nations—
a wilderness, a dry land, a desert.
13Because of the LORD's anger she will not be inhabited
but will be completely desolate.
All who pass Babylon will be horrified and scoff
because of all her wounds.

14"Take up your positions around Babylon,
all you who draw the bow.
Shoot at her! Spare no arrows,
for she has sinned against the LORD.
15Shout against her on every side!

[m]1 Or *Chaldeans*; also in verses 8, 25, 35 and 45 [n]10 Or *Chaldea*

She surrenders, her towers fall,
her walls are torn down.
Since this is the vengeance of the LORD,
take vengeance on her;
do to her as she has done to others.
16Cut off from Babylon the sower,
and the reaper with his sickle at harvest.
Because of the sword of the oppressor
let everyone return to his own people,
let everyone flee to his own land.

17"Israel is a scattered flock
that lions have chased away.
The first to devour him
was the king of Assyria;
the last to crush his bones
was Nebuchadnezzar king of Babylon."

18Therefore this is what the LORD Almighty, the God of Israel, says:

"I will punish the king of Babylon and his land
as I punished the king of Assyria.
19But I will bring Israel back to his own pasture
and he will graze on Carmel and Bashan;
his appetite will be satisfied
on the hills of Ephraim and Gilead.
20In those days, at that time,"
declares the LORD,
"search will be made for Israel's guilt,
but there will be none,
and for the sins of Judah,
but none will be found,
for I will forgive the remnant I spare.

Discovering the Word 1. What is going to happen to Babylon (vv. 1–3, 9–10, 14–16, 18)? 2. When God comes to their rescue, how will Israel respond (vv. 4–5)? 3. How had Babylon gotten the upper hand (vv. 6–7)? 4. Why is God so angry with Babylon (vv. 11–15)? 5. How will God vindicate Israel (v. 20)?

Applying the Word 1. What are some ways that you feel wrong is triumphing over right? 2. In what areas are you tempted to gloat over others who have fallen?

Responding in Prayer Commit to the Lord any situations where you feel wrong is gloating over right. Confess any ways that you gloat over others. Thank the Lord that even in failure he remembers you.

Jeremiah 50:21—51:64

21"Attack the land of Merathaim
and those who live in Pekod.
Pursue, kill and completely destroy[o] them,"
declares the LORD.
"Do everything I have commanded you.
22The noise of battle is in the land,
the noise of great destruction!
23How broken and shattered
is the hammer of the whole earth!
How desolate is Babylon
among the nations!
24I set a trap for you, O Babylon,
and you were caught before you knew it;
you were found and captured
because you opposed the LORD.
25The LORD has opened his arsenal
and brought out the weapons of his wrath,
for the Sovereign LORD Almighty has work to do
in the land of the Babylonians.
26Come against her from afar.
Break open her granaries;
pile her up like heaps of grain.
Completely destroy her
and leave her no remnant.
27Kill all her young bulls;
let them go down to the slaughter!
Woe to them! For their day has come,
the time for them to be punished.
28Listen to the fugitives and refugees from Babylon
declaring in Zion
how the LORD our God has taken vengeance,
vengeance for his temple.
29"Summon archers against Babylon,
all those who draw the bow.
Encamp all around her;
let no one escape.

[o]21 The Hebrew term refers to the irrevocable giving over of things or persons to the LORD, often by totally destroying them; also in verse 26.

Repay her for her deeds;
do to her as she has done.
For she has defied the LORD,
the Holy One of Israel.
30Therefore, her young men will fall in the streets;
all her soldiers will be silenced in that day,"
declares the LORD.
31"See, I am against you, O arrogant one,"
declares the Lord, the LORD Almighty,
"for your day has come,
the time for you to be punished.
32The arrogant one will stumble and fall
and no one will help her up;
I will kindle a fire in her towns
that will consume all who are around her."

33This is what the LORD Almighty says:
"The people of Israel are oppressed,
and the people of Judah as well.
All their captors hold them fast,
refusing to let them go.
34Yet their Redeemer is strong;
the LORD Almighty is his name.
He will vigorously defend their cause
so that he may bring rest to their land,
but unrest to those who live in Babylon.

35"A sword against the Babylonians!"
declares the LORD—
"against those who live in Babylon
and against her officials and wise men!
36A sword against her false prophets!
They will become fools.
A sword against her warriors!
They will be filled with terror.
37A sword against her horses and chariots
and all the foreigners in her ranks!
They will become women.
A sword against her treasures!
They will be plundered.
38A drought on[p] her waters!
They will dry up.
For it is a land of idols,
idols that will go mad with terror.

39"So desert creatures and hyenas will live there,
and there the owl will dwell.
It will never again be inhabited
or lived in from generation to generation.
40As God overthrew Sodom and Gomorrah
along with their neighboring towns,"
declares the LORD,
"so no one will live there;
no man will dwell in it.

41"Look! An army is coming from the north;
a great nation and many kings
are being stirred up from the ends of the earth.
42They are armed with bows and spears;
they are cruel and without mercy.
They sound like the roaring sea
as they ride on their horses;
they come like men in battle formation
to attack you, O Daughter of Babylon.
43The king of Babylon has heard reports about them,
and his hands hang limp.
Anguish has gripped him,
pain like that of a woman in labor.
44Like a lion coming up from Jordan's thickets
to a rich pastureland,
I will chase Babylon from its land in an instant.
Who is the chosen one I will appoint for this?
Who is like me and who can challenge me?
And what shepherd can stand against me?"
45Therefore, hear what the LORD has planned
against Babylon,
what he has purposed against the land of
the Babylonians:
The young of the flock will be dragged away;
he will completely destroy their pasture
because of them.
46At the sound of Babylon's capture the earth
will tremble;
its cry will resound among the nations.

51 This is what the LORD says:
"See, I will stir up the spirit of a destroyer
against Babylon and the people of Leb Kamai.[q]
2I will send foreigners to Babylon
to winnow her and to devastate her land;
they will oppose her on every side
in the day of her disaster.
3Let not the archer string his bow,
nor let him put on his armor.

[p]38 Or *A sword against* [q]1 *Leb Kamai* is a cryptogram for Chaldea, that is, Babylonia.

Do not spare her young men;
completely destroy[r] her army.
4They will fall down slain in Babylon,[s]
fatally wounded in her streets.
5For Israel and Judah have not been forsaken
by their God, the LORD Almighty,
though their land[t] is full of guilt
before the Holy One of Israel.

6"Flee from Babylon!
Run for your lives!
Do not be destroyed because of her sins.
It is time for the LORD's vengeance;
he will pay her what she deserves.
7Babylon was a gold cup in the LORD's hand;
she made the whole earth drunk.
The nations drank her wine;
therefore they have now gone mad.
8Babylon will suddenly fall and be broken.
Wail over her!
Get balm for her pain;
perhaps she can be healed.

9" 'We would have healed Babylon,
but she cannot be healed;
let us leave her and each go to his own land,
for her judgment reaches to the skies,
it rises as high as the clouds.'

10" 'The LORD has vindicated us;
come, let us tell in Zion
what the LORD our God has done.'

11"Sharpen the arrows,
take up the shields!
The LORD has stirred up the kings of the
Medes,
because his purpose is to destroy Babylon.
The LORD will take vengeance,
vengeance for his temple.
12Lift up a banner against the walls of Babylon!
Reinforce the guard,
station the watchmen,
prepare an ambush!
The LORD will carry out his purpose,
his decree against the people of Babylon.
13You who live by many waters
and are rich in treasures,
your end has come,
the time for you to be cut off.
14The LORD Almighty has sworn by himself:
I will surely fill you with men, as with a
swarm of locusts,
and they will shout in triumph over you.

15"He made the earth by his power;
he founded the world by his wisdom
and stretched out the heavens by his
understanding.
16When he thunders, the waters in the heavens
roar;
he makes clouds rise from the ends of the
earth.
He sends lightning with the rain
and brings out the wind from his
storehouses.

17"Every man is senseless and without
knowledge;
every goldsmith is shamed by his idols.
His images are a fraud;
they have no breath in them.
18They are worthless, the objects of mockery;
when their judgment comes, they will
perish.
19He who is the Portion of Jacob is not like
these,
for he is the Maker of all things,
including the tribe of his inheritance—
the LORD Almighty is his name.

20"You are my war club,
my weapon for battle—
with you I shatter nations,
with you I destroy kingdoms,
21with you I shatter horse and rider,
with you I shatter chariot and driver,
22with you I shatter man and woman,
with you I shatter old man and youth,
with you I shatter young man and maiden,
23with you I shatter shepherd and flock,
with you I shatter farmer and oxen,
with you I shatter governors and officials.

24"Before your eyes I will repay Babylon and all who live in Babylonia[u] for all the wrong they have done in Zion," declares the LORD.

25"I am against you, O destroying mountain,
you who destroy the whole earth,"
declares the LORD.
"I will stretch out my hand against you,
roll you off the cliffs,
and make you a burned-out mountain.
26No rock will be taken from you for a
cornerstone,

[r]3 The Hebrew term refers to the irrevocable giving over of things or persons to the LORD, often by totally destroying them. [s]4 Or *Chaldea* [t]5 Or */ and the land ⌞of the Babylonians⌟* [u]24 Or *Chaldea*; also in verse 35

nor any stone for a foundation,
for you will be desolate forever,"
declares the LORD.

27"Lift up a banner in the land!
Blow the trumpet among the nations!
Prepare the nations for battle against her;
summon against her these kingdoms:
Ararat, Minni and Ashkenaz.
Appoint a commander against her;
send up horses like a swarm of locusts.
28Prepare the nations for battle against her—
the kings of the Medes,
their governors and all their officials,
and all the countries they rule.
29The land trembles and writhes,
for the LORD's purposes against Babylon
stand—
to lay waste the land of Babylon
so that no one will live there.
30Babylon's warriors have stopped fighting;
they remain in their strongholds.
Their strength is exhausted;
they have become like women.
Her dwellings are set on fire;
the bars of her gates are broken.
31One courier follows another
and messenger follows messenger
to announce to the king of Babylon
that his entire city is captured,
32the river crossings seized,
the marshes set on fire,
and the soldiers terrified."

33This is what the LORD Almighty, the God of Israel, says:

"The Daughter of Babylon is like a threshing
floor
at the time it is trampled;
the time to harvest her will soon come."

34"Nebuchadnezzar king of Babylon has
devoured us,
he has thrown us into confusion,
he has made us an empty jar.
Like a serpent he has swallowed us
and filled his stomach with our delicacies,
and then has spewed us out.
35May the violence done to our flesh[v] be upon
Babylon,"
say the inhabitants of Zion.
"May our blood be on those who live in
Babylonia,"
says Jerusalem.

36Therefore, this is what the LORD says:

"See, I will defend your cause
and avenge you;
I will dry up her sea
and make her springs dry.
37Babylon will be a heap of ruins,
a haunt of jackals,
an object of horror and scorn,
a place where no one lives.
38Her people all roar like young lions,
they growl like lion cubs.
39But while they are aroused,
I will set out a feast for them
and make them drunk,
so that they shout with laughter—
then sleep forever and not awake,"
declares the LORD.
40"I will bring them down
like lambs to the slaughter,
like rams and goats.

41"How Sheshach[w] will be captured,
the boast of the whole earth seized!
What a horror Babylon will be
among the nations!
42The sea will rise over Babylon;
its roaring waves will cover her.
43Her towns will be desolate,
a dry and desert land,
a land where no one lives,
through which no man travels.
44I will punish Bel in Babylon
and make him spew out what he has
swallowed.
The nations will no longer stream to him.
And the wall of Babylon will fall.

45"Come out of her, my people!
Run for your lives!
Run from the fierce anger of the LORD.
46Do not lose heart or be afraid
when rumors are heard in the land;
one rumor comes this year, another the next,
rumors of violence in the land
and of ruler against ruler.
47For the time will surely come
when I will punish the idols of Babylon;
her whole land will be disgraced
and her slain will all lie fallen within her.

[v]35 Or *done to us and to our children* [w]41 *Sheshach* is a cryptogram for Babylon.

[48]Then heaven and earth and all that is in them
will shout for joy over Babylon,
for out of the north
destroyers will attack her,"
declares the LORD.

[49]"Babylon must fall because of Israel's slain,
just as the slain in all the earth
have fallen because of Babylon.
[50]You who have escaped the sword,
leave and do not linger!
Remember the LORD in a distant land,
and think on Jerusalem."

[51]"We are disgraced,
for we have been insulted
and shame covers our faces,
because foreigners have entered
the holy places of the LORD's house."

[52]"But days are coming," declares the LORD,
"when I will punish her idols,
and throughout her land
the wounded will groan.
[53]Even if Babylon reaches the sky
and fortifies her lofty stronghold,
I will send destroyers against her,"
declares the LORD.

[54]"The sound of a cry comes from Babylon,
the sound of great destruction
from the land of the Babylonians.[x]
[55]The LORD will destroy Babylon;
he will silence her noisy din.
Waves ⌞of enemies⌟ will rage like great waters;
the roar of their voices will resound.
[56]A destroyer will come against Babylon;
her warriors will be captured,
and their bows will be broken.
For the LORD is a God of retribution;
he will repay in full.
[57]I will make her officials and wise men drunk,
her governors, officers and warriors as well;
they will sleep forever and not awake,"
declares the King, whose name is the LORD
Almighty.

[58]This is what the LORD Almighty says:

"Babylon's thick wall will be leveled
and her high gates set on fire;
the peoples exhaust themselves for nothing,
the nations' labor is only fuel for the
flames."

[59]This is the message Jeremiah gave to the staff
officer Seraiah son of Neriah, the son of Mahse-
iah, when he went to Babylon with Zedekiah king
of Judah in the fourth year of his reign. [60]Jere-
miah had written on a scroll about all the disas-
ters that would come upon Babylon—all that had
been recorded concerning Babylon. [61]He said to
Seraiah, "When you get to Babylon, see that you
read all these words aloud. [62]Then say, 'O LORD,
you have said you will destroy this place, so that
neither man nor animal will live in it; it will be
desolate forever.' [63]When you finish reading this
scroll, tie a stone to it and throw it into the Eu-
phrates. [64]Then say, 'So will Babylon sink to rise
no more because of the disaster I will bring upon
her. And her people will fall.' "

The words of Jeremiah end here.

[x]54 Or *Chaldeans*

24 / *Jeremiah 52*
Jerusalem Plundered

THE MOVERS CAME while our friend was at work. She knew they were coming, of course, but still it was a shock when she opened the front door and found all the rooms bare. She admits she broke down and cried. How much worse if she had been robbed of everything against her will as Jerusalem was.

Warming Up to God When do you feel that the Lord has taken away something you counted on? What was that like?

Read Jeremiah 52.

52

Zedekiah was twenty-one years old
when he became king, and he
reigned in Jerusalem eleven years.
His mother's name was Hamutal daughter of Jere-
miah; she was from Libnah. 2He did evil in the
eyes of the LORD, just as Jehoiakim had done. 3It
was because of the LORD's anger that all this hap-
pened to Jerusalem and Judah, and in the end he
thrust them from his presence.

Now Zedekiah rebelled against the king of Bab-
ylon.

4So in the ninth year of Zedekiah's reign, on the
tenth day of the tenth month, Nebuchadnezzar
king of Babylon marched against Jerusalem with
his whole army. They camped outside the city
and built siege works all around it. 5The city was
kept under siege until the eleventh year of King
Zedekiah.

6By the ninth day of the fourth month the fam-
ine in the city had become so severe that there
was no food for the people to eat. 7Then the city
wall was broken through, and the whole army
fled. They left the city at night through the gate
between the two walls near the king's garden,
though the Babylonians[y] were surrounding the
city. They fled toward the Arabah,[z] 8but the Bab-
ylonian[a] army pursued King Zedekiah and over-
took him in the plains of Jericho. All his soldiers
were separated from him and scattered, 9and he
was captured.

He was taken to the king of Babylon at Riblah
in the land of Hamath, where he pronounced sen-
tence on him. 10There at Riblah the king of Bab-
ylon slaughtered the sons of Zedekiah before his
eyes; he also killed all the officials of Judah.
11Then he put out Zedekiah's eyes, bound him
with bronze shackles and took him to Babylon,
where he put him in prison till the day of his
death.

12On the tenth day of the fifth month, in the
nineteenth year of Nebuchadnezzar king of Bab-
ylon, Nebuzaradan commander of the imperial
guard, who served the king of Babylon, came to
Jerusalem. 13He set fire to the temple of the LORD,
the royal palace and all the houses of Jerusalem.
Every important building he burned down. 14The
whole Babylonian army under the commander of
the imperial guard broke down all the walls
around Jerusalem. 15Nebuzaradan the com-
mander of the guard carried into exile some of the
poorest people and those who remained in the
city, along with the rest of the craftsmen[b] and
those who had gone over to the king of Babylon.
16But Nebuzaradan left behind the rest of the
poorest people of the land to work the vineyards
and fields.

17The Babylonians broke up the bronze pillars,
the movable stands and the bronze Sea that were
at the temple of the LORD and they carried all the
bronze to Babylon. 18They also took away the
pots, shovels, wick trimmers, sprinkling bowls,
dishes and all the bronze articles used in the tem-
ple service. 19The commander of the imperial
guard took away the basins, censers, sprinkling
bowls, pots, lampstands, dishes and bowls used
for drink offerings—all that were made of pure
gold or silver.

20The bronze from the two pillars, the Sea and
the twelve bronze bulls under it, and the movable
stands, which King Solomon had made for the
temple of the LORD, was more than could be
weighed. 21Each of the pillars was eighteen cubits
high and twelve cubits in circumference[c]; each
was four fingers thick, and hollow. 22The bronze
capital on top of the one pillar was five cubits[d]
high and was decorated with a network and
pomegranates of bronze all around. The other pil-
lar, with its pomegranates, was similar. 23There
were ninety-six pomegranates on the sides; the
total number of pomegranates above the sur-
rounding network was a hundred.

24The commander of the guard took as prison-
ers Seraiah the chief priest, Zephaniah the priest
next in rank and the three doorkeepers. 25Of
those still in the city, he took the officer in charge
of the fighting men, and seven royal advisers. He
also took the secretary who was chief officer in
charge of conscripting the people of the land and
sixty of his men who were found in the city.
26Nebuzaradan the commander took them all and
brought them to the king of Babylon at Riblah.
27There at Riblah, in the land of Hamath, the king
had them executed.

So Judah went into captivity, away from her
land. 28This is the number of the people Nebu-
chadnezzar carried into exile:

in the seventh year, 3,023 Jews;
29in Nebuchadnezzar's eighteenth year,
832 people from Jerusalem;
30in his twenty-third year,

[y]7 Or *Chaldeans*; also in verse 17 [z]7 Or *the Jordan Valley*
[a]8 Or *Chaldean*; also in verse 14 [b]15 Or *populace* [c]21 That is,
about 27 feet (about 8.1 meters) high and 18 feet (about 5.4 meters) in
circumference [d]22 That is, about 7 1/2 feet (about 2.3 meters)

745 Jews taken into exile by Nebuzaradan
the commander of the imperial guard.
There were 4,600 people in all.

31 In the thirty-seventh year of the exile of Jehoiachin king of Judah, in the year Evil-Merodach[e] became king of Babylon, he released Jehoiachin king of Judah and freed him from prison on the twenty-fifth day of the twelfth month.
32 He spoke kindly to him and gave him a seat of honor higher than those of the other kings who were with him in Babylon.
33 So Jehoiachin put aside his prison clothes and for the rest of his life ate regularly at the king's table.
34 Day by day the king of Babylon gave Jehoiachin a regular allowance as long as he lived, till the day of his death.

[e]31 Also called *Amel-Marduk*

**Discovering the Word** 1. Chapter 51 tells us that Jeremiah's words end there. How does the writer of chapter 52 describe what happened to the city of Jerusalem at the hands of the king of Babylon? 2. What explanation is given for the disaster (vv. 1–3)? 3. There was an excruciatingly long siege by the Babylonian army against Jerusalem. What were some results of it (vv. 4–11)? 4. How did the Babylonian commander treat the sacred items in the Lord's temple (vv. 12–23)? 5. What became of the priests and other Jewish officials (vv. 24–27)? 6. What surprising turn of events happened to Jehoiachin, the young previous king of Judah who had been deposed (vv. 31–34)?

Applying the Word 1. Why does a major loss sometimes shock people into returning to the Lord? 2. Why do you think it sometimes takes a major blow to bring people back? 3. How do you respond to big losses?

Responding in Prayer Pray about any wrenching losses you have had or which you fear happening. Ask the Lord what you should learn through losing. Trust him to restore what he wishes in his own time.

Lamentations

Lamentations is a book that grips our emotions, not just our intellect. It is a personal account of the author's mourning over the fall of Jerusalem in 586 B.C. and the exile of the Jewish people to Babylon. But it is more than a book of grieving; it offers hope in the midst of suffering.

The title *Lamentations* is the translation of a Greek word that means "to cry aloud," aptly summarizing the content. This book has a different structure from other Bible books. It is composed of five melancholy poems (one per chapter) with a limping meter that was used for funeral dirges. In the Hebrew, the second line of two parallel lines is one beat short of the first one, thus producing a limp in the meter. In addition, four of the poems are written as acrostics. In chapters 1, 2 and 4 each verse starts with a word that begins with a letter of the Hebrew alphabet, progressing in order. In chapter 3 three verses go with each letter.

These poems focus on the events described in 2 Kings 25 when the Babylonian army invaded Jerusalem and razed the city, carrying away most of the population. They also provide a sequel to the book of Jeremiah that warns about the coming invasion and fall of the city. Because of the similarity in events described, some commentators believe that Jeremiah was the author. However, since it is anonymous, we cannot be sure.

But Lamentations is more than one man's reaction to the loss of his home. It gives us a biblical approach to suffering. The author teaches us that we can't deal with suffering by ignoring it, pretending it doesn't exist, trying to get out of it, or minimizing its pain. Instead, we have to go through it, remembering that God is with us in it.

Outline

1/ Lamentations 1—2 — *Mourning Over Sin*

2/ Lamentations 3 — *Hope in the Midst of Suffering*

3/ Lamentations 4—5 — *Suffering Is Not Forever*

1 / *Lamentations 1—2*
Mourning Over Sin

"SIN WOULD HAVE few takers if its consequences occurred immediately," said W. T. Purkiser. The history of the Jewish people certainly illustrates this saying. They sinned for years before experiencing the consequences of exile and destruction of their holy city, Jerusalem, as the author described in Lamentations.

Warming Up to God How do you react when you suffer consequences of your sins? Talk to God about your reactions and ask him to show you what he wants to teach you.

Read Lamentations 1—2.

1 [a]How deserted lies the city,
once so full of people!
How like a widow is she,
who once was great among the nations!
She who was queen among the provinces
has now become a slave.

2Bitterly she weeps at night,
tears are upon her cheeks.
Among all her lovers
there is none to comfort her.
All her friends have betrayed her;
they have become her enemies.

3After affliction and harsh labor,
Judah has gone into exile.
She dwells among the nations;
she finds no resting place.
All who pursue her have overtaken her
in the midst of her distress.

4The roads to Zion mourn,
for no one comes to her appointed feasts.
All her gateways are desolate,
her priests groan,
her maidens grieve,
and she is in bitter anguish.

5Her foes have become her masters;
her enemies are at ease.
The LORD has brought her grief
because of her many sins.
Her children have gone into exile,
captive before the foe.

6All the splendor has departed
from the Daughter of Zion.
Her princes are like deer
that find no pasture;
in weakness they have fled
before the pursuer.

7In the days of her affliction and wandering
Jerusalem remembers all the treasures
that were hers in days of old.
When her people fell into enemy hands,
there was no one to help her.
Her enemies looked at her
and laughed at her destruction.

8Jerusalem has sinned greatly
and so has become unclean.
All who honored her despise her,
for they have seen her nakedness;
she herself groans
and turns away.

9Her filthiness clung to her skirts;
she did not consider her future.
Her fall was astounding;
there was none to comfort her.
"Look, O LORD, on my affliction,
for the enemy has triumphed."

10The enemy laid hands
on all her treasures;
she saw pagan nations
enter her sanctuary—
those you had forbidden
to enter your assembly.

11All her people groan
as they search for bread;
they barter their treasures for food
to keep themselves alive.
"Look, O LORD, and consider,
for I am despised."

12"Is it nothing to you, all you who pass by?
Look around and see.
Is any suffering like my suffering
that was inflicted on me,

[a]This chapter is an acrostic poem, the verses of which begin with the successive letters of the Hebrew alphabet.

that the LORD brought on me
in the day of his fierce anger?

13"From on high he sent fire,
sent it down into my bones.
He spread a net for my feet
and turned me back.
He made me desolate,
faint all the day long.

14"My sins have been bound into a yoke[b];
by his hands they were woven together.
They have come upon my neck
and the Lord has sapped my strength.
He has handed me over
to those I cannot withstand.

15"The Lord has rejected
all the warriors in my midst;
he has summoned an army against me
to[c] crush my young men.
In his winepress the Lord has trampled
the Virgin Daughter of Judah.

16"This is why I weep
and my eyes overflow with tears.
No one is near to comfort me,
no one to restore my spirit.
My children are destitute
because the enemy has prevailed."

17Zion stretches out her hands,
but there is no one to comfort her.
The LORD has decreed for Jacob
that his neighbors become his foes;
Jerusalem has become
an unclean thing among them.

18"The LORD is righteous,
yet I rebelled against his command.
Listen, all you peoples;
look upon my suffering.
My young men and maidens
have gone into exile.

19"I called to my allies
but they betrayed me.
My priests and my elders
perished in the city
while they searched for food
to keep themselves alive.

20"See, O LORD, how distressed I am!
I am in torment within,
and in my heart I am disturbed,
for I have been most rebellious.
Outside, the sword bereaves;
inside, there is only death.

21"People have heard my groaning,
but there is no one to comfort me.
All my enemies have heard of my distress;
they rejoice at what you have done.
May you bring the day you have announced
so they may become like me.

22"Let all their wickedness come before you;
deal with them
as you have dealt with me
because of all my sins.
My groans are many
and my heart is faint."

2

[d]How the Lord has covered the
Daughter of Zion
with the cloud of his anger[e]!
He has hurled down the splendor of Israel
from heaven to earth;
he has not remembered his footstool
in the day of his anger.

2Without pity the Lord has swallowed up
all the dwellings of Jacob;
in his wrath he has torn down
the strongholds of the Daughter of Judah.
He has brought her kingdom and its princes
down to the ground in dishonor.

3In fierce anger he has cut off
every horn[f] of Israel.
He has withdrawn his right hand
at the approach of the enemy.
He has burned in Jacob like a flaming fire
that consumes everything around it.

4Like an enemy he has strung his bow;
his right hand is ready.
Like a foe he has slain
all who were pleasing to the eye;
he has poured out his wrath like fire
on the tent of the Daughter of Zion.

5The Lord is like an enemy;
he has swallowed up Israel.
He has swallowed up all her palaces
and destroyed her strongholds.

[b]14 Most Hebrew manuscripts; Septuagint *He kept watch over my sins*
[c]15 Or *has set a time for me / when he will* [d]This chapter is an acrostic poem, the verses of which begin with the successive letters of the Hebrew alphabet. [e]1 Or *How the Lord in his anger / has treated the Daughter of Zion with contempt* [f]3 Or */ all the strength*; or *every king*; *horn* here symbolizes strength.

He has multiplied mourning and lamentation
for the Daughter of Judah.

6He has laid waste his dwelling like a garden;
he has destroyed his place of meeting.
The LORD has made Zion forget
her appointed feasts and her Sabbaths;
in his fierce anger he has spurned
both king and priest.

7The Lord has rejected his altar
and abandoned his sanctuary.
He has handed over to the enemy
the walls of her palaces;
they have raised a shout in the house of the LORD
as on the day of an appointed feast.

8The LORD determined to tear down
the wall around the Daughter of Zion.
He stretched out a measuring line
and did not withhold his hand from destroying.
He made ramparts and walls lament;
together they wasted away.

9Her gates have sunk into the ground;
their bars he has broken and destroyed.
Her king and her princes are exiled among the nations,
the law is no more,
and her prophets no longer find
visions from the LORD.

10The elders of the Daughter of Zion
sit on the ground in silence;
they have sprinkled dust on their heads
and put on sackcloth.
The young women of Jerusalem
have bowed their heads to the ground.

11My eyes fail from weeping,
I am in torment within,
my heart is poured out on the ground
because my people are destroyed,
because children and infants faint
in the streets of the city.

12They say to their mothers,
"Where is bread and wine?"
as they faint like wounded men
in the streets of the city,
as their lives ebb away
in their mothers' arms.

13What can I say for you?
With what can I compare you,
O Daughter of Jerusalem?
To what can I liken you,
that I may comfort you,
O Virgin Daughter of Zion?
Your wound is as deep as the sea.
Who can heal you?

14The visions of your prophets
were false and worthless;
they did not expose your sin
to ward off your captivity.
The oracles they gave you
were false and misleading.

15All who pass your way
clap their hands at you;
they scoff and shake their heads
at the Daughter of Jerusalem:
"Is this the city that was called
the perfection of beauty,
the joy of the whole earth?"

16All your enemies open their mouths
wide against you;
they scoff and gnash their teeth
and say, "We have swallowed her up.
This is the day we have waited for;
we have lived to see it."

17The LORD has done what he planned;
he has fulfilled his word,
which he decreed long ago.
He has overthrown you without pity,
he has let the enemy gloat over you,
he has exalted the horn[g] of your foes.

18The hearts of the people
cry out to the Lord.
O wall of the Daughter of Zion,
let your tears flow like a river
day and night;
give yourself no relief,
your eyes no rest.

19Arise, cry out in the night,
as the watches of the night begin;
pour out your heart like water
in the presence of the Lord.
Lift up your hands to him
for the lives of your children,
who faint from hunger
at the head of every street.

g17 *Horn* here symbolizes strength.

20"Look, O LORD, and consider:
Whom have you ever treated like this?
Should women eat their offspring,
the children they have cared for?
Should priest and prophet be killed
in the sanctuary of the Lord?

21"Young and old lie together
in the dust of the streets;
my young men and maidens
have fallen by the sword.
You have slain them in the day of your
anger;
you have slaughtered them without pity.

22"As you summon to a feast day,
so you summoned against me terrors on
every side.
In the day of the LORD's anger
no one escaped or survived;
those I cared for and reared,
my enemy has destroyed."

Discovering the Word 1. What words and images in chapter 1 describe Jerusalem's misery? 2. How did the author describe God's judgments on the nation (2:1-10)? 3. What various emotions is the author feeling as he writes this (2:11-22)? 4. How did the author view God in this situation (1:5, 18; 2:17)? 5. What do you learn about the cause and effect of sin from these chapters?

Applying the Word 1. Recalling your own experiences with the aftermath of sin, in what ways can you identify with the description of Jerusalem's misery in chapter 1? 2. In what ways, if any, has Christ made your experience with sin different from what is described here? 3. When have you felt like the author in regard to the sins of those around you?

Responding in Prayer Ask God to give you a desire to obey him in one area you are struggling with right now.

2 / *Lamentations 3*
Hope in the Midst of Suffering

HOPE IS SUCH an elusive quality. It's easy to be hopeful when life is going well. But it's harder to hang on to hope when trouble obscures our focus. In the midst of horrible suffering, however, the author of Lamentations learned how to experience hope when everything seemed hopeless.

Warming Up to God What experiences feel hopeless to you? Ask God to show you how you can have hope as you meet him in this chapter.

Read Lamentations 3.

3 [h]I am the man who has seen affliction
by the rod of his wrath.
2He has driven me away and made me
walk
in darkness rather than light;
3indeed, he has turned his hand against me
again and again, all day long.

4He has made my skin and my flesh grow old
and has broken my bones.
5He has besieged me and surrounded me
with bitterness and hardship.
6He has made me dwell in darkness
like those long dead.

7He has walled me in so I cannot escape;
he has weighed me down with chains.
8Even when I call out or cry for help,
he shuts out my prayer.
9He has barred my way with blocks of stone;
he has made my paths crooked.

10Like a bear lying in wait,
like a lion in hiding,

[h] This chapter is an acrostic poem; the verses of each stanza begin with the successive letters of the Hebrew alphabet, and the verses within each stanza begin with the same letter.

[11]he dragged me from the path and mangled me
and left me without help.
[12]He drew his bow
and made me the target for his arrows.

[13]He pierced my heart
with arrows from his quiver.
[14]I became the laughingstock of all my people;
they mock me in song all day long.
[15]He has filled me with bitter herbs
and sated me with gall.

[16]He has broken my teeth with gravel;
he has trampled me in the dust.
[17]I have been deprived of peace;
I have forgotten what prosperity is.
[18]So I say, "My splendor is gone
and all that I had hoped from the LORD."

[19]I remember my affliction and my wandering,
the bitterness and the gall.
[20]I well remember them,
and my soul is downcast within me.
[21]Yet this I call to mind
and therefore I have hope:

[22]Because of the LORD's great love we are not consumed,
for his compassions never fail.
[23]They are new every morning;
great is your faithfulness.
[24]I say to myself, "The LORD is my portion;
therefore I will wait for him."

[25]The LORD is good to those whose hope is in him,
to the one who seeks him;
[26]it is good to wait quietly
for the salvation of the LORD.
[27]It is good for a man to bear the yoke
while he is young.

[28]Let him sit alone in silence,
for the LORD has laid it on him.
[29]Let him bury his face in the dust—
there may yet be hope.
[30]Let him offer his cheek to one who would strike him,
and let him be filled with disgrace.

[31]For men are not cast off
by the Lord forever.
[32]Though he brings grief, he will show compassion,
so great is his unfailing love.
[33]For he does not willingly bring affliction
or grief to the children of men.

[34]To crush underfoot
all prisoners in the land,
[35]to deny a man his rights
before the Most High,
[36]to deprive a man of justice—
would not the Lord see such things?

[37]Who can speak and have it happen
if the Lord has not decreed it?
[38]Is it not from the mouth of the Most High
that both calamities and good things come?
[39]Why should any living man complain
when punished for his sins?

[40]Let us examine our ways and test them,
and let us return to the LORD.
[41]Let us lift up our hearts and our hands
to God in heaven, and say:
[42]"We have sinned and rebelled
and you have not forgiven.

[43]"You have covered yourself with anger and pursued us;
you have slain without pity.
[44]You have covered yourself with a cloud
so that no prayer can get through.
[45]You have made us scum and refuse
among the nations.

[46]"All our enemies have opened their mouths
wide against us.
[47]We have suffered terror and pitfalls,
ruin and destruction."
[48]Streams of tears flow from my eyes
because my people are destroyed.

[49]My eyes will flow unceasingly,
without relief,
[50]until the LORD looks down
from heaven and sees.
[51]What I see brings grief to my soul
because of all the women of my city.

[52]Those who were my enemies without cause
hunted me like a bird.
[53]They tried to end my life in a pit
and threw stones at me;
[54]the waters closed over my head,
and I thought I was about to be cut off.

[55]I called on your name, O LORD,
from the depths of the pit.
[56]You heard my plea: "Do not close your ears

to my cry for relief."
[57]You came near when I called you,
and you said, "Do not fear."

[58]O Lord, you took up my case;
you redeemed my life.
[59]You have seen, O LORD, the wrong done to me.
Uphold my cause!
[60]You have seen the depth of their vengeance,
all their plots against me.

[61]O LORD, you have heard their insults,
all their plots against me—
[62]what my enemies whisper and mutter
against me all day long.
[63]Look at them! Sitting or standing,
they mock me in their songs.

[64]Pay them back what they deserve, O LORD,
for what their hands have done.
[65]Put a veil over their hearts,
and may your curse be on them!
[66]Pursue them in anger and destroy them
from under the heavens of the LORD.

Discovering the Word 1. Why did the author feel so hopeless (vv. 1–18)? 2. Why did his hopelessness turn to hope (vv. 19–24)? 3. What did he remember about God that changed his perspective on suffering (vv. 25–39)? 4. How did the author's prayer relate to his suffering (vv. 40–66)? 5. What do you learn in this chapter about the relationship between God's judgment and his love?

Applying the Word 1. In what ways has God been faithful to you? 2. One way to deal with hopelessness is to be reminded of the character of God. How can you get to know God better?

Responding in Prayer Praise God for his specific attributes that can give you hope in the midst of suffering. Ask him to help you remember these the next time you hit hard times.

3 / *Lamentations 4—5*
Suffering Is Not Forever

WHEN SOMEONE WE know dies, when a spouse departs, when a dream is snatched away, we go through a grieving process. It isn't pleasant, but it's necessary for our emotional healing. Those are not the only times we need to mourn. Lamentations teaches us that grieving over our sins and confessing them to God is important for our spiritual health. As the author ended this book, he focused on steps beyond the grief.

Warming Up to God How do you talk to God when you are suffering? Are you open with God? Are you afraid to voice certain questions? Do you tend to blame God? Evaluate yourself before you turn to the Scripture text.

Read Lamentations 4—5.

4 [1]How the gold has lost its luster,[i]
the fine gold become dull!
The sacred gems are scattered
at the head of every street.

[2]How the precious sons of Zion,
once worth their weight in gold,
are now considered as pots of clay,
the work of a potter's hands!

[3]Even jackals offer their breasts
to nurse their young,
but my people have become heartless
like ostriches in the desert.
[4]Because of thirst the infant's tongue
sticks to the roof of its mouth;
the children beg for bread,
but no one gives it to them.

[5]Those who once ate delicacies
are destitute in the streets.
Those nurtured in purple

[i]This chapter is an acrostic poem, the verses of which begin with the successive letters of the Hebrew alphabet.

now lie on ash heaps.

6The punishment of my people
is greater than that of Sodom,
which was overthrown in a moment
without a hand turned to help her.

7Their princes were brighter than snow
and whiter than milk,
their bodies more ruddy than rubies,
their appearance like sapphires.[j]

8But now they are blacker than soot;
they are not recognized in the streets.
Their skin has shriveled on their bones;
it has become as dry as a stick.

9Those killed by the sword are better off
than those who die of famine;
racked with hunger, they waste away
for lack of food from the field.

10With their own hands compassionate women
have cooked their own children,
who became their food
when my people were destroyed.

11The LORD has given full vent to his wrath;
he has poured out his fierce anger.
He kindled a fire in Zion
that consumed her foundations.

12The kings of the earth did not believe,
nor did any of the world's people,
that enemies and foes could enter
the gates of Jerusalem.

13But it happened because of the sins of her prophets
and the iniquities of her priests,
who shed within her
the blood of the righteous.

14Now they grope through the streets
like men who are blind.
They are so defiled with blood
that no one dares to touch their garments.

15"Go away! You are unclean!" men cry to them.
"Away! Away! Don't touch us!"
When they flee and wander about,
people among the nations say,
"They can stay here no longer."

16The LORD himself has scattered them;
he no longer watches over them.
The priests are shown no honor,
the elders no favor.

17Moreover, our eyes failed,
looking in vain for help;
from our towers we watched
for a nation that could not save us.

18Men stalked us at every step,
so we could not walk in our streets.
Our end was near, our days were numbered,
for our end had come.

19Our pursuers were swifter
than eagles in the sky;
they chased us over the mountains
and lay in wait for us in the desert.

20The LORD's anointed, our very life breath,
was caught in their traps.
We thought that under his shadow
we would live among the nations.

21Rejoice and be glad, O Daughter of Edom,
you who live in the land of Uz.
But to you also the cup will be passed;
you will be drunk and stripped naked.

22O Daughter of Zion, your punishment will end;
he will not prolong your exile.
But, O Daughter of Edom, he will punish your sin
and expose your wickedness.

5 Remember, O LORD, what has happened to us;
look, and see our disgrace.
2Our inheritance has been turned over to aliens,
our homes to foreigners.
3We have become orphans and fatherless,
our mothers like widows.
4We must buy the water we drink;
our wood can be had only at a price.
5Those who pursue us are at our heels;
we are weary and find no rest.
6We submitted to Egypt and Assyria
to get enough bread.
7Our fathers sinned and are no more,
and we bear their punishment.
8Slaves rule over us,

j7 Or *lapis lazuli*

and there is none to free us from their
hands.
9 We get our bread at the risk of our lives
because of the sword in the desert.
10 Our skin is hot as an oven,
feverish from hunger.
11 Women have been ravished in Zion,
and virgins in the towns of Judah.
12 Princes have been hung up by their hands;
elders are shown no respect.
13 Young men toil at the millstones;
boys stagger under loads of wood.
14 The elders are gone from the city gate;
the young men have stopped their
music.
15 Joy is gone from our hearts;
our dancing has turned to mourning.
16 The crown has fallen from our head.
Woe to us, for we have sinned!
17 Because of this our hearts are faint,
because of these things our eyes grow dim
18 for Mount Zion, which lies desolate,
with jackals prowling over it.

19 You, O LORD, reign forever;
your throne endures from generation to
generation.
20 Why do you always forget us?
Why do you forsake us so long?
21 Restore us to yourself, O LORD, that we may
return;
renew our days as of old
22 unless you have utterly rejected us
and are angry with us beyond measure.

Discovering the Word 1. Contrast the people before and after Jerusalem's fall (4:1-12). 2. In what areas did the fall and captivity affect them (4:1-20)? 3. Why did God allow his people to be overtaken by their enemies (4:13-22)? 4. What did the author confess to God (5:1-18)? 5. How does the tone change at the end of this book (5:19-22)? Why?

Applying the Word 1. What part does prayer play in mourning the consequences of your sin? 2. How can talking to God be a help in the midst of suffering? 3. What do you need to confess to God today?

Responding in Prayer Confess whatever sins God brought to mind. Then focus on the miracle of grace that he offers, letting that be the source of your praise.

Ezekiel

"That you may know that I am the LORD" is a phrase that occurs sixty-six times in the book of Ezekiel. It captures the essence of the visions, parables and allegories that comprise this remarkable Old Testament book. It also locates our deepest need: to become increasingly aware of the glory of God as the ultimate reality.

Like Ezekiel, who wrote and ministered in exile in faraway Babylon after 597 B.C., we live an exilic existence in this world, longing for our ultimate homeland—heaven. Ezekiel and his compatriots were surrounded by the seductions of a sophisticated but pagan foreign culture. What they needed was not mere words about God but an empowering vision that would fortify their imagination and evoke their faith. This book is a revelation of God through images, signs and metaphors of God's glory, appealing to faith *through* the imagination. Ezekiel is hard for us to understand precisely because we are so alienated from a full biblical spirituality that includes a redeemed imagination.

But Ezekiel has another important reason for framing his message in allegories, metaphors and parables. His message is one of judgment and hope for Jerusalem—the church of his day. He prophesied not *to* Jerusalem but *of* Jerusalem to his fellow exiles who still lived for Jerusalem and home. News of Jerusalem was the supreme factor in the life of the exiles. Indeed, the book easily is divided between prophecies given before the final collapse of Jerusalem (chapters 1—24) and those given after (chapters 25—48).

But Ezekiel's message about Jerusalem would be hard to speak and harder still to hear. The people who remained in Jerusalem after the first deportation that took Ezekiel and his wife to Babylon in 597 B.C. were given to idolatrous and perverted imaginations. The people were like an unfaithful spouse. The leaders no longer led. The nation was like a valley of dry bones. To communicate the tragedy, as well as the hope of God's covenanted people, Ezekiel needed art to catch the people's attention and draw them into a divine perspective on the matter.

At times Ezekiel becomes an incarnated audio-visual aid when he lies on his side outside his house for part of each day for a year, makes models of Jerusalem with siege works and even forgoes mourning the death of his wife. In these things, too, Ezekiel's passion was that the people should "know that I am the LORD." For even in judging the church of that day, God will reveal himself as a faithful covenant partner. He will lead his own people when the leaders fail to shepherd the sheep. He will resurrect the dead bones of his own house. He will empower his people in exile to live godly lives by showing them the glory of his heavenly temple and his determination to renew the land and bring his whole creation to a worthy end.

Ezekiel is full of apocalyptic end-times visions and prophecies and therefore offers us an important perspective: a short-range pessimism and a long-range optimism. It is not surprising therefore that Ezekiel is a major source of images and metaphors for the "revelation of Jesus Christ" in the last book of the Bible (Rev 1:1). Besides this Ezekiel contains themes that are crucial to our ministry in the modern world: the desperate need for purification in both the outward ethical life and the inner imagination, the recovery of covenantal relationship with God, the restoration of pastoral leadership, the fundamental role of hope in the spiritual life, the wonderful destiny of the created order, and the primacy of the glory of God as the central motive for mission.

It is this passion for the glory of God and this appeal to our redeemed imagination that gives this book its universal and timeless quality. Like Ezekiel we are away from home, longing for our true homeland, distressed that the community that bears God's glory on earth does so in such a tawdry way, and wondering what will come of it all. The word we need, as it turns out, is not so much a word as a vision of the magnificence of God who is absolutely determined to glorify himself and to be known. So these visions, allegories and parables are, as Calvin Seerveld once said, like the sign given to Noah long before: rainbows for the fallen world.

Outline

1/ Ezekiel 1 ———— *Envisioning the Glory of God*

2/ Ezekiel 2:1—3:15 ———— *Experiencing the Call of God*

3/ Ezekiel 4—5 ———— *Warning the People of God*

4/ Ezekiel 6—7 ———— *Living in the End Times*

5/ Ezekiel 8 ———— *The Darkened Inner Eye*

6/ Ezekiel 11 ———— *When Human Leaders Fail*

7/ Ezekiel 16 ———— *The Bride of God*

8/ Ezekiel 18 ———— *Assuming Personal Responsibility*

9/ Ezekiel 24:15–27 ———— *Losing One's Beloved*

10/ Ezekiel 27—28 ———— *National Pride—National Downfall*

11/ Ezekiel 33 ———— *The Watchman*

12/ Ezekiel 34 ———— *Past and Future Shepherds*

13/ Ezekiel 37 ———— *Can These Bones Live?*

14/ Ezekiel 40—41 ———— *The New Temple*

15/ Ezekiel 43:1–12 ———— *The God Who Dwells with His People*

16/ Ezekiel 47:1–12 ———— *The Vision of a Renewed Creation*

Ezekiel's Temple

A. Wall (40:5,16-20)
B. East gate (40:6-14,16)
C. Portico (40:8)
D. Outer court (40:17)
E. Pavement (40:17)
F. Inner court (40:19)
G. North gate (40:20-22)
H. Inner court (40:23)
I. South gate (40:24-26)
J. South inner court (40:27)
K. Gateway (40:28-31)
L. Gateway (40:32-34)
M. Gateway (40:35-38)
N. Priests' rooms (40:44-45)
O. Court (40:47)
P. Temple portico (40:48-49)
Q. Outer sanctuary (41:1-2)
R. Most Holy Place (41:3-4)
S. Temple walls (41:5-7,9,11)
T. Base (41:8)
U. Open area (41:10)
V. West building (41:12)
W. Priests' rooms (42:1-10)
X. Altar (43:13-17)
AA. Rooms for preparing sacrifices (40:39-43)
BB. Ovens (46:19-20)
CC. Kitchens (46:21-24)

Ezekiel uses a long or "royal" cubit, 20.4 inches or 51.81 cm ("cubit and a handbreadth," Eze 40:5) as opposed to the standard Hebrew cubit of 17.6 inches or 44.7 cm.

Scripture describes a floor plan, but provides few height dimensions. This artwork shows an upward projection of the temple over the floor plan. This temple existed only in a vision of Ezekiel (Eze 40:2), and has never actually been built as were the temples of Solomon, Zerubbabel and Herod.

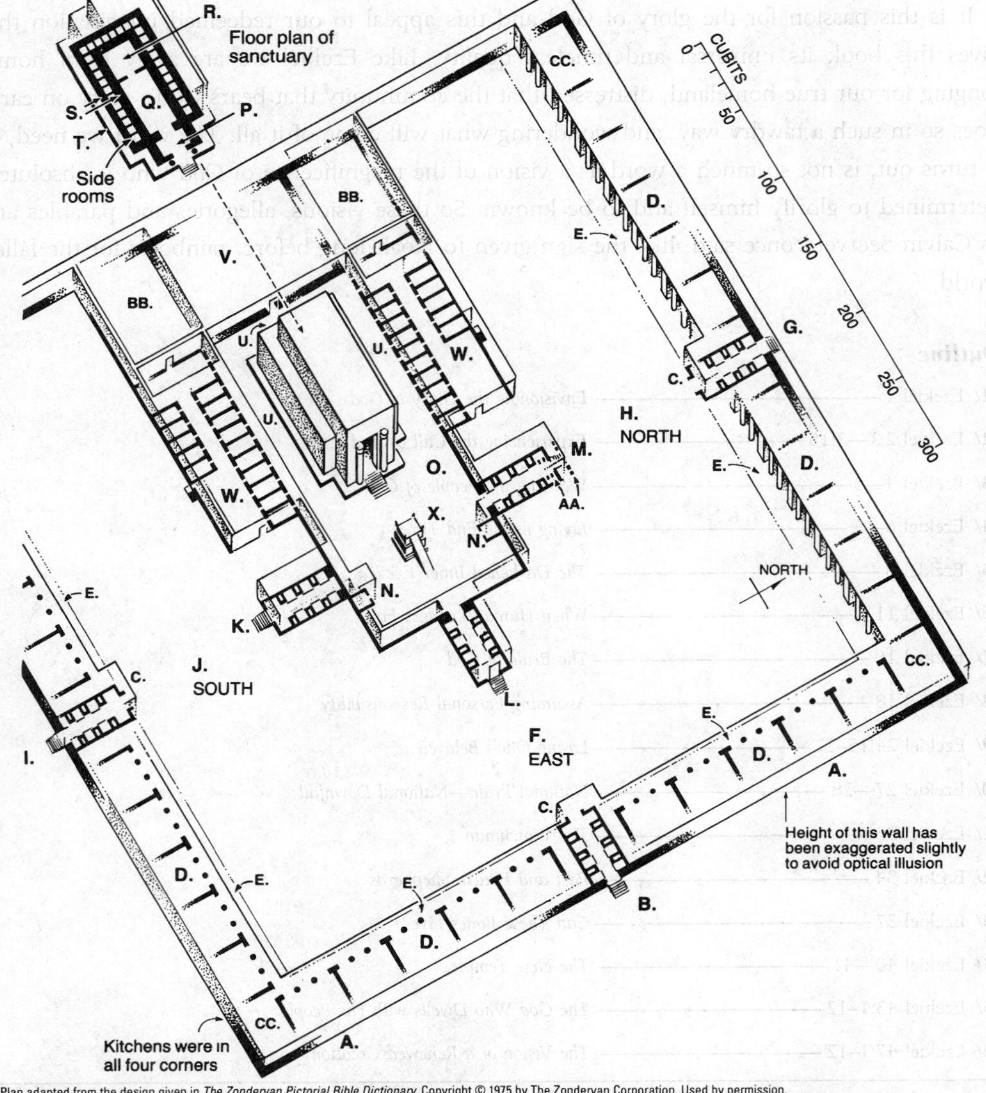

1/ *Ezekiel 1*
Envisioning the Glory of God

NO ONE CAN experience someone else's encounter with God. Therefore, Ezekiel's verbal record of his vision is, in one sense, unique to this prophet. But there are universal elements in Ezekiel's experience which can awaken our own faith if we are willing to not only think about the concept of God's glory, but also allow our imaginations to become a vehicle for faith-response to God's glory through this inspired word picture. We might then say, along with the theologian Karl Barth, "God is beautiful."

Warming Up to God What pictures, if any, have you had when you have thought about or experienced God's greatness?

Read Ezekiel 1.

1 In the[a] thirtieth year, in the fourth month on the fifth day, while I was among the exiles by the Kebar River, the heavens were opened and I saw visions of God.

2On the fifth of the month—it was the fifth year of the exile of King Jehoiachin— 3the word of the LORD came to Ezekiel the priest, the son of Buzi,[b] by the Kebar River in the land of the Babylonians.[c] There the hand of the LORD was upon him.

4I looked, and I saw a windstorm coming out of the north—an immense cloud with flashing lightning and surrounded by brilliant light. The center of the fire looked like glowing metal, 5and in the fire was what looked like four living creatures. In appearance their form was that of a man, 6but each of them had four faces and four wings. 7Their legs were straight; their feet were like those of a calf and gleamed like burnished bronze. 8Under their wings on their four sides they had the hands of a man. All four of them had faces and wings, 9and their wings touched one another. Each one went straight ahead; they did not turn as they moved.

10Their faces looked like this: Each of the four had the face of a man, and on the right side each had the face of a lion, and on the left the face of an ox; each also had the face of an eagle. 11Such were their faces. Their wings were spread out upward; each had two wings, one touching the wing of another creature on either side, and two wings covering its body. 12Each one went straight ahead. Wherever the spirit would go, they would go, without turning as they went. 13The appearance of the living creatures was like burning coals of fire or like torches. Fire moved back and forth among the creatures; it was bright, and lightning flashed out of it. 14The creatures sped back and forth like flashes of lightning.

15As I looked at the living creatures, I saw a wheel on the ground beside each creature with its four faces. 16This was the appearance and structure of the wheels: They sparkled like chrysolite, and all four looked alike. Each appeared to be made like a wheel intersecting a wheel. 17As they moved, they would go in any one of the four directions the creatures faced; the wheels did not turn about[d] as the creatures went. 18Their rims were high and awesome, and all four rims were full of eyes all around.

19When the living creatures moved, the wheels beside them moved; and when the living creatures rose from the ground, the wheels also rose. 20Wherever the spirit would go, they would go, and the wheels would rise along with them, because the spirit of the living creatures was in the wheels. 21When the creatures moved, they also moved; when the creatures stood still, they also stood still; and when the creatures rose from the ground, the wheels rose along with them, because the spirit of the living creatures was in the wheels.

22Spread out above the heads of the living creatures was what looked like an expanse, sparkling like ice, and awesome. 23Under the expanse their wings were stretched out one toward the other, and each had two wings covering its body. 24When the creatures moved, I heard the sound of their wings, like the roar of rushing waters, like the voice of the Almighty,[e] like the tumult of an army. When they stood still, they lowered their wings.

[a]1 Or ⌞my⌟ [b]3 Or *Ezekiel son of Buzi the priest* [c]3 Or *Chaldeans* [d]17 Or *aside* [e]24 Hebrew *Shaddai*

[25]Then there came a voice from above the expanse over their heads as they stood with lowered wings. [26]Above the expanse over their heads was what looked like a throne of sapphire,[f] and high above on the throne was a figure like that of a man. [27]I saw that from what appeared to be his waist up he looked like glowing metal, as if full of fire, and that from there down he looked like fire; and brilliant light surrounded him. [28]Like the appearance of a rainbow in the clouds on a rainy day, so was the radiance around him.

This was the appearance of the likeness of the glory of the LORD. When I saw it, I fell facedown, and I heard the voice of one speaking.

f26 Or lapis lazuli

Discovering the Word 1. Ezekiel is by the Kebar River in faraway Babylonian exile. It is five years after he and his compatriots were forcibly removed from Jerusalem. You may find it helpful to close your eyes and allow each new dimension of the vision to unfold. Record your impressions of colors, changing light, sounds, movement and symbols. 2. In this vision of God what do we learn about the relationship between God and his creation (vv. 4–21)? 3. What do verses 4–21 suggest about the character of God? 4. As Ezekiel is directed from creation to Creator (vv. 22–28), what further images and sounds create a sense of the glory of God? 5. Why would no form but the human form be appropriate to represent God visually?

Applying the Word 1. That the God of Zion would appear to Ezekiel in far-off Babylon amidst the sordid heathenism must have been an immense encouragement to Ezekiel. What does this mean for your personal life and your church life? 2. What aspects of the vision point to new frontiers in your experience of God?

Responding in Prayer As you pray, allow God to redeem your imagination to envision the glory of God. (There are some thoughts on the use of the imagination in the introduction.)

2 / *Ezekiel 2:1—3:15*
Experiencing the Call of God

MENTION THE PHRASE "called of God" and most think of those special few, God's chosen prophets, preachers and missionaries. That was certainly the case under the old covenant (before Christ) even though the people of God as a *people* were called (Hos 11:1). But under the new covenant every Christian is called in three ways: to belong to God, to live a holy life and to serve God's purposes in the world (Eph 4:1). Ezekiel's call was special, setting him apart from the people as God's spokesperson. But we can learn much from it. In chapter one we see that Ezekiel's call is first to Someone. Then, in chapter two, he is called to something. The order is crucial.

Warming Up to God What would it be like if God never called us and merely left us to make of our lives what we could?

Read Ezekiel 2:1—3:15.

2 He said to me, "Son of man, stand up on your feet and I will speak to you." [2]As he spoke, the Spirit came into me and raised me to my feet, and I heard him speaking to me.

[3]He said: "Son of man, I am sending you to the Israelites, to a rebellious nation that has rebelled against me; they and their fathers have been in revolt against me to this very day. [4]The people to whom I am sending you are obstinate and stubborn. Say to them, 'This is what the Sovereign LORD says.' [5]And whether they listen or fail to listen—for they are a rebellious house—they will know that a prophet has been among them. [6]And you, son of man, do not be afraid of them or their words. Do not be afraid, though briers and thorns are all around you and you live among scorpions. Do not be afraid of what they say or terrified by them, though they are a rebellious house. [7]You must speak my words to them, whether they listen or fail to listen, for they are rebellious. [8]But you, son of man, listen to what I say to you. Do

not rebel like that rebellious house; open your mouth and eat what I give you."

9Then I looked, and I saw a hand stretched out to me. In it was a scroll, 10which he unrolled before me. On both sides of it were written words of lament and mourning and woe.

3 And he said to me, "Son of man, eat what is before you, eat this scroll; then go and speak to the house of Israel." 2So I opened my mouth, and he gave me the scroll to eat.

3Then he said to me, "Son of man, eat this scroll I am giving you and fill your stomach with it." So I ate it, and it tasted as sweet as honey in my mouth.

4He then said to me: "Son of man, go now to the house of Israel and speak my words to them. 5You are not being sent to a people of obscure speech and difficult language, but to the house of Israel— 6not to many peoples of obscure speech and difficult language, whose words you cannot understand. Surely if I had sent you to them, they would have listened to you. 7But the house of Israel is not willing to listen to you because they are not willing to listen to me, for the whole house of Israel is hardened and obstinate. 8But I will make you as unyielding and hardened as they are. 9I will make your forehead like the hardest stone, harder than flint. Do not be afraid of them or terrified by them, though they are a rebellious house."

10And he said to me, "Son of man, listen carefully and take to heart all the words I speak to you. 11Go now to your countrymen in exile and speak to them. Say to them, 'This is what the Sovereign LORD says,' whether they listen or fail to listen."

12Then the Spirit lifted me up, and I heard behind me a loud rumbling sound—May the glory of the LORD be praised in his dwelling place!— 13the sound of the wings of the living creatures brushing against each other and the sound of the wheels beside them, a loud rumbling sound. 14The Spirit then lifted me up and took me away, and I went in bitterness and in the anger of my spirit, with the strong hand of the LORD upon me. 15I came to the exiles who lived at Tel Abib near the Kebar River. And there, where they were living, I sat among them for seven days—overwhelmed.

Discovering the Word 1. What indications are there in the passage that Ezekiel heard God's call not only as an obligation but also as an empowering and motivating reality (2:2; 3:12–15)? 2. Why does God want Ezekiel to go on speaking God's word even though the people will not listen (2:5)? 3. What might keep Ezekiel from fulfilling God's call, and how does God deal with this (2:6–8)? 4. In the vision the scroll of God's word is given to Ezekiel. Why would "eating" the scroll (2:8; 3:2) be so important for God's spokesperson? 5. Ezekiel is overwhelmed (3:15). What do you think is happening to this servant of God while he sits among the exiles for seven days?

Applying the Word 1. Why do you think being a missionary to the church (God's people) will be harder than being a missionary to the strangers outside (3:5–9)? 2. Ezekiel found both sweetness and bitterness in being a called person. In what ways is your experience of Christian vocation (or calling) similar? 3. What have you learned that will help you be faithful in witnessing even to those who are obstinately opposed to the gospel or where there is no evident success?

Responding in Prayer Thank God that he now issues his call through Christ to each and every member of his family. Pray for grace to live out the whole of your life in response to God's call and with the provision of his Spirit.

Ezekiel 3:16–27

16At the end of seven days the word of the LORD came to me: 17"Son of man, I have made you a watchman for the house of Israel; so hear the word I speak and give them warning from me. 18When I say to a wicked man, 'You will surely die,' and you do not warn him or speak out to dissuade him from his evil ways in order to save his life, that wicked man will die for[g] his sin, and I will hold you accountable for his blood. 19But if you do warn the wicked man and he does

g18 Or *in*; also in verses 19 and 20

not turn from his wickedness or from his evil ways, he will die for his sin; but you will have saved yourself.

[20]"Again, when a righteous man turns from his righteousness and does evil, and I put a stumbling block before him, he will die. Since you did not warn him, he will die for his sin. The righteous things he did will not be remembered, and I will hold you accountable for his blood. [21]But if you do warn the righteous man not to sin and he does not sin, he will surely live because he took warning, and you will have saved yourself."

[22]The hand of the LORD was upon me there, and he said to me, "Get up and go out to the plain, and there I will speak to you." [23]So I got up and went out to the plain. And the glory of the LORD was standing there, like the glory I had seen by the Kebar River, and I fell facedown.

[24]Then the Spirit came into me and raised me to my feet. He spoke to me and said: "Go, shut yourself inside your house. [25]And you, son of man, they will tie with ropes; you will be bound so that you cannot go out among the people. [26]I will make your tongue stick to the roof of your mouth so that you will be silent and unable to rebuke them, though they are a rebellious house. [27]But when I speak to you, I will open your mouth and you shall say to them, 'This is what the Sovereign LORD says.' Whoever will listen let him listen, and whoever will refuse let him refuse; for they are a rebellious house.

3 / *Ezekiel 4—5*
Warning the People of God

HARDLY ANYONE THINKS of the wrath of God as a positive thing. Most think of it as a divine temper tantrum. But the wrath of God is God's giving people up to experience the results of their own choice (Ro 1:24, 26, 28). It is like a wood plane which if used with the grain produces a smooth surface, but if used against the grain tears up all the fibers even though it is the same tool and the same block of wood.

Ezekiel has a hard message for his people. In far-off Babylon, with hearts still focused on their beloved Jerusalem, the people must be warned about what is going to happen to the holy city. Under King Zedekiah Jerusalem had recovered some of its strength, and false prophets were predicting a time of favor (Jer 28:1–4). The truth was otherwise. If they repent, they will know God's grace; if they do not, they will know his wrath. Much later in history God's own Son bore the wrath they and we deserve outside the walls of that same city.

Warming Up to God Think of a time in your life when you had a hard but good warning. What made it a good thing even though it hurt at the time?

Read Ezekiel 4—5.

4 "Now, son of man, take a clay tablet, put it in front of you and draw the city of Jerusalem on it. [2]Then lay siege to it: Erect siege works against it, build a ramp up to it, set up camps against it and put battering rams around it. [3]Then take an iron pan, place it as an iron wall between you and the city and turn your face toward it. It will be under siege, and you shall besiege it. This will be a sign to the house of Israel.

[4]"Then lie on your left side and put the sin of the house of Israel upon yourself.[h] You are to bear their sin for the number of days you lie on your side. [5]I have assigned you the same number of days as the years of their sin. So for 390 days you will bear the sin of the house of Israel.

[6]"After you have finished this, lie down again, this time on your right side, and bear the sin of the house of Judah. I have assigned you 40 days, a day for each year. [7]Turn your face toward the siege of Jerusalem and with bared arm prophesy against her. [8]I will tie you up with ropes so that you cannot turn from one side to the other until you have finished the days of your siege.

[9]"Take wheat and barley, beans and lentils, millet and spelt; put them in a storage jar and use them to make bread for yourself. You are to eat it

[h]4 Or *your side*

during the 390 days you lie on your side. 10Weigh out twenty shekels[i] of food to eat each day and eat it at set times. 11Also measure out a sixth of a hin[j] of water and drink it at set times. 12Eat the food as you would a barley cake; bake it in the sight of the people, using human excrement for fuel." 13The LORD said, "In this way the people of Israel will eat defiled food among the nations where I will drive them."

14Then I said, "Not so, Sovereign LORD! I have never defiled myself. From my youth until now I have never eaten anything found dead or torn by wild animals. No unclean meat has ever entered my mouth."

15"Very well," he said, "I will let you bake your bread over cow manure instead of human excrement."

16He then said to me: "Son of man, I will cut off the supply of food in Jerusalem. The people will eat rationed food in anxiety and drink rationed water in despair, 17for food and water will be scarce. They will be appalled at the sight of each other and will waste away because of[k] their sin.

5 "Now, son of man, take a sharp sword and use it as a barber's razor to shave your head and your beard. Then take a set of scales and divide up the hair. 2When the days of your siege come to an end, burn a third of the hair with fire inside the city. Take a third and strike it with the sword all around the city. And scatter a third to the wind. For I will pursue them with drawn sword. 3But take a few strands of hair and tuck them away in the folds of your garment. 4Again, take a few of these and throw them into the fire and burn them up. A fire will spread from there to the whole house of Israel.

5"This is what the Sovereign LORD says: This is Jerusalem, which I have set in the center of the nations, with countries all around her. 6Yet in her wickedness she has rebelled against my laws and decrees more than the nations and countries around her. She has rejected my laws and has not followed my decrees.

7"Therefore this is what the Sovereign LORD says: You have been more unruly than the nations around you and have not followed my decrees or kept my laws. You have not even[l] conformed to the standards of the nations around you.

8"Therefore this is what the Sovereign LORD says: I myself am against you, Jerusalem, and I will inflict punishment on you in the sight of the nations. 9Because of all your detestable idols, I will do to you what I have never done before and will never do again. 10Therefore in your midst fathers will eat their children, and children will eat their fathers. I will inflict punishment on you and will scatter all your survivors to the winds. 11Therefore as surely as I live, declares the Sovereign LORD, because you have defiled my sanctuary with all your vile images and detestable practices, I myself will withdraw my favor; I will not look on you with pity or spare you. 12A third of your people will die of the plague or perish by famine inside you; a third will fall by the sword outside your walls; and a third I will scatter to the winds and pursue with drawn sword.

13"Then my anger will cease and my wrath against them will subside, and I will be avenged. And when I have spent my wrath upon them, they will know that I the LORD have spoken in my zeal.

14"I will make you a ruin and a reproach among the nations around you, in the sight of all who pass by. 15You will be a reproach and a taunt, a warning and an object of horror to the nations around you when I inflict punishment on you in anger and in wrath and with stinging rebuke. I the LORD have spoken. 16When I shoot at you with my deadly and destructive arrows of famine, I will shoot to destroy you. I will bring more and more famine upon you and cut off your supply of food. 17I will send famine and wild beasts against you, and they will leave you childless. Plague and bloodshed will sweep through you, and I will bring the sword against you. I the LORD have spoken."

[i]10 That is, about 8 ounces (about 0.2 kilogram) [j]11 That is, about 2/3 quart (about 0.6 liter) [k]17 Or *away in* [l]7 Most Hebrew manuscripts; some Hebrew manuscripts and Syriac *You have*

Discovering the Word 1. What audio-visual aids and personal dramatic acts is Ezekiel instructed to use to communicate what God intended to do with Jerusalem? 2. The prophet is called to bear the sin of the people on his side (4:4–8). What could Ezekiel be communicating through this? 3. What does 4:9–15 reveal about the relationship between Ezekiel and God? 4. What reason does God give for his drastic action with Jerusalem (5:6–7, 11)? 5. How does the punishment fit the crime (5:8–17)? 6. What do you learn in this passage about God's zeal for righteousness (5:13)?

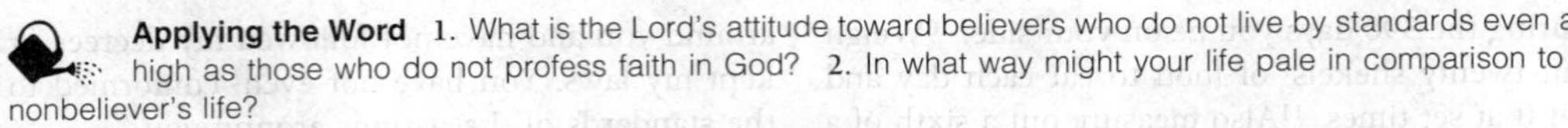

Applying the Word 1. What is the Lord's attitude toward believers who do not live by standards even as high as those who do not profess faith in God? 2. In what way might your life pale in comparison to a nonbeliever's life?

Responding in Prayer Ask the Lord to give you his perspective on what is happening in the world and in your life. Praise God that there is hope in his judgment.

4 / *Ezekiel 6—7*
Living in the End Times

THE FRENCH EXISTENTIALIST Albert Camus once said that he would wait for the judgment of God resolutely because he had known something far worse: the judgment of human beings. With men and women there are no extenuating circumstances. But with God there is hope, often signaled in the Bible by a "but" as in Ezekiel 6:8. Israel was called to be a kingdom of priests (Ex 19:6), declaring God's Word to the world that all may "know the LORD" (2Ki 19:19). In the end people expected the nations to be judged and Israel saved. But in this passage God's final judgment has begun and judgment begins at the house of God.

Warming Up to God What do you most fear and most long for when you hear that God is bringing history to a conclusion with a final judgment?

Read Ezekiel 6—7.

6 The word of the LORD came to me: 2"Son
of man, set your face against the moun-
tains of Israel; prophesy against them
3and say: 'O mountains of Israel, hear the word of
the Sovereign LORD. This is what the Sovereign
LORD says to the mountains and hills, to the ra-
vines and valleys: I am about to bring a sword
against you, and I will destroy your high places.
4Your altars will be demolished and your incense
altars will be smashed; and I will slay your people
in front of your idols. 5I will lay the dead bodies
of the Israelites in front of their idols, and I will
scatter your bones around your altars. 6Wherever
you live, the towns will be laid waste and the high
places demolished, so that your altars will be laid
waste and devastated, your idols smashed and ru-
ined, your incense altars broken down, and what
you have made wiped out. 7Your people will fall
slain among you, and you will know that I am the
LORD.

8" 'But I will spare some, for some of you will
escape the sword when you are scattered among
the lands and nations. 9Then in the nations where
they have been carried captive, those who escape
will remember me—how I have been grieved by
their adulterous hearts, which have turned away
from me, and by their eyes, which have lusted
after their idols. They will loathe themselves for
the evil they have done and for all their detestable
practices. 10And they will know that I am the
LORD; I did not threaten in vain to bring this ca-
lamity on them.

11" 'This is what the Sovereign LORD says: Strike
your hands together and stamp your feet and cry
out "Alas!" because of all the wicked and detest-
able practices of the house of Israel, for they will
fall by the sword, famine and plague. 12He that is
far away will die of the plague, and he that is near
will fall by the sword, and he that survives and
is spared will die of famine. So will I spend my
wrath upon them. 13And they will know that I am
the LORD, when their people lie slain among their
idols around their altars, on every high hill and
on all the mountaintops, under every spreading
tree and every leafy oak—places where they of-
fered fragrant incense to all their idols. 14And I
will stretch out my hand against them and make
the land a desolate waste from the desert to Dib-

lah[m]—wherever they live. Then they will know that I am the LORD.' "

7 The word of the LORD came to me: 2"Son of man, this is what the Sovereign LORD says to the land of Israel: The end! The end has come upon the four corners of the land. 3The end is now upon you and I will unleash my anger against you. I will judge you according to your conduct and repay you for all your detestable practices. 4I will not look on you with pity or spare you; I will surely repay you for your conduct and the detestable practices among you. Then you will know that I am the LORD.

5"This is what the Sovereign LORD says: Disaster! An unheard-of[n] disaster is coming. 6The end has come! The end has come! It has roused itself against you. It has come! 7Doom has come upon you—you who dwell in the land. The time has come, the day is near; there is panic, not joy, upon the mountains. 8I am about to pour out my wrath on you and spend my anger against you; I will judge you according to your conduct and repay you for all your detestable practices. 9I will not look on you with pity or spare you; I will repay you in accordance with your conduct and the detestable practices among you. Then you will know that it is I the LORD who strikes the blow.

10"The day is here! It has come! Doom has burst forth, the rod has budded, arrogance has blossomed! 11Violence has grown into[o] a rod to punish wickedness; none of the people will be left, none of that crowd—no wealth, nothing of value. 12The time has come, the day has arrived. Let not the buyer rejoice nor the seller grieve, for wrath is upon the whole crowd. 13The seller will not recover the land he has sold as long as both of them live, for the vision concerning the whole crowd will not be reversed. Because of their sins, not one of them will preserve his life. 14Though they blow the trumpet and get everything ready, no one will go into battle, for my wrath is upon the whole crowd.

15"Outside is the sword, inside are plague and famine; those in the country will die by the sword, and those in the city will be devoured by famine and plague. 16All who survive and escape will be in the mountains, moaning like doves of the valleys, each because of his sins. 17Every hand will go limp, and every knee will become as weak as water. 18They will put on sackcloth and be clothed with terror. Their faces will be covered with shame and their heads will be shaved. 19They will throw their silver into the streets, and their gold will be an unclean thing. Their silver and gold will not be able to save them in the day of the LORD's wrath. They will not satisfy their hunger or fill their stomachs with it, for it has made them stumble into sin. 20They were proud of their beautiful jewelry and used it to make their detestable idols and vile images. Therefore I will turn these into an unclean thing for them. 21I will hand it all over as plunder to foreigners and as loot to the wicked of the earth, and they will defile it. 22I will turn my face away from them, and they will desecrate my treasured place; robbers will enter it and desecrate it.

23"Prepare chains, because the land is full of bloodshed and the city is full of violence. 24I will bring the most wicked of the nations to take possession of their houses; I will put an end to the pride of the mighty, and their sanctuaries will be desecrated. 25When terror comes, they will seek peace, but there will be none. 26Calamity upon calamity will come, and rumor upon rumor. They will try to get a vision from the prophet; the teaching of the law by the priest will be lost, as will the counsel of the elders. 27The king will mourn, the prince will be clothed with despair, and the hands of the people of the land will tremble. I will deal with them according to their conduct, and by their own standards I will judge them. Then they will know that I am the LORD."

[m]14 Most Hebrew manuscripts; a few Hebrew manuscripts *Riblah*
[n]5 Most Hebrew manuscripts; some Hebrew manuscripts and Syriac *Disaster after* [o]11 Or *The violent one has become*

Discovering the Word 1. Ezekiel now turns from God's condemnation of Jerusalem to Israel as a whole, especially the mountains of Israel (6:2) where the pagan shrines ("high places") and idol worship were located. What sins brings God's judgment on his own people? 2. Trace the various dimensions of God's wrath in chapters 6 and 7 where Ezekiel claims the season of final reckoning is upon them. What patterns do you see? (For example, why is God's judgment of their use of wealth fitting [7:9, 19–22]?) 3. What judgment in 7:25–27 will be particularly distressing (see also Ps 74:9)? 4. In what way could the silence of God in responding to prayers and initiating revelation be a further way in which they could know that God is God (7:4)? 5. What word of comfort and hope does Ezekiel's message contain for the exiles living dispersed in a foreign land far away from Jerusalem (6:8–10)?

Applying the Word 1. What sins addressed by Ezekiel are found also in our contemporary society and church? 2. First Peter 4:17 tells us that God's people will be the first to be judged. What does this mean to you as you think about your life?

Responding in Prayer Ask God to reveal in what ways you have been taken in by the pollution of God's people and the world around you. Pray for a true spirit of repentance that finds hope in God's mercy.

5 / *Ezekiel 8*
The Darkened Inner Eye

IN THE OPENING vision Ezekiel was overwhelmed by the glory of God (1:28). But now as he is taken in a vision not only inside beloved Jerusalem but inside the hearts of God's people in Jerusalem, Ezekiel is overwhelmed by the sin of God's people. The root sin that concerns Ezekiel is not moral failures but the perversion of the human imagination so that people are wooed away from single-minded love of God. This passage reveals the truth that as people imagine in their hearts, so they will be.

Warming Up to God Consider the ways in which imagination is being used in our contemporary culture. What aspects would be troubling to God?

Read Ezekiel 8.

8 In the sixth year, in the sixth month on
the fifth day, while I was sitting in my
house and the elders of Judah were sitting
before me, the hand of the Sovereign LORD came
upon me there. 2 I looked, and I saw a figure like
that of a man.[p] From what appeared to be his
waist down he was like fire, and from there up his
appearance was as bright as glowing metal. 3 He
stretched out what looked like a hand and took
me by the hair of my head. The Spirit lifted me up
between earth and heaven and in visions of God
he took me to Jerusalem, to the entrance to the
north gate of the inner court, where the idol that
provokes to jealousy stood. 4 And there before me
was the glory of the God of Israel, as in the vision
I had seen in the plain.

5 Then he said to me, "Son of man, look toward
the north." So I looked, and in the entrance north
of the gate of the altar I saw this idol of jealousy.

6 And he said to me, "Son of man, do you see
what they are doing—the utterly detestable
things the house of Israel is doing here, things
that will drive me far from my sanctuary? But you
will see things that are even more detestable."

7 Then he brought me to the entrance to the
court. I looked, and I saw a hole in the wall. 8 He
said to me, "Son of man, now dig into the wall."
So I dug into the wall and saw a doorway there.

9 And he said to me, "Go in and see the wicked
and detestable things they are doing here." 10 So I
went in and looked, and I saw portrayed all over
the walls all kinds of crawling things and detest-
able animals and all the idols of the house of Is-
rael. 11 In front of them stood seventy elders of the
house of Israel, and Jaazaniah son of Shaphan was
standing among them. Each had a censer in his
hand, and a fragrant cloud of incense was rising.

12 He said to me, "Son of man, have you seen
what the elders of the house of Israel are doing in
the darkness, each at the shrine of his own idol?
They say, 'The LORD does not see us; the LORD has
forsaken the land.' " 13 Again, he said, "You will
see them doing things that are even more detest-
able."

14 Then he brought me to the entrance to the
north gate of the house of the LORD, and I saw
women sitting there, mourning for Tammuz. 15 He
said to me, "Do you see this, son of man? You will
see things that are even more detestable than
this."

p2 Or *saw a fiery figure*

16He then brought me into the inner court of the house of the LORD, and there at the entrance to the temple, between the portico and the altar, were about twenty-five men. With their backs toward the temple of the LORD and their faces toward the east, they were bowing down to the sun in the east.

17He said to me, "Have you seen this, son of man? Is it a trivial matter for the house of Judah to do the detestable things they are doing here? Must they also fill the land with violence and continually provoke me to anger? Look at them putting the branch to their nose! 18Therefore I will deal with them in anger; I will not look on them with pity or spare them. Although they shout in my ears, I will not listen to them."

Discovering the Word 1. Fourteen months after the opening vision of the glory of God Ezekiel is caught up in another prophetic trance. While the glory of God is still there (v. 4), what in contrast does Ezekiel now see (vv. 5-6, 10-16)? 2. The "idol that provokes to jealousy" (vv. 3, 5-6) is probably the wooden image of Asherah, the Canaanite goddess that Manasseh had put in the temple (2Ki 21:7), which seems to have been returned to the prestigious northern gate next to the royal palace. "All kinds of crawling things and detestable animals" (v. 10) were likely serpent deities that had been part of Egyptian, Canaanite and Babylonian religions. "Mourning for Tammuz" (v. 14) refers to a Sumerian god of vegetation who died and became the god of the underworld and is worshiped here in a mourning ritual. Why do you think spiritual pollution, which so offended Ezekiel, is as serious as social sins and breaches in social justice? 3. Verse 12 tells us even the leaders are worshiping idols. What is the connection between what is happening on the inside of the minds of the leaders and what is taking place in the corporate life of the nation? 4. Why is the vision of the twenty-five men (v. 16), later called elders (9:6), the ultimate detestable picture?

Applying the Word 1. The leaders explain their private imaginative life by the words "the LORD does not see us" (v. 12). How does this same explanation help you understand the downfall of significant Christian leaders today? 2. What perversions of the imagination are threats to healthy spirituality for you? 3. One remarkable fact in this vision is the presence of the glory of God in the midst of spiritual perversion (v. 4). In what way is this both an encouragement and a warning to you as you struggle to have a pure thought life?

Responding in Prayer Pray that your vision of the glory of God will purify your imagination so that every thought will be taken captive.

Ezekiel 9—10

9 Then I heard him call out in a loud voice, "Bring the guards of the city here, each with a weapon in his hand." 2And I saw six men coming from the direction of the upper gate, which faces north, each with a deadly weapon in his hand. With them was a man clothed in linen who had a writing kit at his side. They came in and stood beside the bronze altar.

3Now the glory of the God of Israel went up from above the cherubim, where it had been, and moved to the threshold of the temple. Then the LORD called to the man clothed in linen who had the writing kit at his side 4and said to him, "Go throughout the city of Jerusalem and put a mark on the foreheads of those who grieve and lament over all the detestable things that are done in it."

5As I listened, he said to the others, "Follow him through the city and kill, without showing pity or compassion. 6Slaughter old men, young men and maidens, women and children, but do not touch anyone who has the mark. Begin at my sanctuary." So they began with the elders who were in front of the temple.

7Then he said to them, "Defile the temple and fill the courts with the slain. Go!" So they went out and began killing throughout the city. 8While they were killing and I was left alone, I fell facedown, crying out, "Ah, Sovereign LORD! Are you going to destroy the entire remnant of Israel in this outpouring of your wrath on Jerusalem?"

9He answered me, "The sin of the house of Israel and Judah is exceedingly great; the land is full of bloodshed and the city is full of injustice. They say, 'The LORD has forsaken the land; the LORD does not see.' 10So I will not look on them with pity or spare them, but I will bring down on their own heads what they have done."

11Then the man in linen with the writing kit at

his side brought back word, saying, "I have done as you commanded."

10 I looked, and I saw the likeness of a throne of sapphire[q] above the expanse that was over the heads of the cherubim. [2]The LORD said to the man clothed in linen, "Go in among the wheels beneath the cherubim. Fill your hands with burning coals from among the cherubim and scatter them over the city." And as I watched, he went in.

[3]Now the cherubim were standing on the south side of the temple when the man went in, and a cloud filled the inner court. [4]Then the glory of the LORD rose from above the cherubim and moved to the threshold of the temple. The cloud filled the temple, and the court was full of the radiance of the glory of the LORD. [5]The sound of the wings of the cherubim could be heard as far away as the outer court, like the voice of God Almighty[r] when he speaks.

[6]When the LORD commanded the man in linen, "Take fire from among the wheels, from among the cherubim," the man went in and stood beside a wheel. [7]Then one of the cherubim reached out his hand to the fire that was among them. He took up some of it and put it into the hands of the man in linen, who took it and went out. [8](Under the wings of the cherubim could be seen what looked like the hands of a man.)

[9]I looked, and I saw beside the cherubim four wheels, one beside each of the cherubim; the wheels sparkled like chrysolite. [10]As for their appearance, the four of them looked alike; each was like a wheel intersecting a wheel. [11]As they moved, they would go in any one of the four directions the cherubim faced; the wheels did not turn about[s] as the cherubim went. The cherubim went in whatever direction the head faced, without turning as they went. [12]Their entire bodies, including their backs, their hands and their wings, were completely full of eyes, as were their four wheels. [13]I heard the wheels being called "the whirling wheels." [14]Each of the cherubim had four faces: One face was that of a cherub, the second the face of a man, the third the face of a lion, and the fourth the face of an eagle.

[15]Then the cherubim rose upward. These were the living creatures I had seen by the Kebar River. [16]When the cherubim moved, the wheels beside them moved; and when the cherubim spread their wings to rise from the ground, the wheels did not leave their side. [17]When the cherubim stood still, they also stood still; and when the cherubim rose, they rose with them, because the spirit of the living creatures was in them.

[18]Then the glory of the LORD departed from over the threshold of the temple and stopped above the cherubim. [19]While I watched, the cherubim spread their wings and rose from the ground, and as they went, the wheels went with them. They stopped at the entrance to the east gate of the LORD's house, and the glory of the God of Israel was above them.

[20]These were the living creatures I had seen beneath the God of Israel by the Kebar River, and I realized that they were cherubim. [21]Each had four faces and four wings, and under their wings was what looked like the hands of a man. [22]Their faces had the same appearance as those I had seen by the Kebar River. Each one went straight ahead.

q1 Or *lapis lazuli* r5 Hebrew *El-Shaddai* s11 Or *aside*

6/ *Ezekiel 11*
When Human Leaders Fail

BECOMING DISILLUSIONED WITH leaders, whether in the realm of politics or the media, is always a painful experience. But the keenest loss of respect is most often associated with religious leaders who, instead of leading people to put their trust in God, gain trust for themselves and then lead their followers astray. In Ezekiel's case his pain at seeing the deceitful heart of Jerusalem's leadership is more than matched by the Lord's word of encouragement. Chapter 11 brings to a conclusion the vision given to Ezekiel that started in chapter 8. The fulfillment of his word of judgment came in 2 Kings 25:18–21 and of his word of hope with the restored kingdom (Ezra/Nehemiah) and the coming of Christ.

Warming Up to God Recall an experience of seeing a Christian leader prove to be proud, self-confident or deceitful. What did it do to your relationship with God?

Read Ezekiel 11.

11

Then the Spirit lifted me up and
brought me to the gate of the house
of the LORD that faces east. There at
the entrance to the gate were twenty-five men,
and I saw among them Jaazaniah son of Azzur
and Pelatiah son of Benaiah, leaders of the people.
2The LORD said to me, "Son of man, these are the
men who are plotting evil and giving wicked ad-
vice in this city. 3They say, 'Will it not soon be
time to build houses?[t] This city is a cooking pot,
and we are the meat.' 4Therefore prophesy against
them; prophesy, son of man."
5Then the Spirit of the LORD came upon me,
and he told me to say: "This is what the LORD says:
That is what you are saying, O house of Israel, but
I know what is going through your mind. 6You
have killed many people in this city and filled its
streets with the dead.
7"Therefore this is what the Sovereign LORD
says: The bodies you have thrown there are the
meat and this city is the pot, but I will drive you
out of it. 8You fear the sword, and the sword is
what I will bring against you, declares the Sover-
eign LORD. 9I will drive you out of the city and
hand you over to foreigners and inflict punish-
ment on you. 10You will fall by the sword, and I
will execute judgment on you at the borders of
Israel. Then you will know that I am the LORD.
11This city will not be a pot for you, nor will you
be the meat in it; I will execute judgment on you
at the borders of Israel. 12And you will know that
I am the LORD, for you have not followed my de-
crees or kept my laws but have conformed to the
standards of the nations around you."
13Now as I was prophesying, Pelatiah son of
Benaiah died. Then I fell facedown and cried out
in a loud voice, "Ah, Sovereign LORD! Will you
completely destroy the remnant of Israel?"
14The word of the LORD came to me: 15"Son of
man, your brothers—your brothers who are your
blood relatives[u] and the whole house of Israel—
are those of whom the people of Jerusalem have
said, 'They are[v] far away from the LORD; this land
was given to us as our possession.'
16"Therefore say: 'This is what the Sovereign
LORD says: Although I sent them far away among
the nations and scattered them among the coun-
tries, yet for a little while I have been a sanctuary
for them in the countries where they have gone.'
17"Therefore say: 'This is what the Sovereign
LORD says: I will gather you from the nations and
bring you back from the countries where you
have been scattered, and I will give you back the
land of Israel again.'
18"They will return to it and remove all its vile
images and detestable idols. 19I will give them an
undivided heart and put a new spirit in them; I
will remove from them their heart of stone and
give them a heart of flesh. 20Then they will follow
my decrees and be careful to keep my laws. They
will be my people, and I will be their God. 21But
as for those whose hearts are devoted to their vile
images and detestable idols, I will bring down on
their own heads what they have done, declares
the Sovereign LORD."
22Then the cherubim, with the wheels beside
them, spread their wings, and the glory of the
God of Israel was above them. 23The glory of the
LORD went up from within the city and stopped
above the mountain east of it. 24The Spirit lifted
me up and brought me to the exiles in Babylo-
nia[w] in the vision given by the Spirit of God.
Then the vision I had seen went up from me,
25and I told the exiles everything the LORD had
shown me.

[t]3 Or *This is not the time to build houses.* [u]15 Or *are in exile with you* (see Septuagint and Syriac) [v]15 Or *those to whom the people of Jerusalem have said, 'Stay* [w]24 Or *Chaldea*

Discovering the Word 1. Ezekiel is given a vision of twenty-five leaders by the gate to the temple who were a political pressure group led by the nobility that was left in Jerusalem. In what specific ways were they leading the people astray (vv. 1–13)? 2. The leaders claimed that the people were as safe in Jerusalem as meat kept from the fire in a pot (vv. 3, 11). Why is this reckless course so dangerous (see also Jer 21:8–10)? 3. The death of one of the leaders, Pelatiah (v. 13), provoked a deep crisis for Ezekiel. What insight do we gain about Ezekiel's spirituality (see also 9:8)? 4. What hopeful message does the Lord have for the people scattered in Babylon (vv. 14–25)? 5. The people felt God-forsaken (because they were away from the temple) and spiritually helpless. In what way does Ezekiel now see things differently?

Applying the Word 1. What help do you gain from this chapter on how to relate to leaders? 2. In what ways does the comforting message to the exiles bring hope for times when you feel God-forsaken and spiritually helpless?

Responding in Prayer Thank God that he is your sanctuary (v. 17), that his presence will go with you everywhere, and that your covenantal relationship with God (v. 20) through Christ is secure.

Ezekiel 12—15

12 The word of the LORD came to me:
2“Son of man, you are living among
a rebellious people. They have eyes
to see but do not see and ears to hear but do not
hear, for they are a rebellious people.
3“Therefore, son of man, pack your belongings
for exile and in the daytime, as they watch, set
out and go from where you are to another place.
Perhaps they will understand, though they are a
rebellious house. 4During the daytime, while they
watch, bring out your belongings packed for ex-
ile. Then in the evening, while they are watching,
go out like those who go into exile. 5While they
watch, dig through the wall and take your be-
longings out through it. 6Put them on your shoul-
der as they are watching and carry them out at
dusk. Cover your face so that you cannot see the
land, for I have made you a sign to the house of
Israel.”
7So I did as I was commanded. During the day
I brought out my things packed for exile. Then
in the evening I dug through the wall with my
hands. I took my belongings out at dusk, carrying
them on my shoulders while they watched.
8In the morning the word of the LORD came to
me: 9“Son of man, did not that rebellious house of
Israel ask you, ‘What are you doing?’
10“Say to them, ‘This is what the Sovereign
LORD says: This oracle concerns the prince in Je-
rusalem and the whole house of Israel who are
there.’ 11Say to them, ‘I am a sign to you.’
“As I have done, so it will be done to them.
They will go into exile as captives.
12“The prince among them will put his things
on his shoulder at dusk and leave, and a hole will
be dug in the wall for him to go through. He will
cover his face so that he cannot see the land. 13I
will spread my net for him, and he will be caught
in my snare; I will bring him to Babylonia, the
land of the Chaldeans, but he will not see it, and
there he will die. 14I will scatter to the winds all
those around him—his staff and all his troops—
and I will pursue them with drawn sword.
15“They will know that I am the LORD, when I
disperse them among the nations and scatter
them through the countries. 16But I will spare a
few of them from the sword, famine and plague,
so that in the nations where they go they may
acknowledge all their detestable practices. Then
they will know that I am the LORD.”
17The word of the LORD came to me: 18“Son of
man, tremble as you eat your food, and shudder
in fear as you drink your water. 19Say to the peo-
ple of the land: ‘This is what the Sovereign LORD
says about those living in Jerusalem and in the
land of Israel: They will eat their food in anxiety
and drink their water in despair, for their land
will be stripped of everything in it because of the
violence of all who live there. 20The inhabited
towns will be laid waste and the land will be des-
olate. Then you will know that I am the LORD.’ ”
21The word of the LORD came to me: 22“Son of
man, what is this proverb you have in the land of
Israel: ‘The days go by and every vision comes to
nothing’? 23Say to them, ‘This is what the Sover-
eign LORD says: I am going to put an end to this
proverb, and they will no longer quote it in Is-
rael.’ Say to them, ‘The days are near when every
vision will be fulfilled. 24For there will be no
more false visions or flattering divinations among
the people of Israel. 25But I the LORD will speak
what I will, and it shall be fulfilled without delay.
For in your days, you rebellious house, I will ful-
fill whatever I say, declares the Sovereign LORD.’ ”
26The word of the LORD came to me: 27“Son of
man, the house of Israel is saying, ‘The vision he
sees is for many years from now, and he prophe-
sies about the distant future.’

28“Therefore say to them, ‘This is what the Sov-
ereign LORD says: None of my words will be de-
layed any longer; whatever I say will be fulfilled,
declares the Sovereign LORD.’ ”

13

The word of the LORD came to me:
2“Son of man, prophesy against the
prophets of Israel who are now
prophesying. Say to those who prophesy out of
their own imagination: ‘Hear the word of the
LORD! 3This is what the Sovereign LORD says: Woe
to the foolish[x] prophets who follow their own
spirit and have seen nothing! 4Your prophets, O
Israel, are like jackals among ruins. 5You have not
gone up to the breaks in the wall to repair it for
the house of Israel so that it will stand firm in the
battle on the day of the LORD. 6Their visions are
false and their divinations a lie. They say, “The
LORD declares,” when the LORD has not sent them;
yet they expect their words to be fulfilled. 7Have
you not seen false visions and uttered lying divi-
nations when you say, “The LORD declares,”
though I have not spoken?

8“ ‘Therefore this is what the Sovereign LORD
says: Because of your false words and lying vi-
sions, I am against you, declares the Sovereign
LORD. 9My hand will be against the prophets who
see false visions and utter lying divinations. They
will not belong to the council of my people or be
listed in the records of the house of Israel, nor
will they enter the land of Israel. Then you will
know that I am the Sovereign LORD.

10“ ‘Because they lead my people astray, saying,
“Peace,” when there is no peace, and because,
when a flimsy wall is built, they cover it with
whitewash, 11therefore tell those who cover it
with whitewash that it is going to fall. Rain will
come in torrents, and I will send hailstones hur-
tling down, and violent winds will burst forth.
12When the wall collapses, will people not ask
you, “Where is the whitewash you covered it
with?”

13“ ‘Therefore this is what the Sovereign LORD
says: In my wrath I will unleash a violent wind,
and in my anger hailstones and torrents of rain
will fall with destructive fury. 14I will tear down
the wall you have covered with whitewash and
will level it to the ground so that its foundation
will be laid bare. When it[y] falls, you will be de-
stroyed in it; and you will know that I am the
LORD. 15So I will spend my wrath against the wall
and against those who covered it with whitewash.
I will say to you, “The wall is gone and so are
those who whitewashed it, 16those prophets of
Israel who prophesied to Jerusalem and saw vi-
sions of peace for her when there was no peace,
declares the Sovereign LORD.” ’

17“Now, son of man, set your face against the
daughters of your people who prophesy out of
their own imagination. Prophesy against them
18and say, ‘This is what the Sovereign LORD says:
Woe to the women who sew magic charms on all
their wrists and make veils of various lengths for
their heads in order to ensnare people. Will you
ensnare the lives of my people but preserve your
own? 19You have profaned me among my people
for a few handfuls of barley and scraps of bread.
By lying to my people, who listen to lies, you
have killed those who should not have died and
have spared those who should not live.

20“ ‘Therefore this is what the Sovereign LORD
says: I am against your magic charms with which
you ensnare people like birds and I will tear them
from your arms; I will set free the people that you
ensnare like birds. 21I will tear off your veils and
save my people from your hands, and they will no
longer fall prey to your power. Then you will
know that I am the LORD. 22Because you disheart-
ened the righteous with your lies, when I had
brought them no grief, and because you encour-
aged the wicked not to turn from their evil ways
and so save their lives, 23therefore you will no
longer see false visions or practice divination. I
will save my people from your hands. And then
you will know that I am the LORD.’ ”

14

Some of the elders of Israel came to
me and sat down in front of me.
2Then the word of the LORD came to
me: 3“Son of man, these men have set up idols in
their hearts and put wicked stumbling blocks be-
fore their faces. Should I let them inquire of me at
all? 4Therefore speak to them and tell them, ‘This
is what the Sovereign LORD says: When any Israel-
ite sets up idols in his heart and puts a wicked
stumbling block before his face and then goes to
a prophet, I the LORD will answer him myself in
keeping with his great idolatry. 5I will do this to
recapture the hearts of the people of Israel, who
have all deserted me for their idols.’

6“Therefore say to the house of Israel, ‘This is
what the Sovereign LORD says: Repent! Turn from
your idols and renounce all your detestable prac-
tices!

[x]3 Or *wicked* [y]14 Or *the city*

7" 'When any Israelite or any alien living in Is-
rael separates himself from me and sets up idols
in his heart and puts a wicked stumbling block
before his face and then goes to a prophet to in-
quire of me, I the LORD will answer him myself. 8I
will set my face against that man and make him
an example and a byword. I will cut him off from
my people. Then you will know that I am the
LORD.

9" 'And if the prophet is enticed to utter a
prophecy, I the LORD have enticed that prophet,
and I will stretch out my hand against him and
destroy him from among my people Israel. 10They
will bear their guilt—the prophet will be as guilty
as the one who consults him. 11Then the people
of Israel will no longer stray from me, nor will
they defile themselves anymore with all their sins.
They will be my people, and I will be their God,
declares the Sovereign LORD.' "

12The word of the LORD came to me: 13"Son of
man, if a country sins against me by being un-
faithful and I stretch out my hand against it to cut
off its food supply and send famine upon it and
kill its men and their animals, 14even if these
three men—Noah, Daniel[z] and Job—were in it,
they could save only themselves by their righ-
teousness, declares the Sovereign LORD.

15"Or if I send wild beasts through that country
and they leave it childless and it becomes desolate
so that no one can pass through it because of the
beasts, 16as surely as I live, declares the Sovereign
LORD, even if these three men were in it, they
could not save their own sons or daughters. They
alone would be saved, but the land would be des-
olate.

17"Or if I bring a sword against that country
and say, 'Let the sword pass throughout the land,'
and I kill its men and their animals, 18as surely as
I live, declares the Sovereign LORD, even if these
three men were in it, they could not save their
own sons or daughters. They alone would be
saved.

19"Or if I send a plague into that land and pour
out my wrath upon it through bloodshed, killing
its men and their animals, 20as surely as I live,
declares the Sovereign LORD, even if Noah, Daniel
and Job were in it, they could save neither son
nor daughter. They would save only themselves
by their righteousness.

21"For this is what the Sovereign LORD says:
How much worse will it be when I send against
Jerusalem my four dreadful judgments—sword
and famine and wild beasts and plague—to kill
its men and their animals! 22Yet there will be
some survivors—sons and daughters who will be
brought out of it. They will come to you, and
when you see their conduct and their actions, you
will be consoled regarding the disaster I have
brought upon Jerusalem—every disaster I have
brought upon it. 23You will be consoled when you
see their conduct and their actions, for you will
know that I have done nothing in it without
cause, declares the Sovereign LORD."

15

The word of the LORD came to me:
2"Son of man, how is the wood of a
vine better than that of a branch on
any of the trees in the forest? 3Is wood ever taken
from it to make anything useful? Do they make
pegs from it to hang things on? 4And after it is
thrown on the fire as fuel and the fire burns both
ends and chars the middle, is it then useful for
anything? 5If it was not useful for anything when
it was whole, how much less can it be made into
something useful when the fire has burned it and
it is charred?

6"Therefore this is what the Sovereign LORD
says: As I have given the wood of the vine among
the trees of the forest as fuel for the fire, so will I
treat the people living in Jerusalem. 7I will set my
face against them. Although they have come out
of the fire, the fire will yet consume them. And
when I set my face against them, you will know
that I am the LORD. 8I will make the land desolate
because they have been unfaithful, declares the
Sovereign LORD."

[z]14 Or *Danel*; the Hebrew spelling may suggest a person other than the prophet Daniel; also in verse 20.

7 / *Ezekiel 16*
The Bride of God

JESUS CHOSE PARABLES to express the deepest truths of God, and once even used a parable about the death warrant on himself (Mt 21:33–41) as an appeal to his executioners to have faith. In a similar way Ezekiel uses allegory to express the fundamental problem of Israel's relationship with God. He intends that his readers will eventually come to the conclusion that "he is talking about us!" Unlike a parable, which normally makes a single point, an allegory is intended to have symbolic meaning through every detail. By using a rags-to-riches story of a homeless waif who becomes a much-loved bride, Ezekiel makes an artistic and eloquent appeal to the source of true spirituality: gratitude. And he shows through this story how the heinous sin of ingratitude would be unforgivable but for the unconditional covenant love of the God of Israel, the God and Father of Jesus Christ.

Warming Up to God What feelings do you have when you hear of the sexual unfaithfulness of people you know and love?

Read Ezekiel 16.

16 The word of the LORD came to me:
2"Son of man, confront Jerusalem
with her detestable practices 3and
say, 'This is what the Sovereign LORD says to Jeru-
salem: Your ancestry and birth were in the land of
the Canaanites; your father was an Amorite and
your mother a Hittite. 4On the day you were born
your cord was not cut, nor were you washed with
water to make you clean, nor were you rubbed
with salt or wrapped in cloths. 5No one looked on
you with pity or had compassion enough to do
any of these things for you. Rather, you were
thrown out into the open field, for on the day you
were born you were despised.
6" 'Then I passed by and saw you kicking about
in your blood, and as you lay there in your blood
I said to you, "Live!"[a] 7I made you grow like a
plant of the field. You grew up and developed
and became the most beautiful of jewels.[b] Your
breasts were formed and your hair grew, you who
were naked and bare.
8" 'Later I passed by, and when I looked at you
and saw that you were old enough for love, I
spread the corner of my garment over you and
covered your nakedness. I gave you my solemn
oath and entered into a covenant with you, de-
clares the Sovereign LORD, and you became mine.
9" 'I bathed[c] you with water and washed the
blood from you and put ointments on you. 10I
clothed you with an embroidered dress and put
leather sandals on you. I dressed you in fine linen
and covered you with costly garments. 11I
adorned you with jewelry: I put bracelets on your
arms and a necklace around your neck, 12and I
put a ring on your nose, earrings on your ears and
a beautiful crown on your head. 13So you were
adorned with gold and silver; your clothes were
of fine linen and costly fabric and embroidered
cloth. Your food was fine flour, honey and olive
oil. You became very beautiful and rose to be a
queen. 14And your fame spread among the na-
tions on account of your beauty, because the
splendor I had given you made your beauty per-
fect, declares the Sovereign LORD.
15" 'But you trusted in your beauty and used
your fame to become a prostitute. You lavished
your favors on anyone who passed by and your
beauty became his.[d] 16You took some of your
garments to make gaudy high places, where you
carried on your prostitution. Such things should
not happen, nor should they ever occur. 17You
also took the fine jewelry I gave you, the jewelry
made of my gold and silver, and you made for
yourself male idols and engaged in prostitution
with them. 18And you took your embroidered
clothes to put on them, and you offered my oil
and incense before them. 19Also the food I pro-
vided for you—the fine flour, olive oil and honey
I gave you to eat—you offered as fragrant incense
before them. That is what happened, declares the
Sovereign LORD.
20" 'And you took your sons and daughters
whom you bore to me and sacrificed them as food
to the idols. Was your prostitution not enough?
21You slaughtered my children and sacrificed

[a]6 A few Hebrew manuscripts, Septuagint and Syriac; most Hebrew manuscripts *"Live!" And as you lay there in your blood I said to you, "Live!"* [b]7 Or *became mature* [c]9 Or *I had bathed* [d]15 Most Hebrew manuscripts; one Hebrew manuscript (see some Septuagint manuscripts) *by. Such a thing should not happen*

them[e] to the idols. 22In all your detestable practices and your prostitution you did not remember the days of your youth, when you were naked and bare, kicking about in your blood.

23" 'Woe! Woe to you, declares the Sovereign LORD. In addition to all your other wickedness, 24you built a mound for yourself and made a lofty shrine in every public square. 25At the head of every street you built your lofty shrines and degraded your beauty, offering your body with increasing promiscuity to anyone who passed by. 26You engaged in prostitution with the Egyptians, your lustful neighbors, and provoked me to anger with your increasing promiscuity. 27So I stretched out my hand against you and reduced your territory; I gave you over to the greed of your enemies, the daughters of the Philistines, who were shocked by your lewd conduct. 28You engaged in prostitution with the Assyrians too, because you were insatiable; and even after that, you still were not satisfied. 29Then you increased your promiscuity to include Babylonia,[f] a land of merchants, but even with this you were not satisfied.

30" 'How weak-willed you are, declares the Sovereign LORD, when you do all these things, acting like a brazen prostitute! 31When you built your mounds at the head of every street and made your lofty shrines in every public square, you were unlike a prostitute, because you scorned payment.

32" 'You adulterous wife! You prefer strangers to your own husband! 33Every prostitute receives a fee, but you give gifts to all your lovers, bribing them to come to you from everywhere for your illicit favors. 34So in your prostitution you are the opposite of others; no one runs after you for your favors. You are the very opposite, for you give payment and none is given to you.

35" 'Therefore, you prostitute, hear the word of the LORD! 36This is what the Sovereign LORD says: Because you poured out your wealth[g] and exposed your nakedness in your promiscuity with your lovers, and because of all your detestable idols, and because you gave them your children's blood, 37therefore I am going to gather all your lovers, with whom you found pleasure, those you loved as well as those you hated. I will gather them against you from all around and will strip you in front of them, and they will see all your nakedness. 38I will sentence you to the punishment of women who commit adultery and who shed blood; I will bring upon you the blood vengeance of my wrath and jealous anger. 39Then I will hand you over to your lovers, and they will tear down your mounds and destroy your lofty shrines. They will strip you of your clothes and take your fine jewelry and leave you naked and bare. 40They will bring a mob against you, who will stone you and hack you to pieces with their swords. 41They will burn down your houses and inflict punishment on you in the sight of many women. I will put a stop to your prostitution, and you will no longer pay your lovers. 42Then my wrath against you will subside and my jealous anger will turn away from you; I will be calm and no longer angry.

43" 'Because you did not remember the days of your youth but enraged me with all these things, I will surely bring down on your head what you have done, declares the Sovereign LORD. Did you not add lewdness to all your other detestable practices?

44" 'Everyone who quotes proverbs will quote this proverb about you: "Like mother, like daughter." 45You are a true daughter of your mother, who despised her husband and her children; and you are a true sister of your sisters, who despised their husbands and their children. Your mother was a Hittite and your father an Amorite. 46Your older sister was Samaria, who lived to the north of you with her daughters; and your younger sister, who lived to the south of you with her daughters, was Sodom. 47You not only walked in their ways and copied their detestable practices, but in all your ways you soon became more depraved than they. 48As surely as I live, declares the Sovereign LORD, your sister Sodom and her daughters never did what you and your daughters have done.

49" 'Now this was the sin of your sister Sodom: She and her daughters were arrogant, overfed and unconcerned; they did not help the poor and needy. 50They were haughty and did detestable things before me. Therefore I did away with them as you have seen. 51Samaria did not commit half the sins you did. You have done more detestable things than they, and have made your sisters seem righteous by all these things you have done. 52Bear your disgrace, for you have furnished some justification for your sisters. Because your sins were more vile than theirs, they appear more righteous than you. So then, be ashamed and bear

[e]21 Or *and made them pass through ⌞the fire⌟* [f]29 Or *Chaldea*
[g]36 Or *lust*

your disgrace, for you have made your sisters ap-
pear righteous.
53“ ‘However, I will restore the fortunes of
Sodom and her daughters and of Samaria and her
daughters, and your fortunes along with them,
54so that you may bear your disgrace and be
ashamed of all you have done in giving them
comfort. 55And your sisters, Sodom with her
daughters and Samaria with her daughters, will
return to what they were before; and you and
your daughters will return to what you were be-
fore. 56You would not even mention your sister
Sodom in the day of your pride, 57before your
wickedness was uncovered. Even so, you are now
scorned by the daughters of Edom[h] and all her
neighbors and the daughters of the Philistines—
all those around you who despise you. 58You will
bear the consequences of your lewdness and your
detestable practices, declares the LORD.

59“ ‘This is what the Sovereign LORD says: I will
deal with you as you deserve, because you have
despised my oath by breaking the covenant. 60Yet
I will remember the covenant I made with you in
the days of your youth, and I will establish an
everlasting covenant with you. 61Then you will
remember your ways and be ashamed when you
receive your sisters, both those who are older
than you and those who are younger. I will give
them to you as daughters, but not on the basis of
my covenant with you. 62So I will establish my
covenant with you, and you will know that I am
the LORD. 63Then, when I make atonement for you
for all you have done, you will remember and be
ashamed and never again open your mouth be-
cause of your humiliation, declares the Sovereign
LORD.’ ”

[h]57 Many Hebrew manuscripts and Syriac; most Hebrew manuscripts, Septuagint and Vulgate *Aram*

Discovering the Word 1. The allegory is best studied in three parts. First, look at verses 1–43. The term *Canaanite* (v. 3) was a byword for “moral degradation,” thus the proverb in verse 44. While Israel was born of pure Aramean stock, the nation had assimilated the culture of its surrounding neighbors. What historical events of the nation’s history are recounted in this allegory? 2. In the second part, verses 44–58, Ezekiel links a new allegory of two sisters to the old one. If the mother is seen as Jerusalem and the daughters its suburbs, what further point is Ezekiel now making? 3. In the last section, verses 59–63, the allegory takes a surprising turn, signaled by the word *yet* (v. 60). What does covenant faithfulness require of God and his reluctant bride? 5. While Hosea had been the first prophet to explain the relationship between the Lord and his people as a marriage covenant, Ezekiel develops this metaphor (v. 8) in his allegory. In what way does the covenant metaphor reveal that the sin of Israel is even more inexcusable than merely law-breaking? 6. It appears that this triumphant covenant love presupposed the fall of Jerusalem, which for Ezekiel was inevitable. What hope should this allegory inspire as the exiles wondered about their own future?

Applying the Word 1. What does the covenant allegory inspire in you as you consider the future of Christianity? 2. In what way can this chapter help you deal with a person who is truly converted but has fallen back into sin? 3. What light does this allegory shed on the need for continuous gratitude?

Responding in Prayer Take a few minutes and walk through your life in the Lord’s presence. Reflect on God’s faithfulness and thank God for his covenant love.

Ezekiel 17

17 The word of the LORD came to me:
2“Son of man, set forth an allegory
and tell the house of Israel a para-
ble. 3Say to them, ‘This is what the Sovereign LORD
says: A great eagle with powerful wings, long
feathers and full plumage of varied colors came to
Lebanon. Taking hold of the top of a cedar, 4he
broke off its topmost shoot and carried it away to
a land of merchants, where he planted it in a city
of traders.

5“ ‘He took some of the seed of your land and
put it in fertile soil. He planted it like a willow by
abundant water, 6and it sprouted and became a
low, spreading vine. Its branches turned toward
him, but its roots remained under it. So it became
a vine and produced branches and put out leafy
boughs.
7“ ‘But there was another great eagle with pow-
erful wings and full plumage. The vine now sent
out its roots toward him from the plot where it

was planted and stretched out its branches to him
for water. 8It had been planted in good soil by
abundant water so that it would produce
branches, bear fruit and become a splendid vine.'
9"Say to them, 'This is what the Sovereign LORD
says: Will it thrive? Will it not be uprooted and
stripped of its fruit so that it withers? All its new
growth will wither. It will not take a strong arm
or many people to pull it up by the roots. 10Even
if it is transplanted, will it thrive? Will it not
wither completely when the east wind strikes it—
wither away in the plot where it grew?' "
11Then the word of the LORD came to me: 12"Say
to this rebellious house, 'Do you not know what
these things mean?' Say to them: 'The king of
Babylon went to Jerusalem and carried off her
king and her nobles, bringing them back with
him to Babylon. 13Then he took a member of the
royal family and made a treaty with him, putting
him under oath. He also carried away the leading
men of the land, 14so that the kingdom would be
brought low, unable to rise again, surviving only
by keeping his treaty. 15But the king rebelled
against him by sending his envoys to Egypt to get
horses and a large army. Will he succeed? Will he
who does such things escape? Will he break the
treaty and yet escape?
16" 'As surely as I live, declares the Sovereign
LORD, he shall die in Babylon, in the land of the
king who put him on the throne, whose oath he
despised and whose treaty he broke. 17Pharaoh
with his mighty army and great horde will be of
no help to him in war, when ramps are built and
siege works erected to destroy many lives. 18He
despised the oath by breaking the covenant. Be-
cause he had given his hand in pledge and yet did
all these things, he shall not escape.
19" 'Therefore this is what the Sovereign LORD
says: As surely as I live, I will bring down on his
head my oath that he despised and my covenant
that he broke. 20I will spread my net for him, and
he will be caught in my snare. I will bring him to
Babylon and execute judgment upon him there
because he was unfaithful to me. 21All his fleeing
troops will fall by the sword, and the survivors
will be scattered to the winds. Then you will
know that I the LORD have spoken.
22" 'This is what the Sovereign LORD says: I my-
self will take a shoot from the very top of a cedar
and plant it; I will break off a tender sprig from its
topmost shoots and plant it on a high and lofty
mountain. 23On the mountain heights of Israel I
will plant it; it will produce branches and bear
fruit and become a splendid cedar. Birds of every
kind will nest in it; they will find shelter in the
shade of its branches. 24All the trees of the field
will know that I the LORD bring down the tall tree
and make the low tree grow tall. I dry up the
green tree and make the dry tree flourish.
" 'I the LORD have spoken, and I will do it.' "

8 / *Ezekiel 18*
Assuming Personal Responsibility

"THE DEVIL MADE me do it" is one extreme statement of passing responsibility to someone else. Sometimes we try to excuse ourselves by the company we keep, as Adam did long ago (Ge 3:12). Up until now the prophet has been explaining how national sin will lead to national punishment. But what about God's dealings with individuals? Do good people suffer with the bad for sins they never condoned? In this chapter Ezekiel focuses on individual responsibility.

Warming Up to God Recall an incident when you got blamed for something done by others. What was especially difficult to accept?

Read Ezekiel 18.

18

The word of the LORD came to me: 2“What do you people mean by quoting this proverb about the land of Israel:

“ ‘The fathers eat sour grapes,
and the children’s teeth are set on edge’?

3“As surely as I live, declares the Sovereign LORD, you will no longer quote this proverb in Israel. 4For every living soul belongs to me, the father as well as the son—both alike belong to me. The soul who sins is the one who will die.

5“Suppose there is a righteous man
who does what is just and right.
6He does not eat at the mountain shrines
or look to the idols of the house of Israel.
He does not defile his neighbor’s wife
or lie with a woman during her period.
7He does not oppress anyone,
but returns what he took in pledge for a loan.
He does not commit robbery
but gives his food to the hungry
and provides clothing for the naked.
8He does not lend at usury
or take excessive interest.[i]
He withholds his hand from doing wrong
and judges fairly between man and man.
9He follows my decrees
and faithfully keeps my laws.
That man is righteous;
he will surely live,
declares the Sovereign LORD.

10“Suppose he has a violent son, who sheds blood or does any of these other things[j] 11(though the father has done none of them):

“He eats at the mountain shrines.
He defiles his neighbor’s wife.
12He oppresses the poor and needy.
He commits robbery.
He does not return what he took in pledge.
He looks to the idols.
He does detestable things.
13He lends at usury and takes excessive interest.

Will such a man live? He will not! Because he has done all these detestable things, he will surely be put to death and his blood will be on his own head.

14“But suppose this son has a son who sees all the sins his father commits, and though he sees them, he does not do such things:

15“He does not eat at the mountain shrines
or look to the idols of the house of Israel.
He does not defile his neighbor’s wife.
16He does not oppress anyone
or require a pledge for a loan.
He does not commit robbery
but gives his food to the hungry
and provides clothing for the naked.
17He withholds his hand from sin[k]
and takes no usury or excessive interest.
He keeps my laws and follows my decrees.

He will not die for his father’s sin; he will surely live. 18But his father will die for his own sin, because he practiced extortion, robbed his brother and did what was wrong among his people.

19“Yet you ask, ‘Why does the son not share the guilt of his father?’ Since the son has done what is just and right and has been careful to keep all my decrees, he will surely live. 20The soul who sins is the one who will die. The son will not share the guilt of the father, nor will the father share the guilt of the son. The righteousness of the righteous man will be credited to him, and the wickedness of the wicked will be charged against him.

21“But if a wicked man turns away from all the sins he has committed and keeps all my decrees and does what is just and right, he will surely live; he will not die. 22None of the offenses he has committed will be remembered against him. Because of the righteous things he has done, he will live. 23Do I take any pleasure in the death of the wicked? declares the Sovereign LORD. Rather, am I not pleased when they turn from their ways and live?

24“But if a righteous man turns from his righteousness and commits sin and does the same detestable things the wicked man does, will he live? None of the righteous things he has done will be remembered. Because of the unfaithfulness he is guilty of and because of the sins he has committed, he will die.

25“Yet you say, ‘The way of the Lord is not just.’ Hear, O house of Israel: Is my way unjust? Is it not your ways that are unjust? 26If a righteous man turns from his righteousness and commits sin, he will die for it; because of the sin he has

[i] 8 Or *take interest*; similarly in verses 13 and 17 [j] 10 Or *things to a brother* [k] 17 Septuagint (see also verse 8); Hebrew *from the poor*

committed he will die. 27But if a wicked man
turns away from the wickedness he has commit-
ted and does what is just and right, he will save
his life. 28Because he considers all the offenses he
has committed and turns away from them, he will
surely live; he will not die. 29Yet the house of
Israel says, 'The way of the Lord is not just.' Are
my ways unjust, O house of Israel? Is it not your
ways that are unjust?

30"Therefore, O house of Israel, I will judge
you, each one according to his ways, declares the
Sovereign LORD. Repent! Turn away from all your
offenses; then sin will not be your downfall. 31Rid
yourselves of all the offenses you have commit-
ted, and get a new heart and a new spirit. Why
will you die, O house of Israel? 32For I take no
pleasure in the death of anyone, declares the Sov-
ereign LORD. Repent and live!

Discovering the Word 1. In this chapter Ezekiel compares the fates of unrighteous sons with righteous fathers (vv. 5–13), and righteous sons with unrighteous fathers (vv. 14–18). What are the outward marks of righteousness and unrighteousness? 2. How does Ezekiel answer the question "Why does the son not share in the guilt of his father" (vv. 19–20)? 3. In this chapter Ezekiel gives several fundamental principles about the way God relates to people (vv. 4, 20, 22, 24, 26, 30). Put these in your own words. 4. What hope is there for the righteous and the unrighteous? 5. What is revealed about the heart of God in his treatment of individuals (v. 23)? 6. What makes repentance a desirable alternative (vv. 30–32)?

Applying the Word 1. What answer do you now have for the common complaint "God is not fair"? 2. In what way does this chapter give you confidence to face God daily and finally on the day of judgment?

Responding in Prayer Pray that you may have God's perspective when you speak to others about the judgment of God, namely that God prefers people to turn and have life, not wanting anyone to perish (2Pe 3:9).

Ezekiel 19:1—24:14

19 "Take up a lament concerning the princes of Israel 2and say:

" 'What a lioness was your mother
among the lions!
She lay down among the young lions
and reared her cubs.
3She brought up one of her cubs,
and he became a strong lion.
He learned to tear the prey
and he devoured men.
4The nations heard about him,
and he was trapped in their pit.
They led him with hooks
to the land of Egypt.

5" 'When she saw her hope unfulfilled,
her expectation gone,
she took another of her cubs
and made him a strong lion.
6He prowled among the lions,
for he was now a strong lion.
He learned to tear the prey
and he devoured men.
7He broke down[l] their strongholds
and devastated their towns.
The land and all who were in it
were terrified by his roaring.
8Then the nations came against him,
those from regions round about.
They spread their net for him,
and he was trapped in their pit.
9With hooks they pulled him into a cage
and brought him to the king of Babylon.
They put him in prison,
so his roar was heard no longer
on the mountains of Israel.

10" 'Your mother was like a vine in your
vineyard[m]
planted by the water;
it was fruitful and full of branches
because of abundant water.
11Its branches were strong,
fit for a ruler's scepter.
It towered high
above the thick foliage,
conspicuous for its height

[l]7 Targum (see Septuagint); Hebrew *He knew* [m]10 Two Hebrew manuscripts; most Hebrew manuscripts *your blood*

and for its many branches.
12But it was uprooted in fury
and thrown to the ground.
The east wind made it shrivel,
it was stripped of its fruit;
its strong branches withered
and fire consumed them.
13Now it is planted in the desert,
in a dry and thirsty land.
14Fire spread from one of its main[n] branches
and consumed its fruit.
No strong branch is left on it
fit for a ruler's scepter.'

This is a lament and is to be used as a lament."

20 In the seventh year, in the fifth
month on the tenth day, some of
the elders of Israel came to inquire
of the LORD, and they sat down in front of me.
2Then the word of the LORD came to me: 3"Son
of man, speak to the elders of Israel and say to
them, 'This is what the Sovereign LORD says: Have
you come to inquire of me? As surely as I live, I
will not let you inquire of me, declares the Sover-
eign LORD.'
4"Will you judge them? Will you judge them,
son of man? Then confront them with the detest-
able practices of their fathers 5and say to them:
'This is what the Sovereign LORD says: On the day
I chose Israel, I swore with uplifted hand to the
descendants of the house of Jacob and revealed
myself to them in Egypt. With uplifted hand I
said to them, "I am the LORD your God." 6On that
day I swore to them that I would bring them out
of Egypt into a land I had searched out for them,
a land flowing with milk and honey, the most
beautiful of all lands. 7And I said to them, "Each
of you, get rid of the vile images you have set
your eyes on, and do not defile yourselves with
the idols of Egypt. I am the LORD your God."
8" 'But they rebelled against me and would not
listen to me; they did not get rid of the vile im-
ages they had set their eyes on, nor did they for-
sake the idols of Egypt. So I said I would pour out
my wrath on them and spend my anger against
them in Egypt. 9But for the sake of my name I did
what would keep it from being profaned in the
eyes of the nations they lived among and in
whose sight I had revealed myself to the Israelites
by bringing them out of Egypt. 10Therefore I led
them out of Egypt and brought them into the
desert. 11I gave them my decrees and made
known to them my laws, for the man who obeys
them will live by them. 12Also I gave them my
Sabbaths as a sign between us, so they would
know that I the LORD made them holy.
13" 'Yet the people of Israel rebelled against me
in the desert. They did not follow my decrees but
rejected my laws—although the man who obeys
them will live by them—and they utterly dese-
crated my Sabbaths. So I said I would pour out
my wrath on them and destroy them in the
desert. 14But for the sake of my name I did what
would keep it from being profaned in the eyes of
the nations in whose sight I had brought them
out. 15Also with uplifted hand I swore to them in
the desert that I would not bring them into the
land I had given them—a land flowing with milk
and honey, most beautiful of all lands— 16be-
cause they rejected my laws and did not follow
my decrees and desecrated my Sabbaths. For their
hearts were devoted to their idols. 17Yet I looked
on them with pity and did not destroy them or
put an end to them in the desert. 18I said to their
children in the desert, "Do not follow the statutes
of your fathers or keep their laws or defile your-
selves with their idols. 19I am the LORD your God;
follow my decrees and be careful to keep my laws.
20Keep my Sabbaths holy, that they may be a sign
between us. Then you will know that I am the
LORD your God."
21" 'But the children rebelled against me: They
did not follow my decrees, they were not careful
to keep my laws—although the man who obeys
them will live by them—and they desecrated my
Sabbaths. So I said I would pour out my wrath on
them and spend my anger against them in the
desert. 22But I withheld my hand, and for the sake
of my name I did what would keep it from being
profaned in the eyes of the nations in whose sight
I had brought them out. 23Also with uplifted hand
I swore to them in the desert that I would dis-
perse them among the nations and scatter them
through the countries, 24because they had not
obeyed my laws but had rejected my decrees and
desecrated my Sabbaths, and their eyes ⌊lusted⌋
after their fathers' idols. 25I also gave them over to
statutes that were not good and laws they could
not live by; 26I let them become defiled through
their gifts—the sacrifice of every firstborn[o]—
that I might fill them with horror so they would
know that I am the LORD.'

[n] 14 *Or from under its*
[o] 26 *Or —making every firstborn pass through ⌊the fire⌋*

27“Therefore, son of man, speak to the people of Israel and say to them, ‘This is what the Sovereign LORD says: In this also your fathers blasphemed me by forsaking me: 28When I brought them into the land I had sworn to give them and they saw any high hill or any leafy tree, there they offered their sacrifices, made offerings that provoked me to anger, presented their fragrant incense and poured out their drink offerings. 29Then I said to them: What is this high place you go to?’ ” (It is called Bamah[p] to this day.)

30“Therefore say to the house of Israel: ‘This is what the Sovereign LORD says: Will you defile yourselves the way your fathers did and lust after their vile images? 31When you offer your gifts—the sacrifice of your sons in[q] the fire—you continue to defile yourselves with all your idols to this day. Am I to let you inquire of me, O house of Israel? As surely as I live, declares the Sovereign LORD, I will not let you inquire of me.

32“ ‘You say, “We want to be like the nations, like the peoples of the world, who serve wood and stone.” But what you have in mind will never happen. 33As surely as I live, declares the Sovereign LORD, I will rule over you with a mighty hand and an outstretched arm and with outpoured wrath. 34I will bring you from the nations and gather you from the countries where you have been scattered—with a mighty hand and an outstretched arm and with outpoured wrath. 35I will bring you into the desert of the nations and there, face to face, I will execute judgment upon you. 36As I judged your fathers in the desert of the land of Egypt, so I will judge you, declares the Sovereign LORD. 37I will take note of you as you pass under my rod, and I will bring you into the bond of the covenant. 38I will purge you of those who revolt and rebel against me. Although I will bring them out of the land where they are living, yet they will not enter the land of Israel. Then you will know that I am the LORD.

39“ ‘As for you, O house of Israel, this is what the Sovereign LORD says: Go and serve your idols, every one of you! But afterward you will surely listen to me and no longer profane my holy name with your gifts and idols. 40For on my holy mountain, the high mountain of Israel, declares the Sovereign LORD, there in the land the entire house of Israel will serve me, and there I will accept them. There I will require your offerings and your choice gifts,[r] along with all your holy sacrifices. 41I will accept you as fragrant incense when I bring you out from the nations and gather you from the countries where you have been scattered, and I will show myself holy among you in the sight of the nations. 42Then you will know that I am the LORD, when I bring you into the land of Israel, the land I had sworn with uplifted hand to give to your fathers. 43There you will remember your conduct and all the actions by which you have defiled yourselves, and you will loathe yourselves for all the evil you have done. 44You will know that I am the LORD, when I deal with you for my name’s sake and not according to your evil ways and your corrupt practices, O house of Israel, declares the Sovereign LORD.’ ”

45The word of the LORD came to me: 46“Son of man, set your face toward the south; preach against the south and prophesy against the forest of the southland. 47Say to the southern forest: ‘Hear the word of the LORD. This is what the Sovereign LORD says: I am about to set fire to you, and it will consume all your trees, both green and dry. The blazing flame will not be quenched, and every face from south to north will be scorched by it. 48Everyone will see that I the LORD have kindled it; it will not be quenched.’ ”

49Then I said, “Ah, Sovereign LORD! They are saying of me, ‘Isn’t he just telling parables?’ ”

21

The word of the LORD came to me: 2“Son of man, set your face against Jerusalem and preach against the sanctuary. Prophesy against the land of Israel 3and say to her: ‘This is what the LORD says: I am against you. I will draw my sword from its scabbard and cut off from you both the righteous and the wicked. 4Because I am going to cut off the righteous and the wicked, my sword will be unsheathed against everyone from south to north. 5Then all people will know that I the LORD have drawn my sword from its scabbard; it will not return again.’

6“Therefore groan, son of man! Groan before them with broken heart and bitter grief. 7And when they ask you, ‘Why are you groaning?’ you shall say, ‘Because of the news that is coming. Every heart will melt and every hand go limp; every spirit will become faint and every knee become as weak as water.’ It is coming! It will surely take place, declares the Sovereign LORD.”

8The word of the LORD came to me: 9“Son of

[p]29 *Bamah means high place.* [q]31 Or *—making your sons pass through* [r]40 Or *and the gifts of your firstfruits*

man, prophesy and say, 'This is what the Lord
says:

" 'A sword, a sword,
sharpened and polished—
[10]sharpened for the slaughter,
polished to flash like lightning!

" 'Shall we rejoice in the scepter of my son ⌞Ju-
dah⌟? The sword despises every such stick.

[11]" 'The sword is appointed to be polished,
to be grasped with the hand;
it is sharpened and polished,
made ready for the hand of the slayer.
[12]Cry out and wail, son of man,
for it is against my people;
it is against all the princes of Israel.
They are thrown to the sword
along with my people.
Therefore beat your breast.

[13]" 'Testing will surely come. And what if the
scepter ⌞of Judah⌟, which the sword despises,
does not continue? declares the Sovereign LORD.'

[14]"So then, son of man, prophesy
and strike your hands together.
Let the sword strike twice,
even three times.
It is a sword for slaughter—
a sword for great slaughter,
closing in on them from every side.
[15]So that hearts may melt
and the fallen be many,
I have stationed the sword for slaughter[s]
at all their gates.
Oh! It is made to flash like lightning,
it is grasped for slaughter.
[16]O sword, slash to the right,
then to the left,
wherever your blade is turned.
[17]I too will strike my hands together,
and my wrath will subside.
I the LORD have spoken."

[18]The word of the LORD came to me: [19]"Son of
man, mark out two roads for the sword of the
king of Babylon to take, both starting from the
same country. Make a signpost where the road
branches off to the city. [20]Mark out one road for
the sword to come against Rabbah of the Ammon-
ites and another against Judah and fortified Jeru-
salem. [21]For the king of Babylon will stop at the
fork in the road, at the junction of the two roads,
to seek an omen: He will cast lots with arrows, he
will consult his idols, he will examine the liver.
[22]Into his right hand will come the lot for Jerusa-
lem, where he is to set up battering rams, to give
the command to slaughter, to sound the battle
cry, to set battering rams against the gates, to
build a ramp and to erect siege works. [23]It will
seem like a false omen to those who have sworn
allegiance to him, but he will remind them of
their guilt and take them captive.

[24]"Therefore this is what the Sovereign LORD
says: 'Because you people have brought to mind
your guilt by your open rebellion, revealing your
sins in all that you do—because you have done
this, you will be taken captive.

[25]" 'O profane and wicked prince of Israel,
whose day has come, whose time of punishment
has reached its climax, [26]this is what the Sover-
eign LORD says: Take off the turban, remove the
crown. It will not be as it was: The lowly will be
exalted and the exalted will be brought low. [27]A
ruin! A ruin! I will make it a ruin! It will not be
restored until he comes to whom it rightfully be-
longs; to him I will give it.'

[28]"And you, son of man, prophesy and say,
'This is what the Sovereign LORD says about the
Ammonites and their insults:

" 'A sword, a sword,
drawn for the slaughter,
polished to consume
and to flash like lightning!
[29]Despite false visions concerning you
and lying divinations about you,
it will be laid on the necks
of the wicked who are to be slain,
whose day has come,
whose time of punishment has reached its
climax.
[30]Return the sword to its scabbard.
In the place where you were created,
in the land of your ancestry,
I will judge you.
[31]I will pour out my wrath upon you
and breathe out my fiery anger against you;
I will hand you over to brutal men,
men skilled in destruction.
[32]You will be fuel for the fire,
your blood will be shed in your land,
you will be remembered no more;
for I the LORD have spoken.' "

[s]*15* Septuagint; the meaning of the Hebrew for this word is uncertain.

22

The word of the LORD came to me: 2“Son of man, will you judge her? Will you judge this city of bloodshed? Then confront her with all her detestable practices 3and say: ‘This is what the Sovereign LORD says: O city that brings on herself doom by shedding blood in her midst and defiles herself by making idols, 4you have become guilty because of the blood you have shed and have become defiled by the idols you have made. You have brought your days to a close, and the end of your years has come. Therefore I will make you an object of scorn to the nations and a laughingstock to all the countries. 5Those who are near and those who are far away will mock you, O infamous city, full of turmoil.

6“ ‘See how each of the princes of Israel who are in you uses his power to shed blood. 7In you they have treated father and mother with contempt; in you they have oppressed the alien and mistreated the fatherless and the widow. 8You have despised my holy things and desecrated my Sabbaths. 9In you are slanderous men bent on shedding blood; in you are those who eat at the mountain shrines and commit lewd acts. 10In you are those who dishonor their fathers’ bed; in you are those who violate women during their period, when they are ceremonially unclean. 11In you one man commits a detestable offense with his neighbor’s wife, another shamefully defiles his daughter-in-law, and another violates his sister, his own father’s daughter. 12In you men accept bribes to shed blood; you take usury and excessive interest[t] and make unjust gain from your neighbors by extortion. And you have forgotten me, declares the Sovereign LORD.

13“ ‘I will surely strike my hands together at the unjust gain you have made and at the blood you have shed in your midst. 14Will your courage endure or your hands be strong in the day I deal with you? I the LORD have spoken, and I will do it. 15I will disperse you among the nations and scatter you through the countries; and I will put an end to your uncleanness. 16When you have been defiled[u] in the eyes of the nations, you will know that I am the LORD.’ ”

17Then the word of the LORD came to me: 18“Son of man, the house of Israel has become dross to me; all of them are the copper, tin, iron and lead left inside a furnace. They are but the dross of silver. 19Therefore this is what the Sovereign LORD says: ‘Because you have all become dross, I will gather you into Jerusalem. 20As men gather silver, copper, iron, lead and tin into a furnace to melt it with a fiery blast, so will I gather you in my anger and my wrath and put you inside the city and melt you. 21I will gather you and I will blow on you with my fiery wrath, and you will be melted inside her. 22As silver is melted in a furnace, so you will be melted inside her, and you will know that I the LORD have poured out my wrath upon you.’ ”

23Again the word of the LORD came to me: 24“Son of man, say to the land, ‘You are a land that has had no rain or showers[v] in the day of wrath.’ 25There is a conspiracy of her princes[w] within her like a roaring lion tearing its prey; they devour people, take treasures and precious things and make many widows within her. 26Her priests do violence to my law and profane my holy things; they do not distinguish between the holy and the common; they teach that there is no difference between the unclean and the clean; and they shut their eyes to the keeping of my Sabbaths, so that I am profaned among them. 27Her officials within her are like wolves tearing their prey; they shed blood and kill people to make unjust gain. 28Her prophets whitewash these deeds for them by false visions and lying divinations. They say, ‘This is what the Sovereign LORD says’—when the LORD has not spoken. 29The people of the land practice extortion and commit robbery; they oppress the poor and needy and mistreat the alien, denying them justice.

30“I looked for a man among them who would build up the wall and stand before me in the gap on behalf of the land so I would not have to destroy it, but I found none. 31So I will pour out my wrath on them and consume them with my fiery anger, bringing down on their own heads all they have done, declares the Sovereign LORD.”

23

The word of the LORD came to me: 2“Son of man, there were two women, daughters of the same mother. 3They became prostitutes in Egypt, engaging in prostitution from their youth. In that land their breasts were fondled and their virgin bosoms caressed. 4The older was named Oholah, and her sister was Oholibah. They were mine and gave birth to sons and daughters. Oholah is Samaria, and Oholibah is Jerusalem.

[t]12 Or *usury and interest* [u]16 Or *When I have allotted you your inheritance* [v]24 Septuagint; Hebrew *has not been cleansed or rained on* [w]25 Septuagint; Hebrew *prophets*

5"Oholah engaged in prostitution while she was still mine; and she lusted after her lovers, the Assyrians—warriors 6clothed in blue, governors and commanders, all of them handsome young men, and mounted horsemen. 7She gave herself as a prostitute to all the elite of the Assyrians and defiled herself with all the idols of everyone she lusted after. 8She did not give up the prostitution she began in Egypt, when during her youth men slept with her, caressed her virgin bosom and poured out their lust upon her.

9"Therefore I handed her over to her lovers, the Assyrians, for whom she lusted. 10They stripped her naked, took away her sons and daughters and killed her with the sword. She became a byword among women, and punishment was inflicted on her.

11"Her sister Oholibah saw this, yet in her lust and prostitution she was more depraved than her sister. 12She too lusted after the Assyrians—governors and commanders, warriors in full dress, mounted horsemen, all handsome young men. 13I saw that she too defiled herself; both of them went the same way.

14"But she carried her prostitution still further. She saw men portrayed on a wall, figures of Chaldeans[x] portrayed in red, 15with belts around their waists and flowing turbans on their heads; all of them looked like Babylonian chariot officers, natives of Chaldea.[y] 16As soon as she saw them, she lusted after them and sent messengers to them in Chaldea. 17Then the Babylonians came to her, to the bed of love, and in their lust they defiled her. After she had been defiled by them, she turned away from them in disgust. 18When she carried on her prostitution openly and exposed her nakedness, I turned away from her in disgust, just as I had turned away from her sister. 19Yet she became more and more promiscuous as she recalled the days of her youth, when she was a prostitute in Egypt. 20There she lusted after her lovers, whose genitals were like those of donkeys and whose emission was like that of horses. 21So you longed for the lewdness of your youth, when in Egypt your bosom was caressed and your young breasts fondled.[z]

22"Therefore, Oholibah, this is what the Sovereign LORD says: I will stir up your lovers against you, those you turned away from in disgust, and I will bring them against you from every side—23the Babylonians and all the Chaldeans, the men of Pekod and Shoa and Koa, and all the Assyrians with them, handsome young men, all of them governors and commanders, chariot officers and men of high rank, all mounted on horses. 24They will come against you with weapons,[a] chariots and wagons and with a throng of people; they will take up positions against you on every side with large and small shields and with helmets. I will turn you over to them for punishment, and they will punish you according to their standards. 25I will direct my jealous anger against you, and they will deal with you in fury. They will cut off your noses and your ears, and those of you who are left will fall by the sword. They will take away your sons and daughters, and those of you who are left will be consumed by fire. 26They will also strip you of your clothes and take your fine jewelry. 27So I will put a stop to the lewdness and prostitution you began in Egypt. You will not look on these things with longing or remember Egypt anymore.

28"For this is what the Sovereign LORD says: I am about to hand you over to those you hate, to those you turned away from in disgust. 29They will deal with you in hatred and take away everything you have worked for. They will leave you naked and bare, and the shame of your prostitution will be exposed. Your lewdness and promiscuity 30have brought this upon you, because you lusted after the nations and defiled yourself with their idols. 31You have gone the way of your sister; so I will put her cup into your hand.

32"This is what the Sovereign LORD says:

"You will drink your sister's cup,
a cup large and deep;
it will bring scorn and derision,
for it holds so much.
33You will be filled with drunkenness and sorrow,
the cup of ruin and desolation,
the cup of your sister Samaria.
34You will drink it and drain it dry;
you will dash it to pieces
and tear your breasts.

I have spoken, declares the Sovereign LORD.

35"Therefore this is what the Sovereign LORD says: Since you have forgotten me and thrust me behind your back, you must bear the consequences of your lewdness and prostitution."

x14 Or *Babylonians* y15 Or *Babylonia*; also in verse 16
z21 Syriac (see also verse 3); Hebrew *caressed because of your young breasts* a24 The meaning of the Hebrew for this word is uncertain.

36The LORD said to me: "Son of man, will you judge Oholah and Oholibah? Then confront them with their detestable practices, 37for they have committed adultery and blood is on their hands. They committed adultery with their idols; they even sacrificed their children, whom they bore to me,[b] as food for them. 38They have also done this to me: At that same time they defiled my sanctuary and desecrated my Sabbaths. 39On the very day they sacrificed their children to their idols, they entered my sanctuary and desecrated it. That is what they did in my house.

40"They even sent messengers for men who came from far away, and when they arrived you bathed yourself for them, painted your eyes and put on your jewelry. 41You sat on an elegant couch, with a table spread before it on which you had placed the incense and oil that belonged to me.

42"The noise of a carefree crowd was around her; Sabeans[c] were brought from the desert along with men from the rabble, and they put bracelets on the arms of the woman and her sister and beautiful crowns on their heads. 43Then I said about the one worn out by adultery, 'Now let them use her as a prostitute, for that is all she is.' 44And they slept with her. As men sleep with a prostitute, so they slept with those lewd women, Oholah and Oholibah. 45But righteous men will sentence them to the punishment of women who commit adultery and shed blood, because they are adulterous and blood is on their hands.

46"This is what the Sovereign LORD says: Bring a mob against them and give them over to terror and plunder. 47The mob will stone them and cut them down with their swords; they will kill their sons and daughters and burn down their houses.

48"So I will put an end to lewdness in the land, that all women may take warning and not imitate you. 49You will suffer the penalty for your lewdness and bear the consequences of your sins of idolatry. Then you will know that I am the Sovereign LORD."

24

In the ninth year, in the tenth month on the tenth day, the word of the LORD came to me: 2"Son of man, record this date, this very date, because the king of Babylon has laid siege to Jerusalem this very day. 3Tell this rebellious house a parable and say to them: 'This is what the Sovereign LORD says:

" 'Put on the cooking pot; put it on
and pour water into it.
4Put into it the pieces of meat,
all the choice pieces—the leg and the shoulder.
Fill it with the best of these bones;
5take the pick of the flock.
Pile wood beneath it for the bones;
bring it to a boil
and cook the bones in it.

6" 'For this is what the Sovereign LORD says:

" 'Woe to the city of bloodshed,
to the pot now encrusted,
whose deposit will not go away!
Empty it piece by piece
without casting lots for them.

7" 'For the blood she shed is in her midst:
She poured it on the bare rock;
she did not pour it on the ground,
where the dust would cover it.
8To stir up wrath and take revenge
I put her blood on the bare rock,
so that it would not be covered.

9" 'Therefore this is what the Sovereign LORD says:

" 'Woe to the city of bloodshed!
I, too, will pile the wood high.
10So heap on the wood
and kindle the fire.
Cook the meat well,
mixing in the spices;
and let the bones be charred.
11Then set the empty pot on the coals
till it becomes hot and its copper glows
so its impurities may be melted
and its deposit burned away.
12It has frustrated all efforts;
its heavy deposit has not been removed,
not even by fire.

13" 'Now your impurity is lewdness. Because I tried to cleanse you but you would not be cleansed from your impurity, you will not be clean again until my wrath against you has subsided.

14" 'I the LORD have spoken. The time has come

[b]37 Or *even made the children they bore to me pass through* ⌞*the fire*⌟
[c]42 Or *drunkards*

for me to act. I will not hold back; I will not have pity, nor will I relent. You will be judged according to your conduct and your actions, declares the Sovereign LORD.' "

9 / *Ezekiel 24:15–27*
Losing One's Beloved

"UNTIL DEATH DO us part" are some of the hardest words to utter in the marriage vows. The words stick in our throats not only because of the enduring length of the covenant implied, but also because they remind us that death will rob us of our beloved. In this chapter we see Ezekiel in a new light, not bringing God's searing (but hopeful) judgment on the people, but mourning the loss of his own wife. Ezekiel's marriage was to be a parable for the people. They too must lose their beloved temple in Jerusalem. The chapter opens with the date of the inauguration of the final siege of Jerusalem (January 15, 588 B.C.). It ends with the people being instructed how to mourn the loss of the epicenter of their faith. As always, the purpose is that "they will know that I am the LORD" (v. 27).

Warming Up to God Reflect on the vow "until death us do part." What inner pain or loss does it bring to mind?

Read Ezekiel 24:15–27.

[15]The word of the LORD came to me: [16]"Son of
man, with one blow I am about to take away from
you the delight of your eyes. Yet do not lament or
weep or shed any tears. [17]Groan quietly; do not
mourn for the dead. Keep your turban fastened and your sandals on your feet; do not cover the lower part of your face or eat the customary food ⌞of mourners⌟."
[18]So I spoke to the people in the morning, and in the evening my wife died. The next morning I did as I had been commanded.
[19]Then the people asked me, "Won't you tell us what these things have to do with us?"
[20]So I said to them, "The word of the LORD
came to me: [21]Say to the house of Israel, 'This is what the Sovereign LORD says: I am about to desecrate my sanctuary—the stronghold in which you take pride, the delight of your eyes, the object of your affection. The sons and daughters you left
behind will fall by the sword. [22]And you will do as I have done. You will not cover the lower part of your face or eat the customary food ⌞of mourners⌟.
[23]You will keep your turbans on your heads and your sandals on your feet. You will not mourn or weep but will waste away because of[d] your sins and groan among yourselves.
[24]Ezekiel will be a sign to you; you will do just as he has done. When this happens, you will know that I am the Sovereign LORD.'
[25]"And you, son of man, on the day I take away their stronghold, their joy and glory, the delight of their eyes, their heart's desire, and their sons and daughters as well— [26]on that day a fugitive
will come to tell you the news. [27]At that time your
mouth will be opened; you will speak with him and will no longer be silent. So you will be a sign to them, and they will know that I am the LORD."

[d]23 Or *away in*

Discovering the Word 1. What words does the Lord use to describe Ezekiel's affection for his wife (v. 16) and the people's affection for the temple sanctuary in Jerusalem (vv. 21, 25)? 2. What actions is Ezekiel told to forego in verses 16–17? 3. These were the normal practices of public mourning. What do Ezekiel's words to the people tell you about why God asked him to do this (vv. 20–27)? 4. This would have been very hard for Ezekiel. How did his painful experience become a ministry to the people? 5. The refusal to weep was for both Ezekiel and the Israelites a reflection of a tragedy so deep that any expression of grief would be too inadequate. What does God want to accomplish in all this?

Applying the Word 1. Paul advises the Corinthians that "because of the present crisis" and the shortness of time "those who have wives should live as if they had none; those who mourn, as if they did not" (1Co 7:26, 29-30). In what way does Ezekiel give us a model of putting God first while still loving his family? 2. Why is it spiritually dangerous to live for others, even a family member? 3. How can you better strike a balance between family and spiritual responsibility?

Responding in Prayer Pray that in both life and death, in plenty and loss, you may glorify God and seek first his kingdom.

Ezekiel 25—26

25 The word of the LORD came to me:
2"Son of man, set your face against
the Ammonites and prophesy
against them. 3Say to them, 'Hear the word of the
Sovereign LORD. This is what the Sovereign LORD
says: Because you said "Aha!" over my sanctuary
when it was desecrated and over the land of Israel
when it was laid waste and over the people of
Judah when they went into exile, 4therefore I am
going to give you to the people of the East as a
possession. They will set up their camps and
pitch their tents among you; they will eat your
fruit and drink your milk. 5I will turn Rabbah
into a pasture for camels and Ammon into a resting place for sheep. Then you will know that I am
the LORD. 6For this is what the Sovereign LORD
says: Because you have clapped your hands and
stamped your feet, rejoicing with all the malice of
your heart against the land of Israel, 7therefore I
will stretch out my hand against you and give you
as plunder to the nations. I will cut you off from
the nations and exterminate you from the countries. I will destroy you, and you will know that I
am the LORD.' "

8"This is what the Sovereign LORD says: 'Because Moab and Seir said, "Look, the house of
Judah has become like all the other nations,"
9therefore I will expose the flank of Moab, beginning at its frontier towns—Beth Jeshimoth, Baal
Meon and Kiriathaim—the glory of that land. 10I
will give Moab along with the Ammonites to the
people of the East as a possession, so that the
Ammonites will not be remembered among the
nations; 11and I will inflict punishment on Moab.
Then they will know that I am the LORD.' "

12"This is what the Sovereign LORD says: 'Because Edom took revenge on the house of Judah
and became very guilty by doing so, 13therefore
this is what the Sovereign LORD says: I will stretch
out my hand against Edom and kill its men and
their animals. I will lay it waste, and from Teman
to Dedan they will fall by the sword. 14I will take
vengeance on Edom by the hand of my people
Israel, and they will deal with Edom in accordance with my anger and my wrath; they will
know my vengeance, declares the Sovereign
LORD.' "

15"This is what the Sovereign LORD says: 'Because the Philistines acted in vengeance and took
revenge with malice in their hearts, and with ancient hostility sought to destroy Judah, 16therefore this is what the Sovereign LORD says: I am
about to stretch out my hand against the Philistines, and I will cut off the Kerethites and destroy
those remaining along the coast. 17I will carry out
great vengeance on them and punish them in my
wrath. Then they will know that I am the LORD,
when I take vengeance on them.' "

26 In the eleventh year, on the first
day of the month, the word of the
LORD came to me: 2"Son of man, because Tyre has said of Jerusalem, 'Aha! The gate
to the nations is broken, and its doors have
swung open to me; now that she lies in ruins I
will prosper,' 3therefore this is what the Sovereign
LORD says: I am against you, O Tyre, and I will
bring many nations against you, like the sea casting up its waves. 4They will destroy the walls of
Tyre and pull down her towers; I will scrape away
her rubble and make her a bare rock. 5Out in the
sea she will become a place to spread fishnets, for
I have spoken, declares the Sovereign LORD. She
will become plunder for the nations, 6and her settlements on the mainland will be ravaged by the
sword. Then they will know that I am the LORD.

7"For this is what the Sovereign LORD says:
From the north I am going to bring against Tyre
Nebuchadnezzar[e] king of Babylon, king of kings,

[e]7 Hebrew *Nebuchadrezzar,* of which *Nebuchadnezzar* is a variant; here and often in Ezekiel and Jeremiah

with horses and chariots, with horsemen and a
great army. 8He will ravage your settlements on
the mainland with the sword; he will set up siege
works against you, build a ramp up to your walls
and raise his shields against you. 9He will direct
the blows of his battering rams against your walls
and demolish your towers with his weapons.
10His horses will be so many that they will cover
you with dust. Your walls will tremble at the
noise of the war horses, wagons and chariots
when he enters your gates as men enter a city
whose walls have been broken through. 11The
hoofs of his horses will trample all your streets;
he will kill your people with the sword, and your
strong pillars will fall to the ground. 12They will
plunder your wealth and loot your merchandise;
they will break down your walls and demolish
your fine houses and throw your stones, timber
and rubble into the sea. 13I will put an end to
your noisy songs, and the music of your harps
will be heard no more. 14I will make you a bare
rock, and you will become a place to spread fish-
nets. You will never be rebuilt, for I the LORD have
spoken, declares the Sovereign LORD.
15"This is what the Sovereign LORD says to Tyre:
Will not the coastlands tremble at the sound of
your fall, when the wounded groan and the
slaughter takes place in you? 16Then all the
princes of the coast will step down from their
thrones and lay aside their robes and take off
their embroidered garments. Clothed with terror,
they will sit on the ground, trembling every mo-
ment, appalled at you. 17Then they will take up a
lament concerning you and say to you:

" 'How you are destroyed, O city of renown,
peopled by men of the sea!
You were a power on the seas,
you and your citizens;
you put your terror
on all who lived there.
18Now the coastlands tremble
on the day of your fall;
the islands in the sea
are terrified at your collapse.'

19"This is what the Sovereign LORD says: When
I make you a desolate city, like cities no longer
inhabited, and when I bring the ocean depths
over you and its vast waters cover you, 20then I
will bring you down with those who go down to
the pit, to the people of long ago. I will make you
dwell in the earth below, as in ancient ruins, with
those who go down to the pit, and you will not
return or take your place[f] in the land of the
living. 21I will bring you to a horrible end and you
will be no more. You will be sought, but you will
never again be found, declares the Sovereign
LORD."

f20 Septuagint; Hebrew *return, and I will give glory*

10 / *Ezekiel 27—28*
National Pride—National Downfall

TYPICALLY CHRISTIANS ASSUME that God is interested only in individuals and the church. The newspaper and the Bible seem to be worlds apart. But the prophecies of Ezekiel show that in all things, even in national histories, God will reveal his holy nature. God's judgment of Jerusalem is part of his divine sovereignty over all nations and follows the same pattern. There exists not only personal sin, but national sin, not only personal grace, but national grace. The case we will study is Tyre, but Ezekiel's survey in chapters 25—32 includes all his other neighbors.

Warming Up to God Why do you think it is so hard to discern God's divine purpose in the affairs of nations when you read the newspaper?

Read Ezekiel 27—28.

27 The word of the LORD came to me:
2“Son of man, take up a lament
concerning Tyre. 3Say to Tyre, situ-
ated at the gateway to the sea, merchant of peo-
ples on many coasts, ‘This is what the Sovereign
LORD says:

“ ‘You say, O Tyre,
“I am perfect in beauty.”
4Your domain was on the high seas;
your builders brought your beauty to
perfection.
5They made all your timbers
of pine trees from Senir[g];
they took a cedar from Lebanon
to make a mast for you.
6Of oaks from Bashan
they made your oars;
of cypress wood[h] from the coasts of
Cyprus[i]
they made your deck, inlaid with ivory.
7Fine embroidered linen from Egypt was your
sail
and served as your banner;
your awnings were of blue and purple
from the coasts of Elishah.
8Men of Sidon and Arvad were your oarsmen;
your skilled men, O Tyre, were aboard as
your seamen.
9Veteran craftsmen of Gebal[j] were on board
as shipwrights to caulk your seams.
All the ships of the sea and their sailors
came alongside to trade for your wares.

10“ ‘Men of Persia, Lydia and Put
served as soldiers in your army.
They hung their shields and helmets on your
walls,
bringing you splendor.
11Men of Arvad and Helech
manned your walls on every side;
men of Gammad
were in your towers.
They hung their shields around your walls;
they brought your beauty to perfection.

12“ ‘Tarshish did business with you because of
your great wealth of goods; they exchanged silver,
iron, tin and lead for your merchandise.
13“ ‘Greece, Tubal and Meshech traded with
you; they exchanged slaves and articles of bronze
for your wares.
14“ ‘Men of Beth Togarmah exchanged work
horses, war horses and mules for your merchan-
dise.
15“ ‘The men of Rhodes[k] traded with you, and
many coastlands were your customers; they paid
you with ivory tusks and ebony.
16“ ‘Aram[l] did business with you because of
your many products; they exchanged turquoise,
purple fabric, embroidered work, fine linen, coral
and rubies for your merchandise.
17“ ‘Judah and Israel traded with you; they ex-
changed wheat from Minnith and confections,[m]
honey, oil and balm for your wares.
18“ ‘Damascus, because of your many products
and great wealth of goods, did business with you
in wine from Helbon and wool from Zahar.
19“ ‘Danites and Greeks from Uzal bought your
merchandise; they exchanged wrought iron, cas-
sia and calamus for your wares.
20“ ‘Dedan traded in saddle blankets with you.
21“ ‘Arabia and all the princes of Kedar were
your customers; they did business with you in
lambs, rams and goats.
22“ ‘The merchants of Sheba and Raamah
traded with you; for your merchandise they ex-
changed the finest of all kinds of spices and pre-
cious stones, and gold.
23“ ‘Haran, Canneh and Eden and merchants of
Sheba, Asshur and Kilmad traded with you. 24In
your marketplace they traded with you beautiful
garments, blue fabric, embroidered work and
multicolored rugs with cords twisted and tightly
knotted.

25“ ‘The ships of Tarshish serve
as carriers for your wares.
You are filled with heavy cargo
in the heart of the sea.
26Your oarsmen take you
out to the high seas.
But the east wind will break you to pieces
in the heart of the sea.
27Your wealth, merchandise and wares,
your mariners, seamen and shipwrights,
your merchants and all your soldiers,
and everyone else on board
will sink into the heart of the sea
on the day of your shipwreck.
28The shorelands will quake

[g]5 That is, Hermon [h]6 Targum; the Masoretic Text has a different division of the consonants. [i]6 Hebrew *Kittim* [j]9 That is, Byblos [k]15 Septuagint; Hebrew *Dedan* [l]16 Most Hebrew manuscripts; some Hebrew manuscripts and Syriac *Edom* [m]17 The meaning of the Hebrew for this word is uncertain.

when your seamen cry out.
29All who handle the oars
will abandon their ships;
the mariners and all the seamen
will stand on the shore.
30They will raise their voice
and cry bitterly over you;
they will sprinkle dust on their heads
and roll in ashes.
31They will shave their heads because of you
and will put on sackcloth.
They will weep over you with anguish of soul
and with bitter mourning.
32As they wail and mourn over you,
they will take up a lament concerning you:
"Who was ever silenced like Tyre,
surrounded by the sea?"
33When your merchandise went out on the seas,
you satisfied many nations;
with your great wealth and your wares
you enriched the kings of the earth.
34Now you are shattered by the sea
in the depths of the waters;
your wares and all your company
have gone down with you.
35All who live in the coastlands
are appalled at you;
their kings shudder with horror
and their faces are distorted with fear.
36The merchants among the nations hiss at you;
you have come to a horrible end
and will be no more.' "

28

The word of the LORD came to me:
2"Son of man, say to the ruler of
Tyre, 'This is what the Sovereign
LORD says:

" 'In the pride of your heart
you say, "I am a god;
I sit on the throne of a god
in the heart of the seas."
But you are a man and not a god,
though you think you are as wise as a god.
3Are you wiser than Daniel[n]?
Is no secret hidden from you?
4By your wisdom and understanding
you have gained wealth for yourself
and amassed gold and silver
in your treasuries.
5By your great skill in trading
you have increased your wealth,
and because of your wealth
your heart has grown proud.

6" 'Therefore this is what the Sovereign LORD says:

" 'Because you think you are wise,
as wise as a god,
7I am going to bring foreigners against you,
the most ruthless of nations;
they will draw their swords against your beauty and wisdom
and pierce your shining splendor.
8They will bring you down to the pit,
and you will die a violent death
in the heart of the seas.
9Will you then say, "I am a god,"
in the presence of those who kill you?
You will be but a man, not a god,
in the hands of those who slay you.
10You will die the death of the uncircumcised
at the hands of foreigners.

I have spoken, declares the Sovereign LORD.' "

11The word of the LORD came to me: 12"Son of
man, take up a lament concerning the king of
Tyre and say to him: 'This is what the Sovereign
LORD says:

" 'You were the model of perfection,
full of wisdom and perfect in beauty.
13You were in Eden,
the garden of God;
every precious stone adorned you:
ruby, topaz and emerald,
chrysolite, onyx and jasper,
sapphire,[o] turquoise and beryl.[p]
Your settings and mountings[q] were made of gold;
on the day you were created they were prepared.
14You were anointed as a guardian cherub,
for so I ordained you.
You were on the holy mount of God;
you walked among the fiery stones.
15You were blameless in your ways
from the day you were created
till wickedness was found in you.
16Through your widespread trade
you were filled with violence,

[n]3 Or *Danel*; the Hebrew spelling may suggest a person other than the prophet Daniel. [o]13 Or *lapis lazuli* [p]13 The precise identification of some of these precious stones is uncertain. [q]13 The meaning of the Hebrew for this phrase is uncertain.

and you sinned.
So I drove you in disgrace from the mount of God,
and I expelled you, O guardian cherub,
from among the fiery stones.
17Your heart became proud
on account of your beauty,
and you corrupted your wisdom
because of your splendor.
So I threw you to the earth;
I made a spectacle of you before kings.
18By your many sins and dishonest trade
you have desecrated your sanctuaries.
So I made a fire come out from you,
and it consumed you,
and I reduced you to ashes on the ground
in the sight of all who were watching.
19All the nations who knew you
are appalled at you;
you have come to a horrible end
and will be no more.' "

20The word of the LORD came to me: 21"Son
of man, set your face against Sidon; prophesy
against her 22and say: 'This is what the Sovereign
LORD says:

" 'I am against you, O Sidon,
and I will gain glory within you.
They will know that I am the LORD,
when I inflict punishment on her
and show myself holy within her.
23I will send a plague upon her
and make blood flow in her streets.
The slain will fall within her,
with the sword against her on every side.
Then they will know that I am the LORD.

24" 'No longer will the people of Israel have ma-
licious neighbors who are painful briers and
sharp thorns. Then they will know that I am the
Sovereign LORD.
25" 'This is what the Sovereign LORD says: When
I gather the people of Israel from the nations
where they have been scattered, I will show my-
self holy among them in the sight of the nations.
Then they will live in their own land, which I
gave to my servant Jacob. 26They will live there in
safety and will build houses and plant vineyards;
they will live in safety when I inflict punishment
on all their neighbors who maligned them. Then
they will know that I am the LORD their God.' "

Discovering the Word 1. King Nebuchadnezzar's next move after laying siege to Jerusalem was to lay siege to Tyre. The exiles in Babylon would be concerned to know whether this strong and affluent nation would receive the same moral treatment as God's people. What do the people of Tyre think of themselves (27:3), and what do others think of Tyre (27:4, 33)? 2. How do Tyre's trading partners respond to the demise of this "invincible" nation (27:28–36)? 3. What is Tyre's consuming sin (28:1–10)? 4. God calls the prophet to take up a lament over Tyre (28:12–19). What does this suggest about God's attitude toward this arrogant nation? 5. What is God's method and purpose in executing judgment on Tyre (28:24–26)?

Applying the Word 1. The apostle Paul says that God has made the nations of the earth and determined "the times set for them and the exact places where they should live. God did this so that men should seek him and perhaps reach out for him" (Ac 17:26–27). Ezekiel's fellow exiles were invited to seek God through the national and international events of his day. What national and international events of our day similarly invite us to seek the Lord? 2. When is national pride a good thing, and when does it become idolatrous?

Responding in Prayer Pray, as Paul instructed, with requests, intercession and thanksgiving for kings and those in authority, "that we may live peaceful and quiet lives in all godliness and holiness." Do so knowing that this is both good and pleasing to God (1Ti 2:1–3).

Ezekiel 29—32

29 In the tenth year, in the tenth month on the twelfth day, the word of the LORD came to me: 2"Son of man, set your face against Pharaoh king of Egypt and prophesy against him and against all Egypt. 3Speak to him and say: 'This is what the Sovereign LORD says:

" 'I am against you, Pharaoh king of Egypt,
you great monster lying among your streams.
You say, "The Nile is mine;
I made it for myself."
4But I will put hooks in your jaws
and make the fish of your streams stick to your scales.
I will pull you out from among your streams,
with all the fish sticking to your scales.
5I will leave you in the desert,
you and all the fish of your streams.
You will fall on the open field
and not be gathered or picked up.
I will give you as food
to the beasts of the earth and the birds of the air.

6Then all who live in Egypt will know that I am the LORD.

" 'You have been a staff of reed for the house of Israel. 7When they grasped you with their hands, you splintered and you tore open their shoulders; when they leaned on you, you broke and their backs were wrenched.[r]

8" 'Therefore this is what the Sovereign LORD says: I will bring a sword against you and kill your men and their animals. 9Egypt will become a desolate wasteland. Then they will know that I am the LORD.

" 'Because you said, "The Nile is mine; I made it," 10therefore I am against you and against your streams, and I will make the land of Egypt a ruin and a desolate waste from Migdol to Aswan, as far as the border of Cush.[s] 11No foot of man or animal will pass through it; no one will live there for forty years. 12I will make the land of Egypt desolate among devastated lands, and her cities will lie desolate forty years among ruined cities. And I will disperse the Egyptians among the nations and scatter them through the countries.

13" 'Yet this is what the Sovereign LORD says: At the end of forty years I will gather the Egyptians from the nations where they were scattered. 14I will bring them back from captivity and return them to Upper Egypt,[t] the land of their ancestry. There they will be a lowly kingdom. 15It will be the lowliest of kingdoms and will never again exalt itself above the other nations. I will make it so weak that it will never again rule over the nations. 16Egypt will no longer be a source of confidence for the people of Israel but will be a reminder of their sin in turning to her for help. Then they will know that I am the Sovereign LORD.' "

17In the twenty-seventh year, in the first month on the first day, the word of the LORD came to me: 18"Son of man, Nebuchadnezzar king of Babylon drove his army in a hard campaign against Tyre; every head was rubbed bare and every shoulder made raw. Yet he and his army got no reward from the campaign he led against Tyre. 19Therefore this is what the Sovereign LORD says: I am going to give Egypt to Nebuchadnezzar king of Babylon, and he will carry off its wealth. He will loot and plunder the land as pay for his army. 20I have given him Egypt as a reward for his efforts because he and his army did it for me, declares the Sovereign LORD.

21"On that day I will make a horn[u] grow for the house of Israel, and I will open your mouth among them. Then they will know that I am the LORD."

30 The word of the LORD came to me: 2"Son of man, prophesy and say: 'This is what the Sovereign LORD says:

" 'Wail and say,
"Alas for that day!"
3For the day is near,
the day of the LORD is near—
a day of clouds,
a time of doom for the nations.
4A sword will come against Egypt,
and anguish will come upon Cush.[v]

[r]7 Syriac (see also Septuagint and Vulgate); Hebrew *and you caused their backs to stand* [s]10 That is, the upper Nile region [t]14 Hebrew *to Pathros* [u]21 *Horn* here symbolizes strength. [v]4 That is, the upper Nile region; also in verses 5 and 9

When the slain fall in Egypt,
her wealth will be carried away
and her foundations torn down.
5Cush and Put, Lydia and all Arabia, Libya[w] and
the people of the covenant land will fall by the
sword along with Egypt.
6" 'This is what the LORD says:

" 'The allies of Egypt will fall
and her proud strength will fail.
From Migdol to Aswan
they will fall by the sword within her,
declares the Sovereign LORD.
7" 'They will be desolate
among desolate lands,
and their cities will lie
among ruined cities.
8Then they will know that I am the LORD,
when I set fire to Egypt
and all her helpers are crushed.

9" 'On that day messengers will go out from me
in ships to frighten Cush out of her complacency.
Anguish will take hold of them on the day of
Egypt's doom, for it is sure to come.

10" 'This is what the Sovereign LORD says:

" 'I will put an end to the hordes of Egypt
by the hand of Nebuchadnezzar king of
Babylon.
11He and his army—the most ruthless of
nations—
will be brought in to destroy the land.
They will draw their swords against Egypt
and fill the land with the slain.
12I will dry up the streams of the Nile
and sell the land to evil men;
by the hand of foreigners
I will lay waste the land and everything in
it.

I the LORD have spoken.

13" 'This is what the Sovereign LORD says:

" 'I will destroy the idols
and put an end to the images in
Memphis.[x]
No longer will there be a prince in Egypt,
and I will spread fear throughout the land.
14I will lay waste Upper Egypt,[y]
set fire to Zoan
and inflict punishment on Thebes.[z]
15I will pour out my wrath on Pelusium,[a]
the stronghold of Egypt,
and cut off the hordes of Thebes.
16I will set fire to Egypt;
Pelusium will writhe in agony.
Thebes will be taken by storm;
Memphis will be in constant distress.
17The young men of Heliopolis[b] and Bubastis[c]
will fall by the sword,
and the cities themselves will go into
captivity.
18Dark will be the day at Tahpanhes
when I break the yoke of Egypt;
there her proud strength will come to an
end.
She will be covered with clouds,
and her villages will go into captivity.
19So I will inflict punishment on Egypt,
and they will know that I am the LORD.' "

20In the eleventh year, in the first month on the
seventh day, the word of the LORD came to me:
21"Son of man, I have broken the arm of Pharaoh
king of Egypt. It has not been bound up for heal-
ing or put in a splint so as to become strong
enough to hold a sword. 22Therefore this is what
the Sovereign LORD says: I am against Pharaoh
king of Egypt. I will break both his arms, the
good arm as well as the broken one, and make the
sword fall from his hand. 23I will disperse the
Egyptians among the nations and scatter them
through the countries. 24I will strengthen the
arms of the king of Babylon and put my sword in
his hand, but I will break the arms of Pharaoh,
and he will groan before him like a mortally
wounded man. 25I will strengthen the arms of the
king of Babylon, but the arms of Pharaoh will fall
limp. Then they will know that I am the LORD,
when I put my sword into the hand of the king of
Babylon and he brandishes it against Egypt. 26I
will disperse the Egyptians among the nations
and scatter them through the countries. Then
they will know that I am the LORD."

31

In the eleventh year, in the third
month on the first day, the word of
the LORD came to me: 2"Son of man,
say to Pharaoh king of Egypt and to his hordes:

" 'Who can be compared with you in majesty?
3Consider Assyria, once a cedar in Lebanon,

[w]5 Hebrew *Cub* [x]13 Hebrew *Noph*; also in verse 16
[y]14 Hebrew *waste Pathros* [z]14 Hebrew *No*; also in verses 15 and
16 [a]15 Hebrew *Sin*; also in verse 16 [b]17 Hebrew *Awen* (or *On*)
[c]17 Hebrew *Pi Beseth*

with beautiful branches overshadowing the forest;
it towered on high,
its top above the thick foliage.
4The waters nourished it,
deep springs made it grow tall;
their streams flowed
all around its base
and sent their channels
to all the trees of the field.
5So it towered higher
than all the trees of the field;
its boughs increased
and its branches grew long,
spreading because of abundant waters.
6All the birds of the air
nested in its boughs,
all the beasts of the field
gave birth under its branches;
all the great nations
lived in its shade.
7It was majestic in beauty,
with its spreading boughs,
for its roots went down
to abundant waters.
8The cedars in the garden of God
could not rival it,
nor could the pine trees
equal its boughs,
nor could the plane trees
compare with its branches—
no tree in the garden of God
could match its beauty.
9I made it beautiful
with abundant branches,
the envy of all the trees of Eden
in the garden of God.

10" 'Therefore this is what the Sovereign LORD
says: Because it towered on high, lifting its top
above the thick foliage, and because it was proud
of its height, 11I handed it over to the ruler of the
nations, for him to deal with according to its
wickedness. I cast it aside, 12and the most ruth-
less of foreign nations cut it down and left it. Its
boughs fell on the mountains and in all the val-
leys; its branches lay broken in all the ravines of
the land. All the nations of the earth came out
from under its shade and left it. 13All the birds of
the air settled on the fallen tree, and all the beasts
of the field were among its branches. 14Therefore
no other trees by the waters are ever to tower
proudly on high, lifting their tops above the thick
foliage. No other trees so well-watered are ever
to reach such a height; they are all destined for
death, for the earth below, among mortal men,
with those who go down to the pit.

15" 'This is what the Sovereign LORD says: On
the day it was brought down to the grave[d] I cov-
ered the deep springs with mourning for it; I held
back its streams, and its abundant waters were
restrained. Because of it I clothed Lebanon with
gloom, and all the trees of the field withered
away. 16I made the nations tremble at the sound
of its fall when I brought it down to the grave
with those who go down to the pit. Then all the
trees of Eden, the choicest and best of Lebanon,
all the trees that were well-watered, were con-
soled in the earth below. 17Those who lived in its
shade, its allies among the nations, had also gone
down to the grave with it, joining those killed by
the sword.

18" 'Which of the trees of Eden can be com-
pared with you in splendor and majesty? Yet you,
too, will be brought down with the trees of Eden
to the earth below; you will lie among the uncir-
cumcised, with those killed by the sword.

" 'This is Pharaoh and all his hordes, declares
the Sovereign LORD.' "

32

In the twelfth year, in the twelfth
month on the first day, the word of
the LORD came to me: 2"Son of man,
take up a lament concerning Pharaoh king of
Egypt and say to him:

" 'You are like a lion among the nations;
you are like a monster in the seas
thrashing about in your streams,
churning the water with your feet
and muddying the streams.

3" 'This is what the Sovereign LORD says:

" 'With a great throng of people
I will cast my net over you,
and they will haul you up in my net.
4I will throw you on the land
and hurl you on the open field.
I will let all the birds of the air settle on you
and all the beasts of the earth gorge
themselves on you.
5I will spread your flesh on the mountains
and fill the valleys with your remains.

d15 Hebrew *Sheol*; also in verses 16 and 17

6I will drench the land with your flowing
blood
all the way to the mountains,
and the ravines will be filled with your
flesh.
7When I snuff you out, I will cover the
heavens
and darken their stars;
I will cover the sun with a cloud,
and the moon will not give its light.
8All the shining lights in the heavens
I will darken over you;
I will bring darkness over your land,
declares the Sovereign LORD.
9I will trouble the hearts of many peoples
when I bring about your destruction among
the nations,
among[e] lands you have not known.
10I will cause many peoples to be appalled at
you,
and their kings will shudder with horror
because of you
when I brandish my sword before them.
On the day of your downfall
each of them will tremble
every moment for his life.

11" 'For this is what the Sovereign LORD says:

" 'The sword of the king of Babylon
will come against you.
12I will cause your hordes to fall
by the swords of mighty men—
the most ruthless of all nations.
They will shatter the pride of Egypt,
and all her hordes will be overthrown.
13I will destroy all her cattle
from beside abundant waters
no longer to be stirred by the foot of man
or muddied by the hoofs of cattle.
14Then I will let her waters settle
and make her streams flow like oil,
declares the Sovereign LORD.
15When I make Egypt desolate
and strip the land of everything in it,
when I strike down all who live there,
then they will know that I am the LORD.'

16"This is the lament they will chant for her.
The daughters of the nations will chant it; for
Egypt and all her hordes they will chant it, de-
clares the Sovereign LORD."

17In the twelfth year, on the fifteenth day of the
month, the word of the LORD came to me: 18"Son
of man, wail for the hordes of Egypt and consign
to the earth below both her and the daughters of
mighty nations, with those who go down to the
pit. 19Say to them, 'Are you more favored than
others? Go down and be laid among the uncir-
cumcised.' 20They will fall among those killed by
the sword. The sword is drawn; let her be dragged
off with all her hordes. 21From within the grave[f]
the mighty leaders will say of Egypt and her al-
lies, 'They have come down and they lie with the
uncircumcised, with those killed by the sword.'

22"Assyria is there with her whole army; she is
surrounded by the graves of all her slain, all who
have fallen by the sword. 23Their graves are in the
depths of the pit and her army lies around her
grave. All who had spread terror in the land of the
living are slain, fallen by the sword.

24"Elam is there, with all her hordes around her
grave. All of them are slain, fallen by the sword.
All who had spread terror in the land of the living
went down uncircumcised to the earth below.
They bear their shame with those who go down
to the pit. 25A bed is made for her among the
slain, with all her hordes around her grave. All of
them are uncircumcised, killed by the sword. Be-
cause their terror had spread in the land of the
living, they bear their shame with those who go
down to the pit; they are laid among the slain.

26"Meshech and Tubal are there, with all their
hordes around their graves. All of them are uncir-
cumcised, killed by the sword because they
spread their terror in the land of the living. 27Do
they not lie with the other uncircumcised war-
riors who have fallen, who went down to the
grave with their weapons of war, whose swords
were placed under their heads? The punishment
for their sins rested on their bones, though the
terror of these warriors had stalked through the
land of the living.

28"You too, O Pharaoh, will be broken and will
lie among the uncircumcised, with those killed by
the sword.

29"Edom is there, her kings and all her princes;
despite their power, they are laid with those
killed by the sword. They lie with the uncircum-
cised, with those who go down to the pit.

30"All the princes of the north and all the Sido-
nians are there; they went down with the slain in
disgrace despite the terror caused by their power.

[e]9 Hebrew; Septuagint *bring you into captivity among the nations, / to*
[f]21 Hebrew *Sheol*; also in verse 27

They lie uncircumcised with those killed by the sword and bear their shame with those who go down to the pit.

[31]"Pharaoh—he and all his army—will see them and he will be consoled for all his hordes that were killed by the sword, declares the Sovereign LORD. [32]Although I had him spread terror in the land of the living, Pharaoh and all his hordes will be laid among the uncircumcised, with those killed by the sword, declares the Sovereign LORD."

11 / *Ezekiel 33* The Watchman

THE FIRST TWENTY-FOUR chapters of Ezekiel contain his prophecies *before* the fall of Jerusalem. They are concerned with what will happen to the spiritual epicenter of the Lord's people. Then Jerusalem falls and the temple is destroyed. In the interlude (chapters 25—32) Ezekiel surveys what God is doing with the surrounding nations. Now, in chapters 33—48, Ezekiel turns from the Jerusalem that was to the Jerusalem that will be. In this matter Ezekiel has, once again, a lonely role.

Warming Up to God Think of a time when you stood alone for God's purposes or standards. What comforted you when you were not supported by others?

Read Ezekiel 33.

33 The word of the LORD came to me:
[2]"Son of man, speak to your coun-
trymen and say to them: 'When I
bring the sword against a land, and the people of
the land choose one of their men and make him
their watchman, [3]and he sees the sword coming
against the land and blows the trumpet to warn
the people, [4]then if anyone hears the trumpet
but does not take warning and the sword comes
and takes his life, his blood will be on his own
head. [5]Since he heard the sound of the trumpet
but did not take warning, his blood will be
on his own head. If he had taken warning, he
would have saved himself. [6]But if the watch-
man sees the sword coming and does not blow
the trumpet to warn the people and the sword
comes and takes the life of one of them, that
man will be taken away because of his sin, but I
will hold the watchman accountable for his
blood.'

[7]"Son of man, I have made you a watchman for
the house of Israel; so hear the word I speak and
give them warning from me. [8]When I say to the
wicked, 'O wicked man, you will surely die,' and
you do not speak out to dissuade him from his
ways, that wicked man will die for[g] his sin, and
I will hold you accountable for his blood. [9]But if
you do warn the wicked man to turn from his
ways and he does not do so, he will die for his sin,
but you will have saved yourself.

[10]"Son of man, say to the house of Israel, 'This
is what you are saying: "Our offenses and sins
weigh us down, and we are wasting away because
of[h] them. How then can we live?"' [11]Say to
them, 'As surely as I live, declares the Sovereign
LORD, I take no pleasure in the death of the
wicked, but rather that they turn from their ways
and live. Turn! Turn from your evil ways! Why
will you die, O house of Israel?'

[12]"Therefore, son of man, say to your country-
men, 'The righteousness of the righteous man will
not save him when he disobeys, and the wicked-
ness of the wicked man will not cause him to fall
when he turns from it. The righteous man, if he
sins, will not be allowed to live because of his
former righteousness.' [13]If I tell the righteous man
that he will surely live, but then he trusts in his
righteousness and does evil, none of the righteous
things he has done will be remembered; he will
die for the evil he has done. [14]And if I say to the
wicked man, 'You will surely die,' but he then
turns away from his sin and does what is just and
right— [15]if he gives back what he took in pledge
for a loan, returns what he has stolen, follows the
decrees that give life, and does no evil, he will

[g]8 Or *in*; also in verse 9 [h]10 Or *away in*

surely live; he will not die. 16None of the sins he
has committed will be remembered against him.
He has done what is just and right; he will surely
live.

17"Yet your countrymen say, 'The way of the
Lord is not just.' But it is their way that is not
just. 18If a righteous man turns from his righ-
teousness and does evil, he will die for it. 19And if
a wicked man turns away from his wickedness
and does what is just and right, he will live by
doing so. 20Yet, O house of Israel, you say, 'The
way of the Lord is not just.' But I will judge each
of you according to his own ways."

21In the twelfth year of our exile, in the tenth
month on the fifth day, a man who had escaped
from Jerusalem came to me and said, "The city
has fallen!" 22Now the evening before the man
arrived, the hand of the LORD was upon me, and
he opened my mouth before the man came to me
in the morning. So my mouth was opened and I
was no longer silent.

23Then the word of the LORD came to me:
24"Son of man, the people living in those ruins in
the land of Israel are saying, 'Abraham was only
one man, yet he possessed the land. But we are
many; surely the land has been given to us as our
possession.' 25Therefore say to them, 'This is what
the Sovereign LORD says: Since you eat meat with
the blood still in it and look to your idols and
shed blood, should you then possess the land?
26You rely on your sword, you do detestable
things, and each of you defiles his neighbor's
wife. Should you then possess the land?'

27"Say this to them: 'This is what the Sovereign
LORD says: As surely as I live, those who are left in
the ruins will fall by the sword, those out in the
country I will give to the wild animals to be de-
voured, and those in strongholds and caves will
die of a plague. 28I will make the land a desolate
waste, and her proud strength will come to an
end, and the mountains of Israel will become des-
olate so that no one will cross them. 29Then they
will know that I am the LORD, when I have made
the land a desolate waste because of all the detest-
able things they have done.'

30"As for you, son of man, your countrymen
are talking together about you by the walls and at
the doors of the houses, saying to each other,
'Come and hear the message that has come from
the LORD.' 31My people come to you, as they usu-
ally do, and sit before you to listen to your words,
but they do not put them into practice. With their
mouths they express devotion, but their hearts
are greedy for unjust gain. 32Indeed, to them you
are nothing more than one who sings love songs
with a beautiful voice and plays an instrument
well, for they hear your words but do not put
them into practice.

33"When all this comes true—and it surely
will—then they will know that a prophet has
been among them."

Discovering the Word 1. In what ways is Ezekiel's role with God's people like that of a watchman on the walls of a city (vv. 1–20; 3:16–21)? 2. With what words will Ezekiel encourage the exiles who feel their sins are unforgivable and their punishment so final that there can be no deliverance (vv. 10–11)? 3. Why will Ezekiel's role as a watchman be especially important now that the news of Jerusalem's fall has arrived (v. 21)? 4. What apparently do the people assume they will be able to do (v. 24), and how must Ezekiel warn them (vv. 25–26)? 5. Why must Ezekiel keep speaking even though his words apparently have little effect (vv. 30–32; Mt 7:26–27)?

Applying the Word 1. In what way is the response of Ezekiel's contemporaries (vv. 30–32) similar to the response of church congregations to the weekly experience of listening to sermons? 2. On what issues of our day might God be calling you to stand apart from others? 3. What fears will you need to overcome to stand as a faithful watchman?

Responding in Prayer Pray for Spirit-empowered boldness in standing for God and his righteousness on the issues of our day (Eph 6:19–20).

12/ *Ezekiel 34*
Past and Future Shepherds

SELF-INTEREST SHOULD NOT be the primary motivation of a spiritual leader. When an outstanding Christian leader is found to be sexually unfaithful, consumed with greed or on a power trip, not only are non-Christians tempted to become cynical; even the insiders wonder if there is any reality to the faith. Into such situations Ezekiel was called to speak God's word with searing honesty and triumphant hope. In choosing to address the leadership question by using the metaphor of shepherd, Ezekiel was using an image that was common in the Ancient Near East and is threaded through the Bible (Isa 44:28; Jer 10:21; Mic 5:4-5; Zec 11:4-17), one that can speak to us today.

Warming Up to God Recall a pastor or Christian leader who has truly cared for you and helped you find strength in God. What were his or her characteristics?

Read Ezekiel 34.

34 The word of the LORD came to me:
2"Son of man, prophesy against the
shepherds of Israel; prophesy and
say to them: 'This is what the Sovereign LORD
says: Woe to the shepherds of Israel who only
take care of themselves! Should not shepherds
take care of the flock? 3You eat the curds, clothe
yourselves with the wool and slaughter the choice
animals, but you do not take care of the flock.
4You have not strengthened the weak or healed
the sick or bound up the injured. You have not
brought back the strays or searched for the lost.
You have ruled them harshly and brutally. 5So
they were scattered because there was no shep-
herd, and when they were scattered they became
food for all the wild animals. 6My sheep wan-
dered over all the mountains and on every high
hill. They were scattered over the whole earth,
and no one searched or looked for them.

7" 'Therefore, you shepherds, hear the word of
the LORD: 8As surely as I live, declares the Sover-
eign LORD, because my flock lacks a shepherd and
so has been plundered and has become food for
all the wild animals, and because my shepherds
did not search for my flock but cared for them-
selves rather than for my flock, 9therefore,
O shepherds, hear the word of the LORD: 10This is
what the Sovereign LORD says: I am against the
shepherds and will hold them accountable for my
flock. I will remove them from tending the flock
so that the shepherds can no longer feed them-
selves. I will rescue my flock from their mouths,
and it will no longer be food for them.

11" 'For this is what the Sovereign LORD says: I
myself will search for my sheep and look after
them. 12As a shepherd looks after his scattered
flock when he is with them, so will I look after
my sheep. I will rescue them from all the places
where they were scattered on a day of clouds and
darkness. 13I will bring them out from the nations
and gather them from the countries, and I will
bring them into their own land. I will pasture
them on the mountains of Israel, in the ravines
and in all the settlements in the land. 14I will tend
them in a good pasture, and the mountain heights
of Israel will be their grazing land. There they will
lie down in good grazing land, and there they will
feed in a rich pasture on the mountains of Israel.
15I myself will tend my sheep and have them lie
down, declares the Sovereign LORD. 16I will search
for the lost and bring back the strays. I will bind
up the injured and strengthen the weak, but the
sleek and the strong I will destroy. I will shepherd
the flock with justice.

17" 'As for you, my flock, this is what the Sover-
eign LORD says: I will judge between one sheep
and another, and between rams and goats. 18Is it
not enough for you to feed on the good pasture?
Must you also trample the rest of your pasture
with your feet? Is it not enough for you to drink
clear water? Must you also muddy the rest with
your feet? 19Must my flock feed on what you have
trampled and drink what you have muddied with
your feet?

20" 'Therefore this is what the Sovereign LORD
says to them: See, I myself will judge between the
fat sheep and the lean sheep. 21Because you shove
with flank and shoulder, butting all the weak
sheep with your horns until you have driven
them away, 22I will save my flock, and they will

no longer be plundered. I will judge between one
sheep and another. 23I will place over them one
shepherd, my servant David, and he will tend
them; he will tend them and be their shepherd.
24I the LORD will be their God, and my servant
David will be prince among them. I the LORD have
spoken.
25" 'I will make a covenant of peace with them
and rid the land of wild beasts so that they may
live in the desert and sleep in the forests in safety.
26I will bless them and the places surrounding my
hill.[i] I will send down showers in season; there
will be showers of blessing. 27The trees of the
field will yield their fruit and the ground will
yield its crops; the people will be secure in their
land. They will know that I am the LORD, when I
break the bars of their yoke and rescue them from
the hands of those who enslaved them. 28They
will no longer be plundered by the nations, nor
will wild animals devour them. They will live in
safety, and no one will make them afraid. 29I will
provide for them a land renowned for its crops,
and they will no longer be victims of famine in
the land or bear the scorn of the nations. 30Then
they will know that I, the LORD their God, am
with them and that they, the house of Israel, are
my people, declares the Sovereign LORD. 31You my
sheep, the sheep of my pasture, are people, and I
am your God, declares the Sovereign LORD.' "

[i]26 Or *I will make them and the places surrounding my hill a blessing*

Discovering the Word 1. By reciting the failures of the kings and spiritual leaders before the exile, Ezekiel gives us several descriptions of what should and should not be done by good leaders. What are the characteristics of both? 2. Instead of proposing a leaderless community, Ezekiel offers an inspired vision of the Good Shepherd (vv. 10–16) in a remarkable foreshadowing of the parable of the lost sheep (Jn 10:1–21). What does God as Shepherd do that his human servant-leaders refuse to do? 3. Ezekiel switches the metaphor from shepherd as leader/feeder to shepherd as judge. The flock must be purified not only of bad leaders but also of bad members (vv. 17–22; Mt 25:31–46). Why are both leaders and members tested more by their care of the weak than of the strong and healthy? 4. Many of Ezekiel's visions are presented to us in a kind of dissolve-fade sequence. In verses 23–31 Ezekiel envisions the ultimate hope for the scattered exiles in Babylon. How does he describe it?

Applying the Word 1. Should Christians today long for such judgment by human shepherd-leaders? Why or why not? 2. In what ways does your own relationship with the weak and needy members of God's people express the justice desired by the Good Shepherd and true leader of the church? 3. Who needs your assistance?

Responding in Prayer Reflect on what "the LORD is [your] shepherd" (Ps 23:1) means to you, and turn this reflection into thanksgiving prayer.

Ezekiel 35—36

35 The word of the LORD came to me:
2"Son of man, set your face against
Mount Seir; prophesy against it
3and say: 'This is what the Sovereign LORD says: I
am against you, Mount Seir, and I will stretch out
my hand against you and make you a desolate
waste. 4I will turn your towns into ruins and you
will be desolate. Then you will know that I am
the LORD.
5" 'Because you harbored an ancient hostility
and delivered the Israelites over to the sword at
the time of their calamity, the time their punish-
ment reached its climax, 6therefore as surely as I
live, declares the Sovereign LORD, I will give you
over to bloodshed and it will pursue you. Since
you did not hate bloodshed, bloodshed will pur-
sue you. 7I will make Mount Seir a desolate waste
and cut off from it all who come and go. 8I will fill
your mountains with the slain; those killed by the
sword will fall on your hills and in your valleys
and in all your ravines. 9I will make you desolate
forever; your towns will not be inhabited. Then
you will know that I am the LORD.
10" 'Because you have said, "These two nations
and countries will be ours and we will take pos-
session of them," even though I the LORD was
there, 11therefore as surely as I live, declares the
Sovereign LORD, I will treat you in accordance
with the anger and jealousy you showed in your
hatred of them and I will make myself known

among them when I judge you. 12Then you will
know that I the LORD have heard all the contempt-
ible things you have said against the mountains of
Israel. You said, "They have been laid waste and
have been given over to us to devour." 13You
boasted against me and spoke against me without
restraint, and I heard it. 14This is what the Sover-
eign LORD says: While the whole earth rejoices, I
will make you desolate. 15Because you rejoiced
when the inheritance of the house of Israel be-
came desolate, that is how I will treat you. You
will be desolate, O Mount Seir, you and all of
Edom. Then they will know that I am the LORD.' "

36 "Son of man, prophesy to the
mountains of Israel and say,
'O mountains of Israel, hear the
word of the LORD. 2This is what the Sovereign
LORD says: The enemy said of you, "Aha! The an-
cient heights have become our possession." '
3Therefore prophesy and say, 'This is what the
Sovereign LORD says: Because they ravaged and
hounded you from every side so that you became
the possession of the rest of the nations and the
object of people's malicious talk and slander,
4therefore, O mountains of Israel, hear the word
of the Sovereign LORD: This is what the Sovereign
LORD says to the mountains and hills, to the ra-
vines and valleys, to the desolate ruins and the
deserted towns that have been plundered and rid-
iculed by the rest of the nations around you—
5this is what the Sovereign LORD says: In my burn-
ing zeal I have spoken against the rest of the na-
tions, and against all Edom, for with glee and
with malice in their hearts they made my land
their own possession so that they might plunder
its pastureland.' 6Therefore prophesy concerning
the land of Israel and say to the mountains and
hills, to the ravines and valleys: 'This is what the
Sovereign LORD says: I speak in my jealous wrath
because you have suffered the scorn of the na-
tions. 7Therefore this is what the Sovereign LORD
says: I swear with uplifted hand that the nations
around you will also suffer scorn.

8" 'But you, O mountains of Israel, will pro-
duce branches and fruit for my people Israel, for
they will soon come home. 9I am concerned for
you and will look on you with favor; you will be
plowed and sown, 10and I will multiply the num-
ber of people upon you, even the whole house of
Israel. The towns will be inhabited and the ruins
rebuilt. 11I will increase the number of men and
animals upon you, and they will be fruitful and
become numerous. I will settle people on you as
in the past and will make you prosper more than
before. Then you will know that I am the LORD. 12I
will cause people, my people Israel, to walk upon
you. They will possess you, and you will be their
inheritance; you will never again deprive them of
their children.

13" 'This is what the Sovereign LORD says: Be-
cause people say to you, "You devour men and
deprive your nation of its children," 14therefore
you will no longer devour men or make your na-
tion childless, declares the Sovereign LORD. 15No
longer will I make you hear the taunts of the
nations, and no longer will you suffer the scorn of
the peoples or cause your nation to fall, declares
the Sovereign LORD.' "

16Again the word of the LORD came to me:
17"Son of man, when the people of Israel were
living in their own land, they defiled it by their
conduct and their actions. Their conduct was like
a woman's monthly uncleanness in my sight. 18So
I poured out my wrath on them because they had
shed blood in the land and because they had de-
filed it with their idols. 19I dispersed them among
the nations, and they were scattered through the
countries; I judged them according to their con-
duct and their actions. 20And wherever they went
among the nations they profaned my holy name,
for it was said of them, 'These are the LORD's peo-
ple, and yet they had to leave his land.' 21I had
concern for my holy name, which the house of
Israel profaned among the nations where they
had gone.

22"Therefore say to the house of Israel, 'This is
what the Sovereign LORD says: It is not for your
sake, O house of Israel, that I am going to do
these things, but for the sake of my holy name,
which you have profaned among the nations
where you have gone. 23I will show the holiness
of my great name, which has been profaned
among the nations, the name you have profaned
among them. Then the nations will know that I
am the LORD, declares the Sovereign LORD, when I
show myself holy through you before their eyes.

24" 'For I will take you out of the nations; I will
gather you from all the countries and bring you
back into your own land. 25I will sprinkle clean
water on you, and you will be clean; I will cleanse
you from all your impurities and from all your
idols. 26I will give you a new heart and put a new
spirit in you; I will remove from you your heart of

stone and give you a heart of flesh. [27]And I will put my Spirit in you and move you to follow my decrees and be careful to keep my laws. [28]You will live in the land I gave your forefathers; you will be my people, and I will be your God. [29]I will save you from all your uncleanness. I will call for the grain and make it plentiful and will not bring famine upon you. [30]I will increase the fruit of the trees and the crops of the field, so that you will no longer suffer disgrace among the nations because of famine. [31]Then you will remember your evil ways and wicked deeds, and you will loathe yourselves for your sins and detestable practices. [32]I want you to know that I am not doing this for your sake, declares the Sovereign LORD. Be ashamed and disgraced for your conduct, O house of Israel!

[33]" 'This is what the Sovereign LORD says: On the day I cleanse you from all your sins, I will resettle your towns, and the ruins will be rebuilt. [34]The desolate land will be cultivated instead of lying desolate in the sight of all who pass through it. [35]They will say, "This land that was laid waste has become like the garden of Eden; the cities that were lying in ruins, desolate and destroyed, are now fortified and inhabited." [36]Then the nations around you that remain will know that I the LORD have rebuilt what was destroyed and have replanted what was desolate. I the LORD have spoken, and I will do it.'

[37]"This is what the Sovereign LORD says: Once again I will yield to the plea of the house of Israel and do this for them: I will make their people as numerous as sheep, [38]as numerous as the flocks for offerings at Jerusalem during her appointed feasts. So will the ruined cities be filled with flocks of people. Then they will know that I am the LORD."

13 / *Ezekiel 37*
Can These Bones Live?

IMAGINATION IS THE vehicle through which faith finds expression, allowing us, as Cheryl Forbes says, "to complete the story." We have a profound need to see the conclusion of it all, especially what will come of God's own people. It is impossible for God to *tell* us the future. So he *shows* us. But an inspired vision of the end is different from invented endings. Ezekiel's word pictures envision what God will actually do, thereby feeding faith rather than fancy.

Warming Up to God What anxiety do you have about your future days and years? Pause to voice your fears to God.

Read Ezekiel 37.

37 The hand of the LORD was upon me, and he brought me out by the Spirit of the LORD and set me in the middle of a valley; it was full of bones. [2]He led me back and forth among them, and I saw a great many bones on the floor of the valley, bones that were very dry. [3]He asked me, "Son of man, can these bones live?"

I said, "O Sovereign LORD, you alone know."

[4]Then he said to me, "Prophesy to these bones and say to them, 'Dry bones, hear the word of the LORD! [5]This is what the Sovereign LORD says to these bones: I will make breath[j] enter you, and you will come to life. [6]I will attach tendons to you and make flesh come upon you and cover you with skin; I will put breath in you, and you will come to life. Then you will know that I am the LORD.' "

[7]So I prophesied as I was commanded. And as I was prophesying, there was a noise, a rattling sound, and the bones came together, bone to bone. [8]I looked, and tendons and flesh appeared on them and skin covered them, but there was no breath in them.

[9]Then he said to me, "Prophesy to the breath; prophesy, son of man, and say to it, 'This is what

j5 The Hebrew for this word can also mean *wind* or *spirit* (see verses 6-14).

the Sovereign LORD says: Come from the four winds, O breath, and breathe into these slain, that they may live.' " 10So I prophesied as he commanded me, and breath entered them; they came to life and stood up on their feet—a vast army.

11Then he said to me: "Son of man, these bones are the whole house of Israel. They say, 'Our bones are dried up and our hope is gone; we are cut off.' 12Therefore prophesy and say to them: 'This is what the Sovereign LORD says: O my people, I am going to open your graves and bring you up from them; I will bring you back to the land of Israel. 13Then you, my people, will know that I am the LORD, when I open your graves and bring you up from them. 14I will put my Spirit in you and you will live, and I will settle you in your own land. Then you will know that I the LORD have spoken, and I have done it, declares the LORD.' "

15The word of the LORD came to me: 16"Son of man, take a stick of wood and write on it, 'Belonging to Judah and the Israelites associated with him.' Then take another stick of wood, and write on it, 'Ephraim's stick, belonging to Joseph and all the house of Israel associated with him.' 17Join them together into one stick so that they will become one in your hand.

18"When your countrymen ask you, 'Won't you tell us what you mean by this?' 19say to them, 'This is what the Sovereign LORD says: I am going to take the stick of Joseph—which is in Ephraim's hand—and of the Israelite tribes associated with him, and join it to Judah's stick, making them a single stick of wood, and they will become one in my hand.' 20Hold before their eyes the sticks you have written on 21and say to them, 'This is what the Sovereign LORD says: I will take the Israelites out of the nations where they have gone. I will gather them from all around and bring them back into their own land. 22I will make them one nation in the land, on the mountains of Israel. There will be one king over all of them and they will never again be two nations or be divided into two kingdoms. 23They will no longer defile themselves with their idols and vile images or with any of their offenses, for I will save them from all their sinful backsliding,[k] and I will cleanse them. They will be my people, and I will be their God.

24" 'My servant David will be king over them, and they will all have one shepherd. They will follow my laws and be careful to keep my decrees. 25They will live in the land I gave to my servant Jacob, the land where your fathers lived. They and their children and their children's children will live there forever, and David my servant will be their prince forever. 26I will make a covenant of peace with them; it will be an everlasting covenant. I will establish them and increase their numbers, and I will put my sanctuary among them forever. 27My dwelling place will be with them; I will be their God, and they will be my people. 28Then the nations will know that I the LORD make Israel holy, when my sanctuary is among them forever.' "

[k]23 Many Hebrew manuscripts (see also Septuagint); most Hebrew manuscripts *all their dwelling places where they sinned*

Discovering the Word 1. What future does God present through both the vision (vv. 1–14) and the acted parable (vv. 15–23)? 2. To what condition of the people (vv. 11, 16–17) and of the prophet himself (v. 3) does this message minister? 3. Many people have interpreted verses 1–14 as an Old Testament doctrine of bodily resurrection or an allegory of individual spiritual regeneration in Christ. But in the context of Ezekiel's teachings after the fall of Jerusalem, why do you think "Can these bones live?" (v. 3) is an important question for the Lord to ask the prophet? 4. It appears that Ezekiel has the knowledge that God could resurrect his people, but not faith to believe God will do it. Why is it important for Ezekiel to be asked to speak to the dead bones (vv. 4, 7)? 5. The second part of Israel's resurrection in verses 15–28 is a development of the heart transplant image of 36:26–27. What further statements indicate that God has more in mind than the mere physical restoration of the nation of Israel (vv. 24–28)? 6. In 36:22 God says, "It is not for your sake, O house of Israel, that I am going to do these things, but for the sake of my holy name." Three times in the vision God says he will do this so that "you will know that I am the LORD" (37:6, 13, 14). Why is God's settled decision to renew his own people so crucial to the declaration of God's glory in the world?

Applying the Word 1. What hope does this vision give for Christians today who, viewing the state of the church, say, "Our bones are dried up and our hope is gone" (v. 11)? 2. For a host of skeletons to be turned into an effective army, God must work a miracle. Note the crucial role played by the prophet in the future of God's people. How could preaching and prayer on the part of the church today be part of our renewal process?

Responding in Prayer Pray for the unity of the church (vv. 15–23). Pray for the renewal of God's people (v. 24; 36:26–27). Pray that God's people will delight in being the sanctuary of God (v. 27). Pray that God's people will communicate the glory of God to the nations through mission (v. 28).

Ezekiel 38—39

38 The word of the LORD came to me: 2“Son of man, set your face against Gog, of the land of Magog, the chief prince of[l] Meshech and Tubal; prophesy against him 3and say: ‘This is what the Sovereign LORD says: I am against you, O Gog, chief prince of[m] Meshech and Tubal. 4I will turn you around, put hooks in your jaws and bring you out with your whole army—your horses, your horsemen fully armed, and a great horde with large and small shields, all of them brandishing their swords. 5Persia, Cush[n] and Put will be with them, all with shields and helmets, 6also Gomer with all its troops, and Beth Togarmah from the far north with all its troops—the many nations with you.

7“ ‘Get ready; be prepared, you and all the hordes gathered about you, and take command of them. 8After many days you will be called to arms. In future years you will invade a land that has recovered from war, whose people were gathered from many nations to the mountains of Israel, which had long been desolate. They had been brought out from the nations, and now all of them live in safety. 9You and all your troops and the many nations with you will go up, advancing like a storm; you will be like a cloud covering the land.

10“ ‘This is what the Sovereign LORD says: On that day thoughts will come into your mind and you will devise an evil scheme. 11You will say, “I will invade a land of unwalled villages; I will attack a peaceful and unsuspecting people—all of them living without walls and without gates and bars. 12I will plunder and loot and turn my hand against the resettled ruins and the people gathered from the nations, rich in livestock and goods, living at the center of the land.” 13Sheba and Dedan and the merchants of Tarshish and all her villages[o] will say to you, “Have you come to plunder? Have you gathered your hordes to loot, to carry off silver and gold, to take away livestock and goods and to seize much plunder?” ’

14“Therefore, son of man, prophesy and say to Gog: ‘This is what the Sovereign LORD says: In that day, when my people Israel are living in safety, will you not take notice of it? 15You will come from your place in the far north, you and many nations with you, all of them riding on horses, a great horde, a mighty army. 16You will advance against my people Israel like a cloud that covers the land. In days to come, O Gog, I will bring you against my land, so that the nations may know me when I show myself holy through you before their eyes.

17“ ‘This is what the Sovereign LORD says: Are you not the one I spoke of in former days by my servants the prophets of Israel? At that time they prophesied for years that I would bring you against them. 18This is what will happen in that day: When Gog attacks the land of Israel, my hot anger will be aroused, declares the Sovereign LORD. 19In my zeal and fiery wrath I declare that at that time there shall be a great earthquake in the land of Israel. 20The fish of the sea, the birds of the air, the beasts of the field, every creature that moves along the ground, and all the people on the face of the earth will tremble at my presence. The mountains will be overturned, the cliffs will crumble and every wall will fall to the ground. 21I will summon a sword against Gog on all my mountains, declares the Sovereign LORD. Every man's sword will be against his brother. 22I will execute judgment upon him with plague and bloodshed; I will pour down torrents of rain, hailstones and burning sulfur on him and on his troops and on the many nations with him. 23And so I will show my greatness and my holiness, and I will make myself known in the sight of many nations. Then they will know that I am the LORD.’

39 “Son of man, prophesy against Gog and say: ‘This is what the Sovereign LORD says: I am against you, O Gog, chief prince of[m] Meshech and Tubal. 2I will turn you around and drag you along. I will bring you from the far north and send you against the mountains of Israel. 3Then I will strike your bow

[l]2 Or *the prince of Rosh,* [m]3,1 Or *Gog, prince of Rosh,* [n]5 That is, the upper Nile region [o]13 Or *her strong lions*

from your left hand and make your arrows drop
from your right hand. 4On the mountains of Is-
rael you will fall, you and all your troops and the
nations with you. I will give you as food to all
kinds of carrion birds and to the wild animals.
5You will fall in the open field, for I have spoken,
declares the Sovereign LORD. 6I will send fire on
Magog and on those who live in safety in the
coastlands, and they will know that I am the
LORD.

7" 'I will make known my holy name among my
people Israel. I will no longer let my holy name
be profaned, and the nations will know that I the
LORD am the Holy One in Israel. 8It is coming!
It will surely take place, declares the Sovereign
LORD. This is the day I have spoken of.

9" 'Then those who live in the towns of Israel
will go out and use the weapons for fuel and burn
them up—the small and large shields, the bows
and arrows, the war clubs and spears. For seven
years they will use them for fuel. 10They will not
need to gather wood from the fields or cut it from
the forests, because they will use the weapons for
fuel. And they will plunder those who plundered
them and loot those who looted them, declares
the Sovereign LORD.

11" 'On that day I will give Gog a burial place in
Israel, in the valley of those who travel east to-
ward[p] the Sea.[q] It will block the way of travel-
ers, because Gog and all his hordes will be buried
there. So it will be called the Valley of Hamon
Gog.[r]

12" 'For seven months the house of Israel will
be burying them in order to cleanse the land.
13All the people of the land will bury them, and
the day I am glorified will be a memorable day for
them, declares the Sovereign LORD.

14" 'Men will be regularly employed to cleanse
the land. Some will go throughout the land and,
in addition to them, others will bury those that
remain on the ground. At the end of the seven
months they will begin their search. 15As they go
through the land and one of them sees a human
bone, he will set up a marker beside it until the
gravediggers have buried it in the Valley of Ha-
mon Gog. 16(Also a town called Hamonah[s] will
be there.) And so they will cleanse the land.'

17"Son of man, this is what the Sovereign LORD
says: Call out to every kind of bird and all the
wild animals: 'Assemble and come together from
all around to the sacrifice I am preparing for you,
the great sacrifice on the mountains of Israel.
There you will eat flesh and drink blood. 18You
will eat the flesh of mighty men and drink the
blood of the princes of the earth as if they were
rams and lambs, goats and bulls—all of them fat-
tened animals from Bashan. 19At the sacrifice I am
preparing for you, you will eat fat till you are
glutted and drink blood till you are drunk. 20At
my table you will eat your fill of horses and rid-
ers, mighty men and soldiers of every kind,' de-
clares the Sovereign LORD.

21"I will display my glory among the nations,
and all the nations will see the punishment I in-
flict and the hand I lay upon them. 22From that
day forward the house of Israel will know that I
am the LORD their God. 23And the nations will
know that the people of Israel went into exile for
their sin, because they were unfaithful to me. So
I hid my face from them and handed them over to
their enemies, and they all fell by the sword. 24I
dealt with them according to their uncleanness
and their offenses, and I hid my face from them.

25"Therefore this is what the Sovereign LORD
says: I will now bring Jacob back from captivity[t]
and will have compassion on all the people of
Israel, and I will be zealous for my holy name.
26They will forget their shame and all the unfaith-
fulness they showed toward me when they lived
in safety in their land with no one to make them
afraid. 27When I have brought them back from
the nations and have gathered them from the
countries of their enemies, I will show myself
holy through them in the sight of many nations.
28Then they will know that I am the LORD their
God, for though I sent them into exile among the
nations, I will gather them to their own land, not
leaving any behind. 29I will no longer hide my
face from them, for I will pour out my Spirit on
the house of Israel, declares the Sovereign LORD."

[p]11 Or *of* [q]11 That is, the Dead Sea [r]11 *Hamon Gog* means *hordes of Gog.* [s]16 *Hamonah* means *horde.* [t]25 Or *now restore the fortunes of Jacob*

14 / *Ezekiel 40—41*
The New Temple

EZEKIEL'S SPIRITUAL PILGRIMAGE was a parable of the experience of the Israelites in exile. He was removed from his ministry as priest in the temple and plunged into exile. There, stripped of his old securities, he was led by God to consider in parable, allegory and vision, the sin of Jerusalem, the holiness and otherness of God. Then Ezekiel suffered the loss of his beloved wife (24:15-24), a prophetic symbol of the speechless grief to be experienced by the exiles when their beloved Jerusalem would finally fall in 587 B.C. Now there was nothing left but God himself, the greatest treasure of all. So the last section of the book, chapters 40—48, is pure contemplation. The vision of the restored temple, the ideal Jerusalem and the renewed creation take us beyond "the things of God" to attend to God himself.

Warming Up to God What comes to your mind when you think of heaven?

Read Ezekiel 40—41.

40 In the twenty-fifth year of our exile, at the beginning of the year, on the tenth of the month, in the fourteenth year after the fall of the city—on that very day the hand of the LORD was upon me and he took me there. 2 In visions of God he took me to the land of Israel and set me on a very high mountain, on whose south side were some buildings that looked like a city. 3 He took me there, and I saw a man whose appearance was like bronze; he was standing in the gateway with a linen cord and a measuring rod in his hand. 4 The man said to me, "Son of man, look with your eyes and hear with your ears and pay attention to everything I am going to show you, for that is why you have been brought here. Tell the house of Israel everything you see."

5 I saw a wall completely surrounding the temple area. The length of the measuring rod in the man's hand was six long cubits, each of which was a cubit[u] and a handbreadth.[v] He measured the wall; it was one measuring rod thick and one rod high.

6 Then he went to the gate facing east. He climbed its steps and measured the threshold of the gate; it was one rod deep.[w] 7 The alcoves for the guards were one rod long and one rod wide, and the projecting walls between the alcoves were five cubits thick. And the threshold of the gate next to the portico facing the temple was one rod deep.

8 Then he measured the portico of the gateway; 9 it[x] was eight cubits deep and its jambs were two cubits thick. The portico of the gateway faced the temple.

10 Inside the east gate were three alcoves on each side; the three had the same measurements, and the faces of the projecting walls on each side had the same measurements. 11 Then he measured the width of the entrance to the gateway; it was ten cubits and its length was thirteen cubits. 12 In front of each alcove was a wall one cubit high, and the alcoves were six cubits square. 13 Then he measured the gateway from the top of the rear wall of one alcove to the top of the opposite one; the distance was twenty-five cubits from one parapet opening to the opposite one. 14 He measured along the faces of the projecting walls all around the inside of the gateway—sixty cubits. The measurement was up to the portico[y] facing the courtyard.[z] 15 The distance from the entrance of the gateway to the far end of its portico was fifty cubits. 16 The alcoves and the projecting walls inside the gateway were surmounted by narrow parapet openings all around, as was the portico; the openings all around faced inward. The faces of the projecting walls were decorated with palm trees.

17 Then he brought me into the outer court. There I saw some rooms and a pavement that had been constructed all around the court; there were thirty rooms along the pavement. 18 It abutted the sides of the gateways and was as wide as they were long; this was the lower pavement. 19 Then he measured the distance from the inside of the

[u]5 The common cubit was about 1 1/2 feet (about 0.5 meter). [v]5 That is, about 3 inches (about 8 centimeters) [w]6 Septuagint; Hebrew *deep, the first threshold, one rod deep* [x]8,9 Many Hebrew manuscripts, Septuagint, Vulgate and Syriac; most Hebrew manuscripts *gateway facing the temple; it was one rod deep. 9Then he measured the portico of the gateway; it* [y]14 Septuagint; Hebrew *projecting wall* [z]14 The meaning of the Hebrew for this verse is uncertain.

lower gateway to the outside of the inner court; it
was a hundred cubits on the east side as well as
on the north.
20Then he measured the length and width of
the gate facing north, leading into the outer court.
21Its alcoves—three on each side—its projecting
walls and its portico had the same measurements
as those of the first gateway. It was fifty cubits
long and twenty-five cubits wide. 22Its openings,
its portico and its palm tree decorations had the
same measurements as those of the gate facing
east. Seven steps led up to it, with its portico
opposite them. 23There was a gate to the inner
court facing the north gate, just as there was on
the east. He measured from one gate to the oppo-
site one; it was a hundred cubits.
24Then he led me to the south side and I saw a
gate facing south. He measured its jambs and its
portico, and they had the same measurements as
the others. 25The gateway and its portico had nar-
row openings all around, like the openings of the
others. It was fifty cubits long and twenty-five
cubits wide. 26Seven steps led up to it, with its
portico opposite them; it had palm tree decora-
tions on the faces of the projecting walls on each
side. 27The inner court also had a gate facing
south, and he measured from this gate to the
outer gate on the south side; it was a hundred
cubits.
28Then he brought me into the inner court
through the south gate, and he measured the
south gate; it had the same measurements as the
others. 29Its alcoves, its projecting walls and its
portico had the same measurements as the others.
The gateway and its portico had openings all
around. It was fifty cubits long and twenty-five
cubits wide. 30(The porticoes of the gateways
around the inner court were twenty-five cubits
wide and five cubits deep.) 31Its portico faced the
outer court; palm trees decorated its jambs, and
eight steps led up to it.
32Then he brought me to the inner court on the
east side, and he measured the gateway; it had the
same measurements as the others. 33Its alcoves,
its projecting walls and its portico had the same
measurements as the others. The gateway and its
portico had openings all around. It was fifty cu-
bits long and twenty-five cubits wide. 34Its por-
tico faced the outer court; palm trees decorated
the jambs on either side, and eight steps led up
to it.
35Then he brought me to the north gate and
measured it. It had the same measurements as the
others, 36as did its alcoves, its projecting walls
and its portico, and it had openings all around. It
was fifty cubits long and twenty-five cubits wide.
37Its portico[a] faced the outer court; palm trees
decorated the jambs on either side, and eight
steps led up to it.
38A room with a doorway was by the portico in
each of the inner gateways, where the burnt offer-
ings were washed. 39In the portico of the gateway
were two tables on each side, on which the burnt
offerings, sin offerings and guilt offerings were
slaughtered. 40By the outside wall of the portico
of the gateway, near the steps at the entrance to
the north gateway were two tables, and on the
other side of the steps were two tables. 41So there
were four tables on one side of the gateway and
four on the other—eight tables in all—on which
the sacrifices were slaughtered. 42There were also
four tables of dressed stone for the burnt offer-
ings, each a cubit and a half long, a cubit and a
half wide and a cubit high. On them were placed
the utensils for slaughtering the burnt offerings
and the other sacrifices. 43And double-pronged
hooks, each a handbreadth long, were attached to
the wall all around. The tables were for the flesh
of the offerings.
44Outside the inner gate, within the inner
court, were two rooms, one[b] at the side of the
north gate and facing south, and another at the
side of the south[c] gate and facing north. 45He
said to me, "The room facing south is for the
priests who have charge of the temple, 46and the
room facing north is for the priests who have
charge of the altar. These are the sons of Zadok,
who are the only Levites who may draw near to
the LORD to minister before him."
47Then he measured the court: It was square—
a hundred cubits long and a hundred cubits wide.
And the altar was in front of the temple.
48He brought me to the portico of the temple
and measured the jambs of the portico; they were
five cubits wide on either side. The width of the
entrance was fourteen cubits and its projecting
walls were[d] three cubits wide on either side.
49The portico was twenty cubits wide, and
twelve[e] cubits from front to back. It was reached

[a] 37 Septuagint (see also verses 31 and 34); Hebrew *jambs*
[b] 44 Septuagint; Hebrew *were rooms for singers, which were*
[c] 44 Septuagint; Hebrew *east*
[d] 48 Septuagint; Hebrew *entrance was*
[e] 49 Septuagint; Hebrew *eleven*

by a flight of stairs,[f] and there were pillars on each side of the jambs.

41

Then the man brought me to the outer sanctuary and measured the jambs; the width of the jambs was six cubits[g] on each side.[h] 2The entrance was ten cubits wide, and the projecting walls on each side of it were five cubits wide. He also measured the outer sanctuary; it was forty cubits long and twenty cubits wide.

3Then he went into the inner sanctuary and measured the jambs of the entrance; each was two cubits wide. The entrance was six cubits wide, and the projecting walls on each side of it were seven cubits wide. 4And he measured the length of the inner sanctuary; it was twenty cubits, and its width was twenty cubits across the end of the outer sanctuary. He said to me, "This is the Most Holy Place."

5Then he measured the wall of the temple; it was six cubits thick, and each side room around the temple was four cubits wide. 6The side rooms were on three levels, one above another, thirty on each level. There were ledges all around the wall of the temple to serve as supports for the side rooms, so that the supports were not inserted into the wall of the temple. 7The side rooms all around the temple were wider at each successive level. The structure surrounding the temple was built in ascending stages, so that the rooms widened as one went upward. A stairway went up from the lowest floor to the top floor through the middle floor.

8I saw that the temple had a raised base all around it, forming the foundation of the side rooms. It was the length of the rod, six long cubits. 9The outer wall of the side rooms was five cubits thick. The open area between the side rooms of the temple 10and the ⌞priests'⌟ rooms was twenty cubits wide all around the temple. 11There were entrances to the side rooms from the open area, one on the north and another on the south; and the base adjoining the open area was five cubits wide all around.

12The building facing the temple courtyard on the west side was seventy cubits wide. The wall of the building was five cubits thick all around, and its length was ninety cubits.

13Then he measured the temple; it was a hundred cubits long, and the temple courtyard and the building with its walls were also a hundred cubits long. 14The width of the temple courtyard on the east, including the front of the temple, was a hundred cubits.

15Then he measured the length of the building facing the courtyard at the rear of the temple, including its galleries on each side; it was a hundred cubits.

The outer sanctuary, the inner sanctuary and the portico facing the court, 16as well as the thresholds and the narrow windows and galleries around the three of them—everything beyond and including the threshold was covered with wood. The floor, the wall up to the windows, and the windows were covered. 17In the space above the outside of the entrance to the inner sanctuary and on the walls at regular intervals all around the inner and outer sanctuary 18were carved cherubim and palm trees. Palm trees alternated with cherubim. Each cherub had two faces: 19the face of a man toward the palm tree on one side and the face of a lion toward the palm tree on the other. They were carved all around the whole temple. 20From the floor to the area above the entrance, cherubim and palm trees were carved on the wall of the outer sanctuary.

21The outer sanctuary had a rectangular doorframe, and the one at the front of the Most Holy Place was similar. 22There was a wooden altar three cubits high and two cubits square[i]; its corners, its base[j] and its sides were of wood. The man said to me, "This is the table that is before the LORD." 23Both the outer sanctuary and the Most Holy Place had double doors. 24Each door had two leaves—two hinged leaves for each door. 25And on the doors of the outer sanctuary were carved cherubim and palm trees like those carved on the walls, and there was a wooden overhang on the front of the portico. 26On the sidewalls of the portico were narrow windows with palm trees carved on each side. The side rooms of the temple also had overhangs.

f49 Hebrew; Septuagint *Ten steps led up to it* g1 The common cubit was about 1 1/2 feet (about 0.5 meter). h1 One Hebrew manuscript and Septuagint; most Hebrew manuscripts *side, the width of the tent* i22 Septuagint; Hebrew *long* j22 Septuagint; Hebrew *length*

Discovering the Word 1. To better picture the temple take a look at the diagram in the introduction. The renewed temple of Ezekiel's vision was perfectly symmetrical and designed to exalt the holiness of God. Everything was a perfect fit in this ideal dwelling place for God. For whose benefit is Ezekiel shown this vision? 2. Take a look at the temple diagram. What is striking to you about the temple? 3. How would this physical space encourage worship? 4. The elaborate description of the temple has been interpreted by Christians in four ways: (1) as a prophetic blueprint of what Ezekiel intended to have rebuilt when the exiles would finally return to Jerusalem, (2) as symbolic of the spiritual reality of the Christian church, (3) as a literal future temple that will be built in the last times when Israel is consummated in the kingdom age with Jesus, and (4) as an accepted apocalyptic piece of literature which uses highly symbolic language to express realities that will be experienced when the story of God's people is brought to a worthy end with the coming of the Messiah. What would a vision like this have meant to the first readers? 5. Which interpretation does justice to the timelessness of Scripture, having a message for the Israelites in exile and Christians today longing for heaven?

Applying the Word 1. Revelation 21—22 draws heavily from the imagery of the new Jerusalem pictured in Ezekiel 40—48, but *without* the temple. Why would a future with a temple be essential for an Israelite "heaven," but a future without one be even more appropriate for followers of Jesus who want to dwell with him forever (Rev 21:22)? 2. What new meaning does this study bring to the Christian prayer "Come, Lord Jesus"?

Responding in Prayer In light of this passage, pray, "Your kingdom come, your will be done on earth as it is in heaven" (Mt 6:10).

Ezekiel 42

42 Then the man led me northward
into the outer court and brought
me to the rooms opposite the tem-
ple courtyard and opposite the outer wall on the
north side. 2The building whose door faced north
was a hundred cubits[k] long and fifty cubits wide.
3Both in the section twenty cubits from the inner
court and in the section opposite the pavement of
the outer court, gallery faced gallery at the three
levels. 4In front of the rooms was an inner pas-
sageway ten cubits wide and a hundred cubits[l]
long. Their doors were on the north. 5Now the
upper rooms were narrower, for the galleries took
more space from them than from the rooms on
the lower and middle floors of the building. 6The
rooms on the third floor had no pillars, as the
courts had; so they were smaller in floor space
than those on the lower and middle floors. 7There
was an outer wall parallel to the rooms and the
outer court; it extended in front of the rooms for
fifty cubits. 8While the row of rooms on the side
next to the outer court was fifty cubits long, the
row on the side nearest the sanctuary was a hun-
dred cubits long. 9The lower rooms had an en-
trance on the east side as one enters them from
the outer court.

10On the south side[m] along the length of the
wall of the outer court, adjoining the temple
courtyard and opposite the outer wall, were
rooms 11with a passageway in front of them.
These were like the rooms on the north; they had
the same length and width, with similar exits and
dimensions. Similar to the doorways on the north
12were the doorways of the rooms on the south.
There was a doorway at the beginning of the pas-
sageway that was parallel to the corresponding
wall extending eastward, by which one enters the
rooms.

13Then he said to me, "The north and south
rooms facing the temple courtyard are the priests'
rooms, where the priests who approach the LORD
will eat the most holy offerings. There they will
put the most holy offerings—the grain offerings,
the sin offerings and the guilt offerings—for the
place is holy. 14Once the priests enter the holy
precincts, they are not to go into the outer court
until they leave behind the garments in which
they minister, for these are holy. They are to put
on other clothes before they go near the places
that are for the people."

15When he had finished measuring what was
inside the temple area, he led me out by the east
gate and measured the area all around: 16He mea-
sured the east side with the measuring rod; it was
five hundred cubits.[n] 17He measured the north

[k]2 The common cubit was about 1 1/2 feet (about 0.5 meter).
[l]4 Septuagint and Syriac; Hebrew *and one cubit* [m]10 Septuagint; Hebrew *Eastward* [n]16 See Septuagint of verse 17; Hebrew *rods*; also in verses 18 and 19.

side; it was five hundred cubits[o] by the measuring rod. [18]He measured the south side; it was five hundred cubits by the measuring rod. [19]Then he turned to the west side and measured; it was five hundred cubits by the measuring rod. [20]So he measured the area on all four sides. It had a wall around it, five hundred cubits long and five hundred cubits wide, to separate the holy from the common.

[o]17 Septuagint; Hebrew *rods*

15 / *Ezekiel 43:1–12* The God Who Dwells with His People

NINETEEN YEARS EARLIER (10:18–22; 11:22–24) Ezekiel had seen the glory of the Lord leaving the temple. Then the temple was destroyed. God gave Ezekiel an empowering vision of a renewed temple. But the building would be an empty shell without God's presence. Ezekiel's faith would also be empty without direct experience of God. So Ezekiel is given a second direct encounter with God like the one at the Kebar River in Babylon. As with all true encounters with God, this one means more than getting a personal blessing.

Warming Up to God Does the thought of firsthand encounter with God frighten you or attract you? Why?

Read Ezekiel 43:1–12.

43 Then the man brought me to the gate facing east, [2]and I saw the glory of the God of Israel coming from the east. His voice was like the roar of rushing waters, and the land was radiant with his glory. [3]The vision I saw was like the vision I had seen when he[p] came to destroy the city and like the visions I had seen by the Kebar River, and I fell facedown. [4]The glory of the LORD entered the temple through the gate facing east. [5]Then the Spirit lifted me up and brought me into the inner court, and the glory of the LORD filled the temple.

[6]While the man was standing beside me, I heard someone speaking to me from inside the temple. [7]He said: "Son of man, this is the place of my throne and the place for the soles of my feet. This is where I will live among the Israelites forever. The house of Israel will never again defile my holy name—neither they nor their kings—by their prostitution[q] and the lifeless idols[r] of their kings at their high places. [8]When they placed their threshold next to my threshold and their doorposts beside my doorposts, with only a wall between me and them, they defiled my holy name by their detestable practices. So I destroyed them in my anger. [9]Now let them put away from me their prostitution and the lifeless idols of their kings, and I will live among them forever.

[10]"Son of man, describe the temple to the people of Israel, that they may be ashamed of their sins. Let them consider the plan, [11]and if they are ashamed of all they have done, make known to them the design of the temple—its arrangement, its exits and entrances—its whole design and all its regulations[s] and laws. Write these down before them so that they may be faithful to its design and follow all its regulations.

[12]"This is the law of the temple: All the surrounding area on top of the mountain will be most holy. Such is the law of the temple.

[p]3 Some Hebrew manuscripts and Vulgate; most Hebrew manuscripts *I* [q]7 Or *their spiritual adultery*; also in verse 9 [r]7 Or *the corpses*; also in verse 9 [s]11 Some Hebrew manuscripts and Septuagint; most Hebrew manuscripts *regulations and its whole design*

Discovering the Word 1. What sights, sounds, words and movement contribute to Ezekiel's sense of overpowering awe (vv. 1–5)? 2. What does God say to Ezekiel (vv. 6–9)? 3. What is God's declared reason for trusting this vision to Ezekiel (vv. 10–12)? 4. What needs among the Israelites in exile would be met by the Lord's summary statement "This is where I will live among the Israelites forever" (v. 7)? 5. The law of the temple

(v. 12) is the principle of holiness. From what we have studied in Ezekiel thus far, what will dwelling with God require of those who hunger for God's presence?

Applying the Word 1. Malcolm Muggeridge said, "Only the heavenly-minded are of real earthly use. Those who made the most difference in this world are precisely those who longed most for the next." Do you agree or disagree? Why? 2. The holiness of the temple was secured by courts, walls, barriers and restrictions. Now that the barriers have been removed in Christ, on what conditions may we draw near to God in his glory (Heb 7:24–25; 10:14; 1Pe 2:5)? 3. What conditions for drawing near God remain (Heb 10:19–25)?

Responding in Prayer Pray that you will know the Lord better, drawing near with a sincere heart and being prepared to put aside all that disgraces God's holiness.

Ezekiel 43:13—46:24

13"These are the measurements of the altar in long cubits, that cubit being a cubit[t] and a handbreadth[u]: Its gutter is a cubit deep and a cubit wide, with a rim of one span[v] around the edge. And this is the height of the altar: 14From the gutter on the ground up to the lower ledge it is two cubits high and a cubit wide, and from the smaller ledge up to the larger ledge it is four cubits high and a cubit wide. 15The altar hearth is four cubits high, and four horns project upward from the hearth. 16The altar hearth is square, twelve cubits long and twelve cubits wide. 17The upper ledge also is square, fourteen cubits long and fourteen cubits wide, with a rim of half a cubit and a gutter of a cubit all around. The steps of the altar face east."

18Then he said to me, "Son of man, this is what the Sovereign LORD says: These will be the regulations for sacrificing burnt offerings and sprinkling blood upon the altar when it is built: 19You are to give a young bull as a sin offering to the priests, who are Levites, of the family of Zadok, who come near to minister before me, declares the Sovereign LORD. 20You are to take some of its blood and put it on the four horns of the altar and on the four corners of the upper ledge and all around the rim, and so purify the altar and make atonement for it. 21You are to take the bull for the sin offering and burn it in the designated part of the temple area outside the sanctuary.

22"On the second day you are to offer a male goat without defect for a sin offering, and the altar is to be purified as it was purified with the bull. 23When you have finished purifying it, you are to offer a young bull and a ram from the flock, both without defect. 24You are to offer them before the LORD, and the priests are to sprinkle salt on them and sacrifice them as a burnt offering to the LORD.

25"For seven days you are to provide a male goat daily for a sin offering; you are also to provide a young bull and a ram from the flock, both without defect. 26For seven days they are to make atonement for the altar and cleanse it; thus they will dedicate it. 27At the end of these days, from the eighth day on, the priests are to present your burnt offerings and fellowship offerings[w] on the altar. Then I will accept you, declares the Sovereign LORD."

44

Then the man brought me back to the outer gate of the sanctuary, the one facing east, and it was shut. 2The LORD said to me, "This gate is to remain shut. It must not be opened; no one may enter through it. It is to remain shut because the LORD, the God of Israel, has entered through it. 3The prince himself is the only one who may sit inside the gateway to eat in the presence of the LORD. He is to enter by way of the portico of the gateway and go out the same way."

4Then the man brought me by way of the north gate to the front of the temple. I looked and saw the glory of the LORD filling the temple of the LORD, and I fell facedown.

5The LORD said to me, "Son of man, look carefully, listen closely and give attention to everything I tell you concerning all the regulations regarding the temple of the LORD. Give attention to the entrance of the temple and all the exits of the sanctuary. 6Say to the rebellious house of Israel, 'This is what the Sovereign LORD says: Enough of your detestable practices, O house of Israel! 7In

[t] 13 The common cubit was about 1 1/2 feet (about 0.5 meter).
[u] 13 That is, about 3 inches (about 8 centimeters) [v] 13 That is, about 9 inches (about 22 centimeters) [w] 27 Traditionally *peace offerings*

addition to all your other detestable practices, you brought foreigners uncircumcised in heart and flesh into my sanctuary, desecrating my temple while you offered me food, fat and blood, and you broke my covenant. 8Instead of carrying out your duty in regard to my holy things, you put others in charge of my sanctuary. 9This is what the Sovereign LORD says: No foreigner uncircumcised in heart and flesh is to enter my sanctuary, not even the foreigners who live among the Israelites.

10" 'The Levites who went far from me when Israel went astray and who wandered from me after their idols must bear the consequences of their sin. 11They may serve in my sanctuary, having charge of the gates of the temple and serving in it; they may slaughter the burnt offerings and sacrifices for the people and stand before the people and serve them. 12But because they served them in the presence of their idols and made the house of Israel fall into sin, therefore I have sworn with uplifted hand that they must bear the consequences of their sin, declares the Sovereign LORD. 13They are not to come near to serve me as priests or come near any of my holy things or my most holy offerings; they must bear the shame of their detestable practices. 14Yet I will put them in charge of the duties of the temple and all the work that is to be done in it.

15" 'But the priests, who are Levites and descendants of Zadok and who faithfully carried out the duties of my sanctuary when the Israelites went astray from me, are to come near to minister before me; they are to stand before me to offer sacrifices of fat and blood, declares the Sovereign LORD. 16They alone are to enter my sanctuary; they alone are to come near my table to minister before me and perform my service.

17" 'When they enter the gates of the inner court, they are to wear linen clothes; they must not wear any woolen garment while ministering at the gates of the inner court or inside the temple. 18They are to wear linen turbans on their heads and linen undergarments around their waists. They must not wear anything that makes them perspire. 19When they go out into the outer court where the people are, they are to take off the clothes they have been ministering in and are to leave them in the sacred rooms, and put on other clothes, so that they do not consecrate the people by means of their garments.

20" 'They must not shave their heads or let their hair grow long, but they are to keep the hair of their heads trimmed. 21No priest is to drink wine when he enters the inner court. 22They must not marry widows or divorced women; they may marry only virgins of Israelite descent or widows of priests. 23They are to teach my people the difference between the holy and the common and show them how to distinguish between the unclean and the clean.

24" 'In any dispute, the priests are to serve as judges and decide it according to my ordinances. They are to keep my laws and my decrees for all my appointed feasts, and they are to keep my Sabbaths holy.

25" 'A priest must not defile himself by going near a dead person; however, if the dead person was his father or mother, son or daughter, brother or unmarried sister, then he may defile himself. 26After he is cleansed, he must wait seven days. 27On the day he goes into the inner court of the sanctuary to minister in the sanctuary, he is to offer a sin offering for himself, declares the Sovereign LORD.

28" 'I am to be the only inheritance the priests have. You are to give them no possession in Israel; I will be their possession. 29They will eat the grain offerings, the sin offerings and the guilt offerings; and everything in Israel devoted[x] to the LORD will belong to them. 30The best of all the firstfruits and of all your special gifts will belong to the priests. You are to give them the first portion of your ground meal so that a blessing may rest on your household. 31The priests must not eat anything, bird or animal, found dead or torn by wild animals.

45

" 'When you allot the land as an inheritance, you are to present to the LORD a portion of the land as a sacred district, 25,000 cubits long and 20,000[y] cubits wide; the entire area will be holy. 2Of this, a section 500 cubits square is to be for the sanctuary, with 50 cubits around it for open land. 3In the sacred district, measure off a section 25,000 cubits[z] long and 10,000 cubits[a] wide. In it will be the sanctuary, the Most Holy Place. 4It will be the sacred portion of the land for the priests, who minister in the sanctuary and who draw near to minister before the LORD. It will be a place for their houses as well as a holy place for the sanctu-

x29 The Hebrew term refers to the irrevocable giving over of things or persons to the LORD. y1 Septuagint (see also verses 3 and 5 and 48:9); Hebrew *10,000* z3 That is, about 7 miles (about 12 kilometers) a3 That is, about 3 miles (about 5 kilometers)

ary. 5An area 25,000 cubits long and 10,000 cubits wide will belong to the Levites, who serve in the temple, as their possession for towns to live in.[b]

6" 'You are to give the city as its property an area 5,000 cubits wide and 25,000 cubits long, adjoining the sacred portion; it will belong to the whole house of Israel.

7" 'The prince will have the land bordering each side of the area formed by the sacred district and the property of the city. It will extend westward from the west side and eastward from the east side, running lengthwise from the western to the eastern border parallel to one of the tribal portions. 8This land will be his possession in Israel. And my princes will no longer oppress my people but will allow the house of Israel to possess the land according to their tribes.

9" 'This is what the Sovereign LORD says: You have gone far enough, O princes of Israel! Give up your violence and oppression and do what is just and right. Stop dispossessing my people, declares the Sovereign LORD. 10You are to use accurate scales, an accurate ephah[c] and an accurate bath.[d] 11The ephah and the bath are to be the same size, the bath containing a tenth of a homer[e] and the ephah a tenth of a homer; the homer is to be the standard measure for both. 12The shekel[f] is to consist of twenty gerahs. Twenty shekels plus twenty-five shekels plus fifteen shekels equal one mina.[g]

13" 'This is the special gift you are to offer: a sixth of an ephah from each homer of wheat and a sixth of an ephah from each homer of barley. 14The prescribed portion of oil, measured by the bath, is a tenth of a bath from each cor (which consists of ten baths or one homer, for ten baths are equivalent to a homer). 15Also one sheep is to be taken from every flock of two hundred from the well-watered pastures of Israel. These will be used for the grain offerings, burnt offerings and fellowship offerings[h] to make atonement for the people, declares the Sovereign LORD. 16All the people of the land will participate in this special gift for the use of the prince in Israel. 17It will be the duty of the prince to provide the burnt offerings, grain offerings and drink offerings at the festivals, the New Moons and the Sabbaths—at all the appointed feasts of the house of Israel. He will provide the sin offerings, grain offerings, burnt offerings and fellowship offerings to make atonement for the house of Israel.

18" 'This is what the Sovereign LORD says: In the first month on the first day you are to take a young bull without defect and purify the sanctuary. 19The priest is to take some of the blood of the sin offering and put it on the doorposts of the temple, on the four corners of the upper ledge of the altar and on the gateposts of the inner court. 20You are to do the same on the seventh day of the month for anyone who sins unintentionally or through ignorance; so you are to make atonement for the temple.

21" 'In the first month on the fourteenth day you are to observe the Passover, a feast lasting seven days, during which you shall eat bread made without yeast. 22On that day the prince is to provide a bull as a sin offering for himself and for all the people of the land. 23Every day during the seven days of the Feast he is to provide seven bulls and seven rams without defect as a burnt offering to the LORD, and a male goat for a sin offering. 24He is to provide as a grain offering an ephah for each bull and an ephah for each ram, along with a hin[i] of oil for each ephah.

25" 'During the seven days of the Feast, which begins in the seventh month on the fifteenth day, he is to make the same provision for sin offerings, burnt offerings, grain offerings and oil.

46

" 'This is what the Sovereign LORD says: The gate of the inner court facing east is to be shut on the six working days, but on the Sabbath day and on the day of the New Moon it is to be opened. 2The prince is to enter from the outside through the portico of the gateway and stand by the gatepost. The priests are to sacrifice his burnt offering and his fellowship offerings.[j] He is to worship at the threshold of the gateway and then go out, but the gate will not be shut until evening. 3On the Sabbaths and New Moons the people of the land are to worship in the presence of the LORD at the entrance to that gateway. 4The burnt offering the prince brings to the LORD on the Sabbath day is to be six male lambs and a ram, all without defect. 5The grain offering given with the ram is to be an ephah,[k] and the grain offering with the lambs is to be as much as he pleases, along with a hin[l] of

[b]5 Septuagint; Hebrew *temple; they will have as their possession 20 rooms* [c]*10* An ephah was a dry measure. [d]*10* A bath was a liquid measure. [e]*11* A homer was a dry measure. [f]*12* A shekel weighed about 2/5 ounce (about 11.5 grams). [g]*12* That is, 60 shekels; the common mina was 50 shekels. [h]*15* Traditionally *peace offerings*; also in verse 17 [i]*24,5* That is, probably about 4 quarts (about 4 liters) [j]*2* Traditionally *peace offerings*; also in verse 12 [k]*5* That is, probably about 3/5 bushel (about 22 liters)

oil for each ephah. 6On the day of the New Moon he is to offer a young bull, six lambs and a ram, all without defect. 7He is to provide as a grain offering one ephah with the bull, one ephah with the ram, and with the lambs as much as he wants to give, along with a hin of oil with each ephah. 8When the prince enters, he is to go in through the portico of the gateway, and he is to come out the same way.

9" 'When the people of the land come before the LORD at the appointed feasts, whoever enters by the north gate to worship is to go out the south gate; and whoever enters by the south gate is to go out the north gate. No one is to return through the gate by which he entered, but each is to go out the opposite gate. 10The prince is to be among them, going in when they go in and going out when they go out.

11" 'At the festivals and the appointed feasts, the grain offering is to be an ephah with a bull, an ephah with a ram, and with the lambs as much as one pleases, along with a hin of oil for each ephah. 12When the prince provides a freewill offering to the LORD—whether a burnt offering or fellowship offerings—the gate facing east is to be opened for him. He shall offer his burnt offering or his fellowship offerings as he does on the Sabbath day. Then he shall go out, and after he has gone out, the gate will be shut.

13" 'Every day you are to provide a year-old lamb without defect for a burnt offering to the LORD; morning by morning you shall provide it. 14You are also to provide with it morning by morning a grain offering, consisting of a sixth of an ephah with a third of a hin of oil to moisten the flour. The presenting of this grain offering to the LORD is a lasting ordinance. 15So the lamb and the grain offering and the oil shall be provided morning by morning for a regular burnt offering.

16" 'This is what the Sovereign LORD says: If the prince makes a gift from his inheritance to one of his sons, it will also belong to his descendants; it is to be their property by inheritance. 17If, however, he makes a gift from his inheritance to one of his servants, the servant may keep it until the year of freedom; then it will revert to the prince. His inheritance belongs to his sons only; it is theirs. 18The prince must not take any of the inheritance of the people, driving them off their property. He is to give his sons their inheritance out of his own property, so that none of my people will be separated from his property.' "

19Then the man brought me through the entrance at the side of the gate to the sacred rooms facing north, which belonged to the priests, and showed me a place at the western end. 20He said to me, "This is the place where the priests will cook the guilt offering and the sin offering and bake the grain offering, to avoid bringing them into the outer court and consecrating the people."

21He then brought me to the outer court and led me around to its four corners, and I saw in each corner another court. 22In the four corners of the outer court were enclosed[l] courts, forty cubits long and thirty cubits wide; each of the courts in the four corners was the same size. 23Around the inside of each of the four courts was a ledge of stone, with places for fire built all around under the ledge. 24He said to me, "These are the kitchens where those who minister at the temple will cook the sacrifices of the people."

[l]22 The meaning of the Hebrew for this word is uncertain.

16/ *Ezekiel 47:1–12*
The Vision of a Renewed Creation

GEORGE BERNARD SHAW'S character Don Juan said, "Heaven is all right, of course. But for meeting old friends and acquaintances, you can't beat hell." He thus shows a complete misunderstanding of the attractiveness of heaven. In reality, heaven is no mere "pie in the sky by and by" but our true homeland: a total life in a total environment with the presence of God as the center and source of everything. Ezekiel's vision of the ultimate Temple, the new Jerusalem and the Israelites resettled in the redesigned land of Israel was the ultimate Old Testament hope. But drawing heavily on the imagery of Ezekiel, in Revelation 21—22 John depicts a completely renewed creation.

Warming Up to God What fears and hopes do you have when you consider the future of planet Earth?

Read Ezekiel 47:1-12.

47 The man brought me back to the
entrance of the temple, and I saw
water coming out from under the
threshold of the temple toward the east (for the
temple faced east). The water was coming down
from under the south side of the temple, south of
the altar. 2He then brought me out through the
north gate and led me around the outside to the
outer gate facing east, and the water was flowing
from the south side.
3As the man went eastward with a measuring
line in his hand, he measured off a thousand cu-
bits[m] and then led me through water that was
ankle-deep. 4He measured off another thousand
cubits and led me through water that was knee-
deep. He measured off another thousand and led
me through water that was up to the waist. 5He
measured off another thousand, but now it was a
river that I could not cross, because the water had
risen and was deep enough to swim in—a river
that no one could cross. 6He asked me, "Son of
man, do you see this?"
Then he led me back to the bank of the river.
7When I arrived there, I saw a great number of
trees on each side of the river. 8He said to me,
"This water flows toward the eastern region and
goes down into the Arabah,[n] where it enters the
Sea.[o] When it empties into the Sea,[o] the water
there becomes fresh. 9Swarms of living creatures
will live wherever the river flows. There will be
large numbers of fish, because this water flows
there and makes the salt water fresh; so where the
river flows everything will live. 10Fishermen will
stand along the shore; from En Gedi to En Eglaim
there will be places for spreading nets. The fish
will be of many kinds—like the fish of the Great
Sea.[p] 11But the swamps and marshes will not be-
come fresh; they will be left for salt. 12Fruit trees
of all kinds will grow on both banks of the river.
Their leaves will not wither, nor will their fruit
fail. Every month they will bear, because the wa-
ter from the sanctuary flows to them. Their fruit
will serve for food and their leaves for healing."

[m]3 That is, about 1,500 feet (about 450 meters) [n]8 Or *the Jordan Valley* [o]8 That is, the Dead Sea [p]10 That is, the Mediterranean; also in verses 15, 19 and 20

Discovering the Word 1. This passage is part of a larger section (43:13—48:35) which describes the arrangements for temple worship, the prince, Levites and priests, the division of the land with a kind of "green belt" separating the holy and the profane. What different elements of God's creation are a part of this picture of the temple? 2. What significant truths are communicated by this exquisitely beautiful vision? 3. Read Revelation 22:1-3. How does John draw on Ezekiel's vision now that Christ has been fully and finally revealed? 4. What evidence do we have that John is not giving us a literal description of the renewed land but a highly symbolic one: a figurative account of a literal future reality?

Applying the Word 1. What difference should this vision of a renewed creation (and not merely a renewed worship center) make to our stewardship of the created world? 2. How has this study changed your attitude toward heaven as your ultimate homeland? 3. How has your study of Ezekiel affected what it means to you "to know the Lord"?

Responding in Prayer Jesus says, "I am making everything new" (Rev 21:5), words which Ezekiel would have welcomed with all his heart. Thank God that he is determined to renew you, his people, and the entire creation.

Ezekiel 47:13—48:35

13This is what the Sovereign LORD says: "These are the boundaries by which you are to divide the land for an inheritance among the twelve tribes of Israel, with two portions for Joseph. 14You are to divide it equally among them. Because I swore with uplifted hand to give it to your forefathers, this land will become your inheritance.

15"This is to be the boundary of the land:

"On the north side it will run from the Great Sea by the Hethlon road past Lebo[q] Hamath to Zedad, 16Berothah[r] and Sibraim (which lies on the border between Damascus and Hamath), as far as Hazer Hatticon, which is on the border of Hauran. 17The boundary will extend from the sea to Hazar Enan,[s] along the northern border of Damascus, with the border of Hamath to the north. This will be the north boundary.

18"On the east side the boundary will run between Hauran and Damascus, along the Jordan between Gilead and the land of Israel, to the eastern sea and as far as Tamar.[t] This will be the east boundary.

19"On the south side it will run from Tamar as far as the waters of Meribah Kadesh, then along the Wadi ⌞of Egypt⌟ to the Great Sea. This will be the south boundary.

20"On the west side, the Great Sea will be the boundary to a point opposite Lebo[u] Hamath. This will be the west boundary.

21"You are to distribute this land among yourselves according to the tribes of Israel. 22You are to allot it as an inheritance for yourselves and for the aliens who have settled among you and who have children. You are to consider them as native-born Israelites; along with you they are to be allotted an inheritance among the tribes of Israel. 23In whatever tribe the alien settles, there you are to give him his inheritance," declares the Sovereign LORD.

48 "These are the tribes, listed by name: At the northern frontier, Dan will have one portion; it will follow the Hethlon road to Lebo[v] Hamath; Hazar Enan and the northern border of Damascus next to Hamath will be part of its border from the east side to the west side.

2"Asher will have one portion; it will border the territory of Dan from east to west.

3"Naphtali will have one portion; it will border the territory of Asher from east to west.

4"Manasseh will have one portion; it will border the territory of Naphtali from east to west.

5"Ephraim will have one portion; it will border the territory of Manasseh from east to west.

6"Reuben will have one portion; it will border the territory of Ephraim from east to west.

7"Judah will have one portion; it will border the territory of Reuben from east to west.

8"Bordering the territory of Judah from east to west will be the portion you are to present as a special gift. It will be 25,000 cubits[w] wide, and its length from east to west will equal one of the tribal portions; the sanctuary will be in the center of it.

9"The special portion you are to offer to the LORD will be 25,000 cubits long and 10,000 cubits[x] wide. 10This will be the sacred portion for the priests. It will be 25,000 cubits long on the north side, 10,000 cubits wide on the west side, 10,000 cubits wide on the east side and 25,000 cubits long on the south side. In the center of it will be the sanctuary of the LORD. 11This will be for the consecrated priests, the Zadokites, who were faithful in serving me and did not go astray as the Levites did when the Israelites went astray. 12It will be a special gift to them from the sacred portion of the land, a most holy portion, bordering the territory of the Levites.

13"Alongside the territory of the priests, the Levites will have an allotment 25,000 cubits long and 10,000 cubits wide. Its total length will be 25,000 cubits and its width 10,000 cubits. 14They must not sell or exchange any of it. This is the best of the land and must not pass into other hands, because it is holy to the LORD.

15"The remaining area, 5,000 cubits wide and 25,000 cubits long, will be for the common use of the city, for houses and for pastureland. The city will be in the center of it 16and will have these measurements: the north side 4,500 cubits, the south side 4,500 cubits, the east side 4,500 cubits,

q15 Or *past the entrance to* r15,16 See Septuagint and Ezekiel 48:1; Hebrew *road to go into Zedad, 16Hamath, Berothah* s17 Hebrew *Enon,* a variant of *Enan* t18 Septuagint and Syriac; Hebrew *Israel. You will measure to the eastern sea* u20 Or *opposite the entrance to* v1 Or *to the entrance to* w8 That is, about 7 miles (about 12 kilometers) x9 That is, about 3 miles (about 5 kilometers)

and the west side 4,500 cubits. 17The pastureland for the city will be 250 cubits on the north, 250 cubits on the south, 250 cubits on the east, and 250 cubits on the west. 18What remains of the area, bordering on the sacred portion and running the length of it, will be 10,000 cubits on the east side and 10,000 cubits on the west side. Its produce will supply food for the workers of the city. 19The workers from the city who farm it will come from all the tribes of Israel. 20The entire portion will be a square, 25,000 cubits on each side. As a special gift you will set aside the sacred portion, along with the property of the city.

21"What remains on both sides of the area formed by the sacred portion and the city property will belong to the prince. It will extend eastward from the 25,000 cubits of the sacred portion to the eastern border, and westward from the 25,000 cubits to the western border. Both these areas running the length of the tribal portions will belong to the prince, and the sacred portion with the temple sanctuary will be in the center of them. 22So the property of the Levites and the property of the city will lie in the center of the area that belongs to the prince. The area belonging to the prince will lie between the border of Judah and the border of Benjamin.

23"As for the rest of the tribes: Benjamin will have one portion; it will extend from the east side to the west side.

24"Simeon will have one portion; it will border the territory of Benjamin from east to west.

25"Issachar will have one portion; it will border the territory of Simeon from east to west.

26"Zebulun will have one portion; it will border the territory of Issachar from east to west.

27"Gad will have one portion; it will border the territory of Zebulun from east to west.

28"The southern boundary of Gad will run south from Tamar to the waters of Meribah Kadesh, then along the Wadi ⌞of Egypt⌟ to the Great Sea.[y]

29"This is the land you are to allot as an inheritance to the tribes of Israel, and these will be their portions," declares the Sovereign LORD.

30"These will be the exits of the city: Beginning on the north side, which is 4,500 cubits long, 31the gates of the city will be named after the tribes of Israel. The three gates on the north side will be the gate of Reuben, the gate of Judah and the gate of Levi.

32"On the east side, which is 4,500 cubits long, will be three gates: the gate of Joseph, the gate of Benjamin and the gate of Dan.

33"On the south side, which measures 4,500 cubits, will be three gates: the gate of Simeon, the gate of Issachar and the gate of Zebulun.

34"On the west side, which is 4,500 cubits long, will be three gates: the gate of Gad, the gate of Asher and the gate of Naphtali.

35"The distance all around will be 18,000 cubits.

"And the name of the city from that time on will be:

THE LORD IS THERE."

y28 That is, the Mediterranean

Daniel

In the sweep of great world empires, the impact of military conquest on individual people is usually overlooked. For example, the fall of Jerusalem into the hands of Babylon six hundred years before Christ probably did not make much of a stir in the ancient world. It was an event so insignificant to the Babylonians that it wasn't even worth mentioning in their official chronicles.

This was the first of three defeats that those in Judah would suffer from the king of Babylon, Nebuchadnezzar. He simply established Babylonian authority over Judah and left. On the surface not much changed. But behind the scenes some Jewish families and especially some young Jewish men were deeply affected. A number of gifted young men from the families of the Jewish nobility were taken from their homes to a new land. They were thrust into a new lifestyle. Every effort was made to break down their former convictions. They had to make a difficult choice. Would they hold to their faith and to a life of obedience to the Lord God, or would they flow into the new culture? It was a time of crisis for these young men, including the man we will be studying together—Daniel.

It is precisely at this point that we identify with Daniel. Regardless of how sheltered our existence has been as children or how often we were taken to Sunday school, there comes a time when we are thrust into a pagan world. We are confronted in a modern university or on the job or in society with a lifestyle radically different from what is taught in the Bible. At each turn we have to make difficult decisions. Will we obey God regardless of the consequences, or will we become part of the surrounding culture?

Daniel gives us practical and personal help in our struggle. He was a man who rose to a position of great power and prestige in the world system but who never compromised essential biblical principles. He shows us how to live a life of spiritual integrity in the crush of a secular world. Anyone who has been tempted to cave in to such pressures will learn much from him.

The Historical Framework of the Book

Israel's great king Solomon died in 931 B.C. Solomon's son Rehoboam foolishly provoked the leaders of the northern part of the nation, and they split off from the south. The northern tribes (ten of them) were called Israel. They existed until 722 B.C. when they were destroyed by the Assyrians. The southern two tribes were called Judah. God spared Judah until 586 B.C. when the Babylonian armies crushed the nation.

Nebuchadnezzar, the Babylonian commander, had come to Judah and Jerusalem twice before to put down Jewish rebellion against the authority of the empire. In 605 B.C. the Jews had been treated fairly well. A few young men (including Daniel) from the leading families had been taken as hostages, but the nation was left relatively undisturbed. In 597 B.C. the treatment was harsher. More people were deported to Babylon, including the king, Jehoiachin, and the prophet Ezekiel. Finally, in 586 B.C. the Babylonian patience was exhausted. The temple of God was burned, the walls of Jerusalem were broken down, and the people were virtually all killed or deported to Babylon. A summary of these three "conquests" can be found in 2 Kings 24—25 and 2 Chronicles 36.

God judged Judah for seventy years (from 605 B.C. to 536 B.C.)—a period called the Babylonian captivity. In 536 B.C. Babylon was defeated by a new world power, Persia. Cyrus, the Persian ruler, allowed the Jews to return to Judah.

Daniel's ministry in Babylon extended through the entire seventy-year Babylonian captivity and on into the reign of the Persians. Daniel lived well into his eighties or nineties! His primary prophetic focus was on the Gentiles. Even during the period of Judah's humiliation God's voice was heard in the courtroom of the emperor.

The Theological Focus of the Book

If you read the book of Daniel and see only a den of lions and strange visions, you have missed the main character in the book—a sovereign God! Daniel wrote this book not to glorify himself but to exalt the Lord. In every circumstance, in every crisis, Daniel points us to a God who is sovereignly at work in human history.

To say that God is sovereign simply means that nothing happens that is not planned or permitted by God. That is true of kingdoms, and it is true in our lives. Daniel's God is not a weak, frustrated deity who sits in heaven, wringing his hands, hoping everything will turn out all right. He is a God who orders all events according to his own will.

The book of Daniel is apocalyptic literature designed to speak to us in those times when God seems to be absent. The crushed people of Judah in Daniel's day were saying, "Where is God?" Daniel answers their questions by showing them that, even in a national catastrophe, God is working out his purpose and plan.

Daniel is able to resist compromise because of his relationship to a sovereign God. His obedience was simply an expression of God's kingship in his life. Daniel's courage to proclaim God's message came from his allegiance to a sovereign God. He saw the Lord as the one who was King over the earthly kings of Babylon. Be prepared, then, in these quiet times to see God in a new way! It will be a stretching, convicting but life-changing adventure.

Daniel and the Future

The second part of the book of Daniel is less well known and markedly more difficult to understand than the first part of the book. But it is no less profitable! In Daniel 1—6 the focus is primarily on the life and character of Daniel as a *man* of God. In Daniel 7—12 the focus is on Daniel as the *messenger* of God. These chapters consist of a series of visions given to Daniel—visions of the future of the Gentile nations and of the nation of Israel.

The visions of Daniel are a source of controversy among students of the Bible. The first area of controversy centers around the *integrity* of the visions. Liberal and critical scholars maintain that what is recorded in these chapters is not prophecy at all. Instead the writer wrote after the events (sometime in the second century B.C.) but cast what he wrote in the literary form of predictions given by God to a wise man in Babylon four hundred years earlier. According to this view, these chapters record *history* (a record of events that have already transpired) and not *prophecy* (a prediction of events in the future).

For those who accept the Bible as God's revelation, this controversy is settled by the claims of the book itself and by the defense of those claims mounted by evangelical scholars. We also have Jesus' own confirmation of Daniel. In Matthew 24:15 he referred to Daniel as a real person and called him "the prophet." Jesus quoted from these later chapters of Daniel and took them as authoritative revelation from God (see Mt 24:30; Lk 21:27).

The second area of controversy centers on their *interpretation*. Even those who agree on the historical integrity of Daniel disagree on how these visions should be interpreted. Our objective in this guide is not to defend one particular prophetic system but rather to try to understand what Daniel says. Therefore, while we will refer to other biblical passages, the emphasis of each study will be on what we can learn from this book about God's program for human history. Not all the answers about the future will be found in one part of God's truth. If we understand this part, however, we will have a better understanding of the whole as we attempt to develop a biblical framework for future events. We will gain far more from Daniel if we try to learn what is revealed here rather than seeking to defend a preconceived idea of what we want Daniel to say.

While Daniel 7—12 is not an easy section of Scripture, it is just as much the Word of God as the rest. Therefore, it is profitable to us for instruction and correction. After spending many hours in these chapters, I can tell you that they expand not only our understanding of God's program for the future of the world, but also our capacity to trust a sovereign God for our own future. His cosmic, eternal plan includes us!

Outline

1/ Daniel 1 ——— *Have You Got What It Takes?*

2/ Daniel 2:1–30 ——— *A Disturbing Dream*

3/ Daniel 2:31–49 ——— *The Future from a Divine Perspective*

4/ Daniel 3 ——— *Bow or Burn!*

5/ Daniel 4 ——— *The Sovereign God Rules*

6/ Daniel 5 ——— *The Handwriting on the Wall*

7/ Daniel 6 ——— *On the Menu at the Lions' Club*

8/ Daniel 7 ——— *A Prophetic Panorama*

9/ Daniel 8 ——— *World Powers in Conflict*

10/ Daniel 9 ——— *Prayer and Prediction*

11/ Daniel 10:1—11:35 ——— *Another Vision of the Future*

12/ Daniel 11:36—12:13 ——— *A Dark Day and a Brilliant End*

1 / *Daniel 1*
Have You Got What It Takes?

HOW DID YOU feel when you first moved away from home and were launched out on your own? Daniel and his friends were torn from their land and taken to Babylon as young men. They were probably only twelve to fourteen years old. In Babylon they were placed in a three-year training program to prepare them to oversee Jewish affairs in the Babylonian Empire. A crisis of conscience erupted when the first meal was served.

Warming Up to God In what way are you currently feeling pressured by culture? Talk openly with God about your struggles.

Read Daniel 1.

1 In the third year of the reign of Jehoiakim king of Judah, Nebuchadnezzar king of Babylon came to Jerusalem and besieged it. 2And the Lord delivered Jehoiakim king of Judah into his hand, along with some of the articles from the temple of God. These he carried off to the temple of his god in Babylonia[a] and put in the treasure house of his god.

3Then the king ordered Ashpenaz, chief of his court officials, to bring in some of the Israelites from the royal family and the nobility— 4young men without any physical defect, handsome, showing aptitude for every kind of learning, well informed, quick to understand, and qualified to serve in the king's palace. He was to teach them the language and literature of the Babylonians.[b] 5The king assigned them a daily amount of food and wine from the king's table. They were to be trained for three years, and after that they were to enter the king's service.

6Among these were some from Judah: Daniel, Hananiah, Mishael and Azariah. 7The chief official gave them new names: to Daniel, the name Belteshazzar; to Hananiah, Shadrach; to Mishael, Meshach; and to Azariah, Abednego.

8But Daniel resolved not to defile himself with the royal food and wine, and he asked the chief official for permission not to defile himself this way. 9Now God had caused the official to show favor and sympathy to Daniel, 10but the official told Daniel, "I am afraid of my lord the king, who has assigned your[c] food and drink. Why should he see you looking worse than the other young men your age? The king would then have my head because of you."

11Daniel then said to the guard whom the chief official had appointed over Daniel, Hananiah, Mishael and Azariah, 12"Please test your servants for ten days: Give us nothing but vegetables to eat and water to drink. 13Then compare our appearance with that of the young men who eat the royal food, and treat your servants in accordance with what you see." 14So he agreed to this and tested them for ten days.

15At the end of the ten days they looked healthier and better nourished than any of the young men who ate the royal food. 16So the guard took away their choice food and the wine they were to drink and gave them vegetables instead.

17To these four young men God gave knowledge and understanding of all kinds of literature and learning. And Daniel could understand visions and dreams of all kinds.

18At the end of the time set by the king to bring them in, the chief official presented them to Nebuchadnezzar. 19The king talked with them, and he found none equal to Daniel, Hananiah, Mishael and Azariah; so they entered the king's service. 20In every matter of wisdom and understanding about which the king questioned them, he found them ten times better than all the magicians and enchanters in his whole kingdom.

21And Daniel remained there until the first year of King Cyrus.

[a]2 Hebrew *Shinar* [b]4 Or *Chaldeans* [c]10 The Hebrew for *your* and *you* in this verse is plural.

Discovering the Word 1. What specific tactics were used to give these young Jews a new Babylonian orientation (vv. 3–7)? 2. Why were the food regulations of the Old Testament Law so important to Daniel (vv. 8–10)? 3. Do you think he was making a big issue out of a minor problem? Explain. 4. What steps did Daniel take to provide a creative alternative to the king's plan (vv. 11–14)? 5. What factors combined to produce the exceptional ability of Daniel and his friends?

Applying the Word 1. What criteria can Christians use today to determine which activities we will engage in and which we won't? 2. What can we learn from Daniel's attitude and actions when our biblical convictions are challenged?

Responding in Prayer Pray for refreshment and insight regarding the struggles you face.

2 / *Daniel 2:1–30*
A Disturbing Dream

IN *THE VOYAGE of the Dawn Treader* C. S. Lewis describes an island where dreams come true. "'This is the island I've been looking for this long time,' said one of the sailors. . . . 'Fools!' said a man from the island, stamping his foot with rage. 'That's the sort of talk that brought me here, and I'd better have been drowned or never born.' " Suddenly every man began rowing as they never had before, "for it had taken everyone just that half-minute to remember certain dreams they had had—dreams that make you afraid to sleep again." In Daniel 2 Nebuchadnezzar had such a dream, a dream that was both troubling and true.

Warming Up to God Have you ever had a dream that was so real that it almost seemed true? How did you feel when you woke up?

Read Daniel 2:1–30.

2 In the second year of his reign, Nebu-
chadnezzar had dreams; his mind was
troubled and he could not sleep. 2So the
king summoned the magicians, enchanters, sor-
cerers and astrologers[d] to tell him what he had
dreamed. When they came in and stood before
the king, 3he said to them, "I have had a dream
that troubles me and I want to know what it
means.[e]"
4Then the astrologers answered the king in Ar-
amaic,[f] "O king, live forever! Tell your servants
the dream, and we will interpret it."
5The king replied to the astrologers, "This is
what I have firmly decided: If you do not tell me
what my dream was and interpret it, I will have
you cut into pieces and your houses turned into
piles of rubble. 6But if you tell me the dream and
explain it, you will receive from me gifts and re-
wards and great honor. So tell me the dream and
interpret it for me."
7Once more they replied, "Let the king tell his
servants the dream, and we will interpret it."
8Then the king answered, "I am certain that
you are trying to gain time, because you realize
that this is what I have firmly decided: 9If you do
not tell me the dream, there is just one penalty for
you. You have conspired to tell me misleading
and wicked things, hoping the situation will
change. So then, tell me the dream, and I will
know that you can interpret it for me."
10The astrologers answered the king, "There is
not a man on earth who can do what the king
asks! No king, however great and mighty, has
ever asked such a thing of any magician or en-
chanter or astrologer. 11What the king asks is too
difficult. No one can reveal it to the king except
the gods, and they do not live among men."
12This made the king so angry and furious that
he ordered the execution of all the wise men of
Babylon. 13So the decree was issued to put the
wise men to death, and men were sent to look for
Daniel and his friends to put them to death.
14When Arioch, the commander of the king's
guard, had gone out to put to death the wise men
of Babylon, Daniel spoke to him with wisdom and
tact. 15He asked the king's officer, "Why did the
king issue such a harsh decree?" Arioch then ex-
plained the matter to Daniel. 16At this, Daniel

[d]2 Or *Chaldeans*; also in verses 4, 5 and 10 [e]3 Or *was* [f]4 The text from here through chapter 7 is in Aramaic.

went in to the king and asked for time, so that he
might interpret the dream for him.
17Then Daniel returned to his house and ex-
plained the matter to his friends Hananiah, Mish-
ael and Azariah. 18He urged them to plead for
mercy from the God of heaven concerning this
mystery, so that he and his friends might not be
executed with the rest of the wise men of Bab-
ylon. 19During the night the mystery was revealed
to Daniel in a vision. Then Daniel praised the
God of heaven 20and said:

"Praise be to the name of God for ever and
ever;
wisdom and power are his.
21He changes times and seasons;
he sets up kings and deposes them.
He gives wisdom to the wise
and knowledge to the discerning.
22He reveals deep and hidden things;
he knows what lies in darkness,
and light dwells with him.
23I thank and praise you, O God of my fathers:
You have given me wisdom and power,
you have made known to me what we asked
of you,
you have made known to us the dream of
the king."

24Then Daniel went to Arioch, whom the king
had appointed to execute the wise men of Bab-
ylon, and said to him, "Do not execute the wise
men of Babylon. Take me to the king, and I will
interpret his dream for him."
25Arioch took Daniel to the king at once and
said, "I have found a man among the exiles from
Judah who can tell the king what his dream
means."
26The king asked Daniel (also called Belteshaz-
zar), "Are you able to tell me what I saw in my
dream and interpret it?"
27Daniel replied, "No wise man, enchanter, ma-
gician or diviner can explain to the king the mys-
tery he has asked about, 28but there is a God in
heaven who reveals mysteries. He has shown
King Nebuchadnezzar what will happen in days
to come. Your dream and the visions that passed
through your mind as you lay on your bed are
these:
29"As you were lying there, O king, your mind
turned to things to come, and the revealer of mys-
teries showed you what is going to happen. 30As
for me, this mystery has been revealed to me, not
because I have greater wisdom than other living
men, but so that you, O king, may know the in-
terpretation and that you may understand what
went through your mind.

Discovering the Word 1. Why do you think Nebuchadnezzar demanded to know the content of his dream as well as its interpretation (vv. 1–13)? 2. What can we learn from Daniel's example about how we should react to a personal crisis (vv. 14–18)? 3. What do verses 19–23 tell you about how to respond to answered prayer? 4. Verses 20–23 have often been called "Daniel's psalm." What aspects of God's character are emphasized in these verses? 5. How did Daniel's knowledge of God's character reveal itself in his remarks to King Nebuchadnezzar (vv. 27–30)?

Applying the Word 1. It is common to feel like we are at the mercy of the people and circumstances around us. How should a knowledge of God's wisdom, sovereignty and power affect our view of the people and circumstances in our lives? 2. Three aspects of Daniel's spiritual maturity stand out in this chapter: his *wisdom* in response to a crisis, his *prayer* in response to a problem and his *praise* in response to God's work in his life. How can Daniel's example help you grow in one of these areas?

Responding in Prayer Pray that your character will be remade in God's image.

3 / *Daniel 2:31–49*
The Future from a Divine Perspective

DANIEL 2 IS one of the most amazing prophetic passages in the Bible. It was written in 600 B.C., yet it predicted the future rise and fall of four great world empires! Some of Daniel 2 may seem like so much ancient history to us, but it was all future to Daniel. This passage gives us a long look at the sovereign authority of God, who not only has a plan for human history but is also carrying out that plan perfectly.

Warming Up to God What experiences in your life have led you to put your trust in God?

Read Daniel 2:31–49.

31"You looked, O king, and there before you
stood a large statue—an enormous, dazzling
statue, awesome in appearance. 32The head of the
statue was made of pure gold, its chest and arms
of silver, its belly and thighs of bronze, 33its legs
of iron, its feet partly of iron and partly of baked
clay. 34While you were watching, a rock was cut
out, but not by human hands. It struck the statue
on its feet of iron and clay and smashed them.
35Then the iron, the clay, the bronze, the silver
and the gold were broken to pieces at the same
time and became like chaff on a threshing floor in
the summer. The wind swept them away without
leaving a trace. But the rock that struck the statue
became a huge mountain and filled the whole
earth.

36"This was the dream, and now we will inter-
pret it to the king. 37You, O king, are the king of
kings. The God of heaven has given you domin-
ion and power and might and glory; 38in your
hands he has placed mankind and the beasts of
the field and the birds of the air. Wherever they
live, he has made you ruler over them all. You are
that head of gold.

39"After you, another kingdom will rise, infe-
rior to yours. Next, a third kingdom, one of
bronze, will rule over the whole earth. 40Finally,
there will be a fourth kingdom, strong as iron—
for iron breaks and smashes everything—and as
iron breaks things to pieces, so it will crush and
break all the others. 41Just as you saw that the feet
and toes were partly of baked clay and partly of
iron, so this will be a divided kingdom; yet it will
have some of the strength of iron in it, even as
you saw iron mixed with clay. 42As the toes were
partly iron and partly clay, so this kingdom will
be partly strong and partly brittle. 43And just as
you saw the iron mixed with baked clay, so the
people will be a mixture and will not remain
united, any more than iron mixes with clay.

44"In the time of those kings, the God of
heaven will set up a kingdom that will never be
destroyed, nor will it be left to another people. It
will crush all those kingdoms and bring them to
an end, but it will itself endure forever. 45This is
the meaning of the vision of the rock cut out of a
mountain, but not by human hands—a rock that
broke the iron, the bronze, the clay, the silver and
the gold to pieces.

"The great God has shown the king what will
take place in the future. The dream is true and the
interpretation is trustworthy."

46Then King Nebuchadnezzar fell prostrate be-
fore Daniel and paid him honor and ordered that
an offering and incense be presented to him.
47The king said to Daniel, "Surely your God is the
God of gods and the Lord of kings and a revealer
of mysteries, for you were able to reveal this mys-
tery."

48Then the king placed Daniel in a high posi-
tion and lavished many gifts on him. He made
him ruler over the entire province of Babylon and
placed him in charge of all its wise men. 49More-
over, at Daniel's request the king appointed Sha-
drach, Meshach and Abednego administrators
over the province of Babylon, while Daniel him-
self remained at the royal court.

Discovering the Word 1. As you think about Daniel's description of the dream in verses 31–35 (not the interpretation of the dream in later verses), what was it about the dream that may have caused Nebuchadnezzar to be troubled (see v. 1)? 2. The interpretation of the dream begins in verse 36. Why do you think God referred to Nebuchadnezzar as the head of gold (vv. 36–38)? 3. While Daniel does not say who the future kingdoms are, we can identify them as Medo-Persia (silver), Greece (bronze) and Rome (iron). What does Daniel say about the relative nature and power of these kingdoms (vv. 36–43)? 4. What is the significance of the mixture of clay (ceramic) with iron (vv. 41–43)? 5. Verse 44 says that "in the time of those kings [the ones represented by the toes] the God of heaven will set up a kingdom." What characteristics of the kingdom of God are described in verses 44–45?

Applying the Word 1. What does this chapter teach you about God's activity in the course of human history? 2. How can the portrait of God in this chapter encourage us to trust God with our life and circumstances?

Responding in Prayer Take time to thank God for his control over the present and the future.

4 / *Daniel 3*
Bow or Burn!

THE STORY OF Shadrach, Meshach and Abednego in the fiery furnace ranks with Daniel in the lion's den and David and Goliath as one of the best-known and most exciting Bible stories. One of the problems with a story that's so familiar is that we tend to forget that it really happened. It is not a myth. It is history! It is also a very practical chapter for men and women who are trying to live for God in a secular society. We face the same pressure these three faced—the pressure to compromise what is right before God in order to be accepted by others.

Warming Up to God In what ways are you tempted to compromise your faith in order to be accepted by others?

Read Daniel 3.

3 King Nebuchadnezzar made an image of
gold, ninety feet high and nine feet[g]
wide, and set it up on the plain of Dura in
the province of Babylon. 2He then summoned the
satraps, prefects, governors, advisers, treasurers,
judges, magistrates and all the other provincial
officials to come to the dedication of the image he
had set up. 3So the satraps, prefects, governors,
advisers, treasurers, judges, magistrates and all
the other provincial officials assembled for the
dedication of the image that King Nebuchadnez-
zar had set up, and they stood before it.
4Then the herald loudly proclaimed, "This is
what you are commanded to do, O peoples, na-
tions and men of every language: 5As soon as you
hear the sound of the horn, flute, zither, lyre,
harp, pipes and all kinds of music, you must fall
down and worship the image of gold that King
Nebuchadnezzar has set up. 6Whoever does not
fall down and worship will immediately be
thrown into a blazing furnace."
7Therefore, as soon as they heard the sound of
the horn, flute, zither, lyre, harp and all kinds of
music, all the peoples, nations and men of every
language fell down and worshiped the image of
gold that King Nebuchadnezzar had set up.
8At this time some astrologers[h] came forward
and denounced the Jews. 9They said to King Neb-
uchadnezzar, "O king, live forever! 10You have
issued a decree, O king, that everyone who hears
the sound of the horn, flute, zither, lyre, harp,
pipes and all kinds of music must fall down and
worship the image of gold, 11and that whoever
does not fall down and worship will be thrown
into a blazing furnace. 12But there are some Jews
whom you have set over the affairs of the prov-
ince of Babylon—Shadrach, Meshach and Abed-

g1 Aramaic *sixty cubits high and six cubits wide* (about 27 meters high and 2.7 meters wide) h8 Or *Chaldeans*

nego—who pay no attention to you, O king.
They neither serve your gods nor worship the im-
age of gold you have set up."
13Furious with rage, Nebuchadnezzar sum-
moned Shadrach, Meshach and Abednego. So
these men were brought before the king, 14and
Nebuchadnezzar said to them, "Is it true, Sha-
drach, Meshach and Abednego, that you do not
serve my gods or worship the image of gold I
have set up? 15Now when you hear the sound of
the horn, flute, zither, lyre, harp, pipes and all
kinds of music, if you are ready to fall down and
worship the image I made, very good. But if you
do not worship it, you will be thrown immedi-
ately into a blazing furnace. Then what god will
be able to rescue you from my hand?"
16Shadrach, Meshach and Abednego replied to
the king, "O Nebuchadnezzar, we do not need to
defend ourselves before you in this matter. 17If we
are thrown into the blazing furnace, the God we
serve is able to save us from it, and he will rescue
us from your hand, O king. 18But even if he does
not, we want you to know, O king, that we will
not serve your gods or worship the image of gold
you have set up."
19Then Nebuchadnezzar was furious with Sha-
drach, Meshach and Abednego, and his attitude
toward them changed. He ordered the furnace
heated seven times hotter than usual 20and com-
manded some of the strongest soldiers in his
army to tie up Shadrach, Meshach and Abednego
and throw them into the blazing furnace. 21So
these men, wearing their robes, trousers, turbans
and other clothes, were bound and thrown into
the blazing furnace. 22The king's command was
so urgent and the furnace so hot that the flames
of the fire killed the soldiers who took up Sha-
drach, Meshach and Abednego, 23and these three
men, firmly tied, fell into the blazing furnace.
24Then King Nebuchadnezzar leaped to his feet
in amazement and asked his advisers, "Weren't
there three men that we tied up and threw into
the fire?"
They replied, "Certainly, O king."
25He said, "Look! I see four men walking
around in the fire, unbound and unharmed, and
the fourth looks like a son of the gods."
26Nebuchadnezzar then approached the open-
ing of the blazing furnace and shouted, "Sha-
drach, Meshach and Abednego, servants of the
Most High God, come out! Come here!"
So Shadrach, Meshach and Abednego came out
of the fire, 27and the satraps, prefects, governors
and royal advisers crowded around them. They
saw that the fire had not harmed their bodies, nor
was a hair of their heads singed; their robes were
not scorched, and there was no smell of fire on
them.
28Then Nebuchadnezzar said, "Praise be to the
God of Shadrach, Meshach and Abednego, who
has sent his angel and rescued his servants! They
trusted in him and defied the king's command
and were willing to give up their lives rather than
serve or worship any god except their own God.
29Therefore I decree that the people of any nation
or language who say anything against the God of
Shadrach, Meshach and Abednego be cut into
pieces and their houses be turned into piles of
rubble, for no other god can save in this way."
30Then the king promoted Shadrach, Meshach
and Abednego in the province of Babylon.

Discovering the Word 1. What do you think motivated Nebuchadnezzar to build this image of gold (vv. 1–7)? 2. Why do you think the astrologers reported the disobedience of Shadrach, Meshach and Abednego to Nebuchadnezzar (vv. 8–12)? 3. What temptations do you think Shadrach, Meshach and Abednego faced when they were brought before the king (vv. 13–15)? 4. What impresses you most about their response to these temptations (vv. 16–18)? 5. As you look at Nebuchadnezzar's response (vv. 13–15, 19–23), what evidence do you see that his basic conflict was with God rather than with these three men? 6. What specific actions did God take to bring assurance to the three men and to demonstrate his power to Nebuchadnezzar (vv. 24–30)?

Applying the Word 1. Some Christians claim that pain or sickness or trial are always the result of sin or lack of faith. How would you respond to that claim in light of this passage? 2. As you look back over this chapter, what lessons about the risks and rewards of obedience are most significant to you personally?

Responding in Prayer What commitments can you make to God today that will prepare you to face the pressures of a secular world? Speak to the Lord with honesty.

5 / *Daniel 4*
The Sovereign God Rules

WE ARE NOT accustomed to hearing our national leaders describe their sins in public. That's why Daniel 4 is such an unusual chapter! Nebuchadnezzar, the great, proud, powerful king of Babylon, writes a letter to the world describing in detail how God humiliated him for seven years and then graciously restored him.

Warming Up to God When have you been publicly humiliated?

Read Daniel 4.

4 King Nebuchadnezzar,

To the peoples, nations and men of every language, who live in all the world:

May you prosper greatly!

2It is my pleasure to tell you about the miraculous signs and wonders that the Most High God has performed for me.

3How great are his signs,
how mighty his wonders!
His kingdom is an eternal kingdom;
his dominion endures from generation to generation.

4I, Nebuchadnezzar, was at home in my palace, contented and prosperous. 5I had a dream that made me afraid. As I was lying in my bed, the images and visions that passed through my mind terrified me. 6So I commanded that all the wise men of Babylon be brought before me to interpret the dream for me. 7When the magicians, enchanters, astrologers[i] and diviners came, I told them the dream, but they could not interpret it for me. 8Finally, Daniel came into my presence and I told him the dream. (He is called Belteshazzar, after the name of my god, and the spirit of the holy gods is in him.)

9I said, "Belteshazzar, chief of the magicians, I know that the spirit of the holy gods is in you, and no mystery is too difficult for you. Here is my dream; interpret it for me. 10These are the visions I saw while lying in my bed: I looked, and there before me stood a tree in the middle of the land. Its height was enormous. 11The tree grew large and strong and its top touched the sky; it was visible to the ends of the earth. 12Its leaves were beautiful, its fruit abundant, and on it was food for all. Under it the beasts of the field found shelter, and the birds of the air lived in its branches; from it every creature was fed.

13"In the visions I saw while lying in my bed, I looked, and there before me was a messenger,[j] a holy one, coming down from heaven. 14He called in a loud voice: 'Cut down the tree and trim off its branches; strip off its leaves and scatter its fruit. Let the animals flee from under it and the birds from its branches. 15But let the stump and its roots, bound with iron and bronze, remain in the ground, in the grass of the field.

" 'Let him be drenched with the dew of heaven, and let him live with the animals among the plants of the earth. 16Let his mind be changed from that of a man and let him be given the mind of an animal, till seven times[k] pass by for him.

17" 'The decision is announced by messengers, the holy ones declare the verdict, so that the living may know that the Most High is sovereign over the kingdoms of men and gives them to anyone he wishes and sets over them the lowliest of men.'

18"This is the dream that I, King Nebuchadnezzar, had. Now, Belteshazzar, tell me what it means, for none of the wise men in my kingdom can interpret it for me. But you can, because the spirit of the holy gods is in you."

19Then Daniel (also called Belteshazzar) was greatly perplexed for a time, and his thoughts terrified him. So the king said,

[i]7 Or *Chaldeans* [j]13 Or *watchman*; also in verses 17 and 23
[k]16 Or *years*; also in verses 23, 25 and 32

"Belteshazzar, do not let the dream or its
meaning alarm you."
Belteshazzar answered, "My lord, if only
the dream applied to your enemies and its
meaning to your adversaries! 20The tree you
saw, which grew large and strong, with its
top touching the sky, visible to the whole
earth, 21with beautiful leaves and abundant
fruit, providing food for all, giving shelter to
the beasts of the field, and having nesting
places in its branches for the birds of the
air— 22you, O king, are that tree! You have
become great and strong; your greatness has
grown until it reaches the sky, and your do-
minion extends to distant parts of the earth.
23"You, O king, saw a messenger, a holy
one, coming down from heaven and saying,
'Cut down the tree and destroy it, but leave
the stump, bound with iron and bronze, in
the grass of the field, while its roots remain
in the ground. Let him be drenched with the
dew of heaven; let him live like the wild ani-
mals, until seven times pass by for him.'
24"This is the interpretation, O king, and
this is the decree the Most High has issued
against my lord the king: 25You will be
driven away from people and will live with
the wild animals; you will eat grass like cat-
tle and be drenched with the dew of heaven.
Seven times will pass by for you until you
acknowledge that the Most High is sovereign
over the kingdoms of men and gives them to
anyone he wishes. 26The command to leave
the stump of the tree with its roots means
that your kingdom will be restored to you
when you acknowledge that Heaven rules.
27Therefore, O king, be pleased to accept my
advice: Renounce your sins by doing what is
right, and your wickedness by being kind to
the oppressed. It may be that then your pros-
perity will continue."

28All this happened to King Nebuchadnez-
zar. 29Twelve months later, as the king was
walking on the roof of the royal palace of
Babylon, 30he said, "Is not this the great Bab-
ylon I have built as the royal residence, by
my mighty power and for the glory of my
majesty?"
31The words were still on his lips when a
voice came from heaven, "This is what is de-
creed for you, King Nebuchadnezzar: Your
royal authority has been taken from you.
32You will be driven away from people and
will live with the wild animals; you will eat
grass like cattle. Seven times will pass by for
you until you acknowledge that the Most
High is sovereign over the kingdoms of men
and gives them to anyone he wishes."
33Immediately what had been said about
Nebuchadnezzar was fulfilled. He was driven
away from people and ate grass like cattle.
His body was drenched with the dew of
heaven until his hair grew like the feathers of
an eagle and his nails like the claws of a bird.
34At the end of that time, I, Nebuchadnez-
zar, raised my eyes toward heaven, and my
sanity was restored. Then I praised the Most
High; I honored and glorified him who lives
forever.

His dominion is an eternal dominion;
his kingdom endures from generation to
generation.
35All the peoples of the earth
are regarded as nothing.
He does as he pleases
with the powers of heaven
and the peoples of the earth.
No one can hold back his hand
or say to him: "What have you done?"

36At the same time that my sanity was re-
stored, my honor and splendor were re-
turned to me for the glory of my kingdom.
My advisers and nobles sought me out, and I
was restored to my throne and became even
greater than before. 37Now I, Nebuchadnez-
zar, praise and exalt and glorify the King of
heaven, because everything he does is right
and all his ways are just. And those who
walk in pride he is able to humble.

Discovering the Word 1. How does Nebuchadnezzar's proclamation in 4:1–3 differ from what he expressed in Daniel 3:28–29? 2. As you read Nebuchadnezzar's description of the dream (vv. 9–18), what aspects of the dream might have caused the king to be "terrified" (v. 5)? 3. Three times in this chapter God's purpose for giving the dream is repeated (vv. 17, 25, 32). Why do you think God was so intent on impressing Nebuchadnezzar with his sovereign authority instead of his grace or his love? 4. If Nebuchadnezzar had repented of his sins as Daniel advised, do you think God would have withheld his judgment, or was his decision irrevocable at this point (vv. 24–27)? Explain. 5. What specific steps did God take to humble Nebuchadnezzar (vv. 31–33)?

Applying the Word 1. What does Nebuchadnezzar's experience teach us about the dangers of pride? 2. Sometimes we gain fresh insight into God's character and ways as we wrestle with a hard aspect of God's truth. What is the hardest thing about this chapter for you to accept? 3. What does that hard lesson teach you about how God works in our lives to bring us to Christlikeness?

Responding in Prayer It can be scary to have God at work in our lives. Talk to God about how you are feeling about his role in your life.

6 / *Daniel 5*
The Handwriting on the Wall

NEVER UNDERESTIMATE THE influence of one godly life! As chapter 5 opens, Daniel is an old man—more than eighty years old. The successors to Nebuchadnezzar's throne have ignored him. He has been shuffled off into some obscure office in the Babylonian bureaucracy. But when the king finds himself in trouble, he calls for God's man. Daniel shows us how to stand for God over the long haul.

Warming Up to God Whose life has been an example to you? Thank God for that person's role in your life.

Read Daniel 5.

5 King Belshazzar gave a great banquet for a
thousand of his nobles and drank wine
with them. 2While Belshazzar was drink-
ing his wine, he gave orders to bring in the gold
and silver goblets that Nebuchadnezzar his fa-
ther[l] had taken from the temple in Jerusalem, so
that the king and his nobles, his wives and his
concubines might drink from them. 3So they
brought in the gold goblets that had been taken
from the temple of God in Jerusalem, and the
king and his nobles, his wives and his concubines
drank from them. 4As they drank the wine, they
praised the gods of gold and silver, of bronze,
iron, wood and stone.
5Suddenly the fingers of a human hand ap-
peared and wrote on the plaster of the wall, near
the lampstand in the royal palace. The king
watched the hand as it wrote. 6His face turned
pale and he was so frightened that his knees
knocked together and his legs gave way.
7The king called out for the enchanters, astrol-
ogers[m] and diviners to be brought and said to
these wise men of Babylon, "Whoever reads this
writing and tells me what it means will be clothed
in purple and have a gold chain placed around his
neck, and he will be made the third highest ruler
in the kingdom."
8Then all the king's wise men came in, but they
could not read the writing or tell the king what it
meant. 9So King Belshazzar became even more
terrified and his face grew more pale. His nobles
were baffled.
10The queen,[n] hearing the voices of the king
and his nobles, came into the banquet hall.
"O king, live forever!" she said. "Don't be
alarmed! Don't look so pale! 11There is a man in
your kingdom who has the spirit of the holy gods
in him. In the time of your father he was found to
have insight and intelligence and wisdom like
that of the gods. King Nebuchadnezzar your fa-
ther—your father the king, I say—appointed him
chief of the magicians, enchanters, astrologers
and diviners. 12This man Daniel, whom the king
called Belteshazzar, was found to have a keen
mind and knowledge and understanding, and also
the ability to interpret dreams, explain riddles
and solve difficult problems. Call for Daniel, and
he will tell you what the writing means."
13So Daniel was brought before the king, and

[l]2 Or *ancestor*; or *predecessor*; also in verses 11, 13 and 18 [m]7 Or *Chaldeans*; also in verse 11 [n]10 Or *queen mother*

the king said to him, "Are you Daniel, one of the
exiles my father the king brought from Judah? 14I
have heard that the spirit of the gods is in you
and that you have insight, intelligence and out-
standing wisdom. 15The wise men and enchanters
were brought before me to read this writing and
tell me what it means, but they could not explain
it. 16Now I have heard that you are able to give
interpretations and to solve difficult problems. If
you can read this writing and tell me what it
means, you will be clothed in purple and have a
gold chain placed around your neck, and you will
be made the third highest ruler in the kingdom."
17Then Daniel answered the king, "You may
keep your gifts for yourself and give your rewards
to someone else. Nevertheless, I will read the
writing for the king and tell him what it means.
18"O king, the Most High God gave your father
Nebuchadnezzar sovereignty and greatness and
glory and splendor. 19Because of the high position
he gave him, all the peoples and nations and men
of every language dreaded and feared him. Those
the king wanted to put to death, he put to death;
those he wanted to spare, he spared; those he
wanted to promote, he promoted; and those he
wanted to humble, he humbled. 20But when his
heart became arrogant and hardened with pride,
he was deposed from his royal throne and
stripped of his glory. 21He was driven away from
people and given the mind of an animal; he lived
with the wild donkeys and ate grass like cattle;
and his body was drenched with the dew of
heaven, until he acknowledged that the Most
High God is sovereign over the kingdoms of men
and sets over them anyone he wishes.
22"But you his son,[o] O Belshazzar, have not
humbled yourself, though you knew all this. 23In-
stead, you have set yourself up against the Lord
of heaven. You had the goblets from his temple
brought to you, and you and your nobles, your
wives and your concubines drank wine from
them. You praised the gods of silver and gold, of
bronze, iron, wood and stone, which cannot see
or hear or understand. But you did not honor the
God who holds in his hand your life and all your
ways. 24Therefore he sent the hand that wrote the
inscription.
25"This is the inscription that was written:

MENE, MENE, TEKEL, PARSIN[p]

26"This is what these words mean:

Mene[q]: God has numbered the days of
your reign and brought it to an
end.
27*Tekel*[r]: You have been weighed on the
scales and found wanting.
28*Peres*[s]: Your kingdom is divided and
given to the Medes and Persians."

29Then at Belshazzar's command, Daniel was
clothed in purple, a gold chain was placed around
his neck, and he was proclaimed the third highest
ruler in the kingdom.
30That very night Belshazzar, king of the Bab-
ylonians,[t] was slain, 31and Darius the Mede took
over the kingdom, at the age of sixty-two.

[o]22 Or *descendant*; or *successor* [p]25 Aramaic *UPARSIN* (that is, *AND PARSIN*) [q]26 *Mene* can mean *numbered* or *mina* (a unit of money). [r]27 *Tekel* can mean *weighed* or *shekel*. [s]28 *Peres* (the singular of *Parsin*) can mean *divided* or *Persia* or *a half mina* or *a half shekel*. [t]30 Or *Chaldeans*

Discovering the Word 1. The chapter begins with a party! As you read verses 1–4, what actions and attitudes on the part of Belshazzar and his guests do you think would have provoked the Lord's anger? 2. Three times Daniel has recorded the failure of the "wise men" of Babylon to interpret the message of God. What point is Daniel trying to make (vv. 7–9)? 3. Why do you think Daniel reminds Belshazzar of how God dealt with Nebuchadnezzar (vv. 18–21)? 4. What insights into the nature of Belshazzar's sins can you find in verses 22–23? 5. Based on what is recorded in verses 29–30, do you think Belshazzar accepted Daniel's interpretation as the authoritative message of the true God? Explain. 6. How has this chapter demonstrated that seventy years of life under Babylon's influence had not broken down Daniel's convictions?

Applying the Word 1. In what areas might you be tempted to be proud or arrogant? 2. How can Daniel's words to Belshazzar help you become more humble and thankful to God (vv. 18–24)?

Responding in Prayer Ask God to make you an influencer.

7 / *Daniel 6*
On the Menu at the Lions' Club

DANIEL IN THE lions' den is a story that we never get tired of hearing. As a child, I was impressed by this story because Daniel was not thrown into the lion's den for being bad. He was thrown in for being godly! That is an important point to keep in mind as we study. We usually expect that when we do wrong we ought to be punished, and when we do right we ought to be praised. That is certainly the ideal, but it doesn't always work out that way. Sometimes those who do wrong are rewarded, and those who do right are persecuted. This chapter demonstrates that godliness can be costly.

Warming Up to God How would you feel if the people you work with decided to watch everything about your public and private life?

Read Daniel 6.

6 It pleased Darius to appoint 120 satraps to rule throughout the kingdom, [2]with three administrators over them, one of whom was Daniel. The satraps were made accountable to them so that the king might not suffer loss. [3]Now Daniel so distinguished himself among the administrators and the satraps by his exceptional qualities that the king planned to set him over the whole kingdom. [4]At this, the administrators and the satraps tried to find grounds for charges against Daniel in his conduct of government affairs, but they were unable to do so. They could find no corruption in him, because he was trustworthy and neither corrupt nor negligent. [5]Finally these men said, "We will never find any basis for charges against this man Daniel unless it has something to do with the law of his God."

[6]So the administrators and the satraps went as a group to the king and said: "O King Darius, live forever! [7]The royal administrators, prefects, satraps, advisers and governors have all agreed that the king should issue an edict and enforce the decree that anyone who prays to any god or man during the next thirty days, except to you, O king, shall be thrown into the lions' den. [8]Now, O king, issue the decree and put it in writing so that it cannot be altered—in accordance with the laws of the Medes and Persians, which cannot be repealed." [9]So King Darius put the decree in writing.

[10]Now when Daniel learned that the decree had been published, he went home to his upstairs room where the windows opened toward Jerusalem. Three times a day he got down on his knees and prayed, giving thanks to his God, just as he had done before. [11]Then these men went as a group and found Daniel praying and asking God for help. [12]So they went to the king and spoke to him about his royal decree: "Did you not publish a decree that during the next thirty days anyone who prays to any god or man except to you, O king, would be thrown into the lions' den?"

The king answered, "The decree stands—in accordance with the laws of the Medes and Persians, which cannot be repealed."

[13]Then they said to the king, "Daniel, who is one of the exiles from Judah, pays no attention to you, O king, or to the decree you put in writing. He still prays three times a day." [14]When the king heard this, he was greatly distressed; he was determined to rescue Daniel and made every effort until sundown to save him.

[15]Then the men went as a group to the king and said to him, "Remember, O king, that according to the law of the Medes and Persians no decree or edict that the king issues can be changed."

[16]So the king gave the order, and they brought Daniel and threw him into the lions' den. The king said to Daniel, "May your God, whom you serve continually, rescue you!"

[17]A stone was brought and placed over the mouth of the den, and the king sealed it with his own signet ring and with the rings of his nobles, so that Daniel's situation might not be changed. [18]Then the king returned to his palace and spent the night without eating and without any entertainment being brought to him. And he could not sleep.

[19]At the first light of dawn, the king got up and hurried to the lions' den. [20]When he came near

the den, he called to Daniel in an anguished
voice, "Daniel, servant of the living God, has your
God, whom you serve continually, been able to
rescue you from the lions?"
21 Daniel answered, "O king, live forever! 22 My
God sent his angel, and he shut the mouths of
the lions. They have not hurt me, because I was
found innocent in his sight. Nor have I ever done
any wrong before you, O king."
23 The king was overjoyed and gave orders to
lift Daniel out of the den. And when Daniel was
lifted from the den, no wound was found on him,
because he had trusted in his God.
24 At the king's command, the men who had
falsely accused Daniel were brought in and
thrown into the lions' den, along with their wives
and children. And before they reached the floor of
the den, the lions overpowered them and crushed
all their bones.
25 Then King Darius wrote to all the peoples,
nations and men of every language throughout
the land:

"May you prosper greatly!

26 "I issue a decree that in every part of my
kingdom people must fear and reverence the
God of Daniel.

"For he is the living God
 and he endures forever;
his kingdom will not be destroyed,
 his dominion will never end.
27 He rescues and he saves;
 he performs signs and wonders
 in the heavens and on the earth.
He has rescued Daniel
 from the power of the lions."

28 So Daniel prospered during the reign of Da-
rius and the reign of Cyrus[u] the Persian.

[u]28 Or *Darius, that is, the reign of Cyrus*

Discovering the Word 1. What do we learn about Daniel's character from the results of the investigation by his enemies (vv. 1–5)? 2. King Darius willingly signed the document prohibiting prayer to anyone but him (vv. 6–9). How does this action resemble the sins of his predecessors? 3. What specific evidences do you find in verse 10 of Daniel's consistent obedience to God? 4. How do verses 14–20 underscore the impact Daniel's life had on the king? 5. In what ways would the miracle Darius witnessed have reinforced Daniel's personal example (vv. 21–24)?

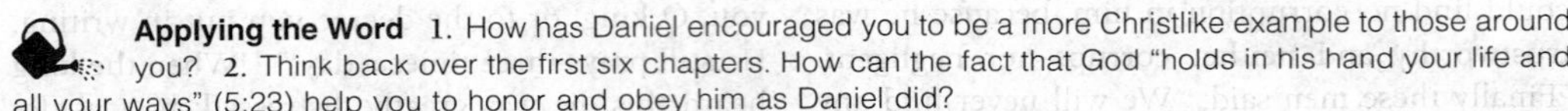

Applying the Word 1. How has Daniel encouraged you to be a more Christlike example to those around you? 2. Think back over the first six chapters. How can the fact that God "holds in his hand your life and all your ways" (5:23) help you to honor and obey him as Daniel did?

Responding in Prayer Make your prayer one of praise for the qualities of God you have been learning about like Daniel did (vv. 25–27).

8 / *Daniel 7*
A Prophetic Panorama

HAVE YOU EVER wondered if there was any order or plan to the course of human history? Nations and empires rise, expand, degenerate and fall. Leaders live, rule and die. But where is everything headed? Some in despair say that human history is going nowhere. Others try to sound optimistic and say that history is going wherever the human race takes it. Christians who know their God and his Word, however, realize that history does have a plan. That's the assurance God gave Daniel in what at first appeared to be a terrifying night vision!

Warming Up to God What questions do you have today about God's plan for you or for the world? Present your questions to the Lord, and ask him to use this text to give you greater understanding.

Read Daniel 7.

7 In the first year of Belshazzar king of Bab-
ylon, Daniel had a dream, and visions
passed through his mind as he was lying
on his bed. He wrote down the substance of his
dream.
2Daniel said: "In my vision at night I looked,
and there before me were the four winds of
heaven churning up the great sea. 3Four great
beasts, each different from the others, came up
out of the sea.
4"The first was like a lion, and it had the wings
of an eagle. I watched until its wings were torn off
and it was lifted from the ground so that it stood
on two feet like a man, and the heart of a man
was given to it.
5"And there before me was a second beast,
which looked like a bear. It was raised up on one
of its sides, and it had three ribs in its mouth
between its teeth. It was told, 'Get up and eat
your fill of flesh!'
6"After that, I looked, and there before me was
another beast, one that looked like a leopard. And
on its back it had four wings like those of a bird.
This beast had four heads, and it was given au-
thority to rule.
7"After that, in my vision at night I looked, and
there before me was a fourth beast—terrifying
and frightening and very powerful. It had large
iron teeth; it crushed and devoured its victims
and trampled underfoot whatever was left. It was
different from all the former beasts, and it had ten
horns.
8"While I was thinking about the horns, there
before me was another horn, a little one, which
came up among them; and three of the first horns
were uprooted before it. This horn had eyes like
the eyes of a man and a mouth that spoke boast-
fully.
9"As I looked,

"thrones were set in place,
  and the Ancient of Days took his seat.
His clothing was as white as snow;
  the hair of his head was white like wool.
His throne was flaming with fire,
  and its wheels were all ablaze.
10A river of fire was flowing,
  coming out from before him.
Thousands upon thousands attended him;
  ten thousand times ten thousand stood
    before him.
The court was seated,
  and the books were opened.

11"Then I continued to watch because of the
boastful words the horn was speaking. I kept
looking until the beast was slain and its body de-
stroyed and thrown into the blazing fire. 12(The
other beasts had been stripped of their authority,
but were allowed to live for a period of time.)
13"In my vision at night I looked, and there
before me was one like a son of man, coming with
the clouds of heaven. He approached the Ancient
of Days and was led into his presence. 14He was
given authority, glory and sovereign power; all
peoples, nations and men of every language wor-
shiped him. His dominion is an everlasting do-
minion that will not pass away, and his kingdom
is one that will never be destroyed.
15"I, Daniel, was troubled in spirit, and the vi-
sions that passed through my mind disturbed me.
16I approached one of those standing there and
asked him the true meaning of all this.
"So he told me and gave me the interpretation
of these things: 17'The four great beasts are four
kingdoms that will rise from the earth. 18But the
saints of the Most High will receive the kingdom
and will possess it forever—yes, for ever and
ever.'
19"Then I wanted to know the true meaning of
the fourth beast, which was different from all the
others and most terrifying, with its iron teeth and
bronze claws—the beast that crushed and de-
voured its victims and trampled underfoot what-
ever was left. 20I also wanted to know about the
ten horns on its head and about the other horn
that came up, before which three of them fell—
the horn that looked more imposing than the oth-
ers and that had eyes and a mouth that spoke
boastfully. 21As I watched, this horn was waging
war against the saints and defeating them, 22until
the Ancient of Days came and pronounced judg-
ment in favor of the saints of the Most High, and
the time came when they possessed the kingdom.
23"He gave me this explanation: 'The fourth
beast is a fourth kingdom that will appear on
earth. It will be different from all the other king-
doms and will devour the whole earth, trampling
it down and crushing it. 24The ten horns are ten
kings who will come from this kingdom. After
them another king will arise, different from the
earlier ones; he will subdue three kings. 25He will
speak against the Most High and oppress his
saints and try to change the set times and the

laws. The saints will be handed over to him for a time, times and half a time.[v]

26" 'But the court will sit, and his power will be taken away and completely destroyed forever. 27Then the sovereignty, power and greatness of the kingdoms under the whole heaven will be handed over to the saints, the people of the Most High. His kingdom will be an everlasting kingdom, and all rulers will worship and obey him.'

28"This is the end of the matter. I, Daniel, was deeply troubled by my thoughts, and my face turned pale, but I kept the matter to myself."

[v]25 *Or for a year, two years and half a year*

Discovering the Word 1. The sea is used in many prophetic passages to represent the nations of the world (see, for example, Is 17:12–13; 57:20 and Lk 21:25). If that is the picture here, how would you explain verses 2–3? 2. Daniel sees four beasts which, according to verse 17, represent four kingdoms. The lionlike appearance of the first beast may represent that kingdom's strength and majesty. What characteristics of the second, third and fourth kingdoms are suggested by verses 5–7? 3. What aspects of God's nature and power are suggested by Daniel's description of the Ancient of Days in verses 9–10? How can this vision of God give us hope and stability when the nations (or our lives) are in turmoil? 4. The final figure to appear in Daniel's vision is "one like a son of man" (vv. 13–14)—an apparent description of the Lord Jesus. Why do you think all the kings and kingdoms of the world are pictured as beasts but Christ looks like a son of man? 5. After the four kingdoms rise, "the saints of the Most High will receive the kingdom" (vv. 17–18). How is their conquest different from that of the four kingdoms? 6. Describe the political and military power of the "other horn" from the information found in this chapter (vv. 19–26).

Applying the Word 1. How does reading this passage affect your attitude toward the future? 2. Daniel is told that the saints of the Most High will share in the kingdom with the Son of man. What do you find most appealing about Daniel's description of God's kingdom (vv. 13–14, 27), and why?

Responding in Prayer Pray for those nations that are currently in turmoil. Ask God to bring hope to the people there.

9 / *Daniel 8*
World Powers in Conflict

GOD GAVE DANIEL the unique opportunity of looking at the future. But in chapter 8 that future gets very personal. The first seven chapters stressed the destinies of the Gentile world powers. In chapters 8—12, the emphasis is on the destiny of Israel.

Warming Up to God Reflect on the current state of your country. What aspects of your nation's future concern you? Take time right now to pray for the future of your nation.

Read Daniel 8.

8 In the third year of King Belshazzar's reign, I, Daniel, had a vision, after the one that had already appeared to me. 2In my vision I saw myself in the citadel of Susa in the province of Elam; in the vision I was beside the Ulai Canal. 3I looked up, and there before me was a ram with two horns, standing beside the canal, and the horns were long. One of the horns was longer than the other but grew up later. 4I watched the ram as he charged toward the west and the north and the south. No animal could stand against him, and none could rescue from his power. He did as he pleased and became great.

5As I was thinking about this, suddenly a goat with a prominent horn between his eyes came from the west, crossing the whole earth without touching the ground. 6He came toward the two-horned ram I had seen standing beside the canal and charged at him in great rage. 7I saw him attack the ram furiously, striking the ram and shat-

tering his two horns. The ram was powerless to
stand against him; the goat knocked him to the
ground and trampled on him, and none could
rescue the ram from his power. 8The goat became
very great, but at the height of his power his large
horn was broken off, and in its place four promi-
nent horns grew up toward the four winds of
heaven.
9Out of one of them came another horn, which
started small but grew in power to the south and
to the east and toward the Beautiful Land. 10It
grew until it reached the host of the heavens, and
it threw some of the starry host down to the earth
and trampled on them. 11It set itself up to be as
great as the Prince of the host; it took away the
daily sacrifice from him, and the place of his
sanctuary was brought low. 12Because of rebel-
lion, the host ⌞of the saints⌟[w] and the daily sacri-
fice were given over to it. It prospered in every-
thing it did, and truth was thrown to the ground.
13Then I heard a holy one speaking, and an-
other holy one said to him, "How long will it take
for the vision to be fulfilled—the vision concern-
ing the daily sacrifice, the rebellion that causes
desolation, and the surrender of the sanctuary
and of the host that will be trampled underfoot?"
14He said to me, "It will take 2,300 evenings
and mornings; then the sanctuary will be reconse-
crated."
15While I, Daniel, was watching the vision and
trying to understand it, there before me stood one
who looked like a man. 16And I heard a man's
voice from the Ulai calling, "Gabriel, tell this man
the meaning of the vision."
17As he came near the place where I was stand-
ing, I was terrified and fell prostrate. "Son of
man," he said to me, "understand that the vision
concerns the time of the end."
18While he was speaking to me, I was in a deep
sleep, with my face to the ground. Then he
touched me and raised me to my feet.
19He said: "I am going to tell you what will
happen later in the time of wrath, because the
vision concerns the appointed time of the end.[x]
20The two-horned ram that you saw represents
the kings of Media and Persia. 21The shaggy goat
is the king of Greece, and the large horn between
his eyes is the first king. 22The four horns that
replaced the one that was broken off represent
four kingdoms that will emerge from his nation
but will not have the same power.
23"In the latter part of their reign, when rebels
have become completely wicked, a stern-faced
king, a master of intrigue, will arise. 24He will
become very strong, but not by his own power.
He will cause astounding devastation and will
succeed in whatever he does. He will destroy the
mighty men and the holy people. 25He will cause
deceit to prosper, and he will consider himself
superior. When they feel secure, he will destroy
many and take his stand against the Prince of
princes. Yet he will be destroyed, but not by hu-
man power.
26"The vision of the evenings and mornings
that has been given you is true, but seal up the
vision, for it concerns the distant future."
27I, Daniel, was exhausted and lay ill for several
days. Then I got up and went about the king's
business. I was appalled by the vision; it was be-
yond understanding.

[w]12 Or *rebellion, the armies* [x]19 Or *because the end will be at the appointed time*

Discovering the Word 1. Daniel is first given a rather strange vision involving a ram and a goat (vv. 1–14). No interpretation is given until after the scene has passed. Why do you think God chose to communicate future events to Daniel in this way? (Why not simply tell him the historical facts?) 2. In verse 20 Daniel is told that the ram represents the kings of the Medo-Persian Empire. From the events portrayed in verses 3–4, how would you expect this kingdom to come on the world scene? 3. The goat with one large horn is a symbol of the Greek Empire and their notable first king, Alexander the Great (v. 21). From the scene in verses 5–8, how would you describe the clash of these two empires? 4. From your experience and knowledge gained thus far in the "interpretation of visions," with Daniel as a guide, how would you interpret the symbolism of verses 9–12? 5. The "stern-faced king" (v. 23) whom Gabriel describes is probably Antiochus Epiphanes, who ruled Syria and Palestine from 175 to 164 B.C. He hated the Jews and their God. His most infamous act was desecrating the temple in Jerusalem in 168 B.C. For just over three years ("2,300 evenings and mornings," v. 14), no sacrifices to God were permitted. Finally, the Jews were able to drive Antiochus out of Israel and reclaim the temple. If you had been a Jew living under the tyranny of Antiochus, how would it have made you feel to read Daniel's prophetic prediction of the very events you were experiencing?

Applying the Word 1. In what ways can this chapter be an encouragement to you as you face emotional discouragement or spiritual attack (or even political tyranny)? 2. How does this chapter fit with Daniel's main theme of God's sovereignty? 3. What perspective does this chapter give us in understanding how a good God can permit evil?

Responding in Prayer Ask God to make his ways known to you as you seek to understand who he is and how he works in the world.

10 / *Daniel 9*
Prayer and Prediction

ONE MORNING, SHORTLY after the Medes and the Persians had conquered Babylon, Daniel was reading the book of the prophet Jeremiah. Jeremiah had been a prophet in Jerusalem when Daniel was a boy. As he read the prophet's words, a couple of passages seemed to leap off the page (Jer 25:8–12; 29:10–11). God promised that Israel's captivity would last seventy years, and then God would bring them back to the land. Daniel began to add up the years since his deportation and realized that the captivity was almost over! As Daniel's mind was gripped by the written Word of God, the urge to pray was born. God's answer to Daniel's prayer was swift—and surprising! This passage not only teaches us about Daniel's response to God's Word; we also learn how we should respond to God's promises to us.

Warming Up to God In times of deep personal crisis, men and women are often driven to pray. When have you experienced such a time in your life?

Read Daniel 9.

9 In the first year of Darius son of Xerxes[y]
(a Mede by descent), who was made ruler
over the Babylonian[z] kingdom— [2]in the
first year of his reign, I, Daniel, understood from
the Scriptures, according to the word of the LORD
given to Jeremiah the prophet, that the desolation
of Jerusalem would last seventy years. [3]So I
turned to the Lord God and pleaded with him in
prayer and petition, in fasting, and in sackcloth
and ashes.

[4]I prayed to the LORD my God and confessed:

"O Lord, the great and awesome God,
who keeps his covenant of love with all who
love him and obey his commands, [5]we have
sinned and done wrong. We have been
wicked and have rebelled; we have turned
away from your commands and laws. [6]We
have not listened to your servants the proph-
ets, who spoke in your name to our kings,
our princes and our fathers, and to all the
people of the land.

[7]"Lord, you are righteous, but this day we
are covered with shame—the men of Judah
and people of Jerusalem and all Israel, both
near and far, in all the countries where you
have scattered us because of our unfaithful-
ness to you. [8]O LORD, we and our kings, our
princes and our fathers are covered with
shame because we have sinned against you.
[9]The Lord our God is merciful and forgiving,
even though we have rebelled against him;
[10]we have not obeyed the LORD our God or
kept the laws he gave us through his servants
the prophets. [11]All Israel has transgressed
your law and turned away, refusing to obey
you.

"Therefore the curses and sworn judg-
ments written in the Law of Moses, the ser-
vant of God, have been poured out on us,
because we have sinned against you. [12]You
have fulfilled the words spoken against us
and against our rulers by bringing upon us
great disaster. Under the whole heaven noth-
ing has ever been done like what has been
done to Jerusalem. [13]Just as it is written in
the Law of Moses, all this disaster has come
upon us, yet we have not sought the favor of
the LORD our God by turning from our sins
and giving attention to your truth. [14]The

y1 Hebrew *Ahasuerus* z1 Or *Chaldean*

Lord did not hesitate to bring the disaster upon us, for the Lord our God is righteous in everything he does; yet we have not obeyed him.

15“Now, O Lord our God, who brought your people out of Egypt with a mighty hand and who made for yourself a name that endures to this day, we have sinned, we have done wrong. 16O Lord, in keeping with all your righteous acts, turn away your anger and your wrath from Jerusalem, your city, your holy hill. Our sins and the iniquities of our fathers have made Jerusalem and your people an object of scorn to all those around us.

17“Now, our God, hear the prayers and petitions of your servant. For your sake, O Lord, look with favor on your desolate sanctuary. 18Give ear, O God, and hear; open your eyes and see the desolation of the city that bears your Name. We do not make requests of you because we are righteous, but because of your great mercy. 19O Lord, listen! O Lord, forgive! O Lord, hear and act! For your sake, O my God, do not delay, because your city and your people bear your Name.”

20While I was speaking and praying, confessing my sin and the sin of my people Israel and making my request to the Lord my God for his holy hill— 21while I was still in prayer, Gabriel, the man I had seen in the earlier vision, came to me in swift flight about the time of the evening sacrifice. 22He instructed me and said to me, “Daniel, I have now come to give you insight and understanding. 23As soon as you began to pray, an answer was given, which I have come to tell you, for you are highly esteemed. Therefore, consider the message and understand the vision:

24“Seventy ‘sevens’[a] are decreed for your people and your holy city to finish[b] transgression, to put an end to sin, to atone for wickedness, to bring in everlasting righteousness, to seal up vision and prophecy and to anoint the most holy.[c]

25“Know and understand this: From the issuing of the decree[d] to restore and rebuild Jerusalem until the Anointed One,[e] the ruler, comes, there will be seven ‘sevens,’ and sixty-two ‘sevens.’ It will be rebuilt with streets and a trench, but in times of trouble. 26After the sixty-two ‘sevens,’ the Anointed One will be cut off and will have nothing.[f] The people of the ruler who will come will destroy the city and the sanctuary. The end will come like a flood: War will continue until the end, and desolations have been decreed. 27He will confirm a covenant with many for one ‘seven.’[g] In the middle of the ‘seven’[g] he will put an end to sacrifice and offering. And on a wing ⌞of the temple⌟ he will set up an abomination that causes desolation, until the end that is decreed is poured out on him.[h]”[i]

[a]24 Or *‘weeks’*; also in verses 25 and 26 [b]24 Or *restrain* [c]24 Or *Most Holy Place; or most holy One* [d]25 Or *word* [e]25 Or *an anointed one*; also in verse 26 [f]26 Or *off and will have no one; or off, but not for himself* [g]27 Or *‘week’* [h]27 Or *it* [i]27 Or *And one who causes desolation will come upon the pinnacle of the abominable ⌞temple⌟, until the end that is decreed is poured out on the desolated ⌞city⌟*

Discovering the Word 1. In verses 4–19, which aspects of God’s character did Daniel appeal to as the basis of his requests? 2. Daniel consistently uses the plural pronoun *we* throughout the prayer. Why do you think Daniel could confess for the whole nation? 3. In verse 24 Gabriel mentions six things that will happen for the people of Israel and the holy city of Jerusalem within seventy “sevens” (usually interpreted as 490 years; see Lev 25:8–24). What do you think these things mean individually and collectively? 4. Verse 26 states that “the people of the ruler who will come will destroy the city and the sanctuary.” The Romans destroyed Jerusalem and its temple in A.D. 70. According to verse 27, how would you describe the course of events during the final “seven,” or period of seven years?

Applying the Word 1. What aspects of God’s character have you been learning about, and how? 2. What specific insights about your prayer life can you glean from Daniel’s prayer?

Responding in Prayer Consider your church and your nation. What corporate sins do you need to confess?

11 / *Daniel 10:1—11:35*
Another Vision of the Future

WARS, TERRORISM, ASSASSINATIONS—so often world events seem out of control. We are frustrated and frightened because of our inability to do anything to stop them. The last of four great visions given to Daniel presents God's perspective on world events.

Warming Up to God What recent national or international crisis made you feel insecure or frightened? Explain.

Read Daniel 10:1—11:35.

10 In the third year of Cyrus king of
Persia, a revelation was given to
Daniel (who was called Belteshaz-
zar). Its message was true and it concerned a
great war.[j] The understanding of the message
came to him in a vision.
2At that time I, Daniel, mourned for three
weeks. 3I ate no choice food; no meat or wine
touched my lips; and I used no lotions at all until
the three weeks were over.
4On the twenty-fourth day of the first month,
as I was standing on the bank of the great river,
the Tigris, 5I looked up and there before me was
a man dressed in linen, with a belt of the finest
gold around his waist. 6His body was like chryso-
lite, his face like lightning, his eyes like flaming
torches, his arms and legs like the gleam of bur-
nished bronze, and his voice like the sound of a
multitude.
7I, Daniel, was the only one who saw the vi-
sion; the men with me did not see it, but such
terror overwhelmed them that they fled and hid
themselves. 8So I was left alone, gazing at this
great vision; I had no strength left, my face turned
deathly pale and I was helpless. 9Then I heard
him speaking, and as I listened to him, I fell into
a deep sleep, my face to the ground.
10A hand touched me and set me trembling on
my hands and knees. 11He said, "Daniel, you who
are highly esteemed, consider carefully the words
I am about to speak to you, and stand up, for I
have now been sent to you." And when he said
this to me, I stood up trembling.
12Then he continued, "Do not be afraid, Daniel.
Since the first day that you set your mind to gain
understanding and to humble yourself before
your God, your words were heard, and I have
come in response to them. 13But the prince of the
Persian kingdom resisted me twenty-one days.
Then Michael, one of the chief princes, came to
help me, because I was detained there with the
king of Persia. 14Now I have come to explain to
you what will happen to your people in the fu-
ture, for the vision concerns a time yet to come."
15While he was saying this to me, I bowed with
my face toward the ground and was speechless.
16Then one who looked like a man[k] touched my
lips, and I opened my mouth and began to speak.
I said to the one standing before me, "I am over-
come with anguish because of the vision, my lord,
and I am helpless. 17How can I, your servant, talk
with you, my lord? My strength is gone and I can
hardly breathe."
18Again the one who looked like a man
touched me and gave me strength. 19"Do not be
afraid, O man highly esteemed," he said. "Peace!
Be strong now; be strong."
When he spoke to me, I was strengthened and
said, "Speak, my lord, since you have given me
strength."
20So he said, "Do you know why I have come
to you? Soon I will return to fight against the
prince of Persia, and when I go, the prince of
Greece will come; 21but first I will tell you what
is written in the Book of Truth. (No one supports
me against them except Michael, your prince.
11 1And in the first year of Darius the
Mede, I took my stand to support
and protect him.)
2"Now then, I tell you the truth: Three more
kings will appear in Persia, and then a fourth,
who will be far richer than all the others. When
he has gained power by his wealth, he will stir up
everyone against the kingdom of Greece. 3Then a
mighty king will appear, who will rule with great

j1 Or *true and burdensome* k16 Most manuscripts of the Masoretic Text; one manuscript of the Masoretic Text, Dead Sea Scrolls and Septuagint *Then something that looked like a man's hand*

power and do as he pleases. 4After he has appeared, his empire will be broken up and parceled out toward the four winds of heaven. It will not go to his descendants, nor will it have the power he exercised, because his empire will be uprooted and given to others.

5"The king of the South will become strong, but one of his commanders will become even stronger than he and will rule his own kingdom with great power. 6After some years, they will become allies. The daughter of the king of the South will go to the king of the North to make an alliance, but she will not retain her power, and he and his power[l] will not last. In those days she will be handed over, together with her royal escort and her father[m] and the one who supported her.

7"One from her family line will arise to take her place. He will attack the forces of the king of the North and enter his fortress; he will fight against them and be victorious. 8He will also seize their gods, their metal images and their valuable articles of silver and gold and carry them off to Egypt. For some years he will leave the king of the North alone. 9Then the king of the North will invade the realm of the king of the South but will retreat to his own country. 10His sons will prepare for war and assemble a great army, which will sweep on like an irresistible flood and carry the battle as far as his fortress.

11"Then the king of the South will march out in a rage and fight against the king of the North, who will raise a large army, but it will be defeated. 12When the army is carried off, the king of the South will be filled with pride and will slaughter many thousands, yet he will not remain triumphant. 13For the king of the North will muster another army, larger than the first; and after several years, he will advance with a huge army fully equipped.

14"In those times many will rise against the king of the South. The violent men among your own people will rebel in fulfillment of the vision, but without success. 15Then the king of the North will come and build up siege ramps and will capture a fortified city. The forces of the South will be powerless to resist; even their best troops will not have the strength to stand. 16The invader will do as he pleases; no one will be able to stand against him. He will establish himself in the Beautiful Land and will have the power to destroy it. 17He will determine to come with the might of his entire kingdom and will make an alliance with the king of the South. And he will give him a daughter in marriage in order to overthrow the kingdom, but his plans[n] will not succeed or help him. 18Then he will turn his attention to the coastlands and will take many of them, but a commander will put an end to his insolence and will turn his insolence back upon him. 19After this, he will turn back toward the fortresses of his own country but will stumble and fall, to be seen no more.

20"His successor will send out a tax collector to maintain the royal splendor. In a few years, however, he will be destroyed, yet not in anger or in battle.

21"He will be succeeded by a contemptible person who has not been given the honor of royalty. He will invade the kingdom when its people feel secure, and he will seize it through intrigue. 22Then an overwhelming army will be swept away before him; both it and a prince of the covenant will be destroyed. 23After coming to an agreement with him, he will act deceitfully, and with only a few people he will rise to power. 24When the richest provinces feel secure, he will invade them and will achieve what neither his fathers nor his forefathers did. He will distribute plunder, loot and wealth among his followers. He will plot the overthrow of fortresses—but only for a time.

25"With a large army he will stir up his strength and courage against the king of the South. The king of the South will wage war with a large and very powerful army, but he will not be able to stand because of the plots devised against him. 26Those who eat from the king's provisions will try to destroy him; his army will be swept away, and many will fall in battle. 27The two kings, with their hearts bent on evil, will sit at the same table and lie to each other, but to no avail, because an end will still come at the appointed time. 28The king of the North will return to his own country with great wealth, but his heart will be set against the holy covenant. He will take action against it and then return to his own country.

29"At the appointed time he will invade the South again, but this time the outcome will be different from what it was before. 30Ships of the western coastlands[o] will oppose him, and he will lose heart. Then he will turn back and vent his fury against the holy covenant. He will return and

[l]6 Or *offspring* [m]6 Or *child* (see Vulgate and Syriac) [n]17 Or *but she* [o]30 Hebrew *of Kittim*

show favor to those who forsake the holy cov-
enant.
31"His armed forces will rise up to desecrate the
temple fortress and will abolish the daily sacrifice.
Then they will set up the abomination that causes
desolation. 32With flattery he will corrupt those
who have violated the covenant, but the people
who know their God will firmly resist him.
33"Those who are wise will instruct many,
though for a time they will fall by the sword or be
burned or captured or plundered. 34When they
fall, they will receive a little help, and many who
are not sincere will join them. 35Some of the wise
will stumble, so that they may be refined, purified
and made spotless until the time of the end, for it
will still come at the appointed time.

Discovering the Word 1. Describe the man in Daniel's vision (10:4–6). 2. Why did the vision of verses 4–6 cause Daniel to react the way he did (10:7–11)? 3. What do the angel's words to Daniel tell us about God's response to those who seek him (10:12–14)? 4. In 11:5–35 the conflict between the Syrian division of the Greek Empire ruled by the Seleucid family ("the king of the North") and the Egyptian division of the Greek Empire ruled by the Ptolemies ("the king of the South") is outlined with amazing accuracy. The focus of the passage is on a man we have met in Daniel before—Antiochus Epiphanes. Verses 21–24 describe his conquest of the people of Israel who had regathered in Palestine after the exile. What do we learn from these verses about Antiochus's character and methods of operation? 5. Antiochus invaded Egypt the first time with relative success (11:25–28). The second time he met some new opposition and in his frustration vented his anger on "the holy covenant," the Jewish religion (11:29–31). What can we learn from 11:32–35 about why God may allow genuine believers to suffer under the hand of a godless tyrant?

Applying the Word 1. How might Daniel's experience encourage us to be persistent in prayer? 2. If an evil power could hinder an angel in Daniel's day, what does this indicate about our own need for help against Satan's forces? 3. How can God's sovereign rule help us to stand firm when evil seems to triumph?

Responding in Prayer Offer your praise to the Lord, who is sovereign over history.

12/ *Daniel 11:36—12:13*
A Dark Day and a Brilliant End

I HOPE AS a result of your quiet times in Daniel you have a new appreciation for the sovereign majesty of God—a God who can predict the future in detail, a God who raises up kings and kingdoms and who also brings them to ruin, a God who can protect Daniel in the lion's den, and a God who is just as concerned about us and our lives. The second part of Daniel's final prophetic vision in 11:36—12:13 projects Daniel far into the future to "the time of the end" of world history. The vision focuses on the nation of Israel, but gives us strong encouragement and hope during difficult times.

Warming Up to God In the course of your study in Daniel, what have you learned about the character of God that strengthened you spiritually?

Read Daniel 11:36—12:13.

36"The king will do as he pleases. He will exalt
and magnify himself above every god and will say
unheard-of things against the God of gods. He
will be successful until the time of wrath is com-
pleted, for what has been determined must take
place. 37He will show no regard for the gods of his
fathers or for the one desired by women, nor will
he regard any god, but will exalt himself above
them all. 38Instead of them, he will honor a god of
fortresses; a god unknown to his fathers he will
honor with gold and silver, with precious stones
and costly gifts. 39He will attack the mightiest for-
tresses with the help of a foreign god and will
greatly honor those who acknowledge him. He

will make them rulers over many people and will
distribute the land at a price.[p]
40“At the time of the end the king of the South
will engage him in battle, and the king of the
North will storm out against him with chariots
and cavalry and a great fleet of ships. He will
invade many countries and sweep through them
like a flood. 41He will also invade the Beautiful
Land. Many countries will fall, but Edom, Moab
and the leaders of Ammon will be delivered from
his hand. 42He will extend his power over many
countries; Egypt will not escape. 43He will gain
control of the treasures of gold and silver and all
the riches of Egypt, with the Libyans and Nubians
in submission. 44But reports from the east and the
north will alarm him, and he will set out in a
great rage to destroy and annihilate many. 45He
will pitch his royal tents between the seas at[q] the
beautiful holy mountain. Yet he will come to his
end, and no one will help him.

12 “At that time Michael, the great
prince who protects your people,
will arise. There will be a time of
distress such as has not happened from the begin-
ning of nations until then. But at that time your
people—everyone whose name is found written
in the book—will be delivered. 2Multitudes who
sleep in the dust of the earth will awake: some to
everlasting life, others to shame and everlasting
contempt. 3Those who are wise[r] will shine like
the brightness of the heavens, and those who lead
many to righteousness, like the stars for ever and
ever. 4But you, Daniel, close up and seal the
words of the scroll until the time of the end.
Many will go here and there to increase knowl-
edge.”

5Then I, Daniel, looked, and there before me
stood two others, one on this bank of the river
and one on the opposite bank. 6One of them said
to the man clothed in linen, who was above the
waters of the river, “How long will it be before
these astonishing things are fulfilled?”
7The man clothed in linen, who was above the
waters of the river, lifted his right hand and his
left hand toward heaven, and I heard him swear
by him who lives forever, saying, “It will be for a
time, times and half a time.[s] When the power of
the holy people has been finally broken, all these
things will be completed.”
8I heard, but I did not understand. So I asked,
“My lord, what will the outcome of all this be?”
9He replied, “Go your way, Daniel, because the
words are closed up and sealed until the time of
the end. 10Many will be purified, made spotless
and refined, but the wicked will continue to be
wicked. None of the wicked will understand, but
those who are wise will understand.
11“From the time that the daily sacrifice is abol-
ished and the abomination that causes desolation
is set up, there will be 1,290 days. 12Blessed is the
one who waits for and reaches the end of the
1,335 days.
13“As for you, go your way till the end. You will
rest, and then at the end of the days you will rise
to receive your allotted inheritance.”

p39 Or *land for a reward* q45 Or *the sea and* r3 Or *who impart wisdom* s7 Or *a year, two years and half a year*

Discovering the Word 1. Building from the prototype of the antichrist in Antiochus Epiphanes (11:21–32), the heavenly messenger now describes the final oppressor of Israel who will arise at “the time of the end” (11:35–40). This “king,” following the example of Antiochus, will magnify himself as a god. How would you describe the “religious” character and actions of this king from 11:36–37? 2. From 11:40–43 trace the military career of this future king. 3. The king’s defeat and the deliverance of the godly comes through the intervention of Michael, “the great prince” (12:1). How do you envision this intervention will take place? 4. Why do you think Daniel is given the instruction to seal the scroll “until the time of the end” (12:4, 9)? 5. In 12:9–13, do you think the messenger avoided Daniel’s last question (12:8), or did he answer it? Explain.

Applying the Word 1. The antichrist’s god will be “a god of fortresses”—the ancient god of war and militarism (11:38–39). How do we see the influence of this “god” at work today? 2. How can this victory and the messenger’s description of the resurrection (12:1–3) encourage us during times of tribulation or persecution? 3. As you think back over the book of Daniel, what specific aspect of Daniel’s character or example helped you most to live spiritually in a secular world? In what way?

Responding in Prayer Ask God to continue to teach you what it means to live spiritually in a secular world.

Hosea

Do you think that the problems in our society are because people do not take responsibility for themselves or because the government is not taking responsibility for the people? Hosea's answer would be yes. He saw both as being at fault.

In the eighth century B.C. Hosea began his ministry in the northern kingdom of Israel (which he sometimes calls Ephraim, Jacob or Samaria). He probably preached at about the same time or a little after the prophet Amos during the prosperous reign of Jereboam II. Unfortunately, along with the strong growth of the economy, there were also increases in poverty, social injustice, religious prostitution, sexual immorality and sales of idols.

The century began without the threat of any superpowers in the Middle East. This allowed Jereboam II to consolidate politically and economically. Assyria (in the east) became the dominant military threat, while at the same time to a lesser degree Egypt experienced resurgence in the west. Israel, besides trying to play Egypt and Assyria against each other, utilized its military might to try to force Judah, the southern kingdom, to join them in a revolt against Assyria. This attempt failed and soon after (721 B.C.) Assyria destroyed Israel.

The book tells us little about Hosea's life; it is primarily about his message—a holistic critique of Israel. Using powerful metaphorical language, Hosea attacks theology, morals, economy and politics. God is passionately concerned for both the responsibility of the individual as well as the society to care for and to give justice to the poor. But the message he gives Hosea is not only one of drastic judgment, but also one of his astounding love, mercy and forgiveness. Carefully reading Hosea's message will help you flesh out these great truths.

Outline

1/ Hosea 1:1—2:1 ——— *What's in a Name?*

2/ Hosea 2:2—3:5 ——— *Married to the Lord?*

3/ Hosea 4 ——— *How Not to Love God*

4/ Hosea 5:1—6:11 ——— *Destroying Evil*

5/ Hosea 6:11—8:14 ——— *What Do You See?*

6/ Hosea 9—10 ——— *What Are You Planting?*

7/ Hosea 11:1–11 ——— *Turning Away from God*

8/ Hosea 11:12—13:16 ——— *Chasing the Wind*

9/ Hosea 14 ——— *Who Is Wise?*

1 / *Hosea 1:1—2:1*
What's in a Name?

WHY WERE YOU given the name that you have? Were you named after a relative or a famous person? The names of Hosea's children are chosen by the Lord because of their meaning. When you see their names, you may be grateful that it was your parents who chose your name!

Warming Up to God Jesus' name, as well as Hosea's, means "the Lord saves" in Hebrew. How is the name of Jesus meaningful to you?

Read Hosea 1:1—2:1.

1 The word of the LORD that came to Hosea
son of Beeri during the reigns of Uzziah,
Jotham, Ahaz and Hezekiah, kings of Ju-
dah, and during the reign of Jeroboam son of Je-
hoash[a] king of Israel:
2When the LORD began to speak through Hosea,
the LORD said to him, "Go, take to yourself an
adulterous wife and children of unfaithfulness,
because the land is guilty of the vilest adultery in
departing from the LORD." 3So he married Gomer
daughter of Diblaim, and she conceived and bore
him a son.
4Then the LORD said to Hosea, "Call him Jez-
reel, because I will soon punish the house of Jehu
for the massacre at Jezreel, and I will put an end
to the kingdom of Israel. 5In that day I will break
Israel's bow in the Valley of Jezreel."
6Gomer conceived again and gave birth to a
daughter. Then the LORD said to Hosea, "Call her
Lo-Ruhamah,[b] for I will no longer show love to
the house of Israel, that I should at all forgive
them. 7Yet I will show love to the house of Judah;
and I will save them—not by bow, sword or bat-
tle, or by horses and horsemen, but by the LORD
their God."
8After she had weaned Lo-Ruhamah, Gomer
had another son. 9Then the LORD said, "Call him
Lo-Ammi,[c] for you are not my people, and I am
not your God.
10"Yet the Israelites will be like the sand on the
seashore, which cannot be measured or counted.
In the place where it was said to them, 'You are
not my people,' they will be called 'sons of the
living God.' 11The people of Judah and the people
of Israel will be reunited, and they will appoint
one leader and will come up out of the land, for
great will be the day of Jezreel.

2 "Say of your brothers, 'My people,' and of
your sisters, 'My loved one.'

[a]1 Hebrew *Joash,* a variant of *Jehoash* [b]6 *Lo-Ruhamah* means *not loved.* [c]9 *Lo-Ammi* means *not my people.*

Discovering the Word 1. In 1:1—2:1 how do the names of Hosea's children play a key part in his message and ministry? 2. How do you react to God's calling Hosea to marry an adulterous wife (v. 2, in Hebrew, "a whore")? 3. Hosea names his firstborn Jezreel (vv. 4–5) after a valley where many bloody massacres had taken place. What would it have been like to have a name like Auschwitz, Hiroshima, Wounded Knee or Tiananmen Square? 4. The translation of the name Lo-Ruhamah (v. 6) is "not loved." How would this name speak to the people of Israel? 5. In the midst of the judgment of God, how would the reversal of the names in verses 1:10—2:1 give the people hope?

Applying the Word 1. Some find it offensive that God called Hosea to marry a whore, yet the point was to characterize God's people as being as unfaithful as a prostitute. How are you unfaithful to God? 2. In 1:10—2:1 God's reaction to the unfaithfulness is unexpected. What does it mean to you to be one of God's people? 3. The good news of 1:10—2:1 is realized today in Jesus Christ. Remember that those you meet today are loved by God and that he calls them his children. If you have an opportunity, offer this message of good news to someone else.

Responding in Prayer Each of us is prone to wander away from God at times. Thank God for his love and forgiveness in your life.

2 / *Hosea 2:2—3:5*
Married to the Lord?

DO YOU REMEMBER the adage "Sticks and stones will break my bones but names will never hurt me"? Children know better. They will tell you that words can hurt. Imagine how a wife of many years would react to hearing "You are not my wife, and I am not your husband." In Hosea 2:2 the Lord's words to Israel have much the same meaning.

Warming Up to God In what ways has your unfaithfulness been a source of pain for God?

Read Hosea 2:2—3:5.

2"Rebuke your mother, rebuke her,
for she is not my wife,
and I am not her husband.
Let her remove the adulterous look from her face
and the unfaithfulness from between her breasts.
3Otherwise I will strip her naked
and make her as bare as on the day she was born;
I will make her like a desert,
turn her into a parched land,
and slay her with thirst.
4I will not show my love to her children,
because they are the children of adultery.
5Their mother has been unfaithful
and has conceived them in disgrace.
She said, 'I will go after my lovers,
who give me my food and my water,
my wool and my linen, my oil and my drink.'
6Therefore I will block her path with thornbushes;
I will wall her in so that she cannot find her way.
7She will chase after her lovers but not catch them;
she will look for them but not find them.
Then she will say,
'I will go back to my husband as at first,
for then I was better off than now.'
8She has not acknowledged that I was the one
who gave her the grain, the new wine and oil,
who lavished on her the silver and gold—
which they used for Baal.

9"Therefore I will take away my grain when it ripens,
and my new wine when it is ready.
I will take back my wool and my linen,
intended to cover her nakedness.
10So now I will expose her lewdness
before the eyes of her lovers;
no one will take her out of my hands.
11I will stop all her celebrations:
her yearly festivals, her New Moons,
her Sabbath days—all her appointed feasts.
12I will ruin her vines and her fig trees,
which she said were her pay from her lovers;
I will make them a thicket,
and wild animals will devour them.
13I will punish her for the days
she burned incense to the Baals;
she decked herself with rings and jewelry,
and went after her lovers,
but me she forgot,"
declares the LORD.

14"Therefore I am now going to allure her;
I will lead her into the desert
and speak tenderly to her.
15There I will give her back her vineyards,
and will make the Valley of Achor[d] a door of hope.
There she will sing[e] as in the days of her youth,
as in the day she came up out of Egypt.

16"In that day," declares the LORD,
"you will call me 'my husband';
you will no longer call me 'my master.[f]'
17I will remove the names of the Baals from her lips;
no longer will their names be invoked.
18In that day I will make a covenant for them

[d]15 *Achor* means *trouble.* [e]15 Or *respond* [f]16 Hebrew *baal*

with the beasts of the field and the birds of
the air
and the creatures that move along the
ground.
Bow and sword and battle
I will abolish from the land,
so that all may lie down in safety.
19 I will betroth you to me forever;
I will betroth you in[g] righteousness and
justice,
in[h] love and compassion.
20 I will betroth you in faithfulness,
and you will acknowledge the LORD.

21 "In that day I will respond,"
declares the LORD—
"I will respond to the skies,
and they will respond to the earth;
22 and the earth will respond to the grain,
the new wine and oil,
and they will respond to Jezreel.[i]
23 I will plant her for myself in the land;
I will show my love to the one I called 'Not
my loved one.[j]'
I will say to those called 'Not my people,[k]'
'You are my people';
and they will say, 'You are my God.' "

3 The LORD said to me, "Go, show your love
to your wife again, though she is loved by
another and is an adulteress. Love her as
the LORD loves the Israelites, though they turn to
other gods and love the sacred raisin cakes."
2 So I bought her for fifteen shekels[l] of silver
and about a homer and a lethek[m] of barley.
3 Then I told her, "You are to live with[n] me many
days; you must not be a prostitute or be intimate
with any man, and I will live with[n] you."
4 For the Israelites will live many days without
king or prince, without sacrifice or sacred stones,
without ephod or idol. 5 Afterward the Israelites
will return and seek the LORD their God and David
their king. They will come trembling to the LORD
and to his blessings in the last days.

g19 Or *with*; also in verse 20 h19 Or *with* i22 *Jezreel* means *God plants.* j23 Hebrew *Lo-Ruhamah* k23 Hebrew *Lo-Ammi* l2 That is, about 6 ounces (about 170 grams) m2 That is, probably about 10 bushels (about 330 liters) n3 Or *wait for*

Discovering the Word 1. How does Israel demonstrate that she is not God's wife (2:2–13)? 2. Chapter 2 is organized by four "threats" (vv. 3, 6, 9, 14), each beginning with *otherwise* or *therefore*. What sets the fourth "threat" apart from the other three? 3. After all the unfaithfulness (2:2–13), how can God do what is described in 2:14–23? 4. Baal is a name for a false god and is translated "lord," "husband" or "master." In 2:16–17 Hosea tells the people to stop calling God "Baal" and to call him "my husband" instead. What significance do you see in that name change? 5. What are the characteristics of a good "marriage" to God (2:18–23)? 6. God has Hosea take back his unfaithful wife in chapter 3. How does Hosea's action mirror God's actions toward Israel?

Applying the Word 1. Israel gave credit for her provisions of necessities and luxuries to other gods instead of to the Lord (2:2–13). Who do you give credit to? 2. How is God calling you and your community to the desert (2:14–23)? 3. We live in the "already" of being the bride of Christ, but we look forward to the "not yet" of perfect peace to come. Imagine what it will be like. How does that picture change your perspective on today?

Responding in Prayer Ask God to forgive you for your unfaithfulness and help you to know him as a God who makes you his bride.

3 / *Hosea 4*
How Not to Love God

HOW DO YOU know if you really love God? Look at how you treat God's people (1Jn 4:20). Hosea tells the people of Israel that they do not know God (4:1). This is revealed in the quality of their society and their worship.

Warming Up to God How do your actions confirm or deny your relationship with God?

 **Read Hosea 4.**

4 Hear the word of the LORD, you Israelites,
because the LORD has a charge to bring against you who live in the land:
"There is no faithfulness, no love,
no acknowledgment of God in the land.
2There is only cursing,[o] lying and murder,
stealing and adultery;
they break all bounds,
and bloodshed follows bloodshed.
3Because of this the land mourns,[p]
and all who live in it waste away;
the beasts of the field and the birds of the air
and the fish of the sea are dying.
4"But let no man bring a charge,
let no man accuse another,
for your people are like those
who bring charges against a priest.
5You stumble day and night,
and the prophets stumble with you.
So I will destroy your mother—
6 my people are destroyed from lack of knowledge.

"Because you have rejected knowledge,
I also reject you as my priests;
because you have ignored the law of your God,
I also will ignore your children.
7The more the priests increased,
the more they sinned against me;
they exchanged[q] their[r] Glory for something disgraceful.
8They feed on the sins of my people
and relish their wickedness.
9And it will be: Like people, like priests.
I will punish both of them for their ways
and repay them for their deeds.

10"They will eat but not have enough;
they will engage in prostitution but not increase,
because they have deserted the LORD
to give themselves 11to prostitution,
to old wine and new,
which take away the understanding 12of my people.
They consult a wooden idol
and are answered by a stick of wood.
A spirit of prostitution leads them astray;
they are unfaithful to their God.
13They sacrifice on the mountaintops
and burn offerings on the hills,
under oak, poplar and terebinth,
where the shade is pleasant.
Therefore your daughters turn to prostitution
and your daughters-in-law to adultery.

14"I will not punish your daughters
when they turn to prostitution,
nor your daughters-in-law
when they commit adultery,
because the men themselves consort with harlots
and sacrifice with shrine prostitutes—
a people without understanding will come to ruin!

15"Though you commit adultery, O Israel,
let not Judah become guilty.

"Do not go to Gilgal;
do not go up to Beth Aven.[s]
And do not swear, 'As surely as the LORD lives!'
16The Israelites are stubborn,
like a stubborn heifer.
How then can the LORD pasture them
like lambs in a meadow?
17Ephraim is joined to idols;
leave him alone!
18Even when their drinks are gone,
they continue their prostitution;
their rulers dearly love shameful ways.
19A whirlwind will sweep them away,
and their sacrifices will bring them shame.

[o]2 That is, to pronounce a curse upon [p]3 Or *dries up* [q]7 Syriac and an ancient Hebrew scribal tradition; Masoretic Text *I will exchange* [r]7 Masoretic Text; an ancient Hebrew scribal tradition *my* [s]15 *Beth Aven* means *house of wickedness* (a name for Bethel, which means *house of God*).

Discovering the Word 1. What in verses 1–2 demonstrates that the knowledge of God is absent in Israel? 2. Why is the Lord angry with the priest (vv. 4–6)? 3. One way God provided for the priests was for them to receive a good portion of people's sacrifices. How had the priests corrupted their office (vv. 7–10)? 4. Verses 11–19 describe the people's worship habits. How had they deteriorated? 5. How are knowledge of God and worship interrelated?

Applying the Word 1. The character of the people is described as stubborn in verse 16. In what way are you stubborn before God and his people? 2. The knowledge of God in this chapter is tied up with more than our relationship with the Lord. How can you and your community demonstrate your knowledge of God by your actions today? this year?

Responding in Prayer Ask God to help you reflect on how you can love him more by loving others more.

4 / *Hosea 5:1—6:11*
Destroying Evil

"GOD IS LIKE rot." Wow! Can you imagine describing the Lord that way? Hosea did (5:12). He wanted to make a point about the God who will destroy evil in the community. The image of God as a moth (5:12) eating away at evil can be a source of comfort to us as we experience pain in this world.

Warming Up to God What evil would you like to see put under God's destructive power? Ask God to help you see what a mighty God he is.

Read Hosea 5:1—6:11.

5 "Hear this, you priests!
Pay attention, you Israelites!
Listen, O royal house!
This judgment is against you:
You have been a snare at Mizpah,
a net spread out on Tabor.
2 The rebels are deep in slaughter.
I will discipline all of them.
3 I know all about Ephraim;
Israel is not hidden from me.
Ephraim, you have now turned to prostitution;
Israel is corrupt.

4 "Their deeds do not permit them
to return to their God.
A spirit of prostitution is in their heart;
they do not acknowledge the LORD.
5 Israel's arrogance testifies against them;
the Israelites, even Ephraim, stumble in their sin;
Judah also stumbles with them.
6 When they go with their flocks and herds
to seek the LORD,
they will not find him;
he has withdrawn himself from them.
7 They are unfaithful to the LORD;
they give birth to illegitimate children.
Now their New Moon festivals
will devour them and their fields.

8 "Sound the trumpet in Gibeah,
the horn in Ramah.
Raise the battle cry in Beth Aven[t];
lead on, O Benjamin.
9 Ephraim will be laid waste
on the day of reckoning.
Among the tribes of Israel
I proclaim what is certain.
10 Judah's leaders are like those
who move boundary stones.
I will pour out my wrath on them
like a flood of water.
11 Ephraim is oppressed,
trampled in judgment,
intent on pursuing idols.[u]
12 I am like a moth to Ephraim,

[t] 8 *Beth Aven* means *house of wickedness* (a name for Bethel, which means *house of God*). [u] 11 The meaning of the Hebrew for this word is uncertain.

like rot to the people of Judah.
13"When Ephraim saw his sickness,
and Judah his sores,
then Ephraim turned to Assyria,
and sent to the great king for help.
But he is not able to cure you,
not able to heal your sores.
14For I will be like a lion to Ephraim,
like a great lion to Judah.
I will tear them to pieces and go away;
I will carry them off, with no one to rescue them.
15Then I will go back to my place
until they admit their guilt.
And they will seek my face;
in their misery they will earnestly seek me."

6 "Come, let us return to the LORD.
He has torn us to pieces
but he will heal us;
he has injured us
but he will bind up our wounds.
2After two days he will revive us;
on the third day he will restore us,
that we may live in his presence.
3Let us acknowledge the LORD;
let us press on to acknowledge him.
As surely as the sun rises,
he will appear;
he will come to us like the winter rains,
like the spring rains that water the earth."

4"What can I do with you, Ephraim?
What can I do with you, Judah?
Your love is like the morning mist,
like the early dew that disappears.
5Therefore I cut you in pieces with my prophets,
I killed you with the words of my mouth;
my judgments flashed like lightning upon you.
6For I desire mercy, not sacrifice,
and acknowledgment of God rather than burnt offerings.
7Like Adam,[v] they have broken the covenant—
they were unfaithful to me there.
8Gilead is a city of wicked men,
stained with footprints of blood.
9As marauders lie in ambush for a man,
so do bands of priests;
they murder on the road to Shechem,
committing shameful crimes.
10I have seen a horrible thing
in the house of Israel.
There Ephraim is given to prostitution
and Israel is defiled.

11"Also for you, Judah,
a harvest is appointed.

[v]7 Or *As at Adam*; or *Like men*

Discovering the Word 1. Ephraim/Israel has turned to prostitution (both literally and figuratively). How are the Israelites politically, socially and religiously unfaithful to the Lord in chapters 5—6? 2. What vivid language does Hosea use in these chapters to describe the Lord who is going to punish Israel? 3. Ephraim/Israel sees Assyria (5:13) as the answer to a military threat she faces. How is this unfaithfulness to the Lord? 4. What do you make of the people's call to worship in 6:1–3? 5. How does the Lord respond to their call to worship (6:4–6)?

Applying the Word 1. Thinking creatively, what word pictures would you use to characterize God? 2. How can your deeds hinder your discipleship? 3. While Hosea is not against the sacrificial system, it is clear that he is opposed to the empty religiosity of the people (6:6). How can we be sure that we are not merely going through the motions?

Responding in Prayer Ask God to show you the things that keep you from returning to him. Ask God to cleanse and restore you for his use and glory.

5 / *Hosea 6:11—8:14*
What Do You See?

HAVE YOU EVER looked at yourself in distorted carnival mirrors that make you look extremely tall and thin or incredibly short and fat? In the next few chapters of Hosea it seems that the Israelites had the opposite kinds of mirrors—they saw only the images of themselves that they wanted to see. Through Hosea the Lord tries to get the Israelites to see their reflection as it really is.

Warming Up to God Ask God to open your eyes and your spirit to the truth about yourself.

Read Hosea 6:11—8:14.

"Whenever I would restore the fortunes of my
people,

7 [1]whenever I would heal Israel,
the sins of Ephraim are exposed
and the crimes of Samaria revealed.
They practice deceit,
thieves break into houses,
bandits rob in the streets;
[2]but they do not realize
that I remember all their evil deeds.
Their sins engulf them;
they are always before me.

[3]"They delight the king with their wickedness,
the princes with their lies.
[4]They are all adulterers,
burning like an oven
whose fire the baker need not stir
from the kneading of the dough till it rises.
[5]On the day of the festival of our king
the princes become inflamed with wine,
and he joins hands with the mockers.
[6]Their hearts are like an oven;
they approach him with intrigue.
Their passion smolders all night;
in the morning it blazes like a flaming fire.
[7]All of them are hot as an oven;
they devour their rulers.
All their kings fall,
and none of them calls on me.

[8]"Ephraim mixes with the nations;
Ephraim is a flat cake not turned over.
[9]Foreigners sap his strength,
but he does not realize it.
His hair is sprinkled with gray,
but he does not notice.
[10]Israel's arrogance testifies against him,
but despite all this
he does not return to the LORD his God
or search for him.

[11]"Ephraim is like a dove,
easily deceived and senseless—
now calling to Egypt,
now turning to Assyria.
[12]When they go, I will throw my net over
them;
I will pull them down like birds of the air.
When I hear them flocking together,
I will catch them.
[13]Woe to them,
because they have strayed from me!
Destruction to them,
because they have rebelled against me!
I long to redeem them
but they speak lies against me.
[14]They do not cry out to me from their hearts
but wail upon their beds.
They gather together[w] for grain and new
wine
but turn away from me.
[15]I trained them and strengthened them,
but they plot evil against me.
[16]They do not turn to the Most High;
they are like a faulty bow.
Their leaders will fall by the sword
because of their insolent words.
For this they will be ridiculed
in the land of Egypt.

8 "Put the trumpet to your lips!
An eagle is over the house of the LORD
because the people have broken my
covenant
and rebelled against my law.

[w]14 Most Hebrew manuscripts; some Hebrew manuscripts and Septuagint *They slash themselves*

and now they must bear their guilt.
The LORD will demolish their altars
and destroy their sacred stones.

3Then they will say, "We have no king
because we did not revere the LORD.
But even if we had a king,
what could he do for us?"
4They make many promises,
take false oaths
and make agreements;
therefore lawsuits spring up
like poisonous weeds in a plowed field.
5The people who live in Samaria fear
for the calf-idol of Beth Aven.[z]
Its people will mourn over it,
and so will its idolatrous priests,
those who had rejoiced over its splendor,
because it is taken from them into exile.
6It will be carried to Assyria
as tribute for the great king.
Ephraim will be disgraced;
Israel will be ashamed of its wooden
idols.[a]
7Samaria and its king will float away
like a twig on the surface of the waters.
8The high places of wickedness[b] will be
destroyed—
it is the sin of Israel.
Thorns and thistles will grow up
and cover their altars.
Then they will say to the mountains, "Cover
us!"
and to the hills, "Fall on us!"
9"Since the days of Gibeah, you have sinned,
O Israel,
and there you have remained.[c]
Did not war overtake
the evildoers in Gibeah?
10When I please, I will punish them;
nations will be gathered against them
to put them in bonds for their double sin.
11Ephraim is a trained heifer
that loves to thresh;
so I will put a yoke
on her fair neck.
I will drive Ephraim,
Judah must plow,
and Jacob must break up the ground.
12Sow for yourselves righteousness,
reap the fruit of unfailing love,
and break up your unplowed ground;
for it is time to seek the LORD,
until he comes
and showers righteousness on you.
13But you have planted wickedness,
you have reaped evil,
you have eaten the fruit of deception.
Because you have depended on your own
strength
and on your many warriors,
14the roar of battle will rise against your people,
so that all your fortresses will be
devastated—
as Shalman devastated Beth Arbel on the day
of battle,
when mothers were dashed to the ground
with their children.
15Thus will it happen to you, O Bethel,
because your wickedness is great.
When that day dawns,
the king of Israel will be completely
destroyed.

[z]5 *Beth Aven* means *house of wickedness* (a name for Bethel, which means *house of God*). [a]6 *Or its counsel* [b]8 *Hebrew aven, a reference to Beth Aven (a derogatory name for Bethel)* [c]9 *Or there a stand was taken*

Discovering the Word 1. How do you see the theme of fertility in chapters 9—10? 2. Festival days were to celebrate the Lord's goodness to Israel. Why then would God take away the joy of the celebration? 3. Why was the prophet, God's lookout, considered a fool (9:7–8)? 4. Hosea describes the people using farming metaphors. What images stand out to you (9:10, 13, 16; 10:1, 4, 7, 11–13)? 5. How does the metaphor of planting describe the plight of Israel (10:11–15)?

Applying the Word 1. When do you find yourself focused more on what the Lord has blessed you with than on the Blesser himself? 2. How has the law of the farm—what you sow, you reap—shown itself in your life? 3. No one likes listening to prophets because they call into question those things which make us comfortable. How can we (as individuals and as the church) learn to keep our ears open to the prophets in our lives?

Responding in Prayer Ask God to help you to be a more faithful worker in the fields of your life, the church and the world.

7 / *Hosea 11:1–11*
Turning Away from God

YOU'VE PROBABLY HAD the experience of being nice to someone who did not appreciate it. It can result in a wedge in the relationship you were trying to nurture. But what about the reverse? Has there been a time when someone was nice to you, but you didn't realize it until much later? Your response to that kindness was probably much less than it should have been. Unfortunately for Israel, their response to God was horrible. God had nurtured them for years, but they gave their love to other gods.

Warming Up to God When is it hard for you to experience God's love for you as his child? Ask God to make his love more than head knowledge for you.

Read Hosea 11:1–11.

11 "When Israel was a child, I loved him,
and out of Egypt I called my son.
2But the more I[d] called Israel,
the further they went from me.[e]
They sacrificed to the Baals
and they burned incense to images.
3It was I who taught Ephraim to walk,
taking them by the arms;
but they did not realize
it was I who healed them.
4I led them with cords of human kindness,
with ties of love;
I lifted the yoke from their neck
and bent down to feed them.
5"Will they not return to Egypt
and will not Assyria rule over them
because they refuse to repent?
6Swords will flash in their cities,
will destroy the bars of their gates
and put an end to their plans.
7My people are determined to turn from me.
Even if they call to the Most High,
he will by no means exalt them.
8"How can I give you up, Ephraim?
How can I hand you over, Israel?
How can I treat you like Admah?
How can I make you like Zeboiim?
My heart is changed within me;
all my compassion is aroused.
9I will not carry out my fierce anger,
nor will I turn and devastate Ephraim.
For I am God, and not man—
the Holy One among you.
I will not come in wrath.[f]
10They will follow the LORD;
he will roar like a lion.
When he roars,
his children will come trembling from the west.
11They will come trembling
like birds from Egypt,
like doves from Assyria.
I will settle them in their homes,"
declares the LORD.

[d]2 Some Septuagint manuscripts; Hebrew *they* [e]2 Septuagint; Hebrew *them* [f]9 Or *come against any city*

Discovering the Word 1. What emotions do you sense as you read 11:1–11? 2. How did the Lord treat Israel (vv. 1, 3–4)? 3. Why does Israel respond to the Lord as she does (vv. 1–7)? 4. What do you make of God's anguish as he wrestles with treating Israel like the sister cities of Sodom and Gomorrah (vv. 8–9; Gen 14; Deut 29:23)? 5. Why will the Israelites finally respond to God's call (vv. 10–11)?

Applying the Word 1. How is your experience of God like the Israelites'? 2. What does it mean to you that the Lord is not human? 3. How are you affected by the descriptions of God's emotions?

Responding in Prayer Pray that God will keep you from being determined to turn away. Ask him to help you realize the depth of his love and to give you the same love for him.

8 / *Hosea 11:12—13:16*
Chasing the Wind

IF YOU KNEW that two tornadoes were going to collide, would you stand in the middle of them? Israel did, because she thought she could play the two superpowers against each other. Hosea called this foolish practice "pursuing the wind." (The west wind was Egypt and the east wind was the more terrifying Assyria.) Instead of relying on the Lord, Israel thought she could control her future through foreign policy. History tells us that Israel was destroyed by Assyria.

Warming Up to God Reflect before God on how you control your life and your future.

Read Hosea 11:12—13:16.

12 Ephraim has surrounded me with lies,
the house of Israel with deceit.
And Judah is unruly against God,
even against the faithful Holy One.

12
1 Ephraim feeds on the wind;
he pursues the east wind all day
and multiplies lies and violence.
He makes a treaty with Assyria
and sends olive oil to Egypt.
2 The LORD has a charge to bring against Judah;
he will punish Jacob[g] according to his ways
and repay him according to his deeds.
3 In the womb he grasped his brother's heel;
as a man he struggled with God.
4 He struggled with the angel and overcame him;
he wept and begged for his favor.
He found him at Bethel
and talked with him there—
5 the LORD God Almighty,
the LORD is his name of renown!
6 But you must return to your God;
maintain love and justice,
and wait for your God always.

7 The merchant uses dishonest scales;
he loves to defraud.
8 Ephraim boasts,
"I am very rich; I have become wealthy.
With all my wealth they will not find in me
any iniquity or sin."

9 "I am the LORD your God,
⌞who brought you⌟ out of[h] Egypt;
I will make you live in tents again,
as in the days of your appointed feasts.
10 I spoke to the prophets,
gave them many visions
and told parables through them."

11 Is Gilead wicked?
Its people are worthless!
Do they sacrifice bulls in Gilgal?
Their altars will be like piles of stones
on a plowed field.
12 Jacob fled to the country of Aram[i];
Israel served to get a wife,
and to pay for her he tended sheep.
13 The LORD used a prophet to bring Israel up from Egypt,
by a prophet he cared for him.
14 But Ephraim has bitterly provoked him to anger;
his Lord will leave upon him the guilt of his bloodshed
and will repay him for his contempt.

g2 *Jacob* means *he grasps the heel* (figuratively, *he deceives*). h9 Or *God / ever since you were in* i12 That is, Northwest Mesopotamia

13

When Ephraim spoke, men trembled;
he was exalted in Israel.
But he became guilty of Baal worship and died.
2Now they sin more and more;
they make idols for themselves from their silver,
cleverly fashioned images,
all of them the work of craftsmen.
It is said of these people,
"They offer human sacrifice
and kiss[j] the calf-idols."
3Therefore they will be like the morning mist,
like the early dew that disappears,
like chaff swirling from a threshing floor,
like smoke escaping through a window.

4"But I am the LORD your God,
⌞who brought you⌟ out of[k] Egypt.
You shall acknowledge no God but me,
no Savior except me.
5I cared for you in the desert,
in the land of burning heat.
6When I fed them, they were satisfied;
when they were satisfied, they became proud;
then they forgot me.
7So I will come upon them like a lion,
like a leopard I will lurk by the path.
8Like a bear robbed of her cubs,
I will attack them and rip them open.
Like a lion I will devour them;
a wild animal will tear them apart.

9"You are destroyed, O Israel,
because you are against me, against your helper.
10Where is your king, that he may save you?
Where are your rulers in all your towns,
of whom you said,
'Give me a king and princes'?
11So in my anger I gave you a king,
and in my wrath I took him away.
12The guilt of Ephraim is stored up,
his sins are kept on record.
13Pains as of a woman in childbirth come to him,
but he is a child without wisdom;
when the time arrives,
he does not come to the opening of the womb.

14"I will ransom them from the power of the grave[l];
I will redeem them from death.
Where, O death, are your plagues?
Where, O grave,[l] is your destruction?

"I will have no compassion,
15 even though he thrives among his brothers.
An east wind from the LORD will come,
blowing in from the desert;
his spring will fail
and his well dry up.
His storehouse will be plundered
of all its treasures.
16The people of Samaria must bear their guilt,
because they have rebelled against their God.
They will fall by the sword;
their little ones will be dashed to the ground,
their pregnant women ripped open."

[j]2 Or "*Men who sacrifice / kiss* [k]4 Or *God / ever since you were in*
[l]14 Hebrew *Sheol*

Discovering the Word 1. How is Israel (also called Ephraim, Jacob and Samaria) revealed as lying, deceitful and manipulative in chapters 12 and 13? 2. How does God stand in contrast to Israel (12:5, 6, 9, 10, 13; 13:4–6)? 3. How does Hosea show the silliness of Israel's pride and idolatry (12:8; 13:2, 6, 13)? 4. Why does Hosea keep reminding Israel of what the Lord God did for them in the past? 5. What was the result of Israel's unfaithfulness to God and her manipulation of Assyria (13:15–16)?

Applying the Word 1. How do you lie to or manipulate God, others and yourself? 2. How can you let the Lord poke holes in your pride and idolatry? 3. How does the way God has saved you in the past change the way you look at the present and the future?

Responding in Prayer Pray that you will remember where to put your trust when the wind blows and when it is silent.

9 / *Hosea 14*
Who Is Wise?

SUPPOSE SOMEONE SAID to you, "Well, if you really knew me, I'm not sure that you would tell me that God loves me." What would you say? Have you ever wondered how God could love you? After reading Hosea, it is quite reasonable to wonder how God could love Israel. The Lord knew Israel to be thoroughly corrupt, and yet in chapter 14 God holds out incredible grace to this wicked nation.

Warming Up to God Our sins are often too big for us to handle. When have you felt that your sins were too big even for God to handle?

Read Hosea 14.

14 Return, O Israel, to the LORD your God.
Your sins have been your downfall!
2 Take words with you
and return to the LORD.
Say to him:
"Forgive all our sins
and receive us graciously,
that we may offer the fruit of our lips.[m]
3 Assyria cannot save us;
we will not mount war-horses.
We will never again say 'Our gods'
to what our own hands have made,
for in you the fatherless find compassion."
4 "I will heal their waywardness
and love them freely,
for my anger has turned away from them.
5 I will be like the dew to Israel;
he will blossom like a lily.
Like a cedar of Lebanon
he will send down his roots;
6 his young shoots will grow.
His splendor will be like an olive tree,
his fragrance like a cedar of Lebanon.
7 Men will dwell again in his shade.
He will flourish like the grain.
He will blossom like a vine,
and his fame will be like the wine from Lebanon.
8 O Ephraim, what more have I[n] to do with idols?
I will answer him and care for him.
I am like a green pine tree;
your fruitfulness comes from me."

9 Who is wise? He will realize these things.
Who is discerning? He will understand them.
The ways of the LORD are right;
the righteous walk in them,
but the rebellious stumble in them.

[m]2 Or *offer our lips as sacrifices of bulls* [n]8 Or *What more has Ephraim*

Discovering the Word 1. How does this chapter act as a conclusion to Hosea? 2. What must Israel do to receive God's forgiveness (vv. 1–3)? 3. What promises are held out to a community who rebelled so greatly against the Lord (vv. 4–7)? 4. Israel sought help from other countries and from idols. How does the Lord stand in contrast to these "saviors" (vv. 8–9)?

Applying the Word 1. How do you need to heed and pray verses 1–3 or words like them? 2. In what way do you need to let God love you as he promises in verses 4–8? 3. Understanding and walking in the ways of the Lord are two critical partners for wisdom. How is that partnership of learning and doing manifested in your life? 4. Where should the partnership be strengthened?

Responding in Prayer Thank the Lord for forgiving and healing you. Pray that the Holy Spirit would help you to both know and walk in God's ways.

Joel

In "The Great Stone Face" Nathaniel Hawthorne tells the story of a rock formation on the side of a mountain that resembled a human face. Legend had it that a truly great man resembling the great stone face would someday come to the nearby town. One boy made it his life's goal to study the face and search for its resemblance in others. Over the years he spent countless hours gazing with wonder at that awesome face. As the boy matured into manhood and as life's influences molded him, those around him were amazed to see what he had become—the great stone face!

The people of Judah were not being cautious about where they focused their attention. Joel's role was to warn them that their faces—and hearts—might be turning to stone.

We know little about the man Joel other than the fact that his message was geared toward Judah and that he was probably a resident of Jerusalem. The date of his writing is disputed among scholars. While some say Joel prophesied as late as 400 B.C., many believe he was a contemporary of Jonah and Amos.

Joel's prophecy came in the wake of a devastating locust plague. Joel saw this plague as a sign of God's judgment and warned that unless the people returned to the Lord they would face even greater judgment on the day of the Lord. But to those willing to "rend their hearts" he promised great blessings that would more than repay "the years the locusts have eaten" (2:25).

Outline

1 / *Joel 1*
Responding to a Crisis

A CRISIS CAN capture anyone's attention. But the response to a crisis can vary greatly from person to person. Some become bitter and hardened. Others quietly endure but learn nothing from the experience. A few, however, find their lives are purified, deepened and strengthened. In Joel 1 a major crisis has occurred—a swarm of locusts has invaded the land, with devastating results. In the aftermath of the devastation, Joel appears with a word from the Lord. His word still has the power to purify those who hear it.

Warming Up to God What is the most traumatic event you have seen during your lifetime? Explain.

Read Joel 1.

---

1 The word of the LORD that came to Joel
son of Pethuel.

[2]Hear this, you elders;
listen, all who live in the land.
Has anything like this ever happened in your
days
or in the days of your forefathers?
[3]Tell it to your children,
and let your children tell it to their
children,
and their children to the next generation.
[4]What the locust swarm has left
the great locusts have eaten;
what the great locusts have left
the young locusts have eaten;
what the young locusts have left
other locusts[a] have eaten.

[5]Wake up, you drunkards, and weep!
Wail, all you drinkers of wine;
wail because of the new wine,
for it has been snatched from your lips.
[6]A nation has invaded my land,
powerful and without number;
it has the teeth of a lion,
the fangs of a lioness.
[7]It has laid waste my vines
and ruined my fig trees.
It has stripped off their bark
and thrown it away,
leaving their branches white.

[8]Mourn like a virgin[b] in sackcloth
grieving for the husband[c] of her youth.
[9]Grain offerings and drink offerings
are cut off from the house of the LORD.
The priests are in mourning,
those who minister before the LORD.
[10]The fields are ruined,
the ground is dried up[d];
the grain is destroyed,
the new wine is dried up,
the oil fails.
[11]Despair, you farmers,
wail, you vine growers;
grieve for the wheat and the barley,
because the harvest of the field is
destroyed.
[12]The vine is dried up
and the fig tree is withered;
the pomegranate, the palm and the apple
tree—
all the trees of the field—are dried up.
Surely the joy of mankind
is withered away.

[13]Put on sackcloth, O priests, and mourn;
wail, you who minister before the altar.
Come, spend the night in sackcloth,
you who minister before my God;
for the grain offerings and drink offerings
are withheld from the house of your God.
[14]Declare a holy fast;
call a sacred assembly.
Summon the elders
and all who live in the land
to the house of the LORD your God,
and cry out to the LORD.

[15]Alas for that day!
For the day of the LORD is near;
it will come like destruction from the
Almighty.[e]

[a]4 The precise meaning of the four Hebrew words used here for locusts is uncertain. [b]8 Or *young woman* [c]8 Or *betrothed* [d]10 Or *ground mourns* [e]15 Hebrew *Shaddai*

16Has not the food been cut off
before our very eyes—
joy and gladness
from the house of our God?
17The seeds are shriveled
beneath the clods.[f]
The storehouses are in ruins,
the granaries have been broken down,
for the grain has dried up.
18How the cattle moan!
The herds mill about
because they have no pasture;
even the flocks of sheep are suffering.
19To you, O LORD, I call,
for fire has devoured the open pastures
and flames have burned up all the trees of the field.
20Even the wild animals pant for you;
the streams of water have dried up
and fire has devoured the open pastures.

f17 The meaning of the Hebrew for this word is uncertain.

Discovering the Word 1. Describe the devastation left by the locust plague. 2. How will the plague affect the drunkards (v. 5), the priests (vv. 9, 13) and the farmers (v. 11)? 3. Why do you think these groups are singled out? 4. Joel compares the people of Judah to a virgin mourning for her husband (a fiancé[e] was referred to as *husband* or *wife*) (v. 8). What does this metaphor say about the depth of relationship between God and his people? 5. In verses 13–14 Joel calls the people to repent. How are they to demonstrate their repentance?

Applying the Word 1. In what ways does God discipline his people today, either individually or corporately? 2. In what meaningful ways can you express your repentance today, both individually and corporately?

Responding in Prayer Ask God to show you where your inner life is in crisis and how you need to repent.

2 / *Joel 2:1–27*
Return to the Lord!

IN ORDER TO get to the roses, we must first go through the thorns. The teaching of Joel in the first two chapters is hard. But roses—in the form of the promises of God—lie ahead. Because he loves us, the Father disciplines us when we wander from him. The warnings we see here are God's last resort to bring his people to true repentance—a *heart* relationship rather than one of empty ritual. As we read this chapter, we too must face questions of the heart.

Warming Up to God How do we sometimes serve God outwardly rather than from the heart?

Read Joel 2:1–27.

2 Blow the trumpet in Zion;
sound the alarm on my holy hill.
Let all who live in the land tremble,
for the day of the LORD is coming.
It is close at hand—
2 a day of darkness and gloom,
a day of clouds and blackness.
Like dawn spreading across the mountains
a large and mighty army comes,
such as never was of old
nor ever will be in ages to come.
3Before them fire devours,
behind them a flame blazes.
Before them the land is like the garden of Eden,
behind them, a desert waste—
nothing escapes them.
4They have the appearance of horses;
they gallop along like cavalry.
5With a noise like that of chariots
they leap over the mountaintops,
like a crackling fire consuming stubble,

like a mighty army drawn up for battle.
6At the sight of them, nations are in anguish;
every face turns pale.
7They charge like warriors;
they scale walls like soldiers.
They all march in line,
not swerving from their course.
8They do not jostle each other;
each marches straight ahead.
They plunge through defenses
without breaking ranks.
9They rush upon the city;
they run along the wall.
They climb into the houses;
like thieves they enter through the
windows.
10Before them the earth shakes,
the sky trembles,
the sun and moon are darkened,
and the stars no longer shine.
11The LORD thunders
at the head of his army;
his forces are beyond number,
and mighty are those who obey his
command.
The day of the LORD is great;
it is dreadful.
Who can endure it?

12"Even now," declares the LORD,
"return to me with all your heart,
with fasting and weeping and mourning."
13Rend your heart
and not your garments.
Return to the LORD your God,
for he is gracious and compassionate,
slow to anger and abounding in love,
and he relents from sending calamity.
14Who knows? He may turn and have pity
and leave behind a blessing—
grain offerings and drink offerings
for the LORD your God.

15Blow the trumpet in Zion,
declare a holy fast,
call a sacred assembly.
16Gather the people,
consecrate the assembly;
bring together the elders,
gather the children,
those nursing at the breast.
Let the bridegroom leave his room
and the bride her chamber.
17Let the priests, who minister before the LORD,
weep between the temple porch and the
altar.
Let them say, "Spare your people, O LORD.
Do not make your inheritance an object of
scorn,
a byword among the nations.
Why should they say among the peoples,
'Where is their God?' "

18Then the LORD will be jealous for his land
and take pity on his people.

19The LORD will reply[g] to them:

"I am sending you grain, new wine and oil,
enough to satisfy you fully;
never again will I make you
an object of scorn to the nations.

20"I will drive the northern army far from you,
pushing it into a parched and barren land,
with its front columns going into the eastern
sea[h]
and those in the rear into the western
sea.[i]
And its stench will go up;
its smell will rise."

Surely he has done great things.[j]
21 Be not afraid, O land;
be glad and rejoice.
Surely the LORD has done great things.
22 Be not afraid, O wild animals,
for the open pastures are becoming green.
The trees are bearing their fruit;
the fig tree and the vine yield their riches.
23Be glad, O people of Zion,
rejoice in the LORD your God,
for he has given you
the autumn rains in righteousness.[k]
He sends you abundant showers,
both autumn and spring rains, as before.
24The threshing floors will be filled with grain;
the vats will overflow with new wine and
oil.

25"I will repay you for the years the locusts
have eaten—
the great locust and the young locust,

[g]18,19 Or *LORD was jealous . . . / and took pity . . . / 19The LORD replied* [h]20 That is, the Dead Sea [i]20 That is, the Mediterranean [j]20 Or *rise. / Surely it has done great things."* [k]23 Or */ the teacher for righteousness:*

the other locusts and the locust swarm[l]—
my great army that I sent among you.
26You will have plenty to eat, until you are full,
and you will praise the name of the LORD
your God,
who has worked wonders for you;
never again will my people be shamed.
27Then you will know that I am in Israel,
that I am the LORD your God,
and that there is no other;
never again will my people be shamed.

[l]25 The precise meaning of the four Hebrew words used here for locusts is uncertain.

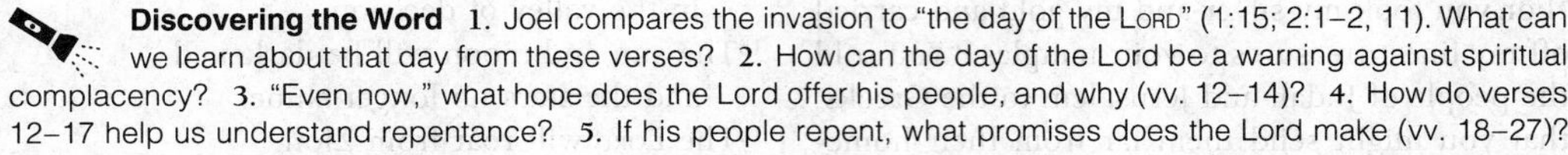

Discovering the Word 1. Joel compares the invasion to "the day of the LORD" (1:15; 2:1–2, 11). What can we learn about that day from these verses? 2. How can the day of the Lord be a warning against spiritual complacency? 3. "Even now," what hope does the Lord offer his people, and why (vv. 12–14)? 4. How do verses 12–17 help us understand repentance? 5. If his people repent, what promises does the Lord make (vv. 18–27)?

Applying the Word 1. In what ways would you like to renew your commitment to the Lord? 2. How have you experienced God's healing through the act of repentance?

Responding in Prayer Take time to "praise the name of the LORD your God" for the wonders he has worked for you (v. 26).

3 / *Joel 2:28—3:21*
The Day of the Lord

CHRISTIANS LONG FOR that great and final day when the Lord will return. But the day of the Lord will not be the same for everyone. For some it will be a day of indescribable joy and blessing. For others it will be a day of judgment and terror. In this final section of his book, Joel looks at both aspects of the day of the Lord.

Warming Up to God When you think of the Lord's return, what images come to mind?

Read Joel 2:28—3:21.

28"And afterward,
I will pour out my Spirit on all people.
Your sons and daughters will prophesy,
your old men will dream dreams,
your young men will see visions.
29Even on my servants, both men and women,
I will pour out my Spirit in those days.
30I will show wonders in the heavens
and on the earth,
blood and fire and billows of smoke.
31The sun will be turned to darkness
and the moon to blood
before the coming of the great and dreadful
day of the LORD.
32And everyone who calls
on the name of the LORD will be saved;
for on Mount Zion and in Jerusalem
there will be deliverance,
as the LORD has said,
among the survivors
whom the LORD calls.

3 "In those days and at that time,
when I restore the fortunes of Judah
and Jerusalem,
2I will gather all nations
and bring them down to the Valley of
Jehoshaphat.[m]
There I will enter into judgment against them
concerning my inheritance, my people
Israel,
for they scattered my people among the
nations
and divided up my land.
3They cast lots for my people

[m]2 *Jehoshaphat* means *the LORD judges*; also in verse 12.

and traded boys for prostitutes;
they sold girls for wine
that they might drink.

4"Now what have you against me, O Tyre and
Sidon and all you regions of Philistia? Are you
repaying me for something I have done? If you
are paying me back, I will swiftly and speedily
return on your own heads what you have done.
5For you took my silver and my gold and carried
off my finest treasures to your temples. 6You sold
the people of Judah and Jerusalem to the Greeks,
that you might send them far from their home-
land.
7"See, I am going to rouse them out of the
places to which you sold them, and I will return
on your own heads what you have done. 8I will
sell your sons and daughters to the people of Ju-
dah, and they will sell them to the Sabeans, a
nation far away." The LORD has spoken.

9Proclaim this among the nations:
Prepare for war!
Rouse the warriors!
Let all the fighting men draw near and attack.
10Beat your plowshares into swords
and your pruning hooks into spears.
Let the weakling say,
"I am strong!"
11Come quickly, all you nations from every side,
and assemble there.

Bring down your warriors, O LORD!

12"Let the nations be roused;
let them advance into the Valley of Jehoshaphat,
for there I will sit
to judge all the nations on every side.
13Swing the sickle,
for the harvest is ripe.
Come, trample the grapes,
for the winepress is full
and the vats overflow—
so great is their wickedness!"

14Multitudes, multitudes
in the valley of decision!
For the day of the LORD is near
in the valley of decision.
15The sun and moon will be darkened,
and the stars no longer shine.
16The LORD will roar from Zion
and thunder from Jerusalem;
the earth and the sky will tremble.
But the LORD will be a refuge for his people,
a stronghold for the people of Israel.

17"Then you will know that I, the LORD your God,
dwell in Zion, my holy hill.
Jerusalem will be holy;
never again will foreigners invade her.

18"In that day the mountains will drip new wine,
and the hills will flow with milk;
all the ravines of Judah will run with water.
A fountain will flow out of the LORD's house
and will water the valley of acacias.[n]
19But Egypt will be desolate,
Edom a desert waste,
because of violence done to the people of Judah,
in whose land they shed innocent blood.
20Judah will be inhabited forever
and Jerusalem through all generations.
21Their bloodguilt, which I have not pardoned,
I will pardon."

The LORD dwells in Zion!

[n]18 Or *Valley of Shittim*

Discovering the Word 1. According to 2:28–31, what signs will precede the "coming of the great and dreadful day of the LORD"? 2. What have the nations done to provoke the Lord's judgment (3:1–8)? 3. The Lord commands the nations to prepare for war (3:9). How does their battle relate to the Lord's judgment (3:9–16)? 4. Joel describes the Lord as a lion, a thunderstorm, a refuge and a stronghold (3:16). What do these images reveal about the God we serve? 5. What blessings does the Lord promise his people (3:16–21)?

Applying the Word 1. Peter claimed Joel's prophecy was fulfilled on the day of Pentecost (Acts 2:17–21, 38–40). How then does Joel's promise of the Spirit and salvation apply to us (2:28–32)? 2. What has Joel taught you about preparing for the day of the Lord? 3. What steps do you need to take to be prepared?

Responding in Prayer Ask God to make you always ready for his return.

Amos

Although Amos was a farmer from Judah, he prophesied to Israel, the northern kingdom, around 760 B.C. During this period the nation was secure and the upper classes prospered. Archaeological discoveries at Megiddo and Samaria have uncovered carved ivory inlays that were used in the furniture and decorative paneling in the homes of the wealthy. But instead of using their wealth to serve the needy, the upper classes were deaf to their cries. In fact, the wealthy maintained their lifestyle by oppressing the poor.

Although the Israelites continued to worship God, their worship was cold and self-serving. Jeroboam had built temples in Bethel and Dan so the people would worship in the north rather than traveling to Jerusalem. But God viewed this worship as idolatrous and declared, "I hate, I despise your religious feasts; I cannot stand your assemblies. Even though you bring me burnt offerings and grain offerings, I will not accept them" (Am 5:21–22).

God's judgment came against Israel in the form of famine, drought and plagues. But because the people failed to return to the Lord, Amos prophesied that all but a remnant would be destroyed. Still the Lord pleaded with Israel, "Seek good, not evil, that you may live!" (Am 5:14).

Amos has a powerful message today. We often seek the wrong things, forgetting the One who is the only source of true life. Amos challenges us to forsake anything and everything that hinders our relationship with God, proclaiming, "Seek the Lord and live!"

Outline

1 / *Amos 1—2*
Judgment & Justice

PICTURE THIS, IF you will. It is about the middle of the eighth century B.C. People are flocking to the worship center at Bethel, people whom we might call "upper middle class." The design of the building is very appealing. The choirs are polished. Several brilliant orators are at hand. It feels good to come here—uplifting music, beautiful surroundings and comforting words. There is even opportunity for the people to placate their consciences by bringing offerings. But wait a minute! Who is that seedy-looking character? He speaks like a shepherd; he looks like a shepherd; he even smells like a shepherd—but he sure doesn't sound like a shepherd!

Warming Up to God Recall something you never thought would happen to you. How did you feel when it *did* happen?

Read Amos 1—2.

1 The words of Amos, one of the shepherds of Tekoa—what he saw concerning Israel two years before the earthquake, when Uzziah was king of Judah and Jeroboam son of Jehoash[a] was king of Israel.

2He said:

"The LORD roars from Zion
and thunders from Jerusalem;
the pastures of the shepherds dry up,[b]
and the top of Carmel withers."

3This is what the LORD says:

"For three sins of Damascus,
even for four, I will not turn back ⌞my wrath⌟.
Because she threshed Gilead
with sledges having iron teeth,
4I will send fire upon the house of Hazael
that will consume the fortresses of Ben-Hadad.
5I will break down the gate of Damascus;
I will destroy the king who is in[c] the Valley of Aven[d]
and the one who holds the scepter in Beth Eden.
The people of Aram will go into exile to Kir,"
says the LORD.

6This is what the LORD says:

"For three sins of Gaza,
even for four, I will not turn back ⌞my wrath⌟.
Because she took captive whole communities
and sold them to Edom,
7I will send fire upon the walls of Gaza
that will consume her fortresses.
8I will destroy the king[e] of Ashdod
and the one who holds the scepter in Ashkelon.
I will turn my hand against Ekron,
till the last of the Philistines is dead,"
says the Sovereign LORD.

9This is what the LORD says:

"For three sins of Tyre,
even for four, I will not turn back ⌞my wrath⌟.
Because she sold whole communities of captives to Edom,
disregarding a treaty of brotherhood,
10I will send fire upon the walls of Tyre
that will consume her fortresses."

11This is what the LORD says:

"For three sins of Edom,
even for four, I will not turn back ⌞my wrath⌟.
Because he pursued his brother with a sword,
stifling all compassion,[f]
because his anger raged continually
and his fury flamed unchecked,
12I will send fire upon Teman
that will consume the fortresses of Bozrah."

13This is what the LORD says:

"For three sins of Ammon,
even for four, I will not turn back ⌞my wrath⌟.

[a]1 Hebrew *Joash,* a variant of *Jehoash* [b]2 Or *shepherds mourn* [c]5 Or *the inhabitants of* [d]5 *Aven* means *wickedness.* [e]8 Or *inhabitants* [f]11 Or *sword / and destroyed his allies*

Because he ripped open the pregnant women
of Gilead
in order to extend his borders,
14I will set fire to the walls of Rabbah
that will consume her fortresses
amid war cries on the day of battle,
amid violent winds on a stormy day.
15Her king[g] will go into exile,
he and his officials together,"
says the LORD.

2 This is what the LORD says:

"For three sins of Moab,
even for four, I will not turn back ⌞my
wrath⌟.
Because he burned, as if to lime,
the bones of Edom's king,
2I will send fire upon Moab
that will consume the fortresses of
Kerioth.[h]
Moab will go down in great tumult
amid war cries and the blast of the trumpet.
3I will destroy her ruler
and kill all her officials with him,"
says the LORD.

4This is what the LORD says:

"For three sins of Judah,
even for four, I will not turn back ⌞my
wrath⌟.
Because they have rejected the law of the
LORD
and have not kept his decrees,
because they have been led astray by false
gods,[i]
the gods[j] their ancestors followed,
5I will send fire upon Judah
that will consume the fortresses of
Jerusalem."

6This is what the LORD says:

"For three sins of Israel,
even for four, I will not turn back ⌞my
wrath⌟.
They sell the righteous for silver,
and the needy for a pair of sandals.
7They trample on the heads of the poor
as upon the dust of the ground
and deny justice to the oppressed.
Father and son use the same girl
and so profane my holy name.
8They lie down beside every altar
on garments taken in pledge.
In the house of their god
they drink wine taken as fines.

9"I destroyed the Amorite before them,
though he was tall as the cedars
and strong as the oaks.
I destroyed his fruit above
and his roots below.

10"I brought you up out of Egypt,
and I led you forty years in the desert
to give you the land of the Amorites.
11I also raised up prophets from among your
sons
and Nazirites from among your young men.
Is this not true, people of Israel?"
declares the LORD.
12"But you made the Nazirites drink wine
and commanded the prophets not to
prophesy.

13"Now then, I will crush you
as a cart crushes when loaded with grain.
14The swift will not escape,
the strong will not muster their strength,
and the warrior will not save his life.
15The archer will not stand his ground,
the fleet-footed soldier will not get away,
and the horseman will not save his life.
16Even the bravest warriors
will flee naked on that day,"
declares the LORD.

g15 Or / *Molech*; Hebrew *malcam* h2 Or *of her cities* i4 Or *by lies* j4 Or *lies*

Discovering the Word 1. How does 1:2 set the tone for Amos's message? 2. Damascus, Gaza, Tyre, Edom, Ammon and Moab all represented enemies of Israel. How would the Israelites feel as they heard prophecies against these nations (1:3—2:3)? 3. The repeated phrase "For three sins . . . even for four" emphasizes God's patience before pronouncing judgment. What kinds of sin do the pagan nations have in common (1:3—2:3)? 4. How are Judah's sins different from those of the pagan nations (2:4–5)? 5. Amos cites a variety of sins of which Israel is guilty (2:6–8, 12). How would you categorize their sins? 6. How are Israel's sins all the more serious in light of their history (2:9–11)?

Applying the Word 1. As Christians, what can we do to bring relief and justice to the righteous, the needy, the poor and the oppressed? 2. How can Amos's warnings to Israel keep us from being presumptuous about our status as God's children?

Responding in Prayer Ask God to grant you humility.

2 / *Amos 3*
Sin & Wealth

A WELL-KNOWN insurance company uses cartoons to advertise their product. One cartoon pictures a piano falling from an upper-story window toward an unsuspecting man below. As it speeds toward its destination, a friend politely asks, "By the way, what's the name of your insurance company?"

"Acme insurance, of course," the man replies. "Why do you ask?"

Disaster often comes unexpectedly. The people of Israel were wealthy, self-centered and complacent. Little did they realize that the full weight of God's judgment was about to fall on them.

Warming Up to God How do you respond to the portrayal of God as judge?

Read Amos 3.

3 Hear this word the LORD has spoken against you, O people of Israel—against the whole family I brought up out of Egypt:

2"You only have I chosen
of all the families of the earth;
therefore I will punish you
for all your sins."

3Do two walk together
unless they have agreed to do so?
4Does a lion roar in the thicket
when he has no prey?
Does he growl in his den
when he has caught nothing?
5Does a bird fall into a trap on the ground
where no snare has been set?
Does a trap spring up from the earth
when there is nothing to catch?
6When a trumpet sounds in a city,
do not the people tremble?
When disaster comes to a city,
has not the LORD caused it?
7Surely the Sovereign LORD does nothing
without revealing his plan
to his servants the prophets.
8The lion has roared—
who will not fear?
The Sovereign LORD has spoken—
who can but prophesy?

9Proclaim to the fortresses of Ashdod
and to the fortresses of Egypt:
"Assemble yourselves on the mountains of Samaria;
see the great unrest within her
and the oppression among her people."

10"They do not know how to do right," declares the LORD,
"who hoard plunder and loot in their fortresses."

11Therefore this is what the Sovereign LORD says:

"An enemy will overrun the land;
he will pull down your strongholds
and plunder your fortresses."

12This is what the LORD says:

"As a shepherd saves from the lion's mouth
only two leg bones or a piece of an ear,
so will the Israelites be saved,
those who sit in Samaria
on the edge of their beds

and in Damascus on their couches.[k]"
[13]"Hear this and testify against the house of Jacob," declares the Lord, the LORD God Almighty.
[14]"On the day I punish Israel for her sins,
I will destroy the altars of Bethel;
the horns of the altar will be cut off
and fall to the ground.
[15]I will tear down the winter house
along with the summer house;
the houses adorned with ivory will be destroyed
and the mansions will be demolished,"
declares the LORD.

[k]12 The meaning of the Hebrew for this line is uncertain.

Discovering the Word 1. The Israelites were confident that Yahweh was their God and they were his chosen people. But how had they misunderstood that call (vv. 1–2)? 2. In verses 3–6 Amos asks several rhetorical questions. How would you summarize what he is trying to say in these verses? 3. What do verses 9–10 say about Israel's morality and lifestyle in comparison with the pagan nations? 4. How would the Lord's judgment against Israel fit their crimes (vv. 10–11, 15)? 5. According to the law, people in danger could find refuge by grasping the horns of the altar (see 1Ki 1:50). How and why would this change (vv. 13–14)? 6. Try to view this chapter from the perspective of those who were oppressed by the wealthy. How would you feel as you heard Amos's prophecy?

Applying the Word 1. What does this chapter teach us about God's character? 2. This passage tells us that privilege brings responsibility. How is that true for you?

Responding in Prayer Ask the Lord to give you the strength of character needed to be responsible as a person of God.

3 / *Amos 4*
Prepare to Meet Your God!

IN 1741 JONATHAN Edwards preached his most famous sermon: "Sinners in the Hands of an Angry God." After using vivid imagery to make non-Christians feel the horror of their position, Edwards concluded: "Therefore, let every one that is out of Christ now awake and fly from the wrath to come!" God used that sermon to bring a powerful awakening to the town of Enfield, in New England. The prophet Amos preaches a similar sermon in this chapter. After warning Israel repeatedly to return to the Lord, he now declares: "Prepare to meet your God!"

Warming Up to God Recall a time when you wandered from God. What brought you back?

Read Amos 4.

4 Hear this word, you cows of Bashan on Mount Samaria,
you women who oppress the poor and crush the needy
and say to your husbands, "Bring us some drinks!"
[2]The Sovereign LORD has sworn by his holiness:
"The time will surely come
when you will be taken away with hooks,
the last of you with fishhooks.
[3]You will each go straight out
through breaks in the wall,
and you will be cast out toward Harmon,[l]"
declares the LORD.
[4]"Go to Bethel and sin;
go to Gilgal and sin yet more.
Bring your sacrifices every morning,
your tithes every three years.[m]
[5]Burn leavened bread as a thank offering
and brag about your freewill offerings—
boast about them, you Israelites,

[l]3 Masoretic Text; with a different word division of the Hebrew (see Septuagint) *out, O mountain of oppression* [m]4 Or *tithes on the third day*

for this is what you love to do,"
declares the Sovereign LORD.

6"I gave you empty stomachs[n] in every city
and lack of bread in every town,
yet you have not returned to me,"
declares the LORD.

7"I also withheld rain from you
when the harvest was still three months away.
I sent rain on one town,
but withheld it from another.
One field had rain;
another had none and dried up.
8People staggered from town to town for water
but did not get enough to drink,
yet you have not returned to me,"
declares the LORD.

9"Many times I struck your gardens and vineyards,
I struck them with blight and mildew.
Locusts devoured your fig and olive trees,
yet you have not returned to me,"
declares the LORD.

10"I sent plagues among you
as I did to Egypt.
I killed your young men with the sword,
along with your captured horses.
I filled your nostrils with the stench of your camps,
yet you have not returned to me,"
declares the LORD.

11"I overthrew some of you
as I[o] overthrew Sodom and Gomorrah.
You were like a burning stick snatched from the fire,
yet you have not returned to me,"
declares the LORD.

12"Therefore this is what I will do to you, Israel,
and because I will do this to you,
prepare to meet your God, O Israel."

13He who forms the mountains,
creates the wind,
and reveals his thoughts to man,
he who turns dawn to darkness,
and treads the high places of the earth—
the LORD God Almighty is his name.

[n] 6 Hebrew *you cleanness of teeth* [o] 11 Hebrew *God*

Discovering the Word 1. The area of Bashan was noted for its fat, sleek cattle. How does the lifestyle of the women of Israel contrast with the judgment the Lord swears to bring upon them (vv. 2–3)? 2. Bethel and Gilgal were centers of worship for the northern kingdom (1Ki 12:26–33; Hos 4:15). What was sinful about Israel's worship at these places (vv. 4–5)? 3. What words would you use to describe each of the judgments the Lord brought on Israel (vv. 6–11)? 4. Amos proclaims to Israel, "Prepare to meet your God" (v. 12). In light of this chapter, what kind of "meeting" could Israel expect this to be? 5. The chapter closes with a brief hymn describing the God Israel would meet in judgment (v. 13). What do we learn about God from each aspect of Amos's description?

Applying the Word 1. How can we keep our worship from becoming empty ritual? 2. God's tenderness, even in the midst of judgment, is evident in the repeated words "yet you have not returned to me" (vv. 6, 8, 9, 10, 11). How have you experienced God's grace in the midst of discipline?

Responding in Prayer Take a few minutes to worship God, using this hymn as the basis for your prayers.

4 / *Amos 5—6*
Seek the Lord and Live!

SUCCESS, WEALTH, POWER, prestige—these are eagerly sought by many today. People are willing to sacrifice their marriages, their families and even their health to obtain these goals. But in the end most discover that the rewards were not worth the cost. How tragic! In chapters 5 and 6 Amos tells us how to avoid this tragedy in our lives—"Seek the Lord and live!"

Warming Up to God Why do you think people are willing to sacrifice so much to obtain the things mentioned above? To what extent are you looking for these things?

Read Amos 5—6.

5 Hear this word, O house of Israel, this lament I take up concerning you:

[2]"Fallen is Virgin Israel,
never to rise again,
deserted in her own land,
with no one to lift her up."

[3]This is what the Sovereign LORD says:

"The city that marches out a thousand strong for Israel
will have only a hundred left;
the town that marches out a hundred strong
will have only ten left."

[4]This is what the LORD says to the house of Israel:

"Seek me and live;
[5] do not seek Bethel,
do not go to Gilgal,
do not journey to Beersheba.
For Gilgal will surely go into exile,
and Bethel will be reduced to nothing.[p]"
[6]Seek the LORD and live,
or he will sweep through the house of Joseph like a fire;
it will devour,
and Bethel will have no one to quench it.

[7]You who turn justice into bitterness
and cast righteousness to the ground
[8](he who made the Pleiades and Orion,
who turns blackness into dawn
and darkens day into night,
who calls for the waters of the sea
and pours them out over the face of the land—
the LORD is his name—
[9]he flashes destruction on the stronghold
and brings the fortified city to ruin),
[10]you hate the one who reproves in court
and despise him who tells the truth.

[11]You trample on the poor
and force him to give you grain.
Therefore, though you have built stone mansions,
you will not live in them;
though you have planted lush vineyards,
you will not drink their wine.
[12]For I know how many are your offenses
and how great your sins.

You oppress the righteous and take bribes
and you deprive the poor of justice in the courts.
[13]Therefore the prudent man keeps quiet in such times,
for the times are evil.

[14]Seek good, not evil,
that you may live.
Then the LORD God Almighty will be with you,
just as you say he is.
[15]Hate evil, love good;
maintain justice in the courts.
Perhaps the LORD God Almighty will have mercy
on the remnant of Joseph.

[16]Therefore this is what the Lord, the LORD God Almighty, says:

"There will be wailing in all the streets
and cries of anguish in every public square.
The farmers will be summoned to weep
and the mourners to wail.
[17]There will be wailing in all the vineyards,
for I will pass through your midst,"
says the LORD.

[18]Woe to you who long
for the day of the LORD!
Why do you long for the day of the LORD?
That day will be darkness, not light.
[19]It will be as though a man fled from a lion
only to meet a bear,
as though he entered his house
and rested his hand on the wall

p5 Or *grief*; or *wickedness*; Hebrew *aven*, a reference to Beth Aven (a derogatory name for Bethel)

only to have a snake bite him.
20Will not the day of the LORD be darkness, not
light—
pitch-dark, without a ray of brightness?

21"I hate, I despise your religious feasts;
I cannot stand your assemblies.
22Even though you bring me burnt offerings
and grain offerings,
I will not accept them.
Though you bring choice fellowship
offerings,[q]
I will have no regard for them.
23Away with the noise of your songs!
I will not listen to the music of your harps.
24But let justice roll on like a river,
righteousness like a never-failing stream!

25"Did you bring me sacrifices and offerings
forty years in the desert, O house of Israel?
26You have lifted up the shrine of your king,
the pedestal of your idols,
the star of your god[r]—
which you made for yourselves.
27Therefore I will send you into exile beyond
Damascus,"
says the LORD, whose name is God
Almighty.

6 Woe to you who are complacent in
Zion,
and to you who feel secure on Mount
Samaria,
you notable men of the foremost nation,
to whom the people of Israel come!
2Go to Calneh and look at it;
go from there to great Hamath,
and then go down to Gath in Philistia.
Are they better off than your two kingdoms?
Is their land larger than yours?
3You put off the evil day
and bring near a reign of terror.
4You lie on beds inlaid with ivory
and lounge on your couches.
You dine on choice lambs
and fattened calves.
5You strum away on your harps like David
and improvise on musical instruments.
6You drink wine by the bowlful
and use the finest lotions,
but you do not grieve over the ruin of
Joseph.
7Therefore you will be among the first to go
into exile;
your feasting and lounging will end.

8The Sovereign LORD has sworn by himself—
the LORD God Almighty declares:

"I abhor the pride of Jacob
and detest his fortresses;
I will deliver up the city
and everything in it."

9If ten men are left in one house, they too will
die. 10And if a relative who is to burn the bodies
comes to carry them out of the house and asks
anyone still hiding there, "Is anyone with you?"
and he says, "No," then he will say, "Hush! We
must not mention the name of the LORD."

11For the LORD has given the command,
and he will smash the great house into
pieces
and the small house into bits.

12Do horses run on the rocky crags?
Does one plow there with oxen?
But you have turned justice into poison
and the fruit of righteousness into
bitterness—
13you who rejoice in the conquest of Lo
Debar[s]
and say, "Did we not take Karnaim[t] by
our own strength?"

14For the LORD God Almighty declares,
"I will stir up a nation against you,
O house of Israel,
that will oppress you all the way
from Lebo[u] Hamath to the valley of the
Arabah."

q22 Traditionally *peace offerings* r26 Or *lifted up Sakkuth your king / and Kaiwan your idols, / your star-gods*; Septuagint *lifted up the shrine of Molech / and the star of your god Rephan, / their idols* s13 *Lo Debar* means *nothing.* t13 *Karnaim* means *horns*; *horn* here symbolizes strength. u14 Or *from the entrance to*

Discovering the Word 1. A *lament* (5:1) was a song or poem mourning someone's death. How does Amos portray the death of Israel (5:2)? 2. What has Israel done to deserve the Lord's judgment (5:7, 10, 11, 12)? 3. The Lord pleads with Israel in verses 4, 6, 14 and 15. In this context, what would it mean for Israel to *seek* the Lord? 4. How were the Israelites mistaken about the day of the Lord (5:18–20)? 5. How does Amos portray the Israelites in 6:1–6? 6. How does the Lord promise to repay those who are complacent and proud (6:7–14)?

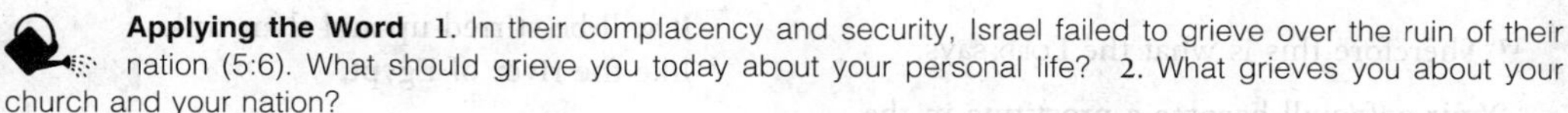

Applying the Word 1. In their complacency and security, Israel failed to grieve over the ruin of their nation (5:6). What should grieve you today about your personal life? 2. What grieves you about your church and your nation?

Responding in Prayer Take time to pray about those things that cause you to grieve. Ask the Lord to help you seek his will in these areas.

5 / *Amos 7—8*
Visions of Judgment

IT IS EASY to side with Amos. After all, his prophecies are part of the Bible! But put yourself in Israel's place. How would you have responded if a farmer came to town and began announcing visions of judgment? In chapters 7—9 we will look at five of Amos's visions and one fairly typical response.

Warming Up to God Think of a time you have been confronted by a street preacher or visiting evangelist who warned of God's judgment. How do you respond to that approach?

Read Amos 7—8.

7 This is what the Sovereign LORD showed
me: He was preparing swarms of locusts
after the king's share had been harvested
and just as the second crop was coming up.
2When they had stripped the land clean, I cried
out, "Sovereign LORD, forgive! How can Jacob sur-
vive? He is so small!"
3So the LORD relented.
"This will not happen," the LORD said.
4This is what the Sovereign LORD showed me:
The Sovereign LORD was calling for judgment by
fire; it dried up the great deep and devoured the
land. 5Then I cried out, "Sovereign LORD, I beg
you, stop! How can Jacob survive? He is so
small!"
6So the LORD relented.
"This will not happen either," the Sovereign
LORD said.

7This is what he showed me: The Lord was
standing by a wall that had been built true to
plumb, with a plumb line in his hand. 8And the
LORD asked me, "What do you see, Amos?"
"A plumb line," I replied.
Then the Lord said, "Look, I am setting a
plumb line among my people Israel; I will spare
them no longer.

9"The high places of Isaac will be destroyed
and the sanctuaries of Israel will be ruined;
with my sword I will rise against the house
of Jeroboam."

10Then Amaziah the priest of Bethel sent a mes-
sage to Jeroboam king of Israel: "Amos is raising
a conspiracy against you in the very heart of Is-
rael. The land cannot bear all his words. 11For
this is what Amos is saying:

" 'Jeroboam will die by the sword,
and Israel will surely go into exile,
away from their native land.' "

12Then Amaziah said to Amos, "Get out, you
seer! Go back to the land of Judah. Earn your
bread there and do your prophesying there.
13Don't prophesy anymore at Bethel, because this
is the king's sanctuary and the temple of the king-
dom."
14Amos answered Amaziah, "I was neither a
prophet nor a prophet's son, but I was a shep-
herd, and I also took care of sycamore-fig trees.
15But the LORD took me from tending the flock
and said to me, 'Go, prophesy to my people Is-
rael.' 16Now then, hear the word of the LORD. You
say,

" 'Do not prophesy against Israel,

and stop preaching against the house of
Isaac.'

17"Therefore this is what the LORD says:

" 'Your wife will become a prostitute in the
city,
and your sons and daughters will fall by
the sword.
Your land will be measured and divided up,
and you yourself will die in a pagan[v]
country.
And Israel will certainly go into exile,
away from their native land.' "

8 This is what the Sovereign LORD showed
me: a basket of ripe fruit. 2"What do you
see, Amos?" he asked.
"A basket of ripe fruit," I answered.
Then the LORD said to me, "The time is ripe for
my people Israel; I will spare them no longer.
3"In that day," declares the Sovereign LORD,
"the songs in the temple will turn to wailing.[w]
Many, many bodies—flung everywhere! Silence!"

4Hear this, you who trample the needy
and do away with the poor of the land,

5saying,

"When will the New Moon be over
that we may sell grain,
and the Sabbath be ended
that we may market wheat?"—
skimping the measure,
boosting the price
and cheating with dishonest scales,
6buying the poor with silver
and the needy for a pair of sandals,
selling even the sweepings with the wheat.

7The LORD has sworn by the Pride of Jacob: "I
will never forget anything they have done.
8"Will not the land tremble for this,
and all who live in it mourn?
The whole land will rise like the Nile;
it will be stirred up and then sink
like the river of Egypt.

9"In that day," declares the Sovereign LORD,

"I will make the sun go down at noon
and darken the earth in broad daylight.
10I will turn your religious feasts into mourning
and all your singing into weeping.
I will make all of you wear sackcloth
and shave your heads.
I will make that time like mourning for an
only son
and the end of it like a bitter day.

11"The days are coming," declares the Sovereign
LORD,
"when I will send a famine through the
land—
not a famine of food or a thirst for water,
but a famine of hearing the words of the
LORD.
12Men will stagger from sea to sea
and wander from north to east,
searching for the word of the LORD,
but they will not find it.

13"In that day

"the lovely young women and strong young
men
will faint because of thirst.
14They who swear by the shame[x] of Samaria,
or say, 'As surely as your god lives, O Dan,'
or, 'As surely as the god[y] of Beersheba
lives'—
they will fall,
never to rise again."

[v] 17 Hebrew *an unclean* [w] 3 Or *"the temple singers will wail*
[x] 14 Or *by Ashima; or by the idol* [y] 14 Or *power*

Discovering the Word 1. What three visions of judgment does the Lord show Amos (7:1, 4, 7)? 2. Why does the Lord "relent" regarding the first two visions (7:1–6)? 3. In verses 10–17, Amos undergoes his own "plumb-line" test. What temptations might he have experienced? 4. How does Amos describe the lifestyle of those who are ripe for judgment (8:4–6)? 5. How does he describe the "harvest" they will experience (8:3–14)?

Applying the Word 1. Even though we can freely read the Bible, how does "famine" evidence itself among God's people? 2. How can the Lord's response to Amos's prayers (7:6) motivate us to pray for our nation? 3. How can Amos's response to Amaziah (7:10–17) be an example to us when we are tempted to compromise our beliefs?

Responding in Prayer Pray that God will use your study in Amos to mold you into the person he wants you to be.

6 / *Amos 9*
Visions of Hope

HOPE IS ONE of the three greatest gifts. It can lift our broken spirits, strengthen our feeble bodies and transform our darkest moments into lighthearted praise. Up to this point Amos has offered little hope to Israel. But in this final chapter, as the pace toward destruction quickens, he brings his prophecy to a surprising conclusion—one that is full of hope, promise and a renewed vision of God.

Warming Up to God How does hope differ from wishful or "positive" thinking?

Read Amos 9.

9 I saw the Lord standing by the altar, and he said:
"Strike the tops of the pillars
so that the thresholds shake.
Bring them down on the heads of all the people;
those who are left I will kill with the sword.
Not one will get away,
none will escape.
2 Though they dig down to the depths of the grave,[z]
from there my hand will take them.
Though they climb up to the heavens,
from there I will bring them down.
3 Though they hide themselves on the top of Carmel,
there I will hunt them down and seize them.
Though they hide from me at the bottom of the sea,
there I will command the serpent to bite them.
4 Though they are driven into exile by their enemies,
there I will command the sword to slay them.
I will fix my eyes upon them
for evil and not for good."

5 The Lord, the LORD Almighty,
he who touches the earth and it melts,
and all who live in it mourn—
the whole land rises like the Nile,
then sinks like the river of Egypt—
6 he who builds his lofty palace[a] in the heavens
and sets its foundation[b] on the earth,
who calls for the waters of the sea
and pours them out over the face of the land—
the LORD is his name.

7 "Are not you Israelites
the same to me as the Cushites[c]?"
declares the LORD.
"Did I not bring Israel up from Egypt,
the Philistines from Caphtor[d]
and the Arameans from Kir?

8 "Surely the eyes of the Sovereign LORD
are on the sinful kingdom.
I will destroy it
from the face of the earth—
yet I will not totally destroy
the house of Jacob,"
declares the LORD.
9 "For I will give the command,
and I will shake the house of Israel
among all the nations
as grain is shaken in a sieve,
and not a pebble will reach the ground.

[z]2 Hebrew *to Sheol* [a]6 The meaning of the Hebrew for this phrase is uncertain. [b]6 The meaning of the Hebrew for this word is uncertain. [c]7 That is, people from the upper Nile region [d]7 That is, Crete

10 All the sinners among my people
will die by the sword,
all those who say,
'Disaster will not overtake or meet us.'

11 "In that day I will restore
David's fallen tent.
I will repair its broken places,
restore its ruins,
and build it as it used to be,
12 so that they may possess the remnant of
Edom
and all the nations that bear my name,[e]"
declares the LORD, who will do these things.

13 "The days are coming," declares the LORD,

"when the reaper will be overtaken by the
plowman
and the planter by the one treading grapes.
New wine will drip from the mountains
and flow from all the hills.
14 I will bring back my exiled[f] people Israel;
they will rebuild the ruined cities and live
in them.
They will plant vineyards and drink their
wine;
they will make gardens and eat their fruit.
15 I will plant Israel in their own land,
never again to be uprooted
from the land I have given them,"

says the LORD your God.

[e]12 Hebrew; Septuagint *so that the remnant of men / and all the nations that bear my name may seek* ⌊*the Lord*⌋ [f]14 Or *will restore the fortunes of my*

Discovering the Word 1. How does Amos describe the fate of those who try to escape (vv. 1–4)? 2. How do you think the description of the Lord in verses 5–6 relates to the pronouncements of the previous verses? 3. The Israelites thought they were superior to other nations because God chose them and delivered them from Egypt. Why would they be shocked by verse 7 and the first part of verse 8? 4. What glimmer of hope does Amos offer the house of Jacob (vv. 8–10)? 5. Suddenly Israel's glimmer of hope begins to shine with intense brightness (vv. 11–15). How does Amos's final prophecy contrast with what he has said before?

Applying the Word 1. When in your life or in the life of your church has the Lord restored what was in ruins (v. 11)? 2. How can this portrait of God give us hope even when things seem hopeless?

Responding in Prayer Pray for hope in your life and in the lives of people you know who may feel hopeless.

Obadiah

It's a little book, the shortest in the Old Testament. Tucked between its more famous neighbors, Amos and Jonah, it is so small you easily miss it. It makes its point briefly in vigorous language, and then it's over. What's more, it is directed to Edom, which most of us can't identify, let alone identify *with.* Yet as we read the prophecy of Obadiah, the words begin to sound strangely familiar. *Pride, exploitation, gloating, justice, deliverance, hope*—they're all here in these few succinct lines.

Who was Obadiah? The name means "servant of God," and there are several Obadiahs mentioned in the Bible from around the time of the book's events. All we know for sure is that this Obadiah received a vision (1:1). It was not a vision for the Jews, but for Edom.

Rivalry between Edom and Israel went way back. Abraham's son Isaac had twin sons, Jacob and Esau. Esau had the important right of firstborn, but in a moment of hunger he sold it to the opportunistic Jacob (Ge 25:27–34). Later Jacob tricked Esau out of their father's blessing (Ge 27). Jacob fled when he found out that Esau planned revenge. It was not till years later that they met again (Ge 33). Though the meeting was emotional, the breach was never entirely healed, and their descendants remained rivals—relatives with an unsettled score.

Esau was called "Edom" as early as Genesis 25:30, and the name is confirmed several times in Genesis 30. There is no doubt that Obadiah was talking about these relatives of Israel when he painted such a grim picture of their fate.

The Edomites had settled south of the Dead Sea, and there were frequent border clashes between Edom and Judah. When the Babylonian king Nebuchadnezzar conquered Jerusalem in 587 B.C. (2Ki 25:8–12), Edom saw their opportunity to move in on the spoils. They joined forces with the Babylonians, cut off the fleeing Judeans and grabbed what they could from the Jews (Ps 137:7). For that sin Obadiah said Edom would be brought down. The Edomites were assimilated into other peoples and never regained their identity as a nation.

In these twenty-one verses Obadiah has a lot to say about contemporary issues: greed, broken families, injustice, profit-taking. We are wise to pay attention to his warnings. If we are victims of those sins, we can take comfort that Obadiah ends on a note of hope—not for Edom, but for Israel. God will bring about justice. God sees the human disaster. God will restore what has been robbed. "And the kingdom will be the LORD's" (Ob 21).

Obadiah 1–21
Compassion for the Fallen

"SHOULD YOU BUY a house that's been repossessed, no matter how cheaply it's offered, or would that be profiting from someone else's misfortune?" To me, the questioner had an overly scrupulous conscience; but perhaps it's good that someone would bother to ask the question. Most of us take advantage of any opportunity that comes along, without caring where it came from.

Warming Up to God When have you found the promise of God's righteous judgment a source of comfort?

Read Obadiah 1–21.

1The vision of Obadiah.

This is what the Sovereign LORD says about Edom—

We have heard a message from the LORD:
An envoy was sent to the nations to say,
"Rise, and let us go against her for battle"—
2"See, I will make you small among the nations;
you will be utterly despised.
3The pride of your heart has deceived you,
you who live in the clefts of the rocks[a]
and make your home on the heights,
you who say to yourself,
'Who can bring me down to the ground?'
4Though you soar like the eagle
and make your nest among the stars,
from there I will bring you down,"
declares the LORD.
5"If thieves came to you,
if robbers in the night—
Oh, what a disaster awaits you—
would they not steal only as much as they wanted?
If grape pickers came to you,
would they not leave a few grapes?
6But how Esau will be ransacked,
his hidden treasures pillaged!
7All your allies will force you to the border;
your friends will deceive and overpower you;
those who eat your bread will set a trap for you,[b]
but you will not detect it.
8"In that day," declares the LORD,
"will I not destroy the wise men of Edom,
men of understanding in the mountains of Esau?
9Your warriors, O Teman, will be terrified,
and everyone in Esau's mountains
will be cut down in the slaughter.
10Because of the violence against your brother Jacob,
you will be covered with shame;
you will be destroyed forever.
11On the day you stood aloof
while strangers carried off his wealth
and foreigners entered his gates
and cast lots for Jerusalem,
you were like one of them.
12You should not look down on your brother
in the day of his misfortune,
nor rejoice over the people of Judah
in the day of their destruction,
nor boast so much
in the day of their trouble.
13You should not march through the gates of my people
in the day of their disaster,
nor look down on them in their calamity
in the day of their disaster,
nor seize their wealth
in the day of their disaster.
14You should not wait at the crossroads
to cut down their fugitives,
nor hand over their survivors
in the day of their trouble.

15"The day of the LORD is near
for all nations.
As you have done, it will be done to you;
your deeds will return upon your own head.

[a]3 Or *of Sela* [b]7 The meaning of the Hebrew for this clause is uncertain.

16 Just as you drank on my holy hill,
so all the nations will drink continually;
they will drink and drink
and be as if they had never been.
17 But on Mount Zion will be deliverance;
it will be holy,
and the house of Jacob
will possess its inheritance.
18 The house of Jacob will be a fire
and the house of Joseph a flame;
the house of Esau will be stubble,
and they will set it on fire and consume it.
There will be no survivors
from the house of Esau."
The LORD has spoken.

19 People from the Negev will occupy
the mountains of Esau,
and people from the foothills will possess
the land of the Philistines.
They will occupy the fields of Ephraim and Samaria,
and Benjamin will possess Gilead.
20 This company of Israelite exiles who are in Canaan
will possess ⌞the land⌟ as far as Zarephath;
the exiles from Jerusalem who are in Sepharad
will possess the towns of the Negev.
21 Deliverers will go up on[c] Mount Zion
to govern the mountains of Esau.
And the kingdom will be the LORD's.

[c]21 Or *from*

Discovering the Word 1. Edom (the descendants of Esau) had taken advantage of the fall of Jerusalem and even participated in its destruction. How did God respond to their actions? 2. What was Edom's attitude toward the future (vv. 3–4)? 3. Why would Edom be destroyed (vv. 10–14)? 4. How would justice be carried out in their downfall (vv. 15–18)? 5. What would be the fate of Edom's lands (vv. 19–21)?

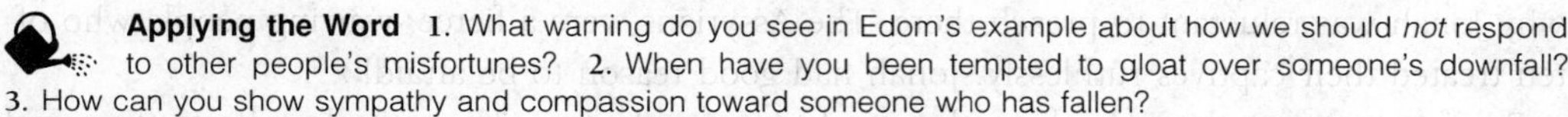

Applying the Word 1. What warning do you see in Edom's example about how we should *not* respond to other people's misfortunes? 2. When have you been tempted to gloat over someone's downfall? 3. How can you show sympathy and compassion toward someone who has fallen?

Responding in Prayer Confess any feeling of superiority over those who have fallen. Ask the Lord to help you see others through his eyes of compassion.

Jonah

A wise professor once said, "What gets your attention, gets you." This is especially true in the book of Jonah. God takes drastic measures to get Jonah's attention. He does so not because he delights in calamity but because he desires our fellowship.

Jonah prophesied in the eighth century B.C., during or shortly before the reign of Jeroboam II (793–753 B.C.). God called him to preach to Nineveh, the capital of Assyria, which was the most powerful nation on earth. The more we know about Assyria, the more we understand why Jonah was reluctant to preach there. The Assyrians were a fierce, warring people who often treated their captives ruthlessly. Jonah had good reason to be afraid!

But fear was not the only thing that made Jonah reluctant. His attitude reflects the racial prejudice common in his day. The "chosen people" could not imagine that God could care about other nations—especially one as vile and idolatrous as Assyria. So the book of Jonah becomes a powerful illustration of the fact that God does not want "anyone to perish, but everyone to come to repentance" (2Pe 3:9).

The story of Jonah has been the subject of much controversy. Many people reject its historicity, preferring to view it as an allegory or parable. However, two things should be noted about this view. First, few people questioned the historicity of Jonah until the nineteenth century, when liberal scholars launched an attack on every book in the Bible. They objected to its historicity primarily because of the incident of Jonah's being swallowed by a fish. However, even from a natural standpoint this incident is quite possible. In his *Introduction to the Old Testament*, R. K. Harrison points out that there are other reliable records of people being swallowed by large fish and surviving. Second, Jesus himself viewed the story of Jonah as history (Mt 12:38–41; Lk 11:29–30, 32), comparing it to the greater miracle of his resurrection.

We can learn from Jonah, knowing there will be times when we run from God's will and need to return to him.

Outline

1/ Jonah 1 ——— *Jonah's Disobedience*

2/ Jonah 2 ——— *Jonah's Prayer*

3/ Jonah 3 ——— *Jonah's Obedience*

4/ Jonah 4 ——— *Jonah's Anger*

1 / *Jonah 1*
Jonah's Disobedience

"DON'T HIT YOUR sister!" Sometimes it takes all the willpower we have to obey. Yet how easy it is to do wrong in the first place. We get mad and we react. That's what it feels like with God sometimes too. He asks us to do things we don't want to do—things that are difficult, uncomfortable or even painful. So politely but firmly we refuse his command and try to put it out of our minds. Yet as Jonah discovered, our disobedience can be even more costly than our obedience.

Warming Up to God Have you ever wanted to turn away from something you knew God wanted you to do? Explain.

Read Jonah 1.

1 The word of the LORD came to Jonah son
of Amittai: 2"Go to the great city of Nine-
veh and preach against it, because its
wickedness has come up before me."
3But Jonah ran away from the LORD and headed
for Tarshish. He went down to Joppa, where he
found a ship bound for that port. After paying the
fare, he went aboard and sailed for Tarshish to
flee from the LORD.
4Then the LORD sent a great wind on the sea,
and such a violent storm arose that the ship
threatened to break up. 5All the sailors were
afraid and each cried out to his own god. And
they threw the cargo into the sea to lighten the
ship.
But Jonah had gone below deck, where he lay
down and fell into a deep sleep. 6The captain
went to him and said, "How can you sleep? Get
up and call on your god! Maybe he will take no-
tice of us, and we will not perish."
7Then the sailors said to each other, "Come,
let us cast lots to find out who is responsible for
this calamity." They cast lots and the lot fell on
Jonah.
8So they asked him, "Tell us, who is responsi-
ble for making all this trouble for us? What do
you do? Where do you come from? What is your
country? From what people are you?"
9He answered, "I am a Hebrew and I worship
the LORD, the God of heaven, who made the sea
and the land."
10This terrified them and they asked, "What
have you done?" (They knew he was running
away from the LORD, because he had already told
them so.)
11The sea was getting rougher and rougher. So
they asked him, "What should we do to you to
make the sea calm down for us?"
12"Pick me up and throw me into the sea," he
replied, "and it will become calm. I know that it
is my fault that this great storm has come upon
you."
13Instead, the men did their best to row back to
land. But they could not, for the sea grew even
wilder than before. 14Then they cried to the LORD,
"O LORD, please do not let us die for taking this
man's life. Do not hold us accountable for killing
an innocent man, for you, O LORD, have done as
you pleased." 15Then they took Jonah and threw
him overboard, and the raging sea grew calm.
16At this the men greatly feared the LORD, and
they offered a sacrifice to the LORD and made vows
to him.
17But the LORD provided a great fish to swallow
Jonah, and Jonah was inside the fish three days
and three nights.

Discovering the Word 1. Nineveh was the capital of Assyria, a nation that was a fierce and powerful enemy of Israel's to the northeast. How does Jonah respond to the Lord's command to preach there (vv. 1–3)? 2. Tarshish, traditionally identified as Spain, was over two thousand miles in the opposite direction. While Jonah was journeying to Tarshish, what kinds of thoughts and feelings might he have experienced? 3. How do you think Jonah felt when the captain urged him to call on God for help (v. 6)? 4. Why do the sailors become even more terrified after they hear Jonah's story (vv. 7–10)? 5. Jonah acknowledges his guilt in verses 11–12. Do you think he is repentant at this point? Explain. 6. How does God use this calamity to demonstrate his grace and mercy (vv. 15–17)?

Applying the Word 1. How does this chapter illustrate the futility of running from God? 2. We run from God in ways that can be as obvious as Jonah's actions and in much more subtle daily ways. In what area of life are you currently running from God?

Responding in Prayer Pray that God will give you courage to be his representative to those he's calling you to minister to.

2 / *Jonah 2*
Jonah's Prayer

IN THE MOVIE *Pinnochio* a kindly woodcutter named Geppetto is swallowed by a whale named Monstro. Inside the dark, damp belly of the whale, Geppetto sits for what seems like an eternity. Then one day the whale violently coughs, and the woodcutter is expelled from his watery grave. Sound familiar? Every Sunday-school child would recognize this retelling of the story of Jonah. But unlike the Disney movie, Jonah's incredible adventure is not fantasy but fact.

Warming Up to God What difficult situation has the Lord delivered you from? Offer your praises to God for his work in your life.

Read Jonah 2.

2 From inside the fish Jonah prayed to the LORD his God. [2]He said:

"In my distress I called to the LORD,
and he answered me.
From the depths of the grave[a] I called for help,
and you listened to my cry.
[3]You hurled me into the deep,
into the very heart of the seas,
and the currents swirled about me;
all your waves and breakers
swept over me.
[4]I said, 'I have been banished
from your sight;
yet I will look again
toward your holy temple.'
[5]The engulfing waters threatened me,[b]
the deep surrounded me;
seaweed was wrapped around my head.
[6]To the roots of the mountains I sank down;
the earth beneath barred me in forever.
But you brought my life up from the pit,
O LORD my God.

[7]"When my life was ebbing away,
I remembered you, LORD,
and my prayer rose to you,
to your holy temple.

[8]"Those who cling to worthless idols
forfeit the grace that could be theirs.
[9]But I, with a song of thanksgiving,
will sacrifice to you.
What I have vowed I will make good.
Salvation comes from the LORD."

[10]And the LORD commanded the fish, and it vomited Jonah onto dry land.

[a]2 Hebrew *Sheol* [b]5 Or *waters were at my throat*

Discovering the Word 1. Describe the terrible sequence of events after Jonah was thrown overboard (vv. 3, 5-6). 2. What initial thoughts and feelings did Jonah have (vv. 3-6)? 3. How did these terrifying events affect Jonah's attitude toward God? 4. Why do you think God answered Jonah's prayer (vv. 2, 6, 9-10)? 5. Why can we be confident God will hear our prayers even if we are suffering the consequences of disobedience?

Applying the Word 1. When have you felt like you were in a deep, dark pit (v. 6), either physically, emotionally or spiritually? 2. Why do you think we sometimes have to sink so low before we remember God?

Responding in Prayer Take time now to thank God for his discipline and his grace. Quietly reaffirm your commitment to obey him.

3 / *Jonah 3*
Jonah's Obedience

GREAT REVIVALS HAVE occurred throughout history—among the Jews in the first century, the tribes of Ireland in the fifth century, the Protestants in the sixteenth century and the people of Wales in the twentieth century. Yet one of the greatest revivals of all time occurred hundreds of years before any of these—the amazing revival in Nineveh described in Jonah 3.

Warming Up to God How have you seen God's compassion expressed when you are obedient?

Read Jonah 3.

3 Then the word of the LORD came to Jonah
a second time: 2"Go to the great city of
Nineveh and proclaim to it the message I
give you."
3Jonah obeyed the word of the LORD and
went to Nineveh. Now Nineveh was a very
important city—a visit required three days.
4On the first day, Jonah started into the city.
He proclaimed: "Forty more days and Nin-
eveh will be overturned." 5The Ninevites be-
lieved God. They declared a fast, and all of
them, from the greatest to the least, put on
sackcloth.
6When the news reached the king of Nineveh,
he rose from his throne, took off his royal robes,
covered himself with sackcloth and sat down in
the dust. 7Then he issued a proclamation in Nine-
veh:

"By the decree of the king and his nobles:

Do not let any man or beast, herd or flock,
taste anything; do not let them eat or drink.
8But let man and beast be covered with sack-
cloth. Let everyone call urgently on God. Let
them give up their evil ways and their vio-
lence. 9Who knows? God may yet relent and
with compassion turn from his fierce anger
so that we will not perish."

10When God saw what they did and how they
turned from their evil ways, he had compassion
and did not bring upon them the destruction he
had threatened.

Discovering the Word 1. If you were Jonah, how would you feel when the word of the Lord came to you a second time (vv. 1–2)? 2. Assyria was one of the most powerful nations on earth, known especially for its military might and brutality. How would this make it difficult for Jonah to proclaim: "Forty more days and Nineveh will be overturned" (vv. 3–4)? 3. What evidence is there that the Ninevites were sincere in their repentance (vv. 5–9)? 4. How and why does the Lord respond to the Ninevites (v. 10)? 5. What view of God do the Ninevites express in this chapter? 6. If a genuine turning to God were to occur in this country, what results would you expect to see?

Applying the Word 1. Describe one area in your life where you feel a need for repentance. 2. What actions can you take to demonstrate the sincerity of your repentance?

Responding in Prayer Spend some time before the Lord expressing your repentance and experiencing God's grace.

4 / *Jonah 4*
Jonah's Anger

LIFE IS FULL of minor joys and irritations. Finding a parking place in rush hour can make us very happy. Finding a flat tire when we return can make us miserable. In chapter 4 we discover that Jonah also cared a great deal about life's little ups and downs. Although his petty passions seem amusing, they also invite us to reexamine what we really care about.

Warming Up to God What little things irritate you or bring you joy?

Read Jonah 4.

4 But Jonah was greatly displeased and be-
came angry. 2He prayed to the LORD,
"O LORD, is this not what I said when I
was still at home? That is why I was so quick
to flee to Tarshish. I knew that you are a gra-
cious and compassionate God, slow to anger
and abounding in love, a God who relents
from sending calamity. 3Now, O LORD, take
away my life, for it is better for me to die than
to live."
4But the LORD replied, "Have you any right to
be angry?"
5Jonah went out and sat down at a place east of
the city. There he made himself a shelter, sat in
its shade and waited to see what would happen to
the city. 6Then the LORD God provided a vine and
made it grow up over Jonah to give shade for his
head to ease his discomfort, and Jonah was very
happy about the vine. 7But at dawn the next day
God provided a worm, which chewed the vine so
that it withered. 8When the sun rose, God pro-
vided a scorching east wind, and the sun blazed
on Jonah's head so that he grew faint. He wanted
to die, and said, "It would be better for me to die
than to live."
9But God said to Jonah, "Do you have a right to
be angry about the vine?"
"I do," he said. "I am angry enough to die."
10But the LORD said, "You have been concerned
about this vine, though you did not tend it or
make it grow. It sprang up overnight and died
overnight. 11But Nineveh has more than a hun-
dred and twenty thousand people who cannot tell
their right hand from their left, and many cattle
as well. Should I not be concerned about that
great city?"

Discovering the Word 1. Why was Jonah greatly displeased and angry (vv. 1-3)? 2. Did these things give him any right to be angry (v. 4)? Explain. 3. Evidently the forty days had already passed (3:10). Why then do you think Jonah still waited to see what would happen to the city (v. 5)? 4. How does the Lord use the vine as an object lesson for Jonah (vv. 6-11)? 5. In what ways are we sometimes more concerned about petty things than about those under God's judgment?

Applying the Word 1. What can we do to begin seeing things more from God's perspective? 2. In your life, how have you seen God demonstrate the qualities Jonah mentions in 4:2? 3. How does God's treatment of you motivate you to reach out to those who don't know him?

Responding in Prayer What have you learned from Jonah? Ask God to impress its message on your heart and life.

Micah

Have you ever learned from someone else's mistakes? We can save ourselves much pain by watching someone suffer the consequences of doing something that we easily could have done. The prophet Micah wonders why Judah does not learn from Israel.

After his death (922 B.C.) Solomon's kingdom was divided. To the north was Israel and to the south, Judah. Micah preaches before, during and after the time when Assyria comes from the east and destroys Israel (722 B.C.).

The society Micah portrays is not much different from what can be seen in the news today. People seize the property of others. The streets are filled with violence; widows and their children are thrown out of their homes. Yet Micah does not point to gangs as the source of the problem, but to the leaders. Prophet, priest and king alike commit wickedness toward those they are to protect. The prideful leaders sell prophecy for a price and cheat justice for a bribe.

Therefore Micah's message is largely one of judgment and doom. He knows that God will not ignore the plight of the innocent, nor will the Lord keep a blind eye toward the wicked. Micah boldly proclaims the impending destruction of God's people for their sins. In the first chapter Micah declares the impending destruction of Israel for her faithlessness. From the second chapter on he warns Judah of impending doom for the same faults as Israel. Yet Micah's message also contains clear messages of hope. At the end of chapters 2 and 7, along with chapters 4 and 5, we see that God will again have mercy on Judah. Micah holds out the promise of both a Messiah and a messianic age when all people will flock to the Lord's house.

Micah is not the first prophet to proclaim God's judgment against his people. He was preceded by Hosea and Amos. We can also be sure that the refugees from Israel, who quadrupled the population of Jerusalem, gave the Judeans eyewitness accounts of how God judged them. Unfortunately, the Judeans did not learn. Will we do any better?

Outline

Micah 1

1 The word of the LORD that came to Micah of Moresheth during the reigns of Jotham, Ahaz and Hezekiah, kings of Judah—the vision he saw concerning Samaria and Jerusalem.

2Hear, O peoples, all of you,
listen, O earth and all who are in it,
that the Sovereign LORD may witness against you,
the Lord from his holy temple.

3Look! The LORD is coming from his dwelling place;
he comes down and treads the high places of the earth.
4The mountains melt beneath him
and the valleys split apart,
like wax before the fire,
like water rushing down a slope.
5All this is because of Jacob's transgression,
because of the sins of the house of Israel.
What is Jacob's transgression?
Is it not Samaria?
What is Judah's high place?
Is it not Jerusalem?

6"Therefore I will make Samaria a heap of rubble,
a place for planting vineyards.
I will pour her stones into the valley
and lay bare her foundations.
7All her idols will be broken to pieces;
all her temple gifts will be burned with fire;
I will destroy all her images.
Since she gathered her gifts from the wages of prostitutes,
as the wages of prostitutes they will again be used."

8Because of this I will weep and wail;
I will go about barefoot and naked.
I will howl like a jackal
and moan like an owl.
9For her wound is incurable;
it has come to Judah.
It[a] has reached the very gate of my people,
even to Jerusalem itself.
10Tell it not in Gath[b];
weep not at all.[c]
In Beth Ophrah[d]
roll in the dust.
11Pass on in nakedness and shame,
you who live in Shaphir.[e]
Those who live in Zaanan[f]
will not come out.
Beth Ezel is in mourning;
its protection is taken from you.
12Those who live in Maroth[g] writhe in pain,
waiting for relief,
because disaster has come from the LORD,
even to the gate of Jerusalem.
13You who live in Lachish,[h]
harness the team to the chariot.
You were the beginning of sin
to the Daughter of Zion,
for the transgressions of Israel
were found in you.
14Therefore you will give parting gifts
to Moresheth Gath.
The town of Aczib[i] will prove deceptive
to the kings of Israel.
15I will bring a conqueror against you
who live in Mareshah.[j]
He who is the glory of Israel
will come to Adullam.
16Shave your heads in mourning
for the children in whom you delight;
make yourselves as bald as the vulture,
for they will go from you into exile.

[a]9 Or *He* [b]10 *Gath* sounds like the Hebrew for *tell.* [c]10 Hebrew; Septuagint may suggest *not in Acco.* The Hebrew for *in Acco* sounds like the Hebrew for *weep.* [d]10 *Beth Ophrah* means *house of dust.* [e]11 *Shaphir* means *pleasant.* [f]11 *Zaanan* sounds like the Hebrew for *come out.* [g]12 *Maroth* sounds like the Hebrew for *bitter.* [h]13 *Lachish* sounds like the Hebrew for *team.* [i]14 *Aczib* means *deception.* [j]15 *Mareshah* sounds like the Hebrew for *conqueror.*

1 / *Micah 2*
Who Do You Listen To?

JUST BECAUSE YOU have ears on your head does not mean that you listen. "Skilled incompetence" is a phrase that has been coined to characterize those who have become adept at protecting themselves from listening and learning. We practice it because we don't believe that the truth sets us free. Knowing that the truth can hurt, we have insulated ourselves from that pain. We are like those who tell Micah not to preach (v. 6).

Warming Up to God Ask God's Spirit to search you. Are you willing to hear the truth even if it is painful?

Read Micah 2.

---

2 Woe to those who plan iniquity,
to those who plot evil on their beds!
At morning's light they carry it out
because it is in their power to do it.
2They covet fields and seize them,
and houses, and take them.
They defraud a man of his home,
a fellowman of his inheritance.

3Therefore, the LORD says:

"I am planning disaster against this people,
from which you cannot save yourselves.
You will no longer walk proudly,
for it will be a time of calamity.
4In that day men will ridicule you;
they will taunt you with this mournful song:
'We are utterly ruined;
my people's possession is divided up.
He takes it from me!
He assigns our fields to traitors.' "

5Therefore you will have no one in the assembly of the LORD
to divide the land by lot.

6"Do not prophesy," their prophets say.
"Do not prophesy about these things;
disgrace will not overtake us."
7Should it be said, O house of Jacob:
"Is the Spirit of the LORD angry?
Does he do such things?"

"Do not my words do good
to him whose ways are upright?
8Lately my people have risen up
like an enemy.
You strip off the rich robe
from those who pass by without a care,
like men returning from battle.
9You drive the women of my people
from their pleasant homes.
You take away my blessing
from their children forever.
10Get up, go away!
For this is not your resting place,
because it is defiled,
it is ruined, beyond all remedy.
11If a liar and deceiver comes and says,
'I will prophesy for you plenty of wine and beer,'
he would be just the prophet for this people!

12"I will surely gather all of you, O Jacob;
I will surely bring together the remnant of Israel.
I will bring them together like sheep in a pen,
like a flock in its pasture;
the place will throng with people.
13One who breaks open the way will go up before them;
they will break through the gate and go out.
Their king will pass through before them,
the LORD at their head."

Discovering the Word 1. What sort of people is Micah preaching against (vv. 1–3, 8–9)? 2. In verses 1–2 we encounter people who apply the philosophy of modern success literature. It works for the prophet's audience, so why does Micah have a problem with it? 3. How does the punishment in verses 4–5 fit the crime of verses 1–3? 4. In verses 6–7 Micah's audience is offended at his message since they consider themselves quite safe. How does Micah respond to their false confidence? 5. Why does Micah characterize the "perfect prophet" as he does (v. 11)?

Applying the Word 1. God cares about our thoughts and actions. How do you need him to transform you? 2. How can you be better at hearing the truth even when it is painful? 3. In what area do you and your church need to cry out for justice?

Responding in Prayer Ask God to make you rich and successful in doing good. Ask him to help you hear the truth.

2 / *Micah 3*
How Not to Be a Leader

PERHAPS YOU HAVE heard Lord Acton's saying "Power tends to corrupt. Absolute power corrupts absolutely." Yet strangely, God entrusts us with power. Even though his gifts of power can be used for evil (for example, David having Bathsheba's husband Uriah killed), God does not shield us from it. He gives us spiritual gifts, authority in the church and leadership positions in the world.

Warming Up to God Consider the different parts of your life. What power has God given to you?

Read Micah 3.

3 Then I said,

"Listen, you leaders of Jacob,
you rulers of the house of Israel.
Should you not know justice,
2 you who hate good and love evil;
who tear the skin from my people
and the flesh from their bones;
3who eat my people's flesh,
strip off their skin
and break their bones in pieces;
who chop them up like meat for the pan,
like flesh for the pot?"

4Then they will cry out to the LORD,
but he will not answer them.
At that time he will hide his face from them
because of the evil they have done.

5This is what the LORD says:

"As for the prophets
who lead my people astray,
if one feeds them,
they proclaim 'peace';
if he does not,
they prepare to wage war against him.
6Therefore night will come over you, without visions,
and darkness, without divination.
The sun will set for the prophets,
and the day will go dark for them.
7The seers will be ashamed
and the diviners disgraced.
They will all cover their faces
because there is no answer from God."

8But as for me, I am filled with power,
with the Spirit of the LORD,
and with justice and might,
to declare to Jacob his transgression,
to Israel his sin.
9Hear this, you leaders of the house of Jacob,
you rulers of the house of Israel,
who despise justice
and distort all that is right;
10who build Zion with bloodshed,
and Jerusalem with wickedness.
11Her leaders judge for a bribe,
her priests teach for a price,
and her prophets tell fortunes for money.
Yet they lean upon the LORD and say,
"Is not the LORD among us?
No disaster will come upon us."
12Therefore because of you,

Zion will be plowed like a field,
Jerusalem will become a heap of rubble,
the temple hill a mound overgrown with thickets.

Discovering the Word 1. Describe the society and the leaders that Micah so vividly portrays in this chapter. 2. Why might God close his ears to our prayers (vv. 1–4)? 3. In verses 5–7 the prophets do not appear to be pretenders or con artists; rather they have gifts from God that they have turned to their own use. How then will the punishment of verse 6 be effective? 4. How does the Spirit of the Lord help Micah stand against his times (v. 8)? 5. The second half of verse 11 says that the leaders believe that the Lord will protect them. How can they think that?

Applying the Word 1. God sometimes calls us to stand against our culture as Micah did (especially v. 8). Where is he calling you to take a stand? 2. How can you guard yourself from using God's gifts for the wrong purpose? 3. All of us have the ability to be self-deluded like the leaders of Israel (v. 11). How can you guard yourself from thinking this way?

Responding in Prayer As you watch the news or read the newspaper, pray against the evil that you see.

3 / *Micah 4*
Tomorrow and Today

A BUMPER STICKER put it this way: "Life is hard, then you die." At the time of Micah's preaching life was tremendously difficult for the people of Israel. Yet in the midst of suffering Micah gives hope to the people that God will not let devastation be the last word.

Warming Up to God Imagine what it will be like to finally be in God's presence. How does it change the way you look at today?

Read Micah 4.

4 In the last days
the mountain of the LORD's temple will be established
as chief among the mountains;
it will be raised above the hills,
and peoples will stream to it.
2Many nations will come and say,
"Come, let us go up to the mountain of the LORD,
to the house of the God of Jacob.
He will teach us his ways,
so that we may walk in his paths."
The law will go out from Zion,
the word of the LORD from Jerusalem.
3He will judge between many peoples
and will settle disputes for strong nations far and wide.
They will beat their swords into plowshares
and their spears into pruning hooks.
Nation will not take up sword against nation,
nor will they train for war anymore.
4Every man will sit under his own vine
and under his own fig tree,
and no one will make them afraid,
for the LORD Almighty has spoken.
5All the nations may walk
in the name of their gods;
we will walk in the name of the LORD
our God for ever and ever.

6"In that day," declares the LORD,

"I will gather the lame;
I will assemble the exiles
and those I have brought to grief.
7I will make the lame a remnant,
those driven away a strong nation.
The LORD will rule over them in Mount Zion
from that day and forever.

[8]As for you, O watchtower of the flock,
O stronghold[k] of the Daughter of Zion,
the former dominion will be restored to you;
kingship will come to the Daughter of
Jerusalem."
[9]Why do you now cry aloud—
have you no king?
Has your counselor perished,
that pain seizes you like that of a woman in
labor?
[10]Writhe in agony, O Daughter of Zion,
like a woman in labor,
for now you must leave the city
to camp in the open field.
You will go to Babylon;
there you will be rescued.
There the LORD will redeem you
out of the hand of your enemies.

[11]But now many nations
are gathered against you.
They say, "Let her be defiled,
let our eyes gloat over Zion!"
[12]But they do not know
the thoughts of the LORD;
they do not understand his plan,
he who gathers them like sheaves to the
threshing floor.

[13]"Rise and thresh, O Daughter of Zion,
for I will give you horns of iron;
I will give you hoofs of bronze
and you will break to pieces many nations."
You will devote their ill-gotten gains to the
LORD,
their wealth to the Lord of all the earth.

[k]8 Or *hill*

Discovering the Word 1. Notice the movement and tone of the major sections of the chapter (vv. 1–8, 9–11, 12–13). How would it have spoken to the people? 2. The mount on which the temple stands (Zion) is not even near the height of the highest mountains, so what will make it chief among the mountains (vv. 1–2)? 3. What will society be like in those days (vv. 3–8)? 4. The picture of the coming future is interrupted by the coming present. What does the society of Israel look like at this time (vv. 9–10)? 5. What sort of promise does God make to Israel (vv. 11–13)?

Applying the Word 1. How can you and your community better embody the picture in verses 1–5? 2. How can you participate in gathering in the lame, the exiled and the grieving into the body of Christ?

Responding in Prayer Ask God to give you hope that can sustain you in trials and that you can give to those who despair.

4 / *Micah 5*
The Future of Our Enemies

AS CHRISTIANS, WE often do not like to talk about the fact that we have enemies. We hesitate to label someone as an enemy. Yet enemies are real and sometimes quite evil. Dealing with them can occupy much of our time and our thoughts. Unfortunately, there are times when we do not even notice the greatest enemy of God's purpose. In the words of Pogo the cartoon character: "We have met the enemy and he is us."

Warming Up to God What concerns are weighing on your mind? Give God your fears and frustrations.

Read Micah 5.

5 Marshal your troops, O city of
troops,[l]
for a siege is laid against us.
They will strike Israel's ruler
on the cheek with a rod.

[2]"But you, Bethlehem Ephrathah,
though you are small among the clans[m] of
Judah,

[l]1 Or *Strengthen your walls, O walled city* [m]2 Or *rulers*

out of you will come for me
  one who will be ruler over Israel,
whose origins[n] are from of old,
  from ancient times.[o]"

3 Therefore Israel will be abandoned
  until the time when she who is in labor
    gives birth
and the rest of his brothers return
  to join the Israelites.

4 He will stand and shepherd his flock
  in the strength of the LORD,
  in the majesty of the name of the LORD his
    God.
And they will live securely, for then his
    greatness
  will reach to the ends of the earth.
5 And he will be their peace.
When the Assyrian invades our land
  and marches through our fortresses,
we will raise against him seven shepherds,
  even eight leaders of men.
6 They will rule[p] the land of Assyria with the
    sword,
  the land of Nimrod with drawn sword.[q]
He will deliver us from the Assyrian
  when he invades our land
  and marches into our borders.

7 The remnant of Jacob will be
  in the midst of many peoples
like dew from the LORD,
  like showers on the grass,
which do not wait for man
  or linger for mankind.
8 The remnant of Jacob will be among the
    nations,
  in the midst of many peoples,
like a lion among the beasts of the forest,
  like a young lion among flocks of sheep,
which mauls and mangles as it goes,
  and no one can rescue.
9 Your hand will be lifted up in triumph over
    your enemies,
  and all your foes will be destroyed.

10 "In that day," declares the LORD,

"I will destroy your horses from among you
  and demolish your chariots.
11 I will destroy the cities of your land
  and tear down all your strongholds.
12 I will destroy your witchcraft
  and you will no longer cast spells.
13 I will destroy your carved images
  and your sacred stones from among you;
you will no longer bow down
  to the work of your hands.
14 I will uproot from among you your Asherah
    poles[r]
  and demolish your cities.
15 I will take vengeance in anger and wrath
  upon the nations that have not obeyed me."

[n]2 Hebrew *goings out* [o]2 Or *from days of eternity* [p]6 Or *crush* [q]6 Or *Nimrod in its gates* [r]14 That is, symbols of the goddess Asherah

Discovering the Word 1. Contrast the present-day ruler (v. 1) with the ruler who is to come (vv. 2–5). 2. How does the description of the future ruler give you comfort? 3. How does Micah picture Israel's future against Assyria (vv. 5–9)? 4. While Israel feared her enemies that were outside her border, what enemies within her borders did Micah expect destroyed (vv. 10–14)?

Applying the Word 1. We no longer wait for the ruler to come from Bethlehem, so how can he give you hope in the midst of your trials? 2. Often we see others as our enemies, but what inside you is an enemy to God's purposes (vv. 10–14)?

Responding in Prayer Ask God's Spirit to search you and to help you know what opposes his purpose. Confess, and ask God to empower you to change and move on.

5 / *Micah 6*
What God Requires

IMAGINE THAT YOU are handed a summons to appear in court for breaching an agreement. Then to your surprise you read that the one who had initiated the suit is God. This is what happens to Judah in chapter 6. God calls them to court and argues his case by reminding them of his faithful acts and their faithlessness.

Warming Up to God How has God recently shown you his faithfulness?

Read Micah 6.

6 Listen to what the LORD says:

"Stand up, plead your case before the mountains;
let the hills hear what you have to say.
2Hear, O mountains, the LORD's accusation;
listen, you everlasting foundations of the earth.
For the LORD has a case against his people;
he is lodging a charge against Israel.

3"My people, what have I done to you?
How have I burdened you? Answer me.
4I brought you up out of Egypt
and redeemed you from the land of slavery.
I sent Moses to lead you,
also Aaron and Miriam.
5My people, remember
what Balak king of Moab counseled
and what Balaam son of Beor answered.
Remember ⌞your journey⌟ from Shittim to Gilgal,
that you may know the righteous acts of the LORD."

6With what shall I come before the LORD
and bow down before the exalted God?
Shall I come before him with burnt offerings,
with calves a year old?
7Will the LORD be pleased with thousands of rams,
with ten thousand rivers of oil?
Shall I offer my firstborn for my transgression,
the fruit of my body for the sin of my soul?
8He has showed you, O man, what is good.
And what does the LORD require of you?
To act justly and to love mercy
and to walk humbly with your God.

9Listen! The LORD is calling to the city—
and to fear your name is wisdom—
"Heed the rod and the One who appointed it.[s]
10Am I still to forget, O wicked house,
your ill-gotten treasures
and the short ephah,[t] which is accursed?
11Shall I acquit a man with dishonest scales,
with a bag of false weights?
12Her rich men are violent;
her people are liars
and their tongues speak deceitfully.
13Therefore, I have begun to destroy you,
to ruin you because of your sins.
14You will eat but not be satisfied;
your stomach will still be empty.[u]
You will store up but save nothing,
because what you save I will give to the sword.
15You will plant but not harvest;
you will press olives but not use the oil on yourselves,
you will crush grapes but not drink the wine.
16You have observed the statutes of Omri
and all the practices of Ahab's house,
and you have followed their traditions.
Therefore I will give you over to ruin
and your people to derision;
you will bear the scorn of the nations.[v]"

[s] *9* The meaning of the Hebrew for this line is uncertain. [t] *10* An ephah was a dry measure. [u] *14* The meaning of the Hebrew for this word is uncertain. [v] *16* Septuagint; Hebrew *scorn due my people*

Discovering the Word 1. What kinds of complaints against Israel does the Lord list in this chapter? 2. What is the significance of the answer that God gives to his own question (vv. 3–5)? (These verses refer to Ex; Nu 22—24 and Jos 4.) 3. God requires the Israelites to sacrifice in worship. So why does he seem to be against it here (vv. 6–8)? 4. How do the actions of the people (vv. 9–12, 16) contrast with what God requires (v. 8)? 5. What sort of punishment awaits wicked towns or cities (vv. 13–15, 16)?

Applying the Word 1. How can remembering God's saving acts in the Bible and in your life (vv. 4–5) change your attitudes when you want to blame him (v. 3)? 2. Sometimes Christians reduce spirituality to simply doing certain things, like going to church or having consistent quiet times. How does this chapter expand your view? 3. Where is the voice of the Lord crying out (v. 9) against your town or city?

Responding in Prayer Ask God to show you how you can better embody verse 8. Ask the Holy Spirit to help you do so.

6 / *Micah 7*
How Long Will God Be Angry?

CDS ARE ABLE to store an amazing amount of information—from music to videos to entire encyclopedias. Imagine that someone had a complete CD of your life, so complete that they could even access your thoughts and actions with the touch of a button. What would someone find on your CD? What would you like to erase? The truth is that someone has all of that information about you—God.

Warming Up to God Reflect on what a CD of your life would be like—the type of music and the content. What brings you joy and what concerns you as you think of your life in this way?

Read Micah 7.

7 What misery is mine!
I am like one who gathers summer fruit
at the gleaning of the vineyard;
there is no cluster of grapes to eat,
none of the early figs that I crave.
2 The godly have been swept from the land;
not one upright man remains.
All men lie in wait to shed blood;
each hunts his brother with a net.
3 Both hands are skilled in doing evil;
the ruler demands gifts,
the judge accepts bribes,
the powerful dictate what they desire—
they all conspire together.
4 The best of them is like a brier,
the most upright worse than a thorn hedge.
The day of your watchmen has come,
the day God visits you.
Now is the time of their confusion.
5 Do not trust a neighbor;
put no confidence in a friend.
Even with her who lies in your embrace
be careful of your words.
6 For a son dishonors his father,
a daughter rises up against her mother,
a daughter-in-law against her
mother-in-law—
a man's enemies are the members of his
own household.
7 But as for me, I watch in hope for the LORD,
I wait for God my Savior;
my God will hear me.

8 Do not gloat over me, my enemy!
Though I have fallen, I will rise.
Though I sit in darkness,
the LORD will be my light.
9 Because I have sinned against him,
I will bear the LORD's wrath,
until he pleads my case
and establishes my right.
He will bring me out into the light;
I will see his righteousness.
10 Then my enemy will see it
and will be covered with shame,
she who said to me,

"Where is the LORD your God?"
My eyes will see her downfall;
even now she will be trampled underfoot
like mire in the streets.

11 The day for building your walls will come,
the day for extending your boundaries.
12 In that day people will come to you
from Assyria and the cities of Egypt,
even from Egypt to the Euphrates
and from sea to sea
and from mountain to mountain.
13 The earth will become desolate because of its inhabitants,
as the result of their deeds.

14 Shepherd your people with your staff,
the flock of your inheritance,
which lives by itself in a forest,
in fertile pasturelands.[w]
Let them feed in Bashan and Gilead
as in days long ago.

15 "As in the days when you came out of Egypt,
I will show them my wonders."

16 Nations will see and be ashamed,
deprived of all their power.
They will lay their hands on their mouths
and their ears will become deaf.
17 They will lick dust like a snake,
like creatures that crawl on the ground.
They will come trembling out of their dens;
they will turn in fear to the LORD our God
and will be afraid of you.
18 Who is a God like you,
who pardons sin and forgives the transgression
of the remnant of his inheritance?
You do not stay angry forever
but delight to show mercy.
19 You will again have compassion on us;
you will tread our sins underfoot
and hurl all our iniquities into the depths of the sea.
20 You will be true to Jacob,
and show mercy to Abraham,
as you pledged on oath to our fathers
in days long ago.

[w]14 *Or in the middle of Carmel*

Discovering the Word 1. How do verses 1 and 7 frame 2–6? 2. As Jerusalem speaks in verses 8–10, do you think she describes her situation correctly? 3. Do you think Micah agrees with Jerusalem's self-assessment (vv. 8–10) as he speaks of the day to come (vv. 11–17)? 4. The book ends with a powerful description of God. What character traits do you see?

Applying the Word 1. In verses 1–6 Micah describes a society falling apart, yet in the midst of the chaos he is able to hope in God. How can you help others to the same? 2. In Jerusalem's confession (v. 9) she is willing to bear the consequences of her guilt. How do you feel about your guilt? 3. How can you make verses 18–20 a part of your life and the lives of others?

Responding in Prayer Pray through this chapter, in particular verses 18–20. Confess your sins. Allow your heart to respond to God's grace.

Nahum

His name means *consolation*. His message carries little of it.

About the prophet Nahum we know little more than his hometown, Elkosh. His book is a poem of judgment directed to a city destined for judgment. At least a century earlier, Jonah had preached to Nineveh with reluctance. After all, the powerful Assyrian city was a particularly violent one, impaling its enemies and stacking their bodies at the gates. But Jonah's message broke through. Led by a shaken king, the city turned from their wickedness and was spared.

Then shortly before 612 B.C.—the fall of Nineveh—an angrier prophet brought a message of doom. Nahum sees that the city has fallen back into the cycle of wickedness which was their heritage. He prophesies that the Lord will use Babylon as his instrument of destruction. History confirms all of it: Nineveh was never heard from again.

The book is not a warning, but a hopeless prognosis. "The LORD is a jealous and avenging God," begins Nahum (1:2). Nearly every verse rings with the theme of inevitable judgment. "Nothing can heal your wound; your injury is fatal," concludes Nahum. Then he says that outsiders will *applaud* the downfall of the Ninevites (3:19).

What comfort can you gain from Nahum? The book speaks to the ultimate sovereignty of God. He judges those who, through the passage of time, ignore God's laws and persecute others. And despite the relentless prophecy of doom, we are assured, "the LORD is good, a refuge in times of trouble" (1:7). In a world which often seems to reward evil and suppress goodness, Nahum stands as a reminder of the absolute standards of God—and the inevitable fate of those who oppose him.

Outline

1 / *Nahum 1*
The God of Judgment

WHAT IS YOUR favorite of God's attributes? Love? Mercy? Grace? Comfort? Chances are you didn't name *judgment.* Yet that concept, however disquieting, is part of the divine equation. We cannot have a world of justice without judgment. Nahum reminds us that God is indeed just, and that when we break his laws, we break ourselves upon them. This chapter deals with the Lord's anger toward a city full of evil.

Warming Up to God What world conflicts are you currently following in the news? How do you think God feels about some of these?

Read Nahum 1.

1 An oracle concerning Nineveh. The book
of the vision of Nahum the Elkoshite.

2The LORD is a jealous and avenging God;
the LORD takes vengeance and is filled with
wrath.
The LORD takes vengeance on his foes
and maintains his wrath against his
enemies.
3The LORD is slow to anger and great in power;
the LORD will not leave the guilty
unpunished.
His way is in the whirlwind and the storm,
and clouds are the dust of his feet.
4He rebukes the sea and dries it up;
he makes all the rivers run dry.
Bashan and Carmel wither
and the blossoms of Lebanon fade.
5The mountains quake before him
and the hills melt away.
The earth trembles at his presence,
the world and all who live in it.
6Who can withstand his indignation?
Who can endure his fierce anger?
His wrath is poured out like fire;
the rocks are shattered before him.

7The LORD is good,
a refuge in times of trouble.
He cares for those who trust in him,
8 but with an overwhelming flood
he will make an end of ⌊Nineveh⌋;
he will pursue his foes into darkness.

9Whatever they plot against the LORD
he[a] will bring to an end;
trouble will not come a second time.
10They will be entangled among thorns
and drunk from their wine;
they will be consumed like dry stubble.[b]
11From you, ⌊O Nineveh,⌋ has one come forth
who plots evil against the LORD
and counsels wickedness.
12This is what the LORD says:

"Although they have allies and are numerous,
they will be cut off and pass away.
Although I have afflicted you, ⌊O Judah,⌋
I will afflict you no more.
13Now I will break their yoke from your neck
and tear your shackles away."

14The LORD has given a command concerning
you, ⌊Nineveh⌋:
"You will have no descendants to bear your
name.
I will destroy the carved images and cast idols
that are in the temple of your gods.
I will prepare your grave,
for you are vile."

15Look, there on the mountains,
the feet of one who brings good news,
who proclaims peace!
Celebrate your festivals, O Judah,
and fulfill your vows.
No more will the wicked invade you;
they will be completely destroyed.

[a]9 Or *What do you foes plot against the LORD? / He* [b]10 The meaning of the Hebrew for this verse is uncertain.

Discovering the Word 1. Why do you think Nahum uses poetry for such a subject as the anger of God? 2. Which description of God in verses 1–6 is most striking to you? Why? 3. How can you reconcile the statement in verse 7 with the rest of this chapter? 4. What charges against Nineveh are found in verses 9–14? 5. This book was written not directly to the Ninevites, but to Jewish readers. What might Nahum have intended the Jews to gain from hearing these words?

Applying the Word 1. What parallels can you find between Nineveh and today's world? 2. How should you respond today in the context of conditions that anger God? 3. Look again at verse 7. In what way do you need God's refuge from the world?

Responding in Prayer Pray that God will give you his perspective of the world and that you'll be angry toward the things which inspire his anger. Ask him to reassure you that "he cares for those who trust in him" (v. 7).

2/ *Nahum 2*
The Approach of Judgment

IMPENDING CATASTROPHE! THE news is full of it. Scientists warn us about global warming, coming earthquakes, acid rain and other dangers to the natural order. Politicians issue dire warnings about sinister movements and culture wars. Similarly, Nahum writes of a catastrophe soon to befall Nineveh. We see the culmination of the evils described in the first chapter as the Babylonian troops descend on the city.

Warming Up to God What crisis or challenge is on the outskirts of your life at present? How might God be working within this situation?

Read Nahum 2.

2 An attacker advances against you,
⌞Nineveh⌟.
Guard the fortress,
watch the road,
brace yourselves,
marshal all your strength!

2 The LORD will restore the splendor of Jacob
like the splendor of Israel,
though destroyers have laid them waste
and have ruined their vines.

3 The shields of his soldiers are red;
the warriors are clad in scarlet.
The metal on the chariots flashes
on the day they are made ready;
the spears of pine are brandished.[c]
4 The chariots storm through the streets,
rushing back and forth through the squares.
They look like flaming torches;
they dart about like lightning.

5 He summons his picked troops,
yet they stumble on their way.
They dash to the city wall;
the protective shield is put in place.
6 The river gates are thrown open
and the palace collapses.
7 It is decreed[d] that ⌞the city⌟
be exiled and carried away.
Its slave girls moan like doves
and beat upon their breasts.
8 Nineveh is like a pool,
and its water is draining away.
"Stop! Stop!" they cry,
but no one turns back.
9 Plunder the silver!
Plunder the gold!
The supply is endless,
the wealth from all its treasures!
10 She is pillaged, plundered, stripped!
Hearts melt, knees give way,
bodies tremble, every face grows pale.

11 Where now is the lions' den,
the place where they fed their young,
where the lion and lioness went,

c3 Hebrew; Septuagint and Syriac / *the horsemen rush to and fro*
d7 The meaning of the Hebrew for this word is uncertain.

and the cubs, with nothing to fear?
12 The lion killed enough for his cubs
and strangled the prey for his mate,
filling his lairs with the kill
and his dens with the prey.
13 "I am against you,"
declares the LORD Almighty.
"I will burn up your chariots in smoke,
and the sword will devour your young lions.
I will leave you no prey on the earth.
The voices of your messengers
will no longer be heard."

Discovering the Word 1. How does chapter 1, which deals with God's power and anger, set the mood for the first verses of chapter 2? 2. Is Nahum actually warning Nineveh? Explain. 3. Given that moral evil is the cause of Nineveh's fall, what point does this chapter make about armies and power (vv. 3–6)? 4. Exactly how is Nineveh like a pool (v. 8)? 5. Nineveh had many lion sculptures. How is this metaphor turned against them in verses 11–13?

Applying the Word 1. Do you see God moving through political forces today? If so, how? 2. Nahum deals with the plundering of Ninevite wealth (vv. 9–10). How can you begin to better acknowledge God's control over your possessions?

Responding in Prayer In this chapter Nahum has described the thoroughness of God's judgment. Nineveh was never revived. Spend some time meditating on God's awesome power—terrifying yet reassuring. Praise and thank him that his power is always tied to justice.

3 / *Nahum 3*
The Aftermath of Judgment

AFTER TRAGEDY STRIKES, shock sets in. The victims become disoriented as they attempt to cope. Everyone else has an angle and an explanation for the tragedy. The question is pondered: could this have been avoided? Nahum closes with a woeful survey of the "city of blood" (3:1). We catch a glimpse of the sad aftermath of God's judgment.

Warming Up to God Recall the greatest crisis in your life over the last few years. How did you feel the day after it? How was your faith affected?

Read Nahum 3.

3 Woe to the city of blood,
full of lies,
full of plunder,
never without victims!
2 The crack of whips,
the clatter of wheels,
galloping horses
and jolting chariots!
3 Charging cavalry,
flashing swords
and glittering spears!
Many casualties,
piles of dead,
bodies without number,
people stumbling over the corpses—
4 all because of the wanton lust of a harlot,
alluring, the mistress of sorceries,
who enslaved nations by her prostitution
and peoples by her witchcraft.

5 "I am against you," declares the LORD Almighty.
"I will lift your skirts over your face.
I will show the nations your nakedness
and the kingdoms your shame.
6 I will pelt you with filth,
I will treat you with contempt
and make you a spectacle.
7 All who see you will flee from you and say,
'Nineveh is in ruins—who will mourn for her?'

Where can I find anyone to comfort you?"

8Are you better than Thebes,[e]
situated on the Nile,
with water around her?
The river was her defense,
the waters her wall.
9Cush[f] and Egypt were her boundless strength;
Put and Libya were among her allies.
10Yet she was taken captive
and went into exile.
Her infants were dashed to pieces
at the head of every street.
Lots were cast for her nobles,
and all her great men were put in chains.
11You too will become drunk;
you will go into hiding
and seek refuge from the enemy.
12All your fortresses are like fig trees
with their first ripe fruit;
when they are shaken,
the figs fall into the mouth of the eater.
13Look at your troops—
they are all women!
The gates of your land
are wide open to your enemies;
fire has consumed their bars.
14Draw water for the siege,
strengthen your defenses!
Work the clay,
tread the mortar,
repair the brickwork!
15There the fire will devour you;
the sword will cut you down
and, like grasshoppers, consume you.
Multiply like grasshoppers,
multiply like locusts!
16You have increased the number of your merchants
till they are more than the stars of the sky,
but like locusts they strip the land
and then fly away.
17Your guards are like locusts,
your officials like swarms of locusts
that settle in the walls on a cold day—
but when the sun appears they fly away,
and no one knows where.

18O king of Assyria, your shepherds[g] slumber;
your nobles lie down to rest.
Your people are scattered on the mountains
with no one to gather them.
19Nothing can heal your wound;
your injury is fatal.
Everyone who hears the news about you
claps his hands at your fall,
for who has not felt
your endless cruelty?

[e]8 Hebrew *No Amon* [f]9 That is, the upper Nile region [g]18 Or *rulers*

Discovering the Word 1. How would you characterize the tone of this chapter? 2. What sins of Nineveh are recounted in this chapter? 3. Nineveh was famous for temple prostitution. How does Nahum appropriately use this reputation as a metaphor in verses 4–7? 4. What is the sin of the merchants (v. 16)? 5. Nahum often uses a mocking tone. How does verse 19 help explain this?

Applying the Word 1. What current areas of national or international life show the devastation of Nineveh? 2. How can you personally make God's sovereignty better known in your surroundings?

Responding in Prayer Nahum celebrates "the feet of one who brings good news, who proclaims peace!" (1:15). Thank God that in the midst of the most terrible events, God is fulfilling his own purposes. Ask him to empower you to bring good news and proclaim peace today.

Habakkuk

The period in which Habakkuk lived had a lot of international tension. Judah was caught between two treacherous world powers. Prior to the events of the book, the king of Egypt had murdered the king of Judah and set up a puppet government in Judah. The Babylonians were also a world power known for their treachery. They were enemies of the Egyptians. The Babylonians were soon to overthrow the Egyptians, but for Judah this was like going from the frying pan into the fire. Habakkuk wondered what God was going to do in this morass. He did not realize that God also saw Judah as a part of the problem in the world.

Habakkuk was a contemporary of Jeremiah's. Both prophets challenged the nation to give up their idolatry, pride and desire for wealth gained at the expense of the poor and by destroying the land. When Jeremiah delivered this message, he was persecuted for being unpatriotic (Jer 20:1–3).

Outline

1/ Habakkuk 1:1—2:1 ——— *Does God Care About Injustice?*

2/ Habakkuk 2:2–20 ——— *The Log in Our Eyes*

3/ Habakkuk 3 ——— *God's Creation*

1 / *Habakkuk 1:1—2:1*
Does God Care About Injustice?

WHAT IF YOU cried out to God about the injustices in our world—the terrorism and trouble in various places—and God responded: "I am going to do something in your days that you would not believe. I'm raising up the nation you most distrust to sweep across the whole earth and seize dwelling places not their own." In this passage, Habakkuk gets that kind of message from God. Habakkuk had viewed Babylonia (modern-day Iraq) as the incarnation of evil. He was not prepared, therefore, when God announced he would use the Babylonians to judge his nation.

Warming Up to God What injustices in your own life and in world news are on your mind as you begin this quiet time?

Read Habakkuk 1:1—2:1.

1 The oracle that Habakkuk the prophet received.

2How long, O LORD, must I call for help,
but you do not listen?
Or cry out to you, "Violence!"
but you do not save?
3Why do you make me look at injustice?
Why do you tolerate wrong?
Destruction and violence are before me;
there is strife, and conflict abounds.
4Therefore the law is paralyzed,
and justice never prevails.
The wicked hem in the righteous,
so that justice is perverted.

5"Look at the nations and watch—
and be utterly amazed.
For I am going to do something in your days
that you would not believe,
even if you were told.
6I am raising up the Babylonians,[a]
that ruthless and impetuous people,
who sweep across the whole earth
to seize dwelling places not their own.
7They are a feared and dreaded people;
they are a law to themselves
and promote their own honor.
8Their horses are swifter than leopards,
fiercer than wolves at dusk.
Their cavalry gallops headlong;
their horsemen come from afar.
They fly like a vulture swooping to devour;
9 they all come bent on violence.
Their hordes[b] advance like a desert wind
and gather prisoners like sand.
10They deride kings
and scoff at rulers.
They laugh at all fortified cities;
they build earthen ramps and capture them.
11Then they sweep past like the wind and go on—
guilty men, whose own strength is their god."

12O LORD, are you not from everlasting?
My God, my Holy One, we will not die.
O LORD, you have appointed them to execute judgment;
O Rock, you have ordained them to punish.
13Your eyes are too pure to look on evil;
you cannot tolerate wrong.
Why then do you tolerate the treacherous?
Why are you silent while the wicked
swallow up those more righteous than themselves?
14You have made men like fish in the sea,
like sea creatures that have no ruler.
15The wicked foe pulls all of them up with hooks,
he catches them in his net,
he gathers them up in his dragnet;
and so he rejoices and is glad.
16Therefore he sacrifices to his net
and burns incense to his dragnet,
for by his net he lives in luxury
and enjoys the choicest food.
17Is he to keep on emptying his net,
destroying nations without mercy?

[a]6 Or *Chaldeans* [b]9 The meaning of the Hebrew for this word is uncertain.

2 I will stand at my watch
and station myself on the ramparts;
I will look to see what he will say to me,
and what answer I am to give to this complaint.[c]

[c]1 *Or and what to answer when I am rebuked*

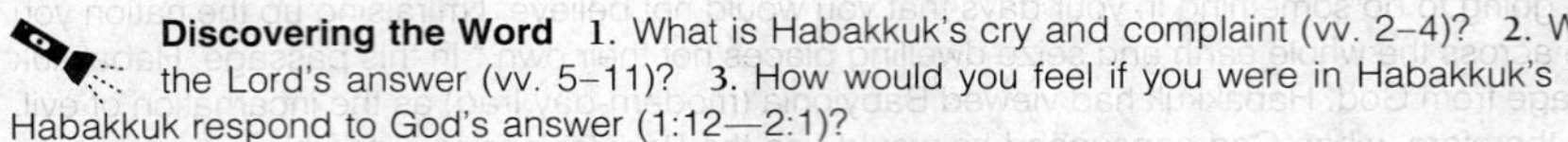

Discovering the Word 1. What is Habakkuk's cry and complaint (vv. 2–4)? 2. What is amazing about the Lord's answer (vv. 5–11)? 3. How would you feel if you were in Habakkuk's shoes? 4. How does Habakkuk respond to God's answer (1:12—2:1)?

Applying the Word 1. Do you ever feel like God doesn't care about the injustice in your life or in the world around you? Explain. 2. What can you learn from Habakkuk's relationship with God?

Responding in Prayer Follow Habakkuk's model and talk openly with God about the injustices you see.

2 / *Habakkuk 2:2–20*
The Log in Our Eyes

ONE OF THE great dangers for anyone who takes evil seriously is that in challenging evil we can begin to think that we are without sin. We can see evil in others much easier than in ourselves. This can result in a self-righteous attitude that denies the power of God in our lives and denies our constant need to seek God's forgiveness.

Warming Up to God When have you found yourself so intent on "the enemy" that you have lost sight of your own sins?

Read Habakkuk 2:2–20.

2Then the LORD replied:

"Write down the revelation
and make it plain on tablets
so that a herald[d] may run with it.
3For the revelation awaits an appointed time;
it speaks of the end
and will not prove false.
Though it linger, wait for it;
it[e] will certainly come and will not delay.

4"See, he is puffed up;
his desires are not upright—
but the righteous will live by his faith[f]—
5indeed, wine betrays him;
he is arrogant and never at rest.
Because he is as greedy as the grave[g]
and like death is never satisfied,
he gathers to himself all the nations
and takes captive all the peoples.

6"Will not all of them taunt him with ridicule and scorn, saying,

" 'Woe to him who piles up stolen goods
and makes himself wealthy by extortion!
How long must this go on?'
7Will not your debtors[h] suddenly arise?
Will they not wake up and make you tremble?
Then you will become their victim.
8Because you have plundered many nations,
the peoples who are left will plunder you.
For you have shed man's blood;
you have destroyed lands and cities and everyone in them.

9"Woe to him who builds his realm by unjust gain
to set his nest on high,
to escape the clutches of ruin!
10You have plotted the ruin of many peoples,
shaming your own house and forfeiting your life.
11The stones of the wall will cry out,

[d]2 *Or so that whoever reads it* [e]3 *Or Though he linger, wait for him; / he* [f]4 *Or faithfulness* [g]5 *Hebrew Sheol* [h]7 *Or creditors*

and the beams of the woodwork will echo
it.

12"Woe to him who builds a city with
bloodshed
and establishes a town by crime!
13Has not the LORD Almighty determined
that the people's labor is only fuel for the
fire,
that the nations exhaust themselves for
nothing?
14For the earth will be filled with the
knowledge of the glory of the LORD,
as the waters cover the sea.

15"Woe to him who gives drink to his
neighbors,
pouring it from the wineskin till they are
drunk,
so that he can gaze on their naked bodies.
16You will be filled with shame instead of glory.
Now it is your turn! Drink and be
exposed[i]!
The cup from the LORD's right hand is coming
around to you,
and disgrace will cover your glory.
17The violence you have done to Lebanon will
overwhelm you,
and your destruction of animals will terrify
you.
For you have shed man's blood;
you have destroyed lands and cities and
everyone in them.

18"Of what value is an idol, since a man has
carved it?
Or an image that teaches lies?
For he who makes it trusts in his own
creation;
he makes idols that cannot speak.
19Woe to him who says to wood, 'Come to life!'
Or to lifeless stone, 'Wake up!'
Can it give guidance?
It is covered with gold and silver;
there is no breath in it.
20But the LORD is in his holy temple;
let all the earth be silent before him."

[i]16 Masoretic Text; Dead Sea Scrolls, Aquila, Vulgate and Syriac (see also Septuagint) *and stagger*

Discovering the Word 1. In verse 2 God begins to explain his answer to Habakkuk. What is the challenge of verses 2–3? 2. Why must one have faith in order to meet the challenge? 3. What is the connection between faith and righteousness (v. 4)? 4. Chapter 2 lists five "woes" (vv. 6, 9, 12, 15, 19). For each, how is the consequence a direct result of the wrong committed? 5. How is the final woe connected to all the rest?

Applying the Word 1. Why is it easier for us to see the idolatry of others than to see our own? 2. What are some of your idols?

Responding in Prayer Pray that God will help you to face your sins of idolatry and self-righteousness.

3 / *Habakkuk 3*
God's Creation

ONE SUMMER NIGHT at a girls' camp I enjoyed a solitary walk in the presence of God's creation. I walked past the beam of a barnyard pole light and out into a grassy meadow shrouded in twilight but still exhaling the warmth of afternoon sun. Myriad meadow insects sang their evening prayers. Tiny feet scurried through their own maze-world so deep in the grass that they barely fluttered the seeded canopy above. Children's voices laughed and sang, near enough to carry music to me, but too distant to bring their ever-present turmoil. A light breeze washed my face clean of sweat.

After hearing the shocking news that the Babylonians would destroy the nation of Judah, Habakkuk meditated on his beautiful land and its upcoming destruction. Then he wrote the prayer in Habakkuk 3.

Warming Up to God When have you seen the wrath of God exercised in a way that surprised or confused you?

Read Habakkuk 3.

3 A prayer of Habakkuk the prophet. On *shigionoth*.[j]

2LORD, I have heard of your fame;
I stand in awe of your deeds, O LORD.
Renew them in our day,
in our time make them known;
in wrath remember mercy.

3God came from Teman,
the Holy One from Mount Paran. *Selah*[k]
His glory covered the heavens
and his praise filled the earth.
4His splendor was like the sunrise;
rays flashed from his hand,
where his power was hidden.
5Plague went before him;
pestilence followed his steps.
6He stood, and shook the earth;
he looked, and made the nations tremble.
The ancient mountains crumbled
and the age-old hills collapsed.
His ways are eternal.
7I saw the tents of Cushan in distress,
the dwellings of Midian in anguish.

8Were you angry with the rivers, O LORD?
Was your wrath against the streams?
Did you rage against the sea
when you rode with your horses
and your victorious chariots?
9You uncovered your bow,
you called for many arrows. *Selah*
You split the earth with rivers;
10 the mountains saw you and writhed.
Torrents of water swept by;
the deep roared
and lifted its waves on high.

11Sun and moon stood still in the heavens
at the glint of your flying arrows,
at the lightning of your flashing spear.
12In wrath you strode through the earth
and in anger you threshed the nations.
13You came out to deliver your people,
to save your anointed one.
You crushed the leader of the land of wickedness,
you stripped him from head to foot. *Selah*
14With his own spear you pierced his head
when his warriors stormed out to scatter us,
gloating as though about to devour
the wretched who were in hiding.
15You trampled the sea with your horses,
churning the great waters.

16I heard and my heart pounded,
my lips quivered at the sound;
decay crept into my bones,
and my legs trembled.
Yet I will wait patiently for the day of calamity
to come on the nation invading us.
17Though the fig tree does not bud
and there are no grapes on the vines,
though the olive crop fails
and the fields produce no food,
though there are no sheep in the pen
and no cattle in the stalls,
18yet I will rejoice in the LORD,
I will be joyful in God my Savior.

19The Sovereign LORD is my strength;
he makes my feet like the feet of a deer,
he enables me to go on the heights.

For the director of music. On my stringed instruments.

[j]1 Probably a literary or musical term [k]3 A word of uncertain meaning; possibly a musical term; also in verses 9 and 13

Discovering the Word 1. Find as many references as you can to the natural environment. 2. What connections did Habakkuk see between God and nature? 3. Habakkuk prayed in verse 2, "In wrath remember mercy." What do you think he meant by that request? 4. Study the last line of verse 6 and the first two lines of verse 13. How might these words help you understand what appears to be senseless destruction? 5. What choices does Habakkuk make in light of his relationship with God (vv. 16–19)?

Applying the Word 1. If you could somehow know that your own nation would soon look like the description in Habakkuk 3, how do you think you would respond to God? 2. How does Habakkuk's prayer encourage you to continue worshiping God even when his actions confuse you?

Responding in Prayer Pray for God's mercy on your land and people.

Zephaniah

Old Testament prophets majored on the themes of God's coming judgment and future blessing. They often blended the near future with events that were so far distant they have yet to happen. Zephaniah was one of those prophets.

Zephaniah prophesied during King Josiah's reign over Judah, around 625–635 B.C. His messages focused on God's judgments on Judah, fulfilled when Babylon conquered the nation and carried most of the people into exile, and their restoration as a nation. Plus he spoke about the coming "day of the Lord," which is also a still-future time when God will judge the heathen nations and usher in the messianic kingdom of peace and blessing.

Even though it was written over 2600 years ago, Zephaniah's book is relevant to our times. He warned people of God's judgment on sins like materialism and injustice that are prevalent today. But he also offered hope of a better time to come, a message we also need to hear.

Outline

1 / *Zephaniah 1*
Complacent to the End

SOMEONE ONCE SAID: "Complacency is a blight that saps energy, dulls attitudes, and causes a drain on the brain. The first symptom is satisfaction with things as they are. The second is rejection of things as they might be. 'Good enough' becomes today's watchword and tomorrow's standard." And as Zephaniah wrote, it gets in the way of spiritual progress.

Warming Up to God What image comes to mind when someone mentions complacency? Ask God to show you from this chapter how dangerous it can be.

Read Zephaniah 1.

1 The word of the LORD that came to Zepha-
niah son of Cushi, the son of Gedaliah,
the son of Amariah, the son of Hezekiah,
during the reign of Josiah son of Amon king of
Judah:

2"I will sweep away everything
from the face of the earth,"
declares the LORD.
3"I will sweep away both men and animals;
I will sweep away the birds of the air
and the fish of the sea.
The wicked will have only heaps of rubble[a]
when I cut off man from the face of the earth,"
declares the LORD.

4"I will stretch out my hand against Judah
and against all who live in Jerusalem.
I will cut off from this place every remnant of Baal,
the names of the pagan and the idolatrous priests—
5those who bow down on the roofs
to worship the starry host,
those who bow down and swear by the LORD
and who also swear by Molech,[b]
6those who turn back from following the LORD
and neither seek the LORD nor inquire of him.
7Be silent before the Sovereign LORD,
for the day of the LORD is near.
The LORD has prepared a sacrifice;
he has consecrated those he has invited.
8On the day of the LORD's sacrifice
I will punish the princes
and the king's sons
and all those clad
in foreign clothes.
9On that day I will punish
all who avoid stepping on the threshold,[c]
who fill the temple of their gods
with violence and deceit.

10"On that day," declares the LORD,
"a cry will go up from the Fish Gate,
wailing from the New Quarter,
and a loud crash from the hills.
11Wail, you who live in the market district[d];
all your merchants will be wiped out,
all who trade with[e] silver will be ruined.
12At that time I will search Jerusalem with lamps
and punish those who are complacent,
who are like wine left on its dregs,
who think, 'The LORD will do nothing,
either good or bad.'
13Their wealth will be plundered,
their houses demolished.
They will build houses
but not live in them;
they will plant vineyards
but not drink the wine.

14"The great day of the LORD is near—
near and coming quickly.
Listen! The cry on the day of the LORD will be bitter,
the shouting of the warrior there.
15That day will be a day of wrath,
a day of distress and anguish,
a day of trouble and ruin,
a day of darkness and gloom,
a day of clouds and blackness,
16a day of trumpet and battle cry
against the fortified cities

[a]3 The meaning of the Hebrew for this line is uncertain. [b]5 Hebrew *Malcam*, that is, Milcom [c]9 See 1 Samuel 5:5. [d]11 Or *the Mortar* [e]11 Or *in*

and against the corner towers.
17I will bring distress on the people
and they will walk like blind men,
because they have sinned against the
LORD.
Their blood will be poured out like dust
and their entrails like filth.
18Neither their silver nor their gold
will be able to save them
on the day of the LORD's wrath.
In the fire of his jealousy
the whole world will be consumed,
for he will make a sudden end
of all who live in the earth."

Discovering the Word 1. What did Zephaniah declare about God's coming judgment (vv. 1–3)? 2. For what sins would God judge his people (vv. 4–13)? 3. God's people responded to him with complacency. How did that attitude affect them (vv. 12–13)? 4. How did Zephaniah describe the coming day of the Lord (vv. 14–18)? 5. If you had been one of the people who received this message, how would you have reacted to it? Why?

Applying the Word 1. In what areas do you tend to be complacent? 2. What would help you to overcome complacency in one area?

Responding in Prayer Ask God to help you trust him and to stretch you spiritually instead of being satisfied with your present comfort zone.

2 / *Zephaniah 2*
Judgment to Come

OUR NEEDS AND problems often keep us focused on ourselves. Sure we're going to heaven someday. But what about the people we know who do not have this assurance? Just as God fulfilled Zephaniah's warning to the nations around Judah, he will judge sinners as he declared in other portions of the Bible.

Warming Up to God How often do you think about the judgment your unsaved friends and relatives will endure? Ask God to show you the seriousness of the judgment to come as you study this passage.

Read Zephaniah 2.

2 Gather together, gather together,
O shameful nation,
2before the appointed time arrives
and that day sweeps on like chaff,
before the fierce anger of the LORD comes
upon you,
before the day of the LORD's wrath comes
upon you.
3Seek the LORD, all you humble of the land,
you who do what he commands.
Seek righteousness, seek humility;
perhaps you will be sheltered
on the day of the LORD's anger.

4Gaza will be abandoned
and Ashkelon left in ruins.
At midday Ashdod will be emptied
and Ekron uprooted.
5Woe to you who live by the sea,
O Kerethite people;
the word of the LORD is against you,
O Canaan, land of the Philistines.

"I will destroy you,
and none will be left."
6The land by the sea, where the Kerethites[f]
dwell,
will be a place for shepherds and sheep
pens.
7It will belong to the remnant of the house of
Judah;
there they will find pasture.
In the evening they will lie down
in the houses of Ashkelon.

f6 The meaning of the Hebrew for this word is uncertain.

The LORD their God will care for them;
he will restore their fortunes.[g]

8"I have heard the insults of Moab
and the taunts of the Ammonites,
who insulted my people
and made threats against their land.
9Therefore, as surely as I live,"
declares the LORD Almighty, the God of Israel,
"surely Moab will become like Sodom,
the Ammonites like Gomorrah—
a place of weeds and salt pits,
a wasteland forever.
The remnant of my people will plunder them;
the survivors of my nation will inherit their land."
10This is what they will get in return for their pride,
for insulting and mocking the people of the LORD Almighty.
11The LORD will be awesome to them
when he destroys all the gods of the land.
The nations on every shore will worship him,
every one in its own land.

12"You too, O Cushites,[h]
will be slain by my sword."

13He will stretch out his hand against the north
and destroy Assyria,
leaving Nineveh utterly desolate
and dry as the desert.
14Flocks and herds will lie down there,
creatures of every kind.
The desert owl and the screech owl
will roost on her columns.
Their calls will echo through the windows,
rubble will be in the doorways,
the beams of cedar will be exposed.
15This is the carefree city
that lived in safety.
She said to herself,
"I am, and there is none besides me."
What a ruin she has become,
a lair for wild beasts!
All who pass by her scoff
and shake their fists.

g7 Or *will bring back their captives* h12 That is, people from the upper Nile region

Discovering the Word 1. What did Zephaniah tell the people to do in order to avoid God's anger (vv. 1–3)? 2. What would God do to those who punished his people (vv. 4–15)? 3. What sins had the nations around Judah committed (vv. 4–15)? 4. What hope did Zephaniah offer God's people in the midst of this judgment (vv. 6–7)? 5. According to this chapter, what would the nations learn about God?

Applying the Word 1. In what ways is your nation in danger of God's judgment? 2. Reread verse 3. How can you seek the Lord today?

Responding in Prayer Ask God for opportunities this week to tell others about him.

3 / *Zephaniah 3*
Better Days Are Coming

WHEN YOU THINK about the future, what comes to mind? Next year? Retirement? Heaven? Escape from the frustrations of today? No matter what you are going through now, you can look forward to some wonderful things, as God made clear through Zephaniah's prophecy.

Warming Up to God If you were in charge of the future, what would you like to have happen?

Read Zephaniah 3.

3 Woe to the city of oppressors,
rebellious and defiled!
[2]She obeys no one,
she accepts no correction.
She does not trust in the LORD,
she does not draw near to her God.
[3]Her officials are roaring lions,
her rulers are evening wolves,
who leave nothing for the morning.
[4]Her prophets are arrogant;
they are treacherous men.
Her priests profane the sanctuary
and do violence to the law.
[5]The LORD within her is righteous;
he does no wrong.
Morning by morning he dispenses his justice,
and every new day he does not fail,
yet the unrighteous know no shame.

[6]"I have cut off nations;
their strongholds are demolished.
I have left their streets deserted,
with no one passing through.
Their cities are destroyed;
no one will be left—no one at all.
[7]I said to the city,
'Surely you will fear me
and accept correction!'
Then her dwelling would not be cut off,
nor all my punishments come upon her.
But they were still eager
to act corruptly in all they did.
[8]Therefore wait for me," declares the LORD,
"for the day I will stand up to testify.[i]
I have decided to assemble the nations,
to gather the kingdoms
and to pour out my wrath on them—
all my fierce anger.
The whole world will be consumed
by the fire of my jealous anger.

[9]"Then will I purify the lips of the peoples,
that all of them may call on the name of the LORD
and serve him shoulder to shoulder.
[10]From beyond the rivers of Cush[j]
my worshipers, my scattered people,
will bring me offerings.
[11]On that day you will not be put to shame
for all the wrongs you have done to me,
because I will remove from this city
those who rejoice in their pride.
Never again will you be haughty
on my holy hill.
[12]But I will leave within you
the meek and humble,
who trust in the name of the LORD.
[13]The remnant of Israel will do no wrong;
they will speak no lies,
nor will deceit be found in their mouths.
They will eat and lie down
and no one will make them afraid."

[14]Sing, O Daughter of Zion;
shout aloud, O Israel!
Be glad and rejoice with all your heart,
O Daughter of Jerusalem!
[15]The LORD has taken away your punishment,
he has turned back your enemy.
The LORD, the King of Israel, is with you;
never again will you fear any harm.
[16]On that day they will say to Jerusalem,
"Do not fear, O Zion;
do not let your hands hang limp.
[17]The LORD your God is with you,
he is mighty to save.
He will take great delight in you,
he will quiet you with his love,
he will rejoice over you with singing."

[18]"The sorrows for the appointed feasts
I will remove from you;
they are a burden and a reproach to you.[k]
[19]At that time I will deal
with all who oppressed you;
I will rescue the lame
and gather those who have been scattered.
I will give them praise and honor
in every land where they were put to shame.
[20]At that time I will gather you;
at that time I will bring you home.
I will give you honor and praise
among all the peoples of the earth
when I restore your fortunes[l]
before your very eyes,"
says the LORD.

[i]8 Septuagint and Syriac; Hebrew *will rise up to plunder* [j]10 That is, the upper Nile region [k]18 Or *"I will gather you who mourn for the appointed feasts; / your reproach is a burden to you* [l]20 Or *I bring back your captives*

Discovering the Word 1. After pronouncing judgments on the nations, Zephaniah came back to Judah. Why did God warn his people about judgment to come (vv. 1–7)? 2. How did the people respond to God's warning (v. 7)? 3. What did God promise his people in the future (vv. 8–20)? 4. What do you learn about God from this chapter?

Applying the Word 1. Which promise are you looking forward to the most? Why? 2. Which description of God do you need to remember today as you wait for what he has promised in the future?

Responding in Prayer Look again at the sins mentioned in verse 2, and confess any sins God is warning you about. Thank him for what is to come in the future.

Haggai

If you're like most believers, you're pulled in a myriad of directions. Full schedules, necessary and worthwhile activities, family members, friends, other people, distractions and interruptions all clamor for attention. But where is God in the midst of our priorities? This is an ancient struggle that Haggai addressed over 2500 years ago.

To understand the messages of Haggai, we need to understand the historical context in which they were given. In 586 B.C. the Babylonians under Nebuchadnezzar defeated the southern kingdom of Judah and razed the city of Jerusalem, including the temple. They took many of the Jewish people captive as God's punishment for their sins, primarily idolatry. In 539 B.C. Cyrus, king of Persia, conquered Babylon, becoming the new ruler of the Jewish people. A year later, he issued a decree that permitted the exiles to return to their land.

The first group of exiles (about 50,000) returned in 536 B.C. under Zerubbabel's leadership to rebuild the temple. Apparently, Haggai was part of this group. After laying the foundation, the exiles quit when their enemies threatened them and hired lawyers to frustrate their work. So the temple rebuilding stopped for fifteen years. These events are recorded in Ezra 1—4.

Then God sent the prophets Haggai and Zechariah to call his people back to this work. Ezra 5 tells about this event while the books of Haggai and Zechariah give us the content of their preaching.

Rebuilding the temple was an important task for the Jewish people. The temple represented their relationship with God. It was the focal point of their worship and fellowship with the God who called them to be his chosen people. But other things had gotten in the way of finishing this task, much like other things—even good things—get in the way of our doing God's will today.

Haggai 1—2
Getting Priorities Straight

IT HAPPENED AGAIN. Even though Nathan had promised his wife their relationship would have greater priority in his schedule, he called to tell her he had to work late for the third night in a row. Then he spent a couple of hours Friday night paying the bills and bemoaning the fact that they didn't have enough money to fulfill their missions pledge. In spite of what we say, our actions are the clues to our priorities. Haggai had some things to say about lining up words and actions.

Warming Up to God What would someone observing you for a week think your priorities are?

Read Haggai 1—2.

1
In the second year of King Darius, on the
first day of the sixth month, the word of
the LORD came through the prophet Hag-
gai to Zerubbabel son of Shealtiel, governor of
Judah, and to Joshua[a] son of Jehozadak, the high
priest:
2This is what the LORD Almighty says: "These
people say, 'The time has not yet come for the
LORD's house to be built.' "
3Then the word of the LORD came through the
prophet Haggai: 4"Is it a time for you yourselves
to be living in your paneled houses, while this
house remains a ruin?"
5Now this is what the LORD Almighty says:
"Give careful thought to your ways. 6You have
planted much, but have harvested little. You eat,
but never have enough. You drink, but never
have your fill. You put on clothes, but are not
warm. You earn wages, only to put them in a
purse with holes in it."
7This is what the LORD Almighty says: "Give
careful thought to your ways. 8Go up into the
mountains and bring down timber and build the
house, so that I may take pleasure in it and be
honored," says the LORD. 9"You expected much,
but see, it turned out to be little. What you
brought home, I blew away. Why?" declares the
LORD Almighty. "Because of my house, which re-
mains a ruin, while each of you is busy with his
own house. 10Therefore, because of you the heav-
ens have withheld their dew and the earth its
crops. 11I called for a drought on the fields and
the mountains, on the grain, the new wine, the oil
and whatever the ground produces, on men and
cattle, and on the labor of your hands."

12Then Zerubbabel son of Shealtiel, Joshua son
of Jehozadak, the high priest, and the whole rem-
nant of the people obeyed the voice of the LORD
their God and the message of the prophet Haggai,
because the LORD their God had sent him. And the
people feared the LORD.
13Then Haggai, the LORD's messenger, gave this
message of the LORD to the people: "I am with
you," declares the LORD. 14So the LORD stirred up
the spirit of Zerubbabel son of Shealtiel, governor
of Judah, and the spirit of Joshua son of Jehoza-
dak, the high priest, and the spirit of the whole
remnant of the people. They came and began to
work on the house of the LORD Almighty, their
God, 15on the twenty-fourth day of the sixth
month in the second year of King Darius.

2
On the twenty-first day of the seventh
month, the word of the LORD came
through the prophet Haggai: 2"Speak to
Zerubbabel son of Shealtiel, governor of Judah, to
Joshua son of Jehozadak, the high priest, and to
the remnant of the people. Ask them, 3'Who of
you is left who saw this house in its former glory?
How does it look to you now? Does it not seem
to you like nothing? 4But now be strong,
O Zerubbabel,' declares the LORD. 'Be strong,
O Joshua son of Jehozadak, the high priest. Be
strong, all you people of the land,' declares the
LORD, 'and work. For I am with you,' declares the
LORD Almighty. 5'This is what I covenanted with
you when you came out of Egypt. And my Spirit
remains among you. Do not fear.'
6"This is what the LORD Almighty says: 'In a
little while I will once more shake the heavens
and the earth, the sea and the dry land. 7I will
shake all nations, and the desired of all nations
will come, and I will fill this house with glory,'

[a] *1* A variant of *Jeshua*; here and elsewhere in Haggai

says the LORD Almighty. 8"The silver is mine and the gold is mine,' declares the LORD Almighty. 9"The glory of this present house will be greater than the glory of the former house,' says the LORD Almighty. 'And in this place I will grant peace,' declares the LORD Almighty."

10On the twenty-fourth day of the ninth month, in the second year of Darius, the word of the LORD came to the prophet Haggai: 11"This is what the LORD Almighty says: 'Ask the priests what the law says: 12If a person carries consecrated meat in the fold of his garment, and that fold touches some bread or stew, some wine, oil or other food, does it become consecrated?' "

The priests answered, "No."

13Then Haggai said, "If a person defiled by contact with a dead body touches one of these things, does it become defiled?"

"Yes," the priests replied, "it becomes defiled."

14Then Haggai said, " 'So it is with this people and this nation in my sight,' declares the LORD. 'Whatever they do and whatever they offer there is defiled.

15" 'Now give careful thought to this from this day on[b]—consider how things were before one stone was laid on another in the LORD's temple. 16When anyone came to a heap of twenty measures, there were only ten. When anyone went to a wine vat to draw fifty measures, there were only twenty. 17I struck all the work of your hands with blight, mildew and hail, yet you did not turn to me,' declares the LORD. 18"From this day on, from this twenty-fourth day of the ninth month, give careful thought to the day when the foundation of the LORD's temple was laid. Give careful thought: 19Is there yet any seed left in the barn? Until now, the vine and the fig tree, the pomegranate and the olive tree have not borne fruit.

" 'From this day on I will bless you.' "

20The word of the LORD came to Haggai a second time on the twenty-fourth day of the month: 21"Tell Zerubbabel governor of Judah that I will shake the heavens and the earth. 22I will overturn royal thrones and shatter the power of the foreign kingdoms. I will overthrow chariots and their drivers; horses and their riders will fall, each by the sword of his brother.

23" 'On that day,' declares the LORD Almighty, 'I will take you, my servant Zerubbabel son of Shealtiel,' declares the LORD, 'and I will make you like my signet ring, for I have chosen you,' declares the LORD Almighty."

[b]15 *Or to the days past*

Discovering the Word 1. Getting priorities straight is not a 20th-century invention. According to chapter 1, what priority problems did the Jewish people have in Haggai's day? 2. What did God have to say about dealing with inappropriate priorities (1:3–8)? 3. What were the results of their wrong priorities (1:9–11)? 4. How did the people respond to Haggai's message (1:12–15)? Why? 5. In chapter 2 God gave Haggai three messages. What promises and warnings did he give his people?

Applying the Word 1. What do you want your priorities to be? List them. 2. What changes do you need to make in your schedule for today to reflect those priorities?

Responding in Prayer Ask God to show you his priorities for you. Then pray that he will help you live them.

Zechariah

When God calls us to complete a task, we know we should be faithful and diligent until it is accomplished. But sometimes we grow tired or discouraged. Obstacles block our path; opponents mock us, and in time we are tempted to give up.

During such times, we need a fresh word from the Lord. He gently rebukes us, then offers us strong encouragement and genuine hope. Most of all, he gives us a renewed vision of how our task fits into his broader plans and purposes in the world.

If you have grown weary doing God's will, then the book of Zechariah can refresh and strengthen you. It was written to the 50,000 Jews who had returned to Jerusalem after the Babylonian captivity. God had called them to rebuild the temple, and initially they responded with great energy and zeal. But as they faced one problem after another, their zeal turned to apathy and the work on the temple ceased. Then God sent the prophet Zechariah (whose name means "The Lord remembers") to turn the people back to the Lord and to the task they needed to complete.

Zechariah is one of the most messianic books in the Bible. In order to encourage his people, the Lord looks beyond their immediate circumstances to the time when all God's enemies will be vanquished, all his purposes fulfilled and the whole earth will acknowledge his rightful rule as King.

Zechariah predicted the Messiah's triumphal entry into Jerusalem (9:9; Mt 21:5), his betrayal for thirty pieces of silver (11:12–13; Mt 26:14–16; 27:1–10), the desertion of his followers (13:7; Mt 26:31), the fact that the Messiah would be pierced (12:10; Jn 19:37) and his glorious return to the Mount of Olives (14:4; Ac 1:9–11). The book of Zechariah is quoted from or alluded to in the New Testament seventy-one times, and apart from Ezekiel had the greatest influence on the book of Revelation.

As you read Zechariah, may the Lord encourage you to complete whatever tasks he has given you and to see them from his eternal perspective.

Outline

1/ Zechariah 1 ——————————— *Return to the Lord*

2/ Zechariah 2—3 ——————————— *Joy and Cleansing*

1 / *Zechariah 1*
Return to the Lord

DO YOU EVER wander from God? When you do things that displease him, does he seem far away? At such times we need to realize that the Lord longs for our return. Like a jealous lover, he wants our undivided loyalty and affection. In Zechariah 1:3 the Lord tells Israel and us, "Return to me . . . and I will return to you."

Warming Up to God When you feel distant from the Lord, what makes you want to return to his love and care?

Read Zechariah 1.

---

1 In the eighth month of the second year of Darius, the word of the LORD came to the prophet Zechariah son of Berekiah, the son of Iddo:

2"The LORD was very angry with your forefathers. 3Therefore tell the people: This is what the LORD Almighty says: 'Return to me,' declares the LORD Almighty, 'and I will return to you,' says the LORD Almighty. 4Do not be like your forefathers, to whom the earlier prophets proclaimed: This is what the LORD Almighty says: 'Turn from your evil ways and your evil practices.' But they would not listen or pay attention to me, declares the LORD. 5Where are your forefathers now? And the prophets, do they live forever? 6But did not my words and my decrees, which I commanded my servants the prophets, overtake your forefathers?

"Then they repented and said, 'The LORD Almighty has done to us what our ways and practices deserve, just as he determined to do.' "

7On the twenty-fourth day of the eleventh month, the month of Shebat, in the second year of Darius, the word of the LORD came to the prophet Zechariah son of Berekiah, the son of Iddo.

8During the night I had a vision—and there before me was a man riding a red horse! He was standing among the myrtle trees in a ravine. Behind him were red, brown and white horses.

9I asked, "What are these, my lord?"

The angel who was talking with me answered, "I will show you what they are."

10Then the man standing among the myrtle trees explained, "They are the ones the LORD has sent to go throughout the earth."

11And they reported to the angel of the LORD, who was standing among the myrtle trees, "We have gone throughout the earth and found the whole world at rest and in peace."

12Then the angel of the LORD said, "LORD Almighty, how long will you withhold mercy from Jerusalem and from the towns of Judah, which you have been angry with these seventy years?" 13So the LORD spoke kind and comforting words to the angel who talked with me.

14Then the angel who was speaking to me said, "Proclaim this word: This is what the LORD Almighty says: 'I am very jealous for Jerusalem and Zion, 15but I am very angry with the nations that feel secure. I was only a little angry, but they added to the calamity.'

16"Therefore, this is what the LORD says: 'I will return to Jerusalem with mercy, and there my house will be rebuilt. And the measuring line will be stretched out over Jerusalem,' declares the LORD Almighty.

17"Proclaim further: This is what the LORD Almighty says: 'My towns will again overflow with prosperity, and the LORD will again comfort Zion and choose Jerusalem.' "

18Then I looked up—and there before me were four horns! 19I asked the angel who was speaking to me, "What are these?"

He answered me, "These are the horns that scattered Judah, Israel and Jerusalem."

20Then the LORD showed me four craftsmen. 21I asked, "What are these coming to do?"

He answered, "These are the horns that scattered Judah so that no one could raise his head, but the craftsmen have come to terrify them and throw down these horns of the nations who lifted up their horns against the land of Judah to scatter its people."

Discovering the Word 1. In verses 1–6 Zechariah asks the people to recall Israel's captivity in Babylon. What lessons do the people need to learn from their forefathers? 2. If we want to return to the Lord, why must we turn from our evil ways (vv. 3–6)? 3. In Zechariah's first vision (vv. 7–17) he sees a horseman who is later identified as the angel of the Lord (v. 11). Why is the angel troubled by the state of the world in contrast to the conditions in Israel (vv. 12–13)? 4. What "comforting words" does the Lord give to the angel and to his people (vv. 13–17)? 5. The "four horns" in verses 18–21 are four rulers or nations "that scattered Judah, Israel and Jerusalem" (v. 19). How will the Lord use four other nations ("craftsmen") to bring justice to his people (vv. 20–21)?

Applying the Word 1. Think of the ways God has disciplined you in the past. How do these experiences make you want to be faithful to him in the present? 2. In what areas do you need to return to the Lord or turn from "evil ways"?

Responding in Prayer Confess any sins that have led you away from God. Ask him to help you return to him, and thank him for his forgiveness and love.

2/ *Zechariah 2—3*
Joy and Cleansing

DO YOU FEEL unclean and unworthy to stand before the Lord? Do your sins seem to be used as evidence against you, proving that you have no right to be called God's child? Zechariah 2—3 offers cleansing to those who feel defiled, hope to those who feel despair and joy to those who are overwhelmed with sorrow.

Warming Up to God Do you ever feel unacceptable to God because of your sins? Express your feelings to the Lord and ask him to use this passage to see yourself as he sees you.

Read Zechariah 2—3.

2 Then I looked up—and there before me was a man with a measuring line in his hand! 2I asked, "Where are you going?"

He answered me, "To measure Jerusalem, to find out how wide and how long it is."

3Then the angel who was speaking to me left, and another angel came to meet him 4and said to him: "Run, tell that young man, 'Jerusalem will be a city without walls because of the great number of men and livestock in it. 5And I myself will be a wall of fire around it,' declares the LORD, 'and I will be its glory within.'

6"Come! Come! Flee from the land of the north," declares the LORD, "for I have scattered you to the four winds of heaven," declares the LORD.

7"Come, O Zion! Escape, you who live in the Daughter of Babylon!" 8For this is what the LORD Almighty says: "After he has honored me and has sent me against the nations that have plundered you—for whoever touches you touches the apple of his eye— 9I will surely raise my hand against them so that their slaves will plunder them.[a] Then you will know that the LORD Almighty has sent me.

10"Shout and be glad, O Daughter of Zion. For I am coming, and I will live among you," declares the LORD. 11"Many nations will be joined with the LORD in that day and will become my people. I will live among you and you will know that the LORD Almighty has sent me to you. 12The LORD will inherit Judah as his portion in the holy land and will again choose Jerusalem. 13Be still before the LORD, all mankind, because he has roused himself from his holy dwelling."

3 Then he showed me Joshua[b] the high priest standing before the angel of the LORD, and Satan[c] standing at his right side to accuse him. 2The LORD said to Satan, "The LORD rebuke you, Satan! The LORD, who has chosen Jerusalem, rebuke you! Is not this man a burning stick snatched from the fire?"

3Now Joshua was dressed in filthy clothes as he stood before the angel. 4The angel said to those

[a] 8,9 Or *says after . . . eye: 9"I . . . plunder them."* [b] 1 A variant of *Jeshua*; here and elsewhere in Zechariah [c] 1 *Satan* means *accuser.*

who were standing before him, "Take off his
filthy clothes."
Then he said to Joshua, "See, I have taken away
your sin, and I will put rich garments on you."
5Then I said, "Put a clean turban on his head."
So they put a clean turban on his head and
clothed him, while the angel of the LORD stood by.
6The angel of the LORD gave this charge to
Joshua: 7"This is what the LORD Almighty says: 'If
you will walk in my ways and keep my require-
ments, then you will govern my house and have
charge of my courts, and I will give you a place
among these standing here.

8" 'Listen, O high priest Joshua and your asso-
ciates seated before you, who are men symbolic of
things to come: I am going to bring my servant,
the Branch. 9See, the stone I have set in front of
Joshua! There are seven eyes[d] on that one stone,
and I will engrave an inscription on it,' says the
LORD Almighty, 'and I will remove the sin of this
land in a single day.
10" 'In that day each of you will invite his
neighbor to sit under his vine and fig tree,' de-
clares the LORD Almighty."

d9 Or *facets*

Discovering the Word 1. At this point in history, Jerusalem lay in ruins because of the Babylonian conquest seventy years earlier. What hope do the angels offer Zechariah about the future of the city (2:1–5)? 2. "The land of the north" (2:6) is Babylon, the place of Israel's former captivity. Why does the Lord command those Israelites who remain there to "flee" and "escape" (2:6–9)? 3. In verses 10–13 the Lord himself promises to come and live among his people. How does this promise compare with the one in Revelation 21:1–4? 4. Joshua the high priest represents the nation of Israel (3:1–5). How does this courtroomlike scene illustrate what Christ has done for us on the cross? 5. Why must those who have been cleansed from their sins respond by walking in God's ways and keeping his requirements (3:6–10)?

Applying the Word 1. How does the promise of living with the Lord forever offer you hope, especially during those times when your life seems to be in ruins? 2. The name Satan means "accuser." When you feel accused and condemned because of your sins, what do you need to remember about what Christ has done for you?

Responding in Prayer Thank God for removing the filth of your sins and dressing you in the spotless clothes of Christ's righteousness. Praise him for his presence in your life and for the hope of living with him forever.

3/ *Zechariah 4—5*
Overcoming Obstacles

SOMETIMES WE FACE obstacles that seem insurmountable. We are confronted by challenges at work, at church or in our communities that are overwhelming. How should we respond in these situations? How can we have the strength to be victorious? This passage tells us: "'Not by might nor by power, but by my Spirit,' says the LORD Almighty" (4:6).

Warming Up to God What situation are you facing that seems overwhelming? Bring that situation to the Lord, asking him for the strength you need.

Read Zechariah 4—5.

4 Then the angel who talked with me re-
turned and wakened me, as a man is wak-
ened from his sleep. 2He asked me, "What
do you see?"
I answered, "I see a solid gold lampstand
with a bowl at the top and seven lights on
it, with seven channels to the lights. 3Also
there are two olive trees by it, one on the

right of the bowl and the other on its left."
4I asked the angel who talked with me, "What
are these, my lord?"
5He answered, "Do you not know what these
are?"
"No, my lord," I replied.
6So he said to me, "This is the word of the LORD
to Zerubbabel: 'Not by might nor by power, but
by my Spirit,' says the LORD Almighty.
7"What[e] are you, O mighty mountain? Before
Zerubbabel you will become level ground. Then
he will bring out the capstone to shouts of 'God
bless it! God bless it!' "
8Then the word of the LORD came to me: 9"The
hands of Zerubbabel have laid the foundation of
this temple; his hands will also complete it. Then
you will know that the LORD Almighty has sent
me to you.
10"Who despises the day of small things? Men
will rejoice when they see the plumb line in the
hand of Zerubbabel.
"(These seven are the eyes of the LORD, which
range throughout the earth.)"
11Then I asked the angel, "What are these two
olive trees on the right and the left of the lamp-
stand?"
12Again I asked him, "What are these two olive
branches beside the two gold pipes that pour out
golden oil?"
13He replied, "Do you not know what these
are?"
"No, my lord," I said.
14So he said, "These are the two who are
anointed to[f] serve the Lord of all the earth."

5 I looked again—and there before me was
a flying scroll!
2He asked me, "What do you see?"
I answered, "I see a flying scroll, thirty feet
long and fifteen feet wide.[g]"
3And he said to me, "This is the curse that is
going out over the whole land; for according to
what it says on one side, every thief will be ban-
ished, and according to what it says on the other,
everyone who swears falsely will be banished.
4The LORD Almighty declares, 'I will send it out,
and it will enter the house of the thief and the
house of him who swears falsely by my name. It
will remain in his house and destroy it, both its
timbers and its stones.' "
5Then the angel who was speaking to me came
forward and said to me, "Look up and see what
this is that is appearing."
6I asked, "What is it?"
He replied, "It is a measuring basket.[h]" And
he added, "This is the iniquity[i] of the people
throughout the land."
7Then the cover of lead was raised, and there
in the basket sat a woman! 8He said, "This is
wickedness," and he pushed her back into the
basket and pushed the lead cover down over its
mouth.
9Then I looked up—and there before me were
two women, with the wind in their wings! They
had wings like those of a stork, and they lifted up
the basket between heaven and earth.
10"Where are they taking the basket?" I asked
the angel who was speaking to me.
11He replied, "To the country of Babylonia[j] to
build a house for it. When it is ready, the basket
will be set there in its place."

[e]7 Or *Who* [f]14 Or *two who bring oil and* [g]2 Hebrew *twenty cubits long and ten cubits wide* (about 9 meters long and 4.5 meters wide) [h]6 Hebrew *an ephah*; also in verses 7-11 [i]6 Or *appearance* [j]11 Hebrew *Shinar*

Discovering the Word 1. Oil is often used in Scripture as a symbol of God's Spirit. As Zerubbabel faces the overwhelming task of rebuilding the temple, what encouragement does the Lord give him (4:1–10)? 2. We may not have human might or power to face our mountains of opposition. How then can we be victorious (4:6–7)? 3. The two olive branches (4:11–14) represent the Lord's anointed servants: Zerubbabel the ruler and Joshua the priest. Why do you think God empowers frail humans to accomplish his mighty tasks? 4. How do the visions of the flying scroll and the woman in a basket challenge the Israelites to repent of their sins (5:1–11)? 5. How can sin become one of the greatest obstacles to accomplishing God's work?

Applying the Word 1. When confronted with overwhelming obstacles, why are we tempted to trust in human might or power? 2. Think of a mountain of difficulty you are currently facing. How can you rely on God's Spirit to level that mountain? 3. Is there any sin in your life that you need to confess and forsake before God anoints you with power?

Responding in Prayer Ask God to level the mountain of difficulty that rises up before you. Thank him for the abundant supply of his spiritual might and power in your life.

4 / *Zechariah 6*
The Priest and King

IN THE OLD Testament priests offered sacrifices and represented the people before God, and kings were divinely appointed leaders and shepherds over Israel. In Zechariah 6 the Lord combines the offices of priest and king. The symbolic crowning of Joshua, the high priest, foreshadows the coming of the ultimate Priest and King—the Messiah himself.

Warming Up to God Like the people in Zechariah's day, we still look forward to the coming of the Messiah—although we anticipate his Second Coming. What do you long for most about the Lord's return? Express your longings to God.

Read Zechariah 6.

---

6 I looked up again—and there before me
were four chariots coming out from be-
tween two mountains—mountains of
bronze! 2The first chariot had red horses, the sec-
ond black, 3the third white, and the fourth dap-
pled—all of them powerful. 4I asked the angel
who was speaking to me, "What are these, my
lord?"
5The angel answered me, "These are the four
spirits[k] of heaven, going out from standing in
the presence of the Lord of the whole world. 6The
one with the black horses is going toward the
north country, the one with the white horses to-
ward the west,[l] and the one with the dappled
horses toward the south."
7When the powerful horses went out, they
were straining to go throughout the earth. And he
said, "Go throughout the earth!" So they went
throughout the earth.
8Then he called to me, "Look, those going to-
ward the north country have given my Spirit[m]
rest in the land of the north."
9The word of the LORD came to me: 10"Take
⌞silver and gold⌟ from the exiles Heldai, Tobijah
and Jedaiah, who have arrived from Babylon. Go
the same day to the house of Josiah son of Zepha-
niah. 11Take the silver and gold and make a
crown, and set it on the head of the high priest,
Joshua son of Jehozadak. 12Tell him this is what
the LORD Almighty says: 'Here is the man whose
name is the Branch, and he will branch out from
his place and build the temple of the LORD. 13It is
he who will build the temple of the LORD, and he
will be clothed with majesty and will sit and rule
on his throne. And he will be a priest on his
throne. And there will be harmony between the
two.' 14The crown will be given to Heldai,[n] Tobi-
jah, Jedaiah and Hen[o] son of Zephaniah as a me-
morial in the temple of the LORD. 15Those who are
far away will come and help to build the temple
of the LORD, and you will know that the LORD
Almighty has sent me to you. This will happen if
you diligently obey the LORD your God."

[k]5 Or *winds* [l]6 Or *horses after them* [m]8 Or *spirit* [n]14 Syriac; Hebrew *Helem* [o]14 Or *and the gracious one, the*

Discovering the Word 1. In Zechariah's eighth and final vision he sees four chariots drawn by various colored horses (vv. 1–8). How does this vision compare with the one in Zechariah 1:7–11 (see also Rev 6:1–8)? 2. The horses and chariots represent divine judgment. How do these chariots give the Lord's Spirit rest (v. 8), especially in the land of the north (Babylon)? 3. What does the Lord command Zechariah to do and to say to Joshua the high priest (vv. 9–13)? 4. Based on Zechariah 3:8 and other Old Testament passages such as Isaiah 11 and Jeremiah 23:5–6 and 33:14–16, we know that "the Branch" (v. 12) is ultimately the Messiah himself. Why is it significant that he will combine the offices of priest and king? 5. Why do you think the promises about the rebuilding of the temple are conditional on the people's obedience (vv. 14–15)?

Applying the Word 1. Why do we need Jesus Christ, our High Priest, to represent us before God? 2. The Lord is also our ruler and king. In what areas do you need to "diligently obey" him this week?

Responding in Prayer Thank the Lord for his loving leadership in your life and for faithfully representing you before the Father. Ask him for the grace and strength to obey him diligently.

5 / *Zecharia h 7*
Justice and Mercy

SOMETIMES OUR ACTIONS may appear to be pious, but our motives are misguided. How can we avoid this kind of hypocrisy? How can we get beyond an external legalism in order to serve the Lord from the heart? In Zechariah 7 the Lord tells his people the kind of obedience that really matters.

Warming Up to God Do you ever feel as though you are merely going through the motions as you serve God? Ask the Lord to purify your motives as you study this passage.

Read Zechariah 7.

---

7 In the fourth year of King Darius, the
word of the LORD came to Zechariah on
the fourth day of the ninth month, the
month of Kislev. 2The people of Bethel had sent
Sharezer and Regem-Melech, together with their
men, to entreat the LORD 3by asking the priests of
the house of the LORD Almighty and the prophets,
"Should I mourn and fast in the fifth month, as I
have done for so many years?"
4Then the word of the LORD Almighty came to
me: 5"Ask all the people of the land and the
priests, 'When you fasted and mourned in the
fifth and seventh months for the past seventy
years, was it really for me that you fasted? 6And
when you were eating and drinking, were you not
just feasting for yourselves? 7Are these not the
words the LORD proclaimed through the earlier
prophets when Jerusalem and its surrounding
towns were at rest and prosperous, and the Negev
and the western foothills were settled?' "
8And the word of the LORD came again to Zech-
ariah: 9"This is what the LORD Almighty says: 'Ad-
minister true justice; show mercy and compas-
sion to one another. 10Do not oppress the widow
or the fatherless, the alien or the poor. In your
hearts do not think evil of each other.'
11"But they refused to pay attention; stubbornly
they turned their backs and stopped up their ears.
12They made their hearts as hard as flint and
would not listen to the law or to the words that
the LORD Almighty had sent by his Spirit through
the earlier prophets. So the LORD Almighty was
very angry.
13" 'When I called, they did not listen; so when
they called, I would not listen,' says the LORD Al-
mighty. 14'I scattered them with a whirlwind
among all the nations, where they were strangers.
The land was left so desolate behind them that no
one could come or go. This is how they made the
pleasant land desolate.' "

Discovering the Word 1. While they were in Babylon, the Israelites observed various fasts to commemorate the destruction of the temple. Now they ask if they need to continue (vv. 1–3). How does the Lord evaluate the seventy years of fasting by the people in exile (vv. 4–7)? 2. Why do you think the people are asking whether they should continue these fasts? 3. How can we know whether our actions are done for the Lord or merely for ourselves? 4. If our motives are pure, what kinds of actions will be evident in our lives (vv. 8–10)? 5. Why is it dangerous to harden our hearts against the Lord and against his Word (vv. 11–14)?

Applying the Word 1. In what areas are you merely practicing religious rituals rather than obeying the Lord from the heart? 2. How do you measure up to Zechariah's four tests of spiritual reality (vv. 8–10)? 3. In what practical ways can you begin to follow these commands?

Responding in Prayer Ask the Lord for insight into the areas of your life where your "obedience" is really self-serving or mere ritual. Pray for opportunities to administer true justice, and show mercy and compassion, while avoiding oppression and thinking evil of others.

6 / *Zechariah 8*
The Lord's Return

HARDSHIPS AND TRIALS often seem as though they will last forever. Our lives seem empty, and our days are dark and filled with pain. But Zechariah 8 offers us great hope. There will be a day when our mourning will be turned into laughter, and our sorrow into joy.

Warming Up to God What do you imagine life will be like when the Lord returns? Thank God for this amazing promise and the great hope it offers.

Read Zechariah 8.

8 Again the word of the LORD Almighty came to me. 2This is what the LORD Almighty says: "I am very jealous for Zion; I am burning with jealousy for her."

3This is what the LORD says: "I will return to Zion and dwell in Jerusalem. Then Jerusalem will be called the City of Truth, and the mountain of the LORD Almighty will be called the Holy Mountain."

4This is what the LORD Almighty says: "Once again men and women of ripe old age will sit in the streets of Jerusalem, each with cane in hand because of his age. 5The city streets will be filled with boys and girls playing there."

6This is what the LORD Almighty says: "It may seem marvelous to the remnant of this people at that time, but will it seem marvelous to me?" declares the LORD Almighty.

7This is what the LORD Almighty says: "I will save my people from the countries of the east and the west. 8I will bring them back to live in Jerusalem; they will be my people, and I will be faithful and righteous to them as their God."

9This is what the LORD Almighty says: "You who now hear these words spoken by the prophets who were there when the foundation was laid for the house of the LORD Almighty, let your hands be strong so that the temple may be built. 10Before that time there were no wages for man or beast. No one could go about his business safely because of his enemy, for I had turned every man against his neighbor. 11But now I will not deal with the remnant of this people as I did in the past," declares the LORD Almighty.

12"The seed will grow well, the vine will yield its fruit, the ground will produce its crops, and the heavens will drop their dew. I will give all these things as an inheritance to the remnant of this people. 13As you have been an object of cursing among the nations, O Judah and Israel, so will I save you, and you will be a blessing. Do not be afraid, but let your hands be strong."

14This is what the LORD Almighty says: "Just as I had determined to bring disaster upon you and showed no pity when your fathers angered me," says the LORD Almighty, 15"so now I have determined to do good again to Jerusalem and Judah. Do not be afraid. 16These are the things you are to do: Speak the truth to each other, and render true and sound judgment in your courts; 17do not plot evil against your neighbor, and do not love to swear falsely. I hate all this," declares the LORD.

18Again the word of the LORD Almighty came to me. 19This is what the LORD Almighty says: "The fasts of the fourth, fifth, seventh and tenth months will become joyful and glad occasions and happy festivals for Judah. Therefore love truth and peace."

20This is what the LORD Almighty says: "Many peoples and the inhabitants of many cities will yet come, 21and the inhabitants of one city will go to another and say, 'Let us go at once to entreat the LORD and seek the LORD Almighty. I myself am going.' 22And many peoples and powerful nations will come to Jerusalem to seek the LORD Almighty and to entreat him."

23This is what the LORD Almighty says: "In those days ten men from all languages and nations will take firm hold of one Jew by the hem of his robe and say, 'Let us go with you, because we have heard that God is with you.'"

Discovering the Word 1. If you were living in war-torn Jerusalem, which was a shadow of its former glory, why would you be encouraged by the Lord's promises in this chapter? 2. When the Lord returns to Jerusalem, what effects will he have on the city and its inhabitants (vv. 1–8)? 3. How will the future days be different from the former days for those who live in the city (vv. 9–13)? 4. How should God's graciousness to us affect us morally and spiritually (vv. 14–19)? 5. Do you think the promises of verses 20–23 were completely fulfilled in Zechariah's day, or do they look forward to a greater fulfillment in the future? Explain.

Applying the Word 1. If we truly know the Lord, why must our actions reflect his character (vv. 16–17)? 2. What are some of the practical ways we can "love truth and peace" (v. 19)?

Responding in Prayer Thank God for the fact that he is already with us through the Holy Spirit. Praise him for the promise of his future return—when he will make all things new.

7 / *Zechariah 9—10*
The Coming of the King

DIFFICULT TIMES DO not last forever, nor do those who oppress us always have the upper hand. Israel had been defeated and humiliated by her enemies. However, in Zechariah 9—10 the Lord promises to conquer those who had conquered Israel and to restore peace to those troubled by war. But the high point of this passage looks beyond Israel's immediate future to the coming of the messianic King.

Warming Up to God When you are in the midst of difficult times or have experienced defeat, how do the Lord's presence and promises give you hope?

Read Zechariah 9—10.

An Oracle

9 The word of the LORD is against the land
of Hadrach
and will rest upon Damascus—
for the eyes of men and all the tribes
of Israel
are on the LORD—[p]
2and upon Hamath too, which borders on it,
and upon Tyre and Sidon, though they are
very skillful.
3Tyre has built herself a stronghold;
she has heaped up silver like dust,
and gold like the dirt of the streets.
4But the Lord will take away her possessions
and destroy her power on the sea,
and she will be consumed by fire.
5Ashkelon will see it and fear;
Gaza will writhe in agony,
and Ekron too, for her hope will
wither.
Gaza will lose her king
and Ashkelon will be deserted.
6Foreigners will occupy Ashdod,
and I will cut off the pride of the
Philistines.
7I will take the blood from their
mouths,
the forbidden food from between their
teeth.
Those who are left will belong to
our God
and become leaders in Judah,
and Ekron will be like the Jebusites.
8But I will defend my house
against marauding forces.
Never again will an oppressor overrun my
people,
for now I am keeping watch.
9Rejoice greatly, O Daughter of Zion!
Shout, Daughter of Jerusalem!
See, your king[q] comes to you,
righteous and having salvation,
gentle and riding on a donkey,
on a colt, the foal of a donkey.

p1 Or *Damascus. / For the eye of the LORD is on all mankind, / as well as on the tribes of Israel,* q9 Or *King*

10I will take away the chariots from
Ephraim
and the war-horses from Jerusalem,
and the battle bow will be broken.
He will proclaim peace to the nations.
His rule will extend from sea to sea
and from the River[r] to the ends of the
earth.[s]
11As for you, because of the blood of my
covenant with you,
I will free your prisoners from the waterless
pit.
12Return to your fortress, O prisoners
of hope;
even now I announce that I will restore
twice as much to you.
13I will bend Judah as I bend my bow
and fill it with Ephraim.
I will rouse your sons, O Zion,
against your sons, O Greece,
and make you like a warrior's sword.
14Then the LORD will appear over them;
his arrow will flash like lightning.
The Sovereign LORD will sound the
trumpet;
he will march in the storms of the
south,
15 and the LORD Almighty will shield
them.
They will destroy
and overcome with slingstones.
They will drink and roar as with wine;
they will be full like a bowl
used for sprinkling[t] the corners of the
altar.
16The LORD their God will save them on that
day
as the flock of his people.
They will sparkle in his land
like jewels in a crown.
17How attractive and beautiful they will be!
Grain will make the young men thrive,
and new wine the young women.

10

Ask the LORD for rain in the
springtime;
it is the LORD who makes the
storm clouds.
He gives showers of rain to men,
and plants of the field to everyone.
2The idols speak deceit,
diviners see visions that lie;
they tell dreams that are false,
they give comfort in vain.
Therefore the people wander like sheep
oppressed for lack of a shepherd.

3"My anger burns against the shepherds,
and I will punish the leaders;
for the LORD Almighty will care
for his flock, the house of Judah,
and make them like a proud horse in
battle.
4From Judah will come the cornerstone,
from him the tent peg,
from him the battle bow,
from him every ruler.
5Together they[u] will be like mighty men
trampling the muddy streets in battle.
Because the LORD is with them,
they will fight and overthrow the
horsemen.

6"I will strengthen the house of Judah
and save the house of Joseph.
I will restore them
because I have compassion on them.
They will be as though
I had not rejected them,
for I am the LORD their God
and I will answer them.
7The Ephraimites will become like mighty
men,
and their hearts will be glad as with
wine.
Their children will see it and be joyful;
their hearts will rejoice in the LORD.
8I will signal for them
and gather them in.
Surely I will redeem them;
they will be as numerous as before.
9Though I scatter them among the peoples,
yet in distant lands they will remember me.
They and their children will survive,
and they will return.
10I will bring them back from Egypt
and gather them from Assyria.
I will bring them to Gilead and Lebanon,
and there will not be room enough for
them.
11They will pass through the sea of trouble;
the surging sea will be subdued

[r] 10 That is, the Euphrates [s] 10 Or *the end of the land*
[t] 15 Or *bowl, / like* [u] 4,5 Or *ruler, all of them together. / [5]They*

and all the depths of the Nile will dry up.
Assyria's pride will be brought down
and Egypt's scepter will pass away.
12I will strengthen them in the LORD
and in his name they will walk,"
declares the LORD.

Discovering the Word 1. In 9:1–8 Zechariah describes the defeat of Israel's enemies, beginning in the north and ending in the south—a prediction fulfilled by Alexander the Great. How does it encourage you to know that the Lord punishes evil? 2. Why will the coming of the great King cause people to shout for joy (9:9–10)? 3. Before the Messiah can establish peace, he must assume the role of the Divine Warrior (9:11–17). How does Zechariah describe the Lord's battles? 4. Why will the Lord punish the shepherds of Israel and become their true Shepherd (10:1–4)? 5. Because the Lord is with his people and cares for them, what future blessings can they expect (10:5–12)?

Applying the Word 1. The prophecy of Zechariah 9:9 was fulfilled during Jesus' triumphal entry into Jerusalem (see Mt 21:1–11). What is it about Christ's kingship that attracts you most? 2. How does it encourage you to know that the Messiah's reign will one day extend "to the ends of the earth" (9:10)? 3. How far does his reign extend in your life today? Explain.

Responding in Prayer Ask the One who is Lord of all to extend his lordship to every area of your life. Thank him for his great promises and his infinite care.

8 / *Zechariah 11*
The Two Shepherds

LIKE SHEEP, GOD'S people need constant care. We need someone to feed us, to seek us when we are lost, and to heal our injuries. Zechariah 11 introduces us to two kinds of shepherds—the Good Shepherd, who represents the Messiah, and the worthless shepherd, who symbolizes all who prey on the flock from perverse motives and for selfish gain. Surprisingly, the prophet tells us that God's people treat both shepherds with equal contempt.

Warming Up to God In what ways do you need the kind of care a sheep receives from a good shepherd? Pray that God will open your eyes to the many ways he expresses his loving care to you.

Read Zechariah 11.

11 Open your doors, O Lebanon,
so that fire may devour your
cedars!
2Wail, O pine tree, for the cedar has fallen;
the stately trees are ruined!
Wail, oaks of Bashan;
the dense forest has been cut down!
3Listen to the wail of the shepherds;
their rich pastures are destroyed!
Listen to the roar of the lions;
the lush thicket of the Jordan is ruined!

4This is what the LORD my God says: "Pasture
the flock marked for slaughter. 5Their buyers
slaughter them and go unpunished. Those who
sell them say, 'Praise the LORD, I am rich!' Their
own shepherds do not spare them. 6For I will no
longer have pity on the people of the land," de-
clares the LORD. "I will hand everyone over to his
neighbor and his king. They will oppress the
land, and I will not rescue them from their
hands."

7So I pastured the flock marked for slaughter,
particularly the oppressed of the flock. Then I
took two staffs and called one Favor and the other
Union, and I pastured the flock. 8In one month I
got rid of the three shepherds.

The flock detested me, and I grew weary
of them 9and said, "I will not be your shep-
herd. Let the dying die, and the perishing per-
ish. Let those who are left eat one another's
flesh."

10Then I took my staff called Favor and broke
it, revoking the covenant I had made with all the
nations. 11It was revoked on that day, and so the

afflicted of the flock who were watching me knew it was the word of the Lord.

12I told them, "If you think it best, give me my pay; but if not, keep it." So they paid me thirty pieces of silver.

13And the Lord said to me, "Throw it to the potter"—the handsome price at which they priced me! So I took the thirty pieces of silver and threw them into the house of the Lord to the potter.

14Then I broke my second staff called Union, breaking the brotherhood between Judah and Israel.

15Then the Lord said to me, "Take again the equipment of a foolish shepherd. 16For I am going to raise up a shepherd over the land who will not care for the lost, or seek the young, or heal the injured, or feed the healthy, but will eat the meat of the choice sheep, tearing off their hoofs.

17"Woe to the worthless shepherd,
who deserts the flock!
May the sword strike his arm and his right eye!
May his arm be completely withered,
his right eye totally blinded!"

Discovering the Word 1. Verses 1–3 can refer either to arrogant nations and their rulers or to the region and people of Syro-Palestine. What is the fate of those described in these verses? 2. The Lord tells Zechariah to assume the role of the good shepherd over his flock—even though they are "marked for slaughter" (v. 4). How had the previous shepherds treated the flock (vv. 5–6)? 3. Even though the good shepherd shows God's favor to his sheep and seeks their unity, they detest him (v. 8). How does the shepherd respond to this abuse (vv. 9–11)? 4. After being rejected, the good shepherd asks for his wages but is paid only the price of a slave (v. 12; see also Ex 21:32 and Mt 27:9–10). How does the shepherd respond to this additional insult (vv. 13–14)? 5. In verse 15 Zechariah is told to assume the role of a foolish shepherd. When we reject God's care, what kind of treatment can we expect (vv. 16–17)?

Applying the Word 1. Which of the sheep's needs listed in verse 16 are areas of need in your life? 2. In what ways has the Good Shepherd met these needs in your life?

Responding in Prayer Ask the Lord to enable you to follow him and to submit to his tender care. Thank him for watching over you like a good and loving shepherd.

9 / *Zechariah 12—13*
Preparing for the Lord

THE LORD'S PEOPLE must be prepared for his return. Zechariah 12—13 describes how God delivers Jerusalem at the end of the age and then brings about national repentance. The passage climaxes with a vision of the pierced Messiah, who causes both mourning and spiritual transformation.

Warming Up to God In what ways is your life different because of your belief in the Lord's return? Ask him to use this passage to prepare your heart for his coming.

Read Zechariah 12—13.

An Oracle

12 This is the word of the Lord concerning Israel. The Lord, who stretches out the heavens, who lays the foundation of the earth, and who forms the spirit of man within him, declares: 2"I am going to make Jerusalem a cup that sends all the surrounding peoples reeling. Judah will be besieged as well as Jerusalem. 3On that day, when all the nations of the earth are gathered against her, I will make Jerusalem an immovable rock for all the nations. All who try to move it will injure themselves. 4On that day I will strike every horse with panic and its rider with madness," declares the Lord. "I will keep a watchful eye over the

house of Judah, but I will blind all the horses of
the nations. 5Then the leaders of Judah will say in
their hearts, 'The people of Jerusalem are strong,
because the LORD Almighty is their God.'

6"On that day I will make the leaders of Judah
like a firepot in a woodpile, like a flaming torch
among sheaves. They will consume right and left
all the surrounding peoples, but Jerusalem will
remain intact in her place.

7"The LORD will save the dwellings of Judah
first, so that the honor of the house of David and
of Jerusalem's inhabitants may not be greater than
that of Judah. 8On that day the LORD will shield
those who live in Jerusalem, so that the feeblest
among them will be like David, and the house of
David will be like God, like the Angel of the LORD
going before them. 9On that day I will set out to
destroy all the nations that attack Jerusalem.

10"And I will pour out on the house of David
and the inhabitants of Jerusalem a spirit[v] of
grace and supplication. They will look on[w] me,
the one they have pierced, and they will mourn
for him as one mourns for an only child, and
grieve bitterly for him as one grieves for a first-
born son. 11On that day the weeping in Jerusalem
will be great, like the weeping of Hadad Rimmon
in the plain of Megiddo. 12The land will mourn,
each clan by itself, with their wives by them-
selves: the clan of the house of David and their
wives, the clan of the house of Nathan and their
wives, 13the clan of the house of Levi and their
wives, the clan of Shimei and their wives, 14and
all the rest of the clans and their wives.

13
"On that day a fountain will be
opened to the house of David and
the inhabitants of Jerusalem, to
cleanse them from sin and impurity.

2"On that day, I will banish the names of the
idols from the land, and they will be remembered
no more," declares the LORD Almighty. "I will re-
move both the prophets and the spirit of impurity
from the land. 3And if anyone still prophesies, his
father and mother, to whom he was born, will say
to him, 'You must die, because you have told lies
in the LORD's name.' When he prophesies, his own
parents will stab him.

4"On that day every prophet will be ashamed
of his prophetic vision. He will not put on a
prophet's garment of hair in order to deceive. 5He
will say, 'I am not a prophet. I am a farmer; the
land has been my livelihood since my youth.[x]'
6If someone asks him, 'What are these wounds on
your body[y]?' he will answer, 'The wounds I was
given at the house of my friends.'

7"Awake, O sword, against my shepherd,
against the man who is close to me!"
declares the LORD Almighty.
"Strike the shepherd,
and the sheep will be scattered,
and I will turn my hand against the little
ones.
8In the whole land," declares the LORD,
"two-thirds will be struck down and perish;
yet one-third will be left in it.
9This third I will bring into the fire;
I will refine them like silver
and test them like gold.
They will call on my name
and I will answer them;
I will say, 'They are my people,'
and they will say, 'The LORD is our God.' "

v10 Or the Spirit *w10 Or to* *x5 Or farmer; a man sold me in my youth* *y6 Or wounds between your hands*

Discovering the Word 1. How would you describe the siege against Jerusalem at the end of the age (12:1–9)? 2. In what ways do God's people discover that "the Lord Almighty is their God" (12:5) during this battle? 3. When Israel looks on (or "to") the one they have pierced, what effect does it have on the nation (12:10–14; see also Jn 19:37)? 4. For generations Israel was plagued by both sin and false prophets. How will the Lord deal with both of these problems (13:1–6)? 5. In 13:7 the scene shifts to a different point in time. How does Zechariah describe both the death of the Messiah and the events that follow (13:7–9; see also Mt 26:31)?

Applying the Word 1. How has looking to the One who was pierced brought both mourning and cleansing in your life? 2. The Lord speaks of a time when he will refine his people "like silver and test them like gold" (13:9). How do trials and testing purify us and make us fit for the Lord's return?

Responding in Prayer Thank the Lord for the great price he paid to cleanse us from sin and impurity. Ask him to purify your life of anything that displeases him so that your life will have the quality of pure silver and gold.

10 / *Zechariah 14*
The Day of the Lord

AT THE BEGINNING of history humanity rebelled against God and rejected his rule. But at the end of history the Lord will return to the earth and reestablish his place as King of kings and Lord of lords. Zechariah 14:1 describes that "day of the LORD" as the climax of both evil and of God's eternal salvation. At that time the Lord will "reign for ever and ever."

Warming Up to God How does it encourage you to know that God is working to reestablish his rule over all the earth?

Read Zechariah 14.

14 A day of the LORD is coming when
your plunder will be divided
among you.
2I will gather all the nations to Jerusalem to
fight against it; the city will be captured, the
houses ransacked, and the women raped. Half of
the city will go into exile, but the rest of the peo-
ple will not be taken from the city.
3Then the LORD will go out and fight against
those nations, as he fights in the day of battle.
4On that day his feet will stand on the Mount of
Olives, east of Jerusalem, and the Mount of Olives
will be split in two from east to west, forming a
great valley, with half of the mountain moving
north and half moving south. 5You will flee by
my mountain valley, for it will extend to Azel.
You will flee as you fled from the earthquake[z]
in the days of Uzziah king of Judah. Then the
LORD my God will come, and all the holy ones
with him.
6On that day there will be no light, no cold or
frost. 7It will be a unique day, without daytime or
nighttime—a day known to the LORD. When eve-
ning comes, there will be light.
8On that day living water will flow out from
Jerusalem, half to the eastern sea[a] and half to the
western sea,[b] in summer and in winter.
9The LORD will be king over the whole earth.
On that day there will be one LORD, and his name
the only name.
10The whole land, from Geba to Rimmon,
south of Jerusalem, will become like the
Arabah. But Jerusalem will be raised up and re-
main in its place, from the Benjamin Gate to the
site of the First Gate, to the Corner Gate,
and from the Tower of Hananel to the royal
winepresses. 11It will be inhabited; never again
will it be destroyed. Jerusalem will be secure.
12This is the plague with which the LORD will
strike all the nations that fought against Jerusa-
lem: Their flesh will rot while they are still stand-
ing on their feet, their eyes will rot in their
sockets, and their tongues will rot in their
mouths. 13On that day men will be stricken
by the LORD with great panic. Each man will
seize the hand of another, and they will attack
each other. 14Judah too will fight at Jerusa-
lem. The wealth of all the surrounding nations
will be collected—great quantities of gold
and silver and clothing. 15A similar plague
will strike the horses and mules, the camels
and donkeys, and all the animals in those
camps.
16Then the survivors from all the nations that
have attacked Jerusalem will go up year after year
to worship the King, the LORD Almighty, and to
celebrate the Feast of Tabernacles. 17If any of the
peoples of the earth do not go up to Jerusalem to
worship the King, the LORD Almighty, they will
have no rain. 18If the Egyptian people do not go
up and take part, they will have no rain. The
LORD[c] will bring on them the plague he inflicts
on the nations that do not go up to celebrate the
Feast of Tabernacles. 19This will be the punish-
ment of Egypt and the punishment of all the na-
tions that do not go up to celebrate the Feast of
Tabernacles.
20On that day HOLY TO THE LORD will be inscribed
on the bells of the horses, and the cooking pots in
the LORD's house will be like the sacred bowls in

[z]5 Or [5]*My mountain valley will be blocked and will extend to Azel. It will be blocked as it was blocked because of the earthquake* [a]8 That is, the Dead Sea [b]8 That is, the Mediterranean [c]18 Or *part, then the* LORD

front of the altar. [21]Every pot in Jerusalem and Judah will be holy to the LORD Almighty, and all who come to sacrifice will take some of the pots and cook in them. And on that day there will no longer be a Canaanite[d] in the house of the LORD Almighty.

[d]21 Or *merchant*

Discovering the Word 1. Verses 1–15 describe the final battle against Jerusalem (see also 12:1–9). Why do you think the Lord allows the city to be plundered before he intervenes (vv. 1–2)? 2. When the Lord returns to the Mount of Olives (v. 4; see also Ac 1:11–12), what dramatic events will occur (vv. 3–11)? 3. How will the Divine Warrior destroy the nations that came against Jerusalem (vv. 12–15)? 4. In what ways will Jerusalem become the geographic and religious center of the earth (vv. 9–21)? 5. Although the Lord will "be king over the whole earth" (v. 9), how does Zechariah's description of life on earth seem less than perfect and complete?

Applying the Word 1. Worship and celebration will be the central events of life on earth after the Lord's return (v. 16). To what extent do these activities characterize your life on earth now? 2. In what ways can you make worship and celebration more central to your daily activities?

Responding in Prayer Worship the Lord now in praise, thanksgiving and prayer. Celebrate the fact that the "king over the whole earth" has already become your King and Savior.

Malachi

It's hard to wait—especially when that wait is open-ended. At first we are edgy and restless, glancing at a watch, adjusting hair and clothing, looking past the door. Then irritation builds. We are annoyed at the delay. We snap or complain to people nearby. Finally we stop waiting. We move on with our schedules but with less precision and enthusiasm. We give up. We believe that what we were waiting for will never happen.

The people of Malachi's era were in a period of waiting. Tragic and wonderful events had happened in the past. Their ancestors had heard the prophets warn of godlessness over and over—with no lasting reform. They had seen their kings subjected, then murdered, their beautiful three-hundred-year-old temple destroyed, their farms pillaged and burned, their friends hustled away as prisoners. They had spent seventy years living in Babylon under foreign rule.

But all that ended. Through the generosity of a Persian king (and God's own kindness), the Hebrew people returned to their homeland. With the help of Ezra and Nehemiah they rebuilt their homes, city walls and temple. They cleared their farmland and slowly resumed life as a worshiping people. Except for one thing. Where was God? They made the usual temple sacrifices, but saw no evidence of his presence. What did they expect? Freedom from poverty? Miracles? Shouting prophets? International respect? God himself? We cannot know. But as the wait grew long, the people grew lax. They married pagans. They took shortcuts in worship and sacrifices. They exploited the weak and poor among them. They prayed—and could not understand why God ignored their prayers.

Then God sent Malachi with a message. God would visit his people, Malachi explained. But they must prepare for his coming. And with these final words of the Old Testament, God showed his people how to wait. When he spoke again, it would be with the startling cry of the infant Jesus.

Outline

1/ Malachi 1:1—2:16 ———————— *How to Offend God*

2/ Malachi 2:17—3:18 ———————— *Me, God's Treasure?*

3/ Malachi 4 ———————— *Last Words*

1 / *Malachi 1:1—2:16*
How to Offend God

SOME OF US walk around under a cloud of guilt. We can't think of any particular sins, but we have a vague feeling that our every breath must offend God. Other people come from an opposite pole. We spend every day hardly aware of God, who establishes what is right and condemns all wrong. A small lie here, a lustful thought there, a brief grinding underfoot of a person at work. Yet on Sunday, we enter church all smiles. The book of Malachi is good for both kinds of people. It does not speak of vague guilt; it speaks of specific offenses against God. And it does not smile at these offenses. But beyond the guilt (or lack of guilt), Malachi speaks of God's power—and his love.

Warming Up to God Meditate for a few moment on God's holiness—and his power. What does this reveal to you about yourself and your relationship to him?

Read Malachi 1:1—2:16.

1 An oracle: The word of the LORD to Israel
through Malachi.[a]
2“I have loved you,” says the LORD.
“But you ask, ‘How have you loved us?’
“Was not Esau Jacob's brother?” the LORD says.
“Yet I have loved Jacob, 3but Esau I have hated,
and I have turned his mountains into a wasteland
and left his inheritance to the desert jackals.”
4Edom may say, “Though we have been
crushed, we will rebuild the ruins.”
But this is what the LORD Almighty says: “They
may build, but I will demolish. They will be
called the Wicked Land, a people always under
the wrath of the LORD. 5You will see it with your
own eyes and say, ‘Great is the LORD—even be-
yond the borders of Israel!’
6“A son honors his father, and a servant his
master. If I am a father, where is the honor due
me? If I am a master, where is the respect
due me?” says the LORD Almighty. “It is you,
O priests, who show contempt for my name.
“But you ask, ‘How have we shown contempt
for your name?’
7“You place defiled food on my altar.
“But you ask, ‘How have we defiled you?’
“By saying that the LORD's table is contemptible.
8When you bring blind animals for sacrifice, is
that not wrong? When you sacrifice crippled or
diseased animals, is that not wrong? Try offering
them to your governor! Would he be pleased with
you? Would he accept you?” says the LORD Al-
mighty.
9“Now implore God to be gracious to us. With
such offerings from your hands, will he accept
you?”—says the LORD Almighty.
10“Oh, that one of you would shut the temple
doors, so that you would not light useless fires on
my altar! I am not pleased with you,” says the
LORD Almighty, “and I will accept no offering
from your hands. 11My name will be great among
the nations, from the rising to the setting of the
sun. In every place incense and pure offerings
will be brought to my name, because my name
will be great among the nations,” says the LORD
Almighty.
12“But you profane it by saying of the Lord's
table, ‘It is defiled,’ and of its food, ‘It is contempt-
ible.’ 13And you say, ‘What a burden!’ and you
sniff at it contemptuously,” says the LORD Al-
mighty.
“When you bring injured, crippled or diseased
animals and offer them as sacrifices, should I ac-
cept them from your hands?” says the LORD.
14“Cursed is the cheat who has an acceptable
male in his flock and vows to give it, but then
sacrifices a blemished animal to the Lord. For I
am a great king,” says the LORD Almighty, “and
my name is to be feared among the nations.
2 “And now this admonition is for you,
O priests. 2If you do not listen, and if you
do not set your heart to honor my name,”
says the LORD Almighty, “I will send a curse upon
you, and I will curse your blessings. Yes, I have
already cursed them, because you have not set
your heart to honor me.
3“Because of you I will rebuke[b] your descen-
dants[c]; I will spread on your faces the offal from
your festival sacrifices, and you will be carried off
with it. 4And you will know that I have sent you
this admonition so that my covenant with Levi

[a]1 *Malachi* means *my messenger.* [b]3 Or *cut off* (see Septuagint)
[c]3 Or *will blight your grain*

may continue," says the LORD Almighty. 5"My covenant was with him, a covenant of life and peace, and I gave them to him; this called for reverence and he revered me and stood in awe of my name. 6True instruction was in his mouth and nothing false was found on his lips. He walked with me in peace and uprightness, and turned many from sin.

7"For the lips of a priest ought to preserve knowledge, and from his mouth men should seek instruction—because he is the messenger of the LORD Almighty. 8But you have turned from the way and by your teaching have caused many to stumble; you have violated the covenant with Levi," says the LORD Almighty. 9"So I have caused you to be despised and humiliated before all the people, because you have not followed my ways but have shown partiality in matters of the law."

10Have we not all one Father[d]? Did not one God create us? Why do we profane the covenant of our fathers by breaking faith with one another?

11Judah has broken faith. A detestable thing has been committed in Israel and in Jerusalem: Judah has desecrated the sanctuary the LORD loves, by marrying the daughter of a foreign god. 12As for the man who does this, whoever he may be, may the LORD cut him off from the tents of Jacob[e]—even though he brings offerings to the LORD Almighty.

13Another thing you do: You flood the LORD's altar with tears. You weep and wail because he no longer pays attention to your offerings or accepts them with pleasure from your hands. 14You ask, "Why?" It is because the LORD is acting as the witness between you and the wife of your youth, because you have broken faith with her, though she is your partner, the wife of your marriage covenant.

15Has not ⌊the LORD⌋ made them one? In flesh and spirit they are his. And why one? Because he was seeking godly offspring.[f] So guard yourself in your spirit, and do not break faith with the wife of your youth.

16"I hate divorce," says the LORD God of Israel, "and I hate a man's covering himself[g] with violence as well as with his garment," says the LORD Almighty.

So guard yourself in your spirit, and do not break faith.

[d]10 Or *father* [e]12 Or *12May the LORD cut off from the tents of Jacob anyone who gives testimony in behalf of the man who does this*
[f]15 Or *15But the one ⌊who is our father⌋ did not do this, not as long as life remained in him. And what was he seeking? An offspring from God*
[g]16 Or *his wife*

Discovering the Word 1. Describe God as he reveals himself in this passage. 2. What warning might God's people heed because of his relationship with the descendants of Esau (1:1–5)? 3. The priests were descendants of Levi with special responsibility to guard the spiritual well-being of the people and lead them in worship. What accusations did God make against these Hebrew priests (1:6—2:9)? 4. What had the people of Judah done that offended God (2:10–16)? 5. What concepts does this passage contribute to biblical teachings on marriage, violence and divorce?

Applying the Word 1. The people of Judah went through the motions of worship, but God declared in 1:10 that it would have been better if they had "shut the temple doors." What flaws in your own worship might be an offense to God? (Consider your weekday behavior and your personal prayers, as well as your worship with other believers.) 2. What is one step you are willing to take toward more holy worship?

Responding in Prayer Confess to God anything in your thoughts or actions that you know is an offense to him. Read the first sentence of Malachi 1:2 and wait quietly as you once again receive his love.

2 / *Malachi 2:17—3:18*
Me, God's Treasure?

"WHERE IS THE God of justice?" the people of Judah asked. Maybe God thinks that all the evil in our nation is fine with him, they thought. Surely if God cared he would pay them a visit. Maybe he would just shake hands and say everything was fine. Or maybe not. Malachi promised that longed-for visit from God, a "messenger," he said. But this messenger would not bring the warm, accepting comfort that they had hoped—except to some.

Warming Up to God If Christ were to visit you today, what would you expect him to say in your home? to your church? to your nation?

Read Malachi 2:17—3:18.

17You have wearied the LORD with your words.
"How have we wearied him?" you ask.
By saying, "All who do evil are good in the eyes
of the LORD, and he is pleased with them" or
"Where is the God of justice?"

3 "See, I will send my messenger, who will
prepare the way before me. Then sud-
denly the Lord you are seeking will come
to his temple; the messenger of the covenant,
whom you desire, will come," says the LORD Al-
mighty.
2But who can endure the day of his coming?
Who can stand when he appears? For he will be
like a refiner's fire or a launderer's soap. 3He will
sit as a refiner and purifier of silver; he will purify
the Levites and refine them like gold and silver.
Then the LORD will have men who will bring of-
ferings in righteousness, 4and the offerings of Ju-
dah and Jerusalem will be acceptable to the LORD,
as in days gone by, as in former years.
5"So I will come near to you for judgment. I
will be quick to testify against sorcerers, adulter-
ers and perjurers, against those who defraud la-
borers of their wages, who oppress the widows
and the fatherless, and deprive aliens of justice,
but do not fear me," says the LORD Almighty.
6"I the LORD do not change. So you,
O descendants of Jacob, are not destroyed. 7Ever
since the time of your forefathers you have turned
away from my decrees and have not kept them.
Return to me, and I will return to you," says the
LORD Almighty.
"But you ask, 'How are we to return?'
8"Will a man rob God? Yet you rob me.
"But you ask, 'How do we rob you?'
"In tithes and offerings. 9You are under a
curse—the whole nation of you—because you
are robbing me. 10Bring the whole tithe into the
storehouse, that there may be food in my house.
Test me in this," says the LORD Almighty, "and see
if I will not throw open the floodgates of heaven
and pour out so much blessing that you will not
have room enough for it. 11I will prevent pests
from devouring your crops, and the vines in your
fields will not cast their fruit," says the LORD Al-
mighty. 12"Then all the nations will call you
blessed, for yours will be a delightful land," says
the LORD Almighty.
13"You have said harsh things against me," says
the LORD.
"Yet you ask, 'What have we said against you?'
14"You have said, 'It is futile to serve God.
What did we gain by carrying out his require-
ments and going about like mourners before the
LORD Almighty? 15But now we call the arrogant
blessed. Certainly the evildoers prosper, and even
those who challenge God escape.' "
16Then those who feared the LORD talked with
each other, and the LORD listened and heard. A
scroll of remembrance was written in his pres-
ence concerning those who feared the LORD and
honored his name.
17"They will be mine," says the LORD Almighty,
"in the day when I make up my treasured posses-
sion.[h] I will spare them, just as in compassion a
man spares his son who serves him. 18And you
will again see the distinction between the righ-
teous and the wicked, between those who serve
God and those who do not.

[h] 17 Or *Almighty, "my treasured possession, in the day when I act*

Discovering the Word 1. Find all the questions in this passage. Give answers to each question based on information in the text. 2. In what ways will God's "messenger" be like soap or like fire (3:1–4)? 3. According to Malachi 3:5, how does God want his people to express their faith in their relationships with other people? 4. What reassurances do you find in Malachi 3:16–18? 5. Of what value might a scroll of remembrance be?

Applying the Word 1. In Malachi 3:17 God speaks of his people as his "treasured possession." Take a look at the day ahead of you: your list of tasks, the potential joys and disappointments. How does knowing that God sees you as his treasured possession influence how you will walk through your day? 2. According to Malachi 3:16, people who feared God got together, talked with each other, and then wrote a scroll. Prepare a "scroll of remembrance" of your own. Record the names of people who have supported your faith. Add a simple statement of your faith and sign your name.

Responding in Prayer In Malachi 3:7 God says, "Return to me, and I will return to you." If it is appropriate, pray a prayer of return to God. If this is not one of your own needs, pray for a friend or family member who you hope will return to God. Ask for his mercy. Picture this person as one of God's treasured possessions and ask that God will bring it about.

3/ *Malachi 4*
Last Words

GOD'S LAST WORDS to readers of the Old Testament are a mixture of hope and warning. They speak of a coming "day of the LORD," a day God's people had long anticipated. But Malachi warns that not everyone will find this a comfortable day.

Warming Up to God Spend a few moments relaxing in God's presence. Invite him into the nooks and crannies of your being. Take inventory of those areas of your life that are warm to God and also those that bristle at his touch. Talk to him about both.

Read Malachi 4.

4 "Surely the day is coming; it will burn
like a furnace. All the arrogant and every
evildoer will be stubble, and that day that
is coming will set them on fire," says the LORD
Almighty. "Not a root or a branch will be left to
them. 2But for you who revere my name, the sun
of righteousness will rise with healing in its
wings. And you will go out and leap like calves
released from the stall. 3Then you will trample
down the wicked; they will be ashes under the
soles of your feet on the day when I do these
things," says the LORD Almighty.
4"Remember the law of my servant Moses, the
decrees and laws I gave him at Horeb for all Israel.
5"See, I will send you the prophet Elijah before
that great and dreadful day of the LORD comes.
6He will turn the hearts of the fathers to their
children, and the hearts of the children to their
fathers; or else I will come and strike the land
with a curse."

Discovering the Word 1. According to Malachi, two kinds of people will be present at the day of the Lord. Who are these people, and how will that day impact each (vv. 1–3)? 2. Imagine yourself in the word pictures in verse 2. What would it be like to be there? 3. Verse 5 speaks of the day of the Lord as both great and dreadful. Why? 4. What part would Elijah (John the Baptist) play in the day of the Lord? 5. These verses may have been the final words of Old Testament writing before Christ's birth some four hundred years later. How do these words prepare us for Jesus?

Applying the Word 1. What personal warnings can you take in the last six verses of the Old Testament? 2. What personal hope do you find?

Responding in Prayer Since you are in the last book of the Old Testament, take time to page backward, noticing familiar passages. Pause at several points and thank God for what he shows you about himself.

THE NEW TESTAMENT

Matthew

What does it mean to be a disciple of Jesus Christ? How can we effectively disciple others? Christian bookstores are full of "how-to" manuals that seek to answer these questions. The early church had a discipling manual too—the book of Matthew. It was written to teach us how to be a disciple of Jesus Christ and how to disciple others. Before looking at current discipling manuals, why not go back to one of the originals?

Discipleship is the application of Christian truth to the present. "What does God want me to do about this relationship?" "How can I deal with anxiety?" We need to know what God expects of us on a daily basis. Discipleship is a very practical matter.

Practical questions are a concern of Matthew's as he writes his book. Matthew is a tax collector, so he knows how important it is to be practical. A tax collector has to know things like how much tax you owe, where you pay and who is authorized to collect it. And when a tax is paid, it must be recorded exactly. Otherwise government authorities tend to become hostile. Very practical stuff.

Matthew draws on all his background as he writes. Your most important need as a disciple is to know what the Lord is like. Matthew will help you. Through his work you will get to know Jesus better as he responds to needy people, handles conflict and faces opposition. You will also see what Jesus is like as a king. How does he handle authority? What type of laws does he give? How does he provide for his subjects?

For your daily living you will discover how to handle anger and envy. You will learn how to strengthen your faith, how to pray and how to grow in humility. You will gain insights into a biblical approach to evangelism. You will find out what attitudes the Lord thinks are important. And you will learn how to handle suffering and grief.

In short, a study of Matthew will help you become a better disciple and disciplemaker.

The contents of Matthew will be covered by dividing it into two equal sections, 1:1—16:20 and 16:21—28:20. The first half is entitled "Discovering the King." It focuses on the identity and authority of Jesus. The second half is entitled "The Rejection and Resurrection of the King." It focuses on Jesus as he encounters opposition and persecution culminating in the cross and resurrection.

From beginning to end Matthew is an exciting and challenging Gospel. Get ready for an adventure!

Outline

Part 1: Discovering the King

Part 2: The Rejection and Resurrection of the King

1 / *Matthew 1—2* In Search of the King

HAVE YOU EVER waited with anticipation for something only to find that when it came it was not what you wanted at all?

The long-awaited birth of the Messiah is recorded in Matthew 1—2. The nation of Israel waited for centuries for God's anointed King to be born. What a wonderful day that was to be. Jesus' birth, however, was not greeted with royal gladness by the nation and its leaders. Instead, there was intrigue and conflict. The political and religious establishment felt threatened by the coming of the Messiah. It was left to foreign leaders to welcome the newborn King.

Warming Up to God Think of something you once strongly desired (a car, TV, stereo, a special relationship or whatever). When you got it, did it fulfill your expectations? Why or why not?

Read Matthew 1—2.

1 A record of the genealogy of Jesus Christ the son of David, the son of Abraham:

2Abraham was the father of Isaac,
Isaac the father of Jacob,
Jacob the father of Judah and his brothers,
3Judah the father of Perez and Zerah, whose mother was Tamar,
Perez the father of Hezron,
Hezron the father of Ram,
4Ram the father of Amminadab,
Amminadab the father of Nahshon,
Nahshon the father of Salmon,
5Salmon the father of Boaz, whose mother was Rahab,
Boaz the father of Obed, whose mother was Ruth,
Obed the father of Jesse,
6and Jesse the father of King David.

David was the father of Solomon, whose mother had been Uriah's wife,
7Solomon the father of Rehoboam,
Rehoboam the father of Abijah,
Abijah the father of Asa,
8Asa the father of Jehoshaphat,
Jehoshaphat the father of Jehoram,
Jehoram the father of Uzziah,
9Uzziah the father of Jotham,
Jotham the father of Ahaz,
Ahaz the father of Hezekiah,
10Hezekiah the father of Manasseh,
Manasseh the father of Amon,
Amon the father of Josiah,
11and Josiah the father of Jeconiah[a] and his brothers at the time of the exile to Babylon.

12After the exile to Babylon:
Jeconiah was the father of Shealtiel,
Shealtiel the father of Zerubbabel,
13Zerubbabel the father of Abiud,
Abiud the father of Eliakim,
Eliakim the father of Azor,
14Azor the father of Zadok,
Zadok the father of Akim,
Akim the father of Eliud,
15Eliud the father of Eleazar,
Eleazar the father of Matthan,
Matthan the father of Jacob,
16and Jacob the father of Joseph, the husband of Mary, of whom was born Jesus, who is called Christ.

17Thus there were fourteen generations in all
from Abraham to David, fourteen from David to
the exile to Babylon, and fourteen from the exile
to the Christ.[b]
18This is how the birth of Jesus Christ came
about: His mother Mary was pledged to be mar-
ried to Joseph, but before they came together, she
was found to be with child through the Holy
Spirit. 19Because Joseph her husband was a right-
eous man and did not want to expose her to
public disgrace, he had in mind to divorce her
quietly.
20But after he had considered this, an angel of
the Lord appeared to him in a dream and said,
"Joseph son of David, do not be afraid to take

[a]11 That is, Jehoiachin; also in verse 12 [b]17 Or *Messiah.* "The Christ" (Greek) and "the Messiah" (Hebrew) both mean "the Anointed One."

Mary home as your wife, because what is con-
ceived in her is from the Holy Spirit. 21She will
give birth to a son, and you are to give him the
name Jesus,[c] because he will save his people
from their sins."
22All this took place to fulfill what the Lord had
said through the prophet: 23"The virgin will be
with child and will give birth to a son, and they
will call him Immanuel"[d]—which means, "God
with us."
24When Joseph woke up, he did what the angel
of the Lord had commanded him and took Mary
home as his wife. 25But he had no union with her
until she gave birth to a son. And he gave him the
name Jesus.

2 After Jesus was born in Bethlehem in Ju-
dea, during the time of King Herod,
Magi[e] from the east came to Jerusalem
2and asked, "Where is the one who has been born
king of the Jews? We saw his star in the east[f]
and have come to worship him."
3When King Herod heard this he was dis-
turbed, and all Jerusalem with him. 4When he
had called together all the people's chief priests
and teachers of the law, he asked them where the
Christ[g] was to be born. 5"In Bethlehem in Ju-
dea," they replied, "for this is what the prophet
has written:

6" 'But you, Bethlehem, in the land of Judah,
are by no means least among the rulers of
Judah;
for out of you will come a ruler
who will be the shepherd of my people
Israel.'[h]"

7Then Herod called the Magi secretly and
found out from them the exact time the star had
appeared. 8He sent them to Bethlehem and said,
"Go and make a careful search for the child. As
soon as you find him, report to me, so that I too
may go and worship him."
9After they had heard the king, they went on
their way, and the star they had seen in the east[i]
went ahead of them until it stopped over the
place where the child was. 10When they saw the
star, they were overjoyed. 11On coming to the
house, they saw the child with his mother Mary,
and they bowed down and worshiped him. Then
they opened their treasures and presented him
with gifts of gold and of incense and of myrrh.
12And having been warned in a dream not to go
back to Herod, they returned to their country by
another route.
13When they had gone, an angel of the Lord
appeared to Joseph in a dream. "Get up," he said,
"take the child and his mother and escape to
Egypt. Stay there until I tell you, for Herod is
going to search for the child to kill him."
14So he got up, took the child and his mother
during the night and left for Egypt, 15where he
stayed until the death of Herod. And so was ful-
filled what the Lord had said through the
prophet: "Out of Egypt I called my son."[j]
16When Herod realized that he had been out-
witted by the Magi, he was furious, and he gave
orders to kill all the boys in Bethlehem and its
vicinity who were two years old and under, in
accordance with the time he had learned from the
Magi. 17Then what was said through the prophet
Jeremiah was fulfilled:

18"A voice is heard in Ramah,
weeping and great mourning,
Rachel weeping for her children
and refusing to be comforted,
because they are no more."[k]

19After Herod died, an angel of the Lord ap-
peared in a dream to Joseph in Egypt 20and said,
"Get up, take the child and his mother and go to
the land of Israel, for those who were trying to
take the child's life are dead."
21So he got up, took the child and his mother
and went to the land of Israel. 22But when he
heard that Archelaus was reigning in Judea in
place of his father Herod, he was afraid to go
there. Having been warned in a dream, he with-
drew to the district of Galilee, 23and he went and
lived in a town called Nazareth. So was fulfilled
what was said through the prophets: "He will be
called a Nazarene."

[c]21 *Jesus* is the Greek form of *Joshua,* which means *the LORD saves.*
[d]23 Isaiah 7:14 [e]1 Traditionally *Wise Men* [f]2 Or *star when it rose* [g]4 Or *Messiah* [h]6 Micah 5:2 [i]9 Or *seen when it rose*
[j]15 Hosea 11:1 [k]18 Jer. 31:15

Discovering the Word 1. Considering Matthew's purpose to portray Jesus as a heavenly king, why would Matthew include a lineage at the very beginning of his book (1:1–17)? 2. Matthew highlights Jesus' birth in 1:18–25. What do these verses tell us about his origin and destiny? 3. In chapter 2, Matthew portrays Jesus' initial reception by the world. How does Jesus the heavenly king contrast with Herod the earthly king? 4. How are the Magi different from the religious leaders in this passage? 5. God is the unseen actor throughout chapter 2. In what ways can we see his "behind-the-scenes" actions (vv. 6, 15, 18 and 23)?

Applying the Word 1. How has knowing Jesus involved you in a search or journey? 2. The responses of the Magi and Herod are typical of the ways people respond to Jesus today. What factors might cause people to respond to Jesus in such radically different ways? 3. The Magi not only found Jesus, but they worshiped him and witnessed to the entire city of Jerusalem concerning his birth (2:2–3). In what ways has your search for the Lord resulted in worshiping him and telling others about him?

Responding in Prayer Spend time worshiping the King of kings. Then ask God to help you tell others about him.

2 / *Matthew 3*
Preparing for the King

IN ANCIENT TIMES the coming of a king required special preparation. A herald was sent ahead to prepare the road on which the king would be traveling. Holes were filled, rough places made smooth and crooked sections straightened. The same thing happened in recent times when Queen Elizabeth II visited the Bahamas. In preparation for her coming, the roads she would be traveling on were completely resurfaced. In Matthew 3, John the Baptist is sent to prepare the way for the coming of the Lord. But his arrival required a very different kind of preparation.

Warming Up to God Spend some time in preparation for meeting the Lord by confessing your sins and listening for God's assurance of forgiveness.

Read Matthew 3.

3 In those days John the Baptist came,
preaching in the Desert of Judea 2and say-
ing, "Repent, for the kingdom of heaven
is near." 3This is he who was spoken of through
the prophet Isaiah:

"A voice of one calling in the desert,
'Prepare the way for the Lord,
make straight paths for him.' "[l]

4John's clothes were made of camel's hair, and
he had a leather belt around his waist. His food
was locusts and wild honey. 5People went out to
him from Jerusalem and all Judea and the whole
region of the Jordan. 6Confessing their sins, they
were baptized by him in the Jordan River.

7But when he saw many of the Pharisees and
Sadducees coming to where he was baptizing, he
said to them: "You brood of vipers! Who warned
you to flee from the coming wrath? 8Produce fruit
in keeping with repentance. 9And do not think
you can say to yourselves, 'We have Abraham as
our father.' I tell you that out of these stones God
can raise up children for Abraham. 10The ax is
already at the root of the trees, and every tree that
does not produce good fruit will be cut down and
thrown into the fire.

11"I baptize you with[m] water for repentance.
But after me will come one who is more powerful
than I, whose sandals I am not fit to carry. He will
baptize you with the Holy Spirit and with fire.
12His winnowing fork is in his hand, and he will
clear his threshing floor, gathering his wheat into
the barn and burning up the chaff with un-
quenchable fire."

13Then Jesus came from Galilee to the Jordan
to be baptized by John. 14But John tried to deter
him, saying, "I need to be baptized by you, and do
you come to me?"

15Jesus replied, "Let it be so now; it is proper

[l]3 Isaiah 40:3 [m]11 Or *in*

for us to do this to fulfill all righteousness." Then
John consented.
[16]As soon as Jesus was baptized, he went up
out of the water. At that moment heaven was
opened, and he saw the Spirit of God descending
like a dove and lighting on him. [17]And a voice
from heaven said, "This is my Son, whom I love;
with him I am well pleased."

Discovering the Word 1. For Israel the desert was a place of both punishment and renewal (recall the wilderness wanderings). How does John's ministry convey both concepts (vv. 1–12)? 2. The religious leaders considered themselves children of Abraham (v. 9). According to verses 7–10, how were they abusing this privilege? 3. John calls us to produce "fruit in keeping with repentance" (v. 8). Give examples of the kind of fruit you think he has in mind. 4. Both John and Jesus have ministries of baptism (vv. 11–12). How are their baptisms similar and different? 5. What does Jesus' willingness to be baptized suggest about him (v. 15)?

Applying the Word 1. The coming of Christ either demands repentance or brings judgment. In what ways do you need to better prepare for his return? 2. Think of people around you who have rough places or valleys in their lives. How can you help them smooth out the rough places or fill in the valleys in preparation for Jesus' coming?

Responding in Prayer Ask God to help you show others how to prepare for Jesus.

3/ *Matthew 4*
The Beginning of the Kingdom

"IS IT TIME yet?" "How much longer?" Those are the questions children ask repeatedly as Christmas approaches. It's hard on them (and their parents) to wait. But when Christmas day comes, it's full of fun and surprises. After weeks of waiting, we all get to open our new gifts. The beginning of Jesus' ministry was like the coming of Christmas. After a long wait, the wrappings came off and the world got to see God's greatest gift.

Warming Up to God All of us have experienced something new—starting a new job, going to a new school, moving to a new community. What did it feel like?

Read Matthew 4.

4 Then Jesus was led by the Spirit into the
desert to be tempted by the devil. [2]After
fasting forty days and forty nights, he was
hungry. [3]The tempter came to him and said, "If
you are the Son of God, tell these stones to be-
come bread."
[4]Jesus answered, "It is written: 'Man does not
live on bread alone, but on every word that comes
from the mouth of God.'[n]"
[5]Then the devil took him to the holy city and
had him stand on the highest point of the temple.
[6]"If you are the Son of God," he said, "throw
yourself down. For it is written:

" 'He will command his angels concerning
you,
and they will lift you up in their hands,
so that you will not strike your foot against a
stone.'[o]"

[7]Jesus answered him, "It is also written: 'Do not
put the Lord your God to the test.'[p]"
[8]Again, the devil took him to a very high
mountain and showed him all the kingdoms of
the world and their splendor. [9]"All this I will give
you," he said, "if you will bow down and wor-
ship me."
[10]Jesus said to him, "Away from me, Satan! For
it is written: 'Worship the Lord your God, and
serve him only.'[q]"
[11]Then the devil left him, and angels came and
attended him.

[n]4 Deut. 8:3 [o]6 Psalm 91:11,12 [p]7 Deut. 6:16 [q]10 Deut. 6:13

[12]When Jesus heard that John had been put in
prison, he returned to Galilee. [13]Leaving Naza-
reth, he went and lived in Capernaum, which was
by the lake in the area of Zebulun and Naphtali—
[14]to fulfill what was said through the prophet Isa-
iah:

[15]"Land of Zebulun and land of Naphtali,
the way to the sea, along the Jordan,
Galilee of the Gentiles—
[16]the people living in darkness
have seen a great light;
on those living in the land of the shadow of
death
a light has dawned."[r]

[17]From that time on Jesus began to preach,
"Repent, for the kingdom of heaven is near."
[18]As Jesus was walking beside the Sea of Gali-
lee, he saw two brothers, Simon called Peter and
his brother Andrew. They were casting a net into
the lake, for they were fishermen. [19]"Come, fol-
low me," Jesus said, "and I will make you fishers
of men." [20]At once they left their nets and fol-
lowed him.
[21]Going on from there, he saw two other broth-
ers, James son of Zebedee and his brother John.
They were in a boat with their father Zebedee,
preparing their nets. Jesus called them, [22]and im-
mediately they left the boat and their father and
followed him.
[23]Jesus went throughout Galilee, teaching in
their synagogues, preaching the good news of the
kingdom, and healing every disease and sickness
among the people. [24]News about him spread all
over Syria, and people brought to him all who
were ill with various diseases, those suffering se-
vere pain, the demon-possessed, those having sei-
zures, and the paralyzed, and he healed them.
[25]Large crowds from Galilee, the Decapolis,[s] Je-
rusalem, Judea and the region across the Jordan
followed him.

[r]16 Isaiah 9:1,2 [s]25 That is, the Ten Cities

Discovering the Word 1. Look over the entire chapter to discover the locations mentioned. What do they tell us about Jesus' ministry? 2. The prerequisite for Jesus' ministry was his ability to resist temptation. What can we discover about Jesus from his encounter with Satan (vv. 1–11)? 3. Look specifically at each temptation (vv. 3–4, 5–7, 8–10). What was Satan trying to accomplish with each of them? 4. How does Jesus demonstrate his message "The kingdom of heaven is near" in verses 18–25? 5. One of Jesus' first functions as heavenly king is calling disciples. From verses 18–22 develop a brief definition of discipleship.

Applying the Word 1. What can we learn about temptation and how to resist it from Jesus' example? 2. Discipleship for the first disciples meant leaving job and family and following Jesus wherever he went. How has discipleship affected your life? 3. Imagine the excitement of the first disciples as they watched Jesus healing and teaching among the crowds. Put yourself in their place and describe how you would feel.

Responding in Prayer Recall the qualities of discipleship you saw. Pray that you will be made a faithful disciple.

4 / *Matthew 5:1—6:18*
The Law of the King (Part 1)

C. S. LEWIS was once criticized for not caring for the Sermon on the Mount. He replied, "As to 'caring for' the Sermon on the Mount, if 'caring for' here means 'liking' or enjoying, I suppose no one 'cares for' it. Who can like being knocked flat on his face by a sledge hammer? I can hardly imagine a more deadly spiritual condition than that of a man who can read that passage with tranquil pleasure" (*God in the Dock* [Grand Rapids, Mich.: Eerdmans, 1970], pp. 181–82).

Lewis was right. Studying the Sermon on the Mount can be a devastating experience. It exposes the depth of our sin and the shallowness of our commitment. But the pain it inflicts is meant to heal, not destroy, us. In fact, the Sermon on the Mount could be called the Christian's job description. It is the most complete summary we have of

Jesus' ethical expectations for his followers. Throughout church history it has been a helpful guide and a convincing challenge.

Warming Up to God When is it hard for you to follow God's law? Talk to God about your struggles with sin.

Read Matthew 5:1—6:18.

5 Now when he saw the crowds, he went up on a mountainside and sat down. His disciples came to him, 2and he began to teach them, saying:

3"Blessed are the poor in spirit,
for theirs is the kingdom of heaven.
4Blessed are those who mourn,
for they will be comforted.
5Blessed are the meek,
for they will inherit the earth.
6Blessed are those who hunger and thirst for righteousness,
for they will be filled.
7Blessed are the merciful,
for they will be shown mercy.
8Blessed are the pure in heart,
for they will see God.
9Blessed are the peacemakers,
for they will be called sons of God.
10Blessed are those who are persecuted because of righteousness,
for theirs is the kingdom of heaven.

11"Blessed are you when people insult you, persecute you and falsely say all kinds of evil against you because of me. 12Rejoice and be glad, because great is your reward in heaven, for in the same way they persecuted the prophets who were before you.

13"You are the salt of the earth. But if the salt loses its saltiness, how can it be made salty again? It is no longer good for anything, except to be thrown out and trampled by men.

14"You are the light of the world. A city on a hill cannot be hidden. 15Neither do people light a lamp and put it under a bowl. Instead they put it on its stand, and it gives light to everyone in the house. 16In the same way, let your light shine before men, that they may see your good deeds and praise your Father in heaven.

17"Do not think that I have come to abolish the Law or the Prophets; I have not come to abolish them but to fulfill them. 18I tell you the truth, until heaven and earth disappear, not the smallest letter, not the least stroke of a pen, will by any means disappear from the Law until everything is accomplished. 19Anyone who breaks one of the least of these commandments and teaches others to do the same will be called least in the kingdom of heaven, but whoever practices and teaches these commands will be called great in the kingdom of heaven. 20For I tell you that unless your righteousness surpasses that of the Pharisees and the teachers of the law, you will certainly not enter the kingdom of heaven.

21"You have heard that it was said to the people long ago, 'Do not murder,[t] and anyone who murders will be subject to judgment.' 22But I tell you that anyone who is angry with his brother[u] will be subject to judgment. Again, anyone who says to his brother, 'Raca,[v]' is answerable to the Sanhedrin. But anyone who says, 'You fool!' will be in danger of the fire of hell.

23"Therefore, if you are offering your gift at the altar and there remember that your brother has something against you, 24leave your gift there in front of the altar. First go and be reconciled to your brother; then come and offer your gift.

25"Settle matters quickly with your adversary who is taking you to court. Do it while you are still with him on the way, or he may hand you over to the judge, and the judge may hand you over to the officer, and you may be thrown into prison. 26I tell you the truth, you will not get out until you have paid the last penny.[w]

27"You have heard that it was said, 'Do not commit adultery.'[x] 28But I tell you that anyone who looks at a woman lustfully has already committed adultery with her in his heart. 29If your right eye causes you to sin, gouge it out and throw it away. It is better for you to lose one part of your body than for your whole body to be thrown into hell. 30And if your right hand causes you to sin, cut it off and throw it away. It is better for you to lose one part of your body than for your whole body to go into hell.

t21 Exodus 20:13 u22 Some manuscripts *brother without cause*
v22 An Aramaic term of contempt w26 Greek *kodrantes*
x27 Exodus 20:14

31"It has been said, 'Anyone who divorces his wife must give her a certificate of divorce.'[y] 32But I tell you that anyone who divorces his wife, except for marital unfaithfulness, causes her to become an adulteress, and anyone who marries the divorced woman commits adultery.

33"Again, you have heard that it was said to the people long ago, 'Do not break your oath, but keep the oaths you have made to the Lord.' 34But I tell you, Do not swear at all: either by heaven, for it is God's throne; 35or by the earth, for it is his footstool; or by Jerusalem, for it is the city of the Great King. 36And do not swear by your head, for you cannot make even one hair white or black. 37Simply let your 'Yes' be 'Yes,' and your 'No,' 'No'; anything beyond this comes from the evil one.

38"You have heard that it was said, 'Eye for eye, and tooth for tooth.'[z] 39But I tell you, Do not resist an evil person. If someone strikes you on the right cheek, turn to him the other also. 40And if someone wants to sue you and take your tunic, let him have your cloak as well. 41If someone forces you to go one mile, go with him two miles. 42Give to the one who asks you, and do not turn away from the one who wants to borrow from you.

43"You have heard that it was said, 'Love your neighbor[a] and hate your enemy.' 44But I tell you: Love your enemies[b] and pray for those who persecute you, 45that you may be sons of your Father in heaven. He causes his sun to rise on the evil and the good, and sends rain on the righteous and the unrighteous. 46If you love those who love you, what reward will you get? Are not even the tax collectors doing that? 47And if you greet only your brothers, what are you doing more than others? Do not even pagans do that? 48Be perfect, therefore, as your heavenly Father is perfect.

6 "Be careful not to do your 'acts of righteousness' before men, to be seen by them. If you do, you will have no reward from your Father in heaven.

2"So when you give to the needy, do not announce it with trumpets, as the hypocrites do in the synagogues and on the streets, to be honored by men. I tell you the truth, they have received their reward in full. 3But when you give to the needy, do not let your left hand know what your right hand is doing, 4so that your giving may be in secret. Then your Father, who sees what is done in secret, will reward you.

5"And when you pray, do not be like the hypocrites, for they love to pray standing in the synagogues and on the street corners to be seen by men. I tell you the truth, they have received their reward in full. 6But when you pray, go into your room, close the door and pray to your Father, who is unseen. Then your Father, who sees what is done in secret, will reward you. 7And when you pray, do not keep on babbling like pagans, for they think they will be heard because of their many words. 8Do not be like them, for your Father knows what you need before you ask him.

9"This, then, is how you should pray:

" 'Our Father in heaven,
hallowed be your name,
10your kingdom come,
your will be done
on earth as it is in heaven.
11Give us today our daily bread.
12Forgive us our debts,
as we also have forgiven our debtors.
13And lead us not into temptation,
but deliver us from the evil one.[c]'

14For if you forgive men when they sin against you, your heavenly Father will also forgive you. 15But if you do not forgive men their sins, your Father will not forgive your sins.

16"When you fast, do not look somber as the hypocrites do, for they disfigure their faces to show men they are fasting. I tell you the truth, they have received their reward in full. 17But when you fast, put oil on your head and wash your face, 18so that it will not be obvious to men that you are fasting, but only to your Father, who is unseen; and your Father, who sees what is done in secret, will reward you.

[y] 31 Deut. 24:1 [z] 38 Exodus 21:24; Lev. 24:20; Deut. 19:21
[a] 43 Lev. 19:18 [b] 44 Some late manuscripts *enemies, bless those who curse you, do good to those who hate you* [c] 13 Or *from evil*; some late manuscripts *one, / for yours is the kingdom and the power and the glory forever. Amen.*

Discovering the Word 1. The Beatitudes describe the qualities Jesus desires in each of his disciples (5:3–12). Give a brief definition of each quality. 2. Jesus compares his followers to salt and light (5:13–16). What do these metaphors suggest about our role in society? 3. In the rest of chapter 5 Jesus discusses various misconceptions we might have about the Law (Old Testament Scriptures). Why do you think that Jesus stresses that he did not come to abolish the Law (5:17–20)? 4. How does Jesus' teaching on murder and adultery (5:21–30) differ from the traditional understanding? 5. How does Jesus want us to respond to evil people and enemies (5:38–47)? 6. What do we learn about proper and improper motives from Jesus' examples about giving, praying and fasting (6:1–18)?

Applying the Word 1. Why are our motives just as important as our religious acts? 2. What does this reveal to you about your motives? 3. In what way do you need to experience Christ's blessing?

Responding in Prayer Pray for Christ's blessing in the areas in which you feel needy.

5 / *Matthew 6:19—7:29*
The Law of the King (Part 2)

JIM ELLIOT, A missionary killed by the Auca Indians, once wrote: "He is no fool who gives what he cannot keep to gain what he cannot lose." His words echo this portion of the Sermon on the Mount. Jesus asks us to choose between two treasures, two masters, two roads and two destinies. But he clearly explains why following him is the only wise choice.

Warming Up to God When are earthly treasures more tempting to you than heavenly ones?

Read Matthew 6:19—7:29.

19"Do not store up for yourselves treasures on earth, where moth and rust destroy, and where thieves break in and steal. 20But store up for yourselves treasures in heaven, where moth and rust do not destroy, and where thieves do not break in and steal. 21For where your treasure is, there your heart will be also.

22"The eye is the lamp of the body. If your eyes are good, your whole body will be full of light. 23But if your eyes are bad, your whole body will be full of darkness. If then the light within you is darkness, how great is that darkness!

24"No one can serve two masters. Either he will hate the one and love the other, or he will be devoted to the one and despise the other. You cannot serve both God and Money.

25"Therefore I tell you, do not worry about your life, what you will eat or drink; or about your body, what you will wear. Is not life more important than food, and the body more important than clothes? 26Look at the birds of the air; they do not sow or reap or store away in barns, and yet your heavenly Father feeds them. Are you not much more valuable than they? 27Who of you by worrying can add a single hour to his life[d]?

28"And why do you worry about clothes? See how the lilies of the field grow. They do not labor or spin. 29Yet I tell you that not even Solomon in all his splendor was dressed like one of these. 30If that is how God clothes the grass of the field, which is here today and tomorrow is thrown into the fire, will he not much more clothe you, O you of little faith? 31So do not worry, saying, 'What shall we eat?' or 'What shall we drink?' or 'What shall we wear?' 32For the pagans run after all these things, and your heavenly Father knows that you need them. 33But seek first his kingdom and his righteousness, and all these things will be given to you as well. 34Therefore do not worry about tomorrow, for tomorrow will worry about itself. Each day has enough trouble of its own.

[d]27 Or *single cubit to his height*

7 "Do not judge, or you too will be judged. 2For in the same way you judge others, you will be judged, and with the measure you use, it will be measured to you.

3"Why do you look at the speck of sawdust in your brother's eye and pay no attention to the plank in your own eye? 4How can you say to your brother, 'Let me take the speck out of your eye,' when all the time there is a plank in your own eye? 5You hypocrite, first take the plank out of your own eye, and then you will see clearly to remove the speck from your brother's eye.

6"Do not give dogs what is sacred; do not throw your pearls to pigs. If you do, they may trample them under their feet, and then turn and tear you to pieces.

7"Ask and it will be given to you; seek and you will find; knock and the door will be opened to you. 8For everyone who asks receives; he who seeks finds; and to him who knocks, the door will be opened.

9"Which of you, if his son asks for bread, will give him a stone? 10Or if he asks for a fish, will give him a snake? 11If you, then, though you are evil, know how to give good gifts to your children, how much more will your Father in heaven give good gifts to those who ask him! 12So in everything, do to others what you would have them do to you, for this sums up the Law and the Prophets.

13"Enter through the narrow gate. For wide is the gate and broad is the road that leads to destruction, and many enter through it. 14But small is the gate and narrow the road that leads to life, and only a few find it.

15"Watch out for false prophets. They come to you in sheep's clothing, but inwardly they are ferocious wolves. 16By their fruit you will recognize them. Do people pick grapes from thornbushes, or figs from thistles? 17Likewise every good tree bears good fruit, but a bad tree bears bad fruit. 18A good tree cannot bear bad fruit, and a bad tree cannot bear good fruit. 19Every tree that does not bear good fruit is cut down and thrown into the fire. 20Thus, by their fruit you will recognize them.

21"Not everyone who says to me, 'Lord, Lord,' will enter the kingdom of heaven, but only he who does the will of my Father who is in heaven. 22Many will say to me on that day, 'Lord, Lord, did we not prophesy in your name, and in your name drive out demons and perform many miracles?' 23Then I will tell them plainly, 'I never knew you. Away from me, you evildoers!'

24"Therefore everyone who hears these words of mine and puts them into practice is like a wise man who built his house on the rock. 25The rain came down, the streams rose, and the winds blew and beat against that house; yet it did not fall, because it had its foundation on the rock. 26But everyone who hears these words of mine and does not put them into practice is like a foolish man who built his house on sand. 27The rain came down, the streams rose, and the winds blew and beat against that house, and it fell with a great crash."

28When Jesus had finished saying these things, the crowds were amazed at his teaching, 29because he taught as one who had authority, and not as their teachers of the law.

Discovering the Word 1. In 6:19–24 Jesus talks about treasures, eyes and masters. What common themes tie these verses together? 2. Worry is a dominant theme in 6:25–34. How can we escape worrying about such things as food and clothes? 3. What is the difference between judging others and being properly discerning (7:1–6)? 4. How should our knowledge of the Father affect our prayers (7:7–11)? 5. In the final section of the Sermon (7:13–27) Jesus talks about narrow and wide gates, good and bad trees, and wise and foolish builders. How do these three metaphors work together to make a common point?

Applying the Word 1. What does seeking first God's kingdom and righteousness (6:33) mean practically for your life? 2. Putting Jesus' words in practice is the way to build a lasting foundation against the day of judgment (7:24–27). What will the practice of Jesus' Sermon require of you?

Responding in Prayer Pray that you will be a person of wisdom and discernment and not of judgment.

6 / *Matthew 8:1—9:34* The Powers of the King

SOMEONE ONCE COMMENTED about a U.S. president: "I don't know where he is going, but I sure like the way he leads."

Leaders must demonstrate authority. But wise leaders know they must not abuse their authority. They know people follow leaders who also demonstrate integrity and compassion. In chapters 8 and 9 Jesus demonstrates that he is a worthy king, one in whom we can safely put our trust.

Warming Up to God How has Jesus' authority been a guide to you in recent days?

Read Matthew 8:1—9:34.

8 When he came down from the mountainside, large crowds followed him. [2]A man with leprosy[e] came and knelt before him and said, "Lord, if you are willing, you can make me clean."

[3]Jesus reached out his hand and touched the man. "I am willing," he said. "Be clean!" Immediately he was cured[f] of his leprosy. [4]Then Jesus said to him, "See that you don't tell anyone. But go, show yourself to the priest and offer the gift Moses commanded, as a testimony to them."

[5]When Jesus had entered Capernaum, a centurion came to him, asking for help. [6]"Lord," he said, "my servant lies at home paralyzed and in terrible suffering."

[7]Jesus said to him, "I will go and heal him."

[8]The centurion replied, "Lord, I do not deserve to have you come under my roof. But just say the word, and my servant will be healed. [9]For I myself am a man under authority, with soldiers under me. I tell this one, 'Go,' and he goes; and that one, 'Come,' and he comes. I say to my servant, 'Do this,' and he does it."

[10]When Jesus heard this, he was astonished and said to those following him, "I tell you the truth, I have not found anyone in Israel with such great faith. [11]I say to you that many will come from the east and the west, and will take their places at the feast with Abraham, Isaac and Jacob in the kingdom of heaven. [12]But the subjects of the kingdom will be thrown outside, into the darkness, where there will be weeping and gnashing of teeth."

[13]Then Jesus said to the centurion, "Go! It will be done just as you believed it would." And his servant was healed at that very hour.

[14]When Jesus came into Peter's house, he saw Peter's mother-in-law lying in bed with a fever. [15]He touched her hand and the fever left her, and she got up and began to wait on him.

[16]When evening came, many who were demon-possessed were brought to him, and he drove out the spirits with a word and healed all the sick. [17]This was to fulfill what was spoken through the prophet Isaiah:

"He took up our infirmities
and carried our diseases."[g]

[18]When Jesus saw the crowd around him, he gave orders to cross to the other side of the lake. [19]Then a teacher of the law came to him and said, "Teacher, I will follow you wherever you go."

[20]Jesus replied, "Foxes have holes and birds of the air have nests, but the Son of Man has no place to lay his head."

[21]Another disciple said to him, "Lord, first let me go and bury my father."

[22]But Jesus told him, "Follow me, and let the dead bury their own dead."

[23]Then he got into the boat and his disciples followed him. [24]Without warning, a furious storm came up on the lake, so that the waves swept over the boat. But Jesus was sleeping. [25]The disciples went and woke him, saying, "Lord, save us! We're going to drown!"

[26]He replied, "You of little faith, why are you so afraid?" Then he got up and rebuked the winds and the waves, and it was completely calm.

[27]The men were amazed and asked, "What kind of man is this? Even the winds and the waves obey him!"

[28]When he arrived at the other side in the re-

[e]2 The Greek word was used for various diseases affecting the skin—not necessarily leprosy. [f]3 Greek *made clean* [g]17 Isaiah 53:4

gion of the Gadarenes,[h] two demon-possessed
men coming from the tombs met him. They were
so violent that no one could pass that way.
29“What do you want with us, Son of God?” they
shouted. “Have you come here to torture us be-
fore the appointed time?”
30Some distance from them a large herd of pigs
was feeding. 31The demons begged Jesus, “If you
drive us out, send us into the herd of pigs.”
32He said to them, “Go!” So they came out and
went into the pigs, and the whole herd rushed
down the steep bank into the lake and died in the
water. 33Those tending the pigs ran off, went into
the town and reported all this, including what
had happened to the demon-possessed men.
34Then the whole town went out to meet Jesus.
And when they saw him, they pleaded with him
to leave their region.

9 Jesus stepped into a boat, crossed over
and came to his own town. 2Some men
brought to him a paralytic, lying on a
mat. When Jesus saw their faith, he said to the
paralytic, “Take heart, son; your sins are for-
given.”
3At this, some of the teachers of the law said to
themselves, “This fellow is blaspheming!”
4Knowing their thoughts, Jesus said, “Why do
you entertain evil thoughts in your hearts?
5Which is easier: to say, ‘Your sins are forgiven,’
or to say, ‘Get up and walk’? 6But so that you may
know that the Son of Man has authority on earth
to forgive sins. . . .” Then he said to the paralytic,
“Get up, take your mat and go home.” 7And the
man got up and went home. 8When the crowd
saw this, they were filled with awe; and they
praised God, who had given such authority to
men.
9As Jesus went on from there, he saw a man
named Matthew sitting at the tax collector’s
booth. “Follow me,” he told him, and Matthew
got up and followed him.
10While Jesus was having dinner at Matthew’s
house, many tax collectors and “sinners” came
and ate with him and his disciples. 11When the
Pharisees saw this, they asked his disciples, “Why
does your teacher eat with tax collectors and ‘sin-
ners’?”
12On hearing this, Jesus said, “It is not the
healthy who need a doctor, but the sick. 13But go
and learn what this means: ‘I desire mercy, not
sacrifice.’[i] For I have not come to call the right-
eous, but sinners.”
14Then John’s disciples came and asked him,
“How is it that we and the Pharisees fast, but your
disciples do not fast?”
15Jesus answered, “How can the guests of the
bridegroom mourn while he is with them? The
time will come when the bridegroom will be
taken from them; then they will fast.
16“No one sews a patch of unshrunk cloth on
an old garment, for the patch will pull away from
the garment, making the tear worse. 17Neither do
men pour new wine into old wineskins. If they
do, the skins will burst, the wine will run out and
the wineskins will be ruined. No, they pour new
wine into new wineskins, and both are pre-
served.”
18While he was saying this, a ruler came and
knelt before him and said, “My daughter has just
died. But come and put your hand on her, and
she will live.” 19Jesus got up and went with him,
and so did his disciples.
20Just then a woman who had been subject to
bleeding for twelve years came up behind him
and touched the edge of his cloak. 21She said to
herself, “If I only touch his cloak, I will be
healed.”
22Jesus turned and saw her. “Take heart,
daughter,” he said, “your faith has healed you.”
And the woman was healed from that mo-
ment.
23When Jesus entered the ruler’s house and saw
the flute players and the noisy crowd, 24he said,
“Go away. The girl is not dead but asleep.” But
they laughed at him. 25After the crowd had been
put outside, he went in and took the girl by the
hand, and she got up. 26News of this spread
through all that region.
27As Jesus went on from there, two blind men
followed him, calling out, “Have mercy on us,
Son of David!”
28When he had gone indoors, the blind men
came to him, and he asked them, “Do you believe
that I am able to do this?”
“Yes, Lord,” they replied.
29Then he touched their eyes and said, “Ac-
cording to your faith will it be done to you”;
30and their sight was restored. Jesus warned them
sternly, “See that no one knows about this.” 31But
they went out and spread the news about him all
over that region.

[h]28 Some manuscripts *Gergesenes*; others *Gerasenes* [i]13 Hosea 6:6

32While they were going out, a man who was demon-possessed and could not talk was brought to Jesus. 33And when the demon was driven out, the man who had been mute spoke. The crowd was amazed and said, "Nothing like this has ever been seen in Israel."

34But the Pharisees said, "It is by the prince of demons that he drives out demons."

Discovering the Word 1. In chapters 8—9 Jesus' miracles occur in three groups, followed by a response, or reaction. Briefly describe how Jesus demonstrates his authority in 8:1–22. 2. In 8:18–22 Jesus begins to attract would-be followers. What do these verses teach us about the cost and urgency of following him? 3. What do we learn about the extent of Jesus' authority in 8:23—9:17? 4. What is the relationship between Jesus' claim to have authority to forgive sins and his healing of the paralytic (9:1–8)? 5. In 9:9–17 Jesus compares himself to a doctor and a bridegroom. Then he discusses garments and wineskins. What do these illustrations teach us about his ministry? 6. How do people respond to Jesus in 9:18–34?

Applying the Word 1. Look back over chapters 8—9. How does Jesus want us to respond to his power and authority? 2. How can a knowledge of Jesus' power and authority strengthen your faith?

Responding in Prayer Spend time praising God for Jesus' leadership.

7 / *Matthew 9:35—11:30*
The Messengers of the King

DURING THE LATE 1800s a wealthy philanthropist decided to give away all his money. He announced he would give five hundred dollars to anyone with a legitimate need. The response was overwhelming! People lined up day after day to receive their gift.

The gospel is a priceless treasure. But as we offer it to people, their response is not always enthusiastic. In this passage Jesus warns us about those who oppose his message and his messengers. But he also encourages us as we reach out to blind and needy people.

Warming Up to God Have you ever known someone who seemed to like you only for what you could give them? What did it feel like?

Read Matthew 9:35—11:30.

35Jesus went through all the towns and villages, teaching in their synagogues, preaching the good news of the kingdom and healing every disease and sickness. 36When he saw the crowds, he had compassion on them, because they were harassed and helpless, like sheep without a shepherd. 37Then he said to his disciples, "The harvest is plentiful but the workers are few. 38Ask the Lord of the harvest, therefore, to send out workers into his harvest field."

10 He called his twelve disciples to him and gave them authority to drive out evil[j] spirits and to heal every disease and sickness.

2These are the names of the twelve apostles: first, Simon (who is called Peter) and his brother Andrew; James son of Zebedee, and his brother John; 3Philip and Bartholomew; Thomas and Matthew the tax collector; James son of Alphaeus, and Thaddaeus; 4Simon the Zealot and Judas Iscariot, who betrayed him.

5These twelve Jesus sent out with the following instructions: "Do not go among the Gentiles or enter any town of the Samaritans. 6Go rather to the lost sheep of Israel. 7As you go, preach this message: 'The kingdom of heaven is near.' 8Heal the sick, raise the dead, cleanse those who have leprosy,[k] drive out demons. Freely you have received, freely give. 9Do not take along any gold or silver or copper in your belts; 10take no bag for

j1 Greek *unclean* k8 The Greek word was used for various diseases affecting the skin—not necessarily leprosy.

the journey, or extra tunic, or sandals or a staff; for the worker is worth his keep.

11"Whatever town or village you enter, search for some worthy person there and stay at his house until you leave. 12As you enter the home, give it your greeting. 13If the home is deserving, let your peace rest on it; if it is not, let your peace return to you. 14If anyone will not welcome you or listen to your words, shake the dust off your feet when you leave that home or town. 15I tell you the truth, it will be more bearable for Sodom and Gomorrah on the day of judgment than for that town. 16I am sending you out like sheep among wolves. Therefore be as shrewd as snakes and as innocent as doves.

17"Be on your guard against men; they will hand you over to the local councils and flog you in their synagogues. 18On my account you will be brought before governors and kings as witnesses to them and to the Gentiles. 19But when they arrest you, do not worry about what to say or how to say it. At that time you will be given what to say, 20for it will not be you speaking, but the Spirit of your Father speaking through you.

21"Brother will betray brother to death, and a father his child; children will rebel against their parents and have them put to death. 22All men will hate you because of me, but he who stands firm to the end will be saved. 23When you are persecuted in one place, flee to another. I tell you the truth, you will not finish going through the cities of Israel before the Son of Man comes.

24"A student is not above his teacher, nor a servant above his master. 25It is enough for the student to be like his teacher, and the servant like his master. If the head of the house has been called Beelzebub,[l] how much more the members of his household!

26"So do not be afraid of them. There is nothing concealed that will not be disclosed, or hidden that will not be made known. 27What I tell you in the dark, speak in the daylight; what is whispered in your ear, proclaim from the roofs. 28Do not be afraid of those who kill the body but cannot kill the soul. Rather, be afraid of the One who can destroy both soul and body in hell. 29Are not two sparrows sold for a penny[m]? Yet not one of them will fall to the ground apart from the will of your Father. 30And even the very hairs of your head are all numbered. 31So don't be afraid; you are worth more than many sparrows.

32"Whoever acknowledges me before men, I will also acknowledge him before my Father in heaven. 33But whoever disowns me before men, I will disown him before my Father in heaven.

34"Do not suppose that I have come to bring peace to the earth. I did not come to bring peace, but a sword. 35For I have come to turn

" 'a man against his father,
a daughter against her mother,
a daughter-in-law against her mother-in-law—
36 a man's enemies will be the members of his own household.'[n]

37"Anyone who loves his father or mother more than me is not worthy of me; anyone who loves his son or daughter more than me is not worthy of me; 38and anyone who does not take his cross and follow me is not worthy of me. 39Whoever finds his life will lose it, and whoever loses his life for my sake will find it.

40"He who receives you receives me, and he who receives me receives the one who sent me. 41Anyone who receives a prophet because he is a prophet will receive a prophet's reward, and anyone who receives a righteous man because he is a righteous man will receive a righteous man's reward. 42And if anyone gives even a cup of cold water to one of these little ones because he is my disciple, I tell you the truth, he will certainly not lose his reward."

11 After Jesus had finished instructing his twelve disciples, he went on from there to teach and preach in the towns of Galilee.[o]

2When John heard in prison what Christ was doing, he sent his disciples 3to ask him, "Are you the one who was to come, or should we expect someone else?"

4Jesus replied, "Go back and report to John what you hear and see: 5The blind receive sight, the lame walk, those who have leprosy[p] are cured, the deaf hear, the dead are raised, and the good news is preached to the poor. 6Blessed is the man who does not fall away on account of me."

7As John's disciples were leaving, Jesus began to speak to the crowd about John: "What did you go out into the desert to see? A reed swayed by the wind? 8If not, what did you go out to see? A man dressed in fine clothes? No, those who wear

[l]25 Greek *Beezeboul* or *Beelzeboul* [m]29 Greek *an assarion*
[n]36 Micah 7:6 [o]1 Greek *in their towns* [p]5 The Greek word was used for various diseases affecting the skin—not necessarily leprosy.

fine clothes are in kings' palaces. [9]Then what did you go out to see? A prophet? Yes, I tell you, and more than a prophet. [10]This is the one about whom it is written:

> " 'I will send my messenger ahead of you,
> who will prepare your way before you.'[q]

[11]I tell you the truth: Among those born of women there has not risen anyone greater than John the Baptist; yet he who is least in the kingdom of heaven is greater than he. [12]From the days of John the Baptist until now, the kingdom of heaven has been forcefully advancing, and forceful men lay hold of it. [13]For all the Prophets and the Law prophesied until John. [14]And if you are willing to accept it, he is the Elijah who was to come. [15]He who has ears, let him hear.

[16]"To what can I compare this generation? They are like children sitting in the marketplaces and calling out to others:

> [17]" 'We played the flute for you,
> and you did not dance;
> we sang a dirge,
> and you did not mourn.'

[18]For John came neither eating nor drinking, and they say, 'He has a demon.' [19]The Son of Man came eating and drinking, and they say, 'Here is a glutton and a drunkard, a friend of tax collectors and "sinners." ' But wisdom is proved right by her actions."

[20]Then Jesus began to denounce the cities in which most of his miracles had been performed, because they did not repent. [21]"Woe to you, Korazin! Woe to you, Bethsaida! If the miracles that were performed in you had been performed in Tyre and Sidon, they would have repented long ago in sackcloth and ashes. [22]But I tell you, it will be more bearable for Tyre and Sidon on the day of judgment than for you. [23]And you, Capernaum, will you be lifted up to the skies? No, you will go down to the depths.[r] If the miracles that were performed in you had been performed in Sodom, it would have remained to this day. [24]But I tell you that it will be more bearable for Sodom on the day of judgment than for you."

[25]At that time Jesus said, "I praise you, Father, Lord of heaven and earth, because you have hidden these things from the wise and learned, and revealed them to little children. [26]Yes, Father, for this was your good pleasure.

[27]"All things have been committed to me by my Father. No one knows the Son except the Father, and no one knows the Father except the Son and those to whom the Son chooses to reveal him.

[28]"Come to me, all you who are weary and burdened, and I will give you rest. [29]Take my yoke upon you and learn from me, for I am gentle and humble in heart, and you will find rest for your souls. [30]For my yoke is easy and my burden is light."

*q*10 Mal. 3:1 *r*23 Greek *Hades*

Discovering the Word 1. How and why does Jesus demonstrate compassion for the crowds (9:35–38)? 2. As a result of his compassion, Jesus sends out the Twelve (10:1–15). Describe their mission. 3. Jesus warns the disciples that their compassionate ministry will not be warmly received (10:16–25). What will they experience? 4. In 10:26–33 Jesus prepares his present and future disciples for opposition. Why shouldn't we be afraid of those who oppose us? 5. What does Jesus promise to those who are receptive to our message (10:40–42)? 6. What does 11:7–19 tell us about John and those who heard his message?

Applying the Word 1. In what ways have you found rest in your life by coming to Jesus? 2. What have you learned about Jesus and the nature of discipleship from this study?

Responding in Prayer Pray for the gift of rest in Jesus.

8 / *Matthew 12* The Leaders and the King

POWER OVER PEOPLE is not easily shared. Wars have been fought, people assassinated and elections rigged in order to gain or maintain power.

The leaders of Israel were becoming concerned over the growing reputation and following of Jesus. Like ripples in a pool of water, the ministry of Jesus and his disciples continued to have a widening impact on the Jewish nation. If Jesus' followers became too numerous, the leaders would end up losing their positions of authority. In Matthew 12 they formulate a strategy to discredit him.

Warming Up to God How would you feel if untrue rumors about you were being spread around?

Read Matthew 12.

12 At that time Jesus went through the
grainfields on the Sabbath. His dis-
ciples were hungry and began to
pick some heads of grain and eat them. 2When
the Pharisees saw this, they said to him, "Look!
Your disciples are doing what is unlawful on the
Sabbath."
3He answered, "Haven't you read what David
did when he and his companions were hungry?
4He entered the house of God, and he and his
companions ate the consecrated bread—which
was not lawful for them to do, but only for the
priests. 5Or haven't you read in the Law that on
the Sabbath the priests in the temple desecrate
the day and yet are innocent? 6I tell you that
one[s] greater than the temple is here. 7If you had
known what these words mean, 'I desire mercy,
not sacrifice,'[t] you would not have condemned
the innocent. 8For the Son of Man is Lord of the
Sabbath."
9Going on from that place, he went into their
synagogue, 10and a man with a shriveled hand
was there. Looking for a reason to accuse Jesus,
they asked him, "Is it lawful to heal on the Sab-
bath?"
11He said to them, "If any of you has a sheep
and it falls into a pit on the Sabbath, will you not
take hold of it and lift it out? 12How much more
valuable is a man than a sheep! Therefore it is
lawful to do good on the Sabbath."
13Then he said to the man, "Stretch out your
hand." So he stretched it out and it was com-
pletely restored, just as sound as the other. 14But
the Pharisees went out and plotted how they
might kill Jesus.
15Aware of this, Jesus withdrew from that
place. Many followed him, and he healed all their
sick, 16warning them not to tell who he was.
17This was to fulfill what was spoken through the
prophet Isaiah:

18"Here is my servant whom I have chosen,
the one I love, in whom I delight;
I will put my Spirit on him,
and he will proclaim justice to the nations.
19He will not quarrel or cry out;
no one will hear his voice in the streets.
20A bruised reed he will not break,
and a smoldering wick he will not snuff
out,
till he leads justice to victory.
21 In his name the nations will put their
hope."[u]

22Then they brought him a demon-possessed
man who was blind and mute, and Jesus healed
him, so that he could both talk and see. 23All the
people were astonished and said, "Could this be
the Son of David?"
24But when the Pharisees heard this, they said,
"It is only by Beelzebub,[v] the prince of demons,
that this fellow drives out demons."
25Jesus knew their thoughts and said to them,
"Every kingdom divided against itself will be ru-
ined, and every city or household divided against
itself will not stand. 26If Satan drives out Satan, he
is divided against himself. How then can his king-
dom stand? 27And if I drive out demons by Beel-
zebub, by whom do your people drive them out?
So then, they will be your judges. 28But if I drive

[s]6 Or *something*; also in verses 41 and 42 [t]7 Hosea 6:6
[u]21 Isaiah 42:1-4 [v]24 Greek *Beezeboul* or *Beelzeboul*; also in verse 27

out demons by the Spirit of God, then the kingdom of God has come upon you.

29 “Or again, how can anyone enter a strong man’s house and carry off his possessions unless he first ties up the strong man? Then he can rob his house.

30 “He who is not with me is against me, and he who does not gather with me scatters. 31 And so I tell you, every sin and blasphemy will be forgiven men, but the blasphemy against the Spirit will not be forgiven. 32 Anyone who speaks a word against the Son of Man will be forgiven, but anyone who speaks against the Holy Spirit will not be forgiven, either in this age or in the age to come.

33 “Make a tree good and its fruit will be good, or make a tree bad and its fruit will be bad, for a tree is recognized by its fruit. 34 You brood of vipers, how can you who are evil say anything good? For out of the overflow of the heart the mouth speaks. 35 The good man brings good things out of the good stored up in him, and the evil man brings evil things out of the evil stored up in him. 36 But I tell you that men will have to give account on the day of judgment for every careless word they have spoken. 37 For by your words you will be acquitted, and by your words you will be condemned.”

38 Then some of the Pharisees and teachers of the law said to him, “Teacher, we want to see a miraculous sign from you.”

39 He answered, “A wicked and adulterous generation asks for a miraculous sign! But none will be given it except the sign of the prophet Jonah. 40 For as Jonah was three days and three nights in the belly of a huge fish, so the Son of Man will be three days and three nights in the heart of the earth. 41 The men of Nineveh will stand up at the judgment with this generation and condemn it; for they repented at the preaching of Jonah, and now one[w] greater than Jonah is here. 42 The Queen of the South will rise at the judgment with this generation and condemn it; for she came from the ends of the earth to listen to Solomon’s wisdom, and now one greater than Solomon is here.

43 “When an evil[x] spirit comes out of a man, it goes through arid places seeking rest and does not find it. 44 Then it says, ‘I will return to the house I left.’ When it arrives, it finds the house unoccupied, swept clean and put in order. 45 Then it goes and takes with it seven other spirits more wicked than itself, and they go in and live there. And the final condition of that man is worse than the first. That is how it will be with this wicked generation.”

46 While Jesus was still talking to the crowd, his mother and brothers stood outside, wanting to speak to him. 47 Someone told him, “Your mother and brothers are standing outside, wanting to speak to you.”[y]

48 He replied to him, “Who is my mother, and who are my brothers?” 49 Pointing to his disciples, he said, “Here are my mother and my brothers. 50 For whoever does the will of my Father in heaven is my brother and sister and mother.”

[w] 41 Or *something;* also in verse 42 [x] 43 Greek *unclean*
[y] 47 Some manuscripts do not have verse 47.

Discovering the Word 1. Consider the ways that religious leaders attacked Jesus in verses 1-14. What was their strategy? 2. As you compare the Pharisees’ second accusation against Jesus (v. 10) with their own response (v. 14), what irony do you see? 3. Notice the startling contrast between the religious leaders’ attitude toward Jesus and God’s attitude (vv. 15-21). How do they differ? 4. In verses 43-45 Jesus tells the Pharisees and teachers of the law a story. What does it reveal about them? 5. Look back over chapter 12. What factors led to the hardness and unbelief of the Pharisees and teachers of the law?

Applying the Word 1. How can we avoid being like the Pharisees and teachers of the law? 2. What area of change in your life does this suggest you consider?

Responding in Prayer Ask God to teach you how to read and understand his Word so that you can use it to his glory.

9 / *Matthew 13*
The Parables of the King

CROWDS ARE FICKLE. One moment they follow with enthusiasm, the next they turn hostile and angry. In Matthew 13 Jesus speaks to a mixed and fickle crowd. Some are hungry to hear his message. Others are suspicious and hostile. In this setting Jesus begins to speak in parables. These stories test our spiritual sight and hearing. They also expose the condition of our hearts.

Warming Up to God Prepare for this study by asking God to open your mind and heart to what is here for you.

Read Matthew 13.

13 That same day Jesus went out of
the house and sat by the lake.
2Such large crowds gathered
around him that he got into a boat and sat in it,
while all the people stood on the shore. 3Then he
told them many things in parables, saying: "A
farmer went out to sow his seed. 4As he was scat-
tering the seed, some fell along the path, and the
birds came and ate it up. 5Some fell on rocky
places, where it did not have much soil. It sprang
up quickly, because the soil was shallow. 6But
when the sun came up, the plants were scorched,
and they withered because they had no root.
7Other seed fell among thorns, which grew up
and choked the plants. 8Still other seed fell on
good soil, where it produced a crop—a hundred,
sixty or thirty times what was sown. 9He who has
ears, let him hear."

10The disciples came to him and asked, "Why
do you speak to the people in parables?"

11He replied, "The knowledge of the secrets of
the kingdom of heaven has been given to you, but
not to them. 12Whoever has will be given more,
and he will have an abundance. Whoever does
not have, even what he has will be taken from
him. 13This is why I speak to them in parables:

"Though seeing, they do not see;
  though hearing, they do not hear or
    understand.

14In them is fulfilled the prophecy of Isaiah:

" 'You will be ever hearing but never
    understanding;
  you will be ever seeing but never
    perceiving.
15For this people's heart has become calloused;
  they hardly hear with their ears,
  and they have closed their eyes.
Otherwise they might see with their eyes,
  hear with their ears,
  understand with their hearts
and turn, and I would heal them.'[z]

16But blessed are your eyes because they see, and
your ears because they hear. 17For I tell you the
truth, many prophets and righteous men longed
to see what you see but did not see it, and to hear
what you hear but did not hear it.

18"Listen then to what the parable of the sower
means: 19When anyone hears the message about
the kingdom and does not understand it, the evil
one comes and snatches away what was sown in
his heart. This is the seed sown along the path.
20The one who received the seed that fell on
rocky places is the man who hears the word and
at once receives it with joy. 21But since he has no
root, he lasts only a short time. When trouble or
persecution comes because of the word, he
quickly falls away. 22The one who received the
seed that fell among the thorns is the man who
hears the word, but the worries of this life and the
deceitfulness of wealth choke it, making it un-
fruitful. 23But the one who received the seed that
fell on good soil is the man who hears the word
and understands it. He produces a crop, yielding
a hundred, sixty or thirty times what was sown."

24Jesus told them another parable: "The king-
dom of heaven is like a man who sowed good
seed in his field. 25But while everyone was sleep-
ing, his enemy came and sowed weeds among the
wheat, and went away. 26When the wheat
sprouted and formed heads, then the weeds also
appeared.

27"The owner's servants came to him and said,

[z] 15 Isaiah 6:9,10

'Sir, didn't you sow good seed in your field?
Where then did the weeds come from?'
28" 'An enemy did this,' he replied.
"The servants asked him, 'Do you want us to go
and pull them up?'
29" 'No,' he answered, 'because while you are
pulling the weeds, you may root up the wheat
with them. 30Let both grow together until the har-
vest. At that time I will tell the harvesters: First
collect the weeds and tie them in bundles to be
burned; then gather the wheat and bring it into
my barn.' "
31He told them another parable: "The kingdom
of heaven is like a mustard seed, which a man
took and planted in his field. 32Though it is the
smallest of all your seeds, yet when it grows, it is
the largest of garden plants and becomes a tree, so
that the birds of the air come and perch in its
branches."
33He told them still another parable: "The king-
dom of heaven is like yeast that a woman took
and mixed into a large amount[a] of flour until it
worked all through the dough."
34Jesus spoke all these things to the crowd in
parables; he did not say anything to them without
using a parable. 35So was fulfilled what was spo-
ken through the prophet:

"I will open my mouth in parables,
I will utter things hidden since the creation
of the world."[b]

36Then he left the crowd and went into the
house. His disciples came to him and said, "Ex-
plain to us the parable of the weeds in the field."
37He answered, "The one who sowed the good
seed is the Son of Man. 38The field is the world,
and the good seed stands for the sons of the king-
dom. The weeds are the sons of the evil one,
39and the enemy who sows them is the devil. The
harvest is the end of the age, and the harvesters
are angels.
40"As the weeds are pulled up and burned in
the fire, so it will be at the end of the age. 41The
Son of Man will send out his angels, and they will
weed out of his kingdom everything that causes
sin and all who do evil. 42They will throw them
into the fiery furnace, where there will be weep-
ing and gnashing of teeth. 43Then the righteous
will shine like the sun in the kingdom of their
Father. He who has ears, let him hear.
44"The kingdom of heaven is like treasure hid-
den in a field. When a man found it, he hid it
again, and then in his joy went and sold all he
had and bought that field.
45"Again, the kingdom of heaven is like a mer-
chant looking for fine pearls. 46When he found
one of great value, he went away and sold every-
thing he had and bought it.
47"Once again, the kingdom of heaven is like a
net that was let down into the lake and caught all
kinds of fish. 48When it was full, the fishermen
pulled it up on the shore. Then they sat down and
collected the good fish in baskets, but threw the
bad away. 49This is how it will be at the end of the
age. The angels will come and separate the
wicked from the righteous 50and throw them into
the fiery furnace, where there will be weeping and
gnashing of teeth.
51"Have you understood all these things?"
Jesus asked.
"Yes," they replied.
52He said to them, "Therefore every teacher of
the law who has been instructed about the king-
dom of heaven is like the owner of a house who
brings out of his storeroom new treasures as well
as old."
53When Jesus had finished these parables, he
moved on from there. 54Coming to his home-
town, he began teaching the people in their syna-
gogue, and they were amazed. "Where did this
man get this wisdom and these miraculous pow-
ers?" they asked. 55"Isn't this the carpenter's son?
Isn't his mother's name Mary, and aren't his
brothers James, Joseph, Simon and Judas?
56Aren't all his sisters with us? Where then did
this man get all these things?" 57And they took
offense at him.
But Jesus said to them, "Only in his hometown
and in his own house is a prophet without
honor."
58And he did not do many miracles there be-
cause of their lack of faith.

[a]33 Greek *three satas* (probably about 1/2 bushel or 22 liters)
[b]35 Psalm 78:2

Discovering the Word 1. According to the parable of the sower, what responses does Jesus expect as he preaches his message of the kingdom (vv. 1–9, 18–23)? 2. In verse 10 the disciples ask Jesus why he speaks to the people in parables. Explain his reply (vv. 11–17). 3. Wheat and weeds look similar until the harvest. How does this parable explain God's delayed judgment of the wicked (vv. 24–30, 36–43)? 4. What do the parables of the mustard seed and yeast suggest about the way the kingdom grows (vv. 31–35)? 5. What do the parables of the hidden treasure and the pearl teach us about the value of the kingdom (vv. 44–46)?

Applying the Word 1. Jesus wants his disciples to understand the parables. How have they enlarged your understanding of the kingdom of heaven? 2. Jesus also wants us to respond to what we have heard and understood. Throughout this chapter, what types of responses does he desire?

Responding in Prayer Ask the Lord to help you respond to him in the ways you observed.

10/ *Matthew 14*
The Revelation of the King (Part 1)

CRISES ARE UNCOMFORTABLE. They force us to make painful decisions, even when we don't want to decide. In Matthew 14 Jesus places the disciples in tough situations where they must act on what they have learned about him. The focus shifts from parables about the kingdom to the identity of the king.

Warming Up to God Teachers use tests during our school years. But tests are not limited to school; God also uses tests throughout our lives. How do you think you've been tested lately?

Read Matthew 14.

14 At that time Herod the tetrarch
heard the reports about Jesus, [2]and
he said to his attendants, "This is
John the Baptist; he has risen from the dead! That
is why miraculous powers are at work in him."
[3]Now Herod had arrested John and bound him
and put him in prison because of Herodias, his
brother Philip's wife, [4]for John had been saying to
him: "It is not lawful for you to have her." [5]Herod
wanted to kill John, but he was afraid of the peo-
ple, because they considered him a prophet.
[6]On Herod's birthday the daughter of Herodias
danced for them and pleased Herod so much [7]that
he promised with an oath to give her whatever
she asked. [8]Prompted by her mother, she said,
"Give me here on a platter the head of John the
Baptist." [9]The king was distressed, but because of
his oaths and his dinner guests, he ordered that
her request be granted [10]and had John beheaded
in the prison. [11]His head was brought in on a
platter and given to the girl, who carried it to her
mother. [12]John's disciples came and took his body
and buried it. Then they went and told Jesus.
[13]When Jesus heard what had happened, he
withdrew by boat privately to a solitary place.
Hearing of this, the crowds followed him on foot
from the towns. [14]When Jesus landed and saw a
large crowd, he had compassion on them and
healed their sick.
[15]As evening approached, the disciples came to
him and said, "This is a remote place, and it's
already getting late. Send the crowds away, so
they can go to the villages and buy themselves
some food."
[16]Jesus replied, "They do not need to go away.
You give them something to eat."
[17]"We have here only five loaves of bread and
two fish," they answered.
[18]"Bring them here to me," he said. [19]And he
directed the people to sit down on the grass. Tak-
ing the five loaves and the two fish and looking
up to heaven, he gave thanks and broke the
loaves. Then he gave them to the disciples, and
the disciples gave them to the people. [20]They all
ate and were satisfied, and the disciples picked up
twelve basketfuls of broken pieces that were left
over. [21]The number of those who ate was about
five thousand men, besides women and children.

22Immediately Jesus made the disciples get into
the boat and go on ahead of him to the other side,
while he dismissed the crowd. 23After he had dis-
missed them, he went up on a mountainside by
himself to pray. When evening came, he was
there alone, 24but the boat was already a consider-
able distance[c] from land, buffeted by the waves
because the wind was against it.

25During the fourth watch of the night Jesus
went out to them, walking on the lake. 26When
the disciples saw him walking on the lake, they
were terrified. "It's a ghost," they said, and cried
out in fear.

27But Jesus immediately said to them: "Take
courage! It is I. Don't be afraid."

28"Lord, if it's you," Peter replied, "tell me to
come to you on the water."

29"Come," he said.

Then Peter got down out of the boat, walked
on the water and came toward Jesus. 30But when
he saw the wind, he was afraid and, beginning to
sink, cried out, "Lord, save me!"

31Immediately Jesus reached out his hand and
caught him. "You of little faith," he said, "why
did you doubt?"

32And when they climbed into the boat, the
wind died down. 33Then those who were in the
boat worshiped him, saying, "Truly you are the
Son of God."

34When they had crossed over, they landed at
Gennesaret. 35And when the men of that place
recognized Jesus, they sent word to all the sur-
rounding country. People brought all their sick to
him 36and begged him to let the sick just touch
the edge of his cloak, and all who touched him
were healed.

c24 Greek *many stadia*

Discovering the Word 1. In verses 1–2 Herod speculates about Jesus' identity. What led him to believe that Jesus is John the Baptist (vv. 3–12)? 2. How is the feeding of the five thousand (vv. 13–21) a test for the disciples? 3. Herod and Jesus, the two kings in this passage, both serve banquets. What does each king's banquet reveal about his character and authority? 4. Imagine you are in the boat with the anxious disciples (vv. 22–26). Describe what you would see, hear and feel. 5. How is Peter's trying experience on the water a vivid picture of faith and doubt (vv. 28–31)?

Applying the Word 1. When are you most tempted to take your eyes off the Lord and to sink in doubt? 2. In verse 33 the disciples worship Jesus and declare, "Truly you are the Son of God." What do you see in this incident that leads you to worship Jesus? 3. How can these things help you to trust Jesus the next time you are tempted to doubt?

Responding in Prayer Spend a few minutes worshiping Jesus, the Son of God.

11 / *Matthew 15:1—16:20*
The Revelation of the King (Part 2)

EUREKA! WHAT A relief and pleasure it is when something we have not quite understood becomes clear to us. In this section of Matthew the disciples come to a supernatural understanding of Jesus. What they thought they knew becomes a new and deeper knowledge. Peter, speaking for the disciples, declares who Jesus really is. Peter's words bring us to the climax of the first half of Matthew.

Warming Up to God When you first recognized who Jesus is and what he offers to you, what were your thoughts and feelings?

Read Matthew 15:1—16:20.

15 Then some Pharisees and teachers
of the law came to Jesus from Jeru-
salem and asked, 2"Why do your
disciples break the tradition of the elders? They
don't wash their hands before they eat!"
3Jesus replied, "And why do you break the
command of God for the sake of your tradition?
4For God said, 'Honor your father and mother'[d]
and 'Anyone who curses his father or mother
must be put to death.'[e] 5But you say that if a man
says to his father or mother, 'Whatever help you
might otherwise have received from me is a gift
devoted to God,' 6he is not to 'honor his father[f]'
with it. Thus you nullify the word of God for the
sake of your tradition. 7You hypocrites! Isaiah
was right when he prophesied about you:

8" 'These people honor me with their lips,
but their hearts are far from me.
9They worship me in vain;
their teachings are but rules taught by
men.'[g]"

10Jesus called the crowd to him and said, "Lis-
ten and understand. 11What goes into a man's
mouth does not make him 'unclean,' but what
comes out of his mouth, that is what makes him
'unclean.' "
12Then the disciples came to him and asked,
"Do you know that the Pharisees were offended
when they heard this?"
13He replied, "Every plant that my heavenly Fa-
ther has not planted will be pulled up by the
roots. 14Leave them; they are blind guides.[h] If a
blind man leads a blind man, both will fall into a
pit."
15Peter said, "Explain the parable to us."
16"Are you still so dull?" Jesus asked them.
17"Don't you see that whatever enters the mouth
goes into the stomach and then out of the body?
18But the things that come out of the mouth come
from the heart, and these make a man 'unclean.'
19For out of the heart come evil thoughts, mur-
der, adultery, sexual immorality, theft, false testi-
mony, slander. 20These are what make a man 'un-
clean'; but eating with unwashed hands does not
make him 'unclean.' "
21Leaving that place, Jesus withdrew to the re-
gion of Tyre and Sidon. 22A Canaanite woman
from that vicinity came to him, crying out, "Lord,
Son of David, have mercy on me! My daughter is
suffering terribly from demon-possession."
23Jesus did not answer a word. So his disciples
came to him and urged him, "Send her away, for
she keeps crying out after us."
24He answered, "I was sent only to the lost
sheep of Israel."
25The woman came and knelt before him.
"Lord, help me!" she said.
26He replied, "It is not right to take the chil-
dren's bread and toss it to their dogs."
27"Yes, Lord," she said, "but even the dogs eat
the crumbs that fall from their masters' table."
28Then Jesus answered, "Woman, you have
great faith! Your request is granted." And her
daughter was healed from that very hour.
29Jesus left there and went along the Sea of Gal-
ilee. Then he went up on a mountainside and sat
down. 30Great crowds came to him, bringing the
lame, the blind, the crippled, the mute and many
others, and laid them at his feet; and he healed
them. 31The people were amazed when they saw
the mute speaking, the crippled made well, the
lame walking and the blind seeing. And they
praised the God of Israel.
32Jesus called his disciples to him and said, "I
have compassion for these people; they have al-
ready been with me three days and have nothing
to eat. I do not want to send them away hungry,
or they may collapse on the way."
33His disciples answered, "Where could we get
enough bread in this remote place to feed such a
crowd?"
34"How many loaves do you have?" Jesus
asked.
"Seven," they replied, "and a few small fish."
35He told the crowd to sit down on the ground.
36Then he took the seven loaves and the fish, and
when he had given thanks, he broke them and
gave them to the disciples, and they in turn to the
people. 37They all ate and were satisfied. After-
ward the disciples picked up seven basketfuls of
broken pieces that were left over. 38The number
of those who ate was four thousand, besides
women and children. 39After Jesus had sent the
crowd away, he got into the boat and went to the
vicinity of Magadan.

16 The Pharisees and Sadducees came
to Jesus and tested him by asking
him to show them a sign from
heaven.
2He replied,[i] "When evening comes, you say,

[d]4 Exodus 20:12; Deut. 5:16 [e]4 Exodus 21:17; Lev. 20:9
[f]6 Some manuscripts *father or his mother* [g]9 Isaiah 29:13
[h]14 Some manuscripts *guides of the blind* [i]2 Some early manuscripts
do not have the rest of verse 2 and all of verse 3.

'It will be fair weather, for the sky is red,' 3and in the morning, 'Today it will be stormy, for the sky is red and overcast.' You know how to interpret the appearance of the sky, but you cannot interpret the signs of the times. 4A wicked and adulterous generation looks for a miraculous sign, but none will be given it except the sign of Jonah." Jesus then left them and went away.

5When they went across the lake, the disciples forgot to take bread. 6"Be careful," Jesus said to them. "Be on your guard against the yeast of the Pharisees and Sadducees."

7They discussed this among themselves and said, "It is because we didn't bring any bread."

8Aware of their discussion, Jesus asked, "You of little faith, why are you talking among yourselves about having no bread? 9Do you still not understand? Don't you remember the five loaves for the five thousand, and how many basketfuls you gathered? 10Or the seven loaves for the four thousand, and how many basketfuls you gathered? 11How is it you don't understand that I was not talking to you about bread? But be on your guard against the yeast of the Pharisees and Sadducees." 12Then they understood that he was not telling them to guard against the yeast used in bread, but against the teaching of the Pharisees and Sadducees.

13When Jesus came to the region of Caesarea Philippi, he asked his disciples, "Who do people say the Son of Man is?"

14They replied, "Some say John the Baptist; others say Elijah; and still others, Jeremiah or one of the prophets."

15"But what about you?" he asked. "Who do you say I am?"

16Simon Peter answered, "You are the Christ,[j] the Son of the living God."

17Jesus replied, "Blessed are you, Simon son of Jonah, for this was not revealed to you by man, but by my Father in heaven. 18And I tell you that you are Peter,[k] and on this rock I will build my church, and the gates of Hades[l] will not overcome it.[m] 19I will give you the keys of the kingdom of heaven; whatever you bind on earth will be[n] bound in heaven, and whatever you loose on earth will be[n] loosed in heaven." 20Then he warned his disciples not to tell anyone that he was the Christ.

j16 Or Messiah; also in verse 20 *k18 Peter means rock.* *l18 Or hell* *m18 Or not prove stronger than it* *n19 Or have been*

Discovering the Word 1. Top religious leaders from Jerusalem oppose Jesus by attacking the disciples (15:1–2). What is their complaint, and what does it suggest about Jesus? 2. How does Jesus respond to their accusation (15:3–20)? 3. How would you account for the unusual interaction between Jesus, the woman and the disciples (15:21–28)? 4. After Jesus heals the sick and feeds the four thousand, the religious leaders ask him for a sign from heaven (16:1). Why do you think Jesus resists them (16:2–4)? 5. In 16:5–12 the disciples misunderstand Jesus' allusion to yeast. How is their misunderstanding related to a lack of faith? 6. In 16:5–12 the disciples couldn't even grasp a simple figure of speech. How then does Peter have enough insight to confess that Jesus is the Christ, the Son of God (16:13–17)?

Applying the Word 1. Are there religious practices in your life that are in danger of becoming outward, empty forms? Explain. 2. How can you avoid this tendency? 3. Jesus' question to Peter is one that everyone will have to respond to at some point. Who do you say Jesus is, and why?

Responding in Prayer Offer praise to Jesus Christ for who he is.

12/ *Matthew 16:21—17:27*
The Work of the King

ONE OF THE rules of good management is "No surprises." While surprises can be fun, they can also be upsetting. Good corporate leadership seeks to eliminate surprises so that everything runs according to plan.

Now that the disciples have been with Jesus for a while, he must prepare them for the true nature of his kingdom. They are shocked at the cost of his mission and his requirements for discipleship.

Warming Up to God Recall an unpleasant surprise you received. How did you handle it?

Read Matthew 16:21—17:27.

21From that time on Jesus began to explain to his disciples that he must go to Jerusalem and suffer many things at the hands of the elders, chief priests and teachers of the law, and that he must be killed and on the third day be raised to life.

22Peter took him aside and began to rebuke him. "Never, Lord!" he said. "This shall never happen to you!"

23Jesus turned and said to Peter, "Get behind me, Satan! You are a stumbling block to me; you do not have in mind the things of God, but the things of men."

24Then Jesus said to his disciples, "If anyone would come after me, he must deny himself and take up his cross and follow me. 25For whoever wants to save his life[o] will lose it, but whoever loses his life for me will find it. 26What good will it be for a man if he gains the whole world, yet forfeits his soul? Or what can a man give in exchange for his soul? 27For the Son of Man is going to come in his Father's glory with his angels, and then he will reward each person according to what he has done. 28I tell you the truth, some who are standing here will not taste death before they see the Son of Man coming in his kingdom."

17 After six days Jesus took with him Peter, James and John the brother of James, and led them up a high mountain by themselves. 2There he was transfigured before them. His face shone like the sun, and his clothes became as white as the light. 3Just then there appeared before them Moses and Elijah, talking with Jesus.

4Peter said to Jesus, "Lord, it is good for us to be here. If you wish, I will put up three shelters—one for you, one for Moses and one for Elijah."

5While he was still speaking, a bright cloud enveloped them, and a voice from the cloud said, "This is my Son, whom I love; with him I am well pleased. Listen to him!"

6When the disciples heard this, they fell facedown to the ground, terrified. 7But Jesus came and touched them. "Get up," he said. "Don't be afraid." 8When they looked up, they saw no one except Jesus.

9As they were coming down the mountain, Jesus instructed them, "Don't tell anyone what you have seen, until the Son of Man has been raised from the dead."

10The disciples asked him, "Why then do the teachers of the law say that Elijah must come first?"

11Jesus replied, "To be sure, Elijah comes and will restore all things. 12But I tell you, Elijah has already come, and they did not recognize him, but have done to him everything they wished. In the same way the Son of Man is going to suffer at their hands." 13Then the disciples understood that he was talking to them about John the Baptist.

14When they came to the crowd, a man approached Jesus and knelt before him. 15"Lord, have mercy on my son," he said. "He has seizures and is suffering greatly. He often falls into the fire or into the water. 16I brought him to your disciples, but they could not heal him."

17"O unbelieving and perverse generation," Jesus replied, "how long shall I stay with you? How long shall I put up with you? Bring the boy here to me." 18Jesus rebuked the demon, and it came out of the boy, and he was healed from that moment.

19Then the disciples came to Jesus in private and asked, "Why couldn't we drive it out?"

20He replied, "Because you have so little faith. I tell you the truth, if you have faith as small as a mustard seed, you can say to this mountain, 'Move from here to there' and it will move. Nothing will be impossible for you.[p]"

22When they came together in Galilee, he said to them, "The Son of Man is going to be betrayed into the hands of men. 23They will kill him, and on the third day he will be raised to life." And the disciples were filled with grief.

24After Jesus and his disciples arrived in Caper-

o25 The Greek word means either *life* or *soul*; also in verse 26.
p20 Some manuscripts *you.* 21*But this kind does not go out except by prayer and fasting.*

naum, the collectors of the two-drachma tax came to Peter and asked, "Doesn't your teacher pay the temple tax[q]?"

[25]"Yes, he does," he replied.

When Peter came into the house, Jesus was the first to speak. "What do you think, Simon?" he asked. "From whom do the kings of the earth collect duty and taxes—from their own sons or from others?"

[26]"From others," Peter answered.

"Then the sons are exempt," Jesus said to him. [27]"But so that we may not offend them, go to the lake and throw out your line. Take the first fish you catch; open its mouth and you will find a four-drachma coin. Take it and give it to them for my tax and yours."

q24 Greek *the two drachmas*

Discovering the Word 1. What were some of the surprises the disciples received? 2. Peter and Jesus seem to be at cross purposes in 16:22-23. Why do you think Jesus addresses Peter as Satan? 3. What does Jesus reveal about the cost and rewards of following him (16:24-28)? 4. What would the disciples learn about Jesus by his transformed appearance, his conversation with Moses and Elijah, and the voice from heaven (17:1-8)? 5. How might this help resolve their confusion about Jesus' impending death? 6. As a result of their powerlessness, what do the disciples learn about faith?

Applying the Word 1. How has following Jesus produced times of confusion for you? 2. We don't always understand life from a heavenly perspective. How can this passage reorient your thinking?

Responding in Prayer Ask God to help you understand his ways so that you can be a better disciple.

13 / *Matthew 18*
The Greatest in the Kingdom

WHO IS GREATEST in the kingdom of God? How can a subject of the kingdom earn true wealth? When should we forgive? These questions dominate the thoughts of the disciples as they approach Jerusalem. They are also important questions for us. How we answer them will directly affect the quality of our discipleship.

Warming Up to God When has someone sinned against you? How did it affect you?

Read Matthew 18.

18 At that time the disciples came to Jesus and asked, "Who is the greatest in the kingdom of heaven?"

[2]He called a little child and had him stand among them. [3]And he said: "I tell you the truth, unless you change and become like little children, you will never enter the kingdom of heaven. [4]Therefore, whoever humbles himself like this child is the greatest in the kingdom of heaven.

[5]"And whoever welcomes a little child like this in my name welcomes me. [6]But if anyone causes one of these little ones who believe in me to sin, it would be better for him to have a large millstone hung around his neck and to be drowned in the depths of the sea.

[7]"Woe to the world because of the things that cause people to sin! Such things must come, but woe to the man through whom they come! [8]If your hand or your foot causes you to sin, cut it off and throw it away. It is better for you to enter life maimed or crippled than to have two hands or two feet and be thrown into eternal fire. [9]And if your eye causes you to sin, gouge it out and throw it away. It is better for you to enter life with one eye than to have two eyes and be thrown into the fire of hell.

10“See that you do not look down on one of
these little ones. For I tell you that their angels in
heaven always see the face of my Father in
heaven.[r]
12“What do you think? If a man owns a hun-
dred sheep, and one of them wanders away, will
he not leave the ninety-nine on the hills and go to
look for the one that wandered off? 13And if he
finds it, I tell you the truth, he is happier about
that one sheep than about the ninety-nine that
did not wander off. 14In the same way your Father
in heaven is not willing that any of these little
ones should be lost.
15“If your brother sins against you,[s] go and
show him his fault, just between the two of you.
If he listens to you, you have won your brother
over. 16But if he will not listen, take one or two
others along, so that ‘every matter may be estab-
lished by the testimony of two or three wit-
nesses.’[t] 17If he refuses to listen to them, tell it to
the church; and if he refuses to listen even to the
church, treat him as you would a pagan or a tax
collector.
18“I tell you the truth, whatever you bind on
earth will be[u] bound in heaven, and whatever
you loose on earth will be[u] loosed in heaven.
19“Again, I tell you that if two of you on earth
agree about anything you ask for, it will be done
for you by my Father in heaven. 20For where two
or three come together in my name, there am I
with them.”
21Then Peter came to Jesus and asked, “Lord,
how many times shall I forgive my brother when
he sins against me? Up to seven times?”
22Jesus answered, “I tell you, not seven times,
but seventy-seven times.[v]
23“Therefore, the kingdom of heaven is like a
king who wanted to settle accounts with his ser-
vants. 24As he began the settlement, a man who
owed him ten thousand talents[w] was brought to
him. 25Since he was not able to pay, the master
ordered that he and his wife and his children and
all that he had be sold to repay the debt.
26“The servant fell on his knees before him. ‘Be
patient with me,’ he begged, ‘and I will pay back
everything.’ 27The servant’s master took pity on
him, canceled the debt and let him go.
28“But when that servant went out, he found
one of his fellow servants who owed him a hun-
dred denarii.[x] He grabbed him and began to
choke him. ‘Pay back what you owe me!’ he de-
manded.
29“His fellow servant fell to his knees and
begged him, ‘Be patient with me, and I will pay
you back.’
30“But he refused. Instead, he went off and had
the man thrown into prison until he could pay
the debt. 31When the other servants saw what had
happened, they were greatly distressed and went
and told their master everything that had hap-
pened.
32“Then the master called the servant in. ‘You
wicked servant,’ he said, ‘I canceled all that debt
of yours because you begged me to. 33Shouldn’t
you have had mercy on your fellow servant just as
I had on you?’ 34In anger his master turned him
over to the jailers to be tortured, until he should
pay back all he owed.
35“This is how my heavenly Father will treat
each of you unless you forgive your brother from
your heart.”

[r] 10 Some manuscripts *heaven.* [11] *The Son of Man came to save what was lost.* [s] 15 Some manuscripts do not have *against you.* [t] 16 Deut. 19:15 [u] 18 Or *have been* [v] 22 Or *seventy times seven* [w] 24 That is, millions of dollars [x] 28 That is, a few dollars

Discovering the Word 1. The disciples want to know who is the greatest in the kingdom of heaven (v. 1). How does Jesus’ appeal to little children answer their question (vv. 2–5)? 2. Spiritually speaking, the “little ones” are those who humble themselves (“become like little children”) and believe in Jesus. What is Jesus’ attitude toward those who cause the little ones to sin (vv. 6–7)? 3. How do verses 10–14 further emphasize the value Jesus places on his “little ones”? 4. Greatness in the kingdom is also dependent on living a life of forgiveness and mercy. What guidelines does Jesus give for dealing with those who sin against us (vv. 15–20)? 5. Forgiving someone once does not always guarantee he or she will not offend us again. How can the parable of the unmerciful servant help us to keep on forgiving (vv. 21–35)?

Applying the Word 1. Children have little status in the eyes of adults. How can we assume the status of children in our circle of friends and coworkers? 2. How should the value Jesus places on his “little ones” affect the way we view ourselves and other believers? 3. How does this chapter challenge your ideas of value and greatness?

 **Responding in Prayer** Ask God to help you forgive those who have hurt you.

14 / *Matthew 19—20*
Life in the Kingdom

WHAT IS REALLY important to you? What makes you feel important? Money? Success? Recognition? These are common answers. The values that Jesus teaches, however, have little to do with such things. In the previous study we learned that to be great in the kingdom, we must become "small." In this study we will see how the values of the kingdom conflict with the world's approach to wealth and leadership.

 **Warming Up to God** What does success mean to you? How does that compare to what our culture says about success?

 **Read Matthew 19—20.**

19 When Jesus had finished saying
these things, he left Galilee and
went into the region of Judea to the
other side of the Jordan. [2]Large crowds followed
him, and he healed them there.
[3]Some Pharisees came to him to test him. They
asked, "Is it lawful for a man to divorce his wife
for any and every reason?"
[4]"Haven't you read," he replied, "that at the
beginning the Creator 'made them male and fe-
male,'[y] [5]and said, 'For this reason a man will
leave his father and mother and be united to his
wife, and the two will become one flesh'[z]? [6]So
they are no longer two, but one. Therefore what
God has joined together, let man not separate."
[7]"Why then," they asked, "did Moses com-
mand that a man give his wife a certificate of
divorce and send her away?"
[8]Jesus replied, "Moses permitted you to divorce
your wives because your hearts were hard. But it
was not this way from the beginning. [9]I tell you
that anyone who divorces his wife, except for
marital unfaithfulness, and marries another
woman commits adultery."
[10]The disciples said to him, "If this is the situa-
tion between a husband and wife, it is better not
to marry."
[11]Jesus replied, "Not everyone can accept this
word, but only those to whom it has been given.
[12]For some are eunuchs because they were born
that way; others were made that way by men; and
others have renounced marriage[a] because of the
kingdom of heaven. The one who can accept this
should accept it."
[13]Then little children were brought to Jesus for
him to place his hands on them and pray for
them. But the disciples rebuked those who
brought them.
[14]Jesus said, "Let the little children come to me,
and do not hinder them, for the kingdom of
heaven belongs to such as these." [15]When he had
placed his hands on them, he went on from there.
[16]Now a man came up to Jesus and asked,
"Teacher, what good thing must I do to get eter-
nal life?"
[17]"Why do you ask me about what is good?"
Jesus replied. "There is only One who is good. If
you want to enter life, obey the commandments."
[18]"Which ones?" the man inquired.
Jesus replied, " 'Do not murder, do not commit
adultery, do not steal, do not give false testimony,
[19]honor your father and mother,'[b] and 'love your
neighbor as yourself.'[c]"
[20]"All these I have kept," the young man said.
"What do I still lack?"
[21]Jesus answered, "If you want to be perfect,
go, sell your possessions and give to the poor, and
you will have treasure in heaven. Then come, fol-
low me."
[22]When the young man heard this, he went
away sad, because he had great wealth.
[23]Then Jesus said to his disciples, "I tell you the
truth, it is hard for a rich man to enter the king-

[y]4 Gen. 1:27 [z]5 Gen. 2:24 [a]12 Or *have made themselves eunuchs* [b]19 Exodus 20:12-16; Deut. 5:16-20 [c]19 Lev. 19:18

dom of heaven. 24Again I tell you, it is easier for
a camel to go through the eye of a needle than for
a rich man to enter the kingdom of God."

25When the disciples heard this, they were
greatly astonished and asked, "Who then can be
saved?"

26Jesus looked at them and said, "With man
this is impossible, but with God all things are
possible."

27Peter answered him, "We have left everything
to follow you! What then will there be for us?"

28Jesus said to them, "I tell you the truth, at the
renewal of all things, when the Son of Man sits on
his glorious throne, you who have followed me
will also sit on twelve thrones, judging the twelve
tribes of Israel. 29And everyone who has left
houses or brothers or sisters or father or
mother[d] or children or fields for my sake will
receive a hundred times as much and will inherit
eternal life. 30But many who are first will be last,
and many who are last will be first.

20 "For the kingdom of heaven is like
a landowner who went out early in
the morning to hire men to work in
his vineyard. 2He agreed to pay them a denarius
for the day and sent them into his vineyard.

3"About the third hour he went out and saw
others standing in the marketplace doing noth-
ing. 4He told them, 'You also go and work in my
vineyard, and I will pay you whatever is right.'
5So they went.

"He went out again about the sixth hour and
the ninth hour and did the same thing. 6About
the eleventh hour he went out and found still
others standing around. He asked them, 'Why
have you been standing here all day long doing
nothing?'

7"'Because no one has hired us,' they an-
swered.

"He said to them, 'You also go and work in my
vineyard.'

8"When evening came, the owner of the vine-
yard said to his foreman, 'Call the workers and
pay them their wages, beginning with the last
ones hired and going on to the first.'

9"The workers who were hired about the elev-
enth hour came and each received a denarius.
10So when those came who were hired first, they
expected to receive more. But each one of them
also received a denarius. 11When they received it,
they began to grumble against the landowner.
12'These men who were hired last worked only
one hour,' they said, 'and you have made them
equal to us who have borne the burden of the
work and the heat of the day.'

13"But he answered one of them, 'Friend, I am
not being unfair to you. Didn't you agree to work
for a denarius? 14Take your pay and go. I want to
give the man who was hired last the same as I
gave you. 15Don't I have the right to do what I
want with my own money? Or are you envious
because I am generous?'

16"So the last will be first, and the first will be
last."

17Now as Jesus was going up to Jerusalem, he
took the twelve disciples aside and said to them,
18"We are going up to Jerusalem, and the Son of
Man will be betrayed to the chief priests and the
teachers of the law. They will condemn him to
death 19and will turn him over to the Gentiles to
be mocked and flogged and crucified. On the
third day he will be raised to life!"

20Then the mother of Zebedee's sons came to
Jesus with her sons and, kneeling down, asked a
favor of him.

21"What is it you want?" he asked.

She said, "Grant that one of these two sons of
mine may sit at your right and the other at your
left in your kingdom."

22"You don't know what you are asking," Jesus
said to them. "Can you drink the cup I am going
to drink?"

"We can," they answered.

23Jesus said to them, "You will indeed drink
from my cup, but to sit at my right or left is not
for me to grant. These places belong to those for
whom they have been prepared by my Father."

24When the ten heard about this, they were in-
dignant with the two brothers. 25Jesus called
them together and said, "You know that the rul-
ers of the Gentiles lord it over them, and their
high officials exercise authority over them. 26Not
so with you. Instead, whoever wants to become
great among you must be your servant, 27and
whoever wants to be first must be your slave—
28just as the Son of Man did not come to be
served, but to serve, and to give his life as a ran-
som for many."

29As Jesus and his disciples were leaving Jeri-
cho, a large crowd followed him. 30Two blind

[d]29 Some manuscripts *mother or wife*

men were sitting by the roadside, and when they heard that Jesus was going by, they shouted, "Lord, Son of David, have mercy on us!"
31The crowd rebuked them and told them to be quiet, but they shouted all the louder, "Lord, Son of David, have mercy on us!"
32Jesus stopped and called them. "What do you want me to do for you?" he asked.
33"Lord," they answered, "we want our sight."
34Jesus had compassion on them and touched their eyes. Immediately they received their sight and followed him.

Discovering the Word 1. How do Jesus' teachings on divorce and remarriage contrast with the values and practices of our culture (19:1–12)? 2. In 19:16–22 a young man struggles between choosing wealth or eternal life. Why do you think Jesus required him to choose? 3. What wealth does Jesus offer those who follow him (vv. 27–30)? 4. What does the parable of the workers teach us about greatness and wealth in the kingdom of God (20:1–16)? 5. In what ways is Jesus a model of the values he teaches in 20:25–28? 6. How does Jesus' interaction with the two blind men illustrate the values he has just taught?

Applying the Word 1. How have you experienced what Jesus describes in 19:29? 2. In what ways has Jesus' teaching on greatness and wealth (Mt 18—20) challenged you?

Responding in Prayer Ask God to give you strength to stand against the world and to make his values your values.

15 / *Matthew 21:1–27*
The King Occupies His Capital

IT IS FASHIONABLE to believe in Jesus. Surveys reveal that millions profess to be Christians. Celebrities claim miraculous, overnight conversions. Politicians boast they are "born again." Religion has become big business.

In Matthew 21 Jesus' popularity reaches its zenith. In the midst of public acclamation he occupies Jerusalem, the capital of the Jewish nation. His clash with the religious leaders reveals the difference between genuine faith and empty profession.

Warming Up to God Today we will see Jesus enter Jerusalem to the praise and acclamation of the crowd. Imagine you have an opportunity to see Jesus. How do you feel? Express your feelings to the Lord.

Read Matthew 21:1-27.

21 As they approached Jerusalem and came to Bethphage on the Mount of Olives, Jesus sent two disciples,
2saying to them, "Go to the village ahead of you, and at once you will find a donkey tied there, with her colt by her. Untie them and bring them to me. 3If anyone says anything to you, tell him that the Lord needs them, and he will send them right away."
4This took place to fulfill what was spoken through the prophet:

5"Say to the Daughter of Zion,
'See, your king comes to you,
gentle and riding on a donkey,
on a colt, the foal of a donkey.' "[e]

6The disciples went and did as Jesus had instructed them. 7They brought the donkey and the colt, placed their cloaks on them, and Jesus sat on them. 8A very large crowd spread their cloaks on the road, while others cut branches from the trees and spread them on the road. 9The crowds that went ahead of him and those that followed shouted,

"Hosanna[f] to the Son of David!"
"Blessed is he who comes in the name of the Lord!"[g]
"Hosanna[f] in the highest!"

[e]5 Zech. 9:9 [f]9 A Hebrew expression meaning "Save!" which became an exclamation of praise; also in verse 15 [g]9 Psalm 118:26

[10]When Jesus entered Jerusalem, the whole city was stirred and asked, "Who is this?"

[11]The crowds answered, "This is Jesus, the prophet from Nazareth in Galilee."

[12]Jesus entered the temple area and drove out all who were buying and selling there. He overturned the tables of the money changers and the benches of those selling doves. [13]"It is written," he said to them, " 'My house will be called a house of prayer,'[h] but you are making it a 'den of robbers.'[i]"

[14]The blind and the lame came to him at the temple, and he healed them. [15]But when the chief priests and the teachers of the law saw the wonderful things he did and the children shouting in the temple area, "Hosanna to the Son of David," they were indignant.

[16]"Do you hear what these children are saying?" they asked him.

"Yes," replied Jesus, "have you never read,

" 'From the lips of children and infants
you have ordained praise'[j]?"

[17]And he left them and went out of the city to Bethany, where he spent the night.

[18]Early in the morning, as he was on his way back to the city, he was hungry. [19]Seeing a fig tree by the road, he went up to it but found nothing on it except leaves. Then he said to it, "May you never bear fruit again!" Immediately the tree withered.

[20]When the disciples saw this, they were amazed. "How did the fig tree wither so quickly?" they asked.

[21]Jesus replied, "I tell you the truth, if you have faith and do not doubt, not only can you do what was done to the fig tree, but also you can say to this mountain, 'Go, throw yourself into the sea,' and it will be done. [22]If you believe, you will receive whatever you ask for in prayer."

[23]Jesus entered the temple courts, and, while he was teaching, the chief priests and the elders of the people came to him. "By what authority are you doing these things?" they asked. "And who gave you this authority?"

[24]Jesus replied, "I will also ask you one question. If you answer me, I will tell you by what authority I am doing these things. [25]John's baptism—where did it come from? Was it from heaven, or from men?"

They discussed it among themselves and said, "If we say, 'From heaven,' he will ask, 'Then why didn't you believe him?' [26]But if we say, 'From men'—we are afraid of the people, for they all hold that John was a prophet."

[27]So they answered Jesus, "We don't know."

Then he said, "Neither will I tell you by what authority I am doing these things.

[h]13 Isaiah 56:7 [i]13 Jer. 7:11 [j]16 Psalm 8:2

Discovering the Word 1. Excitement is building and emotions are intense. What words or phrases communicate something of the electrifying atmosphere? 2. What different perceptions does the crowd have of Jesus (vv. 9–11)? 3. Jesus clears the temple in verses 12–17. How does the condition of the temple contrast with what God intended? 4. A fig tree with leaves usually had fruit. How does Jesus' cursing of the fig tree relate to his clearing the temple (vv. 18–22)? 5. How does Jesus' encounter with the Pharisees (vv. 23–27) illustrate the danger of not responding to the light God gives us?

Applying the Word 1. In what ways do you see the modern church "buying and selling" like those in the temple? 2. Identify one area in which your actions need to be more consistent with your beliefs.

Responding in Prayer Praise God for who Jesus is and what you have seen about him in this passage.

16/ *Matthew 21:28—22:46*
The King Silences the Opposition

CONFRONTATION IS NEVER easy. Yet there are times when the situation demands it. The religious leaders refused to acknowledge that Jesus was God's Messiah sent to rule. Skillfully, Jesus seeks to expose their hardness of heart and bring them to repentance. They respond not in repentance but by plotting a trap for him.

Warming Up to God From time to time we all have been involved in confrontations. How do you feel in these situations?

Read Matthew 21:28—22:46.

28“What do you think? There was a man who
had two sons. He went to the first and said, ‘Son,
go and work today in the vineyard.’
29“ ‘I will not,’ he answered, but later he
changed his mind and went.
30“Then the father went to the other son and
said the same thing. He answered, ‘I will, sir,’ but
he did not go.
31“Which of the two did what his father
wanted?”
“The first,” they answered.
Jesus said to them, “I tell you the truth, the tax
collectors and the prostitutes are entering the
kingdom of God ahead of you. 32For John came to
you to show you the way of righteousness, and
you did not believe him, but the tax collectors
and the prostitutes did. And even after you saw
this, you did not repent and believe him.
33“Listen to another parable: There was a land-
owner who planted a vineyard. He put a wall
around it, dug a winepress in it and built a watch-
tower. Then he rented the vineyard to some farm-
ers and went away on a journey. 34When the har-
vest time approached, he sent his servants to the
tenants to collect his fruit.
35“The tenants seized his servants; they beat
one, killed another, and stoned a third. 36Then he
sent other servants to them, more than the first
time, and the tenants treated them the same way.
37Last of all, he sent his son to them. ‘They will
respect my son,’ he said.
38“But when the tenants saw the son, they said
to each other, ‘This is the heir. Come, let's kill
him and take his inheritance.’ 39So they took him
and threw him out of the vineyard and killed him.
40“Therefore, when the owner of the vineyard
comes, what will he do to those tenants?”
41“He will bring those wretches to a wretched
end,” they replied, “and he will rent the vineyard
to other tenants, who will give him his share of
the crop at harvest time.”
42Jesus said to them, “Have you never read in
the Scriptures:

“ ‘The stone the builders rejected
has become the capstone[k];
the Lord has done this,
and it is marvelous in our eyes’[l]?

43“Therefore I tell you that the kingdom of God
will be taken away from you and given to a peo-
ple who will produce its fruit. 44He who falls on
this stone will be broken to pieces, but he on
whom it falls will be crushed.”[m]
45When the chief priests and the Pharisees
heard Jesus' parables, they knew he was talking
about them. 46They looked for a way to arrest
him, but they were afraid of the crowd because
the people held that he was a prophet.

22 Jesus spoke to them again in para-
bles, saying: 2“The kingdom of
heaven is like a king who prepared
a wedding banquet for his son. 3He sent his ser-
vants to those who had been invited to the ban-
quet to tell them to come, but they refused to
come.
4“Then he sent some more servants and said,
‘Tell those who have been invited that I have pre-
pared my dinner: My oxen and fattened cattle
have been butchered, and everything is ready.
Come to the wedding banquet.’
5“But they paid no attention and went off—one
to his field, another to his business. 6The rest
seized his servants, mistreated them and killed
them. 7The king was enraged. He sent his army
and destroyed those murderers and burned their
city.

[k]42 Or *cornerstone* [l]42 Psalm 118:22,23 [m]44 Some manuscripts do not have verse 44.

8"Then he said to his servants, 'The wedding banquet is ready, but those I invited did not deserve to come. 9Go to the street corners and invite to the banquet anyone you find.' 10So the servants went out into the streets and gathered all the people they could find, both good and bad, and the wedding hall was filled with guests.

11"But when the king came in to see the guests, he noticed a man there who was not wearing wedding clothes. 12'Friend,' he asked, 'how did you get in here without wedding clothes?' The man was speechless.

13"Then the king told the attendants, 'Tie him hand and foot, and throw him outside, into the darkness, where there will be weeping and gnashing of teeth.'

14"For many are invited, but few are chosen."

15Then the Pharisees went out and laid plans to trap him in his words. 16They sent their disciples to him along with the Herodians. "Teacher," they said, "we know you are a man of integrity and that you teach the way of God in accordance with the truth. You aren't swayed by men, because you pay no attention to who they are. 17Tell us then, what is your opinion? Is it right to pay taxes to Caesar or not?"

18But Jesus, knowing their evil intent, said, "You hypocrites, why are you trying to trap me? 19Show me the coin used for paying the tax." They brought him a denarius, 20and he asked them, "Whose portrait is this? And whose inscription?"

21"Caesar's," they replied.

Then he said to them, "Give to Caesar what is Caesar's, and to God what is God's."

22When they heard this, they were amazed. So they left him and went away.

23That same day the Sadducees, who say there is no resurrection, came to him with a question. 24"Teacher," they said, "Moses told us that if a man dies without having children, his brother must marry the widow and have children for him. 25Now there were seven brothers among us. The first one married and died, and since he had no children, he left his wife to his brother. 26The same thing happened to the second and third brother, right on down to the seventh. 27Finally, the woman died. 28Now then, at the resurrection, whose wife will she be of the seven, since all of them were married to her?"

29Jesus replied, "You are in error because you do not know the Scriptures or the power of God. 30At the resurrection people will neither marry nor be given in marriage; they will be like the angels in heaven. 31But about the resurrection of the dead—have you not read what God said to you, 32'I am the God of Abraham, the God of Isaac, and the God of Jacob'[n]? He is not the God of the dead but of the living."

33When the crowds heard this, they were astonished at his teaching.

34Hearing that Jesus had silenced the Sadducees, the Pharisees got together. 35One of them, an expert in the law, tested him with this question: 36"Teacher, which is the greatest commandment in the Law?"

37Jesus replied: " 'Love the Lord your God with all your heart and with all your soul and with all your mind.'[o] 38This is the first and greatest commandment. 39And the second is like it: 'Love your neighbor as yourself.'[p] 40All the Law and the Prophets hang on these two commandments."

41While the Pharisees were gathered together, Jesus asked them, 42"What do you think about the Christ[q]? Whose son is he?"

"The son of David," they replied.

43He said to them, "How is it then that David, speaking by the Spirit, calls him 'Lord'? For he says,

44" 'The Lord said to my Lord:
"Sit at my right hand
until I put your enemies
under your feet." '[r]

45If then David calls him 'Lord,' how can he be his son?" 46No one could say a word in reply, and from that day on no one dared to ask him any more questions.

[n]32 Exodus 3:6 [o]37 Deut. 6:5 [p]39 Lev. 19:18 [q]42 Or *Messiah* [r]44 Psalm 110:1

Discovering the Word 1. What does the parable of the two sons reveal about the chief priests and the elders (21:28–32)? 2. How does the parable of the tenants illustrate the character of the Father, the Son and the religious leaders (21:33–46)? 3. How is the kingdom of heaven like the banquet described in 22:1–14? 4. In 22:23–28 the Sadducees tell Jesus a story designed to refute the resurrection. How does the story illustrate their ignorance of Scripture and God's power (22:29–33)? 5. Love was the foundation of the Old Testament law (22:34–40). Why do you think we have so much trouble equating God's laws with love? 6. Jesus poses a dilemma to the Pharisees that silences them: "How can the Christ be both the son of David and his Lord?" (22:41–46). What does this paradox reveal about the Lord?

Applying the Word 1. What guidance does Jesus give for fulfilling our obligations to God and the government? 2. How can these accounts of Jesus in conflict strengthen our faith in him? 3. What do they teach you about handling conflict?

Responding in Prayer Ask for the help you need for whatever conflict you face today.

17 / *Matthew 23*

The King Condemns the Rebels

INFLUENCE IS A powerful force. Those who influence others are able to change minds and to direct actions. The religious leaders in Israel possessed the power of influence. After they decided to oppose Jesus, they tried to lead others to do the same. In Matthew 23 Jesus condemns them point-blank. They should have been the first to enter the kingdom of God because of their knowledge of Scripture and their standing in the Jewish community. Because they refused, Jesus calls them to judgment. This passage exposes the guilt of those who do not practice what they preach.

Warming Up to God When have you been hurt by inconsistency in the life or teaching of an influential person you respected? Talk to God about any feelings of hurt you still have.

Read Matthew 23.

23 Then Jesus said to the crowds and
to his disciples: 2"The teachers of
the law and the Pharisees sit in Mo-
ses' seat. 3So you must obey them and do every-
thing they tell you. But do not do what they do,
for they do not practice what they preach. 4They
tie up heavy loads and put them on men's shoul-
ders, but they themselves are not willing to lift a
finger to move them.

5"Everything they do is done for men to see:
They make their phylacteries[s] wide and the tas-
sels on their garments long; 6they love the place
of honor at banquets and the most important
seats in the synagogues; 7they love to be greeted
in the marketplaces and to have men call them
'Rabbi.'

8"But you are not to be called 'Rabbi,' for you
have only one Master and you are all brothers.
9And do not call anyone on earth 'father,' for you
have one Father, and he is in heaven. 10Nor are
you to be called 'teacher,' for you have one
Teacher, the Christ.[t] 11The greatest among you
will be your servant. 12For whoever exalts himself
will be humbled, and whoever humbles himself
will be exalted.

13"Woe to you, teachers of the law and Phari-
sees, you hypocrites! You shut the kingdom of
heaven in men's faces. You yourselves do not en-
ter, nor will you let those enter who are trying
to.[u]

15"Woe to you, teachers of the law and Phari-
sees, you hypocrites! You travel over land and sea
to win a single convert, and when he becomes
one, you make him twice as much a son of hell as
you are.

16"Woe to you, blind guides! You say, 'If any-

[s]5 That is, boxes containing Scripture verses, worn on forehead and arm [t]10 Or *Messiah* [u]13 Some manuscripts *to.* [14]*Woe to you, teachers of the law and Pharisees, you hypocrites! You devour widows' houses and for a show make lengthy prayers. Therefore you will be punished more severely.*

one swears by the temple, it means nothing; but if anyone swears by the gold of the temple, he is bound by his oath.' [17]You blind fools! Which is greater: the gold, or the temple that makes the gold sacred? [18]You also say, 'If anyone swears by the altar, it means nothing; but if anyone swears by the gift on it, he is bound by his oath.' [19]You blind men! Which is greater: the gift, or the altar that makes the gift sacred? [20]Therefore, he who swears by the altar swears by it and by everything on it. [21]And he who swears by the temple swears by it and by the one who dwells in it. [22]And he who swears by heaven swears by God's throne and by the one who sits on it.

[23]"Woe to you, teachers of the law and Pharisees, you hypocrites! You give a tenth of your spices—mint, dill and cummin. But you have neglected the more important matters of the law—justice, mercy and faithfulness. You should have practiced the latter, without neglecting the former. [24]You blind guides! You strain out a gnat but swallow a camel.

[25]"Woe to you, teachers of the law and Pharisees, you hypocrites! You clean the outside of the cup and dish, but inside they are full of greed and self-indulgence. [26]Blind Pharisee! First clean the inside of the cup and dish, and then the outside also will be clean.

[27]"Woe to you, teachers of the law and Pharisees, you hypocrites! You are like whitewashed tombs, which look beautiful on the outside but on the inside are full of dead men's bones and everything unclean. [28]In the same way, on the outside you appear to people as righteous but on the inside you are full of hypocrisy and wickedness.

[29]"Woe to you, teachers of the law and Pharisees, you hypocrites! You build tombs for the prophets and decorate the graves of the righteous. [30]And you say, 'If we had lived in the days of our forefathers, we would not have taken part with them in shedding the blood of the prophets.' [31]So you testify against yourselves that you are the descendants of those who murdered the prophets. [32]Fill up, then, the measure of the sin of your forefathers!

[33]"You snakes! You brood of vipers! How will you escape being condemned to hell? [34]Therefore I am sending you prophets and wise men and teachers. Some of them you will kill and crucify; others you will flog in your synagogues and pursue from town to town. [35]And so upon you will come all the righteous blood that has been shed on earth, from the blood of righteous Abel to the blood of Zechariah son of Berekiah, whom you murdered between the temple and the altar. [36]I tell you the truth, all this will come upon this generation.

[37]"O Jerusalem, Jerusalem, you who kill the prophets and stone those sent to you, how often I have longed to gather your children together, as a hen gathers her chicks under her wings, but you were not willing. [38]Look, your house is left to you desolate. [39]For I tell you, you will not see me again until you say, 'Blessed is he who comes in the name of the Lord.'[v]"

[v]39 Psalm 118:26

Discovering the Word 1. What attitude does Jesus teach the people to have toward the religious leaders, and why (vv. 1–4)? 2. Compare the motives of the religious leaders (vv. 5–7) with the motives and attitudes Jesus requires of his followers (vv. 8–12). 3. Jesus pronounces seven woes (judgments) against the teachers of the law and the Pharisees (vv. 13–32). Summarize each one. 4. The entire generation to whom Jesus is speaking is held accountable for the "righteous blood" shed in all previous generations (vv. 33–36). Why do you think they received such a terrible sentence? 5. What responses do you have as you observe Jesus as a judge? 6. In the midst of this overwhelming condemnation, how is the tender compassion of Jesus also evident (vv. 33–39)?

Applying the Word 1. Jesus condemns the religious leaders for confusing inward and outward righteousness (vv. 25–28). In what ways are we inclined to do that today? 2. Where does this point out a place that needs to change in your life?

Responding in Prayer Ask God to make your Christian life consistent with your beliefs.

18 / *Matthew 24*
The Return of the King

WE ALL WANT to be safe and secure. Yet many things can threaten our security—losing our job, our income, our health, our loved ones. Our ability to handle these threats will depend on the source of our security. Matthew 24 focuses on the destruction of Jerusalem and the return of Christ. The true issue of Christ's return is not the "hows" or "whens" that fascinate us. Rather we must learn to live in the present in light of the future. We must learn the true source of our security.

Warming Up to God What gives you a sense of security?

Read Matthew 24.

24 Jesus left the temple and was walking away when his disciples came up to him to call his attention to its buildings. 2"Do you see all these things?" he asked. "I tell you the truth, not one stone here will be left on another; every one will be thrown down."

3As Jesus was sitting on the Mount of Olives, the disciples came to him privately. "Tell us," they said, "when will this happen, and what will be the sign of your coming and of the end of the age?"

4Jesus answered: "Watch out that no one deceives you. 5For many will come in my name, claiming, 'I am the Christ,[w]' and will deceive many. 6You will hear of wars and rumors of wars, but see to it that you are not alarmed. Such things must happen, but the end is still to come. 7Nation will rise against nation, and kingdom against kingdom. There will be famines and earthquakes in various places. 8All these are the beginning of birth pains.

9"Then you will be handed over to be persecuted and put to death, and you will be hated by all nations because of me. 10At that time many will turn away from the faith and will betray and hate each other, 11and many false prophets will appear and deceive many people. 12Because of the increase of wickedness, the love of most will grow cold, 13but he who stands firm to the end will be saved. 14And this gospel of the kingdom will be preached in the whole world as a testimony to all nations, and then the end will come.

15"So when you see standing in the holy place 'the abomination that causes desolation,'[x] spoken of through the prophet Daniel—let the reader understand— 16then let those who are in Judea flee to the mountains. 17Let no one on the roof of his house go down to take anything out of the house. 18Let no one in the field go back to get his cloak. 19How dreadful it will be in those days for pregnant women and nursing mothers! 20Pray that your flight will not take place in winter or on the Sabbath. 21For then there will be great distress, unequaled from the beginning of the world until now—and never to be equaled again. 22If those days had not been cut short, no one would survive, but for the sake of the elect those days will be shortened. 23At that time if anyone says to you, 'Look, here is the Christ!' or, 'There he is!' do not believe it. 24For false Christs and false prophets will appear and perform great signs and miracles to deceive even the elect—if that were possible. 25See, I have told you ahead of time.

26"So if anyone tells you, 'There he is, out in the desert,' do not go out; or, 'Here he is, in the inner rooms,' do not believe it. 27For as lightning that comes from the east is visible even in the west, so will be the coming of the Son of Man. 28Wherever there is a carcass, there the vultures will gather.

29"Immediately after the distress of those days

" 'the sun will be darkened,
and the moon will not give its light;
the stars will fall from the sky,
and the heavenly bodies will be shaken.'[y]

30"At that time the sign of the Son of Man will appear in the sky, and all the nations of the earth will mourn. They will see the Son of Man coming on the clouds of the sky, with power and great glory. 31And he will send his angels with a loud

[w]5 Or *Messiah*; also in verse 23 [x]15 Daniel 9:27; 11:31; 12:11
[y]29 Isaiah 13:10; 34:4

trumpet call, and they will gather his elect from
the four winds, from one end of the heavens to
the other.
32“Now learn this lesson from the fig tree: As
soon as its twigs get tender and its leaves come
out, you know that summer is near. 33Even so,
when you see all these things, you know that it[z]
is near, right at the door. 34I tell you the truth,
this generation[a] will certainly not pass away un-
til all these things have happened. 35Heaven and
earth will pass away, but my words will never
pass away.
36“No one knows about that day or hour, not
even the angels in heaven, nor the Son,[b] but only
the Father. 37As it was in the days of Noah, so it
will be at the coming of the Son of Man. 38For in
the days before the flood, people were eating and
drinking, marrying and giving in marriage, up to
the day Noah entered the ark; 39and they knew
nothing about what would happen until the flood
came and took them all away. That is how it will
be at the coming of the Son of Man. 40Two men
will be in the field; one will be taken and the
other left. 41Two women will be grinding with a
hand mill; one will be taken and the other left.
42“Therefore keep watch, because you do not
know on what day your Lord will come. 43But
understand this: If the owner of the house had
known at what time of night the thief was com-
ing, he would have kept watch and would not
have let his house be broken into. 44So you also
must be ready, because the Son of Man will come
at an hour when you do not expect him.
45“Who then is the faithful and wise servant,
whom the master has put in charge of the ser-
vants in his household to give them their food at
the proper time? 46It will be good for that servant
whose master finds him doing so when he re-
turns. 47I tell you the truth, he will put him in
charge of all his possessions. 48But suppose that
servant is wicked and says to himself, ‘My master
is staying away a long time,’ 49and he then begins
to beat his fellow servants and to eat and drink
with drunkards. 50The master of that servant will
come on a day when he does not expect him and
at an hour he is not aware of. 51He will cut him to
pieces and assign him a place with the hypocrites,
where there will be weeping and gnashing of
teeth.

[z]33 Or *he* [a]34 Or *race* [b]36 Some manuscripts do not have *nor the Son.*

Discovering the Word 1. Following Jesus' statement about the temple's destruction, the disciples ask two questions (v. 3). Look through chapter 24, briefly noting ways that Jesus answers these questions. 2. Throughout history people have set dates for Christ's return and have been mistaken. What events might deceive the disciples into thinking the end is at hand (vv. 4–8)? 3. Before the end comes, what dangers will believers face, and how are we to handle them (vv. 9–14)? 4. In 167 B.C. Antiochus Epiphanes attacked Jerusalem and set up a pagan altar in the temple—an event that anticipated “the abomination that causes desolation” spoken of by Jesus (v. 15). What occurs in the aftermath of this abomination (vv. 15–22)? 5. How will we be able to distinguish false Christs from the true (vv. 23–31)? 6. How do the parables of the thief and the wise and wicked servants (vv. 42–51) emphasize the importance of living in light of Christ's return?

Applying the Word 1. Few of us have ever faced deadly peril for our faith. What types of pressure do you face for your faith in Christ? 2. In what ways do you have need of greater watchfulness and perseverance?

Responding in Prayer Praise God for giving you an unfailing source of security.

19 / *Matthew 25*
Preparation for the King's Return

ACCOUNTABILITY can be uncomfortable and inconvenient. Our desires and preferences are subject to the demands of another. Most of us would prefer to do things our own way. A rule of thumb in management is that people don't do what you expect; they do what you inspect. Jesus is coming back to inspect our lives. He holds us accountable for how we conduct ourselves in his absence. In Matthew 25 he urges us to prepare for his coming.

Warming Up to God Have you ever been in a situation where your work did not meet up to standards when it was reviewed or inspected? How did it affect you?

Read Matthew 25.

25 "At that time the kingdom of
heaven will be like ten virgins who
took their lamps and went out to
meet the bridegroom. 2Five of them were foolish
and five were wise. 3The foolish ones took their
lamps but did not take any oil with them. 4The
wise, however, took oil in jars along with their
lamps. 5The bridegroom was a long time in coming, and they all became drowsy and fell asleep.
6"At midnight the cry rang out: 'Here's the
bridegroom! Come out to meet him!'
7"Then all the virgins woke up and trimmed
their lamps. 8The foolish ones said to the wise,
'Give us some of your oil; our lamps are going
out.'
9" 'No,' they replied, 'there may not be enough
for both us and you. Instead, go to those who sell
oil and buy some for yourselves.'
10"But while they were on their way to buy the
oil, the bridegroom arrived. The virgins who were
ready went in with him to the wedding banquet.
And the door was shut.
11"Later the others also came. 'Sir! Sir!' they
said. 'Open the door for us!'
12"But he replied, 'I tell you the truth, I don't
know you.'
13"Therefore keep watch, because you do not
know the day or the hour.
14"Again, it will be like a man going on a journey, who called his servants and entrusted his
property to them. 15To one he gave five talents[c]
of money, to another two talents, and to another
one talent, each according to his ability. Then he
went on his journey. 16The man who had received
the five talents went at once and put his money to
work and gained five more. 17So also, the one
with the two talents gained two more. 18But the
man who had received the one talent went off,
dug a hole in the ground and hid his master's
money.
19"After a long time the master of those servants returned and settled accounts with them.
20The man who had received the five talents
brought the other five. 'Master,' he said, 'you entrusted me with five talents. See, I have gained
five more.'
21"His master replied, 'Well done, good and
faithful servant! You have been faithful with a few
things; I will put you in charge of many things.
Come and share your master's happiness!'
22"The man with the two talents also came.
'Master,' he said, 'you entrusted me with two talents; see, I have gained two more.'
23"His master replied, 'Well done, good and
faithful servant! You have been faithful with a few
things; I will put you in charge of many things.
Come and share your master's happiness!'
24"Then the man who had received the one talent came. 'Master,' he said, 'I knew that you are a
hard man, harvesting where you have not sown
and gathering where you have not scattered seed.
25So I was afraid and went out and hid your talent
in the ground. See, here is what belongs to you.'
26"His master replied, 'You wicked, lazy servant! So you knew that I harvest where I have not
sown and gather where I have not scattered seed?
27Well then, you should have put my money on
deposit with the bankers, so that when I returned
I would have received it back with interest.
28" 'Take the talent from him and give it to the
one who has the ten talents. 29For everyone who
has will be given more, and he will have an abundance. Whoever does not have, even what he has
will be taken from him. 30And throw that worth-

[c]15 A talent was worth more than a thousand dollars.

less servant outside, into the darkness, where there will be weeping and gnashing of teeth.’

31“When the Son of Man comes in his glory, and all the angels with him, he will sit on his throne in heavenly glory. 32All the nations will be gathered before him, and he will separate the people one from another as a shepherd separates the sheep from the goats. 33He will put the sheep on his right and the goats on his left.

34“Then the King will say to those on his right, ‘Come, you who are blessed by my Father; take your inheritance, the kingdom prepared for you since the creation of the world. 35For I was hungry and you gave me something to eat, I was thirsty and you gave me something to drink, I was a stranger and you invited me in, 36I needed clothes and you clothed me, I was sick and you looked after me, I was in prison and you came to visit me.’

37“Then the righteous will answer him, ‘Lord, when did we see you hungry and feed you, or thirsty and give you something to drink? 38When did we see you a stranger and invite you in, or needing clothes and clothe you? 39When did we see you sick or in prison and go to visit you?’

40“The King will reply, ‘I tell you the truth, whatever you did for one of the least of these brothers of mine, you did for me.’

41“Then he will say to those on his left, ‘Depart from me, you who are cursed, into the eternal fire prepared for the devil and his angels. 42For I was hungry and you gave me nothing to eat, I was thirsty and you gave me nothing to drink, 43I was a stranger and you did not invite me in, I needed clothes and you did not clothe me, I was sick and in prison and you did not look after me.’

44“They also will answer, ‘Lord, when did we see you hungry or thirsty or a stranger or needing clothes or sick or in prison, and did not help you?’

45“He will reply, ‘I tell you the truth, whatever you did not do for one of the least of these, you did not do for me.’

46“Then they will go away to eternal punishment, but the righteous to eternal life.”

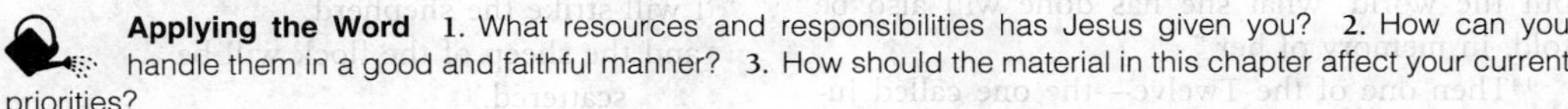

Discovering the Word 1. How does the parable of the ten virgins illustrate the need to prepare for the groom’s delayed return (vv. 1–13)? 2. A talent was a vast sum of money. In the parable of the talents, what were the master’s expectations of his servants (vv. 14–30)? 3. How does the master demonstrate his approval or disapproval? 4. In the parable of the sheep and the goats, identify the King, the sheep, the goats and the “brothers” of the King (vv. 31–46). 5. What criteria does the King use to separate the sheep from the goats? 6. According to Jesus’ teaching in this chapter, what should we be doing until he returns?

Applying the Word 1. What resources and responsibilities has Jesus given you? 2. How can you handle them in a good and faithful manner? 3. How should the material in this chapter affect your current priorities?

Responding in Prayer Ask God to show you how to serve him.

20 / *Matthew 26*
The Betrayal of the King

ON THE DRIZZLY day of October 16, 1555, Hugh Latimer and Nicholas Ridley, two influential English reformers, were tied to the stake and bundles of sticks were piled at their feet. The crowd strained to hear what the two men were saying. Would they recant or would they persist in dying as heretics? As the executioner pushed a torch into the wood, Latimer said, “Be of good comfort, Master Ridley, and play the man; we shall this day light such a candle, by God’s grace, in England, as I trust shall never be put out.” Suffering and temptation reveal the quality of our discipleship. Nowhere is this more evident than in Matthew 26, as we move into the climax of the book.

Warming Up to God Have you ever been tempted to stop following Christ? Explain.

 **Read Matthew 26.**

26

When Jesus had finished saying all these things, he said to his disciples, 2"As you know, the Passover is two days away—and the Son of Man will be handed over to be crucified."

3Then the chief priests and the elders of the people assembled in the palace of the high priest, whose name was Caiaphas, 4and they plotted to arrest Jesus in some sly way and kill him. 5"But not during the Feast," they said, "or there may be a riot among the people."

6While Jesus was in Bethany in the home of a man known as Simon the Leper, 7a woman came to him with an alabaster jar of very expensive perfume, which she poured on his head as he was reclining at the table.

8When the disciples saw this, they were indignant. "Why this waste?" they asked. 9"This perfume could have been sold at a high price and the money given to the poor."

10Aware of this, Jesus said to them, "Why are you bothering this woman? She has done a beautiful thing to me. 11The poor you will always have with you, but you will not always have me. 12When she poured this perfume on my body, she did it to prepare me for burial. 13I tell you the truth, wherever this gospel is preached throughout the world, what she has done will also be told, in memory of her."

14Then one of the Twelve—the one called Judas Iscariot—went to the chief priests 15and asked, "What are you willing to give me if I hand him over to you?" So they counted out for him thirty silver coins. 16From then on Judas watched for an opportunity to hand him over.

17On the first day of the Feast of Unleavened Bread, the disciples came to Jesus and asked, "Where do you want us to make preparations for you to eat the Passover?"

18He replied, "Go into the city to a certain man and tell him, 'The Teacher says: My appointed time is near. I am going to celebrate the Passover with my disciples at your house.' " 19So the disciples did as Jesus had directed them and prepared the Passover.

20When evening came, Jesus was reclining at the table with the Twelve. 21And while they were eating, he said, "I tell you the truth, one of you will betray me."

22They were very sad and began to say to him one after the other, "Surely not I, Lord?"

23Jesus replied, "The one who has dipped his hand into the bowl with me will betray me. 24The Son of Man will go just as it is written about him. But woe to that man who betrays the Son of Man! It would be better for him if he had not been born."

25Then Judas, the one who would betray him, said, "Surely not I, Rabbi?"

Jesus answered, "Yes, it is you."[d]

26While they were eating, Jesus took bread, gave thanks and broke it, and gave it to his disciples, saying, "Take and eat; this is my body."

27Then he took the cup, gave thanks and offered it to them, saying, "Drink from it, all of you. 28This is my blood of the[e] covenant, which is poured out for many for the forgiveness of sins. 29I tell you, I will not drink of this fruit of the vine from now on until that day when I drink it anew with you in my Father's kingdom."

30When they had sung a hymn, they went out to the Mount of Olives.

31Then Jesus told them, "This very night you will all fall away on account of me, for it is written:

" 'I will strike the shepherd,
and the sheep of the flock will be
scattered.'[f]

32But after I have risen, I will go ahead of you into Galilee."

33Peter replied, "Even if all fall away on account of you, I never will."

34"I tell you the truth," Jesus answered, "this very night, before the rooster crows, you will disown me three times."

35But Peter declared, "Even if I have to die with you, I will never disown you." And all the other disciples said the same.

36Then Jesus went with his disciples to a place called Gethsemane, and he said to them, "Sit here while I go over there and pray." 37He took Peter and the two sons of Zebedee along with him, and he began to be sorrowful and troubled. 38Then he said to them, "My soul is overwhelmed with sor-

[d] 25 Or *"You yourself have said it"* [e] 28 Some manuscripts *the new*
[f] 31 Zech. 13:7

row to the point of death. Stay here and keep watch with me."

39Going a little farther, he fell with his face to the ground and prayed, "My Father, if it is possible, may this cup be taken from me. Yet not as I will, but as you will."

40Then he returned to his disciples and found them sleeping. "Could you men not keep watch with me for one hour?" he asked Peter. 41"Watch and pray so that you will not fall into temptation. The spirit is willing, but the body is weak."

42He went away a second time and prayed, "My Father, if it is not possible for this cup to be taken away unless I drink it, may your will be done."

43When he came back, he again found them sleeping, because their eyes were heavy. 44So he left them and went away once more and prayed the third time, saying the same thing.

45Then he returned to the disciples and said to them, "Are you still sleeping and resting? Look, the hour is near, and the Son of Man is betrayed into the hands of sinners. 46Rise, let us go! Here comes my betrayer!"

47While he was still speaking, Judas, one of the Twelve, arrived. With him was a large crowd armed with swords and clubs, sent from the chief priests and the elders of the people. 48Now the betrayer had arranged a signal with them: "The one I kiss is the man; arrest him." 49Going at once to Jesus, Judas said, "Greetings, Rabbi!" and kissed him.

50Jesus replied, "Friend, do what you came for."[g]

Then the men stepped forward, seized Jesus and arrested him. 51With that, one of Jesus' companions reached for his sword, drew it out and struck the servant of the high priest, cutting off his ear.

52"Put your sword back in its place," Jesus said to him, "for all who draw the sword will die by the sword. 53Do you think I cannot call on my Father, and he will at once put at my disposal more than twelve legions of angels? 54But how then would the Scriptures be fulfilled that say it must happen in this way?"

55At that time Jesus said to the crowd, "Am I leading a rebellion, that you have come out with swords and clubs to capture me? Every day I sat in the temple courts teaching, and you did not arrest me. 56But this has all taken place that the writings of the prophets might be fulfilled." Then all the disciples deserted him and fled.

57Those who had arrested Jesus took him to Caiaphas, the high priest, where the teachers of the law and the elders had assembled. 58But Peter followed him at a distance, right up to the courtyard of the high priest. He entered and sat down with the guards to see the outcome.

59The chief priests and the whole Sanhedrin were looking for false evidence against Jesus so that they could put him to death. 60But they did not find any, though many false witnesses came forward.

Finally two came forward 61and declared, "This fellow said, 'I am able to destroy the temple of God and rebuild it in three days.' "

62Then the high priest stood up and said to Jesus, "Are you not going to answer? What is this testimony that these men are bringing against you?" 63But Jesus remained silent.

The high priest said to him, "I charge you under oath by the living God: Tell us if you are the Christ,[h] the Son of God."

64"Yes, it is as you say," Jesus replied. "But I say to all of you: In the future you will see the Son of Man sitting at the right hand of the Mighty One and coming on the clouds of heaven."

65Then the high priest tore his clothes and said, "He has spoken blasphemy! Why do we need any more witnesses? Look, now you have heard the blasphemy. 66What do you think?"

"He is worthy of death," they answered.

67Then they spit in his face and struck him with their fists. Others slapped him 68and said, "Prophesy to us, Christ. Who hit you?"

69Now Peter was sitting out in the courtyard, and a servant girl came to him. "You also were with Jesus of Galilee," she said.

70But he denied it before them all. "I don't know what you're talking about," he said.

71Then he went out to the gateway, where another girl saw him and said to the people there, "This fellow was with Jesus of Nazareth."

72He denied it again, with an oath: "I don't know the man!"

73After a little while, those standing there went up to Peter and said, "Surely you are one of them, for your accent gives you away."

74Then he began to call down curses on himself and he swore to them, "I don't know the man!"

Immediately a rooster crowed. 75Then Peter remembered the word Jesus had spoken: "Before the rooster crows, you will disown me three times." And he went outside and wept bitterly.

[g]50 Or *"Friend, why have you come?"* [h]63 Or *Messiah*; also in verse 68

Discovering the Word 1. How do verses 1–16 set the stage for Jesus' betrayal and death? 2. In verses 17–30 Jesus celebrates the Passover with his disciples. How is this occasion both ominous and hopeful? 3. What insights can we gain about Jesus during his time in Gethsemane (vv. 36–45)? 4. Jesus' betrayal comes at the hand of one of his own disciples (vv. 47–50). As you look over the role of Judas in this chapter, why do you think the religious leaders used him? 5. Why do you think Jesus remained silent during the first part of his trial (vv. 57–63)? 6. In answer to the high priest's question (v. 63), Jesus declares that he is the Christ (alluding to Dan 7:13–14). Describe the immediate—and ultimate—impact of Jesus' words on those present (vv. 65–68).

Applying the Word 1. When have you been confronted with the weakness of your commitment to the Lord? 2. Both Jesus and the disciples faced temptation in this chapter. How can Jesus' example and the disciples' failures help us withstand temptation and testing?

Responding in Prayer Ask God to give you the courage to claim allegiance to Christ.

21 / *Matthew 27*
The Crucifixion of the King

MY GOD, MY God, why have you forsaken me?
Why are you so far from saving me, so far from the words of my groaning?
O my God, I cry out by day, but you do not answer, by night, and am not silent. (Ps 22:1–2)

Do you ever feel that God is absent when you need him most? You pray but receive no answer. You cry but no one seems to care. As Pilate and the religious leaders condemn, mock and crucify God's Son, God himself seems strangely absent. Those who trust in the midst of roaring silence will in the end discover that God was there all along.

Warming Up to God When have you felt as though God were absent when you needed him? Talk to God about how you felt.

Read Matthew 27.

27 Early in the morning, all the chief
priests and the elders of the people
came to the decision to put Jesus to
death. 2They bound him, led him away and
handed him over to Pilate, the governor.
3When Judas, who had betrayed him, saw that
Jesus was condemned, he was seized with re-
morse and returned the thirty silver coins to the
chief priests and the elders. 4"I have sinned," he
said, "for I have betrayed innocent blood."
"What is that to us?" they replied. "That's your
responsibility."
5So Judas threw the money into the temple and
left. Then he went away and hanged himself.
6The chief priests picked up the coins and said,
"It is against the law to put this into the treasury,
since it is blood money." 7So they decided to use
the money to buy the potter's field as a burial
place for foreigners. 8That is why it has been
called the Field of Blood to this day. 9Then what
was spoken by Jeremiah the prophet was fulfilled:
"They took the thirty silver coins, the price set on
him by the people of Israel, 10and they used them
to buy the potter's field, as the Lord commanded
me."[i]
11Meanwhile Jesus stood before the governor,
and the governor asked him, "Are you the king of
the Jews?"
"Yes, it is as you say," Jesus replied.
12When he was accused by the chief priests and
the elders, he gave no answer. 13Then Pilate asked
him, "Don't you hear the testimony they are
bringing against you?" 14But Jesus made no reply,

[i]10 See Zech. 11:12,13; Jer. 19:1-13; 32:6-9.

not even to a single charge—to the great amazement of the governor.

15Now it was the governor's custom at the Feast to release a prisoner chosen by the crowd. 16At that time they had a notorious prisoner, called Barabbas. 17So when the crowd had gathered, Pilate asked them, "Which one do you want me to release to you: Barabbas, or Jesus who is called Christ?" 18For he knew it was out of envy that they had handed Jesus over to him.

19While Pilate was sitting on the judge's seat, his wife sent him this message: "Don't have anything to do with that innocent man, for I have suffered a great deal today in a dream because of him."

20But the chief priests and the elders persuaded the crowd to ask for Barabbas and to have Jesus executed.

21"Which of the two do you want me to release to you?" asked the governor.

"Barabbas," they answered.

22"What shall I do, then, with Jesus who is called Christ?" Pilate asked.

They all answered, "Crucify him!"

23"Why? What crime has he committed?" asked Pilate.

But they shouted all the louder, "Crucify him!"

24When Pilate saw that he was getting nowhere, but that instead an uproar was starting, he took water and washed his hands in front of the crowd. "I am innocent of this man's blood," he said. "It is your responsibility!"

25All the people answered, "Let his blood be on us and on our children!"

26Then he released Barabbas to them. But he had Jesus flogged, and handed him over to be crucified.

27Then the governor's soldiers took Jesus into the Praetorium and gathered the whole company of soldiers around him. 28They stripped him and put a scarlet robe on him, 29and then twisted together a crown of thorns and set it on his head. They put a staff in his right hand and knelt in front of him and mocked him. "Hail, king of the Jews!" they said. 30They spit on him, and took the staff and struck him on the head again and again. 31After they had mocked him, they took off the robe and put his own clothes on him. Then they led him away to crucify him.

32As they were going out, they met a man from Cyrene, named Simon, and they forced him to carry the cross. 33They came to a place called Golgotha (which means The Place of the Skull). 34There they offered Jesus wine to drink, mixed with gall; but after tasting it, he refused to drink it. 35When they had crucified him, they divided up his clothes by casting lots.[j] 36And sitting down, they kept watch over him there. 37Above his head they placed the written charge against him: THIS IS JESUS, THE KING OF THE JEWS. 38Two robbers were crucified with him, one on his right and one on his left. 39Those who passed by hurled insults at him, shaking their heads 40and saying, "You who are going to destroy the temple and build it in three days, save yourself! Come down from the cross, if you are the Son of God!"

41In the same way the chief priests, the teachers of the law and the elders mocked him. 42"He saved others," they said, "but he can't save himself! He's the King of Israel! Let him come down now from the cross, and we will believe in him. 43He trusts in God. Let God rescue him now if he wants him, for he said, 'I am the Son of God.'" 44In the same way the robbers who were crucified with him also heaped insults on him.

45From the sixth hour until the ninth hour darkness came over all the land. 46About the ninth hour Jesus cried out in a loud voice, "*Eloi, Eloi,*[k] *lama sabachthani?*"—which means, "My God, my God, why have you forsaken me?"[l]

47When some of those standing there heard this, they said, "He's calling Elijah."

48Immediately one of them ran and got a sponge. He filled it with wine vinegar, put it on a stick, and offered it to Jesus to drink. 49The rest said, "Now leave him alone. Let's see if Elijah comes to save him."

50And when Jesus had cried out again in a loud voice, he gave up his spirit.

51At that moment the curtain of the temple was torn in two from top to bottom. The earth shook and the rocks split. 52The tombs broke open and the bodies of many holy people who had died were raised to life. 53They came out of the tombs, and after Jesus' resurrection they went into the holy city and appeared to many people.

54When the centurion and those with him who were guarding Jesus saw the earthquake and all that had happened, they were terrified, and exclaimed, "Surely he was the Son[m] of God!"

55Many women were there, watching from a

j35 A few late manuscripts *lots that the word spoken by the prophet might be fulfilled: "They divided my garments among themselves and cast lots for my clothing"* (Psalm 22:18) k46 Some manuscripts *Eli, Eli* l46 Psalm 22:1 m54 Or *a son*

distance. They had followed Jesus from Galilee to
care for his needs. 56Among them were Mary
Magdalene, Mary the mother of James and Joses,
and the mother of Zebedee's sons.
57As evening approached, there came a rich
man from Arimathea, named Joseph, who had
himself become a disciple of Jesus. 58Going to Pi-
late, he asked for Jesus' body, and Pilate ordered
that it be given to him. 59Joseph took the body,
wrapped it in a clean linen cloth, 60and placed it
in his own new tomb that he had cut out of the
rock. He rolled a big stone in front of the entrance
to the tomb and went away. 61Mary Magdalene
and the other Mary were sitting there opposite
the tomb.
62The next day, the one after Preparation Day,
the chief priests and the Pharisees went to Pilate.
63"Sir," they said, "we remember that while he
was still alive that deceiver said, 'After three days
I will rise again.' 64So give the order for the tomb
to be made secure until the third day. Otherwise,
his disciples may come and steal the body and tell
the people that he has been raised from the dead.
This last deception will be worse than the
first."
65"Take a guard," Pilate answered. "Go, make
the tomb as secure as you know how." 66So they
went and made the tomb secure by putting a seal
on the stone and posting the guard.

Discovering the Word 1. After the religious leaders hand Jesus over to Pilate, Judas feels remorse (vv. 1–5). How is remorse different from repentance? 2. Jesus stands before Pilate in verses 11–26. How and why does Pilate seek to avoid sentencing Jesus? 3. The soldiers viciously mock Jesus in verses 27–31. What does their mockery reveal about their knowledge of Jesus? 4. As Jesus hangs on the cross, he is repeatedly mocked and insulted (vv. 32–44). How do these insults reveal the spiritual choices these people have made? 5. As death begins to engulf him, Jesus cries out to God (vv. 45–46). What does his cry, and the overshadowing darkness, reveal about his relationship to the Father during this torment? 6. Observe the role Jesus' followers play during the events of his crucifixion and burial (vv. 55–61). How do you think they felt?

Applying the Word 1. This chapter is filled with irony. Satan's "triumph" is actually his defeat. Christ's "defeat" is actually his triumph. How should this challenge our views about the way God works in our lives?

Responding in Prayer Pray for protection so that you won't succumb to social pressure.

22/ *Matthew 28*
The Resurrection of the King

VICTORY REQUIRES PROCLAMATION! Once a battle has been won, it's time to spread the word. Matthew 28 focuses on the messengers of Jesus' resurrection—the angel tells the women, the women tell the disciples, the disciples tell the nations, even the guards tell the religious leaders. As Matthew concludes his Gospel, we are invited to join with those who throughout history have been witnesses and messengers of Jesus, the victorious resurrected Lord.

Warming Up to God To prepare for this study, recall the joy of an Easter celebration you have experienced. What elements made that joyful for you?

Read Matthew 28.

28 After the Sabbath, at dawn on the
first day of the week, Mary Magda-
lene and the other Mary went to
look at the tomb.
2There was a violent earthquake, for an angel of
the Lord came down from heaven and, going to
the tomb, rolled back the stone and sat on it. 3His
appearance was like lightning, and his clothes
were white as snow. 4The guards were so afraid of
him that they shook and became like dead men.

5The angel said to the women, "Do not be afraid, for I know that you are looking for Jesus, who was crucified. 6He is not here; he has risen, just as he said. Come and see the place where he lay. 7Then go quickly and tell his disciples: 'He has risen from the dead and is going ahead of you into Galilee. There you will see him.' Now I have told you."

8So the women hurried away from the tomb, afraid yet filled with joy, and ran to tell his disciples. 9Suddenly Jesus met them. "Greetings," he said. They came to him, clasped his feet and worshiped him. 10Then Jesus said to them, "Do not be afraid. Go and tell my brothers to go to Galilee; there they will see me."

11While the women were on their way, some of the guards went into the city and reported to the chief priests everything that had happened. 12When the chief priests had met with the elders and devised a plan, they gave the soldiers a large sum of money, 13telling them, "You are to say, 'His disciples came during the night and stole him away while we were asleep.' 14If this report gets to the governor, we will satisfy him and keep you out of trouble." 15So the soldiers took the money and did as they were instructed. And this story has been widely circulated among the Jews to this very day.

16Then the eleven disciples went to Galilee, to the mountain where Jesus had told them to go. 17When they saw him, they worshiped him; but some doubted. 18Then Jesus came to them and said, "All authority in heaven and on earth has been given to me. 19Therefore go and make disciples of all nations, baptizing them in[n] the name of the Father and of the Son and of the Holy Spirit, 20and teaching them to obey everything I have commanded you. And surely I am with you always, to the very end of the age."

n19 Or *into*; see Acts 8:16; 19:5; Romans 6:3; 1 Cor. 1:13; 10:2 and Gal. 3:27.

Discovering the Word 1. The angel is the first messenger of the resurrection (vv. 2–7). What is the significance of his appearance and words? 2. Consider the mission of the women (vv. 1–9). How does it undergo a radical change? 3. The Roman guard and the Jewish leaders are confronted with a miracle. How do they respond, and why? 4. The disciples go to Galilee where they meet with Jesus. Describe the commission he gives to them and us (vv. 16–20). 5. How does Jesus equip them and future disciples to carry out his commission?

Applying the Word 1. What keeps people today from believing that Jesus is the resurrected Lord? 2. As you conclude this study of Matthew, how can you be more involved in making disciples and fulfilling the Great Commission?

Responding in Prayer Pray that God will help you to be faithful to this task.

Mark

Few Americans put much stock in royalty. We have been raised to treasure the spirit of democracy. But democracy, at least on any large scale, is a recent development in human history.

People in other eras were most accustomed to kings. For good or evil, kings and emperors left their mark on daily life. Thus when a new king came to power, whether through natural succession or through victory in battle, questions clamored in people's minds. What would the new king be like? Would he be kind and compassionate or selfish and ruthless? Would he use his power to serve his own ends, or would he seek the welfare of all his subjects?

The Jews of Jesus' day, long oppressed by foreign rulers, yearned for a new king—one whom God himself would anoint and use to establish his own rule of justice and peace, not only over Israel but over all the earth. Imagine the excitement as John the Baptist came announcing the coming of the Lord as king and as Jesus himself announced, "The time has come. The kingdom of God is near." Yet as Jesus continued his ministry, he met a growing wave of opposition. Not everyone was pleased with the kind of kingdom he seemed to be announcing or with who he proclaimed himself to be. The religious rulers especially opposed him, but the common people heard him gladly.

New Testament scholars, with few exceptions, agree that Mark's Gospel is the earliest written account of Jesus' life and ministry. Composed between A.D. 60 and 70, it likely served as the basis for the Gospels of Matthew and Luke. Mark himself, though not one of the Twelve, was probably an early convert (Acts 12:12) and a companion to both Peter (1 Pe 5:13) and Paul. Though Mark had an early falling out with Paul (Acts 15:36–41), the two were clearly reconciled later on (Co 4:10; 2Ti 4:11; Phm 24). Thus Mark is linked to two of the most prominent apostles.

More and more, scholars are coming to believe that Mark was not just a collector of stories about Jesus but that he gave form and shape to these stories to counteract some dangerous distortions of the gospel message. Apparently some Christians so focused on Jesus' deity and glorious resurrection that they began to ignore his humanity and suffering. As a result they expected to be spared suffering in this life and to quickly join Jesus in the glories of heaven. You can well imagine how their faith may have been shaken when Nero took to using some of them as torches!

Mark theologically and pastorally sets out to retell the story of Jesus, showing that the kingdom in its glory comes at the end of the path of suffering and service. While Matthew focuses on Jesus as the teacher from whom we should learn (Mt 11:29; 28:20) and John focuses on him as the Son of God in whom we should believe (Jn 20:31), Mark portrays Jesus principally as the servant-king whom we should follow (Mk 1:17). Thus, if we are to enjoy the glories of the kingdom, we too must follow the road of suffering and service.

May the Lord himself increase your understanding of who he is and the life to which he has called you.

Outline

1 / *Mark 1:1–15*
Gospel Beginnings

DO YOU HAVE any friends who begin mystery novels at the back? Like endings, beginnings tell us a lot. In them writers set the context for what is to come and often drop hints which later prove to be important. The beginning of Mark's Gospel is no exception. This passage introduces several important themes which will be developed in the following chapters.

Warming Up to God What does it mean to you that Jesus is King? What images and feelings does that bring to mind? Meditate on Jesus as King for a while in preparation for reading Mark's Gospel.

Read Mark 1:1–15.

1 The beginning of the gospel about Jesus
Christ, the Son of God.[a]

2It is written in Isaiah the prophet:

"I will send my messenger ahead of you,
who will prepare your way"[b]—
3"a voice of one calling in the desert,
'Prepare the way for the Lord,
make straight paths for him.' "[c]

4And so John came, baptizing in the desert region
and preaching a baptism of repentance for the
forgiveness of sins. 5The whole Judean country-
side and all the people of Jerusalem went out to
him. Confessing their sins, they were baptized by
him in the Jordan River. 6John wore clothing
made of camel's hair, with a leather belt around
his waist, and he ate locusts and wild honey.
7And this was his message: "After me will come
one more powerful than I, the thongs of whose
sandals I am not worthy to stoop down and untie.
8I baptize you with[d] water, but he will baptize
you with the Holy Spirit."

9At that time Jesus came from Nazareth in Gali-
lee and was baptized by John in the Jordan. 10As
Jesus was coming up out of the water, he saw
heaven being torn open and the Spirit descending
on him like a dove. 11And a voice came from
heaven: "You are my Son, whom I love; with you
I am well pleased."

12At once the Spirit sent him out into the
desert, 13and he was in the desert forty days, be-
ing tempted by Satan. He was with the wild ani-
mals, and angels attended him.

14After John was put in prison, Jesus went into
Galilee, proclaiming the good news of God.
15"The time has come," he said. "The kingdom of
God is near. Repent and believe the good news!"

[a]1 Some manuscripts do not have *the Son of God.* [b]2 Mal. 3:1
[c]3 Isaiah 40:3 [d]8 Or *in*

Discovering the Word 1. Verses 2 and 3 combine quotations from Malachi and Isaiah. What do these two quotations have in common? 2. How does John's ministry prepare the way for Jesus? 3. How does John emphasize the greatness of the one who will come after him (vv. 7–8)? 4. Despite his greatness, Jesus came to John for baptism. What does this tell us about Jesus' relationship to us? 5. How do the events surrounding Jesus' baptism prepare him for his temptation in the desert? 6. How does Jesus summarize his mission at the beginning of his ministry?

Applying the Word 1. What temptations are you currently struggling with? 2. What encouragement do you find here for facing your own temptations?

Responding in Prayer Ask God to help you find the encouragement and strength you need to face temptation.

2 / *Mark 1:16–39*
Four Portraits

WE ALL LIVE with authority—whether supervisors, professors, parents or police. And depending on how that authority is exercised, we feel either put upon, trapped and used, or we feel secure, free and useful.

In 1:1–15 Mark has told us that Jesus has come as king to fulfill the Old Testament longings for the Lord's rule over all the earth. But what kind of king is he? Mark, it seems, knows that a picture is worth a thousand words. So, rather than offering an abstract character analysis, he paints four verbal portraits of Jesus in action.

Warming Up to God In this passage we see Jesus going to a solitary place to pray after a busy day of ministry. But even here he is interrupted with more needs. When have you been in that kind of situation? Ask God to help you balance your need to be with him with the needs of others.

Read Mark 1:16–39.

16As Jesus walked beside the Sea of Galilee, he saw Simon and his brother Andrew casting a net into the lake, for they were fishermen. 17"Come, follow me," Jesus said, "and I will make you fishers of men." 18At once they left their nets and followed him.

19When he had gone a little farther, he saw James son of Zebedee and his brother John in a boat, preparing their nets. 20Without delay he called them, and they left their father Zebedee in the boat with the hired men and followed him.

21They went to Capernaum, and when the Sabbath came, Jesus went into the synagogue and began to teach. 22The people were amazed at his teaching, because he taught them as one who had authority, not as the teachers of the law. 23Just then a man in their synagogue who was possessed by an evil[c] spirit cried out, 24"What do you want with us, Jesus of Nazareth? Have you come to destroy us? I know who you are—the Holy One of God!"

25"Be quiet!" said Jesus sternly. "Come out of him!" 26The evil spirit shook the man violently and came out of him with a shriek.

27The people were all so amazed that they asked each other, "What is this? A new teaching—and with authority! He even gives orders to evil spirits and they obey him." 28News about him spread quickly over the whole region of Galilee.

29As soon as they left the synagogue, they went with James and John to the home of Simon and Andrew. 30Simon's mother-in-law was in bed with a fever, and they told Jesus about her. 31So he went to her, took her hand and helped her up. The fever left her and she began to wait on them.

32That evening after sunset the people brought to Jesus all the sick and demon-possessed. 33The whole town gathered at the door, 34and Jesus healed many who had various diseases. He also drove out many demons, but he would not let the demons speak because they knew who he was.

35Very early in the morning, while it was still dark, Jesus got up, left the house and went off to a solitary place, where he prayed. 36Simon and his companions went to look for him, 37and when they found him, they exclaimed: "Everyone is looking for you!"

38Jesus replied, "Let us go somewhere else—to the nearby villages—so I can preach there also. That is why I have come." 39So he traveled throughout Galilee, preaching in their synagogues and driving out demons.

c23 Greek *unclean*; also in verses 26 and 27

Discovering the Word 1. What different factors contributed to the ready response of Simon, Andrew, James and John to Jesus' invitation (vv. 16–20)? (Don't forget 1:1–15!) 2. What might be some of the reasons that Jesus silences the demon about who he is (vv. 21–28)? 3. What impression of Jesus do you get from the portrait of his visit to the home of Simon and Andrew (vv. 29–34)? 4. Thus far we have looked at three portraits of Jesus. What aspects of Jesus' character do we see in them? 5. How does Jesus exercise his authority differently from kings and dictators and other human authorities? 6. The quiet and solitude of verses 35–39 are quite a contrast from the previous events. What do these verses reveal about Jesus' priorities?

Applying the Word 1. How do you respond to Jesus' authority? 2. Jesus' priorities are clear in this passage. What steps do you need to take to bring your priorities more closely in line with his?

Responding in Prayer Ask God to help you reevaluate your priorities in light of Jesus' kingship.

3 / *Mark 1:40—2:17*
The Clean and the Unclean

"UNCLEAN! UNCLEAN!" THE man shouted, and everyone scattered to avoid contact with the leper—everyone except Jesus.

The religious wisdom of the day demanded that a holy man keep away from the common people, the "sinners." So Jesus was bound to encounter resistance as he openly welcomed them. This passage focuses on Christ's compassion toward those we normally avoid.

Warming Up to God What is it about yourself that you feel is "unclean"? Confess your sins to God and hear him declare you to be clean once again.

Read Mark 1:40—2:17.

40A man with leprosy[f] came to him and
begged him on his knees, "If you are willing, you
can make me clean."
41Filled with compassion, Jesus reached out his
hand and touched the man. "I am willing," he
said. "Be clean!" 42Immediately the leprosy left
him and he was cured.
43Jesus sent him away at once with a strong
warning: 44"See that you don't tell this to anyone.
But go, show yourself to the priest and offer the
sacrifices that Moses commanded for your cleans-
ing, as a testimony to them." 45Instead he went
out and began to talk freely, spreading the news.
As a result, Jesus could no longer enter a town
openly but stayed outside in lonely places. Yet the
people still came to him from everywhere.

2 A few days later, when Jesus again en-
tered Capernaum, the people heard that
he had come home. 2So many gathered
that there was no room left, not even outside the
door, and he preached the word to them. 3Some
men came, bringing to him a paralytic, carried by
four of them. 4Since they could not get him to
Jesus because of the crowd, they made an opening
in the roof above Jesus and, after digging through
it, lowered the mat the paralyzed man was lying
on. 5When Jesus saw their faith, he said to the
paralytic, "Son, your sins are forgiven."
6Now some teachers of the law were sitting
there, thinking to themselves, 7"Why does this
fellow talk like that? He's blaspheming! Who can
forgive sins but God alone?"
8Immediately Jesus knew in his spirit that this
was what they were thinking in their hearts, and
he said to them, "Why are you thinking these
things? 9Which is easier: to say to the paralytic,
'Your sins are forgiven,' or to say, 'Get up, take
your mat and walk'? 10But that you may know
that the Son of Man has authority on earth to
forgive sins . . . ." He said to the paralytic, 11"I tell
you, get up, take your mat and go home." 12He
got up, took his mat and walked out in full view
of them all. This amazed everyone and they
praised God, saying, "We have never seen any-
thing like this!"
13Once again Jesus went out beside the lake. A
large crowd came to him, and he began to teach
them. 14As he walked along, he saw Levi son of
Alphaeus sitting at the tax collector's booth. "Fol-
low me," Jesus told him, and Levi got up and
followed him.
15While Jesus was having dinner at Levi's
house, many tax collectors and "sinners" were
eating with him and his disciples, for there were
many who followed him. 16When the teachers of
the law who were Pharisees saw him eating with

f40 The Greek word was used for various diseases affecting the skin—not necessarily leprosy.

the "sinners" and tax collectors, they asked his
disciples: "Why does he eat with tax collectors
and 'sinners'?"

17On hearing this, Jesus said to them, "It is not
the healthy who need a doctor, but the sick. I
have not come to call the righteous, but sinners."

Discovering the Word 1. Leviticus 13:45–46 states that a leper "must wear torn clothes, let his hair be unkempt, cover the lower part of his face and cry out, 'Unclean! Unclean!' As long as he has the infection he remains unclean. He must live alone; he must live outside the camp." What risks did the leper take in coming to Jesus (1:40–45)? 2. What risks did Jesus take in responding to him as he did? 3. How does Jesus respond to the man's total need? 4. Imagine that you are the paralytic being lowered before Jesus (2:1–12). How do you feel, especially when Jesus announces, "Son, your sins are forgiven"? 5. Contrast the Pharisees' attitude toward tax collectors and "sinners" with that of Jesus.

Applying the Word 1. Who do you consider to be some of the "unlovely" or "unreachable" for God's kingdom? 2. What steps can you take to bring your thoughts and actions toward them into line with those of Jesus?

Responding in Prayer Ask Jesus to help you see people as he does and act toward them as he would.

4 / *Mark 2:18—3:35*
Conflict in Galilee

"A TRULY RELIGIOUS person wouldn't do such a thing!"

"Religion is fine, but you're becoming a fanatic!"

Such accusations are commonly leveled at Christians. They are difficult to bear under any circumstances. But when they come from family and friends, the pain is even greater. This passage looks at some of the pressures and privileges of following Jesus.

Warming Up to God In what area of your life are you currently facing pressure or conflict? Ask God to provide you with the strength you need in that situation through his Word and the Holy Spirit.

Read Mark 2:18—3:35.

18Now John's disciples and the Pharisees were
fasting. Some people came and asked Jesus, "How
is it that John's disciples and the disciples of the
Pharisees are fasting, but yours are not?"

19Jesus answered, "How can the guests of the
bridegroom fast while he is with them? They can-
not, so long as they have him with them. 20But
the time will come when the bridegroom will be
taken from them, and on that day they will fast.

21"No one sews a patch of unshrunk cloth on
an old garment. If he does, the new piece will pull
away from the old, making the tear worse. 22And
no one pours new wine into old wineskins. If he
does, the wine will burst the skins, and both the
wine and the wineskins will be ruined. No, he
pours new wine into new wineskins."

23One Sabbath Jesus was going through the
grainfields, and as his disciples walked along,
they began to pick some heads of grain. 24The
Pharisees said to him, "Look, why are they doing
what is unlawful on the Sabbath?"

25He answered, "Have you never read what Da-
vid did when he and his companions were hungry
and in need? 26In the days of Abiathar the high
priest, he entered the house of God and ate the
consecrated bread, which is lawful only for
priests to eat. And he also gave some to his com-
panions."

27Then he said to them, "The Sabbath was
made for man, not man for the Sabbath. 28So the
Son of Man is Lord even of the Sabbath."

3 Another time he went into the synagogue,
and a man with a shriveled hand was
there. 2Some of them were looking for a
reason to accuse Jesus, so they watched him
closely to see if he would heal him on the Sab-
bath. 3Jesus said to the man with the shriveled
hand, "Stand up in front of everyone."
4Then Jesus asked them, "Which is lawful on
the Sabbath: to do good or to do evil, to save life
or to kill?" But they remained silent.
5He looked around at them in anger and,
deeply distressed at their stubborn hearts, said to
the man, "Stretch out your hand." He stretched it
out, and his hand was completely restored. 6Then
the Pharisees went out and began to plot with the
Herodians how they might kill Jesus.
7Jesus withdrew with his disciples to the lake,
and a large crowd from Galilee followed. 8When
they heard all he was doing, many people came to
him from Judea, Jerusalem, Idumea, and the re-
gions across the Jordan and around Tyre and Si-
don. 9Because of the crowd he told his disciples to
have a small boat ready for him, to keep the peo-
ple from crowding him. 10For he had healed
many, so that those with diseases were pushing
forward to touch him. 11Whenever the evil[g] spir-
its saw him, they fell down before him and cried
out, "You are the Son of God." 12But he gave them
strict orders not to tell who he was.
13Jesus went up on a mountainside and called
to him those he wanted, and they came to him.
14He appointed twelve—designating them apos-
tles[h]—that they might be with him and that he
might send them out to preach 15and to have au-
thority to drive out demons. 16These are the
twelve he appointed: Simon (to whom he gave
the name Peter); 17James son of Zebedee and his
brother John (to them he gave the name Boaner-
ges, which means Sons of Thunder); 18Andrew,
Philip, Bartholomew, Matthew, Thomas, James
son of Alphaeus, Thaddaeus, Simon the Zealot
19and Judas Iscariot, who betrayed him.
20Then Jesus entered a house, and again a
crowd gathered, so that he and his disciples were
not even able to eat. 21When his family heard
about this, they went to take charge of him, for
they said, "He is out of his mind."
22And the teachers of the law who came down
from Jerusalem said, "He is possessed by Beelze-
bub[i]! By the prince of demons he is driving out
demons."
23So Jesus called them and spoke to them in
parables: "How can Satan drive out Satan? 24If a
kingdom is divided against itself, that kingdom
cannot stand. 25If a house is divided against itself,
that house cannot stand. 26And if Satan opposes
himself and is divided, he cannot stand; his end
has come. 27In fact, no one can enter a strong
man's house and carry off his possessions unless
he first ties up the strong man. Then he can rob
his house. 28I tell you the truth, all the sins and
blasphemies of men will be forgiven them. 29But
whoever blasphemes against the Holy Spirit will
never be forgiven; he is guilty of an eternal sin."
30He said this because they were saying, "He
has an evil spirit."
31Then Jesus' mother and brothers arrived.
Standing outside, they sent someone in to call
him. 32A crowd was sitting around him, and they
told him, "Your mother and brothers are outside
looking for you."
33"Who are my mother and my brothers?" he
asked.
34Then he looked at those seated in a circle
around him and said, "Here are my mother and
my brothers! 35Whoever does God's will is my
brother and sister and mother."

[g]11 Greek *unclean*; also in verse 30 [h]14 Some manuscripts do not have *designating them apostles.* [i]22 Greek *Beezeboul* or *Beelzeboul*

Discovering the Word 1. On what grounds are Jesus and his disciples criticized in 2:18—3:6? 2. How are Jesus' and the Pharisees' attitudes toward the Sabbath different? 3. While the Pharisees and the Herodians are plotting to kill Jesus, how are the common people responding to him (3:7–12)? 4. What charge do the teachers of the law bring against Jesus in 3:20–30? 5. How does Jesus refute it?

Applying the Word 1. What types of opposition have you encountered as a Christian? 2. How have you dealt with experiences of opposition? 3. When you are opposed or rejected by those who are closest to you, what comfort can you receive from Jesus' words in verses 33–35?

Responding in Prayer Ask God to give you courage to follow him even when others stand against you.

5 / *Mark 4:1–34*
Kingdom Parables

SOME STORIES WEAR their points on their sleeves, as it were. Others, to borrow from P. G. Wodehouse's definition of a parable, keep something up their sleeves "which suddenly pops up and knocks you flat." Among Jesus' stories we find a variety—from those that are easy to understand to those that are so difficult they invite our thought and reflection again and again. The stories in this passage contain vital information about God's kingdom and its subjects—for those who have ears to hear!

Warming Up to God What aspect in your life makes it difficult for you to hear the voice of Christ? Talk to Jesus about the barriers you face and ask him to show you how to remove them.

Read Mark 4:1–34.

4 Again Jesus began to teach by the lake.
The crowd that gathered around him was
so large that he got into a boat and sat in
it out on the lake, while all the people were along
the shore at the water's edge. 2He taught them
many things by parables, and in his teaching said:
3"Listen! A farmer went out to sow his seed. 4As
he was scattering the seed, some fell along the
path, and the birds came and ate it up. 5Some fell
on rocky places, where it did not have much soil.
It sprang up quickly, because the soil was shal-
low. 6But when the sun came up, the plants were
scorched, and they withered because they had no
root. 7Other seed fell among thorns, which grew
up and choked the plants, so that they did not
bear grain. 8Still other seed fell on good soil. It
came up, grew and produced a crop, multiplying
thirty, sixty, or even a hundred times."

9Then Jesus said, "He who has ears to hear, let
him hear."

10When he was alone, the Twelve and the oth-
ers around him asked him about the parables.
11He told them, "The secret of the kingdom of
God has been given to you. But to those on the
outside everything is said in parables 12so that,

" 'they may be ever seeing but never
perceiving,
and ever hearing but never understanding;
otherwise they might turn and be
forgiven!'[j]"

13Then Jesus said to them, "Don't you under-
stand this parable? How then will you understand
any parable? 14The farmer sows the word. 15Some
people are like seed along the path, where the
word is sown. As soon as they hear it, Satan
comes and takes away the word that was sown in
them. 16Others, like seed sown on rocky places,
hear the word and at once receive it with joy.
17But since they have no root, they last only a
short time. When trouble or persecution comes
because of the word, they quickly fall away. 18Still
others, like seed sown among thorns, hear the
word; 19but the worries of this life, the deceitful-
ness of wealth and the desires for other things
come in and choke the word, making it unfruit-
ful. 20Others, like seed sown on good soil, hear
the word, accept it, and produce a crop—thirty,
sixty or even a hundred times what was sown."

21He said to them, "Do you bring in a lamp to
put it under a bowl or a bed? Instead, don't you
put it on its stand? 22For whatever is hidden is
meant to be disclosed, and whatever is concealed
is meant to be brought out into the open. 23If
anyone has ears to hear, let him hear."

24"Consider carefully what you hear," he con-
tinued. "With the measure you use, it will be
measured to you—and even more. 25Whoever
has will be given more; whoever does not have,
even what he has will be taken from him."

26He also said, "This is what the kingdom of
God is like. A man scatters seed on the ground.
27Night and day, whether he sleeps or gets up, the
seed sprouts and grows, though he does not
know how. 28All by itself the soil produces
grain—first the stalk, then the head, then the full
kernel in the head. 29As soon as the grain is ripe,
he puts the sickle to it, because the harvest has
come."

30Again he said, "What shall we say the king-
dom of God is like, or what parable shall we use
to describe it? 31It is like a mustard seed, which is
the smallest seed you plant in the ground. 32Yet

j12 Isaiah 6:9,10

when planted, it grows and becomes the largest of
all garden plants, with such big branches that the
birds of the air can perch in its shade."
[33]With many similar parables Jesus spoke the
word to them, as much as they could understand.
[34]He did not say anything to them without using
a parable. But when he was alone with his own
disciples, he explained everything.

Discovering the Word 1. Watch especially for words and phrases that are repeated in verses 1–25. What idea or ideas seem to dominate these verses? 2. Jesus explains the parable of the sower, or the parable of the soils (vv. 3–8), in verses 14–20. Put this explanation in your own words, describing from your own experience examples of each kind of soil-seed combination. 3. On what grounds are people included or excluded from the secret of the kingdom? 4. How do verses 21–25 help explain verses 11–12? 5. What insights into kingdom growth do the parables of the growing seed and the mustard seed give us (vv. 26–34)?

Applying the Word 1. What kind of soil are you? 2. What can you do to become the kind of soil Jesus is looking for? 3. In this passage we see Jesus both spreading the message of the kingdom and teaching about how the kingdom grows. What lessons can we learn about evangelism both from his example and from his teaching?

Responding in Prayer Ask Jesus to work in you to make you receptive soil.

6/ *Mark 4:35—6:6*
Desperate Straits

"DON'T BE AFRAID; just believe." These words may ring rather hollow when we, and not someone else, face a fearful or life-threatening situation. Yet in the face of real danger we discover just how much faith we have. In this study we find a number of different people in desperate straits. Their experiences with Jesus can help us to trust him with the fearful areas of our own lives.

Warming Up to God When do you feel afraid? Reflect on these words from Isaiah 12:2: "Surely God is my salvation; I will trust and not be afraid." Allow God to comfort you.

Read Mark 4:35—6:6.

[35]That day when evening came, he said to his
disciples, "Let us go over to the other side."
[36]Leaving the crowd behind, they took him along,
just as he was, in the boat. There were also other
boats with him. [37]A furious squall came up, and
the waves broke over the boat, so that it was
nearly swamped. [38]Jesus was in the stern, sleep-
ing on a cushion. The disciples woke him and
said to him, "Teacher, don't you care if we
drown?"

[39]He got up, rebuked the wind and said to the
waves, "Quiet! Be still!" Then the wind died
down and it was completely calm.

[40]He said to his disciples, "Why are you so
afraid? Do you still have no faith?"

[41]They were terrified and asked each other,
"Who is this? Even the wind and the waves obey
him!"

5 They went across the lake to the region of
the Gerasenes.[k] [2]When Jesus got out of
the boat, a man with an evil[l] spirit came
from the tombs to meet him. [3]This man lived in
the tombs, and no one could bind him any more,
not even with a chain. [4]For he had often been
chained hand and foot, but he tore the chains
apart and broke the irons on his feet. No one was
strong enough to subdue him. [5]Night and day
among the tombs and in the hills he would cry
out and cut himself with stones.

[6]When he saw Jesus from a distance, he ran
and fell on his knees in front of him. [7]He shouted

[k] 1 Some manuscripts *Gadarenes*; other manuscripts *Gergesenes*
[l] 2 Greek *unclean*; also in verses 8 and 13

at the top of his voice, "What do you want with me, Jesus, Son of the Most High God? Swear to God that you won't torture me!" 8For Jesus had said to him, "Come out of this man, you evil spirit!"

9Then Jesus asked him, "What is your name?"

"My name is Legion," he replied, "for we are many." 10And he begged Jesus again and again not to send them out of the area.

11A large herd of pigs was feeding on the nearby hillside. 12The demons begged Jesus, "Send us among the pigs; allow us to go into them." 13He gave them permission, and the evil spirits came out and went into the pigs. The herd, about two thousand in number, rushed down the steep bank into the lake and were drowned.

14Those tending the pigs ran off and reported this in the town and countryside, and the people went out to see what had happened. 15When they came to Jesus, they saw the man who had been possessed by the legion of demons, sitting there, dressed and in his right mind; and they were afraid. 16Those who had seen it told the people what had happened to the demon-possessed man—and told about the pigs as well. 17Then the people began to plead with Jesus to leave their region.

18As Jesus was getting into the boat, the man who had been demon-possessed begged to go with him. 19Jesus did not let him, but said, "Go home to your family and tell them how much the Lord has done for you, and how he has had mercy on you." 20So the man went away and began to tell in the Decapolis[m] how much Jesus had done for him. And all the people were amazed.

21When Jesus had again crossed over by boat to the other side of the lake, a large crowd gathered around him while he was by the lake. 22Then one of the synagogue rulers, named Jairus, came there. Seeing Jesus, he fell at his feet 23and pleaded earnestly with him, "My little daughter is dying. Please come and put your hands on her so that she will be healed and live." 24So Jesus went with him.

A large crowd followed and pressed around him. 25And a woman was there who had been subject to bleeding for twelve years. 26She had suffered a great deal under the care of many doctors and had spent all she had, yet instead of getting better she grew worse. 27When she heard about Jesus, she came up behind him in the crowd and touched his cloak, 28because she thought, "If I just touch his clothes, I will be healed." 29Immediately her bleeding stopped and she felt in her body that she was freed from her suffering.

30At once Jesus realized that power had gone out from him. He turned around in the crowd and asked, "Who touched my clothes?"

31"You see the people crowding against you," his disciples answered, "and yet you can ask, 'Who touched me?' "

32But Jesus kept looking around to see who had done it. 33Then the woman, knowing what had happened to her, came and fell at his feet and, trembling with fear, told him the whole truth. 34He said to her, "Daughter, your faith has healed you. Go in peace and be freed from your suffering."

35While Jesus was still speaking, some men came from the house of Jairus, the synagogue ruler. "Your daughter is dead," they said. "Why bother the teacher any more?"

36Ignoring what they said, Jesus told the synagogue ruler, "Don't be afraid; just believe."

37He did not let anyone follow him except Peter, James and John the brother of James. 38When they came to the home of the synagogue ruler, Jesus saw a commotion, with people crying and wailing loudly. 39He went in and said to them, "Why all this commotion and wailing? The child is not dead but asleep." 40But they laughed at him.

After he put them all out, he took the child's father and mother and the disciples who were with him, and went in where the child was. 41He took her by the hand and said to her, "*Talitha koum!*" (which means, "Little girl, I say to you, get up!"). 42Immediately the girl stood up and walked around (she was twelve years old). At this they were completely astonished. 43He gave strict orders not to let anyone know about this, and told them to give her something to eat.

6 Jesus left there and went to his hometown, accompanied by his disciples. 2When the Sabbath came, he began to teach in the synagogue, and many who heard him were amazed.

"Where did this man get these things?" they asked. "What's this wisdom that has been given him, that he even does miracles! 3Isn't this the carpenter? Isn't this Mary's son and the brother of

m20 That is, the Ten Cities

James, Joseph,[n] Judas and Simon? Aren't his sisters here with us?" And they took offense at him.

4Jesus said to them, "Only in his hometown, among his relatives and in his own house is a prophet without honor." 5He could not do any miracles there, except lay his hands on a few sick people and heal them. 6And he was amazed at their lack of faith.

[n]3 Greek *Joses*, a variant of *Joseph*

Discovering the Word 1. In the first incident the disciples are quite naturally afraid of the storm and disturbed that Jesus seems not to be concerned about their drowning. Once Jesus calms the storm, however, they are still terrified. How does their fear after the storm differ from their previous fears? 2. Who in the next incident is afraid and why (5:1–20)? 3. Many people find it hard to understand why Jesus allowed the demons to destroy the pigs. It could have been to prevent a violent exit from the man or to show him visibly that he was now free. Even if we can't pin down exactly why Jesus allowed this, what does the fate of the pigs show about what the demons were trying to do to the man? 4. In 5:21–43 two stories are woven together—that of Jairus's daughter and the woman with a hemorrhage. What sorts of fears are involved in these two incidents? 5. What are the relationships between fear and faith in each of these incidents?

Applying the Word 1. Fear can be a very powerful emotion. What kinds of fear keep you from doing some things you think you should? 2. What keeps you from turning your fears into faith? 3. How can Jesus' authority as shown here calm your fears and strengthen your faith?

Responding in Prayer Pray for your fears to become increased faith.

7/ *Mark 6:6–56*
Beyond Burnout

BURNOUT IS ALL too common an experience among Christians today. One of its most disastrous consequences is a hardened heart that keeps us from being refreshed by our Lord. In this study we see the disciples suffering from burnout and catch a vision of how Jesus can help us to counteract its effects.

Warming Up to God What is pressing on you and taking away your energy? Ask God to refresh your spirit and renew your commitment. Then consider how you could better handle your responsibilities.

Read Mark 6:6–56.

Then Jesus went around teaching from village to village. 7Calling the Twelve to him, he sent them out two by two and gave them authority over evil[o] spirits.

8These were his instructions: "Take nothing for the journey except a staff—no bread, no bag, no money in your belts. 9Wear sandals but not an extra tunic. 10Whenever you enter a house, stay there until you leave that town. 11And if any place will not welcome you or listen to you, shake the dust off your feet when you leave, as a testimony against them."

12They went out and preached that people should repent. 13They drove out many demons and anointed many sick people with oil and healed them.

14King Herod heard about this, for Jesus' name had become well known. Some were saying,[p] "John the Baptist has been raised from the dead, and that is why miraculous powers are at work in him."

15Others said, "He is Elijah."

And still others claimed, "He is a prophet, like one of the prophets of long ago."

16But when Herod heard this, he said, "John, the man I beheaded, has been raised from the dead!"

17For Herod himself had given orders to have

[o]7 Greek *unclean* [p]14 Some early manuscripts *He was saying*

John arrested, and he had him bound and put in prison. He did this because of Herodias, his brother Philip's wife, whom he had married. 18For John had been saying to Herod, "It is not lawful for you to have your brother's wife." 19So Herodias nursed a grudge against John and wanted to kill him. But she was not able to, 20because Herod feared John and protected him, knowing him to be a righteous and holy man. When Herod heard John, he was greatly puzzled[q]; yet he liked to listen to him.

21Finally the opportune time came. On his birthday Herod gave a banquet for his high officials and military commanders and the leading men of Galilee. 22When the daughter of Herodias came in and danced, she pleased Herod and his dinner guests.

The king said to the girl, "Ask me for anything you want, and I'll give it to you." 23And he promised her with an oath, "Whatever you ask I will give you, up to half my kingdom."

24She went out and said to her mother, "What shall I ask for?"

"The head of John the Baptist," she answered.

25At once the girl hurried in to the king with the request: "I want you to give me right now the head of John the Baptist on a platter."

26The king was greatly distressed, but because of his oaths and his dinner guests, he did not want to refuse her. 27So he immediately sent an executioner with orders to bring John's head. The man went, beheaded John in the prison, 28and brought back his head on a platter. He presented it to the girl, and she gave it to her mother. 29On hearing of this, John's disciples came and took his body and laid it in a tomb.

30The apostles gathered around Jesus and reported to him all they had done and taught. 31Then, because so many people were coming and going that they did not even have a chance to eat, he said to them, "Come with me by yourselves to a quiet place and get some rest."

32So they went away by themselves in a boat to a solitary place. 33But many who saw them leaving recognized them and ran on foot from all the towns and got there ahead of them. 34When Jesus landed and saw a large crowd, he had compassion on them, because they were like sheep without a shepherd. So he began teaching them many things.

35By this time it was late in the day, so his disciples came to him. "This is a remote place," they said, "and it's already very late. 36Send the people away so they can go to the surrounding countryside and villages and buy themselves something to eat."

37But he answered, "You give them something to eat."

They said to him, "That would take eight months of a man's wages[r]! Are we to go and spend that much on bread and give it to them to eat?"

38"How many loaves do you have?" he asked. "Go and see."

When they found out, they said, "Five—and two fish."

39Then Jesus directed them to have all the people sit down in groups on the green grass. 40So they sat down in groups of hundreds and fifties. 41Taking the five loaves and the two fish and looking up to heaven, he gave thanks and broke the loaves. Then he gave them to his disciples to set before the people. He also divided the two fish among them all. 42They all ate and were satisfied, 43and the disciples picked up twelve basketfuls of broken pieces of bread and fish. 44The number of the men who had eaten was five thousand.

45Immediately Jesus made his disciples get into the boat and go on ahead of him to Bethsaida, while he dismissed the crowd. 46After leaving them, he went up on a mountainside to pray.

47When evening came, the boat was in the middle of the lake, and he was alone on land. 48He saw the disciples straining at the oars, because the wind was against them. About the fourth watch of the night he went out to them, walking on the lake. He was about to pass by them, 49but when they saw him walking on the lake, they thought he was a ghost. They cried out, 50because they all saw him and were terrified.

Immediately he spoke to them and said, "Take courage! It is I. Don't be afraid." 51Then he climbed into the boat with them, and the wind died down. They were completely amazed, 52for they had not understood about the loaves; their hearts were hardened.

53When they had crossed over, they landed at Gennesaret and anchored there. 54As soon as they got out of the boat, people recognized Jesus. 55They ran throughout that whole region and carried the sick on mats to wherever they heard he was. 56And wherever he went—into villages,

q20 Some early manuscripts *he did many things* r37 Greek *take two hundred denarii* towns or countryside—they placed the sick in the marketplaces. They begged him to let them touch even the edge of his cloak, and all who touched him were healed.

Discovering the Word 1. What do Jesus' instructions to the Twelve tell us about the kind of ministry they were to have (vv. 6–13)? 2. What kind of man was Herod (vv. 14–29)? 3. This flashback to the execution of John the Baptist interrupts the account of Jesus' sending out the Twelve to preach and heal. Why do you suppose Mark recounts it here? 4. What differences are there between Jesus' approach to the crowd and that of his disciples (vv. 30–44)? 5. Jesus and Herod, the two kings in this passage, both serve banquets. Compare the two.

Applying the Word 1. When has tiredness blunted your desire to care for others? 2. Recognizing the contributing factors, what steps can you take to counteract burnout and a hardened heart?

Responding in Prayer Ask God to help you to give of yourself while maintaining balance in your life so that you don't burn out.

8 / *Mark 7*
Violating Tradition

ALL OF US are influenced by traditions of one sort or another—even those of us who *by tradition* don't put much stock in them! But at what point do traditions lose their value or even become counterproductive? When do religious practices become a substitute for really obeying God? In this study Jesus has some rather harsh words for the Pharisees and the traditions they choose to observe.

Warming Up to God Consider your spiritual life. Are there any aspects of your devotional practices that you feel bound to? Consider before God whether you are putting unrealistic expectations on yourself.

Read Mark 7.

7 The Pharisees and some of the teachers of the law who had come from Jerusalem gathered around Jesus and [2]saw some of his disciples eating food with hands that were "unclean," that is, unwashed. [3](The Pharisees and all the Jews do not eat unless they give their hands a ceremonial washing, holding to the tradition of the elders. [4]When they come from the marketplace they do not eat unless they wash. And they observe many other traditions, such as the washing of cups, pitchers and kettles.[s])

[5]So the Pharisees and teachers of the law asked Jesus, "Why don't your disciples live according to the tradition of the elders instead of eating their food with 'unclean' hands?"

[6]He replied, "Isaiah was right when he prophesied about you hypocrites; as it is written:

" 'These people honor me with their lips,
but their hearts are far from me.
[7]They worship me in vain;
their teachings are but rules taught by men.'[t]

[8]You have let go of the commands of God and are holding on to the traditions of men."

[9]And he said to them: "You have a fine way of setting aside the commands of God in order to observe[u] your own traditions! [10]For Moses said, 'Honor your father and your mother,'[v] and, 'Anyone who curses his father or mother must be put to death.'[w] [11]But you say that if a man says to his father or mother: 'Whatever help you might otherwise have received from me is Corban' (that is, a gift devoted to God), [12]then you no longer let him do anything for his father or mother. [13]Thus you nullify the word of God by your tradition that you have handed down. And you do many things like that."

[14]Again Jesus called the crowd to him and said,

[s]4 Some early manuscripts *pitchers, kettles and dining couches* [t]6,7 Isaiah 29:13 [u]9 Some manuscripts *set up* [v]10 Exodus 20:12; Deut. 5:16 [w]10 Exodus 21:17; Lev. 20:9

"Listen to me, everyone, and understand this.
15Nothing outside a man can make him 'unclean'
by going into him. Rather, it is what comes out of
a man that makes him 'unclean.'[x]"

17After he had left the crowd and entered the
house, his disciples asked him about this parable.
18"Are you so dull?" he asked. "Don't you see that
nothing that enters a man from the outside can
make him 'unclean'? 19For it doesn't go into his
heart but into his stomach, and then out of his
body." (In saying this, Jesus declared all foods
"clean.")

20He went on: "What comes out of a man is
what makes him 'unclean.' 21For from within, out
of men's hearts, come evil thoughts, sexual im-
morality, theft, murder, adultery, 22greed, malice,
deceit, lewdness, envy, slander, arrogance and
folly. 23All these evils come from inside and make
a man 'unclean.' "

24Jesus left that place and went to the vicinity
of Tyre.[y] He entered a house and did not want
anyone to know it; yet he could not keep his
presence secret. 25In fact, as soon as she heard
about him, a woman whose little daughter was
possessed by an evil[z] spirit came and fell at his
feet. 26The woman was a Greek, born in Syrian
Phoenicia. She begged Jesus to drive the demon
out of her daughter.
27"First let the children eat all they want," he
told her, "for it is not right to take the children's
bread and toss it to their dogs."
28"Yes, Lord," she replied, "but even the dogs
under the table eat the children's crumbs."
29Then he told her, "For such a reply, you may
go; the demon has left your daughter."
30She went home and found her child lying on
the bed, and the demon gone.
31Then Jesus left the vicinity of Tyre and went
through Sidon, down to the Sea of Galilee and
into the region of the Decapolis.[a] 32There some
people brought to him a man who was deaf and
could hardly talk, and they begged him to place
his hand on the man.
33After he took him aside, away from the
crowd, Jesus put his fingers into the man's ears.
Then he spit and touched the man's tongue. 34He
looked up to heaven and with a deep sigh said to
him, "*Ephphatha!*" (which means, "Be opened!").
35At this, the man's ears were opened, his tongue
was loosened and he began to speak plainly.
36Jesus commanded them not to tell anyone.
But the more he did so, the more they kept talk-
ing about it. 37People were overwhelmed with
amazement. "He has done everything well," they
said. "He even makes the deaf hear and the mute
speak."

x15 Some early manuscripts *'unclean.' 16If anyone has ears to hear, let him hear.* y24 Many early manuscripts *Tyre and Sidon* z25 Greek *unclean* a31 That is, the Ten Cities

Discovering the Word 1. What are the Pharisees concerned about (vv. 1–5)? 2. What specific complaints does Jesus raise against the Pharisees' approach to tradition (vv. 6–13)? 3. How does Jesus' view of becoming "unclean" differ from that of the Pharisees (vv. 14–23)? 4. Jesus responds to the Syrophoenician woman's request with a miniparable about children, bread and dogs (vv. 24–27). What is he actually saying? 5. What does the woman's response reveal about her? 6. The healing of the deaf man takes place in the Decapolis, where Jesus had exorcised the demons from the Gerasene man at the tombs (5:1–20). How do the events here demonstrate that man's success in telling about what Jesus had done for him (vv. 31–37)?

Applying the Word 1. What religious traditions influence your life? Is that influence good or bad? Explain. 2. What sorts of traditions do we observe today that get in the way of really honoring God? 3. In what ways do you sometimes emphasize appearance over internal reality?

Responding in Prayer Now, as then, those who are spiritually deaf—whether through hardness of heart or through substituting traditions for true obedience—can be healed by Jesus. Pray for yourself and others who need Jesus' healing touch.

9 / *Mark 8:1—9:1* Who Do You Say I Am?

"WHO DO YOU say I am?" The whole Gospel of Mark so far has been supplying evidence for answering this question. It's a question Jesus asks each of us, and the answer we give ultimately determines our destiny. But our answer involves more than what we say with our lips. Our real answer is to be found in the way we live our lives.

Warming Up to God What need in your life has God met recently? Spend time praising God and thanking him for meeting your needs.

Read Mark 8:1—9:1.

8 During those days another large crowd
gathered. Since they had nothing to eat,
Jesus called his disciples to him and said,
2"I have compassion for these people; they have
already been with me three days and have nothing to eat. 3If I send them home hungry, they will
collapse on the way, because some of them have
come a long distance."
4His disciples answered, "But where in this remote place can anyone get enough bread to feed
them?"
5"How many loaves do you have?" Jesus asked.
"Seven," they replied.
6He told the crowd to sit down on the ground.
When he had taken the seven loaves and given
thanks, he broke them and gave them to his disciples to set before the people, and they did so.
7They had a few small fish as well; he gave thanks
for them also and told the disciples to distribute
them. 8The people ate and were satisfied. Afterward the disciples picked up seven basketfuls of
broken pieces that were left over. 9About four
thousand men were present. And having sent
them away, 10he got into the boat with his disciples and went to the region of Dalmanutha.
11The Pharisees came and began to question
Jesus. To test him, they asked him for a sign from
heaven. 12He sighed deeply and said, "Why does
this generation ask for a miraculous sign? I tell
you the truth, no sign will be given to it." 13Then
he left them, got back into the boat and crossed to
the other side.
14The disciples had forgotten to bring bread,
except for one loaf they had with them in the
boat. 15"Be careful," Jesus warned them. "Watch
out for the yeast of the Pharisees and that of
Herod."
16They discussed this with one another and
said, "It is because we have no bread."
17Aware of their discussion, Jesus asked them:
"Why are you talking about having no bread? Do
you still not see or understand? Are your hearts
hardened? 18Do you have eyes but fail to see, and
ears but fail to hear? And don't you remember?
19When I broke the five loaves for the five thousand, how many basketfuls of pieces did you
pick up?"
"Twelve," they replied.
20"And when I broke the seven loaves for the
four thousand, how many basketfuls of pieces did
you pick up?"
They answered, "Seven."
21He said to them, "Do you still not understand?"
22They came to Bethsaida, and some people
brought a blind man and begged Jesus to touch
him. 23He took the blind man by the hand and led
him outside the village. When he had spit on the
man's eyes and put his hands on him, Jesus asked,
"Do you see anything?"
24He looked up and said, "I see people; they
look like trees walking around."
25Once more Jesus put his hands on the man's
eyes. Then his eyes were opened, his sight was
restored, and he saw everything clearly. 26Jesus
sent him home, saying, "Don't go into the village.[b]"
27Jesus and his disciples went on to the villages
around Caesarea Philippi. On the way he asked
them, "Who do people say I am?"
28They replied, "Some say John the Baptist;
others say Elijah; and still others, one of the
prophets."
29"But what about you?" he asked. "Who do
you say I am?"

[b]26 Some manuscripts *Don't go and tell anyone in the village*

Peter answered, "You are the Christ.[c]"
30Jesus warned them not to tell anyone about
him.
31He then began to teach them that the Son of
Man must suffer many things and be rejected by
the elders, chief priests and teachers of the law,
and that he must be killed and after three days
rise again. 32He spoke plainly about this, and Pe-
ter took him aside and began to rebuke him.
33But when Jesus turned and looked at his dis-
ciples, he rebuked Peter. "Get behind me, Satan!"
he said. "You do not have in mind the things of
God, but the things of men."
34Then he called the crowd to him along with
his disciples and said: "If anyone would come af-
ter me, he must deny himself and take up his
cross and follow me. 35For whoever wants to save
his life[d] will lose it, but whoever loses his life for
me and for the gospel will save it. 36What good is
it for a man to gain the whole world, yet forfeit
his soul? 37Or what can a man give in exchange
for his soul? 38If anyone is ashamed of me and my
words in this adulterous and sinful generation,
the Son of Man will be ashamed of him when he
comes in his Father's glory with the holy angels."
9 And he said to them, "I tell you the truth,
some who are standing here will not taste
death before they see the kingdom of God
come with power."

[c]29 Or *Messiah.* "The Christ" (Greek) and "the Messiah" (Hebrew) both mean "the Anointed One." [d]35 The Greek word means either *life* or *soul*; also in verse 36.

Discovering the Word 1. Why do you suppose the disciples, having witnessed the feeding of the 5,000, have such a hard time believing Jesus can supply the needs of 4,000 here (8:1–13)? 2. What do the disciples fail to understand in verses 14–21 and why? 3. What unusual thing happens while Jesus is curing the blind man (vv. 22–26)? 4. How is Peter in verses 27–33 like the blind man in verses 22–26? 5. What does Jesus say it means to acknowledge him as the Christ and to follow him?

Applying the Word 1. When have you acted like the disciples in verses 1–13, not expecting God to work just after he has met a need in your life? 2. Is your life characterized more by seeking to lose your life or to save it? Explain. 3. In what way do you need to "lose your life"?

Responding in Prayer Ask Jesus to help you see more clearly those areas where you are not yet following him.

10 / *Mark 9:2–32*
Suffering and Glory

IN A FAMOUS short story, the main character is given the choice of opening one of two doors. Behind one is a beautiful maiden; behind the other, a ferocious tiger. It is easy to identify with the hero of the story, hoping for joy rather than suffering, pleasure rather than pain. But what if we cannot have one without the other? This passage examines the relationship between suffering and glory, human weakness and divine power.

Warming Up to God In this passage God tells the disciples to "listen to" his Son. What does Christ want to say to you today?

Read Mark 9:2–32.

2After six days Jesus took Peter, James and
John with him and led them up a high mountain,
where they were all alone. There he was transfig-
ured before them. 3His clothes became dazzling
white, whiter than anyone in the world could
bleach them. 4And there appeared before them
Elijah and Moses, who were talking with Jesus.
5Peter said to Jesus, "Rabbi, it is good for us to
be here. Let us put up three shelters—one for
you, one for Moses and one for Elijah." 6(He did
not know what to say, they were so frightened.)
7Then a cloud appeared and enveloped them,
and a voice came from the cloud: "This is my Son,
whom I love. Listen to him!"

8Suddenly, when they looked around, they no
longer saw anyone with them except Jesus.
9As they were coming down the mountain,
Jesus gave them orders not to tell anyone what
they had seen until the Son of Man had risen
from the dead. 10They kept the matter to them-
selves, discussing what "rising from the dead"
meant.
11And they asked him, "Why do the teachers of
the law say that Elijah must come first?"
12Jesus replied, "To be sure, Elijah does come
first, and restores all things. Why then is it writ-
ten that the Son of Man must suffer much and be
rejected? 13But I tell you, Elijah has come, and
they have done to him everything they wished,
just as it is written about him."
14When they came to the other disciples, they
saw a large crowd around them and the teachers
of the law arguing with them. 15As soon as all the
people saw Jesus, they were overwhelmed with
wonder and ran to greet him.
16"What are you arguing with them about?" he
asked.
17A man in the crowd answered, "Teacher, I
brought you my son, who is possessed by a spirit
that has robbed him of speech. 18Whenever it
seizes him, it throws him to the ground. He foams
at the mouth, gnashes his teeth and becomes
rigid. I asked your disciples to drive out the spirit,
but they could not."
19"O unbelieving generation," Jesus replied,
"how long shall I stay with you? How long shall
I put up with you? Bring the boy to me."
20So they brought him. When the spirit saw
Jesus, it immediately threw the boy into a convul-
sion. He fell to the ground and rolled around,
foaming at the mouth.
21Jesus asked the boy's father, "How long has
he been like this?"
"From childhood," he answered. 22"It has often
thrown him into fire or water to kill him. But if
you can do anything, take pity on us and
help us."
23" 'If you can'?" said Jesus. "Everything is pos-
sible for him who believes."
24Immediately the boy's father exclaimed, "I do
believe; help me overcome my unbelief!"
25When Jesus saw that a crowd was running to
the scene, he rebuked the evil[e] spirit. "You deaf
and mute spirit," he said, "I command you, come
out of him and never enter him again."
26The spirit shrieked, convulsed him violently
and came out. The boy looked so much like a
corpse that many said, "He's dead." 27But Jesus
took him by the hand and lifted him to his feet,
and he stood up.
28After Jesus had gone indoors, his disciples
asked him privately, "Why couldn't we drive it
out?"
29He replied, "This kind can come out only by
prayer.[f]"
30They left that place and passed through Gali-
lee. Jesus did not want anyone to know where
they were, 31because he was teaching his disci-
ples. He said to them, "The Son of Man is going
to be betrayed into the hands of men. They will
kill him, and after three days he will rise." 32But
they did not understand what he meant and were
afraid to ask him about it.

e25 Greek *unclean* f29 Some manuscripts *prayer and fasting*

Discovering the Word 1. What is the significance of the presence of Elijah and Moses with Jesus on the mount? 2. In verse 7 God's voice is heard for a second time in Mark's Gospel, the first being in 1:11. What purposes are accomplished by God's affirmation here? 3. Jesus descends the mountain and returns to his other disciples, only to find them in hot debate with the teachers of the law over their failure to exorcise a young boy robbed of speech (vv. 14–18). Why do you suppose Jesus is so harsh in verse 19? 4. At the end of this account, Jesus again tells his disciples about his death and resurrection (vv. 30–32). Why do you suppose the disciples failed to understand what he meant? 5. What details in the account of the boy's healing parallel those in Jesus' prediction of his coming suffering and victory?

Applying the Word 1. Which do you struggle with more—believing that Jesus *can* or that he *wants* to answer your prayers? Explain. 2. How can the dialogue between Jesus and the boy's father encourage you when your faith is weak? 3. How can this passage encourage you in the midst of pain and suffering? 4. The statement in verse 7, "Listen to him!" probably alludes to Deuteronomy 18:15–19. Explain how we can listen to Jesus today.

Responding in Prayer Ask God to provide you with the encouragement you need in your life and to make you a channel of his grace to others.

11 / *Mark 9:33–50*
The First and the Last

ALL OF US, I imagine, struggle with the question of status and identity within a group. Where do I fit? How important am I to this group? Who is on our side? Who isn't? In this study we find out how Jesus turns conventional wisdom about status and group identity on its ear.

Warming Up to God When have you put yourself before others? Be vulnerable before God as you consider your selfishness. Let him show you your sin.

Read Mark 9:33–50.

---

33 They came to Capernaum. When he was in
the house, he asked them, "What were you argu-
ing about on the road?" 34 But they kept quiet
because on the way they had argued about who
was the greatest.
35 Sitting down, Jesus called the Twelve and
said, "If anyone wants to be first, he must be the
very last, and the servant of all."
36 He took a little child and had him stand
among them. Taking him in his arms, he said to
them, 37 "Whoever welcomes one of these little
children in my name welcomes me; and whoever
welcomes me does not welcome me but the one
who sent me."
38 "Teacher," said John, "we saw a man driving
out demons in your name and we told him to
stop, because he was not one of us."
39 "Do not stop him," Jesus said. "No one who
does a miracle in my name can in the next mo-
ment say anything bad about me, 40 for whoever is
not against us is for us. 41 I tell you the truth,
anyone who gives you a cup of water in my name
because you belong to Christ will certainly not
lose his reward.
42 "And if anyone causes one of these little ones
who believe in me to sin, it would be better for
him to be thrown into the sea with a large mill-
stone tied around his neck. 43 If your hand causes
you to sin, cut it off. It is better for you to enter
life maimed than with two hands to go into hell,
where the fire never goes out.[g] 45 And if your foot
causes you to sin, cut it off. It is better for you to
enter life crippled than to have two feet and be
thrown into hell.[h] 47 And if your eye causes you
to sin, pluck it out. It is better for you to enter the
kingdom of God with one eye than to have two
eyes and be thrown into hell, 48 where

" 'their worm does not die,
and the fire is not quenched.'[i]

49 Everyone will be salted with fire.
50 "Salt is good, but if it loses its saltiness, how
can you make it salty again? Have salt in your-
selves, and be at peace with each other."

g43 Some manuscripts *out,* 44*where / " 'their worm does not die, / and the fire is not quenched.'* h45 Some manuscripts *hell,* 46*where / " 'their worm does not die, / and the fire is not quenched.'* i48 Isaiah 66:24

Discovering the Word 1. In verses 33–37, what is Jesus trying to get across to the disciples? 2. Why is a child so appropriate an illustration for Jesus' point (vv. 36–37)? 3. What perspective governs Jesus' response to John in verses 39–41? 4. Christian history has known some individuals to take Jesus' words in verses 43–47 quite literally. Why is cutting off a hand or foot or plucking out an eye not radical enough a way to deal with sin? 5. How are Jesus' attitudes about greatness and personal worth radically different from attitudes we often adopt from society?

Applying the Word 1. What individuals or groups are you tempted to silence because they are not one of us? 2. When should you oppose someone in Jesus' name (if ever)? 3. What attitudes and actions does this passage suggest should govern our relationships with rival individuals or groups who act in Jesus' name?

Responding in Prayer Look to God for his wisdom as you consider how to deal with groups and individuals you know who don't uphold the truth as you understand it.

12 / *Mark 10:1–31*
Divorce, Children and Eternal Life

FOR MANY OF us preachin' becomes meddlin' when it impinges on how we live. But Jesus and the New Testament, like the Old Testament before them, never allow religion to be divorced from family life and social relationships. This passage exposes some of the ways the gospel ought to transform these areas of our life.

Warming Up to God Think about a child you know and how that child trusts his or her parents. Compare that picture to how you regard God. Talk to God about what you discover about yourself.

Read Mark 10:1–31.

10 Jesus then left that place and went
into the region of Judea and across
the Jordan. Again crowds of people
came to him, and as was his custom, he taught
them.
2Some Pharisees came and tested him by ask-
ing, "Is it lawful for a man to divorce his wife?"
3"What did Moses command you?" he replied.
4They said, "Moses permitted a man to write a
certificate of divorce and send her away."
5"It was because your hearts were hard that
Moses wrote you this law," Jesus replied. 6"But at
the beginning of creation God 'made them male
and female.'[j] 7'For this reason a man will leave
his father and mother and be united to his wife,[k]
8and the two will become one flesh.'[l] So they are
no longer two, but one. 9Therefore what God has
joined together, let man not separate."
10When they were in the house again, the disci-
ples asked Jesus about this. 11He answered, "Any-
one who divorces his wife and marries another
woman commits adultery against her. 12And if
she divorces her husband and marries another
man, she commits adultery."
13People were bringing little children to Jesus
to have him touch them, but the disciples re-
buked them. 14When Jesus saw this, he was indig-
nant. He said to them, "Let the little children
come to me, and do not hinder them, for the
kingdom of God belongs to such as these. 15I tell
you the truth, anyone who will not receive the
kingdom of God like a little child will never enter
it." 16And he took the children in his arms, put
his hands on them and blessed them.
17As Jesus started on his way, a man ran up to
him and fell on his knees before him. "Good
teacher," he asked, "what must I do to inherit
eternal life?"
18"Why do you call me good?" Jesus answered.
"No one is good—except God alone. 19You know
the commandments: 'Do not murder, do not com-
mit adultery, do not steal, do not give false testi-
mony, do not defraud, honor your father and
mother.'[m]"
20"Teacher," he declared, "all these I have kept
since I was a boy."
21Jesus looked at him and loved him. "One
thing you lack," he said. "Go, sell everything you
have and give to the poor, and you will have trea-
sure in heaven. Then come, follow me."
22At this the man's face fell. He went away sad,
because he had great wealth.
23Jesus looked around and said to his disciples,
"How hard it is for the rich to enter the kingdom
of God!"
24The disciples were amazed at his words. But
Jesus said again, "Children, how hard it is[n] to
enter the kingdom of God! 25It is easier for a
camel to go through the eye of a needle than for
a rich man to enter the kingdom of God."
26The disciples were even more amazed, and
said to each other, "Who then can be saved?"
27Jesus looked at them and said, "With man
this is impossible, but not with God; all things are
possible with God."
28Peter said to him, "We have left everything to
follow you!"
29"I tell you the truth," Jesus replied, "no one
who has left home or brothers or sisters or
mother or father or children or fields for me and
the gospel 30will fail to receive a hundred times as
much in this present age (homes, brothers, sis-

j6 Gen. 1:27 k7 Some early manuscripts do not have *and be united to his wife.* l8 Gen. 2:24 m19 Exodus 20:12-16; Deut. 5:16-20 n24 Some manuscripts *is for those who trust in riches*

ters, mothers, children and fields—and with
them, persecutions) and in the age to come, eter-
nal life. [31]But many who are first will be last, and
the last first."

Discovering the Word 1. What differences in approach to the question of divorce seem evident between Jesus and the Pharisees? 2. On the basis of verses 6–9, some Christian churches have refused to recognize divorce even when a couple has obtained a civil dissolution of their marriage. Do you think this is the intent of Jesus' statement? Why or why not? 3. In verses 13–16 we find that Jesus has used a child or children for the second time to illustrate a spiritual principle. What does it mean to receive the kingdom like a little child? 4. What kind of answer does the rich man expect from Jesus in response to his question (v. 17)? 5. How have the Pharisees (vv. 2–9) and the rich man (vv. 17–25) failed to receive the kingdom like a child (v. 15)?

Applying the Word 1. What obstacles were or are hardest for you to overcome in entering the kingdom? 2. What evidence has there been of God's help in your overcoming these obstacles? 3. In what areas of your life do you most need to express more childlike faith in God? 4. How have you experienced the truth of Jesus' words, "No one who has left home . . . will fail to receive a hundred times as much"?

Responding in Prayer Ask God to make you like a child.

13 / *Mark 10:32–52*
Blindness and Sight

THE BLIND SOMETIMES have uncanny "sight," and the deaf sometimes "hear" what others miss. Spiritual insight and alertness arise from the heart rather than from status or position. In this passage Mark seems to delight in the irony of a blind man who perceives what the sighted cannot see.

Warming Up to God What does God want you to "see" or know? Sit quietly before him and listen for his voice.

Read Mark 10:32–52.

[32]They were on their way up to Jerusalem, with
Jesus leading the way, and the disciples were as-
tonished, while those who followed were afraid.
Again he took the Twelve aside and told them
what was going to happen to him. [33]"We are go-
ing up to Jerusalem," he said, "and the Son of
Man will be betrayed to the chief priests and
teachers of the law. They will condemn him to
death and will hand him over to the Gentiles,
[34]who will mock him and spit on him, flog him
and kill him. Three days later he will rise."
[35]Then James and John, the sons of Zebedee,
came to him. "Teacher," they said, "we want you
to do for us whatever we ask."
[36]"What do you want me to do for you?" he
asked.
[37]They replied, "Let one of us sit at your right
and the other at your left in your glory."
[38]"You don't know what you are asking," Jesus
said. "Can you drink the cup I drink or be bap-
tized with the baptism I am baptized with?"
[39]"We can," they answered.
Jesus said to them, "You will drink the cup I
drink and be baptized with the baptism I am bap-
tized with, [40]but to sit at my right or left is not for
me to grant. These places belong to those for
whom they have been prepared."
[41]When the ten heard about this, they became
indignant with James and John. [42]Jesus called
them together and said, "You know that those
who are regarded as rulers of the Gentiles lord it
over them, and their high officials exercise au-
thority over them. [43]Not so with you. Instead,
whoever wants to become great among you must
be your servant, [44]and whoever wants to be first
must be slave of all. [45]For even the Son of Man
did not come to be served, but to serve, and to
give his life as a ransom for many."

46Then they came to Jericho. As Jesus and his
disciples, together with a large crowd, were leav-
ing the city, a blind man, Bartimaeus (that is, the
Son of Timaeus), was sitting by the roadside beg-
ging. 47When he heard that it was Jesus of Naza-
reth, he began to shout, "Jesus, Son of David,
have mercy on me!"
48Many rebuked him and told him to be quiet,
but he shouted all the more, "Son of David, have
mercy on me!"
49Jesus stopped and said, "Call him."
So they called to the blind man, "Cheer up! On
your feet! He's calling you." 50Throwing his cloak
aside, he jumped to his feet and came to Jesus.
51"What do you want me to do for you?" Jesus
asked him.
The blind man said, "Rabbi, I want to see."
52"Go," said Jesus, "your faith has healed you."
Immediately he received his sight and followed
Jesus along the road.

Discovering the Word 1. Given what Jesus has just said in verses 33–34, what is ironic about James and John's request (vv. 35–37)? 2. What seems to motivate James and John's request? 3. When the other ten apostles hear about this status request, they become indignant. In response, what principle does Jesus bring out again (see 9:35, 10:31 and 10:42–45)? 4. From the brief account in verses 46–52, what kind of man does Bartimaeus seem to be? 5. Why do you suppose Jesus asked Bartimaeus what he wanted him to do for him?

Applying the Word 1. How can your life better conform to Jesus' view of greatness? (Consider what motivates your actions as well as what you do.) 2. Jesus is indeed on the road to glory, but that road will not bypass Jerusalem. Self-sacrifice and service mark the way. What are some present opportunities for you to follow him? 3. What may be some of the costs?

Responding in Prayer Tell God how you want to sacrifice for him.

14 / *Mark 11:1–25*
Palm Sunday

THE TROUBLE WITH righteous anger is that it is so much easier to be angry than righteous. But it is possible to be both. This passage provides an example of how our emotions and attitudes can work toward God's purposes instead of against them.

Warming Up to God When have your emotions "gotten the better of you" lately? Evaluate that experience prayerfully.

Read Mark 11:1–25.

11 As they approached Jerusalem and
came to Bethphage and Bethany at
the Mount of Olives, Jesus sent two
of his disciples, 2saying to them, "Go to the vil-
lage ahead of you, and just as you enter it, you
will find a colt tied there, which no one has ever
ridden. Untie it and bring it here. 3If anyone asks
you, 'Why are you doing this?' tell him, 'The Lord
needs it and will send it back here shortly.' "
4They went and found a colt outside in the
street, tied at a doorway. As they untied it, 5some
people standing there asked, "What are you do-
ing, untying that colt?" 6They answered as Jesus
had told them to, and the people let them go.
7When they brought the colt to Jesus and threw
their cloaks over it, he sat on it. 8Many people
spread their cloaks on the road, while others
spread branches they had cut in the fields. 9Those
who went ahead and those who followed shouted,

"Hosanna![o]"

"Blessed is he who comes in the name of the
Lord!"[p]

[o]9 A Hebrew expression meaning "Save!" which became an exclamation of praise; also in verse 10 [p]9 Psalm 118:25,26

10“Blessed is the coming kingdom of our father
David!”

“Hosanna in the highest!”

11Jesus entered Jerusalem and went to the tem-
ple. He looked around at everything, but since it
was already late, he went out to Bethany with the
Twelve.
12The next day as they were leaving Bethany,
Jesus was hungry. 13Seeing in the distance a fig
tree in leaf, he went to find out if it had any fruit.
When he reached it, he found nothing but leaves,
because it was not the season for figs. 14Then he
said to the tree, “May no one ever eat fruit from
you again.” And his disciples heard him say it.
15On reaching Jerusalem, Jesus entered the
temple area and began driving out those who
were buying and selling there. He overturned the
tables of the money changers and the benches of
those selling doves, 16and would not allow any-
one to carry merchandise through the temple
courts. 17And as he taught them, he said, “Is it not
written:

“ ‘My house will be called
a house of prayer for all nations’[q]?

But you have made it ‘a den of robbers.’[r]”
18The chief priests and the teachers of the law
heard this and began looking for a way to kill
him, for they feared him, because the whole
crowd was amazed at his teaching.
19When evening came, they[s] went out of the
city.
20In the morning, as they went along, they saw
the fig tree withered from the roots. 21Peter re-
membered and said to Jesus, “Rabbi, look! The fig
tree you cursed has withered!”
22“Have[t] faith in God,” Jesus answered. 23“I
tell you the truth, if anyone says to this mountain,
‘Go, throw yourself into the sea,’ and does not
doubt in his heart but believes that what he says
will happen, it will be done for him. 24Therefore
I tell you, whatever you ask for in prayer, believe
that you have received it, and it will be yours.
25And when you stand praying, if you hold any-
thing against anyone, forgive him, so that your
Father in heaven may forgive you your sins.[u]”

[q]17 Isaiah 56:7 [r]17 Jer. 7:11 [s]19 Some early manuscripts *he*
[t]22 Some early manuscripts *If you have* [u]25 Some manuscripts *sins.*
26But if you do not forgive, neither will your Father who is in heaven forgive your sins.

Discovering the Word 1. What progression of moods do you see in this passage? 2. In what ways is the significance of Jesus' entry into Jerusalem reinforced? 3. Why is Jesus so angry with what is taking place in the temple (vv. 15–17)? 4. Why do you suppose Mark has sandwiched this account of Jesus' clearing out of the temple within that of the cursing of the fig tree? 5. What does Jesus teach us about prayer in verses 22–25?

Applying the Word 1. When is anger righteous? 2. Are there activities or attitudes in your church or fellowship which get in the way of God's purposes? 3. What can you do to help eliminate them?

Responding in Prayer Respond to this passage in prayer, praising the King of peace and asking that his kingdom might be established.

15/ *Mark 11:27—12:27*
Tempting Questions

SOME PEOPLE ASK questions because they want to know the answers. Others take malicious delight in posing unanswerable questions or in trying to trip up an opponent. Jesus often asked questions to get his hearers to think deeply for themselves. Learning to look behind questions to motives and learning to pose effective questions can help us all to be better evangelists and servants.

Warming Up to God When is Jesus most real to you? Spend some time meditating on the privilege of having Christ present with you.

Read Mark 11:27—12:27.

27 They arrived again in Jerusalem, and while Jesus was walking in the temple courts, the chief priests, the teachers of the law and the elders came to him. 28 "By what authority are you doing these things?" they asked. "And who gave you authority to do this?"

29 Jesus replied, "I will ask you one question. Answer me, and I will tell you by what authority I am doing these things. 30 John's baptism—was it from heaven, or from men? Tell me!"

31 They discussed it among themselves and said, "If we say, 'From heaven,' he will ask, 'Then why didn't you believe him?' 32 But if we say, 'From men' . . . ." (They feared the people, for everyone held that John really was a prophet.)

33 So they answered Jesus, "We don't know."

Jesus said, "Neither will I tell you by what authority I am doing these things."

12 He then began to speak to them in parables: "A man planted a vineyard. He put a wall around it, dug a pit for the winepress and built a watchtower. Then he rented the vineyard to some farmers and went away on a journey. 2 At harvest time he sent a servant to the tenants to collect from them some of the fruit of the vineyard. 3 But they seized him, beat him and sent him away empty-handed. 4 Then he sent another servant to them; they struck this man on the head and treated him shamefully. 5 He sent still another, and that one they killed. He sent many others; some of them they beat, others they killed.

6 "He had one left to send, a son, whom he loved. He sent him last of all, saying, 'They will respect my son.'

7 "But the tenants said to one another, 'This is the heir. Come, let's kill him, and the inheritance will be ours.' 8 So they took him and killed him, and threw him out of the vineyard.

9 "What then will the owner of the vineyard do? He will come and kill those tenants and give the vineyard to others. 10 Haven't you read this scripture:

" 'The stone the builders rejected
has become the capstone[v];
11 the Lord has done this,
and it is marvelous in our eyes'[w]?"

12 Then they looked for a way to arrest him because they knew he had spoken the parable against them. But they were afraid of the crowd; so they left him and went away.

13 Later they sent some of the Pharisees and Herodians to Jesus to catch him in his words. 14 They came to him and said, "Teacher, we know you are a man of integrity. You aren't swayed by men, because you pay no attention to who they are; but you teach the way of God in accordance with the truth. Is it right to pay taxes to Caesar or not? 15 Should we pay or shouldn't we?"

But Jesus knew their hypocrisy. "Why are you trying to trap me?" he asked. "Bring me a denarius and let me look at it." 16 They brought the coin, and he asked them, "Whose portrait is this? And whose inscription?"

"Caesar's," they replied.

17 Then Jesus said to them, "Give to Caesar what is Caesar's and to God what is God's."

And they were amazed at him.

18 Then the Sadducees, who say there is no resurrection, came to him with a question. 19 "Teacher," they said, "Moses wrote for us that if a man's brother dies and leaves a wife but no children, the man must marry the widow and have children for his brother. 20 Now there were seven brothers. The first one married and died without leaving any children. 21 The second one married the widow, but he also died, leaving no child. It was the same with the third. 22 In fact, none of the seven left any children. Last of all, the woman died too. 23 At the resurrection[x] whose wife will she be, since the seven were married to her?"

24 Jesus replied, "Are you not in error because you do not know the Scriptures or the power of God? 25 When the dead rise, they will neither marry nor be given in marriage; they will be like the angels in heaven. 26 Now about the dead rising—have you not read in the book of Moses, in the account of the bush, how God said to him, 'I am the God of Abraham, the God of Isaac, and the God of Jacob'[y]? 27 He is not the God of the dead, but of the living. You are badly mistaken!"

v10 *Or cornerstone* w11 Psalm 118:22,23 x23 Some manuscripts *resurrection, when men rise from the dead,* y26 Exodus 3:6

Discovering the Word 1. In 11:27 the chief priests, the elders and the teachers of the law come asking a seemingly straightforward question about Jesus' authority. What does Jesus' reply and the subsequent discussion reveal about their motives? 2. The parable of the tenants is rich in meaning. If the tenants are Israel and its religious leaders, who are the owner, the servants and the son? 3. A common enemy can often draw together people who are not otherwise on good terms. In 12:13–17 we find Herodians (supporters of the puppet monarchy) and the Pharisees (ardent nationalists and opponents of Roman rule) joining forces. How does the question they pose to Jesus reflect their conflicting interests? 4. The Sadducees differed from their Jewish contemporaries because they rejected the idea of resurrection. What motives lie behind their question to Jesus (12:18–23)? 5. How do the Sadducees display ignorance of the Scriptures and the power of God?

Applying the Word 1. How are you experiencing the truth of the Scriptures and the power of God? 2. How can we get to know the Scriptures and the power of God better? 3. As we seek to share the good news of Christ and his kingdom, we will meet people with a wide variety of questions and motives. What can we learn about answering and asking questions from this passage?

Responding in Prayer Pray that you will be ready to answer questions about your beliefs.

16/ *Mark 12:28–44*
An End to Questions

PEOPLE ARE MOTIVATED by many things—ambition, money, power, recognition, the desire to please God. In this passage Jesus encounters or comments on a variety of people whose lives are governed by different goals. In so doing he exposes our own motivations to his searching glance.

Warming Up to God What motivates your daily life and future plans? List each motivating factor. Reflect on your list before God.

Read Mark 12:28–44.

28 One of the teachers of the law came and
heard them debating. Noticing that Jesus had
given them a good answer, he asked him, "Of all
the commandments, which is the most impor-
tant?"
29 "The most important one," answered Jesus,
"is this: 'Hear, O Israel, the Lord our God, the
Lord is one.[z] 30 Love the Lord your God with all
your heart and with all your soul and with all
your mind and with all your strength.'[a] 31 The
second is this: 'Love your neighbor as yourself.'[b]
There is no commandment greater than these."
32 "Well said, teacher," the man replied. "You
are right in saying that God is one and there is no
other but him. 33 To love him with all your heart,
with all your understanding and with all your
strength, and to love your neighbor as yourself is
more important than all burnt offerings and sacri-
fices."
34 When Jesus saw that he had answered wisely,
he said to him, "You are not far from the kingdom
of God." And from then on no one dared ask him
any more questions.
35 While Jesus was teaching in the temple
courts, he asked, "How is it that the teachers of
the law say that the Christ[c] is the son of David?
36 David himself, speaking by the Holy Spirit, de-
clared:

" 'The Lord said to my Lord:
"Sit at my right hand
until I put your enemies
under your feet." '[d]

37 David himself calls him 'Lord.' How then can he
be his son?"
The large crowd listened to him with delight.
38 As he taught, Jesus said, "Watch out for the
teachers of the law. They like to walk around in
flowing robes and be greeted in the marketplaces,
39 and have the most important seats in the syna-

[z]29 Or *the Lord our God is one Lord* [a]30 Deut. 6:4,5 [b]31 Lev. 19:18 [c]35 Or *Messiah* [d]36 Psalm 110:1

gogues and the places of honor at banquets.
40They devour widows' houses and for a show
make lengthy prayers. Such men will be punished
most severely."
41Jesus sat down opposite the place where the
offerings were put and watched the crowd putting
their money into the temple treasury. Many rich
people threw in large amounts. 42But a poor
widow came and put in two very small copper
coins,[e] worth only a fraction of a penny.[f]
43Calling his disciples to him, Jesus said, "I tell
you the truth, this poor widow has put more into
the treasury than all the others. 44They all gave
out of their wealth; but she, out of her poverty,
put in everything—all she had to live on."

[e]42 Greek *two lepta* [f]42 Greek *kodrantes*

Discovering the Word 1. Like the chief priests, elders, Pharisees and Sadducees of 11:27—12:27, another teacher of the law comes to Jesus with a pointed question (v. 28). What evidence is there that he is not out to trap Jesus? 2. Though Jesus is only asked for one commandment, in good rabbinic fashion he responds by adding a second to his reply. What relationship does this second commandment bear to the first? 3. To a Jew in Jesus' day a descendant was always inferior to an ancestor. A son might call his father or grandfather "lord," but never vice versa. How *can* Christ be both David's Lord and his descendant (vv. 35-37)? 4. In contrast to the teachers of the law and the rich, what motivates the widow's religious behavior?

Applying the Word 1. If you were to evaluate your daily activities on the basis of love for God and neighbor, how would you fare? Explain. 2. What steps can you take to make the love of God and love of neighbor a higher priority in your life? 3. What implications does the example of the widow have for our giving to the Lord's work?

Responding in Prayer Ask God to give you the attitude of the widow both in your love for him and toward others.

17 / *Mark 13*
Keep Watch

WAITING FOR CHRISTMAS can keep some children excited and on their best behavior for weeks. But what if Christmas never came? To many of us the Second Coming may seem like a Christmas that never comes. In this passage, Jesus answers some questions about the future, both near and far off, but above all he encourages an attitude we all need to develop.

Warming Up to God When is it hard for you to wait for God? Ask him to give you insight and courage as you watch and wait.

Read Mark 13.

13 As he was leaving the temple, one
of his disciples said to him, "Look,
Teacher! What massive stones!
What magnificent buildings!"
2"Do you see all these great buildings?" replied
Jesus. "Not one stone here will be left on another;
every one will be thrown down."
3As Jesus was sitting on the Mount of Olives
opposite the temple, Peter, James, John and An-
drew asked him privately, 4"Tell us, when will
these things happen? And what will be the sign
that they are all about to be fulfilled?"
5Jesus said to them: "Watch out that no one
deceives you. 6Many will come in my name,
claiming, 'I am he,' and will deceive many. 7When
you hear of wars and rumors of wars, do not be
alarmed. Such things must happen, but the end is
still to come. 8Nation will rise against nation, and
kingdom against kingdom. There will be earth-
quakes in various places, and famines. These are
the beginning of birth pains.
9"You must be on your guard. You will be
handed over to the local councils and flogged in
the synagogues. On account of me you will stand

before governors and kings as witnesses to them.
10And the gospel must first be preached to all
nations. 11Whenever you are arrested and
brought to trial, do not worry beforehand about
what to say. Just say whatever is given you at the
time, for it is not you speaking, but the Holy
Spirit.
12"Brother will betray brother to death, and a
father his child. Children will rebel against their
parents and have them put to death. 13All men
will hate you because of me, but he who stands
firm to the end will be saved.
14"When you see 'the abomination that causes
desolation'[g] standing where it[h] does not be-
long—let the reader understand—then let those
who are in Judea flee to the mountains. 15Let no
one on the roof of his house go down or enter the
house to take anything out. 16Let no one in the
field go back to get his cloak. 17How dreadful it
will be in those days for pregnant women and
nursing mothers! 18Pray that this will not take
place in winter, 19because those will be days of
distress unequaled from the beginning, when God
created the world, until now—and never to be
equaled again. 20If the Lord had not cut short
those days, no one would survive. But for the
sake of the elect, whom he has chosen, he has
shortened them. 21At that time if anyone says to
you, 'Look, here is the Christ[i]!' or, 'Look, there
he is!' do not believe it. 22For false Christs and
false prophets will appear and perform signs and
miracles to deceive the elect—if that were possi-
ble. 23So be on your guard; I have told you every-
thing ahead of time.
24"But in those days, following that distress,

" 'the sun will be darkened,
and the moon will not give its light;
25the stars will fall from the sky,
and the heavenly bodies will be shaken.'[j]

26"At that time men will see the Son of Man
coming in clouds with great power and glory.
27And he will send his angels and gather his elect
from the four winds, from the ends of the earth to
the ends of the heavens.
28"Now learn this lesson from the fig tree: As
soon as its twigs get tender and its leaves come
out, you know that summer is near. 29Even so,
when you see these things happening, you know
that it is near, right at the door. 30I tell you the
truth, this generation[k] will certainly not pass
away until all these things have happened.
31Heaven and earth will pass away, but my words
will never pass away.
32"No one knows about that day or hour, not
even the angels in heaven, nor the Son, but only
the Father. 33Be on guard! Be alert[l]! You do not
know when that time will come. 34It's like a man
going away: He leaves his house and puts his ser-
vants in charge, each with his assigned task, and
tells the one at the door to keep watch.
35"Therefore keep watch because you do not
know when the owner of the house will come
back—whether in the evening, or at midnight, or
when the rooster crows, or at dawn. 36If he comes
suddenly, do not let him find you sleeping.
37What I say to you, I say to everyone: 'Watch!' "

g14 Daniel 9:27; 11:31; 12:11 h14 Or *he*; also in verse 29
i21 Or *Messiah* j25 Isaiah 13:10; 34:4 k30 Or *race*
l33 Some manuscripts *alert and pray*

Discovering the Word 1. Jesus doesn't seem to answer the disciples' question directly, at least not at first. What is he concerned about (vv. 5–8)? 2. How would Jesus' warnings and encouragements (vv. 5–13) have helped the disciples in the early years of the church? 3. Christians have sometimes disagreed about how to interpret Jesus' words in verses 14–23. Some think Jesus is talking about the destruction of the temple in A.D. 70 and the events leading up to that. Others think these events are still future. What evidence is there to support each view? 4. How is the distress described in verses 24–27 different from that described in verses 5–23? 5. Many people throughout the ages have tried to make precise predictions about the return of Jesus. How does watching as Jesus urges differ from making such predictions?

Applying the Word 1. What relevance do the warnings and encouragements in verses 5–13 have for us today? 2. In what area of your life do you need to "be on guard"? 3. In what practical ways can we be alert for Jesus' return?

Responding in Prayer Spend some time in praise and thanksgiving for the promises in this passage.

18 / *Mark 14:1–42*
The Betrayer Approaches

IF YOU'VE EVER caught yourself yawning at a critical moment or felt spiritually asleep when the Lord was calling you to a task, you'll have little difficulty in empathizing with the disciples in this account. We now enter into the last few days of Jesus' earthly ministry. The mood is somber as more and more people begin to fail and desert him.

Warming Up to God What task has God been calling you to? Spend some time prayerfully considering what God has for you.

Read Mark 14:1–42.

14 Now the Passover and the Feast of
Unleavened Bread were only two
days away, and the chief priests and
the teachers of the law were looking for some sly
way to arrest Jesus and kill him. 2"But not during
the Feast," they said, "or the people may riot."
3While he was in Bethany, reclining at the table
in the home of a man known as Simon the Leper,
a woman came with an alabaster jar of very ex-
pensive perfume, made of pure nard. She broke
the jar and poured the perfume on his head.
4Some of those present were saying indignantly
to one another, "Why this waste of perfume? 5It
could have been sold for more than a year's
wages[m] and the money given to the poor." And
they rebuked her harshly.
6"Leave her alone," said Jesus. "Why are you
bothering her? She has done a beautiful thing to
me. 7The poor you will always have with you, and
you can help them any time you want. But you
will not always have me. 8She did what she could.
She poured perfume on my body beforehand to
prepare for my burial. 9I tell you the truth, wher-
ever the gospel is preached throughout the world,
what she has done will also be told, in memory of
her."
10Then Judas Iscariot, one of the Twelve, went
to the chief priests to betray Jesus to them. 11They
were delighted to hear this and promised to give
him money. So he watched for an opportunity to
hand him over.
12On the first day of the Feast of Unleavened
Bread, when it was customary to sacrifice the
Passover lamb, Jesus' disciples asked him,
"Where do you want us to go and make prepara-
tions for you to eat the Passover?"
13So he sent two of his disciples, telling them,
"Go into the city, and a man carrying a jar of
water will meet you. Follow him. 14Say to the
owner of the house he enters, 'The Teacher asks:
Where is my guest room, where I may eat the
Passover with my disciples?' 15He will show you a
large upper room, furnished and ready. Make
preparations for us there."
16The disciples left, went into the city and
found things just as Jesus had told them. So they
prepared the Passover.
17When evening came, Jesus arrived with the
Twelve. 18While they were reclining at the table
eating, he said, "I tell you the truth, one of you
will betray me—one who is eating with me."
19They were saddened, and one by one they
said to him, "Surely not I?"
20"It is one of the Twelve," he replied, "one
who dips bread into the bowl with me. 21The Son
of Man will go just as it is written about him. But
woe to that man who betrays the Son of Man! It
would be better for him if he had not been born."
22While they were eating, Jesus took bread,
gave thanks and broke it, and gave it to his disci-
ples, saying, "Take it; this is my body."
23Then he took the cup, gave thanks and of-
fered it to them, and they all drank from it.
24"This is my blood of the[n] covenant, which is
poured out for many," he said to them. 25"I tell
you the truth, I will not drink again of the fruit of
the vine until that day when I drink it anew in the
kingdom of God."
26When they had sung a hymn, they went out
to the Mount of Olives.
27"You will all fall away," Jesus told them, "for
it is written:

" 'I will strike the shepherd,
and the sheep will be scattered.'[o]

[m]5 Greek *than three hundred denarii* [n]24 Some manuscripts *the new*
[o]27 Zech. 13:7

28But after I have risen, I will go ahead of you into
Galilee."
29Peter declared, "Even if all fall away, I will
not."
30"I tell you the truth," Jesus answered, "to-
day—yes, tonight—before the rooster crows
twice[p] you yourself will disown me three times."
31But Peter insisted emphatically, "Even if I
have to die with you, I will never disown you."
And all the others said the same.
32They went to a place called Gethsemane, and
Jesus said to his disciples, "Sit here while I pray."
33He took Peter, James and John along with him,
and he began to be deeply distressed and trou-
bled. 34"My soul is overwhelmed with sorrow to
the point of death," he said to them. "Stay here
and keep watch."
35Going a little farther, he fell to the ground
and prayed that if possible the hour might pass
from him. 36"*Abba*,[q] Father," he said, "every-
thing is possible for you. Take this cup from me.
Yet not what I will, but what you will."
37Then he returned to his disciples and found
them sleeping. "Simon," he said to Peter, "are you
asleep? Could you not keep watch for one hour?
38Watch and pray so that you will not fall into
temptation. The spirit is willing, but the body is
weak."
39Once more he went away and prayed the
same thing. 40When he came back, he again
found them sleeping, because their eyes were
heavy. They did not know what to say to him.
41Returning the third time, he said to them,
"Are you still sleeping and resting? Enough! The
hour has come. Look, the Son of Man is betrayed
into the hands of sinners. 42Rise! Let us go! Here
comes my betrayer!"

p30 Some early manuscripts do not have *twice*. q36 Aramaic for *Father*

Discovering the Word 1. What different motives are present in the conflict that arises at the home of Simon the Leper? 2. During the Passover feast Jesus tells the Twelve that one of them will betray him. What do you think they were feeling as they responded to his announcement (v. 19)? 3. Few words have spawned as much debate regarding their meaning as those Jesus spoke in verses 22–24. Regardless of how literally we take them, what are the bread and cup of the Lord's Supper to symbolize for us? 4. How might verses 32–36 help those who struggle with the question of whether Jesus is the only way to God?

Applying the Word 1. How can the exhortations in verses 34 and 38 make the difference in your own life between resisting or falling into temptation? 2. When have you felt like the disciples must have felt in verse 40? 3. What consolation and encouragement can you draw from the disciples' experience?

Responding in Prayer Thank God for his wonderful provision of forgiveness in Christ.

19 / *Mark 14:43–72*

Betrayed!

THE PERSECUTION OF enemies is one thing, the abandonment of friends another. In this study we find Jesus not only betrayed by one of his disciples but abandoned by all the others and ruefully denied by one of his closest friends. All this added to the cruel and unlawful treatment by the Sanhedrin. This account reveals how intense pressures can test the quality of our discipleship.

Warming Up to God We all betray Christ in the things we say or do. How have you betrayed him recently? Spend time in sincere confession. Hear the words of forgiveness.

Read Mark 14:43–72.

43Just as he was speaking, Judas, one of the
Twelve, appeared. With him was a crowd armed
with swords and clubs, sent from the chief
priests, the teachers of the law, and the elders.
44Now the betrayer had arranged a signal with
them: "The one I kiss is the man; arrest him and
lead him away under guard." 45Going at once to
Jesus, Judas said, "Rabbi!" and kissed him. 46The
men seized Jesus and arrested him. 47Then one of
those standing near drew his sword and struck
the servant of the high priest, cutting off his ear.

48"Am I leading a rebellion," said Jesus, "that
you have come out with swords and clubs to cap-
ture me? 49Every day I was with you, teaching in
the temple courts, and you did not arrest me. But
the Scriptures must be fulfilled." 50Then everyone
deserted him and fled.

51A young man, wearing nothing but a linen
garment, was following Jesus. When they seized
him, 52he fled naked, leaving his garment behind.

53They took Jesus to the high priest, and all the
chief priests, elders and teachers of the law came
together. 54Peter followed him at a distance, right
into the courtyard of the high priest. There he sat
with the guards and warmed himself at the fire.

55The chief priests and the whole Sanhedrin
were looking for evidence against Jesus so that
they could put him to death, but they did not find
any. 56Many testified falsely against him, but their
statements did not agree.

57Then some stood up and gave this false testi-
mony against him: 58"We heard him say, 'I will
destroy this man-made temple and in three days
will build another, not made by man.'" 59Yet even
then their testimony did not agree.

60Then the high priest stood up before them
and asked Jesus, "Are you not going to answer?
What is this testimony that these men are bring-
ing against you?" 61But Jesus remained silent and
gave no answer.

Again the high priest asked him, "Are you the
Christ,[r] the Son of the Blessed One?"

62"I am," said Jesus. "And you will see the Son
of Man sitting at the right hand of the Mighty
One and coming on the clouds of heaven."

63The high priest tore his clothes. "Why do we
need any more witnesses?" he asked. 64"You have
heard the blasphemy. What do you think?"

They all condemned him as worthy of death.
65Then some began to spit at him; they blind-
folded him, struck him with their fists, and said,
"Prophesy!" And the guards took him and beat
him.

66While Peter was below in the courtyard, one
of the servant girls of the high priest came by.
67When she saw Peter warming himself, she
looked closely at him.

"You also were with that Nazarene, Jesus," she
said.

68But he denied it. "I don't know or understand
what you're talking about," he said, and went out
into the entryway.[s]

69When the servant girl saw him there, she said
again to those standing around, "This fellow is
one of them." 70Again he denied it.

After a little while, those standing near said to
Peter, "Surely you are one of them, for you are a
Galilean."

71He began to call down curses on himself, and
he swore to them, "I don't know this man you're
talking about."

72Immediately the rooster crowed the second
time.[t] Then Peter remembered the word Jesus
had spoken to him: "Before the rooster crows
twice[u] you will disown me three times." And he
broke down and wept.

[r]61 Or *Messiah* [s]68 Some early manuscripts *entryway and the rooster crowed* [t]72 Some early manuscripts do not have *the second time.* [u]72 Some early manuscripts do not have *twice.*

Discovering the Word 1. How does Jesus respond to his betrayal? 2. What aspects of Jesus' trial before the Sanhedrin (vv. 53–65) does Mark emphasize? 3. Up until this point Jesus has regularly disguised his identity, but in verse 62 he openly confesses his identity as the Christ. Why do you think he does this now? 4. How is the charge against Jesus both justifiable and unjustifiable? 5. What mix of motives brings Peter into the high priest's courtyard yet keeps him from acknowledging his relationship to Jesus (vv. 66–72)?

Applying the Word 1. How are your motives mixed in following Jesus? 2. In what circumstances are you most tempted to be ashamed of Jesus or to deny him? 3. What warnings and encouragement can you draw from Peter's experience?

Responding in Prayer Ask God to keep you from betrayal.

20 / *Mark 15:1—16:8*
Victory Snatched from Defeat

TRUE GREATNESS, JESUS taught, is found in being a servant: "Whoever wants to be first must be slave of all. For even the Son of Man did not come to be served, but to serve, and to give his life as a ransom for many." Recorded here is the vivid testimony to Jesus' greatness and glory.

Warming Up to God What about death is intimidating to you? Reflect on how Jesus would have felt going to the cross. Spend time responding in prayer.

Read Mark 15:1—16:8.

15 Very early in the morning, the chief
priests, with the elders, the teachers
of the law and the whole Sanhe-
drin, reached a decision. They bound Jesus, led
him away and handed him over to Pilate.
2"Are you the king of the Jews?" asked Pilate.
"Yes, it is as you say," Jesus replied.
3The chief priests accused him of many things.
4So again Pilate asked him, "Aren't you going to
answer? See how many things they are accusing
you of."
5But Jesus still made no reply, and Pilate was
amazed.
6Now it was the custom at the Feast to release
a prisoner whom the people requested. 7A man
called Barabbas was in prison with the insurrec-
tionists who had committed murder in the upris-
ing. 8The crowd came up and asked Pilate to do
for them what he usually did.
9"Do you want me to release to you the king of
the Jews?" asked Pilate, 10knowing it was out of
envy that the chief priests had handed Jesus over
to him. 11But the chief priests stirred up the
crowd to have Pilate release Barabbas instead.
12"What shall I do, then, with the one you call
the king of the Jews?" Pilate asked them.
13"Crucify him!" they shouted.
14"Why? What crime has he committed?"
asked Pilate.
But they shouted all the louder, "Crucify him!"
15Wanting to satisfy the crowd, Pilate released
Barabbas to them. He had Jesus flogged, and
handed him over to be crucified.
16The soldiers led Jesus away into the palace
(that is, the Praetorium) and called together the
whole company of soldiers. 17They put a purple
robe on him, then twisted together a crown of
thorns and set it on him. 18And they began to call
out to him, "Hail, king of the Jews!" 19Again and
again they struck him on the head with a staff and
spit on him. Falling on their knees, they paid
homage to him. 20And when they had mocked
him, they took off the purple robe and put his
own clothes on him. Then they led him out to
crucify him.
21A certain man from Cyrene, Simon, the father
of Alexander and Rufus, was passing by on his
way in from the country, and they forced him to
carry the cross. 22They brought Jesus to the place
called Golgotha (which means The Place of the
Skull). 23Then they offered him wine mixed with
myrrh, but he did not take it. 24And they crucified
him. Dividing up his clothes, they cast lots to see
what each would get.
25It was the third hour when they crucified
him. 26The written notice of the charge against
him read: THE KING OF THE JEWS. 27They crucified
two robbers with him, one on his right and one
on his left.[v] 29Those who passed by hurled in-
sults at him, shaking their heads and saying, "So!
You who are going to destroy the temple and
build it in three days, 30come down from the
cross and save yourself!"
31In the same way the chief priests and the
teachers of the law mocked him among them-
selves. "He saved others," they said, "but he can't
save himself! 32Let this Christ,[w] this King of Is-
rael, come down now from the cross, that we may
see and believe." Those crucified with him also
heaped insults on him.
33At the sixth hour darkness came over the
whole land until the ninth hour. 34And at the
ninth hour Jesus cried out in a loud voice, *"Eloi,
Eloi, lama sabachthani?"*—which means, "My
God, my God, why have you forsaken me?"[x]
35When some of those standing near heard this,
they said, "Listen, he's calling Elijah."
36One man ran, filled a sponge with wine vine-
gar, put it on a stick, and offered it to Jesus to
drink. "Now leave him alone. Let's see if Elijah
comes to take him down," he said.
37With a loud cry, Jesus breathed his last.

[v]27 Some manuscripts *left, 28and the scripture was fulfilled which says, "He was counted with the lawless ones"* (Isaiah 53:12) [w]32 Or *Messiah* [x]34 Psalm 22:1

38The curtain of the temple was torn in two
from top to bottom. 39And when the centurion,
who stood there in front of Jesus, heard his cry
and[y] saw how he died, he said, "Surely this man
was the Son[z] of God!"
40Some women were watching from a distance.
Among them were Mary Magdalene, Mary the
mother of James the younger and of Joses, and
Salome. 41In Galilee these women had followed
him and cared for his needs. Many other women
who had come up with him to Jerusalem were
also there.
42It was Preparation Day (that is, the day before
the Sabbath). So as evening approached, 43Joseph
of Arimathea, a prominent member of the Coun-
cil, who was himself waiting for the kingdom of
God, went boldly to Pilate and asked for Jesus'
body. 44Pilate was surprised to hear that he was
already dead. Summoning the centurion, he
asked him if Jesus had already died. 45When he
learned from the centurion that it was so, he gave
the body to Joseph. 46So Joseph bought some
linen cloth, took down the body, wrapped it in
the linen, and placed it in a tomb cut out of rock.
Then he rolled a stone against the entrance of the
tomb. 47Mary Magdalene and Mary the mother of
Joses saw where he was laid.

16 When the Sabbath was over, Mary
Magdalene, Mary the mother of
James, and Salome bought spices so
that they might go to anoint Jesus' body. 2Very
early on the first day of the week, just after sun-
rise, they were on their way to the tomb 3and they
asked each other, "Who will roll the stone away
from the entrance of the tomb?"
4But when they looked up, they saw that the
stone, which was very large, had been rolled
away. 5As they entered the tomb, they saw a
young man dressed in a white robe sitting on the
right side, and they were alarmed.
6"Don't be alarmed," he said. "You are looking
for Jesus the Nazarene, who was crucified. He has
risen! He is not here. See the place where they
laid him. 7But go, tell his disciples and Peter, 'He
is going ahead of you into Galilee. There you will
see him, just as he told you.' "
8Trembling and bewildered, the women went
out and fled from the tomb. They said nothing to
anyone, because they were afraid.

[The earliest manuscripts and some other ancient witnesses do not have Mark 16:9–20.]

9When Jesus rose early on the first day of the
week, he appeared first to Mary Magdalene, out of
whom he had driven seven demons. 10She went
and told those who had been with him and who
were mourning and weeping. 11When they heard
that Jesus was alive and that she had seen him,
they did not believe it.
12Afterward Jesus appeared in a different form
to two of them while they were walking in the
country. 13These returned and reported it to the
rest; but they did not believe them either.
14Later Jesus appeared to the Eleven as they
were eating; he rebuked them for their lack of
faith and their stubborn refusal to believe those
who had seen him after he had risen.
15He said to them, "Go into all the world and
preach the good news to all creation. 16Whoever
believes and is baptized will be saved, but who-
ever does not believe will be condemned. 17And
these signs will accompany those who believe: In
my name they will drive out demons; they will
speak in new tongues; 18they will pick up snakes
with their hands; and when they drink deadly
poison, it will not hurt them at all; they will place
their hands on sick people, and they will get
well."
19After the Lord Jesus had spoken to them, he
was taken up into heaven and he sat at the right
hand of God. 20Then the disciples went out and
preached everywhere, and the Lord worked with
them and confirmed his word by the signs that
accompanied it.

y39 Some manuscripts do not have *heard his cry and* z39 Or *a son*

Discovering the Word 1. What kind of man is Pilate (vv. 1–15)? 2. What keeps him from doing what is right? 3. What ironies are present in the charges and jeers directed toward Jesus on the cross (vv. 25–32)? 4. Why do you think it was Joseph and the women who had followed Jesus, and not the eleven, who were present when Jesus died and his body needed a tomb (15:42—16:8)? 5. Why is it significant that Peter is mentioned by name in 16:7?

Applying the Word 1. How can we keep from succumbing to the temptation Pilate faced? 2. How can this passage reinforce our commitment to sharing the good news of Christ with others?

Responding in Prayer Spend time in praise and thanksgiving for Christ's sacrifice and for his resurrection over death.

Luke

At coffee break in a Paris conference, a third-year law student approached me with a good question. "You were talking about me when you spoke of church people who are respectfully bored with Jesus. You talk about him as if he's fascinating. How can I see Jesus this way?"

That opener with Jacques led to a fruitful discussion about the basic need to know the earthly life of Jesus Christ. Apart from Revelation 14:4, all references to "following Jesus" are of him as a man living in this world. The Son of God—*yes!* But just as emphatically we must say he is the Son of Humanity, authentically human!

How can we better know and follow Jesus Christ? Master the facts and implications of his earthly life and mission. That is how the first disciples gradually were dispelled of their wrong notions and came to see who Jesus of Nazareth really was—a divine Messiah, the Son of God, the universal Savior. They left behind historical records of his life. You have chosen to study the most comprehensive record of that life, *Luke's good news of new hope and new joy*.

The Uniqueness of Luke

Of the four Gospels, Luke's is the longest. It includes material not found elsewhere—for example, Jesus' childhood, his parables in chapters 10—19, his one-year ministry through Samaria and Berea during his final journey to Jerusalem. It includes unique characters—for instance, Zechariah and Elizabeth, Simeon and Anna, Simon the Pharisee and the prostitute, the Emmaus disciples (note the coupling) and Zaccheus.

Of the four Gospel writers, Luke was the only Gentile. As an initial outsider to God's chosen community, he was intrigued by Jesus' compassionate attention to foreigners (Syrians, Romans, Greeks, Africans) and social outcasts (tax collectors, lepers, prostitutes, beggars).

No other biblical author includes as many women—or as sympathetically as Luke does. No other writer talks about children and describes family life as he does. This is delightfully surprising for one who was apparently a bachelor.

Luke made a rich contribution to apostolic history, the period when the gospel was established in the Roman Empire. As a cosmopolitan traveler, he was admirably suited to become a coworker and "beloved doctor" of Paul, the apostle to the Gentiles. Acts and Paul's letters hint that this companionship had a tempering effect on the fiery apostle who became Christianity's foremost church planter, theologian and statesman.

The Writing of Luke

Luke's Gospel is accurate and well organized. Its formal introduction reflects the writer's Greek literary background (1:1–4). Here he claims to follow the principles for writing dependable history: (1) acquaintance with similar accounts, (2) interviews with primary sources—eyewitnesses and leading personages, (3) investigation of reported events, (4) orderliness in arranging materials, and (5) a stated aim.

Most scholars think that Luke (like Matthew) probably used Mark's older Gospel as the structural basis of his Gospel. When, however, he does use Mark's stories, he often touches them lightly with an extra personal detail. For example, compare the openings of the Jairus story in Mark 5:21–23 and Luke 8:40–42.

Luke addresses his Gospel (and Acts) to Theophilus. We know nothing else about this man. His name, "lover of God," was an aristocratic Roman one, and not uncommon among government officials. He could have been an actual person or a literary representative of this upper class of Gentile readers. According to Luke 1:4, he was either a seeker or a new Christian in need of historical substantiation of the good news.

Characteristics of Luke

Luke writes history like an artist. He employs prose and poetry, dialogue and description. In his choice of events and people he uses rhythm of emphasis, comparisons and contrasts. He uses this last teaching technique especially well with broad subjects—for example, Jesus' compassion for outcasts and his condemnation of the Pharisees, and Jesus' teachings on freedom of life with God and the cost of discipleship.

In transitions Luke is especially artistic. Note how the change of persons and locations in chapter 1 is smoothened by moving from one pregnancy to another. Likewise, his summaries of events also serve as links to the next train of events (for example, 2:39–40 or 5:15–16).

His book overflows with worship, prayer and praise, hope and joy. It begins with Old Testament believers in the temple, worshiping in messianic hope. It ends with New Testament believers also in the temple, rejoicing in resurrection hope. In between we see Jesus interacting personally with the widest range of human beings found in any book of the Bible (or any book in the world)—the old and the young, the very poor and the very rich, Jews and foreigners, national/international leaders and the rejects of society, the highly articulate and the nonarticulate.

Watch for bits of humor (for example, in Jesus' parables and in the Zaccheus story), the role of the Holy Spirit, medical terms, Jesus' habits of prayer, and the "divine necessity" Jesus felt (2:49; 4:43; 13:16, 33; 17:25; 24:26). Luke's portrait of Jesus is strong, warm, compassionate and cosmopolitan—like the writer himself.

My prayer for you as you study comes from Paul the apostle, Luke's friend:

May the God of hope fill you with all joy and peace as you trust in him, so that you may overflow with hope by the power of the Holy Spirit. (Ro 15:13)

Outline

Part 1: Mission in Galilee

Part 2: Mission in Samaria, Berea and Judea

1 / *Luke 1*
People of Hope

LUKE BEGINS HIS story of the extraordinary Christ by introducing some very ordinary people. They live in a small, second-rate country occupied by imperial Rome. It is around 4 B.C. For over 400 years their nation, Israel, has had no prophetic voice from God. Has God forgotten his chosen people? Has he left them to be the perennial pawns of aggressive neighbors? Is he going back on his many promises to send his Messiah to save them?

No. God is about to break into Israel's dark history with new light, and he chooses to do this through an elderly childless couple and a teenaged village girl.

Warming Up to God How do you feel when you are part of a hopeful minority among pessimistic people on a committee or in a group?

Read Luke 1.

1 Many have undertaken to draw up an account of the things that have been fulfilled[a] among us, 2just as they were handed down to us by those who from the first were eyewitnesses and servants of the word. 3Therefore, since I myself have carefully investigated everything from the beginning, it seemed good also to me to write an orderly account for you, most excellent Theophilus, 4so that you may know the certainty of the things you have been taught.

5In the time of Herod king of Judea there was a priest named Zechariah, who belonged to the priestly division of Abijah; his wife Elizabeth was also a descendant of Aaron. 6Both of them were upright in the sight of God, observing all the Lord's commandments and regulations blamelessly. 7But they had no children, because Elizabeth was barren; and they were both well along in years.

8Once when Zechariah's division was on duty and he was serving as priest before God, 9he was chosen by lot, according to the custom of the priesthood, to go into the temple of the Lord and burn incense. 10And when the time for the burning of incense came, all the assembled worshipers were praying outside.

11Then an angel of the Lord appeared to him, standing at the right side of the altar of incense. 12When Zechariah saw him, he was startled and was gripped with fear. 13But the angel said to him: "Do not be afraid, Zechariah; your prayer has been heard. Your wife Elizabeth will bear you a son, and you are to give him the name John. 14He will be a joy and delight to you, and many will rejoice because of his birth, 15for he will be great in the sight of the Lord. He is never to take wine or other fermented drink, and he will be filled with the Holy Spirit even from birth.[b] 16Many of the people of Israel will he bring back to the Lord their God. 17And he will go on before the Lord, in the spirit and power of Elijah, to turn the hearts of the fathers to their children and the disobedient to the wisdom of the righteous—to make ready a people prepared for the Lord."

18Zechariah asked the angel, "How can I be sure of this? I am an old man and my wife is well along in years."

19The angel answered, "I am Gabriel. I stand in the presence of God, and I have been sent to speak to you and to tell you this good news. 20And now you will be silent and not able to speak until the day this happens, because you did not believe my words, which will come true at their proper time."

21Meanwhile, the people were waiting for Zechariah and wondering why he stayed so long in the temple. 22When he came out, he could not speak to them. They realized he had seen a vision in the temple, for he kept making signs to them but remained unable to speak.

23When his time of service was completed, he returned home. 24After this his wife Elizabeth became pregnant and for five months remained in seclusion. 25"The Lord has done this for me," she said. "In these days he has shown his favor and taken away my disgrace among the people."

26In the sixth month, God sent the angel Gabriel to Nazareth, a town in Galilee, 27to a virgin pledged to be married to a man named Joseph, a descendant of David. The virgin's name was

[a]1 *Or been surely believed* [b]15 *Or from his mother's womb*

Mary. 28The angel went to her and said, "Greet-
ings, you who are highly favored! The Lord is
with you."

29Mary was greatly troubled at his words and
wondered what kind of greeting this might be.
30But the angel said to her, "Do not be afraid,
Mary, you have found favor with God. 31You will
be with child and give birth to a son, and you are
to give him the name Jesus. 32He will be great and
will be called the Son of the Most High. The Lord
God will give him the throne of his father David,
33and he will reign over the house of Jacob for-
ever; his kingdom will never end."

34"How will this be," Mary asked the angel,
"since I am a virgin?"

35The angel answered, "The Holy Spirit will
come upon you, and the power of the Most High
will overshadow you. So the holy one to be born
will be called[c] the Son of God. 36Even Elizabeth
your relative is going to have a child in her old
age, and she who was said to be barren is in her
sixth month. 37For nothing is impossible with
God."

38"I am the Lord's servant," Mary answered.
"May it be to me as you have said." Then the
angel left her.

39At that time Mary got ready and hurried to a
town in the hill country of Judea, 40where she
entered Zechariah's home and greeted Elizabeth.
41When Elizabeth heard Mary's greeting, the baby
leaped in her womb, and Elizabeth was filled with
the Holy Spirit. 42In a loud voice she exclaimed:
"Blessed are you among women, and blessed is
the child you will bear! 43But why am I so fa-
vored, that the mother of my Lord should come
to me? 44As soon as the sound of your greeting
reached my ears, the baby in my womb leaped for
joy. 45Blessed is she who has believed that what
the Lord has said to her will be accomplished!"

46And Mary said:

"My soul glorifies the Lord
47 and my spirit rejoices in God my Savior,
48for he has been mindful
of the humble state of his servant.
From now on all generations will call me
blessed,
49 for the Mighty One has done great things
for me—
holy is his name.
50His mercy extends to those who fear him,
from generation to generation.
51He has performed mighty deeds with his arm;
he has scattered those who are proud in
their inmost thoughts.
52He has brought down rulers from their
thrones
but has lifted up the humble.
53He has filled the hungry with good things
but has sent the rich away empty.
54He has helped his servant Israel,
remembering to be merciful
55to Abraham and his descendants forever,
even as he said to our fathers."

56Mary stayed with Elizabeth for about three
months and then returned home.

57When it was time for Elizabeth to have her
baby, she gave birth to a son. 58Her neighbors and
relatives heard that the Lord had shown her great
mercy, and they shared her joy.

59On the eighth day they came to circumcise
the child, and they were going to name him after
his father Zechariah, 60but his mother spoke up
and said, "No! He is to be called John."

61They said to her, "There is no one among
your relatives who has that name."

62Then they made signs to his father, to find
out what he would like to name the child. 63He
asked for a writing tablet, and to everyone's as-
tonishment he wrote, "His name is John." 64Im-
mediately his mouth was opened and his tongue
was loosed, and he began to speak, praising God.
65The neighbors were all filled with awe, and
throughout the hill country of Judea people were
talking about all these things. 66Everyone who
heard this wondered about it, asking, "What then
is this child going to be?" For the Lord's hand was
with him.

67His father Zechariah was filled with the Holy
Spirit and prophesied:

68"Praise be to the Lord, the God of Israel,
because he has come and has redeemed his
people.
69He has raised up a horn[d] of salvation for us
in the house of his servant David
70(as he said through his holy prophets of long
ago),
71salvation from our enemies
and from the hand of all who hate us—
72to show mercy to our fathers
and to remember his holy covenant,

[c]35 Or *So the child to be born will be called holy,* [d]69 *Horn* here symbolizes strength.

73 the oath he swore to our father Abraham:
74to rescue us from the hand of our enemies,
and to enable us to serve him without fear
75 in holiness and righteousness before him all our days.

76And you, my child, will be called a prophet of the Most High;
for you will go on before the Lord to prepare the way for him,
77to give his people the knowledge of salvation
through the forgiveness of their sins,
78because of the tender mercy of our God,
by which the rising sun will come to us from heaven
79to shine on those living in darkness
and in the shadow of death,
to guide our feet into the path of peace."

80And the child grew and became strong in spirit; and he lived in the desert until he appeared publicly to Israel.

Discovering the Word 1. Gabriel announces some astounding facts to Zechariah about his son who is to be born (vv. 11–17). Do you find yourself sympathetic or critical of Zechariah's response of unbelief (vv. 18–22)? Explain. 2. Luke 1:26–56 has Gabriel's second birth announcement. How is it even more extraordinary than the first? 3. The visit to her cousin Elizabeth bolsters Mary's faith for the stupendous event to come. As expressed in her song of response, what kind of God does she believe in (vv. 46–55)? 4. Note the effects of John's birth on neighbors and relatives (vv. 57–66). What might be Luke's purpose in describing their response in such detail? 5. In Zechariah's inspired prophecy he sees (1) the great acts that God's Redeemer will do (vv. 68–75), and (2) his child's unique relation to this Redeemer (vv. 76–79). Suppose you were one of Zechariah's neighbors or relatives listening to him. Which part would have stirred you as a devout Jew? Explain.

Applying the Word 1. When is it difficult for you to hope in God? 2. Zechariah and Mary expressed their hope in God differently. What in their interaction with God gives you hope as you also seek to trust God totally?

Responding in Prayer Thank God for being the only source of true hope.

2 / *Luke 2*
Child of Hope

DID YOU HEAR the one about the woman shopper at Christmas who came upon a nativity scene in the store window? In disgust she exclaimed, "Now look what they're dragging into Christmas. Religion!"

Warming Up to God For you, what is most meaningful at Christmas?

Read Luke 2.

2 In those days Caesar Augustus issued a
decree that a census should be taken of
the entire Roman world. 2(This was the
first census that took place while Quirinius was
governor of Syria.) 3And everyone went to his
own town to register.

4So Joseph also went up from the town of Nazareth in Galilee to Judea, to Bethlehem the town
of David, because he belonged to the house and
line of David. 5He went there to register with
Mary, who was pledged to be married to him and
was expecting a child. 6While they were there, the
time came for the baby to be born, 7and she gave
birth to her firstborn, a son. She wrapped him in
cloths and placed him in a manger, because there
was no room for them in the inn.

8And there were shepherds living out in the
fields nearby, keeping watch over their flocks at
night. 9An angel of the Lord appeared to them,
and the glory of the Lord shone around them, and

they were terrified. 10But the angel said to them,
"Do not be afraid. I bring you good news of great
joy that will be for all the people. 11Today in the
town of David a Savior has been born to you; he
is Christ[e] the Lord. 12This will be a sign to you:
You will find a baby wrapped in cloths and lying
in a manger."

13Suddenly a great company of the heavenly
host appeared with the angel, praising God and
saying,

14"Glory to God in the highest,
and on earth peace to men on whom his
favor rests."

15When the angels had left them and gone into
heaven, the shepherds said to one another, "Let's
go to Bethlehem and see this thing that has hap-
pened, which the Lord has told us about."

16So they hurried off and found Mary and Jo-
seph, and the baby, who was lying in the manger.
17When they had seen him, they spread the word
concerning what had been told them about this
child, 18and all who heard it were amazed at what
the shepherds said to them. 19But Mary treasured
up all these things and pondered them in her
heart. 20The shepherds returned, glorifying and
praising God for all the things they had heard and
seen, which were just as they had been told.

21On the eighth day, when it was time to cir-
cumcise him, he was named Jesus, the name the
angel had given him before he had been con-
ceived.

22When the time of their purification according
to the Law of Moses had been completed, Joseph
and Mary took him to Jerusalem to present him to
the Lord 23(as it is written in the Law of the Lord,
"Every firstborn male is to be consecrated to the
Lord"[f]), 24and to offer a sacrifice in keeping
with what is said in the Law of the Lord: "a pair
of doves or two young pigeons."[g]

25Now there was a man in Jerusalem called
Simeon, who was righteous and devout. He was
waiting for the consolation of Israel, and the Holy
Spirit was upon him. 26It had been revealed to
him by the Holy Spirit that he would not die be-
fore he had seen the Lord's Christ. 27Moved by
the Spirit, he went into the temple courts. When
the parents brought in the child Jesus to do for
him what the custom of the Law required, 28Sim-
eon took him in his arms and praised God, say-
ing:

29"Sovereign Lord, as you have promised,
you now dismiss[h] your servant in peace.
30For my eyes have seen your salvation,
31 which you have prepared in the sight of all
people,
32a light for revelation to the Gentiles
and for glory to your people Israel."

33The child's father and mother marveled at
what was said about him. 34Then Simeon blessed
them and said to Mary, his mother: "This child is
destined to cause the falling and rising of many in
Israel, and to be a sign that will be spoken
against, 35so that the thoughts of many hearts will
be revealed. And a sword will pierce your own
soul too."

36There was also a prophetess, Anna, the
daughter of Phanuel, of the tribe of Asher. She
was very old; she had lived with her husband
seven years after her marriage, 37and then was a
widow until she was eighty-four.[i] She never left
the temple but worshiped night and day, fasting
and praying. 38Coming up to them at that very
moment, she gave thanks to God and spoke about
the child to all who were looking forward to the
redemption of Jerusalem.

39When Joseph and Mary had done everything
required by the Law of the Lord, they returned to
Galilee to their own town of Nazareth. 40And the
child grew and became strong; he was filled with
wisdom, and the grace of God was upon him.

41Every year his parents went to Jerusalem for
the Feast of the Passover. 42When he was twelve
years old, they went up to the Feast, according to
the custom. 43After the Feast was over, while his
parents were returning home, the boy Jesus
stayed behind in Jerusalem, but they were un-
aware of it. 44Thinking he was in their company,
they traveled on for a day. Then they began look-
ing for him among their relatives and friends.
45When they did not find him, they went back to
Jerusalem to look for him. 46After three days they
found him in the temple courts, sitting among the
teachers, listening to them and asking them ques-
tions. 47Everyone who heard him was amazed at
his understanding and his answers. 48When his
parents saw him, they were astonished. His
mother said to him, "Son, why have you treated

[e] 11 Or *Messiah.* "The Christ" (Greek) and "the Messiah" (Hebrew) both mean "the Anointed One"; also in verse 26. [f] 23 Exodus 13:2,12 [g] 24 Lev. 12:8 [h] 29 Or *promised, / now dismiss*
[i] 37 Or *widow for eighty-four years*

us like this? Your father and I have been anx-
iously searching for you."
49"Why were you searching for me?" he asked.
"Didn't you know I had to be in my Father's
house?" 50But they did not understand what he
was saying to them.

51Then he went down to Nazareth with them
and was obedient to them. But his mother trea-
sured all these things in her heart. 52And Jesus
grew in wisdom and stature, and in favor with
God and men.

Discovering the Word 1. As with other strategic events, Luke gives the historical setting of the birth of Jesus (vv. 1–4). What implications does this setting suggest about the world into which Jesus came? 2. Luke gives us few details of Jesus' birth in verses 6–7. But what impression does he leave with you? 3. We like shepherds on Christmas cards. But back then they were an outcast group. So what in the angels' message would be incredible to them (vv. 9–14)? 4. The second and third prophetic events (note that the naming of Jesus was a prophetic event) are closely tied together (2:22–28). In what ways are Simeon and Anna similar? 5. How are their prophetic messages about Jesus similar yet different?

Applying the Word 1. Compare yourself with Jesus' development (vv. 40, 49, 51–52). In which area do you think you need more growth? 2. What can you begin to do to experience that growth?

Responding in Prayer Ask God to mold you into the person he wants you to be.

3 / *Luke 3:1–20*
Public Preparation

SEVERAL YEARS AGO, before Queen Elizabeth arrived in a British Commonwealth country, its people feverishly prepared a royal welcome. They gave special attention to the highway running from the airport to the capital. Each house along the way received from the government a fresh coat of paint—but only on the front of the house!

Superficial changes that people can notice—that's all some Christian leaders seem to ask for. Not so the preaching of John the Baptizer. He asked for radical moral changes, reversals of lifestyle.

Warming Up to God In what way are you likely to be satisfied with superficial changes in your own life?

Read Luke 3:1–20.

3 In the fifteenth year of the reign of Tiber-
ius Caesar—when Pontius Pilate was
governor of Judea, Herod tetrarch of Gali-
lee, his brother Philip tetrarch of Iturea and Trac-
onitis, and Lysanias tetrarch of Abilene— 2during
the high priesthood of Annas and Caiaphas, the
word of God came to John son of Zechariah in the
desert. 3He went into all the country around the
Jordan, preaching a baptism of repentance for
the forgiveness of sins. 4As is written in the book
of the words of Isaiah the prophet:

"A voice of one calling in the desert,
'Prepare the way for the Lord,
make straight paths for him.
5Every valley shall be filled in,
every mountain and hill made low.
The crooked roads shall become straight,
the rough ways smooth.
6And all mankind will see God's salvation.' "[j]

7John said to the crowds coming out to be bap-
tized by him, "You brood of vipers! Who warned
you to flee from the coming wrath? 8Produce fruit
in keeping with repentance. And do not begin to
say to yourselves, 'We have Abraham as our fa-
ther.' For I tell you that out of these stones God
can raise up children for Abraham. 9The ax is
already at the root of the trees, and every tree that

j6 Isaiah 40:3-5

does not produce good fruit will be cut down and thrown into the fire."

10"What should we do then?" the crowd asked.

11John answered, "The man with two tunics should share with him who has none, and the one who has food should do the same."

12Tax collectors also came to be baptized. "Teacher," they asked, "what should we do?"

13"Don't collect any more than you are required to," he told them.

14Then some soldiers asked him, "And what should we do?"

He replied, "Don't extort money and don't accuse people falsely—be content with your pay."

15The people were waiting expectantly and were all wondering in their hearts if John might possibly be the Christ.[k] 16John answered them all, "I baptize you with[l] water. But one more powerful than I will come, the thongs of whose sandals I am not worthy to untie. He will baptize you with the Holy Spirit and with fire. 17His winnowing fork is in his hand to clear his threshing floor and to gather the wheat into his barn, but he will burn up the chaff with unquenchable fire." 18And with many other words John exhorted the people and preached the good news to them.

19But when John rebuked Herod the tetrarch because of Herodias, his brother's wife, and all the other evil things he had done, 20Herod added this to them all: He locked John up in prison.

[k]15 Or *Messiah* [l]16 Or *in*

Discovering the Word 1. Reflect on John's dominant preaching theme in verses 3-9. How would you paraphrase this theme with contemporary relevance? 2. John gladly answers three distinct groups asking about the practical fruits of repentance. What basic sin does John attack in each case (vv. 8-14)? 3. In verses 15-20 John introduces Jesus the Christ. He has been uncompromising about the need for repentance. Now he also refuses to let the crowds think he is the expected Christ. In warning them, what picture of the Christ does he paint? 4. Like repentance, judgment is not a popular topic today among many Christians. Yet how is this also part of "the good news" (v. 18)?

Applying the Word 1. What injustices in your society would John attack? 2. John's message and ministry show what repentance should be. How would you explain repentance to inquirers in terms that make sense to them?

Responding in Prayer Pray for a friend who needs this explanation.

4 / *Luke 3:21—4:13*
Personal Preparation

"THE BEST WAY to get rid of temptation is to give in to it," said Oscar Wilde. He was the brilliant, flamboyant Irish writer of the second half of the nineteenth century. He died young, gifted and dissipated by his unbridled passions.

Jesus also died young and gifted, but disciplined by his passion for God. His discipline began in childhood where we have already observed an early consciousness of his life mission. Now, at thirty, he submits himself to more tests to prepare him further for this goal.

Warming Up to God What would you like to have achieved ten years from now?

Read Luke 3:21—4:13.

21When all the people were being baptized, Jesus was baptized too. And as he was praying, heaven was opened 22and the Holy Spirit descended on him in bodily form like a dove. And a voice came from heaven: "You are my Son, whom I love; with you I am well pleased."

23Now Jesus himself was about thirty years old
when he began his ministry. He was the son, so it
was thought, of Joseph,

the son of Heli, 24the son of Matthat,
the son of Levi, the son of Melki,
the son of Jannai, the son of Joseph,
25the son of Mattathias, the son of Amos,
the son of Nahum, the son of Esli,
the son of Naggai, 26the son of Maath,
the son of Mattathias, the son of Semein,
the son of Josech, the son of Joda,
27the son of Joanan, the son of Rhesa,
the son of Zerubbabel, the son of Shealtiel,
the son of Neri, 28the son of Melki,
the son of Addi, the son of Cosam,
the son of Elmadam, the son of Er,
29the son of Joshua, the son of Eliezer,
the son of Jorim, the son of Matthat,
the son of Levi, 30the son of Simeon,
the son of Judah, the son of Joseph,
the son of Jonam, the son of Eliakim,
31the son of Melea, the son of Menna,
the son of Mattatha, the son of Nathan,
the son of David, 32the son of Jesse,
the son of Obed, the son of Boaz,
the son of Salmon,[m] the son of Nahshon,
33the son of Amminadab, the son of Ram,[n]
the son of Hezron, the son of Perez,
the son of Judah, 34the son of Jacob,
the son of Isaac, the son of Abraham,
the son of Terah, the son of Nahor,
35the son of Serug, the son of Reu,
the son of Peleg, the son of Eber,
the son of Shelah, 36the son of Cainan,
the son of Arphaxad, the son of Shem,
the son of Noah, the son of Lamech,
37the son of Methuselah, the son of Enoch,
the son of Jared, the son of Mahalalel,
the son of Kenan, 38the son of Enosh,
the son of Seth, the son of Adam,
the son of God.

4 Jesus, full of the Holy Spirit, returned
from the Jordan and was led by the Spirit
in the desert, 2where for forty days he was
tempted by the devil. He ate nothing during those
days, and at the end of them he was hungry.
3The devil said to him, "If you are the Son of
God, tell this stone to become bread."
4Jesus answered, "It is written: 'Man does not
live on bread alone.'[o]"
5The devil led him up to a high place and
showed him in an instant all the kingdoms of the
world. 6And he said to him, "I will give you all
their authority and splendor, for it has been given
to me, and I can give it to anyone I want to. 7So
if you worship me, it will all be yours."
8Jesus answered, "It is written: 'Worship the
Lord your God and serve him only.'[p]"
9The devil led him to Jerusalem and had him
stand on the highest point of the temple. "If you
are the Son of God," he said, "throw yourself
down from here. 10For it is written:

" 'He will command his angels concerning you
to guard you carefully;
11they will lift you up in their hands,
so that you will not strike your foot against
a stone.'[q]"

12Jesus answered, "It says: 'Do not put the Lord
your God to the test.'[r]"
13When the devil had finished all this tempting,
he left him until an opportune time.

[m]32 Some early manuscripts *Sala* [n]33 Some manuscripts *Amminadab, the son of Admin, the son of Arni*; other manuscripts vary widely. [o]4 Deut. 8:3 [p]8 Deut. 6:13 [q]11 Psalm 91:11,12 [r]12 Deut. 6:16

Discovering the Word 1. Jesus did not have to be baptized for the forgiveness of his sins (v. 3). But by this public act he identified with our human race in need of repentance and forgiveness. What do Luke's details emphasize about Jesus' baptism? 2. Luke's genealogy of Jesus begins with his father, Joseph, and passing Abraham moves all the way back to "Adam, the son of God" (3:23–38). What does Luke want to bring out about Jesus? 3. Temptations are strong appeals to satisfy legitimate desires in wrong circumstances or by wrong means. What natural desire is the devil trying to get Jesus to satisfy in each appeal? 4. God created these desires. Why then would it become sin if Jesus were to satisfy each desire in his circumstances then?

Applying the Word 1. What do you learn from Jesus about dealing with temptations? 2. If we want to serve God wholeheartedly, we too must undergo tough training. In which area do you feel the greatest need for discipline? 3. What should be your first step in that direction?

Responding in Prayer Pray that God would work in your life to prepare you for the ministry he has for you.

5/ *Luke 4:14—5:16*
Promising Yet Dangerous Beginnings

SOMETIMES PEOPLE SAY, "Everything has been going so well that I feel something awful coming." They know enough about life not to expect good things to continue forever. But we need not be fatalistic. We can be both realistic and positive about expectations in life. We have seen how well Jesus began. We shall also see how realistic he was about fickle human nature and how he drew out the best in people who wanted to follow him.

Warming Up to God When you've felt rejection (on any level), what was your greatest fear?

Read Luke 4:14—5:16.

14Jesus returned to Galilee in the power of the Spirit, and news about him spread through the whole countryside. 15He taught in their synagogues, and everyone praised him.

16He went to Nazareth, where he had been brought up, and on the Sabbath day he went into the synagogue, as was his custom. And he stood up to read. 17The scroll of the prophet Isaiah was handed to him. Unrolling it, he found the place where it is written:

18"The Spirit of the Lord is on me,
because he has anointed me
to preach good news to the poor.
He has sent me to proclaim freedom for the prisoners
and recovery of sight for the blind,
to release the oppressed,
19 to proclaim the year of the Lord's favor."[s]

20Then he rolled up the scroll, gave it back to the attendant and sat down. The eyes of everyone in the synagogue were fastened on him, 21and he began by saying to them, "Today this scripture is fulfilled in your hearing."

22All spoke well of him and were amazed at the gracious words that came from his lips. "Isn't this Joseph's son?" they asked.

23Jesus said to them, "Surely you will quote this proverb to me: 'Physician, heal yourself! Do here in your hometown what we have heard that you did in Capernaum.' "

24"I tell you the truth," he continued, "no prophet is accepted in his hometown. 25I assure you that there were many widows in Israel in Elijah's time, when the sky was shut for three and a half years and there was a severe famine throughout the land. 26Yet Elijah was not sent to any of them, but to a widow in Zarephath in the region of Sidon. 27And there were many in Israel with leprosy[t] in the time of Elisha the prophet, yet not one of them was cleansed—only Naaman the Syrian."

28All the people in the synagogue were furious when they heard this. 29They got up, drove him out of the town, and took him to the brow of the hill on which the town was built, in order to throw him down the cliff. 30But he walked right through the crowd and went on his way.

31Then he went down to Capernaum, a town in Galilee, and on the Sabbath began to teach the people. 32They were amazed at his teaching, because his message had authority.

33In the synagogue there was a man possessed by a demon, an evil[u] spirit. He cried out at the top of his voice, 34"Ha! What do you want with us, Jesus of Nazareth? Have you come to destroy us? I know who you are—the Holy One of God!"

35"Be quiet!" Jesus said sternly. "Come out of him!" Then the demon threw the man down before them all and came out without injuring him.

36All the people were amazed and said to each other, "What is this teaching? With authority and power he gives orders to evil spirits and they come out!" 37And the news about him spread throughout the surrounding area.

38Jesus left the synagogue and went to the home of Simon. Now Simon's mother-in-law was suffering from a high fever, and they asked Jesus to help her. 39So he bent over her and rebuked the fever, and it left her. She got up at once and began to wait on them.

40When the sun was setting, the people brought to Jesus all who had various kinds of sickness, and laying his hands on each one, he

[s]19 Isaiah 61:1,2 [t]27 The Greek word was used for various diseases affecting the skin—not necessarily leprosy. [u]33 Greek *unclean*; also in verse 36

healed them. [41]Moreover, demons came out of many people, shouting, "You are the Son of God!" But he rebuked them and would not allow them to speak, because they knew he was the Christ.[v]

[42]At daybreak Jesus went out to a solitary place. The people were looking for him and when they came to where he was, they tried to keep him from leaving them. [43]But he said, "I must preach the good news of the kingdom of God to the other towns also, because that is why I was sent." [44]And he kept on preaching in the synagogues of Judea.[w]

5 One day as Jesus was standing by the Lake of Gennesaret,[x] with the people crowding around him and listening to the word of God, [2]he saw at the water's edge two boats, left there by the fishermen, who were washing their nets. [3]He got into one of the boats, the one belonging to Simon, and asked him to put out a little from shore. Then he sat down and taught the people from the boat.

[4]When he had finished speaking, he said to Simon, "Put out into deep water, and let down[y] the nets for a catch."

[5]Simon answered, "Master, we've worked hard all night and haven't caught anything. But because you say so, I will let down the nets."

[6]When they had done so, they caught such a large number of fish that their nets began to break. [7]So they signaled their partners in the other boat to come and help them, and they came and filled both boats so full that they began to sink.

[8]When Simon Peter saw this, he fell at Jesus' knees and said, "Go away from me, Lord; I am a sinful man!" [9]For he and all his companions were astonished at the catch of fish they had taken, [10]and so were James and John, the sons of Zebedee, Simon's partners.

Then Jesus said to Simon, "Don't be afraid; from now on you will catch men." [11]So they pulled their boats up on shore, left everything and followed him.

[12]While Jesus was in one of the towns, a man came along who was covered with leprosy.[z] When he saw Jesus, he fell with his face to the ground and begged him, "Lord, if you are willing, you can make me clean."

[13]Jesus reached out his hand and touched the man. "I am willing," he said. "Be clean!" And immediately the leprosy left him.

[14]Then Jesus ordered him, "Don't tell anyone, but go, show yourself to the priest and offer the sacrifices that Moses commanded for your cleansing, as a testimony to them."

[15]Yet the news about him spread all the more, so that crowds of people came to hear him and to be healed of their sicknesses. [16]But Jesus often withdrew to lonely places and prayed.

v *41* Or *Messiah* w *44* Or *the land of the Jews*; some manuscripts *Galilee* x *1* That is, Sea of Galilee y *4* The Greek verb is plural. z *12* The Greek word was used for various diseases affecting the skin—not necessarily leprosy.

Discovering the Word 1. What link do you see between Jesus' temptations and the beginning of his mission (4:14–15)? 2. Watch the people's changing attitudes to Jesus (vv. 14–15, 20–22, 28–29). What has caused the radical change? 3. What prejudices can make people today object to Jesus' good news or perhaps to Jesus himself? How would you respond to these objections? 4. Having been rejected by Nazareth, Jesus now makes Capernaum his base of operations. Here Luke describes what may be a typical work day for Jesus. Identify his activities during that period (4:31–44). 5. Read Luke 5:1–16. Note the progressive steps by which Jesus persuades Simon Peter to leave everything and follow him. When you met Jesus, what tensions arose as you recognized the need to leave everything to follow him?

Applying the Word 1. What can you learn from Jesus' example of dealing with rejection? 2. In its context Jesus' healing of the leper appears to be a personal encounter, typical of his opening ministry. As such then, what do you observe about Jesus as a people helper? 3. Think of your ministry to others. Which of Jesus' ministering qualities do you want to have added to or reinforced in your life?

Responding in Prayer Praise God for such a practical Teacher and Lord!

6 / *Luke 5:17—6:11*
Radical Authority

GOD IS ALWAYS full of surprises. Those who know him delight in this. This, however, upsets people who feel secure only with neatly structured beliefs that are left untouched. One problem for them is that every now and then God chooses to do something new and fresh. Then packaged religions and secure traditions fall apart! This often happened when Jesus came on Israel's religious scene with surprising teaching and authority.

Warming Up to God Do you wish you had more or less authority in your life? Why?

Read Luke 5:17—6:11.

17One day as he was teaching, Pharisees and teachers of the law, who had come from every village of Galilee and from Judea and Jerusalem, were sitting there. And the power of the Lord was present for him to heal the sick. 18Some men came carrying a paralytic on a mat and tried to take him into the house to lay him before Jesus. 19When they could not find a way to do this because of the crowd, they went up on the roof and lowered him on his mat through the tiles into the middle of the crowd, right in front of Jesus.

20When Jesus saw their faith, he said, "Friend, your sins are forgiven."

21The Pharisees and the teachers of the law began thinking to themselves, "Who is this fellow who speaks blasphemy? Who can forgive sins but God alone?"

22Jesus knew what they were thinking and asked, "Why are you thinking these things in your hearts? 23Which is easier: to say, 'Your sins are forgiven,' or to say, 'Get up and walk'? 24But that you may know that the Son of Man has authority on earth to forgive sins. . . ." He said to the paralyzed man, "I tell you, get up, take your mat and go home." 25Immediately he stood up in front of them, took what he had been lying on and went home praising God. 26Everyone was amazed and gave praise to God. They were filled with awe and said, "We have seen remarkable things today."

27After this, Jesus went out and saw a tax collector by the name of Levi sitting at his tax booth. "Follow me," Jesus said to him, 28and Levi got up, left everything and followed him.

29Then Levi held a great banquet for Jesus at his house, and a large crowd of tax collectors and others were eating with them. 30But the Pharisees and the teachers of the law who belonged to their sect complained to his disciples, "Why do you eat and drink with tax collectors and 'sinners'?"

31Jesus answered them, "It is not the healthy who need a doctor, but the sick. 32I have not come to call the righteous, but sinners to repentance."

33They said to him, "John's disciples often fast and pray, and so do the disciples of the Pharisees, but yours go on eating and drinking."

34Jesus answered, "Can you make the guests of the bridegroom fast while he is with them? 35But the time will come when the bridegroom will be taken from them; in those days they will fast."

36He told them this parable: "No one tears a patch from a new garment and sews it on an old one. If he does, he will have torn the new garment, and the patch from the new will not match the old. 37And no one pours new wine into old wineskins. If he does, the new wine will burst the skins, the wine will run out and the wineskins will be ruined. 38No, new wine must be poured into new wineskins. 39And no one after drinking old wine wants the new, for he says, 'The old is better.' "

6 One Sabbath Jesus was going through the grainfields, and his disciples began to pick some heads of grain, rub them in their hands and eat the kernels. 2Some of the Pharisees asked, "Why are you doing what is unlawful on the Sabbath?"

3Jesus answered them, "Have you never read what David did when he and his companions were hungry? 4He entered the house of God, and taking the consecrated bread, he ate what is lawful only for priests to eat. And he also gave some to his companions." 5Then Jesus said to them, "The Son of Man is Lord of the Sabbath."

6On another Sabbath he went into the synagogue and was teaching, and a man was there whose right hand was shriveled. 7The Pharisees and the teachers of the law were looking for a reason to accuse Jesus, so they watched him closely to see if he would heal on the Sabbath. 8But Jesus knew what they were thinking and said to the man with the shriveled hand, "Get up and stand in front of everyone." So he got up and stood there.

9Then Jesus said to them, "I ask you, which is lawful on the Sabbath: to do good or to do evil, to save life or to destroy it?"

10He looked around at them all, and then said to the man, "Stretch out your hand." He did so, and his hand was completely restored. 11But they were furious and began to discuss with one another what they might do to Jesus.

Discovering the Word 1. Imagine yourself a part of the religious establishment mentioned in 5:17. How would you have viewed Jesus' growing popularity? 2. Compare the Pharisees' questions in 5:21, 30, 33; 6:2, 7—criticisms which climax in 6:11. What pattern(s) do you observe? 3. What skills in answering religious critics can you learn from Jesus?

Applying the Word 1. Jesus was relentless in his battle with the religious legalists of his day. He clearly saw that in distorting God's laws they also distorted God's image. What religious legalisms can keep you from enjoying the Lord and his true sabbath? 2. Over which area of your life do you see Jesus exercising authority? 3. Over which area of your life do you sense an absence of Jesus' authority?

Responding in Prayer Ask Jesus to rule over your *whole* life.

7/ *Luke 6:12–49*
Radical Lifestyle

MAHATMA MOHANDAS GANDHI was India's revered leader in the fight for national independence from British colonialism. As a child in India, a student in England and a lawyer in South Africa, he was exposed to Christianity—and racism. He admired the teachings of Jesus, especially the Sermon on the Mount. He admired the life of Jesus, and indeed was inspired to follow his example. But after years of observing Christians, he sadly concluded, "For me to believe in their Redeemer, their lives must show they are redeemed." He never became a Christian.

A Christian's lifestyle matters—not only correct words. The total teaching and example of Jesus demands a lifestyle that is noticeably different from the average person's.

Warming Up to God Describe someone you know who has a truly Christlike lifestyle.

Read Luke 6:12–49.

12One of those days Jesus went out to a mountainside to pray, and spent the night praying to God. 13When morning came, he called his disciples to him and chose twelve of them, whom he also designated apostles: 14Simon (whom he named Peter), his brother Andrew, James, John, Philip, Bartholomew, 15Matthew, Thomas, James son of Alphaeus, Simon who was called the Zealot, 16Judas son of James, and Judas Iscariot, who became a traitor.

17He went down with them and stood on a level place. A large crowd of his disciples was there and a great number of people from all over Judea, from Jerusalem, and from the coast of Tyre and Sidon, 18who had come to hear him and to be healed of their diseases. Those troubled by evil[a] spirits were cured, 19and the people all tried to touch him, because power was coming from him and healing them all.

20Looking at his disciples, he said:

[a]18 Greek *unclean*

"Blessed are you who are poor,
for yours is the kingdom of God.
21Blessed are you who hunger now,
for you will be satisfied.
Blessed are you who weep now,
for you will laugh.
22Blessed are you when men hate you,
when they exclude you and insult you
and reject your name as evil,
because of the Son of Man.

23"Rejoice in that day and leap for joy, because
great is your reward in heaven. For that is how
their fathers treated the prophets.

24"But woe to you who are rich,
for you have already received your comfort.
25Woe to you who are well fed now,
for you will go hungry.
Woe to you who laugh now,
for you will mourn and weep.
26Woe to you when all men speak well of you,
for that is how their fathers treated the
false prophets.

27"But I tell you who hear me: Love your ene-
mies, do good to those who hate you, 28bless
those who curse you, pray for those who mistreat
you. 29If someone strikes you on one cheek, turn
to him the other also. If someone takes your
cloak, do not stop him from taking your tunic.
30Give to everyone who asks you, and if anyone
takes what belongs to you, do not demand it
back. 31Do to others as you would have them do
to you.

32"If you love those who love you, what credit
is that to you? Even 'sinners' love those who love
them. 33And if you do good to those who are good
to you, what credit is that to you? Even 'sinners'
do that. 34And if you lend to those from whom
you expect repayment, what credit is that to you?
Even 'sinners' lend to 'sinners,' expecting to be
repaid in full. 35But love your enemies, do good to
them, and lend to them without expecting to get
anything back. Then your reward will be great,
and you will be sons of the Most High, because he
is kind to the ungrateful and wicked. 36Be merci-
ful, just as your Father is merciful.

37"Do not judge, and you will not be judged.
Do not condemn, and you will not be con-
demned. Forgive, and you will be forgiven.
38Give, and it will be given to you. A good mea-
sure, pressed down, shaken together and running
over, will be poured into your lap. For with the
measure you use, it will be measured to you."

39He also told them this parable: "Can a blind
man lead a blind man? Will they not both fall into
a pit? 40A student is not above his teacher, but
everyone who is fully trained will be like his
teacher.

41"Why do you look at the speck of sawdust in
your brother's eye and pay no attention to the
plank in your own eye? 42How can you say to
your brother, 'Brother, let me take the speck out
of your eye,' when you yourself fail to see the
plank in your own eye? You hypocrite, first take
the plank out of your eye, and then you will see
clearly to remove the speck from your brother's
eye.

43"No good tree bears bad fruit, nor does a bad
tree bear good fruit. 44Each tree is recognized by
its own fruit. People do not pick figs from thorn-
bushes, or grapes from briers. 45The good man
brings good things out of the good stored up in
his heart, and the evil man brings evil things out
of the evil stored up in his heart. For out of the
overflow of his heart his mouth speaks.

46"Why do you call me, 'Lord, Lord,' and do
not do what I say? 47I will show you what he is
like who comes to me and hears my words and
puts them into practice. 48He is like a man build-
ing a house, who dug down deep and laid the
foundation on rock. When a flood came, the tor-
rent struck that house but could not shake it,
because it was well built. 49But the one who hears
my words and does not put them into practice is
like a man who built a house on the ground with-
out a foundation. The moment the torrent struck
that house, it collapsed and its destruction was
complete."

Discovering the Word 1. In verses 17–19 Luke has carefully given us the setting for the "Sermon on the Plain." What kinds of people are in Jesus' audience? 2. Jesus begins with kingdom attitudes that shape one's lifestyle. What contrasts does he draw between his way of personal fulfillment and the world's way (vv. 20–26)? 3. Jesus knows that loving one's enemies is impossible without strong motivation. How does he argue that his disciples can have that motivation (vv. 31–36)? 4. In verse 37 Jesus is probably being facetious, for he knows it is impossible not to judge others. Rather we are to judge with good sense. What guidelines does he give to judge in this way (vv. 37b–42)? 5. Jesus concludes by warning his listeners of the long-term results of their present choice of lifestyle (vv. 43–49). How do his logic and illustrations sharpen his argument?

Applying the Word 1. In what ways have you found Jesus' road to happiness the right one? Or an unsatisfactory one? 2. Loving one's enemies is another aspect of a radical Christian lifestyle. In what ways does your enemy make it hard for you to love him/her? 3. What in this study gives you hope that you can maintain the kind of radical lifestyle Jesus expects of his followers?

Responding in Prayer Pray for the strength and wisdom you need to love your enemies.

8 / *Luke 7*
Five People of Faith

AN ARTIST FRIEND struggled over the exclusive claim of the Christian faith. Is Jesus really the only way to God? Growing up in a pluralistic society had conditioned her to resist such an intolerant position. Because she was still interested, some Christians pressured her to "accept Jesus as your Savior and Lord." She could not. But she privately pursued the Gospels. She began to note how differently people approached Jesus and how personally he treated each of them. Gradually she saw a distinction: There is indeed only one way to God—through Jesus Christ—but there are many ways to Jesus Christ. Today we meet five persons with diverse backgrounds and varying approaches to Jesus—all different in expressing faith in Jesus.

Warming Up to God When is it hard for you to accept the idea that there is only one way to God?

Read Luke 7.

7 When Jesus had finished saying all this in
the hearing of the people, he entered Ca-
pernaum. 2There a centurion's servant,
whom his master valued highly, was sick and
about to die. 3The centurion heard of Jesus and
sent some elders of the Jews to him, asking him to
come and heal his servant. 4When they came to
Jesus, they pleaded earnestly with him, "This man
deserves to have you do this, 5because he loves
our nation and has built our synagogue." 6So
Jesus went with them.

He was not far from the house when the centu-
rion sent friends to say to him: "Lord, don't trou-
ble yourself, for I do not deserve to have you
come under my roof. 7That is why I did not even
consider myself worthy to come to you. But say
the word, and my servant will be healed. 8For I
myself am a man under authority, with soldiers
under me. I tell this one, 'Go,' and he goes; and
that one, 'Come,' and he comes. I say to my ser-
vant, 'Do this,' and he does it."

9When Jesus heard this, he was amazed at him,
and turning to the crowd following him, he said,
"I tell you, I have not found such great faith even
in Israel." 10Then the men who had been sent
returned to the house and found the servant well.

11Soon afterward, Jesus went to a town called
Nain, and his disciples and a large crowd went
along with him. 12As he approached the town
gate, a dead person was being carried out—the
only son of his mother, and she was a widow.
And a large crowd from the town was with her.
13When the Lord saw her, his heart went out to
her and he said, "Don't cry."

14Then he went up and touched the coffin, and
those carrying it stood still. He said, "Young man,
I say to you, get up!" 15The dead man sat up and
began to talk, and Jesus gave him back to his
mother.

16They were all filled with awe and praised
God. "A great prophet has appeared among us,"
they said. "God has come to help his people."
17This news about Jesus spread throughout Ju-
dea[b] and the surrounding country.

18John's disciples told him about all these
things. Calling two of them, 19he sent them to the

[b]17 *Or the land of the Jews*

Lord to ask, "Are you the one who was to come,
or should we expect someone else?"
20When the men came to Jesus, they said,
"John the Baptist sent us to you to ask, 'Are you
the one who was to come, or should we expect
someone else?'"
21At that very time Jesus cured many who had
diseases, sicknesses and evil spirits, and gave
sight to many who were blind. 22So he replied to
the messengers, "Go back and report to John
what you have seen and heard: The blind receive
sight, the lame walk, those who have leprosy[c]
are cured, the deaf hear, the dead are raised, and
the good news is preached to the poor. 23Blessed
is the man who does not fall away on account
of me."
24After John's messengers left, Jesus began to
speak to the crowd about John: "What did you go
out into the desert to see? A reed swayed by the
wind? 25If not, what did you go out to see? A man
dressed in fine clothes? No, those who wear ex-
pensive clothes and indulge in luxury are in pal-
aces. 26But what did you go out to see? A
prophet? Yes, I tell you, and more than a prophet.
27This is the one about whom it is written:

"'I will send my messenger ahead of you,
who will prepare your way before you.'[d]

28I tell you, among those born of women there is
no one greater than John; yet the one who is least
in the kingdom of God is greater than he."
29(All the people, even the tax collectors, when
they heard Jesus' words, acknowledged that God's
way was right, because they had been baptized by
John. 30But the Pharisees and experts in the law
rejected God's purpose for themselves, because
they had not been baptized by John.)
31"To what, then, can I compare the people of
this generation? What are they like? 32They are
like children sitting in the marketplace and call-
ing out to each other:

"'We played the flute for you,
and you did not dance;
we sang a dirge,
and you did not cry.'

33For John the Baptist came neither eating bread
nor drinking wine, and you say, 'He has a demon.'
34The Son of Man came eating and drinking, and
you say, 'Here is a glutton and a drunkard, a
friend of tax collectors and "sinners."' 35But wis-
dom is proved right by all her children."
36Now one of the Pharisees invited Jesus to
have dinner with him, so he went to the Phari-
see's house and reclined at the table. 37When a
woman who had lived a sinful life in that town
learned that Jesus was eating at the Pharisee's
house, she brought an alabaster jar of perfume,
38and as she stood behind him at his feet weeping,
she began to wet his feet with her tears. Then she
wiped them with her hair, kissed them and
poured perfume on them.
39When the Pharisee who had invited him saw
this, he said to himself, "If this man were a
prophet, he would know who is touching him
and what kind of woman she is—that she is a
sinner."
40Jesus answered him, "Simon, I have some-
thing to tell you."
"Tell me, teacher," he said.
41"Two men owed money to a certain money-
lender. One owed him five hundred denarii,[e]
and the other fifty. 42Neither of them had the
money to pay him back, so he canceled the debts
of both. Now which of them will love him more?"
43Simon replied, "I suppose the one who had
the bigger debt canceled."
"You have judged correctly," Jesus said.
44Then he turned toward the woman and said
to Simon, "Do you see this woman? I came into
your house. You did not give me any water for my
feet, but she wet my feet with her tears and wiped
them with her hair. 45You did not give me a kiss,
but this woman, from the time I entered, has not
stopped kissing my feet. 46You did not put oil on
my head, but she has poured perfume on my feet.
47Therefore, I tell you, her many sins have been
forgiven—for she loved much. But he who has
been forgiven little loves little."
48Then Jesus said to her, "Your sins are for-
given."
49The other guests began to say among them-
selves, "Who is this who even forgives sins?"
50Jesus said to the woman, "Your faith has
saved you; go in peace."

[c]22 The Greek word was used for various diseases affecting the skin—not necessarily leprosy. [d]27 Mal. 3:1 [e]41 A denarius was a coin worth about a day's wages.

Discovering the Word 1. Note the distinctive background of each of the five individuals who met Jesus. How are their backgrounds different? 2. What do they all have in common as they relate to Jesus? 3. Picture the two processions in verses 11–13 meeting just outside the town gate. There is no request for help, no sign of faith from the widow. But look at Jesus himself in verses 13–15. What does this focus suggest about another dimension of faith in God's power? 4. Despite the Pharisees' public rejection of Jesus, one of them invites him to dinner. A drama unfolds (vv. 36–50). The woman's faith in Jesus is obvious. But Simon shows signs of some kind of faith in Jesus (vv. 36a, 39, 40b). How does Jesus proceed to draw out his faith? 5. Jesus' interaction with the woman is vastly different from his interaction with Simon. What does this indicate about his understanding of each?

Applying the Word 1. It was physically easy for Jesus to touch the dead man. But in doing so, he ritualistically contaminated himself. In our society what comparable risks might we have to take to help needy people? 2. Of the five people you have looked at, with whom can you more readily identify? How does she/he challenge your faith in Jesus as Friend and Lord?

Responding in Prayer Pray for courage to take risks in reaching out to those around you who are open to learning about Christ.

9 / *Luke 8:1–21*
Taking Care How You Listen

WHEN THE BERLIN Wall fell in 1989, the West rejoiced. For Christians it symbolized evangelistic opportunities in East Europe. At first we heard much of "tremendous openness," "thousands accepting Christ," "demand for Bibles." This was probably true. Then we began hearing about growing materialism and power struggles among some Christian leaders. Journalists began to report that many who came to meetings were mainly eager for Western contacts to worldly opportunities. Wherever the gospel is preached, results vary, because people have different motives for listening and responding. Jesus knew this about his contemporary audience, and he dealt with it in a graphic way.

Warming Up to God What were the two most significant factors that influenced your response to the Christian gospel?

Read Luke 8:1–21.

8 After this, Jesus traveled about from one
town and village to another, proclaiming
the good news of the kingdom of God.
The Twelve were with him, [2]and also some
women who had been cured of evil spirits and
diseases: Mary (called Magdalene) from whom
seven demons had come out; [3]Joanna the wife of
Cuza, the manager of Herod's household; Susanna; and many others. These women were helping to support them out of their own means.
[4]While a large crowd was gathering and people
were coming to Jesus from town after town, he
told this parable: [5]"A farmer went out to sow his
seed. As he was scattering the seed, some fell
along the path; it was trampled on, and the birds
of the air ate it up. [6]Some fell on rock, and when
it came up, the plants withered because they had
no moisture. [7]Other seed fell among thorns,
which grew up with it and choked the plants.
[8]Still other seed fell on good soil. It came up and
yielded a crop, a hundred times more than was
sown."

When he said this, he called out, "He who has ears to hear, let him hear."

[9]His disciples asked him what this parable
meant. [10]He said, "The knowledge of the secrets
of the kingdom of God has been given to you, but
to others I speak in parables, so that,

" 'though seeing, they may not see;
though hearing, they may not
understand.'[f]

[11]"This is the meaning of the parable: The seed
is the word of God. [12]Those along the path are the
ones who hear, and then the devil comes and

f10 Isaiah 6:9

takes away the word from their hearts, so that
they may not believe and be saved. 13Those on the
rock are the ones who receive the word with joy
when they hear it, but they have no root. They
believe for a while, but in the time of testing they
fall away. 14The seed that fell among thorns
stands for those who hear, but as they go on their
way they are choked by life's worries, riches and
pleasures, and they do not mature. 15But the seed
on good soil stands for those with a noble and
good heart, who hear the word, retain it, and by
persevering produce a crop.
16"No one lights a lamp and hides it in a jar or
puts it under a bed. Instead, he puts it on a stand,
so that those who come in can see the light. 17For
there is nothing hidden that will not be disclosed,
and nothing concealed that will not be known or
brought out into the open. 18Therefore consider
carefully how you listen. Whoever has will be
given more; whoever does not have, even what he
thinks he has will be taken from him."
19Now Jesus' mother and brothers came to see
him, but they were not able to get near him be-
cause of the crowd. 20Someone told him, "Your
mother and brothers are standing outside, want-
ing to see you."
21He replied, "My mother and brothers are
those who hear God's word and put it into prac-
tice."

Discovering the Word 1. Luke's description of the women followers in verses 2-3 is unique among the Gospels. What do these verses tell you about the changing nature of Jesus' ministry? 2. In Jesus' first parable the seeds sown are the same, but the soils are different. How are they different? 3. Jesus himself interprets this opening parable. What is his main point (vv. 11-15)? 4. As the crowds grow, Jesus increasingly teaches in parables. He gives his reason for this in verses 8b-10. How is the use of parables effective in testing a listener's sincerity? 5. Luke uses the family episode as a live illustration of listening to God (vv. 19-21). What does Jesus highlight by this illustration?

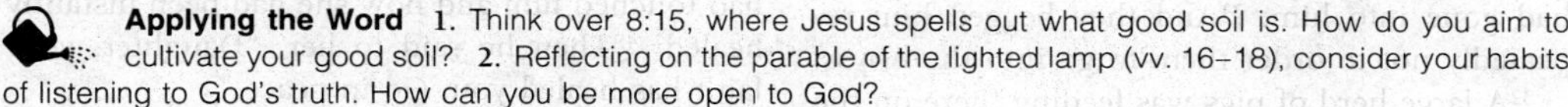

Applying the Word 1. Think over 8:15, where Jesus spells out what good soil is. How do you aim to cultivate your good soil? 2. Reflecting on the parable of the lighted lamp (vv. 16-18), consider your habits of listening to God's truth. How can you be more open to God?

Responding in Prayer Ask God to guide you to his truth and make you always open to what he has to say to you.

10 / *Luke 8:22-56*
Four Signs of Power and Identity

WHEN IS GOD present among people? Worshipers in a village in Portugal, in a village in Yugoslavia and more recently in an Illinois town all said he was present in a unique way. They claimed the Virgin Mary appeared to them, sometimes instructing or comforting and sometimes healing them. These locations drew thousands of people, either seeking the physical reality of God or simply curious. Visions, healing and deliverance services easily draw crowds all over the world. Whether people are believers or skeptics, they want to see, and perhaps experience, God's power—if it's there.

Warming Up to God To what extent do we today need unusual displays of God's power?

Read Luke 8:22-56.

22One day Jesus said to his disciples, "Let's go
over to the other side of the lake." So they got
into a boat and set out. 23As they sailed, he fell
asleep. A squall came down on the lake, so that
the boat was being swamped, and they were in
great danger.
24The disciples went and woke him, saying,
"Master, Master, we're going to drown!"

He got up and rebuked the wind and the raging waters; the storm subsided, and all was calm. 25"Where is your faith?" he asked his disciples.

In fear and amazement they asked one another, "Who is this? He commands even the winds and the water, and they obey him."

26They sailed to the region of the Gerasenes,[g] which is across the lake from Galilee. 27When Jesus stepped ashore, he was met by a demon-possessed man from the town. For a long time this man had not worn clothes or lived in a house, but had lived in the tombs. 28When he saw Jesus, he cried out and fell at his feet, shouting at the top of his voice, "What do you want with me, Jesus, Son of the Most High God? I beg you, don't torture me!" 29For Jesus had commanded the evil[h] spirit to come out of the man. Many times it had seized him, and though he was chained hand and foot and kept under guard, he had broken his chains and had been driven by the demon into solitary places.

30Jesus asked him, "What is your name?"

"Legion," he replied, because many demons had gone into him. 31And they begged him repeatedly not to order them to go into the Abyss.

32A large herd of pigs was feeding there on the hillside. The demons begged Jesus to let them go into them, and he gave them permission. 33When the demons came out of the man, they went into the pigs, and the herd rushed down the steep bank into the lake and was drowned.

34When those tending the pigs saw what had happened, they ran off and reported this in the town and countryside, 35and the people went out to see what had happened. When they came to Jesus, they found the man from whom the demons had gone out, sitting at Jesus' feet, dressed and in his right mind; and they were afraid. 36Those who had seen it told the people how the demon-possessed man had been cured. 37Then all the people of the region of the Gerasenes asked Jesus to leave them, because they were overcome with fear. So he got into the boat and left.

38The man from whom the demons had gone out begged to go with him, but Jesus sent him away, saying, 39"Return home and tell how much God has done for you." So the man went away and told all over town how much Jesus had done for him.

40Now when Jesus returned, a crowd welcomed him, for they were all expecting him. 41Then a man named Jairus, a ruler of the synagogue, came and fell at Jesus' feet, pleading with him to come to his house 42because his only daughter, a girl of about twelve, was dying.

As Jesus was on his way, the crowds almost crushed him. 43And a woman was there who had been subject to bleeding for twelve years,[i] but no one could heal her. 44She came up behind him and touched the edge of his cloak, and immediately her bleeding stopped.

45"Who touched me?" Jesus asked.

When they all denied it, Peter said, "Master, the people are crowding and pressing against you."

46But Jesus said, "Someone touched me; I know that power has gone out from me."

47Then the woman, seeing that she could not go unnoticed, came trembling and fell at his feet. In the presence of all the people, she told why she had touched him and how she had been instantly healed. 48Then he said to her, "Daughter, your faith has healed you. Go in peace."

49While Jesus was still speaking, someone came from the house of Jairus, the synagogue ruler. "Your daughter is dead," he said. "Don't bother the teacher any more."

50Hearing this, Jesus said to Jairus, "Don't be afraid; just believe, and she will be healed."

51When he arrived at the house of Jairus, he did not let anyone go in with him except Peter, John and James, and the child's father and mother. 52Meanwhile, all the people were wailing and mourning for her. "Stop wailing," Jesus said. "She is not dead but asleep."

53They laughed at him, knowing that she was dead. 54But he took her by the hand and said, "My child, get up!" 55Her spirit returned, and at once she stood up. Then Jesus told them to give her something to eat. 56Her parents were astonished, but he ordered them not to tell anyone what had happened.

[g]26 Some manuscripts *Gadarenes*; other manuscripts *Gergesenes*; also in verse 37 [h]29 Greek *unclean* [i]43 Many manuscripts *years, and she had spent all she had on doctors*

Discovering the Word 1. Jesus' Galilean disciples were used to sudden, violent storms on their sea, but this one was ferocious. What emotions do they experience from the beginning to the end of this event (vv. 22–25)? 2. Luke 8:26–39 is the second power encounter—this time in foreign territory. What unusual elements do you observe in the interchange between the man and Jesus? 3. We should not get morbidly curious about the subject of demons. But from this text what can you know about them? 4. Jesus and his disciples are back in home territory, where two more astonishing events take place. How is the healing of the woman different from other Bible healings you know of (vv. 40–56)?

Applying the Word 1. Jesus insists on knowing who touched him. How has it helped to witness publicly to what God has done for you? 2. What signs of God's power in your world move you most to worship and obey Jesus Christ as Lord of the universe?

Responding in Prayer Be thankful that you may worship God, who is both all-powerful and all-loving.

11 / *Luke 9:1–50*
Training for the Twelve

"IT HAS BEEN my experience that superior people are attracted only by challenge. By setting our standards low and making our life soft we have, quite automatically and unconsciously, assured ourselves of mediocre people" (Ambassador MacWhite in *The Ugly American*, referring to his observations in the diplomatic corps). Looking at Jesus' diplomatic corps of twelve, we might wonder about his standards. The Gospels tell us little about their backgrounds, but they tell us much about how Jesus trained them. This is useful for us.

Warming Up to God In what area of your Christian life do you feel that you are growing?

Read Luke 9:1–50.

9 When Jesus had called the Twelve to-
gether, he gave them power and authority
to drive out all demons and to cure dis-
eases, [2]and he sent them out to preach the king-
dom of God and to heal the sick. [3]He told them:
"Take nothing for the journey—no staff, no bag,
no bread, no money, no extra tunic. [4]Whatever
house you enter, stay there until you leave that
town. [5]If people do not welcome you, shake the
dust off your feet when you leave their town, as a
testimony against them." [6]So they set out and
went from village to village, preaching the gospel
and healing people everywhere.

[7]Now Herod the tetrarch heard about all that
was going on. And he was perplexed, because
some were saying that John had been raised from
the dead, [8]others that Elijah had appeared, and
still others that one of the prophets of long ago
had come back to life. [9]But Herod said, "I be-
headed John. Who, then, is this I hear such things
about?" And he tried to see him.

[10]When the apostles returned, they reported to
Jesus what they had done. Then he took them
with him and they withdrew by themselves to a
town called Bethsaida, [11]but the crowds learned
about it and followed him. He welcomed them
and spoke to them about the kingdom of God,
and healed those who needed healing.

[12]Late in the afternoon the Twelve came to him
and said, "Send the crowd away so they can go to
the surrounding villages and countryside and find
food and lodging, because we are in a remote
place here."

[13]He replied, "You give them something to
eat."

They answered, "We have only five loaves of
bread and two fish—unless we go and buy food
for all this crowd." [14](About five thousand men
were there.)

But he said to his disciples, "Have them sit
down in groups of about fifty each." [15]The disci-
ples did so, and everybody sat down. [16]Taking the

five loaves and the two fish and looking up to heaven, he gave thanks and broke them. Then he gave them to the disciples to set before the people. 17They all ate and were satisfied, and the disciples picked up twelve basketfuls of broken pieces that were left over.

18Once when Jesus was praying in private and his disciples were with him, he asked them, "Who do the crowds say I am?"

19They replied, "Some say John the Baptist; others say Elijah; and still others, that one of the prophets of long ago has come back to life."

20"But what about you?" he asked. "Who do you say I am?"

Peter answered, "The Christ[j] of God."

21Jesus strictly warned them not to tell this to anyone. 22And he said, "The Son of Man must suffer many things and be rejected by the elders, chief priests and teachers of the law, and he must be killed and on the third day be raised to life."

23Then he said to them all: "If anyone would come after me, he must deny himself and take up his cross daily and follow me. 24For whoever wants to save his life will lose it, but whoever loses his life for me will save it. 25What good is it for a man to gain the whole world, and yet lose or forfeit his very self? 26If anyone is ashamed of me and my words, the Son of Man will be ashamed of him when he comes in his glory and in the glory of the Father and of the holy angels. 27I tell you the truth, some who are standing here will not taste death before they see the kingdom of God."

28About eight days after Jesus said this, he took Peter, John and James with him and went up onto a mountain to pray. 29As he was praying, the appearance of his face changed, and his clothes became as bright as a flash of lightning. 30Two men, Moses and Elijah, 31appeared in glorious splendor, talking with Jesus. They spoke about his departure, which he was about to bring to fulfillment at Jerusalem. 32Peter and his companions were very sleepy, but when they became fully awake, they saw his glory and the two men standing with him. 33As the men were leaving Jesus, Peter said to him, "Master, it is good for us to be here. Let us put up three shelters—one for you, one for Moses and one for Elijah." (He did not know what he was saying.)

34While he was speaking, a cloud appeared and enveloped them, and they were afraid as they entered the cloud. 35A voice came from the cloud, saying, "This is my Son, whom I have chosen; listen to him." 36When the voice had spoken, they found that Jesus was alone. The disciples kept this to themselves, and told no one at that time what they had seen.

37The next day, when they came down from the mountain, a large crowd met him. 38A man in the crowd called out, "Teacher, I beg you to look at my son, for he is my only child. 39A spirit seizes him and he suddenly screams; it throws him into convulsions so that he foams at the mouth. It scarcely ever leaves him and is destroying him. 40I begged your disciples to drive it out, but they could not."

41"O unbelieving and perverse generation," Jesus replied, "how long shall I stay with you and put up with you? Bring your son here."

42Even while the boy was coming, the demon threw him to the ground in a convulsion. But Jesus rebuked the evil[k] spirit, healed the boy and gave him back to his father. 43And they were all amazed at the greatness of God.

While everyone was marveling at all that Jesus did, he said to his disciples, 44"Listen carefully to what I am about to tell you: The Son of Man is going to be betrayed into the hands of men." 45But they did not understand what this meant. It was hidden from them, so that they did not grasp it, and they were afraid to ask him about it.

46An argument started among the disciples as to which of them would be the greatest. 47Jesus, knowing their thoughts, took a little child and had him stand beside him. 48Then he said to them, "Whoever welcomes this little child in my name welcomes me; and whoever welcomes me welcomes the one who sent me. For he who is least among you all—he is the greatest."

49"Master," said John, "we saw a man driving out demons in your name and we tried to stop him, because he is not one of us."

50"Do not stop him," Jesus said, "for whoever is not against you is for you."

j20 Or *Messiah* k42 Greek *unclean*

Discovering the Word 1. For two years Jesus has been teaching, training and testing the Twelve. In what important ways has Jesus prepared them for this first short-term mission without him (vv. 1–9)? 2. The apostles have just returned from an intense and successful evangelistic mission. Their reluctance to help the crowd is understandable. But Jesus is insistent. What progressive steps do you see him take to involve them in feeding the people (vv. 10–17)? 3. Peter's "Great Confession" of Jesus' true identity is followed by two hard teachings—the first prediction of his ignominious death (vv. 21–22) and the costs of commitment to him as Lord (vv. 23–27). But what does Jesus say are the long-term benefits of these short-term costs? 4. Luke links Jesus' transfiguration to his final trip to Jerusalem, where death awaits (9:30–32, 51ff.). How then is the transfiguration important to Jesus himself and to the disciples? 5. On the plain with the mixed crowd we can sense Jesus' deep feelings. How can he be at once both compassionate and impatient?

Applying the Word 1. When have you felt both God's compassion and impatience? 2. What is one blind spot, or area of spiritual immaturity, that you need to work on?

Responding in Prayer Talk to God about how you want to grow into spiritual maturity.

12 / *Luke 9:51—10:24*
Short-Term Costs for Long-Term Benefits

I THOUGHT ALL my problems would be solved when I became a Christian. But they have increased. Cost? Pain? Sacrifice? These elements don't fit into the American way of life of avoiding discomfort and inconvenience. Instant gratification is the order of the day. No goal could be further from Jesus' way of life for his disciples while here on earth.

Warming Up to God What has been costly for you in following Jesus?

Read Luke 9:51—10:24.

51As the time approached for him to be taken
up to heaven, Jesus resolutely set out for Jerusa-
lem. 52And he sent messengers on ahead, who
went into a Samaritan village to get things ready
for him; 53but the people there did not welcome
him, because he was heading for Jerusalem.
54When the disciples James and John saw this,
they asked, "Lord, do you want us to call fire
down from heaven to destroy them[l]?" 55But
Jesus turned and rebuked them, 56and[m] they
went to another village.

57As they were walking along the road, a
man said to him, "I will follow you wherever
you go."

58Jesus replied, "Foxes have holes and birds of
the air have nests, but the Son of Man has no
place to lay his head."

59He said to another man, "Follow me."

But the man replied, "Lord, first let me go and
bury my father."

60Jesus said to him, "Let the dead bury their
own dead, but you go and proclaim the kingdom
of God."

61Still another said, "I will follow you, Lord;
but first let me go back and say good-by to my
family."

62Jesus replied, "No one who puts his hand to
the plow and looks back is fit for service in the
kingdom of God."

10 After this the Lord appointed sev-
enty-two[n] others and sent them
two by two ahead of him to every
town and place where he was about to go. 2He
told them, "The harvest is plentiful, but the work-
ers are few. Ask the Lord of the harvest, therefore,
to send out workers into his harvest field. 3Go! I
am sending you out like lambs among wolves.
4Do not take a purse or bag or sandals; and do not
greet anyone on the road.

[l]54 Some manuscripts *them, even as Elijah did* [m]55,56 Some manuscripts *them. And he said, "You do not know what kind of spirit you are of, for the Son of Man did not come to destroy men's lives, but to save them."* 56*And* [n]1 Some manuscripts *seventy*; also in verse 17

5“When you enter a house, first say, ‘Peace to this house.’ 6If a man of peace is there, your peace will rest on him; if not, it will return to you. 7Stay in that house, eating and drinking whatever they give you, for the worker deserves his wages. Do not move around from house to house.

8“When you enter a town and are welcomed, eat what is set before you. 9Heal the sick who are there and tell them, ‘The kingdom of God is near you.’ 10But when you enter a town and are not welcomed, go into its streets and say, 11‘Even the dust of your town that sticks to our feet we wipe off against you. Yet be sure of this: The kingdom of God is near.’ 12I tell you, it will be more bearable on that day for Sodom than for that town.

13“Woe to you, Korazin! Woe to you, Bethsaida! For if the miracles that were performed in you had been performed in Tyre and Sidon, they would have repented long ago, sitting in sackcloth and ashes. 14But it will be more bearable for Tyre and Sidon at the judgment than for you. 15And you, Capernaum, will you be lifted up to the skies? No, you will go down to the depths.[o]

16“He who listens to you listens to me; he who rejects you rejects me; but he who rejects me rejects him who sent me.”

17The seventy-two returned with joy and said, “Lord, even the demons submit to us in your name.”

18He replied, “I saw Satan fall like lightning from heaven. 19I have given you authority to trample on snakes and scorpions and to overcome all the power of the enemy; nothing will harm you. 20However, do not rejoice that the spirits submit to you, but rejoice that your names are written in heaven.”

21At that time Jesus, full of joy through the Holy Spirit, said, “I praise you, Father, Lord of heaven and earth, because you have hidden these things from the wise and learned, and revealed them to little children. Yes, Father, for this was your good pleasure.

22“All things have been committed to me by my Father. No one knows who the Son is except the Father, and no one knows who the Father is except the Son and those to whom the Son chooses to reveal him.”

23Then he turned to his disciples and said privately, “Blessed are the eyes that see what you see. 24For I tell you that many prophets and kings wanted to see what you see but did not see it, and to hear what you hear but did not hear it.”

[o]15 Greek *Hades*

Discovering the Word 1. This is the beginning of Jesus’ final, year-long journey to Jerusalem. What impressions of Jesus do the opening statements (9:51–53) leave with you? 2. In 9:56–62 Jesus interviews three would-be disciples. Each encounter reveals the person’s inadequate understanding of what it means to follow Jesus. What issues are at stake for each of these people? 3. From Jesus’ response to each what do you learn about some specific costs of discipleship in his kingdom? 4. How is the mission of the seventy-two in Luke 10:1–16 different from the mission of the Twelve in 9:1–6? 5. Verses 17–24 record a postmission report and evaluation. Of course celebration is in order! For Jesus the success of the seventy-two is a preview of the ultimate overthrow of Satan. But as one of them, how would you have felt on hearing Jesus’ words in verse 20?

Applying the Word 1. Jesus’ every instruction reveals a deep sense of urgency. How do we develop an urgency for mission and evangelism? 2. Jesus’ demands in discipleship and mission are indeed serious (9:57–62; 10:2–12). But he accompanies them with positive appeals—explicit and implicit (9:60b, 62b; 10:2, 16, 18–24). Which of his appeals inspires you to pursue discipleship on his terms?

Responding in Prayer Ask for strength to bear the real cost of discipleship.

13 / *Luke 10:25—11:13*
Marks of Jesus' True Disciples

IT IS SOMETIMES hard to tell who is a real Christian. This is not necessarily because people indiscriminately claim to be Christian. One reason is that many people sincerely live by inherited Christian values and even show fruit of the Spirit. But they have no personal relationship with God. On the other hand, some claim such a relationship to God but do not live by his standards. Among the many who followed Jesus were those who also were not clear about true discipleship. So Jesus makes it absolutely clear what marks a true follower of his.

Warming Up to God If you are not told, how can you tell if a person is a Christian?

Read Luke 10:25—11:13.

25On one occasion an expert in the law stood
up to test Jesus. "Teacher," he asked, "what must
I do to inherit eternal life?"
26"What is written in the Law?" he replied.
"How do you read it?"
27He answered: " 'Love the Lord your God with
all your heart and with all your soul and with all
your strength and with all your mind'[p]; and,
'Love your neighbor as yourself.'[q]"
28"You have answered correctly," Jesus replied.
"Do this and you will live."
29But he wanted to justify himself, so he asked
Jesus, "And who is my neighbor?"
30In reply Jesus said: "A man was going down
from Jerusalem to Jericho, when he fell into the
hands of robbers. They stripped him of his
clothes, beat him and went away, leaving him half
dead. 31A priest happened to be going down the
same road, and when he saw the man, he passed
by on the other side. 32So too, a Levite, when he
came to the place and saw him, passed by on the
other side. 33But a Samaritan, as he traveled, came
where the man was; and when he saw him, he
took pity on him. 34He went to him and bandaged
his wounds, pouring on oil and wine. Then he
put the man on his own donkey, took him to an
inn and took care of him. 35The next day he took
out two silver coins[r] and gave them to the inn-
keeper. 'Look after him,' he said, 'and when I re-
turn, I will reimburse you for any extra expense
you may have.'
36"Which of these three do you think was a
neighbor to the man who fell into the hands of
robbers?"
37The expert in the law replied, "The one who
had mercy on him."
Jesus told him, "Go and do likewise."
38As Jesus and his disciples were on their way,
he came to a village where a woman named Mar-
tha opened her home to him. 39She had a sister
called Mary, who sat at the Lord's feet listening to
what he said. 40But Martha was distracted by all
the preparations that had to be made. She came to
him and asked, "Lord, don't you care that my
sister has left me to do the work by myself? Tell
her to help me!"
41"Martha, Martha," the Lord answered, "you
are worried and upset about many things, 42but
only one thing is needed.[s] Mary has chosen
what is better, and it will not be taken away from
her."

11 One day Jesus was praying in a cer-
tain place. When he finished, one
of his disciples said to him, "Lord,
teach us to pray, just as John taught his disci-
ples."
2He said to them, "When you pray, say:

" 'Father,[t]
hallowed be your name,
your kingdom come.[u]
3Give us each day our daily bread.
4Forgive us our sins,
for we also forgive everyone who sins
against us.[v]
And lead us not into temptation.[w]' "

5Then he said to them, "Suppose one of you
has a friend, and he goes to him at midnight and
says, 'Friend, lend me three loaves of bread, 6be-

p27 Deut. 6:5 q27 Lev. 19:18 r35 Greek *two denarii*
s42 Some manuscripts *but few things are needed—or only one*
t2 Some manuscripts *Our Father in heaven* u2 Some manuscripts *come. May your will be done on earth as it is in heaven.* v4 Greek *everyone who is indebted to us* w4 Some manuscripts *temptation but deliver us from the evil one*

cause a friend of mine on a journey has come to
me, and I have nothing to set before him.’
7“Then the one inside answers, ‘Don’t bother
me. The door is already locked, and my children
are with me in bed. I can’t get up and give you
anything.’ 8I tell you, though he will not get up
and give him the bread because he is his friend,
yet because of the man’s boldness[x] he will get up
and give him as much as he needs.
9“So I say to you: Ask and it will be given to
you; seek and you will find; knock and the door
will be opened to you. 10For everyone who asks
receives; he who seeks finds; and to him who
knocks, the door will be opened.
11“Which of you fathers, if your son asks for[y]
a fish, will give him a snake instead? 12Or if he
asks for an egg, will give him a scorpion? 13If you
then, though you are evil, know how to give good
gifts to your children, how much more will your
Father in heaven give the Holy Spirit to those
who ask him!”

x8 Or *persistence* y11 Some manuscripts *for bread, will give him a stone; or if he asks for*

Discovering the Word 1. The conversation begins with a man who “stood up,” indicating he had been sitting with others listening to Jesus teach. What other facts about this man can you pick up in 10:25–29? 2. What does Jesus perceive about his understanding of the Law (10:25–28)? 3. To challenge the expert Jesus portrays the hero in his parable as a Samaritan. This despised outsider proves obedience to God’s law of love by his actions (first mark). Note the specific ways that he “took pity” on the victim (10:33–35). What could be Jesus’ reasons for including such details? 4. In verse 36 Jesus reverses the expert’s original question in verse 29. If you were the expert, what effect would this have on you? 5. Martha displays both positive and negative qualities (10:38–42). What (second) mark does her sister Mary show? 6. Look at 11:1–13 for the third mark of Jesus’ true disciples—praying. In verses 2–4 Jesus is not giving a prayer merely to be recited. Rather, he is giving prayer headings. What basic needs do these headings cover?

Applying the Word 1. What qualities do you observe in people who, like Mary, “choose what is better”? 2. By parable and commentary Jesus urges his disciples to pray with boldness. We can dare to be bold because of who God is—our Father and our King (vv. 2, 13). How should trust in such a God radicalize your praying?

Responding in Prayer Speak to God boldly and with trust.

14 / *Luke 11:14—12:12*
Jesus the Controversialist

WHEN I THINK of controversialists, Al comes to mind. He was one of the most effective missionaries I’ve known. Yet he stirred up controversy with almost everyone near him—his board, his colleagues, the local church leaders. They didn’t know what to do with him, or what to do without him. But those he was evangelizing loved him!

Some people seem to be born controversialists. They’re happiest when arguing with others, only half alive when the atmosphere is congenial. Jesus was a controversialist. But it was not for his ego that he engaged in fierce debates with the most highly trained Bible scholars of his day. He engaged in controversy because he loved the truth and hated lies.

Warming Up to God How do you respond to controversies? Why?

Read Luke 11:14—12:12.

14Jesus was driving out a demon that was mute.
When the demon left, the man who had been
mute spoke, and the crowd was amazed. 15But
some of them said, “By Beelzebub,[z] the prince of

z15 Greek *Beezeboul* or *Beelzeboul*; also in verses 18 and 19

demons, he is driving out demons." 16Others tested him by asking for a sign from heaven.

17Jesus knew their thoughts and said to them: "Any kingdom divided against itself will be ruined, and a house divided against itself will fall. 18If Satan is divided against himself, how can his kingdom stand? I say this because you claim that I drive out demons by Beelzebub. 19Now if I drive out demons by Beelzebub, by whom do your followers drive them out? So then, they will be your judges. 20But if I drive out demons by the finger of God, then the kingdom of God has come to you.

21"When a strong man, fully armed, guards his own house, his possessions are safe. 22But when someone stronger attacks and overpowers him, he takes away the armor in which the man trusted and divides up the spoils.

23"He who is not with me is against me, and he who does not gather with me, scatters.

24"When an evil[a] spirit comes out of a man, it goes through arid places seeking rest and does not find it. Then it says, 'I will return to the house I left.' 25When it arrives, it finds the house swept clean and put in order. 26Then it goes and takes seven other spirits more wicked than itself, and they go in and live there. And the final condition of that man is worse than the first."

27As Jesus was saying these things, a woman in the crowd called out, "Blessed is the mother who gave you birth and nursed you."

28He replied, "Blessed rather are those who hear the word of God and obey it."

29As the crowds increased, Jesus said, "This is a wicked generation. It asks for a miraculous sign, but none will be given it except the sign of Jonah. 30For as Jonah was a sign to the Ninevites, so also will the Son of Man be to this generation. 31The Queen of the South will rise at the judgment with the men of this generation and condemn them; for she came from the ends of the earth to listen to Solomon's wisdom, and now one[b] greater than Solomon is here. 32The men of Nineveh will stand up at the judgment with this generation and condemn it; for they repented at the preaching of Jonah, and now one greater than Jonah is here.

33"No one lights a lamp and puts it in a place where it will be hidden, or under a bowl. Instead he puts it on its stand, so that those who come in may see the light. 34Your eye is the lamp of your body. When your eyes are good, your whole body also is full of light. But when they are bad, your body also is full of darkness. 35See to it, then, that the light within you is not darkness. 36Therefore, if your whole body is full of light, and no part of it dark, it will be completely lighted, as when the light of a lamp shines on you."

37When Jesus had finished speaking, a Pharisee invited him to eat with him; so he went in and reclined at the table. 38But the Pharisee, noticing that Jesus did not first wash before the meal, was surprised.

39Then the Lord said to him, "Now then, you Pharisees clean the outside of the cup and dish, but inside you are full of greed and wickedness. 40You foolish people! Did not the one who made the outside make the inside also? 41But give what is inside ⌊the dish⌋[c] to the poor, and everything will be clean for you.

42"Woe to you Pharisees, because you give God a tenth of your mint, rue and all other kinds of garden herbs, but you neglect justice and the love of God. You should have practiced the latter without leaving the former undone.

43"Woe to you Pharisees, because you love the most important seats in the synagogues and greetings in the marketplaces.

44"Woe to you, because you are like unmarked graves, which men walk over without knowing it."

45One of the experts in the law answered him, "Teacher, when you say these things, you insult us also."

46Jesus replied, "And you experts in the law, woe to you, because you load people down with burdens they can hardly carry, and you yourselves will not lift one finger to help them.

47"Woe to you, because you build tombs for the prophets, and it was your forefathers who killed them. 48So you testify that you approve of what your forefathers did; they killed the prophets, and you build their tombs. 49Because of this, God in his wisdom said, 'I will send them prophets and apostles, some of whom they will kill and others they will persecute.' 50Therefore this generation will be held responsible for the blood of all the prophets that has been shed since the beginning of the world, 51from the blood of Abel to the blood of Zechariah, who was killed between the altar and the sanctuary. Yes, I tell you, this generation will be held responsible for it all.

52"Woe to you experts in the law, because you

[a]24 Greek *unclean* [b]31 Or *something*; also in verse 32 [c]41 Or *what you have*

have taken away the key to knowledge. You your-
selves have not entered, and you have hindered
those who were entering."
53When Jesus left there, the Pharisees and the
teachers of the law began to oppose him fiercely
and to besiege him with questions, 54waiting to
catch him in something he might say.

12 Meanwhile, when a crowd of many
thousands had gathered, so that
they were trampling on one an-
other, Jesus began to speak first to his disciples,
saying: "Be on your guard against the yeast of the
Pharisees, which is hypocrisy. 2There is nothing
concealed that will not be disclosed, or hidden
that will not be made known. 3What you have
said in the dark will be heard in the daylight, and
what you have whispered in the ear in the inner
rooms will be proclaimed from the roofs.
4"I tell you, my friends, do not be afraid of
those who kill the body and after that can do no
more. 5But I will show you whom you should
fear: Fear him who, after the killing of the body,
has power to throw you into hell. Yes, I tell you,
fear him. 6Are not five sparrows sold for two pen-
nies[d]? Yet not one of them is forgotten by God.
7Indeed, the very hairs of your head are all num-
bered. Don't be afraid; you are worth more than
many sparrows.
8"I tell you, whoever acknowledges me before
men, the Son of Man will also acknowledge him
before the angels of God. 9But he who disowns
me before men will be disowned before the angels
of God. 10And everyone who speaks a word
against the Son of Man will be forgiven, but any-
one who blasphemes against the Holy Spirit will
not be forgiven.
11"When you are brought before synagogues,
rulers and authorities, do not worry about how
you will defend yourselves or what you will say,
12for the Holy Spirit will teach you at that time
what you should say."

[d]6 *Greek two assaria*

Discovering the Word 1. In what two ways do Jesus' critics attack him (11:15–16)? 2. In 11:17–20 Jesus answers the first attack. How does he point out their illogical position? 3. Jesus answers his critics' second attack in 11:29–36. In what way is Jesus comparing himself to Jonah and Solomon? 4. In 11:37–38 the host is surprised that Jesus has not ritually washed his hands after contact with public "uncleanness." Jesus counters that criticism, then adds six more attacks on their religious practices! Of these accusations (11:42, 43, 44, 46, 47, 52), which reminds you of a contemporary practice? In what ways? 5. Jesus must now prepare his disciples for persecution by these same leaders (12:1–12). First, he deals with the fear of these men. How does he help them to distinguish between the wrong kind of fear and the proper kind (12:4–7)?

Applying the Word 1. Few of us would engage in public religious controversy as Jesus did. But we all have occasions when we need to stand against lies and speak the truth. What are your opportunities to do this? 2. In what ways is it difficult for you?

Responding in Prayer Ask the Lord Jesus to give you the help you need to take a stand.

---

15 / *Luke 12:13—13:21*
Greed, Need & Judgment

A CHRISTIAN YUPPIE? Is it possible to be Jesus' disciple on his terms and at the same time be a yuppie, for whom material values and the latest exotica are priorities? Some try to have it both ways and don't make it—either way. One such Christian yuppie described her experience. "For ten years I skillfully juggled both sets of values—Jesus' and Madison Avenue's. Then I collapsed." We are constantly tested in our value system, because we live between earth and heaven, time and eternity. Jesus gives us guidelines and solemn warnings on how to live productively in this creative tension.

Warming Up to God Think about the past few days. In what ways have you been enticed by the material values of the world? Confess them before the Lord.

Read Luke 12:13—13:21.

[13]Someone in the crowd said to him, "Teacher,
tell my brother to divide the inheritance
with me."
[14]Jesus replied, "Man, who appointed me a
judge or an arbiter between you?" [15]Then he said
to them, "Watch out! Be on your guard against all
kinds of greed; a man's life does not consist in the
abundance of his possessions."
[16]And he told them this parable: "The ground
of a certain rich man produced a good crop. [17]He
thought to himself, 'What shall I do? I have no
place to store my crops.'
[18]"Then he said, 'This is what I'll do. I will tear
down my barns and build bigger ones, and there
I will store all my grain and my goods. [19]And I'll
say to myself, "You have plenty of good things
laid up for many years. Take life easy; eat, drink
and be merry." '
[20]"But God said to him, 'You fool! This very
night your life will be demanded from you. Then
who will get what you have prepared for your-
self?'
[21]"This is how it will be with anyone who
stores up things for himself but is not rich toward
God."
[22]Then Jesus said to his disciples: "Therefore I
tell you, do not worry about your life, what you
will eat; or about your body, what you will wear.
[23]Life is more than food, and the body more than
clothes. [24]Consider the ravens: They do not sow
or reap, they have no storeroom or barn; yet God
feeds them. And how much more valuable you
are than birds! [25]Who of you by worrying can add
a single hour to his life[e]? [26]Since you cannot do
this very little thing, why do you worry about the
rest?
[27]"Consider how the lilies grow. They do not
labor or spin. Yet I tell you, not even Solomon in
all his splendor was dressed like one of these. [28]If
that is how God clothes the grass of the field,
which is here today, and tomorrow is thrown into
the fire, how much more will he clothe you, O
you of little faith! [29]And do not set your heart on
what you will eat or drink; do not worry about it.
[30]For the pagan world runs after all such things,
and your Father knows that you need them. [31]But
seek his kingdom, and these things will be given
to you as well.
[32]"Do not be afraid, little flock, for your Father
has been pleased to give you the kingdom. [33]Sell
your possessions and give to the poor. Provide
purses for yourselves that will not wear out, a
treasure in heaven that will not be exhausted,
where no thief comes near and no moth destroys.
[34]For where your treasure is, there your heart will
be also.
[35]"Be dressed ready for service and keep your
lamps burning, [36]like men waiting for their mas-
ter to return from a wedding banquet, so that
when he comes and knocks they can immediately
open the door for him. [37]It will be good for those
servants whose master finds them watching when
he comes. I tell you the truth, he will dress him-
self to serve, will have them recline at the table
and will come and wait on them. [38]It will be good
for those servants whose master finds them ready,
even if he comes in the second or third watch of
the night. [39]But understand this: If the owner of
the house had known at what hour the thief was
coming, he would not have let his house be bro-
ken into. [40]You also must be ready, because the
Son of Man will come at an hour when you do
not expect him."
[41]Peter asked, "Lord, are you telling this para-
ble to us, or to everyone?"
[42]The Lord answered, "Who then is the faithful
and wise manager, whom the master puts in
charge of his servants to give them their food al-
lowance at the proper time? [43]It will be good for
that servant whom the master finds doing so
when he returns. [44]I tell you the truth, he will put
him in charge of all his possessions. [45]But sup-
pose the servant says to himself, 'My master is
taking a long time in coming,' and he then begins
to beat the menservants and maidservants and to
eat and drink and get drunk. [46]The master of that
servant will come on a day when he does not
expect him and at an hour he is not aware of. He
will cut him to pieces and assign him a place with
the unbelievers.
[47]"That servant who knows his master's will
and does not get ready or does not do what his
master wants will be beaten with many blows.
[48]But the one who does not know and does things
deserving punishment will be beaten with few
blows. From everyone who has been given much,
much will be demanded; and from the one who

[e]25 Or *single cubit to his height*

has been entrusted with much, much more will be asked.

49“I have come to bring fire on the earth, and how I wish it were already kindled! 50But I have a baptism to undergo, and how distressed I am until it is completed! 51Do you think I came to bring peace on earth? No, I tell you, but division. 52From now on there will be five in one family divided against each other, three against two and two against three. 53They will be divided, father against son and son against father, mother against daughter and daughter against mother, mother-in-law against daughter-in-law and daughter-in-law against mother-in-law.”

54He said to the crowd: “When you see a cloud rising in the west, immediately you say, ‘It’s going to rain,’ and it does. 55And when the south wind blows, you say, ‘It’s going to be hot,’ and it is. 56Hypocrites! You know how to interpret the appearance of the earth and the sky. How is it that you don’t know how to interpret this present time?

57“Why don’t you judge for yourselves what is right? 58As you are going with your adversary to the magistrate, try hard to be reconciled to him on the way, or he may drag you off to the judge, and the judge turn you over to the officer, and the officer throw you into prison. 59I tell you, you will not get out until you have paid the last penny.[f]”

13

Now there were some present at that time who told Jesus about the Galileans whose blood Pilate had mixed with their sacrifices. 2Jesus answered, “Do you think that these Galileans were worse sinners than all the other Galileans because they suffered this way? 3I tell you, no! But unless you repent, you too will all perish. 4Or those eighteen who died when the tower in Siloam fell on them—do you think they were more guilty than all the others living in Jerusalem? 5I tell you, no! But unless you repent, you too will all perish.”

6Then he told this parable: “A man had a fig tree, planted in his vineyard, and he went to look for fruit on it, but did not find any. 7So he said to the man who took care of the vineyard, ‘For three years now I’ve been coming to look for fruit on this fig tree and haven’t found any. Cut it down! Why should it use up the soil?’

8“ ‘Sir,’ the man replied, ‘leave it alone for one more year, and I’ll dig around it and fertilize it. 9If it bears fruit next year, fine! If not, then cut it down.’ ”

10On a Sabbath Jesus was teaching in one of the synagogues, 11and a woman was there who had been crippled by a spirit for eighteen years. She was bent over and could not straighten up at all. 12When Jesus saw her, he called her forward and said to her, “Woman, you are set free from your infirmity.” 13Then he put his hands on her, and immediately she straightened up and praised God.

14Indignant because Jesus had healed on the Sabbath, the synagogue ruler said to the people, “There are six days for work. So come and be healed on those days, not on the Sabbath.”

15The Lord answered him, “You hypocrites! Doesn’t each of you on the Sabbath untie his ox or donkey from the stall and lead it out to give it water? 16Then should not this woman, a daughter of Abraham, whom Satan has kept bound for eighteen long years, be set free on the Sabbath day from what bound her?”

17When he said this, all his opponents were humiliated, but the people were delighted with all the wonderful things he was doing.

18Then Jesus asked, “What is the kingdom of God like? What shall I compare it to? 19It is like a mustard seed, which a man took and planted in his garden. It grew and became a tree, and the birds of the air perched in its branches.”

20Again he asked, “What shall I compare the kingdom of God to? 21It is like yeast that a woman took and mixed into a large amount[g] of flour until it worked all through the dough.”

*f*59 Greek *lepton* *g*21 Greek *three satas* (probably about 1/2 bushel or 22 liters)

Discovering the Word 1. Nowhere does Jesus condemn possessions. But he has much to say about how to use them. From 12:15, 22–23 and 31, how could you summarize Jesus’ teaching about life and material goods? 2. What view of God do worrying Christians apparently have? 3. The parable in 12:35–48 illustrates priorities Christians should have in view of Jesus’ return after his departure—or in any crisis situation. (That Jesus was referring to his Second Coming would not be obvious to his listeners, as it is to us.) What are these priorities that apply to all servant disciples? 4. All three parables above speak or hint of God’s judgment on the choices we make (12:20, 40, 46–48). The language and imagery of our present text also point to that judgment. In the midst of these warnings, what hope does Jesus offer to the wise (12:57-59)? **5.** Provoked by Jesus' teaching on judgment (13:1-9), some people raise a question about a well-known atrocity. In reply, how does Jesus both correct their wrong assumption and still extend hope? **6.** This is the last time we see Jesus teaching in a synagogue (13:10-21). In what ways does this sabbath conflict with the synagogue ruler summarize the priorities and values of Jesus' total ministry?

Applying the Word 1. The obviously rich are not the only ones in danger of being fools. How do poor and middle-class people also face the same dangers? 2. Recall again your past week's activities and personal concerns. To what extent do they reflect the priorities and values of God's kingdom?

Responding in Prayer Ask God to mold your values and priorities into his own.

16 / *Luke 13:22—14:35*
Are Only a Few People Going to Be Saved?

STILL ANOTHER NEW group has come to our town, attracting scores of disaffected members of other churches. The leaders have convinced them that they alone have the right interpretation of "who is really saved." People in Jesus' day also wanted to be sure about salvation. They asked the question in different ways—"What must I do to inherit eternal life?" "How can a man be born again to enter the kingdom of God?" "Who then can be saved?" Even secular people ask, "Which life goal is right?" No matter the form, it is still an essential question for anyone to ask.

Warming Up to God When are you likely to question your salvation?

Read Luke 13:22—14:35.

22Then Jesus went through the towns and vil-
lages, teaching as he made his way to Jerusalem.
23Someone asked him, "Lord, are only a few peo-
ple going to be saved?"
He said to them, 24"Make every effort to enter
through the narrow door, because many, I tell
you, will try to enter and will not be able to.
25Once the owner of the house gets up and closes
the door, you will stand outside knocking and
pleading, 'Sir, open the door for us.'
"But he will answer, 'I don't know you or
where you come from.'
26"Then you will say, 'We ate and drank with
you, and you taught in our streets.'
27"But he will reply, 'I don't know you or where
you come from. Away from me, all you evildoers!'
28"There will be weeping there, and gnashing
of teeth, when you see Abraham, Isaac and Jacob
and all the prophets in the kingdom of God, but
you yourselves thrown out. 29People will come
from east and west and north and south, and will
take their places at the feast in the kingdom of
God. 30Indeed there are those who are last who
will be first, and first who will be last."
31At that time some Pharisees came to Jesus
and said to him, "Leave this place and go some-
where else. Herod wants to kill you."
32He replied, "Go tell that fox, 'I will drive out
demons and heal people today and tomorrow,
and on the third day I will reach my goal.' 33In
any case, I must keep going today and tomorrow
and the next day—for surely no prophet can die
outside Jerusalem!
34"O Jerusalem, Jerusalem, you who kill the
prophets and stone those sent to you, how often
I have longed to gather your children together, as
a hen gathers her chicks under her wings, but you
were not willing! 35Look, your house is left to you
desolate. I tell you, you will not see me again
until you say, 'Blessed is he who comes in the
name of the Lord.'[h]"

14 One Sabbath, when Jesus went to
eat in the house of a prominent
Pharisee, he was being carefully
watched. 2There in front of him was a man suffer-
ing from dropsy. 3Jesus asked the Pharisees and

h35 Psalm 118:26

experts in the law, "Is it lawful to heal on the
Sabbath or not?" 4But they remained silent. So
taking hold of the man, he healed him and sent
him away.

5Then he asked them, "If one of you has a
son[i] or an ox that falls into a well on the Sab-
bath day, will you not immediately pull him out?"
6And they had nothing to say.

7When he noticed how the guests picked the
places of honor at the table, he told them this
parable: 8"When someone invites you to a wed-
ding feast, do not take the place of honor, for a
person more distinguished than you may have
been invited. 9If so, the host who invited both of
you will come and say to you, 'Give this man your
seat.' Then, humiliated, you will have to take the
least important place. 10But when you are invited,
take the lowest place, so that when your host
comes, he will say to you, 'Friend, move up to a
better place.' Then you will be honored in the
presence of all your fellow guests. 11For everyone
who exalts himself will be humbled, and he who
humbles himself will be exalted."

12Then Jesus said to his host, "When you give
a luncheon or dinner, do not invite your friends,
your brothers or relatives, or your rich neighbors;
if you do, they may invite you back and so you
will be repaid. 13But when you give a banquet,
invite the poor, the crippled, the lame, the blind,
14and you will be blessed. Although they cannot
repay you, you will be repaid at the resurrection
of the righteous."

15When one of those at the table with him
heard this, he said to Jesus, "Blessed is the man
who will eat at the feast in the kingdom of God."

16Jesus replied: "A certain man was preparing a
great banquet and invited many guests. 17At the
time of the banquet he sent his servant to tell
those who had been invited, 'Come, for every-
thing is now ready.'

18"But they all alike began to make excuses.
The first said, 'I have just bought a field, and I
must go and see it. Please excuse me.'

19"Another said, 'I have just bought five yoke of
oxen, and I'm on my way to try them out. Please
excuse me.'

20"Still another said, 'I just got married, so I
can't come.'

21"The servant came back and reported this to
his master. Then the owner of the house became
angry and ordered his servant, 'Go out quickly
into the streets and alleys of the town and bring
in the poor, the crippled, the blind and the lame.'

22" 'Sir,' the servant said, 'what you ordered has
been done, but there is still room.'

23"Then the master told his servant, 'Go out to
the roads and country lanes and make them come
in, so that my house will be full. 24I tell you, not
one of those men who were invited will get a taste
of my banquet.' "

25Large crowds were traveling with Jesus, and
turning to them he said: 26"If anyone comes to me
and does not hate his father and mother, his wife
and children, his brothers and sisters—yes, even
his own life—he cannot be my disciple. 27And
anyone who does not carry his cross and follow
me cannot be my disciple.

28"Suppose one of you wants to build a tower.
Will he not first sit down and estimate the cost to
see if he has enough money to complete it? 29For
if he lays the foundation and is not able to finish
it, everyone who sees it will ridicule him, 30say-
ing, 'This fellow began to build and was not able
to finish.'

31"Or suppose a king is about to go to war
against another king. Will he not first sit down
and consider whether he is able with ten thou-
sand men to oppose the one coming against him
with twenty thousand? 32If he is not able, he will
send a delegation while the other is still a long
way off and will ask for terms of peace. 33In the
same way, any of you who does not give up every-
thing he has cannot be my disciple.

34"Salt is good, but if it loses its saltiness, how
can it be made salty again? 35It is fit neither for
the soil nor for the manure pile; it is thrown out.

"He who has ears to hear, let him hear."

i5 Some manuscripts *donkey*

Discovering the Word 1. Jesus' journeying to Jerusalem gives the setting of our title question (13:22–23). What in Jesus' parable answer would startle his Jewish listeners or perhaps you? 2. The Pharisees' motive for warning Jesus is not clear. They are now allied with the Herodians, their political enemies, against Jesus. But he is fearless (13:31–33). Then he expresses other emotions (vv. 34–35). Why do you think Jesus is so deeply passionate about Jerusalem? 3. What explains the Pharisees' double silence to Jesus' questions (14:4,6)? 4. How does this third parable climax Jesus' answer to our study question of who ultimately will be saved

(14:15–24)? 5. Travelers nearing Jerusalem passed old wooden crosses along the way. Everyone knew their use—for criminal execution. So how would Jesus' fellow travelers understand his words in 14:27?

Applying the Word 1. With two parables he teaches the guests about true honor (14:7–11) and his host about true hospitality (14:12–14). How should Jesus' lessons affect your social life? 2. Jesus lays down his conditions for discipleship by calling into question powerful loyalties—to family and to self. What would be a contemporary example of Christians "hating" their family? 3. Try counting the cost of not following Jesus on his terms. What to you is most sobering?

Responding in Prayer Talk openly with God about how you are experiencing the cost of discipleship.

17 / *Luke 15*
The God Who Likes to Throw Parties

THE TITLE OF Rembrandt's famous painting "Return of the Prodigal Son" focuses on the father's younger son in Jesus' well-known parable. But by composition and lighting, the artist causes us to focus on the father—his face weathered by suffering, his hands lovingly embracing the ragged boy, his whole body bent to his returned son. Some people focus more on the sin and repentance of the young man than on God's compassion and purposes. Repentance is necessary. But Jesus' rejoicing Father completes, indeed dominates, the picture.

Warming Up to God How have you recently experienced the joyful side of God's nature? Praise God for who he is.

Read Luke 15.

15 Now the tax collectors and "sin-
ners" were all gathering around to
hear him. 2But the Pharisees and
the teachers of the law muttered, "This man wel-
comes sinners and eats with them."
3Then Jesus told them this parable: 4"Suppose
one of you has a hundred sheep and loses one of
them. Does he not leave the ninety-nine in the
open country and go after the lost sheep until he
finds it? 5And when he finds it, he joyfully puts it
on his shoulders 6and goes home. Then he calls
his friends and neighbors together and says, 'Re-
joice with me; I have found my lost sheep.' 7I tell
you that in the same way there will be more re-
joicing in heaven over one sinner who repents
than over ninety-nine righteous persons who do
not need to repent.
8"Or suppose a woman has ten silver coins[j]
and loses one. Does she not light a lamp, sweep
the house and search carefully until she finds it?
9And when she finds it, she calls her friends and
neighbors together and says, 'Rejoice with me; I
have found my lost coin.' 10In the same way, I tell
you, there is rejoicing in the presence of the an-
gels of God over one sinner who repents."

11Jesus continued: "There was a man who had
two sons. 12The younger one said to his father,
'Father, give me my share of the estate.' So he
divided his property between them.
13"Not long after that, the younger son got to-
gether all he had, set off for a distant country and
there squandered his wealth in wild living. 14After
he had spent everything, there was a severe fam-
ine in that whole country, and he began to be in
need. 15So he went and hired himself out to a
citizen of that country, who sent him to his fields
to feed pigs. 16He longed to fill his stomach with
the pods that the pigs were eating, but no one
gave him anything.
17"When he came to his senses, he said, 'How
many of my father's hired men have food to spare,
and here I am starving to death! 18I will set out
and go back to my father and say to him: Father,
I have sinned against heaven and against you. 19I
am no longer worthy to be called your son; make
me like one of your hired men.' 20So he got up
and went to his father.
"But while he was still a long way off, his father

j8 Greek *ten drachmas,* each worth about a day's wages

saw him and was filled with compassion for him;
he ran to his son, threw his arms around him and
kissed him.
[21]"The son said to him, 'Father, I have sinned
against heaven and against you. I am no longer
worthy to be called your son.[k]'
[22]"But the father said to his servants, 'Quick!
Bring the best robe and put it on him. Put a ring
on his finger and sandals on his feet. [23]Bring the
fattened calf and kill it. Let's have a feast and
celebrate. [24]For this son of mine was dead and is
alive again; he was lost and is found.' So they
began to celebrate.
[25]"Meanwhile, the older son was in the field.
When he came near the house, he heard music
and dancing. [26]So he called one of the servants
and asked him what was going on. [27]'Your
brother has come,' he replied, 'and your father
has killed the fattened calf because he has him
back safe and sound.'
[28]"The older brother became angry and refused
to go in. So his father went out and pleaded with
him. [29]But he answered his father, 'Look! All
these years I've been slaving for you and never
disobeyed your orders. Yet you never gave me
even a young goat so I could celebrate with my
friends. [30]But when this son of yours who has
squandered your property with prostitutes comes
home, you kill the fattened calf for him!'
[31]" 'My son,' the father said, 'you are always
with me, and everything I have is yours. [32]But we
had to celebrate and be glad, because this brother
of yours was dead and is alive again; he was lost
and is found.' "

[k]21 Some early manuscripts *son. Make me like one of your hired men.*

Discovering the Word 1. What provoked Jesus' parables (vv. 1–2)? 2. In the first two parables the theme of an owner searching for something lost and rejoicing when it is found begins to answer Jesus' critics. The third parable repeats the basic theme. But how is it different from the first two? 3. What steps do you perceive in the young man's 180-degree turnabout? 4. The drama grows as Jesus describes the father in verses 20–24. In the light of verse 2, what does he want his critics to see about this man? 5. In the interaction with his older son, what other dimensions of the father's character and motives appear (vv. 28–32)? 6. The rejoicing nature of God is still foreign if not downright offensive to some religious people (see vv. 2, 6–7, 9–10, 22–24, 32 and 14:16–17). Why?

Applying the Word 1. How do these parables move you to believe in the possibilities of new or fresh changes in your relationship to family members and to God? 2. Which of your friends have like the older son an inadequate or wrong view of God?

Responding in Prayer Pray for an opportunity to share with your friends this appealing portrait of God.

18/ *Luke 16*
Managing Your Money

WE HAVE SUPPOSEDLY left the high-flying 1980s decade of greed. In 1985 Ivan Boesky was commencement speaker at a prestigious school of business administration in California. He said to the graduating class, "Greed is all right, by the way. I want you to know that I think greed is healthy. You can be greedy and still feel good about yourself." Sad, yes. And the response of those young men and women was just as sad. They laughed and applauded. A year and a half later Boesky was in prison for his runaway greed. The two parables in our present chapter show Jesus' judgment on the proper use of money.

Warming Up to God Why do you like money?

Read Luke 16.

16 Jesus told his disciples: "There was
a rich man whose manager was ac-
cused of wasting his possessions.
2So he called him in and asked him, 'What is this
I hear about you? Give an account of your man-
agement, because you cannot be manager any
longer.'

3"The manager said to himself, 'What shall I do
now? My master is taking away my job. I'm not
strong enough to dig, and I'm ashamed to beg—
4I know what I'll do so that, when I lose my job
here, people will welcome me into their houses.'

5"So he called in each one of his master's debt-
ors. He asked the first, 'How much do you owe
my master?'

6" 'Eight hundred gallons[l] of olive oil,' he re-
plied.

"The manager told him, 'Take your bill, sit
down quickly, and make it four hundred.'

7"Then he asked the second, 'And how much
do you owe?'

" 'A thousand bushels[m] of wheat,' he replied.

"He told him, 'Take your bill and make it eight
hundred.'

8"The master commended the dishonest man-
ager because he had acted shrewdly. For the peo-
ple of this world are more shrewd in dealing with
their own kind than are the people of the light. 9I
tell you, use worldly wealth to gain friends for
yourselves, so that when it is gone, you will be
welcomed into eternal dwellings.

10"Whoever can be trusted with very little can
also be trusted with much, and whoever is dis-
honest with very little will also be dishonest with
much. 11So if you have not been trustworthy in
handling worldly wealth, who will trust you with
true riches? 12And if you have not been trustwor-
thy with someone else's property, who will give
you property of your own?

13"No servant can serve two masters. Either he
will hate the one and love the other, or he will be
devoted to the one and despise the other. You
cannot serve both God and Money."

14The Pharisees, who loved money, heard all
this and were sneering at Jesus. 15He said to them,
"You are the ones who justify yourselves in the
eyes of men, but God knows your hearts. What is
highly valued among men is detestable in God's
sight.

16"The Law and the Prophets were proclaimed
until John. Since that time, the good news of the
kingdom of God is being preached, and everyone
is forcing his way into it. 17It is easier for heaven
and earth to disappear than for the least stroke of
a pen to drop out of the Law.

18"Anyone who divorces his wife and marries
another woman commits adultery, and the man
who marries a divorced woman commits adul-
tery.

19"There was a rich man who was dressed in
purple and fine linen and lived in luxury every
day. 20At his gate was laid a beggar named Laza-
rus, covered with sores 21and longing to eat what
fell from the rich man's table. Even the dogs came
and licked his sores.

22"The time came when the beggar died and the
angels carried him to Abraham's side. The rich
man also died and was buried. 23In hell,[n] where
he was in torment, he looked up and saw Abra-
ham far away, with Lazarus by his side. 24So he
called to him, 'Father Abraham, have pity on me
and send Lazarus to dip the tip of his finger in
water and cool my tongue, because I am in agony
in this fire.'

25"But Abraham replied, 'Son, remember that in
your lifetime you received your good things,
while Lazarus received bad things, but now he is
comforted here and you are in agony. 26And be-
sides all this, between us and you a great chasm
has been fixed, so that those who want to go from
here to you cannot, nor can anyone cross over
from there to us.'

27"He answered, 'Then I beg you, father, send
Lazarus to my father's house, 28for I have five
brothers. Let him warn them, so that they will not
also come to this place of torment.'

29"Abraham replied, 'They have Moses and the
Prophets; let them listen to them.'

30" 'No, father Abraham,' he said, 'but if some-
one from the dead goes to them, they will repent.'

31"He said to him, 'If they do not listen to Mo-
ses and the Prophets, they will not be convinced
even if someone rises from the dead.' "

[l]6 Greek *one hundred batous* (probably about 3 kiloliters) [m]7 Greek *one hundred korous* (probably about 35 kiloliters) [n]23 Greek *Hades*

Discovering the Word 1. Jesus' parable in verses 1–18 is quite straightforward. His application, however, seems not as clear (vv. 8b–9). At first reading, how does he seem to be applying the parable to his disciples? 2. Where in the context could you show that Jesus is not condoning greed and dishonesty? 3. According to Jesus in verses 10–15, what does our management of money have to do with our standing before God? 4. In the first part of the parable in verses 19–31 Jesus contrasts the earthly status of Lazarus and the rich man, and then their different eternal states. What does Jesus want the Pharisees to see about the relationship of money in this life and in the life after death? 5. In the second part of the parable we learn more about life after death (vv. 26–31). What facts and implications do you observe about this dimension of existence?

Applying the Word 1. How should these parables affect your present use of money? 2. What practical actions would help you to use your money more effectively?

Responding in Prayer Our relatives and friends are not all skeptics. Pray that Jesus' teaching on life after death may spur you to more personal evangelism with those who are still open.

19 / *Luke 17:1—18:14*

How to Grow Mustard-Seed Faith

AS JESUS, HIS disciples and the crowds draw near Jerusalem, he knows disillusion will set in for them. No one understands his repeated predictions of death by the hands of the nation's leaders. They all expect political glory. Their faith is in a nationalistic, political Messiah come to overthrow the Roman rulers and reinstate their national independence. They had to learn what we also have to learn: Faith is not a complete package one receives at conversion. Our trust is not to be in a set program but in a dynamic Person. Faith is a growing response to God, and grows best in the adversities of life.

Warming Up to God Since you first met Jesus, what disillusionments have you had about him and his way of life?

Read Luke 17:1—18:14

17 Jesus said to his disciples: "Things
that cause people to sin are bound
to come, but woe to that person
through whom they come. [2]It would be better for
him to be thrown into the sea with a millstone
tied around his neck than for him to cause one of
these little ones to sin. [3]So watch yourselves.
"If your brother sins, rebuke him, and if he
repents, forgive him. [4]If he sins against you seven
times in a day, and seven times comes back to
you and says, 'I repent,' forgive him."
[5]The apostles said to the Lord, "Increase our
faith!"
[6]He replied, "If you have faith as small as a
mustard seed, you can say to this mulberry tree,
'Be uprooted and planted in the sea,' and it will
obey you.
[7]"Suppose one of you had a servant plowing or
looking after the sheep. Would he say to the servant
when he comes in from the field, 'Come
along now and sit down to eat'? [8]Would he not
rather say, 'Prepare my supper, get yourself ready
and wait on me while I eat and drink; after that
you may eat and drink'? [9]Would he thank the
servant because he did what he was told to do?
[10]So you also, when you have done everything
you were told to do, should say, 'We are unworthy
servants; we have only done our duty.' "
[11]Now on his way to Jerusalem, Jesus traveled
along the border between Samaria and Galilee.
[12]As he was going into a village, ten men who had
leprosy[o] met him. They stood at a distance [13]and
called out in a loud voice, "Jesus, Master, have
pity on us!"
[14]When he saw them, he said, "Go, show yourselves
to the priests." And as they went, they were
cleansed.
[15]One of them, when he saw he was healed,
came back, praising God in a loud voice. [16]He

[o]12 The Greek word was used for various diseases affecting the skin—not necessarily leprosy.

threw himself at Jesus' feet and thanked him—and he was a Samaritan.

17 Jesus asked, "Were not all ten cleansed? Where are the other nine? 18 Was no one found to return and give praise to God except this foreigner?" 19 Then he said to him, "Rise and go; your faith has made you well."

20 Once, having been asked by the Pharisees when the kingdom of God would come, Jesus replied, "The kingdom of God does not come with your careful observation, 21 nor will people say, 'Here it is,' or 'There it is,' because the kingdom of God is within[p] you."

22 Then he said to his disciples, "The time is coming when you will long to see one of the days of the Son of Man, but you will not see it. 23 Men will tell you, 'There he is!' or 'Here he is!' Do not go running off after them. 24 For the Son of Man in his day[q] will be like the lightning, which flashes and lights up the sky from one end to the other. 25 But first he must suffer many things and be rejected by this generation.

26 "Just as it was in the days of Noah, so also will it be in the days of the Son of Man. 27 People were eating, drinking, marrying and being given in marriage up to the day Noah entered the ark. Then the flood came and destroyed them all.

28 "It was the same in the days of Lot. People were eating and drinking, buying and selling, planting and building. 29 But the day Lot left Sodom, fire and sulfur rained down from heaven and destroyed them all.

30 "It will be just like this on the day the Son of Man is revealed. 31 On that day no one who is on the roof of his house, with his goods inside, should go down to get them. Likewise, no one in the field should go back for anything. 32 Remember Lot's wife! 33 Whoever tries to keep his life will lose it, and whoever loses his life will preserve it. 34 I tell you, on that night two people will be in one bed; one will be taken and the other left. 35 Two women will be grinding grain together; one will be taken and the other left.[r]"

37 "Where, Lord?" they asked.

He replied, "Where there is a dead body, there the vultures will gather."

18 Then Jesus told his disciples a parable to show them that they should always pray and not give up. 2 He said: "In a certain town there was a judge who neither feared God nor cared about men. 3 And there was a widow in that town who kept coming to him with the plea, 'Grant me justice against my adversary.'

4 "For some time he refused. But finally he said to himself, 'Even though I don't fear God or care about men, 5 yet because this widow keeps bothering me, I will see that she gets justice, so that she won't eventually wear me out with her coming!' "

6 And the Lord said, "Listen to what the unjust judge says. 7 And will not God bring about justice for his chosen ones, who cry out to him day and night? Will he keep putting them off? 8 I tell you, he will see that they get justice, and quickly. However, when the Son of Man comes, will he find faith on the earth?"

9 To some who were confident of their own righteousness and looked down on everybody else, Jesus told this parable: 10 "Two men went up to the temple to pray, one a Pharisee and the other a tax collector. 11 The Pharisee stood up and prayed about[s] himself: 'God, I thank you that I am not like other men—robbers, evildoers, adulterers—or even like this tax collector. 12 I fast twice a week and give a tenth of all I get.'

13 "But the tax collector stood at a distance. He would not even look up to heaven, but beat his breast and said, 'God, have mercy on me, a sinner.'

14 "I tell you that this man, rather than the other, went home justified before God. For everyone who exalts himself will be humbled, and he who humbles himself will be exalted."

p21 Or *among*   q24 Some manuscripts do not have *in his day.*
r35 Some manuscripts *left.* 36*Two men will be in the field; one will be taken and the other left.*   s11 Or *to*

Discovering the Word 1. Consider the strong reaction of the disciples in 17:1–5. What has caused this reaction? 2. In the story of the lepers Jesus seems surprised that only one of the ten returned in gratitude for his healing. What relation can you see between faith and gratitude in his final words (17:17–19)? 3. For the Pharisees, what emphasis about the kingdom of God does Jesus make (17:20–21)? Why? 4. To his disciples Jesus stresses the need to be prepared for the coming of the Son of Man (himself). He uses two examples of warning in the Old Testament. Why were those people unprepared for God's judgment (17:22–37)? 5. To encourage us to persist in praying Jesus draws a portrait of a certain judge as a contrast to God. In what ways is God different from the judge (18:6–8)? 6. Persistence in praying is balanced by the caution in the second parable not to be presumptuous about God (18:9–14). Both men address "God." But how do their prayers reveal different concepts of God and their relation to him?

Applying the Word 1. What might your prayers reveal about your concept of God and how you relate to him? 2. Faith often seems abstract and elusive. How has Jesus in this study made it more concrete and attainable for your daily living?

Responding in Prayer Pray from your heart to the God who desires to hear you.

20 / *Luke 18:15—19:10*
The Nobodies God Wants

"ONLY THE LITTLE people pay taxes." This quote comes from the very rich hotel "queen," Leona Helmsley, who is now paying dearly for tax evasion. What a contrast of attitude with God's compassion for "the little people." Our study introduces us to three groups or individuals whom society considered insignificant—little children, a blind beggar and a tax collector. They represent the kind of people he wants in his messianic community.

Warming Up to God Reflect on the past week. Is it possible that you have treated someone as insignificant? If so, confess your sin to the Lord.

Read Luke 18:15—19:10.

15 People were also bringing babies to Jesus to
have him touch them. When the disciples saw
this, they rebuked them. 16 But Jesus called the
children to him and said, "Let the little children
come to me, and do not hinder them, for the
kingdom of God belongs to such as these. 17 I tell
you the truth, anyone who will not receive the
kingdom of God like a little child will never enter it."
18 A certain ruler asked him, "Good teacher,
what must I do to inherit eternal life?"
19 "Why do you call me good?" Jesus answered.
"No one is good—except God alone. 20 You know
the commandments: 'Do not commit adultery, do
not murder, do not steal, do not give false testimony, honor your father and mother.'[t]"
21 "All these I have kept since I was a boy," he
said.
22 When Jesus heard this, he said to him, "You
still lack one thing. Sell everything you have and
give to the poor, and you will have treasure in
heaven. Then come, follow me."
23 When he heard this, he became very sad, because he was a man of great wealth. 24 Jesus
looked at him and said, "How hard it is for the
rich to enter the kingdom of God! 25 Indeed, it is
easier for a camel to go through the eye of a needle than for a rich man to enter the kingdom of God."
26 Those who heard this asked, "Who then can
be saved?"
27 Jesus replied, "What is impossible with men
is possible with God."
28 Peter said to him, "We have left all we had to
follow you!"
29 "I tell you the truth," Jesus said to them, "no
one who has left home or wife or brothers or
parents or children for the sake of the kingdom of
God 30 will fail to receive many times as much in
this age and, in the age to come, eternal life."
31 Jesus took the Twelve aside and told them,
"We are going up to Jerusalem, and everything
that is written by the prophets about the Son of
Man will be fulfilled. 32 He will be handed over to
the Gentiles. They will mock him, insult him, spit
on him, flog him and kill him. 33 On the third day
he will rise again."
34 The disciples did not understand any of this.
Its meaning was hidden from them, and they did
not know what he was talking about.
35 As Jesus approached Jericho, a blind man was

[t]20 Exodus 20:12-16; Deut. 5:16-20

sitting by the roadside begging. [36]When he heard
the crowd going by, he asked what was happen-
ing. [37]They told him, "Jesus of Nazareth is pass-
ing by."

[38]He called out, "Jesus, Son of David, have mercy on me!"

[39]Those who led the way rebuked him and told
him to be quiet, but he shouted all the more, "Son of David, have mercy on me!"

[40]Jesus stopped and ordered the man to be
brought to him. When he came near, Jesus asked
him, [41]"What do you want me to do for you?"

"Lord, I want to see," he replied.

[42]Jesus said to him, "Receive your sight; your
faith has healed you." [43]Immediately he received
his sight and followed Jesus, praising God. When all the people saw it, they also praised God.

19 Jesus entered Jericho and was pass-
ing through. [2]A man was there by
the name of Zacchaeus; he was a chief tax collector and was wealthy. [3]He wanted
to see who Jesus was, but being a short man he
could not, because of the crowd. [4]So he ran ahead
and climbed a sycamore-fig tree to see him, since Jesus was coming that way.

[5]When Jesus reached the spot, he looked up
and said to him, "Zacchaeus, come down immedi-
ately. I must stay at your house today." [6]So he
came down at once and welcomed him gladly.

[7]All the people saw this and began to mutter,
"He has gone to be the guest of a 'sinner.' "

[8]But Zacchaeus stood up and said to the Lord,
"Look, Lord! Here and now I give half of my pos-
sessions to the poor, and if I have cheated any-
body out of anything, I will pay back four times the amount."

[9]Jesus said to him, "Today salvation has come
to this house, because this man, too, is a son of
Abraham. [10]For the Son of Man came to seek and
to save what was lost."

Discovering the Word 1. The disciples represent their society's attitude to children—they're insignificant (18:15). How does Jesus give significance to them? 2. In contrast, 18:18–30 is about a "somebody" who disqualifies himself from the kingdom. He has everything society considers admirable and desirable. But what condition for eternal life does he lack (18:22)? 3. In Luke 18:31–34 Jesus' fourth prediction to the Twelve about his coming violent death again meets with lack of understanding. Their presuppositions about riches and their political agenda (19:11) deafens them to Jesus' intent. Then in 18:35–45 Luke introduces us to someone who represents another group of nobodies. What is unusual about the beggar's attitude and title that catches Jesus' attention? 4. Jericho was a rich agricultural town, a popular resort for royalty and priests. What kind of character would a chief tax collector in such a town likely develop? 5. What other side of Zaccheus surfaces in 19:3–6 and 8?

Applying the Word 1. How does Jesus' example with Zaccheus show you how you might share the gospel? 2. Which outsider or nobody from your circle of acquaintances could you introduce to Jesus?

Responding in Prayer Pray for those who are considered insignificant in your community.

21 / *Luke 19:11–48*
False Hopes About the Kingdom of God

MOST OF MY bosses have been hard drivers who regularly exasperated me. But in the long run we worked together productively. If we respect and like our bosses, we are often willing to work hard and even overtime. If we don't respect or like them, we usually are not willing. Then we probably become unproductive. Likewise our personal view of God affects our working relationship to him. In this case productivity has not just temporal but eternal consequences.

Warming Up to God How has work been for you this week? Talk to God about any frustrations you have experienced.

 **Read Luke 19:11-48.**

11While they were listening to this, he went on
to tell them a parable, because he was near Jerusa-
lem and the people thought that the kingdom of
God was going to appear at once. 12He said: "A
man of noble birth went to a distant country to
have himself appointed king and then to return.
13So he called ten of his servants and gave them
ten minas.[u] 'Put this money to work,' he said,
'until I come back.'

14"But his subjects hated him and sent a delega-
tion after him to say, 'We don't want this man to
be our king.'

15"He was made king, however, and returned
home. Then he sent for the servants to whom he
had given the money, in order to find out what
they had gained with it.

16"The first one came and said, 'Sir, your mina
has earned ten more.'

17" 'Well done, my good servant!' his master
replied. 'Because you have been trustworthy in a
very small matter, take charge of ten cities.'

18"The second came and said, 'Sir, your mina
has earned five more.'

19"His master answered, 'You take charge of
five cities.'

20"Then another servant came and said, 'Sir,
here is your mina; I have kept it laid away in a
piece of cloth. 21I was afraid of you, because you
are a hard man. You take out what you did not
put in and reap what you did not sow.'

22"His master replied, 'I will judge you by your
own words, you wicked servant! You knew, did
you, that I am a hard man, taking out what I did
not put in, and reaping what I did not sow?
23Why then didn't you put my money on deposit,
so that when I came back, I could have collected
it with interest?'

24"Then he said to those standing by, 'Take his
mina away from him and give it to the one who
has ten minas.'

25" 'Sir,' they said, 'he already has ten!'

26"He replied, 'I tell you that to everyone who
has, more will be given, but as for the one who
has nothing, even what he has will be taken away.
27But those enemies of mine who did not want me
to be king over them—bring them here and kill
them in front of me.' "

28After Jesus had said this, he went on ahead,
going up to Jerusalem. 29As he approached Beth-
phage and Bethany at the hill called the Mount of
Olives, he sent two of his disciples, saying to
them, 30"Go to the village ahead of you, and as
you enter it, you will find a colt tied there, which
no one has ever ridden. Untie it and bring it here.
31If anyone asks you, 'Why are you untying it?'
tell him, 'The Lord needs it.' "

32Those who were sent ahead went and found
it just as he had told them. 33As they were unty-
ing the colt, its owners asked them, "Why are you
untying the colt?"

34They replied, "The Lord needs it."

35They brought it to Jesus, threw their cloaks
on the colt and put Jesus on it. 36As he went
along, people spread their cloaks on the road.

37When he came near the place where the road
goes down the Mount of Olives, the whole crowd
of disciples began joyfully to praise God in loud
voices for all the miracles they had seen:

38"Blessed is the king who comes in the name
of the Lord!"[v]

"Peace in heaven and glory in the highest!"

39Some of the Pharisees in the crowd said to
Jesus, "Teacher, rebuke your disciples!"

40"I tell you," he replied, "if they keep quiet,
the stones will cry out."

41As he approached Jerusalem and saw the city,
he wept over it 42and said, "If you, even you, had
only known on this day what would bring you
peace—but now it is hidden from your eyes.
43The days will come upon you when your ene-
mies will build an embankment against you and
encircle you and hem you in on every side.
44They will dash you to the ground, you and the
children within your walls. They will not leave
one stone on another, because you did not recog-
nize the time of God's coming to you."

45Then he entered the temple area and began
driving out those who were selling. 46"It is writ-
ten," he said to them, " 'My house will be a house
of prayer'[w]; but you have made it 'a den of rob-
bers.'[x]"

47Every day he was teaching at the temple. But

[u] *13* A mina was about three months' wages. [v] *38* Psalm 118:26
[w] *46* Isaiah 56:7 [x] *46* Jer. 7:11

the chief priests, the teachers of the law and the leaders among the people were trying to kill him. [48]Yet they could not find any way to do it, because all the people hung on his words.

Discovering the Word 1. Jesus' key words in verse 10 have inflamed the crowd's messianic expectations. Jesus' parable aims to counter any false hopes. In verses 12–15 what comparisons between the nobleman and himself does Jesus highlight? 2. Consider the hour of accountability when the master returns as king (vv. 15–26). The reward of the first two (representative) servants is simple. But the king's dialogue with the third servant is detailed. With this emphasis, what point is Jesus making (keep in mind v. 11)? 3. The adversaries of the nobleman-made-king are mentioned only at the beginning and the end (vv. 14, 27). Whom does Jesus intend them to represent? 4. How does he smash the false hopes of this group? 5. In verses 28–40 we see Jesus in various aspects of his messianic role. In a descriptive word or phrase, what concern of Jesus' do you see as he approaches Jerusalem? 6. What concern of Jesus' do you note as he reflects on Jerusalem (vv. 41–44)?

Applying the Word 1. In this panoramic view of Jesus the Messiah, what do you find hard to understand about him? 2. What about Jesus here can you positively respond to? Why?

Responding in Prayer Worship Jesus the Messiah king with praise, awe and thanksgiving.

22 / *Luke 20:1—21:4*
Final Debates—Clear Rejection

I CAN REMEMBER when a humanist on campus branded the Christians a bunch of losers. He claimed he did not need religion for a crutch as they did. I was reduced to wordlessness by his hostile tone. Then I thought of three perfect answers—late that night in bed.

Most of us are not quick to think on our feet, and certainly not as quick and sharp as Jesus. We have seen him as a fearless controversialist in Galilee. Now we will see him in the capital, taking on four distinct authority groups as each mounts attacks on him.

Warming Up to God When have you felt humiliated because you could not defend your faith?

Read Luke 20:1—21:4.

20 One day as he was teaching the
people in the temple courts and
preaching the gospel, the chief
priests and the teachers of the law, together with
the elders, came up to him. [2]"Tell us by what
authority you are doing these things," they said.
"Who gave you this authority?"
[3]He replied, "I will also ask you a question. Tell
me, [4]John's baptism—was it from heaven, or
from men?"
[5]They discussed it among themselves and said,
"If we say, 'From heaven,' he will ask, 'Why didn't
you believe him?' [6]But if we say, 'From men,' all
the people will stone us, because they are persuaded that John was a prophet."
[7]So they answered, "We don't know where it
was from."
[8]Jesus said, "Neither will I tell you by what
authority I am doing these things."
[9]He went on to tell the people this parable: "A
man planted a vineyard, rented it to some farmers
and went away for a long time. [10]At harvest time
he sent a servant to the tenants so they would
give him some of the fruit of the vineyard. But the
tenants beat him and sent him away emptyhanded. [11]He sent another servant, but that one
also they beat and treated shamefully and sent
away empty-handed. [12]He sent still a third, and
they wounded him and threw him out.
[13]"Then the owner of the vineyard said, 'What

shall I do? I will send my son, whom I love; perhaps they will respect him.’

14“But when the tenants saw him, they talked the matter over. ‘This is the heir,’ they said. ‘Let’s kill him, and the inheritance will be ours.’ 15So they threw him out of the vineyard and killed him.

“What then will the owner of the vineyard do to them? 16He will come and kill those tenants and give the vineyard to others.”

When the people heard this, they said, “May this never be!”

17Jesus looked directly at them and asked, “Then what is the meaning of that which is written:

> “ ‘The stone the builders rejected
> has become the capstone[y]’[z]?

18Everyone who falls on that stone will be broken to pieces, but he on whom it falls will be crushed.”

19The teachers of the law and the chief priests looked for a way to arrest him immediately, because they knew he had spoken this parable against them. But they were afraid of the people.

20Keeping a close watch on him, they sent spies, who pretended to be honest. They hoped to catch Jesus in something he said so that they might hand him over to the power and authority of the governor. 21So the spies questioned him: “Teacher, we know that you speak and teach what is right, and that you do not show partiality but teach the way of God in accordance with the truth. 22Is it right for us to pay taxes to Caesar or not?”

23He saw through their duplicity and said to them, 24“Show me a denarius. Whose portrait and inscription are on it?”

25“Caesar’s,” they replied.

He said to them, “Then give to Caesar what is Caesar’s, and to God what is God’s.”

26They were unable to trap him in what he had said there in public. And astonished by his answer, they became silent.

27Some of the Sadducees, who say there is no resurrection, came to Jesus with a question. 28“Teacher,” they said, “Moses wrote for us that if a man’s brother dies and leaves a wife but no children, the man must marry the widow and have children for his brother. 29Now there were seven brothers. The first one married a woman and died childless. 30The second 31and then the third married her, and in the same way the seven died, leaving no children. 32Finally, the woman died too. 33Now then, at the resurrection whose wife will she be, since the seven were married to her?”

34Jesus replied, “The people of this age marry and are given in marriage. 35But those who are considered worthy of taking part in that age and in the resurrection from the dead will neither marry nor be given in marriage, 36and they can no longer die; for they are like the angels. They are God’s children, since they are children of the resurrection. 37But in the account of the bush, even Moses showed that the dead rise, for he calls the Lord ‘the God of Abraham, and the God of Isaac, and the God of Jacob.’[a] 38He is not the God of the dead, but of the living, for to him all are alive.”

39Some of the teachers of the law responded, “Well said, teacher!” 40And no one dared to ask him any more questions.

41Then Jesus said to them, “How is it that they say the Christ[b] is the Son of David? 42David himself declares in the Book of Psalms:

> “ ‘The Lord said to my Lord:
> “Sit at my right hand
> 43until I make your enemies
> a footstool for your feet.” ’[c]

44David calls him ‘Lord.’ How then can he be his son?”

45While all the people were listening, Jesus said to his disciples, 46“Beware of the teachers of the law. They like to walk around in flowing robes and love to be greeted in the marketplaces and have the most important seats in the synagogues and the places of honor at banquets. 47They devour widows’ houses and for a show make lengthy prayers. Such men will be punished most severely.”

21 As he looked up, Jesus saw the rich putting their gifts into the temple treasury. 2He also saw a poor widow put in two very small copper coins.[d] 3“I tell you the truth,” he said, “this poor widow has put in more than all the others. 4All these people gave their gifts out of their wealth; but she out of her poverty put in all she had to live on.”

y17 Or *cornerstone* z17 Psalm 118:22 a37 Exodus 3:6
b41 Or *Messiah* c43 Psalm 110:1 d2 Greek *two lepta*

Discovering the Word 1. By the end of the debate on Jesus' authority, what has each side achieved (20:1–8)? 2. By parable and commentary Jesus pronounces final judgment on the leaders (20:9–18). How do you respond to his stern characterization of God? 3. The Sadducees accepted only the first five Old Testament books, which they (wrongly) presumed said nothing about life after death. What, therefore, do they expect their hypothetical story to do to belief in the resurrection (20:27–47)? 4. Again Jesus points to wrong assumptions behind their question. What error does he identify in their view of life after death (vv. 34–36)? 5. How refreshing this widow must have been to Jesus after the controversies! What does this tell you about the kind of faith Jesus values (21:1–4)?

Applying the Word 1. All four groups totally reject Jesus as God's Messiah king. After this, there are no more debates on the truth—only arrest and death. Besides valid debates, how can we maintain biblical truth against the enemies of Christianity? 2. What is a political/religious tension for you as a Christian? 3. In what way would you like to be more bold in defending your faith?

Responding in Prayer Pray now for faith like the widow's.

23 / *Luke 21:5–38*
Getting Ready for the End

THE "EVIL EMPIRE" of the once-powerful USSR has disappeared, and its former allies are left dangling for military aid. We praise God for this. But some "scholars" of biblical prophecy have to rewrite their books about who the antichrist is and who the nations that will meet for battle in Magog are. Sensational interpretations of "the last days" can stir up some people, especially when the Middle East is in the news. Others react against what they perceive as scare tactics by avoiding any consideration of biblical prophecies. In today's chapter the Lord Jesus shows us how to keep a balance by being properly informed and obedient to his instructions.

Warming Up to God What feelings does talk about the last days create in you?

Read Luke 21:5–38.

5Some of his disciples were remarking about
how the temple was adorned with beautiful
stones and with gifts dedicated to God. But Jesus
said, 6"As for what you see here, the time will
come when not one stone will be left on another;
every one of them will be thrown down."
7"Teacher," they asked, "when will these things
happen? And what will be the sign that they are
about to take place?"
8He replied: "Watch out that you are not de-
ceived. For many will come in my name, claim-
ing, 'I am he,' and, 'The time is near.' Do not
follow them. 9When you hear of wars and revolu-
tions, do not be frightened. These things must
happen first, but the end will not come right
away."
10Then he said to them: "Nation will rise
against nation, and kingdom against kingdom.
11There will be great earthquakes, famines and
pestilences in various places, and fearful events
and great signs from heaven.
12"But before all this, they will lay hands on
you and persecute you. They will deliver you to
synagogues and prisons, and you will be brought
before kings and governors, and all on account of
my name. 13This will result in your being wit-
nesses to them. 14But make up your mind not to
worry beforehand how you will defend your-
selves. 15For I will give you words and wisdom
that none of your adversaries will be able to resist
or contradict. 16You will be betrayed even by par-
ents, brothers, relatives and friends, and they will
put some of you to death. 17All men will hate you
because of me. 18But not a hair of your head will
perish. 19By standing firm you will gain life.
20"When you see Jerusalem being surrounded
by armies, you will know that its desolation is
near. 21Then let those who are in Judea flee to the

mountains, let those in the city get out, and let those in the country not enter the city. 22For this is the time of punishment in fulfillment of all that has been written. 23How dreadful it will be in those days for pregnant women and nursing mothers! There will be great distress in the land and wrath against this people. 24They will fall by the sword and will be taken as prisoners to all the nations. Jerusalem will be trampled on by the Gentiles until the times of the Gentiles are fulfilled.

25"There will be signs in the sun, moon and stars. On the earth, nations will be in anguish and perplexity at the roaring and tossing of the sea. 26Men will faint from terror, apprehensive of what is coming on the world, for the heavenly bodies will be shaken. 27At that time they will see the Son of Man coming in a cloud with power and great glory. 28When these things begin to take place, stand up and lift up your heads, because your redemption is drawing near."

29He told them this parable: "Look at the fig tree and all the trees. 30When they sprout leaves, you can see for yourselves and know that summer is near. 31Even so, when you see these things happening, you know that the kingdom of God is near.

32"I tell you the truth, this generation[c] will certainly not pass away until all these things have happened. 33Heaven and earth will pass away, but my words will never pass away.

34"Be careful, or your hearts will be weighed down with dissipation, drunkenness and the anxieties of life, and that day will close on you unexpectedly like a trap. 35For it will come upon all those who live on the face of the whole earth. 36Be always on the watch, and pray that you may be able to escape all that is about to happen, and that you may be able to stand before the Son of Man."

37Each day Jesus was teaching at the temple, and each evening he went out to spend the night on the hill called the Mount of Olives, 38and all the people came early in the morning to hear him at the temple.

[c]32 Or *race*

Discovering the Word 1. What are your general impressions of Jesus' discourse on the end of the age? 2. At least three important events are evident. The first is Jesus' delivering this discourse to his disciples in A.D. 30 in Jerusalem. What are the other two (vv. 20–24 and vv. 27–28)? 3. But Jesus also says some positive things will happen during this time (vv. 12–19). (These activities can also be applied between the second and third events.) What in Jesus' message gives you hope for an otherwise uncertain future? 4. In verses 8–9 Jesus has said that certain activities are not signs of the end. But what does he say will be signs of the end when he returns (vv. 25–28, and probably vv. 10–11)? 5. How is Jesus' parable of the fig tree (vv. 29–31) related to his preceding teachings (for example, 19:41–44; 20:16)?

Applying the Word 1. Earthly preoccupation can keep us insensitive to spiritual realities and unprepared "to stand before the Son of Man" (vv. 5, 34–36). What aspects of modern living tempt you this way? 2. Which one of Jesus' promises gives you strong incentive to be well prepared (vv. 14–15, 19, 24, 28, 31, 33)?

Responding in Prayer Pray that you would be made ready.

24 / *Luke 22:1–46*
Jesus' New Passover

NOW WE ENTER deeply into the saddest days of history. With Judas' help the religious leaders, considered the most enlightened men in their nation, complete their plot to kill the Son of God. But these days are also the greatest days on earth for Jesus. He is about to complete his life mission, and he confirms to the eleven remaining that they will carry on that mission. So with them he privately establishes his new Passover to supersede the old Passover.

Warming Up to God Recall your most moving celebration of the Lord's Supper. What made it so?

Read Luke 22:1–46.

22 Now the Feast of Unleavened
Bread, called the Passover, was ap-
proaching, 2and the chief priests
and the teachers of the law were looking for some
way to get rid of Jesus, for they were afraid of the
people. 3Then Satan entered Judas, called Iscariot,
one of the Twelve. 4And Judas went to the chief
priests and the officers of the temple guard and
discussed with them how he might betray Jesus.
5They were delighted and agreed to give him
money. 6He consented, and watched for an op-
portunity to hand Jesus over to them when no
crowd was present.
7Then came the day of Unleavened Bread on
which the Passover lamb had to be sacrificed.
8Jesus sent Peter and John, saying, "Go and make
preparations for us to eat the Passover."
9"Where do you want us to prepare for it?"
they asked.
10He replied, "As you enter the city, a man car-
rying a jar of water will meet you. Follow him to
the house that he enters, 11and say to the owner
of the house, 'The Teacher asks: Where is the
guest room, where I may eat the Passover with
my disciples?' 12He will show you a large upper
room, all furnished. Make preparations there."
13They left and found things just as Jesus had
told them. So they prepared the Passover.
14When the hour came, Jesus and his apostles
reclined at the table. 15And he said to them, "I
have eagerly desired to eat this Passover with you
before I suffer. 16For I tell you, I will not eat it
again until it finds fulfillment in the kingdom of
God."
17After taking the cup, he gave thanks and said,
"Take this and divide it among you. 18For I tell
you I will not drink again of the fruit of the vine
until the kingdom of God comes."
19And he took bread, gave thanks and broke it,
and gave it to them, saying, "This is my body
given for you; do this in remembrance of me."
20In the same way, after the supper he took the
cup, saying, "This cup is the new covenant in my
blood, which is poured out for you. 21But the
hand of him who is going to betray me is with
mine on the table. 22The Son of Man will go as it
has been decreed, but woe to that man who be-
trays him." 23They began to question among
themselves which of them it might be who would
do this.
24Also a dispute arose among them as to which
of them was considered to be greatest. 25Jesus
said to them, "The kings of the Gentiles lord it
over them; and those who exercise authority over
them call themselves Benefactors. 26But you are
not to be like that. Instead, the greatest among
you should be like the youngest, and the one who
rules like the one who serves. 27For who is
greater, the one who is at the table or the one who
serves? Is it not the one who is at the table? But
I am among you as one who serves. 28You are
those who have stood by me in my trials. 29And I
confer on you a kingdom, just as my Father con-
ferred one on me, 30so that you may eat and drink
at my table in my kingdom and sit on thrones,
judging the twelve tribes of Israel.
31"Simon, Simon, Satan has asked to sift you[f]
as wheat. 32But I have prayed for you, Simon, that
your faith may not fail. And when you have
turned back, strengthen your brothers."
33But he replied, "Lord, I am ready to go with
you to prison and to death."
34Jesus answered, "I tell you, Peter, before the
rooster crows today, you will deny three times
that you know me."
35Then Jesus asked them, "When I sent you
without purse, bag or sandals, did you lack any-
thing?"
"Nothing," they answered.
36He said to them, "But now if you have a
purse, take it, and also a bag; and if you don't
have a sword, sell your cloak and buy one. 37It is
written: 'And he was numbered with the trans-
gressors'[g]; and I tell you that this must be ful-
filled in me. Yes, what is written about me is
reaching its fulfillment."
38The disciples said, "See, Lord, here are two
swords."
"That is enough," he replied.
39Jesus went out as usual to the Mount of Ol-
ives, and his disciples followed him. 40On reach-
ing the place, he said to them, "Pray that you will
not fall into temptation." 41He withdrew about a
stone's throw beyond them, knelt down and
prayed, 42"Father, if you are willing, take this cup
from me; yet not my will, but yours be done."

f31 The Greek is plural. *g37* Isaiah 53:12

[43]An angel from heaven appeared to him and
strengthened him. [44]And being in anguish, he
prayed more earnestly, and his sweat was like
drops of blood falling to the ground.[h]
[45]When he rose from prayer and went back to
the disciples, he found them asleep, exhausted
from sorrow. [46]"Why are you sleeping?" he asked
them. "Get up and pray so that you will not fall
into temptation."

[h]44 Some early manuscripts do not have verses 43 and 44.

Discovering the Word 1. What do verses 1–6 tell you about the authorities? 2. Look at verses 7–23, comparing Jesus' plans with the authorities' plans. As you examine his plans, what impresses you about Jesus himself? 3. Jesus chides the disciples for their preoccupation with power and prestige. What lesson does he teach about the kind of leaders he wants to carry on his work (vv. 26–27)? 4. Jesus further prepares them for coming tests. The first preparation is for Peter immediately ahead. The second is for all the apostles in the long run. Like him they would have to face official hostility (vv. 36–38). In either testing what should help them to persevere (vv. 28, 29–30, 31, 32, 35)? 5. What guidelines for praying do you see in each verse of 39–46, showing Jesus' example?

Applying the Word 1. Jesus' institution of his new Passover was interspersed with human weakness and failure. In redeeming his disciples, he used their shortcomings. What weaknesses and failures do you want to acknowledge as you contemplate afresh eating Jesus' new Passover? 2. What new, or renewed, truths about prayer do you discover in Jesus' example (22:39–46)?

Responding in Prayer Follow the guidelines for prayer in Jesus' example.

25 / *Luke 22:47—23:56*
The Message of the Cross

THE SYMBOL OF the cross is used in many ways—on and in Christian churches, by the Red Cross, on many European flags. It is used as jewelry even by non-Christians. But they would never think of wearing a burnished gold miniature of an electric chair around their necks. In the first century the wooden cross meant capital punishment for criminals. Jesus died as a criminal to be the substitute for us sinners. Some old hymns have well retained this essential truth of Jesus' cross. Not many contemporary songs about his death do that. Approach this study with prayer for a deeper understanding of the cross of Jesus.

Warming Up to God What was your first understanding of the Christian cross?

Read Luke 22:47—23:56.

[47]While he was still speaking a crowd came up,
and the man who was called Judas, one of the
Twelve, was leading them. He approached Jesus
to kiss him, [48]but Jesus asked him, "Judas, are
you betraying the Son of Man with a kiss?"
[49]When Jesus' followers saw what was going to
happen, they said, "Lord, should we strike with
our swords?" [50]And one of them struck the ser-
vant of the high priest, cutting off his right ear.
[51]But Jesus answered, "No more of this!" And
he touched the man's ear and healed him.
[52]Then Jesus said to the chief priests, the offi-
cers of the temple guard, and the elders, who had
come for him, "Am I leading a rebellion, that you
have come with swords and clubs? [53]Every day I
was with you in the temple courts, and you did
not lay a hand on me. But this is your hour—
when darkness reigns."
[54]Then seizing him, they led him away and
took him into the house of the high priest. Peter
followed at a distance. [55]But when they had kin-
dled a fire in the middle of the courtyard and had

sat down together, Peter sat down with them. [56]A servant girl saw him seated there in the firelight. She looked closely at him and said, "This man was with him."

[57]But he denied it. "Woman, I don't know him," he said.

[58]A little later someone else saw him and said, "You also are one of them."

"Man, I am not!" Peter replied.

[59]About an hour later another asserted, "Certainly this fellow was with him, for he is a Galilean."

[60]Peter replied, "Man, I don't know what you're talking about!" Just as he was speaking, the rooster crowed. [61]The Lord turned and looked straight at Peter. Then Peter remembered the word the Lord had spoken to him: "Before the rooster crows today, you will disown me three times." [62]And he went outside and wept bitterly.

[63]The men who were guarding Jesus began mocking and beating him. [64]They blindfolded him and demanded, "Prophesy! Who hit you?" [65]And they said many other insulting things to him.

[66]At daybreak the council of the elders of the people, both the chief priests and teachers of the law, met together, and Jesus was led before them. [67]"If you are the Christ,[i]" they said, "tell us."

Jesus answered, "If I tell you, you will not believe me, [68]and if I asked you, you would not answer. [69]But from now on, the Son of Man will be seated at the right hand of the mighty God."

[70]They all asked, "Are you then the Son of God?"

He replied, "You are right in saying I am."

[71]Then they said, "Why do we need any more testimony? We have heard it from his own lips."

23

Then the whole assembly rose and led him off to Pilate. [2]And they began to accuse him, saying, "We have found this man subverting our nation. He opposes payment of taxes to Caesar and claims to be Christ,[j] a king."

[3]So Pilate asked Jesus, "Are you the king of the Jews?"

"Yes, it is as you say," Jesus replied.

[4]Then Pilate announced to the chief priests and the crowd, "I find no basis for a charge against this man."

[5]But they insisted, "He stirs up the people all over Judea[k] by his teaching. He started in Galilee and has come all the way here."

[6]On hearing this, Pilate asked if the man was a Galilean. [7]When he learned that Jesus was under Herod's jurisdiction, he sent him to Herod, who was also in Jerusalem at that time.

[8]When Herod saw Jesus, he was greatly pleased, because for a long time he had been wanting to see him. From what he had heard about him, he hoped to see him perform some miracle. [9]He plied him with many questions, but Jesus gave him no answer. [10]The chief priests and the teachers of the law were standing there, vehemently accusing him. [11]Then Herod and his soldiers ridiculed and mocked him. Dressing him in an elegant robe, they sent him back to Pilate. [12]That day Herod and Pilate became friends—before this they had been enemies.

[13]Pilate called together the chief priests, the rulers and the people, [14]and said to them, "You brought me this man as one who was inciting the people to rebellion. I have examined him in your presence and have found no basis for your charges against him. [15]Neither has Herod, for he sent him back to us; as you can see, he has done nothing to deserve death. [16]Therefore, I will punish him and then release him.[l]"

[18]With one voice they cried out, "Away with this man! Release Barabbas to us!" [19](Barabbas had been thrown into prison for an insurrection in the city, and for murder.)

[20]Wanting to release Jesus, Pilate appealed to them again. [21]But they kept shouting, "Crucify him! Crucify him!"

[22]For the third time he spoke to them: "Why? What crime has this man committed? I have found in him no grounds for the death penalty. Therefore I will have him punished and then release him."

[23]But with loud shouts they insistently demanded that he be crucified, and their shouts prevailed. [24]So Pilate decided to grant their demand. [25]He released the man who had been thrown into prison for insurrection and murder, the one they asked for, and surrendered Jesus to their will.

[26]As they led him away, they seized Simon from Cyrene, who was on his way in from the country, and put the cross on him and made him carry it behind Jesus. [27]A large number of people followed him, including women who mourned and wailed for him. [28]Jesus turned and said to

[i]67 Or *Messiah* [j]2 Or *Messiah*; also in verses 35 and 39 [k]5 Or *over the land of the Jews* [l]16 Some manuscripts *him."* [17]*Now he was obliged to release one man to them at the Feast.*

them, "Daughters of Jerusalem, do not weep for
me; weep for yourselves and for your children.
29For the time will come when you will say,
'Blessed are the barren women, the wombs that
never bore and the breasts that never nursed!'
30Then

" 'they will say to the mountains, "Fall on
us!"
and to the hills, "Cover us!" '[m]

31For if men do these things when the tree is
green, what will happen when it is dry?"
32Two other men, both criminals, were also led
out with him to be executed. 33When they came
to the place called the Skull, there they crucified
him, along with the criminals—one on his right,
the other on his left. 34Jesus said, "Father, forgive
them, for they do not know what they are do-
ing."[n] And they divided up his clothes by casting
lots.
35The people stood watching, and the rulers
even sneered at him. They said, "He saved others;
let him save himself if he is the Christ of God, the
Chosen One."
36The soldiers also came up and mocked him.
They offered him wine vinegar 37and said, "If you
are the king of the Jews, save yourself."
38There was a written notice above him, which
read: THIS IS THE KING OF THE JEWS.
39One of the criminals who hung there hurled
insults at him: "Aren't you the Christ? Save your-
self and us!"
40But the other criminal rebuked him. "Don't
you fear God," he said, "since you are under the
same sentence? 41We are punished justly, for we
are getting what our deeds deserve. But this man
has done nothing wrong."
42Then he said, "Jesus, remember me when you
come into your kingdom.[o]"
43Jesus answered him, "I tell you the truth, to-
day you will be with me in paradise."
44It was now about the sixth hour, and dark-
ness came over the whole land until the ninth
hour, 45for the sun stopped shining. And the cur-
tain of the temple was torn in two. 46Jesus called
out with a loud voice, "Father, into your hands I
commit my spirit." When he had said this, he
breathed his last.
47The centurion, seeing what had happened,
praised God and said, "Surely this was a righteous
man." 48When all the people who had gathered to
witness this sight saw what took place, they beat
their breasts and went away. 49But all those who
knew him, including the women who had fol-
lowed him from Galilee, stood at a distance,
watching these things.
50Now there was a man named Joseph, a mem-
ber of the Council, a good and upright man,
51who had not consented to their decision and
action. He came from the Judean town of Arima-
thea and he was waiting for the kingdom of God.
52Going to Pilate, he asked for Jesus' body. 53Then
he took it down, wrapped it in linen cloth and
placed it in a tomb cut in the rock, one in which
no one had yet been laid. 54It was Preparation
Day, and the Sabbath was about to begin.
55The women who had come with Jesus from
Galilee followed Joseph and saw the tomb and
how his body was laid in it. 56Then they went
home and prepared spices and perfumes. But they
rested on the Sabbath in obedience to the com-
mandment.

[m]30 Hosea 10:8 [n]34 Some early manuscripts do not have this sentence. [o]42 Some manuscripts *come with your kingly power*

Discovering the Word 1. In a word or phrase, what describes the way Jesus relates to each individual or group during his arrest (22:47–62)? 2. Only a few hours after Peter swore loyalty to Jesus, he makes an about-face (vv. 57–60). In what kind of situation are you tempted to avoid identification with Jesus and his cause? 3. Three times Pilate says he finds no valid charge against Jesus, and seeks to release him (23:4, 13–16 and 22). Why then does he ultimately pronounce the death penalty on Jesus? 4. Luke gives few details of Jesus' physical death. Instead he focuses on people's attitudes. What attitude to the man on the center cross does each group or individual reveal (23:32–49)? 5. Throughout his six hours on the cross, Jesus is in touch with his Father. What do his brief words to the Father reflect about their relationship (23:34,46)?

Applying the Word 1. What can you do to make the message of the cross relevant to your needy world? 2. How can the cross become more relevant to you as an individual?

Responding in Prayer Praise God for giving his Son over to this horrible death on the cross for your sake.

26 / *Luke 24*
God Has the Last Word

HOW MIGHT YOU destroy Christianity? Explain away Jesus' resurrection. For instance, you could say the overemotional women at the tomb were deluded. Or argue that they went to the wrong tomb. You might insist that the resurrection was spiritual, not physical, or that the disciples had hallucinations. From that first Easter till now the enemies of the church have tried to get rid of the historical facts (Mt 28:11–15). None has succeeded.

Warming Up to God What does Christ's resurrection mean to you? What would the world lose if Jesus did not rise from death?

Read Luke 24.

---

24 On the first day of the week, very early in the morning, the women took the spices they had prepared and went to the tomb. 2They found the stone rolled away from the tomb, 3but when they entered, they did not find the body of the Lord Jesus. 4While they were wondering about this, suddenly two men in clothes that gleamed like lightning stood beside them. 5In their fright the women bowed down with their faces to the ground, but the men said to them, "Why do you look for the living among the dead? 6He is not here; he has risen! Remember how he told you, while he was still with you in Galilee: 7'The Son of Man must be delivered into the hands of sinful men, be crucified and on the third day be raised again.' " 8Then they remembered his words.

9When they came back from the tomb, they told all these things to the Eleven and to all the others. 10It was Mary Magdalene, Joanna, Mary the mother of James, and the others with them who told this to the apostles. 11But they did not believe the women, because their words seemed to them like nonsense. 12Peter, however, got up and ran to the tomb. Bending over, he saw the strips of linen lying by themselves, and he went away, wondering to himself what had happened.

13Now that same day two of them were going to a village called Emmaus, about seven miles[p] from Jerusalem. 14They were talking with each other about everything that had happened. 15As they talked and discussed these things with each other, Jesus himself came up and walked along with them; 16but they were kept from recognizing him.

17He asked them, "What are you discussing together as you walk along?"

They stood still, their faces downcast. 18One of them, named Cleopas, asked him, "Are you only a visitor to Jerusalem and do not know the things that have happened there in these days?"

19"What things?" he asked.

"About Jesus of Nazareth," they replied. "He was a prophet, powerful in word and deed before God and all the people. 20The chief priests and our rulers handed him over to be sentenced to death, and they crucified him; 21but we had hoped that he was the one who was going to redeem Israel. And what is more, it is the third day since all this took place. 22In addition, some of our women amazed us. They went to the tomb early this morning 23but didn't find his body. They came and told us that they had seen a vision of angels, who said he was alive. 24Then some of our companions went to the tomb and found it just as the women had said, but him they did not see."

25He said to them, "How foolish you are, and how slow of heart to believe all that the prophets have spoken! 26Did not the Christ[q] have to suffer these things and then enter his glory?" 27And beginning with Moses and all the Prophets, he explained to them what was said in all the Scriptures concerning himself.

28As they approached the village to which they were going, Jesus acted as if he were going farther. 29But they urged him strongly, "Stay with us, for it is nearly evening; the day is almost over." So he went in to stay with them.

30When he was at the table with them, he took bread, gave thanks, broke it and began to give it to them. 31Then their eyes were opened and they recognized him, and he disappeared from their sight. 32They asked each other, "Were not our

[p] 13 Greek *sixty stadia* (about 11 kilometers) [q] 26 Or *Messiah*; also in verse 46

hearts burning within us while he talked with
us on the road and opened the Scriptures to
us?"

33They got up and returned at once to Jerusa-
lem. There they found the Eleven and those with
them, assembled together 34and saying, "It is
true! The Lord has risen and has appeared to Si-
mon." 35Then the two told what had happened on
the way, and how Jesus was recognized by them
when he broke the bread.

36While they were still talking about this, Jesus
himself stood among them and said to them,
"Peace be with you."

37They were startled and frightened, thinking
they saw a ghost. 38He said to them, "Why are
you troubled, and why do doubts rise in your
minds? 39Look at my hands and my feet. It is I
myself! Touch me and see; a ghost does not have
flesh and bones, as you see I have."

40When he had said this, he showed them his
hands and feet. 41And while they still did not be-
lieve it because of joy and amazement, he asked
them, "Do you have anything here to eat?" 42They
gave him a piece of broiled fish, 43and he took it
and ate it in their presence.

44He said to them, "This is what I told you
while I was still with you: Everything must be
fulfilled that is written about me in the Law of
Moses, the Prophets and the Psalms."

45Then he opened their minds so they could
understand the Scriptures. 46He told them, "This
is what is written: The Christ will suffer and rise
from the dead on the third day, 47and repentance
and forgiveness of sins will be preached in his
name to all nations, beginning at Jerusalem.
48You are witnesses of these things. 49I am going
to send you what my Father has promised; but
stay in the city until you have been clothed with
power from on high."

50When he had led them out to the vicinity of
Bethany, he lifted up his hands and blessed them.
51While he was blessing them, he left them and
was taken up into heaven. 52Then they worshiped
him and returned to Jerusalem with great joy.
53And they stayed continually at the temple,
praising God.

Discovering the Word 1. The women are a personal link between the cross and the empty tomb. Suppose you are one of them. How do you feel when the men respond with "Nonsense!" (vv. 1–12)? 2. What strikes you about the stranger's dialogue with the disciples (vv. 13–35)? 3. We can sympathize with the disciples' struggle between despair and hope. In his rebuke Jesus identifies the cause of their despair—reluctance to believe the Scriptures about a suffering Messiah (v. 25). How have the Scriptures ever moved you from despair to new hope? 4. Look at verses 36–53 as a seeker inquiring about Jesus' resurrection. Which facts and implications help you to believe his personal reality? 5. For three or so years Jesus has been preparing his disciples to carry on his world mission. He climaxes this mission training by stressing systematic, in-depth Bible understanding (vv. 25–27, 32, 44–47). In what ways can you testify to this importance?

Applying the Word 1. We have been carefully studying the life and mission of Jesus. What would you say are your three greatest incentives to be his "witness of these things"? 2. What a message we have! The Lord Jesus has come to bring new hope and new joy to the world! How can you (and your church or fellowship group) take Jesus' message of new hope and new joy to your community?

Responding in Prayer Pray that you will be a source of joy to many as you bring Jesus' message.

John

The most significant fact in history can be summed up in four words: *Jesus Christ is God!* The great declaration of the Bible is that God in human flesh was born in Bethlehem. It was God in the person of Jesus Christ who astonished the people of his day with his miracles and amazed them with his teaching. It was God who lived a perfect life and then allowed himself to be put to death on a Roman cross for humanity's sins. It was God who three days after he died broke the bonds of death and came out of the grave alive. The deity of Jesus—the fact that he was God in human flesh—is the bottom line of the Christian faith.

When the apostle John sat down to write his Gospel, he was not interested simply in adding one more biography of Jesus to the three already in existence. John wrote his book with a very specific purpose in mind. He tells us in 20:30–31:

> Jesus did many other miraculous signs in the presence of his disciples, which are not recorded in this book. But these are written that you may believe that Jesus is the Christ, the Son of God, and that by believing you may have life in his name.

John's book is not a biography; it's a theological argument. John wants to convince us that Jesus of Nazareth is God the Son. Then he wants to show us how that fact will change our lives in some rather amazing ways. It is by believing in Jesus Christ as the Son of God that we find life—real life, eternal life, a whole new kind of life!

Every event John records is designed to show us that Jesus is God. John pulls from the life of Jesus specific incidents that demonstrate his majesty and deity. Of particular interest to John are the sign miracles of Jesus. In the first twelve chapters of his book, John records seven miracles. These miracles were not performed simply to alleviate human suffering or to meet human need. The miracles were "signs." They pointed to the truth of Jesus' claim to be the Son of God.

John was the last Gospel writer. The best evidence points to a date around A.D. 90 for the composition of his Gospel. The other Gospels had been in circulation for some time. John wrote to add his unique perspective and to fill in some of the details not recorded by the other writers. He assumes his readers are familiar with the other Gospels. John does not mention, for example, the anguish of Jesus in the Garden of Gethsemane. The other writers had adequately described that incident. John does give us the details of Jesus' conversation with his disciples in the upper room. The other writers mention it only briefly.

John never mentions himself by name in the Gospel. He refers to himself simply as "the disciple whom Jesus loved." We have in this Gospel the memories of an intimate friend about the Lord Jesus. Jesus Christ had transformed John's life. I hope you are prepared to have that happen to you! You are about to begin a fascinating study focused on the greatest person who ever lived—Jesus Christ. If you will respond to what John writes in faith and obedience, you, like John, will experience a whole new kind of life.

Outline

Part 1: Jesus, the Living Word of God

1/ John 1 —— *The Master & Five Who Followed*

2/ John 2 —— *Wine & a Whip*

3/ John 3 —— *The New Birth*

4/ John 4 —— *Soul & Body—Saving & Healing*

5/ John 5 —— *Deity on Trial*

6/ John 6 —— *Jesus, the Bread of Life*

7/ John 7:1–52 —— *Confusion over Christ*

8/ John 7:53—8:11 —— *Caught in Adultery*

9/ John 8:12–59 —— *Jesus, the Light of the World*

10/ John 9 —— *A Blind Man Sees the Light*

11/ John 10 —— *The Shepherd & His Sheep*

12/ John 11 —— *Resurrection & Life*

13/ John 12 —— *The King's Last Acts*

Part 2: Jesus, the Living Way to God

14/ John 13:1–17 —— *The Son as a Slave*

15/ John 13:18–38 —— *The Betrayer & the Boaster*

16/ John 14 —— *Comfort for a Troubled Heart*

17/ John 15:1–17 —— *The Secret of Remaining*

18/ John 15:18—16:4 —— *The Cost of Friendship with Jesus*

19/ John 16:5–33 —— *Secrets of the Spirit*

20/ John 17 —— *The Master's Final Prayer*

21/ John 18:1–27 —— *"Jesus, You're Under Arrest!"*

22/ John 18:28—19:16 —— *Pilate on Trial*

23/ John 19:17–42 —— *Obedient to Death*

24/ John 20 —— *The Son Is Up!*

25/ John 21 —— *A Walk with a Resurrected Man*

1 / *John 1*
The Master & Five Who Followed

IT WAS A great day in our history when a man first walked on the moon. But the Bible declares that a far greater event took place two thousand years ago. God walked on the earth in the person of Jesus Christ. John opens his Gospel with a beautiful hymn of exaltation to Christ. It is one of the most profound passages in all the Bible. It is written in simple, straightforward language, yet in studying the depths of its meaning, it is a passage where we never reach bottom. It is an ocean-sized truth, and we have to be content to paddle around in shallow water.

Warming Up to God Consider the miracle of God becoming human. Give him your praise and worship for what he has done for you.

Read John 1.

1 In the beginning was the Word, and the Word was with God, and the Word was God. 2He was with God in the beginning. 3Through him all things were made; without him nothing was made that has been made. 4In him was life, and that life was the light of men. 5The light shines in the darkness, but the darkness has not understood[a] it.

6There came a man who was sent from God; his name was John. 7He came as a witness to testify concerning that light, so that through him all men might believe. 8He himself was not the light; he came only as a witness to the light. 9The true light that gives light to every man was coming into the world.[b]

10He was in the world, and though the world was made through him, the world did not recognize him. 11He came to that which was his own, but his own did not receive him. 12Yet to all who received him, to those who believed in his name, he gave the right to become children of God—13children born not of natural descent,[c] nor of human decision or a husband's will, but born of God.

14The Word became flesh and made his dwelling among us. We have seen his glory, the glory of the One and Only,[d] who came from the Father, full of grace and truth.

15John testifies concerning him. He cries out, saying, "This was he of whom I said, 'He who comes after me has surpassed me because he was before me.' " 16From the fullness of his grace we have all received one blessing after another. 17For the law was given through Moses; grace and truth came through Jesus Christ. 18No one has ever seen God, but God the One and Only,[d,e] who is at the Father's side, has made him known.

19Now this was John's testimony when the Jews of Jerusalem sent priests and Levites to ask him who he was. 20He did not fail to confess, but confessed freely, "I am not the Christ.[f]"

21They asked him, "Then who are you? Are you Elijah?"

He said, "I am not."

"Are you the Prophet?"

He answered, "No."

22Finally they said, "Who are you? Give us an answer to take back to those who sent us. What do you say about yourself?"

23John replied in the words of Isaiah the prophet, "I am the voice of one calling in the desert, 'Make straight the way for the Lord.' "[g]

24Now some Pharisees who had been sent 25questioned him, "Why then do you baptize if you are not the Christ, nor Elijah, nor the Prophet?"

26"I baptize with[h] water," John replied, "but among you stands one you do not know. 27He is the one who comes after me, the thongs of whose sandals I am not worthy to untie."

28This all happened at Bethany on the other side of the Jordan, where John was baptizing.

29The next day John saw Jesus coming toward him and said, "Look, the Lamb of God, who takes away the sin of the world! 30This is the one I meant when I said, 'A man who comes after me has surpassed me because he was before me.' 31I myself did not know him, but the reason I came

[a]5 Or *darkness, and the darkness has not overcome* [b]9 Or *This was the true light that gives light to every man who comes into the world* [c]13 Greek *of bloods* [d]14,18 Or *the Only Begotten* [e]18 Some manuscripts *but the only* (or *only begotten*) *Son* [f]20 Or *Messiah.* "The Christ" (Greek) and "the Messiah" (Hebrew) both mean "the Anointed One"; also in verse 25. [g]23 Isaiah 40:3 [h]26 Or *in;* also in verses 31 and 33

baptizing with water was that he might be re-
vealed to Israel."
32 Then John gave this testimony: "I saw the
Spirit come down from heaven as a dove and re-
main on him. 33 I would not have known him,
except that the one who sent me to baptize with
water told me, 'The man on whom you see the
Spirit come down and remain is he who will bap-
tize with the Holy Spirit.' 34 I have seen and I tes-
tify that this is the Son of God."
35 The next day John was there again with two
of his disciples. 36 When he saw Jesus passing by,
he said, "Look, the Lamb of God!"
37 When the two disciples heard him say this,
they followed Jesus. 38 Turning around, Jesus saw
them following and asked, "What do you want?"
They said, "Rabbi" (which means Teacher),
"where are you staying?"
39 "Come," he replied, "and you will see."
So they went and saw where he was staying,
and spent that day with him. It was about the
tenth hour.
40 Andrew, Simon Peter's brother, was one of
the two who heard what John had said and who
had followed Jesus. 41 The first thing Andrew did
was to find his brother Simon and tell him, "We
have found the Messiah" (that is, the Christ).
42 And he brought him to Jesus.
Jesus looked at him and said, "You are Simon
son of John. You will be called Cephas" (which,
when translated, is Peter[i]).
43 The next day Jesus decided to leave for Gali-
lee. Finding Philip, he said to him, "Follow me."
44 Philip, like Andrew and Peter, was from the
town of Bethsaida. 45 Philip found Nathanael and
told him, "We have found the one Moses wrote
about in the Law, and about whom the prophets
also wrote—Jesus of Nazareth, the son of Jo-
seph."
46 "Nazareth! Can anything good come from
there?" Nathanael asked.
"Come and see," said Philip.
47 When Jesus saw Nathanael approaching, he
said of him, "Here is a true Israelite, in whom
there is nothing false."
48 "How do you know me?" Nathanael asked.
Jesus answered, "I saw you while you were still
under the fig tree before Philip called you."
49 Then Nathanael declared, "Rabbi, you are the
Son of God; you are the King of Israel."
50 Jesus said, "You believe[j] because I told you
I saw you under the fig tree. You shall see greater
things than that." 51 He then added, "I tell you[k]
the truth, you[k] shall see heaven open, and the
angels of God ascending and descending on the
Son of Man."

[i] 42 Both *Cephas* (Aramaic) and *Peter* (Greek) mean *rock*. [j] 50 Or *Do you believe . . . ?* [k] 51 The Greek is plural.

Discovering the Word 1. John records more than a dozen names or descriptions of Jesus in this chapter. What are some of these? 2. In verses 1–3 what facts does John declare to be true of the Word? 3. According to verses 14–18, what specific aspects of God's character are revealed to us through Jesus? 4. What steps did John take to guarantee that people would not look at him but at Christ? 5. In verses 35–51 we are introduced to five men: Andrew, Simon, Philip, Nathanael and one unnamed disciple (John). How did each man respond to the testimony he heard about Jesus?

Applying the Word 1. Which of the names of Jesus has the most significance to you personally? Explain why. 2. What do you hope will happen in your life as a result of studying the Gospel of John?

Responding in Prayer Ask God to bring the light and life of Jesus to you as you study his Word.

2 / *John 2*
Wine & a Whip

AFTER I HAD given a presentation on the claims of Christ, a skeptical student asked: "What proof do you have that Jesus really was who he claimed to be?" People have been asking that question for two thousand years! For John the convincing proof of Jesus' deity was found in his words and deeds. No one but God could say the things Jesus said, and no one but God could do the things Jesus did. In this chapter are two signs that demonstrate that Jesus was the fullness of God clothed in humanity.

Warming Up to God Thank God for revealing himself to you personally.

Read John 2.

2 On the third day a wedding took place at
Cana in Galilee. Jesus' mother was there,
2and Jesus and his disciples had also been
invited to the wedding. 3When the wine was
gone, Jesus' mother said to him, "They have no
more wine."
4"Dear woman, why do you involve me?" Jesus
replied. "My time has not yet come."
5His mother said to the servants, "Do whatever
he tells you."
6Nearby stood six stone water jars, the kind
used by the Jews for ceremonial washing, each
holding from twenty to thirty gallons.[l]
7Jesus said to the servants, "Fill the jars with
water"; so they filled them to the brim.
8Then he told them, "Now draw some out and
take it to the master of the banquet."
They did so, 9and the master of the banquet
tasted the water that had been turned into wine.
He did not realize where it had come from,
though the servants who had drawn the water
knew. Then he called the bridegroom aside 10and
said, "Everyone brings out the choice wine first
and then the cheaper wine after the guests have
had too much to drink; but you have saved the
best till now."
11This, the first of his miraculous signs, Jesus
performed at Cana in Galilee. He thus revealed
his glory, and his disciples put their faith in him.
12After this he went down to Capernaum with
his mother and brothers and his disciples. There
they stayed for a few days.
13When it was almost time for the Jewish Pass-
over, Jesus went up to Jerusalem. 14In the temple
courts he found men selling cattle, sheep and
doves, and others sitting at tables exchanging
money. 15So he made a whip out of cords, and
drove all from the temple area, both sheep and
cattle; he scattered the coins of the money chang-
ers and overturned their tables. 16To those who
sold doves he said, "Get these out of here! How
dare you turn my Father's house into a market!"
17His disciples remembered that it is written:
"Zeal for your house will consume me."[m]
18Then the Jews demanded of him, "What mi-
raculous sign can you show us to prove your au-
thority to do all this?"
19Jesus answered them, "Destroy this temple,
and I will raise it again in three days."
20The Jews replied, "It has taken forty-six years
to build this temple, and you are going to raise it
in three days?" 21But the temple he had spoken of
was his body. 22After he was raised from the dead,
his disciples recalled what he had said. Then they
believed the Scripture and the words that Jesus
had spoken.
23Now while he was in Jerusalem at the Pass-
over Feast, many people saw the miraculous signs
he was doing and believed in his name.[n] 24But
Jesus would not entrust himself to them, for he
knew all men. 25He did not need man's testimony
about man, for he knew what was in a man.

[l]6 Greek *two to three metretes* (probably about 75 to 115 liters)
[m]17 Psalm 69:9 [n]23 Or *and believed in him*

Discovering the Word 1. When the groom's parents ran out of wine for their guests, Jesus' mother asked him to help (v. 3). What do you think Mary expected Jesus to do? (Remember, according to verse 11 Jesus had not yet performed any miracles.) 2. What did Jesus mean by his reply to Mary in verse 4? 3. According to verse 11, the purpose of Jesus' miracle was not to save the groom from embarrassment but to display Christ's glory. What aspects of Christ's glory does this miracle reveal to you? 4. How does John's picture of Jesus in verses 15–16 fit with today's popular concept of him? 5. Only the Messiah had the authority to cleanse the temple. The people recognized that and asked Jesus for a miraculous sign to confirm his identify (v. 18). To what "sign" did Jesus point them (vv. 19–22)? Why do you think that particular sign was so significant in Jesus' mind?

Applying the Word 1. In what practical ways can you demonstrate the same concern that Jesus does toward the holy character of God? 2. How do Jesus' presence and actions at this party serve as a model for you?

Responding in Prayer Ask God to help you to be his representative in everything you do.

3 / *John 3*
The New Birth

I TALKED TODAY to a junior in college who is only one month old. No, she isn't a child genius. Recently a friend explained to her the claims of Christ. As she responded in simple faith, she experienced the joys of spiritual birth.

The most beautiful explanation of the new birth is found here in John 3. It's a passage that children can understand, and one that the greatest saints of God have never fully grasped. It's a message not so much to be analyzed and dissected as it is to be received with joy.

Warming Up to God Do you remember your spiritual birthday? Reflect on what that time meant for you.

Read John 3.

3 Now there was a man of the Pharisees named Nicodemus, a member of the Jewish ruling council. 2He came to Jesus at night and said, "Rabbi, we know you are a teacher who has come from God. For no one could perform the miraculous signs you are doing if God were not with him."

3In reply Jesus declared, "I tell you the truth, no one can see the kingdom of God unless he is born again.[o]"

4"How can a man be born when he is old?" Nicodemus asked. "Surely he cannot enter a second time into his mother's womb to be born!"

5Jesus answered, "I tell you the truth, no one can enter the kingdom of God unless he is born of water and the Spirit. 6Flesh gives birth to flesh, but the Spirit[p] gives birth to spirit. 7You should not be surprised at my saying, 'You[q] must be born again.' 8The wind blows wherever it pleases. You hear its sound, but you cannot tell where it comes from or where it is going. So it is with everyone born of the Spirit."

9"How can this be?" Nicodemus asked.

10"You are Israel's teacher," said Jesus, "and do you not understand these things? 11I tell you the truth, we speak of what we know, and we testify to what we have seen, but still you people do not accept our testimony. 12I have spoken to you of earthly things and you do not believe; how then will you believe if I speak of heavenly things? 13No one has ever gone into heaven except the one who came from heaven—the Son of Man.[r] 14Just as Moses lifted up the snake in the desert, so the Son of Man must be lifted up, 15that everyone who believes in him may have eternal life.[s]

16"For God so loved the world that he gave his one and only Son,[t] that whoever believes in him shall not perish but have eternal life. 17For God did not send his Son into the world to condemn the world, but to save the world through him. 18Whoever believes in him is not condemned, but whoever does not believe stands condemned already because he has not believed in the name of God's one and only Son.[u] 19This is the verdict: Light has come into the world, but men loved darkness instead of light because their deeds were evil. 20Everyone who does evil hates the light, and will not come into the light for fear that his deeds will be exposed. 21But whoever lives by the truth comes into the light, so that it may be seen plainly that what he has done has been done through God."[v]

22After this, Jesus and his disciples went out into the Judean countryside, where he spent some time with them, and baptized. 23Now John also was baptizing at Aenon near Salim, because there was plenty of water, and people were constantly coming to be baptized. 24(This was before John was put in prison.) 25An argument developed between some of John's disciples and a certain Jew[w] over the matter of ceremonial washing.

[o]3 Or *born from above*; also in verse 7 [p]6 Or *but spirit* [q]7 The Greek is plural. [r]13 Some manuscripts *Man, who is in heaven* [s]15 Or *believes may have eternal life in him* [t]16 Or *his only begotten Son* [u]18 Or *God's only begotten Son* [v]21 Some interpreters end the quotation after verse 15. [w]25 Some manuscripts *and certain Jews*

[26]They came to John and said to him, "Rabbi, that
man who was with you on the other side of the
Jordan—the one you testified about—well, he is
baptizing, and everyone is going to him."
[27]To this John replied, "A man can receive only
what is given him from heaven. [28]You yourselves
can testify that I said, 'I am not the Christ[x] but
am sent ahead of him.' [29]The bride belongs to the
bridegroom. The friend who attends the bride-
groom waits and listens for him, and is full of joy
when he hears the bridegroom's voice. That joy is
mine, and it is now complete. [30]He must become
greater; I must become less.
[31]"The one who comes from above is above all;
the one who is from the earth belongs to the
earth, and speaks as one from the earth. The one
who comes from heaven is above all. [32]He testifies
to what he has seen and heard, but no one accepts
his testimony. [33]The man who has accepted it has
certified that God is truthful. [34]For the one whom
God has sent speaks the words of God, for God[y]
gives the Spirit without limit. [35]The Father loves
the Son and has placed everything in his hands.
[36]Whoever believes in the Son has eternal life, but
whoever rejects the Son will not see life, for God's
wrath remains on him."[z]

[x]28 Or *Messiah* [y]34 Greek *he* [z]36 Some interpreters end the quotation after verse 30.

Discovering the Word 1. What is your impression of Nicodemus (vv. 1–21)? 2. Why do you suppose Nicodemus responds to Jesus' explanation of new birth with such amazement (v. 9)? 3. How does the story of Moses lifting up the snake in the desert (vv. 14–15; see Nu 21:4–9) illustrate our need and Christ's offer? 4. How and why does our response to God's Son determine our destiny (vv. 18–21)? 5. How would you summarize John's view of the character and ministry of Jesus (vv. 22–36)?

Applying the Word 1. John made it clear that Jesus was superior to him. What is one way you can demonstrate Christ's superiority in your life? 2. Who do you know that needs to know the truth about God? 3. How can you help that person see God?

Responding in Prayer Ask God to make you ready to testify of the role of Jesus in your life.

4/ *John 4*
Soul & Body—Saving & Healing

"I LOVE HUMANITY; it's people I can't stand!" Those well-known words from a member of the "Peanuts" gang still make us chuckle. But our smiles hide the fact that we sometimes feel exactly like that. John says very little about Jesus' contact with the multitudes. But long sections of the Gospel are devoted to conversations Jesus had with individuals. In John 4 we see Jesus reach out first to a woman, then to his disciples, and finally to a grieving father. Watching Jesus give himself to people with love and compassion will help us care for those God puts in our paths.

Warming Up to God When have you recently felt that you were being mobbed by the multitudes? Ask God to help you take care of yourself even as you try to help others.

Read John 4.

4 The Pharisees heard that Jesus was gain-
ing and baptizing more disciples than
John, [2]although in fact it was not Jesus
who baptized, but his disciples. [3]When the Lord
learned of this, he left Judea and went back once
more to Galilee.
[4]Now he had to go through Samaria. [5]So he
came to a town in Samaria called Sychar, near the
plot of ground Jacob had given to his son Joseph.
[6]Jacob's well was there, and Jesus, tired as he was
from the journey, sat down by the well. It was
about the sixth hour.
[7]When a Samaritan woman came to draw wa-
ter, Jesus said to her, "Will you give me a drink?"
[8](His disciples had gone into the town to buy
food.)

9The Samaritan woman said to him, "You are a Jew and I am a Samaritan woman. How can you ask me for a drink?" (For Jews do not associate with Samaritans.[a])

10Jesus answered her, "If you knew the gift of God and who it is that asks you for a drink, you would have asked him and he would have given you living water."

11"Sir," the woman said, "you have nothing to draw with and the well is deep. Where can you get this living water? 12Are you greater than our father Jacob, who gave us the well and drank from it himself, as did also his sons and his flocks and herds?"

13Jesus answered, "Everyone who drinks this water will be thirsty again, 14but whoever drinks the water I give him will never thirst. Indeed, the water I give him will become in him a spring of water welling up to eternal life."

15The woman said to him, "Sir, give me this water so that I won't get thirsty and have to keep coming here to draw water."

16He told her, "Go, call your husband and come back."

17"I have no husband," she replied.

Jesus said to her, "You are right when you say you have no husband. 18The fact is, you have had five husbands, and the man you now have is not your husband. What you have just said is quite true."

19"Sir," the woman said, "I can see that you are a prophet. 20Our fathers worshiped on this mountain, but you Jews claim that the place where we must worship is in Jerusalem."

21Jesus declared, "Believe me, woman, a time is coming when you will worship the Father neither on this mountain nor in Jerusalem. 22You Samaritans worship what you do not know; we worship what we do know, for salvation is from the Jews. 23Yet a time is coming and has now come when the true worshipers will worship the Father in spirit and truth, for they are the kind of worshipers the Father seeks. 24God is spirit, and his worshipers must worship in spirit and in truth."

25The woman said, "I know that Messiah" (called Christ) "is coming. When he comes, he will explain everything to us."

26Then Jesus declared, "I who speak to you am he."

27Just then his disciples returned and were surprised to find him talking with a woman. But no one asked, "What do you want?" or "Why are you talking with her?"

28Then, leaving her water jar, the woman went back to the town and said to the people, 29"Come, see a man who told me everything I ever did. Could this be the Christ[b]?" 30They came out of the town and made their way toward him.

31Meanwhile his disciples urged him, "Rabbi, eat something."

32But he said to them, "I have food to eat that you know nothing about."

33Then his disciples said to each other, "Could someone have brought him food?"

34"My food," said Jesus, "is to do the will of him who sent me and to finish his work. 35Do you not say, 'Four months more and then the harvest'? I tell you, open your eyes and look at the fields! They are ripe for harvest. 36Even now the reaper draws his wages, even now he harvests the crop for eternal life, so that the sower and the reaper may be glad together. 37Thus the saying 'One sows and another reaps' is true. 38I sent you to reap what you have not worked for. Others have done the hard work, and you have reaped the benefits of their labor."

39Many of the Samaritans from that town believed in him because of the woman's testimony, "He told me everything I ever did." 40So when the Samaritans came to him, they urged him to stay with them, and he stayed two days. 41And because of his words many more became believers.

42They said to the woman, "We no longer believe just because of what you said; now we have heard for ourselves, and we know that this man really is the Savior of the world."

43After the two days he left for Galilee. 44(Now Jesus himself had pointed out that a prophet has no honor in his own country.) 45When he arrived in Galilee, the Galileans welcomed him. They had seen all that he had done in Jerusalem at the Passover Feast, for they also had been there.

46Once more he visited Cana in Galilee, where he had turned the water into wine. And there was a certain royal official whose son lay sick at Capernaum. 47When this man heard that Jesus had arrived in Galilee from Judea, he went to him and begged him to come and heal his son, who was close to death.

48"Unless you people see miraculous signs and

[a]9 *Or do not use dishes Samaritans have used* [b]29 *Or Messiah*

wonders," Jesus told him, "you will never be-
lieve."
49The royal official said, "Sir, come down be-
fore my child dies."
50Jesus replied, "You may go. Your son will
live."
The man took Jesus at his word and departed.
51While he was still on the way, his servants met
him with the news that his boy was living.
52When he inquired as to the time when his son
got better, they said to him, "The fever left him
yesterday at the seventh hour."
53Then the father realized that this was the ex-
act time at which Jesus had said to him, "Your
son will live." So he and all his household be-
lieved.
54This was the second miraculous sign that
Jesus performed, having come from Judea to Gali-
lee.

Discovering the Word 1. What is surprising about Jesus' question to the Samaritan woman (vv. 8–9)? 2. Why does the woman suddenly change the subject and begin talking about the controversy over the proper place of worship (vv. 16–20)? 3. From verses 27–42, do you think the Samaritan woman genuinely believed? What do you see in the passage that supports your position? 4. After his encounter with the Samaritan woman, what specific lessons does Jesus apply to his disciples and to us (vv. 34–38)? 5. What does the "second miraculous sign" Jesus performs (vv. 43–54) reveal about him?

Applying the Word 1. What has Jesus taught you in this chapter about meeting the specific needs of those around you? 2. What present-day situations might arouse the same racial, religious and sexual prejudices as the Samaritan woman did? 3. How could you reach someone who has been rejected by the world, as Jesus did?

Responding in Prayer Ask God to help you be aware of the "Samaritans" around you. Ask him to help you reach out to them.

5 / *John 5*
Deity on Trial

IN MY HIGH-SCHOOL years, I was hooked on television lawyer programs. Those intrepid men and women always found the missing piece of evidence that would rescue the innocent and convict the guilty. I've learned since high-school days that sometimes judges and juries are wrong.

In John chapter five Jesus is on trial. A group of people are forced to make a decision about Jesus in their hearts. They hear all the evidence but make a disastrously wrong decision. Judgments are still made for and against Jesus. Whenever he is presented as Savior and Lord, people decide in their hearts to believe his claims or to turn and walk away.

Warming Up to God How has God recently revealed the truth of his claims as Savior to you? Thank him for his powerful works in your life.

Read John 5.

5 Some time later, Jesus went up to Jerusa-
lem for a feast of the Jews. 2Now there is
in Jerusalem near the Sheep Gate a pool,
which in Aramaic is called Bethesda[c] and which
is surrounded by five covered colonnades. 3Here a
great number of disabled people used to lie—the
blind, the lame, the paralyzed.[d] 5One who was
there had been an invalid for thirty-eight years.
6When Jesus saw him lying there and learned that
he had been in this condition for a long time, he
asked him, "Do you want to get well?"
7"Sir," the invalid replied, "I have no one to
help me into the pool when the water is stirred.

[c]2 Some manuscripts *Bethzatha*; other manuscripts *Bethsaida*
[d]3 Some less important manuscripts *paralyzed—and they waited for the moving of the waters. 4From time to time an angel of the Lord would come down and stir up the waters. The first one into the pool after each such disturbance would be cured of whatever disease he had.*

While I am trying to get in, someone else goes down ahead of me."

[8]Then Jesus said to him, "Get up! Pick up your mat and walk." [9]At once the man was cured; he picked up his mat and walked.

The day on which this took place was a Sabbath, [10]and so the Jews said to the man who had been healed, "It is the Sabbath; the law forbids you to carry your mat."

[11]But he replied, "The man who made me well said to me, 'Pick up your mat and walk.' "

[12]So they asked him, "Who is this fellow who told you to pick it up and walk?"

[13]The man who was healed had no idea who it was, for Jesus had slipped away into the crowd that was there.

[14]Later Jesus found him at the temple and said to him, "See, you are well again. Stop sinning or something worse may happen to you." [15]The man went away and told the Jews that it was Jesus who had made him well.

[16]So, because Jesus was doing these things on the Sabbath, the Jews persecuted him. [17]Jesus said to them, "My Father is always at his work to this very day, and I, too, am working." [18]For this reason the Jews tried all the harder to kill him; not only was he breaking the Sabbath, but he was even calling God his own Father, making himself equal with God.

[19]Jesus gave them this answer: "I tell you the truth, the Son can do nothing by himself; he can do only what he sees his Father doing, because whatever the Father does the Son also does. [20]For the Father loves the Son and shows him all he does. Yes, to your amazement he will show him even greater things than these. [21]For just as the Father raises the dead and gives them life, even so the Son gives life to whom he is pleased to give it. [22]Moreover, the Father judges no one, but has entrusted all judgment to the Son, [23]that all may honor the Son just as they honor the Father. He who does not honor the Son does not honor the Father, who sent him.

[24]"I tell you the truth, whoever hears my word and believes him who sent me has eternal life and will not be condemned; he has crossed over from death to life. [25]I tell you the truth, a time is coming and has now come when the dead will hear the voice of the Son of God and those who hear will live. [26]For as the Father has life in himself, so he has granted the Son to have life in himself. [27]And he has given him authority to judge because he is the Son of Man.

[28]"Do not be amazed at this, for a time is coming when all who are in their graves will hear his voice [29]and come out—those who have done good will rise to live, and those who have done evil will rise to be condemned. [30]By myself I can do nothing; I judge only as I hear, and my judgment is just, for I seek not to please myself but him who sent me.

[31]"If I testify about myself, my testimony is not valid. [32]There is another who testifies in my favor, and I know that his testimony about me is valid.

[33]"You have sent to John and he has testified to the truth. [34]Not that I accept human testimony; but I mention it that you may be saved. [35]John was a lamp that burned and gave light, and you chose for a time to enjoy his light.

[36]"I have testimony weightier than that of John. For the very work that the Father has given me to finish, and which I am doing, testifies that the Father has sent me. [37]And the Father who sent me has himself testified concerning me. You have never heard his voice nor seen his form, [38]nor does his word dwell in you, for you do not believe the one he sent. [39]You diligently study[e] the Scriptures because you think that by them you possess eternal life. These are the Scriptures that testify about me, [40]yet you refuse to come to me to have life.

[41]"I do not accept praise from men, [42]but I know you. I know that you do not have the love of God in your hearts. [43]I have come in my Father's name, and you do not accept me; but if someone else comes in his own name, you will accept him. [44]How can you believe if you accept praise from one another, yet make no effort to obtain the praise that comes from the only God[f]?

[45]"But do not think I will accuse you before the Father. Your accuser is Moses, on whom your hopes are set. [46]If you believed Moses, you would believe me, for he wrote about me. [47]But since you do not believe what he wrote, how are you going to believe what I say?"

[e]39 Or *Study diligently* (the imperative) [f]44 Some early manuscripts *the Only One*

Discovering the Word 1. Based on the scene and conversation around the pool, how would you describe the feelings and attitudes of the invalid (vv. 1–15)? 2. The seventh commandment said: "Remember the Sabbath day by keeping it holy" (see Ex 20:8–11). In their zeal to apply this command, what were the Jews failing to see (vv. 9–15)? 3. What insights do verses 19–23 give us into (a) the Father's devotion to the Son and (b) the Son's dependence on the Father? 4. What "witnesses" does Jesus call forward to testify on his behalf (vv. 31–47)? 5. What counter-accusations does Jesus make against those who are attacking him? 6. According to this chapter, what really influences our verdict for or against Jesus?

Applying the Word 1. When have you been more concerned about a religious activity than the reality behind it? Explain. 2. How can you avoid the kind of religion that is outwardly pious but inwardly bankrupt?

Responding in Prayer Ask God to help you discover true religion.

6 / *John 6*
Jesus, the Bread of Life

DO YOU REALIZE that during your lifetime you will probably spend over thirty-five thousand hours eating? That's the equivalent of eight years of nonstop meals, twelve hours a day! The problem, of course, is that even after a big meal we get hungry again. At best, food only satisfies us for a few hours.

Yet in this chapter, Jesus offers us food that satisfies our hunger forever. You can't buy it in a grocery store. It is found only in Jesus himself.

Warming Up to God How do you usually respond to an "impossible" situation—a problem in your life that doesn't seem to have a solution?

Read John 6.

6 Some time after this, Jesus crossed to the
far shore of the Sea of Galilee (that is, the
Sea of Tiberias), [2]and a great crowd of
people followed him because they saw the mirac-
ulous signs he had performed on the sick. [3]Then
Jesus went up on a mountainside and sat down
with his disciples. [4]The Jewish Passover Feast was
near.
[5]When Jesus looked up and saw a great crowd
coming toward him, he said to Philip, "Where
shall we buy bread for these people to eat?" [6]He
asked this only to test him, for he already had in
mind what he was going to do.
[7]Philip answered him, "Eight months' wages[g]
would not buy enough bread for each one to have
a bite!"
[8]Another of his disciples, Andrew, Simon Pe-
ter's brother, spoke up, [9]"Here is a boy with five
small barley loaves and two small fish, but how
far will they go among so many?"
[10]Jesus said, "Have the people sit down." There
was plenty of grass in that place, and the men sat
down, about five thousand of them. [11]Jesus then
took the loaves, gave thanks, and distributed to
those who were seated as much as they wanted.
He did the same with the fish.
[12]When they had all had enough to eat, he said
to his disciples, "Gather the pieces that are left
over. Let nothing be wasted." [13]So they gathered
them and filled twelve baskets with the pieces of
the five barley loaves left over by those who had
eaten.
[14]After the people saw the miraculous sign that
Jesus did, they began to say, "Surely this is the
Prophet who is to come into the world." [15]Jesus,
knowing that they intended to come and make
him king by force, withdrew again to a mountain
by himself.
[16]When evening came, his disciples went down
to the lake, [17]where they got into a boat and set
off across the lake for Capernaum. By now it was
dark, and Jesus had not yet joined them. [18]A

g7 *Greek two hundred denarii*

strong wind was blowing and the waters grew
rough. 19When they had rowed three or three and
a half miles,[h] they saw Jesus approaching the
boat, walking on the water; and they were terri-
fied. 20But he said to them, "It is I; don't be
afraid." 21Then they were willing to take him into
the boat, and immediately the boat reached the
shore where they were heading.

22The next day the crowd that had stayed on
the opposite shore of the lake realized that only
one boat had been there, and that Jesus had not
entered it with his disciples, but that they had
gone away alone. 23Then some boats from Tibe-
rias landed near the place where the people had
eaten the bread after the Lord had given thanks.
24Once the crowd realized that neither Jesus nor
his disciples were there, they got into the boats
and went to Capernaum in search of Jesus.

25When they found him on the other side of
the lake, they asked him, "Rabbi, when did you
get here?"

26Jesus answered, "I tell you the truth, you are
looking for me, not because you saw miraculous
signs but because you ate the loaves and had your
fill. 27Do not work for food that spoils, but for
food that endures to eternal life, which the Son of
Man will give you. On him God the Father has
placed his seal of approval."

28Then they asked him, "What must we do to
do the works God requires?"

29Jesus answered, "The work of God is this: to
believe in the one he has sent."

30So they asked him, "What miraculous sign
then will you give that we may see it and believe
you? What will you do? 31Our forefathers ate the
manna in the desert; as it is written: 'He gave
them bread from heaven to eat.'[i]"

32Jesus said to them, "I tell you the truth, it is
not Moses who has given you the bread from
heaven, but it is my Father who gives you the true
bread from heaven. 33For the bread of God is he
who comes down from heaven and gives life to
the world."

34"Sir," they said, "from now on give us this
bread."

35Then Jesus declared, "I am the bread of life.
He who comes to me will never go hungry, and
he who believes in me will never be thirsty. 36But
as I told you, you have seen me and still you do
not believe. 37All that the Father gives me will
come to me, and whoever comes to me I will
never drive away. 38For I have come down from
heaven not to do my will but to do the will of him
who sent me. 39And this is the will of him who
sent me, that I shall lose none of all that he has
given me, but raise them up at the last day. 40For
my Father's will is that everyone who looks to the
Son and believes in him shall have eternal life,
and I will raise him up at the last day."

41At this the Jews began to grumble about him
because he said, "I am the bread that came down
from heaven." 42They said, "Is this not Jesus, the
son of Joseph, whose father and mother we
know? How can he now say, 'I came down from
heaven'?"

43"Stop grumbling among yourselves," Jesus
answered. 44"No one can come to me unless the
Father who sent me draws him, and I will raise
him up at the last day. 45It is written in the Proph-
ets: 'They will all be taught by God.'[j] Everyone
who listens to the Father and learns from him
comes to me. 46No one has seen the Father except
the one who is from God; only he has seen the
Father. 47I tell you the truth, he who believes has
everlasting life. 48I am the bread of life. 49Your
forefathers ate the manna in the desert, yet they
died. 50But here is the bread that comes down
from heaven, which a man may eat and not die.
51I am the living bread that came down from
heaven. If anyone eats of this bread, he will live
forever. This bread is my flesh, which I will give
for the life of the world."

52Then the Jews began to argue sharply among
themselves, "How can this man give us his flesh
to eat?"

53Jesus said to them, "I tell you the truth, un-
less you eat the flesh of the Son of Man and drink
his blood, you have no life in you. 54Whoever eats
my flesh and drinks my blood has eternal life, and
I will raise him up at the last day. 55For my flesh
is real food and my blood is real drink. 56Who-
ever eats my flesh and drinks my blood remains
in me, and I in him. 57Just as the living Father
sent me and I live because of the Father, so the
one who feeds on me will live because of me.
58This is the bread that came down from heaven.
Your forefathers ate manna and died, but he who
feeds on this bread will live forever." 59He said
this while teaching in the synagogue in Caper-
naum.

60On hearing it, many of his disciples said,
"This is a hard teaching. Who can accept it?"

[h] 19 Greek *rowed twenty-five or thirty stadia* (about 5 or 6 kilometers)
[i] 31 Exodus 16:4; Neh. 9:15; Psalm 78:24,25 [j] 45 Isaiah 54:13

61Aware that his disciples were grumbling
about this, Jesus said to them, "Does this offend
you? 62What if you see the Son of Man ascend to
where he was before! 63The Spirit gives life; the
flesh counts for nothing. The words I have spo-
ken to you are spirit[k] and they are life. 64Yet
there are some of you who do not believe." For
Jesus had known from the beginning which of
them did not believe and who would betray him.
65He went on to say, "This is why I told you that
no one can come to me unless the Father has
enabled him."
66From this time many of his disciples turned
back and no longer followed him.
67"You do not want to leave too, do you?" Jesus
asked the Twelve.
68Simon Peter answered him, "Lord, to whom
shall we go? You have the words of eternal life.
69We believe and know that you are the Holy One
of God."
70Then Jesus replied, "Have I not chosen you,
the Twelve? Yet one of you is a devil!" 71(He
meant Judas, the son of Simon Iscariot, who,
though one of the Twelve, was later to betray
him.)

[k]63 Or *Spirit*

Discovering the Word 1. How would you characterize Philip's and Andrew's responses to the problem of feeding this enormous crowd (vv. 5–9)? 2. Imagine that you are one of the disciples, rowing the boat in dark, rough waters (vv. 16–21). How would your concept of Jesus have been altered by seeing him walk on water? 3. The next day the people were hungry again, so they came seeking Jesus (vv. 22–25). How does he try to redirect their thinking (vv. 26–33)? 4. Based on the remarks of some in the crowd (vv. 41–42), do you think they finally understood what Jesus was saying? Explain. 5. When Jesus said, "This bread is my flesh," the crowd could think only of cannibalism (v. 52). What do you think it means to eat Jesus' flesh and drink his blood (vv. 53–59)? Is this something we do once for all time, or is it an ongoing process? Explain. 6. In verses 60–71 Jesus turns away from the crowd and focuses on his disciples. How would you describe their responses to his "hard teaching"?

Applying the Word 1. Which response in question 6 best describes your present attitude toward Jesus? Explain. 2. Jesus has contrasted the two appetites found in every person—the appetite for food that perishes and the appetite for food that endures. In what ways has Jesus satisfied the spiritual hunger in your heart?

Responding in Prayer Praise God for satisfying all your needs.

7 / *John 7:1–52*
Confusion over Christ

NOT LONG AGO I had a series of conversations with a young man about Jesus Christ and why faith in him is so important. At first, the young man was interested. He was open to listen to God's Word and to consider Christ's claims. As time went on, however, he became more and more hostile to Christ. Finally, he told me that he didn't want to pursue his investigation any further. He had decided to reject Christ and his offer of salvation.

That is precisely the pattern that John traces in his Gospel. In the early chapters, men and women responded to Jesus with belief. Then some of those who were following him turned away. Now open warfare breaks out between Jesus and his enemies—and yet, some still seek the truth. This chapter will help you respond positively to the wide variety of attitudes toward Jesus today.

Warming Up to God "If anyone is thirsty, let him come to me and drink." These are Jesus' words to us today. In what way do you need Jesus' spiritual refreshment? Be quiet before him and experience the "streams of living water."

Read John 7:1–52.

7 After this, Jesus went around in Galilee, purposely staying away from Judea because the Jews there were waiting to take his life. 2But when the Jewish Feast of Tabernacles was near, 3Jesus' brothers said to him, "You ought to leave here and go to Judea, so that your disciples may see the miracles you do. 4No one who wants to become a public figure acts in secret. Since you are doing these things, show yourself to the world." 5For even his own brothers did not believe in him.

6Therefore Jesus told them, "The right time for me has not yet come; for you any time is right. 7The world cannot hate you, but it hates me because I testify that what it does is evil. 8You go to the Feast. I am not yet[l] going up to this Feast, because for me the right time has not yet come." 9Having said this, he stayed in Galilee.

10However, after his brothers had left for the Feast, he went also, not publicly, but in secret. 11Now at the Feast the Jews were watching for him and asking, "Where is that man?"

12Among the crowds there was widespread whispering about him. Some said, "He is a good man."

Others replied, "No, he deceives the people." 13But no one would say anything publicly about him for fear of the Jews.

14Not until halfway through the Feast did Jesus go up to the temple courts and begin to teach. 15The Jews were amazed and asked, "How did this man get such learning without having studied?"

16Jesus answered, "My teaching is not my own. It comes from him who sent me. 17If anyone chooses to do God's will, he will find out whether my teaching comes from God or whether I speak on my own. 18He who speaks on his own does so to gain honor for himself, but he who works for the honor of the one who sent him is a man of truth; there is nothing false about him. 19Has not Moses given you the law? Yet not one of you keeps the law. Why are you trying to kill me?"

20"You are demon-possessed," the crowd answered. "Who is trying to kill you?"

21Jesus said to them, "I did one miracle, and you are all astonished. 22Yet, because Moses gave you circumcision (though actually it did not come from Moses, but from the patriarchs), you circumcise a child on the Sabbath. 23Now if a child can be circumcised on the Sabbath so that the law of Moses may not be broken, why are you angry with me for healing the whole man on the Sabbath? 24Stop judging by mere appearances, and make a right judgment."

25At that point some of the people of Jerusalem began to ask, "Isn't this the man they are trying to kill? 26Here he is, speaking publicly, and they are not saying a word to him. Have the authorities really concluded that he is the Christ[m]? 27But we know where this man is from; when the Christ comes, no one will know where he is from."

28Then Jesus, still teaching in the temple courts, cried out, "Yes, you know me, and you know where I am from. I am not here on my own, but he who sent me is true. You do not know him, 29but I know him because I am from him and he sent me."

30At this they tried to seize him, but no one laid a hand on him, because his time had not yet come. 31Still, many in the crowd put their faith in him. They said, "When the Christ comes, will he do more miraculous signs than this man?"

32The Pharisees heard the crowd whispering such things about him. Then the chief priests and the Pharisees sent temple guards to arrest him. 33Jesus said, "I am with you for only a short time, and then I go to the one who sent me. 34You will look for me, but you will not find me; and where I am, you cannot come."

35The Jews said to one another, "Where does this man intend to go that we cannot find him? Will he go where our people live scattered among the Greeks, and teach the Greeks? 36What did he mean when he said, 'You will look for me, but you will not find me,' and 'Where I am, you cannot come'?"

37On the last and greatest day of the Feast, Jesus stood and said in a loud voice, "If anyone is thirsty, let him come to me and drink. 38Whoever believes in me, as[n] the Scripture has said, streams of living water will flow from within him." 39By this he meant the Spirit, whom those who believed in him were later to receive. Up to that time the Spirit had not been given, since Jesus had not yet been glorified.

40On hearing his words, some of the people said, "Surely this man is the Prophet."

41Others said, "He is the Christ."

Still others asked, "How can the Christ come from Galilee? 42Does not the Scripture say that

[l] 8 Some early manuscripts do not have *yet*. [m] 26 Or *Messiah*; also in verses 27, 31, 41 and 42 [n] 37,38 Or / *If anyone is thirsty, let him come to me. / And let him drink,* 38*who believes in me. / As*

the Christ will come from David's family[o] and
from Bethlehem, the town where David lived?"
43Thus the people were divided because of Jesus.
44Some wanted to seize him, but no one laid a
hand on him.

45Finally the temple guards went back to the
chief priests and Pharisees, who asked them,
"Why didn't you bring him in?"

46"No one ever spoke the way this man does,"
the guards declared.

47"You mean he has deceived you also?" the
Pharisees retorted. 48"Has any of the rulers or of
the Pharisees believed in him? 49No! But this mob
that knows nothing of the law—there is a curse
on them."

50Nicodemus, who had gone to Jesus earlier
and who was one of their own number, asked,
51"Does our law condemn anyone without first
hearing him to find out what he is doing?"

52They replied, "Are you from Galilee, too?
Look into it, and you will find that a prophet[p]
does not come out of Galilee."

[The earliest manuscripts and many other ancient witnesses do not have John 7:53–8:11.]

o42 Greek *seed* p52 Two early manuscripts *the Prophet*

Discovering the Word 1. The first blast of hostility against Jesus comes from his own family (vv. 1–13). How would you characterize the statements made by Jesus' brothers (vv. 3–5)? 2. When Jesus makes his presence in Jerusalem known, people begin to challenge the origin (and, therefore, the authority) of his teaching. According to Jesus, how can we verify the truth of his teaching (vv. 16–18)? 3. What other opinions or questions do people have about Jesus in verses 20–36? 4. How does Jesus respond to each one? 5. On the last day of the Feast of Tabernacles, large vats of water were poured out on the pavement of the temple court as a reminder of God's provision of water in the wilderness. With that custom in mind, how would you explain the significance of Jesus' remarks in verses 37–39?

Applying the Word 1. What counsel would you give a believer who faces spiritual opposition from his or her family? 2. Which of the opinions about Jesus you have identified in this chapter are still expressed today, and in what way? 3. Based on Jesus' example, what should our response be to such reactions?

Responding in Prayer Pray for wisdom as you face various reactions to Jesus.

8 / *John 7:53—8:11*

Caught in Adultery

NOTHING IS MORE humiliating than being caught in an act of disobedience! Whether it's a child with his hand in the cookie jar or an adult driving over the speed limit, we all know the sinking feeling of being caught. In John 8, a woman is caught in the most awkward of situations—in the very act of adultery. The way Jesus responds to her may surprise you.

Warming Up to God Think of a time when you hurt someone and that person was willing to forgive you. How did it feel to be forgiven? Thank God for extending forgiveness to you.

Read John 7:53—8:11.

53Then each went to his own home.
8 But Jesus went to the Mount of Olives.
2At dawn he appeared again in the temple
courts, where all the people gathered
around him, and he sat down to teach them. 3The
teachers of the law and the Pharisees brought in a
woman caught in adultery. They made her stand
before the group 4and said to Jesus, "Teacher, this
woman was caught in the act of adultery. 5In the
Law Moses commanded us to stone such women.

Now what do you say?" [6]They were using this
question as a trap, in order to have a basis for
accusing him.

But Jesus bent down and started to write on the
ground with his finger. [7]When they kept on ques-
tioning him, he straightened up and said to them,
"If any one of you is without sin, let him be the
first to throw a stone at her." [8]Again he stooped
down and wrote on the ground.

[9]At this, those who heard began to go away one
at a time, the older ones first, until only Jesus was
left, with the woman still standing there. [10]Jesus
straightened up and asked her, "Woman, where
are they? Has no one condemned you?"

[11]"No one, sir," she said.

"Then neither do I condemn you," Jesus de-
clared. "Go now and leave your life of sin."

Discovering the Word 1. What do we know about the character and motives of those who bring this woman to Jesus? 2. While it is obvious that the woman is guilty, what elements of injustice can you find in this situation? 3. The Pharisees and teachers were often very self-righteous. Why do you think they went away rather than stoning the woman (vv. 7–9)? 4. How would you describe Jesus' attitude toward the woman (vv. 10–11)?

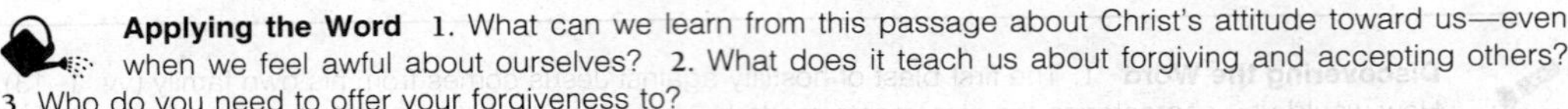

Applying the Word 1. What can we learn from this passage about Christ's attitude toward us—even when we feel awful about ourselves? 2. What does it teach us about forgiving and accepting others? 3. Who do you need to offer your forgiveness to?

Responding in Prayer Ask God to show you what it means to forgive.

9 / *John 8:12–59*
Jesus, the Light of the World

JESUS NEVER SPOKE in public without creating controversy. In fact, he was constantly in trouble! Rather than retreating behind the safety of a pulpit, Jesus spoke in settings where people were bold enough to talk back. In this portion of John's story, Jesus makes a series of claims about himself. Each claim is met by a challenge from his enemies. Each challenge is then answered, and the answer leads to the next claim. Throughout this interchange, Jesus shows us how to speak the truth in the face of hostility. He also reveals some amazing things about himself.

Warming Up to God Have you ever tried to talk about Christ with a family member or coworker who was hostile to your message? How did you feel at the time? Thank God for giving you a Savior who understands everything we experience.

Read John 8:12–59.

[12]When Jesus spoke again to the people, he
said, "I am the light of the world. Whoever fol-
lows me will never walk in darkness, but will
have the light of life."

[13]The Pharisees challenged him, "Here you are,
appearing as your own witness; your testimony is
not valid."

[14]Jesus answered, "Even if I testify on my own
behalf, my testimony is valid, for I know where I
came from and where I am going. But you have
no idea where I come from or where I am going.
[15]You judge by human standards; I pass judgment
on no one. [16]But if I do judge, my decisions are
right, because I am not alone. I stand with the
Father, who sent me. [17]In your own Law it is
written that the testimony of two men is valid. [18]I
am one who testifies for myself; my other witness
is the Father, who sent me."

[19]Then they asked him, "Where is your fa-
ther?"

"You do not know me or my Father," Jesus
replied. "If you knew me, you would know my

Father also." 20He spoke these words while teach-
ing in the temple area near the place where the
offerings were put. Yet no one seized him, be-
cause his time had not yet come.

21Once more Jesus said to them, "I am going
away, and you will look for me, and you will die
in your sin. Where I go, you cannot come."

22This made the Jews ask, "Will he kill himself?
Is that why he says, 'Where I go, you cannot
come'?"

23But he continued, "You are from below; I am
from above. You are of this world; I am not of this
world. 24I told you that you would die in your
sins; if you do not believe that I am ⌊the one I
claim to be⌋,[q] you will indeed die in your sins."

25"Who are you?" they asked.

"Just what I have been claiming all along,"
Jesus replied. 26"I have much to say in judgment
of you. But he who sent me is reliable, and what
I have heard from him I tell the world."

27They did not understand that he was telling
them about his Father. 28So Jesus said, "When
you have lifted up the Son of Man, then you will
know that I am ⌊the one I claim to be⌋ and that I
do nothing on my own but speak just what the
Father has taught me. 29The one who sent me is
with me; he has not left me alone, for I always do
what pleases him." 30Even as he spoke, many put
their faith in him.

31To the Jews who had believed him, Jesus said,
"If you hold to my teaching, you are really my
disciples. 32Then you will know the truth, and the
truth will set you free."

33They answered him, "We are Abraham's
descendants[r] and have never been slaves of any-
one. How can you say that we shall be set free?"

34Jesus replied, "I tell you the truth, everyone
who sins is a slave to sin. 35Now a slave has no
permanent place in the family, but a son belongs
to it forever. 36So if the Son sets you free, you will
be free indeed. 37I know you are Abraham's
descendants. Yet you are ready to kill me, because
you have no room for my word. 38I am telling you
what I have seen in the Father's presence, and
you do what you have heard from your father.[s]"

39"Abraham is our father," they answered.

"If you were Abraham's children," said Jesus,
"then you would[t] do the things Abraham did.
40As it is, you are determined to kill me, a man
who has told you the truth that I heard from God.
Abraham did not do such things. 41You are doing
the things your own father does."

"We are not illegitimate children," they pro-
tested. "The only Father we have is God himself."

42Jesus said to them, "If God were your Father,
you would love me, for I came from God and now
am here. I have not come on my own; but he sent
me. 43Why is my language not clear to you? Be-
cause you are unable to hear what I say. 44You
belong to your father, the devil, and you want to
carry out your father's desire. He was a murderer
from the beginning, not holding to the truth, for
there is no truth in him. When he lies, he speaks
his native language, for he is a liar and the father
of lies. 45Yet because I tell the truth, you do not
believe me! 46Can any of you prove me guilty of
sin? If I am telling the truth, why don't you be-
lieve me? 47He who belongs to God hears what
God says. The reason you do not hear is that you
do not belong to God."

48The Jews answered him, "Aren't we right in
saying that you are a Samaritan and demon-pos-
sessed?"

49"I am not possessed by a demon," said Jesus,
"but I honor my Father and you dishonor me. 50I
am not seeking glory for myself; but there is one
who seeks it, and he is the judge. 51I tell you the
truth, if anyone keeps my word, he will never see
death."

52At this the Jews exclaimed, "Now we know
that you are demon-possessed! Abraham died and
so did the prophets, yet you say that if anyone
keeps your word, he will never taste death. 53Are
you greater than our father Abraham? He died,
and so did the prophets. Who do you think you
are?"

54Jesus replied, "If I glorify myself, my glory
means nothing. My Father, whom you claim as
your God, is the one who glorifies me. 55Though
you do not know him, I know him. If I said I did
not, I would be a liar like you, but I do know him
and keep his word. 56Your father Abraham re-
joiced at the thought of seeing my day; he saw it
and was glad."

57"You are not yet fifty years old," the Jews said
to him, "and you have seen Abraham!"

58"I tell you the truth," Jesus answered, "before
Abraham was born, I am!" 59At this, they picked
up stones to stone him, but Jesus hid himself,
slipping away from the temple grounds.

q24 Or *I am he*; also in verse 28 r33 Greek *seed*; also in verse 37
s38 Or *presence. Therefore do what you have heard from the Father.*
t39 Some early manuscripts *"If you are Abraham's children," said Jesus, "then*

Discovering the Word 1. The Pharisees challenge the validity of Jesus' claim (v. 13). How does Jesus answer their challenge (vv. 14–18)? 2. Jesus' reference to his Father leads to his second claim—that he came from God. How does this claim heighten the tension between Jesus and the Jews (vv. 19–30)? 3. Jesus makes another startling claim in verses 31–32: "If you hold to my teaching . . . then you will know the truth, and the truth will set you free." Why does holding to Jesus' teaching lead to true knowledge and freedom? 4. Jesus' opponents also claim to have both Abraham and God as their father. According to Jesus, how does their conduct contradict their claim (vv. 39–47)?

Applying the Word 1. Why is our conduct the truest test of our beliefs? 2. In what ways does your lifestyle validate (or invalidate) your claim to be a follower of Christ?

Responding in Prayer Ask God to help you change the parts of your life that don't match your beliefs.

10 / *John 9*
A Blind Man Sees the Light

OUR SIGHT IS a wonderful gift from God. We marvel at the fiery colors of a sunset, the rich pastels of spring and the delicate beauty of a flower. How tragic it must be to never see the light of day. Yet there is a far greater tragedy than physical blindness. In this passage Jesus meets a man who has been blind from birth. The man illustrates that those who are blind often see clearly, while those with sight see nothing at all.

Warming Up to God Before you begin this chapter about various kinds of blindness and sight, ask God to open your eyes so that you can see what he has for you.

Read John 9.

9 As he went along, he saw a man blind from birth. 2His disciples asked him, "Rabbi, who sinned, this man or his parents, that he was born blind?"

3"Neither this man nor his parents sinned," said Jesus, "but this happened so that the work of God might be displayed in his life. 4As long as it is day, we must do the work of him who sent me. Night is coming, when no one can work. 5While I am in the world, I am the light of the world."

6Having said this, he spit on the ground, made some mud with the saliva, and put it on the man's eyes. 7"Go," he told him, "wash in the Pool of Siloam" (this word means Sent). So the man went and washed, and came home seeing.

8His neighbors and those who had formerly seen him begging asked, "Isn't this the same man who used to sit and beg?" 9Some claimed that he was.

Others said, "No, he only looks like him."

But he himself insisted, "I am the man."

10"How then were your eyes opened?" they demanded.

11He replied, "The man they call Jesus made some mud and put it on my eyes. He told me to go to Siloam and wash. So I went and washed, and then I could see."

12"Where is this man?" they asked him.

"I don't know," he said.

13They brought to the Pharisees the man who had been blind. 14Now the day on which Jesus had made the mud and opened the man's eyes was a Sabbath. 15Therefore the Pharisees also asked him how he had received his sight. "He put mud on my eyes," the man replied, "and I washed, and now I see."

16Some of the Pharisees said, "This man is not from God, for he does not keep the Sabbath."

But others asked, "How can a sinner do such miraculous signs?" So they were divided.

17Finally they turned again to the blind man, "What have you to say about him? It was your eyes he opened."

The man replied, "He is a prophet."

18The Jews still did not believe that he had been blind and had received his sight until they sent for the man's parents. 19"Is this your son?" they asked. "Is this the one you say was born blind? How is it that now he can see?"

20"We know he is our son," the parents answered, "and we know he was born blind. 21But how he can see now, or who opened his eyes, we don't know. Ask him. He is of age; he will speak for himself." 22His parents said this because they were afraid of the Jews, for already the Jews had decided that anyone who acknowledged that Jesus was the Christ[u] would be put out of the synagogue. 23That was why his parents said, "He is of age; ask him."

24A second time they summoned the man who had been blind. "Give glory to God,[v]" they said. "We know this man is a sinner."

25He replied, "Whether he is a sinner or not, I don't know. One thing I do know. I was blind but now I see!"

26Then they asked him, "What did he do to you? How did he open your eyes?"

27He answered, "I have told you already and you did not listen. Why do you want to hear it again? Do you want to become his disciples, too?"

28Then they hurled insults at him and said, "You are this fellow's disciple! We are disciples of Moses! 29We know that God spoke to Moses, but as for this fellow, we don't even know where he comes from."

30The man answered, "Now that is remarkable! You don't know where he comes from, yet he opened my eyes. 31We know that God does not listen to sinners. He listens to the godly man who does his will. 32Nobody has ever heard of opening the eyes of a man born blind. 33If this man were not from God, he could do nothing."

34To this they replied, "You were steeped in sin at birth; how dare you lecture us!" And they threw him out.

35Jesus heard that they had thrown him out, and when he found him, he said, "Do you believe in the Son of Man?"

36"Who is he, sir?" the man asked. "Tell me so that I may believe in him."

37Jesus said, "You have now seen him; in fact, he is the one speaking with you."

38Then the man said, "Lord, I believe," and he worshiped him.

39Jesus said, "For judgment I have come into this world, so that the blind will see and those who see will become blind."

40Some Pharisees who were with him heard him say this and asked, "What? Are we blind too?"

41Jesus said, "If you were blind, you would not be guilty of sin; but now that you claim you can see, your guilt remains."

[u]22 Or *Messiah* [v]24 A solemn charge to tell the truth (see Joshua 7:19)

Discovering the Word 1. Based on the question the disciples ask Jesus (v. 2), how do they view the relation between sickness and sin? 2. What is Jesus' view of the same issue (vv. 3-5)? 3. Why do you think Jesus goes through the process of making mud and instructing the man to go wash, instead of simply healing him instantly? 4. On what grounds do the Pharisees object to this miracle (vv. 16, 22, 24, 29)? 5. How do the Pharisees react when the genuineness of the miracle becomes undeniable (vv. 28-34)?

Applying the Word 1. When might Christians today exhibit the Pharisees' attitude to a marvelous work of God's grace or power? 2. What principles in this chapter could help you improve your spiritual eyesight?

Responding in Prayer Ask God to strengthen your faith so that you might respond as the man did, "Lord, I believe."

11 / *John 10*
The Shepherd & His Sheep

JESUS WAS A master at using simple, everyday objects or events to illustrate profound spiritual truths. The farmer scattering seed, the vine sustaining the branches, and sparrows falling to the earth all took on a new dimension in Jesus' eyes. In John 10, Jesus uses the scene of a shepherd enclosing his sheep in a sheepfold to give us one of the most moving pictures of our salvation and security in Christ found anywhere in the Bible. If you've ever doubted the love of Christ, Jesus will give you a healthy dose of assurance in this chapter.

Warming Up to God What usually prompts you to have doubts about your salvation or your walk with Christ—your own sin? feelings of unworthiness? personal failures? Be honest with Christ about your doubts.

Read John 10.

10 "I tell you the truth, the man who does not enter the sheep pen by the gate, but climbs in by some other way, is a thief and a robber. 2The man who enters by the gate is the shepherd of his sheep. 3The watchman opens the gate for him, and the sheep listen to his voice. He calls his own sheep by name and leads them out. 4When he has brought out all his own, he goes on ahead of them, and his sheep follow him because they know his voice. 5But they will never follow a stranger; in fact, they will run away from him because they do not recognize a stranger's voice." 6Jesus used this figure of speech, but they did not understand what he was telling them.

7Therefore Jesus said again, "I tell you the truth, I am the gate for the sheep. 8All who ever came before me were thieves and robbers, but the sheep did not listen to them. 9I am the gate; whoever enters through me will be saved.[w] He will come in and go out, and find pasture. 10The thief comes only to steal and kill and destroy; I have come that they may have life, and have it to the full.

11"I am the good shepherd. The good shepherd lays down his life for the sheep. 12The hired hand is not the shepherd who owns the sheep. So when he sees the wolf coming, he abandons the sheep and runs away. Then the wolf attacks the flock and scatters it. 13The man runs away because he is a hired hand and cares nothing for the sheep.

14"I am the good shepherd; I know my sheep and my sheep know me— 15just as the Father knows me and I know the Father—and I lay down my life for the sheep. 16I have other sheep that are not of this sheep pen. I must bring them also. They too will listen to my voice, and there shall be one flock and one shepherd. 17The reason my Father loves me is that I lay down my life—only to take it up again. 18No one takes it from me, but I lay it down of my own accord. I have authority to lay it down and authority to take it up again. This command I received from my Father."

19At these words the Jews were again divided. 20Many of them said, "He is demon-possessed and raving mad. Why listen to him?"

21But others said, "These are not the sayings of a man possessed by a demon. Can a demon open the eyes of the blind?"

22Then came the Feast of Dedication[x] at Jerusalem. It was winter, 23and Jesus was in the temple area walking in Solomon's Colonnade. 24The Jews gathered around him, saying, "How long will you keep us in suspense? If you are the Christ,[y] tell us plainly."

25Jesus answered, "I did tell you, but you do not believe. The miracles I do in my Father's name speak for me, 26but you do not believe because you are not my sheep. 27My sheep listen to my voice; I know them, and they follow me. 28I give them eternal life, and they shall never perish; no one can snatch them out of my hand. 29My Father, who has given them to me, is greater than all[z]; no one can snatch them out of my Father's hand. 30I and the Father are one."

31Again the Jews picked up stones to stone him, 32but Jesus said to them, "I have shown you many great miracles from the Father. For which of these do you stone me?"

[w]9 Or *kept safe* [x]22 That is, Hanukkah [y]24 Or *Messiah*
[z]29 Many early manuscripts *What my Father has given me is greater than all*

33“We are not stoning you for any of these,”
replied the Jews, “but for blasphemy, because
you, a mere man, claim to be God.”
34Jesus answered them, “Is it not written in
your Law, ‘I have said you are gods’[a]? 35If he
called them ‘gods,’ to whom the word of God
came—and the Scripture cannot be broken—
36what about the one whom the Father set apart
as his very own and sent into the world? Why
then do you accuse me of blasphemy because I
said, ‘I am God’s Son’? 37Do not believe me unless
I do what my Father does. 38But if I do it, even
though you do not believe me, believe the mira-
cles, that you may know and understand that the
Father is in me, and I in the Father.” 39Again they
tried to seize him, but he escaped their grasp.
40Then Jesus went back across the Jordan to
the place where John had been baptizing in the
early days. Here he stayed 41and many people
came to him. They said, “Though John never per-
formed a miraculous sign, all that John said about
this man was true.” 42And in that place many be-
lieved in Jesus.

[a]34 Psalm 82:6

Discovering the Word 1. What spiritual truths is Jesus trying to convey in verses 1–5? 2. In verses 11–15 Jesus talks about the shepherd’s care for his sheep. What can you learn from those verses about Jesus’ care and relationship with you? 3. According to Jesus, how are the Jews in this passage different from his sheep (vv. 22–27)? 4. When Jesus claims that he and the Father are one, the Jews pick up stones to stone him (vv. 30–33). Do you think his defense is a denial of his deity (vv. 33–36)? Explain.

Applying the Word 1. How do you respond to promises and assurances Jesus gives his sheep in verses 28–29? 2. Which promise from Jesus in this chapter is most encouraging to you? 3. How can Jesus’ promise help you when you have doubts?

Responding in Prayer Praise God for giving you such a Good Shepherd.

12 / *John 11*
Resurrection & Life

EVER SINCE GOD judged Adam and Eve, death has plagued humanity. It separates us from those we love and looms over our own lives like a menacing spirit. In this chapter Jesus reaches out to a family struggling with the pain of death. He shows us why we need never fear death again.

Warming Up to God When is it difficult for you to feel that God is with you? Talk to God about your feelings of abandonment.

Read John 11.

11 Now a man named Lazarus was
sick. He was from Bethany, the vil-
lage of Mary and her sister Martha.
2This Mary, whose brother Lazarus now lay sick,
was the same one who poured perfume on the
Lord and wiped his feet with her hair. 3So the
sisters sent word to Jesus, “Lord, the one you love
is sick.”
4When he heard this, Jesus said, “This sickness
will not end in death. No, it is for God’s glory so
that God’s Son may be glorified through it.”
5Jesus loved Martha and her sister and Lazarus.
6Yet when he heard that Lazarus was sick, he
stayed where he was two more days.
7Then he said to his disciples, “Let us go back
to Judea.”
8“But Rabbi,” they said, “a short while ago the
Jews tried to stone you, and yet you are going
back there?”
9Jesus answered, “Are there not twelve hours of

daylight? A man who walks by day will not stumble, for he sees by this world's light. 10It is when he walks by night that he stumbles, for he has no light."

11After he had said this, he went on to tell them, "Our friend Lazarus has fallen asleep; but I am going there to wake him up."

12His disciples replied, "Lord, if he sleeps, he will get better." 13Jesus had been speaking of his death, but his disciples thought he meant natural sleep.

14So then he told them plainly, "Lazarus is dead, 15and for your sake I am glad I was not there, so that you may believe. But let us go to him."

16Then Thomas (called Didymus) said to the rest of the disciples, "Let us also go, that we may die with him."

17On his arrival, Jesus found that Lazarus had already been in the tomb for four days. 18Bethany was less than two miles[b] from Jerusalem, 19and many Jews had come to Martha and Mary to comfort them in the loss of their brother. 20When Martha heard that Jesus was coming, she went out to meet him, but Mary stayed at home.

21"Lord," Martha said to Jesus, "if you had been here, my brother would not have died. 22But I know that even now God will give you whatever you ask."

23Jesus said to her, "Your brother will rise again."

24Martha answered, "I know he will rise again in the resurrection at the last day."

25Jesus said to her, "I am the resurrection and the life. He who believes in me will live, even though he dies; 26and whoever lives and believes in me will never die. Do you believe this?"

27"Yes, Lord," she told him, "I believe that you are the Christ,[c] the Son of God, who was to come into the world."

28And after she had said this, she went back and called her sister Mary aside. "The Teacher is here," she said, "and is asking for you." 29When Mary heard this, she got up quickly and went to him. 30Now Jesus had not yet entered the village, but was still at the place where Martha had met him. 31When the Jews who had been with Mary in the house, comforting her, noticed how quickly she got up and went out, they followed her, supposing she was going to the tomb to mourn there.

32When Mary reached the place where Jesus was and saw him, she fell at his feet and said, "Lord, if you had been here, my brother would not have died."

33When Jesus saw her weeping, and the Jews who had come along with her also weeping, he was deeply moved in spirit and troubled. 34"Where have you laid him?" he asked.

"Come and see, Lord," they replied.

35Jesus wept.

36Then the Jews said, "See how he loved him!"

37But some of them said, "Could not he who opened the eyes of the blind man have kept this man from dying?"

38Jesus, once more deeply moved, came to the tomb. It was a cave with a stone laid across the entrance. 39"Take away the stone," he said.

"But, Lord," said Martha, the sister of the dead man, "by this time there is a bad odor, for he has been there four days."

40Then Jesus said, "Did I not tell you that if you believed, you would see the glory of God?"

41So they took away the stone. Then Jesus looked up and said, "Father, I thank you that you have heard me. 42I knew that you always hear me, but I said this for the benefit of the people standing here, that they may believe that you sent me."

43When he had said this, Jesus called in a loud voice, "Lazarus, come out!" 44The dead man came out, his hands and feet wrapped with strips of linen, and a cloth around his face.

Jesus said to them, "Take off the grave clothes and let him go."

45Therefore many of the Jews who had come to visit Mary, and had seen what Jesus did, put their faith in him. 46But some of them went to the Pharisees and told them what Jesus had done. 47Then the chief priests and the Pharisees called a meeting of the Sanhedrin.

"What are we accomplishing?" they asked. "Here is this man performing many miraculous signs. 48If we let him go on like this, everyone will believe in him, and then the Romans will come and take away both our place[d] and our nation."

49Then one of them, named Caiaphas, who was high priest that year, spoke up, "You know nothing at all! 50You do not realize that it is better for you that one man die for the people than that the whole nation perish."

51He did not say this on his own, but as high priest that year he prophesied that Jesus would die for the Jewish nation, 52and not only for that

[b]18 Greek *fifteen stadia* (about 3 kilometers) [c]27 Or *Messiah*
[d]48 Or *temple*

nation but also for the scattered children of God, to bring them together and make them one. [53]So from that day on they plotted to take his life.

[54]Therefore Jesus no longer moved about publicly among the Jews. Instead he withdrew to a region near the desert, to a village called Ephraim, where he stayed with his disciples.

[55]When it was almost time for the Jewish Passover, many went up from the country to Jerusalem for their ceremonial cleansing before the Passover. [56]They kept looking for Jesus, and as they stood in the temple area they asked one another, "What do you think? Isn't he coming to the Feast at all?" [57]But the chief priests and Pharisees had given orders that if anyone found out where Jesus was, he should report it so that they might arrest him.

Discovering the Word 1. How can we resolve the apparent conflict between Jesus' love for Lazarus and his deliberate delay in helping him (vv. 4–6)? 2. What additional insight into God's purposes can we gain from Jesus' statement in verse 15? 3. What elements of doubt and faith do you see in Martha's statements to Jesus (vv. 17–27)? 4. How should Christ's statement in verses 25–26 radically alter our views of life and death? 5. Why do you think John emphasizes that Jesus was deeply moved by Mary's grief and the anguish of those with her (vv. 28–38)? 6. How would you explain the fact that the people who see the same miracle respond in two totally different ways (vv. 45–57)?

Applying the Word 1. How can those verses help us when we feel abandoned by God in a time of great need? 2. In what ways will this chapter change the way you respond to personal difficulty or the apparent delay of God?

Responding in Prayer Thank God for his personal presence with you.

13 / *John 12*
The King's Last Acts

IF YOU HAVE ever felt rejected or misunderstood, you know how Jesus felt as his public ministry came to an end. The hostility against him had risen to a fever pitch. His gentle compassion and abundant miracles were met with oppression and violence. Jesus knew what none of his friends knew—that he was about to die. In spite of the fleeting attempts of the crowd to make him King, Jesus chose the way of the cross.

Warming Up to God If you knew for sure that you had only one week to live, what would you do with that week?

Read John 12.

12 Six days before the Passover, Jesus arrived at Bethany, where Lazarus lived, whom Jesus had raised from the dead. [2]Here a dinner was given in Jesus' honor. Martha served, while Lazarus was among those reclining at the table with him. [3]Then Mary took about a pint[e] of pure nard, an expensive perfume; she poured it on Jesus' feet and wiped his feet with her hair. And the house was filled with the fragrance of the perfume.

[4]But one of his disciples, Judas Iscariot, who was later to betray him, objected, [5]"Why wasn't this perfume sold and the money given to the poor? It was worth a year's wages.[f]" [6]He did not say this because he cared about the poor but because he was a thief; as keeper of the money bag, he used to help himself to what was put into it.

[7]"Leave her alone," Jesus replied. "⌞It was intended⌟ that she should save this perfume for the day of my burial. [8]You will always have the poor among you, but you will not always have me."

[9]Meanwhile a large crowd of Jews found out

[e]3 Greek *a litra* (probably about 0.5 liter) [f]5 Greek *three hundred denarii*

that Jesus was there and came, not only because
of him but also to see Lazarus, whom he had
raised from the dead. 10So the chief priests made
plans to kill Lazarus as well, 11for on account of
him many of the Jews were going over to Jesus
and putting their faith in him.

12The next day the great crowd that had come
for the Feast heard that Jesus was on his way to
Jerusalem. 13They took palm branches and went
out to meet him, shouting,

"Hosanna![g]"

"Blessed is he who comes in the name of the
Lord!"[h]

"Blessed is the King of Israel!"

14Jesus found a young donkey and sat upon it, as
it is written,

15"Do not be afraid, O Daughter of Zion;
see, your king is coming,
seated on a donkey's colt."[i]

16At first his disciples did not understand all
this. Only after Jesus was glorified did they realize
that these things had been written about him and
that they had done these things to him.

17Now the crowd that was with him when he
called Lazarus from the tomb and raised him
from the dead continued to spread the word.
18Many people, because they had heard that he
had given this miraculous sign, went out to meet
him. 19So the Pharisees said to one another, "See,
this is getting us nowhere. Look how the whole
world has gone after him!"

20Now there were some Greeks among those
who went up to worship at the Feast. 21They
came to Philip, who was from Bethsaida in Gali-
lee, with a request. "Sir," they said, "we would
like to see Jesus." 22Philip went to tell Andrew;
Andrew and Philip in turn told Jesus.

23Jesus replied, "The hour has come for the Son
of Man to be glorified. 24I tell you the truth, un-
less a kernel of wheat falls to the ground and dies,
it remains only a single seed. But if it dies, it
produces many seeds. 25The man who loves his
life will lose it, while the man who hates his life
in this world will keep it for eternal life. 26Who-
ever serves me must follow me; and where I am,
my servant also will be. My Father will honor the
one who serves me.

27"Now my heart is troubled, and what shall I
say? 'Father, save me from this hour'? No, it was
for this very reason I came to this hour. 28Father,
glorify your name!"

Then a voice came from heaven, "I have glori-
fied it, and will glorify it again." 29The crowd that
was there and heard it said it had thundered; oth-
ers said an angel had spoken to him.

30Jesus said, "This voice was for your benefit,
not mine. 31Now is the time for judgment on this
world; now the prince of this world will be driven
out. 32But I, when I am lifted up from the earth,
will draw all men to myself." 33He said this to
show the kind of death he was going to die.

34The crowd spoke up, "We have heard from
the Law that the Christ[j] will remain forever, so
how can you say, 'The Son of Man must be lifted
up'? Who is this 'Son of Man'?"

35Then Jesus told them, "You are going to have
the light just a little while longer. Walk while you
have the light, before darkness overtakes you.
The man who walks in the dark does not know
where he is going. 36Put your trust in the light
while you have it, so that you may become sons
of light." When he had finished speaking, Jesus
left and hid himself from them.

37Even after Jesus had done all these miracu-
lous signs in their presence, they still would not
believe in him. 38This was to fulfill the word of
Isaiah the prophet:

"Lord, who has believed our message
and to whom has the arm of the Lord been
revealed?"[k]

39For this reason they could not believe, be-
cause, as Isaiah says elsewhere:

40"He has blinded their eyes
and deadened their hearts,
so they can neither see with their eyes,
nor understand with their hearts,
nor turn—and I would heal them."[l]

41Isaiah said this because he saw Jesus' glory and
spoke about him.

42Yet at the same time many even among the
leaders believed in him. But because of the Phari-
sees they would not confess their faith for fear
they would be put out of the synagogue; 43for
they loved praise from men more than praise
from God.

44Then Jesus cried out, "When a man believes

[g]*13* A Hebrew expression meaning "Save!" which became an exclamation of praise [h]*13* Psalm 118:25, 26 [i]*15* Zech. 9:9 [j]*34* Or *Messiah* [k]*38* Isaiah 53:1 [l]*40* Isaiah 6:10

in me, he does not believe in me only, but in the
one who sent me. 45When he looks at me, he sees
the one who sent me. 46I have come into the
world as a light, so that no one who believes in
me should stay in darkness.
47"As for the person who hears my words but
does not keep them, I do not judge him. For I did
not come to judge the world, but to save it.
48There is a judge for the one who rejects me and
does not accept my words; that very word which
I spoke will condemn him at the last day. 49For I
did not speak of my own accord, but the Father
who sent me commanded me what to say and
how to say it. 50I know that his command leads to
eternal life. So whatever I say is just what the
Father has told me to say."

Discovering the Word 1. What motivates Mary to pour expensive perfume on Jesus' feet? 2. Judas objects to Mary's extravagance. What motives and wrong thinking lie behind his objection (vv. 4–8)? 3. What do the shouts of the crowd tell us about their expectations of Jesus (vv. 12–13)? 4. How do Christ's statements about his mission clash with the crowd's expectations (vv. 23–28)? 5. When we stubbornly refuse to believe, what happens to our spiritual senses, and why (vv. 37–41)? 6. Jesus' last public message to his people is recorded in verses 44–50. What indications do you find that he is still reaching out in love and grace to those who have rejected him?

Applying the Word 1. In what ways should we be extravagant in our devotion to Jesus? 2. How can you apply the example of Jesus to people who reject you or your testimony about Christ?

Responding in Prayer In your own life are you more interested in earthly acclaim and glory or are you willing to lose your life for Christ's sake? Examine your direction and life goals in the light of Jesus' commitment to do the will of the Father.

14 / *John 13:1–17*
The Son as a Slave

THERE WERE TWO things on Jesus' heart the night before his crucifixion—his Father and his disciples. In John 13—17, we have the privilege of listening to his conversations with them both. However, before Jesus can instruct his disciples about his death, he has to act out a lesson in servitude. Jesus also shows us the spirit he expects in those who follow him. Greatness in Christ's eyes does not come from having many servants but from being the servant of many.

Warming Up to God Have you ever been asked to do a demeaning, lowly job? What thoughts went through your mind at that time? Praise God for a Savior who was willing to take on the lowliest task of all.

Read John 13:1–17.

13 It was just before the Passover
Feast. Jesus knew that the time had
come for him to leave this world
and go to the Father. Having loved his own who
were in the world, he now showed them the full
extent of his love.[m]
2The evening meal was being served, and the
devil had already prompted Judas Iscariot, son of
Simon, to betray Jesus. 3Jesus knew that the Fa-
ther had put all things under his power, and that
he had come from God and was returning to God;
4so he got up from the meal, took off his outer
clothing, and wrapped a towel around his waist.
5After that, he poured water into a basin and be-
gan to wash his disciples' feet, drying them with
the towel that was wrapped around him.
6He came to Simon Peter, who said to him,
"Lord, are you going to wash my feet?"
7Jesus replied, "You do not realize now what I
am doing, but later you will understand."
8"No," said Peter, "you shall never wash my
feet."

m1 Or *he loved them to the last*

Jesus answered, “Unless I wash you, you have
no part with me.”
9“Then, Lord,” Simon Peter replied, “not just
my feet but my hands and my head as well!”
10Jesus answered, “A person who has had a
bath needs only to wash his feet; his whole body
is clean. And you are clean, though not every one
of you.” 11For he knew who was going to betray
him, and that was why he said not every one was
clean.
12When he had finished washing their feet, he
put on his clothes and returned to his place. “Do
you understand what I have done for you?” he
asked them. 13“You call me ‘Teacher’ and ‘Lord,’
and rightly so, for that is what I am. 14Now that
I, your Lord and Teacher, have washed your feet,
you also should wash one another’s feet. 15I have
set you an example that you should do as I have
done for you. 16I tell you the truth, no servant is
greater than his master, nor is a messenger
greater than the one who sent him. 17Now that
you know these things, you will be blessed if you
do them.

Discovering the Word 1. According to John, what did Jesus know about himself (vv. 1–3)? In light of that knowledge, what is remarkable about what Jesus did next (vv. 4–5)? 2. Footwashing was normally done by servants or slaves. Why do you think that Jesus washed his disciples’ feet instead of simply talking to them about love? 3. Was Peter simply being humble when he refused to allow Jesus to serve him (vv. 6–8)? Explain. 4. What spiritual truth was Jesus trying to communicate to Peter (and to us) in verses 8–11? 5. Based on Jesus’ words in verse 17, how would you describe the relationship between knowledge, action and joy in the Christian life?

Applying the Word 1. What has this chapter revealed to you about your attitude toward serving? 2. In what specific ways can you model the humility of Jesus toward those with whom you live or work?

Responding in Prayer Ask God to give you a humble spirit.

15 / *John 13:18–38*

The Betrayer & the Boaster

THERE ARE SOME people we just don’t like to be around! They aren’t necessarily our enemies. They simply have the uncanny ability to irritate us. If we had been one of Jesus’ disciples, we would probably have found it difficult to be around Peter. He was blunt and, at times, arrogant. On the other hand, we might have regarded Judas with trust and respect. The only one who saw deeply enough to discern the true character of these men was Jesus.

Warming Up to God Has someone in your life ever hurt you deeply? How have you responded to that hurt? Tell God how you feel about what happened. Allow him to speak to your pain.

Read John 13:18–38.

18“I am not referring to all of you; I know those
I have chosen. But this is to fulfill the scripture:
‘He who shares my bread has lifted up his heel
against me.’[n]
19“I am telling you now before it happens, so
that when it does happen you will believe that I
am He. 20I tell you the truth, whoever accepts
anyone I send accepts me; and whoever accepts
me accepts the one who sent me.”
21After he had said this, Jesus was troubled in
spirit and testified, “I tell you the truth, one of
you is going to betray me.”
22His disciples stared at one another, at a loss
to know which of them he meant. 23One of them,
the disciple whom Jesus loved, was reclining next
to him. 24Simon Peter motioned to this disciple
and said, “Ask him which one he means.”
25Leaning back against Jesus, he asked him,
“Lord, who is it?”

[n]18 Psalm 41:9

[26]Jesus answered, "It is the one to whom I will
give this piece of bread when I have dipped it in
the dish." Then, dipping the piece of bread, he
gave it to Judas Iscariot, son of Simon. [27]As soon
as Judas took the bread, Satan entered into him.
"What you are about to do, do quickly," Jesus
told him, [28]but no one at the meal understood
why Jesus said this to him. [29]Since Judas had
charge of the money, some thought Jesus was tell-
ing him to buy what was needed for the Feast, or
to give something to the poor. [30]As soon as Judas
had taken the bread, he went out. And it was
night.
[31]When he was gone, Jesus said, "Now is the
Son of Man glorified and God is glorified in him.
[32]If God is glorified in him,[o] God will glorify the
Son in himself, and will glorify him at once.
[33]"My children, I will be with you only a little
longer. You will look for me, and just as I told the
Jews, so I tell you now: Where I am going, you
cannot come.
[34]"A new command I give you: Love one an-
other. As I have loved you, so you must love one
another. [35]By this all men will know that you are
my disciples, if you love one another."
[36]Simon Peter asked him, "Lord, where are you
going?"
Jesus replied, "Where I am going, you cannot
follow now, but you will follow later."
[37]Peter asked, "Lord, why can't I follow you
now? I will lay down my life for you."
[38]Then Jesus answered, "Will you really lay
down your life for me? I tell you the truth, before
the rooster crows, you will disown me three
times!

[o]32 Many early manuscripts do not have *If God is glorified in him.*

Discovering the Word 1. Jesus takes this opportunity to predict his betrayal. How would his prediction dispel any doubts the disciples might have and strengthen their faith (v. 19)? 2. Evidently, the disciples did not know who would betray Jesus (v. 22). What does this tell us about how Jesus had treated Judas? 3. Why does the kind of love Jesus describes convince all of humanity that we are Jesus' disciples (v. 35)? 4. Do you think Peter's declaration in verse 37 comes from pride or from sincerity? Explain. 5. Three people stand out in this passage—Jesus, Judas and Peter. What one character quality of each—good or evil—impresses you the most?

Applying the Word 1. How would you have treated Judas if you knew he would eventually betray you? 2. John later wrote: "This is how we know what love is: Jesus Christ laid down his life for us. And we ought to lay down our lives for our brothers" (1 Jn 3:16). In what practical ways can you exhibit this sacrificial love?

Responding in Prayer Pray for a strong faith that won't lead you into betrayal when times are tough.

---

16 / *John 14*
Comfort for a Troubled Heart

THE CALL CAME late at night. A broken sob was followed by these words: "Our son is dying. Will you please come to the hospital?" As I made the trip through darkened streets, I wondered what I could say to bring comfort to these heartbroken parents. Jesus faced that challenge too. In this chapter he comforts eleven disciples who feel like their world is coming unglued.

Warming Up to God What is troubling you? Give it to God, and wait before him to receive his comfort.

Read John 14.

14 "Do not let your hearts be troubled. Trust in God[p]; trust also in me. 2In my Father's house are many rooms; if it were not so, I would have told you. I am going there to prepare a place for you. 3And if I go and prepare a place for you, I will come back and take you to be with me that you also may be where I am. 4You know the way to the place where I am going."

5Thomas said to him, "Lord, we don't know where you are going, so how can we know the way?"

6Jesus answered, "I am the way and the truth and the life. No one comes to the Father except through me. 7If you really knew me, you would know[q] my Father as well. From now on, you do know him and have seen him."

8Philip said, "Lord, show us the Father and that will be enough for us."

9Jesus answered: "Don't you know me, Philip, even after I have been among you such a long time? Anyone who has seen me has seen the Father. How can you say, 'Show us the Father'? 10Don't you believe that I am in the Father, and that the Father is in me? The words I say to you are not just my own. Rather, it is the Father, living in me, who is doing his work. 11Believe me when I say that I am in the Father and the Father is in me; or at least believe on the evidence of the miracles themselves. 12I tell you the truth, anyone who has faith in me will do what I have been doing. He will do even greater things than these, because I am going to the Father. 13And I will do whatever you ask in my name, so that the Son may bring glory to the Father. 14You may ask me for anything in my name, and I will do it.

15"If you love me, you will obey what I command. 16And I will ask the Father, and he will give you another Counselor to be with you forever— 17the Spirit of truth. The world cannot accept him, because it neither sees him nor knows him. But you know him, for he lives with you and will be[r] in you. 18I will not leave you as orphans; I will come to you. 19Before long, the world will not see me anymore, but you will see me. Because I live, you also will live. 20On that day you will realize that I am in my Father, and you are in me, and I am in you. 21Whoever has my commands and obeys them, he is the one who loves me. He who loves me will be loved by my Father, and I too will love him and show myself to him."

22Then Judas (not Judas Iscariot) said, "But, Lord, why do you intend to show yourself to us and not to the world?"

23Jesus replied, "If anyone loves me, he will obey my teaching. My Father will love him, and we will come to him and make our home with him. 24He who does not love me will not obey my teaching. These words you hear are not my own; they belong to the Father who sent me.

25"All this I have spoken while still with you. 26But the Counselor, the Holy Spirit, whom the Father will send in my name, will teach you all things and will remind you of everything I have said to you. 27Peace I leave with you; my peace I give you. I do not give to you as the world gives. Do not let your hearts be troubled and do not be afraid.

28"You heard me say, 'I am going away and I am coming back to you.' If you loved me, you would be glad that I am going to the Father, for the Father is greater than I. 29I have told you now before it happens, so that when it does happen you will believe. 30I will not speak with you much longer, for the prince of this world is coming. He has no hold on me, 31but the world must learn that I love the Father and that I do exactly what my Father has commanded me.

"Come now; let us leave.

p1 Or *You trust in God* q7 Some early manuscripts *If you really have known me, you will know* r17 Some early manuscripts *and is*

Discovering the Word 1. How would the promises Jesus makes in verses 1–4 bring comfort to his disciples? 2. In light of verses 5–14, why is it crucial for our focus to be on Jesus himself? 3. According to Jesus, how will the Spirit bring comfort and help to his followers (vv. 15–27)? 4. What is the relationship between our love and obedience to Jesus and his love and presence in our lives (vv. 15–24)? 5. How does the peace Christ offers differ from that which the world offers (vv. 25–31)?

Applying the Word 1. Think of a friend who is going through a personal crisis. How could this chapter help you to minister to that person? 2. How can Jesus' words help you in a personal crisis or when you have a troubled heart?

Responding in Prayer Ask God to comfort someone you know who is troubled.

17 / *John 15:1–17*
The Secret of Remaining

THE FINAL WEEKEND before Christmas is not the time to visit a shopping mall. If you are fortunate enough to find a parking spot, the press of people inside makes shopping almost impossible. I overheard one mother giving these final instructions to her young son before plunging into the crowd: "Stay close to me and hold my hand all the time. We won't get separated if we hold on to each other."

As Jesus prepared his disciples to face life without his visible presence, he impressed on them the importance of staying close to him spiritually. He said, "Remain in me." If you've ever longed to understand the secret of spiritual growth, you will find it in Jesus' words to us in John 15.

Warming Up to God Have you ever felt far from Christ since becoming a Christian? What circumstances made you feel that way? Be still before God and feel his presence with you now.

Read John 15:1–17.

15 "I am the true vine, and my Father
is the gardener. [2]He cuts off every
branch in me that bears no fruit,
while every branch that does bear fruit he
prunes[s] so that it will be even more fruitful.
[3]You are already clean because of the word I have
spoken to you. [4]Remain in me, and I will remain
in you. No branch can bear fruit by itself; it must
remain in the vine. Neither can you bear fruit
unless you remain in me.
[5]"I am the vine; you are the branches. If a man
remains in me and I in him, he will bear much
fruit; apart from me you can do nothing. [6]If any-
one does not remain in me, he is like a branch
that is thrown away and withers; such branches
are picked up, thrown into the fire and burned.
[7]If you remain in me and my words remain in
you, ask whatever you wish, and it will be given
you. [8]This is to my Father's glory, that you bear
much fruit, showing yourselves to be my disci-
ples.
[9]"As the Father has loved me, so have I loved
you. Now remain in my love. [10]If you obey my
commands, you will remain in my love, just as I
have obeyed my Father's commands and remain
in his love. [11]I have told you this so that my joy
may be in you and that your joy may be complete.
[12]My command is this: Love each other as I have
loved you. [13]Greater love has no one than this,
that he lay down his life for his friends. [14]You are
my friends if you do what I command. [15]I no
longer call you servants, because a servant does
not know his master's business. Instead, I have
called you friends, for everything that I learned
from my Father I have made known to you. [16]You
did not choose me, but I chose you and appointed
you to go and bear fruit—fruit that will last. Then
the Father will give you whatever you ask in my
name. [17]This is my command: Love each other.

[s]2 The Greek for *prunes* also means *cleans.*

Discovering the Word 1. Jesus' instructions to his disciples in this passage revolve around three symbols—the vine, the gardener and the branches. What is Jesus trying to communicate by calling himself the *true vine*? 2. What does it mean to remain in Christ (v. 4)? 3. The Father prunes fruitful branches to make them more fruitful (v. 2). In what ways have you experienced the Father's "pruning"? 4. What spiritual benefits result from remaining in Christ (vv. 7–11)? 5. What are the requirements and benefits of friendship with Christ (vv. 14–17)?

Applying the Word 1. There are three categories of branches described in this passage—those bearing no fruit, those bearing some fruit, and those bearing much fruit. In which category would you place yourself and why? 2. If you are not bearing much fruit, what is Jesus' counsel to you in these verses?

Responding in Prayer Picture yourself as a tree laden with plump, healthy fruit. Ask God to help you become the person he wants you to be.

18 / *John 15:18—16:4*
The Cost of Friendship with Jesus

WHILE ON EARTH, Jesus did not surround himself with a group of students or even a group of followers. He placed himself in the company of friends. To admit that we need friends is a sign of maturity, not immaturity. Close relationships are Christlike! In this passage Jesus shows us what friendship with him is really like. There's both comfort and cost.

Warming Up to God Are you ready to face the cost of following Christ? Talk openly with God about your fears—and excitement.

Read John 15:18—16:4.

18"If the world hates you, keep in mind that it
hated me first. 19If you belonged to the world, it
would love you as its own. As it is, you do not
belong to the world, but I have chosen you out of
the world. That is why the world hates you. 20Re-
member the words I spoke to you: 'No servant is
greater than his master.'[t] If they persecuted me,
they will persecute you also. If they obeyed my
teaching, they will obey yours also. 21They will
treat you this way because of my name, for they
do not know the One who sent me. 22If I had not
come and spoken to them, they would not be
guilty of sin. Now, however, they have no excuse
for their sin. 23He who hates me hates my Father
as well. 24If I had not done among them what no
one else did, they would not be guilty of sin. But
now they have seen these miracles, and yet they
have hated both me and my Father. 25But this is
to fulfill what is written in their Law: 'They hated
me without reason.'[u]
26"When the Counselor comes, whom I will
send to you from the Father, the Spirit of truth
who goes out from the Father, he will testify
about me. 27And you also must testify, for you
have been with me from the beginning.
16 "All this I have told you so that you
will not go astray. 2They will put
you out of the synagogue; in fact, a
time is coming when anyone who kills you will
think he is offering a service to God. 3They will
do such things because they have not known the
Father or me. 4I have told you this, so that when
the time comes you will remember that I warned
you. I did not tell you this at first because I was
with you.

[t]*20* John 13:16 [u]*25* Psalms 35:19; 69:4

Discovering the Word 1. If love is to characterize our relationship with other believers, hate will characterize our relationships with the world. What reasons does Jesus give for the world's hatred? 2. What does Jesus mean when he says that without his coming, his words and his miracles, the world "would not be guilty of sin" (15:22–25)? 3. In what specific ways will the Counselor and the disciples themselves continue the ministry begun by Jesus (15:26–27)? 4. What kind of treatment can the disciples expect from those who do not know Christ (16:1–4)?

Applying the Word 1. What kinds of persecution are more probable for us in our society? Explain. 2. If we as Christians are not persecuted in some way, what might that imply about our spiritual commitment? 3. How are you experiencing the world's hatred as a Christian?

Responding in Prayer Pray for those around the world who face persecution for their faith.

19 / *John 16:5–33*
Secrets of the Spirit

A LOVELY WOMAN in our church died not long ago. She knew for almost a year that, unless the Lord intervened, the cancer in her brain would kill her. That year gave her time of wonderful interaction with her husband and family. Her family had the opportunity to express their love for her, and the dying woman had the privilege of passing on her godly wisdom.

In John 16 Jesus knows that he will die in less than twenty-four hours. When his disciples are faced with that reality, Jesus responds to their concerns by talking about the coming Holy Spirit.

Warming Up to God Think about the people in your life who are important to you. What would you want to tell them if you knew that you had only a short time to live? Ask God to make you ready to hear what Jesus had to say in his last days.

Read John 16:5–33.

5“Now I am going to him who sent me, yet
none of you asks me, ‘Where are you going?’ 6Be-
cause I have said these things, you are filled with
grief. 7But I tell you the truth: It is for your good
that I am going away. Unless I go away, the
Counselor will not come to you; but if I go, I will
send him to you. 8When he comes, he will con-
vict the world of guilt[v] in regard to sin and righ-
teousness and judgment: 9in regard to sin, be-
cause men do not believe in me; 10in regard to
righteousness, because I am going to the Father,
where you can see me no longer; 11and in regard
to judgment, because the prince of this world
now stands condemned.

12“I have much more to say to you, more than
you can now bear. 13But when he, the Spirit of
truth, comes, he will guide you into all truth. He
will not speak on his own; he will speak only
what he hears, and he will tell you what is yet to
come. 14He will bring glory to me by taking from
what is mine and making it known to you. 15All
that belongs to the Father is mine. That is why I
said the Spirit will take from what is mine and
make it known to you.

16“In a little while you will see me no more,
and then after a little while you will see me.”

17Some of his disciples said to one another,
“What does he mean by saying, ‘In a little while
you will see me no more, and then after a little
while you will see me,’ and ‘Because I am going to
the Father’?” 18They kept asking, “What does he
mean by ‘a little while’? We don’t understand
what he is saying.”

19Jesus saw that they wanted to ask him about
this, so he said to them, “Are you asking one
another what I meant when I said, ‘In a little
while you will see me no more, and then after a
little while you will see me’? 20I tell you the truth,
you will weep and mourn while the world re-
joices. You will grieve, but your grief will turn to
joy. 21A woman giving birth to a child has pain
because her time has come; but when her baby is
born she forgets the anguish because of her joy
that a child is born into the world. 22So with you:
Now is your time of grief, but I will see you again
and you will rejoice, and no one will take away
your joy. 23In that day you will no longer ask me
anything. I tell you the truth, my Father will give
you whatever you ask in my name. 24Until now
you have not asked for anything in my name. Ask
and you will receive, and your joy will be com-
plete.

25“Though I have been speaking figuratively, a
time is coming when I will no longer use this
kind of language but will tell you plainly about
my Father. 26In that day you will ask in my name.
I am not saying that I will ask the Father on your
behalf. 27No, the Father himself loves you be-
cause you have loved me and have believed that I
came from God. 28I came from the Father and
entered the world; now I am leaving the world
and going back to the Father.”

29Then Jesus’ disciples said, “Now you are
speaking clearly and without figures of speech.
30Now we can see that you know all things and
that you do not even need to have anyone ask you
questions. This makes us believe that you came
from God.”

31“You believe at last!”[w] Jesus answered.

[v]8 Or *will expose the guilt of the world*   [w]31 Or *“Do you now believe?”*

32"But a time is coming, and has come, when you will be scattered, each to his own home. You will leave me all alone. Yet I am not alone, for my Father is with me.

33"I have told you these things, so that in me you may have peace. In this world you will have trouble. But take heart! I have overcome the world."

Discovering the Word 1. Jesus said that it was for the disciples' good that he go away and that the Counselor come. Why was the Spirit's presence more profitable to the disciples than Jesus' presence? 2. What did Jesus say the Spirit's ministry would be toward the world (vv. 8–11)? 3. The Spirit's ministry is one of communication. What specific things did Jesus say the Spirit would communicate to the disciples (vv. 13–15)? 4. Jesus answers the questions the disciples ask in verses 17–18, not by giving them an explanation but by making them a promise (vv. 19–22). What was the promise? 5. Why would Jesus' promise bring them joy in the midst of their grief and confusion? 6. How would Jesus' assurance of the Father's love help the disciples in the days just ahead of them (vv. 25–33)?

Applying the Word 1. How can this incident help us when our questions to the Lord seemingly go unanswered? 2. How do you respond to the promise in verses 23–24?

Responding in Prayer Give God the desires of your heart, knowing that he wants to make your joy complete.

20/ *John 17*
The Master's Final Prayer

THE APPROACH OF death has a way of bringing our priorities into focus. People who know death is imminent also know what is really important in life and who they really care about. In Jesus' final prayer with his disciples, he prays for himself, for them and for you! Every believer is on Jesus' mind as he faces the greatest trial of his life—the cross.

Warming Up to God Spend some time reflecting on God's glory. To what extent is God's glory foremost in your mind on a daily basis? Explain.

Read John 17.

17 After Jesus said this, he looked toward heaven and prayed:

"Father, the time has come. Glorify your
Son, that your Son may glorify you. 2For you
granted him authority over all people that he
might give eternal life to all those you have
given him. 3Now this is eternal life: that they
may know you, the only true God, and Jesus
Christ, whom you have sent. 4I have brought
you glory on earth by completing the work
you gave me to do. 5And now, Father, glorify
me in your presence with the glory I had
with you before the world began.

6"I have revealed you[x] to those whom
you gave me out of the world. They were
yours; you gave them to me and they have
obeyed your word. 7Now they know that everything you have given me comes from you.
8For I gave them the words you gave me and
they accepted them. They knew with certainty that I came from you, and they believed that you sent me. 9I pray for them. I
am not praying for the world, but for those
you have given me, for they are yours. 10All
I have is yours, and all you have is mine.
And glory has come to me through them. 11I
will remain in the world no longer, but they
are still in the world, and I am coming to
you. Holy Father, protect them by the power
of your name—the name you gave me—so
that they may be one as we are one. 12While
I was with them, I protected them and kept
them safe by that name you gave me. None

[x]6 Greek *your name*; also in verse 26

has been lost except the one doomed to de-
struction so that Scripture would be fulfilled.
13“I am coming to you now, but I say these
things while I am still in the world, so that
they may have the full measure of my joy
within them. 14I have given them your word
and the world has hated them, for they are
not of the world any more than I am of the
world. 15My prayer is not that you take them
out of the world but that you protect them
from the evil one. 16They are not of the
world, even as I am not of it. 17Sanctify[y]
them by the truth; your word is truth. 18As
you sent me into the world, I have sent them
into the world. 19For them I sanctify myself,
that they too may be truly sanctified.
20“My prayer is not for them alone. I pray
also for those who will believe in me through
their message, 21that all of them may be one,
Father, just as you are in me and I am in you.
May they also be in us so that the world may
believe that you have sent me. 22I have given
them the glory that you gave me, that they
may be one as we are one: 23I in them and
you in me. May they be brought to complete
unity to let the world know that you sent me
and have loved them even as you have
loved me.
24“Father, I want those you have given me
to be with me where I am, and to see my
glory, the glory you have given me because
you loved me before the creation of the
world.
25“Righteous Father, though the world
does not know you, I know you, and they
know that you have sent me. 26I have made
you known to them, and will continue to
make you known in order that the love you
have for me may be in them and that I myself
may be in them.”

y17 Greek *hagiazo (set apart for sacred use or make holy)*; also in verse 19

Discovering the Word 1. Jesus makes only one request for himself—that the Father would glorify him so that he might glorify the Father. In what way would each one glorify the other (vv. 1–5)? Why do you think that was so important to Jesus? 2. According to verses 6–19, what specific ministries did Jesus have toward his disciples? 3. Twice Jesus asked the Father to protect his disciples from the evil one (vv. 11, 15). Why would that protection have been so important in Jesus' mind as he faced the cross? 4. Jesus prayed that those who believe in him would be one "so that the world may believe that you have sent me" (vv. 21, 23)? Why is our unity a powerful argument for the reality of Jesus?

Applying the Word 1. Jesus also asked the Father to sanctify his disciples through his word (v. 17). How can we allow God's Word to have that kind of effect on our lives? 2. Jesus obviously prayed this prayer out loud to bring comfort and assurance to his disciples. In what particular ways do Jesus' words encourage or assure you?

Responding in Prayer Ask God to bring unity to your church or fellowship.

21 / *John 18:1–27*

“Jesus, You're Under Arrest!”

MOST OF US would hate the thought of being arrested and brought to trial. If we were guilty of a crime, being arrested would be humiliating. But if we were innocent, it would be devastating. Yet in what should have been a demeaning experience for Jesus, we see again his majesty and glory. Jesus uses an experience of attack, betrayal and abandonment to demonstrate his confident trust in the Father. His calm assurance will help us face life's hurts and injustices with the same trust in the same Father.

Warming Up to God Think about a time when you realized you had committed a deep sin. How did you feel when you took it before Christ? Thank him for his grace to you then and now.

Read John 18:1–27.

18 When he had finished praying, Jesus left with his disciples and crossed the Kidron Valley. On the other side there was an olive grove, and he and his disciples went into it.

[2]Now Judas, who betrayed him, knew the place, because Jesus had often met there with his disciples. [3]So Judas came to the grove, guiding a detachment of soldiers and some officials from the chief priests and Pharisees. They were carrying torches, lanterns and weapons.

[4]Jesus, knowing all that was going to happen to him, went out and asked them, "Who is it you want?"

[5]"Jesus of Nazareth," they replied.

"I am he," Jesus said. (And Judas the traitor was standing there with them.) [6]When Jesus said, "I am he," they drew back and fell to the ground.

[7]Again he asked them, "Who is it you want?"

And they said, "Jesus of Nazareth."

[8]"I told you that I am he," Jesus answered. "If you are looking for me, then let these men go." [9]This happened so that the words he had spoken would be fulfilled: "I have not lost one of those you gave me."[z]

[10]Then Simon Peter, who had a sword, drew it and struck the high priest's servant, cutting off his right ear. (The servant's name was Malchus.)

[11]Jesus commanded Peter, "Put your sword away! Shall I not drink the cup the Father has given me?"

[12]Then the detachment of soldiers with its commander and the Jewish officials arrested Jesus. They bound him [13]and brought him first to Annas, who was the father-in-law of Caiaphas, the high priest that year. [14]Caiaphas was the one who had advised the Jews that it would be good if one man died for the people.

[15]Simon Peter and another disciple were following Jesus. Because this disciple was known to the high priest, he went with Jesus into the high priest's courtyard, [16]but Peter had to wait outside at the door. The other disciple, who was known to the high priest, came back, spoke to the girl on duty there and brought Peter in.

[17]"You are not one of his disciples, are you?" the girl at the door asked Peter.

He replied, "I am not."

[18]It was cold, and the servants and officials stood around a fire they had made to keep warm. Peter also was standing with them, warming himself.

[19]Meanwhile, the high priest questioned Jesus about his disciples and his teaching.

[20]"I have spoken openly to the world," Jesus replied. "I always taught in synagogues or at the temple, where all the Jews come together. I said nothing in secret. [21]Why question me? Ask those who heard me. Surely they know what I said."

[22]When Jesus said this, one of the officials nearby struck him in the face. "Is this the way you answer the high priest?" he demanded.

[23]"If I said something wrong," Jesus replied, "testify as to what is wrong. But if I spoke the truth, why did you strike me?" [24]Then Annas sent him, still bound, to Caiaphas the high priest.[a]

[25]As Simon Peter stood warming himself, he was asked, "You are not one of his disciples, are you?"

He denied it, saying, "I am not."

[26]One of the high priest's servants, a relative of the man whose ear Peter had cut off, challenged him, "Didn't I see you with him in the olive grove?" [27]Again Peter denied it, and at that moment a rooster began to crow.

[z]9 John 6:39 [a]24 Or *(Now Annas had sent him, still bound, to Caiaphas the high priest.)*

Discovering the Word 1. Why would Jesus go to a place where Judas knew he might be found (vv. 1–3)? 2. When the soldiers say they are seeking Jesus of Nazareth, Jesus replies, "I am he" (literally, "I am"; v. 5). How would you explain the reaction of the soldiers (v. 6)? 3. What insight do Peter's action and Jesus' rebuke (v. 11) give you about our attempts at times to "help God out" in our own strength and wisdom? 4. Think back to the deepest sin of your life. How does a look at your own sin change your attitude toward Peter's denial of Jesus? 5. What specific events in this passage display (a) Jesus' courage, (b) his power and (c) his obedience to the Father?

Applying the Word 1. What can we learn from Peter's failure about being ready to stand against the world's challenges? 2. How will this study change the way you will face a time of testing in your own life?

Responding in Prayer Ask God to make you ready to face difficulties with grace.

22 / *John 18:28—19:16*
Pilate on Trial

"CHRIST KILLERS!" THE words made my stomach tighten. Someone had spray-painted the words and a series of swastikas on the Jewish synagogue in our city. Anti-Semitism had raised its ugly head again.

The New Testament does blame the Jewish leaders for condemning Jesus to die. But they weren't acting alone. The Roman governor, Pontius Pilate, also condemned Jesus to die. There is a sense, too, in which we killed Jesus. He died for *our* sins. The most amazing answer to the question of who killed Jesus is that no one did! Jesus said, "No one takes my life from me. I lay it down of my own choice."

Warming Up to God What temptation to compromise your Christian faith or witness are you facing? Ask the One who has faced deep trials to give you strength.

Read John 18:28—19:16.

28Then the Jews led Jesus from Caiaphas to the
palace of the Roman governor. By now it was
early morning, and to avoid ceremonial unclean-
ness the Jews did not enter the palace; they
wanted to be able to eat the Passover. 29So Pilate
came out to them and asked, "What charges are
you bringing against this man?"

30"If he were not a criminal," they replied, "we
would not have handed him over to you."

31Pilate said, "Take him yourselves and judge
him by your own law."

"But we have no right to execute anyone," the
Jews objected. 32This happened so that the words
Jesus had spoken indicating the kind of death he
was going to die would be fulfilled.

33Pilate then went back inside the palace, sum-
moned Jesus and asked him, "Are you the king of
the Jews?"

34"Is that your own idea," Jesus asked, "or did
others talk to you about me?"

35"Am I a Jew?" Pilate replied. "It was your
people and your chief priests who handed you
over to me. What is it you have done?"

36Jesus said, "My kingdom is not of this world.
If it were, my servants would fight to prevent my
arrest by the Jews. But now my kingdom is from
another place."

37"You are a king, then!" said Pilate.

Jesus answered, "You are right in saying I am a
king. In fact, for this reason I was born, and for
this I came into the world, to testify to the truth.
Everyone on the side of truth listens to me."

38"What is truth?" Pilate asked. With this he
went out again to the Jews and said, "I find no
basis for a charge against him. 39But it is your
custom for me to release to you one prisoner at
the time of the Passover. Do you want me to re-
lease 'the king of the Jews'?"

40They shouted back, "No, not him! Give us
Barabbas!" Now Barabbas had taken part in a re-
bellion.

19 Then Pilate took Jesus and had him
flogged. 2The soldiers twisted to-
gether a crown of thorns and put it
on his head. They clothed him in a purple robe
3and went up to him again and again, saying,
"Hail, king of the Jews!" And they struck him in
the face.

4Once more Pilate came out and said to the
Jews, "Look, I am bringing him out to you to let
you know that I find no basis for a charge against
him." 5When Jesus came out wearing the crown
of thorns and the purple robe, Pilate said to them,
"Here is the man!"

6As soon as the chief priests and their officials
saw him, they shouted, "Crucify! Crucify!"

But Pilate answered, "You take him and crucify
him. As for me, I find no basis for a charge against
him."

7The Jews insisted, "We have a law, and ac-
cording to that law he must die, because he
claimed to be the Son of God."

8When Pilate heard this, he was even more
afraid, 9and he went back inside the palace.

“Where do you come from?” he asked Jesus, but Jesus gave him no answer. 10“Do you refuse to speak to me?” Pilate said. “Don’t you realize I have power either to free you or to crucify you?”

11Jesus answered, “You would have no power over me if it were not given to you from above. Therefore the one who handed me over to you is guilty of a greater sin.”

12From then on, Pilate tried to set Jesus free, but the Jews kept shouting, “If you let this man go, you are no friend of Caesar. Anyone who claims to be a king opposes Caesar.”

13When Pilate heard this, he brought Jesus out and sat down on the judge’s seat at a place known as the Stone Pavement (which in Aramaic is Gabbatha). 14It was the day of Preparation of Passover Week, about the sixth hour.

“Here is your king,” Pilate said to the Jews.

15But they shouted, “Take him away! Take him away! Crucify him!”

“Shall I crucify your king?” Pilate asked.

“We have no king but Caesar,” the chief priests answered.

16Finally Pilate handed him over to them to be crucified.

Discovering the Word 1. A Roman trial included four basic elements: the accusation (18:29–31), the interrogation (search for evidence) (18:32–35), the defense (18:36–37) and the verdict (18:38). What events or statements from the text are included in each? 2. Pilate obviously was trying to release Jesus. What specific attempts did he make (18:39; 19:4, 6, 10, 12, 15)? 3. The Jews’ true charge against Jesus comes out in verse 7—“He claimed to be the Son of God.” Why do you think Pilate reacted to that statement as he did (vv. 8–9)? 4. Why didn’t Jesus say more to Pilate (vv. 9–11)? Shouldn’t he have defended himself more vigorously? 5. What can you conclude about Pilate’s character after reading this passage? What kind of man was he?

Applying the Word 1. How can you respond appropriately to Christ’s grace to you? 2. What does this passage tell you about how you should respond when you are treated unjustly?

Responding in Prayer Ask God to help you follow his example of grace when you are under pressure.

23 / *John 19:17–42* Obedient to Death

THERE IS NOTHING pleasant or attractive about an execution. The only one I’ve ever seen was in a televised news report from Vietnam. A captured soldier was shot. It left a knot in my stomach for days.

In Jesus’ day execution was designed to be public and painful. The account of the crucifixion is not easy to read. You may be tempted to think that Jesus’ death was a cruel mistake. It wasn’t. Jesus’ life was not taken from him; he laid it down willingly. It was part of his plan—a plan that included you and me. His cross was in a very real sense our cross.

Warming Up to God When you think about death, what feelings and thoughts come to mind?

Read John 19:17–42.

So the soldiers took charge of Jesus. 17Carrying his own cross, he went out to the place of the Skull (which in Aramaic is called Golgotha). 18Here they crucified him, and with him two others—one on each side and Jesus in the middle.

19Pilate had a notice prepared and fastened to the cross. It read: JESUS OF NAZARETH, THE KING OF THE JEWS. 20Many of the Jews read this sign, for the place where Jesus was crucified was near the city, and the sign was written in Aramaic, Latin and Greek. 21The chief priests of the Jews protested to Pilate, “Do not write ‘The King of the Jews,’ but that this man claimed to be king of the Jews.”

22Pilate answered, "What I have written, I have written."

23When the soldiers crucified Jesus, they took his clothes, dividing them into four shares, one for each of them, with the undergarment remaining. This garment was seamless, woven in one piece from top to bottom.

24"Let's not tear it," they said to one another. "Let's decide by lot who will get it."

This happened that the scripture might be fulfilled which said,

> "They divided my garments among them
> and cast lots for my clothing."[b]

So this is what the soldiers did.

25Near the cross of Jesus stood his mother, his mother's sister, Mary the wife of Clopas, and Mary Magdalene. 26When Jesus saw his mother there, and the disciple whom he loved standing nearby, he said to his mother, "Dear woman, here is your son," 27and to the disciple, "Here is your mother." From that time on, this disciple took her into his home.

28Later, knowing that all was now completed, and so that the Scripture would be fulfilled, Jesus said, "I am thirsty." 29A jar of wine vinegar was there, so they soaked a sponge in it, put the sponge on a stalk of the hyssop plant, and lifted it to Jesus' lips. 30When he had received the drink, Jesus said, "It is finished." With that, he bowed his head and gave up his spirit.

31Now it was the day of Preparation, and the next day was to be a special Sabbath. Because the Jews did not want the bodies left on the crosses during the Sabbath, they asked Pilate to have the legs broken and the bodies taken down. 32The soldiers therefore came and broke the legs of the first man who had been crucified with Jesus, and then those of the other. 33But when they came to Jesus and found that he was already dead, they did not break his legs. 34Instead, one of the soldiers pierced Jesus' side with a spear, bringing a sudden flow of blood and water. 35The man who saw it has given testimony, and his testimony is true. He knows that he tells the truth, and he testifies so that you also may believe. 36These things happened so that the scripture would be fulfilled: "Not one of his bones will be broken,"[c] 37and, as another scripture says, "They will look on the one they have pierced."[d]

38Later, Joseph of Arimathea asked Pilate for the body of Jesus. Now Joseph was a disciple of Jesus, but secretly because he feared the Jews. With Pilate's permission, he came and took the body away. 39He was accompanied by Nicodemus, the man who earlier had visited Jesus at night. Nicodemus brought a mixture of myrrh and aloes, about seventy-five pounds.[e] 40Taking Jesus' body, the two of them wrapped it, with the spices, in strips of linen. This was in accordance with Jewish burial customs. 41At the place where Jesus was crucified, there was a garden, and in the garden a new tomb, in which no one had ever been laid. 42Because it was the Jewish day of Preparation and since the tomb was nearby, they laid Jesus there.

[b]24 Psalm 22:18 [c]36 Exodus 12:46; Num. 9:12; Psalm 34:20
[d]37 Zech. 12:10 [e]39 Greek *a hundred litrai* (about 34 kilograms)

Discovering the Word 1. Three groups were involved in Jesus' death—the soldiers, the Jewish leaders and Pilate. How would you characterize each one's attitude toward Jesus? In what ways do their attitudes toward Jesus parallel those of men and women today? 2. How is Jesus' tender care for Mary evident even while he is dying (vv. 26–27)? 3. What was the significance of Jesus' cry "It is finished" (v. 30; see Jn 17:4)? 4. What evidence does John give that Jesus really died? 5. Why was it so important for John to establish the certainty of Jesus' death?

Applying the Word 1. The disciples are not mentioned at the crucifixion; they were probably not there. When it comes to public identification with Jesus, under what circumstances are you tempted to respond in the same way? 2. What aspect of Jesus' death has made the deepest impression on you, and why?

Responding in Prayer Thank God for providing salvation to you through Christ's death.

24 / *John 20*
The Son Is Up!

THE STORY CIRCULATED for days in the hospital where my brother worked. An orderly was told to take a body to the morgue. Simply out of habit, the orderly felt the man's wrist for a pulse. When he realized his mistake, the orderly quickly dropped the arm, but not before his sensitive fingers told him something his mind struggled to believe. There was a pulse! The doctors were called, and the man revived.

That story may or may not be true. But I know of one account of a man coming back to life that is true. The man lived for years after the event. In fact, he is still alive.

Warming Up to God Imagine being with Joseph of Arimathea and Nicodemus preparing Jesus' body for burial. What thoughts and feelings would have gone through your mind?

Read John 20.

20 Early on the first day of the week,
while it was still dark, Mary Magda-
lene went to the tomb and saw that
the stone had been removed from the entrance.
2So she came running to Simon Peter and the
other disciple, the one Jesus loved, and said,
"They have taken the Lord out of the tomb, and
we don't know where they have put him!"
3So Peter and the other disciple started for the
tomb. 4Both were running, but the other disciple
outran Peter and reached the tomb first. 5He bent
over and looked in at the strips of linen lying
there but did not go in. 6Then Simon Peter, who
was behind him, arrived and went into the tomb.
He saw the strips of linen lying there, 7as well as
the burial cloth that had been around Jesus' head.
The cloth was folded up by itself, separate from
the linen. 8Finally the other disciple, who had
reached the tomb first, also went inside. He saw
and believed. 9(They still did not understand
from Scripture that Jesus had to rise from the
dead.)
10Then the disciples went back to their homes,
11but Mary stood outside the tomb crying. As she
wept, she bent over to look into the tomb 12and
saw two angels in white, seated where Jesus' body
had been, one at the head and the other at the
foot.
13They asked her, "Woman, why are you cry-
ing?"
"They have taken my Lord away," she said,
"and I don't know where they have put him." 14At
this, she turned around and saw Jesus standing
there, but she did not realize that it was Jesus.
15"Woman," he said, "why are you crying?
Who is it you are looking for?"
Thinking he was the gardener, she said, "Sir, if
you have carried him away, tell me where you
have put him, and I will get him."
16Jesus said to her, "Mary."
She turned toward him and cried out in Ara-
maic, "Rabboni!" (which means Teacher).
17Jesus said, "Do not hold on to me, for I have
not yet returned to the Father. Go instead to my
brothers and tell them, 'I am returning to my Fa-
ther and your Father, to my God and your God.' "
18Mary Magdalene went to the disciples with
the news: "I have seen the Lord!" And she told
them that he had said these things to her.
19On the evening of that first day of the week,
when the disciples were together, with the doors
locked for fear of the Jews, Jesus came and stood
among them and said, "Peace be with you!" 20Af-
ter he said this, he showed them his hands and
side. The disciples were overjoyed when they saw
the Lord.
21Again Jesus said, "Peace be with you! As the
Father has sent me, I am sending you." 22And
with that he breathed on them and said, "Receive
the Holy Spirit. 23If you forgive anyone his sins,
they are forgiven; if you do not forgive them, they
are not forgiven."
24Now Thomas (called Didymus), one of the
Twelve, was not with the disciples when Jesus
came. 25So the other disciples told him, "We have
seen the Lord!"
But he said to them, "Unless I see the nail
marks in his hands and put my finger where the
nails were, and put my hand into his side, I will
not believe it."
26A week later his disciples were in the house
again, and Thomas was with them. Though the

doors were locked, Jesus came and stood among
them and said, "Peace be with you!" 27Then he
said to Thomas, "Put your finger here; see my
hands. Reach out your hand and put it into my
side. Stop doubting and believe."
28Thomas said to him, "My Lord and my God!"
29Then Jesus told him, "Because you have seen
me, you have believed; blessed are those who
have not seen and yet have believed."
30Jesus did many other miraculous signs in the
presence of his disciples, which are not recorded
in this book. 31But these are written that you
may[f] believe that Jesus is the Christ, the Son of
God, and that by believing you may have life in
his name.

f31 Some manuscripts *may continue to*

Discovering the Word 1. John records three witnesses to the empty tomb: Mary Magdalene, Peter and "the other disciple" (John himself). What important details do we learn from each one (vv. 1–9)? 2. John also records three appearances of the risen Christ: to Mary, to his disciples and to Thomas. Why do you think Mary doesn't immediately recognize Jesus (vv. 10–15)? 3. After she does recognize him, what impresses you most about their encounter (vv. 16–18)? 4. When Jesus appears to his disciples, what specific gifts and promises does he give them (vv. 19–23)? 5. Finally, Jesus appears to Thomas (vv. 24–29). How does Thomas's attitude—both before and after Jesus appears to him—add credibility to the resurrection?

Applying the Word 1. What do you learn from Jesus' encounter with Thomas about dealing with people who have doubts about Christianity? 2. Who could you help to understand and believe the claims of Christ? 3. John tells us why he has written his Gospel in verses 30–31. Of all the "miraculous signs" John has included, which have been most convincing to you? Why?

Responding in Prayer Praise God for what he has done in Christ.

25 / *John 21*
A Walk with a Resurrected Man

MOST OF US find it easier to forgive than to forget. We may be ready to forgive someone who has hurt us deeply, but we have a hard time trusting that person again. Peter failed Jesus miserably. He promised to give up his life if necessary to protect Jesus, but denied him a few hours later. Peter knew Jesus had forgiven him. But would Jesus still trust him? Could Jesus still use him to bring glory to God? Will Christ still use us after we've failed?

Warming Up to God How do you feel when someone you have hurt refuses to forgive you?

Read John 21.

21 Afterward Jesus appeared again to
his disciples, by the Sea of Tibe-
rias.[g] It happened this way: 2Si-
mon Peter, Thomas (called Didymus), Nathanael
from Cana in Galilee, the sons of Zebedee, and
two other disciples were together. 3"I'm going out
to fish," Simon Peter told them, and they said,
"We'll go with you." So they went out and got
into the boat, but that night they caught noth-
ing.
4Early in the morning, Jesus stood on the
shore, but the disciples did not realize that it was
Jesus.
5He called out to them, "Friends, haven't you
any fish?"
"No," they answered.
6He said, "Throw your net on the right side of
the boat and you will find some." When they did,
they were unable to haul the net in because of the
large number of fish.
7Then the disciple whom Jesus loved said to

g1 That is, Sea of Galilee

Peter, "It is the Lord!" As soon as Simon Peter
heard him say, "It is the Lord," he wrapped his
outer garment around him (for he had taken it
off) and jumped into the water. 8The other disci-
ples followed in the boat, towing the net full of
fish, for they were not far from shore, about a
hundred yards.[h] 9When they landed, they saw a
fire of burning coals there with fish on it, and
some bread.

10Jesus said to them, "Bring some of the fish
you have just caught."

11Simon Peter climbed aboard and dragged the
net ashore. It was full of large fish, 153, but even
with so many the net was not torn. 12Jesus said to
them, "Come and have breakfast." None of the
disciples dared ask him, "Who are you?" They
knew it was the Lord. 13Jesus came, took the
bread and gave it to them, and did the same with
the fish. 14This was now the third time Jesus ap-
peared to his disciples after he was raised from
the dead.

15When they had finished eating, Jesus said to
Simon Peter, "Simon son of John, do you truly
love me more than these?"

"Yes, Lord," he said, "you know that I love
you."

Jesus said, "Feed my lambs."

16Again Jesus said, "Simon son of John, do you
truly love me?"

He answered, "Yes, Lord, you know that I love
you."

Jesus said, "Take care of my sheep."

17The third time he said to him, "Simon son of
John, do you love me?"

Peter was hurt because Jesus asked him the
third time, "Do you love me?" He said, "Lord,
you know all things; you know that I love you."

Jesus said, "Feed my sheep. 18I tell you the
truth, when you were younger you dressed your-
self and went where you wanted; but when you
are old you will stretch out your hands, and
someone else will dress you and lead you where
you do not want to go." 19Jesus said this to indi-
cate the kind of death by which Peter would glo-
rify God. Then he said to him, "Follow me!"

20Peter turned and saw that the disciple whom
Jesus loved was following them. (This was the
one who had leaned back against Jesus at the sup-
per and had said, "Lord, who is going to betray
you?") 21When Peter saw him, he asked, "Lord,
what about him?"

22Jesus answered, "If I want him to remain alive
until I return, what is that to you? You must fol-
low me." 23Because of this, the rumor spread
among the brothers that this disciple would not
die. But Jesus did not say that he would not die;
he only said, "If I want him to remain alive until
I return, what is that to you?"

24This is the disciple who testifies to these
things and who wrote them down. We know that
his testimony is true.

25Jesus did many other things as well. If every
one of them were written down, I suppose that
even the whole world would not have room for
the books that would be written.

[h]8 Greek *about two hundred cubits* (about 90 meters)

Discovering the Word 1. What was Jesus trying to show the disciples by allowing them to catch such a large number of fish (vv. 4–6; see Lk 5:4–11)? 2. When Peter hears that "it is the Lord" (vv. 7–8), he jumps into the water and begins swimming ahead of the boat. What does this reveal about Peter and his relationship with Jesus? 3. What subtle differences do you notice in Jesus' three questions and Peter's responses (vv. 15–17)? 4. Why do you think Jesus chose this particular time to predict the kind of death Peter would die (vv. 18–19)? 5. What does Jesus' rebuke to Peter (v. 22) reveal about the danger of comparing ourselves with other Christians?

Applying the Word 1. What can we learn from this passage about the steps involved in restoring a Christian who has sinned? 2. How does it help to know that you can still serve and glorify God no matter what your past failures have been?

Responding in Prayer Respond to God with your heart and life for what you have learned about Jesus in your study of John.

Acts

The book of Acts should come with a warning label reading, "If you are open to God, this book will call you to new life."

Acts is an extraordinary work. In essence, it is the story of transformed lives—and the difference these lives made in the world.

Just before Acts begins, we see the disciples behind closed doors wallowing in the mire of their fear, self-doubt and personal shame. Apart from their master, they were a pathetic group indeed (Lk 24:11; Jn 20:19). However, by the second chapter of Acts, the same men who abandoned Jesus at Gethsemane have become irrepressible dynamos, preaching with utter conviction—and at great personal risk—"the mighty acts of God."

What changed them? And what impact did they make upon their generation and all subsequent ones? *This* is the story of Acts.

Acts is an important book for us today because it confirms that the power which transformed the disciples' lives is the same power that can transform our lives today! That power is, of course, God himself—coming to us through the Holy Spirit.

There are many benefits to studying Acts:

☐ *Acts serves as a distant mirror.* We will see the dynamics of the earliest church, the nature of their fellowship, the intensity of their prayer life and their out-and-out zeal to declare the saving gospel of Jesus Christ. Through this example, our own situation will be called into question. What does it mean to be the church today—and what are we to be doing?

☐ *Acts emphasizes the primary task of the church—evangelization.* Speaking the gospel is only part of the task. It is the formative process that we see in these earliest communities. In Acts we see the entire process of calling, healing, empowering and sending people forth to love and obey Jesus Christ. Acts will challenge us to a holistic-community spirituality that can renew our churches today.

☐ *Acts calls us to a vital experience with the Holy Spirit.* Jesus promised power to the disciples *after* the Holy Spirit came upon them. And the book of Acts reveals the Holy Spirit as the driving force behind all meaningful ministry in Jesus' name. Where do we look for spiritual power today? Education? Work? Religious heritage? Acts calls us to a Spirit-filled life.

☐ *Acts forges a new sense of identity.* The disciples gradually realized they were no longer Jews (at least from the confessional and ceremonial points of view). They slowly began to understand that they were part of that new community of the Spirit which was prophesied in the Hebrew Scriptures. And they saw the need to call all people—Jews and Gentiles—to repentance and fellowship with this new community—the church. Baptism in the name of the Father, the Son and the Holy Spirit, and the Lord's Supper became the outward signs of the inward grace. The emphasis is on relationships.

The explosive power of this living document will touch you. As you work through these quiet times, may you experience the calling, healing, empowering and sending dynamic of the Holy Spirit.

Outline

1 / *Acts 1*
You Will Be My Witnesses

I REMEMBER TELLING a friend, "If I were dying, what I would most need would be confidence that all I had believed about Jesus was true. I would want you to read Scripture to me, pray with me, and talk to me about Jesus and heaven." This confidence is what I need most not only when I am dying, but also when I am living.

During the days between his resurrection and ascension, Jesus built the confidence of his disciples. He demonstrated and spoke truth about himself. And then he left them with a clearly defined task and the promise of the power to carry out that task. Thus, Luke was able to write with confidence to Theophilus about Jesus.

Warming Up to God Have you had days when you did not feel confident, but fearful? Let God encourage you this day with the power and strength contained in his Word.

Read Acts 1.

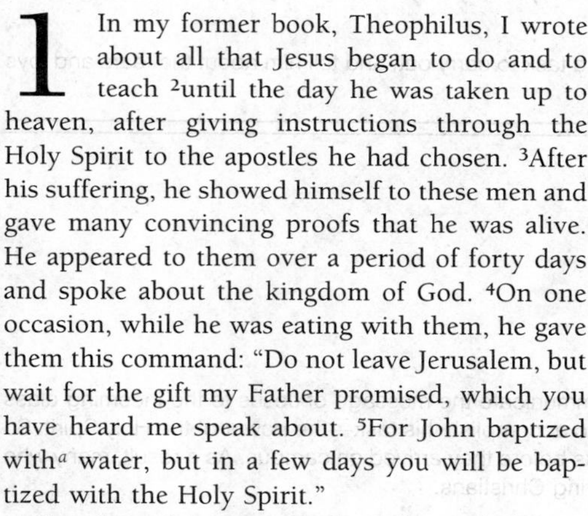

1 In my former book, Theophilus, I wrote
about all that Jesus began to do and to
teach [2]until the day he was taken up to
heaven, after giving instructions through the
Holy Spirit to the apostles he had chosen. [3]After
his suffering, he showed himself to these men and
gave many convincing proofs that he was alive.
He appeared to them over a period of forty days
and spoke about the kingdom of God. [4]On one
occasion, while he was eating with them, he gave
them this command: "Do not leave Jerusalem, but
wait for the gift my Father promised, which you
have heard me speak about. [5]For John baptized
with[a] water, but in a few days you will be bap-
tized with the Holy Spirit."

[6]So when they met together, they asked him,
"Lord, are you at this time going to restore the
kingdom to Israel?"

[7]He said to them: "It is not for you to know the
times or dates the Father has set by his own au-
thority. [8]But you will receive power when the
Holy Spirit comes on you; and you will be my
witnesses in Jerusalem, and in all Judea and Sa-
maria, and to the ends of the earth."

[9]After he said this, he was taken up before their
very eyes, and a cloud hid him from their sight.

[10]They were looking intently up into the sky as
he was going, when suddenly two men dressed in
white stood beside them. [11]"Men of Galilee," they
said, "why do you stand here looking into the
sky? This same Jesus, who has been taken from
you into heaven, will come back in the same way
you have seen him go into heaven."

[12]Then they returned to Jerusalem from the hill
called the Mount of Olives, a Sabbath day's
walk[b] from the city. [13]When they arrived, they
went upstairs to the room where they were stay-
ing. Those present were Peter, John, James and
Andrew; Philip and Thomas, Bartholomew and
Matthew; James son of Alphaeus and Simon the
Zealot, and Judas son of James. [14]They all joined
together constantly in prayer, along with the
women and Mary the mother of Jesus, and with
his brothers.

[15]In those days Peter stood up among the be-
lievers[c] (a group numbering about a hundred
and twenty) [16]and said, "Brothers, the Scripture
had to be fulfilled which the Holy Spirit spoke
long ago through the mouth of David concerning
Judas, who served as guide for those who arrested
Jesus— [17]he was one of our number and shared
in this ministry."

[18](With the reward he got for his wickedness,
Judas bought a field; there he fell headlong, his
body burst open and all his intestines spilled out.
[19]Everyone in Jerusalem heard about this, so they
called that field in their language Akeldama, that
is, Field of Blood.)

[20]"For," said Peter, "it is written in the book of
Psalms,

" 'May his place be deserted;
let there be no one to dwell in it,'[d]

and,

" 'May another take his place of leadership.'[e]

[21]Therefore it is necessary to choose one of the
men who have been with us the whole time the
Lord Jesus went in and out among us, [22]begin-
ning from John's baptism to the time when Jesus

[a]5 Or *in* [b]12 That is, about 3/4 mile (about 1,100 meters)
[c]15 Greek *brothers* [d]20 Psalm 69:25 [e]20 Psalm 109:8

was taken up from us. For one of these must
become a witness with us of his resurrection."
23So they proposed two men: Joseph called Bar-
sabbas (also known as Justus) and Matthias.
24Then they prayed, "Lord, you know everyone's
heart. Show us which of these two you have cho-
sen 25to take over this apostolic ministry, which
Judas left to go where he belongs." 26Then they
cast lots, and the lot fell to Matthias; so he was
added to the eleven apostles.

Discovering the Word 1. What did Luke, the author of Acts, report to Theophilus about Jesus' last days on earth (vv. 1–11)? 2. Put yourself in the shoes of the apostles. How would you feel if you were the first to be given the task described in verse 8? 3. How are we equipped for this task, according to the passage? 4. How did the disciples respond to all that they had seen and heard (vv. 12–26)? 5. Peter goes to Scripture immediately when he speaks. How do these words of David affect their confidence as well as give them direction (v. 20)?

Applying the Word 1. When has your faith in Jesus Christ been encouraged by the words of others? 2. How is your hope and confidence in Jesus affected by what you learn about him in the passage? 3. How are you affected when you pray with other believers—especially as you consider your part in God's mission for the church (v. 14)?

Responding in Prayer Thank God for giving you a task to carry out, and tell him about the fears and joys you feel as his servant.

2 / *Acts 2*
Receiving the Power

AT MY SCHOOL a group of upperclassmen wanted to communicate the message of Jesus to the incoming class of freshmen. They realized that there was only one source to accomplish this task—the power of the Holy Spirit. So they decided to pray for all the new students by name weeks before they arrived on campus. As a result, many who did not know Jesus when they arrived graduated as maturing Christians.

Warming Up to God The Holy Spirit, although at times we do not sense him, is always there to help us. Let him quiet you now and open your heart to what he wants to tell you about himself.

Read Acts 2.

2 When the day of Pentecost came, they
were all together in one place. 2Suddenly
a sound like the blowing of a violent wind
came from heaven and filled the whole house
where they were sitting. 3They saw what seemed
to be tongues of fire that separated and came to
rest on each of them. 4All of them were filled with
the Holy Spirit and began to speak in other
tongues[f] as the Spirit enabled them.
5Now there were staying in Jerusalem God-
fearing Jews from every nation under heaven.
6When they heard this sound, a crowd came to-
gether in bewilderment, because each one heard
them speaking in his own language. 7Utterly
amazed, they asked: "Are not all these men who
are speaking Galileans? 8Then how is it that each
of us hears them in his own native language?
9Parthians, Medes and Elamites; residents of Mes-
opotamia, Judea and Cappadocia, Pontus and
Asia, 10Phrygia and Pamphylia, Egypt and the
parts of Libya near Cyrene; visitors from Rome
11(both Jews and converts to Judaism); Cretans
and Arabs—we hear them declaring the wonders
of God in our own tongues!" 12Amazed and per-
plexed, they asked one another, "What does this
mean?"
13Some, however, made fun of them and said,
"They have had too much wine.[g]"
14Then Peter stood up with the Eleven, raised
his voice and addressed the crowd: "Fellow Jews
and all of you who live in Jerusalem, let me ex-

f4 Or *languages;* also in verse 11 g13 Or *sweet wine*

plain this to you; listen carefully to what I say.
15These men are not drunk, as you suppose. It's
only nine in the morning! 16No, this is what was
spoken by the prophet Joel:

17" 'In the last days, God says,
I will pour out my Spirit on all people.
Your sons and daughters will prophesy,
your young men will see visions,
your old men will dream dreams.
18Even on my servants, both men and women,
I will pour out my Spirit in those days,
and they will prophesy.
19I will show wonders in the heaven above
and signs on the earth below,
blood and fire and billows of smoke.
20The sun will be turned to darkness
and the moon to blood
before the coming of the great and glorious
day of the Lord.
21And everyone who calls
on the name of the Lord will be saved.'[h]

22"Men of Israel, listen to this: Jesus of Naza-
reth was a man accredited by God to you by mira-
cles, wonders and signs, which God did among
you through him, as you yourselves know. 23This
man was handed over to you by God's set purpose
and foreknowledge; and you, with the help of
wicked men,[i] put him to death by nailing him to
the cross. 24But God raised him from the dead,
freeing him from the agony of death, because it
was impossible for death to keep its hold on him.
25David said about him:

" 'I saw the Lord always before me.
Because he is at my right hand,
I will not be shaken.
26Therefore my heart is glad and my tongue
rejoices;
my body also will live in hope,
27because you will not abandon me to the
grave,
nor will you let your Holy One see decay.
28You have made known to me the paths of life;
you will fill me with joy in your
presence.'[j]

29"Brothers, I can tell you confidently that the
patriarch David died and was buried, and his
tomb is here to this day. 30But he was a prophet
and knew that God had promised him on oath
that he would place one of his descendants on his
throne. 31Seeing what was ahead, he spoke of the
resurrection of the Christ,[k] that he was not
abandoned to the grave, nor did his body see de-
cay. 32God has raised this Jesus to life, and we are
all witnesses of the fact. 33Exalted to the right
hand of God, he has received from the Father the
promised Holy Spirit and has poured out what
you now see and hear. 34For David did not ascend
to heaven, and yet he said,

" 'The Lord said to my Lord:
"Sit at my right hand
35until I make your enemies
a footstool for your feet." '[l]

36"Therefore let all Israel be assured of this:
God has made this Jesus, whom you crucified,
both Lord and Christ."
37When the people heard this, they were cut to
the heart and said to Peter and the other apostles,
"Brothers, what shall we do?"
38Peter replied, "Repent and be baptized, every
one of you, in the name of Jesus Christ for the
forgiveness of your sins. And you will receive the
gift of the Holy Spirit. 39The promise is for you
and your children and for all who are far off—for
all whom the Lord our God will call."
40With many other words he warned them; and
he pleaded with them, "Save yourselves from this
corrupt generation." 41Those who accepted his
message were baptized, and about three thousand
were added to their number that day.
42They devoted themselves to the apostles'
teaching and to the fellowship, to the breaking of
bread and to prayer. 43Everyone was filled with
awe, and many wonders and miraculous signs
were done by the apostles. 44All the believers
were together and had everything in common.
45Selling their possessions and goods, they gave
to anyone as he had need. 46Every day they con-
tinued to meet together in the temple courts.
They broke bread in their homes and ate together
with glad and sincere hearts, 47praising God and
enjoying the favor of all the people. And the Lord
added to their number daily those who were be-
ing saved.

[h] 21 Joel 2:28-32 [i] 23 Or *of those not having the law* (that is, Gentiles) [j] 28 Psalm 16:8-11 [k] 31 Or *Messiah.* "The Christ" (Greek) and "the Messiah" (Hebrew) both mean "the Anointed One"; also in verse 36. [l] 35 Psalm 110:1

Discovering the Word 1. How do the Jews respond to the power of the Spirit which they witness (vv. 5–12)? 2. Here we see Peter as a dynamic leader and preacher. It is the power of the Holy Spirit that has changed this man who was once a coward who denied Jesus three times. Scripture, again, is the foundation of Peter's proclamation of truth. What message does the Old Testament book of Joel have for the bewildered crowd (vv. 17–21)? 3. What is there in Peter's sermon that would reassure Theophilus about his faith and help him "know the certainty of the things" that he'd been taught? 4. What does Peter have to offer to those who are responsive to his message (vv. 37–39)? 5. Describe the fellowship of the believers in this young church (vv. 42–47).

Applying the Word 1. Imagine you were there on the day of Pentecost. What do you think it would have been like for you as one of the crowd looking on? 2. How has your life been affected by the gift of the Holy Spirit? 3. How does the life and purpose of your church or Christian fellowship group compare to that of this group?

Responding in Prayer Ask God to make the power of the Holy Spirit come alive in your life, and pray that God will use you through that power.

3 / *Acts 3*
Healing Power

I MET ANNE at the hospital where I was working one evening. She was in an isolation room. She had hepatitis from using contaminated needles to take drugs. In time our relationship grew, and Anne came to know Jesus. She recovered from hepatitis and went off drugs. She worked at healing her relationship with her parents. Later, she married and established a Christian home. Anne's story makes it clear that the power of the Holy Spirit is demonstrated not only through physical healing, but also in the "complete healing" that includes every aspect of our lives.

Warming Up to God Recall a time when you felt broken and in need of healing. Thank God for the ways that he has transformed and healed you since then.

Read Acts 3.

3 One day Peter and John were going up to
the temple at the time of prayer—at three
in the afternoon. 2Now a man crippled
from birth was being carried to the temple gate
called Beautiful, where he was put every day to
beg from those going into the temple courts.
3When he saw Peter and John about to enter, he
asked them for money. 4Peter looked straight at
him, as did John. Then Peter said, "Look at us!"
5So the man gave them his attention, expecting to
get something from them.
6Then Peter said, "Silver or gold I do not have,
but what I have I give you. In the name of Jesus
Christ of Nazareth, walk." 7Taking him by the
right hand, he helped him up, and instantly the
man's feet and ankles became strong. 8He jumped
to his feet and began to walk. Then he went with
them into the temple courts, walking and jumping, and praising God. 9When all the people saw
him walking and praising God, 10they recognized
him as the same man who used to sit begging at
the temple gate called Beautiful, and they were
filled with wonder and amazement at what had
happened to him.
11While the beggar held on to Peter and John,
all the people were astonished and came running
to them in the place called Solomon's Colonnade.
12When Peter saw this, he said to them: "Men of
Israel, why does this surprise you? Why do you
stare at us as if by our own power or godliness we
had made this man walk? 13The God of Abraham,
Isaac and Jacob, the God of our fathers, has glorified his servant Jesus. You handed him over to be
killed, and you disowned him before Pilate,
though he had decided to let him go. 14You disowned the Holy and Righteous One and asked
that a murderer be released to you. 15You killed
the author of life, but God raised him from the
dead. We are witnesses of this. 16By faith in the
name of Jesus, this man whom you see and know
was made strong. It is Jesus' name and the faith

that comes through him that has given this com-
plete healing to him, as you can all see.
17"Now, brothers, I know that you acted in ig-
norance, as did your leaders. 18But this is how
God fulfilled what he had foretold through all the
prophets, saying that his Christ[m] would suffer.
19Repent, then, and turn to God, so that your sins
may be wiped out, that times of refreshing may
come from the Lord, 20and that he may send the
Christ, who has been appointed for you—even
Jesus. 21He must remain in heaven until the time
comes for God to restore everything, as he prom-
ised long ago through his holy prophets. 22For
Moses said, 'The Lord your God will raise up for
you a prophet like me from among your own peo-
ple; you must listen to everything he tells you.
23Anyone who does not listen to him will be com-
pletely cut off from among his people.'[n]
24"Indeed, all the prophets from Samuel on, as
many as have spoken, have foretold these days.
25And you are heirs of the prophets and of the
covenant God made with your fathers. He said to
Abraham, 'Through your offspring all peoples on
earth will be blessed.'[o] 26When God raised up his
servant, he sent him first to you to bless you by
turning each of you from your wicked ways."

[m]18 Or *Messiah*; also in verse 20 [n]23 Deut. 18:15,18,19
[o]25 Gen. 22:18; 26:4

Discovering the Word 1. How does the response of the people to the miracle in verses 6–8 contrast with the beggar's response (vv. 8 and 11–12)? 2. When Peter noticed how the crowd reacted, he saw his opportunity and talked to them about Jesus. According to Peter's message, what had God done to Jesus (vv. 13–15)? What had the Jews done to him? 3. How is the authority of Jesus demonstrated in this miracle (v. 16)? 4. How did Peter explain that all that had happened to Jesus was a part of God's plan (vv. 17–26)?

Applying the Word 1. What healing do you need in your life? 2. How do you respond when you have opportunities like Peter's to talk about Jesus? 3. The "completely" healed man was a powerful testimony to the power of God and the truth of Peter's words. How have you seen the power of God demonstrated in your life and in the lives of others?

Responding in Prayer Thank God for working so powerfully to change your life, and ask him to give you the opportunity to talk about Jesus to one person this week.

4 / *Acts 4:1–31*
Called into Question

A DISABLED PERSON becomes abled! And a one-time burden to society, a beggar, becomes a contributing citizen! How do the religious leaders respond to these miraculous events? Instead of expressing gratitude, they become extremely upset. The two men responsible for the healing are arrested.

Warming Up to God Today, in this new day that God has created, your Savior wants to come to you. With calmness, let the distractions around you—the voices and restless thoughts—slip away. As the spirit of God comes to dwell with you, allow yourself to enjoy his presence in quietness and gratitude.

Read Acts 4:1–31.

4 The priests and the captain of the temple
guard and the Sadducees came up to Peter
and John while they were speaking to the
people. 2They were greatly disturbed because the
apostles were teaching the people and proclaim-
ing in Jesus the resurrection of the dead. 3They
seized Peter and John, and because it was eve-
ning, they put them in jail until the next day.
4But many who heard the message believed,
and the number of men grew to about five thou-
sand.
5The next day the rulers, elders and teachers of
the law met in Jerusalem. 6Annas the high priest
was there, and so were Caiaphas, John, Alexander
and the other men of the high priest's family.
7They had Peter and John brought before them

and began to question them: "By what power or
what name did you do this?"
8Then Peter, filled with the Holy Spirit, said to
them: "Rulers and elders of the people! 9If we are
being called to account today for an act of kind-
ness shown to a cripple and are asked how he was
healed, 10then know this, you and all the people
of Israel: It is by the name of Jesus Christ of Naza-
reth, whom you crucified but whom God raised
from the dead, that this man stands before you
healed. 11He is

" 'the stone you builders rejected,
which has become the capstone.[p,q]

12Salvation is found in no one else, for there is no
other name under heaven given to men by which
we must be saved."
13When they saw the courage of Peter and John
and realized that they were unschooled, ordinary
men, they were astonished and they took note
that these men had been with Jesus. 14But since
they could see the man who had been healed
standing there with them, there was nothing they
could say. 15So they ordered them to withdraw
from the Sanhedrin and then conferred together.
16"What are we going to do with these men?"
they asked. "Everybody living in Jerusalem
knows they have done an outstanding miracle,
and we cannot deny it. 17But to stop this thing
from spreading any further among the people, we
must warn these men to speak no longer to any-
one in this name."
18Then they called them in again and com-
manded them not to speak or teach at all in the
name of Jesus. 19But Peter and John replied,
"Judge for yourselves whether it is right in God's
sight to obey you rather than God. 20For we can-
not help speaking about what we have seen and
heard."
21After further threats they let them go. They
could not decide how to punish them, because all
the people were praising God for what had hap-
pened. 22For the man who was miraculously
healed was over forty years old.
23On their release, Peter and John went back to
their own people and reported all that the chief
priests and elders had said to them. 24When they
heard this, they raised their voices together in
prayer to God. "Sovereign Lord," they said, "you
made the heaven and the earth and the sea, and
everything in them. 25You spoke by the Holy
Spirit through the mouth of your servant, our fa-
ther David:

" 'Why do the nations rage
and the peoples plot in vain?
26The kings of the earth take their stand
and the rulers gather together
against the Lord
and against his Anointed One.'[r,s]

27Indeed Herod and Pontius Pilate met together
with the Gentiles and the people[t] of Israel in
this city to conspire against your holy servant
Jesus, whom you anointed. 28They did what your
power and will had decided beforehand should
happen. 29Now, Lord, consider their threats and
enable your servants to speak your word with
great boldness. 30Stretch out your hand to heal
and perform miraculous signs and wonders
through the name of your holy servant Jesus."
31After they prayed, the place where they were
meeting was shaken. And they were all filled with
the Holy Spirit and spoke the word of God boldly.

p11 Or *cornerstone* q11 Psalm 118:22 r26 That is, Christ or Messiah s26 Psalm 2:1,2 t27 The Greek is plural.

Discovering the Word 1. What has upset the religious leaders (vv. 1–2)? 2. What action did they take (vv. 3–7)? 3. Just a few weeks have passed since Annas and Caiaphas had been involved in the condemnation of Jesus. In his response to their question "By what power or what name did you do this?" Peter is forcing them to encounter Jesus again. What does Peter say about him (vv. 10–12)? 4. In verses 13–22 what made it so difficult for the opposing religious leaders to bring this unacceptable behavior to a halt? 5. What was the reaction of the believers to John and Peter's account (vv. 24–30)? 6. What does their prayer tell you about their faith in the character, power and faithfulness of God (vv. 24–30)?

Applying the Word 1. When has your faith been challenged by others? 2. Imagine that you had been in a group of believers John and Peter returned to and told of what had happened. What would have been your reaction? 3. "After they prayed, the place where they were meeting was shaken. And they were all filled with the Holy Spirit and spoke the word of God boldly." In what ways do you need the power of the Holy Spirit to face the world today?

Responding in Prayer Ask God to fill you with the Spirit as you face constant challenge to the power for and the task of experiencing and communicating the gospel.

5 / *Acts 4:32—5:16*
Oneness of Heart

IT WAS WITH a heavy feeling of dread and pain that I read name after name engraved on the Vietnam Memorial in Washington, D.C. Then I saw that next to the memorial was a statue of three men—a black, a Hispanic and a white soldier. They were standing very close together. The tour guide, a former soldier who fought in Nam, explained the significance of the statue. He said that there were more minorities fighting for the U.S. than ever before. And the reason that they were standing so close together was that in Vietnam they learned, like never before, how very much they needed each other. In this study we will see that when the battle is spiritual, our need for each other is even more critical.

Warming Up to God Who has God given you that meets a need in your life? Thank God for giving you such a valuable and loving gift.

Read Acts 4:32—5:16.

32All the believers were one in heart and mind.
No one claimed that any of his possessions was
his own, but they shared everything they had.
33With great power the apostles continued to tes-
tify to the resurrection of the Lord Jesus, and
much grace was upon them all. 34There were no
needy persons among them. For from time to
time those who owned lands or houses sold them,
brought the money from the sales 35and put it at
the apostles' feet, and it was distributed to anyone
as he had need.

36Joseph, a Levite from Cyprus, whom the
apostles called Barnabas (which means Son of En-
couragement), 37sold a field he owned and
brought the money and put it at the apostles' feet.

5 Now a man named Ananias, together with
his wife Sapphira, also sold a piece of
property. 2With his wife's full knowledge
he kept back part of the money for himself, but
brought the rest and put it at the apostles' feet.

3Then Peter said, "Ananias, how is it that Satan
has so filled your heart that you have lied to the
Holy Spirit and have kept for yourself some of the
money you received for the land? 4Didn't it be-
long to you before it was sold? And after it was
sold, wasn't the money at your disposal? What
made you think of doing such a thing? You have
not lied to men but to God."

5When Ananias heard this, he fell down and
died. And great fear seized all who heard what
had happened. 6Then the young men came for-
ward, wrapped up his body, and carried him out
and buried him.

7About three hours later his wife came in, not
knowing what had happened. 8Peter asked her,
"Tell me, is this the price you and Ananias got for
the land?"

"Yes," she said, "that is the price."

9Peter said to her, "How could you agree to test
the Spirit of the Lord? Look! The feet of the men
who buried your husband are at the door, and
they will carry you out also."

10At that moment she fell down at his feet and
died. Then the young men came in and, finding
her dead, carried her out and buried her beside
her husband. 11Great fear seized the whole
church and all who heard about these events.

12The apostles performed many miraculous
signs and wonders among the people. And all the
believers used to meet together in Solomon's Col-
onnade. 13No one else dared join them, even
though they were highly regarded by the people.
14Nevertheless, more and more men and women
believed in the Lord and were added to their
number. 15As a result, people brought the sick
into the streets and laid them on beds and mats so
that at least Peter's shadow might fall on some of
them as he passed by. 16Crowds gathered also
from the towns around Jerusalem, bringing their
sick and those tormented by evil[u] spirits, and all
of them were healed.

[u]16 Greek *unclean*

Discovering the Word 1. How is oneness of heart and mind demonstrated in 4:32–37? 2. What have Ananias and Sapphira done that is not consistent with Christian community (5:1–2)? 3. Pretend you are watching the interaction between Peter and Ananias and Sapphira (5:3–9). How would you report this incident? 4. Verse 11 states that "great fear seized the whole church and all who heard about these events." How do you think the church was affected by this fear? 5. What are the tangible evidences of the power of the Holy Spirit in this community in 5:12–16?

Applying the Word 1. How does this story demonstrate the high value that God places on truth and unity within the body of Christ? 2. In what ways do we lie to each other today within our Christian communities? 3. How could you begin to help others in your church or fellowship understand what Christian community is about?

Responding in Prayer Ask God to uphold truth in his church and to help you speak the truth before others.

6 / *Acts 5:17—6:7*
Persecution and Expansion

IN 1956 TRAGIC news spread across the world. Five American men—sons, husbands and fathers—were massacred by a tribe of Auca Indians. Their purpose was to take the good news of Jesus Christ to the Aucas. The opposition to this endeavor cost them their lives.

That agonizing loss, which seemed at the time to be such a waste, has turned into great fruit for the kingdom of God. Over the years that same tribe of Indians has been transformed by the power of God. The message of Jesus was taken to them by the loved ones of those five young men. Another visible fruit of this great loss is the many who have gone into the world with the gospel, having been inspired by the lives and deaths of these missionaries. The church of Jesus Christ continues to expand today in spite of great persecution, even as it did in the day of the apostles.

Warming Up to God Although we know that God is in complete control of the universe, we often forget that he also has specific plans for our individual lives. Thank him for being sovereign everywhere, including the secrecy of your own heart.

Read Acts 5:17—6:7.

17 Then the high priest and all his associates,
who were members of the party of the Sadducees,
were filled with jealousy. 18 They arrested the
apostles and put them in the public jail. 19 But
during the night an angel of the Lord opened the
doors of the jail and brought them out. 20 "Go,
stand in the temple courts," he said, "and tell the
people the full message of this new life."
21 At daybreak they entered the temple courts,
as they had been told, and began to teach the
people.
When the high priest and his associates arrived, they called together the Sanhedrin—the
full assembly of the elders of Israel—and sent to
the jail for the apostles. 22 But on arriving at the
jail, the officers did not find them there. So they
went back and reported, 23 "We found the jail securely locked, with the guards standing at the
doors; but when we opened them, we found no
one inside." 24 On hearing this report, the captain
of the temple guard and the chief priests were
puzzled, wondering what would come of this.
25 Then someone came and said, "Look! The
men you put in jail are standing in the temple
courts teaching the people." 26 At that, the captain
went with his officers and brought the apostles.
They did not use force, because they feared that
the people would stone them.
27 Having brought the apostles, they made them
appear before the Sanhedrin to be questioned by
the high priest. 28 "We gave you strict orders not
to teach in this name," he said. "Yet you have
filled Jerusalem with your teaching and are determined to make us guilty of this man's blood."
29 Peter and the other apostles replied: "We
must obey God rather than men! 30 The God of

our fathers raised Jesus from the dead—whom
you had killed by hanging him on a tree. 31God
exalted him to his own right hand as Prince and
Savior that he might give repentance and forgive-
ness of sins to Israel. 32We are witnesses of these
things, and so is the Holy Spirit, whom God has
given to those who obey him."

33When they heard this, they were furious and
wanted to put them to death. 34But a Pharisee
named Gamaliel, a teacher of the law, who was
honored by all the people, stood up in the Sanhe-
drin and ordered that the men be put outside for
a little while. 35Then he addressed them: "Men of
Israel, consider carefully what you intend to do to
these men. 36Some time ago Theudas appeared,
claiming to be somebody, and about four hun-
dred men rallied to him. He was killed, all his
followers were dispersed, and it all came to noth-
ing. 37After him, Judas the Galilean appeared in
the days of the census and led a band of people in
revolt. He too was killed, and all his followers
were scattered. 38Therefore, in the present case I
advise you: Leave these men alone! Let them go!
For if their purpose or activity is of human origin,
it will fail. 39But if it is from God, you will not be
able to stop these men; you will only find your-
selves fighting against God."

40His speech persuaded them. They called the
apostles in and had them flogged. Then they or-
dered them not to speak in the name of Jesus, and
let them go.

41The apostles left the Sanhedrin, rejoicing be-
cause they had been counted worthy of suffering
disgrace for the Name. 42Day after day, in the
temple courts and from house to house, they
never stopped teaching and proclaiming the good
news that Jesus is the Christ.[v]

6 In those days when the number of disci-
ples was increasing, the Grecian Jews
among them complained against the He-
braic Jews because their widows were being over-
looked in the daily distribution of food. 2So the
Twelve gathered all the disciples together and
said, "It would not be right for us to neglect the
ministry of the word of God in order to wait on
tables. 3Brothers, choose seven men from among
you who are known to be full of the Spirit and
wisdom. We will turn this responsibility over to
them 4and will give our attention to prayer and
the ministry of the word."

5This proposal pleased the whole group. They
chose Stephen, a man full of faith and of the Holy
Spirit; also Philip, Procorus, Nicanor, Timon, Par-
menas, and Nicolas from Antioch, a convert to
Judaism. 6They presented these men to the apos-
tles, who prayed and laid their hands on them.

7So the word of God spread. The number of
disciples in Jerusalem increased rapidly, and a
large number of priests became obedient to the
faith.

v42 Or *Messiah*

Discovering the Word 1. List the expressions and causes of emotion throughout verses 5:17–42. 2. Describe the apostles' response, motivation and source of strength throughout this whole episode. 3. What was Gamaliel's message to the religious leaders (5:34–39)? 4. How was his influence in saving the apostles' lives an example of that truth which he spoke? 5. As the number of disciples increased, what practical needs began to present themselves (6:1–6)? 6. How did the Twelve respond to those needs (6:2–6)?

Applying the Word 1. When have you encountered internal and/or external opposition when you have attempted to proclaim the message of Jesus? 2. Is it more difficult for you to deal with internal or external opposition? Why? 3. As you observe the work of the Holy Spirit throughout this passage, what actions do you think you and/or your church should take to ensure his ministry among you?

Responding in Prayer Tell God about the difficulties and struggles you have been facing as a believer in him. Ask him to give you strength and to remind you that his ways are higher than your own.

7 / *Acts 6:8—7:60*
Stephen, Full of Spirit and Wisdom

I AM GLAD for those people in my life who make me long to know God better. God's character in them makes me hunger and thirst for him. That is what happens to me when I am exposed to Stephen. I read about him and I want to know God.

Stephen is described as "full of the Holy Spirit and wisdom, full of God's grace and power." He was a gift to the early church but could not be tolerated by her enemies.

Warming Up to God Think of a person that makes you want to know God better. Reflect on the qualities you see in him or her.

Read Acts 6:8—7:60.

8 Now Stephen, a man full of God's grace and
power, did great wonders and miraculous signs
among the people. 9 Opposition arose, however,
from members of the Synagogue of the Freedmen
(as it was called)—Jews of Cyrene and Alexan-
dria as well as the provinces of Cilicia and Asia.
These men began to argue with Stephen, 10 but
they could not stand up against his wisdom or the
Spirit by whom he spoke.
11 Then they secretly persuaded some men to
say, "We have heard Stephen speak words of blas-
phemy against Moses and against God."
12 So they stirred up the people and the elders
and the teachers of the law. They seized Stephen
and brought him before the Sanhedrin. 13 They
produced false witnesses, who testified, "This fel-
low never stops speaking against this holy place
and against the law. 14 For we have heard him say
that this Jesus of Nazareth will destroy this place
and change the customs Moses handed down
to us."
15 All who were sitting in the Sanhedrin looked
intently at Stephen, and they saw that his face was
like the face of an angel.

7 Then the high priest asked him, "Are
these charges true?"
2 To this he replied: "Brothers and fathers,
listen to me! The God of glory appeared to our
father Abraham while he was still in Mesopota-
mia, before he lived in Haran. 3 'Leave your coun-
try and your people,' God said, 'and go to the land
I will show you.'[w]
4 "So he left the land of the Chaldeans and set-
tled in Haran. After the death of his father, God
sent him to this land where you are now living.
5 He gave him no inheritance here, not even a foot
of ground. But God promised him that he and his
descendants after him would possess the land,
even though at that time Abraham had no child.
6 God spoke to him in this way: 'Your descendants
will be strangers in a country not their own, and
they will be enslaved and mistreated four hun-
dred years. 7 But I will punish the nation they
serve as slaves,' God said, 'and afterward they will
come out of that country and worship me in this
place.'[x] 8 Then he gave Abraham the covenant of
circumcision. And Abraham became the father of
Isaac and circumcised him eight days after his
birth. Later Isaac became the father of Jacob, and
Jacob became the father of the twelve patriarchs.
9 "Because the patriarchs were jealous of Jo-
seph, they sold him as a slave into Egypt. But God
was with him 10 and rescued him from all his trou-
bles. He gave Joseph wisdom and enabled him to
gain the goodwill of Pharaoh king of Egypt; so he
made him ruler over Egypt and all his palace.
11 "Then a famine struck all Egypt and Canaan,
bringing great suffering, and our fathers could
not find food. 12 When Jacob heard that there was
grain in Egypt, he sent our fathers on their first
visit. 13 On their second visit, Joseph told his
brothers who he was, and Pharaoh learned about
Joseph's family. 14 After this, Joseph sent for his
father Jacob and his whole family, seventy-five in
all. 15 Then Jacob went down to Egypt, where he
and our fathers died. 16 Their bodies were brought
back to Shechem and placed in the tomb that
Abraham had bought from the sons of Hamor at
Shechem for a certain sum of money.
17 "As the time drew near for God to fulfill his
promise to Abraham, the number of our people in
Egypt greatly increased. 18 Then another king,
who knew nothing about Joseph, became ruler of

[w] 3 Gen. 12:1 [x] 7 Gen. 15:13,14

Egypt. 19He dealt treacherously with our people
and oppressed our forefathers by forcing them to
throw out their newborn babies so that they
would die.

20"At that time Moses was born, and he was no
ordinary child.[y] For three months he was cared
for in his father's house. 21When he was placed
outside, Pharaoh's daughter took him and
brought him up as her own son. 22Moses was ed-
ucated in all the wisdom of the Egyptians and was
powerful in speech and action.

23"When Moses was forty years old, he decided
to visit his fellow Israelites. 24He saw one of them
being mistreated by an Egyptian, so he went to
his defense and avenged him by killing the Egyp-
tian. 25Moses thought that his own people would
realize that God was using him to rescue them,
but they did not. 26The next day Moses came
upon two Israelites who were fighting. He tried to
reconcile them by saying, 'Men, you are brothers;
why do you want to hurt each other?'

27"But the man who was mistreating the other
pushed Moses aside and said, 'Who made you
ruler and judge over us? 28Do you want to kill me
as you killed the Egyptian yesterday?'[z] 29When
Moses heard this, he fled to Midian, where he
settled as a foreigner and had two sons.

30"After forty years had passed, an angel ap-
peared to Moses in the flames of a burning bush
in the desert near Mount Sinai. 31When he saw
this, he was amazed at the sight. As he went over
to look more closely, he heard the Lord's voice:
32'I am the God of your fathers, the God of Abra-
ham, Isaac and Jacob.'[a] Moses trembled with fear
and did not dare to look.

33"Then the Lord said to him, 'Take off your
sandals; the place where you are standing is holy
ground. 34I have indeed seen the oppression of
my people in Egypt. I have heard their groaning
and have come down to set them free. Now come,
I will send you back to Egypt.'[b]

35"This is the same Moses whom they had re-
jected with the words, 'Who made you ruler and
judge?' He was sent to be their ruler and deliverer
by God himself, through the angel who appeared
to him in the bush. 36He led them out of Egypt
and did wonders and miraculous signs in Egypt,
at the Red Sea[c] and for forty years in the desert.

37"This is that Moses who told the Israelites,
'God will send you a prophet like me from your
own people.'[d] 38He was in the assembly in the
desert, with the angel who spoke to him on
Mount Sinai, and with our fathers; and he re-
ceived living words to pass on to us.

39"But our fathers refused to obey him. Instead,
they rejected him and in their hearts turned back
to Egypt. 40They told Aaron, 'Make us gods who
will go before us. As for this fellow Moses who
led us out of Egypt—we don't know what has
happened to him!'[e] 41That was the time they
made an idol in the form of a calf. They brought
sacrifices to it and held a celebration in honor of
what their hands had made. 42But God turned
away and gave them over to the worship of the
heavenly bodies. This agrees with what is written
in the book of the prophets:

" 'Did you bring me sacrifices and offerings
forty years in the desert, O house of Israel?
43You have lifted up the shrine of Molech
and the star of your god Rephan,
the idols you made to worship.
Therefore I will send you into exile'[f] beyond
Babylon.

44"Our forefathers had the tabernacle of the
Testimony with them in the desert. It had been
made as God directed Moses, according to the
pattern he had seen. 45Having received the taber-
nacle, our fathers under Joshua brought it with
them when they took the land from the nations
God drove out before them. It remained in the
land until the time of David, 46who enjoyed God's
favor and asked that he might provide a dwelling
place for the God of Jacob.[g] 47But it was Solo-
mon who built the house for him.

48"However, the Most High does not live in
houses made by men. As the prophet says:

49" 'Heaven is my throne,
and the earth is my footstool.
What kind of house will you build for me?
says the Lord.
Or where will my resting place be?
50Has not my hand made all these things?'[h]

51"You stiff-necked people, with uncircum-
cised hearts and ears! You are just like your fa-
thers: You always resist the Holy Spirit! 52Was
there ever a prophet your fathers did not perse-
cute? They even killed those who predicted the
coming of the Righteous One. And now you have
betrayed and murdered him— 53you who have

[y]20 Or *was fair in the sight of God* [z]28 Exodus 2:14
[a]32 Exodus 3:6 [b]34 Exodus 3:5,7,8,10 [c]36 That is, Sea of Reeds
[d]37 Deut. 18:15 [e]40 Exodus 32:1 [f]43 Amos 5:25-27
[g]46 Some early manuscripts *the house of Jacob* [h]50 Isaiah 66:1,2

received the law that was put into effect through
angels but have not obeyed it."
54When they heard this, they were furious and
gnashed their teeth at him. 55But Stephen, full of
the Holy Spirit, looked up to heaven and saw the
glory of God, and Jesus standing at the right hand
of God. 56"Look," he said, "I see heaven open and
the Son of Man standing at the right hand of
God."
57At this they covered their ears and, yelling at
the top of their voices, they all rushed at
him, 58dragged him out of the city and began
to stone him. Meanwhile, the witnesses laid
their clothes at the feet of a young man named
Saul.
59While they were stoning him, Stephen
prayed, "Lord Jesus, receive my spirit." 60Then he
fell on his knees and cried out, "Lord, do not hold
this sin against them." When he had said this, he
fell asleep.

Discovering the Word 1. What do you learn about Stephen throughout this passage? 2. What do the accusations against Stephen tell us about why the Jewish religious leaders were so upset (6:13–14)? 3. Sometimes the speech in chapter 7 is called "Stephen's defense," although it is actually a defense of pure Christianity as God's appointed way to worship. What are the main points of this defense? 4. What did God tell Abraham would happen to his descendants, the Hebrews (7:1–7)? 5. What direct application does Stephen make concerning the religious leaders from 7:39–43 (see 7:51–53)?

Applying the Word 1. God told Abraham what would happen to the Hebrews years before it all happened, even before he had a son. How are you affected when you see all that unfolds in history? 2. Throughout this whole passage, we see in Stephen the evidence of being full of the Spirit and wisdom. What are the evidences today of being full of the Spirit and wisdom? 3. In what aspect of your life would you like to reflect more of the Spirit and wisdom?

Responding in Prayer Ask God to fill you with the Spirit and with wisdom.

8 / *Acts 8*
The Power of Suffering

STEPHEN IS DEAD. When he is buried, the people mourn deeply. The church has experienced the tragedy of her first martyr. In this study we meet Philip and Saul. Saul approves of Stephen's death. He is putting all his energy into destroying the rest of Jesus' followers. In contrast, Philip is one of the seven, full of the Spirit and wisdom. His energy goes into the proclamation of the truth about Jesus. People respond. And so both the persecution and the expansion of the church continue.

Warming Up to God Has there been a time recently that you were confused about God's intentions behind the events that he placed in your life? Ask him to give you his understanding and peace.

Read Acts 8.

8 And Saul was there, giving approval to his
death.

On that day a great persecution broke out
against the church at Jerusalem, and all except
the apostles were scattered throughout Judea and
Samaria. 2Godly men buried Stephen and
mourned deeply for him. 3But Saul began to de-
stroy the church. Going from house to house, he
dragged off men and women and put them in
prison.
4Those who had been scattered preached the
word wherever they went. 5Philip went down to a
city in Samaria and proclaimed the Christ[i] there.
6When the crowds heard Philip and saw the mi-
raculous signs he did, they all paid close attention
to what he said. 7With shrieks, evil[j] spirits came

[i]5 Or *Messiah* [j]7 Greek *unclean*

out of many, and many paralytics and cripples
were healed. 8So there was great joy in that city.
9Now for some time a man named Simon had
practiced sorcery in the city and amazed all the
people of Samaria. He boasted that he was some-
one great, 10and all the people, both high and
low, gave him their attention and exclaimed,
"This man is the divine power known as the
Great Power." 11They followed him because he
had amazed them for a long time with his magic.
12But when they believed Philip as he preached
the good news of the kingdom of God and the
name of Jesus Christ, they were baptized, both
men and women. 13Simon himself believed and
was baptized. And he followed Philip everywhere,
astonished by the great signs and miracles he saw.
14When the apostles in Jerusalem heard that
Samaria had accepted the word of God, they sent
Peter and John to them. 15When they arrived,
they prayed for them that they might receive the
Holy Spirit, 16because the Holy Spirit had not yet
come upon any of them; they had simply been
baptized into[k] the name of the Lord Jesus.
17Then Peter and John placed their hands on
them, and they received the Holy Spirit.
18When Simon saw that the Spirit was given at
the laying on of the apostles' hands, he offered
them money 19and said, "Give me also this ability
so that everyone on whom I lay my hands may
receive the Holy Spirit."
20Peter answered: "May your money perish
with you, because you thought you could buy the
gift of God with money! 21You have no part or
share in this ministry, because your heart is not
right before God. 22Repent of this wickedness and
pray to the Lord. Perhaps he will forgive you for
having such a thought in your heart. 23For I see
that you are full of bitterness and captive to sin."
24Then Simon answered, "Pray to the Lord for
me so that nothing you have said may happen
to me."
25When they had testified and proclaimed the
word of the Lord, Peter and John returned to Je-
rusalem, preaching the gospel in many Samaritan
villages.
26Now an angel of the Lord said to Philip, "Go
south to the road—the desert road—that goes
down from Jerusalem to Gaza." 27So he started
out, and on his way he met an Ethiopian[l] eu-
nuch, an important official in charge of all the
treasury of Candace, queen of the Ethiopians.
This man had gone to Jerusalem to worship,
28and on his way home was sitting in his chariot
reading the book of Isaiah the prophet. 29The
Spirit told Philip, "Go to that chariot and stay
near it."
30Then Philip ran up to the chariot and heard
the man reading Isaiah the prophet. "Do you un-
derstand what you are reading?" Philip asked.
31"How can I," he said, "unless someone ex-
plains it to me?" So he invited Philip to come up
and sit with him.
32The eunuch was reading this passage of
Scripture:

"He was led like a sheep to the slaughter,
and as a lamb before the shearer is silent,
so he did not open his mouth.
33In his humiliation he was deprived of justice.
Who can speak of his descendants?
For his life was taken from the earth."[m]

34The eunuch asked Philip, "Tell me, please,
who is the prophet talking about, himself or
someone else?" 35Then Philip began with that
very passage of Scripture and told him the good
news about Jesus.
36As they traveled along the road, they came to
some water and the eunuch said, "Look, here is
water. Why shouldn't I be baptized?"[n] 38And he
gave orders to stop the chariot. Then both Philip
and the eunuch went down into the water and
Philip baptized him. 39When they came up out of
the water, the Spirit of the Lord suddenly took
Philip away, and the eunuch did not see him
again, but went on his way rejoicing. 40Philip,
however, appeared at Azotus and traveled about,
preaching the gospel in all the towns until he
reached Caesarea.

[k]16 Or *in* [l]27 That is, from the upper Nile region [m]33 Isaiah 53:7,8 [n]36 Some late manuscripts *baptized?"* [37]*Philip said, "If you believe with all your heart, you may." The eunuch answered, "I believe that Jesus Christ is the Son of God."*

Discovering the Word 1. In this passage the command to be witnesses in all of Judea and Samaria (Ac 1:8) is fulfilled. What are the causes and extent of the spread of the gospel at this time? 2. Look at the story of Simon the Sorcerer (vv. 9–25). How does he attempt to get spiritual power? What is his motivation for wanting this power (vv. 18–19)? 3. In contrast, what is God's way for his people to receive spiritual power (vv.

20–23)? 4. What are the factors involved in the eunuch's coming to know the Lord (vv. 26–39)? 5. How was Philip's ministry to the eunuch the beginning of the witness "to the ends of the earth" (Ac 1:8)?

Applying the Word 1. The story of Simon the Sorcerer demonstrates that becoming a Christian does not instantly resolve all problems and character flaws. What do you learn from Peter concerning nurturing young believers? 2. What principles of evangelism have you observed throughout this passage? 3. What have you learned from Acts 8 that might make you a more effective witness for Jesus?

Responding in Prayer Ask God for the guidance of his Holy Spirit, and ask him to help you follow the model of evangelism that Philip provides.

9 / *Acts 9:1–31*
Saul's Conversion

WHEN CHUCK COLSON became a Christian in prison, the whole nation reacted with skepticism—Christians and non-Christians alike. Of all the leading characters in the Watergate scandal, he was one of the most notorious. Could such a calculating man sincerely come to God?

Warming Up to God Think back to what your life was like before you met Christ. Thank God for the transformation that he has made in your life—both your instant rebirth into his kingdom and the gradual remolding of your character since then.

Read Acts 9:1–31.

9 Meanwhile, Saul was still breathing out
murderous threats against the Lord's dis-
ciples. He went to the high priest 2and
asked him for letters to the synagogues in Damas-
cus, so that if he found any there who belonged to
the Way, whether men or women, he might take
them as prisoners to Jerusalem. 3As he neared
Damascus on his journey, suddenly a light from
heaven flashed around him. 4He fell to the
ground and heard a voice say to him, "Saul, Saul,
why do you persecute me?"

5"Who are you, Lord?" Saul asked.

"I am Jesus, whom you are persecuting," he
replied. 6"Now get up and go into the city, and
you will be told what you must do."

7The men traveling with Saul stood there
speechless; they heard the sound but did not see
anyone. 8Saul got up from the ground, but when
he opened his eyes he could see nothing. So they
led him by the hand into Damascus. 9For three
days he was blind, and did not eat or drink any-
thing.

10In Damascus there was a disciple named Ana-
nias. The Lord called to him in a vision, "Ana-
nias!"

"Yes, Lord," he answered.

11The Lord told him, "Go to the house of Judas
on Straight Street and ask for a man from Tarsus
named Saul, for he is praying. 12In a vision he has
seen a man named Ananias come and place his
hands on him to restore his sight."

13"Lord," Ananias answered, "I have heard
many reports about this man and all the harm he
has done to your saints in Jerusalem. 14And he
has come here with authority from the chief
priests to arrest all who call on your name."

15But the Lord said to Ananias, "Go! This man
is my chosen instrument to carry my name before
the Gentiles and their kings and before the people
of Israel. 16I will show him how much he must
suffer for my name."

17Then Ananias went to the house and entered
it. Placing his hands on Saul, he said, "Brother
Saul, the Lord—Jesus, who appeared to you on
the road as you were coming here—has sent me
so that you may see again and be filled with the
Holy Spirit." 18Immediately, something like scales
fell from Saul's eyes, and he could see again. He
got up and was baptized, 19and after taking some
food, he regained his strength.

Saul spent several days with the disciples in
Damascus. 20At once he began to preach in the

synagogues that Jesus is the Son of God. [21]All
those who heard him were astonished and asked,
"Isn't he the man who raised havoc in Jerusalem
among those who call on this name? And hasn't
he come here to take them as prisoners to the
chief priests?" [22]Yet Saul grew more and more
powerful and baffled the Jews living in Damascus
by proving that Jesus is the Christ.[o]
[23]After many days had gone by, the Jews con-
spired to kill him, [24]but Saul learned of their plan.
Day and night they kept close watch on the city
gates in order to kill him. [25]But his followers took
him by night and lowered him in a basket
through an opening in the wall.
[26]When he came to Jerusalem, he tried to join
the disciples, but they were all afraid of him, not
believing that he really was a disciple. [27]But Bar-
nabas took him and brought him to the apostles.
He told them how Saul on his journey had seen
the Lord and that the Lord had spoken to him,
and how in Damascus he had preached fearlessly
in the name of Jesus. [28]So Saul stayed with them
and moved about freely in Jerusalem, speaking
boldly in the name of the Lord. [29]He talked and
debated with the Grecian Jews, but they tried to
kill him. [30]When the brothers learned of this,
they took him down to Caesarea and sent him off
to Tarsus.
[31]Then the church throughout Judea, Galilee
and Samaria enjoyed a time of peace. It was
strengthened; and encouraged by the Holy Spirit,
it grew in numbers, living in the fear of the Lord.

[o]22 Or *Messiah*

Discovering the Word 1. Review what you know about Saul (7:58—8:3). What further insights do you get about him from 9:1-2? 2. Describe Saul's encounter with Jesus Christ in verses 3-9. (What is the emotional, spiritual, physical and social climate?) 3. Ananias is the second person within three days to have a direct encounter with the Lord. Compare and contrast his encounter (vv. 10-16) with that of Saul. 4. What is the significance of Ananias addressing Saul as "Brother" (v. 17)? 5. What is the response of both believers and nonbelievers to Saul and his ministry (vv. 19-30)? 6. What role does Barnabas play in Saul's life and ministry?

Applying the Word 1. What do you learn about obedience to God through Saul and Ananias? 2. What does Saul's conversion teach us about those in our lives who are most likely not to believe? 3. Consider the people in your life who are most antagonistic to Christianity. How might God use you to bring them to Christ?

Responding in Prayer Pray for the salvation of someone you consider an unlikely convert. Ask God to increase your faith.

10 / *Acts 9:32—10:48*
Salvation for Every Nation

ONCE THE BERLIN Wall seemed impenetrable, and communism powerful and indestructible. For seventy years Christians wondered if Christmas would ever be openly celebrated in Russia. Then, dramatically, the wall fell. Communism collapsed. Nations that had been closed to the gospel for years began to welcome Christians, their help and their message with open arms. The historic breakthrough was like the one the early Christians experienced in this passage. A seemingly impenetrable spiritual wall was broken down. In both situations we see that from God's perspective there is always the potential for reaching every person in all the corners of the world with the wonderful news of Jesus Christ.

Warming Up to God Think of an impossible feat that you have seen God accomplish. Thank him and allow him to show you again that he truly is almighty.

Read Acts 9:32—10:48.

32As Peter traveled about the country, he went
to visit the saints in Lydda. 33There he found a
man named Aeneas, a paralytic who had been
bedridden for eight years. 34"Aeneas," Peter said
to him, "Jesus Christ heals you. Get up and take
care of your mat." Immediately Aeneas got up.
35All those who lived in Lydda and Sharon saw
him and turned to the Lord.

36In Joppa there was a disciple named Tabitha
(which, when translated, is Dorcas[p]), who was
always doing good and helping the poor. 37About
that time she became sick and died, and her body
was washed and placed in an upstairs room.
38Lydda was near Joppa; so when the disciples
heard that Peter was in Lydda, they sent two men
to him and urged him, "Please come at once!"

39Peter went with them, and when he arrived
he was taken upstairs to the room. All the widows
stood around him, crying and showing him the
robes and other clothing that Dorcas had made
while she was still with them.

40Peter sent them all out of the room; then he
got down on his knees and prayed. Turning to-
ward the dead woman, he said, "Tabitha, get up."
She opened her eyes, and seeing Peter she sat up.
41He took her by the hand and helped her to her
feet. Then he called the believers and the widows
and presented her to them alive. 42This became
known all over Joppa, and many people believed
in the Lord. 43Peter stayed in Joppa for some time
with a tanner named Simon.

10 At Caesarea there was a man named
Cornelius, a centurion in what was
known as the Italian Regiment. 2He
and all his family were devout and God-fearing;
he gave generously to those in need and prayed to
God regularly. 3One day at about three in the
afternoon he had a vision. He distinctly saw an
angel of God, who came to him and said, "Cor-
nelius!"

4Cornelius stared at him in fear. "What is it,
Lord?" he asked.

The angel answered, "Your prayers and gifts to
the poor have come up as a memorial offering
before God. 5Now send men to Joppa to bring
back a man named Simon who is called Peter. 6He
is staying with Simon the tanner, whose house is
by the sea."

7When the angel who spoke to him had gone,
Cornelius called two of his servants and a devout
soldier who was one of his attendants. 8He told
them everything that had happened and sent
them to Joppa.

9About noon the following day as they were on
their journey and approaching the city, Peter
went up on the roof to pray. 10He became hungry
and wanted something to eat, and while the meal
was being prepared, he fell into a trance. 11He saw
heaven opened and something like a large sheet
being let down to earth by its four corners. 12It
contained all kinds of four-footed animals, as well
as reptiles of the earth and birds of the air. 13Then
a voice told him, "Get up, Peter. Kill and eat."

14"Surely not, Lord!" Peter replied. "I have
never eaten anything impure or unclean."

15The voice spoke to him a second time, "Do
not call anything impure that God has made
clean."

16This happened three times, and immediately
the sheet was taken back to heaven.

17While Peter was wondering about the mean-
ing of the vision, the men sent by Cornelius
found out where Simon's house was and stopped
at the gate. 18They called out, asking if Simon
who was known as Peter was staying there.

19While Peter was still thinking about the vi-
sion, the Spirit said to him, "Simon, three[q] men
are looking for you. 20So get up and go down-
stairs. Do not hesitate to go with them, for I have
sent them."

21Peter went down and said to the men, "I'm
the one you're looking for. Why have you come?"

22The men replied, "We have come from Cor-
nelius the centurion. He is a righteous and God-
fearing man, who is respected by all the Jewish
people. A holy angel told him to have you come
to his house so that he could hear what you have
to say." 23Then Peter invited the men into the
house to be his guests.

The next day Peter started out with them, and
some of the brothers from Joppa went along.
24The following day he arrived in Caesarea. Cor-
nelius was expecting them and had called to-
gether his relatives and close friends. 25As Peter
entered the house, Cornelius met him and fell at
his feet in reverence. 26But Peter made him get
up. "Stand up," he said, "I am only a man my-
self."

27Talking with him, Peter went inside and
found a large gathering of people. 28He said to

p36 Both *Tabitha* (Aramaic) and *Dorcas* (Greek) mean *gazelle*.
q19 One early manuscript *two*; other manuscripts do not have the number.

them: "You are well aware that it is against our
law for a Jew to associate with a Gentile or visit
him. But God has shown me that I should not call
any man impure or unclean. 29So when I was sent
for, I came without raising any objection. May I
ask why you sent for me?"

30Cornelius answered: "Four days ago I was in
my house praying at this hour, at three in the
afternoon. Suddenly a man in shining clothes
stood before me 31and said, 'Cornelius, God has
heard your prayer and remembered your gifts to
the poor. 32Send to Joppa for Simon who is called
Peter. He is a guest in the home of Simon the
tanner, who lives by the sea.' 33So I sent for you
immediately, and it was good of you to come.
Now we are all here in the presence of God to
listen to everything the Lord has commanded you
to tell us."

34Then Peter began to speak: "I now realize
how true it is that God does not show favoritism
35but accepts men from every nation who fear
him and do what is right. 36You know the mes-
sage God sent to the people of Israel, telling the
good news of peace through Jesus Christ, who is
Lord of all. 37You know what has happened
throughout Judea, beginning in Galilee after the
baptism that John preached— 38how God
anointed Jesus of Nazareth with the Holy Spirit
and power, and how he went around doing good
and healing all who were under the power of the
devil, because God was with him.

39"We are witnesses of everything he did in the
country of the Jews and in Jerusalem. They killed
him by hanging him on a tree, 40but God raised
him from the dead on the third day and caused
him to be seen. 41He was not seen by all the peo-
ple, but by witnesses whom God had already cho-
sen—by us who ate and drank with him after he
rose from the dead. 42He commanded us to
preach to the people and to testify that he is the
one whom God appointed as judge of the living
and the dead. 43All the prophets testify about him
that everyone who believes in him receives for-
giveness of sins through his name."

44While Peter was still speaking these words,
the Holy Spirit came on all who heard the mes-
sage. 45The circumcised believers who had come
with Peter were astonished that the gift of the
Holy Spirit had been poured out even on the Gen-
tiles. 46For they heard them speaking in
tongues[r] and praising God.

Then Peter said, 47"Can anyone keep these peo-
ple from being baptized with water? They have
received the Holy Spirit just as we have." 48So he
ordered that they be baptized in the name of Jesus
Christ. Then they asked Peter to stay with them
for a few days.

r46 *Or other languages*

Discovering the Word 1. How is God's power demonstrated in 9:32–43? 2. This is the first time Peter has been involved in raising someone from the dead. How might this prepare him for what happens in chapter 10? 3. How did God prepare Cornelius for Peter (10:1–8)? 4. In what ways did God prepare Peter for Cornelius (10:9–33)? 5. What evidence is there that Cornelius expected God to work (10:24–26)?

Applying the Word 1. What lessons do we learn from Cornelius's life? 2. In summary, how do you see God's purpose, as stated in Acts 1:8, "You will receive power when the Holy Spirit comes on you; and you will be my witnesses in Jerusalem, and in all Judea and Samaria, and to the ends of the earth," being fulfilled in this passage? 3. In what ways could you grow in relating to people of other cultures and races?

Responding in Prayer Ask God to use your experiences in life and knowledge of him to bring others to Christ.

11/ *Acts 11*
The First Jewish-Gentile Church

LUKE SET UP the stories of Peter and Cornelius and Ananias with amazing symmetry. The Holy Spirit simultaneously prepared the hearts of Ananias and of Saul—as he simultaneously prepared those of Peter and Cornelius. Peter questioned and hesitated, as did Ananias. Peter doubted whether he could be friends with the Gentiles,

Ananias whether he could approach the enemy of the church. Both obey without hesitation when God makes his divine will known. These stories come together in today's study. Peter defends his ministry to Cornelius to the church at Jerusalem. He convinces them of God's work in the Gentiles. It is also here that Saul, the one-time enemy of the church, reappears as a minister to the church in Antioch, a church filled with both Jewish and Gentile Christians.

Warming Up to God In the face of change, how do you handle the need for a new perspective? Resistance? Excitement? Uncertainty? Do you face a change now? Take time to put your response, whatever it is, in God's hands.

Read Acts 11.

11 The apostles and the brothers
throughout Judea heard that the
Gentiles also had received the word
of God. 2So when Peter went up to Jerusalem, the
circumcised believers criticized him 3and said,
"You went into the house of uncircumcised men
and ate with them."

4Peter began and explained everything to them
precisely as it had happened: 5"I was in the city of
Joppa praying, and in a trance I saw a vision. I
saw something like a large sheet being let down
from heaven by its four corners, and it came
down to where I was. 6I looked into it and saw
four-footed animals of the earth, wild beasts, rep-
tiles, and birds of the air. 7Then I heard a voice
telling me, 'Get up, Peter. Kill and eat.'

8"I replied, 'Surely not, Lord! Nothing impure
or unclean has ever entered my mouth.'

9"The voice spoke from heaven a second time,
'Do not call anything impure that God has made
clean.' 10This happened three times, and then it
was all pulled up to heaven again.

11"Right then three men who had been sent to
me from Caesarea stopped at the house where I
was staying. 12The Spirit told me to have no hesi-
tation about going with them. These six brothers
also went with me, and we entered the man's
house. 13He told us how he had seen an angel
appear in his house and say, 'Send to Joppa for
Simon who is called Peter. 14He will bring you a
message through which you and all your house-
hold will be saved.'

15"As I began to speak, the Holy Spirit came on
them as he had come on us at the beginning.
16Then I remembered what the Lord had said:
'John baptized with[s] water, but you will be bap-
tized with the Holy Spirit.' 17So if God gave them
the same gift as he gave us, who believed in the
Lord Jesus Christ, who was I to think that I could
oppose God?"

18When they heard this, they had no further
objections and praised God, saying, "So then,
God has granted even the Gentiles repentance
unto life."

19Now those who had been scattered by the
persecution in connection with Stephen traveled
as far as Phoenicia, Cyprus and Antioch, telling
the message only to Jews. 20Some of them, how-
ever, men from Cyprus and Cyrene, went to Anti-
och and began to speak to Greeks also, telling
them the good news about the Lord Jesus.
21The Lord's hand was with them, and a great
number of people believed and turned to the
Lord.

22News of this reached the ears of the church at
Jerusalem, and they sent Barnabas to Antioch.
23When he arrived and saw the evidence of the
grace of God, he was glad and encouraged them
all to remain true to the Lord with all their hearts.
24He was a good man, full of the Holy Spirit and
faith, and a great number of people were brought
to the Lord.

25Then Barnabas went to Tarsus to look for
Saul, 26and when he found him, he brought him
to Antioch. So for a whole year Barnabas and Saul
met with the church and taught great numbers of
people. The disciples were called Christians first
at Antioch.

27During this time some prophets came down
from Jerusalem to Antioch. 28One of them, named
Agabus, stood up and through the Spirit pre-
dicted that a severe famine would spread over the
entire Roman world. (This happened during the
reign of Claudius.) 29The disciples, each accord-
ing to his ability, decided to provide help for
the brothers living in Judea. 30This they did,
sending their gift to the elders by Barnabas and
Saul.

[s] 16 Or *in*

Discovering the Word 1. What kind of reception was awaiting Peter when he went back up to Jerusalem (vv. 1–3)? 2. What seemed to be the final and most convincing proof to Peter of God's working in the Gentiles (vv. 15–17)? Why? 3. In the meantime the gospel is spreading to Gentiles at a tremendous rate in Antioch. What kind of care is provided for new believers (vv. 22–30)? 4. What was the reason for, and what were the results of, Barnabas's trip to Antioch (vv. 22–30)?

Applying the Word 1. What can we learn from the way Peter responded to his critics? 2. How does our care for new believers compare and contrast to the care given here? 3. How do you see in this passage the true meaning of "Christian" being more fully discovered and lived out in a multicultural church?

Responding in Prayer Ask God to help you be more open and flexible to the changes that he desires to bring about in your life.

12 / *Acts 12*
Miraculous Escape

HUDSON TAYLOR, FAMOUS missionary to China, said, "Man is moved by God through prayer alone." We see the power of God demonstrated in this passage in response to the prayers of his people.

Warming Up to God Recall a time when God answered one of your prayers. Thank him for the joy and encouragement you received from his gracious blessing upon you.

Read Acts 12.

12 It was about this time that King
Herod arrested some who belonged
to the church, intending to perse-
cute them. 2He had James, the brother of John,
put to death with the sword. 3When he saw that
this pleased the Jews, he proceeded to seize Peter
also. This happened during the Feast of Unleav-
ened Bread. 4After arresting him, he put him in
prison, handing him over to be guarded by four
squads of four soldiers each. Herod intended to
bring him out for public trial after the Passover.
5So Peter was kept in prison, but the church
was earnestly praying to God for him.
6The night before Herod was to bring him to
trial, Peter was sleeping between two soldiers,
bound with two chains, and sentries stood guard
at the entrance. 7Suddenly an angel of the Lord
appeared and a light shone in the cell. He struck
Peter on the side and woke him up. "Quick, get
up!" he said, and the chains fell off Peter's wrists.
8Then the angel said to him, "Put on your
clothes and sandals." And Peter did so. "Wrap
your cloak around you and follow me," the angel
told him. 9Peter followed him out of the prison,
but he had no idea that what the angel was doing
was really happening; he thought he was seeing a
vision. 10They passed the first and second guards
and came to the iron gate leading to the city. It
opened for them by itself, and they went through
it. When they had walked the length of one street,
suddenly the angel left him.
11Then Peter came to himself and said, "Now I
know without a doubt that the Lord sent his an-
gel and rescued me from Herod's clutches and
from everything the Jewish people were anticipat-
ing."
12When this had dawned on him, he went to
the house of Mary the mother of John, also called
Mark, where many people had gathered and were
praying. 13Peter knocked at the outer entrance,
and a servant girl named Rhoda came to answer
the door. 14When she recognized Peter's voice,
she was so overjoyed she ran back without open-
ing it and exclaimed, "Peter is at the door!"
15"You're out of your mind," they told her.
When she kept insisting that it was so, they said,
"It must be his angel."
16But Peter kept on knocking, and when they
opened the door and saw him, they were aston-
ished. 17Peter motioned with his hand for them to
be quiet and described how the Lord had brought
him out of prison. "Tell James and the brothers

about this," he said, and then he left for another
place.
[18]In the morning, there was no small commo-
tion among the soldiers as to what had become of
Peter. [19]After Herod had a thorough search made
for him and did not find him, he cross-examined
the guards and ordered that they be executed.
Then Herod went from Judea to Caesarea and
stayed there a while. [20]He had been quarreling
with the people of Tyre and Sidon; they now
joined together and sought an audience with him.
Having secured the support of Blastus, a trusted
personal servant of the king, they asked for peace,
because they depended on the king's country for
their food supply.
[21]On the appointed day Herod, wearing his
royal robes, sat on his throne and delivered a
public address to the people. [22]They shouted,
"This is the voice of a god, not of a man." [23]Im-
mediately, because Herod did not give praise to
God, an angel of the Lord struck him down, and
he was eaten by worms and died.
[24]But the word of God continued to increase
and spread.
[25]When Barnabas and Saul had finished their
mission, they returned from[t] Jerusalem, taking
with them John, also called Mark.

[t]25 Some manuscripts *to*

Discovering the Word 1. Describe the main characters in this passage. How do they respond to what is happening to and around them? 2. What seems to motivate Herod's actions (vv. 1–5)? 3. What does the church's response to James's death and Peter's being in prison (vv. 5 and 12) demonstrate about prayer? 4. Why was Herod struck down (vv. 21–23)? 5. Contrast Herod's end with what happened with the Word of God (vv. 19–24).

Applying the Word 1. How have you seen God respond to a group of people who were earnestly praying? 2. Why do you think the praying Christians reacted as they did to Peter's return? 3. The earnest prayer of the church significantly affected the outcome of the events of this chapter. How is your motivation to pray influenced by this truth?

Responding in Prayer Think of an "impossible" prayer request or need that you have. Place it before God and ask him to give you the faith to believe that he will answer your prayer and give you "the desires of your heart."

13/ *Acts 13—14*
Paul's First Missionary Journey

PETER HAS DISAPPEARED. We do not know where he is hiding. Luke is ushering Peter from the stage while Paul steps to the forefront. Peter, the apostle to the Jews, has played his part well and prepared the way for Paul, the apostle to the Gentiles. Paul and Barnabas have completed their mission of mercy in Jerusalem on behalf of the church in Antioch (11:29) and have returned to Antioch with John Mark. In this study we will look at Paul's first missionary journey—the beginning of his master plan of evangelism.

Warming Up to God Do you feel distant from God as you try to approach the Scriptures? Remember that God in his great mercy has come to us first and wants to meet us here. He longs to care for us, his little sheep, and capture us in his arms.

Read Acts 13—14.

13 In the church at Antioch there were
prophets and teachers: Barnabas,
Simeon called Niger, Lucius of Cy-
rene, Manaen (who had been brought up with
Herod the tetrarch) and Saul. [2]While they were
worshiping the Lord and fasting, the Holy Spirit
said, "Set apart for me Barnabas and Saul for the
work to which I have called them." [3]So after they

had fasted and prayed, they placed their hands on them and sent them off.

4The two of them, sent on their way by the Holy Spirit, went down to Seleucia and sailed from there to Cyprus. 5When they arrived at Salamis, they proclaimed the word of God in the Jewish synagogues. John was with them as their helper.

6They traveled through the whole island until they came to Paphos. There they met a Jewish sorcerer and false prophet named Bar-Jesus, 7who was an attendant of the proconsul, Sergius Paulus. The proconsul, an intelligent man, sent for Barnabas and Saul because he wanted to hear the word of God. 8But Elymas the sorcerer (for that is what his name means) opposed them and tried to turn the proconsul from the faith. 9Then Saul, who was also called Paul, filled with the Holy Spirit, looked straight at Elymas and said, 10"You are a child of the devil and an enemy of everything that is right! You are full of all kinds of deceit and trickery. Will you never stop perverting the right ways of the Lord? 11Now the hand of the Lord is against you. You are going to be blind, and for a time you will be unable to see the light of the sun."

Immediately mist and darkness came over him, and he groped about, seeking someone to lead him by the hand. 12When the proconsul saw what had happened, he believed, for he was amazed at the teaching about the Lord.

13From Paphos, Paul and his companions sailed to Perga in Pamphylia, where John left them to return to Jerusalem. 14From Perga they went on to Pisidian Antioch. On the Sabbath they entered the synagogue and sat down. 15After the reading from the Law and the Prophets, the synagogue rulers sent word to them, saying, "Brothers, if you have a message of encouragement for the people, please speak."

16Standing up, Paul motioned with his hand and said: "Men of Israel and you Gentiles who worship God, listen to me! 17The God of the people of Israel chose our fathers; he made the people prosper during their stay in Egypt, with mighty power he led them out of that country, 18he endured their conduct[u] for about forty years in the desert, 19he overthrew seven nations in Canaan and gave their land to his people as their inheritance. 20All this took about 450 years.

"After this, God gave them judges until the time of Samuel the prophet. 21Then the people asked for a king, and he gave them Saul son of Kish, of the tribe of Benjamin, who ruled forty years. 22After removing Saul, he made David their king. He testified concerning him: 'I have found David son of Jesse a man after my own heart; he will do everything I want him to do.'

23"From this man's descendants God has brought to Israel the Savior Jesus, as he promised. 24Before the coming of Jesus, John preached repentance and baptism to all the people of Israel. 25As John was completing his work, he said: 'Who do you think I am? I am not that one. No, but he is coming after me, whose sandals I am not worthy to untie.'

26"Brothers, children of Abraham, and you God-fearing Gentiles, it is to us that this message of salvation has been sent. 27The people of Jerusalem and their rulers did not recognize Jesus, yet in condemning him they fulfilled the words of the prophets that are read every Sabbath. 28Though they found no proper ground for a death sentence, they asked Pilate to have him executed. 29When they had carried out all that was written about him, they took him down from the tree and laid him in a tomb. 30But God raised him from the dead, 31and for many days he was seen by those who had traveled with him from Galilee to Jerusalem. They are now his witnesses to our people.

32"We tell you the good news: What God promised our fathers 33he has fulfilled for us, their children, by raising up Jesus. As it is written in the second Psalm:

" 'You are my Son;
today I have become your Father.'[v][w]

34The fact that God raised him from the dead, never to decay, is stated in these words:

" 'I will give you the holy and sure blessings
promised to David.'[x]

35So it is stated elsewhere:

" 'You will not let your Holy One see decay.'[y]

36"For when David had served God's purpose in his own generation, he fell asleep; he was buried with his fathers and his body decayed. 37But the one whom God raised from the dead did not see decay.

38"Therefore, my brothers, I want you to know that through Jesus the forgiveness of sins is pro-

[u]18 Some manuscripts *and cared for them* [v]33 Or *have begotten you* [w]33 Psalm 2:7 [x]34 Isaiah 55:3 [y]35 Psalm 16:10

claimed to you. 39Through him everyone who be-
lieves is justified from everything you could not
be justified from by the law of Moses. 40Take care
that what the prophets have said does not happen
to you:

41" 'Look, you scoffers,
wonder and perish,
for I am going to do something in your days
that you would never believe,
even if someone told you.'[z]"

42As Paul and Barnabas were leaving the syna-
gogue, the people invited them to speak further
about these things on the next Sabbath. 43When
the congregation was dismissed, many of the Jews
and devout converts to Judaism followed Paul
and Barnabas, who talked with them and urged
them to continue in the grace of God.
44On the next Sabbath almost the whole city
gathered to hear the word of the Lord. 45When
the Jews saw the crowds, they were filled with
jealousy and talked abusively against what Paul
was saying.
46Then Paul and Barnabas answered them
boldly: "We had to speak the word of God to you
first. Since you reject it and do not consider your-
selves worthy of eternal life, we now turn to the
Gentiles. 47For this is what the Lord has com-
manded us:

" 'I have made you[a] a light for the Gentiles,
that you[a] may bring salvation to the ends
of the earth.'[b]"

48When the Gentiles heard this, they were glad
and honored the word of the Lord; and all who
were appointed for eternal life believed.
49The word of the Lord spread through the
whole region. 50But the Jews incited the God-fear-
ing women of high standing and the leading men
of the city. They stirred up persecution against
Paul and Barnabas, and expelled them from their
region. 51So they shook the dust from their feet in
protest against them and went to Iconium. 52And
the disciples were filled with joy and with the
Holy Spirit.

14 At Iconium Paul and Barnabas went
as usual into the Jewish synagogue.
There they spoke so effectively that
a great number of Jews and Gentiles believed.
2But the Jews who refused to believe stirred up
the Gentiles and poisoned their minds against the
brothers. 3So Paul and Barnabas spent consider-
able time there, speaking boldly for the Lord, who
confirmed the message of his grace by enabling
them to do miraculous signs and wonders. 4The
people of the city were divided; some sided with
the Jews, others with the apostles. 5There was a
plot afoot among the Gentiles and Jews, together
with their leaders, to mistreat them and stone
them. 6But they found out about it and fled to the
Lycaonian cities of Lystra and Derbe and to the
surrounding country, 7where they continued to
preach the good news.
8In Lystra there sat a man crippled in his feet,
who was lame from birth and had never walked.
9He listened to Paul as he was speaking. Paul
looked directly at him, saw that he had faith to be
healed 10and called out, "Stand up on your feet!"
At that, the man jumped up and began to walk.
11When the crowd saw what Paul had done,
they shouted in the Lycaonian language, "The
gods have come down to us in human form!"
12Barnabas they called Zeus, and Paul they called
Hermes because he was the chief speaker. 13The
priest of Zeus, whose temple was just outside the
city, brought bulls and wreaths to the city gates
because he and the crowd wanted to offer sacri-
fices to them.
14But when the apostles Barnabas and Paul
heard of this, they tore their clothes and rushed
out into the crowd, shouting: 15"Men, why are
you doing this? We too are only men, human like
you. We are bringing you good news, telling you
to turn from these worthless things to the living
God, who made heaven and earth and sea and
everything in them. 16In the past, he let all na-
tions go their own way. 17Yet he has not left him-
self without testimony: He has shown kindness
by giving you rain from heaven and crops in their
seasons; he provides you with plenty of food and
fills your hearts with joy." 18Even with these
words, they had difficulty keeping the crowd
from sacrificing to them.
19Then some Jews came from Antioch and Ico-
nium and won the crowd over. They stoned Paul
and dragged him outside the city, thinking he was
dead. 20But after the disciples had gathered
around him, he got up and went back into the
city. The next day he and Barnabas left for Derbe.
21They preached the good news in that city and
won a large number of disciples. Then they re-
turned to Lystra, Iconium and Antioch,

[z]41 Hab. 1:5 [a]47 The Greek is singular. [b]47 Isaiah 49:6

22strengthening the disciples and encouraging
them to remain true to the faith. "We must go
through many hardships to enter the kingdom of
God," they said. 23Paul and Barnabas appointed
elders[c] for them in each church and, with prayer
and fasting, committed them to the Lord, in
whom they had put their trust. 24After going
through Pisidia, they came into Pamphylia, 25and
when they had preached the word in Perga, they
went down to Attalia.
26From Attalia they sailed back to Antioch,
where they had been committed to the grace of
God for the work they had now completed. 27On
arriving there, they gathered the church together
and reported all that God had done through them
and how he had opened the door of faith to the
Gentiles. 28And they stayed there a long time with
the disciples.

[c]23 Or *Barnabas ordained elders;* or *Barnabas had elders elected*

Discovering the Word 1. Antioch was the second greatest metropolis of the church and the mother of Gentile Christianity. What role did the church of Antioch play in Paul's first missionary journey (13:1–3; 14:26–28)? 2. Review Paul's message in the synagogue in Pisidian Antioch (13:16–41). What truths of the gospel are communicated? 3. How does Paul's message show sensitivity to his audience and the context? 4. List the different responses to the gospel (13:7–8, 13, 42–45, 48, 52; 14:1–5) that you see throughout this passage. 5. How did Paul respond to those who rejected the gospel (13:9–11, 46, 51)? to those who believed (14:9–10, 21–23)?

Applying the Word 1. People today are not apt to offer sacrifices to those who bring the good news of Jesus. However, in what ways are we faced with the temptation to be "God" in another's life or to take credit for what God has done? 2. How can we help one another when in the midst of such temptations? 3. Consider the qualities you see in Paul and Barnabas that made them effective in their ministry. Which of these qualities do you want God to develop in you to make you more effective in communicating the gospel?

Responding in Prayer Is there a way God wants to change you? Talk to God about it.

14 / *Acts 15*
Conflict in the Church

IN MOST AREAS of life, I think I am pretty realistic. When it comes to conflict among believers, however, I tend to be an idealist. I believe that unity is something that God requires of us. Believers should be able to talk, pray and work through conflict—just the way it was worked through by the church at Jerusalem. However, I am becoming a little more realistic about this. I have been in several situations in which I felt like I did everything within my power to bring about reconciliation—but failed.

This seems to be the case with Paul and Barnabas. These two men who were used by God to keep a church from splitting could not resolve their own differences and ended up going separate ways. The late Kenneth Strachan of Latin American Mission said, "We all need to live and serve in the constant recognition of our own humanity."

Warming Up to God Has there been a time recently when you were in conflict with someone? Tell God about it and let his peace and compassion wash over you as he teaches you.

Read Acts 15.

15 Some men came down from Judea
to Antioch and were teaching the
brothers: "Unless you are circum-
cised, according to the custom taught by Moses,
you cannot be saved." 2This brought Paul and
Barnabas into sharp dispute and debate with
them. So Paul and Barnabas were appointed,
along with some other believers, to go up to Jeru-
salem to see the apostles and elders about this
question. 3The church sent them on their way,
and as they traveled through Phoenicia and Sa-
maria, they told how the Gentiles had been con-

verted. This news made all the brothers very glad. 4When they came to Jerusalem, they were welcomed by the church and the apostles and elders, to whom they reported everything God had done through them.

5Then some of the believers who belonged to the party of the Pharisees stood up and said, "The Gentiles must be circumcised and required to obey the law of Moses."

6The apostles and elders met to consider this question. 7After much discussion, Peter got up and addressed them: "Brothers, you know that some time ago God made a choice among you that the Gentiles might hear from my lips the message of the gospel and believe. 8God, who knows the heart, showed that he accepted them by giving the Holy Spirit to them, just as he did to us. 9He made no distinction between us and them, for he purified their hearts by faith. 10Now then, why do you try to test God by putting on the necks of the disciples a yoke that neither we nor our fathers have been able to bear? 11No! We believe it is through the grace of our Lord Jesus that we are saved, just as they are."

12The whole assembly became silent as they listened to Barnabas and Paul telling about the miraculous signs and wonders God had done among the Gentiles through them. 13When they finished, James spoke up: "Brothers, listen to me. 14Simon[d] has described to us how God at first showed his concern by taking from the Gentiles a people for himself. 15The words of the prophets are in agreement with this, as it is written:

16" 'After this I will return
and rebuild David's fallen tent.
Its ruins I will rebuild,
and I will restore it,
17that the remnant of men may seek the Lord,
and all the Gentiles who bear my name,
says the Lord, who does these things'[e]
18 that have been known for ages.[f]

19"It is my judgment, therefore, that we should not make it difficult for the Gentiles who are turning to God. 20Instead we should write to them, telling them to abstain from food polluted by idols, from sexual immorality, from the meat of strangled animals and from blood. 21For Moses has been preached in every city from the earliest times and is read in the synagogues on every Sabbath."

22Then the apostles and elders, with the whole church, decided to choose some of their own men and send them to Antioch with Paul and Barnabas. They chose Judas (called Barsabbas) and Silas, two men who were leaders among the brothers. 23With them they sent the following letter:

The apostles and elders, your brothers,

To the Gentile believers in Antioch, Syria and Cilicia:

Greetings.

24We have heard that some went out from us without our authorization and disturbed you, troubling your minds by what they said. 25So we all agreed to choose some men and send them to you with our dear friends Barnabas and Paul— 26men who have risked their lives for the name of our Lord Jesus Christ. 27Therefore we are sending Judas and Silas to confirm by word of mouth what we are writing. 28It seemed good to the Holy Spirit and to us not to burden you with anything beyond the following requirements: 29You are to abstain from food sacrificed to idols, from blood, from the meat of strangled animals and from sexual immorality. You will do well to avoid these things.

Farewell.

30The men were sent off and went down to Antioch, where they gathered the church together and delivered the letter. 31The people read it and were glad for its encouraging message. 32Judas and Silas, who themselves were prophets, said much to encourage and strengthen the brothers. 33After spending some time there, they were sent off by the brothers with the blessing of peace to return to those who had sent them.[g] 35But Paul and Barnabas remained in Antioch, where they and many others taught and preached the word of the Lord.

36Some time later Paul said to Barnabas, "Let us go back and visit the brothers in all the towns where we preached the word of the Lord and see how they are doing." 37Barnabas wanted to take John, also called Mark, with them, 38but Paul did not think it wise to take him, because he had deserted them in Pamphylia and had not contin-

d14 Greek *Simeon*, a variant of *Simon*; that is, Peter e17 Amos 9:11,12 f17,18 Some manuscripts *things'— / 18known to the Lord for ages is his work* g33 Some manuscripts *them, 34but Silas decided to remain there*

ued with them in the work. 39They had such a
sharp disagreement that they parted company.
Barnabas took Mark and sailed for Cyprus, 40but
Paul chose Silas and left, commended by the
brothers to the grace of the Lord. 41He went
through Syria and Cilicia, strengthening the
churches.

Discovering the Word 1. Describe the conflict that arises between the Christians (vv. 1–35). 2. Describe the spirit of those involved and the steps that were taken to resolve this conflict. 3. What were the results? 4. In what ways do you see (or can you assume) unity between Paul and Barnabas (vv. 36–41)? 5. Paul and Barnabas came to the point of "agreeing to disagree" and going their separate ways. What were the benefits of this temporary solution?

Applying the Word 1. What principles do you observe that are vital to follow as we face conflict with others in our Christian community? 2. Which of these principles do you struggle with implementing the most? 3. Both Paul and Barnabas seemed to have strong cases for their points of view. Under what kinds of circumstances should we surrender deep convictions when they are challenged by another? 4. No matter how strongly we feel about an issue, we do not see the whole picture. How should that affect the way we respond to people with whom we are in conflict?

Responding in Prayer Ask God to give you discernment as you face conflict in both the church and in your personal life.

15 / *Acts 16*
What Must I Do?

THE MEMORY IS still vivid. The event was InterVarsity's Urbana Missionary Conference. The place, a dormitory room. The person, a young lady from the Bible study group that I led. I sensed the prompting of the Holy Spirit to stop by Susan's room. As I walked in to say "hi" she looked up from the booklet she was reading and said, "I would like to become a Christian. Will you help me?" This dormitory setting was not quite as dramatic as the Philippian jail. But it was just as exciting to hear Susan's words, as it was for Paul and Silas to hear the jailer's cry, "Sirs, what must I do to be saved?"

Warming Up to God Think back to the time you uttered those words, either to a friend or to God himself. Praise God for creating a desire for him in you and thank him for giving his precious salvation to you.

Read Acts 16.

16 He came to Derbe and then to Lys-
tra, where a disciple named Timo-
thy lived, whose mother was a Jew-
ess and a believer, but whose father was a Greek.
2The brothers at Lystra and Iconium spoke well
of him. 3Paul wanted to take him along on the
journey, so he circumcised him because of the
Jews who lived in that area, for they all knew that
his father was a Greek. 4As they traveled from
town to town, they delivered the decisions
reached by the apostles and elders in Jerusalem
for the people to obey. 5So the churches were
strengthened in the faith and grew daily in num-
bers.
6Paul and his companions traveled throughout
the region of Phrygia and Galatia, having been
kept by the Holy Spirit from preaching the word
in the province of Asia. 7When they came to the
border of Mysia, they tried to enter Bithynia, but
the Spirit of Jesus would not allow them to. 8So
they passed by Mysia and went down to Troas.
9During the night Paul had a vision of a man of
Macedonia standing and begging him, "Come
over to Macedonia and help us." 10After Paul had
seen the vision, we got ready at once to leave for
Macedonia, concluding that God had called us to
preach the gospel to them.
11From Troas we put out to sea and sailed

straight for Samothrace, and the next day on to
Neapolis. 12From there we traveled to Philippi, a
Roman colony and the leading city of that district
of Macedonia. And we stayed there several days.
13On the Sabbath we went outside the city gate
to the river, where we expected to find a place of
prayer. We sat down and began to speak to the
women who had gathered there. 14One of those
listening was a woman named Lydia, a dealer in
purple cloth from the city of Thyatira, who was a
worshiper of God. The Lord opened her heart to
respond to Paul's message. 15When she and the
members of her household were baptized, she in-
vited us to her home. "If you consider me a be-
liever in the Lord," she said, "come and stay at
my house." And she persuaded us.
16Once when we were going to the place of
prayer, we were met by a slave girl who had a
spirit by which she predicted the future. She
earned a great deal of money for her owners by
fortune-telling. 17This girl followed Paul and the
rest of us, shouting, "These men are servants of
the Most High God, who are telling you the way
to be saved." 18She kept this up for many days.
Finally Paul became so troubled that he turned
around and said to the spirit, "In the name of
Jesus Christ I command you to come out of her!"
At that moment the spirit left her.
19When the owners of the slave girl realized
that their hope of making money was gone, they
seized Paul and Silas and dragged them into the
marketplace to face the authorities. 20They
brought them before the magistrates and said,
"These men are Jews, and are throwing our city
into an uproar 21by advocating customs unlawful
for us Romans to accept or practice."
22The crowd joined in the attack against Paul
and Silas, and the magistrates ordered them to be
stripped and beaten. 23After they had been se-
verely flogged, they were thrown into prison, and
the jailer was commanded to guard them care-
fully. 24Upon receiving such orders, he put them
in the inner cell and fastened their feet in the
stocks.
25About midnight Paul and Silas were praying
and singing hymns to God, and the other prison-
ers were listening to them. 26Suddenly there was
such a violent earthquake that the foundations of
the prison were shaken. At once all the prison
doors flew open, and everybody's chains came
loose. 27The jailer woke up, and when he saw the
prison doors open, he drew his sword and was
about to kill himself because he thought the pris-
oners had escaped. 28But Paul shouted, "Don't
harm yourself! We are all here!"
29The jailer called for lights, rushed in and fell
trembling before Paul and Silas. 30He then
brought them out and asked, "Sirs, what must I
do to be saved?"
31They replied, "Believe in the Lord Jesus, and
you will be saved—you and your household."
32Then they spoke the word of the Lord to him
and to all the others in his house. 33At that hour
of the night the jailer took them and washed their
wounds; then immediately he and all his family
were baptized. 34The jailer brought them into his
house and set a meal before them; he was filled
with joy because he had come to believe in
God—he and his whole family.
35When it was daylight, the magistrates sent
their officers to the jailer with the order: "Release
those men." 36The jailer told Paul, "The magis-
trates have ordered that you and Silas be released.
Now you can leave. Go in peace."
37But Paul said to the officers: "They beat us
publicly without a trial, even though we are Ro-
man citizens, and threw us into prison. And now
do they want to get rid of us quietly? No! Let
them come themselves and escort us out."
38The officers reported this to the magistrates,
and when they heard that Paul and Silas were
Roman citizens, they were alarmed. 39They came
to appease them and escorted them from the
prison, requesting them to leave the city. 40After
Paul and Silas came out of the prison, they went
to Lydia's house, where they met with the broth-
ers and encouraged them. Then they left.

Discovering the Word 1. In verses 6–10 how is Paul directed concerning where he should go? 2. What principles of guidance do you see in verses 6–10? 3. Paul responded immediately to God's message. How was his obedience confirmed on arriving in Macedonia (vv. 11–15)? 4. The slaveowners had Paul and Silas jailed. Their response to being in jail and being beaten was to pray and sing hymns. Describe the events that led up the jailer's question "What must I do to be saved?" (vv. 23–30). 5. It is clear in the book of Acts that God is concerned about the world and the nations being reached with the gospel. But he is also concerned about reaching individuals. What individuals were affected by Paul's obedience to God's leading (vv. 14, 18, 30–31)? How?

Applying the Word 1. How does your response to opposition to and suffering for the gospel compare and contrast to that of Paul and Silas (v. 25)? 2. Paul and Silas speak the truth of the gospel as well as living it out. How do you give both a verbal and a living witness to Jesus? 3. Is there a person or task to which God is calling you? What steps do you need to take for immediate and unreserved obedience?

Responding in Prayer Ask God to give you courage as you step in faith to obey him, to tell those around you about the good news that has transformed your life.

16 / *Acts 17*
An Unknown God

ONLY A FEW short decades ago, Christians in the West could assume that most people they met belonged to a church or at least based their lives on Judeo-Christian values. Today, Christians in the West face what Christians in the East have had to cope with for centuries—a wide variety of religious beliefs and practices that often have little in common with Christianity. The world's major religions, Hinduism, Buddhism and Islam, are making inroads as are a variety of cults, New Age philosophies, occultic activities and even traditional paganism. How do we cope with a world that knows or cares so little about the truth of Jesus Christ? Paul left us a helpful model when he visited the world center of pagan philosophy and religion—Athens.

Warming Up to God Do you often feel overwhelmed by the dismal spiritual conditions of this world? Remember and even savor the knowledge that Jesus is Lord over it all—the sin, deceit and pain around us are all subject to his will.

Read Acts 17.

17 When they had passed through
Amphipolis and Apollonia, they
came to Thessalonica, where there
was a Jewish synagogue. 2As his custom was, Paul
went into the synagogue, and on three Sabbath
days he reasoned with them from the Scriptures,
3explaining and proving that the Christ[h] had to
suffer and rise from the dead. "This Jesus I am
proclaiming to you is the Christ,[h]" he said.
4Some of the Jews were persuaded and joined
Paul and Silas, as did a large number of God-fear-
ing Greeks and not a few prominent women.
5But the Jews were jealous; so they rounded up
some bad characters from the marketplace,
formed a mob and started a riot in the city. They
rushed to Jason's house in search of Paul and Silas
in order to bring them out to the crowd.[i] 6But
when they did not find them, they dragged Jason
and some other brothers before the city officials,
shouting: "These men who have caused trouble
all over the world have now come here, 7and Ja-
son has welcomed them into his house. They are
all defying Caesar's decrees, saying that there is
another king, one called Jesus." 8When they
heard this, the crowd and the city officials were
thrown into turmoil. 9Then they made Jason and
the others post bond and let them go.
10As soon as it was night, the brothers sent Paul
and Silas away to Berea. On arriving there, they
went to the Jewish synagogue. 11Now the Bereans
were of more noble character than the Thessalo-
nians, for they received the message with great
eagerness and examined the Scriptures every day
to see if what Paul said was true. 12Many of the
Jews believed, as did also a number of prominent
Greek women and many Greek men.
13When the Jews in Thessalonica learned that
Paul was preaching the word of God at Berea,
they went there too, agitating the crowds and stir-
ring them up. 14The brothers immediately sent
Paul to the coast, but Silas and Timothy stayed at
Berea. 15The men who escorted Paul brought him
to Athens and then left with instructions for Silas
and Timothy to join him as soon as possible.
16While Paul was waiting for them in Athens,
he was greatly distressed to see that the city was
full of idols. 17So he reasoned in the synagogue
with the Jews and the God-fearing Greeks, as well
as in the marketplace day by day with those who

[h]3 Or *Messiah* [i]5 Or *the assembly of the people*

happened to be there. 18A group of Epicurean and Stoic philosophers began to dispute with him. Some of them asked, "What is this babbler trying to say?" Others remarked, "He seems to be advocating foreign gods." They said this because Paul was preaching the good news about Jesus and the resurrection. 19Then they took him and brought him to a meeting of the Areopagus, where they said to him, "May we know what this new teaching is that you are presenting? 20You are bringing some strange ideas to our ears, and we want to know what they mean." 21(All the Athenians and the foreigners who lived there spent their time doing nothing but talking about and listening to the latest ideas.)

22Paul then stood up in the meeting of the Areopagus and said: "Men of Athens! I see that in every way you are very religious. 23For as I walked around and looked carefully at your objects of worship, I even found an altar with this inscription: TO AN UNKNOWN GOD. Now what you worship as something unknown I am going to proclaim to you.

24"The God who made the world and everything in it is the Lord of heaven and earth and does not live in temples built by hands. 25And he is not served by human hands, as if he needed anything, because he himself gives all men life and breath and everything else. 26From one man he made every nation of men, that they should inhabit the whole earth; and he determined the times set for them and the exact places where they should live. 27God did this so that men would seek him and perhaps reach out for him and find him, though he is not far from each one of us. 28'For in him we live and move and have our being.' As some of your own poets have said, 'We are his offspring.'

29"Therefore since we are God's offspring, we should not think that the divine being is like gold or silver or stone—an image made by man's design and skill. 30In the past God overlooked such ignorance, but now he commands all people everywhere to repent. 31For he has set a day when he will judge the world with justice by the man he has appointed. He has given proof of this to all men by raising him from the dead."

32When they heard about the resurrection of the dead, some of them sneered, but others said, "We want to hear you again on this subject." 33At that, Paul left the Council. 34A few men became followers of Paul and believed. Among them was Dionysius, a member of the Areopagus, also a woman named Damaris, and a number of others.

Discovering the Word 1. In this chapter Paul interacts with three cities and three different cultures. Compare and contrast Paul's ministry in Thessalonica and Berea. (What approach did he take? How was his message received by the people? What kind of results did he have?) 2. In Thessalonica and Berea, as in most places, Paul makes his contacts in the synagogues and speaks almost exclusively from Scripture. How does his ministry in Athens differ from this? 3. How do the people respond to his teaching in Athens? 4. Though Paul approaches people differently, some points in the content of his message are very consistent. Identify these (vv. 3, 18, 24–28, 30–31).

Applying the Word 1. In his lecture in Athens, Paul mentions "the objects of your worship." What are some of the objects of worship for people in our culture? 2. In Athens Paul begins to tell them about the living God with an inscription from one of their altars—"to an unknown god." What are the "points of truth" from which you can start to communicate the gospel to those in your world? 3. What are ways that you might be tempted to compromise the message of the gospel as you communicate it to certain people? 4. How do you need to better prepare yourself to effectively communicate the gospel of Jesus Christ to those to whom God has called you to minister?

Responding in Prayer Ask God to show you what you have in common with the non-Christians in your life.

17 / *Acts 18*
Companions in Ministry

JUST RECENTLY, I visited my childhood pastor and his wife. As I left them, my heart was full of gratitude. Gratitude not only for the Wrights, but also for the others past and present who have prepared me for outreach. I am thankful for those who have prayed for me, been my friends, walked along with me, listened to me, loved me and cared about my walk with God and my service to others, who have encouraged me and corrected me. I enjoy thinking about the people who have touched my life and who have been companions in ministry. I am not alone in this need for companionship. In this study we will look at some of the people in Paul's life who were his companions in ministry.

Warming Up to God Close your eyes and think about one person who profoundly affects your life. Tell God how grateful you are to know such a wonderful friend and thank God for loving you through that person.

Read Acts 18.

18 After this, Paul left Athens and
went to Corinth. 2There he met a
Jew named Aquila, a native of Pon-
tus, who had recently come from Italy with his
wife Priscilla, because Claudius had ordered all
the Jews to leave Rome. Paul went to see them,
3and because he was a tentmaker as they were, he
stayed and worked with them. 4Every Sabbath he
reasoned in the synagogue, trying to persuade
Jews and Greeks.

5When Silas and Timothy came from Macedo-
nia, Paul devoted himself exclusively to preach-
ing, testifying to the Jews that Jesus was the
Christ.[j] 6But when the Jews opposed Paul and
became abusive, he shook out his clothes in pro-
test and said to them, "Your blood be on your
own heads! I am clear of my responsibility. From
now on I will go to the Gentiles."

7Then Paul left the synagogue and went next
door to the house of Titius Justus, a worshiper of
God. 8Crispus, the synagogue ruler, and his entire
household believed in the Lord; and many of the
Corinthians who heard him believed and were
baptized.

9One night the Lord spoke to Paul in a vision:
"Do not be afraid; keep on speaking, do not be
silent. 10For I am with you, and no one is going to
attack and harm you, because I have many people
in this city." 11So Paul stayed for a year and a half,
teaching them the word of God.

12While Gallio was proconsul of Achaia, the
Jews made a united attack on Paul and brought
him into court. 13"This man," they charged, "is
persuading the people to worship God in ways
contrary to the law."

14Just as Paul was about to speak, Gallio said to
the Jews, "If you Jews were making a complaint
about some misdemeanor or serious crime, it
would be reasonable for me to listen to you. 15But
since it involves questions about words and
names and your own law—settle the matter your-
selves. I will not be a judge of such things." 16So
he had them ejected from the court. 17Then they
all turned on Sosthenes the synagogue ruler and
beat him in front of the court. But Gallio showed
no concern whatever.

18Paul stayed on in Corinth for some time.
Then he left the brothers and sailed for Syria,
accompanied by Priscilla and Aquila. Before he
sailed, he had his hair cut off at Cenchrea because
of a vow he had taken. 19They arrived at Ephesus,
where Paul left Priscilla and Aquila. He himself
went into the synagogue and reasoned with the
Jews. 20When they asked him to spend more time
with them, he declined. 21But as he left, he prom-
ised, "I will come back if it is God's will." Then he
set sail from Ephesus. 22When he landed at Caes-
area, he went up and greeted the church and then
went down to Antioch.

23After spending some time in Antioch, Paul set
out from there and traveled from place to place
throughout the region of Galatia and Phrygia,
strengthening all the disciples.

24Meanwhile a Jew named Apollos, a native of
Alexandria, came to Ephesus. He was a learned
man, with a thorough knowledge of the Scrip-
tures. 25He had been instructed in the way of the
Lord, and he spoke with great fervor[k] and taught

[j]5 Or *Messiah;* also in verse 28 [k]25 Or *with fervor in the Spirit*

about Jesus accurately, though he knew only the baptism of John. 26He began to speak boldly in the synagogue. When Priscilla and Aquila heard him, they invited him to their home and explained to him the way of God more adequately.

27When Apollos wanted to go to Achaia, the brothers encouraged him and wrote to the disciples there to welcome him. On arriving, he was a great help to those who by grace had believed. 28For he vigorously refuted the Jews in public debate, proving from the Scriptures that Jesus was the Christ.

Discovering the Word 1. List the people in Paul's life that you see in this passage. 2. What did Silas and Timothy contribute to Paul's life and ministry (v. 5)? 3. In verses 18–23 what do you learn about Paul's relationships? 4. Describe Apollos (vv. 24–26). 5. How was Apollos's ministry affected by his relationship with Aquila and Priscilla (vv. 27–28)?

Applying the Word 1. When has someone encouraged you with good news of God's work elsewhere, entered into your ministry, shared themselves or their home with you, or supported you financially or in other ways? 2. What keeps you from allowing others to enter into your life and ministry in such ways? 3. As you review this passage, what ways do you recognize in which you need to develop, build and nurture relationships that will contribute to your spiritual growth and outreach?

Responding in Prayer Who are your companions in ministry? Thank God for their presence in your life as good gifts from him.

18 / *Acts 19:1—20:12*
In the Name of Jesus

WE LEFT PAUL in chapter 18 traveling throughout Galatia and Phrygia "strengthening all the disciples." In this chapter he returns to Ephesus, where he settles for two and a half years. Great work is done there during this time, and it radiates out to other cities in the province of Asia. Luke vividly portrays the effect of Paul's ministry in just a few scenes in this chapter.

Warming Up to God Often we feel that reading the Bible is our time to give to God. But he dearly wants to come to us as we study Scripture and pray. Lay aside your effort right now and commit yourself to accepting God's grace. Let God be your companion while you study the Word.

Read Acts 19:1—20:12.

19 While Apollos was at Corinth, Paul took the road through the interior and arrived at Ephesus. There he found some disciples 2and asked them, "Did you receive the Holy Spirit when[l] you believed?"

They answered, "No, we have not even heard that there is a Holy Spirit."

3So Paul asked, "Then what baptism did you receive?"

"John's baptism," they replied.

4Paul said, "John's baptism was a baptism of repentance. He told the people to believe in the one coming after him, that is, in Jesus." 5On hearing this, they were baptized into[m] the name of the Lord Jesus. 6When Paul placed his hands on them, the Holy Spirit came on them, and they spoke in tongues[n] and prophesied. 7There were about twelve men in all.

8Paul entered the synagogue and spoke boldly there for three months, arguing persuasively about the kingdom of God. 9But some of them became obstinate; they refused to believe and publicly maligned the Way. So Paul left them. He took the disciples with him and had discussions daily in the lecture hall of Tyrannus. 10This went on for two years, so that all the Jews and Greeks who lived in the province of Asia heard the word of the Lord.

11God did extraordinary miracles through Paul,

[l] 2 Or *after* [m] 5 Or *in* [n] 6 Or *other languages*

12so that even handkerchiefs and aprons that had touched him were taken to the sick, and their illnesses were cured and the evil spirits left them.

13Some Jews who went around driving out evil spirits tried to invoke the name of the Lord Jesus over those who were demon-possessed. They would say, "In the name of Jesus, whom Paul preaches, I command you to come out." 14Seven sons of Sceva, a Jewish chief priest, were doing this. 15⌊One day⌋ the evil spirit answered them, "Jesus I know, and I know about Paul, but who are you?" 16Then the man who had the evil spirit jumped on them and overpowered them all. He gave them such a beating that they ran out of the house naked and bleeding.

17When this became known to the Jews and Greeks living in Ephesus, they were all seized with fear, and the name of the Lord Jesus was held in high honor. 18Many of those who believed now came and openly confessed their evil deeds. 19A number who had practiced sorcery brought their scrolls together and burned them publicly. When they calculated the value of the scrolls, the total came to fifty thousand drachmas.[o] 20In this way the word of the Lord spread widely and grew in power.

21After all this had happened, Paul decided to go to Jerusalem, passing through Macedonia and Achaia. "After I have been there," he said, "I must visit Rome also." 22He sent two of his helpers, Timothy and Erastus, to Macedonia, while he stayed in the province of Asia a little longer.

23About that time there arose a great disturbance about the Way. 24A silversmith named Demetrius, who made silver shrines of Artemis, brought in no little business for the craftsmen. 25He called them together, along with the workmen in related trades, and said: "Men, you know we receive a good income from this business. 26And you see and hear how this fellow Paul has convinced and led astray large numbers of people here in Ephesus and in practically the whole province of Asia. He says that man-made gods are no gods at all. 27There is danger not only that our trade will lose its good name, but also that the temple of the great goddess Artemis will be discredited, and the goddess herself, who is worshiped throughout the province of Asia and the world, will be robbed of her divine majesty."

28When they heard this, they were furious and began shouting: "Great is Artemis of the Ephesians!" 29Soon the whole city was in an uproar. The people seized Gaius and Aristarchus, Paul's traveling companions from Macedonia, and rushed as one man into the theater. 30Paul wanted to appear before the crowd, but the disciples would not let him. 31Even some of the officials of the province, friends of Paul, sent him a message begging him not to venture into the theater.

32The assembly was in confusion: Some were shouting one thing, some another. Most of the people did not even know why they were there. 33The Jews pushed Alexander to the front, and some of the crowd shouted instructions to him. He motioned for silence in order to make a defense before the people. 34But when they realized he was a Jew, they all shouted in unison for about two hours: "Great is Artemis of the Ephesians!"

35The city clerk quieted the crowd and said: "Men of Ephesus, doesn't all the world know that the city of Ephesus is the guardian of the temple of the great Artemis and of her image, which fell from heaven? 36Therefore, since these facts are undeniable, you ought to be quiet and not do anything rash. 37You have brought these men here, though they have neither robbed temples nor blasphemed our goddess. 38If, then, Demetrius and his fellow craftsmen have a grievance against anybody, the courts are open and there are proconsuls. They can press charges. 39If there is anything further you want to bring up, it must be settled in a legal assembly. 40As it is, we are in danger of being charged with rioting because of today's events. In that case we would not be able to account for this commotion, since there is no reason for it." 41After he had said this, he dismissed the assembly.

20 When the uproar had ended, Paul sent for the disciples and, after encouraging them, said good-by and set out for Macedonia. 2He traveled through that area, speaking many words of encouragement to the people, and finally arrived in Greece, 3where he stayed three months. Because the Jews made a plot against him just as he was about to sail for Syria, he decided to go back through Macedonia. 4He was accompanied by Sopater son of Pyrrhus from Berea, Aristarchus and Secundus from Thessalonica, Gaius from Derbe, Timothy also, and Tychicus and Trophimus from the province of Asia. 5These men went on ahead and waited for us at Troas. 6But we sailed from Philippi after the

o19 A drachma was a silver coin worth about a day's wages.

Feast of Unleavened Bread, and five days later joined the others at Troas, where we stayed seven days.

7On the first day of the week we came together to break bread. Paul spoke to the people and, because he intended to leave the next day, kept on talking until midnight. 8There were many lamps in the upstairs room where we were meeting. 9Seated in a window was a young man named Eutychus, who was sinking into a deep sleep as Paul talked on and on. When he was sound asleep, he fell to the ground from the third story and was picked up dead. 10Paul went down, threw himself on the young man and put his arms around him. "Don't be alarmed," he said. "He's alive!" 11Then he went upstairs again and broke bread and ate. After talking until daylight, he left. 12The people took the young man home alive and were greatly comforted.

Discovering the Word 1. Scan chapter 19. Where do you see God's power revealed? 2. In 19:1–7 Paul encounters some disciples. What did he do to interact with them effectively? 3. Throughout this entire passage it is evident that Paul has a strategy for communicating the gospel. Specifically, what strategy does Paul have for his ministry in Ephesus (19:8–10)? 4. What is the cause of the riot in Ephesus (19:23–41)? How was it settled? 5. Paul continued to travel and encourage believers as he preached the gospel. What effect did the episode in 20:7–12 have on the crowd?

Applying the Word 1. What do you see in Paul's relationship with the disciples that might help you in relating to young Christians or your non-Christian friends? 2. What kind of plan for communicating the gospel would be helpful in your world? 3. How can you prepare yourself for both positive and negative responses as you are a part of communicating the gospel of Christ?

Responding in Prayer Thank God for the amazing fact that he uses us, sinful humanity, to spread the gospel and advance his kingdom. Thank him for using you.

19 / *Acts 20:13–38*
Paul's Farewell

"I WILL SEE you in heaven." I nodded, gave him a hug and a kiss and walked away from his bedside. When I left the room, I wept. Although it was twenty years ago that I said goodby to Pop Z, the memory is still deep in my heart. In this chapter we will enter into weeping as Paul says his final goodby to the elders at Ephesus. He knows that more hardship and prison await him in Jerusalem. And he will never see the faces of these elders again.

Warming Up to God Is the busyness of the world around you crowding you as you seek the face of God? Thank God that he has given you the grace that brought you to his Word right now, and ask him to still your restless heart as he comes to sit with you.

Read Acts 20:13–38.

13We went on ahead to the ship and sailed for Assos, where we were going to take Paul aboard. He had made this arrangement because he was going there on foot. 14When he met us at Assos, we took him aboard and went on to Mitylene. 15The next day we set sail from there and arrived off Kios. The day after that we crossed over to Samos, and on the following day arrived at Miletus. 16Paul had decided to sail past Ephesus to avoid spending time in the province of Asia, for he was in a hurry to reach Jerusalem, if possible, by the day of Pentecost.

17From Miletus, Paul sent to Ephesus for the elders of the church. 18When they arrived, he said to them: "You know how I lived the whole time I was with you, from the first day I came into the province of Asia. 19I served the Lord with great humility and with tears, although I was severely tested by the plots of the Jews. 20You know that I have not hesitated to preach anything that would

be helpful to you but have taught you publicly
and from house to house. 21I have declared to
both Jews and Greeks that they must turn to God
in repentance and have faith in our Lord Jesus.
22"And now, compelled by the Spirit, I am go-
ing to Jerusalem, not knowing what will happen
to me there. 23I only know that in every city the
Holy Spirit warns me that prison and hardships
are facing me. 24However, I consider my life
worth nothing to me, if only I may finish the race
and complete the task the Lord Jesus has given
me—the task of testifying to the gospel of God's
grace.
25"Now I know that none of you among whom
I have gone about preaching the kingdom will
ever see me again. 26Therefore, I declare to you
today that I am innocent of the blood of all men.
27For I have not hesitated to proclaim to you the
whole will of God. 28Keep watch over yourselves
and all the flock of which the Holy Spirit has
made you overseers.[p] Be shepherds of the
church of God,[q] which he bought with his own
blood. 29I know that after I leave, savage wolves
will come in among you and will not spare the
flock. 30Even from your own number men will
arise and distort the truth in order to draw away
disciples after them. 31So be on your guard! Re-
member that for three years I never stopped
warning each of you night and day with tears.
32"Now I commit you to God and to the word
of his grace, which can build you up and give you
an inheritance among all those who are sancti-
fied. 33I have not coveted anyone's silver or gold
or clothing. 34You yourselves know that these
hands of mine have supplied my own needs and
the needs of my companions. 35In everything I
did, I showed you that by this kind of hard work
we must help the weak, remembering the words
the Lord Jesus himself said: 'It is more blessed to
give than to receive.'"
36When he had said this, he knelt down with
all of them and prayed. 37They all wept as they
embraced him and kissed him. 38What grieved
them most was his statement that they would
never see his face again. Then they accompanied
him to the ship.

p28 Traditionally *bishops* q28 Many manuscripts *of the Lord*

Discovering the Word 1. What does Paul say about his ministry to the Ephesians (vv. 18–21, 26–27, 31, 33–35)? 2. What are Paul's priorities (vv. 22–25)? 3. What instructions did Paul give to the leaders of the church at Ephesus (vv. 28–31)? 4. According to verse 32, why can Paul leave them with confidence? 5. In summary, according to this passage, why would Paul be able to say with integrity and humility to these leaders, "Follow my example. Do as I have done"?

Applying the Word 1. Who is in your spiritual care? 2. How are you preparing those that you nurture spiritually so that you can leave them with this same confidence? 3. Paul and the Ephesian elders were given the rare and special gift of being able to say goodby. What would you want to say to those in your spiritual care if you knew that you were going to die? Take time to express your hope and your love to that person in the near future.

Responding in Prayer Ask God for the courage to say these most important words to those you love and for whom you care deeply.

20/ *Acts 21:1—22:21*
Facing Opposition

AS THEY WENT to their death, taking the gospel of Jesus Christ to the Auca Indians, five young men sang:

We go in faith, our own great weakness feeling,
And needing more each day Thy grace to know:
Yet from our hearts a song of triumph pealing;
We rest on Thee, and in Thy name we go.

We rest on Thee our Shield and our Defender!
Thine is the battle, thine shall be the praise
When passing through the gates of pearly splendor,
Victors—we rest with Thee, through endless days.

Like Paul, knowing that death was a very real possibility, they did not turn aside from what they knew God wanted them to do.

Warming Up to God There are times when we do not feel courageous about our faith, but question it. However, God is just as real when we doubt or fear as when our faith is strong. Let him come to you now in the midst of your fear and allow him to stretch your vision of how powerful he truly is.

Read Acts 21:1—22:21.

21 After we had torn ourselves away
from them, we put out to sea and
sailed straight to Cos. The next day
we went to Rhodes and from there to Patara. 2We
found a ship crossing over to Phoenicia, went on
board and set sail. 3After sighting Cyprus and
passing to the south of it, we sailed on to Syria.
We landed at Tyre, where our ship was to unload
its cargo. 4Finding the disciples there, we stayed
with them seven days. Through the Spirit they
urged Paul not to go on to Jerusalem. 5But when
our time was up, we left and continued on our
way. All the disciples and their wives and chil-
dren accompanied us out of the city, and there on
the beach we knelt to pray. 6After saying good-by
to each other, we went aboard the ship, and they
returned home.

7We continued our voyage from Tyre and
landed at Ptolemais, where we greeted the broth-
ers and stayed with them for a day. 8Leaving the
next day, we reached Caesarea and stayed at the
house of Philip the evangelist, one of the Seven.
9He had four unmarried daughters who prophe-
sied.

10After we had been there a number of days, a
prophet named Agabus came down from Judea.
11Coming over to us, he took Paul's belt, tied his
own hands and feet with it and said, "The Holy
Spirit says, 'In this way the Jews of Jerusalem will
bind the owner of this belt and will hand him
over to the Gentiles.' "

12When we heard this, we and the people there
pleaded with Paul not to go up to Jerusalem.
13Then Paul answered, "Why are you weeping
and breaking my heart? I am ready not only to be
bound, but also to die in Jerusalem for the name
of the Lord Jesus." 14When he would not be dis-
suaded, we gave up and said, "The Lord's will be
done."

15After this, we got ready and went up to Jeru-
salem. 16Some of the disciples from Caesarea ac-
companied us and brought us to the home of
Mnason, where we were to stay. He was a man
from Cyprus and one of the early disciples.

17When we arrived at Jerusalem, the brothers
received us warmly. 18The next day Paul and the
rest of us went to see James, and all the elders
were present. 19Paul greeted them and reported in
detail what God had done among the Gentiles
through his ministry.

20When they heard this, they praised God.
Then they said to Paul: "You see, brother, how
many thousands of Jews have believed, and all of
them are zealous for the law. 21They have been
informed that you teach all the Jews who live
among the Gentiles to turn away from Moses,
telling them not to circumcise their children or
live according to our customs. 22What shall we
do? They will certainly hear that you have come,
23so do what we tell you. There are four men with
us who have made a vow. 24Take these men, join
in their purification rites and pay their expenses,
so that they can have their heads shaved. Then
everybody will know there is no truth in these
reports about you, but that you yourself are living
in obedience to the law. 25As for the Gentile be-
lievers, we have written to them our decision that
they should abstain from food sacrificed to idols,
from blood, from the meat of strangled animals
and from sexual immorality."

26The next day Paul took the men and purified
himself along with them. Then he went to the
temple to give notice of the date when the days of
purification would end and the offering would be
made for each of them.

27When the seven days were nearly over, some
Jews from the province of Asia saw Paul at the
temple. They stirred up the whole crowd and
seized him, 28shouting, "Men of Israel, help us!
This is the man who teaches all men everywhere

against our people and our law and this place.
And besides, he has brought Greeks into the tem-
ple area and defiled this holy place." 29(They had
previously seen Trophimus the Ephesian in the
city with Paul and assumed that Paul had brought
him into the temple area.)

30The whole city was aroused, and the people
came running from all directions. Seizing Paul,
they dragged him from the temple, and immedi-
ately the gates were shut. 31While they were try-
ing to kill him, news reached the commander of
the Roman troops that the whole city of Jerusa-
lem was in an uproar. 32He at once took some
officers and soldiers and ran down to the crowd.
When the rioters saw the commander and his sol-
diers, they stopped beating Paul.

33The commander came up and arrested him
and ordered him to be bound with two chains.
Then he asked who he was and what he had
done. 34Some in the crowd shouted one thing and
some another, and since the commander could
not get at the truth because of the uproar, he
ordered that Paul be taken into the barracks.
35When Paul reached the steps, the violence of
the mob was so great he had to be carried by the
soldiers. 36The crowd that followed kept shout-
ing, "Away with him!"

37As the soldiers were about to take Paul into
the barracks, he asked the commander, "May I
say something to you?"

"Do you speak Greek?" he replied. 38"Aren't
you the Egyptian who started a revolt and led
four thousand terrorists out into the desert some
time ago?"

39Paul answered, "I am a Jew, from Tarsus in
Cilicia, a citizen of no ordinary city. Please let me
speak to the people."

40Having received the commander's permis-
sion, Paul stood on the steps and motioned to the
crowd. When they were all silent, he said to them

22

in Aramaic[r]: 1"Brothers and fathers,
listen now to my defense."

2When they heard him speak to
them in Aramaic, they became very quiet.

Then Paul said: 3"I am a Jew, born in Tarsus of
Cilicia, but brought up in this city. Under Gama-
liel I was thoroughly trained in the law of our
fathers and was just as zealous for God as any of
you are today. 4I persecuted the followers of this
Way to their death, arresting both men and
women and throwing them into prison, 5as also
the high priest and all the Council can testify. I
even obtained letters from them to their brothers
in Damascus, and went there to bring these peo-
ple as prisoners to Jerusalem to be punished.

6"About noon as I came near Damascus, sud-
denly a bright light from heaven flashed around
me. 7I fell to the ground and heard a voice say to
me, 'Saul! Saul! Why do you persecute me?'

8" 'Who are you, Lord?' I asked.

" 'I am Jesus of Nazareth, whom you are perse-
cuting,' he replied. 9My companions saw the
light, but they did not understand the voice of
him who was speaking to me.

10" 'What shall I do, Lord?' I asked.

" 'Get up,' the Lord said, 'and go into Damas-
cus. There you will be told all that you have been
assigned to do.' 11My companions led me by the
hand into Damascus, because the brilliance of the
light had blinded me.

12"A man named Ananias came to see me. He
was a devout observer of the law and highly re-
spected by all the Jews living there. 13He stood
beside me and said, 'Brother Saul, receive your
sight!' And at that very moment I was able to see
him.

14"Then he said: 'The God of our fathers has
chosen you to know his will and to see the Righ-
teous One and to hear words from his mouth.
15You will be his witness to all men of what you
have seen and heard. 16And now what are you
waiting for? Get up, be baptized and wash your
sins away, calling on his name.'

17"When I returned to Jerusalem and was pray-
ing at the temple, I fell into a trance 18and saw the
Lord speaking. 'Quick!' he said to me. 'Leave Je-
rusalem immediately, because they will not ac-
cept your testimony about me.'

19" 'Lord,' I replied, 'these men know that I
went from one synagogue to another to imprison
and beat those who believe in you. 20And when
the blood of your martyr[s] Stephen was shed, I
stood there giving my approval and guarding the
clothes of those who were killing him.'

21"Then the Lord said to me, 'Go; I will send
you far away to the Gentiles.' "

[r] 40 Or possibly *Hebrew*; also in 22:2 [s] 20 Or *witness*

Discovering the Word 1. Describe the warnings to Paul concerning going to Jerusalem (21:4, 10–12). 2. How did Paul respond to these warnings (21:5, 13)? 3. Paul arrives in Jerusalem, is greeted by the elders and reports what God has done through his ministry. What are the elders concerned about for Paul (21:20–25)? 4. How does Paul demonstrate his desire to be at one with the Jewish Christians (21:26)? 5. Note how Paul was treated with mob hysteria, assumption and false evidence (21:27–36, 38). How does he respond to all of this (21:37—22:21)?

Applying the Word 1. Think of a person you know who is focused on obeying God. How are you affected by his/her obedience? 2. How do you usually respond when you find yourself in conflict with others as a result of your obedience to God? 3. What have you seen in this passage that will help you become more single-minded in your obedience to God's will?

Responding in Prayer Tell God of your desire to be obedient, but admit the difficulties you face because of your sin. Ask him again to cleanse you and help you run the race with fervor.

21 / *Acts 22:22—23:35*
God at Work

BEING UNDER GOD'S protection is not a guarantee of physical safety. Being under his protection does guarantee that our Father is with us and has a purpose for us and that nothing happens to us that does not come through his hands. We can live with confidence that our life on earth will not end until that purpose for us is complete. And that ultimately we will end up safe and protected in heaven. Paul was so sure of God's hand in his life that he continued to move out boldly with the message of Jesus Christ in spite of physical danger intensifying.

Warming Up to God The protection of the Father's strong arms is always around us. Thank him for his mighty but unseen acts that keep you safe and secure as you walk through this life.

Read Acts 22:22—23:35.

22The crowd listened to Paul until he said this.
Then they raised their voices and shouted, "Rid
the earth of him! He's not fit to live!"
23As they were shouting and throwing off their
cloaks and flinging dust into the air, 24the com-
mander ordered Paul to be taken into the bar-
racks. He directed that he be flogged and ques-
tioned in order to find out why the people were
shouting at him like this. 25As they stretched him
out to flog him, Paul said to the centurion stand-
ing there, "Is it legal for you to flog a Roman
citizen who hasn't even been found guilty?"
26When the centurion heard this, he went to
the commander and reported it. "What are you
going to do?" he asked. "This man is a Roman
citizen."
27The commander went to Paul and asked,
"Tell me, are you a Roman citizen?"
"Yes, I am," he answered.
28Then the commander said, "I had to pay a big
price for my citizenship."
"But I was born a citizen," Paul replied.
29Those who were about to question him with-
drew immediately. The commander himself was
alarmed when he realized that he had put Paul, a
Roman citizen, in chains.
30The next day, since the commander wanted
to find out exactly why Paul was being accused by
the Jews, he released him and ordered the chief
priests and all the Sanhedrin to assemble. Then
he brought Paul and had him stand before them.
23 Paul looked straight at the Sanhe-
drin and said, "My brothers, I have
fulfilled my duty to God in all good
conscience to this day." 2At this the high priest
Ananias ordered those standing near Paul to
strike him on the mouth. 3Then Paul said to him,
"God will strike you, you whitewashed wall! You
sit there to judge me according to the law, yet you
yourself violate the law by commanding that I be
struck!"
4Those who were standing near Paul said, "You
dare to insult God's high priest?"
5Paul replied, "Brothers, I did not realize that

he was the high priest; for it is written: 'Do not speak evil about the ruler of your people.'[t]"

6Then Paul, knowing that some of them were Sadducees and the others Pharisees, called out in the Sanhedrin, "My brothers, I am a Pharisee, the son of a Pharisee. I stand on trial because of my hope in the resurrection of the dead." 7When he said this, a dispute broke out between the Pharisees and the Sadducees, and the assembly was divided. 8(The Sadducees say that there is no resurrection, and that there are neither angels nor spirits, but the Pharisees acknowledge them all.)

9There was a great uproar, and some of the teachers of the law who were Pharisees stood up and argued vigorously. "We find nothing wrong with this man," they said. "What if a spirit or an angel has spoken to him?" 10The dispute became so violent that the commander was afraid Paul would be torn to pieces by them. He ordered the troops to go down and take him away from them by force and bring him into the barracks.

11The following night the Lord stood near Paul and said, "Take courage! As you have testified about me in Jerusalem, so you must also testify in Rome."

12The next morning the Jews formed a conspiracy and bound themselves with an oath not to eat or drink until they had killed Paul. 13More than forty men were involved in this plot. 14They went to the chief priests and elders and said, "We have taken a solemn oath not to eat anything until we have killed Paul. 15Now then, you and the Sanhedrin petition the commander to bring him before you on the pretext of wanting more accurate information about his case. We are ready to kill him before he gets here."

16But when the son of Paul's sister heard of this plot, he went into the barracks and told Paul. 17Then Paul called one of the centurions and said, "Take this young man to the commander; he has something to tell him." 18So he took him to the commander.

The centurion said, "Paul, the prisoner, sent for me and asked me to bring this young man to you because he has something to tell you."

19The commander took the young man by the hand, drew him aside and asked, "What is it you want to tell me?"

20He said: "The Jews have agreed to ask you to bring Paul before the Sanhedrin tomorrow on the pretext of wanting more accurate information about him. 21Don't give in to them, because more than forty of them are waiting in ambush for him. They have taken an oath not to eat or drink until they have killed him. They are ready now, waiting for your consent to their request."

22The commander dismissed the young man and cautioned him, "Don't tell anyone that you have reported this to me."

23Then he called two of his centurions and ordered them, "Get ready a detachment of two hundred soldiers, seventy horsemen and two hundred spearmen[u] to go to Caesarea at nine tonight. 24Provide mounts for Paul so that he may be taken safely to Governor Felix."

25He wrote a letter as follows:

26Claudius Lysias,

To His Excellency, Governor Felix:

Greetings.

27This man was seized by the Jews and they were about to kill him, but I came with my troops and rescued him, for I had learned that he is a Roman citizen. 28I wanted to know why they were accusing him, so I brought him to their Sanhedrin. 29I found that the accusation had to do with questions about their law, but there was no charge against him that deserved death or imprisonment. 30When I was informed of a plot to be carried out against the man, I sent him to you at once. I also ordered his accusers to present to you their case against him.

31So the soldiers, carrying out their orders, took Paul with them during the night and brought him as far as Antipatris. 32The next day they let the cavalry go on with him, while they returned to the barracks. 33When the cavalry arrived in Caesarea, they delivered the letter to the governor and handed Paul over to him. 34The governor read the letter and asked what province he was from. Learning that he was from Cilicia, 35he said, "I will hear your case when your accusers get here." Then he ordered that Paul be kept under guard in Herod's palace.

[t]5 Exodus 22:28 [u]23 The meaning of the Greek for this word is uncertain.

Discovering the Word 1. Throughout this passage, we can see God's hand in the circumstances of Paul's life, protecting and directing him. In Acts 22:22–29 what is the source of the conflict? What is it that protects Paul? 2. In 23:1–10 what is the source of the conflict? How is Paul protected? 3. Why was Paul struck on the mouth for saying, "My brothers, I have fulfilled my duty to God in all good conscience to this day" (23:1)? 4. In Acts 23:12–25 the Jews are frustrated because they cannot get rid of Paul through the law, so they decide to ambush and kill him on their own. How is Paul protected? 5. We have observed God's protection of Paul. How do we see God's care for Paul in a more direct and supernatural way in 23:11?

Applying the Word 1. Think about God's hand in your life and ministry. How have you seen him work to protect and direct you toward his will? 2. In what ways do you need to grow in humbly acknowledging God's hand in your life? 3. How has your hope for God's will to be done in you been affected by looking at God's hand in Paul's life?

Responding in Prayer Ask God to show you his active hand in your life.

22 / *Acts 24:1—25:12*
Falsely Accused

OUR DEAR FRIEND George was falsely accused and on trial for heresy. My husband prayed fervently that God would shut the accusers' mouths, that he would bind their efforts, and that truth would prevail and bring freedom. He asked God to confound their actions so that their own words would bring out the truth and show up their false accusations. God chose to do what Andy asked for, and George was exonerated in a dramatic fashion. The words of the accusers brought condemnation on them. The defense did not even have to present their case. The pain, however, of being falsely accused is great. And the damage was not easily repaired. But George's consistent godly response throughout the whole ordeal reminded me of Jesus and Paul when they were falsely accused.

Warming Up to God Remember that today has been given to you by God, and he desires to be with you as you walk through it. Let him come to you now, knowing that he will show you more of himself through his Word.

Read Acts 24:1—25:12.

24 Five days later the high priest Ananias went down to Caesarea with some of the elders and a lawyer named Tertullus, and they brought their charges against Paul before the governor. 2When Paul was called in, Tertullus presented his case before Felix: "We have enjoyed a long period of peace under you, and your foresight has brought about reforms in this nation. 3Everywhere and in every way, most excellent Felix, we acknowledge this with profound gratitude. 4But in order not to weary you further, I would request that you be kind enough to hear us briefly.

5"We have found this man to be a troublemaker, stirring up riots among the Jews all over the world. He is a ringleader of the Nazarene sect 6and even tried to desecrate the temple; so we seized him. 8By[v] examining him yourself you will be able to learn the truth about all these charges we are bringing against him."

9The Jews joined in the accusation, asserting that these things were true.

10When the governor motioned for him to speak, Paul replied: "I know that for a number of years you have been a judge over this nation; so I gladly make my defense. 11You can easily verify that no more than twelve days ago I went up to Jerusalem to worship. 12My accusers did not find me arguing with anyone at the temple, or stirring up a crowd in the synagogues or anywhere else in the city. 13And they cannot prove to you the charges they are now making against me. 14However, I admit that I worship the God of our fathers

v6-8 Some manuscripts *him and wanted to judge him according to our law. 7But the commander, Lysias, came and with the use of much force snatched him from our hands 8and ordered his accusers to come before you. By*

as a follower of the Way, which they call a sect. I believe everything that agrees with the Law and that is written in the Prophets, 15and I have the same hope in God as these men, that there will be a resurrection of both the righteous and the wicked. 16So I strive always to keep my conscience clear before God and man.

17"After an absence of several years, I came to Jerusalem to bring my people gifts for the poor and to present offerings. 18I was ceremonially clean when they found me in the temple courts doing this. There was no crowd with me, nor was I involved in any disturbance. 19But there are some Jews from the province of Asia, who ought to be here before you and bring charges if they have anything against me. 20Or these who are here should state what crime they found in me when I stood before the Sanhedrin— 21unless it was this one thing I shouted as I stood in their presence: 'It is concerning the resurrection of the dead that I am on trial before you today.' "

22Then Felix, who was well acquainted with the Way, adjourned the proceedings. "When Lysias the commander comes," he said, "I will decide your case." 23He ordered the centurion to keep Paul under guard but to give him some freedom and permit his friends to take care of his needs.

24Several days later Felix came with his wife Drusilla, who was a Jewess. He sent for Paul and listened to him as he spoke about faith in Christ Jesus. 25As Paul discoursed on righteousness, self-control and the judgment to come, Felix was afraid and said, "That's enough for now! You may leave. When I find it convenient, I will send for you." 26At the same time he was hoping that Paul would offer him a bribe, so he sent for him frequently and talked with him.

27When two years had passed, Felix was succeeded by Porcius Festus, but because Felix wanted to grant a favor to the Jews, he left Paul in prison.

25 Three days after arriving in the province, Festus went up from Caesarea to Jerusalem, 2where the chief priests and Jewish leaders appeared before him and presented the charges against Paul. 3They urgently requested Festus, as a favor to them, to have Paul transferred to Jerusalem, for they were preparing an ambush to kill him along the way. 4Festus answered, "Paul is being held at Caesarea, and I myself am going there soon. 5Let some of your leaders come with me and press charges against the man there, if he has done anything wrong."

6After spending eight or ten days with them, he went down to Caesarea, and the next day he convened the court and ordered that Paul be brought before him. 7When Paul appeared, the Jews who had come down from Jerusalem stood around him, bringing many serious charges against him, which they could not prove.

8Then Paul made his defense: "I have done nothing wrong against the law of the Jews or against the temple or against Caesar."

9Festus, wishing to do the Jews a favor, said to Paul, "Are you willing to go up to Jerusalem and stand trial before me there on these charges?"

10Paul answered: "I am now standing before Caesar's court, where I ought to be tried. I have not done any wrong to the Jews, as you yourself know very well. 11If, however, I am guilty of doing anything deserving death, I do not refuse to die. But if the charges brought against me by these Jews are not true, no one has the right to hand me over to them. I appeal to Caesar!"

12After Festus had conferred with his council, he declared: "You have appealed to Caesar. To Caesar you will go!"

Discovering the Word 1. What are the accusations brought against Paul by the Jews (24:1–27)? 2. How would you describe Paul's defense? (Consider the content and the attitude and tone.) 3. What do you think is the significance of the fact that Felix was well acquainted with the Way (v. 22)? 4. In Acts 25:1–12 two years have passed since his trial, and Festus has become the new governor. The Jews have not given up. They continue to plot to kill Paul and ask Festus to have him transferred to Jerusalem. Festus refuses and tells the Jewish leaders to come to Caesarea for the trial. What evidence is there in this passage that Festus knows that Paul is innocent? 5. Why does Festus suggest that Paul go back to Jerusalem to be on trial?

Applying the Word 1. When have you known someone to respond to the proclamation of the gospel as Felix did? What might this mean? 2. Describe a time you have been falsely accused because of your faith. 3. What can you learn about how to respond to accusers from the way Paul responded to his accusers?

Responding in Prayer Ask God to give you patience and a heart of love for the people who surround you—your coworkers, family—people you can show the example of Christ.

23 / *Acts 25:13—26:32*
Testimony Before Agrippa

THOUGH HIS INNOCENCE has been clearly stated many times, Paul remains a prisoner. He repeatedly has to face the unfair charges of the Jewish leaders. He has made his defense with integrity and power, and in return he gets only threats of death. In it all Paul's witness remains consistent. His greatest desire is that his accusers and those in judgment over him will become Christians.

Warming Up to God How do you respond to the unfairness in the world around you—poverty, homelessness, the unfairness in your own life? It is difficult to assume an attitude like Paul's in the face of injustice. But God sees and knows what is right, and he understands the anger we feel. Express your thoughts and feelings to him. Let him calm the stirring in your heart with his gentle words.

Read Acts 25:13—26:32.

13A few days later King Agrippa and Bernice arrived at Caesarea to pay their respects to Festus. 14Since they were spending many days there, Festus discussed Paul's case with the king. He said: "There is a man here whom Felix left as a prisoner. 15When I went to Jerusalem, the chief priests and elders of the Jews brought charges against him and asked that he be condemned.

16"I told them that it is not the Roman custom to hand over any man before he has faced his accusers and has had an opportunity to defend himself against their charges. 17When they came here with me, I did not delay the case, but convened the court the next day and ordered the man to be brought in. 18When his accusers got up to speak, they did not charge him with any of the crimes I had expected. 19Instead, they had some points of dispute with him about their own religion and about a dead man named Jesus who Paul claimed was alive. 20I was at a loss how to investigate such matters; so I asked if he would be willing to go to Jerusalem and stand trial there on these charges. 21When Paul made his appeal to be held over for the Emperor's decision, I ordered him held until I could send him to Caesar."

22Then Agrippa said to Festus, "I would like to hear this man myself."

He replied, "Tomorrow you will hear him."

23The next day Agrippa and Bernice came with great pomp and entered the audience room with the high ranking officers and the leading men of the city. At the command of Festus, Paul was brought in. 24Festus said: "King Agrippa, and all who are present with us, you see this man! The whole Jewish community has petitioned me about him in Jerusalem and here in Caesarea, shouting that he ought not to live any longer. 25I found he had done nothing deserving of death, but because he made his appeal to the Emperor I decided to send him to Rome. 26But I have nothing definite to write to His Majesty about him. Therefore I have brought him before all of you, and especially before you, King Agrippa, so that as a result of this investigation I may have something to write. 27For I think it is unreasonable to send on a prisoner without specifying the charges against him."

26 Then Agrippa said to Paul, "You have permission to speak for yourself."

So Paul motioned with his hand and began his defense: 2"King Agrippa, I consider myself fortunate to stand before you today as I make my defense against all the accusations of the Jews, 3and especially so because you are well acquainted with all the Jewish customs and controversies. Therefore, I beg you to listen to me patiently.

4"The Jews all know the way I have lived ever since I was a child, from the beginning of my life in my own country, and also in Jerusalem. 5They have known me for a long time and can testify, if they are willing, that according to the strictest sect of our religion, I lived as a Pharisee. 6And now it is because of my hope in what God has promised our fathers that I am on trial today. 7This is the promise our twelve tribes are hoping to see fulfilled as they earnestly serve God day and night. O king, it is because of this hope that the Jews are accusing me. 8Why should any of you consider it incredible that God raises the dead?

9"I too was convinced that I ought to do all that was possible to oppose the name of Jesus of Nazareth. 10And that is just what I did in Jerusalem. On the authority of the chief priests I put many of the saints in prison, and when they were put to death, I cast my vote against them. 11Many a time I went from one synagogue to another to have them punished, and I tried to force them to blaspheme. In my obsession against them, I even went to foreign cities to persecute them.

12"On one of these journeys I was going to Damascus with the authority and commission of the chief priests. 13About noon, O king, as I was on the road, I saw a light from heaven, brighter than the sun, blazing around me and my companions. 14We all fell to the ground, and I heard a voice saying to me in Aramaic,[w] 'Saul, Saul, why do you persecute me? It is hard for you to kick against the goads.'

15"Then I asked, 'Who are you, Lord?'

" 'I am Jesus, whom you are persecuting,' the Lord replied. 16'Now get up and stand on your feet. I have appeared to you to appoint you as a servant and as a witness of what you have seen of me and what I will show you. 17I will rescue you from your own people and from the Gentiles. I am sending you to them 18to open their eyes and turn them from darkness to light, and from the power of Satan to God, so that they may receive forgiveness of sins and a place among those who are sanctified by faith in me.'

19"So then, King Agrippa, I was not disobedient to the vision from heaven. 20First to those in Damascus, then to those in Jerusalem and in all Judea, and to the Gentiles also, I preached that they should repent and turn to God and prove their repentance by their deeds. 21That is why the Jews seized me in the temple courts and tried to kill me. 22But I have had God's help to this very day, and so I stand here and testify to small and great alike. I am saying nothing beyond what the prophets and Moses said would happen— 23that the Christ[x] would suffer and, as the first to rise from the dead, would proclaim light to his own people and to the Gentiles."

24At this point Festus interrupted Paul's defense. "You are out of your mind, Paul!" he shouted. "Your great learning is driving you insane."

25"I am not insane, most excellent Festus," Paul replied. "What I am saying is true and reasonable. 26The king is familiar with these things, and I can speak freely to him. I am convinced that none of this has escaped his notice, because it was not done in a corner. 27King Agrippa, do you believe the prophets? I know you do."

28Then Agrippa said to Paul, "Do you think that in such a short time you can persuade me to be a Christian?"

29Paul replied, "Short time or long—I pray God that not only you but all who are listening to me today may become what I am, except for these chains."

30The king rose, and with him the governor and Bernice and those sitting with them. 31They left the room, and while talking with one another, they said, "This man is not doing anything that deserves death or imprisonment."

32Agrippa said to Festus, "This man could have been set free if he had not appealed to Caesar."

w14 Or *Hebrew* x23 Or *Messiah*

Discovering the Word 1. Describe the nature and content of Festus's report to Agrippa (25:13–22). 2. What are the main points about himself that Paul presents in his defense (26:1–23)? 3. Why does Paul say he is on trial (26:6–8)? 4. Contrast the commission of the Sanhedrin (26:9–11) to the commission of Christ (26:15–18). 5. Describe Paul's final interaction with King Agrippa (26:26–29).

Applying the Word 1. What motivates you to tell non-Christians about Jesus? 2. How does Paul's desire for King Agrippa compare or contrast with your desire for those around you who do not know Christ? 3. How might you move closer to where Paul was in this desire?

Responding in Prayer Ask God to give you the proper response to injustice and a heart that is soft toward those who do not know him.

24 / *Acts 27—28*
Paul in Rome!

ROME AT LAST! Paul was innocent. He could have been a free man. But he had appealed to Caesar—and to Caesar he was to go. As we look at these last two chapters of Acts and complete our study of the life of this marvelous servant of God, it might be worthwhile to ask the questions "Who was really free, and who were the real prisoners?"

Warming Up to God Sit quietly for a few moments, without trying to force your thoughts to move in any direction. Let silence reign in your heart before you look to Scripture.

Read Acts 27—28.

27 When it was decided that we would
sail for Italy, Paul and some other
prisoners were handed over to a
centurion named Julius, who belonged to the Im-
perial Regiment. 2We boarded a ship from Adra-
myttium about to sail for ports along the coast of
the province of Asia, and we put out to sea. Aris-
tarchus, a Macedonian from Thessalonica, was
with us.
3The next day we landed at Sidon; and Julius,
in kindness to Paul, allowed him to go to his
friends so they might provide for his needs.
4From there we put out to sea again and passed to
the lee of Cyprus because the winds were against
us. 5When we had sailed across the open sea off
the coast of Cilicia and Pamphylia, we landed at
Myra in Lycia. 6There the centurion found an Al-
exandrian ship sailing for Italy and put us on
board. 7We made slow headway for many days
and had difficulty arriving off Cnidus. When the
wind did not allow us to hold our course, we
sailed to the lee of Crete, opposite Salmone. 8We
moved along the coast with difficulty and came to
a place called Fair Havens, near the town of La-
sea.
9Much time had been lost, and sailing had al-
ready become dangerous because by now it was
after the Fast.[y] So Paul warned them, 10"Men, I
can see that our voyage is going to be disastrous
and bring great loss to ship and cargo, and to our
own lives also." 11But the centurion, instead of
listening to what Paul said, followed the advice of
the pilot and of the owner of the ship. 12Since the
harbor was unsuitable to winter in, the majority
decided that we should sail on, hoping to reach
Phoenix and winter there. This was a harbor in
Crete, facing both southwest and northwest.
13When a gentle south wind began to blow,
they thought they had obtained what they
wanted; so they weighed anchor and sailed along
the shore of Crete. 14Before very long, a wind of
hurricane force, called the "northeaster," swept
down from the island. 15The ship was caught by
the storm and could not head into the wind; so
we gave way to it and were driven along. 16As we
passed to the lee of a small island called Cauda,
we were hardly able to make the lifeboat secure.
17When the men had hoisted it aboard, they
passed ropes under the ship itself to hold it to-
gether. Fearing that they would run aground on
the sandbars of Syrtis, they lowered the sea an-
chor and let the ship be driven along. 18We took
such a violent battering from the storm that the
next day they began to throw the cargo over-
board. 19On the third day, they threw the ship's
tackle overboard with their own hands. 20When
neither sun nor stars appeared for many days and
the storm continued raging, we finally gave up all
hope of being saved.
21After the men had gone a long time without
food, Paul stood up before them and said: "Men,
you should have taken my advice not to sail from
Crete; then you would have spared yourselves
this damage and loss. 22But now I urge you to
keep up your courage, because not one of you
will be lost; only the ship will be destroyed. 23Last
night an angel of the God whose I am and whom
I serve stood beside me 24and said, 'Do not be
afraid, Paul. You must stand trial before Caesar;
and God has graciously given you the lives of all
who sail with you.' 25So keep up your courage,
men, for I have faith in God that it will happen
just as he told me. 26Nevertheless, we must run
aground on some island."
27On the fourteenth night we were still being

y9 That is, the Day of Atonement (Yom Kippur)

driven across the Adriatic[z] Sea, when about midnight the sailors sensed they were approaching land. 28They took soundings and found that the water was a hundred and twenty feet[a] deep. A short time later they took soundings again and found it was ninety feet[b] deep. 29Fearing that we would be dashed against the rocks, they dropped four anchors from the stern and prayed for daylight. 30In an attempt to escape from the ship, the sailors let the lifeboat down into the sea, pretending they were going to lower some anchors from the bow. 31Then Paul said to the centurion and the soldiers, "Unless these men stay with the ship, you cannot be saved." 32So the soldiers cut the ropes that held the lifeboat and let it fall away.

33Just before dawn Paul urged them all to eat. "For the last fourteen days," he said, "you have been in constant suspense and have gone without food—you haven't eaten anything. 34Now I urge you to take some food. You need it to survive. Not one of you will lose a single hair from his head." 35After he said this, he took some bread and gave thanks to God in front of them all. Then he broke it and began to eat. 36They were all encouraged and ate some food themselves. 37Altogether there were 276 of us on board. 38When they had eaten as much as they wanted, they lightened the ship by throwing the grain into the sea.

39When daylight came, they did not recognize the land, but they saw a bay with a sandy beach, where they decided to run the ship aground if they could. 40Cutting loose the anchors, they left them in the sea and at the same time untied the ropes that held the rudders. Then they hoisted the foresail to the wind and made for the beach. 41But the ship struck a sandbar and ran aground. The bow stuck fast and would not move, and the stern was broken to pieces by the pounding of the surf.

42The soldiers planned to kill the prisoners to prevent any of them from swimming away and escaping. 43But the centurion wanted to spare Paul's life and kept them from carrying out their plan. He ordered those who could swim to jump overboard first and get to land. 44The rest were to get there on planks or on pieces of the ship. In this way everyone reached land in safety.

28 Once safely on shore, we found out that the island was called Malta. 2The islanders showed us unusual kindness. They built a fire and welcomed us all because it was raining and cold. 3Paul gathered a pile of brushwood and, as he put it on the fire, a viper, driven out by the heat, fastened itself on his hand. 4When the islanders saw the snake hanging from his hand, they said to each other, "This man must be a murderer; for though he escaped from the sea, Justice has not allowed him to live." 5But Paul shook the snake off into the fire and suffered no ill effects. 6The people expected him to swell up or suddenly fall dead, but after waiting a long time and seeing nothing unusual happen to him, they changed their minds and said he was a god.

7There was an estate nearby that belonged to Publius, the chief official of the island. He welcomed us to his home and for three days entertained us hospitably. 8His father was sick in bed, suffering from fever and dysentery. Paul went in to see him and, after prayer, placed his hands on him and healed him. 9When this had happened, the rest of the sick on the island came and were cured. 10They honored us in many ways and when we were ready to sail, they furnished us with the supplies we needed.

11After three months we put out to sea in a ship that had wintered in the island. It was an Alexandrian ship with the figurehead of the twin gods Castor and Pollux. 12We put in at Syracuse and stayed there three days. 13From there we set sail and arrived at Rhegium. The next day the south wind came up, and on the following day we reached Puteoli. 14There we found some brothers who invited us to spend a week with them. And so we came to Rome. 15The brothers there had heard that we were coming, and they traveled as far as the Forum of Appius and the Three Taverns to meet us. At the sight of these men Paul thanked God and was encouraged. 16When we got to Rome, Paul was allowed to live by himself, with a soldier to guard him.

17Three days later he called together the leaders of the Jews. When they had assembled, Paul said to them: "My brothers, although I have done nothing against our people or against the customs of our ancestors, I was arrested in Jerusalem and handed over to the Romans. 18They examined me and wanted to release me, because I was not guilty of any crime deserving death. 19But when the Jews objected, I was compelled to appeal to Caesar—not that I had any charge to bring

[z]27 In ancient times the name referred to an area extending well south of Italy. [a]28 Greek *twenty orguias* (about 37 meters) [b]28 Greek *fifteen orguias* (about 27 meters)

against my own people. 20For this reason I have
asked to see you and talk with you. It is because
of the hope of Israel that I am bound with this
chain."

21They replied, "We have not received any let-
ters from Judea concerning you, and none of the
brothers who have come from there has reported
or said anything bad about you. 22But we want to
hear what your views are, for we know that peo-
ple everywhere are talking against this sect."

23They arranged to meet Paul on a certain day,
and came in even larger numbers to the place
where he was staying. From morning till evening
he explained and declared to them the kingdom
of God and tried to convince them about Jesus
from the Law of Moses and from the Prophets.
24Some were convinced by what he said, but oth-
ers would not believe. 25They disagreed among
themselves and began to leave after Paul had
made this final statement: "The Holy Spirit spoke
the truth to your forefathers when he said
through Isaiah the prophet:

26" 'Go to this people and say,
"You will be ever hearing but never
understanding;
you will be ever seeing but never
perceiving."
27For this people's heart has become calloused;
they hardly hear with their ears,
and they have closed their eyes.
Otherwise they might see with their eyes,
hear with their ears,
understand with their hearts
and turn, and I would heal them.'[c]

28"Therefore I want you to know that God's
salvation has been sent to the Gentiles, and they
will listen!"[d]

30For two whole years Paul stayed there in his
own rented house and welcomed all who came to
see him. 31Boldly and without hindrance he
preached the kingdom of God and taught about
the Lord Jesus Christ.

[c]27 Isaiah 6:9,10 [d]28 Some manuscripts *listen!"* 29*After he said this, the Jews left, arguing vigorously among themselves.*

Discovering the Word 1. Though Paul had every reason by this time to become very self-centered, how do you see him continuing to minister to others throughout these two chapters (27:9–10, 21–25, 31–38, 42–43; 28:3, 8–9, 17–20, 23–31)? 2. What do you see of Paul's compassion as he ministers? 3. What do you think it says about Paul that Julius let him go see his friends (27:3)? 4. What do you see of Paul's confidence in God throughout this passage? 5. In conclusion, what from the book of Acts motivates and equips you to be a witness "to the ends of the earth" (1:8)?

Applying the Word 1. What are the situations or relationships in your life with non-Christians in which you are tempted to give up on your proclamation of the gospel? 2. What truths from this study of Acts encourage you to not give up? 3. The words "Boldly and without hindrance he preached the kingdom of God and taught about the Lord Jesus Christ" (28:31) summarize not only Paul's two years in Rome, but his whole Christian life. To what degree would you like this to be a summary of your life? Explain.

Responding in Prayer Thank God for the ways that he has taught you through the book of Acts. Ask him to continue to teach you as you try to live out the lessons you have learned.

Romans

Romans may be the most important letter you will ever read. It is Paul's masterpiece, the clearest and fullest explanation of the gospel in the Bible. John Calvin said that "if a man understands it, he has a sure road opened for him to the understanding of the whole Scripture." William Tyndale, the father of English Bible translators, believed that every Christian should learn it by heart. "The more it is studied," he wrote, "the easier it is; the more it is chewed, the pleasanter it is" (prologue to Romans in his 1534 English New Testament).

But watch out! Those who study Romans are rarely the same afterward. For example, in the summer of A.D. 386 Augustine sat weeping in the garden of his friend Alypius. He wanted to begin a new life but lacked the strength to break with the old. Taking up a scroll of Romans, he read, "Clothe yourselves with the Lord Jesus Christ, and do not think about how to gratify the desires of the sinful nature." "No further would I read," he tells us, "nor had I any need; instantly at the end of this sentence, a clear light flooded my heart and all the darkness of doubt vanished away."

In 1515 Martin Luther began to teach the book of Romans to his students. He wrote, "Night and day I pondered until . . . I grasped the truth that the righteousness of God is that righteousness whereby, through grace and sheer mercy, he justifies us by faith. Thereupon I felt myself to be reborn and to have gone through open doors into paradise. The whole scripture took on new meaning, and whereas before the 'righteousness of God' had filled me with hate, now it became to me inexpressibly sweet in greater love. This passage in Paul became to me a gateway to heaven." Two years later he nailed his ninety-five theses to the door of the castle church in Wittenberg, and the Protestant Reformation began!

The evening of May 24, 1738, John Wesley "went very unwillingly to a society in Aldersgate Street, where one was reading Luther's preface to the Epistle to the Romans. About a quarter before nine," he wrote in his journal, "while he was describing the change which God works in the heart through faith in Christ, I felt my heart strangely warmed. I felt I did trust in Christ, Christ alone, for my salvation; and an assurance was given me that he had taken *my* sins away, even *mine*; and saved me from the law of sin and death." This event in Wesley's life helped to launch the great Evangelical Revival of the eighteenth century.

We need to grasp the message of Romans in our day as well. Many are preaching a gospel that lacks clarity and substance. People are told to "invite Jesus into their heart" or simply to "follow Christ" without understanding the meaning of his death and resurrection.

We cannot correct this problem merely by memorizing gospel outlines or canned presentations. We need to immerse ourselves in Scripture through diligent study and thoughtful reflection. Only when the gospel grips us as it did Augustine, Luther and Wesley will we realize why "it is the power of God for the salvation of everyone who believes" (Ro 1:16).

Romans is different from most of Paul's letters. He did not found the church in Rome; in fact, he had never been there. It has been suggested that the church in Rome was founded by some of those who were present on the day of Pentecost (Acts 2:10). However, Paul had met some of the Roman Christians, such as Priscilla and Aquila (Ro 16), during his missionary journeys to other cities.

Other letters were written to address specific problems within the churches. Romans seems relatively free of problems. Their only major "problem" was that they had never met the apostle. Therefore, Paul felt a need to fully explain to them in a letter what he would have said in person.

Paul probably wrote Romans between A.D. 57–58 while he was at Corinth in the home of his friend and convert Gaius. He planned to go first to Jerusalem to deliver a gift of money from the Gentile churches to the poor in Jerusalem. Then he hoped to visit Rome on his way to Spain. His hopes were later realized, but not as he had expected. When he finally arrived in Rome in early A.D. 60, he was a prisoner under house arrest (Acts 28:11–31).

May you be encouraged and challenged by the new life and the new lifestyle we have in Christ!

Outline

Part 1: A New Life

Part 2: A New Lifestyle

1 / *Romans 1:1–17*
Good News from God

"I'M ENGAGED!"

"I got a raise!"

"My wife's having a baby!"

What is our immediate response to good news? We tell others! We feel we will burst unless we share our joy with those around us.

Paul felt that way about the gospel, the good news about Jesus Christ. As we read these opening verses in his letter to the Romans, we find his excitement is contagious.

Warming Up to God Our days and weeks are often filled with bad news. Think of all the *good* news you can, and praise God for it.

Read Romans 1:1–17.

1 Paul, a servant of Christ Jesus, called to
be an apostle and set apart for the gospel
of God— 2the gospel he promised before-
hand through his prophets in the Holy Scriptures
3regarding his Son, who as to his human nature
was a descendant of David, 4and who through the
Spirit[a] of holiness was declared with power to be
the Son of God[b] by his resurrection from the
dead: Jesus Christ our Lord. 5Through him and
for his name's sake, we received grace and apos-
tleship to call people from among all the Gentiles
to the obedience that comes from faith. 6And you
also are among those who are called to belong to
Jesus Christ.

7To all in Rome who are loved by God and
called to be saints:

Grace and peace to you from God our Father
and from the Lord Jesus Christ.

8First, I thank my God through Jesus Christ for
all of you, because your faith is being reported all
over the world. 9God, whom I serve with my
whole heart in preaching the gospel of his Son, is
my witness how constantly I remember you 10in
my prayers at all times; and I pray that now at last
by God's will the way may be opened for me to
come to you.

11I long to see you so that I may impart to you
some spiritual gift to make you strong— 12that is,
that you and I may be mutually encouraged by
each other's faith. 13I do not want you to be un-
aware, brothers, that I planned many times to
come to you (but have been prevented from do-
ing so until now) in order that I might have a
harvest among you, just as I have had among the
other Gentiles.

14I am obligated both to Greeks and non-
Greeks, both to the wise and the foolish. 15That is
why I am so eager to preach the gospel also to
you who are at Rome.

16I am not ashamed of the gospel, because it is
the power of God for the salvation of everyone
who believes: first for the Jew, then for the Gen-
tile. 17For in the gospel a righteousness from God
is revealed, a righteousness that is by faith from
first to last,[c] just as it is written: "The righteous
will live by faith."[d]

[a]4 *Or who as to his spirit* [b]4 *Or was appointed to be the Son of God with power* [c]17 *Or is from faith to faith* [d]17 Hab. 2:4

Discovering the Word 1. Imagine that verses 1 and 5 are the only information you possess about Paul. Describe everything you would know about him. 2. In verses 1–5 Paul gives a summary of the gospel for which he had been set apart. What do we learn about the gospel from these verses? 3. What do verses 8–13 reveal about Paul's attitude toward the Romans? 4. Paul says we can be eager to preach the gospel or be ashamed of it (vv. 15–16). What might lead us to adopt one attitude or the other?

Applying the Word 1. Because he was an apostle ("one who is sent"), Paul felt obligated to preach the gospel to everyone (v. 14). Whom do you have the greatest opportunity of reaching with the gospel? 2. What steps can you take to reach them?

Responding in Prayer Pray that God will use Romans to give you Paul's attitude toward the gospel and toward those who need its message.

2 / *Romans 1:18–32*
The Wrath of God

"HOW ARE YOU?" someone asks. "I'm fine," we reply. But are we really, or do our words mask our true condition? In this passage Paul tells us that we are not fine—neither we nor our friends nor society. Something is dreadfully wrong.

Warming Up to God Usually we have to admit we need help before we can be helped. Why do we often find it so difficult to admit a need? Give your needs to God's care.

Read Romans 1:18–32.

[18]The wrath of God is being revealed from heaven against all the godlessness and wickedness of men who suppress the truth by their wickedness, [19]since what may be known about God is plain to them, because God has made it plain to them. [20]For since the creation of the world God's invisible qualities—his eternal power and divine nature—have been clearly seen, being understood from what has been made, so that men are without excuse.

[21]For although they knew God, they neither glorified him as God nor gave thanks to him, but their thinking became futile and their foolish hearts were darkened. [22]Although they claimed to be wise, they became fools [23]and exchanged the glory of the immortal God for images made to look like mortal man and birds and animals and reptiles.

[24]Therefore God gave them over in the sinful desires of their hearts to sexual impurity for the degrading of their bodies with one another. [25]They exchanged the truth of God for a lie, and worshiped and served created things rather than the Creator—who is forever praised. Amen.

[26]Because of this, God gave them over to shameful lusts. Even their women exchanged natural relations for unnatural ones. [27]In the same way the men also abandoned natural relations with women and were inflamed with lust for one another. Men committed indecent acts with other men, and received in themselves the due penalty for their perversion.

[28]Furthermore, since they did not think it worthwhile to retain the knowledge of God, he gave them over to a depraved mind, to do what ought not to be done. [29]They have become filled with every kind of wickedness, evil, greed and depravity. They are full of envy, murder, strife, deceit and malice. They are gossips, [30]slanderers, God-haters, insolent, arrogant and boastful; they invent ways of doing evil; they disobey their parents; [31]they are senseless, faithless, heartless, ruthless. [32]Although they know God's righteous decree that those who do such things deserve death, they not only continue to do these very things but also approve of those who practice them.

Discovering the Word 1. John Stott defines God's wrath (v. 18) as "his righteous reaction to evil, his implacable hostility to it, his refusal to condone it, and his judgment upon it" (John R. W. Stott, "God's Judgment," in *Believing and Obeying Jesus Christ*). According to this definition, how would God's wrath differ from the sinful anger or violent temper condemned by Scripture? 2. What does everyone know about God, according to verses 19–20? 3. Verses 21–32 describe the downward spiral of sin experienced by people who rebel against God. How would you summarize each level of their descent? 4. How might each level lead to the next? 5. People often raise the question of how God could condemn those who have never heard of him. How does this passage address this question?

Applying the Word 1. What evidence do you see of this moral and spiritual degeneration today? 2. How might this passage make you less ashamed of the gospel and more eager to preach it?

Responding in Prayer Pray that God would be revealed powerfully to those who are rejecting him.

3/ *Romans 2*
The Judgment of God

PROSTITUTES, DRUG ADDICTS, thieves—it's easy to see why these people need the gospel. But what about "respectable" people: doctors, business executives, the family next door? They seem so contented, so fulfilled, so . . . *nice*!

In Romans 1:18–32 Paul described the depravity of those who reject God. Now he imagines someone saying, "You're absolutely right, Paul. Such people are wicked and deserve everything that's coming to them! But of course *we* would never do such things and would be very critical of anyone who did." In this passage Paul shows why even "nice" people need the gospel.

Warming Up to God Have you ever wondered whether some non-Christians really need the gospel? Explain. Ask God to open your heart to understand what place he has in each of our lives.

Read Romans 2.

2 You, therefore, have no excuse, you who pass judgment on someone else, for at whatever point you judge the other, you are condemning yourself, because you who pass judgment do the same things. [2]Now we know that God's judgment against those who do such things is based on truth. [3]So when you, a mere man, pass judgment on them and yet do the same things, do you think you will escape God's judgment? [4]Or do you show contempt for the riches of his kindness, tolerance and patience, not realizing that God's kindness leads you toward repentance?

[5]But because of your stubbornness and your unrepentant heart, you are storing up wrath against yourself for the day of God's wrath, when his righteous judgment will be revealed. [6]God "will give to each person according to what he has done."[e] [7]To those who by persistence in doing good seek glory, honor and immortality, he will give eternal life. [8]But for those who are self-seeking and who reject the truth and follow evil, there will be wrath and anger. [9]There will be trouble and distress for every human being who does evil: first for the Jew, then for the Gentile; [10]but glory, honor and peace for everyone who does good: first for the Jew, then for the Gentile. [11]For God does not show favoritism.

[12]All who sin apart from the law will also perish apart from the law, and all who sin under the law will be judged by the law. [13]For it is not those who hear the law who are righteous in God's sight, but it is those who obey the law who will be declared righteous. [14](Indeed, when Gentiles, who do not have the law, do by nature things required by the law, they are a law for themselves, even though they do not have the law, [15]since they show that the requirements of the law are written on their hearts, their consciences also bearing witness, and their thoughts now accusing, now even defending them.) [16]This will take place on the day when God will judge men's secrets through Jesus Christ, as my gospel declares.

[17]Now you, if you call yourself a Jew; if you rely on the law and brag about your relationship to God; [18]if you know his will and approve of what is superior because you are instructed by the law; [19]if you are convinced that you are a guide for the blind, a light for those who are in the dark, [20]an instructor of the foolish, a teacher of infants, because you have in the law the embodiment of knowledge and truth— [21]you, then, who teach others, do you not teach yourself? You who preach against stealing, do you steal? [22]You who

[e]6 Psalm 62:12; Prov. 24:12

say that people should not commit adultery, do
you commit adultery? You who abhor idols, do
you rob temples? [23]You who brag about the law,
do you dishonor God by breaking the law? [24]As it
is written: "God's name is blasphemed among the
Gentiles because of you."[f]

[25]Circumcision has value if you observe the
law, but if you break the law, you have become as
though you had not been circumcised. [26]If those
who are not circumcised keep the law's require-
ments, will they not be regarded as though they
were circumcised? [27]The one who is not circum-
cised physically and yet obeys the law will con-
demn you who, even though you have the[g] writ-
ten code and circumcision, are a lawbreaker.

[28]A man is not a Jew if he is only one out-
wardly, nor is circumcision merely outward and
physical. [29]No, a man is a Jew if he is one in-
wardly; and circumcision is circumcision of the
heart, by the Spirit, not by the written code. Such
a man's praise is not from men, but from God.

[f]24 Isaiah 52:5; Ezek. 36:22 [g]27 Or *who, by means of a*

Discovering the Word 1. When people are judgmental, how do they reveal both an understanding and a misunderstanding of God's judgment (vv. 1–4)? 2. Verses 5–16 describe a future day of judgment known as "the day of God's wrath" (v. 5). What will God consider important and unimportant on that day? 3. How are God's standards of judgment both similar and different for the two groups described in verses 12–16? 4. In verses 17–29 Paul focuses his attention on a hypocritical Jew. How does such a person view himself and others (vv. 17–20)? 5. Jews placed great value on circumcision because it was the visible sign that they were God's people. How had some of them confused the sign with what it signified (vv. 25–29)?

Applying the Word 1. How has religious hypocrisy hurt the cause of Christ in our day? 2. Many non-Christians have high moral standards. How can we use their own standards to help them see their need of Christ? 3. How can this chapter help you to more effectively share the gospel with respectable, religious or moral non-Christians?

Responding in Prayer Ask God to make you bold in talking with a non-Christian.

4 / *Romans 3:1–20*
The Verdict

IF YOUR ETERNAL destiny were decided by the quality of your life and the level of your obedience to God, how would you fare? There is one sure way to find out. Take your case to the divine court. The Bible assures us that we will all have our day in court (Ro 2:5–6; 14:10–12). But we need not wait until then to find out the verdict. Paul tells us in advance in this passage.

Warming Up to God Describe some of the thoughts and feelings you might have if you were on trial for committing a serious crime—and you knew you were guilty. Now consider the fact that Christ has set you free despite your guilt. How do you feel?

Read Romans 3:1–20.

3 What advantage, then, is there in being a
Jew, or what value is there in circumci-
sion? [2]Much in every way! First of all,
they have been entrusted with the very words of
God.

[3]What if some did not have faith? Will their
lack of faith nullify God's faithfulness? [4]Not at
all! Let God be true, and every man a liar. As it is
written:

"So that you may be proved right when you
speak
and prevail when you judge."[h]

[h]4 Psalm 51:4

5But if our unrighteousness brings out God's
righteousness more clearly, what shall we say?
That God is unjust in bringing his wrath on us? (I
am using a human argument.) 6Certainly not! If
that were so, how could God judge the world?
7Someone might argue, "If my falsehood en-
hances God's truthfulness and so increases his
glory, why am I still condemned as a sinner?"
8Why not say—as we are being slanderously re-
ported as saying and as some claim that we say—
"Let us do evil that good may result"? Their con-
demnation is deserved.

9What shall we conclude then? Are we any bet-
ter[i]? Not at all! We have already made the
charge that Jews and Gentiles alike are all under
sin. 10As it is written:

"There is no one righteous, not even one;
11 there is no one who understands,
no one who seeks God.
12All have turned away,
they have together become worthless;
there is no one who does good,
not even one."[j]
13"Their throats are open graves;
their tongues practice deceit."[k]
"The poison of vipers is on their lips."[l]
14 "Their mouths are full of cursing and
bitterness."[m]
15"Their feet are swift to shed blood;
16 ruin and misery mark their ways,
17and the way of peace they do not know."[n]
18 "There is no fear of God before their
eyes."[o]

19Now we know that whatever the law says, it
says to those who are under the law, so that every
mouth may be silenced and the whole world held
accountable to God. 20Therefore no one will be
declared righteous in his sight by observing the
law; rather, through the law we become con-
scious of sin.

[i]9 Or *worse* [j]12 Psalms 14:1-3; 53:1-3; Eccles. 7:20 [k]13 Psalm 5:9 [l]13 Psalm 140:3 [m]14 Psalm 10:7 [n]17 Isaiah 59:7,8 [o]18 Psalm 36:1

Discovering the Word 1. Why might some Jews have accused God of unfaithfulness and injustice (vv. 3–8)? 2. How does Paul respond to these accusations? 3. In the role of prosecutor, Paul has charged that Jews and Gentiles alike are under sin (v. 9). How does Scripture support his charge (vv. 10–18)? 4. In verses 13–18 Paul describes how the various parts of our bodies are involved in sin. How does this figurative language graphically illustrate our condition as fallen people? 5. How would you reconcile the statements in verses 10–18 with the fact that some non-Christians *do* seem to seek after God and lead exemplary lives? 6. Imagine a courtroom scene with God as the judge and the world on trial. From what you have learned in Romans 1:18—3:20, summarize the charges against us, the supporting evidence and the verdict.

Applying the Word 1. Paul does not discuss the grace of God (3:21—5:21) until he has discussed the judgment of God (1:18—3:20). He does not proclaim the good news until we have understood the bad news. Why does he follow this order? 2. How should Paul's example affect our evangelism? (Be as specific as possible.)

Responding in Prayer The letter to the Romans could have ended with 3:20. God would be perfectly just to condemn us all and to leave us fearfully awaiting his wrath. Let this fact sink in for a moment, then take time to thank God for being not only just but also merciful and gracious.

5/ *Romans 3:21–31*
The Righteousness from God

LIKE PRISONERS ON death row, people are guilty, condemned and awaiting the execution of God's wrath. They sit silently in the miserable darkness of their cell, all hope extinguished.

Then abruptly, the door swings open and darkness becomes light, death becomes life, and bondage becomes freedom. "You are *pardoned*," a voice tells them. But how? Why? This passage answers these questions.

Warming Up to God Imagine that you are a judge, and someone you love is on trial. Would you be more tempted to compromise your justice or your love? Explain.

Read Romans 3:21-31.

21But now a righteousness from God, apart
from law, has been made known, to which the
Law and the Prophets testify. 22This righteous-
ness from God comes through faith in Jesus
Christ to all who believe. There is no difference,
23for all have sinned and fall short of the glory of
God, 24and are justified freely by his grace
through the redemption that came by Christ
Jesus. 25God presented him as a sacrifice of atone-
ment,[p] through faith in his blood. He did this to
demonstrate his justice, because in his forbear-
ance he had left the sins committed beforehand
unpunished— 26he did it to demonstrate his jus-
tice at the present time, so as to be just and the
one who justifies those who have faith in Jesus.
27Where, then, is boasting? It is excluded. On
what principle? On that of observing the law? No,
but on that of faith. 28For we maintain that a man
is justified by faith apart from observing the law.
29Is God the God of Jews only? Is he not the God
of Gentiles too? Yes, of Gentiles too, 30since there
is only one God, who will justify the circumcised
by faith and the uncircumcised through that same
faith. 31Do we, then, nullify the law by this faith?
Not at all! Rather, we uphold the law.

p25 *Or as the one who would turn aside his wrath, taking away sin*

Discovering the Word 1. How is the righteousness from God (3:22–24) different from righteousness by law (2:5–13)? 2. The word *redemption* (v. 24) is borrowed from the slave market. It means to buy someone out of slavery. From what types of slavery has Christ delivered us? 3. The phrase *sacrifice of atonement* (v. 25) is borrowed from the Old Testament. Animal sacrifices turned away God's wrath from the sinner. Why does Christ's death turn away God's wrath from us? 4. How should we respond, emotionally and spiritually, to the fact that Jesus experienced God's wrath for us? 5. Some people find it difficult to understand how God can be perfectly just and gracious at the same time. How do the justice and grace of God meet at the cross (vv. 25–26)? 6. How does boasting about ourselves betray a fundamental misunderstanding of the gospel (vv. 27–31)?

Applying the Word 1. At times do you still feel unacceptable to God? Explain. 2. In what ways might you feel or act differently if you more fully grasped what Jesus has done for you?

Responding in Prayer Take time to praise and thank God for Jesus Christ.

---

6 / *Romans 4*
The Example of Abraham

"IT'S HOPELESS." NO words are more discouraging than these. Yet sometimes situations appear beyond hope, beyond help. Our natural response during such times is despair and depression.

Abraham knew what it meant to face insurmountable obstacles. He too was hopeless, yet somehow he found renewed reason to hope. For this reason he has become a timeless example and encouragement for us.

Warming Up to God Recall a situation in which you felt hopeless. What restored you to hope?

Read Romans 4.

4 What then shall we say that Abraham, our
forefather, discovered in this matter? 2If,
in fact, Abraham was justified by works,
he had something to boast about—but not before
God. 3What does the Scripture say? "Abraham be-
lieved God, and it was credited to him as righ-
teousness."[q]

4Now when a man works, his wages are not
credited to him as a gift, but as an obligation.
5However, to the man who does not work but
trusts God who justifies the wicked, his faith is
credited as righteousness. 6David says the same
thing when he speaks of the blessedness of the
man to whom God credits righteousness apart
from works:

7"Blessed are they
whose transgressions are forgiven,
whose sins are covered.
8Blessed is the man
whose sin the Lord will never count against
him."[r]

9Is this blessedness only for the circumcised, or
also for the uncircumcised? We have been saying
that Abraham's faith was credited to him as right-
eousness. 10Under what circumstances was it
credited? Was it after he was circumcised, or be-
fore? It was not after, but before! 11And he re-
ceived the sign of circumcision, a seal of the right-
eousness that he had by faith while he was still
uncircumcised. So then, he is the father of all
who believe but have not been circumcised, in
order that righteousness might be credited to
them. 12And he is also the father of the circum-
cised who not only are circumcised but who also
walk in the footsteps of the faith that our father
Abraham had before he was circumcised.

13It was not through law that Abraham and his
offspring received the promise that he would be
heir of the world, but through the righteousness
that comes by faith. 14For if those who live by law
are heirs, faith has no value and the promise is
worthless, 15because law brings wrath. And where
there is no law there is no transgression.

16Therefore, the promise comes by faith, so
that it may be by grace and may be guaranteed to
all Abraham's offspring—not only to those who
are of the law but also to those who are of the
faith of Abraham. He is the father of us all. 17As it
is written: "I have made you a father of many
nations."[s] He is our father in the sight of God, in
whom he believed—the God who gives life to the
dead and calls things that are not as though they
were.

18Against all hope, Abraham in hope believed
and so became the father of many nations, just as
it had been said to him, "So shall your offspring
be."[t] 19Without weakening in his faith, he faced
the fact that his body was as good as dead—since
he was about a hundred years old—and that
Sarah's womb was also dead. 20Yet he did not wa-
ver through unbelief regarding the promise of
God, but was strengthened in his faith and gave
glory to God, 21being fully persuaded that God
had power to do what he had promised. 22This is
why "it was credited to him as righteousness."
23The words "it was credited to him" were written
not for him alone, 24but also for us, to whom God
will credit righteousness—for us who believe in
him who raised Jesus our Lord from the dead.
25He was delivered over to death for our sins and
was raised to life for our justification.

[q]3 Gen. 15:6; also in verse 22 [r]8 Psalm 32:1,2 [s]17 Gen. 17:5
[t]18 Gen. 15:5

Discovering the Word 1. According to Paul, how were Old Testament saints, such as Abraham and David, justified (vv. 1–8)? 2. What are some of the differences between justification by faith and by works (vv. 4–8)? 3. It's easy to feel that God accepts us only when we are good. When we feel this way, how can the examples of Abraham and David give us hope? 4. Some people today claim that unless we are baptized, we have no hope of being saved. How might Abraham's experience refute this claim? 5. God promised that Abraham and his offspring would inherit the world (v. 13). Who are Abraham's offspring (vv. 13–17)? 6. How does Abraham illustrate our own hopeless predicament as non-Christians and the solution provided in Jesus Christ (vv. 18–25)?

Applying the Word 1. What situation are you currently facing that requires faith in the God of resurrection and creation? 2. How can you demonstrate faith and hope in that situation?

Responding in Prayer Know that God wants you to have hope. Pray with that assurance.

7 / *Romans 5*
Reasons to Rejoice

WE ALL LONG to be joyful, to experience the pure delight that life sometimes offers. But life's joys are elusive, momentary, gone as quickly as they come. How can we have an abiding, enduring joy—especially when suffering intrudes into our lives? In Romans 5 Paul gives us several firm and lasting reasons to rejoice.

Warming Up to God What kinds of things make you joyful? If you are in a private place where you feel comfortable, sing a short song of praise to God.

Read Romans 5.

5 Therefore, since we have been justified
through faith, we[u] have peace with God
through our Lord Jesus Christ, 2through
whom we have gained access by faith into this
grace in which we now stand. And we[u] rejoice in
the hope of the glory of God. 3Not only so, but
we[u] also rejoice in our sufferings, because we
know that suffering produces perseverance; 4per-
severance, character; and character, hope. 5And
hope does not disappoint us, because God has
poured out his love into our hearts by the Holy
Spirit, whom he has given us.

6You see, at just the right time, when we were
still powerless, Christ died for the ungodly. 7Very
rarely will anyone die for a righteous man,
though for a good man someone might possibly
dare to die. 8But God demonstrates his own love
for us in this: While we were still sinners, Christ
died for us.

9Since we have now been justified by his blood,
how much more shall we be saved from God's
wrath through him! 10For if, when we were God's
enemies, we were reconciled to him through the
death of his Son, how much more, having been
reconciled, shall we be saved through his life!
11Not only is this so, but we also rejoice in God
through our Lord Jesus Christ, through whom we
have now received reconciliation.

12Therefore, just as sin entered the world
through one man, and death through sin, and in
this way death came to all men, because all
sinned— 13for before the law was given, sin was
in the world. But sin is not taken into account
when there is no law. 14Nevertheless, death
reigned from the time of Adam to the time of
Moses, even over those who did not sin by break-
ing a command, as did Adam, who was a pattern
of the one to come.

15But the gift is not like the trespass. For if the
many died by the trespass of the one man, how
much more did God's grace and the gift that came
by the grace of the one man, Jesus Christ, over-
flow to the many! 16Again, the gift of God is not
like the result of the one man's sin: The judgment
followed one sin and brought condemnation, but
the gift followed many trespasses and brought
justification. 17For if, by the trespass of the one
man, death reigned through that one man, how
much more will those who receive God's abun-
dant provision of grace and of the gift of right-
eousness reign in life through the one man, Jesus
Christ.

18Consequently, just as the result of one tres-
pass was condemnation for all men, so also the
result of one act of righteousness was justification
that brings life for all men. 19For just as through
the disobedience of the one man the many were
made sinners, so also through the obedience of
the one man the many will be made righteous.

20The law was added so that the trespass might
increase. But where sin increased, grace increased
all the more, 21so that, just as sin reigned in
death, so also grace might reign through right-
eousness to bring eternal life through Jesus
Christ our Lord.

[u]1,2,3 *Or let us*

Discovering the Word 1. How has faith in Jesus Christ changed our relationship with God (vv. 1–2)? 2. In verses 2–11 what reasons does Paul give for rejoicing? 3. How does suffering for Christ's sake produce the character changes mentioned in verses 3–4? 4. How do verses 5–8 emphasize the love God has for us? 5. Read verses 12–21. How are Adam and Christ similar (vv. 12, 18–19)? 6. How is Christ's gift different from Adam's trespass (vv. 15–21)?

Applying the Word 1. In what area of your life are you experiencing suffering? 2. How can a knowledge of the process of character change help us to rejoice in our sufferings?

Responding in Prayer This passage gives us many reasons for rejoicing. Spend time thanking and praising God for all we have in Christ Jesus.

8 / *Romans 6:1—7:6*
New Life, New Lifestyle

SUBTLE ALLURE, PERSISTENT urges, passionate desires. Sin entices us in many ways. A thought enters our mind that we dare not acknowledge: "If I give in, I can always be forgiven." Sound familiar? Such thinking can become an excuse for immoral practices. But it betrays a fundamental misunderstanding of God's grace in our lives. In Romans 6:1—7:6 Paul explains why the idea of "sinning so that grace may increase" is unthinkable for Christians.

Warming Up to God When you became a Christian, was the change in your life dramatic, gradual or imperceptible? Explain. Whether it has taken place slowly or quickly, praise God for the change he has worked in your life.

Read Romans 6:1—7:6.

6 What shall we say, then? Shall we go on sinning so that grace may increase? [2]By no means! We died to sin; how can we live in it any longer? [3]Or don't you know that all of us who were baptized into Christ Jesus were baptized into his death? [4]We were therefore buried with him through baptism into death in order that, just as Christ was raised from the dead through the glory of the Father, we too may live a new life.

[5]If we have been united with him like this in his death, we will certainly also be united with him in his resurrection. [6]For we know that our old self was crucified with him so that the body of sin might be done away with,[v] that we should no longer be slaves to sin— [7]because anyone who has died has been freed from sin.

[8]Now if we died with Christ, we believe that we will also live with him. [9]For we know that since Christ was raised from the dead, he cannot die again; death no longer has mastery over him. [10]The death he died, he died to sin once for all; but the life he lives, he lives to God.

[11]In the same way, count yourselves dead to sin but alive to God in Christ Jesus. [12]Therefore do not let sin reign in your mortal body so that you obey its evil desires. [13]Do not offer the parts of your body to sin, as instruments of wickedness, but rather offer yourselves to God, as those who have been brought from death to life; and offer the parts of your body to him as instruments of righteousness. [14]For sin shall not be your master, because you are not under law, but under grace.

[15]What then? Shall we sin because we are not under law but under grace? By no means! [16]Don't you know that when you offer yourselves to someone to obey him as slaves, you are slaves to the one whom you obey—whether you are slaves to sin, which leads to death, or to obedience, which leads to righteousness? [17]But thanks be to God that, though you used to be slaves to sin, you wholeheartedly obeyed the form of teaching to which you were entrusted. [18]You have been set free from sin and have become slaves to righteousness.

[19]I put this in human terms because you are weak in your natural selves. Just as you used to offer the parts of your body in slavery to impurity and to ever-increasing wickedness, so now offer them in slavery to righteousness leading to holiness. [20]When you were slaves to sin, you were free from the control of righteousness. [21]What benefit did you reap at that time from the things

[v]6 Or *be rendered powerless*

you are now ashamed of? Those things result in death! 22But now that you have been set free from sin and have become slaves to God, the benefit you reap leads to holiness, and the result is eternal life. 23For the wages of sin is death, but the gift of God is eternal life in[w] Christ Jesus our Lord.

7 Do you not know, brothers—for I am speaking to men who know the law—that the law has authority over a man only as long as he lives? 2For example, by law a married woman is bound to her husband as long as he is alive, but if her husband dies, she is released from the law of marriage. 3So then, if she marries another man while her husband is still alive, she is called an adulteress. But if her husband dies, she is released from that law and is not an adulteress, even though she marries another man.

4So, my brothers, you also died to the law through the body of Christ, that you might belong to another, to him who was raised from the dead, in order that we might bear fruit to God. 5For when we were controlled by the sinful nature,[x] the sinful passions aroused by the law were at work in our bodies, so that we bore fruit for death. 6But now, by dying to what once bound us, we have been released from the law so that we serve in the new way of the Spirit, and not in the old way of the written code.

[w]23 Or *through* [x]5 Or *the flesh*; also in verse 25

Discovering the Word 1. In what sense was our baptism both a funeral and a resurrection? 2. Our "old self" (6:6) refers to everything we were as non-Christians. When our old self was crucified with Christ, in what sense was sin rendered powerless (6:5–7)? 3. What does it mean to "count yourselves dead to sin but alive to God" (6:11)? 4. Paul compares both our old life and our new to slavery. Why is this analogy appropriate in each case (6:15–18)? 5. How is the principle "that the law has authority over a man only as long as he lives" illustrated by marriage (7:1–3)? 6. In 6:1—7:6 Paul uses baptism, slavery and marriage to illustrate the differences between our old life and our new life. What common themes are emphasized in these illustrations?

Applying the Word 1. What sins are you particularly struggling to free yourself of? 2. What assurance and encouragement is Paul giving you in your struggle against sin?

Responding in Prayer Thank God that you are no longer a slave to sin. Pray that you will live as a slave to righteousness.

9 / *Romans 7:7–25*

Our Struggle with Sin

ARE YOU EVER baffled by your behavior? You know the right thing to do, but you fail to do it. You resolve to avoid certain things, and they become even more attractive and enticing. Why? What keeps us from translating our desires into actions? In Romans 7 Paul explores his own inner struggles to do good and avoid evil. As we look into his mind and heart, we see a reflection of ourselves and the power that opposes us.

Warming Up to God Saying no to a piece of pie we don't need *seems* so simple, but is easier said than done. How have you recently struggled to do what you know you should do?

Read Romans 7:7–25.

7What shall we say, then? Is the law sin? Certainly not! Indeed I would not have known what sin was except through the law. For I would not have known what coveting really was if the law had not said, "Do not covet."[y] 8But sin, seizing the opportunity afforded by the commandment, produced in me every kind of covetous desire. For apart from law, sin is dead. 9Once I was alive apart from law; but when the commandment came, sin sprang to life and I died. 10I found that

[y]7 Exodus 20:17; Deut. 5:21

the very commandment that was intended to
bring life actually brought death. 11For sin, seiz-
ing the opportunity afforded by the command-
ment, deceived me, and through the command-
ment put me to death. 12So then, the law is holy,
and the commandment is holy, righteous and
good.
13Did that which is good, then, become death
to me? By no means! But in order that sin might
be recognized as sin, it produced death in me
through what was good, so that through the com-
mandment sin might become utterly sinful.
14We know that the law is spiritual; but I am
unspiritual, sold as a slave to sin. 15I do not un-
derstand what I do. For what I want to do I do
not do, but what I hate I do. 16And if I do what I
do not want to do, I agree that the law is good.
17As it is, it is no longer I myself who do it, but it
is sin living in me. 18I know that nothing good
lives in me, that is, in my sinful nature.[z] For I
have the desire to do what is good, but I cannot
carry it out. 19For what I do is not the good I want
to do; no, the evil I do not want to do—this I
keep on doing. 20Now if I do what I do not want
to do, it is no longer I who do it, but it is sin
living in me that does it.
21So I find this law at work: When I want to do
good, evil is right there with me. 22For in my
inner being I delight in God's law; 23but I see
another law at work in the members of my body,
waging war against the law of my mind and mak-
ing me a prisoner of the law of sin at work within
my members. 24What a wretched man I am! Who
will rescue me from this body of death? 25Thanks
be to God—through Jesus Christ our Lord!
So then, I myself in my mind am a slave to
God's law, but in the sinful nature a slave to the
law of sin.

[z]18 Or *my flesh*

Discovering the Word 1. How did the law create in Paul a vivid awareness of sin (vv. 7–12)? 2. Why would it be wrong to blame the law for Paul's spiritual death (vv. 13–14)? 3. According to verses 14–20, why does Paul feel so wretched? 4. In chapter 6 Paul stated that Christians are no longer slaves to sin. Yet here he claims he is a slave to sin (v. 14). How would you explain this difference? 5. How can a person's anguish and frustration with sin be beneficial (vv. 24–25)?

Applying the Word 1. To what extent can you identify with Paul's struggles in these verses? Explain. 2. Why is it important to realize that only Christ can rescue you from the power of your sin?

Responding in Prayer When Paul realized that Jesus could rescue him from his wretched condition, he cried out, "Thanks be to God!" If this is your response too, spend time thanking him.

10/ *Romans 8:1–17*
The Spirit Brings Life

IF WE WERE unable to obey God as non-Christians, then how can we as Christians? What has happened to turn our slavery into freedom, our sin into righteousness and our spiritual death into life?

The struggle described in Romans 7 does not end when we become Christians. But there is a new dimension to that struggle that totally changes its outcome. In chapter 8 Paul describes the life-giving effects of the Spirit.

Warming Up to God This chapter is one of celebration. What has the Holy Spirit recently done in you that gives you reason to rejoice?

Read Romans 8:1–17.

8 Therefore, there is now no condemnation for those who are in Christ Jesus,[a] 2because through Christ Jesus the law of the Spirit of life set me free from the law of sin and death. 3For what the law was powerless to do in that it was weakened by the sinful nature,[b] God did by sending his own Son in the likeness of sinful man to be a sin offering.[c] And so he condemned sin in sinful man,[d] 4in order that the righteous requirements of the law might be fully met in us, who do not live according to the sinful nature but according to the Spirit.

5Those who live according to the sinful nature have their minds set on what that nature desires; but those who live in accordance with the Spirit have their minds set on what the Spirit desires. 6The mind of sinful man[e] is death, but the mind controlled by the Spirit is life and peace; 7the sinful mind[f] is hostile to God. It does not submit to God's law, nor can it do so. 8Those controlled by the sinful nature cannot please God.

9You, however, are controlled not by the sinful nature but by the Spirit, if the Spirit of God lives in you. And if anyone does not have the Spirit of Christ, he does not belong to Christ. 10But if Christ is in you, your body is dead because of sin, yet your spirit is alive because of righteousness. 11And if the Spirit of him who raised Jesus from the dead is living in you, he who raised Christ from the dead will also give life to your mortal bodies through his Spirit, who lives in you.

12Therefore, brothers, we have an obligation—but it is not to the sinful nature, to live according to it. 13For if you live according to the sinful nature, you will die; but if by the Spirit you put to death the misdeeds of the body, you will live, 14because those who are led by the Spirit of God are sons of God. 15For you did not receive a spirit that makes you a slave again to fear, but you received the Spirit of sonship.[g] And by him we cry, "*Abba*,[h] Father." 16The Spirit himself testifies with our spirit that we are God's children. 17Now if we are children, then we are heirs—heirs of God and co-heirs with Christ, if indeed we share in his sufferings in order that we may also share in his glory.

[a] 1 Some later manuscripts *Jesus, who do not live according to the sinful nature but according to the Spirit,* [b] 3 Or *the flesh;* also in verses 4, 5, 8, 9, 12 and 13 [c] 3 Or *man, for sin* [d] 3 Or *in the flesh* [e] 6 Or *mind set on the flesh* [f] 7 Or *the mind set on the flesh* [g] 15 Or *adoption* [h] 15 Aramaic for *Father*

Discovering the Word 1. Romans 7 described how the law of sin brought about our spiritual death. What has God done to free us from the law of sin and death (vv. 1–4)? 2. In verses 5–8 Paul divides all of humanity into two categories: those who live according to the sinful nature and those who live according to the Spirit. In your own words, what are some characteristics of each group? 3. There are many professing Christians whose lives seem very different from Paul's description of life in the Spirit. How do you think Paul would account for this fact? 4. In verse 12 Paul concludes that we have an obligation. Describe in your own words the negative and positive aspects of that obligation (vv. 12–14). 5. How do we experience the reality and privileges of being God's children (vv. 15–17)?

Applying the Word 1. What evidence do you see of your life being controlled by the Spirit? 2. Practically speaking, how can we put to death the misdeeds of the body by the Spirit?

Responding in Prayer Spend time thanking God for the gift of the Spirit and the difference he makes in our lives.

11 / *Romans 8:18–39*
Glorious Conquerors

"ROMAN CONQUERORS RETURNING from the wars enjoyed the honor of a triumph, a tumultuous parade. In the procession came trumpeters, musicians and strange animals from the conquered territories, together with carts laden with treasure and captured armaments. The conqueror rode in a triumphal chariot, the dazed prisoners walking in chains before him. Sometimes his children, robed in white, stood with him in the chariot or rode the trace horses. A slave stood behind the conqueror, holding a golden crown and whispering in his ear a warning: that all glory is fleeting." (At the end of the movie *Patton*, these words went through the mind of that famous general.)

In Romans 8 Paul describes Christians as glorious conquerors who by God's grace overcome all forces arrayed against us. But the glory we receive is eternal.

Warming Up to God Why is it often difficult to feel like a glorious conqueror?

Read Romans 8:18–39.

18I consider that our present sufferings are not worth comparing with the glory that will be revealed in us. 19The creation waits in eager expectation for the sons of God to be revealed. 20For the creation was subjected to frustration, not by its own choice, but by the will of the one who subjected it, in hope 21that[i] the creation itself will be liberated from its bondage to decay and brought into the glorious freedom of the children of God.

22We know that the whole creation has been groaning as in the pains of childbirth right up to the present time. 23Not only so, but we ourselves, who have the firstfruits of the Spirit, groan inwardly as we wait eagerly for our adoption as sons, the redemption of our bodies. 24For in this hope we were saved. But hope that is seen is no hope at all. Who hopes for what he already has? 25But if we hope for what we do not yet have, we wait for it patiently.

26In the same way, the Spirit helps us in our weakness. We do not know what we ought to pray for, but the Spirit himself intercedes for us with groans that words cannot express. 27And he who searches our hearts knows the mind of the Spirit, because the Spirit intercedes for the saints in accordance with God's will.

28And we know that in all things God works for the good of those who love him,[j] who[k] have been called according to his purpose. 29For those God foreknew he also predestined to be conformed to the likeness of his Son, that he might be the firstborn among many brothers. 30And those he predestined, he also called; those he called, he also justified; those he justified, he also glorified.

31What, then, shall we say in response to this? If God is for us, who can be against us? 32He who did not spare his own Son, but gave him up for us all—how will he not also, along with him, graciously give us all things? 33Who will bring any charge against those whom God has chosen? It is God who justifies. 34Who is he that condemns? Christ Jesus, who died—more than that, who was raised to life—is at the right hand of God and is also interceding for us. 35Who shall separate us from the love of Christ? Shall trouble or hardship or persecution or famine or nakedness or danger or sword? 36As it is written:

"For your sake we face death all day long;
we are considered as sheep to be
slaughtered."[l]

37No, in all these things we are more than conquerors through him who loved us. 38For I am convinced that neither death nor life, neither angels nor demons,[m] neither the present nor the future, nor any powers, 39neither height nor depth, nor anything else in all creation, will be able to separate us from the love of God that is in Christ Jesus our Lord.

[i]20,21 Or *subjected it in hope.* 21*For* [j]28 Some manuscripts *And we know that all things work together for good to those who love God* [k]28 Or *works together with those who love him to bring about what is good—with those who* [l]36 Psalm 44:22 [m]38 Or *nor heavenly rulers*

Discovering the Word 1. What words and vivid images in these verses underscore the difficulties of the present time? 2. Explain why these difficulties don't compare with the glory that will be revealed in us (vv. 18–25). 3. How can the Spirit's help encourage us (vv. 26–27)? 4. In verse 28 Paul speaks of "the good" and "his purpose." What is God's good purpose for us (v. 29)? 5. How might trouble, hardship, persecution, famine, nakedness, danger or the threat of death cause us to question God's love for us (vv. 35–36)? 6. In spite of these things, why does Paul proclaim that we are "more than conquerors" (vv. 37–39)?

Applying the Word 1. How can eager expectation of glory help us cope with our present problems and sufferings? 2. Look again at the powerful words of verses 38–39. How does this give you courage to persevere?

 **Responding in Prayer** Ask God to make you ready for his future glory.

12 / *Romans 9:1–29*
The Potter and His Clay

"I DON'T BELIEVE in Christ." It grieves us to hear these words. But when they come from close friends or family members, the pain can be unbearable. Why doesn't God open their hearts to the gospel? Why did he save us and not them? Paul felt great pain and perplexity over Israel's unbelief. Their Messiah had come, and they had rejected him. In chapters 9—11 Paul wrestles with these questions.

 **Warming Up to God** Whose unbelief grieves you? Talk openly with God about your concerns.

 **Read Romans 9:1–29.**

9 I speak the truth in Christ—I am not lying, my conscience confirms it in the Holy Spirit— 2I have great sorrow and unceasing anguish in my heart. 3For I could wish that I myself were cursed and cut off from Christ for the sake of my brothers, those of my own race, 4the people of Israel. Theirs is the adoption as sons; theirs the divine glory, the covenants, the receiving of the law, the temple worship and the promises. 5Theirs are the patriarchs, and from them is traced the human ancestry of Christ, who is God over all, forever praised![n] Amen.

6It is not as though God's word had failed. For not all who are descended from Israel are Israel. 7Nor because they are his descendants are they all Abraham's children. On the contrary, "It is through Isaac that your offspring will be reckoned."[o] 8In other words, it is not the natural children who are God's children, but it is the children of the promise who are regarded as Abraham's offspring. 9For this was how the promise was stated: "At the appointed time I will return, and Sarah will have a son."[p]

10Not only that, but Rebekah's children had one and the same father, our father Isaac. 11Yet, before the twins were born or had done anything good or bad—in order that God's purpose in election might stand: 12not by works but by him who calls—she was told, "The older will serve the younger."[q] 13Just as it is written: "Jacob I loved, but Esau I hated."[r]

14What then shall we say? Is God unjust? Not at all! 15For he says to Moses,

> "I will have mercy on whom I have mercy,
> and I will have compassion on whom I have compassion."[s]

16It does not, therefore, depend on man's desire or effort, but on God's mercy. 17For the Scripture says to Pharaoh: "I raised you up for this very purpose, that I might display my power in you and that my name might be proclaimed in all the earth."[t] 18Therefore God has mercy on whom he wants to have mercy, and he hardens whom he wants to harden.

19One of you will say to me: "Then why does God still blame us? For who resists his will?" 20But who are you, O man, to talk back to God? "Shall what is formed say to him who formed it, 'Why did you make me like this?'"[u] 21Does not the potter have the right to make out of the same lump of clay some pottery for noble purposes and some for common use?

22What if God, choosing to show his wrath and make his power known, bore with great patience the objects of his wrath—prepared for destruction? 23What if he did this to make the riches of his glory known to the objects of his mercy, whom he prepared in advance for glory— 24even us, whom he also called, not only from the Jews but also from the Gentiles? 25As he says in Hosea:

> "I will call them 'my people' who are not my people;

[n]5 Or *Christ, who is over all. God be forever praised!* Or *Christ. God who is over all be forever praised!* [o]7 Gen. 21:12
[p]9 Gen. 18:10,14 [q]12 Gen. 25:23 [r]13 Mal. 1:2,3
[s]15 Exodus 33:19 [t]17 Exodus 9:16 [u]20 Isaiah 29:16; 45:9

and I will call her 'my loved one' who is
not my loved one,"[v]

[26]and,

"It will happen that in the very place where it
was said to them,
'You are not my people,'
they will be called 'sons of the living God.' "[w]

[27]Isaiah cries out concerning Israel:

"Though the number of the Israelites be like
the sand by the sea,
only the remnant will be saved.
[28]For the Lord will carry out
his sentence on earth with speed and
finality."[x]

[29]It is just as Isaiah said previously:

"Unless the Lord Almighty
had left us descendants,
we would have become like Sodom,
we would have been like Gomorrah."[y]

[v]25 Hosea 2:23 [w]26 Hosea 1:10 [x]28 Isaiah 10:22,23 [y]29 Isaiah 1:9

Discovering the Word 1. Why does Paul have great sorrow for the people of Israel? 2. How do verses 6–13 demonstrate that God has not failed in his promises and purposes for Israel? 3. Many people feel it is unjust for God to choose some and not others (v. 14). In reply why does Paul speak of God's mercy rather than his justice or injustice (vv. 15–18)? 4. How does the illustration of the potter and his clay help us gain a proper perspective (vv. 20–23)? 5. How is God's mercy and justice revealed in his treatment of the Gentiles and Jews (vv. 24–29)?

Applying the Word 1. How do you respond to the idea of election (v. 11), God's choosing certain people to be the objects of his mercy? 2. When do you feel uncertain about your own salvation? 3. What would help you to feel more secure?

Responding in Prayer Thank God for the fact that although he would have been perfectly just to condemn us all, he mercifully chose to save some.

13 / *Romans 9:30—10:21*
Misguided Zeal

THE WORLD IS full of religious people: Jews, Christians, Muslims, Hindus, Buddhists and many others. Islam alone has over 800 million adherents. Many of these people are zealous, dedicated and sincere. But are zeal and sincerity enough? Are there many paths to God, or just one? In this passage Paul continues to wrestle with the problem of Israel's unbelief. He now focuses on Israel's and on our own responsibility to believe the gospel.

Warming Up to God Have you ever known a sincere and devout non-Christian? How did you respond to his or her zeal?

Read Romans 9:30—10:21

[30]What then shall we say? That the Gentiles,
who did not pursue righteousness, have obtained
it, a righteousness that is by faith; [31]but Israel,
who pursued a law of righteousness, has not at-
tained it. [32]Why not? Because they pursued it not
by faith but as if it were by works. They stumbled
over the "stumbling stone." [33]As it is written:

"See, I lay in Zion a stone that causes men to
stumble
and a rock that makes them fall,
and the one who trusts in him will never be
put to shame."[z]

10 Brothers, my heart's desire and
prayer to God for the Israelites is
that they may be saved. [2]For I can
testify about them that they are zealous for God,
but their zeal is not based on knowledge. [3]Since

[z]33 Isaiah 8:14; 28:16

they did not know the righteousness that comes
from God and sought to establish their own, they
did not submit to God's righteousness. 4Christ is
the end of the law so that there may be righteous-
ness for everyone who believes.
5Moses describes in this way the righteousness
that is by the law: "The man who does these
things will live by them."[a] 6But the righteous-
ness that is by faith says: "Do not say in your
heart, 'Who will ascend into heaven?'[b]" (that is,
to bring Christ down) 7"or 'Who will descend
into the deep?'[c]" (that is, to bring Christ up
from the dead). 8But what does it say? "The word
is near you; it is in your mouth and in your
heart,"[d] that is, the word of faith we are pro-
claiming: 9That if you confess with your mouth,
"Jesus is Lord," and believe in your heart that
God raised him from the dead, you will be saved.
10For it is with your heart that you believe and are
justified, and it is with your mouth that you con-
fess and are saved. 11As the Scripture says, "Any-
one who trusts in him will never be put to
shame."[e] 12For there is no difference between
Jew and Gentile—the same Lord is Lord of all
and richly blesses all who call on him, 13for, "Eve-
ryone who calls on the name of the Lord will be
saved."[f]
14How, then, can they call on the one they have
not believed in? And how can they believe in the
one of whom they have not heard? And how can
they hear without someone preaching to them?
15And how can they preach unless they are sent?
As it is written, "How beautiful are the feet of
those who bring good news!"[g]
16But not all the Israelites accepted the good
news. For Isaiah says, "Lord, who has believed
our message?"[h] 17Consequently, faith comes
from hearing the message, and the message is
heard through the word of Christ. 18But I ask: Did
they not hear? Of course they did:

"Their voice has gone out into all the earth,
their words to the ends of the world."[i]

19Again I ask: Did Israel not understand? First,
Moses says,

"I will make you envious by those who are
not a nation;
I will make you angry by a nation that has
no understanding."[j]

20And Isaiah boldly says,

"I was found by those who did not seek me;
I revealed myself to those who did not ask
for me."[k]

21But concerning Israel he says,

"All day long I have held out my hands
to a disobedient and obstinate people."[l]

[a]5 Lev. 18:5 [b]6 Deut. 30:12 [c]7 Deut. 30:13 [d]8 Deut. 30:14
[e]11 Isaiah 28:16 [f]13 Joel 2:32 [g]15 Isaiah 52:7
[h]16 Isaiah 53:1 [i]18 Psalm 19:4 [j]19 Deut. 32:21
[k]20 Isaiah 65:1 [l]21 Isaiah 65:2

Discovering the Word 1. Why was Jesus Christ more of a stumbling stone to the Jews than to the Gentiles (9:30–33)? 2. Many people believe religious zeal and sincerity are all a person needs to be saved. How would Paul respond to this belief (10:1–4)? 3. How do verses 6–8 stress the simplicity of righteousness by faith? 4. First-century Christians publicly confessed that "Jesus is Lord" at their baptism. Why is public confession important in addition to the belief in one's heart (vv. 9–13)? 5. William Carey, the father of modern missions, once proposed to a group of ministers that they discuss the implications of the Great Commission. Dr. John C. Ryland retorted: "Young man, sit down. When God pleases to convert the heathen, he will do it without your aid or mine!" How does Dr. Ryland's understanding of God's sovereignty mesh with verses 14–15?

Applying the Word 1. Realizing the implications of verses such as Romans 10:14–15, William Carey responded to God's call and went to India. Where do you feel called to go with the gospel? 2. What steps can you take (or have you taken) to be obedient to that call?

Responding in Prayer Israel's unbelief did not stop Paul from praying for them (10:1). Spend time praying for those with whom you have the opportunity of sharing the gospel.

14 / *Romans 11*
The Future of Israel

FOR CENTURIES THE people of Israel awaited their Messiah. But when he came, very few believed in him. This situation has persisted to the point where Christianity is now considered a Gentile religion. What happened to God's promises and plans for Israel? Has God rejected his people? In this chapter Paul answers these questions.

Warming Up to God We all have expectations of how God will work in our lives that come out of our desires rather than God's. In what way do you feel that God has failed to follow your plan? Express to God any feelings of disappointment or discouragement you might have.

Read Romans 11.

---

11 I ask then: Did God reject his people? By no means! I am an Israelite myself, a descendant of Abraham, from the tribe of Benjamin. 2God did not reject his people, whom he foreknew. Don't you know what the Scripture says in the passage about Elijah—how he appealed to God against Israel: 3"Lord, they have killed your prophets and torn down your altars; I am the only one left, and they are trying to kill me"[m]? 4And what was God's answer to him? "I have reserved for myself seven thousand who have not bowed the knee to Baal."[n] 5So too, at the present time there is a remnant chosen by grace. 6And if by grace, then it is no longer by works; if it were, grace would no longer be grace.[o]

7What then? What Israel sought so earnestly it did not obtain, but the elect did. The others were hardened, 8as it is written:

"God gave them a spirit of stupor,
eyes so that they could not see
and ears so that they could not hear,
to this very day."[p]

9And David says:

"May their table become a snare and a trap,
a stumbling block and a retribution for them.
10May their eyes be darkened so they cannot see,
and their backs be bent forever."[q]

11Again I ask: Did they stumble so as to fall beyond recovery? Not at all! Rather, because of their transgression, salvation has come to the Gentiles to make Israel envious. 12But if their transgression means riches for the world, and their loss means riches for the Gentiles, how much greater riches will their fullness bring!

13I am talking to you Gentiles. Inasmuch as I am the apostle to the Gentiles, I make much of my ministry 14in the hope that I may somehow arouse my own people to envy and save some of them. 15For if their rejection is the reconciliation of the world, what will their acceptance be but life from the dead? 16If the part of the dough offered as firstfruits is holy, then the whole batch is holy; if the root is holy, so are the branches.

17If some of the branches have been broken off, and you, though a wild olive shoot, have been grafted in among the others and now share in the nourishing sap from the olive root, 18do not boast over those branches. If you do, consider this: You do not support the root, but the root supports you. 19You will say then, "Branches were broken off so that I could be grafted in." 20Granted. But they were broken off because of unbelief, and you stand by faith. Do not be arrogant, but be afraid. 21For if God did not spare the natural branches, he will not spare you either.

22Consider therefore the kindness and sternness of God: sternness to those who fell, but kindness to you, provided that you continue in his kindness. Otherwise, you also will be cut off. 23And if they do not persist in unbelief, they will be grafted in, for God is able to graft them in again. 24After all, if you were cut out of an olive tree that is wild by nature, and contrary to nature were grafted into a cultivated olive tree, how much more readily will these, the natural branches, be grafted into their own olive tree!

25I do not want you to be ignorant of this mys-

[m]3 1 Kings 19:10,14 [n]4 1 Kings 19:18 [o]6 Some manuscripts *by grace. But if by works, then it is no longer grace; if it were, work would no longer be work.* [p]8 Deut. 29:4; Isaiah 29:10 [q]10 Psalm 69:22,23

tery, brothers, so that you may not be conceited:
Israel has experienced a hardening in part until
the full number of the Gentiles has come in.
26And so all Israel will be saved, as it is written:

"The deliverer will come from Zion;
he will turn godlessness away from Jacob.
27And this is[r] my covenant with them
when I take away their sins."[s]

28As far as the gospel is concerned, they are
enemies on your account; but as far as election is
concerned, they are loved on account of the patri-
archs, 29for God's gifts and his call are irrevoca-
ble. 30Just as you who were at one time disobedi-
ent to God have now received mercy as a result of
their disobedience, 31so they too have now be-
come disobedient in order that they too may
now[t] receive mercy as a result of God's mercy to
you. 32For God has bound all men over to disobe-
dience so that he may have mercy on them all.

33Oh, the depth of the riches of the wisdom
and[u] knowledge of God!
How unsearchable his judgments,
and his paths beyond tracing out!
34"Who has known the mind of the Lord?
Or who has been his counselor?"[v]
35"Who has ever given to God,
that God should repay him?"[w]
36For from him and through him and to him
are all things.
To him be the glory forever! Amen.

[r]27 Or *will be* [s]27 Isaiah 59:20,21; 27:9; Jer. 31:33,34 [t]31 Some manuscripts do not have *now.* [u]33 Or *riches and the wisdom and the* [v]34 Isaiah 40:13 [w]35 Job 41:11

Discovering the Word 1. How does Paul know that God has not rejected his people (vv. 1–6)? 2. What were the spiritual consequences for those Israelites who rejected Jesus Christ (vv. 7–10)? 3. Why are these consequences inevitable for anyone who persistently rejects the gospel? 4. Why is Paul convinced that even greater blessings will come from Israel's acceptance of Christ (vv. 11–16)? 5. Why should Paul's illustration of the olive tree prevent Gentiles from feeling superior to unbelieving Israelites (vv. 17–24)? 6. In this chapter Paul has argued that Israel's unbelief is partial (vv. 1–10), purposeful (vv. 11–16) and temporary (vv. 25–32). How does this make him feel about God (vv. 33–36)?

Applying the Word 1. Why is it foolish for Christians today to feel superior to non-Christians? 2. How can Paul's description of God in verses 33–36 also encourage us to trust and praise him?

Responding in Prayer Thank God that his plans are greater than anything we can conceive.

15 / *Romans 12*
Living Sacrifices

IN THE FIRST eleven chapters Paul has described God's gift of righteousness. In Christ we who were condemned are justified. We who were sinners are sanctified. And we who had no hope will be glorified. But what is our proper response to God's mercy, love and grace? Paul tells us in this and the following chapters.

Warming Up to God Jesus once told a Pharisee that a person who is forgiven little loves little. But a person who is forgiven much loves much (Lk 7:47). Why do you think this is so?

Read Romans 12.

12 Therefore, I urge you, brothers, in
view of God's mercy, to offer your
bodies as living sacrifices, holy and
pleasing to God—this is your spiritual[x] act of
worship. 2Do not conform any longer to the pat-
tern of this world, but be transformed by the re-
newing of your mind. Then you will be able to
test and approve what God's will is—his good,
pleasing and perfect will.
3For by the grace given me I say to every one of

[x]1 Or *reasonable*

you: Do not think of yourself more highly than you ought, but rather think of yourself with sober judgment, in accordance with the measure of faith God has given you. [4]Just as each of us has one body with many members, and these members do not all have the same function, [5]so in Christ we who are many form one body, and each member belongs to all the others. [6]We have different gifts, according to the grace given us. If a man's gift is prophesying, let him use it in proportion to his[y] faith. [7]If it is serving, let him serve; if it is teaching, let him teach; [8]if it is encouraging, let him encourage; if it is contributing to the needs of others, let him give generously; if it is leadership, let him govern diligently; if it is showing mercy, let him do it cheerfully.

[9]Love must be sincere. Hate what is evil; cling to what is good. [10]Be devoted to one another in brotherly love. Honor one another above yourselves. [11]Never be lacking in zeal, but keep your spiritual fervor, serving the Lord. [12]Be joyful in hope, patient in affliction, faithful in prayer. [13]Share with God's people who are in need. Practice hospitality.

[14]Bless those who persecute you; bless and do not curse. [15]Rejoice with those who rejoice; mourn with those who mourn. [16]Live in harmony with one another. Do not be proud, but be willing to associate with people of low position.[z] Do not be conceited.

[17]Do not repay anyone evil for evil. Be careful to do what is right in the eyes of everybody. [18]If it is possible, as far as it depends on you, live at peace with everyone. [19]Do not take revenge, my friends, but leave room for God's wrath, for it is written: "It is mine to avenge; I will repay,"[a] says the Lord. [20]On the contrary:

"If your enemy is hungry, feed him;
if he is thirsty, give him something to drink.
In doing this, you will heap burning coals on his head."[b]

[21]Do not be overcome by evil, but overcome evil with good.

[y]6 Or *in agreement with the* [z]16 Or *willing to do menial work*
[a]19 Deut. 32:35 [b]20 Prov. 25:21,22

Discovering the Word 1. Why do you think Paul uses the imagery of "living sacrifices" to describe our proper response to God's mercy? 2. Sometimes we view God's will as something to be avoided rather than desired. How can the last part of verse 2 correct this distortion? 3. How can the realization that we are members of a body (vv. 3–8) prevent us from thinking too highly of ourselves (v. 3)? 4. How would the kind of love Paul describes in verses 9–16 transform our relationships with other Christians? 5. How would Paul's advice in verses 17-21 help us to overcome our enemies?

Applying the Word 1. What are some ways we can renew our minds (v. 2) and so be transformed? 2. As you think "with sober judgment" about yourself, what gift (or gifts) do you think God has given you (vv. 3–8)? 3. In what ways do you need to begin living more sacrificially before God, other Christians or the world?

Responding in Prayer Ask God to use you in serving the body of Christ.

16 / *Romans 13*
Submitting to Authorities

THE SERGEANT GLARES at a delinquent recruit whose face is now only inches away.

"That's an order!" he barks. "Do you understand?"

"Yes, sir," replies the recruit.

"I can't *hear* you!" shouts the sergeant.

"YES, SIR!" screams the recruit, who has just had his first lesson in military authority.

For many people the word *authority* conjures up images like the one just described. Those in authority are viewed as oppressors, and too often the impression is correct. Paul was no stranger to the abuses of authority. He had experienced much persecution at the hands of civil and religious authorities all around the Mediterranean. In light of this, Paul's view of authority may be surprising.

Warming Up to God What comes into your mind when you hear the word *authority*? Why?

Read Romans 13.

---

13 Everyone must submit himself to
the governing authorities, for there
is no authority except that which
God has established. The authorities that exist
have been established by God. [2]Consequently, he
who rebels against the authority is rebelling
against what God has instituted, and those who
do so will bring judgment on themselves. [3]For
rulers hold no terror for those who do right, but
for those who do wrong. Do you want to be free
from fear of the one in authority? Then do what
is right and he will commend you. [4]For he is
God's servant to do you good. But if you do
wrong, be afraid, for he does not bear the sword
for nothing. He is God's servant, an agent of
wrath to bring punishment on the wrongdoer.
[5]Therefore, it is necessary to submit to the au-
thorities, not only because of possible punish-
ment but also because of conscience.
[6]This is also why you pay taxes, for the author-
ities are God's servants, who give their full time to
governing. [7]Give everyone what you owe him: If
you owe taxes, pay taxes; if revenue, then reve-
nue; if respect, then respect; if honor, then honor.
[8]Let no debt remain outstanding, except the
continuing debt to love one another, for he who
loves his fellowman has fulfilled the law. [9]The
commandments, "Do not commit adultery," "Do
not murder," "Do not steal," "Do not covet,"[c]
and whatever other commandment there may be,
are summed up in this one rule: "Love your
neighbor as yourself."[d] [10]Love does no harm to
its neighbor. Therefore love is the fulfillment of
the law.
[11]And do this, understanding the present time.
The hour has come for you to wake up from your
slumber, because our salvation is nearer now than
when we first believed. [12]The night is nearly over;
the day is almost here. So let us put aside the
deeds of darkness and put on the armor of light.
[13]Let us behave decently, as in the daytime, not in
orgies and drunkenness, not in sexual immorality
and debauchery, not in dissension and jealousy.
[14]Rather, clothe yourselves with the Lord Jesus
Christ, and do not think about how to gratify the
desires of the sinful nature.[e]

[c]9 Exodus 20:13-15,17; Deut. 5:17-19,21 [d]9 Lev. 19:18 [e]14 Or *the flesh*

Discovering the Word 1. What is Paul's view of authority and those who exercise it (vv. 1–5)? 2. How would Paul's view of governing authorities apply to wicked and perverse rulers such as Nero or Hitler? 3. What are some reasons Paul gives for submitting to those in authority (vv. 1–5)? 4. In verse 8 Paul says, "Let no debt remain outstanding." Does this mean Christians should never incur any type of debts (mortgage, car and so on)? 5. In verses 11–14 Paul uses several vivid images to describe "the present time." How does each one give us a picture of how we should (or shouldn't) live?

Applying the Word 1. In verses 6–7 Paul suggests some practical ways we should submit to those in authority. What other examples can you think of? 2. Do you think it is ever appropriate to resist rather than to submit to the authorities? Explain. 3. Think back over this chapter. In what ways do you need to "clothe yourselves with the Lord Jesus Christ"?

Responding in Prayer Submission does not come to us naturally. Pray that you will learn to submit.

17 / *Romans 14*
To Eat or Not to Eat

IN THE LATE 1800s robed choirs were considered worldly by some Christians. More recently going to movies, watching television and drinking wine or beer have been viewed as sinful.

The Bible contains many clear commands. But it is also silent or ambiguous about many moral issues. These "gray" areas have always been a source of dispute and conflict among Christians, even though the specific areas of dispute change from time to time. What principles should guide us when our actions are criticized by others or when we feel critical toward them? Romans 14 helps us answer these questions.

Warming Up to God What types of behavior do Christians disagree about today?

Read Romans 14:1–23.

14 Accept him whose faith is weak, without passing judgment on disputable matters. 2One man's faith allows him to eat everything, but another man, whose faith is weak, eats only vegetables. 3The man who eats everything must not look down on him who does not, and the man who does not eat everything must not condemn the man who does, for God has accepted him. 4Who are you to judge someone else's servant? To his own master he stands or falls. And he will stand, for the Lord is able to make him stand.

5One man considers one day more sacred than another; another man considers every day alike. Each one should be fully convinced in his own mind. 6He who regards one day as special, does so to the Lord. He who eats meat, eats to the Lord, for he gives thanks to God; and he who abstains, does so to the Lord and gives thanks to God. 7For none of us lives to himself alone and none of us dies to himself alone. 8If we live, we live to the Lord; and if we die, we die to the Lord. So, whether we live or die, we belong to the Lord.

9For this very reason, Christ died and returned to life so that he might be the Lord of both the dead and the living. 10You, then, why do you judge your brother? Or why do you look down on your brother? For we will all stand before God's judgment seat. 11It is written:

"'As surely as I live,' says the Lord,
'every knee will bow before me;
every tongue will confess to God.'"[f]

12So then, each of us will give an account of himself to God.

13Therefore let us stop passing judgment on one another. Instead, make up your mind not to put any stumbling block or obstacle in your brother's way. 14As one who is in the Lord Jesus, I am fully convinced that no food[g] is unclean in itself. But if anyone regards something as unclean, then for him it is unclean. 15If your brother is distressed because of what you eat, you are no longer acting in love. Do not by your eating destroy your brother for whom Christ died. 16Do not allow what you consider good to be spoken of as evil. 17For the kingdom of God is not a matter of eating and drinking, but of righteousness, peace and joy in the Holy Spirit, 18because anyone who serves Christ in this way is pleasing to God and approved by men.

19Let us therefore make every effort to do what leads to peace and to mutual edification. 20Do not destroy the work of God for the sake of food. All food is clean, but it is wrong for a man to eat anything that causes someone else to stumble. 21It is better not to eat meat or drink wine or to do anything else that will cause your brother to fall.

22So whatever you believe about these things keep between yourself and God. Blessed is the man who does not condemn himself by what he approves. 23But the man who has doubts is condemned if he eats, because his eating is not from faith; and everything that does not come from faith is sin.

f11 Isaiah 45:23 g14 Or *that nothing*

Discovering the Word 1. What are some areas of dispute between the "weak" and the "strong" in verses 1–6? 2. What attitudes do the weak and the strong tend to have toward each other (vv. 1–4)? Why? 3. What types of Christians are you most likely to judge or look down on? Why? 4. Why is it wrong to pass judgment on other Christians (vv. 1–13)? 5. When we are *not* around those whose faith is weak, what principles should govern our Christian liberty (vv. 5–23)? 6. When we *are* around those whose faith is weak, what principles should guide our actions, and why (vv. 13–21)?

Applying the Word 1. What practices offend you? 2. Which of your own practices might distress or destroy another brother or sister in Christ?

Responding in Prayer Ask God for wisdom to know how to respond in areas in which you are causing offense.

18 / *Romans 15:1–13*
Unity, Hope and Praise

YOU DESERVE THE best. Look out for number one. Pamper yourself. These are the watchwords of our age. But in this chapter Paul urges us to stop gazing at our own reflection. For the first time in Romans he holds up the example of Christ, the one who embodies all the qualities God desires in us.

Warming Up to God When is self-concern appropriate, and when does it turn into selfishness?

Read Romans 15:1–13.

15 We who are strong ought to bear
with the failings of the weak and
not to please ourselves. 2Each of us
should please his neighbor for his good, to build
him up. 3For even Christ did not please himself
but, as it is written: "The insults of those who
insult you have fallen on me."[h] 4For everything
that was written in the past was written to teach
us, so that through endurance and the encourage-
ment of the Scriptures we might have hope.
5May the God who gives endurance and en-
couragement give you a spirit of unity among
yourselves as you follow Christ Jesus, 6so that
with one heart and mouth you may glorify the
God and Father of our Lord Jesus Christ.
7Accept one another, then, just as Christ ac-
cepted you, in order to bring praise to God. 8For
I tell you that Christ has become a servant of the
Jews[i] on behalf of God's truth, to confirm the
promises made to the patriarchs 9so that the Gen-
tiles may glorify God for his mercy, as it is writ-
ten:

"Therefore I will praise you among the
Gentiles;
I will sing hymns to your name."[j]

10Again, it says,

"Rejoice, O Gentiles, with his people."[k]

11And again,

"Praise the Lord, all you Gentiles,
and sing praises to him, all you peoples."[l]

12And again, Isaiah says,

"The Root of Jesse will spring up,
one who will arise to rule over the nations;
the Gentiles will hope in him."[m]

13May the God of hope fill you with all joy and
peace as you trust in him, so that you may over-
flow with hope by the power of the Holy Spirit.

h3 Psalm 69:9 i8 Greek *circumcision* j9 2 Samuel 22:50; Psalm 18:49 k10 Deut. 32:43 l11 Psalm 117:1 m12 Isaiah 11:10

Discovering the Word 1. What personal attitudes might hinder or help us to bear with the failings of the weak (vv. 1–2)? Explain why. 2. If we follow Christ's example in this and other areas of our lives, why will we need endurance, encouragement and hope (vv. 4–5)? 3. In contrast to the discord and possible verbal abuse hinted at in Romans 14, what does God desire of us (vv. 5–6)? 4. In verses 9–12 Paul quotes from four different Old Testament passages. What words and phrases express the dominant mood of these verses? 5. Why is this mood appropriate for all who hope in Jesus?

Applying the Word 1. Keeping in mind the context of verses 1–12, how can we become those whose lives overflow with joy, peace and hope (v. 13)? 2. Paul concludes this passage with a vivid prayer (v. 13). Consider these words, and try to picture this reality. How do you feel?

Responding in Prayer Spend time praising God for the joy, peace and hope we have in Christ.

19 / *Romans 15:14—16:27*
Brothers and Sisters in Christ

IN CHRIST WE have a bond that is stronger than flesh and blood. We are now and will always be brothers and sisters in Christ, members of God's family. This passage introduces us to some of our first-century relatives. As you read about them, notice the care they had for each other.

Warming Up to God What images come to mind when you think of the first-century church?

Read Romans 15:14—16:27.

[14]I myself am convinced, my brothers, that you yourselves are full of goodness, complete in knowledge and competent to instruct one another. [15]I have written you quite boldly on some points, as if to remind you of them again, because of the grace God gave me [16]to be a minister of Christ Jesus to the Gentiles with the priestly duty of proclaiming the gospel of God, so that the Gentiles might become an offering acceptable to God, sanctified by the Holy Spirit.

[17]Therefore I glory in Christ Jesus in my service to God. [18]I will not venture to speak of anything except what Christ has accomplished through me in leading the Gentiles to obey God by what I have said and done— [19]by the power of signs and miracles, through the power of the Spirit. So from Jerusalem all the way around to Illyricum, I have fully proclaimed the gospel of Christ. [20]It has always been my ambition to preach the gospel where Christ was not known, so that I would not be building on someone else's foundation. [21]Rather, as it is written:

"Those who were not told about him will see,
and those who have not heard will
understand."[n]

[22]This is why I have often been hindered from coming to you.

[23]But now that there is no more place for me to work in these regions, and since I have been longing for many years to see you, [24]I plan to do so when I go to Spain. I hope to visit you while passing through and to have you assist me on my journey there, after I have enjoyed your company for a while. [25]Now, however, I am on my way to Jerusalem in the service of the saints there. [26]For Macedonia and Achaia were pleased to make a contribution for the poor among the saints in Jerusalem. [27]They were pleased to do it, and indeed they owe it to them. For if the Gentiles have shared in the Jews' spiritual blessings, they owe it to the Jews to share with them their material blessings. [28]So after I have completed this task and have made sure that they have received this fruit, I will go to Spain and visit you on the way. [29]I know that when I come to you, I will come in the full measure of the blessing of Christ.

[n]21 Isaiah 52:15

[30]I urge you, brothers, by our Lord Jesus Christ
and by the love of the Spirit, to join me in my
struggle by praying to God for me. [31]Pray that I
may be rescued from the unbelievers in Judea and
that my service in Jerusalem may be acceptable to
the saints there, [32]so that by God's will I may
come to you with joy and together with you be
refreshed. [33]The God of peace be with you all.
Amen.

16 I commend to you our sister
Phoebe, a servant[o] of the church
in Cenchrea. [2]I ask you to receive
her in the Lord in a way worthy of the saints and
to give her any help she may need from you, for
she has been a great help to many people, includ-
ing me.

[3]Greet Priscilla[p] and Aquila, my fellow workers
in Christ Jesus. [4]They risked their lives for
me. Not only I but all the churches of the
Gentiles are grateful to them.
[5]Greet also the church that meets at their house.
Greet my dear friend Epenetus, who was the
first convert to Christ in the province of Asia.
[6]Greet Mary, who worked very hard for you.
[7]Greet Andronicus and Junias, my relatives who
have been in prison with me. They are out-
standing among the apostles, and they were
in Christ before I was.
[8]Greet Ampliatus, whom I love in the Lord.
[9]Greet Urbanus, our fellow worker in Christ,
and my dear friend Stachys.
[10]Greet Apelles, tested and approved in Christ.
Greet those who belong to the household of
Aristobulus.
[11]Greet Herodion, my relative.
Greet those in the household of Narcissus who
are in the Lord.
[12]Greet Tryphena and Tryphosa, those women
who work hard in the Lord.
Greet my dear friend Persis, another woman
who has worked very hard in the Lord.
[13]Greet Rufus, chosen in the Lord, and his
mother, who has been a mother to me, too.
[14]Greet Asyncritus, Phlegon, Hermes, Patrobas,
Hermas and the brothers with them.
[15]Greet Philologus, Julia, Nereus and his sister,
and Olympas and all the saints with them.
[16]Greet one another with a holy kiss.
All the churches of Christ send greetings.

[17]I urge you, brothers, to watch out for those
who cause divisions and put obstacles in your
way that are contrary to the teaching you have
learned. Keep away from them. [18]For such people
are not serving our Lord Christ, but their own
appetites. By smooth talk and flattery they de-
ceive the minds of naive people. [19]Everyone has
heard about your obedience, so I am full of joy
over you; but I want you to be wise about what is
good, and innocent about what is evil.
[20]The God of peace will soon crush Satan un-
der your feet.
The grace of our Lord Jesus be with you.
[21]Timothy, my fellow worker, sends his greet-
ings to you, as do Lucius, Jason and Sosipater, my
relatives.
[22]I, Tertius, who wrote down this letter, greet
you in the Lord.
[23]Gaius, whose hospitality I and the whole
church here enjoy, sends you his greetings.
Erastus, who is the city's director of public
works, and our brother Quartus send you their
greetings.[q]
[25]Now to him who is able to establish you by
my gospel and the proclamation of Jesus Christ,
according to the revelation of the mystery hidden
for long ages past, [26]but now revealed and made
known through the prophetic writings by the
command of the eternal God, so that all nations
might believe and obey him— [27]to the only wise
God be glory forever through Jesus Christ! Amen.

o1 *Or deaconess* p3 *Greek Prisca, a variant of Priscilla*
q23 *Some manuscripts their greetings.* [24]*May the grace of our Lord Jesus Christ be with all of you. Amen.*

Discovering the Word 1. What do we learn about Paul's apostolic ministry from 15:22? 2. What are Paul's immediate and future plans (15:23–33)? 3. What does 15:23–33 teach us about relationships among first-century Christians? 4. Use your imagination. From what we know about Paul and the Romans, how might the people in verses 1–16 have "risked their lives," "worked very hard" and "been a great help" to Paul and others? 5. How do the final words of this letter summarize the scope of our salvation (vv. 25–27)?

Applying the Word 1. In what ways can we share material blessings with other Christians? 2. What can you do to strengthen relationships in your spiritual family?

Responding in Prayer Pray for your church and the needs of specific people you know.

1 Corinthians

In 1938, just before World War II, Dietrich Bonhoeffer wrote *Life Together*, a moving little book on the principles of Christian community. Eighteen and a half centuries earlier the apostle Paul wrote what has come to be known as 1 Corinthians, a fascinating commentary on one Christian community that he founded. Why should we bother with either of these books?

Simply because we all have to live together with people, in Christian contexts and otherwise. Whether the situation involves a close friendship, a roommate, a spouse, a small group, a family, an office, a campus club, a neighborhood or a congregation, the challenges of life together will inevitably crop up. Church life is not immune to these problems, and Corinth was particularly susceptible. As a result, we can benefit from Paul's advice to that community.

Are there cliques and power struggles in the communities of which you are a part? Are you plagued by people who think they are spiritually or intellectually superior? How do you handle the immorality that seems so prevalent in the world, especially when it begins to invade the church? What is the proper way to exercise your rights, especially when a friend wrongs you or you feel that a matter of principle is at stake? How do we regulate marriage and singleness in the face of so many attacks on the health of both these life situations? How are we ever going to solve the battle of the sexes? What is the path to respecting one another's personality and gifts? Can eternity make a difference in how we live together today?

If any of these questions are relevant to your life and communities, then 1 Corinthians has something to say to you.

The relationship between Paul and the church at Corinth is a bittersweet chapter in church history. As the apostle traveled down the isthmus joining the two halves of Achaia (Greece) and first spotted the plain surrounding the city and the hill known as the Acrocorinth jutting up behind, he could hardly have imagined the depths and heights that would be reached by the church he left behind eighteen months later (see Acts 18 for the background of this part of Paul's second missionary journey). Nor could Paul have any idea of the depths and heights of emotion to which the members of that church would lead him, their spiritual father, over the next few years of visits and letters.

Both comedy and tragedy are found in the story of the Corinthian church. There was the comedy of a dynamic, gifted Christian community composed of uneducated, uninfluential people. They were plucked out of one of the greatest centers of trade, political authority and pagan religion in the Roman empire. Morals were so bad in that city that its citizens had inspired a word for sexual license—to *Corinthianize!* The existence of a church in such a setting was a reason for comic rejoicing.

However, there was also the tragedy of the Corinthians forgetting their humble roots and placing themselves as kings over one another—even over Paul, their founder and friend. The resulting tensions and schisms would boil over with even greater heartache for Paul in 2 Corinthians.

In the first six chapters of 1 Corinthians Paul begins with the distressing matters he has learned about: factions, incest, court cases and freedom gone wild. In chapters 7—14 he treats a series of topics that the Corinthians have asked him about, from marriage to spiritual gifts, with each new topic signaled by the phrase *Now concerning.* Finally, he sums up the teaching of the book in chapter 15, which is devoted to a theology of the resurrection or "last things."

Understanding why chapter 15 and parts of chapters 1—4 fit into this book is the key to unlocking 1 Corinthians. As always, Paul is not only interested in correcting practice but also in grounding his instruction in theological principles. In fact, the Corinthians had two root problems: premature spirituality (they thought they had everything heaven could offer) and immature spirituality (they forgot that the heart of the gospel is love, servanthood and the cross). Perhaps our communities, too, need correction in both practice and theology.

Outline

1 / *1 Corinthians 1*
Called in Christ

HAVE YOU EVER found a Christian group that doesn't have any problems? If so, don't join it—you'll ruin everything!

The church in Corinth was far from perfect. Paul had heard a long list of complaints about this eager but misguided flock. As he attempted some long-distance pastoring, where would he begin? Paul's starting point is very relevant for problem groups and individuals today.

Warming Up to God When have you been hurt by division within a church or Christian group you were a part of?

Read 1 Corinthians 1.

1 Paul, called to be an apostle of Christ Jesus by the will of God, and our brother Sosthenes,

2To the church of God in Corinth, to those sanctified in Christ Jesus and called to be holy, together with all those everywhere who call on the name of our Lord Jesus Christ—their Lord and ours:

3Grace and peace to you from God our Father and the Lord Jesus Christ.

4I always thank God for you because of his grace given you in Christ Jesus. 5For in him you have been enriched in every way—in all your speaking and in all your knowledge— 6because our testimony about Christ was confirmed in you. 7Therefore you do not lack any spiritual gift as you eagerly wait for our Lord Jesus Christ to be revealed. 8He will keep you strong to the end, so that you will be blameless on the day of our Lord Jesus Christ. 9God, who has called you into fellowship with his Son Jesus Christ our Lord, is faithful.

10I appeal to you, brothers, in the name of our Lord Jesus Christ, that all of you agree with one another so that there may be no divisions among you and that you may be perfectly united in mind and thought. 11My brothers, some from Chloe's household have informed me that there are quarrels among you. 12What I mean is this: One of you says, "I follow Paul"; another, "I follow Apollos"; another, "I follow Cephas[a]"; still another, "I follow Christ."

13Is Christ divided? Was Paul crucified for you? Were you baptized into[b] the name of Paul? 14I am thankful that I did not baptize any of you except Crispus and Gaius, 15so no one can say that you were baptized into my name. 16(Yes, I also baptized the household of Stephanas; beyond that, I don't remember if I baptized anyone else.) 17For Christ did not send me to baptize, but to preach the gospel—not with words of human wisdom, lest the cross of Christ be emptied of its power.

18For the message of the cross is foolishness to those who are perishing, but to us who are being saved it is the power of God. 19For it is written:

"I will destroy the wisdom of the wise;
the intelligence of the intelligent I will frustrate."[c]

20Where is the wise man? Where is the scholar? Where is the philosopher of this age? Has not God made foolish the wisdom of the world? 21For since in the wisdom of God the world through its wisdom did not know him, God was pleased through the foolishness of what was preached to save those who believe. 22Jews demand miraculous signs and Greeks look for wisdom, 23but we preach Christ crucified: a stumbling block to Jews and foolishness to Gentiles, 24but to those whom God has called, both Jews and Greeks, Christ the power of God and the wisdom of God. 25For the foolishness of God is wiser than man's wisdom, and the weakness of God is stronger than man's strength.

26Brothers, think of what you were when you were called. Not many of you were wise by human standards; not many were influential; not many were of noble birth. 27But God chose the foolish things of the world to shame the wise; God chose the weak things of the world to shame the strong. 28He chose the lowly things of this world and the despised things—and the things

[a]*12* That is, Peter [b]*13* Or *in;* also in verse 15 [c]*19* Isaiah 29:14

that are not—to nullify the things that are, 29so
that no one may boast before him. 30It is because
of him that you are in Christ Jesus, who has be-
come for us wisdom from God—that is, our right-
eousness, holiness and redemption. 31Therefore,
as it is written: "Let him who boasts boast in the
Lord."[d]

[d]31 Jer. 9:24

Discovering the Word 1. Before discussing the problems in Corinth, Paul affirms his readers (vv. 1–9). Why is he thankful for them? 2. Why do you think cliques had formed around Paul, Apollos and Cephas (v. 12)? 3. How did Paul conduct himself in Corinth to avoid, if possible, the problem of a personality cult (vv. 14–17)? 4. The Corinthians boasted in worldly wisdom and those who taught it. How does the message of the cross destroy all such boasting (vv. 18–25)? 5. The Corinthians also felt intellectually and spiritually superior to others. What had they forgotten about their past and the reason God chose them (vv. 26–29)? 6. What does it mean to "boast in the Lord" (vv. 30–31)?

Applying the Word 1. As you reflect on your own past, what reasons do you have for being humble rather than proud? 2. How can genuine humility promote unity in your church or fellowship?

Responding in Prayer Take time to thank the Lord for all he has done for you.

2 / *1 Corinthians 2*
Mind of Christ

MANY PEOPLE THINK Christianity is for the mindless and dull. Someone has said, "I feel like unscrewing my head and putting it underneath the pew every time I go to church." Unfortunately, this chapter has been used to support an uneducated, unthinking approach to Christianity. But this misses the point. As Søren Kierkegaard, the Danish philosopher, once said: Christ doesn't destroy reason; he *dethrones* it.

Warming Up to God In what area of your life do you need wisdom?

Read 1 Corinthians 2.

2 When I came to you, brothers, I did not
come with eloquence or superior wisdom
as I proclaimed to you the testimony
about God.[e] 2For I resolved to know nothing
while I was with you except Jesus Christ and him
crucified. 3I came to you in weakness and fear,
and with much trembling. 4My message and my
preaching were not with wise and persuasive
words, but with a demonstration of the Spirit's
power, 5so that your faith might not rest on men's
wisdom, but on God's power.
6We do, however, speak a message of wisdom
among the mature, but not the wisdom of this age
or of the rulers of this age, who are coming to
nothing. 7No, we speak of God's secret wisdom, a
wisdom that has been hidden and that God des-
tined for our glory before time began. 8None of
the rulers of this age understood it, for if they
had, they would not have crucified the Lord of
glory. 9However, as it is written:

"No eye has seen,
no ear has heard,
no mind has conceived
what God has prepared for those who love
him"[f]—

10but God has revealed it to us by his Spirit.
The Spirit searches all things, even the deep
things of God. 11For who among men knows the
thoughts of a man except the man's spirit within
him? In the same way no one knows the thoughts
of God except the Spirit of God. 12We have not

[e]1 Some manuscripts *as I proclaimed to you God's mystery*
[f]9 Isaiah 64:4

received the spirit of the world but the Spirit who
is from God, that we may understand what God
has freely given us. 13This is what we speak, not
in words taught us by human wisdom but in
words taught by the Spirit, expressing spiritual
truths in spiritual words.[g] 14The man without
the Spirit does not accept the things that come
from the Spirit of God, for they are foolishness to
him, and he cannot understand them, because
they are spiritually discerned. 15The spiritual man
makes judgments about all things, but he himself
is not subject to any man's judgment:

16"For who has known the mind of the Lord
that he may instruct him?"[h]

But we have the mind of Christ.

[g]13 Or *Spirit, interpreting spiritual truths to spiritual men*
[h]16 Isaiah 40:13

Discovering the Word 1. Greek philosophers were often polished orators whose eloquence and wisdom dazzled their audiences. How does this contrast with Paul's preaching in Corinth (vv. 1–5)? 2. How is God's wisdom different from the wisdom of this age (vv. 6–10)? 3. Why are *secret* and *hidden* appropriate words to describe this wisdom? 4. When it comes to understanding God's wisdom, how does the person without the Spirit contrast with the spiritual person (vv. 14–16)? 5. Based on this passage, how would you define spiritual maturity?

Applying the Word 1. Who has been an example of spiritual maturity to you? 2. What can you do to become more spiritually mature?

Responding in Prayer Ask that you would be given the true wisdom that comes from the Spirit.

3/ *1 Corinthians 3*
Founded on Christ

THE DUKE OF Windsor, recalling his childhood discipline by George V, then King of England, said that his father used to daily remind him, "Never forget who you are." As the spiritual father of the Corinthians, Paul reminds them in this chapter, "Never forget *whose* you are."

The Corinthians were worldly and quarrelsome because they misunderstood both the message and the messengers of the cross. In chapters one and two, Paul focused on the message—the true wisdom from God. Now he looks at God's messengers. As he does so, Paul reminds the Corinthians and us of our true identity in Christ.

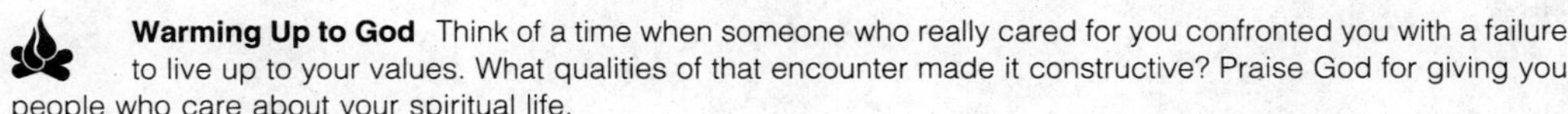

Warming Up to God Think of a time when someone who really cared for you confronted you with a failure to live up to your values. What qualities of that encounter made it constructive? Praise God for giving you people who care about your spiritual life.

Read 1 Corinthians 3.

3 Brothers, I could not address you as spiritual but as worldly—mere infants in
Christ. 2I gave you milk, not solid food,
for you were not yet ready for it. Indeed, you are
still not ready. 3You are still worldly. For since
there is jealousy and quarreling among you, are
you not worldly? Are you not acting like mere
men? 4For when one says, "I follow Paul," and
another, "I follow Apollos," are you not mere
men?

5What, after all, is Apollos? And what is Paul?
Only servants, through whom you came to believe—as the Lord has assigned to each his task.
6I planted the seed, Apollos watered it, but God
made it grow. 7So neither he who plants nor he
who waters is anything, but only God, who
makes things grow. 8The man who plants and the
man who waters have one purpose, and each will
be rewarded according to his own labor. 9For we
are God's fellow workers; you are God's field,
God's building.

10By the grace God has given me, I laid a foun-

dation as an expert builder, and someone else is
building on it. But each one should be careful
how he builds. [11]For no one can lay any founda-
tion other than the one already laid, which is
Jesus Christ. [12]If any man builds on this founda-
tion using gold, silver, costly stones, wood, hay or
straw, [13]his work will be shown for what it is,
because the Day will bring it to light. It will be
revealed with fire, and the fire will test the quality
of each man's work. [14]If what he has built sur-
vives, he will receive his reward. [15]If it is burned
up, he will suffer loss; he himself will be saved,
but only as one escaping through the flames.
[16]Don't you know that you yourselves are
God's temple and that God's Spirit lives in you?
[17]If anyone destroys God's temple, God will de-
stroy him; for God's temple is sacred, and you are
that temple.
[18]Do not deceive yourselves. If any one of you
thinks he is wise by the standards of this age, he
should become a "fool" so that he may become
wise. [19]For the wisdom of this world is foolish-
ness in God's sight. As it is written: "He catches
the wise in their craftiness"[i]; [20]and again, "The
Lord knows that the thoughts of the wise are fu-
tile."[j] [21]So then, no more boasting about men!
All things are yours, [22]whether Paul or Apollos or
Cephas[k] or the world or life or death or the
present or the future—all are yours, [23]and you
are of Christ, and Christ is of God.

[i]19 Job 5:13 [j]20 Psalm 94:11 [k]22 That is, Peter

Discovering the Word 1. Even though the Corinthians had the Spirit, why couldn't they be considered spiritual (vv. 1–4)? 2. What two illustrations does Paul use to describe himself and Apollos (vv. 6–9, 10–15)? 3. In what ways is God's church like a field being planted (vv. 6–9)? 4. In 3:10–15 Paul changes the metaphor from farming to building. Describe the various ways the church is like a building under construction. 5. In verse 3 Paul accused the Corinthians of being worldly. How can he say to the same people, "You are God's temple" and "God's Spirit lives in you" (v. 16)? 6. The Corinthians had initially claimed, "I belong to Paul" or "I belong to Apollos" (1:12 RSV). Paul claims something more important. In what sense do Paul, Apollos and everything else belong to the Corinthians—and to us (vv. 21–23)?

Applying the Word 1. How does this chapter affect your view of your own ministry in the church and that of professional ministers? 2. How does this way of evaluating our lives apply not only to so-called Christian work but also to other aspects of our vocation in Christ: relationships, occupations, avocations, community involvement and so on? 3. In what way are you challenged to "be careful" about how you build?

Responding in Prayer Everything we do must be founded on Christ. Before God, search your attitudes and actions, and pray that this would be true of you.

4 / *1 Corinthians 4*
Servants of Christ

IN THE LAST study Paul called the Corinthians not to forget that they were God's holy temple. Now he calls them and all Christian communities to experience the power of radical servanthood for Christ's sake. St. Francis of Assisi exhibited this when he walked through Muslim battle lines during the Crusades in order to preach to the Sultan. Mother Teresa also is a "fool for Christ" when she bends down to care for a dying beggar in Calcutta. There is power in such actions, even though the wise ones of this age shake their heads in disbelief or wag their tongues in scorn.

Warming Up to God How do you feel when you hear about people like St. Francis who give away all they have to the poor, or Mother Teresa who live sacrificially?

Read 1 Corinthians 4.

4 So then, men ought to regard us as servants of Christ and as those entrusted with the secret things of God. 2Now it is required that those who have been given a trust must prove faithful. 3I care very little if I am judged by you or by any human court; indeed, I do not even judge myself. 4My conscience is clear, but that does not make me innocent. It is the Lord who judges me. 5Therefore judge nothing before the appointed time; wait till the Lord comes. He will bring to light what is hidden in darkness and will expose the motives of men's hearts. At that time each will receive his praise from God.

6Now, brothers, I have applied these things to myself and Apollos for your benefit, so that you may learn from us the meaning of the saying, "Do not go beyond what is written." Then you will not take pride in one man over against another. 7For who makes you different from anyone else? What do you have that you did not receive? And if you did receive it, why do you boast as though you did not?

8Already you have all you want! Already you have become rich! You have become kings—and that without us! How I wish that you really had become kings so that we might be kings with you! 9For it seems to me that God has put us apostles on display at the end of the procession, like men condemned to die in the arena. We have been made a spectacle to the whole universe, to angels as well as to men. 10We are fools for Christ, but you are so wise in Christ! We are weak, but you are strong! You are honored, we are dishonored! 11To this very hour we go hungry and thirsty, we are in rags, we are brutally treated, we are homeless. 12We work hard with our own hands. When we are cursed, we bless; when we are persecuted, we endure it; 13when we are slandered, we answer kindly. Up to this moment we have become the scum of the earth, the refuse of the world.

14I am not writing this to shame you, but to warn you, as my dear children. 15Even though you have ten thousand guardians in Christ, you do not have many fathers, for in Christ Jesus I became your father through the gospel. 16Therefore I urge you to imitate me. 17For this reason I am sending to you Timothy, my son whom I love, who is faithful in the Lord. He will remind you of my way of life in Christ Jesus, which agrees with what I teach everywhere in every church.

18Some of you have become arrogant, as if I were not coming to you. 19But I will come to you very soon, if the Lord is willing, and then I will find out not only how these arrogant people are talking, but what power they have. 20For the kingdom of God is not a matter of talk but of power. 21What do you prefer? Shall I come to you with a whip, or in love and with a gentle spirit?

Discovering the Word 1. In contrast to the hero worship in Corinth, how do Paul and his coworkers wish to be regarded (vv. 1–2)? 2. Paul fears the Corinthians are moving "beyond what was written"—probably a reference to the Old Testament Scriptures. How might going beyond the authority of Scripture result in taking "pride in one man over against another" (v. 6)? 3. Scripture teaches that the suffering of this present age precedes the glory of the age to come. In their own minds, how had the Corinthians taken a shortcut to glory (vv. 8, 10)? 4. How did their "glorious" description of themselves contrast with the experiences of Paul and the other apostles (vv. 9–13)? 5. We receive the first hint in this section that some in Corinth were not only boasting about other leaders but were also putting down Paul. How does the apostle choose to combat these opponents (vv. 18–21)?

Applying the Word 1. How would imitating Paul's way of life (vv. 16–17) require changes in your thinking and actions? 2. In what ways does this passage challenge you to become a "fool for Christ"?

Responding in Prayer Thank God for the leaders who have formed and impacted your Christian faith and walk.

5 / 1 Corinthians 5—6
Members of Christ

THE NEW TESTAMENT church has inspired both exciting and disastrous experiments down through history. Hoping to create the perfect New Testament community, some have tried to design groups where all the gifts are expressed, worship is spontaneous and fellowship is deep. But they forget the common element of all New Testament churches—problems!

In chapters 1—4 Paul dealt with divisions in the church. Now he focuses on serious moral problems in Corinth. Incest and drunkenness during Communion are hardly what we hope to find in church. But we must remember that growing churches are not always filled with well-scrubbed Christians, but rather with a motley collection of sinners being saved.

Warming Up to God How do you react when you hear about serious moral and spiritual problems of people in your church? What about your attitude do you think might be inappropriate or judgmental? Ask God to open your heart to this study.

Read 1 Corinthians 5—6.

5 It is actually reported that there is sexual
immorality among you, and of a kind that
does not occur even among pagans: A
man has his father's wife. 2And you are proud!
Shouldn't you rather have been filled with grief
and have put out of your fellowship the man who
did this? 3Even though I am not physically
present, I am with you in spirit. And I have al-
ready passed judgment on the one who did this,
just as if I were present. 4When you are assem-
bled in the name of our Lord Jesus and I am with
you in spirit, and the power of our Lord Jesus is
present, 5hand this man over to Satan, so that the
sinful nature[l] may be destroyed and his spirit
saved on the day of the Lord.

6Your boasting is not good. Don't you know
that a little yeast works through the whole batch
of dough? 7Get rid of the old yeast that you may
be a new batch without yeast—as you really are.
For Christ, our Passover lamb, has been sacri-
ficed. 8Therefore let us keep the Festival, not with
the old yeast, the yeast of malice and wickedness,
but with bread without yeast, the bread of sincer-
ity and truth.

9I have written you in my letter not to associate
with sexually immoral people— 10not at all
meaning the people of this world who are im-
moral, or the greedy and swindlers, or idolaters.
In that case you would have to leave this world.
11But now I am writing you that you must not
associate with anyone who calls himself a brother
but is sexually immoral or greedy, an idolater or
a slanderer, a drunkard or a swindler. With such
a man do not even eat.

12What business is it of mine to judge those
outside the church? Are you not to judge those
inside? 13God will judge those outside. "Expel the
wicked man from among you."[m]

6 If any of you has a dispute with another,
dare he take it before the ungodly for
judgment instead of before the saints?
2Do you not know that the saints will judge the
world? And if you are to judge the world, are you
not competent to judge trivial cases? 3Do you not
know that we will judge angels? How much more
the things of this life! 4Therefore, if you have dis-
putes about such matters, appoint as judges even
men of little account in the church![n] 5I say this
to shame you. Is it possible that there is nobody
among you wise enough to judge a dispute be-
tween believers? 6But instead, one brother goes to
law against another—and this in front of unbe-
lievers!

7The very fact that you have lawsuits among
you means you have been completely defeated al-
ready. Why not rather be wronged? Why not
rather be cheated? 8Instead, you yourselves cheat
and do wrong, and you do this to your brothers.

9Do you not know that the wicked will not
inherit the kingdom of God? Do not be deceived:
Neither the sexually immoral nor idolaters nor
adulterers nor male prostitutes nor homosexual
offenders 10nor thieves nor the greedy nor drunk-
ards nor slanderers nor swindlers will inherit the
kingdom of God. 11And that is what some of you

l5 Or *that his body*; or *that the flesh* m13 Deut. 17:7; 19:19; 21:21; 22:21,24; 24:7 n4 Or *matters, do you appoint as judges men of little account in the church?*

were. But you were washed, you were sanctified,
you were justified in the name of the Lord Jesus
Christ and by the Spirit of our God.
12“Everything is permissible for me”—but not
everything is beneficial. “Everything is permissi-
ble for me”—but I will not be mastered by any-
thing. 13“Food for the stomach and the stomach
for food”—but God will destroy them both. The
body is not meant for sexual immorality, but for
the Lord, and the Lord for the body. 14By his
power God raised the Lord from the dead, and he
will raise us also. 15Do you not know that your
bodies are members of Christ himself? Shall I
then take the members of Christ and unite them
with a prostitute? Never! 16Do you not know that
he who unites himself with a prostitute is one
with her in body? For it is said, “The two will
become one flesh.”[o] 17But he who unites himself
with the Lord is one with him in spirit.
18Flee from sexual immorality. All other sins a
man commits are outside his body, but he who
sins sexually sins against his own body. 19Do you
not know that your body is a temple of the Holy
Spirit, who is in you, whom you have received
from God? You are not your own; 20you were
bought at a price. Therefore honor God with your
body.

[o]16 Gen. 2:24

Discovering the Word 1. In Greece there was no shame in having sexual relationships before marriage or outside of marriage. What made the sexual problem in this church especially loathsome to Paul? 2. How is Paul's strategy of discipline designed to bring health to both the church and the individual (5:2–5)? 3. Paul compares the Christian life to the Passover and Feast of Unleavened Bread. According to Paul, what do the yeast, the bread without yeast and the Passover lamb symbolize (5:6–8)? 4. Some Christians practice a doctrine of “double separation.” First, they separate themselves from the evil influences in the world. Second, they separate themselves from Christians who have not separated themselves from the world. What type of separation is taught in verses 9–13? 5. What commands and guidelines does Paul give for settling disputes between Christians (vv. 1–8)? Explain. 6. Paul calls the body “a temple of the Holy Spirit” (6:18–20). How does the biblical view of the body presented here contrast with the modern view?

Applying the Word 1. Why do you think so few churches today practice discipline of those who commit an immorality? 2. How can we distinguish between the kinds of people who should be put out of the church (5:2, 9–11; 6:9–10) and those who belong in the church even though they are “worldly” and immature (see 3:1)? 3. How can understanding your body as a temple of the Holy Spirit (v. 19) lead to a healthy balance of bodily control and bodily celebration?

Responding in Prayer Ask God to help you take whatever steps are necessary to maintain both personal and corporate purity.

6 / *1 Corinthians 7*
Devoted to Christ

CORINTH, UNLIKE MOST modern cities today, did not have sex shops, *Playboy* magazines, porn videos and “adult entertainment” centers. But there was so much sexual immorality that the ancients had a word to describe engaging in raw sensual pleasure—to *Corinthianize.* In chapter six Paul dealt with those who justified a permissive lifestyle in the name of Christian freedom. In this chapter he battles on the opposite front. Some Corinthians claimed sex was sinful—or at least a second-class diversion—even in marriage. In response Paul answers questions about marriage, sexuality and singleness.

Warming Up to God How did you learn about sexuality? What attitudes did you learn that have been hurtful to you? Ask God to use this passage to help you better understand marriage and singleness.

Read 1 Corinthians 7.

7 Now for the matters you wrote about: It is good for a man not to marry.[p] 2But since there is so much immorality, each man should have his own wife, and each woman her own husband. 3The husband should fulfill his marital duty to his wife, and likewise the wife to her husband. 4The wife's body does not belong to her alone but also to her husband. In the same way, the husband's body does not belong to him alone but also to his wife. 5Do not deprive each other except by mutual consent and for a time, so that you may devote yourselves to prayer. Then come together again so that Satan will not tempt you because of your lack of self-control. 6I say this as a concession, not as a command. 7I wish that all men were as I am. But each man has his own gift from God; one has this gift, another has that.

8Now to the unmarried and the widows I say: It is good for them to stay unmarried, as I am. 9But if they cannot control themselves, they should marry, for it is better to marry than to burn with passion.

10To the married I give this command (not I, but the Lord): A wife must not separate from her husband. 11But if she does, she must remain unmarried or else be reconciled to her husband. And a husband must not divorce his wife.

12To the rest I say this (I, not the Lord): If any brother has a wife who is not a believer and she is willing to live with him, he must not divorce her. 13And if a woman has a husband who is not a believer and he is willing to live with her, she must not divorce him. 14For the unbelieving husband has been sanctified through his wife, and the unbelieving wife has been sanctified through her believing husband. Otherwise your children would be unclean, but as it is, they are holy.

15But if the unbeliever leaves, let him do so. A believing man or woman is not bound in such circumstances; God has called us to live in peace. 16How do you know, wife, whether you will save your husband? Or, how do you know, husband, whether you will save your wife?

17Nevertheless, each one should retain the place in life that the Lord assigned to him and to which God has called him. This is the rule I lay down in all the churches. 18Was a man already circumcised when he was called? He should not become uncircumcised. Was a man uncircumcised when he was called? He should not be circumcised. 19Circumcision is nothing and uncircumcision is nothing. Keeping God's commands is what counts. 20Each one should remain in the situation which he was in when God called him. 21Were you a slave when you were called? Don't let it trouble you—although if you can gain your freedom, do so. 22For he who was a slave when he was called by the Lord is the Lord's freedman; similarly, he who was a free man when he was called is Christ's slave. 23You were bought at a price; do not become slaves of men. 24Brothers, each man, as responsible to God, should remain in the situation God called him to.

25Now about virgins: I have no command from the Lord, but I give a judgment as one who by the Lord's mercy is trustworthy. 26Because of the present crisis, I think that it is good for you to remain as you are. 27Are you married? Do not seek a divorce. Are you unmarried? Do not look for a wife. 28But if you do marry, you have not sinned; and if a virgin marries, she has not sinned. But those who marry will face many troubles in this life, and I want to spare you this.

29What I mean, brothers, is that the time is short. From now on those who have wives should live as if they had none; 30those who mourn, as if they did not; those who are happy, as if they were not; those who buy something, as if it were not theirs to keep; 31those who use the things of the world, as if not engrossed in them. For this world in its present form is passing away.

32I would like you to be free from concern. An unmarried man is concerned about the Lord's affairs—how he can please the Lord. 33But a married man is concerned about the affairs of this world—how he can please his wife— 34and his interests are divided. An unmarried woman or virgin is concerned about the Lord's affairs: Her aim is to be devoted to the Lord in both body and spirit. But a married woman is concerned about the affairs of this world—how she can please her husband. 35I am saying this for your own good, not to restrict you, but that you may live in a right way in undivided devotion to the Lord.

36If anyone thinks he is acting improperly toward the virgin he is engaged to, and if she is getting along in years and he feels he ought to marry, he should do as he wants. He is not sinning. They should get married. 37But the man who has settled the matter in his own mind, who is under no compulsion but has control over his

p1 Or *"It is good for a man not to have sexual relations with a woman."*

own will, and who has made up his mind not to marry the virgin—this man also does the right thing. 38So then, he who marries the virgin does right, but he who does not marry her does even better.[q]

39A woman is bound to her husband as long as he lives. But if her husband dies, she is free to marry anyone she wishes, but he must belong to the Lord. 40In my judgment, she is happier if she stays as she is—and I think that I too have the Spirit of God.

[q]36-38 Or *36If anyone thinks he is not treating his daughter properly, and if she is getting along in years, and he feels she ought to marry, he should do as he wants. He is not sinning. He should let her get married. 37But the man who has settled the matter in his own mind, who is under no compulsion but has control over his own will, and who has made up his mind to keep the virgin unmarried—this man also does the right thing. 38So then, he who gives his virgin in marriage does right, but he who does not give her in marriage does even better.*

Discovering the Word 1. Although Paul agrees that celibacy is good (v. 1), why is it impractical for most people (vv. 2, 7)? 2. What practical advice does Paul give to the unmarried and the married for avoiding sexual immorality (vv. 2–9)? 3. According to Paul, what are some benefits of remaining in a marriage to a non-Christian (vv. 12–16)? 4. Under what circumstances would Paul seemingly allow for divorce, and why (vv. 15–16)? 5. Paul speaks of God calling us *to* a certain situation (vv. 17, 24) and of God calling us while we were *in* that situation (vv. 18–22). How are these two dimensions of calling different? 6. In verses 24–40 Paul addresses *those considering marriage.* Why does Paul call singleness a "better" way (v. 38) and a "happier" way (v. 40) when he has such a high view of marriage?

Applying the Word 1. What principles from this passage could help us care for Christians who are considering separation or divorce? 2. Whether you are married or single, in what way do you struggle to be faithful to God's calling?

Responding in Prayer Ask God to show you his calling for you.

---

7 / *1 Corinthians 8—9*
Living for Christ

A NOTE TACKED up on a refrigerator had these words: "It is better to be righteous than right!" Today individuals and groups are clamoring and clashing over rights: the right to free speech, the rights of the poor, the right to liberation, women's rights, aboriginal rights, the right not to be bothered by smokers (or nonsmokers), the rights of animals, the rights of blacks, the rights of whites.

So many of the struggles over rights, both legitimate and bogus, seem to revolve around attaining freedom to change the status quo. The apostle Paul, however, appears to be on opposite ground. For him rights and freedoms are unimportant compared to the privilege of living for Christ.

Warming Up to God In what area are you currently struggling with a person or group in opposition to you? Ask God to use this study to show you how to be righteous.

Read 1 Corinthians 8—9.

---

8 Now about food sacrificed to idols: We know that we all possess knowledge.[r] Knowledge puffs up, but love builds up. 2The man who thinks he knows something does not yet know as he ought to know. 3But the man who loves God is known by God.

4So then, about eating food sacrificed to idols: We know that an idol is nothing at all in the world and that there is no God but one. 5For even if there are so-called gods, whether in heaven or on earth (as indeed there are many "gods" and many "lords"), 6yet for us there is but one God, the Father, from whom all things came and for whom we live; and there is but one Lord, Jesus

[r]1 Or *"We all possess knowledge," as you say*

Christ, through whom all things came and
through whom we live.

7But not everyone knows this. Some people are
still so accustomed to idols that when they eat
such food they think of it as having been sacri-
ficed to an idol, and since their conscience is
weak, it is defiled. 8But food does not bring us
near to God; we are no worse if we do not eat,
and no better if we do.

9Be careful, however, that the exercise of your
freedom does not become a stumbling block to
the weak. 10For if anyone with a weak conscience
sees you who have this knowledge eating in an
idol's temple, won't he be emboldened to eat what
has been sacrificed to idols? 11So this weak
brother, for whom Christ died, is destroyed by
your knowledge. 12When you sin against your
brothers in this way and wound their weak con-
science, you sin against Christ. 13Therefore, if
what I eat causes my brother to fall into sin, I will
never eat meat again, so that I will not cause him
to fall.

9 Am I not free? Am I not an apostle? Have
I not seen Jesus our Lord? Are you not
the result of my work in the Lord? 2Even
though I may not be an apostle to others, surely
I am to you! For you are the seal of my apostle-
ship in the Lord.

3This is my defense to those who sit in judg-
ment on me. 4Don't we have the right to food and
drink? 5Don't we have the right to take a believ-
ing wife along with us, as do the other apostles
and the Lord's brothers and Cephas[s]? 6Or is it
only I and Barnabas who must work for a living?

7Who serves as a soldier at his own expense?
Who plants a vineyard and does not eat of its
grapes? Who tends a flock and does not drink of
the milk? 8Do I say this merely from a human
point of view? Doesn't the Law say the same
thing? 9For it is written in the Law of Moses: "Do
not muzzle an ox while it is treading out the
grain."[t] Is it about oxen that God is concerned?
10Surely he says this for us, doesn't he? Yes, this
was written for us, because when the plowman
plows and the thresher threshes, they ought to do
so in the hope of sharing in the harvest. 11If we
have sown spiritual seed among you, is it too
much if we reap a material harvest from you? 12If
others have this right of support from you,
shouldn't we have it all the more?

But we did not use this right. On the contrary,
we put up with anything rather than hinder the
gospel of Christ. 13Don't you know that those
who work in the temple get their food from the
temple, and those who serve at the altar share in
what is offered on the altar? 14In the same way,
the Lord has commanded that those who preach
the gospel should receive their living from the
gospel.

15But I have not used any of these rights. And
I am not writing this in the hope that you will do
such things for me. I would rather die than have
anyone deprive me of this boast. 16Yet when I
preach the gospel, I cannot boast, for I am com-
pelled to preach. Woe to me if I do not preach the
gospel! 17If I preach voluntarily, I have a reward;
if not voluntarily, I am simply discharging the
trust committed to me. 18What then is my re-
ward? Just this: that in preaching the gospel I
may offer it free of charge, and so not make use of
my rights in preaching it.

19Though I am free and belong to no man, I
make myself a slave to everyone, to win as many
as possible. 20To the Jews I became like a Jew, to
win the Jews. To those under the law I became
like one under the law (though I myself am not
under the law), so as to win those under the law.
21To those not having the law I became like one
not having the law (though I am not free from
God's law but am under Christ's law), so as to
win those not having the law. 22To the weak I
became weak, to win the weak. I have become all
things to all men so that by all possible means I
might save some. 23I do all this for the sake of the
gospel, that I may share in its blessings.

24Do you not know that in a race all the run-
ners run, but only one gets the prize? Run in such
a way as to get the prize. 25Everyone who com-
petes in the games goes into strict training. They
do it to get a crown that will not last; but we do
it to get a crown that will last forever. 26Therefore
I do not run like a man running aimlessly; I do
not fight like a man beating the air. 27No, I beat
my body and make it my slave so that after I have
preached to others, I myself will not be disquali-
fied for the prize.

[s]5 That is, Peter [t]9 Deut. 25:4

Discovering the Word 1. Sacrificial animals offered in temples were dedicated to a pagan god, and most of them were sold in the public market. Understandably, many Christians in Corinth wondered whether they should eat such meat. According to Paul, what do mature Christians know about food sacrificed to idols (8:4–6, 8)? 2. What warning does Paul give about this kind of knowledge (8:1–3)? Explain. 3. What does Paul say is more important than exercising the freedom that comes from knowledge (8:9–13)? 4. Paul moves on from rights and freedoms based on *knowledge* to the topic of rights based on *position.* What apostolic rights has Paul given up (9:4–5, 11–12, 14, 18–19)? 5. How and why has Paul given up the freedom to live whatever lifestyle he prefers (9:19–23)? 6. In giving up the rights mentioned in chapters 8—9, how are we like athletes in training (9:24–27)?

Applying the Word 1. In what situations today might our "knowledge" and freedom destroy a weaker brother? 2. What distinguishes actions that challenge the immature to grow from actions that wound them? 3. How might we adjust our lifestyles in order to reach people in various subcultures?

Responding in Prayer Ask God to help you train more rigorously so you will not be disqualified but will receive the victor's crown.

8 / *1 Corinthians 10:1—11:1*
Eating with Christ

SHOULD CHRISTIANS GO to R-rated movies—or any movies, for that matter? Should they drink alcoholic beverages such as beer or wine? Should they wear expensive clothes, makeup and jewelry? Debates over such "questionable" practices are as old as the church. How can we resolve them?

The Corinthians were divided over such issues. Some had overscrupulous consciences. They would not sit down to a meal if the meat had been purchased at a pagan meat market (and therefore offered to a "god"). Others were so "liberated" that they could eat the Lord's Supper and then commit sexual immorality. These liberated Christians regarded baptism and the Eucharist (Communion) as automatic protection against God's judgment. In 1 Corinthians 10 Paul finds a way of reaching both kinds of people: he calls them and us to do everything for the glory of God.

Warming Up to God What "questionable" practices have you wrestled with personally?

Read 1 Corinthians 10:1—11:1.

10 For I do not want you to be igno-
rant of the fact, brothers, that our
forefathers were all under the cloud
and that they all passed through the sea. 2They
were all baptized into Moses in the cloud and in
the sea. 3They all ate the same spiritual food 4and
drank the same spiritual drink; for they drank
from the spiritual rock that accompanied them,
and that rock was Christ. 5Nevertheless, God was
not pleased with most of them; their bodies were
scattered over the desert.

6Now these things occurred as examples[u] to
keep us from setting our hearts on evil things as
they did. 7Do not be idolaters, as some of them
were; as it is written: "The people sat down to eat
and drink and got up to indulge in pagan rev-
elry."[v] 8We should not commit sexual immoral-
ity, as some of them did—and in one day twenty-
three thousand of them died. 9We should not test
the Lord, as some of them did—and were killed
by snakes. 10And do not grumble, as some of
them did—and were killed by the destroying an-
gel.

11These things happened to them as examples
and were written down as warnings for us, on
whom the fulfillment of the ages has come. 12So,
if you think you are standing firm, be careful that
you don't fall! 13No temptation has seized you
except what is common to man. And God is faith-
ful; he will not let you be tempted beyond what
you can bear. But when you are tempted, he will
also provide a way out so that you can stand up
under it.

[u]6 Or *types;* also in verse 11 [v]7 Exodus 32:6

14Therefore, my dear friends, flee from idolatry.
15I speak to sensible people; judge for yourselves
what I say. 16Is not the cup of thanksgiving for
which we give thanks a participation in the blood
of Christ? And is not the bread that we break a
participation in the body of Christ? 17Because
there is one loaf, we, who are many, are one body,
for we all partake of the one loaf.

18Consider the people of Israel: Do not those
who eat the sacrifices participate in the altar?
19Do I mean then that a sacrifice offered to an idol
is anything, or that an idol is anything? 20No, but
the sacrifices of pagans are offered to demons, not
to God, and I do not want you to be participants
with demons. 21You cannot drink the cup of the
Lord and the cup of demons too; you cannot have
a part in both the Lord's table and the table of
demons. 22Are we trying to arouse the Lord's jeal-
ousy? Are we stronger than he?

23"Everything is permissible"—but not every-
thing is beneficial. "Everything is permissible"—
but not everything is constructive. 24Nobody
should seek his own good, but the good of others.
25Eat anything sold in the meat market without
raising questions of conscience, 26for, "The earth
is the Lord's, and everything in it."[w]

27If some unbeliever invites you to a meal and
you want to go, eat whatever is put before you
without raising questions of conscience. 28But if
anyone says to you, "This has been offered in
sacrifice," then do not eat it, both for the sake of
the man who told you and for conscience'
sake[x]— 29the other man's conscience, I mean,
not yours. For why should my freedom be judged
by another's conscience? 30If I take part in the
meal with thankfulness, why am I denounced be-
cause of something I thank God for?

31So whether you eat or drink or whatever you
do, do it all for the glory of God. 32Do not cause
anyone to stumble, whether Jews, Greeks or the
church of God— 33even as I try to please every-
body in every way. For I am not seeking my own
good but the good of many, so that they may be
saved.

11

1Follow my example, as I
follow the example of Christ.

[w]26 Psalm 24:1 [x]28 Some manuscripts *conscience' sake, for "the earth is the Lord's and everything in it"*

Discovering the Word 1. What experiences did all the Israelites have in common when they left Egypt and headed for the Promised Land (vv. 1–10)? 2. Why does Paul remind the Corinthians (and us) of these events (vv. 11–13)? 3. Why are some lifestyles incompatible with celebrating the Lord's Supper (vv. 14–22)? 4. According to verses 23–33, what principles should guide our behavior as Christians? 5. How does Paul apply these principles to the subject of eating meat offered to idols?

Applying the Word 1. Think of one or two areas where you are currently experiencing temptation. In which one of these are you least likely to believe that there is a way of escape? 2. In what way has God provided an escape for your temptation? 3. How can the principles discussed in this passage guide your behavior in areas that might be "permissible" but not beneficial?

Responding in Prayer Ask God to give you courage to flee temptation.

9 / *1 Corinthians 11:2–34*
Headship of Christ

TWO TRENDS IN Western society contrive to make us independent people: the trend to blur the differences between the sexes (androgyny) and the human potential movement. In the movie *Tootsie* a male actor impersonating a woman said to a woman with whom he fell in love, "I was a better man with you when I was a woman than I am a woman with you now that I am a man." Such is the sexual confusion produced by the first trend. Fritz Perls verbalized the second trend this way: "I do my thing and you do your thing and if by chance we meet, it's beautiful."

Both trends work against our newness in Christ. Followers of Jesus are neither independent nor dependent but *inter*dependent. We discover interdependence in Christian worship in this passage.

Warming Up to God When you enter a worship service, do you tend to think mainly of your personal relationship to God or your relationship with your fellow worshipers? Explain.

Read 1 Corinthians 11:2-34.

2I praise you for remembering me in everything and for holding to the teachings,[y] just as I passed them on to you.

3Now I want you to realize that the head of every man is Christ, and the head of the woman is man, and the head of Christ is God. 4Every man who prays or prophesies with his head covered dishonors his head. 5And every woman who prays or prophesies with her head uncovered dishonors her head—it is just as though her head were shaved. 6If a woman does not cover her head, she should have her hair cut off; and if it is a disgrace for a woman to have her hair cut or shaved off, she should cover her head. 7A man ought not to cover his head,[z] since he is the image and glory of God; but the woman is the glory of man. 8For man did not come from woman, but woman from man; 9neither was man created for woman, but woman for man. 10For this reason, and because of the angels, the woman ought to have a sign of authority on her head.

11In the Lord, however, woman is not independent of man, nor is man independent of woman. 12For as woman came from man, so also man is born of woman. But everything comes from God. 13Judge for yourselves: Is it proper for a woman to pray to God with her head uncovered? 14Does not the very nature of things teach you that if a man has long hair, it is a disgrace to him, 15but that if a woman has long hair, it is her glory? For long hair is given to her as a covering. 16If anyone wants to be contentious about this, we have no other practice—nor do the churches of God.

17In the following directives I have no praise for you, for your meetings do more harm than good. 18In the first place, I hear that when you come together as a church, there are divisions among you, and to some extent I believe it. 19No doubt there have to be differences among you to show which of you have God's approval. 20When you come together, it is not the Lord's Supper you eat, 21for as you eat, each of you goes ahead without waiting for anybody else. One remains hungry, another gets drunk. 22Don't you have homes to eat and drink in? Or do you despise the church of God and humiliate those who have nothing? What shall I say to you? Shall I praise you for this? Certainly not!

23For I received from the Lord what I also passed on to you: The Lord Jesus, on the night he was betrayed, took bread, 24and when he had given thanks, he broke it and said, "This is my body, which is for you; do this in remembrance of me." 25In the same way, after supper he took the cup, saying, "This cup is the new covenant in my blood; do this, whenever you drink it, in remembrance of me." 26For whenever you eat this bread and drink this cup, you proclaim the Lord's death until he comes.

27Therefore, whoever eats the bread or drinks the cup of the Lord in an unworthy manner will be guilty of sinning against the body and blood of the Lord. 28A man ought to examine himself before he eats of the bread and drinks of the cup. 29For anyone who eats and drinks without recognizing the body of the Lord eats and drinks judgment on himself. 30That is why many among you are weak and sick, and a number of you have fallen asleep. 31But if we judged ourselves, we would not come under judgment. 32When we are judged by the Lord, we are being disciplined so that we will not be condemned with the world.

33So then, my brothers, when you come together to eat, wait for each other. 34If anyone is hungry, he should eat at home, so that when you meet together it may not result in judgment.

And when I come I will give further directions.

y2 Or *traditions* z4-7 Or *4Every man who prays or prophesies with long hair dishonors his head. 5And every woman who prays or prophesies with no covering* ⌞*of hair*⌟ *on her head dishonors her head—she is just like one of the "shorn women." 6If a woman has no covering, let her be for now with short hair, but since it is a disgrace for a woman to have her hair shorn or shaved, she should grow it again. 7A man ought not to have long hair*

Discovering the Word 1. What seems to be Paul's major concern for the church in this section? 2. The word *head* in verse 3 could mean either "chief" and "ruler" or "source" and "origin" (like the head of a stream). Which understanding of headship best fits Paul's concern here? Explain. 3. In the culture of Corinth a woman signaled that she was in right relationship with her husband either by wearing a veil which covered her hair or by wearing her hair up (rather than letting it fall loose). What reasons does Paul give for continuing this practice (vv. 4–10, 13–16)? 4. Paul balances his previous statements by saying that "in the Lord" man is not independent of woman (vv. 11–12). Why is this balance important? 5. Why would eating and drinking "without recognizing the body of the Lord" be so dangerous (vv. 29–32)? 6. According to Paul, how can we eat and drink the Lord's Supper in a worthy manner (vv. 28–33)?

Applying the Word 1. Although we may not have a cultural equivalent for head coverings, how should appropriate relationships between men and women be expressed in Christian community? 2. What has this chapter taught you about worship that is honoring or dishonoring to God? 3. How do you need to change your pattern of worship?

Responding in Prayer Thank God for making you part of a larger body.

10 / *1 Corinthians 12*
Body of Christ

THE CHURCH TODAY has enormous frozen assets. Only when we thaw these assets and release every member for ministry can the work of God be done in the world. After several decades of "gift" teaching, we have made surprisingly little progress. One reason is that gifts have been co-opted by the human potential movement. We view our gifts as part of our development and fulfillment rather than as one more glorious way to be interdependent in Christ. This passage focuses on the true nature and purpose of spiritual gifts.

Warming Up to God What has God shown you about your gifts and how you should use them in the church?

Read 1 Corinthians 12.

12 Now about spiritual gifts, brothers, I do not want you to be ignorant. 2You know that when you were pagans, somehow or other you were influenced and led astray to mute idols. 3Therefore I tell you that no one who is speaking by the Spirit of God says, "Jesus be cursed," and no one can say, "Jesus is Lord," except by the Holy Spirit.

4There are different kinds of gifts, but the same Spirit. 5There are different kinds of service, but the same Lord. 6There are different kinds of working, but the same God works all of them in all men.

7Now to each one the manifestation of the Spirit is given for the common good. 8To one there is given through the Spirit the message of wisdom, to another the message of knowledge by means of the same Spirit, 9to another faith by the same Spirit, to another gifts of healing by that one Spirit, 10to another miraculous powers, to another prophecy, to another distinguishing between spirits, to another speaking in different kinds of tongues,[a] and to still another the interpretation of tongues.[a] 11All these are the work of one and the same Spirit, and he gives them to each one, just as he determines.

12The body is a unit, though it is made up of many parts; and though all its parts are many, they form one body. So it is with Christ. 13For we were all baptized by[b] one Spirit into one body—whether Jews or Greeks, slave or free—and we were all given the one Spirit to drink.

14Now the body is not made up of one part but of many. 15If the foot should say, "Because I am not a hand, I do not belong to the body," it would not for that reason cease to be part of the body. 16And if the ear should say, "Because I am not an eye, I do not belong to the body," it would not for that reason cease to be part of the body. 17If the whole body were an eye, where would the sense of hearing be? If the whole body were an ear, where would the sense of smell be? 18But in fact God has arranged the parts in the body, every one

[a]10 Or *languages*; also in verse 28 [b]13 Or *with*; or *in*

of them, just as he wanted them to be. [19]If they were all one part, where would the body be? [20]As it is, there are many parts, but one body.

[21]The eye cannot say to the hand, "I don't need you!" And the head cannot say to the feet, "I don't need you!" [22]On the contrary, those parts of the body that seem to be weaker are indispensable, [23]and the parts that we think are less honorable we treat with special honor. And the parts that are unpresentable are treated with special modesty, [24]while our presentable parts need no special treatment. But God has combined the members of the body and has given greater honor to the parts that lacked it, [25]so that there should be no division in the body, but that its parts should have equal concern for each other. [26]If one part suffers, every part suffers with it; if one part is honored, every part rejoices with it.

[27]Now you are the body of Christ, and each one of you is a part of it. [28]And in the church God has appointed first of all apostles, second prophets, third teachers, then workers of miracles, also those having gifts of healing, those able to help others, those with gifts of administration, and those speaking in different kinds of tongues. [29]Are all apostles? Are all prophets? Are all teachers? Do all work miracles? [30]Do all have gifts of healing? Do all speak in tongues[c]? Do all interpret? [31]But eagerly desire[d] the greater gifts.

And now I will show you the most excellent way.

[c]30 Or *other languages* [d]31 Or *But you are eagerly desiring*

Discovering the Word 1. What particular problem in the Corinthian church may have led Paul to offer the "test" in verse 3? 2. What clue does Paul's test give us about the ultimate goal of spiritual gifts? 3. What do verses 4–6 reveal about the unity and diversity of spiritual gifts? 4. What might make some members of your church feel useless or envious of other parts of the body (vv. 12–26)? 5. According to Paul, how can we make every part of the body feel special (vv. 21–26)? 6. Paul does not give us a complete list of gifts in this chapter. What might the words *first, second, third* and *then* (v. 28) indicate?

Applying the Word 1. What can you do to help others in your group or church to discover their giftedness? 2. How would you like to develop and exercise your spiritual gifts?

Responding in Prayer Pray that both you and those you know would use your gifts to God's glory.

11 / *1 Corinthians 13*
Love of Christ

PERHAPS THE MOST abused phrase in the English language is "I love you." Instead of communicating unselfish caring, it often expresses enlightened self-interest, manipulative affection or sheer lust. In 1 Corinthians 13 Paul not only defines love for us but shows us why this is the most excellent way to relate to anyone—especially to members of the family of God.

Warming Up to God Think of a person who has truly loved you. What were the marks of that person's way of relating to you?

Read 1 Corinthians 13.

13 If I speak in the tongues[e] of men and of angels, but have not love, I am only a resounding gong or a clanging cymbal. [2]If I have the gift of prophecy and can fathom all mysteries and all knowledge, and if I have a faith that can move mountains, but have not love, I am nothing. [3]If I give all I possess to the poor and surrender my body to the flames,[f] but have not love, I gain nothing.

[4]Love is patient, love is kind. It does not envy, it does not boast, it is not proud. [5]It is not rude,

[e]1 Or *languages* [f]3 Some early manuscripts *body that I may boast*

it is not self-seeking, it is not easily angered, it keeps no record of wrongs. 6Love does not delight in evil but rejoices with the truth. 7It always protects, always trusts, always hopes, always perseveres.

8Love never fails. But where there are prophecies, they will cease; where there are tongues, they will be stilled; where there is knowledge, it will pass away. 9For we know in part and we prophesy in part, 10but when perfection comes, the imperfect disappears. 11When I was a child, I talked like a child, I thought like a child, I reasoned like a child. When I became a man, I put childish ways behind me. 12Now we see but a poor reflection as in a mirror; then we shall see face to face. Now I know in part; then I shall know fully, even as I am fully known.

13And now these three remain: faith, hope and love. But the greatest of these is love.

Discovering the Word 1. What is so tragic about using our gifts without love (vv. 1-3)? 2. How would you define each of love's qualities (vv. 4-7)? 3. In verses 8-13 Paul summarizes the *supremacy of love.* Compared with love, why do the spiritual gifts have limited value? 4. Some understand the "perfection" in verse 10 as the completed New Testament, thus eliminating the need for tongues or prophecy today. Others understand it as the perfection we will experience when Christ returns. In light of Paul's other comparisons (vv. 11-12), which interpretation seems more likely? Explain. 5. Why is love greater than faith or hope (v. 13)?

Applying the Word 1. How can love lead to healthy interdependence in your relationships rather than unhealthy independence or dependence? 2. Which aspect of love do you most need to develop? 3. Besides telling us what love is, this passage gives us an incidental portrait of Jesus as the ultimate lover. Reread verses 4-7, replacing *love* with *Jesus.* What fresh picture of Jesus' care do you gain through this exercise?

Responding in Prayer Ask Jesus Christ to teach you what it means to love.

12 / *1 Corinthians 14*
Speaking for Christ

WORDS ARE CHEAP today. They can be digitized and processed. With one depressed button on a computer we can eliminate words forever, without even a trace remaining in memory. However, the Bible says words have great power, because they are an extension of our personality. God's Word always accomplishes his purposes, because it is spoken with his personal power. In this chapter Paul focuses on the exciting potential of God-inspired speech in the Christian community.

Warming Up to God Recall a time when something that was shared from the congregation during a worship service (or in a small group) truly encouraged you. What characterized this word ministry?

Read 1 Corinthians 14.

14 Follow the way of love and eagerly desire spiritual gifts, especially the gift of prophecy. 2For anyone who speaks in a tongue[g] does not speak to men but to God. Indeed, no one understands him; he utters mysteries with his spirit.[h] 3But everyone who prophesies speaks to men for their strengthening, encouragement and comfort. 4He who speaks in a tongue edifies himself, but he who prophesies edifies the church. 5I would like every one of you to speak in tongues,[i] but I would rather have you prophesy. He who prophesies is greater than one who speaks in tongues,[i] unless he interprets, so that the church may be edified.

6Now, brothers, if I come to you and speak in tongues, what good will I be to you, unless I bring you some revelation or knowledge or prophecy or word of instruction? 7Even in the case of lifeless

g2 Or *another language;* also in verses 4, 13, 14, 19, 26 and 27
h2 Or *by the Spirit* i5 Or *other languages;* also in verses 6, 18, 22, 23 and 39

things that make sounds, such as the flute or
harp, how will anyone know what tune is being
played unless there is a distinction in the notes?
8Again, if the trumpet does not sound a clear call,
who will get ready for battle? 9So it is with you.
Unless you speak intelligible words with your
tongue, how will anyone know what you are say-
ing? You will just be speaking into the air. 10Un-
doubtedly there are all sorts of languages in the
world, yet none of them is without meaning. 11If
then I do not grasp the meaning of what someone
is saying, I am a foreigner to the speaker, and he
is a foreigner to me. 12So it is with you. Since you
are eager to have spiritual gifts, try to excel in
gifts that build up the church.

13For this reason anyone who speaks in a
tongue should pray that he may interpret what he
says. 14For if I pray in a tongue, my spirit prays,
but my mind is unfruitful. 15So what shall I do? I
will pray with my spirit, but I will also pray with
my mind; I will sing with my spirit, but I will also
sing with my mind. 16If you are praising God with
your spirit, how can one who finds himself
among those who do not understand[j] say
"Amen" to your thanksgiving, since he does not
know what you are saying? 17You may be giving
thanks well enough, but the other man is not
edified.

18I thank God that I speak in tongues more
than all of you. 19But in the church I would rather
speak five intelligible words to instruct others
than ten thousand words in a tongue.

20Brothers, stop thinking like children. In re-
gard to evil be infants, but in your thinking be
adults. 21In the Law it is written:

"Through men of strange tongues
 and through the lips of foreigners
I will speak to this people,
 but even then they will not listen to me,"[k]
says the Lord.

22Tongues, then, are a sign, not for believers
but for unbelievers; prophecy, however, is for be-
lievers, not for unbelievers. 23So if the whole
church comes together and everyone speaks in
tongues, and some who do not understand[l] or
some unbelievers come in, will they not say that
you are out of your mind? 24But if an unbeliever
or someone who does not understand[m] comes in
while everybody is prophesying, he will be con-
vinced by all that he is a sinner and will be judged
by all, 25and the secrets of his heart will be laid
bare. So he will fall down and worship God, ex-
claiming, "God is really among you!"

26What then shall we say, brothers? When you
come together, everyone has a hymn, or a word of
instruction, a revelation, a tongue or an interpre-
tation. All of these must be done for the strength-
ening of the church. 27If anyone speaks in a
tongue, two—or at the most three—should
speak, one at a time, and someone must interpret.
28If there is no interpreter, the speaker should
keep quiet in the church and speak to himself and
God.

29Two or three prophets should speak, and the
others should weigh carefully what is said. 30And
if a revelation comes to someone who is sitting
down, the first speaker should stop. 31For you
can all prophesy in turn so that everyone may be
instructed and encouraged. 32The spirits of
prophets are subject to the control of prophets.
33For God is not a God of disorder but of peace.

As in all the congregations of the saints,
34women should remain silent in the churches.
They are not allowed to speak, but must be in
submission, as the Law says. 35If they want to
inquire about something, they should ask their
own husbands at home; for it is disgraceful for a
woman to speak in the church.

36Did the word of God originate with you? Or
are you the only people it has reached? 37If any-
body thinks he is a prophet or spiritually gifted,
let him acknowledge that what I am writing to
you is the Lord's command. 38If he ignores this,
he himself will be ignored.[n]

39Therefore, my brothers, be eager to prophesy,
and do not forbid speaking in tongues. 40But eve-
rything should be done in a fitting and orderly
way.

[j]16 *Or among the inquirers* [k]21 Isaiah 28:11,12 [l]23 *Or some inquirers* [m]24 *Or or some inquirer* [n]38 Some manuscripts *If he is ignorant of this, let him be ignorant*

Discovering the Word 1. Evidently, the Corinthians placed great value on the gift of tongues. Why does Paul prefer prophecy to uninterpreted tongues (vv. 1–5)? 2. What illustrations does Paul use to show why uninterpreted tongues do not build up the church (vv. 6–12)? 3. What remedy does Paul suggest (vv. 13–19)? 4. What does Paul say about the *purpose* of tongues and of prophecy (vv. 20–25)? 5. What guidelines does Paul give for when someone should speak in tongues and when he should remain silent (vv. 27–28)? 6. How can Paul's statements in verses 33–35 be harmonized with his teaching about women praying and prophesying (11:5)?

Applying the Word 1. In what ways might we be guilty of meaningless or mindless worship today? 2. How can Paul's counsel improve the quality of our worship?

Responding in Prayer Ask that worship in your church might be meaningful and powerful for all who come.

13 / *1 Corinthians 15—16*
Hope in Christ

WHAT HAPPENS AFTER death? Do we live on as disembodied souls, as the Greeks taught? Do we go through countless cycles of reincarnation, as the Hindus believe? Do both body and soul cease to exist, as naturalism maintains?

Because of their Greek heritage, the Corinthians questioned the reality of the resurrection. In this passage Paul challenges their thinking by pointing out the absurd conclusions to which it leads. He reminds us that the resurrection is a crucial aspect of our hope in Christ.

Warming Up to God Have you ever pondered what death will be like for you? How do you feel about it? Express your feelings to Christ. Allow him to prepare you for this study.

Read 1 Corinthians 15—16.

15 Now, brothers, I want to remind
you of the gospel I preached to you,
which you received and on which
you have taken your stand. 2By this gospel you
are saved, if you hold firmly to the word I
preached to you. Otherwise, you have believed in
vain.
3For what I received I passed on to you as of
first importance[o]: that Christ died for our sins
according to the Scriptures, 4that he was buried,
that he was raised on the third day according to
the Scriptures, 5and that he appeared to Peter,[p]
and then to the Twelve. 6After that, he appeared
to more than five hundred of the brothers at the
same time, most of whom are still living, though
some have fallen asleep. 7Then he appeared to
James, then to all the apostles, 8and last of all he
appeared to me also, as to one abnormally born.
9For I am the least of the apostles and do not
even deserve to be called an apostle, because I
persecuted the church of God. 10But by the grace
of God I am what I am, and his grace to me was
not without effect. No, I worked harder than all
of them—yet not I, but the grace of God that was
with me. 11Whether, then, it was I or they, this is
what we preach, and this is what you believed.
12But if it is preached that Christ has been
raised from the dead, how can some of you say
that there is no resurrection of the dead? 13If
there is no resurrection of the dead, then not even
Christ has been raised. 14And if Christ has not
been raised, our preaching is useless and so is
your faith. 15More than that, we are then found to
be false witnesses about God, for we have testified
about God that he raised Christ from the dead.
But he did not raise him if in fact the dead are not
raised. 16For if the dead are not raised, then
Christ has not been raised either. 17And if Christ
has not been raised, your faith is futile; you are
still in your sins. 18Then those also who have
fallen asleep in Christ are lost. 19If only for this
life we have hope in Christ, we are to be pitied
more than all men.
20But Christ has indeed been raised from the
dead, the firstfruits of those who have fallen
asleep. 21For since death came through a man, the
resurrection of the dead comes also through a
man. 22For as in Adam all die, so in Christ all will
be made alive. 23But each in his own turn: Christ,
the firstfruits; then, when he comes, those who
belong to him. 24Then the end will come, when

o3 *Or you at the first* p5 Greek *Cephas*

he hands over the kingdom to God the Father
after he has destroyed all dominion, authority and
power. 25For he must reign until he has put all his
enemies under his feet. 26The last enemy to be
destroyed is death. 27For he "has put everything
under his feet."[q] Now when it says that "every-
thing" has been put under him, it is clear that this
does not include God himself, who put every-
thing under Christ. 28When he has done this,
then the Son himself will be made subject to him
who put everything under him, so that God may
be all in all.

29Now if there is no resurrection, what will
those do who are baptized for the dead? If the
dead are not raised at all, why are people baptized
for them? 30And as for us, why do we endanger
ourselves every hour? 31I die every day—I mean
that, brothers—just as surely as I glory over you
in Christ Jesus our Lord. 32If I fought wild beasts
in Ephesus for merely human reasons, what have
I gained? If the dead are not raised,

"Let us eat and drink,
for tomorrow we die."[r]

33Do not be misled: "Bad company corrupts good
character." 34Come back to your senses as you
ought, and stop sinning; for there are some who
are ignorant of God—I say this to your shame.

35But someone may ask, "How are the dead
raised? With what kind of body will they come?"
36How foolish! What you sow does not come to
life unless it dies. 37When you sow, you do not
plant the body that will be, but just a seed, per-
haps of wheat or of something else. 38But God
gives it a body as he has determined, and to each
kind of seed he gives its own body. 39All flesh is
not the same: Men have one kind of flesh, animals
have another, birds another and fish another.
40There are also heavenly bodies and there are
earthly bodies; but the splendor of the heavenly
bodies is one kind, and the splendor of the
earthly bodies is another. 41The sun has one kind
of splendor, the moon another and the stars an-
other; and star differs from star in splendor.

42So will it be with the resurrection of the dead.
The body that is sown is perishable, it is raised
imperishable; 43it is sown in dishonor, it is raised
in glory; it is sown in weakness, it is raised in
power; 44it is sown a natural body, it is raised a
spiritual body.

If there is a natural body, there is also a spiri-
tual body. 45So it is written: "The first man Adam
became a living being"[s]; the last Adam, a life-
giving spirit. 46The spiritual did not come first,
but the natural, and after that the spiritual. 47The
first man was of the dust of the earth, the second
man from heaven. 48As was the earthly man, so
are those who are of the earth; and as is the man
from heaven, so also are those who are of heaven.
49And just as we have borne the likeness of the
earthly man, so shall we[t] bear the likeness of the
man from heaven.

50I declare to you, brothers, that flesh and
blood cannot inherit the kingdom of God, nor
does the perishable inherit the imperishable.
51Listen, I tell you a mystery: We will not all
sleep, but we will all be changed— 52in a flash, in
the twinkling of an eye, at the last trumpet. For
the trumpet will sound, the dead will be raised
imperishable, and we will be changed. 53For the
perishable must clothe itself with the imperish-
able, and the mortal with immortality. 54When
the perishable has been clothed with the imper-
ishable, and the mortal with immortality, then the
saying that is written will come true: "Death has
been swallowed up in victory."[u]

55"Where, O death, is your victory?
Where, O death, is your sting?"[v]

56The sting of death is sin, and the power of sin is
the law. 57But thanks be to God! He gives us the
victory through our Lord Jesus Christ.

58Therefore, my dear brothers, stand firm. Let
nothing move you. Always give yourselves fully
to the work of the Lord, because you know that
your labor in the Lord is not in vain.

16 Now about the collection for God's
people: Do what I told the Galatian
churches to do. 2On the first day of
every week, each one of you should set aside a
sum of money in keeping with his income, saving
it up, so that when I come no collections will
have to be made. 3Then, when I arrive, I will give
letters of introduction to the men you approve
and send them with your gift to Jerusalem. 4If it
seems advisable for me to go also, they will ac-
company me.

5After I go through Macedonia, I will come to
you—for I will be going through Macedonia.
6Perhaps I will stay with you awhile, or even
spend the winter, so that you can help me on my
journey, wherever I go. 7I do not want to see you

[q]27 Psalm 8:6 [r]32 Isaiah 22:13 [s]45 Gen. 2:7 [t]49 Some early manuscripts *so let us* [u]54 Isaiah 25:8 [v]55 Hosea 13:14

now and make only a passing visit; I hope to
spend some time with you, if the Lord permits.
8But I will stay on at Ephesus until Pentecost,
9because a great door for effective work has
opened to me, and there are many who op-
pose me.
10If Timothy comes, see to it that he has noth-
ing to fear while he is with you, for he is carrying
on the work of the Lord, just as I am. 11No one,
then, should refuse to accept him. Send him on
his way in peace so that he may return to me. I
am expecting him along with the brothers.
12Now about our brother Apollos: I strongly
urged him to go to you with the brothers. He was
quite unwilling to go now, but he will go when he
has the opportunity.
13Be on your guard; stand firm in the faith; be
men of courage; be strong. 14Do everything in
love.
15You know that the household of Stephanas
were the first converts in Achaia, and they have
devoted themselves to the service of the saints. I
urge you, brothers, 16to submit to such as these
and to everyone who joins in the work, and la-
bors at it. 17I was glad when Stephanas, Fortuna-
tus and Achaicus arrived, because they have sup-
plied what was lacking from you. 18For they
refreshed my spirit and yours also. Such men de-
serve recognition.
19The churches in the province of Asia send
you greetings. Aquila and Priscilla[w] greet you
warmly in the Lord, and so does the church that
meets at their house. 20All the brothers here send
you greetings. Greet one another with a holy kiss.
21I, Paul, write this greeting in my own hand.
22If anyone does not love the Lord—a curse be
on him. Come, O Lord[x]!
23The grace of the Lord Jesus be with you.
24My love to all of you in Christ Jesus. Amen.[y]

w19 Greek *Prisca*, a variant of *Priscilla* x22 In Aramaic the expression *Come, O Lord* is *Marana tha.* y24 Some manuscripts do not have *Amen.*

Discovering the Word 1. Paul reminds the Corinthians of the gospel he preached to them. What are the essential elements of the gospel (15:1–11)? 2. If there is no resurrection, what are the consequences for Christ, for Paul and for us (15:12–19)? 3. How does belief or disbelief in the resurrection affect a person's lifestyle (15:29–34)? 4. What illustrations does Paul use to explain why the resurrection is not illogical but makes good sense (15:35–41)? 5. Although the resurrection body is somehow related to the natural body, how is it also radically different (15:42–49)? 6. How does chapter 16 give several illustrations of "the work of the Lord" Paul referred to in 15:58?

Applying the Word 1. To which specific area of service will you give yourself this week, knowing that your labor in the Lord is not in vain? 2. What is the most substantial change that studying 1 Corinthians has brought about in your life?

Responding in Prayer Praise God for what you have learned in 1 Corinthians.

2 Corinthians

Life is relational. We hope and hurt the most about relationships with people who matter to us. A special friend we are in danger of losing, an employer who misunderstands our actions, a spouse who seems distant and cold, a brother in Christ who has spoken behind our back, a family member long estranged are samples of the web of relationships that make up our lives. When a special relationship is hanging by a slender thread, we are often at a loss to know what to say or do. Should we tell the truth even if it hurts? Should we avoid confrontation? Should we share what is going on inside us even if it shows we are weak and struggling, far weaker than we would like others to know?

Second Corinthians is all about relationships—not perfect ones, but real ones. In this letter the apostle Paul reveals that he is struggling deeply in his relationship with the believers in Corinth. Though he founded this church, they have apparently rejected him. This letter is an attempt at reconciliation. What made Paul's relationship more complicated was the seeming contest between Paul and his converts. The Corinthians were enjoying charismatic ecstasy. They had their orators, theologians, super-saints and super-apostles. They were strong, wise and triumphant. Paul, in contrast, was weak, foolish and a seeming failure.

In similar circumstances most people try to use strength and wisdom to win their way back. They create just the right leadership image. But Paul chose to pour out his soul to them, trusting that in the process Christ would be revealed. In this letter Paul is both medium and message. This great Christian leader takes the enormous risk of telling how confused, upset and weak he is. In 1 Corinthians Paul lets us see inside a first-century church. But in 2 Corinthians Paul lets us see inside a first-century Christian, the apostle himself. Through his large heart we see into the heart of God and the heart of the Christian message.

Paul founded the church in Corinth about A.D. 50. It was a lively church composed of first-generation Christians but infected with many of the problems associated with a mission. Corinth was the Las Vegas of the Roman Empire. Some new believers polluted the church with their secular standards in business and sexuality. They argued that all things are permissible in Christ. Others got superspiritual and boasted about their visions, prophecies, words of knowledge and spiritual experiences. In the course of time they wrote Paul asking for advice. Paul write 1 Corinthians in about A.D. 55 to address these questions and various problems.

Then it seems the Corinthians turned against the founding apostle, a crucial fact to know in order to understand 2 Corinthians. This letter was born in hurt.

Paul paid a second "painful visit" (2Co 2:1) and wrote a sorrowful letter, now lost, from Ephesus (2:4). It is highly likely that Paul then came to Macedonia (2Co 7:5), modern Greece, where he was reunited with Titus from Corinth and from which he wrote 2 Corinthians, probably while in Philippi. Later in A.D. 56 Paul visited Corinth again to receive their gifts for the poor Christians in Jerusalem.

As 2 Corinthians was written, Paul had several problems with the Corinthians: he changed his travel plans and did not come when he said he would (2Co 1:12—2:4); they failed to discipline the person who caused a grievous offense (2:5–11); their contributions for his collection for the Jewish Christians had lapsed (2Co 8—9); he had accepted financial support from the Macedonians (Thessalonica and Philippi) but not from the Achaians, especially the Corinthians (11:7–11). Paul also conflicted with newly arrived ministers in Corinth who preached a different gospel, probably a return to a form of Judaism (2:14—7:4; 10:1—13:14). Some individual Corinthians criticized Paul because he was a powerful letter-writer but a weak speaker who was unimpressive in person.

This relational conflict becomes the medium for revealing the distinctive message of this book: Christ meets us at our point of desperate weakness, *not only before we are saved, but after*. Against the false triumphalism of his opponents, Paul proclaims a gospel in which God's power is demonstrated best in human weakness. We have the Christ-treasure in jars of clay or, as Phillips powerfully paraphrases, "in a common earthenware jar." In a day when authentic Christianity seems less attractive than superspirituality or the "gospel of health, wealth and prosperity," Paul's searing honesty offers exactly what the world so deeply hungers for: it tells us how to be really real. As we walk through Paul's relationship with the Corinthians step by step, we discover how God in Christ is prepared to meet our deepest relational needs just as we are and where we are.

Outline

1 / 2 *Corinthians 1:1–11*
Our Comforting God

"LIFE IS DIFFICULT!" With these three words Scott Peck begins his bestselling book *The Road Less Traveled.* But in 2 Corinthians Paul says this and more. Just where life is difficult, where our relationships are strained, where our competence is questioned, where our health and security are threatened, God makes himself known in powerful comfort. We discover that one of the supreme greatnesses of Christianity is that it does not seek a supernatural escape from the difficulties of life. Instead it offers a supernatural use for them. Troubles become triumphs as God makes himself known in our weakness.

Warming Up to God What comfort do you need from God today? Sit and wait for him to visit you with his peace and reassurance.

Read 2 Corinthians 1:1–11.

1 Paul, an apostle of Christ Jesus by the will
of God, and Timothy our brother,

To the church of God in Corinth, together with
all the saints throughout Achaia:

2Grace and peace to you from God our Father
and the Lord Jesus Christ.

3Praise be to the God and Father of our Lord
Jesus Christ, the Father of compassion and the
God of all comfort, 4who comforts us in all our
troubles, so that we can comfort those in any
trouble with the comfort we ourselves have re-
ceived from God. 5For just as the sufferings of
Christ flow over into our lives, so also through
Christ our comfort overflows. 6If we are dis-
tressed, it is for your comfort and salvation; if we
are comforted, it is for your comfort, which pro-
duces in you patient endurance of the same suf-
ferings we suffer. 7And our hope for you is firm,
because we know that just as you share in our
sufferings, so also you share in our comfort.

8We do not want you to be uninformed, broth-
ers, about the hardships we suffered in the prov-
ince of Asia. We were under great pressure, far
beyond our ability to endure, so that we de-
spaired even of life. 9Indeed, in our hearts we felt
the sentence of death. But this happened that we
might not rely on ourselves but on God, who
raises the dead. 10He has delivered us from such a
deadly peril, and he will deliver us. On him we
have set our hope that he will continue to deliver
us, 11as you help us by your prayers. Then many
will give thanks on our[a] behalf for the gracious
favor granted us in answer to the prayers of
many.

[a] 11 Many manuscripts *your*

Discovering the Word 1. After his customary greeting and "signature," Paul breaks into praise. What evokes this spontaneous worship (vv. 3–7)? 2. What is the connection between the sufferings of Christ and the comfort of Christ (vv. 5–6)? 3. Paul's hardships in the province of Asia (modern-day Turkey) were evidently life-threatening. What did he discover about the meaning of such sufferings in the Christian life (vv. 8–11)? 4. How do you think Paul's openness in sharing the realities of his Christian experience affected his relationship with the Corinthians?

Applying the Word 1. In what ways have you experienced God's comfort in a difficult situation? 2. How does your experience of God's comfort enable you to comfort others who are suffering? 3. Based on what you have learned in these first eleven verses, how can hardships draw you closer to God instead of driving you away from him?

Responding in Prayer Think of someone you know who needs to experience God's comfort. Ask God to comfort that person and to use you in offering comfort.

2 / *2 Corinthians 1:12—2:11*
Always Yes in Christ

CONTRARY TO WHAT some misguided Christian parents think, affirming children does not make them proud and self-centered. Rather, it meets a fundamental need of the human personality. But often our attempts to affirm each other backfire.

Such was Paul's experience with the Corinthians. Paul had promised to visit them again, twice, in fact; first as he made his way to Macedonia and then on his way back. But he changed his plans, delaying his visit and deciding to visit only once. This led his opponents to claim that he was unreliable or fickle. In the process of defending his actions, Paul pointed the Corinthians to the ultimate ground of our affirmation: the eternal yes spoken to us by God in Christ.

Warming Up to God Recall an experience of being affirmed by another, possibly a parent or a good friend. What made that word or action especially upbuilding for you?

Read 2 Corinthians 1:12—2:11.

12Now this is our boast: Our conscience testifies that we have conducted ourselves in the world, and especially in our relations with you, in the holiness and sincerity that are from God. We have done so not according to worldly wisdom but according to God's grace. 13For we do not write you anything you cannot read or understand. And I hope that, 14as you have understood us in part, you will come to understand fully that you can boast of us just as we will boast of you in the day of the Lord Jesus.

15Because I was confident of this, I planned to visit you first so that you might benefit twice. 16I planned to visit you on my way to Macedonia and to come back to you from Macedonia, and then to have you send me on my way to Judea. 17When I planned this, did I do it lightly? Or do I make my plans in a worldly manner so that in the same breath I say, "Yes, yes" and "No, no"?

18But as surely as God is faithful, our message to you is not "Yes" and "No." 19For the Son of God, Jesus Christ, who was preached among you by me and Silas[b] and Timothy, was not "Yes" and "No," but in him it has always been "Yes." 20For no matter how many promises God has made, they are "Yes" in Christ. And so through him the "Amen" is spoken by us to the glory of God. 21Now it is God who makes both us and you stand firm in Christ. He anointed us, 22set his seal of ownership on us, and put his Spirit in our hearts as a deposit, guaranteeing what is to come.

23I call God as my witness that it was in order to spare you that I did not return to Corinth. 24Not that we lord it over your faith, but we work with you for your joy, because it is by faith you stand firm.

2 1So I made up my mind that I would not make another painful visit to you. 2For if I grieve you, who is left to make me glad but you whom I have grieved? 3I wrote as I did so that when I came I should not be distressed by those who ought to make me rejoice. I had confidence in all of you, that you would all share my joy. 4For I wrote you out of great distress and anguish of heart and with many tears, not to grieve you but to let you know the depth of my love for you.

5If anyone has caused grief, he has not so much grieved me as he has grieved all of you, to some extent—not to put it too severely. 6The punishment inflicted on him by the majority is sufficient for him. 7Now instead, you ought to forgive and comfort him, so that he will not be overwhelmed by excessive sorrow. 8I urge you, therefore, to reaffirm your love for him. 9The reason I wrote you was to see if you would stand the test and be obedient in everything. 10If you forgive anyone, I also forgive him. And what I have forgiven—if there was anything to forgive—I have forgiven in the sight of Christ for your sake, 11in order that Satan might not outwit us. For we are not unaware of his schemes.

[b]19 Greek *Silvanus*, a variant of *Silas*

Discovering the Word 1. Based on 1:12–22, what do you think Paul's opponents were saying about his motives and ministry style? 2. What reasons does Paul give for maintaining that his change of itinerary was not a change of mind about the Corinthians (1:12, 17)? 3. Why do you think Paul directs their attention away for his travel plans to the unqualified yes or "amen" of the gospel (1:18–20)? 4. What further reason does Paul give for his change of travel plans (1:23—2:4)? 5. In 2:5–11 Paul refers to the discipline of a member of the church, possibly because of a gross sexual sin (see 1Co 5:1). How does Paul's handling of this problem affirm his love not only for the Corinthians but also for the man who had sinned?

Applying the Word 1. What experiences have you had with church discipline? 2. How would Paul's approach to discipline be one that would still allow the person confronted to hear God's affirmation in Christ? 3. What have you learned about the conditions of receiving the affirmation Christ wants us to give?

Responding in Prayer Praise God for his faithful promises and his yes in Christ.

3 / *2 Corinthians 2:12—3:6*

A Letter from Christ

CHRISTIANITY IS ESSENTIALLY a lay movement. But one would not think so while visiting the average church. Often the impression we get is that ministry is for the theologically trained, the polished and proficient. With the professionalism of ministry in our society, many of us question our ability to minister. Like Paul, we ask, "Who is equal to such a task?" (2:16). In this chapter Paul tells us why all believers are competent for ministry in Christ.

Warming Up to God How do you feel about being told that becoming a Christian means becoming a minister? Talk to God about any fears you may have about being a minister.

Read 2 Corinthians 2:12—3:6.

12Now when I went to Troas to preach the gospel of Christ and found that the Lord had opened a door for me, 13I still had no peace of mind, because I did not find my brother Titus there. So I said good-by to them and went on to Macedonia.

14But thanks be to God, who always leads us in triumphal procession in Christ and through us spreads everywhere the fragrance of the knowledge of him. 15For we are to God the aroma of Christ among those who are being saved and those who are perishing. 16To the one we are the smell of death; to the other, the fragrance of life. And who is equal to such a task? 17Unlike so many, we do not peddle the word of God for profit. On the contrary, in Christ we speak before God with sincerity, like men sent from God.

3 Are we beginning to commend ourselves again? Or do we need, like some people, letters of recommendation to you or from you? 2You yourselves are our letter, written on our hearts, known and read by everybody. 3You show that you are a letter from Christ, the result of our ministry, written not with ink but with the Spirit of the living God, not on tablets of stone but on tablets of human hearts.

4Such confidence as this is ours through Christ before God. 5Not that we are competent in ourselves to claim anything for ourselves, but our competence comes from God. 6He has made us competent as ministers of a new covenant—not of the letter but of the Spirit; for the letter kills, but the Spirit gives life.

Discovering the Word 1. Because Paul had no peace of mind in Troas, he couldn't take full advantage of the "door" the Lord had opened for him. How was he able to speak of his triumph in Christ (2:14) in the same breath as confessing his weakness? 2. What do you think Paul means in saying we are "the smell of death" to some and "the fragrance of life" to others (2:15–16)? 3. In contrast to those who boasted about their letters of recommendation, Paul says the Corinthians are his letter (3:1–3). What sort of letter are they? 4. In 2:16 Paul asked, "Who is equal to such a task?" What answer does he give in 3:4–6? 5. According to Paul, how does our ministry under the New Covenant contrast with ministry under the Old (3:3–6)?

Applying the Word 1. When has Christ enabled you to triumph in the midst of a personal struggle? 2. How does the thought that Christianity spreads like a fragrance challenge your church or Christian group? 3. How has this passage encouraged you to feel competent to minister as a disciple of Jesus?

Responding in Prayer You are a letter from Christ. Pray that you would represent Christ to those around you.

4 / 2 Corinthians 3:7–18
Becoming Like Christ

IT SEEMS TO me that it ought to be that Christ is most revealed when we hide ourselves. But that is the Old Covenant with its fading glory, condemnation focus and death-dealing impact. The New Covenant ministry is paradoxically this: as I look at Christ and as I reveal myself, it is not I who am revealed but Christ. I am like a Kodachrome transparency. If I am looked *at,* one will see almost no image at all. But if I am held to the light and looked *through,* a beautiful image begins to appear. In this passage Paul celebrates the revelation that comes with the New Covenant.

Warming Up to God Ask God to reveal that part of himself which is in you. Spend some time seeing yourself through his eyes. Praise him for the beauty he reveals.

Read 2 Corinthians 3:7–18.

7Now if the ministry that brought death, which
was engraved in letters on stone, came with glory,
so that the Israelites could not look steadily at the
face of Moses because of its glory, fading though
it was, 8will not the ministry of the Spirit be even
more glorious? 9If the ministry that condemns
men is glorious, how much more glorious is the
ministry that brings righteousness! 10For what
was glorious has no glory now in comparison
with the surpassing glory. 11And if what was fad-
ing away came with glory, how much greater is
the glory of that which lasts!
12Therefore, since we have such a hope, we are
very bold. 13We are not like Moses, who would
put a veil over his face to keep the Israelites from
gazing at it while the radiance was fading away.
14But their minds were made dull, for to this day
the same veil remains when the old covenant is
read. It has not been removed, because only in
Christ is it taken away. 15Even to this day when
Moses is read, a veil covers their hearts. 16But
whenever anyone turns to the Lord, the veil is
taken away. 17Now the Lord is the Spirit, and
where the Spirit of the Lord is, there is freedom.
18And we, who with unveiled faces all reflect[c]
the Lord's glory, are being transformed into his
likeness with ever-increasing glory, which comes
from the Lord, who is the Spirit.

c18 Or *contemplate*

Discovering the Word 1. How does Paul demonstrate that ministry under the New Covenant is more glorious than under the Old (vv. 7–11)? 2. How are we contrasted with Moses (vv. 12–16)? 3. What does verse 18 reveal about the process and goal of our lives as Christians under the New Covenant? 4. Paul speaks of our boldness (v. 12) and freedom (v. 17). Why should each of these characterize our New Covenant ministry?

Applying the Word 1. What evidence do you see in your life of the glorious transformation (metamorphosis) described in verse 18? 2. Is it easy or difficult for you to recognize God's glory as it is revealed in you? Explain. 3. In what area would you like to be made more like Christ?

 **Responding in Prayer** Praise God for the transformation he has worked and is working in you.

5 / *2 Corinthians 4:1—5:10*
This Treasure, These Jars of Clay

MARGERY WILLIAMS WROTE a delightful children's story about two nursery animals, a Velveteen Rabbit (after which the book is named) and a Skin Horse, who was very old and very wise. "What is real?" asked the Velveteen Rabbit. The Skin Horse said, "Real isn't how you are made, it is a thing that happens when you are loved for a long, long time. Generally, by the time you are real most of your hair has been loved off, and your eyes drop out and you get loose in the joints and very shabby. But these things don't matter at all, because once you are REAL you can't be ugly except to those who don't understand. Once you are real you can't become unreal again. It lasts for always" (Margery Williams, *The Velveteen Rabbit* [New York: Simon & Schuster, Inc., 1975]).

The gospel treasure is contained by people marked by weakness, frailty and a kind of living death. Paradoxically, as we shall see, this life situation serves to enhance the message we bring, not detract from it. Once real in Christ, you can't become ugly or unreal again.

 **Warming Up to God** Do you feel free to be real in your relationship with Christ? Talk to him about the parts of yourself you feel are shabby. Listen for his loving response.

 **Read 2 Corinthians 4:1—5:10.**

4 Therefore, since through God's mercy we
have this ministry, we do not lose heart.
[2]Rather, we have renounced secret and
shameful ways; we do not use deception, nor do
we distort the word of God. On the contrary, by
setting forth the truth plainly we commend our-
selves to every man's conscience in the sight of
God. [3]And even if our gospel is veiled, it is veiled
to those who are perishing. [4]The god of this age
has blinded the minds of unbelievers, so that they
cannot see the light of the gospel of the glory of
Christ, who is the image of God. [5]For we do not
preach ourselves, but Jesus Christ as Lord, and
ourselves as your servants for Jesus' sake. [6]For
God, who said, "Let light shine out of dark-
ness,"[d] made his light shine in our hearts to give
us the light of the knowledge of the glory of God
in the face of Christ.

[7]But we have this treasure in jars of clay to
show that this all-surpassing power is from God
and not from us. [8]We are hard pressed on every
side, but not crushed; perplexed, but not in de-
spair; [9]persecuted, but not abandoned; struck
down, but not destroyed. [10]We always carry
around in our body the death of Jesus, so that the
life of Jesus may also be revealed in our body.
[11]For we who are alive are always being given
over to death for Jesus' sake, so that his life may
be revealed in our mortal body. [12]So then, death
is at work in us, but life is at work in you.

[13]It is written: "I believed; therefore I have spo-
ken."[e] With that same spirit of faith we also be-
lieve and therefore speak, [14]because we know that
the one who raised the Lord Jesus from the dead
will also raise us with Jesus and present us with
you in his presence. [15]All this is for your benefit,
so that the grace that is reaching more and more
people may cause thanksgiving to overflow to the
glory of God.

[16]Therefore we do not lose heart. Though out-
wardly we are wasting away, yet inwardly we are
being renewed day by day. [17]For our light and
momentary troubles are achieving for us an eter-
nal glory that far outweighs them all. [18]So we fix
our eyes not on what is seen, but on what is un-
seen. For what is seen is temporary, but what is
unseen is eternal.

5 Now we know that if the earthly tent we
live in is destroyed, we have a building
from God, an eternal house in heaven,
not built by human hands. [2]Meanwhile we groan,
longing to be clothed with our heavenly dwelling,
[3]because when we are clothed, we will not be
found naked. [4]For while we are in this tent, we
groan and are burdened, because we do not wish

[d]6 Gen. 1:3 [e]13 Psalm 116:10

to be unclothed but to be clothed with our heav-
enly dwelling, so that what is mortal may be swal-
lowed up by life. 5Now it is God who has made us
for this very purpose and has given us the Spirit
as a deposit, guaranteeing what is to come.
6Therefore we are always confident and know
that as long as we are at home in the body we are
away from the Lord. 7We live by faith, not by
sight. 8We are confident, I say, and would prefer
to be away from the body and at home with the
Lord. 9So we make it our goal to please him,
whether we are at home in the body or away from
it. 10For we must all appear before the judgment
seat of Christ, that each one may receive what is
due him for the things done while in the body,
whether good or bad.

Discovering the Word 1. How does Paul's ministry contrast with the practices of evangelists who discredit the gospel (4:2)? 2. What forces does Paul see at work behind those who reject and those who accept his gospel (4:4–6)? 3. In what ways does Paul contrast the glory of the gospel with the weakness of those who preach it (4:7–18)? 4. What images does Paul use to compare the shabbiness of life now with the glory of the life to come (5:1–5)? 5. How does Paul's wonderful destiny in Christ affect his view of life and death (5:6–10)? 6. Reviewing the entire passage, what do you now understand Paul to mean by saying, "we live by faith, not by sight" (5:7)?

Applying the Word 1. We often assume that our weakness will hinder the gospel and detract from it. On the contrary, how does our weakness reveal God's power? 2. How can Paul's perspective help you come to terms with your own weaknesses and mortality?

Responding in Prayer Praise God for what you have learned about yourself through this passage.

6 / 2 *Corinthians 5:11—6:13*
Ambassadors for Christ

DIETRICH BONHOEFFER DESCRIBES the emergence of the super-leader under Hitler:

> It is essential for the image of the Leader that the group does not see the face of the one who goes before, but sees him only from behind as the figure stepping ahead. His humanity is veiled in his Leader's form. (Quoted in Ray Anderson, *Minding God's Business* [Grand Rapids, Mich.: Eerdmans, 1986], p. 5.)

Warming Up to God Think of a time when you defended yourself in the context of a strained relationship. To what did you appeal?

Read 2 Corinthians 5:11—6:13.

11Since, then, we know what it is to fear the
Lord, we try to persuade men. What we are is
plain to God, and I hope it is also plain to your
conscience. 12We are not trying to commend our-
selves to you again, but are giving you an oppor-
tunity to take pride in us, so that you can answer
those who take pride in what is seen rather than
in what is in the heart. 13If we are out of our
mind, it is for the sake of God; if we are in our
right mind, it is for you. 14For Christ's love com-
pels us, because we are convinced that one died
for all, and therefore all died. 15And he died for
all, that those who live should no longer live for
themselves but for him who died for them and
was raised again.
16So from now on we regard no one from a
worldly point of view. Though we once regarded
Christ in this way, we do so no longer. 17There-
fore, if anyone is in Christ, he is a new creation;
the old has gone, the new has come! 18All this is
from God, who reconciled us to himself through
Christ and gave us the ministry of reconciliation:
19that God was reconciling the world to himself
in Christ, not counting men's sins against them.
And he has committed to us the message of rec-
onciliation. 20We are therefore Christ's ambassa-

dors, as though God were making his appeal
through us. We implore you on Christ's behalf:
Be reconciled to God. 21God made him who had
no sin to be sin[f] for us, so that in him we might
become the righteousness of God.

6 As God's fellow workers we urge you not
to receive God's grace in vain. 2For he
says,

"In the time of my favor I heard you,
and in the day of salvation I helped you."[g]

I tell you, now is the time of God's favor, now is
the day of salvation.
3We put no stumbling block in anyone's path,
so that our ministry will not be discredited.
4Rather, as servants of God we commend our-
selves in every way: in great endurance; in trou-
bles, hardships and distresses; 5in beatings, im-
prisonments and riots; in hard work, sleepless
nights and hunger; 6in purity, understanding, pa-
tience and kindness; in the Holy Spirit and in
sincere love; 7in truthful speech and in the power
of God; with weapons of righteousness in the
right hand and in the left; 8through glory and
dishonor, bad report and good report; genuine,
yet regarded as impostors; 9known, yet regarded
as unknown; dying, and yet we live on; beaten,
and yet not killed; 10sorrowful, yet always rejoic-
ing; poor, yet making many rich; having nothing,
and yet possessing everything.
11We have spoken freely to you, Corinthians,
and opened wide our hearts to you. 12We are not
withholding our affection from you, but you are
withholding yours from us. 13As a fair ex-
change—I speak as to my children—open wide
your hearts also.

f21 Or *be a sin offering* g2 Isaiah 49:8

Discovering the Word 1. Paul defends his *ministry* and *message* of reconciliation in this passage. What accusations might Paul's opponents have made about his ministry (5:11–13)? 2. How does Paul explain his true motives and goals (5:11–14)? 3. In describing his message, Paul uses the words *reconciliation* and *reconciled* five times (5:18–20). What does it mean to be reconciled to God? 4. What would it mean for the Corinthians—or us today—to receive the grace of God in vain (6:1)? 5. To what further credentials does Paul point in order to commend himself to the Corinthians (6:3–10)?

Applying the Word 1. How might Paul's example help you be a more effective ambassador, especially to people who are "turned off" by Christianity? 2. Who, specifically, would you like to be an ambassador to? 3. How could you reach that person?

Responding in Prayer Ask God to make you an effective ambassador.

7 / *2 Corinthians 6:14—7:16*
Good Grief

A GREAT THEOLOGIAN once said, "To be a sinner is our distress, but to know it, is our hope!" Paul would say "Amen." We have nothing to lose and everything to gain if we are in Christ and walking into the light. But the Corinthians were tempted to cover up a scandal and not to call it sin. In response, Paul patiently and effectively ministered to the Corinthians, urging them not to cover up the problem. The result was what Paul calls godly sorrow.

Warming Up to God Recall an experience of deep sorrow, possibly a significant loss, hurt or disappointment. What were some of the good things, if any, that came after the sorrow had passed? Praise God for what you learned from that experience.

Read 2 Corinthians 6:14—7:16.

14Do not be yoked together with unbelievers.
For what do righteousness and wickedness have
in common? Or what fellowship can light have
with darkness? 15What harmony is there between
Christ and Belial[h]? What does a believer have in
common with an unbeliever? 16What agreement
is there between the temple of God and idols? For
we are the temple of the living God. As God has
said: "I will live with them and walk among them,
and I will be their God, and they will be my peo-
ple."[i]

17"Therefore come out from them
 and be separate,
 says the Lord.
Touch no unclean thing,
 and I will receive you."[j]
18"I will be a Father to you,
 and you will be my sons and daughters,
 says the Lord Almighty."[k]

7 Since we have these promises, dear
friends, let us purify ourselves from ev-
erything that contaminates body and
spirit, perfecting holiness out of reverence for
God.

2Make room for us in your hearts. We have
wronged no one, we have corrupted no one, we
have exploited no one. 3I do not say this to con-
demn you; I have said before that you have such
a place in our hearts that we would live or die
with you. 4I have great confidence in you; I take
great pride in you. I am greatly encouraged; in all
our troubles my joy knows no bounds.

5For when we came into Macedonia, this body
of ours had no rest, but we were harassed at every
turn—conflicts on the outside, fears within. 6But
God, who comforts the downcast, comforted us
by the coming of Titus, 7and not only by his com-
ing but also by the comfort you had given him.
He told us about your longing for me, your deep
sorrow, your ardent concern for me, so that my
joy was greater than ever.

8Even if I caused you sorrow by my letter, I do
not regret it. Though I did regret it—I see that
my letter hurt you, but only for a little while—
9yet now I am happy, not because you were made
sorry, but because your sorrow led you to repen-
tance. For you became sorrowful as God intended
and so were not harmed in any way by us.
10Godly sorrow brings repentance that leads to
salvation and leaves no regret, but worldly sorrow
brings death. 11See what this godly sorrow has
produced in you: what earnestness, what eager-
ness to clear yourselves, what indignation, what
alarm, what longing, what concern, what readi-
ness to see justice done. At every point you have
proved yourselves to be innocent in this matter.
12So even though I wrote to you, it was not on
account of the one who did the wrong or of the
injured party, but rather that before God you
could see for yourselves how devoted to us you
are. 13By all this we are encouraged.

In addition to our own encouragement, we
were especially delighted to see how happy Titus
was, because his spirit has been refreshed by all of
you. 14I had boasted to him about you, and you
have not embarrassed me. But just as everything
we said to you was true, so our boasting about
you to Titus has proved to be true as well. 15And
his affection for you is all the greater when he
remembers that you were all obedient, receiving
him with fear and trembling. 16I am glad I can
have complete confidence in you.

[h]*15* Greek *Beliar*, a variant of *Belial* [i]*16* Lev. 26:12; Jer. 32:38; Ezek. 37:27 [j]*17* Isaiah 52:11; Ezek. 20:34,41 [k]*18* 2 Samuel 7:14; 7:8

Discovering the Word 1. This passage is usually understood to apply to marriages between believers and unbelievers. However, what other types of close relationships or partnerships might Paul have in mind? 2. What reasons does Paul give for avoiding such unions (6:14–16)? 3. Although we may forfeit certain relationships, what positive promises does the Lord give us (6:16—7:1)? 4. What difference should our relationship with God make when we contemplate marriage or other close relationships (6:17; 7:1)? 5. In 7:2–6 Paul recalls how comforted he was when he met Titus in Macedonia and heard news of the Corinthians. What makes Paul so "confident," "proud" and "encouraged" (7:4) about the Corinthians? 6. Referring to their response to his "sorrowful letter" (7:8), Paul compares worldly sorrow with godly sorrow (7:9–10). What are the positive indications and constructive results of godly sorrow (7:10–11)?

Applying the Word 1. It is often counterproductive to try to persuade someone not to marry a person they deeply love, even if the intended partner is unsuitable. What clues does this passage give us for ministering to someone who is tempted to marry outside the faith? 2. If godly sorrow is so beneficial, why do you think most Christians shrink from the relational work, discipline and tough love that are required to bring it about in others? 3. In what areas of your life are you most in need of godly sorrow?

Responding in Prayer Ask Christ to teach you more about godly sorrow.

8 / 2 *Corinthians 8:1—9:15*
The Need to Give

THE PRIVACY OF the purse makes it extremely difficult for Christians to talk about their money. The fig leaf has slipped from the genitals to the wallet. The problem is compounded by hard-sell media evangelists raising funds for their personal empires. But Paul devotes two whole chapters to the grace of giving, because both he and the Corinthians have a problem in this area.

Warming Up to God Reflect on your own pattern of giving. When is it hard for you?

Read 2 Corinthians 8:1—9:15.

8 And now, brothers, we want you to know
about the grace that God has given the
Macedonian churches. 2Out of the most
severe trial, their overflowing joy and their ex-
treme poverty welled up in rich generosity. 3For I
testify that they gave as much as they were able,
and even beyond their ability. Entirely on their
own, 4they urgently pleaded with us for the privi-
lege of sharing in this service to the saints. 5And
they did not do as we expected, but they gave
themselves first to the Lord and then to us in
keeping with God's will. 6So we urged Titus, since
he had earlier made a beginning, to bring also to
completion this act of grace on your part. 7But
just as you excel in everything—in faith, in
speech, in knowledge, in complete earnestness
and in your love for us[l]—see that you also excel
in this grace of giving.

8I am not commanding you, but I want to test
the sincerity of your love by comparing it with
the earnestness of others. 9For you know the
grace of our Lord Jesus Christ, that though he
was rich, yet for your sakes he became poor, so
that you through his poverty might become rich.

10And here is my advice about what is best for
you in this matter: Last year you were the first not
only to give but also to have the desire to do so.
11Now finish the work, so that your eager willing-
ness to do it may be matched by your completion
of it, according to your means. 12For if the will-
ingness is there, the gift is acceptable according to
what one has, not according to what he does not
have.

13Our desire is not that others might be re-
lieved while you are hard pressed, but that there
might be equality. 14At the present time your
plenty will supply what they need, so that in turn
their plenty will supply what you need. Then
there will be equality, 15as it is written: "He who
gathered much did not have too much, and he
who gathered little did not have too little."[m]

16I thank God, who put into the heart of Titus
the same concern I have for you. 17For Titus not
only welcomed our appeal, but he is coming to
you with much enthusiasm and on his own initia-
tive. 18And we are sending along with him the
brother who is praised by all the churches for his
service to the gospel. 19What is more, he was cho-
sen by the churches to accompany us as we carry
the offering, which we administer in order to
honor the Lord himself and to show our eager-
ness to help. 20We want to avoid any criticism of
the way we administer this liberal gift. 21For we
are taking pains to do what is right, not only in
the eyes of the Lord but also in the eyes of men.

22In addition, we are sending with them our
brother who has often proved to us in many ways
that he is zealous, and now even more so because
of his great confidence in you. 23As for Titus, he

[l]7 Some manuscripts *in our love for you* [m]15 Exodus 16:18

is my partner and fellow worker among you; as
for our brothers, they are representatives of the
churches and an honor to Christ. 24Therefore
show these men the proof of your love and the
reason for our pride in you, so that the churches
can see it.

9 There is no need for me to write to you
about this service to the saints. 2For I
know your eagerness to help, and I have
been boasting about it to the Macedonians, telling
them that since last year you in Achaia were ready
to give; and your enthusiasm has stirred most of
them to action. 3But I am sending the brothers in
order that our boasting about you in this matter
should not prove hollow, but that you may be
ready, as I said you would be. 4For if any Macedo-
nians come with me and find you unprepared,
we—not to say anything about you—would be
ashamed of having been so confident. 5So I
thought it necessary to urge the brothers to visit
you in advance and finish the arrangements for
the generous gift you had promised. Then it will
be ready as a generous gift, not as one grudgingly
given.

6Remember this: Whoever sows sparingly will
also reap sparingly, and whoever sows generously
will also reap generously. 7Each man should give
what he has decided in his heart to give, not re-
luctantly or under compulsion, for God loves a
cheerful giver. 8And God is able to make all grace
abound to you, so that in all things at all times,
having all that you need, you will abound in ev-
ery good work. 9As it is written:

> "He has scattered abroad his gifts to the poor;
> his righteousness endures forever."[n]

10Now he who supplies seed to the sower and
bread for food will also supply and increase your
store of seed and will enlarge the harvest of your
righteousness. 11You will be made rich in every
way so that you can be generous on every occa-
sion, and through us your generosity will result
in thanksgiving to God.

12This service that you perform is not only sup-
plying the needs of God's people but is also over-
flowing in many expressions of thanks to God.
13Because of the service by which you have
proved yourselves, men will praise God for the
obedience that accompanies your confession of
the gospel of Christ, and for your generosity in
sharing with them and with everyone else. 14And
in their prayers for you their hearts will go out to
you, because of the surpassing grace God has
given you. 15Thanks be to God for his indescrib-
able gift!

[n]9 Psalm 112:9

Discovering the Word 1. In what ways are the Macedonians excellent examples of generosity (8:1–5)? 2. In both chapters Paul refrains from using the word *money*. Instead he speaks of *sharing* (8:4; 9:13), *service* (8:4, 18; 9:1, 12–13), *offering* (8:19), *grace* (8:6–7) and *gift* (8:12, 20; 9:5). What insights do these words give us into the nature of giving? 3. Paul never raised money for himself, for his own missionary organization or even for Corinth Community Church. What is the primary goal that governs his appeal for gifts (8:10–15)? 4. What care does Paul take to avoid any suspicion of dishonesty or self-interest as he handles this large gift (8:16–24)? 5. Some people teach that giving money to the Lord's work results in your getting more money yourself. What does Paul say about the personal benefits of giving (9:6–11)?

Applying the Word 1. What positive and negative feelings do you have about people raising money for a Christian cause? 2. Paul encourages *cheerful* giving (9:7). The word is the root of our English *hilarious.* It is the exact opposite of calculated giving under compulsion. According to these two chapters, how could you become a more cheerful giver? 3. What difference will this study make in the stewardship of your resources?

Responding in Prayer Pray for the needs of believers around the world, especially those who suffer persecution.

9 / 2 Corinthians 10
Spiritual Warfare

SOMETIMES WHEN THINGS seem to be getting better we hear news that the situation is worse than we thought. While Paul was writing this letter, or after completing and sending chapters 1—9, he got fresh news that some outside leaders, some so-called super-apostles, had usurped his rightful place. Now Paul engages in spiritual warfare with principalities, powers and persons who oppose not only Paul but Christ himself. Unlike many of us, Paul wants to make peace, not keep the peace by covering over the problem.

Warming Up to God In what area do you feel that you are currently battling evil? What help do you need from God?

Read 2 Corinthians 10.

10 By the meekness and gentleness of
Christ, I appeal to you—I, Paul,
who am "timid" when face to face
with you, but "bold" when away! 2I beg you that
when I come I may not have to be as bold as I
expect to be toward some people who think that
we live by the standards of this world. 3For
though we live in the world, we do not wage war
as the world does. 4The weapons we fight with
are not the weapons of the world. On the con-
trary, they have divine power to demolish strong-
holds. 5We demolish arguments and every pre-
tension that sets itself up against the knowledge
of God, and we take captive every thought to
make it obedient to Christ. 6And we will be ready
to punish every act of disobedience, once your
obedience is complete.

7You are looking only on the surface of
things.[o] If anyone is confident that he belongs to
Christ, he should consider again that we belong
to Christ just as much as he. 8For even if I boast
somewhat freely about the authority the Lord
gave us for building you up rather than pulling
you down, I will not be ashamed of it. 9I do not
want to seem to be trying to frighten you with my
letters. 10For some say, "His letters are weighty
and forceful, but in person he is unimpressive
and his speaking amounts to nothing." 11Such
people should realize that what we are in our let-
ters when we are absent, we will be in our actions
when we are present.

12We do not dare to classify or compare our-
selves with some who commend themselves.
When they measure themselves by themselves
and compare themselves with themselves, they
are not wise. 13We, however, will not boast be-
yond proper limits, but will confine our boasting
to the field God has assigned to us, a field that
reaches even to you. 14We are not going too far in
our boasting, as would be the case if we had not
come to you, for we did get as far as you with the
gospel of Christ. 15Neither do we go beyond our
limits by boasting of work done by others.[p] Our
hope is that, as your faith continues to grow, our
area of activity among you will greatly expand,
16so that we can preach the gospel in the regions
beyond you. For we do not want to boast about
work already done in another man's territory.
17But, "Let him who boasts boast in the Lord."[q]
18For it is not the one who commends himself
who is approved, but the one whom the Lord
commends.

[o]7 Or *Look at the obvious facts* [p]13-15 Or *13We, however, will not boast about things that cannot be measured, but we will boast according to the standard of measurement that the God of measure has assigned us—a measurement that relates even to you. 14 . . . . 15Neither do we boast about things that cannot be measured in regard to the work done by others.* [q]17 Jer. 9:24

Discovering the Word 1. What apparent disadvantages did Paul suffer in comparison to his opponents in Corinth? (See especially verses 1 and 9.) 2. Paul says he is not waging war "as the world does" (v. 3). What types of worldly weapons and strategies do you think he has in mind? 3. What is Paul's strategy in this spiritual warfare (vv. 4-6)? 4. Trace, in verses 7 and 10, the arguments of Paul's opponents. 5. What is wrong with the boasting of Paul's opponents (vv. 7-18)?

Applying the Word 1. In what situations are we tempted to use worldly weapons and strategies today? 2. What similar arguments and pretensions oppose the knowledge of God today? 3. Which of your own thoughts need to be "taken captive" (v. 5) to obedience to Christ?

Responding in Prayer Ask God to guard your words, that your boasting might be only in the Lord.

10 / *2 Corinthians 11*
Super-Apostles, Super-Leaders

IN HIS BOOK *Servant Leadership* Robert K. Greenleaf wrote, "We live in the age of the anti-leader, and our vast educational structure devotes little care to nurturing leaders or to understanding followership" (Robert K. Greenleaf, *Servant Leadership* [New York: Paulist Press, 1977], p. 4).

Warming Up to God Whose leadership are you under? Reflect before Christ on the positive or negative impact of that leadership in your life.

Read 2 Corinthians 11.

11 I hope you will put up with a little
of my foolishness; but you are al-
ready doing that. 2I am jealous for
you with a godly jealousy. I promised you to one
husband, to Christ, so that I might present you as
a pure virgin to him. 3But I am afraid that just as
Eve was deceived by the serpent's cunning, your
minds may somehow be led astray from your sin-
cere and pure devotion to Christ. 4For if someone
comes to you and preaches a Jesus other than the
Jesus we preached, or if you receive a different
spirit from the one you received, or a different
gospel from the one you accepted, you put up
with it easily enough. 5But I do not think I am in
the least inferior to those "super-apostles." 6I may
not be a trained speaker, but I do have knowl-
edge. We have made this perfectly clear to you in
every way.

7Was it a sin for me to lower myself in order to
elevate you by preaching the gospel of God to you
free of charge? 8I robbed other churches by re-
ceiving support from them so as to serve you.
9And when I was with you and needed some-
thing, I was not a burden to anyone, for the
brothers who came from Macedonia supplied
what I needed. I have kept myself from being a
burden to you in any way, and will continue to do
so. 10As surely as the truth of Christ is in me,
nobody in the regions of Achaia will stop this
boasting of mine. 11Why? Because I do not love
you? God knows I do! 12And I will keep on doing
what I am doing in order to cut the ground from
under those who want an opportunity to be con-
sidered equal with us in the things they boast
about.

13For such men are false apostles, deceitful
workmen, masquerading as apostles of Christ.
14And no wonder, for Satan himself masquerades
as an angel of light. 15It is not surprising, then, if
his servants masquerade as servants of righteous-
ness. Their end will be what their actions deserve.

16I repeat: Let no one take me for a fool. But if
you do, then receive me just as you would a fool,
so that I may do a little boasting. 17In this self-
confident boasting I am not talking as the Lord
would, but as a fool. 18Since many are boasting in
the way the world does, I too will boast. 19You
gladly put up with fools since you are so wise!
20In fact, you even put up with anyone who en-
slaves you or exploits you or takes advantage of
you or pushes himself forward or slaps you in the
face. 21To my shame I admit that we were too
weak for that!

What anyone else dares to boast about—I am
speaking as a fool—I also dare to boast about.
22Are they Hebrews? So am I. Are they Israelites?
So am I. Are they Abraham's descendants? So am
I. 23Are they servants of Christ? (I am out of my
mind to talk like this.) I am more. I have worked
much harder, been in prison more frequently,

been flogged more severely, and been exposed to
death again and again. 24Five times I received
from the Jews the forty lashes minus one. 25Three
times I was beaten with rods, once I was stoned,
three times I was shipwrecked, I spent a night
and a day in the open sea, 26I have been con-
stantly on the move. I have been in danger from
rivers, in danger from bandits, in danger from my
own countrymen, in danger from Gentiles; in
danger in the city, in danger in the country, in
danger at sea; and in danger from false brothers.
27I have labored and toiled and have often gone
without sleep; I have known hunger and thirst
and have often gone without food; I have been
cold and naked. 28Besides everything else, I face
daily the pressure of my concern for all the
churches. 29Who is weak, and I do not feel weak?
Who is led into sin, and I do not inwardly burn?
30If I must boast, I will boast of the things that
show my weakness. 31The God and Father of the
Lord Jesus, who is to be praised forever, knows
that I am not lying. 32In Damascus the governor
under King Aretas had the city of the Damascenes
guarded in order to arrest me. 33But I was lowered
in a basket from a window in the wall and slipped
through his hands.

Discovering the Word 1. What are Paul's motives for challenging the so-called super-apostles who are winning over the Corinthians (vv. 1–6)? 2. Why do you think betrothal rather than marriage is such a good image of the goal of Christian ministry (vv. 2–3)? 3. Why do you think Paul's decision to "preach the gospel free of charge" was so important in defending his ministry (vv. 7–12)? 4. Looking at the whole chapter, what marks of the super-apostles justified Paul's description of them as *false, deceitful* and *masquerading*? 5. In contrast, what does Paul boast about as the mark of his own leadership (vv. 16–33)?

Applying the Word 1. What kind of Christian leadership today might fall under the apostle's judgment? 2. What have you learned from this study about the marks of true Christian leadership? 3. What have you learned about being a healthy follower?

Responding in Prayer Pray for your pastor and other Christian leaders.

11 / *2 Corinthians 12*
My Burden Carries Me

UNINTENTIONALLY, A GERMAN philosopher captured the genius of Paul's spirituality with these arresting words: "My burden carries me." Normally we think about the difficulty of carrying our burdens. But in reality our burdens carry us to Christ by convincing us that we are not self-sufficient. They are spiritual assets, not liabilities. "When I am weak, then I am strong" is Paul's final distinction between super-spirituality and the real thing.

Warming Up to God What burdens are you carrying today? Turn them over to Christ one by one. Feel the weight lifted from you.

Read 2 Corinthians 12.

12 I must go on boasting. Although
there is nothing to be gained, I will
go on to visions and revelations
from the Lord. 2I know a man in Christ who four-
teen years ago was caught up to the third heaven.
Whether it was in the body or out of the body I
do not know—God knows. 3And I know that this
man—whether in the body or apart from the
body I do not know, but God knows—4was
caught up to paradise. He heard inexpressible
things, things that man is not permitted to tell. 5I
will boast about a man like that, but I will not
boast about myself, except about my weaknesses.
6Even if I should choose to boast, I would not be
a fool, because I would be speaking the truth. But
I refrain, so no one will think more of me than is
warranted by what I do or say.
7To keep me from becoming conceited because

of these surpassingly great revelations, there was given me a thorn in my flesh, a messenger of Satan, to torment me. 8Three times I pleaded with the Lord to take it away from me. 9But he said to me, "My grace is sufficient for you, for my power is made perfect in weakness." Therefore I will boast all the more gladly about my weaknesses, so that Christ's power may rest on me. 10That is why, for Christ's sake, I delight in weaknesses, in insults, in hardships, in persecutions, in difficulties. For when I am weak, then I am strong.

11I have made a fool of myself, but you drove me to it. I ought to have been commended by you, for I am not in the least inferior to the "super-apostles," even though I am nothing. 12The things that mark an apostle—signs, wonders and miracles—were done among you with great perseverance. 13How were you inferior to the other churches, except that I was never a burden to you? Forgive me this wrong!

14Now I am ready to visit you for the third time, and I will not be a burden to you, because what I want is not your possessions but you. After all, children should not have to save up for their parents, but parents for their children. 15So I will very gladly spend for you everything I have and expend myself as well. If I love you more, will you love me less? 16Be that as it may, I have not been a burden to you. Yet, crafty fellow that I am, I caught you by trickery! 17Did I exploit you through any of the men I sent you? 18I urged Titus to go to you and I sent our brother with him. Titus did not exploit you, did he? Did we not act in the same spirit and follow the same course?

19Have you been thinking all along that we have been defending ourselves to you? We have been speaking in the sight of God as those in Christ; and everything we do, dear friends, is for your strengthening. 20For I am afraid that when I come I may not find you as I want you to be, and you may not find me as you want me to be. I fear that there may be quarreling, jealousy, outbursts of anger, factions, slander, gossip, arrogance and disorder. 21I am afraid that when I come again my God will humble me before you, and I will be grieved over many who have sinned earlier and have not repented of the impurity, sexual sin and debauchery in which they have indulged.

Discovering the Word 1. Paul describes his experience of being caught up to paradise by referring to "a man in Christ" (vv. 1–6). Why do you think he refrains from boasting about such an exalted experience? 2. Opinions concerning Paul's "thorn in my flesh" (v. 7) range from eye disease (Acts 9:9; Gal 4:15) to defective speech to his ever-present opponents. While no conclusive answer can be given about the details, what do we know about this bitter reality Paul faced? 3. How does Paul view Satan's part and God's part in his "thorn"? 4. In contrast to Paul's ecstatic experiences, the simple answer to his prayer (v. 9) is considered to be the summit from which we gain the most complete view of Paul's apostleship. What effect did this answer have on Paul himself? 5. To what credentials does Paul point while pleading for his rightful place in the Corinthians' hearts (vv. 11–21)?

Applying the Word 1. Reflecting on the whole chapter, what kind of weaknesses or problems can we legitimately expect God to transform into a means of grace? 2. What kinds of problems or weaknesses should we not expect God to transform? 3. How does this help you to understand an ongoing problem in your life?

Responding in Prayer Pray that you will be made strong even in your weak places, that you might serve Christ.

12 / *2 Corinthians 13*
Examine Yourselves

IMAGINE LIFE WITHOUT a final examination. At first it strikes us as a wonderful vacation, like school without tests and report cards. But without accountability life quickly loses its meaning. The whole Bible looks toward the final Day with vibrant hope. Those genuinely in Christ have nothing to fear and everything to anticipate. But what of those who are not sure, or who like the Corinthians might have false confidence about the outcome of the final exam? Paul deals with this matter in his final passionate plea.

Warming Up to God When is God's power real to you?

Read 2 Corinthians 13.

13 This will be my third visit to you.
"Every matter must be established
by the testimony of two or three
witnesses."[r] 2I already gave you a warning when
I was with you the second time. I now repeat it
while absent: On my return I will not spare those
who sinned earlier or any of the others, 3since
you are demanding proof that Christ is speaking
through me. He is not weak in dealing with you,
but is powerful among you. 4For to be sure, he
was crucified in weakness, yet he lives by God's
power. Likewise, we are weak in him, yet by
God's power we will live with him to serve you.
5Examine yourselves to see whether you are in
the faith; test yourselves. Do you not realize that
Christ Jesus is in you—unless, of course, you fail
the test? 6And I trust that you will discover that
we have not failed the test. 7Now we pray to God
that you will not do anything wrong. Not that
people will see that we have stood the test but
that you will do what is right even though we
may seem to have failed. 8For we cannot do any-
thing against the truth, but only for the truth.
9We are glad whenever we are weak but you are
strong; and our prayer is for your perfection.
10This is why I write these things when I am ab-
sent, that when I come I may not have to be harsh
in my use of authority—the authority the Lord
gave me for building you up, not for tearing you
down.

11Finally, brothers, good-by. Aim for perfec-
tion, listen to my appeal, be of one mind, live in
peace. And the God of love and peace will be with
you.

12Greet one another with a holy kiss. 13All the
saints send their greetings.

14May the grace of the Lord Jesus Christ, and
the love of God, and the fellowship of the Holy
Spirit be with you all.

r1 Deut. 19:15

Discovering the Word 1. What can the Corinthians expect from Paul's third visit (vv. 1–3, 10)? 2. Verse 4 sums up the whole book. Why does the cross represent the heart of what Paul has been saying to the Corinthians? 3. Paul asks them to examine themselves not so much in their doctrine as in their experience (vv. 5–6). How could the Corinthians know experientially that they truly belonged to Christ? 4. In what ways does Paul show that he cares more for *their* passing the test than for *his* seeming to pass the test in the eyes of others (vv. 7–9)? 5. In what specific ways does Paul pray they will be built up (vv. 11–14)?

Applying the Word 1. In what ways do you shrink from your daily cross and find your power elsewhere? 2. If you are unsure of your position in Christ, what can you do about it in light of this chapter?

Responding in Prayer Pray for courage to take up your cross and follow Christ.

Galatians

We all want to be accepted—by our family, by our friends and most of all by God. But so often people accept us only *if* we are attractive, smart, wealthy or powerful. So we work hard to project the right image and to conceal our faults.

We often transfer this attitude to our relationship with God. We feel we must earn his acceptance. If we could only work harder, live better, pray longer, witness to more people—then we might get on God's good side.

In Galatians Paul challenges this kind of thinking. He exposes the futility of trying to earn God's acceptance when we are already accepted in Christ. His message frees us from living out of a sense of guilt. We find fresh assurance of God's love and renewed power to serve him.

Galatians was written by Paul sometime between A.D. 48–49. It was probably addressed to the churches in Antioch, Iconium, Lystra and Derbe, which were located in the Roman province of Galatia. Paul and Barnabas visited these cities during their first missionary journey. Their reception was unforgettable. Acts 13—14 tells us that they were driven out of Antioch, that they fled from Iconium and that Paul was stoned in Lystra! Yet in spite of the opposition against Paul and Barnabas, people believed the gospel and churches were formed.

The real threat arose shortly thereafter. Certain people infiltrated the new churches with a different message. "Paul omitted an important part of the gospel," they claimed. "You must also be circumcised and keep the law of Moses if you want to be saved" (see Acts 15:1). Their arguments were impressive and the religious zeal was undeniable. The Galatians were almost persuaded when Paul received word of what was happening. Quickly he dictated this letter and sent it to be read in each of the churches. Centuries later it still radiates the heat of Paul's anger. These preachers were impostors. Their gospel was perverted. The Galatians were in grave danger!

Outline

1 / *Galatians 1:1–10*
Good News and Bad

THE CHURCH HAS always been plagued by false teachers, heretics and followers of various cults. Usually such people have an aggressive program for winning new converts. How are we to respond to those who preach or accept a twisted gospel? Paul gives us an example in this passage.

Warming Up to God Read and reflect on Galatians 1:3–5. Allow these verses to speak to you. Let them soak into your mind and heart. Praise God for what he has done in Christ.

Read Galatians 1:1–10.

1 Paul, an apostle—sent not from men nor
by man, but by Jesus Christ and God the
Father, who raised him from the dead—
2and all the brothers with me,

To the churches in Galatia:

3Grace and peace to you from God our Father
and the Lord Jesus Christ, 4who gave himself for
our sins to rescue us from the present evil age,
according to the will of our God and Father, 5to
whom be glory for ever and ever. Amen.

6I am astonished that you are so quickly desert-
ing the one who called you by the grace of Christ
and are turning to a different gospel— 7which is
really no gospel at all. Evidently some people are
throwing you into confusion and are trying to
pervert the gospel of Christ. 8But even if we or an
angel from heaven should preach a gospel other
than the one we preached to you, let him be eter-
nally condemned! 9As we have already said, so
now I say again: If anybody is preaching to you a
gospel other than what you accepted, let him be
eternally condemned!
10Am I now trying to win the approval of men,
or of God? Or am I trying to please men? If I were
still trying to please men, I would not be a servant
of Christ.

Discovering the Word 1. In three brief verses (3–5) Paul tells us an enormous amount about the gospel. What do we learn? 2. In verses 6–7 Paul summarizes the problem that caused him to write this letter. What was happening in the Galatian churches? 3. Verse 6 implies that if we desert the gospel, we also desert God. Why would this be true? 4. Why do you think Paul is so harsh in his judgment of those who preach a different gospel (vv. 8–9)? 5. How might the way we present the gospel be different if we were seeking the approval of people instead of God (v. 10)?

Applying the Word 1. What are some ways the gospel is being perverted today? 2. According to this passage, how can we ensure that the gospel we believe and preach is the true gospel? 3. What can you do to increase your understanding of the gospel?

Responding in Prayer Confess before God the ways in which you are seeking the approval of others before him. Ask God to help you turn your priorities around.

2 / *Galatians 1:11—2:10*
Why Believe the Gospel?

HAVE YOU EVER been talking with someone about the gospel when suddenly he or she says, "But that's just *your* opinion!"? This raises an important question. If the gospel is merely our opinion, then why should they listen to us? There are many other religions in the world, each one claiming to be a path to God. Who are we to assert that the gospel is the only true message of salvation? This objection isn't new. Paul's opponents questioned the authenticity of the gospel he preached.

Warming Up to God We all struggle to believe at times. When is belief difficult for you? Don't be afraid to talk to God about it. Express your struggles and doubts to him.

Read Galatians 1:11—2:10.

---

[11]I want you to know, brothers, that the gospel I preached is not something that man made up. [12]I did not receive it from any man, nor was I taught it; rather, I received it by revelation from Jesus Christ.

[13]For you have heard of my previous way of life in Judaism, how intensely I persecuted the church of God and tried to destroy it. [14]I was advancing in Judaism beyond many Jews of my own age and was extremely zealous for the traditions of my fathers. [15]But when God, who set me apart from birth[a] and called me by his grace, was pleased [16]to reveal his Son in me so that I might preach him among the Gentiles, I did not consult any man, [17]nor did I go up to Jerusalem to see those who were apostles before I was, but I went immediately into Arabia and later returned to Damascus.

[18]Then after three years, I went up to Jerusalem to get acquainted with Peter[b] and stayed with him fifteen days. [19]I saw none of the other apostles—only James, the Lord's brother. [20]I assure you before God that what I am writing you is no lie. [21]Later I went to Syria and Cilicia. [22]I was personally unknown to the churches of Judea that are in Christ. [23]They only heard the report: "The man who formerly persecuted us is now preaching the faith he once tried to destroy." [24]And they praised God because of me.

2 Fourteen years later I went up again to Jerusalem, this time with Barnabas. I took Titus along also. [2]I went in response to a revelation and set before them the gospel that I preach among the Gentiles. But I did this privately to those who seemed to be leaders, for fear that I was running or had run my race in vain. [3]Yet not even Titus, who was with me, was compelled to be circumcised, even though he was a Greek. [4]⌊This matter arose⌋ because some false brothers had infiltrated our ranks to spy on the freedom we have in Christ Jesus and to make us slaves. [5]We did not give in to them for a moment, so that the truth of the gospel might remain with you.

[6]As for those who seemed to be important—whatever they were makes no difference to me; God does not judge by external appearance—those men added nothing to my message. [7]On the contrary, they saw that I had been entrusted with the task of preaching the gospel to the Gentiles,[c] just as Peter had been to the Jews.[d] [8]For God, who was at work in the ministry of Peter as an apostle to the Jews, was also at work in my ministry as an apostle to the Gentiles. [9]James, Peter[e] and John, those reputed to be pillars, gave me and Barnabas the right hand of fellowship when they recognized the grace given to me. They agreed that we should go to the Gentiles, and they to the Jews. [10]All they asked was that we should continue to remember the poor, the very thing I was eager to do.

[a]15 Or *from my mother's womb* [b]18 Greek *Cephas* [c]7 Greek *uncircumcised* [d]7 Greek *circumcised*; also in verses 8 and 9 [e]9 Greek *Cephas*; also in verses 11 and 14

Discovering the Word 1. In 1:11–12 Paul claims he received the gospel from Jesus Christ, not people. How does his brief autobiography in 1:13–24 confirm this claim? 2. Paul obviously did not need human authorization to preach the gospel. Why then did he present his gospel to the leaders in Jerusalem (2:1–2)? 3. Why was it significant that Titus (a Gentile) was not compelled to be circumcised (the sign of becoming a Jew) (2:3–5)? 4. Paul refused to give in to false brothers on the matter of circumcision "so that the truth of the gospel might remain with you" (2:5). How do you show your concern to preserve the gospel? 5. How did the leaders in Jerusalem respond to Paul's message and ministry (2:6–10)?

Applying the Word 1. The apostles were not simply zealous to preserve the gospel. They also felt called to proclaim the gospel (2:7–10). To whom do you feel called to bring the gospel? 2. What step can you take this week to bring the good news to someone? 3. How can Paul's testimony in this passage increase our confidence in the truth of the gospel?

Responding in Prayer Ask God to help you be a bearer of the good news.

3 / *Galatians 2:11–21*
Accepting Others

HAVE YOU EVER felt like avoiding certain types of Christians? Perhaps you don't like their theology. You may disapprove of their lifestyle. Or you may prefer to avoid people of their race, nationality or economic background. This passage helps us see why such attitudes conflict with the basic message of the gospel.

Warming Up to God We have been justified by faith and are no longer under the law. In this way we have been accepted by God. How does God's acceptance help you feel good about who you are?

Read Galatians 2:11–21.

[11]When Peter came to Antioch, I opposed him
to his face, because he was clearly in the wrong.
[12]Before certain men came from James, he used to
eat with the Gentiles. But when they arrived, he
began to draw back and separate himself from the
Gentiles because he was afraid of those who be-
longed to the circumcision group. [13]The other
Jews joined him in his hypocrisy, so that by their
hypocrisy even Barnabas was led astray.
[14]When I saw that they were not acting in line
with the truth of the gospel, I said to Peter in
front of them all, "You are a Jew, yet you live like
a Gentile and not like a Jew. How is it, then, that
you force Gentiles to follow Jewish customs?
[15]"We who are Jews by birth and not 'Gentile
sinners' [16]know that a man is not justified by ob-
serving the law, but by faith in Jesus Christ. So
we, too, have put our faith in Christ Jesus that we
may be justified by faith in Christ and not by
observing the law, because by observing the law
no one will be justified.
[17]"If, while we seek to be justified in Christ, it
becomes evident that we ourselves are sinners,
does that mean that Christ promotes sin? Abso-
lutely not! [18]If I rebuild what I destroyed, I prove
that I am a lawbreaker. [19]For through the law I
died to the law so that I might live for God. [20]I
have been crucified with Christ and I no longer
live, but Christ lives in me. The life I live in the
body, I live by faith in the Son of God, who loved
me and gave himself for me. [21]I do not set aside
the grace of God, for if righteousness could be
gained through the law, Christ died for noth-
ing!"[f]

[f]21 Some interpreters end the quotation after verse 14.

Discovering the Word 1. How were Peter and the other Jews not "acting in line with the truth of the gospel" (vv. 11–14)? 2. How might their actions have forced "Gentiles to follow Jewish customs" (v. 14)? 3. Why is it wrong to make such customs a basis for fellowship (vv. 15–16)? 4. How does Paul refute the accusation that Christ promotes sin (vv. 17–19)? 5. How has Christ enabled us to die to the law and to live for God (v. 20)?

Applying the Word 1. What nonessential customs do Christians sometimes force on each other? (For example, certain ways of praying, certain dress at worship, certain lifestyle habits and so on.) 2. Which of these are you most likely to be concerned about? 3. How can God's acceptance of you help you to be more accepting of others?

Responding in Prayer Pray for discernment about your own attitudes toward others, asking God to make you more accepting.

4 / *Galatians 3:1–14*
Why God Accepts Us

WE ALL WANT to be accepted. We do everything we can to win people's approval and avoid their rejection. But if we work so hard to please people, then what about God? How can we possibly meet his standards? The Galatians felt these inner struggles. They wanted to be fully accepted by God. But they seemed to forget that God had already accepted them. They also forgot *why*.

Warming Up to God When have you felt unacceptable to God recently? Describe your feelings to God. Listen for his reassurance.

Read Galatians 3:1–14.

---

3 You foolish Galatians! Who has be-
witched you? Before your very eyes Jesus
Christ was clearly portrayed as crucified.
2I would like to learn just one thing from you:
Did you receive the Spirit by observing the law, or
by believing what you heard? 3Are you so foolish?
After beginning with the Spirit, are you now try-
ing to attain your goal by human effort? 4Have
you suffered so much for nothing—if it really was
for nothing? 5Does God give you his Spirit and
work miracles among you because you observe
the law, or because you believe what you heard?
6Consider Abraham: "He believed God, and it
was credited to him as righteousness."[g] 7Under-
stand, then, that those who believe are children of
Abraham. 8The Scripture foresaw that God would
justify the Gentiles by faith, and announced the
gospel in advance to Abraham: "All nations will
be blessed through you."[h] 9So those who have
faith are blessed along with Abraham, the man of
faith.
10All who rely on observing the law are under
a curse, for it is written: "Cursed is everyone who
does not continue to do everything written in the
Book of the Law."[i] 11Clearly no one is justified
before God by the law, because, "The righteous
will live by faith."[j] 12The law is not based on
faith; on the contrary, "The man who does these
things will live by them."[k] 13Christ redeemed us
from the curse of the law by becoming a curse for
us, for it is written: "Cursed is everyone who is
hung on a tree."[l] 14He redeemed us in order that
the blessing given to Abraham might come to the
Gentiles through Christ Jesus, so that by faith we
might receive the promise of the Spirit.

g6 Gen. 15:6 h8 Gen. 12:3; 18:18; 22:18 i10 Deut. 27:26
j11 Hab. 2:4 k12 Lev. 18:5 l13 Deut. 21:23

Discovering the Word 1. From verses 1–5 try to reconstruct in chronological order the Galatians' spiritual biography. 2. In what ways did the Galatians' behavior seem "bewitched" and "foolish" according to verses 1–5? 3. When we follow the example of Abraham's faith, what are the results (vv. 6–9)? 4. How does Abraham's experience contrast with that of the person who seeks to earn God's acceptance (vv. 10–12)? 5. How does the gift of the Spirit affirm that God accepts us completely in Christ?

Applying the Word 1. In what ways do we sometimes try to earn God's favor by what we do? 2. How can a vivid image of Christ's crucifixion (v. 1) guard us from this warped way of thinking? 3. How have you been blessed by the Spirit's presence in your life?

Responding in Prayer Spend some time thanking God for what Christ has done for us as described in these verses.

5 / *Galatians 3:15–29*
Exposing Our Needs

"HONEY," JILL CALLED out, "you'd better call the repairman. Our TV is on the blink again."

"Who needs a repairman!" Ron replied confidently. "I can fix this myself."

Four hours later. "There, that should do it." As he plugs it in, there's a loud buzzing noise, smoke rises from the TV, the lights begin to flicker, then darkness blacks out the room.

"Uh . . . maybe you're right, dear," Ron said sheepishly. "I suppose calling a repairman couldn't hurt."

People must admit they need help before they can receive it. Yet often this is very difficult. In Galatians 3:15–29 Paul tells us how God exposes our need for Christ.

Warming Up to God What needs are pressing on you right now? Give them to God one by one.

Read Galatians 3:15–29.

15Brothers, let me take an example from everyday life. Just as no one can set aside or add to a human covenant that has been duly established, so it is in this case. 16The promises were spoken to Abraham and to his seed. The Scripture does not say "and to seeds," meaning many people, but "and to your seed,"[m] meaning one person, who is Christ. 17What I mean is this: The law, introduced 430 years later, does not set aside the covenant previously established by God and thus do away with the promise. 18For if the inheritance depends on the law, then it no longer depends on a promise; but God in his grace gave it to Abraham through a promise.

19What, then, was the purpose of the law? It was added because of transgressions until the Seed to whom the promise referred had come. The law was put into effect through angels by a mediator. 20A mediator, however, does not represent just one party; but God is one.

21Is the law, therefore, opposed to the promises of God? Absolutely not! For if a law had been given that could impart life, then righteousness would certainly have come by the law. 22But the Scripture declares that the whole world is a prisoner of sin, so that what was promised, being given through faith in Jesus Christ, might be given to those who believe.

23Before this faith came, we were held prisoners by the law, locked up until faith should be revealed. 24So the law was put in charge to lead us to Christ[n] that we might be justified by faith. 25Now that faith has come, we are no longer under the supervision of the law.

26You are all sons of God through faith in Christ Jesus, 27for all of you who were baptized into Christ have clothed yourselves with Christ. 28There is neither Jew nor Greek, slave nor free, male nor female, for you are all one in Christ Jesus. 29If you belong to Christ, then you are Abraham's seed, and heirs according to the promise.

[m] 16 Gen. 12:7; 13:15; 24:7 [n] 24 Or *charge until Christ came*

Discovering the Word 1. Why is the law unable to set aside or add to the promises spoken to Abraham (vv. 15–18)? 2. If the law did not set aside or add to the promises given to Abraham, then why was it given (vv. 19–25)? 3. How does a clear grasp of God's law help us to realize our need for Christ (vv. 22–25)? 4. In verse 28 Paul lists several ways in which people have been categorized. How have these categories sometimes functioned as barriers? 5. In light of the context, how have these barriers been broken down in Christ?

Applying the Word 1. When is it difficult for you to admit to God that you have a need or problem? 2. When is it difficult for you to ask others for help? 3. What would help you allow both God and others to help you?

Responding in Prayer Ask God to help you put aside your pride and expose your needs to him and to your Christian friends and church family.

6 / *Galatians 4:1–20*
The Joys of Growing Up

HAVE YOU EVER longed to be a child again—to be free from work, mortgage payments, bills and taxes? Remember the carefree days, when from morning till night your job was to play? The Galatians did. They longed to return to the spiritual childhood of the law. But aren't we forgetting something? Just think of all the things we *couldn't* do as children. In Galatians 4:1–20 Paul reminds us of the joys of growing up.

Warming Up to God What is frustrating you today? Take time to journal or talk to God about how you are feeling and why. Work at it until your mind is clear and you are ready to study.

Read Galatians 4:1–20.

4 What I am saying is that as long as the
heir is a child, he is no different from a
slave, although he owns the whole estate.
2He is subject to guardians and trustees until the
time set by his father. 3So also, when we were
children, we were in slavery under the basic prin-
ciples of the world. 4But when the time had fully
come, God sent his Son, born of a woman, born
under law, 5to redeem those under law, that we
might receive the full rights of sons. 6Because you
are sons, God sent the Spirit of his Son into our
hearts, the Spirit who calls out, "*Abba*,[o] Father."
7So you are no longer a slave, but a son; and since
you are a son, God has made you also an heir.
8Formerly, when you did not know God, you
were slaves to those who by nature are not gods.
9But now that you know God—or rather are
known by God—how is it that you are turning
back to those weak and miserable principles? Do
you wish to be enslaved by them all over again?
10You are observing special days and months and
seasons and years! 11I fear for you, that somehow
I have wasted my efforts on you.
12I plead with you, brothers, become like me,
for I became like you. You have done me no
wrong. 13As you know, it was because of an ill-
ness that I first preached the gospel to you.
14Even though my illness was a trial to you, you
did not treat me with contempt or scorn. Instead,
you welcomed me as if I were an angel of God, as
if I were Christ Jesus himself. 15What has hap-
pened to all your joy? I can testify that, if you
could have done so, you would have torn out
your eyes and given them to me. 16Have I now
become your enemy by telling you the truth?
17Those people are zealous to win you over, but
for no good. What they want is to alienate you
⌞from us⌟, so that you may be zealous for them.
18It is fine to be zealous, provided the purpose is
good, and to be so always and not just when I am
with you. 19My dear children, for whom I am
again in the pains of childbirth until Christ is
formed in you, 20how I wish I could be with you
now and change my tone, because I am perplexed
about you!

[o]6 Aramaic for *Father*

Discovering the Word 1. How was life under the law like spiritual childhood (vv. 3–7)? 2. Verse 4 states, "When the time had fully come, God sent his Son." How did things change because of his coming (vv. 4–7)? 3. In view of Paul's discussion in verses 1–7, how does the Galatians' behavior seem incredible (vv. 8–11)? 4. How and why had the Galatians' attitude toward Paul changed (vv. 12–20)? 5. What do these verses reveal about Paul's feelings toward the Galatians? 6. How do verses 12–20 illustrate the care and concern we should have for other members of God's family?

Applying the Word 1. In what ways do you sometimes act like a spiritual slave? 2. How can you begin acting more like God's beloved son or daughter?

Responding in Prayer Spend a few minutes of intimate prayer with the Father, thanking him for the privileges of being a member of his family.

7 / *Galatians 4:21—5:1*
Do-It-Yourself Religion

TRUSTING GOD CAN seem risky. What if he lets us down? Still worse, what if our faith is simply foolishness? When such thoughts enter our minds, it's easy to panic. We are tempted to take back what we have entrusted to God. We feel safer taking matters into our own hands. Abraham felt these struggles while waiting for God's promise of a son. He rushed God's plan and had a son through his slave Hagar. Later, even though he and Sarah were very old, the promised son was born. This story has become a timeless illustration of do-it-yourself religion versus trust in the promises of God.

Warming Up to God What promises has God kept with you? Spend time in reflection, thanksgiving and worship.

Read Galatians 4:21—5:1.

21 Tell me, you who want to be under the law,
are you not aware of what the law says? 22 For it
is written that Abraham had two sons, one by the
slave woman and the other by the free woman.
23 His son by the slave woman was born in the
ordinary way; but his son by the free woman was
born as the result of a promise.
24 These things may be taken figuratively, for
the women represent two covenants. One cov-
enant is from Mount Sinai and bears children
who are to be slaves: This is Hagar. 25 Now Hagar
stands for Mount Sinai in Arabia and corresponds
to the present city of Jerusalem, because she is in
slavery with her children. 26 But the Jerusalem
that is above is free, and she is our mother. 27 For
it is written:

"Be glad, O barren woman,
who bears no children;
break forth and cry aloud,
you who have no labor pains;
because more are the children of the desolate
woman
than of her who has a husband."[p]

28 Now you, brothers, like Isaac, are children of
promise. 29 At that time the son born in the ordi-
nary way persecuted the son born by the power of
the Spirit. It is the same now. 30 But what does the
Scripture say? "Get rid of the slave woman and
her son, for the slave woman's son will never
share in the inheritance with the free woman's
son."[q] 31 Therefore, brothers, we are not children
of the slave woman, but of the free woman.

5 It is for freedom that Christ has set us
free. Stand firm, then, and do not let
yourselves be burdened again by a yoke of
slavery.

p27 Isaiah 54:1 q30 Gen. 21:10

Discovering the Word 1. What does Paul mean when he says that the son of the slave woman was born the "ordinary way" but the son of the free woman was "the result of a promise" (v. 23; see also v. 29)? 2. In verse 24 Paul says that the story of Hagar and Sarah may be understood "figuratively." What do Hagar, the covenant from Sinai and "the present city of Jerusalem" have in common (vv. 24–25)? 3. How is Sarah (who, although unnamed, is the other woman in the story) similar to the new covenant and to the Jerusalem that is above (vv. 26–27)? 4. How does Paul describe the ultimate fate of the slave woman's and the free woman's spiritual descendants (v. 30)? 5. In 5:1 Paul states that Christ set us free so that we could experience freedom! Given the thrust of Galatians 1—4, what does Paul mean when he says we are free?

Applying the Word 1. The spiritual principle described in this passage has broad application. Throughout Scripture God promises to accomplish that which we cannot do on our own. Think of Abraham, Moses, Joshua, Gideon, the apostles and others. In what areas are you trusting in the promises of God and the power of the Spirit to accomplish the extraordinary? 2. What are some present-day threats to our spiritual freedom? 3. What are some practical ways we can "stand firm" against them?

Responding in Prayer Ask God to help you stand against any threat to spiritual freedom in society and in your life.

8 / *Galatians 5:2–15*
Heavenly Help

"HELP!" THE MAN cried as he dangled helplessly from the edge of a cliff. "Can anyone up there help me?"

"Yes," answered a heavenly voice, "I'll help you. But first you must let go."

"Let go!" gasped the man. "But then I'd fall!"

"I'll catch you," replied the voice.

There was a long pause, then the man cried out, "Can anyone *else* up there help me?"

If we want Christ to save us, we must let go of the idea that we can save ourselves—even a little.

Warming Up to God In what area of your life are you ignoring the help that God is offering? Humble yourself before the Lord as you give him this area of concern.

Read Galatians 5:2–15.

2Mark my words! I, Paul, tell you that if you let
yourselves be circumcised, Christ will be of no
value to you at all. 3Again I declare to every man
who lets himself be circumcised that he is obli-
gated to obey the whole law. 4You who are trying
to be justified by law have been alienated from
Christ; you have fallen away from grace. 5But by
faith we eagerly await through the Spirit the right-
eousness for which we hope. 6For in Christ Jesus
neither circumcision nor uncircumcision has any
value. The only thing that counts is faith express-
ing itself through love.

7You were running a good race. Who cut in on
you and kept you from obeying the truth? 8That
kind of persuasion does not come from the one
who calls you. 9"A little yeast works through the
whole batch of dough." 10I am confident in the
Lord that you will take no other view. The one
who is throwing you into confusion will pay the
penalty, whoever he may be. 11Brothers, if I am
still preaching circumcision, why am I still being
persecuted? In that case the offense of the cross
has been abolished. 12As for those agitators, I
wish they would go the whole way and emascu-
late themselves!

13You, my brothers, were called to be free. But
do not use your freedom to indulge the sinful
nature[r]; rather, serve one another in love. 14The
entire law is summed up in a single command:
"Love your neighbor as yourself."[s] 15If you keep
on biting and devouring each other, watch out or
you will be destroyed by each other.

[r] 13 Or *the flesh*; also in verses 16, 17, 19 and 24 [s] 14 Lev. 19:18

Discovering the Word 1. What were the Judaizers (those preaching against Paul) urging the Galatians to do and why (vv. 2–4)? 2. In verses 2–4 Paul gave stern warnings to those who desired to be circumcised. Now he says, "neither circumcision nor uncircumcision has any value" (v. 6). How can both of these views be true? 3. Paul compares the Galatians to runners in a race and to a batch of dough (vv. 7–9). How do these comparisons illustrate the nature and perils of the Christian life? 4. In verses 10–12 Paul makes some severe statements about those who are troubling the Galatians (especially v. 12!). Even by today's standards they are harsh. Why was he so upset? 5. What is the difference between the two concepts of freedom described in verses 13–14?

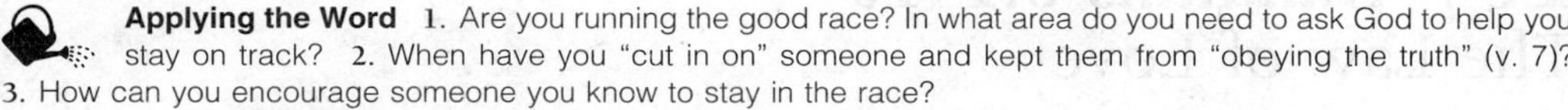

Applying the Word 1. Are you running the good race? In what area do you need to ask God to help you stay on track? 2. When have you "cut in on" someone and kept them from "obeying the truth" (v. 7)? 3. How can you encourage someone you know to stay in the race?

Responding in Prayer Ask God to help you be both a good runner and a good companion in the race.

9 / *Galatians 5:16–26*
Living by the Spirit

IF CHRIST HAS set us free, then why not live as we please? Why not grab all the money, sex and power we can get? Afterward, we can simply ask for forgiveness! Paul challenges this kind of thinking with the true meaning of Christian freedom.

Warming Up to God Spend some time in quiet before the Lord, opening yourself to what he wants to say to you in prayer and through the Scripture.

Read Galatians 5:16–26.

16So I say, live by the Spirit, and you will not
gratify the desires of the sinful nature. 17For the
sinful nature desires what is contrary to the
Spirit, and the Spirit what is contrary to the sinful
nature. They are in conflict with each other, so
that you do not do what you want. 18But if you
are led by the Spirit, you are not under law.
19The acts of the sinful nature are obvious: sex-
ual immorality, impurity and debauchery; 20idola-
try and witchcraft; hatred, discord, jealousy, fits
of rage, selfish ambition, dissensions, factions
21and envy; drunkenness, orgies, and the like. I
warn you, as I did before, that those who live like
this will not inherit the kingdom of God.
22But the fruit of the Spirit is love, joy, peace,
patience, kindness, goodness, faithfulness, 23gen-
tleness and self-control. Against such things there
is no law. 24Those who belong to Christ Jesus
have crucified the sinful nature with its passions
and desires. 25Since we live by the Spirit, let us
keep in step with the Spirit. 26Let us not become
conceited, provoking and envying each other.

Discovering the Word 1. What does it mean to "live by the Spirit" (v. 16)? 2. How is being led by the Spirit different from living under law (v. 18)? 3. Why is it so easy to recognize the acts of the sinful nature (vv. 19–21)? 4. How can Paul's warning in verse 21 be reconciled with his emphasis on justification by faith? 5. Why is *fruit* a good description of the Spirit's work in us (vv. 22–23)?

Applying the Word 1. Paul assumes that even though all Christians live by the Spirit, we do not always keep in step with the Spirit (vv. 25–26). In what ways do you struggle to keep in step with the Spirit? 2. In what ways do you see the Spirit's fruit ripening in your life? 3. What fruit would you like to cultivate more?

Responding in Prayer Spend time thanking God for the Spirit's work in your life. Pray for the Spirit's help in those areas where you feel out of step.

10 / *Galatians 6:1–10*
The Law of Love

THE FRUIT OF the Spirit is most clearly demonstrated in our relationships with others. They are a visible and practical measure of our spirituality. In this passage Paul describes how we should relate to the family of believers and to all people.

Warming Up to God This is a passage about relationships. Who are you having difficulty loving right now? Talk to God about it.

Read Galatians 6:1–10.

6 Brothers, if someone is caught in a sin,
you who are spiritual should restore him
gently. But watch yourself, or you also
may be tempted. 2Carry each other's burdens, and
in this way you will fulfill the law of Christ. 3If
anyone thinks he is something when he is noth-
ing, he deceives himself. 4Each one should test
his own actions. Then he can take pride in him-
self, without comparing himself to somebody
else, 5for each one should carry his own load.
6Anyone who receives instruction in the word
must share all good things with his instructor.
7Do not be deceived: God cannot be mocked. A
man reaps what he sows. 8The one who sows to
please his sinful nature, from that nature[t] will
reap destruction; the one who sows to please the
Spirit, from the Spirit will reap eternal life. 9Let us
not become weary in doing good, for at the
proper time we will reap a harvest if we do not
give up. 10Therefore, as we have opportunity, let
us do good to all people, especially to those who
belong to the family of believers.

[t]8 Or *his flesh, from the flesh*

Discovering the Word 1. What guidelines does Paul offer for dealing with a person who is "caught in a sin," and why is each important (v. 1)? 2. How does the law of Christ (v. 2) differ from the kind of law-keeping urged by Paul's opponents? 3. The sins or burdens of others can lead us to feel superior. How can proper methods of self-examination correct this attitude (vv. 3–5)? 4. What other application of the principle of sowing and reaping does Paul make in verses 9 and 10?

Applying the Word 1. What burdens are people you know carrying? 2. What are some ways you can help a friend carry these? 3. What are one or two new ways you could begin sowing to please the Spirit (a) personally, (b) in relationships with other Christians and (c) in relationships with non-Christians?

Responding in Prayer Ask God to help you "do good to all people," especially to those in the family of God.

11 / *Galatians 6:11–18*
Getting Motivated

PEER PRESSURE CAN exert a powerful influence on us. The style of our clothes, the kind of music we listen to, our vocabulary, even the soft drinks we buy are affected by what others do and say. We are often tempted to change our behavior so others will accept us. But such approval can have a high price tag. In this final passage Paul helps us to consider whose approval we desire most.

Warming Up to God In what areas are you feeling cultural pressure? Consider work, family, Christian and non-Christian friendships, how you dress, what you do or don't buy and so on. Bring each of these pressures to God.

Read Galatians 6:11–18.

11See what large letters I use as I write to you
with my own hand!
12Those who want to make a good impression
outwardly are trying to compel you to be circum-
cised. The only reason they do this is to avoid
being persecuted for the cross of Christ. 13Not
even those who are circumcised obey the law, yet
they want you to be circumcised that they may
boast about your flesh. 14May I never boast except
in the cross of our Lord Jesus Christ, through
which[u] the world has been crucified to me, and
I to the world. 15Neither circumcision nor uncir-
cumcision means anything; what counts is a new
creation. 16Peace and mercy to all who follow this
rule, even to the Israel of God.

[u]14 Or *whom*

17Finally, let no one cause me trouble, for I bear on my body the marks of Jesus.

18The grace of our Lord Jesus Christ be with your spirit, brothers. Amen.

Discovering the Word 1. What do verses 12–13 reveal about the motives of Paul's opponents? 2. How will boasting in the cross affect our desire for the world's approval (v. 14)? 3. Why does the new creation have value in contrast to the worthlessness of circumcision or uncircumcision (v. 15)? 4. In Paul's closing blessing and benediction he mentions peace, mercy and the grace of our Lord Jesus Christ (vv. 16, 18). Why is each of these appropriate for those who follow the "rule" of verses 14–15?

Applying the Word 1. In what situations are you tempted to hide your Christianity in order to "make a good impression outwardly"? 2. Paul bore on his body the marks of Jesus (the evidence of faithful service). What are the "marks of Jesus" in your life? 3. How has this passage helped to purify your motives and goals in life?

Responding in Prayer Ask God to make the "marks of Jesus" more evident in your life.

Ephesians

Let's face it. Most of us are problem centered. How will I get all my work done on time? What can I do to be a better witness? Why do I get angry so easily?

Solving all these problems is good. But so often we lack a broader perspective. We put Band-Aids over gaping wounds instead of looking for long-term solutions. We lack vision, so we fail to ask why we are involved in certain activities at all.

I have enjoyed going back again and again to Paul's letter to the Ephesians because it communicates the Christian vision more powerfully and succinctly than any of his other letters. Most of Paul's other letters are directed to the particular problems of a given church. For example, he wrote to the Galatians about the threat of legalism. He addressed a variety of problems at the church at Corinth. But his letter to the Ephesians is blissfully free from turmoil.

Some believe the letter has this quality because it was not written solely for the church at Ephesus. Rather, it was probably a circular letter sent to the Christian communities of Asia and other provinces, especially where Paul was not personally known. While most of his letters are full of personal greetings, no individuals are mentioned here or greeted by name. In fact some early manuscripts even lack the words "in Ephesus" (1:1). They are addressed generally "to the saints who are also faithful in Christ Jesus." But at an early date the letter became associated with the Ephesian church, so most later manuscripts have "to the saints in Ephesus, the faithful in Christ Jesus."

Ultimately, however, this letter is written to us, whoever the original readers were. It enables us to see the full sweep of God's program from before creation to the ultimate union of everyone and everything in Jesus Christ. It puts our problems and our entire lives in the context of eternity.

May Ephesians expand your vision of what God is doing in history and give you wholeness in this broken world.

Outline

3/ Ephesians 2:1–10 ——— *Amazing Grace*

4/ Ephesians 2:11–22 ——— *We Are One*

5/ Ephesians 3 ——— *Prisoner and Preacher*

6/ Ephesians 4:1–16 ——— *Unity and Uniqueness*

7/ Ephesians 4:17–32 ——— *Something Old, Something New*

8/ Ephesians 5:1–20 ——— *Live in Love, Live in Light*

9/ Ephesians 5:21–33 ——— *Wives and Husbands*

10/ Ephesians 6:1–9 ——— *Children, Parents, Slaves, Masters*

11/ Ephesians 6:10–24 ——— *Prayer Wars*

1 / *Ephesians 1:1–14*
The Purpose of God

WE HAVE A love-hate relationship with God's will. We dearly want to discover it and obey it, to be secure in knowing we are following the path he desires. On the other hand, we definitely don't want to find out what he wants, because deep down we suspect it may not be to our liking. In this study, we'll see what Paul says about God's will.

Warming Up to God Reflect on the ways that God has revealed his will to you over the course of your life. What patterns do you see? Thank God for his guidance.

Read Ephesians 1:1–14.

1 Paul, an apostle of Christ Jesus by the will
of God,
To the saints in Ephesus,[a] the faithful[b] in
Christ Jesus:

2Grace and peace to you from God our Father
and the Lord Jesus Christ.

3Praise be to the God and Father of our Lord
Jesus Christ, who has blessed us in the heavenly
realms with every spiritual blessing in Christ.
4For he chose us in him before the creation of the
world to be holy and blameless in his sight. In
love 5he[c] predestined us to be adopted as his
sons through Jesus Christ, in accordance with his
pleasure and will— 6to the praise of his glorious
grace, which he has freely given us in the One he
loves. 7In him we have redemption through his
blood, the forgiveness of sins, in accordance with
the riches of God's grace 8that he lavished on us
with all wisdom and understanding. 9And he[d]
made known to us the mystery of his will accord-
ing to his good pleasure, which he purposed in
Christ, 10to be put into effect when the times will
have reached their fulfillment—to bring all things
in heaven and on earth together under one head,
even Christ.

11In him we were also chosen,[e] having been
predestined according to the plan of him who
works out everything in conformity with the pur-
pose of his will, 12in order that we, who were the
first to hope in Christ, might be for the praise of
his glory. 13And you also were included in Christ
when you heard the word of truth, the gospel of
your salvation. Having believed, you were marked
in him with a seal, the promised Holy Spirit,
14who is a deposit guaranteeing our inheritance
until the redemption of those who are God's pos-
session—to the praise of his glory.

[a]1 Some early manuscripts do not have *in Ephesus.* [b]1 *Or believers who are* [c]4,5 *Or sight in love.* [5]*He* [d]8,9 *Or us. With all wisdom and understanding,* [9]*he* [e]11 *Or were made heirs*

Discovering the Word 1. According to verses 3–6, what blessings are ours from the Father? 2. What other blessings, according to verses 7–12, do we have in Jesus Christ? 3. From the information given in 1:1–14 alone, try to formulate a clear statement of what it means to be chosen by God. 4. What additional blessings do we receive through the Holy Spirit (vv. 13–14)? 5. What does it mean to live "to the praise of his glory" (vv. 6, 12, 14)?

Applying the Word 1. How do you respond emotionally to knowing you are chosen by God? 2. How has this passage increased your sense of participation in God's total purpose for the universe? 3. How could your life be more in keeping with the phrase "to the praise of his glory"?

Responding in Prayer Spend time in praise to the God and Father of our Lord Jesus Christ who has blessed us with every spiritual blessing.

2 / *Ephesians 1:15–23*
"I Keep Asking"

SOMETIMES PRAYER CAN be like pushing a full wheelbarrow—with no wheel. At other times it's like rushing down the rapids of a mountain river. What makes the difference? In this passage, we'll see why Paul's prayers overflow with praise and thanksgiving.

Warming Up to God Talk to God about the times prayer was hard for you. Describe your disappointment or pain. Take time to allow him to listen to you fully.

Read Ephesians 1:15–23.

15For this reason, ever since I heard about your
faith in the Lord Jesus and your love for all the
saints, 16I have not stopped giving thanks for you,
remembering you in my prayers. 17I keep asking
that the God of our Lord Jesus Christ, the glori-
ous Father, may give you the Spirit[f] of wisdom
and revelation, so that you may know him better.
18I pray also that the eyes of your heart may be
enlightened in order that you may know the hope
to which he has called you, the riches of his glori-
ous inheritance in the saints, 19and his incompa-
rably great power for us who believe. That power
is like the working of his mighty strength,
20which he exerted in Christ when he raised him
from the dead and seated him at his right hand in
the heavenly realms, 21far above all rule and au-
thority, power and dominion, and every title that
can be given, not only in the present age but also
in the one to come. 22And God placed all things
under his feet and appointed him to be head over
everything for the church, 23which is his body,
the fullness of him who fills everything in every
way.

f17 Or a spirit

Discovering the Word 1. How do Paul's prayers for his readers throughout this passage cover the past, the present and the future? 2. How does Paul emphasize the tremendous power available "for us who believe" (v. 19)? 3. How do verses 20–23 expand on Paul's discussion of Christ's headship begun in verses 9–10? 4. How is the church, the body of believers, central to God's plans for the universe (vv. 22–23)?

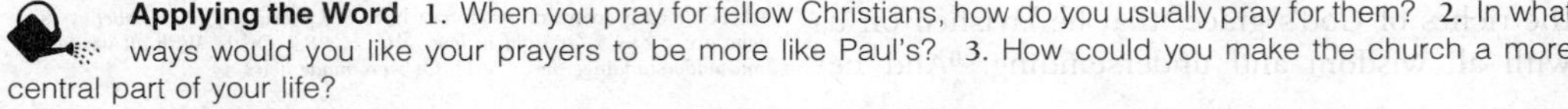

Applying the Word 1. When you pray for fellow Christians, how do you usually pray for them? 2. In what ways would you like your prayers to be more like Paul's? 3. How could you make the church a more central part of your life?

Responding in Prayer Pray for Christ's church and individuals in your church, following Paul's example.

3 / *Ephesians 2:1–10*
Amazing Grace

ONE OF THE best-known verses in the book of Ephesians is 2:8, "By grace you have been saved, through faith." Grace has often been defined by the acrostic God's Riches At Christ's Expense. With this passage, we'll consider some of the riches we have been given in Christ.

Warming Up to God Focus on God's graciousness to you in the past days, weeks and months. Allow yourself to experience the depth of his goodness. Respond to him in prayer and praise.

Read Ephesians 2:1–10.

2 As for you, you were dead in your transgressions and sins, 2in which you used to live when you followed the ways of this world and of the ruler of the kingdom of the air, the spirit who is now at work in those who are disobedient. 3All of us also lived among them at one time, gratifying the cravings of our sinful nature[g] and following its desires and thoughts. Like the rest, we were by nature objects of wrath. 4But because of his great love for us, God, who is rich in mercy, 5made us alive with Christ even when we were dead in transgressions—it is by grace you have been saved. 6And God raised us up with Christ and seated us with him in the heavenly realms in Christ Jesus, 7in order that in the coming ages he might show the incomparable riches of his grace, expressed in his kindness to us in Christ Jesus. 8For it is by grace you have been saved, through faith—and this not from yourselves, it is the gift of God— 9not by works, so that no one can boast. 10For we are God's workmanship, created in Christ Jesus to do good works, which God prepared in advance for us to do.

g3 Or *our flesh*

Discovering the Word 1. In verse 1 Paul says, "You were dead in your transgressions and sins." How does sin kill? 2. In verses 2–3 Paul mentions three negative influences on our lives, which the church later put into the formula of "the world, the flesh and the devil." According to Paul, how did each of these affect our lives as non-Christians? 3. What does Paul mean when he says we have been "made alive," "raised" and "seated" with Christ (vv. 5–6)? 4. When Paul says that our salvation is not from ourselves (vv. 8–9), is he saying that we play no role in our salvation? Explain. 5. What do you learn about God's grace from verses 4–10?

Applying the Word 1. What good works has God prepared you to do? 2. What has hindered you from doing these?

Responding in Prayer Thank God specifically for some of the many ways he has been gracious to you. Ask him to remove the barriers to the good works he has created for you to do.

4 / *Ephesians 2:11–22*
We Are One

MANY OF US have sung, "We are one in the Spirit; we are one in the Lord." But we also continue to find ourselves at odds with Christians who believe or live differently than we do. Such problems were just as common in Paul's day as in ours.

Warming Up to God Consider what groups of Christians you disagree with or have trouble getting along with. Reflect on what causes these tensions. Ask God to open your mind and heart so that you can develop understanding.

Read Ephesians 2:11–22.

11Therefore, remember that formerly you who are Gentiles by birth and called "uncircumcised" by those who call themselves "the circumcision" (that done in the body by the hands of men)— 12remember that at that time you were separate from Christ, excluded from citizenship in Israel and foreigners to the covenants of the promise, without hope and without God in the world. 13But now in Christ Jesus you who once were far away have been brought near through the blood of Christ.

14For he himself is our peace, who has made the two one and has destroyed the barrier, the dividing wall of hostility, 15by abolishing in his flesh the law with its commandments and regulations. His purpose was to create in himself one new man out of the two, thus making peace, 16and in this one body to reconcile both of them

to God through the cross, by which he put to
death their hostility. [17]He came and preached
peace to you who were far away and peace to
those who were near. [18]For through him we both
have access to the Father by one Spirit.

[19]Consequently, you are no longer foreigners
and aliens, but fellow citizens with God's people
and members of God's household, [20]built on the
foundation of the apostles and prophets, with
Christ Jesus himself as the chief cornerstone. [21]In
him the whole building is joined together and
rises to become a holy temple in the Lord. [22]And
in him you too are being built together to become
a dwelling in which God lives by his Spirit.

Discovering the Word 1. Paul uses vivid imagery in this passage. What are some of these images? 2. What divided Gentiles from Jews (vv. 11–13)? 3. How are the two reconciliations Christ achieves related (vv. 14–18)? 4. How do the images Paul uses in verses 19–22 emphasize the unity Christians have with one another?

Applying the Word 1. What kinds of name-calling (perhaps even using biblical terms) do Christians in your church engage in? 2. What rules and requirements would you be inclined to enforce (like the law in verse 15) that might hinder people from coming into the kingdom? 3. What practical first step toward unity with another Christian can you take in the next week?

Responding in Prayer Pray for unity in the church, that people would not be turned away from Christ by Christians who don't get along with each other.

5 / *Ephesians 3*
Prisoner and Preacher

WHAT DO YOU think of when you hear the word *church*? A building on the corner? A stuffy group of religious hypocrites? A vibrant fellowship? Paul's special ministry enables him to enlarge our conception of the church. In this passage he clarifies and exalts its place in God's plan.

Warming Up to God When have you had a particularly powerful experience in the church? It might have been worship, teaching or fellowship. Reflect on what made it special and thank God for it.

Read Ephesians 3.

3 For this reason I, Paul, the prisoner of
Christ Jesus for the sake of you Gen-
tiles—

[2]Surely you have heard about the administra-
tion of God's grace that was given to me for you,
[3]that is, the mystery made known to me by reve-
lation, as I have already written briefly. [4]In read-
ing this, then, you will be able to understand my
insight into the mystery of Christ, [5]which was not
made known to men in other generations as it has
now been revealed by the Spirit to God's holy
apostles and prophets. [6]This mystery is that
through the gospel the Gentiles are heirs together
with Israel, members together of one body, and
sharers together in the promise in Christ Jesus.

[7]I became a servant of this gospel by the gift of
God's grace given me through the working of his
power. [8]Although I am less than the least of all
God's people, this grace was given me: to preach
to the Gentiles the unsearchable riches of Christ,
[9]and to make plain to everyone the administra-
tion of this mystery, which for ages past was kept
hidden in God, who created all things. [10]His in-
tent was that now, through the church, the mani-
fold wisdom of God should be made known to
the rulers and authorities in the heavenly realms,
[11]according to his eternal purpose which he ac-
complished in Christ Jesus our Lord. [12]In him
and through faith in him we may approach God
with freedom and confidence. [13]I ask you, there-
fore, not to be discouraged because of my suffer-
ings for you, which are your glory.

14For this reason I kneel before the Father,
15from whom his whole family[h] in heaven and
on earth derives its name. 16I pray that out of his
glorious riches he may strengthen you with
power through his Spirit in your inner being, 17so
that Christ may dwell in your hearts through
faith. And I pray that you, being rooted and estab-
lished in love, 18may have power, together with
all the saints, to grasp how wide and long and
high and deep is the love of Christ, 19and to know
this love that surpasses knowledge—that you
may be filled to the measure of all the fullness of
God.

20Now to him who is able to do immeasurably
more than all we ask or imagine, according to his
power that is at work within us, 21to him be glory
in the church and in Christ Jesus throughout all
generations, for ever and ever! Amen.

[h]15 Or *whom all fatherhood*

Discovering the Word 1. What gifts of God's grace does Paul say he has received (vv. 2–3, 8)? 2. Explain the meaning of the mystery revealed to Paul (vv. 2–6). 3. How is the mystery connected with the ministry given to him (vv. 7–13)? 4. Three times in verses 14–21 Paul mentions "love" and "power." What do we learn about power and love in these verses? 5. How does the benediction in verses 20–21 tie together the main themes that have run through the first three chapters of Ephesians?

Applying the Word 1. What is your attitude toward the church? 2. What about your attitude matches Paul's? 3. What about your attitude would you like to change?

Responding in Prayer Choose at least one item from Paul's prayer and make it a prayer of your own, for yourself and your church.

6 / *Ephesians 4:1–16*
Unity and Uniqueness

WHILE EPHESIANS 1—3 provides a doctrinal foundation, Ephesians 4—6 shows in practical detail how to give glory to God in the church. Paul now considers the quality of life that is demanded of believers individually and in the fellowship of Christ's church.

Warming Up to God Ephesians 4:2 reads, "Be completely humble and gentle; be patient, bearing with one another in love." Reflect on these words. Measure your recent behavior against them. Talk to God about what you discover.

Read Ephesians 4:1–16.

4 As a prisoner for the Lord, then, I urge
you to live a life worthy of the calling you
have received. 2Be completely humble
and gentle; be patient, bearing with one another
in love. 3Make every effort to keep the unity of
the Spirit through the bond of peace. 4There is
one body and one Spirit—just as you were called
to one hope when you were called— 5one Lord,
one faith, one baptism; 6one God and Father of
all, who is over all and through all and in all.

7But to each one of us grace has been given as
Christ apportioned it. 8This is why it[i] says:

"When he ascended on high,
he led captives in his train
and gave gifts to men."[j]

9(What does "he ascended" mean except that he
also descended to the lower, earthly regions[k]?
10He who descended is the very one who as-
cended higher than all the heavens, in order to fill
the whole universe.) 11It was he who gave some
to be apostles, some to be prophets, some to be
evangelists, and some to be pastors and teachers,
12to prepare God's people for works of service, so
that the body of Christ may be built up 13until we
all reach unity in the faith and in the knowledge

[i]8 Or *God* [j]8 Psalm 68:18 [k]9 Or *the depths of the earth*

of the Son of God and become mature, attaining to the whole measure of the fullness of Christ.

14Then we will no longer be infants, tossed back and forth by the waves, and blown here and there by every wind of teaching and by the cunning and craftiness of men in their deceitful scheming. 15Instead, speaking the truth in love, we will in all things grow up into him who is the Head, that is, Christ. 16From him the whole body, joined and held together by every supporting ligament, grows and builds itself up in love, as each part does its work.

Discovering the Word 1. What are the characteristics of a life that is worthy of our calling (vv. 1–3)? 2. Paul says we have one body, one Spirit, one hope, one Lord, one faith, one baptism, and one God and Father of all. How do these seven "ones" contribute to actually living out true unity? 3. In verses 8–10 Christ is compared to a conquering hero whose victory parade fills "the whole universe," from the highest heaven to the lowest earth. He then generously distributes gifts (the spoils of victory) to his loyal followers. What is the nature and purpose of these gifts (vv. 11–13)? 4. How does spiritual infancy differ from spiritual maturity (vv. 14–16)?

Applying the Word 1. What spiritual gifts do you think you might have? 2. How do they fulfill the purposes described in verses 11–13? 3. In verse 16 Paul says that the body "grows and builds itself up in love, as each part does its work." What steps must you take to more fully work toward this goal?

Responding in Prayer Pray that your spiritual gifts will be used to help others grow in Christ and to build the church.

7 / *Ephesians 4:17–32*
Something Old, Something New

ALREADY AND NOT YET. That's how we experience Christ. Already we have come out of spiritual darkness and into his light. Already we have received his grace and come to know him. But not yet do we live completely the way God wants. We have not yet arrived. Still, Jesus is right beside us on this journey.

Warming Up to God When have you felt that you were lost in the darkness? What brought you into the light? Spend time praising God for his redemption.

Read Ephesians 4:17–32.

17So I tell you this, and insist on it in the Lord, that you must no longer live as the Gentiles do, in the futility of their thinking. 18They are darkened in their understanding and separated from the life of God because of the ignorance that is in them due to the hardening of their hearts. 19Having lost all sensitivity, they have given themselves over to sensuality so as to indulge in every kind of impurity, with a continual lust for more.

20You, however, did not come to know Christ that way. 21Surely you heard of him and were taught in him in accordance with the truth that is in Jesus. 22You were taught, with regard to your former way of life, to put off your old self, which is being corrupted by its deceitful desires; 23to be made new in the attitude of your minds; 24and to put on the new self, created to be like God in true righteousness and holiness.

25Therefore each of you must put off falsehood and speak truthfully to his neighbor, for we are all members of one body. 26"In your anger do not sin"[l]: Do not let the sun go down while you are still angry, 27and do not give the devil a foothold. 28He who has been stealing must steal no longer, but must work, doing something useful with his own hands, that he may have something to share with those in need.

29Do not let any unwholesome talk come out of your mouths, but only what is helpful for building others up according to their needs, that it may benefit those who listen. 30And do not grieve the

[l]26 Psalm 4:4

Holy Spirit of God, with whom you were sealed for the day of redemption. [31]Get rid of all bitterness, rage and anger, brawling and slander, along with every form of malice. [32]Be kind and compassionate to one another, forgiving each other, just as in Christ God forgave you.

Discovering the Word 1. How does Paul contrast the life of the Gentile (unbeliever) with that of a true believer throughout these verses? 2. What are the effects of hard-heartedness (vv. 17–19)? 3. What does it mean to put off the old self (v. 22)? 4. In verses 25–32 what does Paul tell us to put off, what does he say to put on and what reason does he give (or imply) for doing these things?

Applying the Word 1. Which of the commands in verses 25–32 do you have the most difficulty following? Explain. 2. What practical steps could you take this week to improve your relationships with others in this area of difficulty? 3. Which of the commands in verses 25–32 have you seen God strengthen you to obey?

Responding in Prayer Spend time praising God for his work in your life, and pray that he will give you grace in the areas needing improvement.

8 / *Ephesians 5:1–20*
Live in Love, Live in Light

NOT DOING WHAT is wrong is one thing. But sometimes it can be even more difficult to do what is right. In Ephesians 5 Paul continues to outline what it means "to live a life worthy of the calling you have received" (4:1). He does this by considering ways we shouldn't act and ways we should.

Warming Up to God Spend some time singing and making music in your heart to the Lord with "psalms, hymns and spiritual songs" (5:19).

Read Ephesians 5:1–20.

5 Be imitators of God, therefore, as dearly loved children [2]and live a life of love, just as Christ loved us and gave himself up for us as a fragrant offering and sacrifice to God.

[3]But among you there must not be even a hint of sexual immorality, or of any kind of impurity, or of greed, because these are improper for God's holy people. [4]Nor should there be obscenity, foolish talk or coarse joking, which are out of place, but rather thanksgiving. [5]For of this you can be sure: No immoral, impure or greedy person—such a man is an idolater—has any inheritance in the kingdom of Christ and of God.[m] [6]Let no one deceive you with empty words, for because of such things God's wrath comes on those who are disobedient. [7]Therefore do not be partners with them.

[8]For you were once darkness, but now you are light in the Lord. Live as children of light [9](for the fruit of the light consists in all goodness, righteousness and truth) [10]and find out what pleases the Lord. [11]Have nothing to do with the fruitless deeds of darkness, but rather expose them. [12]For it is shameful even to mention what the disobedient do in secret. [13]But everything exposed by the light becomes visible, [14]for it is light that makes everything visible. This is why it is said:

"Wake up, O sleeper,
rise from the dead,
and Christ will shine on you."

[15]Be very careful, then, how you live—not as unwise but as wise, [16]making the most of every opportunity, because the days are evil. [17]Therefore do not be foolish, but understand what the Lord's will is. [18]Do not get drunk on wine, which leads to debauchery. Instead, be filled with the Spirit. [19]Speak to one another with psalms,

m5 Or *kingdom of the Christ and God*

hymns and spiritual songs. Sing and make music
in your heart to the Lord, [20]always giving thanks
to God the Father for everything, in the name of
our Lord Jesus Christ.

Discovering the Word 1. How is Christ the perfect example of what Paul asks of us (v. 2)? 2. How is thanksgiving an appropriate replacement for the behavior Paul condemnns in verses 2–4? 3. Why will immoral, impure or greedy people be unable to inherit the kingdom (vv. 5–7)? 4. In verses 8–14 Paul contrasts light and darkness to say more about holy living. According to these verses, what does it mean to "live as children of light"? 5. Verses 19–20 describe several beneficial results of being filled with the Spirit. In your own words, explain the characteristics of those who are filled with the Spirit.

Applying the Word 1. Look again at verses 1–2. What have you observed about God that you have begun or could begin to imitate? 2. Looking again at verses 3–4, how could you use thanksgiving to replace improper behavior in your life? 3. According to the characteristics in verses 15–17, how could you live more wisely?

Responding in Prayer Talk to God as a child to a father. Tell him how you would like to imitate him.

9 / *Ephesians 5:21–33*
Wives and Husbands

A LOT OF emotion and misunderstanding surrounds the word *submit.* So try to come to this text as if you had never seen it before. Try to set aside your own biases and see what Paul really has to say on the subject of submission.

Warming Up to God How has God shown you that he is faithful and trustworthy? Express your thanksgiving for his care.

Read Ephesians 5:21–33.

[21]Submit to one another out of reverence for
Christ.
[22]Wives, submit to your husbands as to the
Lord. [23]For the husband is the head of the wife as
Christ is the head of the church, his body, of
which he is the Savior. [24]Now as the church sub-
mits to Christ, so also wives should submit to
their husbands in everything.
[25]Husbands, love your wives, just as Christ
loved the church and gave himself up for her [26]to
make her holy, cleansing[n] her by the washing
with water through the word, [27]and to present
her to himself as a radiant church, without stain
or wrinkle or any other blemish, but holy and
blameless. [28]In this same way, husbands ought to
love their wives as their own bodies. He who
loves his wife loves himself. [29]After all, no one
ever hated his own body, but he feeds and cares
for it, just as Christ does the church— [30]for we
are members of his body. [31]"For this reason a
man will leave his father and mother and be
united to his wife, and the two will become one
flesh."[o] [32]This is a profound mystery—but I am
talking about Christ and the church. [33]However,
each one of you also must love his wife as he
loves himself, and the wife must respect her hus-
band.

[n]26 Or *having cleansed* [o]31 Gen. 2:24

Discovering the Word 1. How does verse 21 set the tone for this passage? 2. Why is the church's submission to the Lord a helpful illustration of a wife's submission to her husband (vv. 22–24)? 3. How are husbands to show love for their wives (vv. 25–30)? 4. Why do you think Paul calls on wives to respect their husbands while he calls on husbands to love their wives (v. 33)? 5. How do verses 31–33 summarize his teaching on the unity that is to exist between wives and husbands?

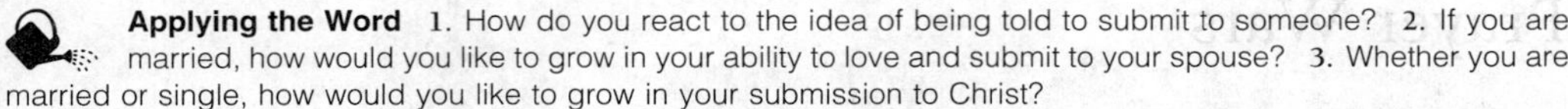

Applying the Word 1. How do you react to the idea of being told to submit to someone? 2. If you are married, how would you like to grow in your ability to love and submit to your spouse? 3. Whether you are married or single, how would you like to grow in your submission to Christ?

Responding in Prayer Tell Christ how you would like to more fully submit your life to him.

10 / *Ephesians 6:1–9*
Children, Parents, Slaves, Masters

HOW MUCH OUR parents mean to us—yet how difficult they can be! How much we love our children—yet how exasperating they are at times! In nine packed verses Paul delves not only into these important relationships but into those of the work world as well.

Warming Up to God Reflect on the finest qualities of your parents (or of parenting in general). Consider which of these qualities you have experienced in your relationship with God and thank him.

Read Ephesians 6:1–9.

6 Children, obey your parents in the Lord,
for this is right. [2]"Honor your father and
mother"—which is the first command-
ment with a promise— [3]"that it may go well with
you and that you may enjoy long life on the
earth."[p]
[4]Fathers, do not exasperate your children; in-
stead, bring them up in the training and instruc-
tion of the Lord.
[5]Slaves, obey your earthly masters with respect
and fear, and with sincerity of heart, just as you
would obey Christ. [6]Obey them not only to win
their favor when their eye is on you, but like
slaves of Christ, doing the will of God from your
heart. [7]Serve wholeheartedly, as if you were serv-
ing the Lord, not men, [8]because you know that
the Lord will reward everyone for whatever good
he does, whether he is slave or free.
[9]And masters, treat your slaves in the same
way. Do not threaten them, since you know that
he who is both their Master and yours is in
heaven, and there is no favoritism with him.

p3 Deut 5:16

Discovering the Word 1. What reasons are given for obeying and honoring parents (vv. 1–3)? 2. Why does Paul contrast making children exasperated with bringing "them up in the training and instruction of the Lord" (v. 4)? 3. What is implied about the way slaves normally worked for their masters (vv. 5–8)? 4. Paul says masters should treat slaves the way slaves should treat masters because both have the same Master in heaven. Why should this make a difference in how slaves are treated? 5. How do verses 1–9 contribute to the theme of the church glorifying God through visible unity?

Applying the Word 1. What are some practical ways you can obey or honor your parents? 2. If you are a parent, what can you do this week to follow verse 4 more closely? (If you are not a parent, how have you seen verse 4 in action?) 3. How could the principles Paul considers in verses 5–9 be lived out in situations you have been in or are in?

Responding in Prayer Pray that in all you do you would serve "wholeheartedly, as if you were serving the Lord."

11 / *Ephesians 6:10–24*
Prayer Wars

IN A WAR of bullets, careful aim and heavy armor win battles. In a war of words, eloquent speech and sharp pens overcome the opposition. But if the fight is outside the realm of sight, sound and touch, how are victories won?

Warming Up to God How have you recently seen God protecting you as you face spiritual battles?

Read Ephesians 6:10–24.

10Finally, be strong in the Lord and in his
mighty power. 11Put on the full armor of God so
that you can take your stand against the devil's
schemes. 12For our struggle is not against flesh
and blood, but against the rulers, against the authorities, against the powers of this dark world
and against the spiritual forces of evil in the heavenly realms. 13Therefore put on the full armor of
God, so that when the day of evil comes, you may
be able to stand your ground, and after you have
done everything, to stand. 14Stand firm then, with
the belt of truth buckled around your waist, with
the breastplate of righteousness in place, 15and
with your feet fitted with the readiness that
comes from the gospel of peace. 16In addition to
all this, take up the shield of faith, with which
you can extinguish all the flaming arrows of the
evil one. 17Take the helmet of salvation and the
sword of the Spirit, which is the word of God.
18And pray in the Spirit on all occasions with all
kinds of prayers and requests. With this in mind,
be alert and always keep on praying for all the
saints.

19Pray also for me, that whenever I open my
mouth, words may be given me so that I will
fearlessly make known the mystery of the gospel,
20for which I am an ambassador in chains. Pray
that I may declare it fearlessly, as I should.

21Tychicus, the dear brother and faithful servant in the Lord, will tell you everything, so that
you also may know how I am and what I am
doing. 22I am sending him to you for this very
purpose, that you may know how we are, and
that he may encourage you.

23Peace to the brothers, and love with faith
from God the Father and the Lord Jesus Christ.
24Grace to all who love our Lord Jesus Christ with
an undying love.

Discovering the Word 1. Four times in verses 10–14 Paul urges his readers to stand firm in the battle against the devil's stratagems. How are we as Christians susceptible to instability? 2. How does the "armor of God" (vv. 13–17) prepare us for spiritual battle? 3. In verses 18–20 Paul urges all kinds of prayers. How has he been a model prayer warrior throughout this letter?

Applying the Word 1. How do you sense a battle around you with more than physical forces and foes? 2. Which piece of armor do you need most to fight your spiritual battles? Explain. 3. What main obstacle do you face in fighting the battle of prayer more effectively?

Responding in Prayer Take time now to pray about your fight in spiritual warfare.

Philippians

"Rejoice in the Lord always," the author of Philippians exhorts us, "I will say it again: Rejoice!" Coming from most people, such words might sound trite and simplistic, but this is the apostle Paul speaking, a man who was not writing from a padded-leather office chair surrounded by books on how to be happy. On the contrary, he was a prisoner awaiting news that could result in his death. It isn't hard to get behind the words of Philippians and see the tension and uncertainty there. Yet through all this we see the example of a man whose life is filled with joy.

As we study Philippians, we discover Paul's secret: that a life lived for the glory of God will overflow with joy. What a message for our hurting world!

Philippi was an important city because it straddled the great east-west highway known as the Egnatian Way. The population of this city was cosmopolitan, being made up of Tracians, Greeks, Romans and a few Jews. In the center of the city was a large forum surrounded by temples, a library, fountains, monuments and public baths.

In 42 B.C. Antony and Octavian defeated Brutus and Cassius near Philippi. In honor of his victory, Antony made Philippi a Roman colony. This provided the Philippians with special rights and privileges as Roman citizens, and they responded with a great deal of pride and loyalty. Women enjoyed a high status in Philippi—taking an active part in both public and business life. Because of this, women also had important responsibilities in the Philippian church.

Paul founded this church sometime around the year A.D. 50, during his second missionary journey (Acts 16:12-40). From the letter to the Philippians we learn that this church was taking its share of suffering (1:29), it was in some danger of division (1:27; 2:2; 4:2), it may have been leaning toward a doctrine of perfectionism (3:12-13), and it was threatened by the teaching of Judaizers—a group which insisted that all Christians adhere to Jewish laws and customs. But despite these problems, Paul's love for this church was obvious. He sincerely rejoiced at the progress they were making.

We know that Paul was writing to the Philippians from prison (1:12-14). Unfortunately, it is not clear which prison he was writing from. If he was writing during his imprisonment in Rome, then the letter can be dated sometime between A.D. 61-63. However, many scholars have pointed out that the conditions which Paul describes seem much harsher than what we know of the Roman imprisonment (Acts 28:16, 30-31). It could be that there was an earlier imprisonment not recorded in Acts. A good case has been made for Ephesus. If this is true, Philippians would have been written about A.D. 54.

Paul had several reasons for writing this letter. He wanted to explain why he was sending a man named Epaphroditus back to Philippi. He also wanted to thank the Philippians for the gift of money they had sent and to reassure his friends of his condition. Also, the news Paul had received concerning the Philippians made him long to encourage and advise a church he loved.

I hope that these quiet times will help you learn and apply Paul's secret to joyful living.

Outline

1 / *Philippians 1:1–11*
A Church Is Born

HAVE ANY OF your good friends ever told you what they appreciate about you? Have you ever listened while others prayed for you? If so, you know what a warm feeling it is to be assured that others care. In Philippians 1:1–11 Paul prays and thanks God for his friends in Philippi. As you read the passage, try to imagine yourself sitting with the Philippian Christians as this letter is read for the first time. You might be meeting in the home of Lydia, a Christian businesswoman. Perhaps you would be seated next to the jailer who heard about Christ while guarding Paul and Silas.

Warming Up to God When has someone encouraged you by praying for you?

Read Philippians 1:1–11.

1 Paul and Timothy, servants of Christ Jesus,

To all the saints in Christ Jesus at Philippi, together with the overseers[a] and deacons:

2Grace and peace to you from God our Father and the Lord Jesus Christ.

3I thank my God every time I remember you.
4In all my prayers for all of you, I always pray
with joy 5because of your partnership in the gos-
pel from the first day until now, 6being confident
of this, that he who began a good work in you will carry it on to completion until the day of Christ Jesus.

7It is right for me to feel this way about all of you, since I have you in my heart; for whether I am in chains or defending and confirming the gospel, all of you share in God's grace with me.
8God can testify how I long for all of you with the affection of Christ Jesus.

9And this is my prayer: that your love may abound more and more in knowledge and depth
of insight, 10so that you may be able to discern what is best and may be pure and blameless until
the day of Christ, 11filled with the fruit of righteousness that comes through Jesus Christ—to the glory and praise of God.

[a]1 Traditionally *bishops*

Discovering the Word 1. What are Paul's feelings toward the Philippians (vv. 3–8)? 2. Why does he feel this way about them? 3. What do verses 3–8 reveal about healthy Christian relationships? 4. What are Paul's prayer requests for the Philippians (vv. 9–11)? 5. Why would each of these qualities be essential to spiritual maturity?

Applying the Word 1. How can your present relationships be strengthened to become more like what is described in verses 3–8? 2. What does Paul's prayer teach about how we should pray for others?

Responding in Prayer Using Paul's prayer as a model, spend a few minutes thanking God and praying for someone you love in Christ.

2 / *Philippians 1:12–30*
A Joyful Imprisonment

IN THIS PASSAGE we discover that Paul is writing to the Philippians from prison. This puts a whole new perspective on the joyful mood of the letter. While Paul is writing, he is experiencing what most of us would describe as awful circumstances. Yet even at a time like this, Paul's first concern is that Christ is praised. This passage can teach us how to honor Christ in a difficult situation.

Warming Up to God What people or things in life bring you the greatest joy?

Read Philippians 1:12–30.

12Now I want you to know, brothers, that what
has happened to me has really served to advance
the gospel. 13As a result, it has become clear
throughout the whole palace guard[b] and to every-
one else that I am in chains for Christ. 14Be-
cause of my chains, most of the brothers in the
Lord have been encouraged to speak the word of
God more courageously and fearlessly.
15It is true that some preach Christ out of envy
and rivalry, but others out of goodwill. 16The lat-
ter do so in love, knowing that I am put here for
the defense of the gospel. 17The former preach
Christ out of selfish ambition, not sincerely, sup-
posing that they can stir up trouble for me while
I am in chains.[c] 18But what does it matter? The
important thing is that in every way, whether
from false motives or true, Christ is preached.
And because of this I rejoice.
Yes, and I will continue to rejoice, 19for I know
that through your prayers and the help given by
the Spirit of Jesus Christ, what has happened to
me will turn out for my deliverance.[d] 20I eagerly
expect and hope that I will in no way be ashamed,
but will have sufficient courage so that now as
always Christ will be exalted in my body, whether
by life or by death. 21For to me, to live is Christ
and to die is gain. 22If I am to go on living in the
body, this will mean fruitful labor for me. Yet
what shall I choose? I do not know! 23I am torn
between the two: I desire to depart and be with
Christ, which is better by far; 24but it is more
necessary for you that I remain in the body.
25Convinced of this, I know that I will remain,
and I will continue with all of you for your prog-
ress and joy in the faith, 26so that through my
being with you again your joy in Christ Jesus will
overflow on account of me.
27Whatever happens, conduct yourselves in a
manner worthy of the gospel of Christ. Then,
whether I come and see you or only hear about
you in my absence, I will know that you stand
firm in one spirit, contending as one man for the
faith of the gospel 28without being frightened in
any way by those who oppose you. This is a sign
to them that they will be destroyed, but that you
will be saved—and that by God. 29For it has been
granted to you on behalf of Christ not only to
believe on him, but also to suffer for him, 30since
you are going through the same struggle you saw
I had, and now hear that I still have.

[b]13 Or *whole palace* [c]16,17 Some late manuscripts have verses 16 and 17 in reverse order. [d]19 Or *salvation*

Discovering the Word 1. What does Paul say has happened as a result of his imprisonment (vv. 12–14)? 2. Compare the motives of the two groups described in verses 15–18. 3. What are Paul's considerations in choosing between life and death (vv. 20–26)? 4. What does it mean to conduct ourselves in a manner worthy of the gospel (vv. 27–30)?

Applying the Word 1. To what extent have you adopted Paul's attitude toward life and death? 2. What are the most difficult circumstances you are presently facing? 3. How can Christ be exalted in that situation?

Responding in Prayer Pray that you would learn to experience the joy that can emerge amidst sorrow.

3 / *Philippians 2:1–18*
The Path of Humility

IS IT POSSIBLE to have a good self-image and still be humble? Can a person want to be the best without being conceited? In Philippians 2:1–18 Paul directs us to Jesus Christ, a person equal with God yet whose incarnation and life are the supreme example of humility. This passage urges us to imitate Christ's attitude.

Warming Up to God What is the difference between humility and a poor self-image?

Read Philippians 2:1–18.

2 If you have any encouragement from be-
ing united with Christ, if any comfort
from his love, if any fellowship with the
Spirit, if any tenderness and compassion, 2then
make my joy complete by being like-minded,
having the same love, being one in spirit and pur-
pose. 3Do nothing out of selfish ambition or vain
conceit, but in humility consider others better
than yourselves. 4Each of you should look not
only to your own interests, but also to the inter-
ests of others.

5Your attitude should be the same as that of
Christ Jesus:

6Who, being in very nature[e] God,
did not consider equality with God
something to be grasped,
7but made himself nothing,
taking the very nature[f] of a servant,
being made in human likeness.
8And being found in appearance as a man,
he humbled himself
and became obedient to death—
even death on a cross!
9Therefore God exalted him to the highest
place
and gave him the name that is above every
name,
10that at the name of Jesus every knee should
bow,
in heaven and on earth and under the
earth,
11and every tongue confess that Jesus Christ is
Lord,
to the glory of God the Father.

12Therefore, my dear friends, as you have al-
ways obeyed—not only in my presence, but now
much more in my absence—continue to work
out your salvation with fear and trembling, 13for
it is God who works in you to will and to act
according to his good purpose.

14Do everything without complaining or argu-
ing, 15so that you may become blameless and
pure, children of God without fault in a crooked
and depraved generation, in which you shine like
stars in the universe 16as you hold out[g] the word
of life—in order that I may boast on the day of
Christ that I did not run or labor for nothing.
17But even if I am being poured out like a drink
offering on the sacrifice and service coming from
your faith, I am glad and rejoice with all of you.
18So you too should be glad and rejoice with me.

[e]6 Or *in the form of* [f]7 Or *the form* [g]16 Or *hold on to*

Discovering the Word 1. How can our experience of Christ and his Spirit (v. 1) help us to achieve the unity Paul desires in verse 2? 2. How do verses 3–4 help us to understand the nature of humility? 3. How did each of Christ's actions illustrate humility and a concern for the interests of others (vv. 6–8)? 4. In your own words, describe God's response to Jesus' humility (vv. 9–11). 5. In verses 12–13 Paul says you are to "work out your salvation" because God "works in you." How are these ideas related?

Applying the Word 1. Who might you be tempted to impress during the next few days? 2. What act of humble service could you do for this person instead?

Responding in Prayer Pray for the opportunity to serve others as Christ has served you.

4 / *Philippians 2:19–30*
Servants of Christ

WHEN THE PHILIPPIANS heard that Paul was in prison, they sent one of their members—a man named Epaphroditus—to Paul with a gift of money. It was his job to help Paul in any way necessary. Epaphroditus returned home carrying the letter to the Philippians.

In this section of the letter, Paul outlines his future plans and explains why he is sending Epaphroditus back. The passage gives several beautiful examples of Christian service as displayed in the lives of Timothy, Epaphroditus, Paul and the Philippians.

Warming Up to God What do you enjoy most and least about serving others?

Read Philippians 2:19–30.

[19]I hope in the Lord Jesus to send Timothy to
you soon, that I also may be cheered when I re-
ceive news about you. [20]I have no one else like
him, who takes a genuine interest in your welfare.
[21]For everyone looks out for his own interests,
not those of Jesus Christ. [22]But you know that
Timothy has proved himself, because as a son
with his father he has served with me in the work
of the gospel. [23]I hope, therefore, to send him as
soon as I see how things go with me. [24]And I am
confident in the Lord that I myself will come
soon.
[25]But I think it is necessary to send back to you
Epaphroditus, my brother, fellow worker and fel-
low soldier, who is also your messenger, whom
you sent to take care of my needs. [26]For he longs
for all of you and is distressed because you heard
he was ill. [27]Indeed he was ill, and almost died.
But God had mercy on him, and not on him only
but also on me, to spare me sorrow upon sorrow.
[28]Therefore I am all the more eager to send him,
so that when you see him again you may be glad
and I may have less anxiety. [29]Welcome him in
the Lord with great joy, and honor men like him,
[30]because he almost died for the work of Christ,
risking his life to make up for the help you could
not give me.

Discovering the Word 1. Imagine that Timothy is being sent to visit your church or fellowship group. What might he do to help you? 2. Why is Paul sending Epaphroditus back to Philippi (vv. 25–28)? 3. How is Christ's attitude evident in the relationships among Paul, Epaphroditus and the Philippians (vv. 25–30)? 4. Why is it important to honor people like Epaphroditus, especially in light of Christ's exaltation (2:9–11)?

Applying the Word 1. Examine your plans and goals during the coming week. How can you bring your own interests into closer harmony with those of Jesus Christ? 2. What are some practical ways you can serve those around you during the coming week?

Responding in Prayer Pray that Christ will continue to give you the heart of a servant.

5 / *Philippians 3*
Rejoice in the Lord

HAVE YOU EVER become excited about an idea only to be deflated by the realities of making it work? Sometimes trying to live a Christian life is like that. We start off very excited about knowing the Lord, but it isn't long before the pressure of keeping "all the right rules" drains us of our joy. Unfortunately, we can then swing too far in the other direction and decide, "I'm not going to be concerned about Christian conduct. If Jesus has saved me, then it doesn't matter how I live." This attitude will destroy our joy as quickly as the first. So what is the solution? Paul tells us in this passage.

Warming Up to God What are some of your most important goals in life?

Read Philippians 3.

3 Finally, my brothers, rejoice in the Lord!
It is no trouble for me to write the same
things to you again, and it is a safeguard
for you.
2Watch out for those dogs, those men who do
evil, those mutilators of the flesh. 3For it is we
who are the circumcision, we who worship by the
Spirit of God, who glory in Christ Jesus, and who
put no confidence in the flesh— 4though I myself
have reasons for such confidence.
If anyone else thinks he has reasons to put con-
fidence in the flesh, I have more: 5circumcised on
the eighth day, of the people of Israel, of the tribe
of Benjamin, a Hebrew of Hebrews; in regard to
the law, a Pharisee; 6as for zeal, persecuting the
church; as for legalistic righteousness, faultless.
7But whatever was to my profit I now consider
loss for the sake of Christ. 8What is more, I con-
sider everything a loss compared to the surpass-
ing greatness of knowing Christ Jesus my Lord,
for whose sake I have lost all things. I consider
them rubbish, that I may gain Christ 9and be
found in him, not having a righteousness of my
own that comes from the law, but that which is
through faith in Christ—the righteousness that
comes from God and is by faith. 10I want to know
Christ and the power of his resurrection and
the fellowship of sharing in his sufferings,
becoming like him in his death, 11and so, some-
how, to attain to the resurrection from the
dead.
12Not that I have already obtained all this, or
have already been made perfect, but I press on to
take hold of that for which Christ Jesus took hold
of me. 13Brothers, I do not consider myself yet to
have taken hold of it. But one thing I do: Forget-
ting what is behind and straining toward what is
ahead, 14I press on toward the goal to win the
prize for which God has called me heavenward in
Christ Jesus.
15All of us who are mature should take such a
view of things. And if on some point you think
differently, that too God will make clear to you.
16Only let us live up to what we have already
attained.
17Join with others in following my example,
brothers, and take note of those who live accord-
ing to the pattern we gave you. 18For, as I have
often told you before and now say again even
with tears, many live as enemies of the cross of
Christ. 19Their destiny is destruction, their god is
their stomach, and their glory is in their shame.
Their mind is on earthly things. 20But our citizen-
ship is in heaven. And we eagerly await a Savior
from there, the Lord Jesus Christ, 21who, by the
power that enables him to bring everything under
his control, will transform our lowly bodies so
that they will be like his glorious body.

Discovering the Word 1. How does rejoicing in the Lord (v. 1) differ from other reasons for joy? 2. Why were the people Paul warns against in verses 2–3 so dangerous? 3. Contrast Paul the Pharisee (vv. 4–6) with Paul the Christian (vv. 7–11). How have his reasons for confidence changed? 4. In verses 12–14 Paul compares himself to an athlete who is running a race. Why is this such an appropriate description of the Christian life? 5. In verses 17–21 Paul contrasts Christians with "enemies of the cross." What are the concerns and destiny of each group?

Applying the Word 1. Have you ever placed your confidence in something, thinking it would bring you closer to God, that you now consider to be rubbish? Explain. 2. In verse 6 Paul speaks of "legalistic righteousness." What legalisms are today's Christians pressured to keep? 3. How do these legalisms get in the way of knowing Christ and rejoicing in the Lord?

Responding in Prayer Reflect on Paul's words "We eagerly await . . . the Lord Jesus Christ." Worship Christ with your anticipation of his return.

6 / *Philippians 4:1–9*
Stand Firm in the Lord

TAKE A MOMENT to think of the people you care about most. What is your greatest desire for these people? As Paul thinks of the Philippians, his greatest desire is that they will stand firm in what they have been taught. But he is also aware of some problems which may cause their faith to weaken. He writes to warn them that in order to stand firm they must put an end to disagreements, rejoice always and fill their thoughts with good things.

Warming Up to God Do you find your stand in the Lord to be firmer or weaker than it was a year ago? What has made the difference?

Read Philippians 4:1–9.

4 Therefore, my brothers, you whom I love
and long for, my joy and crown, that is
how you should stand firm in the Lord,
dear friends!
[2]I plead with Euodia and I plead with Syntyche
to agree with each other in the Lord. [3]Yes, and I
ask you, loyal yokefellow,[h] help these women
who have contended at my side in the cause of
the gospel, along with Clement and the rest of my
fellow workers, whose names are in the book of
life.
[4]Rejoice in the Lord always. I will say it again:
Rejoice! [5]Let your gentleness be evident to all.
The Lord is near. [6]Do not be anxious about any-
thing, but in everything, by prayer and petition,
with thanksgiving, present your requests to God.
[7]And the peace of God, which transcends all un-
derstanding, will guard your hearts and your
minds in Christ Jesus.
[8]Finally, brothers, whatever is true, whatever is
noble, whatever is right, whatever is pure, what-
ever is lovely, whatever is admirable—if anything
is excellent or praiseworthy—think about such
things. [9]Whatever you have learned or received or
heard from me, or seen in me—put it into prac-
tice. And the God of peace will be with you.

[h]3 Or *loyal Syzygus*

Discovering the Word 1. Paul opens this chapter with the statement "that is how you should stand firm in the Lord." Look back at 3:12–21. How are we to stand firm in the Lord? 2. In verse 2 Paul pleads with Euodia and Syntyche "to agree with each other in the Lord." Why do you think he is so concerned about their relationship? 3. How can each of the promises and commands listed in verses 4–7 help you to be joyful, peaceful and free from anxiety? 4. How can improper thoughts rob us of the peace God desires for us? 5. How can true, noble, right, pure, lovely, admirable, excellent or praiseworthy thoughts help to cleanse our minds and restore our tranquility (v. 8)?

Applying the Word 1. What should be your response to disagreements within your church or fellowship group? 2. In verse 9 Paul tells us that the God of peace will be with us as we practice what we have learned. What have you learned in this passage that you need to put into practice?

Responding in Prayer Ask God to show you the thoughts and attitudes which are robbing you of joy and weakening your faith.

7 / *Philippians 4:10–23*
Paul's Thank-You Note

WE'VE ALL WRITTEN thank-you notes for gifts received for a birthday or for Christmas. Such notes usually include rather conventional phrases about the thankfulness of the recipient and the thoughtfulness of the giver. In Philippians 4 Paul thanks the Philippians for a gift of money they sent. However, it is a most unusual thank-you note. First he breaks the conventional rules by waiting until the very end of the letter to say thank you. Then he writes as though he didn't really need the gift!

Warming Up to God Have you thanked God for his many gifts to you lately? Take time to do so before you begin.

Read Philippians 4:10–23.

10I rejoice greatly in the Lord that at last you
have renewed your concern for me. Indeed, you
have been concerned, but you had no opportu-
nity to show it. 11I am not saying this because I
am in need, for I have learned to be content what-
ever the circumstances. 12I know what it is to be
in need, and I know what it is to have plenty. I
have learned the secret of being content in any
and every situation, whether well fed or hungry,
whether living in plenty or in want. 13I can do
everything through him who gives me strength.
14Yet it was good of you to share in my trou-
bles. 15Moreover, as you Philippians know, in the
early days of your acquaintance with the gospel,
when I set out from Macedonia, not one church
shared with me in the matter of giving and receiv-
ing, except you only; 16for even when I was in
Thessalonica, you sent me aid again and again
when I was in need. 17Not that I am looking for a
gift, but I am looking for what may be credited to
your account. 18I have received full payment and
even more; I am amply supplied, now that I have
received from Epaphroditus the gifts you sent.
They are a fragrant offering, an acceptable sacri-
fice, pleasing to God. 19And my God will meet all
your needs according to his glorious riches in
Christ Jesus.
20To our God and Father be glory for ever and
ever. Amen.

21Greet all the saints in Christ Jesus. The broth-
ers who are with me send greetings. 22All the
saints send you greetings, especially those who
belong to Caesar's household.
23The grace of the Lord Jesus Christ be with
your spirit. Amen.[i]

[i]23 Some manuscripts do not have *Amen.*

Discovering the Word 1. Paul thanks the Philippians not for the money but for the concern they have shown (v. 10). Why would this have been more important to Paul? 2. Many people believe they can only be content once they have reached a certain level of economic prosperity. How does their view differ from Paul's secret of contentment (vv. 11–13)? 3. How had the Philippians helped Paul both in the past and the present (vv. 14–18)? 4. What benefits does Paul expect the Philippians to receive from their giving (vv. 17–19)?

Applying the Word 1. Many people complain that missionaries are always asking for money. How does this passage provide a model for both missionaries and those who support them? 2. How will this passage affect your giving?

Responding in Prayer Pray for Christian workers you know, that they would have the emotional and financial support they need.

Colossians

"More! More!" urged our son John when I laid down the spoon after feeding him.
"Again! Again!" pleaded our daughter Sara as I turned the last page in the book I was reading to her.

Their cries for more pudding or stories are echoed in our culture's search for more—more power, more money, more knowledge, more gadgets, more furniture, more clothes—more everything!

Books on self-improvement and success flood the market. Gurus gain eager followers by offering enlightenment, power and secret wisdom. Millions read horoscopes every day.

We cry for "more" not only in our society but also in the church. If only we had more wisdom, more maturity, more power, more faith. To fill these needs we attend seminars, go to concerts, hear celebrity speakers and read their latest books.

Colossians was written to Christians with similar longings. They didn't know who and what they already had. False teachers urged them to add rules, ascetic practices and new philosophies to their Christian faith. Then they would have fullness of life. Paul writes to satisfy their desire for more by showing that they already had fullness in Christ.

Paul never traveled to Colossae, a city in the Lycus River valley about a hundred miles east of Ephesus and twelve miles from Laodicea. But somehow he met Epaphras, the man who had taken the gospel to Colossae, and Philemon, the host for the local house church. While in prison in Rome, Paul learned from Epaphras about the Colossian church and the pressures threatening their peace and stability.

These "faithful brothers" had not turned away from faith in Christ. Paul's warm, friendly letter affirms their positive qualities and the changes in their lives. But he warns them against being deceived by "fine-sounding arguments" (2:4) or being captured by "hollow and deceptive philosophy, which depends on human tradition and on the basic principles of this world rather than on Christ" (2:8).

The temptation to add ascetic practices, regulations or "superior knowledge" threatened their dependence on Christ alone for the fullness of life they wanted. The early Gnostics boasted about a spiritual "fullness" not previously experienced. They promised to complete and perfect the simple and elementary faith introduced by Paul and Epaphras. They emphasized a deeper knowledge of God, reserved for a special few, and an experience of greater power.

Colossians is Paul's strongest declaration of the uniqueness and sufficiency of Christ, his full authority over all powers, and the fullness of life he gives. Paul spells out the implications of this fullness of life again and again in the letter.

Like the Colossians, we are bombarded by longings for something more. But Paul thunders in Colossians, You already have fullness in Christ. Enjoy it! "For in Christ all the fullness of the Deity lives in bodily form, and you have been given fullness in Christ" (2:9–10). The purpose of these quiet times is to help you discover the scope, reality and implications of the fullness of life you have in Christ. Paul's letter to Philemon gives principles for mending broken relationships that apply to us as well.

Outline

1 / *Colossians 1:1–14*
Thanks and Prayer

"GOD BLESS JENNIFER today" may be a typical prayer for a friend as she comes to mind. But what am I specifically asking for? How will I know if my prayer is answered? What difference would it make in Jennifer's life? Paul begins his letter by telling the Colossians why he is thankful for them and what he asks God to do in them. Paul's example gives us a model for encouraging and praying for one another.

Warming Up to God How does it make you feel when a friend tells you the specific things he or she notices and appreciates about you?

Read Colossians 1:1–14.

1 Paul, an apostle of Christ Jesus by the will
of God, and Timothy our brother,

2 To the holy and faithful[a] brothers in Christ at
Colosse:

Grace and peace to you from God our Father.[b]

3 We always thank God, the Father of our Lord
Jesus Christ, when we pray for you, 4 because we
have heard of your faith in Christ Jesus and of the
love you have for all the saints— 5 the faith and
love that spring from the hope that is stored up
for you in heaven and that you have already heard
about in the word of truth, the gospel 6 that has
come to you. All over the world this gospel is
bearing fruit and growing, just as it has been do-
ing among you since the day you heard it and
understood God's grace in all its truth. 7 You
learned it from Epaphras, our dear fellow servant,
who is a faithful minister of Christ on our[c] be-
half, 8 and who also told us of your love in the
Spirit.

9 For this reason, since the day we heard about
you, we have not stopped praying for you and
asking God to fill you with the knowledge of his
will through all spiritual wisdom and understand-
ing. 10 And we pray this in order that you may live
a life worthy of the Lord and may please him in
every way: bearing fruit in every good work,
growing in the knowledge of God, 11 being
strengthened with all power according to his glo-
rious might so that you may have great endurance
and patience, and joyfully 12 giving thanks to the
Father, who has qualified you[d] to share in the
inheritance of the saints in the kingdom of light.
13 For he has rescued us from the dominion of
darkness and brought us into the kingdom of the
Son he loves, 14 in whom we have redemption,[e]
the forgiveness of sins.

[a] 2 Or *believing* [b] 2 Some manuscripts *Father and the Lord Jesus Christ* [c] 7 Some manuscripts *your* [d] 12 Some manuscripts *us* [e] 14 A few late manuscripts *redemption through his blood*

Discovering the Word 1. What characteristics of the Colossians cause Paul to always be thankful for them (vv. 3–6)? 2. What impresses you about how the gospel was spreading (vv. 5–8)? 3. After affirming their strengths, Paul tells the Colossians what he prays for them. What are Paul's requests for how they think and act? 4. How might spiritual wisdom and understanding help us to understand God's will (v. 9)? 5. According to Paul, true knowledge leads to a "life worthy of the Lord" (v. 10). What qualities does such a life include (vv. 10–12)? How are these qualities related to each other?

Applying the Word 1. In what specific ways do you see the qualities in verses 10–12 developing in your life? 2. Reread verses 12–14, putting your name in each sentence. How would meditating on these verses help you to appreciate what God has done for you?

Responding in Prayer Take time to pray for your church or fellowship group, using verses 9–14 as your model.

2 / *Colossians 1:15–23*
Jesus Is Supreme

WE FREQUENTLY HEAR: "All roads lead to God. Everyone is trying to get to the same place. That belief is fine for you, but I don't buy it for myself. Only bigots and fanatics label belief *true* or *false*."

The Colossians heard, "Worship Jesus, but not exclusively. Jesus is just one spirit among many to be worshiped." In this passage we'll study Paul's adamant declaration of Christ's supremacy over every being and idea which invites our attention.

Warming Up to God What problems have you encountered in helping someone understand why Jesus is the only way to God?

Read Colossians 1:15–23.

[15]He is the image of the invisible God, the first-
born over all creation. [16]For by him all things
were created: things in heaven and on earth,
visible and invisible, whether thrones or pow-
ers or rulers or authorities; all things were
created by him and for him. [17]He is before all
things, and in him all things hold together.
[18]And he is the head of the body, the church; he
is the beginning and the firstborn from among
the dead, so that in everything he might
have the supremacy. [19]For God was pleased
to have all his fullness dwell in him, [20]and
through him to reconcile to himself all things,
whether things on earth or things in heaven,
by making peace through his blood, shed on the
cross.
[21]Once you were alienated from God and were
enemies in your minds because of[f] your evil be-
havior. [22]But now he has reconciled you by
Christ's physical body through death to present
you holy in his sight, without blemish and free
from accusation— [23] if you continue in your faith,
established and firm, not moved from the hope
held out in the gospel. This is the gospel that you
heard and that has been proclaimed to every crea-
ture under heaven, and of which I, Paul, have
become a servant.

f21 *Or minds, as shown by*

Discovering the Word 1. Make as many statements as you can about why Jesus is supreme (vv. 15–18). Begin each with "Christ is . . ." 2. What does it mean that Christ is the "head of the body, the church" (v. 18)? 3. What actions was God pleased to take to reconcile us to himself (vv. 19–22)? 4. How does understanding God's actions help you explain why Jesus is the only way to God?

Applying the Word 1. How do the words *reconciled, holy in his sight, without blemish* and *free from accusation* (vv. 22–23) motivate you to continue firm in your faith in Christ? 2. How might those words appeal to unspoken needs of the friends you want to introduce to Jesus? 3. How did some recent choice you made about your time or money reflect Christ's supreme place in your life?

Responding in Prayer Spend some time worshiping Jesus Christ for who he is and what he has done for you and your friends who don't yet know him.

3 / *Colossians 1:24—2:5*
Struggles for Maturity

FOR A WHOLE year a young man lived in isolation on a remote Arctic mountain. He risked his life on the flight in and on trails over thin ice (which gave way when he struggled under a heavy backpack). He shared his cold tent with mice and mosquitoes. He experimented with a diet of boiled, fried or charred mice. Why would anyone willingly subject himself to such hardships? Farley Mowat had a goal. He wanted to learn the relationship between wolves and the diminishing caribou herds. In this study Paul describes his compelling goal, his struggles and his resources to reach it.

Warming Up to God Recall a time when a goal was compelling enough to cause you to suffer for it. What helped you to keep going?

Read Colossians 1:24—2:5.

24Now I rejoice in what was suffered for you,
and I fill up in my flesh what is still lacking in
regard to Christ's afflictions, for the sake of his
body, which is the church. 25I have become its
servant by the commission God gave me to
present to you the word of God in its fullness—
26the mystery that has been kept hidden for ages
and generations, but is now disclosed to the
saints. 27To them God has chosen to make known
among the Gentiles the glorious riches of this
mystery, which is Christ in you, the hope of
glory.
28We proclaim him, admonishing and teaching
everyone with all wisdom, so that we may present
everyone perfect in Christ. 29To this end I labor,
struggling with all his energy, which so power-
fully works in me.

2 I want you to know how much I am
struggling for you and for those at Laodi-
cea, and for all who have not met me per-
sonally. 2My purpose is that they may be encour-
aged in heart and united in love, so that they may
have the full riches of complete understanding, in
order that they may know the mystery of God,
namely, Christ, 3in whom are hidden all the trea-
sures of wisdom and knowledge. 4I tell you this
so that no one may deceive you by fine-sounding
arguments. 5For though I am absent from you in
body, I am present with you in spirit and delight
to see how orderly you are and how firm your
faith in Christ is.

Discovering the Word 1. How does Paul define God's commission to him (1:24–29)? 2. In the New Testament the term *mystery* refers not to something mysterious but to something previously hidden which God now wishes to make clear. What is the mystery that represents the "word of God in its fullness" (1:26–27; 2:2–3)? 3. According to Paul, what are the marks of Christian maturity (2:2–5)? 5. The Gnostics taught that their secret knowledge was the key to salvation. How would Paul's description of Christ (2:3–4) protect the Colossians from the "fine-sounding arguments" of the Gnostics?

Applying the Word 1. What "fine-sounding arguments" today lure us away from Christ and hinder our spiritual maturity? 2. What can you do to refocus your attention on Christ and on his goals for you?

Responding in Prayer Thank God for the people who labored to help you mature in Christ. Pray for friends who need to be encouraged in heart and united in love. Ask God to increase your awareness of the wisdom and knowledge in Jesus Christ.

4 / *Colossians 2:6–23*
No Additions Needed

KIM YENG AND his family celebrated the day they became American citizens. Now they were no longer refugees but free citizens with full privileges and endless opportunities. But soon the neighbors began to question Kim. "Why are you making your kids superpatriots? They don't have to wear flags on their shirts every day." "Why did you spend all that money installing a tall flagpole in your yard?" "Don't you know that making your family eat hamburgers instead of eggrolls doesn't make you a better citizen?" In this study Paul questions the Colossians about the foolish human additions they are trying to add to all they have in Christ.

Warming Up to God How would you finish the following sentence? "I would feel fulfilled if . . ."

Read Colossians 2:6–23.

[6]So then, just as you received Christ Jesus as Lord, continue to live in him, [7]rooted and built up in him, strengthened in the faith as you were taught, and overflowing with thankfulness.

[8]See to it that no one takes you captive through hollow and deceptive philosophy, which depends on human tradition and the basic principles of this world rather than on Christ.

[9]For in Christ all the fullness of the Deity lives in bodily form, [10]and you have been given fullness in Christ, who is the head over every power and authority. [11]In him you were also circumcised, in the putting off of the sinful nature,[g] not with a circumcision done by the hands of men but with the circumcision done by Christ, [12]having been buried with him in baptism and raised with him through your faith in the power of God, who raised him from the dead.

[13]When you were dead in your sins and in the uncircumcision of your sinful nature,[h] God made you[i] alive with Christ. He forgave us all our sins, [14]having canceled the written code, with its regulations, that was against us and that stood opposed to us; he took it away, nailing it to the cross. [15]And having disarmed the powers and authorities, he made a public spectacle of them, triumphing over them by the cross.[j]

[16]Therefore do not let anyone judge you by what you eat or drink, or with regard to a religious festival, a New Moon celebration or a Sabbath day. [17]These are a shadow of the things that were to come; the reality, however, is found in Christ. [18]Do not let anyone who delights in false humility and the worship of angels disqualify you for the prize. Such a person goes into great detail about what he has seen, and his unspiritual mind puffs him up with idle notions. [19]He has lost connection with the Head, from whom the whole body, supported and held together by its ligaments and sinews, grows as God causes it to grow.

[20]Since you died with Christ to the basic principles of this world, why, as though you still belonged to it, do you submit to its rules: [21]"Do not handle! Do not taste! Do not touch!"? [22]These are all destined to perish with use, because they are based on human commands and teachings. [23]Such regulations indeed have an appearance of wisdom, with their self-imposed worship, their false humility and their harsh treatment of the body, but they lack any value in restraining sensual indulgence.

g11 Or *the flesh* h13 Or *your flesh* i13 Some manuscripts *us* j15 Or *them in him*

Discovering the Word 1. How do each of the images *rooted, built up, strengthened* and *overflowing* (v. 7) help us understand how we should continue to live in Christ? 2. In verse 8 we get the first real glimpse of the heresy being taught to the Colossians. What do we learn about it? 3. How would Paul's two statements about fullness in Christ (vv. 9–10) protect the Colossians from those deceptive ideas? 4. In verses 11–15 Paul describes some of what "fullness in Christ" includes. Which of our basic needs did Jesus' death, burial and resurrection meet? 5. What "shadows" were the Colossians adding to the "reality" they had found in Christ (vv. 16–17, 20–23)?

Applying the Word 1. Silently reread verses 9–15, inserting your name every time Paul says *you* or *us*. How do these facts affect your view of yourself? 2. What "shadows" are we tempted to add today?

Responding in Prayer Consider the fact that we are made complete in Christ. Allow your prayer and praise to arise out of that fact.

5 / *Colossians 3:1–11*
New Life, New Lifestyle (Part 1)

HAVE YOU SEEN pictures of marathon runners? Concentration and determination seem to ooze from every pore. These people set their hearts and minds on one thing—finish this race. They focus on the next step, the next checkpoint, until the race is complete. They shed pounds, unnecessary clothing or anything else that might slow them down. Attach their official number and they are ready to run.

As Christians, we are to live like marathon runners. We are to take off anything that slows us down and set our hearts and minds on the finish line.

Warming Up to God As a child, how did setting your heart on a certain toy or gift affect how you acted and what you thought about?

Read Colossians 3:1–11.

3 Since, then, you have been raised with
Christ, set your hearts on things above,
where Christ is seated at the right hand of
God. 2Set your minds on things above, not on
earthly things. 3For you died, and your life is now
hidden with Christ in God. 4When Christ, who is
your[k] life, appears, then you also will appear
with him in glory.
5Put to death, therefore, whatever belongs to
your earthly nature: sexual immorality, impurity,
lust, evil desires and greed, which is idolatry. 6Be-
cause of these, the wrath of God is coming.[l]
7You used to walk in these ways, in the life you
once lived. 8But now you must rid yourselves of
all such things as these: anger, rage, malice, slan-
der, and filthy language from your lips. 9Do not
lie to each other, since you have taken off your
old self with its practices 10and have put on the
new self, which is being renewed in knowledge in
the image of its Creator. 11Here there is no Greek
or Jew, circumcised or uncircumcised, barbarian,
Scythian, slave or free, but Christ is all, and is in
all.

[k]4 Some manuscripts *our* [l]6 Some early manuscripts *coming on those who are disobedient*

Discovering the Word 1. What do you think Paul means by *things above* and *earthly things* (vv. 1–2)? 2. How can we set our hearts and minds on things above rather than on earthly things? 3. What do the things we are to "put to death" have in common (v. 5)? 4. Our old ways of reacting are compared to a garment we took off at conversion (vv. 8–10). Why is each type of behavior inconsistent with our new life in Christ? 5. Although we may still struggle with these sins, what resources for change do we now have (vv. 9–11)?

Applying the Word 1. How can we keep God's perspective on immorality and greed when our culture accepts them as the norm? 2. What has been the effect on you and others when you have fallen back into these old motives or actions (vv. 5, 8–9)? 3. In verse 11 Paul lists the distressing divisions between people in the Colossian culture. How would becoming aware of Christ in other Christians help us to eliminate our cultural divisions?

Responding in Prayer Paul has shown the necessary blending of our emotions, mind and will in order to live like people who have been raised with Christ. Pray for help in the area where you feel weak. Spend time thanking God for the changes he has already made in you.

6 / *Colossians 3:12–17*
New Life, New Lifestyle (Part 2)

MARATHON RUNNERS NOT only shed anything that might slow them down, they also dress carefully. They choose the best running shoes and the most comfortable shorts and shirt possible. After telling us what to get rid of, Paul now speaks about the new clothes we are to wear because of our new life in Christ.

Warming Up to God When you were a child, what was one behavior your parents insisted on just because you were a member of their family?

Read Colossians 3:12–17.

12Therefore, as God's chosen people, holy and
dearly loved, clothe yourselves with compassion,
kindness, humility, gentleness and patience.
13Bear with each other and forgive whatever
grievances you may have against one another.
Forgive as the Lord forgave you. 14And over all
these virtues put on love, which binds them all
together in perfect unity.
15Let the peace of Christ rule in your hearts,
since as members of one body you were called to
peace. And be thankful. 16Let the word of Christ
dwell in you richly as you teach and admonish
one another with all wisdom, and as you sing
psalms, hymns and spiritual songs with gratitude
in your hearts to God. 17And whatever you do,
whether in word or deed, do it all in the name of
the Lord Jesus, giving thanks to God the Father
through him.

Discovering the Word 1. Why does Paul begin by reminding us of who we are in God's sight (v. 12)? 2. Why is the description "God's chosen people, holy and dearly loved" (v. 12) not dependent on our feelings or efforts (1:12–14; 2:9–10)? 3. Paul recognizes that grievances occur even in the church. How are his instructions for handling grievances different from the way our culture handles them (vv. 13–14)? 4. Paul also recognizes that Christians conflict with each other. How could conflicts be better managed with peace ruling (literally, "functioning like an umpire") in our hearts (v. 15)? 5. What does it mean to let the word of Christ "dwell" in us richly (v. 16; see also Eph 5:18–20)?

Applying the Word 1. What "new clothes" (v. 12) would you like to put on? 2. How would doing everything "in the name of the Lord Jesus" transform what you have to say and do today (v. 17)?

Responding in Prayer Let your prayer grow out of the need to put on specific "new clothes." If there is someone you need to forgive, confess that and ask for power and determination to forgive.

7 / *Colossians 3:18—4:1*
At Home and On the Job

FACTORY WORKERS IN the Philippines had been meeting for months for a lunch-hour Bible study. One day the supervisor came to the leader and asked, "Could you start some more Bible studies in the factory? The men in the study have become the best workers on my shift."

That wouldn't have surprised the apostle Paul. In this section he instructs us about the distinctive attitudes and behavior that should mark Christians at home and on the job.

Warming Up to God When is it easiest for you to have a "Christian" attitude toward your work?

Read Colossians 3:18—4:1.

18 Wives, submit to your husbands, as is fitting
in the Lord.
19 Husbands, love your wives and do not be
harsh with them.
20 Children, obey your parents in everything,
for this pleases the Lord.
21 Fathers, do not embitter your children, or
they will become discouraged.
22 Slaves, obey your earthly masters in every-
thing; and do it, not only when their eye is on you
and to win their favor, but with sincerity of heart
and reverence for the Lord. 23 Whatever you do,
work at it with all your heart, as working for the
Lord, not for men, 24 since you know that you will
receive an inheritance from the Lord as a reward.
It is the Lord Christ you are serving. 25 Anyone
who does wrong will be repaid for his wrong, and
there is no favoritism.

4 Masters, provide your slaves with what is
right and fair, because you know that you
also have a Master in heaven.

Discovering the Word 1. How do Paul's commands to wives/husbands, children/fathers and slaves/masters address our tendency to do the opposite? 2. The wife is to submit to the husband "as is fitting in the Lord" (v. 18). From what you learned in 3:5–17, what would that kind of submission include? What would it not include? 3. The husband is to love his wife and not be harsh with her (v. 19). How would 3:12–17 help him understand what that love should be like in actions and attitudes? 4. What attitudes and actions of parents embitter or discourage their children? 5. When and how are slaves to obey their masters (vv. 22–25)? With what motives? 6. What would it demand of a master to "provide your slaves with what is right and fair" (4:1)?

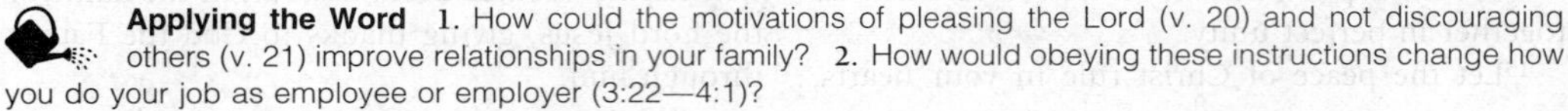

Applying the Word 1. How could the motivations of pleasing the Lord (v. 20) and not discouraging others (v. 21) improve relationships in your family? 2. How would obeying these instructions change how you do your job as employee or employer (3:22—4:1)?

Responding in Prayer Ask God to show you any attitudes or actions toward your family or at work that you need to change. Ask for grace to begin making one small change today.

8 / *Colossians 4:2–18*
Making the Most of Opportunities

NO ONE EVER becomes a Christian by just watching how a Christian lives. An observer might think the Christian is earning his way to heaven by trying to be good. How could anyone ever guess how to become a Christian? Debating if what we say or how we live is more important in witnessing is like asking which leg is more important for walking. In this study Paul shows that witnessing is an interplay between prayer, living and speaking. His closing greetings illustrate many ways Christians help and encourage each other.

Warming Up to God What one piece of advice about witnessing would you give to a younger Christian?

Read Colossians 4:2–18.

2 Devote yourselves to prayer, being watchful
and thankful. 3 And pray for us, too, that God may
open a door for our message, so that we may
proclaim the mystery of Christ, for which I am in
chains. 4 Pray that I may proclaim it clearly, as I
should. 5 Be wise in the way you act toward out-
siders; make the most of every opportunity. 6 Let
your conversation be always full of grace, sea-
soned with salt, so that you may know how to
answer everyone.
7 Tychicus will tell you all the news about me.
He is a dear brother, a faithful minister and fellow
servant in the Lord. 8 I am sending him to you for
the express purpose that you may know about
our[m] circumstances and that he may encourage

[m]8 Some manuscripts *that he may know about your*

your hearts. [9]He is coming with Onesimus, our faithful and dear brother, who is one of you. They will tell you everything that is happening here.

[10]My fellow prisoner Aristarchus sends you his greetings, as does Mark, the cousin of Barnabas. (You have received instructions about him; if he comes to you, welcome him.) [11]Jesus, who is called Justus, also sends greetings. These are the only Jews among my fellow workers for the kingdom of God, and they have proved a comfort to me. [12]Epaphras, who is one of you and a servant of Christ Jesus, sends greetings. He is always wrestling in prayer for you, that you may stand firm in all the will of God, mature and fully assured. [13]I vouch for him that he is working hard for you and for those at Laodicea and Hierapolis. [14]Our dear friend Luke, the doctor, and Demas send greetings. [15]Give my greetings to the brothers at Laodicea, and to Nympha and the church in her house.

[16]After this letter has been read to you, see that it is also read in the church of the Laodiceans and that you in turn read the letter from Laodicea.

[17]Tell Archippus: "See to it that you complete the work you have received in the Lord."

[18]I, Paul, write this greeting in my own hand. Remember my chains. Grace be with you.

Discovering the Word 1. In verses 2–6 Paul teaches us how to speak to God about people and how to speak to people about God. Why would he tell us to *devote* ourselves to prayer (v. 2)? 2. Paul might have asked the church to pray for his release from prison. What requests does he make instead (vv. 3–4)? Why? 3. What advice does Paul give us about the way we live and converse with non-Christians (vv. 5–6)? 4. Paul concludes this letter with numerous personal messages and greetings. What qualities in people does Paul affirm, and why (vv. 7–18)?

Applying the Word 1. In what ways might you "be wise in the way you act toward outsiders" and "make the most of every opportunity" (v. 5)? 2. How could you encourage or comfort a fellow Christian this week by following the example of someone named here?

Responding in Prayer Use verses 3–4 to pray for yourself, your church leaders and missionaries. Ask God to make you aware of every opportunity to influence nonbelievers to consider Jesus.

1 Thessalonians

Conventional wisdom tells us that nothing is certain except death and taxes, but for most of us that is not enough. Wouldn't you like to be just as sure about where you stand with God? That's what the Thessalonians were looking for, and Paul's letters to them can help you find that assurance as well.

In the year A.D. 50, Paul entered Thessalonica while on his second missionary journey. He preached there for three weeks and was able to establish a church. However, a group of jealous Jews interpreted Paul's message to mean that he was proclaiming another ruler in opposition to the Roman emperor, and he was forced to leave town (Acts 17:1–10).

Because of Paul's concern for this young church, he sent his coworker, Timothy, to learn how the Thessalonians were doing. Timothy reported that the Christians' faith remained strong but that they continued to be persecuted by those who had banished Paul. Timothy also brought back questions which Paul had not had time to answer during his short stay.

First Thessalonians was Paul's first attempt at offering encouragement and answering questions—in fact it was probably the first of Paul's epistles. It was written from Corinth only a few months after Paul had left Thessalonica.

In 1 Thessalonians Paul offers encouragement in four major areas: (1) How can I be sure that I will be with Jesus after death? (2) How can I be sure that Jesus is coming again? (3) How can I be sure that Jesus hasn't forgotten me when I am suffering persecution? (4) How can I be sure that my life is pleasing to God?

Through your study of these letters, it is my hope that you will become sure of your faith and of your salvation and that, as a result, you will be able to "encourage each other with these words" (1Th 4:18).

Outline

1/ 1 Thessalonians 1 —— *Faith That Shows*

2/ 1 Thessalonians 2:1–16 —— *Gentle Evangelism*

3/ 1 Thessalonians 2:17—3:13 —— *Unmistakable Love*

4/ 1 Thessalonians 4:1–12 —— *A Life That Pleases God*

5/ 1 Thessalonians 4:13—5:11 —— *The Hope of Christ's Coming*

6/ 1 Thessalonians 5:12–28 —— *Life Among Friends*

1 / *1 Thessalonians 1*
Faith That Shows

A LIGHTHOUSE HAS become a common analogy for a church. Just as a lighthouse stands in a dark and dangerous spot flashing its message of warning and pointing to safe harbor, a church should also be a prominent and unmistakable sign to the community in which it exists. How can you help your church or fellowship group become such a shining light? This passage describes how the church in Thessalonica was able to do it.

Warming Up to God What is the reputation of your church or fellowship group throughout the community?

Read 1 Thessalonians 1.

---

1 Paul, Silas[a] and Timothy,
To the church of the Thessalonians in
God the Father and the Lord Jesus Christ:

Grace and peace to you.[b]

2We always thank God for all of you, mention-
ing you in our prayers. 3We continually remem-
ber before our God and Father your work pro-
duced by faith, your labor prompted by love, and
your endurance inspired by hope in our Lord
Jesus Christ.
4For we know, brothers loved by God, that he
has chosen you, 5because our gospel came to you
not simply with words, but also with power, with
the Holy Spirit and with deep conviction. You
know how we lived among you for your sake.
6You became imitators of us and of the Lord; in
spite of severe suffering, you welcomed the mes-
sage with the joy given by the Holy Spirit. 7And
so you became a model to all the believers in
Macedonia and Achaia. 8The Lord's message rang
out from you not only in Macedonia and
Achaia—your faith in God has become known
everywhere. Therefore we do not need to say any-
thing about it, 9for they themselves report what
kind of reception you gave us. They tell how you
turned to God from idols to serve the living and
true God, 10and to wait for his Son from heaven,
whom he raised from the dead—Jesus, who res-
cues us from the coming wrath.

[a] 1 Greek *Silvanus*, a variant of *Silas* [b] 1 Some early manuscripts *you from God our Father and the Lord Jesus Christ*

Discovering the Word 1. Paul writes that he remembers the Thessalonians' "work produced by faith," "labor prompted by love" and "endurance inspired by hope" (v. 3). How do you think he could tell that faith, love and hope were behind their actions? 2. What role has the Holy Spirit played in the Thessalonians' faith (vv. 5-6)? 3. What role did Paul, Silas and Timothy have in the Thessalonians' conversion (v. 6)? 4. When is it wise and when is it unwise to imitate another Christian (vv. 6-7)? 5. What were the results of the Thessalonians' strong faith (vv. 8-10)?

Applying the Word 1. What do you think your reputation is with non-Christians? 2. How can your faith (and the faith of your church or fellowship group) become more of a witness to others?

Responding in Prayer Ask to be made a genuine witness, and pray for the witness of your church.

2 / 1 Thessalonians 2:1–16
Gentle Evangelism

WHAT THOUGHTS COME to your mind when you hear the word *evangelism*? Pushy people trying to get you to see things their way? Guilt for not saying enough about your Savior? People swarming down the aisles at a gigantic rally? Or friends sharing the excitement of the good news with each other? For Paul, evangelism was always delightful and exciting. In this passage he tells us why talking about Christ is such a positive experience for him.

Warming Up to God How do you feel about telling others about your faith? Talk with God about any fears or guilt you experience.

Read 1 Thessalonians 2:1–16.

2 You know, brothers, that our visit to you
was not a failure. 2We had previously suf-
fered and been insulted in Philippi, as you
know, but with the help of our God we dared to
tell you his gospel in spite of strong opposition.
3For the appeal we make does not spring from
error or impure motives, nor are we trying to
trick you. 4On the contrary, we speak as men ap-
proved by God to be entrusted with the gospel.
We are not trying to please men but God, who
tests our hearts. 5You know we never used flat-
tery, nor did we put on a mask to cover up
greed—God is our witness. 6We were not looking
for praise from men, not from you or anyone else.
As apostles of Christ we could have been a bur-
den to you, 7but we were gentle among you, like
a mother caring for her little children. 8We loved
you so much that we were delighted to share with
you not only the gospel of God but our lives as
well, because you had become so dear to us.
9Surely you remember, brothers, our toil and
hardship; we worked night and day in order not
to be a burden to anyone while we preached the
gospel of God to you.
10You are witnesses, and so is God, of how
holy, righteous and blameless we were among
you who believed. 11For you know that we dealt
with each of you as a father deals with his own
children, 12encouraging, comforting and urging
you to live lives worthy of God, who calls you
into his kingdom and glory.
13And we also thank God continually because,
when you received the word of God, which you
heard from us, you accepted it not as the word of
men, but as it actually is, the word of God, which
is at work in you who believe. 14For you, broth-
ers, became imitators of God's churches in Judea,
which are in Christ Jesus: You suffered from your
own countrymen the same things those churches
suffered from the Jews, 15who killed the Lord
Jesus and the prophets and also drove us out.
They displease God and are hostile to all men 16in
their effort to keep us from speaking to the Gen-
tiles so that they may be saved. In this way they
always heap up their sins to the limit. The wrath
of God has come upon them at last.[c]

[c]16 Or *them fully*

Discovering the Word 1. What excuses might Paul have had not to preach to the Thessalonians (vv. 1–2)? 2. What attitudes enable Paul to continue preaching despite opposition (vv. 3–6)? 3. What does this teach you about proper and improper reasons for witnessing to others? 4. Paul claims to have been "holy, righteous and blameless" (v. 10) among the Thessalonians. If this is important, how can imperfect people dare to do evangelism? 5. How is a father dealing with his children a good example of an evangelist (vv. 11–12)?

Applying the Word 1. In what specific ways can gentleness and caring become more a part of your evangelistic efforts? 2. In what ways have you found evangelism to be difficult? 3. What ideas and encouragement from this passage can help you to overcome these difficulties?

Responding in Prayer Ask God to give you encouragement to be a gentle evangelist.

3 / 1 Thessalonians 2:17—3:13
Unmistakable Love

STUDIES SHOW THAT more people leave their churches today for lack of love than for any other reason (Win Arn, Carroll Nyquist and Charles Arn, *Who Cares About Love?* [Pasadena, Calif.: Church Growth Press, 1986], p. 7). It is indeed sad that even those who are committed to the Lord of love are unable to offer that love to others. How can your church become a place where love will "increase and overflow for each other and for everyone else" (1Th 3:12)? This passage provides some practical examples.

Warming Up to God On a scale of 1 to 10, how loved do you feel by the members of your church or fellowship group?

Read 1 Thessalonians 2:17—3:13.

---

[17]But, brothers, when we were torn away from
you for a short time (in person, not in thought),
out of our intense longing we made every effort to
see you. [18]For we wanted to come to you—cer-
tainly I, Paul, did, again and again—but Satan
stopped us. [19]For what is our hope, our joy, or
the crown in which we will glory in the presence
of our Lord Jesus when he comes? Is it not you?
[20]Indeed, you are our glory and joy.

3 So when we could stand it no longer, we
thought it best to be left by ourselves in
Athens. [2]We sent Timothy, who is our
brother and God's fellow worker[d] in spreading
the gospel of Christ, to strengthen and encourage
you in your faith, [3]so that no one would be unset-
tled by these trials. You know quite well that we
were destined for them. [4]In fact, when we were
with you, we kept telling you that we would be
persecuted. And it turned out that way, as you
well know. [5]For this reason, when I could stand it
no longer, I sent to find out about your faith. I
was afraid that in some way the tempter might
have tempted you and our efforts might have
been useless.

[6]But Timothy has just now come to us from
you and has brought good news about your faith
and love. He has told us that you always have
pleasant memories of us and that you long to see
us, just as we also long to see you. [7]Therefore,
brothers, in all our distress and persecution we
were encouraged about you because of your faith.
[8]For now we really live, since you are standing
firm in the Lord. [9]How can we thank God enough
for you in return for all the joy we have in the
presence of our God because of you? [10]Night and
day we pray most earnestly that we may see you
again and supply what is lacking in your faith.
[11]Now may our God and Father himself and
our Lord Jesus clear the way for us to come to
you. [12]May the Lord make your love increase and
overflow for each other and for everyone else, just
as ours does for you. [13]May he strengthen your
hearts so that you will be blameless and holy in
the presence of our God and Father when our
Lord Jesus comes with all his holy ones.

[d]2 Some manuscripts *brother and fellow worker*; other manuscripts *brother and God's servant*

Discovering the Word 1. What evidence do you find in this passage that Paul really did love the Thessalonians (2:17, 20; 3:2, 5, 10)? 2. What phrases does Paul use to express his love (2:17–18; 3:5)? 3. What fears caused Paul to send Timothy to Thessalonica (3:2–5)? 4. What are Paul's desires for the Thessalonians (3:10–13)? 5. How do these desires reflect Paul's love and caring?

Applying the Word 1. How do you most often express your love for others? 2. What ideas from this passage can help you become even better at expressing love? 3. How can you (as an individual or group) help love increase within your church or fellowship group?

Responding in Prayer Ask God to help you show love to someone in your church this week.

4 / *1 Thessalonians 4:1–12*
A Life That Pleases God

ALL OF US want to please the people we love the most. That is why a wife will surprise her husband with his favorite meal, a husband will plan a special evening at a concert he knows will excite his wife, or a child will pick a bouquet of dandelions to present to Mom and Dad. What can Christians do to please God, whom they love so dearly?

Warming Up to God If a Christian brother or sister asked you for advice on how to make their life more pleasing to God, what is the first thing you would say?

Read 1 Thessalonians 4:1–12.

---

4 Finally, brothers, we instructed you how
to live in order to please God, as in fact
you are living. Now we ask you and urge
you in the Lord Jesus to do this more and more.
2For you know what instructions we gave you by
the authority of the Lord Jesus.
3It is God's will that you should be sanctified:
that you should avoid sexual immorality; 4that
each of you should learn to control his own
body[e] in a way that is holy and honorable, 5not
in passionate lust like the heathen, who do not
know God; 6and that in this matter no one should
wrong his brother or take advantage of him. The
Lord will punish men for all such sins, as we have
already told you and warned you. 7For God did
not call us to be impure, but to live a holy life.
8Therefore, he who rejects this instruction does
not reject man but God, who gives you his Holy
Spirit.
9Now about brotherly love we do not need to
write to you, for you yourselves have been taught
by God to love each other. 10And in fact, you do
love all the brothers throughout Macedonia. Yet
we urge you, brothers, to do so more and more.
11Make it your ambition to lead a quiet life, to
mind your own business and to work with your
hands, just as we told you, 12so that your daily life
may win the respect of outsiders and so that you
will not be dependent on anybody.

e4 *Or learn to live with his own wife; or learn to acquire a wife*

Discovering the Word 1. Why would Paul give these instructions on holy living to people whom he says are already living a life which pleases God (vv. 1,10)? 2. What clues does this passage give as to how Paul would define sexual immorality (vv. 3–6)? 3. How does sexual immorality "wrong" or "take advantage of" a brother (v. 6)? 4. Scholars agree that verses 11 and 12 were directed toward members of the church who had quit working and were relying on the kindness of their fellow Christians to provide them with necessities. Why would Paul have been concerned about the effect this attitude was having on outsiders?

Applying the Word 1. What work habits detract from your Christian witness? 2. How can this passage help you to resist sexual temptation? 3. Paul has given commands in this passage concerning sexual immorality, love for fellow Christians and work. What can you do this week to become more obedient in one of these areas?

Responding in Prayer Give your life to the Lord, praying that it will be made pleasing to him.

5 / *1 Thessalonians 4:13—5:11*
The Hope of Christ's Coming

A CRISIS OCCURRED in the Thessalonian church when one of their members died. Since they had expected to all be alive when Christ returned, they were now confused. Did this mean their friend would miss out on Christ's coming? Had this person died because God was angry with them? How much longer would it be before Christ finally did return? Maybe you have fears about what will happen when you die or when Christ returns. In this passage, Paul seeks to calm our fears and encourage us to look forward to the day we meet our Maker.

Warming Up to God What fears do you have about death?

Read 1 Thessalonians 4:13—5:11.

13Brothers, we do not want you to be ignorant
about those who fall asleep, or to grieve like the
rest of men, who have no hope. 14We believe that
Jesus died and rose again and so we believe that
God will bring with Jesus those who have fallen
asleep in him. 15According to the Lord's own
word, we tell you that we who are still alive, who
are left till the coming of the Lord, will certainly
not precede those who have fallen asleep. 16For
the Lord himself will come down from heaven,
with a loud command, with the voice of the arch-
angel and with the trumpet call of God, and the
dead in Christ will rise first. 17After that, we who
are still alive and are left will be caught up to-
gether with them in the clouds to meet the Lord
in the air. And so we will be with the Lord for-
ever. 18Therefore encourage each other with these
words.

5 Now, brothers, about times and dates we
do not need to write to you, 2for you
know very well that the day of the Lord
will come like a thief in the night. 3While peo-
ple are saying, "Peace and safety," destruction
will come on them suddenly, as labor pains
on a pregnant woman, and they will not
escape.

4But you, brothers, are not in darkness so that
this day should surprise you like a thief. 5You are
all sons of the light and sons of the day. We do
not belong to the night or to the darkness. 6So
then, let us not be like others, who are asleep, but
let us be alert and self-controlled. 7For those who
sleep, sleep at night, and those who get drunk, get
drunk at night. 8But since we belong to the day,
let us be self-controlled, putting on faith and love
as a breastplate, and the hope of salvation as a
helmet. 9For God did not appoint us to suffer
wrath but to receive salvation through our Lord
Jesus Christ. 10He died for us so that, whether we
are awake or asleep, we may live together with
him. 11Therefore encourage one another and
build each other up, just as in fact you are
doing.

Discovering the Word 1. In what ways is grief different for a Christian than it is for a non-Christian (4:13)? 2. What sequence of events does Paul say will occur when Christ returns (4:16–17)? 3. Why are the examples of a thief (5:2) and labor pains (5:3) good analogies of what will happen on the day of the Lord? 4. What dangers are associated with living in darkness (5:5–7)? 5. What instructions does Paul give for living in the light (5:8)?

Applying the Word 1. How do Paul's words help you to face your own fears about death? 2. Paul tells us that our defensive weapons against darkness are faith, love and hope (v. 8). What are some practical ways in which these virtues can defend you?

Responding in Prayer Pray that you will be made ready for the day of the Lord.

6 / 1 Thessalonians 5:12–28
Life Among Friends

ANY GROUP OF people needs rules for getting along, and the church is no exception. Paul so wants the Thessalonians to "live in peace with each other" (1Th 5:13) that he closes his first letter to them with several instructions on how they can do this. These are instructions which have never gone out of date and can still be used to end the quarrels, hurt feelings and resentments in your church or fellowship group.

Warming Up to God If you had the power to make one rule for helping people get along, what would it be?

Read 1 Thessalonians 5:12–28.

---

[12]Now we ask you, brothers, to respect those
who work hard among you, who are over you in
the Lord and who admonish you. [13]Hold them in
the highest regard in love because of their work.
Live in peace with each other. [14]And we urge you,
brothers, warn those who are idle, encourage the
timid, help the weak, be patient with everyone.
[15]Make sure that nobody pays back wrong for
wrong, but always try to be kind to each other
and to everyone else.
[16]Be joyful always; [17]pray continually; [18]give
thanks in all circumstances, for this is God's will
for you in Christ Jesus.
[19]Do not put out the Spirit's fire; [20]do not treat
prophecies with contempt. [21]Test everything.
Hold on to the good. [22]Avoid every kind of evil.
[23]May God himself, the God of peace, sanctify
you through and through. May your whole spirit,
soul and body be kept blameless at the coming of
our Lord Jesus Christ. [24]The one who calls you is
faithful and he will do it.

[25]Brothers, pray for us. [26]Greet all the brothers
with a holy kiss. [27]I charge you before the Lord to
have this letter read to all the brothers.
[28]The grace of our Lord Jesus Christ be with
you.

Discovering the Word 1. What does it mean for someone to be "over you in the Lord" (v. 12)? 2. How can you warn a person about something they are doing wrong (v. 14) or prevent them from taking revenge (v. 15) and still live in peace with them? 3. What does it mean to be joyful "always," pray "continually" and give thanks "in all circumstances" (vv. 16–18)? 4. How can you test things like prophecy or teaching to find out if they are good or evil (vv. 19–22)? 5. Look through the passage again and pick out the actions and attitudes (stated or implied) which are displeasing to God. What are they?

Applying the Word 1. When have you found God faithful in keeping you from sin (v. 24)? 2. In what way do you currently need God's faithfulness to keep you from sin?

Responding in Prayer Follow the discipline of giving thanks in all circumstances by finding as many things in your life as you can to be thankful for.

2 Thessalonians

Second Thessalonians was written a short time after 1 Thessalonians to clear up misconceptions about the Second Coming that the first letter had failed to answer.

Although the letter was written to Gentiles, it assumes some knowledge of the Old Testament. According to Donald Guthrie, this was typical of early Christian teaching (*New Testament Introduction,* rev. ed. [Downers Grove, Ill.: InterVarsity Press, 1990], p. 596).

Paul most likely wrote the letter from Corinth. In addition to clarifying their understanding about Christ's return, Paul addressed some ongoing problems in the church in dealing with idleness. This book offered its readers comfort and insight about faith and end times, as well as a call to take responsibility. May it both challenge and encourage you as well.

Outline

1 / 2 Thessalonians 1
Evidence of Faith

CAN I KNOW for sure that I will go to heaven?

This is a question that plagued the Thessalonians to such an extent that even after the comfort of his first letter, Paul has to write again and give further encouragement. It was difficult for these young Christians to believe that the suffering of their present life would really be followed by the eternal joy of heaven. Perhaps you also wonder if heaven really exists and if you can be sure of going there. If so, you will find Paul writing this passage directly to you.

Warming Up to God Have you ever met a person and gone away thinking, "They must be a Christian." What gave you that impression?

Read 2 Thessalonians 1.

1 Paul, Silas[a] and Timothy,
To the church of the Thessalonians in
God our Father and the Lord Jesus Christ:
2Grace and peace to you from God the Father
and the Lord Jesus Christ.
3We ought always to thank God for you, broth-
ers, and rightly so, because your faith is growing
more and more, and the love every one of you has
for each other is increasing. 4Therefore, among
God's churches we boast about your perseverance
and faith in all the persecutions and trials you are
enduring.
5All this is evidence that God's judgment is
right, and as a result you will be counted worthy
of the kingdom of God, for which you are suffer-
ing. 6God is just: He will pay back trouble to
those who trouble you 7and give relief to you who
are troubled, and to us as well. This will happen
when the Lord Jesus is revealed from heaven in
blazing fire with his powerful angels. 8He will
punish those who do not know God and do not
obey the gospel of our Lord Jesus. 9They will be
punished with everlasting destruction and shut
out from the presence of the Lord and from the
majesty of his power 10on the day he comes to be
glorified in his holy people and to be marveled at
among all those who have believed. This includes
you, because you believed our testimony to you.
11With this in mind, we constantly pray for
you, that our God may count you worthy of his
calling, and that by his power he may fulfill every
good purpose of yours and every act prompted by
your faith. 12We pray this so that the name of our
Lord Jesus may be glorified in you, and you in
him, according to the grace of our God and the
Lord Jesus Christ.[b]

[a]1 Greek *Silvanus*, a variant of *Silas* [b]12 Or *God and Lord, Jesus Christ*

Discovering the Word 1. What good things does Paul notice about the lives of the Thessalonians (vv. 3–4)? 2. Why do you think that in times of persecution, some people's faith and love grow while others' fail (v. 4)? 3. Paul proclaims that "God is just." How does he describe God's justice (vv. 5–10)? 4. According to this passage, what makes a person "worthy of the kingdom" (v. 5) or "worthy of [God's] calling" (v. 11)? 5. In light of his teaching about God's judgment, why does Paul pray as he does in verses 11–12?

Applying the Word 1. How can God's justice encourage you when things are "just not fair"? 2. If someone were to pray for you as Paul did in verses 11–12, what is one specific way in which you would want God to change your life?

Responding in Prayer Pray that God's justice would be done in your life and throughout the world.

2 / 2 Thessalonians 2
Lawlessness on the Loose

HOW WILL THE world end? Will there be nuclear war? An evil empire? The destruction of civilization? Paul advises us that Satan has yet to attack us with the worst he has, and when he does, it will be a fearful time to be alive. However, Paul also promises that God will always be in control.

Warming Up to God What potential threats to the safety of the world do you see right now (for example, attitudes, weapon building, warfare and so on)? What personal fears or concerns do you have about that?

Read 2 Thessalonians 2.

---

2 Concerning the coming of our Lord Jesus Christ and our being gathered to him, we ask you, brothers, 2not to become easily unsettled or alarmed by some prophecy, report or letter supposed to have come from us, saying that the day of the Lord has already come. 3Don't let anyone deceive you in any way, for ⌊that day will not come⌋ until the rebellion occurs and the man of lawlessness[c] is revealed, the man doomed to destruction. 4He will oppose and will exalt himself over everything that is called God or is worshiped, so that he sets himself up in God's temple, proclaiming himself to be God.

5Don't you remember that when I was with you I used to tell you these things? 6And now you know what is holding him back, so that he may be revealed at the proper time. 7For the secret power of lawlessness is already at work; but the one who now holds it back will continue to do so till he is taken out of the way. 8And then the lawless one will be revealed, whom the Lord Jesus will overthrow with the breath of his mouth and destroy by the splendor of his coming. 9The coming of the lawless one will be in accordance with the work of Satan displayed in all kinds of counterfeit miracles, signs and wonders, 10and in every sort of evil that deceives those who are perishing. They perish because they refused to love the truth and so be saved. 11For this reason God sends them a powerful delusion so that they will believe the lie 12and so that all will be condemned who have not believed the truth but have delighted in wickedness.

13But we ought always to thank God for you, brothers loved by the Lord, because from the beginning God chose you[d] to be saved through the sanctifying work of the Spirit and through belief in the truth. 14He called you to this through our gospel, that you might share in the glory of our Lord Jesus Christ. 15So then, brothers, stand firm and hold to the teachings[e] we passed on to you, whether by word of mouth or by letter.

16May our Lord Jesus Christ himself and God our Father, who loved us and by his grace gave us eternal encouragement and good hope, 17encourage your hearts and strengthen you in every good deed and word.

c3 Some manuscripts *sin* d13 Some manuscripts *because God chose you as his firstfruits* e15 Or *traditions*

Discovering the Word 1. In 1 Thessalonians 4:13–18 Paul responded to the fears of the Thessalonians that if they died before Christ returned, they would miss the joy Christ had for them. Apparently, after Paul sent the first letter, someone tried to convince the Thessalonians that the day of the Lord had already come. What is Paul's proof that the day of the Lord has not come (vv. 3, 9)? 2. What can you learn about the "man of lawlessness" from this passage (vv. 3–4, 7–10)? 3. In what ways have you noticed the "secret power of lawlessness" (v. 7) to be already at work? 4. What contrasts do you find between those whom God condemns (vv. 10–12) and those whom he chooses for salvation (vv. 13–17)?

Applying the Word 1. Even for Christians, the lawless one will bring fear and testing. What can you do to prepare yourself to withstand him? 2. How can this passage encourage you about facing the future?

Responding in Prayer Talk openly with God about any fears or concerns you have regarding the future.

3 / 2 Thessalonians 3
Lazy Christians

MEMBERS OF THE Thessalonian church were refusing to take responsibility. Some had quit working because they thought Jesus would be back any moment and didn't see any reason to exert themselves. Others relaxed because there were plenty of wealthier members in the church who were always willing to share. Regardless of the reason, Paul was abhorred by such laziness, and set the rule "If a man will not work, he shall not eat." How can our laziness affect the work of Christ? What can we do about the laziness of others? Paul addresses those questions in this study.

Warming Up to God When is it hard for you to feel motivated to do the work of your church?

Read 2 Thessalonians 3.

3 Finally, brothers, pray for us that the
message of the Lord may spread rapidly
and be honored, just as it was with you.
2And pray that we may be delivered from wicked
and evil men, for not everyone has faith. 3But the
Lord is faithful, and he will strengthen and pro-
tect you from the evil one. 4We have confidence
in the Lord that you are doing and will continue
to do the things we command. 5May the Lord
direct your hearts into God's love and Christ's
perseverance.
6In the name of the Lord Jesus Christ, we com-
mand you, brothers, to keep away from every
brother who is idle and does not live according to
the teaching[f] you received from us. 7For you
yourselves know how you ought to follow our
example. We were not idle when we were with
you, 8nor did we eat anyone's food without pay-
ing for it. On the contrary, we worked night and
day, laboring and toiling so that we would not be
a burden to any of you. 9We did this, not because
we do not have the right to such help, but in
order to make ourselves a model for you to fol-
low. 10For even when we were with you, we gave
you this rule: "If a man will not work, he shall not
eat."
11We hear that some among you are idle. They
are not busy; they are busybodies. 12Such people
we command and urge in the Lord Jesus Christ to
settle down and earn the bread they eat. 13And as
for you, brothers, never tire of doing what is
right.
14If anyone does not obey our instruction in
this letter, take special note of him. Do not associ-
ate with him, in order that he may feel ashamed.
15Yet do not regard him as an enemy, but warn
him as a brother.
16Now may the Lord of peace himself give you
peace at all times and in every way. The Lord be
with all of you.
17I, Paul, write this greeting in my own hand,
which is the distinguishing mark in all my letters.
This is how I write.
18The grace of our Lord Jesus Christ be with
you all.

f6 Or *tradition*

Discovering the Word 1. In what ways did Paul expect that his ministry could be enhanced because of the Thessalonians' prayer (vv. 1–2)? 2. How is Paul's confidence in the Lord expressed in this request for prayer (vv. 3–5)? 3. How would you describe the problem the Thessalonian church was experiencing (v. 11)? 4. How did Paul make himself an example of the proper attitude toward work (vv. 7–9)? 5. What actions are to be taken against those who refuse to work (vv. 12–15)?

Applying the Word 1. What encouragement and ideas do these verses give you concerning your own prayer life? 2. In what ways do lazy Christians still continue to take advantage of the work of others? 3. What principles for discipline that could be applied in the church today do you find in this passage?

Responding in Prayer Pray that like Paul you will be a good example to others in your attitude toward work.

1 Timothy

Ephesus, a key seaport for Asia Minor, was a swinging commercial center. Without an army, it maintained its place in the world through deal-making. It was the crowded home of about 350,000 people.

Dominating the economy of Ephesus was the temple of Artemis, "goddess of the Ephesians." It was regarded as one of the seven wonders of the ancient world. A huge structure of solid marble, it was the largest temple in the world outside Egypt, and the biggest *bank* east of Rome! You can read in Acts 19 about the riot Paul's preaching triggered among the guilds that depended on temple business. Artemis herself was a 37-breasted fertility goddess who stood for bringing prosperity out of constant change.

And change there was.

Various cultures mixed in Ephesus. Its heritage was Greek, but Romans pushed in when it became part of the Empire. A sizeable Jewish community took root, as well as smaller communities of many ethnic groups. Different religions, philosophies and ethics coexisted while everybody sought some piece of the economic action.

Sports were a major entertainment. The Greeks had two gymnasia built for athletic contests, while the Romans built a stadium for gladiator combat. By the mid-second century, the Roman approach of spectacular violence won the day over the Greek ideal of simple competition.

Sex was also big business. Art depicting various sex acts adorned the garden walls of large villas. Bestiality and homosexuality were celebrated. The Romans built baths—a kind of ancient country club where the upper-class members of both sexes went nude. Prostitution, divorce, multiple marriages, abandoned children and neglect of the elderly were common. Religious opinion ranged from advocating deviant sex to shunning sex totally.

A confusing mix of religions existed in the shadow of the dominant Artemis. The large Jewish community coexisted with it. Smaller ethnic groups had their own religions but didn't seek prominence. The Romans argued the case to rename Artemis as Diana, while thinking Greeks argued over mystical experiences and whether the names of gods were just diverse labels for the "One Prime Mover."

Although Artemis ruled in the public square, magic influenced the personal lives of most people and invaded all of the formal religions. A striking example is the account in Acts

19:13–17, which involved even the family of the Jewish high priest. In magic, the Ephesian spirit of deal-making was applied to spirituality. Ephesian magic became famous throughout the Roman world.

Paul, for his part, saw Ephesus as a great place to preach the gospel. He began with preaching to his fellow Jews on his second missionary journey. On his third journey, he invested two solid years evangelizing and developing Christian leaders. Christian faith became so popular that the magic trade and temple business fell sharply.

Paul's farewell message (Acts 20), however, shows that he was bracing for a spiritual counterattack on the Christian community. He predicted even some of his converts would set themselves up as Christian "gurus" and carve out followings around their own blend of Scripture, the gospel and mystical teachings. The issue Paul saw as crucial was spiritual authority: When should we accept spiritual teachings? When should we reject them? How do we know if Christian teachers are trustworthy? This, in fact, was just the situation when Paul wrote his first letter to Timothy.

Paul had turned over the leadership of the church in Ephesus, the most strategic in Asia Minor, to Timothy, a bright, sensitive associate. Timothy was about forty years old at that time, which was considered young for such leadership. False teaching was coming from people within the church. Since some of these were leaders (see Acts 20:30), Paul could not write to the church at Ephesus directly, but instead went through Timothy whom he had confidence in (Gordon Fee, "Issues in Evangelical Hermeneutics," *Crux* 26, no. 4 [December 1990]). Timothy's mission was to deal with false teaching, and it seems he was a capable teacher.

From references in 1 and 2 Corinthians, Acts, and the letters to Timothy, we know Timothy was a committed, but very human, person with some insecurities. Hebrews 13:23 shows that he spent some time in prison for his faith. We don't know what finally happened to Timothy, but we do know that John became the leader of the church not too long after these letters were written.

In these letters we can see Paul coaching the younger leader. In the process he raises issues which bear on us all—leaders or not.

Outline

1/ 1 Timothy 1 — *What Difference Does It Make?*

2/ 1 Timothy 2 — *Barriers to Renewal*

3/ 1 Timothy 3 — *Who Can Lead?*

4/ 1 Timothy 4 — *True and False Ministry*

5/ 1 Timothy 5:1—6:2 — *Implementing Spiritual Teaching*

6/ 1 Timothy 6:3–20 — *Find Your Riches in Christ*

1 / 1 Timothy 1
What Difference Does It Make?

"CHRIST CONSCIOUSNESS—MYSTICAL Teaching in the Bible," advertises a poster. "The mystical core of Christ's teaching has been obscured by centuries of dogma," it announces, inviting Christians to come to lectures by a young lady who follows a Hindu sect. And at the other extreme, some Christian leaders, dismayed by a low level of commitment, seek to create high-intensity groups with special teachings on top of the gospel and extra rules that regulate the social lives of their members. These modern examples are the kinds of thing that were rampant in the church at Ephesus; Paul sent Timothy to Ephesus to deal with them.

Warming Up to God How do you distinguish between true and false spirituality?

Read 1 Timothy 1.

1 Paul, an apostle of Christ Jesus by the
command of God our Savior and of Christ
Jesus our hope,

2To Timothy my true son in the faith:

Grace, mercy and peace from God the Father
and Christ Jesus our Lord.

3As I urged you when I went into Macedonia,
stay there in Ephesus so that you may command
certain men not to teach false doctrines any
longer 4nor to devote themselves to myths and
endless genealogies. These promote controversies
rather than God's work—which is by faith. 5The
goal of this command is love, which comes from
a pure heart and a good conscience and a sincere
faith. 6Some have wandered away from these and
turned to meaningless talk. 7They want to be
teachers of the law, but they do not know what
they are talking about or what they so confidently
affirm.
8We know that the law is good if one uses it
properly. 9We also know that law[a] is made not
for the righteous but for lawbreakers and rebels,
the ungodly and sinful, the unholy and irreligious;
for those who kill their fathers or mothers,
for murderers, 10for adulterers and perverts, for
slave traders and liars and perjurers—and for
whatever else is contrary to the sound doctrine
11that conforms to the glorious gospel of the
blessed God, which he entrusted to me.
12I thank Christ Jesus our Lord, who has given
me strength, that he considered me faithful, appointing
me to his service. 13Even though I was
once a blasphemer and a persecutor and a violent
man, I was shown mercy because I acted in ignorance
and unbelief. 14The grace of our Lord was
poured out on me abundantly, along with the
faith and love that are in Christ Jesus.
15Here is a trustworthy saying that deserves full
acceptance: Christ Jesus came into the world to
save sinners—of whom I am the worst. 16But for
that very reason I was shown mercy so that in me,
the worst of sinners, Christ Jesus might display
his unlimited patience as an example for those
who would believe on him and receive eternal
life. 17Now to the King eternal, immortal, invisible,
the only God, be honor and glory for ever
and ever. Amen.
18Timothy, my son, I give you this instruction
in keeping with the prophecies once made about
you, so that by following them you may fight the
good fight, 19holding on to faith and a good conscience.
Some have rejected these and so have
shipwrecked their faith. 20Among them are Hymenaeus
and Alexander, whom I have handed
over to Satan to be taught not to blaspheme.

[a]9 *Or that the law*

Discovering the Word 1. How does Paul describe Timothy's job (vv. 3–5)? 2. Finding hidden meanings in the Old Testament was big business in first-century religion. False teachers here tried to mix these "secret teachings" with the gospel. What results were the false teachers getting for their efforts (vv. 4–6)? 3. From what Paul says about the proper use of the law, how does it seem that the false teachers use it (vv. 8–11)? 4. In what ways was Paul himself like the false teachers before his conversion (vv. 12–17)? 5. Note the places where the word *conscience* comes up (vv. 5, 19). When we speculate and theorize instead of dealing with our own issues of sin, what happens to conscience?

Applying the Word 1. How can the kind of faith Paul shows in verse 15 help you face your own issues of conscience? 2. As in Paul's day, Christians can wander into groups that make unusual claims and demands. They may have impressive features, but engage in certain practices and pressures which make members feel uneasy. A lot of energy goes into keeping faith and conscience apart in these groups. Are you involved with some "spiritual" activities which bother your own conscience? (Be as honest as possible.)

Responding in Prayer Close in prayer by putting your own name in place of the general word *sinners* in verse 15. Now read verses 16–17 as your own prayer of thanks to God.

2 / *1 Timothy 2*
Barriers to Renewal

DO YOU EVER have difficulty approaching God in prayer? The Christians in Ephesus did. The barriers to prayer described here are anger, an over-emphasis on appearance, and an inappropriate role for women. Having sized up the situation and reminded Timothy of his mission, Paul outlines first steps to dealing with the needs of the church.

Warming Up to God When do you find prayer difficult?

Read 1 Timothy 2.

2 I urge, then, first of all, that requests,
prayers, intercession and thanksgiving be
made for everyone— [2]for kings and all
those in authority, that we may live peaceful and
quiet lives in all godliness and holiness. [3]This is
good, and pleases God our Savior, [4]who wants all
men to be saved and to come to a knowledge of
the truth. [5]For there is one God and one mediator
between God and men, the man Christ Jesus,
[6]who gave himself as a ransom for all men—the
testimony given in its proper time. [7]And for this
purpose I was appointed a herald and an apos-
tle—I am telling the truth, I am not lying—and a
teacher of the true faith to the Gentiles.
[8]I want men everywhere to lift up holy hands
in prayer, without anger or disputing.
[9]I also want women to dress modestly, with
decency and propriety, not with braided hair or
gold or pearls or expensive clothes, [10]but with
good deeds, appropriate for women who profess
to worship God.
[11]A woman should learn in quietness and full
submission. [12]I do not permit a woman to teach
or to have authority over a man; she must be
silent. [13]For Adam was formed first, then Eve.
[14]And Adam was not the one deceived; it was the
woman who was deceived and became a sinner.
[15]But women[b] will be saved[c] through child-
bearing—if they continue in faith, love and holi-
ness with propriety.

[b]15 Greek *she* [c]15 Or *restored*

Discovering the Word 1. Find all the times Paul says "all" and "everyone" (vv. 1–6). What does the use of these terms communicate about God? 2. Why do you think Paul emphasizes the word *one* in verse 5? 3. This entire chapter deals with worship. The church in Ephesus was probably a network of house churches. Their worship may have been patterned after the Jewish synagogues which separated men and women. What problem hindered the worship by men (v. 8)? 4. What problem hindered the worship by women (v. 9)? 5. In verses 11–12, Paul forbids women to teach men. But in 1 Corinthians 11:5, he tells them how to dress when they preach (or prophesy). How do you reconcile these texts?

Applying the Word 1. According to this passage, what could hinder worship and sharing the gospel? 2. Consider which of those are problems for you. How can you better deal with them?

Responding in Prayer Pray for your church's worship and for your personal worship.

3 / *1 Timothy 3* Who Can Lead?

SOME CHURCHES AND fellowships have a few people who are willing to lead. Those people may end up feeling burdened and alone. Other churches have people who are willing to lead, but not ready. If there are not enough leaders, however, the work of the church will not get done. The church of Ephesus was in the latter category. Those who were willing to lead were immature. And Timothy could not hope to carry out his mission against false teachers unless the leadership was healthy.

Warming Up to God What have your experiences of Christian leadership been like?

Read 1 Timothy 3.

3 Here is a trustworthy saying: If anyone sets his heart on being an overseer,[d] he desires a noble task. 2Now the overseer must be above reproach, the husband of but one wife, temperate, self-controlled, respectable, hospitable, able to teach, 3not given to drunkenness, not violent but gentle, not quarrelsome, not a lover of money. 4He must manage his own family well and see that his children obey him with proper respect. 5(If anyone does not know how to manage his own family, how can he take care of God's church?) 6He must not be a recent convert, or he may become conceited and fall under the same judgment as the devil. 7He must also have a good reputation with outsiders, so that he will not fall into disgrace and into the devil's trap.

8Deacons, likewise, are to be men worthy of respect, sincere, not indulging in much wine, and not pursuing dishonest gain. 9They must keep hold of the deep truths of the faith with a clear conscience. 10They must first be tested; and then if there is nothing against them, let them serve as deacons.

11In the same way, their wives[e] are to be women worthy of respect, not malicious talkers but temperate and trustworthy in everything.

12A deacon must be the husband of but one wife and must manage his children and his household well. 13Those who have served well gain an excellent standing and great assurance in their faith in Christ Jesus.

14Although I hope to come to you soon, I am writing you these instructions so that, 15if I am delayed, you will know how people ought to conduct themselves in God's household, which is the church of the living God, the pillar and foundation of the truth. 16Beyond all question, the mystery of godliness is great:

He[f] appeared in a body,[g]
  was vindicated by the Spirit,
was seen by angels,
  was preached among the nations,
was believed on in the world,
  was taken up in glory.

[d] 1 Traditionally *bishop*; also in verse 2 [e] 11 Or *way, deaconesses*
[f] 16 Some manuscripts *God* [g] 16 Or *in the flesh*

Discovering the Word 1. Consider two categories of qualification—*character* and *ability*. How do the qualities mentioned in these verses divide into these two categories? 2. What do you think is Paul's reason for insisting that a leader's relationships must work in the spheres of both church and family (vv. 5-6)? 3. How have you seen the principle in verse 7 obeyed or disobeyed? 4. "Deacon" simply means "servant." In the passage it seems that deacons deal with the more practical affairs of church life, rather than with teaching. Given that, why do you think the point about doctrine in verse 9 is made with so much emphasis? **5.** What do verses 14–16 tell us about Paul's purpose in writing this letter?

Applying the Word **1.** Verse 16 was probably a hymn sung in the church at Ephesus. The word translated as "deep truths" in verse 9 is rendered "mystery" here. We can say that the result Paul wanted from good Christian leadership was that these truths would be revealed. Therefore, when people look at our fellowship, what should they see? **2.** How can you serve your church through leadership, or encourage others who lead?

Responding in Prayer Pray for your pastor and church leaders.

4 / *1 Timothy 4*
True and False Ministry

WITH THIS CHAPTER Paul's strategy for Timothy starts to emerge clearly. Timothy's mission was to deal with the false teachers. Paul sees, however, that fighting false teachers with ideology alone is fruitless. The real mission is that the church be healthy so that Jesus Christ is communicated through it. So he spoke of prayer and leadership first. With that foundation in place, Timothy will be able to turn his attention directly to the problems at hand.

Warming Up to God Is there an older Christian in your family or church who has given you good advice? What was it?

Read 1 Timothy 4.

4 The Spirit clearly says that in later times
some will abandon the faith and follow
deceiving spirits and things taught by de-
mons. 2Such teachings come through hypocritical
liars, whose consciences have been seared as with
a hot iron. 3They forbid people to marry and or-
der them to abstain from certain foods, which
God created to be received with thanksgiving by
those who believe and who know the truth. 4For
everything God created is good, and nothing is to
be rejected if it is received with thanksgiving, 5be-
cause it is consecrated by the word of God and
prayer.

6If you point these things out to the brothers,
you will be a good minister of Christ Jesus,
brought up in the truths of the faith and of the
good teaching that you have followed. 7Have
nothing to do with godless myths and old
wives' tales; rather, train yourself to be godly.
8For physical training is of some value, but
godliness has value for all things, holding
promise for both the present life and the life
to come.

9This is a trustworthy saying that deserves full
acceptance 10(and for this we labor and strive),
that we have put our hope in the living God, who
is the Savior of all men, and especially of those
who believe.

11Command and teach these things. 12Don't let
anyone look down on you because you are young,
but set an example for the believers in speech, in
life, in love, in faith and in purity. 13Until I come,
devote yourself to the public reading of Scripture,
to preaching and to teaching. 14Do not neglect
your gift, which was given you through a pro-
phetic message when the body of elders laid their
hands on you.

15Be diligent in these matters; give yourself
wholly to them, so that everyone may see your
progress. 16Watch your life and doctrine closely.
Persevere in them, because if you do, you will
save both yourself and your hearers.

Discovering the Word 1. What is the nature of the teachings described in verses 2–3? 2. Why is this teaching—which could seem to be "superspiritual"—really a doctrine of demons (vv. 3–4)? 3. When you think of "false teaching," do you think of teachers who are morally too loose or too strict? Explain. 4. What was Timothy's personal life to be like (vv. 7–16)? 5. How was it to differ from that of the false teachers?

Applying the Word 1. Why do you think you are motivated at some times and *not* motivated at other times for training in godliness (v. 7)? 2. Timothy's primary ministry was teaching. What in this passage encourages you to develop and use your ministry gifts?

Responding in Prayer Pray for those who might be under the hold of false teachers, that the truth would be revealed to them.

5 / *1 Timothy 5:1—6:2*
Implementing Spiritual Teaching

AT ONE TIME or another all of us have probably been in a situation in which we felt that someone in our church or fellowship was sinning. Whether or not we act on the situation and how we communicate to that person have a big effect on the outcome. Often when we rebuke others about their lifestyles, we come off as being judgmental and self-righteous. When Paul tells Timothy about specific persons and groups he needed to confront about certain issues, he is careful to show how to do so in love. Paul's teaching here gives us valuable guidance on being both direct and loving with other Christians.

Warming Up to God When have you found—or seen—rebuke to have a positive impact?

Read 1 Timothy 5:1—6:2.

5 Do not rebuke an older man harshly, but
exhort him as if he were your father.
Treat younger men as brothers, 2older
women as mothers, and younger women as sisters, with absolute purity.
3Give proper recognition to those widows who
are really in need. 4But if a widow has children or
grandchildren, these should learn first of all to
put their religion into practice by caring for their
own family and so repaying their parents and
grandparents, for this is pleasing to God. 5The
widow who is really in need and left all alone puts
her hope in God and continues night and day to
pray and to ask God for help. 6But the widow
who lives for pleasure is dead even while she
lives. 7Give the people these instructions, too, so
that no one may be open to blame. 8If anyone
does not provide for his relatives, and especially
for his immediate family, he has denied the faith
and is worse than an unbeliever.
9No widow may be put on the list of widows
unless she is over sixty, has been faithful to her
husband,[h] 10and is well known for her good
deeds, such as bringing up children, showing
hospitality, washing the feet of the saints, helping
those in trouble and devoting herself to all kinds
of good deeds.
11As for younger widows, do not put them on
such a list. For when their sensual desires overcome their dedication to Christ, they want to
marry. 12Thus they bring judgment on themselves, because they have broken their first
pledge. 13Besides, they get into the habit of being
idle and going about from house to house. And
not only do they become idlers, but also gossips
and busybodies, saying things they ought not to.
14So I counsel younger widows to marry, to have
children, to manage their homes and to give the
enemy no opportunity for slander. 15Some have
in fact already turned away to follow Satan.
16If any woman who is a believer has widows in
her family, she should help them and not let the
church be burdened with them, so that the
church can help those widows who are really in
need.

h9 *Or has had but one husband*

17The elders who direct the affairs of the
church well are worthy of double honor, espe-
cially those whose work is preaching and teach-
ing. 18For the Scripture says, "Do not muzzle the
ox while it is treading out the grain,"[i] and "The
worker deserves his wages."[j] 19Do not entertain
an accusation against an elder unless it is brought
by two or three witnesses. 20Those who sin are to
be rebuked publicly, so that the others may take
warning.

21I charge you, in the sight of God and Christ
Jesus and the elect angels, to keep these instruc-
tions without partiality, and to do nothing out of
favoritism.

22Do not be hasty in the laying on of hands,
and do not share in the sins of others. Keep your-
self pure.

23Stop drinking only water, and use a little
wine because of your stomach and your frequent
illnesses.

24The sins of some men are obvious, reaching
the place of judgment ahead of them; the sins of
others trail behind them. 25In the same way, good
deeds are obvious, and even those that are not
cannot be hidden.

6 All who are under the yoke of slavery
should consider their masters worthy of
full respect, so that God's name and our
teaching may not be slandered. 2Those who have
believing masters are not to show less respect for
them because they are brothers. Instead, they are
to serve them even better, because those who
benefit from their service are believers, and dear
to them. These are the things you are to teach and
urge on them.

[i]18 Deut. 25:4 [j]18 Luke 10:7

Discovering the Word 1. Paul touches on the different age and gender groups Timothy must lead. How is Timothy to regard the people he ministers to? 2. How is a godly widow to be distinguished from an ungodly one (vv. 3–8)? 3. What criteria did a widow need to meet to receive a place on the list of those who received financial aid from the church (vv. 9–10)? 4. Why do you think Paul gives these specific instructions about rebuking an elder in verses 19–20? 5. How have you found verses 24–25 to be true? 6. From 6:1–2 what do you think has been happening when slaves become believers?

Applying the Word 1. How can you rebuke someone in ways that are clear but also affirm the other person as a member of God's family? 2. In affluent Ephesus, like twentieth-century America, many elderly people were evidently abandoned. What obligations do you have to your own parents? 3. What ideas does this passage give you for new areas of ministry?

Responding in Prayer Pray for those in your church who are needy and who may be without family.

6 / *1 Timothy 6:3–20*
Find Your Riches in Christ

SOME WELL-KNOWN Christian teachers and authors tell us that being a Christian means success and prosperity. If we are faithful, God will bless us with wealth. Other Christians advocate a simple lifestyle without interest in material possessions. What does Scripture say about how we are to regard money? In this chapter Paul concludes his agenda of how to lead the powerful and the powerless by addressing the wealthy members of the church.

Warming Up to God What do you believe is the place of money in the life of a Christian?

Read 1 Timothy 6:3–20.

3If anyone teaches false doctrines and does not
agree to the sound instruction of our Lord Jesus
Christ and to godly teaching, 4he is conceited and
understands nothing. He has an unhealthy inter-
est in controversies and quarrels about words that
result in envy, strife, malicious talk, evil suspi-

cions 5and constant friction between men of cor-
rupt mind, who have been robbed of the truth
and who think that godliness is a means to finan-
cial gain.

6But godliness with contentment is great gain.
7For we brought nothing into the world, and we
can take nothing out of it. 8But if we have food
and clothing, we will be content with that. 9Peo-
ple who want to get rich fall into temptation and
a trap and into many foolish and harmful desires
that plunge men into ruin and destruction. 10For
the love of money is a root of all kinds of evil.
Some people, eager for money, have wandered
from the faith and pierced themselves with many
griefs.

11But you, man of God, flee from all this, and
pursue righteousness, godliness, faith, love, en-
durance and gentleness. 12Fight the good fight of
the faith. Take hold of the eternal life to which
you were called when you made your good con-
fession in the presence of many witnesses. 13In
the sight of God, who gives life to everything, and
of Christ Jesus, who while testifying before Pon-
tius Pilate made the good confession, I charge you
14to keep this command without spot or blame
until the appearing of our Lord Jesus Christ,
15which God will bring about in his own time—
God, the blessed and only Ruler, the King of
kings and Lord of lords, 16who alone is immortal
and who lives in unapproachable light, whom no
one has seen or can see. To him be honor and
might forever. Amen.

17Command those who are rich in this present
world not to be arrogant nor to put their hope in
wealth, which is so uncertain, but to put their
hope in God, who richly provides us with every-
thing for our enjoyment. 18Command them to do
good, to be rich in good deeds, and to be gener-
ous and willing to share. 19In this way they will
lay up treasure for themselves as a firm founda-
tion for the coming age, so that they may take
hold of the life that is truly life.

20Timothy, guard what has been entrusted to
your care. Turn away from godless chatter and
the opposing ideas of what is falsely called knowl-
edge, 21which some have professed and in so do-
ing have wandered from the faith.

Grace be with you.

Discovering the Word 1. What do you think Paul means by an "unhealthy interest" (v. 4)? 2. According to verses 6–8, how are we to find contentment? 3. In your own words, how would you explain Paul's teaching on riches in verses 9–10? 4. What was Paul commanding Timothy to do in this context (vv. 11–14)? 5. How is Christ pictured in verses 13–16? 6. Why do you think Paul told Timothy to turn away from "godless chatter" (v. 20)?

Applying the Word 1. In what ways does your Christian life feel like a fight? 2. Describe how you have seen Christians use riches to do good work. 3. What has God entrusted to your care, and how do you guard it?

Responding in Prayer Pray that you would be a good steward of what you have been given.

2 Timothy

Second Timothy is Paul's last letter. He is in prison in Rome again—under Nero. He is an older man and does not expect to get out, but to die in prison (contrast with Php 1:23–25).

Opposition to Paul both inside and outside the church has intensified. Many former associates have deserted him. His loneliness and desire to see Timothy come through clearly. Further, Nero's persecution is under way, and many Christians are facing the choice of suffering or leaving the faith. Much of what he has built is at risk. When Paul's personal resources are at their lowest, he faces the greatest test. In this context he reflects on his own life and gives his final counsel.

This letter has fantastic value for us. It gives us insight into facing persecution and supporting others who are persecuted. It also shows both how to give away leadership and how to assume it at the right time. Finally, it provides encouragement to us in facing our own death.

Outline

1/ 2 Timothy 1 — *Rejected but Not Ashamed*

2/ 2 Timothy 2 — *Pass It On*

3/ 2 Timothy 3 — *How to Recognize God's Voice*

4/ 2 Timothy 4 — *It's Your Turn Now*

1 / 2 *Timothy 1*
Rejected but Not Ashamed

SHAME MEANS BEING revealed to others as weak and inadequate. Rejection is always cause for shame unless we are quite sure of both our ideas and our approach. We are prone to believe what others say about us, especially if they are more successful or in authority. We often need support from our own friends to maintain our dignity even in the face of unjust charges.

It is remarkable but true that when Paul was imprisoned, the church in Rome did not come to Paul's defense. Only one believer came looking for him. The rest probably held back from fear or considered the imprisonment something shameful. But although he has been rejected, Paul tells us he is *not* ashamed.

Warming Up to God When have non-Christian friends or pressures from the world caused you to feel ashamed of the gospel?

Read 2 Timothy 1.

1 Paul, an apostle of Christ Jesus by the will
of God, according to the promise of life
that is in Christ Jesus,

[2]To Timothy, my dear son:

Grace, mercy and peace from God the Father
and Christ Jesus our Lord.

[3]I thank God, whom I serve, as my forefathers
did, with a clear conscience, as night and day I
constantly remember you in my prayers. [4]Recall-
ing your tears, I long to see you, so that I may be
filled with joy. [5]I have been reminded of your
sincere faith, which first lived in your grand-
mother Lois and in your mother Eunice and, I am
persuaded, now lives in you also. [6]For this reason
I remind you to fan into flame the gift of God,
which is in you through the laying on of my
hands. [7]For God did not give us a spirit of timid-
ity, but a spirit of power, of love and of self-disci-
pline.

[8]So do not be ashamed to testify about our
Lord, or ashamed of me his prisoner. But join
with me in suffering for the gospel, by the power
of God, [9]who has saved us and called us to a holy
life—not because of anything we have done but
because of his own purpose and grace. This grace
was given us in Christ Jesus before the beginning
of time, [10]but it has now been revealed through
the appearing of our Savior, Christ Jesus, who has
destroyed death and has brought life and immor-
tality to light through the gospel. [11]And of this
gospel I was appointed a herald and an apostle
and a teacher. [12]That is why I am suffering as I
am. Yet I am not ashamed, because I know whom
I have believed, and am convinced that he is able
to guard what I have entrusted to him for that
day.

[13]What you heard from me, keep as the pattern
of sound teaching, with faith and love in Christ
Jesus. [14]Guard the good deposit that was en-
trusted to you—guard it with the help of the
Holy Spirit who lives in us.

[15]You know that everyone in the province of
Asia has deserted me, including Phygelus and
Hermogenes.

[16]May the Lord show mercy to the household
of Onesiphorus, because he often refreshed me
and was not ashamed of my chains. [17]On the con-
trary, when he was in Rome, he searched hard for
me until he found me. [18]May the Lord grant that
he will find mercy from the Lord on that day! You
know very well in how many ways he helped me
in Ephesus.

Discovering the Word 1. What information are we given about the relationship between Paul and Timothy (vv. 2–6)? 2. What is Paul's situation (vv. 1, 8, 11–12, 15–16)? 3. Find the references to shame (vv. 12, 16). Why would *shame* be a response to Paul's imprisonment? 4. How did Paul reject shame in this situation (vv. 3, 8–12)?

Applying the Word 1. Imprisonment can take many forms beyond the literal example here, such as chronic disease, financial collapse, abuse, or anything that severely restricts your freedom and separates you from people. How can we apply Paul's example of resisting the shame that arises from such situations?

2. Consider Timothy's situation: his mentor has been disgraced; many of his associates have deserted the ministry; many of his church's members are drifting from the faith or cowed by the threat of persecution. How have you struggled or are you struggling with similar situations? 3. How do you believe God is calling you to testify about him in your own situation?

Responding in Prayer With your call to witness in mind, pray through what the text affirms about God in verses 8–12. As you pray, think especially about how you might be ashamed of sharing your faith, and ask for God's help.

2 / *2 Timothy 2*
Pass It On

BARBARA BOYD ONCE said, "Paul had no dead-end disciples." The essence of Paul's ministry was to be certain that the gospel was handed on to other people in such a way that they came to regard this task as their own. This approach, which was very radical in its time, puts the "power" of the movement into the hands of thousands. Paul, having been deserted by many, wants to make sure the gospel won't die when he does—or when Timothy does.

Warming Up to God Think of a time when an older Christian has entrusted some aspect of ministry to you. How did this create growth and maturity in your life?

Read 2 Timothy 2.

2 You then, my son, be strong in the grace
that is in Christ Jesus. 2And the things
you have heard me say in the presence of
many witnesses entrust to reliable men who will
also be qualified to teach others. 3Endure hard-
ship with us like a good soldier of Christ Jesus.
4No one serving as a soldier gets involved in civil-
ian affairs—he wants to please his commanding
officer. 5Similarly, if anyone competes as an ath-
lete, he does not receive the victor's crown unless
he competes according to the rules. 6The hard-
working farmer should be the first to receive a
share of the crops. 7Reflect on what I am saying,
for the Lord will give you insight into all this.
8Remember Jesus Christ, raised from the dead,
descended from David. This is my gospel, 9for
which I am suffering even to the point of being
chained like a criminal. But God's word is not
chained. 10Therefore I endure everything for the
sake of the elect, that they too may obtain the
salvation that is in Christ Jesus, with eternal
glory.
11Here is a trustworthy saying:

If we died with him,
we will also live with him;
12if we endure,
we will also reign with him.
If we disown him,
he will also disown us;
13if we are faithless,
he will remain faithful,
for he cannot disown himself.

14Keep reminding them of these things. Warn
them before God against quarreling about words;
it is of no value, and only ruins those who listen.
15Do your best to present yourself to God as one
approved, a workman who does not need to be
ashamed and who correctly handles the word of
truth. 16Avoid godless chatter, because those who
indulge in it will become more and more un-
godly. 17Their teaching will spread like gangrene.
Among them are Hymenaeus and Philetus, 18who
have wandered away from the truth. They say
that the resurrection has already taken place, and
they destroy the faith of some. 19Nevertheless,
God's solid foundation stands firm, sealed with
this inscription: "The Lord knows those who are
his,"[a] and, "Everyone who confesses the name of
the Lord must turn away from wickedness."
20In a large house there are articles not only of
gold and silver, but also of wood and clay; some
are for noble purposes and some for ignoble. 21If
a man cleanses himself from the latter, he will be

[a] 19 Num. 16:5 (see Septuagint)

an instrument for noble purposes, made holy,
useful to the Master and prepared to do any good
work.
22Flee the evil desires of youth, and pursue
righteousness, faith, love and peace, along with
those who call on the Lord out of a pure heart.
23Don't have anything to do with foolish and stu-
pid arguments, because you know they produce
quarrels. 24And the Lord's servant must not quar-
rel; instead, he must be kind to everyone, able to
teach, not resentful. 25Those who oppose him he
must gently instruct, in the hope that God will
grant them repentance leading them to a knowl-
edge of the truth, 26and that they will come to
their senses and escape from the trap of the devil,
who has taken them captive to do his will.

Discovering the Word 1. Paul begins with the call to Timothy to "be strong in grace." Why does he give that instruction rather than "be strong in your gifts," "be strong in knowledge" or "be strong in willpower"? 2. What does each of the three images in verses 3–7 illustrate about the ministry of entrusting the gospel to others who can pass it on? 3. Why does Paul cite these specific aspects of Christ that Timothy should remember (v. 8)? 4. How does this explain Paul's own confidence even while he is imprisoned (v. 9)? 5. Why does Paul say he endures (vv. 10–13)? 6. What do verses 18–19 say is both the potential and the limitation of false teaching?

Applying the Word 1. Which of the images in verses 3–7 seems most applicable to your life right now? Why? 2. How should the trustworthy saying in verses 11–13 motivate us?

Responding in Prayer Where is your own character being tested as you try to entrust the gospel to others? Pray that God will encourage you and strengthen you in those areas.

3 / *2 Timothy 3*
How to Recognize God's Voice

MOST OF US go through stages in our lives where we are vulnerable to false teachers. Campus cults make their biggest outreaches during the opening days of school and during finals week—when students are under the greatest stress. Life crises are doors of change—for good or evil. In addition, guilt, greed and other lusts often distort judgment and give false teachers their opportunity.

Philetus and Hymanaeus represent a tradition of potent religious falsehood Timothy fought against his whole career. We can expect the same kind of struggle. In spite of the power and appeal of such groups, however, Paul had great confidence in both Scripture and those who live by it. In this chapter he encourages Timothy to have confidence in God's teaching as well.

Warming Up to God What factors do you think would make a person particularly susceptible to heresy?

Read 2 Timothy 3.

3 But mark this: There will be terrible times
in the last days. 2People will be lovers of
themselves, lovers of money, boastful,
proud, abusive, disobedient to their parents, un-
grateful, unholy, 3without love, unforgiving, slan-
derous, without self-control, brutal, not lovers of
the good, 4treacherous, rash, conceited, lovers of
pleasure rather than lovers of God— 5having a
form of godliness but denying its power. Have
nothing to do with them.
6They are the kind who worm their way into
homes and gain control over weak-willed women,
who are loaded down with sins and are swayed by
all kinds of evil desires, 7always learning but
never able to acknowledge the truth. 8Just as Jan-
nes and Jambres opposed Moses, so also these
men oppose the truth—men of depraved minds,
who, as far as the faith is concerned, are rejected.
9But they will not get very far because, as in the
case of those men, their folly will be clear to eve-
ryone.
10You, however, know all about my teaching,

my way of life, my purpose, faith, patience, love,
endurance, [11]persecutions, sufferings—what
kinds of things happened to me in Antioch, Ico-
nium and Lystra, the persecutions I endured. Yet
the Lord rescued me from all of them. [12]In fact,
everyone who wants to live a godly life in Christ
Jesus will be persecuted, [13]while evil men and
impostors will go from bad to worse, deceiving
and being deceived. [14]But as for you, continue in
what you have learned and have become con-
vinced of, because you know those from whom
you learned it, [15]and how from infancy you have
known the holy Scriptures, which are able to
make you wise for salvation through faith in
Christ Jesus. [16]All Scripture is God-breathed and
is useful for teaching, rebuking, correcting and
training in righteousness, [17]so that the man of
God may be thoroughly equipped for every good
work.

Discovering the Word 1. What evidence do we have here that these people are religious? 2. Notice the way those controlled by these religious leaders are described (v. 6). Why are we vulnerable to spiritual manipulation when we are "weak-willed," "loaded down with sins" and "swayed by evil desires"? 3. Why could Timothy trust Paul's spiritual influence (vv. 10–13)? 4. Paul does not expect blind faith from Timothy. What does he expect, and what two reasons does he give for it (vv. 14–15)? 5. Where does Scripture come from, and what is its power (vv. 15–17)?

Applying the Word 1. What would enhance your own trustworthiness among those you influence (children, students, coworkers or employees, and friends)? 2. In Hebrew (conceptually) to hear is to obey and do God's will. During this study, how have you sensed that God wants you to change in order to hear his voice more clearly?

Responding in Prayer Pray that you would hear God's voice and be kept safe from false teaching.

4 / 2 *Timothy 4*
It's Your Turn Now

THE STORY IS told of the umpire who called a strike on Babe Ruth. The Babe turned around and angrily shouted, "Hey, meathead! Me and 40,000 people here know that pitch was a ball!" The umpire replied, "Yeah, and mine is the only opinion that matters."

The gospel is not often popular. As he gears up for ministry, Timothy needs to know that only God's opinion matters. In this passage, the last written words of Paul we have, Paul instructs Timothy to think of eternity.

Warming Up to God How do you respond (inwardly and outwardly) when you see friends turning away from the faith?

Read 2 Timothy 4.

4 In the presence of God and of Christ
Jesus, who will judge the living and the
dead, and in view of his appearing and his
kingdom, I give you this charge: [2]Preach the
Word; be prepared in season and out of season;
correct, rebuke and encourage—with great pa-
tience and careful instruction. [3]For the time will
come when men will not put up with sound doc-
trine. Instead, to suit their own desires, they will
gather around them a great number of teachers to
say what their itching ears want to hear. [4]They
will turn their ears away from the truth and turn
aside to myths. [5]But you, keep your head in all
situations, endure hardship, do the work of an
evangelist, discharge all the duties of your minis-
try.

[6]For I am already being poured out like a drink
offering, and the time has come for my departure.
[7]I have fought the good fight, I have finished the
race, I have kept the faith. [8]Now there is in store

for me the crown of righteousness, which the
Lord, the righteous Judge, will award to me on
that day—and not only to me, but also to all who
have longed for his appearing.

9Do your best to come to me quickly, 10for De-
mas, because he loved this world, has deserted
me and has gone to Thessalonica. Crescens has
gone to Galatia, and Titus to Dalmatia. 11Only
Luke is with me. Get Mark and bring him with
you, because he is helpful to me in my ministry.
12I sent Tychicus to Ephesus. 13When you come,
bring the cloak that I left with Carpus at Troas,
and my scrolls, especially the parchments.

14Alexander the metalworker did me a great
deal of harm. The Lord will repay him for what he
has done. 15You too should be on your guard
against him, because he strongly opposed our
message.

16At my first defense, no one came to my sup-
port, but everyone deserted me. May it not be
held against them. 17But the Lord stood at my
side and gave me strength, so that through me the
message might be fully proclaimed and all the
Gentiles might hear it. And I was delivered from
the lion's mouth. 18The Lord will rescue me from
every evil attack and will bring me safely to his
heavenly kingdom. To him be glory for ever and
ever. Amen.

19Greet Priscilla[b] and Aquila and the house-
hold of Onesiphorus. 20Erastus stayed in Corinth,
and I left Trophimus sick in Miletus. 21Do your
best to get here before winter. Eubulus greets
you, and so do Pudens, Linus, Claudia and all the
brothers.

22The Lord be with your spirit. Grace be with
you.

[b]19 Greek *Prisca,* a variant of *Priscilla*

Discovering the Word 1. What charge was Timothy to keep (vv. 3–5)? 2. Paul is seeing a big part of what he labored so hard to build under God's power dissolve. How can he still feel such satisfaction about his life (vv. 6–8)? 3. What do verses 9–13 reveal about Paul's situation? 4. Rome had a big Christian community, but they shunned Paul when he came to trial (vv. 16–17, see also 1:8, 12, 16–18). Paul could have chosen to burn with resentment. What clues in the passage show why he was not bitter? 5. The names in verses 19–20 denote men, women, Romans, Greeks, nobles and commoners. What comfort would that fact give both Paul and Timothy?

Applying the Word 1. What life tasks do you need to finish in order to share Paul's satisfaction? 2. Who is taking a public stand for the gospel in your community, and how can you support him or her?

Responding in Prayer Pray for the spread of the gospel locally and around the world.

Titus

Titus was no stranger to conflict. He was a long-term companion of Paul who was a valuable aid in two of Paul's greatest crises.

Titus first appears in the New Testament in Galatians 2:1, where Paul says he took Titus along on his trip to Jerusalem with Barnabas. Titus was a Gentile, and the issue at hand was whether Gentiles should have to comply with Jewish ceremonial rites (circumcision, diet restrictions and so on) in order to be full members of the Christian community. With the young Paul at one side and Barnabas at the other, he was essentially "tried" (and acquitted) by the leaders in Jerusalem.

Titus appears again in the middle of Paul's struggle with the church at Corinth. In that deeply divided church, he represented Paul. He had the unwelcome job of delivering what we call the "severe letter," which Paul refers to in 2 Corinthians 2:1–4 and 7:5–13, and then staying there for about a year. Then he delivered the letter we now call 2 Corinthians in which Paul takes on his critics and calls the church to honor an unfulfilled financial pledge.

Titus was in Crete at the time Paul wrote him. Crete was a seaport, a sleazy port of call for cargo ships traversing the Mediterranean. It had been socially backward for 1400 years since the Minoan civilization was destroyed by a devastating earthquake. We do not know exactly when Titus went with Paul to Crete, but one possible scenario places it after Paul's release from his first imprisonment in Rome.

Paul had preached in Crete and was giving Titus the job of following through with developing a healthy church. This letter was sent while he was in the midst of his task and reviews his assignment. It shows Titus as a forceful personality and skilled administrator. It seems he was made of tougher stuff than Timothy, but his assignments were shorter. By the time Paul had written 2 Timothy, the job in Crete was done, and Titus had been sent on to Dalmatia (part of modern Yugoslavia).

This letter gives us two very valuable things: (1) a showcase of Paul's strategy for leadership in the midst of chaos (Timothy was given a long-term assignment in an established church; Titus was sent to follow up an evangelistic movement and give the Christian body some coherence) (2) a model of hope in the face of a very messy situation (Paul's confidence in the power of the gospel shines throughout the letter).

Titus 1—3
Great Expectations

GREAT EXPECTATIONS IS the well-known title of a novel by Charles Dickens. It is the story of a young man's early experiences out in the "real world" as he seeks to gain the fortune he has inherited. Similarly, the book of Titus tells of Paul's expectations for Titus during his first ministry experience on his own. Paul's promise to Titus is that he will become an heir of eternity.

Warming Up to God Think of a person in your life who expects great things from you. How do you feel about that person's expectations? Are they realistic?

Read Titus 1—3.

1 Paul, a servant of God and an apostle of
Jesus Christ for the faith of God's elect
and the knowledge of the truth that leads
to godliness— 2a faith and knowledge resting on
the hope of eternal life, which God, who does not
lie, promised before the beginning of time, 3and
at his appointed season he brought his word to
light through the preaching entrusted to me by
the command of God our Savior,

4To Titus, my true son in our common faith:

Grace and peace from God the Father and
Christ Jesus our Savior.

5The reason I left you in Crete was that you
might straighten out what was left unfinished and
appoint[a] elders in every town, as I directed you.
6An elder must be blameless, the husband of but
one wife, a man whose children believe and are
not open to the charge of being wild and disobe-
dient. 7Since an overseer[b] is entrusted with
God's work, he must be blameless—not overbear-
ing, not quick-tempered, not given to drunken-
ness, not violent, not pursuing dishonest gain.
8Rather he must be hospitable, one who loves
what is good, who is self-controlled, upright, holy
and disciplined. 9He must hold firmly to the
trustworthy message as it has been taught, so that
he can encourage others by sound doctrine and
refute those who oppose it.

10For there are many rebellious people, mere
talkers and deceivers, especially those of the cir-
cumcision group. 11They must be silenced, be-
cause they are ruining whole households by
teaching things they ought not to teach—and
that for the sake of dishonest gain. 12Even one of
their own prophets has said, "Cretans are always
liars, evil brutes, lazy gluttons." 13This testimony
is true. Therefore, rebuke them sharply, so that
they will be sound in the faith 14and will pay no
attention to Jewish myths or to the commands of
those who reject the truth. 15To the pure, all
things are pure, but to those who are corrupted
and do not believe, nothing is pure. In fact, both
their minds and consciences are corrupted.
16They claim to know God, but by their actions
they deny him. They are detestable, disobedient
and unfit for doing anything good.

2 You must teach what is in accord with
sound doctrine. 2Teach the older men to
be temperate, worthy of respect, self-con-
trolled, and sound in faith, in love and in endur-
ance.

3Likewise, teach the older women to be rever-
ent in the way they live, not to be slanderers or
addicted to much wine, but to teach what is good.
4Then they can train the younger women to love
their husbands and children, 5to be self-con-
trolled and pure, to be busy at home, to be kind,
and to be subject to their husbands, so that no
one will malign the word of God.

6Similarly, encourage the young men to be self-
controlled. 7In everything set them an example by
doing what is good. In your teaching show integ-
rity, seriousness 8and soundness of speech that
cannot be condemned, so that those who oppose
you may be ashamed because they have nothing
bad to say about us.

9Teach slaves to be subject to their masters in
everything, to try to please them, not to talk back
to them, 10and not to steal from them, but to
show that they can be fully trusted, so that in
every way they will make the teaching about God
our Savior attractive.

11For the grace of God that brings salvation has
appeared to all men. 12It teaches us to say "No" to

[a]5 Or *ordain* [b]7 Traditionally *bishop*

ungodliness and worldly passions, and to live
self-controlled, upright and godly lives in this
present age, 13while we wait for the blessed
hope—the glorious appearing of our great God
and Savior, Jesus Christ, 14who gave himself for
us to redeem us from all wickedness and to purify
for himself a people that are his very own, eager
to do what is good.

15These, then, are the things you should teach.
Encourage and rebuke with all authority. Do not
let anyone despise you.

3 Remind the people to be subject to rulers
and authorities, to be obedient, to be
ready to do whatever is good, 2to slander
no one, to be peaceable and considerate, and to
show true humility toward all men.

3At one time we too were foolish, disobedient,
deceived and enslaved by all kinds of passions
and pleasures. We lived in malice and envy, being
hated and hating one another. 4But when the
kindness and love of God our Savior appeared,
5he saved us, not because of righteous things we
had done, but because of his mercy. He saved us
through the washing of rebirth and renewal by
the Holy Spirit, 6whom he poured out on us gen-
erously through Jesus Christ our Savior, 7so that,
having been justified by his grace, we might be-
come heirs having the hope of eternal life. 8This is
a trustworthy saying. And I want you to stress
these things, so that those who have trusted in
God may be careful to devote themselves to doing
what is good. These things are excellent and prof-
itable for everyone.

9But avoid foolish controversies and genealo-
gies and arguments and quarrels about the law,
because these are unprofitable and useless.
10Warn a divisive person once, and then warn
him a second time. After that, have nothing to do
with him. 11You may be sure that such a man is
warped and sinful; he is self-condemned.

12As soon as I send Artemas or Tychicus to
you, do your best to come to me at Nicopolis,
because I have decided to winter there. 13Do eve-
rything you can to help Zenas the lawyer and
Apollos on their way and see that they have eve-
rything they need. 14Our people must learn to
devote themselves to doing what is good, in order
that they may provide for daily necessities and
not live unproductive lives.

15Everyone with me sends you greetings. Greet
those who love us in the faith.

Grace be with you all.

Discovering the Word 1. Note all you can from the book about the social situation (family, public and private morality). 2. What do you learn about the economic situation (work, wealth and poverty)? 3. What is revealed about the religious situation (spirituality, doctrine, church life)? 4. Paul expected enormous things of Titus. And he wanted Titus to meet him in Nicopolis (3:12) in about eight months. When it comes to what others expect of us, our first response is often to question whether they are fair. How fair do you think Paul's expectations of Titus were? 5. Paul's expectations were built not only on his knowledge of Titus, but on solid theological grounds as well. What were they (see 1:1-3; 2:11-14; 3:3-7)? 6. Do you think Paul's expectations helped Titus to accomplish his mission? Why or why not?

Applying the Word 1. Do your own Christian leaders expect too much or too little of you? 2. What effect does that have on your own walk with Jesus Christ? 3. At work, home, school or church, whether you are a follower or a leader, you have a responsibility to communicate your expectations. Name one step you could take to do this more effectively.

Responding in Prayer What expectations are you wrestling with? Ask God for insight to know which come from him and which do not.

Philemon

The little book of Philemon is the only surviving letter of Paul to an individual friend and convert about a private matter. In it we learn that Onesimus, one of Philemon's slaves, had stolen from his master and run away to Rome. In that great city he met Paul and became a Christian. Under Roman law, Philemon had the right to brand a returned slave and even kill him.

Paul applies what he wrote in Colossians: "Here there is no Greek or Jew . . . slave or free, but Christ is all, and is in all" (Col 3:11). Philemon and Onesimus are given the chance to participate in a revolutionary new process for reconciliation.

Philemon 1–25
Mending Fractured Relationships

DAVE AND ANDY enjoyed a prosperous business partnership for several years. Their families became closest friends, sharing vacations made possible by their growing computer business. Then one day Andy disappeared, along with the company bank account. Dave lost his friend, his business and his home. Three years later Andy returned, having squandered the money but having found Christ. Could Dave forgive him? Could they ever be friends again?

In Paul's letter to Philemon, you'll find principles for bringing reconciliation between two Christians who know the pain of wronging another and being wronged.

Warming Up to God Recall a time when you wanted to restore a broken relationship. What were some of your fears in approaching the situation?

Read Philemon 1–25.

---

[1]Paul, a prisoner of Christ Jesus, and Timothy our brother,

To Philemon our dear friend and fellow worker, [2]to Apphia our sister, to Archippus our fellow soldier and to the church that meets in your home:

[3]Grace to you and peace from God our Father and the Lord Jesus Christ.

[4]I always thank my God as I remember you in my prayers, [5]because I hear about your faith in the Lord Jesus and your love for all the saints. [6]I pray that you may be active in sharing your faith, so that you will have a full understanding of every good thing we have in Christ. [7]Your love has given me great joy and encouragement, because you, brother, have refreshed the hearts of the saints.

[8]Therefore, although in Christ I could be bold and order you to do what you ought to do, [9]yet I appeal to you on the basis of love. I then, as Paul—an old man and now also a prisoner of Christ Jesus— [10]I appeal to you for my son Onesimus,[a] who became my son while I was in chains. [11]Formerly he was useless to you, but now he has become useful both to you and to me.

[12]I am sending him—who is my very heart—back to you. [13]I would have liked to keep him with me so that he could take your place in helping me while I am in chains for the gospel. [14]But I did not want to do anything without your consent, so that any favor you do will be spontaneous and not forced. [15]Perhaps the reason he was separated from you for a little while was that you might have him back for good— [16]no longer as a slave, but better than a slave, as a dear brother. He is very dear to me but even dearer to you, both as a man and as a brother in the Lord.

[17]So if you consider me a partner, welcome him as you would welcome me. [18]If he has done you any wrong or owes you anything, charge it to me. [19]I, Paul, am writing this with my own hand. I will pay it back—not to mention that you owe me your very self. [20]I do wish, brother, that I may have some benefit from you in the Lord; refresh my heart in Christ. [21]Confident of your obedience, I write to you, knowing that you will do even more than I ask.

[22]And one thing more: Prepare a guest room for me, because I hope to be restored to you in answer to your prayers.

[23]Epaphras, my fellow prisoner in Christ Jesus, sends you greetings. [24]And so do Mark, Aristarchus, Demas and Luke, my fellow workers.

[25]The grace of the Lord Jesus Christ be with your spirit.

[a]*10 Onesimus* means *useful.*

Discovering the Word 1. Based on what you have read, how would you reconstruct the events that led up to this letter? 2. Having described Philemon's loving character, Paul appeals to him on the basis of love (v. 9). Why is love so essential for mending a fractured relationship? 3. In what ways has Onesimus changed since running away from Philemon (vv. 10–16)? 4. What will it require of Onesimus to return to Philemon? 5. What will it require of Philemon to do what Paul asks?

Applying the Word 1. What principles in this letter could you use for mending a fractured relationship? 2. Paul intervened to restore these two brothers in Christ. When might we need the help of a friend or counselor?

Responding in Prayer Pray for God's grace for you to follow these principles in a situation where you may be an Onesimus or Philemon or Paul.

Hebrews

A former Olympic distance runner and veteran missionary wrote the following letter of encouragement to a friend who was caught in the throes of a horrendous personal crisis:

> In this race . . . I suddenly hit a branch of a tree (and) . . . the blow almost knocked me out. . . . It knocked me out of my race, stopped me cold. . . . Somehow I staggered back on the track and stumbled along. . . . I remember one clear conclusion. I must keep going, even if I come in long behind. I must not quit. So I kept going. I won the race. . . . Whatever the difficulty, the blow, we must keep on. God will lead to the result that will glorify him. (Gordon MacDonald, *Rebuilding Your Broken World* [Nashville: Oliver-Nelson, 1988], p. 224.)

The sentence "Whatever . . . the blow, we must keep on" captures the theme of the letter to the Hebrews, which I have entitled "Race to Glory." The author of Hebrews states it very clearly: "Let us run with perseverance the race marked out for us" (12:1).

Throughout, the author emphasizes this chief concern for the readers—that they finish their faith-race with Jesus Christ gloriously and triumphantly. "Pay more careful attention," the author warns, "so that we do not drift away" (2:1). "Let us be careful that none of you be found to have fallen short of it [God's promised rest]" (4:1). "Let us leave the elementary teachings about Christ and go on to maturity," the writer appeals (6:1). "We want each of you to show this same diligence to the very end, in order to make your hope sure" (6:11).

After convincingly showing how Jesus Christ meets all of our needs, the writer cries out, "Let us draw near to God with a sincere heart in full assurance of faith. . . . Let us hold unswervingly to the hope we profess, for he who promised is faithful" (10:22–23). "Do not throw away your confidence. . . . You need to persevere so that when you have done the will of God, you will receive what he has promised" (10:35–36).

The author devotes an entire chapter (11) to drawing the readers to the stories of great heroes who finished the race to glory, people like Moses, Abraham, Noah, Jacob and Joseph. These witnesses are summoned to inspire us onward in our own faith-race.

A friend of mine loves to joke that when he gets to heaven he is going to find out who wrote Hebrews. The letter bears no byline, so scholars have had a field day speculating about its possible authors. Included in this list are Paul, Silas, Titus, Mark, Clement, Luke, Aquila, Priscilla and Barnabas. If you took a poll among these scholars, Luke, Barnabas and Apollos would be strongly favored. At any rate, whoever the author was, he or she knew the Hebrews very well.

The readers were knowledgeable Jews who had converted to faith in Jesus Christ. The entire scaffolding of the letter is Jewish history, theology and practice. These Jews were old enough in the faith to be teachers and to recall older leaders (5:12; 13:7). They had served one another and had suffered (6:10; 10:32–34). Their city can only be guessed at—possibly Jerusalem, Alexandria, Corinth, Ephesus or Rome.

What is completely clear about the audience is their spiritual peril. They were in danger of reverting to Judaism. The letter is chock full of warnings about it. They were being taunted by Jews as apostates from God and renegades from Moses. They were accused of abandoning their law and forfeiting the Old Testament promises.

So the writer goes to great lengths to prove that Jesus Christ is far superior to everything they had left behind for his sake. In that context, he warns them against neglect, unbelief, disobedience, immaturity and rejection. He stands in the grandstand, as it were, wildly cheering them on to stay on the track, not to quit, and to reach the finish line in the power of Jesus Christ.

Today's readers most likely will not have come to faith in Christ out of such a deeply embedded cultural and religious tradition. But every Christian at some time or other is tempted to quit and to ask, "What's the use?" As problems and roadblocks mount, as faith seems unproductive, as doors slam, we find it easy to think about quitting our personal faith-race.

We also need current reminders about the supremacy of Jesus Christ. There is no stronger enticement to stay in the race than to "fix our eyes on Jesus" (12:2). As the Pioneer of our salvation, he brings us to glory (2:10).

We run our faith-race in vital communion with God through prayer, by giving God's Word command of our lives, by faithfully worshiping him and loving fellow Christians, and by knowing and serving Jesus Christ better each day as our daily companion, guide and master.

Outline

1/ Hebrews 1 — *Starting the Race*

2/ Hebrews 2 — *Warning Signs*

3/ Hebrews 3 — *Winning the Race*

4/ Hebrews 4:1–13 — *Receiving God's Blessings*

5/ Hebrews 4:14—5:10 — *Overcoming Weakness*

6/ Hebrews 5:11—6:20 — *The Race to Maturity*

7/ Hebrews 7 — *Eternal Companion*

8/ Hebrews 8 — *God's "New Deal"*

9/ Hebrews 9 — *The Runner's Power*

10/ Hebrews 10 — *Staying in the Race*

11/ Hebrews 11 — *Models of Faith*

12/ Hebrews 12 — *The Runner's Discipline*

13/ Hebrews 13 — *Running by the Rules*

1 / *Hebrews 1*
Starting the Race

WHEN THE ANCIENT church father John Chrysostom, bishop of Constantinople, was summoned by Emperor Arcadius and threatened with banishment, he responded, "You cannot banish me, for the whole world is my Father's kingdom."

"Then I will take away your life," said the emperor.

"You cannot," answered Chrysostom, "for my life is hid with Christ in God."

"I will take away your treasure," roared the emperor.

"You can't," replied Chrysostom, "for my treasure is in heaven, where my heart is."

"Then I will drive you away from all your friends," the emperor said.

"You cannot, for I have one friend from whom you can never separate me. I defy you," said Chrysostom, "because you can do me no harm."

Such conviction grows out of a firm grasp of who Jesus Christ really is. Hebrews 1 will get you started on the race with a look at the majesty, power and glory of Jesus Christ.

Warming Up to God Focus on what you have experienced of the majesty, power and glory of Jesus Christ. Praise Jesus for who he is.

Read Hebrews 1.

1 In the past God spoke to our forefathers
through the prophets at many times and
in various ways, 2but in these last days he
has spoken to us by his Son, whom he appointed
heir of all things, and through whom he made the
universe. 3The Son is the radiance of God's glory
and the exact representation of his being, sustain-
ing all things by his powerful word. After he had
provided purification for sins, he sat down at the
right hand of the Majesty in heaven. 4So he be-
came as much superior to the angels as the name
he has inherited is superior to theirs.
5For to which of the angels did God ever say,

"You are my Son;
today I have become your Father[a]"[b]?

Or again,

"I will be his Father,
and he will be my Son"[c]?

6And again, when God brings his firstborn into the world, he says,

"Let all God's angels worship him."[d]

7In speaking of the angels he says,

"He makes his angels winds,
his servants flames of fire."[e]

8But about the Son he says,

"Your throne, O God, will last for ever and ever,
and righteousness will be the scepter of your kingdom.
9You have loved righteousness and hated wickedness;
therefore God, your God, has set you above your companions
by anointing you with the oil of joy."[f]

10He also says,

"In the beginning, O Lord, you laid the foundations of the earth,
and the heavens are the work of your hands.
11They will perish, but you remain;
they will all wear out like a garment.
12You will roll them up like a robe;
like a garment they will be changed.
But you remain the same,
and your years will never end."[g]

13To which of the angels did God ever say,

"Sit at my right hand
until I make your enemies
a footstool for your feet"[h]?

14Are not all angels ministering spirits sent to serve those who will inherit salvation?

[a]5 Or *have begotten you* [b]5 Psalm 2:7 [c]5 2 Samuel 7:14; 1 Chron. 17:13 [d]6 Deut. 32:43 (see Dead Sea Scrolls and Septuagint) [e]7 Psalm 104:4 [f]9 Psalm 45:6,7 [g]12 Psalm 102:25-27 [h]13 Psalm 110:1

Discovering the Word 1. How do verses 1–3 reveal the essential truth of Christ's supremacy and sufficiency? 2. Based on what we learn in verses 2–3, how would you answer the question "Who is Jesus Christ?" 3. To drive his point home, the author uses seven Old Testament citations. What characteristics or attributes of Jesus does the writer find in the Old Testament to prove his claim that Jesus is superior to angels (vv. 4–14)? 4. Who is the source of all these astounding statements (vv. 5–8, 10, 13)? 5. What do you learn about angels from these verses? 6. Based on what you have observed in verses 5–14, how would you expand your answer to the question "Who is Christ?"

Applying the Word 1. What needs in your life do these qualities of Jesus address? 2. What kind of life should you have because all this is true of Jesus?

Responding in Prayer Pray that your life will reflect your knowledge of Jesus.

2 / *Hebrews 2*
Warning Signs

"WARNING!" A BLACK-and-white lettered sign that I encounter on the Fox River in St. Charles, Illinois, warns me of a dam ahead. In that placid stream it would be easy to drive over the dam. Cigarette packs, cans of weed killer, fences around nuclear power plants—they all carry impressive warnings designed to steer us from life-threatening perils. In Hebrews 2, the writer erects the first of six prominent warning signs in the letter. The first, in effect, alerts us to the danger of drifting off the course of our faith-race. It tells us to concentrate on staying in the race.

Warming Up to God What might cause you to "drive away" from Christ, or to let "such a great salvation" slip away like a loose ring that falls off your finger?

Read Hebrews 2.

2 We must pay more careful attention,
therefore, to what we have heard, so that
we do not drift away. 2For if the message
spoken by angels was binding, and every viola-
tion and disobedience received its just punish-
ment, 3how shall we escape if we ignore such a
great salvation? This salvation, which was first
announced by the Lord, was confirmed to us by
those who heard him. 4God also testified to it by
signs, wonders and various miracles, and gifts of
the Holy Spirit distributed according to his will.

5It is not to angels that he has subjected the
world to come, about which we are speaking.
6But there is a place where someone has testified:

"What is man that you are mindful of him,
the son of man that you care for him?
7You made him a little[i] lower than the
angels;
you crowned him with glory and honor
8 and put everything under his feet."[j]

In putting everything under him, God left noth-
ing that is not subject to him. Yet at present we
do not see everything subject to him. 9But we see
Jesus, who was made a little lower than the an-
gels, now crowned with glory and honor because
he suffered death, so that by the grace of God he
might taste death for everyone.

10In bringing many sons to glory, it was fitting
that God, for whom and through whom every-
thing exists, should make the author of their sal-
vation perfect through suffering. 11Both the one
who makes men holy and those who are made
holy are of the same family. So Jesus is not
ashamed to call them brothers. 12He says,

"I will declare your name to my brothers;
in the presence of the congregation I will
sing your praises."[k]

13And again,

"I will put my trust in him."[l]

And again he says,

[i]7 Or *him for a little while*; also in verse 9 [j]8 Psalm 8:4-6
[k]12 Psalm 22:22 [l]13 Isaiah 8:17

"Here am I, and the children God has given
me."[m]

[14]Since the children have flesh and blood, he
too shared in their humanity so that by his death
he might destroy him who holds the power of
death—that is, the devil—[15]and free those who
all their lives were held in slavery by their fear of
death. [16]For surely it is not angels he helps, but
Abraham's descendants. [17]For this reason he had
to be made like his brothers in every way, in order that he might become a merciful and faithful
high priest in service to God, and that he might
make atonement for[n] the sins of the people.
[18]Because he himself suffered when he was
tempted, he is able to help those who are being
tempted.

[m]13 Isaiah 8:18 [n]17 Or *and that he might turn aside God's wrath, taking away*

Discovering the Word 1. In verse 1 we read, "pay more careful attention . . . to," and in verse 3 we are told not to "ignore." What is it that we are to focus our lives on? 2. What logic does the writer use in verses 2–3 to further focus our attention on the peril of drifting away? 3. How does the writer strengthen the warning that God's salvation in Christ is well worth our most intense obedience (vv. 3–4)? 4. To prove that Jesus is too great and too valuable to neglect, the writer tells us more about him (vv. 5–9). What major facts does he cite here? 5. Why did Jesus have "to be made like his brothers [you and me] in every way" (vv. 16–18)?

Applying the Word 1. How does Jesus help you when you are tempted? 2. What helps you to maintain a warm, life-changing relationship with Jesus? 3. "Be sure your seatbelts are securely fastened," the aircraft's captain warns you because of approaching turbulence. How can you help other believers to be "securely fastened" into Jesus?

Responding in Prayer Ask God to keep you securely fastened to Jesus.

3 / *Hebrews 3*
Winning the Race

COACHES TELL US that what distinguishes average from superior athletes is the will to win. Endowed with equal physical strengths, one reaches the heights of stardom while the other slips into obscurity. In this chapter, the writer describes two equally endowed Christian runners in the faith-race. One succeeded and the other failed. What made the difference? The will to win. One held firmly to Christ, but the other fell by the wayside because of a hard heart.

Warming Up to God What makes the difference between vibrant, growing Christians you know and those who appear to be dull and uninterested in the implications of their profession of faith?

Read Hebrews 3.

3 Therefore, holy brothers, who share in
the heavenly calling, fix your thoughts on
Jesus, the apostle and high priest whom
we confess. [2]He was faithful to the one who appointed him, just as Moses was faithful in all
God's house. [3]Jesus has been found worthy of
greater honor than Moses, just as the builder of a
house has greater honor than the house itself.
[4]For every house is built by someone, but God is
the builder of everything. [5]Moses was faithful as a
servant in all God's house, testifying to what
would be said in the future. [6]But Christ is faithful
as a son over God's house. And we are his house,
if we hold on to our courage and the hope of
which we boast.

[7]So, as the Holy Spirit says:

"Today, if you hear his voice,
8 do not harden your hearts
as you did in the rebellion,
during the time of testing in the desert,
[9]where your fathers tested and tried me

and for forty years saw what I did.
[10]That is why I was angry with that generation,
and I said, 'Their hearts are always going astray,
and they have not known my ways.'
[11]So I declared on oath in my anger,
'They shall never enter my rest.' "[o]

[12]See to it, brothers, that none of you has a
sinful, unbelieving heart that turns away from the
living God. [13]But encourage one another daily, as
long as it is called Today, so that none of you may
be hardened by sin's deceitfulness. [14]We have
come to share in Christ if we hold firmly till the
end the confidence we had at first. [15]As has just
been said:

"Today, if you hear his voice,
do not harden your hearts
as you did in the rebellion."[p]

[16]Who were they who heard and rebelled?
Were they not all those Moses led out of Egypt?
[17]And with whom was he angry for forty years?
Was it not with those who sinned, whose bodies
fell in the desert? [18]And to whom did God swear
that they would never enter his rest if not to those
who disobeyed[q]? [19]So we see that they were not
able to enter, because of their unbelief.

[o]11 Psalm 95:7-11 [p]15 Psalm 95:7,8 [q]18 Or *disbelieved*

Discovering the Word 1. What does the writer emphasize about Jesus in verses 1–6 that would encourage us to "fix [our] thoughts" on him (v. 1) and "hold on" to our courage and hope (v. 6)? 2. In verses 7–11 the writer hoists his second warning—unbelief and disobedience. These verses describe the nation of Israel after they crossed the Red Sea. They refused to obey God's command to take the Promised Land because they were afraid of the military might they would face. So they were forced to wander forty years till that whole generation died off. How does the psalmist describe God's perspective on the Israelites? 3. In what ways might Christians "test and try" God (v. 9)? Why? 4. How did God judge the Israelites whom Moses led out of Egypt (vv. 15–19)? 5. Why did he judge them in this way?

Applying the Word 1. Review the facts about the hardhearted (vv. 8, 10, 12–13, 15–18). Which aspects of this lifestyle come closest to your experience? 2. What are you doing to avoid the peril of "falling in the desert" (v. 17)?

Responding in Prayer Pray for your own salvation.

4 / *Hebrews 4:1–13*
Receiving God's Blessings

AMERICAN BUSINESS TYCOON Roger Babson once observed, "Opportunities are greater today than ever before in history. Young people have greater chances for health, happiness, and prosperity than had the children of any previous generation." The same is true for Christians in God's faith-race.

It was true for God's people, Israel, yet they missed the opportunity for living in God's land of blessing and perished in a wilderness of unbelief and disobedience. This chapter tells Christians in the race that there is something to fear, but also something to strive for—experiencing God's promised rest now.

Warming Up to God Do you need more times of rest in your life? In what areas?

Read Hebrews 4:1–13.

4 Therefore, since the promise of entering
his rest still stands, let us be careful that
none of you be found to have fallen short
of it. 2For we also have had the gospel preached
to us, just as they did; but the message they heard
was of no value to them, because those who heard
did not combine it with faith.[r] 3Now we who
have believed enter that rest, just as God has said,

"So I declared on oath in my anger,
'They shall never enter my rest.'"[s]

And yet his work has been finished since the cre-
ation of the world. 4For somewhere he has spo-
ken about the seventh day in these words: "And
on the seventh day God rested from all his
work."[t] 5And again in the passage above he says,
"They shall never enter my rest."

6It still remains that some will enter that rest,
and those who formerly had the gospel preached
to them did not go in, because of their disobedi-
ence. 7Therefore God again set a certain day, call-
ing it Today, when a long time later he spoke
through David, as was said before:

"Today, if you hear his voice,
do not harden your hearts."[u]

8For if Joshua had given them rest, God would
not have spoken later about another day. 9There
remains, then, a Sabbath-rest for the people of
God; 10for anyone who enters God's rest also rests
from his own work, just as God did from his.
11Let us, therefore, make every effort to enter that
rest, so that no one will fall by following their
example of disobedience.

12For the word of God is living and active.
Sharper than any double-edged sword, it pene-
trates even to dividing soul and spirit, joints and
marrow; it judges the thoughts and attitudes of
the heart. 13Nothing in all creation is hidden from
God's sight. Everything is uncovered and laid
bare before the eyes of him to whom we must
give account.

[r]2 Many manuscripts *because they did not share in the faith of those who obeyed* [s]3 Psalm 95:11; also in verse 5 [t]4 Gen. 2:2 [u]7 Psalm 95:7,8

Discovering the Word 1. What do you think the promise of entering God's rest means in verse 1? 2. The tragic fate of the Israelites who perished in the desert serves as the basis of God's warning to those who have heard the gospel. Why did some who had the gospel preached to them miss their opportunity to receive God's rest (v. 2)? 3. From what you have observed in Hebrews thus far, how would you describe the faith which is required to receive God's rest? 4. We are told to do our best to reach God's rest (3:11, 18; 4:1, 3, 5–6, 9–11). How do you picture such rest? 5. Verses 6–8 refer to the Israelites. How did they refuse to receive God's rest? 6. The "word of God" that judges our thoughts and attitudes (vv. 12–13) is the specific promise of God's rest. How can God's Word show you the condition of your heart?

Applying the Word 1. God rested from all of his work (v. 4), and he offers us a "Sabbath-rest" on the seventh day of the week. What does it mean to you to rest from your work? 2. What role does Scripture have in your life right now? 3. How would you like to deepen or change that relationship?

Responding in Prayer Praise God for the gifts in this passage—of Scripture and of rest.

---

5 / *Hebrews 4:14—5:10*
Overcoming Weakness

THE PULITZER PRIZE-winning book *City of Joy* tells about the intense suffering of a Polish priest in a Calcutta slum. His superiors offered him a comfortable lodging, but he chose to live just like the slum-dwellers. By his suffering he learned what it was like to be a slum-dweller. He could not have learned that any other way. Likewise, the Hebrews needed to be reminded of their God-appointed, suffering high priest, Jesus Christ, so they would hold firmly to him.

Warming Up to God What experiences have you had that have helped you to better understand another person?

Read Hebrews 4:14—5:10.

14Therefore, since we have a great high priest
who has gone through the heavens,[v] Jesus the
Son of God, let us hold firmly to the faith we
profess. 15For we do not have a high priest who is
unable to sympathize with our weaknesses, but
we have one who has been tempted in every way,
just as we are—yet was without sin. 16Let us then
approach the throne of grace with confidence, so
that we may receive mercy and find grace to help
us in our time of need.

5 Every high priest is selected from among
men and is appointed to represent them
in matters related to God, to offer gifts
and sacrifices for sins. 2He is able to deal gently
with those who are ignorant and are going astray,
since he himself is subject to weakness. 3This is
why he has to offer sacrifices for his own sins, as
well as for the sins of the people.
4No one takes this honor upon himself; he
must be called by God, just as Aaron was. 5So
Christ also did not take upon himself the glory of
becoming a high priest. But God said to him,

"You are my Son;
today I have become your Father."[w][x]

6And he says in another place,

"You are a priest forever,
in the order of Melchizedek."[y]

7During the days of Jesus' life on earth, he of-
fered up prayers and petitions with loud cries and
tears to the one who could save him from death,
and he was heard because of his reverent submis-
sion. 8Although he was a son, he learned obedi-
ence from what he suffered 9and, once made per-
fect, he became the source of eternal salvation for
all who obey him 10and was designated by God to
be high priest in the order of Melchizedek.

v14 *Or gone into heaven* w5 *Or have begotten you* x5 Psalm 2:7
y6 Psalm 110:4

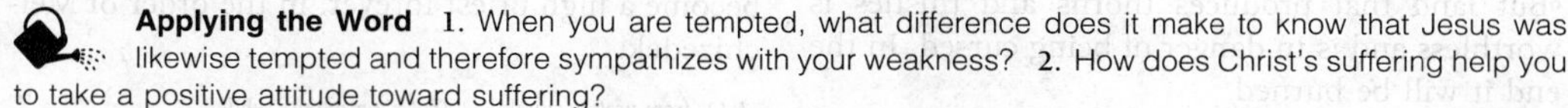

Discovering the Word 1. What commands are given in 4:14 and 16? 2. What is there about the character of Jesus that encourages us to obey these commands? 3. Jesus, as our merciful and faithful high priest, made atonement for our sins. The writer reminds the Hebrews of their earthly high priest in Judaism. What was the high priest like (5:1–4)? 4. How would you compare Jesus' high appointment with the life he lived (5:7–8)? 5. What was the result of Christ's suffering (5:8–10)?

Applying the Word 1. When you are tempted, what difference does it make to know that Jesus was likewise tempted and therefore sympathizes with your weakness? 2. How does Christ's suffering help you to take a positive attitude toward suffering?

Responding in Prayer Pray that your life would reflect your high appointment as the adopted son or daughter of God.

6 / *Hebrews 5:11—6:20* The Race to Maturity

PETER SNELL, FORMER Olympic gold medalist, said that the only way to win a race is to get in front and go flat out. Prior to that, he said, it takes a whole lot of hard training and self-discipline. The Hebrews were in desperate danger of quitting the race, so the writer urged them to go forward. This is a chapter with four strong appeals: "Let us go on to maturity" (v. 1). "Show diligence" (v. 11). "Do not become lazy" (v. 12). "Take hold of the hope " (v. 18).

Warming Up to God When are you most tempted to drop out of the faith-race? Why?

Read Hebrews 5:11—6:20.

11We have much to say about this, but it is hard to explain because you are slow to learn. 12In fact, though by this time you ought to be teachers, you need someone to teach you the elementary truths of God's word all over again. You need milk, not solid food! 13Anyone who lives on milk, being still an infant, is not acquainted with the teaching about righteousness. 14But solid food is for the mature, who by constant use have trained themselves to distinguish good from evil.

6 Therefore let us leave the elementary teachings about Christ and go on to maturity, not laying again the foundation of repentance from acts that lead to death,[z] and of faith in God, 2instruction about baptisms, the laying on of hands, the resurrection of the dead, and eternal judgment. 3And God permitting, we will do so.

4It is impossible for those who have once been enlightened, who have tasted the heavenly gift, who have shared in the Holy Spirit, 5who have tasted the goodness of the word of God and the powers of the coming age, 6if they fall away, to be brought back to repentance, because[a] to their loss they are crucifying the Son of God all over again and subjecting him to public disgrace.

7Land that drinks in the rain often falling on it and that produces a crop useful to those for whom it is farmed receives the blessing of God. 8But land that produces thorns and thistles is worthless and is in danger of being cursed. In the end it will be burned.

9Even though we speak like this, dear friends, we are confident of better things in your case—things that accompany salvation. 10God is not unjust; he will not forget your work and the love you have shown him as you have helped his people and continue to help them. 11We want each of you to show this same diligence to the very end, in order to make your hope sure. 12We do not want you to become lazy, but to imitate those who through faith and patience inherit what has been promised.

13When God made his promise to Abraham, since there was no one greater for him to swear by, he swore by himself, 14saying, "I will surely bless you and give you many descendants."[b] 15And so after waiting patiently, Abraham received what was promised.

16Men swear by someone greater than themselves, and the oath confirms what is said and puts an end to all argument. 17Because God wanted to make the unchanging nature of his purpose very clear to the heirs of what was promised, he confirmed it with an oath. 18God did this so that, by two unchangeable things in which it is impossible for God to lie, we who have fled to take hold of the hope offered to us may be greatly encouraged. 19We have this hope as an anchor for the soul, firm and secure. It enters the inner sanctuary behind the curtain, 20where Jesus, who went before us, has entered on our behalf. He has become a high priest forever, in the order of Melchizedek.

[z] 1 Or *from useless rituals* [a] 6 Or *repentance while*
[b] 14 Gen. 22:17

Discovering the Word 1. How would you describe the failures of the Hebrews (5:11–14)? 2. In view of their resources and opportunities for growth, how do you account for their problems? 3. According to 6:6, why is it absolutely essential to develop Christian maturity? 4. What hope does the writer see for better things to come (vv. 9–10)? Why? 5. What essential part of God's nature encourages the Hebrews to be positive and hopeful about their future (vv. 13–18)?

Applying the Word 1. Two kinds of land production vividly portray the reason to go on to maturity (6:7–8). How does each characterize your life? 2. As you reflect on your track record, of both diligence and laziness (6:11–12), how can you improve? 3. In verses 19–20 the writer returns to the Hebrews' familiar religion of priests and their temple with its holy place curtained off. In other words, it was a picture of a more profound spiritual reality in Christ. How does Jesus fulfill your deepest aspirations and help you to go on to maturity in your faith-race?

Responding in Prayer Ask God to firmly anchor your soul with hope in Christ.

7 / *Hebrews 7*
Eternal Companion

IN THE OLD Testament, religion and priests go hand in hand. Moses had carefully laid out all the rules for the Levites, the priestly clan of Israel. But the Hebrew Christians had departed from their old religion that was centered on priestly functions. Yet some of them hankered to return to their old ways. "Don't turn back," the writer appeals. "You have something far better in Christ." In chapters 7—10 the author tells of Christ's superior priestly origin, his better covenant and his sufficient-for-all-time sacrifice of himself. Regardless of whether we have had to move away from old traditions to find Christ, we all need confidence builders like chapter 7 so that as we run our faith-race, we will stick with Jesus no matter what.

Warming Up to God "He always makes me feel so strong," a church member said of his pastor after a sermon. What relationships strengthen your knowledge of Christ and build you up?

Read Hebrews 7.

7 This Melchizedek was king of Salem and
priest of God Most High. He met Abra-
ham returning from the defeat of the
kings and blessed him, 2and Abraham gave him a
tenth of everything. First, his name means "king
of righteousness"; then also, "king of Salem"
means "king of peace." 3Without father or
mother, without genealogy, without beginning of
days or end of life, like the Son of God he remains
a priest forever.

4Just think how great he was: Even the patri-
arch Abraham gave him a tenth of the plunder!
5Now the law requires the descendants of Levi
who become priests to collect a tenth from the
people—that is, their brothers—even though
their brothers are descended from Abraham.
6This man, however, did not trace his descent
from Levi, yet he collected a tenth from Abraham
and blessed him who had the promises. 7And
without doubt the lesser person is blessed by the
greater. 8In the one case, the tenth is collected by
men who die; but in the other case, by him who
is declared to be living. 9One might even say that
Levi, who collects the tenth, paid the tenth
through Abraham, 10because when Melchizedek
met Abraham, Levi was still in the body of his
ancestor.

11If perfection could have been attained
through the Levitical priesthood (for on the basis
of it the law was given to the people), why was
there still need for another priest to come—one
in the order of Melchizedek, not in the order of
Aaron? 12For when there is a change of the priest-
hood, there must also be a change of the law.
13He of whom these things are said belonged to a
different tribe, and no one from that tribe has
ever served at the altar. 14For it is clear that our
Lord descended from Judah, and in regard to that
tribe Moses said nothing about priests. 15And
what we have said is even more clear if another
priest like Melchizedek appears, 16one who has
become a priest not on the basis of a regulation as
to his ancestry but on the basis of the power of an
indestructible life. 17For it is declared:

"You are a priest forever,
in the order of Melchizedek."[c]

18The former regulation is set aside because it
was weak and useless 19(for the law made nothing
perfect), and a better hope is introduced, by
which we draw near to God.

20And it was not without an oath! Others be-
came priests without any oath, 21but he became a
priest with an oath when God said to him:

"The Lord has sworn
and will not change his mind:
'You are a priest forever.' "[c]

22Because of this oath, Jesus has become the guar-
antee of a better covenant.

23Now there have been many of those priests,
since death prevented them from continuing in
office; 24but because Jesus lives forever, he has a
permanent priesthood. 25Therefore he is able to
save completely[d] those who come to God
through him, because he always lives to intercede
for them.

26Such a high priest meets our need—one who
is holy, blameless, pure, set apart from sinners,

c17,21 Psalm 110:4 d25 Or *forever*

exalted above the heavens. 27Unlike the other high priests, he does not need to offer sacrifices day after day, first for his own sins, and then for the sins of the people. He sacrificed for their sins once for all when he offered himself. 28For the law appoints as high priests men who are weak; but the oath, which came after the law, appointed the Son, who has been made perfect forever.

Discovering the Word 1. Jesus is our high priest, not of the ancient Jewish line of Aaron but of the line of the pre-Aaronic Melchizedek. "Just think how great he [Melchizedek] was," commands the writer (v. 4). What was there about Melchizedek that made him so great (vv. 1–3)? 2. Great as his name and position were, there was one incident that proved Melchizedek's superiority to the Hebrews: Their patriarch Abraham tithed (gave one tenth of his income) to him (v. 4). According to verses 5–10, why does this prove that Jesus' high priesthood is superior to that of Levi (Aaron's son)? 3. Jesus inaugurated a new era and set aside the old because he was not of the priestly tribe (vv. 11–14). On what does his priestly authority rest (vv. 15–17)? 4. In what sense were the ancient rules of the Jews "weak and useless" (vv. 18–19)? 5. God's oath set aside Jesus as a distinctive high priest (vv. 20–21). How does Jesus guarantee our faith-agreement (covenant) with him (vv. 22–25)? 6. What about Christ's character and sacrifice sets him far above other earthly priests (vv. 26–28)?

Applying the Word 1. Twice the writer tells us to come to God through Christ's high priesthood (vv. 19, 25). Why do you need to do this? 2. How can you practice it in your faith-race?

Responding in Prayer Praise God for giving you a high priest over all in Jesus Christ.

8/ *Hebrews 8*
God's "New Deal"

BACK IN 1932, President Franklin Roosevelt sought to rescue the country from the pit of the Great Depression by launching the New Deal. The concept caught the imagination of the people. The time was ripe for a radically new economic and social program. In this chapter, the writer of Hebrews announces God's "new deal"—a covenant, or agreement, between God and humanity. It offers far superior promises to those of the "old deal" (Old Testament laws and regulations).

Warming Up to God What does knowing you are God's child mean to you?

Read Hebrews 8.

8 The point of what we are saying is this: We do have such a high priest, who sat down at the right hand of the throne of the Majesty in heaven, 2and who serves in the sanctuary, the true tabernacle set up by the Lord, not by man.

3Every high priest is appointed to offer both gifts and sacrifices, and so it was necessary for this one also to have something to offer. 4If he were on earth, he would not be a priest, for there are already men who offer the gifts prescribed by the law. 5They serve at a sanctuary that is a copy and shadow of what is in heaven. This is why Moses was warned when he was about to build the tabernacle: "See to it that you make everything according to the pattern shown you on the mountain."[e] 6But the ministry Jesus has received is as superior to theirs as the covenant of which he is mediator is superior to the old one, and it is founded on better promises.

7For if there had been nothing wrong with that first covenant, no place would have been sought for another. 8But God found fault with the people and said[f]:

"The time is coming, declares the Lord,
when I will make a new covenant

[e]5 Exodus 25:40 [f]8 Some manuscripts may be translated *fault and said to the people.*

with the house of Israel
and with the house of Judah.
9It will not be like the covenant
I made with their forefathers
when I took them by the hand
to lead them out of Egypt,
because they did not remain faithful to my
covenant,
and I turned away from them,
declares the Lord.
10This is the covenant I will make with the
house of Israel
after that time, declares the Lord.
I will put my laws in their minds
and write them on their hearts.
I will be their God,
and they will be my people.
11No longer will a man teach his neighbor,
or a man his brother, saying, 'Know the
Lord,'
because they will all know me,
from the least of them to the greatest.
12For I will forgive their wickedness
and will remember their sins no more."[g]

13By calling this covenant "new," he has made
the first one obsolete; and what is obsolete and
aging will soon disappear.

[g]12 Jer. 31:31-34

Discovering the Word 1. "We do have such a high priest" (v. 1) refers to the description of Jesus in 7:23–28. What additional facts do you learn about him (vv. 1–2)? 2. What is Christ's heavenly ministry (vv. 3–6)? 3. Verse 6 looks back to prove Christ's superior ministry and ahead to prove that we have a superior covenant with God. The key is "better promises." What was the problem with the first covenant (vv. 7–12)? 4. What guarantees God's "new deal" (v. 12)? (See also vv. 1–3; 9:14.)

Applying the Word 1. Do you function better under external restraint (the law) or inner constraint (God's Spirit) (v. 10)? Why? 2. What happens to you when you say to God, "Thank you for forgiving and forgetting my sin"? 3. A magazine ad for dishwashers offers more power, more pizzazz and more performance. How could your understanding and application of God's "new deal" offer all of that to you in your walk with him?

Responding in Prayer Ask God to forgive your sins, naming those you can think of specifically.

9 / *Hebrews 9*
The Runner's Power

IN VIEW OF the colossal problems besetting us—drugs, divorce, depression, to name a few—it seems like a gross oversimplification to say that the blood of Jesus Christ is the solution. But, in a different context, the Hebrews faced similar problems of neglect, unbelief and immaturity. They were in danger of dropping out of the race and turning back to their old ways. Seemingly, they lacked the power and purpose to advance and press on in their faith-race. What was the solution given to them? The blood of Jesus. Only a full and perfect knowledge of what Jesus is and does for us can bring us to a full and perfect Christian life.

Warming Up to God When do you feel like dropping out of the race?

Read Hebrews 9.

9 Now the first covenant had regulations
for worship and also an earthly sanctuary.
2A tabernacle was set up. In its first room
were the lampstand, the table and the consecrated
bread; this was called the Holy Place. 3Behind the
second curtain was a room called the Most Holy
Place, 4which had the golden altar of incense and
the gold-covered ark of the covenant. This ark
contained the gold jar of manna, Aaron's staff that
had budded, and the stone tablets of the cov-

enant. 5Above the ark were the cherubim of the Glory, overshadowing the atonement cover.[h] But we cannot discuss these things in detail now.

6When everything had been arranged like this, the priests entered regularly into the outer room to carry on their ministry. 7But only the high priest entered the inner room, and that only once a year, and never without blood, which he offered for himself and for the sins the people had committed in ignorance. 8The Holy Spirit was showing by this that the way into the Most Holy Place had not yet been disclosed as long as the first tabernacle was still standing. 9This is an illustration for the present time, indicating that the gifts and sacrifices being offered were not able to clear the conscience of the worshiper. 10They are only a matter of food and drink and various ceremonial washings—external regulations applying until the time of the new order.

11When Christ came as high priest of the good things that are already here,[i] he went through the greater and more perfect tabernacle that is not man-made, that is to say, not a part of this creation. 12He did not enter by means of the blood of goats and calves; but he entered the Most Holy Place once for all by his own blood, having obtained eternal redemption. 13The blood of goats and bulls and the ashes of a heifer sprinkled on those who are ceremonially unclean sanctify them so that they are outwardly clean. 14How much more, then, will the blood of Christ, who through the eternal Spirit offered himself unblemished to God, cleanse our consciences from acts that lead to death,[j] so that we may serve the living God!

15For this reason Christ is the mediator of a new covenant, that those who are called may receive the promised eternal inheritance—now that he has died as a ransom to set them free from the sins committed under the first covenant.

16In the case of a will,[k] it is necessary to prove the death of the one who made it, 17because a will is in force only when somebody has died; it never takes effect while the one who made it is living. 18This is why even the first covenant was not put into effect without blood. 19When Moses had proclaimed every commandment of the law to all the people, he took the blood of calves, together with water, scarlet wool and branches of hyssop, and sprinkled the scroll and all the people. 20He said, "This is the blood of the covenant, which God has commanded you to keep."[l] 21In the same way, he sprinkled with the blood both the tabernacle and everything used in its ceremonies. 22In fact, the law requires that nearly everything be cleansed with blood, and without the shedding of blood there is no forgiveness.

23It was necessary, then, for the copies of the heavenly things to be purified with these sacrifices, but the heavenly things themselves with better sacrifices than these. 24For Christ did not enter a man-made sanctuary that was only a copy of the true one; he entered heaven itself, now to appear for us in God's presence. 25Nor did he enter heaven to offer himself again and again, the way the high priest enters the Most Holy Place every year with blood that is not his own. 26Then Christ would have had to suffer many times since the creation of the world. But now he has appeared once for all at the end of the ages to do away with sin by the sacrifice of himself. 27Just as man is destined to die once, and after that to face judgment, 28so Christ was sacrificed once to take away the sins of many people; and he will appear a second time, not to bear sin, but to bring salvation to those who are waiting for him.

[h]5 Traditionally *the mercy seat* [i]11 Some early manuscripts *are to come* [j]14 Or *from useless rituals* [k]16 Same Greek word as *covenant*; also in verse 17 [l]20 Exodus 24:8

Discovering the Word 1. Contrast what Jesus did (vv. 11–14) with the old system (vv. 1–10). 2. Why was the shedding of sacrificial blood required even under the old covenant (vv. 16–22)? 3. The writer explains why the offering of Jesus' blood is not only necessary, but also a superior sacrifice. Why is it important to direct our attention to "heavenly things" (v. 23)? 4. What difference would it make to those steeped in Old Testament religion to know that Jesus once-for-all offered his own blood, rather than offering animal blood (vv. 25–26)?

Applying the Word 1. How can you deepen your understanding of and appreciation for Christ's self-sacrifice? 2. Death and judgment are certain. In view of that, how would you encourage someone to face eternity with hope and peace, based on what you have learned in this chapter? 3. Also certain is Jesus' Second Coming (v. 28). In light of his blood offering, how should you spend your time waiting for him?

Responding in Prayer Pray that you will use your time to serve Jesus even as you wait for him.

10 / *Hebrews 10*
Staying in the Race

FACED WITH SEEMINGLY eternal years of schoolwork and a multitude of rules to obey, children get discouraged. When that happens, parents say, "Look at your great opportunities. Take advantage of what you have now. Don't throw it away."

The writer of Hebrews, in chapter 10, reaches the heights of Mt. Everest with a picture of Jesus that offers his readers encouragement. From those lofty heights he tells them to warm up to God, hold their faith in him, and stir up one another in Christian faith and practice.

Warming Up to God Recall an opportunity you missed because it sounded too good. What did you miss by not believing the evidence?

Read Hebrews 10.

10 The law is only a shadow of the
good things that are coming—not
the realities themselves. For this
reason it can never, by the same sacrifices re-
peated endlessly year after year, make perfect
those who draw near to worship. [2]If it could,
would they not have stopped being offered? For
the worshipers would have been cleansed once
for all, and would no longer have felt guilty for
their sins. [3]But those sacrifices are an annual re-
minder of sins, [4]because it is impossible for the
blood of bulls and goats to take away sins.
[5]Therefore, when Christ came into the world,
he said:

"Sacrifice and offering you did not desire,
but a body you prepared for me;
[6]with burnt offerings and sin offerings
you were not pleased.
[7]Then I said, 'Here I am—it is written about
me in the scroll—
I have come to do your will, O God.' "[m]

[8]First he said, "Sacrifices and offerings, burnt of-
ferings and sin offerings you did not desire, nor
were you pleased with them" (although the law
required them to be made). [9]Then he said, "Here
I am, I have come to do your will." He sets aside
the first to establish the second.• [10]And by that
will, we have been made holy through the sacri-
fice of the body of Jesus Christ once for all.
[11]Day after day every priest stands and per-
forms his religious duties; again and again he of-
fers the same sacrifices, which can never take
away sins. [12]But when this priest had offered for
all time one sacrifice for sins, he sat down at the
right hand of God. [13]Since that time he waits for
his enemies to be made his footstool, [14]because by
one sacrifice he has made perfect forever those
who are being made holy.
[15]The Holy Spirit also testifies to us about this.
First he says:

[16]"This is the covenant I will make with them
after that time, says the Lord.
I will put my laws in their hearts,
and I will write them on their minds."[n]

[17]Then he adds:

"Their sins and lawless acts
I will remember no more."[o]

[18]And where these have been forgiven, there is no
longer any sacrifice for sin.
[19]Therefore, brothers, since we have confi-
dence to enter the Most Holy Place by the blood
of Jesus, [20]by a new and living way opened for us
through the curtain, that is, his body, [21]and since
we have a great priest over the house of God, [22]let
us draw near to God with a sincere heart in full
assurance of faith, having our hearts sprinkled to
cleanse us from a guilty conscience and having
our bodies washed with pure water. [23]Let us hold

[m]7 Psalm 40:6-8 (see Septuagint) [n]16 Jer. 31:33 [o]17 Jer. 31:34

unswervingly to the hope we profess, for he who promised is faithful. [24]And let us consider how we may spur one another on toward love and good deeds. [25]Let us not give up meeting together, as some are in the habit of doing, but let us encourage one another—and all the more as you see the Day approaching.

[26]If we deliberately keep on sinning after we have received the knowledge of the truth, no sacrifice for sins is left, [27]but only a fearful expectation of judgment and of raging fire that will consume the enemies of God. [28]Anyone who rejected the law of Moses died without mercy on the testimony of two or three witnesses. [29]How much more severely do you think a man deserves to be punished who has trampled the Son of God under foot, who has treated as an unholy thing the blood of the covenant that sanctified him, and who has insulted the Spirit of grace? [30]For we know him who said, "It is mine to avenge; I will repay,"[p] and again, "The Lord will judge his people."[q] [31]It is a dreadful thing to fall into the hands of the living God.

[32]Remember those earlier days after you had received the light, when you stood your ground in a great contest in the face of suffering. [33]Sometimes you were publicly exposed to insult and persecution; at other times you stood side by side with those who were so treated. [34]You sympathized with those in prison and joyfully accepted the confiscation of your property, because you knew that you yourselves had better and lasting possessions.

[35]So do not throw away your confidence; it will be richly rewarded. [36]You need to persevere so that when you have done the will of God, you will receive what he has promised. [37]For in just a very little while,

"He who is coming will come and will not
delay.
38 But my righteous one[r] will live by faith.
And if he shrinks back,
I will not be pleased with him."[s]

[39]But we are not of those who shrink back and are destroyed, but of those who believe and are saved.

[p]30 Deut. 32:35 [q]30 Deut. 32:36; Psalm 135:14 [r]38 One early manuscript *But the righteous* [s]38 Hab. 2:3,4

Discovering the Word 1. The writer continues to discuss Jesus and the Old Testament offerings. How do verses 1–4 prove that the Old Testament system was a shadow, not the real thing? 2. Contrast Jesus' sacrifice (the reality) with the shadow (vv. 5–10). Why is his sacrifice better? 3. As you meditate on verses 11–18 and the awesome love and power of Jesus to take away your sins, what are the responses in your heart and mind? 4. In light of what God has done for us in Christ (vv. 19–21), what three commands does the writer feel compelled to issue (vv. 22–24)? 5. If we fail to draw near to God, hold fast our faith and stir up one another, what is likely to happen (vv. 25–26, 38–39)?

Applying the Word 1. How can you help hold someone you know "unswervingly" to faith? 2. What purposes could be achieved in your life by both this strong encouragement and this stern warning?

Responding in Prayer Pray for your church, that you would support and encourage one another.

11 / *Hebrews 11*
Models of Faith

PROBABLY NO SUBJECT is so glibly misunderstood as faith. Nearly everyone professes to have some of it. Many people would like to have more. The writer to the Hebrews takes faith out of religious theory and clothes it with flesh and blood. The author does this with what we today call *role models.* These models inspire us to go on believing in Jesus.

Warming Up to God Complete the sentence: "Faith is . . ."

 **Read Hebrews 11.**

11 Now faith is being sure of what we hope for and certain of what we do not see. 2This is what the ancients were commended for.

3By faith we understand that the universe was formed at God's command, so that what is seen was not made out of what was visible.

4By faith Abel offered God a better sacrifice than Cain did. By faith he was commended as a righteous man, when God spoke well of his offerings. And by faith he still speaks, even though he is dead.

5By faith Enoch was taken from this life, so that he did not experience death; he could not be found, because God had taken him away. For before he was taken, he was commended as one who pleased God. 6And without faith it is impossible to please God, because anyone who comes to him must believe that he exists and that he rewards those who earnestly seek him.

7By faith Noah, when warned about things not yet seen, in holy fear built an ark to save his family. By his faith he condemned the world and became heir of the righteousness that comes by faith.

8By faith Abraham, when called to go to a place he would later receive as his inheritance, obeyed and went, even though he did not know where he was going. 9By faith he made his home in the promised land like a stranger in a foreign country; he lived in tents, as did Isaac and Jacob, who were heirs with him of the same promise. 10For he was looking forward to the city with foundations, whose architect and builder is God.

11By faith Abraham, even though he was past age—and Sarah herself was barren—was enabled to become a father because he[t] considered him faithful who had made the promise. 12And so from this one man, and he as good as dead, came descendants as numerous as the stars in the sky and as countless as the sand on the seashore.

13All these people were still living by faith when they died. They did not receive the things promised; they only saw them and welcomed them from a distance. And they admitted that they were aliens and strangers on earth. 14People who say such things show that they are looking for a country of their own. 15If they had been thinking of the country they had left, they would have had opportunity to return. 16Instead, they were longing for a better country—a heavenly one. Therefore God is not ashamed to be called their God, for he has prepared a city for them.

17By faith Abraham, when God tested him, offered Isaac as a sacrifice. He who had received the promises was about to sacrifice his one and only son, 18even though God had said to him, "It is through Isaac that your offspring[u] will be reckoned."[v] 19Abraham reasoned that God could raise the dead, and figuratively speaking, he did receive Isaac back from death.

20By faith Isaac blessed Jacob and Esau in regard to their future.

21By faith Jacob, when he was dying, blessed each of Joseph's sons, and worshiped as he leaned on the top of his staff.

22By faith Joseph, when his end was near, spoke about the exodus of the Israelites from Egypt and gave instructions about his bones.

23By faith Moses' parents hid him for three months after he was born, because they saw he was no ordinary child, and they were not afraid of the king's edict.

24By faith Moses, when he had grown up, refused to be known as the son of Pharaoh's daughter. 25He chose to be mistreated along with the people of God rather than to enjoy the pleasures of sin for a short time. 26He regarded disgrace for the sake of Christ as of greater value than the treasures of Egypt, because he was looking ahead to his reward. 27By faith he left Egypt, not fearing the king's anger; he persevered because he saw him who is invisible. 28By faith he kept the Passover and the sprinkling of blood, so that the destroyer of the firstborn would not touch the firstborn of Israel.

29By faith the people passed through the Red Sea[w] as on dry land; but when the Egyptians tried to do so, they were drowned.

30By faith the walls of Jericho fell, after the people had marched around them for seven days.

31By faith the prostitute Rahab, because she welcomed the spies, was not killed with those who were disobedient.[x]

32And what more shall I say? I do not have time

[t] *11* Or *By faith even Sarah, who was past age, was enabled to bear children because she* [u] *18* Greek *seed* [v] *18* Gen. 21:12
[w] *29* That is, Sea of Reeds [x] *31* Or *unbelieving*

to tell about Gideon, Barak, Samson, Jephthah, David, Samuel and the prophets, [33]who through faith conquered kingdoms, administered justice, and gained what was promised; who shut the mouths of lions, [34]quenched the fury of the flames, and escaped the edge of the sword; whose weakness was turned to strength; and who became powerful in battle and routed foreign armies. [35]Women received back their dead, raised to life again. Others were tortured and refused to be released, so that they might gain a better resurrection. [36]Some faced jeers and flogging, while still others were chained and put in prison. [37]They were stoned[y]; they were sawed in two; they were put to death by the sword. They went about in sheepskins and goatskins, destitute, persecuted and mistreated— [38]the world was not worthy of them. They wandered in deserts and mountains, and in caves and holes in the ground.

[39]These were all commended for their faith, yet none of them received what had been promised. [40]God had planned something better for us so that only together with us would they be made perfect.

[y]37 Some early manuscripts *stoned; they were put to the test;*

Discovering the Word 1. Look for both assured confidence and calm expectation (v. 1) in the role models of faith in this chapter. How did Abel, Enoch and Noah express their faith (vv. 4–7)? 2. Considering the foolishness of his choices by human standards, what do you think Abraham's emotions were like (vv. 8–10)? 3. How does the promise of a heavenly country help us to keep our faith, even when we don't see our hopes fulfilled immediately (vv. 13–16)? 4. Why do you think Abraham's faith triumphed when he was asked to give up Isaac (vv. 17–19)? 5. How would you compare the faith of the named heroes and heroines who achieved greatness (vv. 20–35) with those unnamed persons who suffered grievously (vv. 35–38)? 6. Some Christians believe that faith always leads to material and physical blessing. What does this passage tell you about the role of both blessing and suffering for the faithful?

Applying the Word 1. In tough circumstances, what connection do you make between your faith and the certainty of resurrection (v. 35)? 2. What unseen certainties have guided you in making fundamental, life-changing decisions?

Responding in Prayer Pray for the faith you need in your life right now to do God's will.

12 / *Hebrews 12*
The Runner's Discipline

WE OFTEN WONDER why thousands of marathoners seem to enjoy punishing themselves in grueling races. Certainly, for most, it's not the hope of winning. What is it then? Explaining it to his readers, writer Art Carey said, "The real joy of the Boston Marathon is just finishing, just winning the contest with yourself—doing what you have set out to do." That's the attitude the Hebrews were supposed to have: Stay in the faith-race to the end.

Warming Up to God Who has been a model of perseverance and endurance for you? Thank God for that person.

Read Hebrews 12.

12 Therefore, since we are surrounded by such a great cloud of witnesses, let us throw off everything that hinders and the sin that so easily entangles, and let us run with perseverance the race marked out for us. [2]Let us fix our eyes on Jesus, the author and perfecter of our faith, who for the joy set before him endured the cross, scorning its shame, and sat down at the right hand of the throne of God. [3]Consider him who endured such opposition from sinful men, so that you will not grow weary and lose heart.

4In your struggle against sin, you have not yet resisted to the point of shedding your blood. 5And you have forgotten that word of encouragement that addresses you as sons:

"My son, do not make light of the Lord's
discipline,
and do not lose heart when he rebukes
you,
6because the Lord disciplines those he loves,
and he punishes everyone he accepts as a
son."[z]

7Endure hardship as discipline; God is treating you as sons. For what son is not disciplined by his father? 8If you are not disciplined (and everyone undergoes discipline), then you are illegitimate children and not true sons. 9Moreover, we have all had human fathers who disciplined us and we respected them for it. How much more should we submit to the Father of our spirits and live! 10Our fathers disciplined us for a little while as they thought best; but God disciplines us for our good, that we may share in his holiness. 11No discipline seems pleasant at the time, but painful. Later on, however, it produces a harvest of righteousness and peace for those who have been trained by it.

12Therefore, strengthen your feeble arms and weak knees. 13"Make level paths for your feet,"[a] so that the lame may not be disabled, but rather healed.

14Make every effort to live in peace with all men and to be holy; without holiness no one will see the Lord. 15See to it that no one misses the grace of God and that no bitter root grows up to cause trouble and defile many. 16See that no one is sexually immoral, or is godless like Esau, who for a single meal sold his inheritance rights as the oldest son. 17Afterward, as you know, when he wanted to inherit this blessing, he was rejected. He could bring about no change of mind, though he sought the blessing with tears.

18You have not come to a mountain that can be touched and that is burning with fire; to darkness, gloom and storm; 19to a trumpet blast or to such a voice speaking words that those who heard it begged that no further word be spoken to them, 20because they could not bear what was commanded: "If even an animal touches the mountain, it must be stoned."[b] 21The sight was so terrifying that Moses said, "I am trembling with fear."[c]

22But you have come to Mount Zion, to the heavenly Jerusalem, the city of the living God. You have come to thousands upon thousands of angels in joyful assembly, 23to the church of the firstborn, whose names are written in heaven. You have come to God, the judge of all men, to the spirits of righteous men made perfect, 24to Jesus the mediator of a new covenant, and to the sprinkled blood that speaks a better word than the blood of Abel.

25See to it that you do not refuse him who speaks. If they did not escape when they refused him who warned them on earth, how much less will we, if we turn away from him who warns us from heaven? 26At that time his voice shook the earth, but now he has promised, "Once more I will shake not only the earth but also the heavens."[d] 27The words "once more" indicate the removing of what can be shaken—that is, created things—so that what cannot be shaken may remain.

28Therefore, since we are receiving a kingdom that cannot be shaken, let us be thankful, and so worship God acceptably with reverence and awe, 29for our "God is a consuming fire."[e]

[z]6 Prov. 3:11,12 [a]13 Prov. 4:26 [b]20 Exodus 19:12,13
[c]21 Deut. 9:19 [d]26 Haggai 2:6 [e]29 Deut. 4:24

Discovering the Word 1. Of what value is it to keep your eyes on Jesus (vv. 2–3)? 2. What discipline of the Hebrews do you think the writer alludes to (vv. 3–4, 7; 11:35–38)? 3. How do the values of God's discipline cited here help us to respond positively to discipline (vv. 10–12)? 4. Identify the writer's specific instructions in verses 14–17. On what principles are they based? 5. How could you identify a "bitter root" or a "godless Esau" in your life (vv. 15–16)? 6. We've all been tempted to drop out of the race. Why would the warning of verses 25–29 cause us to reconsider?

Applying the Word 1. What hindrances and entanglements get in the way of your Christian faith-race (v. 1)? Why? 2. What encouragement do you find in verses 18–24 to run the faith-race with perseverance?

Responding in Prayer Let your prayer be one of worship for the God who is a "consuming fire."

13 / *Hebrews 13*
Running by the Rules

BEN JOHNSON OF Canada was stripped of the Olympic gold medals he won at Seoul in 1988 because he broke the rules about drug use. Similarly, the Christian's faith-race is much more than a sprint to the finish line. It's a race which brings glory to God by the way the runners behave. In the concluding chapter, the writer to the Hebrews sketches a variety of duties to God and humanity. Together they reveal an exalted level of personal morality and duty.

Warming Up to God Consider your attitude to God's law. At what times do you find it a burden? When does it help you?

Read Hebrews 13.

13 Keep on loving each other as brothers. 2Do not forget to entertain strangers, for by so doing some people have entertained angels without knowing it. 3Remember those in prison as if you were their fellow prisoners, and those who are mistreated as if you yourselves were suffering.

4Marriage should be honored by all, and the marriage bed kept pure, for God will judge the adulterer and all the sexually immoral. 5Keep your lives free from the love of money and be content with what you have, because God has said,

"Never will I leave you;
never will I forsake you."[f]

6So we say with confidence,

"The Lord is my helper; I will not be afraid.
What can man do to me?"[g]

7Remember your leaders, who spoke the word of God to you. Consider the outcome of their way of life and imitate their faith. 8Jesus Christ is the same yesterday and today and forever.

9Do not be carried away by all kinds of strange teachings. It is good for our hearts to be strengthened by grace, not by ceremonial foods, which are of no value to those who eat them. 10We have an altar from which those who minister at the tabernacle have no right to eat.

11The high priest carries the blood of animals into the Most Holy Place as a sin offering, but the bodies are burned outside the camp. 12And so Jesus also suffered outside the city gate to make the people holy through his own blood. 13Let us, then, go to him outside the camp, bearing the disgrace he bore. 14For here we do not have an enduring city, but we are looking for the city that is to come.

15Through Jesus, therefore, let us continually offer to God a sacrifice of praise—the fruit of lips that confess his name. 16And do not forget to do good and to share with others, for with such sacrifices God is pleased.

17Obey your leaders and submit to their authority. They keep watch over you as men who must give an account. Obey them so that their work will be a joy, not a burden, for that would be of no advantage to you.

18Pray for us. We are sure that we have a clear conscience and desire to live honorably in every way. 19I particularly urge you to pray so that I may be restored to you soon.

20May the God of peace, who through the blood of the eternal covenant brought back from the dead our Lord Jesus, that great Shepherd of the sheep, 21equip you with everything good for doing his will, and may he work in us what is pleasing to him, through Jesus Christ, to whom be glory for ever and ever. Amen.

22Brothers, I urge you to bear with my word of exhortation, for I have written you only a short letter.

23I want you to know that our brother Timothy has been released. If he arrives soon, I will come with him to see you.

24Greet all your leaders and all God's people. Those from Italy send you their greetings.

25Grace be with you all.

f5 Deut. 31:6 g6 Psalm 118:6,7

Discovering the Word 1. Verses 1–3 tie in with verse 16. In what sense should loving others, doing good, sharing, entertaining strangers, and helping the prisoners and the mistreated be considered "sacrifices" to God? 2. Sexual purity is one of God's absolutes (v. 4). How do you account for sexual impurity among professing Christians—some of them well-known public figures? 3. What facts about God help to keep you from loving money (vv. 5–6)? 4. Obligation to spiritual leaders are laid out in verses 7, 17–18. What is here that we should follow? 5. In what sense is our praise a sacrifice to God (v. 15)?

Applying the Word 1. Which of these exhortations do you need to apply to yourself? 2. On the basis of your study of Hebrews, what do you think God would like to "work" in you that would please him?

Responding in Prayer Verses 20–21 are a benediction, a summary prayer. Make that your prayer for yourself.

James

What does James have to say to me? James is practical.

Take problems. James knows nobody's perfect. So he doesn't tell us how to live trouble-free. He tells us how to live when troubles hit. Do I complain? Or do I use difficulties as an opportunity for growth?

Take words. We all talk. And sometimes we say things we wish we hadn't. James helps us use words more carefully, more positively. Do my words hurt others? Do they advance God's kingdom? Are they truthful? Are they loving?

Take money. It flows around us (despite our complaints about tight budgets and taxes). Do I withhold my money when others are in need? Do I put more value on worldly things than on the things of God?

Take time. If we have enough money, we know we never have enough time. We do all we can to get the most out of each hour of each day, filling our calendars with activity. But am I missing God's will and perspective in the midst of schedule making?

James is practical—maybe too practical! So expect these quiet times to be challenging—not because they will be hard to understand but because they will be all too easy to understand.

Who is this fellow James? There are several people in the New Testament called James, including two apostles. Though they have never been completely certain, most church scholars have believed that a third man, James the brother of Jesus (Mt 13:55; Mk 6:3), wrote this letter. While he probably joined the others in Jesus' family in rejecting Jesus during his earthly ministry, James certainly started following Jesus after his resurrection. In fact, James soon became the head of the church in Jerusalem.

He probably led the first church council in Jerusalem (Acts 15), which decided that Gentiles did not have to become Jews before they could be saved. This is an important factor in assessing James's view of faith and works (which is to be noted in light of 2:14–16).

Yet James was aware of the very Jewish makeup of the church in Jerusalem and required Paul to squelch the rumor that he, Paul, was telling Jews to abandon the law of Moses. James himself apparently followed Jewish law closely, enough so that he was known as "James the Just." He died a martyr in A.D. 62.

James addresses his letter to "the twelve tribes scattered among the nations." "Twelve tribes" could refer to Jewish Christians who through exile, enslavement and trade were spread throughout the entire Mediterranean basin. More likely it refers simply to Christians, since the New Testament compares the church to Israel (Gal 6:16 RSV; 1Pe 2:9–10). In any case, the letter is not addressed to one specific congregation, as Paul's letters were. It is therefore called a general, or catholic, epistle.

These quiet times will help you face squarely James's call for a consistent Christian life, for a practical faith—a faith that works.

Outline

1/ James 1:1–18 ———— *Dependable or Double-minded?*

2/ James 1:19–27 ———— *Words, Words, Words*

3/ James 2:1–13 ———— *Who's the Judge?*

4/ James 2:14–26 ———— *Just Works*

5/ James 3:1–12 ———— *Preventing Forest Fires*

6/ James 3:13—4:10 ———— *Keeping the Peace*

7/ James 4:11–17 ———— *Getting Perspective*

8/ James 5:1–11 ———— *What Awaits*

9/ James 5:12–20 ———— *Making Others Whole*

1 / *James 1:1–18*
Dependable or Double-minded?

NO PAIN, NO gain. Or so the saying goes. Athletes remind themselves of this to get their best possible performance. Sometimes they have to go through grueling training. Without it there is no improvement. James suggests it is the same for Christians.

Warming Up to God Enduring pain is not pleasant! What fears do you have as you think about what it means to face trials? Be honest with yourself. Describe your fears to God. Allow him to comfort you.

Read James 1:1–18.

1 James, a servant of God and of the Lord
Jesus Christ,

To the twelve tribes scattered among the na-
tions:

Greetings.

2Consider it pure joy, my brothers, whenever
you face trials of many kinds, 3because you know
that the testing of your faith develops persever-
ance. 4Perseverance must finish its work so that
you may be mature and complete, not lacking
anything. 5If any of you lacks wisdom, he should
ask God, who gives generously to all without
finding fault, and it will be given to him. 6But
when he asks, he must believe and not doubt,
because he who doubts is like a wave of the sea,
blown and tossed by the wind. 7That man should
not think he will receive anything from the Lord;
8he is a double-minded man, unstable in all he
does.
9The brother in humble circumstances ought to
take pride in his high position. 10But the one who
is rich should take pride in his low position, be-
cause he will pass away like a wild flower. 11For
the sun rises with scorching heat and withers the
plant; its blossom falls and its beauty is destroyed.
In the same way, the rich man will fade away
even while he goes about his business.
12Blessed is the man who perseveres under
trial, because when he has stood the test, he will
receive the crown of life that God has promised to
those who love him.
13When tempted, no one should say, "God is
tempting me." For God cannot be tempted by
evil, nor does he tempt anyone; 14but each one is
tempted when, by his own evil desire, he is
dragged away and enticed. 15Then, after desire
has conceived, it gives birth to sin; and sin, when
it is full-grown, gives birth to death.
16Don't be deceived, my dear brothers. 17Every
good and perfect gift is from above, coming down
from the Father of the heavenly lights, who does
not change like shifting shadows. 18He chose to
give us birth through the word of truth, that we
might be a kind of firstfruits of all he created.

Discovering the Word 1. How are perseverance and maturity developed in us by enduring trials (vv. 3–4)? 2. Under pressure, how does the faithful Christian (described in vv. 5–6) contrast with the person described in verses 6–8? 3. In the context of trials and perseverance, why does James contrast rich and poor Christians (vv. 9–11)? 4. How are temptations different from trials (vv. 2–16)? 5. How is God the ultimate example of goodness and dependability (vv. 16–18)?

Applying the Word 1. What difficult experiences have increased your perseverance and maturity? 2. In what ways do you tend to rely on your possessions? 3. Think of trials or temptations you are currently facing. How can this passage encourage you to depend on God?

Responding in Prayer Take time now to talk to God about your needs. Ask him to help you be like him in his goodness and dependability.

2 / *James 1:19–27*
Words, Words, Words

WE ALL DO it. It's as common as flies around a horse. While someone else is talking, we're thinking about what we're going to say next instead of about what is being said to us. We know others are worth more care and attention. But the habit is hard to break.

God wants us to slow down and listen too. But even when we've really listened to him, we're still not done. This study gives us practical help on listening and more.

Warming Up to God There's so much to listen to all around us. What different voices and messages are on your mind? Tell God about them and ask him to help you clear your mind and focus on his Word.

Read James 1:19–27.

19My dear brothers, take note of this: Everyone
should be quick to listen, slow to speak and slow
to become angry, 20for man's anger does not bring
about the righteous life that God desires. 21There-
fore, get rid of all moral filth and the evil that is
so prevalent and humbly accept the word planted
in you, which can save you.
22Do not merely listen to the word, and so de-
ceive yourselves. Do what it says. 23Anyone who
listens to the word but does not do what it says is
like a man who looks at his face in a mirror 24and,
after looking at himself, goes away and immedi-
ately forgets what he looks like. 25But the man
who looks intently into the perfect law that gives
freedom, and continues to do this, not forgetting
what he has heard, but doing it—he will be
blessed in what he does.
26If anyone considers himself religious and yet
does not keep a tight rein on his tongue, he de-
ceives himself and his religion is worthless. 27Re-
ligion that God our Father accepts as pure and
faultless is this: to look after orphans and widows
in their distress and to keep oneself from being
polluted by the world.

Discovering the Word 1. How can being quick to listen and slow to speak help us to be slow to become angry (v. 19)? 2. James tells us that God's Word was planted in us. What weeds can choke that Word and keep it from growing (v. 21)? Explain. 3. In your own words explain how the person who merely listens to God's Word is different from the one who puts it into practice (vv. 22–25). 4. According to verses 26 and 27, how do people who think they are religious differ from those who are truly religious? 5. Based on what you've read in this chapter, do you think James would be satisfied with good works apart from our listening to and receiving God's Word? Explain.

Applying the Word 1. When is it hard for you to listen to God? 2. Sometimes we do listen to God's Word, but we still don't follow it. How is this true for you? 3. How would you like your religion to be more "pure and faultless"?

Responding in Prayer Ask God to help you become a better listener and doer of his Word.

3 / *James 2:1–13*
Who's the Judge?

LABELS AREN'T JUST found on soup cans. We put them on people all the time. Funny or dull. Smart or thick-headed. Friendly or cold. There are all kinds of ways we can categorize people. And our categories can have a profound influence on the way we treat people. As you might suspect, James has a few words to say about favoritism.

Warming Up to God Reflect on judgmental words and thoughts you have had this week. Confess them to God. Allow yourself to experience his mercy.

Read James 2:1–13.

---

2 My brothers, as believers in our glorious
Lord Jesus Christ, don't show favoritism.
[2]Suppose a man comes into your meeting
wearing a gold ring and fine clothes, and a poor
man in shabby clothes also comes in. [3]If you
show special attention to the man wearing fine
clothes and say, "Here's a good seat for you," but
say to the poor man, "You stand there" or "Sit on
the floor by my feet," [4]have you not discriminated
among yourselves and become judges with evil
thoughts?
[5]Listen, my dear brothers: Has not God chosen
those who are poor in the eyes of the world to be
rich in faith and to inherit the kingdom he prom-
ised those who love him? [6]But you have insulted
the poor. Is it not the rich who are exploiting
you? Are they not the ones who are dragging you
into court? [7]Are they not the ones who are slan-
dering the noble name of him to whom you be-
long?
[8]If you really keep the royal law found in Scrip-
ture, "Love your neighbor as yourself,"[a] you are
doing right. [9]But if you show favoritism, you sin
and are convicted by the law as lawbreakers.
[10]For whoever keeps the whole law and yet stum-
bles at just one point is guilty of breaking all of it.
[11]For he who said, "Do not commit adultery,"[b]
also said, "Do not murder."[c] If you do not com-
mit adultery but do commit murder, you have
become a lawbreaker.
[12]Speak and act as those who are going to be
judged by the law that gives freedom, [13]because
judgment without mercy will be shown to anyone
who has not been merciful. Mercy triumphs over
judgment!

[a]8 Lev. 19:18 [b]11 Exodus 20:14; Deut. 5:18 [c]11 Exodus 20:13; Deut. 5:17

Discovering the Word 1. How would you react if someone came into your church who wore sloppy clothes, was dirty or had body odor (vv. 2–4)? 2. Why is it wrong to give preferential treatment to those who have money (vv. 5–7)? 3. Verse 5 says God has chosen the poor to be rich in faith. Is God guilty of showing favoritism in this way? Explain. 4. How can "the royal law" (v. 8) guide our treatment of both poor and rich? 5. In what sense is violating one law as serious as breaking every law (vv. 9–11)?

Applying the Word 1. Toward what people or groups do you show favoritism? 2. How can you change your attitude and actions?

Responding in Prayer Ask God to work in your heart and mind to help you see beneath the surface as you relate to people.

---

4 / *James 2:14–26*
Just Works

"IT IS EASIER said than done" is a cliché that certainly applies to our Christian life. It is much easier to talk about God than to obey him. James said that even the demons believe there is one God. But that certainly does not make them Christians! That's why someone can have all his or her doctrine perfectly straight and still have missed out on God's will. James helps us stay on target.

Warming Up to God What has God been asking you to do that you have been ignoring? Talk to him about it.

Read James 2:14–26.

14What good is it, my brothers, if a man claims
to have faith but has no deeds? Can such faith
save him? 15Suppose a brother or sister is without
clothes and daily food. 16If one of you says to
him, "Go, I wish you well; keep warm and well
fed," but does nothing about his physical needs,
what good is it? 17In the same way, faith by itself,
if it is not accompanied by action, is dead.

18But someone will say, "You have faith; I have
deeds."

Show me your faith without deeds, and I will
show you my faith by what I do. 19You believe
that there is one God. Good! Even the demons
believe that—and shudder.

20You foolish man, do you want evidence that
faith without deeds is useless[d]? 21Was not our
ancestor Abraham considered righteous for what
he did when he offered his son Isaac on the altar?
22You see that his faith and his actions were
working together, and his faith was made com-
plete by what he did. 23And the scripture was
fulfilled that says, "Abraham believed God, and it
was credited to him as righteousness,"[e] and he
was called God's friend. 24You see that a person is
justified by what he does and not by faith alone.

25In the same way, was not even Rahab the
prostitute considered righteous for what she did
when she gave lodging to the spies and sent them
off in a different direction? 26As the body without
the spirit is dead, so faith without deeds is dead.

[d]20 Some early manuscripts *dead* [e]23 Gen. 15:6

Discovering the Word 1. According to James, what good is faith without deeds (vv. 14–17)? Explain why he says this. 2. How does James answer the objection "You have faith; I have deeds" (vv. 18–19)? 3. James gives two Old Testament examples of faith in action. The first is the familiar story of God testing Abraham by asking him to sacrifice his son Isaac. Abraham obeyed but was stopped by an angel at the last minute. How was Abraham's faith made complete by what he did (vv. 21–24)? 4. The second Old Testament example is Rahab, the prostitute who hid two Israelite spies sent to Jericho before Israel's attack. How did Rahab's belief affect her (v. 25)? 5. How does James's closing analogy (v. 26) summarize his teaching on faith and actions?

Applying the Word 1. How do your actions demonstrate the reality of your faith? 2. In what ways can you bring your actions more in line with your beliefs?

Responding in Prayer Ask God to help you follow through with the works that will reveal your true faith.

5 / *James 3:1–12*
Preventing Forest Fires

ONE OF THE most distressing crises is a fire out of control. The pain of seeing the destruction can be almost unbearable. Personal belongings going up in smoke. The beauty of nature destroyed. Even loss of life itself. In this passage James compares the destructive power of the tongue to that of a forest fire.

Warming Up to God How have you been hurt by someone's destructive words recently? Give your pain to God. Let him comfort you.

Read James 3:1–12.

3 Not many of you should presume to be
teachers, my brothers, because you know
that we who teach will be judged more
strictly. 2We all stumble in many ways. If anyone
is never at fault in what he says, he is a perfect
man, able to keep his whole body in check.
3When we put bits into the mouths of horses to
make them obey us, we can turn the whole ani-
mal. 4Or take ships as an example. Although they
are so large and are driven by strong winds, they
are steered by a very small rudder wherever the
pilot wants to go. 5Likewise the tongue is a small
part of the body, but it makes great boasts. Con-
sider what a great forest is set on fire by a small

spark. 6The tongue also is a fire, a world of evil
among the parts of the body. It corrupts the
whole person, sets the whole course of his life on
fire, and is itself set on fire by hell.
7All kinds of animals, birds, reptiles and crea-
tures of the sea are being tamed and have been
tamed by man, 8but no man can tame the tongue.
It is a restless evil, full of deadly poison.
9With the tongue we praise our Lord and Fa-
ther, and with it we curse men, who have been
made in God's likeness. 10Out of the same mouth
come praise and cursing. My brothers, this
should not be. 11Can both fresh water and salt[f]
water flow from the same spring? 12My brothers,
can a fig tree bear olives, or a grapevine bear figs?
Neither can a salt spring produce fresh water.

[f]11 Greek *bitter* (see also verse 14)

Discovering the Word 1. James compares the tongue (the words we speak) to a bit and a rudder (vv. 3–4). Why do you think the tongue has such control over our lives? 2. James also compares the tongue to a fire and to a world of evil (vv. 5–6). What is the point of these two comparisons? 3. Verses 7–8 emphasize what a challenge it is to control the tongue. What makes this so difficult? 4. In what ways can the tongue poison people and relationships? 5. In verses 9–12 James uses a series of analogies from nature (springs, trees, vines). How do they highlight the inconsistencies of the tongue?

Applying the Word 1. What damage has your tongue done recently? 2. What in this text gives you added strength and motivation to be more careful with your words? 3. What can you do to give God more praise? Be specific. 4. How can you give more affirmation to those you come in contact with each day?

Responding in Prayer Ask God to help you to be self-controlled about the ways that you speak to others.

6 / *James 3:13—4:10*
Keeping the Peace

WHY DO PEOPLE who love each other the most often fight the most too? Husbands and wives, parents and children, brothers and sisters—it's all too common. James offers a valuable remedy for this sickness.

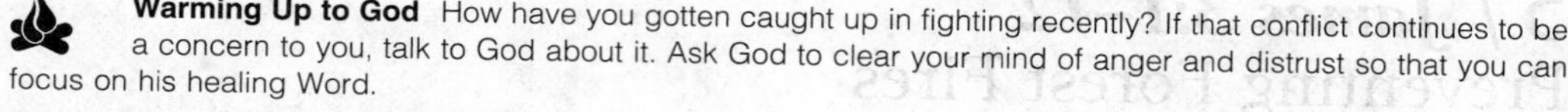

Warming Up to God How have you gotten caught up in fighting recently? If that conflict continues to be a concern to you, talk to God about it. Ask God to clear your mind of anger and distrust so that you can focus on his healing Word.

Read James 3:13—4:10.

13Who is wise and understanding among you?
Let him show it by his good life, by deeds done in
the humility that comes from wisdom. 14But if
you harbor bitter envy and selfish ambition in
your hearts, do not boast about it or deny the
truth. 15Such "wisdom" does not come down
from heaven but is earthly, unspiritual, of the
devil. 16For where you have envy and selfish am-
bition, there you find disorder and every evil
practice.
17But the wisdom that comes from heaven is
first of all pure; then peace-loving, considerate,
submissive, full of mercy and good fruit, impar-
tial and sincere. 18Peacemakers who sow in peace
raise a harvest of righteousness.

4 What causes fights and quarrels among
you? Don't they come from your desires
that battle within you? 2You want some-
thing but don't get it. You kill and covet, but you
cannot have what you want. You quarrel and
fight. You do not have, because you do not ask
God. 3When you ask, you do not receive, because
you ask with wrong motives, that you may spend
what you get on your pleasures.
4You adulterous people, don't you know that
friendship with the world is hatred toward God?

Anyone who chooses to be a friend of the world
becomes an enemy of God. 5Or do you think
Scripture says without reason that the spirit he
caused to live in us envies intensely?[g] 6But he
gives us more grace. That is why Scripture says:

"God opposes the proud
but gives grace to the humble."[h]

7Submit yourselves, then, to God. Resist the
devil, and he will flee from you. 8Come near to
God and he will come near to you. Wash your
hands, you sinners, and purify your hearts, you
double-minded. 9Grieve, mourn and wail.
Change your laughter to mourning and your joy
to gloom. 10Humble yourselves before the Lord,
and he will lift you up.

g5 *Or that God jealously longs for the spirit that he made to live in us; or that the Spirit he caused to live in us longs jealously* h6 Prov. 3:34

Discovering the Word 1. In 3:13–18 James discusses earthly and heavenly wisdom. What are the characteristics of each? 2. What does James say is the source of quarrels (4:1–2)? 3. What does James say is necessary to come to God in prayer (vv. 3–10)? 4. What does it mean to be humble, to submit to God (vv. 6–7)? 5. In verses 7–10 James gives several suggestions for humbling ourselves before God. How does each contribute to a humble spirit?

Applying the Word 1. As you look at 4:3, what might be examples of right and wrong motives in your prayer? 2. In what area are you an enemy of God (see v. 4 and consider your attitude toward material possessions, friends, study or work, and leisure time)? How can you restore your relationship to him? 3. In what situations could humility help you become a source of peace? Explain.

Responding in Prayer Take a few minutes to quietly humble yourself before God. Ask him to help you become a peacemaker.

7 / *James 4:11–17*
Getting Perspective

"I AM THE master of my fate. I am the captain of my soul." How subtly we convince ourselves that we control our lives. Sometimes only a crisis or even death itself convinces us otherwise. If we are truly wise and humble, we will listen carefully when James says, "You are a mist that appears for a little while and then vanishes."

Warming Up to God How have you been trying to control your life? Confess it to God and experience the freedom of giving him control.

Read James 4:11–17.

11Brothers, do not slander one another. Anyone
who speaks against his brother or judges him
speaks against the law and judges it. When you
judge the law, you are not keeping it, but sitting
in judgment on it. 12There is only one Lawgiver
and Judge, the one who is able to save and de-
stroy. But you—who are you to judge your neigh-
bor?

13Now listen, you who say, "Today or tomor-
row we will go to this or that city, spend a year
there, carry on business and make money."
14Why, you do not even know what will happen
tomorrow. What is your life? You are a mist that
appears for a little while and then vanishes. 15In-
stead, you ought to say, "If it is the Lord's will, we
will live and do this or that." 16As it is, you boast
and brag. All such boasting is evil. 17Anyone,
then, who knows the good he ought to do and
doesn't do it, sins.

Discovering the Word 1. Why does James say we shouldn't slander or speak against a Christian brother or sister (vv. 11–12)? 2. If we judge the law, what does this say about our attitude toward the lawgiver (v. 11)? 3. How can a proper attitude toward God (v. 12) enable us to have a proper attitude toward others? 4. How would you describe the two attitudes toward the future found in verses 13–17? 5. If our life is like a mist, what should be our attitude toward tomorrow?

Applying the Word 1. If you knew you were going to die tomorrow, how would your attitude toward life today be different? 2. What future plans do you often dwell on? 3. In what area of your life do you need to turn your plans over to God's will?

Responding in Prayer Ask God to help you love those around you rather than judge them. Humbly commit your future plans to the Lord.

8 / *James 5:1–11*
What Awaits

YOU HAVE PROBABLY heard of the young man who cried out, "Lord, I want patience and I want it now!" James encourages us in this passage to wait on God and to be patient, and warns us against wanting it all now.

Warming Up to God God wants to know your concerns and frustrations. Tell God what has been making you impatient lately.

Read James 5:1–11.

5 Now listen, you rich people, weep and
wail because of the misery that is coming
upon you. [2]Your wealth has rotted, and
moths have eaten your clothes. [3]Your gold and
silver are corroded. Their corrosion will testify
against you and eat your flesh like fire. You have
hoarded wealth in the last days. [4]Look! The
wages you failed to pay the workmen who mowed
your fields are crying out against you. The cries of
the harvesters have reached the ears of the Lord
Almighty. [5]You have lived on earth in luxury and
self-indulgence. You have fattened yourselves in
the day of slaughter.[i] [6]You have condemned and
murdered innocent men, who were not opposing
you.
[7]Be patient, then, brothers, until the Lord's
coming. See how the farmer waits for the land to
yield its valuable crop and how patient he is for
the autumn and spring rains. [8]You too, be patient
and stand firm, because the Lord's coming is near.
[9]Don't grumble against each other, brothers, or
you will be judged. The Judge is standing at the
door!
[10]Brothers, as an example of patience in the
face of suffering, take the prophets who spoke in
the name of the Lord. [11]As you know, we con-
sider blessed those who have persevered. You
have heard of Job's perseverance and have seen
what the Lord finally brought about. The Lord is
full of compassion and mercy.

[i]5 Or *yourselves as in a day of feasting*

Discovering the Word 1. James declares that misery awaits rich people. What crimes have they committed (vv. 1–6)? 2. Is James condemning all rich people? Explain. 3. James goes on to give three examples of patient people: a farmer, the prophets and Job. How is each an example of patience? 4. What different reactions would you expect the rich and those who suffer to have to the prospect of the Lord's return (vv. 7–9)? 5. How is piling up riches the opposite of patience that waits in faith for God to provide?

Applying the Word 1. When are you tempted to hoard rather than to give and wait on God? 2. In what areas of your life are you impatient? 3. What do you learn about patience from the examples James mentions?

Responding in Prayer Pray that God would make you a person who can wait for God to answer prayer.

9 / *James 5:12–20* Making Others Whole

BROKEN HOMES, shattered relationships, damaged emotions—we live in a fragmented and hurting world. As we see all the wounded people around us, we long to help, to offer a healing touch. James gives us very practical suggestions for helping people become whole.

Warming Up to God God wants you to be whole. In what area are you struggling with emotional pain? Tell God how you want him to help you.

Read James 5:12–20.

12Above all, my brothers, do not swear—not by
heaven or by earth or by anything else. Let your
"Yes" be yes, and your "No," no, or you will be
condemned.
13Is any one of you in trouble? He should pray.
Is anyone happy? Let him sing songs of praise.
14Is any one of you sick? He should call the elders
of the church to pray over him and anoint him
with oil in the name of the Lord. 15And the prayer
offered in faith will make the sick person well; the
Lord will raise him up. If he has sinned, he will be
forgiven. 16Therefore confess your sins to each
other and pray for each other so that you may be
healed. The prayer of a righteous man is powerful
and effective.
17Elijah was a man just like us. He prayed ear-
nestly that it would not rain, and it did not rain
on the land for three and a half years. 18Again he
prayed, and the heavens gave rain, and the earth
produced its crops.
19My brothers, if one of you should wander
from the truth and someone should bring him
back, 20remember this: Whoever turns a sinner
from the error of his way will save him from
death and cover over a multitude of sins.

Discovering the Word 1. What different types of prayer are mentioned in verses 13–18? 2. In verses 14–16 James discusses physical and spiritual healing. What are the steps in this process? 3. How is physical healing connected with the forgiveness of sins? 4. How does the Old Testament prophet Elijah illustrate the effectiveness of prayer (vv. 17–18)? 5. According to verses 19–20, how, if at all, are we our brother's keeper?

Applying the Word 1. Do you pray more when you are in trouble or when things are going well? Explain. 2. How could you make one of the types of prayer James describes more a part of your life? 3. How can you help others become whole physically, emotionally or spiritually?

Responding in Prayer Ask God for grace as you minister to others.

1 Peter

It was a shaky time for Christians in the Roman Empire. In A.D. 68 Emperor Nero saw himself surrounded by political enemies and took the easy way out: suicide. In the next year three emperors, in rapid succession, took his place, but couldn't hold the job. So in A.D. 69 troops proclaimed the military leader Vespasian as emperor—and saw that he stayed there.

Vespasian hated Jews, and he counted Christians among them. Prior to becoming emperor, his goal had been to trample Judea and erase it from existence. As emperor, he sent his oldest son, Titus, to finish the job. Titus put Jerusalem under siege for three months. Then he tightened the noose. Troops leveled buildings to the ground. The temple became a crumble of stones. Jerusalem fell. Jews (and Christians) became Roman captives.

Aftershocks vibrated throughout the Roman Empire, blending with the general persecution against "atheists" (people who refused to worship Roman gods) that Nero had begun. Christians everywhere suffered. They were driven from their homes, deported to the outer borders of the empire, forbidden to worship openly and, worse yet, splintered by their own internal doctrinal disputes.

It is possible that the apostle Paul was martyred under Nero. And Peter was martyred as well—crucified upside-down, tradition says, because he felt unworthy to die in the same position as his Lord. It was a dark season for Christians.

How were they to endure?

Peter, through God's inspiration, sensed this coming darkness. If conservative scholars are correct, Peter's first letter can be dated about A.D. 64, written probably from the city of Rome —which Peter called Babylon in 5:13.

This is not a bleak letter. Indeed, it is full of hope and practical counsel on how to endure. It tells us to balance holy living with correct doctrine, to nurture spiritual growth, to work within existing authority structures, and to take care of each other.

This letter, sent with prophetic love to first-century Christians, still lives today. It provides a compass for our own dark road.

Outline

1 / *1 Peter 1:1–12*
Strangers in the World

A SMALL YOUNG man stood in the front of my classroom and spoke anxiously of home. He pointed to South Korean newspaper clippings that hinted of takeover by the North. He worried that the end was near: Ten years? Five? Two? If he is correct, Christians in South Korea have a right to feel nervous. Will they still have a church five years from now? Will they still have Bibles? Will they have to shutter their windows and lower their voices when they pray with their children?

How can a believer prepare for that kind of suffering? And what is it, anyway, that makes Christians strangers to the rest of the world?

Warming Up to God If you knew you were about to enter a difficult set of circumstances that would test your faith, how would you prepare yourself?

Read 1 Peter 1:1–12.

---

1 Peter, an apostle of Jesus Christ,

To God's elect, strangers in the world, scattered throughout Pontus, Galatia, Cappadocia, Asia and Bithynia, [2]who have been chosen according to the foreknowledge of God the Father, through the sanctifying work of the Spirit, for obedience to Jesus Christ and sprinkling by his blood:

Grace and peace be yours in abundance.

[3]Praise be to the God and Father of our Lord Jesus Christ! In his great mercy he has given us new birth into a living hope through the resurrection of Jesus Christ from the dead, [4]and into an inheritance that can never perish, spoil or fade—kept in heaven for you, [5]who through faith are shielded by God's power until the coming of the salvation that is ready to be revealed in the last time. [6]In this you greatly rejoice, though now for a little while you may have had to suffer grief in all kinds of trials. [7]These have come so that your faith—of greater worth than gold, which perishes even though refined by fire—may be proved genuine and may result in praise, glory and honor when Jesus Christ is revealed. [8]Though you have not seen him, you love him; and even though you do not see him now, you believe in him and are filled with an inexpressible and glorious joy, [9]for you are receiving the goal of your faith, the salvation of your souls.

[10]Concerning this salvation, the prophets, who spoke of the grace that was to come to you, searched intently and with the greatest care, [11]trying to find out the time and circumstances to which the Spirit of Christ in them was pointing when he predicted the sufferings of Christ and the glories that would follow. [12]It was revealed to them that they were not serving themselves but you, when they spoke of the things that have now been told you by those who have preached the gospel to you by the Holy Spirit sent from heaven. Even angels long to look into these things.

Discovering the Word 1. Study Peter's description of the people who were about to receive his letter (vv. 1–2). How does his description of them help explain why they were "strangers in the world"? 2. Peter says in verse 6, "Now for a little while you may have had to suffer grief in all kinds of trials." If you were to hear that kind of message, what information in this paragraph might help you through the suffering (vv. 3–9)? 3. What did Peter believe to be true of genuine faith (vv. 7–9)? 4. By what different routes did news of salvation come to the readers of Peter's letter (vv. 10–12)?

Applying the Word 1. How does the future, as Peter describes it here, offer you hope in your own setting? 2. When have you seen Jesus (through a person or event) in a way that increased your faith? 3. Peter refers to new birth, or salvation, throughout this passage as a central difference between Christians and the world. What tensions have you experienced because of this difference?

Responding in Prayer Praise God for his gift of salvation that can help us cope with tensions with the world.

2 / *1 Peter 1:13–25*
Called to Be Different

I GREW UP in a church of fervent Christians. We knelt to pray, carried Bibles to school, wore "modest" clothes—even to gym class—and talked a lot about Jesus. Needless to say, kids from our church never made the "most popular" lists at the local public high school. Instead, we feared the taunt "Holy Roller."

It's possible that our attempts to be separate and holy did more to close people out of our beliefs than to invite them in. Yet God does call his people to be different; different from what they would be if they did not believe in Jesus and different from the unbelievers around them.

Warming Up to God Think of a Christian you admire. In what ways does that person resemble Christ? Praise God for what you learn about him through others.

Read 1 Peter 1:13–25.

13Therefore, prepare your minds for action; be
self-controlled; set your hope fully on the grace to
be given you when Jesus Christ is revealed. 14As
obedient children, do not conform to the evil de-
sires you had when you lived in ignorance. 15But
just as he who called you is holy, so be holy in all
you do; 16for it is written: "Be holy, because I am
holy."[a]
17Since you call on a Father who judges each
man's work impartially, live your lives as strang-
ers here in reverent fear. 18For you know that it
was not with perishable things such as silver or
gold that you were redeemed from the empty way
of life handed down to you from your forefathers,
19but with the precious blood of Christ, a lamb
without blemish or defect. 20He was chosen be-
fore the creation of the world, but was revealed in
these last times for your sake. 21Through him you
believe in God, who raised him from the dead and
glorified him, and so your faith and hope are in
God.
22Now that you have purified yourselves by
obeying the truth so that you have sincere love
for your brothers, love one another deeply, from
the heart.[b] 23For you have been born again, not
of perishable seed, but of imperishable, through
the living and enduring word of God. 24For,

"All men are like grass,
and all their glory is like the flowers of the field;
the grass withers and the flowers fall,
25 but the word of the Lord stands forever."[c]

And this is the word that was preached to you.

[a]16 Lev. 11:44,45; 19:2; 20:7 [b]22 Some early manuscripts *from a pure heart* [c]25 Isaiah 40:6-8

Discovering the Word 1. Peter lists several ways that followers of Jesus ought to respond to his gift of salvation. Define each of these responses more fully (vv. 13–16). 2. Select one of these responses. If you were to put that response on the "front burner" of your priorities, what changes would you have to make in your life? 3. What events from the past would help the recipients of Peter's letter to appreciate God's concern for them (vv. 18–21)? 4. How could the conditions that Peter describes in verses 21–25 promote sincere love among Christians? 5. Peter links the Word of God with salvation and new birth. (Compare verses 10, 12, 23 and 25.) What do you think Peter meant when he said that this Word is "enduring" and "stands forever"?

Applying the Word 1. How might an honest attempt to "be holy" improve your relationships with people close to you? 2. In what situations might it make you, as verse 17 says, more like a stranger? 3. Jot a quick list of all you have to do today (or tomorrow). How could you begin to tackle this list with the goal "Be holy in all you do"?

Responding in Prayer Pray specifically from your list that you would be holy and would improve relationships with those around you.

3/ *1 Peter 2:1–12*
Do I Want to Grow Up?

"WOULD YOU SEND me to school?" [Peter] inquired craftily.

"Yes . . ."

"I don't want to go to school and learn solemn things," he told her passionately. "I don't want to be a man. O Wendy's mother, if was to wake up and feel there was a beard!"

"Peter," said Wendy the comforter, "I should love you in a beard." Mrs. Darling stretched out her arms to him. "Keep back, lady, no one is going to catch me and make me a man." (James M. Barrie, *Peter Pan* [New York: Charles Scribner's Sons, 1911], p. 228.)

Warming Up to God In what ways are you tempted to follow Peter Pan's approach to life?

Read 1 Peter 2:1–12.

2 Therefore, rid yourselves of all malice and
all deceit, hypocrisy, envy, and slander of
every kind. 2Like newborn babies, crave
pure spiritual milk, so that by it you may grow up
in your salvation, 3now that you have tasted that
the Lord is good.
4As you come to him, the living Stone—re-
jected by men but chosen by God and precious to
him— 5you also, like living stones, are being
built into a spiritual house to be a holy priest-
hood, offering spiritual sacrifices acceptable to
God through Jesus Christ. 6For in Scripture it
says:

"See, I lay a stone in Zion,
a chosen and precious cornerstone,
and the one who trusts in him
will never be put to shame."[d]

7Now to you who believe, this stone is precious.
But to those who do not believe,

"The stone the builders rejected
has become the capstone,[e]"[f]

8and,

"A stone that causes men to stumble
and a rock that makes them fall."[g]

They stumble because they disobey the mes-
sage—which is also what they were destined for.
9But you are a chosen people, a royal priest-
hood, a holy nation, a people belonging to God,
that you may declare the praises of him who
called you out of darkness into his wonderful
light. 10Once you were not a people, but now you
are the people of God; once you had not received
mercy, but now you have received mercy.
11Dear friends, I urge you, as aliens and strang-
ers in the world, to abstain from sinful desires,
which war against your soul. 12Live such good
lives among the pagans that, though they accuse
you of doing wrong, they may see your good
deeds and glorify God on the day he visits us.

[d]6 Isaiah 28:16 [e]7 Or *cornerstone* [f]7 Psalm 118:22
[g]8 Isaiah 8:14

Discovering the Word 1. Peter speaks here of two aspects of Christian growth: individual and corporate. How might the five inner sins of verse 1 damage outer relationships with other believers? 2. What does the metaphor in verses 2–3 contribute to your understanding of how to nurture spiritual growth? 3. How does belief or unbelief influence the way a person understands Jesus, the "living Stone" (vv. 4–8)? 4. What reasons do the people here have to praise God (vv. 9–10)? 5. Verse 11 repeats a now familiar theme in 1 Peter—that Christians are aliens and strangers in the world. How might living up to the description of verse 9 cause a Christian to be alienated from the world?

Applying the Word 1. The *New Bible Commentary* interprets verse 12, "the day [God] visits us," as "the day God will visit the earth and search out man's hearts in judgment." If this were to occur in your lifetime, what evidence would you want God to find of your own spiritual growth? 2. How could today's passage help you overcome a tendency to become a spiritual Peter Pan?

Responding in Prayer Ask God to rid you of "all malice and all deceit, hypocrisy, envy, and slander of every kind."

4 / *1 Peter 2:13—3:7*
In His Steps

IN THE LATE 1800s a young social worker tramped the streets of Topeka, Kansas. Disguised as an unemployed printer, he begged for food, work, hope. The social-worker-turned-tramp was a believer in Jesus and knew the giving, caring moral code that Jesus lived and taught. So he assumed that fellow Christians, even though they could not see through his disguise, would be among the first to help. He was wrong. He found that a tramp's life was tough—and that Christians didn't make it any easier.

Charles Sheldon went home to write a book about his experience—a novel that introduced a dying tramp to the Reverend Henry Maxwell and his congregation. In it, a body of believers begins to see the submissive suffering of Jesus and what it means to walk *In His Steps.*

Warming Up to God If you were to rate your natural inclination for being submissive on a scale of one to ten, where would you place yourself and why? (One is a mud-covered doormat; ten is a banner-waving firebrand.)

Read 1 Peter 2:13—3:7.

13Submit yourselves for the Lord's sake to every authority instituted among men: whether to the king, as the supreme authority, 14or to governors, who are sent by him to punish those who do wrong and to commend those who do right. 15For it is God's will that by doing good you should silence the ignorant talk of foolish men. 16Live as free men, but do not use your freedom as a cover-up for evil; live as servants of God. 17Show proper respect to everyone: Love the brotherhood of believers, fear God, honor the king.

18Slaves, submit yourselves to your masters with all respect, not only to those who are good and considerate, but also to those who are harsh. 19For it is commendable if a man bears up under the pain of unjust suffering because he is conscious of God. 20But how is it to your credit if you receive a beating for doing wrong and endure it? But if you suffer for doing good and you endure it, this is commendable before God. 21To this you were called, because Christ suffered for you, leaving you an example, that you should follow in his steps.

22"He committed no sin,
and no deceit was found in his mouth."[h]

23When they hurled their insults at him, he did not retaliate; when he suffered, he made no threats. Instead, he entrusted himself to him who judges justly. 24He himself bore our sins in his body on the tree, so that we might die to sins and live for righteousness; by his wounds you have been healed. 25For you were like sheep going astray, but now you have returned to the Shepherd and Overseer of your souls.

3 Wives, in the same way be submissive to your husbands so that, if any of them do not believe the word, they may be won over without words by the behavior of their wives, 2when they see the purity and reverence of your lives. 3Your beauty should not come from outward adornment, such as braided hair and the wearing of gold jewelry and fine clothes. 4Instead, it should be that of your inner self, the unfading beauty of a gentle and quiet spirit, which is of great worth in God's sight. 5For this is the way the holy women of the past who put their hope in God used to make themselves beautiful. They were submissive to their own husbands, 6like Sarah, who obeyed Abraham and called him her master. You are her daughters if you do what is right and do not give way to fear.

7Husbands, in the same way be considerate as you live with your wives, and treat them with respect as the weaker partner and as heirs with you of the gracious gift of life, so that nothing will hinder your prayers.

[h]22 Isaiah 53:9

Discovering the Word 1. According to Peter, why should Christians treat their governing leaders with respect (2:13–15)? 2. How could the teachings of 2:16–17 keep you from becoming a "muddy doormat" to your government? 3. How might being a Christian bring some meaning to the suffering that comes from being a slave (2:18–21)? 4. 2:23 says that in his suffering, Jesus "entrusted himself to him who judges justly." How might a similar trust in God help you to submit to the necessary suffering that has come into your own life?

Applying the Word 1. Finding a balance between responsible action for healthy change and submission to authority is a constant tension for the Christian who wants to obey this passage. How can you draw together both ends of this tension? (In what situations would you take action? At what point would you submit?) 2. How do you balance the tension of submission versus responsible action in your job? in your marriage? in other relationships?

Responding in Prayer Pray for courage to walk "in his steps" even in the face of suffering.

5/ *1 Peter 3:8–22*

If I'm Living Right, Then Why Do I Hurt So Much?

WE OFTEN ASSUME a direct connection between "right living" and "easy living." It's an added pat on the back when life runs smoothly. But it is an unspoken accusation when trauma strikes. Peter contemplated this connection—even added a link or two to the chain. (Sure there are ways to live that will decrease our chances for unjust conflict.) But Peter made no promises of easy living. Sometimes suffering comes—whether or not we earn it. It came to Jesus.

Warming Up to God When in your life has suffering been hard to understand?

Read 1 Peter 3:8–22.

8 Finally, all of you, live in harmony with one
another; be sympathetic, love as brothers, be
compassionate and humble. 9 Do not repay evil
with evil or insult with insult, but with blessing,
because to this you were called so that you may
inherit a blessing. 10 For,

"Whoever would love life
and see good days
must keep his tongue from evil
and his lips from deceitful speech.
11 He must turn from evil and do good;
he must seek peace and pursue it.
12 For the eyes of the Lord are on the righteous
and his ears are attentive to their prayer,
but the face of the Lord is against those who
do evil."[i]

13 Who is going to harm you if you are eager to
do good? 14 But even if you should suffer for what
is right, you are blessed. "Do not fear what they
fear[j]; do not be frightened."[k] 15 But in your
hearts set apart Christ as Lord. Always be prepared
to give an answer to everyone who asks you
to give the reason for the hope that you have. But
do this with gentleness and respect, 16 keeping a
clear conscience, so that those who speak maliciously
against your good behavior in Christ may
be ashamed of their slander. 17 It is better, if it is
God's will, to suffer for doing good than for doing
evil. 18 For Christ died for sins once for all, the
righteous for the unrighteous, to bring you to
God. He was put to death in the body but made
alive by the Spirit, 19 through whom[l] also he
went and preached to the spirits in prison 20 who
disobeyed long ago when God waited patiently in
the days of Noah while the ark was being built. In
it only a few people, eight in all, were saved
through water, 21 and this water symbolizes bap-

[i] 12 Psalm 34:12-16 [j] 14 Or *not fear their threats* [k] 14 Isaiah 8:12
[l] 18,19 Or *alive in the spirit,* 19 *through which*

tism that now saves you also—not the removal of
dirt from the body but the pledge[m] of a good
conscience toward God. It saves you by the resur-
rection of Jesus Christ, 22who has gone into
heaven and is at God's right hand—with angels,
authorities and powers in submission to him.

[m]21 Or *response*

Discovering the Word 1. Find as many phrases as you can in verses 8–12 that describe what a Christian ought to be and do. 2. What do you find difficult about the way of life described in verses 8–12? 3. In spite of godly living, Peter knew that Christians may encounter hardship. What counsel does Peter offer for coping with suffering (vv. 13–17)? 4. Why might unbelievers be willing to listen to reasons for hope from a person who is living the way Peter describes (vv. 15–17)? 5. Verse 18 is a "capsule" description of Christ's work and purpose. What all can you know from this verse about why Jesus came and what he accomplished?

Applying the Word 1. How could setting apart Christ as Lord, as verse 15 commands, help you endure suffering? 2. Our world is often unjust. Bring to mind some of your past or current sufferings. In the context of these sufferings, how can the picture of Christ portrayed by this passage bring you hope?

Responding in Prayer Thank God for the hope we have been given in Christ.

6 / *1 Peter 4*
The Christian Path of Nails

SHUSAKO ENDO, THE Japanese novelist, tells the story of two missionary priests in *Silence.* The priests came from Portugal to Japan in the mid–1600s. At that time the Christian faith in Japan was one hundred years old. It had some 300,000 followers, a cluster of colleges, seminaries, hospitals and local clergy. But persecution had struck the church. A fragmented government united under a single cause: to become truly Japanese. And that meant erasing foreign religion, especially Christianity. Christians suffered horrible deaths. Endo's book asks why. Why the suffering? Why did God appear to sit through it in silence? And these questions are just as relevant for us today as we continue to suffer because of our beliefs.

Warming Up to God When you learn of Christians suffering because of their faith, what questions come to your mind? Voice your questions to God.

Read 1 Peter 4.

4 Therefore, since Christ suffered in his
body, arm yourselves also with the same
attitude, because he who has suffered in
his body is done with sin. 2As a result, he does
not live the rest of his earthly life for evil human
desires, but rather for the will of God. 3For you
have spent enough time in the past doing what
pagans choose to do—living in debauchery, lust,
drunkenness, orgies, carousing and detestable
idolatry. 4They think it strange that you do not
plunge with them into the same flood of dissipa-
tion, and they heap abuse on you. 5But they will
have to give account to him who is ready to judge
the living and the dead. 6For this is the reason the
gospel was preached even to those who are now
dead, so that they might be judged according to
men in regard to the body, but live according to
God in regard to the spirit.

7The end of all things is near. Therefore be
clear minded and self-controlled so that you can
pray. 8Above all, love each other deeply, because
love covers over a multitude of sins. 9Offer hospi-
tality to one another without grumbling. 10Each
one should use whatever gift he has received to
serve others, faithfully administering God's grace
in its various forms. 11If anyone speaks, he should
do it as one speaking the very words of God. If
anyone serves, he should do it with the strength
God provides, so that in all things God may be

praised through Jesus Christ. To him be the glory
and the power for ever and ever. Amen.
12Dear friends, do not be surprised at the pain-
ful trial you are suffering, as though something
strange were happening to you. 13But rejoice that
you participate in the sufferings of Christ, so that
you may be overjoyed when his glory is revealed.
14If you are insulted because of the name of
Christ, you are blessed, for the Spirit of glory and
of God rests on you. 15If you suffer, it should not
be as a murderer or thief or any other kind of
criminal, or even as a meddler. 16However, if you
suffer as a Christian, do not be ashamed, but
praise God that you bear that name. 17For it is
time for judgment to begin with the family of
God; and if it begins with us, what will the out-
come be for those who do not obey the gospel of
God? 18And,

> "If it is hard for the righteous to be saved,
> what will become of the ungodly and the sinner?"[n]

19So then, those who suffer according to God's
will should commit themselves to their faithful
Creator and continue to do good.

[n] 18 Prov. 11:31

Discovering the Word 1. According to this passage, how is a Christian different from a pagan (vv. 1–6)? (Note attitudes as well as actions.) 2. Our doubts may sometimes taunt us, "Of what use is your Christian faith? God does not protect you. When your time comes, you die like the rest." How might the information in verses 4–6 help us deal with those doubts? 3. What specific instructions does Peter give suffering Christians who are aware that the end of all things is coming (vv. 7–11)? 4. Of what spitirual and practical value are these instructions? 5. Verse 11 speaks of two forms of leadership in the early church: those who speak (teach) and those who serve. How would the purpose of church leadership as it is described here prevent a misuse of power between Christians? 6. According to verses 12–19, what are some right and wrong ways for a Christian to suffer?

Applying the Word 1. Think back to the questions you posed in question one. How do Peter's teachings help you deal with these questions? 2. How might verse 19 become both a comfort and a challenge to you when you suffer because of your faith?

Responding in Prayer Pray for Christians in many parts of the world who face suffering for their beliefs.

7 / 1 Peter 5
TLC for Trying Times

RELATIONSHIPS BRING COLOR to life. Sure, the mountaintop hermit has a spectacular view outside the window. But the colors inside the cabin are browns and grays. It is people who bring sparkle and fire to existence.

When Peter concluded his first letter, a work frequently pointing to suffering, he did not tell his readers to escape to the isolation of a spiritual or literal mountaintop. Instead, he pointed to their relationships and said, "Here's how to take care of each other."

Warming Up to God What has been one of your most valuable relationships, and what made it valuable?

Read 1 Peter 5.

5 To the elders among you, I appeal as a
fellow elder, a witness of Christ's suffer-
ings and one who also will share in the
glory to be revealed: 2Be shepherds of God's flock
that is under your care, serving as overseers—not
because you must, but because you are willing, as
God wants you to be; not greedy for money, but
eager to serve; 3not lording it over those entrusted
to you, but being examples to the flock. 4And
when the Chief Shepherd appears, you will re-

ceive the crown of glory that will never fade
away.
5Young men, in the same way be submissive to
those who are older. All of you, clothe yourselves
with humility toward one another, because,

"God opposes the proud
but gives grace to the humble."[o]

6Humble yourselves, therefore, under God's
mighty hand, that he may lift you up in due time.
7Cast all your anxiety on him because he cares for
you.
8Be self-controlled and alert. Your enemy the
devil prowls around like a roaring lion looking
for someone to devour. 9Resist him, standing firm
in the faith, because you know that your brothers
throughout the world are undergoing the same
kind of sufferings.
10And the God of all grace, who called you to
his eternal glory in Christ, after you have suffered
a little while, will himself restore you and make
you strong, firm and steadfast. 11To him be the
power for ever and ever. Amen.

12With the help of Silas,[p] whom I regard as a
faithful brother, I have written to you briefly, en-
couraging you and testifying that this is the true
grace of God. Stand fast in it.
13She who is in Babylon, chosen together with
you, sends you her greetings, and so does my son
Mark. 14Greet one another with a kiss of love.
Peace to all of you who are in Christ.

[o]5 Prov. 3:34 [p]12 Greek *Silvanus*, a variant of *Silas*

Discovering the Word 1. Peter speaks, in verse 1, to his fellow elders. In what ways did Peter see himself as like the elders he was writing to (vv. 1–4)? 2. When have you appreciated a person who acted toward you as a spiritual elder? 3. With what different beings or groups do these verses describe a Christian's relationships (vv. 5–11)? 4. What reasons did Peter give for following each of the commands in verses 5–9? 5. Peter points out three sets of relationships for all Christians—relationships with other believers, relationship with Satan, relationship with God. How would you summarize Peter's ideal for each of these?

Applying the Word 1. God's Word speaks to us in a variety of ways. What joy, comfort or warning do Peter's instructions in verses 5–11 point to in your own experience? 2. How could Peter's teachings about relationships in this chapter help you to "stand fast" in your own faith?

Responding in Prayer Ask God to comfort you, and wait before him to experience his care.

2 Peter

Peter's second letter refers appreciatively to Paul's letters in 3:15–16, but bears no hint that Paul is dead. On the other hand, Peter seems to anticipate his own death. Soon (see 1:13–14). Scholars therefore date this letter in the same decade of the sixties as 1 Peter—but closer to the end.

This letter does not tell us how to escape suffering, but instead to expect it. It shows us that throughout suffering we can enjoy our fellowship with other believers and look forward to a new heaven and a new earth, a "home of righteousness," with an end to pain.

Outline

1/ 2 Peter 1:1–11 —— *The Long Way Home*

2/ 2 Peter 1:12–21 —— *If I Should Die . . .*

3/ 2 Peter 2 —— *Follow Which Leader?*

4/ 2 Peter 3 —— *The Fire Next Time*

1 / *2 Peter 1:1–11*
The Long Way Home

HOW DOES A person get to heaven? Is it by proper knowledge of Christian doctrines? Or by godly living? Is it by faith in Christ's gift of salvation? Or by working according to Christ's goals and principles? Is it by God's call to us to be his own? Or by our own endurance with God until the day we die? Weighty issues. And with them, Peter opens his second letter.

Warming Up to God Reflect on your life. What qualities of godliness is God developing within you?

Read 2 Peter 1:1–11.

1 Simon Peter, a servant and apostle of
Jesus Christ,

To those who through the righteousness of our
God and Savior Jesus Christ have received a faith
as precious as ours:

2Grace and peace be yours in abundance
through the knowledge of God and of Jesus our
Lord.

3His divine power has given us everything we
need for life and godliness through our knowl-
edge of him who called us by his own glory and
goodness. 4Through these he has given us his
very great and precious promises, so that through
them you may participate in the divine nature
and escape the corruption in the world caused by
evil desires.

5For this very reason, make every effort to add
to your faith goodness; and to goodness, knowl-
edge; 6and to knowledge, self-control; and to self-
control, perseverance; and to perseverance, godli-
ness; 7and to godliness, brotherly kindness; and
to brotherly kindness, love. 8For if you possess
these qualities in increasing measure, they will
keep you from being ineffective and unproductive
in your knowledge of our Lord Jesus Christ. 9But
if anyone does not have them, he is nearsighted
and blind, and has forgotten that he has been
cleansed from his past sins.

10Therefore, my brothers, be all the more eager
to make your calling and election sure. For if you
do these things, you will never fall, 11and you will
receive a rich welcome into the eternal kingdom
of our Lord and Savior Jesus Christ.

Discovering the Word 1. In verses 1–2 we are told that we will receive the gifts of faith, grace and peace through Christ's righteousness and knowledge of God. How does your own spiritual well-being depend in part on Christ's righteousness and in part on your knowledge of God? 2. Verse 3 speaks of both knowledge and holy living as a part of the Christian life. Think of the balance between knowledge of Jesus and holy living that you have seen in Christians. What happens if one area or the other is weak? 3. Peter writes in verse 4 that because of God's promises, Christians "may participate in the divine nature and escape the corruption in the world." What does he then expect believers to do to nurture their own holy living (vv. 5–7)? 4. How are knowledge of Jesus and godly living related to each other (vv. 8–9)? 5. What do you think it means for a person to be called and elected by God (vv. 10–11)?

Applying the Word 1. Select one of the Christian qualities mentioned in verses 5–7 that you would like to become more prominent in your own life. If you were to practice this quality more faithfully, how would it help you escape the pollution of evil influences around you? 2. Verse 3 says that the divine power of Jesus has given us everything we need for godliness here and also for eternal life. If you were to draw more fully on this power that Jesus makes available to you, what changes would you hope to see in yourself?

Responding in Prayer Pray for the changes you think God is calling for within you.

2 / *2 Peter 1:12–21*
If I Should Die . . .

IN 1976 JOE Bayly lay on a gurney outside an operating room at the Mayo Clinic's Methodist Hospital. He was scheduled for a minor operation. He'd probably be shuffling through the hospital hallway in a couple of days. But what if he just didn't wake up?

Joe's musings on that possibility left readers with a small thought-provoking book titled, appropriately, *Heaven.* In it he speaks of his faith in Jesus Christ and his hope here—and hereafter. It has influenced children and adults, believers and nonbelievers to follow Christ. Ten years later, Joe again lay on a gurney outside the operating room. The operation was a little more serious this time—his heart. But still, at Mayo, it was routine. But in 1986, when Joe woke up, it was hereafter.

Warming Up to God As you think back over why you believe what you believe, who or what were the major influences in your life? Praise God for the privilege of knowing him.

Read 2 Peter 1:12–21.

12So I will always remind you of these things,
even though you know them and are firmly estab-
lished in the truth you now have. 13I think it is
right to refresh your memory as long as I live in
the tent of this body, 14because I know that I will
soon put it aside, as our Lord Jesus Christ has
made clear to me. 15And I will make every effort
to see that after my departure you will always be
able to remember these things.
16We did not follow cleverly invented stories
when we told you about the power and coming of
our Lord Jesus Christ, but we were eyewitnesses
of his majesty. 17For he received honor and glory
from God the Father when the voice came to him
from the Majestic Glory, saying, "This is my Son,
whom I love; with him I am well pleased."[a] 18We
ourselves heard this voice that came from heaven
when we were with him on the sacred mountain.
19And we have the word of the prophets made
more certain, and you will do well to pay atten-
tion to it, as to a light shining in a dark place,
until the day dawns and the morning star rises in
your hearts. 20Above all, you must understand
that no prophecy of Scripture came about by the
prophet's own interpretation. 21For prophecy
never had its origin in the will of man, but men
spoke from God as they were carried along by the
Holy Spirit.

[a]17 Matt. 17:5; Mark 9:7; Luke 9:35

Discovering the Word 1. What phrases here create a picture of Peter's view of death (vv. 13–15)? 2. Based on these phrases, how would you describe Peter's attitude about death? 3. What difference would it make to those who knew Peter that his teachings about Jesus came from an "eyewitness of his majesty" (v. 16)? 4. What do verses 19–21 show about the origin and purpose of Scripture?

Applying the Word 1. What do you hope will be your own feelings when you approach death? 2. What could you be doing during your lifetime to build toward a "good death"? 3. Peter did not want his readers to be so dependent on him that their faith would fall apart after his death. Who would you like to influence with your faith in your lifetime, and how can you best go about it?

Responding in Prayer Thank God for the gift of Scripture and the ways in which it increases our faith.

3 / 2 Peter 2
Follow Which Leader?

"I HUGGED HER, and it was like hugging a statue. I looked into her eyes, and I felt that 'the lights were on, but no one was home.' She had been my best friend in a Christian college! What happened?"

For months my friend puzzled over this strange reunion with her college housemate. Later the puzzle pieces fell into place. A cult. "Someone got to her," she said later. "That person had to be very persuasive, and very tricky. My friend knew the Bible, and she wasn't dumb. I wish I knew what happened."

Warming Up to God Jesus Christ is always faithful to his promises. Reflect on that fact and allow praise to well up within you in response.

Read 2 Peter 2.

2 But there were also false prophets among the people, just as there will be false teachers among you. They will secretly introduce destructive heresies, even denying the sovereign Lord who bought them—bringing swift destruction on themselves. 2Many will follow their shameful ways and will bring the way of truth into disrepute. 3In their greed these teachers will exploit you with stories they have made up. Their condemnation has long been hanging over them, and their destruction has not been sleeping.

4For if God did not spare angels when they sinned, but sent them to hell,[b] putting them into gloomy dungeons[c] to be held for judgment; 5if he did not spare the ancient world when he brought the flood on its ungodly people, but protected Noah, a preacher of righteousness, and seven others; 6if he condemned the cities of Sodom and Gomorrah by burning them to ashes, and made them an example of what is going to happen to the ungodly; 7and if he rescued Lot, a righteous man, who was distressed by the filthy lives of lawless men 8(for that righteous man, living among them day after day, was tormented in his righteous soul by the lawless deeds he saw and heard)— 9if this is so, then the Lord knows how to rescue godly men from trials and to hold the unrighteous for the day of judgment, while continuing their punishment.[d] 10This is especially true of those who follow the corrupt desire of the sinful nature[e] and despise authority.

Bold and arrogant, these men are not afraid to slander celestial beings; 11yet even angels, although they are stronger and more powerful, do not bring slanderous accusations against such beings in the presence of the Lord. 12But these men blaspheme in matters they do not understand. They are like brute beasts, creatures of instinct, born only to be caught and destroyed, and like beasts they too will perish.

13They will be paid back with harm for the harm they have done. Their idea of pleasure is to carouse in broad daylight. They are blots and blemishes, reveling in their pleasures while they feast with you.[f] 14With eyes full of adultery, they never stop sinning; they seduce the unstable; they are experts in greed—an accursed brood! 15They have left the straight way and wandered off to follow the way of Balaam son of Beor, who loved the wages of wickedness. 16But he was rebuked for his wrongdoing by a donkey—a beast without speech—who spoke with a man's voice and restrained the prophet's madness.

17These men are springs without water and mists driven by a storm. Blackest darkness is reserved for them. 18For they mouth empty, boastful words and, by appealing to the lustful desires of sinful human nature, they entice people who are just escaping from those who live in error. 19They promise them freedom, while they themselves are slaves of depravity—for a man is a slave to whatever has mastered him. 20If they have escaped the corruption of the world by knowing our Lord and Savior Jesus Christ and are again entangled in it and overcome, they are worse off at the end than they were at the beginning. 21It would have been better for them not to have

[b]4 Greek *Tartarus* [c]4 Some manuscripts *into chains of darkness* [d]9 Or *unrighteous for punishment until the day of judgment* [e]10 Or *the flesh* [f]13 Some manuscripts *in their love feasts*

known the way of righteousness, than to have known it and then to turn their backs on the sacred command that was passed on to them. [22]Of them the proverbs are true: "A dog returns to its vomit,"[g] and, "A sow that is washed goes back to her wallowing in the mud."

[g]22 Prov. 26:11

Discovering the Word 1. Why are false teachers dangerous (2:1-3, also 1:20-21)? 2. Study verses 4-9. What did Peter want his readers to learn from these Old Testament events? 3. What characteristics should alert us that we are encountering a false teacher (vv. 10-19)? 4. Why might some people be attracted to teachers with these characteristics? 5. Why might it be better if a false teacher had never known the truth (vv. 20-22)?

Applying the Word 1. How can you protect yourself from the influence of false teachers? 2. What cautions can you institute to keep from becoming a false teacher yourself?

Responding in Prayer Pray for those who are victims of false teachers.

4 / 2 *Peter* 3
The Fire Next Time

AS A TEEN and young adult, when someone mentioned the end of the world, I shuddered and hoped, "Not yet." I wanted to graduate, fall in love, get married, raise children, work at a career—not necessarily in that order. At the very least I wanted to see how the weekend's date turned out. My sunsets looked like sunrise. And God's promised end of the world seemed a cruel interruption.

But at this writing, my twenty-two-year-old daughter and her unborn child lie cold in a country cemetery, a teenage son struggles with severe depression in a nearby psychiatric ward, my husband's colleague of over twenty years just revealed a secret life that includes distributing drugs to teens. My sunrises long for sunset. And the end of the world promises welcome relief.

Warming Up to God When are you likely to wish the world would end? Explain.

Read 2 Peter 3.

3 Dear friends, this is now my second letter
to you. I have written both of them as
reminders to stimulate you to wholesome
thinking. [2]I want you to recall the words spoken
in the past by the holy prophets and the command given by our Lord and Savior through your apostles.

[3]First of all, you must understand that in the
last days scoffers will come, scoffing and following their own evil desires. [4]They will say, "Where
is this 'coming' he promised? Ever since our fathers died, everything goes on as it has since the
beginning of creation." [5]But they deliberately forget that long ago by God's word the heavens existed and the earth was formed out of water and
by water. [6]By these waters also the world of that
time was deluged and destroyed. [7]By the same
word the present heavens and earth are reserved for fire, being kept for the day of judgment and destruction of ungodly men.

[8]But do not forget this one thing, dear friends:
With the Lord a day is like a thousand years, and
a thousand years are like a day. [9]The Lord is not
slow in keeping his promise, as some understand slowness. He is patient with you, not wanting anyone to perish, but everyone to come to repentance.

[10]But the day of the Lord will come like a thief.
The heavens will disappear with a roar; the elements will be destroyed by fire, and the earth and everything in it will be laid bare.[h]

[h]10 Some manuscripts *be burned up*

[11]Since everything will be destroyed in this
way, what kind of people ought you to be? You
ought to live holy and godly lives [12]as you look
forward to the day of God and speed its com-
ing.[i] That day will bring about the destruction
of the heavens by fire, and the elements will melt
in the heat. [13]But in keeping with his promise we
are looking forward to a new heaven and a new
earth, the home of righteousness.

[14]So then, dear friends, since you are looking
forward to this, make every effort to be found
spotless, blameless and at peace with him. [15]Bear
in mind that our Lord's patience means salvation,
just as our dear brother Paul also wrote you with
the wisdom that God gave him. [16]He writes the
same way in all his letters, speaking in them of
these matters. His letters contain some things that
are hard to understand, which ignorant and un-
stable people distort, as they do the other Scrip-
tures, to their own destruction.

[17]Therefore, dear friends, since you already
know this, be on your guard so that you may not
be carried away by the error of lawless men and
fall from your secure position. [18]But grow in the
grace and knowledge of our Lord and Savior Jesus
Christ. To him be glory both now and forever!
Amen.

[i]12 *Or as you wait eagerly for the day of God to come*

Discovering the Word 1. What reasons did Peter give his readers to pay attention to this writing? (Look especially at verses 1–3 and 15–18.) 2. What mistakes will the last-day scoffers make (vv. 4–7)? 3. What reasons does Peter offer for a delay in Christ's return (vv. 8–9, 15)? 4. Compare and contrast the use of fire and water in this passage. What is the significance of each? 5. Notice the question of verse 11, "What kind of people ought you to be?" What answers can you find through the remainder of the chapter?

Applying the Word 1. If the day of the Lord were to come in your lifetime, what would you like to accomplish first? 2. In what condition would you like God to find your work? 3. How would you like God to find your relationships?

Responding in Prayer Pray that you will be always ready for Christ's return.

1 John

Today many people claim to be Christians. In fact, a 1986 Gallup Survey revealed that ninety-four percent of adult Americans believe in God, and that seventy-six percent believe that Jesus is either God or the Son of God. Furthermore, when the question "Would you describe yourself as a 'born again' Christian or not?" was asked, thirty-three percent said yes.

The problem, of course, is that actions speak louder than words. The same survey revealed that many of the mainline Protestant denominations have experienced sharp losses in membership since the mid sixties. For example, only forty percent told Gallup that they had attended church in the last week, and only ten percent claimed to read the Bible on a daily basis.

This credibility problem is intensified when we move from the pew to the pulpit. A shocking number of Christian leaders have been found guilty of sexual sin or financial misconduct. Sadly, their moral failures have been brought to our national attention by the secular news media, anxious to expose such blatant hypocrisy. If such leaders are representative of the church in general, it seems that we are indeed experiencing a period of unprecedented moral decline.

How are we to respond to this kind of situation? How can we tell the difference between genuine Christians and those who merely profess to know Christ?

John's letters were written for that very purpose. John writes to expose the false claims of those whose conduct contradicts their claims. He also provides strong assurance to those whose lifestyle is consistent with their Christian faith.

First John was written between A.D. 85 and 95 by the apostle John, the author of the Gospel of John and Revelation. Evidently the letter was circulated among a number of churches in Asia who were threatened by false teachers.

These false teachers embraced an early form of heresy known as Gnosticism. They taught that matter was entirely evil and spirit was entirely good. This teaching resulted in two fundamental errors:

A "new" theology. This centered in a denial of the incarnation. Since God could not be contaminated by a human body, these false teachers did not believe God became man in Jesus Christ. Some taught that he merely seemed to have a body, a view known as Docetism. Others claimed that the divine Christ descended on Jesus at his baptism but departed before the crucifixion, a view known as Cerinthianism. This latter view seems to be in the background of much of 1 John.

A *"new" morality*. These false teachers also claimed "to have reached such an advanced stage in spiritual experience that they were 'beyond good and evil.' They maintained that they had no sin, not in the sense that they had attained moral perfection but in the sense that what might be sin for people at a less mature stage of inner development was no longer sin for the completely 'spiritual' man. For him ethical distinctions had ceased to be relevant" (F. F. Bruce, *The Epistles of John* [Grand Rapids, Mich.: Eerdmans, 1978], p. 26).

What intensified this problem was that these false teachers had once been an active part of the fellowship which John's readers were continuing to enjoy (see 2:19). But because their "new" teaching was so contrary to the apostolic truths of the gospel, they had to part company with the faithful. As you can well imagine, those who remained in the true fellowship were unsettled and shaken by the defection of these new teachers and needed to be reassured. But in the process, the others also needed to be exposed for what they truly were—unbelieving heretics.

In order to accomplish both purposes, John provides a series of tests for distinguishing between genuine Christians and those who falsely claim to know Christ. In response to the "new" theology, he provides us with a doctrinal test: What does the person believe about Christ? In response to the "new" morality, he provides us with a moral test: How does the person respond to the commandments of Christ? Finally, he provides us with a social test: Does the person love other Christians?

In fact, John's entire first letter is structured around these three tests, each of which appears in three separate groups, or cycles, in the letter. After the prologue (1:1–4), there is the first cycle (1:5—2:27), followed by the second (2:28—4:6) and third (4:7—5:12). Then in the conclusion (5:13–21) John again emphasizes his theme of Christian assurance.

In view of this purpose and structure, it is important to realize that the contrasts in John's letter are not between two types of Christians but between genuine Christians and those who merely claim to be Christians. For in the words of John Stott: "John's argument is double-edged. If he seeks to bring believers to the knowledge that they have eternal life, he is equally at pains to show that unbelievers have not. His purpose is to destroy the false assurance of the counterfeit as well as to confirm the right assurance of the genuine" (John Stott, *The Epistles of John* [Grand Rapids, Mich.: Eerdmans, 1964], p. 52).

Outline

1 / *1 John 1*
Fellowship & Forgiveness

CHRISTIANS EVERYWHERE SEEM to be interested in fellowship. They gather in fellowship halls, attend fellowship dinners and participate in well-organized activities with fellow believers. But what really constitutes biblical fellowship? A covered-dish supper? Coffee and doughnuts? Social events and activities? Perhaps more than any other passage of Scripture, these opening verses of 1 John establish the basis of true fellowship that is to be enjoyed and experienced by all Christians. More importantly, they enable us to understand how we can know we have fellowship with God.

Warming Up to God What thoughts and feelings come to your mind when you think of Christian fellowship?

Read 1 John 1.

1 That which was from the beginning,
which we have heard, which we have
seen with our eyes, which we have looked
at and our hands have touched—this we pro-
claim concerning the Word of life. 2The life ap-
peared; we have seen it and testify to it, and we
proclaim to you the eternal life, which was with
the Father and has appeared to us. 3We proclaim
to you what we have seen and heard, so that you
also may have fellowship with us. And our fellow-
ship is with the Father and with his Son, Jesus
Christ. 4We write this to make our[a] joy com-
plete.
5This is the message we have heard from him
and declare to you: God is light; in him there is
no darkness at all. 6If we claim to have fellowship
with him yet walk in the darkness, we lie and do
not live by the truth. 7But if we walk in the light,
as he is in the light, we have fellowship with one
another, and the blood of Jesus, his Son, purifies
us from all[b] sin.
8If we claim to be without sin, we deceive our-
selves and the truth is not in us. 9If we confess
our sins, he is faithful and just and will forgive us
our sins and purify us from all unrighteousness.
10If we claim we have not sinned, we make him
out to be a liar and his word has no place in our
lives.

[a]4 Some manuscripts *your* [b]7 Or *every*

Discovering the Word 1. John begins this chapter by announcing an apostolic message. What is the content of that message (vv. 1–2)? 2. What are John's reasons for announcing his message (vv. 3–4)? 3. John provides a test by which we can know if we have fellowship with God (vv. 5–10). 4. The first part of John's test concerns the way we live or "walk" (vv. 6–7). What is the relationship between our conduct and our claim to have fellowship with God? 5. The second part of John's test concerns our attitude toward sin (vv. 8–10). What does our denial or confession of sin reveal about the reality of our relationship with God? 6. Based on your study of this passage, what does it mean to have fellowship with God—and each other?

Applying the Word 1. Does John's test strengthen or weaken your assurance of fellowship with God? Explain. 2. How can we enjoy a greater fellowship with those who know the Father and the Son?

Responding in Prayer Pray that the level of fellowship in your church would be deepened and enriched.

2/ *1 John 2:1–11*

Talking & Walking the Truth

FROM THE VERY beginning of Jesus' ministry, he emphasized that it is not what we profess but what we *possess* that counts for eternity. In his first major message he declared, "By their fruit you will recognize them." He then went on to teach, "Not everyone who says to me, 'Lord, Lord,' will enter the kingdom of heaven, but only he who does the will of my Father who is in heaven" (Mt 7:20–21). In the same way, John emphasizes that our claim to know Jesus must be backed by our conduct. This is necessary if we are to be certain about the reality of our faith.

Warming Up to God When have you been impacted by someone saying one thing and doing another?

Read 1 John 2:1–11.

2 My dear children, I write this to you so
that you will not sin. But if anybody does
sin, we have one who speaks to the Father
in our defense—Jesus Christ, the Righteous One.
2He is the atoning sacrifice for our sins, and not
only for ours but also for[c] the sins of the whole
world.
3We know that we have come to know him if
we obey his commands. 4The man who says, "I
know him," but does not do what he commands
is a liar, and the truth is not in him. 5But if any-
one obeys his word, God's love[d] is truly made
complete in him. This is how we know we are in
him: 6Whoever claims to live in him must walk as
Jesus did.
7Dear friends, I am not writing you a new com-
mand but an old one, which you have had since
the beginning. This old command is the message
you have heard. 8Yet I am writing you a new com-
mand; its truth is seen in him and you, because
the darkness is passing and the true light is al-
ready shining.
9Anyone who claims to be in the light but hates
his brother is still in the darkness. 10Whoever
loves his brother lives in the light, and there is
nothing in him[e] to make him stumble. 11But
whoever hates his brother is in the darkness and
walks around in the darkness; he does not know
where he is going, because the darkness has
blinded him.

[c]2 Or *He is the one who turns aside God's wrath, taking away our sins, and not only ours but also* [d]5 Or *word, love for God* [e]10 Or *it*

Discovering the Word 1. According to John, how can we tell whether we truly know Christ or merely claim to know him (vv. 3–6)? 2. Practically speaking, what does it mean to "walk as Jesus did" (v. 6)? 3. In verses 7–11, John focuses on one of the commands. How can this command be both old and new (vv. 7–8)? 4. Why would love for our brother rather than love for God serve as a test of being in the light (vv. 9–11)? 5. In view of the overall context of this passage, what does it mean to *live* in the light (v. 10)? to live in Christ (v. 6)?

Applying the Word 1. Although John does not want us to sin, he knows that we sometimes do (vv. 1–2). How does the realization that Jesus speaks "in our defense" provide comfort and assurance when you sin? 2. How does this passage encourage you to obey Christ and love other members of his body?

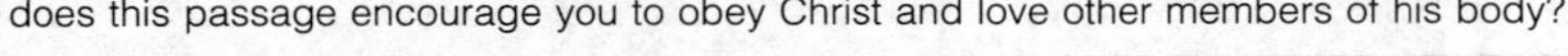

Responding in Prayer Ask that your life would reflect the integrity of Christ.

3 / 1 John 2:12–17
Encouragement & Warning

PILGRIM'S PROGRESS IS the classic tale of Christian's escape from the City of Destruction to the Heavenly City. It is true to experience because all of us can identify with his encounters along the way. In the Valley of Humiliation he enters into combat with Apollyon, his fiercest foe. At the Hill of Difficulty he meets Adam-the-First and his three daughters: Lust-of-the-Flesh, Lust-of-the-Eyes and Pride-of-Life. In the town of Folly he narrowly escapes its greatest attraction, Vanity Fair. These encounters are John Bunyan's well-known descriptions of the threefold arena of all Christian conflict—the world, the flesh and the devil. They are the same three foes that appear here in 1 John.

Warming Up to God How far did you progress as a Christian before you became aware of these three foes? Explain.

Read 1 John 2:12–17.

12I write to you, dear children,
because your sins have been forgiven on
account of his name.
13I write to you, fathers,
because you have known him who is from
the beginning.
I write to you, young men,
because you have overcome the evil one.
I write to you, dear children,
because you have known the Father.
14I write to you, fathers,
because you have known him who is from
the beginning.
I write to you, young men,
because you are strong,
and the word of God lives in you,
and you have overcome the evil one.

15Do not love the world or anything in the
world. If anyone loves the world, the love of the
Father is not in him. 16For everything in the
world—the cravings of sinful man, the lust of his
eyes and the boasting of what he has and does—
comes not from the Father but from the world.
17The world and its desires pass away, but the
man who does the will of God lives forever.

Discovering the Word 1. Who is represented by the three groups being addressed (vv. 12–14)? 2. What is the source of our victory over the evil one (vv. 13–14)? 3. Why can there be no middle ground between our love for God and love for the world (vv. 15–17)? 4. What are the reasons we are to resist such temptations (vv. 15–17)? 5. How does the realization that the world is passing away (v. 17) lessen its appeal in your life?

Applying the Word 1. How does this passage help us gain a better understanding of our spiritual battle? 2. On a daily basis, how can that truth help us overcome the tactics and schemes of the evil one?

Responding in Prayer Praise God for giving you the strength you need to overcome the evil one.

4 / 1 John 2:18–27
How Important Is Theology?

THERE IS AN increasingly popular mindset within the church today that seeks to divorce Christian teaching from Christian living. "We don't want more theology," we are told, "just more about Jesus." But how can we learn more about Jesus apart from a proper understanding of who he is and what he has accomplished? The fact is, there is nothing more basic to Christianity than the person and work of Christ. Apart from understanding Christ, there can be no real Christian living. That is why John goes to great lengths to protect his "dear children" from false views about Christ and to instruct them in the truth.

Warming Up to God What have you been learning about the person and work of Christ recently?

Read 1 John 2:18–27.

18Dear children, this is the last hour; and as
you have heard that the antichrist is coming, even
now many antichrists have come. This is how we
know it is the last hour. 19They went out from us,
but they did not really belong to us. For if they
had belonged to us, they would have remained
with us; but their going showed that none of
them belonged to us.
20But you have an anointing from the Holy
One, and all of you know the truth.[f] 21I do not
write to you because you do not know the truth,
but because you do know it and because no lie
comes from the truth. 22Who is the liar? It is the
man who denies that Jesus is the Christ. Such a
man is the antichrist—he denies the Father and
the Son. 23No one who denies the Son has the
Father; whoever acknowledges the Son has the
Father also.
24See that what you have heard from the begin-
ning remains in you. If it does, you also will re-
main in the Son and in the Father. 25And this is
what he promised us—even eternal life.
26I am writing these things to you about those
who are trying to lead you astray. 27As for you,
the anointing you received from him remains in
you, and you do not need anyone to teach you.
But as his anointing teaches you about all things
and as that anointing is real, not counterfeit—
just as it has taught you, remain in him.

f20 Some manuscripts *and you know all things*

Discovering the Word 1. What characteristics of false teachers and their teaching is John exposing in these verses? 2. All the New Testament authors viewed the first coming of Christ as the event which marked the beginning of the end—"the last hour." What are some of the signs of the last hour (vv. 18–19)? 3. To deny that "Jesus is the Christ" (v. 22) is to deny that the man Jesus is the eternal, divine Christ—the God-Man. Why is John so harsh toward those who believe and teach such a view (vv. 22–23)? 4. Why is remaining in the truth so important in the Christian life (vv. 24–25)? 5. How does his instruction (v. 27) help us understand what it means to remain in Christ?

Applying the Word 1. What does this passage teach us about the Holy Spirit's ministry of *preserving* us from error? 2. What does it teach about our responsibility of *persevering* in the truth?

Responding in Prayer Ask God to fill your heart and mind with truth about himself.

5/ *1 John 2:28—3:10*
Like Father, Like Son

A NUMBER OF years ago *Newsweek* featured an article on the increasing amount of people within our society who are claiming to be "born again." The article included the following report:

> According to a recent Gallup survey based on personal interviews with 1,553 Americans of voting age, half of all Protestants—and a third of all Americans—say they have been "born again." That figure comes to nearly 50 million adult Americans who claim to have experienced a turning point in their lives by making a personal commitment to Jesus Christ as their Savior. ("Born Again," *Newsweek*, October 25, 1976, p. 68.)

How would we go about discovering if the results of that survey were true? Where would we turn in God's Word to validate such a claim? Without question, 1 John 2:28—3:10 provides one of the clearest tests in Scripture for determining whether one who claims to be a Christian has truly been born of God.

Warming Up to God What do you think your local community would be like if one third of everyone who lived there was born again?

Read 1 John 2:28—3:10.

28And now, dear children, continue in him, so
that when he appears we may be confident and
unashamed before him at his coming.
29If you know that he is righteous, you know
that everyone who does what is right has been
born of him.

3 How great is the love the Father has lav-
ished on us, that we should be called chil-
dren of God! And that is what we are!
The reason the world does not know us is that it
did not know him. 2Dear friends, now we are
children of God, and what we will be has not yet
been made known. But we know that when he
appears,[g] we shall be like him, for we shall see
him as he is. 3Everyone who has this hope in him
purifies himself, just as he is pure.
4Everyone who sins breaks the law; in fact, sin
is lawlessness. 5But you know that he appeared so
that he might take away our sins. And in him is
no sin. 6No one who lives in him keeps on sin-
ning. No one who continues to sin has either seen
him or known him.
7Dear children, do not let anyone lead you
astray. He who does what is right is righteous,
just as he is righteous. 8He who does what is sin-
ful is of the devil, because the devil has been sin-
ning from the beginning. The reason the Son of
God appeared was to destroy the devil's work.
9No one who is born of God will continue to sin,
because God's seed remains in him; he cannot go
on sinning, because he has been born of God.
10This is how we know who the children of God
are and who the children of the devil are: Anyone
who does not do what is right is not a child of
God; nor is anyone who does not love his
brother.

g2 Or *when it is made known*

Discovering the Word 1. Based on John's emphasis at the beginning and the end of the passage (2:28–29; 3:9–10), what test is he using to validate a person's claim of being born again? 2. Throughout this passage John teaches that God's children resemble their Father. In what ways does he reinforce this principle (2:29—3:10)? 3. How does John's definition of sin (v. 4) compare with some of the viewpoints people have today? 4. Although Christians can and do sin, how does knowing Christ change our relationship to sin (v. 6)? 5. Why does the new birth make it impossible for God's children to have a life characterized by sin (v. 9)?

Applying the Word 1. As one who has been born of God, what are some ways you see the family traits of obedience and love developing in your life? 2. In what area would you like to be more obedient?

Responding in Prayer Pray that your family resemblance to God and to Christ would be increased.

6/ *1 John 3:11–24*
Blessed Assurance

IN HIS CLASSIC book *Holiness* J. C. Ryle expresses concern for believers who doubt: "I heartily wish that assurance was more sought after than it is. Too many among those who believe begin doubting and go on doubting, live doubting and die doubting, and go to heaven in a kind of mist" (J. C. Ryle, *Holiness* [Grand Rapids, Mich.: Baker, 1979], p. 158). He goes on to say:

> Doubts and fears have power to spoil much of the happiness of a true believer in Christ. Uncertainty and suspense are bad enough in any condition—in the matter of our health, our property, our families, our affections, our earthly callings—but never so bad as in the affairs of our souls. (Ryle, *Holiness*, p. 159.)

Without question, doubt and fear have robbed many of the joys of Christian assurance. That is why this passage is so important for Christian living. It overflows with the confidence and assurance that ought to characterize every member of God's family.

Warming Up to God Have you ever questioned whether you were a member of God's family? Explain.

Read 1 John 3:11–24.

11This is the message you heard from the be-
ginning: We should love one another. 12Do not be
like Cain, who belonged to the evil one and mur-
dered his brother. And why did he murder him?
Because his own actions were evil and his
brother's were righteous. 13Do not be surprised,
my brothers, if the world hates you. 14We know
that we have passed from death to life, because
we love our brothers. Anyone who does not love
remains in death. 15Anyone who hates his brother
is a murderer, and you know that no murderer
has eternal life in him.
16This is how we know what love is: Jesus
Christ laid down his life for us. And we ought to
lay down our lives for our brothers. 17If anyone
has material possessions and sees his brother in
need but has no pity on him, how can the love of
God be in him? 18Dear children, let us not love
with words or tongue but with actions and in
truth. 19This then is how we know that we belong
to the truth, and how we set our hearts at rest in
his presence 20whenever our hearts condemn us.
For God is greater than our hearts, and he knows
everything.
21Dear friends, if our hearts do not condemn
us, we have confidence before God 22and receive
from him anything we ask, because we obey his
commands and do what pleases him. 23And this is
his command: to believe in the name of his Son,
Jesus Christ, and to love one another as he com-
manded us. 24Those who obey his commands live
in him, and he in them. And this is how we know
that he lives in us: We know it by the Spirit he
gave us.

Discovering the Word 1. John begins this passage by talking about love and hate. How do Cain and Abel illustrate the two basic categories of humanity (vv. 11–15)? 2. Why is Christ's death on the cross the supreme example of love (v. 16)? 3. How can John's assurances in verses 19–20 help us deal with times of doubt? 4. Why would our obedience to God's commands affect our confidence in prayer (vv. 21–22)? 5. Why do you think John reduces the commandments to a single command to be obeyed (v. 23)?

Applying the Word 1. In verse 17 John mentions one specific way we can follow Christ's example. How have you and those in your church sought to love those with material needs? 2. In what other practical ways might we "lay down our lives" for each other? 3. Based on this passage, how would you counsel someone who lacked assurance that he or she was a Christian?

Responding in Prayer Pray about the needs on your heart with confidence before God.

7 / 1 John 4:1–12
Discernment & Devotion

EVERY CHRISTIAN VIRTUE bears within itself the seeds of its own destruction. A zeal for the truth, for example, if not tempered by love and compassion can cause us to become arrogant, harsh and cold. Likewise, love for others if unchecked by the truth can cause us to be wishy-washy and even tolerant toward sin. If one of these virtues is not governed by the other, it can become a liability and not a strength. Like everything else, obtaining a proper balance is of utmost importance. In this passage, both doctrinal discernment and devotion to other Christians are held before us in perfect balance. They are not either/or, but both/and. One without the other is not enough.

Warming Up to God Which of these two aspects of the Christian life do you tend to emphasize above the other? Why?

Read 1 John 4:1-12.

---

4 Dear friends, do not believe every spirit,
but test the spirits to see whether they are
from God, because many false prophets
have gone out into the world. 2This is how you
can recognize the Spirit of God: Every spirit that
acknowledges that Jesus Christ has come in the
flesh is from God, 3but every spirit that does not
acknowledge Jesus is not from God. This is the
spirit of the antichrist, which you have heard is
coming and even now is already in the world.
4You, dear children, are from God and have
overcome them, because the one who is in you is
greater than the one who is in the world. 5They
are from the world and therefore speak from the
viewpoint of the world, and the world listens to
them. 6We are from God, and whoever knows
God listens to us; but whoever is not from God
does not listen to us. This is how we recognize
the Spirit[h] of truth and the spirit of falsehood.
7Dear friends, let us love one another, for love
comes from God. Everyone who loves has been
born of God and knows God. 8Whoever does not
love does not know God, because God is love.
9This is how God showed his love among us: He
sent his one and only Son[i] into the world that
we might live through him. 10This is love: not
that we loved God, but that he loved us and sent
his Son as an atoning sacrifice for[j] our sins.
11Dear friends, since God so loved us, we also
ought to love one another. 12No one has ever seen
God; but if we love one another, God lives in us
and his love is made complete in us.

[h]6 *Or spirit* [i]9 *Or his only begotten Son* [j]10 *Or as the one who would turn aside his wrath, taking away*

Discovering the Word 1. Why is there such a great need for Christians to be discerning (v. 1)? 2. What test does John give us for determining whether a person's teaching is from "the Spirit of God" or the "spirit of the antichrist" (vv. 2-3)? 3. As Christians, how can we overcome the doctrinal errors that continually confront us (vv. 4-6)? 4. Why must we be diligent in our devotion to one another (vv. 7-8)? 5. How does our love for each other make the invisible God visible in our midst (v. 12)?

Applying the Word 1. How does God's love for you motivate you to love others (v. 11)? 2. In what practical way can you show love this week to a brother or sister in Christ?

Responding in Prayer Ask that you would be filled with love.

---

8 / *1 John 4:13-21*
Fear's Remedy

IN THE SEQUEL to *Pilgrim's Progress*, Mr. Great-Heart and Father Honest engage in a conversation about an old friend, Mr. Fearing. At one point in the dialogue he is portrayed in the following way: "He was a man that had the root of the matter in him, but he was one of the most troublesome Pilgrims that I ever met with in all my days."

That is Bunyan's way of describing many who are on the road to heaven: thoroughly sincere (the root of the matter is in them) yet so overloaded with doubts and fears that their pilgrimage is indeed "troublesome." How is Mr. Fearing to fare in this life? How does he, and how do we, overcome this kind of problem? The answer, in part, lies within this passage in 1 John.

Warming Up to God In what ways do you feel burdened by fear? Pause to voice your fears to God and listen for his assurance.

Read 1 John 4:13-21.

13We know that we live in him and he in us,
because he has given us of his Spirit. 14And we
have seen and testify that the Father has sent his
Son to be the Savior of the world. 15If anyone
acknowledges that Jesus is the Son of God, God
lives in him and he in God. 16And so we know
and rely on the love God has for us.

God is love. Whoever lives in love lives in God,
and God in him. 17In this way, love is made com-
plete among us so that we will have confidence
on the day of judgment, because in this world we
are like him. 18There is no fear in love. But perfect
love drives out fear, because fear has to do with
punishment. The one who fears is not made per-
fect in love.

19We love because he first loved us. 20If anyone
says, "I love God," yet hates his brother, he is a
liar. For anyone who does not love his brother,
whom he has seen, cannot love God, whom he
has not seen. 21And he has given us this com-
mand: Whoever loves God must also love his
brother.

Discovering the Word 1. What three tests does John give for determining whether "we live in him and he in us" (vv. 13–16)? 2. How is our experience of God's love related to our ability to love others (vv. 16, 19)? 3. What insights does verse 18 give us into why we sometimes fear God and others? 4. Why is it impossible to love God and yet hate one of the members of his family (vv. 19–21)?

Applying the Word 1. How can the principle "perfect love drives out fear" (v. 18) help you overcome your fears? 2. In what ways can this passage strengthen our confidence before God?

Responding in Prayer Ask God to fill you with love for someone whom you find difficult to love.

9 / *1 John 5:1–12*
Faith Is the Victory

CHRISTIANS WITH A variety of theological views have wholeheartedly sung the words to the well-known hymn:

Faith is the victory! Faith is the victory!
O glorious victory, That overcomes the world.

But in light of the daily battles in the Christian life, not all agree on what this victory is, when it is accomplished, or how we go about achieving it. In this passage John clears up some of our confusion. He focuses our attention on not only the victory we have in Christ, but also on Christ himself. For, first and foremost, an overcoming faith is one that is centered in a correct understanding of who Christ is.

Warming Up to God What spiritual battles are the focus of your attention?

Read 1 John 5:1–12.

5 Everyone who believes that Jesus is the
Christ is born of God, and everyone who
loves the father loves his child as well.
2This is how we know that we love the children
of God: by loving God and carrying out his com-
mands. 3This is love for God: to obey his com-
mands. And his commands are not burdensome,
4for everyone born of God overcomes the world.
This is the victory that has overcome the world,
even our faith. 5Who is it that overcomes the
world? Only he who believes that Jesus is the Son
of God.
6This is the one who came by water and
blood—Jesus Christ. He did not come by water
only, but by water and blood. And it is the Spirit
who testifies, because the Spirit is the truth. 7For
there are three that testify: 8the[k] Spirit, the water

[k]7,8 Late manuscripts of the Vulgate *testify in heaven: the Father, the Word and the Holy Spirit, and these three are one. 8And there are three that testify on earth: the* (not found in any Greek manuscript before the sixteenth century)

and the blood; and the three are in agreement.
9We accept man's testimony, but God's testimony
is greater because it is the testimony of God,
which he has given about his Son. 10Anyone who
believes in the Son of God has this testimony in
his heart. Anyone who does not believe God has
made him out to be a liar, because he has not
believed the testimony God has given about his
Son. 11And this is the testimony: God has given
us eternal life, and this life is in his Son. 12He who
has the Son has life; he who does not have the
Son of God does not have life.

Discovering the Word 1. What are some inevitable results of the new birth (vv. 1–2)? 2. Why is obedience to God's commandments not burdensome for Christians (v. 3)? 3. How then can we explain the struggle we sometimes have to obey? 4. Reflect for a moment on the two major characteristics of the world described earlier (see 2:15–17; 4:1–6). What then does it mean for us to "overcome the world" (vv. 4–5)? 5. The heretics of John's day taught that the divine Christ descended on Jesus at his baptism but left *before* his death (v. 6). What is wrong with this view? 6. The Old Testament law required two or three witnesses to prove a claim. Who are John's three witnesses, and what do they testify (vv. 7–8)?

Applying the Word 1. What evidence of the victory over the world do you see in your life? 2. How does your own experience confirm the truth that eternal life is found in Jesus (vv. 10–12)?

Responding in Prayer Take time to thank God for his son, and for the victory and eternal life we have in him.

10/ *1 John 5:13–21*
What We Know as Christians

ALMOST IMMEDIATELY AFTER his well-known conversion experience at Aldersgate Street, John Wesley struggled for months over the uncertainty of his own salvation. Receiving little help from his friends or his church, his thoughts began to turn inward. Focusing on his sinful failures, he became increasingly despondent and dejected. He sought relief by opening passages within the Bible at random, but when that also proved unfruitful he continued his downward spiral. Finally he sank to such depths of despair that he made the following shocking notation in his journal: "My friends affirm that I am mad because I said I was not a Christian a year ago. I affirm I am not a Christian now" (Arnold A. Dallimore, *George Whitefield*, Vol. I [Carlisle, Penn.: Banner of Truth, 1975], p. 196).

What was Wesley's problem? Unfortunately, it is the same problem that afflicts many sincere Christians today—a lack of knowledge. There are certain truths that all of us as Christians must know if we are to avoid an experience like his. Those truths are found in this passage.

Warming Up to God How well can you relate to Wesley's experience? Explain.

Read 1 John 5:13–21.

13I write these things to you who believe in the
name of the Son of God so that you may know
that you have eternal life. 14This is the confidence
we have in approaching God: that if we ask
anything according to his will, he hears us.
15And if we know that he hears us—whatever
we ask—we know that we have what we asked
of him.

16If anyone sees his brother commit a sin that
does not lead to death, he should pray and God
will give him life. I refer to those whose sin does
not lead to death. There is a sin that leads to
death. I am not saying that he should pray about
that. 17All wrongdoing is sin, and there is sin that
does not lead to death.

18We know that anyone born of God does not
continue to sin; the one who was born of God
keeps him safe, and the evil one cannot harm
him. 19We know that we are children of God, and
that the whole world is under the control of the

evil one. [20]We know also that the Son of God has
come and has given us understanding, so that we
may know him who is true. And we are in him
who is true—even in his Son Jesus Christ. He is
the true God and eternal life.
[21]Dear children, keep yourselves from idols.

Discovering the Word 1. What assurance does John give us in these verses? 2. Verse 13 is a summary statement of purpose for the entire epistle. What then are those "things" which assure us we have eternal life? 3. How can we get to the point where we want what God wants (vv. 14–15)? 4. In light of the whole context of this epistle, what might be the distinction between the sin that does not lead to death and the one that does (vv. 16–17)? 5. How does the coming of God's Son enable us to know the true God in contrast to the false conceptions of God that continually surround us (vv. 20–21)?

Applying the Word 1. What certainties in this passage are the most encouraging to you? 2. In what way do you need greater assurance from God?

Responding in Prayer Pray that God will make your desires his own will.

2 John

Like 1 John, 2 John was written by the apostle John between A.D. 85 and 95. It was written to provide guidance about hospitality. During the first century, traveling evangelists relied on the hospitality of church members. Because inns were few and unsafe, believers would take such people into their homes and then give them provisions for their journey. Since Gnostic teachers also relied on hospitality, John warned his readers against taking such people into their homes lest they participate in spreading heresy.

2 John 1–13
Truth & Love

THERE ARE TWO equally extreme misconceptions many people have concerning what it means to be a Christian or to live the Christian life. One view says, "It doesn't matter what you believe as long as you are sincere and loving." The other one says, "It doesn't matter how you live as long as you believe the truth." The reason why both views are just as wrong is because the Word of God binds both truth and love inseparably together. They are friends, not enemies. Nowhere will you see this perspective more clearly than in John's second epistle. His major purpose is to demonstrate how love and truth are designed to support and complement one another as only good friends can.

Warming Up to God Have you ever been in a situation where you felt you were torn between doing the right thing and the loving thing? Explain.

Read 2 John 1–13.

---

1 The elder,

To the chosen lady and her children, whom I
love in the truth—and not I only, but also all who
know the truth— 2 because of the truth, which
lives in us and will be with us forever:

3 Grace, mercy and peace from God the Father
and from Jesus Christ, the Father's Son, will be
with us in truth and love.

4 It has given me great joy to find some of your
children walking in the truth, just as the Father
commanded us. 5 And now, dear lady, I am not
writing you a new command but one we have had
from the beginning. I ask that we love one an-
other. 6 And this is love: that we walk in obedi-
ence to his commands. As you have heard from
the beginning, his command is that you walk in
love.
7 Many deceivers, who do not acknowledge
Jesus Christ as coming in the flesh, have gone out
into the world. Any such person is the deceiver
and the antichrist. 8 Watch out that you do not
lose what you have worked for, but that you may
be rewarded fully. 9 Anyone who runs ahead and
does not continue in the teaching of Christ does
not have God; whoever continues in the teaching
has both the Father and the Son. 10 If anyone
comes to you and does not bring this teaching, do
not take him into your house or welcome him.
11 Anyone who welcomes him shares in his
wicked work.
12 I have much to write to you, but I do not
want to use paper and ink. Instead, I hope to visit
you and talk with you face to face, so that our joy
may be complete.

13 The children of your chosen sister send their
greetings.

Discovering the Word 1. In the brief introductory address and greeting (vv. 1–3), notice how many times *truth* and *love* are mentioned together. What does it mean to love someone "in the truth" (v. 1)? 2. We tend to love only those Christians who agree with us or who we feel are compatible with us. But what does it mean to love them "because of the truth" (v. 2)? 3. In verses 4–6 the unity of truth and love is applied to our relationships within the church. What distinction is made between the *commandment* and the *commandments*? 4. In verses 7–11 the unity of truth and love is applied to our relationships outside the church. By denying that Christ had come in the flesh (v. 7), what fundamental truths were the false teachers rejecting? 5. Obtaining a future reward for faithful service was a strong motivation for John (v. 8). In what sense does the prospect of receiving a reward from Jesus Christ motivate you to walk in truth and love?

Applying the Word 1. Would you identify yourself as someone whose truth needs to be balanced by love or whose love needs to be balanced by truth? Explain. 2. What can you do to gain a better balance?

Responding in Prayer Pray that your life would reveal an understanding of both truth and love.

3 John

Like 2 John, 3 John was written to provide us with guidance about hospitality, but in a much more positive way. Whereas 2 John tells us what we are *not* to do, 3 John emphasizes what we *are* to do. For those genuine teachers who are totally dependent upon the body of Christ for all of their needs, we are to open not only our hearts but also our homes. This instruction is primarily found in John's commendation of Gaius, who has done this very thing, and in his denunciation of Diotrephes, who has refused. These two men become living examples of good and evil, truth and error.

It is my hope that these studies will encourage and assure you that you "walk in the truth."

3 John 1–14
Opening Our Hearts & Homes

IMAGINE LIVING IN a world where there were no bed-and-breakfasts, no hotels and headwaiters. If traveling evangelists and teachers were to come to your town, you would have the privilege of inviting them into your home for the night and giving them provisions for their journey. Such was the world of John and his readers. Their hospitality was one of the clearest testimonies of their love for the brethren and obedience to God.

The same is true today. For in the words of Helga Henry, wife of noted theologian Carl F. H. Henry, "Christian hospitality is not a matter of choice; it is not a matter of money; it is not a matter of age, social standing, sex, or personality. Christian hospitality is a matter of obedience to God" (V. A. Hall, *Be My Guest* [Chicago: Moody Press, 1979], p. 9). For that reason the instruction concerning hospitality in this letter takes on added significance.

Warming Up to God When is showing hospitality difficult?

Read 3 John 1–14.

1The elder,

To my dear friend Gaius, whom I love in the
truth.

2Dear friend, I pray that you may enjoy good
health and that all may go well with you, even as
your soul is getting along well. 3It gave me great
joy to have some brothers come and tell about
your faithfulness to the truth and how you con-
tinue to walk in the truth. 4I have no greater joy
than to hear that my children are walking in the
truth.

5Dear friend, you are faithful in what you are
doing for the brothers, even though they are
strangers to you. 6They have told the church
about your love. You will do well to send them on
their way in a manner worthy of God. 7It was for
the sake of the Name that they went out, receiv-
ing no help from the pagans. 8We ought therefore
to show hospitality to such men so that we may
work together for the truth.

9I wrote to the church, but Diotrephes, who
loves to be first, will have nothing to do with us.
10So if I come, I will call attention to what he is
doing, gossiping maliciously about us. Not satis-
fied with that, he refuses to welcome the broth-
ers. He also stops those who want to do so and
puts them out of the church.

11Dear friend, do not imitate what is evil but
what is good. Anyone who does what is good is
from God. Anyone who does what is evil has not
seen God. 12Demetrius is well spoken of by every-
one—and even by the truth itself. We also speak
well of him, and you know that our testimony is
true.

13I have much to write you, but I do not want
to do so with pen and ink. 14I hope to see you
soon, and we will talk face to face.

Peace to you. The friends here send their greet-
ings. Greet the friends there by name.

Discovering the Word 1. Why is Gaius an especially good example for us to follow? 2. How are both love and faithfulness demonstrated in Christian hospitality (vv. 5–6)? 3. Why do you think Christian workers are to look to Christians for support and not to non-Christians (vv. 7–8)? 4. In addition to hospitality, how else can we "work together" with such people? 5. How are the actions of Diotrephes consistent with his true heart's desire (vv. 9–11)?

Applying the Word 1. In contrast to Diotrephes, Demetrius was "well spoken of by everyone" (v. 12). If those who know you best were asked about your love and hospitality, what might they say? 2. In light of this passage, what practical steps could you take to develop more of a ministry of hospitality?

Responding in Prayer Pray for an open heart that will lead you to an open home.

Jude

Jude wrote in the same era as Peter. In fact, much of the information in Jude is found also in 2 Peter 2.

Jude was the brother of James and the half-brother of Jesus. Both Matthew 13:55 and Mark 6:3 speak of James and Jude (along with Joseph and Simon) as brothers of Jesus. Though, according to John 7:5, Christ's brothers were not believers in him during his lifetime, these two at least became converts after his death.

James became a leader in the early church. We see him in action in 1 Corinthians 15:7; Acts 12:17 and 15:13; Galatians 1:19 and 2:9, 12; and Acts 21:18. We hear from Jude only in this book, except perhaps in 1 Corinthians 9:5. It is interesting to note that while Jude claims James as brother, both he and James refer to themselves as servants of Jesus.

The book of Jude was written to oppose false teachers who were sexually immoral and were teaching arrogantly. This letter would have been used as a sermon in the writer's absence (Craig S. Keener, *The IVP Bible Background Commentary: New Testament* [Downers Grove, Ill.: InterVarsity Press, 1993], pp. 752–53).

Jude 1–25
The Twisted Fate of Twisted Faith

IN NOVEMBER OF 1978, in a jungle clearing in Guyana, more than nine hundred people committed suicide by drinking cyanide-treated punch. Those too young to act on their own were given the punch by their parents. The Jonestown massacre sends a shudder through all Christians—and well it should—because Jim Jones, who prescribed this "White Night" of death, at one time claimed to be among us. It's enough to cause Christians to take a hard, critical look at the life and faith of their leaders—and themselves. The book of Jude shows us how.

Warming Up to God How do you think that people get tricked into perverted versions of the Christian faith?

Read Jude 1–25.

1Jude, a servant of Jesus Christ and a brother of
James,

To those who have been called, who are loved
by God the Father and kept by[a] Jesus Christ:

2Mercy, peace and love be yours in abundance.

3Dear friends, although I was very eager to
write to you about the salvation we share, I felt I
had to write and urge you to contend for the faith
that was once for all entrusted to the saints. 4For
certain men whose condemnation was written
about[b] long ago have secretly slipped in among
you. They are godless men, who change the grace
of our God into a license for immorality and deny
Jesus Christ our only Sovereign and Lord.
5Though you already know all this, I want to
remind you that the Lord[c] delivered his people
out of Egypt, but later destroyed those who did
not believe. 6And the angels who did not keep
their positions of authority but abandoned their
own home—these he has kept in darkness,
bound with everlasting chains for judgment on
the great Day. 7In a similar way, Sodom and Go-
morrah and the surrounding towns gave them-
selves up to sexual immorality and perversion.
They serve as an example of those who suffer the
punishment of eternal fire.
8In the very same way, these dreamers pollute
their own bodies, reject authority and slander ce-
lestial beings. 9But even the archangel Michael,
when he was disputing with the devil about the
body of Moses, did not dare to bring a slanderous
accusation against him, but said, "The Lord re-
buke you!" 10Yet these men speak abusively
against whatever they do not understand; and
what things they do understand by instinct, like
unreasoning animals—these are the very things
that destroy them.
11Woe to them! They have taken the way of
Cain; they have rushed for profit into Balaam's
error; they have been destroyed in Korah's rebel-
lion.
12These men are blemishes at your love feasts,
eating with you without the slightest qualm—
shepherds who feed only themselves. They are
clouds without rain, blown along by the wind;
autumn trees, without fruit and uprooted—twice
dead. 13They are wild waves of the sea, foaming
up their shame; wandering stars, for whom black-
est darkness has been reserved forever.
14Enoch, the seventh from Adam, prophesied
about these men: "See, the Lord is coming with
thousands upon thousands of his holy ones 15to
judge everyone, and to convict all the ungodly of
all the ungodly acts they have done in the un-
godly way, and of all the harsh words ungodly
sinners have spoken against him." 16These men
are grumblers and faultfinders; they follow their
own evil desires; they boast about themselves and
flatter others for their own advantage.
17But, dear friends, remember what the apostles
of our Lord Jesus Christ foretold. 18They said to
you, "In the last times there will be scoffers who
will follow their own ungodly desires." 19These
are the men who divide you, who follow mere
natural instincts and do not have the Spirit.
20But you, dear friends, build yourselves up in
your most holy faith and pray in the Holy Spirit.
21Keep yourselves in God's love as you wait for
the mercy of our Lord Jesus Christ to bring you to
eternal life.

[a] 1 Or *for;* or *in* [b] 4 Or *men who were marked out for condemnation*
[c] 5 Some early manuscripts *Jesus*

[22]Be merciful to those who doubt; [23]snatch oth-
ers from the fire and save them; to others show
mercy, mixed with fear—hating even the clothing
stained by corrupted flesh.
[24]To him who is able to keep you from falling
and to present you before his glorious presence
without fault and with great joy— [25]to the only
God our Savior be glory, majesty, power and au-
thority, through Jesus Christ our Lord, before all
ages, now and forevermore! Amen.

Discovering the Word 1. What can you know of the circumstances of the people receiving this letter and of Jude's purpose in writing to them (vv. 3–4)? 2. Find as many words and phrases as you can in this letter that describe those "certain men" who have "secretly slipped in among you." 3. What harm could people like these do within a body of believers? 4. Jude used a series of six metaphors in verses 12–13. How does each illustrate the danger of teachers who have perverted the gospel? 5. In the face of this problem, Jude gives his readers two sets of instructions: "Remember" (v. 17) and "Build yourselves up" (v. 20). Notice the specific instructions under each of these. How would remembering, in the way Jude describes, help believers keep the essential ingredients of the Christian faith? 6. How would building ourselves up in the ways Jude outlines (vv. 17–23) help us keep on living in a way that is true to our faith?

Applying the Word 1. What errors in faith and life do you see as subtle dangers to today's Christians? 2. How can you protect yourself, and other believers whose lives you touch, from falling into these errors?

Responding in Prayer Pray that you and your church would be protected from false religion.

Revelation

The human spirit is like a little child on a long journey asking, "Are we almost there?" Yet today many of us have stopped thinking about the future. Fear of the bomb and an unthinkable holocaust drives us to squeeze what we can from the present. We become obsessed with momentary gratification. This erodes our capacity to plan and build for the future—if there is one—and paralyzes us from living faithfully in the present.

Unlike people today, New Testament Christians eagerly awaited and longed for the future. They believed the complete reign of Christ on earth was a more certain reality than the seeming victory of evil. Jesus gave John the strangely beautiful vision recorded in the book of Revelation to give us hope. Of the three Christian virtues—faith, hope and love—the one most needing attention today is hope. Revelation touches us at the point of our despair, our world-weariness, our future shock, our fear of persecution, our collaboration with a sick (though friendly) society. It is quite possibly the most relevant book of the Bible for this moment in history.

But how are we to understand this highly symbolic book? Since Revelation was meant to be read at one sitting (1:3), we do well to put aside the charts, sermons and films we have seen that claim to unravel its mysteries. It is better just to read it. A child might understand Revelation better than adults who approach it with preconceived systems. If a child were to hear this as a story and were to conclude, "I'm so glad the Lamb won over the awful beast," he or she would have truly heard it and taken to heart what is written in it (1:3).

Two Common Misconceptions

Many people misunderstand the book because of two commonly held misconceptions. First, Revelation is not difficult to understand. Though it is highly symbolic, it is not a lock whose key has been lost. The major reason we have difficulty decoding the symbolism of this book is that, unlike the first readers, we are largely illiterate when it comes to the Bible.

The Old Testament provides the most important clues for decoding Revelation. Of the 404 verses in Revelation, 278 allude to the Old Testament (though not one direct citation is actually quoted). The book is a biblical implosion. Old Testament ideas, symbols, names and themes have been powerfully pulled together through the inspiration of the Spirit to form a collage, a kaleidoscopic effect in the message John brings.

For example, a phrase like "God will wipe away every tear from their eyes" (7:17) is a creative adaptation of Isaiah 25:8. Proper names like "Balaam," "Jerusalem" and "Sodom" and concepts like "the tree of life" are adapted from John's Bible. Numbers like "forty-two months" are used symbolically, as numbers like "seven" are in the Old Testament (Dan 9:27). This book above all others in the New Testament must be interpreted by Scripture.

Second, we misunderstand Revelation when we treat it as a book of predictions. It is not so much a prediction of future events as it is an exposé of spiritual realities that affect us now and will bring the events of history to a worthy end. John shows us how the world looks to someone in the Spirit.

John wrote Revelation between A.D. 90 and 95 from his place of exile on Patmos Island. Tradition tells us that prior to his exile John left Israel to live in Ephesus, capital of the Roman province of Asia. The seven churches to whom this book is addressed were visited by a courier traveling on the circular road through modern Turkey. His letter described John's vision of Christ as Lord of the churches (1:12–3:22), as the Lamb on the throne (5:1–14), as the liberating Word of God (19:11–16) and as the Leader in the new creation (21—22). This book is truly *the Revelation of Jesus Christ* (1:1).

John says, "Blessed is the one who reads the words of this prophecy, and blessed are those who hear it" (1:3). Look forward to this blessing as you study Revelation.

Outline

1/ Revelation 1:1–8 — *The Illustrated Letter*

2/ Revelation 1:9–20 — *Surprised by Magnificence*

3/ Revelation 2 — *Pardon My Speaking the Truth*

4/ Revelation 3 — *My Dear Compromised People*

5/ Revelation 4—5 — *Worship the Omnipotent Lamb*

6/ Revelation 6 — *The Beautiful Wrath of God*

7/ Revelation 7 — *Living Faithfully Through the Holocaust*

8/ Revelation 8—9 — *The Message of the Angels*

9/ Revelation 10—11 — *God's Messenger*

10/ Revelation 12 — *Conflict with the Accuser*

11/ Revelation 13 — *The Beast*

12/ Revelation 14—15 — *Tale of Two Choices*

13/ Revelation 16 — *Who's to Blame?*

14/ Revelation 17—18 — *Beneath the Surface*

15/ Revelation 19 — *Are You Going to the Wedding?*

16/ Revelation 20 — *The Last Battle*

17/ Revelation 21—22 — *God Dwelling with His People*

1 / *Revelation 1:1–8*
The Illustrated Letter

PERSECUTION, IMPRISONMENT, MARTYRDOM. These seem far removed from the lives of many Christians today. Yet we do suffer. Who can witness the breakup of families, the death of unborn children, the threat of war and the plight of the poor without crying out, "Come, Lord Jesus"? In this passage he does come in a vision to give us hope in a suffering world.

Warming Up to God Following Jesus brings many benefits. It also causes new pressures and problems. In what ways have you found being a Christian difficult?

Read Revelation 1:1–8.

1 The revelation of Jesus Christ, which God
gave him to show his servants what must
soon take place. He made it known by
sending his angel to his servant John, 2who testi-
fies to everything he saw—that is, the word of
God and the testimony of Jesus Christ. 3Blessed is
the one who reads the words of this prophecy,
and blessed are those who hear it and take to
heart what is written in it, because the time is
near.

4John,

To the seven churches in the province of Asia:

Grace and peace to you from him who is, and
who was, and who is to come, and from the seven
spirits[a] before his throne, 5and from Jesus
Christ, who is the faithful witness, the firstborn
from the dead, and the ruler of the kings of the
earth.

To him who loves us and has freed us from our
sins by his blood, 6and has made us to be a king-
dom and priests to serve his God and Father—to
him be glory and power for ever and ever! Amen.

7Look, he is coming with the clouds,
and every eye will see him,
even those who pierced him;
and all the peoples of the earth will mourn
because of him.
So shall it be! Amen.

8"I am the Alpha and the Omega," says the
Lord God, "who is, and who was, and who is to
come, the Almighty."

[a]4 *Or the sevenfold Spirit*

Discovering the Word 1. The word *reveal* means "to bring to light what was formerly hidden, veiled and secret." Who and what will be unveiled by the revelation given to John (vv. 1–3)? 2. How would John's description of God be a comfort to his readers (vv. 4–5)? 3. Why would it help discouraged believers to know they are "a kingdom and priests to serve his God and Father" (v. 6)? 4. John presents a vision of Jesus as both coming (v. 7) and already and always here (v. 8). What would it be like to have only one of these two perspectives?

Applying the Word 1. In what ways has a knowledge of Christ's coming encouraged you in the midst of suffering? 2. John states that we will be blessed if we hear his message and take it to heart (v. 3). In what ways do you think he expects us to take this message to heart?

Responding in Prayer Ask God to fill your heart with hope.

2 / *Revelation 1:9–20*
Surprised by Magnificence

THE EXPERIENCE OF meeting a famous person is sometimes disconcerting. He or she may be less impressive than we had imagined. But when John sees Jesus face to face, he is overwhelmed with his magnificence. John's experience challenges us to ask whether we have ever met the same Person. Or do we follow a pale, distorted copy of the real Lord?

Warming Up to God From all that you have read or experienced before opening Revelation, what images or pictures do you have of Jesus?

Read Revelation 1:9–20.

---

9 I, John, your brother and companion in the
suffering and kingdom and patient endurance
that are ours in Jesus, was on the island of Patmos
because of the word of God and the testimony of
Jesus. 10 On the Lord's Day I was in the Spirit, and
I heard behind me a loud voice like a trumpet,
11 which said: "Write on a scroll what you see and
send it to the seven churches: to Ephesus,
Smyrna, Pergamum, Thyatira, Sardis, Philadel-
phia and Laodicea."
12 I turned around to see the voice that was
speaking to me. And when I turned I saw seven
golden lampstands, 13 and among the lampstands
was someone "like a son of man,"[b] dressed in a
robe reaching down to his feet and with a golden
sash around his chest. 14 His head and hair were
white like wool, as white as snow, and his eyes
were like blazing fire. 15 His feet were like bronze
glowing in a furnace, and his voice was like the
sound of rushing waters. 16 In his right hand he
held seven stars, and out of his mouth came a
sharp double-edged sword. His face was like the
sun shining in all its brilliance.
17 When I saw him, I fell at his feet as though
dead. Then he placed his right hand on me and
said: "Do not be afraid. I am the First and the
Last. 18 I am the Living One; I was dead, and be-
hold I am alive for ever and ever! And I hold the
keys of death and Hades.
19 "Write, therefore, what you have seen, what
is now and what will take place later. 20 The mys-
tery of the seven stars that you saw in my right
hand and of the seven golden lampstands is this:
The seven stars are the angels[c] of the seven
churches, and the seven lampstands are the seven
churches.

[b] 13 Daniel 7:13 [c] 20 Or *messengers*

Discovering the Word 1. John pictures the seven churches as seven golden lampstands (to hold oil lamps). What does John's picture tell us about the function of the churches? 2. How would Jesus' relationship to these churches (v. 13) encourage them to fulfill their function during hard times? 3. John's vision of Jesus is rich with biblical symbolism. Instead of trying to picture all these characteristics at once, allow them to impress you one at a time, like a slide presentation. Which images impress you most with the magnificence of Jesus, and why (vv. 13–16)? 4. Why do you think a godly person like John would be so powerfully overcome by the presence of the One he loved (v. 17)? 5. How would Jesus' words encourage John not to be fearful in his presence (vv. 17–18)?

Applying the Word 1. Revelation was written to churches persecuted under a totalitarian regime. Our society seems more friendly. Yet how is it hostile to us both morally and spiritually? 2. How has this passage enlarged your vision of who Jesus is? 3. How can this vision of Jesus encourage us to resist the seductions of our society?

Responding in Prayer Praise Jesus for who he is and for what you have learned about him here.

3 / *Revelation 2*
Pardon My Speaking the Truth

WHAT CAN WE do to help a fellow Christian who is ready to cave in under pressure? Usually we wouldn't say that things are going to get worse before they get better! But that's what Christ does in the seven letters to churches in Asia (Rev 2—3). He confronts believers who have compromised morally and spiritually. But he also encourages them. This kind of tough love is essential for spiritual health.

Warming Up to God In what area of your life do you feel pressured (spiritually or otherwise)?

Read Revelation 2.

2 "To the angel[d] of the church in Ephesus
write:

These are the words of him who holds the
seven stars in his right hand and walks
among the seven golden lampstands: 2I
know your deeds, your hard work and your
perseverance. I know that you cannot toler-
ate wicked men, that you have tested those
who claim to be apostles but are not, and
have found them false. 3You have persevered
and have endured hardships for my name,
and have not grown weary.
4Yet I hold this against you: You have for-
saken your first love. 5Remember the height
from which you have fallen! Repent and do
the things you did at first. If you do not re-
pent, I will come to you and remove your
lampstand from its place. 6But you have this
in your favor: You hate the practices of the
Nicolaitans, which I also hate.
7He who has an ear, let him hear what the
Spirit says to the churches. To him who
overcomes, I will give the right to eat from
the tree of life, which is in the paradise of
God.

8"To the angel of the church in Smyrna write:

These are the words of him who is the
First and the Last, who died and came to life
again. 9I know your afflictions and your pov-
erty—yet you are rich! I know the slander of
those who say they are Jews and are not, but
are a synagogue of Satan. 10Do not be afraid
of what you are about to suffer. I tell you, the
devil will put some of you in prison to test
you, and you will suffer persecution for ten
days. Be faithful, even to the point of death,
and I will give you the crown of life.
11He who has an ear, let him hear what the
Spirit says to the churches. He who over-
comes will not be hurt at all by the second
death.

12"To the angel of the church in Pergamum write:

These are the words of him who has the
sharp, double-edged sword. 13I know where
you live—where Satan has his throne. Yet
you remain true to my name. You did not
renounce your faith in me, even in the days
of Antipas, my faithful witness, who was put
to death in your city—where Satan lives.
14Nevertheless, I have a few things against
you: You have people there who hold to the
teaching of Balaam, who taught Balak to en-
tice the Israelites to sin by eating food sacri-
ficed to idols and by committing sexual im-
morality. 15Likewise you also have those
who hold to the teaching of the Nicolaitans.
16Repent therefore! Otherwise, I will soon
come to you and will fight against them with
the sword of my mouth.
17He who has an ear, let him hear what the
Spirit says to the churches. To him who
overcomes, I will give some of the hidden
manna. I will also give him a white stone
with a new name written on it, known only
to him who receives it.

18"To the angel of the church in Thyatira write:

These are the words of the Son of God,
whose eyes are like blazing fire and whose
feet are like burnished bronze. 19I know your
deeds, your love and faith, your service and

[d]1 Or *messenger*; also in verses 8, 12 and 18

perseverance, and that you are now doing
more than you did at first.
20Nevertheless, I have this against you:
You tolerate that woman Jezebel, who calls
herself a prophetess. By her teaching she
misleads my servants into sexual immorality
and the eating of food sacrificed to idols. 21I
have given her time to repent of her immo-
rality, but she is unwilling. 22So I will cast
her on a bed of suffering, and I will make
those who commit adultery with her suffer
intensely, unless they repent of her ways. 23I
will strike her children dead. Then all the
churches will know that I am he who
searches hearts and minds, and I will repay
each of you according to your deeds. 24Now
I say to the rest of you in Thyatira, to you
who do not hold to her teaching and have
not learned Satan's so-called deep secrets (I
will not impose any other burden on you):
25Only hold on to what you have until I
come.
26To him who overcomes and does my
will to the end, I will give authority over the
nations—

27'He will rule them with an iron scepter;
he will dash them to pieces like
pottery'[e]—

just as I have received authority from my
Father. 28I will also give him the morning
star. 29He who has an ear, let him hear what
the Spirit says to the churches.

[e]27 Psalm 2:9

Discovering the Word 1. Why would forsaking "your first love" (v. 4) be so tragic for the church at Ephesus? 2. Why do you think Christ's judgment would be so severe if they did not repent (v. 5)? 3. Smyrna was noted for emperor worship. Refusal to worship the emperor brought martyrdom to some Christians. What does Jesus know about the believers in Smyrna (vv. 8–11)? 4. The letter to Smyrna is the only one of the seven that mentions no problem and gives no warning. What role does affirmation play in helping Christians who are under spiritual pressure? 5. Pergamum was also a center of emperor worship. This may be why it is called the place "where Satan has his throne." In addition, temple prostitution was prevalent. How had the church responded to the lure of these temptations (vv. 12–17)? 6. Jezebel (v. 20) is an Old Testament character who symbolizes spiritual adultery (1 Kings 16:31). How was the so-called prophetess in Thyatira like her namesake (vv. 18–29)?

Applying the Word 1. Jesus charges the godly and loving church at Thyatira with being too tolerant of evil in their midst. In what areas are Christians today too tolerant? 2. Each of the letters (except the one to Smyrna) contains an affirmation, a problem, a warning and a promise. How might Jesus' example guide us as we care for a brother or sister ready to cave in under pressure?

Responding in Prayer Pray for someone you know who is under pressure to compromise.

4/ *Revelation 3*
My Dear Compromised People

EXPERTS TELL US we are exposed to fourteen hundred advertisements a day. It takes an enormous act of will not to be conformed to our environment, to be in but not of the world. The remaining three churches in the crownlike array of towns in Asia would be visited by a postal courier completing his circuit in the exact order of John's letters. Each letter helps us resist this powerful threat of being conformed to the world.

Warming Up to God In what ways do Christian groups and churches you know resemble the surrounding culture?

Read Revelation 3.

3 "To the angel[f] of the church in Sardis
write:

These are the words of him who holds the
seven spirits[g] of God and the seven stars. I
know your deeds; you have a reputation of
being alive, but you are dead. 2Wake up!
Strengthen what remains and is about to die,
for I have not found your deeds complete in
the sight of my God. 3Remember, therefore,
what you have received and heard; obey it,
and repent. But if you do not wake up, I will
come like a thief, and you will not know at
what time I will come to you.
4Yet you have a few people in Sardis who
have not soiled their clothes. They will walk
with me, dressed in white, for they are wor-
thy. 5He who overcomes will, like them, be
dressed in white. I will never blot out his
name from the book of life, but will ac-
knowledge his name before my Father and
his angels. 6He who has an ear, let him hear
what the Spirit says to the churches.

7"To the angel of the church in Philadelphia
write:

These are the words of him who is holy
and true, who holds the key of David. What
he opens no one can shut, and what he shuts
no one can open. 8I know your deeds. See, I
have placed before you an open door that no
one can shut. I know that you have little
strength, yet you have kept my word and
have not denied my name. 9I will make those
who are of the synagogue of Satan, who
claim to be Jews though they are not, but are
liars—I will make them come and fall down
at your feet and acknowledge that I have
loved you. 10Since you have kept my com-
mand to endure patiently, I will also keep
you from the hour of trial that is going to
come upon the whole world to test those
who live on the earth.
11I am coming soon. Hold on to what you
have, so that no one will take your crown.
12Him who overcomes I will make a pillar in
the temple of my God. Never again will he
leave it. I will write on him the name of my
God and the name of the city of my God, the
new Jerusalem, which is coming down out of
heaven from my God; and I will also write
on him my new name. 13He who has an ear,
let him hear what the Spirit says to the
churches.

14"To the angel of the church in Laodicea write:

These are the words of the Amen, the
faithful and true witness, the ruler of God's
creation. 15I know your deeds, that you are
neither cold nor hot. I wish you were either
one or the other! 16So, because you are luke-
warm—neither hot nor cold—I am about to
spit you out of my mouth. 17You say, 'I am
rich; I have acquired wealth and do not need
a thing.' But you do not realize that you are
wretched, pitiful, poor, blind and naked. 18I
counsel you to buy from me gold refined in
the fire, so you can become rich; and white
clothes to wear, so you can cover your
shameful nakedness; and salve to put on
your eyes, so you can see.
19Those whom I love I rebuke and disci-
pline. So be earnest, and repent. 20Here I am!
I stand at the door and knock. If anyone
hears my voice and opens the door, I will
come in and eat with him, and he with me.
21To him who overcomes, I will give the
right to sit with me on my throne, just as I
overcame and sat down with my Father on
his throne. 22He who has an ear, let him hear
what the Spirit says to the churches."

f1 Or *messenger*; also in verses 7 and 14 g1 Or *the sevenfold Spirit*

Discovering the Word 1. In the first century, Sardis exhibited a stark contrast between its past splendor as a Persian capital and its current decay. What indications does the Lord give that the church's reputation does not match its reality (vv. 1–6)? Why is this such a serious problem? 2. Of the seven churches, only the church in Philadelphia received nothing but praise and promises. Why would a weak church be encouraged by Jesus' promise of an open door of opportunity (v. 8)? 3. As the Philadelphian church faced opposition, how would Jesus' other promises encourage them (vv. 9–13)? 4. Laodicea's northern neighbor, Hierapolis, had famous hot springs. Its southern neighbor, Colossae, had refreshing cool water. A six-mile aqueduct brought water to Laodicea, but by the time it arrived it was lukewarm. How does this help us understand Christ's statements in verses 14–16? 5. Laodicea was so self-sufficient that when they suffered an earthquake in A.D. 60 they rejected help from Rome. How did this attitude affect them spiritually?

Applying the Word 1. Many churches today feel weak, insignificant and discouraged. What can we learn from Christ's words to the Philadelphians? 2. As you review all seven letters (Rev 2—3), what has the Spirit taught you about being an overcomer?

Responding in Prayer Pray that the church would be a powerful force in the world.

5/ *Revelation 4—5*
Worship the Omnipotent Lamb

IN A PLAY by George Bernard Shaw, Don Juan says, "Heaven is all right, of course, but for meeting old friends and acquaintances you can't beat hell." There is a powerful truth in this facetious remark. While most people *say* they want to go to heaven, they might prefer hell if heaven is like the picture given in these two chapters. People concerned only about themselves would find the ceaseless praise of God and the Lamb intolerable. Worship on earth, a foretaste of heaven, is just as unpalatable. But worship is the deepest need of the seven churches just described. And it is our deepest need too, as this study will show.

Warming Up to God What was the most significant worship experience you have ever had, and what made it so special?

Read Revelation 4—5.

4 After this I looked, and there before me
was a door standing open in heaven. And
the voice I had first heard speaking to me
like a trumpet said, "Come up here, and I will
show you what must take place after this." 2At
once I was in the Spirit, and there before me was
a throne in heaven with someone sitting on it.
3And the one who sat there had the appearance of
jasper and carnelian. A rainbow, resembling an
emerald, encircled the throne. 4Surrounding the
throne were twenty-four other thrones, and
seated on them were twenty-four elders. They
were dressed in white and had crowns of gold on
their heads. 5From the throne came flashes of
lightning, rumblings and peals of thunder. Before
the throne, seven lamps were blazing. These are
the seven spirits[h] of God. 6Also before the throne
there was what looked like a sea of glass, clear as
crystal.

In the center, around the throne, were four liv-
ing creatures, and they were covered with eyes, in
front and in back. 7The first living creature was
like a lion, the second was like an ox, the third
had a face like a man, the fourth was like a flying
eagle. 8Each of the four living creatures had six
wings and was covered with eyes all around, even
under his wings. Day and night they never stop
saying:

"Holy, holy, holy
is the Lord God Almighty,
who was, and is, and is to come."

9Whenever the living creatures give glory, honor
and thanks to him who sits on the throne and
who lives for ever and ever, 10the twenty-four el-
ders fall down before him who sits on the throne,
and worship him who lives for ever and ever.
They lay their crowns before the throne and say:

11"You are worthy, our Lord and God,
to receive glory and honor and power,
for you created all things,
and by your will they were created
and have their being."

5 Then I saw in the right hand of him who
sat on the throne a scroll with writing on
both sides and sealed with seven seals.
2And I saw a mighty angel proclaiming in a loud
voice, "Who is worthy to break the seals and
open the scroll?" 3But no one in heaven or on
earth or under the earth could open the scroll or
even look inside it. 4I wept and wept because no
one was found who was worthy to open the scroll
or look inside. 5Then one of the elders said to me,

h5 Or *the sevenfold Spirit*

"Do not weep! See, the Lion of the tribe of Judah,
the Root of David, has triumphed. He is able to
open the scroll and its seven seals."
[6]Then I saw a Lamb, looking as if it had been
slain, standing in the center of the throne, encir-
cled by the four living creatures and the elders.
He had seven horns and seven eyes, which are the
seven spirits[l] of God sent out into all the earth.
[7]He came and took the scroll from the right hand
of him who sat on the throne. [8]And when he had
taken it, the four living creatures and the twenty-
four elders fell down before the Lamb. Each one
had a harp and they were holding golden bowls
full of incense, which are the prayers of the
saints. [9]And they sang a new song:

"You are worthy to take the scroll
 and to open its seals,
because you were slain,
 and with your blood you purchased men
  for God
 from every tribe and language and people
  and nation.
[10]You have made them to be a kingdom and
  priests to serve our God,
 and they will reign on the earth."

[11]Then I looked and heard the voice of many
angels, numbering thousands upon thousands,
and ten thousand times ten thousand. They encir-
cled the throne and the living creatures and the
elders. [12]In a loud voice they sang:

"Worthy is the Lamb, who was slain,
 to receive power and wealth and wisdom and
  strength
 and honor and glory and praise!"

[13]Then I heard every creature in heaven and on
earth and under the earth and on the sea, and all
that is in them, singing:

"To him who sits on the throne and to the
  Lamb
 be praise and honor and glory and power,
  for ever and ever!"

[14]The four living creatures said, "Amen," and the
elders fell down and worshiped.

[l]6 *Or the sevenfold Spirit*

Discovering the Word 1. Instead of trying to decode every part of the throne room of God, try to imagine what can be seen and heard. What are some of your initial impressions of God's glory as envisioned here (Rev 4)? 2. How do the four creatures and the twenty-four elders respond to God's glory (vv. 8, 10-11)? 3. How does their reaction help us define and practice worship? 4. While John leaves us in suspense about the contents of the scroll and its seals, there is no doubt about the central figure in the unfolding drama. Why do you think he superimposes the image of the Lamb on the image of the Lion (5:5-6)? 5. The heavenly choir gets larger and larger as the scene unfolds (5:8, 11, 13). What do we see in this vision of heavenly worship that is timelessly relevant?

Applying the Word 1. Worship is not an action but a reaction, a response evoked by a vision of God's glory. If we have difficulty worshiping God, what might we need to do? 2. If earthly worship is to be modeled after heavenly, what is most lacking in your experience of worship?

Responding in Prayer Take time now to worship the Lamb and the One who sits on the throne.

6 / *Revelation 6*
The Beautiful Wrath of God

JUDGMENT IS NOT something we normally long for. But if we are suffering unjustly in an evil social system, God's judgment—far from being a dreaded prospect—is our only hope. Like a wood plane that is used against the grain rather than with it, so wrath is how people opposing the rule of God will experience his grace.

In Revelation 6—19 there is a complicated and rather confusing pattern of disaster and suffering. If we seek to unravel these pictures as a timetable for the future, we will be disappointed and perplexed. But if we want to learn how to live in the present and find hope for the future, there is much here to encourage us. These chapters inspire trust in a God who is faithful and just.

Warming Up to God As you approach the subject of God's wrath, what thoughts and feelings do you have? Explain.

Read Revelation 6.

6

I watched as the Lamb opened the first of the seven seals. Then I heard one of the four living creatures say in a voice like thunder, "Come!" [2]I looked, and there before me was a white horse! Its rider held a bow, and he was given a crown, and he rode out as a conqueror bent on conquest.

[3]When the Lamb opened the second seal, I heard the second living creature say, "Come!" [4]Then another horse came out, a fiery red one. Its rider was given power to take peace from the earth and to make men slay each other. To him was given a large sword.

[5]When the Lamb opened the third seal, I heard the third living creature say, "Come!" I looked, and there before me was a black horse! Its rider was holding a pair of scales in his hand. [6]Then I heard what sounded like a voice among the four living creatures, saying, "A quart[j] of wheat for a day's wages,[k] and three quarts of barley for a day's wages,[k] and do not damage the oil and the wine!"

[7]When the Lamb opened the fourth seal, I heard the voice of the fourth living creature say, "Come!" [8]I looked, and there before me was a pale horse! Its rider was named Death, and Hades was following close behind him. They were given power over a fourth of the earth to kill by sword, famine and plague, and by the wild beasts of the earth.

[9]When he opened the fifth seal, I saw under the altar the souls of those who had been slain because of the word of God and the testimony they had maintained. [10]They called out in a loud voice, "How long, Sovereign Lord, holy and true, until you judge the inhabitants of the earth and avenge our blood?" [11]Then each of them was given a white robe, and they were told to wait a little longer, until the number of their fellow servants and brothers who were to be killed as they had been was completed.

[12]I watched as he opened the sixth seal. There was a great earthquake. The sun turned black like sackcloth made of goat hair, the whole moon turned blood red, [13]and the stars in the sky fell to earth, as late figs drop from a fig tree when shaken by a strong wind. [14]The sky receded like a scroll, rolling up, and every mountain and island was removed from its place.

[15]Then the kings of the earth, the princes, the generals, the rich, the mighty, and every slave and every free man hid in caves and among the rocks of the mountains. [16]They called to the mountains and the rocks, "Fall on us and hide us from the face of him who sits on the throne and from the wrath of the Lamb! [17]For the great day of their wrath has come, and who can stand?"

[j]6 Greek *a choinix* (probably about a liter) [k]6 Greek *a denarius*

Discovering the Word 1. The scene shifts back to earth as the Lamb opens the book of destiny. Summarize the events during the first four seals (vv. 1–8). 2. Are the events during the seals normal bad times (compare vv. 1–8 with vv. 12–14)? Explain. 3. How does the experience of the saints (vv. 9–11) contrast with that of the unbelievers (vv. 15–17) as they anticipate the impending wrath of God? 4. What evidence, if any, do you see of this contrast among people today?

Applying the Word 1. If we realize that the wrath of God will one day be fully expressed, what difference should it make in our attitude toward sin? 2. In our attitude toward unjust suffering? 3. In our attitude toward non-Christians?

Responding in Prayer Pray for non-Christians you know, that they would come to know the love of the Lord.

7/ *Revelation 7*
Living Faithfully Through the Holocaust

SOME PREACHERS SPEAK of the Christian life as one great success story. They say that if we attend church, live right, tithe and exercise faith, we will prosper financially and be free of illness and distress.

But the relative peace some of us enjoy at this moment is exceptional in the world and in history. From the ascension of Christ to his return, the normal lot of believers is tribulation.

Most of the Christians John pictures for us are martyrs. They are dead to the threats of this life but gloriously alive to God. Their experience reminds us that the call to discipleship is a call to radical obedience.

Warming Up to God What feelings do you have when you hear of Christians today who lose their jobs, are thrown into prison or are martyred for Christ?

Read Revelation 7.

7 After this I saw four angels standing at the
four corners of the earth, holding back
the four winds of the earth to prevent any
wind from blowing on the land or on the sea or
on any tree. 2Then I saw another angel coming up
from the east, having the seal of the living God.
He called out in a loud voice to the four angels
who had been given power to harm the land and
the sea: 3"Do not harm the land or the sea or the
trees until we put a seal on the foreheads of the
servants of our God." 4Then I heard the number
of those who were sealed: 144,000 from all the
tribes of Israel.

5From the tribe of Judah 12,000 were sealed,
from the tribe of Reuben 12,000,
from the tribe of Gad 12,000,
6from the tribe of Asher 12,000,
from the tribe of Naphtali 12,000,
from the tribe of Manasseh 12,000,
7from the tribe of Simeon 12,000,
from the tribe of Levi 12,000,
from the tribe of Issachar 12,000,
8from the tribe of Zebulun 12,000,
from the tribe of Joseph 12,000,
from the tribe of Benjamin 12,000.

9After this I looked and there before me was a
great multitude that no one could count, from
every nation, tribe, people and language, standing
before the throne and in front of the Lamb. They
were wearing white robes and were holding palm
branches in their hands. 10And they cried out in a
loud voice:

"Salvation belongs to our God,
who sits on the throne,
and to the Lamb."

11All the angels were standing around the throne
and around the elders and the four living crea-
tures. They fell down on their faces before the
throne and worshiped God, 12saying:

"Amen!
Praise and glory
and wisdom and thanks and honor
and power and strength
be to our God for ever and ever.
Amen!"

13Then one of the elders asked me, "These in
white robes—who are they, and where did they
come from?"

14I answered, "Sir, you know."

And he said, "These are they who have come
out of the great tribulation; they have washed
their robes and made them white in the blood of
the Lamb. 15Therefore,

"they are before the throne of God
and serve him day and night in his temple;
and he who sits on the throne will spread his
tent over them.
16Never again will they hunger;
never again will they thirst.
The sun will not beat upon them,
nor any scorching heat.
17For the Lamb at the center of the throne will
be their shepherd;
he will lead them to springs of living water.
And God will wipe away every tear from their
eyes."

Discovering the Word 1. In verses 1–8 an angel seals 144,000 people. What do you think "the seal of the living God" means (7:2; 9:4)? 2. In verse 9 the scene shifts from earth to heaven. How did the great multitude in verse 9 come to stand before the Lamb? 3. Why does the multitude cry out with praise, worship and thanksgiving (vv. 10–12)? 4. How do the blessings these martyred Christians enjoy compare with the tribulations they suffered (vv. 13–17)? 5. How does their experience help us understand the ultimate benefit of being a faithful Christian?

Applying the Word 1. In the first century, persecution of Christians came from three basic sources: emperor worshipers, heretics and those whose commercial interests were threatened by the radical lifestyle of Christians. Why might faithful Christians suffer today? 2. This vision comes at the point of maximum dramatic intensity: between the sixth and seventh seals. How can the vision encourage us to be faithful no matter what happens in the world?

Responding in Prayer Pray for those who suffer for their faith.

8 / *Revelation 8—9*
The Message of the Angels

ANGELS ARE QUITE popular these days. We see them depicted on T-shirts, mugs and cards. You can get little pins picturing charming angels. And there's a growing category of books available to show you how to get in touch with your "inner angels" and other such things. None of this has much to do with the angels we meet in Scripture. In the next few passages you will meet some of God's angels—and you will be confronted with their terrible power.

Warming Up to God What positive feelings or experiences have you had about angels?

Read Revelation 8—9.

8 When he opened the seventh seal, there
was silence in heaven for about half an
hour.
[2]And I saw the seven angels who stand before
God, and to them were given seven trumpets.
[3]Another angel, who had a golden censer, came
and stood at the altar. He was given much incense
to offer, with the prayers of all the saints, on the
golden altar before the throne. [4]The smoke of the
incense, together with the prayers of the saints,
went up before God from the angel's hand. [5]Then
the angel took the censer, filled it with fire from
the altar, and hurled it on the earth; and there
came peals of thunder, rumblings, flashes of
lightning and an earthquake.
[6]Then the seven angels who had the seven
trumpets prepared to sound them.
[7]The first angel sounded his trumpet, and there
came hail and fire mixed with blood, and it was
hurled down upon the earth. A third of the earth
was burned up, a third of the trees were burned
up, and all the green grass was burned up.
[8]The second angel sounded his trumpet, and
something like a huge mountain, all ablaze, was
thrown into the sea. A third of the sea turned into
blood, [9]a third of the living creatures in the sea
died, and a third of the ships were destroyed.
[10]The third angel sounded his trumpet, and a
great star, blazing like a torch, fell from the sky
on a third of the rivers and on the springs of
water— [11]the name of the star is Wormwood.[l]
A third of the waters turned bitter, and many
people died from the waters that had become
bitter.
[12]The fourth angel sounded his trumpet, and a
third of the sun was struck, a third of the moon,
and a third of the stars, so that a third of them
turned dark. A third of the day was without light,
and also a third of the night.
[13]As I watched, I heard an eagle that was flying
in midair call out in a loud voice: "Woe! Woe!

[l]*11* That is, Bitterness

Woe to the inhabitants of the earth, because of the trumpet blasts about to be sounded by the other three angels!"

9 The fifth angel sounded his trumpet, and I saw a star that had fallen from the sky to the earth. The star was given the key to the shaft of the Abyss. [2]When he opened the Abyss, smoke rose from it like the smoke from a gigantic furnace. The sun and sky were darkened by the smoke from the Abyss. [3]And out of the smoke locusts came down upon the earth and were given power like that of scorpions of the earth. [4]They were told not to harm the grass of the earth or any plant or tree, but only those people who did not have the seal of God on their foreheads. [5]They were not given power to kill them, but only to torture them for five months. And the agony they suffered was like that of the sting of a scorpion when it strikes a man. [6]During those days men will seek death, but will not find it; they will long to die, but death will elude them.

[7]The locusts looked like horses prepared for battle. On their heads they wore something like crowns of gold, and their faces resembled human faces. [8]Their hair was like women's hair, and their teeth were like lions' teeth. [9]They had breastplates like breastplates of iron, and the sound of their wings was like the thundering of many horses and chariots rushing into battle. [10]They had tails and stings like scorpions, and in their tails they had power to torment people for five months. [11]They had as king over them the angel of the Abyss, whose name in Hebrew is Abaddon, and in Greek, Apollyon.[m]

[12]The first woe is past; two other woes are yet to come.

[13]The sixth angel sounded his trumpet, and I heard a voice coming from the horns[n] of the golden altar that is before God. [14]It said to the sixth angel who had the trumpet, "Release the four angels who are bound at the great river Euphrates." [15]And the four angels who had been kept ready for this very hour and day and month and year were released to kill a third of mankind. [16]The number of the mounted troops was two hundred million. I heard their number.

[17]The horses and riders I saw in my vision looked like this: Their breastplates were fiery red, dark blue, and yellow as sulfur. The heads of the horses resembled the heads of lions, and out of their mouths came fire, smoke and sulfur. [18]A third of mankind was killed by the three plagues of fire, smoke and sulfur that came out of their mouths. [19]The power of the horses was in their mouths and in their tails; for their tails were like snakes, having heads with which they inflict injury.

[20]The rest of mankind that were not killed by these plagues still did not repent of the work of their hands; they did not stop worshiping demons, and idols of gold, silver, bronze, stone and wood—idols that cannot see or hear or walk. [21]Nor did they repent of their murders, their magic arts, their sexual immorality or their thefts.

[m]*11* *Abaddon* and *Apollyon* mean *Destroyer*. [n]*13* That is, projections

Discovering the Word 1. List the events that happen when each of the angels blows his trumpet. 2. What similarities do you note between all of these events? 3. The seventh seal (8:1–5) contains the seven trumpet judgments (8:6—11:15). What apparently is God's purpose in allowing these judgments to fall on the whole creation (9:20–21)? 4. Does such a response by God seem justified? Explain. 5. It is sometimes maintained that Christians are removed from the world before God's wrath falls. What alternate view is possibly suggested by 9:4 (see also 7:3)?

Applying the Word 1. Those mentioned in 9:20–21 did not repent. How do our sins today compare to theirs? 2. Where do you see yourself in this list of sins? 3. In what way do you feel that you need to be ready for the judgment that takes place here?

Responding in Prayer Repent of your sins before God.

9/ *Revelation 10—11*
God's Messenger

IN THE OLD Testament, God often used specific persons to deliver a message to another person, or sometimes to entire groups. Sometimes these messages were positive and easy to hear. However, they were often condemnations of the way things were, and those who delivered the messages, the prophets, were often ridiculed or threatened. In chapter 10, John is given a message which is not easy to deliver.

In chapter 11, two of God's prophets have a life experience which roughly parallels Jesus' time on earth. Their example can give us hope that the God who calls us to be a light in the darkness is also the one who will vindicate us.

Warming Up to God When has God used someone else to give you a message? How did you react to the message and the messenger?

Read Revelation 10—11.

---

10 Then I saw another mighty angel
coming down from heaven. He was
robed in a cloud, with a rainbow
above his head; his face was like the sun, and
his legs were like fiery pillars. 2He was holding
a little scroll, which lay open in his hand. He
planted his right foot on the sea and his left foot
on the land, 3and he gave a loud shout like
the roar of a lion. When he shouted, the voices
of the seven thunders spoke. 4And when the
seven thunders spoke, I was about to write; but
I heard a voice from heaven say, "Seal up what
the seven thunders have said and do not write it
down."
5Then the angel I had seen standing on the sea
and on the land raised his right hand to heaven.
6And he swore by him who lives for ever and
ever, who created the heavens and all that is in
them, the earth and all that is in it, and the sea
and all that is in it, and said, "There will be no
more delay! 7But in the days when the seventh
angel is about to sound his trumpet, the mystery
of God will be accomplished, just as he announced to his servants the prophets."
8Then the voice that I had heard from heaven
spoke to me once more: "Go, take the scroll that
lies open in the hand of the angel who is standing
on the sea and on the land."
9So I went to the angel and asked him to
give me the little scroll. He said to me, "Take it
and eat it. It will turn your stomach sour, but
in your mouth it will be as sweet as honey."
10I took the little scroll from the angel's hand
and ate it. It tasted as sweet as honey in my
mouth, but when I had eaten it, my stomach
turned sour. 11Then I was told, "You must prophesy again about many peoples, nations, languages
and kings."

11 I was given a reed like a measuring
rod and was told, "Go and measure
the temple of God and the altar,
and count the worshipers there. 2But exclude the
outer court; do not measure it, because it has
been given to the Gentiles. They will trample on
the holy city for 42 months. 3And I will give
power to my two witnesses, and they will prophesy for 1,260 days, clothed in sackcloth." 4These
are the two olive trees and the two lampstands
that stand before the Lord of the earth. 5If anyone
tries to harm them, fire comes from their mouths
and devours their enemies. This is how anyone
who wants to harm them must die. 6These men
have power to shut up the sky so that it will not
rain during the time they are prophesying; and
they have power to turn the waters into blood
and to strike the earth with every kind of plague
as often as they want.
7Now when they have finished their testimony,
the beast that comes up from the Abyss will attack them, and overpower and kill them. 8Their
bodies will lie in the street of the great city, which
is figuratively called Sodom and Egypt, where
also their Lord was crucified. 9For three and a
half days men from every people, tribe, language
and nation will gaze on their bodies and refuse
them burial. 10The inhabitants of the earth will
gloat over them and will celebrate by sending
each other gifts, because these two prophets had
tormented those who live on the earth.
11But after the three and a half days a breath of
life from God entered them, and they stood on

their feet, and terror struck those who saw them.
12 Then they heard a loud voice from heaven say-
ing to them, "Come up here." And they went
up to heaven in a cloud, while their enemies
looked on.
13 At that very hour there was a severe earth-
quake and a tenth of the city collapsed. Seven
thousand people were killed in the earthquake,
and the survivors were terrified and gave glory to
the God of heaven.
14 The second woe has passed; the third woe is
coming soon.
15 The seventh angel sounded his trumpet, and
there were loud voices in heaven, which said:

"The kingdom of the world has become the
kingdom of our Lord and of his Christ,
and he will reign for ever and ever."

16 And the twenty-four elders, who were seated on
their thrones before God, fell on their faces and
worshiped God, 17 saying:

"We give thanks to you, Lord God Almighty,
the One who is and who was,
because you have taken your great power
and have begun to reign.
18 The nations were angry;
and your wrath has come.
The time has come for judging the dead,
and for rewarding your servants the prophets
and your saints and those who reverence your name,
both small and great—
and for destroying those who destroy the earth."

19 Then God's temple in heaven was opened,
and within his temple was seen the ark of his
covenant. And there came flashes of lightning,
rumblings, peals of thunder, an earthquake and a
great hailstorm.

Discovering the Word 1. What are the actions of the "mighty angel" introduced in 10:1? 2. What is the significance of the mystery of God which will be revealed without further delay (10:6–7)? 3. What happens to the two witnesses empowered by God (11:3–14)? 4. Why do you think the witnesses caused such turmoil? 5. What happens when the seventh trumpet is blown (11:15–19)?

Applying the Word 1. The "little scroll" that John eats (10:8–11) probably refers to the gospel. When has the gospel tasted like honey or turned your stomach sour? 2. 11:10 says that the two witnesses had "tormented those who live on the earth." When have you felt that God was calling you to deliver a message of bad news? 3. What feelings about God and his actions do you have after reading the description of worship in 11:15–19?

Responding in Prayer Pray that you will be willing to be God's messenger to those around you.

10 / *Revelation 12*
Conflict with the Accuser

DRAGONS SYMBOLIZE ALL that is terrifying, evil and loathsome. In Revelation 12 Satan appears as an enormous red dragon, full of rage. Knowing that his time is short, he unleashes his fury as never before. During such dark moments of history, it seems as though God is absent and Satan is victorious. Yet in this passage John describes a heavenly vision that puts all earthly tribulation in proper perspective.

Warming Up to God In what ways are you experiencing the reality of spiritual warfare?

Read Revelation 12.

12 A great and wondrous sign ap-
peared in heaven: a woman clothed
with the sun, with the moon under
her feet and a crown of twelve stars on her head.
2She was pregnant and cried out in pain as she
was about to give birth. 3Then another sign ap-
peared in heaven: an enormous red dragon with
seven heads and ten horns and seven crowns on
his heads. 4His tail swept a third of the stars out
of the sky and flung them to the earth. The
dragon stood in front of the woman who was
about to give birth, so that he might devour her
child the moment it was born. 5She gave birth to
a son, a male child, who will rule all the nations
with an iron scepter. And her child was snatched
up to God and to his throne. 6The woman fled
into the desert to a place prepared for her by God,
where she might be taken care of for 1,260 days.
7And there was war in heaven. Michael and his
angels fought against the dragon, and the dragon
and his angels fought back. 8But he was not
strong enough, and they lost their place in
heaven. 9The great dragon was hurled down—
that ancient serpent called the devil, or Satan,
who leads the whole world astray. He was hurled
to the earth, and his angels with him.
10Then I heard a loud voice in heaven say:

"Now have come the salvation and the power
and the kingdom of our God,
and the authority of his Christ.
For the accuser of our brothers,
who accuses them before our God day and night,
has been hurled down.
11They overcame him
by the blood of the Lamb
and by the word of their testimony;
they did not love their lives so much
as to shrink from death.
12Therefore rejoice, you heavens
and you who dwell in them!
But woe to the earth and the sea,
because the devil has gone down to you!
He is filled with fury,
because he knows that his time is short."

13When the dragon saw that he had been
hurled to the earth, he pursued the woman who
had given birth to the male child. 14The woman
was given the two wings of a great eagle, so that
she might fly to the place prepared for her in the
desert, where she would be taken care of for a
time, times and half a time, out of the serpent's
reach. 15Then from his mouth the serpent spewed
water like a river, to overtake the woman and
sweep her away with the torrent. 16But the earth
helped the woman by opening its mouth and
swallowing the river that the dragon had spewed
out of his mouth. 17Then the dragon was enraged
at the woman and went off to make war against
the rest of her offspring—those who obey God's
commandments and hold to the testimony of
Jesus.

Discovering the Word 1. Three of the characters in this chapter are the woman (perhaps the Lord's people or the Holy Spirit), the red dragon (Satan) and the male child (the Lord Jesus). What conflict does John observe among them (vv. 1–6)? 2. In verses 7–9 John describes a war in heaven. What does the war reveal about the dragon? 3. What does the dragon's defeat mean in heaven (vv. 10, 12) and on earth (vv. 12–17)? 4. What does it mean to overcome Satan's accusations by the blood of the Lamb and the word of our testimony (v. 11)?

Applying the Word 1. How can we help a fellow Christian who is no longer under God's condemnation but who still feels condemned and defeated? 2. In what other ways do we experience Satan's attacks? 3. How can the victory of Christ help us face these battles and struggles of the Christian life?

Responding in Prayer Pray for those who are struggling against Satan.

11/ *Revelation 13*
The Beast

IN *BRAVE NEW World* Aldous Huxley described a future too close for comfort: "As political and economic freedom diminishes, sexual freedom tends compensatingly to increase. And the dictator will do well to encourage that freedom." Faithful Christianity inevitably involves conflict, tension and suffering for followers of Jesus. We cannot be fully at home in our own culture. Even where we do not face open hostility, we are pressured—indeed seduced—by a seemingly friendly society. Revelation 13 demonstrates that the church must always deal with radical evil. In these visions John unmasks the powers of darkness at work in everyday life and at the end of history.

Warming Up to God Why do you think it is so difficult for believers to make substantial changes in society? (For example, in the areas of justice, protection of the unborn or making peace.)

Read Revelation 13.

13 1And the dragon[o] stood on the
shore of the sea.
And I saw a beast coming out of the
sea. He had ten horns and seven heads, with ten
crowns on his horns, and on each head a blasphe-
mous name. 2The beast I saw resembled a leop-
ard, but had feet like those of a bear and a mouth
like that of a lion. The dragon gave the beast his
power and his throne and great authority. 3One of
the heads of the beast seemed to have had a fatal
wound, but the fatal wound had been healed. The
whole world was astonished and followed the
beast. 4Men worshiped the dragon because he had
given authority to the beast, and they also wor-
shiped the beast and asked, "Who is like the
beast? Who can make war against him?"
5The beast was given a mouth to utter proud
words and blasphemies and to exercise his au-
thority for forty-two months. 6He opened his
mouth to blaspheme God, and to slander his
name and his dwelling place and those who live
in heaven. 7He was given power to make war
against the saints and to conquer them. And he
was given authority over every tribe, people, lan-
guage and nation. 8All inhabitants of the earth
will worship the beast—all whose names have
not been written in the book of life belonging to
the Lamb that was slain from the creation of the
world.[p]
9He who has an ear, let him hear.
10If anyone is to go into captivity,
into captivity he will go.
If anyone is to be killed[q] with the sword,
with the sword he will be killed.

This calls for patient endurance and faithfulness
on the part of the saints.
11Then I saw another beast, coming out of the
earth. He had two horns like a lamb, but he spoke
like a dragon. 12He exercised all the authority of
the first beast on his behalf, and made the earth
and its inhabitants worship the first beast, whose
fatal wound had been healed. 13And he performed
great and miraculous signs, even causing fire to
come down from heaven to earth in full view of
men. 14Because of the signs he was given power to
do on behalf of the first beast, he deceived the
inhabitants of the earth. He ordered them to set
up an image in honor of the beast who was
wounded by the sword and yet lived. 15He was
given power to give breath to the image of the
first beast, so that it could speak and cause all
who refused to worship the image to be killed.
16He also forced everyone, small and great, rich
and poor, free and slave, to receive a mark on his
right hand or on his forehead, 17so that no one
could buy or sell unless he had the mark, which
is the name of the beast or the number of his
name.
18This calls for wisdom. If anyone has insight,
let him calculate the number of the beast, for it is
man's number. His number is 666.

[o] 1 Some late manuscripts *And I* [p] 8 Or *written from the creation of the world in the book of life belonging to the Lamb that was slain* [q] 10 Some manuscripts *anyone kills*

13 / *Revelation 16*
Who's to Blame?

WHEN SOMETHING GOES wrong, who do we blame? Often, God's name is among the first to come up. When we are inclined to blame God, we must ask ourselves what it is we expect out of life. Do we feel that we have an innate right to health, wealth and happiness? In understanding God's working in the world it's important that we learn to see beyond our private world to God's vast creation.

Warming Up to God Be honest with yourself about your feelings toward God. When are you inclined to place blame on God for events in your life?

Read Revelation 16.

16 Then I heard a loud voice from the
temple saying to the seven angels,
"Go, pour out the seven bowls of
God's wrath on the earth."
2The first angel went and poured out his bowl
on the land, and ugly and painful sores broke out
on the people who had the mark of the beast and
worshiped his image.
3The second angel poured out his bowl on the
sea, and it turned into blood like that of a dead
man, and every living thing in the sea died.
4The third angel poured out his bowl on the
rivers and springs of water, and they became
blood. 5Then I heard the angel in charge of the
waters say:

"You are just in these judgments,
you who are and who were, the Holy One,
because you have so judged;
6for they have shed the blood of your saints
and prophets,
and you have given them blood to drink as
they deserve."

7And I heard the altar respond:

"Yes, Lord God Almighty,
true and just are your judgments."

8The fourth angel poured out his bowl on the
sun, and the sun was given power to scorch peo-
ple with fire. 9They were seared by the intense
heat and they cursed the name of God, who had
control over these plagues, but they refused to
repent and glorify him.
10The fifth angel poured out his bowl on the
throne of the beast, and his kingdom was plunged
into darkness. Men gnawed their tongues in ag-
ony 11and cursed the God of heaven because of
their pains and their sores, but they refused to
repent of what they had done.
12The sixth angel poured out his bowl on the
great river Euphrates, and its water was dried up
to prepare the way for the kings from the East.
13Then I saw three evil[t] spirits that looked like
frogs; they came out of the mouth of the dragon,
out of the mouth of the beast and out of the
mouth of the false prophet. 14They are spirits of
demons performing miraculous signs, and they
go out to the kings of the whole world, to gather
them for the battle on the great day of God Al-
mighty.
15"Behold, I come like a thief! Blessed is he
who stays awake and keeps his clothes with him,
so that he may not go naked and be shamefully
exposed."
16Then they gathered the kings together to the
place that in Hebrew is called Armageddon.
17The seventh angel poured out his bowl into
the air, and out of the temple came a loud voice
from the throne, saying, "It is done!" 18Then
there came flashes of lightning, rumblings, peals
of thunder and a severe earthquake. No earth-
quake like it has ever occurred since man has
been on earth, so tremendous was the quake.
19The great city split into three parts, and the cit-
ies of the nations collapsed. God remembered
Babylon the Great and gave her the cup filled
with the wine of the fury of his wrath. 20Every
island fled away and the mountains could not be
found. 21From the sky huge hailstones of about a
hundred pounds each fell upon men. And they
cursed God on account of the plague of hail, be-
cause the plague was so terrible.

[t]13 Greek *unclean*

Discovering the Word 1. Note the similarity between these plagues and those brought on Egypt (blood, frogs, gnats, flies, livestock, boils, hail, locusts, darkness, firstborn). What might be meant by this comparison? 2. How could the same events lead to worship on the part of some (vv. 5–7) and cursing on the part of others (vv. 9, 21)? 3. How can we see this happening in our culture? 4. What is the result of the plagues (vv. 19–21)?

Applying the Word 1. When has God's judgment been a source of praise for you? 2. When has God's judgment caused you to curse or blame God?

Responding in Prayer Talk honestly with God about any feelings of blame and responsibility that have been revealed to you during this study.

14 / *Revelation 17—18*
Beneath the Surface

IN EVERY AGE there is at least one symbol for everything that goes against God. For several of the Old Testament writers it was Babylon, the beautiful city that held captive God's chosen people. Babylon represented everything that was evil and unsightly about humanity. John uses this powerful symbol to interpret his own age and the powers that opposed God in his generation. In these two chapters we see not only John's vision of how those powers opposed God, but the ultimate outcome of that opposition.

Warming Up to God When have you noticed someone or something that looked appealing, but upon closer scrutiny was unappealing or revolting?

Read Revelation 17—18.

17 One of the seven angels who had
the seven bowls came and said to
me, "Come, I will show you the
punishment of the great prostitute, who sits on
many waters. 2With her the kings of the earth
committed adultery and the inhabitants of the
earth were intoxicated with the wine of her adulteries."
3Then the angel carried me away in the Spirit
into a desert. There I saw a woman sitting on a
scarlet beast that was covered with blasphemous
names and had seven heads and ten horns. 4The
woman was dressed in purple and scarlet, and
was glittering with gold, precious stones and
pearls. She held a golden cup in her hand, filled
with abominable things and the filth of her adulteries.
5This title was written on her forehead:

MYSTERY
BABYLON THE GREAT
THE MOTHER OF PROSTITUTES
AND OF THE ABOMINATIONS OF THE EARTH.

6I saw that the woman was drunk with the blood
of the saints, the blood of those who bore testimony to Jesus.

When I saw her, I was greatly astonished.
7Then the angel said to me: "Why are you astonished? I will explain to you the mystery of the
woman and of the beast she rides, which has the
seven heads and ten horns. 8The beast, which you
saw, once was, now is not, and will come up out
of the Abyss and go to his destruction. The inhabitants of the earth whose names have not been
written in the book of life from the creation of the
world will be astonished when they see the beast,
because he once was, now is not, and yet will
come.
9"This calls for a mind with wisdom. The seven
heads are seven hills on which the woman sits.
10They are also seven kings. Five have fallen, one
is, the other has not yet come; but when he does
come, he must remain for a little while. 11The
beast who once was, and now is not, is an eighth
king. He belongs to the seven and is going to his
destruction.
12"The ten horns you saw are ten kings who
have not yet received a kingdom, but who for one
hour will receive authority as kings along with
the beast. 13They have one purpose and will give
their power and authority to the beast. 14They

will make war against the Lamb, but the Lamb will overcome them because he is Lord of lords and King of kings—and with him will be his called, chosen and faithful followers."
15Then the angel said to me, "The waters you saw, where the prostitute sits, are peoples, multitudes, nations and languages. 16The beast and the ten horns you saw will hate the prostitute. They will bring her to ruin and leave her naked; they will eat her flesh and burn her with fire. 17For God has put it into their hearts to accomplish his purpose by agreeing to give the beast their power to rule, until God's words are fulfilled. 18The woman you saw is the great city that rules over the kings of the earth."

18 After this I saw another angel coming down from heaven. He had great authority, and the earth was illuminated by his splendor. 2With a mighty voice he shouted:

"Fallen! Fallen is Babylon the Great!
She has become a home for demons
and a haunt for every evil[u] spirit,
a haunt for every unclean and detestable bird.
3For all the nations have drunk
the maddening wine of her adulteries.
The kings of the earth committed adultery with her,
and the merchants of the earth grew rich from her excessive luxuries."

4Then I heard another voice from heaven say:
"Come out of her, my people,
so that you will not share in her sins,
so that you will not receive any of her plagues;
5for her sins are piled up to heaven,
and God has remembered her crimes.
6Give back to her as she has given;
pay her back double for what she has done.
Mix her a double portion from her own cup.
7Give her as much torture and grief
as the glory and luxury she gave herself.
In her heart she boasts,
'I sit as queen; I am not a widow,
and I will never mourn.'
8Therefore in one day her plagues will overtake her:
death, mourning and famine.
She will be consumed by fire,
for mighty is the Lord God who judges her.

9"When the kings of the earth who committed adultery with her and shared her luxury see the smoke of her burning, they will weep and mourn over her. 10Terrified at her torment, they will stand far off and cry:

" 'Woe! Woe, O great city,
O Babylon, city of power!
In one hour your doom has come!'

11"The merchants of the earth will weep and mourn over her because no one buys their cargoes any more— 12cargoes of gold, silver, precious stones and pearls; fine linen, purple, silk and scarlet cloth; every sort of citron wood, and articles of every kind made of ivory, costly wood, bronze, iron and marble; 13cargoes of cinnamon and spice, of incense, myrrh and frankincense, of wine and olive oil, of fine flour and wheat; cattle and sheep; horses and carriages; and bodies and souls of men.
14"They will say, 'The fruit you longed for is gone from you. All your riches and splendor have vanished, never to be recovered.' 15The merchants who sold these things and gained their wealth from her will stand far off, terrified at her torment. They will weep and mourn 16and cry out:

" 'Woe! Woe, O great city,
dressed in fine linen, purple and scarlet,
and glittering with gold, precious stones and pearls!
17In one hour such great wealth has been brought to ruin!'

"Every sea captain, and all who travel by ship, the sailors, and all who earn their living from the sea, will stand far off. 18When they see the smoke of her burning, they will exclaim, 'Was there ever a city like this great city?' 19They will throw dust on their heads, and with weeping and mourning cry out:

" 'Woe! Woe, O great city,
where all who had ships on the sea
became rich through her wealth!
In one hour she has been brought to ruin!
20Rejoice over her, O heaven!
Rejoice, saints and apostles and prophets!

[u]2 Greek *unclean*

God has judged her for the way she treated
you.'"

21Then a mighty angel picked up a boulder the size of a large millstone and threw it into the sea, and said:

"With such violence
the great city of Babylon will be thrown
down,
never to be found again.
22The music of harpists and musicians, flute
players and trumpeters,
will never be heard in you again.
No workman of any trade
will ever be found in you again.
The sound of a millstone
will never be heard in you again.
23The light of a lamp
will never shine in you again.
The voice of bridegroom and bride
will never be heard in you again.
Your merchants were the world's great men.
By your magic spell all the nations were led
astray.
24In her was found the blood of prophets and
of the saints,
and of all who have been killed on the
earth."

Discovering the Word 1. Who or what do you think John had in mind when he described the prostitute (17:3–6)? 2. What is the relationship between the prostitute and the beast, and how does it change (chapter 17)? 3. What are the crimes of the prostitute, identified as Babylon (17:3–6; 18:1–3)? 4. How does the prostitute see herself (18:7–8)? 5. What is the reaction of the kings (18:9–10), merchants (18:11–17a) and sea captains (18:17b–20) to the fall of Babylon?

Applying the Word 1. Who or what is a contemporary parallel to the prostitute? 2. In what ways is the modern "prostitute" a temptation to you? 3. How can you avoid this temptation?

Responding in Prayer Ask God for protection from the temptations of those who are prideful and oppose God.

15 / *Revelation 19*
Are You Going to the Wedding?

JOHN USES A metaphor that has lost much of its meaning in our generation—marriage. In this day of interchangeable marriage roles, five-year renewable relationships and serial monogamy, it is difficult to grasp the splendor of marriage as God intends it. John chooses a wedding to describe the consummation of the deepest longing of the human soul: Christ's coming to receive us. Our present engagement (betrothal) to Christ will be followed by the wedding service and a joyous feast. Then and only then can we experience complete unity with Christ. This vision seems a welcome relief after the long passage on tribulation and judgment (chapters 6—18). In fact, the marriage is the logical result of all that has gone before, as we shall see.

Warming Up to God In your opinion, what are some of the best things about marriage?

Read Revelation 19.

19 After this I heard what sounded like the roar of a great multitude in heaven shouting:

"Hallelujah!
Salvation and glory and power belong to our
God,
2 for true and just are his judgments.
He has condemned the great prostitute
who corrupted the earth by her adulteries.
He has avenged on her the blood of his
servants."

3And again they shouted:

"Hallelujah!
The smoke from her goes up for ever and
ever."

[4]The twenty-four elders and the four living creatures fell down and worshiped God, who was seated on the throne. And they cried:

"Amen, Hallelujah!"

[5]Then a voice came from the throne, saying:

"Praise our God,
all you his servants,
you who fear him,
both small and great!"

[6]Then I heard what sounded like a great multitude, like the roar of rushing waters and like loud peals of thunder, shouting:

"Hallelujah!
For our Lord God Almighty reigns.
[7]Let us rejoice and be glad
and give him glory!
For the wedding of the Lamb has come,
and his bride has made herself ready.
[8]Fine linen, bright and clean,
was given her to wear."
(Fine linen stands for the righteous acts of the saints.)

[9]Then the angel said to me, "Write: 'Blessed are those who are invited to the wedding supper of the Lamb!' " And he added, "These are the true words of God."

[10]At this I fell at his feet to worship him. But he said to me, "Do not do it! I am a fellow servant with you and with your brothers who hold to the testimony of Jesus. Worship God! For the testimony of Jesus is the spirit of prophecy."

[11]I saw heaven standing open and there before me was a white horse, whose rider is called Faithful and True. With justice he judges and makes war. [12]His eyes are like blazing fire, and on his head are many crowns. He has a name written on him that no one knows but he himself. [13]He is dressed in a robe dipped in blood, and his name is the Word of God. [14]The armies of heaven were following him, riding on white horses and dressed in fine linen, white and clean. [15]Out of his mouth comes a sharp sword with which to strike down the nations. "He will rule them with an iron scepter."[v] He treads the winepress of the fury of the wrath of God Almighty. [16]On his robe and on his thigh he has this name written:

KING OF KINGS AND LORD OF LORDS.

[17]And I saw an angel standing in the sun, who cried in a loud voice to all the birds flying in midair, "Come, gather together for the great supper of God, [18]so that you may eat the flesh of kings, generals, and mighty men, of horses and their riders, and the flesh of all people, free and slave, small and great."

[19]Then I saw the beast and the kings of the earth and their armies gathered together to make war against the rider on the horse and his army. [20]But the beast was captured, and with him the false prophet who had performed the miraculous signs on his behalf. With these signs he had deluded those who had received the mark of the beast and worshiped his image. The two of them were thrown alive into the fiery lake of burning sulfur. [21]The rest of them were killed with the sword that came out of the mouth of the rider on the horse, and all the birds gorged themselves on their flesh.

[v]*15* Psalm 2:9

Discovering the Word 1. Why is the great multitude shouting praise in heaven? 2. John does not describe the details of the marriage, he simply proclaims it. Why is marriage such a good image for the believer's hope (vv. 7–9)? 3. Like a champion ready for battle, Jesus appears on horseback. What do we learn about him (vv. 11–16)? 4. Why must this battle take place before the marriage can begin and the kingdom of God can fully come (vv. 17–21)?

Applying the Word 1. In what ways would you like to see Christ triumph in your life or in the world around you? 2. How can we confidently know we are invited to the "wedding supper of the Lamb"?

Responding in Prayer Allow praise for this future celebration to flow forth out of your prayer.

16 / *Revelation 20*
The Last Battle

FINALITY IS SOMETHING we crave and which God graciously provides. A relationship needs to be broken, an assignment needs to be completed, an extended friendship needs to become a committed marriage—all require closure. The previous study explored our inexpressible hope to be reunited with our Lord. This chapter enlarges our appreciation of God's master plan: his settled decision to be with us forever and to establish his glorious rule over everything.

Warming Up to God What do you look forward to most about Christ's return?

Read Revelation 20.

20 And I saw an angel coming down
out of heaven, having the key to the
Abyss and holding in his hand a
great chain. 2He seized the dragon, that ancient
serpent, who is the devil, or Satan, and bound
him for a thousand years. 3He threw him into the
Abyss, and locked and sealed it over him, to keep
him from deceiving the nations anymore until the
thousand years were ended. After that, he must
be set free for a short time.
4I saw thrones on which were seated those who
had been given authority to judge. And I saw the
souls of those who had been beheaded because of
their testimony for Jesus and because of the word
of God. They had not worshiped the beast or his
image and had not received his mark on their
foreheads or their hands. They came to life and
reigned with Christ a thousand years. 5(The rest
of the dead did not come to life until the thou-
sand years were ended.) This is the first resurrec-
tion. 6Blessed and holy are those who have part in
the first resurrection. The second death has no
power over them, but they will be priests of God
and of Christ and will reign with him for a thou-
sand years.
7When the thousand years are over, Satan will
be released from his prison 8and will go out to
deceive the nations in the four corners of the
earth—Gog and Magog—to gather them for bat-
tle. In number they are like the sand on the sea-
shore. 9They marched across the breadth of the
earth and surrounded the camp of God's people,
the city he loves. But fire came down from heaven
and devoured them. 10And the devil, who de-
ceived them, was thrown into the lake of burning
sulfur, where the beast and the false prophet had
been thrown. They will be tormented day and
night for ever and ever.
11Then I saw a great white throne and him who
was seated on it. Earth and sky fled from his pres-
ence, and there was no place for them. 12And I
saw the dead, great and small, standing before the
throne, and books were opened. Another book
was opened, which is the book of life. The dead
were judged according to what they had done as
recorded in the books. 13The sea gave up the dead
that were in it, and death and Hades gave up the
dead that were in them, and each person was
judged according to what he had done. 14Then
death and Hades were thrown into the lake of
fire. The lake of fire is the second death. 15If any-
one's name was not found written in the book of
life, he was thrown into the lake of fire.

Discovering the Word 1. This chapter, out of the whole book, has sparked the greatest controversy. Why is Satan, previously thrown to earth (12:9), now bound (20:1-3)? 2. The thousand-year reign of Christ (vv. 4-6) has been interpreted as referring to: (a) a period of righteousness and peace on earth *before* Christ's return; (b) Christ's reign in heaven *between* his First and Second Coming; (c) Christ's reign on earth *after* his return. Which view (if any) do you think best fits this passage and the book of Revelation? 3. What is the nature and outcome of Satan's last fling (vv. 7-10)? 4. Who will be judged at the great-white-throne judgment (vv. 11-15)? 5. What does it say about God's character that he should keep a record of each person's deeds?

Applying the Word 1. How can verses 4-6 help us to see life and death in proper perspective? 2. How should the ultimate judgment of evil and the reward of faithfulness affect the way we live now?

 **Responding in Prayer** Pray that you will be made faithful in every way.

17 / *Revelation 21—22*
God Dwelling with His People

W. H. AUDEN said, "Nobody is ever sent to hell; he or she insists on going there." Could the same be said of heaven? Far from being "pie in the sky by and by" or a hedonistic longing for pleasure, John's vision of God dwelling with his people is the consummation of faith. Creation is renewed. Evil is finally excluded. The face of God is seen. But John's vision is, at the same time, unsettling to the normal view held by Christians about "last things." It goes beyond not only our imagination but even our faith.

 **Warming Up to God** What do you think about when you hear the word *heaven?*

 **Read Revelation 21—22.**

21 Then I saw a new heaven and a new
earth, for the first heaven and the
first earth had passed away, and
there was no longer any sea. 2I saw the Holy City,
the new Jerusalem, coming down out of heaven
from God, prepared as a bride beautifully dressed
for her husband. 3And I heard a loud voice from
the throne saying, "Now the dwelling of God is
with men, and he will live with them. They will
be his people, and God himself will be with them
and be their God. 4He will wipe every tear from
their eyes. There will be no more death or mourning or crying or pain, for the old order of things
has passed away."

5He who was seated on the throne said, "I am
making everything new!" Then he said, "Write
this down, for these words are trustworthy and
true."

6He said to me: "It is done. I am the Alpha and
the Omega, the Beginning and the End. To him
who is thirsty I will give to drink without cost
from the spring of the water of life. 7He who overcomes will inherit all this, and I will be his God
and he will be my son. 8But the cowardly, the
unbelieving, the vile, the murderers, the sexually
immoral, those who practice magic arts, the idolaters and all liars—their place will be in the fiery
lake of burning sulfur. This is the second death."

9One of the seven angels who had the seven
bowls full of the seven last plagues came and said
to me, "Come, I will show you the bride, the wife
of the Lamb." 10And he carried me away in the
Spirit to a mountain great and high, and showed
me the Holy City, Jerusalem, coming down out of
heaven from God. 11It shone with the glory of
God, and its brilliance was like that of a very
precious jewel, like a jasper, clear as crystal. 12It
had a great, high wall with twelve gates, and with
twelve angels at the gates. On the gates were written the names of the twelve tribes of Israel.
13There were three gates on the east, three on the
north, three on the south and three on the west.
14The wall of the city had twelve foundations, and
on them were the names of the twelve apostles of
the Lamb.

15The angel who talked with me had a measuring rod of gold to measure the city, its gates and
its walls. 16The city was laid out like a square, as
long as it was wide. He measured the city with the
rod and found it to be 12,000 stadia[w] in length,
and as wide and high as it is long. 17He measured
its wall and it was 144 cubits[x] thick,[y] by man's
measurement, which the angel was using. 18The
wall was made of jasper, and the city of pure gold,
as pure as glass. 19The foundations of the city
walls were decorated with every kind of precious
stone. The first foundation was jasper, the second
sapphire, the third chalcedony, the fourth emerald, 20the fifth sardonyx, the sixth carnelian, the

[w] *16* That is, about 1,400 miles (about 2,200 kilometers) [x] *17* That is, about 200 feet (about 65 meters) [y] *17* Or *high*

seventh chrysolite, the eighth beryl, the ninth topaz, the tenth chrysoprase, the eleventh jacinth, and the twelfth amethyst.[z] 21The twelve gates were twelve pearls, each gate made of a single pearl. The great street of the city was of pure gold, like transparent glass.

22I did not see a temple in the city, because the Lord God Almighty and the Lamb are its temple. 23The city does not need the sun or the moon to shine on it, for the glory of God gives it light, and the Lamb is its lamp. 24The nations will walk by its light, and the kings of the earth will bring their splendor into it. 25On no day will its gates ever be shut, for there will be no night there. 26The glory and honor of the nations will be brought into it. 27Nothing impure will ever enter it, nor will anyone who does what is shameful or deceitful, but only those whose names are written in the Lamb's book of life.

22 Then the angel showed me the river of the water of life, as clear as crystal, flowing from the throne of God and of the Lamb 2down the middle of the great street of the city. On each side of the river stood the tree of life, bearing twelve crops of fruit, yielding its fruit every month. And the leaves of the tree are for the healing of the nations. 3No longer will there be any curse. The throne of God and of the Lamb will be in the city, and his servants will serve him. 4They will see his face, and his name will be on their foreheads. 5There will be no more night. They will not need the light of a lamp or the light of the sun, for the Lord God will give them light. And they will reign for ever and ever.

6The angel said to me, "These words are trustworthy and true. The Lord, the God of the spirits of the prophets, sent his angel to show his servants the things that must soon take place."

7"Behold, I am coming soon! Blessed is he who keeps the words of the prophecy in this book."

8I, John, am the one who heard and saw these things. And when I had heard and seen them, I fell down to worship at the feet of the angel who had been showing them to me. 9But he said to me, "Do not do it! I am a fellow servant with you and with your brothers the prophets and of all who keep the words of this book. Worship God!"

10Then he told me, "Do not seal up the words of the prophecy of this book, because the time is near. 11Let him who does wrong continue to do wrong; let him who is vile continue to be vile; let him who does right continue to do right; and let him who is holy continue to be holy."

12"Behold, I am coming soon! My reward is with me, and I will give to everyone according to what he has done. 13I am the Alpha and the Omega, the First and the Last, the Beginning and the End.

14"Blessed are those who wash their robes, that they may have the right to the tree of life and may go through the gates into the city. 15Outside are the dogs, those who practice magic arts, the sexually immoral, the murderers, the idolaters and everyone who loves and practices falsehood.

16"I, Jesus, have sent my angel to give you[a] this testimony for the churches. I am the Root and the Offspring of David, and the bright Morning Star."

17The Spirit and the bride say, "Come!" And let him who hears say, "Come!" Whoever is thirsty, let him come; and whoever wishes, let him take the free gift of the water of life.

18I warn everyone who hears the words of the prophecy of this book: If anyone adds anything to them, God will add to him the plagues described in this book. 19And if anyone takes words away from this book of prophecy, God will take away from him his share in the tree of life and in the holy city, which are described in this book.

20He who testifies to these things says, "Yes, I am coming soon."

Amen. Come, Lord Jesus.

21The grace of the Lord Jesus be with God's people. Amen.

[z] *20* The precise identification of some of these precious stones is uncertain. [a] *16* The Greek is plural.

Discovering the Word 1. What aspects of the "old order" must be eliminated before God can fully dwell with his people (21:1–5)? 2. What in the passage suggests that the new Jerusalem is nothing other than the church in its final, consummated life (21:10)? 3. Why do you think John gives such a detailed description of the splendor of the city (21:11–21)? 4. Why do you think a city (rather than a glorious garden like Eden) is used to describe our final home? 5. Taken together, chapters 21 and 22 describe a place of exquisite beauty. Yet what statements indicate that the real significance of the city lies in something else (22:1–21)? 6. What are the requirements for entering the city (21:6–7, 27; 22:12, 14)?

Applying the Word 1. Why must the requirements for entering the city be met during the times of testing we experience in this life? 2. As you review what you have learned in Revelation, what new insight do you have into the early Christian prayer "Come, Lord Jesus!"?

Responding in Prayer Pray for Jesus' coming.

ACKNOWLEDGMENTS

The following articles were revised and adapted from InterVarsity Press publications:

"Why Have a Quiet Time?" by John White, from pp. 136-43 of *The Race* ©1984 by InterVarsity Christian Fellowship of the United States of America.

"How to Have a Quiet Time" by Stephen D. Eyre, from pp. 3-12 and 28-31 of *Quiet Time Dynamics* © 1989 by InterVarsity Press.

"How to Study the Bible" by James F. Nyquist and Jack Kuhatschek, from pages 25-35 of *Leading Bible Discussions,* 2d ed. © 1985 by InterVarsity Christian Fellowship of the United States of America.

"Prayer and Journaling" by Bill Hybels, from pages 39-44 and 59-60 of *Too Busy Not to Pray* © 1988 by InterVarsity Christian Fellowship of the United States of America.

The quiet times in the following books of the Bible were adapted from InterVarsity Press LifeGuide® Bible Studies:

Genesis by Charles and Anne Hummel © 1985 by InterVarsity Christian Fellowship of the United States of America.

Exodus © 1989 by James Reapsome.

Deuteronomy by Stephen Eyre. LifeGuide® Bible Study to be published in 1998.

Joshua © 1988 by Donald Baker.

Judges © 1995 by Donald Baker.

Nehemiah by Don Fields © 1994 by InterVarsity Christian Fellowship of the United States of America.

Esther © 1995 by Patty Pell.

Job © 1995 by R. Paul Stevens.

Psalms © 1987 by Eugene H. Peterson. Introduction and quiet times 1-3, 6-7, 16, 39, 47, 52, 60, 76 and 83.

Psalms II © 1995 by Juanita Ryan. Quiet times 34, 41-45, 50-51, 54, 59, 74, 78.

Proverbs © 1990 by William Mouser.

Ecclesiastes © 1992 by Bill and Teresa Syrios

Isaiah © 1991 by Howard Peskett.

Jeremiah © 1996 by Stephen Eyre. Introduction and quiet times 1, 4, 7, 9, 11-15, 18-19 and 21.

Daniel by Douglas Connelly © 1986 by InterVarsity Christian Fellowship of the United States of America.

Jonah, Joel & Amos © 1988 by Doug and Doris Haugen.

Matthew © 1987 by Stephen and Jacalyn Eyre.

Mark by James Hoover © 1985 by InterVarsity Christian Fellowship of the United States of America.

Luke © 1992 by Ada Lum.

John © 1990 by Douglas Connelly.

Acts © 1992 by Phyllis J. Le Peau.

Romans by Jack Kuhatschek © 1986 by InterVarsity Christian Fellowship of the United States of America.

1 Corinthians © 1988 by Paul Stevens and Dan Williams.

2 Corinthians © 1990 by Paul Stevens.

Galatians by Jack Kuhatschek © 1986 by InterVarsity Christian Fellowship of the United States of America.

Ephesians by Andrew T. and Phyllis J. Le Peau © 1985 by InterVarsity Christian Fellowship of the United States of America.

Philippians by Donald Baker © 1985 by InterVarsity Christian Fellowship of the United States of America.

Colossians & Philemon © 1989 by Martha Reapsome.

1 & 2 Thessalonians © 1991 by Donald E. Baker.

1 & 2 Timothy and Titus © 1991 by Pete Sommer.

Hebrews © 1991 by James Reapsome.

James by Andrew T. and Phyllis J. Le Peau, rev. ed. © 1987.

1 & 2 Peter and Jude © 1992 by Carolyn Nystrom.

John's Letters © 1990 by Ron Blankley.

Revelation © 1987 by R. Paul Stevens. (Quiet times 9, 12 and 14 of Revelation are by Scott Hotaling.)

Quiet times in the Psalms are taken from the following sources (all titles are published by InterVarsity Press):

Quiet times 13, 15, 17, 36, 49, 53, 55-57, 64-65, 67, 70-71, 75 and 82 are by Dietrich Gruen.

Quiet times 21-32 taken from *Waiting on the Lord* by Stephen D. and Jacalyn Eyre © 1994.

Quiet times 20 and 35 are by Linda Gehrs.

Quiet times 38 and 72 are by Cindy Bunch.

Quiet time 4 taken from *Healing for Broken People* © 1990 by Dan Harrison.

Quiet time 5 taken from *Prayer* © 1994 by David Healey.

Quiet times 8, 9 and 12 taken from *Recovery from Abuse* © 1990 by Dale and Juanita Ryan.

Quiet time 10 taken from *Pursuing Holiness* © 1992 by Carolyn Nystrom.

Quiet time 11 taken from *Created Male* © 1993 by Brian M. Wallace and Cindy Bunch.

Quiet time 14 taken from *Resources for Caring People* © 1991 by Phyllis J. Le Peau and NCF.

Quiet time 19 taken from *Suffering* © 1992 by Jack Kuhatschek.

Quiet time 33 taken from *Caring for Emotional Needs* © 1991 by Phyllis J. Le Peau and NCF.

Quiet time 37 taken from *Entering God's Presence* © 1992 by Stephen D. Eyre.

Quiet times 40 and 66 taken from *Recovery from Family Dysfunctions* © 1990 by Dale and Juanita Ryan.

Quiet time 46 taken from *Multi-Ethnicity* © 1990 by Isaac Canales.

Quiet time 48 taken from *Women Facing Temptation* © 1993 by Cindy Bunch.

Quiet time 58 taken from *Recovery from Distorted Images of Self* by Juanita and Dale Ryan © 1993.

Quiet time 61 taken from *Loving the World* © 1992 by Carolyn Nystrom.
Quiet time 62 taken from *The Fruit of the Spirit* by Hazel Offner, revised ed. © 1987.
Quiet time 63 taken from *Recovery from Bitterness* © 1990 by Dale and Juanita Ryan.
Quiet time 68 taken from *Deciding Wisely* © 1992 by Bill Syrios.
Quiet times 69 and 79 taken from *Recovery: A Lifelong Journey* © 1993 by Juanita and Dale Ryan.
Quiet time 73 taken from *People and Technology* © 1990 by Mary Fisher.
Quiet time 77 taken from *Self-Esteem* © 1990 by Jack Kuhatschek.
Quiet time 80 taken from *Recovery from Distorted Images of God* © 1990 by Dale and Juanita Ryan.
Quiet time 81 taken from *Recovery from Depression* © 1993 by Juanita and Dale Ryan.

Other quiet times are from the following sources (all titles are published by InterVarsity Press unless otherwise noted):
Leviticus: Introduction and quiet times 1-3, 5-6 and 8 by Dale and Sandy Larsen. Quiet time 4 taken from *Pursuing Holiness* by Carolyn Nystrom © 1992. Quiet time 7 taken from *Environmental Stewardship* © 1990 by Ruth Goring Stewart.
Numbers: Introduction and quiet times 1-3 and 6-10 by Rob Suggs. Quiet time 4 taken from *Women of the Old Testament* by Gladys Hunt © 1990. Quiet time 5 taken from *Staying Faithful* by Andrea Sterk Louthan and Howard Louthan.
Ruth: Taken from *Women of the Old Testament* © 1990 by Gladys Hunt.
1 Samuel: Introduction and quiet times 6-7, 9-11 and 13 taken from *David* © 1990 by Jack Kuhatshek. Quiet times 2 and 5 taken from *Old Testament Characters* © 1988 by Peter Scazzero. Quiet time 2 taken from *Fruit of the Spirit,* revised edition © 1987 by Hazel Offner.
2 Samuel: Quiet times 1-2 and 4-5 taken from *David* © 1990 by Jack Kuhatshek. Quiet times 3 and 7-8 taken from *Created Male* © 1993 by Brian Wallace and Cindy Bunch. Quiet time 6 taken from *Sexual Wholeness* © 1993 by Cindy Bunch and Scott Hotaling. Introduction by Cindy Bunch.
1 Kings: Introduction and quiet times 1-3 and 8 taken from *Old Testament Kings,* revised edition © 1993 by Carolyn Nystrom. Quiet time 5 taken from *Old Testament Characters* © 1988 by Peter Scazzero. Quiet time 6 taken from *Caring for Emotional Needs* © 1991 by Phyllis J. Le Peau and NCF. Quiet time 7 taken from *Women Facing Temptation* © 1993 by Cindy Bunch. Quiet time 4 taken from *Following God Together* © 1993 by Cindy Bunch and Scott Hotaling.
2 Kings: Introduction and quiet times 7-8 and 11-13 taken from *Old Testament Kings,* revised edition © 1993 by Carolyn Nystrom. Quiet times 1 and 4-6 taken from *Characters and Kings,* Part 2 by Carolyn Nystrom (Grand Rapids, Mich.: Zondervan, 1985) and used by permission of the author. Quiet times 9-10 taken from *Staying Faithful* © 1992 by Andrea Sterk Louthan and Howard Louthan. Quiet time 2 taken from *Women of the Old Testament* © 1990 by Gladys Hunt. Quiet time 3 taken from *Caing for Physical Needs* © 1991 by Phyllis J. Le Peau and NCF.
1 Chronicles: Introduction and quiet times 1-4 and 6 by Dale and Sandy Larsen. Quiet times 5 and 7 taken from *David* © 1990 by Jack Kuhatschek.
2 Chronicles: Quiet times 3 and 5 taken from *Old Testament Kings* by Carolyn Nystrom rev. ed. © 1993. Quiet time 2 taken from *Characters and Kings,* Part 1 by Carolyn Nystrom (Grand Rapids, Mich.: Zondervan, 1985) and used by permission of the author. Quiet time 6 taken from *Characters and Kings,* Part 2 by Carolyn Nystrom (Grand Rapids, Mich.: Zondervan, 1985) and used by permission of the author. Quiet time 7 taken from *Following God Together* © 1993 by Cindy Bunch and Scott Hotaling. Introduction and quiet times 3 and 5 by Dale and Sandy Larsen.
Ezra: Introduction and quiet times by Tom Parker.
Song of Songs: Adapted from *Sexual Wholeness* by Cindy Bunch and Scott Hotaling © 1993 and *Created for Relationships* by Cindy Bunch and Scott Hotaling.
Jeremiah: Quiet times 2-3, 5-6, 8, 10, 16-17, 20 and 22-24 by Dale and Sandy Larsen.
Lamentations: Introduction and quiet times by Lin Johnson.
Ezekiel: Introduction and quiet times by Paul Stevens.
Hosea: Introduction and quiet times by Tom Parker.
Obadiah: Introduction and quiet times by Dale and Sandy Larsen.
Micah: Introduction and quiet times by Tom Parker.
Nahum: Introduction and quiet times by Rob Suggs.
Habakkuk: Introduction and quiet times 1-2 taken from *Loving Justice* © 1990 by Bob and Carol Hunter. Quiet time 3 taken from *Loving the World* © 1992 by Carolyn Nystrom.
Zephaniah: Introduction and quiet times by Lin Johnson.
Haggai: Introduction and quiet time by Lin Johnson.
Zechariah: Introduction and quiet times by Jack Kuhatschek.
Malachi: Introduction and quiet times by Carolyn Nystrom.

INDEX OF QUIET TIME SUBJECTS